Principles of GERIATRIC MEDICINE and GERONTOLOGY

NOTICE

THIRD EDITION

Principles of GERIATRIC MEDICINE and GERONTOLOGY

EDITORS

William R. Hazzard, M.D.

Professor and Chairman, Department of Internal Medicine
Director, J. Paul Sticht Center on Aging
Bowman Gray School of Medicine, Wake Forest University

Edwin L. Bierman, M.D.

Professor of Medicine
Head, Division of Metabolism, Endocrinology, and Nutrition
University of Washington School of Medicine

John P. Blass, M.D., Ph.D.

Winifred Masterson Burke Professor of Neurology and Medicine
Cornell University Medical College
Director, Dementia Research Service, Burke Medical Research Institute

Walter H. Ettinger, Jr., M.D.

Associate Professor of Internal Medicine and Public Health Sciences
Bowman Gray School of Medicine, Wake Forest University

Jeffrey B. Halter, M.D.

Professor of Internal Medicine
Chief, Division of Geriatric Medicine
Director, Geriatrics Center
Medical Director, Institute of Gerontology, University of Michigan
Director, Geriatric Research Education and Clinical Center
DVA Medical Center

EDITOR EMERITUS

Reubin Andres, M.D.

Chief, Clinical Physiology Branch
Gerontology Research Center, National Institutes of Health

McGraw-Hill, Inc.

HEALTH PROFESSIONS DIVISION

New York St. Louis San Francisco Auckland Bogotá
Caracas Lisbon London Madrid Mexico City Milan
Montreal New Delhi San Juan Singapore
Sydney Tokyo Toronto

Principles of Geriatric Medicine and Gerontology

4567890 KGP KGP 98765

ISBN 0-07-027501-7

This book was set in New Baskerville by York Graphic Services, Inc.
The editors were J. Dereck Jeffers and Susan Finn;
the production supervisor was Richard Ruzycka;
the cover designer was Marsha Cohen/Parallelogram.
Arcata Graphics/Kingsport was printer and binder.
The book is printed on acid-free paper

Library of Congress Cataloging-in-Publication Data

Principles of geriatric medicine and gerontology / [edited by]
William R. Hazzard . . . [et al.].—3d ed.
p. cm.
Includes bibliographical references and index.
ISBN 0-07-027501-7 (alk. paper):
1. Geriatrics. I. Hazzard, William R., (date).
[DNLM: 1. Geriatrics. WT 100 P9575 1994]
RC952.P752 1994
618.97—dc20
DNLM/DLC
for Library of Congress 93-32986
CIP

CONTENTS

Contributors xiii
Preface xxi
Introduction xxiii

Part One PRINCIPLES OF GERONTOLOGY

1. The Biology of Aging and Longevity 3
Richard A. Miller

2. Genetics of Human Disease, Longevity, and Aging 19
George M. Martin and Mitchell S. Turker

3. The Sex Differential in Longevity 37
William R. Hazzard

4. Nutrition and Aging 49
Irwin H. Rosenberg

5. Clinical Immunology and Aging 61
William H. Adler and James E. Nagel

6. Oncology and Aging: General Principles of Cancer in the Elderly 77
Harvey Jay Cohen

7. Exercise in the Elderly: Physiologic and Functional Effects 91
Robert S. Schwartz and David M. Buchner

8. Personality and Aging 107
Paul T. Costa, Jr., and Robert R. McCrae

9. Sexuality and Aging 115
Judith A. Levy

10. Sociology of Aging 125
George L. Maddox

11. The Epidemiology of Aging 135
Maurice B. Mittelmark

12. Risk Factors for Morbidity and Mortality in Older Populations: An Epidemiologic Approach 153
Trudy L. Bush, Susan R. Miller, Michael H. Criqui, and Elizabeth Barrett-Connor

13. Health Care Implications of an Aging Population 167
L. Gregory Pawlson

14. Aging in Different Cultures: Implications for Postponement of Aging 177
Alvar Svanborg and Leopold Selker

15. Preventive Gerontology: Strategies for Attenuation of the Chronic Diseases of Aging 187
Edwin L. Bierman and William R. Hazzard

Part Two PRINCIPLES OF GERIATRICS

16. Clinical Management of the Elderly Patient 195
Mark E. Williams

17. Comprehensive Geriatric Assessment 203
Albert L. Siu, David B. Reuben, and Alison A. Moore

18. Promoting Health and Function Among Older Adults 213
Risa Lavizzo-Mourey

19. Neuropsychiatric Assessment of Syndromes of Altered Mental State 221
Marshal F. Folstein and Susan E. Folstein

20. Caring for the Older Adult: The Role of the Family 229
Robert C. Intrieri and Stephen R. Rapp

21. Appropriate Use of New Diagnostic Techniques in Older Persons 235
Eric B. Larson

22. Acute Hospital Care for Frail Older Patients 241
Marsha Duke Fretwell

23. Contemporary Geriatric Nursing 249
Terry T. Fulmer and Mathy D. Mezey

24. Clinical Pharmacology 259
Janice B. Schwartz

25. Perioperative Management of the Older Patient 277
Joseph Francis

26. Anesthesia for the Elderly Patient 287
Raymond C. Roy

27. Surgery in the Elderly 301
Ronnie Ann Rosenthal and Dana K. Andersen

28. Pain Management in the Elderly 317
Kathleen M. Foley

29. Enteral/Parenteral Alimentation 333
Edward W. Lipkin

30. Principles of Rehabilitation in Older Persons 343
T. Franklin Williams and Leo M. Cooney, Jr.

31. Rehabilitation of Specific Conditions 349
Leo M. Cooney, Jr., and T. Franklin Williams

32. Nursing Home Care 357
Joseph G. Ouslander

33. Community-Based Long-Term Care 375
Thomas E. Finucane and John R. Burton

34. The Care of the Dying Patient 383
Phyllis Schmitz, Joanne Lynn, and Elizabeth Cobbs

35. **Legal Aspects of Geriatric Medicine** 391
Kate Mewhinney

36. **Ethical Issues in Geriatric Care** 397
Robert A. Pearlman

Part Three DISEASES OF THE ORGAN SYSTEMS IN THE ELDERLY

37. **Aging of the Skin** 411
Michael S. Kaminer and Barbara A. Gilchrest

38. **The Oral Cavity** 431
Bruce J. Baum and Jonathan A. Ship

39. **The Eye** 441
David D. Michaels

40. **Auditory and Vestibular Dysfunction** 457
Thomas S. Rees, Larry G. Duckert, and Henry A. Milczuk

41. **Geriatric Gynecology** 473
Howard D. Homesley

42. **Breast Cancer** 481
Hyman B. Muss

SECTION A: THE CARDIOVASCULAR SYSTEM

43. **Alterations in Circulatory Function** 493
Edward G. Lakatta

44. **Aging and Atherosclerosis** 509
Edwin L. Bierman

45. **Disorders of the Heart** 517
Jeanne Y. Wei

46. **Peripheral Vascular Disease** 533
Brian L. Thiele and D. Eugene Strandness, Jr.

47. **Hypertension** 541
William B. Applegate

SECTION B: THE RESPIRATORY SYSTEM

48. **Aging of the Respiratory System** 555
Melvyn S. Tockman

49. **Pneumonia** 565
John G. Bartlett

50. **Tuberculosis: A Special Problem in the Elderly** 575
William W. Stead and Asim K. Dutt

51. **Chronic Airflow Obstruction and Respiratory Failure** 583
Norman Adair

52. **Interstitial Lung Disease, Hypersensitivity Pneumonitis, and Pulmonary Vascular Disease** 597
Gary W. Hunninghake

53. **Lung Cancer** 607
Michael C. Perry

SECTION C: THE RENAL SYSTEM AND URINARY TRACT

54. **Aging Changes in Renal Function** 615
Laurence H. Beck

55. **Urinary Tract Infections** 625
Allan R. Tunkel and Donald Kaye

56. **Renal Diseases** 637
John M. Burkart and Vincent J. Canzanello

57. **Disorders of the Prostate** 657
Charles B. Brendler

SECTION D: THE GASTROINTESTINAL SYSTEM

58. **Aging of the Gastrointestinal System** 665
Michael J. Baime, James B. Nelson, and Donald O. Castell

59. **Disorders of the Esophagus** 683
Wallace C. Wu

60. **Disorders of the Stomach and Duodenum** 693
Robert M. Kerr

61. **Hepatobiliary Disorders** 707
John H. Gilliam

62. **Pancreatic Disorders** 717
John H. Gilliam

63. **Colonic Disorders** 723
Lawrence J. Cheskin and Marvin M. Schuster

SECTION E: THE HEMATOLOGIC SYSTEM

64. **Aging of the Hematopoietic System** 733
D. A. Lipschitz

65. **Anemia** 741
D. A. Lipschitz

66. **White Cell Disorders** 749
Gerald Rothstein

67. **Malignant Lymphoma, Hodgkin's Disease, and Multiple Myeloma** 763
William B. Ershler

68. **Thrombotic and Hemorrhagic Disorders in the Elderly** 775
John Owen

SECTION F: THE ENDOCRINE SYSTEM AND METABOLISM

69. **Aging of the Endocrine System** 791
L. Cass Terry and Jeffrey B. Halter

70. **Thyroid Diseases** 807
Robert I. Gregerman and Michael S. Katz

71. **Diabetes Mellitus and Glucose Metabolism in the Elderly** 825
Andrew P. Goldberg and Patricia J. Coon

72. **Mortality and Obesity: The Rationale for Age-Specific Height-Weight Tables** 844
Reubin Andres

73. **Dyslipoproteinemia** 855
William R. Hazzard

74. **The Menopause and Hormone Replacement Therapy** 867
Paul B. Marshburn and Bruce R. Carr

SECTION G: DISORDERS OF BONE AND MINERAL METABOLISM

75. **Calcium and Bone Homeostasis and Changes with Aging** 879
David J. Baylink and John C. Jennings

76. **Osteoporosis** 897
Charles H. Chesnut III

77. **Osteomalacia** 911
David J. Baylink

78. **Hyperparathyroidism** 923
Kenneth W. Lyles

79. **Paget's Disease of Bone** 929
Frederick R. Singer

SECTION H: THE MUSCULOSKELETAL AND JOINT SYSTEM

80. **Aging and the Musculoskeletal System** 935
David Hamerman

81. **Nonsteroidal Anti-Inflammatory Drugs** 947
Jeffrey L. Carson and Brian L. Strom

82. **Polymyalgia Rheumatica and Giant Cell Arteritis** 955
Gerald M. Eisenberg

83. **Polymyositis, Dermatomyositis, and Inclusion Body Myositis** 961
Gerald M. Eisenberg

84. **Rheumatoid Arthritis and the Autoimmune Rheumatic Diseases in the Older Patient** 965
Evan Calkins, John D. Reinhard, and Adrian O. Vladutiu

85. **Osteoarthritis** 981
Rose S. Fife

86. **Gout and Pyrophosphate Gout (Chondrocalcinosis)** 987
J. Edwin Seegmiller

87. **Bursitis, Tendinitis, and Related Disorders** 995
Elliott L. Semble

SECTION I: THE NERVOUS SYSTEM

88. **Neurochemistry of the Aging Human Brain** 1005
Judes Poirier and Caleb E. Finch

89. **Cognition and Aging** 1013
Marilyn S. Albert

90. **Delirium (Acute Confusional States)** 1021
Zbigniew J. Lipowski

91. **Stroke** 1027
John C.M. Brust

92. **Alzheimer's Disease** 1035
Richard Mayeux and Peter W. Schofield

93. **Parkinson's Disease and Related Disorders** 1051
Fletcher H. McDowell

94. **Other Degenerative Disorders of the Nervous System** 1063
Samuel E. Gandy

95. **Infections of the Central Nervous System** 1071
Suzanne F. Bradley and Carol A. Kauffman

96. **Head Injury** 1079
Dennis G. Vollmer and Marc E. Eichler

97. **Seizures and Epilepsy** 1089
John W. Miller and James A. Ferrendelli

98. **Brain Tumors in the Elderly** 1095
Charisse D. Litchman and Jerome B. Posner

99. **Depression** 1103
Dan G. Blazer

100. **Paraphrenias and Other Psychoses** 1111
Leila B. Laitman and Kenneth L. Davis

101. **Aging of the Chronically Neuropsychologically Impaired** 1119
Steven R. Gambert

102. **Chemical Dependency** 1125
Patricia P. Barry

103. **Personality Disorders** 1131
Suzanne Holroyd and Peter V. Rabins

104. **Psychopharmacology and Psychotherapy** 1137
Kimberly A. Sherrill, Christopher C. Colenda III, and Burton V. Reifler

Part Four GERIATRIC SYNDROMES AND SPECIAL PROBLEMS OF ELDERLY PATIENTS

105. **Frailty** 1149
Linda P. Fried

106. **Approach to the Diagnosis and Treatment of the Infected Older Adult** 1157
Thomas T. Yoshikawa

107. **Dizziness and Syncope** 1165
Palmi V. Jonsson and Lewis A. Lipsitz

108. **Disorders of Fluid Balance: Dehydration and Hyponatremia** 1183
Kenneth M. Davis and Kenneth L. Minaker

109. **Disorders of Temperature Regulation** 1191
Itamar B. Abrass

110. **Syndromes of Altered Mental State** 1197
Marshal F. Folstein and Susan E. Folstein

111. **Failure to Thrive** 1205
Roy B. Verdery

112. **Sleep Problems** 1213
Edward F. Haponik

113. **Incontinence** 1229
Joseph G. Ouslander

114. **Erectile Dysfunction (Impotence)** 1251
Stanley G. Korenman

115. **Eating and Swallowing Disorders** 1259
Donald O. Castell

116. **Constipation** 1267
Lawrence J. Cheskin and Marvin M. Schuster

117. **Diarrhea** 1275
Richard G. Bennett and William B. Greenough

118. **Spinal and Peripheral Nerve Syndromes: Back Pain and Weakness** 1285
Mindy Aisen

119. **Common Foot Problems** 1297
Jeffrey A. Holman, Gary G. Poehling, and David F. Martin

120. **Immobility** 1307
Walter H. Ettinger, Jr.

121. **Falls** 1313
Mary E. Tinetti

122. **Hip Fractures** 1321
Jeane Ann Grisso and Frederick Kaplan

123. **Pressure Ulcers** 1329
Richard M. Allman

Index 1337

CONTRIBUTORS

Itamar B. Abrass, M.D. [109]
Professor of Medicine
Head, Division of Gerontology and Geriatric Medicine
University of Washington, Harborview Medical Center
Seattle, Washington

Norman E. Adair, M.D. [51]
Associate Professor of Internal Medicine
Pulmonary/Critical Care Medicine
Bowman Gray School of Medicine
Wake Forest University
Winston-Salem, North Carolina

William H. Adler, M.D. [5]
Chief of Clinical Immunology Section
Gerontology Research Center
Baltimore, Maryland

Mindy Lipson Aisen, M.D. [118]
Burke Rehabilitation Hospital
White Plains, New York

Marilyn S. Albert, Ph.D. [89]
Department of Psychiatry
Massachusetts General Hospital
Boston, Massachusetts

Richard M. Allman, M.D. [123]
Associate Professor of Internal Medicine
Director, Division of Gerontology and Geriatric Medicine
University of Alabama at Birmingham
Chief, Geriatrics Center
Birmingham Veterans Affairs Medical Center
Birmingham, Alabama

Dana K. Andersen, M.D. [27]
Professor of Surgery and Medicine
University of Chicago, Pritzker School of Medicine
Attending Surgeon, University of Chicago Hospitals and Clinics
Chicago, Illinois

Reubin Andres, M.D. [72]
Chief, Clinical Physiology Branch
Gerontology Research Center, NIH
Baltimore, Maryland

William B. Applegate, M.D., M.P.H. [47]
Professor of Preventive Medicine
University of Tennessee, Memphis
Memphis, Tennessee

Michael J. Baime, M.D. [58]
Chief, Division of Internal Medicine
Department of Internal Medicine
The Graduate Hospital
Philadelphia, Pennsylvania

Elizabeth Barrett-Connor, M.D. [12]
Professor and Chair, Division of Epidemiology
Department of Community and Family Medicine
University of California School of Medicine
La Jolla, California

Patricia P. Barry, M.D., M.P.H. [102]
Chief, Geriatrics Section
Director, Home Medical Services
Director, Gerontology Center
Boston University School of Medicine
Boston, Massachusetts

John G. Bartlett, M.D. [49]
Stanhope Bayne Jones Professor of Medicine
Chief, Division of Infectious Diseases
The Johns Hopkins University School of Medicine
Baltimore, Maryland

Bruce J. Baum, D.M.D., Ph.D. [38]
Clinical Director and Chief
Clinical Investigation Patient Care Branch
National Institute of Dental Research, NIH
Bethesda, Maryland

David J. Baylink [75, 77]
Distinguished Professor of Medicine
Loma Linda University School of Medicine
Chief, Mineral Metabolism
Jerry L. Pettis Veterans Administration Hospital
Loma Linda, California

Lawrence H. Beck, M.D. [54]
Executive Vice President, Geisinger Clinic
Danville, Pennsylvania

Richard G. Bennett, M.D. [117]
Assistant Professor of Medicine
Francis Scott Key Medical Center
The Johns Hopkins University School of Medicine
Baltimore, Maryland

Edwin L. Bierman, M.D. [15, 44]
Professor of Medicine
Head, Division of Metabolism, Endocrinology, and Nutrition
University of Washington School of Medicine
Seattle, Washington

John P. Blass, M.D. Ph.D.
Winifred Masterson Burke Professor of Neurology & Medicine
Cornell University Medical College
Director, Dementia Research Service
Burke Medical Research Institute
White Plains, New York

The numbers in brackets following the contributor name refer to chapter(s) authored or coauthored by the contributor.

Dan G. Blazer, M.D. Ph.D. [99]
J.P. Gibbons Professor of Psychiatry
Dean of Medical Education
Duke University Medical Center
Durham, North Carolina

Suzanne F. Bradley [95]
Assistant Professor of Internal Medicine
University of Michigan Medical School
Ann Arbor, Michigan

Charles B. Brendler, M.D. [57]
Professor & Chief, Section of Urology
University of Chicago Medical Center
Chicago, Illinois

John C.M. Brust, M.D. [91]
Professor of Clinical Neurology
Columbia University College of Physicians and Surgeons
Director, Department of Neurology
Harlem Hospital Medical Center
New York, New York

David M. Buchner, M.D., M.P.H. [7]
Associate Professor of Health Services and Medicine
University of Washington School of Medicine
Research Coordinator, Northwest HSR&D Field Program
Seattle VA Medical Center
Seattle, Washington

John M. Burkart, M.D. [56]
Associate Professor of Internal Medicine
Section on Nephrology
Bowman Gray School of Medicine
Wake Forest University
Winston-Salem, North Carolina

John R. Burton, M.D. [33]
Professor of Medicine and Clinical Director Division of Geriatric Medicine and Gerontology
The Johns Hopkins University School of Medicine
Director of Geriatric Medicine
Francis Scott Key Medical Center
Baltimore, Maryland

Trudy L. Bush, Ph.D., M.H.S. [12]
Associate Professor
The Johns Hopkins University
School of Hygiene and Public Health
Baltimore, Maryland

Evan Calkins, M.D. [84]
Professor of Medicine and Family Medicine
State University of New York, Buffalo Health Care Plan
Buffalo, New York

Vincent J. Canzanello, M.D. [57]
Senior Associate Consultant
Division of Hypertension and Internal Medicine
The Mayo Clinic
Rochester, Minnesota

Bruce R. Carr, M.D. [74]
Paul C. MacDonald Professor of Obstetrics and Gynecology
Director, Division of Reproductive Endocrinology
University of Texas, Southwestern Medical Center at Dallas
Dallas, Texas

Jeffrey L. Carson, M.D. [81]
Associate Professor and Chief, Division of General Internal Medicine
University of Medicine and Dentistry of New Jersey
Robert Wood Johnson Medical School
New Brunswick, New Jersey

Donald O. Castell, M.D. [58, 115]
Kimbel Professor and Chairman
Department of Medicine, The Graduate Hospital
University of Pennsylvania School of Medicine and School of Dental Medicine
Philadelphia, Pennsylvania

Lawrence J. Cheskin, M.D. [63, 116]
Assistant Professor of Medicine
The Johns Hopkins University School of Medicine
Francis Scott Key Medical Center
Baltimore, Maryland

Charles H. Chesnut, III, M.D. [76]
Professor of Medicine and Radiology
University of Washington School of Medicine
Seattle, Washington

Elizabeth Cobbs, M.D. [34]
Assistant Professor of Health Care Sciences and Medicine
Director, Division for Aging Studies and Services
George Washington University Medical Center
Washington, D.C.

Harvey J. Cohen, M.D. [6]
Director, Geriatric Research Education and Clinical Center
Veterans Administration Medical Center
Director, Center for the Study of Aging and Human Development
Duke University Medical School
Durham, North Carolina

Christopher C. Colenda, III, M.D., M.P.H. [104]
Associate Professor of Psychiatry
Bowman Gray School of Medicine
Wake Forest University
Winston-Salem, North Carolina

Patricia J. Coon, M.D. [71]
Billings Clinic
Billings, Montana

Leo M. Cooney, Jr., M.D. [30, 31]
Humana Foundation Professor of Geriatric Medicine
Yale University School of Medicine
New Haven, Connecticut

Paul T. Costa, Jr., Ph.D. [8]
Research Psychologist and Chief
Laboratory of Personality and Cognition
Gerontology Research Center
National Institute on Aging
Baltimore, Maryland

Michael H. Criqui, M.D., M.P.H. [12]
Professor of Community and Family Medicine
Division of Epidemiology, University of California
La Jolla, California

Kenneth L. Davis, M.D. [100, 108]
Chairman, Department of Psychiatry
Mount Sinai Medical School
New York, New York

Larry G. Duckert, M.D., Ph.D. [40]
Professor of Otolaryngology–Head and Neck Surgery
University of Washington School of Medicine
Seattle, Washington

Asim K. Dutt, M.D. [50]
Chief, Medical Service
Professor and Vice Chairman
Department of Medicine, Meharry Medical College
Murfreesboro, Tennessee

Marc E. Eichler, M.D. [96]
Department of Neurosurgery, Barnes Hospital
Washington University School of Medicine
St. Louis, Missouri

Gerald M. Eisenberg, M.D. [82, 83]
Director of Rheumatology, Lutheran General Hospital
Park Ridge, Illinois
Clinical Associate Professor of Medicine
University of Chicago, Pritzker School of Medicine
Chicago, Illinois

William B. Ershler, M.D. [67]
Professor of Internal Medicine
Director, Institute on Aging
Director, Madison VA GRECC
University of Wisconsin
Madison, Wisconsin

Walter H. Ettinger, Jr., M.D. [120]
Associate Professor of Internal Medicine and Public Health Sciences
Bowman Gray School of Medicine
Wake Forest University
Winston-Salem, North Carolina

James A. Ferrendelli, M.D. [97]
Professor of Pharmacology and Neurology
Seay Professor of Clinical Neuropharmacology
Department of Neurology
Washington University School of Medicine
St. Louis, Missouri

Rose S. Fife, M.D. [85]
Professor of Medicine, Biochemistry and Molecular Biology
Assistant Dean for Research
Indiana University School of Medicine
Indianapolis, Indiana

Caleb E. Finch, Ph.D. [88]
Professor, Neurobiology of Aging
Andrus Gerontology Center
University of Southern California
Los Angeles, California

Thomas E. Finucane, M.D. [33]
Associate Professor of Medicine
The Johns Hopkins University School of Medicine
Director, Elder Housecall Program
Francis Scott Key Medical Center
Baltimore, Maryland

Kathleen M. Foley, M.D. [28]
Professor of Neurology, Neuroscience, and Clinical Pharmacology
Cornell University Medical College
Chief, Pain Service, Department of Neurology
Memorial Sloan-Kettering Cancer Center
New York, New York

Marshal F. Folstein, M.D. [19, 110]
Chairman and Professor of Psychiatry
Tufts University School of Medicine
Psychiatrist-in-Chief, New England Medical Center
Department of Psychiatry
Boston, Massachusetts

Susan E. Folstein, M.D. [19, 110]
Director of Research
Department of Psychiatry
New England Medical Center Hospital
Boston, Massachusetts

Joseph Francis, M.D., M.P.H. [25]
Assistant Professor of Medicine and Preventive Medicine
VA Medical Center
University of Tennessee, Memphis
Memphis, Tennessee

Marsha D. Fretwell, M.D. [22]
Clinical Associate Professor of Community Health
Brown University School of Medicine
Medical Director, Aging 2000
Boston, Massachusetts

Linda P. Fried, M.D., M.P.H. [105]
Director, Geriatric Assessment Center and Functional Status Laboratory
The Johns Hopkins Medical Institutions
Baltimore, Maryland

Terry Fulmer, R.N., Ph.D., F.A.A.N. [23]
Anna C. Maxwell Professor in Nursing Research
Associate Dean for Research
Columbia University School of Nursing
New York, New York

Steven R. Gambert, M.D. [101]
Professor of Medicine
Associate Dean of Academic Programs
New York Medical College
Valhalla, New York

Samuel E. Gandy, M.D., Ph.D. [94]
Associate Professor of Neurology and Neuroscience
Cornell University Medical College
New York, New York

Barbara A. Gilchrest, M.D. [37]
Professor and Chairman, Department of Dermatology
Boston University School of Medicine
Boston, Massachusetts

John H. Gilliam, M.D. [61, 62]
Associate Professor of Internal Medicine
Section on Gastroenterology
Bowman Gray School of Medicine
Wake Forest University
Winston-Salem, North Carolina

Andrew P. Goldberg, M.D. [71]
Professor of Medicine
Head, Division of Gerontology, Department of Medicine
University of Maryland
Director, GRECC
ACOS Geriatrics and Extended Care
VA Medical Center Geriatrics Service
Baltimore, Maryland

William B. Greenough, III, M.D. [117]
Professor of Medicine
Francis Scott Key Medical Center
The Johns Hopkins University School of Medicine
Baltimore, Maryland

Robert I. Gregerman, M.D. [70]
Professor of Medicine
The Johns Hopkins University School of Medicine
Head, Division of Endocrinology and Metabolism
Francis Scott Key Medical Center
Guest Scientist
Gerontology Research Center
Baltimore, Maryland

Jeane Ann Grisso, M.D., M.SC. [122]
Associate Professor of Medicine
Center for Clinical Epidemiology and Biostatistics
Division of General Internal Medicine
University of Pennsylvania Medical Center
Philadelphia, Pennsylvania

Jeffrey B. Halter, M.D. [69]
Professor of Internal Medicine
Chief, Division of Geriatric Medicine
Director, Geriatrics Center
Medical Director, Institute of Gerontology
Univesity of Michigan
Director, Geriatric Research Education & Clinical Center
DVA Medical Center
Ann Arbor, Michigan

David Hamerman, M.D. [80]
Director, Resnick Gerontology Center
Department of Medicine, Division of Geriatrics
Albert Einstein College of Medicine
Montefiore Medical Center
Bronx, New York

Edward F. Haponik, M.D. [112]
Professor of Internal Medicine
Clinical Director, Section on Pulmonary/
Critical Care Medicine
Bowman Gray School of Medicine
Wake Forest University
Winston-Salem, North Carolina

William R. Hazzard, M.D. [3, 15, 73]
Professor and Chairman
Department of Internal Medicine
Director, J. Paul Sticht Center on Aging
Bowman Gray School of Medicine
Wake Forest University
Winston-Salem, North Carolina

Jeffery A. Holman, M.D. [119]
Santa Barbara Medical Foundation Clinic
Santa Barbara, California

Suzanne Holroyd, M.D. [103]
Assistant Professor of Psychiatry
The Johns Hopkins University School of Medicine
Baltimore, Maryland

Howard D. Homesley, M.D. [41]
Professor and Head, Section on Gynecologic Oncology
Department of Obstetrics and Gynecology
Bowman Gray School of Medicine
Wake Forest University
Winston-Salem, North Carolina

Gary W. Hunninghake, M.D. [52]
Professor of Internal Medicine
Director, Pulmonary Disease Division
University of Iowa College of Medicine
Iowa City, Iowa

Robert C. Intrieri, Ph.D. [20]
Research Associate, School of Nursing
College of Health and Human Development
The Pennsylvania State University
University Park, Pennsylvania

John C. Jennings, M.D. [75]
Associate Professor of Internal Medicine
Loma Linda University Medical School
Chief, Endocrinology and Metabolism
Jerry L. Pettis VA
Loma Linda, California

Palmi V. Jonsson, M.D. [107]
Attending and Consultant, Geriatrics
Reykjavik City Hospital
University of Iceland School of Medicine Teaching Hospital
Reykjavik, Iceland

Michael S. Kaminer, M.D. [37]
Department of Dermatology
Boston University School of Medicine
Boston, Massachusetts

Frederick S. Kaplan, M.D. [122]
Associate Professor of Orthopaedic Surgery
University of Pennsylvania Medical Center
Philadelphia, Pennsylvania

Michael S. Katz, M.D. [70]
Professor and Chief, Division of Geriatrics and Gerontology, Department of Medicine
University of Texas Health Science Center at San Antonio
Geriatric Research, Education and Clinical Center
Director and Associate Chief of Staff / Extended Care
Audie L. Murphy Memorial Veterans Hospital
San Antonio, Texas

Carol A. Kauffman, M.D. [95]
Chief of Infectious Diseases, VA Medical Center
Ann Arbor, Michigan

Donald Kaye, M.D. [55]
Professor and Chairman
Department of Medicine
Medical College of Pennsylvania
Philadelphia, Pennsylvania

Robert M. Kerr, M.D. [60]
Associate Professor of Internal Medicine
Section on Gastroenterology
Bowman Gray School of Medicine
Wake Forest University
Winston-Salem, North Carolina

Stanley G. Korenman, M.D. [114]
Associate Dean and Professor of Medicine
Chief, Division of Endocrinology
UCLA School of Medicine
Los Angeles, California

Leila B. Laitman, M.D. [100]
Department of Psychiatry
Mount Sinai School of Medicine
New York, New York

Edward G. Lakatta, M.D. [43]
Chief, Laboratory of Cardiovascular Science
Gerontology Research Center
National Institute on Aging, NIH
Professor of Medicine
The Johns Hopkins School of Medicine
Professor of Physiology
University of Maryland School of Medicine
Baltimore, Maryland

Eric B. Larson, M.D., M.P.H. [21]
Professor of Medicine
Medical Director, University of Washington Medical Center
Associate Dean, University of Washington School of Medicine
Seattle, Washington

Risa Lavizzo-Mourey, M.D., M.B.A. [18]
Deputy Administrator
Agency for Health Care Policy and Research
Associate Professor of Medicine
University of Pennsylvania
Philadelphia, Pennsylvania

Judith A. Levy, Ph.D. [9]
Associate Professor of Health Resources Management
School of Public Health, University of Illinois
Chicago, Illinois

Charisse D. Lichtman, M.D. [98]
Department of Neurology and Neuroscience
Cornell University Medical College
New York, New York

Edward W. Lipkin, M.D., Ph.D. [29]
Associate Professor of Medicine
Division of Metabolism, Endocrinology and Nutrition
University of Washington School of Medicine
Seattle, Washington

Zbigniew J. Lipowski, M.D., F.R.P.C. [90]
Professor Emeritus of Psychiatry
University of Toronto
Toronto, Ontario, Canada

David A. Lipschitz, M.D., Ph.D. [64, 65]
Director, Geriatric Research Education and Clinical Center (GRECC)
John L. McClellan Memorial Veterans Hospital
Professor of Medicine, Physiology, and Biophysics
Director, Division on Aging
University of Arkansas for Medical Sciences
Little Rock, Arkansas

Lewis A. Lipsitz, M.D. [107]
Assistant Professor of Medicine
Harvard Medical School
USEN Director Medical Research
Research and Training Institute
Hebrew Rehabilitation Center for Aged
Director, Harvard Geriatric Fellowship Program
Boston, Massachusetts

Kenneth W. Lyles, M.D. [78]
Associate Professor of Medicine
Geriatrics Division
Duke University Medical Center
Durham, North Carolina

Joanne Lynn, M.D., M.A. [34]
Professor of Medicine and Community and Family Medicine
Associate Director, Center for the Aging
Senior Associate, Center for the Evaluative Clinical Sciences
Dartmouth-Hitchcock Medical Center
Hanover, New Hampshire

George L. Maddox, Ph.D. [10]
Professor of Sociology and Medical Sociology (Psychiatry)
Senior Fellow, Center for the Study on Aging and Human Development
Duke University
Durham, North Carolina

Paul B. Marshburn, M.D. [74]
Assistant Professor of Obstetrics and Gynecology
Division of Reproductive Endocrinology and Infertility
University of Texas Southwestern Medical Center
Dallas, Texas

David F. Martin, M.D. [119]
Assistant Professor of Orthopaedic Surgery
Bowman Gray School of Medicine
Wake Forest University
Winston-Salem, North Carolina

George M. Martin, M.D. [2]
Professor of Pathology
Director, Alzheimer's Disease Research Center
University of Washington School of Medicine
Seattle, Washington

Richard Mayeux, M.D. [92]
Gertrude H. Sergievsky Professor of Neurology, Psychiatry and Public Health (Epidemiology)
Columbia University College of Physicians and Surgeons
Director, Sergievsky Center
New York, New York

Robert R. McCrae, Ph.D. [8]
Research Psychologist
Personality, Stress and Coping Section
Laboratory of Personality and Cognition
Gerontology Research Center
National Institute on Aging
Baltimore, Maryland

Fletcher H. McDowell, M.D. [93]
Executive Medical Director
Burke Rehabilitation Hospital
Winifred Masterson Burke Professor of Rehabilitation Medicine
Cornell University Medical College
White Plains, New York

Kate Mewhinney, J.D. [35]
Assistant Clinical Professor
Wake Forest University School of Law
Managing Attorney, Legal Clinic for the Elderly
J. Paul Sticht Center on Aging
Bowman Gray School of Medicine
Winston-Salem, North Carolina

Mathy Mezey, EdN, RN, FAAN [23]
Independence Professor of Nursing
Division of Nursing, New York University
New York, New York

David D. Michaels, M.D. [39]
Professor of Opthalmology
UCLA School of Medicine
Los Angeles, California

Henry A. Milczuk, M.D. [40]
Senior Fellow, Department of Otolaryngology
Children's Hospital Medical Center
Seattle, Washington

John W. Miller, M.D., Ph.D. [97]
Assistant Professor of Neurology
Washington University School of Medicine
St. Louis, Missouri

Richard A. Miller, M.D., Ph.D. [1]
Professor of Pathology
University of Michigan School of Medicine
Research Scientist
University of Michigan Institute of Gerontology
Research Scientist, GRECC, Ann Arbor VA Medical Center
Associate Director, University of Michigan Geriatrics Center
Ann Arbor, Michigan

Susan R. Miller, M.P.H., Sc.D. [12]
Research Study Coordinator
The Johns Hopkins University
Women's Research Center
Lutherville, Maryland

Kenneth L. Minaker, M.D., F.R.C.P., G.S.C. [108]
Associate Professor in Medicine
Harvard Medical School
Director, Brockton/West Roxbury Division of The Boston Area GRECC
Chief, Geriatrics and Extended Care
Brockton/West Roxbury VAMC
Boston, Massachusetts

Maurice B. Mittelmark, Ph.D. [11]
Associate Professor of Public Health Sciences
Bowman Gray School of Medicine
Wake Forest University
Associate Director for Public Health Sciences
J. Paul Sticht Center on Aging
Winston-Salem, North Carolina

Alison A. Moore, M.D., M.P.H. [17]
Robert Wood Johnson Clinical Scholar
UCLA Department of Medicine
Los Angeles, California

Hyman Bernard Muss, M.D. [42]
Professor of Medicine
Bowman Gray School of Medicine
Associate Director for Clinical Research
Comprehensive Cancer Center of Wake Forest University
Winston-Salem, North Carolina

James E. Nagel, M.D. [5]
Senior Clinical Associate
Clinical Immunology Section
National Institute on Aging, NIH
Bethesda, Maryland

James B. Nelson, M.D. [58]
Clinical Associate Professor of Internal Medicine
University of North Carolina-Chapel Hill
Charlotte Medical Clinic
Charlotte, North Carolina

Joseph G. Ouslander, M.D. [32, 113]
Associate Professor
UCLA Multicampus Program of Geriatric Medicine and Gerontology
Vice President of Medical Affairs
Jewish Home for the Aging of Greater Los Angeles
Reseda, California

John Owen, M.D. [68]
Professor of Internal Medicine
Section on Hematology/Oncology
Bowman Gray School of Medicine
Wake Forest University
Winston-Salem, North Carolina

L. Gregory Pawlson, M.D., M.P.H. [13]
Professor and Chairman, Department of Health Care Sciences
George Washington University School of Medicine and Health Sciences
Washington, D.C.

Robert A. Pearlman, M.D., M.P.H. [36]
Associate Professor of Medicine and Health Services, Geriatric Medicine and Gerontology
VA Medical Center
University of Washington School of Medicine
Seattle, Washington

Michael C. Perry, M.D., F.A.C.P. [53]
Professor of Medicine
Senior Associate Dean
University of Missouri-Columbia School of Medicine
Medical Director, Ellis Fischel Cancer Center
Columbia, Missouri

Gary G. Poehling, M.D. [119]
Professor and Chairman
Department of Orthopaedic Surgery
Bowman Gray School of Medicine
Wake Forest University
Winston-Salem, North Carolina

Judes Poirier, Ph.D. [88]
Associate Director
Centre for Studies in Aging
McGill University
Douglas Hospital Research Centre
Verbun, PQ, Canada

Jerome B. Posner, M.D. [98]
Chairman, Department of Neurology
Memorial Sloan-Kettering Cancer Center
New York, New York

Peter V. Rabins, M.D., M.P.H. [103]
Professor of Psychiatry
Department of Psychiatry and Behavioral Sciences
The Johns Hopkins University School of Medicine
Baltimore, Maryland

Stephen R. Rapp, Ph.D. [20]
Associate Professor of Psychiatry
Department of Psychiatry and Behavioral Medicine
Bowman Gray School of Medicine
Wake Forest University
Winston-Salem, North Carolina

Thomas S. Rees, Ph.D. [40]
Associate Professor of Otolaryngology—Head and Neck Surgery
University of Washington School of Medicine
Seattle, Washington

Burton Reifler, M.D., M.P.H. [104]
Chairman, Department of Psychiatry
Bowman Gray School of Medicine
Wake Forest University
Winston-Salem, North Carolina

John D'Arcy Reinhard, M.D. [84]
Clinical Assistant Professor of Medicine
State University of New York at Buffalo
Buffalo, New York

David B. Reuben, M.D. [17]
Associate Professor of Medicine
Chief, Division of Geriatrics Department of Medicine
UCLA School of Medicine
Los Angeles, California

Irwin H. Rosenberg, M.D. [4]
Director, United States Department of Agriculture
Human Nutrition Research Center on Aging at Tufts University
Boston, Massachusetts

Ronnie Ann Rosenthal, M.D. [27]
Associate Professor of Clinical Surgery
University of Chicago Hospitals
Chicago, Illinois

Gerald Rothstein, M.D. [66]
Professor of Medicine and Pediatrics
Director, Salt Lake City Geriatric Research, Education, and Clinical Center
Department of Veterans Affairs
Chief, Division of Human Development and Aging
University of Utah School of Medicine
Salt Lake City, Utah

Raymond C. Roy, M.D., Ph.D. [26]
Professor and Chairman, Department of Anesthesiology
Medical University of South Carolina
Charleston, South Carolina

Phyllis Schmitz, RN, MSN [34]
Washington Home and Hospice
Washington, D.C.

Peter W. Schofield, M.D. [92]
Fellow, Behavioral Neurology
College of Physicians and Surgeons
Columbia University
New York, New York

Marvin M. Schuster, M.D. [63, 116]
Professor of Medicine and Psychiatry
The Johns Hopkins University School of Medicine
Director, Division of Digestive Diseases
Francis Scott Key Medical Center
Baltimore, Maryland

Janice B. Schwartz, M.D. [24]
Associate Professor of Medicine, Pharmacy and the Cardiovascular Research Institute
Director, UCSF Gerontology and Geriatric Medicine Research Program
University of California, San Francisco
San Francisco, California

Robert S. Schwartz, M.D. [7]
Associate Professor of Medicine
Division of Gerontology and Geriatric Medicine
Harborview Medical Center
Seattle, Washington

Edwin J. Seegmiller, M.D. [86]
Associate Director, Sam and Rose Stein Institute for Research on Aging
Professor Emeritus, Department of Medicine
University of California at San Diego
La Jolla, California

Leopold Selker, Ph.D. [14]
Professor of Medical Social Work and Physical Therapy
Dean of Associate Health Professions
University of Illinois at Chicago
Chicago, Illinois

Elliott Semble, M.D. [87]
Associate Professor of Internal Medicine
Section on Rheumatology
Bowman Gray School of Medicine
Wake Forest University
Winston-Salem, North Carolina

Kimberly A. Sherrill, M.D. [104]
Department of Psychiatry
Bowman Gray School of Medicine
Wake Forest University
Winston-Salem, North Carolina

Jonathan A. Ship, D.M.D. [38]
Associate Professor and Director, Hospital Dentistry
Department of Oral Medicine, Pathology, and Surgery
University of Michigan School of Dentistry
Ann Arbor, Michigan

Frederick R. Singer, M.D. [79]
Medical Director
Osteoporosis/Metabolic Bone Disease Program
Saint John's Hospital and Health Center
Director, Skeletal Biology Laboratory
John Wayne Cancer Institute
Los Angeles, California

Albert L. Siu, M.D., M.S.P.H. [17]
Deputy Commissioner
New York State Department of Health
Albany, New York

William W. Stead, M.D. [50]
Director, Tuberculosis Program
Arkansas Department of Health, Professor of Medicine
University of Arkansas School of Medicine
Little Rock, Arkansas

D. Eugene Strandness, Jr., M.D. [46]
Professor of Surgery
University of Washington School of Medicine
Seattle, Washington

Brian L. Strom, M.D., M.P.H. [81]
Professor of Medicine and Pharmacology
Director, Center for Clinical Epidemiology and Biostatistics
University of Pennsylvania School of Medicine
Philadelphia, Pennsylvania

Alvar Svanborg, M.D., Ph.D. [14]
Professor of Medicine
Chief, Section of Geriatric Medicine
Clinical Director of Research in Gerontology
University of Illinois at Chicago
Chicago, Illinois

L. Cass Terry, Pharm. D., M.D., Ph.D. [69]
Professor and Chairman, Department of Neurology
Medical College of Wisconsin
Milwaukee, Wisconsin

Brian L. Thiele, M.D. [46]
Professor of Surgery and Chief of Vascular Surgery
Milton S. Hershey Medical Center
Hershey, Pennsylvania

Mary E. Tinetti, M.D. [121]
Associate Professor of Medicine
Yale University School of Medicine
Associate Director, Continuing Care Unit
Yale-New Haven Hospital
New Haven, Connecticut

Melvyn S. Tockman, M.D., Ph.D. [48]
Associate Professor of Environmental Sciences
The Johns Hopkins University
School of Hygiene and Public Health
Baltimore, Maryland

Allan Tunkel, M.D. [55]
Associate Professor of Medicine
Medical College of Pennsylvania
Philadelphia, Pennsylvania

Mitchell S. Turker, Ph.D. [2]
Assistant Professor of Pathology
Merkey Cancer Center
University of Kentucky College of Medicine
Lexington, Kentucky

Roy B. Verdery, M.D., Ph.D. [111]
Associate Professor of Medicine
Arizona Center on Aging
University of Arizona
Tucson, Arizona

Adrian O. Vladutiu, M.D., Ph.D., F.A.C.P. [84]
Professor of Pathology, Microbiology and Medicine
State University of New York at Buffalo
Director of Clinical Laboratories
The Buffalo General Hospital
Buffalo, New York

Dennis G. Volmer [96]
Assistant Professor of Neurosurgery
Washington University School of Medicine
St. Louis, Missouri

Jeanne Y. Wei, M.D., Ph.D. [45]
Director, Division of Aging
Harvard Medical School
Staff Physician, Geriatric Research, Education, and Clinical Center
Brockton-West Roxbury Department of Veterans Affairs Medical Center; and Chief Gerontology Division, Beth Israel Hospital
Boston, Massachusetts

Mark E. Williams, M.D. [16]
Associate Professor of Medicine
Director, Program on Aging, School of Medicine
University of North Carolina-Chapel Hill
Chapel Hill, North Carolina

T. Franklin Williams, M.D. [30, 31]
Professor of Medicine Emeritus
University of Rochester School of Medicine
Attending Physician, Monroe Community Hospital
Rochester, New York

Wallace C. Wu, M.B., B.S. [59]
Professor of Internal Medicine
Section on Gastroenterology
Bowman Gray School of Medicine
Wake Forest University
Winston-Salem, North Carolina

Thomas T. Yoshikawa, M.D. [106]
Assistant Chief Medical Director for Geriatrics and Extended Care
U.S. Department of Veterans Affairs
Adjunct Professor of Health Care Sciences
George Washington University School of Medicine
Washington, D.C.

PREFACE

The third edition of *Principles of Geriatric Medicine and Gerontology* appears at a critical juncture in the evolution of the American health care system. The contemporary focus on health care is driven by the twin concerns that health care in the United States has not only become unaffordable for many citizens (and unavailable to an unacceptable number), but also may have lost that important balance between scientific/technical expertise and the essential humanistic dimension of quality patient care. In 1994, the American public, through its business and political leaders, appears determined to rectify this imbalance, instill fiscal responsibility, and restore confidence that the health care system will serve all Americans well at a cost that we can afford.

It should be clear to readers of this textbook, who have special concern for the health care needs of the elderly, that the principles and practice of expert geriatric medicine are central to any reform in health care that truly addresses the future needs of the American public. The elderly constitute, inexorably, the fastest growing segment of the American population, the oldest segments within the elderly population are growing at the fastest rates of all, and health care requirements (and, as currently practiced, costs) escalate exponentially with ever-advancing age. Given that a substantial fraction of all Medicare expenditures are directed to those persons in the final stages of life (nearly half for those in their last two months), these twin concerns have become "confocused" in the public debate: clearly the tension and the imbalance between excessive cost and insufficient humanism is most excruciating in the care of our oldest citizens.

The editors have carefully considered the dimensions of this dilemma in crafting this third edition: we are confident that the information contained in the 123 chapters and the manner and tone with which it has been presented represent appropriate balances between frontier science and technology and practical, common sense approaches to those problems; between reductionistic strategies in geriatric research and patient care and the polydimensional, often intuitive thinking that defines the essence of expert care in geriatrics; between bold action by the decisive practitioner and cautious, expectant reflection and appreciation of the many daunting and often uncontrollable forces that determine the course and outcome in our older patients; between the contributions of the physician and those essential and frequently dominant efforts of other health care professionals (family members and other friends and advocates of the patient); and between the dimensions of the daily ethical dilemmas that we face in our practice. This edition also extends the tradition of the first two in providing both up-to-date information on those elements of geriatrics that are changing while at the same time informing, reassuring, and giving comfort and confidence to the adult learner about those elements that are changeless.

The organization and design of the third edition have been largely retained from the second, a structure that appeared to lead to its widespread acceptance by geriatric physicians both in the United States and, increasingly, abroad. The volume begins with 15 chapters on the Principles of Gerontology (the study of aging), solid summaries of an exploding literature that is bedrock information for the well-rounded geriatrician and, especially, for fellows in geriatric medicine, the teachers and role models for future generations of students, residents, and practicing geriatric generalists and specialists. Part Two features 21 chapters on the Principles of Geriatrics (the health and social care of the elderly), equally fundamental and eminently practical basic information for the geriatric clinician as well as the academician. Part Three remains the core of geriatric medicine that most closely parallels our classic parent textbook (*Harrison's Principles of Internal Medicine*), 68 chapters each designed to be information-dense, largely self-contained treatises on the complete spectrum of geriatric organ system diseases and featuring 17 chapters on the nervous system disorders that so distinguish (and often define) geriatric practice. Finally, 19 chapters in Part Four in Geriatric Syndromes and Special Problems complete this edition, chapters that capture the essence of our art, chapters that provide practical, immediate assistance to the practitioner struggling to address the subtleties of our craft, chapters that perhaps best answer that perennial question most vexing to the geriatrician who continues to struggle for recognition and identity, "But what do you do that is different?" What do we do best that is different? Try Failure to Thrive (Chapter 113); Impotence (Chapter 117); Falls (Chapter 121); Hip Fractures (Chapter 122); and Pressure Ulcers (Chapter 123). To which your questioner may finally respond, "Oh, hmm, I see."

Just as the publication of the third edition coincides with the dawn of American health care reform, so also does it but shortly precede the fourth (and final) examination offered jointly by the American Board of Internal Medicine and the American Board of Family Practice leading to the Certificate of Added Qualifications in Geriatrics. But even as such certificates beyond 1994 will be awarded only to those with accredited geriatric fellowship training, this and future editions of this textbook will continue to stress the core elements of geriatrics, the main dishes, as it were, that must be the concern of all physicians who care for the elderly. It seems clear that the care of older citizens in the American health care system of the future, just as at present, will not be the province of a select cadre of geriatric specialists but instead remain in the hands primarily of generalists (internists and family physicians) supported as appropriate by specialists (who, by the way, are evolving subspecialties and cross-disciplinary specialties such as geriatric psychiatry, geriatric neurology, geriatric cardiology, geriatric physiatry, etc., especially in academic centers to address the learning needs of medical students and residents in parent specialties and subspecialties).

Thus the third edition remains targeted to all students of medicine, of all ages and at all stages, who would address with competence and confidence the burgeoning needs of their aging patients, just as the numbers and aggregate needs of such patients will increasingly dominate the American health care system as the "demographic imperative" of the twenty-first century becomes a reality.

As with previous editions, assembly of the third has proved an exciting and fulfilling challenge. To address this challenge, the editorial board has been strengthened through addition of new members (Walter H. Ettinger, Jr., and Jeffrey B. Halter), while our founding editor, Reubin Andres, achieves emeritus status. As ever we have been assisted in our mission by skilled, dedicated, and patient staff absolutely essential to the success of this venture: Ellen Meyer in support of Edwin L. Bierman at the University of Washington; Carol Montanaro, Mirna Pantoja, and Nina Martin in support of John P. Blass at Burke Rehabilitation Center/Cornell Westchester Division; Allyson Edwards and Maria Montgomery in support of Walter H. Ettinger at the Bowman Gray School of Medicine of Wake Forest University; Ann Pine and Judith A. Seeger in support of Jeffrey B. Halter at the University of Michigan; and Nancy Woolard in support of William R. Hazzard, also at Bowman Gray. As Chief Editorial Assistant (both supported in turn by the advice and encouragement of Ellen B. Hazzard, Chief Editorial Assistant of the first two editions), Ms. Woolard has been the final common pathway of communication and quality control for all chapters as well as for liaison with staff at McGraw-Hill (notably Dereck Jeffers as supported by Susan Finn); to her, the editors offer special thanks and recognition.

A special attribute of geriatrics that adds to its excitement and appeal is, perhaps ironically, its relative youth. Even in 1994 it remains an adolescent if no longer infant discipline, one that will be on center stage as we adapt to our maturing population, part of the solution to the challenges facing our health care system. The editorial board and McGraw-Hill are committed to keeping the *Principles of Geriatric Medicine and Gerontology* continuously current and useful, an essential tool in meeting those challenges and making the practice of geriatric medicine ever-stimulating and ever-satisfying to physicians and other professionals who provide quality health care to the elderly.

William R. Hazzard

INTRODUCTION

The Practice of Geriatric Medicine

The changing distribution of the American population by age which has characterized the latter half of the twentieth century (often called the "graying of America" or "the demographic imperative") has given special meaning to the interrelated disciplines of gerontology and geriatric medicine and an urgency to the mastery of both by physicians and other health care practitioners. For the purposes of this text we shall define *gerontology* as the study of aging, *geriatrics* as the health and social care of the elderly, and *geriatric medicine* as that subdiscipline within geriatrics specifically devoted to the medical care of the elderly.

Geriatric medicine can be described by the nature of its clientele, elderly patients, and the characteristics of its practitioners and their activities. Its clientele has been traditionally defined by demographers, insurers, and employers as those over the age of 65. In those nations where geriatric medicine has emerged as a distinct specialty, the age of 75 is more often employed, with flexibility about that age depending upon the specific age of the patient in question and the capacity of the geriatric health care system to meet his or her specific needs. Hence, in such countries, geriatricians may care for certain chronically disabled patients even below age 65. It is clear that those over 75 years of age, however, have generally accumulated the multiple problems which distinguish the elderly. Perhaps no age definition is truly desirable given the variable rates of aging and disease accumulation by different persons. As this area of interest expands, however, geriatricians must often define and defend their specific area of expertise. To the question as to "What is the typical geriatric patient?", this author responds, "Think of your oldest, sickest, most complicated and frail patient."

Such a patient encompasses the problems most often encountered by the geriatrician. He or, more frequently, she often presents with multiple disabilities, covert as well as overt. Thus while signs and symptoms might suggest, for example, pneumonia as in the younger patient, limited physiologic reserves in multiple systems may lead to complications and all too often a cascade of complications vastly reducing the remaining life span of the patient. The elderly patient often also presents atypically; e.g., infection may present without fever, myocardial infarction without pain, or hyperthyroidism without evidence of hypermetabolism. This aspect of geriatric practice is often overdrawn, however, nor are there many conditions which present uniquely in the elderly (e.g., polymyalgia rheumatica is rare except in the geriatric patient). Thus these atypical presentations and diseases are unusual even in the elderly and do not comprise a large fraction of the practice of the geriatrician. More demanding of the physician's time are the chronic, progressive, only partially reversible problems which are typical in the elderly patient once the health care system is encountered. Management of such enduring problems defines geriatric medicine as primary care medicine in the elderly in this nation, as opposed to the role of consultant that has been reserved for the geriatrician in countries such as the United Kingdom, where geriatrics has been defined as a hospital-based specialty. Another characteristic of geriatric practice in the U.S. health care system is overlap among and necessary consideration of multiple dimensions of the patient's life, which are the rule in defining the presentation of impairment or the ability to live with the disability that is imposed. Thus, multidisciplinary assessment is essential, emphasizing not only physical and mental parameters but also social, economic, and most importantly, functional measures. Therapeutic planning must be similarly multidimensional, and multiple persons become involved. Health practitioners from numerous fields, notably medicine, psychiatry, neurology, nursing, social work, dentistry, pharmacy, rehabilitation medicine, and the related therapies, occupational, physical, recreational, must collaborate with supporters, especially friends and family, in assisting patients to maximize their independence for as long as possible in whatever setting they may reside. In this circumstance, the physician is usually called upon to be a team leader, administrator, and coordinator. Specific medical expertise is crucial, but diplomacy and clear definition of spheres of responsibility and tasks to be performed are essential. Leadership in a corporate sense rather than the image of the solo practitioner of old is a distinguishing characteristic of the modern geriatrician.

The coincidence of multiple problems in the elderly patient often produces blurring of diagnostic categories, and nonspecific presentations and courses are common. This has led some to define geriatric medicine by its emphasis upon specific problem complexes ("The 5 I's"): Iatrogenic disease, (mental) Incompetence, Incontinence, Immobility, and Impaired homeostasis. Each of these syndromes is dealt with in detail elsewhere in this volume and thus no summary will be attempted here. However, their mastery is essential to the successful practice of geriatric medicine. Of the five, perhaps iatrogenic disease is of the greatest concern to the geriatrician, given the primary role of the physician in its genesis. In this regard it would appear that the therapeutic ratio for almost any modality of diagnosis or therapy narrows in the elderly and may even become negative. This appears especially true for pharmacological interventions, and the tendency for multiple problems to be treated with multiple drugs compounds that risk in exponential fashion. Thus a cardinal principle of geriatric medicine, especially when the course of a patient turns suddenly for the worse, is to ask first, "What have I done to the patient?" rather than what the environment or the given disease process has done.

A final cardinal feature of disease and disability in the elderly is their tendency to be chronic and often progressive. Thus the primary care physician caring for the elderly patient becomes an expert in the management of chronic disease across the spectrum of levels of health care, including long-term institutional care. In this practice the geriatrician learns to use the dimension of time in the diagnostic and treatment process perhaps more than his or her acute care colleague. This may both reduce risk by minimizing aggressive and invasive diagnostic efforts and also allow the constant tailoring of therapy to the changing needs of the patient through time. A subjective estimate of the time remaining in the patient's life is also constantly kept in mind. A major proportion of the geriatrician's efforts are devoted to those in the final stages of life. Some, such as those with terminal malignancies, are clearly dying: the courses of others, when a terminal cause is not evident, are not so clearly capable of delineation. Given that a substantial fraction of the total health care resources consumed by an individual during his or her lifetime is expanded in the final year, the geriatrician must also bear in mind the inordinate cost of the care delivered under his or her direction. Questions of life and death, of the efficacy, risk, and ethics of diagnosis and treatment are a major concern of the geriatrician, and he or she must continuously consult with the patient, supporters, and other members of the health care team (on occasion including clergy, lawyers, ethicists) as to the wisdom or folly of therapeutic efforts. The geriatrician must always bear in mind that prolongation of the dying process is to be avoided, while preservation of comfort and dignity is a primary goal. Inherent in these considerations is the special role of patience and humility in the make-up of the consummate geriatrician. Given that the upper limit of the human life span is relatively fixed and that most patients will be approaching that limit, the geriatrician must respect a limited ability to intervene when that barrier is approached. Thus art and compassion are the essence of geriatric medicine, and wisdom plays a greater role in its practice than technical knowledge or skill.

In what ways is gerontology related to geriatric medicine? An appreciation of the aging process in all its stages is of both theoretical and practical importance to geriatrician. Knowledge of the multiple dimensions of physiological decline which precede the presentation of the elderly patient is essential to the geriatrician. Appreciation of the interaction of these declines with specific diseases will help define the course of individual patients. The art of individualizing such knowledge to the given patient combines a subjective assessment of the point in that person's life course at which the encounter with the health care system has taken place and a clinical estimate of the trajectory of the patient's future course and its remediable and irremediable components. When to intervene with all the technology and resources of the health care system and when to observe and support without resorting to that technology is critical to the practice of expert geriatric medicine. Finally, appreciation of the areas of physiology and psychology which do not decline or which become stronger by virtue of time and the aging process is also important to the geriatrician. The elderly are themselves an enormous resource in their own health care and the care of others, and the knowledge and trust built between the physician and the elderly patient constitute an important resource in both the diagnostic and therapeutic processes.

Given these characteristics of elderly patients and their physicians, just who should practice geriatric medicine? It would appear most likely that in the pluralistic health care system prevailing in the United States that the majority of geriatric medicine will be practiced by generalists, be they family physicians or internists. A small proportion of such physicians may choose to devote all of their practice to the care of the elderly. Another minority may elect to obtain additional training through continuing medical education, preceptorships in divisions of geriatric medicine, or through fellowship training which emphasizes those aspects of medicine especially pertinent to the care of the elderly. However, to define geriatric medicine as a narrow specialty to be practiced only by those with specific training therein would be to both overwhelm the extant geriatric training programs and also ignore the enormous existing resource in the form of well-trained and experienced generalists within the medical profession. To assure that all physicians will be prepared to meet the demands that the demographic imperative will place upon their professional capabilities, the principles of gerontology and geriatric medicine should be incorporated within all levels of the medical school and postgraduate and continuing education curricula, especially those for the internist, family physician, psychiatrist, neurologist, and physiatrist. Indeed, no physician, even the pediatrician or obstetrician (whose patients' lives are likely to be affected by the expanding burden of care for elderly family themselves), should lack such knowledge. Hence this text is directed toward students of medicine at all levels, given the increasing attention to the health care needs of the elderly which will be brought about by their growing proportion and absolute numbers within our population, their greater vulnerability to disease and disability, and the greater per capita expenditure of health care resources on their behalf. The charge to physicians of the future is clear: *care* for your elderly patients, in every sense of this word. To do otherwise would be to neglect a basic challenge to the medical profession. This text is assembled to assist the physician in meeting that challenge by presenting in one volume the current body of knowledge regarding the aging process and its implications to the care of the elderly, in so doing also serving to lend credibility and respect to the practice of geriatric medicine.

WILLIAM R. HAZZARD

PART ONE

PRINCIPLES OF GERONTOLOGY

Chapter 1

THE BIOLOGY OF AGING AND LONGEVITY

Richard A. Miller

Aging is a process that converts healthy adults into frail ones, with diminished reserves in most physiological systems and an exponentially increasing vulnerability to most diseases and to death. Aging is a mystery, in the sense that cancer, heredity, development, and infection were once mysteries and cognition still is: a process so poorly understood that we cannot yet be sure how to go about seeking an explanation. The impact of aging on health and well-being dwarfs that of any single category of illness, because aging is itself the principal risk factor for most important diseases. The ability to modify the aging rate in humans to the degree that is now routine in mice and some other animals would be of greater benefit to the health of individuals than the total abolition of cancer, cardiovascular diseases, and diabetes.

The central goal of this chapter is to provide a brief overview of what is now known or suspected about the basic biological processes of aging: what aging is, what aging does, why aging occurs at all (from an evolutionary perspective), and what biochemical processes seem likely to contribute to age-associated decline. The chapter ends with an annotated selection of some promising research areas in basic gerontology.

A brief essay on a topic this broad must rely heavily on generalizations rather than data and on review articles in place of specific citations. Readers interested in deeper and broader introductions may turn to several monographs and review collections.[1–5]

MATTERS OF TERMINOLOGY AND RECOMMENDED DEFINITIONS

Although lay persons and physicians alike can tell young people apart from old people and although researchers generate hundreds of papers each year describing the effects of age at ever finer levels of cellular and molecular detail, the fundamental processes that control the rate at which people age and that can explain how aging leads to the diseases of aging are still essentially unknown. Experimental work over the last 30 years has, however, ruled out theories of aging that once seemed promising while providing new support for several others. Before we delve into these results, however, it may be helpful to focus first on a set of working definitions.

The definition that began this chapter—aging as a process that converts healthy adults into frail ones with diminished reserves in most physiological systems and an exponentially increasing vulnerability to diseases and death—was proposed to help focus attention on uniform, broadly based, deteriorative changes as the fundamental concern of experimental gerontology. Some authorities have argued that aging should be viewed as an extension of the normal developmental process that turns fertilized eggs into reproductively mature adults. This idea seems seriously flawed: although there may well be senescent processes that begin in early life or that depend upon embryogenic and maturational processes, there is no good reason to suspect that the mechanisms that convert zygotes into adults will closely resemble those that turn adults into 90-year-olds. Factories that convert steel and glass into new automobiles are usually not also involved in the production of used cars from new ones.

A second set of confusions arises from borrowed terminology—the use of common terms to describe more than one biological phenomenon. Thus the term *senescence,* in addition to denoting the effects of aging on whole animals, has been used to describe annual leaf abcission from deciduous plants, the removal of erythrocytes from the circulation, and the conversion of proliferative cell cultures to differentiated, nondividing progeny. While it is possible that important insights into organismal aging can be gained from the study of such models (see the discussion of clonal senescence, below), it is important to avoid the temptation to assume that study of "senescence" in these senses will necessarily prove relevant to the study of senescent change in intact multicellular organisms. The same caveat can be applied to the analysis of various forms of programmed (apoptotic) "cell death," which are neither more nor less likely to reveal important insights into aging than other major biological processes with less suggestive names.

A more serious set of confusions arises from our inability to measure aging directly, as it occurs, in any single individual. We can measure a huge variety of age-sensitive outcomes—including gray hair, skin wrinkles, collagen cross-linking, maximum work output and endurance, antibody responses, and so on in individual subjects—but each of these and most (perhaps all) other indirect indices of aging are also influenced by genetic and environmental factors besides aging per se. It is tempting to argue from this perspective that there is no single process worth calling "aging," since no two people age in exactly the same way, and to argue that gerontologists are studying the effects of a variety of diseases that afflict some, but not all, old people. We have not, however, abandoned the idea of a unified process of embryogenesis simply because newborns differ from one another. One 70-year-old may be hard of hearing, another vulnerable to complications of influenza, and a third no longer able to climb five flights of stairs, but it is rare to find a 20-year-old with any of these problems and rare to find a 90-year-old who has avoided all of them. It is also unlikely to be merely coincidental that a spectrum of disabilities, including declines in cardiovascular reserve, neurosensory function, immune response, and resistance to neoplastic and degenerative diseases affects old mice, old horses, and old dogs in patterns recognizably similar to those seen in aging humans. The challenge of measuring the "biological age" of an individual in the face of age-independent variation in all age-dependent outcomes will be taken up later in this chapter in the context of biomarkers.

The relationship between aging and disease can be seen as a special case of the question of interindividual differences just discussed. The details of how aging contributes to and alters various diseases will be addressed in most of the other chapters in this text. Here, however, we confront a more general issue: Which age-dependent changes can be considered a part of "normal" aging and which are aspects of disease? The matter is not merely semantic: researchers who wish to measure the effects of "normal" aging on some end point (immune function, perhaps, or speed in the 100-m dash) typically try to compare disease-free young and old subjects so as to avoid the objection that any differences seen might be due not to aging per se but instead to diseases present in a proportion of the elderly subject pool. This makes excellent sense. A group of 80-year-olds of whom 10 percent are cardiac patients and another 10 percent suffer from Alzheimer's disease is unlikely to produce a representative average time in the 100-m dash. On the other hand, classification of an 80-year-old as "disease-free" is itself problematic. An 80-year-old who has osteoporosis but no broken bones, prostatic hypertrophy but no malignancy, coronary atherosclerosis but no angina may be classified "disease-free" by some conventions and for some purposes, but it is clear that the dividing line, wherever drawn, will be arbitrary from the perspective of basic biology. If one does locate a group of 80-year-olds who meet a rigorous set of exclusion criteria, is it reasonable to allow this highly atypical group to represent the "typical" aged human?

One way to deal with this chronic debate is to acknowledge that while it may not always be possible to decide whether a specific condition (loss of visual acuity, or atheromatous change, etc.) represents an effect of aging with variable expression in different individuals or is instead a disease that accompanies aging in some but not all people, it is in practice often possible to discern an effect of aging despite the confounding effects of age-related disease. It is important to realize that while the effects of aging may not become obvious until the last quarter of life, the process by which aging produces 70-year-olds acts on adults throughout life. Thus changes that occur progressively and (almost) universally throughout the middle half of life are likely to be reflections of aging rather than of illness. The challenge for the research gerontologist is to identify the processes that create the elderly person. These processes are far less likely to be confused with the effects of disease than are events that are detectable only at ages at which a large fraction of the surviving population has latent or apparent illness.

FUNDAMENTAL OBSERVATIONS

We know a great deal about the phenotype of the aged but far less about the aging process itself. Three fundamental results seem central to any comprehensive model of aging. First, we know that the general *pattern* of aging across nearly all mammalian species is recognizably similar. Second, we know that the *rate* of aging is determined by genes that vary across species. Third, we know that the rate of aging can be *decreased* by caloric restriction, at least in rodents. These three generalities constitute the central "core" observations that will need to be explained by any comprehensive model of the aging process. We will consider them in turn.

Generality 1 Aged mice, dogs, and humans share a common loss of physiological reserve over a wide range of measures and share an exponentially increasing vulnerability to most forms of life-threatening illnesses. The details differ from species to species and indeed from strain to strain: some rodents are more susceptible than others to kidney degeneration and others are more susceptible to lymphomas, while none seems at risk for the neurological signs and deficits seen in human Alzheimer's disease. Yet in each of these species aging brings recognizable changes in phenotype—alterations in hair coloration, loss of immune function, decline in cardiovascular capabilities, alterations in collagen and crystallin structure, increases in lipofuscin deposition, changes in protein synthesis and degradation rates, among many others—that occur in rough synchrony within each species and over time scales proportional to rates of change in disease incidence and mortality risks.

There are instructive exceptions to this general parallelism. Some strains of rats and mice are genetically predisposed to specific diseases that occur at ages younger than the age at which unaffected members of the species begin to experience high risks of mortality. The leukemia that affects AKR/J and B10.F mice, for example, tends to kill members of these strains within the first 18 months of life. It seems sensible to consider these situations as examples in which the development of late-life aging changes has been precluded by a lethal early-life disease. Similarly, strains of mice, such as (NZB × NZW)F_1 and MRL/lpr, in which lethal autoimmune disease develops relatively early in life, are probably unsuitable for studies of the aging process per se. Semelparous species, such as Pacific salmon and marsupial mice, in which a single burst of reproductive effort is followed by synchronized death, provide natural examples of species in which aging is inaccessible to study. A more typical, gradual senescent process is observable in salmon that are restrained from breeding,[6] consistent with the idea that the sequence of events that lead to postreproductive death are unlikely to resemble aging in useful detail.

Generality 2 The second of these three fundamental principles is that the rate of aging varies across species; in other words, that the rate of aging is under genetic control. Since the rate of aging is not itself directly measurable by current techniques, surrogate measures have traditionally relied on life table analysis, in which the age at death is recorded for each member of a test population. The two most accepted indices of interspecies differences in aging rate are the maximum life-span potential (MLP) and the rate of increase in the mortality rate over time. MLP (i.e., the life span of the longest-lived member of a very large, optimally protected population) varies in mammals over a 30-fold range, from 3 to 5 years in rodents to about 115 years in humans.[1,2] MLP is a better measure of aging than other values, such as mean or median life span, because the latter statistics are influenced greatly by factors that induce (or decrease) early and midlife illnesses. The very large increase in human mean longevity over the last few centuries, for example, has been due to factors that do not influence aging itself and has not been accompanied by any change in MLP. In experimental work, alteration of the MLP has been the "gold standard" by which to judge manipulations alleged to affect the aging process itself.

The other commonly accepted measure of aging rate within a species or subspecies is the rate at which the mortality risk increases over time. The method of life table analysis developed by Gompertz breaks down the risk of mortality at any adult age [$R_m(t)$] into at least two components: an initial mortality rate M_o that is unrelated to age, and a second component that increases exponentially with age, according to the equation:

$$R_m(t) = M_o + A \exp(Gt)$$

where M_o is a measure of the mortality rate at the age of lowest mortality risk and A and G are constants chosen to optimize the fit of the line to the experimental data. Equations of this form have been shown to describe the adult survival curves of a remarkable range of invertebrate and vertebrate species.[1] Populations with a high value of G will show a large increase in mortality risk over any given time interval and can, in this sense, be said to age rapidly. A related, recent reformulation[1] of these relationships emphasizes that species can differ both in their initial mortality rate (IMR) (defined as the mortality risk at its nadir, typically at puberty) and in the mortality rate doubling time (MRDT). The MRDT of humans (8 years), for example, is much higher than that of mice (4 months). There are some cases, however, in which differences among species in longevity seem largely to reflect differences in IMR, rather than MRDT, or to reflect a combination of both factors. Among primates, for example, macaque monkeys have a maximum life span about threefold less than that of humans, but this seems to represent differences in IMR rather than in MRDT, which is about 8 years in each species. These distinctions, which are reviewed at length by Finch,[1,7] may eventually prove quite important, particularly if the genes that modify MRDT prove to be distinct from those that modify initial mortality rates. The species-specific MRDT seems to be very stable even in environments where the mortality rate is substantially higher than under optimal conditions (Fig. 1-1).

However, we do not yet have good ideas about either the number or the nature of the genetic differences that account for differences in longevity among species. The problem of how evolutionary forces act upon genes that affect longevity will be discussed later in this chapter. The question of whether there are or are not genetic differences in aging rate between members of the same species will be reserved for the discussion of biomarker research below.

Generality 3 The third central challenge for any general model of the aging process is to account for the effect of calorie restriction (CR), the only method known to retard most aspects of aging in mammals (Fig. 1-2). This effect, first described by McKay et al.[8] and recently reviewed briefly by Masoro[9] and at length by Weindruch and Walford,[10] can lead to an extension of both mean and maximum life span by as much as 30 to 40 percent. The appearance of most age-related disease is retarded roughly in parallel to the increase in longevity, and about 90 percent of the indices of age-associated physiological and biochemical change show a similar retardation. Many different regimens for CR seem to work about equally well (e.g., smaller daily portions or every-other-day feeding), as long as the total calorie intake is reduced to about 60 percent of the ad libitum intake and as long as protein, vitamins, and micronutrients are provided in amounts adequate to prevent malnutrition. Calorie restriction imposed at the time of weaning has the

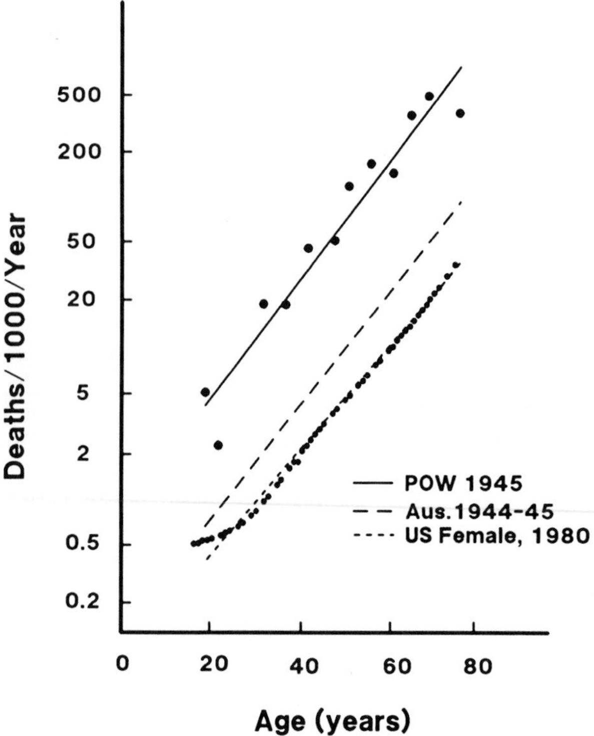

FIGURE 1-1
Mortality rates as a function of age in three human populations. Note that harsh conditions, such as those that prevail in a prisoner-of-war camp (POW curve), can increase mortality risk without any effect on the mortality rate doubling time, or by inference, the aging rate. (*From Finch et al,[7] with permission.*)

largest effect, but substantial effects both on longevity and on physiological measures of aging can also be seen in rodents placed on a low-calorie diet in midlife.[9,11] The degree of CR is severe enough to delay or prevent sexual maturation[12] and is thus unlikely to resemble dietary conditions encountered by free-living wild rodent populations, for which delayed sexual competence would lead to extinction. It is not yet clear whether a similar degree of CR will delay age-related changes in primates.[13] While the side effects of the CR regimen, including stunted growth and diminished reproductive function, preclude its direct application to humans, an improved understanding of the biochemical and physiological basis for the effect would have profound implications for fundamental gerontology and might well have implications for public health. Clever exploitation of the CR effect has helped to eliminate several previously attractive general models for aging while providing supportive evidence in favor of others, as described in more detail below.

The most general goal, then, for a comprehensive model of aging is to answer the basic question: What times aging? That is, what molecular mechanisms account for the synchrony of structural and functional change in different cells and tissues of each member of a given species? Which genes and which processes set the aging rate differently in different species, and how does CR slow this rate? Biochemists and physiologists have proposed a number of different answers to these related questions, and we will consider these mechanistic models below.

THEORIES OF AGING

Books and review articles on aging published 20 years ago often began with a list of general "theories" that had been proposed to explain the process of aging in mechanistic terms; aside from shifts in vocabulary, these lists were quite similar to lists proposed 200 and even 2000 years ago. We do not yet have a good general theory of aging, in the sense that we did acquire good general theories of infection in the nineteenth

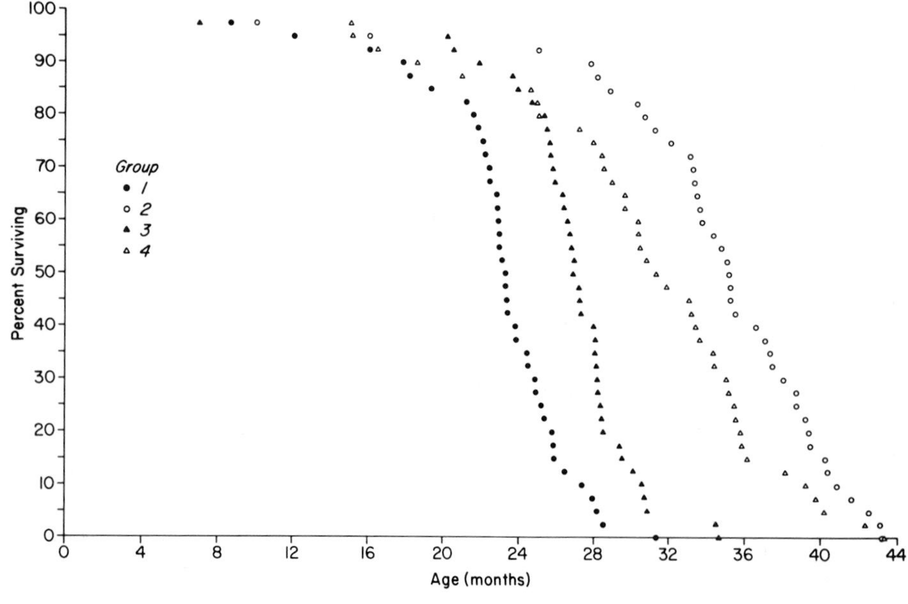

FIGURE 1-2
Effect of calorie restriction on longevity in rats. Note that food restriction both from midlife (curve 4) and in early life (curve 3) has partial effects as compared with lifelong restriction (curve 2). 1, not food restricted; 2, food restricted from 6 weeks; 3, food restricted, 6 weeks to 6 months; 4, food restricted from 6 months. (*From Yu et al, J Gerontol 40:657, 1985, with permission.*)

century, of heredity in the last 100 years, and of cancer and immune function in the last 20 to 30 years. On the other hand, experimental work in basic gerontology has succeeded over the last 20 years in eliminating from serious consideration a number of theories that once seemed plausible. These rejected theories include:

1. The "error catastrophe" model first elaborated in detail by Orgel.[14] This idea held that perhaps errors in DNA transcription or RNA translation might be self-amplifying through a kind of positive feedback. Initial evidence seemed to support this idea by showing that proteins produced in cells from older people did exhibit structural alterations, but later work showed that these alterations did not include changes in the sequence of amino acids, thus arguing strongly against the error cascade model.[15] The observation that aging does lead to an accumulation of altered proteins and data showing that the alterations often reflect posttranslational changes in protein conformation or adduct formation are still receiving careful attention as a possible cause of senescent changes.[16]

2. The "rate of living" idea of Pearl[17] and his followers emerged from observations that, in general, smaller mammals tended to have a high metabolic rate (adjusted for size) and also tended to die earlier than larger animals. This theory, in its crudest form, suggested that each individual was allowed to burn a given number of calories (per gram of tissue) and then ran out of life span. Systematic studies of metabolic rate and MLP have, however, shown extremely wide ranges in the amount of calories consumed per gram of tissue in different species of mammals and have identified groups of mammals that have both long lives and high rates of energy expenditure (bats) and others (marsupials) with short lives despite low metabolic rates.[18] The rate-of-living and related metabolic theories, though clearly incorrect in detail, have helped to focus attention on questions of antioxidant defenses, discussed more extensively below.

3. The "glucocorticoid" hypothesis[19] proposed that the feedback system by which the hypothalamus regulates secretion of adrenal glucocorticoid hormones might be damaged gradually over the life span by repeated stress, leading, at older ages, to an unregulated increase in glucocorticoids with consequent effects on immune function, tissue repair, and other aspects of homeostasis. Although the matter is still controversial, recent study of normal and CR rats[20] has placed these ideas in doubt. These studies used round-the-clock measurements of corticosterone production to show (a) an increase in free corticosterone in the longer-lived CR group and (b) the lack of an increase in hormone levels in the last third of life. Each of these observations is contrary to the prediction of the glucocorticoid cascade hypothesis. Further work in this area, however, is likely to provide important insights into the effects of aging on neuroendocrine regulation and age-related changes in neuronal vulnerability to glucose deprivation.

4. Szilard,[21] among others, has speculated that aging might result from somatic mutations or other forms of DNA damage. In this formulation, differences in longevity among species might be attributable to variations in the rate at which DNA damage occurs or is repaired. However, there is little experimental evidence in support of this idea.[22,23]

CURRENTLY PLAUSIBLE THEORIES OF AGING

Many theories of aging which are still plausible are of the "master clock" form—i.e., suggestions that mammals have an organ, cell type, or perhaps intracellular molecule that loses function over time and that is coupled to, entrains, and helps to time age-dependent changes in a whole range of secondary organs and cell types. Many research gerontologists subscribe to some variation of this idea. Unfortunately, there is no good evidence about where this timing mechanism might lie or how it might control aging in so many subsidiary areas. Somatic mutations in DNA, cross-linking of extracellular connective tissue fibers, changes in the composition and fluidity of the plasma membrane, changes in mitochondrial function, alterations in immune surveillance, alterations in the rate of protein degradation and synthesis, programmed loss of mitotic capacity in fibroblasts, velocity of DNA repair enzymes, and changes in hypothalamic, pineal, or pituitary cell function have all from time to time been nominated as potential timers for the aging process, often (not surprisingly) by scientists who had dedicated much effort to the study of the system in question. Testable (i.e., refutable) theories that explain convincingly just how a given master clock could control the rate of decline in so many tissues have been much rarer, and none of the specific hypotheses has earned as great a reputation for explanatory power as, say, the germ theory of infection or the DNA theory of heredity. It is not an easy matter to determine which of the many age-dependent alterations in extracellular, intracellular, and multicellular function are primary, (i.e., tightly linked to some fundamental control system) and which change secondarily as a consequence of other age-dependent changes.

Further progress in sorting out these competing claims may require comparisons between animals that age at different rates. If a proposed master clock has any claim to such a title, it ought at a minimum to tick at different rates in animals that age slowly as opposed to those that age rapidly. Thus, tests among rival ideas are likely to depend upon investigations of different species, or comparisons of CR animals and controls fed ad libitum. A third possible approach involves the multisystem comparison of genetically heterogeneous animals, if it can be established that allelic differences within a species lead to alterations in aging rates.

A detailed analysis of each of the plausible theories is beyond the scope of this brief review, but there is space to mention a few of the most provocative suggestions, with citations to allow further study.

1. The "free radical" theory of aging[24] suggests that the highly reactive by-products of oxidative metabolism can react with key cellular constituents—including proteins, DNA, and lipids—to generate long-lived dysfunctional molecules that interfere with cellular function. There is indeed some evidence that such altered macromolecules do accumulate with age, but there is relatively little evidence yet that their accumulation leads to functional decline or that alteration between species explains species-specific aging rates. Several of the lines of argument that originally supported this theory have now been substantially undermined. Thus the proposed relationship between high metabolic rates and lower maximum life span has been shown not to apply as broadly as originally thought and also to be well explained by evolutionary considerations.[18] The suggestion that CR altered longevity via an effect on metabolic rate has been refuted by data showing that there is no effect of caloric restriction on metabolic rate per gram of metabolizing tissue.[25] The claim that antioxidant diets retard aging has been hard to demonstrate reproducibly[26] and now seems likely to represent diminished food intake by rodents forced to consume the unpalatable antioxidant-containing diet. Nonetheless, several lines of evidence suggest that calorie restriction may render rodents less susceptible to the damaging effects of oxidants.[27] Furthermore, transgenic or selectively bred flies that have unusually high levels of antioxidant protection seem to live longer than controls.[28,29] A body of evidence that oxidative modification of cellular proteins is implicated in aging has been summarized by Stadtman.[30] On balance, therefore, it is still possible that alterations in oxidant production and control of oxidant-mediated damage may eventually be shown to account for some portion of interspecies differences in aging rate.

2. The "glycosylation" theory[31] suggests that nonenzymatic glycosylation can create modified forms of proteins and perhaps other macromolecules that accumulate and cause dysfunction in aging animals. Glycosylated forms of human collagen accumulate with age in tendon and skin,[32,33] although other long-lived proteins[34] change very little with age. Evidence that CR rats have lower blood glucose levels and thus might accumulate these advanced glycosylation products more slowly has lent some additional credence to the glycosylation hypothesis.[35] A good deal of additional work is still needed, however, to make even a prima facie case that glycosylated proteins contribute to a wide range of age-related defects, in both stem cells and postmitotic cell types, or to produce evidence that interspecies differences in aging rates are related to changes in glycosylation pathways.

3. The work of Hart and Setlow[36] showed a pattern of interspecies differences in the rate of repair of damage in cultured fibroblasts induced by ultraviolet (UV) light. Fibroblasts from species with long maximum life spans showed a greater rate of DNA repair, with correlations demonstrable across several orders of mammals[36] (see Fig. 1-3*A*). A similar relationship, though with a different slope, was found to describe life span and DNA repair within primates.[37] This work and many related studies have been reviewed.[24] The extent to which such differences reflect alterations in the repair enzymes themselves (or in nucleotide pools), the extent to which similar differences apply to other cell types in vitro or any cell type in vivo, the relevance to age-related changes in tissues that are not exposed to UV light, and the way in which such repair processes might lead to physiological decline will all require further work. Some forms of DNA damage do seem to accumulate with age, but in general they seem to involve large-scale chromosomal rearrangements rather than the smaller-scale changes ordinarily associated with repair of damage induced by UV light.

4. Work in other laboratories has also documented other striking interspecies correlations between MLP and some other measurement, such as the ability to metabolize the carcinogen benzo(a)pyrene[38] and the maximum achievable in vitro passage number for cultured diploid fibroblasts[39] (see Figs. 1-3*B* and 1-3*C*). It is tempting to see in such interspecies correlations the hint of a general theory, in which, for example, differences in DNA repair, anticarcinogen defenses, fibroblast expansion potential, and so on account for differences in longevity among the species studied. In these and similar cases, however, it is difficult to know whether the observed correlation reflects an authentic protective mechanism, evolved by long-lived species to protect them from environmental damage that would otherwise be incompatible with long life spans, or whether the relationship reflects the effects of some other, underlying factor, in the way that the relationship between metabolic rate and life span can be attributed in larger mammals to their common linkage to slow reproductive schedules.[18]

Many other "general" models for aging also still seem worthy of further attention. Age-dependent alterations have been noted in plasma membrane viscosity,[40] protein synthesis and degradation rates,[15] telomere length,[41] mitochondrial function,[42] and other end points. Each such finding can be used to support a plausible causative hypothesis linking the alteration in cell physiology to senescent changes. In most of these cases a comprehensive analysis, involving several distinct cell types over a wide range of species, is still lacking, as are suggestions for distinguishing primary from secondary effects.

AN EVOLUTIONARY MODEL FOR AGING

Evolutionary biologists have, over the last 35 years, produced a convincing picture of the way in which evolutionary pressures lead to the development of aging, a picture that explains how longevity is distrib-

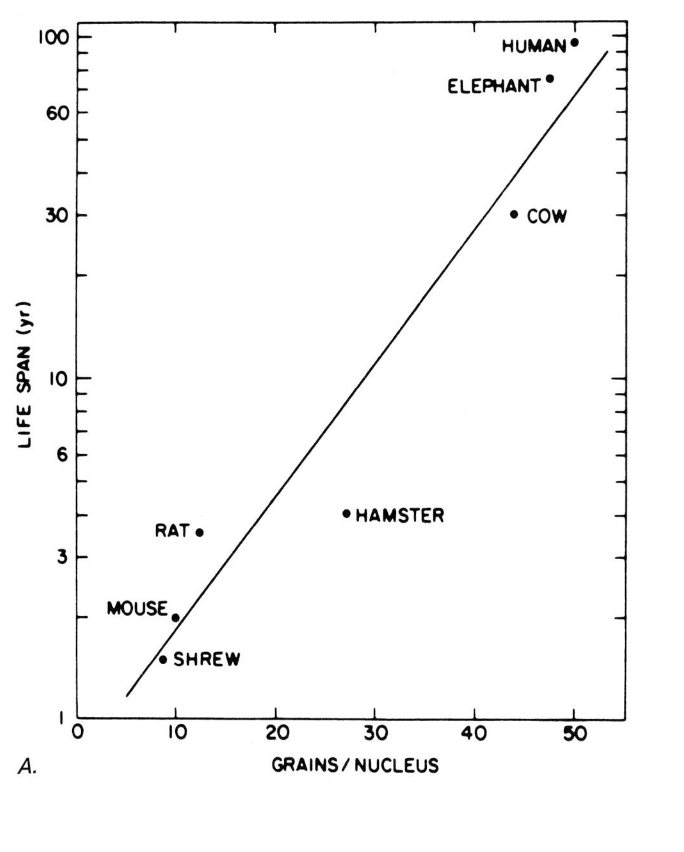

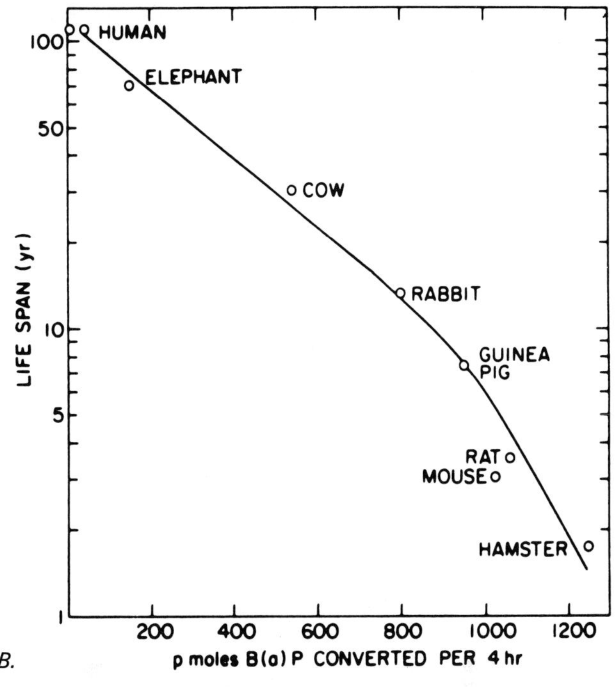

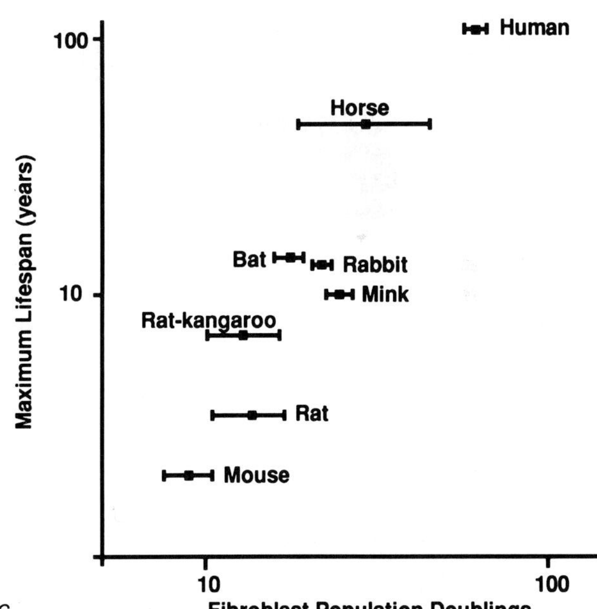

FIGURE 1-3

Correlations between biochemical and physiological measurements and species maximum longevity. *A.* Repair of unscheduled DNA synthesis. *B.* Metabolic conversion of benzo(a)pyrene. *C.* Maximum passage number of fibroblasts in vitro. (*A and B from Handbook of the Biology of Aging, 2d ed, Van Nostrand Reinhold, 1985; C from Finch,[1] with permission.*)

uted across species and makes predictions that can be (and have been) tested in laboratory and "field" situations. The modern evolutionary theory of aging, based on ideas of Medawar and Haldane, fully stated by G. Williams in 1957, and then developed quantitatively by Charlesworth and his colleagues, has been thoroughly reviewed[43]; a less technical summary is also available.[44]

The naive intuition that aging evolves in order to remove old individuals and thus prevent them from competing with their offspring does not have merit: there is no evolutionary advantage in ceasing to produce offspring at an age when others of the same species, lacking the gene(s) that induce senescence, are still reproductively active. Instead, the modern model begins from the observation that individuals would have a substantial probability of dying even in the absence of any effect of aging. In the absence of aging, the mortality rate would be unrelated to chronological age, and the survival curve would resemble the familiar exponential decay curve of radioisotopes. Thus members of a nonaging population are in no sense immortal, even though they do not exhibit the characteristic age-related exponential increase in mortality risk. In a hypothetical nonaging population, in which half the individuals die each year due to predation, starvation, infection, or other ill fortune, the fraction of individuals surviving to the fifth year will be small, and the fraction of those surviving to 15 years will be vanishingly so.

In this nonaging population, there would be very little selection pressure against genes whose harmful effects are "late" relative to ages at which most individuals are likely already to have died. There would, in addition, be strong pressure in favor of genes that were beneficial early in life, even if these genes carried with them harmful effects later in the life span. (Genes of the latter type are said to exhibit "antagonistic pleiotropy.") In a species in which half the individuals die each year, for example, a mutant gene that prevents some degenerative disease that only affects 50-year-old members of the species will have no chance of fixation, since there will not be any 50-year-old member present in the population. On the contrary, genes that increase the fitness of 1-year-olds and 2-year-olds would be highly favored, even if as a side effect they led to lethal diseases in 5- and 10-year-olds, since they have a good chance of "saving" some lucky recipients and little chance of doing any harm by killing a 10-year-old (since 10-year-olds are very rare). Both these pressures favor the evolution of genes whose negative effects are postponed until late in life—i.e., genes that cause aging.

Thus evolutionary considerations predict that nearly all species (or, more precisely, species in which the germline cells can be distinguished from somatic tissues) will evolve an aging phenotype in which the risk of mortality increases with time as a consequence of (1) selective pressures for genes whose beneficial early effects more than compensate for any injurious late life effects and (2) a lack of selection pressure against genes whose effects, though entirely negative, are delayed until very late in life. It is not hard to suggest plausible examples. A gene that leads to calcium deposition, for example, may promote the rapid development of the bones needed to support independent locomotion and yet predispose to arterial calcification in later life. A gene that promotes rapid cell division in embryogenesis may also render an animal vulnerable, in later life, to rapid growth of neoplastic tissue.

There will, of course, also be strong selective pressures for genes that diminish vulnerability in both old and young individuals—for example, by inducing the formation of limbs, eyes, antibodies, and other desiderata. Many of these are likely to produce increases in longevity along with increases in reproductive success. The power of selective pressures on genes that have distinct effects on reproductive fitness in young and old individuals is likely to depend on the details of that species' life history. Animals subjected to high predation pressures as adults, for example, may tend to evolve genomes that favor rapid production of large litters. Diminished selection pressures (e.g., as a consequence of size, fierceness, habitat, or speed), or lifestyles that require intensive protection or education of juveniles by adults, may diminish the pressures for rapid reproduction and increase the reproductive value of the later stages of adult life.

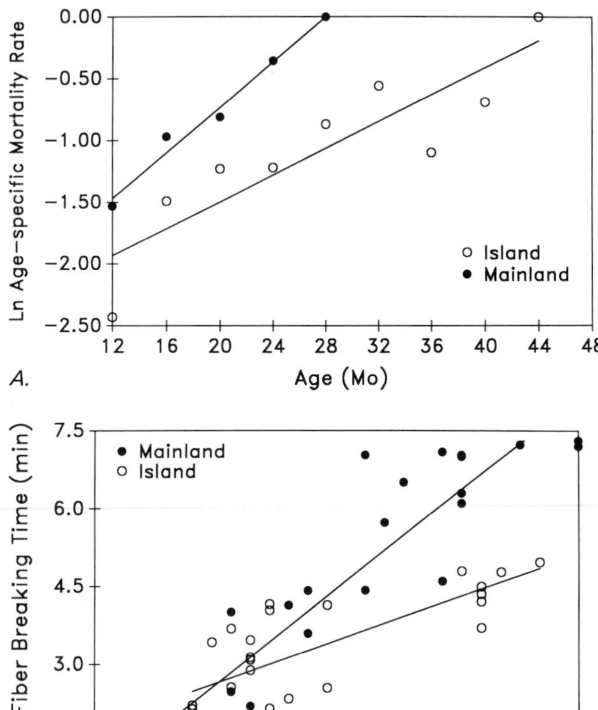

FIGURE 1-4

Differential aging in two closely related species of opossums. *A.* Gompertz analysis shows lower aging rate in island opossums. *B.* Island opossums show a slower rate of collagen cross-linking as measured by tail tendon break time. (*Figure courtesy Dr. S. Austad.*)

Laboratory and fieldwork have illustrated these principles in action. Rose and his co-workers[45] have found evidence for genes in fruit flies that accelerate reproduction (and are hence usually highly favored) but also accelerate the aging process. Artificial selection for flies that could produce eggs late in life created, over many generations, a population that was less "fit," in the Darwinian sense that it produced fewer total offspring than the starting group, but lived longer. Biochemical studies of these flies and their shorter-lived relatives may produce some insights into the aging process, at least as it affects flies.

It is not yet clear if similar breeding schemes will work in mammals; this will depend in part on whether a given species retains allelic differences that could contribute to increased longevity even at the expense of impaired reproductive fitness. However, such polymorphisms are likely to have been retained by natural mammalian populations. Austad[46] has compared survival and reproduction in two groups of closely related opossums, one population of which has lived for 4500 years on an island unconnected to the mainland and thus been subject to greatly diminished lev-

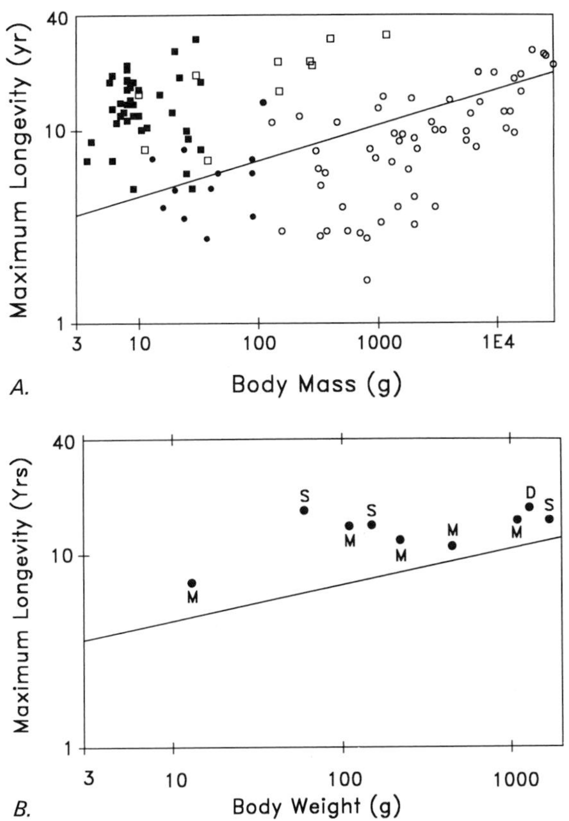

FIGURE 1-5
Relationship of body mass to maximum longevity: comparison across orders of mammals. *A* shows that bats tend to live longer, and marsupials less long, than comparatively sized eutherian mammals. Squares = bats; circles = marsupials; open symbols = homeotherms. *B* shows that among nonflying mammals, those with an aerial (sailing) lifestyle tend to live longer than those without such protective abilities. S = squirrels; M = marsupials; D = dermopteran. (*From Austad and Fischer,*[18] *with permission.*)

els of predation pressure—that is, with less selection for extremely rapid reproduction. In good agreement with the evolutionary ideas, the island population was found to age more slowly than the mainland animals, as measured both by longevity and by alterations in collagen biochemistry (see Fig. 1-4) and to devote a diminished amount of effort to early reproduction. This study suggests that selective pressures can lead fairly quickly to changes in the frequency of genes that alter aging rate in mammals. Studies of the genetic and physiological differences between these two closely related groups of opposums, or between populations of mice selectively bred for differences in reproductive scheduling, could provide important insights into the control of the aging rate.

Analyses of the distribution of longevity among species have also generated support for predictions of the evolutionary model. Among mammals, for example, bats are remarkably long-lived compared to nonflying mammals of similar mass[18]; gliding mammals also tend to have longer maximum life spans than closely related nongliding species (see Fig. 1-5). It is worth noting that this relationship between life span and reduced predation pressure is *not* the trivial result of increased death by predation per se but rather an evolved, intrinsic change induced by differences in selective pressures but demonstrable in predator-free environments. The exceptional longevity of birds and turtles may also reflect, in part, their relative invulnerability to predation.

Biochemists and cell physiologists have been lamentably slow in beginning to exploit these insights from comparative biology. Birds that live five to ten times longer than comparably sized mammals have apparently evolved protective mechanisms (e.g., antioxidant pathways, controls on oncogene expression, etc.) that account for their resistance to age-related pathology and dysfunction and which might well be worth careful molecular analysis.

"HOT TOPICS" IN EXPERIMENTAL GERONTOLOGY

A brief introductory chapter cannot list all of the experimental models that are receiving attention in biogerontology laboratories but can provide only a somewhat arbitrary sample of some of the more interesting areas. Studies aimed specifically at diseases of aging are covered elsewhere in this text, and hence omitted here in favor of work on the biology of the aging process itself.

Nematodes The unusual genetic properties of the soil nematode *Caenorhabditis elegans* have made it a very powerful tool for molecular studies of development. Studies of this worm have provided support for two important theoretical principles. First, Johnson[47] has established by selective breeding that populations of worms contain polymorphic alleles that, in different combinations, can lead to significant increases in MLP; this finding is in good agreement with selective breeding studies in fruit flies discussed earlier in the context of evolutionary ideas about aging. More recently, Johnson[48] and his colleagues have characterized a single-gene mutation, *age-1,* that leads to increased maximum longevity in this species, along with an alteration of the slope of the Gompertz plot (Fig. 1-6). This group is now attempting to map and then to clone and sequence one or more of these age-retarding alleles in the hopes of learning more about the physiological basis for altered aging rate and perhaps even of identifying mammalian homologues with analogous function. The initial studies of *age-1* suggested that the gene might lead to a decline in fertility along with an increased longevity, in accord with the predictions of the evolutionary theory. However, subsequent genetic analysis showed that the change in reproductive success was associated not with *age-1* itself but instead with a second, closely

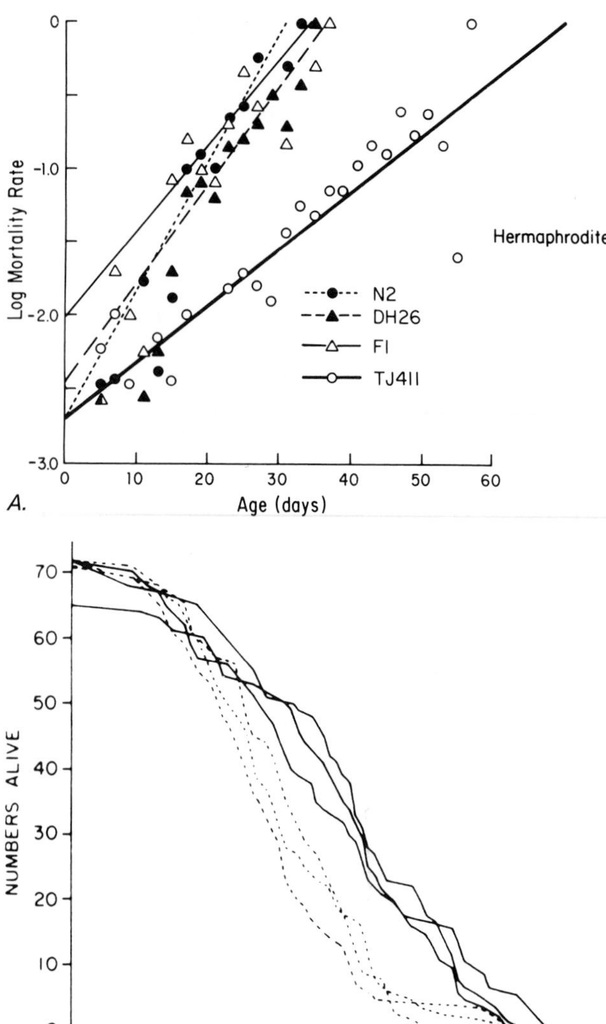

FIGURE 1-6

Production of long-lived invertebrates by mutation or selection. *A* shows the extended longevity of a mutant strain of the nematode *C. elegans* (bold line) in comparison to various controls. *B* shows extended longevity of three lines of fruit flies *D. melanogaster* (solid lines) selected for delayed egg-laying. (*From Finch,[1] with permission.*)

linked gene.[49] Other geneticists are using *C. elegans* to search for mutations that alter neurogenesis, programmed cell death, and other aspects of development; these studies may well identify genes whose mammalian homologues contribute to aging or to age-related degenerative diseases.

Diploid Cell Lines in Vitro The famous observation of Hayflick[50] that human diploid fibroblasts cease to grow in culture after a limited number of population doublings has sparked a line of experimentation that continues to provide important insights into the molecular basis of cell growth, differentiation, and neoplastic transformation. For reasons still undetermined, a population of diploid fibroblasts kept in continuous tissue culture will continue to divide only until approximately 50 "doublings" have occurred, after which the remaining cells can survive, in a healthy but nondividing state, for many months.[51] At any passage level, individual cells display a wide range of replicative potential, with the number of cells able to produce large progeny populations declining to zero at later passages.[52] This "Hayflick model" seemed to a generation of biogerontologists the most attractive approach to the biochemical, cellular, and genetic analysis of the aging process and thus led to a large body of work on the chromosomal, enzymatic, and proliferative capacities of cells at various passage levels. More recent developments—including isolation of genes preferentially expressed by late passage fibroblasts, identification of chromosomes that control the late passage cessation of growth, and demonstrations that late passage cells contain both RNA and proteins that can limit DNA synthesis of early passage cells—have been reviewed by Goldstein.[53] Several other cell types, including endothelial cells, have also been shown to have limited capacities for in vitro expansion and have begun to provide insights into the basis for this growth limitation.[54]

The question of whether this model of "in vitro senescence" actually provides important insights into aging in intact animals is, and deserves to be, controversial. The root of the controversy lies in the objection that "real" aging is not in any obvious way connected to growth cessation, and that the use of the term *senescence* to describe what happens in late passage cell cultures may be simply an unfortunate and misleading choice of words. (A fibroblast culture containing 2^{50} cells, for example, would weigh approximately 10,000 kg.) For example, there is little or no evidence that cells present in, or freshly isolated from, the skin of old people resemble late passage cells and little reason to believe that the developmental changes that convert early to late passage cells in culture are related to changes that convert young adults to old adults. Several authors have argued persuasively that the conversion of proliferating to nonproliferating cells in late passage cultures represents a form of cellular differentiation analogous to that which occurs through fetal and adult life in many different tissues.[55,56] Perhaps the strongest evidence supporting the potential relevance of in vitro growth cessation to aging in intact organisms are the data suggesting that cell lines established from younger donors tend to have a greater in vitro expansion potential than cell lines established from older donors.[57] This trend, however, is considerably less strong, though still statistically significant, when one considers only cell lines derived from young and old adults, eliminating those from neonates and young children. The positive correlation between species longevity and in vitro expansion potential of fibroblasts[39] also supports the idea that the timing of in vitro clonal senescence may reflect some critical interspecies difference in aging rate, perhaps related to the need for greater protection against neoplasia in animals with longer life expectancies.

Senescence in Yeast, Paramecia, and Fungi Many one-celled life forms also exhibit a kind of "senescence" that resembles to some extent the phenomenon of growth cessation in diploid fibroblasts. The budding yeast *Saccharomyces cerevisiae* divides asymmetrically, with large "mother" cells producing a series of smaller "daughter" cells that eventually detach, individually, to initiate clones of their own. Each mother cell, however, has only a limited capacity to produce new daughter cells and exhibits an age-specific decline in the rate at which new daughters are generated. Work of Jazwinski[58] and his colleagues has shown that the number of daughters produced before cessation of reproduction and the rate at which reproductive speed declines are both subject to control by alleles at one or more loci. Identification of these loci will permit a search for homologous mammalian genes whose relevance to the aging process in multicellular animals will then need to be examined.

Similarly, paramecia that are restrained from sexual conjugation proliferate in culture, but only up to a species-specific limit of population doublings.[59] Exchange of genetic material, followed by meiosis, "resets the clock" to permit an additional series of nonmeiotic divisions. Germ cells of all species, from protozoans to porcupines, must be nonsenescent (in the sense in which diploid fibroblasts exhibit clonal senescence): there is no limit (short of species extinction) on their indefinite potential for proliferation. Studies of paramecia, yeast, and other species that possess only a limited capacity for vegetative growth may provide useful insights into the role of processes that reverse epigenetic change in genome function.

A series of studies of senescent change in the filamentous fungus *Podospora anserina*[60] has shown that loss of viability in this species is clearly related to alterations in mitochondrial cytochrome oxidase expression, which are themselves related to overexpression of a free, plasmidlike DNA sequence derived from the cytochrome oxidase gene itself. The extent to which similar alterations in mitochondria occur in mammals and other multicellular eukaryotes is currently under investigation.

Short-Term Tissue Culture: T Lymphocytes A wide range of tissue culture systems have been exploited to study age-sensitive functions of specific mammalian cell types ex vivo. The general goal of these short-term tissue cultures is to provide better access and better control than is possible in intact animals while avoiding to some extent the possible artifacts, including cell selection and adaptation, that complicate interpretation of long-term culture models. From the many useful systems of this kind, two representative examples—the T lymphocyte and the salivary acinar cell—will be used to illustrate the insights that can be obtained.

T-cell immune function declines with age in mice, rats, and humans and probably contributes to the vulnerability of the elderly to infection and cancer. Compared to many systems—brains, bones, and kidneys, for example—T cells are easy to study since they will often do in tissue culture what they do in the intact organism. Work with T cells[61] has shown that the decline in protective T-cell immunity involves both a loss in the ability to produce specific growth and activation factors, including the T-cell growth factor interleukin-2 (IL-2), and also a loss in the ability to express the receptors needed to respond to IL-2. Other functions of T cells—including their capacity to provide help for B-cell antibody production, to generate antiviral and antitumor cytotoxic cells, and to proliferate into expanded clones of memory and effector cells—all decline with age in mice and humans. Work in mice has suggested that the decline in T-cell responses probably involves at least two factors: (1) a shift in the relative proportion of different T-cell subtypes, resulting in relatively fewer naive cells and more memory cells, and (2) alterations in several of the earliest biochemical processes that prepare resting T cells for entry into the cell cycle, including the production of intracellular calcium signals and the activation of protein kinases. The biochemical basis for T-cell dysfunction seems to differ to some extent between humans and mice.[62] It is not yet possible to decide whether these differences are due to technical differences in assay methodology or instead represent important distinctions in the mode of immune senescence in long- and shorter-lived species.

Cell transplantation studies[63] have shown that the defects in T-cell responsiveness are in the main intrinsic to the T cells themselves: T cells from old mice continue to perform poorly even after transplantation into young recipients, while T cells from young donors continue to function well even after transplant into old hosts. The immune status of old animals can be restored for a significant though not indefinite period by administration of young bone marrow together with engraftment of a neonatal thymus gland.[64] Old bone marrow also works in such a reconstitution model, but somewhat less well than marrow from young donors under some conditions.[65,66]

It is plausible to assume that the diminished proportion of newly generated naive T cells reflects a loss of function of the involuted thymus, but definitive evidence for this is lacking, and changes in the self-renewal capacity of the peripheral T-cell pool[67] may also play a significant role. Further work in this system is likely to provide new insights into how shifts in cellular subpopulations and changes in gene activation pathways contribute to decline in a key protective system in the elderly.

Salivary Acinar Cells in Culture The work of Roth and his colleagues[68] has provided a good deal of insight into age-associated changes in a second ex vivo model: dissociated clusters of salivary gland acinar cells from rats. Diminished secretory responses to physiological agonists have been traced to alterations in the ability to produce an internal calcium signal; these have, in turn, been attributed to changes in the pathway by which inositol phosphates release calcium from intracellular stores. Roth[69] has compiled a list of over 20 cell types in which aging seems to lead to an alteration in the generation of calcium signals and in which there is some evidence that pharmacological manipulation of calcium transport, usually by means of a calcium ionophore, can ameliorate the functional defect in vitro. It remains to be seen if some or all of these changes reflect similar underlying mechanisms, but the strategy of seeking common biochemical factors to explain age-related pathology in disparate organ systems seems likely to provide important insights into both basic aging processes and the pathogenesis of degenerative diseases.

Neuroendocrine Control of Ovarian Function Finch and his colleagues[70] have studied the basis for midlife failure of female reproductive function in mice. In brief, they have found that the timing of ovarian failure depends not simply on intrinsic alterations in ovarian function per se but instead on an ovary-driven effect on hypothalamic function. Transplantation studies were used to show that young ovaries continued to cycle after transplantation into young but not into old recipients. Old recipients who had been ovariectomized while young—and who had therefore not undergone the same number of estrous cycles as similarly aged, nonoperated controls—were found, surprisingly, to be able to support the estrous function of transplanted ovaries. These data, and other follow-up studies, were interpreted as evidence for a feedback circuit in which hypothalamic structures were able to support only a limited number of ovarian cycles. The hypothalamus, in a sense, "counts" the number of completed cycles—a count that is interrupted by ovariectomy but which then resumes upon transplantation. In principle, similar feedback interactions between components of the central nervous system and other peripheral tissues might eventually be shown to regulate the pace of senescent change. There are numerous examples of age-dependent alterations in hormone levels and hormone responsiveness[71] and evidence that hormone supplementation can in some cases restore age-associated losses in function of muscle[72] or immune function,[73] among others. As yet, however, there is no comprehensive, detailed model to explain these observations, let alone to account for interspecies differences in aging rate.

Differential Gene Expression While it seems plausible to suppose that differences in gene expression may account for at least some of the differences between young and old adults, experiments to flesh out this hypothesis have in general proven disappointing. RNA subtraction and differential screening approaches, designed to search for mRNA species that are present in old but not in young tissues (or vice versa), have failed to identify new genes plausibly connected to basic aging processes. For example, one study of 50,000 RNA-bearing phage clones yielded only five candidate genes,[74] of which four were found to represent well-known products: a urinary protein, an actin gene, an allele of the H-2 histocompatibility locus, and the enzyme creatine kinase. An analogous study produced similarly disappointing results.[75] In retrospect, this frustration seems attributable to several factors, including the cellular complexity of the tissues analyzed and the likelihood that products of key controlling genes, if there are any, may be active at very low abundance, and then only in very few cell types. A survey of *Drosophila* proteins, using two-dimensional electrophoresis, found no evidence for any qualitative differences between young and old flies in over 500 proteins evaluated,[76] while a more quantitative analysis of a subset of 100 proteins found that only 10 differed by as much as twofold between young and old flies. It seems likely that productive work will require methods that consider individual cell types (rather than whole organisms or complex tissues) and do so at a level of resolution that can identify changes in expression of genes expressed at very low levels. Even so, the effects of disease and of compensatory interactions among different cell types and organ systems may render data of this kind exceptionally hard to interpret.

Nonetheless, two approaches to differential gene expression have already begun to yield provocative initial findings. In the first of these, detailed analyses of immunoglobulin gene expression by B lymphocytes have shown two kinds of age-dependent change: (1) the preferential use by aged B cells, in response to antigens of *Pneumococcus*, of some antibody variable region genes that are not utilized by B cells of young donors,[77] and (2) changes with age in the patterns of D-region gene segments used for antibody synthesis.[78] It remains to be seen to what extent these and similar alterations might contribute to altered immune responses in old age.

A second set of studies has examined the effects of aging on the status of X-chromosome genes stochastically inactivated in early embryonic life in females. There are now two reports[79,80] demonstrating a progressive reactivation, in middle and late life, of X-linked genes on the inactive chromosome. Two other reports, however,[81,82] in analyses of different genetic loci, have been unable to document such an effect. A systematic examination of gene reactivation from sex chromosomes and autosomes will be needed to assess the generality and implications of these initial, provocative reports.

Telomere Shortening Mammalian chromosomes have specialized structures called telomeres at the ends of each chromosomal arm, stretches of noncoding DNA that permit RNA-primed replication of chromosomal 5′ ends and which are thought to prevent certain forms of chromosomal aberration. In humans, telomere length in blood cells seems to diminish in proportion to age.[41] Germ cells and fetal tissues were found to have longer telomeres than somatic tissues from adults, while colon tumor cells were found to have shorter telomeres than normal colonic mucosa. These observations suggest that there may be an age-related decline in telomere length, at least in proliferative tissues, which could contribute to oncogenesis by generating chromosomes unprotected by the telomere structure. Interestingly, telomere length is also reported to decline as a function of culture passage level in diploid fibroblasts.[83] Studies of telomere length in mice, however, have so far produced a more confusing picture, with no obvious relationships among telomere length, age, and species-specific longevity. Additional work will be needed to extend and clarify the importance of this line of research.

Progeroid Diseases The fancied resemblance of two very rare human diseases, Hutchinson-Guilford syndrome (progeria) and Werner's syndrome, has brought these illnesses to both popular and medical attention as possible examples of premature or accelerated aging. More critical analyses[84,85] have noted both similarities and differences between these syndromes and the normal aging process. Modern work has classified these and many other human maladies (including most notably Down's trisomy 21) as "segmental" progeroid syndromes that may well provide useful insights into the pathogenesis of some of the important changes in tissue structure and physiological function that accompany normal aging. Demonstrations that both Werner's and Hutchinson-Guilford patients exhibit abnormal patterns of hyaluronidate metabolism,[84] for example, may help to focus attention on this aspect of connective tissue aging and its role in degenerative cardiovascular diseases, while studies of neuropathology in Down's syndrome patients may shed light on similar changes in Alzheimer's disease.[86]

Genetic Control of Aging Rate The offspring of long-lived parents tend themselves to have longer than average life spans. However, it is very difficult to discriminate, in the available human data sets, the effects of inherited early- and midlife diseases from postulated genetic effects on the aging rate itself. Perhaps the best previous study in mammals[87] utilized sets of "recombinant inbred" mice, in which groups of approximately 20 genetically identical animals in each of 20 related inbred strains were followed until natural death. Comparison of the mortality patterns of each strain to its known genetic composition showed that at least 16 percent, and perhaps as many as 44 percent, of the individual polymorphic alleles had a detectable effect on longevity. In a study of this kind, each of the detectable allelic differences actually serves as a marker for large regions of the genome, including perhaps as many as 1000 individual genes, an unknown proportion of which have effects on life span. This analysis also showed that only 29 percent of the variability among these mice in life expectancy could be explained by genetic factors, even in this highly regulated laboratory environment. Environmental variation in a natural setting might be expected to influence longevity to an even greater degree. This important study helps to set in perspective reports (for example, Ref. 88) that demonstrate an effect on life span of single polymorphic loci: the work of Gelman et al.[87] suggest that as many as 44 percent of randomly chosen marker loci might be expected to show a similar correlation with life span. Nonetheless, this study of recombinant inbred mouse lines has a serious flaw in that the statistical test used to detect interstrain variations, which is sensitive to any change in the shape or position of the mortality curve, could well be influenced by midlife illness and thus does not provide reliable information about MLP. Indeed, generation of useful data on MLP of a large number of genetically disparate strains is likely to require sample sizes well beyond current funding horizons.

A related and perhaps more promising approach is illustrated by the studies of Covelli et al.[89] This group made use of noninbred lines of mice, originally bred selectively for high and low early-life immune responsiveness. Unexpectedly, lines of mice bred for low immune responses have been found to have substantially lower life expectancy than lines of mice bred for high levels of immunity. Backcross analysis has shown that as few as three to nine genetic loci are likely to be responsible for the interline differences in immunity. Life table analysis has shown that the genetic differences affect survival at both early and late time intervals along the life span, including estimates of MLP, while necropsy data show that members of both the short- and long-lived lines exhibit a wide range of pathologies at death, refuting the idea that the selective breeding regimen has simply produced in the "low immunity" lines a tendency to early development of a specific illness. Selection based on either T-cell-mediated or humoral immunity has been found to be equally efficacious in producing lines of differing longevity.[90] This set of studies, though provocative, has serious flaws, most notably the lack of any "control" strain bred without selection, the short life expectancy of the low-immunity strains, and the lack of reported information about husbandry standards (including prevalence of infectious illness). Nonetheless, this work suggests that it may be possible to generate closely related lines of rodents that differ in a limited number of genes with major effects on aging. A field study of opossums,[46] discussed above, is also consistent with the hypothesis that shifts at a relatively small number of genetic loci may have substantial effects on aging in mammals.

Biomarkers for Aging The goal of biomarker research is to provide an innocuous assay—or more likely a set of such assays—that can detect differences in the rate of aging among individual members of the same species. The basic challenge is to find ways to measure the rate of a process—aging—which cannot itself be directly measured and whose effects are on end points (skin elasticity, T-cell subsets, muscle power, hormone levels) that themselves can be influenced by many causes besides aging.

The discovery of a useful set of biomarkers for rodents or humans would have important implications, both practical and theoretical. As a practical matter, a battery of biomarkers would greatly facilitate studies of interventions (drug treatments, selective breeding, etc.) hypothesized, like caloric restriction, to alter the aging rate. At present the only acceptable test of such a maneuver is to carry out a life table analysis on a suitably large group of subjects to see if the intervention alters MLP. Such studies are extremely expensive in rodents and virtually impossible in humans. One objective of biomarker research is to overcome this obstacle to aging research by allowing investigators to measure the rate of aging in individuals over periods substantially shorter than the life span. In addition, the age at death is itself an exceptionally poor (though unfortunately the best available) index of the aging rate. A set of biomarkers, once validated by comparison to life table results, would allow experimentalists to test potential interventions at far greater speed and far lower expense and help to free them of relying on age at death as the sole estimator of the underlying aging rate.

The theoretical implications of biomarker research are of perhaps equal importance. The fundamental assumptions behind the idea that biomarkers may exist are twofold: (1) that the signs of aging result either from a single primary biological process or else from several parallel processes that are tightly linked in rate, and (2) that individual members of a species differ—because of differences in genotype, environmental influences, or both—in the rate at which the process operates. It is not yet clear, for example, if individuals who exhibit more rapid than average loss of immune function in adult life also tend to be those who lose muscle function, exhibit declines in hormone levels, generate cross-linked collagen, and have a greater risk of death from a wide range of causes. The development of a robust set of biomarkers, well correlated with physiological senescence and mortality risk across a range of genotypes, environments, and perhaps even species, would provide strong support for the underlying postulate that the many signs of aging are uniformly coupled, with varying degrees of elasticity, to an underlying process that proceeds at a species-specific rate.

ACKNOWLEDGMENTS

Preparation of this review was supported by grants provided by the National Institute on Aging (AG08808, AG03978, and AG09801). I am grateful to Dr. Thomas Johnson and Dr. David Harrison for their comments on an early draft of the manuscript.

REFERENCES

1. Finch CE: *Longevity, Senescence, and the Genome.* Chicago, University of Chicago Press, 1990.
2. Comfort A: *The Biology of Senescence,* 3d ed. New York, Elsevier North Holland, 1979.
3. Schneider EL, Rowe RW: *Handbook of the Biology of Aging,* 3d ed. San Diego, Academic Press, 1990.
4. Finch CE, Schneider EL: *Handbook of the Biology of Aging,* 2d ed. New York, Van Nostrand Reinhold, 1985.
5. Finch CE, Hayflick L: *Handbook of the Biology of Aging.* New York, Van Nostrand Reinhold, 1977.
6. Diamond JM: Big-bang reproduction and ageing in male marsupial mice (news). *Nature* 298:115, 1982.
7. Finch CE, Pike MC, Witten M: Slow mortality rate accelerations during aging in some animals approximate that of humans. *Science* 249:902, 1990.
8. McCay CM, Crowell MF, Maynard LA: The effect of retarded growth upon the life span and upon ultimate body size. *J Nutr* 10:63, 1935.
9. Masoro EJ: Food restriction in rodents: An evaluation of its role in the study of aging. *J Gerontol* 43:B59, 1988.
10. Weindruch R, Walford RL: *The Retardation of Aging and Disease by Dietary Restriction.* Springfield, IL, Charles C Thomas, 1988.
11. Weindruch R, Walford RL: Dietary restriction in mice beginning at 1 year of age: Effect on life span and spontaneous cancer incidence. *Science* 215:1415, 1982.
12. Merry BJ, Holehan AM: Onset of puberty and duration of fertility in rats fed a restricted diet. *J Reprod Fertil* 57:253, 1979.
13. Cutler RG, Davis BJ, Ingram DK, Roth GS: Plasma concentrations of glucose, insulin, and percent glycosylated hemoglobin are unaltered by food restriction in rhesus and squirrel monkeys. *J Gerontol Biol Sci* 47:B9, 1992.
14. Orgel LE: The maintenance of the accuracy of protein synthesis and its relevance to aging. *Proc Natl Acad Sci USA* 49:517, 1963.
15. Reff ME: RNA and protein metabolism, in Finch CE, Schneider EL (eds): *Handbook of the Biology of Aging.* New York, Van Nostrand Reinhold, 1985, p 225.
16. Gafni A: Altered protein metabolism in aging. *Annu Rev Gerontol Geriatr* 10:117, 1990.
17. Pearl R: *The Rate of Living.* London, England, University of London Press, 1928.
18. Austad SN, Fischer KE: Mammalian aging, metabolism, and ecology: Evidence from the bats and marsupials. *J Gerontol Biol Sci* 46:B47, 1991.
19. Sapolsky R, Krey L, McEwan B: The neuroendocrinology of stress and aging: The glucocorticoid cascade hypothesis. *Endocr Rev* 7:284, 1986.
20. Sabatino F, Masoro EJ, McMahan CA, Kuhn RW: Assessment of the role of the glucocorticoid system in aging processes and in the action of food restriction. *J Gerontol Biol Sci* 46:B171, 1991.
21. Szilard L: On the nature of the aging process. *Proc Natl Acad Sci USA* 45:30, 1959.
22. Tice RR, Setlow RB: DNA repair and replication in aging organisms and cells, in Finch CE, Schneider EL (eds): *Handbook of the Biology of Aging.* New York, Van Nostrand Reinhold, 1985, p 173.
23. Clark AM, Rubin MA: The modification by x-irradiation of the life span of haploids and diploids of the wasp, *Habrobracon* sp. *Rad Res* 15:244, 1961.
24. Harmon D: Aging: A theory based on free radical and radiation chemistry. *J Gerontol* 11:298, 1956.

25. McCarter R, Masoro EJ, Yu BP: Does food restriction retard aging by reducing the metabolic rate? *Am J Physiol* 248:E488, 1985.
26. Balin AK: Testing the free radical theory of aging, in Adelman RC, Roth GS (eds): *Testing the Theories of Aging*. Boca Raton, FL, CRC Press, 1983, p 137.
27. Yu BP, Lee DW, Marler CG, Choi JH: Mechanism of food restriction: Protection of cellular homeostasis. *Proc Soc Exp Biol Med* 193:13, 1990.
28. Arking R, Buck S, Berrios A, et al: Elevated paraquat resistance can be used as a bioassay for longevity in a genetically based long-lived strain of *Drosophila. Dev Genet* 12:362, 1991.
29. Reveillaud I, Niedzwiecki A, Bensch KG, Fleming JE: Expression of bovine superoxide dismutase in *Drosophila melanogaster* augments resistance of oxidative stress. *Mol Cell Biol* 11:632, 1991.
30. Stadtman ER: Protein oxidation and aging. *Science* 257:1220, 1992.
31. Monnier VM: Nonenzymatic glycosylation, the Maillard reaction and the aging process. *J Gerontol* 45:B105, 1990.
32. Sell DR, Monnier VM: End-stage renal disease and diabetes catalyze the formation of a pentose-derived cross-link from aging human collagen. *J Clin Invest* 85:380, 1990.
33. Schnider SL, Kohn RR: Glucosylation of human collagen in aging and diabetes mellitus. *J Clin Invest* 66:1179, 1980.
34. Patrick JS, Thorpe SR, Baynes JW: Nonenzymatic glycosylation of protein does not increase with age in normal human lenses. *J Gerontol* 45:B18, 1990.
35. Masoro EJ, McCarter RJM, Katz MS, McMahan CA: Dietary restriction alters characteristics of glucose fuel use. *J Gerontol Biol Sci* 47:1992.
36. Hart RW, Setlow RB: Correlation between deoxyribonucleic acid excision repair and lifespan in a number of mammalian species. *Proc Natl Acad Sci USA* 71:2169, 1974.
37. Hart RW, Daniel FB: Genetic stability in vitro and in vivo. *Adv Pathobiol* 7:123, 1980.
38. Moore CJ, Schwartz AG: Inverse correlation between species lifespan and capacity of cultured fibroblasts to convert benzo(a)pyrene to water-soluble metabolites. *Exp Cell Res* 116:359, 1978.
39. Rohme D: Evidence for a relationship between longevity of mammalian species and life-spans of normal fibroblasts in vitro and erythrocytes in vivo. *Proc Natl Acad Sci USA* 78:5009, 1981.
40. Rivnay B, Bergman S, Shinitzky M, Globerson A: Correlations between membrane viscosity, serum cholesterol, lymphocyte activation and aging in man. *Mech Ageing Dev* 12:119, 1980.
41. Hastie ND, Dempster M, Dunlop MG, et al: Telomere reduction in human colorectal carcinoma and with ageing. *Nature* 346:866, 1990.
42. Wallace DC: Mitochondrial genetics: A paradigm for aging and degenerative diseases? *Science* 256:628, 1992.
43. Rose MR: *Evolutionary Biology of Aging*. New York, Oxford University Press, 1991.
44. Kirkwood TBL: Comparative and evolutionary aspects of longevity, in Finch CE, Schneider EL (eds): *Handbook of the Biology of Aging*. New York, Van Nostrand Reinhold, 1985, p 27.
45. Hutchinson EW, Shaw AJ, Rose MR: Quantitative genetics of postponed aging in *Drosophila melanogaster:* II. Analysis of selected lines. *Genetics* 127:729, 1991.
46. Austad SN: Retarded aging rate in an insular population of opossums. *J Zool,* in press, 1993.
47. Johnson TE: Aging can be genetically dissected into component processes using long-lived lines of *Caenorhabditis elegans. Proc Natl Acad Sci USA* 84:3777, 1987.
48. Johnson TE: Increased life-span of *age-1* mutants in *Caenorhabditis elegans* and lower Gompertz rate of aging. *Science* 249:908, 1990.
49. Johnson TE, Friedman DB, Foltz N, et al: Genetic variants and mutations of *Caenorhabditis elegans* provide tools for dissecting the aging process, in Harrison DE (ed): *Genetic Effects on Aging II*. Caldwell, NJ, Telford Press, 1990, p 101.
50. Hayflick L, Moorhead PS: The serial cultivation of human diploid cell strains. *Exp Cell Res* 25:585, 1961.
51. Matsumura T, Zerrudo Z, Hayflick L: Senescent human diploid cells in culture: Survival, DNA synthesis and morphology. *J Gerontol* 34:328, 1979.
52. Smith JR, Pereira-Smith OM, Schneider EL: Colony size distributions as a measure of in vivo and in vitro aging. *Proc Natl Acad Sci USA* 75:1353, 1978.
53. Goldstein S: Replicative senescence: The human fibroblast comes of age. *Science* 249:1129, 1990.
54. Maier JA, Voulalas P, Roeder D, Maciag T: Extension of the life-span of human endothelial cells by an interleukin-1 alpha antisense oligomer. *Science* 249:1570, 1990.
55. Seshadri T, Campisi J: Repression of c-fos transcription and an altered genetic program in senescent human fibroblasts. *Science* 247:205, 1990.
56. Beyreuther K, Rodemann HP, Hommel R, et al: Human skin fibroblasts in vitro differentiate along a terminal cell lineage. *Proc Natl Acad Sci USA* 85:5112, 1988.
57. Martin GM, Sprague CA, Epstein CJ: Replicative lifespan of cultivated human cells. Effects of donor's age, tissue, and genotype. *Lab Invest* 23:86, 1970.
58. Jazwinski SM: An experimental system for the molecular analysis of the aging process: The budding yeast *Saccharomyces cerevisiae. J Gerontol* 45:B68, 1990.
59. Smith-Sonneborn J: Aging in unicellular organisms, in Finch CE, Schneider EL (eds): *Handbook of the Biology of Aging*. New York, Van Nostrand Reinhold, 1985, p 79.
60. Tudzynski P, Esser K: Chromosomal and extrachromosomal control of senescence in the ascomycete *Podospora anserina. Mol Gen Genet* 173:71, 1979.
61. Miller RA: Aging and immune function. *Int Rev Cytol* 124:187, 1991.
62. Miller RA: Accumulation of hyporesponsive, calcium extruding memory T cells as a key feature of age-dependent immune dysfunction. *Clin Immunol Immunopathol* 58:305, 1991.
63. Harrison DE: Cell and tissue transplantation: A means of studying the aging process, in Finch CE, Schneider EL (eds): *Handbook of the Biology of Aging*. New York, Van Nostrand Reinhold, 1985, p 322.
64. Hirokawa K, Utsuyama M: The effect of sequential multiple grafting of syngeneic newborn thymus on the immune functions and life expectancy of aging mice. *Mech Ageing Dev* 28:111, 1984.
65. Averill LE, Wolf NS: The decline in murine splenic

PHA and LPS responsiveness with age is primarily due to an intrinsic mechanism. *J Immunol* 134:3859, 1985.
66. Eren R, Zharhary D, Abel L, Globerson A: Age-related changes in the capacity of bone marrow cells to differentiate in thymic organ cultures. *Cell Immunol* 112:449, 1988.
67. Rocha BB: Population kinetics of precursors of IL 2-producing peripheral T lymphocytes: Evidence for short life expectancy, continuous renewal, and post-thymic expansion. *J Immunol* 139:365, 1987.
68. Ambudkar IS, Kuyatt BL, Roth GS, Baum BJ: Modification of ATP-dependent Ca^{2+} transport in rat parotid basolateral membranes during aging. *Mech Ageing Dev* 43:45, 1988.
69. Roth GS: Mechanisms of altered hormone-neurotransmitter action during aging: From receptors to calcium mobilization. *Annu Rev Gerontol Geriatr* 10:132, 1991.
70. Finch CE, Felicio LS, Mobbs CV, Nelson JF: Ovarian and steroidal influences on neuroendocrine aging processes in female rodents. *Endocr Rev* 5:467, 1984.
71. Minaker KL, Meneilly GS, Rowe JW: Endocrine systems, in Finch CE, Schneider EL (eds): *Handbook of the Biology of Aging.* New York, Van Nostrand Reinhold, 1985, p 433.
72. Rudman D, Feller AG, Nagraj HS, et al: Effects of human growth hormone in men over 60 years old. *N Engl J Med* 323:1, 1990.
73. Daynes RA, Araneo BA: Prevention and reversal of some age-associated changes in immunologic responses by supplemental dehydroepiandrosterone sulfate therapy. *Aging: Immunol Infect Dis* 3:135, 1992.
74. Friedman V, Wagner J, Danner DB: Isolation and identification of aging-related cDNAs in the mouse. *Mech Ageing Dev* 52:27, 1990.
75. Sierra F, Fey GH, Guigoz Y: T-kininogen gene expression is induced during aging. *Mol Cell Biol* 9:5610, 1989.
76. Fleming JE, Quattrocki E, Latter G, et al: Age-dependent changes in proteins of *Drosophila melanogaster. Science* 231:1157, 1986.
77. Riley SC, Froscher BG, Linton PJ, et al: Altered V_h gene segment utilization in the response to phosphorylcholine of aged mice. *J Immunol* 143:3798, 1989.
78. Bangs LA, Sanz IE, Teale JM: Comparison of D, J_h, and junctional diversity in the fetal, adult, and aged B cell repertoires. *J Immunol* 146:1996, 1991.
79. Wareham KA, Lyon MF, Glenister PH, Williams ED: Age related reactivation of an X-linked gene. *Nature* 327:725, 1987.
80. Cattanach BM: Position effect variegation in the mouse. *Genet Res* 23:291, 1974.
81. Migeon BR et al: Effect of aging on reactivation of the human X-linked HPRT locus. *Nature* 335:93, 1988.
82. Tsukada M et al: Stable lyonization of X-linked pgk-1 gene during aging in normal tissues and tumors of mice carrying Searle's translocation. *J Gerontol Biol Sci* 46:B213, 1991.
83. Harley CB, Futcher AB, Greider CW: Telomeres shorten during ageing of human fibroblasts. *Nature* 345:458, 1990.
84. Brown WT: Genetic diseases of premature aging as models of senescence. *Annu Rev Gerontol Geriatr* 10:23, 1991.
85. Martin GM: Genetic syndromes in man with potential relevance to the pathobiology of aging, in Bergsma D, Harrison DE (eds): *Genetic Effects on Aging.* New York, Liss, 1978, p 5.
86. Mann DM: The pathological association between Down syndrome and Alzheimer disease. *Mech Ageing Dev* 43:99, 1988.
87. Gelman R, Watson A, Bronson R, Yunis E: Murine chromosomal regions correlated with longevity. *Genetics* 118:693, 1988.
88. Smith GS, Walford RL: Influence of the main histocompatibility complex on aging in mice. *Nature* 270:727, 1977.
89. Covelli V, Mouton D, Di Majo V, et al: Inheritance of immune responsiveness, life span, and disease incidence in interline crosses of mice selected for high or low multispecific antibody production. *J Immunol* 142:1224, 1989.
90. Covelli V, De Majo V, Bassani B, et al: Spontaneous lymphomas in mice genetically selected for high or low phytohemagglutinin responsiveness. *J Natl Cancer Inst* 75:1083, 1985.

Chapter 2

GENETICS OF HUMAN DISEASE, LONGEVITY, AND AGING

George M. Martin and Mitchell S. Turker

The physician may be called upon to respond to a variety of questions concerning the relationships between human genetics and the pathobiology of aging. While some questions are of purely theoretical interest, others have important implications for patient management. In this review, we shall deal with examples of both categories of questions. We shall begin with an overview of some basic issues regarding genetics and aging, several of which are dealt with, from different points of view, in other chapters. This overview will lead naturally into a discussion of the human progeroid syndromes.

Although most of this chapter is concerned with the effects of aging on human *somatic cells,* we shall conclude with a brief consideration of the clinically and biologically important topic of the effects of parental age upon reproductive performance, in which the focus is upon qualitative aspects of the *germ line.*

A major thesis of this chapter is that, to a considerable extent, future progress in geriatric medicine is likely to be coupled to progress in basic and medical genetics. A few basic terms of genetics have been defined in the body of the text. For those seeking a more comprehensive glossary, we suggest the work of King and Stansfield.[1]

SOME BASIC CONSIDERATIONS OF GENETICS AND AGING

The Role of Gene Action in Explaining Interspecific and Intraspecific Variations in Life Span

When a new species evolves, an array of phenotypic variations appears involving intrinsic or constitutional properties including qualitative and quantitative alterations in development, maturational structure and function, and the pattern of aging. A given species thus can be characterized by a typical range of life spans. Among mammalian species, these vary by at least a factor of 30, strong evidence of the importance of the constitutional genotype in modulating life span potential. It is a misconception, however, to state that genes *program* the life span, at least for iteroparous organisms (those, like mammals, that have multiple episodes of reproduction). There is no evidence that certain sets of genes are turned on or turned off (as they are during development) in order to initiate a program of aging. On the other hand, it is clear that genes can *modulate* rates of aging, probably, in part, by varying efficiencies of the metabolic machineries that prevent, repair, or compensate for a wide range of macromolecular and cellular injuries. According to current evolutionary theory,[2] these variations can be viewed as *by-products* or *epiphenomena* of gene action concerned with earlier life events. Recent research with exceptionally large populations of insects have, in fact, challenged the conventional view that there is a specific limit to the life span[3,4] and raise the question that the maximum potential life span of human beings may be substantially greater than the current figure of about 115 to 120 years. While it is possible that—given increasing population sizes, improvements in disease prevention and management, and increasing genetic and environmental diversity—physicians will be seeing more supracentenarians, it would take many centuries of natural or artificial selection to achieve life spans approaching the wild predictions of the popular press.

Heritability of Longevity

When one considers the complex interactions of each person's set of genes involved in the determination of life span, combined with multiple differences in environmental factors influencing their expression, it is clear why attempts to examine the heritability of longevity in humans are tenuous at best. Even studies with inbred strains of research mice, whose environment and genetic variability can be reasonably controlled, are confounded by complex survival and disease patterns. How then are we to assess the impact of a single gene, or a given set of genes, on longevity of humans?

A logical approach is to examine aging in monozygotic twins, since their genetic constitutions, with the exception of those genes whose final structures are developmentally regulated (e.g., immunoglobin genes), are identical. A comparison of aging in such twin pairs with dizygotic twin pairs indicated that the intrapair difference in the age of death was smaller for the monozygotic twins than for the dizygotic twins (14.5 versus 18.6 years). Perhaps the more salient point, however, is the large mean difference in the age of death in both cases,[5,6] suggesting a role for environmental factors. Classic examples of environmental factors influencing aspects of aging in humans include alcohol,[7] smoking,[8] and exposure to sun.[9] In rodents, caloric restriction is known to increase longevity and to delay the onset of age-related diseases.[10] A novel observation of the influence of environment on mortality was that male prisoners in French jails had lower mortality rates for all types of natural deaths than males in the general French population.[11]

A second approach, used at times in this chapter, is to examine in different kindreds the expression of a single mutant allele (an *allele* is simply an alternative form of a gene) associated with an age-related onset of clinical symptoms. This approach has allowed us to conclude that a number of family-specific traits interact with the mutant allele to influence the age of disease onset.

A third approach is to search for "private markers"[12] in persons with unusual longevities, such as nonagenerians and centenarians. In a study of such populations, a positive correlation for HLA-DR1 and a negative correlation for HLA-DRw9 was found.[13] The presence of HLA-DRw9 has been positively correlated with the presence of autoimmune antibodies. The appearance of these antibodies increases as a function of age.[14] A genetic study of purported high-longevity populations in the Georgian Republic of the Soviet Union failed to find any significant deviation in the observed genotypic frequencies from those predicted by the Hardy-Weinberg equation for the red-cell enzyme markers adenylate kinase, esterase D, phosphoglucomutase I, acid phosphatase, 6-phosphogluconate dehydrogenase, glutamate pyruvate transaminase, phosphoglycolate phosphatase, phosphohexose isomerase, and the serum proteins haptoglobin, Gc-component, and transferrin.[15] (The Hardy-Weinberg expression describes the genotypic equilibrium produced by a static gene pool. In a large, randomly mating population, both the gene frequencies and the genotype frequencies are constant from generation to generation in the absence of mutations, migration, or selection.)

A fourth approach is to search for genetic polymorphisms that may be present in families with unusual susceptibility to some age-related alteration. One potential example is genetic variation for the alpha$_1$-antitrypsin locus. This locus codes for a glycoprotein that inhibits neutrophil elastase, a proteolytic enzyme capable of degrading multiple components of connective tissue. Approximately 35 different genetic variants have been described, with the normal M type being found at a gene frequency of 0.9. Other variants include S and Z, with gene frequencies of 0.02 to 0.04 and 0.01 to 0.02, respectively. MZ and SZ heterozygotes are prone to develop chronic obstructive pulmonary disease as they age,[12] with a variable age of onset; clinically evident emphysema is commonly not observable until after age 50.[16,17] In the latter study, the oldest apparent heterozygote studied who exhibited pulmonary dysfunction was a 70-year-old male with a positive smoking history.

A final approach attempts to determine the heritability of longevity in nonmammalian model systems.[18] For example, an excellent series of experiments has been carried out with the nematode *Caenorhabditis elegans* in which the component of life span variation due to genetic rather than environmental factors was estimated to be as high as 50 percent and as low as 20 percent. A single mutant locus has been identified which confers a significantly increased longevity. Another interesting system involves maternal inheritance of senescence in the ascomycete fungus *Podospora anserina.* A maternal component for longevity in humans has also been reported.[19]

Estimate of the Number of Genetic Loci Involved in Aging in Humans

There have been two general approaches to the question of the number of genetic loci involved in aging in humans. Sacher[20] and Cutler[21] estimated the rates of evolution of maximum life span potential (MLSP) from hominoid precursors. Judging from the known rates of amino acid substitutions in proteins, Sacher concluded: "If on the order of a few hundred loci were involved in the transition from *Australopithecus* to *Homo sapiens,* then a considerably smaller number of genes might be able to effect notable improvements in general vigor or intelligence in an evolutionarily natural way." Cutler concluded: "Assuming 4×10^4 genes per genome, it is predicted that about 250 genes or 0.6% of the total functional genes have received base substitutions leading to one or more adaptive amino-acid changes in 10,000 generations of hominid evolution." These interesting and ingenious estimates suggest that a comparatively small proportion of genes are of crucial importance in modulating life span potential. The relative importance of various potential genetic mechanisms of hominid evolution, however, have not yet been established. It is conceivable that point mutations played a comparatively minor role compared to chromosomal rearrangements. The latter have the potential, via position effects, to regulate the extent of expression of many hundreds or thousands of genes.

The second approach involved a determination of the proportion of the known spontaneous genetic variation in humans that has the potential to modulate one or more aspects of the senescent phenotype or that involves loci thought to be of significance to the pathobiology of aging.[22] An example of the latter would be the locus controlling the extent of inducibility of aryl hydrocarbon hydroxylase enzymes (mixed function oxidases) which can convert premutagenic and precarcinogenic compounds to proximal mutagens and carcinogens. Examples of loci that have the potential to modulate the rates of development of certain components of the senescent phenotype are given in a later section of this chapter that deals with human progeroid syndromes. It was concluded that the probable upper limit for the proportion of the human genome of relevance to the pathobiology of aging is approximately 7 percent. Assuming an upper limit of about 100,000 informational genes in humans, this would give up to 7000 loci, different alleles of which could differentially modulate the rates of development of particular subsets of the senescent phenotype. The majority of the loci identified, however, certainly could not be assumed to regularly influence major aspects of the phenotype in most individuals. A reasonable crude estimate would be that perhaps only 1 percent of the total might eventually be characterized as major aging genes, giving about 70 such genes.[22] It remains to be seen how far such crude estimates are from reality. It is important to realize, however, that given the number of possible permutations and combinations, even as few as 70 major genes can result in an extraordinarily rich variety of aging phenotypes. Consider the fact, for example, that with the amount of genetic variation already known for the major histocompatibility complex of humans [at least 30 alleles at each of the major (A and B) subloci, 7 or 8 at the C sublocus, and at least 10 at the D region], there is enough information to code for up to a billion unique phenotypes. When we add to this equation the vast number of possibilities of different interactions with humanity's ever-changing and enormously varied environment, one has to conclude that no two human beings, even identical twins, have ever aged or will ever age in precisely the same fashion.

Sex Differences in Longevity

There is as yet no evidence that the MLSP of human females is greater than that of human males. The currently best-accepted longevity record (113 years and 100 days) is, as a matter of fact, held by a male.[23] There is ample evidence, however, that other life-table parameters, such as mean life span and average life expectancy, indicate greater longevity for most females. Early on in life, males are at a numerical advantage, with approximately 115 males conceived for each 100 females. By birth, this ratio has dropped to somewhere between 105 and 100 and continues to drop until age 30, at which age the sex ratio is equal.[24] In each successive age group, the surviving female cohort increasingly outnumbers the corresponding surviving male cohort until, by age 65, 84 percent of females compared with 70 percent of males are still alive.[25] There are several arguments that indicate an important genetic contribution to this phenomenon which, to an increasing degree, poses serious social problems for the more advanced societies. First of all, preferential survival of the female is observed not only in the United States but also in all the advanced societies.[25] Such a finding could, of course, be largely attributable to common elements in the environment and lifestyle. This possibility will be addressed at the end of this section. A more persuasive argument is that the bulk of the evidence, although still incomplete, seems to indicate that the female advantage is widespread among the animal kingdom.[26] An even more cogent argument, however, would depend upon documentation that it was not femaleness per se that was correlated with enhanced survival but rather a sex chromosomal constitution that was *homogametic.* In humans and other mammals, the female is homogametic, having two X chromosomes that segregate during meiosis. The mammalian male is *heterogametic,* since he has one X chromosome and one Y chromosome, each of his sperm bearing either one or the other. Thus, the male is at a potential disadvantage, in that sex-linked recessive alleles would be expressed. Although there is good evidence for dosage compensation in the female via inactivation during early development of one of her two X chromosomes, such inactivation is random and clonally inherited, so that she is, in effect, a fine-grained somatic mosaic. Since, on the average, only half of her cells would be transcribing information from the X chromosome bearing a given recessive mutation, many such mutations (for example, the classic hemophilias and a rare sex-linked recessive form of parkinsonism) are in fact not expressed. It is, furthermore, important to note that not *all* X-linked genes are subject to complete inactivation in the human female. A well-documented example is the gene coding for steroid sulfatase,[27] a deficiency of which results in a sex-linked skin disorder, ichthyosis vulgaris.

Recent evidence indicates that in mice a particular locus on the inactivated X chromosome may be reactivated during aging.[28] If such observations can be generalized for the case of multiple X-linked loci and other mammalian species (an initial study indicates that it may *not* obtain for a different locus on the human X chromosome),[29] this could create, via abnormal gene dosage, an actual disadvantage for the female.

Differences in longevity have also been attributed to genes located on the Y chromosome. An Amish kindred has been identified in which the men are missing a portion of the long arm of the Y chromosome and outlive their wives by 5 years (82.3 versus 77.4 years).[24]

The limited data available indicate that there is no dosage compensation for sex-linked loci in avian species.[30] Therefore, one might expect the homogametic sex to exhibit a survival advantage, in that unfavorable recessive alleles would not be expressed. In birds, the male is the homogametic sex. Do male birds thus tend to have greater life spans? If so, we will have provided an important test of the genetic hypothesis for the female advantage in our species. Most of the old data on this subject are not of much use, as they deal with very small numbers of birds and mainly measure short-term survival.[26] Reasonable although still incomplete data are available for Japanese quail (*Coturnix coturnix japonica*),[31] and these life tables quite clearly point to a substantially greater life span for males.

Finally, it is important to consider that sex differences in longevity reflect a complex interaction of biological, behavioral, and sociocultural characteristics. In societies where men and women share similar lifestyles, such as the society of a kibbutz in Israel, the difference in life span between males and females is lessened.[32] Similarly, it has been shown that the difference in the mean age of death between male and female Seventh-Day Adventists, whose adherents do not smoke and have relatively prudent diets (i.e., low-fat, high-fiber), is relatively small.[33] In both of the above cases, however, the women still outlive the men. Therefore, intrinsic biological differences cannot be ignored. For example, it has been postulated that the more efficient metabolism of lipoproteins by women may be due to their higher levels of estrogen[34] and that women are protected from free-radical damage because of their menstrual loss of iron.[35] Combined with differences in lifestyle in most cultures, these biological factors may be critical in determining a shorter life span for men than women. Such differences might include greater male exposure, in some societies, to ethanol[36] and to tobacco smoke.[37] These important issues are dealt with in greater detail elsewhere in this text.

Gene Action and Aging

What might be the mechanisms whereby heredity influences MLSP and the rates of aging in various tissues and organs? Most of what can be said about this most crucial of all gerontological questions remains in the realm of speculation; however, we can certainly begin to see areas in which further research is likely to prove productive.

It is convenient, first of all, to consider two broad domains of gene action—one related to the *development* of the organism and the other related to the *maintenance* of the structural and functional integrity of the mature organism. These two are clearly related, as a failure of proper development of a given system must certainly cause subsequent difficulties for the maintenance system designed for it. Hutchinson-Gilford syndrome, which is described in a later section, may reflect this relationship. Although various genetic systems will be described in this chapter in which apparently normal development is followed by late onset of disease, it should be noted that more than 90 percent of genetic diseases are expressed prior to the onset of puberty.[38] Changes in the rate of development may have played important roles in evolution, as a slowing of this rate, a process sometimes referred to as "fetalization," has been postulated as an important mechanism in the evolution of primates.[39]

Genetic control of the kinetics of cellular proliferation must also be considered in the domain of maintenance of structure and function. It is now well established that cultures of human and other animal diploid somatic cells from embryos and adults undergo a process of clonal attenuation,[40] whereby there is a gradual and variable loss of the growth potential of all individual clones of cells. This restriction of growth potential is often referred to as the "Hayflick limit," after the scientist who first quantitatively documented the phenomenon.[41] Such processes can be assumed to be taking place in vivo and must surely be under genetic control. The implication is that differential gene action could lead to differential degrees of cellular reserve and, ultimately, tissue atrophy among various subjects. The situation is surely much more complicated, however. While tissue atrophy is a common observation in senescent mammals, a major aspect of the senescent phenotype is in fact an inappropriate and multifocal *proliferation* of many somatic cell types.[42] It is possible that such age-related hyperplasias play important roles in the pathogenesis of cancer and of atherosclerosis.[42,43]

Most of the current research on gene action and the maintenance of structure and function in adult organisms, however, focuses upon the concept of "longevity assurance genes."[44] The function of such genes is presumed to be the maintenance of appropriate gene expression throughout the life span. Thus, those who advocate the free-radical theory of aging[45] would argue that the genes controlling the baseline activities and the efficiency of induction of the enzymes that protect cells from free-radical-mediated injury are of seminal importance. Among these are the genes for cytoplasmic and mitochondrial forms of superoxide dismutase, hydrogen peroxidase, catalase, glutathione peroxidase, and glutathione reductase. Comparable lists of genes can be devised for other theories of aging. For the intrinsic mutagenesis theory,[46] the several DNA-dependent DNA polymerases would be most prominent, since the basic idea is that the enzymes of long-lived organisms copy DNA more faithfully than those of short-lived organisms, thus minimizing the accumulation of somatic mutations. DNA repair enzymes would also figure prominently. For the protein synthesis error-catastrophe theory,[47] the key genes would be those that are responsible for the accuracy of gene transcription and gene translation as well as those that control the synthesis of proteolytic enzymes capable of recognizing and of degrading abnormal proteins. A number of laboratories have now reported the accumulation of abnormal proteins with aging, which is largely attributable to posttranscriptional modifications and to impaired protein degradation[48]; an important role for biosynthetic errors has not been established.

A recent theory has suggested that age-related nonmutational changes in gene expression may be of critical importance,[49] including changes in DNA methylation patterns. Increased DNA methylation has been linked to X-chromosome inactivation and to changes in gene expression for autosomal loci. Therefore, age-related alterations in DNA methylase and a putative mechanism to remove methylated bases may also have important consequences.

An important approach to testing these theories would be to examine the various gene products in detail, comparing those from species of various MLSPs. Moreover, it would be useful to determine if such gene products are altered (i.e., mutant) or if they exhibit normal amino acid sequences with abnormal posttranslational modifications. A study such as this should also determine if the gene products are expressed at appropriate times and in appropriate cell types. Another approach is to investigate the pathogenetic mechanisms responsible for putative progeroid and "antiprogeroid" syndromes. We shall now turn our attention to certain of these entities in humans.

GENETIC SYNDROMES THAT MODULATE ASPECTS OF THE SENESCENT PHENOTYPE

Progeroid Syndromes (Table 2-1)

The suffix *-oid* (a term borrowed from the Greek language meaning "like" or "resembling") is among the most venerable and popular linguistic tools of pathologists, who use it to communicate their uncertainty regarding a diagnostic or descriptive term. For example, Virchow coined the term *amyloid* ("like starch") because such tissue deposits stain purple when treated with iodine and sulfuric acid. To what extent the various *progeroid* ("like premature senility") syndromes prove useful as model systems for various aspects of the senescent phenotype, or as probes of the pathogenesis of various age-related disorders, awaits further research. However, any clues that can provide a molecular understanding of unusual pathways—leading, for example, to accumulations of lipofuscins, amyloids, or paired helical filaments—can provide us with the keys to the discovery of the usual pathways.

Segmental Progeroid Syndromes

While there is no single hereditary disorder that brings forward in time all of the signs and symptoms of aging, there are several which appear to involve multiple aspects; hence the term *segmental progeroid syndrome.*[22]

Werner's Syndrome[50,51] Werner's syndrome (WS) represents a particularly informative segmental progeroid syndrome because of its potential to link a specific biochemical lesion with the pathogenesis of several of the major age-related disorders of humans, including atherosclerosis, cancer, osteoporosis, diabetes, and cataracts.

Werner's syndrome is inherited as an autosomal recessive, suggesting that it is most likely attributable to a deficiency of a single enzyme, although an abnormality in gene regulation is also a possibility.[52] The frequency of heterozygotes has been estimated at 1 to 5 per 1000 and for homozygotes at 1 to 25 per million. The gene defect for WS has recently been mapped to chromosome 8 (8p12).[53]

Werner's syndrome heterozygotes are generally considered to be asymptomatic, with the possible exceptions of premature graying and increased incidence of cancer. Homozygotes appear to be normal at birth and during childhood, although they tend to be smaller than unaffected sibs. A few patients have exhibited symptoms such as graying hair, skin changes, and cataracts as early as 6 to 8 years of age. The first obvious signal of a clinical problem, however, is the failure to undergo the usual adolescent growth spurt. Graying of the hair, hair loss, and atrophic changes of the skin appear during the early twenties. The voice takes on a peculiar and high-pitched squeaky quality. By about age 30, the patient may consult an ophthalmologist because of visual symptoms. The combination of short stature, gray hair, atrophic skin, high-pitched voice, and cataracts should prompt the ophthalmologist to make the diagnosis of WS. By the mid-thirties, skin atrophy and an apparently disproportionate loss of subcutaneous fat of the limbs is often associated with chronic leg ulcers. Diabetes mellitus and progressive osteoporosis (especially of distal limbs) begin to be evident. Fertility is reduced for both males and females; this reduction is associated with severe hyalinization of seminiferous tubules in the male (the histological picture being that of normal senescence in the male) and loss of primary follicles in the ovaries of the female. Death typically occurs in the late forties from either degenerative vascular disease or neoplasia. Approximately 10 percent of the patients develop neoplasms, with a particularly high frequency of sarcomas, meningiomas, and thyroid carcinomas. Finally, WS patients excrete relatively large amounts of hyaluronic acid. This clinical feature is shared with patients suffering from the Hutchinson-Gilford syndrome.

Cultured fibroblasts from WS patients have several interesting features that prompted the classification of WS as a chromosomal instability syndrome. The chromosomes in these cells show a propensity to undergo reciprocal translocations, resulting in a large variety of pseudodiploid cells (variegated translocation mosaicism). Moreover, these cells show a mutator phenotype characterized by an elevated frequency of mutant cells when compared with cells derived from

TABLE 2-1

Selected Major Criteria for the Identification of Genetic Progeroid Syndromes of Humans

	Syndromes	
Criteria	**Unimodal**	**Segmental**
Increased susceptibility to one or more types of neoplasms of relevance to aging	Polyposis, intestinal, type III	Ataxia telangiectasia
Increased frequencies of nonconstitutional chromosomal aberrations	Porokeratosis of Mibelli	Werner's
Dementia and/or relevant degenerative neuropathology	Alzheimer's disease of brain	Down's
Premature graying or loss of hair	White hair, prematurely	Progeria
Amyloid depositions	Amyloid, type III (cardiac form)	Down's
Increased depositions of lipofuscin pigments	Neuronal ceroid lipofuscinosis (Parry type)	?Cockayne's
Diabetes mellitus	Diabetes mellitus, autosomal dominant (mild juvenile form)	Seip's
Disorder of lipid metabolism	Familial hypercholesterolemia	Cervical lipodysplasia, familial
Hypogonadism	Kallmann's syndrome	Myotonic dystrophy
Autoimmunity	Thyroid autoantibodies	Down's
Hypertension	Hypertension, essential	Turner's
Degenerative vascular disease	Amyloidosis, cerebral, arterial	Werner's
Osteoporosis	Osteoporosis, juvenile	Klinefelter's
Cataracts	Cataract, nuclear total	Werner's
Regional fibrosis	Antitrypsin deficiency of plasma with chronic obstructive pulmonary disease	Werner's
Variations in amounts and/or distributions of adipose tissue	Adiposis dolorosa	Progeria

SOURCE: Adapted from Martin.[73]

age-matched normal controls. At the molecular level, most of the mutations are relatively large-scale deletion events.[54] The fibroblasts from WS patients also have a greatly diminished replicative potential in comparison with others from age-matched controls. In terms of these three characteristics, WS fibroblasts (mutator phenotype, chromosomal rearrangement, and diminished in vitro life span) are strikingly similar to fibroblasts from patients with Bloom's syndrome, which is associated with a defect in DNA ligase I.[55,56] The common cellular phenotypes observed in WS and Bloom's syndrome raise the possibility that the WS genetic defect may be involved in DNA replication or repair-related enzyme. The discovery of an increased duration of the S phase of the cell cycle is consistent with this hypothesis.[57]

Hutchinson-Gilford Syndrome[58] Hutchinson and Gilford were both pediatricians, which should help us to remember that the syndrome they described was "progeria of childhood," in contrast to the generally later onset of WS; Hutchinson-Gilford syndrome is often simply referred to as "progeria." The absence of consanguinity among parents of children with progeria, the low frequency of recurrence in families, and an increased average age for fathers of progeroid children suggest that progeria is a sporadic autosomal dominant. Occasional familial reports of progeria are most likely due to misdiagnosis rather than a second form of progeria with an autosomal recessive mode of inheritance (W. T. Brown, personal communication). Progeria occurs at a frequency of 1 in 8 million in the general population. As of 1990, however, there were only 17 known living patients.

At birth, Hutchinson-Gilford patients are usually considered to be normal, which sets progeria apart from the "neonatal progeroid syndrome" (Wiedemann-Rautenstrauch syndrome), in which depletion of subcutaneous fat, sparse hair, small size, and progeroid facies are quite obvious at birth. In Hutchinson-Gilford patients, profound growth retardation is evident within a year after birth, and there is so little hair and subcutaneous fat over the scalp that the scalp veins become remarkably prominent; patients have been described as having a "plucked-bird" appearance. Nonetheless, they have normal to above-normal intelligence. Other distinctive characteristics include coxa valga, which results in a "horse-riding" stance and a shuffling, wide-base gait; a weak, high-pitched voice; and an elevated basal metabolic rate. As with WS, there is no evidence of central nervous system (CNS) pathology. The median age of death for progeria patients is 12 years, with a range of 7 to 27 years. In 75 to 80 percent of cases, death is due to myocardial infarction or congestive heart failure. The accompanying atherosclerosis is histologically indistinguishable from that which accompanies normal aging. Other cardiovascular degenerative changes in individuals with progeria include calcification of heart rings, cardiomyopathy, arteriosclerosis, and arterial aneurysms.

A biochemical defect that is specific to both progeria and WS but not to other genetic disorders is increased excretion of urinary hyaluronic acid. The increase is 7 to 14 times that seen in normal age-matched controls. Interestingly, hyaluronic acid excretion also increases with normal aging. Hyaluronic acid appears to act as an antiangiogenesis factor, whereas partial degradation products of hyaluronic acid act to stimulate angiogenesis. Therefore, altered hyaluronic acid metabolism may have significant impact on development and growth. Recently, several attempts have been made to increase growth in two progeria patients by treatment with recombinant human growth hormone. Both patients exhibited increased linear growth rates and decreased basal metabolic rates. Therefore, a potential treatment to ameliorate some of the symptoms of progeria may be available. However, a true test of this treatment is complicated by both the rarity of progeria and the accompanying delay in diagnosis.

Ataxia Telangiectasia[59–61] Patients with ataxia telangiectasia (AT), an autosomal, recessively inherited disorder, develop a progressive cerebellar ataxia in early childhood and are frequently confined to a wheelchair by adolescence. Whereas ordinary human subjects exhibit a gradual loss of Purkinje's cells as they age, with about a 25 percent loss by the tenth decade,[62] this cell loss is vastly accelerated in AT patients. Other clinical features include additional degenerative neuropathological changes, including cerebral cortical cell loss and demyelination of the posterior column of the spinal cord, immunological defects, premature graying of hair, increased levels of serum albumin, a high propensity to develop tumors, increased levels of serum alpha-fetoprotein, and glucose intolerance. The patients are not retarded, but their IQ scores tend to decline as the ataxia progresses. Most patients who do not die of cancer will eventually succumb to chronic pulmonary disease. Exposed skin and skin subjected to friction undergo premature atrophic changes, together with hyper- and hypopigmentation and telangiectasia. Hypogonadism is striking, with depletion of ovarian follicles and testicular atrophy. Consistent with the immunological deficiency, the thymus is described as hypoplastic or even absent.

The cells of AT patients show an unusually high sensitivity to ionizing radiation. Approximately 10 percent of AT homozygotes develop a malignancy in childhood or early childhood. A minority of these tumors are epithelial cell cancers with an unusually high predisposition to stomach carcinoma. The vast majority of these tumors are lymphoid in origin, with a 70-fold and 250-fold increase, respectively, for leukemias and lymphomas. Chromosomal instability in lymphocytes is a hallmark of AT, with translocations involving chromosomes 7 and 14 being particularly noted in AT leukemias. In addition, an elevated frequency of somatic cell mutations of lymphocytes has been demonstrated in vivo in AT homozygotes.[63]

Although AT is an autosomal recessive condition, evidence has been obtained indicating that heterozygotes have an increased susceptibility to neoplasia.[64] This is particularly true for breast cancer. Since it has been suggested that 1 percent of the general population is heterozygous for AT, perhaps 10 percent of all breast cancers occur in AT heterozygotes. Moreover, occupational or diagnostic exposure to ionizing radiation may increase the risk of breast cancer.

The underlying enzymatic defect in AT has not been determined. It may involve an aberration in the control of a "checkpoint" in the cell cycle.[65] The AT locus has been mapped to chromosome 11q22-23,[66] in a region associated with neurological and immune function. Four to five complementation groups have been reported, of which three map to the 11q22-23 region.

Down's Syndrome[51] Down's syndrome (DS) is a leading candidate as a segmental progeroid syndrome. Symptoms include premature graying of hair and hair loss, premature deposits of tissue lipofuscin, neurodegenerative changes, hypogonadism, autoimmunity, degenerative vascular disease (exclusive of atherosclerosis), and cataracts. A decline in immune function is believed to contribute to high mortality due to infections and to certain malignancies.

The chromosomal abnormality specific for DS is trisomy 21, with trisomy for region 21q22.2-3 believed to play the major role in producing the DS phenotype.[67,68] Trisomy for other regions of chromosome 21 and diploidy for 21q22.2-3 will often have recognizable phenotypes, but without the specific stigmata of DS. It is significant to note that the 21q22.2-3 region does not include either the amyloid precursor protein gene (*APP*), which plays a significant role in the neuropathology of DS and Alzheimer's disease (AD), or CuZn-superoxide dismutase (*SOD1*). Trisomy for *SOD1* could result in an increase in hydrogen peroxide, leading to an elevated level of free radicals in DS patients.[69] Therefore, it remains to be determined if the senescent phenotype in DS is due to a gene or genes in the DS region (21q22.2-3), in the proximal regions containing *APP* (21q21.2), *SOD1* (21q22.1), or in other presently unidentified regions, including those that regulate the expression of genes in other chromosomes.

Perhaps the most striking observation concerning DS is that the brains from more than 96 percent of patients over the age of 36 to 40 display AD-type neuropathology. This includes two of the basic hallmarks for AD, neuritic plaques with amyloid cores and neurofibrillary tangles. This morphological relationship has been strengthened by the chemical demonstration that the amyloid found in the affected brains of both AD and DS patients is identical.[70] It is still not known if DS patients who are not trisomic for the *APP* gene will display AD-type neuropathology.

The neuropathological similarities between AD and DS have led to the suggestion that DS is a genetic model for AD. Therefore, a number of studies have investigated the relationship between age of DS patients and signs of dementia. A consensus for an age-related increase in dementia has been reached, although there is some disagreement as to the percentage of patients affected for a given age group and the severity of the dementia. Perhaps more importantly, a consensus has also been reached that in a subset of DS patients, many of the pathological hallmarks of AD can be present in the absence of clinical dementia. No clinical pathologic correlations have yet been reported, however, for what may be the most significant indicator of dementia—the loss of synapses.[71]

Other Segmental Progeroid Syndromes Martin has listed other hereditary disorders deserving of further investigation as models for the study of genetic control of multiple aspects of the senescent phenotype.[22] Two of them (familial cervical lipodysplasia and the Seip syndrome) are of special interest because they were initially identified as a result of a deliberate search for conditions characterized by aberrations in the amounts and/or distributions of adipose tissue.

In addition to DS, two other constitutional aneuploidies (the Klinefelter and Turner syndromes) were cited as exhibiting multiple features suggestive of premature aging, thus underscoring the importance of abnormalities in gene dosage. Myotonic dystrophy (Steinert disease) was also mentioned in a list of the 10 leading candidates of segmental progeroid syndromes. The molecular basis of this disease has been shown to be a variable expansion of a trinucleotide repeat sequence (CTG) in a chromosome-19 gene coding for a member of the protein kinase family.[72]

Unimodal Progeroid Syndromes

Equally important conceptually are a group of hereditary disorders that accelerate predominantly a particular aspect of the senescent phenotype. Investigations of such genetic diseases[73] provide the potential for a more fine-grained analysis of the biochemical genetic basis of various aspects of aging. We can give only a few examples here.

Familial Hypercholesterolemia[74–76] Familial hypercholesterolemia (FH) results from a variety of mutations in the gene coding for the cell surface receptor controlling the degradation of low-density lipoprotein (LDL). The LDL receptor regulates plasma cholesterol by mediating endocytosis of LDL, the major cholesterol transport protein in humans. Although not usually thought about in the context of accelerated aging, it is apparent that the predominant feature of this disorder, premature atherosclerosis, qualifies FH as a unimodal progeroid syndrome. Quantitative evidence that atherosclerosis is a marker of aging in humans came from extensive population studies (review in Ref. 43). While the rate of increase in the lesions varies substantially among different geographic-ethnic groups, all populations studied thus far show steady (typically linear) age-related increments. Familial hypercholesterolemia is likely to serve as a prototype of unimodal progeroid syndromes because of the detailed molecular understanding of its pathogenesis and underlying genetic defects. In contrast, the specific gene or genes that predispose the general population to atherosclerosis remain to be determined.[77]

Approximately 180 mutations in the LDL receptor gene have been identified, including base-pair substitutions, deletions, duplications, and unequal crossing-over events. These mutations result in five distinct classes of LDL receptor phenotypes: class 1, null alleles that do not encode a protein; class 2, transport-defective alleles that encode proteins blocked in transport between the endoplasmic reticulum and Golgi complex; class 3, binding-defective alleles that encode proteins that are transported to the cell surface but cannot bind LDL; class 4, internalization-defective alleles that encode proteins binding LDL but cannot cluster in clatherin-coated pits and thus do not internalize LDL; and class 5, recycling-defective alleles that encode receptors binding and internalizing LDL in clatherin-coated pits but fail to discharge the LDL into the endosome and to recycle to the cell surface.

The severity of the FH phenotype is dependent upon the number of mutant alleles borne by the affected individuals. Familial hypercholesterolemia heterozygotes, who are present in the population at a frequency of 1 in 500, exhibit various symptoms in an age-dependent manner. Hypercholesterolemia is present virtually from birth, with a cholesterol level of 300 to 500 mg/dl. Arcus cornea and tendinous xanthomas appear in the latter part of the second decade, each being present in about half of the patients by the third decade. Coronary heart disease appears by the fourth decade. Homozygotes are far more severely affected, with all of the above symptoms present in childhood; their cholesterol levels are 600 to 1200 mg/dl. Most die of myocardial infarction before age 30, and many die before age 20. Therefore, FH is not a true autosomal dominant disease. Homozygotes are simply more affected than heterozygotes.

Two observations have suggested that expression of the FH phenotype can be partially modulated by other alleles. The first is the observation that two unrelated individuals homozygous for a mutation abolishing the LDL receptor RNA and protein had markedly different outcomes. One person did not exhibit symptoms of coronary atherosclerosis until the age of 17. Although she had long-standing and severe angina pectoris, her death at age 33 was due to malignant melanoma, not coronary heart disease. In contrast, a second person with the identical mutation died of myocardial infarction at the age of 3. The second observation comes from a family in which expression of the FH phenotype in heterozygotes is apparently under the influence of a second dominant gene. Family members harboring both a mutant LDL receptor gene and the second putative gene have normal LDL cholesterol levels.[78] This second gene may act to suppress the FH phenotype.[79]

Hereditary Amyloidosis[80] *Amyloidosis* is a generic term for a heterogeneous group of conditions associated with the multifocal accumulations of various types of polypeptides having certain physicochemical commonalities. A hallmark of these amyloid proteins is their dichroic (two-color) appearance when stained with congo red and examined with rotating polarized light. A variety of precursor proteins are now known to give rise to amyloidosis; many will be considered in another chapter of this book. Mutations in the transthyretin gene (*TTR*) that give rise to amyloid deposition will be considered in this section. The *TTR* gene, which has been mapped to chromosome 18, has proven to be a useful model for examining the relationship between mutation and late-onset genetic disease.

Hereditary amyloidosis due to *TTR* mutation is inherited as an autosomal dominant disease with virtually complete penetrance (i.e., all carriers of a single gene copy of the mutant gene develop some degree of deposition of amyloid in their tissues as they age). Most affected individuals carry a copy of both a mutant allele and a wild-type allele, resulting in the production of approximately equal amounts of the normal and abnormal protein. A few individuals with homozygous deficiencies have been identified. Their phenotypes are similar to those of individuals with heterozygous deficiencies, confirming that hereditary amyloidosis is a true autosomal dominant. The circulating transthyretin protein, which functions as a carrier for thyroxin and retinol, is a tetramer of four identical subunits of 127 amino acids each. It is believed that one or more abnormal proteins in the tetramer will allow the molecule to participate in the formation of an amyloid fibril. At least 15 separate mutant *TTR* genes have been identified, with each mutation conferring a specific phenotype. Affected organs and tissues include the heart, eye, kidney, and autonomic nervous system. Molecular probes for each of these mutations are now available, allowing prenatal diagnosis and identification of persons at risk. An interesting observation is that for a specific mutation, the tissue-specific distribution of amyloid fibrils, and hence the resulting phenotype, can vary in different kindreds. For example, a mutation resulting in the substitution of a methionine for valine at position 30 (Met30) has been found in families in Portugal, Sweden, Japan, Italy, Greece, England, and the United States. In the affected English and American kindreds this mutation results in cardiomyopathy, whereas affected Swedish individuals usually suffer kidney disease.

The age of onset of symptoms for hereditary amyloidosis varies widely and is often dependent upon the mutation that an individual carries. A mutation identified recently at position 55 can affect individuals in their teenage years,[81] whereas a mutation involving position 60 is normally not expressed until after age 60. However, the age of onset for specific mutations can also have a familial component. For the Met30 mutation, the average age of onset is earliest in Portuguese families and latest in Swedish families. This observation suggests that additional genetic or environmental factors can influence the expression of a mutant *TTR* gene.

The ability to identify asymptomatic patients who carry mutant *TTR* genes has allowed a determination of when amyloid deposition occurs.[82] A family with a mutation at position 84 was identified whose first recognizable disease symptom is carpal tunnel syndrome. This symptom affects individuals in their mid to late 30s or early 40s. In a study of 12 family members who have not yet exhibited symptoms, six who carried the mutation were identified. Carpal ligament biopsies were conducted on four of these individuals (ages 26 to 34), but all were negative for the presence of amyloid. Therefore, the possibility that amyloid deposition accumulates throughout the life span, with a threshold effect leading to the presence of symptoms, appears unlikely. Moreover, the presence of abnormal proteins is not solely responsible for amyloid deposition. Therefore, other factors must be present that contribute to amyloid deposition, and the expression of these factors must have an age-related component. In this regard it is useful to recall that a variety of abnormal proteins are found to accumulate even with normal aging. The recent development of transgenic mice containing the position-30 mutation, which exhibit amyloid deposition beginning at age 6 months, may prove useful in addressing the relationship between the presence of abnormal TTR protein and the age-related accumulation of TTR amyloid fibrils.[83]

Familial Alzheimer's Disease Some 200 families are now being investigated worldwide in which there is variable evidence for a hereditary basis of dementia of the Alzheimer type (familial Alzheimer's disease, FAD). In many such families there has been at least one histologically confirmed case.[84] (The pathology of Alzheimer's disease will be described in a separate chapter.) In most pedigrees, the best interpretation is that a single autosomal dominant gene segregates, leading to a high probability that dementia will be expressed if the subject bearing the mutant allele lives long enough. Research into the molecular biology and genetics of senile dementia of the Alzheimer type (SDAT) and FAD has increased at a rapid rate in the 1980s, leading to a number of significant observations.[85] The gene coding for a protein with properties of a cell membrane receptor, a portion of which forms the amyloid found in the brains of SDAT, FAD, and DS patients, has been cloned and localized to chromosome 21, most likely in the region bordering between 21q21 and 21q22.[86,87] As discussed previously, this region has been implicated in the DS phenotype. For some early-onset pedigrees, those with a familial mean age of onset at or below age 60, an FAD gene was thought to be localized to chromosome 21 at 21q11, in a region close to the centromere.[88] It now appears, however, that the great majority of early-onset FAD families can be linked to a dominant mutation on the long arm of chromosome 14.[89] A lesser proportion of early-onset pedigrees has been linked to various point mutations in the structural gene for the β-amyloid precursor protein.[90] A third group of early-onset pedigrees with FAD, all of whom can be traced to a small region of Russia inhabited by Volga Germans, is not linked to any of the above loci. These families may provide a unique opportunity to examine a founder effect for FAD.[91]

For late-onset families, there is evidence, yet to be confirmed, of a linkage to the long arm of chromosome 19.[92] Thus, the picture that has emerged is one of genetic heterogeneity (Table 2-2). Genetic heterogeneity, however, does not necessarily indicate mechanistic heterogeneity. For example, there is a distinct possibility that all of the genetic loci so far implicated fit into a pathogenetic mechanism based upon the metabolism of the β-amyloid precursor protein. Thus, not only the structural gene on chromosome 21 but also genes determining the structure or the regulation of various competing proteases and protease inhibitors could also play key roles in determining if an individual is likely to develop cognitive decline in the fifth decade or in the ninth decade (Fig. 2-1).

On the other hand, one could take the view that there are only a limited number of ways in which the human nervous system can react to injury. A number of pathogenetically distinct mechanisms might then

TABLE 2-2

Genetic Linkages to Familial Forms of Alzheimer's Disease

Chromosome Localization	Mutant Gene	Onset
21q21	β-amyloid precursor protein	Early*
14q24.3	Unknown	Early
?21q11	Unknown	Early
?19q13	Unknown	Late†
Unknown	Unknown	Early‡

*Early onset arbitrarily defined as mean familial age of ≤60 years.
†Late onset arbitrarily defined as mean familial age of >60 years.
‡"Volga German" families for which linkage to regions listed has been excluded.

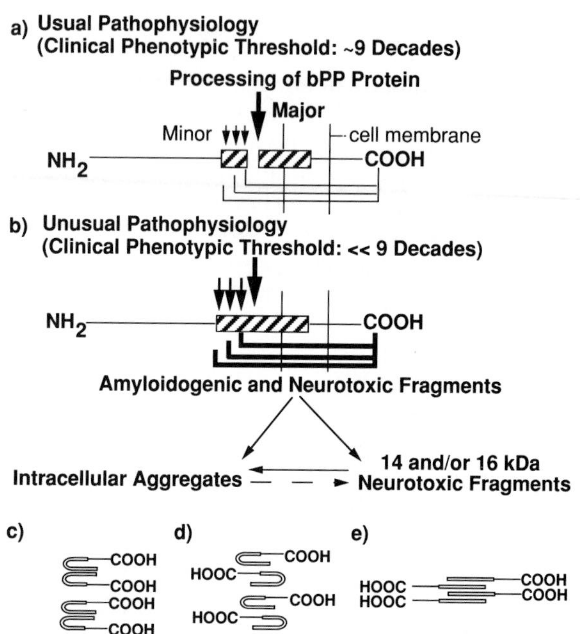

FIGURE 2-1

A. Unified hypothesis for β-amyloidogenesis. β-amyloid precursor protein is mostly cleaved near the middle of the β-amyloid sequence, excluding this proteolytic pathway as a source of the β-amyloid protein. *B.* Altered metabolism of β-amyloid precursor protein, such as the overproduction of β-amyloid precursor protein, mutation in the β-amyloid precursor protein, or an imbalance of proteases and protease inhibitors, may lead to an increased rate of amyloidogenic proteolysis. These amyloidogenic fragments may be associated with neurotoxicity. Our experimental results (*Fukuchi K et al: Biochem Biophys Res Commun 182:165, 1992*) suggest that C-terminal fragments of β-amyloid precursor protein are involved in the intracellular formation of amyloid protein aggregates and are associated with neurotoxicity. *C, D,* and *E.* Three schematic models for the aggregation of the C-terminal fragments are deduced from observations in several sources. (*Kirschner DA et al, Proc Natl Acad Sci USA 84:6953, 1987; Hilbich C et al, J Mol Biol 218:149, 1991; Dyrks T et al, EMBO J 7:949, 1988; and Fukuchi K et al, Biochem Biophys Res Commun 182:165, 1992.*) [*After Martin GM, Fukuchi K: Current Sci* (*India*) *63:410, 1992.*]

lead to the plaques, tangles, amyloid, and synaptic losses characteristic of Alzheimer's disease, including some in which β-amyloid deposits are merely epiphenomena.

Huntington's Disease[93] Huntington's disease (HD) is a progressive neurodegenerative disorder characterized by both motor abnormalities (chorea and athetosis) and intellectual deterioration. These symptoms result from premature neuronal death, particularly for the neurons of the basal ganglia. Selective, regional neuronal death also occurs during normal aging.

HD is inherited as an autosomal dominant condition with a mean age of onset between 35 and 42 years. The disease then progresses relatively slowly for an approximately 10- to 20-year period, ultimately leading to death. Juvenile onset of HD (before the age of 15) is observed in approximately 3 percent of cases and is associated with a more rapid progression lasting 8 to 10 years. Moreover, in a striking break from Mendelian inheritance, 80 to 95 percent of individuals suffering from juvenile-onset HD have inherited the mutant allele from their fathers. The possibility of a protective effect from the mother's mitochondrial genome has been ruled out. A current hypothesis to explain the preponderance of paternal transmission is genomic imprinting of either the HD allele or of a modifying allele. Genomic imprinting is an epigenetic process in which expression of specific alleles is a function of the contributing parent's gender. Late-onset cases of HD have also been reported in which individuals do not begin exhibiting symptoms until past the age of 60. Progression in these cases is relatively slow. A possible relationship between late-onset disease and maternal inheritance has been suggested, but the data are more equivocal than those reported for juvenile onset and paternal inheritance.

HD provides a useful paradigm for exploring the relationship between a specific gene mutation and age of disease onset. An extensive kindred of 10,000 individuals has been identified in the Lake Maracaibo region of Venezuela which includes 358 patients, 1227 persons at 50 percent risk, and 2885 persons at 25 percent risk. All HD patients in this kindred have inherited a single mutant HD allele from a common ancestor. A few individuals with homozygous deficiencies have been identified whose clinical course is similar to that of those individuals with heterozygous deficiencies. Therefore, HD is a true autosomal dominant disease. If the phenotypic characteristics for HD were strictly a function of the mutant allele, it would be predicted that affected members of this kindred would have similar phenotypes, including age of onset. Instead, a wide range of phenotypic variability has been noted for the Venezuelan family. However, in a study of monozygotic twins with HD that were raised apart, the onset (35 years) and progression of the disease (14 years) was found to be remarkably similar.[94] In contrast, the affected father and uncle of these siblings, who both presumably shared the same mutant allele, had markedly different ages of onset and times of progression. These observations suggest two related possibilities for phenotypic variability in HD. The first is that the severity of HD is affected by a modifying gene or genes that can differ for different members of a kindred but not for monozygotic twins. The second possibility is that genomic imprinting and/or other developmentally regulated phenomena can establish the level of phenotypic expression during embryonic development. The HD gene has recently been identified. Similar to myotonic dystrophy, the genetic defect appears to be due to expansion of a trinucleotide sequence (CAG).[95]

Spongiform Encephalopathies[96] Three diseases in humans—kuru, Creutzfeldt-Jakob disease (CJD), and Gerstmann-Staussler-Scheinker syndrome (GSS)—are neurodegenerative disorders characterized by progressive vacuolation in the dendritic and axonal processes and cell bodies of neurons. To a lesser extent, vacuolation is also noted in astrocytes and oligodendrocytes. Extensive neuronal loss is accompanied by astroglial hypertrophy in the brains of affected patients. Additional clinical features for these diseases include variable ages of onset and duration of illness. The age of onset for kuru is 5 to 40 years, with a duration of 3 to 9 months; for CJD, the age of onset is 50 to 75 years, with a duration of 2 to 5 months; and for GSS, the age of onset is 35 to 55 years, with a duration of 2 to 8 years. Although the human spongiform encephalopathies are relatively rare, they are nonetheless a fascinating group of diseases that in many cases result from infectious particles lacking an apparent nucleic acid component. The possibility that the infectious agent is a protein has led to the term *prion.* Amyloid deposition of the prion protein is one of the hallmarks of the prion diseases. Prion diseases have also been described in sheep (scrapie), cattle (bovine spongiform encephalopathy), and mink (mink encephalopathy).

One of the more remarkable aspects of prion diseases is that they can be either infectious or inherited. The prion proteins are encoded by species-specific cellular genes (*PrP* genes). The human gene, termed *PRNP,* has been mapped to the short arm of chromosome 20. Mutations in this gene have been linked to both GSS and CJD, the former being exclusively a genetic disease with an autosomal dominant mode of inheritance. Amino acid substitutions at positions 102 and 117 have been described in GSS patients, with the position 102 mutation associated with ataxia and the position 117 mutation associated with dementia. Although only 5 to 10 percent of CJD cases are familial, at least three distinct mutations in the *PRNP* gene have been linked to CJD. One is an amino acid substitution at position 200 and the other two are insertions of 96 or 144 base pairs (bp) that begin at position 53. An individual homozygous for the position 200 mutation has been described whose clinical course was similar to that of heterozygous individuals.[97] This result confirms that CJD is a true autosomal dominant disorder. Most of the remainder of CJD cases are sporadic and of unknown etiology. However, a few cases are due to iatrogenic transmission, such as corneal transplants from affected donors. The infectious nature of the prion particle is best revealed in kuru disease, which was essentially confined to natives living in the mountainous interior of Papua, New Guinea. The route of infection for this disease was through the ritualistic handling and consumption of brain tissue from dead kinsmen. By stopping this practice, kuru has virtually been eliminated.

The development of animal models, including transgenic mice,[98] to study the prion diseases has provided additional insight into their nature. One of the more surprising observations has been that the infectious forms of the prions are dependent upon the host *PrP* gene rather than the donor gene. For example, if the scrapie prion is transferred to hamsters, the prion particles found in infected animals contain the hamster protein. Likewise, if the hamster prion is transferred to mice, the infectious prion particles now contain the mouse protein. It has also been shown that transfer of the hamster *PrP* gene into mice results in the production of the hamster PrP protein when the transgenic animals are infected with hamster prions. Additional genetic studies have demonstrated that spongiform encephalopathy occurs in transgenic mice containing a mutation specific to GSS and that the PrP protein is not necessary for normal development.

The newest chapter in this fascinating group of late-onset neurodegenerative disorders deals with a rare form of insomnia ("fatal familial insomnia"), which has been associated with a mutation in codon 178 of the *PrP* gene.[99]

Mitochondrial Disease[100] In the late 1970s, maternally inherited senescence in the fungus *Podospora anserina* was found to be correlated with deterioration of its mitochondrial genome. It is now apparent that a relationship exists between mitochondrial function, mutation, and aging in humans as well. The human mitochondrial genome is 16,569 bp in size. It encodes 13 genes essential for oxidative phosphorylation (i.e., cellular energy production) as well as genes for transfer RNA (tRNA) and ribosomal RNA (rRNA). At least three factors contribute to a role for mitochondrial genomes in aging, particularly in persons inheriting mitochondrial mutations. One factor is an age-related decline in oxidative phosphorylation.[101] A second factor is the apparent lack of DNA repair pathways for the mitochondrial genome and the concomitant age-related accumulation of mutations.[102] This accumulation includes an enrichment for mutant mitochondrial genomes containing partial deletions. A third factor is the creation of highly reactive oxygen radicals at several steps in the oxidative phosphorylation pathway. These reactive molecules are likely to contribute to the mutational load in the mitochondrial genome. It has also been reported that hypoxemia, which occurs in ischemic tissues, will further increase the level of mitochondrial mutation induced by oxygen radicals.[103] It has been hypothesized that random accumulation of mitochondrial mutations is the major contributing factor in the age-related decrease in the capacity for oxidative phosphorylation.

Most genetically inherited mitochondrial diseases have an age-related onset of symptoms. The severity of these symptoms increases progressively. The rare genetic disease myoclonic epilepsy associated with ragged red fibers (MERRF) provides an example of the relationship between aging and mitochondrial point mutation. This disease is due to a base-pair substitution in $tRNA^{lys}$ that decreases the translational efficiency for affected mitochondrial genomes. The mitochondria of most affected individuals contain a mixture of both wild-type and mutant genomes, with a protective effect afforded by a relatively small percentage of the wild-type genomes. For individuals less than 20 years of age, the mutant genomes must comprise more than 95 percent of the mitochondria for the complete MERRF phenotype to be expressed. Individuals younger than 20 years of age with less than 85 percent mutant genomes are clinically normal. In contrast, individuals over 60 years of age with 85 percent mutant mitochondrial genomes exhibit the complete MERRF phenotype, and mild symptoms are observed in individuals with only 63 percent mutant genomes. This age-related shift in expression of the MERRF phenotype is believed to be due to the age-related decrease in oxidative phosphorylation that occurs in all individuals.

Other mitochondrial diseases, such as ocular myopathy, are due to spontaneous deletion events. If the deletion event occurs very early in development, a variable tissue distribution for the mutant genomes will be noted. It is believed that the mutant genomes are at a replicative advantage, allowing them to accumulate over the individual's lifetime. Not surprisingly, diseases associated with mitochondrial deletion mutations also progress with age. In these cases, it may be the combination of accumulating mutant genomes and decreasing capacity for oxidative phosphorylation that accounts for the progressive severity in phenotype.

Antigeroid Syndromes

The progeroid syndromes were defined as having resulted from gene mutations that resulted in the premature onsets and/or the accelerated rates of development of specific components of the senescent phenotype. We now consider the logical alternative situation, in which certain allelic forms of genes at particular loci act to defer or to ameliorate such phenotypes. Individuals who are lucky enough to have inherited such genes could be diagnosed as having "antigeroid" syndromes! Unfortunately, physicians generally do not investigate pedigrees in which there is evidence of unusually good preservation of structure and function in older individuals. This is clearly a high priority for future research.

Neonatal familial hyperalphalipoproteinemia and hypobetalipoproteinemia may represent examples of unimodal antigeroid syndromes.[104,105] Affected individuals have elevations of high-density lipoproteins. At least in some pedigrees, this elevation may be associated with reduced cardiac mortality and morbidity and prolonged life expectancy, presumably by virtue of the ability of high-density lipoproteins to mediate mobilization of cholesterol from the arterial wall and hence to diminish the rate of development of atherosclerosis. Although these neonatal conditions were originally thought to be inherited by an individual as a simple autosomal dominant, subsequent studies suggested a polygenic determination[106] and questioned the generality of a relationship to enhanced life expectancy.[107]

PARENTAL AGE AND MUTATION

Paternal Age and Point Mutation

Since the normal male remains fertile throughout most of his life span, the quality of his gametes provides an important bioassay of the effects of age upon the rate of genetic mutations. For dominant mutations with complete penetrance, such calculations can be determined directly and provide clear evidence that older fathers are more likely to sire children bearing certain types of deleterious mutations.[108] For example, for the case of achondroplasia, the risk for a father in his late forties may be up to nine times that for a father in his mid-twenties. The absolute risk, however, remains comparatively small for the ages so far studied (mainly lower than age 50); for the case of achondroplasia, the mutation rate in the general population is of the order of one mutant per 100,000 gametes.[108] This relatively mild impact of paternal age is in contrast to the clinically significant problem of the increase in the risk of chromosomal aneuploidy with advanced maternal age, as described below.

It is of considerable theoretical interest that some dominant mutations do not increase in incidence with advancing paternal age; examples include osteogenesis imperfecta, neurofibromatosis, and tuberous sclerosis. Vogel has argued that such mutations may derive from mechanisms other than point mutation—for example, from insertional types of mutagenesis.[109]

Maternal Age and Aneuploidy

Knowledge of this subject is now of medical and legal importance, as a physician may be subject to a malpractice suit if he or she fails to inform pregnant patients who will deliver when they are over the age of 35 ("advanced maternal age") of the availability of prenatal tests for chromosomally abnormal fetuses. With the exception of the classic variety of the Turner syndrome (45,X), all of the major aneuploid syndromes that are compatible with a live birth dramatically increase in frequency as a function of advancing maternal age and, to a more limited extent, as a function of advancing paternal age.[110] For example, the frequency of births of infants with trisomy 21 (Down's syndrome) for a 20-year-old mother is about 1 in 2000; for mothers over the age of 45, the frequency is about 1 in 35. A cytogenetic analysis of over 2200 spontaneous abortions has also revealed an age-related increase for trisomy for most of the human chromosomes. For those chromosomes in which an increase was noted, the increased frequency was usually modest until approximately 32 to 33 years of age, after which the frequencies of trisomic abortuses increased dramatically. An unusual pattern for chromosome 16 was observed, the increase being linear after age 20. Trisomies for the A+B group chromosomes showed little or no increase with maternal age, nor did sex chromosome monosomy or polyploidy.[111] These various patterns, of course, reflect the combined forces of etiologic factors and selective abortion. The usual explanation is that the probability of meiotic nondisjunction increases as a function of maternal age. The observation, in mice, that the number of chromosomal chiasmata (sites of prolonged association of homologous chromosomes, where crossing over takes place) declines with maternal age could be interpreted as support for this hypothesis.[112]

Additional experiments with mice have demonstrated that unilateral ovariectomy, which leads to a premature loss of fecundity, caused an earlier-than-normal rise in aneuploidy in embryos examined at 3.5 days. The authors concluded that biological rather than chronological age of the reproductive system was the determining factor in the increase in aneuploidy and suggested that unilateral ovariectomy in women might be an additional risk factor for Down's syndrome.[113]

A number of theories have been proposed to explain the association between maternal age and trisomy. Possibilities include decay of spindle components during the prolonged meiotic prophase, environmental insults, dissolution of the nucleolus, or predetermination of trisomy by the order of formation of oocytes during development.[113] An additional hypothesis to explain an increase in Down's syndrome with maternal age, termed *relaxed selection,* proposes that a putative mechanism to spontaneously abort chromosomally abnormal embryos begins to fail with age.[114,115] In addition to an increase in the percentage of live-birth trisomies with maternal age, however, there is an increase in the percentage of spontaneously aborted trisomies. Moreover, the ratio of live births to spontaneously aborted trisomies decreases with age,[111] in contradiction to the predictions of this theory.

CONCLUSIONS

We have only begun to dissect out the genetic basis for individual variations in patterns of aging. Progress has been particularly gratifying for the case of genetic loci involved in familial Alzheimer's disease and for abnormalities in lipid metabolism associated with atherogenesis. A reasonable hypothesis is that these and numerous other age-related disorders have the potential to inform us about underlying aging processes that *set the stage* for late-onset disabilities. Such research should also lead to the identification of alleles that provide unusual *resistance* to particular aging processes and their associated diseases.

Genes, of course, do not act in a vacuum. All phenotypes are the result of nature-nurture interactions. There is thus the potential for preventive and therapeutic interventions using "phenotype engineering." Such interventions will have to be tailored to the special vulnerabilities and strengths of the individual patient.

REFERENCES

1. King RC, Stansfield WA: *A Dictionary of Genetics,* 14th ed. New York, Oxford, Oxford University Press, 1990.
2. Rose MR: *Evolutionary Biology of Aging.* New York, Oxford University Press, 1991.
3. Carey JR et al: Slowing of mortality rates at older ages in large medfly cohorts. *Science* 258:457, 1992.
4. Curtsinger JW et al: Demography of genotypes: Failure of the limited life-span paradigm in *Drosophila melanogaster. Science* 258:461, 1992.
5. Jarvik LF et al: Survival trends in senescent twin populations. *Am J Hum Genet* 12:170, 1960.
6. Hauge M et al: The Danish twin register. *Acta Genet Med Gemellol* 17:315, 1968.
7. Leber WR, Parsons OA: Premature aging and alcoholism. *Int J Addict* 17:61, 1982.
8. Read RC: Systemic effects of smoking. *Am J Surg* 148:706, 1984.
9. Kligman LH: Photoaging: Manifestations, prevention, and treatment. *Dermatol Clin* 4:517, 1986.
10. Masoro EJ: Minireview: Food restriction in rodents: An evaluation of its role in the study of aging. *J Gerontol* 43:B59, 1988.
11. Clavel F et al: Decreased mortality among male prisoners. *Lancet* 2:1012, 1987.
12. Martin GM: Constitutional genetic markers of aging. *Exp Gerontol* 23:257, 1988.
13. Takata H et al: Influence of major histocompatibility complex region genes on human longevity in Okinawan-Japanese centenarians and nonagenarians. *Lancet* 2:824, 1987.
14. Martin GM: Interactions of aging and environmental agents: The gerontological perspective, in Baker SR, Rogul M (eds): *Environmental Toxicity and the Aging Processes.* New York, Liss, 1987, p 25.
15. Lelashvili NG, Dalakishvili SM: Genetic study of high longevity index populations. *Mech Ageing Dev* 28:261, 1984.
16. Lieberman J: Heterozygous and homozygous alpha$_1$-antitrypsin deficiency in patients with pulmonary emphysema. *N Engl J Med* 281:279, 1969.
17. Stevens PM et al: Pathophysiology of hereditary emphysema. *Ann Intern Med* 74:672, 1971.
18. Martin GM, Turker MS: Model systems for the genetic analysis of mechanisms of aging. *J Gerontol* 43:B33, 1988.
19. Brand FN et al: Family patterns of coronary heart disease mortality: The Framingham Longevity Study. *J Clin Epidemiol* 45:169, 1992.
20. Sacher GA: Maturation and longevity in relation to cranial capacity in hominid evolution, in Tuttle R (ed): *Antecedents of Man and After,* vol 1, *Primates: Functional Morphology and Evolution.* The Hague, Mouton, 1975, p 417.
21. Cutler RG: Evolution of human longevity and the genetic complexity governing aging rate. *Proc Natl Acad Sci USA* 72:4664, 1975.
22. Martin GM: Genetic syndromes in man with potential relevance to the pathobiology of aging, in Bergsma D, Harrison DE (eds): *Genetic Effects on Aging. Birth Defects: Original Article Series,* vol XIV, no. 1. New York, Liss, 1978, p 5.
23. Comfort A: *The Biology of Senescence.* New York, Elsevier, 1979.
24. Holden C: Why do women live longer than men? *Science* 238:158, 1987.
25. Brody JA, Brock DB: Epidemiologic and statistical characteristics of the United States elderly population, in Finch CE, Schneider EL (eds): *Handbook of the Biology of Aging,* 2d ed. New York, Van Nostrand Reinhold, 1985, p 3.
26. Hamilton JB: The role of testicular secretions as indicated by the effects of castration in man and the short lifespan associated with maleness. *Recent Prog Horm Res* 3:257, 1948.
27. Migeon BR et al: Differential expression of steroid sulfatase locus on active and inactive human X chromosomes. *Nature* 299:838, 1982.
28. Wareham KA et al: Age-related reactivation of an X-linked gene. *Nature* 327:725, 1987.
29. Migeon BR et al: Effects of ageing on reactivation of the human X-linked HPRT locus. *Nature* 335:93, 1988.
30. Cock AG: Dosage compensation and sex-chromatin in nonmammals. *Genet Res* 5:354, 1964.
31. Cherkin A, Eckardt MJ: Effects of dimethylaminoethanol upon life-span and behavior of aged Japanese quail. *J Gerontol* 32:38, 1977.

32. Leviatan V, Cohen J: Gender differences in life expectancy among kibbutz members. *Soc Sci Med* 21:545, 1985.
33. Berkel J, de Waard F: Mortality pattern and life expectancy of Seventh-Day Adventists in the Netherlands. *Int J Epidemiol* 12:455, 1983.
34. Hazzard WR: Biological basis of the sex differential in longevity. *J Am Geriatr Soc* 34:455, 1986.
35. Seely S: The gender gap: Why do women live longer than men? *Int J Cardiol* 29:113, 1990.
36. McDonnel R, Maynard A: Estimation of life years lost from alcohol-related premature death. *Alcohol Alcohol* 20:435, 1985.
37. Holden C: Can smoking explain the ultimate gender gap? *Science* 221:1034, 1983.
38. Childs B, Schriver CR: Age at onset and causes of disease. *Perspect Biol Med* 29:437, 1986.
39. Gould S: *Ontogeny and Phylogeny*. Cambridge, MA, Harvard University Press, 1977.
40. Martin GM et al: Clonal selection, attenuation and differentiation in an *in-vitro* model of hyperplasia. *Am J Pathol* 74:137, 1974.
41. Hayflick L, Moorhead PS: The serial cultivation of human diploid cell strains. *Exp Cell Res* 25:585, 1961.
42. Martin GM: Genetic and evolutionary aspects of aging. *Fed Proc* 38:1962, 1979.
43. Martin G et al: Senescence and vascular disease. *Adv Exp Med Biol* 61:163, 1975.
44. Cutler RG: On the nature of aging and life maintenance processes, in Cutler RG (ed): *Interdisciplinary Topics in Gerontology,* vol 9. Basel, Karger, 1976, p 83.
45. Harman D: The aging process. *Proc Natl Acad Sci USA* 78:7124, 1981.
46. Burnet M: *Intrinsic Mutagenesis: A Genetic Approach to Ageing*. New York, Wiley, 1974.
47. Orgel LE: The maintenance of the accuracy of protein synthesis and its relevance to ageing. *Proc Natl Acad Sci USA* 49:517, 1963.
48. Gracy RW et al: Impaired protein degradation may account for the accumulation of "abnormal" proteins in aging cells, in Adelman RC, Dekker EE (eds): *Modification of Proteins during Aging,* vol 7. New York, Liss, 1985, p 1.
49. Holliday R: The inheritance of epigenetic defects. *Science* 238:163, 1987.
50. Salk D et al: *Werner's Syndrome and Human Aging*. New York, Plenum Press, 1985.
51. Brown WT: Genetic diseases of premature aging as models of senescence. *Annu Rev Geriatr Gerontol* 10:23, 1990.
52. Goldstein S et al: Werner syndrome: A molecular genetic hypothesis. *J Gerontol* 45:B3, 1990.
53. Goto M et al: Genetic linkage of Werner's syndrome to five markers on chromosome 8. *Nature* 355:735, 1992.
54. Fukuchi K et al: Mutator phenotype of Werner syndrome is characterized by extensive deletions. *Proc Natl Acad Sci USA* 86:5893, 1989.
55. Chan JYH et al: Altered DNA ligase I activity in Bloom's syndrome cells. *Nature* 325:357, 1987.
56. Willis AE, Lindahl T: DNA ligase I deficiency in Bloom's syndrome. *Nature* 325:355, 1987.
57. Poot M et al: Impaired S-phase transit of Werner syndrome cells expressed in lymphoblastoid cell lines. *Exp Cell Res* 202:267, 1992.
58. Brown WT: Progeria: A human-disease model of accelerated aging. *Am J Clin Nutr* 55:1222S, 1992.
59. Taylor AMR: Ataxia telangiectasia genes and predisposition of leukaemia, lymphoma, and breast cancer. *Brit J Cancer* 66:5, 1992.
60. McKinnon PJ: Ataxia-telangiectasia: An inherited disorder of ionizing radiation sensitivity in man. *Hum Genet* 75:197, 1987.
61. Nyhan WL, Sakati NA: *Diagnostic Recognition of Genetic Disease*. Philadelphia, Lea & Febiger, 1987, p 613.
62. Hall TC et al: Variations in the human Purkinje cell population according to age and sex. *Neuropathol Appl Neurobiol* 1:267, 1975.
63. Bigbee WL et al: Evidence for an elevated frequency of in vivo somatic cell mutations in ataxia telangiectasia. *Am J Hum Genet* 44:402, 1989.
64. Swift M et al: 1991 Incidence of cancer in 161 families affected by ataxia telangiectasia. *N Engl J Med* 325:1831, 1991.
65. Hartwell L: Defects in a cell cycle checkpoint may be responsible for the genomic instability of cancer cells. *Cell* 71:543, 1992.
66. Gatti R et al: Localization of an ataxia telangiectasia gene to chromosome 11q22-23. *Nature* 336:577, 1988.
67. Rahmani Z et al: Down syndrome critical region D21S55 on proximal 21q22.3. *Am J Med Genet* 7:98, 1990.
68. Korenberg JR et al: Down syndrome: Toward a molecular definition of the phenotype. *Am J Med Genet* 7:91, 1990.
69. Sinet PM: Metabolism of oxygen derivatives in Down's syndrome. *Ann NY Acad Sci* 396:83, 1982.
70. Glenner GG, Wong CW: Alzheimer's disease and Down's syndrome: Sharing of a unique cerebrovascular amyloid fibril protein. *Biochem Biophys Res Commun* 122:1131, 1984.
71. Terry RD et al: Physical basis of cognitive alterations in Alzheimer's disease: Synapse loss is the major correlate of cognitive impairment. *Ann Neurol* 30:572, 1991.
72. Brook JD et al: Molecular basis of myotonic dystrophy: Expansion of a trinucleotide (CTG) repeat at the 3′ end of a transcript encoding a protein kinase family member. *Cell* 68:799, 1992.
73. Martin GM: Syndromes of accelerated aging. *Natl Cancer Inst Monogr* 60:241, 1982.
74. Hobbs HH et al: The LDL receptor locus in familial hypercholesterolemia: Mutational analysis of a membrane protein. *Annu Rev Genet* 24:133, 1990.
75. Goldstein JL, Brown MS: Familial hypercholesterolemia, in Scriver CR et al (eds): *The Metabolic Basis of Inherited Disease,* 6th ed. New York, McGraw Hill, 1989, p 1215.
76. Goldstein JL, Brown MS: The LDL receptor defect in familial hypercholesterolemia: Implications for pathogenesis and therapy. *Med Clin North Am* 66:335, 1982.
77. Sing CF, Moll PP: Genetics of atherosclerosis. *Annu Rev Genet* 24:171, 1990.
78. Hobbs HH et al: Evidence for a dominant gene that suppresses hypercholesterolemia in a family with defective low density lipoprotein receptors. *J Clin Invest* 84:656, 1989.

79. Vega GL et al: Low density lipoprotein kinetics in a family having defective low density lipoprotein receptors in which hypercholesterolemia is suppressed. *Arterioscler Thromb* 11:578, 1991.
80. Jacobson DR, Buxbaum JN: Genetic aspects of amyloidosis. *Adv Hum Genet* 20:69, 1991.
81. Jacobson DR et al: Transthyretin Pro[55], a variant associated with early-onset, aggressive, diffuse amyloidosis with cardiac and neurologic involvement. *Hum Genet* 89:353, 1992.
82. Harats N et al: Hereditary amyloidosis: Evidence against early amyloid deposition. *Arth Rheum* 32:1474, 1989.
83. Yi S et al: Systemic amyloidosis in transgenic mice carrying the human mutant transthyretin (Met30) gene. *Am J Pathol* 138:403, 1991.
84. Cook RH et al: Studies in aging of the brain: IV. Familial Alzheimer disease: Relation to transmissible dementia, aneuploidy, and microtubular defects. *Neurology* 29:1402, 1979.
85. Glenner GG: Alzheimer's disease: Its proteins and genes. *Cell* 52:307, 1988.
86. Tanzi RE et al: Amyloid beta protein gene: cDNA, mRNA distribution, and genetic linkage near the Alzheimer locus. *Science* 235:880, 1987.
87. Van Broekhoven C et al: Failure of familial Alzheimer's disease to segregate with the A4-amyloid gene in several European families. *Nature* 329:153, 1987.
88. St. George-Hyslop PH et al: The genetic defect causing familial Alzheimer's disease maps on chromosome 21. *Science* 235:885, 1987.
89. Schellenberg GD et al: Genetic linkage evidence for a familial Alzheimer's disease locus on chromosome 14. *Science* 258:668, 1992.
90. Hardy J: Framing β-amyloid. *Nature Genet* 1:233, 1992.
91. Bird TD et al: Familial Alzheimer's disease in American descendants of the Volga Germans: Probable genetic founder effect. *Ann Neurol* 23:25, 1988.
92. Pericak-Vance MA et al: Linkage studies in familial Alzheimer disease: Evidence for chromosome 19 linkage. *Am J Hum Genet* 48:1034, 1991.
93. Harper PS: The epidemiology of Huntington's disease. *Hum Genet* 89:365, 1992.
94. Sudarsky L et al: Huntington's disease in monozygotic twins reared apart. *J Med Genet* 20:408, 1983.
95. The Huntington's Disease Collaborative Research Group: A novel gene containing a trinucleotide repeat that is expanded and unstable on Huntington's disease chromosomes. *Cell* 72:971, 1993.
96. Prusiner SB: Molecular biology of prion diseases. *Science* 252:1515, 1991.
97. Hsiao KK et al: Mutation of the prion protein in Libyan Jews with Creutzfeldt-Jakob disease. *N Engl J Med* 324:1091, 1991.
98. Bueler H et al: Normal development and behavior of mice lacking the neuronal cell-surface PrP protein. *Nature* 356:577, 1992.
99. Medori R et al: Fatal familial insomnia, a prion disease with a mutation at codon 178 of the prion protein gene. *N Engl J Med* 326:444, 1992.
100. Wallace DC: Diseases of the mitochondrial DNA. *Annu Rev Biochem* 61:1175, 1992.
101. Trounce I et al: Decline in skeletal muscle mitochondrial respiratory chain function: Possible factors in ageing. *Lancet* 1:637, 1989.
102. Cortopassi GA et al: A pattern of accumulation of a somatic deletion of mitochondrial DNA in aging human tissues. *Proc Natl Acad Sci USA* 89:7370, 1992.
103. Corral-Debrinski M et al: Hypoxemia is associated with mitochondrial DNA damage and gene induction: Implications for cardiac disease. *JAMA* 266:1812, 1991.
104. Glueck CJ et al: Familial hyper-alpha-lipoproteinemia: Studies in eighteen kindreds. *Metabolism* 24:1243, 1975.
105. Glueck CJ et al: Longevity syndromes: Familial hypobeta and familial hyperalpha lipoproteinemia. *J Lab Clin Med* 88:941, 1976.
106. Iselius L, Lalouel JM: Complex segregation analysis of hyperalphalipoproteinemia. *Metabolism* 31:521, 1982.
107. Heckers H et al: Hyper-alpha-lipoproteinemia and hypo-beta-lipoproteinemia are not markers for a high life expectancy. Serum lipid and lipoprotein findings in 103 randomly selected nonagenarians. *Gerontology* 28:176, 1982.
108. Vogel F et al: Spontaneous mutation in man. *Adv Hum Genet* 5:223, 1975.
109. Vogel F: Aging and reproductive performance: Models for the study of age-related chromosomal and point mutations. Paternal age and point mutations, in Schimke RT (ed): *Biological Mechanisms in Aging.* Bethesda, MD, DHHS (NIH) 81-2194, 1981, p 55.
110. Kram D, Schneider EL: Parental-age effects: Increased frequencies of genetically abnormal offspring, in Schneider EL (ed): *The Genetics of Aging.* New York, Plenum Press, 1978, p 225.
111. Hassold T, Chiu P: Maternal age-specific rates of numerical chromosomal abnormalities with specific reference to trisomy. *Hum Genet* 70:11, 1985.
112. Henderson SA, Edwards RG: Chiasma frequency and maternal age in mammals. *Nature* 218:22, 1968.
113. Brook JD et al: Maternal ageing and aneuploid embryos—Evidence from the mouse that biological age and not chronological age is the important influence. *Hum Genet* 66:41, 1984.
114. Erickson JD: Down syndrome, paternal age, maternal age and birth order. *Ann Hum Genet* 41:289, 1978.
115. Sved JA, Sandler L: Relation of maternal age effect in Down syndrome to nondisjunction, in del la Cruz FF, Gerald PS (eds): *Trisomy 21 (Down Syndrome): Research Perspective.* Baltimore, MD, University Park Press, 1981, p 95.

ADDITIONAL READING

Bergsma D, Harrison DE (ed): *Genetic Effects on Aging, Birth Defects: Original Article Series,* vol XIV, no 1. New York, Liss, 1978.

Holliday R (ed): *Genes, Proteins, and Cellular Aging.* New York, Van Nostrand Reinhold, 1986.

Lints FA: *Genetics and Ageing.* Basel, Karger, 1978.

Rose MR: *Evolutionary Biology of Aging.* New York, Oxford University Press, 1991.

Rothstein M (ed): *Review of Biological Research in Aging,* vol 3. New York, Liss, 1987.

Schneider EL (ed): *The Genetics of Aging.* New York, Plenum Press, 1978.

Sohol RS et al (eds): *Molecular Biology of Aging: Gene Stability and Gene Expression,* vol 29. New York, Raven Press, 1985.

Chapter 3

THE SEX DIFFERENTIAL IN LONGEVITY

William R. Hazzard

A visit to almost any long-term-care facility (except those of the Department of Veterans Affairs) will prompt the same question from even the most casual observer: "Where are the men?" This treatise will attempt to answer this intriguing question on the basis of both practical and theoretical considerations, though the data base for the speculations and conclusions is only now beginning to be assembled.

DIMENSIONS OF THE SEX DIFFERENTIAL IN LONGEVITY

The sex differential for longevity at birth in contemporary American society is between 7 and 8 years (Table 3-1). This can be contrasted with that in this country at the beginning of the twentieth century, when the nation was largely undeveloped, and in developing nations today, with expected longevity at birth being almost equal between the sexes in both circumstances. Thus the sex differential in longevity has arisen historically as a simultaneous by-product of socioeconomic and industrial development together with increasing longevity of both sexes, attributable to improved education levels, nutrition, housing, sanitation, public health, etc. Except for a dip at the time of the influenza epidemic in 1918, the sex ratio in mortality figure in the United States has risen progressively throughout the twentieth century (Fig. 3-1), only recently appearing to reach a plateau.[1] Intriguingly, as shown in Fig. 3-2, the gender differential in years of expected life at birth had begun to decline in the 1980s (see below for further discussion). To a certain extent this reflects the improved status of females that accompanies socioeconomic development (less sex discrimination in access to food and health care during childhood, better prenatal and obstetrical

TABLE 3-1

Average Life Expectancy at Given Ages for Adult Whites, United States, 1980, Presented by Sex

	Life Expectancy, Years		
	Male	**Female**	**Male/Female Ratio, %**
At birth	70.7	78.1	90.5
At 60 years	17.5	22.4	78.1
At 65 years	14.2	18.5	76.8
At 70 years	11.3	14.8	76.4
At 75 years	8.8	11.5	76.5
At 80 years	6.7	8.6	77.0
At 85 years	5.0	6.3	79.4

SOURCE: From Wylie, Ref. 2.

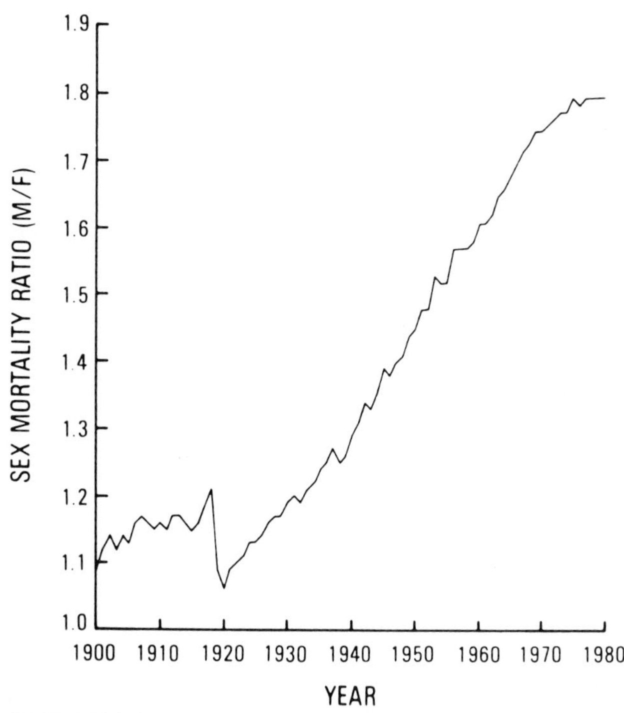

FIGURE 3-1

Sex mortality ratio (M/F), United States 1900–1980. Based on mortality rates age-adjusted to the 1940 total US population. (*From Wingard.*[1])

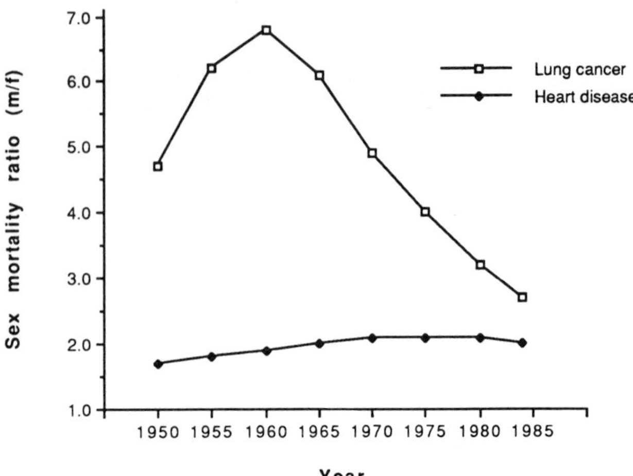

FIGURE 3-2

Secular trends in the sex mortality ratio (M/F) for lung cancer and heart disease, United States, 1950 to 1985. (*Reproduced with permission from Wingard DL, Cohn BA: Variations in disease-specific sex morbidity and mortality ratios in the United States, in Ory MG, Warner HR (eds): Gender, Health, and Longevity. New York, Springer Verlag, 1990, p 29.*)

care, increased employment opportunities, etc). This has allowed a greater proportion of female infants to escape the hazards of growth, development, and childbearing and to survive into middle and old age, when the chronic diseases that preferentially afflict men progressively dominate the list of causes of death.

When in the life cycle does the greater mortality of males begin? Apparently at conception (Fig. 3-3), when the ratio of male to female zygotes may be as high as 170 to 100 (for reasons that are unclear, Y-bearing sperm are more likely to fertilize an egg than those with the X chromosome). At 10 to 12 weeks, the sex ratio among abortuses is approximately 130:100. By birth, this has declined to 106:100. Parity between the sexes is reached near adolescence. At all points beyond that era, females outnumber males, and since the sex ratio at any given age is the cumulative result of the sex ratio in mortality at all previous ages, the gender gap grows progressively throughout the remainder of the life span. This is in spite of a progressive *decrease* in the absolute difference in remaining longevity between the sexes,[2] which declines to just over 1 year at age 85 (Table 3-1; this may be a minimum estimate, however, since a man who has survived to age 85 may be considerably hardier than a woman survivor of the same age). Interestingly, the ratio between the sexes in average remaining longevity is relatively constant beyond middle age, the man having 75 to 80 percent of the expected longevity of the woman of comparable age.

The sex ratio in long-term care facilities is thus due in part to the sex ratio in survival to advanced ages (which is approximately 3:2). However, the dependency (reflecting primarily marital status) of elderly women is also a major contributor: about 80 percent of men over 65 are married and 40 percent of women over 65 are married. The majority of the women are widows, and the ratio of widows to widowers is 4:1. Thus the elderly man requiring social and health care support is likely to have the help and company of his wife (who is also usually younger and more vigorous), whereas the elderly woman requiring such care is much less likely to have an able spouse in attendance, and long-term institutional care is thus a far more likely outcome.

BIOLOGICAL BASIS OF THE SEX DIFFERENTIAL IN LONGEVITY

The greater longevity of females versus males appears to have a fundamental biological basis. Studies of comparative zoology suggest that greater female longevity is virtually universal. Only when strains are inbred for lethal diseases selectively afflicting females does this general rule of zoology not apply, e.g., murine strains inbred for systemic lupus erythematosus

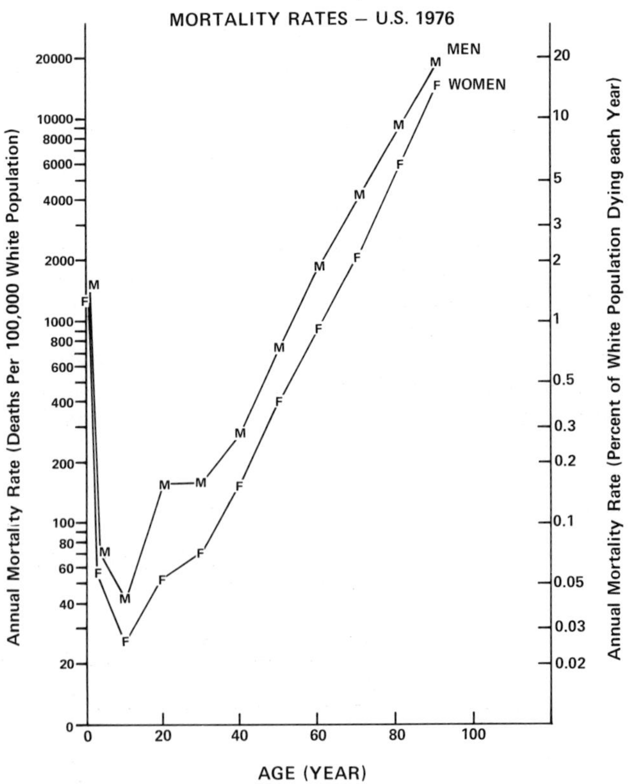

FIGURE 3-3

Mortality rates by sex, United States, 1976. (*Compiled from data presented in Gee EM, Veevers JE: Accelerating sex differentials in mortality: An analysis of contributing factors. Soc Biol 30:75, 1984.*)

in females. Thus it is logical to examine genetics to search for the basis of the sex differential in longevity.

To date, however, this approach has been largely unrewarding, whether at the level of molecular or population genetics. Clearly the burden of reduced longevity represented by all the known X-linked recessive disorders can account for but a tiny fraction of the sex differential in longevity. Studies of the Y chromosome (which bears but a few identified genes) and of the X chromosome have also thus far not yielded clues as to the greater hardiness of the XX genotype (there is no evidence for reactivation of the X chromosome inactivated by lyonization at the time of fertilization to replace X chromosome DNA damaged later in life, for instance). Further, studies (admittedly preliminary) of somatic cell longevity (population doublings or plating efficiency in culture) have failed to identify greater inherent longevity or hardiness of those with the XX genotype. Nevertheless, the possibility of a genetic basis for greater female longevity remains both an attractive hypothesis and an investigative opportunity.

Another line of investigation also bears consideration. A basic principle of gerontology holds that because decline in no single organ system is sufficient to account for the upper limit of the human life span, one should examine the function of integrating systems for decreased efficiencies with aging that may produce a synergistic effect among other systems, leading to a terminal cascade that ends in death by a maximum of 120 years. Specifically, these effects might occur in the neural, endocrine, or immune systems or at linkages among the three.

On superficial examination, this approach is a highly attractive way to explain the sex differential in longevity in both nonhuman and human species. Clearly there are major sex differentials in behavior, evident in both veterinary and human medicine, and preliminary anatomical evidence suggests sexual dimorphism in the human brain very early in life. Clear-cut sex differentials exist in areas of both normal intellectual function (e.g., a majority of boys perform better than girls on mathematical tasks and a majority of girls better than boys on verbal tests of the Scholastic Aptitude Test) and abnormal psychological performance (a pronounced male predilection is evident for such disorders as stuttering, hyperactivity/inattention, and dyslexia). It thus seems logical to hypothesize that the sex differential in behavior that underlies much of the sex differential in the major causes of death across the life span (see below) has as its root cause a sex differential in the neuroendocrine system, perhaps based, in turn, upon sexual dimorphism in sex steroid secretion at critical periods in development—intrauterine, infancy, and adolescence. However, perhaps because such an approach seems overly simplistic and becomes entangled in the long-standing scientific struggle between "nature versus nurture" and "culture versus biology," this area of investigation remains curiously unpursued, reflecting the historical gulf in communication between social and biological scientists that only recently has begun to be bridged.[1,3] That the sex hormones confer a sex differential in the risk factors to the major chronic diseases of middle and old age is incontrovertible, however, and this evidence constitutes the major thrust of this treatise (see below).

Equally attractive (and equally scientifically neglected) is the possibility that a sex differential in immune regulation (also probably conferred by the sex differential in sex hormones) underlies the sex differential in longevity. Most research and clinical evidence to date have focused upon the greater vulnerability of women than men to most of the autoimmune diseases (rheumatoid arthritis, systemic lupus erythematosus, and autoimmune thyroiditis are three notable examples) and to the rise in titer of many autoantibodies that accompanies aging. Indeed, such evidence of immune dysfunction may underlie the substantial female excess in many of the chronic diseases across the adult life span that account for greater *morbidity* among women (without commensurate increases in mortality), arthritis being the prime example. Put another way, there is no set of mortality-increasing diseases that is more common in women than men other than the autoimmune disorders (save for those virtually unique to the female, such as breast cancer). However, the collective prevalence of such disorders is not sufficient to narrow even slightly the overall sex differential in longevity.

Less clear-cut, but potentially more relevant to that differential, is what has been considered the other side of the coin of immunology, isoimmune regulation (the recognition of and reaction to foreign antigens), the declining function of which has been advanced as a fundamental theory of aging.[4] Here—though this is poorly documented—males may be at a disadvantage. Clearly males are at increased risk of death from infection across the entire life span, and the greater vulnerability of men than women to death from cancer may reflect a greater impairment in immune surveillance (this, too, is compounded by the sex differential in traditional "male behaviors" that increase risk of oncogenesis). Overall, however, like the sex differential in neuroendocrinology, the sex differential in immunology has been largely unexplored, though preliminary results suggesting modulation of immune function by certain sex steroids are intriguing.[5,6]

CAUSE-SPECIFIC SEX DIFFERENTIALS IN MORTALITY

A more empirical approach to the sex differential in human longevity begins with inspection of the sex ratio in longevity across the life span (Fig. 3-4). This configuration, with a peak of about 3:1 at age 20 and a plateau of about 2:1 in late middle age, is seen not only in the United States but also in nearly all developed nations.[1]

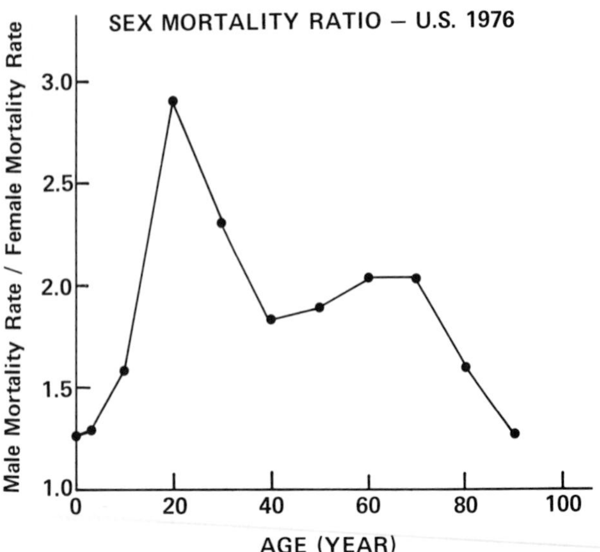

FIGURE 3-4

Sex mortality ratio, US 1976. (*Compiled from data presented in Gee EM, Veevers JE: Accelerating sex differentials in mortality: An analysis of contributing factors. Soc Biol 30:75, 1984.*)

Inspection of the sex ratio by cause of death (Table 3-2 and Fig. 3-5) reinforces the universality of the higher *age-adjusted* death rate of men versus women for all causes, both major and minor, with the single clear exception of diabetes, for which men and women are at virtually identical risk (see below). However, such inspection also readily allows grouping of these causes into those that are common in adolescence and young adulthood—dominated by violence and the risks of a youthful lifestyle—and those that are prevalent in middle and old age, the chronic and progressive "degenerative" diseases of complex etiology. In the first group, neurobehavioral sex differentials are clearly causative—"macho" behavior involving considerable risk being the most obvious factor increasing male vulnerability. Once again, however, the possibility that such behavior is determined at least in part by hormonal factors should not be dismissed, though modification—exaggeration or dampening—by sociocultural forces is clearly important. This risk-taking behavior also extends to sex differentials in drug abuse and sexual practices, with consequences that could have a dramatic impact upon the sex differential in longevity if the AIDS epidemic continues to affect men more than women. (However, narrowing in the sex differential in HIV-related deaths has recently become apparent as the viral infection spreads to women by heterosexual contact and intravenous drug abuse. Indeed, HIV is now the fastest-growing cause of death in young adult American women.)

The causality of the diseases clustered under the plateau of greater male mortality in later life is certain to prove multifactorial. An attractive hypothesis advanced principally by social scientists has, as with the spike in youth, focused upon behavioral-cultural factors. Men in Western societies have traditionally adopted lifestyles of greater risk to health: more miles driven, more alcohol consumed, more cigarettes smoked, less focus upon health promotion and disease prevention. Men have also traditionally made fewer visits to physicians and taken fewer prescription drugs. These latter phenomena have tended to confound the issue of gender and health: Women have greater morbidity (often reported in terms of encoun-

TABLE 3-2

Sex-Specific Mortality Rates and Sex Differentials for the 12 Leading Causes of Death, United States, 1980[a]

Cause	*Age-Adjusted Mortality Rate*[b] Males	Females	Sex Ratio, M/F	Sex Difference, M/F	% of Difference
Diseases of the heart	280.4	140.3	1.99	140.1	40.7
Malignant neoplasms	165.5	109.2	1.51	56.3	16.3
Respiratory system	59.7	18.3	3.43	41.4	12.0
Cerebrovascular diseases	44.9	37.6	1.19	7.3	2.1
Accidents	64.0	21.8	2.93	42.2	12.2
Motor vehicle	34.3	11.8	2.90	22.5	6.5
Other	29.6	10.0	2.96	19.6	5.7
Chronic obstructive pulmonary disease	26.1	8.9	2.93	17.2	5.0
Pneumonia and influenza	17.4	9.8	1.77	7.6	2.2
Diabetes mellitus	10.2	10.0	1.02	0.2	0.1
Cirrhosis of the liver	17.1	7.9	2.16	9.2	2.7
Atherosclerosis	6.6	5.0	1.32	1.6	0.5
Suicide	18.0	5.4	3.33	12.6	3.7
Homicide	17.4	4.5	3.86	12.9	3.7
Certain causes in infancy	11.1	8.7	1.27	2.4	0.7
All other causes	98.5	63.5	1.55	35.0	10.1
All causes	777.2	432.6	1.79	344.6	—

[a] Rank based on number of deaths.
[b] Per 100,000, direct standardization to the 1940 total U.S. population.
SOURCE: Calculated from data from the National Center for Health Statistics, 1983.

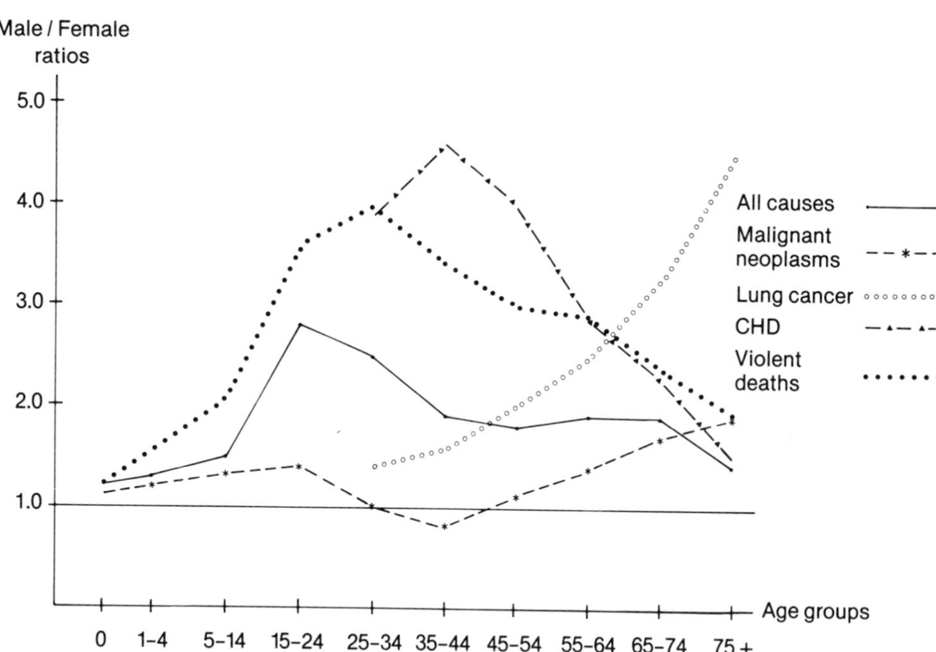

FIGURE 3-5
Sex mortality ratios for specific causes of death by age in the United States according to WHO statistics. (World Health Statistics Annual: Vital statistics and causes of death. World Health Organization, Geneva, 1986.) (*Reprinted with permission from Johnasson S: Longevity in women, in Douglas P (ed): Heart Disease in Women. Philadelphia, Davis, 1989, p 8.*)

ters with the health care system) but men have greater mortality.[2] The bases for these sex differentials in health behavior have been widely investigated (though with relatively little correlation with quantitative biomarkers of disease risk or measurements of sex hormone transport or effects) and have been reviewed elsewhere.[1,3]

The behavior with greatest potential impact upon the sex differential in longevity—and that behavior currently in greatest flux—relates to cigarette smoking. To illustrate this point, it has been reported that mortality in middle-aged nonsmoking men exceeds that in women by only 30 percent, compared with a male excess of greater than 120 percent for the total population studied.[7] Cigarette smoking became fashionable in this country in the twentieth century and until recently was predominantly a masculine habit, reinforced by the encouragement of cigarette smoking during the World Wars. The clear parallel between increases in male cigarette smoking and the rising sex ratio in mortality during the present century cannot be ignored. Indeed, it has been estimated by consensus that the historical sex differential in cigarette smoking behavior may account for as much as 4 years of the 7-year differential in expected longevity at birth.[8]

In this context it is relevant to examine recent trends in cigarette smoking in both sexes and parallel trends in mortality rates from diseases related to smoking. Cigarette smoking reached its peak prevalence in the United States shortly after World War II, when nearly half the adult population were smokers. At that time not only did more men than women smoke but also heavy cigarette use was far more prevalent in men. From that point through the present, cigarette smoking has declined, a decline that has accelerated progressively since the landmark Surgeon General's *Report on Smoking and Health* in 1963, the first clear public statement linking cigarette smoking to lung cancer and other diseases. Initially the decline in smoking appeared to be greater in men than in women, but by the late 1960s women were also giving up smoking. The decline was most notable among those over 35 years of age in both sexes. Hence by 1974, when the decline in coronary heart disease (CHD) mortality first received public attention (the "epidemic" having reached its peak about 1963, coincident with the Surgeon General's report), a significant proportion of that decrease was attributed to the decline in cigarette smoking.[9]

Interestingly, the relative decline in CHD mortality (which has continued to progress to the present) has been equivalent between the sexes, mortality among women declining by the same percentage (approximately 35 percent) as among men (the decline among women was shown actually to have begun far earlier, however). Nevertheless, because the absolute levels of CHD mortality were much higher in men, their absolute decrease in CHD deaths has been greater. Similarly, because the absolute level of cigarette smoking in men was higher than in women, their absolute reduction in cigarette "consumption" has been greater. Hence recent trends have shown a decrease in the difference in the number of CHD deaths in men versus women in parallel with the decrease in the number of cigarettes smoked by men as opposed to women. And, ominously, the sex differentials in certain clear-cut consequences of chronic cigarette abuse, such as lung cancer (which now surpasses breast cancer as the most common cause of cancer-related death in women), chronic obstructive lung disease, and peptic ulcer disease, appear to have narrowed in recent years.

The plateau (Fig. 3-1) in the previously escalating sex ratio in total mortality may reflect these changing patterns of cigarette smoking behavior between the sexes. This is further illustrated by the declining gender ratio in deaths from lung cancer (Fig. 3-2), the cause of which is most clearly related to cigarette smoking. If working women adopt (or retain) the heavy cigarette smoking behavior historically characteristic of men, a popular hypothesis related to changing lifestyles of women in the second half of the twentieth century may be borne out; namely, that the increased participation of women in the work force characteristic of this era (and their penetration into work domains traditionally dominated by men) will result in increased female mortality from diseases traditionally considered masculine, and a consequent narrowing in the sex differential in longevity will occur. Indeed, the modest decline in the sex differential in expected longevity recorded in the 1980s suggests that such a narrowing may have already begun.

However, the extant (but clearly imperfect and preliminary) data on this contentious subject provide no evidence to date to suggest that women working outside the home suffer increased morbidity or mortality; quite to the contrary, these women clearly enjoy improved health, with fewer days of disability and fewer physician visits than women who are not thus employed.[3] Just as clearly, however, these trends will bear close surveillance as the full impact through time of changing lifestyles between the genders becomes evident over the next several decades.

THE SEX DIFFERENTIAL IN ATHEROSCLEROSIS: THE DOMINANT FACTOR

Review of the leading causes of death (Table 3-2) clearly places atherosclerosis at the center of any consideration of the sex differential in longevity. It has been estimated, for instance, that elimination of atherosclerotic disease in its various manifestations, notably CHD, cerebrovascular disease, and peripheral arterial disease, could add more than 10 years to average longevity above age 65 in the United States,[9] raising the mean age at death to over 85 years. Furthermore, by deferring death among men beyond late middle age, reduction in the sex ratio in mortality and narrowing between the sexes (and between marriage partners) in their ages at death would be by-products.

Reference to Table 3-2 allows estimation of the potential reduction in the sex differential in mortality were these leading causes of death to be eliminated; it is readily apparent that elimination of atherosclerosis-related deaths would reduce the sex differential in longevity by nearly half, close to that potentially achievable through elimination of all the other leading causes combined.

While sex differentials may exist in the most basic aspects of atherogenesis (e.g., arterial intimal integrity, vasomotor response, lipoprotein uptake, or other aspects of arterial wall biology), evidence for all such possibilities must at present be considered preliminary, albeit intriguing (see below). A more practical approach is to review the traditional atherosclerosis risk factors as to possible sex differentials across the life span. Population studies suggest at least subtle differentials. Median systolic and diastolic blood pressure levels are lower in women than in men until middle age, when a crossover occurs such that hypertension (especially isolated systolic hypertension) is more common in older women than in men. After administration of oral glucose, blood sugar levels show a similar pattern. By contrast, blood lipids (cholesterol and triglyceride) change with age in a biphasic pattern, increasing in both sexes (albeit at lower levels in women than in men) until middle age and declining thereafter. Except for the abrupt increase in cholesterol levels in women beyond age 50, these changes in blood lipid levels (and the increase in blood pressure and in glycemic levels after administration of glucose in the first half of adult life only) have been thought to be mediated by changes in relative body weight (Fig. 3-6). These increases normally continue until middle age, when a plateau is reached. A decline during old age follows (the continued increases in blood pressure and blood glucose beyond middle age require a different explanation).

Close inspection of these curves reveals subtly different patterns in men as opposed to women: the

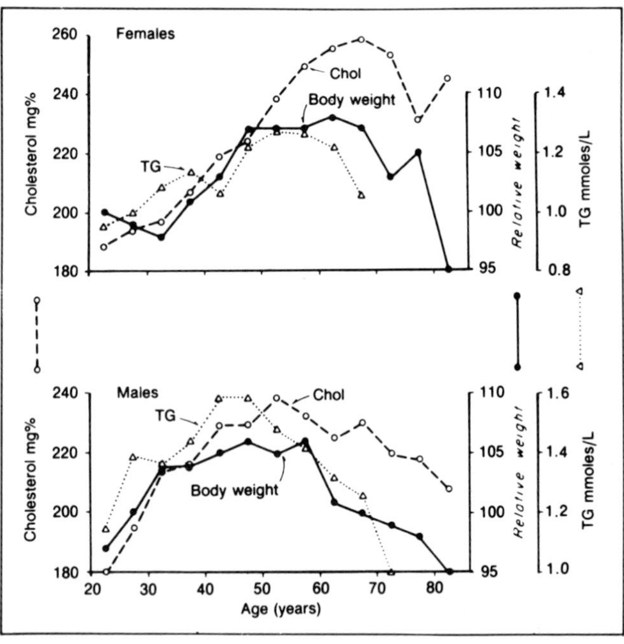

FIGURE 3-6

Median plasma cholesterol (Chol), triglyceride (TG), and relative body weight values as a function of age in Tecumseh (cholesterol and relative weights) and Stockholm (TG) community studies. (*Reprinted with permission from Williams RDH (ed): Textbook of Endocrinology, 5th ed. Philadelphia, Saunders, 1974.*)

increases from ages 20 to 50 are concave downward in men and convex downward in women, the middle-age-weight plateau being achieved approximately a decade later in women than in men (during the sixties rather than the fifties). Thus a slower accretion of weight and a later achievement of peak weight in women than in men may explain in part the more favorable cardiovascular risk profiles of women prior to age 50 and the infrequency of CHD in women prior to that age, a benefit that may carry over into the succeeding era by virtue of the slower rate of atherogenesis in women to that point.

The sex differential in regional patterns of weight gain is another possible explanation of lower cardiovascular risk in women, a topic of intense contemporary investigation (see Chaps. 15 and 72). Women prototypically gain adipose mass during childhood, preferentially about the hips and buttocks (so-called "lower-body," "pear-shaped," or "gynoid" obesity), while men add fat about the waist ("upper-body," "apple-shaped," or "android" obesity). The latter has been shown to confer extra cardiovascular risk, exaggerating the known interaction between relative body weight and the traditional risk factors in population studies such as in Framingham. Moreover, women who atypically demonstrate upper-body obesity have cardiovascular risk profiles (and relative sex steroid patterns) resembling those of men and are at substantially increased risk of type II diabetes mellitus (perhaps by virtue of increased insulin resistance and compensatory hyperinsulinism conferred by their relative androgenicity). This topic is of special interest in a review of the sex differential in longevity, given that diabetes mellitus is the one clear exception to the rule of greater male mortality (Table 3-2). Diabetes is, in fact, a relatively more ominous disease in women than in men, since it eliminates the relative immunity to death enjoyed by women in other spheres. Interestingly, the greater risk of diabetes and CHD posed by upper-body adiposity in women also appears to extend to an increased chance of developing breast cancer.[10]

Additional insight into the sex differential in atherosclerotic disease may be afforded by inspection of the sex ratio in cardiovascular mortality across the adult life span (Fig. 3-5). This demonstrates a major decline with advancing age, from nearly 5:1 at age 35 to approximately 1.2:1 at age 85 (it never dips below unity). Thus the pattern is far from static with advancing age. Viewed from another perspective, women enjoy an approximately 10-year relative immunity to cardiovascular disease compared with their male counterparts (the rate in women aged 55 to 64 being equivalent to that in men aged 45 to 54, for instance).[11–13] This immunity is even evident in the presence of a major monogenic disorder vastly accelerating atherogenesis (heterozygous familial hypercholesterolemia), in which a simply inherited approximately 50 percent reduction in low-density lipoprotein (LDL) receptors doubles the normal LDL cholesterol levels. Women with this disorder, present in about 1 in 500 in the American population, develop clinical atherosclerosis approximately a decade later than their similarly affected male siblings.[12]

A further clue to the mechanism of this protection is afforded in the greater incidence of ischemic heart disease in pre- versus postmenopausal women of comparable age (who are still at lower risk than men of the same age, however).[12] This suggests that the differential sex hormone status of premenopausal women may underlie their relative immunity to cardiovascular disease.

To consider this further, it becomes appropriate to review the hierarchy of cardiovascular risk factors by gender in middle and old age.[13] This clearly identifies the high-density lipoprotein (HDL) cholesterol as the most powerful risk factor (albeit in a negative, protective fashion), followed by the LDL cholesterol, positively associated with risk, and the other traditional factors. Of note, triglyceride levels and relative body weight each appear to be positively associated with cardiovascular disease only in women and only on univariate analysis, but this disappears in both instances on multivariate analysis. This reflects the inverse relationships between HDL cholesterol and both triglyceride and relative body weight. Thus obese, hypertriglyceridemic women may be at increased cardiovascular risk if their HDL cholesterol levels are depressed; if, however, their HDL levels remain normal in the presence of obesity and hypertriglyceridemia, they remain at normal risk.

Mean population levels of LDL cholesterol, HDL cholesterol, and the LDL/HDL ratio (a convenient index of net lipid-associated risk) across the adult life span are summarized in Fig. 3-7. These data from the 11-population hyperlipidemia prevalence surveys of the Lipid Research Clinics in the 1970s[14] reveal distinct differences between the genders. Lipid levels are equivalent in both sexes until puberty. At that time (and in parallel with the Tanner scale of pubertal development), HDL levels decline in boys, average levels staying lower in men than in women throughout remainder of the adult life span. Thus it would seem most likely that androgens physiologically suppress HDL levels. This hypothesis has received direct experimental support in studies of normal men temporarily rendered hypogonadal with a gonadotropin releasing hormone (GnRH) antagonist, in whom HDL levels rose (an increase prevented by simultaneous testosterone replacement).[15]

With regard to LDL, whereas mean levels rise in both sexes between puberty and the menopause, they remain substantially lower in women than in men until the menopausal era, when they rise significantly, average levels in postmenopausal women exceeding those in men of comparable age. These trends in women seem most likely to be attributable to the effects of estrogen in premenopausal women and the lack of estrogen beyond the menopause. Thus, it seems logical to hypothesize that physiological levels of androgens do not raise LDL levels; rather, estrogens lower LDL more than androgens do. (This contrasts with pharmacological types and doses of androgens, including androgenic progestins in combination

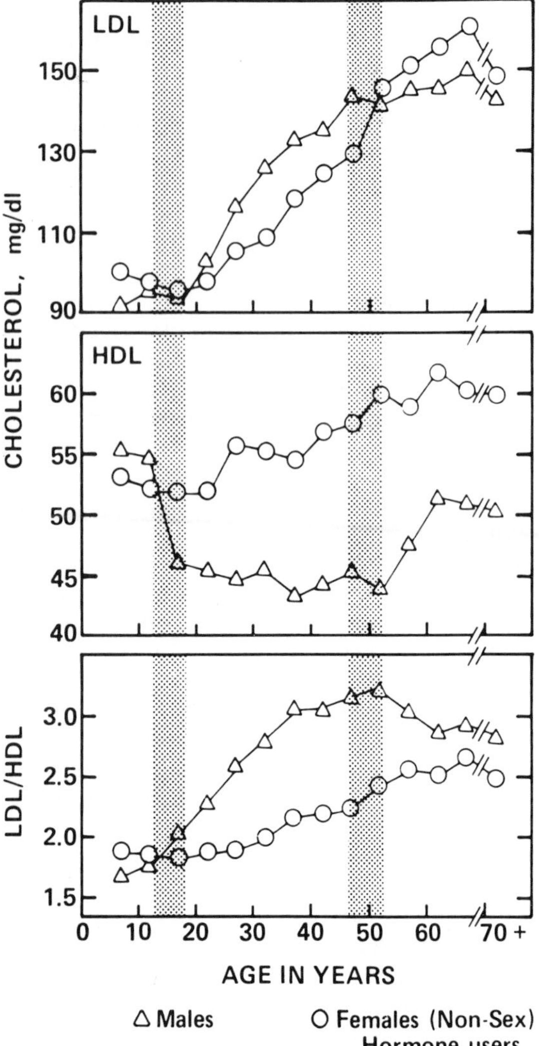

FIGURE 3-7

Median North American population high-density lipoprotein (HDL) cholesterol, low-density lipoprotein (LDL) cholesterol, and the ratio between the two versus age in white subjects. (*Data from Lipid Research Clinic Prevalence Survey.*)

oral contraceptives, which are associated with elevated LDL cholesterol levels.) Because the continuing differential in HDL levels exceeds that in LDL in the postmenopausal era, the mean LDL/HDL ratio remains higher in men than in women beyond the menopause, but the magnitude of the differential is lower among older persons.

Thus (1) the adult male/female ratio in cardiovascular disease is greater than unity at all ages, but it declines with advancing age, and (2) the adult male/female ratio in LDL/HDL is greater than unity at all ages, but it, too, declines with advancing age coincident with lesser estrogen secretion by postmenopausal women. Given these parallel trends, a simplistic hypothesis emerges, namely, that the sex differential in sex hormone secretion determines the sex differential in longevity in Western societies.

Can this, however, account for the entire sex differential in atherosclerosis? Not entirely, it would appear, yet nevertheless for a substantial fraction. Thus, in the lower three quintiles of the ratio of the total cholesterol to HDL (as an approximation of the LDL/HDL) in the Framingham study, women at a given ratio were still at lower risk than men.[13] However, in the upper two quintiles of this ratio (in which the majority of cardiovascular events were clustered), women were at equivalent risk with men.

Direct evidence linking sex hormone status with LDL or HDL levels has been hard to obtain, however; no study to date clearly links plasma levels of testosterone, the several estrogens, or progesterone with plasma levels of the lipoproteins. Estimation of the concentrations of free steroid hormone levels after measurement of the levels of the sex hormone-binding globulin (SHBG) probably represents the most promising approach to this issue.[16]

The most compelling evidence to date, lying in the association of exogenous sex hormone therapy with alterations in mean lipoprotein lipid levels, is increasingly persuasive. In the same Lipid Research Clinics surveys (Fig. 3-8), postmenopausal women taking estrogen replacement therapy (overwhelmingly consisting of Premarin, 0.625 or 1.25 mg daily) had higher HDL and lower LDL levels than those not taking estrogens.[14] Contrasting patterns were evident in premenopausal women taking combination oral contraceptives: their mean LDL cholesterol levels were higher than in women not taking exogenous hormones, presumably reflecting the androgenic effects of the progestational components, usually derived from 19-nor-testosterone, while average HDL levels were unaffected. Closer analysis of the latter data, however,[17] revealed that women taking oral contraceptives with a high estrogen/(androgenic) progestin ratio had increased average HDL levels, whereas those consuming combinations with a low estrogen/progestin ratio had decreased average HDL levels compared to those in women not taking these oral contraceptives. A number of other population-based studies have shown similar results (see Ref. 18 and Chap. 12).

These effects of exogenous estrogens have been confirmed in carefully controlled metabolic studies of postmenopausal women maintained on a diet of constant composition enriched in cholesterol content 84 days, in the middle 28 days of which ethinyl estradiol in a dosage averaging 0.06 mg/day was added.[19] These studies revealed rapid, reproducible, and dramatic changes in blood lipids with estrogen: average triglyceride levels rose (by 57 percent), total and LDL cholesterol levels fell (by 13 and 26 percent, respectively), and HDL levels rose (by 21 percent, albeit somewhat more sluggishly), the latter rising selectively in the more cholesterol-rich, buoyant, putatively more antiatherogenic HDL_2 subfraction (by 42 percent). The mean LDL/HDL ratio in these women declined by nearly 40 percent, from 2.5 to 1.5 (a cur-

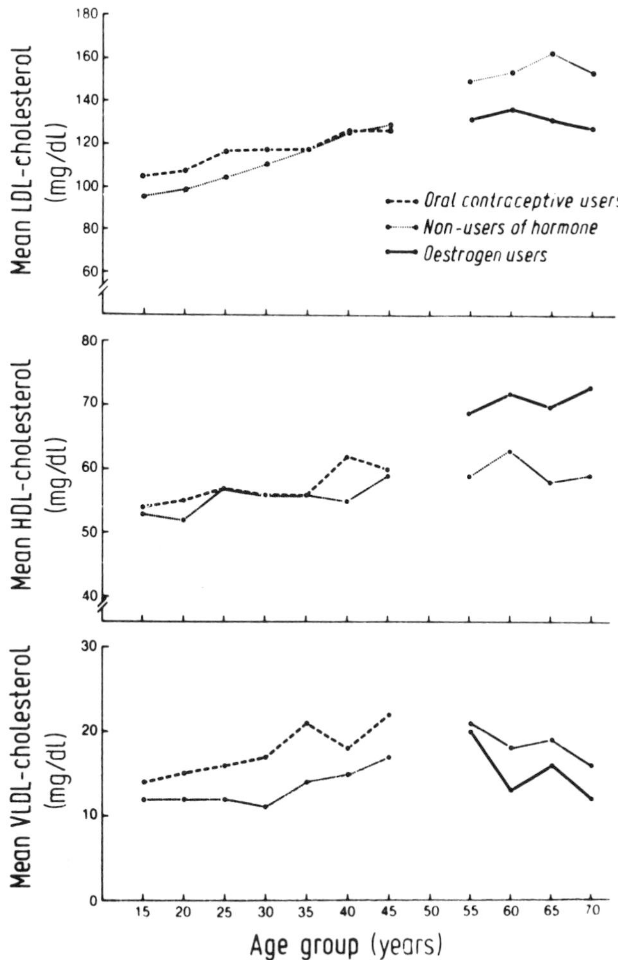

FIGURE 3-8

Plasma lipoprotein cholesterol levels in users and nonusers of oral contraceptives and estrogens. (*Reprinted with permission from Wallace RB et al: Altered plasma lipid and lipoprotein levels associated with oral contraceptives and oestrogen use. Lancet 2:11, 1979.*)

rent popular threshold for considering hypolipidemic therapy is 3.0). All changes were rapidly reversed upon estrogen withdrawal. Mean levels of the carrier apolipoproteins changed in the expected fashion: apo B fell, whereas apo A-I increased. These effects of exogenous estrogens upon plasma lipoproteins have now been widely reproduced in both normal subjects and dyslipoproteinemic women, and they are increasingly recognized by clinicians as having potential therapeutic value. Currently estrogens are receiving consideration by those crafting recommendations for the management of lipoprotein disorders in postmenopausal women, possibly even as first-line pharmacological therapy (see Chap. 73). Here an important caveat must be registered: estrogen may exaggerate hypertriglyceridemia specifically when of familial origin, raising triglyceride levels to concentrations exceeding 1000 mg/dl and thus risking hyperlipemic pancreatitis.

The other side of the sex steroid story, also relying on exogenous hormone administration, is seen in persons taking androgenic anabolic steroids. One such study[20] of postmenopausal osteoporotic women disclosed the dramatic effects of stanozolol in a therapeutic dosage of 6 mg/day: LDL rose (by 21 percent), HDL declined (by 53 percent), and the mean LDL/HDL ratio rose from 2.5 to 6.8, the latter clearly in the range of theoretically high risk. Moreover, the HDL_2 cholesterol fraction fell most dramatically (by 85 percent). HDL_3 cholesterol and apo A-I and A-II levels also declined, but more modestly.

A detailed study of a single volunteer confirmed those effects of ethinyl estradiol and stanozolol[21] estrogen dramatically and reproducibly raised HDL and lowered LDL cholesterol levels; stanozolol exerted opposite effects. Interestingly, the LDL and HDL levels of this woman were the same on the combination of both drugs as they were off both hormones.

Thus, exogenous estrogens and androgens produce changes in lipoprotein lipids which are at least a *caricature* of those in men and women under physiological conditions. Estrogens lower LDL and raise HDL (selectively HDL_2), while androgens raise LDL and lower HDL (selectively HDL_2). The mechanism of the fall in LDL (and in apo B and E levels) with estrogens is likely to relate to enhanced LDL (apo B and apo E) receptor function directly demonstrated in animals treated with estrogens[22,23] (and implied acceleration of LDL removal); whether androgens down-regulate the LDL receptor in reciprocal fashion is unknown. The mechanism of the increase in HDL with estrogen is likely to reflect retarded HDL catabolism[21] (though increased synthesis is also likely).[24] Androgens in mirror-image fashion lower HDL, most likely by accelerating HDL catabolism.[25]

Whether these pharmacological effects of sex steroids are relevant to the physiological effects of such hormones upon lipoprotein lipids, much less upon the sex differential in cardiovascular risk and longevity, is speculative. As noted, simple measurements of the sex hormones and their binding proteins do not provide a clear pattern of the expected correlations with lipoprotein lipids.

It is increasingly clear that the effects of sex hormones upon those lipids cannot account for the entire sex differential in cardiovascular disease. Indeed, it is currently estimated that the changes in lipoprotein lipids associated with postmenopausal estrogen replacement therapy can account for but 25 to 50 percent of the remarkable, at least 50 percent, reduction in CHD events in women who take such therapy (Ref. 26 and Chap. 12). This discrepancy has fueled recent research as to alternative mechanisms whereby estrogens may exert their cardioprotective effect, notably by means not reflected in plasma lipids and lipoproteins. Intriguing early results have been reported. For example, estrogens given to oophorectomized monkeys maintained on a hypercholesterolemic diet reduce uptake of LDL by coronary arteries of such animals[27] and acutely reduce the paradoxical vasoconstrictive effect of acetylcholine in their atherosclerotic coronary vessels.[28]

Still, an important clinical paradox remains unexplained. Estrogen given to men in middle and early old age has been associated with *increased,* not decreased, cardiovascular events. In a VA cooperative study of older men with noninvasive prostatic carcinoma, estrogen increased the death rate, attributable to a rise in cardiovascular deaths.[29] Estrogen (Premarin in a high dosage of 5.0 mg) also increased recurrent myocardial infarction (despite lowering cholesterol levels) in the Coronary Drug Project, a secondary prevention trial.[30] These results have led to caution in the possible translation of favorable estrogen-induced LDL/HDL changes into widespread use of estrogens, especially in men, since "what is good for the goose may *not* be good for the gander." Nevertheless, the consistently favorable CHD experience of postmenopausal women to estrogen replacement has reopened the possibility that men treated with *low-dose* estrogen or perhaps estrogen analogues with weak feminizing effects might still enjoy net cardioprotection.

Finally, a comment regarding the potential cardiovascular effects of the current widespread postmenopausal sex steroid replacement therapy (covered elsewhere in Chaps. 12, 74, and 76, the last with special reference to preservation of bone mineral content). The well-known increased risk of endometrial carcinoma in such women (with intact uteri) dictates cyclic progestational therapy to avoid the risks of unopposed estrogen treatment. Perhaps fortuitously, the progestin currently in widest use (and reported to eliminate such risk) is medroxyprogesterone acetate (Provera), a weakly androgenic progestin (not a 19-nor-testosterone derivative) that has no measurable effects upon lipoprotein lipids in the doses currently recommended. Thus clinicians can be reassured that the clear benefits of reduced CHD risk in postmenopausal women taking estrogen replacement therapy will not be nullified by concomitant continuous or cyclic progestin treatment in currently recommended regimens.

IMPLICATIONS OF THE SEX DIFFERENTIAL TO GERIATRICS: PRESENT AND FUTURE

Given the concentration of geriatric care in the most frail and dependent segment of the population, geriatricians care predominantly for elderly women. Nowhere is this more evident than in long-term institutional care, in which women constitute about 85 percent of the resident population and the gender ratio of 7:1 far exceeds that in the free-living population of comparable age. Current trends suggest at last that this sex differential in mortality is beginning to diminish as the twentieth century nears its end. However, this is occurring as death rates for both sexes are continuing to decline, and notably so at advanced ages. The gains in longevity among American males are currently exceeding those among females and may reflect the greater potential for reductions in the leading causes of death among men (especially CHD). There may be relatively less opportunity ("room") for extension of average longevity among women, given the "barrier to immortality" that defines the upper limit of the lifespan for our species. Ironically, however, the most obvious and, to date, most powerful life-extending intervention, estrogen replacement therapy, is currently only practically applicable to women. Thus, should long-term estrogen replacement therapy become nearly universal among postmenopausal women in America, the gender gap in average longevity could widen once again in the twenty-first century. It may be equally probable, however, that men in the future will continue to enjoy further reductions in premature mortality as they become more health conscious and adopt behaviors that are both less risky (e.g., cigarette smoking cessation) and more healthy (e.g., low-fat diets and exercise). Thus the difference in average longevity between the sexes should continue to decline in the twenty-first century even as average longevity continues to rise in both.

REFERENCES

1. Wingard DL: The sex differential in morbidity, mortality and lifestyle. *Ann Rev Public Health* 5:433, 1984.
2. Wylie CM: Contrasts in the health of elderly men and women: An analysis of recent data for whites in the United States. *J Am Geriatr Soc* 32:670, 1984.
3. Nathanson CA, Lorenz G: Women and health: The social dimensions of biomedical data, in Giele JZ (ed): *Women in the Middle Years.* New York, Wiley, 1982, p 37.
4. Weksler ME: A possible role for the immune system in the gender-longevity differential, in Ory MG, Warner HG (eds): *Gender, Health, and Longevity.* New York, Springer Verlag, 1990, pp 109–115.
5. Lahita RG: Sex steroids and autoimmune disease. *Arth Rheum* 28:121, 1985.
6. Sthoeger ZM, Chiorazzi N, Lahita RG: Regulation of the immune response by sex steroids: In vitro effects of estradiol and testosterone on pokeweed-nitrogen induced human B cell differentiation. *J Immunol* 141:91, 1988.
7. Waldron I: Why do women live longer than men? *J Human Stress* 2:2, 1976.
8. Holden C: Can smoking explain the ultimate gender gap? *Science* 221:1034, 1983.
9. Stern MP: The recent decline in ischemic heart disease mortality. *Ann Intern Med* 91:630, 1979.

10. Schapiro DV, Kumar NB, Lyman GH, Cox CE: Abdominal obesity and breast cancer risk. *Ann Intern Med* 112:182, 1990.
11. Brock DB, Brody JA: Statistical and epidemiological characteristics, in Andres R, Bierman E, Hazzard W (eds): *Principles of Geriatric Medicine.* New York, McGraw-Hill, 1984, chap. 6.
12. Sullivan JL: The sex differential in ischemic heart disease. *Persp Biol Med* 26:657, 1983.
13. Kannel WB, Brand FN: Cardiovascular risk factors in the elderly, in Andres R, Bierman E, Hazzard W (eds): *Principles of Geriatric Medicine.* New York, McGraw-Hill, 1984, chap. 10.
14. The Lipid Research Clinics: *Population Studies Data Book,* vol 1: *The Prevalence Study.* DHHS (NIH) 80:1527, 1980.
15. Bagatell CR, Knopp RH, Vale WW, et al: Physiologic testosterone levels in normal men suppress high density lipoprotein cholesterol levels. *Ann Intern Med* 116:967, 1992.
16. Godsland IF, Wynn V, Crook D, Miller NE: Sex, plasma lipoproteins, and atherosclerosis: Prevailing assumptions and outstanding questions. *Am Heart J* 114:1467, 1987.
17. Knopp RH, Walden CE, Wahl PW, et al: Oral contraceptive and postmenopausal estrogen effects on lipoprotein triglyceride and cholesterol in an adult female population: Relationships to estrogen and progestin potency. *J Clin Endocrinol Metab* 53:1123, 1981.
18. Bradley DD, Wingard J, Petit DB, et al: Serum high density lipoprotein cholesterol in women using oral contraceptives, estrogens, and progestins. *N Engl J Med* 299:17, 1978.
19. Applebaum-Bowden D, Hazzard W, McLean P, et al: Estrogen reduces LDL cholesterol on high cholesterol diet in post-menopausal women (abstract). *Arteriosclerosis* 2:415A, 1982.
20. Taggart H McA, Applebaum-Bowden D, Haffner S, et al: Reduction in high density lipoproteins by anabolic steroid (stanozolol) therapy for post-menopausal osteoporosis. *Metabolism* 31:1147, 1982.
21. Hazzard WR, Haffner SM, Kushwaha RS, et al: Preliminary report: Kinetic studies on the modulation of high-density lipoprotein, apolipoprotein, and subfraction metabolism by sex steroids in a post-menopausal woman. *Metabolism* 33:779, 1984.
22. Windler E, Kovanen Y, Chao S, et al: The estradiol simulated lipoprotein receptor of rat liver: A binding site that mediates the uptake of rat lipoproteins containing apoproteins B & E. *J Biol Chem* 255:10464, 1980.
23. Ma PT, Yamamoto T, Goldstein JL, Brown MS: Increased mRNA for low density lipoprotein receptor in liver of rabbits treated with 17-alpha ethinyl estradiol. *Proc Natl Acad Sci USA* 83:792, 1986.
24. Schaefer EJ, Foster DM, Zech LA, et al: The effects of estrogen administration on plasma lipoprotein metabolism in premenopausal females. *J Clin Endocrinol Metab* 57:262, 1983.
25. Haffner SM, Kushwaha RS, Foster DM et al: Studies on the metabolic mechanism of reduced high density lipoproteins during anabolic steroid therapy. *Metabolism* 32:413, 1983.
26. Barrett-Connor E, Bush TL: Estrogen and coronary heart disease in women. *JAMA* 265:1861, 1991.
27. Wagner JD, Clarkson TB, St. Clair RW, et al: Estrogen and progesterone replacement therapy reduces low-density lipoprotein accumulation in the coronary arteries of surgically postmenopausal cynomolgus monkey. *J Clin Invest* 88:1995, 1991.
28. Williams JK, Adams MR, Klopfenstein S: Estrogen modulates response of atherosclerotic coronary arteries. *Circulation* 81:1680, 1990.
29. The Veterans Administration Cooperative Urological Research Group: Treatment and survival of patients with cancer of the prostate. *Surg Gynecol Obstet* 124:1011, 1967.
30. Coronary Drug Project Research Group. The coronary drug project: Initial findings leading to modifications of research protocol. *JAMA* 214:1301, 1970.

Chapter 4

NUTRITION AND AGING

Irwin H. Rosenberg

Nutritional considerations are fundamental to our understanding of healthy development and successful aging. Our knowledge relating diet and nutrition to disease prevention and health maintenance has reached levels that mandate nutritional assessment and planning as integral to patient management. Earlier population surveys of the nutritional status of institutionalized elderly demonstrated the prevalence of calorie-protein and micronutrient malnutrition, often reflecting and also adding to the clinical burden of concurrent chronic disease. These deprivations are, as well, frequently associated with social and economic characteristics of the aged.[1,2] Surveys performed in the past decade in North America and Europe[3–5] have emphasized the modest prevalence of undernutrition among the noninstitutionalized, free-living elderly. The focus on nutrition and aging has expanded beyond the prevention of poverty and undernutrition to the critical role of diet and nutritional factors in successful aging and the prevention of declining function and disease associated with age.

This chapter will present an approach to nutritional elements of patient care by providing a conceptual basis for recommending dietary and nutritional goals based on the special needs and physiologic changes experienced by the aging individual. Dietary and nutritional strategy for the generally well, aging adult or for the patient with chronic disease must be designed to lessen the progression or risk of degenerative diseases of the cardiovascular, nervous, musculoskeletal, visual, and gastrointestinal systems while also ameliorating the impact of chronic disease on nutritional status and function. There is scant justification for excluding this essential focus on diet and nutrition in patient management when the goal is no less than the maintenance of the greatest possible function and quality of life over the enlarging life span.

Changing Nutritional Requirements with Aging

Dietary and nutritional management of aging adults must be based upon an understanding of the physiologic changes that are occurring in association with aging and the impact of these changes on nutritional needs. In the past, few studies have been directed specifically to the dietary goals and requirements of the elderly, as researchers have been dependent upon extrapolating from recommendations for younger adults, as in the case of the recommended dietary allowances (RDAs) in the United States. The volume of available information relevant to the dietary requirements of the elderly is growing rapidly, as more studies focus on the elderly population. Table 4-1 enumerates some of the changes in body composition and physiologic function with age that influence changing nutritional requirements.

TABLE 4-1

Age-Related Changes in Physiologic Function That Influence Nutrient Needs

- Energy requirements decline as the muscle mass of the aging person decreases; fewer calories are used in physical activity.
- Peripheral tissues of older persons take up fat-soluble vitamins at slower rates, thus vitamin A intake in elderly people results in higher circulating levels of vitamin A.
- There is a decline in immune function with age that may be responsible in part for the increased susceptibility to conditions such as infection and malignancy. At the same time, there is evidence that increased vitamin and mineral intake, including zinc, may counteract this age-related change.
- While the efficiency of nutrient absorption is relatively well maintained during aging, intestinal absorption of calcium declines.
- Skin synthesis of vitamin D diminishes.
- Metabolic utilization of vitamin B_6 in older subjects is less efficient.
- One-third of individuals over age 70 lose entirely or have a significantly diminished capacity to secrete stomach acid. The effect of lower stomach acid on the absorption of vitamin B_{12}, calcium, iron, folic acid, and possibly zinc appears to explain some of the increased tendency for depletion of some of those micronutrients with age and the possible need for increased intake by diet or the use of supplements.
- Both the senses of smell and taste decline with age.

Changes in Body Composition: Loss of Lean Mass

Some of the most dramatic changes that we see with age are changes in body composition (see Chap. 44). Figure 4-1 plots the decline in lean body mass over the age span for both men and women.[6] If one projects these changes beyond age 80, they become further accelerated. The average woman's lean body mass is always less, but the decline is just as striking. Some studies show accelerated decline after the menopause. The condition or state of sarcopenia, literally deficiency of flesh or muscle,[7] strongly influences muscle strength and mobility and contributes to falls and frailty.

This age-related change is even more dramatic if one measures the decline in muscle mass as opposed to total lean body mass. A cross-sectional study of 959 healthy men aged 20 to 97 years[8] examined their 24-hour creatinine excretion as a measure of muscle mass. As shown in Fig. 4-2, the decline by decade is particularly dramatic after age 60. Direct regional assessments of the cross-sectional area of skeletal muscle may be made by analyzing images yielded by computed tomography (CT) of the area of interest. At the level of the midthigh, for example, muscle accounts for 90 percent of the cross-sectional area in active young men but only 30 percent in frail elderly women, as exemplified by this typical scan in a 90-year-old woman[9] (Fig. 4-3).

The nutritional implications of this change in body composition are many. The simplest is that energy requirements diminish by about 100 calories per decade as basal metabolism strongly reflects the lean, metabolizing component of body mass. With a lower energy intake, it becomes very difficult for the older person to satisfy all his or her micronutrient requirements through diet alone.

The functional significance of these changes in the muscle portion of the lean body compartment is substantial. In an ongoing study of resistance training and nutritional supplementation in frail nursing home residents,[9] baseline relationships between body composition and muscle function have been characterized in 31 volunteers aged 72 to 99 years (mean = 87 ± 7). Several different techniques were used to partition body mass into fat and fat-free components in these subjects, since techniques of measuring body composition have not previously been well validated

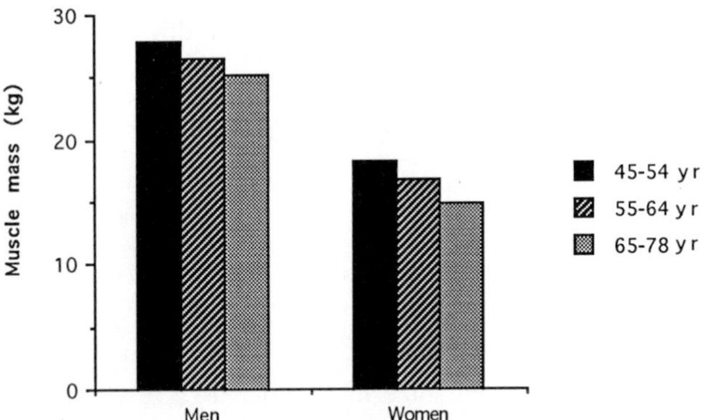

FIGURE 4-1
Declining muscle mass with increasing age (*From Frontera et al.*[6] *Reproduced by permission.*)

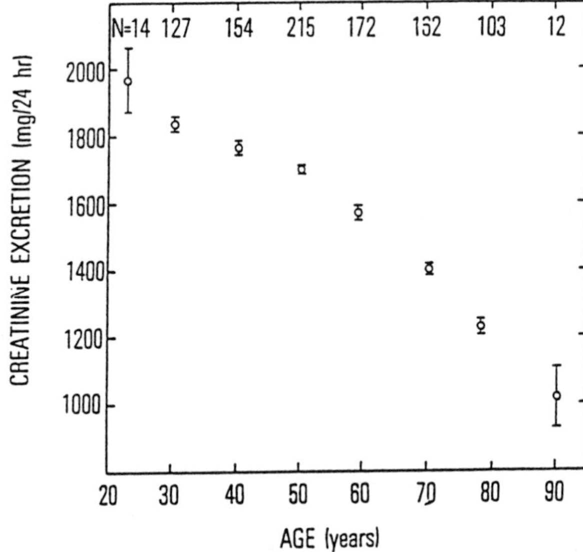

FIGURE 4-2
Creatinine excretion reflects declining muscle mass. (*From Tzankoff et al.*[8] *Reproduced by permission.*)

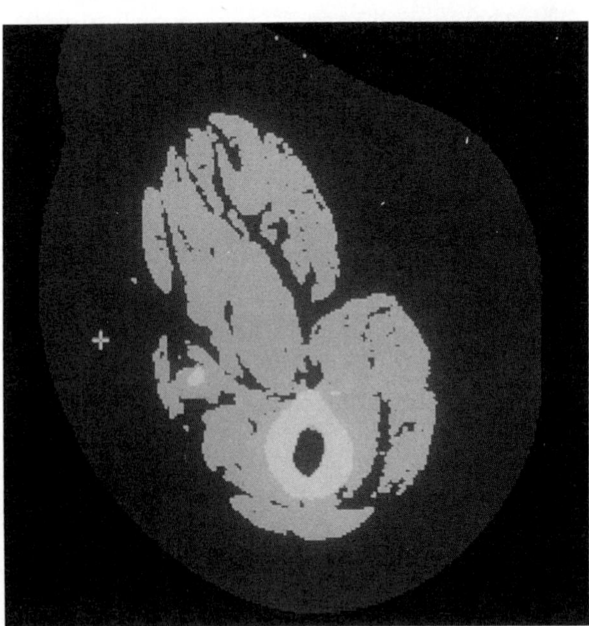

FIGURE 4-3
Computed tomography of the thigh of a 90-year-old woman. (*From Maria Fiatarone. Reproduced by permission.*)

in this population. Preservation of the fat-free compartment appears to be highly predictive of muscle function and mobility in the very old. It is clear that consideration of body composition is critical to any discussion of nutrient requirements and physical functioning in the elderly.

In a cross-sectional study, Frontera et al.[6] investigated muscle strength and mass in 45- to 78-year-old men and women. Strength in all muscle groups was lower in the oldest group. Absolute strength of women ranged from 42 to 62 percent that of men. When strength was expressed per kilogram of muscle mass, these gender differences were smaller and/or not present. This study indicates that muscle mass is the major determinant of the age- and gender-related differences in muscle strength. Therefore, if muscle mass can be preserved into old age, one would hypothesize that muscle strength could also be preserved.

Exercise is extremely important throughout life for women as well as for men, especially with regard to the changes in body composition and muscle function. Resistance training (weight lifting) is a form of exercise which specifically targets the decrements in muscle mass and function typically seen in sedentary individuals. There is now evidence that it is never too late to start such exercise, even among frail, institutionalized women up to 100 years of age.[10] When previously sedentary nonagenarians began a resistance training program for the lower extremities, Fiatarone and her colleagues demonstrated that they were able to increase the cross-sectional muscle area of the midthigh on CT scan by 9 percent and to increase maximal muscle strength by 174 percent on average.

This finding has a number of other important implications for nutrition. Increased muscle mass may be associated with greater insulin sensitivity, since skeletal muscle is the largest repository for glucose disposal. Maintenance of lean body mass through exercise may also prevent the reduced consumption of calories with aging that is related to a lowered basal metabolic rate.[11,12] Micronutrient deficiencies are most likely to arise in the setting of reduced total energy intake in extremely sedentary elderly subjects with low body mass who reside in nursing homes.[10] Among the micronutrients, vitamin D, magnesium, calcium, and zinc intakes are most substantially below the RDA in these sarcopenic individuals as studied by 3-day food weighing.

Declining Bone Density and Skin Synthesis of Vitamin D

Women have lower total bone mass, or total body calcium, than men. Over a lifetime, women lose about 40 percent of their skeletal calcium; of this, approximately half occurs in the first 5 years after menopause. During the 5-year period following ovarian failure, it is not possible to prevent bone mineral loss with calcium supplementation alone.[13–15] On the other hand, older postmenopausal women with the widely prevalent low calcium intakes (under 400 mg/day) benefit significantly at the femoral neck, spine, and radius from calcium supplementation.[15] In those with intakes in the intermediate range of 400 to 650 mg, the effect of supplementation with calcium to the level of the RDA, 800 mg per day, is less striking.

Inadequate vitamin D intake can lead to bone loss and increased risk of osteoporosis (see Chaps. 76 and 77). It has long been known that serum levels of 25-hydroxyvitamin D, the best clinical index of vitamin D status, are higher in summer and fall than in winter and spring.[16] In addition to the general finding of seasonal variation in 25-hydroxyvitamin D, levels of this metabolite decline with age.[17] Reduced levels of 25-hydroxyvitamin D in the elderly result from declining intake, decreased sun exposure, and, perhaps most importantly, less efficient skin synthesis of vitamin D.[18] Dawson-Hughes and coworkers[19] reported recently that, among healthy postmenopausal women, 25-hydroxyvitamin D levels were lower in winter only in those with vitamin D intakes under 220 IU daily. Those with low vitamin D intakes had parathyroid hormone levels that were higher although still within the normal range. Treatment of this population with a 400-IU vitamin D supplement prevented significant seasonal variation in either 25-hydroxyvitamin D or parathyroid hormone and, more importantly, reduced wintertime bone loss from the spine.[20] During this vitamin D trial, both the placebo and supplemented groups had significant and similar gains in bone density of the spine and whole body in the summer/fall. Overall, there was a significant net benefit at the spine from supplementation with vitamin D.

Those exhibiting seasonal bone changes (increases in summer/fall, decreases in winter/spring) also had seasonal changes of similar magnitude in lean tissue mass. As indicated earlier, moderate changes in body composition can have a significant impact on level of function in the elderly. Much is to be learned about why bone, lean, and also fat tissues fluctuate with the seasons. Potential contributors to these circannual changes include seasonal changes in exercise, nutrition, and blood levels of hormones that are known to affect the metabolism of these three tissue compartments.

Immunity, Nutrition, and Aging

From the involution of the adenoids in childhood and the thymus in early adult life and throughout the remainder of life, there is a continuing decline in the mass of immune tissue which is associated with some decline in immune function.[21] The decline in the mass of the immune system represents a substantial element of age-related decline in lean tissue mass, since the immune system is one of the largest in the body, representing 8 percent of the lean mass.[22] Since immune function depends critically upon adequate macro- and micronutrient nutrition, a general assessment of nutritional status often utilizes measures of immune function. Assessments range from total lymphocyte count to delayed hypersensitivity reactions in the skin and may include a measure of lymphocyte function, such as the proliferative response to mitogens or the stimulated elaboration of lymphocytic cytokines such as interleukins and tumor necrosis factor. The age-related increase in susceptibility to infection and certain cancers may be related to this decline in immune function.

Figure 4-4 depicts the interrelationships of nutritional factors and infectious and inflammatory diseases that are mediated by immunocyte-produced cytokines.[21] Adequate protein, vitamin, and mineral intake is essential for the maintenance of immune function. Moreover, the quality of immune function may be influenced by the nature of lipids in the diet, which act as precursors for eicosanoids, prostaglandins, and leukotrienes. Prostaglandins and leukotrienes are highly active substances that play an important role in the regulation of immune and inflammatory responses. Eicosanoid synthesis can also be modified by dietary antioxidant nutrients such as vitamin E, selenium, vitamin C, and copper. This can, in turn, influence cytokine production as well as other aspects of the immune and inflammatory response. Cytokine production by peripheral blood monocytes is impaired in patients with protein deficiency. Cytokines also are modulated by various micronutrients. The age-associated decline in T-cell-mediated function has been attributed to defective interleukin-2 production and responsiveness. Healthy elderly people supplemented with 800 IU of vitamin E for 30 days had a significantly greater increase in production of interleukin-2 than those consuming a placebo.[23] Chandra[24] has shown that nutritional supplementation with a multivitamin/multimineral preparation has resulted not only in improved in vitro tests of lymphocyte function but also in a decreased incidence of infections.

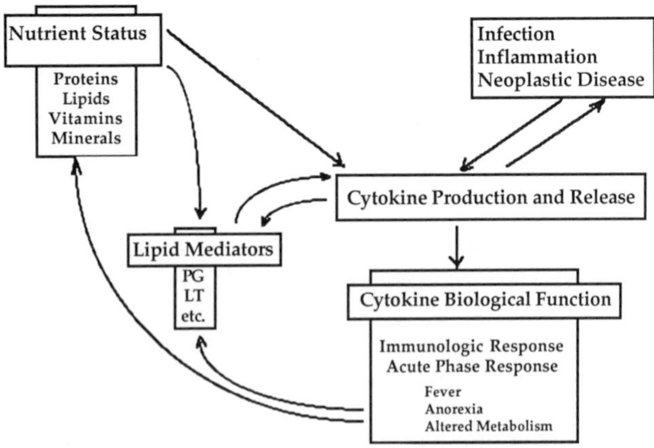

FIGURE 4-4

Interrelationships and mediators of nutrition and immunity. (*From Meydani S: Dietary modulation of cytokine production and biologic functions. Nutr Rev 48:361, 1990. Reproduced by permission.*)

Vitamin B_6 depletion in healthy elderly subjects causes significant reduction in interleukin-2 production, which returns to baseline following vitamin B_6 repletion.[25] Zinc deficiency in rats[26] and humans[27] is associated with impaired T-cell-mediated function. Thus, protein malnutrition, zinc deficiency, vitamin B_6 deficiency, and inadequate antioxidant intake—all conditions for which the aging are at greater risk—may negatively influence the function of the immune system. This adds additional emphasis to the importance of good nutritional status in the maintenance of critical functions over the age span. It has been argued that a significant proportion of the age-related decline in immune function could be prevented by more vigorous attention to the supportive and immunomodulatory effects of diet and nutrition on that system.[28]

Nutrition and the Aging Vascular System

The associations between dietary fat, cholesterol, and heart disease are widely recognized and highly relevant to the age-related changes in the vascular system. Atherosclerotic cardiovascular disease and nutrition are closely related (see Chap. 44). One relatively new entry into the spectrum of nutritional relationships with vascular disease and aging is homocysteine. Very high levels of homocysteine, a non-protein-forming sulfur amino acid, result from certain genetic defects. This disorder is associated with premature vascular disease and mental retardation.[29] More recent studies indicate that moderate elevations in homocysteine associated with aging[30] may increase the risk of vascular disease.[31,32,33] Homocysteine is believed to be a risk factor for cardiovascular and cerebrovascular disease in both women and men. There is also evidence in women that homocysteinemia is a potent predictor of premature peripheral occlusive vascular disease.[34] The reasons why high circulating levels of homocysteine in the blood result in cardiovascular disease are not fully understood, but it does appear that there are effects both on thrombogenesis and on the vascular wall. The lower risk of vascular disease among premenopausal versus postmenopausal women is reflected in homocysteine levels. The lower homocysteine levels among premenopausal women may be due to their higher levels of estrogens or to better nutritional status. Support for the first hypothesis is provided by data showing a reduced homocysteine level during pregnancy,[35] when estrogens are notably elevated.

Homocysteine metabolism is also regulated by vitamins, including folate, vitamin B_6, and vitamin B_{12}.[36] A greater response of homocysteine levels to folate therapy in elderly men and postmenopausal women[37] suggests that the higher homocysteine levels may also be due in part to subclinical vitamin deficiency. Lowered vitamin B_{12} status, with resulting higher homocysteine levels, may also result from atrophic gastritis, which is present in approximately 35 percent of men and women by age 80.[38] Resulting achlorhydria impairs the intestinal absorption of food-bound vitamin B_{12} by altering gastric acidity.

Changes in neurocognitive function in the elderly may be related to moderate elevations in homocysteine as well. Lindenbaum et al.[39] have shown that vitamin B_{12} therapy, which reduces homocysteine levels, also improves neurologic function in impaired individuals, often in the absence of hematologic signs of vitamin deficiency.

TABLE 4-2

Neurologic and Behavioral Effects of Vitamin Deficiencies

Vitamin	Presentation
1. Thiamin (B_1)	Beri-beri, Wernicke-Korsakoff's psychosis
2. Niacin (B_3)	Pellagra, dementia
3. Pantothenic acid	Myelin degeneration
4. Pyridoxine (B_6)	Peripheral neuropathy, convulsions
5. Folate	Irritability, depression
6. Cobalamin (B_{12})	Peripheral neuropathy, subacute combined system degeneration, dementia
7. Vitamin E	Spinocerebellar degeneration, peripheral axonopathy

Nutrition and Cognitive Function

Elsewhere in this text, the effect of aging on central nervous system (CNS) function is discussed (Chap. 87). There are many factors that influence the changes in CNS function with age. For our purposes, we will refer to some of the nutritional interactions that may explain and possibly help to reverse some of these declining functions.

No other organ system of the body depends more minutely on its nutrient supply than the CNS. In turn, that system has profound effects on dietary intake. Current theories describe functions of brain receptors for cholecystokinin, opioid-like endorphins,[40] and serotonin that appear to influence eating behavior and satiety. In animal studies, the number and function of such receptors have been found to decline with age. But the importance of these observations with respect to declining appetite in the elderly is uncertain. In addition, there are well-documented declines in olfactory function and less dramatic declines in taste function that may influence eating behavior and the hedonic threshold of the elderly.[41]

In addition to the minute-to-minute requirement for glucose by the CNS, almost all essential nutrients are required for adequate brain function and maintenance. Table 4-2 describes the various nutrients that are required for CNS function. In most people, overt vitamin and mineral deficiencies are uncommon. It is possible though, that milder, subclinical vitamin deficiencies play a role in the pathogenesis of declining neurocognitive function with aging.[42] Healthy elderly subjects with low blood levels of certain vitamins score less well on tests of memory and nonverbal abstract thinking.[43] Some recent evidence focuses more attention again on vitamins B_{12}, B_6, and folate. Declining vitamin status for these water-soluble vitamins has been reported in cross-sectional studies of aging populations, and, in the case of vitamin B_{12}, reversal of both cognitive and peripheral nervous system deficits has been observed even in the absence of any evidence of hematologic abnormalities of vitamin B_{12} deficiency.[39] These three vitamins, as noted earlier, are also involved in the modulation of homocysteine metabolism and circulating levels in the blood, and there is now compelling evidence that high levels of homocysteine represent an independent risk factor for cerebrovascular disease.[32] Twenty percent of the elderly cohort of the Framingham Heart Study (age 69 to 96) have elevated homocysteine levels, and these levels are associated with low circulating levels of folate, vitamin B_{12}, or vitamin B_6.[30] Elevated blood levels of homocysteine are strong predictors of occlusive carotid arteriosclerosis.[44] Thus, in addition to the direct CNS and/or behavioral effects of dietary factors and vitamins, there is the possibility that selected vitamins are important in the maintenance of normal levels of blood homocysteine, thereby functioning to limit the risk of cerebrovascular disease with its associated changes in cognitive function.

Nutrition and Vision

Of all the functions that determine the quality of life of the older person, none is more important than vision, and no functional impairment is more common than visual impairment. In a large cohort study, nearly half of the population between ages 75 and 85 had a history of significant visual loss because of cataract.[45] Fortunately, loss of vision due to cataract is usually correctable by surgery, and cataract removal is the most common operation performed in the elderly age group (Chap. 39). There is growing evidence that onset of cataract can be retarded in many cases by attention to behavioral and nutritional factors.[46] Since excessive light exposure and smoking are risk factors, avoidance of these oxidative stresses would diminish risk of developing cataract. Even in the face of oxidative stress induced by ultraviolet exposure, the presence of adequate levels of antioxidant nutrients in and around the lens of the eye may be protective.[47,48] Several observational and case-control studies have now documented a protective effect of increasing levels of vitamin C, vitamin E, and beta carotene in the diet and as measured in the circulation. Intervention studies are under way which should provide more discrete information about the levels of intake that confer protection.

Evidence is also accumulating in regard to the potential protective effect of antioxidant nutrients and macular degeneration, the most common irreversible cause of blindness in the elderly population.[49] Information linking the etiology of age-related macular degeneration to oxidation and indications that antioxidants may prolong retinal function are less well defined than in the case of cataract. Macular degeneration affects almost 30 percent of Americans over the age of 65, and that proportion increases with age.[45] The common form of macular degeneration characterized by slow, insidious atrophy of the photoreceptors in the retinal pigment epithelium severely compromises normal visual tasks such as reading, face recognition, and depth perception. Particular emphasis has been placed on photooxidative damage, since the photoreceptors in retinal pigment epithelial cells exist in a highly oxidative environment subject to bright illumination. If the pathogenesis of macular degeneration involves oxidative and free-radical damage, it is plausible that antioxidants that decrease this damage may provide protection. Protection by antioxidant nutrients has been observed in animal studies, and correlations between nutrient status and macular degeneration in human cohorts have begun to appear.[50] Taken together, these data clearly indicate correlations between photooxidative insult and loss of function of the lens and the retina. Until dose response and intervention studies provide guidance for recommended intakes of antioxidant nutrients by food and/or supplement, it will be prudent to recommend increased dietary intake of yellow and orange fruits and vegetables, with antioxidant nutrient supplementation for those unable to achieve adequate dietary intakes.

Nutritional Assessment

The nutritional assessment of the patient is an integral part of the patient evaluation and assessment of risk or presence of disease. All elements of patient evaluation are employed: history, physical exam, laboratory tests, and other diagnostic evaluation.

A carefully performed history may be the most valuable means of screening for patients at particular risk as well as for identifying symptoms that suggest nutritional deficiency. Some of the findings in the medical history suggesting increased risk of nutrient deficiency are listed in Table 4-3. There is broad consensus that unintentional loss of 10 pounds or more of body weight in the preceding 6 months is strongly indicative of nutritional risk and morbidity. A weight gain of 10 pounds or more in the preceding 6 months is also worthy of further evaluation. Weight change as an indicator of change in body composition will be further assessed, as noted below, by simply anthropometric evaluation of height and weight and the derived body mass index (BMI).

TABLE 4-3

Findings in the Medical History Suggesting Increased Risk of Nutrient Deficiency

- Recent weight loss
- Restricted dietary intake (limited variety)
  - Limited variety, food avoidances
- Psychosocial situation
  - Depression, cognitive impairment, isolation, economic difficulties
- Problems with eating, chewing, swallowing
- Previous surgery
- Increased losses due to GI disorders such as malabsorption and diarrhea
- Systemic disease interfering with appetite or eating (chronic lung, liver, heart and renal disease, abdominal angina, cancer)
- Excessive alcohol use
- Medications that interfere with appetite and/or nutrient metabolism

The history should include a qualitative assessment of diet that includes a description of the usual dietary pattern; problems in eating, chewing, swallowing, or bowel function; and description of food avoidances as well as drug use that may influence appetite or nutrient utilization (Table 4-4). The number of daily servings of breads, cereals, legumes, and fruits and vegetables, along with frequency of intake of meat, fish, and poultry, will provide an overview of the dietary pattern. The use of dietary supplements should be noted.

While the patient's weight is an essential part of any physical examination, it is important to measure height whenever possible, since the discriminatory and prognostic importance of the BMI that is derived from weight and height can be a highly useful tool for assessing and following nutrition and health status. Figure 4-5 provides a nomogram for the calculation of BMI from height and weight. Table 4-5 lists the signs on physical examination that suggest the possibility of nutritional deficiency and therefore should result in further quantitative evaluation of diet and nutrition-related risks. Table 4-6 provides a description of the desirable BMI levels according to age. These numbers are derived from data, elaborated elsewhere in this book (Chap. 72), showing that the relationship of BMI to mortality is a U-shaped curve, with increased mortality being associated with BMIs both below and above the "ideal" range.[51]

In addition to the central importance of BMI in the assessment of nutritional status, other anthropometric indicators have been used to further elaborate the information on body composition. The goal of these assessments is to determine the status of the muscle mass or lean body mass relative to norms or the patient's own pattern and also to determine the extent of fat as an indicator of obesity risk. Midarm muscle circumference and triceps skinfold measure-

TABLE 4-4

Common Drugs and Drug Classes That May Cause Nutritional Depletion and Deficiency

Drug Class	Drug	Deficiency
Antacids	Sodium bicarbonate, aluminum hydroxide	Folate, phosphate, calcium, copper
Anticonvulsants	Phenytoin, phenobarbital, primidone	Vitamins D and K
	Valproic acid	Carnitine
Antibiotics	Tetracycline	Calcium
	Gentamicin	Potassium, magnesium
	Neomycin	Fat, nitrogen
Antibacterial agents	Boric acid	Riboflavin
	Trimethoprim	Folate
	Isoniazid	Vitamin B_6, niacin, vitamin D
Antimalarials	Pyrimethamine	Folate
Anti-inflammatory agents	Sulfasalazine	Folate
	Colchicine	Fat, Vitamin B_{12}
Anticancer drugs	Methotrexate	Folate, calcium
	Cisplatin	Magnesium
Anticoagulants	Warfarin	Vitamin K
Antihypertensive agents	Hydralazine	Vitamin B_6
Diuretics	Thiazides	Potassium, magnesium
	Furosemide	Potassium, calcium, magnesium
	Triamterene	Folate
H_2-receptor antagonists	Cimetidine	Vitamin B_{12}
	Ranitidine	
Cholesterol-lowering agents	Cholestyramine	Fat
	Colestipol	Vitamin K, vitamin A, folate, vitamin B_{12}
Laxatives	Mineral oil	Carotene, retinol, vitamins D and K
	Phenolphthalein	
	Senna	Potassium, fat, calcium
Oral contraceptives	Estrogens, progestogens	Vitamin B_6, folate, vitamin C
Tranquilizers	Chlorpromazine	Riboflavin

ments, when compared to age-adjusted standards,[52] give some indication of relative muscle size and amounts of fat (Table 4-7). The triceps fat fold measures subcutaneous fat and is fairly well correlated with overall body fatness in younger adults; however, in older people, beyond age 75, the distribution and composition of body fat and skinfolds changes. These measurements are sometimes useful but often time-consuming and not highly dependable, particularly in individuals over the age of 75. Moreover, the total body fat may not be as important prognostically as fat distribution; therefore waist-to-hip circumference ratios adjusted for age, which measure the preponderance of visceral fat as a predictor of risk of diabetes and vascular disease, are more useful.

In the laboratory screens, a serum albumin level below 3.5 g/dl suggests the possibility of visceral protein depletion, although there is evidence of an age-related decline in serum albumin even in the absence of protein malnutrition. It is important to remember that assuming the recumbent position may cause up to a 0.5 g/dl fall in serum albumin in some individuals because of fluid redistribution. Low cholesterol levels are correlated with increased mortality in the long-term-care setting and may be an additional indicator of nutritional depletion. A total lymphocyte count under 1500/cm^3 may also be indicative of calorie-protein malnutrition.

Assessment of the results from the complete blood count as well as the total lymphocyte count may be useful in identifying people at risk. Newer data from the Framingham Heart Study has now extended our information about the risk of low or borderline status for folate and vitamin B_{12} to populations over age 75. Previous findings of the National Health and Nutrition Examination Survey (NHANES) and others that assessed status in individuals up to the age of 75 failed to show significant numbers of free-living elderly with deficiency. However, an extension of those surveys to older populations and the use of more discriminating measures of status suggest that the risk of folate and vitamin B_{12} deficiency is increased with age and may reach 20 percent of the elderly with borderline or low vitamin B_{12} status. Thus, changes in the mean corpuscular volume should be noted and additional measurements of folate or vitamin B_{12} should

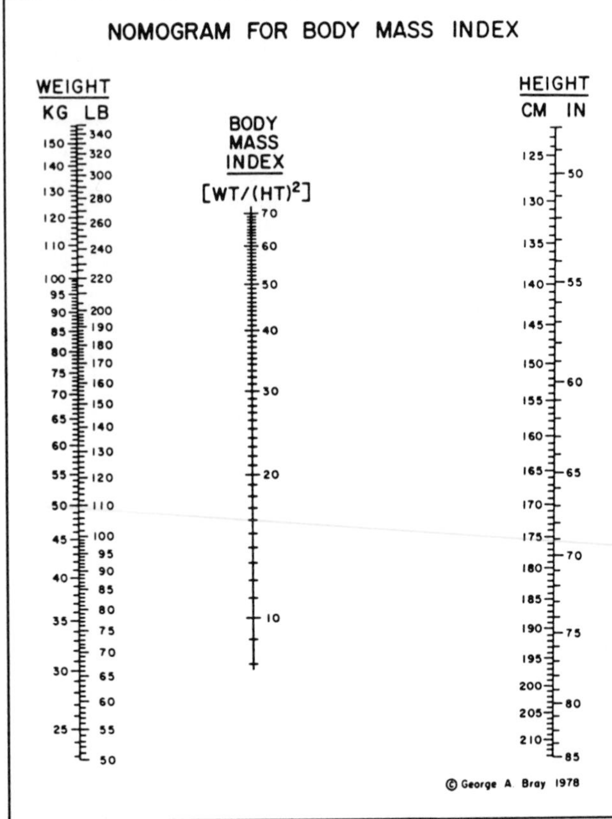

FIGURE 4-5

Nomogram for calculating body mass index (BMI). *(From Bray GA: The Obese Patient: Major Problems in Internal Medicine. Philadelphia, Saunders, 1976. Reproduced by permission.)*

be made in the presence of increased mean corpuscular volume or unexplained neurologic or cognitive impairment. Of special note is the observation that vitamin B_{12} deficiency may present in the elderly as a pure neurologic deficit even without any evidence of hematologic abnormalities.

The importance of considering vitamin D as well as calcium status in the evaluation of patients with symptoms or signs of osteoporosis has been emphasized. Recent studies showing the importance of dietary intake of vitamin D in the range of 10 μg (400 IU), particularly in individuals living in the upper tier of North America and Europe, where sunlight-generated vitamin D synthesis in the skin is nearly absent during all the winter months, emphasize that assessment of 25-hydroxy vitamin D should be considered as well.

Formulating a Nutritional Plan

With the goal of preventing disability, maintaining independence, and ensuring a satisfying quality of

TABLE 4-5

Signs Caused by Nutritional Deficiencies

Nutrient	Physical Signs of Deficiency
Calories (energy)	Weight loss, loss of subcutaneous fat, muscle wasting, growth retardation
Protein	Muscle wasting, edema, skin and hair changes, depigmentation, hepatomegaly
Essential fatty acids	Scaly, eczematoid skin rash on face and extremities, hepatomegaly
Calcium	Tetany, convulsions, growth failure
Phosphorus	Weakness, osteomalacia
Magnesium	Weakness, tremor, tetany
Iron	Pallor, anemia, weakness, lingual atrophy, koilonychia
Zinc	Hypogeusia, acrodermatitis, slow wound healing, growth failure, hypogonadism, delayed puberty
Copper	Bone marrow suppression
Chromium	Glucose intolerance
Thiamine	Beriberi, muscle weakness, hypesthesia, tachycardia, heart failure
Riboflavin	Angular stomatitis, cheilosis, corneal vascularization, dermatoses
Niacin	Pellagra, glossitis, dermatosis, dementia, diarrhea
Vitamin B_6	Nasolabial seborrhea, peripheral neuropathy
Biotin	Organic aciduria
Folic acid	Macrocytosis, megaloblastic anemia, glossitis
Vitamin B_{12}	Megaloblastic anemia, paresthesias, mental changes, combined systems degeneration
Vitamin A	Xerophthalmia, hyperkeratosis of skin
Vitamin D	Bone pain, bone loss, muscle weakness
Vitamin K	Bleeding, ecchymoses
Vitamin E	Cerebellar ataxia, areflexia

TABLE 4-6

Desirable Body Mass Index Range in Relation to Age

Age Group (Years)	BMI (kg/m^2)
19–24	19–24
25–34	20–25
35–44	21–26
45–54	22–27
55–64	23–28
65+	24–29

TABLE 4-7

Norms of Upper-Limb Fat and Muscle Areas for Assessment of Nutritional Status

	Men		*Women*	
Percentile	**Age 55–65**	**Age 65–75**	**Age 55–65**	**Age 65–75**
	Arm circumference (cm)			
10th	27.3	26.3	25.7	25.2
50th	31.7	30.7	30.3	29.9
95th	36.9	35.5	38.5	37.3
	Arm muscle circumference (cm)			
10th	24.5	23.5	19.6	19.5
50th	27.8	26.8	22.5	22.5
95th	32.0	30.6	28.0	27.9
	Triceps skinfold (mm)			
10th	6.0	6.0	16.0	14.0
50th	11.0	11.0	25.0	24.0
95th	22.0	22.0	38.0	36.0

life, the information from the nutritional assessment can be used to formulate a nutritional plan or prescription based on the special physiologic changes and needs of the aging patient as presented earlier. The plan should be quantitative as well as qualitative and may need to involve other resources and services, such as dietitians and social agencies.

For the generally well aging person with minimal evidence of nutritional deficiency, nutritional prescription should be directed to health maintenance and disease prevention. Older as well as younger Americans need to consume sufficient nutrients and calories and achieve levels of physical activity that maintain a desirable body weight. For the sedentary individual, that may mean counseling on techniques and methods that may increase physical activity and caloric expenditure. It is important to emphasize that physical activity should include strength-training exercise as well as aerobic exercise, since the former is more effective for the maintenance of lean body mass and muscle strength.

While appetite, dietary intake, and caloric requirements decrease modestly with increasing age, particularly in association with declining lean body mass, it is important to maintain the balanced dietary intake associated with a lessened risk of vascular disease and cancer, including four to five servings of fruits and vegetables daily, breads, cereals and grains. For the small or frail person with reduced total caloric intake, the ability to achieve a balanced nutritional intake from diet alone is increasingly compromised and the need to consider supplementation certainly increases, as noted in the section on nutrient requirements, below.

The principles of general dietary recommendations should apply. A diet based on grains, vegetables, and fruits, with moderate quantities of lean meat and dairy products and a modest intake of fats and sweets, is consistent with national dietary guidelines and recommendations. The requirement of the body for the 40 different nutrients for good health and disease prevention can best be met by eating a variety of foods. This recommendation consists of the following guides to daily intake:

1. Breads, cereals, rice, and pasta: 6 to 11 servings
2. Vegetables: 3 to 5 servings
3. Fruits: 2 to 4 servings
4. Milk, yogurt, and cheese: 2 to 3 servings
5. Meat, poultry, fish, dried beans, eggs, and nuts: 2 to 3 servings
6. Fats, oils, and sweets: to be eaten sparingly

Alcohol, if used, should be consumed in moderation (i.e., not more than 1 to 2 ounces per day). The serving sizes for these recommended numbers of servings and the total numbers will need to be adjusted according to body size and activity levels. It should be emphasized that increased physical activity will increase caloric needs and appetite, with the associated increase in intake of other nutrients as well as energy sources alone.

Of all the recommendations, those relating to increased intake of vegetables, fruits, and grain products may be most important from the point of view of intake of micronutrients (folate, vitamin B_6, vitamin C, beta carotene, vitamin E, and fiber). For those who do not or cannot consume adequate amounts of nutrients from food sources and those who have dietary, biochemical, or clinical evidence of inadequate intake, the possibility of supplementation with vitamins and minerals should be considered.

As discussed previously, certain micronutrients deserve special attention in the aging adult, as these requirements may not be as readily met. Among these problem nutrients are vitamin D, vitamin B_{12}, vitamin B_6, folate, calcium, and zinc. For those with risk factors relating to cardiovascular disease, cancer, or cataract, the use of increased amounts of micronutrients is associated with some diminished risk of these conditions. A good diet is also essential. Multivitamin and/or mineral preparations that include the dosage ranges in Table 4-8 are recommended.

Correction of Undernutrition

For those patients whose nutritional assessment indicates abnormalities in body mass or laboratory values indicative of undernutrition, special attention to nutritional counseling and intervention is mandatory. Quantitative evaluation of diet could be carried out in consultation with dietitians. Special attention should be paid to medication use and nutrient-drug interactions. Underlying diseases that influence nutritional intake, appetite, and nutrient utilization need to be addressed and treated. In some circumstances, social isolation, problems with mental health, and difficulty

TABLE 4-8

Ranges of Vitamin Doses for Prevention and Treatment of More Common Deficiencies with Aging

Vitamin	Prevention	Treatment
Vitamin A (μg)	1000	5000
Vitamin D (μg)	10	10–20
Vitamin E (mg)	10–20	100–800
Ascorbic acid (mg)	60–120	250–500
Vitamin B_6 (mg)	2.0	5–25
Folic acid (μg)	400	1000
Vitamin B_{12} (μg)	3–10	1000 (IM) per month or 1000 (PO) daily

in ambulation, shopping, and activities of daily living may require the additional involvement of supportive and social service agencies.

In the presence of accelerated loss of body weight and lean body mass or in the face of severe difficulty in dietary intake, the use of special enteral or even parenteral nutrition support techniques may be indicated, as discussed in Chap. 29.

REFERENCES

1. Vir SC, Love AGH: Nutritional status of institutionalized and non-institutionalized aged in Belfast, Northern Ireland. *Am J Clin Nutr* 32:1934, 1979.
2. Baker H et al: Vitamin profiles in elderly persons living at home or in nursing homes versus profiles in healthy subjects. *J Am Geriatr Soc* 29:444, 1979.
3. Hartz SC et al: *Nutrition in the Elderly: The Boston Nutritional Status Survey*. London, Smith-Gordon, 1992.
4. Garry PJ et al: Nutritional status in an elderly population: Dietary and supplemental status. *Am J Clin Nutr* 36:319, 1982.
5. deGroot LCPGM et al: Euronut-Seneca Nutrition and the elderly in Europe. *Eur J Clin Nutr* 45(suppl 3), 1991.
6. Frontera WR et al: A cross-sectional study of muscle strength and mass in 45- to 78-yr-old men and women. *J Appl Physiol* 71(2):644, 1991.
7. Rosenberg IH: Summary comments: Epidemiological and methodological problems in determining nutritional status of older persons. *Am J Clin Nutr* 50:1231, 1989.
8. Tzankoff SP, Norris AH: Effect of muscle mass decrease on age-related BMR changes. *J Appl Physiol* 43:1001, 1977.
9. Fiatarone M et al: Body composition and muscle function in the very old. *Med Sci Sports Exerc* 23:S20, 1991.
10. Fiatarone MA et al: High-intensity strength training in nonagenarians: Effects on skeletal muscle. *JAMA* 263:3029, 1990.
11. Shock NW: Energy metabolism, caloric intake and physical activity of the aging, in Carson LA (ed): *Nutrition in Old Age, Symposia of the Swedish Nutrition Foundation, 10*. Uppsala, Almqvist & Wiksell, 1972.
12. Tzankoff SP, Norris AH: Longitudinal changes in basal metabolism in man. *J Appl Physiol* 45:536, 1978.
13. Riis B et al: Does calcium supplementation prevent postmenopausal bone loss? A double-blind, controlled clinical study. *N Engl J Med* 316:173, 1987.
14. Ettinger B et al: Postmenopausal bone loss is prevented by treatment with low-dosage estrogen with calcium. *Ann Intern Med* 106:40, 1987.
15. Dawson-Hughes B et al: A controlled trial of the effect of calcium supplementation on bone density in postmenopausal women. *N Engl J Med* 323:878, 1990.
16. Stamp TC, Round JM: Seasonal changes in human plasma levels of 25-hydroxyvitamin D. *Nature* 247:563, 1974.
17. Tsai KS et al: Effect of aging on vitamin D stores and bone density in women. *Calcif Tissue Int* 40:241, 1987.
18. Webb AR et al: Influence of season and latitude on the cutaneous synthesis of vitamin D_3: Exposure to winter sunlight in Boston and Edmonton will not promote vitamin D_3 synthesis in human skin. *J Clin Endocrinol Metab* 61:373, 1988.
19. Krall EA et al: Effect of vitamin D intake on seasonal variations in parathyroid hormone secretion in postmenopausal women. *N Engl J Med* 321:1777, 1989.
20. Dawson-Hughes B et al: Effect of vitamin D supplementation on wintertime and overall bone loss in healthy postmenopausal women. *Ann Intern Med* 115:505, 1991.
21. Thomas ML, Weigle WO: The cellular and subcellular basis of immunosenescence. *Adv Immunol* 46:221, 1989.
22. Makinodan T, Kay MMB: Age influences on the immune system. *Adv Immunol* 29:287, 1980.
23. Meydani SN et al: Effect of vitamin E supplementation on immune responsiveness of the aged. *Ann NY Acad Sci* 510:283, 1989.
24. Chandra RK: Effect of vitamin and trace-element supplementation on immune responses and infection in elderly subjects. *Lancet* 340(2):1124, 1992.
25. Meydani SN et al: Effect of vitamin B_6 on immune responses of healthy elderly. *Ann NY Acad Sci* 587:303, 1990.
26. Dowd PS et al: T-lymphocyte subsets and interleukin-

2 production in zinc deficient rats. *Br J Nutr* 55:59, 1986.
27. Prasad AS et al: Serum thymulin in human zinc deficiency. *J Clin Invest* 82:1201, 1988.
28. Chandra RK: Nutritional regulation of immunity and risk of illness in old age. *Immunology* 67:141, 1989.
29. McCully KS: Micronutrients, homocysteine metabolism and atherosclerosis, in Bendich A, Butterworth CE (eds): *Micronutrients in Health and in Disease Prevention.* New York, Dekker, pp 69–93.
30. Selhub J et al: Vitamin status and intake as primary determinants of homocysteinemia in the elderly. Submitted.
31. Ueland PM, Refsum H: Plasma homocysteine, a risk factor for vascular disease: Plasma levels in health, disease, and drug therapy. *J Lab Clin Med* 114(5):473, 1989.
32. Clark R et al: Hyperhomocysteinemia: An independent risk factor for vascular disease. *N Engl J Med* 324(17):1149, 1991.
33. Genest JJ et al: Plasma homocysteine levels in men with premature coronary artery disease. *J Am Coll Cardiol* 16:1114, 1990.
34. Boers GHJ et al: Heterozygosity of homocysteinuria in premature peripheral and cerebral occlusive vascular disease. *N Engl J Med* 313:709, 1985.
35. Kang SS et al: Homocysteinemia due to folate deficiency. *Metabolism* 36:458, 1986.
36. Selhub J, Miller JW: The pathogenesis of homocysteinemia: Interruption of the coordinate regulation by s-adenosyl methionine of the remethylation and transsulfuration of homocysteine. *Am J Clin Nutr* 55:131, 1991.
37. Brattstrom LE et al: Folic acid responsive postmenopausal homocysteinemia. *Metabolism* 34:1073, 1985.
38. Krasinski SD et al: Fundic atrophic gastritis in an elderly population: Effect on hemoglobin and several serum nutritional indicators. *J Am Geriatr Soc* 34:800, 1986.
39. Lindenbaum J et al: Neuropsychiatric disorders caused by cobalamin deficiency in the absence of anemia or macrocytosis. *N Engl J Med* 318:1720, 1988.
40. Morley JE et al: Opioid modulation of appetite. *Neurosci Biobehav Rev* 7:281, 1983.
41. Schiffman SS et al: Increased taste thresholds of amino acids with age. *Am J Clin Nutr* 32:1622, 1979.
42. Rosenberg IH, Miller JW: Nutritional factors in physical and cognitive function in the elderly. *Am J Clin Nutr* 55:1237S, 1992.
43. Goodwin JS et al: Association between nutritional status and cognitive functioning in a healthy elderly population. *JAMA* 249:2917, 1983.
44. Selhub J et al: Elevated levels of plasma homocysteine are associated with carotid artery stenosis: Results from the Framingham Heart Study. Submitted.
45. Kahn HA et al: The Framingham Eye Study: I. Outline and major prevalence findings. *Am J Epidemiol* 106:17, 1977.
46. Taylor A: Role of nutrients in delaying cataracts. *Ann NY Acad Sci* 669:111, 1992.
47. Jacques PF, Chylack LT Jr: Epidemiologic evidence of a role for the antioxidant vitamins and carotenoids in cataract prevention. *Am J Clin Nutr* 53:352S, 1991.
48. Taylor A et al: Oxidation and aging: Impact on vision. *Journ Toxicol Industr Health* 9:349, 1993.
49. Taylor A et al: Relationship in humans between ascorbic acid consumption and levels of total and reduced ascorbic acid in lens, aqueous acid in lens, aqueous humor, and plasma. *Curr Eye Res* 10:751, 1991.
50. Taylor HR et al: Visible light and risk of age-related macular degeneration. *Trans Am Ophthalmol Soc* 88:163, 1990.
51. US Department of Agriculture, US Department of Health and Human Services: *Nutrition and Your Health: Dietary Guidelines for Americans,* 3rd ed. Washington, DC, US Government Printing Office, 1990, p 9.
52. Frisancho AR: New norms of upper limb fat and muscle areas for assessment of nutritional status. *Am J Clin Nutr* 34:2540, 1981.

Chapter 5

CLINICAL IMMUNOLOGY AND AGING

William H. Adler and James E. Nagel

The immune system is composed of a group of mechanisms that allow individuals to resist pathogens within their environments. Because of the variety of potentially harmful encounters, the immune system has to be extremely adaptable and able to respond quickly and appropriately. Age has a profound effect on immune function and host defense mechanisms; however, precisely defining the effects of age and the mechanisms by which age alters immune function are difficult. Many factors such as nutrition, environmental chemicals, ultraviolet radiation, genetics, previous illnesses, anatomic variations, and the neuropsychoendocrine system also influence immune function and modulate the effects of age.

Two well-established generalizations are that physiologic functions show a high degree of variability among individuals regardless of age, and interpopulation variability increases with age. While one can find among even the oldest old a few individuals with levels of immune function similar to that seen in many individuals decades younger, in general, aging produces increasing numbers of individuals with decreasing levels of immune function. To the clinician faced with the care of an elderly patient, the assumption can be made that one is dealing with an individual with defective host defenses, who is at a greater risk for developing an infectious disease, and who will have greater morbidity and mortality from that infection. Immunosenescence markedly affects the outcomes of many illnesses that have an age-related increased incidence such as emphysema, postoperative infections, urinary tract infections, diabetes, bowel inflammation, and infections in areas with decreased blood perfusion. Similarly, behavioral or lifestyle factors such as smoking, chronic stress, drug and alcohol abuse, and lifelong obesity contribute to the incidence, morbidity, and mortality of diseases associated with aging. While some feel that the decreased immune function of many elderly individuals can be entirely attributed to the diseases that accompany aging, we feel that a reasonably comprehensive picture of the effects of age on immune function can be determined by studying elderly individuals who either are free of known illness or have only minor diseases that have no significant influence on immune function.

Data that describe the immunodeficiency associated with aging have utilized elderly individuals from a variety of sources. Some studies have used ambulatory healthy individuals, others nursing home residents, and still others residents of chronic-care hospital facilities. The results obtained on these populations differ, although it is interesting to note the similarities. Since clinicians must deal with both healthy and ill elderly patients, it is important to recognize the various changes in immune function that occur in diverse populations. In general, differences in immune function between healthy versus ill elderly individuals concern the degree of loss rather than the loss of specific activities. The part of the immune system that is most influenced by age is T cells.[2] This would be expected if thymic involution has a long-term effect since the development of immunocompetence depends on the presence of a functioning thymus. As dramatically demonstrated in the AIDS epidemic, the T-cell system is of paramount importance in regulating immune responsiveness and in the development of cell-mediated immunity.

ORGANIZATION OF THE IMMUNE SYSTEM

The immune system is one component of the host defense system. Composed of a variety of both cells and soluble factors, these systems provide "tools" or "weapons" that enable individuals to deal effectively with their environments. While specific defenses acquired from previous natural exposure or through immunization are generally more effective in protecting an individual against pathogens, there are many nonspecific mechanisms that are highly critical. Before considering specific age-related defects of the immune system, it would be useful to review in a general way the host defense mechanisms that contribute to the maintenance of health.

The primary consideration in the interaction between a pathogen and host in determining whether the host will become ill and might possibly die is the element of time. For the most part, the nonspecific defense systems of a healthy individual are always ready to function and require minimal time before they are fully operational. In contrast, an immune response takes time. If an individual has a primary encounter with a pathogen, the infection can be well established before there is an adequate immune reaction. The immune response, if adequate, can then generally limit the infection, leading to the recovery of the patient. If the immune response is inadequate, the infection can progress and possibly cause death or become chronic and cause serious ongoing problems. It is the element of time that may be the most important consideration in the discussion of age-related immunodeficiencies. Since most age-related changes in immune function are ones of degree rather than an absolute, it is necessary to understand what half-normal levels of function mean when one considers the element of time. It has been repeatedly demonstrated that both the morbidity and the mortality of most infectious illnesses are increased in the elderly. However, a defective immune response is not the only cause of these findings. The first lines of host defense—granulocytes, complement, acute-phase reactants, natural killer cells, and fixed and circulating monocytes—are more important in the early response to a pathogen than an immune response. Cytotoxic antibody, lytic destruction of the pathogen, and phagocytosis of antibody-coupled (opsonized) pathogens are critical. The role of granulocytes in this process cannot be overemphasized. Normal T- and B-lymphocyte function on its own is ineffective in preventing bacterial infection. Individuals with deficiencies in specific complement components also have difficulty with infections despite the presence of normal levels of cellular immune function. In most elderly adult patients, a complete lack of a factor or cell or antibody is unusual, and since there are extensive interactions within the immune system among cells, antibodies, growth factors, inflammatory molecules, complement, and reticuloendothelial tissues, it is generally difficult to establish a direct cause-and-effect relationship between a quantitative change in function and a disease. Because of this, the basic causes of immune dysfunction in elderly persons are a central issue in aging research. Much of the past knowledge linking the fields of immunology, host defense, and aging is descriptive, but recently the mechanisms of age-related changes have begun to be actively investigated and scrutinized. A concise review of the normal immune system will help in understanding the changes seen with aging.

NORMAL IMMUNE FUNCTION AND HOST DEFENSE MECHANISMS

The immune system relies on the functioning of immunocytes in the lymph nodes, spleen, bone marrow, tonsils, and thymus, and localized lymphoid tissue associated with the respiratory and gastrointestinal tract. These tissues are composed of cells that either provide regulatory function or cell-mediated immunity or differentiate into antibody-forming plasma cells. Many lymphocytes, mostly of the T (thymus-derived) series, also circulate in the peripheral blood and in lymph channels, traveling throughout the body and trafficking through the solid lymphoid tissue. Regional lymphoid tissue, the lymph nodes, responds rapidly to antigens introduced into their region. The architecture of lymph node and splenic tissue is distinct—with the T cells residing in interstitial reticular areas and the B cells in germinal centers. The T lymphocytes, which depend on thymic influence for their differentiation and development from precursor to immunocompetent units, can be further subdivided into function subclasses based on identifiable membrane markers (Table 5-1). The subclasses include inducer-helper cells and suppressor-cytotoxic cells. These classifications can have some functional overlap depending on the assays employed. B cells can also be subdivided based on their stage of development, so that precursor, activated, immunoglobulin-synthesizing, and memory B cells are all identifiable stages in the B cell. Furthermore immunoglobulin-synthesizing cells can be subclassified by the types of light chains and heavy chains they synthesize. The membrane markers and membrane and cytoplasmic immunoglobulin can be identified using monoclonal antibodies. Serum antibody and immunoprotein can also be identified using various methods that utilize antisera, radial diffusion, radioimmunoassay, enzyme-linked immunosorbent assay (ELISA), and solid-state immunoassays. Immunoglobulin-synthesizing B cells can also be defined based on their usage of the variable and constant areas for the immunoglobulin gene.

Another subset of lymphoid cells which carry unique membrane markers are associated with a specific functional assay. They are the natural killer (NK) cells. These cells have the ability to lyse tumor cell lines in vitro without the necessity for a preceding immunization procedure. The role of NK cells in host defense is still being defined, but NK cells can kill some bacteria without a requirement for a preceding immunization. How these cells recognize a target as a foreign organism or a tumor cell without the aid of membrane immunoglobulin, Fc receptors, or T-cell antigen receptors is still not fully understood, but the in vitro assay for NK cell activity clearly shows that they have this ability.

The various cellular components of the immune system can interact through both cell-to-cell contact and the release of factors that can modulate their activities. Factors can supply obligatory signals for cellular differentiation or proliferation, facilitate the development of immunocompetency in concert with other factors or antigen, initiate an inflammatory response, or turn off an immune response. In many cases the cells that can respond to a factor need to express membrane receptors for the factor as part of a development or activation process. In the laboratory

TABLE 5-1

Human Leukocyte Cell Surface Antigens

Antigen Cluster	Other Names	Cell Types	Specificity
CD2	OKT11, Leu 5b, 9.6, T11	Thymocytes T cells	E rosette receptor Leukocyte function Antigen 3 (LFA-3)
CD3	OKT3, Leu 4, T3	Mature T cells Thymocytes	Associated with T-cell receptor (TCR)
CD4	OKT4, Leu 3, T4	T cells Thymocytes Monocytes	Helper-inducer T cells MHC class II receptor
CD8	OKT8, Leu 2, T8	T cells Thymocytes	Cytotoxic-suppressor T cells MHC class I
CD16	Leu 11, 3G8	NK cells Granulocytes Macrophages	IgG Fc III receptor (RIII)
CD19	B4, Leu 12	Pan B cells	
CD23	Leu 20	Activated B cells Macrophages	Low-affinity IgE receptor (Fc ϵII receptor)
CD25	Tac, 7G7, B1	Activated T cells	p55 IL2 receptor subunit
CD56	HNK-1, Leu 7	Large granular lymphocytes (NK cells)	Isoform of N-CAM

it is possible to assay factor production, receptor expression, mRNA accumulation for the factor and for the receptor, and the modulation of the receptor complex on the cell membrane. It is also possible to determine the membrane expression of structures associated with cellular activation, as well as the changes in RNA and DNA content which occur as the cell enters the division cycle. Using molecular biological techniques it is possible to determine the rearrangement of the genes for the T-cell antigen receptor and for the immunoglobulin molecule that are crucial steps in the differentiation of both T and B cells, respectively. A partial listing of some of the important factors, lymphokines, and cytokines inducing immune cell differentiation and their proposed function can be found in Table 5-2.

The initiation of an immune response requires the recognition of an antigen by immunocompetent lymphocytes. This recognition may require both a T cell and a B cell as well as an accessory cell (monocyte-macrophage) that functions in the presentation or processing of the antigen. The T cell may recognize a separate binding site (epitope) on the whole antigen (usually larger than that recognized by the B cell). After the recognition step, there is an activation process which involves the intracellular transduction of signals to the cytoplasm and nucleus. This results in the up regulation of mRNAs for several protooncogenes and receptor components and the expression of new molecules on the cell membrane. Some of these structures are involved with the recognition of the B cell by the T cell, while others function as high-affinity receptors for growth factors. The activated T cell releases newly synthesized factors that will result in an expansion of the clone of T cells that recognize the antigen to form a specific clone, while other factors influence the development of B cells into antibody-synthesizing units. There are other factors that can be synthesized and released which downregulate T- and B-cell function. The control of this response is dependent on several elements: the amount and type of antigen present, the activity of T-helper and T-suppressor cells, the synthesis of anti-idiotypic antibody, the number of antigen-sensitive cells involved in the response (which is most important in secondary response), the presence of factors which initiate an inflammatory response such as endotoxin, and the age of the individual. As antigen is depleted and the anti-idiotype network expands, the response subsides, leaving an expanded population of memory cells, mostly B cells, that are ready to respond in an accelerated fashion to the next contact with the same or related antigen.

Host defenses other than immune reactions also depend on cellular and protein factors. In most cases the first lines of defense are granulocytes and monocytic cells with membrane receptors (Fc receptors) for immunoprotein (usually IgG). Both these cell types have the ability to phagocytose organisms, but granulocytes can function in the absence of a specific trigger such as antibody to the organism, while the monocytes are better able to function if they encounter an antibody-coated organism. Accompanying phagocytosis there is a burst of metabolic activity and the release of cytoplasmic enzymes that lead to the destruction of the organism. Granulocytes are very efficient in this activity and provide the most important first line of defense against infection.

The role of allergic reactions in host defense and, in particular, in immune responses is not fully known. In certain parasitic diseases an allergic response to the parasite may participate in the initiation of a beneficial inflammatory response. The immediate reactivity to an antigen with the release of a variety of very po-

TABLE 5-2

Cytokines

Name	Other Names	Biological Actions	Principal Source
Interleukin 1α Interleukin 1β	Lymphocyte-activating factor (LAF) Hematopoietin 1 (HP-1) Endogenous pyrogen (EP) Mononuclear cell factor (MCF) Leukocyte endogenous pyrogen (LEP) B-cell activating factor (BAF)	Activates T-cell growth Enhances differentiation of B cells Induces resorption of bone Induces fever	Macrophages Epithelial cells Keratinocytes Astrocytes EBV-transformed B cells Kupfer cells
Interleukin 2	T-cell growth factor (TCGF or TCGF-I) Killer helper factor (KHF)	Promotes growth and differentiation of T cells and monocytes Induces cytotoxic T cells Stimulates NK cell activity	Helper T cells
Interleukin 3	Colony-stimulating factor (CSF) Multi-colony-stimulating factor (multi-CSF) Mast cell growth factor I (MCGF-I) Hematopoietic cell growth factor (HCGF) Burst-promoting activity (BPA) Thy-1-inducing factor	Promotes growth and differentiation of hematopoietic stem cells Mast cell growth factor	Activated T cells Mast cells
Interleukin 4	B-cell stimulating factor 1 (BSF-1) B-cell growth factor I (BCGF-I) Mast cell growth factor II (MCGF-II) Macrophage fusion factor (MFF) Macrophage-activating factor (MAF) T-cell growth factor II (TCGF-II)	Promotes activation, growth, and differentiation of B cells and mast cells Induces Ig synthesis by B cells Induces expression of class II MHC antigens Synergizes with CSF to promote growth of hematopoietic cells	Activated T cells Mast cells Bone marrow stromal cells
Interleukin 5	T-cell replacing factor (TRF) B-cell growth factor II (BCGF-II) Eosinophil-differentiating factor (EDF) IgA-enhancing factor (IgA-EF) B-cell differentiation factor μ (BCDFμ)	Promotes growth and differentiation of eosinophils Enhances IL-2-mediated killer cell activity	T cells Mast cells B cells?
Interleukin 6	B-cell-stimulating factor 2 (BSF-2) Interferon β_2 (IFN-β_2) Hybridoma plasmacytoma growth factor (HPGF) B-cell-differentiating factor (BCDF) Hepatocyte-stimulating factor (HSF) Monocyte granulocyte inducer type 2 (MGI-2) 26-kDa protein	Activates T cells Induces Ig synthesis by B cells Induces hematopoiesis	Monocytes Activated T cells Fibroblasts Variety of tumors
Interleukin 7	Lymphopoietin (LP-1)	Promotes proliferation and maintenance of B- and T-cell progenitors Induces tumoricidal activity in monocytes and macrophages Inhibits proliferation of some ALL cells	Bone marrow Thymus
Interleukin 8	Leukocyte adhesion inhibitor (LAI) Neutrophil-activating peptide 1 (NAP-1) Neutrophil chemotactic factor (NCF) Monocyte-derived neutrophil-chemotactic factor (MDNCF) Monocyte-derived neutrophil-activating peptide (MONAP) Neutrophil-activating factor (NAF) Lymphocyte-derived neutrophil-activating peptide (LYNAP)	Chemattractant for neutrophils Increases expression of CD18 (Mac-1) and CR1 Stimulates neutrophil degranulation Attenuates leukocyte adhesion to endothelial cells	Monocytes Endotheial cells Fibroblasts Chondrocytes Synovial cells Keratinocytes
Interleukin 9	Mast cell growth-enhancing activity (MEA) T-cell growth factor III (TCGF-III)	Enhances IL3-dependent mast cell growth	T cells
Interleukin 10	Cytokine synthesis inhibitory factor (CSIF)	Increases class II MHC antigen expression on B cells Autocrine growth factor for B cells? Inhibits cytokine synthesis, esp. IFN-γ by Th 1 cells Coregulates T and mast cell growth	T helper cells
Interleukin 11	Adipogenesis inhibitory factor (AGIF)	Synergizes with IL3 to support megakaryocyte colony formation Stimulates plasma cell proliferation Stimulates development of T-cell-dependent Ig-producing B cells	Stromal cells
Interleukin 12	Cytotoxic lymphocyte maturation factor (CLMF) Natural killer cell stimulatory factor (NKSF)	Stimulates T-cell proliferation Synergizes with IL-2 to induce LAK cells Induces IFN-γ Enhances cytotoxicity of NK cells	Lymphoblastoid B cells
Interferon γ		Inhibits virus replication in many cell types Modulates expression of class I and II MHC antigens Primes macrophages for tumoricidal and microbicidal activity Inhibits cell growth Induces differentiation of myeloid cells Increases expression of Fcγ receptors	T cells
TNF-α	Cachectin	Induces differentiation of myeloid cells Activates neutrophils Synergizes with IFN-γ to kill viruses Kills tumor cells Induces many acute-phase reactants	Monocytes and macrophages
TNF-β	Lymphotoxin Cytotoxic factor	Activates osteoclasts Growth factor for activated B cells Activates expression of MHC and adhesion molecule genes Induces DNA fragmentation Kills tumor cells Most activities of TNF-α	T and B lymphocytes Astrocytes

tent chemical mediators would putatively be an effective immune-inflammatory reaction, but most information on the allergic system demonstrates that this reactivity is against nonpathogen-associated antigens, and the inflammatory response due to the release of mediators can cause serious disease.

Another system whose importance in providing protection has been questioned is the secretory immune system mediated through IgA. While IgA and IgA-type antibody can be found in tears, saliva, milk, gastrointestinal secretions, and pulmonary tract secretions, it is still not clear what benefit they provide. In ataxia-telangiectasia, a condition with an associated immune deficit, there is a lack of IgA. However, in 10 percent of the population there is also a deficiency of IgA with few or no clinical signs or symptoms of an immune deficiency. Since the secretory IgA is found on epithelial surfaces, it should, in theory, be able to serve as a primary deterrent to infection. Therefore, the IgA (secretory IgA) system has been the target of topical vaccines administered by aerosol and designed to provide local mucosal immunity. While specific IgA antibody can be induced in this manner, there is still debate as to the efficacy of this antibody in preventing illness. A major consideration in determining the role of IgA is that it does not fix complement and therefore cannot provide a lytic or opsonization component for dealing with a pathogen. On the other hand, there are data that show that aerosol influenza vaccines, which provoke local IgA antibody responses, can provide protection, although these vaccines also induce serum antibody. This continues to be an important area for research on vaccine development for the elderly.

The immune system, since it is an adaptive system, not only interacts with various components of itself, but as a physiologic system is influenced by other systems within and outside of the individual. Sorting out the role of age in the decline of immune function seen during a lifespan of an individual requires careful scrutiny of the individual for the presence of confounding factors. Since many elderly individuals experience diseases, therapies, chronic pain, and altered nutritional states, which can influence immune function, as well as anatomic problems and disability, which can lead to an increase in susceptibility to infection, it is equally important to recognize that elderly persons have an immunodeficiency, and on a clinical basis whether it is primary or secondary to age is unimportant. With this in mind, the following section will detail what is known about the changes seen in immune function with aging and in older patients with disease.

ASSESSMENT OF IMMUNE FUNCTION IN ELDERLY PERSONS

Research on the effects of aging on immune function has been concerned with the description of the differences seen in the examination of cellular function using cells from young and old donors. The desire to move these investigations forward by employing techniques in molecular biology in order to understand the mechanisms responsible for changes in cellular activity has in most cases succeeded only in providing more descriptive information rather than an understanding of the basis for the changes. It was known over 20 years ago that lymphocytes from old donors would not proliferate to the same extent as those from young donors. In the 20 years since that realization, we have found that the cells from the old donors secrete less interleukin 2 (IL-2), a T-cell growth factor, than do the cells from young donors. In addition, cells from elderly donors do not express the receptor for IL-2 to the same extent or transcribe the mRNA for IL-2 or the IL-2R to the same extent. Studies of intracellular signal transduction pathways have shown that calcium mobilization, protein phosphorylation, kinase activation, and gene activation for cell cycle progression are all different for the cells from old donors compared with cells from young donors. As elegant as these studies are, they still leave unanswered the question as to the cause of aging effects on immune function. However, these investigations are headed in the right direction, and as the onion continues to be peeled, the field comes closer to the core. Nonetheless, there have been major advancements in the understanding of the aging process as it affects immune function. These include the knowledge that with age there is a heterogeneity of cellular function. There is a population of T lymphocytes that functions poorly or not at all, but this does not mean there are not cells in elderly persons that function well. Understanding this finding alone (i.e., why some cells seem perfectly normal while others are markedly impaired) could provide the basis for future therapeutic strategies. Other studies have shown that the genes responsible for the synthesis of growth factors such as IL-2 are not inactivated or mutated in the cells from elderly donors. Their expression, however, seems to be altered because of a defect in the activation pathways that connect a membrane event with a nuclear activation. Certain of the activation pathways are not influenced by age while others are dysfunctional. Cellular activation itself results in a different pattern of responsiveness by the cells from the old donors. While some cells from an old donor may not release IL-2 upon activation, they will release higher levels of other factors such as interferon-γ, tumor necrosis factor α (TNF-α), IL-1, IL-6, and tumor growth factor (TGF) than seen with cells from young donors. These cells are activated, but their response is different. The changes in the function of the immune system seen in an aging host are more complicated than envisioned in the past. Thus there is a loss of functional cells, a change in the ability to respond to an activation event, and basic changes in the pattern of the response to the activation event. As these complicated changes are understood, there actually is a better chance of developing strategies for the maintenance of the system than had been previously realized.

Assays of immune function, like all diagnostic laboratory examinations, vary in their usefulness in the clinical care of patients. Some tests are useful for diagnosis or monitoring the progress of a disease, while others serve mainly as research tools. Because older individuals often have complex multisystem medical problems, their laboratory results frequently fall outside the range of normal for young persons and raise the question as to whether these values truly represent "disease." Because clinicians are aware that numerous diseases are accompanied by or produce altered immune function, the clinical use of costly immunologic testing has increased. However, it should be kept in mind that few diseases, especially among the elderly population, have a primary immunologic cause. Many laboratory assays to evaluate immune function have become very complex and therefore are not readily available to clinicians or interpretable by them. Further, many in vitro tests of immune function take considerable time to perform, especially if they involve cell culture. This means that the results of these assays are frequently not available for use in clinical diagnosis or management for several days or perhaps weeks.

However, considerable useful information regarding the adequacy of an elderly individual's immune system can be obtained from several generally available laboratory studies (Table 5-3). When immune deficiencies were first recognized over 40 years ago, laboratory tests were introduced to identify patients with those disorders. Most of these patients were children with genetically determined sex-linked hypogammaglobulinemia or the Swiss-type thymic deficiency, or variations such as the DiGeorge syndrome with the absence of brachial arch development. Diagnosis of these disorders was concerned with the description of a lack of a function such as an inability to make antibody, a lack of immunoglobulin, or a lack of lymphocytes. In most cases there was an absolute loss or lack of a function, but this is not the case with age-associated immune dysfunction. With aging there is usually a decline of a function to some level below the level seen in young adults. It is frequently difficult to understand the significance of these changes in a clinical setting. What does a 10 percent drop in the number of T cells mean? For example, what does a titer half the value seen in young adults mean? Are these changes of sufficient magnitude to allow the patient to become ill? These are the questions that make the interpretation of the laboratory results so difficult. Since it is clear that age is associated with increased morbidity and mortality due to infectious disease, it is necessary to develop assays that reflect the clinical status of the patient. For example, a study comparing immunization-induced type-specific pneumococcal polysaccharide antigen titers with several in vitro assays of immune function showed in a healthy elderly population that the percentage of T lymphocytes in the peripheral blood was the only test that was correlated with in vivo antibody-forming ability. This finding may be related to the assessments now being used in HIV-infected individuals in whom CD4+ cells are routinely enumerated and used to determine the progression of the infection. However, there are a number of laboratory assays that are used in an attempt to determine the status of the immune system in elderly patients or those patients with a secondarily acquired immune defect. These studies, usually directed toward precisely identifying the cause of a defect found through use of the widely available tests, are done in the research laboratory (Table 5-4).

Preliminary evaluation of immune function begins with the determination of the number of immunocompetent cells in an individual's peripheral circulation. While the total number of peripheral blood white blood cells, as well as the major morphologic components including lymphocytes, monocytes, and neutrophils, appears to be remarkably stable throughout the adult life span, two points deserve mention. First, longitudinal studies indicate that the number of leukocytes in a particular individual is unique and relatively constant during adult life. When studied over a 25-year span, most healthy individuals display little fluctuation in their total white cell count or in the number of lymphocytes. While some healthy individuals consistently maintain baseline white counts of 10,000 to 12,000 cells/mm^3, other equally healthy persons have counts in the 3000 to

TABLE 5-3

Readily Available Tests of Immune Function

Complete blood count and differential
Quantitative measurement of immunoglobulins (IgG, IgA, IgM)
Intradermal skin testing for delayed hypersensitivity responses
Measurement of antibody titers to common pathogens or vaccine antigens (i.e., rubella, rubeola, polio, influenza, diphtheria, tetanus)
Measurement of isohemagglutinins
Pre- and postimmunization antibody titers
Determination of complement activity and quantification of C3 and CH_{50}
Nitroblue tetrazolium (NBT) dye reduction test
HIV antibody determination

TABLE 5-4

Evaluation of Immune Function in a Research Setting

Enumerate T-cell subpopulations with monoclonal antibodies
Determine proliferative ability of lymphocytes following activation by phytohemagglutinin, concanavalin A, pokeweed mitogen, allogeneic cells, and anti-CD3.
Assay NK cell activity.
Assay cytotoxic T cell activity.
Assay in vitro lymphokine production by activated cells.
Quantify mRNA for cytokines.
Quantify serum immunoglobulins, IgG subclasses, and k/λ ratio.

4000 cells/mm^3 range. There are racial differences. Many members of the African-American community have low white blood cell counts and yet are healthy. Second, there appears to be a subtle, yet definite, decrease in the number of circulating lymphoid cells during the few years immediately preceding death.[2] This is a decrease from the "norm" of a particular individual that occurs before any overt signs of terminal illness can be appreciated. The subtlety of this finding does not make it clinically useful to predict impending death but is a point that certainly deserves recognition when interpreting serial longitudinal lymphocyte data in the elderly population.

One useful technique to determine immune function in vivo is the delayed hypersensitivity skin reaction that develops in sensitized individuals 12 to 48 hours after an intradermal injection of antigens such as purified protein derivative (tuberculin) (PPD), streptokinase-streptodornase (SK-SD), *Candida,* or *Trichophyton.* While the information that this test provides concerning cell-mediated immunity (CMI) and T-cell function is unquestionably useful, the actual performance of the test on an elderly person frequently creates a number of practical difficulties. With the exception of PPD, the clinician often finds that appropriate and clinically useful delayed hypersensitivity skin-testing materials are not readily available. While preparations of *Candida* and *Trichophyton* can be obtained from companies marketing materials for allergy diagnosis and therapy, the efficacy of these antigens in provoking a delayed response varies widely by manufacturer and lot number. Additionally, intradermal injection of the antigen is often difficult in elderly persons with thin, easily traumatized skin. Even when the antigen is applied by an experienced individual using a fine, short-bevel needle, it is not uncommon in elderly individuals to inject subcutaneously or to cause hematoma formation, which makes reading the reaction difficult and possibly invalid. Recently a disposable, plastic puncture device (Multitest CMI) preloaded with seven standardized antigens has become available. This device has been extensively evaluated in all adult age groups and appears to be a solution to many of the problems mentioned.[1,3]

Useful data regarding delayed hypersensitivity reactivity in normal elderly individuals is difficult to obtain because the results of many studies from the 1960s and 1970s are significantly influenced by patient selection. Recent studies using multiple standardized antigens indicate that while the area of induration decreases with age, total anergy is uncommon even in quite elderly persons. The amount of reactivity also varies at different sites such as the volar surface of the forearm and the triceps area on the same individual. Nonreactivity to tuberculin now appears to be commonplace among persons admitted to nursing homes, a finding that differs significantly from that of earlier generations.[4]

Age-related alterations in the number and/or function of T lymphocytes is unquestionably the most widely studied area of immunosenescence and has been the topic of several recent reviews.[5] In general, results in this area are characterized by a lack of consensus as to precisely what changes occur. Perhaps the most influential factor accounting for the different results in studies of cell-mediated immunity and aging is related to the selection criteria for the study population. The health status of participants in various studies ranges from uncategorized nursing home residents, through persons studied on multiple visits over many years,[6] to individuals chosen on the basis of rigid clinical and laboratory exclusion criteria such as those associated with the SENIEUR protocol of EURAGE.[7]

Older laboratory methods that relied on techniques such as rosetting with sheep erythrocytes to identify and quantify T lymphocytes and T-cell subsets have now been replaced by immunofluorescence with monoclonal antibodies that identify developmental and functional markers on T cells. The recent introduction of flow cytometers with multicolor analysis capabilities into many laboratories provides the ability to phenotypically identify very small subpopulations of immunocompetent cells. There are now hundreds of commercial, and an indeterminate number of noncommercial, anti–human T-cell monoclonal antibodies, many with similar specificities, available for clinical research, diagnosis, or therapy. The once widely used commercial designations such as OKT and Leu should now be abandoned in favor of a system developed by the International Workshop of Human Leukocyte Differentiation Antigens that groups the antibodies and the cells that they identify into functional groups or antigen clusters designated by CD (cluster designation) numbers (Table 5-1).[8] While the identification and quantification of cell populations with individual monoclonal antibodies has become commonplace in oncology, transplantation monitoring, and the diagnosis of AIDS, the value of this information in the evaluation of elderly patients generally remains unproved.

There is a slight decrease with age in the absolute number of CD3+ T cells.[6,9] The changes in the functional subsets that account for this decline remain uncertain since both CD4+ helper-inducer and CD8+ cytotoxic-suppressor cell populations are reported to increase or decrease with age.[6,10,11] Recent research has complicated this point by making it clear that both the CD4+ and the CD8+ T-cell populations are functionally heterogeneous.

The overwhelmingly predominant technique to assess T-cell function continues to be mitogen reactivity. The ability of peripheral blood T lymphocytes to proliferate following activation with plant lectins such as phytohemagglutinin or concanavalin A, monoclonal antibodies such as anti-CD3, or allogeneic cells (MLC) decreases with advancing age.[12–14] Although they are a minority in each population, one can find apparently healthy young individuals whose cells respond quite poorly and robust elderly persons whose cells respond very well. The mitogen assay is very sensitive to the presence of concurrent illness. This makes assay results obtained at a single point in time on a clinically ill patient of dubious value in establishing the level of the individual's T-cell function.

Since the decline in T-cell function with age is preceded by the involution of the thymus, it is attractive to hypothesize that these events are associated, although there is presently no direct evidence that this is the case. Thymic involution begins during adolescence and progresses fairly rapidly so that almost complete involution is present at an age when no significant change in T-cell numbers in the peripheral blood of humans or in the solid lymphoreticular tissues of mice can be appreciated. Present data relating thymic hormone levels [α and β thymosins, facteur thymique serique (FTS), thymopoietin, thymopentin] to age indicate that the levels decrease with age and become undectable after the age of 50 to 60 years.[15] Over 20 years have passed since the first description of a thymic hormone, and there still is no clear evidence that there is a preparation that has any clinical use in elderly patients.

As previously mentioned, the mechanisms underlying the age-associated decrease in the proliferative ability of T cells continue to remain elusive. While elderly individuals synthesize and respond less to the proliferation-inducing lymphokine IL-2,[16] synthesis of and response to this protein are clearly only symptoms rather than causes of the problem. The addition of even large quantities of exogenous IL-2 does not fully reconstitute in vitro proliferative ability, and studies of IL-2 receptors indicate that the proliferating cells from both young and old persons have similar numbers of signal-transducing high-affinity IL-2 receptors.[17] While age-related changes in the amounts of IL-2 mRNAs have been reported,[18] this defect appears more closely linked to an inability to respond to a particular activation stimulus rather than to a genetic incapacity to produce IL-2. If appropriate stimuli are used, cells from young and elderly persons respond similarly. An important secondary defect of T cells from elderly humans is the inability of a portion of these cells to be activated, since once activated the T lymphocytes from both young and old persons proliferate similarly, although there may be less proliferative ability for the daughter cells from the original reacting population from the elderly persons. With this in mind, research is shifting toward the investigation of cell activation, which unlike proliferation that involves a myriad of signals and biochemical processes, may be controlled by a single, possibly unique, on-off signal. Research areas being actively pursued in search of an activation defect include modifications of transmembrane signal transmission via intracellular second messengers such as the serine-threonine protein kinases and inositol lipid metabolites, changes in intracellular calcium levels and pH, defects in the expression or control of regulatory protooncogenes, and alterations in guanine nucleotide–binding regulatory proteins (G proteins).

For the clinician, evaluation of B-cell function is best accomplished by quantitative measurement of serum immunoglobulin levels. Additionally, quantification of antibody titers to common bacteria or viruses (i.e., tetanus, measles, influenza, poliovirus) and isohemagglutinins can provide useful information about the individual's ability to make specific antibody. Age-related changes in serum levels of various immunoglobulins have been reported, although the significance is difficult to establish since all studies are cross-sectional and various exclusionary selection criteria have been applied to the participants. Available data indicate that serum levels of IgM and IgD decrease modestly with age, while serum and secretory IgA values rise.[19] Although there is not universal agreement, serum IgG levels appear to increase slightly with age, which could be due to the effects on mean values of a few elderly individuals with monoclonal gammopathies. IgE levels decline sharply with age in atopic individuals, possibly partially accounting for the decline in pollen- and dander-induced allergic symptoms observed in elderly persons. Despite these decreases, serum IgG, IgA, and IgM values remain well above the levels generally considered to represent an immunodeficiency.

Available information indicates that both primary and to a lesser degree secondary specific antibody responses decrease with age. The mechanism responsible for this decrease is likely related to decreased helper T-cell activity as well as defective B-cell responsiveness. Regardless of the cause, two important clinical considerations are that booster injections of common vaccines are certainly more effective when administered at an age when immune function remains fairly normal, and single-dose immunization of elderly persons may not produce the expected rises in protective antibody. A decline in titer to the hepatitis B virus has been shown to occur in the third decade compared with titers in persons in the second decade, so the onset of age-related problems in inducing high titers is not a feature seen only in elderly individuals.

In the elderly person it is not unusual to find a monoclonal immunoglobulin (M component) in the serum.[20] This monoclonal serum immunoprotein is thought to arise through a series of events that involves both a deregulation of normal cell differentiation and chronic antigenic stimulation. During this process a cell of the B-lymphocyte lineage escapes normal control at the pre–plasma cell stage and is driven to terminal differentiation by chronic antigen stimulation. The finding of a monoclonal immunoglobulin spike has been given a variety of generally interchangeable names including monoclonal gammopathy, paraproteinemia, plasma cell dyscrasia, and dysproteinemia. Whatever one chooses to term the homogeneous immunoglobulin, it produces a family of clinical diseases that includes multiple myeloma (monoclonal IgG, IgA, IgD, IgE, or light chain), Waldenström's macroglobulinemia (monoclonal IgM), primary amyloidosis (polymerized light chain fragments), and heavy chain disease (IgG, IgA, or IgM heavy chains with Fd region deleted). While there is an increased incidence of these monoclonal B-cell neoplasms in the elderly, it is also not uncommon to detect high levels of monoclonal serum immunoglobulin without the associated findings of recurrent infections, anemia, hyperviscosity, lymphadenopathy, hepatosplenomegaly, renal failure, lytic bone lesions, or hypercalcemia. Whereas high levels of monoclonal immunoglobulin in the young and middle-aged adult are almost certainly indicative of a neoplastic process, older individuals may have homogeneous serum immunoprotein without apparent serious disease. It is interesting to note that in young mice it is possible to induce a monoclonal gammopathy using procedures to ablate thymic function and then inducing inflammation by administering endotoxin. In effect these conditions would replicate those seen in elderly humans. This condition, formerly termed benign monoclonal gammopathy (BMG), is now generally referred to as monoclonal gammopathy of uncertain significance (MGUS).[21] It is found in approximately 3 percent of persons over 70 years old living in Sweden, France, and the United States, making it more common in elderly persons than multiple myeloma. Despite a higher incidence of multiple myeloma in the black population, the incidence of M proteins is about the same as in the white population.[22] While the lack of physical findings and negative laboratory studies (<30 g of M component per liter, no Bence-Jones proteins in the urine, <5 percent bone marrow plasmacytosis, and a thymidine-labeling index <1 percent) usually permit MGUS to be differentiated from so-called smoldering multiple myeloma (SMM), approximately 10 percent of the cases eventually (usually within the first year) display neoplastic behavior. Another point to be kept in mind is that immunoglobulin catabolism is regulated by serum immunoglobulin levels. As a result, individuals with large M components, particularly of the IgG class, are often frankly hypogammaglobulinemic in respect to the normal types of functioning serum immunoglobulin, a condition also seen in many hypergammaglobulinemic AIDS patients.

In addition to monoclonal gammopathies, many studies have noted that the serum from 10 to 15 percent of elderly individuals contains some type of autoimmune antibodies. These autoantibodies in elderly patients are additional evidence of disordered T-cell immunoregulation, since terminal B-cell differentiation is controlled by a balance between suppressor and helper T cells that recognize self-antigens. While autoantibodies to DNA, IgG, thyroid tissue, gastric parietal cells, erythrocytes, lymphocytes, cardiolipids, and cytoskeletal proteins may be found in elderly persons, it remains uncertain whether the incidence of autoantibodies other than anti-IgG-specific IgM (i.e., rheumatoid factor) is greater than that found in younger individuals.[23] The important clinical consideration is that the presence of autoantibodies in elderly persons is seldom associated with manifestations of autoimmune disease. The frequent finding of serum autoantibodies among elderly persons is the basis of the *autoimmune theory of aging,* in which these antibodies are thought to be involved with causing the aging process. Based on Burnet's clonal selection theory, the hypothesis proposes that autoantibodies cause aging through immune complex and antibody- and immune complex–induced tissue damage. While disease from failure to eliminate so-called forbidden clones that produce self-directed antibodies is certainly worth consideration, present knowledge of the function of the immune system makes this concept outdated. While previously the receptor for self was postulated as the cause of autoimmune disease, present models (also based on Jerne's network theory) implicate the receptor for self as a regulator that restrains potentially disease-causing T and B lymphocytes that are spontaneously and randomly generated by the immune system.

There is considerable current interest in a specific type of autoantibody. The unique portion of the variable region of the immunoglobulin molecule (the region responsible for antigen binding) is called the *idiotype,* and antibodies reactive with this region are called anti-idiotype antibodies. Formation of autologous anti-idiotype antibodies is clearly part of the normal immune response, and it appears likely that these antibodies function as an off signal for antibody synthesis.[24] It is easily recognized that if there is a defect in idiotype–anti-idiotype interaction, B-cell hyperreactivity will result. Anti-idiotype antibodies also appear important in the pathogenesis of many clinical autoimmune diseases.[25] However, the presence of autoantibodies in elderly persons in the absence of autoimmune disease provides a warning light to the use of procedures to augment or restore immune function in elderly individuals. It may be that by restoration of effector mechanisms it would be possible to provide the elderly individual with the means necessary for the induction of autoimmune disease.

While there may be the impression that all components of the immune system deteriorate with advancing age, this is not universally the case. NK cells, Fc receptor–positive large granular lymphocytes, are recognized as having an effector role in immune surveillance against tumor and virus-infected cells and in the regulation of hematopoiesis. Unlike T-cell proliferative responses, NK cell function does not show any age-related defect. In fact, NK activity appears to be slightly enhanced in men over 80 years of age.[26] Additionally the number of cells expressing the CD56 and CD16 antigens, phenotypic markers for NK cells, are maintained with advancing age.[27] However, there is evidence that gender, cigarette smoking, and alcohol consumption all influence the level of NK cell activity, variables which could influence the interpretation of assay results.

As previously outlined, granulocytes play an important role in host defense against disease. Even in individuals who are hypogammaglobulinemic, normal phagocytic cell function prevents the development of most bacterial diseases. In general, there must be a profound decrease in the number of granulocytes, to perhaps less than 10 percent of normal, before an increased susceptibility to infection is apparent. The number of granulocytes in the peripheral blood does not change with age, and neither do assays of granulocyte metabolic or bactericidal activity. Decreased phagocytic ability by a portion of the granulocytes of elderly persons has been reported.[28]

Monocytes and macrophages, especially as secretors of bioactive immunoregulatory proteins, play important roles in many diverse types of immune reactions.[29] Although the macrophage has been long recognized as the secretor of IL-1 or endogenous pyrogen, other important lymphokines such as IL-2, IL-8, and TNF are also products of the macrophage. Unfortunately, the effects of aging on monocyte-macrophage function remain largely unstudied, although it is reasonable to infer from both clinical observations (decreased fever response in the elderly) and the research laboratory (alterations in cell growth and proliferation) that these cells have age-associated defects. Many factors which are associated with an inflammatory response and are able to be induced by endotoxin or concanavalin A, such as interferon γ, TGF-β, IL-1, IL-6, and TNF, are synthesized at higher levels by the cells from old animals and humans when compared with the amount made by cells from young and middle-aged individuals. The reason for this and the significance of this are not known, but these factors are immunosuppressive and antiproliferative and have been shown to regulate the expression of transcription factor genes such as the protooncogenes.

It can be readily appreciated that there are a large number of defects, many of which may not be relevant to patient care, found in the immune system of elderly persons. The more generally agreed upon changes are summarized in Table 5-5.

TABLE 5-5

Summary of Changes in Immune Function in Elderly Persons

Decreased production of thymic hormones
Diminished in vitro responsiveness to IL2
Decreased cell proliferation in response to mitogenic stimulation
Decreased cell-mediated cytotoxicity
Enhanced cellular sensitivity to prostaglandin E_2
Increased synthesis of anti-idiotype antibodies
Decreased levels of specific antibody response
Increased presence of autoimmune antibodies
Increased incidence of serum monoclonal immunoproteins
No change in NK cell function
Decreased representation of peripheral blood B lymphocytes in men
Diminished delayed hypersensitivity
No change in numbers of peripheral blood lymphocytes
Enhanced ability to synthesize IFN-γ, IL-6, and TNF-α

CLINICAL CARE OF AN ELDERLY PATIENT WITH AN INFECTIOUS DISEASE AND AUGMENTATION OF THE IMMUNE RESPONSE

With the appreciation that the immune system of an elderly individual functions at a lower level than the immune system of a younger person, it is important to consider various ways to deal with the situation. In a broad sense there are two solutions: one is to treat the elderly person with an infection as one does any individual with an immunodeficiency, and the other is to consider procedures for augmenting immune responsiveness and retarding its deterioration.

As previously discussed, a major clinical feature of many immunodeficient individuals is a suboptimal or lack of an early response to infection. This point is relevant to elderly patients in whom because of a combination of immunosenescence, age-related loss of CNS thermal control, decreased vasoconstriction to cooling, and the loss of muscle mass and shivering ability, classic manifestations of sepsis, like fever and chills, occur less frequently.[30] Among elderly patients, up to 25 percent of individuals are hypothermic or fail to develop a fever greater than 100°F (<37.6°C) during the initial stages of a septic episode. Subtle signs, such as alterations in mental status, disorientation, and tachypnea, may be the only changes initially noted in a septic elderly person. Septicemia is the thirteenth leading cause of death in the United States, and although septicemia rates increased for all age groups over the past decade, the greatest increase was among persons ≥65 years of age.[31] One may argue that this increase can be attributed to increases in both the proportion of the U.S. population ≥65 years old and the number of elderly persons that were hospitalized. However, age adjustments of these rates still resulted in a 111 percent increase in the septicemia rate for persons ≥65 years old in the period 1979 to 1987.

Elderly persons have many age-related risk factors making them more susceptible to infection (Table 5-6). Among normal elderly individuals, approximately 60 percent of infections leading to septic shock are caused by gram-negative bacteria infecting the gastrointestinal tract, gall bladder, genitourinary tract, or lungs, and the responsible organisms are usually the normal commensuals found in the gastrointestinal flora. Gram-positive organisms such as pneumococci, streptococci, and staphylococci account for another 30 percent of cases, mainly those involving the respiratory tract and skin. However, one should be mindful that among elderly patients who have debilitating diseases or who are otherwise immunocompromised, 30 percent or more of the cases of sepsis occur without a readily identifiable primary focus of infection and without detectable organisms on blood culture. In the elderly patient the bedside diagnosis of a bacterial infection is often difficult be-

TABLE 5-6

Age-Related Risk Factors That Increase Susceptibility to Infection

Decreased pulmonary function and cough reflex
Decreased gastric acidity and GI motility
Atherosclerosis and decreased capillary blood flow
Thin, easily traumatized skin
Decreased activity secondary to motor and balance problems
Impaired host defense mechanisms
Inadequate nutrition and hydration
Lack of recent immunization against preventable diseases
Neuropsychological diseases and mental deterioration
Chronic use of medications
Chronic diseases (diabetes, cardiac disease, renal disease, alcoholism)
Previous exposures to hazardous materials (asbestos, chemicals, dusts)
Hospitalization and residence in long-term care facilities
Invasive devices (urinary catheters, nasogastic tubes)

cause elderly patients frequently have enigmatic symptoms and common laboratory tests are difficult to interpret. For example, 50 percent of frail elderly patients have their oropharynx colonized with aerobic gram-negative bacteria, and 15 to 25 percent of women 65 years or older are bacteruric at any given time.[32] Therefore, a high degree of suspicion and the rapid use of appropriate bactericidal antibiotics is critical. Even a trivial infection can lead to septic shock (i.e., sepsis, evidence of decreased organ perfusion, and hypotension) and multiple organ failure. If possible, blood and other appropriate cultures should be obtained, but this should not delay the institution of antibiotic therapy. Similarly, time and effort should not be spent performing complex radiographic, CT, or MRI studies in a potentially septic elderly patient who requires stabilization and treatment. The greatest error is to allow the patient with suspected sepsis to go untreated. In the absence of a microbiological diagnosis, the selection of antibiotics is best guided by the presumed or identified site or portal of infection, and initially bactericidal antibiotics or combinations of bactericidal antibiotics with activity against both gram-positive and gram-negative organisms should be chosen. Knowledge of local patterns of antibiotic resistance is helpful in antibiotic selection since in many institutional settings an increasing number of organisms now require the use of aminoglycosides or second- or third-generation cephalosporins. In addition to treating the suspected bacterial infection, it is important to maintain both adequate tissue perfusion and oxygenation of vital organs. This is generally best accomplished by the rapid expansion of intravascular volume, a complicated problem in elderly individuals who may have serious underlying cardiovascular and pulmonary disease. Toward this end, the use of intravenous immunoglobulin preparations should be considered. Fresh-frozen plasma preparations are also a good source of IgM antibody that in addition to providing protein to a debilitated patient also supplies effective antibacterial antibody. It is also well to recognize that serum albumin levels decrease with age, and these decreases may alter antibiotic distribution and metabolism in an elderly patient.

The clinical manifestations of severe sepsis are the result of the interactions of bacterial endotoxins with the complement and coagulation systems, as well as with specific immunocompetent cells such as macrophages that in response to these products synthesize and release cytokines such as IL-1, IL-6, IL-8, and TNF-α. Evidence indicates that endogenously produced cytokines, notably TNF-α and IL-1, mediate the lethality of experimental endotoxemia, and several clinical studies have demonstrated that in patients with gram-negative bacteremia, serum IL-1, IL-6, and TNF-α levels are elevated and correlate with the severity of sepsis.[33,34] More importantly, elderly individuals appear to have an enhanced ability to synthesize some of the proinflammatory cytokines such as TNF-α, IL-6, TGF-β, and interferon-γ. Conversely, frail elderly patients have decreased IL-1 production as well as an inability to respond to it as an endogenous pyrogen. One treatment approach for sepsis that has undergone several clinical trials for effectiveness is the use of polyclonal and now monoclonal antibodies against endotoxin.[35] Unfortunately, while these antibodies do appear to reduce mortality in patients with gram-negative bacteremia, they are not effective in patients with shock, suggesting that other treatment strategies or agents are needed. Granulocyte colony-stimulating factor (G-CSF) is being explored as a down-regulator of TNF-α synthesis,[36] and IL-4 as an inhibitor of IL-1 and IL-6 production.[37] Since IL-1 activity is regulated at the level of its receptor, pharmacologic agents that bind to this receptor could potentially inhibit the actions of IL-1. One naturally occurring agent, termed IL-1 receptor agonist (IL-1ra), has been isolated, reproduced by recombinant technology, and is now undergoing clinical trials. Phase I trials are also underway with a monoclonal antibody to TNF-α for the treatment of sepsis. However, since TNF-α has important effects on tumor cells and tumor vasculature as well as upon mineral metabolism, hematopoietic precursors, and monocyte cytotoxicity, its inhibition may prove harmful.[38]

The vast majority of clinical procedures that have been designed to modulate immune activity involve down-regulating responsiveness (immunosuppression). This can be seen with the therapy for allergic diseases, organ transplantation, and autoimmune disorders. This therapy is becoming increasingly effective and now employs a wide range of agents that interfere with T-cell function, protein synthesis, and the production of inflammation-inducing mediators. Principally in the area of cancer therapy, new strategies employing both specific and nonspecific targeted effector cells [NK, lymphokine-activated killer (LAK), and tumor-infiltrating lymphocytes (TILs)] are undergoing clinical trials. At this point, however, none of these agents or strategies have specifically been examined for their effect on enhancing the immune response of elderly individuals.

Despite the obvious attractiveness of rejuvenating the immune system in elderly patients, there are a number of issues related to basic immunology that must be considered and dealt with if one is to be successful. First, it is important that the proposed agent or treatment have well-defined effective functions whose benefits clearly outweigh any side effects it might induce. Also, if one wishes to augment T-cell activity, then one must consider if all T cells are to be stimulated, or just a helper or suppressor subset, or only those cells that have specificity to a particular antigen. Recently a number of individuals have suggested the use of IL-2 as a general T-cell stimulant in elderly patients. However, we should point out that IL-2 only augments those cells that have already responded to an activation signal. Furthermore, in vitro experiments have shown that IL-2 alone can only reconstitute the responses of a portion of the T cells from elderly individuals and that this responsive cell population declines and the nonresponsive population increases with advancing age. Finally in suggesting IL-2 as a therapeutic agent for elderly patients, one must keep in mind the large amount of clinical experience and data obtained from the use of IL-2 in experimental cancer treatment protocols. While admittedly very large doses were used and most toxicity associated with IL-2 use is dose-related and probably schedule-dependent, it is unquestionable that the administration of IL-2 is routinely accompanied by significant, potentially life-threatening, side effects such as shock, pulmonary edema, and massive fluid retention due to a loss of vascular integrity.[39] Another consideration is that many of the side effects (and possibly the benefits as well) of IL-2 therapy seem to result from the IL-2-induced elaboration of other cytokines such as IL-1, IL-4, IL-6, TNF, and interferon γ. Also, as shown in Table 5-2, the actions of all the cytokines are manifold, making the enhancement of a single feature using an unmodified product impossible.

If one wishes to augment B-cell activity, the same problems would be present. Should all B cells be augmented or just specific clones? What would be the effect if anti-idiotype clones were activated? The transformation of specific clones of B cells is the process that leads to multiple myeloma, and anti-idiotype antibodies down-regulate responsiveness rather than enhancing it. There is also the possibility that the indiscriminate activation of certain clones of B cells would induce the synthesis of autoantibodies.

While many cell growth factors have been described over the past decade, none are considered as general immune system-enhancing agents. The problem is that rarely, if ever, do cytokines appear to have a single, well-defined activity, but rather have multiple potential mechanisms and act in concert with a variety of other cytokines. The FDA-approved growth factors, which regulate the production of red blood cells (epo), neutrophils (G-CSF), and neutrophils and monocytes-macrophages [granulocyte-macrophage colony-stimulating factor (GM-CSF)][40] have been approved for treating the anemia of renal failure, reducing chemotherapy-induced neutropenia, and enhancing recovery from autologous bone marrow transplantation for lymphoma, respectively. Additional uses of these and other cytokines seems forthcoming. For example, recently G-CSF has been reported as a treatment for idiopathic neutropenia of elderly patients,[41] and other factors, such as IL-1, IL-3, IL-6, and stem cell factor (c-*kit* ligand), are now in clinical trials. At this point, experience with these agents is limited, and their potential and optimal uses, as well as their interactions with each other, need further definition. When this information becomes available, it may be possible to use specific cytokines or to engineer new agents suitable for treating specific clinical conditions including immunosenescence.

The use of general immunomodulating agents, such as thymic hormone, for the promotion of T-cell development is an attractive consideration. Conceptually, the idea that with age, thymic involution produces a loss of continued T-cell development seems logical. The problem with all thymic hormone preparations tested to date is that in contrast to expectations, they produce very little or no in vivo immunologic reconstitution.[42] There is some indication that thymosin α_1 may have an effect on IL-2 production and IL-2 receptor expression, but how these findings relate to T-cell ontogeny is unclear. In addition to thymic hormones, reports continue of various compounds [levamisole, isoprinosine, NPT 15392, Krestin, Lentinan, diethyldithiocarbamate (DTC), FK565, azimexon, Imreg, and others] with alleged immunostimulating abilities. Some of these agents are widely available in foreign markets, and a few have undergone limited clinical trials in the United States. While the dosage and administration schedules used may have been less than optimal, the results of these trials have produced little enthusiasm in the United States for any of these drugs in elderly patients.[42]

Since growth hormone production is known to decline after age 50 and may be associated with the decrease in muscle and bone mass and increase in adipose tissue that accompany aging, considerable interest (and controversy) was generated by a report of the rejuvenating effects of human growth hormone administration in a group of elderly men.[43] While the effect of recombinant human growth hormone (rHGH) on immune function was not examined in the study, attempts by our laboratory and others to document improved immune function in elderly adults receiving rHGH have been unsuccessful. Although disputed, data from pediatric hypopituitary dwarfs treated with rHGH indicate that rHGH therapy is associated with decreases in some immune functions.[44]

There are mechanisms for augmenting a specific immune response. The use of adjuvants has been shown to be effective in augmenting responsiveness to specific antigens administered simultaneously.

This strategy appears particularly useful in designing vaccines for use in elderly patients. However, this approach does not provide a general "tonic" for the immune system of elderly persons, since adjuvants work by expanding specific antigen-sensitive clones. Vaccines that are given with IL-2 or which contain the IL-2 gene coupled to the antigen have been shown to be effective in producing a normal immune response in T-cell deficient nude mice. Viral-mediated gene transfer, which relies on splicing the genes for a specific antigen and for IL-2 into a carrier, but incomplete, virus, seems ideal for producing long-term expression of the recombinant genes since viral infections are generally highly efficient and many viruses become stably integrated into the host DNA. One of several problems with this system is that because the carrier virus must infect the cells of the individual (obviating the need for the host cells to multiply) to transfer the desired genes, it is necessary that the individual not be immune to the carrier virus or else there will not be an infection and the recombinant genes will not be transferred. To date, almost all the clinical trials using viral vectors have employed retroviruses since it is possible to separate the packaging of the recombinant gene from the process of producing virus. Despite extensive testing, there is ongoing concern regarding the long-term safety of the retroviral vectors. Also, while viral-mediated gene transfer may be useful for providing protection against antigenically stable pathogens, it is probably not the best method for dealing with others such as influenza virus that frequently change their antigenic signature. Another variant on this theme relevant to geriatrics is the use of somatic gene therapy to provide hormones that are deficient because of acquired diseases such as type I diabetes or to increase the expression of hormones such as growth or thymic hormones to alter the aging process.

Another important consideration in treating the declining immune system is whether it is better to reconstitute the immune system or to maintain it and prevent it from declining in activity. Clinical experience in which a severe immunodeficiency has spontaneously corrected itself or was corrected by the transplantation of appropriate stem cells has shown that in some cases the correction was followed by a severe disease resembling an autoimmune disease. It appears that during the period of immunodeficiency, ineffectively controlled viral infections allow the development of cell surface viral antigens. Upon the return of T-cell function, these antigens on the host cells are recognized and a severe illness is produced while the viral antigen–bearing cells are eliminated. Experiments in animals with lymphocytic choriomeningitis virus support this hypothesis. Therefore, it may be better to consider strategies to prevent the decline in immune function and to maintain it in later life than to pursue reconstitution.

Perhaps in considering how to preserve host defenses throughout life, we should list those possibilities that are currently available and those that would be ideal. The ideal would be to provide a continuous supply of immunocompetent T cells throughout life. Agents and techniques to do this do not presently exist. Because of graft rejection, transplantation of thymus tissue older than approximately 8 weeks of gestation does not work in humans, although there is evidence in syngeneic mice that multiple fetal thymus transplants are effective in reconstituting the immune system of elderly animals.[45]

The maintenance of an "ideal" diet may be beneficial, but even here there are difficulties. First, there is no generally accepted definition of a "good" diet that maintains immune function. Elderly individuals are susceptible to a variety of nutritional deficiencies. While low levels of vitamin D may have implications for a disease like osteoporosis, whether levels of specific nutrients have any relationship to the causation of immunodeficiency remains generally unproved. Clinical research has demonstrated an association between low levels of vitamin B_6 and pyridoxine and decreased lymphocyte responsiveness in elderly individuals.[46] Other studies suggest an inverse association between megadoses of vitamin E and immune function.[47] In experimental animals caloric restriction appears associated with an extension of life span.[48] However, controlled studies of lifelong caloric restriction in humans are probably not realistic and thus cannot be evaluated for extending human life span. There is also considerable interest in the effects of specific diets such as low-fat and high-fiber diets for the prevention of breast or colon cancer, respectively, and in the effects of vitamin A and β-carotene supplementation in cancer prevention. While the clinical implications for the prevention of coronary artery disease remain unknown, oral (n-3) fatty acid substitution in older women causes suppression of the synthesis of several cytokines including IL-1β, IL-2, IL-6, and TNF-α as well as in vitro lymphocyte proliferation.[49] There is evidence in mice that zinc restores the ability of old animals to synthesize some cytokines and to maintain antibody production at levels seen in young mice.[50] Comparable studies have not been done in humans; however, mean serum zinc concentrations in elderly persons are generally above accepted minimal standards. Possibly because nutrient surveys suggest that a high proportion of elderly persons are at risk of deficiency for several minerals, including zinc, magnesium, and calcium, many over-the-counter vitamin and mineral preparations marketed for the elderly contain zinc.

One area in which the practitioner can intervene is routinely to administer vaccines against common pathogens such as tetanus, pneumococcus, and influenza. Despite its availability in the United States for over 15 years, polyvalent pneumococcal polysaccharide vaccine remains underutilized. Many practitioners appear uncertain of vaccines' efficacies, and, wishing not to be bothered by patient complaints of side effects such as myalgia, low-grade fever, or sore arms, do not encourage pneumococcal immunization. Two recent studies have finally shown pneumococcal vaccine to be both efficacious and cost-effective, especially among immunocompromised individuals.[51,52]

Although data are still being gathered on this point, booster pneumococcal immunizations appear to be needed at approximately 5- to 6-year intervals and perhaps more frequently in immunocompromised individuals.

Since secondary immune responses remain relatively intact in elderly persons, it is prudent to begin a yearly program of influenza immunization around age 50 so that a library of responses to the various influenza antigens can be built up and expanded when needed. Like the pneumococcal vaccine, influenza vaccine is underutilized in elderly persons. All older adults, especially those in nursing homes or residential care facilities, should receive influenza vaccine annually.

Despite the fact that up to 95 percent of adults have antibodies to varicella-zoster (VZ), symptomatic recurrence of the infection increases with age, reaching a peak in the fifth to the seventh decades (see Chap. 11). A live virus vaccine to VZ was developed in the 1970s but has yet to be endorsed by immunization advisory agencies or the government. Recently there has been renewed interest in this vaccine for use in normal children; however, its potential use among adults has not been defined. One concern with the vaccine is that herpesviruses (e.g., VZ) are excellent examples of latent infections. Following an initial infection the virus persists in nerve root ganglia for years without producing disease but later may emerge to produce clinical symptoms. While the precise mechanisms leading to reactivation to produce herpes zoster in elderly persons is unknown, age-associated decreases in cell-mediated immunity seem likely to contribute.

In summary, the immune system is a complicated interplay of many different cells and factors. At this time there is no experimentally verified way to forestall deterioration or to reconstitute in a general way the diminished function of the immune system. Future work in this area will need to focus on these issues to understand what specific parts of the system require augmentation and how this can best be accomplished without producing disease.

REFERENCES

1. Marrie TJ et al: H: Cell-mediated immunity of healthy adult Nova Scotians in various age groups compared with nursing home and hospitalized senior citizens. *J Allergy Clin Immunol* 81:836, 1988.
2. Bender BS et al: Absolute peripheral blood lymphocyte count and subsequent mortality in elderly men: The Baltimore Longitudinal Study of Aging. *J Am Geriatr Soc* 34:649, 1986.
3. Kniker WT et al: Multitest CMI for standardized measurement of delayed cutaneous hypersensitivity and cell mediated immunity: Normal values and proposed scoring system for healthy adults in the USA. *Ann Allergy* 52:75, 1984.
4. Stead WW et al: Tuberculosis as an endemic and nosocomial infection among the elderly in nursing homes. *N Engl J Med* 312:1483, 1985.
5. Jones KH, Ennist DL: Mechanisms of age-related changes in cell mediated immunity. *Rev Biol Res Aging* 2:155, 1985.
6. Nagel JE et al: Monoclonal antibody analysis of T-lymphocyte subsets in young and aged adults. *Immunol Commun* 12:223, 1983.
7. Ligthart GJ et al: Admission criteria for immunogerontological studies in man: The SENIEUR protocol. *Mech Ageing Dev* 28:47, 1984.
8. Pallesen G, Plesner T: The Third International Workshop and Conference on Human Leukocyte Differentiation Antigens with an up-to-date overview of the CD nomenclature. *Leukemia* 1:231, 1987.
9. Nagel JE et al: Enumeration of T-lymphocyte subsets by monoclonal antibodies in young and aged humans. *J Immunol* 121:2086, 1981.
10. Mascart-Lemone F et al: Characterization of immunoregulatory T lymphocytes during aging by monoclonal antibodies. *Clin Exp Immunol* 48:148, 1982.
11. Traill KN et al: Age-related changes in lymphocyte subset proportions, surface differentiation antigen density and plasma membrane fluidity: Application of the Eurage SENIEUR protocol admission criteria. *Mech Ageing Dev* 33:39, 1985.
12. Adler WH et al: Effect of age upon primary alloantigen recognition by mouse spleen cells. *J Immunol* 107:1351, 1971.
13. Makinodan T, Adler WH: The effects of aging on the differentiation and proliferation potentials of cells of the immune system. *Fed Proc* 34:153, 1975.
14. Nagel JE et al: Activity of 12-*O*-tetradecanoyl phorbol-13-acetate on peripheral blood lymphocytes from young and elderly adults. *Clin Exp Immunol* 49:217, 1982.
15. Lewis VM et al: Age, thymic involution and circulating thymic hormone activity. *J Clin Endocrinol Metab* 47:145, 1978.
16. Gillis S et al: Immunological studies of aging: Decreased production of and response to T cell growth factor by lymphocytes from aged humans. *J Clin Invest* 67:937, 1981.
17. Nagel JE et al: Effect of age on the human high affinity interleukin a receptor of phytohemagglutinin-stimulated peripheral blood lymphocytes. *Clin Exp Immunol* 75:286, 1989.
18. Nagel JE et al: Decreased proliferation, interleukin 2 synthesis, and interleukin 2 receptor expression is accompanied by decreased mRNA expression in phytohemagglutinin-stimulated cells from elderly donors. *J Clin Invest* 81:1096, 1988.
19. Buckley CE III, Dorsey FC: Effect of aging on human serum immunoglobulin concentrations. *J Immunol* 105:964, 1970.
20. Radl J: Age-related monoclonal gammapathies: Clini-

cal lessons from the aging C58B1 mouse. *Immunol Today* 11:234, 1990.
21. Kyle RA: Monoclonal gammopathy of undetermined significance and smoldering multiple myeloma. *Eur J Haematol* 43(suppl 51):79, 1989.
22. Singh J et al: Increased incidence of monoclonal gammopathy of undetermined significance in blacks and its age-related differences with whites on the basis of a study of 397 men and women in a hospital setting. *J Lab Clin Med* 116:785, 1990.
23. Silvestris F et al: Discrepancy in the expression of autoantibodies in healthy aged individuals. *Clin Immunol Immunopathol* 35:234, 1985.
24. Nisonoff A: Idiotypes: concepts and applications. *J Immunol* 147:2429, 1991.
25. Buskila D, Shoenfeld Y: Anti-DNA idiotypes: Their pathogenic role in autoimmunity. *Concepts Immunopathol* 8:85, 1992.
26. Robertson MJ, Ritz J: Biology and clinical relevance of human natural killer cells. *Blood* 76:2421, 1990.
27. Bender BS et al: Phenotypic expression of natural killer cell associated membrane antigens and cytolytic function of purified blood cells from different aged humans. *J Clin Lab Immunol* 21:31, 1986.
28. Nagel JE et al: Oxidative metabolism and bactericidal capacity of polymorphonuclear leukocytes from normal young and aged adults. *J Gerontol* 37:529, 1986.
29. Unanue E, Allen PM: The basis for the immunoregulatory role of macrophages and other accessory cells. *Science* 236:551, 1987.
30. Gleckman R, Hibert D: Afebrile bacteremia: A phenomena in geriatric patients. *JAMA* 248:1478, 1981.
31. Centers for Disease Control: Increase in national hospital discharge survey rates for septicemia—United States, 1979–1987. *MMWR* 39:31, 1987.
32. Boscia JA et al: Therapy vs no therapy for bacteriuria in elderly ambulatory nonhospitalized women. *JAMA* 257:1067, 1987.
33. Damas P et al: Cytokine serum level during severe sepsis in human IL-6 as a marker of severity. *Ann Surg* 215:356, 1992.
34. Calandra T et al: High circulating levels of interleukin-6 in patients with septic shock: Evolution during sepsis, prognostic value, and interplay with other cytokines. The Swiss-Dutch J5 Immunoglobulin Study Group. *Am J Med* 91:23, 1991.
35. Smith CR et al: HA-1A. A human monoclonal antibody for the treatment of gram-negative sepsis. *Infect Dis Clin North Am* 6:253, 1992.
36. Görgen I et al: Granulocyte colony-stimulating factor treatment protects rodents against lipopolysaccharide-induced toxicity via suppression of systemic tumor necrosis factor-α. *J Immunol* 149:918, 1992.
37. Fenton MJ et al: IL-4 reciprocally regulates IL-1 and IL-1 receptor antagonist expression in human monocytes. *J Immunol* 149:1283, 1992.
38. Bone RC: A critical evaluation of new agents for the treatment of sepsis. *JAMA* 266:1686, 1991.
39. Lotze MT: T-cell growth factors and the treatment of patients with cancer. *Clin Immunol Immunopathol* 62:S47, 1992.
40. Lieschke GJ, Burgess AW: Granulocyte colony-stimulating factor and granulocyte-macrophage colony-stimulating factor. *N Engl J Med* 1992:327, 28 & 99, 1992.
41. Sonoda Y et al: Treatment of idiopathic neutropenia in the elderly with recombinant human granulocyte colony-stimulating factor. *Acta Haematol* 85:146, 1991.
42. Hadden JW: Therapeutic immunopharmacology. *Curr Opin Immunol* 2:258, 1989.
43. Rudman D et al: Effects of human growth hormone in men over 60 years old. *N Engl J Med* 323:1, 1990.
44. Rapaport R et al: Suppression of immune function in growth hormone–deficient children during treatment with human growth hormone. *J Pediatr* 109:434, 1986.
45. Hirokawa K et al: Restoration of impaired immune function in aging animals: II. Effect of syngeneic thymus and bone marrow grafts. *Clin Immunol Immunopathol* 5:371, 1976.
46. Payette H et al: Nutrition factors in relation to cellular and regulatory immune variables in a free-living elderly population. *Am J Clin Nutr* 52:927, 1990.
47. Goodwin JS, Garry PJ: Lack or correlation between indices of nutritional status and immunologic function in elderly humans. *J Gerontol* 43:M46, 1988.
48. Weindruch R et al: Modification of age-related immune decline in mice dietarily restricted from or after midadulthood. *Proc Natl Acad Sci USA* 79:898, 1982.
49. Meydani SN et al: Oral (n-3) fatty acid supplementation suppresses cytokine production and lymphocyte proliferation: Comparison between young and old women. *J Nutr* 121:547, 1991.
50. Winchurch RA et al: Supplemental zinc restores antibody formation in cultures of aged spleen cells: III. Impairment of IL-2-mediated responses. *Clin Immunol Immunopathol* 49:215, 1988.
51. Shapiro ED et al: The protective efficacy of polyvalent pneumococcal polysaccharide vaccine. *N Engl J Med* 325:1506, 1991.
52. Gable CB et al: Pneumococcal vaccine. Efficacy and associated cost savings. *JAMA* 264:2910, 1990.

Chapter 6

ONCOLOGY AND AGING: GENERAL PRINCIPLES OF CANCER IN THE ELDERLY

Harvey Jay Cohen

This chapter will discuss many of the general relationships of oncology and aging. It will focus on the epidemiologic, basic etiologic, and biologic relationships between the processes of aging and neoplasia, and the generalizable aspects of management of malignant disease in the elderly patient. This chapter will also discuss clinical management of individual malignancies only as an example of general principles. The approach to specific malignancies will be covered in subsequent chapters related to the appropriate organ system.

It is now well-recognized that cancer is a major problem for elderly individuals.[1,2] It is the second leading cause of death after heart disease in the United States, and one-half of all cancers occur in the 11 percent of the population over the age of 65.[3,4] What may not be as well appreciated is the magnitude of the problem for the elderly individual as well as for the physicians caring for this population. If one examines incidence and mortality data obtained from the National Cancer Institute's Surveillance, Epidemiology, and End Results (SEER) Program (Fig. 6-1),[5] one sees that the total cancer incidence rises progressively through the middle years and then falls off in the later years. However, the age-specific cancer incidence rises progressively throughout the age range. Thus, while the rate of increase diminishes somewhat in the oldest age groups, the risk of developing cancer continues to rise for an individual throughout life. Since the number of people in this country above the age of 65 is rising rapidly and the oldest of the old—i.e., over the age of 85—are increasing at the greatest rate, geriatricians, generalists, and internists will be encountering increasing numbers of elderly individuals with cancer in their practices.

Not only does cancer occur at an increased rate in older individuals, but it makes a significant impact on such people's lives, from the standpoint of both increasing morbidity and mortality. Thus, as Fig. 6-1 also demonstrates, the age-specific cancer mortality continues to rise as a function of age, as does incidence. In support of this observation is the report from the SEER Program that 5-year survivals for most types of cancer decrease with advancing age.[6,7]

Though the overall pattern for the incidence of age-specific cancer shows a rise with age, this is not uniform for individual cancers. Moreover, for some malignancies there is an apparent decrease in incidence in people over the age of 80. This may be due to a number of factors, including underreporting or a natural selection which would allow the less-cancer-prone population to survive. However, cohort effects may have the most significant impact.[8] Figure 6-2*A* demonstrates age-specific annual cancer incidence rates from the SEER Program with a fall in incidence in the oldest age groups for both prostate and lung cancer. Figure 6-2*B* shows data corrected for certain known risk factors. Thus, for prostate cancer when only men are considered in the base population at risk, the incidence continues to rise into the oldest age groups. For lung cancer, an apparent decrease in lung cancer incidence in the older age groups might be explained by a smaller high-risk population because of decreased prevalence of smoking in the older age groups. When data derived from the Lung Cancer Early Detection Project[9] for annual cancer incidence in male smokers over the age of 45 are used, one notes a continuing increase into advanced age. There is little change in the case of colorectal cancer because the entire population appears to be at risk. For women with breast cancer, data shown here indicate an incidence that continues to rise slowly into advanced age. It has been suggested that data from the most recent survey showing a decrease in breast cancer risk at older ages (>75 years) may be an artifact of recent increases in breast cancer screening in the United States.[10] For other gynecologic malignancies there does appear to be a decrease, perhaps due to different interactions of hormonal status and neoplasia in hormonally responsive target organs.

Other types of patterns in age-specific incidence may also be seen.[8] Thus, for example, Hodgkin's disease has a distinct bimodal distribution in incidence with a peak in the early years and another peak after

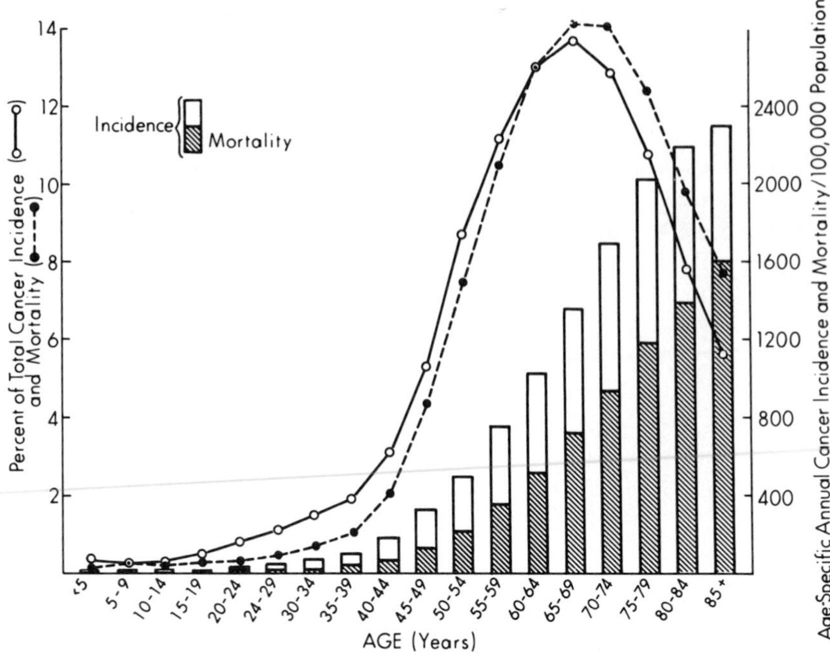

FIGURE 6-1
Comparison of age with the percentage of total cancer incidence and mortality versus the age-specific cancer incidence and mortality. Data compiled from the SEER Program, 1973–1977, all areas except Puerto Rico. (*From Crawford and Cohen.*[8])

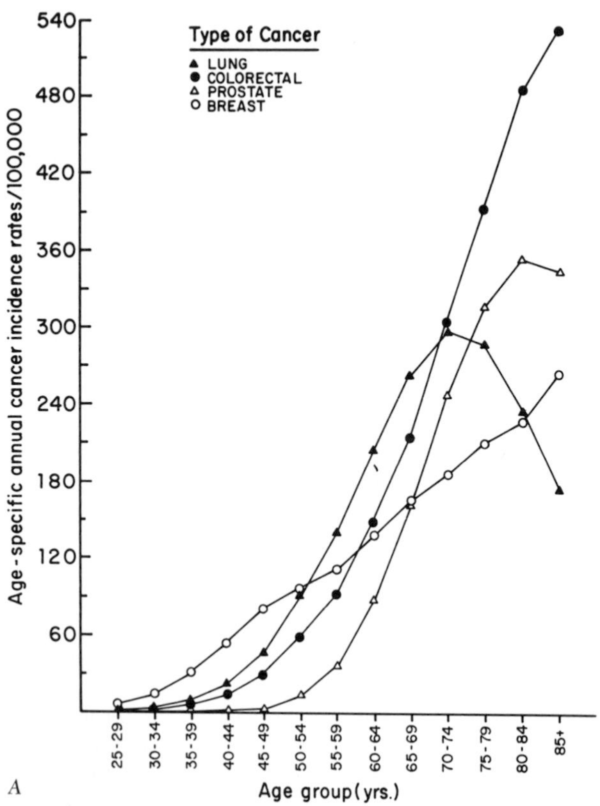

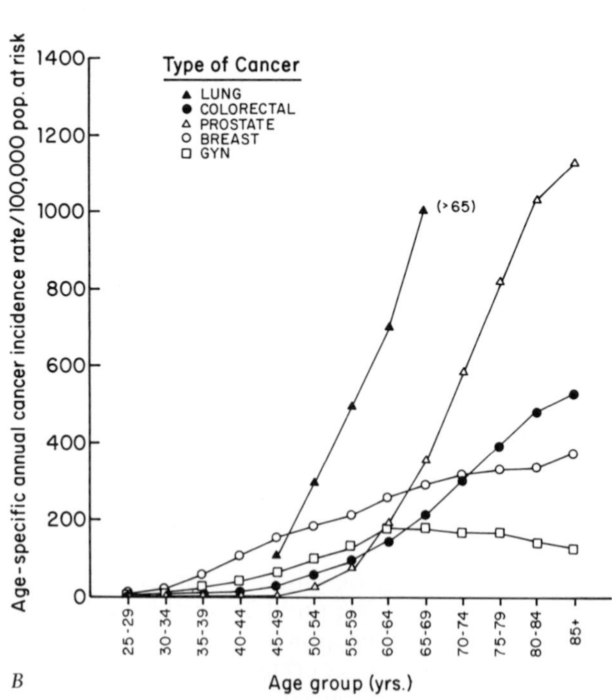

FIGURE 6-2
A. Age-specific annual cancer incidence rates, SEER Program, all races, both sexes, 1978-1981. *B.* Age- and population-specific annual cancer incidence rates. Tabulated from the SEER Program, 1978-1981: colorectal, all races, both sexes; prostate, males only; breast and gynecologic, females only. Compiled from Lung Cancer Early Detection Program: lung cancer, male smokers only. (*From Crawford and Cohen.*[8])

late middle age. This has led to the suggestion that there actually may be two different diseases involved, one in the young individual and one in the older one, but that they assume similar morphologic features, so that with current technologies we are unable to tell them apart. This impression is further substantiated by the markedly different response to treatment in younger and older groups of individuals with this disease. On the other hand, the most common leukemias and lymphomas in elderly patients are those derived from the B-lymphocyte arm of the immune system. These, including chronic lymphocytic leukemia and multiple myeloma, rise dramatically in incidence throughout life with the great majority of these disorders found in elderly individuals. Whether this dramatic relationship is due to an enhanced susceptibility of the B lymphocyte to neoplastic transformation in older individuals is a question relevant to the entire issue of the relationship between the aging process and the neoplastic process—a subject which will be considered next.

RELATIONSHIP OF AGING AND NEOPLASIA

It is difficult to discuss a relationship between two processes both of which are incompletely understood at this time, i.e., aging (senescence) and neoplastic transformation. In order to explore the relationship, however, we must first briefly describe the current understanding of the process of carcinogenesis. Figure 6-3 shows the current concept of the multistep nature of cancer development, which includes the major stages of initiation, promotion, and progression.[8,11,12] The first stage of cancer development is known as *initiation.* In this process, chemical or physical carcinogens, or certain viruses, cause a change in the cell that predisposes it to a subsequent malignant transformation. This change appears to be an irreversible lesion in the genomic DNA of a stem cell; the lesion may remain stable for a long period of time. It is not clear whether such an initiated cell can be recognized clinically, but certain disorders such as preleukemia, or carcinoma-in-situ may be a manifestation of this phenomenon.

The next stage of carcinogenesis is called *promotion* and involves a proliferative phase. *Promoters* are agents which can induce mitogenesis, or cell division, in an initiated cell. Whereas it appears that a single initiating event is sufficient to begin the process, promotion appears to be most successful when it is repetitive. This may occur shortly after initiation or after a prolonged delay and appears to be dose-dependent as well as reversible. For this reason researchers believe that cessation of cigarette smoking (containing both initiators and promoters) reduces the incidence of cancer in former smokers compared with those who continue to smoke.

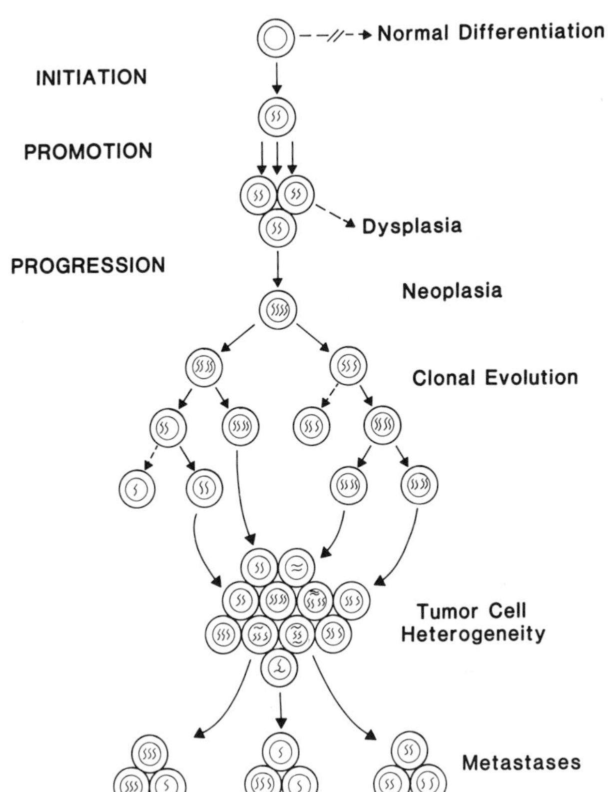

FIGURE 6-3

Stages of Carcinogenesis. (*From Crawford and Cohen.*[8])

The final stage of cancer development in this model is *progression.* This is actually multiphasic itself and involves the transformation of a cell from a premalignant to a malignant state, the potential clonal evolution of a subset of such cells, and the potential development of metastasis. The latter two phenomena are quite important and have led to the concept of tumor cell heterogeneity. While we believe that tumors arise from a single "clone of cells," tumor cells are genetically more unstable than normal cells, yielding progeny with variable proliferative and metastatic potential. Thus, not all cells within a given tumor are the same. Clinically, this may explain such diversity as variable chemosensitivity of tumor cells, the selection of resistant cells, the differential behavior of different metastatic lesions compared with the original tumor and with other metastatic lesions, and the sometimes unpredictable behavior of a particular cancer.

In recent years there has been an explosion of information concerning the role of cellular genetics in neoplastic evolution.[13,14] There are two major classes of such genes—oncogenes and tumor suppressor genes.[15,16] *Oncogenes,* or cancer genes, were initially described as viral genes capable of transforming normal cells to malignant ones. It was subsequently found that these viral oncogenes have normal cellular counterparts, i.e., a normal cellular gene important to the physiologic regulation of cellular processes. It is now felt that such genes have the potential of causing malignant transformation of a normal cell, if the genetic information is altered or expressed inappropriately, as with the application of mutagenic or carcinogenic stimuli as noted in the previous section. Though it is not clear what the precise interaction of oncogenes with other aspects of the carcinogenic process is, the genes may also play a role during the latter stages of progression of neoplasia.

A large number of oncogenes have been described.[15,16] They appear to have the potential for growth-enhancing activity at a series of steps along the mitogenic pathway, including activating signal transduction at the cell surface, producing endogenous growth factors at the cytoplasmic level (e.g., *ras*-like), and increasing the sensitivity of the cell to exogenous (or endogenous) growth factors at the nuclear level (e.g., *myc*-like). Recently, another oncogene, *bcl*-2, has been shown to code for an inner mitrochondrial protein which blocks apoptosis, or programmed cell death.[17] This mechanism may be of particular interest in the context of senescence since it may operate by increasing cell longevity rather than proliferation. Increased cellular oncogenic expression has been noted in many tumors and can be mimicked experimentally by altering the DNA encoding for the oncogene, usually at or near the promoter. Thus, it is possible that the chromosomal damage noted in neoplasia during the initiation and promotion phases, if it occurred near the region of an oncogene, could result in transformation and clonal evolution of the cancer. The evolutions noted in Burkitt's lymphoma and chronic granulocytic leukemia may be examples of this process. The expression of more than one oncogene is necessary to cause transformation.

In recent years a number of *tumor suppressor genes* have been described.[18] The normal function of such genes appears to be to prevent uncontrolled growth as a result of the action of various growth-promoting factors. It has even been suggested that senescence may act as a form of tumor suppression.[19] The inactivation of tumor suppressor genes can result in the development of neoplasia. However, it is likely that alterations in both oncogenes and tumor suppressor genes are necessary in many cases to achieve full malignant potential.

How then might the aging process influence the process of neoplastic transformation to result in the markedly increased rates of cancer in older people.[20–22] General aspects of the aging process have been covered in Chap. 1, and only certain specific aspects relevant to the process under discussion will be reiterated here. The types of theories which appear relevant to an explanation of the striking epidemiologic relationship are given in Table 6-1. First, it is possible that aging simply allows the time necessary for the accumulation of cellular events to develop into a clinical neoplasm. There is evidence for age-related accumulation and expression of genetic damage.[8,21] Somatic mutations are felt to occur at the rate of approximately 1 in 10^6 cell divisions with approximately 10^{16} cell divisions occurring in a lifetime of a human being. Certainly the complex set of events required in the multistep process of carcinogenesis, for example as described for colon cancer in humans,[23] does occur over time. The passage of time alone, however, is not likely to explain the phenomenon, since the time for a mutated cell to become a malignant cell and then subsequently to become a detectable tumor has been estimated to be approximately 10 to 30 percent of the maximum life span for a given animal species, which may vary from just a few years to over 100 years. Second, there may be altered susceptibility of aging cells to a given amount of carcinogenic exposure. Data in this area are somewhat contradictory.[8,22] In some cases the incidence of skin tumors in mice produced with benzpyrene has been more related to dose than to age, while in other models accelerated carcinogenesis as a function of age has been demonstrated, as, for example, when dimethylbenzanthracene (DMBA) was applied to skin grafts of young and old mice.[21] In addition, an age-related increase in the sensitivity of lymphocytes to cell cycle arrest and chromosome damage after radiation has been demonstrated.[24] It is also possible that there are alterations in carcinogen metabolism with age, but the findings from such studies have also been contradictory.[25] Third, it is possible that damage once initiated is more difficult to repair in older cells. A number of studies have demonstrated decreased DNA repair as a function of age following damage by carcinogens as well as radiation.[8,26] Such repair failures may also be reflected in increased karyotypic abnormalities in aged normal cells as well as in older patients with neoplastic disease. Fourth, oncogene activation or amplification might be increased in the older host resulting either in increased initiation or promotion or in differential clonal evolution. Though evidence is currently limited, there have been observations of increased amplification of proto-oncogenes and their products in aging fibroblasts in vitro as well as evidence for increased c-*myc* transcript levels in the livers of aging mice.[27,28] Alternatively such factors as genetic alterations or DNA damage could lead to inactivation of cancer suppressor genes. Since age-related mutations frequently appear to result in the loss of function, alterations in tumor suppressor genes may prove to be an important mechanism. Finally, a decrease in immune surveillance, or immunosenescence, could contribute to the increased incidence. This phenomenon has been described in detail in Chap. 5. However, with respect to tumor-related immunity, there is a considerable amount of

TABLE 6-1

Cancer: Aging Theories

1. Longer duration of carcinogenic exposure
2. Increased susceptibility of cells to carcinogens
3. Decreased ability to repair DNA
4. Oncogene activation or amplification; tumor suppressor gene loss
5. Decreased immune surveillance

evidence for a loss of tumor-specific immunity with progressive age, in animal models.[8,29] This includes the altered capacity of old mice to reject transplanted tumors, the close relationship between susceptibility to malignant melanomas and the rate of age-related T-cell-dependent immune function decline, and the ability by immunopharmacologic manipulation to increase age-depressed tumoricidal immune function and to decrease the incidence of spontaneous tumors. The evidence linking such data to age-associated immune deficiency and the rise of cancer incidence in humans, however, is mainly circumstantial.

Probably the explanation for the increased incidence of neoplasia that occurs with advancing age in humans will be multifactorial and will include a number of these factors as well as others yet to be discovered. It is also likely that through research at the basic level concerning the interactions of aging and neoplasia we will learn a great deal about the fundamental basis of each. Such information will hopefully enhance our ability to engage in prevention at the primary and secondary levels.

Current information suggests that a large proportion of cancers are potentially preventable.[30] The most obviously available modalities in this regard are avoidance of known and suspected carcinogenic exposures such as tobacco smoke, occupational and environmental chemicals, excessive sunlight, and dietary factors such as excessive fat and smoked, salted, and pickled foods. While older individuals have potentially acquired a lifetime exposure to such carcinogens, they should still accrue benefits from modifying these behaviors as well as from engaging in positive ones such as the suggested intake of fiber, vitamins, and fresh vegetables.[31,32] In recent years there has been increased interest in cancer prevention through chemopreventive approaches. Several trials have indicated the potential for such an approach, but results have not been consistent.[30] However, in this situation elderly individuals may be the most appropriate candidates since their risk is highest and thus the benefit per intervention could be the greatest. This is exemplified by the recently initiated tamoxifen trial for the prevention of breast cancer, in which the most eligible subjects are older postmenopausal women.[33] More definitive word awaits the final outcome of these trials.

CLINICAL PRESENTATIONS AND DISEASE BEHAVIOR

Screening in Asymptomatic Individuals

The situations in which periodic routine screening are recommended for all individuals regardless of age are relatively few. A number of organizations have made recommendations, and there is some variation among them.[34] It should be recognized that when applied to elderly persons, especially those over 75, such information is largely empirically derived.[34] These recommendations are directed at mass screening of populations. When applied to individuals within a physician's office or other practice, they serve only as general guidelines for decisions which may be modified by many other factors. The current guidelines of the American Cancer Society[35] relevant to the older adult, those of the U.S. Preventive Health Task Force, a synthesized recommendation by the authors, and Medicare reimbursement are shown in Table 6-2 from Oddone et al.[34] Most of these recommendations do not directly address alterations in strategy for people at more advanced ages. Screening recommendations for colorectal cancer and prostate cancer are relatively straightforward, with prostate cancer covered by the recommended yearly digital rectal examination. Evidence for the use of prostate-specific antigen (PSA) is not sufficient to recommend it for general screening.[34] The difficulty in arriving at a specific recommendation for breast cancer screening in older women has been extensively reviewed recently.[36] In addition to the lack of specific outcome data for women over 75 years of age, factors such as increased mammographic detectability of cancers in older women because of the increase in fatty tissue of the breast with age, contrasted with the increased prevalence of comorbid disease, make decision making difficult. In general, breast cancer screening should be a lifelong activity, though cessation has been suggested if life expectancy is less than 5 years.[34] While there are no specific outcome data to support breast self-examination in older women, if it is practiced, it should be made clear that it is not a substitute for mammography and clinical examination. In the past, recommendations concerning cervical cancer and the Pap test have been controversial. The effectiveness of this screening modality is widely accepted. Controversy has been centered more around the frequency of testing required and whether testing could be suspended either at a certain age or after a certain number of negative tests. The current American Cancer Society guideline for detection of cervical cancer in asymptomatic women appears to be a consensus position which should adequately address the issue. The guideline states that "all women who are, or who have been, sexually active, or have reached age 18 years, have an annual Pap test and pelvic examination. After a women has three or more consecutive satisfactory normal annual examinations, the Pap test may be performed less frequently at the discretion of her physician." It is to be noted that this recommendation has no specific upper-age limitation, and the discussion of these recommendations contains a reminder that "mature women—those over 65—also require testing." This is considered to be critical if such women have not had a history of regular Pap testing in their younger years. Thus, we would recommend that for the older patient whose history of previous screening is not clear, Pap testing be done until the recommendations have been fulfilled.

TABLE 6-2

Recommendations for Cancer Screening in Elderly Patients

Disease	Test	ACS Guideline	USPSTF Guideline	Authors' Recommendation	Medicare Reimbursement
Breast	1. Breast self-exam	Monthly	None	None	N/A
	2. Breast physical exam	Annual	Annual	Annual	Part of office exam
	3. Mammography	Annual	Biennial; stop age 75	Biennial	Yes
Cervical	Pap test	Annual until 3 or more smears normal	Every 1–3 years until age 65; stop if normal	Include if previously unscreened	Yes, if no Medicare-covered test within 3 years
Skin	Skin inspection	Annual	None for normal risk	Annual for high-risk patients	None as screening tool
Oral	Mouth inspection and palpation	Annual	None for normal risk	Annual for high-risk patients	None as screening tool
Colon	1. Digital rectal exam	Annual	No recommendation for or against any modality	Annual	1. Part of office exam
	2. Fecal occult blood test	Annual		Annual	2. None as screening tool
	3. Sigmoidoscopy	Every 3–5 years		Every 5 years	3. None as screening tool
Prostate	Digital rectal exam	Annual	No recommendation	Annual	Part of office exam
Lung	1. Chest x-ray film	Not recommended	Not recommended	Not recommended in any group	1. None as screening tool
	2. Sputum cytology	Not recommended	Not recommended	Not recommended in any group	2. None as screening tool

SOURCE: From Oddone et al.[34]

For one of the most common malignancies in both sexes, i.e., lung cancer, specific mass screening is not recommended. This is based on a lack of demonstrated cost-benefit efficacy, even in high-risk smoking groups.[37] However, with the relatively few elderly patients involved in the large screening trials on which these recommendations have been based and given the very high cancer incidence in the older smoker and evidence (to be described later) that this malignancy may present at an earlier stage in older patients, there exists some rationale for the potential usefulness of screening in individual patients in the older age group.

Despite these widely disseminated recommendations, many individuals do not follow them.[38] This appears to relate to both physician- and patient-derived factors. Despite the increased risk of cancer in the older age group, such individuals appear to avail themselves of routine screening even less frequently than their younger counterparts.[39] The physician, and other health care professionals in a position to do so, should ensure that the older individual is aware of the importance of screening, that the opportunity for such examinations is provided, and that fears and anxieties about these tests are allayed to as great an extent as possible.

Initial Presentation

As an extension of the screening concept, the goal for initial cancer detection is to make the diagnosis as early as possible with the hope that treatment at the earliest stages of disease would yield the best survival rates. Therefore, it is of great importance that both patient and physician pay attention to symptoms that may herald the onset of the neoplastic process. Though information on "warning signs of cancer" has been widely disseminated by the American Cancer Society and others, it is often ignored. This may be due in part to a lack of knowledge of what the implications of such warning signs are. Indeed some studies have indicated that elderly persons know less about potential cancer symptoms and their significance than young individials, which might lead to a delay in presentation.[40] Another factor that might interfere with early diagnosis is what might be called "cancer symptom confusion"; that is, not the specific failure to know that a particular symptom might indicate a neoplastic process but a tendency to write off the symptom as simply another change due to the aging process. Examples of such possibilities are listed in Table 6-3. Physicians and patients alike may be prone to

TABLE 6-3

Cancer Symptom Confusion

Symptom or Sign	Possible Malignancy	Aging "Explanation"
Increase in skin pigment	Melanoma, squamous cell	"Age spots"
Rectal bleeding	Colon or rectum	Hemorrhoids
Constipation	Rectal	"Old age"
Dyspnea	Lung	Getting old, out of shape
Decrease in urinary stream	Prostate	"Dribbling"—benign prostatic hypertrophy (BPH)
Breast contour change	Breast	"Normal" atrophy, fibrosis
Fatigue	Metastatic or other	Loss of energy due to "aging"
Bone pain	Metastatic or other	Arthritis: "aches and pains of aging"

such assumptions and should be alerted to the fact that a new symptom or a change in symptoms should be appropriately pursued in the elderly individual.

Current evidence suggests that once having noticed a symptom that appears to be related to cancer, older individuals do not delay appreciably in seeking medical help. Thus, in both a study of a Rhode Island population and a population-based study in New Mexico, older individuals were no more likely than younger ones to delay seeking medical attention once the symptom was noted.[40,41] Physicians, however, may be guilty of delaying further diagnostic pursuits in elderly patients. In one study of factors affecting the delay in the ultimate diagnosis of breast cancer, there was somewhat of a longer delay in diagnosis from the time of presentation for older patients than for younger, but the greatest part of this delay was due to factors for which the physician was responsible rather than those for which patients were responsible.[42] Part of the problem may lie in a failure to recognize some of the new signs and symptoms in patients with multiple disease processes. It is easy to attribute such symptoms as anorexia, weight loss, or decrease in performance status to social or psychological changes. The increasing prevalence of processes such as anemia in elderly patients may lower the index of suspicion for attributing the factor to a new specific neoplastic process. The remarkable age-related increase in cancer incidence described above should be sufficient to maintain vigilance in this regard, though it must be balanced by judgment concerning the risk/benefit ratio for diagnostic evaluations in individual patients depending on their other medical status. Thus, the initial discovery of a new symptom in a previously totally well, active 80-year-old may be pursued rather differently than a similar discovery in a severely demented, bedbound individual with severe congestive heart failure, diabetes, and pulmonary failure.

Biologic Behavior of Tumors in the Elderly Host

The effect of the aging process on the clinical course of cancer—or to put it another way, whether cancer behaves differently in the older individual—is not clear-cut.[43,44] While the SEER data noted previously suggested that in many cancers the 5-year survival rate is lower for older people, it is possible that this is related more to comorbid disease and other factors rather than simply to aging per se. On the other hand, there is a widespread belief that cancers may behave more indolently in elderly patients. These are important issues since they may affect decisions regarding treatment to a considerable degree. In fact there is both clinical and experimental evidence to support both sides of this issue, and it is likely that there is a spectrum of responses dependent upon initial tumor types as well as individual host status. One indicator of the phenomenon is the extent of disease at presentation. For most cancers examined there has been no consistent difference in the stage of disease or presentation for different age groups.[40] For those which have been determined, the directions are not always the same.[45] Thus, for malignant melanoma, older patients have been consistently found to have more advanced stage local disease with deeper penetrating lesions at presentation.[46,47] For breast cancer, some studies show a greater proportion of older patients with distant metastatic spread at presentation,[48] while for lung cancer the opposite has been found, and older patients have been noted to present with localized disease in a greater proportion of cases.[49,50] Uterine and cervical cancers have in some cases been noted to be later in the course of disease at presentation in older individuals.[45] Of course, even these differences might be related to such phenomena as delay in the patient's presenting for diagnosis (which does not appear to be the case), delay in pursuing the diagnosis, and/or intensity of diagnostic endeavors, or, on the other hand, a greater chance for a serendipitous finding because of more frequent visits to physicians.

Another biologic factor that may influence neoplastic behavior in differently aged hosts is the histologic subtype of the tumor. Thus, while thyroid cancer overall appears to behave more aggressively in the older host, it is also true that a larger proportion of thyroid neoplasia in elderly patients is made up by anaplastic carcinoma, which at any age has more aggresive behavior.[51,52] In addition, however, there may be a poorer overall prognosis for older individuals with thyroid cancer even independent of histologic type.[53] Similarly, for malignant melanoma, while there is an increased proportion of older people who have melanomas of poor prognostic histologic type and location at presentation, older individuals have a poorer prognosis for survival than do younger ones independent of this phenomenon even for localized disease.[47] Similarly, for lung cancer the increased proportion of elderly patients with squamous carcinoma of the lung—which is the histologic subset most likely to present as localized disease—partially, but not completely, explains some of the findings noted above.[54–56] Such biologic differences may be manifested in other ways, as in the case of breast cancer, in which older women have an increased frequency of estrogen-receptor-positive breast cancer, probably related to hormonal influences of the postmenopausal state.[57] Since estrogen-receptor positivity is associated with better prognosis, with more slowly growing tumors and with longer disease-free survivals, this phenomenon, rather than age per se, might explain the reason why the cancer appears to behave more indolently in an older individual.[58]

Experimental data in animal models likewise show this spectrum in rate of tumor growth and progression as a function of age.[59] Most such studies have assessed the ability of animals to resist the growth and/or spread of transplanted or infused tumors. In these studies the ability to contain tumor growth depends on the particular host tumor system used, thus mimicking the clinical situation to some extent. A potential explanation for the situation in which the older host more effectively controls the rate of tumor growth has been proposed to rest in a paradoxical effect of decreasing immune function with age, i.e., decreased activity of those cells in the old host's immune system which, under the stimulation of the neoplastic process, produce tumor-enhancing factors such as angiogenesis factor.[59–61] When this occurs, tumor growth might be expected to be diminished. To what extent these various factors play a role in the biologic behavior of neoplasia in the human aging host remains a fascinating puzzle to be unraveled.

MANAGEMENT

This section will examine the utility of the major modalities of cancer treatment in the elderly individual. The use of such modalities is heavily conditioned by the initial decision-making process, i.e., whether to screen, whether to pursue diagnostic workups, whether to treat at all, and how intensively to treat. In such decisions the physician is often placed in the position of weighing benefits versus risks of diagnostic and therapeutic interventions. This is as it should be, and the physician should take into account the various biologic, psychological, and social factors involved in the patient's well-being. Of great importance in this regard is the patient's own assessment of the value of both quantity and quality of potential survival during and after the treatment for malignancy. In this process there is a clear need to individualize such decisions, and a decision made for a "wellderly" patient may be appropriately different than that for a "frailderly" patient. Currently it would appear that age bias in diagnostic and treatment decisions for older patients with cancer does exist. Thus, it has been reported that despite the presentation of older patients with higher proportion of localized lung cancer, such patients more infrequently received potentially curative surgical therapy.[50] Though this study did not address the appropriateness of such decisions, another study of patients with breast cancer did and revealed that older women with breast cancer received appropriate therapy, be it surgical, hormonal, chemotherapy, etc., less frequently than did younger women.[62] Other studies have confirmed these variations in treatment decisions on the basis of the patient's age.[63–66] Differences in decisions may be entirely appropriate in certain situations but must be based on specific individualized patient information not on categorical decisions made on the basis of chronological age.

We have proposed one framework in which the general aspects of such decision making can be considered for the individual patient.[67] This is shown in Fig. 6-4 and is called the Comprehensive Geriatric Model. It graphically presents a number of the concepts critical to the care of the elderly, i.e., the fact that there is a decreased functional reserve and, as an extension of Engel's Bio-Psycho-Social Model, that all these various aspects of the individual's background must be taken into account when making decisions about the new process—i.e., the cancer. Thus, each of these levels, e.g., biologic or psychological, can create interactions which influence both the cancer and the host, and likewise any intervention directed at the cancer may influence both the cancer and each of these levels of the host's function. Conversely, each of these levels of function, when compromised by the aging process or other comorbid diseases, may influence the ability to deliver these various interventions. Thus, in a sense, a conceptual checklist is presented in which a four-way street of various interacting factors can be systematically considered when making such decisions. In this concept, chronological age per se plays a role only by having defined the potentially decreased functional reserve in any of these areas that the older patients may exhibit, but once this is factored into the system, subsequent decisions are dependent more upon those capabilities actually still remaining in the social, psychological, and biologic spheres for the individual patient. We would suggest that such considerations be the ones that more directly weigh upon subsequent management decisions for utilization of diagnostic as well as therapeutic technologies for the elderly patient with cancer.

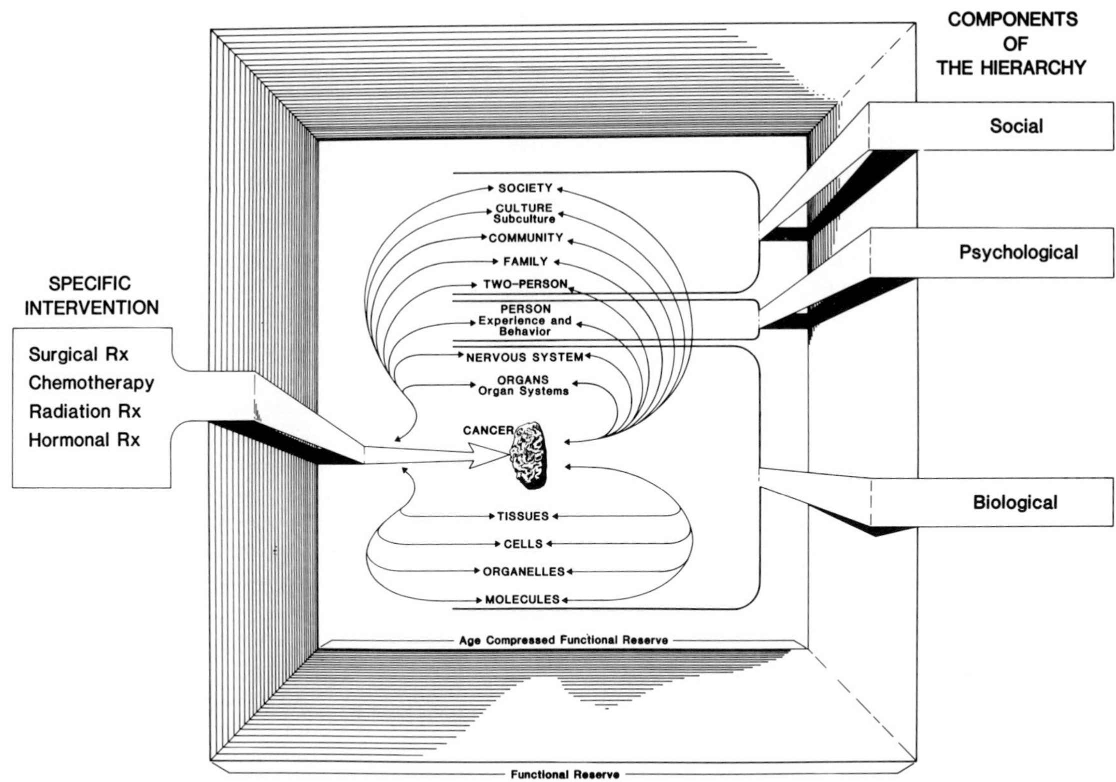

FIGURE 6-4
Comprehensive Geriatric Model. (*From Cohen and Demaria.*[67])

Major Therapeutic Modalities

Surgery

Surgery and other invasive procedures are frequently involved in initial diagnostic as well as therapeutic approaches to the elderly patient with cancer. The general aspects of surgery in the elderly patient will be discussed thoroughly in Chap. 27. Suffice it to say here that a number of studies have demonstrated that cancer surgery may be accomplished in elderly patients with mortality and morbidity rates which are similar in many cases to those for younger patients and appear to be conditioned more by the extent of comorbid disease and declines in measurable physiologic functions than by chronological age. In comparing potential alternative modalities, it is well to remember that the acute and time-limited stress of surgery may be preferable to many older patients than the more chronic or protracted courses of therapy frequently involved in radiation therapy and/or chemotherapy.

Radiation Therapy

Radiation therapy is used in the treatment of malignancies with both curative and palliative intent.[68] In an attempt to cure local or regional disease, since both radiation therapy and surgery might be considered, one must consider whether the cure rate is equivalent and whether there are differences in morbidity or mortality between the procedures that would cause one to favor one over the other. Radiation therapy has the advantage of having no appreciable acute mortality; it is generally not contraindicated by associated medical conditions; and it may allow maintenance of function of the organ in which the tumor arises. For example, for an elderly person, radiating laryngeal carcinoma and maintaining speech, rather than requiring the learning of laryngeal speech postoperatively, may be of considerable advantage. On the other hand, radiation treatment frequently involves a protracted course of therapy.

Radiation therapy is also utilized as an effective adjunct to surgery and/or chemotherapy. For those surgical procedures with high operative mortality, utilizing adjunct radiation therapy to reduce the degree of surgery required may be especially attractive to an elderly patient. The results for adjunct radiation therapy and approaches such as quadrantectomy in breast cancer or lymph node excision in head or neck cancer have been demonstrated to be equivalent to more extensive surgical procedures.[68,69] Palliatively radiation therapy can be extremely effective in providing relief from pain from bone metastases, the effects of brain metastases, control of local obstructive symptoms, and spinal cord compromise. Such treatments can frequently be delivered in courses of 1 to 2 weeks' duration rather than the longer courses of therapy that may be more difficult to tolerate. However, short courses of high-dose radiation may be associated with a higher incidence of acute side effects. The results of treatment, as well as the incidence of complications, are highly dependent upon the technology available and its correct application. Thus, the frequency of complications is directly related to excessive target volume dose and the volume of tissue radiated. Megavoltage equipment, such as the linear accelerator and cobalt 60, are more penetrating than older orthovoltage conventional x rays, thus sparing the skin when treating deep-seated malignancies. The linear accelerator, which has very high output, straight-beam edges, and excellent localizability is the most desirable and has been associated with improved therapeutic responses. Thus, for example, in prostate cancer, local recurrences occurred in only 10 percent of those patients treated with 6-MeV, or greater, equipment, but in those treated with cobalt machines recurrence was 20 percent. Similarly, there were fewer recurrences for both cervical cancer and Hodgkin's disease in treatment facilities utilizing a linear accelerator rather than a cobalt unit.[70]

The side effects of therapy may create problems for the older patient. The radiation effect on normal tissue is said to be enhanced approximately 10 to 15 percent in the elderly patient.[71] Logically, those organs with more marked physiologic decline would be at greatest risk. Radiation to the oral pharynx and oral cavity can produce a loss of taste, dryness of mucous membranes, and involution of salivary glands, which when combined with a precarious nutritional intake in a frail and elderly individual might be lethal, or certainly contribute a considerable amount of morbidity, if not recognized.[72] Moreover, if daily treatment is tolerated poorly due to nausea or weakness, treatment may be compromised because of the decreased daily doses, patient's unscheduled absences, or decrease in the total planned dose. Since radiation therapy is frequently used in the treatment of lung cancer, pulmonary complications may be of particular importance. In one study, severe radiation pneumonitis was noted more frequently in elderly individuals than in younger ones regardless of field size and other therapies.[73] Alterations in schedule can be made and still deliver potentially curative radiation therapy to older individuals. This must be done with care, however; although decreasing the daily fraction has not been shown to be detrimental to local control of neck and head cancer, split-dose schedules have been associated with significantly lower control rates for some tumor sites.[68,70]

Chemotherapy and Hormonal Therapy

A thorough discussion of the principles of pharmacology in elderly persons can be found in Chap. 24. There have been few direct studies of the effect of age on the pharmacokinetics of orally or parenterally administered chemotherapeutic agents.[74,75] There has been no clear demonstration of differences in the responsiveness of malignant cells per se to chemotherapy in the older versus younger host. The delivery of equivalent doses of the drug to the tumor site, however, may be conditioned by the alterations in pharmacokinetics and pharmacodynamics which may be seen in the elderly individual.

The potential for response and degree of toxicity for various regimens in elderly patients appears to constitute a spectrum depending predominantly upon the aggressiveness of the therapeutic regimen.[76–78] The major limiting factor for most drugs is bone marrow reserve. Decreased reserve capacity has been demonstrated in both experimental animals and humans,[79,80] but clinical toxicity would depend upon the degree to which bone marrow reserve is stressed. Other toxicities, such as the pulmonary toxicity of bleomycin, the cardiotoxicity of doxorubicin, and the peripheral nerve toxicity of vincristine, also appear to be increased somewhat, though again depending upon the aggressiveness of the regimen.[74,75] Thus, in one clinical study of treatment for metastatic lung, breast, and colorectal carcinoma, the responses of the elderly patients were equivalent to those of the younger ones with no substantial increase in toxicity.[81] For these relatively unaggressive treatment regimens, excessive toxicity was seen with only two drugs. One was methotrexate. For this drug, however, apparently age-related excesses in toxicity have been shown to be more related to, and limitable by adjustment for, decrements in renal function.[82] The other drug was semustine, which may have rather profound and long-lasting effects on marrow stem cells. However, in another treatment trial of combination chemotherapy of a moderately aggressive nature for multiple myeloma, including another nitrosourea, carmustine, equivalent success rates in terms of response and survival were obtained for elderly patients with no increase in bone marrow or other toxicities.[83]

When one considers somewhat more aggressive combination chemotherapy, such as for small-cell carcinoma of the lung, equivalent response rates have been obtained for older individuals, but this has come at the cost of increased marrow toxicity.[84] Likewise, multiagent chemotherapy approaches for Hodgkin's disease and for non-Hodgkin's lymphoma have been associated with markedly increased toxicity, increased numbers of early deaths, and therefore decreased survival for elderly patients.[85–89] This phenomenon is seen to the maximal extent in elderly patients treated with the most aggressive regimens for acute nonlymphocytic leukemia, wherein excessive early treatment-related deaths severely constrain the use of such approaches.[90–92]

For the hormonally responsive cancers, such as prostate cancer and breast cancer, hormonal therapy is purported to be at least as good in elderly patients as it is in younger patients, and it may be actively employed alone or in combination with other modalities for effective palliative treatment.[70]

When approaching decisions about chemotherapy in treating the elderly patient, the clinician must use those modalities which in the prescribed dosages have acceptable responses with acceptable levels of toxicity, while in the case of those tumor types which require extremely aggressive therapy, the physician must seek modifications and new approaches in order to achieve lower levels of toxicity for the results achieved.[93] In making these decisions, an effective dialogue between the patient and physician is critically important. We must be wary of the phenomenon of "risk aversion" leading to underdosing, in which, in an attempt to avoid toxicities, we effectively abrogate any chance of a therapeutic response. Such a phenomenon may explain the initial reports of the failure of adjuvant chemotherapy for breast cancer to have an effect in elderly women.[94] Upon reanalysis of this information, it appears that no effect had been seen in those elderly women who had lower than the prescribed dosage of adjuvant therapy, presumably in an attempt to avoid toxicities, while in those older women who had received equivalent doses of therapy as the younger women, an equal effect was noted.

Supportive Care

The effects of cancer and its treatment may be devastating to elderly patients and may require substantial supportive care.[95] The goal of such therapy is to maximize the ability of patients to tolerate the treatment as well as the disease. Underlying problems requiring symptomatic relief need to be actively sought by the physician since elderly patients more frequently underreport their symptoms. Many of the specific aspects of supportive care will be covered in other chapters and are only mentioned here to stress their importance for the management of the elderly cancer patient. These include the extreme importance of effective pain management (see Chap. 28), maintenance of appropriate nutritional support (see Chap. 29), the supportive role of nursing (see Chap. 23), the importance of patient, physician, and family discussions concerning decisions regarding terminal care and other issues (see Chaps. 34 and 36), and the utility of hospice care (see Chap. 34).

One complication frequently seen in treatment of the cancer patient, i.e., nausea and vomiting, has not been discussed in this volume. These side effects can seriously compromise the ability to deliver effective chemotherapy, and they create a considerable degree of morbidity. It is interesting that elderly patients appear to experience less nausea and vomiting than younger ones.[96] Nevertheless, it is wise to attempt to prevent this occurrence in the first place and correct it when possible. Patients should be kept well hydrated, and an attempt should be made to eliminate environmental factors, such as food and other odors, which may trigger vomiting. Oral feedings with dry bland foods are generally well tolerated, but high-protein diets are not. Antiemetic drugs may be required for control.[96,97] Phenothiazines have been the mainstay of antiemetic therapy. Elderly patients appear to be more susceptible to the side effects of these drugs, including excessive sedation, hypertension, and extrapyramidal reactions. Benzodiazepines, such as lorazepam, may be useful in preventing anticipatory nausea and vomiting, which is a conditioned response in patients with previous chemotherapy reactions. For very severely emetogenic chemotherapy, such as cis-platinum, metoclopramide has proved to be effective, and steroids may be beneficial when utilized in combination with other antiemetics. Ondansetron, the first of a new class of serotonin antagonists, appears to be at least as effective as metoclopramide for severe nausea and vomiting.[97]

Elderly patients may be particularly predisposed to constipation, especially as a side effect of such drugs as vincristine, and both preventive and treatment approaches to this problem should be borne in mind at all times. Because of the bone marrow suppressive effects of most cancer chemotherapies, significant cytopenias may result and should be treated with blood products. Because of decreased functional reserve, as well as other comorbid processes, maintenance of an effective and appropriate hemoglobin level should be approached with prophylactic and maintenance transfusion during the period of cytopenia. Hematopoietic growth stimulants such as granulocyte colony–stimulating factor (GCSF), granulocyte macrophage colony–stimulating factor (GMCSF), and erythropoietin are receiving increasing attention for the amelioration of such side effects, but their ultimate role in the care of the older cancer patient is yet to be fully established.[98]

Thus, cancer is a disease seen with great frequency in elderly patients. The relationship of cancer to aging poses a challenge to our scientific understanding of these processes as well as to our clinical approach to the elderly patient. Further research will be required to resolve the former,[99] but a systematic, logically developed diagnostic and treatment plan can produce effective and gratifying results in the latter.

REFERENCES

1. Crawford J, Cohen HJ: Aging and neoplasia. *Annu Rev Gerontol Geriatr,* 4:3, 1984.
2. Lipschitz DA et al: Cancer in the elderly: Basic science and clinical aspects. *Ann Intern Med* 102:218, 1985.
3. Baranovsky A, Myers MH: Cancer incidence and survival in patients 65 years of age and older. *CA* 36:26, 1986.
4. Cancer statistics, 1992. *CA* 42:21, 1992.
5. Young JL et al: Surveillance, epidemiology, and end results: Incidence and mortality data, 1973–1977. *Natl Cancer Inst Monogr* 57:1981.
6. Ries LG et al: Cancer patient survival: Surveillance, epidemiology, and end results program, 1973–79. *J Natl Cancer Inst* 70:693, 1983.

7. Ries LAG et al: *Cancer Statistics Review 1973–88*. NIH Publication 91-2789. National Cancer Institute, 1991.
8. Crawford J, Cohen HJ: Relationship of cancer and aging. *Clin Geriatr Med* 3:419, 1987.
9. Melamed MR et al: Screening for lung cancer: Results of the Memorial Sloan Kettering study in New York. *Chest* 86:44, 1984.
10. Kessler LG: The relationship between age and incidence of breast cancer. *Cancer* 69(suppl):1896, 1992.
11. Farber E: The multistep nature of cancer development. *Cancer Res* 44:4217, 1984.
12. Harris CC: Chemical and physical carcinogenesis: Advances and perspectives for the 1990s. *Cancer Res* 51(suppl):5023s, 1991.
13. Bishop JM: The molecular genetics of cancer. *Science* 235:305, 1987.
14. Solomon E et al: Chromosomal aberrations and cancer. *Science* 254:1153, 1991.
15. Friend SH et al: Onogenes and tumor-suppressor genes. *N Engl J Med* 318:618, 1988.
16. Weinberg RA: A short guide to oncogenes and tumor-suppressor genes. *J NIH Res* 3:45, 1991.
17. Williams GT: Programmed cell death. Apoptosis and oncogenesis. *Cell* 65:1097, 1991.
18. Weinberg RA: Tumor suppressor genes. *Science* 254:1138, 1991.
19. Sager R: Senescence as a mode of tumor suppression. *Environ Health Perspect* 93:59, 1991.
20. Anisimov VN: Age-related mechanisms of susceptibility to carcinogenesis. *Semin Oncol* 16:10, 1989.
21. Ebbesen P: Cancer and normal aging. *Mech Ageing Dev* 25:269, 1984.
22. Macieira-Coelho A: Review article cancer and aging. *Exp Gerontol* 21:483, 1986.
23. Vogelstein B et al: Genetic alterations during colorectal tumor development. *N Engl J Med* 319:525, 1988.
24. Staiano-Coico L et al: Increased sensitivity of lymphocytes from people over 65 to cell cycle arrest and chromosomal damage. *Science* 219:1335, 1983.
25. Birnbaum LS: Age-related changes in carcinogen metabolism. *J Am Geriatr Soc* 35:51, 1987.
26. Neidermuller H: Age dependency of DNA repair in rats after DNA damage by carcinogens. *Mech Ageing Dev* 19:259, 1982.
27. Srivastava A et al: C-Ha-ras-1 protooncogene amplification and overexpression during the limited replicative life span of normal human fibroblasts. *J Biocommun* 260:6404, 1985.
28. Matocha MF et al: Selective elevation of c-myc transcript levels in the liver of the aging Fischer-344 rat. *Biochem Biophys Res Commun* 147:1, 1987.
29. Makinodan T et al: Age-associated immunodeficiency and cancer, in Mathe G, Reizenstein P (eds): *Pathophysiological Aspects of Cancer Epidemiology*. Elmsford, NY, Pergamon, 1985.
30. Weinstein IB: Cancer prevention: Recent progress and future opportunities. *Cancer Res* 51(suppl):5080s, 1991.
31. Meyskens FL: Strategies for prevention of cancer in humans. Oncology 6(suppl):15, 1992.
32. Yates JW: Cancer prevention in older adults, in Balducci L (ed): *Geriatric Oncology*. Philadelphia, Lippincott, 1992, p 99.
33. Love RR: Prospects for antiestrogen chemoprevention of breast cancer. *J Natl Cancer Inst* 82:18, 1990.
34. Oddone EZ et al: Can screening older patients for cancer save lives? *Clin Geriatr Med* 8:51, 1992.
35. American Cancer Society: Update January 1992: The American Cancer Society guidelines for the cancer-related check-up, *CA* 42:44, 1992.
36. Breast Cancer Screening in Older Women. *J Gerontol* (special issue: Mary Costanza, guest ed.), vol. 47, November, 1992.
37. Early Lung Cancer Cooperative Study: Early lung cancer detection: Summary and conclusions. *Am Rev Respir Dis* 130:565, 1984.
38. Hayward RA et al: Who gets screened for cervical and breast cancer? *Arch Intern Med* 148:1177, 1988.
39. Brown JT, Hulka GS: Screening mammography in the elderly: A case-control study. *J Gen Intern Med* 3:126, 1988.
40. Mor V: Malignant disease and the elderly, in Evered D, Whelan J (eds.): *Research and the Ageing Population*. Chichester, Wiley (Ciba Foundation Symposium 134), p 160, 1988.
41. Samet JM et al: Delay in seeking care for cancer symptoms: A population-based study of elderly New Mexicans. *J Natl Cancer Inst* 80:432, 1988.
42. Robinson E et al: Factors affecting delay in diagnosis of breast cancer: Relationship of delay of disease. *Isr J Med Sci* 22:333, 1986.
43. Holmes FF: Clinical evidence for a change in tumor aggressiveness with age. *Semin Oncol* 16:34, 1989.
44. Ershler WB: Geriatric correlates of experimental tumor biology. *Oncology* 6(suppl):58, 1992.
45. Goodwin JS et al: Stage at diagnosis of cancer varies with the age of the patient. *J Am Geriatr Soc* 43:20, 1986.
46. Levine J et al: Correlation of thickness of superficial spreading malignant melanomas and ages of patients. *J Dermatol Surg Oncol* 7:311, 1981.
47. Cohen HJ et al: Malignant melanoma in the elderly. *J Clin Oncol* 5:100, 1987.
48. Allen C et al: Breast cancer in the elderly: Current patterns of care. *J Am Geriatr Soc* 34:637, 1986.
49. DeMaria LC, Cohen HJ: Characteristics of lung cancer in elderly patients. *J Gerontol* 452:540, 1987.
50. O'Rourke M et al: Age trends of lung cancer stage at diagnosis: Implications for lung cancer screening in the elderly. *JAMA* 258:921, 1987.
51. Cady R: Risk factor analysis in differentiated thyroid cancer. *Cancer* 43:810, 1979.
52. Schelfhout LJDM et al: Multivariate analysis of survival in differentiated thyroid cancer: The prognostic significance of the age factor. *Eur J Cancer* 24(2):331, 1988.
53. Joensuu H et al: Survival and prognostic factors in thyroid carcinoma. *Acta Radiol [Oncol]* 25 (1986) Fasc 4–6, 243.
54. Teeter SM et al: Lung carcinoma in the elderly population: Influence of histology on the inverse relationship of stage to age. *Cancer* 60:1331, 1987.
55. Crawford J et al: Age factors in the management of lung cancer, in Yancik R, Yates JW (Eds): *Cancer in the Elderly*. New York, Springer, 1989 p 177.
56. Dodds L et al: A population based study of lung can-

cer incidence trends by histologic type, 1974–81. *J Natl Cancer Inst* 76:21, 1986.
57. McCarty KS Jr et al: Relationship of age and menopausal status to estrogen receptor content in primary carcinoma of the breast. *Ann Surg* 197:123, 1983.
58. Cox EB: Breast cancer in the elderly. Cancer II: Specific neoplasms. *Clin Geriatr Med* 695, 1987.
59. Kaesberg PR, Ershler WB: The change in tumor aggressiveness with age: Lessons from experimental animals. *Semin Oncol* 16:28, 1989.
60. Hadar EJ et al: Lymphocyte-induced angiogenesis factor is produced by L3T4 murine T lymphocytes, and its production declines with age. *Cancer Immunol Immunother* 26:31, 1988.
61. Volk MJ, Ershler WB: The influence of immunosenescence on tumor growth and spread: Lessons from animal models. *Cancer Cells* 3:13, 1991.
62. Greenfield S et al: Patterns of care related to age of breast cancer patients. *JAMA* 257:2766, 1987.
63. Greenberg ER et al: Social and economic factors in the choice of lung cancer treatment. *N Engl J Med* 318:612, 1988.
64. Chu J et al: The effect of age on the care of women with breast cancer in community hospitals. *J Gerontol* 42:185, 1987.
65. Ganz PA: Does (should) chronologic age influence the choice of cancer treatment? *Oncology* 6(suppl):45s, 1992.
66. Bennett CL et al: Patterns of care related to age of men with prostate cancer. *Cancer* 67:2633, 1991.
67. Cohen HJ, DeMaria L: Comprehensive cancer care: Special problems of the elderly, in Laszlo J (ed): *Physician's Guide to Cancer Care Complications.* New York, Dekker, 1986.
68. Crocker I, Prosnitz L: Radiation therapy of the elderly. *Clin Geriatr Med* 3:473, 1987.
69. Parsons J et al: The influence of excisional or incisional biopsy of metastatic neck nodes on the management of head and neck cancer. *Int J Radiat Oncol Biol Phys* 11:1447, 1985.
70. Hertler AA et al: Cancer in the elderly, in Ham R (ed): *Geriatric Medicine Annual,* 1989. Oradell, NJ, Medical Economics Books.
71. Gunn WG: Radiation therapy for the aging patient. *Cancer* 30:337, 1980.
72. Strohl RA: The elderly patient receiving radiation therapy: Treatment sequelae and nursing care. *Geriatr Nursing* 3:153, 1992.
73. Koga K et al: Age factor relevant to the development of radiation pneumonitis in radiotherapy of lung cancer. *Int J Radiat Oncol Biol Phys* 14:367, 1988.
74. Hutchins LF, Lipschitz DA: Cancer, clinical pharmacology and aging. *Clin Geriatr Med* 3:483, 1987.
75. Balducci L, Mowry K: Pharmacology and organ toxicity of chemotherapy in older patients. *Oncology* 6(suppl):62, 1992.
76. Walsh SJ et al: Cancer chemotherapy in the elderly. *Semin Oncol* 16:66, 1989.
77. Einhorn LH: Approaches to drug therapy in older cancer patients. *Oncology* 6(suppl):69s, 1992.
78. Leslie WT: Chemotherapy in older patients. *Oncology* 6(suppl):74s, 1992.
79. Rothstein G et al: Kinetic evaluation of the pool sizes and proliferative response of neutrophils in bacterially challenged aging mice. *Blood* 70:1836, 1987.
80. Lipschitz DA et al: Effect of age on hematopoiesis in man. *Blood* 63:502, 1984.
81. Begg CB, Carbone PP: Clinical trials and drug toxicity in the elderly. *Cancer* 52:1986, 1983.
82. Gelman RS, Taylor SG: Cyclophosphamide, methotrexate, and 5-fluorouracil chemotherapy in women more than 65 years old with advanced breast cancer: The elimination of age trends in toxicity by using doses based on creatinine clearance. *J Clin Oncol* 2:1404, 1984.
83. Cohen HJ, Bartolucci A: Influence of age on response to treatment and survival in multiple myeloma. *J Am Geriatr Soc* 31:272, 1983.
84. Poplin E et al: Small cell carcinoma of the lung: Influence of age on treatment outcome. *Cancer Treat Rep* 71:291, 1987.
85. Armitage JO, Potter JF: Aggressive chemotherapy for diffuse histiocytic lymphoma in the elderly: Increased complications with advancing age. *J Am Geriatr Soc* 32:269, 1984.
86. Dixon DO et al: Effect of age on therapeutic outcome in advanced diffuse histiocytic lymphoma: The Southwest Oncology Group experience. *J Clin Oncol* 4:295, 1986.
87. Connors JM: Infusions, age, and drug dosages: Learning about large-cell lymphoma. *J Clin Oncol* 6:407, 1988.
88. Erdkamp FL et al: Hodgkin's disease in the elderly. *Cancer* 70:830, 1992.
89. Solal-Celigny P et al: Age as the main prognostic factor in adult aggressive non-Hodgkin's lymphoma. *Am J Med* 83:1075, 1987.
90. Arlin AZ, Clarkson BD: The treatment of acute nonlymphoblastic leukemia in adults. *Adv Intern Med* 28:303, 1983.
91. Kahn SB et al: Full dose versus attenuated dose daunorubicin, cytosine arabinoside, and 6-thioguanine in the treatment of acute nonlymphocytic leukemia in the elderly. *J Clin Oncol* 2:865, 1984.
92. Walters RS et al: Intensive treatment of acute leukemia in adults 70 years of age and older. *Cancer* 60:149, 1987.
93. Kennedy BJ: Needed: Clinical trials for older patients. *J Clin Oncol* 9:718, 1991.
94. Bonadonna G, Valagussa P: Dose-response effect of adjuvant chemotherapy in breast cancer. *N Engl J Med* 304:10, 1981.
95. Dugar SO, Scallion LM: Nursing care of elderly persons throughout the cancer experience: A quality of life framework. *Clin Geriatr Med* 3:517, 1987.
96. Triozzi PL et al: Supportive care of the patient with cancer. *Clin Geriatr Med* 3:505, 1987.
97. Pisters KNW, Kris MG: Management of nausea and vomiting caused by anticancer drugs: State of the art. *Oncology* 6(suppl):99, 1992.
98. Heinemann V, John V: Acute myeloid leukemia in the elderly: Biologic features and search for adequate treatment. *Ann Hematol* 63:179, 1991.
99. McCachren SS, Cohen HJ: Cancer, in Cooper RL et al (eds): *Aging and Environmental Toxicology.* Baltimore, Johns Hopkins University Press, p 56, 1989.

Chapter 7

EXERCISE IN THE ELDERLY: PHYSIOLOGIC AND FUNCTIONAL EFFECTS

Robert S. Schwartz and David M. Buchner

AGING, DISUSE, AND DISEASE

A common belief among the lay public and many health care professionals is that much of the disease and loss of function which commonly accompanies aging is inevitable and due to the "aging process" itself. However, it has become clear that at least some of the physical decline and reduced physiologic reserve previously blamed on aging is in fact due to the complex interactions of true genetically determined aging, disease (often subtle or subclinical), and disuse.[1]

The myriad of possible interrelationships among true aging changes, disease, and disuse make it difficult to ascribe specific causality for the loss of physical vigor or function in many cases. Thus, for example, preconceived societal notions about aging may predispose to greatly reduced expectations with regard to physical as well as mental performance. Such preconceptions may promote inactivity and disuse in women at an even earlier age than in men.[2] With years of ensuing inactivity, disuse not only enhances the true age-related loss of endurance, strength, and flexibility, leading to further inactivity and disuse, but may also exacerbate previously subtle or subclinical diseases such as intraabdominal obesity, glucose intolerance, osteopenia, hypertension, dyslipemia, and coronary artery disease. These physiologic disorders, the drugs used in their treatments, and the associated functional impairments may in turn further limit activity and continue the vicious downhill spiral. Using physiochemical concepts, Bortz[1] has emphasized the possible role that activity, as reflected by active energy flow, may play in mitigating the age-related drift toward entropic decay. Although not conclusive, evidence that activity level is inversely related to the risk for mortality and is associated with a greater average life span (about 2 years in human studies[2–4]) supports this concept.

In this chapter we will rcview the physiologic effects of aging and exercise training on the most common measures of physical fitness: (1) endurance, or maximum aerobic exercise capacity; (2) skeletal muscle strength; and (3) body composition. We will then review the effects of aging and activity on several disorders commonly observed in geriatric patients. Next, we will investigate the theoretical relationship between fitness and functional status, reviewing the available, albeit limited, data on the effect of increased activity on functional performance. Last, we will discuss the risks associated with exercising and make some suggestions with respect to prescribing an exercise program for older individuals.

AGING AND EXERCISE

Endurance (Aerobic) Exercise Capacity

Aging-Associated Changes in Endurance Exercise Capacity

The best physiologic measure of an individual's endurance work capacity is the amount of oxygen consumed at maximal exercise (maximal aerobic power or $\dot{V}O_2max$). For more than 50 years, cross-sectional studies have repeatedly demonstrated a significant age-related decrement in $\dot{V}O_2max$ in both men and women.[5,6] Together, these cross-sectional data suggest that exercise capacity declines by approximately 1 percent per year when $\dot{V}O_2max$ is expressed as milliliters of oxygen consumed per minute and corrected for kilograms of body weight (e.g., $ml \cdot min^{-1} \cdot kg^{-1}$). Longitudinal data in this area are somewhat more confusing,[6,7] probably owing to (1) variation in the initial level of fitness of the subject populations, (2) spontaneous modifications in activity level between test periods, (3) alterations in body weight and composition, and (4) intervening illness. It is possible that the data are further influenced by a nonlinear decline

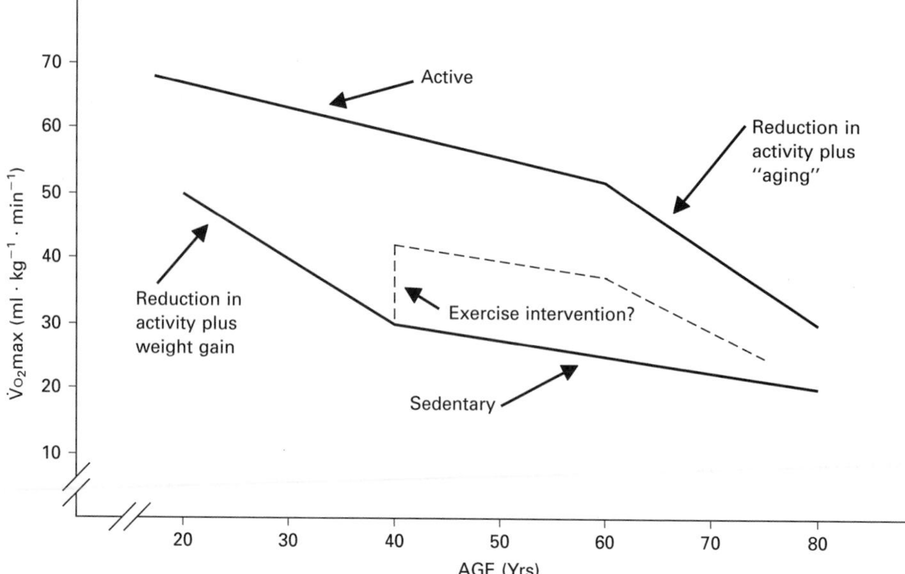

FIGURE 7-1

Possible interindividual differences in the age-related decline in $\dot{V}O_2$max. The possible effects of regular physical activity (or lack thereof) and the inevitable decline at advanced age are depicted. (*From Buskirk with permission.*[8])

over time (Fig. 7-1), with a more rapid decline in $\dot{V}O_2$max in early adulthood in sedentary individuals followed by a less steep decline later in life.[8]

Both cross-sectional and longitudinal studies[6,9,10] have attempted to assess whether continued endurance training can mitigate the age-related decline in $\dot{V}O_2$max. As reviewed by Hagberg,[11] there appears to be a reduction in the slope of the regression line for age-related decline in $\dot{V}O_2$max in habitually active men when compared to their more sedentary counterparts. In fact, continued exercise appears to reduce the observed decline by up to 50 percent (0.5 percent versus 1.0 percent per year[10]). In one study, no decline in $\dot{V}O_2$max was detected in master athletes who maintained their competitive training over a 10-year period.[9] It must be noted, however, that despite their continued competitive training, $\dot{V}O_2$max did not improve in these older athletes over time. Nevertheless, even if there is no difference in the rate of decline in $\dot{V}O_2$max between active and sedentary individuals, the higher initial starting fitness level in active individuals may afford them some protection in later life by allowing them to remain above the threshold of exercise capacity necessary to remain functionally active.

The Peripheral Components of Endurance Exercise Capacity $\dot{V}O_2$max is equal to the product of maximal cardiac output (Q_{max}) and the maximal ability of muscle to extract oxygen from the blood (a − V_{O_2} difference), and thus is determined by both central (cardiovascular) and peripheral (primarily muscle) components. Studies have almost uniformly detected significant changes in body composition associated with aging (see the following section on body composition), including increases in fat mass and decreases in fat-free mass (FFM) or lean body mass (LBM). Furthermore, it appears that with aging, muscle mass comprises a lesser percentage of what is usually measured as FFM.[12] Therefore, it is possible that some of the age-related decline in $\dot{V}O_2$max is due merely to a decrement in the mass muscle which can extract and then consume oxygen. This notion has been investigated in very healthy men and women between 22 and 87 years of age.[13] Muscle mass, as reflected by 24-h creatinine excretion, was found to decline 23 percent between ages 30 and 70, and when normalized for this decrease in muscle mass, the slope of the decline in $\dot{V}O_2$max with age flattened significantly. Thus, the predicted decline in $\dot{V}O_2$max between the ages of 30 and 70 was lessened in both men (39 percent versus 18 percent) and women (30 percent versus 14 percent). Approximately half of the previous age-related decline in $\dot{V}O_2$max could be explained by the age-associated loss of muscle mass. It must be stressed, however, that muscle mass and $\dot{V}O_2$max are not independent. Thus, more active individuals may develop and/or maintain a larger muscle mass. Another study of carefully screened older subjects confirmed that differences in FFM could explain some (30 percent in this study) of the age-related differences in $\dot{V}O_2$max.[14] Additional peripheral mechanisms might also account for some of the age-related decrement in $\dot{V}O_2$max by attenuating the a − V_{O_2} difference, including a reduced ability to direct blood flow to the working muscles or a diminished ability of muscle cells in older (inactive) individuals to utilize oxygen.

The Central (Cardiovascular) Component of Endurance Capacity (See Chap. 43) Deficits in the central (cardiovascular) component contribute substantially to the age-related reduction in $\dot{V}O_2$max. In the absence of hypertension or coronary artery disease (clinical or asymptomatic), studies consistently find that resting cardiac output, heart rate, and heart size are normal in older individuals.[15,16] However, as illustrated in Fig. 7-2, a number of age-related

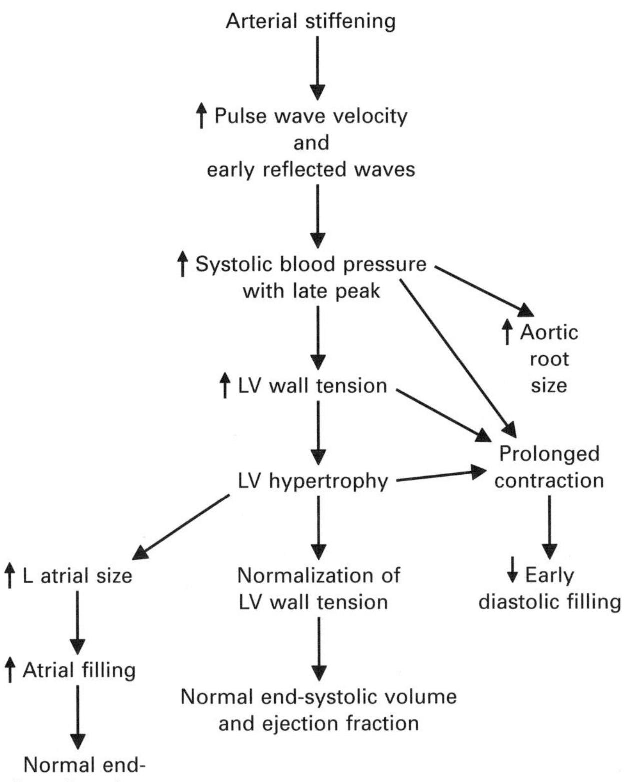

FIGURE 7-2

The interplay of vascular changes and adaptive cardiac changes that occur to varying degrees with aging in otherwise healthy individuals. (*Reproduced from Lakatta,*[15] *with permission.*)

changes in resting cardiac function have been defined.[15] These cardiovascular changes detected at rest in the elderly are quite similar to those observed with hypertension. Indeed, it has been hypothesized that mild vascular stiffness and ensuing subclinical hypertension may initiate this group of resting compensatory responses.[15]

As with most age-related abnormalities, the alterations in cardiovascular physiology are most apparent and most clinically relevant during stress, such as physical exercise. In the setting of maximal exercise, and a three- to fourfold increase in cardiac output, striking differences between young and older individuals become apparent. By far the most salient and consistently found is the marked decline in maximal heart rate with age.[14,16] Beyond this one finding, however, there is at present little agreement. While some studies suggest that most of the age-related decrement in $\dot{V}O_2max$ is explained by a decline in cardiac output,[14,17] others detect no significant decrease in maximal cardiac output with age.[13]

The study which found no significant decline in maximal cardiac output supports a compensatory increase in stroke volume mediated by the Frank-Starling mechanism and an increase in left ventricular end-diastolic volume. These investigators suggest that this physiologic profile is similar to that observed with beta-adrenergic blockade.[15] This explanation is appealing, given the plethora of data demonstrating reduced cardiovascular responses to beta-adrenergic-agonist stimulation in the elderly.[16,18] These findings suggest that most of the decline in $\dot{V}O_2max$ in the elderly is related to peripheral mechanisms.[13] The investigators propose that their findings differ from other studies, which detect a diminished cardiac output with age, because they had more meticulously excluded subjects with occult heart disease. However, recent data from our laboratory,[19] using similar stringent screening criteria, found a substantial difference in peak cardiac index between healthy young and older men despite no significant differences at baseline. In fact, the majority of studies[14,17,19] now support the concept that diminished central responses to maximal exercise substantially contribute to the reduced $\dot{V}O_2max$ with aging. The degree to which this defect can be explained by a slower maximal heart rate or a reduced stroke volume response to exercise remains unclear, as does the role of diminished beta-adrenergic sensitivity.

The Physiologic Effects of Endurance Exercise Training

Effect on $\dot{V}O_2max$ Although it has been known for many years that certain individuals (e.g., master athletes) can maintain a reasonably high endurance capacity into old age, it had previously been assumed that the ability to train previously sedentary older individuals, as compared with younger persons, was quite limited. In fact, the results of endurance training studies in previously sedentary older individuals are quite variable. This is understandable in light of the numerous factors which can affect the response to a training program, including (1) the intensity and duration of the program, (2) the baseline health of the subjects, (3) the testing methods used, and (4) subjects' baseline level of fitness. It has now been clearly demonstrated that the fitness response to an endurance training program in previously sedentary, healthy older individuals is comparable to that in younger subjects.[20,21] Depending on the type and duration of exercise employed, the improvement in $\dot{V}O_2max$ varies between 10 and 30 percent, with similar responses in both men and women.[22] Furthermore, when young and older subjects are trained in the same program at the same relative intensity, their increments in $\dot{V}O_2max$ are similar.[21]

Healthy older individuals can tolerate endurance training at relatively intense levels [e.g., 85 percent of heart reserve; HHR = 0.85 (HR max − HR rest) + HR rest] with acceptable attrition rates and few if any significant injuries.[20–22] Indeed, it appears that speed is a more important determinant of injury than the actual intensity of the exercise.[23] A clinically more salient question is whether qualitatively similar adaptive responses can occur with lower-intensity training. Although not all studies agree, it appears that substantial improvement can be obtained with low- to moderate-intensity programs, where subjects train at less than 50 percent of HRR.[24]

Effect on Body Composition As noted above, with aging there is a significant loss of FFM or LBM, mostly due to a reduction in muscle mass. This decline has been estimated to be approximately 6 percent per decade between ages 30 and 80.[13] Despite the loss of LBM, body weight may be sustained due to the accumulation of adipose tissue. More importantly, with age, fat is preferentially accumulated in a central distribution.[25] This centralization of body fat seems to occur continuously with age in adult men, but in women a significant increase in central adiposity first occurs following menopause.[26] This central distribution of adipose mass is a risk factor for many obesity- and age-related metabolic abnormalities, and is independent of relative weight or other measures of obesity or fat distribution.[27]

In cross-sectional studies comparing highly physically active older individuals with more sedentary controls, the active group is consistently leaner and, in fact, similar to active younger individuals. This is true for both men and women, with the physically active groups having about 10 percent less body fat than sedentary controls.[14] Furthermore, there is an inverse correlation between $\dot{V}O_2max$ and central adiposity, as defined by waist:hip ratio (WHR), within a population of healthy older men.[28] However, little difference in FFM or LBM has been observed in active compared to sedentary healthy elderly. Thus, despite being highly trained, older individuals still have significantly less LBM than younger individuals.

Longitudinal endurance training studies in previously sedentary individuals support these cross-sectional findings. Endurance training has repeatedly produced small but significant decrements in percent body fat and overall fat mass in older men and women. The two most recent studies[21,22] were in close agreement, with a loss of 2.5 percent body fat and 1.5 to 3 kg of fat mass following a 6- to 12-month intensive endurance training program. Associated with this statistically significant but modest decrement in overall adiposity was a preferential decrease in the central distribution of fat. In fact, our laboratory demonstrated, following endurance training in older men, not only a fall in WHR but a 20 percent decline in the intraabdominal fat depot as measured by computed tomography. In contrast to this decrement in adiposity, little or no change in overall FFM has been detected following even intensive endurance training in the elderly. The lack of improvement in overall FFM may be countered by significant changes in specific muscle groups. Thus, in our study, cross-sectional mid-thigh muscle mass, measured by computed tomography, increased 10 percent in older men despite no change in overall FFM. This finding suggests a redistribution of FFM with intensive endurance training in older men.

Although highly trained athletes are leaner than less active controls, the loss of weight or fat with endurance training is small when compared to dieting. The importance, however, may be magnified by the preferential loss of central and specifically intraabdominal fat with endurance training.[21,22] Endurance training can increase the usually low resting metabolic rate in the elderly by about 10 percent, even when corrected for any change in FFM.[29] Training is also associated with a lower rate of long-term recidivism in subjects participating in a dietary weight reduction program.[30]

Effect on Cardiac Function While cross-sectional studies suggest a significant age-related decline in cardiac output (see previous discussion), training status appears to positively affect this measurement, with a greater cardiac output found in well-trained older men and women when compared to matched sedentary controls.[14] In fact, most of the higher $\dot{V}O_2max$ in trained older individuals can be explained by their higher cardiac output. The higher cardiac output is, in turn, explained by a larger stroke volume, whereas no difference in maximal heart rate is detected between trained and untrained groups. Longitudinal studies of endurance training in previously sedentary older subjects have provided conflicting results. Some have found no improvement in estimated cardiac output or systolic time intervals following either low- or high-intensity endurance training.[31,32] However, studies using more sensitive methods provide evidence of enhanced cardiac output due to increases in stroke volume and ejection fraction.[19,33]

Skeletal Muscle Strength

Strength can be defined as the maximum force exerted by a muscle. Strength is not defined by muscle tissue alone but also involves intact neurologic function. Consequently, as discussed in more detail below, strength can be increased by improving muscular function (e.g., muscle cell hypertrophy) or by improving neurologic function (e.g., learning).

Strength assessment depends upon the conditions of measurement, specifically the speed of muscular contraction, whether the muscle is shortening or lengthening during the contraction, and the conditions of mechanical leverage. *Isometric* strength is the maximum force that can be exerted against a fixed object. *Isotonic* strength is the largest weight that can be lifted against gravity through the full range of motion of a joint. *Isokinetic* strength is the maximum torque that can be developed at a given muscle speed.

Aging-Associated Changes in Muscle Strength

For over 100 years, cross-sectional studies have demonstrated that strength declines with age. After peak strength is reached sometime around age 30, cross-sectional studies show about a 30 to 40 percent reduction in strength by age 80.[34,35] Longitudinal studies suggest that the true rate of decline is underestimated by the cross-sectional data. For example, a longitudinal study estimated a 60 percent loss of hand grip strength between ages 30 and 80, while a cross-sectional analysis of the same data estimated loss at 40 percent.[36] Strength loss appears even more rapid at greater ages. For example, longitudinal studies report about a 10 to 25 percent loss in quadriceps strength within only 5 to 7 years in 70-year-old adults.[37,38]

Muscle Mass A close relationship exists between the size of a muscle, measured as cross-sectional area, and its ability to generate force. One would predict, then, that a decline in muscle strength should be accompanied by a decline in muscle mass of a roughly equal amount—about 30 to 40 percent. This is the case,[34,35,39] and just as strength loss is more rapid at greater ages, loss of muscle mass is also reported as becoming more rapid with age.

The simultaneous loss of strength and muscle mass is somewhat more complicated, however. First, there are well-documented differences among individuals in the strength per unit of cross-sectional muscle area, presumably due in part to differences among individuals in the relative proportions of the muscle fiber types. Second, some studies report that in older adults, strength loss exceeds the loss in muscle mass.[37,40,41] These findings naturally lead to questions about how muscle fiber function and composition change with aging.

Muscle Fibers Wilmore[39] provides a clear summary of the anatomic structure and physiologic function of muscle. Skeletal muscle comprises bunches of individual muscle *fibers*. These fibers contain myofibrils, which are, in turn, composed of a number of myofilaments. The myofilaments contain the proteins actin and myosin and are arranged to form *sarcomeres*—the contractile units of muscle.

There are two major types of muscle fibers: *slow-twitch* and *fast-twitch*. Further, there are at least three subtypes of fast-twitch fibers: a, b, and c. The fast-twitch fibers are variously referred to either as FTa, FTb, and FTc or as type 2a, type 2b, and type 2c. The slow-twitch fibers are referred to as ST or type 1 fibers. Type 1 fibers can sustain tension for long periods, are slow to fatigue, and have high oxidative (aerobic) capacity. Type 2 fibers can rapidly develop high tension, but only for short periods of time, and have high glycolytic (anaerobic) capacity. Type 2a, type 2b, and type 2c fibers all differ in their relative oxidative capacity.

There is general agreement that the metabolic potential of muscle does not change with age. However, in humans, there is a loss in the number of muscle fibers with age. Whether some fiber types are lost more rapidly with age is controversial. Some evidence suggests that type 2 fibers are lost more rapidly than type 1.[41] Opposing evidence suggests a more rapid reduction in type 2 fiber size with age but not a more rapid reduction in the total number of type 2 fibers.[42]

One factor that may contribute to the variation in these findings is the tremendous plasticity of skeletal muscle.[39] Fiber cross-sectional area, and even the relative proportion of fiber types, may predominantly reflect the response to existing or recent physical activity patterns. That is, type 2 fiber loss and/or atrophy could be due to an age-related change in activity patterns. As older adults perform fewer activities requiring rapid development of muscular force, they may have selective reduction in the type 2 fibers that are required for such activities.

Motor Units Muscle function depends on the coordinated activity of groups of muscle fibers and the motor neuron which innervates them, i.e., the motor unit. The motor neuron appears to control the size, contraction time, resistance to fatigue, and enzyme activity of the muscle fibers it innervates.[43] Hence, neuronal mechanisms could account for many age-related changes in muscle fibers. There is growing evidence that the number of motor units decreases with age. This conclusion is supported by electromyographic studies that suggest a loss of functional motor neurons with age. Indeed, the loss of motor units may even exceed the loss of neurons.[42,44]

Disuse versus Aging There is some epidemiological evidence that regular physical activity may prevent some of the age-related loss in strength.[38,45] However, when activities are classified as to their expected effect on muscle strength, epidemiologic studies have probably focused on a relatively narrow range of activity near the middle of the continuum. At one end of the continuum is bed rest. Bed rest is associated with a dramatic loss of strength—estimated as high as 1 to 5 percent *per day*.[46] At the other end of the continuum is vigorous strengthening exercise (discussed below), which produces substantial gains in strength in older adults.

It is this perspective, integrating findings from studies of bed rest, epidemiology, and experimental interventions, that most clearly suggests that age-related losses in strength are mainly due to age-related changes in physical activity. As a corollary, epidemiologic studies of adults with similar activity at all ages should show little or no loss in strength. Indeed, a cross-sectional study of workers at a machine shop showed no decline in grip strength between the ages of 20 and 60.[47] But aging per se appears to have some role in loss of strength, as, at some point during life, strength will begin to decline despite continued activity patterns.

The Physiologic Effects of Strength Training

Strength training (resistance exercise) can be done in several ways. Unfortunately at present there is no standard and little agreement on a preferred method. Analogous to the way in which strength can be measured, strength training can use isokinetic, isometric, or isotonic exercise. A typical isotonic protocol may have 20 to 30 repetitions of the exercise divided into two or three sets of 8 to 10 repetitions, with the subject resting between sets. Most commonly, the maximal weight that the subject can lift once (called the one-repetition maximum or 1RM) is determined. In each set, the subject lifts a certain percentage of that 1RM. With *progressive resistance exercise,* as described almost 50 years ago by DeLorme,[48] each set involves lifting a higher weight than the previous set. *Fixed resistance exercise* uses the same weight—for example, 70 percent of the 1RM—for all sets. Progression occurs as the percent of the 1RM is increased and by intermittent retesting to determine a new, higher, 1RM. Other possible protocols are *progressive rate training,* where the weight is constant but the speed of exercise is increased, and the *"Oxford" technique,* where the heaviest weight is lifted in the first set and lighter weights in the subsequent set(s).

Effect on Muscular Strength There are fewer studies of the effect of strengthening exercise than of aerobic exercise in older adults. Studies have used primarily isotonic, fixed-resistance exercise and trained subjects for 2 to 6 months. Though almost all studies report that resistance training increases the strength of older adults,[49] there is tremendous variability in the magnitude of the reported strength gains (from a few percent to almost 200 percent). A number of factors could account for the variability, including the method of measuring strength, the duration of training, the exercise intensity, and characteristics of the study sample.

A metaanalysis[50] suggests that intensity of training is the most important factor affecting study results. Some studies used low- and moderate-intensity resistance training and reported only modest increases (10 to 25 percent) in strength. Other studies in healthy adults, physically unfit adults, and even frail adults have utilized more vigorous strength training, where resistance is set as high as 80 percent of the 1RM.[51–54] These studies report substantially larger strength gains (50 to 200 percent). Expressed in terms of the cross-sectional distribution of strength in the study samples, subjects improve from 1.0 to 3.5 standard deviations in strength over just a few months with these vigorous training protocols.[50]

Duration of training also affects strength gain. Studies have reported weekly measurements of 1RMs, and strength continues to increase throughout the training interval—at least up to 6 months.[51,54] Most studies of strengthening exercise have failed to comment on the fact that their results show substantial variability in how older adults respond to strength training.[50] The observed variability occurs despite the use of standard training protocols administered in highly supervised research settings. The causes of this variability remain to be explained.

Physiologic Mechanisms Explaining Gains in Strength with Exercise An early study argued that, although older adults did increase strength with exercise, their muscles did not hypertrophy. Rather, neural factors apparently accounted for the increased strength.[55] Later studies showed that resistance exercise does cause muscular hypertrophy in older adults,[51,53,56] and muscle biopsies show hypertrophy of both type 1 and type 2 fibers.[51]

However, 10 to 20 percent increases in muscle mass are accompanied by much larger (50 to 200 percent) increases in strength. This situation apparently violates the "rule" that muscle cross-sectional area is highly correlated with muscle strength. Actually, it is true in both older and younger adults that, after short-term strength training, there is a discrepancy between the increases in strength and muscle cross-sectional area. Some consider the increase in strength, which cannot be accounted for by hypertrophy, as due to increased neural discharge. In younger adults, the discrepancy is temporary, as highly trained individuals show a normal ratio of strength to cross-sectional area. In older adults, it is unclear how the ratio of strength to cross-sectional area changes over the course of prolonged strength training.

EXERCISE AND FUNCTIONAL STATUS

The question "Can exercise prevent or reverse functional impairment in older adults?" is of great importance to public health. In discussing the question, the distinction between *physiology* and *functional status* is critical. Physiology deals with biological structure and function, whereas functional status deals with behavior. Herein, *disability* and *functional impairment* are synonymous. The consensus definition of disability is a "restriction or lack . . . of ability to perform an activity in the manner or within the range considered normal for a human being."[57] An older person is commonly regarded as functionally impaired if he or she cannot handle the normal activities of daily life required for independent living.

There is no consensus definition of *frail health* or *frailty.* Some use the term to describe adults with functional impairment; others use it to emphasize the potential to lose functional status. A recently proposed definition of frailty is ". . . the state of reduced physiologic reserve associated with increased susceptibility to disability."[58] This definition avoids a tautologic relationship with disability, since frailty is defined and measured independently of disability.

The argument that exercise improves functional status is then as follows: "Exercise produces physiologic effects (reduces frailty), which, in turn, improve functional status." As discussed above, there is substantial evidence that exercise produces desirable physiologic effects in older adults. As discussed below, there is far less evidence that these physiologic changes lead to improved function, and there is at present inadequate theoretical work to guide research in this area.

Theoretical Relationship between Fitness and Functional Status

The more common explanation of why exercise should improve function focuses on aerobic capacity.[59,60] In the laboratory, it is possible to measure the energy needed to do a given task by measuring oxygen consumption during steady-state performance of the task. For example, walking on a level grade at 5 km/h requires 3.2 METS (1 MET = 3.5 ml O_2/kg/min). With illness or inactivity, aerobic capacity falls below the level required for daily tasks. Because exercise can increase aerobic capacity, it should improve functional status when aerobic capacity is below the threshold needed for normal daily function.

A less common, parallel explanation focuses on strength.[60,61] The amount of strength needed to perform a task can be estimated from biomechanical studies. For example, a typical adult needs about 120 Newton-meters of knee torque to stand up from a chair.[62] With illness or inactivity, strength can drop below that required amount, and standing would then become difficult. Because exercise can increase strength, it should theoretically improve function when strength is below the threshold needed for normal function.

A key feature of both explanations is that the effect of exercise on function depends upon the amount of *physiologic reserve*. Physiologic reserve is the physiologic capacity not normally used during routine daily activities, which usually require only submaximal effort. Physiologic reserve is important for responding to stress and is entirely used, by definition, during activities that require maximal effort.

It follows that the relationship between fitness and functional status is likely to be curvilinear: above a certain threshold level of adequate physiologic reserve, functional status is normal; below the threshold, function is impaired (Fig. 7-3). The implication is that the effect of exercise on functional outcome depends upon the target group. In frail adults with little or no physiologic reserve, exercise theoretically produces a large improvement in function. In healthy adults with adequate physiologic reserve, exercise theoretically cannot improve function; it only increases physiologic reserve.

The possibility of a curvilinear relationship between physiologic measures and functional status measures is not widely recognized,[49] though it is intuitive. After all, if strength were linearly related to walking speed, highly trained weight lifters would walk ridiculously fast (10 to 20 mph), since they are several times as strong as normal adults who walk at around 3 mph. The curvilinear relationship explains why cross-sectional studies in healthy adults can fail to find an association between fitness and function. For example, in a study of mainly healthy, community dwelling adults, the correlation between leg strength and walking speed was not statistically significant.[63]

However, the pathogenesis of disability in older adults is complex and poorly understood. Further theoretical work is needed, for example, to address issues such as how and when to adjust physiologic measures for body habitus,[64] How to deal with hierarchical relationships among variables in statistical models, and how to deal with interactions over time among psychosocial, environmental, and host factors.

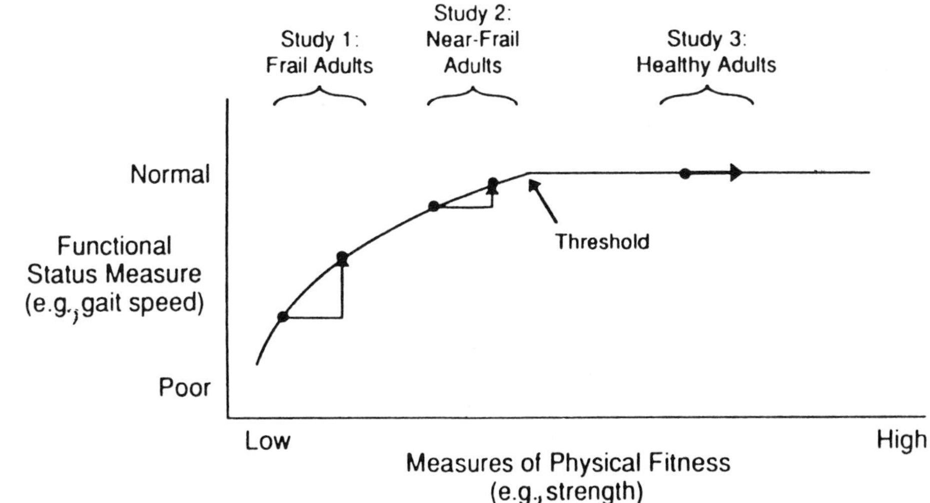

FIGURE 7-3
Theoretical relationship between physical fitness and functional status. The curvilinear relationship shows a threshold effect: above the threshold level of fitness, functional status is normal; below it, function is impaired. A curvilinear relationship implies that the benefit from exercise depends upon the target group. Three hypothetical exercise studies are shown. Each study produces the same absolute improvement in fitness. In the frail adults of study 1, exercise produces a large improvement in functional status. In the healthy adults of study 3, no benefit is seen. Study 2 shows intermediate benefits. (*Reproduced with permission from Buchner.[49]*)

Evidence That Exercise Improves Function

Based on a review[49] of 12 studies of the effect of exercise on gait, balance, and physical function, the authors concluded that the evidence that exercise improves functional status is promising but presently inconclusive. While most studies showed positive effects on functional status outcomes, the evidence was inconclusive due to a variety of problems. These include a lack of randomized trials; a lack of studies having comprehensive functional status outcome measures; a lack of evidence that the exercise stimulus was sufficient to produce physiologic effects; inadequate statistical power; and failure to target the frail, physically unfit individuals who theoretically would improve most with exercise. Furthermore, there are no studies demonstrating that exercise and functional status effects can be sustained over long periods of time—a critical issue to the public health importance of exercise.

The National Institute on Aging (NIA) has made research on functional impairment a priority. The issue of exercise and functional status is being addressed by ongoing studies funded under the Older Adult Independence Center initiative ("Claude Pepper Centers"), and the FICSIT (Frailty and Injuries: Cooperative Studies of Intervention Techniques) initiative. Future studies should also address how the type and intensity of exercise affect bone strength and whether exercise reduces fracture rates.

EXERCISE AND COMMON GERIATRIC DISORDERS

Insulin Resistance and Glucose Intolerance

Because aging is frequently associated with inactivity, increased adiposity, and a central distribution of fat and each of these potentially interrelated parameters can be associated with insulin resistance and glucose intolerance, the importance of aging alone has been unclear (see Chap. 71). Indeed, when secondary factors such as relative weight (e.g., body mass index), central adiposity, and hypertension were statistically accounted for, age itself was not a significant independent determinant of the insulin resistance and glucose intolerance associated with aging.[65]

Immobilization or inactivity is known to be associated with a decline in insulin sensitivity and glucose tolerance.[66] An important effect of physical activity on glucose and insulin metabolism with age is supported by cross-sectional studies finding normal or near normal insulin sensitivity and glucose tolerance in physically well-trained older individuals.[67] More recently, prospective studies have investigated the effects of endurance exercise training on glucose and insulin metabolism in older individuals.[20,68,69] For example, following a 6-month intensive endurance training program, no change in fasting glucose or the oral glucose response curve was observed (Fig. 7-4).[68] However, both fasting insulin and the insulin response to the oral glucose challenge declined, suggesting improved insulin sensitivity. Although quantitative measurement demonstrated a 36 percent improvement in insulin sensitivity, the sensitivity of the older men remained 30 to 60 percent lower than that of normal young controls. Because the improvement in insulin sensitivity was balanced by a reciprocal change in insulin secretion, overall glucose tolerance was unchanged.

There are at present no prospective studies which have evaluated the effect of endurance exercise training in older patients with non-insulin-dependent diabetes (NIDDM). However, studies in middle-aged patients suggest modest improvements in glucose tolerance associated with increased insulin sensitivity.[70] It is now generally agreed that most of the metabolic effects of exercise training are transitory and that

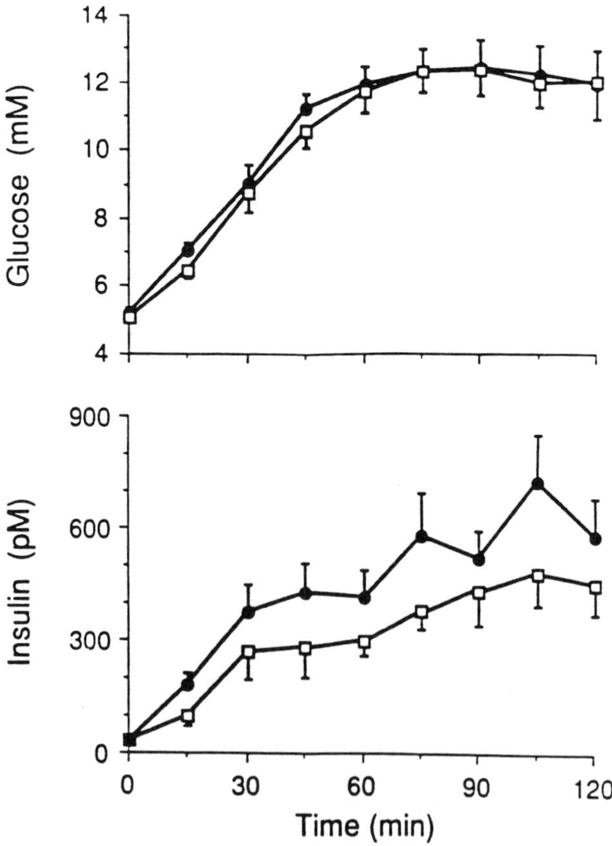

FIGURE 7-4

Glucose and insulin responses after 100-g oral glucose load in 13 older subjects before (●) and after (□) 6-month exercise training. Data points, means ± SE. (*Reproduced with permission from Kahn.[68]*)

most of the observed changes are related more to the effects of repeated acute bouts of exercise rather than a more sustained training effect.[71]

Thus, it appears that endurance training in older individuals produces a response similar to that noted in younger subjects. Insulin sensitivity is improved, as reflected by a decline in plasma insulin levels. Glucose tolerance improves modestly in non-insulin-dependent diabetics but little or not at all in older subjects with normal or impaired glucose tolerance. Although there are much fewer data for strength training, the qualitative and quantitative responses may be similar.[72] It is as yet unclear whether these changes are related indirectly to alterations in body fat, fat distribution, and/or FFM, or whether they are directly related to the training itself through changes in muscle capillary density or blood flow, fiber type, enzymes or glucose transporters. Despite relatively unimpressive effects of exercise on adiposity or glucose tolerance, exercise-induced changes could be important in the long term, given the accumulating data linking insulin resistance and hyperinsulinemia to diabetes mellitus, hypertension, dyslipemia, and atherosclerosis.[73]

Dyslipidemia

Dyslipidemia is common in the elderly population (see Chap. 73). However, it is not known to what degree this may be related to inactivity; secondary factors such as abnormal body composition; pathological processes such as diabetes mellitus, thyroid, renal or liver disease; or drugs such as thiazide diuretics, beta adrenergic blockers, or glucocorticoids. Furthermore, the relationship between measured plasma lipid abnormalities and mortality may be more complicated with age.[74]

Higher levels of physical activity are associated with less atherogenic lipoprotein profiles in cross-sectional studies in young and middle-aged individuals.[75] Reduced plasma triglyceride (TG), very low density lipoprotein (VLDL) TG concentrations, and higher HDL-C, HDL_2-C, and apolipoprotein A-I levels are consistently observed in trained subjects when compared to sedentary controls. Of interest is the apparent lack of effect of activity on total and LDL cholesterol levels. These cross-sectional findings are supported by studies of enforced inactivity[75] as well as prospective endurance training studies in young and middle-aged subjects.[75,76] Although most of the studies detecting improvement in the lipoprotein profile involved rather intensive endurance exercise programs, qualitatively similar improvements have been detected in some moderate or even light exercise studies.[77,78] It is noteworthy that there appears to be a difference in the effect of training on plasma lipoproteins between men and women, with women often demonstrating little or no improvement.[79] The reason for this gender-related difference in response is not entirely clear but may relate to better baseline lipoprotein concentrations in premenopausal women or to differences in training effects on body composition between men and women. Indeed, there is evidence that the exercise-related reduction in body composition (fat loss), or more specifically, in central fat distribution, may account for some[76] but not all[80,81] of the exercise effect on plasma lipoproteins. The mechanisms for exercise-related improvement in plasma lipoproteins are unclear but have been hypothesized to involve (1) lipoprotein lipase–induced enhancement of VLDL-TG removal and subsequent production of HDL particles; (2) increased lecithin cholesterol acyl transferase (LCAT) activity, leading to greater reverse cholesterol transport; or (3) reduced hepatic clearance of HDL particles due to inhibition of hepatic TG lipase activity.

There are far less data on the effects of activity on lipoprotein profiles in older individuals. Studies of trained older adults and lean and nonlean untrained older men have demonstrated that total and LDL-C levels are more related to body fatness than to physical training. In contrast, HDL-C is higher and the total cholesterol/HDL-C ratio lower in trained elderly men even after correcting for fatness.[82,83] HDL-C concentrations in healthy older men appear to be more closely related to fitness, body composition (percent of body fat), and fat distribution (WHR) than to age.[84,85] Prospective studies of the effects of endurance training on lipoprotein profiles in older individuals demonstrate no changes in lipoprotein concentrations with low-intensity training. Consistent with studies in younger individuals, TG decreases and HDL-C increases following high-intensity training, but no changes are observed in total or LDL cholesterol.[30,86] There are at present no published studies on the effects of strength or resistance training on lipoprotein profiles in elderly individuals. Although there is some disagreement, studies in young and middle-aged individuals fail to show any significant response.[72]

Hypertension

Drug treatment of hypertension in the elderly produces long-term benefits, with reductions in stroke, atherosclerotic cardiovascular disease, or both (see Chap. 47). Despite the known benefits of antihypertensive therapy, the side-effect profile of many of the drug therapies, especially in the elderly, has led to a resurgence of interest in nonpharmacologic treatments (e.g., weight loss, low-sodium diet and endurance exercise), especially in patients with mild to moderate hypertension.[87] In particular, the effect of exercise on blood pressure has been the subject of many individual studies as well as several good reviews.[88–90] The majority of cross-sectional and cohort studies find modestly lower systolic and diastolic blood pressures (about 5 to 10 mmHg) in active subjects, but the magnitude of the difference is dependent on the type and intensity of exercise as well as the position in which the blood pressure was measured (there are greater differences when the patient is supine). As a whole, the studies also suggest a greater exercise effect in older subjects and those with mild to moderate hypertension. Two large prospective cohort studies demonstrated that both leisure-time activity[91] and increased fitness, measured by $\dot{V}O_2max$ testing,[92] were protective against the development of hypertension, with the effect being independent of age, obesity, and family history. Not all such studies agree, however.[4]

Cross-sectional studies have detected little difference in resting blood pressure between healthy trained and sedentary individuals, especially when differences in adiposity or relative weight were accounted for. Similarly, exercise intervention studies in older individuals have detected little or no decrement in resting blood pressure, even following intensive endurance training.[16,31] In contrast, a training-related decrease in the blood pressure response to acute submaximal exercise has been detected in both cross-sectional and prospective training studies in older individuals.[31,82,93]

There is at present no agreement on the possible etiology of any of the exercise-related effects on blood pressure in older individuals, though changes in body composition, fat distribution, sympathetic nervous system activity, and insulinemia have all been postulated. The available data on the effect of strength training on blood pressure is more limited and at present there is no consensus.[72,94]

Atherosclerotic Cardiovascular Disease and Overall Mortality

The relationship between atherosclerotic cardiovascular disease and regular exercise has been extensively investigated. As reviewed by Schneider et al.,[95] an important effect of activity in reducing the risk of atherosclerotic cardiovascular disease is supported by (1) population studies demonstrating a low prevalence of ischemic heart disease in extremely active societies; (2) retrospective studies comparing rates of heart disease in workers with active versus sedentary jobs; and (3) studies where activity mitigated the deleterious effects of a diet high in saturated fat and cholesterol in monkeys. Several prospective cohort studies in humans also support this hypothesis.[4,96–98] Paffenberger's[96] classic study in Harvard alumni found a greater than 50 percent reduction in risk for heart attack in subjects expending more than 2000 kcal per week in leisure-time physical activity. Furthermore, it was present, not college, activity level that was inversely related to risk. Findings of a more recent 2-year follow-up study in older subjects suggest that initiation of exercise, even late in life, may be cardio-protective, although most of the end points in this study were arrhythmias, not angina or myocardial infarctions.

Given the previously discussed effects of exercise training on cardiovascular risk factors, the observed relationship with atherosclerotic cardiovascular disease end points is not unexpected. However, recent prospective cohort studies have also demonstrated that physical activity is also associated with a significant reduction in all-cause mortality in men and women[2–4] even when adjusted for other known risk factors. Furthermore, the protective effect of exercise was more pronounced in the older subjects. Some of this independent exercise-related protection may be due to newly recognized cardiac risk factors, such as fibrinolytic variables, which are improved with exercise.[99]

In reviewing the available data on the effects of exercise on coronary artery disease, the median relative risk between the least and the most active groups was approximately 2.0, similar to that for blood pressure (2.1), hypercholesterolemia (2.4), and smoking (2.5).[100] It remains unclear from this body of literature what level of exercise is most beneficial, but the benefit with regard to all-cause mortality has been observed to become asymptotic beyond a $\dot{V}O_2max$ of approximately 35 ml/kg/min.[2] It should be noted that all of the above studies involved endurance exercise, and we are aware of no published studies assessing the relationship between atherosclerotic cardiovascular disease or all-cause mortality and strength training.

Arthritis

Arthritis is an important cause of functional impairment in older adults. A description of age-related changes in joint function, and the impact of arthritis on function in older adults is given in Chaps. 84 and 85. Until recently, exercise was considered as possibly harmful to arthritis patients. Arthritis patients were cautioned to avoid vigorous exercise in involved joints, especially during flares in arthritic symptoms. However, several randomized controlled trials have demonstrated that exercise, even vigorous exercise, is probably beneficial in arthritis. These studies have enrolled both young and old adults and have included functional status outcomes. Exercise has included endurance training, such as riding a stationary bicycle, and strength training using weights.

The exercise trials in arthritis patients report 10 to 25 percent improvement in functional status outcomes.[101–104] Improvements include faster gait, improvement in physical activity, lower depression scores, less pain, and less frequent use of pain medications. Importantly, exercise did not increase pain. Improvements have persisted as long as 9 months after discharge from supervised exercise classes.[101] As a group, these studies provide strong evidence of a beneficial effect of exercise on functional status in patients with mild to moderate arthritis (both rheumatoid and osteoarthritis).

Osteoporosis

The decline in bone mineral density with age is well recognized (see Chap. 75). A fracture threshold is hypothesized, and most older adults are below this theoretical threshold. The result is an epidemic of osteoporotic fractures that affects women more than men and primarily involves vertebral, wrist, and hip fractures.

The concept that mechanical loads are important to the integrity of the skeleton is more than 100 years old. Animal studies have not only confirmed the importance of mechanical strain to bone remodeling but have shed some light on the intensity and type of loading which produces the greatest effects. The greatest bone response (increases of 30 to 40 percent compared to a disuse control) was seen with high peak strains used intermittently and with relatively few (36) loading cycles.[105] Artificial loading also reduced the loss of bone in a calcium-deficient avian model.

There have been numerous cross-sectional studies in humans which have investigated the effect of exercise on bone mass. Interpretation of many of these studies is limited because the area of bone density measurement frequently did not correspond to the bones that would be expected to receive the bulk of the mechanical stress from the given exercise. Since there is no known systemic effect of mechanical stress, measurement of radial bone mass in runners versus non-runners is unlikely to be very conclusive. However, one particularly well-conceived study found that the humerus in the dominant arm of tennis players had approximately 30 percent greater cortical bone thickness when compared to the non-dominant arm.[106] Studies using more sensitive and reproducible methodologies, capable of assessing weight-bearing bone (hip and spine), have found a 10 percent higher trabecular bone density in eumenorrheic runners when compared with eumenorrheic nonrunning women.[107] These data suggest that exercise in younger individuals may increase peak bone mass—an important negative risk factor for osteopenia in older women.

Several prospective studies on the effects of exercise on bone mass in postmenopausal women have been difficult to interpret due to small numbers of subjects, short duration of the intervention, or, as noted above, a mismatch between the area of measurement and the bone that is loaded by the intervention. However, studies in postmenopausal women, using better designs and measurement techniques, have detected exercise-related increases in bone density of 6 to 9 percent compared to nonexercising controls.[108] The majority of the available prospective studies have used an endurance exercise intervention. Although there are theoretical reasons why strength training may be a preferable intervention to increase bone mass, the few published studies to date have been inconsistent. Therefore, at this time the utility of strength training in the treatment of osteopenia remains open to question and, one hopes, open to additional investigation.

RISKS ASSOCIATED WITH EXERCISE

Despite the recognition of exercise as a major public health concern and objective[109] for our entire population, there has been little systematic assessment of the health risks of exercise. This lack of information may be due to the complex interplay of factors that may or may not predispose to injury:[110] (1) host factors such as age, sex, fitness level, gait, balance, health status and body weight; (2) exercise factors such as frequency, intensity, speed, duration, and proper use of warm-up/cool-down periods; and (3) environmental factors such as surface, location, temperature, weather conditions, and use of proper supportive and protective equipment.

By far the majority of the injuries are due to "overuse" and involve soft tissues. In a recent survey, approximately 10 percent of individuals (16 to 65 years old) participating in active sports or recreation reported having an injury within the last 4 weeks, with half of the incidents causing limitations in activity and 15 percent causing a hospital visit.[111] Although the number of injuries might be expected to be reduced with less intensive and competitive activity, it is also likely to be greater with increasing age. As noted previously, the speed of an activity may be a greater risk for injury than the intensity of the activity. Thus fewer injuries would be expected from walking uphill as compared to jogging on a flat surface.[23] Evidence also suggests that eccentric exercise (e.g., lowering a weight that has been lifted) may predispose to muscle injury.[112] Patients with osteoporosis are at increased risk for fracture if they fall while exercising.

A rigorous review of the potential exercise risks in an older population is outside the scope of this chapter, but two specific areas require more detailed coverage. The risk of an untoward cardiovascular event has been carefully addressed in an important study, which found a significant transient increase in the risk of sudden death occurring during a bout of vigorous exercise, especially in previously sedentary individuals.[97] However, the reduction in risk during the nonexercising period of the day more than makes up for the transient increase during exercise, producing an overall risk of sudden death in active men that is 30 percent of that in sedentary men. These data are supported by studies describing lower cardiovascular-related and overall mortality in active individuals.[2–4,96] It should be emphasized that the relationship between the type, intensity, and duration of exercise and the reduction in cardiac risk remains unclear.

Exercise in older patients with diabetes mellitus also deserves additional comments and has been reviewed.[70] Careful attention to the possibility of both immediate and delayed episodes of exercise-induced hypoglycemia are critical, because of the sustained improvement in insulin sensitivity (24 to 48 h) associated with vigorous exercise. Transient worsening of orthostatic hypotension can also occur following vigorous exercise, especially in hot weather. Meticulous foot care and supportive, well-fitted shoes are particularly critical for the exercising diabetic patient. Patients with proliferative retinopathy should avoid anaerobic (specifically isometric) exercise, such as power lifting, because of the increased ocular and systemic pressure occurring with the Valsalva maneuver. Diabetes is an important risk factor for ischemic heart disease, and its presence also puts the diabetic patient in a higher risk category with respect to exercise-associated cardiovascular events (see discussion below[113]).

RECOMMENDATIONS

There is now ample evidence strongly supporting the beneficial effects of exercise in the elderly on several important health-related end points. It is also clear, however, that we do not yet know enough about different types of exercise regimens to accurately prescribe a specific program which can be aimed at a specific disorder. Most previous exercise recommendations have been based on the stimulus known to improve endurance capacity.[114] However it is possible, even likely, that other health benefits may be accrued by different exercise stimuli which produce relatively little or even no improvement in cardiovascular fitness. Examples include low-intensity endurance training (50 to 60 percent of HRR) and strength training. In the future, the use of exercise to prevent and/or treat chronic disease will depend upon studies that can specifically define the exercise stimulus to match the therapeutic need. Thus, the American College of Sports Medicine recommendation for maintaining cardiovascular fitness (exercising at 70 percent of maximum heart rate for at least 20 min, three times a week) should be viewed only as a general guideline. Individual modifications will be necessary, particularly for frail older adults, for whom both the risks and potential benefits of an exercise program may be substantial.

Although specific recommendations are beyond the scope of this chapter, general guidelines can be given. For reasons of safety, most experts strongly recommend a pre-exercise assessment, including a complete history and physical examination, as well as an exercise stress test for men over age 40 and women over age 50. However, it is clear that the substantial cost of such an evaluation would affect the practicality of using exercise as a public health measure and could limit the participation of many older individuals in an exercise program. Furthermore, many older individuals have safely participated in community-based exercise programs for years with no such evaluation. The American College of Sports Medicine suggests that for those without symptoms of coronary disease, a formal medical examination and exercise testing may not be necessary if moderate noncompetitive exercise is performed in a supervised setting.[113] The geriatric medicine axiom of "start low and go slow" should certainly be applied to beginning an exercise program. It is appropriate for patients to at least notify their physicians of their intent to begin an exercise program, since adjustments in medications or dosages may be necessary.

An appropriate exercise program for an elderly population would include heart rate monitoring, with a target heart rate starting at 50 percent of maximum and with gradual increases, as tolerated, every 2 to 4 weeks up to 70 to 80 percent of maximum heart rate. The maximum heart rate can be most accurately obtained during a maximal exercise test, but it can also be estimated from the formula "220 minus age." Endurance exercise should involve large muscle groups in large arcs and can potentially be complemented by low-resistance, high-repetition strength training. Appropriate warm-up and cool-down periods, as well as emphasis on stretching and flexibility, are likely to be especially important in reducing soft tissue injury in an older population.

Changes in lifestyle are difficult to maintain at any age and dropout rates for exercise programs are high. This problem may be reduced by (1) careful attention to warm-up periods and slow progression in an effort to reduce early injuries, (2) enthusiastic leadership, (3) regular assessment of improvement with personalized feedback and praise, (4) spousal and family support for participation, (5) flexible goals (time rather than distance) set by the participant, and (6) use of distraction techniques such as music. Since it is inevitable that a participant will at some time have a setback, it is important to provide strategies for coping with this stress at the beginning of the exercise program.

REFERENCES

1. Bortz WM II: Redefining human aging. *J Am Geriatr Soc* 37:1092, 1989.
2. Blair SN, Kohl HW, Paffenberger RS, et al: Physical fitness and all-cause mortality: A prospective study of healthy men and women. *JAMA* 262:2395, 1989.
3. Paffenberger RS Jr, Hyde RT, Wing AC, Hsiek C-C: Physical activity, all-cause mortality, and longevity of college alumni. *N Engl J Med* 314:605, 1986.
4. Pekkanen J, Marti B, Nissinen A, Tuomilehto J: Reduction of premature mortality by high physical activity: A 20 year follow-up of middle-aged Finnish men. *Lancet* 1:1473, 1987.
5. Robinson S: Experimental studies of physical fitness in relation to age. *Arbeitsphysiologie* 10:251, 1938.
6. Dehn MM, Bruce RA: Longitudinal variations in maximal oxygen uptake with age and physical activity. *J Appl Physiol* 33:805, 1972.
7. Kasch FW, Wallace JP, VanCamp SP: Effects of 18 years of endurance exercise on the physical work capacity of older men. *J Cardiac Rehabil* 5:308, 1985.
8. Buskirk ER, Hodgson JL: Age and aerobic power: The rate of change in men and women. *Fed Proc* 46:1824, 1987.
9. Pollock ML, Foster C, Knapp D, et al: Effect of age, training and competition on aerobic capacity and body composition of masters athletes. *J Appl Physiol* 62:725, 1987.
10. Rogers MA, Hagberg JM, Martin WH, et al: Decline in $\dot{V}O_2$max with aging in masters athletes and sedentary men. *J Appl Physiol* 68:2195, 1990.
11. Hagberg JM: Effect of training on the decline of $\dot{V}O_2$max with aging. *Fed Proc* 46:1830, 1987.
12. Cohn SH, Vartsky D, Yasumura S, et al: Compartmental body composition bsaed on total-body nitrogen, potassium and calcium. *Am J Physiol* 239:E524, 1980.
13. Fleg JL, Lakatta EG: Role of muscle loss in the age associated reduction in $\dot{V}O_2$max. *J Appl Physiol* 65:1147, 1988.
14. Ogawa T, Schechtman KB, Spina RJ, et al: Effects of aging, sex and physical training on cardiovascular responses to exercise. *Circulation* 86:494, 1992.
15. Lakatta EG: Changes in cardiovascular function with aging. *Eur Heart J* 11(suppl C):22, 1990.
16. Stratton JR, Cerqueira MD, Schwartz RS, et al: Differences in cardiovascular responses to isoproterenol in relation to age and exercise training in healthy men. *Circulation* 86:504, 1992.
17. Higginbotham MS, Morris KG, Williams RS, et al: Physiologic basis for the age-related decline in aerobic work capacity. *Am J Cardiol* 57:1374, 1986.
18. Lakatta EG: Catecholamines and cardiovascular functions in aging, in Sacktor B (ed): *Endocrinology and Metabolism Clinics of North America.* Philadelphia, Saunders, 1987, pp 877–891.
19. Levy WC, Cerqueira MD, Abrass IB, et al: Exercise training enhances cardiac dilatation at peak exercise in healthy older males compared to young males. *Circulation* 86:I-670, 1992.
20. Seals DR, Hagberg JM, Hurley BF, et al: Effects of endurance training on glucose tolerance and plasma lipids in older men and women. *JAMA* 252:645, 1984.
21. Schwartz RS, Shuman WP, Larson V, et al: The effect of intensive endurance training on body fat distribution in young and older subjects. *Metabolism* 40:545, 1991.
22. Kohrt WM, Obert KA, Holloszy JO: Exercise training improves fat distributions patterns in 60- to 70-year-old men and women. *J Gerontol* 47:M99, 1992.
23. Carroll JF, Pollock ML, Graves JE, et al: Incidence of injury during moderate- and high-intensity walking training in the elderly. *J Gerontol* 47:M61, 1992.
24. Posner JD, Gorman KM, Windsor-Landsberg L, et al: Low to moderate intensity endurance training in healthy older adults: physiological responses after four months. *J Am Geriatr Soc* 40:1, 1992.
25. Schwartz RS, Shuman WD, Bradbury VL, et al: Body fat distribution in healthy young and older men. *J Gerontol* 45:M181, 1990.
26. Shimokata H, Tobin JD, Muller DC, et al: Studies in the distribution of body fat: I. Effects of age, sex and obesity. *J Gerontol* 44:M66, 1989.
27. Peiris A, Sothmann MS, Hoffmann RG, et al: Adiposity, fat distribution and cardiovascular risk. *Ann Intern Med* 110:867, 1989.
28. Meyers DA, Goldberg AP, Bleeker ML, et al: Relationship of obesity and physical fitness to cardiopulmonary and metabolic function in healthy older men. *J Gerontol* 46:M57, 1991.
29. Poehlman ET, Danforth E Jr: Endurance training increases metabolic rate and norepinephrine appearance rate in older individuals. *Am J Physiol* 261:E233, 1991.
30. Pavlou CN, Krey S, Steffee WP: Exercise as an adjunct to weight loss and maintenance in moderately obese subjects. *Am J Clin Nutr* 49:1115, 1989.
31. Seals DR, Hagberg JM, Hurley BF, et al: Endurance training in older men and women: I. Cardiovascular responses to exercise. *J Appl Physiol* 57:1024, 1984.
32. Shocken DD, Blumenthal JA, Port S, et al: Physical conditioning and left ventricular performance in the elderly: Assessment by radionucleotide angiocardiography. *Am J Cardiol* 52:359, 1983.
33. Ehsani AA, Ogawa T, Miller TR, et al: Exercise training improves left ventricular systolic functions in older men. *Circulation* 83:96, 1991.
34. Grimby G: Muscle changes and trainability in the elderly. *Top Geriatr Rehabil* 5:54, 1990.
35. Stamford BA: Exercise and the elderly. *Exerc Sport Sci Rev* 1988:341–379.
36. Clement FJ: Longitudinal and cross-sectional assessments of age changes in physical strength as relate to sex, social class, and mental ability. *J Gerontol* 29:423, 1974.
37. Aniansson A, Hedberg M, Henning GB, Grimby G: Muscle morphology, enzymatic activity, and muscle strength in elderly men: A follow-up study. *Muscle Nerve* 9:585, 1986.
38. Aniansson A, Sperling L, Rundgren A, Lehnberg E: Muscle function in 75-year-old men and women: A longitudinal study. *Scand J Rehabil Med* 9(suppl):92, 1983.

39. Wilmore JH: The aging of bone and muscle. *Clin Sports Med* 10:231, 1991.
40. MacLennan WJ, Hall MRP, Timothy JI, Robinson M: Is weakness in old age due to muscle wasting? *Age Ageing* 9:188, 1980.
41. Larsson L: Morphological and functional characteristics of aging skeletal muscle in man. *Acta Physiol Scand (Suppl)* 457:1, 1978.
42. Grimby G, Saltin B: Mini-review: The ageing muscle. *Clin Physiol* 3:209, 1983.
43. Kovanen V: Effects of ageing and physical training on rat skeletal muscle. *Acta Physiol Scand* 135(suppl):1, 1989.
44. Green HJ: Characteristics of aging human skeletal muscle, in Sutton JR, Brock RM (eds): *Sports Medicine for the Mature Athlete.* Indianapolis, IN, Benchmark Press, 1986, pp 16–26.
45. Sandler RB, Burdett R. Zaleskiewicz M, et al: Muscle strength as an indicator of the habitual level of physical activity. *Med Sci Sports Exerc* 23:1375, 1991.
46. Harper CM, Lyles YM: Physiology and complications of bed rest. *J Am Geriatr Soc* 36:1047, 1988.
47. Petrofsky JS, Lind AR: Aging, isometric strength and endurance, and cardiovascular responses to static effort. *J Appl Physiol* 38:91, 1975.
48. DeLorme TL: Restoration of muscle power by heavy-resistance exercise. *J Bone Joint Surg* 27:645, 1945.
49. Buchner DM, Beresford SAA, Larson EB, et al: Effects of physical activity on health status in older adults. II. Intervention studies. *Annu Rev Public Health* 13:469, 1992.
50. Buchner DM: Understanding variability in studies of strength training in older adults: A meta-analytic perspective. *Top Geriatr Rehabil* 8:1, 1993.
51. Frontera WR, Meredith CN, O'Reilly KP, et al: Strength conditioning in older men: Skeletal muscle hypertrophy and improved function. *J Appl Physiol* 64:1038, 1988.
52. Charette SL, McEvoy L, Pyka G, et al: Muscle hypertrophy response to resistance training in older women. *J Appl Physiol* 70:1912, 1991.
53. Meredith CN, Fronter WR, O'Reilly KP, Evans WJ: Body composition in elderly men: Effect of dietary modification during strength training. *J Am Geriatr Soc* 40:155, 1992.
54. Buchner DM, Cress ME, de Lateur BJ, Wagner EH: Variability in the effect of strength training on skeletal muscle strength in older adults. *Facts Res Gerontol* 7:143, 1993.
55. Moritani T, deVries HA: Neural factors versus hypertrophy in the time course of muscle strength gain. *Am J Phys Med* 58:115, 1979.
56. Fiatarone MA, Marks EC, Ryan ND, et al: High-intensity strength training in nonagenarians. *JAMA* 263:3029, 1990.
57. Chamie M: The status and use of the International Classification of Impairments, Disabilities and Handicaps (ICIDH). *World Health Stat Q* 43:273, 1990.
58. Buchner DM, Wagner EH: Preventing frail health. *Clin Geriatr Med* 8:1, 1992.
59. Shephard RJ: The scientific basis of exercise prescribing for the very old. *J Am Geriatr Soc* 38:62, 1990.
60. Young A: Exercise physiology in geriatric practice. *Acta Med Scand* (Suppl) 711:227, 1986.
61. Buchner DM, de Lateur BJ: The importance of skeletal muscle strength to physical function in older adults. *Ann Behav Med* 13:91, 1991.
62. Kelley DL, Dainis A, Wood GK: Mechanics and muscular dynamics of rising from a seated position, in Komi PV (ed): *Biomechanics,* vol 1, Baltimore, MD, University Park Press, 1976, pp 127–134.
63. Danneskiold-Samsoe B, Kofod V, Munter J, et al: Muscle strength and functional capacity in 78–81 year old men and women. *Eur J Appl Physiol* 52:310, 1984.
64. Buchner DM, Cress ME, Wagner EH, de Lateur BJ: The role of exercise in fall prevention: Developing targeting criteria for exercise programs, in Vellas B, et al (eds): *Falls, Balance and Gait Disorders in the Elderly.* Paris, Elsevier, 1992, pp 55–67.
65. Coon PJ, Rogus EM, Drinkwater D, et al: Role of body fat distribution in the decline in insulin sensitivity and glucose intolerance with age. *J Clin Endocrinol Metab* 75:1125, 1992.
66. Lipman RL, Raskin P, Love T, et al: Glucose intolerance during decreased physical activity in man. *Diabetes* 21:101, 1972.
67. Seals DR, Hagberg JM, Allen WK, et al: Glucose tolerance in young and older athletes and sedentary men. *J Appl Physiol* 56:1521, 1984.
68. Kahn SE, Larson VG, Beard JC, et al: Effect of exercise on insulin action, glucose intolerance and insulin secretion in aging. *Am J Physiol* 258:E937, 1990.
69. Tonino RP: Effect of physical training on the insulin resistance of aging. *Am J Physiol* 256:E352, 1989.
70. Schwartz RS: Exercise training in the treatment of diabetes mellitus in elderly patients. *Diabetes Care* 13(suppl 2):77, 1990.
71. Schneider GH, Ruderman RH, Amorosa LF, et al: Studies on the mechanism of improved glucose control during regular exercise in type 2 (non-insulin-dependent) diabetes. *Diabetologia* 26:355, 1984.
72. Smutok MA, Reece C, Kokkinos PF, et al: Aerobic vs strength training for risk factor intervention in middle-age men at high risk for coronary heart disease. *Metabolism,* in press.
73. DeFronzo RA, Ferrannini E: Insulin resistance: A multi-faceted syndrome responsible for NIDDM, obesity, hypertension, dyslipemia and atherosclerotic cardiovascular disease. *Diabetes Care* 14:173, 1991.
74. Rubin SM, Sidney S, Black DM, et al: High blood cholesterol in elderly men and the excess risk for coronary heart disease. *Ann Intern Med* 113:916, 1990.
75. Haskell WL: The influence of exercise training on plasma lipids and lipoproteins in health and disease. *Acta Med Scand* (suppl 711):25, 1986.
76. Woods PD, Stefanick ML, Dreon DM, et al: Changes in lipids and lipoproteins in overweight men during weight loss through dieting as compared to exercise. *N Engl J Med* 319:1173, 1988.
77. Huttenen JK, Lansimies E, Vontilainess E, et al: Effect of moderate physical exercise on serum lipoproteins: A controlled clinical trial with special reference to serums high-density lipoproteins. *Circulation* 60:1220, 1979.
78. Cook TC, Laporte RE, Washburn RA, et al: Chronic low level physical activity as a determinant of high

density lipoprotein cholesterol and subfractions. *Med Sci Sports Exerc* 18:653, 1986.
79. Bassett-Frey MA, Doerr BM, Laubach LL, et al: Exercise does not change high density lipoprotein cholesterol in women after ten weeks of training. *Metabolism* 31:1142, 1982.
80. Schwartz RS: Independent effects of dietary weight loss and aerobic training on high density lipoproteins and apolipoproteins in obese men. *Metabolism* 36:165, 1987.
81. Williams PT, Krauss RM, Vranizan KM, Woods PDS: Changes in lipoprotein subfractions during diet-induced and exercise-induced weight loss in moderately overweight men. *Circulation* 81:1293, 1990.
82. Seals DR, Allen WK, Hurley BF, et al: Elevated high-density lipoprotein cholesterol levels in older endurance athletes. *Am J Cardiol* 54:390, 1984.
83. Tamai T, Nakai T, Kakai H, et al: The effects of physical exercise on plasma lipoprotein and apolipoprotein metabolism in elderly men. *J Gerontol* 43:M75, 1988.
84. Coon PJ, Bleecker ER, Drinkwater DT, et al: Effects of body composition and exercise capacity on glucose tolerance, insulin and lipoprotein lipids in healthy older men: A cross-sectional and longitudinal study. *Metabolism* 38:1201, 1989.
85. Houmard JA, Wheeler WS, McCammon MR, et al: Effects of fitness level and regional distribution of fat on carbohydrate metabolism and plasma lipids in middle- to older-aged men. *Metabolism* 40:714, 1991.
86. Schwartz RS, Cain KC, Shuman WP, et al: Effect of intensive endurance training on lipoprotein profiles in young and older men. *Metabolism* 41:649, 1992.
87. Applegate WB: High blood pressure treatment in the elderly. *Clin Geriatr Med* 8:103, 1992.
88. Tipton CM: Exercise, training and hypertension. *Exerc Sport Sci Rev* 12:245, 1984.
89. Hagberg TM, Seals DR: Exercise training and hypertension. *Acta Med Scand* (suppl 711):131, 1986.
90. Bjorntorp P: Effects of physical training on blood pressure in hypertension. *Eur Heart J* 8(suppl B):71, 1987.
91. Paffenberger RS, Wing AL, Hyde RT, Jung DL: Physical activity and indicence of hypertension in college alumni. *Am J Epidemiol* 117:245, 1983.
92. Blair SN, Goodyear NN, Gibbons LW, Cooper KH: Physical fitness and incidence of hypertension in healthy normotensive men and women. *JAMA* 252:487, 1984.
93. Hagberg JM, Montain SJ, Martin WH, Ehsam AA: Effect of exercise training in 60- to 69-year old persons with essential hypertension. *Am J Cardiol* 64:348, 1989.
94. Reid CM, Yeates RA, Ullrich IH: Weight training and strength, cardiorespiratory functioning and body composition of men. *Brit J Sports Med* 21:40, 1987.
95. Schneider SH, Vitug A, Ruderman N: Atherosclerosis and physical exercise. *Diabetes/Metab Rev* 1:513, 1986.
96. Paffenberger RS Jr, Wing AL, Hyde RT: Physical activity as an index of heart attack risk in college alumni. *Am J Epidemiol* 108:161, 1978.
97. Siscovick DS, Weiss NS, Fletcher RH, Lasky T: The incidence of primary cardiac arrest during vigorous exercise. *N Engl J Med* 311:874, 1984.
98. Posner JD, Gorman KM, Gitlin LN, et al: Effects of exercise training in the elderly on the occurrence and time to onset of cardiovascular diagnoses. *J Am Geriatr Soc* 38:205, 1990.
99. Stratton JR, Chandler WL, Schwartz RS, et al: Effects of physical conditioning on fibrinolytic variables and fibrinogens in young and old healthy adults. *Circulation* 83:1692, 1991.
100. Powell KE, Caspersen CJ, Koplan JP, Ford ES: Physical activity and chronic disease. *Am J Clin Nutr* 49:999, 1989.
101. Minor MA, Hewett JE, Webel RR, et al: Efficacy of physical conditioning exercise in patients with rheumatoid arthritis and osteoarthritis. *Arthr Rheum* 32:1396, 1989.
102. Ekdahl C, Andersson SI, Moritz U, Svensson B: Dynamic versus static training in patients with rheumatoid arthritis. *Scand J Rheumatol* 19:17, 1990.
103. Fisher NM, Pendergast DR, Gresham GE, Calkins E: Muscle rehabilitation: Its effect on muscular and functional performance of patients with knee osteoarthritis. *Arch Physiol Med Rehabil* 72:367, 1991.
104. Kovar PA, Allegrante JP, MacKenzie CR, et al: Supervised fitness walking in patients with osteoarthritis of the knee: A randomized controlled trial. *Ann Intern Med* 116:529, 1992.
105. Lanyon LE: Strain-related bone modeling and remodeling. *Top Geriatr Rehabil* 4:13, 1989.
106. Jones JJ, Priest JD, Hayes WC: Humeral hypertrophy in response to exercise. *J Bone Joint Surg* 59:204, 1977.
107. Drinkwater BL, Nilson K, Chestnut CH, et al: Bone mineral content of amenorrheic and eumeonorrheic athletes. *N Engl J Med* 311:277, 1984.
108. Dalsky GP: The role of exercise in the prevention of osteoporosis. *Comp Ther* 15:30, 1989.
109. *Healthy People 2000: National Health Promotion and Disease Prevention Objectives.* U.S. Dept of Health and Human Services, Public Health Service, DHHS Publication No (PHS) 91-50212, Washington, DC, 1990.
110. Koplan JP, Siscovick DS, Goldbaum GM: The risks of exercise: A public health view of injuries and hazards. *Public Health Rep* 100:189, 1985.
111. Nicholl JP, Coleman P, Williams BT: Pilot study of the epidemiology of sports injuries and exercise-related morbidity. *Br J Sports Med* 25:61, 1991.
112. Friden J, Lieber RL: Structural and mechanical basis of exercise-induced muscle injury. *Med Sci Sports Exerc* 24:521, 1992.
113. American College of Sports Medicine: *Guidelines for Exercise Testing and Prescription,* 4th ed. Philadelphia, Lea and Febiger, 1991.
114. Haskell WL: Physical activity and health: Need to define the required stimulus. *Am J Cardiol* 55:4D, 1985.

Chapter 8

PERSONALITY AND AGING

Paul T. Costa, Jr. and Robert R. McCrae

Aging is devalued in our society, and physicians are not immune to negative stereotypes. It is widely believed that older individuals are hypochondriacs, prone to depression, and unable to adapt to change,[1] and some of these generalizations appear to be confirmed by clinical experience. When, however, standardized measures of personality are used in unselected samples, the influence of age on personality is seen to be very slight. A more objective view of personality in aging men and women can provide a more informed basis for dealing with older patients. This chapter provides an overview of recent research on age and personality and discusses some of the implications most relevant to geriatric medicine.

A DEFINITION OF PERSONALITY

Psychiatry is the medical specialty most directly concerned with personality, and historically, psychiatric approaches to personality were dominated by psychoanalytic concepts like *id, ego,* and *superego.* Both psychopathology and normal personality were discussed in terms of instinctual impulses and unconscious defensive processes. Because the major determinants of personality were thought to be unconscious, the individual's own conception of himself or herself could not be trusted as a source of data: A skilled clinician, perhaps using inkblots or other projective tests, was seen as the only legitimate judge of personality.

In the past few decades the psychoanalytic position has fallen from favor with most personality psychologists and psychiatrists, and alternative views, especially biological and trait approaches, have been widely adopted.[2] Self-report instruments have shown their utility in thousands of applications, and a recent review[3] comparing self-reports with expert ratings found that the former were equal or superior to the latter in predicting a variety of important criteria. Psychometric sophistication has also increased over the years, and self-report measures of anxiety,[4] depression,[5] and symptoms of personality disorders[6] are now widely used as part of the comprehensive psychiatric evaluation of individuals. Personality ratings, whether from experts or from acquaintances or family members, remain an important adjunct to self-reports.

When questionnaire data collected from large samples of subjects become the focus of psychological study, the implicit definition of personality changes. Instead of evidence of internal conflict, symbolic distortion, and neurotic defense, researchers look for consistent patterns of response that distinguish one individual from others. Personality *traits*—characteristic emotional, interpersonal, experiential, and motivational styles—emerge as the basic elements of personality.[7,8]

In their extreme form, personality traits are readily recognizable on even casual observation. In clinical practice, some individuals are silent and reserved, taking the medical interview with great seriousness. Others are talkative, informal, and lighthearted. Again, some patients chronically minimize their medical problems, while others complain long and loud about relatively minor symptoms. Inferences about personality are almost inevitable in these cases. It is, however, essential to note that behavior in the special situation of a visit to a physician or hospital may not be characteristic of the individual. Standard psychological tests, perhaps taken at home, would provide a much better guide to the individual and could set in context the particular reactions seen by the physician during an examination.

The Five-Factor Model

The English language contains thousands of words to describe individuals, and psychologists have created hundreds of scales to measure theoretically important traits. The clinician or researcher is faced with the problem of selecting the most appropriate of these, and, until recently, there was little basis for the selection. Several independent lines of research[9–12] have now begun to converge on the five-factor model of personality, according to which most traits can be seen as aspects of neuroticism, extraversion, open-

TABLE 8-1

Examples of Traits from the Five Personality Factors

Factor	Characteristic: Low Scorer	Characteristic: High Scorer
Neuroticism	Calm	Worrying
	Even-tempered	Temperamental
	Self-satisfied	Self-pitying
	Comfortable	Self-conscious
	Unemotional	Emotional
	Hardy	Vulnerable
Extraversion	Reserved	Affectionate
	Loner	Joiner
	Quiet	Talkative
	Passive	Active
	Sober	Fun-loving
	Unfeeling	Passionate
Openness	Down-to-earth	Imaginative
	Uncreative	Creative
	Conventional	Original
	Prefers routine	Prefers variety
	Uncurious	Curious
	Conservative	Liberal
Agreeableness	Ruthless	Soft-hearted
	Suspicious	Trusting
	Stingy	Generous
	Antagonistic	Acquiescent
	Critical	Lenient
	Irritable	Good-natured
Conscientiousness	Negligent	Conscientious
	Lazy	Hard-working
	Disorganized	Well-organized
	Late	Punctual
	Aimless	Ambitious
	Quitting	Persevering

SOURCE: PT Costa Jr, RR McCrae: Personality stability and its implications for clinical psychology. *Clin Psychol Rev* 6:407, 1986.

ness, agreeableness, or conscientiousness. Table 8-1 gives examples of some of the adjectives that characterize these five broad domains of personality. The same dimensions have been found in analyses of questionnaire scales[12] and adjective checklists,[10] in self-reports and observer ratings,[13] in men and women, and in English and other languages.[14] These five factors appear to be fundamental to the description of normal personality and form a comprehensive basis for systematic research and assessment.

Of course, five scores do not exhaustively characterize an individual's personality. Recent research has emphasized measurement of more specific traits within each of the five factors or domains.[12] For example, distinctions may be made within the domain of conscientiousness between such traits as competence, order, and achievement striving. For general medical purposes, however, it is often sufficient to characterize the patient at the broad level of the five factors.

PERSONALITY AND AGING: STABILITY OR CHANGE?

Throughout most of history, adulthood has been considered a kind of plateau between the growth of childhood and the decline of old age. Erikson's work on psychosocial development[15] signaled a new approach, in which theorists began to look for ways in which individuals continued to develop across the life span. A wide range of theories was proposed: Age might bring increased introversion and interiority,[16] growth and maturity,[17] or a reversal of sex-role-linked characteristics.[18] Elaborate theories of stages of adult development have been advanced,[19] and the view that individuals undergo a period of tumultuous personal reassessment around age 40—the so-called midlife crisis—has become the conventional wisdom. These theories often conflict with each other, but all concur in suggesting that the period of adulthood is not a plateau but a period of dynamic growth and change in personality.

Mean Level Differences in Personality Traits

When put to empirical test, however, a very different picture emerges. The theories described would suggest that, on the average, predictable changes in personality traits should occur with age, and that, other things being equal, these changes should appear as mean level differences in cross-sectional studies. Early cross-sectional studies on small samples yielded a variety of small and inconsistent results.[20] However, when short scales measuring the three dimensions of neuroticism, extraversion, and openness to experience were examined in a national sample with more than 10,000 respondents, the results were clear.[21] There was very little difference in these three aspects of personality for adults between the ages of 35 and 84. Declines, although statistically significant, were quite small in magnitude. Further, there was no evidence that personality scores are different for individuals around the time of the hypothesized "midlife crisis" or around the age of retirement, as might be suggested by some role-based theories of personality.

Regardless of the sample, all cross-sectional studies are limited by the confounding of generational differences with age differences. The small age differences described above, for example, might be due to changes in patterns of child rearing over the past century. For that reason, the results of longitudinal studies, in which the same individuals are retested at different ages, are particularly important. A number of longitudinal studies have reported analysis of longitudinal changes using a variety of standard personality instruments.[22–25] Although changes between adolescence and adulthood are often seen[23] and occasional age changes are reported for older adults—e.g., a small decline in activity level[22]—the great majority of studies report little or no change in the average level of personality traits after about age 30. Some of the studies include individuals tested up to age 90; again, there is no consistent evidence of change in the average level of most personality traits even in advanced age.

Stability of Individual Differences

The fact that average levels of a variable do not change over time does not necessarily mean that the variable is constant within the individual: some people may have increased while others declined. Indeed, one of the oldest theories of personality development[26] held that such complementary changes *should* be seen as each individual developed, in late life, the aspects of personality that had been dormant in early life. Cross-sectional studies cannot speak to these issues, but longitudinal research can. The degree to which individuals maintain the same relative order is assessed by the correlation coefficient; positive correlations imply stability of individual differences, whereas low or negative correlations suggest that there have been substantial changes in the individual over the retest interval.

A recent study[25] addressed this question using the NEO Personality Inventory,[27] a questionnaire measure of the five-factor model. Self-report data from a 6-year retest were available for 398 men and women, initially aged 25 to 84, on the neuroticism, extraversion, and openness scales; 3-year retest data were available for 360 men and women on the agreeableness and conscientiousness scales. Retest correlations ranged from .63 to .83, and equally high correlations were found for younger and older subjects as well as for men and women. These correlations are almost as high as the short-term retest reliability of the scales and strongly suggest that all five of the major dimensions of personality are highly stable in adulthood.

It has sometimes been argued that such high stability might be due to a crystallized self-concept[28]; that is, individuals may develop a picture of themselves early in life and retain this image despite actual changes in personality. One way to test this hypothesis is by examining stability or change in descriptions made by external observers. In a 7-year longitudinal study of peer ratings,[29] retest correlations for the five factors ranged from .63 to .84, again supporting the view that individual differences in personality are in fact highly stable.

These findings are consistent with a large body of longitudinal results, using a variety of personality tests in diverse samples and over intervals of up to 30 years.[29–32] Studies of adolescents traced into adulthood show somewhat lower levels of stability,[23,33] but there is clear evidence of at least some continuity in personality from childhood on. Combined with the evidence of little or no change in mean levels, these studies suggest that by about age 30, men and women have attained their adult personality, and—barring therapeutic interventions or catastrophic events or illnesses—they maintain these characteristics for the rest of their lives. This can be seen graphically in Fig. 8-1, which shows personality profiles for two men who completed the Guilford-Zimmerman Temperament Survey on five occasions over a 30-year period.

These findings make it necessary to reexamine many of the popular theories of aging. Some people are prone to experience periods of personal crisis; when they are at midlife, the crisis is likely to take the form of concerns over career choice, impending physical decline, and discontent with marriage. A period of personal problems during these years may resemble the legendary "midlife crisis," but only a small portion of the population is likely to experience such a crisis.[34] Higher levels of neuroticism predispose in-

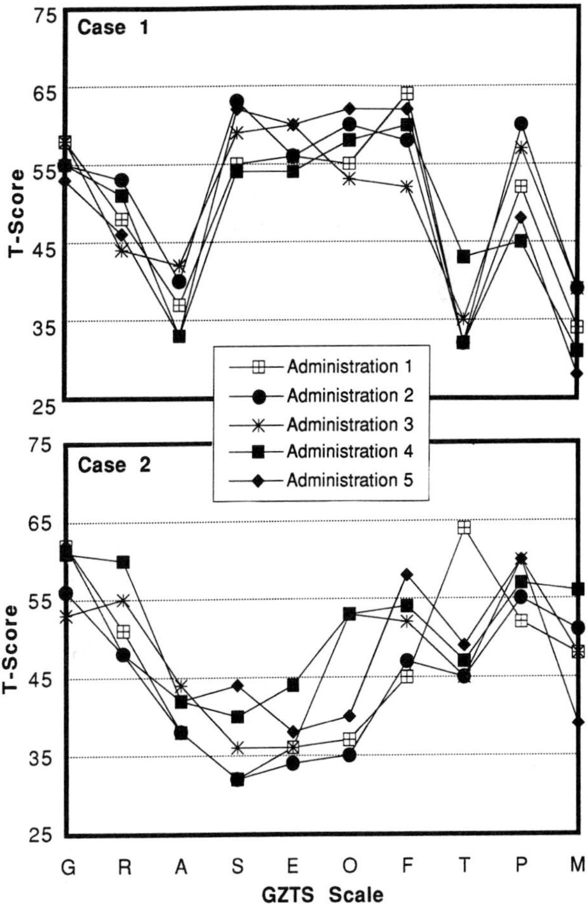

FIGURE 8-1

Personality profiles of two men tested on five occasions over a 30-year period. (*Adapted from Costa and McCrae.*[29])

dividuals to have crises at all ages.[35] Again, Erikson's famous stages of adult life may represent meaningful changes in social roles and expectations, but they do not imply changes in the underlying personality of the individual.

SOME IMPLICATIONS OF PERSONALITY STABILITY

Gerontologists sometimes assume that gerontology is the study of what changes with age; if personality does not change, why study personality and aging? This is surely a narrow view of the field. The question the gerontologist really asks is, "What happens to a variable as individuals age?" If the answer is "It remains constant," that is a potentially important finding in itself. When age changes are found, the next question is, what mechanisms are responsible for the change, and how might interventions affect the rate of change? The stability of personality suggests different but equally basic questions: How does personality remain stable despite changes in social roles, cognitive and physical declines, and the accumulation of a lifetime of experience? What kind of interventions would be needed to alter undesirable aspects of personality?

In a broader context, the stability of personality is important to gerontology and geriatrics because personality itself is important in many areas of life. Personality profoundly affects psychological well-being and morale,[36] vocational choices,[37] coping styles,[38] interpersonal relations,[39] health perceptions, and health behaviors.[40,41] The knowledge that these effects are likely to persist throughout adulthood provides a deeper perspective on all these areas.

Implications for the Individual

The finding that personality is generally stable in adulthood is often viewed with dismay by humanistic psychologists and others who would prefer to imagine limitless possibilities for human growth. Conversely, it is welcomed by those who fear that age must bring depression, isolation, and rigidity. Clearly, how one evaluates the fact depends on one's expectations; it also depends on how satisfied one is with one's current personality. Individuals who are well-adjusted and happy should be pleased to learn that they are likely to remain so. Those who are less happy with themselves should learn to accept the fact that they are likely to remain unhappy unless they take concrete steps, including perhaps professional counseling, to change. The mere passage of time is unlikely to improve their condition.

The stability of personality traits, styles, and motives contributes to the individual's sense of identity and gives continuity and coherence to the course of adult life. Stable individual differences provide a basis for realistic long-term planning. Why would people go through the rigors of medical school unless they believed that their interest in medicine would persist? Why would anyone marry without some faith that the spouse would retain the characteristics that now make him or her lovable? How could people meaningfully plan for a peaceful or exciting or a productive retirement if they were unsure whether they would continue to prefer tranquillity, adventure, or achievement? Age stereotypes provide a poor basis for future planning. At all ages, the range of individual differences is large, and men and women preserve their individuality throughout old age.

Implications for Psychiatry

Other chapters in this volume are devoted to a discussion of psychiatric conditions and their diagnosis and treatment in the elderly. It should be pointed out, however, that the distinction between normal personality traits and psychiatric conditions is often one of degree.[2] Personality disorders, in particular, can be viewed as maladaptive forms of familiar traits, and one focus of contemporary research is on linking DSM Axis II disorders with the five-factor model of normal personality.[42] Anxiety and depression are also clinical conditions that may reflect lifelong predispositions to experience these affects.

Findings on the stability of personality are therefore relevant to the diagnosis of psychiatric conditions in the elderly. Psychiatric problems may be reactions to recent stressors like bereavement, reflections of organic pathology, or continuations of lifelong patterns of maladjustment, but they are not likely to be attributable to aging itself. Depression, in particular, is not an inevitable or even common[43] feature of normal aging and should be regarded as a mental health problem in individuals of any age.

Against the background of normative constancy, marked changes in personality may be indicative of pathology. For example, family members may note personality changes in individuals with dementing disorders.[44] Apparent changes in personality might also be due to sensory problems or to reactions to medication; any marked change should alert the physician to the need for a careful evaluation.

A word on prognosis is also appropriate. Historically, psychiatrists were reluctant to undertake therapy with the elderly both because the shortness of remaining life did not seem to justify it and because the elderly were believed to be unable to benefit. An increasing number of geropsychiatrists[45] and psychotherapists[46] dispute both these claims, and research suggests that older individuals are able to adapt to even the most stressful events. Although death of a spouse is associated with a slightly higher risk of mortality in the year following bereavement (notably among widowers),[47] the great majority of widows and widowers continue their lives, and, in the long run, show little or no evidence of psychological impairment.[48] Older men and women show a remarkable degree of psychological resilience.

Implications for Medical Evaluation and Treatment

For many years, the chief relevance of personality to physicians was believed to be its etiological significance in certain diseases. Specific intrapsychic conflicts[49] were thought to give rise to particular forms of pathology, but these views have found little empirical support.[50] The type A behavior pattern, which was officially recognized by the National Heart, Lung, and Blood Institute as a risk factor for coronary heart disease (CHD) a few years ago,[51] has in subsequent studies failed to predict CHD morbidity or mortality.[52] However, there is some evidence that one aspect of the type A pattern, antagonistic hostility,[53] is a predictor of CHD, and this may explain why early studies using global measures of type A found significant associations. Although it is widely believed that anger, anxiety, and depression are etiological factors in the development of coronary artery disease, cancer, and a variety of other illnesses,[54] the evidence at present is very mixed, and critical interpretations cast doubt on the link between these aspects of personality and objective indicators of disease.[41] Psychosomatic medicine continues to be an important, if controversial, topic for research, and one which presupposes the stability of personality. If traits were not chronic conditions, they would be unlikely to exert much long-term effect on physical health. Finally, it should be pointed out that the five-factor model of personality offers a comprehensive framework in which links between personality and disease can be systematically assessed.[55]

Whatever the role of personality in objective medical conditions, there is little doubt that the dimension of neuroticism plays a prominent role in subjective health status. Individuals high in neuroticism—that is, people who are characteristically anxious, frustrated, depressed, and unable to cope with stress—consistently report more medical complaints and make a disproportionate number of visits to physicians and medical clinics.[40] In the extreme, these individuals are considered hypochondriacs, but the same phenomenon—the magnification of minor pains or other physical sensations as signs of disease—can be seen in psychiatrically normal individuals high in neuroticism.[40]

The association of medical complaints with neuroticism and the stability of neuroticism across the adult life span together suggest that styles of symptom reporting should themselves be stable, and longitudinal studies generally confirm this hypothesis. Total physical complaints on the Cornell Medical Index showed a 6-year stability coefficient of .74 in a sample of 386 men in the Baltimore Longitudinal Study of Aging,[40] and analyses of mean level changes showed predictable increases in cardiovascular, genitourinary, and sensory systems but no consistent changes in other systems. Subjects higher in neuroticism showed higher scores on all physical and psychiatric sections, regardless of age.

There are two conclusions to be drawn from these findings. First, the widespread belief that individuals become hypochondriacs as they age is not supported. The increased use of medical treatment by older men and women is a rational response to their greater objective health problems, and somatic complaints should never be discounted simply because the patient is old.

Second, physicians should be aware that there are enduring individual differences in styles of perceiving, recalling, and reporting medical symptoms. A knowledge of the individual's personality traits and history of symptom reporting can give insight into current complaints. Individuals high in neuroticism may exaggerate reports of pain, leading to inappropriate diagnoses[41]; in these cases, more extensive objective testing may be indicated. Individuals particularly low in neuroticism also require special attention because they may be inclined to minimize problems, and they may not seek the routine screenings that frequent clinic visitors experience.[56] In this way, early signs of disease may be missed.

Although there has been less research on the relevance of the other four dimensions of personality to health behavior, there is reason to suspect that they, too, will be important. Patients high in openness to experience may be more inquisitive and more willing to try novel approaches to therapy; however, they may also be less deferential to medical authority and more likely to seek a second opinion. The dimension of conscientiousness is of particular interest in regard to health practices. Conscientious patients should be better able to maintain diet and exercise regimens and should be more scrupulous about taking medications as prescribed. Patients who are very low in conscientiousness may need extra motivation from and monitoring by the physician.

SUMMARY

Personality can be defined in terms of enduring individual differences in emotional, interpersonal, experiential, attitudinal, and motivational styles. Five major domains of personality have been identified: neuroticism, extraversion, openness, agreeableness, and conscientiousness. Both large-scale cross-sectional studies and longitudinal research demonstrate that personality traits in all five domains are highly stable after about age 30. Enduring dispositions give a sense of identity to the individual and provide a basis for future planning. The stability of normal personality traits provides a context for the evaluation of psychiatric disorders, which may reflect recent stressors or organic pathology or may instead be continuations of lifelong patterns of maladjustment. The five-factor model provides a basis for systematic research in psychosomatic medicine, and knowledge of personality traits can assist the physician in the interpretation of somatic complaints at all ages.

REFERENCES

1. Friedman SA et al: *The Doctors' Guide to Growing Older.* New York, New American Library, 1980.
2. McHugh PR, Slavney PR: *The Perspectives of Psychiatry.* Baltimore, MD, Johns Hopkins University Press, 1983.
3. Shrauger JS, Osberg TM: The relative accuracy of self-predictions and judgments by others in psychological assessment. *Psychol Bull* 90:322, 1981.
4. Spielberger CD et al: *Manual for the State-Trait Anxiety Inventory.* Palo Alto, CA, Consulting Psychologists Press, 1983.
5. Zung WW: A self-report depression scale. *Arch Gen Psychiatry* 12:63, 1965.
6. Millon T: *Millon Clinical Multiaxial Inventory Manual,* 3rd ed. Minneapolis, MN, Interpretive Scoring Systems, 1983.
7. McCrae RR, Costa PT Jr: *Personality in Adulthood.* New York, Guilford, 1990.
8. Buss AH: Personality as traits. *Am Psychol* 44:1378, 1989.
9. Digman JM, Inouye J: Further specification of the five robust factors of personality. *J Pers Soc Psychol* 50:116, 1986.
10. Goldberg LR: An alternative "description of personality": The big-five factor structure. *J Pers Soc Psychol* 59:1216, 1990.
11. Hogan RT: Socioanalytic theory of personality, in Page MM (ed): *Nebraska Symposium on Motivation: Personality—Current Theory and Research.* Lincoln, NE, University of Nebraska Press, 1983, pp 55–89.
12. Costa PT Jr et al: Facet scales for agreeableness and conscientiousness: A revision of the NEO Personality Inventory. *Pers Indiv Dif* 12:887, 1991.
13. McCrae RR, Costa PT Jr: Validation of the five-factor model across instruments and observers. *J Pers Soc Psychol* 52:81, 1987.
14. John OP et al: Better than the alphabet: Taxonomies of personality-descriptive terms in English, Dutch, and German, in Bonarius HJC et al (eds): *Personality Psychology in Europe: Theoretical and Empirical Developments.* Lisse, Switzerland, Swets & Zeitlinger, 1984, pp 83–100.
15. Erikson EH: *Childhood and Society.* New York, Norton, 1950.
16. Neugarten BL: *Personality in Middle and Later Life.* New York, Atherton, 1964.
17. Vaillant GE: *Adaptation to Life.* Boston, Little, Brown, 1977.
18. Gutmann DL: An exploration of ego configurations in middle and later life, in Neugarten BL (ed): *Personality in Middle and Later Life.* New York, Atherton, 1964, pp 114–148.
19. Levinson DJ et al: *The Seasons of a Man's Life.* New York, Knopf, 1978.
20. Neugarten BL: Personality and aging, in Birren JE, Schaie KW (eds): *Handbook of the Psychology of Aging,* 1st ed. New York, Van Nostrand Reinhold, 1977, pp 626–649.
21. Costa PT Jr et al: Cross-sectional studies of personality in a national sample: 2. Stability in neuroticism, extraversion, and openness. *Psychol Aging* 1:144, 1986.
22. Douglas K, Arenberg D: Age changes, cohort differences, and cultural change on the Guilford-Zimmerman Temperament Survey. *J Gerontol* 33:737, 1978.
23. Mortimer JT et al: Persistence and change in development: The multi-dimensional self-concept, in Baltes PB, Brim OG Jr (eds): *Life-span Development and Behavior,* vol 4. New York: Academic Press, 1982, pp 264–315.
24. Siegler IC et al: Cross-sequential analysis of adult personality. *Dev Psychol* 15:350, 1979.
25. Costa PT Jr, McCrae RR: Personality in adulthood: A six-year longitudinal study of self-reports and spouse ratings on the NEO Personality Inventory. *J Pers Soc Psychol* 54:853, 1988.
26. Jung CG: *Psychological Types.* Princeton, NJ, Princeton University Press, 1923/1971.
27. Costa PT Jr, McCrae RR: *The NEO Personality Inventory Manual.* Odessa, FL, Psychological Assessment Resources, 1985.
28. McCrae RR, Costa PT Jr: Self-concept and the stability of personality: Cross-sectional comparisons of self-reports and ratings. *J Pers Soc Psychol* 43:1282, 1982.
29. Costa PT Jr, McCrae RR: Trait psychology comes of age, in Sonderegger TB (ed): *Nebraska Symposium on Motivation: Psychology and Aging.* Lincoln, NE, University of Nebraska Press, 1992, pp 169–204.
30. Costa PT Jr et al: Enduring dispositions in adult males. *J Pers Soc Psychol* 38:793, 1980.
31. Leon GR et al: Personality stability and change over a 30 year period—Middle age to old age. *J Consult Clin Psychol* 47:517, 1979.
32. Conley JJ: Longitudinal stability of personality traits: A multitrait-multimethod-multioccasion analysis. *J Pers Soc Psychol* 49:1266, 1985.
33. Helson R, Moane G: Personality change in women from college to midlife. *J Pers Soc Psychol* 53:176, 1987.
34. Farrell MP, Rosenberg SD: *Men at Midlife.* Boston, Auburn House, 1981.
35. Costa PT Jr, McCrae RR: Objective personality assessment, in Storandt M et al (eds): *The Clinical Psychology of Aging.* New York, Plenum Press, 1978, pp 119–143.
36. McCrae RR, Costa PT Jr: Adding *Liebe und Arbeit:* The full five-factor model and well-being. *Pers Soc Psychol Bull* 17:227, 1991.
37. Costa PT Jr et al: Personality and vocational interests in an adult sample. *J Applied Psychol* 69:390, 1984.
38. McCrae RR, Costa PT Jr: Personality, coping, and

coping effectiveness in an adult sample. *J Pers* 54:385, 1986.
39. Wiggins JS: A psychological taxonomy of trait-descriptive terms: The interpersonal domain. *J Pers Soc Psychol* 37:395, 1979.
40. Costa PT Jr, McCrae RR: Hypochondriasis, neuroticism, and aging: When are somatic complaints unfounded? *Am Psychol* 40:19, 1985.
41. Costa PT Jr, McCrae RR: Neuroticism, somatic complaints, and disease: Is the bark worse than the bite? *J Pers* 55:299, 1987.
42. Trull TJ: DSM-III-R personality disorders and the five-factor model of personality: An empirical comparison. *J Abnorm Psychol* 101:553, 1992.
43. Costa PT Jr et al: Personality variables in the NHANES-I Followup, in Cornoni-Huntley JC et al (eds): *Health Status and Well-being of the Elderly: National Health and Nutrition Examination Survey I Epidemiologic Follow-up Study.* New York, Oxford University Press, 1990, pp 210–220.
44. Siegler IC et al: Ratings of personality change in patients being evaluated for memory disorders. *Alzheimer Dis Assoc Disord* 5:240, 1991.
45. Ruskin PE: Geropsychiatric consultation in a university hospital: A report on 67 referrals. *Am J Psychiatry* 412:333, 1985.
46. Thompson LW et al: Comparative effectiveness of psychotherapies for depressed elders. *J Consult Clin Psychol* 55:385, 1987.
47. Stroebe M, Stroebe W: *Bereavement and Health.* New York, Cambridge University Press, 1987.
48. McCrae RR, Costa PT Jr: Psychological resilience among widowed men and women: A 10-year follow-up of a national sample. *J Soc Issues* 44:129, 1988.
49. Alexander F: *Psychosomatic Medicine.* New York, Norton, 1950.
50. Luborsky L et al: Onset conditions for psychosomatic symptoms: A comparative review of immediate observation with retrospective research. *Psychosom Med* 35:187, 1973.
51. Cooper T et al: Coronary-prone behavior and coronary heart disease: A critical review. *Circulation* 263:1199, 1981.
52. Costa PT Jr et al: Hostility, agreeableness-antagonism, and coronary heart disease. *Holistic Med* 2:161, 1987.
53. Costa PT Jr et al: Agreeableness vs. antagonism: Explication of a potential risk factor for CHD, in Siegman A, Dembroski TM (eds): *In Search of Coronary Behavior: Beyond Type A.* Hillsdale, NJ, Erlbaum, 1989, pp 41–63.
54. Friedman HS, Booth-Kewley S: The "disease-prone personality": A meta-analytic view of the construct. *Am Psychol* 42:539, 1987.
55. Costa PT Jr, McCrae RR: Personality assessment in psychosomatic medicine: Value of a trait taxonomy, in Fava GA, Wise TN (eds): *Advances in Psychosomatic Medicine,* vol 17: *Research Paradigms in Psychosomatic Medicine.* Basel, Karger, 1987, pp 71–82.
56. Berglund G et al: Personality and reporting of symptoms in normo- and hypertensive 50 year old males. *J Psychosom Res* 19:139, 1975.

Chapter 9

SEXUALITY AND AGING

Judith A. Levy

Aging is marked by a series of psychosocial and physiological changes including decline in the capacity and desire for sexual functioning. The timing, pace, and degree to which aging affects sexual behavior differs by individual, and the process is shaped by such factors as gender, age cohort, previous sexual history, physical and social well-being, partnering opportunities, and libido. The challenge for physicians is to differentiate "normal" changes in sexual behavior from those related to disease, injury, or psychological barriers.[1] Meeting this challenge requires understanding of what constitutes a healthy trajectory of sexual aging and knowing how it differs when transformed by pathologic conditions. Toward this end, this chapter examines the effects of social, psychological, and biological factors on the sexual attitudes, beliefs, and behaviors of older adults.

SEXUAL BEHAVIOR IN LATER LIFE

Although research on the topic is sparse and riddled with methodological problems,[2] a growing body of findings reveals that most people engage in some form of sexual behavior well into old age. These practices form a sexual continuum ranging from purely mental fantasies to a variety of physical practices that may or may not involve a partner. For example, Kinsey found that most of the males and two-thirds of the females who participated in his classic study reported experiencing erotic dreams.[3,4] Masturbation is a common form of sexual pleasure and release for older people, particularly for those without access to a sexual partner.[5,6] Meanwhile, a recent national survey found that nearly one-third of persons over 70 had engaged in at least one act of sexual intercourse over the previous year.[7] Moreover, some individuals find that sexual interest and enjoyment increase with advancing age.[8]

While these studies point to the continued importance of sex and sexuality in late adulthood, mounting evidence also reveals a less positive side from the standpoint of the older person's ability to maintain previous levels of sexual activity. Besides documenting lifelong sexual interest among his respondents, Kinsey's study also discovered a general decline in the reported frequency of sexual activity with age.[3,4] Although the study's small sampling of older adults limits the generalizability of his findings, women appeared to be less sexually responsive after age 50, and men in the study reported similar declines. Approximately 18 percent of the white men that he sampled had experienced erectile failure by age 60; this percentage increased to 75 percent by age 80.

Other, more recent studies support Kinsey's finding that sexual activity declines in frequency with age. For example, the Duke Longitudinal Study assessment of 20 men over the age of 68 showed that the percentage of men who reported engaging in sexual intercourse dropped from 70 percent at the onset of the study to 25 percent over a 10-year period.[9] The Baltimore Longitudinal Study of Aging found that the number of men who reported being partially or totally impotent increased from 7 percent at age 20 to 57 percent at ages 70 to 79.[10] National Opinion Research Center findings from the 1989 General Social Survey showed that the percentage of respondents who reported abstinence over the preceding year grew steadily from 13 percent among respondents under age 30 to 68 percent at age 70 or older.[7]

When these and other research findings are considered, it appears that sex and sexuality are an integral part of older people's lives even with reported reductions in the frequency of coitus with age.[11–13] Also, cumulative evidence indicates that older persons are not homogeneous in their sexual appetites or behavior. Marked variability in interest and capacity is apparent within age groups.[9] Some older men and women are celibate in late adulthood, while others engage in various levels of behavior that, in some cases, may not differ significantly from those when they were younger.[14] Indeed, continuity appears to be the best predictor of a person's sexual activity in later life. Repeated findings show that people who are sexually active in youth are more likely than their less active counterparts to maintain this interest and functioning in old age.[15–18] Similarly, lifelong or prolonged celibacy has been found to be associated with diminished or complete lack of sexual interest in later life.[12] Among those who do remain sexually active, many report that their sexual lives are as good as or better than at an earlier age.[11,14,19] Given this variability, what social and biological factors explain the reported differences in sexual interest, activity, and enjoyment as people age?

SOCIAL FACTORS AFFECTING SEXUAL INTEREST AND BEHAVIOR

At least three social factors contribute to whether or not a person engages in sex in later life. First, to remain sexually active, the individual must feel some desire to do so. Self-perceptions of being sexually attractive appear critical in shaping such libido. Individuals who feel good about their bodies and who perceive themselves as appealing to a sexual partner are more likely to report being sexually interested than those with negative self-images.[20] Older men appear to have the advantage over older women in this regard. Popular judgments about appearance and sexual desirability typically define overt signs of physical aging more harshly in women than in men. Consequently, older women are more likely to view themselves and be viewed by others as less desirable than their male counterparts of the same age.[21]

Most people bring the same beliefs, values, and behaviors to old age that organized their lives at earlier life stages.[22] This patterning holds true for sexual interest and activity. For instance, the attitudes and behaviors of older people born during the early decades of the twentieth century largely were shaped by a social climate of young adulthood in which sexuality was less openly discussed in conversation, the media, or literature. Moreover, birth control was not as readily available or reliable during this period. Because of these factors, many adults born in these older age cohorts grew up viewing sexual activity as appropriately furtive in nature, and they were taught to regard sex as a practice linked closely with procreation. For these individuals, the image of enjoying sex in old age solely for recreational purposes may conflict with long-established personal norms and values. This image of sex as the prerogative of fertile youth and midadulthood is reinforced widely through the media and popular stereotypes of love, romance, and sexual attractiveness.[23] Meanwhile, few positive role models exist for older people who wish to remain sexually active. Indeed, some older adults may need reassurance that sexual desire is normal for persons of any age and that sexual gratification constitutes one of life's enduring entitlements and pleasures.[19]

A second factor affecting sexual activity in old age relates to having access to a sexually functional partner. Because of their greater longevity and tendency to marry men somewhat older than themselves, women are more likely than men to be without a sexual partner in old age due to the death of their spouse.[24] Also for the same reasons, women are the more likely of the two sexes to be the caretaker for a marital or romantic partner who is sexually incapacitated because of advanced age or chronic illness.[25] Among older married and cohabiting couples, both sexes report male sexual dysfunction as the prime reason for not engaging in sexual intercourse.[12,14,19]

Peers and family members also affect the older person's partnering opportunities by encouraging or discouraging an older person's attempts at courtship and by conveying or withholding permission to engage in sex. Some adult children, for example, discourage their widowed or divorced parents from becoming sexually involved because of the potential problems that they perceive will ensue. Their reasons for dampening a parent's sexual liaisons include worries about loss of inheritance, belief that sex in old age is morally offensive, loyalty to the deceased parent, and the wish to avoid potential conflicts that might evolve.[26–29] The opinion of friends, meanwhile, can powerfully influence the older person's conception of appropriate sexual behavior by supporting or deriding the interest.[30]

Having access to a conducive environment that offers both privacy and lacks interference is the third social factor influencing sexual behavior in later life. Although most older people live alone or as part of a marital dyad, those who reside with children or in other joint household arrangements frequently lack the secluded personal space necessary to permit sexual involvement. Similarly, residents of long-term care facilities historically have been subject to prohibitive institutional norms, negative staff attitudes, and environmental barriers that inhibit rather than support or encourage sexual expression. For example, until recently most nursing homes commonly separated married or courting couples.[31] Older persons who wished to maintain marital sexual relations or socially pursue a potential partner were ridiculed, isolated, or punished. Although current legislation now guarantees older residents the right to privacy and the privileges of sexual interaction, a legacy of prejudice and other barriers that limit residents' sexual behavior often remains.[32]

BIOLOGICAL FACTORS AFFECTING SEXUAL INTEREST AND BEHAVIOR

As characterized by Masters and Johnson, the human sexual response cycle normally consists of four phases: desire, excitement, orgasm, and resolution.[12] The revised third edition of the *Diagnostic and Statistical Manual of Mental Disorders* (*DSM* III-R) defines sexual dysfunction as a disruption or inhibition of this cycle. Unfortunately from the standpoint of identifying sexual problems among older people, the discrete boundaries dividing normal age-related changes from functional impairment have not been clearly established.

As men age, the duration and intensity of their sexual response cycle change even in the absence of pathologic conditions.[12] During the *excitement phase,* older men may require several minutes rather than the several seconds of their youth to achieve an erection. Response to visual and tactile stimuli is reduced,[33] and men commonly report being less easily aroused even though desire may remain at levels similar to those when they were younger.[12] During the *plateau stage,* myotonia is less pronounced and the testes may not elevate as close to the perineum as in earlier years. The *orgasm phase* may shorten and feel less urgent; the expulsive force and volume of seminal fluid decrease. By age 60, many men report ejaculating at every second or third act of coitus rather than with every instance. In the *resolution phase* in older men, detumescence occurs more rapidly and the refractory period lengthens before another erection can be attained.

All phases of the response cycle continue among women but with less intensity.[12] In contrast to the 10 to 30 seconds experienced during early adulthood, vaginal expansion and lubrication during the *excitement phase* in older women may take several minutes to produce. During the *plateau phase,* the uterus elevates to a lesser degree for those women who have completed menopause. The duration and intensity of physiological responses to sexual stimulation diminish, and longer stimulation may be required during intercourse to reach orgasm. During the *orgasm phase,* contractions of the orgasmic platform and the uterus continue to occur, but their numbers lessen. Painful contractions may occur during orgasm because of uterine atrophy, but multiple orgasms remain possible.[34] Postmenopausal women typically enter the *resolution phase* more rapidly than their younger counterparts.

The role of hormones in maintaining sexual interest and desire in either sex is unclear. Among women, current thinking holds that estrogens and progesterones do not directly affect libido. Although low estrogen levels are associated with reduced coital activity, it appears that the "hot flashes," loss of vaginal lubrication, and emotional lability of menopausal discomfort are the culprit, not a decrease in sexual drive stemming directly from the hormone itself.[12] While administered estrogen has been found to enhance orgasm, this effect may reflect relief from menopausal symptoms rather than direct hormonal stimulation. Progestin treatment, which is used to protect against the adverse effects of estrogen replacement therapy, appears to exert little or no influence on sexual functioning.[35] While the research findings are somewhat conflicting, a small number of studies point to the influence of androgens in promoting sexual interest in women although the mechanism through which they work is unknown.[36] In the absence of an adequate theoretical rationale to explain the phenomenon and without a larger body of supportive data to justify its use, the efficacy of combining estrogen and androgen to treat sexual dysfunction in menopausal women remains unclear.

The processes that influence sexual desire in men result from the role of psychosocial, hormonal, neural, and vascular mechanisms in mediating both the response cycle and reproductive capacities of men as they grow older.[36] Primary testicular changes that are clearly associated with hormonal aging include reduction in daily sperm production[37] and reduced sperm motility.[38] Leydig cell mass is reduced and nocturnal penile tumescence (NPT) decreases in frequency, rigidity, and duration.[39,40] Many men, however, remain sexually active and have regular intercourse in the presence of marked decrements in erectile capacity as measured by NPT.[41] Age-related alterations of the central neurotransmitter activity also result in disturbance of the circadian rhythmicity of endocrine secretions including circulating testosterone.[42] Total, free, and bioavailable plasma testosterone concentrations appear to decline with age accompanied by alterations in the CNS pituitary mechanisms controlling gonadal function.[43]

Although it is tempting and theoretically defensible to posit that reduced testosterone levels contribute to male declines in sexual activity and NPT, this relationship has yet to be experimentally demonstrated.[36] Indeed, some current research findings counter this theory. For example, some older men produce testosterone in levels typical of younger men. Yet a study of such men found the same declines in sexual functioning usually associated with aging and common to reduced testosterone output.[39] Similarly, a study of 220 men that correlated questionnaire data with hormonal levels found that only a small part of the self-reported declines in sexual functioning were attributable to reductions in free testosterone levels and none to total testosterone levels.[44] These findings, coupled with results from other studies, suggest that testosterone plays a secondary and minor role compared with other factors in explaining reduced sexual capabilities. Although the relationships have yet to be empirically demonstrated, two competing hypotheses speculate that either an impairment of monoaminergic pathways to the brain or cell desensitization to the effects of androgen may be responsible.[45] Without substantiating evidence, however, administering androgens to offset the latter effect is not recommended except with clearly hypogonadal men.

MENOPAUSE IN WOMEN

Menopause, with its connotations of "the change of life," commonly is regarded as a sociobiological event marking a woman's entry into a new, but older life phase. Culturally, depending upon the norms and expectations of the society in which she lives, becoming menopausal confers or negates certain socially prescribed privileges and roles for women. Medically, menopause largely has been viewed as a disease entity because of the psychosocial and physiological problems associated with it.[46] For most women, menopause begins and ends between ages 45 and 55. A woman is considered menopausal when her menses has ceased for a full year. Thus, the completion of menopause can only be determined after the fact.[47]

Prior to the turn of the century, fewer than half the female babies born in the United States survived childhood infectious diseases or maternal morbidity to enter middle age and experience menopause. Because of the increased longevity that results from postindustrial living, the majority of today's women will experience a climacteric. An increasing number of these women will enter menopause at a comparatively early age because of the increased number of hysterectomies performed in contemporary society. Thus, a large portion of American women will live a third or more of their lives while postmenopausal.[48]

Menopause itself, which involves a complex set of biological and psychological processes and symptoms, exerts its influence on sexuality in a number of ways. Commonly held beliefs about menopause equate its occurrence with declining libido and a loss of "womanliness." These negative associations help perpetuate an image of menopause as heralding the end of a woman's desirability and sexual identity.[47] Biologically, severe drops in estrogen and progesterone associated with cessation of ovarian functioning can produce increased irritability, moodiness, sleeplessness, and depression in some but not all women.[46] This lability in turn can affect sexual responsiveness and enjoyment.[49] Also, the rate and quantity of vaginal mucus secretion during sexual arousal typically is reduced.[50] Inadequate lubrication can result in dyspareunia (painful intercourse) and vulvovaginitis. Vaginismus, or the involuntary constriction of the outer one-third of the vaginal barrel, may arise secondary to dyspareunia or other causes, thus making penile penetration impossible.[12] Due to thinning of the vaginal wall and an increased propensity to tearing of the vaginal tissue, older women may need to urinate more frequently and in large volumes to avoid cystitis related to prolonged coital friction.[51] The problem of vaginal dryness can be alleviated by using a water-solution lubricant and also the use of topical or oral estrogen replacement when desired and warranted.[12] Regular vaginal exercises have been found effective in treating vaginismus.[49]

Although little research has examined how women view the influence of menopause on their sexuality, the few data that are available suggest that their experiences vary widely.[48] Some women report experiencing a loss of libido and reduced involvement beginning with the arrival of menopause. Others report that their sexual interests and practices remain unaffected. Still others report enhanced sexual feelings and enjoyment. Regardless of response, women frequently cite two positive advantages to menopause.[53] First, the cessation of menses can bring welcome relief from the bodily discomforts and hygienic concerns related to managing monthly periods. Second, a large proportion of women also appreciate that menopause frees them from worrying about family planning and unwanted pregnancies.

"MENOPAUSE" IN MEN

Middle age for men often is marked by dissatisfaction with previous life choices and a search for more satisfying alternatives. Having devoted their primary energies to work and job achievements, many men at midlife discover a new appreciation for affective affiliations and the positive value of developing new aspects of their lives and personalities.[54] The self-reflections and concerns about the future that sometimes accompany this life stage can manifest themselves in worries about aging, fears of reduced sexual performance, and general regret for life opportunities that have gone unrealized. These feelings can mobilize small to major changes in the man's life. Culturally, although lacking the dramatic physical transformations associated with the climacteric in women, such instances of "male menopause" have been the subject of popular humor and deprecating anecdotes. It must be emphasized, however, that the scientific and clinical characterization of this syndrome remain largely anecdotal and that it represents the exception rather than the rule in middle-aged men, most of whom experience the midlife passage without any dramatic change in sexual life trajectory.

Clinically male menopause, also known as the *male climacteric syndrome,* refers to a rare condition among middle-aged men who experience the symptoms associated with female menopause at a level producing serious interpersonal or psychological consequences. Symptoms of the male climacteric include irritability, memory loss, changes in libido, and depression.[55] There are several causes of this disorder. In line with the propensity for midlife changes, the most common psychological explanation holds that the syndrome stems directly from the middle-aged man's confrontation with growing older, recognition of life's unmet expectations and limitations, and an awareness of reduced sexual functioning that sparks fears of sexual failure.[48] Biological explanations point to reduced hormonal production as the causal agent resulting in a range of psychosocial complaints, loss of libido, and severe alterations of the sexual response cycle.[12,56] A third perspective attributes the syndrome to an interaction of both biological and social influences. In the absence of a body of research to definitively support any of these hypotheses, psychological therapy typically is recommended to address the psychosocial symptoms of the disorder if not its underlying cause.

THE EFFECTS OF HEALTH, ILLNESS, AND MEDICATION ON SEXUALITY

Despite the appeal of assuming that good health enhances sexual capabilities, research findings that attempt to link physical well-being with the propensity to engage in sexual intercourse often are inconclusive or contradictory. Two studies offer cases in point. Evidence from the Duke Longitudinal Study of Aging, supports the position that better physical health increases the likelihood of a person's engaging in a sexual act.[57] Among men 65 to 79, basal metabolic rates, maximum breathing capacity, and serum cholesterol concentrations were found to correlate with differences in sexual activity.[10] Conversely, physical health was not a significant factor separating the celibate from the sexually active in a study of 70-year-olds in Sweden.[58] Rather, good ratings of mental health, positive attitudes toward sex, and high sexual drive when younger were associated with increased levels of sexual activity in later life.

While it is unclear if good health promotes sexual behavior, poor health clearly dampens libido and negatively alters the sexual response.[36] Surgical or traumatic damage to the spinal cord, peripheral nerves, or reproductive organs often is found to impair sexual response and inhibit orgasm. Similarly, surgery related to pelvic cancer or reconstruction of the vagina reduces sexual response by producing genital numbness in some women. Neurological diseases, such as multiple sclerosis, can alter sexual capabilities by affecting the spinal cord or peripheral nerve. Further, type II diabetes, which is particularly prevalent among older persons, is known to impair both sexual arousal and the sexual response cycle in both sexes. This also is true of both endocrine and metabolic disorders.

Impotence, or the persistent inability to attain or maintain an erection that permits satisfactory sexual relations, is a common presenting symptom among older men (see Chap. 114). The likelihood of impotence increases with age and is believed to affect 10 to 20 million men in the United States.[59] Despite worries to the contrary, enlargement of the prostate gland, which is common in older men, does not appear to be a limiting factor.[60] Neither does prostatic surgery in the absence of psychological trauma and when conducted with special efforts to preserve sexual function. Generally with such surgery, the nerve and blood supply to the penis are not affected, although expulsion of semen into the bladder is a common side effect. Diabetes mellitus is, perhaps, the most common physical disorder associated with male erectile dysfunction.[36] Psychosocial influences also are believed to exert a major influence.[56]

Disease and illness that disfigure the body or negatively alter the person's body image also can reduce libido and discourage sexual activity.[60] For instance, individuals who have undergone mastectomy or colostomy must cope with both the side effects of treatment and the possibility of rejection by a sexual partner. Although hysterectomy does not appear to have adverse physiological effects,[60] it does have psychological consequences when the woman equates desirability and sexual satisfaction with procreative capability.[62] Men who have experienced prostate surgery sometimes confront similar threats to their sexual self-esteem and confidence.[12] Meanwhile, incontinence can rob both men and women of a satisfactory sex life.[63] Incontinence affects a large proportion of older adults, with mature women at particularly high risk because of previous perinatal damage to the supporting tissues of the pelvic floor.[64] Its presence is a source of embarrassment, distress, and depression. Involuntary urine loss, particularly when precipitated by sexual exertion, can lead to avoidance of sexual activity by the person and possible rejection by a partner.

Beside physical difficulties, mental disorders also should be included among diseases that transform sexual behavior.[36] Particularly in hospitals and long-term care facilities where lack of privacy limits intimate behaviors, senility produces behavior considered sexually offensive when older people forget to keep their bodies covered or no longer remember social injunctions against masturbating in public view. Mental depression also is commonly associated with lowered sexual drive at any age. Because depression is more common among women than men, they are the more likely of the two sexes to be affected.[64] Declines in sexual responsiveness and orgasmic function also can be attributed to the use of antidepressants and beta blockers. Their ubiquity in the treatment of clinical depression, however, confounds attempts to determine how much of an observed decline in sensual interest or behavior is due to the mental disorder and how much to its treatment.[65]

Finally, in terms of the indirect impact of illness of sexuality, drugs and alcohol are potential inhibitors of sexual relations.[34] In general, older people are heavy users of prescription drugs and over-the-counter medications.[65] They frequently combine these substances with the consumption of alcohol. Narcotics and barbiturates inhibit sexual behavior by delaying or eliminating orgasmic capacity.[34] Sleeping pills reduce alertness and may blunt interest in sex at bedtime. Antihistamines used as nasal decongestants sometimes dry the vagina, thus increasing the likelihood of painful coitus. Hypertensive medications potentially affect sexual capacity in both sexes by depleting catecholamines in the central nervous system. Antihypertensive agents can impair female sexual capacity through their influence on the peripheral nerves involved in vaginal congestion.

COUNSELING THE OLDER PATIENT

In an older person, any dramatic transformation of sexual interest or behavior that has become problematic or is inconsistent with earlier life patterning warrants investigation and possible intervention. From a diagnostic standpoint, sexual decline or dysfunction may be symptomatic of an existing illness. When it arises from the side effect of medication such as antidepressants or antihypertensives, regaining sexual capacity may call for the use of an alternative treatment with fewer or no inhibiting properties. Patient reports of sexual difficulties also may signal the unintended misuse of prescribed drugs, overmedication, or harmful lifestyle practices such as alcoholism and illegal drug use. Finally, sexual dysfunction may warn of undiagnosed medical problems.

As is true of adults of all ages, older people differ in their openness to sexual counseling, obtaining treatment, or making major life changes. The practice of geriatric medicine includes providing older adults with the clinical information or medical intervention needed to maintain or achieve a rewarding sex life. Meeting this responsibility begins with establishing an open and encouraging atmosphere in which sexuality is considered a natural part of older people's lives. It involves making a commitment to provide the time and effort needed to work with patients in communicating and identifying their sexual problems to achieve satisfactory outcomes.

In general, health professionals tend to be uncomfortable talking about sex with patients of any age.[66] Many avoid discussing sexual matters with their older patients because of time demands and the erroneous belief that people over 60 aren't interested.[67] This neglect is particularly unfortunate in cases in which surgery or illness, such as diabetes or myocardial infarction, call for accurate information and practical guidelines for maintaining or resuming sexual activity.[21] In addressing such problems, medical and nursing staff may benefit from in-service training aimed at dispelling the myths that bias their reaction to sexuality among those who are older. Counseling or workshops designed to educate family members also can yield greater acceptance of the older person's sexual identity and practices.[68]

Sexual behavior at any age requires an investment of time, psychosocial involvement, and energy. As is true for all age groups, the daily pressures and competing demands of living can interfere with the older person's pursuit or enjoyment of a sexual relationship. Sometimes clinical intervention can be as simple as successfully encouraging the older person to rearrange daily schedules to permit more opportunities to initiate and savor romance. This advice may be especially salient in cases in which overfamiliarity and sexual monotony have reduced romantic interest between long-term partners.[19] Establishing new behavioral patterns, such as engaging in sex in new locations or indulging in neglected or untried techniques, may break the monotony and rekindle interest. Referral to sexual enhancement programs for older adults can help those who wish to develop a more creative and rewarding sexual life.[68] Typically these programs focus on communication exercises and sexual techniques.[68,69] By overtly condoning sexual interest and activity, such programs help counter the myth that to be old is to be sexless. Also by delivering factual information about aging and sexuality, enhancement programs provide a forum for promoting useful strategies and techniques for dealing with age-related sexual problems and concerns.[70]

In some instances, courtship may be one of the areas perceived as troubling. Many older people find themselves single for the first time in decades, through either divorce or the death of a spouse. Given how much dating etiquette and the person are likely to have changed since earlier courtship, dating after so long a period of inactivity may be psychologically threatening. The widowed or divorced person may benefit from being encouraged to seek a potential partner or from suggestions on how to locate one. Toward this end, a number of excellent advice books on dating and sexuality in later life are available at bookstores.[71,72] These primers provide practical advice on a wide range of topics including tips on finding a partner, reassurance about embarrassment concerning an aging body, fears about sexually transmitted diseases, and guidelines for establishing a rewarding sexual relationship. For the most part, later life provides an opportunity for exploring untried sexual options and forging new patterns of social relationships that many older people appreciate. Some of these options may differ considerably from earlier life choices. For example, some older people prefer to practice nonmarital sex rather than marrying for various reasons including inheritance concerns, tax status, and social security eligibility advantages.[7]

Not all expressions of sexuality, of course, require access to another person. Masturbation, enjoyment of visual erotica, and sexual fantasizing can be practiced solo. Moreover, not only does engaging in these pursuits increase sexual appetite, but masturbation contributes to the maintenance of aging genitalia.[73] Unfortunately from the standpoint of the rewards that these practices offer, many older adults were reared to believe that these actions are morally wrong.[74] Older individuals, and possibly concerned family members, may need reassurance that sexual fantasies, interests, and actions in later life are not unnatural.

Many older people confuse a normal decline in sexual responses with permanent functional loss. Yet slower arousal and less frequent sexual ejaculation is normal to the aging process. Because older men may interpret these declines as signs of impending impotence or fear the loss of orgasmic capabilities, education to understand these changes may help allay unnecessary fears. For the most part, men vary considerably in the timing and extent to which they personally experience or are troubled by such changes.[73] Unfortunately, their declines can have a ripple effect that adds to worry in a relationship. A woman may interpret impotence or slower excitation in her partner as a sign that he is sexually bored with her or that she is no longer sexually desirable.[74] Explaining the process of normal sexual aging while also highlighting its potential for greater emotional fulfillment and intimacy may ameliorate some of this fear. In short, men need to know that sexual changes related to aging are normal; women need to know that such changes in male partners are not caused by themselves.

The limitations and side effects of a severe illness pose a series of challenges for the older person who wants to remain sexually active. Older adults need information about the possible side effects of medication they are taking so that they can report problems that occur. Following surgery or with physical impairment, new positions or activities may be necessary to compensate for pain or frailty, or to avoid further injury. Fantasies and masturbation are rich outlets when hospitalization or the person's physical condition rule out intercourse or other forms of coupled sex. Illness also can dampen interest in sexual relations by creating strife, tension, or misunderstandings. For example, a patient's feeling of helplessness or a partner's response to the demands of care giving can interfere with sexual exchanges. Cerebrovascular accidents, which may involve mental and physical impairment, can raise worries about being sexually appealing to a partner. So can the management of incontinence or colostomy because of the external devices needed to control body wastes. Similarly, surgery and treatment that visually alter or disfigure the body may engender fears of rejection that result in the person's avoiding sex. Reassurance and useful coping strategies often are gained by participation in a self-help group of people with similar conditions and concerns.

Following illness, some older people may avoid sexual intercourse because they fear triggering an illness episode through strenuous activity.[75] Such worries are particularly common with myocardial infarction, as both the patient and spouse may be afraid that sexual activity will prompt a second infarction or death. Typically, it is safe to recommend that sexual relations gradually be resumed after 3 months, though male patients should avoid using a push-up position above their partner.[75] Psychosocially, some men who practice abstinence following a major health incidence may experience functional difficulties when resuming activities. In others, the difficulties in retrospect may have preceded the incident, a situation discovered in one study of men who complained of erectile problems following myocardial infarction.[76] For some men, particularly those who equate virility with rapid erections and hurried intercourse, illness may relieve self-induced pressure to perform at youthful levels that they no longer can sustain.[9] Similarly, women who have never enjoyed sex or intercourse sometimes use illness to justify avoiding or abandoning sexual activity altogether.

Even when sexual interest is high, resumption of sexual activity following an extended period of abstinence can be difficult. "Disuse attrition" describes any condition in which prolonged celibacy or infrequent intercourse results in reduced sexual capability. Some older women who have sex less than once a month, for example, report discomfort at penetration.[60] Among older men, "widower's syndrome" refers to a condition of temporary impotence experienced when attempting to resume sexual intercourse with a new partner following the death of a spouse.[11,62] This syndrome is most likely to occur when the former wife's illness demanded a long period of sexual abstinence.

Lifestyle choices and personal habits also affect sexual interest and capabilities. Negative influences include lack of exercise, reduced lung capacity from smoking, poor nutrition, and excessive drug or alcohol consumption. The latter abuse can become more pronounced following retirement, as some older adults use social or private drinking to fill unstructured time. As is true for any age, low or moderate levels of alcohol consumption can heighten desire by reducing some of the fear or anxiety that might inhibit a sexual encounter. At higher levels, however, reduced vasocongestion typically impairs sexual response.[34]

Getting older also is associated with changes in sleep patterns including an increased number of arousals and wakeful periods after sleep onset, poorer sleep efficiency, and less time spent in slow wave sleep (see Chap. 112).[40] Although the effects of these disturbances on sexuality have not been systematically evaluated, they are believed to contribute to erectile failure in men and loss of sexual interest due to tiredness in both sexes. The "hot flashes" that often accompany menopause are a common culprit in producing sleep disturbances in middle-aged women, although the problem persists for a small proportion of women for the remainder of their lives.[48] Hot flash episodes, which reflect acute changes in cardiovascular and neurovascular function, can be treated by stabilizing hypothalamic functioning through estrogen replacement therapy.[77] Stress reduction and biofeedback techniques that counter the flushing experience have also shown promise.[78] Some women also benefit from taking 400 units of vitamin E twice a day.[79]

Because of the low incidence and possible undetected presence of sexually transmitted diseases (STDs) in older populations, most physicians do not screen for these disorders among their elderly patients.[80] Evidence indicates, however, that older adults are sexually active both inside and outside long-term stable relationships.[2] Also, rising rates of marital separation and divorce among older age cohorts increase the likelihood of exposure to infection through newly acquired partners. Among women, reduced lubrication, thinning of the epithelium, and narrowing of the vaginal canal common to aging add to their susceptibility to STD infection.[80] Moreover, 10 percent of all AIDS cases each year over the last decade occurred among people 55 years of age or older.[81] Most of these cases resulted from receiving blood transfusions before effective screening procedures were developed. Nonetheless, because of the extended latency of the virus, the number of sexually transmitted cases of AIDS among older persons can be expected to grow as young and middle-aged adults who are infected with the virus move into later life stages.[82] Thus, STDs including AIDS may become increasingly more common among older adults.

If old age brings a loss of certain forms of sexual capacity, it also heralds opportunities and advantages for new forms of sexual expression. Often, grown children have left home to establish their own households, giving the couple added privacy. Postmenopausal infertility frees many women to feel more responsive without fear of unwanted pregnancy. The longer period needed for most men to develop an erection and to reach climax can result in greater foreplay, communication, and sharing. Intimacy and affection are enhanced through greater attention to hugging, kissing, and caressing.[18,19] Indeed sex may be better than ever.

REFERENCES

1. Schiavi RC: Sexuality and aging in men. *Soc Sci Study Sex* 1:227, 1990.
2. Levy JA, Albrecht GA: Methodological considerations in research on sexual behavior and AIDS among older people, in Riley M et al (eds): *AIDS in an Aging Society.* New York, Springer, 1989, 96.
3. Kinsey AC et al: *Sexual Behavior in the Human Male.* Philadelphia, Saunders, 1948.
4. Kinsey AC et al: *Sexual Behavior in the Human Female.* Philadelphia, Saunders, 1953.
5. Downey L: Intergenerational change in sexual behavior: A belated look at Kinsey's males. *Arch Sex Behav* 9:297, 1980.
6. Doress PB, Siegal D: The potential of the second half of life, in Doress D et al (eds): *Ourselves, Growing Older.* New York, Simon, Brown, 1987, p xxi.
7. Smith RW: Adult sexual behavior in 1989: Number of partners, frequency of intercourse and risk of AIDS. *Fam Plann Perspect* 3:102, 1991.
8. George LK, Weiler SJ: Sexuality in middle and late life. *Arch Gen Psychiatry* 38:919, 1981.
9. Pfeiffer E et al: Sexual behavior in aged men and women. *Arch Gen Psychiatry* 19:753, 1988.
10. Martin CE: Factors affecting sexual functioning in 60–79 year old married males. *Arch Sex Behav* 10:399, 1981.
11. Butler RN, Lewis MI: *Aging and Mental Health,* 2d ed. St. Louis, Mosby, 1977, 112.
12. Masters WH, Johnson VE: *Human Sexual Response.* Boston, Little, Brown, 1966, p 233.
13. Kaluger G, Kaluger MF: *Human Development: The Span of Life,* 2d ed. St. Louis, Mosby, 1979, p 441.
14. Starr BD, Weiner MB: *The Starr-Weiner Report on Sex and Sexuality in the Mature Years.* New York, Briarcliff Manor, 1981.
15. Pfeiffer E, Davis G: Determinants of sexual behavior in middle and old age. *J Am Geriatr Soc* 20:151, 1972.
16. Irwin T: Sexuality in later years. *Physician's World* 1:53, 1973.
17. Corbett L: The 1st sexual taboo: Sex in old age. *Med Aspects Hum Sexuality* 15:117, 1981.
18. White CB: Sexual interest, attitudes, knowledge, and sexual history in relation to sexual behavior in the institutionalized aged. *Arch Sex Behav* 11(1):11, 1982.
19. Comfort A: Sexuality in later life, in Birren JE, Sloane RB (eds): *A Handbook of Health and Aging.* Englewood Cliffs, NJ, Prentice-Hall, 1980, p 885.
20. Stimpson A et al: Sexuality and self-esteem among the elderly. *Res Aging* 3:228, 1981.
21. Byers JP: Sexuality and the elderly. *Geriatr Nursing* 1293, 1983.
22. Neugarten BL: Personality change in late life: A developmental perspective, in Eisendorfer C, Lawton MP (eds): *The Psychology of Adult Development and Aging.* Washington, DC, American Psychological Association, 1973, p 311.
23. Demos V, Jache A: When you care enough: An analysis of attitudes towards aging in humorous birthday cards. *Gerontologist* 21:209,
24. Riley MW: Women, men, and the lengthening life course, in Rossi A (ed): *Gender and the Life Course.* Hawthorne, NY, Aldine, 1985, p 333.
25. Chappell N: Aging and social care, in Binstock RH, George LK (eds): *Handbook of Aging and the Social Science.* San Diego, Academic, 1990, p 438.
26. Stanford D: Sexuality and aging, in Eisendorfer et al (eds): *Mental Health and the Elderly.* New York, Grune & Stratton, 1984.
27. Rubin I: Sexual life after forty and before seventy, in Brecher R, Brecher E (eds): *Analysis of Human Sexual Response.* Boston, Little, Brown, 1965, p 251.
28. Woods N: Human sexuality and the healthy elderly, in Brown E (ed): *Readings in Gerontology,* 2d ed. St. Louis, Mosby, 1978, p 84.
29. Robinson PK: The sociological perspective, in Weg RB (ed): *Sexuality in the Later Years: Roles and Behavior.* New York, Academic, 1983, p 82.
30. Costello MK: Intimacy and aging. *Am J Nursing* 75:1330, 1973.
31. Falk G, Falk U: Sexuality and the aged. *Nursing Outlook* 28:51, 1980.
32. Patients Rights Section, Marital Privacy, 405 1121

(K(14)), in Kander ML, May K (eds): *Federal Regulations Guidelines for Directors of Nursing.* Owings Mill, MD, National Law Publishing, p 710.
33. Pearlman CK: Slower sexual response of the aged. *Med Aspects Hum Sexuality* 11:119, 1977.
34. Sultan FE, Chambless DL: Sexual functioning, in Blechman EA, Brownell KD (eds): *Handbook of Behavioral Medicine for Women.* New York, Pergamon, 1988, p 92.
35. Dennerstein L et al: Hormones and sexuality: Effect of estrogen and progestogen. *Obstet Gynecol* 56:316, 1980.
36. Schiavi RC: Impact of chronic disease and medication on sexual functioning. Invited paper for the McArthur Foundation Research Network on Successful Mid-Life Development Meeting, New York, 1992.
37. Neaves WB et al: Leydig cell numbers, daily sperm production and serum gonadotropin levels in aging men. *J Clin Endocrinol Metab* 59:756, 1984.
38. Nieschlag E et al: Reproductive functions in young fathers and grandfathers. *J Clin Endocrinol* 23:527, 1982.
39. Harman SM et al: Reproductive hormones in aging men: I. Measurement of sex steroids, basal luteinizing hormone and Leydig cell response to human chorionic gonadotropin. *J Clin Endocrinol Metab* 51:35, 1980.
40. Harman SM et al: Reproductive hormones in aging men: II. Basal pituitary gonadotropins and gondadotropin responses to basal luteinizing hormone–releasing hormone. *J Clin Endocrinol Metab* 54:547, 1982.
41. Shiavi RC et al: The relationship between pituitary-gonadal function and sexual behavior in healthy aging men. *Psychosomatic Med* 53:363, 1991.
42. McGinty D et al: Circadian and sleep-related modulation of hormone levels: Changes with aging, in Sowers JR, Felicetta, JV (eds): *The Endocrinology of Aging.* New York: Raven, 1988.
43. Winters S et al: The gonadotropin-suppressive activity of androgen is increased in elderly men. *Metabolism* 33:1052, 1984.
44. Tsitouras PD et al: Relationship of serum testosterone to sexual activity in healthy elderly men. *J Gerontol* 37:288, 1982.
45. Davidson JM: Sexuality and aging, in Hazzard WR et al: *Principles of Geriatric Medicine and Gerontology,* 2d ed. New York, McGraw-Hill, 1989, p 108.
46. Goodman M: Toward a biology of menopause. *J Women Culture Society* 5:739, 1980.
47. Sheehy G: *The Silent Passage.* New York, Random House, 1991.
48. Strickland B: Menopause, in Blechman EA, Brownell KD (eds): *Handbook of Behavioral Medicine for Women.* New York, Pergamon, 1988, p 41.
49. McCoy NW et al: Relationship among sexual behavior, hot flashes, and hormone levels in premenopausal women. *Arch Sex Behav* 14:385, 1985.
50. Semmens JP et al: Effects of estrogen on vaginal function in postmenopausal women. *JAMA* 248:445, 1982.
51. Charatan FB: Sexual function in old age. *Med Aspects Hum Sexuality* 12:151, 1978.
52. Kegel A: Sexual functions of the pubococcygeus muscle. *West J Surg Obstet Gynecol* 60:521, 1952.
53. McKinlay S, McKinlay J: Selected Studies on the Menopause. *J Biosoc Sci* 5:533, 1973.
54. Levinson DJ: *The Seasons of a Man's Life.* New York, Knopf, 1978.
55. Lear MW: Is there a male menopause? in Gordon C, Johnson G (eds): *Readings in Human Sexuality.* New York, Harper & Row, 1980, p 273.
56. Kolodny R et al: *Textbook of Sexual Medicine.* St Louis, Little, Brown, 1979.
57. Pfeiffer E, Davis G: Determinants of sexual behavior in middle and old age. *J Am Geriatr Soc* 20:151, 1972.
58. Persson G: Sexuality in a 70 year old urban population. *J Psychosomat Res* 24:335,
59. Furlow WL: Prevalence of impotence in the United States. *Med Aspects Hum Sex* 19:13, 1985.
60. Riportella-Muller R: Sexuality in the elderly: A review, in McKinney K, Sprecher S (eds): *Human Sexuality: The Societal and Interpersonal Context.* Norwood, NJ, Ablex, 1989, p 210.
61. Marron KR: Sexuality with aging. *Geriatrics* 37:135, 1982.
62. Sarrel LJ, Sarrel PM: *Sexual Turning Points: The Seven Stages of Adult Sexuality.* New York, Macmillan, 1984.
63. Jeter KF, Wayne DP: Incontinence in the American home: A survey of 35,000 people. *J Am Geriatr Soc* 379, 1990.
64. Wisochki PA, Keuthen NK: Later life, in Blechman EA, Brownell KD (eds): *Handbook of Behavioral Medicine for Women.* New York, Pergamon, 1988, p 48.
65. Capel W, Stewart G: The management of drug abuse in aging populations: New Orleans findings. *J Drug Issues* 1:114, 1971.
66. Rienzo BA: The impact of aging on human sexuality. *J Sch Health* 55:66, 1985.
67. Shover LR. *Prime Time: Sexual Health for Men over Fifty.* New York, Holt, 1984.
68. Driver JD, Detrich D: Elders and sexuality. *Nurs Care* Feb:8, 1982.
69. White C et al: Sexual education for aged people, people who work with the aged, and families of aged people. *Final Report to the Andrus Foundation,* 1980.
70. Rowland KF, Haynes SN: A sexual enhancement program for elderly couples. *J Sex Marital Ther* 4:91, 1978.
71. Grice J: *How to Find Romance after 40.* New York, Evans, 1985.
72. Gresehnfeld M, Newman J: *Love, Sex, and Intimacy after 50.* New York, Fawcett Combine, 1991.
73. Weg R: Beyond babies and orgasms, in Hess E, Markson E (eds): *Growing Old in America* 1985, p 206.
74. Smith J, Smith L: Co-marital sex and the sexual freedom movement. *J Sex Res* 6:131, 1989.
75. Griggs W: Staying well while growing old: Sex and the elderly. *Am J Nurs* 78:1353, 1978.
76. Dhabuwala CB et al: Myocardial infarction and its influence on male sexual function. *Arch Sex Behav* 15:599, 1986.
77. Brecher E: *Love, Sex, and Aging.* Boston, Little, Brown, 1984.
78. Stevenson DW, Delprato DJ: Multiple component self-control program for menopausal hot flashes. *J Behav Ther Exp Psychiatry* 10:137, 1983.
79. Nachtigall L, Heilman J: *Estrogen: The Facts Can Change Your Life.* New York, Harper & Row, 1987.
80. Ehrhardt AA, Wasserheit JN: Age, gender, and sexual

risk behaviors for sexually transmitted diseases in the United States, in Wasserheit SO et al (eds): *Research Issues in Human Behavior and Sexually Transmitted Disease in the AIDS Era.* Washington, DC, American Society for Microbiology, 1991, p 97.
81. Stall R et al: The social epidemiology of AIDS and HIV infection among older Americans, in Riley MW et al (eds): *AIDS in an Aging Society.* New York, Springer, 1989, p 60.
82. Riley MW: AIDS and older people: The overlooked segment of the population, in Riley MW et al (eds): *AIDS in an Aging Society.* New York, Springer, 1989, p 3.

Chapter 10

SOCIOLOGY OF AGING

George L. Maddox

The perspective of gerontologists and geriatricians on the processes and outcomes of human aging has been persistently and distinctively multidisciplinary and action-oriented over the history of these relatively new fields of inquiry and practice. Four decades of research and scholarship have reinforced the perceived utility of studying aging as a synergistic product of interacting biological, behavioral, and social factors. Each type of factor is known to be diverse and, to a degree yet to be fully determined, modifiable. Gerontologists and geriatricians have, however, already illustrated in research and demonstrations the relevance of a venerable maxim of experimental and clinical sciences: If you want to understand something, try to change it.

In gerontology and geriatrics, the understanding required for realistic and responsible testing of the modifiability of aging processes and outcomes necessarily involves not only the research of biological scientists but also the research of behavioral and social scientists. Commitment among gerontologists and geriatricians to the intellectual interdependence of the specific disciplines which share an interest in human aging remains deep and persistent. Research and scholarship in the social sciences generally, and in sociology in particular, have continued to complement the work of biological gerontologists and geriatricians who themselves tend to perceive and acknowledge that in understanding human development, biology reveals what is possible in human life, not just what is necessary.

Four propositions that summarize a contemporary sociological perspective in aging outline the argument which will be developed in this chapter.

1. The well-documented diversity of aging processes and outcomes can be satisfactorily explained only by inclusion of contextual factors external to individuals; the material and social resources available to and differentially distributed over the life course by societies constitute key externalities affecting human development over the life course.
2. In human development, past does tend to be prologue. Consequently, the roots of differential aging are found early in the life course and suggest the wisdom of identifying and assessing early in life the risks factors not only for survival but also for well-being in later life.
3. The potential for modifying the processes and outcomes of aging by social policy is suggested generally by the observed effects of social resource allocations on morbidity, mortality, and well-being in later life and specifically by the demonstrable beneficial effects of particular public policy initiatives.
4. Public policy intended to shape the future of how one ages may be usefully informed by scientific information; but, in the final analysis, effective public policy regarding aging tends to reflect and reinforce the dominant values and preferences of society and the political feasibility of the particular policy proposals regarding the distribution of resources across the life course.

Critical overviews of gerontological research underlying these propositions are conveniently summarized in articles by Rowe and Kahn[1] and by Maddox.[2] These articles, in turn, reference a large and diverse multidisciplinary literature relevant to this chapter. Additionally, *The Annual Review of Gerontology and Geriatrics*[3] focuses specifically on documenting and discussing the theoretical issues, and it illustrates a wide variety of practical implications of diversity in the processes and experience of human aging from the perspective of economists, epidemiologists, sociologists, and public policy analysts.

DIVERSITY IN AGING

As normally practiced and taught, scientific research places considerable emphasis on empirically derived succinct generalizations about various phenomena under study and, consequently, tends to be reductionistic. Although scientific investigators are aware that every statistical mean summarizing a complex array of values in a data set inexorably has a companion estimate of variance around the mean, measures of central tendency appear to be more interesting and memorable than measures of dispersion in reports of scientific inquiry. The neglect of measures of dispersion reflects in part a concern that variance may be attributable to errors in measurement as well as real substantive differences in the phenomena observed. While measurement error is a legitimate concern, there is no longer reason to doubt substantial intraspecies diversity in the processes and outcomes of aging among all animals or that the diversity in human aging explained by contextual factors external to the individual is substantial.

Societies are Natural Experiments

Societies are large-scale natural experiments in the effects of differential availability and allocation of material and social resources on the processes and outcomes of aging. These effects appear at three different levels: *macro* (societal), *meso* (institutional), and *micro* (milieu).[4]

Macrosocial Effects

Macrosocial (societal) effects can be illustrated in at least two ways. One illustration of the effects of resource availability on aging focuses on implications of the distinction between societies which are more or less developed. The other notes the implications of socioeconomic differentiation in resource distribution within a society.

Differential Resources Both historical and contemporary demographic and epidemiology evidence document (see Chap. 11) convincingly that survival to old age as an average expectation at birth is a recent achievement. This is an achievement explained initially by the differential ability of societies to provide a stable supply of food and water and the basic elements of public sanitation and more recently by advances in medical sciences which have increased age-specific life expectancy in adulthood generally and specifically for individuals 80 years and older. In the United States in the twentieth century, the average life expectancy at birth increased from about 50 years in 1900 to the mid-70s in 1985—a demographic achievement not far behind those of the world's leaders, the Nordic countries and Japan. Average life expectancy at birth in the United States in the 1980s was 74.7 years overall, and 71.9 years for white males, 78.7 years for white females. Even at age 85, age-specific expected years of life remaining were estimated to be 6.0 to 5.1 for white males, and 6.4 years for white females.[5] Such achievements cannot be taken for granted. In a few developing nations average life expectancy continues to be about the same as that in the United States at the turn of the century. Estimated life expectancy for all less developed nations in 1980 was, for example, 55 years and specifically for Africa, 48.6 years. Average life expectancy at birth in the year 2020 is now estimated to be 70.4 years for less developed countries and 78.7 for more developed countries.[6]

The differential success of societies in achieving long life as an average expectation continues, although less dramatically between less and more developed nations as the availability of the essential resources which this distinction implies changes. Patterns of disease and illness remain expectedly different in developing and developed nations. The epidemiology of a developing nation documents that one is most likely to experience nutritional deprivation or acute, epidemic disease typically of viral or bacterial origin; the epidemiology of a developed nation (Chap. 11) is, in contrast, more likely to highlight chronic disease, to involve the gradual deterioration and failure of one or another biological system, and to be influenced by personal behavior and lifestyle characteristics.[4]

Socioeconomic Differentiation Differential availability of resources occurs within as well as between societies. Within a given society, even if adequate resources to meet overall societal needs are assumed to be available, material and social resources are not inevitably distributed equally. In fact, the evidence indicates that unequal distribution of resources within a society in relation to socioeconomic status is the norm. The rationale for observed unequal distribution is found in societal values and preferences regarding rules of equity. All societies generate systems of differential rewards of goods, status, honor, and power. The process and outcome of consensual differences about distribution of resources is what is meant by social stratification. In any society, to be at the top of the system of stratification means more than the prospects of having access to material and social rewards such as prestigious occupation, higher pay, and a maximum degree of self-determination. These rewards, in turn, change patterns of morbidity and mortality in a favorable direction and increase the prospects of perceived well-being in later life. Social status continues, given such correlates, to be one of the most powerful predictor variables in epidemiologic research.[7] Growing old poor, uneducated, and socially isolated clearly is not the same as growing old rich, educated, and socially integrated.

The ingenuity of social groups to differentiate members for purposes of special treatment does not end with general status differentiation. Social groups can and do differentiate individuals complexly on the basis of race, nationality, or religion or simply as male or female. Growing old as a member of a racial or ethnic minority or as a member of a majority group in a society typically is quite different. Life expectancy at birth varied by as much as 6 years for minority and majority individuals in the United States in 1985. For women, who appear to be biologically programmed for longer life than men, the fact that women have an elevated risk of poverty is explained better socially than biologically,[3] and poor women have a shorter life expectancy at birth than nonpoor women and a greater risk of functional impairment.

The relationship between the distribution of social resources and differential outcomes of aging has been demonstrated with special effectiveness in a

Canadian study by Wilkins and Adams.[8] In this study, the authors develop the concepts of *health expectancy* (i.e., disability-free life expectancy at birth) and *quality-adjusted life expectancy* (i.e., a weighted measure to indicate the probability of capacity for self-care in a noninstitutional setting) and apply these to the experience of Canada; for similar evidence from the United States, see Katz et al.[9] These concepts make an important distinction differentiating living personally and socially satisfying and adequate lives from simply surviving. Table 10-1 provides classic illustrations of diversity of aging outcomes in relation to both income level and residence in a poor versus a middle-class neighborhood. The almost 5-year average differential in life expectancy at birth between those with lowest and highest income is overshadowed by the even larger income-related differentials in quality-adjusted life expectancy (7.7 years) and disability-free life expectancy (11 years). Residential location, which by implication adds adequate housing and degree of social integration to income as predictors, also has the expected effect on survival. Life expectancy at birth is 9.1 years greater for those residing in a middle-class neighborhood than for those in a poor neighborhood. The differential favoring those in a middle-class neighborhood for quality-adjusted life expectancy is 10.8 years and for disability-free years, 13.3. The effects of socioeconomic status on survival and quality of life are consistently less dramatic for females than for males. Socioeconomic factors modify the persistent effects of biological differences on survival and also have an effect on the quality-adjusted life expectancy of females.

In sum, whether one survives into later life and how one grows old are substantially affected by external macrosocial factors. The operation of these factors is illustrated both through the effectiveness with which a society controls its food supply and sanitation and through its internal allocation of resources in terms of implicit and explicit values and related social policy regarding the perceived differential worth of individuals.

Mesosocial Effects

At the mesosocial (institutional) level, societies are also natural experiments in the effects of alternative institutionalized arrangements for providing and maintaining income in adulthood, delivering health care, and structuring living environments. The social roles traditionally allocated to women and the effects of this allocation on economic security in later life illustrate this point particular well. In a comparative analysis of the incomes of older women and men in both the United States and Sweden, Angela O'Rand documents the inferior economic outcomes for older women compared with older men in both societies and explains why this outcome is observed.[10] The explanation reflects similar institutional arrangements in both societies regarding family responsibility, careers within the workplace, and public policy regarding the indexing of pension income to income during the working years. In both societies, although more so in the United States than in Sweden, women have continued to have more extensive responsibilities than men for child rearing. These responsibilities, in turn, affect entry into and continuation in the work force, influence career advancement and related income, and determine the probability of working in industries likely to provide additional private pensions in retirement. Consequently, women in both societies tend to have lower average incomes in retirement than men. Gender in a society, then, has social connotations for economic security as well as for survival. Social roles related to gender become proxies for shared understandings about social obligations which, as they are met, have consequences for careers and the level of resources available in the postretire-

TABLE 10-1

Life Expectancy, Disability-Free Expectancy, and Quality-Adjusted Life Expectancy at Birth in Years by Gender, Income Level, and Socioeconomic Status of Residential Area, Canada, 1978

	Life expectancy			*Disability-free expectancy*			*Quality-adjusted expectancy*		
Quartile	**M**	**F**	**Total**	**M**	**F**	**Total**	**M**	**F**	**Total**
Income Level									
Lowest	67.1	76.6	71.9	50.0	59.9	54.9	59.4	69.7	64.6
Second	70.1	77.6	73.8	57.9	61.8	59.9	64.8	71.1	68.0
Third	70.9	78.5	74.7	61.1	64.3	62.7	66.8	72.7	69.8
Fourth	72.0	79.0	75.5	62.6	63.5	63.1	68.1	72.8	70.5
Highest	73.4	79.4	76.4	64.3	67.5	65.9	69.7	74.8	72.3
Residential Neighborhood									
Poor	61.4	70.9	66.1	49.2	54.0	51.6	56.1	63.9	60.0
Middle-class	72.2	78.2	75.2	62.9	66.9	64.9	68.2	73.5	70.8

SOURCE: From Wilkins and Adams.[8]

ment years. Therefore, explanation of differential incomes for older men and women is found substantially in a society's preferred institutional arrangements.

The effects of preferred societal arrangements for organizing and financing health care are also easily illustrated with evidence from the experience of older adults in North America (see also Chap. 13). In critical reviews of a large body of empirical evidence about the health and health care of older adults, Wolinsky and Arnold[11] and Shapiro[12] have documented the incorrectness of generalizations such as "older adults have poor health and high rates of health care utilization." In fact, a minority of older adults have a disabling chronic illness, and only a relatively small proportion of them have extraordinarily high rates of utilization, such high rates occurring particularly in the last year of life. These elevated rates of disability and care utilization of a subpopulation and the related high health care costs generated are a reflection not only of age-related biological decrement but also of public policy which ensures that chronic and particularly terminal illnesses will be treated in the high-technology environments of hospitals or some other institutional setting. In societies whose populations are aging, these policy decisions ensure that large concentrations of older adults in high-cost medical settings will achieve very high social visibility, particularly if the treatment involves public expenditure. Consequently, a society's institutional arrangements which determine where older adults are treated, what kind of care they receive, and who pays for that care contribute significantly to whether a population is really concerned about population aging and the expressed nature of that concern. Medicare and Medicaid legislation in the United States in 1965 literally laid the groundwork for creating in the private sector a new component of the health care industry—the nursing home. This industry has come to dominate thinking about long-term care to the degree that long-term care is inappropriately, even if inadvertently, frequently equated with nursing home care.

The National Long Term Care Survey (see Manton[13]) provides the estimate that in 1984, 5.5 percent of persons 65 and older in the United States were institutionalized, primarily in nursing homes. But, this survey also reinforces other evidence which documents the diversity of older adults as the risk of disability increases. More than twice the proportion of impaired elderly who are institutionalized continue to reside in communities in spite of high levels of disabilities similar to those observed among institutionalized persons. Whether disabled elderly persons continue to live in a community or move to an institution is obviously not simply a matter of the presence or absence of disability, although the level of disability is demonstrably an important factor. Other factors which affect the risk of whether one is institutionalized include marital status, living arrangements, socioeconomic status, and public policy regarding institutionalization. One finds that holding the level of disability constant, women are more likely to be institutionalized than men, in part because women are more likely than men to be single or widowed and to live alone. The shorter average life expectancy of men increases the likelihood that a spouse will provide care. As one surveys across societies in which older impaired individuals currently live out their lives, the effects of alternative living arrangements, socioeconomic status, and public policy are also evident. Canada and a number of countries in Western Europe, which include long-term care as a basic component of their national health financing schemes, have relatively high rates of disabled older adults in special settings.[14] The United States, as a matter of policy, has concentrated on nursing homes for impaired older adults rather than a continuum of sheltered housing environments or community-based care and has required nonindigent individuals to pay for long-term care (as distinct from relatively brief posthospital care). Consequently, long-term care in the United States tends for all practical purposes to be equated with nursing home care. In 1985, 55 percent of the national total of $35.2 million spent on nursing home care in the United States was paid by individuals. Of the 47 percent of the total paid by federal and state governments, the great majority (42 of the 47 percent) was paid by Medicaid in behalf of persons qualifying as indigent either prior to institutionalization or as a result of depletion of private resources following extended personal payment for care.[15] Informed observers speculate that current long-term care policy in the United States is likely to continue because of the estimate of the high cost of public financing and a lack of a clear national consensus about the balance of public versus private financing of long-term care.[16] Neither the United States nor Canada has developed a continuum of special housing for disabled older adults of the kind found in the United Kingdom, Sweden, Norway, or the Netherlands, where from 9 to 11 percent of older adults are housed in specially designed and managed group quarters in addition to nursing homes.

Similarly, whether an older adult receives care from health professionals who have received special training in geriatrics and in settings which emphasize the special problems of older adults reflects public policy and related societal investments in gerontological and geriatric programs. The United Kingdom and Sweden have had designated medical consultants and special assessment units in geriatrics for several decades. In the United States both federal agencies and private foundations have increased their investment in promoting geriatrics as a subspecialty in medicine and psychiatry and more recently as a specialty in nursing and social work.[17] In short, the type of person who responds to the health and welfare needs of older adults, the competence of such a caregiver, and the locale of the service are all functions of social preferences and public policy.

Microsocial Effects

Microsocial (milieu) factors affecting the processes and outcomes of aging are illustrated when individuals are easily observed in the various milieus recognizable in everyday life. Irving Rosow[18] summarized a broad range of early research on the effects of milieu in its most common form—residential location and living arrangement—on the well-being of older adults (see also Lawton[19]). Specifically Rosow hypothesized that in a society inclined to prejudice toward aging and discrimination toward the aged, older adults would lack positive models of adaptation to aging. His research suggested that age and socioeconomic homogeneity of neighborhoods increase the probability of supportive interaction and, in turn, perceived well-being of older adults. While this conclusion suggested to some observers an unacceptable argument for age segregation, Rosow's sociological point is valid: The meaning of and responses to aging are not independent of one's social milieu. Powell Lawton and Lucille Nahemow[20] generalized Rosow's basic point in the development of the concept of person–environment fitting—that is, the matching of personal capabilities and preferences with the demands and opportunities of different milieus. The observed competence of an older adult from this perspective is substantially dependent on the types and levels of competences expected or required in a particular milieu and the compensatory resources available to reduce the effects of impairments. Lawton and Nahemow argued that milieus can be both over- and underdemanding and can provide many or few compensatory aids.

The research of Rudolph Moos,[21] an environmental psychologist, also addresses the issue of person–environment fitting in a useful way by analyzing physical, social, and organizational milieus in terms of their positive or negative contributions to therapeutic outcomes. His analysis of the behavioral consequences of physical as well as organizational barriers in institutional settings makes a point that is now becoming better understood in our society as we have become sensitive about the kinds of modifiable barriers which make ordinary personal and interpersonal behavior difficult if not impossible. That is, different milieus in which older adults live are differentially handicapping for individuals with the same level of impairment and disability. For example, Judith Rodin and colleagues[22] have written about long-term care environments which encourage personal disengagement from personal responsibility for self-care and thereby exaggerate dependency. This sort of institutionalized encouragement to disengage from self-care responsibility is well-known in care settings which may define the good resident as passive, nondemanding, and compliant. Rodin's research (see also Arnetz[23]) indicates there are behavioral techniques for increasing the appropriate self-reliance of disabled older adults. Having demonstrated that the potential personal initiative is greater than one may observe, Rodin's work suggests, but answers only implicitly, the next question: If the level of dependency or self-care is manipulable and dependent on the presence or absence of stimuli and incentives in the milieu, then the construction of appropriately stimulating milieus should be a function of the training of caregivers, the philosophy of care among caregivers, and the organizational policies which affect the selection and supervision of caregivers.

CONTINUITIES OF THE LIFE COURSE

The importance of the milieus in which individuals age provides a transition to the second basic proposition of this chapter. Aging processes illustrate important continuities in the way individuals interact with milieus as they age. This person–milieu interaction creates not only recognizable biographies but also patterns of behavior and lifestyle which affect survival and well-being. There are discontinuities and surprises in processes of aging. But longitudinal research in aging has demonstrated repeatedly that the best predictor of a variable in aging is the value of that variable at an earlier time. For example, research in the social sciences on patterns of physical and social activity in adulthood demonstrates that even as levels of activity tend to decline with age, individuals who are rank-ordered on the basis of levels and types of activity tend to hold their rank in relation to peers over time. Similarly, the perception of subjective well-being among adults as excellent or poor tends to remain fairly stable in the later years even though the components of well-being may change. That is, two basic components of well-being—affect (happiness) and satisfaction (realized expectations)—may reflect a changing balance with age so that age-related declines in positive affect may be countered by increases in the sense of satisfaction with life accomplishments to achieve the observed continuity of perceived well-being in later life.[2]

Risk Factors and Cohorts

Two concepts widely used by demographers and epidemiologists are particularly useful in illustrating continuities in the human life course. These concepts are risk factor and cohort. The concept *risk factor* has been popularized in discussions of the etiology of cardiovascular disease. The argument proceeds like this: If one smokes cigarettes; indulges in a diet that includes large quantities of salt, sugar, and fat; ignores the importance of exercise; and handles stress poorly, over time the probability (risk) of cardiovascular illness increases. This sort of argument has interesting sociological implications. The factors most commonly identified which reportedly change the probability of an unwanted outcome are all related to learned, socially reinforced behaviors. Cumulatively these behaviors may pattern as healthy or unhealthy lifestyles reflecting shared, reinforced preferences for living. It is worth noting that research evidence indicates that unhealthy lifestyles are more commonly found in persons of lower socioeconomic status and that, in at least some surveys, older adults tend to display relatively healthy lifestyles.[24] The latter observation may reflect the probability that surveyed older adults have survived in part because their lifestyles are healthy. In any case, discussion of risk factors for survival and well-being reminds one that one's past behavior is a prologue to one's later years.

The second concept of interest is *cohort*. This concept has been introduced by demographers and social scientists to take account of the expected differential experiences of individuals born at different times. The timing of birth possibly exposes individuals to distinctively different environmental circumstances, events, or milieus initially and over the course of their development. Eras characterized by overpopulation, war, or economic depression immediately come to mind. The concept also permits the possibility of intracohort variation occasioned by socioeconomic or other social differences affecting person–milieu interaction over the life course (see Ref. 25). To be born in a less developed nation in contrast to a developed nation has easily understandable implications for survival because "less developed" in this case is a proxy for levels of public sanitation, food and water supplied, and health care, which are known to predict survival. Similarly, to be born into a family of lower rather than higher socioeconomic status at a point in time in a particular society is associated with a higher probability of minimal education, low income, and social isolation. Or, in contrast, individuals born in the United States in the mid-1920s have been appropriately characterized as one of the most advantaged cohorts in human history. Born at the beginning of a depression, this cohort was relatively small. Most survived World War II, and their small number inherited a milieu of postwar affluence in which they competed with great success for extensive social and economic resources such as education, income, housing, and eventually public policies intended to secure their retirement income and health care. This cohort of adults are the parents of the Baby Boomers, a very large cohort which succeeded their affluent parents, inherited much more intense competition for social resources, and predictably exhibited elevated rates of social maladjustment (see, e.g., Ref. 26). For worse as well as for better, members of cohorts interact with milieus in the process of development in ways which generate identifiable differences in the problems encountered and the personal and social responses developed.

Several important practical implications of understanding risk factors and cohorts follow. One is that late life is best understood as a later but continuous part of the human life course. The processes and experience of aging do not occur in a vacuum. Individuals as the result of circumstances of birth (e.g., born in a developing or developed country, born in lower or higher socioeconomic status) will age and experience their aging differently. Second, different learned patterns of behavior and lifestyles developed and continued over the life course change the probabilities of survival and well-being in later life. If learned behavior can be presumed to be modifiable, one thinks of potentially beneficial interventions to modify aging processes. The modification of unhealthy lifestyles and the promotion of healthy lifestyles not just in adulthood but also early in life would appear sensible in the interest of well-being in later life. From this perspective, discussions of generational equity which suggest that older adults are being supported at the expense of children as though the distribution is only a matter of equity miss an important point. The social and economic deprivation of children has predictable long-range implications for the aging of future cohorts. The benefits of reducing risk factors early in life by avoiding exposure to dangerous drugs, improving the diet, increasing the amount of exercise, and managing stress more effectively seem obvious enough. One needs, however, to add that equally powerful or more powerful factors affecting well-being over the entire life course are social and societal in origin—ignorance, poverty, and social isolation. These social factors affect the processes of aging and the experience of aging as powerfully as the biomedical and lifestyle factors more frequently discussed. These social factors in aging are also demonstrably modifiable by public policy.

MODIFIABILITY OF AGING PROCESSES

As it is normally taught and practiced, scientific investigation, we reiterate, emphasizes the search for predictable relationships between variables and, in seeking economical explanations, tends to be reductionistic. Biological theories of aging which have tended to conceptualize aging processes of decline which are intrinsic and hence inevitable are increasingly countered by longitudinal evidence. The issue of differential rates of age-related biological change observed and the explanation of these differences has received less attention. The observed differences in aging processes and the experience of aging are precisely what we have stressed in this chapter. We have stressed them because we believe the observed differences are the outcome of a synergistic interaction of internal biological potential and the activation of this potential through interaction with the externalities we index as milieu; the social resources and institutional arrangements for meeting needs; and the distribution of social and material resources available to and distributed within a society.

In an earlier literature, gerontologists and geriatricians attempted to distinguish between primary and secondary aging. This distinction was meant to differentiate intrinsic biological forces of development from those aspects of development affected by externalities. This, we argue, is a false dichotomy rejected by both contemporary biology and the social sciences. In the contemporary view, biology specifies what genetic potential makes possible in various contexts, not just what genetic structure makes necessary. The social sciences, in turn, index and trace the consequences of the exposure of individuals and cohorts of individuals to different milieus over the course of development.

A first obvious move away from the perception of necessary biological process of decline in gerontology and geriatrics was evident at least a decade ago with the emergence of what might be called "therapeutic optimism." This designation was meant to contrast with an earlier orientation designated "therapeutic nihilism" which focused on a biology of inevitable decline,[4] or, as Rowe and Khan[1] observe, one needs to distinguish between "usual" and "successful" aging, as research has increasingly demonstrated that later life is not adequately characterized as a period of uniform decline in biological and related functional capacities. In fact, recent research on the risk and course of impairment in later life is documenting both the differential experience of socially defined subpopulations (e.g., by sex, race, and socioeconomic status) and dynamic changes in impairment status.[27,13]

The beneficial effects of a variety of social and societal interventions on the quality of life in later adulthood have been suggested and sometimes effectively demonstrated. The health benefits of not smoking cigarettes in particular or cessation of all forms of smoking are now well documented and widely known. Access to adequate social and material resources changes the risk of morbidity and mortality favorably whether one is comparing less developed nations which do or do not experience development or comparing socioeconomically deprived individuals who do or do not receive economic, health, and social interventions. As adequate food, water, and sanitation are increasingly available worldwide, there is every reason to expect that life expectancy at birth and age-specific life expectancy in adults will continue to increase in all societies, and this is what one now observes worldwide. This achievement, sometimes referred to as the "First Revolution in Health," ensures the necessity in every society of a Second Revolution as populations age and chronic disease replaces acute disease as a primary health concern. This Second Revolution in health must focus on lifestyle and environmental issues, which are so central to the understanding of and in the response to age-related chronic impairments, disabilities, and handicaps.[4]

At the mesosocial (institutional) level of intervention, public policy to modify institutional arrangements for income and access to health care has been demonstrably affected in beneficial ways in the United States in the past two decades.[28–30,11] And at the microsocial level of milieu and lifestyle modification, the available evidence indicates that promoting healthy lifestyles has apparently been increasingly effective in achieving beneficial change at least among educated adults (e.g., Berkman[24]). The effects of public policy regarding income maintenance in later adulthood is a story of successful public policy, although the success is far from complete.

Social security policy and improved private pensions in the United States have halved the rate of poverty among older adults in less than two decades from 25 to 12 percent (Table 10-2). The reduction is sufficient to produce a rate of poverty among older adults which is slightly below that of children. This fact has caused concern about generational equity. There is no obvious answer to questions about generational equity, and it is more appropriate here to note the limited success of national income policy for older women in the United States. For older unmarried women in 1984, 20.6 percent were in poverty. For elderly persons with one or more limitations in activities of daily living (ADL), 34.1 percent were poor and another 27.6 percent "near poor." Women were found to be two and a half times more likely than men to be poor or near poor.[31]

The upshot of such evidence of modifiability of the experience of aging is that in gerontology and geriatrics, a reaffirmation of a venerable maxim of clinical and experimental science is observed: If you want to understand something, try to change it. The benefits of aerobic exercise on cardiovascular efficiency and possibly the mood of older adults have been suggested[32]; the possible restoration of some cognitive functioning through retraining illustrated[33]; and increased self-respect and greater personal responsibility for self-care through modest behavioral interventions demonstrated.[22] Lifestyles affect risks for survival and quality of life.[24] The social milieus of housing, living arrangements, and neighborhoods affect the sense of well-being and the effective expression of independence in later life.[22]

The demonstrated potential for change indicates a realistic basis for optimism without, however, identifying the feasible and reasonable limits of change in aging processes. We therefore do not know the limits of desirable change even when change is feasible. In

TABLE 10-2

Proportion of Elderly Persons below Selected Income Thresholds, 1969–1986

	Percent of elderly persons below:		
Year	**The Poverty Threshold**	**125% of Poverty**	**150% of Poverty**
1969	25.1	35.2	43.3
1975	15.3	25.4	34.9
1980	15.7	25.7	34.4
1983	14.1	22.5	30.2
1986	12.4	20.5	28.0

SOURCE: From Moon.[29]

any case, what is feasible is a scientific question; i.e., what is desirable is an ethical and political question. Whether we should expect to delay the onset of morbidity and to what degree we should expect to delay it are clearly debatable. The issue will continue to be debated, particularly in the absence of definitive evidence. But there is no question that public policy on sanitation; institutional arrangements for income maintenance, health care, and housing; and the demonstrably beneficial modification of milieus to enhance the functioning of older adults have had profoundly beneficial effects on both the objective and subjective well-being of older adults, not only in the United States but in all developed nations.

THE IMPORTANCE OF PUBLIC POLICY

The fourth proposition noted at the beginning of the chapter follows inevitably from the validity of the first three: Societal consensus about allocating resources over the life course affects how individuals age and experience their aging. Resource availability and allocation affect functional capacity and perceived well-being as well as survival. Institutional arrangements affect who wins and who loses in gaining access to income, health care, and the amenities of lifestyle which make growing old a very different experience for the rich and the poor, for the socially integrated and the isolated elderly, for the informed and the ignorant.

In this chapter the focus on the societal externalities involved in understanding how we grow older has important practical implications for geriatric physicians and, more generally, for all geriatric practitioners. First, observed diversity cautions practitioners to be wary about generalizations regarding the elderly. Contemporary older adults literally are not what they were or will be. This is an obvious implication of the concept of cohort differences discussed above. The changing probability of cohorts of individuals developing and aging differently is obvious enough. Yet the pressure to simplify our thinking about aging processes and aging persons with facile stereotypes is persistently powerful. Stereotyping encourages inappropriate projection of personal, socially reinforced expectations about later life. "What do you expect at your age?" clinicians may ask an older patient or client even when they probably do not have a large and definitive factual basis for answering that question. Factual evidence indicates that there are many different answers to that question.

But there is an even more significant reason for gerontological and geriatric practitioners to study how externalities affect aging processes and the experience of aging. In their comparative study of long-term care in three Canadian provinces, Kane and Kane[34] noted the persistent tension between two competing perspectives on long-term care: One is that the disabling functional impairments of later life are most adequately viewed as the domain of medicine and hospitals, although with some need for social interventions. The competing perspective is that geriatric care is more adequately perceived as basically a social process best pursued in a community setting with appropriate assistance from health practitioners. The attractiveness of these alternative viewpoints and the probability of acting on one or the other is very much dependent on sociocultural values and how the preferences related to these values are embedded in the training of professional caregivers and the expectations of laypersons.

In the United States, in fact in Western industrial countries generally, the care of older adults has been primarily a medical affair and resources have been concentrated in the institutional context of hospitals and nursing homes. Experienced geriatricians, one suspects, recognize that one of their greatest and necessary skills may be as care managers who take into consideration the reality that the externalities of income, housing, and social support have a great deal to do with determining well-being in later life. But different societies are clearly pursuing with more or less confidence and vigor quite different facets of issues and problems related to the aging of populations.[17] For example, the United Kingdom and Sweden have maintained strong medically oriented and hospital-based geriatricians. Both are advanced welfare states with well-developed income maintenance programs for older citizens, established traditions of integrated social and medical services, and a broad range of alternative housing other than nursing homes for dependent elderly. Geriatric care in Britain and Sweden is unambiguously primarily the responsibility of the public sector.

The United States, in contrast to the United Kingdom and Sweden, has continued to assert the private sector's primacy in responsibility for aging populations, particularly in regard to health care. This has continued to be the case even as public investment in geriatric care has escalated upward in the past two decades. Public policy regarding geriatric care remains ambiguous and without obvious consensus, however, regarding the preferred mix of public and private responsibility. Certainly there is little evidence of political consensus about a national health service or a national health insurance system, or the systematic integration of health and social services. Issues related to long-term care illustrate the ambiguities and ambivalence in the United States regarding public policy on geriatric care.

Even though relatively high cost nursing homes have not ensured quality care, no consensus has emerged for alternatives to the institutionalization of dependent older adults. Community-based care has not emerged as more than a theoretically cost-effective alternative to institutionalization[35] because no politically acceptable alternative to a fragmented health and welfare system has been identified. Consequently, long-term care remains the last great risk of life that has remained inadequately insured even for most middle- and upper-income individuals.[36] Even in 1985 slightly more than half of the expenditures for long-term care were paid for privately. Most of the public sector payment for care (42 of 47 percent) was provided by Medicaid, clearly a public welfare mechanism in the United States. In the late 1980s, legislation ostensibly creating protection against catastrophic illness in later life proved to be protection against acute medical illness in hospital settings. This financial risk is demonstrably secondary to the much greater financial risk of the average older adult for long-term care in a nursing home setting at an average cost of $22,000 per year in 1988.

An analysis by researchers at the Brookings Institution[16] reaches a pessimistic conclusion regarding a change of national public policy regarding long-term care in the United States. Under realistic assumptions about the current and future cost of care and personal economic resources of adults, no more than 30 to 40 percent of adults will be able to afford to insure long-term care adequately. The great majority (60 to 70 percent) will have to depend on public provision of care, a provision which the Brookings researchers conclude is likely to continue to be the existing Medicaid procedure requiring certification of indigence as a condition of eligibility.

Two publications of the Institute of Medicine, National Academy of Sciences provide some basis for optimism in forecasting the future of aging in the United States. A review of evidence regarding the possibility of preventing or minimizing excessive disability associated with chronic disease explicitly uses older adults as a particularly important population for testing the potential of purposive interventions.[37] The proposed national research agenda clearly recognizes the relevance of the social factors discussed in this chapter and makes a case for purposive interventions.[38]

Attention to long-term care is not given with the intention to view with alarm the current situation in the United States or to suggest an easy solution. The point rather is to make clear that a basic issue in care and welfare in later life remains a matter of achieving political consensus regarding objectives and responsibilities and the related political will to act on that consensus. The future of welfare in later life will, for better or worse, be invented by thoughtful political action or inherited by default. It is not "Nature" so much as the preferences of effective political groups in a society which determine how populations grow older and deal with their aging and how health and welfare institutions serving older adults are staffed and managed.

REFERENCES

1. Rowe J, Kahn R: Human aging: Usual and successful. *Science* 237:143, 1987.
2. Maddox GL: Aging differently. *Gerontologist* 27(5):557, 1987.
3. Maddox G, Lawton P: *Varieties in Aging: Annual Review of Gerontology and Geriatrics.* New York, Springer, 1988, vol 8.
4. Maddox GL: Modifying the social environment, in Holland W et al (eds): *Oxford Textbook of Public Health.* London, Oxford University Press, 1985, vol 2.
5. Metropolitan Life: New longevity record in the United States, *Statistical Bulletin,* July-September 1988, p 10.
6. Myers G: Demography of aging, in Binstock R, George L (eds): *Handbook of Aging and the Social Sciences,* 3d ed. New York, Academic, 1990, p 19.
7. Syme SL, Berkman LF: Social class, susceptibility and sickness. *Am J Epidemiol* 104:1, 1976.
8. Wilkins R, Adams O: *Healthfulness of Life: A Unified View of Mortality, Institutionalization and Non-institutionalized Disability Research.* Montreal, Institute for Research in Public Policy, 1978.
9. Katz S et al: Active life expectancy. *N Engl J Med* 309:1218, 1983.
10. O'Rand A: Convergence, institutionalization and bifurcation: Gender and the pension acquisition process, in Maddox G, Lawton P (eds): *Varieties in Aging: Annual Review of Gerontology and Geriatrics.* New York, Springer, 1988, vol 8, chap 5.
11. Wolinsky F, Arnold L: A different perspective on health and health service utilization, in Maddox G, Lawton P (eds): *Varieties in Aging: Annual Review of Gerontology and Geriatrics.* New York, Springer, 1988, vol 8, chap 3.
12. Shapiro E: The relevance of research on aging to policy making and planning: Evidence from the Manitoba longitudinal studies of aging, in Brody J, Maddox G (eds): *Epidemiology and Aging.* New York, Springer, 1988, p 167.
13. Manton K: Planning long-term care for heterogeneous populations, in Maddox G, Lawton P (eds): *Varieties in Aging: Annual Review of Gerontology and Geriatrics.* New York, Springer, 1988, vol 8, chap 8.
14. Rabin D, Stockton P: *Long Term Care for the Elderly: A Factbook.* New York, Oxford University Press, 1987, chap 12.
15. Swan J et al: State Medicaid reimbursement for nursing homes, 1978–86. *Health Care Financ Rev* 9:3, 33, 1988.
16. Rivlin A et al: Insuring long-term care, in Maddox G, Lawton P (eds): *Varieties in Aging: Annual Review of Gerontology and Geriatrics.* New York, Springer, 1988, vol 8, chap 9.
17. Eisdorfer C, Maddox G: *The Role of Hospitals in Geriatric Care.* New York, Springer, 1988.
18. Rosow I: *Social Integration of the Aged.* New York, Free Press, 1967.
19. Lawton P: Housing and living environments of older people, in Binstock R, Shanas E (eds): *Handbook of Aging and the Social Sciences,* 2nd ed. New York, Van Nostrand Reinhold, 1985, p 450.

20. Lawton P, Nahemow L: Ecology and the aging process, in Eisdorfer C, Lawton P (eds): *Psychology of Adult Development and Aging.* Washington, American Psychological Association, 1973.
21. Moos R: Specialized living arrangements for older people, *J Soc Issues* 36:75, 1980.
22. Rodin J et al: The construct of control, in Lawton P, Maddox G (eds): *Annual Review of Gerontology and Geriatrics.* New York, Springer, 1985, vol 5, p 3.
23. Arnetz B: Interaction of biomedical and psychosocial factors in research on aging, in Lawton P, Maddox G (eds): *Annual Review of Gerontology and Geriatrics.* New York, Springer, 1985, vol 5, p 56.
24. Berkman L: The changing and heterogeneous nature of aging and longevity: A social and biomedical perspective, in Maddox G, Lawton P (eds): *Varieties in Aging: Annual Review of Gerontology and Geriatrics.* New York, Springer, 1988, vol 8, chap 2.
25. Maddox G, Campbell R: Scope, concepts and methods in the study of aging, in Binstock R, Shanas E (eds): *Handbook of Aging and the Social Sciences,* 2nd ed. New York, Van Nostrand Reinhold, 1985, p 3.
26. Easterlin R: *Birth and Fortune.* New York, Basic Books, 1980.
27. Maddox G, Clark D: Trajectories of functional impairment in later life. *J Health Soc Behav* 33:114, 1992.
28. Clark R, Maddox G et al: *The Economic Well-being of the Elderly.* Baltimore, Johns Hopkins University Press, 1984.
29. Moon M: The economic situation of older Americans: Emerging wealth and continuing hardship, in Maddox G, Lawton P (eds): *Varieties in Aging: Annual Review of Gerontology and Geriatrics.* New York, Springer, 1988, vol 8, chap 4.
30. Chen Y-P: Better options for work and retirement: Some suggestions for improving economic security mechanisms for old age, in Maddox G, Lawton P (eds): *Varieties in Aging: Annual Review of Gerontology and Geriatrics.* New York, Springer, 1988, vol 8, chap 7.
31. *Medicare's Poor: A Report of the Commission on Elderly People Living Alone.* New York, Commonwealth Fund, November 20, 1987.
32. Blumenthal J et al: Psychological and physiological effects of physical conditioning on the elderly. *J Psychosom Res* 26(5):505, 1982.
33. Schaie W, Willis S: Can decline in intellectual functioning be reversed? *Dev Psychol* 22:223, 1986.
34. Kane R, Kane R: *A Will and a Way: What the United States Can Learn from Canada about Caring for the Elderly.* New York, Columbia University Press, 1985.
35. Maddox GL, Glass T: The continuum of care: Movement toward the community, in Busse E, Blazer D (eds): *Handbook of Geriatric Psychiatry,* rev ed. New York, Van Nostrand Reinhold, 1989.
36. Somers AR: Insurance for long-term care. *N Engl J Med* 317:23, 1982.
37. Pope A, Tarlov A: *Disability in America: Toward a National Agenda for Prevention.* Washington, DC, Institute of Medicine, National Academy of Sciences Press, 1991.
38. Lonergan E: *Extending Life, Enhancing Life: A National Research Agenda on Aging.* Washington, DC, Institute of Medicine, National Academy of Sciences Press, 1991.

Chapter 11

THE EPIDEMIOLOGY OF AGING

Maurice B. Mittelmark

The health issues that most occupy society vary systematically across the life span. Accident and injury are prominent concerns in childhood, adolescence, and early adulthood; developing chronic diseases are a central feature of middle adulthood; morbidity and mortality from chronic diseases characterize the period around retirement; and deterioration in functioning, disability, and dependency are concerns mainly at old and very old age.

Thus, the epidemiology of aging includes a focus not only on diseases that cause morbidity and mortality but also on the principal conditions that cause disability and subsequent decline in independent functioning.

As well, the epidemiology of aging includes an emphasis on demography that is not usual when the health and illness patterns of younger persons are considered. The composition of the population in the United States and elsewhere is at the beginning of a period of significant change, resulting in a sharp increase in the proportionate size of the older adult population. With this change, the health concerns of the elderly are becoming more and more the health concerns of the entire population, who share the responsibility of providing for the needs of older adults. Reflecting these realities, this chapter begins with an overview of demographic trends, and there is considerable emphasis throughout on risk factors, conditions, and diseases that figure prominently in the health concerns of the older adult patient population.

As a final introductory note, it is hoped that the material of this chapter will provide the reader with a realistic view of the overall health status of the older adult population. Medical professionals, whose time with older adults may well be spent mostly with those who are ill and needy, tend to overestimate the extent of illness and disability in the general population of older adults. The fact is that the large majority of older adults are healthy and independent as well as vigorous contributors to the society in which we live.

DEMOGRAPHY

The population of the United States, in comparison with other countries, contains a small proportion of elderly.[1] Yet in numbers, the United States has the third largest population of elderly (age 60 and older) in the world, behind China and India, and is second only to China in the size of the population aged 80 and older.[1]

Growth in the U.S. population during the next several decades will be modest by international standards but greater than average for developed countries. The projected percent increase in the population aged 60 and above by the year 2020 is 159 percent in less developed countries, 59 percent in developed countries, and 69 percent in the United States.[1] The projected growth by the year 2050 in the population of American women is twice that of men (Fig. 11-1).[2] Women at all ages are projected to have substantially higher dependency rates than men, and by the year 2050, the age/sex group with the largest number of dependent persons will be women 92 years of age and older (Fig. 11-2).[2]

EPIDEMIOLOGY

Mortality

The trend in proportionate mortality over the past 40 years has been one of increasing rates of death due to malignant neoplasms and chronic obstructive pulmonary disease, decreasing rates of death due to cerebrovascular disease, injuries, and perinatal conditions, and little change in the proportion of deaths due to cardiovascular diseases, pneumonia, and influenza.[3] Among the elderly, the trend in proportionate mortality due to cardiovascular diseases is decreasing except among the oldest old, yet cardiovascular diseases

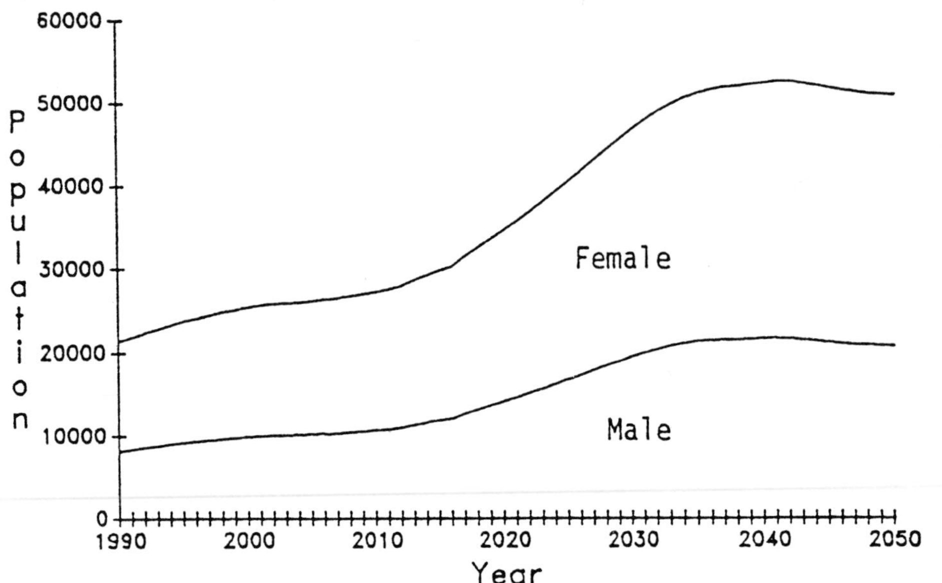

FIGURE 11-1
Sex-specific projected population aged 70 and over. United States, 1990–2050 (population in thousands). (*U.S. Bureau of the Census, 1989, middle series.*) (*From Rogers RG et al: Active life among the elderly in the United States: Multistate life table estimates and population projections. Milbank Q 67:370, 1989. Reprinted with permission.*)

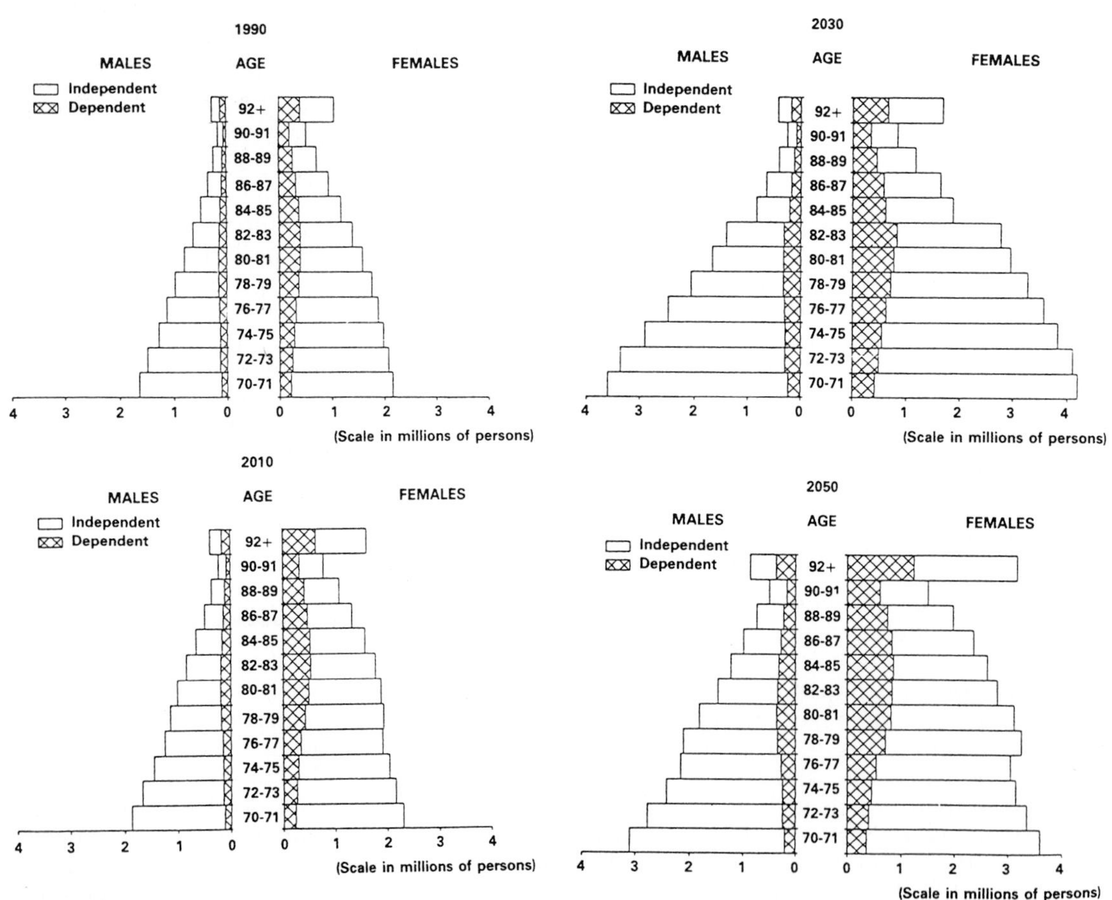

FIGURE 11-2
Population pyramids for individuals aged 70 and over by functional status. Selected years, United States. (*Calculations based on LSOA data, U.S. Department of Health and Human Services, 1988. Reprinted with permission.*)

remain the leading cause of death among those aged 65 and above (Fig. 11-3).[3]

Death rate trends for the ten leading causes of death among persons 65 years of age and older are shown in Table 11-1.[4] In 1982, diseases of the heart, cerebrovascular disease, and atherosclerosis together accounted for 48 percent of all deaths among those 65 to 74 years old and 66 percent of all deaths among those aged 85 and older (Table 11-1). Conversely, malignant neoplasms accounted for 29 percent of all deaths among those 65 to 74 years old and 11 percent of all deaths among those aged 85 and older (Table 11-1).

Morbidity

Detailed data on a wide range of chronic and acute conditions in the U.S. population aged 65 and older are available from the 1991 National Health Interview Survey.[5] Tables 11-2 and 11-3 present core data from that report on age-sex- and age-race-specific prevalences of skin and musculoskeletal, digestive, circulatory, respiratory, and other conditions as well as impairments in hearing, vision, and speech.

Disability

Disability, as the term is used here, refers to limitations in the capacity to perform the normal activities of daily living, such as managing personal hygiene. In 1985, it was estimated that 80 percent of the American older adult population was not disabled, but due to the changing demographic profile of the elderly, the proportion of nondisabled elderly is projected to drop to about 70 percent by the year 2060.[6] Nevertheless, even the most cautious projections of the fu-

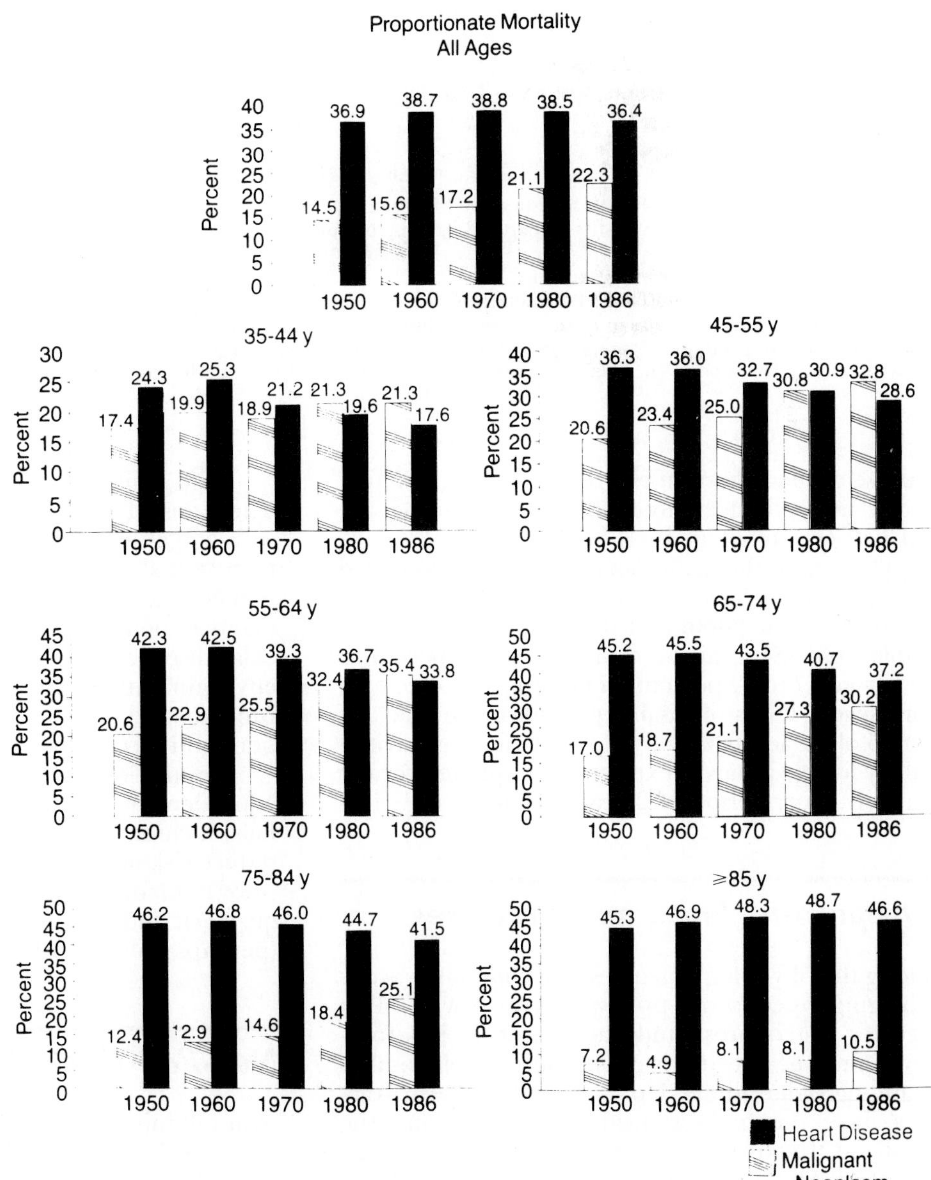

FIGURE 11-3
Proportionate mortality of heart disease and malignant neoplasms: 1950 through 1986. (*From Sutherland JE et al: Proportionate mortality trends: 1950 through 1986. JAMA 264:3178, 1990. Reprinted with permission.*)

TABLE 11-1

Death Rates for the Ten Leading Causes of Death among Persons 65 Years and Over: 1970, 1975, 1978, 1982 (by rank order and by age for 1982)[a,b]

Cause of Death and ICD Code		1970	1975	1978	1982			
					65 and over	65–74	75–84	85 and over
All causes		5892.1	5432.4	5293.5	5048.9	2885.2	6329.8	15,048.3
Diseases of heart	390–398 402 404–429	2683.3	2403.9	2231.1	2223.9	1156.4	2801.4	7341.8
Malignant neoplasms, including neoplasms of lymphatic and hematopoietic tissues	140–208	923.4	961.1	1002.4	1022.0	824.9	1238.7	1598.6
Cerebrovsacular disease	430–438	847.5	729.7	622.0	505.7	193.5	675.1	2000.8
Chronic obstructive pulmonary disease and allied conditions[c]	490–496	102.2	80.5	66.1	176.8	131.1	236.0	278.0
Pneumonia and influenza[c]	480–487	200.4	187.1	193.2	152.9	47.6	183.4	747.8
Atherosclerosis	440	149.7	123.0	115.0	95.2	20.6	102.9	563.0
Diabetes mellitus	250	131.4	112.9	101.3	94.0	60.1	125.4	212.1
Accidents	E-800-E949	135.9	109.6	100.3	85.8	50.9	103.9	255.9
Motor vehicle accidents	E-810-E825	36.2	25.3	24.5	20.4	17.5	25.2	23.7
All other accidents	E-800-E807 E-826-E949	99.7	84.3	75.8	65.4	33.4	78.7	232.2
Nephritis, nephrotic syndrome and nephrosis[c]	580–589	23.7	23.2	25.6	53.5	25.8	69.7	182.8
Chronic liver disease and cirrhosis	571	37.1	36.6	36.3	35.3	40.1	31.1	17.9
All other causes	Residual	657.5	664.9	700.6	603.4	334.1	762.2	1849.6

[a] Data from National Center for Health Statistics: *Vital Statistics of the United States*, 2, 1970, 1975, and 1978; *Advance Report of Final Mortality Statistics*, 1982, Monthly Vital Statistics Report, 33:9, Supplement. DHHS Pub. No. (PHS) 85-1120. Public Health Service, Hyattsville, Md., 1984.

[b] Rates per 100,000 population in age group.

[c] Cause-of-death titles and numbers are based on the *Ninth Revision International Classification of Diseases*. Because of decennial revision of the classification nad changes in rules of cause-of-death coding, the 1982 rates in this table are not comparable to those prior to 1980 for those causes indicated by a footnote. Pneumonia and influenza trends are subject to large fluctuations due to epidemic in some years.

SOURCE: Brody JA, Brock DB, Williams TF: Trends in the health of the elderly population. *Annu Rev Public Health* 8:211, 1987.

ture size of the American elderly disabled population predict more than a threefold increase during the next half century (Fig. 11-4).[7]

The size of the institutionalized population aged 65 and older is projected to increase from 5 to 7 percent by the year 2060, and the proportion of those disabled but living in the community is expected to grow from 17 to 22 percent.[6] The progression to ever more severe levels of disability is not inexorable. Of every 5 older adults with five or six limits on activities of daily living, 1 may be expected to improve over the relatively short period of 2 years (Table 11-4).[8]

Osteoporosis, Falls, and Fractures

Among the physiologic changes that commonly occur with aging, osteoporosis predisposes those who fall to fractures. Osteoporosis and fractures of the hip, forearm, humerus, and pelvis cause considerable disability among older adults. Up to age 80, forearm fractures have the highest incidence, but among the oldest old, fractures of the hip are by far the most common.[9] The incidence rate of hip fracture falls off only after age 90 or 95.[10]

The prime risk factor for bone fracture is falls. The rates of injury and death due to falls increase with age and are higher among women than among men.[11] Risk factors for falls include advancing age; female sex; chronic ailments; gait and balance abnormalities; neurologic, cerebrovascular, and cardiovascular disorders, decline in strength and coordination, environmental hazards, poor vision, impaired mental function and depression, use of psychotropic medication, and alcohol use.[9–13]

Population-based strategies to reduce the loss of bone density (which underlies hip fractures due to falls) include increased physical activity (which could reduce risk of hip fracture by half), smoking cessation prior to menopause (with potential to reduce risk by a quarter), and postmenopausal estrogen replacement (perhaps halving risk of hip fracture).[12]

Non-Fall Injury

Non-fall injuries, with an incidence rate of 7 percent annually in the elderly, are an important cause of morbidity and mortality in this group. The following synopsis of the epidemiology of non-fall injury is ex-

TABLE 11-2

Number of Selected Reported Chronic Conditions per 1000 persons, by Sex and Age: United States, 1991 (Data are based on household interviews of the civilian noninstitutionalized population)

Type of Chronic Condition	*Male*					*Female*				
			65 Years and Over					*65 Years and Over*		
	Under 45 Years	45–64 Years	Total	65–74 Years	75 Years and Over	Under 45 Years	45–64 Years	Total	65–74 Years	75 Years and Over
Selected skin and musculoskeletal conditions										
Arthritis	24.8	193.2	387.0	335.5	481.3	34.9	284.7	555.0	498.4	630.9
Gout, including gouty arthritis	3.6	23.3	43.6	45.5	40.5	1.3	12.6	18.7	12.7	26.7
Intervertebral disc disorders	15.1	47.4	31.8	34.1	27.5	9.1	40.6	24.6	28.7	19.1
Bone spur or tendinitis, unspecified	4.9	18.3	15.0	18.6	8.5	5.4	24.4	21.4	20.1	23.3
Disorders of bone or cartilage	3.3	5.2	10.0	13.6	3.4	2.9	15.2	29.4	24.1	36.6
Trouble with bunions	1.7	4.5	10.3	8.8	12.8	9.4	29.1	43.6	36.3	53.4
Bursitis, unclassified	6.8	38.0	32.2	39.7	18.3	11.0	43.9	35.3	40.2	28.7
Sebaceous skin cyst	4.7	3.0	8.8	10.5	5.8	4.0	8.0	2.0	3.5	—
Trouble with acne	24.6	4.6	2.8	4.4	—	31.2	5.3	0.7	—	1.6
Psoriasis	7.6	16.7	14.9	11.9	20.4	6.7	14.1	11.2	11.3	11.3
Dermatitis	26.9	33.6	26.1	32.4	14.3	46.7	39.9	34.3	36.7	31.0
Trouble with dry (itching) skin, unclassified	13.6	21.7	42.1	29.7	64.9	18.3	24.6	32.0	20.2	48.0
Trouble with ingrown nails	17.3	26.3	43.7	40.9	48.8	18.6	26.8	58.3	57.6	59.3
Trouble with corns and calluses	9.2	23.3	23.9	18.1	34.7	12.1	42.4	63.5	58.6	70.1
Impairments										
Visual impairment	27.0	63.5	94.2	72.6	133.8	12.2	32.7	68.4	44.0	101.2
Color blindness	14.7	25.3	25.9	21.9	33.3	2.1	2.0	3.6	4.0	3.1
Cataracts	1.6	16.1	139.2	105.0	202.1	3.1	23.9	197.3	146.0	266.3
Glaucoma	2.1	13.4	48.9	40.7	64.0	1.3	10.5	62.9	50.2	79.9
Hearing impairment	44.0	178.5	368.0	330.6	436.6	29.7	107.0	286.5	214.1	383.9
Tinnitus	9.8	57.5	99.3	118.9	63.3	9.2	43.4	70.3	76.3	62.2
Speech impairment	16.4	9.6	12.6	8.6	19.9	7.0	10.5	8.6	4.2	14.6
Absence of extremities (excludes tips of fingers or toes only)	4.7	16.4	33.7	32.6	35.6	1.1	3.8	4.8	2.8	7.6
Paralysis of extremities, complete or partial	3.5	9.5	13.8	8.8	23.3	2.4	4.8	14.1	7.8	22.6
Deformity or orthopedic impairment	94.0	159.6	167.9	168.5	166.7	93.7	149.5	184.5	166.0	209.1
Back	56.3	101.6	89.6	98.4	73.4	61.6	97.3	100.9	93.8	110.5
Upper extremities	10.7	26.6	32.0	33.9	28.6	7.5	18.0	25.5	26.9	23.5
Lower extremities	37.4	60.3	58.3	55.8	62.7	31.8	55.6	84.4	78.4	92.7
Selected digestive conditions										
Ulcer	9.9	25.2	32.0	26.0	43.0	9.5	27.1	23.4	23.1	23.8
Hernia of abdominal cavity	8.0	41.4	53.0	51.2	56.2	5.9	39.9	63.1	58.1	69.9
Gastritis or duodenitis	7.0	12.7	12.6	12.5	13.0	8.9	27.2	26.2	29.6	21.8
Frequent indigestion	17.8	37.7	43.6	34.0	61.3	15.1	32.3	40.2	43.4	36.0
Enteritis or colitis	5.0	9.4	11.5	11.7	11.2	6.8	13.8	28.7	22.0	37.6
Spastic colon	2.3	3.0	2.5	3.8	—	8.8	18.5	11.1	14.6	6.2
Diverticula of intestines	0.7	7.5	32.5	36.5	25.1	1.0	16.7	39.7	42.5	35.9
Frequent constipation	6.1	8.1	44.3	29.6	71.4	16.0	29.3	70.7	50.9	97.4
Selected conditions of the genitourinary, nervous, endocrine, metabolic, and blood and blood-forming systems										
Goiter or other disorders of the thyroid	1.6	4.4	14.1	13.7	14.8	10.9	50.4	61.6	71.8	47.9
Diabetes	7.6	57.9	96.4	97.3	95.1	10.0	57.0	101.4	109.0	91.1
Anemias	3.0	2.0	20.9	14.9	32.0	21.9	23.6	29.8	28.7	31.2
Epilepsy	6.4	5.9	7.5	5.6	11.0	5.2	5.0	4.9	5.8	3.6
Migraine headache	24.0	26.4	7.9	9.5	5.1	54.0	66.3	29.8	27.8	32.4
Neuralgia or neuritis, unspecified	0.4	4.0	2.7	1.3	5.4	1.0	2.4	8.0	9.3	6.5
Kidney trouble	5.8	16.7	20.0	18.0	23.7	12.5	17.9	28.7	27.9	29.9
Bladder disorders	1.4	6.3	24.4	12.8	45.6	19.7	24.1	51.9	44.9	61.3
Diseases of prostate	1.8	25.5	83.8	86.8	78.3	. . .	. . .	. . .	. . .	. . .
Diseases of female genital organs	. . .	. . .	. . .	. . .	. . .	39.7	46.8	16.6	24.2	6.4
Selected circulatory conditions										
Rheumatic fever with or without heart disease	3.1	8.0	9.2	10.6	6.5	9.7	21.5	15.7	16.5	14.6
Heart disease	24.3	152.7	302.3	290.4	324.2	37.3	116.9	290.1	229.1	372.2
Ischemic heart disease	2.1	87.9	175.9	162.9	199.8	1.4	36.4	111.3	98.2	128.8
Heart rhythm disorders	18.2	30.8	53.0	53.0	52.8	27.7	53.1	98.1	76.3	127.5
Tachycardia or rapid heart	2.0	11.5	14.1	15.9	11.2	4.5	18.8	35.8	30.7	42.7
Heart murmurs	14.3	9.5	16.0	15.4	17.2	20.7	27.5	24.2	22.4	26.6
Other and unspecified heart rhythm disorders	1.8	9.9	22.7	21.8	24.6	2.5	6.8	38.1	23.1	58.2
Other selected diseases of heart, excluding hypertension	4.0	34.0	73.4	74.3	71.8	8.1	27.3	80.7	54.5	115.9
High blood pressure (hypertension)	30.7	242.4	306.0	319.4	281.0	27.9	245.4	419.8	422.8	415.6
Cerebrovascular disease	1.0	12.9	68.2	63.4	77.0	1.2	19.0	59.3	54.1	66.3
Hardening of the arteries	0.4	12.0	45.7	40.8	54.6	0.3	10.3	40.5	32.9	50.7
Vericose veins of lower extremities	5.1	26.1	37.1	48.0	17.2	27.1	88.7	109.9	124.7	89.9
Hemorrhoids	19.4	72.0	56.9	70.4	32.2	27.8	64.6	75.1	80.1	68.3
Selected respiratory conditions										
Chronic bronchitis	41.9	41.6	50.6	56.2	40.3	56.4	65.2	53.8	56.2	50.5
Asthma	53.2	33.7	32.7	34.1	30.2	48.2	47.2	40.4	41.2	39.4
Hay fever or allergic rhinitis without asthma	95.8	98.0	76.1	81.3	66.7	102.6	115.5	70.6	78.0	60.6
Chronic sinusitis	99.1	148.0	111.2	119.5	96.0	132.9	192.5	159.8	186.2	124.3
Deviated nasal septum	6.8	13.0	3.7	4.5	2.2	5.2	2.6	4.5	4.5	4.5
Chronic disease of tonsils or adenoids	13.5	1.2	2.0	3.1	—	17.1	1.0	3.5	4.0	2.8
Emphysema	0.1	17.2	51.9	52.8	50.3	0.6	8.6	18.4	16.5	20.9

SOURCE: U.S. Department of Health and Human Services Public Health Service, National Center for Health Statistics, Vital and Health Statistics, series 10, no. 184, December 1992.

TABLE 11-3

Number of Selected Reported Chronic Conditions per 1000 persons, by Race and Age: United States, 1991
(Data are based on household interviews of the civilian noninstitutionalized population)

	White					*Black*				
			65 Years and Over					*65 Years and Over*		
Type of Chronic Condition	**Under 45 Years**	**45–64 Years**	**Total**	**65–74 Years**	**75 Years and Over**	**Under 45 Years**	**45–64 Years**	**Total**	**65–74 Years**	**75 Years and Over**
Selected skin and musculoskeletal conditions										
Arthritis	31.1	241.7	489.1	430.4	577.3	26.0	258.8	468.2	434.4	525.2
Gout, including gouty arthritis	2.8	16.6	27.0	24.2	31.2	—	33.5	57.4	64.6	45.1
Intervertebral disc disorders	14.1	44.9	28.3	32.5	22.1	2.0	44.8	18.7	24.2	9.4
Bone spur or tendinitis, unspecified	5.5	24.6	20.3	21.4	18.8	2.6	2.1	5.9	3.7	9.4
Disorders of bone or cartilage	3.4	11.6	22.7	20.1	26.7	2.3	1.9	10.5	16.8	—
Trouble with bunions	6.2	16.5	30.2	25.0	38.0	2.1	27.8	21.8	13.1	36.7
Bursitis, unclassified	9.8	41.9	36.3	43.2	25.9	6.1	40.9	16.4	16.2	16.8
Sebaceous skin cyst	4.7	6.5	5.4	7.4	2.4	4.0	—	—	—	—
Trouble with acne	28.8	5.2	1.8	2.2	1.1	18.9	—	—	—	—
Psoriasis	8.0	16.5	13.3	12.9	14.0	2.8	7.2	—	—	—
Dermatitis	37.4	36.7	32.4	36.5	26.2	28.1	32.5	11.7	18.6	—
Trouble with dry (itching) skin, unclassified	16.1	21.5	37.4	23.5	58.3	15.3	33.5	31.2	39.2	18.9
Trouble with ingrown nails	19.7	26.6	50.2	50.2	50.1	9.0	33.9	81.2	55.9	123.7
Trouble with corns and calluses	9.1	33.0	46.4	39.3	57.1	20.2	42.0	54.6	57.8	49.3
Impairments										
Visual impairment	20.5	47.3	77.9	56.0	110.9	14.9	62.7	99.9	70.9	148.8
Color blindness	9.4	14.1	13.6	12.7	15.0	3.9	10.1	8.2	7.5	9.4
Cataracts	2.7	20.1	174.9	129.8	242.7	0.9	25.3	166.6	113.1	256.8
Glaucoma	1.9	11.7	53.6	42.8	70.0	0.7	17.3	96.8	89.5	109.0
Hearing impairment	39.1	147.5	330.3	275.5	412.5	24.1	102.4	216.9	171.5	292.5
Tinnitus	9.0	51.9	83.9	97.2	63.9	11.6	42.6	70.2	83.3	48.2
Speech impairment	11.0	8.3	9.9	5.8	16.1	16.8	25.7	16.0	10.6	25.2
Absence of extremities (excludes tips of fingers or toes only)	3.0	10.6	16.4	16.2	16.6	2.1	4.7	25.4	18.6	36.7
Paralysis of extremities, complete or partial	3.0	6.6	13.8	7.5	23.2	3.2	9.1	19.5	18.0	22.0
Deformity or orthopedic impairment	100.9	157.9	178.5	168.3	193.9	61.8	152.2	160.0	151.6	174.0
Back	64.8	103.4	98.1	98.5	97.6	27.6	80.8	55.4	48.5	67.1
Upper extremities	9.5	21.7	28.0	29.8	25.2	9.5	25.9	32.4	37.9	23.1
Lower extremities	36.5	55.5	72.9	65.6	83.8	28.7	92.2	81.9	89.5	69.2
Selected digestive conditions										
Ulcer	10.4	25.5	26.9	23.6	31.8	6.5	35.8	33.9	37.9	27.3
Hernia of abdominal cavity	7.3	44.1	62.8	58.7	68.9	6.8	18.9	19.5	13.7	28.3
Gastritis or duodenitis	8.3	20.5	20.2	22.3	17.1	6.6	16.9	24.6	23.0	26.2
Frequent indigestion	18.2	34.1	40.5	38.4	43.6	10.9	48.1	51.5	55.9	45.1
Enteritis or colitis	6.9	12.9	21.3	18.0	26.4	1.1	0.8	13.3	8.7	21.0
Spastic colon	6.6	11.8	8.3	11.0	4.3	1.1	6.4	—	—	—
Diverticula of intestines	0.9	13.2	40.0	43.8	34.2	1.1	8.0	9.0	8.7	10.5
Frequent constipation	11.6	17.0	58.0	38.8	86.8	10.5	38.1	69.1	46.0	106.9
Selected conditions of the genitourinary, nervous, endocrine, metabolic, and blood and blood-forming systems										
Goiter or other disorders of the thyroid	6.9	29.8	44.0	47.6	38.5	2.2	17.9	21.5	30.5	6.3
Diabetes	8.7	53.5	90.8	91.2	90.2	8.5	97.7	179.1	219.4	111.1
Anemias	11.1	12.6	26.5	22.9	31.8	20.7	23.5	27.3	24.2	32.5
Epilepsy	6.0	4.9	5.3	5.6	4.9	5.5	11.3	14.0	8.1	24.1
Migraine headache	41.0	50.4	21.5	19.5	24.6	25.0	29.6	10.5	16.8	—
Neuralgia or neuritis, unspecified	0.7	3.2	5.7	5.1	6.6	0.3	—	2.7	4.4	—
Kidney trouble	9.3	18.3	22.7	22.7	22.8	8.4	10.3	37.1	14.3	75.5
Bladder disorders	11.4	15.0	42.1	32.5	56.6	8.6	25.5	21.5	3.7	51.4
Diseases of prostate	0.9	12.3	36.7	41.9	29.1	.0.7	13.8	19.1	16.2	24.1
Diseases of female genital organs	20.9	25.0	10.8	15.0	4.4	15.8	24.9	—	—	—
Selected circulatory conditions										
Rheumatic fever with or without heart disease	7.0	14.9	11.3	12.3	9.9	2.8	16.3	28.5	26.1	32.5
Heart disease	31.8	136.8	301.2	261.3	361.0	29.4	138.0	263.0	225.0	327.0
Ischemic heart disease	1.9	63.9	143.9	132.2	161.4	0.8	51.0	87.0	80.2	98.5
Heart rhythm disorders	22.9	43.7	80.8	67.9	100.1	25.9	38.9	74.5	52.8	111.1
Tachycardia or rapid heart	3.5	14.6	27.2	25.7	29.3	2.9	19.1	23.4	5.6	54.5
Heart murmurs	17.5	20.2	20.0	18.4	22.3	19.2	14.2	33.9	32.3	35.6
Other and unspecified heart rhythm disorders	2.0	9.0	33.6	23.8	48.6	3.8	5.6	16.8	14.9	21.0
Other selected diseases of heart, excluding hypertension	6.9	29.1	76.5	61.2	99.4	2.8	48.1	101.4	92.6	117.4
High blood pressure (hypertension)	27.1	229.3	367.0	370.6	361.4	48.5	386.1	447.5	446.9	448.6
Cerebrovascular disease	1.2	15.2	61.8	57.3	68.5	0.9	29.4	79.6	65.9	102.7
Hardening of the arteries	0.2	12.3	44.5	38.5	53.5	1.1	5.3	31.6	23.6	45.1
Vericose veins of lower extremities	18.3	62.1	82.7	93.2	66.8	6.9	32.3	53.1	67.7	28.3
Hemorrhoids	25.0	73.2	70.5	80.6	55.5	20.2	34.1	44.5	36.7	57.7
Selected respiratory conditions										
Chronic bronchitis	52.2	54.8	55.3	58.6	50.3	38.6	56.6	27.3	37.9	9.4
Asthma	49.6	41.6	37.2	36.5	38.3	62.3	40.1	32.4	42.9	14.7
Hay fever or allergic rhinitis without asthma	106.5	107.1	73.2	80.7	62.1	58.6	98.5	55.0	53.4	56.6
Chronic sinusitis	121.3	177.2	136.7	151.6	114.5	106.3	165.8	153.3	185.2	99.6
Deviated nasal septum	6.6	8.8	4.7	5.1	4.0	2.3	—	—	—	—
Chronic disease of tonsils or adenoids	17.0	0.9	3.1	4.0	1.9	9.6	3.5	—	—	—
Emphysema	0.5	13.4	34.8	35.6	33.7	—	11.7	9.4	5.0	16.8

SOURCE: U.S. Department of Health and Human Services Public Health Service, National Center for Health Statistics, Vital and Health Statistics, series 10, no. 184, December 1992.

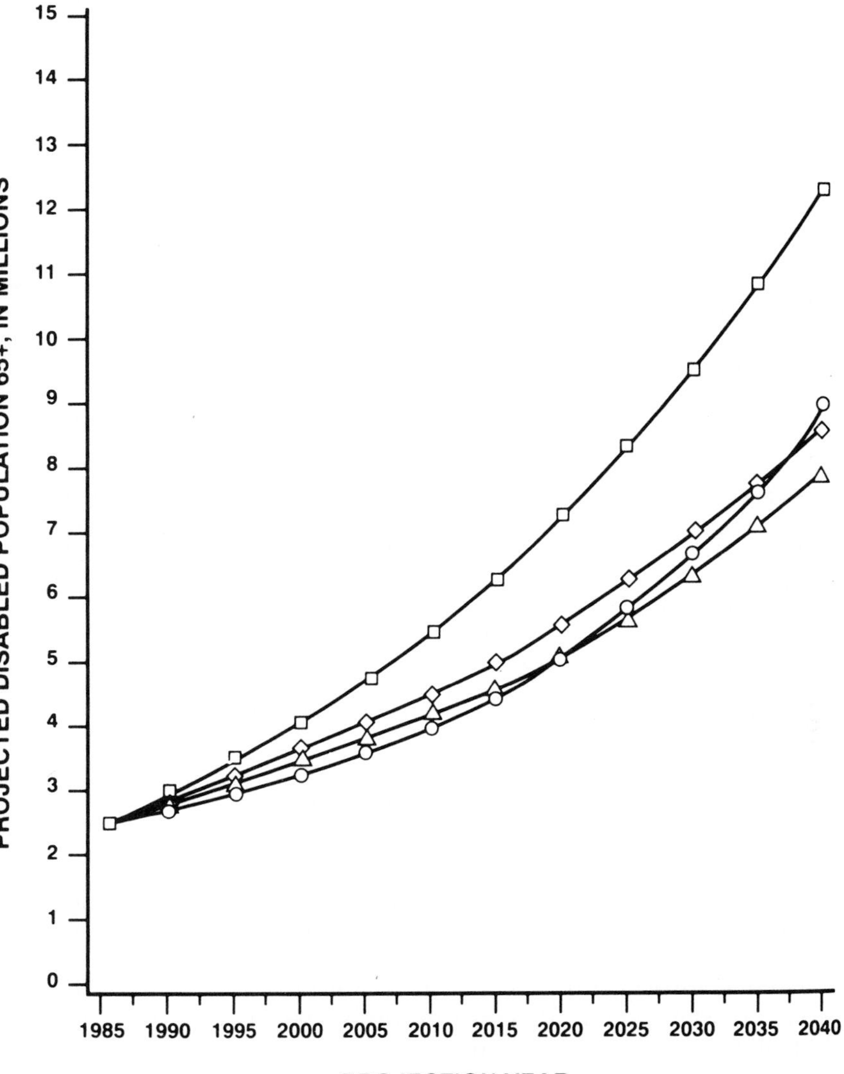

FIGURE 11-4
Total projected population aged 65 and older with severe disability (in millions), 1986–2040. Key to different mortality and disability assumptions: △ constant; ○ longer life, less disability; □ longer life, higher disability; ◇ moderately longer life, moderately higher disability. (*From Kunkel SR, Applebaum RA: Estimating the prevalence of long-term disability for an aging society. J Gerontol 47:S253, 1992. Reprinted with permission.*)

tracted from Wolf and Rivara's comprehensive review of the epidemiology of non-fall injuries among the elderly.[14]

Motor Vehicle Crashes

Motor vehicle accidents are the leading cause of injury and death among older adults, and those 85 years of age and older have the highest crash rate per miles of travel of any age group, including teenagers.[14] The risk factors for motor vehicle accidents in the elderly are not well characterized and preventive measures are correspondingly broad, including occupant protection, driver education, and more frequent license renewal for older drivers.

Suicide

Age trends in the incidence of suicide are widely disparate for men and women, with rates for older men two to seven times those for older women.[14] There is little systematic evidence about risk factors for suicide among older persons, although social isolation, physical and mental illness, and the availability of means (gunshot is the most common means of suicide among older men) have been suggested as among the most important. Older adults represent at most 2 percent of the caseloads of suicide prevention centers. The primary medical care setting may offer special opportunities for prevention, since the majority of older adult suicides are preceded by a visit to a physician.

Burns

The rate of fatal burns, 90 percent of which are caused by residential fires, is much greater among persons 75 years of age and older than among any other age group; also, at all ages, men are at greater risk than women.[14] Conversely, the incidence of nonfatal burn injuries is lower among the elderly than others. Poverty is one of the strongest risk factors for fatality in a residential fire, and cigarettes cause almost half of all fires and a quarter to a half of residential fire deaths. The potential for preventive efforts is

TABLE 11-4

Percent Distributions of Weighted Population in Disability Groups in 1984 by Disability Level in 1982 among Persons Aged 65+: 1982 and 1984 National Long-Term Care Survey Samples

	1984 Status				
1982 Status	**Lower Disability Level**	**Same Disability Level**	**Higher Disability Level**	**Institutionalized**	**Died**
Nondisabled		81.6 (9,880)	8.8 (1,196)	1.5 (190)	8.1 (1,020)
Difficulty with:					
IADL[c] only	9.3 (183)[a]	40.8 (682)	29.0 (494)	5.7 (100)	15.2 (258)
1–2 ADL[d]	18.2 (343)	34.4 (663)	19.1 (368)	7.7 (151)	20.7 (398)
3–4 ADL	23.6 (194)	22.8 (190)	19.7 (165)	10.0 (85)	24.0 (202)
5–6 ADL	22.2 (206)	30.9 (291)	—	9.7 (93)	37.2 (352)
Institutionalized	6.2[b] (100)			54.2 (1071)	40.6 (810)

[a] Numbers in parentheses are unweighted counts. These sum to 95.8 percent (the response rate) of the 20,451 persons in the longitudinal sample.
[b] Returned to community distributed approximately uniformly across ADL/IADL range.
[c] IADL = instrumental activity of daily living
[d] ADL = activity of daily living
SOURCE: Liu K, Manton KG, Liu BM: Morbidity, disability, and long-term care of the elderly: Implications for insurance financing. *Milbank Q* 68:445, 1990.

substantial: many fire deaths are caused by smoke inhalation, and smoke detectors reduce the potential of death or severe injury in 8 out of 10 fires. Fire-safe cigarettes, for which the technology is already available, have the potential to reduce deaths by 2000 and burn injuries by 6000 annually.

Incontinence

Estimates of the prevalence of incontinence, both urinary and fecal, vary widely due to lack of consistent methods for defining and measuring incontinence.[15] Self-reports underestimate true prevalence due to the embarrassing nature of the condition. Estimates of the prevalence of severe (at least weekly episodes) urinary incontinence among the elderly range from 3 to 11 percent.[15]

Arthritis

Extensive data on the epidemiology of arthritis are available from the National Health and Nutrition Examination Survey.[16] The prevalence of moderate to severe abnormality in the knee among older women is more than three times that among older men (7 percent compared to 2 percent), but there is little difference between the sexes in prevalence of moderate to severe abnormality in the hip (1 percent among women and 2 percent among men).[16]

Little is known as yet about the etiology of arthritis, factors related to its progression, or effective preventive measures. Genetic and nongenetic factors have been investigated in etiologic studies of arthritis: twin studies support a role for genetics, but the level of discordance in monozygotic twins points to the importance of nongenetic factors. There is little evidence supporting a role for infectious agents, and oral contraceptive use appears to alter the course but not prevent the occurrence of the disease.[17] Patients with arthritis experience excess mortality compared to the U.S. population as a whole; this is due mainly to infection, renal disease, respiratory disease, rheumatoid arthritis, and gastrointestinal disease.[17]

Cardiovascular Diseases

Coronary Heart Disease

Among diseases of the heart, coronary heart disease (CHD) remains the leading cause of death and disability in the older adult population, despite the fact that CHD death rates have declined steadily over the past two decades for all U.S. age, race, and sex groups.[18] Incidence rates of CHD are higher with age for all race and sex groups, with rates for women lagging behind those for men by about 10 years.[19]

The age-adjusted incidence of CHD among older (white) men and women respectively is 110 and 64 per 10,000 person-years.[19] Age-specific CHD incidence rates are given in Fig. 11-5 and data on relative

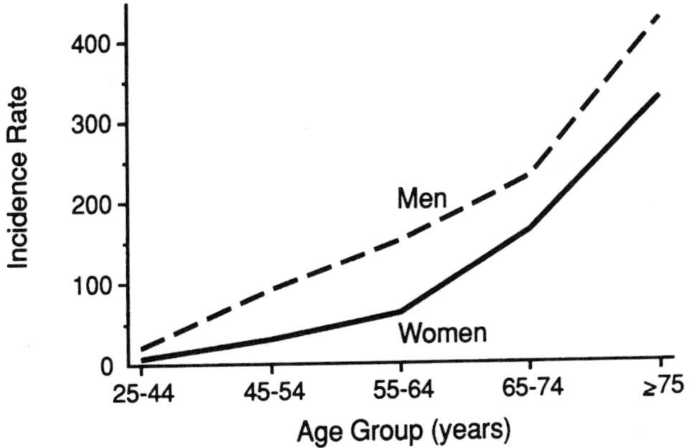

FIGURE 11-5

Coronary heart disease incidence rate by sex and age group—epidemiologic follow-up study of the First National Health and Nutrition Examination Survey. (*From: Coronary heart disease incidence, by sex—United States, 1971–1987.* Morb Mortal Wkly Rep *526, 1992.*)

risk associated with selected risk factors are presented in Table 11-5.

There is controversy about the importance for older adults of the established CHD risk factors, including tobacco use, hypertension, and hypercholesterolemia, among others. Major studies are under way to explore this issue (e.g., the Cardiovascular Health Study).[20] The best available data are from the 10-year follow-up examination of a nationally representative sample first examined in the National Health and Nutrition Examination Survey (NHANES I).[21] In this sample, free of CHD until at least age 55, the most consistently significant predictors of incident CHD were age, systolic blood pressure, smoking, diabetes, and educational level (Tables 11-6 and 11-7).[21] The findings of the NHANES I follow-up study are consistent with those of the Framingham Study for the risk factors of age, systolic blood pressure, and cholesterol but not for tobacco use or obesity.[22]

Electrocardiographic Abnormalities

The prevalence of specific major electrocardiographic abnormalities among older adults ranges from a low of 3 percent for atrial fibrillation to 9 percent for ventricular conduction defects; the prevalence of any major abnormality is 29 percent (Table 11-8).[23]

Lipids

The influence of total blood cholesterol level on the incidence of CHD diminishes with age for men but not for women. This is not true for the high-density lipoprotein (HDL) and low-density lipoprotein (LDL) components of total blood cholesterol, with high HDL and low LDL imparting a protective effect for men and women of all ages.[22] Evidence collected over the past two decades suggests an improving lipid profile for older Americans (Fig. 11-6).[24] Nevertheless, up to two-fifths of older adults may meet the National Cholesterol Education Program's definition of borderline high risk (200–239 mg/dl total cholesterol) and one-quarter may be in the high-risk range (≥ 200 mg/dl total cholesterol).[24]

Stroke

The prevalence and the incidence of stroke rise with age among both men and women (Table 11-9).[25] However, mortality trends show declining age-specific stroke mortality rates for both men and women.[26] In concert with these trends, the rate of discharge diagnoses for acute stroke decreased significantly for men and women from 1970 to 1985.[26]

TABLE 11-5

Relative Risk for Coronary Heart Disease, by Sex, Comparing the Presence of Each Factor to Its Absence and Controlling for All Others—Epidemiologic Follow-up Study of the First National Health and Nutrition Examination Survey, 1982–84, 1986, and 1987[a]

	Men		*Women*	
Risk Factor	**RR**[b]	**(95% CI**[c]**)**	**RR**	**(95% CI)**
Education[d]				
≤8th grade	1.3	(1.1–1.6)	1.6	(1.3–2.0)
9th–12th grade	1.1	(0.9–1.3)	1.1	(0.9–1.4)
Hypertension	1.5	(1.3–1.7)	1.5	(1.3–1.8)
High cholesterol	1.4	(1.2–1.6)	1.1	(0.9–1.2)
Diabetes	1.9	(1.5–2.5)	2.4	(1.9–3.0)
Overweight	1.3	(1.1–1.5)	1.4	(1.2–1.6)
Cigarette smoking	1.6	(1.4–1.8)	1.8	(1.5–2.1)

[a] Because of the small number of persons of other races in the sample, this includes only the 12,402 white participants.
[b] Relative risk.
[c] Confidence interval.
[d] Compared with persons having completed at least some college education.
SOURCE: Coronary heart disease incidence, by sex—United States, 1971–1987. *Morb Mortal Wkly Rep* 526, 1992.

TABLE 11-6

Relationship between Baseline (NHANES I) Measures and Risk of a Coronary Heart Disease Event over a 10-Year Interval for White Men and Women: Multivariate Logistic Coefficients

	Coefficient for Indicated Group					
	Men			Women		
Characteristic	**55–64**	**65–74**	**55–74**	**55–64**	**65–74**	**55–74**
Age	0.032	0.035	0.044[a]	0.106[a]	0.055[a]	0.101[a]
Systolic blood pressure	0.013[a]	0.009[a]	0.010[a]	0.006	0.010[a]	0.010[a]
Serum cholesterol	0.001	0.002	0.002	−0.004	0	−0.001
Cigarette smoking	0.453	0.396[a]	0.408[a]	0.527	0.546[a]	0.538[a]
Diabetes	0.775	0.688[a]	0.719[a]	0.638	0.794[a]	0.794[a]
Body mass index	0.029	0.004	0.013	−0.016	0.018	0.013
Alcohol	0.004	−0.005	0	−0.013	−0.038	−0.029
Education[b]	−0.326[a]	−0.169[a]	−0.220[a]	−0.477[a]	−0.241[a]	−0.279[a]

[a] Significant at $p < .05$; t-test.
[b] In computing mean years of education, the following scale was used: 0 = 0–4 years; 1 = 5–8 years; 2 = 9–11 years; 3 = ≥12 years.
SOURCE: Leaverton PE, Havlik RJ, Ingster-Moore LM, et al: Coronary heart disease and hypertension, in Cornoni-Huntley JC, Huntley RR, Feldman JJ (eds): *Health Status and Well-Being of the Elderly*. New York, Oxford University Press, 1990, chap 4, pp 53–70.

TABLE 11-7

Relationship between Baseline (NHANES I) Measures and Risk of a Coronary Heart Disease Event over a 10-Year Interval for Black Men and Women: Multivariate Logistic Coefficients

	Coefficient for Indicated Group					
	Men			Women		
Characteristic	**55–64**	**65–74**	**55–74**	**55–64**	**65–74**	**55–74**
Age	—	0.065	0.076[a]	—	0.009	0.070[a]
Systolic blood pressure	—	0.017[a]	0.016[a]	—	0.004	0.004
Serum cholesterol	—	0.007	0.005	—	0.003	0.003
Cigarette smoking	—	−0.729	−0.662	—	0.369	−0.605
Diabetes	—	−0.858	−0.944	—	1.518[a]	1.367[a]
Body mass index	—	−0.008	0.019	—	−0.068[a]	−0.048[a]
Alcohol	—	0.009	0.010	—	0.051	0.047
Education[b]	—	−0.041	−0.160	—	−0.403[a]	−0.448[a]

[a] Significant at $p < .05$; t-test.
[b] In computing mean years of education, the following scale was used: 0 = 0–4 years; 1 = 5–8 years; 2 = 9–11 years; 3 = ≥12 years.
SOURCE: Leaverton PE, Havlik RJ, Ingster-Moore LM, et al: Coronary heart disease and hypertension, in Cornoni-Huntley JC, Huntley RR, Feldman JJ (eds): *Health Status and Well-Being of the Elderly*. New York, Oxford University Press, 1990, chap 4, pp 53–70.

TABLE 11-8

Prevalence of Major Electrocardiographic Abnormalities among Elderly Men and Women

	Women, n = 2940		*Men, n = 2210*		*Total, n = 5150*	
	No.	**(%)**	**No.**	**(%)**	**No.**	**(%)**
Major Q/QS waves	107	(3.6)	162	(7.3)	269	(5.2)[a]
Left ventricular hypertrophy	122	(4.1)	95	(4.3)	217	(4.2)
Isolated major ST-T wave abnormalities	200	(6.8)	122	(5.5)	322	(6.3)
Atrial fibrillation	75	(2.6)	88	(4.0)	163	(3.2)[a]
First-degree atrioventricular block	93	(3.2)	180	(8.1)	273	(5.3)[a]
Ventricular conduction defects	158	(5.4)	288	(13.0)	446	(8.7)[a]
Left bundle branch block	52	(1.8)	35	(1.6)	87	(1.7)
Right bundle branch block	72	(2.4)	150	(6.8)	222	(4.3)[a]
Intraventricular block of indeterminate type	34	(1.2)	103	(4.7)	137	(2.7)[a]
Any	688	(23.4)	789	(35.7)	1477	(28.7)[a]

[a] p value <.01 for a test of equal proportions of men and women with each abnormality.
SOURCE: Furberg CD, Manolio TA, Psaty BM, et al: Major electrocardiographic abnormalities in persons aged 65 years and older (the Cardiovascular Health Study). *Am J Cardiol* 69:1329, 1992.

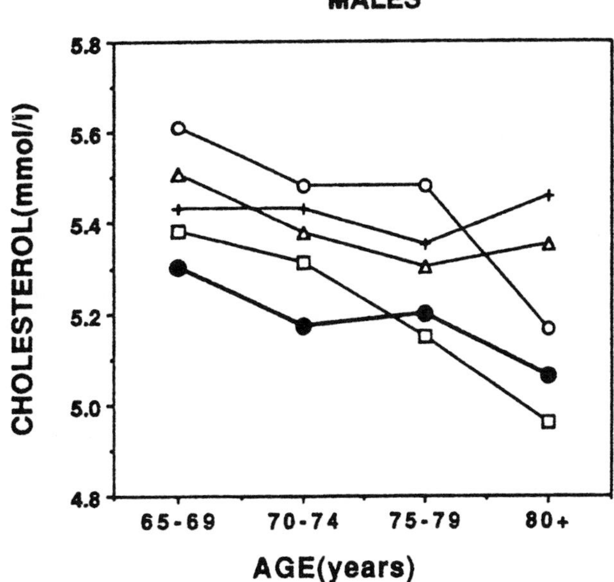

FIGURE 11-6

Comparison among five epidemiological studies of total plasma cholesterol concentrations, stratified by sex. Values for persons 80 to 84 and ≥ 85 years old are combined for the Cardiovascular Health Study (●), the Framingham Heart Study (○), and the Minnesota Heart Health Program (□) to allow comparison with results from the Lipid Research Clinics (△) and Honolulu Heart Study (+). (*From Ettinger WH et al: Lipoprotein lipids in older people—Results from the Cardiovascular Health Study.* Circulation *86:858, 1992. Reprinted with permission.*)

Much of the improvement in stroke morbidity and mortality is due to improved control of hypertension.[27] Stroke epidemiology becomes more complex as new diagnostic procedures are developed and as stroke subtypes (thrombotic, embolic, hemorrhagic) are separately investigated—serum cholesterol, for example, is inversely related with death from hemorrhagic stroke but positively related with death from nonhemorrhagic stroke.[27] Nevertheless, there is considerable consensus that important stroke risk factors include hypertension, tobacco use, high-fat diet, alcohol use, inactivity, obesity, elevated hematocrit, oral contraceptive use, and sickle cell anemia.[28]

TABLE 11-9

Prevalence of History of Prior Stroke Reported at Baseline (NHANES I)

	No. with stroke/No. examined (%)	
Age	**Men**	**Women**
35–44	5/928 (0.5%)	17/2013 (0.8%)
45–54	14/1058 (1.3%)	8/1220 (0.6%)
55–64	24/861 (2.8%)	28/962 (2.9%)
65–69	48/1067 (4.5%)	47/1148 (4.1%)
70	44/769 (5.7%)	48/870 (5.5%)

SOURCE: White LR, Losonczy KG, Wolf PA: Cerebrovascular disease, in Cornoni-Huntely JC, Huntley RR, Feldman JJ (eds): *Health Status and Well-Being of the Elderly.* New York, Oxford University Press, 1990, chap 6, pp 115–135.

Congestive Heart Failure

Relatively little is known about the epidemiology of congestive heart failure (CHF). It has been estimated from several studies that the prevalence of CHF increases from about 3 percent in middle-aged persons to 10 percent in those aged 75 and older, but methodological limitations in the studies are such that these estimates are probably too conservative.[29] The best available data are from the Framingham cohort. Over 30 years of follow-up, the incidence of CHF rose with age, with the sharpest rise occurring among the oldest old [the highest rate being 9 percent among 85- to 94-year-old men (Fig. 11-7)].[30] The highest mortality risk due to CHF occurs during the year after the patient comes under treatment; after this, life expectancy returns to normal.[29]

Lower-Extremity Arterial Disease

The prevalence in the adult population of lower extremity arterial disease (LEAD) as determined by abnormal ankle/brachial blood pressure index (ABI) ranges between 13 and 25 percent in Europe and the United States, with little difference between men and women.[31] Symptomatic LEAD presenting as self-reported intermittent claudication is observed in 14 percent of the elderly population.[32] Recognized risk factors for LEAD include cigarette smoking, diabetes and impaired glucose metabolism, and elevated systolic blood pressure; the role of lipids in LEAD is uncertain.[31] Smoking plays a particularly important role in the progression of the disease, with the ABI worsening over time in smokers versus nonsmokers.[31] Myocardial ischemia is the main cause of death in patients with LEAD (up to 70 percent of all deaths in this group), followed by cerebrovascular diseases, ruptured aneurysms, and visceral infarction.[31]

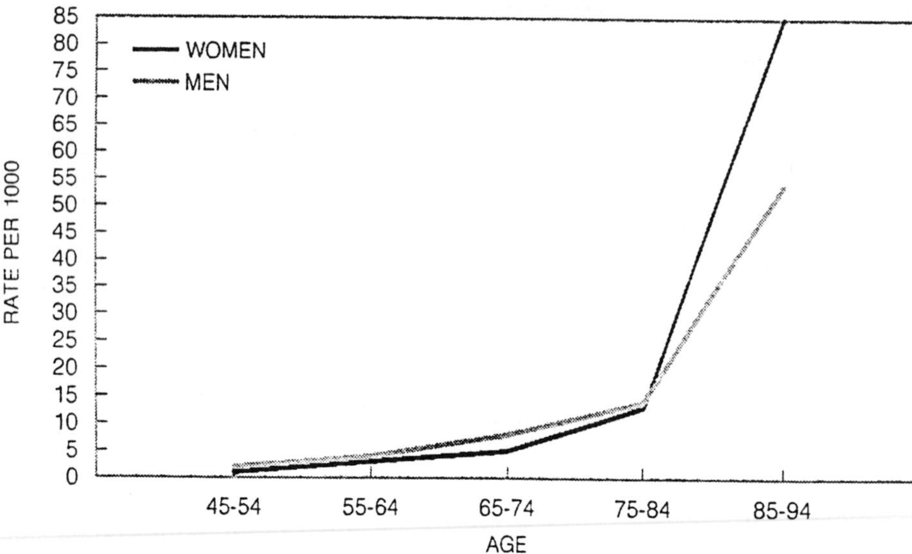

FIGURE 11-7
Incidence of cardiac failure by age and sex. Framingham Study, 30-year follow-up. (*From Kannel WB: Epidemiological aspects of heart failure. Cardiol Clin 7:1, 1989. Reprinted with permission.*)

Hypertension

Systolic and diastolic blood pressures commonly rise with age until the fifties and sixties, after which the rise in systolic pressure continues while levels of diastolic pressure tend to fall.[33] The result is increased prevalence of isolated systolic hypertension (ISH) with age[34]—important because ISH is a preeminent predictor of morbidity and mortality among the elderly.[33] The pharmacologic treatment of ISH in the elderly is now of demonstrated value.[35] However, less than one-fifth of the total burden of hypertension in the elderly population is due to ISH (Table 11-10).[21] Elevated diastolic blood pressure is a potent risk factor at all ages. For all levels of systolic blood pressure, risk increases with increases in diastolic blood pressure.[33] In addition to the evidence from the Systolic Hypertension in the Elderly Program, data from other investigations both in the United States and abroad suggest that the benefits of treating hypertension at all ages are demonstrable.[36]

Diabetes

As for many other chronic conditions, there is great regional variability in the prevalence of diabetes in the older adult population; worldwide, the prevalence of diabetes ranges from a high of 50 percent or more among Pima indians to a low of 2 percent in En-

TABLE 11-10

Rate of Hypertension by Traditional Categories According to Race, Gender, and Age at Follow-up (NHEFS) (in percent)

Group	Sample Size	Borderline	Isolated Systolic	Definite by Blood Pressure	Treated	Total Definite[a]
Age 55–64						
White men	698	19.2	1.9	6.6	26.2	34.7
White women	879	12.6	2.1	3.5	32.1	37.7
Black men	95	13.7	5.3	11.6	34.7	51.6
Black women	136	11.0	3.7	8.1	44.9	56.7
Age 65–74						
White men	522	19.4	4.0	4.6	33.0	41.6
White women	632	14.6	4.8	3.0	42.6	50.4
Black men	67	14.9	7.5	9.0	43.3	59.8
Black women	109	16.5	2.8	3.7	58.7	65.2
Age 75–86						
White men	641	22.2	8.9	5.0	30.6	44.5
White women	963	17.3	7.3	2.2	49.1	58.6
Black men	107	18.7	7.5	5.6	44.9	58.0
Black women	161	14.3	9.9	4.4	59.0	73.3

[a] Includes isolated systolic, definite by blood pressure, and treated categories.
SOURCE: Leaverton PE, Havlik RJ, Ingster-Moore LM, et al: Coronary heart disease and hypertension, in Cornoni-Huntley JC, Huntley RR, Feldman JJ (eds): *Health Status and Well-Being of the Elderly.* New York, Oxford University Press, 1990, chap 4, pp 53–70.

gland.[37] In the United States, African-Americans 65 to 74 years of age experience diabetes at twice the rate of same-aged whites; in the group aged 75 and older, the rate is 1.7 times greater among African-Americans (Table 11-3). There is little difference in the prevalence of diabetes between older men and women (99 and 98 per 1000, respectively; Table 11-2). The prevalence of occult diabetes among older adults has been investigated in relatively few studies. Most of these have used the oral glucose tolerance test, but diagnostic criteria vary considerably. Across many definitions of fasting hyperglycemia, the highest reported prevalence of newly diagnosed diabetes among those aged 60 and older is 26 percent, in Danish women, and the lowest prevalence is 1 percent or less, in Australian men and women.[37]

Cancer

The incidence of cancer (all sites combined) increases with age, with only a slight moderation in this trend among those aged 85 and older.[4] Exceptions to this pattern are lung and uterine cancer, for which peak incidence occurs in the age group 75 to 79. Cancer incidence rates in general have risen over time, the exceptions being stomach cancer and the leukemias. Of intense interest is the observation in many studies of an inverse relationship between blood cholesterol level and risk of cancer. The newest evidence supporting this relationship is from NHANES I and the Epidemiologic Follow-up Study. Data from a nationally representative sample were used to examine the hypothesis that lower cholesterol in those with cancer results from a preclinical effect of cancer on cholesterol (e.g., that cancer is a risk factor for lowered cholesterol, rather than the other way around). The finding, consistent with several other studies, was that the inverse relationship between cholesterol and all incident cancer in men held for several years after cholesterol was measured (and held in women for smoking-related cancers).[38] This suggests that a preclinical cancer effect is at best a partial explanation of the cancer/cholesterol association.

Pneumonia and Influenza

Several influenza outbreaks occur almost every year in the United States. Mortality experienced due to influenza and pneumonia has been summarized as follows by the National Center for Health Statistics[39]:

1. Mortality due to pneumonia and influenza has risen steadily during the past two decades, from about 11 to about 13 per 100,000 population.
2. Among the elderly (age 75 and older), the rates are much higher—472 and 318 per 100,000 for men and women, respectively.
3. Among the oldest old (age 85 and older), the rates are 1,067 and 711 per 100,000 for men and women.
4. The large majority of deaths in this category are due to pneumonia.
5. There is large regional variability in mortality in the United States, ranging from a high of 96 per 100,000 population among men of age 45 and older in the District of Columbia to a low of 19 per 100,000 among women of age 45 and older in Delaware (the U.S. averages for men and women at or above age 45 are 55 and 30 per 100,000, respectively).

While pneumonia is the leading cause of infection-caused death among the elderly, it accounts for less than half of all deaths from infection among those aged 65 and older (Table 11-11).[40]

TABLE 11-11

Mortality Rates for Deaths Associated with Infectious Diseases at 12 Years of Follow-up According to Gender and Age at Baseline (NHANES I)[a]

		Men			*Women*		
			Age Group			*Age Group*	
Type of Infection/ICD9 Code		**Total, n = 2605**	**55–64, n = 836**	**≥65, n = 1769**	**Total, n = 2869**	**55–64, n = 927**	**≥65, n = 1942**
Pneumonia	480–486	55.2 (101)	29.4 (18)	68.7 (83)	22.7 (35)	6.2 (4)	31.2 (31)
Septicemia	038–038.9	13.0 (23)	2.8 (2)	18.5 (21)	15.9 (25)	5.6 (5)	20.9 (20)
Herpes zoster	053–053.9	4.1 (9)	2.6 (2)	4.9 (7)	3.0 (6)	1.1 (1)	3.8 (5)
Kidney	590–590.9	3.6 (6)	0 (0)	5.5 (6)	2.7 (7)	1.2 (1)	3.5 (6)
Gangrene	785.4	3.4 (6)	1.3 (1)	4.5 (5)	3.1 (6)	3.2 (1)	3.1 (5)
Miscellaneous infectious diseases	001–139.8	120.0 (224)	57.9 (39)	151.4 (185)	71.7 (141)	35.4 (26)	89.0 (115)
Total mortality all causes[b]		486.1 (1019)	249.2 (184)	564.4 (835)	305.7 (679)	134.3 (100)	378.0 (579)

[a] Rates presented are cumulative event rates at 12 years of follow-up computed from Kaplan-Meier survival curves; number of events are in parenthese.

[b] Includes 37 deaths among men and 39 deaths among women, where no death certificate has been obtained.

SOURCE: Lacroix AZ, Lipson S, White LR: Infectious diseases, in Cornoni-Huntley JC, Huntley RR, Feldman JJ (eds): *Health Status and Well-Being of the Elderly.* New York, Oxford University Press, 1990, chap 3, pp 41–52.

Dementia, Alzheimer's Disease, and Depression

The epidemiology of late-life dementia is not well developed. International comparisons of prevalence rates show a consistent pattern of sharply increased prevalence of moderate and severe dementia with age, with peak prevalence reaching 20 to 30 percent among the oldest old.[41] Data on the incidence of dementia, which are very scarce, suggest a peak of 2 to 3 percent annually in the ninth decade of life, followed by a sharp fall in incidence rates thereafter.[41]

Alzheimer's disease is the most prevalent cause of dementia. Internationally, there is wide variation in the prevalence of Alzheimer's disease, probably due in large part to methodological differences; prevalence is high (the disease is present in almost 50 percent of those 90 and older) when diagnosis is based only on psychometric testing, while prevalence is low (5 to 10 percent among those 90 and older) when diagnosis requires the presence of functional impairments.[42] Age-specific incidence rates are remarkably similar in several countries in Europe and in the United States, rising exponentially from less than 5 per 1000 person-years among the young old to 15 or more per 1000 person years among the oldest old.[42] Research on the etiology of Alzheimer's disease is in its infancy; except for age and a positive family history of dementia, no definite risk factors for Alzheimer's disease have yet been identified.[42]

The study of the epidemiology of late-life depression advanced with the establishment in 1980 of diagnostic criteria for major depressive disorders; investigations that have used these criteria have consistently observed that the peak prevalence of depression is during young or middle adulthood.[43] For those aged 65 and older, the pattern for depression is parallel for men and women and rates are among the lowest experienced in the life span. The pattern for dysphoria is sharply divergent, with prevalence decreasing with age among men and increasing sharply among women.[43] The reasons for these differences are not known.

Parkinson's Disease

Parkinson's disease is relatively rare and difficult to study epidemiologically because no definitive diagnostic tests exist.[44] Nevertheless, there is substantial consistency among studies that both prevalence and incidence rates rise steadily with age.[44] In the United States, the prevalence of Parkinson's disease has been observed to double with each decade of age from the fifties on; it is diagnosed in about 1 percent of those aged 80 or older.[44]

HEALTH HABITS

The health habits and risk profiles of the U.S. population have improved steadily since the mid-1960s, and this has been true of older women and men as well (Table 11-12).[45]

Tobacco Use

There are large regional differences in patterns of tobacco use by older adults. For example, smoking rates among persons aged 65 and older in Boston have been reported to be twice the rates in Iowa (25 versus 13 percent among men and 20 versus 9 percent among women).[46] However, there is a clear decrease in use with age, with only 1 to 7 percent of those aged 85 and older reporting tobacco use.[46] This is due to early mortality among smokers and an increase in smoking cessation with age. The effect of tobacco use on mortality in the elderly is the same as among younger people: elderly smokers experience much higher mortality rates than do nonsmokers.[47] The evidence on the importance of smoking cessation by the elderly is compelling—demonstrated benefits of cessation among elderly smokers include lowered CHD mortality rate, gain in life expectancy, and improved pulmonary function.[47]

Physical Activity

Physical activity levels tend to decline with advancing age, although for many people in the United States, lifelong activity levels are low. Factors related to decreased activity include illness and fear of injury.[48] It is now recognized that people of all ages may benefit from regular physical activity; in the elderly (including those who are ill), exercise improves strength, aerobic capacity, gait, balance, and mobility.[49]

Alcohol

As for tobacco use, there is great regional variation in alcohol use patterns among the elderly—not a surprising finding, since smoking and drinking alcohol are companion behaviors for many. As an example of regional variation, alcohol use rates (30-day prevalence) among persons aged 65 and older were reported in Iowa to be two-thirds to half the rates observed in Boston (46 versus 68 percent among men and 23 versus 47 percent among women).[46] As with smoking, the prevalence of alcohol use declines with age, but not as markedly.[50]

TABLE 11-12

Cigarette Smoking, Definite Elevated Blood Pressure, and High-Risk Serum Cholesterol Levels According to Sex and Age: United States for Selected Years[a]

	Current Smoker[b]				Former Smoker			
Sex and Age	**1965**	**1976**	**1983**	**1987**	**1965**	**1976**	**1983**	**1987**
Cigarette smoking								
Male								
20 years and over, age adjusted	52.1	41.6	35.4	31.5	20.3	29.6	31.1	31.4
65 years and over	28.5	23.0	22.0	17.2	28.1	44.4	48.1	53.4
Female								
20 years and over, age adjusted	34.2	32.5	29.9	27.0	8.2	13.9	16.4	18.0
65 years and over	9.6	12.8	13.1	13.7	4.5	11.7	18.7	19.8
	1960–62	1971–74	1976–80					
Definite elevated blood pressure[c]								
Both sexes								
Age adjusted, 25–74 years	20.9	21.7	20.1					
65–74 years	48.7	40.9	34.5					
Male								
Age adjusted, 25–74 years	20.7	22.9	23.0					
65–74 years	40.5	36.4	33.3					
Female								
Age adjusted, 25–74 years	21.0	20.4	17.4					
65–74 years	55.4	44.4	35.5					
	1960–62	1971–74	1976–80					
High-risk serum cholesterol levels[d]								
Both sexes								
Age adjusted, 25–74 years	26.9	23.2	21.9					
65–74 years	37.3	31.3	27.2					
Male								
Age adjusted, 25–74 years	24.1	22.1	20.1					
65–74 years	20.8	19.9	18.1					
Female								
Age adjusted, 25–74 years	29.3	24.0	23.3					
65–74 years	50.8	40.0	34.3					

[a] Data from National Center for Health Statistics. 1989. *Health, United States, 1988.* DHHS pub. no. (PHS) 89-1232, 96, 100, 101. Washington. Data expressed in percent.
[b] A current smoker is a person who has smoked at least 100 cigarettes and who now smokes; includes occasional smokers.
[c] Systolic pressure ≥160 mmHg or diastolic pressure ≥95 mmHg, or both.
[d] Risk range: 20–29 years: >200 mg/dl; 30–39 years: >240 mg/dl; 40+ years: >260 mg/dl.
SOURCE: Manton KG: The dynamics of population aging: Demography and policy analysis. *Milbank Q* 69:309, 1991.

CHALLENGES IN THE EPIDEMIOLOGIC STUDY OF THE ELDERLY

The past several decades of epidemiologic study in the United States have been characterized by many as a period of concentration on the diseases and conditions most salient to the health of men, especially middle-aged men. This is often attributed to the fact that most investigators have themselves been middle-aged men, and that they have been preoccupied with thoughts of their own vulnerability.

Fortunately, current directions in epidemiologic research are emphasizing the health of the broader population, including ethnic groups other than those of European origin, women, and older adults. There are now under way a good number of major epidemiologic studies of the elderly, some of which are referenced in this chapter.

Nevertheless, past systematic exclusion of older adults from epidemiologic investigations has resulted in a current dearth of data on the elderly. In the near future, cautious extrapolation from the findings of studies that have not included participants in their seventies and older will continue to be a necessity.

As more epidemiologic studies of the elderly are undertaken, researchers will encounter issues in study design and data collection that are somewhat unique to the study of older adults. With the elderly, it can be difficult to differentiate specific disease processes from normal, global aging processes in terms of their relative influence on physical and mental functioning and on morbidity and mortality patterns. Ascertaining the health status of older adults in epidemiologic surveys may be considerably complicated by some respondents' inability to report reliably about medical conditions and treatments because of long medical history, diminished diagnostic efforts for elderly patients, cognitive impairment, and other limits.[51]

Other challenges to survey researchers working with older adults include sampling problems—persons in poorer health may be less likely to participate—and the use of secondhand reports obtained from proxy respondents complicates the interpretation of data, to mention but two issues among many. Special considerations in the epidemiologic study of the elderly have been addressed recently in a comprehensive collection of papers on this topic.[52]

REFERENCES

1. U.S. Department of Commerce Economics and Statistics Administration Bureau of the Census, Global Aging—Comparative Indicators and Future Trends, September 1991.
2. Rogers RG, Rogers A, Belanger A: Active life among the elderly in the United States: Multistate life-table estimates and population projections. *Milbank Q* 67:370, 1989.
3. Sutherland JE, Persky VW, Brody JA: Proportionate mortality trends: 1950 through 1986. *JAMA* 264:3178, 1990.
4. Brody JA, Brock DB, Williams TF: Trends in the health of the elderly population. *Annu Rev Public Health* 8:211, 1987.
5. National Center for Health Statistics: *Current Estimates from the National Health Interview Survey, 1991.* Series 10: Data from the National Health Survey No. 184. Vital and Health Statistics, USDHHS, PHS, CDC, NCHS, Hyattsville, Maryland, December, 1992, DHHS Publication No. (PHS) 93-1512.
6. Manton KG: Epidemiological, demographic, and social correlates of disability among the elderly. *Milbank Q* 67:13, 1989.
7. Kunkel SR, Applebaum RA: Estimating the prevalence of long-term disability for an aging society. *J Gerontol* 47:S253, 1992.
8. Liu K, Manton KG, Liu BM: Morbidity, disability, and long-term care of the elderly: Implications for insurance financing. *Milbank Q* 68:445, 1990.
9. Cummings SR, Kelsey JL, Nevitt MC, O'Dowd KJ: Epidemiology of osteoporosis and osteoporotic fractures. *Epidemiol Rev* 7:178, 1985.
10. Jacobsen SJ, Goldberg J, Miles TP, et al: Hip fracture incidence among the old and very old: A population-based study of 745,435 cases. *Am J Public Health* 80:871, 1990.
11. Sattin RW: Falls among older persons: A public health perspective. *Annu Rev Public Health* 13:489, 1992.
12. Law MR, Wald NJ, Meade TW: Strategies for prevention of osteoporosis and hip fracture. *Br Med J* 303:453, 1991.
13. Grisso JA, Kelsey JL, Strom BL, et al: Risk factors for falls as a cause of hip fracture in women. *N Engl J Med* 324:1326, 1991.
14. Wolf ME, Rivara FP: Nonfall injuries in older adults. *Annu Rev Public Health* 13:509, 1992.
15. Herzog AR, Fultz NH: Prevalence and incidence of urinary incontinence in community-dwelling populations. *J Am Gerontol Soc* 38:273, 1990.
16. Lawrence RC, Everett DF, Hochberg MC: Arthritis, in Cornoni-Huntley JC, Huntley RR, Feldman JJ (eds): *Health Status and Well-Being of the Elderly.* New York, Oxford University Press, 1990, chap 7, pp 136–154.
17. Hochberg MC, Spector TD: Epidemiology of rheumatoid arthritis: Update. *Epidemiol Rev* 12:247, 1990.
18. Feinleib M, Gillum RF: Coronary heart disease in the elderly: The magnitude of the problem in the United States, in Wenger NK, Furberg CD, Pitt E (eds): *Coronary Heart Disease in the Elderly.* New York, Elsevier, 1986, chap 3, pp 29–59.
19. Coronary heart disease incidence, by sex—United States, 1971–1987. *Morb Mortal Wkly Rep* 526, 1992.
20. Fried LP, Borhani NO, Enright P, et al: The Cardiovascular health study: Design and rationale. *Ann Epidemiol* 1:263, 1991.
21. Leaverton PE, Havlik RJ, Ingester-Moore LM, et al: Coronary heart disease and hypertension, in Cornoni-Huntley JC, Huntley RR, Feldman JJ (eds): *Health Status and Well-Being of the Elderly.* Oxford University Press, 1990, chap 4, pp 53–70.
22. Kannel WB, Vokonas PS: Primary risk factors for coronary heart disease in the elderly: The Framingham Study, in Wenger NK, Furberg CD, Pitt E (eds): *Coronary Heart Disease in the Elderly.* New York, Elsevier, 1986, chap 4, pp 60–95.
23. Furberg CD, Manolio TA, Psaty BM, et al: Major Electrocardiographic abnormalities in persons aged 65 years and older (the Cardiovascular Health Study). *Am J Cardiol* 69:1329, 1992.
24. Ettinger WH, Wahl PW, Kuller LH, et al: Lipoprotein lipids in older people—Results from the Cardiovascular Health Study. *Circulation* 86:858, 1992.
25. White LR, Losonczy KG, Wolf PA: Cerebrovascular disease, in Cornoni-Huntley JC, Huntley RR, Feldman JJ (eds): *Health Status and Well-Being of the Elderly.* New York, Oxford University Press, 1990, chap 6, pp 115–135.
26. McGovern PG, Burke GL, Sprafka JM, et al: Trends in mortality, morbidity, and risk factor levels for stroke from 1960 through 1990. *JAMA* 268:753, 1992.
27. Ostfeld AM, Wilk E: Epidemiology of stroke, 1980–1990: A progress report. *Epidemiol Rev* 12:253, 1990.
28. Dyken ML, Wolf PA, Barnett JJ, et al: Risk factors in stroke: A statement for physicians by the Subcommittee on Risk Factors and Stroke of the Stroke Council. *Stroke* 15:1105, 1984.
29. Luchi RJ, Taffet GE, Teasdale TA: Congestive heart failure in the elderly. *J Am Gerontol Soc* 39:810, 1991.

30. Kannel WB: Epidemiological aspects of heart failure. *Cardiol Clin* 7:1, 1989.
31. Vogt MT, Wolfson SK, Kuller LH: Lower extremity arterial disease and the aging process: A review. *J Clin Epidemiol* 45:529, 1992.
32. Hale WE, Marks RG, May FE: Epidemiology of intermittent claudication: Evaluation of risk factors. *Age Ageing* 17:57, 1988.
33. Bulpitt CJ: Blood pressure in the elderly, in Marmot M, Elliott P (eds): *Coronary Heart Disease Epidemiology—From Aetiology to Public Health.* New York, Oxford University Press, 1992, chap 7, pp 103–113.
34. Psaty BM, Furberg CD, Kuller LH, et al: Isolated systolic hypertension and subclinical cardiovascular disease in the elderly—Initial findings from the Cardiovascular Health Study. *JAMA* 268:1287, 1992.
35. SHEP Cooperative Research Group: Prevention of stroke by antihypertensive drug treatment in older persons with isolated systolic hypertension—Final results of the Systolic Hypertension in the Elderly Program (SHEP). *JAMA* 265:3255, 1991.
36. Smith WM: Epidemiology of hypertension in older patients. *Am J Med* 85:2, 1988.
37. Damsgaard EMS: Known diabetes and fasting hyperglycaemia in the elderly. *Dan Med Bull* 37:530, 1990.
38. Schatzkin A, Jones DY, Harris TB, et al: Cancer, in Cornoni-Huntley JC, Huntley RR, Feldman JJ (eds): *Health Status and Well-Being of the Elderly.* New York, Oxford University Press, 1990, chap 5, pp 71–114.
39. Metropolitan Insurance Companies: Pneumonia and Influenza Mortality on the Increase. Statistical Bulletin 68 (2):10, 1987.
40. Lacroix AZ, Lipson S, White LR: Infectious diseases, in Cornoni-Huntley JC, Huntley RR, Feldman JJ (eds): *Health Status and Well-Being of the Elderly.* New York, Oxford University Press, 1990, chap 3, pp 41–52.
41. Mortimer JA: Epidemiology of dementia: International comparisons, in Brody JA, Maddox GL (eds): *Epidemiology and Aging—An International Perspective.* New York, Springer Verlag, 1988, chap 10, pp 150–164.
42. Breteler MMB, Claus JJ, van Duijin CM, et al: Epidemiology of Alzheimer's disease. *Epidemiol Rev* 14:59, 1992.
43. Leaf PJ, Berkman CS, Weissman MM, et al: The epidemiology of late-life depression, in Brody JA, Maddox GL (eds): *Epidemiology and Aging—An International Perspective.* New York, Springer Verlag, 1988, chap 8, pp 117–133.
44. Tanner CM: Epidemiology of Parkinson's disease. *Neurol Clin* 10:317, 1992.
45. Manton KG: The Dynamics of population aging: Demography and policy analysis. *Milbank Q* 69:309, 1991.
46. Cornoni-Huntley J, Brock DB, Ostfeld AM, et al: *Established Populations for Epidemiologic Studies of the Elderly Resource Data Book.* U.S. Department of Health and Human Services, Public Health Service, National Institutes of Health, NIH Publication No. 86-2443.
47. The Surgeon General's 1990 Report on the Health Benefits of Smoking Cessation, Executive Summary. *MNUR* 1990:39(12), 1.
48. Wagner EH, LaCroix AZ, Buchner DM, Larson EB: Effects of physical activity on health status in older adults: I. Observational studies. *Annu Rev Public Health* 13:451, 1992.
49. Buchner DM, Beresford SA, Larson EB, et al: Effects of physical activity on health status in older adults: II. Intervention studies. *Annu Rev Public Health* 13:469, 1992.
50. Dufour MC, Colliver J, Grigson MB, Stinson F: Use of alcohol and tobacco, in Cornoni-Huntley JC, Huntley RR, Feldman JJ (eds): *Health Status and Well-Being of the Elderly.* New York, Oxford University Press, 1990, chap 9, pp 172–183.
51. Mittelmark MB, Psaty BM, Rautaharju PM, et al: Prevalence of cardiovascular diseases among older adults: The Cardiovascular Health Study. *Am J Epidemiol* 137:311, 1993.
52. Wallace RB, Woolson RF (eds): *The Epidemiologic Study of the Elderly.* New York, Oxford University Press, 1992.

Chapter 12

RISK FACTORS FOR MORBIDITY AND MORTALITY IN OLDER POPULATIONS: AN EPIDEMIOLOGIC APPROACH

Trudy L. Bush, Susan R. Miller, Michael H. Criqui, and Elizabeth Barrett-Connor

This chapter discusses risk factors for morbidity (nonfatal conditions and disability) and mortality in older persons. *Risk factors* may be defined as innate or acquired characteristics of individuals which are associated with an increased likelihood of a disease or condition. Of particular importance are those factors which are amenable to change and/or treatment, since it may be possible to alter the risk of morbid and mortal events by altering the risk factor.

It may be argued that the identification of risk factors for mortality in older individuals is less important than in younger persons, since it is possible only to delay death. The biologic limit to the human life span now appears to be around 100 years of age. However, our goal as physicians and public health practitioners is to postpone death, enabling more persons to live out their full life spans, that is, to prevent the deaths occurring in individuals in their seventh and eighth decades.

Perhaps even more important than the potential to delay death is the potential to delay or even avoid morbidity and disability. Consequently, the identification of risk factors for nonfatal conditions associated with serious sequelae may, in the long run, enable older persons to live out that full life span in good health. Even if we are unable to extend life, the prevention of morbid events, including impairments, disabilities, and handicaps, is a most worthy goal.

Until recently, the principal purpose of identifying risk factors has been to prevent "premature" mortality and morbidity, with the definition of a premature event as one which occurs in persons younger than 60 years of age. Thus, the majority of major studies on antecedents of coronary heart disease, cancers, and other common conditions has included primarily middle-aged individuals as participants. Moreover, because most such conditions pass the clinical horizon earlier in men than in women, those studies have perforce focused on diseases more prevalent and causing more deaths in men. Few studies have looked exclusively or even primarily at antecedents of fatal and nonfatal events in older people.

As a result of that historical emphasis on premature mortality and morbidity, we are left with serious deficiencies in knowledge regarding the cause and prevention of diseases incident in old age, to the disadvantage of practitioners who care for elderly patients. Furthermore, since many of the studies on "premature" morbidity and mortality were conducted in men, we are also left with descrepancies in knowledge about prevention in older women, who constitute a disproportionate share of the elderly population. Fortunately these deficiencies are being increasingly widely appreciated, and there is a growing interest in the conduct of both epidemiologic research and clinical trials in the elderly, notably including older women. This reflects a growing recognition that women have been understudied and that the old definition of a "premature" event is outdated. In the last two decades the marked decline in death rates from coronary heart disease and stroke in both men and women over 65 years of age provided empirical evidence that mortality can be delayed in older individuals. It may be argued now that a conservative definition of a "premature" death is one that occurs in either gender before age 75.

Conventional wisdom holds that traditional risk factors for morbidity and mortality (e.g., smoking, elevated blood pressure, elevated serum cholesterol levels) are less important, or even unimportant, in older persons. The implication of this "wisdom" is that there is little personal or public health benefit to be gained by modifying risk factors in older people. However, this view has been inferred from information which is both dated and limited.

As an example, many studies have found no association between smoking and mortality in older adults. However, these reports have failed to consider that the negative results may represent methodologic problems of insufficient statistical power, survivorship bias, or a cohort effect. That is, smoking may appear not to be associated with increased mortality in older people because insufficient numbers of older persons who had smoked survived into old age, because too few older persons smoked, at least for long or intensively enough, or because studies included too few other persons for the association to be clear. As an example of how such notions may become disproven with larger and more sophisticated studies, however, smoking has recently been shown to carry substantial risk to health in epidemiologic research targeted to older populations.[1]

In this chapter we examine known and suspected risk factors for coronary heart disease, stroke, cancer, and fractures in older people. These specific conditions were chosen because they are (1) common in older individuals, (2) the major causes of death and of functional disability in older persons, and (3) associated with significant health care costs. In addition, risk factors for these conditions have been identified in younger individuals, and modification of these risk factors results in a reduced risk of death or morbidity in younger people, suggesting that similar risk reduction in older persons might confer similar benefits.

Currently there is no consensus on the definition of older persons, although individuals 65 years and older are, by convention, considered to be older. Of necessity, however, some of the data discussed here will be from studies of individuals over 55 or 60 years of age.

AGE AND SEX AS RISK FACTORS

Age

Chronologic age is the most consistent and robust predictor of morbidity and mortality in both sexes across the entire life span. In other words, the age of an individual is the best indicator of his or her risk of dying and/or having a chronic disease or disability.

Figure 12-1 presents all-cause death rates by 5-year age groups for men and women 40 and older in the United States in 1987.[2] (Mortality data on persons older than 84 years of age are not available in 5-year increments.) As evident from this figure, there is an exponential increase in mortality with increasing chronologic age. This association of age with mortality is consistent across the entire age span, with each 5-year increase in age associated with an approximately 50 percent increased risk of death. This reality, well appreciated by gerontologists since the age of Gompertz (and by the lay public since at least biblical times), is often masked in research designed to focus on other forces that increase risk of death, especially "premature" death. Thus the critical reader is well advised to look for "age-adjusted" in tables or figure legends of morbidity and mortality associations and consider the data in that context.

An increase in disability and morbidity is also associated with increasing chronologic age. Figure 12-2 presents the proportion of the noninstitutionalized elderly population having difficulty performing selected activities of daily living by age groups.[3] As can be seen in this figure, the prevalence of all disabilities is higher at each successive age; each 10-year increase in age is associated with a 50 to 100 percent increase in the prevalence of a specific disability.

The percentage of older persons with selected chronic conditions and sensory impairments (loss of hearing or visual acuity) by age is presented in Fig. 12-3. These data, from a geriatric screening program located in Dunedin, Florida (the Florida Geriatric Research Program), clearly indicate that increasing age is associated with higher prevalence of morbid conditions. The aggregate burden of morbid conditions by age is underestimated even in such carefully conducted research, however, since comorbidity (the presence of multiple chronic conditions) also increases with increasing age.

Sex

Next to chronologic age, an individual's sex is the most important predictor of mortality (see Chap. 3). Men at every age, even the oldest ages, have mortality rates 60 to 80 percent higher than those of women (Fig. 12-4). On average, death rates in women lag behind those in men by approximately 8 years.

A common misconception is that the female advantage in mortality is rapidly lost after menopause, and that at advanced ages women "catch up" to men vis à vis their mortality. However, the data do not support this thesis. Younger women (in their forties and fifties) have mortality rates about 45 percent lower than men of the same ages; in postmenopausal women in their sixties and seventies, mortality rates also are 45 percent lower than those of similarly aged men. Even at the oldest ages (i.e., 85 years and older), women have death rates 22 percent lower than those of men.[2]

While female sex is protective against death at the older ages, this same protection is not afforded for disabilities and morbidity (Figs. 12-5 and 12-6). Compared with men of similar ages, women over 65 years of age have more difficulty performing more activities of daily living. For example, as seen in Fig. 12-5, women have more difficulty walking, bathing, dressing, going outside, getting out of a bed or chair, and using a toilet than do men.[2]

Likewise, women do not have any apparent advantage in actual burden of disease. As demonstrated

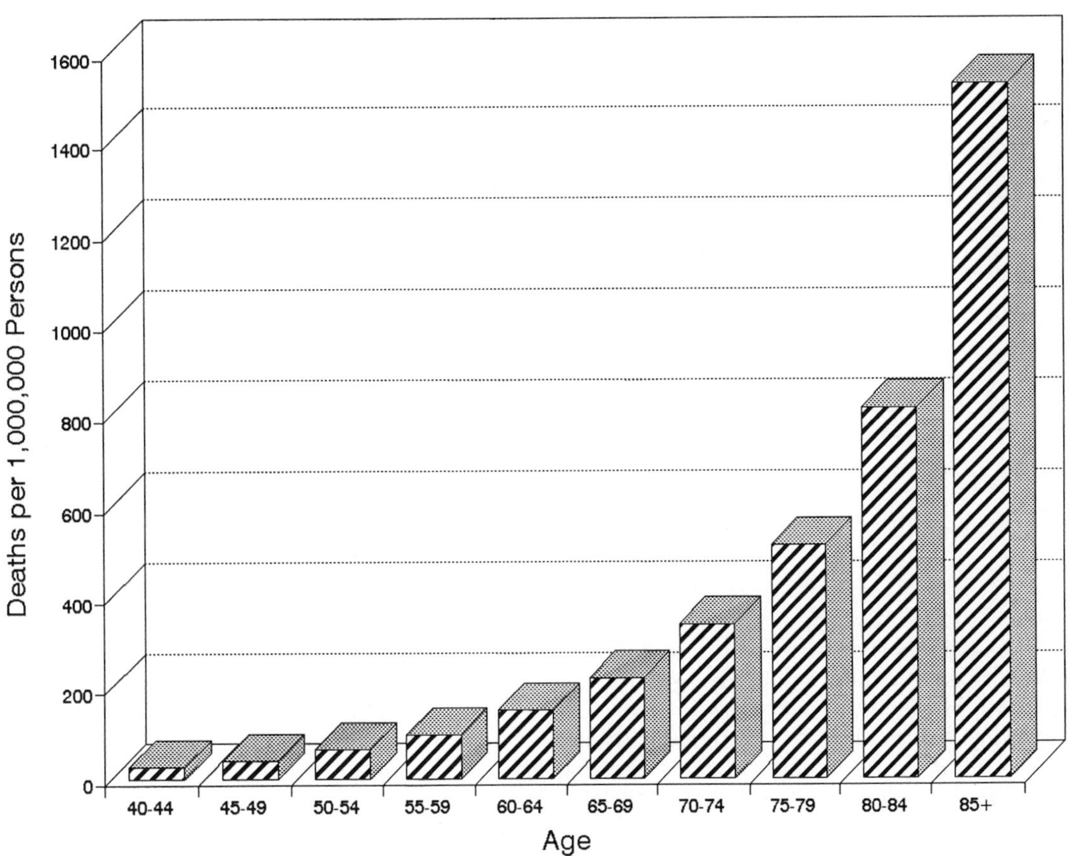

FIGURE 12-1

Death rates by age, United States, 1987. (*From National Center for Health Statistics, Vital Health Statistics of the United States, 1987, Washington, DC, Public Health Service, 1990, vol 2, part A.*)

by data from the Florida Geriatric Research Program (Fig. 12-6), women and men have about an equal prevalence of diabetes, sensory deprivation, and gastrointestinal problems, men are somewhat more likely than women to have cardiovascular disease and cancer, and women are more likely to have bone and joint conditions and hypertension.

In summary, both age and sex are consistent and immutable risk factors for mortality across the entire life span, including old age. Increasing chronologic

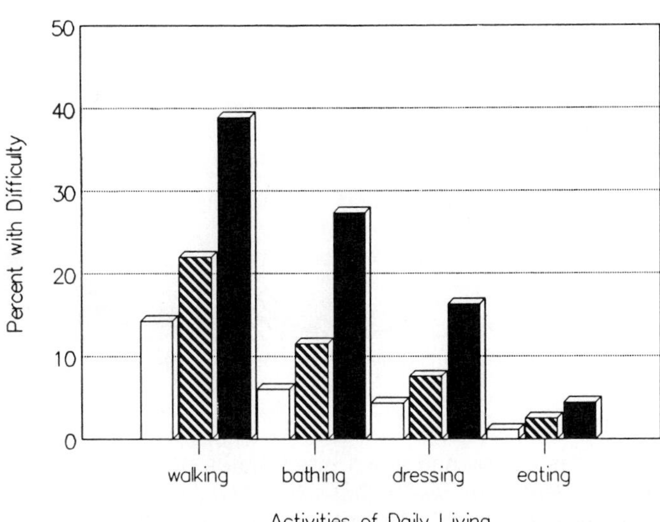

FIGURE 12-2

Percentage of older persons with difficulty doing daily activities, by age (□ 65–74; ▧ 75–84; ■ 85+).

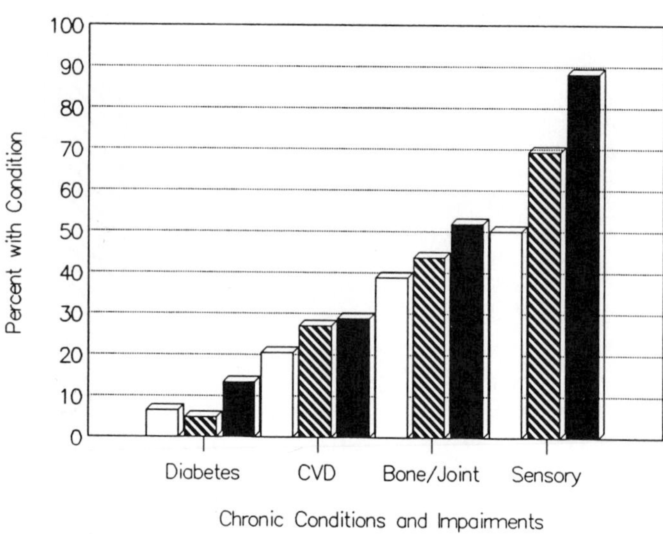

FIGURE 12-3

Percentage of older persons with selected chronic conditions, by age (□ 65–74; ▧ 75–84; ■ 85+). (*From Newschafer CJ et al: Am J Epidemiol 136:23, 1992.*)

age is associated with increasing risk of death, with the risk increasing exponentially by age after age 13 for each sex. However, at every age, women have a clear advantage in risk of death compared with men. Nonetheless, older women tend to have somewhat greater disability than older men and about the same burden of chronic conditions. As a result women with a heavy burden of chronic disabilities, notably immobility (see Chap. 120), and functional limitations are heavily represented among the "oldest old" (those over 85) and especially outnumber men (by approximately 6:1) in long-term care institutions.

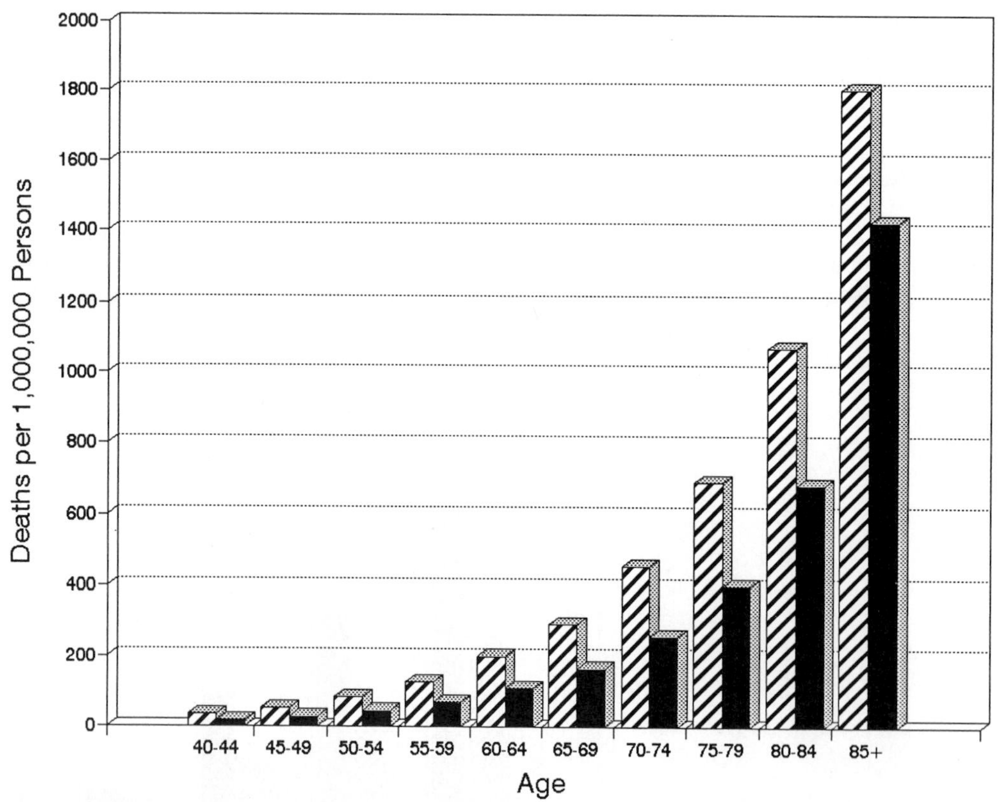

FIGURE 12-4

Death rates by sex and age, United States, 1987 (▨, men; ■, women). (*From National Center for Health Statistics, Vital Health Statistics of the United States, 1987, Washington, DC, Public Health Service, 1990, part A.*)

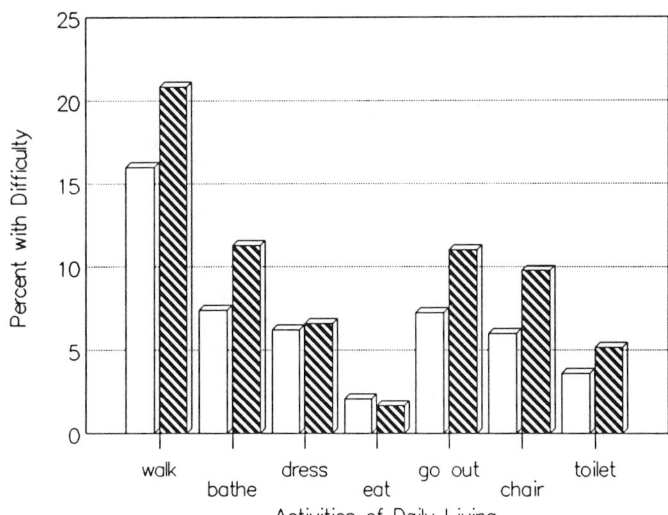

FIGURE 12-5
Percentage of older persons with difficulty doing daily activities, by sex (□, men; ▨, women).

RISK FACTORS FOR SELECTED CONDITIONS

Coronary Heart Disease

Coronary heart disease (CHD) is the major killer of older people,[2] accounting for 31 percent of all deaths in both men and women over 65 years of age. CHD also accounts for significant health costs and is the second leading cause of disability (after arthritis) in older people. A 40 percent increase in the prevalence of CHD, as well as limitations in activities as a result of the disease, has occurred during the past two decades.[3–5] This is attributable principally to increasing average age of the population and the high proportion of elderly persons, in whom CHD prevalence and incidence are the highest of any age group.

Somewhat paradoxically, since the mid-1960s, mortality from CHD has been declining at all ages, including the oldest ages.[3] Even in recent years (between 1979 and 1984), there has been a substantial further decline in coronary deaths in older people (Table 12-1). This recent decline is substantial (7 percent) in those over 85 years and in the younger elderly (65–74 years) (13 percent). This finding suggests that both medical-surgical interventions and changes in lifestyle may have contributed to this decline in mortality.[6] Even the most aggressive sorts of interventions appear generally well tolerated in carefully selected patients over 75 (especially if urgent or emergent surgery can be avoided), with good long-term survival and improvement in symptoms.[7] Thus while diagnostic and therapeutic advances have reduced mortality from CHD, they concomitantly contribute to the increasing prevalence of CHD among older persons who have survived into an age of higher risk with or without previous CHD.

These observations of decreasing CHD mortality in the elderly population are compatible with the the-

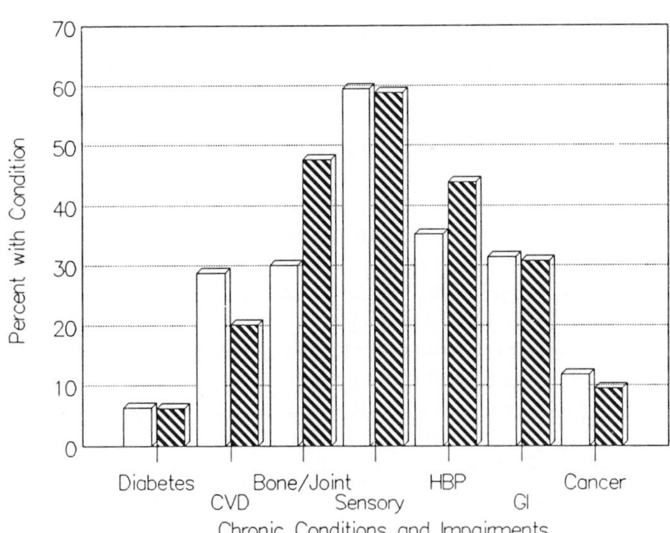

FIGURE 12-6
Percentage of older persons with selected chronic conditions, by sex (□, men; ▨, women). (CVD = cardiovascular disease; HBP = high blood pressure; and GI = gastrointestional.)

TABLE 12-1

Percentage Decline in Mortality from Ischemic Heart Disease, 1984–1987, by Age and Sex

Age	Men, %	Women, %
65–74	−13.3	−12.3
75–84	−11.3	−10.6
85+	−8.2	−6.0

SOURCE: National Center for Health Statistics: Vital Statistics of the United States, 1987. Washington, DC, Public Health Service, 1990, vol 2, part A.

sis that risk factors and risk factor changes can affect the risk of CHD mortality even at the oldest ages. A growing body of evidence suggests that CHD is not an inevitable expression of normal senescence but is a disease process in persons of all ages (see Chap. 45). Some data from earlier studies suggested that the traditional risk factors for CHD are weaker at the advanced ages. However, even if this were the case (i.e., that a risk factor demonstrated a lesser relative effect in persons of older ages), the high prevalence of risk factors and the high incidence of CHD at older ages means that the absolute impact of risk factor reduction would be greater in that age range.[8] Further, there is mounting evidence, reviewed below, that risk factors which predict CHD in midlife also predict CHD at the older ages.[9–12]

Lipids and Lipoproteins (See Chap. 73)

In younger individuals, levels of total cholesterol, high-density lipoproteins (HDLs), and low-density lipoproteins (LDLs) are all major predictors of CHD. However, in older individuals the data are both limited and conflicting. The prevalance of hyperlipidemia is lower in older people, which may reflect (1) a survivorship effect (persons with hyperlipidemia on average die younger), (2) a cohort effect (persons born earlier in the century have lower lipid levels), (3) an effect of other illnesses on lipid levels, or (4) a true marker of the aging process in its final phase. Prospective studies (e.g., the Baltimore Longitudinal Study of Aging, and the Dunedin Study[13]), have suggested a decline in mean cholesterol levels at advanced ages prior to any decline in function or advent of clear-cut disease, compatible with the fourth option, but the third is clearly also possible, since those at lower cholesterol levels (most clearly evident below 140 to 160 mg/dl) appear at increased risk of illness and death, even before disease becomes evident clinically[14] (see Chaps. 73 and 14).

Total Serum Cholesterol Data from five large prospective studies, the Framingham Study,[9] Rancho Bernardo,[12] the Lipid Research Clinics' (LRC) Follow-Up Study,[11] the Honolulu Heart Program,[15] and the Kaiser Permanente Coronary Heart Disease in the Elderly Study,[16] suggest that the total cholesterol level continues to be a risk factor for CHD in individuals over 65 years of age. Other studies have also demonstrated that elevated cholesterol levels are associated with an increased risk of CHD in persons over 60 years of age.[10,17]

In the Framingham study, an increased total cholesterol level was statistically significantly associated with an increased risk of CHD in older women. In that 30-year follow-up, women who had total cholesterol levels over 295 mg/dl had CHD rates approximately 75 percent higher than women with cholesterol levels less than 205 mg/dl. Although the association between total cholesterol levels and CHD in the Framingham men was not statistically significant, men with clearly elevated total cholesterol levels (over 295 mg/dl) had CHD rates over 70 percent higher than men with more desirable levels (under 205 mg/dl).

Total cholesterol levels were significantly predictive of CHD mortality among men and women aged 65 to 79 years in the Rancho Bernardo study.[12] Men and women in the highest quintile of cholesterol levels had death rates 40 to 50 percent higher than those in the lowest quintile.

In the LRC Program Follow-Up Study, total cholesterol levels were significantly predictive of subsequent CHD mortality in both men and women over 65 years of age. Among the men, each 20 mg/dl increase in the total cholesterol level was associated with a 10 percent increased risk of CHD death. Among the older women the association was somewhat stronger, with each 20 mg/dl increase in total cholesterol levels associated with a 29 percent increased risk of CHD mortality.

In the Kaiser Permanente Study of men 60 to 79 years of age, the CHD mortality risk of those in the highest cholesterol quartile compared with those in the lower three quartiles was increased 50 percent (with no significant change with age), but because of the great increase in CHD mortality with age, the excess mortality attributable to elevated cholesterol levels was increased over fivefold across this 20-year age span.[16]

HDL and LDL Cholesterol Data from both the Framingham and the LRC studies support the thesis that HDL and LDL cholesterol levels are significant determinants of CHD in elderly persons. In Framingham participants between the ages of 50 and 82 years, the HDL cholesterol level was strongly and inversely associated with the risk of developing CHD in both men and women.[18] In this same cohort, the LDL cholesterol level was positively and significantly associated with CHD incidence in both men and women. For both sexes HDL was the stronger predictor of CHD.

In the LRC study, the LDL level was positively and significantly associated with CHD death in both older men and older women; an increase of 20 mg/dl of LDL cholesterol was associated with a 17 percent increased risk of CHD death in older men and a 32 percent increased risk of CHD death in older women.

However, the HDL level was only significantly (inversely) associated with CHD death in women.

Smoking

The adverse health consequences of smoking are clearly established in younger individuals. However, the health effects of smoking in older persons are less well defined. The prevalence of smoking is lowest in the oldest ages, which may be partly explained by a survivorship effect. Nonetheless, recent estimates indicate that 20 percent of elderly men and 13 percent of elderly women currently smoke. Among these men and women, 53 percent and 21 percent, respectively, are former smokers.[3]

Currently, cigarette smoking is a major risk factor for cardiovascular disease mortality and morbidity in both men and women under 65 years of age. Further, there is clear evidence of a dose-response association between the number of cigarettes smoked and the risk of CHD at these ages.[9,10,19]

Among older people, the association between smoking and CHD is less clear. In the Framingham study there was no significant association between smoking and CHD incidence in men or women aged 65 to 94 years, although older men smoking more than two packs a day had CHD rates 40 percent higher than nonsmokers.[9] Several other large studies (American Cancer Society and the Canadian Veterans Study) also found no significantly increased risk among older smokers.

In contrast, other studies have reported an increased risk of CHD in older smokers, although the findings are not always concordant by sex. Results from the British Physicians Study indicated that smoking clearly increased the risk of CHD among female physicians of all ages; however, smoking was not a predictor for CHD in the older male physicians. Likewise, elderly women living in Massachusetts who smoked had an increased risk of death compared with nonsmokers; among men there was no association between smoking and mortality.[20] An analysis of pilot data from the Systolic Hypertension in the Elderly Program (SHEP) found that smoking was a significant predictor of first cardiovascular event, myocardial infarction, and sudden death.[21] And, in a large prospective study of over 2500 poor men aged 65 and 74 years, current smokers compared with ex-smokers or to those who had never smoked had a 52 percent excess risk of CHD death.[22]

A more recent study has clearly identified smoking as a cause of increased mortality in older men and women.[1] This prospective study of persons over 65 years of age without a history of myocardial infarction, stroke, or cancer living in three communities reported prevalence rates of smoking between 5.2 and 17.8 percent among women and 14.2 and 25.8 percent among men. Total mortality was increased twofold in smokers versus never-smokers (2.1 in men, 1.8 in women). CHD mortality was likewise doubled (2.0 for men, 1.6 for women), as was cancer (2.4-fold for men and women). Of special relevance for the potential of risk factor reduction to reduce risk in older persons, former smokers had rates of CHD mortality no greater than never-smokers, though smoking-related cancer risk remained elevated.

Hypertension (See Chap. 47)

High blood pressure is very common in people over 65 years of age in the United States; 41 percent of women and 33 percent of men aged 65 to 74 years and 48 percent of women and 29 percent of men over 75 years reported hypertension (systolic >160 mmHg and/or diastolic >95 mmHg).[3] Isolated systolic hypertension (systolic >160 mmHg and diastolic <90 mmHg) is seen less frequently and has been estimated to occur in 7 percent of older persons.[23]

Unlike other risk factors for CHD in the elderly population, the evidence regarding hypertension as a risk factor for CHD at older ages is strong. Elevations of both systolic and diastolic blood pressures are associated with an increased risk of CHD in both men and women. In the Framingham study, for example, men and women 65 to 94 years old with systolic pressures >180 mmHg had a risk of CHD 300 to 400 percent higher than those with systolic pressures <120 mmHg. Likewise, men and women with diastolic pressures >105 mmHg had a risk of CHD nearly 200 to 300 percent higher than those with diastolic pressures <75 mmHg.[9] Other studies in different populations generally support the Framingham results.[10,24] However, a recent study from Finland suggests that after age 85, lower blood pressure may be associated with an increased risk of cardiovascular death.[25]

Isolated systolic hypertension also appears to be associated with a significantly increased risk of CHD. Framingham participants aged 55 to 74 years with isolated systolic hypertension had a 200 to 500 percent excess risk of cardiovascular death during a 2-year follow-up.[26] The 1979 Build and Blood Pressure Study reported that insured persons with isolated systolic hypertension had mortality rates 51 percent higher than insured normotensive individuals.[27] Additionally, a cohort study of upper middle class individuals living in California found a 200 to 300 percent increased risk of cardiovascular death among those persons 60 years or older with isolated systolic hypertension.[28]

There is also a body of evidence suggesting that treating diastolic hypertension in older persons reduces the risk of CHD. Data from both the U.S.-based Hypertension Detection and Follow-Up Program and the Australian National Blood Pressure Study show that antihypertensive therapy in persons 60 to 69 years of age significantly reduces the risk of cardiovascular morbidity and mortality.[29,30] Additionally, the European Working Party on High Blood Pressure in the Elderly Trial reported a 38 percent reduction in fatal cardiac events among persons over 60 years of age randomized to antihypertensive therapy.[31] However, one moderate-sized (n = 884) randomized trial in persons 60 to 79 years found no benefit of antihypertensive therapy in preventing coronary disease, although a significant reduction in stroke was observed.[32] A recent study reported that effective treatment of elderly hypertensive patients with verapamil or atenolol (plus chlorthalidone when necessary) reduced left ventricular mass and diastolic dysfunction.[33] Even more directly relevant to the potential for reducing risk in elderly hypertensive patients, the recently concluded Systolic Hypertension in the Elderly Program (SHEP) clearly demonstrated diminished morbidity and mortality in older persons with blood pressures >160/<90 treated with atenolol and chlorthalidone[34] (see Chap. 47).

Physical Activity

A recent review of the effects of physical activity on disease risk concluded that habitual exercise was inversely related to the risk of CHD at all ages.[35] Further, it was suggested that elderly people, as a group, might benefit significantly by increasing their levels of habitual physical activity. Unfortunately, most of the data on physical activity and CHD risk in both younger and older persons come from observational studies. Thus, it remains uncertain whether physical activity appears beneficial for CHD because healthier people are more likely to exercise, or if physical activity prevents CHD.

Physical activity has been found to be inversely related to CHD risk in older individuals in several (but not all) studies. In the Alameda County study, in which persons 60 to 94 years of age were followed for 17 years, a relatively crude measure of low physical activity, i.e., "having little leisure time for physical activity," was significantly associated with the risk of death.[36]

Similarly, in a study of Harvard alumni, the risk of death decreased with increasing levels of exercise, even at the oldest ages (70 to 84 years) and after adjusting for preexisting illness.[37] However, not all studies have demonstrated a protective effect of physical activity. In a 5-year follow-up study of people over 65 years in Massachusetts, physical activity did not predict risk of death or CHD once preexisting illnesses were considered.[20]

Physical activity could impact directly on the risk of CHD or could affect the occurrence of CHD by altering other CHD risk factors. One study reported that older people who exercised were more likely to be nonsmokers and to have better weight control than more sedentary people.[38] In a large group of men over 60 years of age, both serum cholesterol levels and blood pressure were inversely related to leisure time activity.[39] Physical activity has also been associated with improvement in glucose tolerance, insulin resistance, and neuropsychological functioning in older individuals.[40–42]

There is also evidence suggesting that older people, even those who had been previously sedentary, can become conditioned by a regular exercise program.[40] One report of 112 men 52 to 87 years of age found significant improvement in several physiologic measures, particularly oxygen transport capacity, after as little as 6 weeks of vigorous training.[43] Another study found significant improvements in maximum workload and maximum oxygen uptake in eight women and four men (mean age, 71 years) who trained for 3 months on a bicycle ergometer.[44] Further, there is some agreement among cardiologists that exercise training (cardiac rehabilitation) is appropriate for older persons with clinical manifestations of CHD.[45–47] However, this view remains controversial.[48]

Obesity (See Chaps. 72 and 111)

The positive association between overweight, obesity, and risk of CHD is generally accepted for younger individuals.[49] However, the association between overweight, obesity, and CHD in older persons is less well studied and remains controversial.[50,51]

In 597 nonsmoking men and 1126 nonsmoking women over 65 years of age followed for up to 23 years in the Framingham study,[52] the risk of cardiovascular mortality among the heaviest was increased. Women with body mass greater than the 70th percentile had about twice the risk of dying from cardiovascular disease that women whose body mass was between the 30th and 49th percentile had. In men, an increase in body mass was also associated with a 40 percent increased risk of cardiovascular death; however, only the results in women were statistically significant.

These results are compared with a very large Norwegian study (n = 236,000)[53] which reported on the association between body mass and mortality among men and women aged 65 and older. Among the men, a slightly increased risk of death (approximately 10 percent) was seen for those whose body mass index (BMI) was greater than 29 kg/m^2. Among the younger women (65 to 79 years), an increased risk of mortality (approximately 15 percent) was observed for those whose BMI was greater than 31 kg/m^2. However, there was no association between BMI and risk of death in the oldest women (those over 80 years of age).

In a follow-up study of very old persons (over 85 years) living in Finland, BMI was found to be negatively associated with subsequent risk of mortality.[54] The lowest 5-year mortality rate was seen in the group of persons with a BMI greater than 30 kg/m^2, leading the authors to conclude that "moderate overweight may . . . be a sign of good health."

In all three studies cited above, thinness was strongly associated with subsequent risk of death in older persons. In Framingham, the thinnest men and women were nearly twice as likely to die from cardiovascular disease than more "normal" sized (30th < BMI < 49th percentile) persons. Likewise in the Norwegian study, men with a BMI less than 21 kg/m^2 and women with a BMI less than 23 kg/m^2 were at an increased risk of death. In the Finnish study, the highest 5-year mortality rates were observed for persons with a BMI less than 20 kg/m^2. These results support the hypothesis that there is a U-shaped association between body mass and mortality in older people.

Estrogen Use (See also Chaps. 3, 73, and 74)

In virtually all published studies, estrogen replacement therapy appears to protect against the development of fatal and nonfatal CHD among older women. However, of the two published reports from the Framingham Study, one shows no effect of estrogen use on CHD risk in women over 60,[55] and the other shows a slight increased risk.[56] In two large prospective studies[57,58] unopposed estrogen therapy was associated with a dramatic (greater than 50 percent) reduction in the risk of CHD in women over 70 years of age. The recently analyzed Nurses' Health Study confirmed the major reduction in CHD among those taking postmenopausal estrogen replacement,[59] generating consensus that such therapy probably confers net benefits in diminished CHD (and total mortality) risk.[60] However, the lack of evidence from a randomized clinical trial has prevented the emergence of definitive medical opinion on this subject (women who take estrogen generally being of higher socioeconomic and health status than those who don't) and led to the Women's Health Initiative study currently being implemented. It has been suggested that estrogen-altered lipoprotein fractions account for up to half (25 to 50 percent) of the reduced CHD risk,[57] stimulating much contemporary research to identify additional beneficial effects of estrogen on vascular function.

Stroke

Cerebrovascular disease is primarily a disease of older individuals.[61] The death rates from stroke increase exponentially with age and are higher in men than in women (Fig. 12-7). Stroke is the third leading cause of death in older Americans, accounting for more than 150,000 deaths each year. Nonfatal strokes are common (7 percent of persons over 65 have had a stroke) and may be associated with significant disability.[62]

Stroke mortality has been declining in the United States since as early as 1915. The downward trend had remained relatively constant until the early 1970s, when the rates began to decline even more steeply.[63] This decline in stroke mortality has continued and is seen for both men and women at all ages (Table 12-2). The identification and treatment of hy-

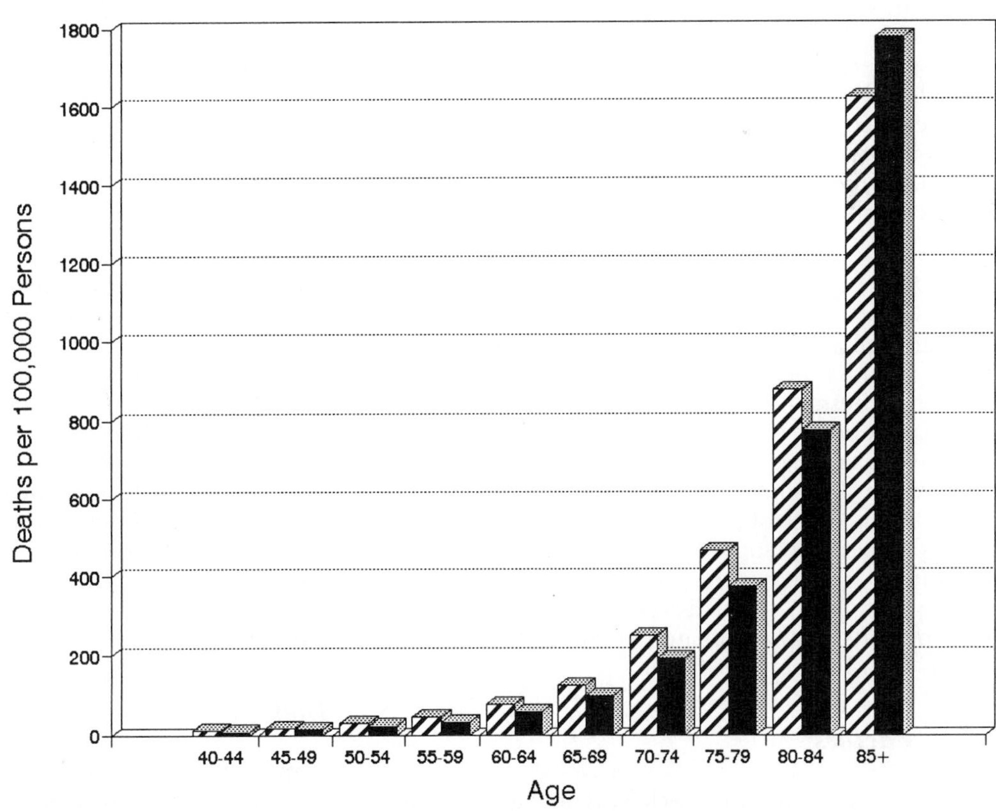

FIGURE 12-7
Death rates from stroke, United States, 1987, by sex and age group (▨, men; ■, women). (*From National Center for Health Statistics, Vital Health Statistics of the United States, 1987, Washington, DC, Public Health Service, 1990, part A.*)

TABLE 12-2

Percentage Decline in Mortality from Stroke, 1984–1987, by Age and Sex

Age	Men, %	Women, %
65–74	−12.8	−9.1
75–84	−10.0	−10.4
85+	−9.6	−7.5

SOURCE: National Center for Health Statistics: Vital Statistics of the United States, 1987. Washington, DC, Public Health Service, 1990, vol 2, part A.

pertensive persons has been suggested to account for most of the more recent observed decline.[63]

Hypertension

Both diastolic and isolated systolic hypertension increase the risk of stroke. Further, the risk of stroke increases almost linearly for all levels of systolic and diastolic pressures.[63] Most observational studies find that individuals with systolic blood pressures over 160 mmHg and/or diastolic pressures over 95 mmHg have a two- to threefold increased risk of stroke compared with normotensive individuals.

Treatment of hypertension in elderly persons has been demonstrated to reduce the risk of stroke. In the European Working Party on High Blood Pressure in the Elderly Trial, cerebrovascular mortality was reduced 32 percent in the treated group compared with controls.[31] In a second randomized trial, fatal strokes were reduced to 30 percent, and all strokes (fatal and nonfatal) were reduced 58 percent in the group treated for their hypertension.[32] This was confirmed in Americans in the recent SHEP trial.[34]

Diabetes

Clinical diabetes is also a suspected risk factor for stroke in older persons, although the data are not consistent. Results from the Framingham study indicate that diabetic compared with nondiabetic individuals have over twice the risk of stroke. Data from the Chicago Stroke Study also found a significantly increased risk of stroke (approximately 65 percent) among diabetic persons.[64] Of particular concern are individuals who have the common combination of both hypertension and diabetes. The risk of stroke in these persons is approximately six times that in individuals with neither risk factor.[65]

Other Factors

Other risk factors for atherosclerosis, including smoking, serum lipid and lipoprotein levels, exercise, personality characteristics, and obesity, have not been shown to be consistent predictors of stroke. While hypertension appears to be the strongest predictor of stroke occurrence, the decline in stroke mortality seen in this country occurred long before effective antihypertensive therapy was available. This latter observation suggests that additional risk factors, perhaps dietary, are influencing the occurrence of stroke. Two dietary candidates include sodium intake (hypothesized to be positively associated with hypertension) and potassium intake (shown to be negatively associated with stroke occurrence).[65]

Cancer

Cancers are the second leading cause of mortality in older persons, accounting for almost 20 percent of all deaths in individuals over 65 years of age. Although only 12 percent of the U.S. population is over 65 years of age, 65 percent of all cancer fatalities occur in this group.[2] Unfortunately, relatively few studies have specifically examined risk factors for cancers in elderly individuals.

Risk factors for cancer at all ages include smoking, diet, environmental exposures, and family history. However, the most important risk factors for cancer in older persons are probably smoking and diet.[66] The most commonly occurring tumors in older persons are lung, colon, and breast. Thus, the risk factors briefly reviewed below (smoking and diet) are somewhat specific to these tumor sites.

Smoking

It has been suggested that 25 to 35 percent of all cancers occurring in the United States are the result of cigarette smoking, with the majority of these tumors being cancer of the lung. Further, lung cancers occur most frequently in older people; 60 percent of all lung cancer deaths occur in persons over 65 years of age (Fig. 12-8). In men over 65 years of age, smoking is associated with a 12-fold increased risk of lung cancer.[67] Among older women, the risk of lung cancer in smokers compared with nonsmokers ranges from a three- to a fivefold excess risk.[68]

Smoking has also been shown to be significantly associated with tumors of other sites in older men. Compared with nonsmokers, men smoking cigarettes had excess risk for dying from kidney cancer [relative risk (RR) = 1.6], bladder cancer (RR = 3.0), esophageal cancer (RR = 1.7), cancer of the larynx (RR = 9.0), and cancer of the buccal cavity (RR = 2.9).[67]

Diet

Many nutrients have been suggested to increase or decrease the risk of cancer.[69,70] These nutrients include fiber, vitamin C, vitamin A and retinoids, vitamin E, trace minerals, alcohol, and fats. Again, very few studies have specifically looked at dietary factors as predictors of death in older persons.

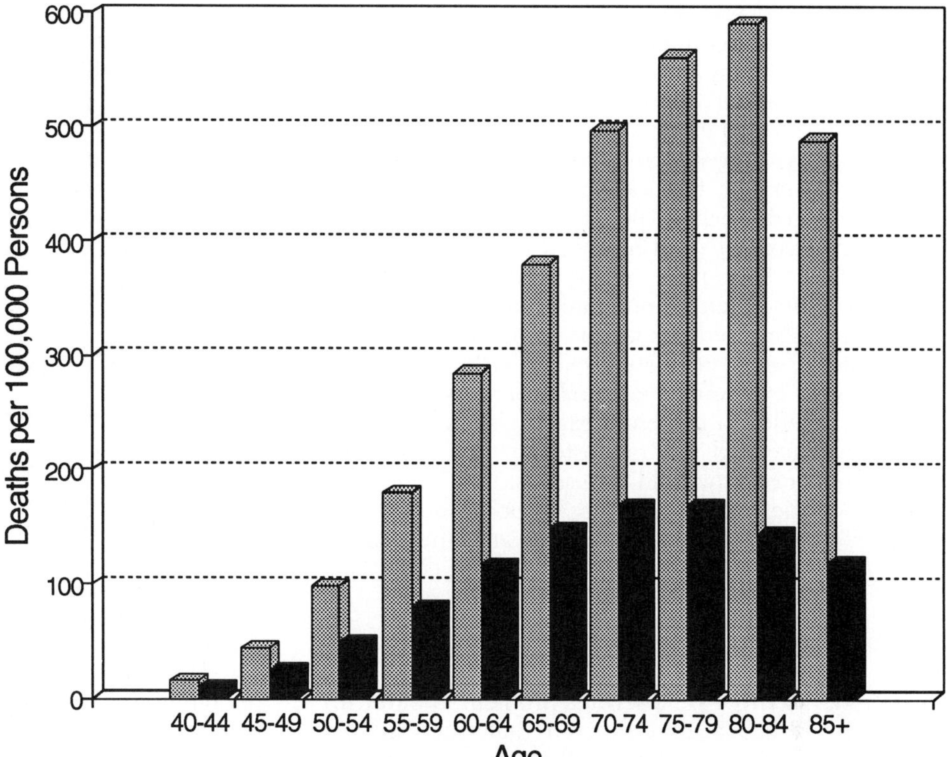

FIGURE 12-8
Death rates from lung cancer, United States, 1987, by sex and age group (▩, men; ■, women). (*From National Center for Health Statistics, Vital Health Statistics of the United States, 1987, Washington, DC, Public Health Service, 1990, part A.*)

One study, however, reported on 1271 residents of Massachusetts over 65 years of age who were followed for 5 years.[71] Persons in the highest quintile of intake of green and yellow vegetables had a significantly reduced risk for all cancer mortality (RR = 0.3) and all-cause mortality (RR = 0.5) compared with persons in the lowest quintile. The authors attribute this apparent protective effect to the provitamin A content of the vegetables. In contrast, another found no association between vitamin supplementation and mortality in a group of health-conscious older people.[72]

It has been suggested that dietary fat increases the risk for both colon cancer and breast cancers.[69,70] However, the epidemiologic data on the association between fat intake and these tumors in humans are inconsistent.

For colon cancer, there is reason to suspect an association with fat intake for two reasons. The animal studies are remarkably consistent, as animals fed increased amounts of saturated and unsaturated fats and cholesterol all had increased rates of colon tumors.[69,70] Second, individuals at high risk of colon cancer, with colon cancer, and with colonic polyps all have increased fecal concentrations of bile acids, which are the by-products of diets high in fat and which act as tumor promoters.[69,70]

The suggested link between dietary fat and breast cancer in humans has not been well studied, though there are extensive animal data which would support such a hypothesis. However, most of the evidence which points toward a causal role for dietary fat in the pathogenesis of breast cancer (vis à vis a hormonal mechanism) appears to be limited to premenopausal women.[69,70]

Falls, Fractures, and Osteoporosis

Fractures are a significant cause of morbidity and mortality in older persons. The two most commonly occurring fractures in older persons are hip and vertebral. Falls are a major risk factor for these fractures and by themselves are associated with risk of increased morbidity (restricted activity, soft tissue injury, nursing home admissions) and mortality. Falls account for the majority of deaths related to injuries in aged persons and are the sixth leading cause of death in persons over 65 years of age.[73]

Risk Factors for Falls

About 30 percent of community-dwelling elderly persons fall each year,[74–76] and between 2 and 6 percent of all falls are associated with a fracture.[74,77] Approximately 24 percent of fallers incur serious injury.[74] Women appear to be twice as likely to fall as men.[76,78] In addition the risk of fall-related injury increases exponentially with age among elderly persons, reaching a high for those aged 85 years or over of 136 per 1000 in men and 159 per 1000 in women.[79] Fear of falling, moreover, represents a leading cause of apprehensiveness,[80] exacerbating the functional limitations associated with falls and representing a major psychological impediment to effective rehabilitation.

One of the most consistent predictors of falls appears to be sedative use[74,76,81]; in one longitudinal study, the risk of falling was 28 times higher in persons using sedatives than in individuals not using them.[74] Other risk factors for falls include environmental hazards such as poor lighting, worn carpet, and electric cords.[73,77] It has been suggested that between 35 and 50 percent of home falls are associated with accidents or environmental causes.[77]

Other identified risk factors for falls include cognitive impairment (a fivefold excess risk), disabilities of the lower extremities (a fourfold excess risk), palmomental reflex (a threefold excess risk), abnormalities of balance and gait (a twofold excess risk), and foot problems (a twofold excess risk).[74] There also appears to be a dose-response association between number of risk factors for falling and the risk of falling.[74]

Osteoporosis and Fractures

As noted, fractures are a serious problem in older individuals. It has been estimated that one-third of women over 65 years of age will have vertebral fractures.[82] Hip fracture, which increases dramatically with age, leads to death in 12 to 20 percent of cases; an additional 25 percent of hip fracture patients require long-term nursing home care, and ultimately 50 percent are unable to walk without help.[83]

Osteoporosis is considered the major risk factor for fracture. The epidemiologic determinants of osteoporosis include advanced age, female sex, geographic location, white race, and estrogen deficiency.[83] Some researchers have suggested that calcium consumption is inversely associated with risk of osteoporosis and fracture.[84,85] Smoking, high alcohol consumption, and lean body mass have also been suggested to increase the risk of osteoporosis and fracture.[84]

Physical activity has also been suggested as a protective risk factor for bone loss and fracture. In an extensive review, exercise was clearly shown to increase bone mass in elderly persons.[84] In the Florida Geriatric Research Program, men and women walking at least 1 mile three or more times per week had a reduced risk of subsequent fracture (RR = 0.5 in men and 0.6 in women).[86]

Perhaps the most potent predictor of osteoporosis and osteoporotic fracture in women is estrogen deficiency. One study has found that estrogen deficiency and not age per se is responsible for the loss of bone mass which occurs in the two decades after menopause.[87] Further, estrogen replacement therapy in peri- and postmenopausal women is a powerful determinant of bone loss and fracture risk.[83,88,89] It has been estimated that 50 percent of hip fractures (not to mention fractures of other sites) could be prevented by a more widespread use of estrogen therapy.[90]

SUMMARY AND CONCLUSIONS

In this chapter we have briefly reviewed risk factors for the major causes of death and disability in older persons. We are limited in any definitive conclusions we may want to draw about most of the factors addressed here simply because of the paucity of studies of risk factors in older people. However, two general points have emerged.

First, there is good evidence that disease in older people is not the inevitable consequence of biologic aging, but is in fact a pathological process with identifiable risk factors. Thus, the potential exists to modify the occurrence of disease in older people by modifying their risk factor profiles. Most of the risk factors for death and morbidity which operate at midlife also continue to predict events at the advanced ages. This suggests that general hygienic interventions such as improved diet, smoking cessation, weight control, and exercise could improve the health of older people.

Second, there is a direct evidence that therapeutic interventions in older persons can reduce morbidity and mortality. Clearly, pharmacologic treatment of hypertension leads to a reduced risk of stroke and possibly CHD, and the use of estrogen replacement therapy probably reduces the risk of CHD and clearly does decrease the risk of fracture. Whether other therapeutic interventions such as pharmacologic treatment of hyperlipidemia are effective in this age group remains to be seen, although there is no compelling reason to suppose that this would not be the case.

In summary, there is sufficient evidence at this time to encourage both primary and secondary prevention of disease in older persons by hygienic measures and, if appropriate, with pharmacologic treatments. Such measures will prevent "premature" mortality and enable persons to live healthier lives.

REFERENCES

1. La Croix AZ et al: Smoking and mortality among older men and women in 3 communities. *N Engl J Med* 324:1619, 1991.
2. National Center for Health Statistics: *Vital Statistics of the United States, 1984.* DHHS publication (PHS) 87-1122 and 87-1114. Public Health Service. Washington, DC, Government Printing Office, 1987, Vol 2, parts A and B.
3. National Center for Health Statistics et al: *Health Statistics on Older Persons, United States, 1986.* Vital and

Health Statistics, Series 3, No. 25, DHHS Publication (PHS) 87-1409, Public Health Service. Washington, DC, Government Printing Office, 1987.

4. Verbrugge L: Longer life but worsening health? Trends in health and mortality of middle-aged and older persons. *Milband Mem Fund Q* 62:475, 1984.
5. Weinstein MC et al: Forecasting coronary heart disease incidence, mortality, and cost: The coronary heart disease policy model. *Am J Public Health* 77:1417, 1987.
6. Gillum R et al: Decline in coronary heart disease mortality. Old questions and new facts. *Am J Med* 76:1055, 1984.
7. Hosvalls K et al: Favorable results of coronary artery bypass grafting in patients older than 75 years. *J Thorac Cardiovasc Surg* 99:92, 1990.
8. Rose G: Strategy of prevention: Lessons from cardiovascular disease. *Br Med J* 282:1847, 1981.
9. Kannel W et al: Primary risk factors for coronary heart disease in the elderly: The Framingham study, in Wenger N et al (eds): *Coronary Heart Disease in the Elderly: Working Conference on the Recognition and Management of Coronary Heart Disease in the Elderly.* New York, Elsevier, 1986.
10. The Pooling Project Research Group: Relationship of blood pressure, serum cholesterol, smoking habit, relative weight, and ECG abnormalities to incidence of major coronary events: Final report of the Pooling Project. *J Chronic Dis* 31:201, 1978.
11. Bush TL et al: Total and LDL cholesterol as predictors of CHD death in elderly men: The Lipid Research Clinics' Program Follow-Up Study. *CVD Epidemiol Newslett* 43:22, 1988.
12. Barrett-Connor E et al: Ischemic heart disease risk factors after age 50. *J Chronic Dis* 37:903, 1984.
13. Newschafer CJ et al: Aging and total cholesterol levels: Cohort, period, and survivorship levels. *Am J Epidemiol* 136:23, 1992.
14. Verdery RB, Goldberg AP: Hypocholesterolemia as a predictor of death: A prospective study of 224 nursing home residents. *J Gerontol* M84, 1991.
15. Benfante R, Reed D: Is elevated serum cholesterol level a risk factor for coronary heart disease in the elderly? *JAMA* 263:393, 1990.
16. Rubin SM et al: High blood cholesterol in elderly men and the excess risk for coronary heart disease. *Ann Intern Med* 113:916, 1990.
17. Abramson JH et al: Risk markers for mortality among elderly men: A community study in Jerusalem. *J Chronic Dis* 35:565, 1982.
18. Kannel WB et al: Prevention of cardiovascular disease in the elderly. *J Am Coll Cardiol* 10:25A, 1987.
19. Criqui MH et al: Lipoproteins as mediators for the effects of alcohol consumption and cigarette smoking on cardiovascular mortality: Results from the Lipid Research Clinics' Follow-Up Study. *Am J Epidemiol* 126:629, 1987.
20. Branch LG et al: Personal health practices and mortality among the elderly. *Am J Public Health* 74:1126, 1984.
21. Siegel D et al: Predictors of cardiovascular events and mortality in the Systolic Hypertension in the Elderly pilot project. *Am J Epidemiol* 126:385, 1987.
22. Jajick CL et al: Smoking and coronary heart disease mortality in the elderly. *JAMA* 252:2831, 1984.
23. Curb JD et al: Isolated systolic hypertension in 14 communities. *Am J Epidemiol* 121:362, 1985.
24. Chapman JM et al: The interrelationship of serum cholesterol, hypertension, body weight, and risk of coronary disease. The results of the first ten years of follow-up in the Los Angeles Heart Study. *J Chronic Dis* 17:1933, 1964.
25. Mattila K et al: Blood pressure and five year survival in the very old. *Br Med J* 296:887, 1988.
26. Kannel WB: Implications of Framingham study data for treatment of hypertension: Impact of other risk factors, in Laragh JH et al (eds): *Frontiers in Hypertension Research.* New York, Springer-Verlag, 1981.
27. *Build Study 1979.* Chicago, Society of Actuaries and the Association of Life Insurance Medical Directors of America, 1980.
28. Garland C et al: Isolated systolic hypertension and mortality after age 60 years: A prospective population-based study. *Am J Epidemiol* 118:365, 1983.
29. Hypertension Detection and Follow-up Program Cooperative Group: Five-year findings of the Hypertension Detection and Follow-up Program: II. Mortality by race, sex, and age. *JAMA* 242:2572, 1979.
30. National Heart Foundation of Australia: Treatment of mild hypertension in the elderly: Report by the Management Committee. *Med J Aust* 2:398, 1981.
31. Amery A et al: Mortality and morbidity results from the European Working Party on High Blood Pressure in the Elderly Trial. *Lancet* 1:1349, 1985.
32. Coope J et al: Randomised trial of treatment of hypertension in elderly patients in primary care. *Br Med J* 293:1145, 1986.
33. Schulman SP et al: The effects of antihypertensive therapy on left ventricular mass in elderly patients. *N Engl J Med* 322:1350, 1990.
34. SHEP Cooperative Research Group. Prevention of stroke by antihypertensive drug treatment in older persons with isolated septolet hypertension. *JAMA* 265:325, 1991.
35. Siscovick DS et al: The disease-specific benefits and risks of physical activity and exercise. *Public Health Rep* 100:180, 1985.
36. Kaplan GA et al: Mortality among the elderly in the Almeda County Study: Behavioral and demographic risk factors. *Am J Public Health* 77:307, 1987.
37. Paffenbarger RS et al: Physical activity, all-cause mortality, and longevity of college alumni. *N Engl J Med* 314:605, 1986.
38. Blair SN et al: Relationships between exercise or physical activity and other health behaviors. *Public Health Rep* 100:172, 1985.
39. Hickey N et al: Study of coronary risk factors related to physical activity in 15,171 men. *Br Med J* 3:507, 1975.
40. Fitzgerald PL: Exercise for the elderly. *Med Clin North Am* 69:189, 1985.
41. Rowe JW et al: Human aging: Usual and successful. *Science* 237:143, 1987.
42. Dustman RE et al: Aerobic exercise training and improved neuropsychological function of older individuals. *Neurobiol Aging* 5:35, 1984.
43. deVries HA: Physiological effects of an exercise training regimen upon men aged 52–88. *J Gerontol* 25:325, 1970.
44. Haber P et al: Effects in elderly people 67–76 years of age of three-month endurance training on a bicycle ergometer. *Eur Heart J* 5(suppl E):37, 1984.

45. Oldridge NB et al: Cardiac rehabilitation after myocardial infarction. Combined experience of randomized clinical trials. *JAMA* 260:945, 1988.
46. Herd JA: Management of coronary heart disease in the elderly: Education and rehabilitation, in Wenger N et al (eds): *Coronary Heart Disease in the Elderly. Working Conference on the Recognition and Management of Coronary Heart Disease in the Elderly.* New York, Elsevier, 1986.
47. Williams MA et al: Early exercise training in patients older than age 65 years compared with that in younger patients after acute myocardial infarction or coronary artery bypass grafting. *Am J Cardiol* 55:263, 1985.
48. Froelicher C: *Exercise Testing and Training.* New York, LeJacq, 1982.
49. Kannel WB et al: Physiological and medical concomitants of obesity: The Framingham Study, in Bray GA (ed): *Obesity in America.* (NIH) 79-359. Washington, DC, Government Printing Office, 1979.
50. Jarret RJ et al: Weight and mortality in the Whitehall study. *Br Med J* 285:535, 1982.
51. Andres R et al: Impact of age on weight goals. *Ann Intern Med* 103:1030, 1985.
52. Harris T et al: Body mass index and mortality among nonsmoking older persons. *JAMA* 259:1520, 1988.
53. Waaler HT: Height, weight and mortality: The Norwegian experience. *Acta Med Scand* 679(suppl):1, 1984.
54. Mattila K et al: Body mass index and mortality in the elderly. *Br Med J* 292:867, 1986.
55. Eaker ED et al: Coronary heart disease and its risk factors among women in the Framingham Study, in Eaker ED (ed): *Coronary Heart Disease in Women.* Proceedings of an NIH Workshop. New York, Haymarket Doyma, 1987, p 123.
56. Wilson PWF et al: Postmenopausal estrogen use, cigarette smoking, and cardiovascular morbidity in women over 50. *N Engl J Med* 313:1308, 1985.
57. Bush TL et al: Cardiovascular mortality and noncontraceptive use of estrogen in women: Results from the Lipid Research Clinics' Program Follow-up Study. *Circulation* 75:1102, 1987.
58. Henderson BE et al: Estrogen use and cardiovascular disease. *Am J Obstet Gynecol* 154:1181, 1986.
59. Stampfer MJ et al: Postmenopausal estrogen therapy and cardiovascular disease. Ten-year follow-up from the Nurses' Health Study. *N Engl J Med* 325, 756, 1991.
60. American College of Physicians: Guidelines for counseling postmenopausal women about preventative hormone therapy. *Ann Intern Med* 117:1038, 1992.
61. Weinfeld FD: The national survey of stroke. National Institute of Neurological and Communicative Disorders and Stroke. *Stroke* 12(suppl):IL, 1981.
62. Smith W: *Cardiovascular Disease. A Profile of Health and Disease in America.* New York, Facts on File, 1987.
63. Ostfeld AM: A review of stroke epidemiology. *Epidemiol Rev* 2:136, 1980.
64. Ostfeld AM et al: Epidemiology of stroke in an elderly welfare population. *Am J Public Health* 64:450, 1974.
65. Khaw K-T et al: Dietary potassium and stroke-associated mortality. A 12-year prospective population study. *N Engl J Med* 316:235, 1987.
66. Balducci L et al: Nutrition, cancer, and aging: An annotated review: I. Diet, carcinogenesis, and aging. *J Am Geriatr Soc* 34:127, 1986.
67. Hammond EC: Smoking in relation to the death rates of one million men and women. *Natl Cancer Inst Monogr* 19:126, 1966.
68. Garfinkel L, Stellman SD: Smoking and lung cancer in women: Findings in a prospective study. *Cancer Res* 48:6951, 1988.
69. Willett WC et al: Diet and cancer—an overview (first of two parts). *N Engl J Med* 310:633, 1984.
70. Willett WC et al: Diet and cancer—an overview (second of two parts). *N Engl J Med* 310:697, 1984.
71. Colditz GA et al: Increased green and yellow vegetable intake and lowered cancer deaths in an elderly population. *Am J Clin Nutr* 41:32, 1985.
72. Enstrom JE et al: Mortality among health-conscious elderly Californians. *Proc Natl Acad Sci* 79:6023, 1982.
73. Baker SL: The preventability of falls, in Gray JAM (ed): *Prevention of Disease in the Elderly.* New York, Churchill Livingstone, 1985, p 114.
74. Tinetti ME et al: Risk factors for falls among elderly persons living in the community. *N Engl J Med* 319:1701, 1988.
75. Campbell AJ et al: Falls in old age: A study of frequency and related clinical factors. *Age Ageing* 10:264, 1981.
76. Prudham D, Evans JG: Factors associated with falls in the elderly: A community study. *Age Ageing* 10:141, 1981.
77. Rubenstein LZ et al: Falls and instability in the elderly. *J Am Geriatr Soc* 36:266, 1988.
78. Perry BC: Falls among the elderly: A review of the methods and conclusions of epidemiologic studies. *J Am Geriatr Soc* 30:367, 1982.
79. Satteir RW et al: The incidence of fall injury events among the elderly in a defined population. *Am J Epidemiol* 131:1028, 1990.
80. Walker JE, Howland J: Falls and fear of falling among elderly persons living in the community: Occupational therapy interventions. *Am J Occup Ther* 45:119, 1991.
81. Ray WA et al: Psychotropic drug use and the risk of hip fracture. *N Engl J Med* 316:363, 1987.
82. Riggs BL et al: Osteroporosis and age-related fracture syndromes, in Evered D, Whelan J (eds): *Research and the Ageing Population.* Chichester, Wiley (Ciba Foundation Symposium 134), 1988, p 129.
83. Cummings SR et al: Osteoporosis and osteoporotic fractures. *Epidemiol Rev* 7:178, 1985.
84. Rodysill KJ: Postmenopausal osteoporosis—intervention and prophylaxis. A review. *J Chronic Dis* 40:743, 1987.
85. Holbrook TL et al: Dietary calcium and risk of hip fracture: 14-year prospective population study. *Lancet* 2:1046, 1988.
86. Sorock GS et al: Physical activity and fracture risk in a free-living elderly cohort. *J Gerontol* 43:M134, 1988.
87. Richelson LS et al: Relative contributions of aging and estrogen deficiency to postmenopausal bone loss. *N Engl J Med* 311:1273, 1984.
88. Kiel DP et al: HIp fracture and the use of estrogens in postmenopausal women. The Framingham Study. *N Engl J Med* 317:1169, 1987.
89. Lindsay R: Prevention of osteoporosis, in Gray JAM (ed): *Prevention of Disease in the Elderly.* New York, Churchill Livingstone, 1985.
90. Brody JA et al: Diseases and disorders of aging: An hypothesis. *J Chronic Dis* 39:871, 1986.

Chapter 13

HEALTH CARE IMPLICATIONS OF AN AGING POPULATION

L. Gregory Pawlson

Despite the magnitude of the demographic changes outlined in Chap. 11, the impact of those changes on the utilization, cost, financing, and delivery of health services is only slowly being recognized. The large number of "baby boomers" entering the work force over the last 20 years has significantly reduced the apparent effect of enhanced longevity on the use and cost of services. The most pronounced effect of the baby-boomer phenomenon has been to dilute the burden of increasing cost of health care of retirees by spreading the financing over a larger base. Even so, the public origin of financing for a significant proportion of the care of those over 65 and the gradual realization of the eventual effect of the aging of the baby-boom generation itself have resulted in increasing attention to this area.[1–3] In this chapter we will explore in depth the effect of the changing age structure of our population on the utilization, costs, and financing of health care. Then we will briefly examine the related areas of quality assessment, service organization, and manpower. In each area, we will first review changes which appear to be related to the aging of our population over the last 25 years together with current patterns and then attempt to ascertain what changes are likely over the next 50 to 75 years. The reader is cautioned that projections of more than a year or two in the future are subject to errors that multiply with time and do not take into account "catastrophic" changes that can occur.

UTILIZATION

Both the absolute amount and rates of utilization of health care services are important in understanding the impact of changes in the population on the need for health care.[4–7] Table 13-1 provides information on the utilization of different types of health services by age. Clearly, the age dependency of nursing home and home care utilization is greater than that of hospital use, with physician use varying the least. A recent trend indicates an increasing rate of visits to physicians and home health agencies, with steady or declining rates of use of nursing homes and hospitals.[6,7] Data on home care use is incomplete, except for services provided as part of the Medicare benefit and the home care benefit under Medicaid.

One of the most difficult issues in projecting future use is to predict whether past changes in rates will increase, decrease, or stabilize, especially in those instances where rates appear to be highly variable. Our projections for utilization in the period from 1990 to 2050 (Fig. 13-1) are based on the assumption of stable rates. In essence, these projections tell us what utilization would be today if our current population had the demographic structure we will have at various times in the future. The years between 2010 and 2040 pose an especially interesting challenge to our health care system. Even when expressed in terms of absolute number and rates for the entire population, taking into account the reduction in the number of persons under 65 that will occur in the period, hospital utilization increases by 65 percent in absolute terms and 22 percent in days per 1000, and nursing home use by 200 percent and 100 percent, respectively.

While the aging of the population may be of considerable importance in the future, it has accounted for less than 10 percent of the increase in utilization in the past 30 years. The Rand Health Insurance Study[8] provides evidence that decreases in deductibles and copayments or covering deductibles and coinsurance with "supplemental" private insurance (as is common with Medicare) are likely to increase utilization. Another factor that has not been widely studied is the effect of the increasing relative wealth of the elderly as compared to that of the younger population on health care utilization. Most studies have suggested that medical care utilization varies considerably with income. Since 1965 the number of elderly living under the poverty line has decreased by 50 percent and the average income of households headed by

TABLE 13-1

Utilization of Health Services

	Hospital Bed Days/1000*	Physician Office Visits Per Year†	Nursing Home Residents/1000‡	Home Care Visits per 1000 Medicare Enrollees§
15–44	481	2.3	0.1	
45–64	903	3.1	1.6	
65–74	2115	4.6	12	858
75–84	4087¶	5.4¶	57	1194
>85	NA	NA	220	1612
Percent of change				
<65 to >65	350%	85%	3500%	NA
65–74 to >85	90%¶	17%¶	1800%	88%

SOURCES: *Ref. 7, Table 72; †Ref. 7, Table 69; ‡Ref. 7, Table 80; §*Health Care Financing Review* 12:120, 1990. (This underestimates the use and differences, since only Medicare-reimbursed home care services are recorded.)
¶Patients aged 75 and above.

persons over 65 has increased in relation to the average for those under 65. Educational level, which is positively correlated to utilization of health services, is also increasing with each new cohort of persons over 65. Another factor that may be increasing health care utilization is the increasing supply of physicians in the United States. While there is still controversy as to whether physicians can "induce" demand in health services, it seems likely that easier access to the services of physicians results in increased use of those services. Our changing attitudes toward aging and older persons and the increasing political power of nearly 30 million retirees may also be contributing to the increasing use of medical care services in this age group.

As yet unanticipated technologies that may cure or control chronic illnesses, further changes in family structure and function, or changes in the absolute and relative wealth of future cohorts of elderly are all factors that could affect the use of health services in the future. It is instructive to note that our history over the last 30 years is toward ever-increasing per capita use of health care services for those over 65.[6]

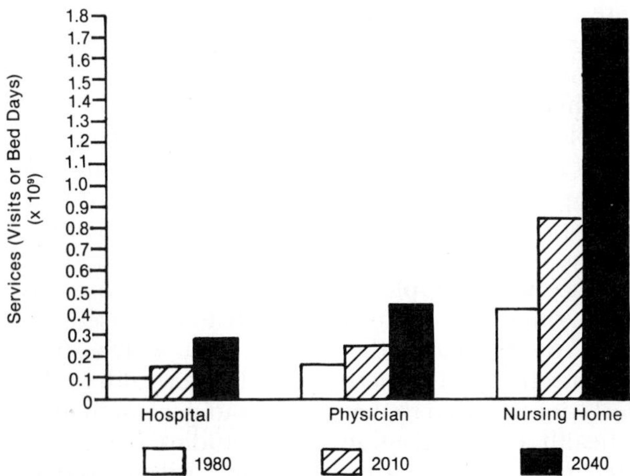

FIGURE 13-1

Growth in health care services for persons over 65, 1980–2040.

The increasing knowledge and concerns about the causes of increased utilization may eventually have an impact on utilization itself. For example, the studies of variation in the use of medical services have shown that the rate of some surgical procedures varies by over 100 percent in comparable health service areas.[9–11] A more recent study from researchers at the Rand Corporation found a 50 to 200 percent variation in the rates of some procedures (carotid enarterectomy, coronary arteriogram, and endoscopy) in different states.[12] In addition, the study found that the proportion of procedures that were judged by an expert panel to have been done for appropriate reasons was only in the 30 to 50 percent range. Moreover, only a small part of the differences in appropriateness were explained by the variations of the utilization rates in different areas. If utilization and costs continue to rise, these and similar studies will accelerate efforts to reduce utilization rates by eliminating procedures that are ineffective.[13] Another area of inquiry is whether alteration in the use of one service can reduce the use of other more costly services. It has been shown that comprehensive geriatric assessment can reduce the rate of nursing home utilization.[14] Unfortunately, in many studies of service substitution, overall costs actually increased. The "Social HMO" demonstration project may provide us with better information in this area.[15] Other programs such as preadmission screening of nursing home applicants have been implemented with varying success.[16]

COSTS

The term *cost* is used in a variety of contexts with confusing results. In this text we will use it in the sense of denoting the product of volume and prices of inputs needed to produce health care services. The term *expenditures* will be used to refer to the amount paid by individuals or insurance for services.

Causes of Increasing Expenditures

Expenditures for medical care in the aggregate are the product of utilization by service category and price. In the case of expenditures for persons over 65—even if there were neither inflation in the general or medical care economy nor new technologies—the increased utilization due to demographic changes would result in increased costs. However, our experience in this country over the last 30 years is that there has been marked inflation in the medical care sector that has consistently outpaced that in the economy in general, and a plethora of new technologies has been developed that has increased the volume of services. Expenditures for medical care services for those over 65 have increased at an accelerating pace (Fig. 13-2).[6,17,18] An analysis of the causes of increased expenditures in the Medicare program reveals that only a small proportion (about 8 percent) of the increase has been due to increases in the numbers of Medicare enrollees. In the 10 years from 1975 to 1984, general inflation in the economy accounted for nearly 50 percent of the total rise in Medicare expenditures.[18] However, over the past 8 years, with moderation in general inflation, inflation in medical care prices (30 percent) and increases in service volume and intensity (45 percent) explain a far greater proportion of the continued rise in expenditures.

Some of the reasons for increased volume or intensity of services per Medicare enrollee were discussed in the preceding section. An additional factor is new technologies that add to, rather than replace, existing services. For example, the use of thallium scans as an adjunct to the diagnosis and management of angina has not produced a concomitant reduction in the use of electrocardiograms or coronary arteriograms. Most new technologies also increase costs through a factor termed *intensity of service.* For example, in the hospital treatment of myocardial infarction, multiple new technologies have been added in the treatment of such patients, including both diagnostic and monitoring devices (e.g., radionuclide scanning and pulmonary wedge pressure monitoring) and therapeutic modalities (coronary angioplasty and thrombolytic therapy). These new technologies result in increases in the "intensity" and costs of a given service (in our example, the service is hospital treatment for myocardial infarction).[19] In addition, the specialized personnel needed to provide some of these technologies further accelerate hospital labor costs.

Another factor which appears to have contributed to increasing expenditures for medical care services for older persons is the reimbursement structure of Medicare. Prior to 1983, hospitals were reimbursed on the basis of their costs (i.e., the amount they re-

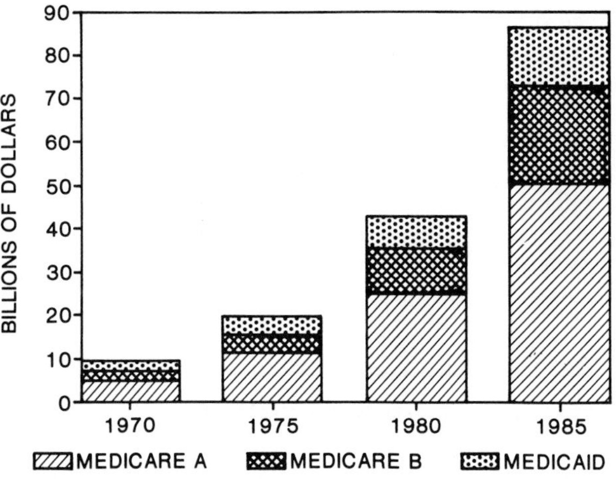

FIGURE 13-2

Medicare and Medicaid expenditures for persons 65 and older.

ported spending in providing health services). Further, there were few, if any, controls on the appropriateness of admissions or on the length of stay. This resulted in an incentive for hospitals to acquire expensive new technologies and to allow increased labor costs since the costs could simply be "passed on" to Medicare for reimbursement. In addition, the "costs" that were recognized included costs of depreciation of capital (including that acquired through charity or government grants) and the costs of graduate medical education. Many felt that a reasonable portion of the increase in Medicare expenditures for hospital services was a result of the cost-based reimbursement system.[20] The radical change of incentives and controls on admissions imposed by the prospective payment system (PPS) using diagnosis-related groupings (DRGs) and the use of peer review organizations (PROs) has resulted in a reduction of both length of stay and admissions.[6] While most observers agree that expenditures for hospital services have increased at a slower rate than they otherwise may have, some of the "savings" have been displaced by concurrent increases in the use of ambulatory services such as outpatient surgery and home care.[6]

Medicare utilization and expenditures for physician services have been rising faster than hospital or nursing home payments.[21] The use of a Medicare reimbursement system that paid physicians based on the lesser of their actual, usual, or average charges was felt to be a major factor driving cost and utilization. In 1989, Congress passed legislation which will, over the course of several years, change the basis of physician payment from charges submitted to a Medicare-determined fee schedule, based in part on the relative costs of inputs used in producing a given service (resource-based relative value system or RBRVS).[22] Recognizing that the volume of services is also critical in driving cost, Congress also stipulated that the volume of services in a given year would be compared to predicted increases (volume performance standard or VPS). Any increase in volume over expected levels would result in a downward adjustment in the annual adjustments that Congress might make to the fee schedule. An increased utilization has been predicted as a result of lower costs to the patient (by the provision in the legislation that placed controls on balance billing by physician) and by lower payments to many physicians. Whether the new payment system controls expenditures or utilization and how it will affect quality and access remains to be seen.[23]

Distribution of Expenditures

The distribution of the use of health care services and expenditures for these services by those over 65 is highly skewed.[4,24] The skewness is especially marked for care in a nursing home, somewhat less so for hospital care, and least, but still substantially, for physician and drug costs. It has been shown, for example, that only 10 percent of Medicare enrollees account for over 70 percent of the overall program expenditures. At the other extreme, approximately 35 percent of Medicare enrollees have no reimbursable expenses in a given year.[18] Even in the group of persons over 85, there are still over 20 percent who do not expend Medicare funds. Persons who resided in the community for less than the full year (i.e., those who died or were institutionalized), while representing only 5 percent of the group, accounted for 22 percent of total expenditures. Of those residing in the community for the full year, 12 percent incurred expenses of more than $3000 and accounted for nearly 60 percent of all expenditures. Thus, 17 percent of the overall group accounted for over 80 percent of the expenditures.[4] Other analyses have focused on expenditures for care in the last year of life. The 5.9 percent of Medicare patients who die each year account for nearly 30 percent of total program expenditures. Within the group of decedents, less than 6 percent account for nearly 30 percent of the expenditures (this 0.4 percent of Medicare recipients account for over 10 percent of total program costs).[25] However, since it is difficult to predict in advance which persons who are sick will die, it is not clear how these observations may be useful in addressing the problem of cost increases. Clearly, a major portion of expenditures are concentrated in a relatively small number of older persons. As we shall see, the skewness also has important implications for financing care for the elderly.

Future Trend in Expenditures

Barring a major depression, increases in costs of health care and expenditures for this care will continue.[5] Indeed, as noted, it is likely that increases may be even greater in the years ahead than they have been in the recent past. The development of low-risk, high-cost procedures such as magnetic resonance imaging (MRI) is likely to further increase the rate of expenditures, since the MRI can be applied in situations of low marginal benefit.[26] This is especially true in older persons where there is a high prevalence of disease but a high risk of complication from more invasive procedures. Furthermore, many of the trends cited—such as increasing wealth and educational attainment of the elderly, enhanced supply of physicians (and perhaps of geriatricians), and the development of new but "additive" costly technologies—are likely to continue in the future.

It should be noted that all increases in expenditures and utilization for medical care services for the elderly are not inherently undesirable. Indeed, some of the increase has occurred because we have delayed the onset of some disease from the preretirement years to the postretirement years and extended life expectancy. Unfortunately, most attempts at cost containment directed toward the elderly have resulted primarily in shifting costs or reducing services.[27,28] Thus, as medical care expenditures for those over 65 continue to rise as a proportion of the gross national product (GNP), questions as to whether the benefits that we gain for additional health services for our older citizens are comparable in value to those that would be gained by investing more in areas such as perinatal care, education, highway improvement, defense, or energy research will intensify. This is especially true because of the way in which we currently finance the care of our older citizens, a topic addressed in the next section.

FINANCING

The continuing conflict in our society between the values of ensuring reasonable access for all to health care and our history of favoring "free enterprise" and private insurance over government programs and social insurance have been nowhere more manifest than in decisions concerning the financing of health care for our elderly and disabled citizens. Since the current system of financing health care for the elderly has grown with no coherent plan, it is not surprising that the sources of financing are fragmented and inconsistent from service to service (Fig. 13-3) and among different socioeconomic groups. We will consider each of the major financing mechanisms, beginning with the public programs.

In 1965, prior to the implementation of Medicare, over 25 percent of those 65 and over had incomes below the federal poverty line. While about 60 percent had some form of private insurance for hospital care, many of those policies were inadequate. Thus, a significant proportion of the elderly were forced to rely on charity or were denied access to care. The growing effectiveness and increased cost of hospital care gave a major impetus toward recognition of the need for more comprehensive insurance. In part

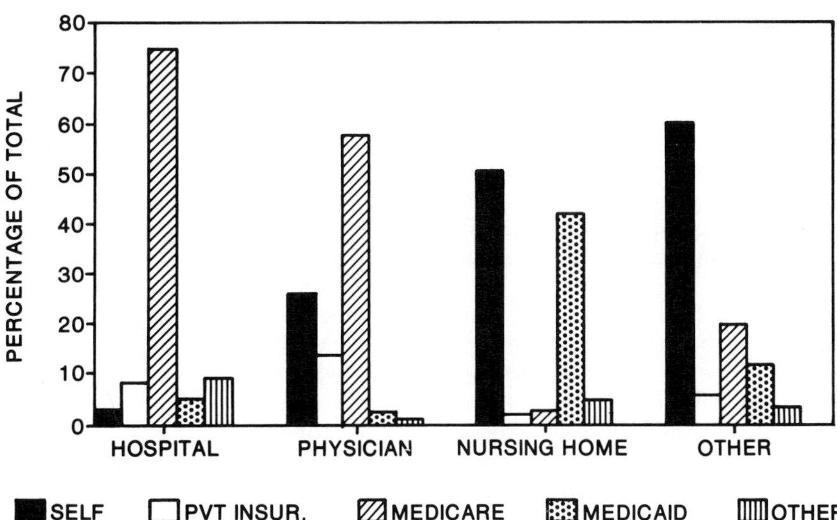

FIGURE 13-3
Source of payment for health care services for persons 65 and older.

because the elderly were a less significant political force in 1965 than they are today, it was necessary in proposing a social insurance program to make major concessions to hospitals and physicians. These concessions formed the basis of some of the cost and utilization problems which followed the implementation of the Medicare program.

The financing of the Medicare program is dichotomous because the program itself was put together from at least two separate and largely unrelated concepts.[29] Medicare Part A, which covers the hospitals and rehabilitation-oriented skilled nursing home and home care, was modeled after the social security program. Funds from a specially designated portion of the social security tax are placed in a trust fund (the Hospital Trust Fund) from which payments to providers are disbursed. Participation in the program is linked with social security eligibility and is essentially universal. The tie to the concepts of the social security system is important for a variety of reasons. Social security is viewed by many as an entitlement which is guaranteed on retirement for those who have contributed to the program during their working years. A key element is that, while there is some linkage between benefits per month and preretirement income, there is no direct link between the actual amounts contributed to the program and any benefit received. Thus, in reality, both the social security program and Part A of Medicare are transfers of income from those currently employed to pay for benefits for those who are retired.

By contrast, Part B of the Medicare program was introduced by the American Medical Association (AMA) and the Republican members of Congress opposed to social insurance as an alternative to Medicare Part A.[28] It was originally funded 50 percent from general tax revenues and 50 percent from a premium paid by participants. It was and remains a voluntary program, although over 95 percent of persons 65 and older participate. The use of general tax revenues reflected the problem that, with the large proportion of elderly below the poverty line in 1965, many individuals would not be able to afford the premiums necessary to fund the entire program. Because of the rapid rise in the costs of Part B and the growing political power of the elderly, the proportion of costs of Part B funded by the premium declined to less than 25 percent of total costs before Congress in 1988 specified that the level of premium would be set so as to cover 25 percent of expenditures.[15]

The Medicaid program has become an important element in the financing of health care for the elderly largely by default. Like Medicare Part B, Medicaid was originally formulated as an alternative to a universal social health insurance program.[29] Unlike Medicare, which is a purely federally controlled program, Medicaid has joint state/federal funding and control. Eligibility for Medicaid is based first on membership in a specified group (as those eligible for Aid to Families with Dependent Children, or those who are blind, disabled, or aged). Persons who are in a specified group must then be below state-set thresholds (with federal guidelines) for the amount of the income and assets they have. There are different thresholds for different groups. States also determine, again within federal guidelines, the specific benefits to which eligible persons are entitled. In creating Medicaid, one of the benefits that Congress required the states to offer was coverage of skilled long-term nursing home care (with coverage of intermediate-care facilities being an optional benefit but one which essentially all states offer). With the inclusion of persons who are blind, disabled, or aged in the Medicaid program and increasing nursing home charges—coupled with the lack of Medicare or private insurance coverage for nursing home care—Medicaid became the primary source of nursing home financing. In 1992, 70 percent of those persons in nursing homes had all or part of their expenses paid for by the Medicaid program. In terms of expenditures for nursing home care, the Medicaid program accounted for 45 percent, self-pay for 50 percent,

Medicare for 2 percent, private insurance for 1 percent, and other sources (such as the Veterans Administration) for another 4 percent (Fig 13-3).[7]

Medicaid financing of long-term care of older persons presents a number of difficult problems. Although this was intended as a welfare program to provide comprehensive health benefits to the poor, over 40 percent of Medicaid payments now go to support nursing home care. At the same time, coverage for the poor in many states has been markedly reduced, with fewer than 50 percent of persons under 65 who are below the poverty line being eligible for Medicaid and the use of low reimbursement rates (which are solely determined by states) for medical care services. These low rates adversely affect access even for those who are eligible. While older persons are eligible for coverage, many of them find it is humiliating to have to impoverish themselves by income and asset depletion to qualify for the program. Other older persons with substantial assets and income have legally evaded this provision by transferring assets and income to other family members—a practice which clearly subverts the intent of the Medicaid program.

Private insurance has played a limited role in the financing of health care for retired persons in this country. In the period before the development of Medicare and Medicaid, private insurance coverage for retirees was constrained by the high prevalence of poverty among the elderly and the relatively small number of employers providing health insurance to their retirees. With the emergence of the political and economic power of retirees (and especially those in the 55- to 70-year-old group) there was a proliferation of both self-purchased and employer-sponsored private insurance. The self-purchase insurance often took the form of "Medigap" coverage—that is, coverage of the "gaps" in the Medicare program. Nearly 70 percent of the Medicare-covered population have some form of Medigap coverage.[17] Most of the policies cover some or all of the Medicare physician and hospital deductible and copay, and a few cover areas such as prescription drugs, which are not addressed by the Medicare program. The focus of many Medigap policies on first-dollar coverage of deductibles and copayments may result in overutilization of some services.[30] However, there are still major gaps in coverage, the most notable being in long-term care. For example, while private insurance finances about 10 percent of hospital expenses and 25 percent of physician's fees of persons over 65, it accounts for less than 1 percent of long-term care expenses (Fig. 13-3).

In addition, there is evidence of what some feel is exploitation of the elderly by a few private insurers. While those policies actually labeled "Medicare supplemental" have to adhere to certain specified principles, other policies do not. As a result, some older persons have purchased multiple policies with overlapping coverages and policies that return less than 50 cents per dollar of premium in the form of benefits paid to the policyholders. In most cases the most flagrant abuses appear to emanate from policies sold directly to individuals via the mail or door-to-door merchandizing.

While avoiding some of the problems of policies sold to individuals, private insurance provided by former employers shares the problem of offering policies of limited scope, often directed to first-dollar coverage. Coverage of retiree health benefits is largely confined to large manufacturing sector employers, who offered what in the short term was a relatively inexpensive benefit, often to mollify unions or to encourage early retirement. However, the cumulative burden of these retiree health benefits presents a major long-range fiscal crisis for many of these businesses. Because of tax laws, only a small portion of the benefits are funded in advance. With time and increasing longevity, the number of retirees increases and the cost of these benefits per unit of production rises as a consequence. At present and long before the adverse demographics of the period 2020 to 2050, the unfunded retiree health benefits of some corporations exceed their net worth. Cost shifting by Medicare has added to the problem, and many corporations have serious concerns as to the long-range effects of this obligation. Attempts to reduce benefits to current retirees have been largely unsuccessful due to legal opinions which, in effect, limit the reductions to future retirees.[31]

The problems resulting from the pattern of use and benefits provided in the public programs and private insurance are most apparent when we consider the distribution of payments made by individuals for uninsured expenses (Fig. 13-3). These problems include the following:

1. As a result of the limit on the number of days of hospital care and the presence of a copayment which increases as the use of hospital days increases in Medicare Part A, elderly persons with prolonged high-cost hospitalization pay a much higher proportion of their expenses as out-of-pocket payment than do those with less severe illness.[17]
2. Despite the imposition of a limit of balance billing to 15 percent over the Medicare fee schedule, some older individuals still face substantial out-of-pocket expenses for high-cost surgery. Many of these individuals are likely to have substantial out-of-pocket expenses for the hospital deductible and outpatient drug use.
3. Because of lack of insurance coverage for certain items like prescription drugs or chronic long-term care, those with a need for these services account for nearly 80 percent of those with high levels of out-of-pocket expenses.[32]

These variations in the sources of financing for different types and intensities of services have produced an uneven pattern of out-of-pocket expenses for older persons. An especially vexatious problem is that not only the absolute amount but also the proportion of expenses paid directly by the patient actually increases with very high-cost illness. Thus, persons who have the most severe illness often have self-pay expenses that are "catastrophic," either in absolute terms (for example greater than $10,000) or in relative terms (costs which exceed 20 percent of income). Most affected are individuals with incomes or assets too high to qualify for Medicaid but too low to afford adequate private insurance. While the average out-of-pocket expenses of the elderly are approximately $1500 or slightly more than one-quarter of total expenses, this average, like many others, is very misleading. Twelve percent of the elderly had self-pay expenses of more than $500 per year, and those who did averaged nearly $5000 and accounted for nearly 50 percent of all self-pay expenditures. By contrast, the nearly 75 percent of enrollees who do not incur hospital or long-term-care expenses average less than $700 per year for all self-pay expenses, including premiums for private insurance and Medicare Part B.[4]

Several demographic changes will have a major impact on the current financing mechanisms. The trends toward increasing educational level and earlier retirement substantially reduce the ratio between time in the work force and time prior to work-force entry or in retirement. This, together with increasing longevity and the graying of the baby-boom generation, will have a dramatic effect on programs such as Medicare Part A, which rely on transfers of income from those in the work force to retirees. Reliance on general tax revenues is less affected, although a substantial portion of the income and benefits received by retirees, such as half of the social security benefit, is not subject to federal or state income tax. This problem will be most acute during the period from 2010 until 2060, when the ratio of persons in the work force to retirees will be less than two to one, as compared to four to one at present, or nearly eight to one in 1932, when social security was implemented. Given the increased costs of health care for retirees due just to the size of population, this would translate into a need for a three- to fourfold increase in the 2.9 percent (1.45 percent each for employer and employee) social security tax currently used to fund Medicare Part A. (Note that this assumes no future expansion of Medicare benefits.)

The marked reduction in poverty among the elderly between 1965 and the present has led some to suggest that the elderly should pay a greater share of either current or future health care costs.[33] Incomes among the elderly show an almost bimodal distribution, with the largest proportion (nearly 50 percent) clustered below 1½ times the poverty level and a small but growing population with incomes over $30,000 per year. Attempting to increase the share paid by the elderly by increasing direct self-pay (i.e., uncovered, copay, or deductible) expenses seems self-defeating, since, as was noted, those who are very old are often the most ill, and have low to moderate incomes, and they already face a staggering burden of self-financed health care costs.

In 1987, Congress passed what was intended to be a major expansion of the Medicare program with elimination of the copay and limit on days covered in prolonged hospitalizations, coverage (with a $600 deductible) of prescription drugs, and a modest expansion of skilled home and nursing home coverage. Given the relative gains in income of the elderly relative to others in the population, a decision was made not to finance the new benefit through the usual Part A mechanism of social security taxes. Rather, the new benefit was to have been financed by the elderly themselves through a combination of an increased basic premium and a new premium, the size of which was to be related to the person's income. Growing opposition to the tax-based premium from wealthy older persons, the lack of any new benefit to the substantial number of persons with employer-based retiree health benefits, the fear that the financing undermined the promise of the social security program, and strong opposition from the pharmaceutical industry resulted in repeal of the so-called catastrophic insurance program in 1988. The political turmoil surrounding the repeal of this program resulted in a major retrenchment in the willingness of Congress and the Bush Administration to address health care reform for those over 65.

Despite the negative experience of the Medicare Catastrophic Care Program, the provision of adequate and equitable financing for long-term care—the need for which is becoming increasingly obvious—is a matter that will require careful consideration of both current necessity and future demographics. The use of a public social insurance program such as Medicare Part A, which relies largely on the employed population to fund retiree benefits, will further add to the problems of health care financing which face this country in the period from 2020 to 2050. The use of private insurance, which is essentially a form of prepayment (i.e., reserves are set aside now to cover future expenses), is on the surface an attractive option.[34] However, it is not clear that many persons in their forties or fifties will be willing to pay premiums of several hundred dollars a year to provide for an event that is most likely to occur 30 to 40 years later. In addition, because of the fear among private insurance companies of assuming what could be an almost open-ended risk at a time far in the future, most currently available long-term-care policies limit benefits to a set total payout or a flat amount per month. A few very expensive policies do provide an inflation-adjusted premium or a services-based benefit. Given our past history of the medical care sector, it is unclear how much protection a $50/day benefit might provide 30 years hence. Finally, due to the problem of adverse selection, the cost of long-term-care insurance to those already at high risk of needing such care is beyond the means of the vast majority of such individuals. Other solutions that have been advanced include full public financing through a Medicare expansion financed by increased social security taxes,[35] an expansion of the current, time-limited Medicare nursing home benefit, and a program financed by estate tax and an income-related premium and existing Medicaid revenues to provide coverage after a 2-year period. This program would be augmented by private insurance purchased by employee groups at or prior to the time of retirement.[36]

A recent proposal, implemented in Connecticut, would allow individuals who purchase private long-term-care insurance to exclude from the Medicaid limit on assets the amount of the benefit paid by the private insurance. As yet, none of these proposals has reached a level of consensus necessary for broad implementation.

HEALTH CARE PERSONNEL AND ORGANIZATION

Implicit in the discussion of the use of health care resources by our aging population is the issue of the distribution of the health care work force. Obviously, in view of the greater proportion of our population over 65, our needs for physicians will change, since there will be a higher relative demand for internists and ophthalmologists and a lower relative demand for pediatricians and obstetricians. While a number of sources have predicted a relative surplus of physicians in the future, the earlier projections did not take into account the apparent increases in the rate of physician utilization by those over 65 or the differential impact of a higher average age within the over-65 group on demand.[37] What role the emergence of geriatric medicine as a specialty, subspecialty, or area of "additional qualifications" will have is unclear. Estimates of the "need" for geriatricians are highly subjective and are dependent on assumptions about the amount of direct patient care assumed by geriatricians—whether the care will be in the form of consultation or primary care and whether patients will actually prefer the care offered by geriatric specialists to that supplied by general internists or family practitioners. Assumptions about supply hinge on how much interest medical students and house staff have developed or will acquire in the area of geriatric medicine and reimbursement issues and on what training opportunities are available in the area.[38]

Given the large differences in the utilization of nursing homes, hospitals, and home care by our older population, the demand for professional nurses, for allied health personnel, and for those who assist in personal care is likely to increase substantially. The problem in nursing is likely to be especially critical given a relative shortage of nursing personnel at all levels and the seemingly low appeal of chronic care nursing, especially in nursing homes. The efforts at controlling the costs of nursing home and home care are likely to conflict with the need to increase nursing and allied health salaries to attract more persons into these fields. It is probable that we will see the emergence of new types of providers in these areas as well as redistribution of tasks to those in lower-paying positions. How such changes will affect the access to care or the cost and quality of health services for the elderly is unclear.

The cost and diversity of health care services required by some older persons is also beginning to have an impact on the organization of health services in this country. While the original intent of Medicare was to ensure access for the elderly to the existing health care system, a number of observers have begun to question whether older persons, most especially those with severe chronic disease and functional impairments, might not benefit from a more organized health care system. The impetus for this experimentation has come mostly from efforts to control costs. However, in some instances, the innovation has resulted in better outcomes, but at the same or even greater costs than the baseline situation. Geriatric assessment and management,[14] life care at home, and social health maintenance organizations[15] are just a few examples that have been advanced.

The growth of consumer-, industry-, or government-based organized care systems such as HMOs and PPOs (preferred provider organizations) oriented toward the older member is a trend that is also likely to continue. It is important to remember, however, that at present a smaller proportion of those over 65 are enrolled in such organizations than persons under 65. This is not surprising given the tendency of those with chronic illness to stay with their usual source of care. It is likely that future cohorts of retired persons will be more favorably disposed toward alternative forms of practice since more of them will have had direct experience with those alternatives during their years of employment. Whether organized practices can indeed better serve the needs of the elderly is unproved both in the health care research community as well as in the minds of the older population.

QUALITY OF CARE

The impact of our aging population on considerations of the quality and distribution of health care is less obvious than the impact on utilization, cost, and financing. Yet what we consider "quality" care is dependent on the type and purpose of the care being rendered. To take an extreme example, it is foolish to measure the quality of care in a hospice by mortality rates or the number of years of survival. Even in the acute care setting, the quality of care of persons with chronic illness and markedly limited life expectancy is more difficult to discern and measure than quality measures for the treatment of a person with an acute disease. The problem is especially marked in the area of long-term-care services. The excellent monograph by Kane and Kane[39] provides an extensive discussion of the difficult task of assigning a value and determining the quality of long-term-care services. The need to develop and test quality monitoring measures that accurately define and efficiently and effectively measure changes in functional ability, attitudes, moods, and overall quality of life is paramount.

Despite the difficulty, the growing numbers of older individuals in nursing homes and home care settings will force us into better definitions and standards of quality of care in those areas. The passage and implementation of the nursing home provisions contained in the Omnibus Reconciliation Act of 1987 ("OBRA 87") have placed new demands on the practice of medicine in nursing homes. Provisions relating to the rights of residents to be free of chemical and physical restraints have resulted in a series of specific guidelines which must be followed if physical restraints or psychotropic drugs are used. Other provisions set minimum levels of training for nursing assistants, define initial and ongoing resident assessment (minimum data set), suggest standardized approaches to investigation of patient problems (resident assessment protocols), and require an active quality assessment process.[40] Whether any resulting improvement in the quality of care in nursing homes will be worth the increased cost and time needed to adhere to these requirements is as yet unknown.

COST-QUALITY TRADE-OFFS AND ALLOCATION OF HEALTH CARE

The issues of what constitutes quality of care and how to place a value on care for elderly persons are hidden elements in most debates about cost. Since the dollars that are spent by individuals and by society in providing health care benefits for the elderly presumably could be used in other ways, it is appropriate for our society to ask questions about the quality and value of the services received by the elderly in relation to other goods and services. As we have a larger proportion of our population in the age group where the need for health care services is high, with costs that exceed the ability of the individual (or the elderly as a group) to pay, these questions will become more pressing.[41,42]

Our task is just as difficult when we try to compare the benefits within the health care sector, such as providing a more humane dying process in a hospice as opposed to providing prenatal education, a liver transplant, or the use of a pediatric neonatal intensive care unit. While some commentators have been concerned with possible "rationing," it would seem that their concerns are misplaced. Rationing already occurs both on the basis of ability to pay and on degree of benefit.[43] We do not send every patient with a headache for a CT scan, and we do not provide a heart transplant to an 85-year-old severely demented patient dying from congestive heart failure. Those with generous health care insurance receive more coronary bypass operations than those with limited or no insurance. The question is not whether we should or should not ration health care but rather at what level we ration, what criteria are used to ration, and whether the rationing is implicit or explicit. In considering the value of a service to the elderly, it is important that we avoid overt age biases and base our choices on criteria such as life expectancy or severity of chronic illness, which are applicable to broader groups.[44] In the final analysis, an important measure of the humaneness of our society is the equity and openness of the processes by which we decide how to address the problem of health care for our older citizens.

REFERENCES

1. Mechanic D: Cost containment and the quality of medical care: Rationing strategies in an era of constrained resources. *Milbank Mem Fund Q* 63(3):453, 1985.
2. Aaron HJ, Schwartz WB: *The Painful Prescription: Rationing Health Care.* Washington, Brookings Institute, 1984.
3. Blumenthal D et al: Special report—The future of medicare. *N Engl J Med* 314(11):722, 1986.
4. Kovar MG: Expenditures for the medical care of elderly people living in the community in 1980. *Milbank Mem Fund Q* 64(1):100, 1986.
5. Division of National Cost Estimates, Office of the Actuary, Health Care Financing Administration: National health expenditures, 1986–2000. *Health Care Financ Rev* 8(4):1, summer 1987.
6. Office of Research and Demonstrations: *Health Care Financing, Program Statistics, Medicare and Medicaid Data Book, 1990* (HCFA Pub. No. 03314). Baltimore, MD, U.S. Dept. of Health and Human Services, Health Care Financing Administration, March 1991.
7. National Center for Health Statistics: *Health, United States, 1990* (DHHS Pub. No. PHS 91-1232). Hyattsville, MD, Public Health Service, 1991.
8. *Med Care* supplement 24(9): September 1986.
9. Pasley B et al: Geographic variations in elderly hospital and surgical discharge rates, New York State. *Am J Public Health* 77(6):6, 679, 1987.
10. McPherson K et al: Small-area variations in the use of common surgical procedures: An international comparison of New England, England, and Norway. *N Engl J Med* 307(21):1310, 1982.
11. Greenspan AM et al: Incidence of unwarranted implantation of permanent cardiac pacemakers in a large medical population. *N Engl J Med* 318(3):158, 1988.
12. Chassin MR et al: Does inappropriate use explain geographic variations in the use of health care services? *JAMA* 258(18):2533, 1987.
13. Wennberg JE: Dealing with medical practice variations: A proposal for action. *Health Aff (Millwood)* summer 1984, p 6.
14. Applegate WB et al: A randomized controlled trial of a geriatric assessment unit in a community rehabilitation hospital. *N Engl J Med* 322(22):1572, May 31, 1990.
15. Leutz W et al: Targeting expanded care to the aged: Early SHMO experience. *Gerontologist* 28(1):4, 1988.
16. Polich CL, Iversen LH: State preadmission screening

programs for controlling utilization of long-term care. *Health Care Financ Rev* 9(1):43, fall 1987.
17. Christensen S et al: Acute health care costs for the aged Medicare population: Overview and policy options. *Milbank Mem Fund Q* 65(3):397, 1987.
18. Gornick M et al: Twenty years of Medicare and Medicaid: Covered populations, use of benefits, and program expenditures. *Health Care Financ Rev* (annual supplement) 1985, p 13.
19. Sawitz E et al: The use of in-hospital physician services for acute myocardial infarction—Changes in volume and complexity over time. *JAMA* 259(16):2419, 1988.
20. Freeland MS, Schendler CE: Health spending in the 1980's: Integration of clinical practice patterns with management. *Health Care Financ Rev* 5(3):1, spring 1984.
21. Berenson R, Holahan J: Sources of the growth in medicare physician expenditures. *JAMA* 267(5):687, 1992.
22. "Medicare Physician Payment: An Agenda for Reform," *Annual Report to Congress,* Physician Payment Review Commission, March 1, 1987.
23. Blumenthal D, Epstein AM: Physician-payment reform—Unfinished business. *N Engl J Med* 326(20): 1330, 1992.
24. Roos NP et al: Aging and the demand for health services: Which aged and whose demand? *Gerontologist* 24(1):31, 1984.
25. Riley G et al: The use and costs of Medicare services by cause of death. *Inquiry* 24:233, fall 1987.
26. Kent DL, Larson EB: Magnetic resonance imaging of the brain and spine—Is clinical efficacy established after the first decade? *Ann Intern Med* 108(3):402, 1988.
27. Schwartz WB: The inevitable failure of current cost-containment strategies—Why they can provide only temporary relief. *JAMA* 257(2):220, 1987.
28. Estes CL: Cost containment and the elderly: Conflict or challenge? *J Am Geriatr Soc* 36(1):68, 1988.
29. Cohen WJ: Reflections on enactment of Medicare and Medicaid. *Health Care Financ Rev* (annual supplement) 6:3, 1985.
30. "An Aging Society—Meeting the Needs of the Elderly While Responding to Rising Federal Costs," *Report to the Chairman, Subcommittee on Intergovernmental Relations and Human Resources, Committee on Government Operations, House of Representatives.* Washington, HRD-86-135, U.S. General Accounting Office, September 1986.
31. Birnbaum H, Reilly H: Retiree health care costs demand attention. *Business Health,* March 1988, p 28.
32. Rice T, Gabel J: Protecting the elderly against high health care costs. *Health Affairs,* fall 1986, p 5.
33. Longman P: Justice between generations. *The Atlantic Monthly,* June 1985, p 73.
34. Task Force on Long-Term Health Care Policies, U.S. Department of Health and Human Services: *Report to Congress and the Secretary.* Washington, September 21, 1987.
35. Rivlin AM, Weiner J: *Caring for the Disabled Elderly: Who Will Pay.* Washington, Brookings Institute, 1988.
36. Pawlson LG, Lavizzo-Mourey RJ: Financing long-term care: An insurance based approach. *J Am Geriatr Soc* 38:696, 1990.
37. Schwartz WB et al: Why there will be little or no physician surplus between now and the year 2000. *N Engl J Med* 318(14):892, April 7, 1988.
38. Vivell S et al: Medical education responds to the 20th century's success story. *J Am Geriatr Soc* 35(12):1107, 1987.
39. Kane RL, Kane RA: *Values and Long-Term Care.* Lexington, MA, Heath, 1982.
40. Elon R, Pawlson LG: The impact of OBRA on medical practice within nursing facilities. *J Am Geriatr Soc* 40(9):958, 1992.
41. Churchill LR: Should we ration health care by age? *J Am Geriatr Soc* 36:644, 1988.
42. Jecker NS, Pearlman RA: Ethical constraints on rationing medical care by age. *J Am Geriatr Soc* 37:1067, 1989.
43. Wikler D: Ethics and rationing: "Whether," "how," or "how much?" *J Am Geriatr Soc* 40:398, 1992.
44. Eddy DM: The Individual vs. society: Resolving the conflict. *JAMA* 265(18):2399, 1991.

Chapter 14

AGING IN DIFFERENT CULTURES: IMPLICATIONS FOR POSTPONEMENT OF AGING

Alvar Svanborg and Leopold Selker

The main aim of this chapter is to throw light on the dimly recognized fact that the rate of aging per se and its functional consequences are influenced by lifestyle, environmental factors, and the availability of health care. To what extent would a better understanding of differences in aging in different cultures contribute to the development of programs aimed at prolonging the period of life characterized by good vitality and health? The aim is not to survey the differences in morbidity in different parts of the world or in different segments of the population of a country but to illustrate findings that show a relationship between lifestyle and vitality and possibilities for postponing the negative consequences of aging.

DEMOGRAPHIC PERSPECTIVES

Global inequalities in life expectancy are real. Differences in longevity are observable across different countries, with developed countries typically showing longer average life spans than developing countries. Even in developing countries where the average life span is shorter, people reach advanced ages. Yet in many developing countries, only the fittest survive to advanced age. Thus, life expectancy after age 65 for this latter group may well be similar to that of those who have attained advanced age in developed countries. In countries with a low life expectancy at birth, the average life expectancy at age 45 can be only 2 to 2 1/2 years less than in Japan and Sweden, and at age 65, less than a year shorter than in Japan and Sweden. In these two countries, more than 80 percent of the persons born today can expect to live to age 65 or more. Table 14-1 illustrates not only total life expectancy in selected populations but also further life expectancy after age 65. Unfortunately, the available statistics are not drawn from the same year, which accounts for some of the differences. In certain countries where infant mortality is already low and nowadays declining only slowly, the main reason for the increase in total life span is a prolongation of further life expectancy at the age of, say, 70 years.

Developing countries are today home to over one-half of the world's population of older persons, a proportion expected to increase to over two-thirds by the year 2000 and to nearly three-quarters by the year 2020.[1] While almost half of today's older people reside in four countries—China, India, the former Soviet Union, and the United States (Fig. 14-1)—China and India (see Fig. 14-2) will almost certainly be the main contributors to growth anticipated by the year 2020.[1] Indeed, Asia alone will contribute nearly half of the world's population of older persons by as soon as the year 2000, having doubled its elderly population in the 20-year interval since 1980.[2]

Of immediate concern is the fact that over half of the fastest growing segment of the world's aging population, the oldest old, will reside in developing countries before the turn of the century, where resources, for example, for medical support, are limited.[1] As people age, their predominant health needs may shift from acute diseases such as infections, for example, to long-standing diseases and disorders. The higher

TABLE 14-1

Life Expectancy (Years) at Ages 0, 1, and 65

Country	Year	0	1	65
Suriname	1985	63.6	64.8	13.6
USSR	1990	64.2	64.8	12.4
Hungary	1990	65.1	65.2	12.1
USA	1988	71.6	71.4	15.0
UK	1990	73.0	72.6	14.2
Japan	1989	76.2	75.5	16.5

SOURCE: *WHO Health Statistics Annual*, 1991

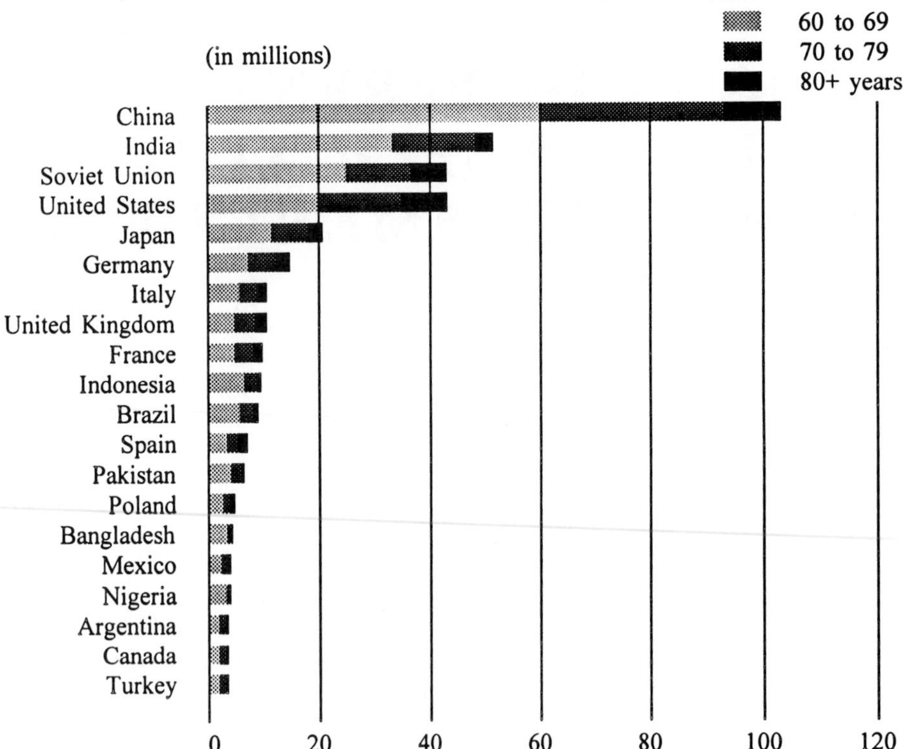

FIGURE 14-1
The world's largest elderly populations: 1991. [From *Global Aging: Comparative Indicators and Future Trends,* U.S. Department of Commerce, Economics and Statistics Administration, Bureau of Census (1991)].

rates of chronic disease and higher needs for assistance with activities of daily living that characterize the frail subpopulation of the oldest old may easily dwarf the ability of a health service system to respond, particularly as these large cohorts of older persons arrive at 80+ years of age. Thus, the problems confronting the frail elderly and the development of appropriate preventive interventions are, indeed, global problems.

In developed countries, availability of medical services, the healthy lifestyle of the individual, and environmental factors have become major contributors to the vitality and functional consequences of aging. The expectation is that this trend will also

FIGURE 14-2
The world's oldest countries: 1991 (Percent of population ages 60 and over). [From *Global Aging: Comparative Indicators and Future Trends,* U.S. Department of Commerce, Economics and Statistics Administration, Bureau of Census (1991)].

TABLE 14-2

Life Expectancy (Years) at Ages 0, 1, and 65

Country	Year	0	1	65
Denmark	1990	72.2	71.8	14.0
Finland	1989	70.9	70.4	13.9
Iceland	1990	75.4	75.0	16.4
Norway	1989	73.3	73.0	14.7
Sweden	1988	74.2	73.7	15.0

SOURCE: *WHO Health Statistics Annual*, 1991

come to developing countries, where infectious diseases are currently a major threat to health at advanced ages. Developing countries, where additional life expectancy after age 65 already parallels aging in developed countries, are likely in the future to approach the lifestyle and environmental focus that now typifies aging in developed countries.

Table 14-2 illustrates that in populations with very similar health programs for children and younger and older adults and similar rates of prevalence for diseases, e.g., cardiovascular disease and cancer, there are marked differences in longevity. The implication is that people grow old in different ways in these societies. As in the previous table, the World Health Organization (WHO) statistics are not available for the same year.

In addition to the differences in longevity across countries, expected length of life also varies among social strata within a given genetic base and within ethnic groupings over time.[3] Chronological age thus does not mean the same as "functional" age in different societies and ethnic groups around the world. Different life situations imply different functional consequences of growing old.

The global perspective on these demographics emphasizes the urgent need for a better understanding of causative relationships between environmental factors and aging. To what extent can societal planning for future generations take advantage of knowledge about exogenous factors influencing aging and use such knowledge in the development of public health programs!

LIFESTYLE, ENVIRONMENT, AND AGING

There are many reports in the literature that not just the availability of health services but also the lifestyle of the individual and the social environment seem to influence the vitality of older people and their quality of life. For many decades leading up to the 1980s, Sweden has had the longest-living population in the world. This implies also that a higher percentage have reached old age. Theoretically, since the Swedes should be more marked by aging than other populations, it should be possible to predict or anticipate health and vitality in coming older generations in other countries, such as the United States, when their populations attain the same survival rates. Results from a detailed study of vitality, functional performance, and state of health (i.e., the Gothenburg longitudinal study of 70-year-olds)[4–7] have shown, for example, that smokers and alcohol abusers grow old faster in certain ways than nonsmokers and those who do not abuse alcohol. Both these groups were found to have lower muscle strength and lower bone density.[8–10] Previous research in Sweden has also shown that the menopause occurs earlier in smokers than in nonsmokers,[11] and tobacco smoking has also been shown to influence gonadal steroid hormone balance[9] in a way indicative of earlier gonadal aging.

BONE AND MUSCLE

There is clear evidence that if abundant skeletal tissue or bone is developed at younger ages and the peak bone mass is achieved at about age 23, one has a much better start in weathering the negative consequences of bone loss at advanced age. There is also indirect evidence that physical activity with reasonable loading and weight bearing by the skeleton will postpone age-related osteoporosis. The stimulatory effect of physical loading and weight bearing on the density and stability of the skeleton seems to last over most of the life span,[12,13] not only during childhood and adolescence. Available information indicates that this stimulatory effect is definitely of importance for women after the menopause, when osteoporosis is advancing and the risk of fractures successively increases. Older people in developed countries thus may be at greater risk of osteoporosis, due to modern lifestyles with lower levels of physical activity. Furthermore, a more sedentary lifestyle increases the need for adjusting the intake of nutrients (e.g., calcium and vitamin D) to daily requirements in order to maintain quality nutrition.

The later phases of aging are accompanied by a slow decline in the number of cells in striated muscles as well as in their strength and speed of contraction.[14] Yet systematic training can result in improvement both in strength and speed[15] even at advanced ages. There is also evidence that, for muscle tissue, physical loading preserves muscle strength and quality of muscle function—possibly also muscle mass—and postpones aging-related declines in functional performance.

There are, on the other hand, muscle tissue compartments for which there is no clear evidence of a possible postponement of aging-related functional decline. At the same time as the previously described changes occur in muscle cells, a relative increase occurs in the connective tissue part of the muscle. During aging, tissue compliance—or distensibility—declines, mainly due to aging of the connective tissue.[16] The potential for preventing the loss of compliance and "retraining" for improved muscle tissue compliance is not known, although certain recent reports[17] suggest that systematic endurance training would slow age-related changes in the relative proportion of collagen fibers with good elastic properties. Aging-related changes in innervation and in the vascularization responsible for nutritional blood flow to the striated muscles are also well documented. The extent to which age-related declines in innervation and vascularization can be postponed by systematic training is not proven.

Nonetheless, available information regarding postponement of the negative impact of aging on physical performance indicates that, overall, a reasonable degree of physical activity would have clear positive effects.

The extent to which variations in vitality between nations and between social and ethnic groups are caused by variations in such factors as lifestyle has not been systematically studied. There are, however, several epidemiological studies which show that in developed countries the age-matched incidence of hip fractures increases considerably faster than can be explained by the ongoing increases in age.[18] This trend portends a threat further illustrated by the fact that, if it persists, a doubling of the number of hip fractures beyond those explained by chronological aging of the population would occur by the beginning of the next century. Studies showing that hip fractures are more common in urban than in rural areas of the same nation (for review, see Ref. 18) indicate that factors other than tobacco smoking and alcohol abuse, such as physical activity, are of pathogenetic importance. The extent to which similar trends occur in developing countries is not known. Older people in developing countries may be at a lower risk of osteoporosis due to higher levels of activity and a less sedentary lifestyle.[19]

It is important to emphasize that "skeletal" training through physical activation does not necessarily imply a recommendation to start with heavy lifting and mechanically stressing body-building activities with related risks for skeletal injuries. Available information indicates that systematic "loading" and weight bearing in the form of daily walking would give skeletal stimulation at least to the spinal column and lower extremities.

The negative functional consequences due to aging of striated muscles thus can also be postponed by systematic maintenance of a reasonable degree of physical activity during the life span. The striated muscles, unlike the skeleton, may possibly be "retrained" despite life events that have endangered vitality; that is, functional performance may well be improved even at ages above 70 or 80. A guiding principle is that programs aimed either at postponing the negative functional consequences of aging or at "reactivation" of older patients after debilitating medical or social events have to be more carefully planned and systematically implemented the more limited the individual's functional reserves have become.

These examples illustrate the general principle that reasonable activity at the cell, organ, and organ system levels is vitalizing. There is no clear evidence that such a "reasonable" loading of different organs would provoke premature aging.

SENSORY DEPRIVATION

Even though marked visual deficits are less common among older persons than is generally thought, vision problems do indeed exist. Population studies indicate that "only" around 5 percent of people at the age of 70 have such visual impairment that they are not able to read the text in common telephone directories. On the other hand, at these ages more light is needed for comfortable reading, and also more indirect illumination of the living areas in order to avoid accidents and to stimulate use of the whole home, not only a few small areas with adequate light. In order to stimulate reading and intellectual activity, it is also important to recommend both the use of higher-wattage bulbs and the use of lamps that do not cause disturbing reflections which impair the contour of written material.

A common reason for accidents among older people is the increased adaptation time for changes from darkness to light or vice versa. Many older persons are not aware that they need to be patient and let the adaptation process take its time.

Most medical staff personnel know that presbyacusis is a very common problem accompanying aging and that one should speak slowly, distinctly, not too loudly, and face to face with the older person. It is not uncommon for these common hearing defects to cause inactivity and social isolation. It is also one of the reasons why the "awareness" of some older persons of what is happening around them is reduced. When we are young, we have the capacity to register quickly and precisely from which direction sounds are coming—for example, to localize what is happening in traffic nearby. With increasing presbyacusis, this ability is reduced, which implies risks for accidents and possible fear of participation in the intensely pulsating modern life typical of developed countries.

Since aging of vision and hearing obviously cannot be prevented, the availability of modern illumination technology and hearing aids is important. Information for older patients about their hearing and visual defects should include information not only about the risks involved but also about the advantages of careful attempts to compensate for these disabilities.

COGNITION

Several studies indicate that healthy older people keep their cognitive ability almost unchanged to very advanced ages, but with one exception: psychomotor speed decreases.[20,21] The reserves we need to mobilize in stressful situations are diminished when we are older. To what extent cognition can be preserved by sustained activity levels has not been demonstrated in longitudinal studies of representative populations. Nonetheless, there is indirect evidence supporting the conclusion that systematic intellectual training would slow down age-related declines in psychomotor speed and that inactivity, both intellectual and physical, lowers the psychomotor speed.

NUTRITION

From a lifelong perspective, the positive potential for nutritional modulation of aging processes is currently a topic of focused discussion.[22] The only nutritional manipulation that has been shown to slow the aging process, if an increase in maximum life span potential is used as the criterion, is food restriction in laboratory rodents. To what extent such manipulation also would influence life expectancy in humans is not known. There is, however, clear evidence, as already mentioned, that the amount of bone produced during childhood and adolescence will influence skeletal stability and aging-related osteoporosis later in life.

Aging-related alterations in the gastrointestinal (GI) tract are known to exist (e.g., commonly occurring atrophy of the gastric mucosa with reduced gastric secretion). Aging-related alterations in the GI capacity to absorb nutrients are not pronounced over most of the life span. Constipation is more common in older people. However, the impact of aging per se on GI motility is not well known. The extent to which aging-related changes in the GI tract are of sufficient dimension and practical consequence that attempts to postpone them really would be urgent is also not clear.

There is not enough information about aging-related changes in the nutritional requirements of older people. When making dietary recommendations to older people, the health care provider thus should be aware that factors other than aging of the GI tract dominate the nutritional problems older people encounter. These factors include decreased physical activity and emotional stimulation of GI motility, drug effects, and changes like diverticulosis of the colon. Moreover, isolation and depression may reduce appetite and increase the risk of nutrient deficiency. Furthermore, age-associated changes in taste, odor sensation, and flavor perception actually influence food preference.

In general, a low-fat diet rich in nutrients is important for people who engage in little physical activity, which is the case for most older persons. Screening of their dietary habits is, therefore, essential. Concerning the "traditional" risk factors for heart disease influenced by the diet, recent epidemiological studies indicate that a higher than average cholesterol level after about age 70 no longer seems to imply a significant threat, but that a spontaneously declining cholesterol level is associated with a higher risk of dying. A high triglyceride level is, however, still a risk factor for cardiovascular disease and mortality at ages above 70.

The recommendations for intake of calcium vary in different countries. An intake of up to 1000 to 1500 mg/day does not seem to have any unwanted side effects and would produce a positive calcium balance in older people. With the exception of supplementation of calcium and vitamin D, there is little evidence to suggest the value of either widespread use of general-purpose vitamins or the use of large doses of vitamin supplements. On the other hand, the combination of aging-related disability and morbidity implies risks for specific dietary deficiencies. Again, the generally lower levels of physical activity in developed countries may place older people at higher risk of inadequate nutrition. The diet must be planned more carefully, especially if it is already low in calories. Thus, higher levels of physical activity in developing countries may be a positive factor in the attainment of adequate nutrition—that is, when food is available. Issues related to the nutrition of older people have recently been reviewed in greater detail by Munro and Schlierf.[23]

ORAL HEALTH

Loss of teeth, changes in the gingiva, and altered saliva production often lead not only to physical discomfort and changes in eating habits but also to psychological problems that may precipitate reduced social interaction and reduced stimulation as well as declines in appetite and physical mobility. The equal importance of oral hygiene in the older person and in the young is often not recognized. But gingival resistance to infection and to mechanical injuries is lower in the older person—even more so in those with dentures. Health providers are more accustomed to assisting with hygiene in the pelvic area than in the mouth.

Many older persons with chewing problems and dry mouth increase their consumption of sugary sweets, even though the intake of starches and simple sugars is known to aggravate decay and increase tooth loss. Tobacco smoking also implies increased risk for loss of teeth. While fiber-rich food may be most desirable, older people with dentures often select from the soft food category, which may make it more difficult to attain an adequate diet. Most importantly, both quality and quantity of food influence digestion. Older people do not need teeth to obtain an adequate intake of calories and nutrients; but the absence of teeth may make it difficult to ingest enough calories or to ingest enough fiber-rich foods to avoid constipation and other negative consequences of a diet poor in fibers. This must be more problematic in developing countries, where the prevalence of older persons without teeth is greater.

Available data suggest that aging in itself does not markedly lower the production of saliva to the point that it influences chewing[24] (see Chap. 38). Older people, however, often complain about having a dry mouth, which might illustrate a lowered secretion of saliva between meals and especially during the night. Many commonly used drugs dry out the mouth and place older people at increased risk for caries, particularly on dental surfaces uncovered by enamel. Such drugs can dry out the mouth to such an extent that chewing becomes influenced. Since older women produce less saliva than older men, they are at greater risk of drug-induced reduction in chewing-stimulated saliva production.

INFECTIOUS DISEASE/ IMMUNIZATION

Older people in general are more susceptible to infections. This is obviously due in part to the presence of other conditions influencing surface membrane resistance, circulation, and nutrition but also in part due to aging-related changes in immune response (see Chap. 5). The possibility that the population of older people in developing countries, having survived a higher incidence of infections earlier in life, will have accumulated a better resistance toward infections later in life, reflected in readiness of memory T and B cells, is theoretically attractive.

A positive response to vaccination is proven but may be less efficient in older people. In developed countries, influenza and pneumonia are leading causes of death in older people. In developing countries, the same threat is a reality, but older people there are also facing high risks of tuberculosis and GI infections.

Even in the face of poorer antibody response to vaccinations in older people as compared with the young, vaccinations should be considered, especially in the frail and sick. Institutionalized older persons are typically at greater risk of exposure to infectious diseases than older persons living in the community.

Adequate nutrition is of great importance to the immune system, a phenomenon well known in infants and children. We are beginning to understand that in older people also, well-defined nutritional deficiency may be responsible for general or selective immunodeficiency states. Adequate protein intake is of great importance for the immune system, and the risks for protein deficiency is more common in developing countries. In developed countries, improvements in immunological function (e.g., enhanced delayed cutaneous hypersensitivity, increased CD4 T cells, improved natural killer cell activity, mitogen-induced lymphocyte proliferation, interleukin-2 production) have been reported[25] after correction of the diet in older persons with nutritional deficiency.

In the frail older person, illness often leads to the development of malnutrition. Acute infections increase the demand for calories and nutrients. If adequate improvements in diet are not made, long-standing infections can lead not only to malnutrition but also to impaired immune response. It is also known that prolonged trace metal deficiency (e.g., zinc, copper, manganese, magnesium, or selenium) can significantly impair immune competence.

The bulk of experimental and clinical data thus show the definite influence of nutritional status on both immune competence and risk of infectious disease worldwide in older people.

SMOKING

As already mentioned, tobacco smoking has been shown to have certain negative consequences with respect to aging, through earlier initiation of the decline in density of the skeleton and the onset of menopause. The aging context for smoking also includes additional reduction in the respiratory capacity beyond aging-related shortness of breath. Besides the well-known increased risks in older persons for, for example, peptic ulcers and coronary heart disease as well as cancer, the further lowering of the respiratory capacity beyond that caused by aging constitutes another strong argument to advise older patients to stop smoking. The improved respiratory function due to smoking cessation is often substantial and experienced almost immediately. The trend toward a shift of mass advertising for smoking from developed to developing countries is thus distressing not only because of the risks for disease that accompany tobacco smoking but also because of the known negative influences on aging.

FALLS

Certain factors influencing balance appear to be due to aging itself and are, presumably, not preventable. The amplitude of swaying when standing still increases markedly at ages above 60 to 70, and this declining ability to correct and realign oneself to midline may in itself be one reason why so many older persons complain of "dizziness" and feelings of disturbed balance. Many other factors such as decreased physical fitness and speed of muscle contraction, and orthostatic reactions partly caused by aging but often further potentiated by dehydration or drug treatment constitute common risk factors for falls and are examples of risk factors that to a certain extent can be avoided.

Falls, frequently resulting in fractures and other traumatic injuries, increase with age, especially in women. The majority of these falls are caused by a combination of health-related, activity-related, pharmacological, or environmental factors. Poor illumination is a common risk factor in both developing and developed countries. It is important to know that most accidents occur in the older person's home, and that fear of falls and fractures unfortunately too often leads to inactivity and a lowering of the physical performance, which only further contributes to the threat of falling. Balance retraining after episodes of disease should be more systematically considered, as well as active programs aimed at lowering the feelings of insecurity and progressive instability which many older persons are experiencing.

The overall higher levels of physical activity of older people in developing countries may in itself result in lower risks for falling. From this perspective, systematic comparison is needed in order to eliminate causative and related factors which imply risks for falls, a common threat to older people all over the world.

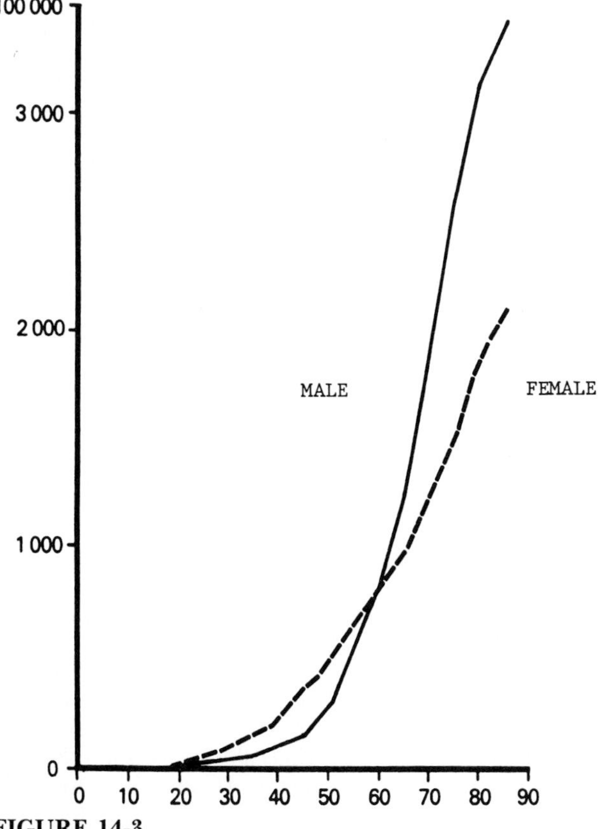

FIGURE 14-3

Age specific incidence of all cancer forms in Sweden in 1982.

MALIGNANT DISEASE

Figure 14-3 shows the relationship between age and the incidence of cancer in a population with high longevity and a reliable registration of malignant disorders. The figure also illustrates the sex difference in this incidence. Cancer is indeed a leading cause of death among older people. From the perspective of possibilities for prevention/postponement, it is important to emphasize that many forms of cancer may not be a consequence of cell and organ aging. Instead, the longer we live, the longer we are exposed to carcinogenic compounds. More and more data, thus, indicate that many of the usual forms of cancer are not necessarily related to "aging in itself." Avoidance of exposure to carcinogenic factors, therefore, could be of great importance to the vitality and health of older persons. A better understanding of why the spectrum of malignancy is so different in different populations is also needed. From a worldwide perspective, lung, breast, prostate, colorectal, and pancreas cancers are the most common in older people.

The present reality is that early detection and intervention is essential but usually more and more difficult the older the patient. Simple, inexpensive, and widely applicable screening tests (e.g., the recently available serological tests for prostatic cancer) would be important, and even more so in developing countries.

SOCIAL INTERACTIONS

Meaningful social interaction often becomes even more important at ages when vigor declines. Social isolation and inactivity have been shown to cause greater tiredness and fatigue, more reports of physical and psychological symptoms, more frequent visits to physicians, and increased drug use. The most drastic example of what effect a sudden change in the social situation of older persons can have is illustrated by the relationship between loss of spouse and subsequent vitality and state of health. In certain developed countries, the risk of dying has been shown to be 50 percent higher among widowers during the first 3 months of bereavement than among males of the same age still living with their spouse, and for widows the mortality rate was 20 percent higher.[26] To what extent this sudden decline in vitality and health would be influenced by supportive interventions is not clear.

In developed countries compulsory retirement often leads to a sudden contraction of the social network, which may well lead to negative health consequences. A better use of the productive contributions of the older person could result in postponement of the declines in functional performance that are an inevitable consequence of aging.

STRATEGIES FOR POSTPONEMENT OF THE NEGATIVE FUNCTIONAL CONSEQUENCES OF AGING

Indirect evidence has accumulated indicating that measures taken to postpone aging-related functional decline are realistic. There are no systematic prospective lifelong intervention programs providing the scientific evidence necessary for the formulation of preventive interventions that can guarantee success.

More and more data are available indicating that preventive or postponing measures would be meaningful also when they are initiated at ages when the aging-related impediments to functional performance become obvious. Geriatric physicians and other health providers need resources to systematically identify high-risk older people and to intervene as a part of good public health practice.

The main concepts governing such programs both in developing and developed countries are:

- Adequate physical activity, intellectual performance, emotional engagement, and social integration can all preserve vitality and in many situations reduce the negative impact of disease. Preservation of the autonomy of older persons may be integral to this outcome.
- Personal lifestyle has significant influence on aging-related changes in performance and state of health. This influence becomes even more pertinent at ages when the reserve capacity is reduced.
- Because of decline in functional reserves, early detection of disease and earliest possible intervention is generally of even greater importance in the older than in the younger person.
- Special risk groups need to be identified and given special attention. Two examples are lonely persons and newly bereaved persons. Due to lack of stimulation, not disease, many *lonely* older persons are more tired, have a more negative estimation of their health, and have been found to visit physicians more often. They also run a high risk of being overdiagnosed and overtreated with drugs. Much more can be done for these older persons, even without drugs. Even in frail and sick patients of advanced age, available literature shows that good results can be achieved through a combination of psychosocial interactions and medical treatment. *Bereaved* older persons constitute another risk group with an enhanced threat of morbidity and mortality, especially during the first 3 to 6 months after the death of a spouse.
- The possibility of retraining or *reactivation* of older patients after episodes of disease causing functional decline is generally much better than previously considered. Too many older persons, adequately cured of acute disease, are left without adequate help to regain previous functional performance level. Systematic studies now show that muscle strength and quality of muscle function can be regained and not only allow better quality of life but also less dependence on others and lower risk for disability induced by negative life events.

This chapter has repeatedly underscored the central observation that the rate of aging per se, and its functional consequences, are indeed influenced by lifestyle, environmental factors, and the availability of health care. Acknowledging that aging in different cultures is different and contrasting how aging may differ in developed and developing countries, it is hoped that a better understanding of these perspectives will, in the end, lead to improved programs for the prolongation of the period of life characterized by vitality and good health.

REFERENCES

1. *Global Aging: Comparative Indicators and Future Trends.* Washington, DC, US Department of Commerce, Economics and Statistics Administration, Bureau of the Census, 1991.
2. Martin LG: Census data for study in elderly population. *Asia-Pacific Popul J* 2(2):69; 1987.
3. Gibson RC: Age-by-race differences in the health and functioning of elderly persons. *J Aging Health* 3:335, 1991.
4. Rinder L et al: 70-year-old people in Gothenburg: A population study in an industrialized Swedish city: I. General presentation of the study. *Acta Med Scand* 198:297, 1975.
5. Svanborg A: Seventy-year-old people in Gothenburg: A population study in an industrialized Swedish city: General presentation of social and medical conditions. *Acta Med Scand Suppl* 611:5, 1977.
6. Svanborg A et al: Possibilities of preserving physical and mental fitness and autonomy in old age, in Hafner H, Mosche G, Sartorius N (eds): *Mental Health in the Elderly. A Review of the Present State of Research.* Berlin-Heidelberg, Springer-Verlag, 1986, pp 195–202.
7. Svanborg A: The health of the elderly population: Results from longitudinal studies with age cohort comparisons, in Evered D (organizer), Whelan J (ed): *Research and the Aging Population,* Ciba Foundation Symposium no. 134. New York, Wiley, 1988, pp 3–16.
8. Mellström D et al: Previous alcohol consumption and its consequences for aging, morbidity and mortality in men aged 70–75. *Age Aging* 10:277, 1981.
9. Mellström D et al: Tobacco smoking, aging and health among the elderly: A longitudinal population study of 70-year-olds and an age cohort comparison. *Age Aging* 11:45, 1982.

10. Mellström D, Svanborg A: Tobacco smoking—A major cause of sex differences in health. *Compr Gerontol* A(1):34, 1987.
11. Lindquist O, Bengstsson C: Menopausal age in relation to smoking. *Acta Med Scand* 205:73, 1979.
12. Rundgren Å et al: Effects of a training programme for elderly people on mineral content of the heel bone. *Arch Gerontol Geriatr* 3:243, 1984.
13. Suominen H et al: Mineral density of calcaneus in men at different ages: A population study with special reference to life-style factors. *Age Aging* 13:273, 1984.
14. Grimby G, Saltin B: Mini-review: The aging muscle. *Clin Physiol* 3:209, 1983.
15. Aniansson A, Gustafsson E: Physical training in elderly men with special reference to quadriceps muscle strength and morphology. *Clin Physiol* 1:87, 1981.
16. Labat-Robert J, Robert L: Mini-review: Aging of the extracellular matrix and its pathology. *Exper Gerontol* 23:5, 1988.
17. Kovanen V, Suominen H: Age- and training-related changes in the collagen metabolism of rat skeletal muscle. *Eur J Appl Physiol* 58:765, 1989.
18. Mannius S et al: Incidence of hip fracture in Western Sweden 1974–1982. *Acta Orthop Scand* 58:38, 1987.
19. Morley JE: International aging: Why does the United States do so poorly? *J Am Geriatr Soc* 39:836, 1991.
20. Schaie KW, Parham IA: Cohort-sequential analyses of adult intellectual development. *Dev Psychol* 13:649, 1977.
21. Berg S et al: Behavioural and clinical aspects: Longitudinal studies, in Wattis J, Hindmarch I (eds): *Psychological Assessment of the Elderly.* New York, Churchill Livingston, Longman Group UK Limited, 1988, pp 47–60.
22. Ingram DK et al: *The Potential for Nutritional Modulation of Aging Processes.* Trumbull, CT, Food & Nutrition Press, 1991.
23. Munro H, Schlierf G (eds): *Nutrition of the Elderly.* Nestle Nutrition Workshop Series, vol. 29. New York, Raven Press, 1991.
24. Osterberg T et al: Longitudinal study of stimulated whole saliva in an elderly population. *Scand J Dent Res* 100(6):340, 1992.
25. Chandra RK: Nutrition-immunity-infection interactions in old age, in Chandra RK (ed): *Nutrition, Immunity and Illness in the Elderly,* sec. III. New York, Pergamon Press, 1985, pp 87–96.
26. Mellström D et al: Mortality among the widowed in Sweden. *Scand J Soc Med* 10:33, 1982.

Chapter 15

PREVENTIVE GERONTOLOGY: STRATEGIES FOR ATTENUATION OF THE CHRONIC DISEASES OF AGING

Edwin L. Bierman and William R. Hazzard

The most striking feature of disorders afflicting individuals in old age is the progressive emergence of chronic diseases. These "diseases of aging" (or, more accurately, time-related diseases), such as atherosclerotic coronary or cerebrovascular disease, osteoarthritis, hypertension, chronic lung disease, and non-insulin-dependent diabetes mellitus, tend to be highly prevalent in Westernized societies. Characteristically, they remain subclinical for long periods, reaching the clinical horizon (i.e., onset of symptoms) sometime during "middle age" or "old age."

Since these chronic diseases require time for their expression, and time is inextricably linked to aging, prevention or attenuation of the chronic diseases of aging should be the ultimate goal of medical practice in the interests of a healthy, vigorous, and satisfying old age. It must be stressed, however, that this most often requires intervention during middle age or earlier. Thus, given that the upper limit of life span presumably is fixed, prevention of the chronic diseases of old age can be defined as a delay in the onset of their clinical expression until the upper limit of the human life span is reached. A practical consequence and realistic goal for many of the chronic diseases discussed in this chapter is the shortening of the period of symptoms and disability that exists between the delayed onset of the disease and the current practical upper limit of the human life span (the "compression of morbidity").[1] However, at the present time we are far from this goal. Since the number of very old individuals is increasing and mean life expectancy is increasing,[2] it appears that the average period of disability is also lengthening and chronic diseases will probably occupy a larger proportion of the life span unless multiple preventive strategies are instituted on a broad scale. This has implications for both individual health and health care policy, since, if current trends continue, the fastest growing segment of the population (i.e., the group over age 85) is the one most susceptible to chronic diseases.[2]

The chronic disorders of the elderly are, as a rule, multifactorial in etiology. They result from complex, interacting forces, both genetic and environmental, linked to the variable rate of biological aging in individuals who may share in common only their chronological age. Since preventive genetics (genetic engineering) is not currently practical, and intervention to slow the rate of intrinsic aging remains only a future possibility, the primary strategy for prevention must be an alteration of the environmental and lifestyle factors that contribute to chronic disease.

Unfortunately, possible measures for prevention or attenuation of chronic diseases of old age (Table 15-1) require, during middle age or earlier, the personal rejection of many aspects of a way of life which is still accepted by the majority of individuals in Westernized societies. Considerations of personal freedom of choice, lack of conclusive proof (in some instances) of cause and effect (i.e., that a modification of lifestyle will, in fact, prevent or attenuate a chronic disease), and powerful social and economic forces leave the burden of modification of a popular way of life on the individual and his or her supporters, including the physician. Thus, while a multifaceted strategy designed to defer or totally prevent the common disorders of old age through lifestyle modification in middle age can be articulated (Table 15-1), putting such a strategy into place requires determination and an ethic of self-denial in the interest of future health, which is a mind-set at odds with common contemporary lifestyles. However, the recent inroads into the social acceptability and public perceptions of cigarette

TABLE 15-1

Common Chronic Diseases of Aging Potentially Modifiable in Middle Age through Personal Changes in Lifestyle

Disorder	Preventive Strategy
Hypertension	Reduction of dietary sodium Reduction of body weight
Atherosclerotic cardiovascular disease (CAD; stroke)	Treatment of hypertension Cessation of cigarette smoking Reduction of excess body weight Reduction of dietary saturated fat and cholesterol Increased aerobic exercise
Cancers	Cessation of cigarette smoking Reduction of dietary fat Reduction of salt- or smoke-cured food intake Minimization of radiation exposure Minimization of sun exposure
Chronic obstructive pulmonary disease	Cessation of cigarette smoking
Diabetes mellitus (type II)	Reduction of excess body weight Diet consistent with atherosclerosis prevention
Osteoporosis	Maintenance of dietary calcium Regular exercise Cessation of cigarette smoking Avoidance of alcohol excess
Osteoarthritis	Reduction of body weight
Cholelithiasis	Reduction of body weight

*Gallstones may be precipitated during active weight loss; this may be prevented by concurrent ursochenodeoxycholic acid treatment.

smoking in the United States suggest that important aspects of lifestyle can be modified across all segments of the population.

CIGARETTE SMOKING

The adverse health consequences of cigarette smoking and, to a much lesser extent, cigar and pipe smoking are well documented in terms of their associations with chronic bronchopulmonary disease, atherosclerotic coronary heart disease, and peripheral arterial insufficiency, aside from their clear role in the pathogenesis of bronchogenic, oral, and other cancers. Cigarette smoking is the most important cause of chronic obstructive pulmonary disease among adults in the United States; even younger smokers and those nonsmokers living or working in close proximity with smokers have demonstrable reduction in pulmonary function. From the standpoint of preventive strategy, evidence is accumulating that cessation or appreciable reduction of cigarette smoking can decrease morbidity from these chronic diseases.[3] Progress in overcoming this single most clear-cut threat to health in middle and old age has been substantial, even to the extent that young smokers have decreased per capita cigarette consumption in recent years. Starting with the unequivocal message from the scientific community that smoking may be dangerous to health, there has been progressive social pressure to curb smoking on an individual and populationwide basis. The dramatic progress of the past two decades in this most difficult campaign justifies optimism that other lifestyle modifications once considered unpopular and peculiar may become widespread, a current example being the popularity of running and other aerobic exercise.

OBESITY

Among the multiplicity of factors involved in the causation of chronic diseases, obesity, especially when an individual is more than 30 percent above the age-, height-, and sex-specific population average (or when the body-mass index, kg weight/m height^2, exceeds 27) is a clear risk factor (see Chap. 72). Excess morbidity in such individuals is attributable mainly to atherosclerotic disorders, hypertension and its complications, cholelithiasis, endometrial cancer, and non-insulin-dependent diabetes mellitus.[4] With regard to atherosclerosis in particular, obesity is associated with at least six identifiable risk factors; i.e., hypertension, non-insulin-dependent diabetes mellitus, hyperinsulinemia, hypercholesterolemia, hypertriglyceridemia, and reduced high-density lipoprotein (HDL) cholesterol levels. It is now appreciated that there are two major types of obesity, central (abdominal or "android") and peripheral (lower-body or "gynoid"). The obesity-linked risk factors for atherosclerotic coronary heart disease are associated with only one type, abdominal obesity[5] ("middle-age spread"), simply estimated by the waist/hip circumference ratio. [Obesity-linked risk factors are most likely when the waist/hip ratio (WHR) exceeds 1.0 for males and 0.85 for females]. Actually, risk is most closely related to visceral abdominal fat rather than subcutaneous adipose tissue, but since CT measurements are required, its estimation is still less practical than the WHR. It has been suggested that measures to attenuate the effects of obesity in predisposing to atherosclerosis should be focused on those individuals with abdominal obesity, those who have gained excessive weight after age 25, and those who have a family history of familial combined hyperlipidemia or non-insulin-dependent diabetes).[6] Abdominal obesity should be amenable to the preventive strategy of long-term caloric restriction and increased energy expenditure through regular exercise. However, this lifestyle change is not easy to make in an environment in which food is readily available, attractive, and convenient and in which labor-saving devices and automation continue to proliferate. Nevertheless, the recent popularity of voluntary aerobic exercise programs suggests that social forces may encourage an increase in energy expenditure and thus help attenuate or prevent adult-onset abdominal adiposity and its long-term sequelae. Regular aerobic exercise in adult life may also contribute its own benefits to maintenance of cardiovascular health in the elderly.[7]

ATHEROSCLEROSIS

Other dietary modifications are also attractive as preventive strategies during the middle years. Reduction of dietary sodium may be very effective among the (unknown proportion of) individuals in the population whose blood pressure is sensitive to variations in dietary sodium intake. Reduction of dietary fat (particularly saturated fat and cholesterol) to 30 percent of total calories or less has been associated with lowered plasma levels of cholesterol and triglyceride, and these, in turn, are associated with reduced atherosclerosis risk (see Chap. 44). In addition, reduction of calorically dense fat-rich foods may make caloric restriction easier. While not all skeptics have been convinced of the efficacy of this preventive strategy and individual variation in response will remain great, such a personal program of dietary modification appears safe and hygienic, and recent statistics of food consumption in the United States suggest a populationwide secular trend in the direction of these alterations.

CANCER

Partly as a result of a comprehensive study by the National Academy of Sciences,[8] it has become apparent that many common cancers, notably breast and colon, may be influenced by diet. The evidence was deemed strong enough to warrant recommendation of dietary modifications designed to reduce the risks of developing these malignancies. Such measures include reduction of total fat intake (both saturated and unsaturated) to about 30 percent of daily calories; increased ingestion of fruits, vegetables, and whole-grain cereal products (especially those high in vitamin C and carotene, which is converted in the body to vitamin A); marked reduction of intake of salt-cured, salt-pickled, and smoked foods; and alcohol drinking in moderation. Although it is clearly not possible to design a diet that protects all people from all forms of cancer, the clear associations from epidemiological studies would seem to warrant a dietary preventive strategy for cancer which is remarkably similar to that suggested for atherosclerosis prevention.

Preventable nondietary factors other than cigarette smoking also contribute to certain cancers. The most common cancers of all, skin cancers, markedly increased in prevalence among the elderly, can be prevented by reduction of sun exposure earlier in life.

OSTEOPOROSIS

Dietary modifications during the middle years and earlier may also influence the development of osteoporosis. A lifelong increase in calcium intake, especially among white and Asian females (who are at greatest risk), appears to be warranted. When translated into particular foodstuffs, conflicts may be produced in the achievement of certain goals. For example, though milk is a rich source of calcium and protein, it is also high in saturated fat and calories. Modified foods, such as low-fat or skim milk in this example, may represent appropriate compromises. The interaction with other aspects of lifestyle modification should also be recognized: exercise enhances lean body mass (including bony mineral) retention, and avoidance of cigarette smoking appears to defer menopause by several years. Hence, the important effect of endogenous estrogens upon bone mineral content is prolonged.

ALCOHOL

The watchword in regard to alcohol is *moderation.* Clearly alcoholic cirrhosis and the other morbid sequelae of alcohol excess can be prevented by lifelong abstinence. There can be no alcoholism without alcohol. However, despite the burden to the population represented by all the adverse associations with alcohol abuse, there is little current enthusiasm for revival of the Eighteenth Amendment; to the contrary, the per capita consumption of alcohol steadily increased in the decades following World War II, plateauing in more recent years. This coincided with epidemiological evidence of minimal mortality being associated with modest alcohol intake, not with abstinence.[9] This "protective effect" of alcohol appears to be mediated principally by a reduction in cardiovascular disease mortality among those imbibing modestly. This relationship holds despite the inclusion of an important subset of hypertensives whose high blood pressure is induced or accentuated by alcohol. While the exact mechanism of the apparent protective effect of moderate alcohol intake remains unclear, a possible link may be the connection between alcohol intake and serum HDL cholesterol levels[10] in a manner suggesting a dose-response effect and demonstrable in controlled metabolic studies. Above a weekly intake of about 10 to 15 oz of alcohol (one to two drinks per day), however, the mortality rate climbs rapidly, and any potential benefits in the cardiovascular realm are outweighed by adverse effects all too familiar to the clinician. Thus the decision as to whether to drink alcohol is a personal one and should depend on the ability of the individual to drink only in moderation. That this decision is a difficult one is suggested by the close correlation demonstrated in many societies between the average per capita alcohol consumption and the prevalence of alcohol-related diseases and costs, both personal and societal.[11]

DISCUSSION AND CONCLUSIONS

Life involves a continuing series of choices. As improvements in standard of living and associated changes in the environment make death in childhood uncommon, these choices increasingly relate to the future health of those who will survive into middle and old age. While advances in medical technology would clearly seem to have contributed to the decline in many diseases, it is generally accepted that changes, often subtle, in lifestyle and the environment have had the greatest impact upon the prevalence and incidence of the major diseases of adulthood: The decline in tuberculosis preceded the advent of specific antimicrobial agents; the decrease in rheumatic heart disease has been more clearly related to better housing than to penicillin; most recently, the decline in cardiovascular mortality is more attributable to changing patterns of diet, cigarette smoking, and the diagnosis and treatment of hypertension than to acute coronary care or coronary artery bypass surgery or angioplasty.

From the perspective of the epidemiologist, the greatest impact upon the burden of chronic disease in the population can be made through widespread adherence to the guidelines for the prevention of these diseases detailed earlier. This is perhaps best achieved through public education, utilizing the talents and technology of those in the communications media and perhaps involving physicians only in a supportive capacity as role models and sources of expertise. Such mass preventive strategies require acceptance of differential benefit on the part of the participants in such a program. Since all are not at equal risk, all will not derive equal benefit, and many will incur only marginal advantage over their less compliant counterparts. Some, in fact, will still suffer premature coronary disease, cancer, osteoporosis, and other chronic illnesses which this strategy is designed to prevent. In this connection, quantification of potential benefit through individualized risk factor assessment and prescription of specific lifestyle modifications will involve the physician in an important professional role. The physician will also remain a critical supporter of the afflicted whether or not a prevention strategy has been part of the patient's lifestyle. The two approaches—mass versus individualized intervention strategies[12]—are often mutually reinforcing, the physician (and his or her team) having only to reinforce the tenets of prevention already known to the patient by the time of their medical encounter.

This should not suggest that all is known in this area. Clearly this is not the case, and future research will disclose surprises (e.g., reduced osteoporosis among persons taking thiazide diuretics) as well as quantify risk/benefit ratios and clarify mechanisms. An important element of such research, highlighted in the current focus on cholesterol, is the timing of such preventive strategies: When should they begin? In childhood? Young adulthood? Middle age? And, equally important, when should they cease, if ever? Should hypercholesterolemia be treated in old age? Clearly there will come a time in each person's life when the benefit of such treatment will no longer justify the effort and perhaps even the risk. Thus *preventive gerontology* must be distinguished from *preventive geriatrics* (the subject of Chap. 18), which focuses on health maintenance/disease prevention once old age has been reached. And the balanced application of both will be a hallmark of "successful aging."

Research must also address behavioral issues related to the barriers to compliance and improved techniques of "behavioral modification." Nevertheless, the direction of future trends is clear: What has happened already in developed nations, the near elimination of death in childhood and that related to childbearing, is likely to be followed by a reduction in morbidity and premature death from atherosclerosis and, it is to be hoped, other chronic diseases of middle and old age as well. When this occurs, the dream of "rectangularization" of the human survival curve and its possible corollary, "the compression of morbidity," will have been achieved, and death from "old age" (multiple, interacting, perhaps nonspecific causes) will once again achieve respectability and prominence.[1]

REFERENCES

1. Fries J: Aging, natural death, and the compression of morbidity. *N Engl J Med* 303:130, 1980.
2. Schneider EL, Brody JA: Sounding board: Aging, natural death, and the compression of morbidity: Another view. *N Engl J Med* 309:854, 1983.
3. Friedman GD et al: Mortality in cigarette smokers and quitters. *N Engl J Med* 304:1407, 1981.
4. Lew EA, Garfinkel L: Variation in mortality by weight among 750,000 men and women. *J Chron Dis* 32:563, 1979.

5. Stern MP, Haffner SM: Body fat distribution and hyperinsulinemia as risk factors for diabetes and cardiovascular disease. *Arteriosclerosis* 6:123, 1986.
6. Brunzell J: Obesity and coronary heart disease, a targeted approach. *Arteriosclerosis* 4:180, 1984.
7. Larson EB, Bruce RA: Health benefits of exercise in an aging society. *Arch Intern Med* 147:353, 1987.
8. Committee on Diet and Health, Food and Nutrition Board, Commission on Life Sciences, National Research Council: *Diet and Health.* Washington, DC, National Academy Press, 1989.
9. Friedman GD, Siegelaub AB: Alcohol and mortality: The ten year Kaiser-Permanente experience. *Ann Intern Med* 95:139, 1981.
10. Ernst N et al: The association of plasma high-density lipoprotein cholesterol with dietary intake and alcohol consumption. *Circulation* 62(suppl IV):31, 1980.
11. Gordis E et al: Regulation of alcohol consumption. *Am J Med* 74:322, 1983.
12. Rose G: Sick individuals and sick populations. *Int J Epidemiol* 14:32, 1985.

PART TWO

PRINCIPLES OF GERIATRICS

Chapter 16

CLINICAL MANAGEMENT OF THE ELDERLY PATIENT

Mark E. Williams

The increasing biologic uniqueness of older persons requires an individualized approach to their care. The physician must understand the clinically relevant differences between young and old people, including how older persons behave when they are ill and how to interpret a changing constellation of multiple disease possibilities and interrelationships. The physician must be aware of his or her own attitudes and beliefs regarding aging and death and how these views influence the physician-patient relationship. The physician requires knowledge, skills, and the willingness to evaluate each individual situation carefully and to formulate a specifically tailored plan of care. Because of the magnitude and complexity of medical, psychological, and social problems in older persons, the physician must cooperate with other members of the health care team. The accumulation and constant refinement of these skills defines the maturity and scientific grounding of the physician. This chapter will specifically address these issues.

CLINICALLY SIGNIFICANT DIFFERENCES BETWEEN YOUNG AND OLD PEOPLE

Aging is a ubiquitous biologic process characterized by a progressive, predictable, inevitable evolution and maturation of an organism until death. Aging is not the accumulation of disease, although aging and disease are related in subtle and complex ways. Whereas it is conveniently quantified in chronologic terms, aging occurs at different rates for different persons and for different biologic processes and organ systems within an individual.

Normal aging in the absence of disease is a remarkably benign process. In physiologic terms, normal aging involves the steady erosion of organ system reserves and homeostatic controls. This erosion may be evident only during periods of maximal exertion or stress. The maximal limits of homeostatic maintenance eventually reach a critical point (usually in very advanced age) such that relatively minimal insults cannot be overcome, resulting in the person's death over a relatively short time. Consequently, the morbidity apparent to the person is usually compressed into the last period of life.[1,2] Deviations from this ideal represent the effects of superimposed disease.

An additional aspect of normal aging is the occurrence of changes in body composition and in the structural elements of tissues. Between the ages of 25 and 75, the lipid compartment expands from 14 to 30 percent of the total body weight, while total body water (mainly extracellular water) and lean muscle mass decline.[3] This change in body composition has important implications for nutritional planning, metabolic activity, and the use of drugs by older persons. For example, lipid-soluble compounds such as diazepam remain in the bodies of older persons for a much longer time than they remain in younger persons.[4] Aging changes have been documented in various tissues and in the isomeric forms of structural proteins.[5,6] The implications of these changes and the establishment of biologic markers of aging are the focus of considerable research interest.[7]

What are the clinically relevant implications of these age-related physiologic changes? First, variation among individuals is a central feature of aging, since advancing age results in increasing differentiation and biologic uniqueness.[8,9] As a result of this increasing differentiation with age, algorithmic approaches, triage techniques, and other strategies of diagnostic investigation and resource allocation are likely to be less than optimal if they are based solely on age.

The second implication of growing older is that biologic systems minimally affected by age are often profoundly influenced by lifestyle circumstances such as cigarette smoking, physical activity, nutritional intake, or economic advantage. Although the precise mechanisms by which these environmental and lifestyle factors induce physiologic changes are unknown, some exposures seem to accelerate physiologic aging. The potential interactions of environmental and physiologic conditions are shown in Fig. 16-1.[10] The upper curve represents the maximal po-

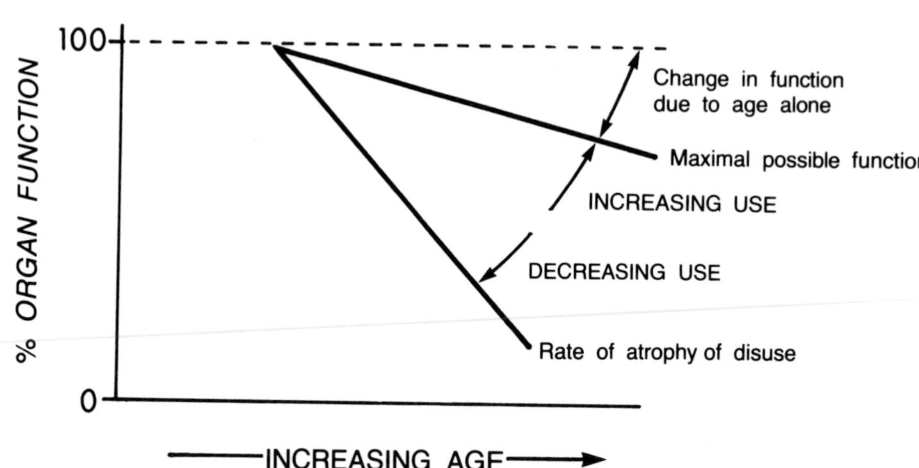

FIGURE 16-1
Effect of conditioning and increasing age on organ function. The upper curve represents the maximal possible performance of a given organ system, whereas the lower curve shows the rate of atrophy when the system is never stressed. Organ function always occurs at some point between the two curves. The slope of the upper curve defines the change in function resulting from aging.

tential performance for a given system (e.g., musculoskeletal or cardiovascular). Ideally, this curve is almost horizontal, with minimal decrements in maximal performance occurring over time. The position and slope of this curve may be affected by various environmental factors. For example, cigarette smoking in youth may reduce optimal respiratory potential in later years. The lower curve represents the rate of atrophy when the system is put to complete rest (never stressed). The system always functions at some point between the two curves.

Three inferences can be drawn from the curves. First, age-related physiologic changes are generally of a lesser magnitude than environmental and conditioning factors. Second, self-maintenance of a given function becomes more important with increasing age because of the divergence of the curves over time. In other words, the possibility of significant decline increases as a person ages. Finally, unless a person is in near optimal condition, advancing age suggests a greater chance for improvement. As a result, the prevalent pessimism regarding aging cannot be supported by the available evidence.

Failure to appreciate the relationship between aging and functional performance often results in inconsistent medical decisions. For example, the life expectancy of a 45-year-old man surviving an acute myocardial infarction but manifesting left ventricular dysfunction, ventricular ectopy, and residual ischemia is approximately 3 years.[11] Aggressive health interventions, including monitoring in an intensive care unit, are indicated and usually offered in this setting. Certainly, the same attitudes about health care resources should prevail for the average 80-year-old, who enjoys more than twice this life expectancy.[12]

The third consequence of aging physiology is the prospect of living with diminishing resources with which to meet increasingly complicated environmental demands. The decline of functional reserve is often compounded by losses of social status, income, family support (e.g., through death), and self-esteem. Disease processes may reduce physical and mental capabilities. The changes in capacity may appear magnified by rapidly changing societal expectations. For example, knowledge of computer systems and multiple computer languages is becoming an increasingly important social skill. Computer literacy is a virtual prerequisite for some employment opportunities, regardless of experience or previous contributions. The complexity of changing social expectations may be especially problematic for persons who have accepted a self-reliant lifestyle and self-image. In addition, some older persons may be victims of changes in the physical environment. Some neighborhoods, fashionable decades ago, may have deteriorated into high-crime areas.

PRESENTATION OF ILLNESS IN OLDER PERSONS

Three factors influence the presentation of disease in an older person: the underreporting of illness, changes in the patterns of illness, and altered responses to illness. A common myth is that older persons are hypochondriacal and frequently burden the health care system with trivial complaints. In fact, older people may underreport significant symptoms of illness. The reasons for underutilization of health care services by older persons may result from personal attitudes and social isolation. One prevalent attitude is ageism: the belief that old age is inextricably linked with disability and morbidity.[13] This belief reduces the demand for health care, since the manifestations of disease may be dismissed as age-related changes, leading people to say "What do you expect at my age?" A second factor contributing to the underreporting of illness by older persons is the perception of an unresponsive system of care. This apparent unresponsiveness may take several forms, such as inconvenient office locations, inadequate parking facilities, abbreviated encounters with physicians, and apparently disinterested or discourteous health personnel. Depression is another factor limiting the desire in some older persons for interaction with the health care system. This condition reduces the desire for improvement—"What do I have to gain?" Depression is a significant geriatric illness because it is both prevalent and treatable.[14] Denial, another reason suggested for the underreporting of illness by older persons, may result from fear of economic, social, or functional consequences. Economic fears may be justified because of the high cost of clinical encounters, especially to persons who saved their resources without planning for unstable economic trends. A final relevant psychosocial factor is the isolation often experienced by many older persons. Isolation reduces opportunities for receiving reactions to personal appearance, state of health, ideas, or attitudes.

The second factor influencing the presentation of illness in some older persons is an altered pattern or distribution of illness. Some conditions such as hip fracture, Parkinson's disease, or polymyalgia rheumatica are virtually confined to the later stages of life. In addition, some disease processes are more prevalent in old age. Examples of conditions with an increased prevalence in older persons include cardiovascular disorders, malignancy, malnutrition, myxedema, and tuberculosis. Because of these altered patterns of illness, the physician must understand these epidemiologic implications in the interpretation of various signs and symptoms. For example, jaundice, a sign often suggesting viral hepatitis in young people, usually results from gallbladder disease or malignancy in an older person.

The accumulation of multiple chronic disorders is another special feature of illness presentation in older persons. Four of every five older persons have at least one chronic illness.[15] Symptoms of one condition may either exacerbate or mask symptoms of another, frequently complicating clinical evaluation.[16] For example, symptomatic arthritis may mask the expression of severe cardiovascular disease if a person, by limiting physical activity, does not stress the heart.

Altered response of older persons to illness is yet another dimension of geriatric health behaviors. A person's perception of illness may be modified by attitudinal factors, social factors, and changes in the sensory organs. Manifestations of clinically important disease may be attenuated in older persons, particularly those that are frail and disabled. For example, angina pectoris may be absent or less dramatic in older persons with ischemic cardiac disease. A final factor relevant to geriatric physical diagnosis is that symptoms in one organ system may reflect abnormalities in another. An acutely ill older person frequently presents with confusion, anorexia, urinary incontinence, unsteady gait (or the effects of a fall), or combinations of these symptoms and other symptoms. For example, an older person with a urinary tract infection may present with confusion and disorientation. As a result of this nonspecific presentation of illness, the physician must exercise meticulous attention to expeditiously evaluate acute changes in an older person's health status.

CHANGES IN THE CLINICAL PERSPECTIVE

How critical is it for the physician to determine the precise nature of the underlying disease when helping an elderly person cope with illness? Certainly, the quest to define the disease causing a person's distress is important when the disease is reversible, remediable, or both. Almost by definition, this search is not a dominant issue in the management of many chronic conditions, such as heart failure or chronic arthritides. Nonetheless, the clinical algorithm that mandates the initial "ruling out" of the remediable disease permeates clinical teaching and practice. Since the seventeenth century, a first principle of medical practice has been the mandate to define the one disease that underlies a patient's distress.[17] Treatment directed at this underlying disease represents the most direct and effective way to alleviate symptoms. Despite the overwhelming success of this disease-illness paradigm, its limitations cannot be disregarded: some features of illness (the manifestations or symptoms of distress) are independent of disease (the anatomic or physiologic derangement). Many diseases do not necessarily produce illness, and the quality of the illness may not be predictable from knowledge of the disease. For example, knowing the extent of disease in a patient with rheumatoid arthritis does not allow one to predict confidently that patient's capacity to work.[18] The search for reversible disease, although important, is a secondary issue in the management of chronic illness and may even be detrimental if the physician-patient relationship is predicated on uncovering reversible disease.

Three arguments that favor precise determination of the underlying disease are particularly compelling: (1) identifying reversible or remediable disease is obviously rewarding, (2) clinical uncertainty is thereby reduced, and (3) accurate prognosis through an understanding of the condition's natural history should be useful. But do these arguments pertain to chronic illness in an elderly person?

The discovery of reversible disease in chronically ill elderly patients remains an important medical responsibility. However, this search for remediable disease should not be the focus of the clinical encounter. If it is the focus, what is the basis of the doctor-patient relationship when all reversible diseases have been excluded? Contrary to the situation in acute illness, in which the expeditious discovery of remediable disease is an imperative, the search for reversible disease in chronically ill people can be pursued in a more leisurely manner. Most experienced physicians readily define and treat remediable conditions in their elderly patients. Often, iatrogenic problems (especially drug toxicities and abuse of physical restraints) are the reversible processes identified.

A disease-specific focus, however, deemphasizes the dominant issue in the management of chronic illness, which is the maximization of the patient's productivity, creativity, well-being, and happiness. This goal of improving patient function and satisfaction to the utmost is usually achieved without curing the underlying disease.

The need to reduce clinical uncertainty, to leave no stone unturned, is another rationale for defining disease in the setting of chronic illness. A common argument is that a patient may be spared unnecessary diagnostic procedures once the underlying condition is totally defined. The decision about how far to proceed with diagnostic evaluation is ultimately a joint contract between the patient and physician. The benefit of a diagnostic procedure derives from the likelihood that it will yield meaningful information. In chronic illness in elderly people, information meaningful in the definition of disease is elusive. Diagnostic tests are an exercise reflecting more the need to allay clinicians' anxiety than to resolve clinical uncertainty, and they are often counterproductive. If it is justifiable to make illness the primary concern of both participants, many diagnostic tests become irrelevant.

The third argument for defining disease in chronically ill people is to allow accurate prognosis. Because prognosis generally involves estimating the remaining life span, its value is maximal in diseases that markedly influence longevity. For such diseases, prognostic estimates facilitate therapeutic decisions. For example, treatment regimens that are especially toxic or risky are usually reserved for circumstances in which longevity is immediately threatened. Small reductions in life expectancy are a less important concern in the management of chronic disease and become nearly irrelevant for many elderly people. Even for some less chronic problems, many patients seem to prefer improved quality of life over extended life span.[19]

Another factor that limits the utility and accuracy of prognostic estimates in geriatric patients relates to the constancy of the human life span.[1] As Fries and Crapo[2] have suggested, if the age at which patients have their first infirmity continues to increase, then the overall period of infirmity must decrease, assuming that life span remains constant. In view of this compressed morbidity, delaying the onset or progression of chronic illness becomes as important as curing the underlying chronic disease. Furthermore, most of the disability experienced by the elderly results from diseases (such as atherosclerosis, diabetes mellitus, osteoarthritis, or chronic obstructive pulmonary disease) that represent exaggerations of normal age-related physiologic decline, thus raising them above a clinical threshold.[2,20] Because the problem is one of the rate, not the fact of decline, a "cure" would require defining the determinants of the threshold. For example, what specific factors determine the clinical threshold above which a physician should prescribe medications for elderly patients with glucose intolerance? Does the maintenance of a euglycemic state with medications constitute a cure? Defining these threshold determinants and their relation to the quality of illness is a matter of some urgency. Otherwise, "prognosis" will continue to predict the number of chronic diseases at death—hardly an overriding patient concern. Even such a limited prognostic inference is confounded because elderly persons manifest such wide biologic variability.

Understanding the difference between illness and disease is part of the treatment of elderly people, with function rather than disease as the focus. The effective physician appreciates that an increase in diagnostic capability does not substitute for care. And diagnostic efficiency does not necessarily improve the patient's quality of life or life expectancy. In fact, functioning can often be improved without knowledge of what disease the patient has; but knowledge of the illness can provide the necessary information. For example, treatment of urinary incontinence due to detrusor instability focuses on reduction of bladder contractions, increasing of bladder capacity, and improvement of confidence and self-esteem.[21] Treatment does not depend on knowing whether the bladder instability is due to brain trauma, cerebrovascular accidents, dementia caused by Alzheimer's disease, or any other irreversible process. Knowledge of the illness, rather than the underlying disease, allows the physician to help the patient to a greater degree. When the patient is treated in this way, both physician and patient avoid the disappointment and frustration of not being able to define or cure the primary disease that underlies the illness of urinary incontinence.

When a diagnosis does need to be made, it can usually be made more effectively in the elderly patient by reversing the usual order of the diagnostic thought process.[22] In younger patients, there are four basic parts to the diagnostic formulation: The first is etiology, which may range from bacteria to poverty; the second is anatomy, i.e., what would be seen if the body were dissected today; the third is pathophysiology; and the fourth is the functioning of the patient. In elderly people, the key points remain the same, but the order of importance—the order in which these factors need to be considered—tends to be reversed. Functioning is the first step to consider.

THE IMPORTANCE OF FUNCTION

The ability to continue living independently is a critical issue for all elderly persons. Loss of this ability is a serious "illness," which, in this country, often leads to institutionalization.[23] In some instances, the loss of independence is a manifestation of overt organ-system dysfunction (such as severe heart failure), but that is the exception.[24] Why should an elderly person with reasonably well-preserved visceral, mental, and musculoskeletal function be afflicted with the illness of loss of independence?

Manual dexterity, extensively validated in numerous studies, appears to be intimately and principally associated with the ability to live independently.[25–28] Manual function is quantified by timing the performance of 27 simple tasks (such as writing a sentence, opening a door, or stacking checkers). In one study, the least sensitive of the 27 manual tasks surpassed in sensitivity any other traditional measure studied, including a battery of standard assessments and findings on physical examination.[25] The quantification of manual inefficiency in elderly patients provides important information for making clinical decisions that relate to the probability that the patient will lose independence. This inference holds in spite of the enormous differences in other characteristics within the three groups.

An important implication of these observations is that measurements of illness, when they are properly quantitated, are superior to strictly disease-oriented indices in defining certain health needs. Because of the ubiquity of chronic disease and the lack of objective physiologic markers of aging, most geriatric assessments use measurements of disability (or illness). Even in the studies just described, no difference in pathoanatomic state (disease) could be discerned in the functioning of the rheumatologic, neurologic, ophthalmologic, or other organ systems. We do not know how to account for the difference in manual ability; yet, in this population, the measurement reflects the risk of the loss of independence, and the impairment in hand function may even be responsible for this loss.

FROM PRESENTATION TO EVALUATION

One complicated case shows both how the presence of multiple diseases is a complicating factor and how a change in the physician's emphasis—from diagnosis of disease to functioning of the patient—can change the patient's course if not the course of his or her diseases.

An 81-year-old woman presented with a long history of poorly controlled hypertension and diabetes. Some 4 years previous, she had experienced an extensive myocardial infarction; 6 months previous, she had suffered another. The hospitalization was complicated by congestive heart failure that was difficult to manage. Medication to treat the heart failure led to progressive renal damage. After several weeks in the hospital, she was discharged, and she slowly returned to her previous level of functioning. In later interviews with the patient at our geriatric evaluation clinic, it was found that she was an active and enthusiastic gardener who had won many awards. After the second heart attack, the patient had returned to gardening. She dug, planted, seeded, weeded, bent down, and lifted with her arms and hands, and, of course, stressed her cardiac system. Three months after the second heart attack, she was hospitalized again for shortness of breath and extensive peripheral edema. The admitting diagnosis was ischemic cardiomyopathy.

After the last episode in the hospital, the patient was placed on several new medications and was not able to return to her previous level of functioning. Over the ensuing 6 weeks, she began to accumulate fluid, became short of breath, and was easily fatigued. She was readmitted, and the physician diagnosed a terminal cardiomyopathy.

The patient was then referred to a teaching hospital. A ventricular aneurysm and very poor cardiac function were documented, and the patient was put on another medication trial, which included digitalis, to improve heart function. Adjustments were made, and the patient improved enough to return home but was bedfast and on a regimen of multiple medications. The family accepted the local physician's pronouncement that the patient was in a terminal stage, which was confirmed by the teaching hospital physicians, and the diagnostic issues seemed resolved.

The patient was referred to our geriatric evaluation clinic when she complained that she was becoming increasingly anxious staying in bed. When the patient was interviewed, the cardiac problems seen previously were confirmed. The patient—an extremely pleasant, alert woman—had no recent pedal edema, and examination revealed signs of moderate congestive heart failure. There were also other problems that had not been noted previously. She had lost considerable lean body weight and was blind in one eye because of a cataract. She had an enlarged thyroid gland and bilateral pleural effusions one-third of the way up the chest on each side. The patient also had a stool specimen positive for occult blood. Results of a neurologic exam were normal. Laboratory studies showed blood glucose levels over 400 mg/dl and dangerously low potassium, magnesium, and phosphorus levels; her hematocrit was very low (26 percent), and her thyroid function revealed significant hypothyroidism with elevated thyroid-stimulating hormone (TSH).

Essentially, this patient had been "written off" by her local physician and by the teaching hospital because she had so many objective signs of significant heart disease. Unfortunately, they had not appreciated that other problems might be contributing to and complicating the heart disease. As a result, these other factors were not addressed. The single most important factor that they had missed was the patient's high level of functioning after the second heart attack. Once that level of functioning was recognized, the diagnosis of terminal heart disease seemed unlikely despite the evidence of a ventricular aneurysm and poor cardiac output. In retrospect, the well-intended medications may have worsened the problem. Control of the complicating factors (hyperglycemia, electrolyte imbalance, hypothyroidism, anemia, and medication toxicity) reduced the cardiac symptoms and allowed the patient to return to her gardening.

Here is another example that underscores the necessity of addressing the patient's needs and ability to function rather than the disease or diseases from which he or she suffers. A 77-year-old man with extreme malnutrition and a significant weight loss presented at the hospital. Diagnosis was no challenge; metastatic prostate cancer was obvious. Discussion at the hospital centered on palliative treatment of the malignancy: chemotherapy and radiation.

When the patient was seen by a geriatrician, the discussion centered on his level of functioning. It was clear that he had been sick for some time and that he knew he had a serious problem, probably cancer. Why had he entered the hospital at that time? What made him seek help at that particular moment? What had changed? Further history that included social factors showed that the man was a widower. His wife had recently died, and he lived alone in a shack in a remote area. His real concern—his chief presenting complaint—was fear of loss of independence. His physical symptoms were of far less concern to him. The major focus of medical attention was not the treatment of the cancer but the arrangement of care and the help needed to maintain his independence or adjust to the loss of it. Obviously, the malignancy was not ignored in his management, but its presence, and possible treatment, were not the dominant issues.

PERFORMING THE GERIATRIC ASSESSMENT

Geriatric assessment means getting to know the older person. The basic principles of the assessment are to (1) use observational skills; (2) avoid causing discomfort or indignity; (3) evaluate physical, mental, and social function; (4) uncover signs of disease; and (5) eliminate iatrogenic factors.

The assessment process begins when the physician first sees the patient. The clinician's overall impression of the older person's health is an important aspect of the preliminary examination. The way a person walks into the room and sits down, the nature of the handshake, the manner of dress, the type of language, and the many other specific observations all combine to produce a general impression of the elderly person's health.

Important inferences regarding functional cardiovascular and respiratory capacity and basic nutritional status can be made from observations of exposed skin at the hands, arms, face, and head. Skin and nails often reveal signs of systemic disease, vitamin deficiency, and occupational trauma or hypertrophy. Recent loss of weight can be judged from clothing that is too large, especially at the collar and the waist. Other useful, specific observations are detailed elsewhere.[29]

While taking the history, the physician can make important observations regarding visual acuity, hearing, articulation, vocabulary, manner of delivery, and mental status. If carefully structured and attentively pursued, the interview can serve as the physical examination of the intellect. The physician uses the patient's language and behavior during the history taking to assess his or her degree of mental resiliency, flexibility, attentiveness, and general attitude. Any change from expected behavior or from previous patient behavior should be noted.

THE PHYSICAL EXAMINATION

The technique of physical examination in an older person does not differ substantially from that in a younger patient, although the type and nature of abnormalities pursued are often different. Sensitivity to modesty is especially important. Regardless of the organ system or part of the body being evaluated, it is often rewarding to direct special attention to uncovering signs of degeneration, ischemia, chronic infection, and neoplasm. Certain examination features that are frequently evaluated only superficially in younger persons may require detailed investigation in older persons. For example, careful examination of the foot is an especially important component of the geriatric physical examination.

Quantification of the functional reserve of an organ system can also often provide useful information. Astute geriatricians often watch the patient dress and undress, stand up from a sitting position, walk down the hall, turn around, and perform other physical maneuvers to observe functional performance. Persons who require excessive time or effort to perform daily activities may require increased help from others and more intensive planning for the future.[25]

SUMMARY

In summary, the approach to the elderly person requires a perspective different from that needed for the medical evaluation of younger persons. The spectrum of complaints is different; the manifestations of distress are more subtle; the implications for function are more important; and improvements are sometimes less dramatic and slower to appear. The differential diagnosis of various problems is often different in older people, and presentations are frequently nonspecific (for example, mental status changes, behavioral changes, urinary incontinence, gait disturbance, or weight loss). Symptoms may be very difficult to interpret. The crucial issue is the elderly person's ability to function: although many factors influence the possibilities for "total cure" for a person with a given geriatric problem, the discomfort and disability produced by incurable conditions can often be modified.

Understanding the difference between illness and disease is a prerequisite to the care of patients affected by incurable disorders. Educated palliation in the absence of substantive information regarding this discrepancy is the art of medicine. Because elderly patients often present with several chronic diseases, many of which are irreversible, cure-oriented physicians caring for the elderly are especially vulnerable to frequent disappointments. Multiple influences—such as psychological, social, environmental, and iatrogenic factors—may also substantially limit the possibilities for "total cure." More important, even though many chronic conditions are incurable, the discomfort or disability they produce may be substantially modified. If this concept is not realized and addressed, elderly patients with irreversible chronic diseases may receive less than optimal care from physicians seeking cures. Studies need to be directed at defining and quantifying specific interactions between illness and disease and discovering risk factors for chronic disability.

The degree to which we as physicians can assist chronically ill people may reflect our understanding of human discomfort and our sensitivity to personal distress. If we maintain a purely disease-specific focus, we may have difficulty thinking about strategies to serve the patient. Defining pathologic entities may be less complicated than intervening in the illness of the patient, but the latter constitutes healing.

REFERENCES

1. Fries JF: Aging, natural death and the compression of morbidity. *N Engl J Med* 303:130, 1980.
2. Fries JF, Crapo LM: *Vitality and Aging: Implications of the Rectangular Curve.* San Francisco, Freeman, 1981.
3. Goldman R: Speculation on vascular changes with age. *J Am Geriatr Soc* 18:765, 1970.
4. Greenblatt DJ, Sellers EM, Shader RI: Drug disposition in old age. *N Engl J Med* 306:1081, 1982.
5. Williams ME: Aging of tissues and organs, in Beck J (ed): *Geriatric Review Syllabus: A Core Curriculum in Geriatric Medicine.* New York, American Geriatrics Society, 1991, pp 11–17.
6. Hoffman PM, Bada JL: Aspartic acid racemization in dentine as a measure of aging. *Nature* 262:279, 1976.
7. Reff ME, Schneider EL (eds): *Biological Markers of Aging.* (U.S. Department of Health and Human Services, NIH publication 82-2221.) Washington, DC, US Government Printing Office, 1982.
8. Shock NW: Current trends in research on the physiological aspects of aging. *J Am Geriatr Soc* 15:995, 1967.
9. Rowe JW: Clinical research on aging: Strategies and directions. *N Engl J Med* 297:1331, 1977.
10. Berman R, Corwin E, Davidson ME, et al: Update on the basic science of aging. *Patient Care* 13:24, 1979.
11. Multicenter Postinfarction Research Group: Risk stratification and survival after myocardial infarction. *N Engl J Med* 309:331, 1983.
12. Rothenberg R, Lentzer HR, Parker RA: Population aging patterns: The expansion of mortality. *J Gerontol* 46:S66, 1991.
13. Butler RN: Age-ism: another form of bigotry. *Gerontologist* 9:243, 1969.
14. Diagnosis and treatment of depression in late life. (Reprinted from NIH Consensus Development Conference Consensus Statement Nov 4–6, 1991) 9(3): 1991.
15. Fowles DG: A profile of older Americans. Washington, DC, American Association of Retired Persons, Administration on Aging, 1991.
16. Portnoi VA: Diagnostic dilemma of the aged. *Arch Intern Med* 141:734, 1981.
17. Williams ME, Hadler NM: The illness as the focus of geriatric medicine. *N Engl J Med* 308:1357, 1983.
18. Yelin E, Meenan R, Nevitt M, Epstein W: Work disability in rheumatoid arthritis: Effects of disease, social, and work factors. *Ann Intern Med* 93:551, 1980.
19. McNeil BJ, Weichselbaum R, Pauker SG: Speech and survival: tradeoffs between quality and quantity of life in laryngeal cancer. *N Engl J Med* 305:982, 1981.
20. Limitation of activity due to chronic conditions, U.S. 1974. Rockville, MD: National Center for Health Statistics, 1977. (DHEW publication no. HRA 77-1537.)
21. Williams ME, Pannill FC: Urinary incontinence in the elderly: Physiology, pathophysiology, diagnosis, and treatment. *Ann Intern Med* 97:895, 1982.
22. Lipkin M: *The Care of Patients.* New Haven, CT, Yale University Press, 1987.
23. Williams ME, Williams TF: Assessment of the elderly for long-term care. *J Am Geriatr Soc* 30:71, 1982.
24. Weissert WG: Toward a continuum of care for the elderly: A note of caution. *Public Policy* 29:331, 1981.
25. Williams ME, Hadler NM, Earp JAL: Manual ability as a marker of dependency in geriatric women. *J Chronic Dis* 35:115, 1982.
26. Williams ME: Identifying the older person likely to require long-term care services. *J Am Geriatr Soc* 35:761, 1987.
27. Ostwald SK, Snowdon DA, Del Marie Rysavy S, et al: Manual dexterity as a correlate of dependency in the elderly. *J Am Geriatr Soc* 37:963, 1989.
28. Scholer SG, Potter JF, Burke WJ: Does the Williams manual test predict service use among subjects undergoing geriatric assessment? *J Am Geriatr Soc* 38:767, 1990.
29. Braverman IM: *Skin Signs of Systemic Disease.* Philadelphia, Saunders, 1980.

Chapter 17

COMPREHENSIVE GERIATRIC ASSESSMENT

Albert L. Siu, David B. Reuben, and Alison A. Moore

The processes and techniques of comprehensive geriatric assessment (CGA) derive from initial efforts to formalize such assessments in the United Kingdom in the 1930s. For the next several decades, the techniques evolved in parallel with the growth of geriatric medicine as a specialty. In North America, the recognition of CGA as a distinct service was further stimulated by a series of studies that illustrated the health benefits of this procedure when performed in specialized geriatric evaluation units. Meanwhile, it has become recognized that such units are not the only means of providing geriatric assessment. This has led to further evolution and variation of the CGA model to accommodate the needs of different subgroups of older patients and the resources available in different practice settings. This chapter reviews the rationale and evidence of the effectiveness of CGA as well as the general methods for performing it. The chapter emphasizes the screening and assessment process that is central to the mission of CGA; however, it should be recognized that CGA is only a starting point and that it will be fruitless unless identified problems are also effectively diagnosed and managed. The diagnosis and management of these specific problems is covered in other chapters.

RATIONALE AND EVIDENCE OF EFFECTIVENESS

Comprehensive geriatric assessment may be defined as an interdisciplinary approach to the screening and diagnosis of physical and psychosocial impairments and functional disabilities in frail older patients. Such assessments are made in order to develop a comprehensive plan for prevention, treatment, and rehabilitation. The term *impairment* is used here to describe an abnormality of psychological, physiological, and/or anatomical structure or function, whereas the term *disability* is used to describe any restriction or lack of ability to perform certain activities as a result of an impairment.[1]

Programs of CGA have been established in recognition of the complex medical and psychosocial impairments and functional disabilities of many frail elderly patients. In contrast to the many older persons who have aged successfully and may have no or only single organ system disease, the typical frail patient seen in CGA usually has multiple and sometimes interacting medical and psychosocial impairments. One important goal of CGA is to identify these problems and develop a comprehensive and interdisciplinary management plan that emphasizes patient function more than, or at least as much as, diagnosis and treatment of specific diseases.[2] The complexity of problems in frail older patients also increases the risk of adverse iatrogenic events, and another goal of CGA is to identify and modify factors that increase the risk of these adverse events. Thus, the goal of CGA is to improve the function and health, living situation, and possibly survival of the frail older patient through prevention of iatrogenesis, improved diagnosis of potentially treatable reversible problems, and coordinated interdisciplinary treatment and rehabilitation.

The value of comprehensive geriatric assessment has been evaluated in the inpatient, outpatient, and home settings. These studies[3–20] have demonstrated that geriatric assessment can improve selected aspects of the medical care provided to the frail elderly (see Table 17-1). In some studies, it has been shown that these assessments, compared to a standard physician evaluation, lead to the identification of previously unrecognized medical and psychosocial problems and that CGA often leads to more frequent medication changes, psychosocial evaluation, and use of community services.

In addition to better diagnosis and management, CGA often leads to improved patient outcomes. Some but not all studies have shown improved residential placement, and no study has shown worsened placement.[3] Similarly, although a number of studies have failed to show that CGA leads to improved functional status, improvements in patient function have been documented in several controlled studies, and no study has shown that CGA leads to worsening in functional status. Although individual studies have reported varying results in terms of survival, a meta-

TABLE 17-1

Significant Benefits of Geriatric Assessment Programs*

Type of Benefit	Form of Benefits
Process of care	New diagnoses/problems uncovered[4–7]
	Reduced medications[5,8]
Patient outcomes	Improved scores on functional status tests[4,6,9–12]
	Improved scores on affective or cognitive function tests[4,5,13,14]
	Prolonged survival[4,5,11–13,15,16]
Nursing home use	Improved placement[4,8–10,12,17]
	Reduction in mean days in nursing homes[4,8,9,12,15,17,18]
Health care use/costs	Increased use of home healthcare[8,13,15,19,20]
	Reduced use of hospital services (mean days or hospitalization rates)[4,6,10,13,15–17]
	Reduced medical care costs[4,15,16,20]

SOURCE: Rubenstein LZ et al.[3]

analysis[3] that pooled the results from available controlled studies showed that various forms of inpatient CGA improved survival. The effect of ambulatory or outpatient CGA on survival is less clear.

Variation in the effectiveness of different CGA programs can be attributed to differences in study design, study populations, various programmatic factors, and outcome measures. For example, implementation of the recommendations that result from CGA varies among programs. Programs that do not have direct and continuing control of patients may have difficulty obtaining full implementation of assessment recommendations. Indeed, in some trials of geriatric assessment, over a quarter of the recommendations were never implemented. Additionally, the effectiveness of CGA may also be influenced by whether or not assessment is accompanied by continuing follow-up and reassessment of patients at periodic intervals.

The effectiveness of CGA may also vary depending on how carefully patients are selected or targeted to receive such services. Patients who are acutely ill or who are suffering from irreversible end-stage disease (e.g., severe dementia) may not benefit from assessment. Similarly, it may be difficult to show benefit from CGA in older healthy patients. Even when CGA has been carefully targeted to specific classes of patients, subgroups of this targeted group may benefit more than others.[4,12,21] Consequently, it has been argued that CGA should be targeted and limited to older patients who have potentially improvable function. However, the optimal targeting criteria have not been established, and the criteria are likely to vary by program and clinical setting. Furthermore, in many cases, excluding nontargeted patients would not be practical; it may be difficult to refuse a referral from another physician or from a burdened family. For this reason appropriate targeting should perhaps be thought of as matching the components and intensity of geriatric assessment to the specific patient's needs, prognosis, and treatment goals. Thus, a bed-bound patient with advanced dementia may not have the potential for improved physical function; however, the assessment can still legitimately focus on reducing iatrogenic complications and hospital readmissions in such a patient.

THE COMPONENTS OF CGA

Comprehensive geriatric assessment has been employed in hospital settings with or without designated beds or units, in rehabilitation units, in outpatient clinics or practices, in geriatric day-hospital settings, and in home care programs. Regardless of the setting, the basic components of CGA include a set of assessment protocols that focus on screening for various physical and psychosocial impairments and disabilities. The traditional medical examination is supplemented with specific assessments to detect impairments that are particularly prevalent and important in the frail elderly. These include impairments of cognition, affect, mobility, gait, balance, continence, nutrition, vision, and hearing. In some populations of older persons, screening for alcoholism or other selected disorders may be indicated. To complement these assessments, a variety of measures are generally included to assess various dimensions of disability and functional status. This most commonly includes scales that assess performance of activities of daily living (ADL) and the more complex range of activities commonly referred to as instrumental activities of daily living (IADLs). However, these assessments may also include measures of pain, social functioning, general well-being, and role functioning. Assessments also generally include consideration of the patient's living situation—its adequacy and safety—as well as other available social and economic needs and resources. In most circumstances, the assessment should include a discussion with the patient and family regarding preferences for future medical care. Apart from assessment, which is at the core of CGA programs, CGA programs also may have other secondary objectives, including outreach and case finding, intensive rehabilitation, primary care of frail older patients, and evaluation for long-term-care placement and services.

The classical model of CGA employs an interdisciplinary team to make these assessments and to develop a diagnosis and treatment plan.[3] Generally each member of the team sees every patient. The teams typically include a physician, a nurse or nurse practitioner, and a social worker; however, most programs will employ a variety of other disciplines, including physical and occupational therapy, psychology or psychiatry, rehabilitation medicine, audiology, clinical pharmacy, dentistry, podiatry, nutrition, and other medical or surgical subspecialties (such as ophthalmology) on a consulting basis. Depending upon the patient population and any secondary program goals (e.g., post–acute hospital care or nursing home placement evaluation), the CGA program will differ in the emphasis placed on these various disciplines.

This classical interdisciplinary model of CGA has been instituted in many Veterans Administration hospitals and academic medical centers in North America. The full and more widespread diffusion of this model of CGA, however, has been limited by a number of factors. Principal among these is inadequate reimbursement for these services and a shortage of health care professionals trained in geriatric medicine, geropsychiatry, and the related disciplines. Because many of the CGA models have been based in inpatient settings, CGA has also become increasingly difficult to conduct because of the declining length of hospital stay since the early 1980s. In practical terms, this has meant that some patients are discharged before interdisciplinary assessment can be completed or before all recommendations can be implemented. Additionally, the more effective models of geriatric assessment have involved programs that assumed actual control over patient care. Because many patients have existing long-term relationships with primary care physicians, it is sometimes difficult to blend the classical nonconsultative interdisciplinary CGA model with this existing relationship.

For these and other reasons, variations on the classical CGA model have been developed in recent years. These variations adapt the classical model to the needs of the patient population, the reality of local practice arrangements, and the availability of financial and nonfinancial resources. The variations have generally attempted to incorporate parts of or abbreviated versions of CGA into clinical practice in medicine or other specialties. The resulting shorter and simpler procedures may be particularly useful for selected healthier patient populations and clinical settings where the classical model of CGA is impractical. It should be kept in mind, however, that the ability of these abbreviated versions to confer the same benefits as the classical model has yet to be demonstrated.

True to the core function of CGA, these variations on the classical CGA model have focused on simplifying and refining techniques for screening for impairment and functional disability. Methods have been developed to administer functional status assessment measures in physician office practice.[22–24] Another group has attempted to adapt CGA to physician office practice by using very brief screening techniques and measures to detect common impairments and functional disabilities that might be missed with conventional histories and physical examinations (see Table 17-2). The procedure also includes questioning patients and caregivers about the adequacy of the home environment and the social support system.[25]

SCREENING ASSESSMENTS USED IN CGA

Either in the classical or the many more abbreviated models of CGA, careful screening is particularly indicated for cognitive impairment, depression, problems of mobility (including gait and balance), poor nutrition or undernutrition, vision and hearing, and overall functional status. For each of these areas of impairment or disability, a variety of screening methods and instruments have been developed and validated. The following section focuses on some of the more commonly used screening methods (alternatives are described in some of the referenced citations). Because these are screening instruments, more detailed diagnostic testing very often may be required either in place of or as a supplement to the described procedures.

Cognitive Impairment

Screening and management of patients with cognitive impairment is one of the more common issues encountered in the care of older patients. Although dementia is common, mild or even moderate dementia may frequently go unrecognized by physicians. Some cases of dementia are potentially treatable or reversible, whereas other dementia patients will have chronic medical problems that can be more optimally treated.[26] Whether treatable or not, it is important to identify patients with dementia to plan for future care (including decision making) and needs. This emphasizes the importance of screening for cognitive impairment in the type of patients commonly seen in CGA.

As with all screening tests, the value of screening measures for cognitive impairment depends on the overall prevalence of the problem in the population or the clinician's estimate of prior probability of impairment. After having estimated the prior probability of cognitive impairment (or any other impairment), the results of the screening test(s) can help the clinician revise that probability downward or upward. Depending on the prior probability of disease and the properties of the diagnostic test, a disease or impairment can, with confidence, be said to be present or not.

The consideration of prior probabilities is particularly important given that the prevalence of cognitive impairment varies greatly by age of the patient and by clinical setting. Thus, for community-dwelling patients over age 65, the prevalence of Alzheimer's disease may be as high as 10 percent; for those over 85, the prevalence may be as high as 47 percent.[27] This probability of impairment rises among hospitalized patients and is even greater in institutionalized

TABLE 17-2

Procedure for Functional Assessment Screening in the Elderly

Target Area	Assessment Procedure	Abnormal Result
Vision	Test each eye with Jaeger card while patient wears corrective lenses (if applicable).	Inability to read better than 20/40
Hearing	Whisper a short, easily answered question such as "What is your name?" in each ear while the examiner's face is out of direct view.	Inability to answer question
Arm	Proximal: "Touch the back of your head with both hands." Distal: "Pick up the spoon."	Inability to do task
Leg	Observe the patient after asking: "Rise from your chair, walk 10 feet, return, sit down."	Inability to walk to or transfer out of chair
Urinary incontinence	Ask: "Do you ever lose your urine and get wet?"	Yes
Nutrition	Weigh the patient. Measure height.	Weight is below acceptable range for height
Mental status	Instruct: "I am going to name three objects (pencil, truck, book). I will ask you to repeat their names now and then again in a few minutes from now."	Inability to recall all three objects after 1 minute
Depression	Ask: "Do you often feel sad or depressed?"	Yes
ADL-IADL*	Ask: "Can you get out of bed yourself?" "Can you make your own meals?" "Can you do your own shopping?"	No to any question
Home environment	Ask: "Do you have trouble with stairs inside or outside of your home?" Ask about potential hazards inside the home with bathtubs, rugs, or lighting.	Yes
Social support	Ask: "Who would be able to help you in case of illness or emergency?"	Not applicable

*ADL-IADL = activities of daily living-instrumental activities of daily living.
SOURCE: Lachs et al.[25]

populations. In each setting, the probability rises with advancing age.

A number of screening tools for detecting cognitive impairment are available to the clinician. These tools include a number of brief screening questions (such as three-item recall or serial sevens) which in some patients will be useful in reducing the probability of cognitive impairment if the response is normal. As a rule, however, these tests do not establish the presence of cognitive impairment if the results are abnormal.

For this reason, a number of more extensive screening batteries for cognitive impairment have been developed. Of these tests, the most commonly used is the Mini-Mental State Examination (MMSE) (see Chap. 19). The MMSE is an abbreviated structured mental status examination that takes approximately 5 to 10 min to administer. Points are awarded for correct responses to questions, up to a maximum score of 30. This test has been extensively validated. A score of 20 or less greatly increases the chances of cognitive impairment, and a score of 26 or more greatly decreases the chances of such impairment.[28] Intermediate values of 21 to 25 are less helpful diagnostically. The patient's level of education affects the results on this and other screening tests of cognition, and previous education should be taken into consideration when the results of the MMSE are interpreted.

Other common screening tests for cognitive impairment include the Mental Status Questionnaire, the Short Portable Mental Status Questionnaire, the Set Test, the Cognitive Capacity Screening Examination, the Short Test of Mental Status, and the Blessed Information–Memory Concentration Test and its modifications. These screening instruments have not been as extensively studied as the MMSE. As is the case with any screening instrument, a positive test indicates the need for further evaluation. Depending upon the circumstances (whether or not a change in cognitive impairment is suspected), the screen should either be repeated at a later date or a more extensive diagnostic evaluation should be initiated to establish the diagnosis of dementia based on the criteria of the American Psychological Association's *Diagnostic and Statistical Manual,* third edition, revised (DSM-III-R) and to determine the specific etiology of dementia.

In some cases, it will be important to assess the severity of a known cognitive impairment rather than to screen for the presence of cognitive impairment. In these cases, a variety of other assessment instruments are available. Although it is too lengthy to be considered a true screening instrument, the best-characterized scale of this type is the Dementia Rating Scale, which includes assessments of the domains of attention, initiation and perseveration, construction, conceptualization, and memory.[29]

Depression

As with cognitive impairment, impairment related to affect is common in the elderly. These impairments range from depressive symptoms to major depression and bipolar disease, as described in Chap. 99. Impairment related to depression may also be unrecognized unless specific attempts are made to screen for it.

To screen for depression, a variety of assessment instruments are available. Although many of these were initially developed for use with adults of all ages,[22] some instruments have been developed with formats that are useful specifically for frail older patients. One of these instruments is the Geriatric Depression Scale, a 30-item instrument that asks for yes/no responses to a series of questions covering symptoms and the manifestations of depression. This instrument takes approximately 10 to 15 min to administer. Scores of 11 or more on this 30-point instrument substantially increase the probability of depression, and scores of less than 11 greatly decrease this probability. Scores of 14 or over or scores of less than 9 more greatly increase or decrease, respectively, the probability of depression.[31] More recently, a shorter 15-item version of this scale has been developed,[32] but the diagnostic accuracy of this shorter version is less certain.

Other common screening tests for depression include the Center for Epidemiological Studies Depression Scale and the Beck Depression Inventory.[33] Many of these instruments (including the Geriatric Depression Scale) have one important disadvantage for CGA involving frail elderly patients—they are difficult to use in patients with concomitant cognitive impairment. For these patients, measures have been developed that screen for depression without a heavy reliance on patient self-report. The Cornell Scale is one such measure. This scale includes 19 items wherein the caregiver is asked a variety of questions about the presence of a number of symptoms and manifestations of depression. This is followed by a confirmatory interview and examination of the patient. This measure has been shown to be useful in screening for major depression in both demented and nondemented patients.[34,35]

Although we have focused on cognitive impairment and depression, clinicians must be aware of other aspects of mental status that are not included in these two domains. Clinicians must also be attentive to problems relating to delirium, anxiety, hostility, psychosis, and behavioral problems.

Musculoskeletal Impairment and Immobility

Mobility impairment (such as unsteadiness or abnormality in sitting or getting up from a chair, turning or walking, or step height) increases the risk of falling in older persons.[36] Just as with impairments in mental status, mobility impairment is often undetected in the standard history and physical (including neuromuscular) examination.[37] This is the rationale for adding screening for mobility impairment to examinations of the nervous system in CGA.

To screen for musculoskeletal impairment and mobility, measures are available that focus on upper-extremity mobility, manual dexterity, lower-extremity mobility, or a combination of both. One commonly used method to assess upper-extremity mobility and manual dexterity is a test of timed manual performance. This test involves timed measures of the opening and closing of a variety of fasteners (such as a padlock or door latch) and assessment of five manual skills that include writing a short sentence, turning over cards, picking up small objects, stacking checkers, and simulating eating. Performance on this test has been found to be a predictor of the level of dependency and risk of subsequent institutionalization.[38,39]

Among tests of lower-extremity mobility, the timed "Up & Go"[40] test and balance and gait evaluations[36] are commonly used. The Up & Go test is a test of the time required to rise from a chair, walk 10 feet, turn, and return to the sitting position; performance on this test is correlated with abnormalities of gait that are associated with an increased risk of falling. The balance and gait evaluation (see Table 17-3) includes standardized criteria for scoring a number of balance maneuvers (such as sitting and standing balance) and features of the patient's gait (such as step length, step height, step continuity, and symmetry). Abnormalities in the overall evaluation and in three or more balance or gait items are associated with an increased risk of falling.[36,37]

The appropriate screening measure for mobility impairment will vary greatly depending on the purpose and patient population involved in CGA. In

TABLE 17-3

Evaluations of Balance and Gait

*Balance Measures**
Sitting balance†
Rising from a chair‡
Immediate standing balance (first 5 s)§
Prolonged standing balance§
Withstanding nudge on chest§
Standing balance with eyes closed†
Turning balance (360°)§
Sitting down†

*Gait Observations**
Initiation of gait§
Step length§
Step height (whether foot clears floor)§
Step continuity§
Step symmetry‡
Walking stance†
Amount of trunk sway‡
Path deviation§

*Criteria for scoring subjects available from author
†Scored 0 to 1
‡Scored 0 to 4
§Scored 0, 1, or 2
SOURCE: Tinetti et al.[36]

some circumstances, measures that combine screening for upper- and lower-extremity mobility are preferred.[41,42] In other cases, screening for mobility impairment might be more appropriately conducted using the standard assessments performed by physical and occupational therapists or physiatrists.

Malnutrition

The elderly may be at increased risk for poor nutritional status because of chronic disease, poverty, social isolation, cognitive impairment, and/or functional disability. Various indicators of poor nutrition have been associated with impaired wound healing, increased surgical complications, and increased mortality.[43–45] Thus, screening for poor nutrition or undernutrition is an important component of CGA.

Although many indicators of poor nutritional status exist, a more definitive screening assessment for malnutrition is being developed.[46] A body weight of 100 pounds or less is highly sensitive for the diagnosis of malnutrition in older ambulatory patients,[47] but malnutrition also occurs in patients who weigh more than 100 pounds. Historical clues (e.g., involuntary weight loss of 10 percent or more of body weight) should be sought, along with physical findings such as cheilosis, glossitis, loss of subcutaneous body fat, muscle wasting, and edema.[48] Laboratory tests (such as serum albumin) and physical measurements (such as the body mass index, midarm circumference, or triceps skinfolds) may also be helpful in some circumstances. Where the patient's height cannot be easily measured due to skeletal impairments or immobility, arm span may be used to approximate the measurement of height in the elderly.[49]

Visual and Hearing Impairment

Visual impairment is encountered in approximately 13 percent of older persons, and hearing impairment is reported by nearly one in four adults age 65 to 74 and nearly half of those of age 85 and above.[50] These impairments may increase the risk of injury, contribute to disabilities in physical and psychosocial function, and adversely affect quality of life. Because these impairments may not be detected in routine history and physical examinations, specific screening may be justified in the context of CGA.

Although a variety of screening methods are available for visual impairment, the methods available to primary care physicians and geriatricians have limitations. The sensitivity and specificity of screening tests of visual acuity have not been established in older adults. Similarly, there are limitations to the diagnostic accuracy of glaucoma screening (e.g., tonometry), and the performance of these tests by primary care physicians may not be particularly accurate. Nevertheless, vision screening by the CGA team or primary care physician should be performed, given that the services of an eye specialist for routine screening are not likely to be available in most programs. Screening by the CGA team can be performed using the Snellen test or other tests of visual acuity. This should be combined with specific questioning of the patient about functional disability that might be due to poor vision.

For hearing impairment, screening can be performed with a hand-held audioscope,[51] a $500 instrument that delivers 40-dB tones at 500, 1000, 2000, and 4000 Hz. The audioscope examination can be performed in 90 s, and the sensitivity and specificity of the instrument in physicians' offices are 94 percent and 72 percent, respectively.[52] The accuracy of the test may also be enhanced when it is combined with a short questionnaire on functional disability associated with hearing impairment.[52] Physical examination techniques such as the whispered voice or finger rub tests also are available for hearing screening. Although the diagnostic performance of these latter tests is comparable to audioscopy in some instances, they may be subject to greater variation in technique between examiners and between examining conditions.

Functional Disability

Physicians often have an inaccurate impression of their patients' functional status.[53] Given that older patients have a particularly high prevalence of functional limitations, functional status screening is an important component of CGA. Evaluation of functional disability is useful as a complement to screening for specific impairments, to guide treatment and other management decisions, to plan long-term-care services, and to monitor the effectiveness of interventions.[54] In this section, a few examples of the many instruments which assess functional disability will be highlighted.[22] The choice between the various methods and instruments to measure function depends on the frailty of the patient population, the time available for assessment, the staffing of the CGA team, the purposes of the assessment, and the intended use and user of the functional status information.

The Katz Scale of ADLs is one of the original methods for measuring function,[55] and it remains in wide use today. This scale and other similar measures[22] focus on basic ADLs such as bathing, dressing, toileting, transferring, continence, and feeding. To supplement information on basic ADLs, various measures of instrumental ADLs (IADLs) are used in CGA programs.[56,57] These scales generally focus on more complex activities that are important for independent living in the community, including ability to use the telephone, shopping, food preparation, housekeeping, transportation in the community, taking medications, and handling finances. More advanced functional activities have been defined, including ability to perform heavy work around the house, walk half a mile, go out for social activities,[58] and participate in physical exercise.[59] Assessing ability to perform these more advanced activities may be valuable in monitoring functional status in healthy older persons who are independent in ADLs and IADLs.

Although assessment of basic and instrumental ADLs is at the core, CGA typically focuses on additional dimensions of functional status and disability. A number of measurement techniques have been developed to assess these multiple dimensions. The Older American's Resources and Services Multidimensional Functional Assessment Questionnaire (OMFAQ)[60] is an example of such a multidimensional instrument, as are the Functional Assessment Instrument (FAI) and the Comprehensive Older Persons' Evaluation (COPE) scale[61] derived from it. The OMFAQ, the FAI, and the COPE scales take approximately 60, 35, and 15 min, respectively, to administer.[61] In addition to ADLs, these instruments include measures of mental status, social resources, economic resources, mental health, and physical health. These instruments have been used extensively in aging-related research and practice.

Multidimensional measures initially developed and used in nongeriatric populations also have become increasingly used in CGA. It must be emphasized, however, that many of these instruments rely on patient self-report, and different results may be obtained when the information is obtained from patient proxies. These short-form health status measures include self-rated subscales that summarize the respondent's overall health, pain, physical function, mental function, social function, and role function.[62] A related instrument is the Functional Status Questionnaire, which includes subscales for basic and intermediate ADLs, social activities, psychological functioning, role function, social function, bed days, restricted days, sexual relationships, and overall health.[24] Another noteworthy instrument is the COOP Chart, comprising cartoonlike drawings of different levels of physical, emotional, social, and other dimensions of functioning.[23] These measures have been used in clinical settings to provide physicians with reports on the functioning of their patients. The instruments can be easily administered, and various aspects of their validity have been demonstrated.

More recently, performance-based tests of function have been validated and used in ambulatory,[42] hospital,[63] and nursing home[64] settings. Although these measures have primarily been used in research, they may eventually have clinical utility. Compared to self-report measures, these measures provide the advantage of obtaining more observational information and reducing difficulties related to language barriers.

CONCLUSION

Comprehensive Geriatric Assessment has been advanced as a means to more effectively diagnose and manage the complex medical problems of the frail elderly; the components of CGA and some of the screening measures used to assess impairments and disabilities in these programs are described above. Taken alone, few of these individual screening tests have been shown to be effective in improving health outcomes either in geriatric or in nongeriatric patient populations. When combined with other aspects of CGA, however, the resulting geriatric assessment program has been shown to effectively improve the health of older subjects in some programs and settings. As the screening techniques improve in the future, these improved tests should replace previous assessments used in CGA programs and may enhance the efficiency and effectiveness of CGA. Just as CGA programs today bear only limited resemblance to the initial programs over half a century ago in the United Kingdom, CGA programs 10 years from now will use a new generation of screening assessments. The effectiveness of these future programs will be accordingly enhanced.

REFERENCES

1. World Health Organization: *International Classification of Impairments, Disabilities, and Handicaps: A Manual of Classification Relating to the Consequences of Disease.* Twenty-ninth World Health Assembly, May 1976. Geneva, Switzerland, WHO, 1980.
2. Williams ME, Hadler NM: The illness as the focus of geriatric medicine. *N Engl J Med* 308:1357, 1983.
3. Rubenstein LZ et al: Impacts of geriatric evaluation and management programs on defined outcomes: Overview of the evidence. *J Am Geriatr Soc* 39 (suppl):8S, 1991.
4. Rubenstein LZ et al: Effectiveness of a geriatric evaluation unit: A randomized clinical trial. *N Engl J Med* 311:1664, 1984.
5. Hogan DB et al: Effect of a geriatric consultation service on management of patients in an acute care hospital. *Can Med Assoc J* 136:713, 1987.
6. Tulloch AH, Moore V: A randomized controlled trial of geriatric screening and surveillance in general practice. *J R Coll Gen Pract* 29:733, 1979.
7. Gilchrist WJ et al: Prospective randomized study of an orthopaedic geriatric inpatient service. *Br Med J* 297:1116, 1988.
8. Popplewell PY, Henschke PJ: What is the value of a geriatric assessment unit in a teaching hospital? A comparative study. *Aust Health Rev* 6:23, 1983.
9. Lefton E et al: Success with an inpatient geriatric unit: A controlled study. *J Am Geriatr Soc* 31:149, 1983.
10. Kennie DC et al: Effectiveness of geriatric rehabilitative care after fractures of the proximal femur in elderly women: A randomized clinical trial. *Br Med J* 297:1083, 1988.
11. Hogan DB, Fox RA: A prospective controlled trial of a geriatric consultation team in an acute-care hospital. *Age Ageing* 19:107, 1990.
12. Applegate WB et al: A randomized, controlled trial of a geriatric assessment unit in a community rehabilitation hospital. *N Engl J Med* 322:1527, 1990.
13. Vetter NJ et al: Effects of health visitors working with elderly patients in general practice: A randomized controlled trial. *Br Med J* 288:369, 1984.
14. Epstein AM et al: Consultative geriatric assessment for ambulatory patients: A randomized trial in a health maintenance organization. *JAMA* 263:538, 1990.
15. Hendriksen C et al: Consequences of assessment and intervention among elderly people: Three-year randomized controlled trial. *Br Med J* 289:1522, 1984.
16. Collard AF et al: Acute care delivery for the geriatric patient: An innovative approach. *Qual Rev Bull* (June):180, 1985.
17. Schuman JE et al: The impact of a new geriatric program in a hospital for the chronically ill. *Can Med Assoc J* 118:639, 1978.
18. Reid J, Kennie DC: Geriatric rehabilitative care after fractures of the proximal femur: One-year follow-up of a randomized clinical trial. *Br Med J* 299:25, 1989.
19. Berkman B et al: Geriatric consultation teams: Alternate approach to social work discharge planning. *J Gerontol Soc Work* 5:77, 1983.
20. Williams ME et al: How does the team approach to outpatient geriatric evaluation compare with traditional care: A report of a randomized controlled trial. *J Am Geriatr Soc* 35:1071, 1987.
21. Rubenstein LZ et al: Improved survival for frail elderly inpatients in a geriatric evaluation unit: Who benefits? *J Clin Epidemiol* 41:441, 1988.
22. Applegate WB et al: Instruments for the functional assessment of older patients. *N Engl J Med* 322:1207, 1990.
23. Nelson EC et al: The functional status of patients: How can it be measured in physicians' offices? *Med Care* 28:1111, 1990.
24. Jette AM et al: The functional status questionnaire: Reliability and validity when used in primary care. *J Gen Intern Med* 1:143, 1986.
25. Lachs MS et al: A simple procedure for general screening for functional disability in elderly patients. *Ann Intern Med* 112:699, 1990.
26. Clarfield AM: The reversible dementias: Do they reverse? *Ann Intern Med* 109:476, 1988.
27. Evans DA et al: Prevalence of Alzheimer's disease in a community population of older persons. *JAMA* 262:2551, 1989.
28. Siu AL: Screening for dementia and investigating its causes. *Ann Intern Med* 115:122, 1991.
29. Vitaliano PP et al: The clinical utility of the dementia rating scale for assessing Alzheimer patients. *J Chron Dis* 37:743, 1984.
30. Koenig HG et al: Self-rated depression scales and screening for major depression in the older hospitalized patient with medical illness. *J Am Geriatr Soc* 36:699, 1988.
31. Brink TL et al: Screening tests for geriatric depression. *Clin Gerontol* 1:37, 1982.
32. Sheikh JL, Yesavage JA: Geriatric depression scale (GDS): Recent evidence and development of a shorter version. *Clin Gerontol* 5:165, 1986.
33. Gallagher D: Assessing affect in the elderly. *Clin Geriatr Med* 3:65, 1987.
34. Alexopoulos GS et al: Cornell scale for depression in dementia. *Biol Psychiatry* 23:271, 1988.
35. Alexopoulos GS et al: Use of the Cornell scale in nondemented patients. *J Am Geriatr Soc* 36:230, 1988.
36. Tinetti ME et al: Fall risk index for elderly patients based on number of chronic disabilities. *Am J Med* 80:429, 1986.
37. Tinetti ME, Ginter SF: Identifying mobility dysfunctions in elderly patients. *JAMA* 259:1190, 1988.
38. Williams ME, Hornberger JC: A quantitative method of identifying older persons at risk for increasing long term care services. *J Chron Dis* 37:705, 1984.
39. Williams ME et al: Manual ability as a marker of dependency in geriatric women. *J Chron Dis* 35:113, 1982.
40. Podsiadlo D, Richardson S: The timed "up & go": A test of basic functional mobility for frail elderly persons. *J Am Geriatr Soc* 39:142, 1991.
41. Kuriansky J, Gurland B: The performance test of activities of daily living. *Int J Aging Hum Dev* 7:343, 1976.
42. Reuben DB, Siu AL: An objective measure of physical function of elderly outpatients: The physical performance test. *J Am Geriatr Soc* 38:1105, 1990.

43. Harris T et al: Body mass index and mortality among nonsmoking older persons. *JAMA* 259:1520, 1988.
44. Rudman D, Feller AG: Protein-calorie undernutrition in the nursing home. *J Am Geriatr Soc* 37:173, 1989.
45. Klonoff-Cohen H et al: Albumin levels as a predictor of mortality in the healthy elderly. *J Clin Epidemiol* 45:207, 1992.
46. White JV et al: Consensus of the nutrition screening initiative: Risk factors and indicators of poor nutritional status in older Americans. *J Am Dietetic Assoc* 91:783, 1991.
47. Manson A, Shea S: Malnutrition in elderly ambulatory medical patients. *Am J Pub Health* 81:1195, 1991.
48. Baker JP et al: A comparison of clinical judgment and objective measurements. *N Engl J Med* 306:969, 1982.
49. Kwok T, Whitelaw MN: The use of armspan in nutritional assessment of the elderly. *J Am Geriatr Soc* 39:492, 1991.
50. Havlik RJ: Aging in the eighties, impaired senses for sound and light in persons age 65 years and over: Preliminary data from the supplement on aging to the National Health Interview Survey: United States, January–June 1984, *Advance Data, Vital and Health Statistics of the National Center for Health Sciences,* No. 125. Washington, DC, US Government Printing Office, September 19, 1986.
51. Mulrow CD, Lichtenstein MJ: Screening for hearing impairment in the elderly: Rationale and strategy. *J Gen Intern Med* 6:249, 1991.
52. Lichtenstein MJ: Validation of screening tools for identifying hearing-impaired elderly in primary care. *JAMA* 259:2875, 1988.
53. Nelson E et al: Functional health status levels of primary care patients. *JAMA* 249:3331, 1983.
54. Rubenstein LV et al: Health status assessment for elderly patients: Report of the society of general internal medicine task force on health assessment. *J Am Geriatr Soc* 37:562, 1988.
55. Katz S et al: Studies of illness in the aged. *J Am Geriatr Soc* 185:94, 1963.
56. Lawton MP, Brody EM: Assessment of older people: Self-maintaining and instrumental activities of daily living. *Gerontologist* 9:179, 1969.
57. Fillenbaum GG: Screening the elderly: A brief instrumental activities of daily living measure. *J Am Geriatr Soc* 33:698, 1985.
58. Rosow I, Breslau N: A Guttman health scale for the aged. *J Gerontol* 21:556, 1966.
59. Reuben DB et al: A hierarchical exercise scale to measure function at the advanced activities of daily living (AADL) level. *J Am Geriatr Soc* 38:855, 1990.
60. Fillenbaum GG, Smyer MA: The development, validity, and reliability of the OARS multidimensional functional assessment questionnaire. *J Gerontol* 36:428, 1981.
61. Pearlman RA: Development of a functional assessment questionnaire for geriatric patients: The comprehensive older persons' evaluation (COPE). *J Chron Dis* 40:85S, 1987.
62. Stewart AL et al: The MOS short-form general health survey: Reliability and validity in a patient population. *Med Care* 26:724, 1988.
63. Sager MA et al: Measurement of activities of daily living in hospitalized elderly: A comparison of self-report and performance-based methods. *J Am Geriatr Soc* 40:457, 1992.
64. Gerety MB et al: Development and validation of a physical performance instrument for the functionally impaired elderly: The Physical Disability Index (PDI). *J Gerontol: Med Sci* 48:33, 1993.

Chapter 18

PROMOTING HEALTH AND FUNCTION AMONG OLDER ADULTS

Risa Lavizzo-Mourey

This chapter defines the goal of health promotion among older adults as the prevention of avoidable decline, fragility, and dependence. Although health promotion is usually coupled with disease prevention, it is not particularly useful to link the two concepts for older adults. Other conceptual frameworks better represent the goals of health promotion in this population. Many older adults already have the diseases that health promotion and preventive medicine generally strive to avoid. Similarly, the primary outcome of some traditional strategies is increased life expectancy, while the more relevant outcomes for older adults are reducing the rate of functional decline, preventing fragility, and staving off dependency. Also, the traditional conceptualization of prevention into primary prevention (those interventions which are aimed at preventing disease) and secondary prevention (those interventions aimed at detecting early, asymptomatic, and presumably more treatable disease) is not complete enough for older adults. Therefore an alternate framework is presented below. Most of the chapter is devoted to specific recommendations and the evidence underlying them. Unfortunately, evidence is wanted in a number of areas, either because the studies are inadequate or they have not been extended to all age, racial, and ethnic groups and, where appropriate, to both men and women. These areas will be highlighted as requiring sound clinical judgment—particularly consideration of the patient's functional status.

CONCEPTUAL FRAMEWORK

A conceptual framework is useful because preventive care for older adults, more then any other group, must be individualized. The mix of preventive interventions and, more importantly, the emphasis placed on particular strategies will vary depending on age, functional status, and patient preference. Without a conceptual framework, the dozens of age-specific recommendations (which are sometimes conflicting) can be overwhelming to clinician and patient alike. Two conceptual models will be presented, one based on the World Health Organization (WHO) International Classification of Impairments, Disabilities, and Handicaps[1] and the other based on the concept of preventing fragility.[2]

The Institute of Medicine proposes functional status as the principal outcome measure for prevention in older adults.[1] Using the WHO classification system, the model describes a progression of the consequences of diseases along a linear continuum, as shown in Table 18-1. Diseases or injuries lead to impairments, which in turn progress to disabilities and then to handicaps. An impairment is an abnormality at the organ or organ-system level, whereas a disability is a disturbance in the behavior or functioning of an individual that has an adverse effect. Handicaps are barriers to fulfilling roles or carrying out activities because of an impairment or disability. The consequences of untreated hypertension provides an illustration in Fig. 18-1. Untreated hypertension is known to cause cerebral vascular accidents, which may result in a host of other impairments at the organ or organ-system level. Should an individual suffer a stroke, a number of disabilities such as dysarthria, hemiparesis, and depression are likely to ensue. Such disabilities can limit the stroke victim's ability to carry out activities of daily living and to engage in meaningful social relationships.

The WHO model offers several advantages in conceptualizing the purpose and timing of preventive interventions for older people. First, the model has a realistic starting point for many older adults—the presence of disease or injury. A model which considers disease or injury as the preventable end point rather than the starting point conveys a sense of futility to the millions of elders who already have the disease or injury in question. Second, the WHO model is consistent with the overall goal: to maximize func-

TABLE 18-1

Preventing Functional Loss as a Conceptual Loss

Classification level	Disease (or injuries or congenital abnormality)	Impairment	Disability	Handicap
Planes of experience		Exteriorized	Objectified	Socialized
	General Progression of the Consequences of Disease			
Example:	Hypertension	Stroke	Dysarthria Hemiparesis Depression	Social isolation, mobility and independence handicaps

SOURCE: From World Health Organization's International Classification of Impairments, Disabilities and Handicaps. Adapted from *The Second Fifty Years.* Washington, DC, National Academy Press, 1990.

tioning by preventing progression to the next level and, where possible, reversing the direction of the trend. Third, it provides a structure for formulating disease-specific strategies and interventions.

However, as is the case with any model, it has limitations. Conditions characterized by a variable natural history do not fit easily into this model. For example, on the basis of the WHO model, it would prove difficult to develop a preventive strategy for an individual with Alzheimer's disease. In addition, the chain of events leading to impairment is often complicated by multiple interacting conditions. Finally, the linkages from one state to another are poorly understood and poorly described for the vast majority of diseases and injuries.

Another conceptualization, less dependent on specific diseases because it focuses on preventing fragility, is described by Buchner and Wagner.[2] In this

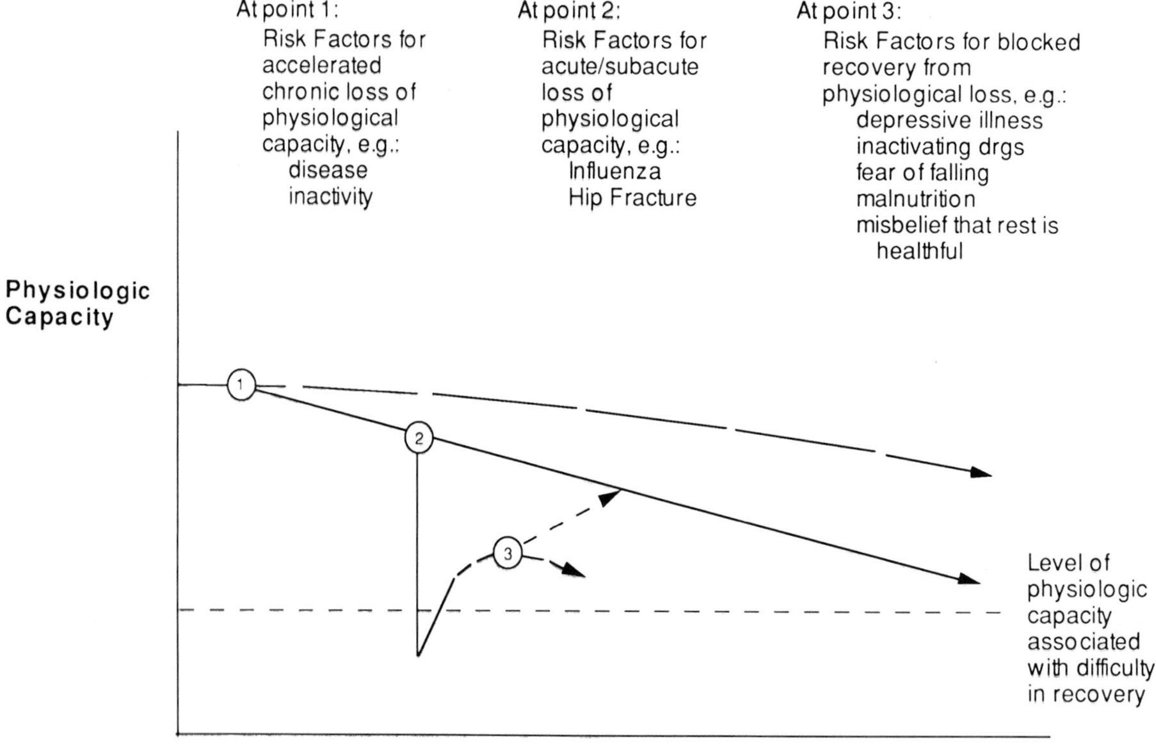

FIGURE 18-1

Conceptual model of risk factors for frailty. (*Reprinted with permission from Ref. 2.*)

framework, depicted in Fig. 18-1, a number of factors interact along the path to disability. For the purposes of this discussion on prevention, maintaining physiological capacity as a means of avoiding fragility is most important. Buchner and Wagner suggest that "fragility describes a physiological state that (1) is the result of combined effects of biologic aging, disease and disuse; (2) predicts disability; and (3) is modifiable by appropriate interventions." The authors describe three types of risk factors that increase an individual's level of fragility. First, factors that accelerate chronic loss of physiological capacity, such as chronic diseases and inactivity. Many common chronic diseases—including hypertension, coronary artery disease, and diabetes, among others—reduce physiological capacity. Similarly, numerous studies have demonstrated that the rate decline in aerobic capacity, muscular strength, and bone mass is greater in inactive, sedentary older adults than in their more active peers.[3–5] Second, factors that cause acute or subacute loss in physiological capacity are described. Examples include acute illnesses such as influenza or myocardial infarction as well as injuries such as hip fracture. These factors can dramatically reduce physiological capacity. However, since these are acute or subacute events, they are expected to resolve after a recovery period. Finally, factors that might impede recovery from a physiological loss are described. Examples include depression, malnutrition, and iatrogenic conditions. These three sets of factors work in concert to reduce physiological capacity toward the level associated with fragility. The goal of preventive strategies is to reduce or eliminate those factors that threaten physiological capacity.

This conceptualization is appealing for several reasons. First, it provides a theoretical underpinning for an individualized preventive strategy irrespective of functional status. The challenge is to identify which factors in each category potentially threaten the physiological capacity of an individual and to modify those factors. In the case of relatively fit older adults, most preventive measures will be aimed at reducing those factors that accelerate the loss of physiological capacity. Measures to prevent acute or subacute losses in physiological capacity will be appropriate for virtually all elders. Among those who are already frail, the clinician will focus on those factors known to impede recovery.

Before using the frailty prevention framework to review health promoting measures, the importance of individualizing preventive strategies must be emphasized. The heterogeneity of functional ability and capacity increases with age. Most geriatricians are accustomed to individualizing their treatment plans on the basis of this concept of heterogeneity. However, preventive strategies must be individualized with respect to culture as well. The U.S. population has a multitude of racial and ethnic groups whose differences affect clinical practice. Among some racial and ethnic groups, the prevalence of particular diseases is much higher than among others, implying that the clinician should have a lower threshold for screening. Attempts to modify medication behaviors, diet, and levels of exercise may well fail if they are not seen within the contexts of an individual's culture. An understanding of the influence that culture has on health beliefs, attitudes, and behaviors is important in all of health care, particularly health promotion.

MEASURES TO MODIFY ACCELERATED LOSS OF PHYSIOLOGICAL CAPACITY

This section will provide recommendations in several areas known to threaten physiological capacity among older adults, including screening for sensory loss, cancer, cardiovascular and thyroid disease, smoking, and physical inactivity.

Screening

In the asymptomatic patient, early screening to detect diseases can limit illnesses that accelerate loss of physiological capacity. In general, screening for a particular condition is considered worthwhile if it meets five criteria.[6] First, the condition must be associated with enough morbidity to warrant attempting to avert the illness. Second, the condition must have an asymptomatic period during which initiation of treatment results in a better outcome than treatment later in the disease. Third, an acceptable treatment must be available. Fourth, incidence in the population under consideration must be high enough to justify screening. Finally, a screening test with acceptable levels of sensitivity must be available at a reasonable cost.

Screening Test Recommendations

Screening for chronic illness which might accelerate the loss of physiologic capacity is critical to preventing fragility. Screening recommendations of the U.S. Preventive Services Task Force are summarized in Table 18-2.[7,8] These recommendations assume that the individual is asymptomatic and, except where indicated, they are based on objective data from the literature rather than expert opinion. Differences between the recommendations of the U.S. Preventive Task Force and those of other groups are highlighted.

Coronary Artery Disease

Coronary artery disease is a leading cause of death, particularly among older adults.[7–9] In addition, it causes considerable morbidity and loss of function. Multiple cardiac risk factors including male gender, family history, smoking, hypertension, hypercholesterolemia, diabetes, and obesity; all of these increase the risk of coronary artery disease. Smoking, hypertension, hypercholesterolemia, and, to a lesser extent, obesity are modifiable risk factors in young and middle-aged populations. Task Force recommendations on all of these areas are shown in Table 18-2.

Treatment of hypercholesterolemia among the asymptomatic elder is controversial. While the beneficial effects on mortality of lowered cholesterol levels have been demonstrated in middle-aged populations, these findings have not been extended to persons over age 65—particularly women.[10,11] The Task Force does not recommend screening for asymptomatic elders. However, among those with known coronary artery disease, the lowering of cholesterol levels leads to demonstrable regressions of coronary stenosis. The Expert Panel on Detection, Evaluation and Treatment of High Blood Cholesterol recommends routine screening for all adults over age 18, and *Healthy People 2000* has a goal to increase the proportion of adults screened.[9,12] It should be noted that despite the high prevalence of coronary artery disease in these groups, fewer African Americans and Hispanic/Latinos (39 and 35 percent, respectively) as compared to whites (59 percent) have ever been screened.[9] In short, there are few data to support routine cholesterol screening and subsequent intervention for the asymptomatic elderly, particularly those over age 75, but clinical judgment should guide decision making in cases where coronary artery disease is or may be present.

Obesity—a risk factor for hypertension, diabetes, and hyperlipidemia as well as osteoarthritis and limitations in functional status—is documented in between 25 to 38 percent of older persons,[7,8,13] with a higher prevalence among minority women.[9] Thus, routine weight measurements and initiation of appropriate intervention for individuals more than 20 percent over ideal body weight (body mass index >29) is recommended. The prevalence of obesity decreases after age 70, and there is no evidence for the extension of routine weighing to detect obesity beyond age 74.[7–9]

Cerebral Vascular Disease

Strokes account for at least 86 percent of the deaths occurring among those over age 65. Even when they are not fatal, cerebral vascular accidents account for significant limitations in functional status as well as depression and prolonged rehabilitation or long-term care.[7,8] Screening measures related to hypercholesterolemia and hypertension are recommended, but screening for carotid stenosis with carotid auscultation and noninvasive tests is not recommended.[7,8] However, the Task Force did suggest carotid auscultation for symptomatic patients and those with several risk factors for coronary artery disease or cerebral vascular disease—including hypertension, smoking, very advanced age, atrial fibrillation, diabetes, and previous transient ischemic attacks or stroke.

Cancer Screening

The vast majority of cancers afflict older people, with the incidence and mortality rates of breast, cervical,

TABLE 18-2

Screening Tests: Summary of Recommendations of the U.S. Preventive Services Task Force

Tests Considered	*Recommendation*
Coronary Artery Disease	
BP measurement, total	Every 2 years; normotensive—diastolic <85, systolic <140 mg
Cholesterol lipid measurement	Venous sample every 5 years; <240 or 200–239 mg/dl and two risk factors need intervention
Resting and stress electrocardiogram (ECG)	Resting not recommended, Stress ECG if starting a vigorous exercise program
Obesity	
Measurement of limb circumference Skin-fold thickness Body weight and height	Measure weight routinely; intervention if body mass index ≥27.8 in men or 27.3 in women
Cerebral Vascular Disease	
Auscultation for carotid stenosis Noninvasive arterial studies	Not recommended for asymptomatic individuals
Breast Cancer	
Clinical breast exam	Every 1–2 years
Mammography	Every 1–2 years
Self-examination	Not specifically recommended
Colorectal Cancer	
Digital rectal exam	Not sufficient
Fecal occult blood test	Clinical judgment
Sigmoidoscopy	Clinical judgment
Colonoscopy	High-risk only
Cervical cancer	
Papanicolaou smears	Every 1–3 years; may discontinue at 65 if adequate screening has occurred at younger ages
Skin Cancer	
Self-examination	Use clinical judgment and perform in conjunction with physical exam
Prostate Cancer	
Digital rectal exam	Clinical judgment
Transrectal ultrasound	Not recommended
Serum Prostate-specific antigen	Not recommended
Lung Cancer	
Chest x-ray	
Sputum cytology	Not recommended
Pancreatic cancer	Not recommended
Ovarian cancer	Not recommended
Oral Cancer	Routine for high-risk only
Inspection	

TABLE 18-2 (continued)

Tests Considered	*Recommendation*
Thyroid Disease	
T4, free T4 index, or TSH	Use clinical judgment
Physical exam	Annually if history of upper-body radiation
Sensory Loss	
Visual Acuity and glaucoma	Routinely by eye specialist
Audiometry	Yes, if evidence of impairment
Osteoporosis	
Radiographs	Not recommended routinely
Absorptiometer (single photon, dual photon, dual energy, and quantified computerized)	Screening for decreased bone mineral content may be clinically useful in high-risk women

colon, prostate, lung, skin, and oral cancers increasing after age 50 and dramatically so after age 65. Despite these statistics, there is not sufficient information to make definitive statements about screening for all cancers. Clinical judgment which takes into account the individual risks factors, other medical problems, and the morbidity associated with diagnostic tests indicated by a positive screening test is essential.

Breast The U.S. Preventive Services Task Force recommendations are shown in Table 18-2.[7,8] Screening for breast cancer using low-dose mammography is recommended every 1 to 2 years up to age 75. Beyond age 75, clinical judgment is necessary. The incidence of breast cancer continues to rise. Therefore, the American Cancer Society and others recommend continuing to screen as long as the patient's life expectancy exceeds 5 years.[14]

Mammography continues to be underutilized for older women. Only 25 percent of all women of age 50 or older received breast cancer screening in the 2 years preceding 1987, with the percentage being even smaller, 18 to 19 percent, for African American and Hispanic/Latino women.[9]

Colon Colorectal cancer is the second most common malignancy in the United States, with the vast majority of new cases occurring in persons over 75 years of age. Routine screening for colorectal cancer requires clinical judgment for several reasons. First, screening only by testing for occult blood has a very high false positive rate and is not sensitive at detecting precancerous lesions. Second, although sigmoidoscopy in combination with occult blood testing is reasonably efficacious in detecting precancerous lesions, a decrease in mortality from screening has not been demonstrated.[14]

The American Cancer Society recommends digital rectal examination and occult blood tests annually, with sigmoidoscopy every 3 to 5 years for persons over age 50. For patients with a high risk of colon cancer (those with a strong family history; a history of inflammatory bowel disease, adenomatous polyps, or previous colon cancer; as well as those with a history of endometrial, ovarian, or breast cancer) a periodic colonoscopy is recommended.[15]

Cervix Because the rate of progression from dysplasia to carcinoma is very slow in cervical cancer, screening with Papanicolaou smears can be discontinued at age 65.[14] This assumes regular screening and normal results before age 65. However, nearly half of women over age 65 have never been screened.[9] The need is even greater in low-income women, making screening particularly cost-effective in this population.[16]

Prostate Prostate cancer is the most common cancer among men, and virtually all of the deaths occur after age 65. Yet the literature on available screening tests caused the U.S. Preventive Task Force to recommend the use of clinical judgment in performing such tests routinely. The American Cancer Society recommends an annual digital rectal exam.[7–9,14,15] This test (when performed by a urologist) has a sensitivity of 69 percent and a specificity of 89 percent as compared to prostate biopsy. The sensitivity and specificity of transrectal ultrasonography and prostate-specific antigen (PSA) yield unacceptably low positive predictive values. Ultrasound appears to offer no advantage over digital examination, and the positive predictive value of an abnormal PSA is only 40 percent.[17–19] Nonetheless, use of serum PSA is becoming more common and is recommended as a screening test by some.

Lung Lung cancer continues to be a deadly disease and the leading cause of cancer deaths among all populations in the United States. However, routine screening by chest x-ray or sputum cytology does not reduce mortality rates. The risk of lung cancer is reduced with long-term smoking cessation. Therefore even elderly patients should be counseled about the benefits of smoking cessation.[1,8,9,13,20]

Skin Although skin cancer does not account for a larger number of cancer deaths each year, many of these cancers are extremely amenable to treatment. Clinical examination of the entire body of individuals at risk is recommended. Individuals with a family or past history of skin cancer, evidence of precursor lesions, and high levels of sun exposure are considered to be at high risk. Even though skin cancer is much less common in nonwhite racial groups, it does occur; therefore, the same criteria for determining risk status should be used.[7,8]

Oral There are approximately 30,000 new cases of oral cancer annually, half of which occur in those over age 65. Persons who have been heavy users of alcohol, tobacco, and smokeless tobacco are at particularly high risk. The U.S. Preventive Task Force recommends routine screening by oral inspection for high-risk individuals.[7–9,14] The American Cancer Society, on the other hand, recommends annual screening for all individuals.[14]

Other Despite the fact that ovarian and pancreatic cancer are devastating diseases, there is little evidence that routine screening increases survival, and it is not recommended.[7,8,14]

Screening for Other Chronic Illnesses

Screening criteria for other conditions that potentially decrease physiological capacity—such as thyroid disease, vision loss, and hearing loss—are shown in Table 18-1. Thyroid failure increases with age, can be insidious, and produces a wide variety of nonspecific signs and symptoms. Screening annually or biannually is considered useful. Similar recommendations are made for hearing and vision screening.[1,7,8,13]

MODIFICATION OF HEALTH HABITS

Exercise

Most Americans over 65 years of age are sedentary; only 30 percent report routine physical activity.[9] The price of inactivity in older adults is high. Increased blood pressure, total peripheral resistance, total cholesterol, obesity, risk of glucose intolerance, and rate of bone loss have all been associated with physical inactivity.[1,5,21] Similarly, a decrease in cardiac output, maximal oxygen consumption, and muscle strength are other sequelae of inactivity.[1,5,13] Even short-term inactivity such as that associated with acute illness has been shown to produce measurable decrements in the above physiological measures.[2] The benefits of an aerobic exercise program, even among elders who have been sedentary most of their lives, are well documented.[1,21]

Persons who get regular vigorous exercise have decreased mortality, particularly from cardiovascular disease, in addition to other benefits. Men and women reporting regular exercise have significantly higher high-density lipoprotein levels and lower triglycerides than those who do not get regular exercise.[22] Exercise has been shown to decrease abdominal fat in men and to increase the amount of lean body mass.[23] In women, regular exercise retards bone loss and may even be associated with the accrual of new bone in osteoporotic women.[4]

Realizing the benefits of regular exercise does not require marathon levels of training. The clinician must bear in mind that there are two principal goals of exercise: (1) to improve cardiopulmonary and muscular fitness and (2) to improve or preserve functional ability. Any exercise prescription that can meet these goals must be tailored to the individual, and must take into account the tremendous variability in physical abilities and cultural attitudes toward exercise. The following parameters should be used in developing an individualized program: (1) the overall goal is to reach 70 to 80 percent of the maximal heart rate reserve for 20 min three times a week; (2) it is best to build up the duration and intensity of exercise slowly (in the beginning, an individual should only strive to reach 60 percent of the maximal heart rate; (3) patients should be advised to warm up and cool down for 5 min at the beginning and end of the exercise session; (4) patients may be told to take advantage of routine activities such as climbing stairs, gardening, and walks in a shopping mall; (5) patients may benefit from help in developing ways to stay motivated.[13,21]

Whether an exercise tolerance test is required prior to starting an exercise program is controversial. Although it has been routinely recommended for persons over age 40 who are beginning an exercise program, several studies have questioned its necessity. In fact, cardiac rehabilitation programs have noted relatively few cardiac complications among the elderly.[21] The best recommendation at this time is to determine the necessity of an exercise tolerance test on the basis of the individual patient's risk for coronary artery disease and the presence of other comorbidities which might increase the risk associated with exercise.

Smoking

Although the benefits of smoking cessation are well recognized in younger persons, many clinicians still have a fatalistic attitude toward smoking cessation among older people. The prevalence of smoking among older adults has decreased over the last 20 years, but 1987 data indicate that 17.2 percent of older men and 13.7 percent of older women continue to smoke.[9] The risks of smoking are cumulative and go beyond increased mortality. Smoking cessation is recommended to all older adults as a means of decreasing morbidity and increasing physiological capacity.[13,20]

Smoking cessation reduces morbidity due to cardiovascular disease. A recent study demonstrated that among men and women over the age of 65 with documented coronary artery disease, the risk of reinfarction was reduced after smoking cessation.[24] In this study, the reduction in mortality rate is measurable within 1 year after quitting.

With regard to stroke, the risk associated with smoking decreases with age to a relative risk of 1.1 among those over age 75.[25] Smoking cessation does not alter the risk of stroke in older adults.

Physiological measures of respiratory function improve with smoking cessation but do not return to the peak expiratory rates observed in nonsmokers.[26] It must be emphasized that the symptoms associated with smoking–such as coughing, wheezing, and sputum production—improve with smoking cessation.[27] Similarly, the risk of death from pneumonia and influenza decreases from 2.0 in male and 3.0 in female smokers to 1.3 and 1.2 respectively.[28] Finally, the risk of hip fracture is higher (1.5 to 2 times greater) among smokers than among nonsmokers.[20] However, there is no strong evidence that smoking cessation reduces the risk of osteoporosis or hip fracture.

Smoking cessation is beneficial to older adults. Therefore, clinicians should strongly urge patients to stop smoking. The most effective modalities to achieve smoking cessation in older adults have not been definitively shown, necessitating clinical judgment and extrapolation from effective modalities for younger populations.

PREVENTING ACUTE AND SUBACUTE LOSSES OF PHYSIOLOGIC CAPACITY

Injury Prevention

Injuries, particularly those due to falls, motor vehicle accidents, and burns, cause significant morbidity among older adults. The recovery period can be long, with many elders reporting continuing functional impairment several months after a fall. Moreover, falls are associated with significant mortality—18/100,000 among persons aged 65 to 84 and 131.2/100,000 among those over age 85.[9] There are both intrinsic and extrinsic factors associated with falling.

Intrinsic factors include lower-extremity weakness; postural blood pressure decline of more than 20 mmHg; certain medications such as benzodiazepines, tricyclic antidepressants, and some antipsychotics; alcohol use; and abnormalities in balance.[1,9,29] Extrinsic factors include poor lighting (especially in the bathroom and on the stairs), rickety stairs or loose banisters, faulty flooring or loose rugs, and cluttered paths (particularly between the bed and bathroom).[29] Counseling older adults about these intrinsic and extrinsic factors is a recommended part of preventive practice.

Although driving is a source of great independence for anyone, the risk of motor vehicle accidents may warrant restricting automobile use if significant impairments in functional status exist. Sensory and cognitive losses can affect driving skills and increase the risk of an accident. Older drivers have a greater risk of crashing per mile driven than younger drivers.[9] In the author's view, recommending routine retesting (both the written and the road test) is a logical way to detect early problems and to reassure patients and family members.

With regard to burns, two areas deserve attention—house fires and scaldings. House fires are significant cause of injury-related death, with older adults, minority populations, the poor, and very young children bearing most of the burden.[9,29] The use of smoke detectors is especially important, because diminished sense of smell and limited mobility can conspire to slow an older person's evacuation in case of fire. Counseling patients to have an evacuation plan coupled with reduction of behaviors such as smoking and excess use of alcohol are recommended. In addition, the risk of scalding burns can be reduced by turning the temperature of the hot water heater from the usual 65°C (150°F) to a range of 43° to 49°C (110° to 120°F).[29]

Chemoprophylaxis and Immunization

Since myocardial infarction, stroke, and upper respiratory infection are serious, acute threats to physiological capacity and safe, effective prophylactic treatments are available, it is recommended that older men and women take low-dose aspirin daily and receive pneumococcal and influenza immunization at appropriate intervals.

A series of studies indicate that aspirin in low doses, 325 mg daily or every other day, reduces the risk of myocardial infarction by 32 to 44 percent over a 5- to 6-year follow-up periods. The studies included persons up to 84 years old and the effect was seen in those over 50 years of age. The weight of evidence indicates that aspirin is also beneficial in patients with TIAs or a history of stroke. Since most of the studies conducted in the United States used doses of 1 to 3 g/day, the current recommendation is for 1 g/day. Based on British studies, 325 mg/day is probably sufficient. Similarly, aspirin has been shown to reduce the risk of embolic stroke by 49 percent in patients with atrial fibrillation. Aspirin has not been conclusively shown to slow the rate of progression in multi-infarct dementia.[30] The side effects of low-dose aspirin are minimal: minor bleeding, epistaxis, and occult gastrointestinal bleeding. Gastrointestinal symptoms such as dyspepsia occur at the same rate among those receiving aspirin as among those receiving a placebo.[30]

Hospitalization and death rates for influenza and pneumococcal disease are several times higher among older adults than among the young and middle-aged.[31] Pneumococcal vaccine reduces the risk of pneumococcal infection and pneumonia, and hospitalization and death have been reported to have much higher relative risks (2.4 to 5.6) among elderly not receiving influenza vaccine.[31,32] Accordingly, all older adults should receive the 23-valent pneumococcal vaccine once and an annual influenza shot in the late fall. Since the side effects of reimmunizing for pneumococcal disease are mild, patients with unknown immunization status should be immunized.

SUMMARY

Individualized health promotion strategies should maximize functional capacity and prevent frailty among older adults. The evidence that this can be accomplished is strong and mounting, especially in screening for hypertension, sensory loss, and breast and cervical cancer. Similarly, the benefits of exercise, smoking cessation and immunizations are extensive. Yet these health-promoting practices continue to be underutilized.[9,33] Developing innovative and culturally relevant ways to improve older adults' motivation to change behaviors while simultaneously improving clinicians' reminder systems and knowledge may reverse the unhealthy underutilization of health promotion among this nation's elders.[34]

REFERENCES

1. Berg RL, Cassells JS: *The Second Fifty Years: Promoting Health and Preventing Disability.* Washington, DC, National Academy Press, 1990.
2. Buchner DM, Wagner EH: Preventing frail health. *Clin Geriatr Med* 8(1):1, 1992.
3. Conference CD: Prophylaxis and treatment of osteoporosis. *Am J Med* 90:107, 1991.
4. Kasch FW, Boyer JL, Van Camp SP, et al: The effect of physical activity and inactivity on aerobic power in older men. *Phys Sports Med* 18:73, 1990.
5. Astrand P: Exercise physiology and its role in disease prevention and in rehabilitation. *Arch Physiol Med Rehabil* 68:305, 1987.
6. Day SC: Principles of Screening, in Lavizzo-Mourey (ed): *Practicing Prevention for the Elderly.* Philadelphia, Hanley and Belfus, 1989.
7. Woolf SH, Kamerow DB, Lawrence RS, et al: The periodic health examination of older adults: The recommendations of the U.S. Preventive Services Task Force (part 1). *J Am Geriatr Soc* 38(7):817, 1990.
8. Woolf SH, Kamerow DB, Lawrence RS, et al: The periodic health examination of older adults: The recommendations of the U.S. Preventive Services Task Force (part 2). *J Am Geriatr Soc* 38(8):933, 1990.
9. U.S. Department of Health and Human Services: Healthy People 2000: National health promotion and disease prevention objectives. Washington, DC, Department of Health and Human Services, 1991.
10. Garber AM, Littenberg B, Sox HC, et al: Cost and health consequences of cholesterol screening for asymptomatic older Americans. *Arch Intern Med* 151:1089, 1991.
11. Hazzard W: Dyslipoproteinemia in the elderly: Should it be treated? *Clin Geriatr Med* 8(1):89, 1992.
12. National Heart, Lung, and Blood Institute: Report of the Expert Panel on Detection Evaluation and Treatment of High Blood Cholesterol. Washington, DC, U.S. Department of Health and Human Services, 1988.
13. Lavizzo-Mourey R, Day S, Diserens D, Grisso JA: *Practicing prevention for the elderly.* Philadelphia, Hanley and Belfus, 1989, p 252.
14. Oddon EZ, Feussner JR, Cohen HJ: Can screening older patients for cancer save lives? *Clin Geriatr Med* 8(1):51, 1992.
15. American Cancer Society: Guidelines for cancer related checkup. *CA* 30:194, 1980.
16. Mandelblatt JS, Fahs MC: Cost-effectiveness of cervical cancer screening for low-income elderly women. *JAMA* 259(16):2409, 1988.
17. Diagnostic and Therapeutic Technology Assessment (DATTA): Transrectal ultrasonography in prostate cancer. *JAMA* 259:2757, 1988.
18. Brawer MK, Lange PH: Prostate-specific antigen and premalignant change. *CA* 39:361, 1989.
19. Catalona WJ, Smith DS, Ratliff TL, et al: Measurement of prostate-specific antigen in serum as a screening test for prostate cancer. *N Engl J Med* 324:1156, 1991.
20. LaCroix AZ, Omenn GS: Older adults and smoking. *Clin Geriatr Med* 8(1):69, 1992.
21. Elward K, Larson EB: Benefits of exercise for older adults: A review of existing evidence and current recommendations for the general population. *Clin Geriatr Med* 8(1):35, 1992.
22. Reaven PD, McPhillips JB, Barrett-Connor EL, et al: Leisure time exercise and lipid and lipoprotein levels in an older population. *J Am Geriatr Soc* 38:847, 1990.
23. Schwartz RS, Larson V: The effect of intensive endurance exercise training on body fat distribution in young and older men. *Metabolism* 80:545, 1991.
24. Hermanson B, Omenn GS, Kronmal RA, et al: Beneficial 6-year outcome of smoking cessation in older men and women with coronary artery disease. *N Engl J Med* 319:1365, 1990.
25. Shinton R: Meta-analysis of relation between cigarettes smoking and stroke. *Br Med J* 298:789, 1989.
26. Cook NR, Evans DA, Scherr PA et al: Peak expiratory flow rate in an elderly population. *Am J Epidemiol* 130:66, 1989.
27. Colsher PL, Wallace RB, Pomrehn PR et al: Demographic and health characteristics of elderly smokers: Results from established populations for epidemiologic studies of the elderly. *Am J Prev Med* 6:61, 1990.
28. U.S. Department of Health and Human Services: The health benefits of smoking cessation. DHHS Publication no. (CDC) 90-8416. Washington, DC, Centers for Disease Control and Prevention, 1990.
29. Grisso JA, Mezey MD: Preventing dependence and injury: An approach to sensory changes, in Lavizzo-Mourey (ed): *Practicing Prevention for the Elderly.* Philadelphia, Hanley and Belfus, 1989.
30. Dalen JE, Goldberg RJ: Prophylactic aspirin and the elderly. *Clin Geriatr Med* 8(1):119, 1992.
31. Sims R: Immunization in the elderly, in Lavizzo-Mourey (ed): *Practicing Prevention for the Elderly.* Philadelphia, Hanley and Belfus, 1989.
32. Sims RV, Steinman WC, McConville JC, et al: The clinical effectiveness of pneumococcal vaccine in the elderly. *Ann Intern Med* 108:653, 1988.
33. Schwartz JS, Lewis CF, Clancy C, et al: Internist's practices in health promotion and disease prevention. *Ann Intern Med* 114(1):46, 1991.
34. Pascucci MA: Measuring incentives to health promotion in older adults. *Clin Geriatr Med* 18(3):16, 1992.

Chapter 19

NEUROPSYCHIATRIC ASSESSMENT OF SYNDROMES OF ALTERED MENTAL STATE

Marshal F. Folstein and Susan E. Folstein

The term *altered mental state* means *a change in the patient's usual premorbid state of mind.* Although it is sometimes used to mean delirium or dementia, the definition used here includes alterations in *emotions* and *behavior* as well as *cognition.* To diagnose an altered mental state, it is necessary to establish the patient's premorbid mental state and the nature and associations of any change. This requires that a history be taken from both the patient and another informant and that the patient's mental state be examined. Neurological and physical examinations, appropriate laboratory tests, and sometimes repeated examinations over a period of months are needed to complete the diagnostic process.

This chapter lays out the neuropsychiatric approach to the patient with an altered mental state. The neuropsychiatric approach assumes that the physician desires to give complete care to the patient with a minimum of referral to other physicians. For this reason the physician caring for patients with altered mental states should be equipped to evaluate their neurological causes and also to evaluate and manage the psychiatric symptoms which often need care and reassessment over many years. Since disorders presenting as alterations of mental state are so common, affecting 25 to 30 percent of medical inpatients and 90 percent of nursing home residents, and because they are even more frequent in the elderly, the general physician and geriatrician must be able to diagnose and treat them.[1,2]

The aims of the neuropsychiatric history and mental state and neurological examinations are the (1) documentation of the onset, progression, and current state of abnormal cognition, mood, behaviors, and motor signs and (2) the identification of these psychological and motor signs and symptoms with recognizable syndromes and disease entities. The case is formulated so that the symptoms, syndromes, and diseases are viewed in relation to the individual patient, taking into account the patient's particular vulnerabilities and situation. Out of this formulation emerges the prognosis and treatment plan. The treatment plan may include a rational therapy or, if none is known, empirical and empathic approaches to the patient and his or her family. For the geriatric patient, the treatment plan may range from definitive therapy through palliative pharmacotherapy to advice about living circumstances, competence, and finances.[3]

NEUROPSYCHIATRIC HISTORY TAKING

Diagnosis derives almost entirely from the history because of the importance to etiology of the progression of the signs and symptoms over time. Of equal importance to the history of present illness is the history of elements of the individual's past. These include the family illness history and the early life history of the patient as it reveals his or her capacity to obtain an education, to participate in family life, and to remain employed. The history should be taken both from the patient and from a family member or friend who knows the patient well. This is essential if the patient is cognitively impaired but provides valuable information for every patient assessed for any kind of alteration in mental state. Begin by taking the history from the patient, even though he or she may have a cognitive impairment. Patients may have a different point of view about their symptoms than do their families or caregivers, and asking them for their views will enhance their self-respect and increase their willingness to cooperate with the examination.

Chief Complaint By examining the patient in a quiet room and maintaining a helping attitude, the physician can further improve the patient's cooperation. After introducing himself or herself, the physician begins by asking "What is your major problem?" or "Why are you here?" in order to elicit the patient's perception of the chief complaint, and proceeds on the basis of the reply. The nature of the patient's account, vague and disconnected or clear and sequential, will give clues to the presence of cognitive impairment.

Personal History The physician then asks the patient about personal history. This has two purposes. First, assessment of the patient's education, occupation, and family life supplies baseline of expected general knowledge and sophistication as well as current social supports. Second, the clarity of the account is useful in assessing the presence of cognitive impairment.

Family History The physician should question the patient about a history of illnesses in other family members, including Alzheimer's disease (memory trouble, died in a nursing home, didn't recognize people, couldn't dress self), stroke, and depression. The family history is especially useful in patients with dementia, since at least 40 percent of patients with Alzheimer's disease will have an affected first-degree relative. Obtaining an accurate family history from an elderly person requires the use of prompts to guide the memory of the patient or family member. Thus it is helpful to ask for the name and birth and death dates of the patient's father, mother, and sibs. This focuses the informant on his or her memories of the life events of each family member separately and helps in the recall of illnesses. The place of death is often useful, since institutionalization late in life is usually indicative of cognitive impairment severe enough to interfere with social function.

Review of Systems An accurate account should be taken of all current medications (ask families to bring all medications to the clinic), since these alone can be responsible for cognitive impairment or depression. When inquiring about past treatments, include treatment for psychiatric disorders. Of particular relevance for patients complaining of cognitive decline is a past history of head trauma and alcohol use. Families should be asked about recent falls, eating patterns, behaviors such as abnormal sleep patterns, irritability, and apathy. Facts about the current social milieu are also relevant and should be elicited, including questions about safety issues such as driving and using kitchen appliances as well as inquiries about caregiving arrangements and the patient's ability to function in various situations.

Onset of Symptoms The timing and circumstances of the onset of symptoms can best be documented by asking about it in relation to other events occurring at the same time. It is often difficult for families to recall the time of onset when it occurred at some time in the past. The accuracy of timing is improved by asking the informant to relate the onset to holidays, birth of a grandchild, or other relevant life events. Important circumstances to inquire about are the association of onset of the mental state change with head trauma, loss of consciousness, paralysis, fever or other evidence of infection, or a change in medication.

ASSESSMENT OF DISABILITY

Impairment, Disability, and Competence An aspect of the history that needs special emphasis is the assessment of the patient's disability. It is useful to distinguish impairment from disability. *Impairment* is the defect of a part, function, or organ; for example, a patient may have a visual, motor, or cognitive impairment. A *disability* is the incapacity of an individual with an impairment to function in a particular social environment. Impairments may or may not be associated with disability in a particular environment.

The impact of cognitive or emotional impairment on social function can be estimated by asking the informant about the patient's ability to function in daily activities relative to his or her normal baseline. Patients tend to underestimate their disability or may be unaware of it. Examples of such questions are: Can the patient still function adequately at work? Balance a checkbook? Find the way home when driving or walking? Use the telephone and remember previously familiar phone numbers? Does the patient leave pots on the stove when cooking or forget to turn off the gas? Can the patient dress himself or herself? Recognize family members? Eat if food is provided? Remember how to use the bathroom?

Impairments of cognition, emotion, perception, or mobility may all lead to an incapacity to perform tasks in the same social environments. Thus, a patient may be unable to climb stairs because of apraxia, blindness, or arthritis. Disabilities can range in severity from an incapacity to perform a high-level job or manage the complex finances of a large corporation to being unable to survive unsupported because of inability to eat without assistance. Since disabilities are defined in terms of environments, the same impairment can be more or less disabling in different environments. A microbiologist who develops a mild cognitive impairment may be able to function well at home but not be able to work. A change of job might even remove the occupational disability. On the other hand, cognitive impairments that appear to be mild on formal testing may be associated with severe disability. For example, individuals with Huntington's disease or Pick's disease may score normally on an intelligence test but be unable to care for themselves because of apathy and inertia.

Disability should also be distinguished from incompetence. Disability is the inability to perform certain functions because of any one of a variety of impairments. *Incompetence* is a term assigned by the legal system to limit an individual's freedom to manage self and property. While a person judged incompetent is ordinarily disabled in one or more ways, disabled persons are not necessarily incompetent to manage their affairs. These concepts are discussed in the book *Disability in America* (Pope and Tarlov, Academic Press, 1991).

Disability Scales The documentation of the ability to function in daily life, or its opposite, disability, is an aspect of history-taking that can be quantified by standard scales. Disability scales are useful adjuncts to history taking and are also used in research and for administrative purposes by the Social Security Disability Administration and nursing homes. The many scales available can be divided into two general types. Pure disability scales (Powell, Katz) assess instrumental activities (e.g., the capacity to use instruments such as a telephone or checkbook) or activities of daily living (the capacity to dress, bathe and feed oneself).[4,5] This type of scale makes it possible to systematize one aspect of history-taking and to study the effects of cognition, emotion, or physical mobility on the ability to function. In the other type of scale, the assessment of disability is mixed with other dimensions such as cognition, mood, and personality. Examples of this type are the Sickness Impact Scale, the Blessed Dementia Scale, which correlates with the numbers of plaques and tangles in Alzheimer's disease, and the Psychogeriatric Dependency Rating Scale (PGDRS), which predicts the amount of nursing time needed for nursing home patients.[6,7]

THE MENTAL STATE EXAMINATION

This part of the medical examination assesses the patient's mental experience and capacity at the time of the examination. It is thus distinguished from history taking, which covers distressing mental experiences or behavior that have taken place in the past. The history and the manner in which it is related can give clues about the patient's current mental state, but a separate procedure is needed to determine and document the present mental state per se. It includes an examination of the patient's appearance, talk, mood, and cognitive state and the presence of delusions, hallucinations, phobias, and obsessions.

The mental state examination is introduced by an explanation of the necessity for an examination and a request for the patient's permission and cooperation. For example, the physician asks, "As a routine part of the examination, I would like to ask you some questions about how you feel and how you think." The examination is conducted in a supportive manner, but direct questions are asked in order to elicit the patient's experiences. For example, the patient may be asked, "Do you hear voices?" Ambiguous or uncertain responses are followed with further questioning to determine whether the patient is reporting on an experience that meets the definition of the phenomenon. For example "Are the voices as clear as mine?" "Do you hear them through your ears?"

The mental state examination is well accepted by patients if it is conducted calmly and supportively. If patients say they do hear voices or believe people are following them, the physician should make an interested but not surprised or disbelieving response. For example, the examiner might say, "That must have been frightening. Tell me more about these voices. What did they say?" The cognitive examination must also be conducted supportively in order to avoid an emotional response to failure (catastrophic reaction), which in itself can worsen performance. In particular, if the patient gives an incorrect response, do not correct him or her. If the patient fails to respond at all, go to another topic (after having ascertained that the patient heard the question).

The Clinical Mental State Examination

The mental state examination is conventionally divided into the following sections:

Appearance The patient's dress and grooming are assessed with attention to evidence of self-neglect or inability to dress, perhaps due to apraxia. The physician notes the patient's level of activity (e.g., agitation or motor slowing); whether the patient walks normally, is wearing a hearing aid and glasses, or appears lethargic or inattentive, as in delirium or confusional states.

Talk The physician listens for the form of talk and notes whether the patient's talk is normally coherent; whether it is fast (as in mania), or slow (as in depression or dementia); whether speech is clear or slurred (as in dysarthria secondary to stroke or parkinsonism); and whether there is evidence of trouble with naming or the appearance of jargon words (as in aphasia due to stroke or Alzheimer's disease). A language disorder is rarely seen in old-age-onset schizophrenia.

Mood The physician asks, "How are your spirits?" or "How is your mood?" followed, if necessary by asking the patient if he or she feels depressed, hopeless, worthless, or guilty; or, alternatively, unduly cheerful, optimistic, or overconfident. Abnormal mood states are often associated with disturbances of appetite and sleep, which can be queried at this point. A sense of dread or impending doom, as seen in attacks of panic or anxiety, may also be queried. In the elderly, a lack of feeling, apathy, or a feeling of general irritability can be prominent features of a depressed mood. Suicidal thoughts and intentions must be assessed in elderly persons, since suicide rates in this group are high, particularly in depressed elderly males with physical impairments. The physician asks, "Have you thought of harming yourself or doing away with yourself?" If the patient indicates the presence of suicidal thinking, an inquiry is made as to whether the patient has thought about any specific plan or method. Psychiatric hospitalization is indicated for the depressed patient with suicidal thoughts.

Delusions Delusions are false, fixed, idiosyncratic, and preoccupying beliefs. The physician may ask, "Is anyone harassing you or trying to harm you?" Other common delusions involve the patient's belief that he or she is poverty-stricken (do you have enough money to get along?), the victim of theft (is anyone stealing from you?), or attempts to poison the food. In Alzheimer's disease, delusions are frequent but are rarely identified as such by the family, so that they should be inquired about directly. In addition to the delusions mentioned above, these patients also suffer from delusions related to misidentification (that they are not living in their own house) or loss of the sense of time (believing relatives are alive; and that they themselves are a different age). Since delusions are significant predictors of aggressive behavior, it is important to detect them.

Delusions (as they occur in late-life schizophrenia or paraphrenia) should be distinguished from overvalued ideas, which may be expressed as a hobby that preoccupies a person's life to the exclusion of other activities, and from culturally determined beliefs such as religious, superstitious, or magical ideas that, while not widely held, are part of the patient's immediate culture.

Delusions should be distinguished also from obsessions or hypochondriacal preoccupations which are not idiosyncratic and which appear to arise from obsessive character traits or in the context of a depressive mood disorder.

Obsessions and Compulsions Obsessions are recurrent, unwanted thoughts that the patient tries unsuccessfully to resist. Compulsions are recurrent, unwanted behaviors such as hand washing or checking locks or the stove repeatedly. The physician asks, "Do you have thoughts that keep coming back that you can't get out of your mind?" "Are the thoughts sensible or do they seem foolish?" "Do you have to do a certain thing in order to get them out of your mind?"

Hallucinations Hallucinations are false *perceptions* in the visual, auditory, olfactory, or tactile realms. The physician asks such questions as, "Do you see visions of people?" "Any buzzing or ringing in your ears?" "Are there voices talking about you?" "Are they as clear as my voice?" "Do you smell anything unusual?" "Do you feel things crawling on your skin?" Hallucinations are prominent in delirium, dementia, and schizophrenia and may occur in late-life depression and occasionally in bereavement.

Phobias Phobias are irrational fears of particular places, things, or situations that are severe enough to cause the person to avoid them. For example, the patient may stay in the house because of fears of going out or avoid high buildings because of a fear of elevators. The appearance of phobias as well as obsessions and compulsions in the elderly can be the first signs of a severe depression. They often occur with anxiety and a sense of impending doom and may be associated with autonomic signs of palpitations, trouble swallowing, or trouble breathing.

Cognition Cognition is the capacity to think in order to know the world. The level of cognition at any given time is related, in part, to premorbid intelligence, mood, and level of consciousness (delirium) as well as the presence of dementia. Assessment of cognition traditionally involves testing orientation, attention, memory, and language functions. Cognition is best tested through a quantitative procedure, such as the one described below, that ensures a systematic assessment and the clear documentation of change due to illness or to its treatment.

Mental State Screening Tests

The clinical mental state examination can be supplemented with quantified procedures that are also useful for patient follow-up or case finding in the hospital, clinic, or community. In some cases these quantified aids to the examination can be used to buttress a clinical opinion that an impairment exists. These brief, quantified measures can be used at the bedside by physicians, nurses, social workers, or technicians. These measures can be used as grade severity along a dimension but, in addition, have established specificities and sensitivities so that they can be used for case detection in the hospital or community. It is important to emphasize, however, that these quantified aids to the clinical examination do not make a diagnosis but rather signal the likely presence of a cognitive or emotional impairment that needs to be assessed by the clinician.

If physicians review the results of brief screening tests administered by technicians, their recognition of emotional and cognitive disorders improves and their practice is altered. They are more likely to further evaluate any detected cognitive impairment, to discuss emotional problems with the patient and family, and to make any appropriate interventions or referrals.

Mini Mental State Examination (MMSE) Among the several quantified measures, MMSE is a useful screen for cognitive impairment in the elderly.[8] The MMSE has been found reliable and valid in field studies and hospital settings. Of elderly community-dwelling subjects over age 65, 95 percent score 24 or higher out of a total of 30 possible points on this test. Scores below 24 occur in delirium or dementia; they can also occur in severe depression in the elderly and in mental retardation. Although the sensitivity and specificity adequately detect dementia in elderly community or hospital populations, many additional persons with no diagnosable neurological or psychiatric conditions attain low scores. The reasons for these low scores are not understood, but despite the lack of a diagnosable psychiatric or neurological condition, these persons are more disabled than persons with higher MMSE scores, and they have more physical illnesses and take more medicines. In general, individuals who have had little education score lower; race and sex do not appear to influence scores if level of education is taken into account.[9,10]

Screening Tests for Abnormal Mood States Quantified aids to the examination are also available for some noncognitive functions of the elderly patient, particularly depression. Some, like the

Zung Depression Scale and the General Health Questionnaire (GHQ),[11] are self-rated, and others are observer-rated, such as the Montgomery Asberg Scale and the Hamilton Depression Scale. Both types are equally useful in non-cognitively impaired populations, but the observer-rated types should be used for patients with cognitive impairment.

NEUROPSYCHOLOGICAL ASSESSMENT

In the age of the computerized head scan, it is appropriate to consider the rationale for carrying out neuropsychological assessment for clinical purposes. Like the mental state examination, neuropsychological testing serves two major functions. The first function is the deduction of pathology and etiology from the test scores. In this way the neuropsychological tests can provide a probability that a brain lesion is present in a particular location. The accuracy of this type of localization is constantly debated in the field, and clinicians do not draw conclusions about lesion location from neuropsychological test results without scanning. The second function is to make predictions and recommendations from the test results about the subject's ability to carry out social functions that depend on particular cognitive functions for their safe and accurate completion. Although subjects' strengths and weakness in *particular cognitive functions* can be identified by a neuropsychological assessment, the ability of these results to predict patients' capacities to perform *particular social functions* has been little studied epidemiologically. For example, a patient's capacity to drive a car or to prepare a meal has not been directly related to particular patterns of neuropsychological test performance. The interpretation results are limited by the lack of standard normative values for neuropsychological testing in very old and poorly educated individuals.

In spite of its limitations, assessment can be useful now and can serve as the standard for the development of new tests that are designed to tap functional aspects of behavior. For these reasons some of the basic tests will now be discussed.

The Wechsler Adult Intelligence Scale (WAIS) The WAIS is a battery of tests that cover a wide range of verbal and nonverbal abilities. The standard scores on these tests are summed to provide an estimate of overall cognitive ability. They have been given to many thousands of people, and norms exist for persons up through age 65. The scores on the WAIS decline in relation to many brain diseases such as stroke and Alzheimer's disease but are also affected by depression and anxiety.

Tests of Memory There are many tests of verbal memory (assessing the patient's ability to learn and recall lists of words, events, or text) and a few of visual memory (assessing ability to recall drawings or a series of shapes). Memory tests for the position of an object in an array or for the appearance of a new object in the array have also been devised.

Language Tests Language testing includes an evaluation of the patient's ability to retrieve words in a particular category (such as foods or animals) or that begin with a given letter of the alphabet. This type of testing is usually called "verbal fluency," but it also involves verbal memory and attention. The ability to recognize and name objects can be tested using real objects, as it usually is clinically, or by naming line drawings of objects, as with the Boston Naming Test. The Token Test assesses the ability of patients to understand and carry out verbal commands of varying complexity. Experimental protocols are available for other aspects of language, such as pragmatics and prosody, but these are not usually included in clinical neuropsychological batteries.

Reading Many different reading tests have been developed for use with children and adolescents. There are norms for adults for some of these, including the Gray Oral Reading Test (GORT) which includes tests of word recognition and comprehension of the meaning of a passage. It is important to estimate reading level when assessing a patient's competence for making a will or consenting to medical treatment.

Visuospatial Perception Patients are usually tested using the Rey-Osterich figure drawing test. The figure is a complex geometric drawing that the patient copies and then is asked to redraw from memory.

Executive Functions A number of tests have been developed to assess the patient's ability to carry out complicated, multistep tasks, some of which involve judgment or planning. These tests have been said to test frontal-striatal function. While the tests are not specific to this neural system, they are useful in assessing patients' ability to maintain attention on a complex task, change from one thinking set to another, and plan a strategy. Examples of tests of executive function include the Wisconsin Card Sorting Test, which requires patients to sort cards according to unpredictably changing rules. In the Trail Making Test, subjects must "connect the dots," first from one number to the next and then, in the second part, from alternating letters and numbers. The Stroop Test requires patients to respond to stimuli with conflicting features (e.g., the word *blue* written in red ink).

THE NEUROLOGICAL EXAMINATION IN COGNITIVELY IMPAIRED PATIENTS

Elderly individuals often suffer from several diseases simultaneously, so that a complete physical and neurological examination is needed in every case, even though the major cause of the altered mental state may be apparent in the first minutes of the interview. The physical examination should be repeated at follow-up visits to determine the reliability of initial findings and in some cases, such as Alzheimer's disease, to assess the validity of the diagnosis, which is often uncertain early in the disease course. Patients and families are also reassured by repeated examinations, even when the diagnosis is clear. A precipitous decline in the mental state of a patient with stroke or Alzheimer's disease can be caused by the onset of some new condition that may be treatable, such as infection or cardiac failure. Regular examination will aid in prompt detection and prescription of appropriate treatment.

The neurological examination consists of a series of clinical tests designed to demonstrate the function or defect in particular motor and sensory areas of the nervous system. The neurological examination is only one part of the general physical examination, which should be completed prior to the neurological components. All aspects of the neurological examination components of an awake patient require the patient's cooperation. Thus, it is important to place the patient in a standard position, such as sitting on an examining table, so that the examiner can elicit the patient's performance in the same manner each time. The patient should be comfortable and the examiner should place the patient at ease by asking if he or she is comfortable and explaining that the testing will be brief and not painful. The examination should always be performed in the same order so that the maximum of information can be obtained without asking the patient to change position more than necessary and so that each task is always performed with the patient in the same position. Many reflexes will change depending on the patient's exact position. The complete neurological examination can be very lengthy. This section will review those components that are frequently abnormal in disorders that produce the common dementia syndromes.

Head and Neck The head, neck, and spine are examined for tenderness. Head trauma and temporal vasculitis are accompanied by local tenderness. The neck is examined for carotid bruits and also for evidence of cervical arthritis or disc disease, which can influence the deep tendon reflexes.

Cranial Nerves Olfaction is tested by asking the patient to smell and identify nonnoxious odors. Thus, the patient can be examined with a scratch-and-sniff card[12] or vials of odorants. Ammonia should not be used, since the substance can be detected by the fifth nerve. Patients with Alzheimer's disease and Huntington's disease have decreased olfaction, as do patients with frontal meningiomas. Head trauma which damages the olfactory bulb and tracts can also interfere with the ability to smell.

Visual acuity is tested with an eye chart, and visual fields are tested with confrontation maneuvers at the bedside and, if indicated, with more sophisticated measures in the laboratory. Visual loss can be due to optic nerve atrophy in syphilis or to vitamin deficiency. Visual fields can be affected by focal brain diseases which interfere with the transmission from the retina to the occipital pole. In Alzheimer's disease, patients often have decreased acuity as well as visual agnosia. Visual agnosia is distinguished from decreased acuity because patients can detect the presence of an object but cannot recognize what it is.

Ocular movements are frequently affected in dementing diseases and in delirium. The abnormalities include slowed and jerky movements of the eyes as they look back and forth between two peripheral stimuli—i.e., saccadic eye movements. This abnormality occurs in many subcortical conditions such as Huntington's disease. Visual pursuit movements may also be abnormal, as in schizophrenia. Limitation of the full range of vertical movement is seen in supranuclear palsy. Thiamine deficiency also produces abnormal eye movements and limitations of the range of movement.

Facial strength is diminished by lesions of the pyramidal system and is seen commonly in bilateral corticobulbar disease in patients with multi-infarct disease and multiple sclerosis. In these conditions, facial weakness is accompanied by dysarthria, dysphagia, and pathological emotional lability. This cluster of symptoms is called pseudobulbar palsy.

Hearing loss follows lesions of the eighth nerve and of the ear. It is often accompanied by a simple hallucination of buzzing or ringing in the ears called tinnitus. Vertigo, a sensation that the patient or the room is spinning or moving, often accompanies eighth nerve disease.

The Motor System The functions of the voluntary and involuntary motor system are examined. Observing the patient walk down the hall reveals many abnormalities including weakness of one side or abnormal posture and gait. In Parkinson's disease, the gait is stooped with short accelerating steps, while in frontal lobe or cerebellar disease, the feet are held wide apart—i.e., gait is wide-based. The observation of gait is refined by asking the patient to tandem walk, touching the heel to the toe with each step. Patients can also be asked to walk on their heels or toes. During walking, the writhing movements of choreoathetosis or dystonic movements of the arms and hands can be seen. The speed of walking is slowed in many conditions such as Parkinson's disease, which involves voluntary as well as involuntary movements. Gait disorders, abnormalities of tone and tremor are seen in subcortical diseases such as Parkinson's disease, Huntington's disease, and hydrocephalus. Late-stage Alzheimer's disease is also characterized by a gait disorder, with increased motor tone and pathological reflexes indicating frontal disease.

Voluntary movement is examined by testing the patient's initiation, strength, rhythm, and rapidity of movement. The patient is first asked to hold his or her arms outstretched with wrist extended and fingers held wide apart. In this posture the symmetry of strength can be observed as well as the presence of tremor. Fine motor movement, preserved in cortical disease and slowed in subcortical disease, is tested by asking the patient to tap the index finger rapidly on the thumb and to perform rapid alternating movements by alternately slapping the palm and back of one hand onto the palm of the other. These movements are also affected by apraxia, in which case the patient will have difficulty understanding how to execute the movement. Cerebellar disease produces dysrhythmic movements.

Involuntary aspects of movement include adventitious movements such as tremor, myoclonus, tics, chorea, or asterixis. Abnormalities of tone such as flaccidity, spasticity, or rigidity can also be included here. Motor reflexes are involuntary movements which are produced after a particular stimulus, such as stretching a tendon or scratching the lateral aspect of the sole. Pathological reflexes include grasp and suck reflexes, which indicate frontal disease, and the Myerson's sign seen in Parkinson's disease, the inability to suppress eye blinks when the forehead between the eyes is tapped by the examiner.

The Sensory System The sensory examination in the elderly is not well standardized. Some decreased vibratory sense in the feet is expected, but its etiology is not known. Severe vitamin B_{12} deficiency causes spinal cord degeneration and peripheral sensory disorder with decreased position and vibration sense as well as dementia.

LABORATORY EXAMINATIONS

Imaging The syndrome of dementia is usually accompanied by changes in the structure of the brain which can be visualized by modern neuroimaging techniques. Magnetic resonance imaging (MRI) produces the most detailed anatomic images of the brain at all levels. Cerebral atrophy, ventricular enlargement, and abnormalities in the density of the white matter produced by mass lesions and infarcts are easily seen without the injection of radioactive material. When quantified, these scans can demonstrate a progression of atrophy characteristic of Alzheimer's disease. Computed tomography (CT) of the brain is less sensitive than MRI but shows similar lesions and atrophy.

Single photon emission computed tomography (SPECT) is a brain scan taken following the injection of an isotope which is then detected by a camera which scans the head. Computers are used to indicate the location of the isotope in the brain. With currently available isotopes, these scans produce a sensitive image of blood flow. In Alzheimer's disease, blood flow can be decreased in a temporal parietal pattern. Multi-infarct disease appears as a pattern of patchy hypoperfusion.

Positron emission tomography (PET) is an experimental technique which uses short-acting positron-emitting isotopes to label ligands of interest which can bind to particular brain receptors. Other ligands are used to label glucose and used to indicate areas of hypometabolism. Although these methods are sensitive, quantitative, and of higher resolution than SPECT scans, they are expensive, invasive, and not widely available.

Electroencephalography (EEG) The EEG is a noninvasive, inexpensive procedure which is useful in the differential diagnosis of cognitive impairment of the elderly. The EEG records changes in voltage across the scalp. Fast waves or spikes are seen over regions of the brain which are irritable and potentially epileptogenic. Slow waves are seen over focal lesions such as strokes and tumors and also diffusely over the brain in metabolic disorders and diffuse degenerative diseases like Alzheimer's disease. The EEG is often slow in delirium and thus aids the differential between delirium and depression in the elderly. Although there is diffuse slowing in Alzheimer's disease, a superimposed intoxication or delirium will slow the record further.

PITFALLS IN THE INTERPRETATION OF EXAMINATIONS AND TESTS

The most commonly encountered pitfall in the use of the mental state examination is the common attribution by physicians of observations of cognitive or emotional impairment to a particular cause before completely evaluating the observations. For example, a low MMSE score may be attributed to aging or to a lack of education, prematurely excluding the possibility of a dementia syndrome from diagnostic consideration. Observations of a depressed mood in an isolated elderly person may be interpreted as an understandable, meaningful response to a sad situation before consideration is given to the possible relationship of the mood to a concurrent stroke or parkinsonism, both of which are associated with high rates of depression. Depressed mood, combined with cognitive impairment, is frequently ascribed to old age, and the physician fails to ask about a family or personal history of affective disorder which may be a treatable cause of the patient's symptoms.

Another inappropriate use of examination and tests results from the belief that the result of any single examination, such as a screening test or a laboratory test, implies a particular diagnosis. For example, psychological test results indicating impairment or a CT scan showing atrophy are often used to make a diagnosis of Alzheimer's disease. Diagnosis requires the combining of all sources of information and rarely depends on only one examination or test.

CONCLUSION

The neuropsychiatric assessment of the elderly patient requires a knowledge of the individual situation of the patient and family and of the diagnosis derived from a complete medical, psychiatric, and social history as well as the examination of the mental and physical state. The formulation of a treatment plan requires a knowledge of the patient's diagnosis, other complicating medical conditions, the patient's level of disability, the nature of his or her social supports, and the appreciation of behaviors and symptoms that, while not crucial to diagnosis, may need treatment. The careful history and physical examination provide the details on which to base a personal supportive relationship with even the most cognitively impaired patient and his or her family. This relationship provides hope even in the face of a relentlessly deteriorating condition.

REFERENCES

1. Rocca RP et al: Deementia among medical inpatients. *Arch Int Med* 146:1923, 1986.
2. Knights EB, Folstein MF: Unsuspected emotional and cognitive disturbance in medical patients. *Ann Int Med* 87:723, 1977.
3. Folstein MF, McHigh PR: Phenomenological approach to the treatment of organic psychiatric syndromes, in Wolman BB (ed): *The Therapist Handbook: Treatment Methods of Mental Disorders.* New York, Van Nostrand Reinhold, 1976, p. 279.
4. Lawton PM, Brody EM: Assessment of older people: Self-maintaining and instrumental activities of daily living. *Gerontologist* 9:179, 1969.
5. Katz S et al: Studies of illness in the aged. The index of ADL: A standardized measure of biological and psychological functions. *JAMA* 185:914, 1963.
6. Blessed G et al: Blessed Dementia Scale. *Br J Psychiat* 114:797, 1986.
7. Wilkinson IM, Graham-White J: Psychogeriatric Dependency Rating Scale (PGDRS): A method of assessment for use by nurses. *Br J Psychiat* 137:558, 1980.
8. Folstein MF et al: "Mini-Mental State": A practical method for grading the cognitive state of patients for the clinician. *J Psychiatr Res* 12:189, 1975.
9. Folstein MF et al: Meaning of cognitive impairment in the elderly. *J Amer Geriatr Soc* 33:228, 1985.
10. Anthony JC et al: Limits of the mini-mental state as a screening test for demtnai and delerium among hospital patients. *Psychol Med* 12:397, 1982.
11. Goldberg DP: *The Detection of Psychiatric Illness by Questionnaire.* New York, Oxford University Press, 1972.
12. Carrasco M, Ridout JB: Olfactory perception and imagery: A multidimensional analysis. *J Exptl Psychol Hum Perc Perf* 19:287, 1993.

Chapter 20

CARING FOR THE OLDER ADULT: THE ROLE OF THE FAMILY

Robert C. Intrieri and Stephen R. Rapp

For most elderly Americans, the family is the center of their support system, a system that provides a variety of services including instrumental assistance, financial assistance, decision making, and emotional support. The role of the family in the life of an older adult intensifies when disability occurs. Frailty in one of its members is a serious challenge to a family's coping resources. Families vary in how well they are able to cope with major life challenges.

Health care providers and other members of the "formal" support system, such as public and private home health agencies, are called upon to complement the care provided by families. How well they understand and work with families to eliminate, reduce, and/or manage disability will have a significant influence on the quality of life of their older patients. It is useful, therefore, to learn more about today's family caregivers. The objective of this chapter is to offer a brief overview of the research on caregiving of the elderly. We will explore several key issues including (1) the structure of today's American families, (2) the level of care older adults require, (3) who provides this care, (4) the impact on the caregivers of providing care, and (5) the services available to assist caregivers. While an exhaustive treatment of these topics is beyond the scope of this chapter, it is hoped that this overview will stimulate greater interest among health care providers in the older adult's caregiving system.

THE STRUCTURE OF FAMILIES IN AMERICA TODAY

Contemporary families are intergenerational and qualitatively and quantitatively different from those of previous generations.[1] In the 1990s, it is much more likely that an elderly person will be part of a four- or five-generation family that is made up of fewer members per generation than a family would have been in the first half of the twentieth century.[2] For example, 20 percent of women who died at age 80 in the early 1900s were great-great-grandmothers.[3] Moreover, the number of years that aging people spend in families has increased since the early nineteenth century. The elderly today may spend up to 50 years with their children[4] as compared to 20 or 30 years in the 1800s. Changes in the structure and extensiveness of these roles and relationships may be attributed to at least three demographic factors: (1) the decline in mortality during the last century[5]; (2) the decline in fertility, with the number of children per female declining from 3.7 in 1900 to 1.8 in 1986[6]; and (3) the increasing number of women versus men.

As a consequence of declining mortality and fertility, the structure of intergenerational families in North America has come to resemble a "beanpole."[7] This is due to the extended life of the living generations within families and the steady reduction in the number of offspring. The result is a decreasing number of family members per generation.[2] Hagestad[2] suggests that, unlike earlier decades where individuals were more likely to have a variety of horizontal intragenerational family ties, current and future generations will have more vertical ties between generations. Further, due to shifts in mortality and fertility, the balance between old and young has changed, so that families have more older members than younger ones. As a result of these changes, it is likely that their active child-rearing activities will be over by the time women become grandmothers.

Fewer children in the family and longer life spans have increased the time individuals spend within the intergenerational family[8] and will change how care is provided to the elderly by the family. For example, grandparents may be 20 to 30 years older than their children, so that when they reach old age their children will be in late middle age. Further, as a result of the decrease in family size, the pool of potential caregivers to the dependent, frail elderly is limited. There are fewer siblings, intragenerationally, to share care responsibilities. And the smaller size of the eligible pool conflicts with the extended survival of the elderly.[9]

Not only have parent and child intergenerational structures changed, but now grandparenthood has become an expanded and clearly delineated role that is separate from parenthood.[10] Increased longevity allows one to see a grandchild through most of life's developmental transitions. Though clear data are lacking, the median age of transition to grandparenthood is estimated to be around 45.[11] Given this estimate and the current life expectancy of 75 years,[12] a person can expect to be a grandparent for nearly one-half of his or her life.

Increase in a *verticalized* family and changes in the duration of the intergenerational family roles are not the only changes resulting from an altered population structure. Demographic changes have created family structures that promote age-condensed, age-gapped, truncated, matrilineal, and stepfamily models. *Age-condensed* intergenerational patterns are found when teenage pregnancy occurs across multiple generations, changing the family structure and relationships in three ways. First, in age-condensed families, generations are as little as 15 years apart. Second, boundary blurs occur when mother and daughter perceive themselves to be more like sisters than parent and child. Third, an early, unwanted transition to grandparenthood results. Child-care responsibilities usually assumed by the grandmother are transferred to the great-grandmother. As a result, the great-grandmother usually has care responsibilities for multiple generations.[7] *Age-gapped* intergenerational patterns occur when women postpone childbearing until their mid- to late thirties. If this has been a familial pattern, large gaps in the family structure are created, with the following implications for intergenerational relations. First, transition to grandparenthood may occur much later in life and, as a result, individuals may not experience grandparenthood for as long a period. Second, intergenerational strains may occur as a result of the increased age gap, and developmental bonds may not be as strong. Third, late childbearing usually produces fewer children, thus reducing the caregiver pool to a greater extent than would be the case in verticalized ("beanpole") families. Childlessness, though the choice of many couples in today's society, creates a *truncated* family structure, and the options for childless older adults to receive care within the family are therefore limited. Typically, the childless elderly establish bonds with the extended family (nieces, nephews) or promote liaisons with family friends. However, this strategy for kin building may become increasingly more limited because of the dramatically decreased fertility rate. *Matrilineal* intergenerational structures are based on out-of-wedlock childbearing and the creation of single-parent families headed by mothers. In 1986, nearly one-half (49 percent) of all out-of-wedlock births were to African-American women not married at the time of this survey[6]; as a result, many older black women find themselves serving as surrogate parents.[13] Because of the increased economic pressures, single mothers may be more likely to share households with their own mothers.[14] Stepfamily models largely evolve from the many divorces among young and middle-age adults.[6] Intergenerational families are affected because of the disruptions in the usual social interactions occurring between grandparent and grandchild. Non-custodial grandparents do not have the same opportunities for involvement in the lives of their grandchildren because their relationships with their former daughters- or sons-in-law and their families is severely curtailed. In addition, remarriage usually means the blending of several families, and further complexity results from the integration of stepchildren into the new family structure.[15]

Unprecedented changes in the structure of American families will continue to affect the type and availability of services families provide to their frail older adult members. As a result of these changes, the role played by formal care providers could also change. We now turn to the question of need for services.

CARE NEEDS OF OLDER PEOPLE

American society is aging. For example, while the general population tripled from 1900 to 1980, the age segment over age 65 increased 10 times, and projections through the year 2020 suggest that this segment will grow to about 17 times the 1900 population level.[16,17] More compelling has been the growth of that segment of the population labeled the oldest old (persons of age 75 or older). By 1980, this group made up 38 percent of the population over age 65. By 1990, that figure had risen to 41.7 percent.[16,17] By all accounts, this segment of American society will grow faster than any other segment over the next several decades.

Altered mortality patterns have increased the life span of the average adult. As a result, not only duration of life but the family's responsibility to the aging person have concomitantly expanded. Death has become more an event of late life, with about 80 percent of all deaths in the United States occurring in people aged 65 and older. Morbidity has also increased in relation to the lengthening life span, so that more people require care and treatment for chronic disease states. Cross-sectional data show that chronic disease states increase dramatically with age. Current estimates suggest that more than 80 percent of those above age 65 have at least one chronic illness for which they are receiving continuing medical care.[12] Also, medical comorbidity is much more prevalent among older adults, and the probability of having two or more of these chronic conditions increases with age. Despite these data, information compiled by the National Center for Health Statistics shows that over 71 percent of the community-dwelling elderly rate their health as excellent, very good, or good compared to noninstitutionalized same-age peers; only 29 percent rated their health as fair or poor.[18]

The severity of chronic disease is highly variable in the older population. As a result, the consequences of the diseases also vary. Functional disability—commonly defined as difficulty in performing the activities of daily living (ADLs; e.g., bathing, dressing, transferring, toiletting, or indoor mobility) or instrumental activities of daily living (IADLs; e.g., cooking, shopping, housecleaning, transportation, handling finances, or doing laundry)—affects an estimated 3 to 7 million American families. One-quarter of the elderly population has difficulty with at least one ADL or one IADL. The proportion of people who have difficulty with either ADLs or IADLs increases significantly with age.[19,21]

Confinement may be considered another measure of physical limitation. While 62 percent of all elderly spend no days in bed due to disease, approximately 1 percent of older adults aged 65 to 74 and 3 percent of adults over 85 years of age are permanently confined to bed.[12] At any given time, only 5 percent of older adults are institutionalized in nursing homes. The remaining portion of the frail elderly population is cared for at home, often with assistance provided by a family member. These caregivers represent a growing population. They have received increased attention lately, as more research has focused on the social impact of age-related disease and disability. Before reviewing data on the impact of providing care, we will first briefly describe the persons providing care to the elderly.

WHO ARE TODAY'S CAREGIVERS?

Two recent national surveys of caregivers for noninstitutionalized older adults[20,21] provide us with a profile of caregivers. In the survey conducted by Stone et al.,[20] based on the 1982 National Long Term Care Survey, caregiving was defined as providing unpaid assistance (i.e., personal assistance, directive assistance, or supervision) to someone 65 years old or older who had difficulty with at least one ADL or one IADL. Highlights of the Stone survey are presented below. The interested reader is referred to it for additional detail.

Stone et al.[20] found that caregivers were predominantly middle-aged (mean age, 57 years), married (70 percent), and female (72 percent). Most (70 percent) were "primary" caregivers; that is, they had major responsibility and received little or no help from others, family or otherwise. One-third of caregivers in this survey were elderly themselves, with 10 percent of the sample aged 75 or older.

More than 35 percent of the caregivers were spouses, 29 percent were adult daughters, 8.5 percent were adult sons, and friends, relatives, or others comprised the remaining 27 percent of caregivers for these noninstitutionalized older adults.[20]

Competing work and familial obligations were common among the caregivers surveyed. Some 25 percent of caregiving children and 33 percent of nonspousal caregivers had children under 18 years of age in their households. Of the caregiving children, 40 percent were in the labor force. Another 9 percent reported that they had left work to care for an elderly relative. Daughters were about 2.5 times more likely to quit their jobs than sons, which is consistent with the data, reported by Brody et al.,[22] which found that daughters were expected to quit or alter their work schedules in order to provide parent care. Of caregiving children, 29 percent had some conflict over work and caregiving responsibilities.

The care recipients in the survey of Stone et al.[20] were typically females (60 percent). Most were either married (51 percent) or widowed (41 percent). They were elderly, averaging 78 years of age, with 20 percent above age 85. Not surprisingly, most (69 percent) of the care recipients described their health as fair or poor and 57 percent had three or more ADL deficits.

Caregiving can be described both in terms of the amount of time spent in this activity and the amounts and types of services provided. The Stone et al.[20] survey revealed that caregiving is often an ongoing responsibility. Over 80 percent of caregivers surveyed provided assistance seven days a week, and 20 percent had been in the caregiving role longer than 5 years. The tasks performed by the caregivers included a variety of activities: assisting with personal hygiene (67 percent), mobility (45 percent), medication administration (53 percent), household tasks (80 percent), shopping/transportation (86 percent), and handling finances (49 percent). Despite the heavy workload, fewer than 10 percent of the caregivers surveyed used paid services of any kind.

The AARP/Travelers survey[21] included caregivers for persons 50 years of age or older; thus several statistics were different from those of the survey by Stone et al. Nevertheless, the overall picture was quite similar. Both surveys found middle-aged, married women to be the most typical caregivers. Special attention was given to the effects of caregiving on working individuals. About half of the respondents to the AARP/Travelers survey were employed outside the home while also spending an average of 10 hours per week in caregiving; 38 percent had lost time from work because of their caregiving responsibilities; and 20 percent reported having lost some benefits as a result.

Several interesting trends from both national surveys and related studies are noteworthy. First, most caregiving is done by women including wives and daughters.[23] Second, most caregiving is done by a single primary caregiver. Third, the tasks caregivers perform are varied, regular, and demanding of their time and energy. Finally, a growing number of caregivers work outside the home, and their dual roles often conflict with each other. Next we will examine the available data on the impact that caregiving has on family members' psychological, physical, and financial well-being.

THE IMPACT OF CAREGIVING

Caregiving by family members is provided despite the high potential for emotional, physical, and financial burdens (for reviews, see Refs. 24 to 27). A large and growing number of studies point to the adverse effects of acute and chronic stressors associated with caregiving. Biegel et al.[26] provide an excellent review of the literature on the impact of caregiving associated with different diseases. Much of the existing research on the consequences of providing daily care to a disabled older adult has focused on persons caring for patients with dementia, so we will highlight these findings.

Emotional Impact There is evidence that caregivers report higher levels of psychiatric distress symptoms than noncaregivers, especially depressive symptoms.[26,27] Cross-sectional as well as longitudinal studies document higher rates of self-reported depressive symptomatology among help-seeking caregivers than among noncaregivers. Even in studies using more rigorous clinical assessments, the prevalence of depression can be quite high, ranging between 30 and 50 percent.[27–29] As a reflection of their higher than normal levels of psychological distress, caregivers are also more likely than noncaregivers to be taking psychotropic medications.[30] Thus many studies suggest that the stressors associated with their role can lead at least some caregivers of dementia patients to develop significant psychiatric morbidity.

Physical Impact Less is known about the impact of caregiving on physical health because of the paucity of carefully controlled studies and the inherent difficulties in isolating single causal factors related to health.[26,27] A consistent finding in studies of help-seeking caregivers, however, is that they describe their health as poorer than that of noncaregivers.[20,26,27,31] Recent work has begun to explore possible biological mediators of psychological stress associated with caregiving. Keicolt-Glaser and her associates[32] reported poorer immune responsivity and higher depression among caregivers compared to noncaregivers. Caregivers had lower percentages of total T-lymphocytes and helper T-lymphocytes and lower helper-suppressor cell ratios than did noncaregivers. Even though methodological complexities have precluded definitive studies in this area, research data do suggest that for some people poorer health may be a cost of providing care. More research in this area is needed to clarify the role of caregiving in physical health.

Economic Impact Almost half of American caregivers are in the labor force, and between one-quarter and one-third of these caregivers report that their roles as care providers conflict with their jobs.[21] Out-of-pocket expenditures can be substantial. According to the AARP/Travelers national survey of caregivers[21] almost half report incurring additional personal and family expenditures and 11 percent of them spend over 50 percent of their monthly income on care. The majority of these expenditures are for hospital care and in-home nursing services. In addition to out-of-pocket expenses, working caregivers may miss work and lose benefits as a result of caring for their disabled family members.[21]

Taken together, these findings highlight the possibility that caregiving may have a negative psychological, physical, and financial impact on some individuals.

SERVICES ARE AVAILABLE FOR THE CAREGIVER

We have presented data showing that care for frail older adults in America is provided predominantly by family members and that the biopsychosocial consequences to the caregiver can be significant. In this section we will describe several types of services intended to help caregivers. While research into the effectiveness of these services is increasing, little can be said at this time about the relative advantages of one type of service over another.

In their review of interventions specifically for primary caregivers, Gallagher et al.[29] describe four broad categories. *Respite care programs* include day care, day treatment, time-limited inpatient respite, and in-home services. The goals of respite care are to provide time-limited relief from caregiving by temporarily shifting responsibility for care from the family member to professionals and paraprofessionals. Day care, day treatment, and partial hospitalization programs all involve bringing the frail older person to a central location where he or she is looked after for a limited time each day. By contrast, inpatient respite enables the care recipient to receive full-time care for a number of days. Typically, inpatient care is reserved for more functionally impaired individuals, whereas day treatment is offered to mildly to moderately impaired adults. *In-home services* include sitting, home-health nursing services, and homemaker services. The effectiveness of respite services is uncertain, and it is not known whether they improve or maintain functional status or prevent institutionalization. In a recent randomized control study[33] in which a group of caregivers receiving respite services (a combination of day care, inpatient care, and in-home services) was compared to a control group of caregivers offered no services, the results showed that caregivers receiving respite services maintained their disabled family member in the community longer than did the control caregivers.

Peer- and professional-led *support groups* are another popular service available to caregivers. Typically caregivers in these groups are offered general information about illnesses such as dementia and told about community resources; they are also given emotional support. Support groups are varyingly sponsored by public or private agencies, churches, and individuals. Perhaps the best-known network of support groups is that affiliated with the Alzheimer's Disease and Related Disorders Association (ADRDA). Local chapters of the ADRDA, now found in many communities, offer regular support-group meetings for caregivers of individuals with dementia. Despite their increasing numbers and the intuitive appeal of support groups, little is known about whether they really help or how they work. A recent review of 29 studies of support groups[34] highlighted vast differences in group composition and goals and, not surprisingly, outcomes as well. It was found that caregivers frequently rated groups as helpful and satisfying even if their distress levels were not reduced. Thus support groups do hold some promise for caregivers.

Counseling and psychotherapy involve psychologically based treatment delivered to the individual by a professional therapist. This may be done on an individual basis or in the form of group therapy. Several structured psychological interventions specifically designed for caregivers have been studied and will be mentioned briefly. The interested reader is encouraged to consult primary sources for greater detail.

Pinkston and Linsk[35,36] examined the effect of teaching behavior management techniques to caregivers of family members with disordered behavior. Typical behaviors targeted for change included bizarre conduct, repetitive behaviors (e.g., question asking), incontinence, poor self-care, social isolation, and other behaviors that threaten independent living. During 10 to 15 training sessions, a therapist provided instructions to the caregiver in his or her home. The therapist showed the caregiver how to measure and monitor behavior, how to identify behavioral treatment goals, and how to alter environmental cues and consequences to change the targeted behavior. In addition, caregivers received information about available community resources. The intervention's effectiveness has been documented in studies showing improvement in 76 percent of the targeted behaviors and high caregiver satisfaction.[35,37]

Taking a different approach, Gallagher and her associates developed a psychoeducational treatment package to teach self-change skills to caregivers.[38,29] In a randomized controlled study, caregivers were assigned to one of two experimental groups or a waiting-list control group. Caregivers in the experimental groups were taught either methods for increasing the frequency of pleasant activities or strategies for solving problems. In the first condition, pleasant events/activities were first identified and then systematically programmed into the caregiver's daily or weekly routine. Those taught problem solving were shown how to specify problems, "brainstorm" solutions, systematically evaluate the relative advantages and disadvantages of each solution, and evaluate the effectiveness of the implemented solution. Both skill-building groups showed significant decreases in depression levels and increases in morale relative to the control group. Thus, for some caregivers, formal psychotherapeutic interventions can be effective in reducing distress associated with caregiving.

As is evident from this brief overview, professional and nonprofessional services specifically intended to help caregivers to cope with the stresses associated with caregiving are quite varied in nature. Some services aim at reducing or temporarily relieving family caregivers of their responsibilities, while others aim at trying to enhance the caregiver's effectiveness. Access to currently available services varies widely from community to community and state to state. There is currently no national agenda for addressing this complex family issue. Some communities enjoy a broad continuum of services, while others offer few if any. The costs associated with the different types of services also vary, with some services being provided free of charge (e.g., support groups) while others may be costly (e.g., respite, psychotherapy). Responsibility for providing caregiver services is equally broad-ranging. Federal, state, and local government as well as private initiatives may be involved. Discovering which specialized services are available in a community is the first step to assisting caregivers to access them; many caregivers find such assistance very helpful.

CONCLUSION

The provision of continuous, quality care to frail older adults is a goal shared by American families and health care providers. As more and more Americans live longer with chronic and disabling conditions, both formal and informal care providers are increasingly challenged to provide more and better-coordinated services. Many factors will continue to influence the attainment of this goal. The changing structure of American families is precipitating changes in the caregiving experience and will continue to do so well into the next century. The sometimes devastating impact of providing care to a frail family member can undermine the caregiver's physical, emotional, and financial well-being. There is some promise in the success of interventions tailored for caregivers; however, more research is needed. Finally, public policy which utilizes the personal commitment and skills of American caregivers and promotes the integration of formal and informal service delivery is greatly needed.

REFERENCES

1. Cherlin AJ, Furstenburg FF: *The New American Grandparent.* New York, Basic Books, 1986.
2. Hagestad GO: The aging society as a context for family life. *Daedalus* 115:119, 1986.
3. Hagestad GO: Demographic changes and the life course: Some emerging trends in the family realm. *Fam Relat* 37:405, 1988.
4. Preston S: Children and the elderly: Divergent paths for America's dependent. *Demography* 21:435, 1984.
5. U.S. Bureau of the Census: *Demographic and Socioeconomic Aspects of Aging in the United States.* Current Population Reports (series P-23, no. 138). Washington, DC, U.S. Government Printing Office, 1984.
6. U.S. Bureau of the Census: *Fertility of American Women: June 1986.* Current Population Reports (series P-20, no. 421). Washington, DC, U.S. Government Printing Office, 1987.
7. Bengston VL et al: Families and aging: Diversity and heterogeneity, in Binstock RH, George LK (eds): *Handbook of Aging and the Social Sciences,* 3rd ed. San Diego, CA, Academic Press, 1990, pp. 263–287.
8. Hagestad GO: Problems and promises in the social psychology of intergenerational relations, in Fogel R, Hatfield E, Kiesler SB, Shanas E (eds): *Aging Stability and Change in the Family.* New York, Academic Press, 1981, pp 11–46.
9. Treas J, Bengtson VL: Family in the later years, in Sussman M, Steinmetz S (eds): *Handbook on Marriage and the Family.* New York, Plenum Press, 1987, pp 625–648.
10. Hagestad GO, Burton LM: Grandparenthood, life context, and family development. *Am Behav Sci* 29:471, 1985.
11. Sweet JA, Bumpas LL: *American Families and Households.* New York, Russell Sage Foundation, 1987.
12. U.S. Senate Special Committee on Aging: *Aging America: Trends and Projections.* Washington, DC, U.S. Government Printing Office, 1989.
13. Burton LM: Teenage childbearing as an alternative life course strategy in multigenerational black families. *Hum Nature* 1:123, 1990.
14. Wilson MN: The black extended family: An analytical consideration. *Develop Psychol* 22:246, 1986.
15. Matthews SH: Perception of fairness in the division of responsibilities for old parents. *Soc Jus Rev* 1:425, 1987.
16. U.S. Bureau of the Census: *Projections of the Population of the United States by Age, Sex, and Race: 1988 to 2080.* Current Population Reports (series P-25, no. 1018). Washington, DC, U.S. Government Printing Office, 1989.
17. U.S. Senate Special Committee on Aging: *Aging America: Trends and Projections.* Washington, DC, U.S. Government Printing Office, 1991.
18. National Center for Health Statistics: *Current Estimates from the National Health Interview Survey, 1989.* Vital and Health Statistics, series 10, no. 176. Hyattsville, MD, DHHS publication no. (PHS) 90-1504, 1990.
19. Stone RI, Murtaugh CM: The elderly population with chronic functional disability: Implications for home care eligibility. *Gerontologist* 30:491, 1990.
20. Stone R et al: Caregivers of the frail elderly: A national profile. *Gerontologist* 27:616, 1987.
21. American Association of Retired Persons & The Travelers Companies Foundation: *A National Survey of Caregivers: Working Caregivers Report.* Washington, DC, American Association of Retired Persons, 1989.
22. Brody EM et al: Women's changing roles and help to the elderly: Attitudes of three generations of women. *J Gerontol* 38:597, 1983.
23. Brody EM: Parent care as a normative family stress. *Gerontologist* 25:19, 1985.
24. Horowitz A: Family caregiving to the frail elderly. *Annu Rev Gerontol Geriatr* 5:194, 1985.
25. George LK: Caregiver stress studies—There really is more to learn. *Gerontologist* 30:580, 1990.
26. Biegel DE, Sales E, Schulz R: *Family Caregiving in Chronic Illness.* Newbury Park, CA, Sage Publications, 1991.
27. Schulz R et al: Psychiatric and physical morbidity effects of caregiving. *J Gerontol* 45:P181, 1990.
28. Dura JR et al: Anxiety and depressive disorders in adult children caring for demented parents. *Psychol Aging* 6:467, 1991.
29. Gallagher D et al: Interventions with caregivers of frail elderly persons, in Ory M, Bond K (eds): *Aging and Health Care: Social Science and Policy Perspectives.* New York, Routledge, 1989, pp 167–190.
30. George LK, Gwyther LP: Caregiver well-being: A multidimensional examination of family caregivers of demented adults. *Gerontologist* 26:253, 1986.
31. Haley WE et al: Psychological, social, and health consequences of caring for a relative with senile dementia. *J Am Geriatr Soc* 35:405, 1987.
32. Kiecolt-Glaser JK et al: Chronic stress and immunity in family caregivers of Alzheimer's disease victims: *Psychosom Med* 49:523, 1987.
33. Lawton MP et al: A controlled study of respite service for caregivers of Alzheimer's patients. *Gerontologist* 29:8, 1989.
34. Toseland RW, Rossiter CM: Group interventions to support family caregiver: A review and analysis. *Gerontologist* 29(4):438, 1989.
35. Pinkston EM, Linsk NL: *Care of the Elderly: A Family Approach.* New York, Pergamon Press, 1984.
36. Pinkston EM, Linsk NL: Behavioral family intervention with the impaired elderly. *Gerontologist* 24(6):576, 1984.
37. Pinkston EM et al: Home-based behavioral family treatment of the impaired elderly. *Behav Ther* 19(3):331, 1988.
38. Lovett S, Gallagher D: Psychoeducational interventions for family caregivers: Preliminary efficacy data. *Behav Ther* 19(3):321, 1988.

Chapter 21

APPROPRIATE USE OF NEW DIAGNOSTIC TECHNIQUES IN OLDER PERSONS

Eric B. Larson

The clinician practicing in the 1990s may choose from an array of diagnostic technologies which can provide valuable information about patients. The quality of information which helps us diagnose and treat patients has improved dramatically in the last three or four decades. It is likely that newer diagnostic techniques will regularly appear, offering clinicians further opportunities to more effectively diagnose and treat patients. However, diagnostic advances are not without their attendant problems. Most noteworthy is their high cost. Much attention has been justifiably focused on high-cost, widely applied imaging devices[1] like computed tomography (CT), magnetic resonance imaging (MRI), and now positron emission tomography (PET). Equally important in the generation of costs are the frequently used low-cost tests (so-called little-ticket items) which, because of their frequency, constitute a major source of expense.[2]

Problems also occur because physicians are misled or may misinterpret diagnostic information[3,4] or because diagnostic tests are under- or overutilized.[3,5] Problems relating to the interpretation and use of diagnostic tests are probably more common with newer diagnostic technologies; these may be particularly troublesome in relation to geriatric patients due to the effects of increased underlying biologic variation, existence of age-related change, and the presence of multiple diseases in older persons.

The purpose of this chapter is to review clinical epidemiologic principles regarding medical diagnosis and the evaluation of diagnostic tests. The chapter also describes a general framework for the evaluation of new diagnostic tests. This can provide a basis for general principles regarding the selection and use of new diagnostic tests as well as ideas about how these tests can be expected to benefit our patients and medical practices.

PURPOSE OF DIAGNOSTIC TESTS

Most of the time clinicians see patients because the patients are sick and seek help. Patients present with clusters of symptoms and signs which characterize their illness. The act of clinical diagnosis focuses on the signs and symptoms of the patient's illness in order to classify it as a disease or target disorder.[6] The purpose of the classification is to enable us to offer advice, give treatments, or institute other clinical strategies which, based on previous experience with that condition, will maximize the patient's health.

In proceeding from the illness to the disease or target disorder, experienced and effective clinicians use a so-called hypotheticodeductive process, frequently unconsciously. As we listen to and examine patients, we are processing bits of information and constantly refining (reinforcing or rejecting) diagnostic hypotheses. Typically, a clinician entertains no more than three hypotheses and is frequently working on just one.[6,7] This process occurs whether we are actively diagnosing the target disorder, following a patient for health maintenance, or monitoring response to therapy.

Diagnostic tests are used to help clinicians navigate the process more effectively, the ultimate goal being better patient well-being. In most cases, we diagnose by pattern recognition from multiple sources. The result of pattern recognition may be so distinctive that little information beyond what can be achieved at the patient's side (or even over the phone) is necessary. Diagnostic tests are needed when we lack sufficient certainty about a particular diagnosis to proceed or to monitor the process of care.

The gathering of diagnostic data is, therefore, typically viewed as part of an effort to make a diagnosis. The same data are also used for four different but interrelated processes: to judge the severity of an illness, to predict patient's subsequent course and prognosis, to estimate likely responsiveness to treatment, and to determine actual response to therapy.[8] Regardless of the reason, the overriding criterion for seeking diagnostic information will be the usefulness of the given piece of data to the clinician who seeks it and the patient who generates it. Because of this, it is the individual clinician who has the task of critically appraising which individual diagnostic data are helpful and who faces the daunting task—given the rate at which new diagnostic tests and whole new diagnostic technologies are developing—of incorporating these tests into practice.

The group at McMaster[9] has described eight guides for evaluating the clinical usefulness of a diagnostic test—these are presented in Table 21-1.

Each of these issues has potentially important effects on the overall usefulness of a diagnostic test to a given patient and clinician. Several such issues are particularly relevant to geriatrics. For example, the value of diagnostic tests for demented elderly patients was inferred on the basis of data collected from referral populations who were predominantly below age 65. This led clinicians to overvalue and even misinterpret the results of CT scanning, a new technology, because influential papers (Ref. 10, for example) mistakenly assume that subdural hematoma, normal pressure hydrocephalus, and resectable brain tumor were more common than they actually are in elderly demented patients. In fact, Alzheimer's disease and multi-infarct dementia are overwhelmingly the most common types of dementia in the elderly population.[11]

The definition of *normal*[12] can be particularly challenging in geriatrics. Using the same example of neuroimaging for dementia, both CT and MRI were frequently misinterpreted in their early use among older patients; for CT, there was a mistaken notion that brain atrophy with prominent sulci and ventricles was equivalent to Alzheimer's disease whereas, in fact, these signs are more strongly associated with aging.[13] For both CT and MRI, there was also failure to appreciate that so-called periventricular lucencies—although similar to changes resulting from stroke—can be seen in persons with "normal" aging and thus do not constitute a criterion for diagnosing multi-infarct dementia.[14]

Finally, the ultimate criterion for any clinical maneuver, including a diagnostic test, is whether a patient is better off for it.[8] This may seem like a tall order for new tests, but it will predictably become increasingly important. As we become more concerned about the costs and benefits of medical care and our ability to pay for that care, increasing attention is being focused on diagnostic tests and their ability to contribute to overall patient well-being.[1,15] In geriatrics, where the bulk of treatment is directed toward chronic diseases, palliation, and health promotion to optimize patient function—not the complete cure or prevention of disease—there are potentially limitless opportunities to apply diagnostic tests. Knowledge of the effect that diagnostic tests may have on outcome will likely become increasingly important. For example, Deyo et al.[16] randomized patients with apparently innocent low back pain to receive immediate x-rays (a common practice) or an informative discussion with a nonphysician about low back pain and the risks and benefits of x-rays. Those receiving x-rays ended up no less symptomatic or more satisfied than those in the education group. The geriatric caregiver will need to seek increasingly good evidence of test utility, especially as we see progressive escalation of test costs. This is clearly exemplified by what has occurred in neuroimaging, where CT has been succeeded by MRI. Now PET is the latest technology that may be utilized in the care of elderly patients with central nervous system disorders.

TABLE 21-1

Eight Guides for Deciding the Clinical Usefulness of a Diagnostic Test

1. Has there been an independent, "blind" comparison with a "gold standard" of diagnosis?
2. Has the diagnostic test been evaluated in a patient sample that included an appropriate spectrum of mild and severe, treated and untreated disease, plus individuals with different but commonly confused disorders?
3. Was the setting for this evaluation, as well as the filter through which study patients passed, adequately described?
4. Have the reproducibility of the test result (precision) and its interpretation (observer variation) been determined?
5. Has the term *normal* been defined sensibly as it applied to this test?
6. If the test is advocated as part of a cluster or sequence of tests, has its individual contribution to the overall validity of the cluster or sequence been determined?
7. Have the tactics for carrying out the test been described in sufficient detail to permit their exact replication?
8. Has the utility of the test been determined?

SOURCE: From Sackett et al.[19]
Reproduced by permission.

FEATURES OF DIAGNOSTIC TEST PERFORMANCE

Establishing a diagnosis from a cluster of symptoms and signs is a process that results in a probability of correctness. Although clinicians tend to think and act on the basis of diagnoses as categorical certainties, there is uncertainty or error in medical diagnosis. The traditional relationship between diagnosis and test results is shown in Fig. 21-1. Two of the four possible outcomes are correct and two are wrong. Assessment of accuracy ("the truth") is based on a "gold standard."

Test performance is defined on the basis of the preceding two-by-two accuracy table (Fig. 21-1).[17] The most commonly described characteristics of test performance are sensitivity and specificity. The key rates (false positive, true positive, false negative, true negative) and positive and negative predictive values can be described once one knows sensitivity and specificity and the prevalence of disease, as shown in Fig. 21-2.

		Disease	
		Present	Absent
Test	Positive	True Positive	False Positive
	Negative	False Negative	True Negative

FIGURE 21-1
The relationship between a diagnostic test result and the occurrence of disease. There are two possibilities for the result to be correct (true positive and true negative) and two possibilities for the result to be incorrect (false positive and false negative). *(From Fletcher et al.[17] Reproduced by permission.)*

Sensitivity is the probability that a test will be positive in the patient with disease; it is also called the true-positive rate.[6,8,17] The false-negative rate is the probability that a test will be negative in a patient with disease. The *specificity* is the probability that a test will be negative in patients without disease; it is also called the true-negative rate. The false-positive rate is the probability that a test will be positive in a patient without disease. The *positive predictive value* is the probability that the given disease will be present in a patient with a positive test result. The *negative predictive value* is the probability that the given disease will not be present in a patient with a negative test result. A perfect test would be highly sensitive and highly specific. However, typically, there is a trade-off between sensitivity and specificity—especially when a test has a continuous scale—for example, the serum test for thyroid-stimulating hormone (TSH). When a test is sensitive but not specific, the clinician pays a penalty of a relatively large number of patients with false-positive test results. In geriatrics, the main problem with diagnostic tests is the relatively high frequency of false-positive results. This occurs because of the increased biologic variability with aging and because of the increased frequency of so-called incidental positive results, especially in imaging tests.

The properties that help a clinician select which test to use are sensitivity and specificity.[8,17] However, once the results of a test are known, its predictive value is the probability of interest. The predictive value is determined by the sensitivity and specificity of the test as well as the prevalence of the disease in the population being tested. Predictive value is calculated according to Bayes' theorem of probability:

$$+PV = \frac{(Se)(P)}{(Se)(P) + (1 - Sp)(1 - P)}$$

where: Se = sensitivity;
Sp = specificity;
P = prevalence;
+PV = positive predictive value.

When a test is more sensitive, the negative predictive value is better and the clinician can be more confident that a patient with a negative test result does not have the disease. By contrast, the more specific the test is, the more confident the clinician will be that the positive test result indicates disease—that is, the better the positive predictive value.

Clinicians have difficulty incorporating the effect of prevalence on predictive value, especially in the

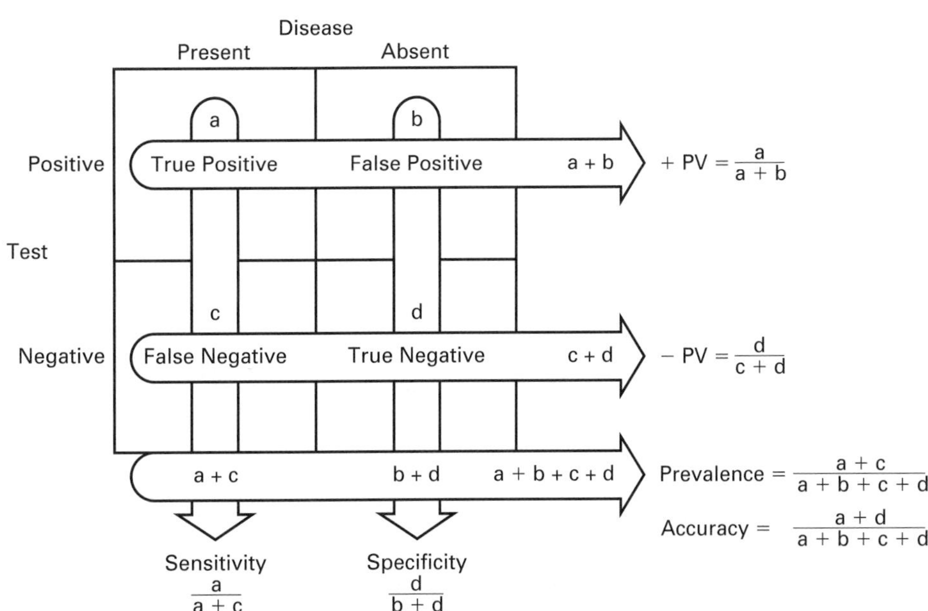

FIGURE 21-2
Diagnostic test characteristics and definitions. (Design courtesy of the Department of Clinical Epidemiology and Biostatistics, McMaster Health Sciences Centre.) *(From Fletcher et al.[17] Reproduced by permission.)*

case of rare diseases. For example, when the test is applied to patients among whom the prevalence of a given disease is low, "positive" results may be largely false-positive results. The relationship between the effect of prevalence on positive predictive value for a test with high sensitivity and specificity (0.9) is shown in Fig. 21-3. This can be further demonstrated for an extremely common disease in elderly men—prostatic carcinoma. That is, Watson and Teng[18] reported that in the general population where the prevalence of prostatic carcinoma is 35 cases per 100,000, the positive predictive value of an abnormal prostatic acid phosphatase is 0.4 percent; whereas in men aged 75 or older, where the prevalence is 500 per 100,000, the positive predictive value is still only 5.6 percent. By contrast, when a patient has a clinically suspicious prostatic nodule and the prevalence is 50,000 cases per 100,000, the positive predictive value of an abnormal acid phosphatase is 93 percent.

Summary test performance characteristics are the so-called *likelihood ratio* statistics.[19] *The likelihood ratio for a positive test* is the likelihood of a positive test in a patient with disease divided by the probability of a positive test result in a patient who does not have the disease. Thus, the likelihood ratio is sensitivity (or true-positive rate) divided by false-positive rate (or 1 minus specificity). The *likelihood ratio for a negative test* is the likelihood of a negative test in a patient who does have the disease divided by the likelihood of a negative test in a patient who does not have the disease. This value is computed by dividing the false-negative rate (1 minus sensitivity) by the true-negative rate (specificity). The most effective tests will have high likelihood ratios for positive tests (greater than 10 to 20) and lower likelihood ratios for negative tests (less than 0.2). Such tests will have the greatest effect on posttest probability for a target disorder compared to diagnostic tests with intermediate values of likelihood ratios. Likelihood ratios are often published in critical reviews or so-called meta-analyses of diagnostic test efficacy.

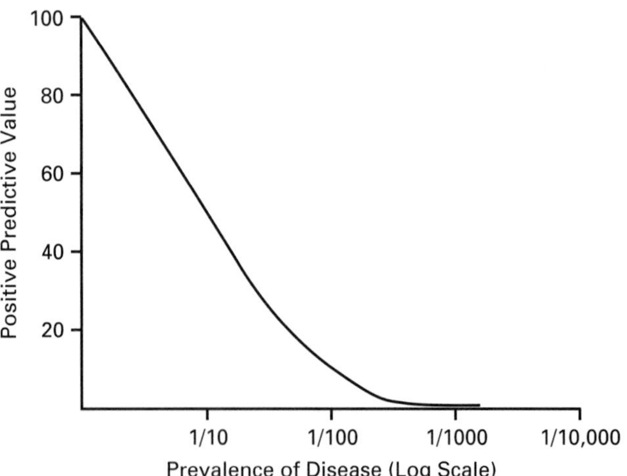

FIGURE 21-3

The relationship between prevalence and positive predictive value (where sensitivity = 90 percent and specificity = 90 percent). *(From Fletcher et al.*[17] *Reproduced by permission.)*

PRINCIPLES OF DIAGNOSTIC TECHNOLOGY ASSESSMENT

In the wake of societal concerns about the high cost of diagnostic technologies, taxonomies of diagnostic efficacy have been developed. The most commonly cited taxonomy describes a hierarchy of five levels consisting of technologic capacity, diagnostic accuracy, diagnostic impact, therapeutic impact, and patient outcomes.[20,21] Ideally, a new diagnostic technology will have clinical research and development describing its effect in all five levels. In fact, there are very few instances when we have evidence of a diagnostic technology favorably affecting patient outcomes.

Technologic capacity deals with the capacity for a diagnostic technique to measure a phenomenon with accuracy. In imaging, this capacity is measured by such variables as image quality and reliability. *Diagnostic accuracy* refers to the technology's ability to detect and classify pathology accurately. These properties are measured by the diagnostic test performance variables described earlier, including sensitivity, specificity, and true-positive and false-positive rates. *Diagnostic impact* refers to the accuracy and clinical value of a new technique compared to the alternative diagnostic test. This impact is typically measured in the same properties used to measure diagnostic accuracy but, at this level, these properties are compared with some alternative and not simply described in isolation.

Therapeutic impact relates to the effect of diagnostic technology on patient care. Desirable effects would be to reduce risk and discomfort to patients, improve treatment selection by clinicians, and perhaps provide more reassurance to patients or clinicians. Finally, *patient outcome* refers to whether a diagnostic test leads to a longer life, relief of pain and suffering, or improved functional status. These outcomes are difficult to prove but are certainly important when one is considering widely used tests like screening tests. Nonetheless, it is certainly not unreasonable to expect that well-established diagnostic tests should have fairly good information on the first four levels of efficacy.

USE AND SELECTION OF NEW DIAGNOSTIC TESTS

Clinicians tend to develop practice patterns that "work" to solve problems for them and their patients. New diagnostic tests can be viewed as offering added efficiencies in solving clinical problems or in enhancing the quality of information available to the physician. The principles described in the preceding section should be helpful in deciding whether to use a new test, in whom, and how to interpret the results.

Health services research has demonstrated considerable variation among physicians in the use of diagnostic tests. In general, the variation in test ordering leads to widespread differences in the costs generated by those tests without any measurable difference in value to patients. This has led to increased efforts to establish practice standards or guidelines for common clinical problems. Such efforts occur at all levels, from local hospital or clinic practice guidelines, to specialty society standard settings, to efforts sanctioned by national governments to establish national guidelines. One example is the U.S. NIH Consensus Development Conference on Differential Diagnosis of Dementia[22] and a similar effort in Canada[23] which proposed guidelines for evaluating and diagnosing dementia, including the use of older and newer diagnostic tests (see Table 21-2). Both the United States and Canada have also charged ongoing task forces to describe those elements of the periodic health exam that have been demonstrated to be effi-

TABLE 21-2

Diagnostic Tests Recommended by Consensus for Evaluation of Patients with Newly Diagnosed Dementia[22,23]

	NIH Consensus Development Conference Statement[22]		*Canadian Consensus Conference Statement*[23]	
	Recommended for All Patients	**Recommended for Selected Patients**	**Recommended for All Patients**	**Recommended for Selected Patients**
First Test				
Careful history physical and mental status examination	x		x	
Second Test (laboratory)				
Thyroid function tests	x		x	
Complete blood count	x		x	
Screening metabolic panel	x			
Calcium, glucose			x	
B_{12}, folate	x			x
Syphilis serology	x			x
HIV antibodies		x		x
Urinalysis	x			x
Electrocardiogram	x			x
Chest x-ray	x			x
CT scan[a]		x		x
Drug levels		x		x
Electro-encephalogram		x		x
Others[b]		x		x

[a] NIH recommends neuroimaging in "presence of history suggestive of a mass or focal neurologic signs, or in dementia of brief duration." The Canadian conference notes that the following suggests referral for neuroimaging: age less than 60 years, anticoagulants or bleeding disorder, recent head trauma, history of carcinoma that metastasizes to brain, unexplained neurologic symptoms (new onset headache, seizures), rapid decline, short duration (<2 years), history of incontinence and gait disturbance early in the course, localizing signs, gait ataxia.

[b] Both groups advocate careful approach to differential diagnosis with use of other diagnostic tests (lumbar puncture, etc.) based on limited selective indications rather than simply routine use. Neither group endorses any formal mental status or functional status rating scales but both note that assessment of both was important in the evaluation of demented patients. Both groups emphasized the need for ongoing assessment after diagnosis.

cacious. These guidelines are formulated to assist physicians in using diagnostic tests effectively and were designed to help produce more standardized and cost-effective practice patterns.

New tests pose a particular challenge to practicing physicians, since most clinicians will not have experienced new tests in a training situation. The eight guides[8] described in Table 21-1, earlier in this chapter, should be helpful to clinicians in determining the extent to which a test's value has been demonstrated and will thus likely be of value for patients. In addition, given the vastness of the medical literature, groups like the Clinical Efficacy Assessment Project (CEAP) of the American College of Physicians[21] have commissioned clinical reviews of carefully peer-reviewed statements of clinical efficacy to help clinicians determine those clinical instances when a new test—for example, MRI of the brain and spine[24]—will be valuable. The most useful reviews are likely to be those which use principles of clinical epidemiology and so-called rules of evidence to determine value rather than those which rely solely on expert opinion or the enthusiastic reports of a test's developer.

REFERENCES

1. Hiatt HH: Protecting the medical commons: Who is responsible? *N Engl J Med* 293:235, 1975.
2. Maloney TW, Rogers DE: Medical technology: A different view of the contentious debate over tests. *N Engl J Med* 301:1413, 1979.
3. Larson EB: Ignorance is not bliss: Knowledge, information and the diagnostic technology problem. *Am J Roentgenol* 145:1124, 1985.
4. Casscells W et al: Interpretation by physicians of clinical laboratory results. *N Engl J Med* 299:999, 1979.
5. Griner PF et al: Selection and interpretation of diagnostic tests. *Ann Intern Med* 94:557, 1981.
6. Sackett DL et al: *Clinical Epidemiology: A Basic Science for Clinical Medicine,* 2d ed. Boston, Little, Brown, 1991, pp 3–18.
7. Elstein AS et al: *Medical Problem Solving: An Analysis of Clinical Reasoning*. Cambridge, MA, Harvard University Press, 1978.
8. Sackett DL et al: *Clinical Epidemiology: A Basic Science for Clinical Medicine,* 2d ed. Boston, Little Brown, 1991, pp 41–68.
9. Sackett DL et al: *Clinical Epidemiology: A Basic Science for Clinical Medicine,* 2d ed. Boston, Little, Brown, 1991, p 52.
10. Beck JC et al: Dementia in the elderly: The silent epidemic. *Ann Intern Med* 97:231, 1982.
11. Larson EB et al: Dementia in elderly out patients: A prospective study. *Ann Intern Med* 100:417, 1984.
12. Galen RS, Gambino ST: *Beyond Normality: The Predictive Value and Efficiency of Medical Diagnosis.* New York, Wiley, 1975.
13. Yarby MS et al: A new method for measuring brain atrophy: The effect of aging in its application to diagnosing dementia. *Neurology* 35:1316, 1985.
14. McCormick WC, Larson EB: Dementia, in Panzer RJ, Black ER, Griner PF (eds): *Diagnostic Strategies in Common Medical Problems.* Philadelphia, American College of Physicians, 1992, pp 499–509.
15. Evans RW: Health care technology and the inevitability of resource allocations and rationing decisions. *JAMA* 249:2208, 1983.
16. Deyo RA et al: Reducing roentgenography use: Can patient expectations be altered? *Ann Intern Med* 147:141, 1987.
17. Fletcher RN et al: *Clinical Epidemiology—The Essentials.* Baltimore, Williams & Wilkins, 1982, pp 41–58.
18. Watson RA, Tang DB: The predictive value of prostatic acid phosphatase as a screening test for prostate cancer. *N Engl J Med* 303:497, 1980.
19. Sackett DL et al: *Clinical Epidemiology: A Basic Science for Clinical Medicine,* 2d ed. Boston, Little, Brown, 1991, pp 119–139.
20. Institute of Medicine: *Assessing Medical Technologies.* Washington, DC, National Academy Press, 1985, pp 73–79.
21. Kent DL, Larson EB: Disease, level of impact and quality of research methods. *Invest Radiol* 27:245, 1992.
22. NIH Consensus Development Conference Statement, vol 6, no 11, July 6–8, 1987: Differential diagnosis of dementia. *Alz Dis Assoc Dis* 2:4, 1988.
23. Canadian Consensus Conference on the Assessment of Dementia. Toronto, Canadian Printing Office, 1991.
24. Kent DL, Larson EB: Magnetic resonance imaging of the brain and spine: Is clinical efficacy established after the first decade? *Ann Intern Med* 108:402, 1988.

Chapter 22

ACUTE HOSPITAL CARE FOR FRAIL OLDER PATIENTS

Marsha Duke Fretwell

The best overall approach to acute hospital care for older adults is to emphasize preventive health and early detection of illness in order to minimize the need for hospitalization. However, older patients enter acute care hospitals more frequently, stay longer, and experience more adverse consequences than younger patients. Subsequently, they are discharged more frequently to another health care facility.[1]

This chapter will focus on the experience of frail older patients in the acute care hospital. Interindividual variation among older patients prevents us from using any single marker, such as age, diagnosis, or functional disability, as an accurate predictor of biologic or physiologic frailty.[2] For this discussion, *frailty* in an individual will be defined as an inherent vulnerability to challenge from the environment. It would most likely be seen in the oldest patients or in those "younger" old patients who have a combination of diseases or functional impairments that reduce their capacity to adapt to the stress of acute illness and its treatment in the hospital. Following a review of the factors in the patient and in the hospital environment that appear to influence the outcomes of acute medical care, a description of the results of this interaction between frail older patients and the environment is presented. The chapter concludes with a discussion of a prospective approach to acute hospital care that promotes optimal management of serious illness in frail older patients.

DESCRIPTION OF THE FRAIL PATIENT

The most important demographic change that will influence the frequency of utilization of and the risk associated with acute hospital care is the rapidly increasing proportion of the older population that is very old, i.e., over the age of 85.[3] This group, on average, has a larger burden of chronic illness and functional disability. It is important to note, however, that even though a portion of these patients may not have any clinical or subclinical organ disease or any abnormalities in physiologic parameters under resting circumstances, these very old individuals may nevertheless deteriorate under circumstances of stress.[4] The stress of illness in an individual patient usually manifests itself first, and most prominently, in the organ of that patient with the least functional reserve—often, the brain. Thus, the very old patient who has been functioning well in the community may come into the hospital with pneumonia and suddenly appear extremely agitated and confused.

The additive effect of extreme age and such age-associated conditions as dementia, hip fracture, cerebrovascular accidents, arthritis, and visual disorders on a person's overall ability to withstand environmental challenge has not been clarified, but is probably significant. Additionally, a larger proportion of this group's burden of disease and functional impairment may be irreversible or only very slowly reversible by current therapy. Interindividual variation creates uncertainty in decision making. Generalizations about treatment are unproductive and may even be counterproductive, as in the case in which the presence of one condition greatly influences treatment of another. If we are to understand and achieve optimal outcomes in these frail individuals, we must identify the entire spectrum of their multiple organ diseases. If we do not do so, any subsequent diagnostic or therapeutic maneuver may very likely bring with it unexpected adverse effects.

This shift in focus from attempting to pinpoint a single disease underlying the acute illness to a study of the interaction between the acute illness and the individual's entire burden of disease and disability is one of the major changes that our aging population has brought to the clinical and research agenda of medicine. We now see that the outcome of any acute illness is more dependent upon various attributes of the host, positive or negative, than the absolute virulence of the infecting organism or the progressive nature of the acute disease. Added to this complexity is the fact that in older patients acute illnesses may first present in a vague and nonspecific manner, perhaps only by a functional decline in an unrelated organ system.[5] This may lead, especially in cognitively impaired patients, to a missed or late diagnosis, delayed referral for treatment, and subsequent higher than average severity of illness on presentation to the acute care hospital.[6]

Cohort studies examining both admission and outcome information about older patients show that the patient's functional status at admission, the burden of comorbid conditions, and the estimate of the severity of the presenting illness most accurately predict the outcome from a particular episode of illness.[7–9] Subgroup analysis of those over 70 years old demonstrated that those with cognitive impairment were older, sicker, and less physiologically stable than the cognitively "intact." These individuals experienced approximately three times the hospital morbidity and mortality of those who were cognitively intact.[6] Another study showed that approximately 70 percent of those over 75 years were cognitively impaired at admission, suggesting that this variable alone may select the most vulnerable individuals.[9] Finally, it appears that entering the hospital from a nursing home is, in most cases, associated with many of the attributes predicting a poor outcome in the acute hospital.[8]

DESCRIPTION OF THE TREATMENT AND ENVIRONMENT

Hospital care, with its increased use of medications, invasive catheters and lines, diagnostic tests, and nosocomial infections, may be best thought of as a significant source of physiologic stress for the older patient. Studies examining the complications of medical and surgical treatments in the acute hospital have shown older patients to be at increased risk for clinical iatrogenesis.[10–12] One study compared patients who were over 65 years of age with those who were not yet 65 on both medical and surgical wards of a VA hospital.[10] The complication rate for the older group was 45 percent versus 29 percent for the younger group. The most common cause of complications was drugs, but compared with younger patients, older patients also had more infections and trauma in addition to more adverse drug reactions. The rate of procedure-related complications was the same in both old and young. Psychiatric decompensation occurred in nearly 20 percent of the older and in none of the younger patients, suggesting that changes in the location of care and in the providers of that care as well as changes in routine and loss of familiar daily schedules all add up to a major source of psychological stress for older patients in the acute hospital. An earlier study on the medical service of a teaching hospital documented a clinical iatrogenesis rate of 36 percent and noted the associated factors to be increased age, poor condition, increased numbers of drugs, admission from an institution, and increased length of stay.[12]

Another study of general medical patients for evidence of complications that may be considered a side effect of hospitalization itself (i.e., separate from side effects of diagnosis or treatment) suggests that as many as 40.5 percent of persons over the age of 70 years experience loss of mental and physical function unrelated to their admitting diagnosis.[13] This is in contrast to 8.5 percent of patients under 70 years. The current disease-oriented model of acute medical care promotes a sequential approach to diagnosis and treatment which generally ignores the practices of restorative care until after the patient is discharged from the hospital. This approach, in combination with the high rate of delirium and psychological decompensation, can result in excessive bed rest, with accompanying loss of mobility, tendency to fall, and increased confusion, incontinence, and aphagia.[13,14]

As a result, additional medical interventions are then focused upon these symptoms. These interventions often include physical restraints, psychotropic medications, nasogastric tube or hand feedings, and Foley catheters. Finally, complications of these interventions may lead to delirium, agitation, constipation, nosocomial urinary tract infection, aspiration pneumonia, bacteremia, and pressure sores. Figure 22-1 illustrates the hypothesized pathway of development of these functional complications of hospitalization.[13]

Another consideration in the management of acutely ill older patients is the impact of depressive symptoms that come *after* the illness. Studies evaluating older patients entering medical rehabilitation units have documented that 50 to 80 percent of these previsously independent patients suffer from such depression.[15,16] These older patients share several characteristics which contributed to a loss of their functional independence: severe illnesses, illnesses of long duration with poor prognosis, chronic pain, and prolonged bed rest. In these studies, patients whose mood improved also improved in physical and mental function, whereas 75 percent of those whose mood did not improve failed to make any headway in regaining function.

Thus, the common experience of frail older patients in the acute care hospital has several dimensions, each of which may have an adverse impact on the overall outcome of the illness. The very old patient may arrive at the hospital at a later and more severe stage of the illness, may have other chronic conditions that complicate diagnosis and treatment of the presenting illness, may be unable to adapt to a new environment, and may experience additional new problems in that setting which are related to the treatment of the original or presenting illness. The combination of unpredictable physiolgic and psychosocial stressors over which a frail patient has little or no control provides a setting conducive to the development of emotional and cognitive decompensations that further impair recovery from acute illness. The emerging literature on the direct effect of psychosocial factors on physiologic processes in humans pro-

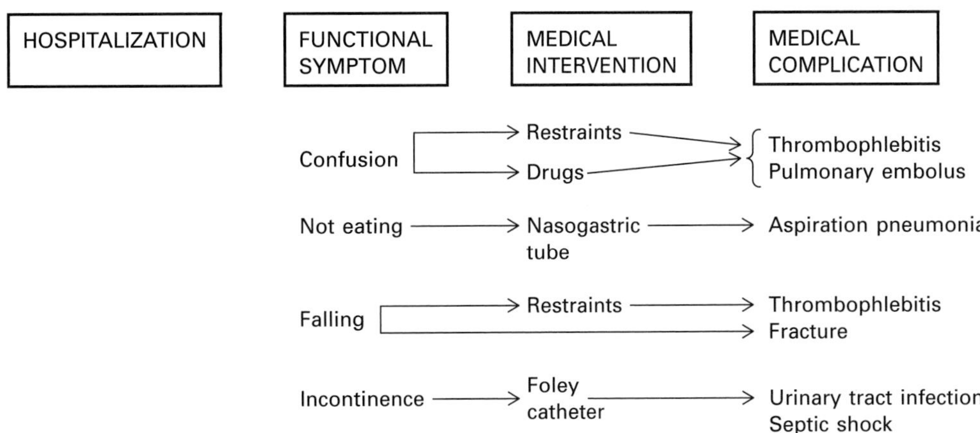

FIGURE 22-1

Hypothesized pathway of development of complications of hospitalization. *(From Gillick et al.[13] Printed in Great Britain. All rights reserved. Reprinted by permission of the author.)*

vides further support for this conceptual framework, especially in relation to issues of immunologic function, resistance to infection, and disease outcome.[17]

THE CASCADE OF ILLNESS AND FUNCTIONAL DECLINE: THE INTERACTION OF THE FRAIL OLDER PERSON AND THE STRESS OF ACUTE HOSPITAL CARE

The experience of some frail older patients in the acute care hospital might best be thought of as a *cascade,* a word used to describe a process that, once started, proceeds stepwise to its full, seemingly inevitable, conclusion. Often, despite effective treatment of their acute medical illnesses, these individuals decline in functional abilities, developing problems associated with confusion, immobility, incontinence, and malnutrition. Figure 22-2 shows the hypothetical hospital course of a frail older patient. It illustrates how medications that have the capacity to impair mental function can interact with the patient's anxiety at having been relocated in a strange, new, and admittedly bewildering environment to set off a complex series of events leading to acute loss of mental and physical function.[18] Additional medical and nursing interventions (Foley catheters, physical restraints, feeding tubes, broad-spectrum antibiotics, anticoagulants, and antipsychotic drugs) are required, adding to the numbers of medications and to the potential for clinical and functional iatrogenesis. It is important to note that this diagram does not include the impact of any specific diagnostic tests or therapies that would be utilized for management of the initial illness. Nor does this example address the influence of the physician's anxiety, which, as it interacts with the concerns of the patient or the family, may be an important catalyst for continuing the cascade of diagnosis, treatment, and functional decline.[19]

In this model, an elderly person, perhaps with a mild cognitive deficit, can become confused, immobile, and incontinent within a few days after admission. As this process continues, it becomes increasingly difficult to determine cause and effect and to intervene appropriately. Each of these succeeding complications, i.e., delirium, urinary tract infection, constipation, aspiration pneumonia, and malnutrition, carries with it additional physiologic and psychological stress. Never recovering completely from one complication, the patient has a diminished likelihood of recovering from successive complications.

A frequent outcome of this cascade, even if the patient becomes physiologically stable, is a complex of symptoms including anorexia, lack of motivation, difficulty sleeping, and a feeling of depletion and hopelessness. Although this "failure to thrive" syndrome is often referred to as a "depression" because of this cluster of somatic or vegetative symptoms, diagnosis and treatment may be missed because the patient denies any feelings of depression or because the patient's behavior is felt to be an appropriate response to the situation of the illness.[21] In the cascade of illness and functional decline, isolated vegetative symptoms at the end of acute hospitalization may best be understood as both a causal factor, accelerating the decline of function, and, if not treated, a final outcome of the hospitalization. In other words, the functional decline is the result of this vegetative state; it is the response of a physiologically frail individual to the recurrent and unpredictable stress of treatment.[18]

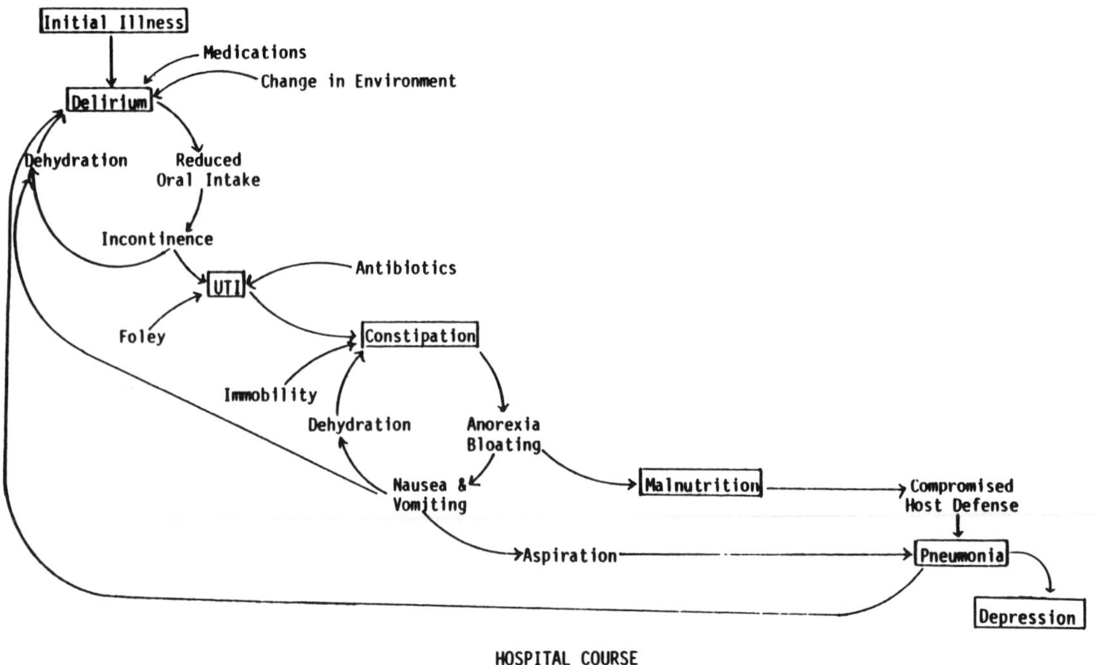

FIGURE 22-2
Cascade of illness and functional decline.

IMPROVING THE QUALITY OF ACUTE HOSPITAL CARE

There are many factors that may interact in a complex fashion in an older person's life to influence health outcomes and our efforts to provide excellent hospital care. These include physiological, cognitive, emotional, physical, social, and environmental factors. This multiplicity of factors influencing health outcomes requires that we shift the focus of our admitting histories and physical examinations to routinely include more comprehensive information about the older patient's cognitive, emotional, and physical function. This complex mixture of factors increases interindividual variation among older individuals of a given chronological age and necessitates that we tailor each older person's care plan to address specific limitations of their physical and cognitive function as well as their personal preference for treatments.

With aging, individuals may have reduced capacity to respond effectively to environmental stress. This suggests the importance of increased emphasis on early detection of acute illness and the delivery of medical treatments in the least stressful site of care. For those elderly individuals who have experienced irreversible declines in functional capacity, a shift in our definition of excellent or quality hospital care may be most appropriate: from survival at all costs to a focus on improving the patient's functional outcomes.[22]

Comprehensive Geriatric Assessment

Comprehensive geriatric assessment (CGA) is a systematic approach to the collection of patient data that allows evaluation of the frail older patient's health status and functional impairments in multiple areas or domains (see Chap. 17). Based on an evaluation of consultative geriatric assessment in 236 acutely ill patients over the age of 75 years,[23] nine major domains or areas of concern have emerged as essential in comprehensive geriatric assessment (see Table 22-1). A careful review of these domains or areas of concern provides the physician with full knowledge of coexisting medical problems, complete medication lists, nutritional status, cognitive and emotional function, and mobility and continence problems. Once informed,

TABLE 22-1

Health Status Domains or Areas of Concern

Diagnoses
Medications
Nutrition
Continence
Defecation
Cognition
Emotion
Mobility
Cooperation with care plan

the physician may use the information to (1) prospectively identify patients at high risk for a poor outcome during hospitalization, (2) assist in organizing the more complex problem list of the frail older patient, and (3) target areas that are of particular concern to the individual patient.

In the inpatient setting, CGA can be carried out in specialized geriatric assessment units. Controlled trials have demonstrated the effectiveness of geriatric assessment units in the care of selected groups of patients at the end of acute hospitalization. Care in such units involves the creation of individualized treatment plans that not only improve functional outcomes but also reduce placement in nursing homes, improve patient survival, and reduce overall costs of care (also see Chap. 17).[24] Additionally, one study comparing lengths of stay in a group of hospitalized frail older patients who were cared for by either general internists or a group of geriatricians showed a statistically significant reduction of hospital days in the group cared for by the latter group of doctors.[25] Despite an older age in this group managed by the geriatricians, there was no increase in readmission rates or in mortality after the hospital stay. Presumably an understanding of the principles of geriatric care may therefore allow physicians to provide care for a select group of older patients that involves lower costs without a reduction in the quality of patient outcomes.

Respecting the Patient's Preferences for Treatment

In December 1991, the Patient Self-Determination Act was implemented in acute care hospitals and other institutions reimbursed by Medicare, Medicaid, or both. This law was designed to increase patient involvement in decisions regarding life-sustaining treatment. Its purpose is to help implement a right that has been universally recognized: the right to refuse any and all medical interventions, even life-sustaining interventions. The act requires that the hospital, in some fashion, ask all new patients whether they have prepared an advanced directive and include this information in the patient's chart.[26] Unfortunately, if a person has not completed an advanced directive, the act does not require that a directive be actually initiated during that hospitalization.

There are two issues critical to the discussion of medical directives in frail older patients: the timing of the discussion and the breadth of areas of preference to be explored. First, the older and more frail the patient is on admission to the acute care hospital, the more likely the patient will have an accompanying delirium or acute confusional state and therefore be incapable of stating preferences for treatment. Second, because of the intimate interaction between social and medical problems in frail older patients, identifying the personal preferences for treatment must go beyond the completion of advanced medical directives to include other preferences such as choice of caretaker, site of residence, and site of treatment of acute illness. Thus, in frail older patients, the discussion of preferences for treatment should be both prospective, i.e., before they become acutely ill, and relevant to their particular concerns, both medical and social.

Prevention of Functional Decline Associated with the Treatment of Illness in the Acute Care Hospital

The health status domains or areas of concern in Table 22-1 offer a comprehensive and convenient checklist by which the physician can monitor the complex events of the patient's hospital stay and thereby prevent unnecessary functional decline. Because much of the therapy directed at preservation of function falls within the realm of excellent nursing care, a close collaborative relationship must be established between the physician, the nurse, and the patient's family. A first step is to review with the nurse the areas of particular concern for each individual patient. By evaluating the older patient's physical and cognitive vulnerabilities and strengths before initiation of therapy, the nurse can help institute a care plan that allows the patient maximal levels of self-care, personal control, and mobility and thereby optimize the outcome of the medical therapy in progress. Making the nursing staff aware of baseline and admission cognitive and emotional status allows them to act as competent early detectors of delirium and other adverse effects of medications. Knowledge of continence and bowel status before hospitalization allows them to design bladder and bowel protocols that are individualized to the patient's needs.

Diagnosis

It is important to clarify the specific medical goals of acute hospitalization for the individual patient. Because the outcome of any illness is dependent upon various attributes of the patient, it is important to have a complete listing of all medical and surgical diagnoses and some estimate of their severity, their reversibility, and their impact on the patient's physical, cognitive, and emotional function. This information can be used to prioritize medical therapies (reversible problems that significantly influence patient function should be addressed first) and to help the patient and family establish appropriate guidelines for the use of extraordinary means during this particular episode of illness.

Medications

All medications including over-the-counter drugs should be listed, the list should be kept up to date, and the list reviewed to ensure that patients are actually taking the drugs listed. Blood levels of medications should be obtained as appropriate. If acute illness has altered the patient's renal function, dosages of previously prescribed medications as well as those prescribed in the hospital should be adjusted. If the patient is taking more than two or three medications that require hepatic metabolism, drug interactions are likely and blood levels should be monitored, particularly if new medications are added.

Before starting any new medication, its impact on the patient's current physical (this includes nutrition, bladder and bowel function, and mobility), cognitive, and emotional function should be considered. If a patient experiences decline in any of these functions, medications initiated during the hospitalization and/or their interaction with existing medications should be suspected. Functional decline caused by medications should be both preventable and reversible.

Narcotics should be avoided in frail older patients, especially those with cognitive impairments. Adequate pain control can often be achieved with acetaminophen administered orally or rectally around the clock. Blood levels of acetaminophen can be obtained.

Nutrition

The stress of acute illness and the use of glucose as the primary source of nutrition during the early stages of hospital care for patients who are not eating will result in nitrogen wasting and can contribute to protein malnutrition. Monitoring of serum albumin levels, provision of vitamin supplements as needed, and attention to calorie intake can reduce this risk. Depression, medications that influence appetite and bowel function, and the presence of constipation or frank impaction can all contribute to reduced oral intake by older patients. Prospective evaluation and treatment of these common conditions early during the hospitalization can help avoid this unnecessary complication.

Fluid therapy must also be adjusted to account for the reduction in cardiac output and the increase in antidiuretic hormone experienced by many frail older patients in the acute care hospital. Gradual replacement of fluid deficit with careful monitoring for the signs of fluid overload helps prevent treatment-related congestive heart failure.

Continence

Many frail older patients are best described as *compensated incontinent* and any disruption of their carefully maintained compensation strategies (e.g., an acute illness, hospitalization with immobilization in a strange bed in a strange place, introduction of new medications, etc.) may precipitate a new onset of urinary incontinence. Maintenance of the patient's cognitive function and mobility are probably the most important elements of preventing urinary incontinence. Reducing the flow of IV fluids during the night when most older patients are immobilized in bed, careful evaluation for fecal impaction, and avoidance of anticholinergic medications may also help prevent incontinence. If the patient has been continent prior to hospitalization, reassurance that the incontinence is a temporary event can boost morale considerably.

Defecation

Because of chronic illnesses, ongoing medications, and immobility, many older patients are already constipated and have impending or existing fecal impaction on admission to the hospital. If they are very old or cognitively impaired, patients may be unable to give accurate histories or register complaints, and this state may not be addressed until the fourth or fifth day of hospitalization. This situation can lead to urinary incontinence and refusal of food by the patient. Therefore, bowel function should be investigated early during hospitalization and followed carefully to avoid these complications.

Cognition

The onset of delirium in a frail older patient in the acute care hospital is predictive of a higher hospital mortality and rate of discharge to a nursing home.[27] Patients with a chronic cognitive disorder are at highest risk for developing a delirium in the acute care hospital. Other factors consistently associated with delirium in the acute care hospital include abnormal (usually low) serum sodium levels, fever or hypothermia, the use of psychoactive medications, azotemia, and severe medical illness.

Careful attention to maintaining fluid and electrolyte balance, minimization of psychoactive medications, and the use of acetaminophen around the clock for management of fevers and pain may reduce the incidence of delirium in susceptible individuals. Any environmental maneuvers that reduce stress (family members present during the night, etc.) may also be effective.

Delirium is sometimes difficult to diagnose in frail older patients because they may become somnolent or develop psychomotor retardation rather than agitation. Often, it is a new onset of incontinence, the refusal of food, or increased sleeping that herald the onset of delirium. Once delirium is detected and inciting stimuli are removed, recovery of cognitive function may have a slow course, sometimes requiring 5 to 7 days or more. If the patient becomes agitated and disruptive and cannot be managed nonpharmacologically, haloperidol is an effective short-term therapy. A loading dose of 2 to 4 mg given orally in 1–2-mg doses every 2 hours is usually sufficient and should not be exceeded in the acutely ill older patient. The following day the dose can be reduced to 1 mg twice a day; thereafter it can be further tapered by 0.5 mg/day. Patients rarely need to be discharged on haloperidol.

Emotion

The prevalence of depression or depressive symptoms in older hospitalized patients ranges between 20 and 60 percent.[28,29] The association of depression with prolonged functional dependency during the recovery from severe medical illness makes the early detection and treatment of depressive symptoms critical. Treatment with low-dose tricyclic antidepressants can be effective. For patients who are primarily expressing fatigue, desipramine, 20 to 50 mg/day, is effective. For patients experiencing significant anxiety or agitation, nortriptyline, 20 to 50 mg/day, is more useful and less disruptive to cognitive function than the benzodiazepines.

Mobility

The loss of physical mobility in the acute care environment is usually multifactorial. Patients at highest risk are those with acute and chronic cognitive impairments and those with depression. Anxiety or fear of falling in the unknown environment of the hospital may seriously inhibit ambulatory function. Careful review of the patient's history and physical examination and medications may also reveal the cause of the new-onset immobility. If no physical diagnoses are discovered, the depression should be treated and physical therapy engaged to remobilize the patient, as expeditiously as possible.

Cooperation with Care Plan

Frail older patients who become uncooperative with the treatment care plan may be experiencing a delirium or a depression in the setting of their acute medical illness. Attention to preserving each patient's cognitive and emotional function during the treatment of acute medical illness is an essential first step toward preventing unnecessary functional decline.

SUMMARY

This chapter has outlined an approach to the hospital care of frail older patients that focuses on the maintenance and restoration of the individual's mental and physical function as one of the critical measures of the overall quality of the care received. The interrelationships between the patient's physiologic and functional status at admission, events in the hospital, and the discharge functional outcomes and cost merit further description and analysis. The argument is made that additional attention should and can be directed toward identifying and reducing the recurrent and unpredictable challenges of the environment and modalities of treatment for each of these frail individuals in the acute care hospital. In this way, the quality of the experience and the outcomes of the illnesses can be improved.

REFERENCES

1. Garnick DW, Short T: Utilization of hospital inpatient services by elderly Americans, in *Hospital Studies Program.* DHHS (PHS)85-3351, June 1985, p 3.
2. Costa PT, McCrae RR: Concepts of functional or biological age: A critical review, in Andres R et al (eds): *Principles of Geriatric Medicine.* New York, McGraw-Hill, 1985, p. 30.
3. Davis K: Aging and the health care system: Economics and structural issues in the aging society. *J Am Acad Arts Sci* Winter 1986, p 229.
4. Williams TF: The future of aging. John Stanley Soulter Lecture. *Arch Phys Med Rehabil* 68:335, 1987.
5. Gilcrist BA, Rowe JW: The biology of aging, in Rowe JW, Besdine RW (eds): *Health and Disease in Old Age.* Boston, Little, Brown, 1982, p. 15.
6. Fields SD et al: Cognitive impairment: Can it predict the course of hospitalized patients? *J Am Geriatr Soc* 34:579, 1986.
7. Charlson ME et al: Morbidity during hospitalization: Can we predict it? *J Chron Dis* 40:705, 1987.
8. Pompei P et al: Clinical assessments as predictors of one year survival after hospitalization: Implications for prognostic stratification. *J Clin Epidemiol* 41:275, 1988.
9. Narain P et al: Predictors of immediate and 6-month outcomes in hospitalized elderly patients: The importance of functional status. *J Am Geriatr Soc* 36:775, 1988.
10. Jahnigen D et al: Iatrogenic disease in hospitalized elderly veterans. *J Am Geriatr Soc* 30:387, 1982.
11. Barry PP: Iatrogenic disorders in the elderly: Preventive techniques. *Geriatrics* 41:42, 1986.
12. Steele K: Iatrogenic disease on a medical service. *J Am Geriatr Soc* 32:445, 1984.
13. Gillick MR et al: Adverse consequences of hospitalization in the elderly. *Soc Sci Med* 16:1033, 1982.
14. Miller MB: Iatrogenic and nurisgenic effects of prolonged immobilization of the ill aged. *J Am Geriatr Soc* 23:360, 1975.
15. Lakshmanan M et al: Effective low dose tricyclic antidepressant treatment for depressed geriatric rehabilitation patients: A double-blind study. *J Am Geriatr Soc* 34:421, 1986.
16. Harris RE et al: Severe illness in older patients: The association between depressive disorders and functional dependency during the recovery phase. *J Am Geriatr Soc* 36(10):890, 1988.
17. Rowe JW, Kahn RL: Human aging: Usual and successful. *Science* 237:143, 1987.
18. Fretwell MD: Management in the acute care setting, in Kelley WN (ed): *Textbook of Internal Medicine.* Philadelphia, Lippincott, 1988, p 2619.

19. Mold JW, Stein HF: Sounding board: The cascade effect in the clinical care of patients. *N Engl J Med* February 20:512, 1986.
20. Palmer RM: "Failure to thrive" in the elderly: Diagnosis and Management. *Geriatrics* 45:47, 1990.
21. Fogel B, Fretwell MD: Reclassification of depression in the elderly. *J Am Geriatr Soc* 33:446, 1985.
22. Fretwell MF: The frail elderly: Creating standards of care, in B. Spilker (ed): *Quality of Life Assessments in Clinical Trials.* Raven, New York, 1990.
23. Fretwell MD et al: The Senior Care Study: A controlled trial of a consultation/unit-based geriatric assessment program in acute care. *J Am Geriatr Soc* 38:1073, 1990.
24. Rubenstein L: Effectiveness of a geriatric evaluation unit. *N Engl J Med* 311:26, 1984.
25. Pawlson LG: Hospital length of stay of frail elderly patients. *J Am Geriatr Soc* 36:202, 1988.
26. Greco PJ et al: The patient self-determination act and the future of advanced directives. *Ann Intern Med* 115:639, 1991.
27. Francis J et al: A prospective study of delirium in hospitalized elderly. *JAMA* 263:1097, 1990.
28. Kitchell MA et al: Screening for depression in hospitalized medical patients. *J Am Geriatr Soc* 30:179, 1982.
29. Magni G et al: Depression in geriatric and adult medical inpatients. *J Clin Psychol* 41:337, 1985.

Chapter 23

CONTEMPORARY GERIATRIC NURSING

Terry T. Fulmer and Mathy D. Mezey

OVERVIEW

The history of geriatric nursing in the United States is notable for the speed with which it has responded to the burgeoning demands of the elderly and their families. Burnside divides the evolution of geriatric nursing into two eras: prior to 1940 and 1940 to the present.[1] The paucity of historical information about all health professionals' interest in care of the elderly prior to 1940 reflects the relatively short life span of most Americans in the early part of the twentieth century. Geriatric nursing during the early part of this century means primarily nursing practice in the early almshouses.[2]

The American Nurses Association (ANA) convened its first focus group on gerontological nursing in 1962; the first gerontological practice group convened in 1966. In 1968, the Geriatric Division of the ANA published the first geriatric nursing standards, followed shortly by ANA certification of the first gerontological nurses. This flurry of activity coincides with the attention generated by Titles 18 and 19 of the Social Security Act, which established Medicare and Medicaid.

The first gerontological master's program in nursing was established at Duke University in 1966 under the direction of Virginia Stone.[1] Since then, the increased number of elderly, the changing face of American health care, and substantial shifts in health policy and funding have helped to shape geriatric nursing education, research, and practice. This chapter provides an in-depth look at the preparation of nurses to care for the elderly, the focus of geriatric nursing research, and the influence of geriatric nurses on the care provided elderly Americans. Although the ANA emphasizes the term *gerontological nursing* for this area of special expertise and knowledge, the term *geriatric nursing* is equivalent and will be used interchangeably in this chapter.

EDUCATIONAL PREPARATION FOR GERIATRIC NURSING

Basic Preparation of Nurses

Associate degree, diploma, and baccalaureate programs offer nurses basic preparation to function as generalists in ambulatory settings, home care, hospitals, and nursing homes. Irrespective of preparation, all new nurses sit for the same licensure examination to become registered nurses (RNs). Hospital-based diploma programs vary from 2 to 3 years in length. Associate degree programs require 2 years of study in junior colleges or 4-year universities. Baccalaureate programs, which in 1991 graduated over 27 percent of all new nurses, require 4 years of study in a college or university.

The patterns of geriatric nursing education and the preparation, focus, and work of geriatric nurses are shown in Tables 23-1 and 23-2. Traditionally, basic nursing programs have included very little geriatric nursing content. Some have rotations in nursing homes, where students learn basic nursing skills: bathing, feeding, and positioning patients. In hospital rotations, students care primarily for elderly patients. Unfortunately, because most faculty lack preparation in geriatric nursing, they focus on patients' general nursing and medical conditions rather than aspects of care—for example, function and cognition—which are the hallmark of geriatric practice.

More recently, however, several initiatives have supported the expansion of geriatric content in nursing programs. The Kellogg Foundation funded a national initiative, the Community College–Nursing Home Partnership, to prepare nursing students in associate degree programs to work in nursing homes.[3] The six schools that participated in this project developed curriculum models which have been widely disseminated and have published competen-

TABLE 23-1

Preparation, Focus, and Work of Gerontological Nurses

License	Length of Preparation	Focus of Preparation	Primary Work Setting	Primary and Secondary Roles
Licensed practical nurse	12 months	Technical basic skills	Nursing home, MD's office, hospital	Technical (basic task nursing) work under supervision of RN
Registered nurse (ADN)	2 years	Entry level for basic technical nursing care	Hospital, nursing home, MD's office, home care	Direct patient care
Diploma	3 years	Entry level for basic care, technical and professional	Hospital, nursing home, MD's office, home care	Direct patient care
Baccalaureate (BSN, BS)	4 years	Entry level for professional nursing	Hospital, public health, home care, private practice	Direct patient care, supervisory position
Generic master's (MSN)	2–3 years			
Nursing doctorate (ND)	3 years			
Master's (MS, MA, MN, MSN)	1–2 years	Advanced practice clinical specialist, nurse practitioner	Hospital, private practice, education, community-based agency	Expert clinical practice Specialty practice
Doctorate (PhD, DNSc)	3–7 years	Research, teaching, add to body of knowledge	School of nursing, federal/state agency	Teaching, research, policy, administration, clinical practice (independent or joint)

SOURCE: Johnson MA, Connelly JR: *Nursing and Gerontology: Status Report.* Washington, DC, Association for Gerontology in Higher Education Advisory Committee on Nursing and Gerontology, 1990. Reproduced by permission.

TABLE 23-2

Patterns of Gerontological Nursing Education

	Undergraduate	Master's	Doctorate
Degree	ADN, diploma, BS, BA, BSN, generic master's, ND	MS, MN, MSN, MA	PhD, DNSc
Level	Entry level	Postbaccalaureate Clinical specialization	Post-master's
Focus	Generalist, beginning practitioner, "safe" practitioner	Functional role and leadership	Research, add to body of nursing knowledge or specialization
Method of entry	Licensure as RN	Graduation and/or advanced licensure certification (optional)	Graduation
Scope	Plan health care with elderly, use strengths of person, maximize capabilities, manage care	In-depth theory of aging Dynamics of aging Independent or collaborative practice Not setting-specific May be in two specialty areas: e.g., gerontology and administration	Public policy issues, clinical and theoretical research, independent or collaborative practice
Role	Registered nurse	GNP (clinician), GCNS, teacher, administrator	Researcher, nurse executive, educator, practitioner
Course work	Medical-surgical, pediatrics, obstetrics, community mental health	Cognate, core (all master's), clinical-specific, functional role	Cognate, core, original scholarship

SOURCE: Johnson MA, Connelly JR: *Nursing and Gerontology: Status Report.* Washington, DC, Association for Gerontology in Higher Education Advisory Committee on Nursing and Gerontology, 1990. Reproduced by permission.

cies in geriatric nursing for students in associate, bachelor's, and master's programs.

The impetus to increase geriatric content in baccalaureate programs has come from several sources. The Association for Gerontology in Higher Education has published recommendations related to outcomes and objectives for basic and advanced preparation in geriatric nursing and strategies for increasing geriatric content in nursing education.[4] The Teaching Nursing Home Program, a national initiative funded by the Robert Wood Johnson Foundation, encouraged 11 baccalaureate schools of nursing to increase geriatric content in their curricula and to create clinical teaching sites for students in 12 affiliated nursing homes.[5,6] The project results indicate that, under favorable circumstances, students can have positive learning experiences in nursing homes. Over the course of the project, approximately 600 undergraduate students and over 300 graduate students had clinical rotations in the nursing homes. Undergraduate geriatric nursing for-credit courses increased from 3 to 12; graduate courses doubled.[7]

The changing pool of applicants has also had a favorable effect on incorporation of geriatric content within schools of nursing. Increasingly, new applicants to nursing programs hold a second and at times a third nonnursing degree.[8] Fully 32 percent of students enrolled in baccalaureate programs in 1990 were over 25 years of age, with 15 percent over age 30. Many baccalaureate programs encourage these mature students and RN students to accelerate their study toward a master's degree in nursing (BSN/MSN combined programs or generic master's programs) or toward a nursing doctorate (ND), modeled after the JD and MD degrees. These students, many of whom have cared for elderly relatives, are sophisticated as to the changing demographics, enthusiastic about didactic geriatric content, and often seek out clinical experiences with elderly patients.

Initiatives to improve the geriatric preparation of the generalist nurse have been further supported by the American Nurses Association's (ANA) national certification process.[9] The ANA offers three levels of certification in gerontological nursing: gerontological nurse, geriatric nurse practitioner, and gerontological clinical nurse specialist. Certification as a gerontological nurse is open to all RNs irrespective of academic preparation. Some schools of nursing encourage interested undergraduate students to prepare for this certification on graduation. Nursing homes and hospitals wishing to upgrade nurses' geriatric skills offer courses to encourage nurses to become certified as gerontological nurses.

While the aforementioned activities are encouraging, geriatric nursing continues to lag behind other areas of interest in generic nursing programs. Few baccalaureate programs offer a required course in geriatric nursing. Even within the Teaching Nursing Home Program, only 3 of the 11 participating schools had a required undergraduate geriatric nursing course.[7] When geriatric content is integrated into traditional medical and surgical nursing courses, which is most often the case, the quality of the content is very dependent on the preparation of the faculty teaching the course. Preparation of geriatric nursing faculty continues to be of grave concern. In one study, close to 60 percent of students' clinical experience involved patients of age 65 and over, yet less than 25 percent of faculty reported any preparation in care of the elderly.[10]

Preparation for Advanced Clinical Practice

Professional nurses wishing to specialize for advanced clinical practice complete a master's program which involves from 1 to 2 years of full-time study. There are currently over 72,000 nurses with advanced clinical preparation. By the year 2000, the total supply is expected to reach 87,500, or twice the 1988 supply. Yet this number will fall far short of the estimated need for 259,000 nurses with advanced clinical skills.[11]

University master's programs produce two streams of graduates prepared to assume advanced clinical positions: nurse practitioners and clinical specialists. Geriatric nurse practitioners (GNPs), geriatric clinical specialists (GNCs), and geropsychiatric clinicians complete a formal educational program in care of the elderly and are certified for expanded practice by the American Nurses Association and/or state boards of nursing.[12]

The curriculum for most programs preparing nurses for advanced practice in geriatrics is based on the American Nurses Association's Standards and Scope of Gerontological Nursing Practice and the Standards of Practice for the Primary Health Care Nurse Practitioner and the Clinical Specialist. All programs teach physical, functional, and psychosocial assessment, physiology and pathophysiology, pharmacology, and recognition and management of physical and behavioral conditions associated with aging. Geriatric nurse practitioner and geriatric fellowship programs have been shown to teach similar content related to geriatric assessment.[13] While GNP programs are directed by nurse faculty, geriatricians, geriatric social workers, and other professionals participate in the presentation of content and supervision of students in clinical agencies.

In addition to didactic (classroom) content, all programs require clinical rotations. Clinical practicums vary as to number of required hours; anecdotal data suggest that most programs require between 12 and 16 h of practice per week.

Academic institutions are currently reassessing their preparation of nurses for advanced practice. Nurse practitioners have traditionally been prepared to provide a broad range of direct services to patients and families,[14–17] while clinical specialists are prepared to provide primarily consultation and education about discrete clinical problems (i.e., renal disease, cancer, ostomy care) to patients, families, and staff in hospitals.[18] Despite these distinctions, recent objective comparisons suggest striking similarities and very few areas of difference in both the preparation and function of nurse practitioners and clinical specialists, especially those in geriatric practice. With the exception of pharmacology, the preparation of GNPs closely resembles that of GNCs.[19] Geriatric nurse practitioners and GNCs often function interchangeably in hospitals, long-term care facilities, and home care. The Omnibus Reconciliation Act of 1991 recognizes both GNPs and GNCs as eligible for reimbursement under Medicare and Medicaid. In 1991, the ANA's Councils of Clinical Nurse Specialist and Primary Health Care Nurse Practitioners became one Council of Advanced Nursing Practice. Thus, in the foreseeable future, GNP and GNC preparation will in all likelihood merge into one program.

Geriatric nurse practitioners were introduced in the mid-seventies. In 1990, 28 academic programs prepared GNPs.[20] Both graduate and certificate programs average 1 year in length. In the 17 GNP programs funded by the Division of Nursing of the Public Health Service in 1987, the average age of students was 31.5 years; 75 percent of students had 4 or more years of professional nursing experience prior to admission. After graduation, approximately 40 percent were employed either by nursing homes or by physicians with practices in nursing homes. Thirty-five percent worked in facilities in the inner city and 20 percent in rural areas.

Preparation of GNPs and evaluation of their performance has received extensive support from the federal government and private foundations.[14,21] Since 1980, Congress has appropriated $1.3 million annually for the education of GNPs; the Department of Veterans Affairs has provided scholarships for candidates since 1982. Beginning in 1976, with funding from the Kellogg Foundation, the Mountain States Health Corporation trained, placed, and evaluated the effectiveness of 172 GNPs in over 200 nursing homes in 18 western states.[22–24]

In contrast to GNPs, less information is available about the preparation and number of geriatric clinical nurse specialists (GNCs) and geropsychiatric clinical nurse specialists. The Division of Nursing currently funds 11 GNC programs. Many GNCs, however, have been prepared in adult clinical specialist programs which have electives or clinical options for gerontological specialization. There are three programs specifically preparing geropsychiatric clinical specialists currently funded by the Division of Nursing, but other programs preparing psychiatric nurse specialists also offer courses in geropsychiatric nursing. Three hundred nurses report a specialization in geropsychiatric nursing according to the ANA membership data; but given the number of nurses who are nonmembers, it is difficult to know the final number.

The ANA offers national certification as either a GNP or a GNC.[9] There is no certification exam for the geropsychiatric clinical nurse specialist. Many states require certification by the ANA for recognition for advanced practice, including reimbursement. As of 1990, 1210 GNPs were certified by the ANA. The total number of practicing GNPs, however, exceeds those with certification by the ANA, since some have prepared as adult and family nurse practitioners and others practice in states which use criteria other than that of the ANA to establish practice eligibility. The ANA certification for geriatric clinical nurse specialist was offered for the first time in 1991.[9]

The federal government has extended third-party reimbursement for nurses with advanced preparation practicing in rural health settings (The Rural Health Act) and for dependents of military personnel through the Civilian Health and Medical Program of the Uniformed Service (CHAMPUS). As of 1992, Medicare, which had previously reimbursed for services provided by nurse midwives and nurse anesthetists, extended reimbursement to GNPs and GNCs for services currently reimbursed to physicians for care of nursing home residents. Geropsychiatric nurse specialists are not currently eligible for Medicare reimbursement. Designation of which nurses are eligible for such reimbursement is determined by each state through its nurse practice act.

All states have mechanisms for authorizing advanced nursing practice, either through specific regulations by state boards of nursing (34 states), regulation by both boards of nursing and medicine (8 states), or a broad nurse practice act permitting considerable scope of practice (8 states).[12] Legislative authority to prescribe has been granted to nurse practitioners in 28 states.[12]

GERIATRIC NURSING RESEARCH

Nursing research is conducted primarily by doctorally prepared faculty [PhD, EdD, or DNSc (doctorate of nursing science)]. As of 1988, there were 5302 doctorally prepared nurses, 47 of whom listed geriatrics as their primary area of preparation.[25] As in other disciplines, faculty without specific credentials in geriatric nursing also conduct studies involving the elderly.

Federal grants can serve as a barometer against which to measure geriatric nursing research. From 1955 to 1986, federal support for nursing research came from the Division of Nursing, Public Health Service, Department of Health and Human Services (and its forerunners). In that span of time, 618 grants were awarded for nurses' training and nursing research. Of these, only 24 (4 percent) were directly related to geriatric nursing. In 1986, the National Center for Nursing Research (NCNR) was established within the National Institutes of Health to promote excellence in the knowledge base of the profession.[26] Establishment of the NCNR represents a turning point in nursing research, leading to a substantial increase in the number of funded research studies overall and geriatric nursing research in particular. The NCNR has placed a special emphasis on improving care for the elderly through its three branches: (1) Health Promotion-Disease Prevention, (2) Acute and Chronic Illness, and (3) Nursing Systems. The NCNR's nursing home initiative is expected to spark research in that important area and to build upon community-based care programs. The NCNR has a continuing interest in research that improves the health, well-being, and long-term care of the elderly.

Since 1986, of the 270 grants awarded by NCNR 44 (16 percent) have explicitly addressed geriatric nursing. In fiscal year 1992, the NCNR had 201 active research grants, 25 (12 percent) of which were explicitly related to aging. Of the 86 active NCNR and Division of Nursing fellowship and training grants for fiscal year 1992, 25 (13 percent) were explicitly related to aging. For both research and training, many additional federally funded nursing projects—such as studies of cerebral vascular accidents, myocardial infarction, and cancer and coping—implicitly benefit the elderly.

The National Institute on Aging (NIA), the National Institute of Mental Health (NIMH), and the Agency for Health Care Policy Research (AHCPR) provide additional sources of federal funding for nurse researchers. Recent examples of studies being conducted by geriatric nurses with NIA funding include a study which examines interventions for agitated behavior in elderly people with cognitive impairment, a study to determine the feasibility of reducing the use of physical restraints in elderly nursing home residents, a study which explores reasons why elderly patients are transferred from nursing homes to hospitals, and a study of caregiver stress.

PRACTICE MODELS FOR SPECIALIZATION IN GERIATRIC NURSING

Geriatric nurses with advanced clinical preparation provide high-quality care in long-term-care facilities, hospitals, life-care communities, and in ambulatory health maintenance organizations (HMOs), home health agencies, and senior housing sites. There is substantive evidence that, in each of the settings where they work, nurses with geriatric specialization provide a comprehensive and rehabilitative approach to care for patients experiencing chronic and acute illnesses. These nurse specialists conduct assessments and provide direct care to patients; educate and counsel patients, families, and professional and nonprofessional nursing staff; develop programs to promote health or to prevent excess disabilities, such as immunization and fall prevention programs; work collaboratively with physicians and other health professionals; supervise professional and nonprofessional staff; and oversee quality assurance.[5,23]

Advanced Geriatric Practice in Nursing Homes

On any given day, over 1.5 million residents are cared for in nursing homes by 1,200,000 full-time-equivalent (FTE) employees. Of these, 700,000 FTEs are personnel who provide some form of nursing or personal care. Nursing aides and orderlies account for over 40 percent of a home's total FTEs. RNs, on the other hand, make up less than 7 percent of a nursing home's total FTE employees[27] and less than 20 percent of a facility's total nursing staff. Of the estimated 1.5 million employed nurses in the United States only about 83,300 are employed in nursing homes.

Regulations are such that very few nursing homes (5.6 percent) are required to have an RN on duty around the clock.[28] Consequently, because available staff are distributed over a 24-h period, for every 100 nursing home beds, the average staffing is one RN, who is most likely to be the director of nursing; 1.5 LPNs; and 6.5 nursing assistants. Nursing homes have on average fewer than three RNs among 41 full-time employees. This translates, on average, to one RN for every 49 patients in a nursing home, as compared to a ratio of 1:4 in a hospital.[22] The median amount of RN time per resident per day across all nursing homes in 1985 was 12 min or less, and nearly 40 percent of nursing homes (7402 homes) reported 6 min or less of RN time per resident per day.[28] This staffing pattern persists despite a sicker case mix in nursing homes since the introduction of the prospective payment system (PPS).[29]

As a result of this relative paucity of RNs in nursing homes, the RNs who are there spend most of their time on administrative and supervisory tasks and very little or no time in direct care.[28] Further intensifying the lack of professional supervision of patients, primary care physicians spend less than 1.5 h per month in a nursing home.[29] Such a system fosters inadequate on-site decision making and delayed communication between nurses in the nursing home and off-site physicians, thus heightening the potential for medical conditions to go unmonitored and untreated.

It is this relative absence of professional nurses and physicians that makes nurses specialized in care of the elderly such effective providers in nursing homes. Over 1000 GNPs work in long-term care. Numerous demonstrations have yielded convincing evidence of GNP and GNC effectiveness in nursing homes. The Health Care Financing Administration (HCFA) supported the evaluation of two demonstration projects: the Robert Wood Johnson Foundation Teaching Nursing Home Program[5] and the Nursing Home Connection (Massachusetts 1115: Case Managed Medical Care for Nursing Home Patients), in which 16 provider teams of physicians and nonphysicians, 75 percent of whom were nurse practitioners, cared for 2000 patients in 100 nursing homes. Evaluation of the mountain states program to place GNPs in nursing homes was supported by the Kellogg Foundation.[24,30]

Together, these evaluations confirm that nurses with advanced preparation in care of the elderly decrease unnecessary hospitalizations and use of emergency rooms, improve admission and ongoing patient assessment, provide better illness prevention and case finding, decrease incontinence, lower the use of psychotropic medications and physical restraints, and generally improve the overall management of chronic and acute health problems.[5,24,31] These improvements in care occur without incurring additional costs and in some instances at a reduced cost.[5,30]

While direct care is important in explaining these impressive outcomes, the outcomes are in good part attributable to GNP and GNC teaching and supervision of professional and nonprofessional nursing staff and the decentralization of nursing services, which encourages decision making at the unit level.[5] Documentation in medical records indicates that, by working directly with GNPs or GNCs, RNs and LPNs conduct more comprehensive patient assessments, have earlier contact with physicians, provide physicians with more complete information, and institute treatment in a more effective and timely manner.

Partly as a result of these demonstrations, Medicare now reimburses for GNP and GNC care to nursing home residents. Unfortunately, geropsychiatric clinical specialists, who have been shown to be highly effective in providing care to residents in nursing homes,[5] are not currently eligible for Medicare reimbursement. Nevertheless, the recent legislation, coupled with new regulations requiring RN-supervised assessments and the growing recognition of their effectiveness by corporations which operate nursing homes, should substantially expand the use of master's-prepared nurses in nursing homes.

In addition to overall improvements for nursing home residents, geriatric nurse specialists and faculty have taken a leadership role in fostering research aimed at further understanding and amelioration of the common problems experienced by nursing home residents: urinary incontinence,[31] decubiti,[32] the overuse of physical restraints,[33] and management of difficult behaviors evidenced by residents with dementia. Nurses have played a pivotal role in legislation to reduce restraint use. Similarly, a geriatric nurse, recognized for her research on decubiti, chaired the committee which developed the AHCPR guidelines for the prediction and prevention of pressure ulcers in adults.[32]

Advanced Geriatric Practice in Hospitals

Long-term-care facilities provide a limited view of the niche for nurses with advanced preparation in geriatrics. The bulk of patients who use acute care hospitals are elderly. Almost all models for quality care of these patients rely on the use of specially prepared geriatric nurses.

The elderly are admitted to hospitals approximately three times as often as the overall population, and 42 percent of all acute care hospital days represent care for people aged 65 and over.[34] The level of complexity of elderly patients is evidenced by their average length of stay, which is 8.9 days, as opposed to 5.6 days for younger patients. Since PPS was first introduced, shortened lengths of hospital stays for Medicare beneficiaries have contributed to a sicker case mix in hospitals. Thus, nurses are caring for elderly patients who are sicker because they both stay less time in the hospital and have multiple chronic physical, functional, and mental health problems.

A substantial number of hospitals are employing geriatric clinical nurse experts. Increasingly, such specialists are unit-based and provide a combination of direct and indirect care. On selected hospital units in which the case load of elderly patients is especially complex (e.g., geriatric assessment units, medical and orthopedic units, alternate level of care units, and hospital-based skilled nursing care units), hospitals are experimenting with new staffing patterns which use master's-prepared geriatric nurses as case managers. These nurses provide direct care, oversee the care of elderly patients with special needs (such as delirium, for example) and coordinate and oversee the activities of professional and nonprofessional nursing staff.[35–38] To meet the needs of these and other nurses, the first geriatric textbook specifically prepared for nurses working in acute care was recently published.[39] As is the case in nursing homes, the care provided by these nurses has been shown to be of high quality, to result in improved patient outcomes, to be well received by patients, and to be cost-effective.[35,40,41]

Practice protocols for geriatric syndromes have been used in selected acute care hospitals. Their aim is to improve nurses' ability to manage problems commonly seen in older people during the course of a hospital stay, with their ultimate purpose being to decrease the prevalence of such problems on any given unit. Practice protocols are tailored to the institution as well as the unit and are most effective when developed by nursing staff working together. The most important aspects of protocols are that they be accurate, effective, and used, not stored in file cabinets.

Assessment, treatments, and target outcomes have also been developed for nursing diagnoses commonly encountered in the hospitalized elderly. Examples of nursing diagnoses include impaired skin integrity, sleep pattern disturbances, sexual dysfunction, and altered thought process.

Fundamental to the success of improving nursing care for the elderly are practice models which assist primary, bedside nurses to develop their skills and knowledge in geriatric nursing. The Hospital Outcome Project for the Elderly (HOPE), funded by the John A. Hartford Foundation, tested three such approaches.[41] The geriatric resource nurse (GRN) model is an example of such a practice model.[42,43] The GRN is a primary nurse who volunteers time within regular working hours to learn principles of geriatric nursing under the tutelage of a geriatric clinical nurse specialist. Such a program is based on the tenets that (1) primary nurses know the most about day-to-day patterns and problems of the elderly, (2) primary nurses are more likely to integrate new behaviors into their practice, and (3) a GRN program provides recognition of talent and fosters clinical advancement.

The GRN serves as a consultant to peers on the unit with regard to common problems of the elderly. Geriatric resource nurses address six baseline problems: *s*leep disorders, *p*oor nutrition, *i*ncontinence, *c*onfusion, *e*vidence of falls, and/or *s*kin breakdown (acronym: SPICES). From this base, GRNs can work with staff on other problems not listed in this paradigm. Each problem in the SPICES model triggers a practice protocol. For example, incontinence triggers a protocol which guides nursing practice relative to toileting schedules, patterns of fluid intake, appropriate administration of diuretics over a 24-h period, and so on. Problems deemed complex by the primary nurse are referred to the GNC and/or the physician. Table 23-3 is an example of outcomes anticipated from institution of a practice protocol for a patient with delirium.

TABLE 23-3

Anticipated Outcomes for a Patient with Delirium

Hours of sleep at night should increase and episodes of confused night awakening should decrease.
Resident's weight should stabilize or increase without special supplements. Food intake from tray will increase and caloric expenditure will decrease as pacing and agitation disappear.
Episodes of combative behavior will be eliminated. Agitated episodes will diminish or be eliminated.
Resident's socialization will increase, including voluntary participation in small-group activities.
Functional level may improve briefly as excess disability disappears.
Needs for sedatives and tranquilizers will decrease.
Once families understand the care program, satisfaction with care and empathy with staff will increase.

SOURCE: Maas, Buckwalter, and Hardy: *Nursing Diagnoses and Interventions for the Elderly.* Reading, MA, Addison-Wesley, 1991. Reproduced by permission.

A second model in the HOPE project provides GNC consultation and education to the bedside nurse in order to improve the nurse's accuracy and speed in detecting and managing delirium in hospitalized elderly patients.[41] Specifically, nurses are taught (1) the use and interpretation of simple bedside tests for assessing cognition; (2) the clinical features that distinguish delirium, dementia, and depression; (3) when and how to communicate symptoms to physicians; (4) common causes of delirium in this patient population; (5) independent, interdependent, and dependent strategies for preventing and managing delirium; and (6) how to document findings in the hospital record. In addition, the model provides for consultation with the GNC.

In yet a third HOPE model, a newly renovated 29-bed medical-surgical nursing unit, named the Acute Care of the Elderly (ACE), was designed with special attention to the physical environment, collaborative team building, and development of nurse-initiated clinical protocols of care.[41] Unlike other geriatric units which use geriatric experts as consultants, in this model the geriatric medical director and clinical nurse specialist hold dual roles.

These three models are evidence of the evolution of geriatric nursing practice from a unidimensional to a multidimensional sphere where a variety of models are developing based on clinical practice demands. In addition to attempts to improve care for elderly patients while in the hospital, several nurse researchers have examined ways to improve discharge planning and prevent unnecessary readmissions. One such model uses GNCs and GNPs who first contact an elderly patient soon after admission, follow the patient and family throughout the hospital stay, and continue to have telephone contact at specified times following discharge from the hospital.[40]

Advanced Geriatric Practice in Ambulatory Settings

Geriatric nurse practitioners, GNCs, and geropsychiatric clinical specialists are employed in a multitude of ambulatory settings. In traditional ambulatory sites such as clinics in public health, municipal and Department of Veterans Affairs facilities, and private physicians offices, GNPs carry both their own caseloads and collaborative caseloads of patients with physicians. Continuing care retirement communities (CCRCs) encompass a continuum of care from independent living to nursing home placement. There are over 500 CCRCs nationwide. In these settings, GNPs and GNCs have been shown to be highly effective, providing health promotion and illness surveillance to the independent-living elderly and supervision of residents needing long-term care.[20]

Geriatric nurse practitioners and faculty have also developed specialty ambulatory practices and research directed at common problems afflicting older people living in the community. Geriatric nurses assess and treat elderly patients with urinary incontinence in established clinics, urologists' offices, nurse-managed offices, and patients' homes.[44–46] Evidence suggests that nurse-managed care is comparable to care with more extensive physician involvement.[46] Studies by geriatric nurse researchers have yielded the knowledge necessary to recognize and intervene in elder abuse.[47,48] Geriatric nurse practitioners and GNCs have developed specialty practices for patients following a cerebral vascular accident; case-management for patients with complex functional, physical, and psychiatric disorders; and immunization programs in senior centers and housing.

Home care agencies are only now beginning to consider using a GNP or GNC to assist in the care of elderly patients. It is estimated that over 12,000 home care agencies nationally deliver services to patients who are primarily elderly. In 1988, the 5600 home care agencies certified to receive Medicare reimbursement made over 38 million visits to approximately 1.6 million Medicare beneficiaries. Some 52 percent of these were nursing visits, while another approximately 30 percent were for nursing aide services.[49] In New York City, for example, over 200 organizations offer some form of home care service to the elderly. On any given day, the four major home care providers alone serve over 60,000 older persons. Early evidence of the effectiveness of geriatric nurse specialists in home care is expected to spur increased demands for their services.

In summary, over the past 10 years, the role of nurses with advanced geriatric preparation who work in nursing homes has been clearly defined and shown to be highly beneficial for patients. Documentation as to the effectiveness of the hospital-based geriatric nurse specialist, while less substantial, is still impressive. In ambulatory practice, GNP and GNC effectiveness is consistent with the positive outcomes attributable to nurse practitioners overall.[15] Home care agencies are just beginning to explore the potential benefits of geriatric nurse specialists. Future trends in care of elderly patients in ambulatory settings, nursing homes, hospitals, and home care have the potential to markedly increase both the demand and use of master's-prepared geriatric nurses.

THE INTERDISCIPLINARY MANDATE IN GERIATRIC NURSING

An interdisciplinary approach to the care of geriatric patients has been forcefully argued for many years.[50–52] With few exceptions, geriatric nurses practice in collaboration with physicians and other disciplines. Nevertheless, objective evidence that interdisciplinary care improves outcomes for the elderly has proved elusive. It would seem self-evident that the convergence of clinical assessment by several disciplines produces complementary information and thus fosters effective patient care. For example, in the case of urinary incontinence in the elderly, the physician or nurse is able to describe the type of urinary incontinence. Nursing practice also focuses on the behavioral aspects of the urinary incontinence and the environmental influences that mediate its correction. A physical therapist adds an evaluation of motor skills and an appropriate exercise regimen necessary to maintain continence, and a social worker is able to provide an analysis of the family context in order to ascertain whether the demands of the medical problem outweigh available supports.

While the interdisciplinary dimension of geriatrics began in the clinical setting, it is also evident in the education of health professionals.[14,16] In some universities, introductory courses in gerontology are offered to students from a variety of disciplines. There are instances where clinical courses which focus on the history and physical assessment of older adults are taught jointly to nursing and medical students. An increasing number of geriatric research studies involve coinvestigators from several disciplines. The convergence of faculty and students fostered by interdisciplinary courses and research may be an important basis for future clinical and research collaboration.

THE FUTURE DIRECTION OF GERIATRIC NURSING

All evidence confirms that the health care environment of the next 20 years will create an increasing need for better preparation of the bedside nurse in care of the elderly and for the advanced skills of the geriatric nurse specialist. By the year 2030, 18 percent of the population in the United States will be over age 65. Some 10 percent of the population will be over 75 years of age, and 50 percent of these individuals will be over 80. The population aged 85 and over is expected to triple within the next 50 years.[49]

These changes in demographics will markedly affect how we deliver acute, long-term, and home care. Residents in nursing homes are already "patients." Their care far exceeds the ability of family members to manage at home. The greatest proportion of residents, 39 percent, are admitted to nursing homes directly from general or short-stay hospitals.[53] Half of new admissions to nursing homes are reimbursed by Medicare,[54] and these admissions are substantially sicker than was the case prior to the introduction of PPS. As an example, the length of hospital stay for elderly hip fracture patients is half what it was prior to PPS. At the same time, the probability that an elderly hip fracture patient will be transferred to a nursing home following hospitalization jumped from 17 percent in 1983 to 25 percent in 1985.[55] Programs seeking to improve care to this sicker case mix of nursing home residents rely heavily on bedside nurses with minimum competencies in geriatric nursing and on master's-prepared geriatric nurse specialists.[13,56]

Hospitals also care for large numbers of elderly patients, many of whom are sicker at the point of entry, undergo more complex procedures, and have shorter lengths of stay than in the past. The degree to which these patients' functional, physical, and mental disabilities negatively impact on their recovery during and following a hospital stay is of increasing concern to clinicians and administrators. For example, surgery in centenarians, including procedures unheard of just a few years ago, is now regularly reported in professional journals. The most promising models to improve care to the hospitalized elderly (case management, targeted geriatric units, unit-based training and support for bedside nurses, and programs to bridge hospital and community care) all involve the use of master's-prepared nurses with clinical specialization in care of the elderly.[35–41]

Finally, many very sick elderly persons remain at home. At best, their care is complex. They require on-site monitoring to prevent excess disability and to promote optimum function. Often, an acute illness compounds the functional, physical, and psychological declines brought on by multiple chronic illnesses. At such times, care may involve several sophisticated technologies. Such care exceeds the ability of most home-care nurses unless they have specialized training or can call on the backup of a geriatric nurse specialist.

In summary, the maturation of educational programs and advances in research have redefined the scope of geriatric nursing practice. Professional practice and the health policy influence of geriatric nursing research and education are already helping reshape health care for the current generation of older adults. There is no reason to believe the next decade will be any less exciting.

REFERENCES

1. Burnside I: *Nursing and the Aged: A Self Care Approach,* 3rd ed. St Louis, Mosby, 1988.
2. Dock L: Quoted in *Am J Nurs* 48(9):680, 1948.
3. National League for Nursing: *Gerontology in the Nursing Curriculum.* New York, National League for Nursing, 1991.
4. Johnson MA, Connelly JR: *Nursing and Gerontology: Status Report.* Washington, DC, Association for Gerontology in Higher Education, 1990.
5. Mezey M, Lynaugh J: The teaching nursing home program: Outcomes of care. *Nurs Clin North Am* 24:769, 1989.
6. Aiken H, Mullinex CF: The nurse shortage—Myth or reality. *N Engl J Med* 317(1):641, 1987.
7. Mezey J, Lynaugh J, Cartier M (eds): Aging and academia: The teaching nursing home experience. New York, Springer, 1988.
8. Rogers B et al: Employment and salary characteristics of nurse practitioners. *Nurse Pract* 14:58, 1989.
9. American Nurses Association: Credentialing/Recertification Catalog. Washington, DC, American Nurses' Association, 1992.
10. Strumpf N et al: Gerontological education for baccalaureate nursing students. *Gerontol Geriatr Ed.*
11. Hill B: The development of a master's degree program based on perceived future practice needs. *J Nurs Ed* 28:307, 1989.
12. Bullough B: The state nurse practice acts, in Mezey M, McGivern D (eds): *Nurses, Nurse Practitioners: The Evolution to Advanced Practice.* New York, Springer, 1993.
13. Lavizzo-Mourey R et al: Completeness of resident's admission assessments in teaching nursing homes. *J Am Geriatr Soc* 39:433, 1991.
14. Ebersole P: Gerontological nurse practitioners past and present. *Geriatr Nurs* 6:219, 1985.
15. U.S. Congress, Office of Technology Assessment: Nurse practitioners, physician assistants, and certified nurse midwives: A policy analysis, in *Health Technology Case Study 37,* OTA-HCS-37. Washington DC, US Government Printing Office, December 1986.
16. Sultz H et al: Nurse practitioners: A decade of change, Part III. *Nurs Outlook* 31:266, 1983.
17. Grey M, Flint S: 1988 NAPNAP membership survey: Characteristics of members' practice. *J Pediatr Health Care* 3:336, 1989.
18. Reilly CH: The consultative role of the gerontological nurse specialist in hospitals. *Nurs Clin North Am* 24:3, 1989.
19. Forbes K et al: Clinical nurse specialist and nurse practitioner core curricular survey results. *Nurse Pract* 15, 45, 1990.
20. Kummerer-Butler J, in Mezey M, McGivern D: *Nurses, Nurse Practitioners: The Evolution to Advanced Practice.* New York, Springer, 1993.
21. Special anniversary issue: 25 years later. *Nurse Pract* 15:9, 1990.
22. Mezey M: Care in nursing homes: Patients' needs, nursings' response, in Aiken L, Fagin C (eds): *Nursing in the 90's.* Philadelphia, Lippincott, 1992.
23. Kane RL et al: Effect of the geriatric nurse practitioner on the process and outcomes of nursing home care. *Am J Public Health* 79:1271, 1989.
24. Garrard J et al: The impact of nurse practitioners on the care of nursing home residents, in Katz P, Kane R, Mezey M (eds): *Advances in Long-Term Care,* vol 1. New York, Springer, 1991, p 169.
25. Moses E: The RN population: Findings from a national sample survey of RN's. DHHS Division of Nursing, March 1988.
26. Hinshaw AS: National Center for Nursing Research—

A commitment to excellence in science, in McCloskey JC, Grace HK (eds): *Current Issues in Nursing*. St Louis, Mosby, 1990, p 357.
27. Strahan G: Characteristics of registered nurses in nursing homes, preliminary data from the 1985 National Nursing Home Survey. *Advance Data from Vital and Health Statistics*, no. 152. DHHS pub no (PHS) 88-1250. Hyattsville, MD, Public Health Service, 1988.
28. Jones D et al: Analysis of the environment for recruitment and retention of registered nurses in nursing homes. USDDHS, PHS, HRSA, Bureau of Health Professions, Division of Nursing, Washington, DC, U.S. Government Printing Office, 1987.
29. Kanda K, Mezey M: Registered nurse staffing in Pennsylvania nursing homes: A comparison before and after the implementation of the medicare prospective payment system. *Gerontologist* 31:3, 318, 1991.
30. Buchanan J et al: Assessing cost effects of nursing-home-based geriatric nurse practitioners. *Health Care Financing Review* 11:67, Spring 1990.
31. Collings J: Educating nurses to care for the incontinent patient, in McCormick K (ed): Incontinence in the elderly. *Nurs Clin North Am* 3:240, 1988.
32. U.S. Department of Health and Human Services: *Pressure Ulcers in Adults: Prediction and Prevention*. Clinical Practice Guideline #3. Rockville, MD, Public Health Service Agency for Health Care Policy and Research. AHCPR pub no. 92-0047, May 1992.
33. Evans LK, Strumpf NE: Tying down the elderly: A review of the literature on physical restraint. *J Am Geriatr Soc* 37:65, 1989.
34. National Center for Health Statistics: *Health United States, 1991*. Hyattsville, MD, Public Health Service, 1992.
35. Rubenstein LZ et al: Effectiveness of a geriatric evaluation unit: A randomized clinical trial. *N Engl J Med* 311:26, 1984.
36. Jones LC: In-patient nurse practitioners. *Nurse Pract* 10:48, 1985.
37. Sullivan EM et al: Nursing assessment, management of delirium in the elderly. *Am Op Rm Nurses J* 53:3, 1991.
38. Ake J et al: The nursing initiative program: Practice-based models for care in hospitals, in *American Academy of Nursing: Differentiating Nursing Practice into the Twenty-First Century*. Washington, DC, American Academy of Nursing, 1991.
39. Fulmer T, Walker M (eds): Critical care nursing of the elderly. New York, Springer, 1992.
40. Naylor MD: Comprehensive discharge planning for hospitalized elderly: A pilot study. *Nurs Res* 39:3, 1990.
41. Foreman M et al: Nursing models for the HOPE Project. *Geriatr Nurs* (in press).
42. Fulmer T: A new model for implementing the role of the geriatric nurse specialist in acute care settings. *Nurs Mgt* 22:3, 1991.
43. Fulmer T: Grow your own experts in hospital elder care. *Geriatr Nurs* 12:2, May/June 1991.
44. Newman DK et al: Restoring urinary incontinence. *Am J Nurs* 45:28, 1991.
45. Brink C et al: A continence clinic for the aged. *J Gerontol Nurs* 9:652, 1983.
46. Wanich C et al: Continence services for the ambulatory elderly: A comparison of cost of care outcomes between geriatric nurse clinician (GNC) and GNC-MD team managed care. *Gerontologist* 31SS:218, 1991.
47. Fulmer T et al: Abuse, neglect, abandonment, violence and exploitation: An analysis of all elderly patients seen in one ED during a six-month period. *J Emerg Nurs* (in press).
48. Phillips L, Rempusheski V: A decision-making model for diagnosing and intervening in elder abuse and neglect. *Nurs Res* 34:3, 1985.
49. U.S. Special Committee on Aging: *Aging in America: Trends and Projections*, 1991 ed.
50. Fulmer T, Walker M (eds): *Critical Care Nursing of the Elderly*. New York, Springer, 1992.
51. Appelgate WB et al: Instruments for the functional assessment of older patients. *N Engl J Med* 322:1207, 1990.
52. Kane RA, Kane RL: *Assessing the Elderly: A Practical Guide to Measurement*. Lexington, MA, Lexington Books, 1988.
53. National Center for Health Statistics: Nursing home characteristics, preliminary data from the 1985 National Nursing Home Survey, in *Advance Data from Vital and Health Statistics*, no. 131 [DHHS pub no. (PHS) 87-1250]. Hyattsville, MD: Public Health Service, 1987.
54. Lewis A et al: The initial effects of the prospective payment system on nursing home patients. *Am J Public Health* 77:819, 1987.
55. Fitzgerald J et al: The care of elderly patients with hip fracture: Changes since implementation of the prospective payment system. *N Engl J Med* 319:1392, 1988.
56. Zimmer J et al: Nursing homes as acute care providers. *J Am Gerontol Soc* 36:124, 1988.

Chapter 24

CLINICAL PHARMACOLOGY

Janice B. Schwartz

The effects of drug administration to an individual are the net result of many complex processes. These processes are often considered in two major categories: pharmacokinetics and pharmacodynamics. Pharmacokinetic parameters include drug bioavailability, volume of distribution, clearance rate, and elimination half-life ($t_{1/2}$). Pharmacodynamics relates the drug dose or concentration to measures of effect. In addition, both pharmacokinetics and pharmacodynamics are modulated by the unique physiologic status of the patient (normal physiology vs. disease state vs. age alterations). To rationally approach pharmacologic therapy for the geriatric patient, one must have a working knowledge of the basic concepts of pharmacokinetics, pharmacodynamics, and the potential age-related alterations in these processes. Appreciation of alterations due to common disease processes of aging will also aid in selection of optimal therapeutic regimens, and recognition of the limitations of current knowledge will help to lead to awareness that any pharmacologic intervention has a potential for unexpected as well as expected outcomes. The purpose of this chapter is to present an overview of the current state of knowledge regarding pharmacokinetics in elderly patients, pharmacodynamics in elderly patients, and the complexity of drug therapy in elderly patients. Common models used to study age-related changes will be presented in each section to allow interpretation of the anticipated expansion of knowledge in these areas. Finally a description of the current drug evaluation process in the United States as it relates to drug evaluation in elderly persons will be presented.

PHARMACOKINETICS

Pharmacokinetic processes determine the rate of appearance of drugs in the body, distribution throughout the tissues, and disappearance from the body. As shown in Fig. 24-1, the major kinetic terms which describe these processes are (1) bioavailability, (2) distribution, and (3) clearance.

Bioavailability

Bioavailability is defined as the fraction of drug reaching the circulation following administration. By definition, intravascular (IV) administration of a drug results in a bioavailability of 1, or 100%. For the common oral route of drug administration, the bioavailability depends on the chemical properties of the drug, the amount of drug absorbed from the stomach or intestine, and the amount of drug metabolized in the liver or excreted in the bile before it reaches the arterial circulation and organ distribution. Similarly, bioavailability after percutaneous drug administration depends on the lipid solubility of the drug and absorption through the skin into the venous circulation before it reaches the arterial circulation and the remainder of the body. The bioavailability of extravascular (EV) routes of drug administration are usually determined for humans by comparisons of the area under the curve (AUC) of drug concentration versus the time following (EV) administration divided by the area under the curve of the concentration versus time after IV dosage.

$$\text{Bioavailability} = \frac{\text{AUC}_{\text{EV}}}{\text{AUC}_{\text{IV}}}$$

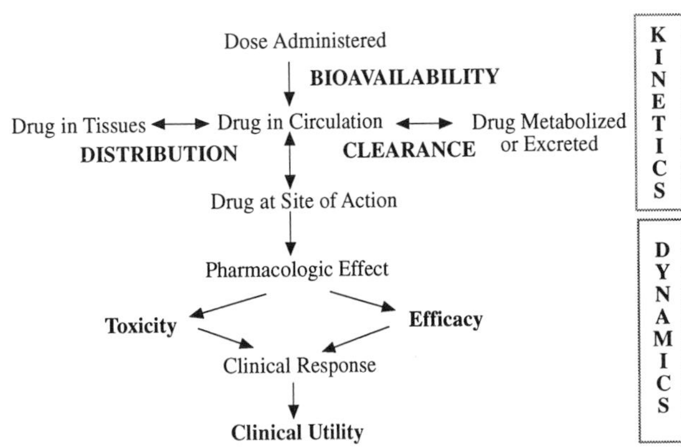

FIGURE 24-1

A schematic representation of the pharmacokinetic and pharmacodynamic processes that relate a drug to the effects produced.

This EV/IV ratio is the bioavailability expressed as a fraction or as a percentage. The clinical application of this principle is that bioavailability defines the dose adjustment between intravascular and EV drug administration. Low-bioavailability drugs require much greater EV versus IV doses. For example, a single IV dose of verapamil is about 5 to 15 mg, while single oral doses range from 80 to 240 mg.

Age-Related Changes

Age-related changes in bioavailability depend on the route of drug administration and age-related changes in the organs of absorption, as well as changes in hepatic drug metabolism during the first pass of the drug through the liver. Gastric pH, gastrointestinal motility, blood flow, and active membrane transport processes are altered to a variable extent by aging. The decreased acid secretion, decreased perfusion of the gastrointestinal tract, and possibly decreased membrane transport activity could be anticipated to lead to lesser drug absorption. These age-related changes would, however, be counterbalanced by the longer gastrointestinal transit time providing longer times for drug absorption.

A model compound used to study intestinal absorption is D-xylose, a water-soluble monosaccharide which is absorbed passively. D-Xylose absorption tests usually measure urinary excretion of xylose following oral administration of a known dose of drug and are corrected for age-related changes in renal excretion (see renal clearance below). Studies of aging effects on D-xylose absorption have shown that although the extent of D-xylose absorbed for a given dose is not altered with aging, the rate of absorption is slower.[1–3] Most drug absorption from the gastrointestinal tract is by passive diffusion, and to date, most studies suggest little clinically significant age-related changes in the rate or extent of drug absorption from the gastrointestinal tract.[4] For traditional oral formulations, net drug absorption can be considered relatively unaffected by age. Slow-release preparations, however, have undergone limited to no study of potential age-related changes in drug delivery rates. Similarly, data regarding transdermal, transbuccal, and transbronchial drug administration are too limited to allow conclusions regarding age-related changes in drug absorption via those routes.[5,6]

Distribution

The volume of distribution terms relate the amount of drug in the body to the concentration measured. A common way of determining the volume of distribution of a drug in humans is to administer an IV bolus of a known amount of drug and then measure the concentration immediately following drug administration:

$$\text{Volume of distribution} = \frac{\text{Drug dose}}{\text{Concentration}}$$

This pharmacokinetic calculation of the volume of distribution of a drug does not represent a "real" volume but an approximation of the volume that would be necessary if the drug were equally distributed throughout the body. Thus, although the total body water for a 70-kg human is about 42 liters, distribution volumes of drugs have been reported to range from 7 to 30,000 liters per 70-kg human.

Major determinants of the volume of distribution of a drug are the binding of the drug to the plasma proteins, the lipid to water partition coefficient, and the binding of the drug to the tissues. Drugs which are highly bound in the circulation form a drug–protein complex which is large and thus less able to cross membranes into tissues and, in general, have volumes of distribution related to vascular volumes. The major drug-binding proteins are albumin for acidic drugs and alpha-1-acid glycoprotein for basic drugs.

Distribution rates into peripheral tissues and organs are also dependent on the blood flow to the organ or tissue. For example, fat is relatively poorly perfused, so distribution of drug into fat occurs slowly. In contrast, drugs distribute into highly perfused organs such as the heart and kidney at a faster rate. Once the drug reaches an organ, if a drug is highly bound to tissue proteins, distribution volumes will be large. An example of such a drug is digoxin, which distributes into and binds to muscle.

The volume of distribution is an especially important concept for drugs which require loading doses. Clinically, the volume of distribution defines the loading dose of a drug. Calculations of loading doses are based on the concentration desired and the volume of distribution of the drug.

$$\text{Loading dose} = \text{desired concentration} \times \text{volume of drug distribution}$$

Age-Related Changes in Volume of Distribution

Body composition changes with senescence and also varies with gender. Changes especially relevant to drug distribution are the decline in lean body muscle mass and decreased total body water seen with advanced age.[7,8] These changes lead to decreased volumes of distribution for some drugs. The consequence of a decrease in drug volume of distribution would be higher initial concentrations after administration unless dosages were reduced. A clinically important example is the calculation of the initial loading doses of antibiotics (polar drugs which usually distribute only in body water). For aminoglycosides, much of the toxicity is related to peak concentrations, and age adjustment of loading doses is necessary to avoid toxicity. It is also now recognized that the increased effects of alcohol (or decreased tolerance) seen in elderly persons and in women are due to the reduced distribution volume leading to higher alcohol concentrations for a given amount consumed.[9] Another practical point regarding age-related considerations is that since cardiac output and organ blood flow may be reduced with aging, even for drugs without changes in steady-state distribution volumes, loading doses may need to be given at a slower rate or in divided doses to avoid potentially high or toxic initial concentrations.

Plasma protein concentrations are also known to be altered with advancing age. In particular, the serum albumin concentration may decrease, especially in the presence of disease.[10–13] It had been suggested that this would result in decreased protein binding of drugs and greater amounts of unbound drug present in elderly patients. The decrease in albumin levels, however, appears to be partially counterbalanced by an increase in alpha-1-acid-glycoprotein levels with age, and acute illnesses with clinically important age-related changes in protein binding of drugs have been largely absent.[10,12] One important exception is warfarin. This anticoagulant is very highly protein-bound (about 99 percent), and even small changes in albumin levels result in significant increases of free drug available to inhibit clotting factors and produce anticoagulant effect.

Clearance

Total body drug clearance CL_t is defined as the rate of removal of a drug from the body. It is usually described as a unit of volume cleared of drug per unit time. Total body clearance is the sum of all organ drug clearances. The two major sites of drug clearance in humans are the kidney and the liver. Total body clearance is commonly expressed as

$$CL_t = CL_{renal} + CL_{hepatic} + CL_{other}$$

Estimates of CL_t are necessary since to maintain a constant drug concentration, input must equal output, or clearance. Thus, clinically clearance defines the drug dosing rate. A pharmacokinetic estimate of total clearance following IV drug administration is often obtained by dividing the dose administered by the resulting area under the concentration versus time curve.

For several newer drug compounds which are analogues of natural transmitters or naturally occurring substances, such as adenosine, rapid metabolism occurs by enzymes present in the blood. As new drugs more closely resemble hormones, agonists, and naturally occurring pharmacologic substances, metabolic and deactivation pathways throughout the body will assume more importance to clinical pharmacology. For now, knowledge of renal and hepatic elimination suffices for an understanding of the pharmacology of most drugs administered to the geriatric patient.

Renal Drug Clearance

Drugs can undergo three processes of elimination in the kidney: (1) glomerular filtration, (2) tubular secretion, and (3) tubular reabsorption. Appearance of a drug in the urine is the net result of filtration, secretion, and reabsorption. Glomerular filtration is perhaps the best understood, since it can be reasonably well approximated clinically by estimates of creatinine clearance. Creatinine clearance is defined as

$$\frac{U \times V}{P}$$

where U = creatinine concentration, V = urine volume per time, and P = plasma creatinine concentration. It should be noted that creatinine is also actively secreted to an extent which is balanced by reabsorption. More specific measures of glomerular filtration utilize tests of exogenously administered substances, such as inulin, which do not undergo secretion. Only unbound drug can be filtered (both creatinine and inulin are unbound).

Before a drug is excreted into the urine, the drug must be presented to the kidney. Renal perfusion or blood flow is about 25 percent of the total cardiac output, and 10 percent of this is filtered at the glomerulus. Renal blood flow and changes in renal blood flow can be estimated by para-amino hippuric acid (PAH) clearance from plasma.

Renal secretion is detected in vivo when renal clearance of a substance exceeds clearance rates by filtration. Secretion is an active process, and separate processes exist for acids and bases. Secretion efficiently eliminates protein-bound drugs. Significant tubular reabsorption is detected when urinary excretion of a compound is less than filtration rates. For the majority of drugs, reabsorption is passive and can be effected markedly by urine flow and by changes in pH.

Age-Related Changes in Renal Function Affecting Drug Clearance Alterations in renal function with aging were among the first age-related physiologic changes to be investigated and are among the most consistent of reported age-related changes.[14–16] There is a decrease in renal blood flow to the kidney with aging, and a decrease in renal mass, and creatinine clearance has been shown to decrease about 10 percent per decade after age 20 (see Fig. 24-2). Algorithms to estimate creatinine clearance based on subject age, gender, and serum creatinine levels have been shown to provide accurate estimates of the glomerular filtration rate and have widespread clinical applications. It is important to note that serum creatinine concentrations alone will not accurately reflect creatinine clearance in elderly persons, since muscle mass is decreased and, therefore, the rate of formation of creatinine is decreased. Thus, a normal serum creatinine level may be seen when a significant reduction of creatinine clearance or glomerular filtration is present at the renal level. This can be demonstrated by examination of the most commonly used formula for estimation of creatinine clearance[17] where

$$\text{Creatinine clearance} = \frac{140 - \text{age(yr)} \times \text{lean body weight (kg)}^*}{72 \times \text{serum creatinine}}$$

*For females multiply by 0.85.

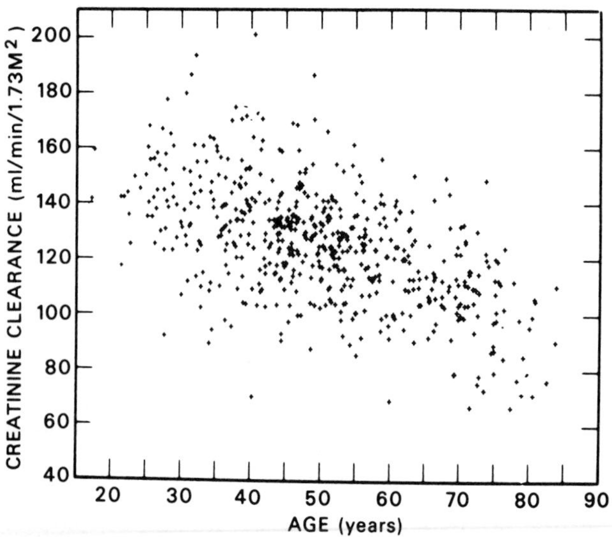

FIGURE 24-2

Creatinine clearance data normalized for body surface area are plotted vs. subject age. Data are from a cross-sectional population analysis in 548 normal subjects. (*Reprinted by permission from Rowe et al,*[15] *p 158.*)

Lean body weight can be estimated for males as 50 kg + 2.3 kg/inch over a height of 5 feet; for females, lean body weight is equal to 45.5 kg + 2.3 kg/inch over 5 feet.

Clinical examples of the need to use such algorithms are for determining doses of drugs which are renally excreted and have narrow therapeutic ranges and toxicities closely related to concentration. Digoxin clearance has also been shown to correlate closely with creatinine clearance and requires dosage adjustments in elderly patients.[18] Similarly, aminoglycoside antibiotics require dosage adjustments based on creatinine clearance.

Disease- and Drug-Related Changes The effects of renal insufficiency add to the underlying age-related physiologic decrease in renal drug elimination with aging. Hypertension, diabetes, and atherosclerosis are common in elderly persons and can produce further decrements in renal function. Fortunately, creatinine clearance algorithms are accurate in these disease states except during periods of acute changes in status. Renal disease or insufficiency can also lead to alterations in drug absorption and changes in plasma proteins which may alter drug pharmacokinetics in a manner not predicted by creatinine clearance algorithms.

Renal blood flow is decreased with aging, and regulation of intrarenal perfusion may also be altered. It has been reported that renal blood flow in elderly persons may be more dependent on prostaglandin regulation than in younger individuals. Nonsteroidal anti-inflammatory drugs (NSAIDs) can decrease the production of vasodilating renal prostaglandins which help to maintain renal perfusion in disease states such as congestive heart failure, cirrhosis, and dehydration, and with aging. NSAID inhibition of cyclooxygenase has been postulated to be the underlying mechanism responsible for the variable azotemia seen during the administration of NSAIDs in elderly patients.[19,20]

Angiotensin-converting enzyme (ACE) inhibitors decrease blood pressure and in the presence of renal artery disease may result in a reduction of renal perfusion pressure. In addition, ACE inhibitors can block the production of angiotensin II, which is responsible for dilation of the efferent arteriole, and alter the balance between afferent and efferent arteriolar resistance such that perfusion through the glomerulus may decrease. This can result in clinically significant decreases in glomerular filtration (and creatinine clearance) and increases in serum potassium levels, especially in elderly patients.

Hepatic Drug Clearance

The rate and extent of hepatic drug metabolism depends on extrahepatic and intrahepatic factors. For example, hepatic blood flow determines the delivery of a drug to the liver and hepatic enzyme numbers, affinity, and activity rate determine hepatic drug metabolism.

A simplified view of hepatic drug clearance divides drugs into "high" clearance and "low" clearance drugs. A high-clearance drug is efficiently and usually rapidly metabolized by the liver. A high-clearance drug can be conceptualized as one whose removal is limited only by the rate of drug presentation to the liver. Thus, the hepatic metabolism of a high-clearance drug is affected by changes in hepatic blood flow, such as decreases in cardiac output with congestive failure, which result in decreased hepatic drug clearance, while changes in hepatic size or enzyme content (unless extreme) do not markedly affect drug clearance. Another correlate is that significant amounts of a high-clearance drug may also be removed during the first pass of the drug through the liver, and these drugs usually have lower systemic bioavailability. Examples of high-clearance drugs are lidocaine, verapamil, and propranolol. For a low-clearance drug, the rate of removal is limited by hepatic enzymatic processes. These processes can further be induced or inhibited. Hepatic disease processes leading to decreased liver enzyme content, damage, or fibrosis have a major impact on hepatic metabolism of low-clearance drugs. An example of a low-clearance drug is phenytoin.

To evaluate changes in hepatic drug clearance or drug interactions, several model compounds for hepatic processes are used. The plasma clearance of indocyanine green—a compound which undergoes little to no hepatic metabolism—can be used to estimate hepatic blood flow and, therefore, approximates hepatic clearance of a high-clearance drug. Antipyrine is a compound which undergoes extensive hepatic metabolism via several major hepatic oxidative cytochrome P_{450} metabolic pathways. Antipyrine clearance can be used to estimate hepatic oxidative P_{450}

enzyme activity and approximates hepatic clearance of low-clearance drugs eliminated by those cytochrome P_{450} pathways.[21,22]

Most hepatic drug clearance does not result in removal of the drug from the body but results in drug inactivation by oxidative drug biotransformation, largely via the cytochrome P_{450} pathway. The parent drug compound is usually transformed in phase I by oxidation, reduction, or hydrolysis to a less lipophilic metabolite; this metabolite has sites to which more polar groups can be conjugated in phase II, resulting in a compound that can be eliminated more efficiently by the kidney. Metabolites, however, can be active or inactive. In addition, several drugs are also currently administered in the prodrug form and are biotransformed in the liver to the active drug. Then, hepatic clearance determines the rate of appearance of the drug rather than its inactivation. An example of a commonly administered prodrug is the ACE inhibitor enalapril.

The cytochrome P_{450} family has a number of isoforms which differ by species as well as race and are to a large extent genetically determined. Phenotyping for hepatic metabolic pathways can be estimated by the use of model drug compounds known to be metabolized via a certain oxidative pathway. For example, the study of the elimination of debrisoquine can estimate the activity of a recessively inherited P_{450} mixed-function oxidase system. Debrisoquine was the first drug shown to exhibit genetic polymorphism but is not the only drug displaying polymorphism. Knowledge in this area is rapidly expanding. The development of specific antibodies for many of the cytochrome P_{450} isoenzymes has been progressing, and clones are being developed which may be useful for the study of metabolic processes; for the screening of new drugs for the isoenzyme responsible for metabolism and its distribution in the population as well as genetic phenotyping; and possibly for more accurate predictions of drug metabolism in vivo.

Hepatic drug metabolism is far more variable than renal drug clearance, and reliable algorithms to estimate hepatic drug clearance have not been developed. The marked variability of factors influencing hepatic clearance, such as hepatic blood flow, hepatic size, hepatic enzyme inducibility, genetic polymorphism between individuals, and cumulative and differential exposures to modulating environmental influences, has limited progress in this area.

Age-Related Changes in Hepatic Drug Clearance

Variability in the conclusions of studies investigating age-related changes in hepatic drug metabolism is as common as variability in the parameters of hepatic drug metabolism. There is general agreement regarding changes in several of the extrahepatic influences on hepatic drug clearance. Hepatic blood flow parallels cardiac output and has been shown to decrease with age[23–26] This decrease in hepatic blood flow would be anticipated to result in age-related decreases in hepatic drug clearance of high-clearance drugs. In most studies, reduced clearance of high-clearance drugs, such as lidocaine, verapamil, and propranolol, has been seen with increasing age. Variability is marked, however, and gender and smoking history may influence the results.[27–31]

Intrahepatic influences on hepatic drug metabolism also display some general age-related trends. Hepatic size has been shown to decrease with age, and in animal species, hepatic enzyme content per gram of tissue also declines.[24,25] Declines in phases I and II oxidative pathways have been noted, while conjugation pathways have been generally unaffected by age. The relevance of such declines to in vivo drug metabolism, however, has been recently questioned. Data from in vivo experiments with tissues from rodent models of aging show marked and consistent declines in hepatic enzyme affinity and metabolic rates, while changes in antipyrine clearance with age in humans are less marked (see Fig. 24-3). In addition, recent evidence from human liver biopsy tissues fail to demonstrate age-related declines, suggesting differences in age-related hepatic enzyme changes in the rodent compared with humans.[22,29,32–34] This would also suggest that most clinically observed and demonstrated decreases in hepatic drug clearance are related to changes in hepatic blood flow or circulating proteins or hormonal changes with aging. Evidence does exist, however, for a decline in the inducibility of human hepatic mixed-function oxidase enzyme activity with increasing age.[29,31,35,36] Inducibility occurs in aged hepatic tissue, but the extent of inducibility may be less than that seen in younger individuals.

Further complexity results from the recognition of the impact on stereoselective hepatic metabolism on conclusions regarding age-related changes. Many drugs are available as the racemic mixture of the naturally occurring dextro [*d*, or *r*(+)] and levo [*l*, or *s*(−)] rotatory isomers. The variation in pharmacologic potency of the two enantiomers is termed *stereoselectivity*. Metabolism may also be stereoselective. Data regarding total clearance of a racemic drug reflect the net clearances for the more and less potent isomers. Recent evidence suggests that aging may result in stereoselective effects on drug clearance that can be dependent on gender.[37,38] Selective inhibition of clearance of the more potent isomer with aging would lead to greater amounts of more active drug at the same total plasma concentration in elderly patients. The clinical relevance of such a process could be increased drug effects seen at the same racemic drug concentrations in elderly patients and lower dosage requirements and circulating concentrations necessary for equivalent drug effects. Although these concepts are scientifically valid and some evidence exists for age-related changes in stereoselective drug elimination, the clinical importance has yet to be well defined.

The clinical implication is that, in general, drug dosage of hepatically metabolized drugs should be reduced in elderly patients since decreases in hepatic clearance can be anticipated but the exact extent cannot be precisely quantitated.

Recognition of the inducibility of hepatic enzyme activity is particularly relevant to the use of several drugs which are prescribed for very elderly patients

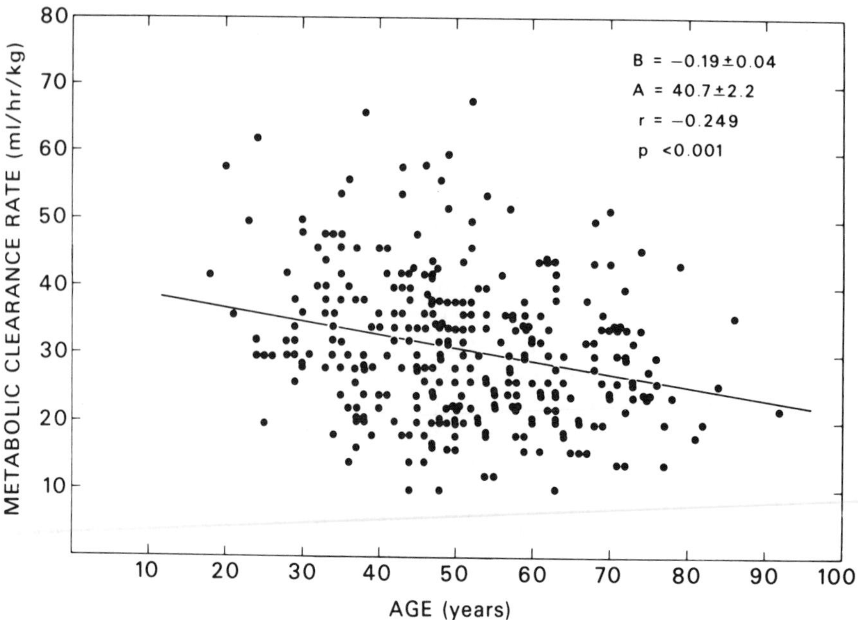

FIGURE 24-3
Clearance rates of antipyrine corrected for subject weight are plotted vs. subject age. Data are from a cross-sectional population analysis. Note that the intersubject variability is large and the age-related trend is not as pronounced as that seen in Fig. 24-2 for creatinine clearance. (*Reprinted by permission from Vestal et al.*[22])

or the nursing home population. The antituberculous drug rifampin has recently been shown to be the most potent inducer of hepatic microsomal oxidase system activity.[39] It is far more potent in this effect than phenobarbital, the prior prototype for hepatic mixed oxidase function enzyme induction. When rifampin is administered to patients, profound increases in hepatic drug clearance of hepatically metabolized drugs have been seen, and concentrations of coadministered drugs undergoing hepatic metabolism can become negligible, although this effect may not be as great in elderly persons.[36] Therefore, dosages of coadministered drugs may need to be increased during rifampin coadministration *and* decreased upon discontinuation of rifampin. Conversely, considerations regarding hepatic drug enzyme inhibitors are also pertinent to elderly patients. During the initial use of one of the histaminergic receptor blocking drugs, cimetidine, profound elevations of serum lidocaine and propranolol concentrations were seen in elderly patients receiving these drugs in combination with cimetidine.[40,41] Cimetidine both decreases hepatic blood flow and inhibits microsomal oxidase system activity and can produce profound decrements in hepatic drug clearance. Dosages of coadministered hepatically metabolized drugs must be decreased to avoid toxicity. Newer antihistaminergic blocking drugs such as ranitidine and famotidine have lesser affinities for the cytochrome P_{450} system and, in general, lesser inhibition of hepatic drug metabolism. Dosage adjustment may not be necessary for drugs coadministered with ranitidine or famotidine. Because of the generally higher cost of the new agents, however, cimetidine is still frequently prescribed, and knowledge of this potential drug interaction is crucial to avoid drug toxicity with multidrug administration, especially in elderly patients.

Elimination Half-life

The $t_{1/2}$ of a drug is described as the time it takes for the amount of drug in the body to decrease by half. Clinically the $t_{1/2}$ usually refers to the terminal elimination $t_{1/2}$ of the drug or the time it takes for the drug concentration to decrease by half after drug distribution has occurred throughout the body (the loglinear phase). The drug elimination $t_{1/2}$ depends on the relationship between drug volume of distribution and clearance as depicted by

$$t_{1/2} = \frac{0.693(\text{volume})}{\text{Clearance}}$$

The $t_{1/2}$, therefore, is a dependent variable, and changes in drug $t_{1/2}$ can occur secondary to changes in drug distribution, drug clearance, or distribution and clearance. Following drug administration, another method of estimating drug elimination $t_{1/2}$ is by determining the slope of the concentration-versus-time plot during the terminal loglinear portion of the relationship (see Fig. 24-4).

The $t_{1/2}$ is a clinically useful kinetic parameter because it represents the amount of time required to reach 50 percent of steady-state drug concentrations in the body as well as the amount of time for concentrations to decrease by 50 percent. The clinical rule of thumb is that it takes approximately 3.3 $t_{1/2}$ of a drug to reach 90 percent of steady-state concentrations or to remove 90 percent of the drug from the body. Therefore, the $t_{1/2}$ provides information necessary to determine the time between dosage adjustments or the time necessary for stabilization or reduction in effects of the drug related to drug concentrations.

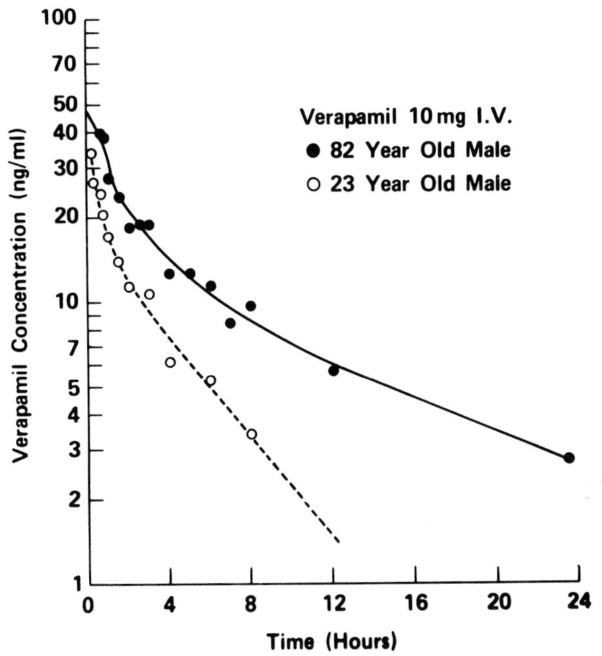

FIGURE 24-4

An example of typical concentration-vs.-time data from which pharmacokinetic parameters can be estimated. Drug concentration data vs. time following an IV infusion in a young and an elderly hypertensive individual are shown. The steeper decline in concentrations from 3 to 24 hours after drug administration in the younger individual indicates a more rapid elimination rate, or $t_{1/2}$. The total area under the concentration-vs.-time curve is also smaller in the young individual, representing a faster clearance rate (since CL_t = dose/AUC).

Age-Related Effects on Elimination Half-Lives

The elimination $t_{1/2}$ has been reported to increase with age for a number of drugs (Table 24-1). Because it can reflect changes in drug clearance and/or distribution, the $t_{1/2}$ provides no information on the underlying mechanism of the effect and may not be easily predicted. When age-related increases in terminal elimination $t_{1/2}$ are seen, it is important that the time between dosage adjustments be increased to allow evaluation of drug efficacy for a given drug dosage. In the setting of potential drug toxicity which frequently manifests as altered mental status in the elderly, it is also important to allow adequate time for drug elimination before concluding effects to be irreversible or non-drug-related.

Summary of Clinical Pharmacokinetics

The clinical relevance of individual pharmacokinetic parameters can be summarized as follows:

- The clearance defines the amount or dose of drug given per unit time.
- The half-life defines the dosing interval.
- The bioavailability defines dose adjustments between intravascular and oral drug administration.
- The volume of distribution determines loading doses.

Age-related changes have been reliably found and estimated for renal drug clearance, but changes in hepatic drug clearance, half-life, bioavailability, and distribution are less predictable. Another consistent finding in all parameters measured is increased variability with increasing age. In general, one should reduce drug dosages in elderly individuals and titrate drug dosages slowly. The current state of knowledge is limited by the paucity of investigations in female subjects and in the old-old and by the paucity of studies of pharmacokinetics in target patient populations. A summary of the literature available on drugs commonly prescribed in geriatric patients with suggested dosage adjustments is found in Table 24-1.

PHARMACODYNAMICS

Pharmacodynamic models attempt to approximate the relationship of drug dose or concentration to the intensity of response at an effect site. Most pharmacologic models assume steady-state conditions. The models used have evolved from drug receptor theory.

The E_{max} Model

The maximum effect (E_{max}) model is one of the simplest which adequately describes drug (or agonist) effect over a range of concentrations. It predicts no effect when the drug concentration is zero and the maximum effect a drug can achieve when "infinite" drug is present. It is based on the premise that drug combines reversibly with a receptor to form a drug–receptor complex which then produces an effect. It can be depicted as

$$\text{Drug} + \text{receptor} \leftrightarrow \text{activated receptor drug complex} \rightarrow \text{effect}$$

The measured effect is proportional to the fraction of occupied receptors. This model is frequently used in various forms: in enzyme kinetic analyses as the Michaelis-Menten equation and in physiology as the Langsmuir saturation isotherm equation. Graphically, this relationship takes the form of a hyperbola, and the parameters estimated are the maximum effect (or rate) and the concentration at which half-maximal effect is seen k_d or C_{50}). A minor modification of the E_{max} model creates the sigmoidal E_{max}

TABLE 24-1

Commonly Prescribed Drugs in Elderly Patients and Reported Age-Related Alterations in Pharmacokinetics

	Route of Elimination	Age effects*			
		Clearance	Volume	$t_{1/2}$	Dose Adjustment
A. Cardiovascular					
Furosemide[42]	Hepatic, Renal	↓	? ↓	? ↑	↓§
Hydrochlorothiazide	Renal	? N.A.	N.A.	N.A.	↓§
Chlorthalidone	Renal	N.A.	N.A.	N.A.	↓§
Digoxin[18]	Renal	↓	↓, ↔	↑	↓
Quinidine[43]	Hepatic	↓	?	↑	↓
Lidocaine[44]	Hepatic	↓, ↔	↔, ↑	↑	↓
Procainamide + NAPA[45,46]	Renal	↓	N.A.	↑	↓
Beta Blockers					
Propranolol[31,47]	Hepatic	↓ (males)	↔	↑	↓
Metoprolol[48]	Hepatic	↑, ↔	N.A.	↑, ↔	↓, ↔
Atenolol	Renal	Slight ↓	N.A.	↔	↔
Calcium Antagonists					
Verapamil[49]	Hepatic	↓, ↔	↔	↑, ↔	↓
Diltiazem[50,51]	Hepatic	↓, ↔	↔	↑,↔	↓
Nifedipine[†,52]	Hepatic	↓	↔	↑	↓
Nisoldipine[53,54]	Hepatic	↓, ↔	N.A.	↑, ↔	↓, ↔
Amlodipine[55,56]	Hepatic	↓	↔	↑	↓
Nicardipine[57]	Hepatic	↔, ↑	↔	↔	↔, ↓
Alpha-adrenergic blockers					
Clonidine[58]	Renal & Hepatic	↓	N.A.	N.A.	↓§
Prazosin[59]	Hepatic	↓, ↔	↔	↑	↓, ↔§
Terazosin[60]	Hepatic, Renal	↓, ↔	N.A.	↔, ↓	↔, ↓§
Alpha methyldopa[58]	Hepatic, Renal	↓	N.A.	? ↑	↓
Labetalol[61,62]	Hepatic	↓, ↔	N.A.	↑, ↔	? ↓
ACE Inhibitors					
Captopril[63]	Renal	↓	N.A.	↑	↓
Enalapril[64,65†]	Hepatic	↓	N.A.	↑	↓
Lisinopril[66]	Renal	↓	N.A.	↑	↓
B. Hypoglycemic Agents					
Glipizide[67–69]	Hepatic	↔	N.A.	↔	↔, ?
Chlorpropamide[70]	Renal	↓	↑	↑	↓
Glyburide[71]	Hepatic, Renal	↔	↑	↑	↔
C. Sedative-Hypnotics					
Lorazepam[72]	Hepatic	↔	N.A.	↔	↓§
Diazepam[72]	Hepatic	↓	?	↑	↓
Triazolam[73]	Hepatic	↓	N.A.	↔	↓
D. Antituberculous					
Isoniazid (INH)[74,75]					
Slow acetylators	Hepatic	↔	↔	↔	↔
Rapid acetylators	Hepatic	↓, ↔	↔	↑	↓
Rifampin[36,39]	Hepatic	N.A.	N.A.	N.A.	?
E. Antibiotics					
Erythromycin[76]	Hepatic	↓	↔	↑	↓
Gentamycin[77]	Renal	↓, ↔	↑, ↔	↑, ↔	↓
Ampicillin[78]	Renal	↓	↔	↑	↓
Amoxicillin	Renal	N.A.	N.A.	N.A.	?↓
Ciprofloxacin[79]	Renal	↓	?	↑	↓

*N.A. = not available.

†Active drug is metabolite enalaprilat, which is renally excreted.

‡Decreased plasma binding → ↑ effect.

§Aging effects on specific pharmacokinetic parameters have not been well studied, but clinical efficacy has been observed with reduced doses in the elderly.

TABLE 24-1 (continued)

	Route of Elimination	Age effects* Clearance	Volume	$t_{1/2}$	Dose Adjustment
F. Antiarthritics					
Acetaminophen[80–83]	Hepatic	↔, ↓	↓, ↔	↔	↔
Aspirin[84,85]	Hepatic	↑, ↔	↑	↑	↓, ↔
Naproxen[83]	Renal	↓	N.A.	↑	↓
Ibuprofen[83]	Renal	↔, or ↓ in males	N.A.	↔ in males	↔ or ↓ in males
Salicylic acid[83,85]	Hepatic	↔	N.A.	↔ or ↑	↔
G. Histaminergic Blockers					
Cimetidine[86–88]	Hepatic, Renal	↓	N.A.	↑	↓
Ranitidine[89]	Hepatic, Renal	↓	N.A.	↑	↓
Terfenadine[90]	Hepatic	? ↑	N.A.	↑	↓
H. Antiulcer					
Misoprostol[91]	Renal?	↔	N.A.	Slight ↑	↔
I. Miscellaneous					
Levothyroxine	Hepatic	N.A.	N.A.	N.A.	§
Conjugated estrogen	Hepatic	N.A.	N.A.	N.A.	N.A.
L-dopa[92]	Hepatic + Other	↓	↓	↔	↓
Lithium[93]	? Renal	↓	?	↑	↓
Warfarin[94]	Hepatic	↔	↔	↔	↓ ‡,§

model, also known as the Hill equation.[95] This model is useful since it often approximates clinical conditions. The sigmoidal E_{max} model predicts a sigmoidal response curve in which no effect is seen at zero drug concentration *and* at lower concentrations until a concentration is reached at which a steep rise is seen in the effect-response. The steeply rising portion of the response curve is approximately linear throughout the 20 to 80 percent response range and then levels off somewhat as it more slowly approaches maximal effect.

The equations for the E_{max} and sigmoidal E_{max} models and idealized concentration-versus-response curves are shown in Fig. 24-5. Derived parameters for the sigmoidal E_{max} model are the maximal effect (E_{max}), the concentration at which half-maximal effect is seen (C_{50}), and a steepness or slope factor n. These parameters can be determined experimentally and have clinical applications. The E_{max} can be used to estimate maximal effects for comparisons between drugs or between individuals. The C_{50} or k_d can be thought of as an estimate or representation of the sensitivity of an individual or group to a drug (or affinity for a receptor). The slope factor describing the steepness of responses predicts the amount of change anticipated due to changes in drug concentration and, to some extent, the wideness or narrowness of the therapeutic range of a drug.

These basic models can take more complex forms to accommodate for the known physiologic conditions of tolerance, nonproportionality of response, multiple drugs and multiple receptors, and non-steady-state conditions; these more complex forms have been recently reviewed.[96,97]

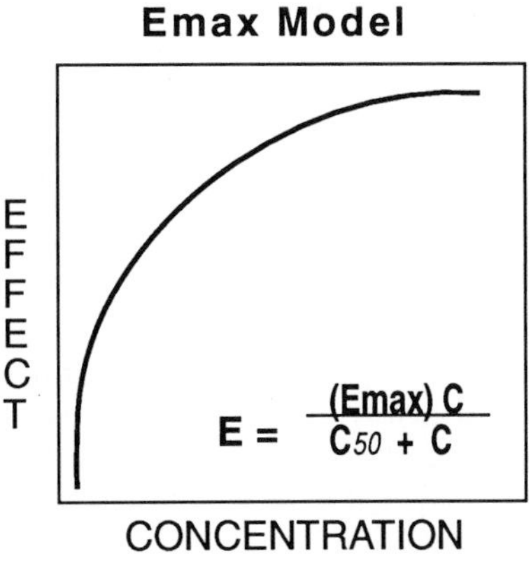

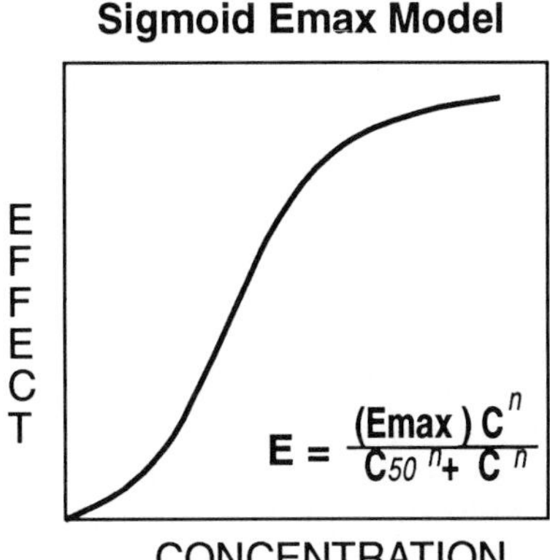

FIGURE 24-5
The effect-vs.-concentration relationship for the maximal effect (E_{max}) model is shown in the left panel and for the sigmoidal E_{max} model in the right panel. The models differ in the hyperbolic-vs.-sigmoid shape, and in the initial rate of rise of the relationship.

A Linear Model

In clinical applications, the administration of drugs at dosages that produce maximal effects is often impractical because of potential toxicity or undesired effects. For example, following the administration of an antihypertensive agent, one would not want to reduce blood pressure to zero. In dose- or concentration-versus-response studies not attaining maximal effect, the linear portion of the relationship is often approximated using simple linear regression where

$$\text{Effect} = (\text{slope})(\text{concentration}) + \text{basal value}$$
$$\text{or} \quad y = mx + b$$

This simplified model allows appreciation of the steepness of response or the slope, and this can be used as an index of sensitivity to the drug for between-group and between-drug comparisons and desired concentration guidelines.

A number of challenges are presented in the clinical design and interpretation of pharmacodynamic measures. A basic assumption is that the plasma or serum concentration measured reflects the active compound and concentrations at the site of effect and is related to the effect, and that the proper effect measure is chosen.

For many drug compounds that are found in nature, such as quinidine (cinchona bark) or digoxin (foxglove), and local anesthetics (cocaine), a linear concentration-versus-response relationship, with toxicity at increased concentrations, is observed. For receptor agonist and antagonist drugs (i.e., alpha, beta, and calcium receptor blocking drugs) and enzyme-inhibiting drugs (i.e., ACE inhibitors), the E_{max}-type models better approximate the concentration-versus-response relationship. New concepts in drug design which attempt targeted organ delivery or inhibition of intracellular phenomena will require new pharmacodynamic models.

For the study of pharmacologic properties, an easily measurable effect is often chosen. This may be a "surrogate" effect measure for the clinically described response. For example, heart rate suppression by a beta blocker may be measured as a drug effect, yet drugs may not have equal potency on different effect measures. For beta blockers, heart rate suppression correlates with angina relief but not with blood pressure reduction. The clinician must interpret results of pharmacodynamic studies with this factor in mind. This is also of particular importance when one attempts to extrapolate from the results of blood pressure reduction with one agent to the prolongation of life associated with blood pressure reduction with another class of drugs which lower blood pressure. In the geriatric population, another frequent issue is whether a measured "statistically" significant change in performance on a cognitive test results in improved function.

Indirect Drug Effects–Reflex Responses

The pharmacodynamic models described above assume that all effects seen are related to direct drug effects. This assumption is valid in vitro, but in vivo, homeostatic or reflex mechanisms often counter direct drug effects. Reflex responses can be considered indirect drug effects. Thus, a more realistic representation of a drug effect is similar to that of total drug clearance. This can be expressed as

$$\text{Total or net effect} = \text{direct effect} + \text{indirect effect}$$

The modulation of observed effects by reflex responses is of especial importance in understanding responses to many vasoactive drugs in the elderly.

Age-Related Changes in Pharmacodynamics

To accurately evaluate age effects on drug pharmacodynamics, equivalent concentration-versus-response studies should be utilized rather than dose-versus-response relationships to eliminate differences which might be secondary to age-related changes in pharmacokinetics, potentially resulting in greater concentrations of drug for a given dose. Interpretation of studies of dose-versus response do not allow differentiation between altered pharmacokinetics and altered pharmacodynamics.

Age alterations in dynamic responses appear to be well-established for beta$_1$-adrenergic autonomic responses and central nervous system sedation. Decreased responses of heart rate, contractility, and vasodilation are seen following isoproterenol administration in animal and human models of aging.[98,99] In Fig. 24-6, the decreased beta$_1$-adrenergic responsiveness with aging results in a shift of the concentration-versus-response relationship to the right—higher concentrations are necessary for any given effect, and the C_{50} is higher. The maximal effect is also reduced, suggesting an age-related decrease in receptor numbers as well. Analogously, the decrease in heart rate following beta$_1$-adrenergic-blocking drug administration to humans is also less in older subjects. Similar shifts in the response curves can then be anticipated for any beta$_1$-adrenergic agonist or antagonist response in aged subjects. This decreased β_1-adrenergic responsiveness contributes to the alterations in baroflex responses to hypotension. In studies of hypotensive responses following vasodilator administration to older versus younger individuals, variable results and age-related differences in response may be partially due to altered reflex or indirect drug effects as well as to the direct drug effect. For example, elderly patients may be observed to have greater de-

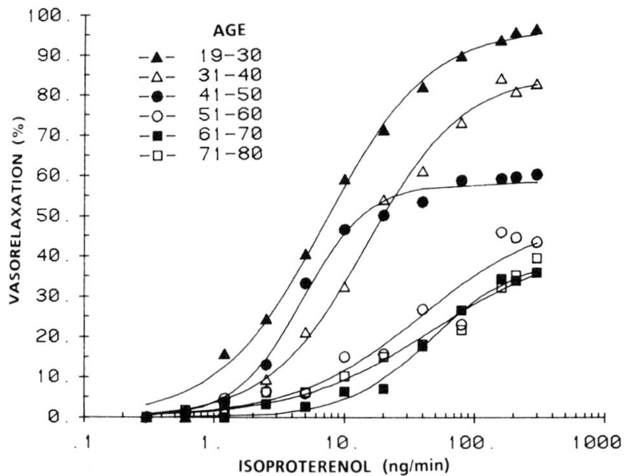

FIGURE 24-6
The vasodilatory responses to isoproterenol (a beta$_1$-adrenergic agonist) infusion into preconstricted hand veins of subjects ranging in age from 19 to 80 years are shown. The lines represent the model fit using a variation of the sigmoid E_{max} model. Decreased response or less effect was seen as age increased. (*Reprinted by permission from Pan et al.*[100])

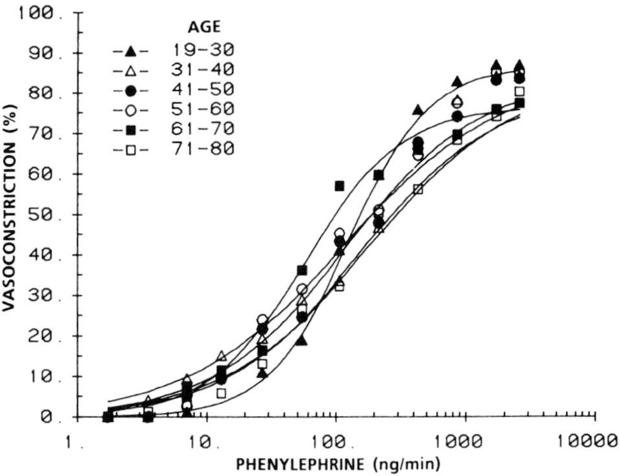

FIGURE 24-7
The vasoconstrictive responses to phenylephrine infusion into hand veins of subjects ranging in age from 19 to 80 years are shown. The lines represent the model fit using a variation of the sigmoid E_{max} model. No age-related differences in vasoconstriction were detected in contrast to the altered beta$_1$-adrenergic responses in the same subjects shown in Fig. 24-6. (*Reprinted by permission from Pan et al.*[100])

creases in blood pressure following alpha-adrenergic-blocking drug administration when compared with younger subjects. When alpha-adrenergic drugs are infused directly into vessels at doses which do not produce systemic effects, however, no age-related differences in vessel responses are seen (see Fig. 24-7).[100] These data suggest that the age-related increase in hypotensive responses following systemic alpha-blocking drug administration may be mostly secondary to differences in indirect reflex responses to direct hypotensive effects.

While age-alterations in beta$_1$-adrenergic responses appear similar in central and peripheral tissues, a disparity for age-related differences in peripheral versus central dynamic responses to parasympathetic blocking agents has been reported. Decreased sensitivity and responses to parasympathetic agonists and antagonists are seen at the cardiac level, while increased central nervous system adverse effects are frequently seen in elderly patients following the administration of drugs with anticholinergic effects.

Central nervous system responses to benzodiazepines have been shown to be enhanced in senescent animals when brain concentrations of benzodiazepines have been related to effects.[101] Results of studies in elderly versus younger humans also show pharmacokinetic differences with higher plasma benzodiazepine concentrations in elderly persons, and these differences have been thought to contribute to the enhanced sedative effects of benzodiazepines in the elderly persons studied (see Fig. 24-8).[72,102]

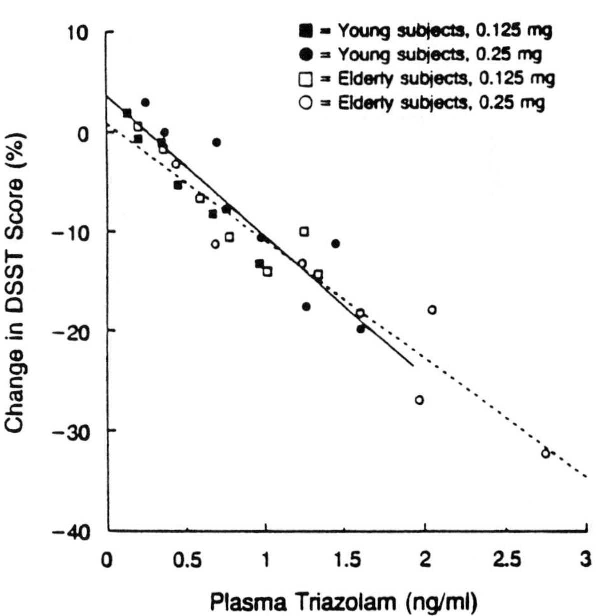

FIGURE 24-8
Effects following triazolam administration to young and elderly subjects are shown. The effect measure [changes in digit-symbol substitution test (DSST)] is plotted vs. the plasma triazolam concentration. The lines represent the results of linear regression analyses for the younger (solid) and elderly (dashed) subject groups. No age-related differences were noted in the slopes of the regression lines. (*Reprinted by permission from Greenblatt et al.*[73])

Summary

Age-related changes in pharmacodynamics have been much less extensively studied than pharmacokinetic changes but contribute to clinical effects following drug administration. Variability in dynamic responses, like variability in pharmacokinetics, is greater in elderly persons. The increasing development and therapeutic use of drugs which act as receptor agonists and antagonists will make investigations of age-related changes in the dynamics of receptor-based systems of growing importance to drug therapy in the elderly population.

ADVERSE DRUG EFFECTS

The prevalence of chronic and multiple diseases increases with age and leads to polypharmacy in elderly patients. Several national data bases follow drug utilization in U.S. hospitals (Hospital Data Services data base of Pharmaceutical Data Services, Scottsdale, Arizona), pharmacies (National Prescription Audit, IMS America), and physician office-based practices (National Disease and Therapeutic Index, IMS America). From these sources, data on drug use in the elderly population are periodically compiled [*Drug Utilization in the United States, Annual Reviews, U.S. Food and Drug Administration,* available from National Technical Information Service (NTIS), Springfield, Virginia]. The categories of drugs most frequently prescribed in both hospitalized and nonhospitalized elderly patients are cardiovascular and diuretic agents. Therapeutic classes specifically cited in ≥2 percent of outpatient encounters with elderly patients are antihypertensives, beta and alpha-beta blockers, coronary vasodilators, calcium blockers, digitalis preparations, diuretics, anti-infectives, ophthalmics, analgesics, antiarthritics, diabetes therapy (oral therapy and insulin), psychotherapeutics, bronchial therapy, corticoids, antispasmodics, nutrients and supplements, and cough and cold products. It is more difficult to accurately assess the number of concomitant drugs used per person in the community, but it has been estimated that older North Americans take an average of 4.5 medications at any one time.[103] A recent population-based study of community elderly persons also demonstrated that most patients use both prescription drugs and over-the-counter drugs.[104] Data available regarding drug use in institutionalized elderly persons show a mean of three to eight drugs administered daily,[105–108] with a somewhat higher use of psychotropics compared with outpatient elderly persons.[109]

Although the frequency of adverse drug reactions in elderly patients had often been thought to correlate with the age of the patient, recent strikingly consistent observations demonstrate that age is not the major determinant of adverse drug effects. Rather, it is the number of drugs administered that is directly related to the risk of adverse drug-related events.[94,110,111] Thus, in the elderly patient, the altered pharmacokinetics, pharmacodynamics, and presence of multiple disease states combine to increase the complexities of therapeutic decision making and the risk of adverse drug-related events. Most, if not all, drugs have the potential for adverse drug reactions in the elderly patient, and all relevant points cannot be addressed here. The general clinical rules of optimal geriatric prescribing are to

1. Start at low dosages
2. Increase doses at a slow rate and at small increments
3. Be observant for toxicity

Several additional points unique to the care of the elderly should also be made:

1. Drugs with narrow therapeutic ranges need to be particularly closely monitored—these include drugs such as digitalis, theophylline, warfarin, lithium, lidocaine, quinidine, and aminoglycoside antibiotics.
2. Drugs with central nervous system effects or side effects may significantly affect the quality of life, mentation, and functional status—these include drugs such as the long-acting hypnotics, histaminergic- and alpha-blocking drugs, and drugs with anticholinergic effects such as disopyramide and antihistamines.
3. Drug-related adverse effects may present "atypically" as a change in mental status. Thus, a high index of suspicion must always be present. An example is digitalis excess presenting as altered mental status.

Improved knowledge of age-related changes in pharmacokinetics and pharmacodynamics should alter the incidence of adverse drug effects, but minimizing the number of drugs administered could potentially have an even greater impact. Several approaches to optimizing drug usage in elderly patients are being evaluated. These include prospective programs of targeted physician education on specific drug categories thought to be inappropriately overutilized ("academic drug detailing"), clinical pharmacist pre-hospital-discharge counseling, and the use of specialized geriatric patient care units. Each approach has been associated with improvement in measures of patient care, but all are expensive and time-consuming and may show only transient alterations in prescribing patterns. The best overall method to optimize medication use in elderly patients will likely need to incorporate greater educational efforts in university curriculums, hospitals, pharmacies, nursing homes, and the community.

THE DRUG DEVELOPMENT AND APPROVAL PROCESS

In the United States, approval of a new drug for clinical use follows a series of developmental and evaluative steps under an Investigational New Drug Application (IND), which precedes submission of a New Drug Application (NDA) for marketing approval from the Food and Drug Administration (FDA). The process is divided into preclinical and three clinical investigational phases followed by NDA review by the FDA (see Fig. 24-9).[112]

Preclinical Studies

Preclinical studies are usually performed in animals to address biological activity, toxicity and safety data, and collection of pharmacokinetic and pharmacodynamic data to assist in developing initial human dosing regimens.

Clinical Studies

Phase 1 studies are performed in healthy volunteers and patients to define initial toxicity parameters, the tolerated dose range, and pharmacokinetics and pharmacodynamics in humans. Special patient target populations (such as the elderly) may be evaluated, and different methods of drug formulation or delivery systems may be tested. Phase 2 studies test clinical efficacy or therapeutic effectiveness and are designed to provide dose- or concentration-versus-response relationships in closely monitored patient groups of limited numbers. Results aid in the design of studies in phase 3. Phase 3 studies are patient studies to document clinical safety and efficacy, further define the dose- or concentration-versus-response relationships, and assess adverse drug reaction rates. Larger numbers of patients are usually studied in phase 3 compared with phase 2; however, phase 2 and phase 3 studies are often conducted simultaneously. Phase 4 trials are postmarketing approval surveillance trials and are variable in design and objective.

Until *very recently,* elderly groups were commonly excluded from both preclinical and clinical studies. Factors contributing to the exclusion of elderly subjects were the complexity of interpreting pharmacokinetic and pharmacodynamic data in elderly subjects, the presence of multiple diseases in the elderly subjects and the frequent administration of additional medications, the greater variability in investigational parameters in the elderly subjects requiring larger sample sizes, a greater likelihood of death during a long-term study in an elderly individual compared with a younger one, and a theoretically greater risk of adverse effects due to altered homeostatic mechanisms in the elderly subjects. Nonetheless, with the growing recognition that elderly patients would be the largest target population and consumers of most drugs immediately after marketing release, guidelines for the inclusion of elderly subjects in the drug evaluation process were developed and circulated in 1989 after a series of policy conferences and scientific exchanges between industry, academia, and the FDA.[113] These are intended as a supplement to the previously published FDA guidelines for drug evaluation.[114]

The 1989 guidelines focus largely on the evaluation of potential pharmacokinetic differences between younger and older people for a number of reasons. These stated reasons are that (1) pharmacokinetic differences are known to occur, (2) pharmacokinetic differences are more frequent than pharmacodynamic differences, (3) pharmacokinetic differ-

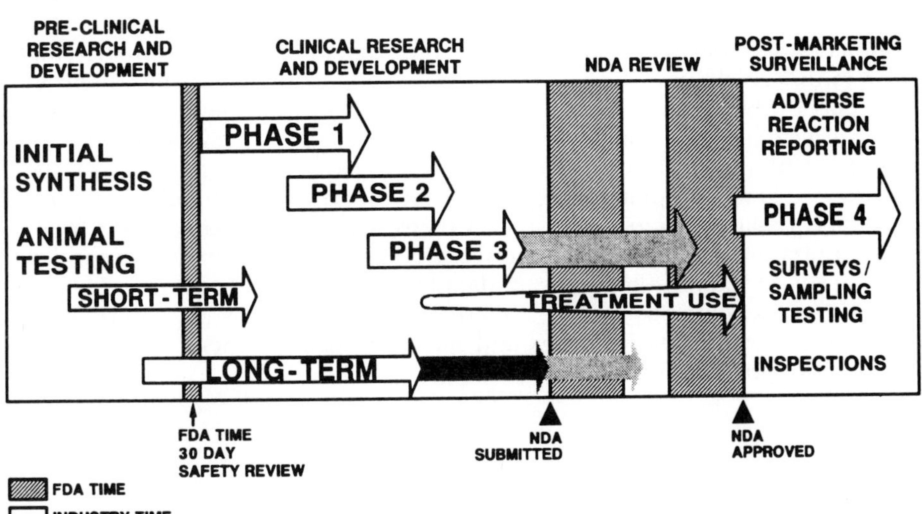

FIGURE 24-9
A schematic of the steps involved in the drug development and approval process in the United States. (*Reprinted with permission from Peck et al.*[112])

ences are relatively easy to discover, (4) good dose- or concentration-versus-response information may not be readily accessible (i.e., depression or anxiety), and (5) pharmacokinetic studies must precede the design of pharmacodynamic studies.[113] It is also recommended that drug interactions be evaluated for drugs which can be anticipated to be frequently coadministered. The inclusion of elderly patients in clinical trials is stressed especially in phase 3 and especially for the >75-year-old population. It is anticipated that significant pharmacodynamic differences will be detected during analyses of clinical trials, which might then indicate the need for more detailed pharmacodynamic studies. Guidelines and recommendations for the design of clinical trials in elderly subjects have also been recently reviewed and the ethical arguments for studies in the elderly presented in the scientific literature.[115–118]

The current recommendations from the FDA are that elderly subjects and patients be studied during the drug evaluation when it can be reasonably anticipated that elderly patients will be a target population for drug administration based on estimates of disease prevalence by age. For example, the high prescribing rates of antihypertensive drugs, cardiovascular drugs, and antiarthritic drugs in elderly patients reflect the prevalence of these diseases in the elderly population. It is also obvious that drugs developed for diseases unique to elderly persons should be tested in an elderly population (i.e., a drug for benign prostatic hypertrophy or the treatment of Alzheimer's disease). A recent FDA review of NDAs has shown that significant progress has been made in including elderly target populations.[119] Nonetheless, the reader should be aware that for most drugs currently on the market, evaluation in elderly subjects was *not* performed prior to marketing. At least some of the adverse effects of drug use in elderly patients could be due to the lack of data on which to base therapeutic regimens when drugs were released. Furthermore, postmarketing surveillance has been notoriously poor for discovery of adverse or unexpected effects since it is based on voluntary reporting of suspected drug-related adverse events. This is especially difficult in the elderly population since such adverse effects are often attributed to disease processes.

The problem of detection of drug-related adverse effects has contributed to the emergence of a new field of pharmacologic study, pharmacoepidemiology. Pharmacoepidemiology uses the survey methods of epidemiologic data base review to analyze drug utilization and drug-related effects. For example, recent reviews of the Medicaid data base identified the increased risk of hip fractures in elderly patients receiving sedative drugs and increased risk of peptic ulcer disease in patients receiving NSAIDs.[120,121] Pharmacoepidemiologic studies of the Medicare and Health Care Finance Administration data bases have been proposed for inclusion in the design of proposed new drug dispensing and reimbursement regimens.[118]

The drug evaluation process and postmarketing surveillance policy are currently undergoing review, and changes in the process have been recommended.[112] Anticipated changes are an increased emphasis on drug concentration data, concentration-versus-effect and toxicity studies, and studies of special populations such as the elderly during clinical testing phases 1 through 3. A prior limitation to the collection of concentration data for pharmacokinetic and pharmacodynamic analysis had been the requirement for frequent sampling of blood or plasma following drug administration in a given individual. An alternative method called a *population pharmacokinetic screen* has been proposed and is being utilized. The population pharmacokinetic screen involves the collection of limited numbers of plasma or blood samples from an individual but the collection of samples from large populations of patients receiving the drug. These concentration data can be modeled to determine estimates of "population" clearance and half-life and volume estimates with subanalysis of influences such as age, disease, gender, and concomitant medications on the derived parameters. This method of evaluation[96,97,122,123] could be of special utility in studies of geriatric patients since anemia and concomitant diseases often exclude them from more traditional pharmacokinetic-pharmacodynamic study designs requiring multiple blood samples and effect measures. Another suggestion that would have an impact on the geriatric population is the recommendation that studies evaluate a *no-anticipated-effect* dose and estimate the lowest useful concentration. Previously, dosages known to produce a substantial effect in normal individuals or younger patients were chosen for testing. There have been numerous examples in which the optimal clinical regimens have later been shown to require significantly lower dosing regimens. Prospective study of lower dosing regimens would be anticipated to be of major importance in the testing of drugs for the elderly.

The underlying principle behind the recommended changes in the drug evaluation process is the belief that a full understanding of the pharmacokinetics and pharmacodynamics of a new drug in preclinical animal studies and human testing provides a framework for efficient and rational drug development. The corollary is that a full understanding of a drug and its effects in target patient populations such as the elderly will lead to improved therapeutic regimens and decreased drug toxicity.

REFERENCES

1. Johnson SL et al: Xylose disposition in humans as a function of age. *Clin Pharmacol Ther* 39:697, 1986.
2. Mayersohn M: The "xylose test" to assess gastrointestinal absorption in the elderly; a pharmacokinetic evaluation of the literature. *J Gerontol* 37:300, 1982.
3. Johnson SL et al: Gastrointestinal absorption as a function of age: Xylose absorption in healthy adults. *Clin Pharmacol Ther* 38:331, 1985.
4. Castleden CM et al: The effect of ageing on drug absorption from the gut. *Age Ageing* 6:138, 1977.
5. Roskos KV et al: The effect of aging on percutaneous absorption in man. *J Pharmacokinet Biopharm* 17:617, 1989.
6. Ameer B et al: Systemic absorption of topical lidocaine in elderly and young adults undergoing bronchoscopy. *Pharmacotherapy* 9:74, 1989.
7. Forbes GB, Reina JC: Adult lean body mass declines with age: Some longitudinal observations. *Metabolism* 19:653, 1970.
8. Bruce A et al: Body composition: Prediction of normal body potassium, body water and body fat in adults on the basis of body height, body weight and age. *Scand J Clin Lab Invest* 40:461, 1980.
9. Vestal RE et al: Aging and methanol metabolism. *Clin Pharmacol Ther* 21:343, 1977.
10. Veering BT et al: The effect of age on serum concentrations of albumin and alpha 1-acid glycoprotein. *Br J Clin Pharmacol* 29:201, 1990.
11. Greenblatt DJ: Reduced serum albumin concentration in the elderly: A report from the Boston Collaborative Drug Surveillance Program. *J Am Geriatr Soc* 27:20, 1979.
12. Abernethy DR, Kerzner L: Age effects on alpha-1 glycoprotein concentration and imipramine plasma protein binding. *J Am Geriatr Soc* 32:705, 1984.
13. Campion EW et al: The effect of age on serum albumin in healthy males: Report from the normative aging study. *J Gerontol* 43:M18, 1988.
14. Davies DF, Shock NW: Age changes in glomerular filtration rate, effective renal plasma flow and tubular excretory capacity in adult males. *J Clin Invest* 29:496, 1950.
15. Rowe JW et al: The effect of age on creatinine clearance in men: Cross-section and longitudinal study. *J Gerontol* 31:155, 1976.
16. Bennett WM: Geriatric pharmacokinetics and the kidney. *Am J Kidney Dis* 16:283, 1990.
17. Cockcroft DW, Gault MH: Prediction of creatinine clearance from serum creatinine. *Nephron* 16:31, 1976.
18. Ewy GA et al: Digoxin metabolism in the elderly. *Circulation* 39:449, 1969.
19. Gurwitz JH et al: Nonsteroidal anti-inflammatory drug–associated azotemia in the very old. *JAMA* 264:471, 1990.
20. Menkes CJ: Renal and hepatic effects of NSAIDs in the elderly. *Scand J Rheumatol* 83(suppl):11, 1989.
21. Greenblatt DJ et al: Antipyrine kinetics in the elderly: Prediction of age-related changes in benzodiazepine oxidizing capacity. *J Pharmacol Exp Ther* 220:120, 1982.
22. Vestal RE et al: Antipyrine metabolism in man: Influence of age. *Clin Pharmacol Ther* 18:425, 1975.
23. Wynne HA et al: Hepatic clearance: The effect of age using indocyanine green as a model compound. *Br J Clin Pharmacol* 30:634, 1990.
24. Geokas MC, Haverback BJ: The aging gastrointestinal tract. *Am J Surg* 117:881, 1969.
25. Wynne HA et al: The effect of age upon liver volume and apparent liver bloodflow in healthy man. *Hepatology* 9:297, 1989.
26. Woodhouse KW, Wynne HA: Age-related changes in liver size and hepatic blood flow: The influence on drug metabolism in the elderly. *Clin Pharmacokinet* 15:287, 1988.
27. Woodhouse KW, James OFW: Hepatic drug metabolism and ageing. *Br Med Bull* 46:22, 1990.
28. Kitani K: Aging and the liver. *Prog Liver Dis* 9:603, 1990.
29. Wood AJJ et al: Effect of aging and cigarette smoking on antipyrine and indocyanine green elimination. *Clin Pharmacol Ther* 26:16, 1979.
30. Wynne HA et al: The association of age and frailty with paracetamol conjugation in man. *Age Ageing* 19:419, 1990.
31. Vestal RE et al: Effects of age and cigarette smoking on propranolol disposition. *Clin Pharmacol Ther* 26:8, 1979.
32. Adelman RC: An age dependent modification of enzyme regulation. *J Biol Chem* 245:1032, 1970.
33. Wynne HA et al: The effect of age upon the affinity of microsomal mono-oxygenase enzymes for substrate in human liver. *Age Ageing* 17:401, 1988.
34. Schmucker DL et al: Effects of age and gender on in vitro properties of human liver microsomal monooxygenases. *Clin Pharmacol Ther* 48:365, 1990.
35. Twum-Barima Y et al: Impaired enzyme induction by rifampicin in the elderly. *Br J Clin Pharmacol* 17:595, 1984.
36. Smith DA et al: Age-dependent stereoselective increase in the oral clearance of hexobarbitone isomers caused by rifampicin. *Br J Clin Pharmacol* 32:735, 1991.
37. Chandler MHH et al: Age-associated stereoselective alterations in hexobarbital metabolism. *Clin Pharmacol Ther* 43:436, 1988.
38. Hooper WD, Qing MS: The influence of age and gender on the stereoselective metabolism and pharmacokinetics of mephobarbital in humans. *Clin Pharmacol Ther* 48:633, 1990.
39. Baciewicz AM, Self TH: Rifampin drug interactions. *Arch Intern Med* 144:1667, 1984.
40. Feeley J et al: Increased toxicity and reduced clearance of lidocaine by cimetidine. *Ann Intern Med* 96:592, 1982.
41. Somogyi A, Gugler R: Drug interactions with cimetidine. *Clin Pharmacokinet* 7:23, 1982.
42. Muhlberg W: Pharmacokinetics of diuretics in geriatric patients. *Arch Gerontol Geriatr:* 9(3):283, 1989.
43. Ochs HR et al: Reduced quinidine clearance in elderly persons. *Am J Cardiol* 42:481, 1978.
44. Nation RL et al: Lignocaine kinetics in cardiac pa-

tients and aged subjects. *Br J Clin Pharmacol* 4:439, 1977.
45. Reidenberg MM et al: Aging and renal clearance of procainamide and acetylprocainamide. *Clin Pharmacol Ther* 28:732, 1980.
46. Bauer LA et al: Influence of age, renal function and heart failure on procainamide clearance and *n*-acetylprocainamide serum concentrations. *Int J Clin Pharmacol Ther Toxicol* 27:213, 1989.
47. Castelden CM, George CF: The effect of age on the hepatic clearance of propranolol. *Br J Clin Pharmacol* 7:49, 1979.
48. Kendall MJ et al: Plasma metoprolol concentrations in young, old and hypertensive subjects. *Br J Clin Pharmacol* 4:497, 1977.
49. Abernethy DR et al: Verapamil pharmacodynamics and disposition in young and elderly hypertensive patients: Altered electrocardiographic and hypotensive responses. *Ann Intern Med* 105:329, 1986.
50. Schwartz JB, Abernethy DR: Responses to intravenous and oral diltiazem in elderly and younger patients with systemic hypertension. *Am J Cardiol* 59:1111, 1987.
51. Montamat SC, Abernethy DR: Calcium antagonists in geriatric patients: Diltiazem in elderly persons with hypertension: *Clin Pharmacol Ther* 45:682, 1989.
52. Robertson DRC et al: Age-related changes in the pharmacokinetics and pharmacodynamics of nifedipine. *Br J Clin Pharmacol* 25:297, 1988.
53. Van Harten J et al: Single- and multiple-dose nisoldipine kinetics and effects in the young, the middle-aged, and the elderly. *Clin Pharmacol Ther* 45:600, 1989.
54. Baksi AK et al: A comparison of the pharmacokinetics of nisoldipine in elderly and young subjects. *Br J Clin Pharmacol* 31:367, 1991.
55. Abernethy DR et al: Effects of amlodipine, a long-acting dihydropyridine calcium antagonist in aging hypertension: Pharmacodynamics in relation to disposition. *Clin Pharmacol Ther* 48:76, 1990.
56. Abernethy DR et al: Amlodipine in elderly hypertensive patients: Pharmacokinetics and pharmacodynamics. *J Cardiovasc Pharmacol* 12(suppl):S67, 1988.
57. Forette F et al: Effect of nicardipine in elderly hypertensive patients. *Br J Clin Pharmacol* 20:125S, 1985.
58. Piepho RW, Fendler KJ: Antihypertensive therapy in the aged patient: Clinical pharmacokinetic considerations. *Drugs Aging* 1:194, 1991.
59. Rubin PC et al: Prazosin disposition in young and elderly subjects. *Br J Clin Pharmacol* 12:401, 1981.
60. Somberg JC et al: Terazosin: Pharmacokinetics and the effect of age and dose on the incidence of adverse events. *Am Heart J* 122(3):901, 1991.
61. Abernethy DR et al: Comparison in young and elderly patients of pharmacodynamics and disposition of labetalol in systemic hypertension. *Am J Cardiol* 60:697, 1987.
62. Rocci ML et al: Pharmacokinetics and pharmacodynamics of labetalol in elderly and young hypertensive patients following single and multiple doses. *Pharmacotherapy* 10:92, 1990.
63. Creasey WA et al: Pharmacokinetics of captopril in elderly healthy male volunteers. *J Clin Pharmacol* 26:264, 1986.
64. Hockings N et al: Age and the pharmacokinetics and pharmacodynamics of chronic enalapril treatment. *Clin Pharmacol Ther* 41:597, 1987.
65. Lees KR, Reid JL: Age and the pharmacokinetics and pharmacodynamics of chronic enalapril treatment. *Clin Pharmacol Ther* 41:597, 1987.
66. Cirillo VJ et al: Effect of age on lisinopril pharmacokinetics. *Clin Pharmacol Ther* 39:187, 1986.
67. Kobayashi KA et al: Glipizide pharmacokinetics in young and elderly volunteers. *Clin Pharm* 7:224, 1988.
68. Balant L et al: Pharmacokinetics of glipizide in man: Influence of renal insufficiency. *Diabetologia* 9(suppl):331, 1973.
69. Balant L et al: The pharmacokinetics of glipizide and glibenclamide in man. *Eur J Clin Pharmacol* 8:63, 1975.
70. Arrigoni L et al: Chlorpropamide pharmacokinetics in young healthy adults and older diabetic patients. *Clin Pharm* 6:162, 1987.
71. Schwinghammer TL et al: Pharmacokinetics and pharmacodynamics of glyburide in young and elderly nondiabetic adults. *Clin Pharm* 10(7):532, 538, 1991.
72. Greenblatt JD et al: Clinical pharmacokinetics of anxiolytics and hypnotics in the elderly. *Clin Pharmacokinet* 21:262, 1991.
73. Greenblatt DJ et al: Sensitivity to triazolam in the elderly. *N Engl J Med* 324:1691, 1991.
74. Advenier C et al: Pharmacokinetics of isoniazid in the elderly. *Br Clin Pharmacol* 10:167, 1980.
75. Farrah F et al: Hepatic drug acetylation and oxidation: Effect of aging in man. *Br Med J* 2:155, 1977.
76. Miglioli PA et al: Effect of age on single- and multiple-dose pharmacokinetics of erythromycin. *Eur J Clin Pharmacol* 39:161, 1990.
77. Lumholtz B et al: Dose-regimen of kanamycin and gentamycin. *Acta Med Scand* 190:521, 1974.
78. Triggs et al: Absorption and disposition of ampicillin in the elderly. *Eur J Clin Pharmacol* 18:195, 1980.
79. LeBel M et al: Pharmacokinetics of ciprofloxacin in elderly subjects. *Pharmacotherapy* 6:87, 1986.
80. Divoll M et al: Acetaminophen kinetics in the elderly. *Clin Pharmacol Ther* 31:151, 1982.
81. Divoll M et al: Age does not alter acetaminophen absorption. *J Am Geriatr Soc* 30:240, 1982.
82. Briant RH et al: The rate of acetaminophen metabolism in the elderly and the young. *J Am Geriatr Soc* 24:359, 1976.
83. Cusack BJ: Drug metabolism in the elderly. *J Clin Pharmacol* 28:571, 1988.
84. Cuny G et al: Pharmacokinetics of salicylates in elderly. *Gerontology* 25:49, 1979.
85. Netter P et al: Salicylate kinetics in old age. *Clin Pharmacol Ther* 38:6, 1985.
86. Gugler R, Somogy A: Reduced cimetidine clearance with age. *N Engl J Med* 301:435, 1979.
87. Schentag JJ et al: Pharmacokinetic and clinical studies in patients with cimetidine-associated mental confusion. *Lancet* 1:177, 1979.
88. Drayer DE et al: Age and renal clearance of cimetidine. *Clin Pharmacol Ther* 31:45, 1982.
89. Platt D et al: Pharmacokinetics of ranitidine in geriatric patients with multiple diseases. *Arch Gerontol Geriatr* 8(2):139, 1989.
90. Simons KJ et al: Pharmacokinetics and pharmacody-

namics of terfenadine and chlorpheniramine in the elderly. *J Allergy Clin Immunol* 85:540, 1990.

91. Nicholson PA et al: Pharmacokinetics of misoprostol in the elderly, in patients with renal failure and when coadministered with NSAID or antipyrine, propranolol or diazepam. *J Rheumatol* 17:33, 1990.
92. Robertson DRC et al: The effect of age on the pharmacodynamics of levodopa administered alone and in the presence of carbidopa. *Br J Clin Pharmacol* 28:61, 1989.
93. Simko A: Guidelines for the use of psychopharmacia in geriatric cases. *Ther Hung* 37(4):187, 1989.
94. Gurwitz JH, Avorn J: The ambiguous relationship between aging and adverse drug reactions. *Ann Intern Med* 114:956, 1991.
95. Hill AV: The possible effects of the aggregation of the molecules of haemoglobin on its dissociation curves. *J Physiol (Lond)* 40:4, 1910.
96. Beal SL, Sheiner LB: Estimating population kinetics. *CRC Crit Rev Biomed Eng* 8:195, 1982.
97. Beal SL, Sheiner LB: Methodology of population pharmacokinetics, in Garrett ER, Hirtz JL (eds): *Drug Fate and Metabolism—Methods and Techniques.* New York, Dekker, 1985.
98. Lakatta EG: Altered autonomic modulation of cardiovascular function with adult aging: Perspectives from studies ranging from man to cell, in Stone and Weglicki (eds): *Pathobiology of Cardiovascular Injury.* Boston, Nijhoff, p 441, 1985.
99. Goldberg PB et al: Effects of age on the adrenergic cardiac neuroeffector junction. *Life Sci* 35:2585, 1984.
100. Pan HYM et al: Decline in beta adrenergic receptor–mediated vascular relaxation with aging in man. *J Pharmacol Exp Ther* 239:802, 1986.
101. Guthrie S et al: Pharmacodynamics and pharmacokinetics of ethanol, diazepam, and pentobarbital in young and aged rats. *Pharmacol Toxicol* 61:308, 1987.
102. Greenblatt DJ et al: Implications of altered drug disposition in the elderly: Studies of benzodiazepines. *J Clin Pharmacol* 29:866, 1989.
103. Beers MH, Ouslander JG: Risk factors in geriatric drug prescribing: A practical guide to avoiding problems. *Drugs* 37:105, 1989.
104. Chrischilles EA et al: Use of medications by persons 65 and over: Data from the Established Populations for Epidemiologic Studies of the Elderly. *Gerontol Med Sci* 47:M137, 1992.
105. Brown MM et al: Drug–drug interactions among residents in homes for the elderly. *Nurs Res* 26:47, 1977.
106. Nolan L, O'Malley K: The need for a more rational approach to drug prescribing for elderly people in nursing homes. *Age Ageing* 18:52, 1989.
107. Johnson RE, Vollmer WM: Comparing sources of drug data about the elderly. *J Am Geriatr Soc* 39:1079, 1991.
108. Gurwitz JH et al: Improving medication prescribing and utilization in the nursing home. *J Am Geriatr Soc* 38:542, 1990.
109. Ray WA et al: The study of antipsychotic use in nursing homes: Epidemiologic evidence suggesting misuse. *Am J Public Health* 70:485, 1980.
110. Hutchinson TA et al: Frequency, severity, and risk factors for adverse drug reactions in adult outpatients: A prospective study. *J Chronic Dis* 39:533, 1986.
111. Carbonin P et al: Is age an independent risk factor of adverse drug reactions in hospitalized medical patients? *J Am Geriatr Soc* 39:1093, 1991.
112. Peck CC et al: Opportunities for integration of pharmacokinetics, pharmacodynamics, and toxicokinetics in rational drug development. *Clin Pharmacol Ther* 51:465, 1992.
113. *Guidelines for the Study of Drugs Likely to be Used in the Elderly.* Dept. of Health and Human Services. Public Health Service. Food and Drug Administration. Center for Drug Evaluation and Research. November, 1989.
114. FDA: *General Considerations for the Clinical Evaluation of Drugs.* Washington, DC, HEW (FDA), 1977.
115. Applegate WB, Curb JD: Designing and executing randomized clinical trials involving elderly persons. *J Am Geriatr Soc* 38:943, 1990.
116. Abernethy DR, Azarnoff DL: Pharmacokinetic investigations in elderly patients: Clinical and Ethical considerations. *Clin Pharmacokinet* 19:89, 1990.
117. Turner P: Clinical trials in elderly subjects. *Postgrad Med J* 65:218, 1989.
118. Institute of Medicine (IOM): *Report of a Workshop: Drug Development for the Geriatric Population.* Washington, DC, National Academy Press, 1990.
119. Temple R: Perspectives on drug testing in the elderly. Presented at Annual Meeting of American Society for Clinical Pharmacology, Orlando, Florida, March, 1992; available from Hour Glass Recording, Tampa, Fla.
120. Ray WA et al: Psychotropic drug use and the risk of hip fracture. *N Engl J Med* 316:363, 1987.
121. Griffin MR et al: Nonsteroidal inflammatory drug use and increased risk for peptic ulcer disease in elderly persons. *Ann Intern Med* 114:257, 1991.
122. Laplanche R et al: Exploratory analysis of population pharmacokinetic data from clinical trials with application to isradipine. *Clin Pharmacol Ther* 50:39, 1991.
123. Blychert E et al: A population study of the pharmacokinetics of felodipine. *Br J Clin Pharmacol* 31:15, 1991.

Additional Reading

Rowland M, Tozer TN: *Clinical Pharmacokinetics: Concepts and Applications,* 2d ed. Philadelphia, Lea & Febiger, 1989.

Yuen GJ: Altered pharmacokinetics in the elderly. *Clin Geriatr Med* 6:257, 1990.

Feely J, Coakely D: Altered pharmacodynamics in the elderly. *Clin Geriatr Med* 6:269, 1990.

Chapter 25

PERIOPERATIVE MANAGEMENT OF THE OLDER PATIENT

Joseph Francis

Rates of surgical procedures among older persons have risen dramatically since 1980. During the same period, surgical mortality has fallen, and even persons 85 and older who undergo major surgery now have long-term survival rates that equal or surpass those of the general population.[1] Since advanced age no longer makes surgery impractical, clinicians can expect to become increasingly involved in the perioperative care of their older patients.

The physiologic changes of aging can influence operative outcomes, but comorbid medical conditions remain the strongest predictors of risk. Eighty percent of older surgical patients have significant preoperative medical problems, and nearly one-third have three or more problems.[2] Many of these conditions are unrecognized prior to surgery. This complexity makes perioperative medicine in the older patient uniquely challenging but also provides greater opportunity for meaningful interventions.

AGING AND SURGICAL RISK

The physiologic changes of "normal aging" that have the potential to increase the likelihood or severity of postoperative complications are summarized in Table 25-1. For example, impaired renal and hepatic function predispose to drug toxicity, and impaired cardiac compensatory mechanisms increase the likelihood of hypotension. Aging may also alter the presentation of disease—for instance, significant renal insufficiency may be present despite a normal serum creatinine, and diabetes may present without glycosuria. Other changes are more directly related to surgical outcome—for instance, slower wound healing.

The clinical impact of aging physiology may not be evident except during periods of maximal stress. For example, cardiac output can be maintained in healthy older persons, despite a lower peak heart rate, by increases in stroke volume. However, anesthetic-induced venodilation, third-space fluid shifts, or blood loss during surgery may cause circulatory collapse in older patients, because less compliant hearts are more dependent upon adequate preload.[3]

Despite these theoretical considerations, the actual contribution of "normal aging" to surgical risk remains unclear. The degree of organ decline that accompanies aging is relatively small compared to the effects of chronic disease and lifestyle. For example, forced expiratory volume in 1 second (FEV_1) decreases by 200 ml per decade after age 20, leaving the average nonsmoking 80-year-old man with an FEV_1 greater than 2 liters, which is above the threshold believed to confer increased risk for pulmonary complications. Smoking, however, doubles or triples the rate of decline in FEV_1 and contributes to a higher risk of perioperative pulmonary complications[4] (see Chap. 48). Furthermore, studies of surgical risk that control for underlying chronic disease often fail to demonstrate an independent effect of age on surgical risk. In settings where the effect of age cannot be "adjusted away" by statistical control of confounding chronic illness, it is still possible that it is acting as a surrogate for underlying chronic diseases that are unrecognized or cannot be measured with great precision.[5]

ASSESSING RISK DUE TO CHRONIC DISEASE

Overall Mortality Risk

Since normal aging cannot account for the bulk of operative risk, the clinician's task is to identify underlying illnesses and their impact on postoperative mortality and complications. One attempt to do so is represented by the American Society of Anesthesiologists' Classification System, a global assessment of the burden of disease that has been shown to correlate with overall perioperative mortal-

TABLE 25-1

Selected Physiologic Changes of Aging and Their Significance for Perioperative Complications

System	Change	Significance
General	Decreased total body water and lean mass	Increased drug toxicity
	Decreased thermoregulatory response	Increased risk of hypothermia
Skin	Slower reepithelialization, fewer dermal blood vessels	Slower wound healing Possibly increased risk of pressure sores
Cardiac	Fibrosis and degeneration of pacemaking and conducting tissue	Increased risk for conduction disturbances
	Impaired early diastolic filling due to: Mitral valve thickening Decreased ventricular compliance Prolonged isovolumic relaxation	Increased risk of hypotension with dehydration, tachyarrhythmias, vasodilators
	Decreased arterial compliance	Leads to systolic hypertension and ventricular hypertrophy Possibly increased susceptibility to loss of plasma volume
	Impaired compensatory mechanisms Decreased baroreceptor sensitivity Decreased target-organ response to β-adrenergic stimulation Decreased renin, angiotensin, and aldosterone	Decreased heart rate response to stress Increased risk of hypotension
	Resting cardiac output is maintained	Cardiac risk determined more by disease than age
	Exercise cardiac output maintained by increased stroke volume, since maximum attainable heart rate is less	Circulatory status dependent on adequate preload/volume
Pulmonary	Altered mechanics of ventilation: Loss of elastic recoil Stiffening of chest wall Increased ventilation-perfusion mismatch	Airway closure (FEV_1 falls by 0.2 L per decade after age 20); decreased vital capacity and pulmonary reserve; increased reliance on diaphragmatic breathing; arterial hypoxemia (Po_2 falls 4 mm per decade after age 20)
	Decreased ventilatory response to hypercapnia	Greater potential for ventilatory failure (e.g., with sedative drugs)
	Decreased airway protection: Cough, laryngeal reflexes impaired Slower mucociliary clearance	Risk of aspiration and infection
Renal	Nephron "drop out" with loss of glomerular filtration rate	Prolonged half-life of drugs cleared by kidney
	Creatinine production declines due to fall in muscle mass	Glomerular filtration rate diminished despite "normal" serum creatinine
	Delayed response to sodium deficiency	Increased risk of volume depletion
	Reduced capacity to excrete salt and water	Risk of fluid overload and hyponatremia
	Increased renal threshold for glycosuria	Urine glucoses unreliable
Immune	Thymus gland involution	Increased risk for infection
	Impaired T-cell function	
Hepatic	Decreased blood flow and microsomal oxidation	Prolonged half-life of some drugs metabolized by liver
Endocrine	Decreased secretion and action of insulin	Hyperglycemia in response to glucose loads in nondiabetics
Other	Prostatic hypertrophy	Risk of urinary retention

ity.[6] Unfortunately, this classification is subjective and prone to considerable interobserver disagreement.[7]

Relatively few studies have attempted to quantify overall perioperative mortality in terms of objective indicators of risk. In one study of older male veterans, in-hospital deaths were predicted by three factors: history of hypertension, creatinine clearance less than 50 ml/min, and limited physical activity (bed- or chair-bound). Patients with two or more of these factors experienced 20 percent in-hospital mortality. Two-year mortality in this same population was predicted by four factors: diagnosis of cancer, impaired renal function, history of congestive heart failure, and use of bronchodilator medication. Mortality was 7 percent when none of these factors were present and 64 percent when three or more were present. Age was not a significant predictor of short- or long-term mortality in these multivariable analyses.[8]

Cardiac Complications

Because 25 to 30 percent of perioperative deaths are attributed to cardiac causes, much of perioperative risk assessment has focused on predicting cardiac complications. Goldman's Cardiac Risk Index (Table 25-2) was first described in 1977 and has been widely used since then.[9] Advanced age is an independent predictor of risk in this index, possibly because other chronic conditions are not assessed. Several investigators have attempted, independently, to validate the Cardiac Risk Index in elderly surgical populations. The index has predictive value, making it useful for preoperative assessment. However, in some studies it may fail to identify as many as 70 percent of patients prone to serious cardiac complications.[10]

This poor performance reflects, in part, the high prevalence of coronary artery disease that is masked in older persons by inactivity or other factors. Autopsy studies show significant stenosis in at least one coronary artery in nearly 75 percent of subjects over 60 years old, but only about half of these cases are clinically recognized.[3] In the Framingham Study, nearly a quarter of myocardial infarctions were initially unrecognized, a proportion that increased with age in males.[11] Although the clinical importance of all forms of silent coronary disease is not established, patients with asymptomatic ischemia during preoperative ambulatory electrocardiographic monitoring have a higher risk of postoperative cardiac events.[12]

Noninvasive testing can identify patients with occult coronary artery disease and stratify older persons according to cardiac risk. Because exercise testing is often impractical in such individuals, modalities such as gated nuclear scans, dipyridamole-thallium imaging, dipyridamole echocardiography, and ambulatory electrocardiographic monitoring for ischemia have been used to assess cardiac performance or ischemic burden. These techniques can provide predictive information beyond that of the clinical assessment, although their impact on outcome has not been established.[13] Until further data become available, it is recommended that the clinical evaluation be used to identify patients requiring further testing to assess cardiac risk. Older patients with low risk (e.g., nonvascular surgery patients without diabetes who can walk two blocks at a normal pace without developing angina) probably require no further testing. Patients deemed to have an intermediate risk (e.g., the vascular surgery patient who denies angina but is unable to walk) may benefit from further risk stratification with dipyridamole-thallium imaging or preoperative monitoring for silent myocardial ischemia.[14] Recommendations for managing the high-risk patient are discussed below.

TABLE 25-2

Cardiac Risk Index

Risk Factors	Points
History:	
a. Age > 70 years	5
b. MI in previous 6 months	10
Physical examination:	
a. S3 gallop or JVD	11
b. significant aortic stenosis	3
Electrocardiogram:	
a. Rhythm other than sinus or PACs	7
b. >5 PVCs/min	7
Poor general status:*	3
Operation:	
a. Intraperitoneal, intrathoracic, or aortic	3
b. Emergency	4
Total possible	53

Point-Total	Risk Classification	Life-threatening Complications, %	Cardiac Deaths, %
0–5	I	0.7	0.2
6–12	II	5	2
13–25	III	11	2
≥26	IV	22	56

*Defined as presence of one of the following: $Po_2 < 60$ or $Pco_2 > 50$ mmHg; $K < 3.0$ or $HCO_3 < 20$ meq/liter; BUN > 50 to Cr > 3.0 mg/dl; abnormal SGOT; chronic liver disease; or bedridden.
SOURCE: Goldman et al.[9]

Pulmonary Complications

In older patients, most postoperative deaths are noncardiac and are often due to pulmonary complications, including pneumonia, aspiration, adult respiratory distress syndrome, and pulmonary embolism. The frequency of postoperative pneumonia, atelectasis, hypoxemia, and prolonged mechanical ventilation depends on factors such as smoking history, prior respiratory disease (especially obstructive lung disease), severity of airflow obstruction, and the type and duration of surgery. Pulmonary function abnormalities that potentially confer risk for respiratory complications and mortality include maximal breathing capacity less than 50 percent of predicted, FEV_1 less than 2 liters, and an arterial Pco_2 greater than 45 mmHg.[15] Except for patients undergoing pneumonectomy, pulmonary function tests appear to add little predictive information beyond the clinical assessment.[16] For noncardiothoracic surgery, even patients with severe obstructive pulmonary disease (FEV_1 less than 50 percent of predicted) appear to have an acceptable operative risk. In one series, combined mortality and nonfatal ventilatory failure were less than 3 percent.[17]

Functional Impairment and Operative Risk

Functional impairment is a useful index of the severity of chronic disease, which may make it the most easily measured predictor of operative risk. Gerson[10] found that the ability to exercise for 2 minutes or longer on a bicycle had better sensitivity and specificity for predicting cardiac complications than Goldman's Cardiac Risk Index. The mechanism by which inability to exercise predicted cardiac complications was unclear, since patients were primarily limited by joint problems, dementia, or weakness rather than claudication or angina, and ischemic EKG changes were uncommon. Poor performance on bicycle ergometry also predicted postoperative pulmonary complications.[18]

Functional assessment need not require specialized testing. Simple performance-based tests such as walking or stair climbing may identify patients at higher risk for pulmonary and other postoperative complications.[19] Information obtained from interview can also be valuable. Seymour[20] found that "active" elderly (defined as those who reported leaving their homes at least twice weekly) had fewer respiratory, cardiac, and wound complications than the homebound. Poor premorbid functional status such as inability to perform one or more activities of daily living or instrumental activities also identifies those hip fracture patients who are at risk for mortality, postoperative complications, and loss of independence.[21]

Period of Risk

Although patients and physicians may fear intraoperative or anesthetic-related death, such events are now rare. Anesthesia appears to be exceptionally safe: in a review of 100,000 anesthetic procedures, 7-day mortality was related to patient and surgical factors but not to duration of anesthesia or experience of the anesthesiologist. Although spinal anesthesia in this study was associated with decreased mortality compared with inhalational techniques, type of anesthesia failed to predict outcome once patient and surgical characteristics were considered.[22]

It is after surgery that the vast majority of deaths occur; in one series of patients undergoing noncardiac surgery, half of postoperative deaths occurred 3 or more weeks after surgery.[8] For some patients, the period of risk after surgery may be quite long. For instance, patients experiencing postoperative myocardial ischemia or infarction had an increased risk of subsequent cardiac complications for at least the next 2 years.[23]

PREOPERATIVE MANAGEMENT

History and Physical

The medical management of the older surgical patient does not differ in principle from that of any patient with similar underlying disease. The crux of the preoperative evaluation remains the comprehensive history and physical. Although the history is perceived to be less useful in geriatric patients—due to the atypical presentation of disease, sensory loss, and cognitive impairment—valuable information still is available to the astute clinician. For instance, mildly demented patients living in the community can give valid reports of symptoms.[24] However, informants should be sought out for further data if impairment is profound.

The medical interview should also assess physical function, cognitive ability, competency, and the availability of social supports. Functional impairment is common but often missed by physicians, so it must be specifically assessed either by asking about activities of daily living and instrumental activities or by incorporating performance-based functional assessment into the physical examination. Because impaired cognition identifies patients at risk for postoperative delirium, mortality, and prolonged hospitalization, preoperative mental status should be determined with a brief, screening mental status examination, such as the Mini-Mental State Examination (Chap. 19). However, cognitive screening tests do not constitute an adequate test of decision-making competency, which requires directly assessing the patient's ability to communicate and his or her understanding of the risks, benefits, and consequences of a proposed surgical procedure and its alternatives (Chap. 35).

Finally, since patients with few family or friends are at risk for functional decline after surgery, the availability of supports should be determined. Elderly patients at risk because of poor physical function, impaired cognition, or few social supports may benefit from further evaluation by a social worker with experience in geriatrics.

The physical examination is modified by age and concomitant disease, particularly in the assessment of cardiac status. Systolic blood pressure should be confirmed by palpation, since an "auscultatory gap" is often present in older patients with stiff vessels and systolic hypertension. Systolic ejection murmurs at the base of the heart may represent aortic valve cusp sclerosis rather than hemodynamically significant valvular obstruction. Conversely, markers of severe aortic stenosis, such as a diminished S2 or delayed carotid upstrokes, may be falsely normal in older patients with significant aortic valve obstruction. Echocardiography and Doppler studies may be necessary to establish a diagnosis, particularly when murmurs are long, late peaking, or transmitted to the carotids,[3] because patients with hemodynamically significant aortic stenosis are at increased risk for cardiac complications.[9]

Medications

The initial preoperative encounter provides an ideal opportunity to review medications the patient is receiving, eliminating those that have no clear benefit or might contribute to complications. Aspirin, for instance, can increase risk of perioperative hemorrhage, so discontinuation at least 7 days prior to elective surgery is recommended.[25] If this is not possible, a bleeding time should be checked. Use of nonsteroidal anti-inflammatory agents may also increase postoperative bleeding and should be discontinued 48 hours prior to surgery.[26] Medications that may contribute to risk for postoperative delirium, such as anticholinergic agents, should be discontinued unless absolutely necessary. Sedative drugs such as benzodiazepines should be tapered rather than suddenly discontinued because of the risk of withdrawal symptoms. If volume overload is absent, one should consider holding diuretics 48 hours prior to surgery. Finally, oral hypoglycemic agents should be discontinued the night before surgery (3 days preoperatively for the longer-acting chlorpropamide) to reduce risk of perioperative hypoglycemia; glucoses above 250 mg/dl can then be safely managed with sliding-scale subcutaneous or constant intravenous infusion of short-acting, regular insulin.[25]

Provisions must be made to continue essential medications throughout the perioperative period. Patients on antiepileptic, cardiovascular, and antihypertensive drugs can take their morning dose with small sips of water several hours before surgery; then appropriate parenteral alternatives should be used until oral intake is resumed. Abrupt discontinuation of beta blockers and clonidine must be avoided; intravenous propranolol and transdermal clonidine are useful to prevent withdrawal syndromes if patients cannot ingest anything for more than 24 hours. Stable diabetics on insulin should receive one-half of their usual dose of intermediate-acting insulin subcutaneously on the morning of surgery and be provided with 5% dextrose intravenously. Finally, patients at risk for adrenal suppression due to recent chronic corticosteroid use should receive stress coverage (e.g., hydrocortisone 100 mg intravenously every 6 hours beginning the night prior to surgery, tapering to the usual maintenance dose of steroid after 3 to 5 days).[25]

Preoperative Testing

The yield of abnormalities from routine blood tests, electrocardiography, and chest x-ray is said to be considerably higher for older patients, but few studies address whether these abnormalities alter management or outcome. One way to eliminate unnecessary screening tests is to rely on the results of recent prior laboratory testing. In one study of older veterans undergoing elective surgery, nearly half of "routine" preoperative laboratory tests (CBC, electrolytes, creatinine, PT and PTT) duplicated tests performed in the same patient during the previous year. It was rare for repeat values to lie outside a range considered acceptable for surgery if the initial test was normal; the few exceptions could be predicted from the patient's history.[27]

Managing Cardiac Risk

Patients judged to be at high risk for cardiac complications based on clinical assessment (e.g., vascular surgery patient with a Goldman Index greater than 12 or high ischemic burden on dipyridamole-thallium imaging) or who are severely symptomatic have several options. The procedure can be canceled or a lower-risk surgical approach selected. If surgery cannot be postponed, then perioperative electrocardiographic and hemodynamic monitoring (including pulmonary artery catheterization) is recommended; fluids, inotropic agents, nitrates, and vasodilators can then be titrated to obtain optimal perfusion.[13]

For some patients, it may be prudent to delay surgery to allow for coronary arteriography and possible myocardial revascularization. Unfortunately, data to guide this decision are limited. Percutaneous transluminal coronary angioplasty prior to surgery has had little study. In descriptive, nonrandomized studies, vascular surgery patients who have undergone prophylactic coronary artery bypass grafting (CABG) have a mortality of 2 percent or less, compared with 7 percent mortality for vascular surgery not preceded by CABG. However, the 5 percent mortality associated with CABG in patients with peripheral vascular disease offsets the improved short-term mortality for subsequent surgery.[28] If there is benefit to prophylactic revascularization, it may consist primarily of reduction in long-term cardiac complications.

Finally, some older patients may be felt to face a high cardiac risk due to critical aortic stenosis. If valvular surgery is not an option, they may be able to undergo noncardiac surgery safely with careful intraoperative hemodynamic monitoring or after balloon valvuloplasty.[29]

Nutrition

Malnutrition, evident in approximately 20 percent of older hospital patients, impairs wound healing and increases postoperative complications. Measurement of the serum albumin is recommended to assess nutritional state, despite its complex relationship to nutritional status and operative outcome, since it predicts complications, mortality, and long-term outcome much better than other indicators of nutritional status—such as triceps skinfold thickness, midarm circumference, creatinine-height index, transferrin, and lymphocyte count—which do not discriminate accurately between well and malnourished elderly or lack appropriate normal standards for this age group.[30]

Unfortunately, existing data do not provide firm support for most preoperative nutritional interventions. For instance, perioperative parenteral nutrition has little effect on postoperative complications, although there may be some potential benefit to the severely malnourished (albumin < 2.8 g/dl or weight loss of 20 percent).[31] Enteral feeding through small-bore, soft catheters has been suggested as an alternative to parenteral hyperalimentation in patients without gastrointestinal contraindications but can lead to agitation, diarrhea with resultant dehydration, and aspiration in older patients. A trial of nighttime nasogastric feedings in malnourished elderly with hip fractures demonstrated modest improvements in albumin, shorter hospital stays, and a trend toward lower hospital mortality in the supplemented group. However, 22 percent of patients allocated to receive overnight supplements were unable to tolerate tube feedings.[32] Simple oral nutritional supplements in patients able to swallow may have similar beneficial effects, without the complications of nasogastric intubation.[33] Even less is known about the influence of micronutrients (e.g., zinc supplementation) upon surgical outcome in the elderly.

In the absence of data, recommendations on nutritional support in the elderly surgical patient are difficult to establish. Preoperative nutritional support should be considered in severely malnourished patients if delays in surgery are not anticipated to worsen outcome. Chronic diseases contributing to hypoalbuminemia should be addressed. In the perioperative period, patients should receive sufficient levels of protein, calories, and micronutrients to correct potential deficiencies and maintain balance under conditions of stress, but enthusiasm for enteral or parenteral feeding must be tempered by consideration of potential complications.

Other Preventive Measures

Patients who are identified to have chronic obstructive lung disease, either clinically or through spirometry, should begin measures to reduce postoperative pulmonary complications. Smoking is the strongest risk factor for obstructive lung disease, but to reduce postoperative complications, smoking cessation should occur at least 8 weeks before surgery. Other important measures include preoperative education in the importance of deep-breathing maneuvers, coughing, and use of incentive spirometry; bronchodilators; and, where appropriate, antibiotics, steroids, and intravenous aminophylline. Since many elderly do not use metered dose inhalers correctly, bronchodilator medication should be delivered via nebulization. Patients who are wheeze-free or improve their pulmonary function during the preoperative "tune-up" are believed to have a better prognosis. Chest physiotherapy may provoke bronchospasm in some patients, so it should be limited to patients producing more than 30 ml of sputum daily or those with lobar atelectasis.[14]

Intravascular volume status is critical in older patients because of the greater dependence of cardiac output on adequate preload. Patients with congestive heart failure, for instance, must not be overtreated with diuretics. Risk of postoperative congestive heart failure might actually be increased if patients sustain hypotension due to inadequate intraoperative fluid status. Although routine hemodynamic evaluation will probably prevent relatively few postoperative complications if used nonselectively in older patients,[34] those with significant cardiopulmonary problems (e.g., ejection fraction under 40 percent) or uncertain volume status should be considered for intraoperative pulmonary artery catheterization and optimization of hemodynamics through fluid loading, afterload reduction, and/or inotropic support.[35]

Risk for deep venous thrombosis increases with age and is high in certain procedures commonly performed in older persons, such as hip replacement and urologic surgery. Pulmonary embolism may be responsible for nearly one-third of postoperative deaths in older patients, so appropriate prophylaxis should always be provided. For low- to moderate-risk procedures, low-dose subcutaneous heparin (begun 12 to 24 hours before surgery) or external pneumatic compression (applied immediately before surgery) is recommended and should be continued until time of discharge. High-risk procedures such as elective hip surgery require warfarin begun several days preoperatively and adjusted to prolong the prothrombin time to an International Normalized Ratio of 2.0 to 3.0 (corresponding to 1.3 to 1.5 times control using North American thromboplastin). Because of its potential to induce fluid overload, intravenous dextran is usually avoided in older patients with diminished cardiac reserve.[36]

Finally, endocarditis is increasingly a problem of the elderly, due to the high prevalence of degenerative valvular disease and the large numbers of older patients undergoing oral, bowel, urinary, biliary, and pulmonary procedures, which can result in bacteremia. If a murmur, implying turbulent blood flow, is present, antibiotic prophylaxis, summarized in Table 25-3, should be provided.[37]

POSTOPERATIVE MANAGEMENT

Because complications of surgery are not limited to the first few postoperative days, physicians should follow their older surgical patients throughout the hospitalization and be prepared to intervene in the

TABLE 25-3

Recommended Prophylactic Regimens for Patients at Risk for Bacterial Endocarditis

	Not allergic to penicillin		*Allergic to penicillin*	
Procedure	**Oral Regimen**	**Parenteral Regimen, IM or IV, unless specified**	**Oral Regimen**	**Parenteral Regimen, IM or IV, unless specified**
Dental, oral, or upper respiratory tract procedures	Amoxicillin 3.0 g 1 h before procedure, then 1.5 g 6 h after initial dose*	High-risk patients: ampicillin 2.0 g plus gentamicin 1.5 mg/kg (up to 80 mg) 30 min before procedure; either amoxicillin 1.5 g orally 6 h after initial dose or repeat parenteral regimen 8 h after initial dose	Erythromycin 1.0 g 2 h before procedure or clindamycin 300 mg 1 h before procedure; then half dose 6 h after initial dose	Clindamycin 300 mg IV 30 min before procedure; then 150 mg orally or IV 6 h after initial dose High-risk patients: vancomycin 1.0 g over 1 h, starting 1 h before procedure
Genitourinary or gastrointestinal procedures	Amoxicillin as above (low-risk patients only)	Ampicillin, gentamicin, and amoxicillin as above*	Not applicable	Vancomycin 1.0 g over 1 h plus gentamicin 1.5 mg/kg (up to 80 mg) 1 h before procedure; may repeat 8 h after initial dose

*Standard regimen
SOURCE: Dajani AS et al.[37]

home—or nursing home, where convalescence is now more likely to take place.

Pain Control

Considerable evidence suggests that pain is undertreated in older patients, which may be due to misconceptions that pain sensation is diminished in old age or that older persons cannot tolerate narcotic analgesics. Postoperative patients should be directly queried about their pain at frequent intervals (not less than every 2 to 4 hours for the first 24 hours), and analgesics should be given according to anticipated needs rather than "as needed" (see Chap. 28). Improved postoperative pain control can enhance mobilization and may reduce myocardial ischemia.[38]

Older persons are more sensitive to the pain-relieving properties of opiates and are at higher risk for sedation or acute confusion, so smaller doses of these drugs are needed than in younger patients. Meperidine should be avoided in older persons, since its metabolite, normeperidine, has considerable central nervous system toxicity and can accumulate when renal insufficiency is present.[39] Patients with intact cognition should be considered for patient-controlled analgesia, which has been shown to provide significantly better pain relief and lower risk of postoperative confusion and pulmonary complications than intramuscular narcotic dosing.[40]

Mobilization

Prompt mobilization from bed is vital in order to reduce the risk of venous thromboembolism and to prevent loss of the ability to walk. Bed rest leads to cardiovascular deconditioning, increased risk of orthostatic hypotension, decreased coordination and balance, loss of muscle mass (as much as 5 percent per day), and joint contractures, all of which threaten independent ambulation. Recumbency also contributes to urinary retention, fecal impaction, atelectasis, and pneumonia.[41] In the patient whose condition precludes full activity, range-of-motion exercises and maintenance of upright position (e.g., sitting in chair) can reduce the severity and frequency of these complications.

Catheters

Voiding problems frequently accompany surgery in the elderly and are often managed with indwelling catheters, which predispose to urinary tract infection and gram-negative sepsis. Very short-term use of indwelling catheters in the elderly (e.g., removal by the morning after surgery) may reduce the incidence of urinary retention and bladder overdistension without increasing the rate of urinary tract infection.[42] In general, use of catheters beyond 48 hours should be avoided except when urinary retention cannot be practically managed by conservative measures (early mobilization; intermittent catheterization) or when wounds or pressure ulcers are being contaminated by incontinent urine. Patients who require short-term postoperative catheterization (more than 2 days but less than 2 weeks) may benefit from antibiotic prophylaxis[43]; this is not recommended, however, for patients who are anticipated to require long-term catheterization.

Postoperative Delirium

Acute confusion occurs in 10 to 15 percent of older general surgical patients, 30 percent of cardiac surgery patients, and over 50 percent of patients treated for hip fracture, making it perhaps the most frequently observed postoperative complication. Factors that increase risk of delirium during surgery include dementia, Parkinson's disease, low cardiac output, perioperative hypotension, postoperative hypoxia, and use of anticholinergic drugs. Type of anesthesia (general versus regional) does not appear to be an important determinant of delirium after the first postoperative day. Delirium is important because it may be the only manifestation of serious postoperative illness, such as sepsis or myocardial infarction, and identifies patients at risk for higher mortality, longer hospital stays, and poorer functional outcomes.[44]

Postoperative delirium is often missed by physicians, so it is important to be alert to subtle mental changes. Brief tests of attention, such as serial subtraction or digit span (immediate recall of a string of numbers) should be considered in patients at high risk. Delirium fluctuates and may not be evident during a single visit to the bedside, so nursing staff and family members should be asked about cognitive and behavioral changes. Delirium often does not present with agitation; patients who manifest inattention with acute onset and fluctuating course and have either disorganized thinking or altered level of consciousness should be considered to have delirium.[44]

Delirium often threatens to compromise postoperative care. Ideally, the approach to such patients is to ascertain the etiology of the disturbance, treat the underlying cause of delirium, and control behavior with environmental measures, which include use of a bedside sitter or family members to gently reorient the patient, providing orientating stimuli such as calendars and items from home, minimizing abrupt relocations, and leaving lights on at night to decrease frightening hallucinations.[44]

Occasionally, prompt symptomatic control is needed to control agitation and prevent harm to the patient or others. There is no ideal drug to accomplish this for older persons, although low-dose (0.5 mg) haloperidol is generally accepted as a safe and reliable regimen for short-term use, with little risk for hypotension or arrhythmias. In the severely disruptive, benzodiazepines (e.g., lorazepam 0.5 to 1 mg intravenously) may work synergistically with haloperidol, blunting extrapyramidal side effects and prompting sedation. Because they restrict mobility and many adverse effects are associated with their use, physical restraints should be considered only if these more conservative measures have failed.[44]

Other Complications

In patients at high cardiac risk, continuous postoperative electrocardiographic monitoring may identify silent ischemia that predisposes to subsequent cardiac complications, but it is unknown if interventions based on discovering such ischemia can alter outcomes. Routine 12-lead electrocardiograms are not indicated postoperatively and often provide confusing information. For instance, one-fifth of older men undergoing transurethral prostate resection developed ECG changes within the first 3 postoperative days in one study of 206 men, but none had enzymatic evidence of myocardial infarction.[45]

Ventricular arrhythmias (frequent ventricular ectopic beats; nonsustained ventricular tachycardia) may occur in over one-third of high-risk patients after noncardiac surgery, primarily in those with preoperative arrhythmias; but in most instances, risk for more serious cardiac events is low.[46] Addressing contributing factors such as pain, myocardial ischemia, hypoxia, and electrolyte disturbances (especially hypokalemia and hypomagnesemia) is warranted. Due to their proarrhythmic actions and potential for greater side effects in older persons, prophylactic use of antiarrhythmic agents is not justified.

Hemoglobin levels often fall after major surgery. Although transfusion has been recommended in the past for hemoglobin levels below 10 g/dl, many older patients can tolerate lower hemoglobin levels. Transfusions should be reserved for patients with symptoms and those with hemoglobin levels under 7 g/dl; a single-unit transfusion may be adequate and is less likely to produce volume overload.[47] It has also become common to treat patients routinely with oral iron after surgery. However, in a randomized, controlled study of iron supplementation in hip surgery patients, use of oral iron did not hasten recovery of hemoglobin values in patients demonstrated to have adequate tissue iron stores.[48] Routine postoperative iron supplementation, therefore, is not recommended.

SUMMARY

Age per se should not be used as a criterion for deciding whether or not a patient should have surgery. Chronic disease is a much stronger determinant of operative risk, but even patients with substantial medical comorbidity can successfully undergo major surgery. Specific recommendations for perioperative management made in this chapter are summarized in Table 25-4. Perioperative care of the older patient requires an astute medical evaluation and optimal treatment of underlying conditions affecting risk. Although some preoperative interventions (e.g., parenteral nutrition, prophylactic coronary artery bypass) may be useful in selected patients, the prudent clinician needs to weigh their uncertain risks and benefits carefully against the potential risks of surgical delay. Postoperatively, special attention should be directed toward pain control, mobilization, mental status, and prompt removal of indwelling catheters. Risk is not limited to the immediate perioperative period, requiring that management continue throughout the hospital stay and extend into long-term-care or home settings.

TABLE 25-4

Recommendations for Perioperative Management of Older Patients

Do not use age as a criterion for performing surgery.
Assess comorbid medical conditions and optimize their treatment.
Assess functional and cognitive ability, competency, and availability of supports.
Consider noninvasive assessment of coronary artery disease for high-risk patients.
Ensure patient is not dehydrated; use hemodynamic monitoring in high-risk patients.
Utilize appropriate preventive measures for thromboembolism and endocarditis.
Review all medications preoperatively and eliminate the unnecessary.
Provide nutritional support to the malnourished if surgery can be safely delayed.
Monitor for complications through the hospital stay and after discharge.
Ask about pain often; use scheduled or patient-controlled analgesic dosing.
Mobilize promptly; remove urinary catheters within 48 hours whenever possible.
Be alert to postoperative delirium.

REFERENCES

1. Hosking MP et al: Outcomes of surgery in patients 90 years of age and older. *JAMA* 261:1909, 1989.
2. Vaz FG, Seymour DG: A prospective study of elderly general surgical patients: I. Pre-operative medical problems. *Age Ageing* 18:309, 1989.
3. Wei JY, Gersh BJ: Heart disease in the elderly. *Curr Probl Cardiol* 12:1, 1987.
4. Sparrow D, Weiss ST: Respiratory physiology. *Annu Rev Gerontol Geriatr* 6:197, 1986.
5. Manolio TA, Furberg CD: Age as a predictor of outcome: What role does it play? *Am J Med* 92:1, 1992.
6. Djokovic JL, Hedley-Whyte J: Prediction of outcome of surgery and anesthesia in patients over 80. *JAMA* 242:2301, 1979.
7. Owens WD et al: ASA physical status classifications: A study of consistency of ratings. *Anesthesiology* 49:239, 1978.
8. Browner WS et al: In-hospital and long-term mortality in male veterans following noncardiac surgery. *JAMA* 268:228, 1992.
9. Goldman L et al: Multifactorial index of cardiac risk in noncardiac surgical procedures. *N Engl J Med* 297:845, 1977.
10. Gerson MC et al: Cardiac prognosis in noncardiac geriatric surgery. *Ann Intern Med* 103:832, 1985.
11. Kannel WB, Abbott RD: Incidence and prognosis of unrecognized myocardial infarction: An update on the Framingham study. *N Engl J Med* 311:1144, 1984.
12. Raby KE et al: Correlation between preoperative ischemia and major cardiac events after peripheral vascular surgery. *N Engl J Med* 321:1296, 1989.
13. Gersh BJ et al: Evaluation and management of patients with both peripheral vascular and coronary artery disease. *J Am Coll Cardiol* 18:203, 1991.
14. Wong T, Detsky AS: Preoperative cardiac risk assessment for patients having peripheral vascular surgery. *Ann Intern Med* 116:743, 1992.
15. Jackson CV: Preoperative pulmonary evaluation. *Arch Intern Med* 148:2120, 1988.
16. Zibrak JD et al: Indications for pulmonary function testing. *Ann Intern Med* 112:763, 1990.
17. Kroenke K et al: Operative risk in patients with severe obstructive pulmonary disease. *Arch Intern Med* 152:967, 1992.
18. Gerson MC et al: Prediction of cardiac and pulmonary complications related to elective abdominal and noncardiac thoracic surgery in geriatric patients. *Am J Med* 88:101, 1990.
19. Williams-Russo P et al: Predicting postoperative pulmonary complications: Is it a real problem? *Arch Intern Med* 152:1209, 1992.
20. Seymour DG, Pringle R: Post-operative complications in the elderly surgical patient. *Gerontology* 29:262, 1983.

21. Magaziner J et al: Predictors of functional recovery one year following hospital discharge for hip fracture: A prospective study. *J Gerontol* 45:M101, 1990.
22. Cohen MM et al: Does anesthesia contribute to operative mortality? *JAMA* 260:2859, 1988.
23. Mangano DT et al: Long-term cardiac prognosis following noncardiac surgery. *JAMA* 268:233, 1992.
24. Davis PB, Robins LN: History-taking in the elderly with and without cognitive impairment. *J Am Geriatr Soc* 37:249, 1989.
25. Cygan R, Waitzkin H: Stopping and restarting medications in the perioperative period. *J Gen Intern Med* 2:270, 1987.
26. Connelly CS, Panush RS: Should nonsteroidal anti-inflammatory drugs be stopped before elective surgery? *Arch Intern Med* 151:1963, 1991.
27. MacPherson DS et al: Preoperative screening: Value of previous tests. *Ann Intern Med* 113:969, 1990.
28. Granieri R, MacPherson DS: Perioperative care of the vascular surgery patient: The perspective of the internist. *J Gen Intern Med* 7:102, 1992.
29. Hayes SN et al: Palliative percutaneous aortic balloon valvuloplasty before noncardiac operations and invasive diagnostic procedures. *Mayo Clin Proc* 64:753, 1989.
30. Finucane P et al: Markers of the nutritional status in acutely ill elderly patients. *Gerontology* 34:304, 1988.
31. Veterans Affairs Total Parenteral Nutrition Cooperative Study Group: Perioperative total parenteral nutrition in surgical patients. *N Engl J Med* 325:525, 1991.
32. Bastow MD et al: Benefits of supplementary tube feeding after fractured neck of femur: A randomized controlled trial. *Br Med J* 287:1589, 1983.
33. Delmi M et al: Dietary supplementation in elderly patients with fractured neck of the femur. *Lancet* 335:1013, 1990.
34. Schrader LL et al: Is routine preoperative hemodynamic evaluation of nonagenarians necessary? *J Am Geriatr Soc* 39:1, 1991.
35. Berlauk JF et al: Preoperative optimization of cardiovascular hemodynamics improves outcome in peripheral vascular surgery: A prospective, randomized clinical trial. *Ann Surg* 214:289, 1991.
36. Hyers TM et al: Antithrombotic therapy for venous thromboembolic disease. *Chest* 95(suppl):37, 1989.
37. Dajani AS et al: Prevention of bacterial endocarditis: Recommendations by the American Heart Association. *JAMA* 264:2919, 1990.
38. Mangano DT et al: Postoperative myocardial ischemia: Therapeutic trials using intensive analgesia following surgery. *Anesthesiology* 76:342, 1992.
39. Kaiko RF et al: Central nervous system excitatory effects of meperidine in cancer patients. *Ann Neurol* 13:180, 1983.
40. Egbert AM et al: Randomized trial of postoperative patient-controlled analgesia vs. intramuscular narcotics in frail elderly men. *Arch Intern Med* 150:1897, 1990.
41. Harper CM, Lyles YM: Physiology and complications of bed rest. *J Am Geriatr Soc* 36:1047, 1988.
42. Michelson JD et al: Urinary-bladder management after total joint-replacement surgery. *N Engl J Med* 319:321, 1988.
43. van der Wall E et al: Prophylactic ciprofloxacin for catheter-associated urinary-tract infection. *Lancet* 339:946, 1992.
44. Francis J: Delirium in older patients. *J Am Geriatr Soc* 40:829, 1992.
45. Ashton CM et al: The frequency and significance of ECG changes after transurethral prostate resection. *J Am Geriatr Soc* 39:575, 1991.
46. O'Kelly B et al: Ventricular arrhythmias in patients undergoing noncardiac surgery. *JAMA* 268:217, 1992.
47. Welch HG et al: Prudent strategies for elective red blood cell transfusion. *Ann Intern Med* 116:393, 1992.
48. Zauber NP et al: Iron supplementation after femoral head replacement for patients with normal iron stores. *JAMA* 267:525, 1992.

Chapter 26

ANESTHESIA FOR THE ELDERLY PATIENT

Raymond C. Roy

It has never been my bad fortune to lose a patient from the effects of ether. And yet this unqualified statement should not be made. Those who advocate the use of ether as an anaesthetic agent maintain that the deaths due to ether, do not, as a rule, occur with the patient on the operating table, but that pneumonia or bronchitis, or renal disturbance that finally carries the patient off, may be traced back to the anaesthetic. But inasmuch as these same visceral changes are produced by septic influences connected with the operations performed under ether, there will still remain a doubt in the minds of all advocates of ether, as to the relative part played by the ether and the operation in the fatal result. A profitable study of statistics relating to alleged ether deaths might put the profession in a better position to defend or to refute the charge that ether is not so safe an anaesthetic as most surgeons are disposed to believe.

JD Rushmore[1]

The challenge made in the opening quote from the turn of the century has finally been accepted. Recent studies have addressed the contribution anesthesia makes to perioperative mortality and morbidity. In this chapter three questions related to this issue will be addressed. What is an anesthesia-related complication (ARC)? Will reducing the number of ARCs significantly reduce perioperative mortality and morbidity? What are the biases of anesthesiologists in those areas of overlapping responsibility for perioperative care? The purpose of this chapter is to help the general physician understand how an anesthesiologist approaches care of a geriatric patient.

OPERATIVE RISK IN PERSPECTIVE

The overall mortality and morbidity associated with any operative procedure depends on four major risk factors: chronologic age, coexisting disease, the surgical procedure itself, and perioperative care which includes anesthetic management.

Perioperative mortality increases with advancing age (Fig. 26-1).[2] Is age the significant risk factor, or is it a marker for physiologic impairment secondary to chronic disease states? The question is relevant because chronologic age cannot be altered, but disease may be prevented or treated. Evans clearly delineates the relationship between age, physiological impairment, and morbidity. "On average, unselected groups of older patients do less well after hazardous medical or surgical interventions than younger patients—because on average physiological impairment increases with age. But at no age will impairment affect everyone equally. If enough is known about a person's physiological status age contributes little to the prediction of outcome—only about 4 percent of the variance in outcome from intensive care, for example."[3]

A more important risk factor than age is the presence and severity of coexisting disease. In a study of 2391 deaths associated with 108,878 anesthetics, mortality rates for elective surgical procedures were increased 25-fold in the presence of congestive heart

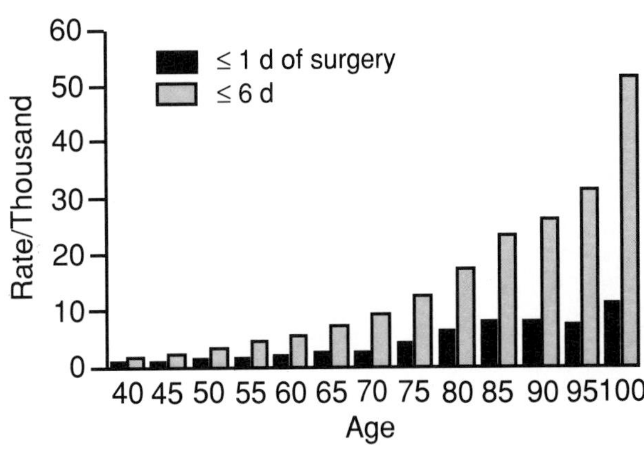

FIGURE 26-1

Perioperative death rates in the United States (1979–1984 data). More patients die after postoperative day 1 than before postoperative day 2. (*Modified from Lichtor.*[2])

failure, 15-fold by chronic renal failure, 12-fold by ischemic heart disease, and 8-fold with chronic obstructive pulmonary disease.[4] The presence of disease is not a fixed risk, i.e., the risk is greater with advanced disease than with early disease, with critical lesions than with noncritical ones. In a study of 10,120 patients presenting for coronary artery bypass surgery, serum creatine levels >1.8 mg/dl, severe left ventricular dysfunction, reoperation, mitral insufficiency, chronic obstructive pulmonary disease, and anemia were risk factors more powerful than age in predicting mortality and morbidity in patients less than 75 years old.[5] Several studies have shown similar mortality and morbidity for the same operation in patients of different ages but equivalent physiologic states.[6]

Not all operations are associated with the same risks. Surgical procedures may be divided into those which are likely to increase perioperative ischemia above the patient's normal pattern—e.g., vascular procedures involving aortic cross-clamping or infrainguinal arterial bypass, and intraabdominal and intrathoracic surgery—and those which do not appear to increase the risk of myocardial ischemia above the patient's normal pattern, e.g., transurethral resection of the prostate, total hip replacement, and ophthalmologic operations.[7] The mortality statistics presented in Table 26-1 for surgery performed on patients 90 years of age or older at the Mayo Clinic reflect an increasing mortality for those procedures which cause the greatest physiologic derangement.[8]

The above arguments suggest that if one were to weight the the four major risk factors in terms of their relative contribution to perioperative mortality and morbidity, severity of coexisting disease would rank first, the surgical procedure next, and chronologic age last. Where does anesthesia, the other risk factor, fit into all of this?

ANESTHETIC RISK

Keenan defines anesthetic risk as follows: "Anesthesia, by itself, does not improve a patient's health. Anesthesia is useful only because it makes possible otherwise painful and dangerous procedures. . . Thus the goals of anesthesia are not therapeutic, but protective: to protect patients from pain and harm. . . An acceptable anesthesia outcome. . . must be defined. . . as one in which the patient suffered no unnecessary (that is, preventable) pain or harm. . . However, the definition changes with time. . . A downward adjustment of what is considered necessary pain and harm should be expected as progress is made."[9]

TABLE 26-1

Percentage of Perioperative Mortality in Patients ≥90 Years of Age (n = 301)

Type of Surgery	Mortality after 2 Days, %	Mortality after 30 Days, %
Major vascular	20.0	20.0
Thoracotomy	12.5	37.5
Biliary, liver	6.7	26.7
Bowel, rectal, anal	3.8	23.8
Hip	2.7	8.2
Transurethral prostatic resection, eye	0.0	0.0

SOURCE: From Warner et al.[8]

Because anesthesia enables surgery to be performed, the agreement to provide anesthesia should be interpreted as a willingness to share responsibility for morbid and mortal events occurring in the perioperative period. Although it is inappropriate for anesthesiologists to bear the full burden of this responsibility, the message of the chapter-opening quote and the Keenan definition suggests that it is equally inappropriate for them to abstain from any responsibility for untoward events which occur in association with the surgery and convalescence.

Anesthetic risk can thus be divided into two categories—obvious and subtle. A subtle increase in anesthetic risk is defined as an increase in risk that results from choosing an anesthetic technique that provides less protection from postoperative complications than one which may provide more protection. But anesthetic agents also interfere with the physiological mechanisms that the body utilizes to maintain hemostasis. Obvious ARCs are defined as those complications which arise from direct interference by the anesthetic technique and which are inadequately compensated for by the actions of anesthetists.

An anesthetist is the individual who actually administers the anesthetic agents. In the United States anesthesia is administered by anesthesiologists (MDs), certified registered nurse anesthetists (CRNAs) supervised by an MD (usually an anesthesiologist), or physician's assistants in anesthesia, always supervised by an anesthesiologist.

Obvious Anesthetic Risk

The cleanest definition of an obvious ARC would be a complication arising from the administration of anesthesia without surgery to healthy 30-year-old volunteers. The monitoring standards approved by the House of Delegates of the American Society of Anesthesiologists suggest consensus definitions of obvious ARCs. Standard II demands continuous assessment of oxygenation, ventilation, and circulation and ready availability of temperature monitoring. Thus, complications related to hypoxia, hypoventilation (including aspiration and loss of airway), cardiac arrest, hypoperfusion, hypertension, hypothermia, and hyperthermia are usually classified as obvious ARCs.[10] These are the complications commonly delineated in lay terms on the anesthesia consent form (Fig. 26-2) and addressed in closed claims studies.[11]

I understand that in addition to the risks of surgery, anesthesia carries its own risks, but I request the use of anesthetics for my own protection and pain relief. I realize that the type and form of anesthesia may have to be changed before or during the surgery, possibly without explanation to me. Such changes would be made for my own protection and benefit.

A doctor from the anesthesia department has explained to me that there may be complications resulting from the use of *any* anesthetic, and I understand that these complications may include AMONG OTHERS the following:

1. Nausea and vomiting
2. Headache
3. Back pain
4. Damage to blood vessels
5. Dental damage
6. Damage to eyes, nose, or skin
7. Sore throat
8. Vocal cord injury
9. Windpipe injury
10. Respiratory problems
11. Drug reactions
12. Infection
13. Nerve injury
14. Paralysis
15. Brain damage
16. Heart injury
17. Death
18. Damage to baby if you are pregnant now

I understand that medical care is not an exact science and that no guarantee is made as to the outcome of the administration of anesthesia. I have been given an explanation of the proposed plan of anesthesia and have been given the opportunity to ask questions about it as well as alternative forms of anesthesia. I have been given an explanation of the procedures and techniques to be used, as well as the risks and hazards involved, and I believe that I have sufficient information to give this informed consent.

I certify that this form has been fully explained to me, that I have read it or have had it read to me, and that I understand its contents.

________________________ ________________________

Patient or person authorized to consent for patient — Date and time

I have discussed the contents of this form with the patient, as well as the risks, hazards, and potential complications of anesthesia, in addition to the alternatives to anesthesia.

________________________ ________________________

Physician Signature — Date and time

FIGURE 26-2
Anesthesia consent form.

In seven recent well-conducted studies, the incidence of serious obvious ARCs was very low compared with the overall perioperative mortality and morbidity rates. For example, in one study only 83 episodes of aspiration were observed during 185,358 anesthetic procedures (0.04 percent), and only 4 of these episodes resulted in death (0.002 percent).[12] At the Mayo Clinic 62 aspirations occurred in 215,488 patients (0.03 percent). Of these patients, one died intraoperatively from exsanguination unrelated to the aspiration, 40 did not develop respiratory sequelae, 21 were observed in the intensive care unit, and only 3 died as a result of the aspiration (0.001 percent).[13]

In two investigations the incidence of intraoperative cardiac arrest was 79 occurrences in 112,721 operations (0.07 percent)[14] and 170 events during 250,543 procedures (0.07 percent).[15] The Confidential Enquiry into Perioperative Deaths (CEPOD) from the United Kingdom reported only 3 deaths in 555,258 anesthetic procedures as solely attributed to anesthetic misadventure (0.0005 percent).[16] The incidence of major complications partially or totally related to anesthesia (aspiration, postoperative respiratory depression, intubation problems, anaphylactoid shock, severe arrhythmias, myocardial infarction, cardiac arrest, pulmonary edema, coma, and death) was 268 events during 198,103 administrations in a French study.[17]

Finally, when a Canadian study of 100,007 patients asked the question, "Does anesthesia contribute to operative mortality?" it clearly demonstrated that the patient's physical status (a function of the severity of disease or injury) and surgical risk factors are much more important in determining 7-day mortality than anesthesia risk factors.[18] In quality assurance studies from Australia[19] and the United Kingdom,[20] the obvious contribution of anesthesia to perioperative mortality was estimated to be 10 percent, surgery 20 percent, and disease 70 percent. In healthy patients, the major anesthetic complication rate increases very little as the population ages so that it remains less than 0.02 percent. As the number and severity of coexisting diseases increase, which tends to occur with advancing age, the likelihood of an obvious ARC increases to around 1 percent. Thus, a 5- to 6-fold increase in complication rate is seen with the acquisition of chronic disease compared with a 1.5-fold increase associated with aging in the absence of disease (Fig. 26-3).[17] To prioritize contributions to perioperative risk: disease > surgery > anesthesia > age.

There are five major consequences of the low occurrence rates for obvious ARCs.

1. No patient should be denied surgery based on a perceived inability to tolerate anesthesia. Coexisting disease and surgery are more important factors. Does this patient have enough reserve to withstand postoperative stresses? This is the real question (see below).
2. The statistical impact of the low ARC rate is that while the elimination of all ARCs would improve the outcome in hundreds of patients, it would make very little difference in the national perioperative mortality rate.
3. Because the obvious anesthesia complication rate is so low, when a complication does occur, there is a tendency to imply fault. In fact most obvious ARCs are felt to be related to human error. In a recent closed claims study of deaths during spinal anesthesia, a "new" or "unappreciated" mechanism for untoward outcome was proposed.[21] An *Anesthesiology* editorial by Keats applauded the concept that not all events leading to bad outcomes are as yet fully understood.[22] But letters appeared disagreeing and supporting the view that these events were entirely avoidable errors in management.[23–26] Anesthesiologists reviewing medical records are more accusatory and fault-finding when they know a bad outcome has occurred than when they do not know the outcome.[27]

   This author believes a more rational view of the relationship between untoward events and malpractice is presented in Fig. 26-4. Central to this view is the concept that reasonable clinical judgment acknowledges that not all events can be anticipated, that it is neither cost-effective nor safe to aggressively and invasively monitor for infrequent or unlikely events, and that not all treatment, however appropriate and timely, is 100 percent effective.
4. Routine prophylaxis for rare events is not cost-effective. For example, it has become common practice to routinely administer drugs to reduce the pH and volume of gastric contents prior to the induction of anesthesia with the admirable intent of reducing the incidence of aspiration or the severity of sequelae if aspiration should occur. However, the incidence of side effects from prophylaxis with H_2 blockers, metoclopramide, and antacids is about the same as the incidence of aspiration. Also, prophylaxis with these drugs is too expensive to be administered to all geriatric patients preoperatively in hopes of preventing an event which occurs so rarely. Thus, aspiration prophylaxis should be confined to that very small subset of patients at increased risk, i.e., those presenting for emergency surgery with full stomachs in whom a difficult intubation is anticipated, and those with significant gastric reflux symptoms.
5. Because disease and surgery make such important contributions to perioperative mortality and morbidity, these need to be taken into consideration in efforts to decide which of two different anesthetic techniques is safer. The study population should be made as homogeneous as possible by including only patients with the same disease, occurring with the same severity, undergoing the identical operation. If one wanted to randomize patients presenting for surgery associated with a mortality rate of 1 percent to a variation in technique that reduced mortality from 1 to 0.5 percent, 7400 patients would have to be studied with the population composition restrictions described above.[28] The requirement for large numbers of patients means that studies have to be either multicenter or single center with long study periods. But anesthesia approaches change with time and are different from center to center, no matter how rigorous clinical researchers try to be. Because of the logistics and expense of such large

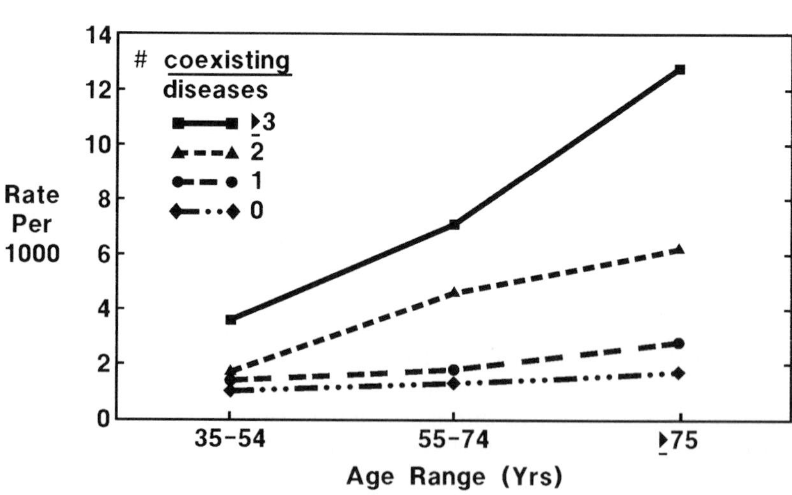

FIGURE 26-3
The anesthetic complication rate increases very little with advancing age in the absence of coexisting disease. It increases markedly as the number and severity of coexisting diseases increase. (*Constructed from data presented by Tiret et al.*[17])

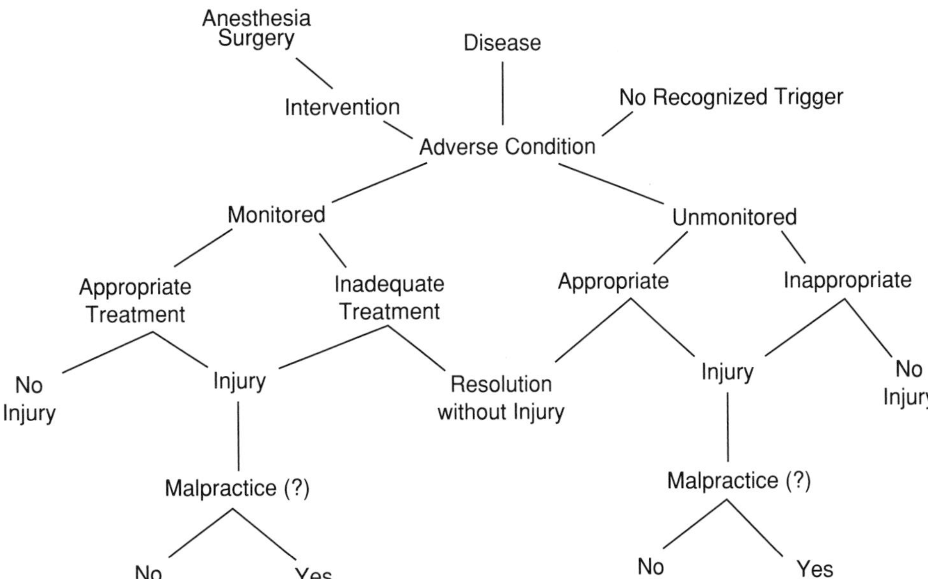

FIGURE 26-4
Relationship between injury, treatment, monitoring, and malpractice.

studies and the changes associated with the continual introduction of new drugs into anesthetic practice, it seems unlikely that any one reasonable technique will emerge as superior to another based on traditional obvious ARCs.

An investigation by Yeager et al. is an important example of how to reduce the required size of a study population by expanding the number of outcome markers.[29] Using mortality alone, they were unable to conclude statistically that the combination of "light" general anesthesia with epidural anesthesia intraoperatively and epidural analgesia postoperatively was safer than general anesthesia with conventional parenteral on-demand postoperative pain management. However, when other outcome markers were included, such as congestive heart failure, wound dehiscence, and mandatory ventilatory support, they were able to draw the statistically significant, clinically relevant conclusion with just 60 patients that light general anesthesia combined with epidural anesthesia and analgesia was better. Although the study is still criticized for being too small and for including patients whose disease states were too variable, they were among the first to suggest that the type of postoperative analgesia makes a real difference in clinical outcome. They also were among the first to assume that anesthesia could contribute to complications not traditionally associated with anesthesia, i.e., subtle ARCs.

Subtle Anesthetic Risk

There are two broad categories of subtle anesthetic risk. The first is risk that results from the choice of one technique which provides less protection from a premorbid or morbid event. The second is risk that results from the choice of a technique which increases the physiologic stress of the perioperative experience more than another. In either situation it is important to realize that the two techniques being compared are reasonable and acceptable approaches but that one may be better than another for certain patients with specific disease states for one particular surgical procedure. The vagueness of the above definition is a reflection of a subject in evolution and of old views being challenged. What is considered a nonanesthetic risk today may have an anesthetic component tomorrow. Part of the problem in discussing subtle anesthetic risk is that the outcome markers tend to be in the postoperative period, where there is considerable overlap in responsibility.

Research into anesthetic risk is being directed toward four areas (1) identifying less (or more) protective anesthetic techniques (always defined relative to another), e.g., postoperative ischemia is reduced in patients with prolonged intensive postoperative analgesia;[30] (2) persistent but previously unappreciated continuation of anesthetic effects into the postoperative period, e.g., the substitution of nitrogen (air) for nitrous oxide reduced the time required for full return of gastrointestinal function after colon resection and shortened the patients' length of stay,[31] (3) physiologically destructive anesthetic agents, e.g., limiting the use of succinylcholine and halothane, which have destructive effects on muscle and liver cells, respectively, and from which the patient must recover[32,33]; and (4) gray zones in which anesthesia risk is potentiated by other risk factors, e.g., ARCs increase with increasing severity of illness or intensity of surgery (Fig. 26-3).[17]

WHEN DO ARCS OCCUR?

Obvious ARCs tend to occur in the operating room or in the postanesthesia care unit (PACU, the former

TABLE 26-2

Results of a Prospective Study of 20,802 Patients Determining When Postoperative Complications Occur

Complication	Median Day
Cardiac failure	2
Myocardial infarction	1
Pneumonia	2
Pulmonary edema	2
Atelectasis	2
Cerebral stroke	3
Pulmonary embolism	3

SOURCE: Johannessen et al.[35]

recovery room). In a review of all deaths within 24 hours of surgery in Australia between 1970 and 1985, poor preoperative preparation was implicated in 40 percent of the cases in which anesthesia or surgery contributed to death.[19] Similarly, in the CEPOD study, poor preoperative preparation was implicated in one-third of the deaths.[20] The most important aspect of preoperative preparation is the restoration of normal intravascular volume in patients who are hypovolemic because of dehydration, bowel disorders, sepsis, or blood loss or who are hypervolemic because of congestive heart failure.

The differences between the 1-day and 6-day mortality rates in Fig. 26-1 and the 2-day and 30-day mortality rates in Table 26-1 demonstrate that much of the mortality occurs postoperatively. More patients die after postoperative day 1 than before postoperative day 2. Subtle ARCs tend to become manifest in the postoperative period in which there is considerable overlapping of physician responsibility. Several of the most common cardiac, pulmonary, neurologic, and psychiatric complications seen in the perioperative period appear most frequently in the first postoperative week, i.e., between the first and fifth postoperative days (see Table 26-2), well after the direct effects of anesthetic agents are gone.[34–37]

BASIC PRINCIPLES

This author's 10 basic principles in the anesthetic management of the elderly patient are as follows: (1) choose drug doses carefully because of a variable, most likely decreased, requirement and an increased variability and unpredictability in response; (2) recognize that each patient is different physiologically pre-, intra-, and postoperatively; (3) be prepared for greater hemodynamic instability than in a younger patient; (4) avoid hypothermia; (5) think regional anesthesia, but be prepared to resuscitate or to administer a general anesthetic; (6) extend monitoring well into the postoperative period and respond to subclinical events; (7) remember that signs and symptoms of untoward events are often nonspecific in elderly patients; (8) allow time for the elderly patient to respond to questions, requests, and drugs administered; (9) remember that bad outcomes can occur despite good care; and (10) give good informed consent to patients and their families.

Drug Response

There are four major effects of advancing age on drug response: (1) increased variability; (2) decreased requirements for most anesthetic agents; (3) increased length of redosing interval and (4) increased requirements for both α- and β-adrenergic agonists.[38,39]

The increased variability (see Fig. 26-5) is the result of the influence of aging and chronic disease processes on pharmacokinetics and pharmacodynamics. Compared with younger patients, elderly patients generally require lower levels of inhalational anesthesia[40] and lower doses of both opioids[41] and intravenous agents[42] to reach the same electroencephalographic endpoints. For those intravenous agents which bind to receptors, such as narcotics, benzodiazepines, and ketamine, the explanation for the reduced dose requirement is generally a pharmacodynamic one. For those intravenous agents which do not have specific binding sites, such as barbiturates, etomidate, and propofol, the reduced requirement tends to have a pharmacokinetic explanation, usually a decreased volume of distribution. There is no change in the initial dose of muscle relaxants compared with that of younger patients, but there is an increased time before a redose is necessary.[43]

Prolonged emergence from anesthesia is a problem which develops intraoperatively in the elderly patient, usually from having been given an initial dose of a drug which would have been more appropriate for a younger patient or from having been redosed at

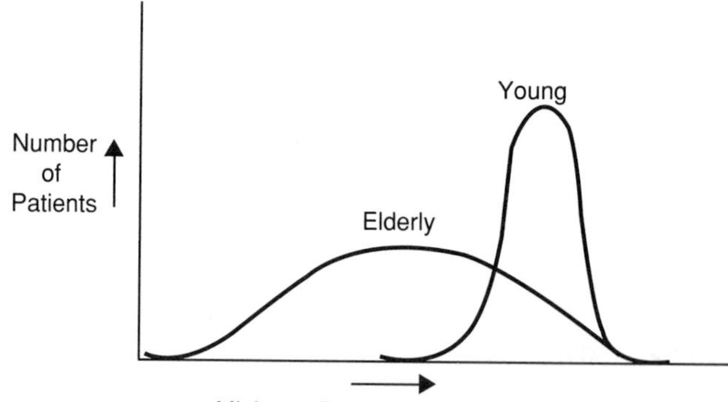

FIGURE 26-5

Dose-response curves in elderly patients are broader than those of younger patients and are centered at lower doses.

too short an interval, with too high a dose, or too close to the end of the procedure. There are specific reversal agents for both opioids [e.g., naloxone (Narcan)] and benzodiazepines [i.e., flumazenil (Mazicon)]. Preoperative medication with scopolamine and the intraoperative administration of atropine have also been associated with postoperative somnolence or confusion. Fortunately, there exists both a substitute, glycopyrrolate, which does not cross the blood-brain barrier, and a reversal agent, physostigmine (Antilirium).

With all reversal agents it is important to make sure the patient is hemodynamically stable and adequately oxygenated and ventilated before the agents are given. Otherwise, cardiac arrests have been reported to occur. Likewise, it is important to give smaller incremental doses rather than a larger bolus to minimize the degree of hypertension and tachycardia and subsequent arrhythmias, myocardial ischemia, pulmonary edema, bronchospasm, nausea and vomiting, or seizures that can occur. Finally, the durations of action of the reversal agents are shorter than those of the drugs they are given to reverse. To avoid possible unwitnessed "renarcotization" or "recurarization" with potential hypoventilation, oxygen desaturation, loss of the airway, and respiratory arrest, patients given these agents should be carefully watched for at least 1 hour after the administration of a reversal agent, usually in the PACU. Most anesthesiologists feel it is better to omit sedative preoperative medication and to reduce the dose of anesthetic agents in those patients they are planning to extubate at the end of the procedure rather than to add routinely one more potentially dangerous drug to the pharmacologic regimen of the elderly patient.[44]

Changing Physiologic States

Each patient who is anesthetized is actually three different patients. The preoperative patient is different from the same patient intraoperatively and postoperatively. Metabolic demands[45] and ventilatory requirements[46] are greatest postoperatively, less preoperatively, and least intraoperatively. The incidence of myocardial ischemic events show the same pattern.[36,47] The adverse effect of abdominal surgery on pulmonary function persists for days postoperatively.[48] Anesthesia with surgery does not produce the same responses without surgery.[34] Surgical incisions activate the stress response with varying intensity depending on the procedure. Anesthesia attenuates this response to varying degrees depending on the technique chosen. Postoperatively the stress continues, but the anesthesia is withdrawn. Evidence is now appearing that outcomes are improved if normothermia is maintained intraoperatively (see below), if attenuation of the stress response persists well into the postoperative period with the maintenance of intensive postoperative analgesia,[30,49] if the metabolic demands of ventilation are eliminated by mechanical ventilation in select patients,[50,51] if the adverse hemodynamic effects of the stress response are detected early with invasive monitoring and aggressively treated well into the postoperative period,[52] and if hormonal and nutritional support is provided.[53]

Hemodynamic Instability

General Anesthesia

An example of the hemodynamic problems with which elderly patients confront anesthesiologists is depicted in Fig. 26-6. At equivalent depths of anesthesia, elderly patients, when compared with younger ones, show greater falls in blood pressure in the absence of surgical stimulation and greater increases in blood pressure in response to surgical incision.[54] It is not uncommon to use nonanesthetic agents, such as beta blockers and nitroglycerin, to treat intraoperative hypertension if adequate doses of anesthetic agent have been given. The swings in blood pressure are intensified in the untreated hypertensive patient. It is very important that patients' regular antihypertensive medications, including their diuretics, be considered part of the anesthesia preoperative medication. In addition, supplemental doses of beta blockers or clonidine are advocated to attenuate intraoperative hypertension and to reduce the incidence of perioperative myocardial ischemia.[55,56] In this regard, it is important to consider that, although sensitivity to beta agonists is reduced in elderly patients, sensitivity to beta antagonists is increased. Interestingly, chronic treatment with calcium channel blockers does not reduce the incidence of perioperative ischemia.[57]

Regional Anesthesia

Significant cardiovascular changes also occur during spinal and epidural anesthesia. Both involve a major

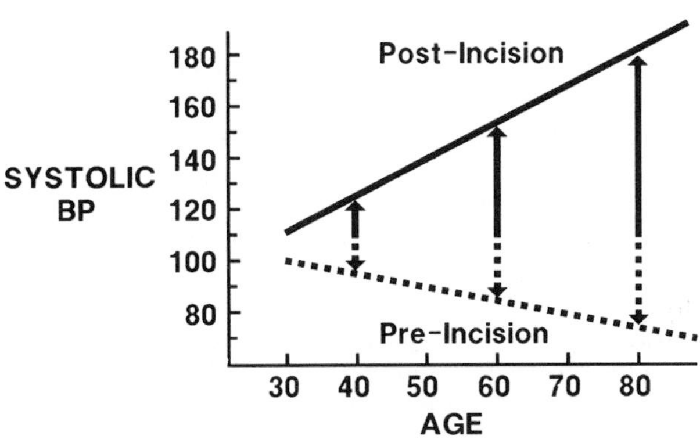

FIGURE 26-6

At equivalent depths of anesthesia, elderly patients, when compared with younger ones, show greater falls in blood pressure in the absence of surgical stimulation and greater increases in blood pressure in response to surgical incision. (*Constructed from data presented by Roizen et al.*[54])

redistribution of blood volume and frequent hypotension. Patients who are hypovolemic, hypertensive, or elderly (or combinations thereof) are especially likely to become hypotensive. The definition of, and response to, this hypotension in normovolemic patients has come under scrutiny recently. In 65-year-old patients with coronary artery disease without hypertension or heart failure, epidural anesthesia which reduced mean arterial pressure (MAP) from 102 to 79 mmHg increased the ejection fraction and improved left ventricular wall motion. When 500 ml of fluid was infused to restore the MAP, the ejection fraction decreased and the wall motion deteriorated.[58] In patients with poor left ventricular function, epidural anesthesia improved the ejection fraction from 32 to 41 percent as the MAP decreased from 95 to 79 mmHg. But when ephedrine was administered to restore the MAP, the ejection fraction fell.[59] Thus, the commonly held view that one should keep the blood pressure intraoperatively the same as when the patient was not complaining of angina preoperatively clearly needs to be reevaluated. MAPs around 70 mmHg are well tolerated. In fact, a successful technique lowering MAPs to 50 mmHg for hip surgery in elderly hypertensive patients with epidural anesthesia, maintaining a normal cardiac output with low-dose dopamine or epinephrine infusions, was recently reported.[60]

During spinal anesthesia when hypotension (<70 mmHg systolic pressure) and bradycardia (<40 beats per minute) are not corrected with a head-down tilt, epinephrine is required to avoid a cardiac arrest.[21] Atropine takes too long to act in the elderly patients, especially if cardiac output is low, and yields an unreliable response. A rapid infusion of crystalloid may be required, but it also may take too long to administer to prevent a cardiac arrest.

The main point is that significant hemodynamic changes do occur with spinal and epidural anesthesia. The response to deviations from what is perceived to be appropriate hemodynamics is not always clear. Occasionally it may be necessary to insert arterial, central venous pressure, or even pulmonary artery catheters to help make these decisions. Generally, this author prefers less volume loading in elderly patients prior to spinal or epidural anesthesia (none in patients with heart failure or undergoing transurethral resection of the prostate), dopamine or ephedrine for hypotension in patients with heart failure or during epidural anesthesia (to offset the effects of systemically absorbed local anesthesia), and phenylephrine infusions to improve perfusion pressure in patients with left ventricular hypertrophy, tight coronary artery stenosis, or extracranial cerebrovascular disease.

Renal Insufficiency

Deliberate or controlled hypotension is an accepted anesthetic technique to reduce intraoperative blood loss. Sustained mean arterial blood pressures of 50 mmHg during anesthesia for total hip arthroplasty were not associated with postoperative renal insufficiency, ischemia, confusion, or stroke.[60,61] Unlike inadvertent or uncontrolled hypotension from hemorrhage, dehydration, or low-cardiac-output states, deliberate hypotension is a low-vascular-resistance, normal- to high-cardiac-output state made possible by a normal blood volume. Hydration minimizes the effects of anesthesia on renal hemodynamics and avoids acute oliguria.[62] Moderate hypotension during anesthesia should not be viewed as a causative factor for renal insufficiency, unless it occurs concurrently with other conditions which reduce renal blood flow, such as renal artery stenosis, low cardiac output, aortic cross-clamping, or sepsis. Even when 2114 consecutive medical and noncardiac surgical admissions were screened prospectively for the development or worsening of renal insufficiency, hypotension below 90/60 mmHg (MAP 70 mmHg) was not a predictor of postoperative renal insufficiency.[63]

Hypothermia

Anesthetized patients suffer a fall in temperature for five reasons: (1) redistribution of heat within the body decreasing core temperature and increasing peripheral temperature,[64] (2) decreased heat production, (3) heat loss to warm and humidify dry anesthetic gases, (4) heat loss to the environment, especially from viscera exposed to the ambient temperature of the operating room or cool irrigation fluids, e.g., during transurethral resection of the prostate, and (5) interference with the normal thermoregulatory processes. Elderly patients tend to cool more rapidly and rewarm more slowly than younger patients.[65]

The adverse effects of postoperative hypothermia are manifold. Many of the catabolic effects previously blamed on the stress response activated by surgery can be attenuated by conservation of body heat during surgery. Elderly patients undergoing abdominal and hip surgery who were allowed to cool to 34°C showed greater urinary excretion of urea nitrogen and 3-methylhistidine, an indication of muscle protein breakdown, and a greater decrease in total body potassium, measured as an index of body cell mass, up to 7 days postoperatively, compared with elderly patients who were kept normothermic.[66] The incidence of myocardial ischemia is greater in colder patients, even if they are not actively shivering.[67] Shivering itself can be associated with respiratory acidosis from increased carbon dioxide production, which may lead to respiratory acidosis in the elderly patient already splinting from the incision and whose ventilatory response is inhibited by narcotics and residual anesthesia. Shivering can also be associated with decreased mixed venous oxygen saturation and hypoxia and subsequent myocardial or cerebral ischemia.[68] Other adverse effects of hypothermia include prolongation of prothrombin and activated partial thromboplastin times,[69] increased susceptibility to infection,[70] prolongation of muscle relaxants,[71] and potentiation of the sedative effects of anesthetic agents.

The best way to avoid these problems is to aggressively maintain normothermia intraoperatively, e.g., with forced air warmers. When a patient presents to the PACU or ICU cold, suppression of shivering with meperidine if the patient is extubated,[72] or muscle relaxants if the patient is being mechanically ventilated, and rewarming with forced air warmers is recommended.

Regional Anesthesia

Regional anesthesia runs the gamut from local injections to field blocks to major nerve blocks such as axillary blocks to central axis blocks such as spinal or epidural anesthetics. With most regional anesthesia, except spinal anesthesia, there is significant absorption of local anesthetic into the systemic circulation. Elevated plasma levels of local anesthetics can occur acutely (intravascular injection) or 20 to 30 minutes later (systemic absorption) and cause seizures, arrhythmias, and cardiac arrest. Careful technique tends to eliminate the former; restriction of drug dose, the latter. No regional anesthetic ought to be administered without the capability of cardiopulmonary resuscitation with advanced cardiac life support.

There is a strongly held clinical impression that regional anesthesia is intrinsically safer than general anesthesia in elderly patients when either would be a reasonable choice for a particular operation. Most anesthesiologists themselves prefer a regional anesthetic when possible if they require surgery. This preference is based on the perception that regional anesthesia is associated with minimal physiologic trespass, better attenuation of the stress response during surgery, less invasive monitoring, fewer complications, and better postoperative analgesia. It is worthwhile discussing attempts to demonstrate these theoretical benefits clinically for spinal and epidural anesthesia because to the chagrin of most of us, they have not yet been proved.

Mortality Studies

A widely quoted prospective study in 1978 suggested that the mortality rate after general anesthesia was four times that after spinal anesthesia in elderly patients presenting for hip surgery. Although these statistics were confirmed in a follow-up study from the same institution,[73] the mortality rate for general anesthesia was much higher than that being reported from other centers.[74] Excluding the McLaren study,[73] multiple prospective studies found no statistical difference in the mortality rates between the two techniques (Table 26-3).[75,76] Thus, the reason to choose spinal or epidural over general anesthesia must be based on differences in morbidity, cost, or ease of administration rather than mortality.

TABLE 26-3

Prospective, Randomized Studies of Regional versus General Anesthesia for Hip Surgery

			Mortality after 28 days, %	
Source	**n**	**Age**	**Regional**	**General**
McLaren[73]	116	76	7	28
McKenzie[75]	100	75	10	16
White[75]	40	80	0	0
Davis[75]	132	80	5	13
Wickstrom[75]	169	81	6	6
Valentin[75]	578	79	6	8
Davis[76]	538	80	7	6

Deep Venous Thrombosis and Pulmonary Embolism

After hip surgery the incidence of deep vein thrombosis and pulmonary embolism is the same after regional anesthesia in patients who do not receive heparin prophylaxis as it is after general anesthesia in patients who receive heparin or aspirin prophylaxis.[77]

Blood Loss

A significant advantage of regional anesthesia is that it is consistently associated with less blood loss than general anesthesia in patients presenting for hip surgery,[78] transurethral resection of the prostate,[79] and large bowel anastomosis.[80]

Postoperative Somnolence

There is no question that regional anesthesia without preoperative and intraoperative sedation is associated with less postoperative somnolence than general anesthesia. However, the more sedation that is given, the less this advantage manifests itself. In fact, it is unusual to see patients not receive small doses of midazolam, fentanyl, and/or propofol during these procedures.

Cardiac Complications

The previously discussed beneficial effects of a mean blood pressure of 70 mmHg during spinal and epidural anesthesia can be offset by the administration of volume, vasoconstrictors, or inotropic agents. The incidence of new T-wave inversions not associated with other signs or symptoms of myocardial ischemia is 18 percent after both regional and general anesthesia.[81] The incidence and pattern of myocardial ischemia in patients undergoing elective hip arthroplasty during spinal and epidural anesthesia have recently been described.[47] The incidence of ischemia has been reported to be greater after regional than general anesthesia for lower extremity vascular surgery,[82] but the incidence of congestive heart failure is less after combined general and epidural anesthesia than after general anesthesia for abdominal surgery.[29]

Pulmonary Complications

Pulmonary complications after surgery in comparable groups of patients are primarily dependent on the type of surgery, not the anesthetic technique. Upper abdominal and intrathoracic surgery carry the highest morbidity. When respiratory function after lower extremity surgery in 65-year-old patients who received spinal anesthesia was compared with respiratory function in those who received general anesthesia, there were no significant differences.[82] There was no difference in the incidence of postoperative pneumonia in 65-year-olds who underwent abdominal surgery during general anesthesia followed by systemic analgesia compared with those who had combined general-epidural anesthesia and epidural analgesia postoperatively.[83]

Wound Complications

A retrospective study from the 1970s suggested that there was a greater incidence of dehiscence of large bowel anastomoses after general anesthesia than after a combination of epidural and general anesthesia. However, a prospective study in the 1980s from the same group found no difference.[80] The incidence of wound infection was higher in higher-risk patients after general anesthesia with parenteral narcotic postoperative analgesia than after combined epidural-general anesthesia with postoperative epidural analgesia.[29]

Anesthetic Failure

There are three components to regional anesthesia failures: (1) an inability to deposit local anesthetic in the proper location, (2) an incomplete or absent block despite apparent correct deposition of local anesthetic, and (3) a longer duration or extent of surgery than the duration or level of block. A 10 percent failure rate is probably reasonable.

Summary

Most of the theoretical benefits of regional anesthesia have yet to be clinically demonstrated. Certainly they must hold true when comparing general anesthesia with local anesthetic infiltration for excision of a skin lesion. However, they have been seriously challenged when comparing spinal or epidural anesthesia with general anesthesia. It is the continuing bias of this author that, though the benefits of regional anesthesia are frequently overstated, regional anesthesia, when possible, is associated with lower morbidity in elderly patients. Large prospective studies, however, have yet to demonstrate this superiority. Therefore, if an anesthesiologist prefers general anesthesia in a situation in which the internist or the surgeon suggests spinal or epidural anesthesia, there may be sound reasons for doing so. Clearly, however, whichever route is selected, careful intraoperative and postoperative monitoring needs to be the watchword for ensuring a successful outcome.

Postoperative Care

Significant improvement in perioperative mortality and morbidity can occur if attention is focused on postoperative care. Anesthesiologists have addressed postoperative analgesia. Epidural anesthesia administered intraoperatively but discontinued postoperatively did not attenuate protein breakdown in normothermic general anesthesia controls, but extension of epidural analgesia 24 h into the postoperative period minimized postoperative protein breakdown.[49] Intercostal nerve blocks after cholecystectomy and epidural analgesia after total hip replacement remarkably reduced the high incidence of postoperative arterial desaturation in elderly patients breathing room air.[84] Thoracic epidural analgesia also improved diaphragmatic function after upper abdominal surgery.[85] There is exciting new research exploring the concept of preemptive analgesia. The administration of local anesthetics[86] or epidural opioids[87] prior to incision rather than at the conclusion of surgery significantly reduces subsequent analgesics requirements.

Acute postoperative pain management services now offer patient-controlled analgesia, intermittent or continuous regional infusions of local anesthetics, continuous infusions of epidural local anesthetics and/or narcotics, and subarachnoid narcotics in place of conventional intramuscular narcotics. The common side effects of subarachnoid and epidural narcotics—pruritus, urinary retention, nausea, and vomiting—are all manageable. But there is also a risk of respiratory depression, especially if conventional narcotics and sedatives are administered concurrently. A syringe containing naloxone and a bag-valve-mask system for ventilation should be kept at the bedside. Narcotic and sedative orders must also be cleared with the acute pain service. With these precautions, thoracic epidurals for thoracotomies and upper abdominal surgery and lumbar epidurals for lower abdominal surgery, suprapubic prostatectomies, and total hip and knee replacements are remarkably safe and effective.[88]

Blood Replacement

Acute normovolemic hemodilution to a hemoglobin level of 9.0 g/dl is not tolerated as well in older patients as it is in younger ones.[89] There is also evidence that oxygen transport across stenotic lesions is better at normal hemoglobin levels than at hemoglobin levels between 8 and 10 g/dl.[90,91] Therefore, the recommendation is to keep the transfusion trigger for elderly surgical patients at the traditional 10 g/dl.

Informed Consent

More and more departments of anesthesia require informed consent for anesthesia separate from that for surgery. A copy of the anesthesia consent form used at North Carolina Baptist Hospital is presented in Fig. 26-2. However, the ability of many elderly patients to comprehend the consent information is reduced compared with that of younger patients.[92] Furthermore, physical disorders in the elderly are frequently manifested by signs of an acute confusional state. A signature may be obtained, but truly informed consent may not. In these situations it is prudent for the anesthesia personnel to include family members in the consent process. Discussion of plans to confront risk with patients and their families is essential in transforming the anesthesia consent form from a list of horrors to a list of precautions.

Do-not-resuscitate (DNR) orders are uncomfortable for anesthesiologists to interpret or to comply with in the operating room. Anesthesiologists accept the fact that elderly patients are more likely than younger ones to present with preexisting DNR orders. However, these same patients are the ones who are most susceptible to ARCs (see Fig. 26-3). The primary arguments for suspension of DNR orders by anesthesiologists are first that it is difficult and arbitrary to differentiate standard anesthetic maneuvers, such as endotracheal intubation, mechanical ventilation, and administration of blood and inotropes, from what an internist or geriatrician would call a resuscitation. Second, cardiopulmonary arrests outside the operating room are related to patients' disease states and carry a low chance of successful resuscitation, but arrests in the operating room are more likely to have quickly reversible causes. A separate, or renegotiated, DNR form applicable to the operating room, defining resuscitation and the duration of endotracheal intubation, has been suggested after a discussion with the patient and his or her family, the geriatrician, the surgeon, and the anesthesiologist.[93]

SUMMARY

When perioperative risk factors are prioritized, the presence and severity of disease are the most potent, major surgery next, followed by anesthesia, and then chronologic age. A successful surgical outcome is expected if the patient's reserve organ function is sufficient to restore homeostasis disrupted by the surgery. The anesthesiologist views the elderly patient as one who has less reserve than a younger patient. Reserve is maximized by good preoperative preparation and postoperative care. Surgical stress is attenuated by anesthesia and postoperative analgesia. Most of the perioperative morbidity and mortality occurs postoperatively. The intraoperative maintenance of normovolemia and normothermia, postoperative analgesia, and judicious postoperative monitoring for, and treatment of, likely subclinical events before they become irreversible help to reduce the number of untoward events.

ARCs can be divided into obvious and subtle. The incidence of obvious ARCs is so low that studies comparing anesthetic techniques based on these traditional outcome markers need to be very large. Because of the logistics and expense of large studies and because of the continuous modification in anesthetic approaches, it is unlikely that any one reasonable technique will emerge as superior to another. Regardless of the choice, the obvious anesthetic risk is almost always low enough that the elderly patient should not be denied surgery because of a fear that he or she would not tolerate anesthesia. The definition and significance of subtle anesthetic complications is now actively being studied. It is a sure sign of the maturity of the profession that it is willing to expand its sense of responsibility to include untoward events occurring after the patient leaves the PACU.

REFERENCES

1. Rushmore JD: JAMA 100 years ago. Ether anaesthesia. *JAMA* 267:1427, 1992.
2. Lichtor JL: Sponsored research reveals post-operative mortality stats. *Anesth Patient Safety Found Newsletter* 3(1):9, 1988.
3. Evans JG: Aging and rationing. Physiology not age should determine care. *Br Med J* 303:869, 1991.
4. Fowkes FGR et al: Epidemiology in anaesthesia III: Mortality risk in patients with coexisting disease. *Br J Anaesth* 54:819, 1982.
5. Higgins TL et al: Stratification of morbidity and mortality outcome by preoperative risk factors in coronary artery bypass patients. *JAMA* 267:2344, 1992.
6. Mohr DN: Estimation of surgical risk in the elderly: A correlative review. *J Am Geriatr Soc* 31:99, 1983.
7. Fleisher LA, Barash PG: Preoperative cardiac evaluation for noncardiac surgery: A functional approach. *Anesth Analg* 74:586, 1992.
8. Warner MA et al: Surgical procedures among those >90 years of age. *Ann Surg* 207:380, 1988.
9. Keenan RL: What is known about anesthesia outcome? *Probl Anesth* 5:179, 1991.
10. Eichhorn JH: The role of standards of care. *Probl Anesth* 5:188, 1991.
11. Keats AS: The closed claims study (editorial). *Anesthesiology* 73:199, 1990.
12. Olsson GL et al: Aspiration during anaesthesia: A computer-aided study of 185,358 anaesthetics. *Acta Anaesthesiol Scand* 30:84, 1986.
13. Warner MA: MN county studied intensely for anesthesia complications. *Anesth Patient Safety Found Newsletter* 7(1):7, 1992.

14. Cohen MM et al: A survey of 112,000 anaesthetics at one teaching hospital (1975–83) *Can Anaesth Soc J* 33:22, 1986.
15. Olsson GL et al: Cardiac arrest during anaesthesia. A computer-aided study in 250,543 anaesthetics. *Acta Anaesthesiol Scand* 32:653, 1988.
16. Chopra V et al: Reported significant observations during anaesthesia: A prospective analysis over an 18-month period. *Br J Anaesth* 68:13, 1992.
17. Tiret et al: Complications associated with anaesthesia—a prospective study in France. *Can Anaesth Soc J* 33:336, 1986.
18. Cohen MM et al: Does anesthesia contribute to operative mortality? *JAMA* 260:2859, 1988.
19. Holland R: Anaesthetic mortality in New South Wales. *Br J Anaesth* 59:834, 1987.
20. Spence AA: The lessons of CEPOD (editorial). *Br J Anaesth* 60:753, 1988.
21. Caplan RA et al: Unexpected cardiac arrest during spinal anesthesia: A closed claims analysis of predisposing factors. *Anesthesiology* 68:5, 1988.
22. Keats AS: Anesthesia mortality—A new mechanism (editorial). *Anesthesiology* 68:2, 1988.
23. Abramowitz J: Cardiac arrest during spinal anesthesia: I (letter). *Anesthesiology* 68:970, 1988.
24. Zornow MH et al: Cardiac arrest during spinal anesthesia. II (letter). *Anesthesiology* 68:970, 1988.
25. Brown DL: Cardiac arrest during spinal anesthesia. III (letter). *Anesthesiology* 68: 971, 1988.
26. Knill RL: Cardiac arrests during spinal anesthesia: Unexpected? (letter). *Anesthesiology* 69:629, 1988.
27. Caplan RA et al: Effect of outcome on physician judgments of appropriateness of care. *JAMA* 265:1957, 1991.
28. Brown DL (ed): *Risk and Outcome in Anesthesia.* Philadelphia, Lippincott, 1988, p 24.
29. Yeager MP et al: Epidural anesthesia and analgesia in high-risk surgical patients. *Anesthesiology* 66:729, 1987.
30. Mangano DT et al: Postoperative myocardial ischemia. Therapeutic trials using intensive analgesia following surgery. *Anesthesiology* 76:342, 1992.
31. Scheinin B et al: Peroperative nitrous oxide delays bowel function after colonic surgery. *Br J Anaesth* 64:154, 1990.
32. Asari H et al: The inhibitory effect of intravenous D-tubocurarine and oral dantrolene on halothane-succinylcholine-induced myoglobinemia in children. *Anesthesiology* 61:332, 1984.
33. Hussey AJ et al: Plasma glutathione *S*-transferase levels as a measure of hepatocellular integrity following a single general anaesthetic with halothane, enflurane or isoflurane. *Br J Anaesth* 60:130, 1988.
34. Knill RL et al: Anesthesia with abdominal surgery leads to intense REM sleep during the first postoperative week. *Anesthesiology* 73:52, 1990.
35. Johannessen NW et al: When do most postoperative complications occur? A prospective study of 20,802 patients (abstract). *Anesthesiology* 75:A863, 1991.
36. Mangano DT et al: Association of perioperative myocardial ischemia with cardiac morbidity and mortality in men undergoing noncardiac surgery. *N Engl J Med* 323:1781, 1990.
37. London MJ et al: The "natural history" of segmental wall motion abnormalities in patients undergoing noncardiac surgery. *Anesthesiology* 73:644, 1990.
38. Feldman RD et al: Alterations in leukocyte-receptor affinity with aging: A potential explanation for altered-adrenergic sensitivity in the elderly. *New Engl J Med* 310:815, 1984.
39. Elliott HL et al: Effect of age on the responsiveness to vascular α-adrenoreceptors in man. *J Cardiovasc Pharmacol* 4:388, 1982.
40. Munson ES et al: Use of cyclopropane to test generality of anesthetic requirement in the elderly. *Anesth Analg* 63:998, 1984.
41. Scott JC, Stanski DR: Decreased fentanyl and alfentanil dose requirements with age. A simultaneous pharmacokinetic and pharmacodynamic evaluation. *J Pharmacol Exp Ther* 240:159, 1987.
42. Homer TD, Stanski DR: The effect of increasing age on thiopental disposition and anesthetic requirement. *Anesthesiology* 62:714, 1985.
43. Lien CA et al: Distribution, elimination, and action of vecuronium in the elderly. *Anesth Analg* 73:39, 1991.
44. Roy RC: Rational use of reversal agents. *Anesth Analg* 60:120, 1981.
45. Weissman C: The metabolic response to stress: An overview and update. *Anesthesiology* 73:308, 1990.
46. Elia S et al: Oxygen cost of breathing in postoperative cardiac surgical patients (abstract). *Anesthesiology* 63:A141, 1985.
47. Marsch SCU et al: Perioperative myocardial ischemia in patients undergoing elective hip arthroplasty during lumbar regional anesthesia. *Anesthesiology* 76:518, 1992.
48. Dureuil B et al: Effects of upper and lower abdominal surgery on diaphragmatic function. *Br J Anaesth* 59:1230, 1987.
49. Carli F et al: Protein metabolism after abdominal surgery: Effect of 24-hour extradural block with local anaesthetic. *Br J Anaesth* 67:729, 1991.
50. Field S et al: The oxygen cost of breathing in patients with cardiorespiratory disease. *Am Rev Respir Dis* 126:9, 1982.
51. Hurford WE et al: Myocardial perfusion assessed by thallium-201 scintigraphy during the discontinuation of mechanical ventilation in ventilator-dependent patients. *Anesthesiology* 74:1007, 1991.
52. Rao TLK et al: Reinfarction following anesthesia in patients with myocardial infarction. *Anesthesiology* 59:499, 1983.
53. Wilmore DW: Catabolic illness. Strategies for enhancing recovery. *N Engl J Med* 323:695, 1991.
54. Roizen MF et al: Aging increases hemodynamic responses to induction and incision (abstract). *Anesth Analg* 64:275, 1984.
55. Stone JG et al: Myocardial ischemia in untreated hypertensive patients: Effect of a small oral dose of a beta-adrenergic blocking agent. *Anesthesiology* 68:495, 1988.
56. Ghignone M et al: Anesthesia and ophthalmic surgery in the elderly: The effects of clonidine on intraocular pressure, perioperative hemodynamics, and anesthetic requirement. *Anesthesiology* 68:707, 1988.
57. Slogoff S, Keats AS: Does chronic treatment with calcium entry blocking agents reduce perioperative myocardial ischemia? *Anesthesiology* 68:676, 1988.
58. Baron J-F et al: Left ventricular global and regional function during lumbar epidural anesthesia in pa-

tients with and without angina pectoris. Influence of volume loading. *Anesthesiology* 66:621, 1987.
59. Coriat P et al: Lumbar epidural anesthesia improves ejection fraction in patients with poor left ventricular function (abstract). *Anesthesiology* 67:A259, 1987.
60. Sharrock N et al: Haemodynamic effects and outcome analysis of hypotensive extradural anaesthesia in controlled hypotensive patients undergoing total hip arthroplasty. *Br J Anaesth* 67:17, 1991.
61. Thompson GE et al: Hypotensive anesthesia for total hip arthroplasty. *Anesthesiology* 48:91, 1978.
62. Barry EG et al: Prevention of surgical oliguria and renal hemodynamic suppression by sustained hydration. *N Engl J Med* 270:1371, 1963.
63. Hou SH et al: Hospital-acquired renal insufficiency: A prospective study. *Am J Med* 74:243, 1983.
64. Sessler DI et al: Core temperature changes during N_2O/fentanyl and halothane/O_2 anesthesia. *Anesthesiology* 67:137, 1987.
65. Frank SM et al: Epidural versus general anesthesia, ambient operating room temperature, and patient age as predictors of inadvertent hypothermia. *Anesthesiology* 77:252, 1992.
66. Carli F et al: Effect of preoperative normothermia on postoperative protein metabolism in elderly patients undergoing hip arthroplasty. *Br J Anaesth* 63:276, 1989.
67. Frank SM et al: Unintentional hypothermia is associated with postoperative hypothermia myocardial ischemia. *Anesthesiology* 78:468, 1993.
68. Zwischenberger JB et al: Suppression of shivering decreases oxygen consumption and improves hemodynamic stability during postoperative rewarming. *Ann Thorac Surg* 43:428, 1987.
69. Rohrer MJ, Natale AM: Effect of hypothermia on the coagulation cascade. *Crit Care Med* 20:1402, 1992.
70. Sheffield CW et al: Mild hypothermia during anesthesia decreases resistance to *S. aureus* dermal infection. *Anesthesiology* 77:A1106, 1992.
71. Heier T et al: Mild intraoperative hypothermia increases duration of action and spontaneous recovery of vecuronium blockade during nitrous oxide–isoflurane anesthesia in humans. *Anesthesiology* 74:815, 1991.
72. Pauca AL et al: Effect of pethidine [meperidine], fentanyl and morphine on post-operative shivering in man. *Acta Anaesthesiol Scand* 28:138, 1984.
73. McLaren AD: Mortality studies. *Reg Anesth* 7:S172, 1982.
74. Coleman SA et al: Outcome after general anaesthesia for repair of fractured neck of femur. *Br J Anaesth* 60:43, 1988.
75. Valentin N et al: Spinal or general anaesthesia for surgery of the fractured hip. *Br J Anaesth* 58:284, 1986.
76. Davis FM et al: Prospective, multi-centre trial of mortality following general or spinal anaesthesia for hip fracture in the elderly. *Br J Anaesth* 59:1080, 1987.
77. Davis FM et al: Influence of spinal and general anaesthesia on haemostasis during total hip arthroplasty. *Br J Anaesth* 59:561, 1987.
78. McKenzie PJ, Loach AB: Local anaesthesia for orthopaedic surgery. *Br J Anaesth* 58:779, 1986.
79. Abrams PH et al: Blood loss during transurethral resection of the prostate. *Anesthesia* 37:71, 1982.
80. Worsley MH et al: High spinal nerve block for large bowel anastomosis. *Br J Anaesth* 60:836, 1988.
81. Breslow MJ et al: Changes in T-wave morphology following anesthesia and surgery: A common recovery-room phenomenon. *Anesthesiology* 64:398, 1986.
82. Hedenstierna G, Lofstron J: Effect of anaesthesia on respiratory function after major lower extremity surgery. *Acta Anaesthesiol Scand* 29:55, 1985.
83. Jayr C et al: Postoperative pulmonary complications: Epidural analgesia using bupivacaine and opioids versus parenteral opioids. *Anesthesiology* 78:666, 1993.
84. Catley DM et al: Pronounced, episodic oxygen desaturation in the postoperative period: Its association with ventilatory pattern and analgesic regimen. *Anesthesiology* 63:20, 1985.
85. Mankikian B et al: Improvement of diaphragmatic function by a thoracic epidural block after upper abdominal surgery. *Anesthesiology* 68:379, 1988.
86. Ejlersen E et al: A comparison between preincisional and postincisional lidocaine infiltration and postoperative pain. *Anesth Analg* 74:495, 1992.
87. Katz J et al: Preemptive analgesia. *Anesthesiology* 77:439, 1992.
88. Ready LB et al: Development of an anesthesiology-based postoperative pain management service. *Anesthesiology* 68:100, 1988.
89. Rosburg B, Wulff K: Haemodynamics following normovolemic haemodilution in elderly patients. *Acta Anaesthesiol Scand* 25:402, 1981.
90. Crystal GJ, Salem MR: Myocardial oxygenation in selective hemodilution in dogs: Effect of coronary insufficiency (abstract). *Anesth Analg* 66:S34, 1987.
91. Christopherson R et al: Low postoperative hematocrit is associated with cardiac ischemia in high-risk patients. *Anesthesiology* 75:499, 1991.
92. Stanley B et al: The elderly patient and informed consent. *JAMA* 252:1302, 1984.
93. Cohen CB, Cohen PJ: Do-not-resuscitate orders in the operating room. *N Engl J Med* 325:1879, 1991.

Chapter 27

SURGERY IN THE ELDERLY

Ronnie Ann Rosenthal and Dana K. Andersen

Over the last decade the percentage of operations performed on patients over age 65 has increased from 19 percent of total operations in 1980 to 29 percent in 1989.[1] As the elderly population continues to grow, we can expect an ever-increasing need for surgical care. It is therefore important to gain an understanding of the special issues involved in providing such care to patients in this age group.

For the most common surgical diseases encountered in the older patient, the decision to proceed with surgery is dictated by the circumstance of the illness. Hip fractures and prostatic hypertrophy have been considered surgical diseases of the elderly for many years and there is little controversy about the need to correct these problems. It has been only recently, as the techniques of surgical and anesthetic management have improved, that operative treatment of a far broader range of illnesses has been considered. The decision to proceed with surgery, however, is still more difficult to make in the elective setting than in emergency circumstances. Unfortunately, mortality for emergency procedures is at least three times the mortality for the same procedure performed under elective conditions. To deny surgical treatment on the basis of chronological age alone, is, therefore, no longer acceptable practice. However, "physiologic" age, or the presence of comorbid conditions, is now widely recognized as the important concern. (See Chap. 25, on perioperative assessment.)

In contemplating the need for surgery in the elderly patient, several factors must be considered: the clarity of the surgical indication, including the likelihood of progression of disease; the practical limitations imposed on the patient by the disease process; the degree of expected improvement after surgery; the hazards of the operative procedure; the likelihood of serious postoperative complications; and the need of the patient to maintain a maximum level of activity or productivity.

Unfortunately, at present, many decisions regarding surgery in older patients are made on the basis of speculation and prejudice rather than the guidelines outlined above. This bias in the provision of surgical care is magnified when the benefit of surgery seems small, either because the disability or "risk" of the disease appears to be minor (e.g., biliary colic) or because the prognosis of the disease appears to be poor (e.g., gastrointestinal malignancies). An excellent example of this bias can be found in an analysis of the effect of age on the surgical treatment of patients with breast cancer. Greenfield and colleagues[2] demonstrated that in patients with stage 1 or 2 disease and little or no comorbid illness, a significantly lower percentage of patients aged 70 years or more (83 percent) received appropriate surgery as compared to patients aged 50 to 69 years (96 percent).[2] This age bias subjected older women to a less favorable prognosis than would be expected for their overall state of health and stage of disease.

One further consideration is the quality of life without operation. The limitations imposed by nonsurgical alternatives can diminish independence and deprive patients of activities they previously enjoyed. A truss to control the symptoms of a groin hernia, for example, can limit mobility and be a constant encumbrance, while surgical repair can usually be accomplished easily and safely under local anesthesia. Severe symptoms of correctable peripheral vascular disease can confine an otherwise ambulatory patient to a wheelchair, while surgical repair can often restore flow with acceptably low morbidity and mortality.

A broader acceptance of elective surgery as a tool in the care of the elderly patient will come as we gain a better understanding of indications and outcomes and as we further limit the risks incurred by comorbidity with the development of new technologies.

ABDOMINAL DISORDERS

Alterations occur throughout the gastrointestinal (GI) tract with aging. This results in an increase in both benign and malignant disorders, many of which present as surgical problems. Janzon et al.[3] studied the etiology of acute abdominal complaints of 10,000 patient visits to a surgical emergency room in Sweden and found an age-related increase in the incidence of biliary tract disease, intestinal obstruction, gastrointestinal hemorrhage, hernia, and acute diverticulitis (Table 27-1). Surprisingly, appendicitis, which is usu-

TABLE 27-1

Etiology of Abdominal Complaints in the Elderly

Disorder	Incidence per 1000 Population per Year
Biliary tract diseases	16.0 in women >80
Intestinal obstruction	6.8 in women >80
Acute diverticulitis	3.5 in all patients >70
GI hemorrhage	5.7 in men 70–79
Hernia	4.0–6.0 in men >70
Appendicitis	3.0 in men >70

ally a disease of the second and third decades of life, had a second peak incidence in men over age 80. Reiss et al.[4] reviewed the causes for 1000 consecutive laparotomies in patients over age 70 (Table 27-2). Benign diseases accounted for slightly more than half of the procedures. Biliary tract disorders were the single most common benign diagnosis (46 percent). Obstruction of both the small and large bowels from postoperative adhesions, incarcerated hernia, and malignancy, in that order, accounted for 25 percent of all cases. Peptic ulcer disease accounted for 20 percent of procedures for benign disease, and half of these procedures were performed as emergencies. Tumors of the rectum and colon were the most common malignancies (56 percent), with gastric and esophageal cancer second (23 percent). In the following sections, several of the more common disorders will be discussed. Also, some less common problems with more controversial solutions will be briefly addressed.

Biliary Tract Disease

Biliary tract disease is the single most common cause of acute abdominal complaints and accounts for approximately one-third of all abdominal operations in the elderly.[4–6] Autopsy studies demonstrate a steady rise in the incidence of gallstones with age, which reaches over 50 percent by age 70.[7] The incidence of common bile duct stone also increases, approaching twice the overall incidence by age 60. The complications of calculous disease likewise increases with age, such that 40 to 60 percent of elderly patients treated for biliary stones present with a complication and require emergency surgery, compared to only 7 to 20 percent of patients of all ages.[8,9] Mortality in the emergency setting is 5 to 19 percent, compared to 0 to 3 percent in the elective setting.[5] To date there are no data to suggest which elderly patient with gallstones will develop a complication. For this reason the consideration of elective cholecystectomy is even more relevant in older than younger patients and indications for elective operation should probably be broadened in this age group rather than curtailed.

TABLE 27-2

Operative Procedures Performed in Patients over Age 70

	Cases (%)
Benign cases (n = 547)	
Simple cholecystectomy	162 (30)
Cholecystectomy and choledochotomy	92 (17)
Stomach and duodenum (vagotomy included)	98 (18)
Appendectomy	34 (6)
Lysis of adhesions	43 (8)
Miscellaneous procedures	118 (21)
Malignant cases (n = 453)	
Resections	
Colon and rectum	216 (47)
Stomach and esophagus	66 (14)
Miscellaneous	31 (8)
Palliative procedures	68 (15)
Laparotomy only, with or without biopsy	72 (16)

SOURCE: From Reiss et al.[4]

At present the major indication for elective cholecystectomy is the presence of "symptomatic" gallstones. The concept that "asymptomatic" stones pose little threat was espoused by Gracie and Ransohoff[10] in a frequently quoted study entitled "The Natural History of Silent Gallstones—The Innocent Gallstone Is Not a Myth." The patients in this study were mostly male faculty members of the University of Michigan, mean age 54. "Silent" stones, defined as stones that produced no symptoms, were discovered on screening oral cholecystogram. Patients were followed prospectively for the development of symptoms or complications. Of 123 subjects followed for 20 years, one-third remained asymptomatic, one-quarter had "prophylactic" cholecystectomy, one-quarter died of non-biliary causes, and one-sixth went on to develop symptoms. Nearly 20 percent of patients who became symptomatic developed a complication as well. Life-table analysis suggested a 15 percent risk of developing symptoms at 10 years and an 18 percent risk at both 15 and 20 years. Although a substantial number of subjects in this study did not develop overt manifestations of stone disease, these subjects are clearly not representative of the more diverse elderly population as a whole.

Data more relevant to the elderly can be found in several older studies. Wenckhert and Robertson[11] (1966) described "The Natural Course of Gallstone Disease" in 781 patients followed for 1 to 11 years, of whom 223 were over age 60. During the follow-up period, a significantly larger percent of older patients developed complications (29 versus 14 percent) without the antecedent worsening of symptoms seen in younger patients (18 versus 38 percent). Lund et al.[12] (1960) followed 526 patients with unoperated gallstones for 5 to 20 years. Symptoms or overt complications developed in 50 percent of "asymptomatic" females and 30 percent of "asymptomatic" males. In one quarter of the patients, complications developed without preceding symptoms.

The unreliable nature of biliary symptomatology is further demonstrated by data from McSherry et al.[13] (1985). Of 556 patients with gallstones accompanied by colic, 44 percent required cholecystectomy in a median of 2.5 years from diagnosis. Of these operations, 1 in 5 had to be performed as an emergency, however, due to the sudden occurrence of a complication. The need for a relatively large number of emergency procedures in this series underscores the inability to determine accurately, on the basis of antecedent symptoms, which patient is at high risk for complications. Reliance on symptoms to guide elective therapy for biliary stone disease in the elderly has limited our ability to avoid complications. We have now come to realize that symptoms may be misleading or even absent in spite of significant pathology. The best example of this can be found in a study of the pathophysiology of gallbladder perforation. This entity, which is principally a disease of elderly males, is a dreaded complication, with a mortality of 15 to 23 percent. Roslyn and Busuttil[14] recently reported that in patients with perforation, only 25 percent had a prior history of biliary tract symptoms (Fig. 27-1). On pathological examination of the gallbladder, however, 70 percent had histological evidence of chronic cholecystitis underlying the acute inflammatory changes. Even in the presence of acute inflammation, symptoms can be atypical. In one series of elderly patients with acute cholecystitis, one-quarter had no abdominal tenderness, one-third had no elevation in temperature or white blood cell count, and over one-half had no signs of peritonitis in the right upper quadrant.[15]

Although the risk of death from gallstones is relatively low overall, morbidity and mortality are clearly higher in elderly patients who come to emergency surgery. It has also been shown that of those patients who die from stone disease, 80 percent had been characterized as "asymptomatic."[16] While it is not appropriate to extend the indication for surgery to all elderly patients with gallstones, it is apparent that "silent" stones are not always "innocent" in this age group. Prospective clinical studies to determine what factors predispose to complications of gallstones in elderly patients are needed to appropriately define indications for elective operation.

Recent advances in minimally invasive surgical techniques for cholecystectomy may provide some help in caring for the elderly with gallstones. Laparoscopic operations are well tolerated, with less pain and physical disability than accompanies standard open procedures. Length of stay, hospital costs, and the need for postoperative recovery time and support services can be reduced.[17] Studies on the exact benefits of laparoscopic cholecystectomy in the elderly are currently in progress. In our experience with the first 100 patients, however, we have seen less morbidity, less disability and shorter stays with this technique, which has now become our standard approach.

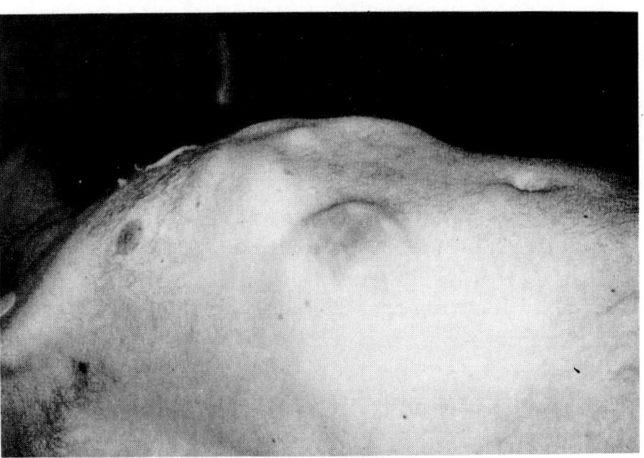

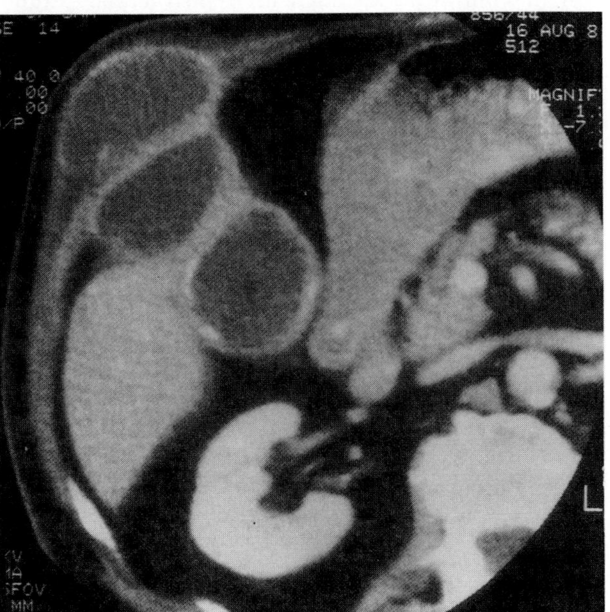

FIGURE 27-1

A. A 75-year-old male presents with a nontender mass in the right upper quadrant, no symptoms or signs of sepsis, and no history of gallstones. *B.* Computed tomography (CT) scan showing perforated gallbladder with abcess eroding through the fascia and into the subcutaneous space. *(From Berger D, Rubenstein J: Gallbladder perforation. Surgical Rounds 8:45, 1989. Reproduced by permission.)*

Pancreatic Disorders

Pancreatic diseases of special concern in elderly patients include acute pancreatitis and pancreatic carcinoma. The diagnosis of each of these entities is particularly challenging due to the inherently nonspecific nature of the signs and symptoms of pancreatic disease combined with the masked manifestations of abdominal disease usually seen in this age group.

Pancreatitis

Although the incidence of acute pancreatitis does not appear to be significantly different in elderly populations, the severity of the disease is usually increased.[18] The hospital mortality rate for acute pancreatitis in patients below the age of 50 is less than 10 percent, but it increases steadily to over 20 percent in patients over 75.[19] Acute pancreatitis in the elderly is most frequently caused by biliary tract disease. The increased incidence of this form of pancreatitis in the sixth, seventh, and eighth decades of life parallels the increased incidence of choledocholithiasis in these age groups. The increased death rate with acute pancreatitis is almost entirely due to coexisting diseases rather than to an increased incidence of complications resulting directly from the pathologic process of acute pancreatitis per se.[19] The treatment of acute pancreatitis in elderly patients should therefore be directed toward the rapid documentation and treatment of biliary tract pathology and the more aggressive prevention of complications such as hypovolemia, pulmonary compromise, and infection.

Pancreatic Carcinoma

Cancer of the pancreas occurs with a peak incidence in the sixth and seventh decades of life.[20] The resectability rate for pancreatic carcinoma remains in the 20 to 25 percent range for all age groups; but until recently, an age above 70 was frequently judged as a relative contraindication for radical pancreatic resection. Over the past decade, mortality and morbidity rates for pancreatic resection have decreased significantly, however, and patients over age 70 are now routinely considered candidates for surgical treatment of pancreatic malignancies.[20–22] The operative mortality rate for pancreatic resection in patients above age 70 is now reported to range from 5 to 10 percent, and postoperative complications are seen in 14 to 28 percent of patients. These results are similar to those seen in younger age groups. Interestingly, the long-term survival of patients after pancreatic resection is largely determined by the histology of the tumor, not the age of the patient. While ductal adenocarcinoma carries a median survival of 12 to 18 months in all age groups, 25 to 30 percent of pancreatic malignancies in elderly patients are found to be of a more favorable histologic type. Successful resection of duodenal and ampullary tumors is associated with a 25 to 60 percent 5-year survival in both younger and older patients.

The decreased incidence of perioperative complications after pancreatic resection has largely been a result of improved perioperative care and the advent of specific pharmacologic agents which inhibit pancreatic function.[23] These agents decrease the incidence of pancreatic leaks by minimizing exocrine output while anastomoses heal. In the absence of severe cardiac or pulmonary disease, elderly patients with pancreatic tumors can be expected to do nearly as well as younger patients and should, therefore, be considered as potential candidates for resection.

Appendicitis

Appendicitis, primarily a disease of the second and third decades of life, also occurs with increased frequency in males over age 80. It deserves special attention because of the disproportionately high mortality of 6 to 10 percent associated with its occurrence in the older age group.[24] As with acute cholecystitis, the increased severity of disease is due largely to the atypical presentation of the signs and symptoms of acute inflammation, which leads to a delay in diagnosis and treatment. The classic sequence of periumbilical pain followed by anorexia, nausea, vomiting, and localization of pain to the right lower quadrant at or near McBurney's point is uncommon in the elderly. Instead, there is a prolonged period of vague abdominal discomfort. Nausea and anorexia are common but vomiting is infrequent. As the inflammatory process progresses and localized peritonitis develops, pain may appear in the right lower quadrant. However, in spite of peritonitis, rebound tenderness and abdominal guarding, so common in the young, are absent in more than half of elderly patients. The indolent nature of the initial symptomatology usually leads to a 40- to 60-hour delay before the elderly patient seeks medical attention. This delay is compounded by a delay in diagnosis once the patient is admitted to the hospital. As many as 40 percent of patients are not operated upon within the first 48 hours of admission.[25]

Pathophysiologic changes of the appendix with aging may contribute to the severity of the disease. Early perforation has been attributed to narrowing of the lumen, which can lead to increased intraluminal pressure. Atherosclerotic changes in the artery to the appendix can result in a blood supply so marginal that even minimal increases in pressure lead to edema, vascular thrombosis, necrosis, and perforation. These changes—combined with the long diagnostic delay—may explain why, at surgery, perforation is present in approximately 70 percent of elderly patients, as compared to only 20 percent of younger patients.[26] Good postoperative results are usually associated with a short duration of symptoms and rapid diagnosis and operation.

Duodenal Ulcer

Duodenal ulcer disease had been thought to be primarily a disease of midlife. More recently, it has been recognized to occur in the elderly with increasing frequency and severity. When duodenal ulcer does occur in this age group, it is more likely to be associated with a complication or death. In one study comparing duodenal ulcers in patients younger and older than age 60, mortality for older patients was significantly higher than for younger patients (15 versus 2 percent) and half the deaths in the older group were directly attributable to ulcer disease.[27] World Health Organization statistics demonstrate that in 1986, over 80 percent of deaths from peptic ulcer in the United States were in patients over age 65.[28]

Duodenal ulcers may occur in the elderly as an exacerbation of long-standing disease or as a new event. When the disease presents de novo in these patients, it tends to be virulent. As many as half of the elderly patients who present with an acute complication of duodenal ulcer disease have no antecedent history of ulcers.

The use of nonsteroidal anti-inflammatory drugs (NSAIDs) has been implicated in the development of ulcer complications in older persons. Watson et al.[29] reported that 40 percent of patients with bleeding and 30 percent of those with perforation had been taking NSAIDs.[29] Others confirm a higher use of NSAIDs in older persons with duodenal ulcer.[30,31] Complications of ulcers, however, are still more common in older patients regardless of the influence of NSAIDs.

The diagnosis of duodenal ulcer disease in the elderly is often difficult to establish because of peculiarities in presentation. The classic symptom of epigastric pain relieved by eating or antacids is often absent. As many as 35 percent of duodenal ulcer patients over age 60 have no pain, compared to 8 percent of those between ages 20 and 50.[32] Instead, older persons present with anorexia and weight loss, nausea and vomiting, hematemesis, melena, or unexplained anemia. In those with anemia, secondary complications—such as changes in mental status, congestive heart failure, or angina—may be the initial complaint.

Once the diagnosis of duodenal ulcer disease is made, initial treatment does not vary with age. However, the incidence of complications requiring surgery is higher in the elderly. The two major complications are bleeding and perforation. In half of the elderly patients who present with hemorrhage, this bleeding is the first symptom of the ulcer disease. Recurrent bleeding is nearly twice as likely in this age group as well.[27] It has also been shown that spontaneous cessation of hemorrhage is less likely in older than in younger patients. In as many as 50 percent of elderly patients who present with bleeding, surgery will be required.[29] Operative mortality correlates with the amount of blood transfused and varies from 7 percent for less than three units to 35 percent for five or more units.[33] Overall operative mortality varies from 10 to 18 percent, although the mortality rate for "nonoperative" treatment is considerably higher.[29,33] (See Table 27-3.)

Perforation has become the most common indication for duodenal ulcer surgery in the elderly. Some series report a recent rise in the incidence of perforation, particularly in elderly women, although the etiology of this trend is not completely defined. As with many other abdominal catastrophes in this age group, the presenting signs and symptoms are often vague and misleading. The classic history of sudden onset of severe epigastric pain followed shortly by the development of a rigid abdomen is the exception rather than the rule. Instead, nausea and vomiting predominate, in association with vague abdominal discomfort. In one series, the initial findings were so nonspecific that over 35 percent of patients were thought to have medical rather than surgical illnesses. In 30 percent of these patients, pain was not a significant complaint. In 40 percent, there was no rigidity, and in 50 percent, there was no guarding.[34] In addition, standard diagnostic tests are often not helpful. Free intraperitoneal air is not seen on 25 to 50 percent of upright chest or left lateral decubitus x-rays.

Once the diagnosis of perforated ulcer is made, there is little doubt that surgery is needed. The choice of procedure varies from simple omentopexy to resection, depending on the time since perforation, the amount of peritoneal contamination, the severity of the ulcer disease, and the general condition of the patient. The mortality following surgery is determined in large part by the length of time from perforation to operation. Surgical mortality has been shown to double if the procedure is performed more than 12 hours after perforation[35] or if shock is present on admission[36] and to increase fivefold if the delay is more than 24 hours.[36] Nonoperative management in this age group is contraindicated because this form of therapy has been associated with mortality rates as high as 100 percent.[29]

Gastric Ulcer

Gastric ulcer is primarily a disease of the elderly. While duodenal ulcer is more common in this age group, gastric ulcer is more lethal. Two-thirds of all ulcer deaths in older patients occur from ulcers that arise in the stomach.[37] Gastric ulcer behaves much like a chronic disorder, with healing followed by episodes of exacerbation. Prior to the introduction of proton pump antagonists, recurrence rates for medical therapy were as high as 40 to 75 percent.[37,38] The impact of H^+-K^+ ATPase inhibitors on late recur-

TABLE 27-3

Surgical versus Nonsurgical Management of Duodenal Ulcer in the Elderly

		Surgical		*Nonsurgical*	
	Total Number of Patients (%)	**Number of Patients (%)**	**Mortality**	**Number of Patients (%)**	**Mortality**
Bleeding	81 (50)	41 (51)	10%	40 (49)	20%
Perforation	47 (29)	43 (92)	21%	4 (8)	100%
Obstruction	8 (5)	7 (88)	0%	1 (12)	0%
Intractability	27 (16)	12 (45)	0%	15 (55)	0%

SOURCE: From Watson et al.[29]

rence, particularly in the elderly, has not yet been determined.

The signs and symptoms of gastric ulcer are as misleading as those of duodenal ulcer. Pain, when present, is often confused with pain of biliary or cardiac origin. Dysphagia and weight loss may predominate, because the location of the ulcer tends to approach the esophagogastric junction with advancing age (Fig. 27-2). The sequelae of chronic blood loss may further confuse the presentation.

The diagnosis of gastric ulcer is made on upper gastrointestinal contrast studies or at endoscopy. Multiple biopsies are indicated to rule out malignancy. The combination of benign appearance on upper-GI series and negative biopsies is accurate in 95 to 99 percent of cases. Follow-up examination to document healing, however, is mandatory. Successful healing on medical therapy is defined as 50 percent reduction in ulcer size at 3 weeks, 90 percent at 6 weeks, and complete healing at 12 weeks. In a large VA cooperative study,[37] 42 percent of patients who healed within this time frame had a recurrence within 2 years. Of those who healed more slowly, 62 percent recurred during the same interval.[39] Healing rates in the elderly have been shown to be prolonged, which leaves this group at increased risk for recurrence.

The outcome from nonsurgical therapy of gastric ulcer in the elderly is poor. Amberg and Zboralske[37] have demonstrated a 40 percent mortality for medically treated gastric ulcer in patients over age 70. Others have shown that of those patients who come to surgery as failures of medical management, 35 percent require emergency operation.[40] It is therefore important to be more aggressive in the consideration of surgical therapy in gastric ulcer disease. Intractability—as indicated by slow healing or recurrence—should be thought of as an indication for elective resection. The mortality for emergency surgery for gastric ulcer in the elderly is as high as 30 percent,[33,37] while elective surgical mortality ranges from 2 to 9 percent[5] and has been reported as low as zero percent in cases where failure to heal was the indication for surgery.[33]

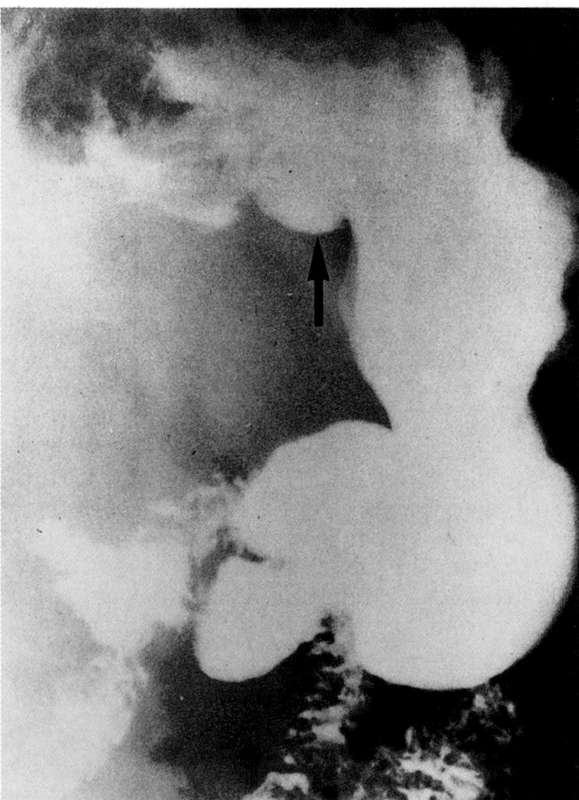

FIGURE 27-2

Upper gastrointestinal series showing a gastric ulcer high on the lesser curvature of the stomach. This ulcer has the typical appearance of a "geriatric ulcer." *(From Amberg and Zboralske.[37] Reproduced by permission.)*

Gastric Cancer

Despite a general decrease in the incidence of gastric cancer, the risk of development of this disease in the elderly has remained unchanged. Histologically, gastric tumors in the elderly are more often well differentiated and tend to occur in the distal two-thirds of the stomach. Early detection of these lesions is made difficult by the nonspecific nature of the symptoms of gastric malignancies. In as many as one-third of elderly patients with this disease, anemia of unknown etiology is the presenting finding. In another third, disorders such as peptic ulcer or cholecystitis are suspected. In only one-third of the patients who are subsequently found to have gastric cancer is the diagnosis established prior to admission.[41] This delay in diagnosis is reflected in the stage of the disease at the time of operation. In a study from Italy, 60 percent of elderly patients with gastric carcinoma were found to have stage IV disease at the time of diagnosis, while none had stage I disease. Only half of the patients had tumors that were resectable at the time of exploration.[42] In Japan, where gastric cancer is endemic and screening is common, approximately 40 percent of elderly patients have been classified as stages I and II.[43]

There is no question that the treatment of choice for gastric adenocarcinoma in younger patients is resection unless there is gross metastatic disease outside the field of operation. The treatment in the elderly should be the same unless coexisting diseases make surgical risks prohibitive or make life expectancy less than 2 years. The extent of operation should depend primarily upon the location of the tumor and the stage of the disease. Several studies confirm that the extent of a potentially curative resection does not significantly alter operative mortality. Even total gastrectomy requiring thoracotomy can be performed safely in patients over age 70 if there is little coexisting impairment. Mortality for total gastrectomy in the elderly varies from 3.3 to 12.2 percent, while mortality for partial gastrectomy is similar and varies from 2.3 to 10.5 percent.[43] By comparison with data from younger patients, the mortality for older patients from total gastrectomy is not different, although younger patients do show a better outcome with partial gastrectomy.[41–43] When total gastrectomy is done for palliation in the elderly, mortality and morbidity are prohibitively high, and other methods of palliation including laser therapy should be considered as alternatives.[44]

Survival for resectable gastric cancer in older patients is actually as good as or better than survival in younger patients. In the study from Italy where a large majority of patients had advanced-stage disease, 5-year survival following resection was 23 percent for older patients and only 11 percent for younger patients. No younger patients with stage IV disease survived 3 years, while several older patients with similarly staged disease were alive at 5 years.[42] In the Japanese studies, survival rates are better overall because of earlier detection. Five-year survival after curative total gastrectomy in one series was 48.6 percent in older patients as compared to 49.4 percent in younger ones.[43]

Lower Gastrointestinal Hemorrhage

Massive hemorrhage from the lower GI tract is not an uncommon occurrence in the elderly. The etiology of lower-GI bleeding in this age group is usually either diverticulosis or angiodysplasia (Fig. 27-3). Differentiating between the two, however, may be difficult, because vascular ectasia and diverticula, respectively, are estimated to be present in 25 and 50 percent of the elderly population.[45,46] In addition, the majority of diverticula occur on the left side of the colon, yet diverticular bleeding usually occurs on the right side in older patients. Therefore, lesions may exist simultaneously on both sides of the colon, and unless bleeding is actually visualized, the source will remain undefined.

The pattern of bleeding from each lesion may help to distinguish the source. Diverticular bleeding occurs from a single vessel and tends to be self-limited. The cessation of bleeding usually means that the offending vessel has clotted, and rebleeding is not common. Angiodysplasia, on the other hand, tends to bleed intermittently. Initially, the bleeding may be slow because it is primarily venous in origin. As the lesion enlarges and true arteriovenous malformations develop, bleeding becomes more massive and recurrence is frequent.

The approach to the diagnosis of lower-GI hemorrhage in the elderly should be aggressive. Localization of the bleeding site is most important. It is first necessary to rule out an upper-GI source. This can be accomplished rapidly by confirming the absence of blood in a bilious nasogastric aspirate. If no bile is present in the aspirate, upper-GI endoscopy should be performed. The next step is a careful digital rectal exam and proctoscopy to promptly rule out an anorectal source. In cases where the bleeding appears to be slow or to have stopped, colonoscopy can provide a rapid assessment of the source of hemorrhage and has the added advantage of providing a potential means of therapy. Colonoscopy may also be useful when bleeding is more rapid,[47] but visualization is often poor and an accurate diagnosis may not be possible. In these cases early radionuclide scanning with both technetium 99m sulfur colloid and red blood cells labeled with technetium 99m can be diagnostic. Sulfur colloid can detect bleeding at approximately 0.1 ml/min but is cleared rapidly from the circulation, so intermittent bleeding can easily be missed. "Tagged" red blood cells persist in the circulation for 24 h, and serial scans over a longer period of time may be helpful.[48] More rapid bleeding, 0.5 to 1.0 ml/min, can be demonstrated with selective injections of contrast agent into the superior mesenteric and inferior mesenteric arteries. When rapid bleeding is from a diverticulum, extravasation of contrast at the point of hemorrhage can be seen on the angiogram in as many as 75 percent of cases. When bleeding is from angiodysplasia, dilated submucosal veins, vascular tufts and an early filling vein may be the only indication of the bleeding site.[46]

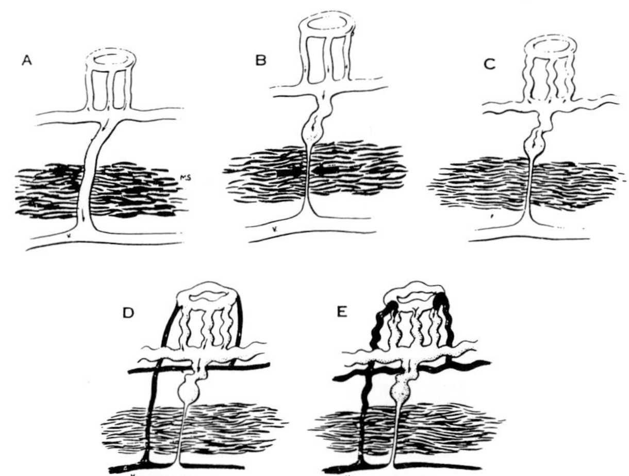

FIGURE 27-3

A diagrammatic illustration of the proposed concept of the development of cecal vascular ectasia. *A.* Normal state of the vein perforating the muscular layers. *B.* With muscular contraction or increased intraluminal pressure, the vein becomes partially obstructed. *C.* After repeated episodes over many years, the submucosal vein becomes dilated and tortuous. *D.* Later the veins and venules draining into the submucosal vein becomes similarly involved. *E.* Ultimately, the capillary ring becomes dilated, the precapillary sphincter becomes incompetent, and a small arteriovenous communication appears. *(From Boley SJ et al: On the nature and etiology of vascular ectasis of the colon. Gastroenterology 72:650, 1977. Reproduced by permission.)*

Although 80 percent of diverticular bleeding is self-limited and will stop with observation, bleeding from angiodysplasia is more persistent. Prolonged attempts to control bleeding nonoperatively are not usually warranted. Mortality and morbidity correlate with the amount of blood transfused and increase dramatically after five or six units. In the majority of elderly patients, the source of bleeding is in the right colon, and right hemicolectomy is sufficient to control the hemorrhage. When no bleeding site has been found preoperatively, a blind total abdominal colectomy is usually indicated. Emergency subtotal colectomy for bleeding carries an operative mortality of from 15 to 50 percent and has been associated with disabling diarrhea in approximately 15 percent of cases.[45] Aggressive attempts at localization and early surgical intervention can therefore limit the extent of resection and the operative mortality and morbidity.

Diverticulitis

Although 50 percent or more of persons in the ninth decade of life have colon diverticula, only 10 to 20 percent will develop symptoms of diverticular disease or diverticulitis.[49] As with other acute inflammatory processes in this age group, the signs and symptoms of diverticulitis may be vague. Abdominal pain in the suprapubic area or left lower quadrant occurs in 70 to 80 percent of patients, but a tender left lower quadrant mass is felt in only a minority of cases. The pain of diverticulitis is often accompanied by a change in bowel habits, with either diarrhea or constipation or both. The inflammatory process may progress to occlude the bowel lumen, resulting in complete obstruction, or it may induce spasm, causing intermittent partial obstruction. Nausea and vomiting occur in about 25 percent of cases. Occasionally signs and symptoms of a fistula may be the presenting findings. In approximately 2 percent of cases, pneumaturia or pyuria and recurrent urinary tract infections will indicate a colovesical fistula. In another 2 percent, a feculent discharge from the vagina will be present.[50] Often these fistulae are the first indication of diverticular disease. Finally, patients may present with signs of sepsis, change in mental status, and diffuse peritonitis from free perforation of a previously contained pericolic abscess.

The vague nature of the symptoms, and the nonspecific physical exam, can lead to difficulty in establishing the diagnosis. Both renal colic and irritable bowel syndrome can easily be confused with diverticulitis. When changes in bowel habits or obstructive symptoms predominate, carcinoma of the left colon is the primary initial diagnosis. Proctosigmoidoscopy as the initial study is useful to rule out rectal pathology when obstruction is the predominant finding. This study should be performed with as little air insufflation as possible. Colonoscopy in the acute setting is not indicated. The diagnostic study of choice is computed tomography (CT) with triple contrast (oral Gastrograffin, rectal Gastrograffin by enema, and intravenous contrast; Fig. 27-4). This study clearly defines the extent of inflammation from phlegmon to abscess, although it cannot distinguish perforated cancer from diverticular infection. It is also less useful in the obstructed patient, where a simple Gastrograffin enema can define the level and completeness of obstruction.

The treatment of diverticulitis in the elderly should be governed by the understanding that serious infection can be present with minimal signs and symptoms. Younger patients with mild diverticulitis and without signs of sepsis (such as fever or elevated white blood cell count) can be treated as outpatients with oral antibiotics and a liquid or low-residue diet. Older patients should be considered for hospitalization if there is the slightest doubt about the severity of disease. With bowel rest, intravenous hydration, and intravenous antibiotics, most episodes of diverticular infection will resolve. Failure of the inflammation to respond to conservative measures is an indication for emergency surgery. The operative goal is to eradicate the infection and divert the fecal stream. In most cases the emergency operative treatment of diverticulitis consists of resection of the involved segment of colon and creation of an end colostomy with a closed rectal pouch (Hartmann's procedure), followed by restoration of bowel continuity several months later. On rare occasions, initial resection may be hazardous either because of the size of extent of the inflammation and abscess or because of the patient's overall condition. In these cases, drainage of the abscess and diverting colostomy is the initial procedure of choice, followed by resection once the infection is under control.

Other indications for surgery in diverticular disease include recurrent acute attacks of diverticulitis, stricture of the involved segment of bowel, fistulae to other organs, and the inability to exclude carcinoma

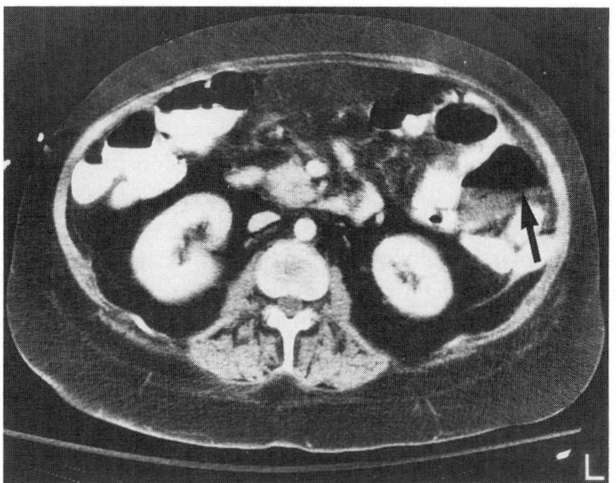

FIGURE 27-4
CT scan with triple contrast showing diverticular abcess with air fluid level adjacent to the sigmoid colon (arrow).

as a cause of the deformity of the involved segment. Elective surgical treatment of diverticular disease is associated with an operative mortality of less than 4 percent in the elderly. This mortality rises to 20 to 30 percent when emergency surgery becomes necessary.[51]

Carcinoma of the Colon and Rectum

The incidence of carcinoma of the colon and rectum increases with age, beginning at age 40. After age 50, the risk climbs sharply, nearly doubling with each successive decade of life.[52] Colorectal cancer is the second and third most common cause of cancer death in men and women respectively. It is reported to account for approximately two-thirds of all gastrointestinal malignancies in patients over age 70 seen recently at Memorial Sloan-Kettering Hospital.[53]

The signs and symptoms of colorectal cancer do not differ significantly with age. The response to these signs and the symptoms, however, may vary considerably. Constipation and other changes in bowel function are such common chronic complaints of the aged that they are often ignored by both the patient and the physician. Vague abdominal discomfort, changes in mental status, and weakness are often the presenting complaints. The diagnosis, therefore, is often not made until a complication occurs. Waldron et al.[54] have shown that emergency surgery is necessary more frequently in older than in younger patients (58 versus 43 percent). In the elective setting, operative mortality is approximately 4 percent (2 to 8 percent), but when emergency surgery is necessary, mortality at least triples.[55]

Establishing a method of early detection of colorectal cancer in the elderly is essential. Screening with fecal occult blood testing is inadequate because false-negative tests are found in nearly two-thirds of patients with early (Dukes' A and B) cancers (Fig. 27-5). In centers where colonoscopic studies are liberally employed, the incidence of Dukes' A and B lesions increases nearly fourfold.[56] At present the recommendations for screening in the younger population have been extended to apply to the elderly; annual digital rectal exam, annual stool guaiac testing, and flexible sigmoidoscopy every 3 years have been advised. More frequent screening with colonoscopy has been recommended for people in high-risk groups, such as those with previous adenomatous polyps, previous cancers, or ulcerative colitis. It may also be appropriate to consider elderly patients with abdominal or colonic symptoms as a high-risk group and use colonoscopic screening more aggressively in these patients as well.

There is general consensus that both the operative mortality and morbidity and the long-term prognosis for surgical treatment of colorectal cancer in the elderly does not differ significantly from the results in younger patients and that age alone should not affect the choice of therapy. Even in patients over age 80,

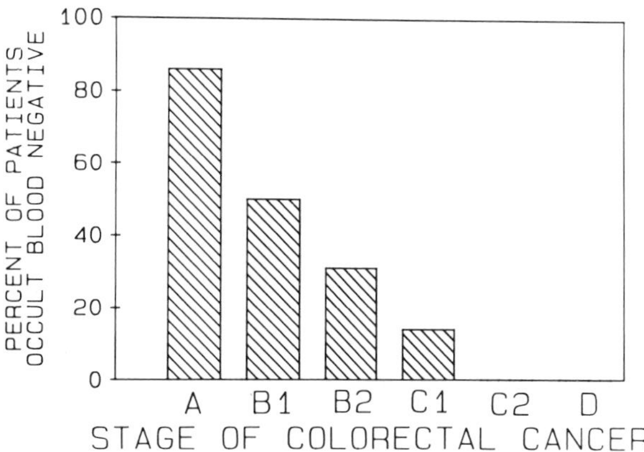

FIGURE 27-5

This graph depicts the percentage of patients with negative tests for occult blood in stool according to the stage of the colorectal tumor found. These results indicate that testing stool for occult blood detects few early colorectal cancers. *(From Longo et al.*[56] *Reproduced by permission.)*

cancer of the abdominal colon can be resected with an operative mortality as low as 2.2 percent and a 3-year survival virtually identical with that of younger patients.[57]

There has been some concern, however, about the ability of elderly patients to tolerate the operative procedures for low rectal cancers. These procedures include abdominoperineal resection, low anterior resection, and, more recently, the sphincter-saving coloanal reconstruction. Alternatives for these procedures—such as transanal excision, transsacral excision, and fulguration—have all been suggested for the highest-risk elderly with short life expectancy. However, for those with few comorbid conditions, resectional procedures can be performed with operative mortality rates that do not differ statistically from those in younger patients.[55,58]

Abdominal Wall Hernia

Approximately one-half million herniorraphies are performed in the United States each year. The incidence of abdominal wall hernia in older males is estimated at 13/1000. The incidence of hernia in older females is approximately one-fourth to one-eighth that in males.[59]

The relative frequency of the various types of hernia changes with increasing age. The incidence of indirect (congenital) hernia falls from 90 percent in young men to 50 to 60 percent in older men, and the incidence of direct hernia rises to about 35 percent. In elderly women, the incidence of femoral hernia rises, although indirect inguinal hernia is still the most common. The exact percentage of each type of hernia in females is difficult to ascertain from the literature.

Some 15 to 30 percent of hernia repairs in patients over age 65 are done as emergencies for incarceration. Incarceration is the cause of one-third of bowel obstructions and is responsible for 10 percent of all abdominal surgical emergencies in this age group.[60] Indirect inguinal hernias in men and femoral hernias in women are the most likely to incarcerate. Umbilical and ventral hernias, although less common, each account for approximately 10 percent of hernias that present as bowel obstruction.

Elective repair of abdominal wall hernias in the elderly can usually be performed under local anesthesia with minimal mortality and morbidity. Recent series report mortality rates for elective procedures approaching zero percent in patients over age 65.[59] Mortality for emergency cases is much higher and averages 15 percent. Data from a large Danish study show crude survival after elective hernia repair in patients over age 70 to be 99.4 percent at 30 days, 98.4 percent at 1 year, and 76.1 percent at 10 years. For emergency repair, however, survival falls to 86.4 percent at 30 days, 81.1 percent at 1 year, and 30.5 percent at 10 years.[61]

A rare but insidious type of hernia, found most often in frail elderly women, occurs through the obturator canal (Fig. 27-6). Relaxation of the pelvic musculature with aging and multiple pregnancies, combined with loss of extraperitoneal fat and increased intraabdominal pressure, are thought to be the etiologic factors. Pain down the medial aspect of the thigh, known as the Howship-Romberg sign, is present in about 50 percent of cases. The lack of external manifestations often makes the diagnosis of obturator hernia difficult. Unfortunately, the obscure nature of these signs and symptoms leads to preoperative delays of from 2 to 7 days. In over two-thirds of cases, the diagnosis is not established until the time of abdominal exploration for bowel obstruction. Strangulation requiring resection is present in 50 percent of cases, and operative mortality is high, ranging from 10 to 20 percent.[62] Awareness of the possibility of incarcerated obturator hernia in a frail elderly female with bowel obstruction of unknown etiology is essential if the need for resection—and mortality—are to be reduced.

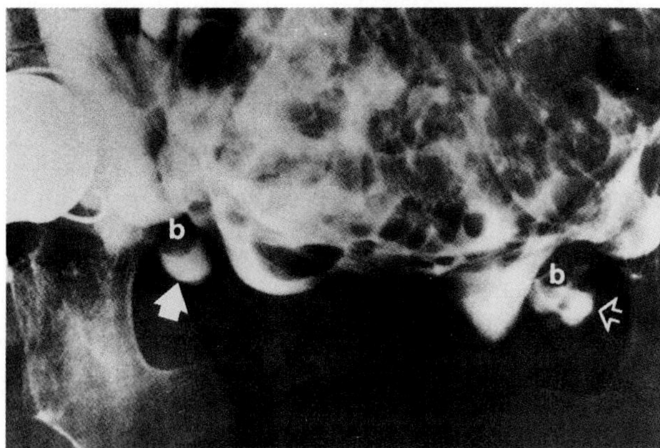

FIGURE 27-6

Herniography showing intraperitoneal contrast agent in bilateral obturator hernial sacs. *(From Persson NH et al: Obturator hernia—Clinical significance of radiologic diagnosis. Acta Chir Scand 153:361, 1987. Reproduced by permission.)*

CARDIAC AND THORACIC SURGERY

Over the past 5 to 10 years, an increasing proportion of patients undergoing cardiac surgery are elderly. Considerable information exists about indications and results of cardiac operations in patients over age 70. More recent studies have begun to address this issue in patients over age 80.[63,64] It is now generally accepted that surgical treatment can be offered almost regardless of age if the overall health of the patient and the nature of the disease process warrant such intervention. Coronary artery disease and valvular dysfunction respond well to surgical treatment, with mortality rates only slightly higher than those seen in younger patients and with comparable functional results. Most studies emphasize that patient selection is important. Best results are seen in patients with few associated disorders who are active, well motivated, and mentally competent.

Noncardiac disorders of the thoracic cavity frequently require surgical intervention in the elderly as well. The incidence of malignancies of both the lung and esophagus increase with age, making thoracotomy for resection a clinically important issue.

Coronary Artery Bypass Grafting

The number of coronary bypass procedures performed on patients over age 65 has risen from 2.6 per 1000 population in 1980 to 10.4 per 1000 population in 1989.[1] This dramatic increase indicates a growing willingness to offer surgical therapy to older patients with reconstructable coronary artery disease. The indications for coronary bypass grafting in the elderly are not different for those in younger patients. Symptomatic major stenosis of the left main (greater than 50 percent) or other coronary arteries (greater than 70 percent) has been considered severe enough to warrant revascularization. In fact, because the results of surgical therapy for left main disease have been shown to be superior to medical therapy, the presence of significant left main stenosis is considered a definite indication for revascularization.[65]

A recent study designed to relate the risk of coronary bypass surgery to the severity of the preoperative illness identified each of the following, including age, as risk factors for mortality: emergency procedure, elevated preoperative creatinine, severe left ventricular dysfunction, anemia (hematocrit below 34 percent) chronic pulmonary disease, prior vascular surgery, reoperation, and mitral insufficiency. Obesity, diabetes mellitus, aortic stenosis, and cerebrovascular disease were found to be additional risk factors for morbidity. For each risk factor an odds ratio, which measured its association with mortality, was calculated and a point score from 1 to 6 was assigned according to the odds ratio. Emergency surgery was the highest, with an odds ratio of 6.25 and a point score of 6, while age 65 to 74 received a point score of 1 and age above 75 a point score of 2. When considered alone, this contribution of age to the increased mortality is small and not sufficient to warrant withholding surgical therapy.[66]

The results of coronary bypass surgery from several recent series are shown in Table 27-4.[67] Even in the series of patients over age 80, coronary artery surgery was associated with an acceptable overall mortality and an elective mortality as low as 2 percent.[64] Early elective operation is clearly preferable, as the mortality for emergency operations is two to ten times higher. Unfortunately, because of a failure to offer elective operations to the very old, as many as 40 percent of elderly patients require urgent or emergent operations.

Morbidity following coronary surgery in the elderly is quite high in many series. Pulmonary failure requiring prolonged intubation, neurologic events including cerebrovascular accident and disorientation, and atrial arrhythmias are more common in this age group than in younger patients. Other complications—including reoperation for bleeding, need for pacemaker insertion, perioperative myocardial infarction, and wound infections—occur with equal frequency in both age groups.

Nonoperative revascularization using the technique of percutaneous transluminal coronary angioplasty (PTCA) has been shown to be effective in patients in the seventh and eighth decades of life with discrete single- or double-vessel disease. Recent mortality in patients over age 65 is less than 1 percent, which is no different from the mortality for younger patients.[68] One-year patency has been reported as approximately 70 percent, compared to the 90 to 95 percent for surgical bypass. PTCA in the very elderly (age 80 or above) has been reported to have a very high rate of mortality and morbidity. This has been attributed to the fact that many of the procedures in this age group are performed as emergencies for unstable angina or myocardial infarction. Although PTCA is a useful adjunct, it should not be thought of as a complete substitute for coronary artery surgery. It does provide a satisfactory alternative to surgery in the appropriately selected older patient for whom the risks of surgery may be prohibitive.

Valvular Disease

Calcific aortic stenosis is a disease of the elderly. Over the past several years, there have been over twenty published series concerning valve replacement in older people. The evolution of the therapy for this ailment in this age group is an excellent example of how considerations of indications and outcome, and improved technology, have led to the widespread acceptance of surgery as the appropriate treatment. In a recent report of aortic valve replacement in patients over age 75, Blakemore et al.[69] chronicled the aging of the valve-replacement patient population. They recount that in 1964, Spencer and colleagues reported a series of four older patients undergoing aortic valve replacement (AVR) whose ages ranged from 54 to 62. In 1969, Ahmad and Starr reported on 91 patients over age 60. In 1980, Starr et al. reported a series of patients over age 75, and in 1989, Fiore et al. published a series of 25 octogenarians receiving valve

TABLE 27-4

Mortality for Coronary Artery Bypass Graftings (CABG)

			CABG Operative Mortality		
First Author	**Age**	**Series Years**	**Overall**	**Elective**	**Emergency**
Hochberg	>70	1971–79	12.0%	6.0%	22.0%
Ennabli	>70	1977–83	6.9%	1.0%	17.0%
Horvath	>75	1977–86	10.8%	3.6%	35.0%
Montague	>70	1978–83	2.7%	2.2%	23.0%
Ivert	>70	1979–85	12.0%	8.6%	25.0%
Acinapura	>70	1981–86	8.0%	N/A	N/A
Noyez	>70	1987–88	2.9%	2.0%	33.0%
Grondin	>70	1987–88	12.0%	4.7%	31.2%
Edwards	>70	1984–89	7.4%	2.9%	22.2%
Naunheim	>80	1980–88	13.0%	2.0%	28.0%
Merrill	>80	1978–89	7.1%	N/A	N/A
Mullany	>80	1977–89	10.7%	7.8%	22.6%

SOURCE: Adapted from Edwards.[67]

replacements. This willingness to offer AVR to older patients comes, in part, from a better understanding of the natural history of aortic valvular disease. It has been shown that once symptoms such as angina or syncope develop, average life expectancy is only 3 to 4 years. Once congestive heart failure occurs, death can be expected in 1.5 to 2 years. Over 80 percent of patients with any of these symptoms will be dead in 4 years.[65] Average life expectancy for a healthy 70-year-old is approximately 12 years, and for an 80-year-old approximately 8 years. Clearly, if AVR could be accomplished with acceptable operative mortality and could restore patients to a more normal state of health, the benefit in increased survival would justify the procedure. In fact, the recent data from many series since 1975 do indicate that AVR can be performed with an acceptable operative mortality of 3 to 10 percent (mean 7.7 percent) and long-term survival of approximately 75 to 80 percent.[65] In addition, the vast majority of elderly patients receiving new aortic valves have great improvements in quality of life. Blakemore reports that preoperatively, 85 percent of elderly patients in his study were classified as New York Heart Association functional class III or IV and postoperatively 68 of 71 long-term survivors were reclassified as class I or II.[69]

Mitral valve disease in the elderly has been less well investigated partly because it is less common but also because the natural history is less well defined and the outcome of surgical therapy is less positive. Mitral valve disease in the elderly is usually rheumatic in origin. Valvular incompetence is the predominant defect in two-thirds of cases, and aortic valvular disease is present as well in nearly half. Left ventricular reserve is compromised in the elderly with mitral insufficiency, and low cardiac output is a particular problem after valve replacement. The recent mortality for isolated mitral valve replacement is from 4.7 to 14 percent, and while it is higher than for aortic valve replacement, it is still acceptable.[65] The increase in mortality seen when mitral valve replacement is part of a cardiac procedure occurs in younger patients as well.

Frequently both aortic and mitral valve replacement is accompanied by additional procedures. Some authors feel that the addition of coronary artery bypass grafting or multiple valve replacements in the very elderly pose a prohibitive risk and they therefore suggest caution in these cases.[70] Others feel that even multiple procedures can be performed with relative safety.[63,64]

Lung Cancer

Bronchogenic carcinoma is the leading cause of cancer deaths in this country, occurring with the greatest frequency between the ages of 55 and 75.[71] Interestingly, data from an analysis of over 6000 patients who underwent surgical staging for lung cancer showed a greater likelihood of localized disease with increasing age. Untreated lung cancer in the elderly population results in a survival of only 7 percent at 1 year.[72] This dismal outcome of nonoperative therapy, together with the higher proportion of elderly patients who have more localized disease, indicates the need for a more aggressive surgical approach to lung cancer in this population. An analysis of over 20,000 new lung cancer cases that were diagnosed and staged at comprehensive cancer centers in the United States between 1977 and 1982, however, revealed that surgery was used to treat nearly 30 percent of those aged 54 or below but only 20 percent of those aged 75 or above.[71]

The increased incidence of coexisting disease in elderly patients raises concern about the increased risk of perioperative morbidity and mortality. This risk may be overestimated, however, as operative mortality after thoracotomy for lung cancer has been shown to range from only 4 to 10 percent in patients over age 70, compared to 2 to 5 percent for younger patients.[73,74] Increased postoperative mortality in elderly patients is almost always due to cardiopulmonary complications; therefore, significant evidence of ischemic heart disease or severely restricted pulmonary function is regarded as a contraindication to thoracotomy. In addition, the location and extent of the pulmonary resection may be an important factor in the outcome of lung surgery in older people. Right pneumonectomy has been shown to have a significantly higher risk of mortality in the elderly than resection of the left lung.[75,76] Interestingly, the incidence of postoperative complications does not vary much with age.

Overall, 5-year survival for patients over age 70 ranges from 27 to 36 percent, compared to 35 to 48 percent for younger patients.[73] Despite the increased operative mortality in the elderly, long-term survival is clearly better with surgical resection than with nonoperative therapy. Further improvements in perioperative mortality are possible when patients are treated with lung-sparing procedures—such as sleeve resections or lobectomy—instead of pneumonectomy. Despite these reduced procedures, there is no evidence that potential for cure is adversely affected.

Esophageal Cancer

Esophageal carcinoma occurs most commonly in the seventh decade of life. Without resection, the survival in all patients at 1 year is only 18 percent.[77–79] Surgical resection, therefore, offers the best hope for long-term survival. Resectability is based on the stage of disease and is similar in young and old patients. While esophageal resection carries a higher mortality risk in elderly patients (7 to 20 percent) compared to younger patients (3 to 14 percent), the actuarial survival of old and young patients with resectable disease is virtually identical at 1 year (40 percent) and 5 years (22 percent).[80] Postoperative morbidity and mortality is largely a consequence of pulmonary complications in all age groups,[77] and severely impaired pulmonary function may serve as an indication for palliative procedures, such as bypass, laser therapy, or intubation. Radiotherapy is useful for palliation of unresectable squamous cancers and for treatment of some small squamous cancers in patients with prohibitive operative risk or short life expectancy. Radiation is ineffective for adenocarcinomas arising from the gastroesophageal junction.

VASCULAR SURGERY

Atherosclerosis is a diffuse process that is rarely limited to one area. It is not unusual to find clinically significant coronary artery or cerebrovascular disease in patients with a chief complaint referable to the peripheral circulation. Unless the peripheral disease is life- or limb-threatening, as is the case with ruptured aneurysm or acute arterial occlusion, the treatment of the peripheral problem can be delayed until an appropriate evaluation of cardiac and cerebrovascular status is completed. Coronary and cerebral vascular disease should be corrected first if they are amenable to surgical therapy.

Cerebrovascular Disease

Stroke is the third leading cause of death in the United States. It occurs with an annual incidence of 1440/100,000 men aged 75 to 84 and a death rate of approximately half that incidence. Nearly half of these strokes appear to be related to atherosclerosis in the extracranial carotid artery. Carotid endarterectomy has, therefore, been a valuable method of stroke prevention in appropriately selected patients.[81]

The guidelines for patient selection are complex and have been comprehensively reviewed elsewhere; however, two important points should be considered.[87] In patients with symptoms of transient ischemic attacks (TIA) and documented high-grade carotid stenosis or ulceration, carotid endarterectomy is recommended as long as the operative mortality and morbidity can be kept below 5 percent. It has been shown that endarterectomy for TIA can reduce the annual incidence of stroke from 5 to 16 percent to 1 to 2 percent.

In patients being considered for other vascular reconstruction, the presence of an audible bruit, even in the absence of symptoms, deserves further evaluation. Duplex scanning of the carotid vessels is an accurate and simple method of screening for significant carotid disease. The demonstration of a stenosis greater than 75 percent warrants still further evaluation for silent cerebral infarcts with CT or magnetic resonance imaging (MRI) of the brain. Endarterectomy for these asymptomatic lesions is recommended if life expectancy is greater than 5 years and the stenosis exceeds 75 percent. If the stenosis is less than 75 percent but is associated with a prior silent stroke in the distribution of the disease, carotid endarterectomy is also advised. In either case, however, the operative mortality and morbidity must be kept below 3 percent. The postoperative rate of neurologic events after endarterectomy for asymptomatic lesions is extremely low, averaging 0.3 percent per year.

Aortic Aneurysm

The natural history of the presenting problem is of importance in choosing the proper therapy for vascular disorders. Aneurysm of the abdominal aorta presents a rather urgent problem, because the natural history of this condition is expansion and rupture. Overall, elective operative mortality for abdominal aortic aneurysmorrhaphy is less than 5 percent. This mortality rises to 25 to 50 percent once rupture has occurred.[82] In their now classic study of abdominal aortic aneurysm, Szilagyi et al.[83] compared 5-year survival in patients with and without operation. Of operative cases, 53 percent survived 5 years, while only 19 percent of those managed nonoperatively were alive at 5 years. Of the deaths in the nonoperative group, 35 percent were from rupture. The incidence of rupture in these patients was related to the size of the aneurysms. For those smaller than 6 cm, the rate of rupture was 20 percent, while in larger aneurysms the rupture rate was 43 percent. Size also influenced operative mortality. For aneurysms smaller than 6 cm, the mortality was 2.7 percent, while for larger aneurysms the death rate was 22.7 percent. Abdominal aortic aneurysms should, therefore, be treated early when both the risk of rupture and the operative mortality are low. In general, aneurysmorrhaphy should be offered to patients with (1) an aneurysm of 4 to 6 cm if the life expectancy is 10 years or greater, (2) an aneurysm of more than 6 cm, (3) a symptomatic or rapidly expanding aneurysm of any size.

Recently, as the number of octogenarians has increased, abdominal aneurysms have become a clinically significant issue in this age group. Increased concern about operative risk in this age group has made surgical therapy less available to these patients. This factor is thought to be responsible for the higher incidence of rupture in patients over age 80 when compared to those under age 80 (33 versus 20 percent).[84] Studies confirm the safety of elective aneurysmorrhaphy in octogenarians; operative mortality rates of as low as 4.7 percent have recently been reported.[85] Mortality from aneurysm rupture in this age group is 60 percent or more. With an 80-year-old person's average life expectancy of approximately 8 years, the risk of rupture is greater that the likelihood of death from other causes. Vascular repair, therefore, is warranted unless the risks imposed by coexisting ailments are prohibitive.

Occlusive Disease

Occlusive disease can be approached somewhat less aggressively because of the relatively benign natural history. In patients with symptoms of lower-extremity claudication alone, amputation rates will be only 6 percent in 2.5 years[86] and 12 percent in 10 years.[87] These patients can usually be treated initially with programs to eliminate risk factors like smoking and to increase the development of collateral blood flow with exercise.

When symptoms progress to ischemic pain at rest or when impeding gangrene or ulcerations are present, limb loss becomes imminent, with a 40 percent chance of major amputation at 1 year.[82] Major amputation in the elderly is a significant risk, both in terms of operative mortality and in the loss of functional independence. Mortality for major amputations has been reported to be as high as 17 percent in patients over age 70,[88] and rehabilitation potential in this age group is poor. For these reasons many have suggested vascular reconstruction as an alternate to amputation even in the ninth and tenth decades of life.

Most commonly, limb-threatening ischemia is caused by occlusive disease below the inguinal ligament. Operative bypass of infrainguinal occlusive disease is usually from the common femoral artery to either the popliteal or infrapopliteal vessels. Success of these bypasses has depended primarily on the graft material used. At any location, autologous saphenous vein is the material of choice. The technique of in situ grafting has made saphenous vein more available even to the level of the dorsalis pedis artery. For bypasses to the above-knee popliteal, patency rates comparable to saphenous vein have been reported using the synthetic graft material polytetrafluoroethylene (PTFE). In a series of vascular reconstructions for limb salvage in patients over the age of 80, Scher et al.[89] demonstrated cumulative life-table graft patency rates of above-knee femoropopliteal bypasses of 95 percent at 1 year and 80 percent at 2 and 3 years. Eighty percent of these grafts were PTFE.

In the below-knee position, saphenous vein is clearly superior, and excellent patency rates have been reported using in situ techniques. When saphenous vein is not available, some controversy exists. Some authors feel that primary amputation is indicated,[82] while Scher et al.[89] feel that an attempt at limb salvage using PTFE in the elderly is indicated because of the high risk and poor results of amputation. They have shown a 48 percent 4-year limb-salvage rate in their patients over age 80 using PTFE when vein was not available.

The overall results of surgical bypass for severe ischemia in the elderly are good, with limb salvage rates, including maintenance of function, of 74 to 80 percent at 2 years. The operative mortality of 6 percent for most series of limb-salvage bypasses is clearly better than the mortality for major amputation.

Aortoiliac disease alone is rarely a cause of severe distal ischemia; however, poor inflow is often found in association with infrainguinal disease. Aortofemoral bypass is a highly successful and durable method to improve inflow; however, it can be a formidable surgical stress. In otherwise healthy elderly patients, it can usually be accomplished with acceptable risk. Modifications of the operative approach, such as retroperitoneal rather than transabdominal exposure of the aorta, have helped to decrease postoperative respiratory and gastrointestinal complications. The primary cardiac and renal stress, however, is related to aortic cross-clamping. It has been shown that, even in high-risk patients, decreasing cross-clamp time can lead to improved results.[90]

Although it is not well documented, it is felt that aortic cross-clamping in the elderly with poor cardiac and renal reserve will result in an unacceptably high mortality. For this reason, extraanatomic bypasses from the axillary to femoral arteries or from one femoral artery to the other have been used as alternatives to direct aortic reconstruction. The long-term patency for axillofemoral grafts, however, is significantly lower than that for aortofemoral bypass. They are reserved, therefore, for only the highest-risk patients with short life expectancy.

Another useful alternative to direct aortic bypass is percutaneous transluminal angioplasty (PTA). This technique is most applicable to short-segment stenosis in the iliac arteries. At this location, the results are good in terms of both improvement in inflow and long-term patency. The technique of PTA has been extended to the femoral and popliteal vessels, but with far less success.

Even in the oldest patients, vascular reconstruction for severe limb ischemia should be considered before accepting amputation as inevitable. This is particularly true if it is likely that the patient would be restored to a good functional status with a well-perfused limb.

REFERENCES

1. Peebles RJ, Schneidman DS (eds): *Socioleconomic Factbook for Surgery* 1991–1992. Chicago, American College of Surgeons, 1991.
2. Greenfield S et al: Patterns of care related to age of breast cancer patients. *JAMA* 257:2766, 1987.
3. Janzon L et al: Acute abdomen in the surgical emergency room: Who is taken care of, when and for what? *Acta Chir Scand* 148:141, 1982.
4. Reiss P et al: Abdominal surgery in elderly patients: Statistical analysis of clinical factors prognostic of mortality in 1,000 cases. *Mt Sinai J Med* 54:135, 1987.
5. Rosenthal RA et al: Abdominal surgery in the elderly,

in Katlic MR (ed): *Geriatric Surgery: Comprehensive Care of the Elderly Patient.* Baltimore, Urban & Schwarzenberg, pp 459–512, 1991.
6. Fenyo G: Acute abdominal disease in the elderly, *Am J Surg* 143:751, 1982.
7. Crump C: The incidence of gallstones and gallbladder diseases (abstract). *Surg Gynecol* 53:447, 1939.
8. Huber DF et al: Cholecystectomy in elderly patients. *Am J Surg* 146:719, 1983.
9. Pigott JP, Williams GB: Cholecystectomy in the elderly. *Am J Surg* 155:408, 1988.
10. Gracie WA, Ransohoff DF: The natural history of silent gallstones. *N Engl J Med* 307:798, 1982.
11. Wenckhert A, Robertson B: The natural course of gallstone disease. *Gastroenterology* 50:376, 1966.
12. Lund J: Surgical indications in cholelithiasis: Prophylactic cholecystectomy elucidated on the basis of long term follow-up on 526 nonoperated cases. *Ann Surg* 151:153, 1960.
13. McSherry CK et al: The natural history of diagnosed gallstone disease in symptomatic and asymptomatic patients. *Ann Surg* 202:59, 1985.
14. Roslyn J, Busuttil RW: Perforation of the gallbladder: A frequently misdiagnosed condition. *Am J Surg* 137:307, 1979.
15. Morrow DJ et al: Acute cholecystitis in the elderly: A surgical emergency. *Arch Surg* 113:1149, 1978.
16. Cucchiaro G et al: Deaths from gallstones: Incidence and associated clinical factors. *Ann Surg* 209:149, 1989.
17. Schirmer B, Dix J: Cost effectiveness of laparoscopic cholecystectomy. *J Lap Endo Surg* 2:145, 1992.
18. Ranson JHC et al: Prognostic signs and the role of operative management in acute pancreatitis. *Surg Gynecol Obstet* 136:69, 1974.
19. Fan ST et al: Influence of age on the mortality from acute pancreatitis. *Br J Surg* 75:463, 1988.
20. Spencer MP et al: Radical pancreatectomy for pancreatic cancer in the elderly: Is it safe and justified? *Ann Surg* 212:140, 1990.
21. Kairaluoma MI et al: Pancreatic resection for carcinoma of the pancreas and the periampullary region in patients over 70 years of age. *Br J Surg* 74:116, 1987.
22. Delcore R et al: Pancreaticoduodenectomy for malignant pancreatic and periampullary neoplasms in elderly patients. *Am J Surg* 162:532, 1991.
23. Buckler M et al: Role of octreotide in the prevention of postoperative complications following pancreatic resection. *Am J Surg* 163:125, 1992.
24. Lau WY et al: Acute appendicitis in the elderly. *Surg Gynecol Obstet* 161:157, 1985.
25. Owens BJ, Hamit HF: Appendicitis in the elderly. *Ann Surg* 187:392, 1978.
26. Hall A, Wright T: Acute appendicitis in the geriatric patient. *Am Surg* 42:147, 1976.
27. Perlmutt RP, Cello JP: Duodenal ulcer disease in hospitalized elderly patients. *Dig Dis Sci* 27:1, 1982.
28. World Health Organization: *World Statistics Annual 1988.* Geneva, World Health Organization, 1988.
29. Watson RJ et al: Duodenal ulcer disease in the elderly: A retrospective study. *Age Ageing* 14:225, 1985.
30. Galinsky NH: Peptic ulcer disease in the elderly. *Surg Clin North Am* 19:255, 1990.
31. Scapa E et al: Duodenal ulcer in the elderly. *J Clin Gastroenterol* 11:502, 1989.
32. Clinch D et al: Absence of abdominal pain in elderly patients with peptic ulcer. *Age Ageing* 13:120, 1985.
33. Kaplan MS et al: Surgical management of peptic ulcer disease in the aged patient. *Arch Surg* 104:667, 1972.
34. Coleman JA, Dinham MJ: Perforation of peptic ulceration in the elderly. *Age Ageing* 9:251, 1980.
35. Stanford CE et al: Complications of peptic ulcer in the aged. *Calif Med* 84:42, 1956.
36. Irvin TT: Mortality and perforated peptic ulcer: A case for risk stratification in elderly patients. *Br J Surg* 76:215, 1989.
37. Amberg JR, Zboralske FF: Gastric ulcer after 70. *Am J Roentegenol* 96:393, 1966.
38. Jordan PH Jr: Gastric ulcer, in Scott WH, Sawyer JL (eds): *Surgery of the Stomach, Duodenum and Small Intestine.* Boston, Blackwell, pp 395–426, 1987.
39. Sun DCH, Stempien SJ: Site and size of the ulcer determinants of outcome: VA cooperative study of gastric ulcer. *Gastroenterology* 61:576, 1971.
40. Adkin RB et al: The management of gastric ulcer: A current review. *Ann Surg* 201:741, 1985.
41. Edelman DS et al: Gastric cancer in the elderly. *Am Surg* 53:170, 1987.
42. Coluccia C et al: Gastric cancer in the elderly: Result of surgical treatment. *Int Surg* 72:4, 1987.
43. Bandoh T et al: Total gastrectomy for gastric cancer in elderly. *Surgery* 109:136, 1991.
44. Habu H, Metsud E: Gastric cancer in elderly patients—Results of surgical treatment. *Hepatogastroenterology* 36:71, 1989.
45. Boley SJ et al: Vascular ectasea of the colon—1986. *Dig Dis Sci* 31(suppl):26S, 1986.
46. Boley SJ et al: Severe lower intestinal bleeding: Diagnosis and treatment. *Clin Gastroenterol* 10:65, 1981.
47. Forde KF: Colonoscopy in acute rectal bleeding. *Gastrointest Endosc* 27:650, 1985.
48. Anotine KV, Wanah DE: Colon bleeding in the elderly. *Clin Geriatr Med* 2:33, 1985.
49. Cheskin LJ et al: Diverticular disease in the elderly. *Gastroenterol Clin North Am* 19:391, 1990.
50. Maty WF et al: Surgical management of diverticulitis in the elderly. *Am Fam Phys* 3:94, 1971.
51. Finlay IG, Carter DC: A comparison of emergency resection of staged management in perforated diverticular disease. *Dis Colon Rectum* 30:929, 1877.
52. Brocklehurst JC: Colonic diseases. *Clin Gastroenterol* 14:725, 1985.
53. Wallach CG, Kurtz RC: Gastro-intestinal cancer in the elderly. *Gastroenterol Clin North Am* 19:419, 1990.
54. Waldron RD et al: Emergency presentation and mortality from colorectal cancer in the elderly. *Br J Surg* 73:214, 1988.
55. Webbes TH: Carcinoma of the colon and rectum in geriatric patients. *Age Ageing* 14:321, 1985.
56. Longo WE et al: Colonoscope detection of early colorectal cancers: Impact of a surgical endoscopy service. *Ann Surg* 207:174, 1988.
57. Hobler KE: Colon surgery for cancer in the very elderly: Cost and 3-year survival. *Am Surg* 203:129, 1986.
58. Huguet C et al: Coloanal anastomosis after resection of low rectal cancer in the elderly. *World J Surg* 14:619, 1990.
59. Deysine M et al: Herniorrhaphy in the elderly: Bene-

fits of a clinic for the treatment of external abdominal wall hernias. *Am J Surg* 146:257, 1987.
60. Feny G: Diagnostic problems of acute abdominal diseases in the aged. *Acta Chir Scand* 140:396, 1974.
61. Anderson BM, Astberg J: Long term prognosis in geriatric surgery: 2–17 year follow-up of 7922 patients. *Am J Geriatr Surg* 20:255, 1972.
62. Temple TF, Miller RE: Incarcerated obturator hernia: Two case reports and review of the literature. *J Natl Med Assoc* 72:513, 1981.
63. Bashour TT et al: Cardiac surgery in patients over the age of 80 years. *Clin Cardiol* 13:267, 1990.
64. Merrill WH et al: Cardiac surgery in patients age 80 years or older. *Ann Surg* 211:772:1990.
65. Hochberg MC: Cardiac surgery in the elderly, in Katlic MR (ed): *Geriatric Surgery: Comprehensive Care of the Elderly Patient.* Baltimore, Urban & Schwarzenberg, pp 445–458, 1990.
66. Higgins TL et al: Stratification of morbidity and mortality outcome by preoperative risk factors in coronary artery bypass patients. *JAMA* 267:2344, 1992.
67. Edwards FH: Current status of coronary artery operation in septuagenarians. *Ann Thorac Surg* 52:365, 1991.
68. Raizner AE et al: Transluminal coronary angioplasty in the elderly. *Am J Cardiol* 57:29, 1986.
69. Blakemore BM et al: Aortic valve replacement in patients 75 years old and older. *Ann Thorac Surg* 44:637, 1987.
70. Fiore AC et al: Valve replacement in octogenarians. *Ann Thorac Surg* 48:104, 1989.
71. O'Rourke MA et al: Age trends of lung cancer stage at diagnosis: Implication for lung cancer screening in the elderly. *JAMA* 258:921, 1987.
72. Evans EWT: Resection for bronchial carcinoma in the elderly. *Thorax* 28:86, 1973.
73. Sherman S, Guidot C: The feasibility of thoracotomy for lung cancer in the elderly. *JAMA* 258:927, 1987.
74. Breyer RH et al: Thoracotomy in patients over age seventy years. *Thorac Cardiovas Surg* 18:187, 1987.
75. Higgins GA, Beebe GW: Bronchogenic carcinoma: Factors in survival. *Arch Surg* 94:539, 1967.
76. Dalton ML et al: The increased risk of right pneumonectomy in elderly patients. *Contemp Surg* 41:81, 1992.
77. Postlethwaite RW: Complications and deaths after operation for oesophageal carcinoma. *J Thorac Cardiovas Surg* 85:827, 1983.
78. Sugimachi K et al: Evaluation of surgical treatment of carcinoma of the esophagus in the elderly: 20 years experience. *Br J Surg* 72:19, 1985.
79. Katlic MR: Thoracic surgery in the elderly, in Katlic MR (ed): *Geriatric Surgery: Comprehensive Care of the Elderly Patient.* Baltimore, Urban & Schwarzenberg, pp 419–443, 1990.
80. Keeling P et al: Oesophageal resection in the elderly. *Ann Roy Coll Surg Eng* 70:34, 1988.
81. Moore WS et al: Carotid endoarterectomy: Practice guidelines. *J Vasc Surg* 15:469, 1992.
82. Atnip RG: Vascular surgery in the elderly, in Katlic MR (ed): *Geriatric Surgery: Comprehensive Care of the Elderly Patient.* Baltimore, Urban & Schwarzenberg, pp 513–540, 1990.
83. Szilagyi DE et al: Contribution of abdominal aortic aneurysmectomy to prolongation of life. *Ann Surg* 164:678, 1966.
84. Treiman RL et al: Aneurysmectomy in the octogenarian. *Am J Surg* 144:194, 1982.
85. ODonnell TF Jr et al: Is 80 years too old for aneurysectomy? *Arch Surg* 111:1250, 1976.
86. Imparato MD et al: Intermittent claudication: Its natural course. *Surgery* 78:795, 1975.
87. Boyd AM: Obstruction of the lower limb arteries. *Proc R Soc Med* 55:519, 1962.
88. Kuhn RB et al: The "geriatric" amputee. *Ann Surg* 176:306, 1972.
89. Scher LA et al: Limb salvage in octogenarians and nonagenarians. *Surgery* 99:160, 1986.
90. Purdy RT et al: Reduced aortic cross clamp time in high risk patients with abdominal aortic aneurysm. *J Vasc Surg* 3:320, 1986.

Chapter 28

PAIN MANAGEMENT IN THE ELDERLY

Kathleen M. Foley

Effective management of pain in the elderly patient presents a difficult clinical problem for physicians. Treatment of the cause of the pain should always be the initial approach, but syndromes which commonly occur in this population are not always amenable to therapy that successfully removes the cause. Further complicating the formulation of a treatment strategy is that drug therapy, which is the mainstay of treatment, has both desirable and undesirable side effects. The goals of effective pain management should be (1) to provide the patients with adequate relief of pain to undergo the necessary diagnostic and therapeutic procedures to define their pain symptoms and (2) to allow patients to function as they choose and (for the seriously ill patient) to die relatively pain-free.

Critical to developing a pain treatment approach for this group of patients is an understanding of the types of pain (somatic, visceral, neuropathic), the temporal aspects (acute or chronic), the types of patients with pain, and the common pain sites and syndromes. The general principles of pain assessment can be used as an approach to categorize patients. Before considering this approach, however, the chapter will provide a brief summary of the epidemiologic aspects of pain in elderly patients.

EPIDEMIOLOGY OF PAIN

There are limited data to assess the prevalence of pain in the elderly population, and there are no extant data on the incidence of acute pain. Pain appears to be common among older people, occurring in 25 to 50 percent of community-dwelling people over age 60.[1] Crook et al. reported that the age-associated morbidity was twofold greater in those over 60 compared with those under 60.[2] In a random survey of survivors of 200 deceased older community residents to assess the role of pain in the last year of life, interviews with a surviving close person revealed that pain increased in the last year of life.[3] One month before death, 66 percent of the deceased residents had reported pain frequently or all the time, compared with a matched comparison group of living persons, of whom only 24 percent had pain. Pain contributed to both "lowered happiness and depression." Of interest, there was no independent impact on hope and interest in the world from this study. In another national survey of 1254 adults, including 200 who were 65 or older, younger people reported more pain than older people, except for joint pain.[4] Conditions like osteoarthritis, rheumatism, rheumatoid arthritis, angina, and precordial pain all appeared to increase in the elderly adults. Low back pain was reported to occur in 23.6 percent of women and 18.4 percent of men in the year prior to an interview study of 3067 rural persons 65 years or older, with the prevalence declining with age.[5] The use of medical and chiropractic services for this symptom was nearly 75 percent; 25 percent had at least one hospitalization related to low back pain, and 5 percent had low back surgery. Fifteen to 40 percent reported limitation in activities of daily living, and 20 percent attributed sleep disturbances to their low back pain.

The prevalence of pain varies with the population studied. In a nursing home population, 97 subjects in a 311-bed multilevel teaching nursing home were interviewed.[6] The data indicate that 71 percent had at least one pain complaint (range 1 to 4); of those with pain, 34 percent described constant (continuous) pain, and 66 percent described intermittent pain. The major sources of pain included low back pain (40 percent), arthritis of an appendicular joint (24 percent), previous fracture sites (14 percent), and neuropathies (11 percent). Pain significantly interfered with the recreational and social activities of this group of individuals. Comparable studies revealed that 83 percent of selected residents in a Canadian multilevel long-term facility had pain.[7]

Other types of pain more common in an elderly population include postherpetic neuralgia, temporal arteritis, polymyalgia rheumatica, and atherosclerotic peripheral vascular disease. Cancer is also more prevalent in older people. One-third of cancer patients in active therapy and two-thirds with advanced disease have significant pain.[8] From a detailed study in hospices in which one-third of patients were 65 or older, 17 percent rated their pain at the most severe level at

6 weeks prior to death, compared with 25 percent within 2 days of death. In short, these data suggest a wide variation in the type of pain, its prevalence, and its impact on the quality of life.

Physical illness is only one of the mechanisms to explain pain complaints in the elderly.[9] From a series of studies, there is no clear relationship between age and pain and depression or hypochondriasis in the elderly pain patient.[10,11] Studies comparing the physical and psychosocial characteristics of elderly and young chronic pain patients showed few factors that distinguish patients on the basis of age. These studies suggest that multidisciplinary treatment for chronic pain should be utilized in both young and elderly populations.[12]

An alternative way to look at pain epidemiology is to look at the use of analgesic medications in elderly persons. Analgesic use falls off with age.[13] The National Nursing Home Survey of 1977 reported that 36.6 percent of residents were receiving analgesic medications.[14] Forty-eight percent of residents with arthritis or rheumatism were receiving analgesics. In a National Hospice study, elderly patients required fewer analgesic medications for terminal cancer pain than did younger patients.[15] For acute postoperative pain, survey data suggests that elderly patients are prescribed less and consume less analgesic medications but that their satisfaction with pain relief provided by a postoperative analgesic is greater.[16,17] As discussed in a later section, changes in both pharmacodynamic and pharmacokinetic effects occur in the elderly persons.

Survey data, as well as studies of experimental pain, have yielded conflicting data about the pain thresholds in the elderly population.[18] There are several hypotheses concerning this observation. One hypothesis is that aging patients may actually experience less pain after a nociceptive stimulus; however, pain thresholds do not appear to change with age.[19] The second hypothesis is that pain may be better controlled in the elderly person because of enhanced efficacy of the analgesic drugs.[20–22] This aspect will be discussed in the following section. A third hypothesis is that elderly patients may simply report less pain and that this may be related to a combination of increased stoicism, slowness to respond to painful stimuli, and/or a mild cognitive deficit. To what extent each of these factors contributes to the perception of pain and its meaning in the elderly patient remains poorly defined. However, this dearth of data clearly indicates the need for careful expert pain assessment in this patient population.

TYPES OF PAIN

Recent advances in the neuroanatomy, neurophysiology, and neuropharmacology of pain have provided a greater understanding of the peripheral and central nervous system mechanisms of pain.[23,24] The elderly patient typically has pain of one or more of three types: somatic, visceral, and neuropathic.

Somatic, or nociceptive pain, occurs as a result of activation of peripheral nociceptors in cutaneous and deep tissues. The pain is typically well localized and is frequently described as aching or gnawing. Examples of somatic pain include joint pain, myofascial and musculoskeletal pain, and, in the cancer patient, bone metastases.

Visceral pain results from infiltration, compression, distension, or stretching of thoracic or abdominal viscera and activation of nociceptors. It may be the result of a primary or metastatic tumor, or it may result from stones in the gallbladder or kidney; it may also occur with gastrointestinal ulceration. Visceral pain, which is often described as deep, squeezing, and pressurelike, is poorly localized and is typically associated with nausea, vomiting, and diaphoresis, particularly when acute. Visceral pain is often referred to cutaneous sites that may be remote from the lesion, as occurs in shoulder pain with diaphragmatic irritation in the patient with liver capsule pain. The pain may also be associated with tenderness in the referred cutaneous site.

Neuropathic pain, the third major type of pain, results from injury to the peripheral and/or central nervous system as a consequence of compression, infiltration, or degeneration of the peripheral nerve or the spinal cord as a result of trauma, chemical injury, or toxic metabolic effect. Examples of neuropathic pain include postherpetic neuralgia, postsurgical pain syndromes, diabetic peripheral neuropathy, and tumor infiltration of the brachial and lumbosacral plexus. Pain resulting from nerve injury is often severe and is different in quality than somatic or visceral pain. It is typically described as a constant, dull ache, often with pressure or a vicelike quality. Superimposed paroxysms of burning or electric shock–like sensations are common. These paroxysms of pain may be associated with spontaneous ectopic activity in either the peripheral nervous system or the central nervous system.

The pathophysiology of these three types of pain is complex and poorly understood,[23] and although these pain types frequently coexist in patients, their recognition often has direct diagnostic and therapeutic implications. For example, both somatic and visceral pains respond to a wide variety of analgesic agents and anesthetic approaches. In contrast, neuropathic pain is not well controlled by opioid analgesics and is only partially ameliorated by the use of anesthetic blocks and/or neurosurgical procedures.[25] Somatic and visceral pain are the most common causes of pain in the elderly population, and neuropathic pain is the most difficult and frustrating to treat in this population because of its lack of response to common analgesic approaches. It is commonly believed that the sympathetic nervous system may be involved in all three of these pain states but that it is most consistently involved in acute visceral and neuropathic pain.

TEMPORAL ASPECTS OF PAIN

Identifying the temporal qualities of pain is useful. The classification of pain into acute pain versus chronic pain is based again on an increased understanding of pain mechanisms and the recognition that the central modulation for these types of pain states may be different. In the clinical setting, awareness of these two types of pain is particularly important in the management of patients, as the response to treatment is often quite different for these two pain groups. Acute pain is relatively easy to recognize, is amenable to many of the therapeutic approaches, and usually follows a self-limited course in which treatment of the cause is an effective treatment for the pain.

The point at which acute pain becomes chronic is not known, but pain lasting for longer than 3 months is usually considered to be chronic pain.[26] With patients in chronic pain, the persistent pain has usually failed to respond to those modalities directed at the cause of the pain. In these patients, the pain has led to significant changes in personality, lifestyle, and functional ability. Such patients need a management approach which encompasses not only the treatment of the cause of the pain, but also the treatment of the complications which have ensued in their functional status, their social lives, and their personality.[27] Postherpetic neuralgia is a good example of this type of chronic pain syndrome in which a persistent pain has led to a demoralization of the patient and marked limitation in physical activity.[28,29]

TYPES OF PATIENTS WITH PAIN

Another aspect that can further help to categorize the elderly patient with pain is the consideration of the types of patients with pain. These are listed in Table 28-1.

The first group includes patients with acute or chronic pain associated with a medical illness, e.g., cancer or diabetes. In this group of patients, pain may be the overriding symptom of the medical illness, and its management should be an integral part of the primary treatment approach. Pain management should facilitate the necessary diagnostic and therapeutic interventions.

The second group consists of patients with chronic nonmalignant pain and a specific pain syndrome, e.g., patients with cervical or lumbar osteoarthritis or patients with lumbar stenosis. For this group of patients, management approaches are directed at the cause of the pain, but therapeutic approaches such as surgery or drug therapy may not give the patient complete relief. Providing patients with psychological support, encouraging them to remain as functional as possible, and using analgesic drug therapy appropriately are the major approaches to treatment of this group of patients.[30] Although psychological factors play a role in this group, they usually do not present a significant management issue. What is problematic is that these patients often have reduced vision or hearing, gait instability, or other symptoms which limit their ability to be distracted from their pain.

The third category of patients include those patients with chronic nonmalignant pain associated with a neuropsychiatric diagnosis, e.g., patients with dementia or patients with depression who complain of pain as an overriding symptom.[31] In this group, patients may present with complaints of a "burning mouth" or "burning vagina." Their pain complaints may also be diffuse, and a careful workup does not reveal the cause. In such patients, careful assessment of an early dementia and careful assessment of a masked depression are critical in order to formulate an approach directed toward the psychological factors, rather than one directed toward specific treatment for an elusive pain syndrome. Table 28-2 lists the common sites of pain in the elderly patient and some of the common pain syndromes that are seen in this group of patients. A discussion of each of these

TABLE 28-1

Types of Patients with Pain

- Patients with chronic pain associated with a medical illness (e.g., cancer or diabetes)
- Patients with chronic nonmalignant pain and a specific pain syndrome (e.g., lumbar osteoarthritis or lumbar stenosis)
- Patients with chronic nonmalignant pain associated with a neuropsychiatric disorder (e.g., depression or dementia)

TABLE 28-2

Common Sites of Nonmalignant Pain in Elderly Patients

Site of Pain	Common Pain Syndromes
Head and neck	Trigeminal neuralgia, cluster headache, temporal arteritis, cervical osteoarthritis
Joints	Shoulder and hip osteoarthritis, rheumatoid arthritis
Lower back	Lumbar disc disease, lumbar stenosis, lumbar osteoarthritis, osteoporosis, vertebral body collapse
Extremities	Peripheral neuropathy, peripheral vascular disease, reflex sympathetic dystrophy
Heart	Angina
Trunk	Postsurgical intercostal neuralgia, diabetic radiculopathy, postherpetic neuralgia
Gastrointestinal	Hiatus hernia, acute cholecystitis, irritable bowel syndrome, chronic constipation

common pain syndromes is beyond the scope of this chapter. However, what is critical as part of the pain assessment in this group of patients is to define carefully the nature of the pain syndrome, distinguishing nonmalignant from malignant syndromes and ascertaining the degree of psychological component in the pain complaint. Table 28-3 presents a useful approach to the assessment of the elderly patient with pain.

CLINICAL ASSESSMENT OF PAIN

Believe the Patient's Pain Complaint

In assessing the patient who complains of pain, it is of utmost importance to respect the complaint. The complaint may represent a pathologic process or may be a somatic delusion or a masked depression. Each of these possible causes must be considered and excluded. The diagnosis of the cause of the pain is not always made on the initial evaluation, and in some instances it may take several months to define the nature of the pain. Therefore, the physician should not draw conclusions too soon or label the patient with a psychiatric diagnosis. Similarly, to misdiagnose a masked depression or to fail to attend to the psychological variables associated with the pain complaint is an equally serious mistake. There is good evidence to suggest that in the majority of elderly patients an organic pathologic condition is the most common cause of pain, with psychological-psychiatric disturbances being a less prominent etiologic agent.[13]

Take a Careful History of the Pain Complaint

There is no substitute for a complete history in helping to define the nature of the pain complaint. History taking should begin with the pain complaint.

TABLE 28-3

The Clinical Assessment of the Elderly Patient with Pain

Believe the patient's pain complaint.
Take a careful history of the pain complaint.
Assess the psychosocial status of the patient.
Perform a careful medical and neurologic examination.
Order and personally review the appropriate diagnostic procedures.
Evaluate the extent of disease in the patient with cancer.
Treat the pain to facilitate the diagnostic study.
Consider alternative methods of pain control during the initial evaluation.
Reassess the pain complaint during the prescribed therapy.
Individualize therapy.

History taking should begin with the patient's description of the site of pain, its quality, the exacerbating or relieving factors, its exact onset, and associated circumstances. All of these factors can help to clarify whether the pain results from an acute or chronic process and help to categorize the specific pain syndrome.

In the patient with multiple pain complaints, each complaint should be identified and considered systematically. Defining how the pain interferes with the patient's activities of daily living, work, and social life can help place the pain complaint in the setting of the patient's illness. In our experience, the majority of pain syndromes in this population of patients can be defined from a careful history, with the medical and neurologic examination confirming the probable diagnosis. The history helps direct the medical and neurologic examination. Awareness of the referral patterns of pain is also of particular importance. Referred pain in the arm or the leg is often the first presentation of tumor infiltration of the brachial lumbar plexus. Commonly, referred pain sites are tender to palpation, and pain is often misdiagnosed as suggesting a local pathologic condition.[32]

It is also critical to verify the history with a family member, particularly in the patient who is unable or unwilling to provide sufficient information. Similarly, in the patient who is a poor historian, the family member may be able to provide essential information that alters the diagnostic approach. For the patient who does not share a common language with the physician, an interpreter should be used. In short, all attempts should be made to obtain a careful history.

Assess the Psychosocial Status of the Patient

As an adjunct to a careful history of the chief complaint, the physician must assess multiple factors, including age, sex, cultural, environmental, and psychological factors, in directing appropriate diagnostic and therapeutic approaches. From our experience in the elderly patient, the complaint of pain can rarely be assigned to psychological influences alone.[12] In a structured interview, information gathered on the patient's prior medical and psychiatric illnesses, the current level of anxiety and depression, suicidal ideation, and the degree of functional incapacity can provide the data required to detect those patients at high risk for decompensating psychologically in the setting of a painful illness.

Perform a Careful Medical and Neurologic Examination

A careful physical and neurologic examination will help provide the necessary data to substantiate the clinical diagnosis. However, if the physical and neurologic examinations are negative, further assessment of the patient should be directed by the clinical history alone. In this particular instance, knowledge of the types of pain syndromes which occur in the elderly population can suggest possible causes of pain and direct early diagnostic intervention. Careful examination of the site of pain may provide sufficient information to make a clinical diagnosis without detailed radiologic examination.

Order and Personally Review the Diagnostic Procedures

The purpose of diagnostic studies is to confirm the clinical diagnosis and to define the area and extent of pathologic lesions. The use of computed axial tomography and magnetic resonance imaging has markedly facilitated the diagnostic workup of the elderly patient. The usefulness of specific procedures must be recognized by the physician ordering such tests.

Evaluate the Extent of Disease in the Patient with Cancer

The onset of pain in the elderly patient with the diagnosis of cancer does not necessarily imply recurrence of disease. An evaluation of the extent of metastatic disease may help to discern the nature of the cancer pain syndrome. For example, in the patient with carcinoma of the lung who develops postthoracotomy pain immediately following a thoracotomy for tumor resection, the presence of recurrent disease may be closely associated with the appearance of this postthoracotomy pain syndrome. In contrast, the postmastectomy pain syndrome, which occurs secondary to interruption of the intercostobrachial nerve, is never associated with recurrent disease. In the patient with previously resected carcinoma of the colon and perineal pain, an abnormal scan or a rising level of carcinogenic embryonic antigen (CEA) may help to confirm the fact that the lumbosacral pain represents local nerve infiltration by tumor, even in the absence of radiologic changes.

Treat the Pain to Facilitate the Diagnostic Studies

The persistence of pain debilitates the patient physically and psychologically. Early treatment with analgesics while investigating the source of pain will markedly improve the patient's ability to participate in the necessary diagnostic procedures. No patient should be inadequately evaluated because of pain. There is no evidence to support the practice of withholding analgesics while the nature of the pain is being established. Adequate pain control will not obscure the diagnosis.

Consider Alternative Methods of Pain Control during the Initial Evaluation

A detailed description of the wide variety of methods of pain control is beyond the scope of this chapter, but those approaches commonly used are detailed in Table 28-4. The choice of the method depends on a careful assessment of the pain. Although medical therapy, specifically drug therapy, represents the mainstay of treatment, alternative methods are essential in managing some of the pain problems which occur. These methods should be considered concurrent with the use of analgesics in the management of

TABLE 28-4

Medical, Anesthetic, Surgical, and Behavioral Approaches to Pain

Type of Approach	Indications
Drug therapy	
Nonopioid analgesics	Mild-to-moderate somatic and visceral pain
Opioid analgesics	Moderate-to-severe somatic and visceral pain
Adjuvant analgesics	Moderate-to-severe neuropathic pain
Anesthetic approaches with local anesthetics	
Trigger-point injections	Local myofascial pain
Joint capsule injections	Local inflammatory joint pain
Nerve blocks:	
Peripheral	Intercostal neuralgia, acute herpes zoster
Epidural	Perioperative and postoperative pain control or peripheral vascular disease
Intrathecal	Perioperative pain control
Autonomic blocks:	
Stellate ganglion	Reflex sympathetic dystrophy with arm pain, V_1 herpes zoster
Lumbar sympathetic	Reflex sympathetic dystrophy, peripheral vascular disease, lumbosacral plexopathy
Celiac plexus block	Abdominal pain from carcinoma of the pancreas

TABLE 28-4

Medical, Anesthetic, Surgical, and Behavioral Approaches to Pain (Continued)

Type of Approach	Indications
Neurosurgical approaches	
Neuroablative:	
Dorsal root entry zone (DREZ) lesions	Neuropathic pain in nerve root distribution
Trigeminal radiofrequency lesions	Trigeminal neuralgia
Cordotomy	Unilateral malignant pain below the T1 area
Neurostimulatory:	
Dorsal column stimulation	Neuropathic pain of spinal cord or peripheral nerve origin
Thalamic stimulation	Unilateral focal neuropathic pain
Neuropharmacologic:	
Epidural and intrathecal opioids	Chronic midline cancer pain, patients who cannot tolerate systemic opioids
Physical therapy approaches	
Bracing, splinting, and mechanical devices	Arm, leg, or joint support to minimize pain and facilitate activity
Transcutaneous nerve stimulation	Management of mild peripheral nerve point pain
Full ROM* and ADL† programs	Reduction of limitations at joints secondary to extremity pain
Behavioral approaches (cognitive-behavioral)	
Relaxation Biofeedback Hypnosis	Comprehensive approach to manage the psychological consequences of pain, the meaning of pain, and pain's impact on mood

*ROM, range of motion.
†ADL, activities of daily living.

pain; the appropriate selection of these approaches depends on the patient's specific pain complaint. For example, in the patient with traumatic injury to a peripheral nerve, the use of autonomic nerve blocks, such as stellate ganglion blocks, can be particularly effective. In the patient with cancer of the colon and unilateral pain in the leg from tumor infiltration of the lumbosacral plexus, cordotomy should be considered as an effective procedure. In the patient with severe osteoarthritis of the hip, surgical replacement of the hip should be considered as the procedure of choice.

Reassess the Pain Complaint during the Prescribed Therapy

Continual reassessment of the response of the patient's pain complaint to the prescribed therapy provides a useful method of validating the accuracy of the original diagnosis. In patients in whom the response to therapy is less than predicted or in whom exacerbation of the pain occurs, reassessment of the approach to treatment or a search for a new cause of pain should be considered. For example, in the patient with osteoporosis and collapse of a vertebral body, a lack of rapid improvement with bed-rest and bracing and the development of radicular symptoms and/or signs of myelopathy should make the physician reconsider the diagnosis and reassess the patient with the concern that the collapse may represent tumor infiltration of the vertebral body which was not apparent on the initial studies.

These general principles of pain assessment encompass the clinically relevant facts that the physician needs in order to clarify the cause of pain. Strict attention to these principles provides the physician with an approach that ensures a careful, respectful assessment of the pain complaint for both the patient and the physician.

MANAGEMENT OF PAIN—DRUG THERAPY

Drug therapy with nonopioid, opioid, and adjuvant drugs is the mainstay of treatment and should be within the armamentarium of the general physician.[33–36] Other approaches, which usually involve referral to appropriate experts, will not be covered in this chapter. Such approaches include the use of anesthetic, surgical, and behavioral treatment (see Table 28-4).

Clinical Pharmacologic Considerations

In the development of specific guidelines for the use of analgesics in elderly patients, the effect of age on pharmacokinetic and pharmacodynamic responses to analgesic medications must be considered.[20,21,37] It is probable that all phases of drug pharmacology—absorption, distribution, metabolism, and excretion—are affected by the aging process.[38] Absorption may be influenced by age-related decreases in gastric acid production, intestinal blood flow, mucosal cell mass, and gastrointestinal motility.[39,40] The use of concurrent medications and the presence of other medical disease may also diminish absorption.[41] Changes in drug distribution can result from reductions in total body water, lean body mass, and serum protein levels, and from an increase in body fat.[39] The effect of these changes on drug distribution depends on the lipid solubility of the specific drug and its degree of protein binding. Metabolism can be affected by diminution in hepatic mass and blood flow, as well as by a reduction in enzymatic activity.[42] These changes are most apparent with medication largely metabolized in the liver, including the opioids. Drug excretion can be influenced by an age-related impairment of renal function. This process, which is often subclinical, slows the clearance of drugs in elderly patients and may result in higher plasma drug concentrations.[22,41]

Pharmacodynamic factors also affect elderly patients. Increased receptor sensitivity and concurrent alterations in mental status may account in part for the increased response of elderly patients to nonopioid and opioid drugs. The existing data demonstrate that elderly patients have a diminished ability to bind nonsteroidal anti-inflammatory drugs (NSAIDs), which are highly protein-bound, resulting in rapidly increasing free-drug concentrations after dosing has begun. Increased free-drug concentration adds to the risk of adverse effects. Eliminations of NSAIDs may also be prolonged in elderly persons.[36]

The effect of age on the clinical pharmacology of patients taking opioids has been studied. Belleville et al. reported greater analgesia in elderly patients, compared with younger patients, after 10-mg and 20-mg doses of morphine.[43] After single-dose morphine studies, Kaiko et al. reported higher plasma levels and slower rates of decline of drug levels, suggesting a decrease in morphine clearance.[21,44] Other studies have observed a reduced volume of distribution in elderly patients, and comparable studies have reported similar changes in drug clearance and distribution with other opioids, including meperidine[45] and alfentanil.[46] In summary, alterations in drug metabolism can augment the elderly patient's sensitivity to analgesic drugs.

The guidelines for the rational use of analgesics in this population are listed in Table 28-5. Before these guidelines are discussed, certain caveats must be emphasized. Excessive use of medication should be discouraged, and the use of each drug should have a specific rationale.[1,47,48] Short-acting medications are preferable to reduce side effects associated with drug accumulation. Detailed instructions to the patient with appropriate pill boxes and calendars can facilitate the proper dispensing of drugs. Lastly, effective pain control requires continuous reassessment of drug effects and side effects with titration that provides analgesia that is acceptable to the patient. Of major importance is the recognition that the individualization of therapy must be the overriding consideration in the management of pain.

TABLE 28-5

Guidelines for the Rational Use of Analgesics

1. Choose a specific drug based on the type of pain, its intensity, patient's age, and prior opioid exposure
2. Know the clinical pharmacology of the drug prescribed:
   - Duration of analgesic effect
   - Pharmacokinetic properties of the drug
   - Equianalgesic doses for the route of administration
3. Administer the analgesic on a regular basis after initial titration
4. Use drug combinations that
   - Provide either additive analgesia or reduce side effects (opioid-nonopioid, opioid + hydroxyzine, opioid + amitriptyline)
   - Have special analgesic effects in certain conditions (amitriptyline, carbamazepine)
5. Avoid drug combinations that increase sedation without enhancing analgesia
6. Adjust the route of administration to the type of pain, patient status, and possible routes
7. Watch and treat the side effects appropriately:
   - Respiratory depression
   - Sedation
   - Nausea and vomiting
   - Constipation
   - Multifocal myoclonus and seizures
8. Know the differences between tolerance, physical dependence, and psychological dependence
9. Manage tolerance:
   - Switch to an alternative opioid analgesic
   - Start with one-half the equianalgesic dose and titrate to pain relief
10. Prevent acute withdrawal:
    - Taper drugs slowly
    - Use diluted doses of naloxone (0.4 mg in 10 ml of saline) to reverse respiratory depression in the physically dependent patient and administer cautiously
11. Do not use placebos to assess the nature of the pain

Guidelines for the Use of Nonopioid and Opioid Analgesics

Analgesic drugs can be classified in a variety of ways as defined by their chemical receptor and pharmacologic properties, their sites and mechanisms of analgesia, and the intensity of pain for which they are generally used. Based on this concept, analgesic drug therapy can be separated into three broadly defined groups: (1) the mild analgesics, including the nonopioid analgesics and certain weak opioid analgesics (e.g., codeine, oxycodone, and propoxyphene), (2) the strong opioid analgesics, including morphine and related opioids, and (3) the adjuvant analgesic drugs, including those drugs that enhance the analgesic effects of the opioids and those which have intrinsic analgesic activity in certain situations (e.g., amitriptyline).

The mild analgesics include both the nonopioids and the weak opioid analgesics. This group, which represents a first-line approach in the management of patients with mild-to-moderate pain, includes acetaminophen, aspirin, and the NSAIDs (see Table 28-6). These drugs are commonly used orally, and tolerance and physical dependence do not occur with repeated administration. However, their analgesic effectiveness is limited by ceiling effects, i.e., escalation of the dose beyond a certain level (e.g., aspirin at 900 to 1300 mg/dose) does not produce additive analgesia. The NSAIDs have analgesic, antipyretic, and anti-inflammatory actions. Acetaminophen is as potent as aspirin as an analgesic and an antipyretic but is less effective than aspirin in inflammatory conditions. Both aspirin and acetaminophen are the drugs of first choice because of their proven efficacy for mild-to-moderate pain at a relatively low cost. Patients allergic to aspirin do not exhibit cross-sensitivity to acetaminophen, and acetaminophen does not have the gastrointestinal, hematopoietic, and renal side effects that occur with aspirin. As a group, the NSAIDs have analgesic effectiveness equal to or greater than that of aspirin and share with aspirin the adverse effects. To date, several NSAIDs have been approved by the Food and Drug Administration for use as analgesics for mild-to-moderate pain. The NSAIDs, e.g., ibuprofen and fenoprofen, differ among themselves in their pharmacokinetic profiles and duration of analgesic action. The short-half-life NSAIDs have the same duration of action as aspirin. Diflunisal and naproxen have longer half-lives and are longer-acting. Agents such as choline magnesium trisalicylate have anti-inflammatory properties without the impact on platelets associated with aspirin. Ketorolac is a newer NSAID with an analgesic potency comparable to that of morphine. It is used orally and parenterally for acute pain management.[49]

In the elderly patient whose major pain symptoms are related to inflammatory joint disease, the use

TABLE 28-6

Analgesics Commonly Used Orally for Mild-to-Moderate Pain

Drug	Equianalgesic Dose, mg*	Starting Oral Dose Range, mg†	Comments
Nonnarcotics			
Aspirin	650	650	Often used in combination with opioid-type analgesics
Acetaminophen	650	650	Minimal anti-inflammatory properties
Ibuprofen (Motrin)	ND‡	200–400	Higher analgesic potential than aspirin
Fenoprofen (Nalfon)	–	200–400	Like ibuprofen
Diflunisal (Dolobid)	ND	500–1000	Longer duration of action than ibuprofen; higher analgesic potential than aspirin
Naproxen (Naprosyn)	ND	250–500	Like diflunisal
Ketorolac	ND	30–60	Higher analgesic potential than aspirin
Morphine-like agonists			
Codeine	32–65	32–65	"Weak" morphine; often used in combination with nonopioid analgesics; biotransformed, in part to morphine
Oxycodone	5	5–10	Shorter-acting; also in combination with nonopioid analgesics (Percodan, Percocet), which limits dose escalation
Meperidine (Demerol)	50	50–100	Shorter-acting; biotransformed to normeperidine, a toxic metabolite
Propoxyphene HCl (Darvon) Propoxyphene napsylate (Darvon-N)	65–130	65–130	"Weak" opioid; often used in combination with nonopioid analgesics; long half-life biotransformed to potentially toxic metabolite (norpropoxyphene)
Mixed agonist-antagonist			
Pentazocine (Talwin)	50	50–100	In combination with nonopioid; in combination with naloxone to discourage parenteral abuse; causes psychotomimetic effects

*For these equianalgesic doses (see Comments) the time of peak analgesia ranges from 1.5 to 2 hours and the duration from 4 to 6 hours. Oxycodone and meperidine are shorter-acting (3 to 5 hours), and diflunisal and naproxen are longer-acting (8 to 12 hours).

†These are the recommended starting doses from which the optimal dose for each patient is determined by titration and the maximal dose limited by adverse effects.

‡ND, not determined.

of NSAIDs for both their analgesic and their anti-inflammatory properties is a common approach. It is recommended that each patient be given an adequate trial of one drug on a regular basis before switching the patient to another drug. If the analgesia is not adequate, a trial of other NSAIDs, one at a time, is appropriate. The concurrent use of two different NSAIDs is discouraged because of the available in vitro data suggesting that such combinations compete with each other for protein binding and therefore have diminished analgesic effectiveness.

A stepwise approach to the use of these drugs in patients, balancing the desirable effects of analgesia with the undesirable effects of gastrointestinal or hematopoietic risks, must be achieved.

In a review of the commonly used NSAIDs, the use of H_2 blockers to reduce the incidence of NSAID-induced gastropathy in elderly patients remains controversial.[50] In the patient who has had an adequate trial of these drugs without achieving adequate analgesia, or in whom the nonopioid analgesic is ineffective or poorly tolerated, an opioid analgesic is considered as an alternative drug to manage such mild-to-moderate pain. In this instance, codeine, oxycodone, and propoxyphene are classified as the mild opioid analgesics, and they all share morphine's spectrum of pharmacologic action. They are most often used in a fixed oral dose mixture with a nonopioid analgesic. They clearly have a higher analgesic potential than the nonopioid drugs, and they serve as a second-line approach in the management of pain. The major advantage of using the combination of a weak opioid with a nonopioid is that there is enhanced additive analgesia.

In order to provide patients with individualized dosing schedules, it is often better to use the components of these mixed combinations separately, e.g., titrating the dose of codeine without increasing the amount of acetaminophen or aspirin the patient is receiving. This is a useful approach to consider in patients taking a mixture of weak opioids and nonopioids because it avoids the problem of escalation of a fixed dose combination in which the additional NSAID may become excessive. The use of these drugs is particularly tailored to the presence of mild-to-moderate pain. In patients with moderate-to-severe pain, it probably is most useful to start with a weak opioid-nonopioid combination and titrate the patient to a strong opioid if inadequate pain relief is obtained. The opioid analgesics that are commonly used for moderate-to-severe pain are listed in Table 28-7. As a group, these drugs are capable of producing analgesia over a wide range of doses. There appears to be no ceiling effect to their analgesia, i.e., as the dose is increased on a logarithmic scale, the increment in analgesia appears to be virtually linear to the point of loss of consciousness.

Choose a Specific Drug for a Specific Type of Pain

All the opioid analgesics work by binding to opiate receptors in the peripheral and central nervous systems. As a group, the opioid drugs can be classified into opioid agonist drugs, which bind to the receptor and produce analgesia, and opioid antagonist drugs, which bind to the receptor and can, in some instances, reverse the effect of morphine at the receptor (e.g., the drug naloxone) or can block the effect of morphine at the receptor but can also produce some degree of analgesia. Table 28-7 lists the commonly available agonist, mixed agonist-antagonist, and partial agonist drugs, and their plasma half-lifes, relative potency, usual starting dose, and pertinent pharmacologic facts. At times it is not clear to the physician when to consider the choice of an appropriate opioid analgesic. The first and most important rule is that *the choice of the drug should be dependent on the type of pain and its intensity*. For example, in those patients with mild-to-moderate pain who have not responded or could not tolerate a nonopioid analgesic, an oral opioid analgesic such as codeine or oxycodone is an appropriate choice. Each drug should be given an adequate trial on a regular basis before it is considered to be ineffective.

The next step is to consider the use of one of a series of strong opioid drugs such as morphine, hydromorphone, methadone, levorphanol, or fentanyl. The choice of one strong opioid over another can be based on a series of pharmacologic and pharmacokinetic factors and available preparations as well as the treating physician's experience in the use of these drugs. The exact choice of the opioid analgesic will depend upon the patient's prior opioid exposure, as well as his or her physical and neurologic status. The effective dose to control pain must be determined for each individual patient, and this is, in fact, one of the most difficult aspects in the management of pain with pharmacologic approaches.

The role of opioid antagonist drugs such as pentazocine, nalbuphine, and butorphanol are limited in the management of patients with chronic pain in whom oral drugs are considered the major approach. These drugs do have a role to play in the acute postoperative management, but their chronic use is not recommended.

Only one drug, buprenorphine, which is a partial agonist-antagonist, is available in an oral form, specifically as a sublingual preparation. It, like the other opioid antagonist drugs, may also precipitate opioid withdrawal in patients receiving opioid analgesics for prolonged periods of time. At the current time, it is available only in Europe, but it has been demonstrated to be effective in both postoperative management and as a first-line agent in the management of patients with mild-to-moderate cancer pain.

Know the Pharmacology of the Drug Prescribed

The next important principle is to know the pharmacology of the drug prescribed. This includes an understanding of the duration of the analgesic effect, which is a result of many factors, including the dose, the intensity of pain, the criteria for analgesia, indi-

TABLE 28-7

Oral and Parenteral Opioid Analgesics for Moderate-to-Severe Pain

	Equianalgesic Dose, mg*	Duration h†	Plasma Half-Life, h	Comments
Narcotic agonists				
Morphine	10 60 PO	4–6 4–7	2–3.5	Standard for comparison; also available in slow-release tablets. Reduce dose in elderly and in renal failure.
Codeine	130 IM 200‡PO	4–6 4–6	3	Biotransformed to morphine; useful as initial opioid analgesic.
Oxycodone	15 IM 30 PO	2–3 3–5	1.5–2 ?	Short-acting; available alone or as 5-mg dose in combination with aspirin and acetaminophen.
Levorphanol (Levo-Dromoran)	2 IM 4 PO	4–6 4–7	12–16	Good oral potency; requires careful titration in initial dosing because of drug accumulation. Use cautiously in elderly.
Hydromorphone (Dilaudid)	1.5 IM 7.5 PO	4–5 4–6	2–3	available in high-potency injectable form (10 mg/ml) for cachectic patients and as rectal suppositories; more soluble than morphine.
Oxymorphone (Numorphan)	1 IM 10 PR	4–6 4–6	2–3	Available in parenteral and rectal-suppository forms only.
Meperidine (Demerol)	75 IM 300‡ PO	3–4 4–6	3–4	Contraindicated in patients with renal disease; accumulation of active toxic metabolite normeperidine (plasma half-life: 12–16 h) produces central nervous system excitation.
Methadone (Dolophine)	10 IM 20 PO	4–6 5–7	15–30	Good oral potency; requires careful titration of the initial dose; drug accumulation occurs.
Fentanyl (Duragesic)	TD	1–2	4–21	Available in transdermal patch.
Mixed agonist-antagonist drugs				
Pentazocine (Talwin)	60 IM 180‡ PO	4–6 4–7	2–3	Limited use for chronic pain; psychotomimetic effects with dose escalation; available only in combination with naloxone, aspirin, or acetaminophen; may precipitate withdrawal in physically dependent patients.
Nalbuphine (Nubain)	10 IM	4–6	5	Not available orally; less severe psychotomimetic effects than pentazocine; may precipitate withdrawal in physically dependent patients.
Butorphanol (Stadol)	2 IM	4–6	2.5–3.5	Not available orally, produces psychotomimetic effects; may precipitate withdrawal in physically dependent patients.
Partial agonists				
Buprenorphine (Temgesic)	0.4 IM 0.8 SL	4–6 5–6	6–8	Not available in United States in SL forms; no psychotomimetic effects; may precipitate withdrawal in tolerant patients.

*IM, intramuscular; PO, oral; PR, rectal; SL, sublingual

†Based on single-dose studies in which an intramuscular dose of each drug listed was compared with morphine to establish the relative potency. Oral doses are those recommended when changing from a parenteral to an oral route. For patients without prior narcotic exposure, the recommended oral starting dose is 30 mg for morphine, 5 mg for methadone, 2 mg for levorphanol, and 4 mg for hydromorphone.

‡The recommended starting doses for these drugs are listed in Table 28-6.

vidual pharmacokinetic variation, and the patient's prior opioid experience. Table 28-7 lists the relative duration for each analgesic at the dose which produced a peak equivalent to that of morphine. It is well-recognized that drugs administered by mouth have a slower onset of action and a longer duration of effect. Drugs given parenterally similarly have a rapid onset of action and a shorter duration of effect. The pharmacokinetics of the drug can vary widely and do not necessarily correlate directly with the analgesic time course. For example, drugs like methadone and levorphanol produce analgesia for 4 to 6 hours, but these drugs accumulate with repetitive dosing, and such accumulation accounts for the untoward effects of sedation and respiratory depression. The plasma half-life for methadone is approximately 14 to 24 hours and for levorphanol is 12 to 16 hours. Adjustments of dose and dosing interval based upon the plasma half-life may be necessary during the introduction of the drug. As well, plasma half-life can be altered by compromised hepatic and renal function, and dose adjustments and dosing intervals must be individualized. In the elderly patient, one-half of the recommended dose should be given initially because of the effect of age on drug clearance.[44]

Know the Equianalgesic Dose and Route of Administration

Knowledge of the equianalgesic doses can also ensure more appropriate drug use, particularly when switching from one opioid analgesic and from one route of administration to another. Patients who have been receiving one opioid analgesic for a long period and then are switched to another opioid to provide better analgesia should be given half the equianalgesic dose of the new drug as the initial starting dose. This is based on the concept that cross-tolerance is incomplete and that the relative potency of some of the opioid analgesics may change with repetitive doses.[51,52]

Administer Analgesics Regularly

Another important consideration is to administer analgesics regularly, which at times may include awakening the patient from sleep. The purpose of this approach is to maintain the patient's pain at a tolerable level. The development of a steady state level may allow a reduction in the total amount of drug taken in a 24-hour period. Patients receiving methadone, for example, require a smaller amount of drug than that initially prescribed to control pain once they reach a steady state level. The pharmacologic rationale for this approach is to maintain the plasma level of the drug above the minimal effective concentration for pain relief. Before a physician accepts the fact that an opioid analgesic is ineffective in a particular patient, the drug should be given on a regular basis with the interval between the doses based on the duration of effect of the drug. The time required to reach steady state depends on the half-life of the drug; for example, with morphine, steady state levels can be reached within five to six doses within a 24-hour period, whereas it may take 5 to 7 days to reach steady state with methadone. Full assessment of the analgesic efficacy of a drug therefore often cannot be completed on the first or second day. In the elderly patient, it is wise to use drugs with short half-lives in order to achieve steady state within a 24-hour period and to assess the full efficacy of the drug's analgesic action. The availability of transdermal patches delivering fentanyl and slow-release oral morphine preparations has facilitated the clinician's ability to provide the patient with continuous analgesia. However, because of their sustained release, these preparations should not be used in the confused or unstable geriatric patient.

Use a Combination of Drugs

Another important consideration is to use a combination of drugs. These are drugs that can either provide additive analgesia, reduce side effects, or reduce the rate of dose escalation of the opioid portion of the combination. Combinations that are known to produce additive analgesic effects include an opioid plus a nonopioid such as aspirin, acetaminophen, or ibuprofen[53,54]; an opioid plus an antihistamine, specifically hydroxyzine 100 mg[55]; and an opioid plus an amphetamine such as intramuscular dextroamphetamine sulfate (Dexedrine) 10 mg.[56] Studies have demonstrated the efficacy of these combinations in single-dose studies using larger doses of hydroxyzine than is often clinically used. In practice, oral hydroxyzine in 25-mg doses has been used on a regular basis with anecdotal observations of its effectiveness. Similarly, dextroamphetamine sulfate in 2.5- to 5-mg oral doses given twice a day and methylphenidate in 5- to 10-mg doses twice a day have been reported to reduce the sedative effects of opioids in patients receiving adequate analgesia but with excessive accompanying sedation.[57] These approaches have been used predominantly in the cancer patient who is chronically receiving an opioid and achieving effective analgesia but with excessive sedation.

Use of Other Adjuvant Drugs

Several other adjuvant drugs that appear to have analgesic properties of their own include the anticonvulsants that have specific analgesic effects in certain pain syndromes.[58] These drugs are most useful in the management of patients with pain of neuropathic origin such as occurs with brachial and lumbosacral plexopathy in cancer, postherpetic neuralgia, diabetic peripheral neuropathy, and postsurgical neuropathic pain syndromes. The mechanism of action of these drugs is suppression of spontaneous neuronal firing which occurs following nerve injury. The minimal effective dose for analgesia has not been determined; phenytoin and carbamazepine are the drugs most commonly used. The dose of carbamazepine is usually begun at 100 mg/day and very slowly titrated to analgesia to a dose of no more than 800 mg/day over a 7- to 10-day period. Elderly patients are very sensitive to this drug, and titration at 100-mg doses should be done cautiously, warning the patient about excessive potential side effects including sedation, ataxia, dizziness, and nausea and vomiting. However, this is the drug of choice for the management of patients with, for example, trigeminal neuralgia or for patients with ticlike pain associated with postherpetic neuralgia. In chronic use with carbamazepine, blood counts should be taken before drug therapy is started, 2 weeks after initiation of therapy, and at regular intervals afterward to assess the degree, if any, of neutropenia. This effect is idiosyncratic but should be watched for when the drug is used on a chronic basis. Several other compounds including baclofen, valproic acid, and mexilitine have been reported in survey studies to provide pain relief in patients with neuropathic pain.[58]

Another group of adjuvant drugs includes the tricyclic antidepressants. These are drugs that have analgesic properties in specific pain conditions characterized by neuropathic pain. The mechanism of their analgesic efficacy is thought to be by increasing levels of serotonin in the central nervous system and in part by affecting norepinephrine modulation of pain. Amitriptyline has been the most widely studied and has been demonstrated to be effective in controlling neuropathic pain in both postherpetic neuralgia and diabetic neuropathy.[59] The dose of amitriptyline as an analgesic varies from 10 to 75 mg. The starting dose is 10 to 25 mg for the elderly patient, with slow titration of the dose to 75 to 100 mg daily, eventually using a single bedtime dose. Of note, these drugs have significant anticholinergic effects and can precipitate acute glaucoma and also produce urinary retention. They should be used with care in the elderly patient, but they do have an important role to play.

Adjust the Route of Administration to the Needs of the Patient

Another important principle of drug therapy is to gear the route of administration to the needs of the patient. The oral route of administration is the most practical, but in patients who require immediate pain relief, parenteral administration, either intramuscular or intravenous, is the route of choice. The rectal route of administration should be considered for patients who cannot take oral drugs or for whom parenteral administration is contraindicated. Several of the more novel routes of drug administration include sublingual administration,[60] transdermal administration,[22] continuous subcutaneous infusions,[61] continuous intravenous infusions,[62] and continuous epidural and intrathecal infusions.[63] Each of these approaches can provide the patient with a continuous dosing regimen that can be maintained both in the hospital and at home. Continuous infusions allow delivery of the minimal effective concentration of drug and facilitate appropriate care at home, particularly in chronic use and particularly in the terminally ill cancer patient.

Treat the Side Effects Appropriately

The use of opioid analgesics can, depending upon the circumstances, have both desirable and undesirable effects. It is the adverse effects that markedly limit the use of the drugs. The most common side effects include respiratory depression, sedation, nausea and vomiting, constipation, urinary retention, and multifocal myoclonus. A host of other side effects, including confusion, hallucinations, nightmares, dizziness, and dysphoria, have been reported by patients acutely and chronically receiving these drugs but are not discussed here in detail.

Respiratory Depression Respiratory depression is potentially the most serious adverse side effect of opioid analgesics. Therapeutic doses of morphine may depress all phases of respiratory activity (rate, minute volume, and tidal exchange). However, as carbon dioxide accumulates, it stimulates the respiratory center, resulting in a compensatory increase in the respiratory rate that masks the degree of respiratory depression. At equianalgesic doses, the morphine-like agonist drugs produce an equivalent degree of respiratory depression. For these reasons, individuals with impaired respiratory function or bronchial asthma are at greater risk of experiencing clinically significant respiratory depression in response to usual doses of these drugs. When respiratory depression occurs it is usually in the opioid-naive patient following acute administration of an opioid and is associated with other signs of central nervous system depression, including sedation and mental clouding. Tolerance to this effect develops rapidly with repeated drug administration, allowing opioid analgesics to be used in the management of chronic cancer pain without significant risk of such depression. When respiratory depression occurs, it can be reversed by the administration of the specific opioid antagonist naloxone. In patients chronically receiving opioids who develop respiratory depression, naloxone, diluted 1 part to 10, should be titrated carefully to prevent the precipitation of severe withdrawal symptoms while reversing the respiratory depression. An endotracheal tube should be placed in the comatose patient before the administration of naloxone to prevent aspiration-associated respiratory compromise with excessive salivation and bronchial spasm.

Sedation and Drowsiness Sedation and drowsiness are also common side effects of the opioid analgesics. These effects will vary with the drug and dose and may occur after both single or repetitive administration of opioid drugs. Although these effects may be useful in certain clinical situations, they usually are not desirable components of analgesia, particularly in the ambulatory patient. The effects are mediated through the activation of opiate receptors in the reticular formation and diffusely throughout the cortex. Management of these effects includes reducing the individual drug dose and prescribing the drug more frequently or switching to an analgesic with a shorter plasma half-life. Amphetamines and methylphenidate in combination with an opioid can be used to counteract these sedative effects. It is critical to discontinue all other drug therapy that might exacerbate the sedative effect of the opioid, including cimetidine, barbiturates, and other anxiolytic medications.

Nausea and Vomiting The opioid analgesics produce nausea and vomiting by an action limited to the medullary chemoreceptor trigger zone. The incidence of nausea and vomiting is markedly increased in ambulatory patients. Tolerance develops to these side effects with repeated administration of the drug. Nausea caused by one drug does not mean that all drugs will produce similar symptoms. To obviate this effect, the patient should be switched to an alternative opioid analgesic or prescribed an antiemetic, e.g., prochlorperazine or metoclopromide, in combination with the opioid.

Constipation This side effect occurs because of the action of these drugs at multiple sites in the gastrointestinal tract and in the spinal cord to produce a decrease in intestinal secretion and peristalsis resulting in a dry stool and constipation. When opioid analgesics are started in the elderly patient, provisions for a regular bowel regimen including cathartics and stool softeners should be instituted. Several bowel regimens have been suggested because of their specific ability to counteract the effect of the opioid drug, but none of these have been studied in a controlled way. Anecdotal survey data suggest that doses far above those for routine bowel management are necessary and that careful attention to dietary factors, combined with the use of a bowel regimen, can reduce patient complaints dramatically. Again, tolerance develops to this effect over time but at a relatively slow rate. This is a critical problem in elderly patients, who often refuse to take pain medications because of concern about developing constipation. Again, aggressive bowel regimens to minimize this side effect can facilitate the patient's ability to obtain analgesia and to prevent the development of severe constipation.

Urinary Retention Urinary retention occurs with all the opioids and appears to be a dose-related effect. It is most common in the elderly male patient with already-compromised bladder function. It is readily reversible with reduction in drug dose and the use of bethanechol chloride (Urecholine).

Multifocal Myoclonus and Seizures Another side effect that has been clearly described with the use of opioid drugs is multifocal myoclonus and seizures. This side effect has been reported in patients receiving multiple doses of meperidine, although signs and symptoms of central nervous system hyperirritability may occur with toxic doses of all the opioid analgesics. In a series of cancer patients receiving meperidine, accumulation of the active metabolite normeperidine was associated with these neurologic signs and symptoms. Management of this hyperirritability includes discontinuing the meperidine, using intravenous diazepam (Valium) if seizures occur, and substituting morphine to control the persistent pain.[64]

Watch for the Development of Tolerance

Tolerance to each of the effects of the opioids develops at different rates, and it occurs in all patients receiving opioids chronically. The hallmark of tolerance is the patient's complaint of a decrease in the duration of the effective analgesia. Increasing the frequency or the dose of the opioid is required to provide continued pain relief. Since the analgesic effect is a logarithmic function of the dose of the opioid, a doubling of the dose may be required to restore full analgesia. There is no limit to tolerance, and with an appropriate adjustment of dose, patients can continue to obtain pain relief. Of note, cross-tolerance is not complete, and switching to an alternative opioid can often provide effective pain relief. Starting with one-half the equianalgesic dose of the alternative drug, the dose should be titrated for the individual patient. Numerous approaches to slow the development of tolerance include the use of oral drugs, particularly combinations of nonopioids and opioids; the use of local anesthetics to manage a focal area of pain; and the use of neurosurgical procedures, e.g., cordotomy, in the terminal cancer patient with unilateral pain below the waist. Physicians should not be concerned with the dose of drug required to manage the patient; rather, the degree of effective analgesia is the most important fact.

The abrupt discontinuation of opioid analgesics in a patient with significant prior opioid experience will result in signs and symptoms of opioid withdrawal. *Physical dependence* is the name for the condition that includes this appearance of withdrawal signs when an opioid is abruptly stopped. The time course of the withdrawal syndrome is a function of the elimination half-life of the opioid used. To prevent this syndrome from appearing, patients should be slowly weaned from the opioid drugs. Experience indicates that the usual daily dose required to prevent withdrawal is equal to one-fourth of the previous daily dose. Physical dependence must be distinguished from psychological dependence, which is a behavioral pattern of drug use characterized by a continued craving for an opioid manifested as compulsive drug-seeking behavior leading to an overwhelming involvement with the use and procurement of the drug. It is this fear of the patient's becoming addicted that limits both physician prescribing patterns and patient use of opioids. Some patients are reluctant to take any small dose because of this concern. Recent surveys in hospitalized medical patients[65] and analysis of patterns of drug use in a series of cancer patients receiving chronic narcotics[52] suggest that medical use of opioids rarely if ever leads to drug abuse or iatrogenic addiction. In the elderly patient, the chance of addiction is negligible.

Do Not Use Placebos to Assess the Nature of the Pain

A positive response to a placebo for pain is a normal response. The majority of patients participating in analgesic studies respond to placebos at various times during their treatment program. A placebo response does not reveal anything about the underlying nature of the pain and does not help to distinguish somatic pain from a somatic delusion. Placebos should not be used unless the patient has been informed of their use.

Conclusion

In summary, drug therapy is the mainstay of treatment for the majority of elderly patients with a wide variety of pain syndromes. However, pain management often may require a multidisciplinary approach, and the numerous approaches are listed in Table 28-4. Each of the approaches requires expertise in the specific area and triaging of care from the primary physician. For example, in the patient with trigeminal neuralgia in whom drug therapy fails, referral to a neurosurgeon is the next reasonable approach. Similarly, in the patient with reflex sympathetic dystrophy, referral to an anesthesiologist for sympathetic blockade is the first step to consider. Triggerpoint injections and various physical therapy approaches can readily be implemented by the primary physician. It is the careful definition of the pain complaint and diagnosis that is the first and most important step. Drug therapy transcends all levels of the diagnostic and therapeutic approach and should be within the armamentarium of the treating physician.

REFERENCES

1. Ferrell BA, Ferrell BR: Principles of pain management in older people. *Compr Ther* 17:53, 1991.
2. Crook J et al: The prevalence of pain complaints in a general population. *Pain* 18:299, 1984.
3. Moss MS et al: The role of pain in the last year of life of older persons. *J Gerontol Psychol Sci* 46:51, 1991.
4. Sternbach RA: Survey of pain in the United States: The Nuprin Pain Report. *J Clin Pain* 2:49, 1986.
5. Lavsky-Shulan V et al: Prevalence and functional correlates of low back pain in the elderly: The Iowa 65+ Rural Health Study. *J Am Geriatr Soc* 33:23, 1985.
6. Ferrell BA et al: Pain in the nursing home. *J Am Geriatr Soc* 38:409, 1990.
7. Roy R, Michael TA: Survey of chronic pain in an elderly population. *Can Fam Physician* 32:513, 1986.
8. Foley KM: Pain syndromes in patients with cancer. *Med Clin North Am* 71:169, 1987.
9. Daut RL, Cleeland CS: The prevalence and severity of pain in cancer. *Cancer* 50:1913, 1982.
10. Mor V: *Hospice Care Systems: Structure, Process, Costs and Outcomes*. New York, Springer, 1987.
11. Magni D et al: Pain as a symptom in elderly depressed patients. *Eur Arch Psychiatr Neurol Sci* 235:143, 1985.
12. Barsky AJ et al: The relation between hypochondriasis and age. *Am J Psychiatry* 148:923, 1991.
13. Sorkin BA et al: Chronic pain in old and young patients: Differences appear less important than similarities. *J Gerontol* 45(2):64, 1990.
14. Portenoy RK, Kanner RM: Patterns of analgesic prescription and consumption in a university-affiliated community hospital. *Arch Intern Med* 145:439, 1985.
15. *Characteristics of Nursing Home Residents, Health Status and Care Received: National Home Survey, 1977*. National Health Survey Series 13, No. 51, DHHS Publications (PHS) 81-1712, April 1981.
16. Goldberg RJ et al: Analgesic use in terminal cancer patients: Report for the national hospice study. *J Chronic Dis* 39:37, 1986.
17. Faherty BS, Grier MR: Analgesic medication for elderly people post-surgery. *Nurs Res* 33:369, 1984.
18. Cauna N: The effect of aging on the receptor organs on the human dermis, in Montagna W (ed): *Advances in Biology of the Skin*. New York, Pergamon, 1965, p 63.
19. Harkins SW et al: Pain and the elderly. *Adv Pain Res Ther* 7:103, 1984.
20. Reidenberg MM: Drugs in the elderly. *Med Clin North Am* 66:1073, 1982.
21. Kaiko RF et al: Narcotics in the elderly. *Med Clin North Am* 66:1079, 1982.
22. Scott JC, Stanski DR: Decreased fentanyl and alfentanil dose requirements with age. A simultaneous pharmacokinetic and pharmacodynamic evaluation. *J Pharm Exp Therap* 240:159, 1987.
23. Bonica JJ: Cancer pain, in Bonica JJ (ed): *The Management of Pain*. Philadelphia, Lea & Febiger, 1990, p 400.
24. Wall PD, Melzack R (eds): *Textbook of Pain*. London, Churchill Livingstone, in press.
25. Boivie J: Hyperalgesia and allodynia in patients with CNS lesions, in Willis W (ed): *Hyperalgesia and Allodynia*. New York, Raven, 1992, p 363.
26. IASP Subcommittee on Taxonomy Pain Terms: A list with definitions and notes on usage. *Pain* 6:249, 1979.
27. Hendler N, Talo S: Role of the pain clinic. *Med Clin North Am* 71:23, 1987.
28. Portenoy RK et al: Acute herpetic and postherpetic neuralgia: Clinical review and current management. *Ann Neurol* 20:651, 1987.
29. Galer BS, Portenoy RK: Acute herpetic neuralgia and postherpetic neuralgia: Clinical features and management. *Mt Sinai J Med* 58:257, 1991.
30. Portenoy RK, Farkash A: Optimal control of nonmalignant pain in the elderly. *Geriatrics* 43:29, 1988.
31. Hurley AC et al: Assessment of discomfort in advanced Alzheimer patients. *Res Geriatr Health*, in press.
32. Kellgren JG: On the distribution of pain arising from deep somatic structures with charts of segmental pain areas. *Clin Sci* 435:303, 1939.
33. American Pain Society: *Principles of Analgesic Use in the Treatment of Acute Pain and Cancer Pain*, 3d ed. Skokie, American Pain Society, 1992.
34. Acute Pain Management Guideline Panel: *Acute Pain Management: Operative or Medical Procedures and Trauma. Clinical Practice Guideline*. AHCPR Pub. No. 92-0032. Rockville, MD, Agency for Health Care Policy and Research, Public Health Service, U.S. Department of Health and Human Services, February 1992.
35. Foley KM: The treatment of cancer pain. *N Engl J Med* 313:84, 1985.
36. Schlegel SE, Paulus H: Non-steroidal and analgesic therapy in the elderly. *Clin Rheum Dis* 12:245, 1986.
37. Cohen JL: Pharmacokinetic changes in aging. *Am J Med* 80 (suppl 5A):31, 1986.
38. Morgan J, Furst DE: Implications of drug therapy in the elderly. *Clin Rheum Dis* 12:227, 244, 1986.
39. Bender AD: The effect of increased age on the distribution of peripheral blood flow in man. *J Am Geriatr Soc* 13:192, 1965.
40. Geokas MC, Haverbck BJ: The aging gastrointestinal tract. *Am J Surg* 117:881, 1969.
41. Goldberg PB, Roberts J: Pharmacologic basis for de-

veloping rational drug regimens for elderly patients. *Med Clin North Am* 67:315, 1983.

42. Rafsky HA, Newman B: Liver function tests in the aged. (The serum cholesterol partition, bromsulphalein, cephalin flocculation and oral and intravenous hippuric acid test.) *Am J Digest Dis* 10:66, 1965.
43. Belleville JW et al: Influence of age on pain relief from analgesics. *JAMA* 217:1835, 1971.
44. Kaiko RF: Age and morphine analgesia in cancer patients with postoperative pain. *Clin Pharmacol Ther* 28:823, 1980.
45. Chan K et al: The effect of aging on plasma pethidine concentration. *Br J Pharmacol* 1:297, 1975.
46. Helmers H et al: Alfentanil used in the aged: A clinical comparison with its use in young patients. *Eur J Anaesth* 2:347, 1985.
47. Portenoy RK: Pain, in Abrams W, Berkow R (eds): *Merck Manual of Geriatrics*, 2d ed. Rahway, NJ, Merck, in press.
48. Thienhaus OJ: Pain in the elderly, in Foley KM, Payne R (eds): *Current Therapy in Pain*. Philadelphia, Decker, 1989, p 82.
49. Forbes JA et al: Evaluation of ketorolac, aspirin, and acetaminophen-codeine combination in postoperative oral surgery pain. *Pharmacotherapy* 10, 1990.
50. Brooks PM, Wood AJJ: Nonsteroidal anti-inflammatory drugs—Differences and similarities. *N Engl J Med* 324:1716, 1991.
51. Galer BS et al: Individual variability in the response to different opioids: Report of five cases. *Pain* 49:87, 1992.
52. Foley KM: Clinical tolerance to opioids, in Basbaum AI, Besson JM (eds): *Towards a New Pharmacotherapy of Pain*. Chichester, Wiley, 1991, p 181.
53. Houde RW et al: Evaluation of analgesics in patients with cancer pain, in Lasagna L (ed): *International Encyclopedia of Pharmacology and Therapeutics*. New York, Pergamon, 1966, vol 1, p 59.
54. Ferrer-Brechner T, Ganza P: Combination therapy with ibuprofen and methadone for chronic cancer pain. *Am J Med* 77:78, 1984.
55. Beaver WT, Feise G: Comparison of analgesic effects of morphine sulfate, hydroxyzine and their combination in patients with postoperative pain. *Adv Pain Res Ther* 1:553, 1976.
56. Forrest WH et al: Dextroamphetamine with morphine for the treatment of postoperative pain. *N Engl J Med* 296:712, 1977.
57. Bruera E et al: Methylphenidate associated with narcotics for the treatment of cancer pain. *Cancer Treat Rep* 71:67, 1987.
58. Foley KM, Macaluso C: Adjuvant analgesic drugs in cancer pain management, in Aronoff GM (ed): *Evaluation and Treatment of Chronic Pain*, 2d ed. Baltimore, Williams & Wilkins, 1992, p 340.
59. Watson CRN et al: Amitriptyline vs placebo in postherpetic neuralgia. *Neurology* 32:671, 1982.
60. Weinberg DS et al: Sublingual absorption of selected opioid analgesics. *Clin Pharmacol Ther* 44:335, 1988.
61. Coyle N et al: Continuous subcutaneous infusions of opiates in cancer patients with pain. *Oncol Nurs Forum* 13:53, 1986.
62. Portenoy RK et al: Intravenous infusions of opioids in cancer pain: Clinical review and guidelines for use. *Cancer Treat Rep* 70:575, 1986.
63. Cousins MJ, Mather LE: Intrathecal and epidural administration of opioids. *Anesthesiology* 61:276, 1984.
64. Kaiko RF et al: Central nervous system excitatory effects of meperidine in cancer patients. *Ann Neurol* 13:180, 1983.
65. Porter J, Jick H: Addiction rare in patients treated with narcotics. *N Engl J Med* 302:123, 1980.

Chapter 29

ENTERAL/PARENTERAL ALIMENTATION

Edward W. Lipkin

Nutritional support for the elderly is becoming more widespread. Although there is no universally accepted definition of the term *elderly*,[1] for the purposes of this chapter it will arbitrarily be taken to designate those over age 65. The recommended dietary allowances (RDAs) look upon adults as being divided into two age categories: those aged 25 to 50 years old and those older than 51.[2] The National Health and Nutrition Examination Surveys (NHANES I and II) recognize a distinct category of the elderly aged 64 to 74.[3,4] The physiological processes of aging, however, do not show a distinct bimodal distribution, and thus these data are a poor means of distinguishing between "adult" and "elderly."

The high prevalence of malnutrition among institutionalized and hospitalized patients and the increasing use of these facilities by the elderly suggest the need for adequate programs to support their nutritional requirements. In designing such a program, several factors, for which there is an emerging body of information, must be taken into consideration. First, the nutritional requirements of this age group must be defined. Second, these requirements must distinguish between the healthy elderly and those with chronic diseases. Third, nutritional assessment techniques must be utilized in determining the nutritional status of this age group, for which "normal" standards have been developed. And fourth, in feeding the elderly, physiological limitations to feeding imposed by the aging process must be recognized and techniques appropriately adjusted for these limitations.

NUTRITIONAL NEEDS OF THE ELDERLY

Lean body mass declines with age and is one of the major determinants of basal metabolic rate (BMR). Therefore, if energy expenditure is expressed per total body mass, energy expenditure declines with age. The classic studies of Harris and Benedict[5] and Fleisch[6] both documented a declining BMR with age. The Harris and Benedict study examined BMR in subjects aged 21 to 70, while Fleisch studied subjects aged 1 to 80. In the Baltimore Longitudinal Study, a significant decline in BMR of 3 to 4 percent per decade and a decline of 5 to 6 percent per decade in total energy expenditure was observed for men aged 20 to 99.[7,8] These data, however, are cross-sectional, and some were not normalized for changes in body mass with age. In examining such data prospectively over 22 years, Keys et al.[9] observed a 3 percent decline in BMR per kilogram body mass per decade in younger men (mean age 21.9 years at start) and a 1 to 2 percent decline in elderly men (mean age 49.4 years at start) that was not statistically significant. Recent studies of resting energy expenditure (REE) in both women[10,11] and men[12] have suggested a small contribution of age to the REE consistent with the earlier study of Keys et al. Any estimate of total energy expenditure must also account for declining activity level with aging, but a precipitous drop in activity level is not considered as either inevitable or desirable for the elderly. The recommended daily allowance (RDA) for calories[2] in the elderly, calculated on the basis of assumptions about the impact of aging on BMR and activity levels, is considerably higher than previous published values and is summarized in Table 29-1.

There is no universal agreement about the protein requirements to maintain nitrogen balance in the healthy elderly, nor are there data about protein requirements in illness.[13] The protein requirements for

TABLE 29-1

Recommended Energy Intake for the Elderly

Sex	Age	Energy Needs, kcal, with Range
Males	25–50	2900 (2320–3480)
	51+	2300 (1840–2760)
Females	25–50	2200 (1760–2640)
	51+	1900 (1520–2280)

the healthy elderly, however, are thought to be about 0.8 to 1.0 g/kg.[14]

The requirements for calories and protein for the elderly in disease are poorly defined, but one intervention study suggests that more calories are needed for maintenance of body cell mass in the malnourished elderly than in younger populations.[15]

The RDAs for vitamins in the age group of 51 + suggest that a significant portion of the elderly fail to consume the RDA for several vitamins.[16–18] Elderly populations, furthermore, often show a significant increment in physiological measures of vitamin sufficiency on supplementation.[19–22] This information is difficult to interpret in light of the low incidence of clinically apparent vitamin deficiencies in this population and the high incidence of routine vitamin use.[23]

NUTRITIONAL ASSESSMENT OF THE ELDERLY

The decision to initiate nutritional support depends on the ability to assess nutritional status (Chap. 4). The mainstays of nutritional assessment consist of (1) anthropometric measures, (2) measures of immune response, (3) measures of visceral proteins, (4) measurements of selected vitamins and micronutrients, and (5) direct measures of body composition.

Anthropometric measures such as weight, weight for height, skinfold thickness, and arm muscle circumference are utilized for nutritional assessment as indirect measures of body composition. A useful measure of change in relative body composition with prognostic significance is the present body weight as a percentage of the usual body weight.[24,25] The distribution of values for ideal or usual weight for height have an inherently large biological variation, as do published measurements of skinfold thickness and arm muscle circumference.[26,27] The ponderal or body mass index (weight in kilograms divided by height in square meters) has been suggested for nutritional assessment in the elderly.[28,29] Other standards have been advocated that rely not on measurements of height but rather on estimates of height based on regressions utilizing knee height[30,31] or forearm length.[32] These estimates have the advantage of eliminating the variable loss in height with aging. Direct measures of body composition by determination of total body potassium,[33] underwater weight,[34] or bioelectrical impedance[35] or by use of multicompartmental measures[36,37] are still largely confined to the research setting. Measures of immune response—such as reaction to skin-test antigens and absolute lymphocyte count—are poorly correlated with nutritional status in the elderly.[38,39] The effects of age per se on the immune system in the healthy elderly not taking medication are poorly defined; studies have suggested either improvement[40–42] or no change[43–45] in immunological status with refeeding or specific nutrient supplementation in the malnourished elderly.

Although it has not been extensively studied, the capacity for visceral protein synthesis does not appear to be impaired in the healthy elderly.[46] Thus, measurements of serum albumin,[24,47] transferrin, and thyroxine-binding prealbumin have the same prognostic significance in the elderly as in other patient populations. Values considered "normal" in the healthy elderly may have to be modified for application to the institutionalized[48] or hospitalized elderly.[49] For example, in hospitalized elderly,[49] serum albumin levels declined as much as 9.7 percent per decade of age.

Serum measures of vitamins and selected micronutrients in the healthy elderly are rarely lower than in younger populations.[3,4,19] For routine nutritional assessment in the elderly, therefore, these measures are rarely helpful. Various functional assays show that vitamin status—as indicated by transketolase activity (thiamine) and erythrocyte glutamate:oxaloacetate transaminase activity (pyridoxine)—is impaired in elderly populations and responds to supplementation.[19] These measures of nutritional status may be useful in assessing the elderly, but their general applicability remains to be established.

Newer studies of nutritional status in the elderly have incorporated assessment of activities of daily living[24,25,50] and underlying medical conditions such as cancer[51] or sepsis.[47] To summarize (see Table 29-2), nutritional status in the elderly can be assessed in the clinical setting through a combination of data obtained by history, physical examination, and selected serum measures. A detailed weight history—including an appreciation of the person's present body weight as a percentage of usual body weight—is essential. A survey of the patient's activities of daily living should be obtained and noted in comparison to the usual baseline for that individual. Medical conditions that predispose to poor outcome, including cancer and sepsis, should also be noted. Measurements of height and forearm length can be utilized for calculation of body mass index and weight for forearm length. Notation of drugs that induce protein catabolism, including steroids, and quantification of excessive losses, such as diarrhea, leading to protein-calorie deficits are useful. A dietary history and physical examination may suggest vitamin or micronutrient deficiencies. Selected measures of visceral protein status, including albumin and transferrin or thyroxine-binding prealbumin, quantify the net protein-calorie balance.

INTERVENTION

If specific deficits have been identified, nutritional support merits consideration. It must be acknowledged that few data document the efficacy of enteral

TABLE 29-2

Summary of Selected Laboratory and Historical Data Useful in Nutritional Assessment*

Degree of Malnutrition	Weight Loss, Percent of Usual Body Weight	Serum Albumin, g/dl	Serum Transferrin, mg/dl	Lymphocyte Count, cells per mm^3
None	0	3.5–4.5	220–350	>2000
Mild	5–10	2.8–3.4	150–200	1200–2000
Moderate	5–10	2.1–2.7	100–150	800–1200
Severe	>10	<2.1	<100	<800

*Other prognostic indicators of poor outcome in the elderly: sepsis, cancer, deteriorating activities of daily living.
SOURCE: Abstracted and reproduced from Blackburn GL et al.[52]

or parenteral nutrition in the elderly, but at least one study[53] showed a reduction in hospital morbidity and mortality, with reduced length of stay, utilizing enteral supplementation of dietary deficits in an elderly population with femoral neck fractures and marked calorie and protein deficits.[54] Several studies have documented gross inadequacy in assessing the nutritional status and providing the appropriate nutritional needs of the hospitalized and nursing home resident elderly.[50,51,55] Many hospitalized and nursing home residents are never evaluated for nutritional status, assistance provided is either not offered or inadequate, and complications are frequent. There is no conceivable medical condition, however, under which a suboptimal (or no) diet is the optimal treatment. In the severely malnourished and compromised elderly patient, furthermore, it is unlikely that deficits will be corrected without appropriate intervention.[50]

A decision must be made in the nutritionally compromised elderly regarding enteral versus parenteral supplementation, and realistic goals must be established. In all instances where the gastrointestinal tract is accessible and usable, the enteral route is preferred. Short-term access to the gastrointestinal tract is established utilizing small-bore nasoenteral tubes. Nasogastric tubes suitable for suction are inappropriate for enteral feeding because their large size and rigidity predispose the patient to the dangers of aspiration and erosion. Optimal placement of a nasoenteral tube to minimize aspiration is in the distal duodenum. Gastric placement of feeding tubes is less optimal but can be utilized. Ileus is no absolute contraindication to enteral feeding provided that close attention is paid to residuals and periodic aspiration of gastric contents. Aspiration of greater than 50 ml should initiate discontinuation of enteral feeding and instillation of the equivalent amount of fresh feeding formula at frequent intervals (every 30 minutes if possible) until absorption resumes. The position of all tubes should be verified prior to use by fluoroscopy or x-ray. Directed placement has been accomplished utilizing endoscopy[56] for verification of position. The only absolute contraindication to enteral support is a distal obstruction. More proximal obstruction may necessitate surgical jejunostomy placement. Malabsorption, fistulas, or a short gut are also not absolute contraindications to enteral support. Increased losses and failure to stabilize weight within 3 to 5 days of enteral feeding, however, should suggest consideration of supplemental parenteral feeding. Initial selection of enteral supplements (see Table 29-3) should emphasize lactose-free products in light of the high incidence of lactose intolerance in the elderly. For chronic nutritional support, however, milk-based or lactose-containing enteral products are often well tolerated and are a good source of essential fatty acids. Furthermore, although relative lactase deficiency is common, it is often of minimal clinical significance. Many institutions utilize fiber-supplemented formulas to decrease the problems associated with poorly formed stool.

Enteral products can be chosen which are either iso- or hyperosmolar. Hyperosmolar tube feedings contain large amounts of osmotically active nutrients such as carbohydrates and amino acids or peptides. Fat does not contribute substantially to the osmolarity of tube feedings. As long as hyperosmolar solutions are delivered into the stomach and there is no increased gastrointestinal transit, these solutions are well tolerated without excessive diarrhea. Hyperosmolar nutrients are not well tolerated, however, if introduced directly into the jejunum. Various sources of carbohydrate, nitrogen, and fat are used to constitute the remainder of the enteral formula (see Table 29-3). Polymeric carbohydrates do not contribute as much to osmolarity as their mono- or disaccharide components. Some experimental evidence supports an increased absorption of di- and tripeptides compared to crystalline amino acids, and intact or partially hydrolyzed protein is much less of an osmolar load than crystalline amino acids. The commonly utilized fat sources (corn, soybean, or safflower oil) all provide sufficient intake of essential fatty acids. Medium- and short-chain triglycerides do not require hydrolysis for absorption and are adequately absorbed even in the presence of severe pancreatic insufficiency. However, medium- and short-chain triglycerides are not capa-

TABLE 29-3

Basic Formulary Choices in Enteral Feedings

I. Options in enteral feeds
  Whole food
  Defined formula
  Elemental
  Partially hydrolyzed
II. Basic enteral formulas
  Isoosmolar
  Hyperosmolar
  Lactose-free
  Lactose-containing
  Fiber-supplemented
III. Nutrient density in enteral formulas
  1.0–2.0 kcal/ml
  Carbohydrate: 115–366 g/liter
  Protein: 9.5–111 g/liter
  Fat: 1.0–91 g/liter
IV. Carbohydrate sources in commercial formulas
  Starch
  Glucose polymers
  Soy polysaccharides
  Disaccharides
  Monosaccharides
V. Protein sources in commercial formulas
  Intact protein
  Hydrolyzed protein
  Crystalline amino acids
VI. Fat sources in commercial formulas
  Butterfat (in milk-based products)
  Corn oil
  Soybean oil
  Safflower oil
  Sesame oil
  Sunflower oil
  Lecithin; mono- and diglycerides
  Medium- and short-chain triglycerides
VII. Specialty enteral formulas
  Liver failure
  Renal failure
  Respiratory failure
  Glucose intolerance

ble of meeting essential fatty acid requirements. Specialty enteral formulas rely on an enriched branched-chain amino acid content (liver failure), essential amino acids only (renal failure), increased fat content (respiratory failure), and high fat content enriched with monounsaturated fatty acids (glucose intolerance). The addition of free water and vitamins to tube feedings may be necessary if the total volume of tube feeding is less than 1800 ml/day, but the vitamin content per volume for many products has been increased to accommodate this possibility. Other micronutrient requirements, including iron and zinc, may need to be adjusted upward. There are very few data to support the use of hypoosmotic enteral solutions.

Given the prolonged convalescence required for recovery from chronic illness in the elderly, early attention should be paid to the possible requirements for long-term enteral or venous access. Thus gastrostomy, jejunostomy, or permanent placement of venous access is often a preferred option for nutritional support in chronic illness. Gastrostomy placement has been facilitated by the use of percutaneous endoscopic procedures,[57,58] thus obviating the need for general anesthesia. Feeding tubes should not be sutured in place to avoid potential self-mutilation by disoriented or combative patients. Restraint is never appropriate. Endoscopically placed gastrostomies are usually well tolerated even by disoriented patients. Gastrostomies must be examined periodically and cared for appropriately to avoid the potentially lethal complication of necrotizing fascitis.[59] Permanent venous access is limited to indwelling, small-bore Silastic catheters, which either exit percutaneously or are attached to subcutaneous reservoirs. Permanent venous access catheters require close monitoring by an appropriately educated and oriented patient, family member, or primary caregiver. Periodic nursing follow-up is considered crucial by most care providers. The disoriented or combative patient is at extreme risk from an indwelling catheter for a potentially fatal air embolus, exsanguination, or infection.

The primary goals of nutritional support in the elderly consist of arresting the depletion of cellular mass associated with starvation, injury, and illness. Goals such as reduction of mortality, morbidity, and length of hospital stay, preoperative management, or adjuvant treatment for chemo- or radiation therapy and bone marrow transplantation are all secondary. A unique consideration in the elderly population with malnutrition is the relatively large proportion of individuals with dementia of the Alzheimer's type.

Alzheimer's disease has been estimated to be the cause of up to 75 percent of all dementias and to have a prevalence of up to 50 percent in all patients admitted to nursing homes[60] (Chap. 92). These patients are at risk for the development of malnutrition and are difficult to feed for a variety of neuropsychiatric and physical reasons. In the early stages of the disease, anxiety, depression, and combative behavior secondary to delusions and hallucinations may result in poor oral intake. Subsequently, aphasia and apraxia may impair patients' ability to express their needs; as a result, nutritional needs may not be met. Agnosia (loss of smell) may depress appetite. Late in the disease, seizures, decortication, and contractures may not only make voluntary oral intake impossible but also contribute substantially to morbidity secondary to aspiration from tube feedings. There are also significant moral and ethical issues involved in the initiation and withdrawal of life support for such patients, and these issues are not easily resolved.

If nutritional support is undertaken in the elderly, how is it most optimally monitored? The problems inherent in performing nitrogen balance studies under steady-state conditions and the interpretation of "positive nitrogen balance" render data obtained from such studies difficult to interpret under routine hospital conditions. If weight loss has been characteristic of the patient's medical condition or can be expected from an inability to sustain an adequate intake of nourishment, a realistic goal is to arrest the inexorable weight loss. On the other hand, attempts to promote weight gain or increase lean body mass are not realistic in the acutely ill patient who is not fully mobile. Under almost all circumstances, any short-term weight gain in such patients reflects accumulation of fluid and not lean body mass.

A change in visceral protein concentration often does not reflect the adequacy of nutritional support. The long half-life of serum albumin (21 days) and its susceptibility to third spacing limit its usefulness as a marker of nutrient repletion. Other serum proteins, such as thyroxine-binding prealbumin and somatomedin-C (IGF-1), reflect net protein-calorie balance more adequately. Serial measurements provide a reasonable assessment of the adequacy of nutrient intake complicated only by the sufficiency of liver function. Other visceral proteins have been advocated as serum markers of nutrient repletion, including retinol-binding protein and serum transferrin levels; however, retinol-binding protein levels are confounded by vitamin A status, and transferrin levels are influenced by iron status and inflammation.

In prescription writing for nutritional support, attention must be paid to requirements for fluid, total calories, protein, essential fatty acids, micronutrients, and trace elements. Several references on enteral and parenteral nutrition have recognized the need for sections dealing specifically with the needs of the elderly and provide comprehensive discussions of the products and techniques required to address these needs.[61,62] Total caloric requirements can be reasonably estimated in the clinical setting on a per-kilogram dry-weight basis, as suggested by Jeejeebhoy[63] (Table 29-4), or as an adjustment of the resting energy expenditure measured directly or estimated from the Harris-Benedict equation, and as proposed by Long et al.[64] (Table 29-5). The RDAs serve as the standard for the provision of other nutrient requirements in the elderly. The RDAs for trace elements have been revised to include copper, manganese, fluoride, chromium, and molybdenum as well as zinc. The requirements for trace elements in the intravenously alimented elderly are poorly defined, but the adult recommendations set by the AMA's Expert Panel[65] (Table 29-6) suffice.

TABLE 29-4

Estimates of Energy Needs Applicable to the Elderly Based on Ideal Body Weight (IBW)

Clinical Status	kcal/kg IBW
Basal state	25–30
Maintenance (ambulatory)	30–35
Mild stress and malnutrition	40
Severe injuries and sepsis	50–70
Extensive burns	80

SOURCE: Summarized from Ref. 63 with permission of the author and publisher.

TABLE 29-5

Estimates of Energy Expenditure in the Elderly Based on Adjustments to the Harris-Benedict Equation

Clinical Condition	Adjustment*
Confined to bed	1.2
Out of bed	1.3
Minor operation	1.2
Skeletal trauma	1.35
Major sepsis	1.60
Severe thermal burn	2.10

*Estimated energy expenditure as a multiple of the basal metabolic rate (BMR) calculated from the Harris-Benedict equations: BMR (men) = 66.47 + 13.75 (W) + 5.0 (H) − 6.76 (A) and BMR (women) = 655.10 + 9.56 (W) + 1.85 (H) − 4.68 (A), where W = weight in kilograms, H = height in centimeters, and A = age in years.
SOURCE: Summarized from Ref. 64 with permission of the author and publisher.

TABLE 29-6

Recommendations for Trace Element Intake Applicable to the Elderly

Trace Element	Oral Dietary Requirement* mg/day	Estimated Intravenous Requirements†
Zinc	12–15	2.5–. . .‡
Copper	1.5–3.0	0.5–1.5
Chromium	0.05–0.2	0.010–0.015§
Manganese	2.0–5.0	0.15–0.8
Fluoride	1.5–4.0	. . . . .
Molybdenum	0.075–0.25	. . . . .

*RDAs for oral intake.
†Abstracted and summarized from Ref. 65 with permission of the publisher. Copyright 1979, American Medical Association.
‡In a catabolic adult, 2.0 mg should be added to this estimate. In the presence of jejunostomy, ileostomy, or diarrheal losses, up to 17 mg/kg output may have to be added to this estimate.
§With increased stool losses, this estimate may have to be increased to 0.020 to maintain balance.

In summary, intervention to supply adequate nutrition to the elderly can be accomplished by utilizing a variety of guidelines developed to support the unique nutritional needs of the elderly.

METABOLIC COMPLICATIONS OF NUTRITIONAL SUPPORT IN THE ELDERLY

The physiological changes that occur with aging impose some unique restraints on nutritional support. The declines in respiratory, cardiac, and renal functions as well as impaired glucose tolerance observed with aging require a conservative and more gradual approach to nutritional repletion than might safely be applied to the younger person. Decreased vital capacity may impair gas exchange and promote CO_2 retention with large calorie intakes. Decreased cardiac output and glomerular filtration may promote fluid, sodium, and nitrogen retention, leading to the development of edema, azotemia, and congestive heart failure. Impaired renal function—including impaired free water excretion, mineral excretion, increased or decreased sodium and potassium excretion—may precipitate more frequent episodes of hypo- or hypernatremia, hypo- or hyperkalemia, hypermagnesemia, and hyperphosphatemia. Acidosis may be more common because of the diminished capacity for renal acidification and impaired respiratory compensation. Impaired glucose tolerance may precipitate hyperosmolarity and difficulties with fluid balance because of the ensuing osmolar diuresis. Hypokalemia may result from excessive urine losses.

Three specific complications of nutritional support of the elderly deserve additional comment. Glucose intolerance, hyponatremia, and diarrhea are common in the tube-fed elderly. Glucose intolerance, however, should always precipitate a search for underlying infection and a reassessment of caloric requirements. Treatment with insulin for glucose intolerance should be reserved to blood glucose levels consistently over 200 mg/dl in the absence of infection or overfeeding. Oral hypoglycemic agents have no place in the management of glucose intolerance in the tube-fed individual.

Hyponatremia in the tube-fed elderly is common and usually results from inappropriate antidiuretic hormone regulation[66–68] or intravascular volume depletion (diuretics, cardiac or liver disease). Treatment usually consists of withdrawing offending drugs, intravascular volume repletion, and limiting free water intake. Chronic serum sodium concentrations greater than 125 mmol/liter are well tolerated and rarely require treatment.

The development of loose and poorly formed stools on tube feeding is common but should not be equated with diarrhea (greater than 500 g stool output per day). Loose stools are cosmetically unpleasant but of little physiological consequence, whereas diarrhea may signify malabsorption, enteric pathogens, or small-bowel and/or pancreatic disease and should initiate a search for these entities. The addition of "fiber" to tube feedings increases stool bulk and decreases frequency in selected individuals but is often overshadowed by other factors, including bacterial overgrowth of the bowel, contamination of the formula, and use of magnesium-containing antacids and nonabsorbable hyperosmolar vehicles for drug delivery.[69] On the other hand, maintaining strict aseptic technique in preparation of solutions, discontinuation of offending antibiotics, antacids, and nonabsorbable vehicles that may be used for medication delivery (e.g., sorbitol), and slowing the infusion rate as well as adding antimotility drugs in the management of selected patients to slow transit time will significantly improve tolerance to tube feedings in many individuals.

All these factors suggest that nutritional repletion in the elderly must be approached conservatively, with close attention to estimated needs and periodic readjustment of intakes depending on clinical response.

CASE STUDIES AND REVIEW OF BASIC CONCEPTS

Case No. 1

A markedly demented 80-year-old woman with Alzheimer's disease is admitted for fever to the hospital from a nursing home. Extensive evaluation suggests that the source of fever is osteomyelitis and a large open sacral decubitus ulcer. By history from the nursing home, the patient was becoming increasingly disoriented and her oral intake decreased dramatically over the 2 weeks prior to admission. The patient was previously able to assist with clothing herself, managing her own toiletries, and was ambulatory, but had lost all of her usual activities of daily living. No weight history was available. On admission, the patient's weight is 60 kg. Physical exam is significant for the open ulcer, diminished muscle bulk and tone, but significant fat stores. Knee height and forearm length are measured and used to predict a height of 160 cm.

The patient is treated with antibiotic coverage and wound care. Despite these measures and resumption of spontaneous oral intake, her diet provides only 800 kcal per day and is deficient in all essential nutrients. The family is contacted and involved in a care conference, including both nursing home and hospital care providers. Apparently the patient at one time was quite obese and weighed 100 kg. The patient's diet had diminished over a number of years because of declining appetite and more and more restricted food preferences. Since there is no living will or physician directive from the patient and a living daughter has durable power of attorney, a care plan was developed with the immediate family. The patient's infection is to be treated and an attempt made to restore the patient to her previous functional status but without resuscitative measures to be undertaken should a cardiac or respiratory arrest occur or dialysis to be undertaken in the event of renal failure. It is the opinion of all the participants that the patient is unlikely to meet her dietary requirements without intervention and a release is signed for elective placement of a feeding tube via percutaneous endoscopic gastrostomy (PEG).

Placement of the PEG is uncomplicated and the patient is started on a lactose-free, high-fiber tube feeding gradually titrated up to meet her estimated nutritional needs. The decubitus ulcer and osteomyelitis heal over the course of the following year, but in the meantime the patient is able to return to her nursing home with some restoration of activities of daily living (ambulation, able to assist with clothes changes and toilet transfer). The patient continues to require gastrostomy feedings to meet her nutritional needs.

Comments This case illustrates the utility of early placement of a PEG for feeding in a patient unable to meet her own nutrient requirements. The healing of osteomyelitis and a decubitus ulcer of this severity is unlikely without provision of adequate nutrition. Since the patient was demented, this case shows how such a decision for an invasive procedure (PEG) is undertaken in these circumstances.

Case No. 2

An unconscious 80-year-old man is found lying on the floor of his apartment by a neighbor. The emergency medical team arrives on the scene and documents a regular heart rhythm and a blood pressure of 60/0. The patient appears grossly dehydrated. An intravenous infusion of normal saline is started, and the patient is transported immediately to the nearest emergency room. In the emergency room, the patient is lethargic but arousable. He appears disheveled and has no known relatives. He is given 100 mg thiamine IV. On examination, he has a right hemiparesis and expressive aphasia. His weight is 55 kg and, according to his driver's license, he is 6 feet tall (183 cm). A previous medical record is located which confirms that he lives alone and has a long-standing history of hypertension. His last documented weight was 64 kg on a routine outpatient visit 6 months prior to the current incident.

The patient is admitted to the hospital, and computed tomography (CT) confirms a left parietal infarct of indeterminate age. A serum albumin level obtained the next day is 2.8 g/dl. The patient, although alert, is incapable of feeding himself, and on the following day a nasoduodenal tube is passed for initiation of enteral feeding. A dietician assesses the patient as "moderately malnourished" and estimates his dietary needs as 1880 to 2260 kcal and 50 to 60 g protein. Feeding is initiated with an isoosmolar solution at one-half the estimated final rate by a continuous drip. The rate is advanced over the next 2 days to the estimated full rate. Three days after admission, the patient develops a pneumonia, and the dietician recommends increasing the rate of supplementation to 2300 to 2600 kcal/day. Following resolution of the pneumonia, the rate of infusion is again decreased. The patient gradually improves neurologically and is gaining approximately 0.5 kg/week in body weight. After the patient regains use of the dominant hand and resumes some voluntary oral intake, tube feedings are decreased to nightly infusions only and then discontinued altogether. After a period of rehabilitation, the patient is discharged to a minimal-care nursing home at his usual body weight with a serum albumin of 3.5 g/dl.

Comments This case illustrates the optimal nutritional management of a patient who is moderately malnourished at presentation, with a reversible neurological deficit making voluntary oral intake impossible for an indefinite period of time. The patient was, appropriately, given thiamine in the emergency room on the possibility of long-standing alcohol abuse and to prevent the development of encephalopathy. A diagnosis of "moderate malnutrition" was made based on several criteria: The patient presented at 86 percent of his usual body weight, which represented a weight loss of 9 kg over 6 months. His present body weight represented 73 percent of "ideal" according to age-adjusted "normals" of medium frame derived from the NHANES I and II surveys,[27] and his body mass index had decreased from 19.1 kg/m^2 to 16.4 kg/m^2. His albumin after hydration was decreased, and although these were not commented on, it would not be surprising to find other obvious physical signs of malnutrition, including decreased muscle bulk and depleted subcutaneous fat stores. The prognosis was indeterminate, but it was obvious that voluntary oral intake would be impossible for an indefinite period of time and that the patient was already malnourished. An appropriate decision was made for early initiation of enteral feedings via a nasoduodenal tube. The estimated needs of such a patient are arrived at by a variety of approaches. The estimated resting energy expenditure (REE) from the Harris-Benedict equation is 1200 kcal/day. The RDA is 1840 to 2760 kcal/day. Since the patient was not infected and was immobile but was moderately malnourished, a reasonable estimate of caloric needs was 25 to 30 kcal/kg ideal body weight (IBW). For this patient of IBW = 67.1 kg, this amounted to 1880 and 2260 kcal, or 1.6 to 1.9 times the estimated REE. Protein needs were calculated as 0.8 to 1.0 g/kg body weight. A standard lactose-free isoosmolar tube feeding was started and rapidly advanced to fulfill estimated requirements. This avoided one of the major pitfalls of tube feedings—the failure to meet estimated needs in a reasonable interval of time. With the development of pneumonia, the patient's requirements were estimated to have increased to 30 to 35 kcal/kg IBW, or 2.2 to 2.5 times the estimated REE. If the same tube feeding is used, this will increase his protein intake to 78 to 88 g/day, or 1.4 to 1.6 g/kg IBW. In this particular case the early institution of tube feeding arrested the patient's malnutrition, which would have worsened with no intake, and resulted in a reasonable weight gain through a period of rehabilitation, with normalization of his visceral proteins.

Case No. 3

A 60-year-old woman presents to the emergency room complaining of palpitations and abdominal pain. The patient is afebrile, but atrial fibrillation is documented, as well as guaiac-positive stool. Abdominal exam is unremarkable except for diffuse pain to deep palpation. An elevated white cell count is noted, and the patient is admitted to the hospital for observation. The patient's heart converts to normal sinus rhythm with treatment, but that night she develops acute abdominal pain and is taken to the operating room for an exploratory laparotomy. During surgery, a cyanotic proximal small bowel is noted, as well as apparent occlusion of the superior mesenteric artery. The majority of the small bowel distal to the ligament of Trietz is resected and the duodenum anastomosed to 60 cm of the remaining jejunum. It is possible to revascularize the ileum and colon. A Hickman catheter is inserted in the brachiocephalic vein, advanced to the juncture of the superior vena cava and right atrium, and exteriorized retrograde through the chest wall at the time of surgery. Immediately after the operation, the patient is begun on intravenous alimentation.

The patient's weight is 59.1 kg, and she is 165 cm tall. Her ideal body weight is 68.2 kg, her body mass index is 21.7 kg/m^2, and her estimated resting energy expenditure from the Harris-Benedict equation is 1200 kcal/day. A dietary consult recommends an alimentation solution consisting of 20% dextrose and 4.25% amino acids to be delivered continuously at a target rate of 80 ml/h. Administration of two 500-ml bottles of 10% lipid emulsion weekly is also suggested to prevent essential fatty acid deficiency, and vitamins, electrolytes, minerals, and trace elements are added to the basic solution. Additional fluid is given to maintain adequate hydration. The patient has an uneventful postoperative recovery and resumes oral intake 7 days postoperatively with small amounts of low-fat solid foods. Diarrhea results but is improved by antimotility agents. The rate of infusion is advanced until all the patient's nutrients are delivered overnight. The patient is encouraged to experiment with her oral intake to develop an awareness of which foods aggravate and which alleviate the diarrhea. She is discharged 3 weeks postoperatively on home parenteral nutrition.

Over the next 2 years, the patient's diet is advanced as tolerated and intravenous feedings are decreased. The patient is able to come off intravenous feeding completely, and the Hickman catheter is removed. During this time her family presents her with two additional grandchildren, and she is able to see several of her grandchildren graduate from college. She dies at age 85 of cerebrovascular accident totally unrelated to her underlying disease.

Comments This case illustrates the optimal nutritional management of an elderly patient with a massive small-bowel resection. Permanent venous access was established at the time of operation with consideration of the long period of convalescence required for recovery from short-bowel syndrome. Intravenous nutrition was started immediately, since the lack of small-bowel absorptive surface and anticipated diarrhea compromise the patient's ability to be sustained on oral intake alone. Oral intake was encouraged to promote residual small-bowel adaptation. Whole food is well tolerated in the form of multiple small feedings provided that rapid gastrointestinal transit can be controlled and pancreatic exocrine function is intact. The findings at laparotomy suggested a good prognosis. It was possible to preserve the ileum, a significant portion of the jejunum, and the ileocecal valve and large intestine. The presence of an ileum and intact ileocecal valve made massive fat or bile salt malabsorption unlikely provided that transit time could be controlled. Age was not a crucial determinant of management strategy but rather the patient's previous premorbid physiological and mental function as well as the potential for return to her premorbid status.

The initial total parenteral nutrition (TPN) prescription was written to supply 1857 kcal/day or 1.5 times the estimated REE based on the Harris-Benedict equation. On a per-weight basis, the prescription provided 31 kcal/kg body weight or 27 kcal/kg ideal body weight. These are reasonable estimates of energy expenditure for a postoperative patient with extensive abdominal surgery who is not infected and is not mobile. The RDA is 1520 to 2280 kcal/day. The patient was also given 1.4 g/kg body weight of crystalline amino acids to meet her protein requirements and 3 percent of her total caloric intake as fat emulsion to meet her requirements for essential fatty acids. The infusion rate was rapidly advanced to convert to cyclic overnight therapy. This allowed the patient greater mobility during the daytime and some time to experiment with oral intake. Home therapy was a reasonable treatment option, given the expected long period of bowel adaptation. Despite catastrophic illness, this patient was rehabilitated and able to lead a fully functional existence for the duration of her natural life span. This patient benefited from medical management that focused on her long-term prognosis and not on her chronological age.

REFERENCES

1. Butler RN, McGuire EAH: Foreword. *Am J Clin Nutr* 36:977, 1982.
2. *Recommended Dietary Allowances,* 10th ed. Subcommittee on the Tenth Edition of the RDAs, Food and Nutrition Board, Commission on Life Sciences, National Research Council. Washington, DC, National Academy Press, 1989.
3. Programs and collection procedures, no. 10, in *Plan and Operation of the National Health and Nutrition Examination Survey, 1971–1973. Vital and Health Statistics,* ser 1. Washington, DC, Government Printing Office, DHEW (HSM) 73-1310, 1975.
4. *Plan and Operation of the Second National Health and Nutrition Examination Survey, 1976–1980. Vital and Health*

Statistics, ser 1, no. 232. Washington, DC, Government Printing Office, DHHS (PHS) 81-1317, 1982.

5. Harris JA, Benedict FG: Biometric studies of basal metabolism in man. Washington, DC, Carnegie Institute of Washington, Publication 279, 1919.
6. Fleisch PA: Le metabolisme basal standard et sa determination au moyen du "metabocalculator." *Helv Med Acta* 18:23, 1986.
7. McGandy RB et al: Nutrient intakes and energy expenditure in men of different ages. *J Gerontol* 21:581, 1966.
8. Munro HN: Nutrient needs and nutritional status in relation to aging. *Drug Nutr Interact* 4:55, 1985.
9. Keys A et al: Basal metabolism and age of adult man. *Metabolism* 22:579, 1973.
10. Owen OE et al: A reappraisal of caloric requirements in healthy women. *Am J Clin Nutr* 44:1, 1986.
11. Boer JO et al: Energy requirements and energy expenditure of lean and overweight women, measured by indirect calorimetry. *Am J Clin Nutr* 46:13, 1987.
12. Owen OE et al: A reappraisal of the caloric requirements of men. *Am J Clin Nutr* 46:875, 1987.
13. Munro HN et al: Protein nutriture of a group of free-living elderly. *Am J Clin Nutr* 46:586, 1987.
14. Munro HN: Protein nutriture and requirement in elderly people, in Comogyi JC, Fioanza F (eds): *Bibl Nutr Dieta,* no 33. Basel, Karger, 1983, p 61.
15. Shizgal HM et al: The effect of age on the caloric requirement of malnourished individuals. *Am J Clin Nutr* 55:783, 1992.
16. Young EA: Evidence relating selected vitamins and minerals to health and disease in the elderly population in the United States: Introduction. *Am J Clin Nutr* 36:979, 1982.
17. U.S. Department of Health and Human Services and U.S. Department of Agriculture: *Nutrition Monitoring in the United States—A Report from the Joint Nutrition Monitoring Evaluation Committee.* DHHS (PHS) 86-1255, Washington, DC, Government Printing Office, July 1986.
18. Delvin EE et al: Vitamin D nutritional status and related biochemical indices in an autonomous elderly population. *Am J Clin Nutr* 48:373, 1988.
19. Suter PM, Russell RM: Vitamin requirements of the elderly. *Am J Clin Nutr* 45:501, 1987.
20. Lowik MRH et al: Dose-response relationships regarding vitamin B-6 in elderly people: A nationwide nutritional survey (Dutch Nutritional Surveillance System). *Am J Clin Nutr* 50:391, 1989.
21. Manore MM et al: Plasma pyridoxal 5′-phosphate concentration and dietary vitamin B-6 intake in free-living, low-income elderly people. *Am J Clin Nutr* 50:339, 1989.
22. Meydani SN et al: Vitamin B-6 deficiency impairs interleukin 2 production and lymphocyte proliferation in elderly adults. *Am J Clin Nutr* 53:1275, 1991.
23. Garry PJ et al: Nutritional status in a healthy elderly population: Dietary and supplemental intakes. *Am J Clin Nutr* 36:319, 1982.
24. Sullivan DH et al: Impact of nutrition status on morbidity and mortality in a select population of geriatric rehabilitation patients. *Am J Clin Nutr* 51:749, 1990.
25. Sullivan DH et al: Protein-energy undernutrition and the risk of mortality within 1 year of hospital discharge in a select population of geriatric rehabilitation patients. *Am J Clin Nutr* 53:599, 1991.
26. Master AM, Lasser RP: Tables of average weight and height of Americans aged 65 to 94 years—Relationship of weight and height to survival. *JAMA* 117:658, 1960.
27. Frisancho AR: New standards of weight and body composition by frame size and height for assessment of nutritional status of adults and the elderly. *Am J Clin Nutr* 40:808, 1984.
28. Kergoat MJ et al: Discriminant biochemical markers for evaluating the nutritional status of elderly patients in long-term care. *Am J Clin Nutr* 46:849, 1987.
29. Rajala SA et al: Body weight and the three-year prognosis in very old people. *Int J Obes* 14:997, 1990.
30. Chumlea WC et al: Estimating stature from knee height for persons 60 to 90 years of age. *J Am Geriatr Soc* 33:116, 1985.
31. Baumgartner RN, Cockram DB: Evaluation of accuracy and reliability of calipers for measuring recumbent knee height in elderly people. *Am J Clin Nutr* 52:397, 1990.
32. Mitchell CO, Lipschitz DA: Arm length measurements as an alternative to height in nutritional assessment of the elderly. *J Parent Ent Nutr* 6:226, 1982.
33. Flynn MA et al: Total body potassium in aging humans: A longitudinal study. *Am J Clin Nutr* 50:713, 1989.
34. Coon PJ et al: Effects of body composition and exercise capacity on glucose tolerance, insulin, and lipoprotein lipids in healthy older men: A cross-sectional and longitudinal intervention study. *Metabolism* 38:1201, 1989.
35. Deurenberg P et al: Assessment of body composition by bioelectrical impedance in a population aged > 60 years. *Am J Clin Nutr* 51:3, 1990.
36. Baumgartner RN et al: Body composition in elderly people: Effect of criterion estimates on predictive equations. *Am J Clin Nutr* 53:1345, 1991.
37. Schwartz RS et al: The effect of intensive endurance exercise training on body fat distribution in young and older men. *Metabolism* 40:545, 1991.
38. Talbott MC et al: Pyridoxine supplementation: Effect on lymphocyte responses in elderly persons. *Am J Clin Nutr* 46:659, 1987.
39. Payette H et al: Nutritional factors in relation to cellular and regulatory immune variables in a free-living elderly population. *Am J Clin Nutr* 52:927, 1990.
40. Lipschitz DA, Mitchell CO: The correctability of the nutritional, immune, and hematopoietic manifestations of protein calorie malnutrition in the elderly. *J Am Coll Nutr* 1:17, 1982.
41. Watson RR et al: Effect of β-carotene on lymphocyte subpopulations in elderly humans: Evidence for a dose-response relationship. *Am J Clin Nutr* 53:90, 1992.
42. Peretz A et al: Lymphocyte response is enhanced by supplementation of elderly subjects with selenium-enriched yeast. *Am J Clin Nutr* 53:1323, 1991.
43. Lipschitz DA et al: Nutritional evaluation and supplementation of elderly subjects participating in a "Meals on Wheels" program. *J Parent Ent Nutr* 9:343, 1985.
44. Swanson CA et al: Zinc status of healthy elderly adults: Response to supplementation. *Am J Clin Nutr* 48:343, 1988.
45. Bogden JD et al: Zinc and immunocompetence in elderly people: Effects of zinc supplementation for 3 months. *Am J Clin Nutr* 48:655, 1988.

46. Morley JE: Nutritional status of the elderly. *Am J Med* 81:679, 1986.
47. Agarwal N et al: Predictive ability of various nutritional variables for mortality in elderly people. *Am J Clin Nutr* 48:1173, 1988.
48. Sahyoun NR et al: Dietary intakes and biochemical indicators of nutritional status in an elderly, institutionalized population. *Am J Clin Nutr* 47:524, 1988.
49. Herrmann F et al: Serum albumin level on admission as a predictor of death, length of stay, and readmission. *Arch Intern Med* 152:125, 1992.
50. Thomas DR et al: A prospective study of outcome from protein-energy malnutrition in nursing home residents. *J Parent Ent Nutr* 15:400, 1991.
51. Sullivan DH et al: Patterns of care: An analysis of the quality of nutritional care routinely provided to elderly hospitalized veterans. *J Parent Ent Nutr* 13:249, 1989.
52. Blackburn GL et al: Nutritional and metabolic assessment of the hospitalized patient. *J Parent Ent Nutr* 1:11, 1977.
53. Delmi M et al: Dietary supplementation in elderly patients with fractured neck of the femur. *Lancet* 1:1013, 1990.
54. Jallut D et al: Energy balance in elderly patients after surgery for a femoral neck fracture. *J Parent Ent Nutr* 14:563, 1990.
55. Maslow K: Total parenteral nutrition and tube feeding for elderly patients: Findings of an OTA study. *J Parent Ent Nutr* 12:425, 1988.
56. Gallo S et al: Endoscopic placement of feeding tubes. *J Parent Ent Nutr* 9:747, 1985.
57. Miller RE et al: Percutaneous endoscopic gastrostomy: Procedure of choice. *Ann Surg* 204:543, 1986.
58. Kirby DF et al: Percutaneous endoscopic gastrostomies: A prospective evaluation and review of the literature. *J Parent Ent Nutr* 10:155, 1986.
59. Martindale R et al: Necrotizing fasciitis as a complication of percutaneous endoscopic gastrostomy. *J Parent Ent Nutr* 11:583, 1987.
60. Pepys MB: Amyloidosis, in Weatherall DJ, Ledingham LCG, Warrell DA (eds): *The Oxford Textbook of Medicine*, 2nd ed. Oxford, England, Oxford University Press, 1987, vol 1, p 9.149.
61. Chernoff R, Lipschitz D: Enteral nutrition and the geriatric patient, in Rombeau JL, Caldwell MD (eds): *Clinical Nutrition: Enteral and Tube Feeding*, 2nd ed. Philadelphia, Saunders, 1990, pp 386–399.
62. Chernoff R, Lipschitz DA: Total parenteral nutrition: Considerations in the elderly, in Rombeau JL, Caldwell MD (eds): *Clinical Nutrition: Parenteral Nutrition*. Philadelphia, Saunders, 1986, pp 648–653.
63. Jeejeebhoy KN: Total parenteral nutrition. *Ann R Coll Phys Surg Can* 9:287, 1976.
64. Long CL et al: Metabolic response to injury and illness: Estimation of energy and protein needs from indirect calorimetry and nitrogen balance. *J Parent Ent Nutr* 3:452, 1979.
65. AMA Department of Foods and Nutrition: Guidelines for essential trace element preparations for parenteral use, Statement by an expert panel. *JAMA* 241:2051, 1979.
66. Helderman JH et al: The response of arginine vasopressin to intravenous ethanol and hypertonic saline in man: The impact of aging. *J Gerontol* 33:39, 1978.
67. Anderson RJ et al: Hyponatremia: A prospective analysis of its epidemiology and the pathogenic role of vasopressin. *Ann Intern Med* 102:104, 1985.
68. Gross PA et al: Pathogenesis of clinical hyponatremia: Observations of vasopressin and fluid intake in 100 hyponatremic medical patients. *Eur J Clin Invest* 17:123, 1987.
69. Scheppach W et al: Addition of dietary fiber to liquid formula diets: The pros and cons. *J Parent Ent Nutr* 14:204, 1990.

Chapter 30

PRINCIPLES OF REHABILITATION IN OLDER PERSONS

T. Franklin Williams and Leo M. Cooney, Jr.

The highest priority for a satisfying quality of life for most older persons is to maintain as much independence as possible—that is, to be able to make their own choices. Or, when independence has been threatened or decreased by some disabling condition, there is the strong desire to regain as much autonomy as possible. These desires define the goals of rehabilitation and indeed the overall goals of geriatric medicine. As has been emphasized elsewhere, a rehabilitative philosophy is at the heart of geriatrics.[1,2]

Many older persons maintain highly functional lives into very late years; but with increasing age they tend to acquire chronic conditions, both medical and psychosocial, which often result in decreased independence. The World Health Organization has adopted a set of terms which have been widely accepted to describe such losses more explicitly. *Impairments* describe losses of physical or mental functions in one or more of the organ systems—due to diseases, disuse, or possibly aging—which nevertheless may not have affected the person's overall ability to function as usual. *Disabilities* are considered to be present when one or more impairments are of such magnitude that overall function is decreased. *Handicaps* consist of disabling conditions which, because of lack of adequate corrective or adaptive measures, are preventing the person from carrying out usual social or societal roles. As Brummel-Smith[3] summarizes it, impairments are losses at the organ level, disabilities are losses at the level of the person, and handicaps are losses at the level of society (i.e., society has not provided the adaptive or replacement services which would enable the disabled person to continue to be independent). The distinctions provided by these terms are important inasmuch as they help to pinpoint the levels at which rehabilitative interventions are needed. In this chapter we will review the physical and psychological aspects of aging relevant to rehabilitation, discuss the general approach to rehabilitation, review where rehabilitation can take place, and consider the types of formal care required in the home by the person who is physically disabled.

PRINCIPLES OF GERONTOLOGY IN REHABILITATION

Careful research in recent years has given us more insights into the characteristics of older persons and has helped both to dispel earlier views and to define our current rehabilitative strategies. Table 30-1 (modified from Ref. 4) lists these characteristics.

First, we now recognize the *immense variabilities* among older individuals in terms of physical, psychological, and social characteristics. People become more, not less, different as they age. This variation must be taken into consideration as we look for explanations for aging-related changes, and the specific, idiosyncratic characteristics of each individual must be the basis for a rehabilitative plan for that person.

Second, as already noted, we now have strong evidence that most organ systems can continue to function at high levels into very late years—contrary to earlier views of inevitable declines with aging. This aspect is addressed in other chapters of this textbook as well but warrants emphasis here. For example, in healthy individuals who have been screened carefully to establish that there is no evidence of coronary or other heart disease, the maximum cardiac output on standard stress testing may be just as high in 80-year-olds as in those in their twenties;[5] considerable vari-

TABLE 30-1

Characteristics of Older Persons Relevant to Rehabilitation

Individual differences increase with age
Physiological capacity decreases with age but is rarely limiting
Chronic disabling conditions become increasingly common in old age
Older persons continue to, and want to, contribute significantly to the welfare of family and society

ability is found, as noted above, but there is no overall decline.

Similarly, brain metabolic function as measured by 2-deoxy glucose uptake on positron emission tomography does not decline with age;[6] in one of the most careful studies of cognitive performance and aging, the majority of healthy older persons performed as well as the average younger person.[7] If one examines the range and variability of results of cognitive testing in the many studies of this function, one finds that, even though the average performance on various measures may decline with age, 20 to 30 percent of older subjects perform as well as the younger adults. In the light of such data, it is hard to claim that age per se is the explanation for differences between individuals. Furthermore, various studies have documented the plasticity of the nervous system, at the cellular level and in terms of cognitive function, even in old age—including the ability to improve cognitive performance through "mental exercises."

The same picture is seen in renal function. Earlier, cross-sectional studies of glomerular filtration rate indicated a progressive decline in function with age. More recent research, using longitudinal measurements in the healthy volunteers of the Baltimore Longitudinal Study on Aging, gives a quite different picture: with each subject serving as his or her own control and with comparative measurements repeated approximately every 2 years for many years, approximately one-third of the subjects showed no change in glomerular filtration rate; another one-third showed a slight progressive decline, and the final one-third showed a more marked decline in renal function.[8]

An individual's personality characteristics are also quite stable throughout the adult years. This fact helps us to predict how a patient may respond to proposed rehabilitative therapies and enables us to adjust our approach.

Neuromuscular function is maintained into very old age provided that active exercise is also maintained. It is true that maximum athletic performance declines; but potential function is of far greater magnitude than would be required for most ordinary activities. Furthermore, as discussed in more detail elsewhere (Chap. 7), muscular function and aerobic capacity in previously sedentary older persons, even very frail 90-year-olds,[9] can be considerably restored through participation in therapeutic exercise programs.[10]

On the other hand, there *are* changes with aging which are intrinsic to our genetic and structural makeup, are seen in virtually everyone, and have significance for rehabilitation. Neuroendocrine changes, such as the menopause in women, result in increased risk of osteoporosis and fractures. Declines in circulating levels of growth hormone and other growth factors are common but not universal. There is a slow, general process of glycosylation of structural proteins which increases the likelihood of stiffness and loss of flexibility. End organs such as cardiac muscle tend to become less responsive to circulating hormones like catecholamines, which may contribute to ultimate limitations in maximum function.

To summarize, there is much intrinsic potential for older persons to continue to maintain high function and to be able to respond to rehabilitative efforts. Furthermore, losses of function are often due to lifestyle factors (sedentary lifestyle, inadequate nutrition, use of tobacco, alcohol, or other drugs), environmental exposures including injuries, and identifiable disease conditions.

The third characteristic of aging relevant to rehabilitation is that older persons are likely to acquire chronic conditions which result in disabilities. Table 30-2[11] lists the most common chronic conditions as self-reported by people in National Health Interview

TABLE 30-2

Top Ten Chronic Conditions for People 65+, by Age and Race: 1989 (number per 1000 people)

	Age				Race (65+)		
Condition	**65+**	**45 to 64**	**65 to 74**	**75+**	**White**	**Black**	**Black as % of white**
Arthritis	483.0	253.8	437.3	554.5	483.2	522.6	108
Hypertension	380.6	229.1	383.8	375.6	367.4	517.7	141
Hearing impairment	286.5	127.7	239.4	360.3	297.4	174.5	59
Heart disease	278.9	118.9	231.6	353.0	286.5	220.5	77
Cataracts	156.8	16.1	107.4	234.3	160.7	139.8	87
Deformity or orthopedic impairment	155.2	155.5	141.4	177.0	156.2	160.8	97
Chronic sinusitis	153.4	173.5	151.8	155.8	157.1	125.2	80
Diabetes	88.2	58.2	89.7	85.7	80.2	165.9	207
Visual impairment	81.9	45.1	69.3	101.7	81.1	77.0	95
Varicose veins	78.1	57.8	72.6	86.6	80.3	64.0	80

SOURCE: National Center for Health Statistics: Current estimates from the National Health Interview Survey, 1989, in *Vital and Health Statistics,* series 10, no. 176, October 1990.

Surveys, including the increasing prevalences with age and differences between races. Arthritis, hypertension, and hearing impairments are most prominent. When we consider the most common causes of disability severe enough to require help from another person every day, we find a somewhat different order of prevalence (Table 30-3).[12] Dementia is the most common cause of severe disability, with high prevalences of arthritis, peripheral vascular disease, strokes, and fractures, in particular of the hip. These data serve to highlight the major challenges for rehabilitation.

A fourth important characteristic of older persons is that most of them do continue to contribute in many ways to the lives and welfare of their families and society; they generally want to continue to do so. Yet ironically, when faced with disabling problems, many older persons as well as their families and physicians will assume that little can be done to restore their independence—their ability to go on being active, contributing members of family and society. As Kemp[13] and others point out, the public as well as professionals need to understand and adopt more positive attitudes.

STEPS IN THE REHABILITATIVE APPROACH

Table 30-4 summarizes the key steps in incorporating a rehabilitative approach into the care of older patients. Of highest importance is the early detection of potentially disabling conditions or circumstances—medical, psychological, or social. This step should be a part of regular screening and preventive care and is discussed elsewhere (Chap. 18).

When a problem or multiple problems threaten loss of independence, a comprehensive evaluation is required, including medical, functional, and psychosocial assessments. A well-prepared general physician can often carry out such an evaluation in relatively simple situations; for the more major and complex problems often seen in older patients, however, there is need for a multidisciplinary team approach involving physician, nurse, social worker, rehabilitative therapists, and often other specialists.[14,15]

TABLE 30-3

Principal Causes of Severe, Chronic Disability among Disabled Persons Aged 85 and Older

Condition	Percent
Dementia	19.43
Arthritis	16.75
Peripheral vascular disease	14.88
Cerebrovascular disease	12.86
Hip and other fractures	8.81
Ischemic heart disease	1.88
Hypertension	1.38
Diabetes	1.01
Cancer	0.91
Emphysema and bronchitis	0.26

TABLE 30-4

Steps in the Rehabilitative Approach

Early detection of potentially disabling conditions
Comprehensive medical, functional, and psychosocial assessment, including home environment
Planning rehabilitative therapies and assistive adaptations

Functional assessment deserves special comment inasmuch as it is key to determining the baseline as well as potential functional capabilities of the patient. Functional assessment should include physical, cognitive, affective, and social information. A number of useful, objective protocols and scales have been developed; Applegate et al.[16] have provided a recent summary of those readily available, and Ramsdell[17] discusses functional assessment in the context of primary medical practice. Basic components include determination of the patient's performance of activities of daily living (ADL), more complex "instrumental" activities of daily living (IADL), mobility status, cognitive status, affective disorders, and a review of social supports, housing, transportation, and economic resources.

Based on the information obtained through a comprehensive evaluation in collaboration with the older person (and family if indicated), a plan for rehabilitative therapy is developed, with explicit goals, tailored to that individual, defined in terms of intended improvements in specific functions, in overall functioning and independence, in the need for and use of assistive devices, and in the need for and means of obtaining supportive services and adaptation of home environment. The participation of a multidisciplinary professional team is usually essential in developing and accomplishing comprehensive rehabilitative therapy for a complexly disabled older patient. There are many studies documenting the value of such a comprehensive approach in terms of functional recovery and independence and in terms of cost-effectiveness.

SITE OF REHABILITATION

The appropriate site of rehabilitation for each patient depends on that patient's ability to participate in an intense rehabilitation process, the progress the patient is expected to make with rehabilitation, and the potential for the patient to return to a noninstitutional setting at discharge. There are a number of rehabilitation options open to elderly patients. While many patients and their families will request the most elaborate and sophisticated program, the intensity of these programs may not be appropriate for each patient. If the patient is placed in too intense a program, he or she may require several transfers from institution to institution and feel that he or she has failed in the rehabilitation effort. An early matching of patient needs to appropriate resources can preclude the failure of expectations, noncoverage of care, and unnecessary transfers.

Patients with such new disabilities as fractured hips, amputations, strokes, or other central nervous system events can undergo rehabilitation in an acute care hospital, on the rehabilitation unit of an acute care hospital, in a rehabilitation hospital, in a skilled nursing facility (one type of nursing home), at home, or in a comprehensive outpatient rehabilitation facility. Rehabilitation hospitals provide a multidisciplinary approach, including a rehabilitation physician, rehabilitation nurses, physical therapists, occupational therapists, speech therapists, social workers, and, usually, the consultative assistance of neuropsychologists, rehabilitation and vocational counselors, and experts in prosthetic and orthotic devices. Rehabilitation units of acute care hospitals supply many of these resources but may be limited by the relatively small size of the unit. Patients in such units or hospitals benefit from the close, cooperative, multidisciplinary approach between the various caregiving personnel as well as from the services provided by each discipline. Comprehensive outpatient rehabilitation facilities provide the same type and extent of care provided in rehabilitation hospitals but in an outpatient setting. Skilled nursing facilities provide primarily nursing care and physical therapy. While occupational therapy may be available, it is usually on an intermittent basis by contract. In most skilled nursing facilities, it is difficult to achieve close coordination between physician, nursing staff, and physical and occupational therapists. Most home health care agencies can provide physical therapy, occupational therapy, speech therapy, social work, and skilled nursing care in the home setting (the patient must be homebound to be eligible for this care). A practical limitation of rehabilitation in this setting is the limited opportunity for multidisciplinary planning, communication, and collaboration.

One cannot practically consider rehabilitation of an elderly person in the United States without taking into account coverage guidelines for Medicare and other insurers. Medicare has very stringent criteria for inpatient hospital stays for rehabilitative care. These guidelines cover both freestanding rehabilitation hospitals and "DRG-exempt" rehabilitation units of acute care hospitals. The DRG-exempt classification means that when a patient with a problem such as a stroke is transferred from an acute care floor to a rehabilitation unit, the hospital can collect per diem charges for the duration of the stay on such a unit in addition to the DRG payment for acute stroke care.

Medicare regulations state that "rehabilitative care in a hospital, rather than in a skilled nursing facility or on an outpatient basis, is reasonable and necessary for a patient who requires a more coordinated, intense program of multiple services than is generally found out of a hospital." To be eligible for reimbursement of such in-hospital care, a patient must fulfill all of the following criteria:

1. Require close medical supervision by a physician trained or experienced in rehabilitation
2. Require around-the-clock rehabilitation nursing
3. Require at least 3 hours per day of physical therapy and occupational therapy in addition to any other required services
4. Require a multidisciplinary team approach to the delivery of the program
5. Require a coordinated program of care
6. Have a good prospect of significant functional improvement
7. Have clearly articulated, realistic goals of therapy

In addition, 75 percent of the patients discharged from the rehabilitation hospital or unit must carry one of the following principal diagnoses: stroke, spinal cord injury, congenital deformity, amputation, major multiple trauma, fracture of the femur, brain injury, polyarthritis, neurological disorders, or burns. Medicare guidelines for reimbursement of care in a skilled nursing facility rehabilitation do not require occupational therapy, 3 hours of daily specific rehabilitative care, the care of a rehabilitation physician, or a multidisciplinary approach. Medicare does require 5 days per week of physical therapy, need for skilled restorative care, and continued significant functional progress.

Thus, as a practical matter, most patients transferred to a rehabilitation unit or hospital must be in one of the ten diagnostic categories above, must be able to tolerate at least 3 hours per day of therapy, must require occupational therapy in addition to physical therapy, and must require close medical supervision by a rehabilitation physician. To qualify for Medicare coverage in a skilled nursing facility, one must go to that facility for the same reason that one was hospitalized, must require daily physical therapy which could not be given in the home, must have significant functional deficits at the time of transfer, and must show continued significant progress toward a higher level of care.

The most essential step in the rehabilitative planning process is the setting of goals prior to the initiation of therapy. Once the physician, therapist, and nurses have made a complete assessment of the extent of the patient's disability, prognostic factors for recovery, general medical status, mental status, response to initial rehabilitation efforts, and motivation, they should be able to predict the recovery expected from a period of inpatient rehabilitation. This recovery can vary. One patient might be expected only to move independently in bed and transfer from bed to chair with the assistance of a family member, while another patient might be expected to achieve complete independence with transfers, walking, stair climbing, and many activities of daily living. The patient and the patient's family must understand the practical goals of inpatient rehabilitation in order to plan for the patient's care needs prior to the time of discharge.

CARE NEEDS

Families must be given guidance about the amount and type of care that a patient will need after hospital discharge. Once the goals of inpatient rehabilitation have been set, one may translate these goals into how much care the patient will need at home. Families cannot be expected to make realistic decisions about their ability to care for patients at home until they know how much care will be expected. The patient's ability to perform the activities of daily living correlates well with the amount of care needed at home. These functions of bathing, dressing, eating, toileting, transferring, ambulating, and maintaining continence of bladder and bowel are measured on such scales as the Katz Index of ADL and the Barthel Index.

Few studies have used these indices in a practical way to assist planning for the care of an elderly patient at home. There are, however, several basic principles which may be helpful in planning care needs. The physical task which is most important for the patient is the ability to transfer in and out of a bed or chair. A patient who cannot transfer from bed to chair or chair to toilet without help cannot be left alone for substantial periods of time. The ability to walk is less important for independence, as patients who are wheelchair-dependent yet able to transfer can often function quite well on their own. Confusion and lack of safety awareness are major problems for the frail elderly patient. The patient who knows and understands his or her own limitations can function much more independently than the patient who consistently attempts tasks that are too difficult. The following guide, although not confirmed by timed studies, has been helpful in predicting the amount of care that patients will need in the home environment.

1. Supervision around the clock
   Patient cannot get from bed to chair or chair to toilet without help.
   Patient cannot make transfers or walk alone safely.
   Patient is incontinent.
2. Supervision 8 hours per day
   Patient cannot eat independently.
3. Supervision 2 to 4 hours per day
   Patient cannot dress independently.
   Patient cannot prepare own meals—can use "Meals-on-Wheels."
4. Daily Supervision
   Help with medications.
   Administration of insulin, etc.
5. Help three times a week
   Patient cannot bathe independently.

THE PHYSICIAN'S ROLE IN REHABILITATION DECISIONS

After a patient has suffered a new disability, families need as much hard information as possible so that they will be able to make difficult decisions regarding care. They need to know how much recovery can be expected from this disability, how long this recovery might take, where this recovery may best proceed, how much of the rehabilitation process will be covered by insurance, how much the patient will be able to do after completion of rehabilitation, what the patient's care needs will then be, and how much care will be needed by the patient at home. While the answers to these questions must be limited to general predictions, there are now enough data in the literature to give a good estimate of the amount of recovery to be expected, the most appropriate site of rehabilitation, the expected goals of rehabilitation, and the amount of care needed after these goals are met. A complete assessment of the extent of the patient's disabilities—including perceptual problems, mental status, prior level of function, motivation, and response to rehabilitation—must be made based on an understanding of those patient and disease factors which predict outcome. The patient and the patient's family, given reasonable expectations for the results of the rehabilitative process, can then make thoughtful and reasonable decisions about the patient's short- and long-term care.

REFERENCES

1. Williams TF (ed): *Rehabilitation in the Aging.* New York, Raven Press, 1984.
2. Williams TF: The future of aging. *Arch Phys Med Rehab* 68:335, 1987.
3. Brummel-Smith K: Introduction, in Kemp B et al (eds): *Geriatric Rehabilitation.* Boston, Little, Brown, 1990.
4. Williams TF: Geriatrics: A perspective on quality of

life and care for older people, in Spilker B (ed): *Quality of Life Assessments in Clinical Trials.* New York, Raven Press, 1990.

5. Rodeheffer RJ et al: Exercise cardiac output is maintained with advancing age in healthy human subjects: Cardiac dilation and increased stroke volume compensate for a diminished heart rate. *Circulation* 69:203, 1984.
6. Creary H et al: The aging human brain. *Ann Neurol* 17:2, 1985.
7. Schaie KW: Perceptual speed in adulthood: Cross-sectional and longitudinal studies. *Psychol Aging* 4:443, 1989.
8. Lindeman RD et al: Longitudinal studies on rate of decline in renal function with age. *J Am Geriatr Soc* 33:278, 1985.
9. Fiatarone M et al: High-intensity strength training in nonagenarians. *JAMA* 236:3029, 1990.
10. Seals DR et al: Endurance training in older men and women: I. Cardiovascular response to exercise. *J Appl Physiol* 57:1024, 1984.
11. National Center for Health Statistics: Current estimates from the National Health Interview Survey, 1989, in *Vital and Health Statistics,* series 10, no. 176. Washington, DC, US Government Printing Office, October, 1990.
12. Health Care Financing Administration: Long-term Care Survey, 1982. Presented by KG Manton at Annual Meeting of American Public Health Association, Washington, DC, 1985.
13. Kemp B: The psychological context of geriatric rehabilitation, in Kemp B et al (eds): *Geriatric Rehabilitation.* Boston, Little, Brown, 1990.
14. Redford JB: Making the team approach work, in Frengley JD et al (eds): *Practicing Rehabilitation with Geriatric Clients.* New York, Springer-Verlag, 1990.
15. Cole KD et al: Issues in interdisciplinary team care, in Kemp B et al (eds): *Geriatric Rehabilitation.* Boston, Little, Brown, 1990.
16. Applegate WB et al: Instruments for the functional assessment of older patients. *N Engl J Med* 322:1207, 1990.
17. Ramsdell JW: A rehabilitation orientation in the workup of general medical problems, in Kemp B: *Geriatric Rehabilitation.* Boston, Little, Brown, 1990.

Chapter 31

REHABILITATION OF SPECIFIC CONDITIONS

Leo M. Cooney, Jr., and T. Franklin Williams

When an older individual suffers a disabling event such as a fractured hip or stroke, the patient and patient's family have a number of questions and concerns. Most importantly, they wish to know how dependent that individual might be on family members and others for care in the future. Predicting that need for care, and directing the patient to the appropriate rehabilitative setting, is an important role for the patient's physician. In this chapter we will review the rehabilitative approaches to specific conditions.

STROKE

Stroke is a major cause of disability for older individuals. The prognosis for both mortality and functional recovery can vary greatly, depending upon the patient's age, other medical conditions, and the type and extent of the stroke and associated neurological deficits. Recognition of those predictive factors can help a family anticipate the expected function of a patient at the end of an acute hospitalization, at the conclusion of a period of inpatient rehabilitation, and after further home and outpatient rehabilitation. These expectations on the part of the family are essential to the realistic planning of care for the patient.

Despite advancements in diagnostic imaging techniques, the predictive value of these studies is still limited in the management of patients with strokes. Because the computed tomography (CT) scan is abnormal on admission in patients with an intracerebral hemorrhage, the severity of the lesion on CT scan—manifested by hemorrhage size, midline shift, and intraventricular spread of the hemorrhage—is associated with increased mortality.[1] For all types of strokes, Miller and Miyamoto[2] found that patients with deep lesions involving the basal ganglia, internal capsule, and thalamus have worse functional outcomes than patients with superficial lesions of the cerebral cortex. Lundgren et al.[3] also found that patients with deep lesions had greater motor impairment than those with cortical lesions. Several other studies,[4,5] however, have not found a significant correlation with outcome with the side, region, size, or presence or absence of enhancement with contrast with CT scans.

Clinical factors, therefore, are the major predictive variables in determining mortality and functional outcome from stroke. Studies of these factors, however, have been limited by patient selection, measurement of outcome, the timing of measurement of predictive factors, and the problem of comparing final functional outcome with changes in function during rehabilitation. Jongbloed[6] reviewed 33 studies which were designed to compare a patient's functional recovery from a stroke with patient characteristics measured earlier in the hospital stay. These studies demonstrated that a prior stroke, older age, urinary and bowel incontinence, and visuospatial deficits were adverse prognostic indicators of function. No relationship was shown between sex, hemisphere of stroke, and functional outcome. A number of problems were identified in these studies, including differences in patient samples, timing of assessments, and criteria by which outcome was measured.

Most studies of stroke outcome have followed patients who have already been selected for rehabilitation. Information on these patients is less relevant to questions raised at the time of the patient's stroke. Family, physicians, and discharge planners need information as soon as possible after the stroke to help with both rehabilitation and care plans. Several studies have identified factors within several days of the onset of stroke which predict both mortality and functional recovery. Fullerton and colleagues[7] followed 206 patients with acute strokes admitted to general hospitals in Belfast, Northern Ireland. They found that increased age, the patient's level of consciousness on admission, urinary incontinence, mental status score, speech difficulties, visual field deficits, decreased limb power and function, and perceptual disorders such as neglect, denial, and disordered spatial orientiation were all associated with decreased function and mortality 6 months after the stroke. When multivariate analysis was carried out, six variables were found to make an independent contribution to outcome: Albert's Test–a measure of perceptual disorders, leg function, level of consciousness, arm power, weighted mental score, and the presence of ST or T-wave changes on the electroencephalogram. Kotila et al.[8] reviewed all stroke patients hospitalized in two Finnish towns and found the following factors at time of presentation of the stroke to be associated with a poor prognosis: age over 65, hemiparesis at onset, lower level of consciousness at onset, impairment of memory and intelligence, visual field deficits, perceptual deficits, and depression. The clinical severity of the stroke at presentation, defined primarily by altered mental status and the presence of aphasia, and any extension of the stroke correlated with poor outcome in a study of all patients admitted to a Veterans Administration Hospital Stroke Unit.[9] These studies all demonstrate that prolonged coma, decreased level of consciousness, altered mental status, incontinence, and visual field deficits are predictors of an adverse outcome which can be identified soon after the onset of the stroke.

The improvement in function that occurs during the first week or two after a stroke can be quite predictive of ultimate outcome. Prescott et al.[10] reviewed patients admitted to an acute stroke unit, excluding those patients unconscious at the onset of stroke or previously dependent in daily activities. Improvements in upper-limb motor function, postural function, and proprioception were associated with subsequent independence. Loewen and Anderson[11] followed patients with strokes throughout their hospital course. They obtained data on admission, 1 week after admission, 1 month after the stroke, and at hospital discharge. They excluded patients in deep coma and those with altered level of consciousness, those in the intensive care unit, and those with previous strokes. They found that balanced sitting, bowel and bladder control, and overall score of motor strength measured one week after the stroke predicted overall functional outcome.

A number of studies have evaluated patients at the time of admission to a rehabilitation unit. These patients have already been selected, in that patients who are either poor candidates for rehabilitation or do not require intensive rehabilitation are excluded. Most of these patients were evaluated 2 to 4 weeks after the onset of stroke. Feigenson[12] found that severe weakness on admission, perceptual or cognitive dysfunction, poor motivation, visual field deficit, and multiple neurologic deficits were all associated with a poor functional outcome. Wade et al.[4] found that increased age, visual field deficits, urinary incontinence, arm weakness, and poor sitting balance predicted a poor functional outcome at 6 months. Kinsella and Ford[13] found that spatial neglect was a particularly important predictor of poor functional recovery. The importance of perceptual and cognitive problems as well as visual field deficits in stroke recovery was pointed out in a study by Reding and Pottes.[14] They studied 95 patients admitted to an inpatient stroke rehabilitation unit, classifying them as having motor deficits alone, motor deficits plus somatosensory deficits, or motor deficit plus somatosensory deficit plus visual field deficit. Over 95 percent of patients with motor deficit alone were able to walk 150 feet 14 weeks after their stroke. Only 35 percent of patients with motor plus somatic sensory deficit reach this goal, and only 3 percent of patients with motor, somatic sensory, and visual field deficits did so.

EVALUATION OF A PATIENT WITH STROKE

Although no study can predict the outcome of an individual patient with stroke, the above studies can guide physicians and families in planning care. Factors which predict a poor functional outcome must be recognized when helping families plan the future care needs of these patients. At the time of presentation, patients with an altered level of consciousness, incontinence, aphasia, and visual field deficits have a poor prognosis and are likely to require a good deal of help in the future, even after a period of rehabilitation. Some 7 to 10 days after the acute stroke, difficulty with sitting balance, one-sided neglect, perceptual and cognitive deficits, abnormal proprioception, and poor position sense all indicate that the patient's functional recovery will be limited and that the patient will need substantial help in the future. At the time of admission to a rehabilitation unit, a low level of function, altered mental status, visual field deficits, neglect, perceptual and cognitive deficits, and speech deficits all indicate that a patient will still require considerable assistance at discharge from that unit.

The full assessment of those factors which predict recovery and the patient's ability to undergo intense rehabilitation must be carried out by a team of individuals, including a physical therapist, occupational therapist, nurse, social worker, and physician. The physical therapist is the individual first called upon to assess patients with strokes. That individual will assess the patient's present functional status, ability to follow simple and complex commands, physical status and endurance, ability to use the involved and uninvolved limbs, and the patient's need for further rehabilitation. This assessment will help predict how successful further rehabilitation will be. An evaluation by an occupational therapist prior to setting goals of rehabilitation is essential. The above studies have pointed out the importance of visual field deficits, cognitive and perceptual deficits, neglect, and abnormal proprioception in the prognosis of patients with strokes. Occupational therapists—who test for cognitive and perceptual deficits, evaluate and treat upper extremity dysfunction, and assist the patient to adapt to the complex daily tasks of dressing, feeding, and bathing—have an essential role in this evaluation process. The patient's nurse must be questioned about such problems as incontinence, nighttime confusion, and the patient's effort level in rehabilitation. While patients might perform reasonably well during one or two physical therapy sessions per day, the ultimate success of rehabilitation will depend on the full effort that the patient makes throughout the day, as determined by the patient's nurse. The social worker or discharge planner must assess the family's commitment and ability to care for the patient after discharge. This commitment can be made only after the patient's expected function at discharge is estimated. Careful attention to the above prognostic factors as well as a complete assessment by physical and occupational therapy should produce a reasonable expectation of need for care at the conclusion of inpatient rehabilitation. The physician must determine the presence and extent of associated diseases, including such conditions as prior strokes, Parkinson's disease, and arthritis, which may affect the progress and success of rehabilitation. He or she must also determine how the patient's cardiac, pulmonary, and general medical condition will affect the patient's ability to undergo an intense period of rehabilitation, which must include 3 hours per day of physical and occupational therapy.

Thus, the overall rehabilitation assessment must include (1) the patient's premorbid level of function; (2) the extent of the present disability and prognosis for recovery; (3) the mental acuity of the patient, especially the ability to follow a therapist's instructions and retain these instructions from one session to the next; (4) the physical ability of the patient to endure an intense rehabilitation program; and (5) the patient's motivation and effort in rehabilitation.

HIP FRACTURE

Fractures of the hip are among the most common causes of serious disability in older persons, with more than 200,000 U.S. hospital admissions per year due to such fractures. The incidence rises exponentially with age beginning in the fifties. The rate of increase is greater in white women than in other racial groups or in men, but the pattern of increase with age is the same. White women who live to age 90 or more have a one-in-three risk of hip fracture.

Clearly the most important approach to this problem is prevention: prevention of falls through addressing the risk factors for falling in older persons and preventing or minimizing the development of osteoporosis. Ongoing research and treatment gives much promise for ultimate success in these preventive efforts; these aspects are discussed elsewhere (Chap. 121).

In persons who do sustain fractures of the hip, a rehabilitative evaluation and plan should be initiated as early as possible—even before reparative surgery. The older person's general medical, mental, functional, and emotional status should be assessed and co-morbidities identified and addressed. There is no age limit for the surgical correction of hip fractures; many persons in their nineties may have successful outcomes.[15] As noted with other disabling conditions, the decision about surgery must be based on individualized judgment by the primary physician, surgeon, and informed patient.

The timing of mobilization after surgery, with walking in parallel bars or with a cane or walker, is influenced by the type of repair but should be initiated as soon as possible. Any sustained period of immobilization results in serious further losses of strength and function; 2 or more days of restorative exercises are required to recover what is lost with each day of immobilization. A plan for long-term maintenance physiotherapy should be a part of the overall rehabilitation approach.

A patient's premorbid mental and functional status, rather than the nature of the fracture itself, is the most important predictive factor in both mortality and functional outcome following a hip fracture. Altered mental status has long been demonstrated to be a predictor of poor outcome in patients with hip fracture. Miller[16] found that 47 percent of patients with "cerebral dysfunction" died within the first year after injury, with only an 18 percent mortality in those patients who were mentally alert and oriented. There was no significant relationship between duration of anesthesia, blood loss, or choice of fixation device and outcome at 1 year. Baker[17] found that 17 of 24 patients with fair to poor mental status had died by 6 months, while only 5 of 26 with good mental status expired in this period. A number of studies have demonstrated the importance of prefracture physical and social function in predicting outcome following hip fracture. Jensen[18] found that mortality in 508 patients with hip fractures was related to the prefracture "social function" of patients, which measured the amount of care patients were receiving prior to their fracture. While age and social dependence before fracture were statistically related to mortality, there was no significant association between mortality and the method of treatment, the type of fracture, and placement after discharge. Ceder et al.[19] found that patients who did their own shopping and had frequent social contacts outside the home had a better outcome following hip fracture. Cobey et al.[20] followed patients who were alert and independent prior to their fracture. These authors found that physical therapists were better predictors of outcome than were nurses or physicians. The therapists found that a patient's motivation, postoperative mental clarity, balance, mental coordination, and stamina were related to independence with ambulation and activities of daily living at 6 months. In addition, there was a good correlation between outcome and the frequency of the patient getting out of the home prior to fracture. Marottoli et al.,[21] in a prospective study of patients followed prior to fracture, found that the substantial decline in physical function associated with fracture was best predicted by prefracture physical function and score on mental status testing. These studies all demonstrate that the type of fracture, type of anesthesia, and mode of fixation of the fracture are much less important than the patient's prefracture mental status and physical function in predicting both mortality and functional recovery following a hip fracture.

The site of rehabilitation of patients with hip fracture has been a source of recent concern. Fitzgerald et al.[22,23] reported on the changing patterns of hip fracture care before and after implementation of the prospective payment system (DRGs). These authors found that the percentage of patients discharged from two hospitals in Indianapolis to nursing homes following hip fractures doubled after the initiation of prospective payment. A substantial number of these patients were still in nursing homes 6 months to 1 year after their fracture. Prospective payment increased the percentage of patients permanently placed in nursing homes from 13 to 39 percent in one study and from 9 to 32 percent in the other. The frequency of transfer of patients from hospital to nursing home following hip fracture does appear to be regional. Fitzgerald found that 48 to 60 percent of patients in Indianapolis were transferred to nursing homes, while Magaziner et al.[24] reported that 39 percent of hip fracture patients admitted from home to seven Baltimore hospitals were transferred to nursing homes. Bonar et al.[25] found that the frequency of discharge to nursing home was 21 percent from the two hospitals in New Haven, Connecticut, in the period following implementation of prospective payment. The Bonar study examined those factors which predicted permanent nursing home placement for hip fracture patients sent to nursing homes for rehabilitation. Those factors were age over 80 years, disorientation, needing assistance with bathing, lack of social supports, and the number of physical therapy hours provided in the nursing home setting.

While fracture of the hip is one of the ten diagnostic categories listed under rehabilitation hospital diagnoses, these patients frequently are not eligible for rehabilitation hospital care. In the absence of coexisting neurological or musculoskeletal problems, it is often difficult to justify intense occupational therapy and the need for a multidisciplinary rehabilitative approach. In many regions, therefore, Medicare guidelines call for the rehabilitation of hip fracture patients in a skilled nursing facility. Fitzgerald's[22,23] studies raise concern about the ability of staff in many skilled nursing facilities to return patients with fractured hips to their own home environment. It is important, therefore, to ensure that nursing homes to which fractured hip patients are discharged are capable of providing intense rehabilitation and good discharge planning.

While there are few published studies on rehabilitation in the nursing home setting, there are some guidelines to follow in arranging rehabilitation in skilled nursing facilities: (1) at least 20 percent of the facility's beds should be directed to short-term rehabilitation; (2) therapists should be on the staff of the facility, not on contract; (3) there must be coordination of the nurses' and therapists' rehabilitative efforts; (4) the facility staff must have the appropriate resources, skills, and experience for comprehensive discharge planning; and (5) a physician with expertise in rehabilitation should be available to the facility on at least a weekly basis. The frequent presence of a physician with experience in rehabilitation and familiarity with the facility's nursing and rehabilitation staff can be essential to the success of rehabilitation in a skilled nursing facility. This physician can evaluate the patient at the bedside, communicate knowledgeably with the referring orthopedic surgeon, and ensure that rehabilitation proceeds at a pace which will fit the needs of each patient.

The approach to a patient with hip fracture typifies some of the difficult decisions that face the elderly patient with rehabilitative needs. The hip fracture patient's potential for returning to an independent existence depends on that patient's prior level of function and independence, mental status, balance, stamina, motivation, and capacity for responding to rehabilitation. The patient's physical therapist is the individual best suited to predict outcome. Those patients with good mental status, rapid return to ambulation in the hospital setting, and limited complications can best be managed by completion of inpatient rehabilitation in the acute care hospital and direct discharge home. Patients whose rehabilitation is complicated by fluctuating mental status, slow return of function, medical problems, or associated physical problems such as prior strokes, Parkinson's disease, and other neurological abnormalities will have the best chance of return to independence and home if placed in a specialized rehabilitation hospital or unit. Those patients who have good mental status, good motivation, and a supportive family but whose return to independence is slowed by limited weight-bearing status, frailty, and other medical or physical factors may benefit from rehabilitation in a skilled nursing facility. Close coordination between the staff of the acute care hospital and the skilled nursing facility, excellent discharge planning at the skilled nursing facility, and participation by physicians with experience in rehabilitation will enhance the nursing facility's ability to return patients with fractured hips to their own homes.

DEMENTIA

As noted in the previous chapter, dementia is the most common principal cause of severe disability and dependency on others. As discussed elsewhere (Chaps. 19 and 92), defining the degree and nature of the dementia and searching for potentially reversible causes is of first importance. But even with patients with the common, progressive dementia of Alzheimer's type, a rehabilitative philosophy and approach is very important.

Chui et al.[26] provide a succinct, practical description of the important features. Key elements include preventing or minimizing additional disability; maintaining as much intellectual, physical, and social activity as possible; and helping the caregiver in her or his role. Emphasis should be placed on avoiding unnecessary medications, in particular anticholinergic drugs, which will likely add to the confused state; providing a simple, regular daily routine in a familiar environment; and searching for correctable causes of agitation. Knowledge of the person's usual daily routines and preferences is needed to help in promoting her or his ease and well-being. Communication with demented persons can be assisted by simple, direct, nonthreatening, face-to-face contact, a nurturing approach, discussion of familiar topics, and, interestingly, encouraging demented persons to communicate with other demented persons, as in a day-care program.[27]

OSTEOARTHRITIS

The general aspects of diagnosis and treatment of this common chronic condition, which increases in prevalence with age, are discussed elsewhere (Chap. 85). From a rehabilitative perspective, the major challenge is to prevent and reverse the trends toward decreased mobility, decreased muscle mass and strength, and social isolation which characterize many persons suffering from painful osteoarthritis in their knees or hips.

Successful rehabilitative intervention requires three components: relief of pain, increasing muscular strength, and maintaining joint flexibility. In addition, in affected persons who are overweight, weight reduction is important. The pain associated with osteoarthritic joints can usually be controlled by low dose anti-inflammatory medications, often helped by the addition of acetaminophen. A recent study suggests that acetaminophen alone may be as helpful as anti-inflammatory drugs for pain relief in this disease.[28] The potential side effects of chronic use of any of these medications (see Chap. 81) must be kept in mind.

Building muscular strength is perhaps the most important and least emphasized component of rehabilitative therapy for osteoarthritis. The muscles which support the functions of an affected joint—knee or hip—when strengthened through regular muscle-building exercises, provide a splinting, protective effect for that joint, adding to the relief and avoidance of pain with use as well as restoring the needed muscular power for mobility. Appropriate use of isometric, isotonic, and isokinetic exercises is needed in a continuing, individualized program developed by a physiotherapist for use at home and/or in an exercise program. The strength and function of the unaffected side must be developed along with that of the affected area. Further details of relevant guidelines for older persons are available.[29]

If a patient with osteoarthritis still suffers from significant pain and limitation of function, joint replacement surgery should be considered. There is no specific age beyond which this is inappropriate and selected very old persons have benefited considerably. Individual factors of risks for surgery, the likelihood of success, and the patient's own informed preference must be considered.

PERIPHERAL VASCULAR DISEASE

Functional limitations and loss of independence due to peripheral vascular disease are more common in old and very old persons than is often appreciated. As noted in the previous chapter, this condition is the third leading cause of severe limitations, requiring help from someone else every day, among persons aged 85 and older. The prevention and general management of this condition are discussed elsewhere (Chap. 46 and Ref. 30).

Consultation with appropriate professionals with special expertise is essential to assure that the patient has comfortable, well-fitting shoes and that an exercise regimen has been prescribed which may extend walking capability but will not be overdone in the face of intermittent claudication. Meticulous skin care is essential, and the appearance of any ulceration requires immediate medical and nursing attention, with regular non-tissue-damaging cleansing of the area, use of antibiotics to treat any infection, and protection against further damage.

CARDIAC REHABILITATION

Symptoms due to cardiac disease, in particular those related to coronary ischemia, while not a common cause of major functional losses are nevertheless common occurrences in older persons. Following the establishment of an effective treatment regimen with medications and/or corrective surgery, it is important to arrange a carefully planned, progressive exercise rehabilitation program. Such programs are described elsewhere.[31,32] The goal is to help the patient regain as much overall functional capability as possible. Even in the first few days after successful surgical intervention and/or in the early recovery period following a myocardial infarction, a program of stepwise increases in physical activity should be initiated, with careful professional monitoring. The patient and family should be educated about the promising potential for functional gains with relative safety. Old age is no limitation to this approach.

OTHER CONDITIONS

Within the properly broad definition of geriatric rehabilitation, the improvement/restoration of function in older persons in essentially any organ system is an appropriate challenge. Efforts to improve pulmonary function in older persons with chronic obstructive pulmonary disease, while not as dramatic as in some other systems, should nevertheless be considered, in cooperation with pulmonary specialists.[33] Restorative prosthetic dental surgery as well as other maxillofacial corrections should be considered in some edentulous older persons.[34,35] Loss of vision and hearing obviously deserve full attempts at restoration and are addressed elsewhere (Chaps. 39, 40). Successful management of urinary incontinence is also addressed (Chap. 113). The improvement of sexual functioning, for problems such as dyspareunia in women and impotence in men, should be considered by appropriate specialists. Several good recent texts on geriatric rehabilitation are available.[36–38]

Other social and institutional causes of loss of freedom to make personal choices should also be seen as subject to rehabilitative approaches for older as well as younger disabled persons. The challenges of persons with lifelong developmental disabilities who are living into older ages are beginning to be addressed more directly. We see important steps toward removing barriers to full societal involvement by disabled persons in the recently passed Americans with Disabilities Act. Another landmark legislative step affecting all residents of nursing and similar facilities is the Nursing Home Reform Law of 1987 (Office of Management and Budget Reconciliation Act 1987), which requires a nursing facility to "provide services and activities to attain or maintain the highest practicable physical, mental and psychosocial well-being of each resident, in accordance with a written plan of care . . . ."

In summary, virtually any loss of personal function, with potential or actual loss of autonomy, of ability to choose, should be considered an appropriate challenge for geriatric rehabilitation.

REFERENCES

1. Daverat P et al: Death and functional outcome after spontaneous intracerebral hemorrhage. *Stroke* 22:1, 1991.
2. Miller LS, Miyamoto AT: Computed tomography: Its potential as a predictor of functional recovery following stroke. *Arch Phys Med Rehabil* 60:108, 1979.
3. Lundgren J et al: Site of brain lesion and functional capacity in rehabilitated hemiplegics. *Scand J Rehabil Med* 14:141, 1982.
4. Wade FT et al: Predicting Barthel ADL score at 6 months after an acute stroke. *Arch Phys Med Rehabil* 64:24, 1983.
5. Hertanu JS et al: Stroke rehabilitation: Correlation and prognostic value of computerized tomography and sequential functional assessments. *Arch Phys Med Rehabil* 65:505, 1984.
6. Jongbloed L: Prediction of function after stroke: A critical review. *Stroke* 17:765, 1986.
7. Fullerton KJ et al: Prognostic indices in stroke. *Q J Med* 250:174, 1988.
8. Kotila M et al: The profile of recovery from stroke and factors influencing outcome. *Stroke* 15:1039, 1984.
9. Dove HG et al: Evaluating and predicting outcome of acute cerebral vascular accident. *Stroke* 15:858, 1984.
10. Prescott RJ et al: Predicting functional outcome following acute stroke using a standard clinical examination. *Stroke* 13:641, 1982.
11. Loewen SC, Anderson BA: Predictors of stroke outcome using objective measurement studies. *Stroke* 21:78, 1990.
12. Feigenson JS: Factors influencing outcome and length of stay in a stroke rehabilitation unit. *Stroke* 8:651, 1977.
13. Kinsella G, Ford B: Acute recovery patterns in stroke patients. *Med J Aust* 2:663, 1980.
14. Reding NJ, Pottes E: Rehabilitation outcome following initial unilateral hemispheric stroke: Life table analysis approach. *Stroke* 19:1354, 1988.
15. Kauffman TL et al: Rehabilitation outcomes after hip fracture in persons 90 years old and older. *Arch Phys Med Rehab* 68:369, 1987.
16. Miller CW: Survival and ambulation following hip fracture. *J Bone Joint Surg* 60-A:930, 1978.
17. Baker BR et al: Mental state and other prognostic factors in femoral fractures of the elderly. *J R Coll Gen Pract* 28:557, 1978.
18. Jensen JS: Determining factors for the mortality following hip fracture. *Injury* 15:411, 1984.
19. Ceder L et al: Statistical prediction of rehabilitation in elderly patients with hip fractures. *Clin Orthop* 152:185, 1980.
20. Cobey JC et al: Indicators of recovery from fractures of the hip. *Clin Orthop* 117:258, 1976.
21. Marottoli RA et al: Decline in physical function following hip fracture. *J Am Geriatr Soc* 40:861, 1992.
22. Fitzgerald JF et al: The care of elderly patients with hip fracture: Changes since implementation of the prospective payment system. *N Engl J Med* 319:1392, 1988.
23. Fitzgerald JF et al: Changing patterns of hip fracture care before and after implementation of the prospective payment system. *JAMA* 258:218, 1987.
24. Magaziner J et al: Survival experience of aged hip fracture patients. *Am J Public Health* 79:274, 1989.
25. Bonar SK et al: Factors associated with short versus long-term skilled nursing facility placement among community-living hip fracture patients. *J Am Geriatr Soc* 38:1139, 1990.
26. Chui HC et al: Rehabilitation of persons with dementia, in Kemp B (ed): *Geriatric Rehabilitation.* Boston, Little, Brown, 1990.
27. Obler LK: Communication therapy and the elderly, in Frengley JD et al (eds): *Practicing Rehabilitation with Geriatric Clients.* New York, Springer-Verlag, 1990.
28. Bradley JD et al: Comparison of an antiinflammatory dose of ibuprofen, an analgesic dose of ibuprofen, and

acetaminophen in the treatment of patients with osteoarthritis of the knee. *N Engl J Med* 325:87, 1991.

29. Hicks JE: Rehabilitation of musculoskeletal disorders in the geriatric population, in Frengley JD et al (eds): *Practicing Rehabilitation with Geriatric Clients.* New York, Springer-Verlag, 1990.
30. Spittell JA Jr: Conservative management of occlusive peripheral vascular disease. *Cardiovasc Clin* 22:209, 1992.
31. Wenger NK: Specific cardiac disorders, in Williams TF (ed): *Rehabilitation in the Aging.* New York, Raven Press, 1984.
32. Wenger NK: Rehabilitation of the elderly coronary patient, in Frengley JD et al (eds): *Practicing Rehabilitation with Geriatric Clients.* New York, Springer-Verlag, 1990.
33. Ries AL: Pulmonary rehabilitation, in Kemp B et al (eds): *Geriatrics Rehabilitation.* Boston, Little, Brown, 1990.
34. Holm-Pedersen P et al (eds): *Geriatric Dentistry.* Copenhagen, Munksgaard, 1986.
35. Papas AS et al (eds): *Geriatric Dentistry: Aging and Oral Health.* St. Louis, Mosby, 1991.
36. Kemp B et al (eds): *Geriatric Rehabilitation.* Boston, Little, Brown, 1990.
37. Frengley JD et al (eds): *Practicing Rehabilitation with Geriatric Clients.* New York, Springer-Verlag, 1990.
38. Williams TF (ed): *Rehabilitation in the Aging.* New York, Raven Press, 1984.

Chapter 32

NURSING HOME CARE

Joseph G. Ouslander

Nursing homes are an integral component of a broad array of long-term care services for elderly and chronically ill, functionally disabled Americans. Other components of the long-term care system are discussed throughout this text (see Chaps. 20, 33, and 34). Despite the desire of most elderly people to remain in their own homes, and the further development of community long-term care services and innovative specialized geriatric units that can prevent or delay nursing home (NH) admission,[1,2] the need and demand for NH care is likely to increase over the next several decades.

Over 1.5 million Americans awaken every day in one of over 18,000 nursing homes.[3] While some NHs provide high-quality care, the poor quality of care in many has been repeatedly documented in the medical literature, congressional testimony, and lay press over the last two decades.[3–8] Some of the most poignant descriptions have come from the perspective of NH residents themselves.[9] Despite this widespread documentation, little has been done to improve the process, quality, and outcomes of NH care. The medical profession must accept much of the responsibility for the poor quality of care in NHs. Most physicians do not care for NH residents, and many of those who do care provide substandard care. The visits of physicians are usually brief and superficial, documentation in medical records is scanty, treatable conditions are underdiagnosed or misdiagnosed, and psychotropic drugs are overused and misused. Misuse of psychotropic drugs is also due in part to the absence of mental health interventions by appropriately trained professionals.[10,11] Only recently has interest developed in the education of physicians, nurses, and other health professionals in long-term care and in basic biomedical, clinical, and health services research focusing on NHs and NH residents.[12–18]

Despite the logistic, economic, and attitudinal barriers that can foster inadequate medical care in the NH, there are many relatively straightforward principles and strategies that can lead to improvements in the quality of medical care provided to NH residents. Fundamental to achieving these improvements is a clear perspective on the goals of NH care, which are in many respects quite different from the goals of medical care in other settings and patient populations.

The objectives of this chapter are to briefly review some demographic aspects of NH care and then to focus in particular on the clinical care of NH residents and the appropriate strategies to improve the care currently provided. While the focus of the chapter is on medical care, this by no means implies that other aspects of the care residents of NHs receive (such as nursing, psychosocial, rehabilitative) are not just as important, if not more important.

NURSING HOMES AND NURSING HOME RESIDENTS

The increasing number of people age 85 and older with functional disabilities, the potential decrease in the availability of family caregivers (due to smaller, more geographically dispersed families and an increase in the number of working women), who currently provide most noninstitutional long-term-care services and continued restrictive eligibility and reimbursement policies for community long-term-care services will all contribute to an increasing demand for NH care over the next several decades (Fig. 32-1).

Close to two-thirds of NHs have fewer than 100 beds, and most are run for profit (Table 32-1).[19] Many nonprofit, often religiously affiliated, institutions provide several different levels of care at the same site. These range from board and care through intermediate and skilled nursing care. Intermediate care facilities (ICFs) and skilled nursing facilities (SNFs) are both referred to as NHs in this chapter. In 1986, an Institute of Medicine report recommended eliminating the distinction between these two levels of care,[4] and subsequent federal regulations implemented this recommendation in 1991. A still small but increasing number of NHs are developing affiliations with medical and nursing schools.[12,14,15–18] Many are becoming "vertically integrated" with other geriatric health and social services through affiliations with acute care hospitals, health maintenance organizations, and life care communities.

Close to 90 percent of NH employees are nursing staff, predominantly nursing assistants, who provide

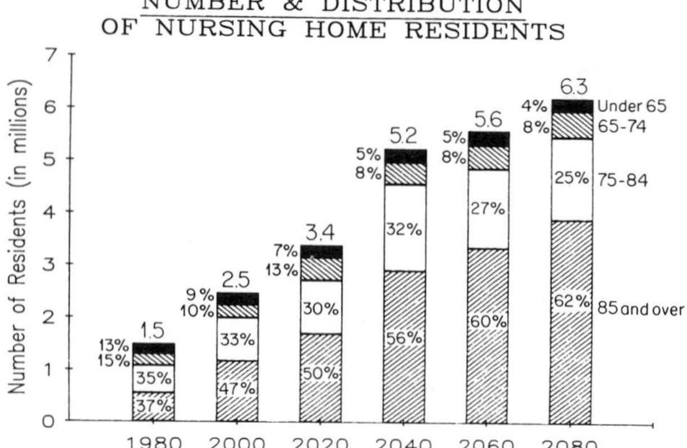

FIGURE 32-1

Demographics of the NH population. *(Reprinted with permission from Ouslander and Martin.[27])*

over 90 percent of hands-on patient care. These individuals are often unlicensed, and their educational background is limited. They frequently do not speak English. The turnover rate for these nursing assistants exceeds 50 percent per year.[20] Less than 20 percent of physicians attend patients at NHs, and those who do frequently make very brief visits.[8,21] Most NHs have only part-time social workers and part-time contract physical, occupational, and recreational therapists.

The dynamics of NH populations have been the subject of several studies.[22–26] At admission, NH residents appear equally distributed between short stayers (1 to 6 months) and long stayers (who may stay several years). At any one time, however, a cross section of NH residents reveals a much higher proportion of long stayers. While most NH discharges occur within the first 3 to 6 months after admission, studies of NH admissions have revealed that only 28 percent of the residents were discharged to their own homes and 33 percent were discharged dead. Moreover, 75 percent had died within 2 years.[23,24] Whichever subpopulation is examined, the typical NH resident is an elderly, white, widowed, functionally disabled woman. Close to two-thirds of NH residents are women. One-third are 85 or older, one-half have significant degrees of dementia, frequently with associated behavioral disorders, and one-half are incontinent. The majority are nonambulatory and require help in most basic activities of daily living.[19]

For the purpose of discussing clinical care in the NH, it is helpful to subdivide NH residents as depicted in Fig. 32-2.[27] The two basic types of NH residents, short stayers and long stayers, can be further subdivided. Short stayers include (1) patients recovering from medical and functional problems after an acute illness who have a reasonable expectation of discharge to a lower level of care (e.g., patients recovering from hip fracture, stroke, pneumonia, or decompensated congestive heart failure with prolonged bed rest) and (2) patients who have end-stage or terminal disease (e.g., cancer, severe brain injury, chronic lung disease, or heart failure) and are expected to die in days to weeks. Long stayers comprise patients with chronic disabilities involving impaired cognitive function (e.g., dementia) or impaired physical function (e.g., stroke, arthritis, multiple sclerosis), or both. The approaches to assessment, the goals for care, and the treatment process differ substantially among these different types of NH residents. The relative proportion of residents of each type can have important programmatic and financial implications for individual NHs as well as for NH chains.

TABLE 32-1

Selected Characteristics of Nursing Homes (1985 Data)

Facility Characteristics	NHs: Number	NHs: Distribution, %	NH Beds Distribution, %
Total	19,000	100	100
Ownership			
Proprietary	14,300	75	69
Voluntary nonprofit	3,800	20	23
Government	1,000	5	8
Certification			
Certified (total)	14,400	76	89
SNF* only	3,500	18	19
SNF/ICF†	5,700	30	45
ICF only	5,300	28	25
Not certified	4,700	24	11
Bed size‡			
<50 beds	6,300	33	9
50–99 beds	6,200	33	27
100–199 beds	5,400	28	43
≥200 beds	1,200	6	20

*SNF: Skilled nursing facility.
†ICF: Intermediate care facility
‡Average bed size is 85 beds.
SOURCE: Adapted from Kane and Kane RI.[19]

THE GOALS OF NURSING HOME CARE

Fundamental to improving the care of NH residents is a clear conception of the goals of care. The key goals of NH care are listed in Table 32-2.[28] While the prevention, identification, and treatment of chronic, subacute, and acute medical conditions are important, most of these goals focus on the functional independence, autonomy, quality of life, comfort, and

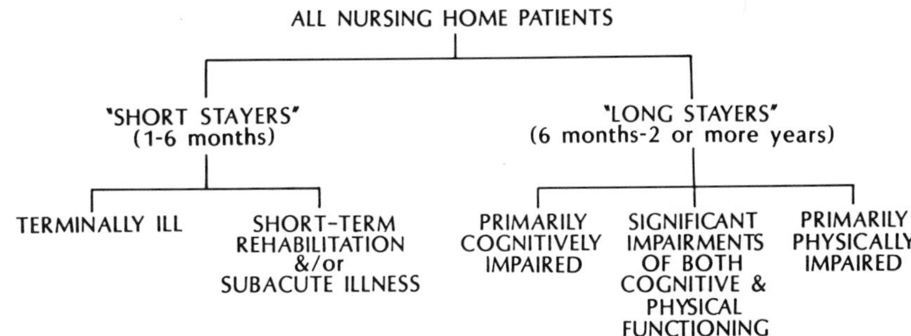

FIGURE 32-2
Basic types of NH patients. *(Reprinted with permission from Ouslander and Martin.[27])*

dignity of the residents. Physicians who care for NH residents must keep these goals in perspective while at the same time addressing the more traditional goals of medical care.

The heterogeneity of the NH population must also be recognized in order to focus and individualize the goals of care. Nursing home residents can be subgrouped into five basic types, as depicted in Fig. 32-2. The focus and goals of care for these five subgroups of NH residents are obviously very different.

Many NHs attempt to isolate these different types of residents geographically. This strategy has several advantages, including the specialized training of staff to care for residents with specific types of problems (e.g., rehabilitation, terminal illness) and the separation of residents with severe dementia and behavioral disturbances from cognitively intact residents. The latter often find interactions with severely demented residents very distressing.

Although it is not always possible to isolate these different types of residents geographically and residents often overlap or change between the types described, subgrouping NH residents in this manner can help the physician and interdisciplinary team focus the care-planning process on the most critical and realistic goals for individual residents.

TABLE 32-2

Key Goals of Nursing Home Care

- Provide a safe and supportive environment for chronically ill and dependent people
- Restore and maintain the highest possible level of functional independence
- Preserve individual autonomy
- Maximize quality of life, perceived well-being, and life satisfaction
- Provide comfort and dignity for terminally ill patients and their loved ones
- Stabilize and delay progression, whenever possible, of chronic medical conditions
- Prevent acute medical and iatrogenic illnesses and identify and treat them rapidly when they do occur

SOURCE: From Ouslander et al,[31] with permission.

CLINICAL ASPECTS OF CARE FOR NURSING HOME RESIDENTS

In addition to the different goals for care in the NH, several factors make the assessment and treatment of NH residents different from that in other settings (Table 32-3). Many of these factors relate to the process of care and are discussed in the following section. A fundamental difference in the NH is that medical evaluation and treatment must be complemented by an assessment and care-planning process involving staff from multiple disciplines. Data on medical conditions and their treatment are integrated with assessments of the functional, mental, and behavioral status of the resident in order to develop a comprehensive data base and individualized plan of care. The Minimum Data Set (MDS), mandated by the Omnibus Reconciliation Act (OBRA) legislation implemented in 1991, is now the basis for this comprehensive assessment (see the section below on the OBRA).

Medical evaluation and clinical decision making for NH residents is complicated for several reasons. Unless the physician has cared for a resident before NH admission, it may be difficult to obtain a comprehensive medical data base. Residents may be unable to accurately relate their medical history or describe their symptoms, and medical records are frequently unavailable or incomplete—especially for residents who have been transferred between NHs and acute care hospitals. When acute changes in status occur, initial assessments are often performed by NH staff with limited skills and are transmitted to physicians by telephone. Even when the diagnoses are known or strongly suspected, many diagnostic and therapeutic procedures have an unacceptably high risk/benefit ratio among NH residents. For example, a barium enema may cause dehydration or severe fecal impaction; nitrates and other cardiovascular drugs may precipitate syncope or disabling falls in frail ambulatory residents with baseline postural hypotension; and adequate control of blood sugar may be extremely difficult to achieve without a high risk for hypoglycemia among diabetic residents with marginal or fluctuating nutritional intake who may not recognize or complain of hypoglycemic symptoms.

TABLE 32-3

Factors That Make Assessment and Treatment in the Nursing Home Different from Those in Other Settings

The goals of care are often different (see Table 32-2).
Specific clinical disorders are prevalent among NH residents (see Table 32-4).
The approach to health maintenance and prevention differs (see Table 32-6).
Mental and functional status are just as important as, if not more important than, medical status.
Assessment must be interdisciplinary, including
- Nursing
- Psychosocial
- Rehabilitation
- Nutritional
- Other (e.g., dental, pharmacy, podiatry, audiology, ophthalmology)

Sources of information are variable:
- Patients often cannot give a precise history.
- Family members and nurse's aides with limited assessment skills may provide the most important information.
- Information is often obtained over the telephone.

Administrative procedures for record keeping in both NHs and acute care hospitals can result in inadequate and disjointed information.
Clinical decision making is complicated for several reasons:
- Many diagnostic and therapeutic procedures are expensive, unavailable, or difficult to obtain and involve higher risks of iatrogenic illness and discomfort than are warranted by the potential outcome.
- The potential long-term benefits of "tight" control of certain chronic illnesses (e.g., diabetes mellitus, congestive heart failure, hypertension) may be outweighed by the risks of iatrogenic illnesses in many very old and functionally disabled residents.
- Many residents are not capable (or questionably capable) of participating in medical decision making, and their personal preferences based on previous decisions are often unknown (see Table 32-8).

The appropriate site for treatment and the level of intensity of such treatment are often difficult decisions that involve medical, emotional, ethical, and legal considerations that may be in conflict with each other in the NH setting.
Logistic considerations, resource constraints, and restrictive reimbursement policies may limit the ability of and incentives for physicians to carry out optimal medical care of NH residents.

SOURCE: From Kane et al,[28] with permission.

Further compounding these difficulties is the inability of many NH residents to effectively participate in important decisions regarding their medical care. Their prior expressed wishes are often not known, and an appropriate or legal surrogate decision maker has often not been appointed. Several strategies described later in this chapter may help to overcome many of these difficulties.

Table 32-4 lists the most commonly encountered clinical disorders in the NH population. They represent a broad spectrum of chronic medical illnesses; neurologic, psychiatric, and behavioral disorders; and problems which are especially prevalent in the frail elderly—such as incontinence, falls, nutritional disorders, and chronic pain syndromes. Although the

TABLE 32-4

Common Clinical Disorders in the Nursing Home Population

- Medical conditions
  - Chronic medical illnesses
  - Congestive heart failure
  - Degenerative joint disease
  - Diabetes mellitus
  - Obstructive lung disease
  - Renal failure
  - Infections
    - Lower respiratory tract
    - Urinary tract
    - Skin (pressure sores, vascular ulcers)
    - Conjunctivitis
    - Gastroenteritis
    - Tuberculosis
  - Gastrointestinal disorders
    - Ulcers
    - Reflux esophagitis
    - Constipation
    - Diarrhea
  - Malignancies
- Neuropsychiatric conditions
  - Dementia
  - Behavioral disorders associated with dementia
    - Wandering
    - Agitation
    - Aggression
  - Depression
  - Neurologic disorders other than dementia
    - Stroke
    - Parkinsonism
    - Multiple sclerosis
    - Brain or spinal cord injury
- Functional disabilities requiring rehabilitation
  - Stroke
  - Hip fracture
  - Joint replacement
  - Amputation
- Geriatric problems
  - Delirium
  - Incontinence
  - Gait disturbances, instability, falls
  - Malnutrition, feeding difficulties, dehydration
  - Pressure sores
  - Insomnia
  - Chronic pain: musculoskeletal conditions, neuropathies, malignancy
  - Iatrogenic disorders
    - Adverse drug reactions
    - Falls
    - Nosocomial infections
    - Induced disabilities—restraints and immobility, catheters, unnecessary help with basic activities of daily living
  - Death and dying

SOURCE: From Kane et al,[28] with permission.

incidence of iatrogenic illnesses has not been systematically studied in NHs, it is likely to be as high as if not higher than in acute hospitals. The management of many of the conditions listed in Table 32-4 is discussed in some detail in other chapters of this text (see Contents and Index regarding specific conditions). Clinicians caring for NH residents should be especially well versed in the unique medical aspects of managing these conditions in the frail dependent elderly patient.

In addition to the numerous factors already mentioned that make the medical assessment and treatment of these conditions different, the process of care in NHs also differs substantially from that in acute hospitals, clinics, and home care settings.

PROCESS OF CARE IN THE NURSING HOME

The process of care in NHs is strongly influenced by numerous state and federal regulations, the highly interdisciplinary nature of NH residents' problems, and the training and skills of the staff that delivers most of the hands-on care. New federal regulations for nursing home care are discussed in a subsequent section of this chapter.

The involvement of the physician in NH care and the nature of the medical assessment and treatment offered to NH residents are often limited by logistical and economic factors. Few physicians have offices based either inside the NH or in close proximity to the facility. Many physicians who do visit NHs care for relatively small numbers of residents, often in several different facilities. Most NHs therefore have numerous physicians who make rounds once or twice per month. Although these physicians are not generally present to evaluate acute changes in the status of a resident, they nevertheless often attempt to assess these changes over the telephone. Many NHs do not have the ready availability of laboratory, radiologic, and pharmaceutical services with the capability of rapid response, which further compounds the logistics of evaluating and treating acute changes in medical status. Thus, NH residents are often sent to hospital emergency rooms where they are evaluated by personnel who are generally not familiar with their baseline status and who frequently lack training and interest in the care of frail and dependent elderly patients.

Restrictive Medicare and Medicaid reimbursement policies may also dictate certain patterns of NH care. While physicians are required to visit NH residents only every 30 to 60 days, many residents require more frequent assessment and monitoring of treatment, especially those patients who have the shorter acute hospital stays brought about by the prospective payment system (diagnosis-related groups). Yet, Medicare will generally only reimburse a physician for one routine visit per month, and perhaps for one additional visit for an acute problem. Reimbursement for the routine visit is hardly adequate for the time that is required to provide good medical care in the NH, including travel to and from the facility, assessment and treatment planning for residents with multiple problems, communication with members of the interdisciplinary team and the resident's family, and proper documentation in the medical record. Activities which are often essential to good care in the NH, such as attendance at interdisciplinary conferences, family meetings, complex assessments of decision-making capacity, and counseling residents and surrogate decision makers on treatment plans in the event of terminal illness, are generally not reimbursable at all. Medicare intermediaries have often restricted reimbursement for rehabilitative services in a variable and inequitable manner, thus limiting the treatment options for many residents.[29] Although Medicaid programs vary considerably, most provide minimal coverage for ancillary services that are critical for optimum medical care, and many restrict reimbursement for several types of drugs which may be especially helpful for NH residents.

Amidst these logistic and economic constraints, expectations for the care of NH residents are high. Table 32-5 outlines the various types of assessments that are generally recommended for the optimal care of NH residents. Physicians are responsible for completing an initial assessment within 48 to 72 hours of admission and for monthly or bimonthly visits thereafter. Licensed nurses assess new residents as soon as they are admitted and on a daily basis, and generally summarize the status of each resident weekly. The extent of involvement of other disciplines in the assessment and care-planning process varies depending on the residents' problems, the availability of various professionals, and state and federal regulations. Federal regulations now mandate that several key sections of the MDS be updated quarterly and that the entire MDS be reviewed whenever there is a major change in clinical status.

Representatives from nursing, social service, dietary, recreational, and rehabilitation (physical and/or occupational) departments should participate in interdisciplinary care-planning meetings. Residents are generally discussed at this meeting within 2 weeks of admission and quarterly thereafter. The product of these meetings is an interdisciplinary care plan, which separately lists interdisciplinary problems (such as restricted mobility, incontinence, wandering, diminished food intake, poor social interaction, etc.), goals for the resident related to the problem, approaches to achieving these goals, target dates for achieving the goals, and assignment of responsibilities for working toward the goals among the various disciplines. The interdisciplinary care-planning process serves as a cornerstone for resident management in many facilities, but it is a difficult and time-consuming process which requires leadership and tremendous interdisciplinary (and interpersonal) cooperation.[30] Staffing limitations in relation to the amount of time and ef-

TABLE 32-5

Important Aspects of Various Types of Assessments in the Nursing Home*

Types of Assessments	Timing	Major Objectives	Important Aspects
Medical			
Initial	Within 48 hours of admission	Verify medical diagnoses Document baseline physical findings, mental and functional status, vital signs, and skin condition Attempt to identify potentially remediable, previously unrecognized medical conditions Get to know the resident and family (if this is a new resident) Establish goals for the admission and a medical treatment plan	Physical examination and a thorough review of medical records are necessary. Relevant medical diagnoses and baseline findings should be clearly and concisely documented in the patient's record. Medication lists should be carefully reviewed and only essential medications continued. Requests for specific types of assessments and inputs from other disciplines should be made. An initial medical problem list should be established.
Periodic	Usually monthly	Monitor progress of active medical conditions Update medical orders Communicate with patient and NH staff	Progress notes should include clinical data relevant to active medical conditions and focus on changes in status. Unnecessary medications, orders for care, and laboratory tests should be discontinued. Mental, functional, and psychosocial status should be reviewed with NH staff, and changes from baseline noted. The medical problem list should be updated.
As needed	When acute changes in status occur	Identify and treat causes of acute changes	On-site clinical assessment by the physician (or nurse practitioner or physicians' assistant), as opposed to telephone consultation, will result in more accurate diagnoses, more appropriate treatment, and fewer unnecessary emergency room visits and hospitalization. Vital signs, food and fluid intake, and mental status often provide essential information. Infection, dehydration, and adverse drug effects should be at the top of the differential diagnosis for acute changes in status.

*Federal rules now mandate the use of the MDS as a component of the assessment of NH residents (see text).
†See Table 32-8; these issues are also discussed in more detail in Chap. 36.
SOURCE: From Ouslander Osterweil et al,[31] with permission.

TABLE 32-5 (continued)

Types of Assessments	Timing	Major Objectives	Important Aspects
Major reassessment	Annual	Identify and document any significant changes in status and new potentially remediable conditions	Targeted physical examination and assessment of mental, functional, and psychosocial status and selected laboratory tests should be done (see Table 32-7).
Nursing	Within hours of admission, and then routinely with monitoring of daily and weekly progress	Identify biopsychosocial and functional status strengths and weaknesses Develop an individualized care plan Document baseline data for ongoing assessments	Particular attention should be given to emotional state, personal preferences, and sensory function. Careful observation during the first few days of admission is important to detect effects of relocation. Potential problems related to other disciplines should be recorded and communicated to appropriate members of the interdisciplinary care team.
Psychosocial	Within 1–2 weeks of admission and as needed thereafter	Identify any potentially serious psychological signs or symptoms and refer to mental health professional, if appropriate Determine past social history, family relationships, and social resources Become familiar with personal preferences regarding living arrangement	Getting to know family members and their preferences and concerns are critical to good NH care. Relevant psychosocial data should be communicated to the interdisciplinary team.
Rehabilitation (physical and occupational therapy)	Within days of admission and daily or weekly thereafter (depending on the rehabilitation program)	Determine functional status as it relates to basic activities of daily living Identify specific goals and time frame for improving specific areas of function Monitor progress toward goals Assess progress in relation to potential for discharge	Small gains in functional status can improve chances for discharges as well as quality of life. Not all residents have areas in which they can reasonably be expected to improve; strategies to maintain function should be developed for these residents. Assessment of and recommendations for modifying the environment can be critically important for improving function and discharge planning.
Nutritional	Within days of admission and then periodically thereafter	Determine nutritional status and needs Identify dietary preferences Plan an appropriate diet	Restrictive diets may not be medically necessary, and can be unappetizing. Weight loss should be identified and reported to nursing and medical staff.

TABLE 32-5 (continued)

Types of Assessments	Timing	Major Objectives	Important Aspects
Interdisciplinary care plan	Within 1–2 weeks of admission and every 3–4 months thereafter	Identify interdisciplinary problems Establish goals and treatment plans Determine when maximum progress toward goals has been reached	Each discipline should prepare specific plans for communication to other team members based on their own assessment.
Capacity for medical decision making†	Within days of admission and then whenever changes in status occur	Determine which types of medical decisions the resident is capable of participating in If resident still is capable, encourage him or her to identify a surrogate decision maker in the event he or she becomes incapable of participation in medical decision making If the resident lacks capacity for many or all decisions, identify appropriate surrogate decision makers (if not already done)	Residents with varying degrees of dementia may still be capable of participating in many decisions regarding their medical care. Attention should be given to potentially reversible factors that can interfere with decision-making capacity (e.g., depression, fear, delirium, metabolic, and drug effects). Family and health professional concerns should be considered, but the resident's desires should be paramount. The resident's capacity may fluctuate over time because of physical and emotional conditions.
Preferences regarding treatment intensity† and NH routines	Within days of admission and periodically thereafter	Determine resident's wishes as to the intensity of treatment he or she would want in the event of acute or chronic progressive illness	Specificity is important (i.e., "No heroic measures" is ambiguous). An attempt to identify the specific procedures the resident would or would not want should be made. This assessment is often made by ascertaining the resident's prior expressed wishes (if known), or through surrogate decision makers (legal guardian, durable power of attorney for health care, family).

fort required make intensive interdisciplinary care planning and teamwork unrealistic in many nursing homes. Although physicians are usually not directly involved in the care-planning meetings in most facilities, they are generally required to review the care plan and may find the team's perspective very valuable in planning subsequent medical care.

STRATEGIES TO IMPROVE MEDICAL CARE IN NURSING HOMES

Several strategies might improve the process of medical care delivered to NH residents. Detailed descriptions of these strategies, as well as the management of common clinical conditions in the NH, can be found in a recently published textbook.[31] Three such strategies will be described briefly: the use of a comprehensive face sheet and documentation standards, the use of nurse practitioners or physicians' assistants, and a systematic approach to screening, health maintenance, and preventive practices for the elderly dependent NH population. In addition to these strategies, the strong leadership of a medical director who is appropriately trained and dedicated to improving the facility's quality of medical care is essential in order to develop, implement, and monitor policies and procedures for medical services. The role of the medical director in the NH is discussed in detail elsewhere.[31,32] He or she should set standards for medical care and serve as an example to the medical staff by caring for some of the residents in the facility. The medical director should also be involved in various committees (representing the pharmacy, infection control, quality assurance) and should involve interested medical staff in these committees as well as educational efforts through formal in-service presentations, teaching rounds, and appropriate documentation procedures.

One of the fundamental problems with the medical care delivered to NH residents is in fact documentation. As already mentioned, NH residents often have multiple coexisting medical problems and long past medical histories. Residents often cannot relate their medical history, and their previous medical records are frequently unavailable or incomplete. Thus, it is difficult, and sometimes impossible, to obtain a comprehensive medical data base. The effort should, however, be invested and not wasted. Critical aspects of the medical data base should be recorded on one page or a face sheet of the medical record. An example of a format for a face sheet is shown in Fig. 32-3. The face sheet should also contain some information on the resident's neuropsychiatric and usual mental status, social information such as individuals to contact at critical times, and information about the resident's treatment status in the event of acute illness. These are data essential to the care of the resident and should be readily available in one place in the record so that when emergencies arise, when medical consultants see the resident, or when members of the interdisciplinary team need an overall perspective, they are easy to locate. The face sheet should be copied and sent to the hospital or other health care facilities to which the resident might be transferred. Time and effort will be required in order to keep the face sheet updated. For facilities with access to computers and/or word processing, incorporating the face sheet into a data base should be relatively easy and will facilitate its rapid completion and periodic updating.

Medical documentation in progress notes for routine visits and assessments of acute changes is frequently scanty and/or illegible. "Stable" or "No change" are sometimes the only documentation for routine visits. Even though time constraints may preclude extensive notes, certain standard information should be documented. The SOAP (subjective, objective, assessment, plan) format for charting routine notes is especially appropriate for NH residents (Table 32-6). In facilities in which microcomputers are available, simple data bases with word-processing capabilities can be used to enable physicians to efficiently produce legible, concise, yet comprehensive, progress notes.

Another area in which medical documentation is often inadequate relates to the residents' decision-making capacity and treatment preferences. These issues are discussed briefly at the end of this chapter as well as in Chap. 6. In addition to placing critical information on the face sheet and other areas (e.g., identifying residents on "No CPR Status" on the front and/or spine of the medical record), physicians must thoroughly and legibly document all discussions they have had with the resident, family, legal guardians, and/or durable power of attorney for health care about these issues. Failure to do so may result not only in poor communication and inappropriate treatment, but in substantial legal liability. Notes about these issues should not be thinned from the medical record and are probably best kept on a separate page behind the face sheet.

TABLE 32-6

SOAP Format for Medical Progress Notes on NH Residents

Subjective	New complaints
	Symptoms related to active medical conditions
	Reports from nursing staff
	Progress in rehabilitative therapy
	Reports of other interdisciplinary team members
Objective	General appearance
	Weight
	Vital signs
	Physical findings relevant to new complaints and active medical conditions
	Laboratory data
	Consultant reports
Assessment	Presumptive diagnosis(es) for new complaints or changes in status
	Stability of active medical conditions
Plans	Changes in medications or diet
	Nursing interventions (e.g., monitoring or vital signs, skin care, etc.)
	Assessments by other disciplines
	Consultants
	Laboratory studies
	Discharge planning (if relevant)

SOURCE: From Ouslander et al,[31] with permission.

A second approach to improving medical care in NHs is the development and implementation of selected screening, health maintenance, and preventive practices. Table 32-7 lists examples of such practices. With few exceptions, the efficacy of these practices has not been well studied in the NH setting. In addition, not all the practices listed in Table 32-7 are relevant for every NH resident. For example, some of the annual screening examinations are not appropriate for short stayers, or for many long-staying residents with end-stage dementia (Fig. 32-2). Thus, the practices outlined in Table 32-7 must be tailored to the specific NH population as well as to the individual resident and must be creatively incorporated into routine care procedures as much as possible in order to be time-efficient, cost-effective, and reimbursable by Medicare.

All long-staying residents should have some type of comprehensive, multidisciplinary reevaluation yearly. The efficacy of a routine standard annual history and physical examination and large panels of laboratory tests has been questioned.[33–37] A targeted physical examination and functional assessment and selected laboratory tests are probably beneficial.[37]

JEWISH HOME FOR THE AGING
MEDICAL FACE SHEET

ACTIVE MEDICAL PROBLEMS

1. ____________________
2. ____________________
3. ____________________
4. ____________________
5. ____________________
6. ____________________
7. ____________________
8. ____________________

NEUROPSYCHIATRIC STATUS

A. Dementia ___Absent ___Present
If present:

___Alzheimer's ___Mixed
___Multi-infarct ___Uncertain/other

B. Psychiatric/behavioral disorders
1. ____________________
2. ____________________

C. Usual mental status
___Alert, oriented, follows simple instructions
___Alert, *disoriented*, but *can* follow simple directions
___Alert, *disoriented*, *cannot* follow simple directions
___Not alert (lethargic, comatose)

D. Most recent Mini Mental State Score
___/30 (Date ______/______/ _____)

PAST HISTORY

A. Acute hospitalizations since admission to JHA

	Diagnoses	Month/Year
1.		___/ ___
2.		___/ ___
3.		___/ ___
4.		___/ ___

B. Major surgical procedures *before* admission to JHA

	Procedure	Year
1.		
2.		
3.		
4.		

C. Allergies
1. ____________________
2. ____________________

FUNCTIONAL STATUS

A. Ambulation
___Unassisted
___With cane
___With walker
___Unable
Transfer: ____Ind ___Dep

B. Continence

	Cont	Inc
Urine	___	___
Stool	___	___

C. Basic ADL

	Ind	Dep
Bathing	___	___
Dressing	___	___
Grooming	___	___
Feeding	___	___

D. Vision
___Adequate for regular print
___Impaired-can see large print
___Highly impaired-but can get around
___Severely impaired-has difficulty getting around

E. Hearing
___Adequate
___Minimal difficulty
___Hears only w/amplifier
Highly impaired-no useful hearing

TREATMENT STATUS (See Treatment Staus Sheet Note Date _____/______/_____)

___Full code ___DNR ___DNR, do not hospitalize ___No tube feeding

This form completed by ______________________________ Date ___/___/ ___

- -

Resident's Name ______ Bldg. ______ Room Number ______ JHA Record No. ______

FIGURE 32-3
Example of a face sheet for NH medical record. The treatment status sheet is used to document all discussions about intensity of care (e.g., no CPR, etc.).

TABLE 32-7

Screening, Health Maintenance, and Preventive Practices in the Nursing Home

Practice	Minimum Recommended Frequency*	Comments
Screening		
History and physical examination	Yearly	Generally required, but yield of routine annual history and physical is debated. Focused exam probably beneficial, including rectal, breast, and in some women pelvic exam.
Weight	Monthly	Generally required. Persistent weight loss should prompt a search for treatable medical, psychiatric, and functional conditions.
Functional status assessment, including gait and mental status testing	Yearly	Functional status usually assessed periodically by nursing staff. Systematic global functional assessment should be done at least yearly in order to detect potentially treatable conditions or prevent complications such as early dementia, gait disturbances, urinary incontinence.
Visual screening	Yearly	Assess acuity, intraocular pressure; identify correctable problems.
Auditory	Yearly	Identify correctable problems.
Dental	Yearly	Assess status of any remaining teeth, fit of dentures; identify any abnormality.
Podiatry	Yearly	More frequently in diabetics and residents with peripheral vascular disease. Identify correctable problems and ensure appropriateness of shoes.
Tuberculosis	On admission and yearly	Test all residents and staff. Control skin tests and booster testing are generally recommended for NH residents (see text).
Laboratory tests Stool for occult blood Complete blood count Fasting glucose Electrolytes Renal function Albumin, calcium, phosphorus Thyroid function [including thyroid-stimulating hormone (TSH) level]	Yearly	These tests appear to have reasonable yield in the NH population (see Ref. 37).

*Frequency may vary depending on resident's condition.
†See Yoshikowa and Norman[46] for detailed recommendations.
SOURCE: From Ouslander et al,[31] with permission.

TABLE 32-7 (continued)

Practice	Minimum Recommended Frequency*	Comments
Monitoring in selected residents		
All residents	Monthly	More often if unstable or subacutely ill.
Vital signs, including weight		
Diabetic residents	Must be individualized	Fingerstick tests may also be useful if staff can perform reliably.
Fasting and postprandial glucose, glycosylated hemoglobin		
Residents on diuretics or with renal insufficiency (residents with creatinine level >2, or BUN > 35)	Every 2–3 months	NH residents are more prone to dehydration, azotemia, hyponatremia, and hypokalemia.
Electrolytes, BUN, creatinine		
Anemic residents who are on iron replacement or who have hemoglobin lower than 10	Monthly until stable, then every 2–3 months	Iron replacement should be discontinued once hemoglobin value stabilizes.
Hemoglobin-hematocrit		
Residents on specific drugs (e.g., digoxin, phenytoin, quinidine, procainamide, theophylline, nortriptyline)	Every 3–6 months	More frequently if drug treatment has just been initiated.
Blood level of drug		
Prevention		
Influenza		
Vaccine	Yearly	All residents and staff with close resident contact should be vaccinated.
Amantadine	Within 24–48 hours of outbreak of suspected influenza type A	Dose should be reduced to 100 mg/day in elderly; further reduction if renal failure present. Unvaccinated residents and staff should be treated throughout outbreak; those vaccinated can be treated until their symptoms resolve.
Pneumococcal pneumonia bacteremia		
Pneumococcal vaccine	Once	Efficacy in NH residents is debated.
Tetanus		
Booster	Every 10 years; every 5 years with tetanus-prone wounds	Many elderly people have not received primary vaccinations; they require tetanus toxoid, 250–500 U of tetanus immunoglobulin, and completion of the immunization series with toxoid injection 4–6 weeks later and then 6–12 months after the second injection.

TABLE 32-7 (continued)

Practice	Minimum Recommended Frequency*	Comments
Tuberculosis		
Isoniazid 300 mg/day for 1 year	Skin test conversion in selected residents	Residents with abnormal chest x-ray film (more than granuloma), diabetes, end-stage renal disease, hematologic malignancies, steroid or immunosuppressive therapy, malnutrition should be treated.
Other Infections		
Antimicrobial prophylaxis for residents at risk†	Generally recommended for dental procedures, genitourinary procedures, and most operative procedures	Chronically catheterized residents should not be treated with continuous prophylaxis (see Chap. 113).
Immobility		
Body positioning and range of motion for immobile residents	Ongoing	Frequent turning of very immobile residents is necessary to prevent pressure sores. Semiupright position is necessary for residents with swallowing disorders or enteral feeding to help prevent aspiration. Range of motion to immobile limbs and joints is necessary to prevent contractures.
Infection control procedures and surveillance	Ongoing	Policies and protocols should be in effect in all NHs. Surveillance of all infections should be continuous to identify outbreaks and resistance patterns.
Environmental safety	Ongoing	Appropriate lighting and colors, and the removal of hazards for falling, are essential in order to prevent accidents. Routine monitoring of potential safety hazards and accidents may lead to alterations which may prevent further accidents.

Because reactivated tuberculosis is relatively common among chronically ill elderly patients, all NH residents should have a skin test (with controls) on admission and yearly (unless they have a known prior positive test).[38] Testing for the "booster phenomenon" has been recommended 10 to 14 days after an initial negative test, because there is some incidence (probably in the range of 5 to 15 percent) of conversion to a positive response during this time period which could be falsely interpreted as conversion upon subsequent annual testing. Many NH residents are anergic, which can create difficulty in detecting active cases. Details about recommendations for tuberculosis screening in NHs can be found elsewhere.[38–41]

Because most NH residents have chronic medical conditions which are being actively treated, monitoring of these conditions and their treatment becomes an important aspect of medical care. Several examples of such monitoring are presented in Table 32-7. It is extremely important to assess vital signs and weight accurately on a routine basis, so that when acute or subacute changes occur, they can be compared with the resident's baseline.

Despite the old age and prevalence of chronic

medical conditions and functional disabilities among the NH population, several preventive health practices may be effective. Most of these are related to infectious diseases (Table 32-7). One important exception relates to body positioning and range of motion for immobile residents, with the hope of preventing pressure sores, contractures, and aspiration pneumonia. The efficacy of exercise in improving or preserving functional status among frail NH residents is currently under investigation. In addition to preventive practices for NH residents, prevention is also relevant for the entire NH staff. All NH staff who have close contact with residents should be vaccinated against influenza annually.[42] The NH staff must also be intensively educated about infection control procedures such as hand washing, wound care, and catheter care.[43–46]

The facility should have sound policies and procedures for infection control and should monitor patterns of infection and antimicrobial susceptibility carefully. Because of the prevalent and often inappropriate use of antimicrobials, resistant organisms and *Clostridia difficile* diarrhea have become important problems in NHs.[47] Another example of facility-wide prevention relates to environmental safety. Recommendations for assessing and altering the home environment in order to prevent falls are also relevant to NHs. Facilities should monitor falls and other accidents and make routine "environmental rounds" in order to identify potential hazards.

The third strategy that may help improve medical care in NHs is the use of nurse practitioners and physicians' assistants. Although the cost effectiveness of this approach has not been well documented, these health professionals may be especially helpful in carrying out specific functions in the NH setting. Although there is substantial overlap in training and skills, nurse practitioners may have a helpful perspective in interacting with nursing staff about the nonmedical aspects of NH resident care. On the other hand, physicians' assistants may be especially helpful in facilities where there is a high concentration of subacutely ill patients who require frequent medical assessment and intervention. Both can be very helpful in implementing some of the screening, monitoring, and preventive practices outlined in Table 32-7 and in communicating with interdisciplinary staff, families, and residents at times when the physician is not in the facility. One of the most appropriate roles for nurse practitioners and physicians' assistants is in the initial assessment of acute or subacute changes in the status of the resident. They can perform a focused history and physical examination and can order appropriate diagnostic studies. Several algorithms have been developed for this purpose,[48] one of which is shown in Fig. 32-4. This strategy enables the on-site assessment of acute change, the detection and treatment of new problems early in their course, more appropriate utilization of acute care hospital emergency rooms, and the rapid identification of residents who need to be hospitalized.

THE NURSING HOME–ACUTE CARE HOSPITAL INTERFACE

NH residents are frequently transferred back and forth between the NH and one or more acute care

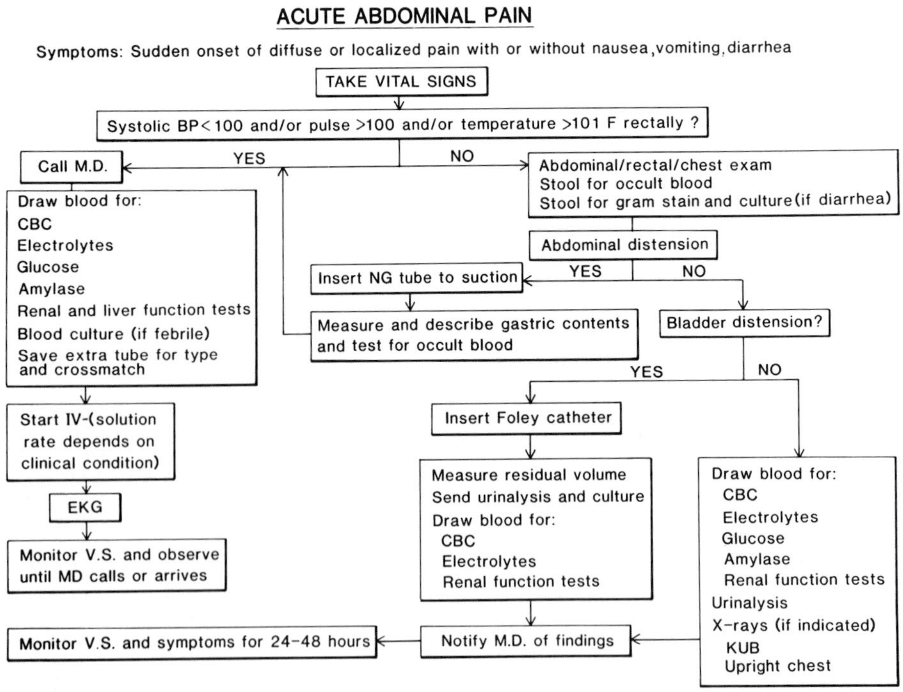

ACUTE ABDOMINAL PAIN

Symptoms: Sudden onset of diffuse or localized pain with or without nausea, vomiting, diarrhea

TAKE VITAL SIGNS

Systolic BP < 100 and/or pulse > 100 and/or temperature > 101 F rectally ?

YES → Call M.D.

Draw blood for:
CBC
Electrolytes
Glucose
Amylase
Renal and liver function tests
Blood culture (if febrile)
Save extra tube for type and crossmatch

Start IV-(solution rate depends on clinical condition)

EKG

Monitor V.S. and observe until MD calls or arrives

NO → Abdominal/rectal/chest exam
Stool for occult blood
Stool for gram stain and culture (if diarrhea)

Abdominal distension

YES → Insert NG tube to suction

Measure and describe gastric contents and test for occult blood

NO → Bladder distension?

YES → Insert Foley catheter

Measure residual volume
Send urinalysis and culture
Draw blood for:
CBC
Electrolytes
Renal function tests

NO → Draw blood for:
CBC
Electrolytes
Glucose
Amylase
Renal function tests
Urinalysis
X-rays (if indicated)
KUB
Upright chest

Notify M.D. of findings

Monitor V.S. and symptoms for 24–48 hours

FIGURE 32-4
Example of an algorithm protocol for the management of acute abdominal pain in the NH by a nurse practitioner or physician's assistant. *(Reprinted with permission from Ouslander et al.[31])*

hospitals. The major reasons for transfer include infection and the need for parenteral antimicrobials and hydration, as well as certain acute cardiovascular conditions and hip fractures. Transfer to an acute care hospital is often a very disruptive process for a chronically ill NH resident. In addition to the effects of the acute illness, NH residents are subject to acute changes in mental status and a myriad of potential iatrogenic problems. Probably the most prevalent of these iatrogenic problems are related to immobility, including deconditioning and difficulty regaining ambulation and/or transfer capabilities, and the development of pressure sores.

Because of the risks of acute hospitalization, those making the decision to hospitalize a NH resident must carefully weigh a number of factors. A variety of medical, administrative, logistic, economic, and ethical issues can influence decisions to hospitalize NH residents. (It is beyond the scope of this chapter to discuss these issues in detail; they are reviewed at length elsewhere.[49–51]) Very often when NH residents become acutely ill, they simply need a few days of close observation with intravenous antimicrobials and hydration, such as for a lower respiratory or urinary tract infection. Decisions about hospitalization in these situations boil down to the capabilities of the physician and NH staff in providing these services in the NH, the preferences of the resident and the family, and the logistic and administrative arrangements for acute hospital care. If, for example, the NH staff has been trained and has the personnel to institute intravenous therapy without detracting from the care of the other residents, and there is a nurse practitioner or a physician's assistant to perform follow-up assessments, the resident with an acute infection who is otherwise medically stable may best be managed in the NH. Many facilities, however, have limited nursing staff; they do not run continuous intravenous infusions, and they do not have nurse practitioners or physicians' assistants and are therefore not capable of managing these situations adequately.

One of the biggest difficulties arising from the frequent transfer of NH residents to acute care hospitals is the disruption in the continuity of medical records at a time when major changes in the residents' status are occurring. Hospitals often receive inadequate information from the NH records upon transfer, and vice versa when the resident is transferred back to the NH. Most NHs begin an entirely new medical record after a resident has been readmitted from an acute care hospital, which further compounds the difficulty in obtaining an adequate medical data base. Utilizing a face sheet similar to the one depicted in Fig. 32-3 helps provide hospital personnel and physicians (who may be covering the primary physician) with critical data and helps update these data when the face sheet is completed at the NH on readmission. The physician's hospital discharge summaries are rarely available within 24 to 48 hours of the resident's NH admission, and standard intrafacility transfer forms often contain incomplete or ambiguous information. The development of a standard discharge summary and NH readmission order forms with data tailored to the needs of the NH greatly improves the transfer of information and the assessment process.

These are just a few of many potential strategies for improving care in NHs. In addition to the need for improved medical care, there is a great unmet need for mental health services.[10] Given the prevalence of dementia, depression, and related behavioral disorders in NHs, it is critical that the availability and quality of mental health services for NH residents be improved as quickly as possible.

ETHICAL ISSUES IN NURSING HOME CARE

Ethical issues arise as much, if not more often, in the day-to-day care of NH residents than in the care of patients in any other setting. Since these issues are discussed at length in Chap. 36, they will be only briefly mentioned here. Several of the most common ethical dilemmas that occur in the NH are outlined in Table 32-8. NHs care for an extraordinarily high concentration of individuals who are unable or questionably capable of participating in decisions about their current and future health care. It is among these same individuals that severe functional disabilities and terminal illness are very prevalent. Thus, questions about individual autonomy, decision-making capacity, surrogate decision makers, and the intensity of treatment that should be given at end of life arise on a daily basis. These questions are both troublesome and complex but must be dealt with in a straightforward and systematic manner in order to provide optimal medical care to NH residents within the context of ethical principles and state and federal laws. Ethics committees have been established in some NHs,[52] and all NHs should be encouraged either to establish such a committee or to become affiliated with an institution that has one that can serve the NH. In addition to Chap. 36, several sources discuss the issues listed in Table 32-8 in considerable detail.[53–65]

FEDERAL RULES AND REGULATIONS FOR NURSING HOME CARE (OBRA 1987)

In 1987, the OBRA contained a comprehensive set of new rules and regulations for NH care. These regulations were largely based on the recommendations made in the Institute of Medicine report on quality of care in NHs.[4] The intent of the new regulations was to revise and consolidate the requirements for long-term care facilities to participate in Medicare and

TABLE 32-8

Common Ethical Issues in the Nursing Home

Ethical Issues*	Examples
Preservation of autonomy	Choices in many areas are limited in most NHs (e.g., meal times, sleeping hours) Families, physicians, and NH staff tend to become paternalistic
Decision-making capacity	Many NH residents are incapable, or questionably capable, of participating in decisions about their care There are no standard methods of assessing decision-making capacity in this population
Surrogate decision making	Many NH residents have not clearly stated their preferences or appointed a surrogate before becoming unable to decide for themselves Family members may be in conflict, have hidden agendas, or be incapable of making decisions or unwilling to make them
Quality of life	This concept is often entered into decision making, but it is difficult to measure—especially among those with dementia Ageist biases can influence perceptions of NH residents' quality of life
Intensity of treatment	A range of options must be considered, including cardiopulmonary resuscitation and mechanical ventilation, hospitalization, treatment of specific conditions (e.g., infection) in the NH without hospitalization, enteral feeding, comfort, or supportive care only

*Approaches to these ethical issues are discussed further in Table 32-5 and Chap. 36.
SOURCE: Ouslander et al,[31] with permission.

Medicaid, and to improve the quality of care provided in NHs. The rules and regulations cover a broad range of administrative and clinical issues, and many specific guidelines are set forth relating to clinical care for such conditions as pressure sores, incontinence and catheter use, malnutrition, behavioral disorders associated with dementia, and drug therapy.

Medical directors, administrators, and directors of nursing should be intimately familiar with the law itself (as implemented in 1991), as well as with the detailed interpretive guidelines promulgated by the Health Care Financing Administration. A detailed summary of aspects of OBRA 1987 relevant to clinicians can be found elsewhere.[31] Three areas of critical importance to clinicians will be briefly reviewed herein: residents' rights, resident assessment, and chemical and physical restraints.

Residents' rights are a major focus of OBRA 1987. The rules and interpretive guidelines repeatedly emphasize that residents have the right to care directed at *restoring and maintaining the highest practicable level of functioning*. Thus, the traditional "custodial care" approach is no longer appropriate. Potentially remediable clinical conditions and functional deficits should be regularly sought and addressed with the above goal in mind whenever identified. The focus on residents' rights also relates to the issue of decision making and informed consent. The regulations emphasize the right of NH residents to participate in decisions about their care and mandate a clear approach to assessing decision-making capacity, proxy decision makers, and informed consent.

New guidelines for resident assessment are a cornerstone of the clinical aspects of OBRA 1987. The mandated assessment includes three components: the MDS, triggers, and resident assessment protocols (RAPs). The MDS is a comprehensive computer-compatible assessment form that covers 13 key clinical areas.[66] It must be completed within 14 days of admission, and most of the assessment must be reviewed and updated quarterly. The MDS protocol identifies multiple "triggers" for the assessment of a variety of conditions using the RAPs. The RAPs are detailed assessments protocols that address 18 clinical areas, including cognitive loss, mood disorders, falls, nutritional status, and incontinence. Though the MDS, triggers, and RAPs outline a high level of clinical assessment and care for NH residents, most typical NHs have neither the resources nor the personnel to make full use of them at the present time. In addition to its potential use in the care of individual NH residents, the MDS will likely be used in the future as a tool for reimbursing NH care based on resident characteristics, as well as for identifying quality-of-care issues in specific NHs.

OBRA's regulations on chemical and physical restraints have been the most contentious among clinicians, probably in large part because they begin to impinge on the practice of medicine and nursing. The regulations define both physical and chemical restraints broadly. Much has been written about untying NH residents and "restraint-free" NH environments—but thus far, few data are available about the risks and appropriateness of restraint use. One recent study suggests that restraints are associated with a higher rate of falls, but the methods do not allow any conclusions about a cause-and-effect relationship.[67] The regulations mandate that physical restraints be used only after a multidisciplinary assessment documents that less restrictive alternatives are not effective; and that when restraints are used a rehabilitative plan of care, including releasing and repositioning the resident every 2 hours, be implemented. At present, the regulations basically define all psychotropic drugs as "chemical restraints." Antipsychotics in particular can only be prescribed for specific conditions identified in the interpretive guidelines. The regulations for chemical restraints, similar to those for physical restraints, mandate that there be ongoing documentation of an attempt at behavioral interventions or other alternatives to drug use and that drug therapy be monitored closely with appropriate dosage reductions and trials off therapy when appropriate.

In sum, OBRA 1987 sets high standards for NH care. If implemented as intended, and monitored appropriately by state and federal agencies, the new rules and regulations are likely to lead to improved care. Other approaches, such as the application of new management strategies that incorporate principles of computerized industrial quality control[68] will be necessary to further improve the quality and outcomes of NH care.

REFERENCES

1. Rubenstein LZ et al: Effectiveness of a geriatric evaluation unit: A randomized clinical trial. *N Engl J Med* 311:1164, 1984.
2. Rubenstein et al (eds): Geriatric assessment. *Clin Geriatr Med* 3 (1): 1987.
3. Vladek B: *Unloving Care: The Nursing Home Tragedy.* New York, Basic Books, 1980.
4. Institute of Medicine: *Improving the Quality of Care in Nursing Homes.* Washington, DC, National Academy Press, 1986.
5. Moss FE, Halamandaris VJ: *Too Old, Too Sick, Too Bad: Nursing Homes in America.* Germantown, PA, Aspen Systems, 1977.
6. Rango N: Nursing home care in the United States: Prevailing conditions and policy implications. *N Engl J Med* 307:883, 1982.
7. Somers AR: Long-term care for the elderly and disabled: A new health priority. *N Engl J Med* 307:221, 1982.
8. Rabin DL: Physician care in nursing homes. *Ann Intern Med* 94:126, 1981.
9. Anonymous: Is anybody listening? Letter to the Los Angeles Times, September 23, 1979.
10. Ray WA et al: A study of antipsychotic drug use in nursing homes: Epidemiologic evidence suggesting misuse. *Am J Public Health* 70(5):485, 1980.
11. Borson S et al: Psychiatry in the nursing home. *Am J Psychiatry* 144:1412, 1987.
12. Aiken LH et al: Teaching nursing homes: Prospects for improving long-term care. *J Am Geriatr Soc* 33:196, 1985.
13. Health and Public Policy Committee, American College of Physicians: Long-term care of the elderly. *Ann Intern Med* 100:760, 1984.
14. Jahnigen DW et al: Academic affiliation with a nursing home: Impact on patient outcome. *J Am Geriatr Soc* 33:472, 1985.
15. Libow LS: The teaching nursing home: Past, present and future. *J Am Geriatr Soc* 32:598, 1984.
16. Schneider EL (ed): *The Teaching Nursing Home: A New Approach to Geriatric Research, Education and Clinical Care.* New York, Raven, 1985.
17. Williams C: Teaching nursing homes: Their impact on public policy, patient care and medical education. *J Am Geriatr Soc* 33:189, 1985.
18. Wieland GD et al: Organizing an academic nursing home: Impacts of institutionalized elderly. *JAMA* 255:2622, 1986.
19. Kane RA, Kane RL: *Long Term Care: Principles, Programs and Policies.* New York, Springer, 1987.
20. Waxman HM et al: Job turnover and job satisfaction among nursing home aides. *Gerontologist* 24:503, 1984.
21. Schwartz TB: How to install a first-rate doctor in a third-rate nursing home. *N Engl J Med* 306:743, 1982.
22. Keeler EB et al: Short and long-term residents of nursing homes. *Med Care* 19:363, 1981.
23. Lewis MA et al: The immediate and subsequent outcomes of nursing home care. *Am J Public Health* 75:758, 1985.
24. Lewis MA et al: The natural history of nursing home patients. *Gerontologist* 25:382, 1985.
25. Liu K, Manton KG: The characteristics and utilization pattern of an admission cohort of nursing home patients. *Gerontologist* 22:92, 1983.
26. Liu K, Manton KG: The characteristics and utilization pattern of an admission cohort of nursing homes patients: II. *Gerontologist* 24:70, 1984.
27. Ouslander JG, Martin SE: Assessment in the nursing home. *Clin Geriatr Med* 3:155, 1987.
28. Kane RL et al: *Essentials of Clinical Geriatrics,* 2d ed. New York, McGraw-Hill, 1988.
29. Smits HL et al: Medicare's nursing-home benefit: Variations in interpretation. *N Engl J Med* 307 (6):353, 1981.
30. Baldwin D, Tuskuda R: Interdisciplinary teams, in Cassel C, Walsh J (eds): *Geriatric Medicine.* New York, Springer-Verlag, 1990, p 668.
31. Ouslander JG et al: *Medical Care in the Nursing Home.* New York, McGraw-Hill, 1991.
32. Levensen S (ed): *Medical Direction in Long Term Care.* Owings Mills, MD, National Health Publishing, 1988.
33. Gambert SR et al: The value of the yearly medical evaluation in a nursing home. *J Chron Dis* 35:65, 1982.
34. Irvine PW et al: The value of annual medical examinations in the nursing home. *J Am Geriatr Soc* 32:540, 1984.
35. Domoto K et al: Yield of routine annual laboratory screening in the institutionalized elderly. *Am J Public Health* 75:243, 1985.
36. Wolf-Klein GP et al: Efficacy of routine annual studies in the care of elderly patients. *J Am Geriatr Soc* 33:325, 1985.
37. Levenstein MR et al: Yield of routine annual laboratory tests in a skilled nursing home population. *JAMA* 258(14):1909, 1987.
38. Stead WW et al: Tuberculosis as an endemic and noso-

comial infection among the elderly in nursing homes. *N Engl J Med* 312:1383, 1985.
39. Cooper JK: Decision analysis for tuberculosis prevention treatment in nursing homes. *J Am Geriatr Soc* 34:814, 1986.
40. Stead WW, To T: The significance of the tuberculin skin test in elderly persons. *Ann Intern Med* 107:837, 1987.
41. Stead WW et al: Benefit-risk considerations in preventive treatment of tuberculosis in elderly persons. *Ann Intern Med* 107:843, 1987.
42. Patriarca PA et al: Prevention and control of type A influenza infections in nursing homes: Benefits and costs of four approaches using vaccination and amantadine. *Ann Intern Med* 107:732, 1987.
43. Garibaldi RA et al: Infections among patients in nursing homes. *N Engl J Med* 305:731, 1981.
44. Crossley KB et al: Infection control practices in Minnesota Nursing Homes. *JAMA* 254:2918, 1985.
45. Warren JW: Catheters and catheter care. *Clin Geriatr Med* 2:857, 1986.
46. Yoshikowa TT, Norman DC: *Aging and Clinical Practice: Infectious Diseases.* New York, Igaku-Shoin, 1987.
47. Zimmer JG et al: Systemic antibiotic use in nursing homes: A quality assessment. *J Am Geriatr Soc* 34(10):703, 1986.
48. Martin SE et al: Assessment and initial management of acute medical problems in a nursing home, in Basku G (ed): *Principles and Practice of Acute Geriatric Medicine.* St. Louis, Mosby, 1988.
49. Zimmer JG et al: Nursing homes as acute care providers: A pilot study of incentives to reduce hospitalizations. *J Am Geriatr Soc* 36:124, 1988.
50. Rubenstein LZ et al: Dynamics and clinical implications of the nursing home–hospital interface. *Clin Geriatr Med* 4:471, 1988.
51. Ouslander JG: Reducing the hospitalization of nursing home residents. *J Am Geriatr Soc* 36:171, 1988.
52. Glasser et al: The ethics committee in the nursing home: Results of a national survey. *J Am Geriatr Soc* 36:150, 1988.
53. Brown NK, Thompson DJ: Nontreatment of fever in extended-care facilities. *N Engl J Med* 300:1246, 1979.
54. Fabiszewski KJ et al: Effect of antibiotic treatment on outcome of fevers in institutionalized Alzheimer patients. *JAMA* 263:3168, 1990.
55. Besdine RW: Decisions to withold treatment from nursing home residents. *J Am Geriatr Soc* 30:602, 1983.
56. Hilfiker D: Allowing the debilitated to die. *N Engl J Med* 308:716, 1983.
57. Lo B, Dornbrand L: Guiding the hand that feeds: Caring for the demented elderly. *N Engl J Med* 311(6):402, 1984.
58. Lo B, Dornbrand L: The case of Claire Conroy: Will administrative review safeguard incompetent patients? *Ann Intern Med* 104:869, 1986.
59. Nevins MA: Analysis of the Supreme Court of New Jersey's decision in the Claire Conroy case. *J Am Geriatr Soc* 34:140, 1986.
60. Volicer L et al: Hospice approach to the treatment of patients with advanced dementia of the Alzheimer's type. *JAMA* 256(16):2210, 1986.
61. Lynn J: Dying and dementia. *JAMA* 156(16):2244, 1986.
62. Lynn J (ed): *By No Extraordinary Means—The Choice to Forgo Life-sustaining Food and Water.* Bloomington, Indiana University Press, 1986.
63. Uhlman RF et al: Medical management decisions in nursing home patients: Principles and policy recommendations. *Ann Intern Med* 106:879, 1987.
64. Steinbrook R, Lo B: Artificial feeding—Solid ground, not a slippery slope. *N Engl J Med* 318:286, 1988.
65. Mott PD, Barker WH: Hospital and medical care use by nursing home patients: The effect of patient care plans. *J Am Geriatr Soc* 36:47, 1988.
66. Morris JN et al: Designing the National Resident Assessment Instrument for Nursing Homes. *Gerontologist* 30:293, 1990.
67. Tinetti ME et al: Mechanical restraint use and fall-related injuries among residents of skilled nursing facilities. *Ann Intern Med* 116:369, 1992.
68. Schnelle JF et al: Assessment and quality control of incontinence care in long-term nursing facilities. *J Am Geriatr Soc* 39:165, 1991.

Chapter 33

COMMUNITY-BASED LONG-TERM CARE

Thomas E. Finucane and John R. Burton

If current trends continue, increasingly large numbers of very old, frail people will develop chronic illness and become dependent on others for basic activities of daily living. At the same time, the number of close family members who now provide care for these individuals will probably decrease. The care that will be required for the frail elderly will not permit clear distinction between medical and social needs. Society in general and the health care system in particular will try to develop strategies that define eligibility in a fair way, meet the needs of the patients, and are cost-effective. To do so presents a formidable challenge and requires a careful rethinking about society's responsibility to its most vulnerable citizens. Community-based long-term care will be part of the solution.

Recently, community-based long-term care has undergone tremendous growth. The home health industry has increased by 20 percent per year for the past 5 years, while the number of nursing home beds have increased by 2 percent annually and acute hospital beds have decreased.[1] An increasing population of elderly people, many of them frail and chronically ill, provides much of the substrate for this growth. In addition, prospective payment for hospitalization creates financial incentives to provide care in the home, and technologic advances make sophisticated diagnostic and therapeutic options portable. Finally, nursing home beds are scarce in several regions of the country, thus forcing long-term care to occur in the home.

This chapter presents data about the frail elderly at home. Research, both experimental and quasi-experimental, about long-term care at home is reviewed. Public programs that finance long-term care are described. A variety of innovative services—including foster care, day care, continuing care communities, and respite care, not yet widely studied—are discussed.

Home health agencies are federally designated organizations eligible to receive Medicare payment. In contrast, the term *home health care* will be used throughout this chapter to refer to any health care delivered in the home. The phrase *community-based long-term care* is generally applied to care for patients who are frail and chronically ill—not to the majority of elderly people who are healthy. This connotation has evolved from an earlier usage of *long-term care* to mean institutional care of people who were simply too frail to remain in the community. *Medical care* differs subtly from *long-term care.* In this chapter the latter term is used to refer to comprehensive health care delivered over an extended interval. *Community-based long-term care* refers to health care provided longitudinally to people not living in institutions. It includes physician home care and a broad variety of programs in the community.

THE FRAIL ELDERLY AT HOME

A U.S. Senate report noted that in 1990 approximately 30 million people living in the community were above age 65, and 4.4 million of these people (about two-thirds of whom were women) experienced difficulties in one or more activities of daily living (ADLs).[2] About 18 percent of people age 65 and over experienced limitations in instrumental activities of daily living (IADLs), most commonly inability to shop and to get around the community independently. This level of dependency makes access to health care especially difficult. Thus, millions of elderly Americans require the help of others to continue living at home. Most of this help is provided by unpaid family and friends, usually adult daughters (29 percent of caregivers), and wives (23 percent).[3] Only a small portion of dependent elderly people living at home utilize any formal services.

To further complicate the provision of coordinated health care for older people in the community, about half of the elderly with ADL limitation had no more than a modest income.[4] Low-income elderly people are more likely to have chronic diseases and to be functionally dependent than the higher-income elderly. Among the near-poor elderly, many are reduced to poverty by their out-of-pocket medical expenses.[5]

The elderly/support ratio (the number of people over 65 years of age compared to the number of people of working age, 18 to 64) is rising dramatically. For example, in 1900, there were 7 elderly for every 100 people of working age; in 1990, there were 20 per 100; and in 2030, this ratio is expected to reach 38 per 100.[6] Declining birthrates and the entry of women into the work force are also important demographic trends which have implications for care of the frail elderly. To illustrate the point, in Britain, "David Eversley has estimated . . . that a hypothetical married couple age 85 and 80, in 1980, married in 1920 would, in 1980, have had 42 female relatives alive, 14 of whom would not have been working. By comparison, a married couple age 55 in 1980, married in 1950, would, by the year 2005, when they will have reached the age of 80, have only 11 female relatives alive, only three of whom would not be working."[7] Thus, developing systems to provide care for a large and growing group of frail, dependent elderly is a serious challenge for society.

EVIDENCE FOR THE EFFECTIVENESS OF COMMUNITY-BASED LONG-TERM CARE

For a frail, elderly person, intermittent office visits to a physician as the only type of service received may be inadequate and inappropriate health care. What is appropriate care for such patients and how should it be financed? Much of the controversy about the answers to these questions is due to the imprecise distinction between social and medical needs. For example, most people would not consider food, shelter, and clothing to be medical issues for a young, healthy adult. For an ill, elderly, isolated person, however, these items may be crucial to health and even survival. American society has been far more willing to try to guarantee medical care than to provide for social needs, yet for the frail elderly the two converge. Research and policy questions have been framed in a way that finesses this basic uncertainty: most large studies of community-based long-term care have used nursing home residents (or applicants to nursing homes) and nursing home costs as reference points.

Nursing homes are a high-cost system of care that, presumably, provides care to the most dependent and vulnerable segment of the population. At the same time most people report a strong desire to avoid living in a nursing home. A survey of elders in the community found that paid in-home services were the first choice among possible long-term care arrangements, while nursing home placement ranked next to last (moving to the home of a relative ranked last).[8] Nursing homes thus make a convenient comparison "treatment" in quasi-experimental studies of community-based long-term care.

Does community-based long-term care "work"? The effort to assess the effectiveness of community care experimentally has encountered serious difficulties in every aspect of experimental design. First, to test whether community-based long-term care is effective, a well-characterized group of subjects should be randomly allocated to different treatment modalities. However, several methodological and ethical problems have prevented studies from providing a definitive answer. Measures of disease severity and patient frailty are primitive and imprecise. In addition, it is difficult to randomize such patients ethically. As a result, treatment and control groups often differ substantially at initiation of treatment. In many studies too there has been a great deal of attrition. Hughes et al.,[9] for example, report that at 4 years, only 18 percent of their treatment group was still alive and receiving care in the community. Finally, studies of community-based long-term care are affected by major changes in the health care system. The nature of nursing home patients has, in fact, changed dramatically during the 1980s—a period when many of the important long-term care demonstrations were conducted. Responding to the prospective payment system, hospitals began to discharge patients to nursing homes "sicker and quicker."[10] Second, a discrete intervention should be applied to the treatment group. Community-based long-term care interventions that have been studied have ranged from a simple in-home emergency alarm and response system[11] to case management with the additional ability to purchase discretionary services, such as foster care, medical equipment, home health aides, etc.[12] Third, treatment and control groups should be compared with respect to predefined outcomes. Outcomes have ranged from cost comparisons to hospital or nursing home utilization to physical health, mental well-being, and mortality.

In the early 1980s, the federal government began a 10-state demonstration project with a randomized experimental design to determine whether community-based long-term care could be a cost-effective alternative to nursing home placement for severely impaired, community-dwelling elderly. Thousands of patients were enrolled and the essential intervention was case management. In the "basic" model, case managers had no control over service availability; they performed an educational, coordinating ("channeling"), and supportive function. In the "complex" model, also known as the "financial control" model, case managers could, in addition, use program funds to purchase services for clients within certain limits.

The results of the demonstration were disappointing. Neither model of case management produced a reduction in the use of nursing homes, hospitals, or physician services. Differences of functional status and perceived life satisfaction were unsubstantial and mortality was unchanged.[13] The major demonstrable benefit accrued to family caregivers, who seemed to feel supported by the intervention. However, in this study and elsewhere,[14] there was little evidence that family caregivers reduced their level of support when paid caregivers were provided. Since institutional and physician use was not reduced by the interventions, however, the costs of the interventions were simply added costs.[12]

In the mid-1980s, the Health Care Financing Administration, with waivers from Medicare and Medicaid, initiated a demonstration project at a different level of analysis. A new form of health plan, the social/health maintenance organization (SHMO), was devised. These plans offer a much wider array of services, chronic and acute, than a standard health maintenance organization (HMO). Nursing home care, personal care, and homemaker services, for example, are included as standard benefits. The SHMO receives a monthly per capita payment (the average adjusted per capita cost, or AAPCC) from Medicare and either a Medicaid payment or, from those who are not eligible for Medicaid, a self-paid premium. This demonstration project is quasi-experimental, as there is no control group. The outcome measures are costs and utilization. Costs of the plans are measured against average costs of all Medicare subscribers, for example.

The question asked by this project is whether managed care can reduce the overall costs of care for an "average" group of elderly people. (Unlike HMOs, SHMOs were allowed to do functional screening of applicants. If the SHMO had already enrolled a percent of disabled applicants that was higher than the percent of disabled in the community at large, the SHMO was allowed to put disabled applicants on a waiting list. In this way an "average" group was enrolled.[15])

After 5 full years of operation, the four SHMO sites were struggling. Start-up costs were higher and enrollments lower than expected. None of the plans achieved a financial break-even point. The plans had fair success at keeping hospital utilization below the national average for Medicare patients, but all "showed a general trend for increased hospital utilization over the 5-year period as their membership aged."[16] Comparative data on chronic care utilization are not yet available.

Pooling results from different studies is another approach that has been used to assess efficacy of long-term care. Weissert et al.[17] identified over 700 citations, reviewed 150 documents, and chose the 27 "most rigorous and generalizable studies." Kemper et al.[18] reviewed 16 demonstration projects (including the "channeling" demonstration) that provided case-managed community-based long-term care to frail elderly via Medicare and Medicaid waivers. Hedrick et al.[19] performed a metaanalysis of all 13 randomized or quasi-experimental studies of home care which measured as outcomes mortality and nursing home placement. The results from these three summaries are remarkably similar.

Both reviews note that there was no demonstrable overall cost-reduction from community-based long-term care, and there often was an increase in total costs. One section of the paper by Weissert et al. is entitled, "Studies which saved money or came close," emphasizing the weakness of evidence. The reduction in nursing home costs (by preventing a few admissions) was less than the increased cost from providing community care to people who would not have gone to a nursing home regardless of services.

In the metaanalysis, analysis of randomized trials found no reduction in nursing home placement. Kemper et al. noted a weak, inconsistent reduction in nursing home placement that was confined solely to the first year. In most studies, the rates of nursing home placement were low in all groups and reductions would have been difficult to detect. Of 27 studies reviewed by Weissert et al., 22 reported nursing home admission rates. In 70 percent of these, fewer than one-quarter of at-risk patients entered nursing homes: most lengths of stay were less than a month.

Both reviews showed little effect on hospitalization rates. This outcome has been less studied and the analysis is weaker, although there probably is not an increase in hospital use as a result of home health care. Effects on functional status, self-reported health, and quality of life were slight, and virtually all positive effects were no longer measurable by 18 months. The metaanalysis found a small, statistically insignificant improvement in mortality for patients receiving home care. The two reviews report equivocal results with little or no survival benefit from home care.

The problem of accurate "targeting" emphasizes the tension in attempting to reconcile various goals of community-based long-term care. If cost-effectiveness is the primary goal, stringently defined groups of patients should be identified for intervention. Patients with light care needs who are on the threshold of nursing home admission are the obvious candidates. From a pure cost point of view, it would be cheapest to ignore people, regardless of their needs, whose likelihood of nursing home admission was low, and to institutionalize those with heavy care needs. This is obviously quite different from a decision to provide care to those who need it.

PUBLIC PROGRAMS

Four major public programs pay for long-term care: Medicare, Medicaid, the Older Americans' Act, and Social Services Block Grants. The economic climate of the 1990s has provided budgetary pressure to limit the cost of these programs, and this has been done by restricting both eligibility for and type of services.

Medicare (Title XVIII of the Social Security Act) was initially intended as an insurance program to provide acute health care for the elderly and to cover a limited period of recovery. As a result, in 1990, only 3 percent of the $108.9 billion Medicare budget was spent for home care services.[20] Medicare coverage is intended for management of and short-term recovery from acute illness. Coverage for the latter applies only when the beneficiary receives skilled nursing care. From 1980 to 1990, Medicare home health expenditures increased from $666 million[21] to $3.27 billion.[20] The program is administered at the state level, and interpretation of criteria for covered services is often variable; intermediaries have considerable latitude in deciding whether to approve payment for cases.[22] In general, Medicare coverage for long-term care either at home or in an institution is limited to a few months. When patients are no longer improving as a result of services, they lose eligibility.

In contrast to Medicare, *Medicaid* (Title XIX of the Social Security Act) is intended as a "welfare" program for poor people regardless of age. Because of stringent eligibility requirements (e.g., a monthly income of less than $384 and liquid assets less than $2,500 for a single person in Maryland in 1992) and highly complex enrollment procedures, many older people of meager means are not eligible for coverage by Medicaid. Nevertheless, Medicaid expenditures for the elderly in 1989 totaled $19.2 billion, of which 69 percent went for institutional long-term care of the elderly.[23] Only about $1.5 billion (8 percent) went for home health care of the elderly.[23] Unlike Medicare, services such as personal care, homemaker help, and chore services may be covered through Medicaid or Medicaid waiver programs. In the latter programs, states offer community-based services designed to reduce institutionalization. Many elderly must "spend down" their assets to eligibility levels in order to become poor enough to receive coverage by Medicaid. Married couples face a particular risk as a result of this policy. If one of the two requires nursing home placement, the spouse may be necessarily impoverished during "spend down." However, legislation effective in 1989 substantially increases the assets and income that a person may retain when the spouse is institutionalized with Medicaid funds.

Social Service Block Grants (Title XX of the Older Americans Act) reimburse states for a variety of social services, such as adult day care, personal care, protective services, and others. The mix of services and eligibility requirements is defined at the state level. Programs are largely directed toward low-income people. Relatively little money is appropriated for these services, and Title XX currently provides only about 5 percent of the public funds for long-term care. The *Older Americans Act* provides funding for a variety of programs, including information and referral services (such as those offered by area offices on aging), congregate and home-delivered meals, and support services similar to those provided under Title XX.

In summary, several programs provide a variety of services with significant overlap. Nursing home expenditures consume by far the greatest share of long-term-care spending, and only a modest amount is therefore available for community-based long-term-care programs. The proper reimbursement structure for community-based long-term care is uncertain and undergoing constant evolution and discussion. Nursing home care is the best reimbursed through Medicaid. Incentive is thus created to move people into institutions. On the other hand, with better reimbursement, community-based long-term care would flourish. As described above, for most recipients, these services would be additional benefits rather than alternatives to nursing home placement. Although many of these people have genuine unmet needs, actual rates of nursing home placement are low. This makes demonstration of cost savings extremely difficulty.

Should society decide to provide in-home service more widely, defining eligibility would be a major requirement. Dependency in an ADL is defined by whether a person needs assistance in bathing. Whether a person is unable or simply unwilling to perform such an activity is not considered. Nonetheless, dependency in ADLs has been the primary basis for eligibility in many of the major bills recently considered by Congress concerning coverage of community-based services.[24] Many of the services under consideration are attractive for anyone (e.g., homemaker and chore services), and inappropriately high utilization is therefore a theoretical possibility.

EXISTING PROGRAMS IN LONG-TERM COMMUNITY CARE

Physician House-Call Programs

A description of several existing physician home care programs is provided to illustrate the different models of delivery of physician services. Physician house calls should be considered an important part of providing community-based long-term care to frail home-bound elders.[25] Even though the number of physician house calls has been declining in recent years, probably because of low reimbursement,[26] house calls remain a vital ingredient in the provision of appropriate comprehensive community-based long-term care. Whether physicians make house calls is largely related to physician attitudes about the value of home visiting and the adequacy of reimbursement. Keenan and colleagues[26,27] note that physicians who spend more time in patient care tend to be more likely to make home visits, so that being "too busy" seems a matter of perception. It is likely that reimbursement rates for house calls in the 1990s will be increased under Medicare. Until that time, physicians can achieve efficiency in performing house calls by clustering calls in certain regions and performing them at the beginning or end of the day.

There are several important reasons for physicians to make house calls[28]: (1) An important and needed service is provided to frail individuals who otherwise would be extremely inconvenienced in seeing a physician or who would not see one at all. (2) The "nonmedical" aspects of care, so important in providing effective health care to the infirm—such as social support, environment, and functional status—are more easily and fully assessed in the home.[29] (3) Physician/patient relations are likely to prosper and better health care will result. (4) Physicians are reminded of their very important role as educators and advisers. This sensitization is critical to the selection of cost-effective diagnostic and management goals that are genuinely patient-sensitive. (5) Physician credibility with and understanding of the many nonphysician professionals and nonprofessionals who are providing home health services will be markedly improved. (6) Not insignificantly, the physician performing the house call is immensely rewarded personally.[30]

Several physician home care programs have been implemented at large medical centers and teaching hospitals. Community-based long-term-care services at the Francis Scott Key Medical Center of the Johns Hopkins Health System in Baltimore began in 1979, when a group of physicians began making home visits to a group of frail elderly patients. The program has evolved to provide care for over 200 extremely frail (annual mortality is about 20 percent) home-bound elderly living in a wide catchment area surrounding the hospital. An attending physician and a patient-care advocate coordinate the work of a geriatric medicine postdoctoral fellow and eight to ten internal medicine residents who provide the physician home visits. A home health agency, under a letter of agreement, provides the nursing and personal care services to those patients who are eligible under Medicare guidelines. Nurses, social workers, physical therapist, postdoctoral fellow, patient-care advocate, and attending physician meet weekly to discuss active patients. The program does not pay for direct costs from fee-for-service billing alone and hospital support is necessary to maintain it.

The Home Medical Service at Boston began in 1875 at the Homeopathic Medical Dispensary. In the 1930s, "obstetrical care and home delivery were commonplace," and in 1950 most of the patients were children. However, by 1980, the mean age of this patient population was 80 years, consistent with demographic changes in our society. About 900 patients are cared for by three teams, each of which includes a nurse coordinator, a social worker, and other support staff. A team of internists as well as a surgeon, neurologist, psychiatrist, and arthritis specialist visits patients in the home. The program has been funded through state demonstration money, as a capitated Medicaid HMO, by the Robert Wood Johnson Foundation and by fee-for-service billings.[31] Other programs have been described in New York, Boston, Chicago, and Milwaukee, as well as Hamilton, Ontario, and Beer Sheva, Israel.[32]

In contrast to physician house call programs, On Lok Senior Health Services in San Francisco began in 1971 without direct physician involvement. Initially a network of community services was developed for the frail elderly. In 1973, a "day health center" was opened. From 1971 through 1978, the program was supported through federal and state grants. In 1979, outpatient medical services were begun. The program is now funded primarily through a Medicare and Medicaid waiver as a capitated, risk-based, community care organization for dependent adults. All community-based long-term-care services are provided.[33] This highly successful program is now being duplicated with support from the Robert Wood Johnson Foundation under the auspices of the Program of All-inclusive Care for the Elderly (PACE). In 1992, six sites were operational and more are planned. The PACE programs differ from SHMOs in the way financial risk is managed. The former manage risk at the level of the individual patient while SHMOs manage risk by enrolling thousands of well and frail elderly.[34]

Adult Day Care

Adult day-care programs have been initiated in recent years to help community-living frail elderly patients and their caregivers. These centers are proliferating rapidly.[35] There are two major types: social and medical. Social day-care centers are largely for the functional elderly. Socialization, educational programs, and activities are sponsored by government, church, or community agencies, usually at little or no cost to the participant. Many of these programs also have a primary medical care component associated with them.

Medical adult day-care centers, in contrast, provide service to a more frail and dependent group of elderly and must provide skilled nursing services. They usually operate on a fee-for-service basis, often utilizing a sliding scale. In these programs, the goal is to relieve the caregiver during some days of the week, to provide services to patients who require a more intense level of care than those in social day-care centers. Services provided in a medical adult day-care center include meals, nursing services for assessment, the administration of medical treatments, personal care services (such as bathing and transportation), and socialization as well as physical and recreational activities. Such centers usually operate 6 to 8 hours a day. Of the entitlement programs, only Medicaid currently provides coverage for these services. The average daily cost is about half that of a nursing home, but costs have often been a major factor limiting utilization. Adult medical day-care centers may be associated with hospitals, nursing homes, life-care communities, churches, or other community-based programs. While there is a paucity of controlled studies on the efficacy of adult medical day-care centers, anecdotal evidence suggests that such programs provide significant relief for caregivers and may delay nursing home placement for some individuals. For example, in one study,[36] a geriatric day-care hospital in a community hospital retrospectively interviewed referring physicians and discovered that, in the opinion of the patients' personal physicians, one-third of such patients would have had to be hospitalized or had a hospital stay prolonged without such a program.

Respite Care

Respite care is nursing home or adult day care[37] that provides caregivers with short-term relief (several days to weeks) from the burdens of caring for an elderly person. Available only rarely a few years ago, respite care is now offered by many nursing homes and adult day-care centers. Caregivers can be relieved of the responsibilities of providing care for any reason. Except for Medicaid recipients, expenses for respite care must be borne by the patient and family. The cost for respite care in a nursing home is between \$100 and \$300 per day. The cost of respite care provided in an adult day-care center is about half of that in a nursing home.

Corporate-Sponsored Health Care Program

While still probably less than 1 percent of U.S. employers offer programs specifically for the elderly, corporate-sponsored care for the elderly is an example of a community-based long-term-care program that is likely to grow in the next several years. An example of such a program is Generation, sponsored by the Southern California Edison Company, for retirees and their dependents.[38] Case management services are coupled with comprehensive geriatric assessment utilizing a multidisciplinary team approach. Programs of health promotion and retirement benefits are provided. Knowledgeable retired employees advise younger individuals and orient them to the available services. Access to other community resources is facilitated and a network is formed to provide coordinated long-term health care to the elderly. Other companies have provided programs where employees can speak with professionals familiar with health care systems in all parts of the country to help coordinate care for aging parents who live in different areas.

Special Housing for the Elderly

Life-care retirement communities or *Continuing-Care Retirement Communities* are proliferating rapidly and in 1991 numbered about 1000.[39] Physicians are commonly asked by patients to provide advice regarding such programs. The basic concept of continuing care retirement communities is to provide an attractive living environment that is adapted for persons with physical disabilities, and to couple housing with congregate meals and social, educational, recreational, and sports programs. An integral part of such life-care communities is a health care program that includes one or more of the following: on-site physician office practice, a personal care program for those individuals who require some supervision in the performance of ADLs or IADLs, and nursing home care for those more severely impaired. As the residents' needs for care change, the appropriate resources are accessible within the community. Ideally, a life-care community is a self-contained health care continuum. The cost of such programs is considerable; therefore they are accessible to only a small portion of the elderly population. Cost varies markedly, depending on location, size of the living unit, number of included services, and financial structure. Residents usually pay a substantial initial fee as well as monthly "rent." In some, the initial fee is rebated in full or in part at death or if the resident moves out of the community.

Patients considering moving to such a facility should be advised by their physicians to analyze the services included carefully, to review the reputation of the facility with the local office on aging, and to be certain that the legal aspects of the contract are fully understood. Individuals who enter life-care communities commonly tout positive aspects of the program, including access to health care, security, avoidance of becoming a burden on their families, socialization, activities, and relief from the burdens of independent home ownership. Other elders who can afford to enter a life-care community are reluctant to do so, disparagingly describing them as expensive ghettos for older people. Many retirement communities require an individual to be highly functional and cognitively intact to enter. This forces an early decision on prospective members.

The concept of continuing care has been adapted to an individual's home environment in several demonstration projects. These new programs are focused in part on affordability and maintenance of a maximum level of independence and personal freedom. One such program is Life Care at Home or Continuing Care without Walls. Prototypical programs were initiated in the last several years with pilot funding from the Robert Wood Johnson Foundation. In 1992, programs are established and functional in Huntington, California, and in a suburb of Philadelphia; others are in development. Depending on the success of these programs, others may become available in other communities in the next several years. The idea of Life Care at Home is to bundle case management services with coordinated health care, including an insurance benefit that covers personal care and nursing home care. These programs may also offer brokered home maintenance services. The initial and monthly fees are typically much lower than that for those of a retirement community. These programs are aimed at making a maximum effort to assist an older person to remain at home, independent and as secure as possible for as long as possible, and to provide an insurance program for nursing home and personal care.

Several other special housing programs are available for older people. Informal adult retirement communities with high concentrations of elderly residents have become nearly de facto continuing-care retirement communities due to the imaginative and persistent efforts of residents. Such communities are likely to grow spontaneously in the next few years with the ever-increasing population of older individuals. Each community has its own characteristics and should be investigated carefully by a prospective resident. In many states, subsidized housing for elders is available. Such programs are usually available on a means-tested basis. These programs, commonly called *congregate, sheltered,* or simply *elder housing,* provide basic housing, on-site health care, and social programs. *Foster homes* are essentially boarding houses. In most foster-care programs for older adults, a few frail elderly people live in the private home of an nonrelative who is reimbursed by the state. One randomized study found that foster care for a segment of the nursing home population is an effective and acceptable alternative.[40]

CONCLUSION

Most elderly Americans are healthy and live in the community. Several million elderly, however, are chronically ill, frail, and dependent. Of these dependent elderly, most are well cared for in the community by informal support systems, primarily family. Several social and demographic trends suggest that these support systems will weaken progressively in the decades to come. At the same time the number of very old people will be increasing dramatically.

The growth in health care spending dwarfs the growth of the national economy. Even in the context of health care spending, however, the growth in home health care spending is rapid. Cost considerations are thus an inevitable factor in thinking about community-based long-term care. A health policy based on economic competition in a free market seems particularly incongruous for this group of people. Providing care to the frail elderly is unlikely to generate a profit, and the payor will often be relying on tax revenues. Fragmentation of care is likely in a free-market model as profitable but circumscribed niches are discovered; fragmentation is particularly undesirable in long-term care.

Nursing homes are expensive. Yet studies comparing community-based long-term care with nursing home care have not shown significant clinical or financial advantages for the former. Thus, national policy for long-term care remains amorphous. Fundamental disagreements remain about the proper definition of eligibility, services to be provided, and payors.

REFERENCES

1. Council on Scientific Affairs, American Medical Association: Home Care in the 1990s. *JAMA* 263:1241, 1990.
2. U.S. Senate Special Committee on Aging: *Aging America—Trends and Projections.* Washington, DC, U.S. Government Printing Office, 1992, p 144.
3. *Ibid.* p 158.
4. Kasper JD: Aging alone: Profiles and projections. Baltimore, MD, The Commonwealth Fund Commission on Elderly People Living Alone, 1988.
5. Pepper Commission, Executive Summary: *A Call for Action.* Washington, DC, U.S. Government Printing Office, 1990.
6. U.S. Senate, Special Committee on Aging. *Aging in America—Trends and Projections.* Washington, DC, U.S. Government Printing Office, 1992, p 18.
7. Bulmer M: *Neighbours: The Work of Philip Abrams.* Cambridge, England, Cambridge University Press, 1986.
8. McAuley WJ, Bleiszner R: Selection of long-term care arrangements by older community residents. *Gerontologist* 25:188, 1985.
9. Hughes SL et al: Impact of long-term home care on mortality, functional status, and unmet meds. *Health Serv Res* 23:269, 1988.
10. Shaughnessy PW, Kramer AM: The increased needs of patients in nursing homes and patients receiving home health care. *N Engl J Med* 322:21, 1990.
11. Ruchlin HS, Morris JN: Cost-benefit analysis of an emergency alarm and response system: A case-study of a long-term care program. *Health Serv Res* 16:65, 1981.
12. Kane RA: The noblest experiment of them all: Learning from the national channeling evaluation. *Health Serv Res* 23:189, 1988.
13. Applebaum RA et al: The evaluation of the National Long Term Care Demonstration: The effect of channeling on mortality, functioning, and well-being. *Health Serv Res* 23:143, 1988.
14. Edelman P, Hughes S: The impact of community care on provision of informal care to homebound elderly persons. *J Gerontol* 45:S74, 1990.
15. Newcomer R et al: Social Health Maintenance Organizations: Assessing their initial experience. *Health Serv Res* 25:425, 1990.
16. Harrington C, Newcomer RJ: Social health maintenance organizations' service use, and costs, 1985–1989. *Health Care Finan Rev* 12:37, 1991.
17. Weissert WG et al: The past and future of home- and community-based long-term care. *Milbank Mem Q* 66:309, 1988.
18. Kemper P et al: Community care demonstrations: What have we learned. *Health Care Finan Rev* 8:87, 1987.
19. Hedrick SC et al: Meta-analysis of home-care effects

on mortality and nursing home placement. *Med Care* 27:1015, 1988.
20. Somers, AR, Livengood WS: Long-term care for the elderly: Major developments of the last 10 years. *Pride Inst J* 11(1):6–17, 1992.
21. *Physician Guide to Home Health Care.* Chicago, American Medical Association, 1989.
22. Smits HL et al: Medicare's nursing home benefit: Variations in interpretation. *N Engl J Med* 307:855, 1982.
23. US Senate, Special Committee on Aging: *Aging America—Trends and Projections.* Washington, DC, US Government Printing Office, 1992, p 138.
24. Kasper JD: Cognitive impairment among functionally-limited elderly people in the community: Future considerations for long-term care policy. *Milbank Mem Q* 68:81, 1990.
25. Keenan JM, Fanale JE: Home care: Past and present, problems and potential. *J Am Geriatr Soc* 37:1076, 1989.
26. Keenan JM et al: The home care practice and attitudes of Minnesota family physicians. *J Am Geriatr Soc* 39:1100, 1992.
27. Boling PA et al: Factors associated with the frequency of house calls by primary care physicians. *J Gen Intern Med* 6:335, 1991.
28. Burton JR: The house call: An important service for the frail elderly. *J Am Geriatr Soc* 33:291, 1985.
29. Ramsdell JW et al: The yield of a home visit in the assessment of geriatric patients. *J Am Geriatr Soc* 37:17, 1989.
30. Galloway RF: House calls. *JAMA* 266:786, 1991.
31. Steel K: Physician-directed long-term home care health care for the elderly—A century-long experience. *J Am Geriatr Soc* 35:264, 1987.
32. Steel K: Home care for the elderly: The new institution. *Arch Intern Med* 151:439, 1991.
33. Eng C: Multidisciplinary approach to medical care: The On Lok model. *Clin Rep Aging* 1:5, 1987.
34. Zawadski RT, Eng C: Case-management in capitated long-term care. *Health Care Finan Rev* 9:75, 1988.
35. Von Behren R: *Adult Day Care in America: Summary of a National Survey.* Washington, DC, The National Council on the Aging, Inc. National Institute on Adult Daycare, October 1988.
36. Morishita L et al: Comprehensive geriatric care in a day hospital: A demonstration of the British model in the United States. *Gerontologist* 29:336, 1989.
37. Strang V, Neufeld A: Adult day care programs: A source of respite. *J Gerontol Nurs* 16:16, 1990.
38. Scharlach AE et al: Generation: A corporate-sponsored retiree health care program. *Gerontologist* 32:265, 1992.
39. Levit KR et al: National health expenditure, 1990. *HCFA Rev* 13:29, 1991.
40. Oktay JS, Volland PJ: Foster home care for the frail elderly as an alternative to nursing home care: An experimental evaluation. *Am J Public Health* 77:1505, 1987.

Chapter 34

THE CARE OF THE DYING PATIENT

Phyllis Schmitz, Joanne Lynn, and Elizabeth Cobbs

To provide the care that ensures that the end of life is meaningful and comfortable is a privilege and a challenge. Success requires compassion, technical expertise, and good teamwork. Medical decision making must seek to craft the best life that is possible for patients burdened by progressive chronic disease that is expected to be fatal. In evaluating the merits of potential alternative futures, the patient's symptoms near death and the approximate timing of the dying are essential considerations. Although predicting how long a dying patient will live is unavoidably uncertain,[1–3] estimating prognosis is essential for planning care.

Hospice care is sometimes the appropriate choice for dying patients. Hospice programs serve those who are beyond cure and provide patient-centered comprehensive care to relieve suffering, alleviate unwarranted symptoms, and enhance life opportunities in a necessarily limited lifespan. Though relatively few facilities exist, the inpatient hospice is a cherished resource for patients with poorly controlled symptoms, inadequate social resources, or temporarily exhausted family caregivers. Outpatient hospice programs provide coordinated services for dying patients who are at home or in long-term care facilities. Some formal hospice services are reimbursable under Medicare and commercial insurance, though with onerous caps and limits.

APPROACH TO THE PATIENT

Identifying the Dying Patient

Identifying a patient as dying is not problematic when the patient has an aggressive malignancy which has failed every possible treatment. However, many elderly patients who are dying are not so easily labeled. Because of the difficulty of precisely predicting the remaining time for such patients, few such patients are referred to hospice programs, though they certainly are appropriate recipients of "hospice-type" care.

Doctor-Patient Relationship

Humankind is unique in knowing that each person will die. Yet denial mechanisms effectively push back concerns about mortality, even among caregivers. Confronting mortality in patients can cause anxiety and precipitate dysfunctional defenses. Only when the physician and other key caregivers learn to confront their own fears can management of the patient be effective and appropriately patient-centered.[4]

The patient needs a doctor whose concern for the patient will be lifelong, even in the absence of curative treatments. The effective physician allows time to listen to individual concerns as well as to explain and discuss care options. In doing so, the physician enhances the patient's quality of life and makes the time remaining as meaningful as possible.

Medical Assessment

Thorough history taking, including review of old medical records, ordinarily is essential for understanding the story of the patient's past and future course of illness. The physical examination is helpful and, if done well, can help avoid unnecessary and burdensome diagnostic interventions. At times, further medical investigations may be indicated even when cure is impossible. For example, a new symptom may be due to another disease process altogether, and perhaps one that is treatable. On the other hand, the symptom may represent a treatable complication of the underlying disease. Documenting the rate of disease progression might help choose interventions for optimal effect. Knowing that time is short, for example, a patient may be willing to spend funds on round-the-clock nursing care.

Psychosocial Aspects of Assessment

Strengths or weaknesses in the psychological or social realms of function may be critical contributors to a patient's general well-being. Patients have vastly differing concerns regarding the process of dying: What has been the patient's previous experience of death? What were the experiences of loved ones the patient has seen die? What are this person's fears about dying? Pain? Isolation? Disfigurement? Helplessness? How has the patient coped with difficult situations in the past? The clinician should know about the immediate family and friends and should make efforts to communicate with them. Often, financial concerns are inextricably bound up with the care of the dying patient. A patient may refuse a costly treatment for fear of bankrupting a spouse or might interfere with needed care by refusing to divulge financial information.

Anticipating the likelihood that the patient will eventually lose the capacity to contribute to decision making, the physician should attempt to make important decisions about future care with the patient and should identify a person who can make decisions as the patient's "surrogate." Commonly, this surrogate will be a close family member, but it may also be a good friend or a professional adviser. The clinician is obliged to be knowledgeable about local legal issues surrounding incompetence and dying in order to counsel patients about durable powers of attorney, living wills, and wills. Durable powers of attorney for health care are especially powerful and flexible and should be used more widely.

The Importance of Teamwork

Optimally, the dying patient will be cared for by an interdisciplinary team of professionals and concerned others. The physician often coordinates and leads this team, which may include nurses, social workers, clergy, volunteers (as patient advocates and friends), rehabilitation therapists, dietitians, and others.

The quality of interaction among the team members will be reflected in the ability of that team to provide smooth, well-coordinated services to the patient. Patient care is optimal when there exists mutual respect among team members and a fair amount of cross-training. Shared information and expertise enables the team to accomplish more than the individuals could acting independently.

Caring for dying people is stressful for all involved. Even the best solutions and remedies to illness and suffering are far from perfect. Despite the most valiant efforts, mistakes are made, shortcomings are perceived. In addition to providing more holistic and better coordinated patient care, the team approach permits mutual support among team members.

DECISION MAKING

When caring for elderly dying patients, questions without clear answers appear often, "How long do I have?" "What will dying be like?" "What has my life amounted to?" and "Why me?" Compassion, honesty, and spiritual counseling may help. However, the question, "What should be done now?" has to have an answer, and finding it requires attention to ethical and social issues as well as medical possibilities.

A General Framework

Ill elderly individuals rarely have one diagnosis that suffices to explain the entire clinical picture. More frequently there will be a multiplicity of chronic and acute problems, historical elements, and physiologic characteristics unique to each patient. When making a decision about care, all must be part of the assessment. The choice of treatment will depend on the patient's overall situation and the goals and desires of that patient. For each patient, there are likely to be several possible "futures" that would constitute reasonable choices. The longest future (i.e., that which puts off death as long as possible) will usually not be the most desirable. The practitioner must avoid basing choices on prejudices about how people should value life with various characteristics.[5]

The physician must also recognize which options are not available. A practitioner is ethically and legally barred from administering a lethal poison to a patient.[6] Certain other options may not be open to the patient because of financial constraints, travel distance, or scarce resources.[7]

Resuscitation

Treatments should always be judged by what good they can do the patient. In the case of cardiopulmonary resuscitation for dying elderly patients, the chances of prolonging meaningful life for that patient are extremely slim. Foregoing resuscitation may become a matter of dismissing treatment that is doomed to fail and that might serve only to prolong suffering.

One must always differentiate a "Do Not Resuscitate" (DNR) order from a "Do Nothing" order. The DNR order does not decide other vigorous interventions such as artificial feeding, intravenous antibiotics, or even surgery. Each of these other decisions must be taken up in its own right and in the context in which it arises, keeping in mind the overall goals of treatment.

Artificial Feeding

Issues of artificial feeding in dying patients come up frequently. Reasonable people differ as to the desirability of feeding dying patients by artificial means, but the following generally are accepted:

- First, that food and water should be provided freely as long as the patient is able to swallow reasonably safely.
- Second, artificial methods of providing nourishment to patients who can no longer swallow food and water are sometimes useful, desirable, or both.
- Third, patients who are dying do not ordinarily experience discomfort from dehydration and insufficient nutrition. Maintaining "normal" levels of hydration in a dying patient might well actually increase the likelihood of pulmonary edema and distressing respiratory secretions.[8,9]
- Fourth, court cases have not required caregivers to administer artificial feedings forcibly to a seriously ill person who objects to such feedings or who would be, on balance, harmed.[10–15]

Each decision should be tailored to the patient and the special circumstances. The patient may have a special event to live for, such as a graduation or the birth of a grandchild. Then, the patient may be motivated to endure the discomfort and added medical monitoring of intravenous hydration in order to survive for that event. In a different patient with a decreasing ability to take oral sustenance, the dying process may be so far progressed that the patient no longer has an interest in pursuing any avenue of aggressive nutritional intervention. The patient or the patient's surrogate may then communicate with the physician that the patient's desire is to forgo artificial feeding and let nature take its course. Like all other treatments, artificial feedings have some associated discomforts and risks.

DESIGNING CARE FOR COMFORT

Each clinician develops a repertoire of techniques for managing unwanted symptoms and maximizing function and comfort. The goal is to design a comprehensive approach for care, utilizing medications, interpersonal interactions, optimal nursing technique, and other resources as appropriate.

General Principles

Routes of Medications

Medications should ordinarily be delivered by the oral route, since that is usually more convenient and the pharmacodynamics are smoother. Parenteral administration usually results in a faster onset but a shorter duration of action. Once a patient is unable to tolerate oral medications, rectal, subcutaneous, intramuscular, or intravenous routes may be used. Constant infusion (intravenous, subcutaneous, or intrathecal) pumps for opioid analgesics have proved to be useful. Age alone should not be a barrier to the utilization of symptom-relieving medications, including narcotics. As for all patients, the individual's response must be monitored closely and the dosage and frequency titrated to response and side effects.

Timing

Most dying patients who are experiencing pain or other troubling symptoms will be more comfortable on a regular, round-the-clock dosing schedule of medication rather than treatment only after the symptoms become apparent. The goal of treatment is to suppress the symptoms and prevent their reemergence between doses. For example, round-the-clock dosing eliminates the "pain behavior" cycle, in which the pain returns in force as the analgesic wears off and the patient must wait until the caregiver can respond and until the medication takes effect. The delay heightens anxiety and exacerbates pain. Pain behavior occurs frequently in the hospital setting, where short-staffed nurses may not be able to respond quickly, resulting in an anxious, frightened, dependent, and hurting patient.

Boosters

When a symptom occasionally becomes poorly controlled, parenteral boosters between regular doses of oral palliative medications can help restore control of a symptom quickly and can also predict how much more medication might be needed regularly.

SYMPTOM COMPLEXES AND TREATMENTS

Pain

Pain is a frequent and complex symptom of dying patients.[16,17] The clinician should be alert to the multiple guises of pain. A patient in chronic pain may present as a demanding, hostile, irritable individual who denies "pain" or as a withdrawn, noncommunicative person. A multidimensional approach that includes history taking, physical examination, and functional and psychological evaluation will result in a more accurate diagnosis and subsequently the most effective intervention.[18] With appropriate treatment an affable, tolerant, and relaxed personality may be restored. Ascertaining etiology may guide treatment. The sensation of pain comprises both the nociception (the perception of the painful stimulus) and the emotional reaction to it.[19] Both may be treated. Understanding the half-life, pharmacokinetics, relative potencies, and mechanisms of action is extremely important to using analgesics correctly. The most commonly used narcotic analgesics are compared in Table 34-1.

TABLE 34-1

Comparison of Selected Narcotic Analgesics

		Starting Range, mg	Usual Duration, h	Approximate Equivalent Dose, mg
Morphine	*Oral immediate release*	5–15	3–5	40
	Tablets 15, 30 mg			
	Solution 10 or 20 mg/5 ml			
	Concentrated solution 100 mg/5 ml			
	Oral sustained release	*	8–12	
	Tablets 30, 60 mg			
	SQ or IM†	2.5–5.0	3–5	10
Hydromorphone	*Oral*	1–2	4–5	7.5
	Tablets 1, 2, 3, 4 mg			
	Rectal	3	6–8	Highly variable
	Suppository 3 mg			
	SQ or IM	0.5–1.5	4–5	1.5
Levorphanol	*Oral*	1–2	4–6	4.0
	Tablets 2 mg			
Methadone	*Oral*	2.5–10.0	3–5	20
	Tablets 5, 10, 40 mg			
	Solution 5 or 10 mg/5 ml			
Codeine	*Oral*	30–60	4–6	200

*Ordinarily convert to sustained release after stabilization on immediate release preparation.
†SQ, subcutaneous; IM, intramuscular.

Nonnarcotic Analgesics

Mild pain may be treated with aspirin (if tolerated) or acetaminophen on a round-the-clock schedule of 650 mg four times daily. If this is insufficient, other nonsteroidal anti-inflammatory drugs (NSAIDs) may be tried, especially for musculoskeletal pain such as bone metastases or disuse contractures. Ketorolac tromethamine (Toradol), a NSAID, has been effective in controlling the acute pain of rheumatoid and osteoarthritis and shows promise in the control of serious cancer pain, mainly because it can be administered parenterally. It probably has no advantage over other oral NSAIDs. If narcotic analgesics are needed, continuing NSAIDs can reduce the dosage required.

Narcotics

If NSAIDs and plain acetaminophen have failed, the fixed combination of codeine and acetaminophen is useful, especially in outpatients, in the dose of 1 to 2 tablets every 3 to 4 hours. The most common side effect is constipation. Oral morphine is the gold standard of narcotic analgesia. The initial dose in a frail elderly person can be as low as 2.5 mg every 4 to 6 hours. The dose and interval can be titrated quickly. Oral morphine comes in tablets, solution, and slow-release tablets. Short-acting preparations are best until pain is under control, and then a regular schedule, using the equivalent dose of longer-acting medications, can be set. A transdermal system for delivering fentanyl, a potent opioid analgesic, over a 72-hour period has been successfully used in ambulatory elderly living at home. The continuous administration of this drug provides a more stable level of analgesia.

Strong opioids commonly cause drowsiness, constipation, and nausea. Patients usually develop a tolerance to the drowsiness within a few days. The constipation should be aggressively treated with laxatives. The nausea may be suppressed with a nonsedative antiemetic such as haloperidol 0.5 mg every 8 hours. In an agitated patient, a mildly sedating antiemetic such as prochlorperazine (Compazine) may be used.

Physical dependence is a concomitant of regular use of narcotics. If discontinuation becomes possible, tapering over 5 to 10 days will prevent withdrawal symptoms.

Tolerance to narcotics also occurs, but increased doses of the narcotic should continue to achieve pain relief. If need be, switching to a different narcotic and using nonnarcotic agents, anesthetic and neurosurgical interventions, or hypnosis and imaging usually allow effective pain control despite tolerance. Hydromorphone HCl (Dilaudid) can be prepared for parenteral use at 100 mg/ml—a dosage which is concentrated enough for virtually any need.

Adjuvant Analgesic Drugs

Some drugs that are marketed for other purposes have been shown to relieve pain. Hydroxyzine (Atarax, Vistaril) appears to produce an analgesic effect that reduces morphine doses by about one-quarter. Serotonergic antidepressants (amitriptyline, doxepin) potentiate the analgesic effect of narcotics but may also hasten the onset of narcotic tolerance. The sedating side effects can be useful when the drug is given at bedtime. Steroids may reduce edema and thereby treat pain in situations such as nerve compression, elevated intracranial pressure, lumen obstruction, bone pain, and possibly lymphedema. Dexamethasone, 4 mg every 6 hours for several days, should provide an adequate trial.

Anesthesia Techniques

For pain in the distribution of a peripheral nerve, afferent input can be interrupted by nerve blocking procedures or transcutaneous nerve stimulation. If the pain source is intraspinal, the patient may benefit from a neurosurgical procedure ablating the affected spinal roots or a part of the spinal cord. An implanted spinal epidural morphine pump for metastatic cancer can deliver the narcotic directly to the nervous system, thereby greatly reducing total doses and possibly reducing side effects. The implantation can be done under epidural anesthesia and requires placement of a subcutaneous abdominal automatic pump that can be refilled percutaneously every few weeks in the outpatient setting. An implanted spinal electrical stimulator can be used for control of pain in the lower trunk and lower extremities.[20]

Noninvasive Measures

A variety of nonpharmacologic methods can be useful strategies for pain relief. The use of heat, cold, and massage, with or without a topically applied substance such as menthol, can relieve tension and be soothing to the individual. Transcutaneous electrical nerve stimulation (TENS) therapy can reduce the discomfort of some neuropathic and musculoskeletal conditions. A variety of alternative techniques such as relaxation, music, prayer, meditation, pets, and recreational activities, used according to the preferences of the patient, can be effective in controlling pain.[21] Life review, the process of looking back over one's life to recall pleasant memories or unresolved conflicts, not only reduces the perception of pain but takes the patient beyond the biophysical and psychological dimension to an understanding of the meaning and purpose of his or her life. This need for spiritual integration is thought to be fundamental at the end of life.[22]

PULMONARY SYMPTOMS

Respiratory Distress

Next to pain, dyspnea is a symptom most feared by patients and caregivers alike. Determining the exact etiology may lead to treatment for dyspnea caused by hypoxemia, poor handling of secretions, anxiety, bronchospasm, or musculoskeletal pain.

Supplemental oxygen, anxiolytics, bronchodilators, analgesics, and drying agents such as atropine may suffice to suppress dyspnea. Morphine and other narcotics dull the sensation of dyspnea from all causes. Control over dyspnea can almost always be achieved through the use of these medications, especially with increasing doses of narcotics. Of course, large doses of sedating drugs may precipitate hypercarbia and respiratory arrest, and so their use is warranted only when these risks are reasonable in light of the patient's other alternatives and discomfort from dyspnea.

Airway Secretions

The most common cause of troubling bronchial secretions in dying patients is intravenous overhydration. If cardiotonic and diuretic drugs are ineffective or if an untreatable cause is suspected, severe respiratory congestion and distress may be treated with morphine sulfate.

Cough

Guaifenesin syrup is often adequate. If cough remains unrelieved, hydrocodeine syrup may suffice. If sedation is undesirable and the cough is dry, benzonatate (Tessalon) can be dramatically effective. The patient should not chew or hold this drug in the mouth because it is a powerful local anesthetic.

Respiratory Depression from Narcotics

Transient oversedation is not uncommon in dying patients treated with narcotics, but most patients have little ill effect. Unexpected respiratory depression in the setting of stable analgesic doses is more likely to result from another cause, such as metabolic derangement or central nervous system disturbance. In any case, moderate overnarcotization rarely needs treatment other than precautions regarding aspiration and the monitoring of vital signs and neurologic status. Reversal of the effect of narcotics with naloxone (Narcan) usually causes unpleasant withdrawal symptoms but may be used if needed.

GASTROINTESTINAL PROBLEMS

Anorexia

Anorexia is common in the last days of many disease processes. Patients often lose interest in food when they are anxious about end-of-life concerns or when they lose the "will to live." However, anorexia also may result from local mouth pain or dysphagia from a treatable cause. Attention to food preferences, aesthetics of surroundings, and the presentation of the food are simple but effective measures. Relaxing dietary restrictions and providing frequent supplemental feedings may contribute greatly to enhancing the patient's enjoyment of remaining life. Pharmacologic stimulation of appetite is not usually successful, though some claim that an alcoholic cocktail prior to meals may be useful. Some patients respond to steroids with improved appetite.[20]

Nausea and Vomiting

Nausea may be caused by local factors (gastritis, obstruction, etc.) or central factors (tumor, raised intracranial pressure, etc). Antacids and H_2 blockers are commonly used to reduce symptoms. Prochlorperazine (Compazine) or small doses of haloperidol (Haldol) are often effective. Gastric paresis or mild functional ileus may respond to the addition of metaclopramide (Reglan) 10 mg orally before meals.

Intestinal Obstruction

Although most physicians are accustomed to giving aggressive treatments to relieve intestinal obstruction, palliative management may sometimes be better in the dying patient. The spasmodic pain can be relieved by diphenoxylate hydrochloride 2.5 mg with atropine sulfate 0.025 mg (Lomotil) or loperamide hydrochloride 2 mg (Imodium), or narcotics. Many patients prefer occasional emesis to nasogastric suction and may actually absorb enough to live comfortably or even unexpectedly reopen the intestines without surgery.

Constipation

Constipation is a common complaint of dying patients. In patients who require large amounts of narcotics and whose activity and diet are restricted, constipation may be a constant concern. Often recognition of the problem is delayed even when the patient is in a hospital and receiving careful medical supervision. Through careful monitoring, trouble can be anticipated or detected early.

Adding water and fiber to the diet to create bulky, hydrated stools would be ideal, but these measures may be impractical for dying elderly patients, especially those with chronic constipation, and this is a situation where stool softeners (docusate, psyllium hydrophic mucilloid) and aggressive treatment with oral cathartics (lactulose, magnesium citrate) should be tried. Before giving psyllium hydrophilic mucilloid or other bulk-forming laxatives for constipation, one must determine if the patient is able to maintain sufficient fluid intake and diet. Poor oral intake combined with this laxative could result in impaction. If all other interventions fail, then manual disimpaction, suppositories, and enemas are in order. Vigilance and persistence are required for prevention and treatment.

Dry Mouth

Anticholinergic medications frequently cause a dry and sore mouth. Radiation therapy may also contribute to this painful condition. Gentle and thorough mouth care can alleviate the discomfort to a great degree despite the continuation of the causative medications and poor hydration. Glycerine and citric acid mouth washes provide soothing comfort. Viscous xylocaine 1% to 2% or artificial saliva (Salivart) may help.

Oral Thrush

Oral candidiasis can be extremely debilitating and may prevent adequate oral intake. Symptoms involving the esophagus are not uncommon. The following mixture has been found to be quite helpful: 1 ounce each of diphenhydramine liquid, liquid antacid, nystatin, and viscous xylocaine 2%, given as a 5 ml swish and swallow, qid. Nystatin (Mycostatin) oral suspension or troche, clotrimazole (Mycelex) troches, or ketoconazole (Nizoral) may be needed for refractory cases and should be continued for 2 to 4 weeks after all clinical signs are gone.

MENTAL STATUS CHANGES

Anxiety

The dying patient who is uncomfortably anxious needs assessment for potentially treatable causes (such as hypoxemia, pain, or fear). Often, a stable and available professional staff will itself greatly relieve anxiety.

The long-acting benzodiazepines (flurazepam, diazepam) are best avoided. Their effects may be paradoxical and their prolonged half-lives prevent rapid adjustment if the patient is intolerant of their effect. Lorazepam (Ativan) or alprazolam (Xanax) are quite short-acting and are preferred.

Other useful drugs for anxiety include diphenhydramine (Benadryl) and hydroxyzine (Atarax, Vistaril), which are ordinarily well tolerated and effective for 4 to 6 hours.

Hallucinations

If a patient is hallucinating, antipsychotics such as haloperidol (Haldol), chlorpromazine (Thorazine), and thioridazine (Mellaril) may be useful in minimizing hallucinatory input to the patient's thought processes and provide sedation as well. It is prudent to begin with very low doses (such as haloperidol 0.5 mg) and gradually increase the dose. Some patients may require very little to achieve the desired effect.

Depression

Methylphenidate (Ritalin) may be useful and can be almost immediately effective. Tricyclic antidepressants are also helpful, with nocturnal sedation often being a welcome side effect. The antidepressant benefits of treatment require at least a few days to become evident.

Skin

Skin Breakdown

Skin breakdown is the scourge of all bedridden patients. Dying people are at special risk since they may encounter all the circumstances that cause skin breakdown: poor nutrition, incontinence of bowel and bladder, decreased mobility, and poor hygiene. Decubitus ulcers are painful and may provide an entry point for deep infection. Thus, they may contribute to further morbidity and early mortality in dying patients.

To reduce risk of skin breakdown, the patient should be turned at least every 2 hours. Minimizing shearing forces on the skin is crucial; a patient should not be pulled across the sheets. A soft bed covering (such as an egg-crate mattress) will reduce shear forces. Pressure-reducing mattresses are beneficial in maintaining skin integrity and relieving pain. Early versions of pressure-relieving mattresses were so expensive that most patients could not afford them. Recently, less expensive products have been developed and appear to be beneficial.

Fungating Tumors

Large tumor masses on the surface sometimes develop areas of necrosis and infection, with painful, malodorous lesions. Local radiation therapy may be effective for temporary control of the lesion. If persistent capillary bleeding is a problem, pads soaked in epinephrine 1:1000 may help. Moderate persistent bleeding may respond to radiotherapy. Persistent foul odor may be controlled with topical tetracycline (by opening a capsule and sprinkling on the affected area).

Pruritus

Medications to suppress itching include diphenhydramine (Benadryl), hydroxyzine (Atarax), or topical Mycolog (nystatin and triamcinolone acetonide) or steroid cream. Skin hydration is helpful and may be achieved with increased fluid intake, lotions, baths, and room humidifiers.

Seizures

Patients dying from central nervous system tumors or with profound metabolic changes may develop seizure activity. Generally, the antiseizure regimen is much the same as in other seizure patients. Phenytoin (Dilantin), phenobarbital, carbamazepine (Tegretol), and primidone (Mysoline) are commonly used.

For status epilepticus, IV diazepam (Valium) is preferred. Intramuscular (IM) diazepam is erratically absorbed. If there is no IV access, IM lorazepam (Ativan) is preferable, as it is reliably absorbed. It may be given in 2-mg increments until the seizures subside. Lorazepam requires refrigerated storage.

Seizures may come from elevated intracranial pressure, which can sometimes be reduced by steroids. Decadron, 4 mg every 4 hours for 2 to 3 days, provides a reasonable trial of treatment.

Genitourinary Tract

Urinary Tract Infection

A patient bothered by urinary tract symptoms such as dysuria or frequency may have an acute urinary tract infection. In light of the bothersome symptoms, it usually is best to treat with the appropriate antibiotics and phenazopyridine (Pyridium).

Urinary Incontinence

Incontinence of urine is a common problem in ill elderly patients. The general disapproving attitude toward chronic indwelling (Foley) catheters for geriatric patients may be safely suspended in dying patients. If pain and dysmobility are prominent problems, the indwelling catheter may permit considerable increase in comfort and prevent skin breakdown.

MANAGING DEATH

Bereavement

The team caring for the patient is in a position to provide much comfort and reassurance to the family and close friends.[21] If there is no ongoing team that ensures bereavement follow-up, the physician should do so.

The family or close friends ordinarily face certain "tasks" during mourning. These tasks need not be performed in any particular order, and there may be significant heterogeneity in the ways different people approach them. The tasks of mourning include:

1. Accepting the reality of the loss.
2. Experiencing the pain of the loss.
3. Adjusting to an environment where the deceased is missing.
4. Withdrawing emotional energy from the deceased and reinvesting that energy in other relationships and activities.

The team can facilitate successful mourning in several ways. Before the patient's death, they can encourage anticipatory grieving and encourage communication between the patient and the family. The family should be allowed to stay with the body after death, an experience that is immensely helpful toward accepting the reality of the death and reducing fears. After the death, the family and friends should be encouraged to talk about the deceased. This is especially effective when done a few days following the death with all members of the immediate family present, perhaps along with a member of the clergy. A wide range of emotions is normal. Profoundly dysfunctional or prolonged grieving should be directed to professional counseling.

Aesthetic Concerns

In general, the team strives to care for the patient in a way that is as pleasing as possible to the patient and to the family. Even in an unresponsive patient, for example, great care should be taken to maintain cleanliness and orderliness of appearance. These measures exhibit a lasting respect for the patient that persists despite the progression of the dying process.

Death at Home

With the help of family, friends, and caregivers, patients may live out their final days at home. So that societal needs are met and families are not overburdened by "procedural tasks" at the time of death, coordination and planning are required. Funeral arrangements should be made in advance. The physician and home care nurse should be available at all times. At the hour of death, the caregiver should notify the physician or nurse so that arrangements can be made for pronouncement of death, notification of the medical examiner (if that is necessary), consideration of autopsy (if not decided in advance), and removal of the body.

REFERENCES

1. Forster L, Lynn J: Predicting life span for applicants to inpatient hospice. *Arch Intern Med* 148:2540, 1988.
2. Parkes CM: Accuracy of predictions of survival in later stages of cancer. *Br Med J* 2:29, 1972.
3. Evans C, McCarthy M: Prognostic uncertainty in terminal care: Can the Karnofsky Index help? *Lancet* 1:204, 1985.
4. Artiss KL, Levine AS: Doctor-patient relation in severe illness. *N Engl J Med* 288:1210, 1974.
5. Pearlman R, Speer J: Quality of life considerations in geriatric care. *J Am Geriatr Soc* 31:113, 1983.
6. The President's Commission for the Study of Ethical Problems in Medicine and Biomedical and Behavioral Research: *Deciding to Forego Life-Sustaining Treatment.* Washington, Government Printing Office, 1983.
7. Lynn J: Legal and ethical issues in palliative health care. *Semin Oncol* 12:476, 1985.
8. Lynn J, Childress JF: Must patients always be given food and water? *Hastings Center Rep* 17:13, 1983.
9. Schmitz P, O'Brien M: Observations on nutrition and hydration in dying cancer patients, in Lynn J (ed): *By No Extraordinary Means: The Choice to Forego Life-Sustaining Food and Water.* Bloomington, Indiana University Press, 1986.
10. Glover J, Lynn J: Update since *Conroy:* 1985–1988, in *By No Extraordinary Means: The Choice to Forego Life-Sustaining Food and Water,* 2d ed. Bloomington, Indiana University Press, 1989.
11. *In re Conroy,* 98 New Jersey, 321, 486, A.2d 1209 (1985).
12. *Bouvia v. County of Riverside,* No. 159780 (California Supreme Court, Riverside County, December 16, 1983).
13. *In re Jobes,* 180 New Jersey, 394, 529 A.2d 434 (1987).
14. *In re Requena,* 213 New Jersey Superior Court 475, 517 A.2d 886 (Superior Court Ch. Division) aff'd 213 N.J. Superior Court 443, 517 A.2d 869 (Superior Court Appelate Division, 1986) (per curiam).
15. *In re Rodas,* No. 86 PR 139 (Colorado District Court Mesa County, January 22, 1987).
16. Foley KM: The treatment of cancer pain. *N Engl J Med* 313:84, 1985.
17. Levy MH: Pain management in advanced cancer. *Semin Oncol* 12:394, 1985.
18. Ferrell BA: Pain management in elderly people. *J Am Geriatr Soc* 39:66, 1991.
19. Hillier R: Terminally ill patient: Medical and nursing care, in Aaronson NK, Beckman J (eds): *The Quality of Life of Cancer Patients.* New York, Raven Press, 1987, p 239.
20. Black P: Neurosurgical management of cancer pain. *Semin Oncol* 12:438, 1985.
21. McCaffery M, Beebe A: Pain in the elderly, in McCaffery M, Beebe A (eds): *Pain: Clinical Manual for Nursing Practice.* St. Louis, MO, Mosby, chap 11, pp 308–323.
22. Missine LE: Death & spiritual concerns. *Generations* 14:45, 1990.
23. Levy MH, Catalano RB: Control of common physical symptoms other than pain in patients with terminal disease. *Semin Oncol* 12:411, 1985.
24. Worden JW: Bereavement. *Semin Oncol* 12:472, 1985.

Chapter 35

LEGAL ASPECTS OF GERIATRIC MEDICINE

Kate Mewhinney

The physician who cares for older adults is likely to encounter certain legal questions. These cover a broad range of subjects, including mental competency, drivers licenses, and "death with dignity." This chapter addresses the physician's role and responsibilities when these legal questions arise. Since there will be variations between the laws of different states, the best course is to become familiar with the state laws where one practices medicine. For advice on a specific case, the reader should obtain legal advice.

Often, the physician is the only professional with whom an older person interacts on a regular basis. Although the physician may not become directly involved in the legal issues affecting a patient, he or she should be able to spot legal needs and refer the patient for appropriate assistance.

COMPETENCY

Informed Consent and the Refusal of Treatment

The term *competency* has many meanings in the law. In the medical context, the term is used to describe a patient's capacity to give informed consent to medical treatment. The requirement of informed consent arises out of the law of battery, which bars unauthorized touching of others, and a constitutional right to privacy.

The physician's primary legal duty, aside from providing good care, is to respect the patient's autonomy and right to self-determination. In the eyes of the law, adults are presumed to be competent to make their own decisions. Thus, it will be up to the physician to begin with this presumption of competence for all patients.

Frequently, the physician will need to determine whether a patient has the mental capacity to consent to or refuse medical treatment. Decisional capacity is not an all-or-nothing proposition: the patient may have the capacity to make simple decisions about medical options, but not more difficult ones. Only occasionally will a patient already have been declared incompetent by a court, and a guardian is appointed to make medical decisions.

If a patient is actually not competent but the physician carelessly fails to determine this and goes ahead with medical treatment, the physician may have committed a battery. It is easy to assume that a nod of the head or simple assent signifies consent, especially since it is assumed that the doctor has the patient's best interests at heart. If a determination of competence is made, the physician should make file notes about how this conclusion was arrived at. While helpful, the results of a mental status exam, such as the Folstein Mini-Mental, would not necessarily indicate that the patient could fully understand and give informed consent.

With all patients, but especially those with declining competence, the physician should initiate a discussion of the patient's views on end-of-life treatment decisions. Courts, health care providers, and surrogates will often need to have this information later, when the patient can no longer express himself or herself. Another important reason to have this discussion is to determine whether the physician would be unwilling to abide by the patient's desires. For example, the physician may be morally opposed to discontinuing artificial nutrition or hydration to a patient who is terminally ill or in a persistent vegetative state. However, that may be exactly what the patient would want. If such a disagreement exists, the patient might consider changing to a physician with more compatible views. (See "Advance Directives" below.)

A physician must scrupulously abide by the decisions of a competent patient to accept or refuse medical treatment. When treating very elderly patients and patients with diminished capacity, there is often a tendency to defer to the patient's family. Technically, in most circumstances the family does not have the legal authority to make medical decisions for the elderly relative. (See "The Role of the Family: Surrogates and Substituted Judgment" below.) The legal role of surrogates is evolving rapidly, however, especially as it relates to end-of-life treatment decisions.

A patient's adamant, sustained refusal of treatment may be difficult for the physician to accept. However, it does not, in and of itself, indicate a lack of decisional capacity. If the physician determines that the patient is competent to refuse treatment, the discussion should be documented in the patient's file.

Unfortunately, the law does not clearly define the competency standard for refusal of treatment. People do have the right to refuse medical treatment, even if the refusal may lead to death. In very limited circumstances, the law of most states will, in emergencies, allow the provision of medical care *without* informed consent.

If the patient's capacity to make medical decisions is in doubt, and there is no properly appointed surrogate, the physician may suggest that the family or social services department file a court action to determine whether a guardian should be appointed to make medical decisions.

Other Competency Issues

As mentioned earlier, the issue of competency comes up in many contexts in the law, not just in the area of informed consent. When asked to render an expert opinion on the mental competence of a patient, the physician will, of course, have to be vigilant about protecting patient confidentiality. At the request of a court, however, or with the patient's permission, an opinion may be given. It is important for the physician to understand the *standard of competency* that is being applied.[1] For example, in some states a person may still be competent to make a will ("have testamentary capacity") despite having been declared incompetent under the guardianship laws.

DRIVERS LICENSES AND THE ELDERLY

Often the first legal issue to arise in treating an elderly patient is the question of what to do about the patient's declining ability to drive safely. The issue of driving may be raised by concerned family members, or it may be precipitated by the patient's involvement in a car accident.

The physician will, first and foremost, be concerned about the patient's future safety. Cautionary instructions and advice to the patient on how to limit driving should be documented in the patient's file.

Only a handful of states have specific restrictions pertaining to all elderly drivers, such as requiring periodic vision tests after a specific age.[2]

Often physicians are concerned about whether they would be liable to an injured third party if they *do not* act to restrict the patient's driving. When patients are competent and refuse to modify their driving habits or to stop driving altogether, physicians will need to determine whether they may breach their duty of confidentiality to their patients and, in fact, whether they are *required* by any law to report such patients to the appropriate authority. (For convenience, the authority licensing drivers will be referred to as the DMV, for the Department of Motor Vehicles, although it may go by other names in some states.)

Physician Reporting Laws. The large majority of states do not require that physicians report patients who may be unsafe drivers. As of 1989, only eight states required physicians to report persons whom they had diagnosed as having specific disorders which may adversely affect their ability to drive safely. Seven additional states gave statutory authorization for, but did not require, physicians to report such cases. In 1991, California became the first state to include Alzheimer's disease and related disorders among the list of conditions that physicians are required to report to their local health department, for purposes of regulating drivers' licensing.[3]

To avoid breaching the physician's duty of confidentiality, it may be best if the patient's family members themselves contacted the DMV. In some jurisdictions, following motor vehicle accidents, law enforcement officers report to the DMV if the officers believe that the driver needs to be called in for a recheck on his or her ability to drive.

Physician Liability to Third Parties. Only a few civil suits against physicians have been filed by individuals who were injured by the dangerous driving of the physician's patients. The injured parties claimed that the physicians should have acted to keep dangerous patients/drivers from driving. The few state courts that have addressed the issue of physician liability are divided. Local legal counsel should be sought when this issue arises in the care of elderly patients.

The decision to recommend that a patient restrict or cease driving is one that should be documented and, when required by state law, reported to the DMV. In the absence of a mandatory reporting law, the duty of confidentiality obligates the physician not to reveal a patient's declining ability to drive. Only if the patient has become a substantial public risk or danger, as shown by a medical examination and increasingly frequent motor vehicle accidents, and has no family member who will contact the licensing authorities should the physician consider reporting a patient to the authorities.

ELDER ABUSE AND NEGLECT

The issue of elder abuse and neglect is receiving increased attention in the medical community. In 1992, the American Medical Association (AMA) established a national resource center and clearinghouse to provide clinical protocols to physicians to diagnose and treat elder abuse.

Already mandatory reporting laws applying to physicians exist in 42 states and the District of Columbia.[4] Failure to report is usually a misdemeanor but may be punishable by a fine or penalty.

Abuse of the elderly is not only of the physical or psychological type. It may also be financial, and the alert physician may detect that this abuse is occurring. Typically, financial abuse is theft or conversion of money or other valuables by an elder's relatives or caregivers.

Patients should be encouraged to obtain legal advice on how to stop or prevent financial abuse. The use of a durable power of attorney, discussed in more detail below, would allow the patient to designate a trustworthy person to handle his or her financial affairs. Also, there are simple procedures to have a "representative payee" appointed to receive social security payments on behalf of a person unable to manage his or her finances. Social Security procedures, derived from federal law, are uniform in all states.

Unfortunately, sometimes it is the agent under a power of attorney, or the representative payee, who is committing the financial abuse. The power of attorney may be revoked by the patient if he or she is competent. Similarly, the patient or patient's family could alert the Social Security Administration if there are questions about the payee's handling of social security payments. If the patient is not competent, it may be possible for a guardianship petition to be filed by the patient's relative or the local department of social services.

Financial abuse of the elderly also occurs when they are the victims of fraudulent and deceptive business practices. Patients who have been taken advantage of should be referred to the Better Business Bureau, the consumer protection division of the state attorney general's office, or legal assistance.

In serious cases of abuse or neglect, either physical or financial, there is the possibility of criminal sanctions or a civil suit against the perpetrator. Additional federal laws apply to patient abuse and neglect in residential health care facilities that receive Medicaid funds. Also, if the abuser is a family member, domestic violence statutes may apply, sometimes providing a quick court hearing in urgent situations.

GUARDIANSHIP AND CONSERVATORSHIP

When a person has not designated another to handle his or her affairs in the event of incapacity, it occasionally becomes necessary to have the courts appoint someone to fulfill this function. Typically, this is done through the filing of a guardianship or conservatorship proceeding. (The term used for the surrogate decision maker varies from state to state; in some states the term *conservator* applies to the person appointed simply to handle financial matters.) The courts distinguish between the management of financial affairs and the management of personal affairs, such as health care or housing, and may appoint a guardian to handle one or both types of decisions.

The basis for appointing a guardian is a finding by the court that the person is incapacitated, or incompetent, due to mental illness, mental deficiency, physical illness or disability, or even, under some statutes, advanced age. Medical evidence of incapacity is generally required to support a determination of incapacity or inability to manage oneself or one's property.[5] Some courts require only the affidavit, or sworn statement, of a physician rather than in-person testimony.

Many, if not most, guardianship proceedings will involve individuals who are clearly incapacitated and urgently in need of a responsible individual to make decisions. On the other hand, some guardianship proceedings are initiated by family members who merely want the power to override the decisions, particularly financial decisions, of an eccentric or feeble elderly person. Thus, more than a cursory evaluation of the putative incompetent is in order. This is especially important when one considers that a person who is under a full guardianship loses the right to decide where to live, to give consent to or refusal of medical treatment, to vote, and to handle his or her property and funds.

ADVANCE DIRECTIVES

Powers of Attorney—Financial and Health Care

In order to avoid the cost and delays associated with guardianship proceedings, a person may give written, advance direction as to who should handle his or her financial and health care decisions when he or she is unable to do so. These "advance directives" usually take the form of a durable power of attorney and a health care power of attorney. *Patients with progressive dementias or illnesses that will lead to incapacity should be counseled by their physicians to obtain legal advice about executing advance directives while they are still mentally competent.* Many patients will say that they have made a power of attorney, when actually they are referring to the executor that they appointed to administer their will after their death. Also, some patients will have a power of attorney, but it will not be *durable,* as explained below.

In a durable power of attorney, provided for by statute in all states, a person (called the principal) appoints another person (called the agent or the attorney-in-fact) to handle all of his or her property and financial affairs. The principal may select a family member to serve as the agent, although this is not required. Usually, this power goes into effect when the document is signed, which means that the agent is empowered to handle the principal's affairs immediately. The agent does not necessarily take control right away, however, unlike a guardian, who actually takes over handling all matters. Rather, the agent may be available in the event the principal needs assistance, whether temporarily or permanently. What makes the power "durable" is a provision stating that the power will continue if the principal becomes incapacitated or incompetent. Some individuals prefer that the agent's powers become effective only when the principal becomes incompetent, and thus they would execute a "springing" power of attorney, which "springs" into effect upon incapacity.

The power of attorney may be revoked by the principal if he or she is still competent. It is also revoked if a guardian is appointed by a court, and upon the death of the principal.

All states either authorize by statute the creation of a *durable power of attorney for health care,* or will honor such a document if executed in another state. This is another important option for all individuals to consider, but especially those with progressive illnesses such as Alzheimer's disease. Most statutes explicitly state that a health are provider is authorized to honor the decisions of a properly appointed health care agent and will not face criminal or civil liability or professional disciplinary action for doing so.

The power of the health care agent is effective whenever the principal is unable to make or communicate health care decisions, whether the inability is temporary or permanent. The principal will usually select a family member to be the health care agent, although a nonrelative may be appointed.

Living Wills

The living will is a document in which a person, while competent, states his or her views on the use of life-sustaining medical treatment if he or she should become unable to communicate those views. As with health care powers of attorney, the state laws on living wills are evolving rapidly. All states, plus the District of Columbia, have statutes authorizing living wills, either as free-standing documents or as part of a health care power of attorney.

Public awareness of living wills was given a boost by the U.S. Supreme Court decision in *Cruzan v. Director, Missouri Dept. of Health,* 110 S. Ct. 2841 (1990). In its first consideration of a "right-to-die" case, the Court held that, where a statutory living will had not been executed, a state could question the legitimacy of a surrogate decision by requiring "clear and convincing evidence" that a patient would have refused treatment.

Implementation of the Patient Self-Determination Act, beginning in December 1991, has also raised public awareness about living wills. This federal law requires most medical facilities to inform adult patients, upon admission, of what the law is in their state on advance health care directives. Patients may not be required to sign these directives, although some may choose to do so.

Living will statutes vary in several important respects. First, the majority of statutes apply only to "terminal conditions" and do not address the individual's right to refuse life-sustaining treatment when in a persistent vegetative state.[6]

Second, the statutes vary as to whether an individual may refuse artificial nutrition and hydration. Some statutes do not address the issue at all, and some explicitly *exclude* artificial hydration and nutrition from the treatments that may be withdrawn unless the patient had clearly expressed directions that such treatments be withdrawn.

Third, only a few state statutes address the question of how health care providers should proceed in the absence of a living will when the patient is unable to communicate and is either terminally ill or in a persistent vegetative state. The few statutes that address this issue allow decision making by a hierarchy of family members, beginning with the spouse (e.g., in North Carolina). The right of the family or other surrogates to make decisions is usually unclear, as discussed below.

If the physician is unwilling to abide by the patient's wishes as expressed in the living will, he or she is obligated under some state statutes to transfer the patient to another facility or else comply with the patient's wishes. In addition, case law and professional ethics may require that the physician assist in transferring the patient who wishes to refuse life-sustaining treatment to the care of a doctor willing to abide by such wishes.

It is important to remember that a living will is not self-executing. In other words, the decision to withhold or discontinue life support must be made by the attending physician before the patient's directions will be honored. The physician's decision, which usually requires the concurrence of a second physician, is expressed in a written "do not resuscitate" (DNR) order. If the patient is still competent, he or she may also be asked to sign the DNR order, signifying concurrence. Most hospitals now have ethics committees that should be consulted when questions arise as to the use of a DNR order. Informal or oral agreements not to resuscitate a patient are unacceptable and could result in legal liability. Similarly, physicians should not participate in a "slow code" or a deliberately slow effort to resuscitate a patient.

THE ROLE OF THE FAMILY: SURROGATES AND SUBSTITUTED JUDGMENT

When no advance directives have been executed, physicians have traditionally turned to the patient's family for consent to provide or terminate treatment.

However, the legal status of the family to give consent is not always clear. Surrogate decision making by family members is authorized by statute or case law in approximately half the states.[7]

In the absence of a family consent statute, a physician justifiably may be uneasy about relying on the authority of the family when making treatment decisions. However, most courts have declined to require judicial intervention as a prerequisite to withdrawal of life-sustaining treatment from an incompetent adult. The physician may proceed if he or she conforms to accepted medical practices and documents the family's informed consent and the ineffectiveness and burdensome nature of further treatment.

Questions about how to proceed become even more difficult in certain situations. There may be no family consensus about the treatment (or nontreatment) plan. Perhaps there is family consensus, but it is to *ignore* the wishes that the incompetent patient had earlier expressed in a valid living will. The family, or a properly appointed surrogate, will sometimes make decisions that may not conform to the patient's best interests. When discussions with the family cannot resolve the impasse, the physician would be well advised to consult with the hospital's ethics committee and with legal counsel before terminating *or* continuing treatment. Ultimately, the case can be put before a court for a decision that will clarify the physician's responsibilities and liabilities. Recommended guidelines have been developed by a multidisciplinary panel of experts to aid state courts in handling such cases. These guidelines are available from the West Publishing Company in Eagan, Minnesota.

Where the physician determines that a medical treatment such as cardiopulmonary resuscitation (CPR) is useless or needlessly prolongs the dying process, he or she is not required by law to continue such treatment. Of course, the futility of such treatment is not always clear cut. Nevertheless, where the family cannot provide an adequate reason for not consenting to a DNR order and where CPR appears to be futile, the physician will probably not face legal difficulties if he or she goes ahead and issues a DNR order.

When life support is burdensome for the patient but not clearly futile, the lack of family consensus on how to proceed poses a difficult problem for the physician. This is particularly true where the patient had not previously expressed to the physician his or her views on life-sustaining medical treatment. If the family cannot reach agreement, it may be advisable for the family, the county social services department, or the health care provider to petition the court to appoint a guardian to act on the patient's behalf.[8,9]

PHYSICIAN AID IN DYING

Along with the development of living will laws have come efforts to enact patients' rights to obtain medical treatments that will bring on death, especially for patients with pain that is not medically manageable. Currently, euthanasia is not legal, although less than half of the states make it a crime to assist someone in committing suicide.

In some states, efforts have been made to permit "physician aid in dying." In Washington state in 1991, voters narrowly defeated a measure that would have permitted physicians to end the life of conscious, competent adults who were terminally ill and who requested such assistance in writing. Physicians debated whether such voluntary euthanasia was contrary to their proper role as healers.[10]

On the November 1992 ballot in California, there was a referendum on the California Death with Dignity Act, which would have permitted terminally ill adults to request and receive physician aid in dying. Had the act become law, California would have become the first jurisdiction in the United States to legalize active euthanasia. However, this referendum was defeated. Nevertheless, similar measures have been introduced in legislatures in a handful of other states, and the issue of physician-assisted suicide, given notoriety by the actions of Dr. Jack Kevorkian in Michigan, has emerged as a major issue of public and professional debate in the present decade.

NURSING HOMES

The most common, broader legal issues in nursing homes are those of mental competency, futility of treatment, and the appropriate role of surrogates or family in decision making. In addition, legal regulation of nursing homes by the state and federal governments has increased significantly in recent years. On the state level, regulation occurs primarily in the licensing of nursing homes and their administrators. To assist nursing home residents and their families, the federal government funds the position of regional ombudsman in all parts of the country.

Most importantly, the federal government has enacted major changes in the quality control of facilities receiving Medicare or Medicaid. These laws are part of the Social Security Act and are administered by the U.S. Department of Health and Human Services through its Health Care Financing Administration (HCFA). Medicare and Medicaid requirements for long-term care are found in the Code of Federal Regulations (CFR), Title 42, Part 483. The regulations are extensive and should be read by physicians who treat nursing home residents. Some of the most important regulations, pertaining to the role of the physician, are listed below.

Standardized assessments of new nursing home residents are now required soon after admission. Physicians must provide an admission diagnosis, medical history, physical exam, medical problem list, and estimate of rehabilitation potential. Visits by a physician are required at prescribed intervals, and specific documentation is mandated.

Physical or chemical restraints may be used only when necessary to treat the residents' medical symptoms and not for purposes of discipline or convenience. For residents who have been able to eat alone or with assistance, nasogastric tubes must not be used for feeding unless the resident's clinical condition makes the use of such a tube unavoidable.

The regulations proscribe the administration of unnecessary drugs, which includes excessive doses, excessive duration, and use without adequate monitoring or without adequate indications for use. Antipsychotic drugs may be used only to treat a specific condition as diagnosed and documented in the clinical record, and residents who receive such drugs must receive gradual dose reductions, together with behavioral interventions, unless these measures are clinically contraindicated.

MEDICAID PLANNING

When patients anticipate needing nursing home care for themselves or for a family member, they will often be concerned about how to pay for such care. The physician should caution patients not to dispose of assets, especially homes, in an attempt to become eligible for Medicaid coverage *until an experienced attorney has been consulted.*

It is legal for families to restructure and even transfer assets in order to become Medicaid-eligible as long as this is disclosed to the Medicaid eligibility workers. However, some transfers may trigger a "penalty" or sanction period during which the Medicaid applicant may be disqualified from receiving Medicaid benefits. Just as with tax planning, Medicaid planning should be done only upon the advice of an attorney knowledgeable about this area of law. Patients may want to consult a Legal Services office for assistance or for a referral, and some traditional estate-planning attorneys may be familiar with Medicaid rules.

CONCLUSION

The legal issues of geriatric medicine are varied and do not always provide clear answers for physicians on how to proceed. By becoming familiar with the laws in one's state and keeping abreast of developments in the areas discussed above, a physician can prevent potential legal problems and provide better service to elderly patients.

REFERENCES

1. Spar JE, Garb AS: Assessing competency to make a will. *Am J Psychiatry* 149:2, 1992.
2. Reuben DB et al: The aging driver: Medicine, policy, and ethics. *J Am Geriatr Soc* 36:1135, 1988.
3. Reuben DB: Dementia and driving (editorial). *J Am Geriatr Soc* 39:11, 1991.
4. Special Committee on Aging, U.S. Senate: *An Advocate's Guide to Laws and Programs Addressing Elder Abuse.* Serial No. 102-1, U.S. Government Printing Office, Washington, DC, 1991, p 13.
5. Legal Counsel for the Elderly: Decision-Making, Incapacity and the Elderly. Legal Counsel for the Elderly, Washington, DC, 1987, chap 6, pp 71–73.
6. Council on Scientific Affairs and Council on Ethical and Judicial Affairs: Persistent vegetative state and the decision to withdraw or withhold life support. *JAMA* 263:426, 1990.
7. Legal Counsel for the Elderly: Decision-Making, Incapacity and the Elderly. Legal Counsel for the Elderly, Washington, DC, 1987, p 110.
8. Hafemeister TL: Guidelines for state court decision making in life-sustaining medical treatment cases. *Issues Law Med* 7:4, 443, 1992. (Available from West Publishing Company, Eagan, MN.)
9. Molloy DW et al: Decision making in the incompetent elderly: "The daughter from California syndrome." *J Am Geriatr Soc* 39:396, 1991.
10. Misbin RI: Sounding board—Physicians' aid in dying. *N Engl J Med* 325:1307, 1991.

Chapter 36

ETHICAL ISSUES IN GERIATRIC CARE

Robert A. Pearlman

The roles and practices of medical providers have evolved throughout history within a context of philosophical and ethical principles. These principles elucidate values and normative standards that define the relationship of medicine to society, the scope of its authority, and the extent of its obligations. Although many of the ethical issues implicit in the relationship between a health care provider and patient are timeless, others, reflecting the capabilities and costs created by recent advances in medical technologies, uniquely challenge the consciences of medical providers. When taken together with profound changes in family structure and in social and economic provisions for health care, these challenges generate unprecedented ethical concerns.

Medical literature over the past decade reflects a heightened awareness of the moral dimensions of medical practice. Controversy and research have been stimulated by questions of what medicine should be doing, for whom, and at what cost. Three recent examples are representative of the issues under debate: Should octogenarians receive open-heart surgery?[1] Should expensive medical care be withheld from those in the last year of life?[2] Should transplantations be restricted so that other health services can be provided?[3] Monographs and journal articles now offer useful insights to the problems faced by practitioners, advice on practical skills for dealing with them, and structured approaches to clinical decision making.[4] Ethical issues are being recognized as crucial in their bearing on the formulation of medical protocols and national policies, particularly as they concern the care of the geriatric patient.

Many of the specific circumstances and characteristics of an aging population are perceived as medical problems. This perception is revealed in commentaries and studies on issues such as quality of life, informed consent, mental incapacitation, rationing of scarce medical resources, and loss of independence and autonomy for the elderly nursing home resident. Biomedical ethics is germane not only to these issues but is also involved in judgments concerning life-sustaining therapies such as "Do-Not-Attempt-Resuscitation" (DNAR) orders, cardiopulmonary resuscitation (CPR) decisions, and artificial nutrition and hydration. Moreover, many of these issues are being paraphrased into legal and political questions about the adequacy, fairness, and costs of health care for the elderly, who need and use health care the most.

THE TEXTURE OF ETHICAL PROBLEMS IN GERIATRICS

The current increase of attention directed toward ethics in the practice of geriatric medicine is explained by several predisposing factors. Within medical practice itself, innovative technological advances have blurred the distinction between life and death. The process of dying has shifted perceptually and in reality from a matter of mystery to one of conscious human management. With the knowledge and capabilities for doing more than they are certain they should, physicians grapple with the moral implications of death defined as a fitting goal of case strategy rather than as a strategy to be avoided at all cost.[5] Respirators, pacemakers, dialysis, and feeding tubes enable some dying or comatose patients to continue living, yet the benefits often do not obviously outweigh the burdens of added suffering and loss of human dignity. In addition, physicians often deliberate about whether life-sustaining treatment is futile in many situations. Another aspect of geriatric medicine that generates ethical concern pertains to quality of care. The provision of excellent care to older patients often requires a comprehensive, longitudinal, and interdisciplinary approach. Yet, health care delivery in the United States does not provide any incentives to encourage or support these characteristics; acute care receives a higher priority than long-term care.

A second set of factors derives from the societal milieu. Cost-containment strategies, competitive interests, and consumerist behaviors imported from the marketplace are being thrust upon providers and patients alike before policies can be formulated that foster a just, explicit rationing of resources.[6] These pressures conflict with many of the central tenets of geriatric care: continuity, comprehensiveness, promotion of maximal independence, and treatment of acute and chronic illnesses. Furthermore, increases in health insurance costs, coinsurance percentages, and deductible payments limit access to health care. This financial limitation conflicts with the attitudes of a majority of Americans, who feel that access to needed health care should not be dependent on ability to pay.[7]

The values and practices of medical practitioners themselves provide a third impetus generating ethical issues. Conflicts between paternalism and the autonomy of the patient are complicated issues of control. Questions over authority and treatment plans are made even more difficult in the face of technological advances which introduce medical as well as moral uncertainty. The physician faces one dilemma if a successful treatment plan inadvertently violates a patient's civil rights and quite another when the success of actions aimed at prolonging life are seen, on balance, to have done more harm than good. What is more, judgments about tests and procedures in individual cases may be affected by generalized concerns over the social costs of medicine. Such accountings are often made in reference to the criteria of patient age, cognitive functioning, quality of life, or expected length of survival. These are external measures of social worth, for which grave concerns have been expressed.[8–10] Furthermore, when physicians give greater importance to societal cost containment than to individual patient benefit without the patient's awareness, they undermine their traditional advocacy role for the patient's well-being and, as a consequence, threaten patient trust in the profession.

Finally, changes in the values, expectations, and capabilities of aging patients are also predisposing factors for many ethical issues in geriatric care. Elderly patients may defer more readily to a physician's authority than younger ones, but they still often desire more information and involvement than physicians provide. As public awareness of technological advances in medicine expands, patients or their families may insist on requesting procedures the physician considers to be not in the best interest of the patient, beyond established medical standards, or simply useless. Moreover, the elderly often have serious limitations in their functional activities and present with cognitive dysfunctions, two predisposing factors for dependence and vulnerability. These circumstances may be compounded by additional factors such as sensory impairment, reduced reaction time, slower speech, and diminished function in response to stress. Care for the elderly can, therefore, impose upon the physician unusual demands and high moral obligation. In the provision of care to the elderly, physicians need to recognize threats to patient autonomy, independence, and individuality, and to avoid these threats if possible. This approach to care should reduce unnecessary patient humiliation and help patients retain their dignity.

REASONING ABOUT DILEMMAS

In a dynamic, pluralistic society, issues of good versus bad, right versus wrong, and just versus unjust are rarely capable of resolution by reference to a single, simple, authoritative standard. Although the specific application of absolute standards for human conduct can seem clear and compelling, centuries of careful reasoning in the Western tradition have proven that such instances are exceedingly rare. Total relativity is not less problematic, even though individual cases differ and circumstances vary tremendously. Our cultural experience in ethical reasoning has shown that neither rigid absolutism nor wide-open situational relativity provides workable, satisfying solutions. The important concerns in medical practice, touching on issues such as human dignity, freedom of choice, and life and death, present moral dilemmas in which no single thing done or left undone can serve all wants or needs and for which there is no unblemished, unambiguous sense of the "best thing to do." A careful process of reasoning can be the most effective means of resolving such cases and ascertaining the "best thing to do."

Moral dilemmas in a medical context commonly involve conflicts either between justifiable principles or between principles and consequences. Under most circumstances, physicians and patients alike consider the outcomes, or consequences, of medical care, and in the majority of situations this approach seems obvious and appropriate to both those giving and receiving care; questions of treatment are answered by what works best or produces the desired results. In morally problematic cases, however, the facts may be unclear or contradictory, or the affected parties may have fundamentally different views on what constitutes the best outcome. Consider two examples: Should a demented patient's refusal of treatment be accepted when his family considers the treatment to be in his best interest? Should a patient who has shown a repeated inability to care for himself be allowed to refuse nursing home placement?

When consequences alone are taken as the measure of best response to dilemmas, three critical limitations occur. First and most obviously, the future is uncertain and unpredictable. Second, it is usually impossible to gauge how far and in what way the consequences of a medical decision may reverberate for the patient. For the practitioner, endpoints for such calculations are usually within the time frame of the present treatment regimen or hospitalization. For the patient, however, the measures keep running. Months or years may pass before the final outcomes are established. Third, the physician and patient may hold different values and opinions about what constitutes a good outcome. Physicians may value a normal range of laboratory and physical measures for disease conditions such as blood sugar for diabetes mellitus, blood pressure for hypertension, and serum levels for many prescribed medications. In contrast, patients often may value their independence, lifestyle, and family interactions to a greater degree than their health. As a result, patients often seem noncompliant with physician recommendations. For example, they take prescribed medications only when it is convenient and often engage in unhealthy activities, such as smoking cigarettes and driving automobiles without seat belts. Consideration of consequences alone, therefore, rarely provides an adequate basis for response to a moral dilemma. Principles must also be weighed.

Resolving moral issues by examining them in terms of important and basic principles, sometimes called deontological, can be a helpful guide for patient management. One significant principle in Western societies is that of autonomy, or self-determination. This principle derives from a fundamental right of privacy under which adults of sound mind are considered to be in control of their own bodies and, by extension, their own fate. Many legal cases have articulated this principle; three deserve special note. In *Schloendorff v. Society of New York Hospital* in 1914, Judge Cordoza stated that "every human being of adult years and sound mind has a right to determine what shall be done with his own body."[11] In 1965, the Supreme Court of the United States supported the rights of a Connecticut married couple to procure a contraceptive device, referring to a right of privacy based on the penumbrae of the First, Third, Fourth, Fifth, and Ninth Amendments.[12] Most recently, in the Supreme Court case involving Nancy Cruzan, the Court assumed a constitutionally protected right, derived from the liberty interest in the due process clause, to refuse life-sustaining treatment, including artificial hydration and nutrition.[13] A second guiding set of principles is beneficence and nonmaleficence; that is, the doing of good and the avoiding of harm. In *Epidemics,* Hippocrates first stated the maxim: *primum non nocere.*[14] Both of these principles are reiterated in medical codes from antiquity to the present. Justice and a commitment to fairness define another important guiding set of principles. These principles play a role in resource allocation determinations and informed consent, but they also apply broadly to discrimination issues in which social worth characteristics of the patient are considered.

These principles are important points of reference in the physician's process of ethical reasoning. Yet a course of action deemed moral by the standard of one principle could be clearly wrong and inappropriate in terms of another. Ethical choice involves more than just the outcome of a decision or course of action. To the physician responding to a moral dilemma, "ethical" should be descriptive of a *process* of reasoning and careful consideration. Careful attention should be directed beyond medical indications to individual preferences, patient-determined quality of life, and contextual features such as insurance and organizational policies.[8] The role of process in responding to ethical issues in geriatric care is especially prominent.

General issues of informed consent, rationing of medical resources, quality of life, and withholding tests or treatments suggest the diversity, frequency, and seriousness of moral questions involving elderly patients. Reasoning about these dilemmas is presented in the section that follows.

INFORMED CONSENT

Although the foundations of informed consent derive from both legal and ethical traditions, the purpose of informed consent also supports the goals of medical care. Properly understood and utilized, informed consent can become a useful means for improving communication between patients and health care providers, educating patients, increasing their responsible investment in their own care, and identifying appropriate goals for medical treatments.

For consent to be meaningful, the individual giving consent must be competent, informed, and free of coercion.[15] Relevant information must be communicated and understood, the responsibility for which falls to the physician.[15] The patient then has, within very broad parameters, the freedom to accept or reject a proposed treatment or diagnostic test. Paraphrased as a question, the patient asks and then decides, "What course of treatment, if any, offers me the chances of achieving the benefit I wish at risks I am willing to take?" Obviously, the question is highly personal and subjective; the answer may have little connection to what, from a strictly medical viewpoint, would be the best thing to do or even to what might seem rational or reasonable. The idea that the patient's response is free of coercion means that a patient should be able to choose any option without feeling intimidated.

The basic elements of informed consent presume the information needs of a reasoning individual.[15] These needs include a clear rationale for the recommended test or procedure, comprising a statement of the underlying problem as well as a statement of the expected benefits and the likelihood of their achievement with each option. The information provided must also include a clear description of the likelihood of any untoward events associated with each option identified as high risk/low probability or low risk/high probability and with the alternatives, including no treatment.

Many studies describe the problems inherent in achieving true informed consent.[16–21] Patients often sign consent forms not knowing or unable to recall the basic medical information. They are uncomfortable assuming responsibility for their course of treatment and may be afraid to ask questions necessary to be enlightened "shoppers." In the elderly patient, comprehension difficulties may be further compounded by specific characteristics such as diminished visual and/or auditory acuity and cognitive dysfunction.

Attitudes and practices of health care professionals may also interfere with effective consent. Time constraints, incomplete communication, lack of understanding of culturally relevant risks to the patient, or minimizing alternatives less acceptable from a medical perspective result in a loss of positive opportunities for creative, effective consent techniques. Documentation by cursory procedures may signify a misunderstanding that consent has low value or is optional. Physicians may brush over risks and alternatives. Furthermore, the consent process may be considered appropriate only for procedures that are risky from a litigation standpoint.

Recommendations for improving consent practices have dealt mainly with the improvement of procedures and forms through simplified language, clearer descriptions, mutual consents between patients and physicians, and two-stage procedures in which confirmation of understanding is obtained before proceeding. A recently proposed recommendation suggests that informed consent become an ongoing process rather than a one-time, event-oriented activity.[22] This recommended reorientation highlights the belief that patients have a unique knowledge of their own history and facts, a unique ability to evaluate their own symptoms, and a responsibility for approving their own health care. A patient who assumes a more active role in the prescribed course of therapy will generally be better prepared to accept the outcome and less likely to blame the physician for any unsatisfactory results. Such improvements of form, matched with improvements of attitude and understanding, encourage prospects for the enhanced protection of the rights and interests of elderly patients.

EQUITABLE DISTRIBUTION OF MEDICAL RESOURCES

A majority of the population maintain that the quality and quantity of health care should be available to everyone and not be provided on the basis of ability to pay,[7] yet conflicting attitudes seem to support the goals of rationing. This conundrum reflects the high costs of medical care, the increasing use of expensive technologies for some patients while millions of Americans either lack health insurance or have inadequate insurance protection, questions about benefits of expenditures made in a patient's last year of life, pressures from large corporate consumers of health care to lower premiums, and pressure by hospitals to minimize unprofitable practices. Furthermore, for physicians the dilemma is heightened because there is no corresponding guarantee that cost containment or selective allocation will lead to a greater good or the promotion of just societal outcomes.

The American Geriatric Society's policy on the allocation of scarce medical resources makes several important points.[23] According to that policy, careful, reasoned, *public* debate, based on an adequate knowledge base, is necessary before any policy decisions can be made to ration health care. Efforts to allocate resources should focus on unnecessary spending and waste in all areas of medical care and must not target a specific area or population, such as the elderly. In this regard, a person's chronological age per se should not be used as a criterion for exclusion from a given therapy. The findings of the Society were that disproportionately greater per capita expenditures for the elderly were appropriate, given the greater need for medical care in that age group. Most importantly for the practitioner, considerations of resource distribution should not outweigh efforts to maximize an individual patient's welfare.

The physician as a trusted, loyal caregiver has a multifaceted role in assuring fair rationing of medical resources. Identifying those patients who would not benefit from treatment, practicing medicine that is cost-effective, planning treatment on the basis of patient goals and health care aspirations, and avoiding wasteful practices are some straightforward measures to implement. The physician may also need to employ decision-analysis methods in order to better understand the diagnostic value of tests in relation to the desired outcomes of patients.

The role of the physician is more complicated when dealing with institutions, but the responsibility remains to encourage development of explicit, understandable, defensible, and fair policies that are open to review, criticism, and revision within the institutional setting. Physicians need to avoid pressures such as premature hospital discharge based on diagnosis-related groups (DRGs) when such pressures conflict with the patient's best interests.[24] The proper place for societal gatekeeping is at the front door of policies throughout the system, not at the bedside of a vulnerable patient.[25] Moreover, physicians need to remember that DRG cutoffs represent mean values. Thus, for a specific medical problem, some patients require more hospital days and some fewer.

A good patient-caregiver relationship can be maintained with consideration given to rationing of resources if such policies are openly discussed with patients. In this way, the trust factor will continue to be a primary consideration.

In contrast to two recently proposed rationing strategies[26,27] based on age, the American College of Physicians (ACP) recommends extensive reform in the overall health care system to reduce the need for rationing.[28] However, the ACP also recommends that a national health care commission establish a global health care budget and determine the benefits to be covered. Thus, this proposed commission would develop strategies to ration (if needed) by criteria that are unspecified at this time.

PHYSICIAN VALUES: OLD AGE AND QUALITY OF LIFE

Age discrimination in the delivery of health care is generally unacceptable. Despite this, physicians often treat older persons differently, even when controlling for stage of disease and comorbidity. Studies have shown that physicians are both less aggressive and less comprehensive with older patients.[29,30] Although advanced age may increase risks from a treatment and reduce the duration of benefit because of limited life expectancy, these are only two factors that influence whether a treatment's benefits outweigh its risks. Chronological age should not be used as a proxy for a negative characteristic such as poor quality of life, nor should it justify withholding efficacious treatment.

Patient quality of life is discussed frequently as a factor affecting life-sustaining medical decisions for chronically ill patients.[2,8,31–38] This factor is particularly relevant in decision making for mentally incapacitated patients without advance care directives. In these circumstances, physicians often try to consider patient quality of life in order to justify the decisions they must make without knowing a patient's wishes.

Many factors make determinations of quality of life difficult to predict. The term *quality of life* has no obvious meaning; it is not clear to which empirical states the term refers, nor is it manifest how any particular person will evaluate those states. In addition, the traditional pressures in acute care facilities for aggressive treatment and the uncertainties of diagnosis and prognosis make predictions of patient quality of life difficult. Other complicating issues include the physician's subjective values relative to the patient's characteristics, inadequate communication between physicians and patients, and basic problems with the measurement of quality of life.[32,34,39,40] In situations in which *quality of life* connotes a vague set of attributes and conditions, the variability of perceptions of a patient's quality of life may be great.

The ambiguous concept of quality of life can be used responsibly when clinicians attune their interactions with patients to the values and goals of the patient. In these contexts, a patient's own evaluation of the quality of his or her life may determine the choice of a therapeutic intervention and what is beneficial or in his or her best interest. An example is when a clinician recommends a walker rather than a nursing home for a patient with irreversible gait instability, in order to comply with the patient's desire to remain independent. A less common example is when a clinician accepts a competent elderly patient's refusal of treatment because from the patient's perspective the proposed intervention will only improve the patient's health and not the overall quality of life. When consideration of a patient's quality of life is grounded in the patient's self-evaluation, ethical concerns are rarely raised.

Using quality of life as a factor in decisions involving life-sustaining procedures, however, can represent a crucial ethical concern in patient care.[33,37] With an informed, competent patient who is able to communicate his or her feelings, respect for patient autonomy should foster respect for the patient's attitudes about the use of life-sustaining procedures. The underlying rationale is that this type of patient is able to determine what is beneficial for himself or herself on the basis of his or her perceived current or future quality of life. This situation requires that a clinician's subjective evaluation of the patient's quality of life generally be secondary to the patient's opinions.[15] Ethical problems appear only when a patient's competency is in doubt or an incompetent patient's family or health care provider proposes that the patient's quality of life does not justify a medical intervention. When a patient is unable to communicate his or her feelings about life-sustaining procedures, quality of life may be considered a decisive factor only if the patient's quality of life falls below a minimum standard and intervention would only preserve this condition or maintain organic life.[8] One definition for minimal threshold of life quality is extreme physical debilitation and a complete loss of sensory and intellectual activity.[8,41] According to this definition, only when the qualities common to human interaction (i.e., ability to reason, experience emotions, and enter into relationships) have been irreversibly lost should the clinician's assessment of the patient's quality of life determine withholding of life-supporting therapy. A more recent and contentious definition of a minimal threshold of life quality (discussed in terms of qualitative futility) is having one's life prolonged by and preoccupied with intensive medical treatment.[42]

Physicians need to be aware of and avoid subjective judgments of poor quality of life based on socioeconomic or other value-laden attributes. This minimum standard reflects respect for personal function, cerebration, the essential qualities of being human, and the sanctity of human life. These guidelines attempt to protect patient autonomy, to ensure justice by preventing capricious decision making based on personal preferences, and to promote beneficial results for patients.

WITHHOLDING AND WITHDRAWING LIFE-SUSTAINING PROCEDURES

Withholding or withdrawing life-sustaining therapies is one of the most troublesome ethical issues in geriatric care and is relevant to concerns about the rationing of medical resources and quality-of-life decisions. These judgments frequently occur under circumstances of medical futility: it becomes apparent to the physician and/or the patient that treatment is not benefiting the patient. Often, orders are written within 24 hours of the patient's death and are associated with such patient characteristics as being elderly, nonambulatory, incontinent, and demented and having resided in a nursing home.[43–45] Physicians may believe they understand the wishes of their patients, but they may inadvertently override them. Research data in fact suggest inadequate physician-patient communication and errors in both excessive overtreatment and undertreatment.[35,46,47] Unfortunately, physician inaccuracy does not appear to improve with either longer patient-physician relationships or comparable ages between patient and physician.[48]

There is great ambiguity in the terminology used to describe the withholding or withdrawing of life-sustaining procedures. For example, the word *euthanasia,* Greek for "good death," has come to describe many different things. Active euthanasia, the affirmative and intentional doing of something to cause the death of an individual, is prohibited by law and condemned by professional standards. When passive, however, euthanasia is described approvingly as simply allowing a patient to die and is considered permissible under certain specified circumstances. Both conceptions of euthanasia apply, at least ideally, to instances in which the patient voluntarily desires death. Interestingly, both also may share the same intentions, justification, motives, methods, and outcomes.[49] "Extraordinary," "heroic," and "imminent" are confusing terms, meaningless outside a narrow and quite selectively biased context, that are used to justify passive, voluntary euthanasia. The American Medical Association's policy statement on euthanasia demonstrates the aforementioned ambiguity: "The cessation of extraordinarily or heroic measures to prolong life is permissible when there is irrefutable evidence that biological death is imminent."[50]

American courts have contributed important insights about professional roles and standards and patients' rights to determine medical care for themselves, including the issues of voluntary, passive euthanasia and withholding therapies.[51] Developing patterns of case law reflect society's stresses in coming to grips with the issues of humanity's increasing ability to "manage" death. Legal decisions resulting from public debate on these topics can provide useful guidance for the making of ethical decisions. The President's Commission for the Study of Ethical Problems in Medicine and Biomedical and Behavioral Research in 1983 also made a number of helpful and influential observations.[9] Some suggestions to keep in mind from these sources are discussed below.

General Recommendations

It is essential that the voluntary choice of a competent and informed patient be allowed to determine whether or not life-sustaining therapy will be undertaken. This respects the principle of autonomy. The right of choice extends to patients incapable of making decisions for whatever reason, including chronic cognitive dysfunction or coma. In these instances, previous expressions of the patient's preferences, even unwritten, can be considered valid signposts and accepted as authentic expressions. Appropriate surrogates for incompetent adults, generally family members, should attempt to replicate decisions the patient would have made. If lack of evidence exists as to wishes, surrogates should seek to protect the patient's best interests. The courts, in their role as protectors of the rights of the individual, should promote surrogate decision making with substituted judgments reflecting the expressed wishes of the patient, and then, if necessary, with determinations of the patient's best interests inferred from patient goals and values. In this regard, while recognizing that patients have rights to reject or accept recommended treatment, and respecting the principle of beneficence, it will be assumed that the interests of most patients will best be served by presuming in favor of sustaining life. As matters both of legal and medical professional responsibility, the primary obligation for ensuring morally justified processes of decision making lies with the physician.

The physician's reasoning about whether a choice that leads to a premature death is acceptable or not should be directed by the degree to which a patient is benefited or burdened by a treatment. Proportionate benefit/burden assessments fall within guidelines of the principles of doing good and avoiding harm and are reasonable approaches to decision making as long as they are patient-centered. It is the responsibility of the physician to assist the patient or surrogate in decisions by providing complete and realistic information regarding prognosis and the potential benefits and risks with various therapeutic options, especially those involving withholding or withdrawing therapy.[52]

In nonemergency cases, patient autonomy or self-determination may be overridden selectively, but only under highly unusual circumstances. One situation is when major depression directly interferes with the ability to make an informed, reasoned decision. Another situation occurs when a state's rights outweigh those of the individual. Both cases would involve judicial review. In theory, an infringement on the patient's autonomy is expected to result in long-term enhancement of the patient's (or his family's) self-determination and well-being.

Serious consideration of patient autonomy and the proportionate benefits and burdens of treatment for a patient may lead to questions about the appropriateness of physician-assisted suicide (PAS) in a particular case. Although public interest in PAS is high and the much publicized case involving Dr. Timothy Quill reflects compassionate care,[53] PAS is not within the scope and standards of the profession.[54] The strongest arguments against a policy allowing PAS include the following:

1. The reasons for patient requests for "aid in dying" may reflect issues such as lack of access to care, inadequate pain control, and being a financial burden on family. If these form the basis of requests for PAS, then a policy endorsing PAS

would be the inappropriate response to these correctable problems in the health care system.
2. A policy allowing PAS might indirectly pressure patients to end their lives.
3. The performance of PAS does not have adequate guidelines or sufficient safeguards to prevent abuses.
4. Minimizing suffering (a common reason in support of PAS) can usually be accomplished without intentionally causing death.
5. Respect for self-determination (another common reason in support of PAS) should not obligate physicians to behave contrary to professional standards.

CPR and DNAR Orders

Several approaches have been suggested recently to promote patient autonomy and maximize the useful applications of the benefit/burden rationale.[9,38,55] An outline of the Commission's approach to decision making is presented in Table 36-1. More recently, however, physicians have suggested that life-sustaining procedures should not have to be offered if they represent futile or meaningless therapy.[36,56] A rational alternative approach to decision making regarding CPR or any other life-sustaining treatment that considers medical futility and patient-derived quality of life is offered by Tomlinson and Brody (see Table 36-2).[37]

Physician communication with the patient should seek to identify patient values where possible, so that when crisis situations occur, the patient's views and preferences can be controlling of outcomes.[36] Discussions regarding CPR should focus on whether it serves the patient's goals, and such discussions should be repeated at various stages of health because patient values may change.[57] Partial codes are appropriate only when they reflect the wishes of the patient or surrogate.[36] Slow codes are not ethically justifiable.

TABLE 36-1

Resuscitation (CPR) of Competent Patients—Physician's Assessment in Relation to Patient's Preference

Physician's Assessment	Patient Favors CPR*	No Preference	Patient Opposes CPR*
CPR would benefit patient	Try CPR	Try CPR	Do not try CPR; review decision†
Benefit of CPR unclear	Try CPR	Try CPR	Do not try CPR
CPR would not benefit patient	Try CPR; review decision†	Do not try CPR	Do not try CPR

*Based on an adequate understanding of the relevant information.
†Such a conflict calls for careful reexamination by both patient and physician. If neither the physician's assessment nor the patient's preference changes, then the competent patient's decision should be honored.
SOURCE: From Decision to forego life-sustaining treatment, in *President's Commission for the Study of Ethical Problems in Medicine and Biomedical and Behavioral Research.* Washington, Government Printing Office, 1983, p 244.

TABLE 36-2

Contrasts among Rationales for DNAR Orders

Rationale	Patient's Values Relevant?	Implications for Other Treatments?
No medical benefit	No	No
Poor quality of life after CPR	Yes	No
Poor quality of life before CPR	Yes	Yes

SOURCE: From Tomlinson T, Brody H: Ethics and communication in Do-Not-Resuscitate orders. *N Engl J Med* 318:44, 1988.

Informed choices about cardiopulmonary resuscitation, as with other interventions, require clear and candid information about benefits (likelihood of in-hospital survival), risks (likelihood of complications such as anoxic encephalopathy, fractured ribs, and death), and alternatives (death if cardiopulmonary arrest occurs).

Current practice for DNAR orders requires that there be written and signed consent forms by either the patient or surrogate decision maker. Although this may appear cumbersome and different from traditional indications for written consent, it helps prevent covert decision making without patient (or surrogate) participation. Advance care directives such as Natural Death Acts, living wills, and durable powers of attorney for health care can allow competent patients to express their values for potential future use under conditions of mental incapacitation. Natural Death Acts are legislatively approved living wills that allow competent patients to direct their physicians to withhold or withdraw life-sustaining procedures under specified conditions. The durable power of attorney for health care allows a competent patient to empower "health care agents" (commonly referred to as proxies or surrogates) to make health care decisions on his or her behalf in the event of becoming mentally incapacitated.

The Patient Self-Determination Act and recent Joint Commission on Accreditation of Health Care Organizations require that patients, on or near admission to hospitals, nursing homes, and other health care programs, be asked whether they are interested in learning about and/or preparing an advance directive.[58,59] This may be the wrong time for an initial discussion of this topic due to the stresses of an acute illness, a change in living situation, or the lack of a long-standing relationship between an admitting physician and the patient. A more appropriate time for these initial discussions is during repeat outpatient visits.

Unfortunately, many policies and recommendations for discussing CPR and the use of other life-sustaining treatment continue to focus on terminally ill, imminently dying patients. Table 36-3 presents an approach that extends the logic and rights regarding care for the dying to other patients. It is oriented to and based upon ethical principles rather than legal considerations and should therefore be discussed with a legal counselor to ascertain the context of legal review in a particular jurisdiction. For example, in several states, withholding artificial hydration and nutrition is prohibited from being part of an advance care directive.[60]

Recently, evidence has been presented suggesting that preferences regarding life-sustaining procedures are not well understood by a patient's physician, nurse, or spouse.[48,61] Furthermore, although a patient's preferences may remain stable over time, they change across both different baseline states of health (e.g., hypothetical stroke, hypothetical dementia) and life-sustaining procedures (CPR; CPR requiring mechanical ventilation, artificial hydration, and nutrition).[57,62] Therefore, new attempts at obtaining advance care directives or eliciting patient values should include inquiries about multiple life-sustaining procedures under several health scenarios. The health scenarios can include the actual present situation as well as conditions that would interfere with the patient's ability to express his or her preferences, such as coma, severe stroke, and dementia. Appropriate inquiries into treatment preferences should include CPR; CPR requiring ventilation, artificial hydration, and nutrition; antibiotics for infection; hospitalization for care; the hospital as a place to die; surgery; dialysis; chemotherapy; cardiovascular drugs; blood; and intensive care unit services. Additional useful information might include the desired duration of mechanical ventilation and artificial hydration and nutrition to sustain life in coma or dementia conditions. An alternative approach to eliciting patient values would inquire about circumstances considered to be worse than death. Because this inquiry can seem daunting, a line of questioning is suggested in Table 36-4.

Another part of an advance care directive should designate a proxy decision maker (surrogate). Without this designation, a common hierarchy to identify a surrogate decision maker will often be imposed. The hierarchy is usually the spouse first and then consensus by all adult children, parents, and siblings. This ordering might not be appropriate for an elderly pa-

TABLE 36-3

Approach to Patients or Their Surrogates Requesting the Witholding or Withdrawing of Life-Sustaining Procedures

	Health Status	
	Terminally Ill or Irreversible Coma	**Not Terminally Ill**
Capable of making a carefully considered specific decision	1. Per patient's wishes. 2. If M.D.-patient disagree, discuss. 3. If irreconcilable disagreement, either defer to patient's wishes or transfer care to another physician.	1. Per patient's wishes. 2. If M.D.-patient disagree, discuss. 3. If irreconcilable disagreement, either transfer care to another physician or evaluate for capacity to make informed choice.
Mentally incapacitated with wishes known	1. Per surrogate's expression of patient's wishes. 2. If M.D.-surrogate disagree, discuss. 3. If irreconcilable disagreement, either defer to surrogate's wishes or transfer care to another physician.	1. Per surrogate's expression of patient's wishes. 2. If M.D.-surrogate disagree, discuss. 3. If irreconcilable disagreement, either defer to surrogate's wishes or transfer care to another physician.
Mentally incapacitated without known wishes	1. Per surrogate's expression of patient's best interests. 2. If M.D.-surrogate disagree, discuss. 3. If irreconcilable disagreement, either defer to surrogate's wishes, transfer care to another physician, or seek guardianship review. 4. If a surrogate does not exist, life-sustaining procedures may be withdrawn or withheld if they are merely futile (i.e., prolong the dying process without any apparent benefit).	1. Seek guardianship review to confirm best interests.

SOURCE: From Pearlman RA, Speer JB: Philosophical and ethical issues, in Kelley WN (ed): *Textbook of Internal Medicine.* Philadelphia, Lippincott, 1988, p 2618.

TABLE 36-4

Proposed Questions to Facilitate Discussions about Advance Care Planning

Question 1: *A.* If you became seriously ill today with a life-threatening problem, what should be the goals of your medical care? To get better? To make you comfortable? *B.* What are the factors that influence your choice? (Here is a good place to explore the patient's feelings about hope for improvement, attitudes about risk-taking/aversion, and posture regarding "fighting" for life.)

Question 2: *A.* If you were facing a life-threatening event, are there any circumstances when all you'd want is just to be kept comfortable? *B.* What are these circumstances? To answer this, it might be helpful to think about any situations on TV, in the news, hearsay, or personal experiences where you've thought to yourself, "I wouldn't want to be kept alive like that." (Here is a good place to explore concerns about "loss of dignity.")

Question 3: *A.* Are there any life-sustaining treatments that you know you would not want under any circumstances? *B.* What is it about these treatments that makes them undesirable? (Sometimes a patient will say that a mechanical ventilator or being fed through tubes is not desired. These responses should promote further questions about the difference between permanent use of these life-sustaining treatments versus short-term "therapeutic trials.")

Question 4: Are there any life-sustaining teatments you would *want* regardless of the situation? At the extreme, if you were in the final stages of an incurable disease and were dying, would you still want these treatments?

Question 5: If you were dying, where would you want to receive medical care? At home? In a hospital? At a hospice center? In a nursing home?

Question 6: Finally, should your current preferences be strictly applied to future situations or serve as a guide for your proxy decision makers?

For each of these questions, you should ask patients why they feel the way they do. The more explicit the patient is in explaining feelings, the greater will be everyone's understanding of what is best for the *patient.* The patient and physician need to remember that there are no right or wrong answers to these questions.

tient without a traditional family structure. The surrogate decision maker should be the individual who knows the patient's values the best and can speak on his or her behalf.

Artificial Hydration and Nutrition

One of the most difficult and controversial issues for withholding care has centered upon artificial means for providing nutrition and hydration. These problems are somewhat different from the life-sustaining treatments discussed earlier, for while nutrition and hydration qualify as life-sustaining procedures, the giving of food and water is often considered a general moral duty, has tremendous symbolic value as a caring gesture, and is sometimes considered basic nursing care. Since all people require food and water, the provision of food and water is considered by some to represent supportive care. Withholding food and water also leads to starvation and dehydration and subsequently to death. As a result, it has been considered by some to be the proximate cause of death.[63,64] The role of health care providers is to sometimes cure, occasionally relieve, and always comfort.[63] Consequently, many physicians support artificial hydration and nutrition because they view it as a comforting gesture.[63,65] Other reservations about withholding the provision of food and water include the appearance of abandonment, the suffering associated with starvation and dehydration, its use as a cost-containment strategy, its capricious use on patients with impaired quality of life, and the fear of a "slippery slope" that undermines the value of life.[63,66,67]

Although several cases reviewed by courts have had conflicting results, the prevailing opinion considers that the use of tubes or intravenous lines (i.e., artificial means) makes the procedures medical care and not routine nursing care.[51,60,68] Therefore, withholding or withdrawing of these procedures should follow the general guidelines discussed in the previous section. Unless a patient explicitly requests not to receive artificial hydration and nutrition, the burdens of providing this care must outweigh the benefits if its withholding or withdrawing is to be considered justifiable. In cases where doubt exists as to the benefits of treatment, trials of support with hydration and nutrition often clarify the burden/benefit balance.[64] Interestingly, medical consensus is developing that dehydration and malnutrition lead to sedation, diminished awareness, and increased pain threshold, which may all reduce suffering prior to death.[69] The only discomfort can be ameliorated with nursing attention to a patient's dry lips and mouth.

MENTAL INCAPACITATION

Persons are presumed to be mentally competent. Mental incompetency is a legal determination which indicates that a patient is incapable of understanding the implications of his or her decisions and choices. Mental incompetence in the law is thus a sliding scale assessment that requires compelling proof and depends greatly on the issues at stake. In many cases, for example, it is easier to prove incompetence to handle financial affairs than it is to reach this finding when what is at stake is the patient's best interest in terms of health and well-being. The best example of this difference is the frequent use of durable power of attorney for VA finances among elderly veterans who have difficulty managing their VA pensions; these durable powers of attorney are rarely also empowered to manage a patient's health care decisions.

A physician may question the competence of patients under many situations, including acute stress, treatment refusal, and coma. Unfortunately, the issue of incompetence or mental incapacitation has frequently been associated with paternalistic actions to override the patient's autonomy. Use of surrogate decision makers is often considered more acceptable with invasive or risky procedures. However, if our society's commitment to personal self-determination is fundamental, then when the stakes regarding the outcome of a patient's decisions get higher, reliance on the surrogate should be more constrained.

The use of durable powers of attorney for health or advance care directives is perhaps the most far-reaching recommendation to facilitate decision making for seemingly incompetent patients. In these situations, respectively, either another individual is empowered to make health care decisions or the patient expresses his or her values and preferences at an earlier point in time. Both of these approaches for enhancing patient self-control have application in many states, and they are especially useful for patients who develop severe dementia or an acute altered mental state and require immediate treatment decisions. It should be noted, however, that the diagnosis of dementia does not necessarily make a patient mentally incapacitated. The judgment should be based on a documented inability to make an informed decision. Furthermore, the elderly are at increased risk of transient episodes of incapacity to make decisions for a variety of reasons (e.g., disease exacerbation, medication side effects, and change in the environment). The potential reversibility of these conditions requires that the physician pursue the cause of altered mental status. For these reasons, and on account of complexities in the family's role as surrogate helpers with decisions, physicians should not automatically seek out a surrogate decision maker for patients who appear to be incapable of making informed choices.

CHALLENGES OF THE INSTITUTIONAL SETTING

Ethical issues are pervasive in this nation's arrangements for long-term care. The physician should be sensitive to issues arising out of the voluntariness of nursing home placement and exercise a careful monitoring role over the patient's transfers from acute to long-term settings. Within these institutions are implicit threats to human dignity and individuality, such as shared rooms and bathrooms, fixed eating times, and scheduled activities that reflect staffing patterns. The physician should be aware of concerns about personal freedom and mobility and about limitations on personal expressions. For example, the use of restraints, both physical and chemical, should be avoided because less restrictive options are usually available. Physicians should know whether the nursing home they recommend has a policy that allows wandering in a protected area or has sufficient volunteers and staff so that physical restraints are not used.

SUGGESTIONS

In this chapter, respect for patient self-determination and the balance between benefits and burdens have been stressed. In addition, the primacy of the physician's responsibility to the patient as a medical care advocate has been emphasized. Care of the elderly is complicated by multiple problems interwoven with physiological, social, functional, and economic complexities. Technology offers blessings and curses, giving the physician the opportunity to ask, "Will this serve my patient's best interests?" Cost concerns have affected medical care and health systems so that the physician also has to ask, "Am I still serving my patient's interests? If not, does the patient know it so that he or she can purchase another package?" If the quality of chronic long-term care is not at the same level as other aspects of care in our health care systems, the physician also ought to ask, "What can I do as an individual? What can my professional organization do? If society knew about the problems that exist, would it approve or would it consider my profession to have been in a conspiracy of silence?"

In conclusion, several suggestions are offered to help avoid and resolve ethical dilemmas. First, physicians should identify the difference between medical and nonmedical problems. Just because ethical or social issues arise in the medical context does not mean that physicians have the knowledge to "treat" them or the social warrant to apply the force of medical expertise. Second, physicians should be aware of personal values that may influence their thoughts about treatment. Age, quality of life, pain, select diagnoses such as cancer or incontinence, and other attributes have been shown to bias physicians' judgment so that they inadvertently act in a discriminatory fashion. Third, dilemmas often seem to exist because no one has talked to the patient. It is only through communication that physicians ascertain patient values, interests, and perceived benefits. An important topic for communication is the patient's preferences regarding the future use of life-sustaining procedures. Fourth, patients usually know their own values, interests, and benefits better than anyone else. Fifth, patient stress, a treatment refusal, or even a diagnosis of dementia are not invariant grounds for mental incapacitation. For example, treatment refusal may merely reflect a difference in the relative value of health as defined by the physician to other values of importance to the patient. Sixth, trained ethics consultants and ethics committees may help health care providers decipher the conflicting issues in a case and promote clearer thinking and ethically reasoned actions. And last, the elderly are at risk for ethical dilemmas arising in the health "care" system. The vulnerability that accrues with their physical disabilities and socioeconomic limitations warrants special attention to prevent any unfair practices.

REFERENCES

1. Edmonds LH et al: Open-heart surgery in octogenarians. *N Engl J Med* 319:131, 1988.
2. Avorn J: Benefit and cost analysis in geriatric care: Turning age discrimination into health policy. *N Engl J Med* 310:1294, 1984.
3. Welch HG, Larson EB: Dealing with limited resources. The Oregon decision to curtail funding for organ transplantation. *N Engl J Med* 319:171, 1988.
4. Jonsen AR et al: The ethics of medicine: An annotated bibliography of recent literature. *Ann Intern Med* 92:136, 1980.
5. Hilfiker D: Allowing the debilitated to die: Facing our ethical choices. *N Engl J Med* 308:716, 1983.
6. Miller FH, Miller GAH: Why saying no to patients in the United States is so hard: Cost containment, justice, and provider autonomy. *N Engl J Med* 314:1380, 1986.
7. Cambridge Reports, Inc. HMQ Survey: A mandate for high quality health care. *Health Manage Q* 4:3, 1986.
8. Jonsen AR et al: *Clinical Ethics: A Practical Approach to Ethical Decisions in Clinical Medicine,* 3d ed. New York, McGraw-Hill, 1992.
9. President's Commission for the Study of Ethical Problems in Medicine and Biomedical and Behavioral Research. Decision to forego life-sustaining treatment. Washington, Government Printing Office, 1983.
10. Fox RC, Swazey JP: *The Courage of Fact.* Chicago, University of Chicago, 1978.
11. *Schloendorff v. Society of New York Hospital* 211 N.Y. 125, 1914.
12. *Griswold v. Connecticut* 381 U.S. 479, 1965.
13. Cruzan, US Supreme Court, June 1990.
14. Sandulescu C: *Primum non nocere:* Philosophical commentaries on a medical aphorism. *Acta Antiqua* (Academiae Scientiarium Hungaricae) 13:359, 1965.
15. President's Commission for the Study of Ethical Problems in Medicine and Biomedical and Behavioral Research. Making health care decisions: The ethical and legal implications of informed consent in the patient-practitioner relationship. Washington, Government Printing Office, 1982, p 38.
16. Meisel A, Roth LH: What we do and do not know about informed consent. *JAMA* 246:2473, 1981.
17. Lidz CW et al: Barriers to informed consent. *Ann Intern Med* 99:539, 1983.
18. Stanley B et al: The elderly patient and informed consent. *JAMA* 252:1302, 1984.
19. Cross AW, Churchill LR: Ethical and cultural dimensions of informed consent: A case study and analysis. *Ann Intern Med* 96:110, 1982.
20. Cassileth BR et al: Informed consent: Why are its goals imperfectly realized? *N Engl J Med* 302:896, 1980.
21. Wu WC, Pearlman RA: Consent in medical decision making: The role of communication. *J Gen Intern Med* 3:9, 1988.
22. Lidz CW et al: Two models of implementing informed consent. *Arch Intern Med* 148:1385, 1988.
23. American Geriatrics Society: Allocation of medical resources. *Am Geriatr Soc Newsletter* 15:5, 1986.
24. Relman AS: Practicing medicine in the new business climate. *N Engl J Med* 316:1150, 1987.
25. Reagan MD: Physicians as gatekeepers: A complex challenge. *N Engl J Med* 317:1731, 1987.
26. Callahan D: *Setting Limits: Medical Goals in an Aging Society.* New York, Simon and Schuster, 1987.
27. Daniels N: *Just Health Care.* New York, Cambridge University Press, 1985.
28. American College of Physicians: Universal insurance for American health care. *Ann Intern Med* 117:511, 1992.
29. Sudnow D: *Passing On.* Englewood Cliffs, NJ, Prentice-Hall, 1967.
30. Wetle T: Age as a risk factor for inadequate treatment. *JAMA* 258:516, 1987.
31. Crane D: *The Sanctity of Social Life: Physician's Treatment of Critically Ill Patients.* New York, Russel Sage, 1975.
32. Pearlman RA et al: Variability in physician bioethical decision-making: A case study of euthanasia. *Ann Intern Med* 97:420, 1982.
33. Pearlman RA, Jonsen A: The use of quality of life considerations in medical decision making. *J Am Geriatr Soc* 33:344,1985.
34. Lo B, Jonsen AR: Clinical decisions to limit treatment. *Ann Intern Med* 93:764, 1980.

35. Starr TJ et al: Quality of life and resuscitation decisions in elderly patients. *J Gen Intern Med* 1:373, 1986.
36. Perkins HS: Ethics at the end of life: Practical principles for making resuscitation decisions. *J Gen Intern Med* 1:170, 1986.
37. Tomlinson T, Brody H: Ethics and communication in Do-Not-Resuscitate orders. *N Engl J Med* 318:43, 1988.
38. Miles SH et al: The do-not-resuscitate order in a teaching hospital: Considerations and a suggested policy. *Ann Intern Med* 96:660, 1982.
39. Spitzer WO et al: Measuring the quality of life of cancer patients: A concise QL-index for use by physicians. *J Chronic Dis* 34:585, 1981.
40. Pearlman RA, Uhlmann RF: Quality of life in chronic diseases: Perceptions of elderly patients. *J Gerontol* 43:M25, 1988.
41. Fletcher J: Four indicators of humanhood: The enquiry matures. *Hastings Cent Rep* 4:4, 1974.
42. Schneiderman LJ et al: Medical futility: Its meaning and ethical implications. *Ann Intern Med* 112:949, 1990.
43. Charlson ME et al: Resuscitation: How do we decide? *JAMA* 255:1316, 1986.
44. Brown NK, Thompson DJ: Nontreatment of fever in extended care facilities. *N Engl J Med* 300:1246, 1979.
45. Farber NJ et al: Cardiopulmonary resuscitation (CPR): Patient factors and decision making. *Arch Intern Med* 144:2229, 1984.
46. Bedell SE, Delbanco TL: Choices about cardiopulmonary resuscitation in the hospital—When do physicians talk with patients? *N Engl J Med* 310:1089, 1984.
47. Shmerling RH et al: Discussing cardiopulmonary resuscitation: A study of elderly outpatients. *J Gen Intern Med* 3:317, 1988.
48. Uhlmann RF et al: Ability of physicians and spouses to predict resuscitation preferences of elderly patients. *J Gerontol* 43:M115, 1988.
49. Rachels J: Active and passive euthanasia. *N Engl J Med* 292:78, 1975.
50. American Medical Association: *Current Opinions of the Council on Ethical and Judicial Affairs of the American Medical Association.* Chicago, American Medical Association, 1986, p 12.
51. Emanuel EJ: A review of the ethical and legal aspects of terminating medical care. *Am J Med* 84:291, 1988.
52. Wanzer SH et al: The physician's responsibility toward helplessly ill patients. *N Engl J Med* 310:955, 1984.
53. Quill TE: Death and dignity. *N Engl J Med* 322:1881, 1990.
54. Gaylin W et al: Doctors must not kill. *JAMA* 259:2139, 1988.
55. Brett AS, McCollough LB: When patients request specific interventions: Defining the limits of the physician's obligation. *N Engl J Med* 315:1347, 1986.
56. Blackhall LJ: Must we always use CPR? *N Engl J Med* 317:1281, 1987.
57. Pearlman RA, Uhlmann RF: Resuscitation preferences: Are they generalizeable? *Gerontologist* 28:105A, 1988.
58. Omnibus Budget Reconciliation Act of 1990.
59. Joint Commission on Accreditation of Health Care Organizations: *Accreditation Manual for Hospitals.* Oak Brook Terrace, Ill, 1992.
60. Steinbrook R, Lo B: Artificial feeding—Solid ground, not a slippery slope. *N Engl J Med* 318:286, 1988.
61. Uhlmann RF et al: Understanding of elderly patients' resuscitation preferences by physicians and nurses. *West J Med* 150:705, 1989.
62. Everhart MA, Pearlman RA: Stability of patient preferences regarding life sustaining treatments: *Clin Res* 36:711A, 1988.
63. Siegler M, Weisbard AJ: Against the emerging stream: Should fluids and nutritional support be discontinued? *Arch Intern Med* 145:129, 1985.
64. Meilaender G: On removing food and water: Against the stream. *Hastings Cent Rep* 14:11, 1984.
65. Micetich KC et al: Are intravenous fluids morally required for a dying patient? *Arch Intern Med* 143:975, 1983.
66. Smith DG, Wigton RS: Modeling decisions to use tube feeding in seriously ill patients. *Arch Intern Med* 147:1242, 1987.
67. Siegler M, Shiedermayer DL: Should fluid and nutritional support be withheld from terminally ill patients? Tube feeding in hospice settings. *Am J Hospice Care* March/April:32, 1987.
68. Lynn J, Childress JF: Must patients always be given food and water? *Hastings Cent Rep* 13:17, 1983.
69. Abrams FR: Withholding treatment when death is not imminent. *Geriatrics* 42:77, 1987.

PART THREE

DISEASES OF THE ORGAN SYSTEMS IN THE ELDERLY

Chapter 37

AGING OF THE SKIN

Michael S. Kaminer and Barbara A. Gilchrest

Human skin has at least three major roles. It is a protective barrier, a highly visible interface with the external environment, and a dynamic component of various immunologic, endocrine, and metabolic systems within the body. Cutaneous integrity is essential to protection from microbial invasion, ultraviolet radiation, extremes of temperature, mechanical trauma, and chemical toxins. It is vital for thermoregulation as well as sensory interactions with the surrounding environment, including both pain and pleasure. As skin ages, it becomes less able to perform these functions. Even subtle changes may significantly affect comfort and function. Because the skin is readily visible, it is also the basis of many first impressions. The cosmetic properties of skin change with age, often with profound psychosocial impact.

The significance of dermatologic problems is evident from the fact that approximately 7 percent of all physician visits are motivated by skin disorders. Moreover, in a study involving 68 noninstitutionalized volunteers aged 50 to 91 years, none of whom had ever consulted a dermatologist, two-thirds had medical concerns about their skin. Of those aged 70 to 80 years, 83 percent complained of cutaneous problems. On examination, all subjects had at least one abnormal skin finding, and almost two-thirds had a clinically significant cutaneous abnormality.[1] These statistics do not include the universal "normal" changes that include both intrinsic aging and chronic sun damage. This high prevalence of previously unrecognized symptomatic skin disease is virtually identical to that recorded for the 65- to 74-year-old cohort in the most recent federal HANES study of more than 20,000 Americans.

Many elderly patients view common skin problems as a normal consequence of the aging process and thus hesitate to mention them to their physician even when they cause considerable discomfort or anxiety. The effect of this reticence on diagnosis and treatment of signficant skin disease in the elderly cannot be overemphasized. As well, the skin serves as a window through which the body reveals much of its internal pathology. Hence the elderly should, as an important part of their comprehensive medical care, be encouraged to draw attention to their skin.

This chapter reviews the age-associated changes in normal skin, differentiates between intrinsic aging and chronic environmental damage, and discusses selected geriatric dermatoses. Common terms are defined in Table 37-1, and unreferenced statements of fact are based on the selected readings at the end of this chapter.

FUNCTIONAL AND MORPHOLOGIC CHANGES IN AGED SKIN

Changes in the appearance and function of normal skin due to the passage of time alone are termed *intrinsic aging* (Table 37-2). In most individuals, however, the majority of unwanted changes are due not to aging alone but to the combination of aging and chronic environmental damage, largely sun exposure. This process is termed *photoaging*.

TABLE 37-1

Definition of Terms

Term	Definition
Macule	Flat lesion ≤3 cm in diameter
Patch	Flat lesion >3 cm in diameter
Papule	Raised solid superficial lesion ≤5 mm in diameter
Plaque	Raised solid superficial lesion >5 mm in diameter
Nodule	Raised solid lesion of any size, deeper than a papule
Vesicle	Fluid-filled lesion ≤5 mm in diameter
Bulla	Fluid-filled lesion >5 mm in diameter
Pustule	Fluid-filled lesion of any size containing pus/leukocytes
Erosion	A superficial wound with loss of all or part of the epidermis
Ulcer	A deep wound with loss of epidermis and some dermis

TABLE 37-2

Skin Changes Associated with Intrinsic Aging

Compartment	Component	Change	Biologic Consequence
Epidermis	Keratinocytes	Decreased proliferative potential	↓ Wound healing, ↓ vitamin D production
	Melanocytes	Decreased 10%–20% per decade	↓ Photoprotection, white hairs
	Langerhans cells	Decreased as much as 40%	↓ Delayed hypersensitivity reactions
	Basement membrane	Decreased surface area	↓ Epidermal-dermal adhesion, ↑ blistering
Dermis	Fibroblasts	Decreased collagen/elastin	↓ Tensile strength, ↓ elasticity
	Blood vessels	Decreased	↓ Thermoregulation, ↓ response to injury
	Mast cells	Decreased	↓ Immediate hypersensitivity reactions
	Neural elements	Decreased by one-third	↓ Sensation, ↑ pain threshold
Subcutis	Fat	Decreased	↓ Mechanical protection and insulation
Appendages	Eccrine glands	Decreased number and output	↓ Thermoregulation
	Apocrine glands	Decreased number and output	Unknown
	Sebaceous glands	Increased size, decreased output	Unknown
	Hair	Decreased number and growth rate	Cosmetic

Intrinsic Cutaneous Aging

Human skin consists of several interrelated functional compartments: the epidermis, the dermis, subcutaneous fat, and the appendages. All change during aging (Fig. 37-1).

Epidermis

The epidermis is the most superficial compartment and serves as the major interface with the external environment. It is composed primarily of keratinocytes (>90 percent of all epidermal cells) and forms the stratum corneum, the major barrier to chemical and microbial insults. It takes approximately 28 days for a proliferative keratinocyte in the basal layer to migrate outward through the 0.1 to 0.2 mm of epidermis; during this transition, it undergoes a carefully regulated program of terminal differentiation. Finally, it is shed from the skin surface. This epidermal turnover time is reduced by approximately 50 percent between the third and eighth decades. With aging, the normally convoluted dermal-epidermal junction is flattened, reducing both the proportion of proliferative basal keratinocytes and the area of contact between the epidermis and dermis.[2] The former is postulated to affect the epidermal wound healing rate and the latter to decrease dermal-epidermal adhesion, reflected in turn by the increased susceptibility of aged skin to blistering or abrasion after mild mechanical trauma.[3]

The epidermis contains two other major cell types, melanocytes and Langerhans cells. Melanocytes comprise 2 to 4 percent of epidermal cells. During embryogenesis, they migrate from the neural crest to the basal layer, where they produce melanin pigment granules and transfer them to surrounding keratinocytes. Melanin determines skin color and tanning capacity and is the skin's major protection against damaging solar radiation. The number of enzymatically active melanocytes decreases by 10 to 20 percent each decade in both sun-protected and sun-exposed skin, although the initial density is far higher in habitually exposed sites. Langerhans cells (1 to 2 percent of epidermal cells) are derived from the bone marrow and are distributed diffusely throughout the epidermis. They are dentritic, immunocompetent cells involved in antigen recognition and presentation. In aged skin, Langerhans cells are reduced in number by as much as 40 percent, a loss that may account for the observed age-associated decrease in delayed hypersensitivity. There is an even greater loss of Langerhans cells in photoaged skin.

A major endocrine function of the skin is vitamin D synthesis. In normal skin, provitamin D_3 is generated from the plasma membrane of keratinocytes and converted to previtamin D_3 by ultraviolet B (UV-B) radiation—290 to 320 nm. Previtamin D_3 is then thermally converted to vitamin D_3 and subsequently translocated to the dermal microvasculature for transport to the liver and kidney, where it is hydroxylated to 1,25-dihydroxyvitamin D, the active form of the vitamin. With advancing age, the amount of provitamin D_3 in the epidermis is markedly reduced.[4] This, in turn, is reflected in a marked reduction in the amount of previtamin D_3 production in elderly skin following UV-B irradiation. Thus, aged skin appears to have a significantly reduced capacity for vitamin D synthesis, a problem often aggravated by a tendency to spend less time outdoors, to expose less skin to the sun, and to avoidance of dairy products, the only dietary source of vitamin D.[5]

Dermis

The dermis consists primarily of connective tissue, in which blood vessels, lymphatics, and nerves are located. Cellular components of the dermis include fibroblasts, macrophages, mast cells, histiocytes, and endothelial cells. Dermal collagen and elastin, pro-

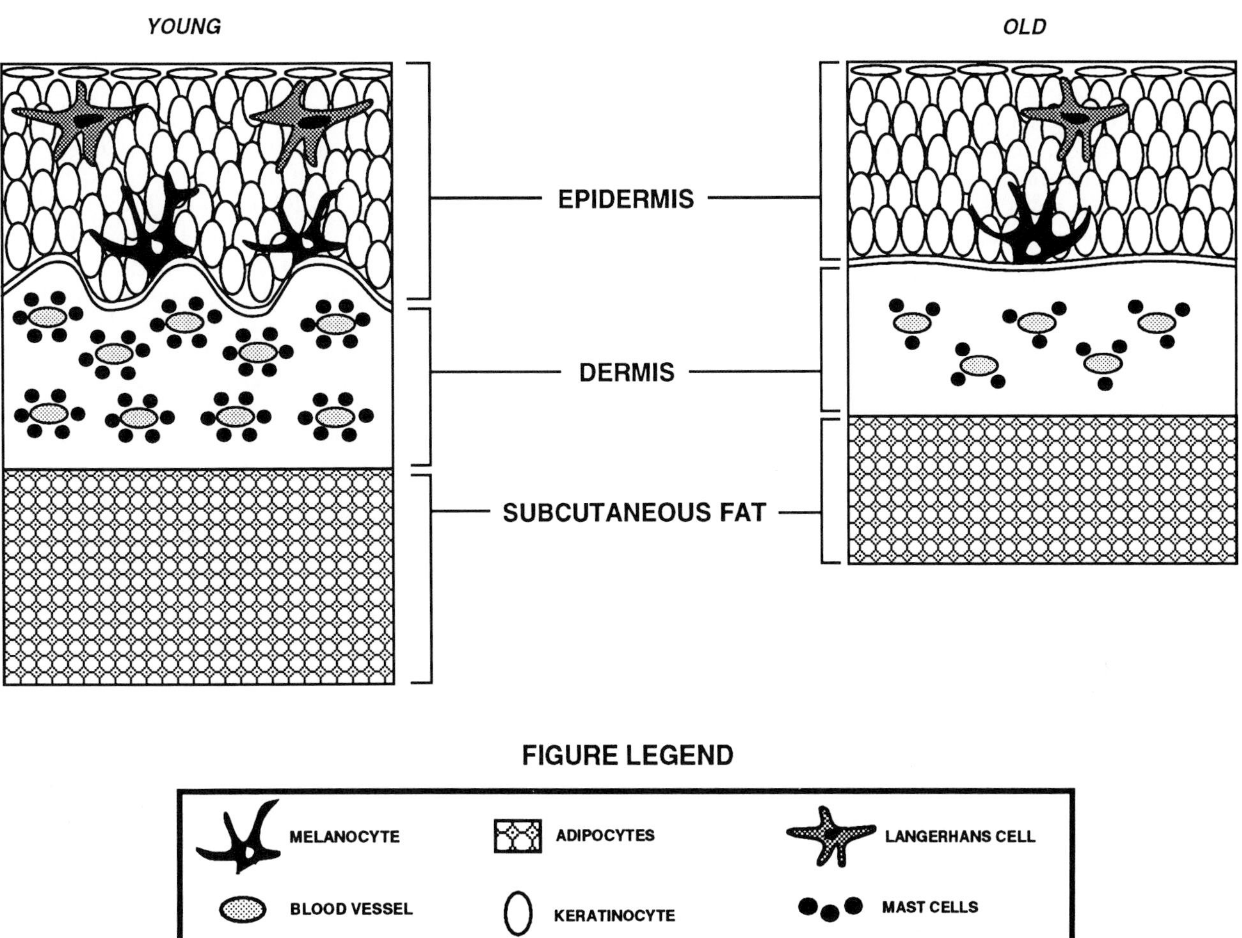

duced by fibroblasts, respectively provide tensile strength and elasticity to the skin. The dermal microvasculature is extensive and involved with thermoregulation and the inflammatory response, as well as the delivery of nutrients and oxygen to the skin.

Age-related changes in the dermis are numerous. The most striking is the approximately 20 percent loss in dermal thickness that may account for the occasionally paper-thin appearance of elderly skin. In addition, the remaining dermis is relatively acellular and avascular. The decrease in the dermal microvasculature, and therefore its thermoregulatory capacity, in part predisposes the elderly to hypothermia and heat stroke during temperature extremes. In addition, arteriole-associated mast cells are decreased by as much as 50 percent. Since the mast cell is the main cell involved in immediate cutaneous hypersensitivity reactions, it is not surprising that the elderly have a diminished capacity to manifest the characteristic wheal-and-flare reaction on exposure to known allergens. The vascular response of old skin to ultraviolet irradiation (sunburn), chemical irritants, and microbial invasion is also frequently reduced. Thus inflammatory reactions may be muted, failing to alert either the patient or the physician to the need for therapy.

One of the major consequences of the changes in elderly skin described above is poor wound healing. The diminished tensile strength of the dermis, flattening of the dermal-epidermal junction (with diminished epidermal proliferative capacity), loss of hair follicles, abrogated inflammatory responsiveness, and reduction of the dermal microvasculature (and thus its ability to deliver blood-borne cellular elements to the healing wound) may all contribute. Elderly individuals are still able to repair major wounds, as evidenced by the number of surgical procedures that are successfully performed; but the wounds take longer to heal and the scars are weaker than in younger patients. It should be stressed that the elderly also tend to have multiple medical problems that themselves compromise wound healing.

Decreased sensory perception is another well-documented feature of aging skin. Meissner's and Pacinian corpuscles—the cutaneous end organs responsible for pressure, vibration, and light touch sensation—decrease to approximately one-third of their initial density between the second and ninth decades. The resulting increase in pain threshold presumably contributes to skin injury.

The subcutaneous fat below the dermis consists

primarily of adipocytes and provides mechanical protection and insulation. Its loss during aging results in parallel reductions in these protective functions.

The cutaneous appendages are eccrine glands, apocrine glands, and pilosebaceous units, composed of hair follicles and sebaceous glands. Eccrine (sweat) glands are present diffusely on the skin surface; evaporation of eccrine sweat aids thermoregulation and is responsible for the "wetness" of axillary sweat. Apocrine glands have no known function in humans but contribute to the odor of axillary sweat. Both types of glands decrease in number and output per gland with aging. Sebaceous glands are androgen-dependent structures found everywhere on the body surface except palms, soles, and proximal nail folds. These glands secrete a lipid-rich substance (sebum) which has no known function. The sebaceous glands increase markedly in size in the elderly, at least on the face, but there is a 40 to 60 percent decrease in sebum production with age in both men and women, attributed to the decreased production of androgens. The clinical effects of decreased sebum production are not known.

The average person has 150,000 hair follicles on the scalp and loses 50 to 100 hairs per day. At birth, an individual has the maximum density of hair follicles; with somatic growth, the follicles become spread out. Hair growth progresses through three cycles: anagen (growth), catagen (involution), and telogen (rest). Each hair follicle goes through these three stages many times. Aging is associated with a gradual reduction in the number of hair follicles as well as a decrease in growth rate, length of the anagen cycle, and diameter of individual hairs. Thus, the hair of older persons is sparse and thin; it fails to grow as rapidly or to the same maximum length as in young adults. With advancing age, there is also an increase in the number of gray or, more correctly, white hairs. By age 50, approximately half of the population will have 50 percent depigmented body hairs and a higher percentage of gray hairs on the scalp. Hair graying is due to progressive loss of melanocytes from the hair bulb, an accentuation of the melanocyte loss also observed in the interfollicular epidermis.

Photoaging

Photoaging consists of those changes in cutaneous appearance and function that are a direct result of repeated sun exposure superimposed on intrinsic aging. Although many physicians and patients perceive no difference between them, photoaging and chronologic aging are two distinct entities. It has been estimated that over 90 percent of cosmetically undesirable skin changes in the elderly are due to photoaging, and more than 90 percent of skin cancer arises in chronically sun-exposed (photoaged) versus sun-protected skin.

Photoaged skin is characterized by wrinkling, yellowing, coarseness, mottled pigmentation, telangiectasia, atrophy, easy bruising, and various premalignant neoplasms. Histologically, the most striking change is dermal elastosis—large aggregates of amorphous elastic fibers. Collagen is diminished, ground substance is increased, activated fibroblasts are numerous, and a mild perivascular infiltrate with degranulating mast cells indicates low-grade inflammation.[6,7] In contrast, intrinsically aged skin is characteristically hypocellular.

Photoaging appears to have the same action spectrum as other forms of sun damage. UV-B (290- to 320-nm) photons, the shortest ultraviolet wavelengths that reach the earth, are potent inducers of sunburn, tanning, damage to deoxyribonucleic acid (DNA), skin cancer, and presumably photoaging.[8] Ultraviolet A (UV-A; 320- to 400-nm) photons are 100 times more abundant in terrestial sunlight than UV-B but are on average only 1/1000 as damaging.[9] However, the longer the wavelength, the greater the depth of penetration into the skin. UV-A photons thus penetrate more deeply into the dermis, site of the most characteristic histologic changes in photodamaged skin.[10] In experimental animal models, both UV-A and UV-B produce histologic changes similar to those present in photoaged skin. In human skin, the relative contribution of UV-A versus UV-B in producing photoaging is unknown.[11] Visible light (400 to 760 nm) is not known to play a role in photoaging or other forms of sun damage in normal skin.

Basal and squamous cell carcinomas account for more than half of all malignancies in the United States, and both epidemiologic data and recent laboratory investigations argue strongly for a direct causal relationship to ultraviolet radiation (UVR). Sunlight also plays a role in human melanoma. In addition to its mutagenic effects on DNA, UVR has been demonstrated to decrease the immune response by increasing CD8+ T suppressor cells, decreasing CD4+ T helper cells, and decreasing epidermal Langerhans cells, which are necessary for antigen presentation.

EVALUATION AND MANAGEMENT OF ELDERLY SKIN

Any physician visit for an elderly patient is an exceptional opportunity to search for cutaneous lesions and complaints. Very few elderly patients consult doctors for dermatologic concerns, even though the vast majority of them have at least some degree of skin pathology. They are often unsure as to the significance of their cutaneous lesions and may feel that their complaints will be viewed as trivial by their physician. In addition, these individuals, especially those over 80 years of age, tend to have a rather limited understanding of proper skin care techniques.[1] The dermatologic needs of the elderly remain largely unmet because of this poor transfer of information from patient to physician and vice versa. It is essential that the physician initiate communication with the patient about his or her dermatologic concerns.

One aspect of cutaneous pathology that has gone largely underrecognized and undertreated is photoaging. Given the vast effects of UVR on human skin, photoprotection is essential. To begin with, there are several misconceptions about sun exposure and photoprotection. A thin cloud cover reduces UVR exposure by only 20 to 40 percent. White sand and cement reflect most UVR; therefore, an umbrella or hat may not afford the level of protection that is anticipated. In addition to clothing, which is the simplest and most practical means of photoprotection, several topical sunscreen preparations are currently available. These preparations act by a variety of mechanisms to block UVR exposure. Most sunscreens offer excellent UV-B protection, and several provide some UV-A protection. Sunscreens should be applied 20 minutes to 2 hours prior to sun exposure and should be reapplied after strenuous exercise or swimming. The amount of photoprotection a sunscreen provides is reflected in its sun protection factor (SPF). This is defined as the ratio of the amount of UV-B energy required to produce minimal erythema through the film of a sunscreen product to the amount of energy required to produce the same amount of erythema without any sunscreen application. A sunscreen with an SPF of 15 will filter more than 92 percent of the UVR responsible for erythema. Therefore, it is recommended that a sunscreen with an SPF of 15 or higher be used by most individuals. It should be noted that the SPF does not quantitate a sunscreen's ability to block UV-A.

A substantial number of skin complaints in the elderly correspond to the effects of photoaging.[12] To date, the most effective nonsurgical, noninvasive method of treating photoaging is the application of topical tretinoin. It has been shown partially to reverse many of the clinical signs of photoaging, including fine and coarse wrinkling, roughness, and lentigenes.[13] Side effects have been limited to an irritant reaction that subsides as the treated skin accommodates. It follows that topical tretinoin can be an effective component of an overall skin care regimen that includes the regular use of sunscreens and moisturizers.

CUTANEOUS DISORDERS

Inflammatory Dermatoses

Xerosis

The term *xerosis* describes the dry quality of the skin that is especially prominent in the elderly. Although previously attributed to an age-associated decrease in the skin's water content or rate of sebum production, its exact etiology remains unknown.[14] It probably reflects minor abnormalities in the keratinocyte maturation process.

Clinically, the skin exhibits a dry scaling and delineation of individual corneocytes; this may resemble "cracked porcelain," especially on the lower extremities (Plate I). Pruritus is often prominent. If untreated, the involved skin may become inflamed, a condition termed *erythema craquelé* or *asteototic eczema*.

Treatment Winter months are especially difficult for patients with xerosis, also known as winter itch, presumably due to the relatively low humidity and increased time spent indoors in heated rooms. Frequent bathing without subsequent application of emollients can also contribute to "dry skin," and the use of mild soaps and/or soapless cleansers can help alleviate the contribution of bathing to xerosis.

Xerosis is best treated prophylactically with frequent use of a topical emollient. Emollient application, the central strategy in the management of xerosis, retards water loss from the epidermis. During bathing, the stratum corneum becomes maximally hydrated, and topical emollients applied immediately after bathing help the skin to retain water. Oils added to the bath also prolong hydration of the stratum corneum, but they coat the surface of the bathtub and thus create a dangerously slippery surface, especially hazardous to the elderly.

Available emollient preparations contain a variety of active ingredients, including lanolin, glycerin, urea 10 to 20 percent and lactic acid 5 or 12 percent. The latter two ingredients loosen retained layers of stratum corneum and thus mitigate the scaliness often associated with xerosis. A mild topical corticosteroid preparation, such as hydrocortisone, expedites the healing process in erythema craquelé.

Stasis Dermatitis/Venous Ulcers

Stasis dermatitis appears as red-brown discoloration of the lower leg (Plate IV). Extremely common in the elderly, stasis dermatitis is caused by chronic venous insufficiency, with subsequent increased hydrostatic pressure and transudation of fluid and red cells. The brown color represents hemosiderin deposition.

A possible sequela of chronic venous stasis is ulceration. Often a result of minor trauma, these ulcers have a predilection for the medial aspect of the distal lower extremity. They can be accompanied by significant morbidity and potentially cost the U.S. economy as much as $1 billion per year, with a loss of 2 million work days annually. While the exact mechanism is unknown, it is hypothesized that venous valvular incompetence increases deep venous pressure, which is then transmitted to the superficial vascular plexus. This in turn causes increased hydrostatic pressure with transudation of fluid and the development of fibrin complexes around the capillaries. Long-standing stasis dermatitis may be associated with liposclerosis, a bound-down quality of the skin. Tissue ischemia and ulceration ensue.[15]

Treatment Stasis dermatitis is best managed by elevation of the legs, reduction of underlying edema, and correction of the venous insufficiency if feasible. The inflammatory, pruritic component of stasis dermatitis responds well to topical corticosteroid ointments, although hyperpigmentation may persist. After symptoms improve, frequent application of an emollient alone is often sufficient. Potent topical steroids should not be used for more than a few weeks. Persistent pruritus should lead the clinician to consider whether contact dermatitis or other problems are also present.

The available therapeutic options for venous stasis ulcers are numerous and include measures ranging from conservative local wound care, including use of hydrocolloid dressings, to cultured epidermal allografting. Ulcers that do not begin to improve within 3 months of initiating conventional therapy should be biopsied because of the approximately 10 percent incidence of basal cell carcinoma in these lesions.[16] Referral to a physician specifically trained in the evaluation and management of venous stasis ulcers is recommended for extensive or persistent lesions.

Contact Dermatitis

There are two types of contact dermatitis: allergic and irritant. Allergic contact dermatitis is a cell-mediated immune response that has as its prerequisite prior contact with the offending agent. Irritant dermatitis refers to a nonimmunologic interaction between the substance and the skin. Any persons sufficiently exposed to the agent will react.

The clinical features of irritant and allergic contact dermatitis are identical, but a careful history will often produce etiologic clues. Acute eruptions tend to be erythematous, pruritic, vesicular, and sometimes linear or geometric in configuration, reflecting the pattern of contact between the skin and the offending agent (Plate III). Low-grade, chronic contact dermatitis, in contrast, tends to be only slightly scaly. Diagnosis in the elderly may be difficult due to the skin's muted inflammatory response.

One specific example of irritant dermatitis is diaper dermatitis, postulated by some but not all authorities to be due to ammonia formed in the wet diaper by bacterial splitting of urea in the feces.[17,18] Diaper dermatitis tends to spare body folds because they are protected by occlusion from the irritant. Differential diagnosis from *Candida albicans* infection is essential (see below).

Treatment Initial treatment of contact dermatitis is always removal of the offending agent. Management of diaper dermatitis specifically focuses on frequent diaper changes and application of topical barrier preparations such as zinc oxide ointment. Application of absorptive powder to the involved area at the time of each diaper change is also helpful.

While identification of the offending agent is not always possible, care should be taken to prevent subsequent exposure of the patient to those agents judged most likely to be the cause of the dermatitis. Patch testing, usually by a dermatologist, is sometimes helpful in identifying the responsible agent in refractory cases. Contact dermatitis usually responds well to potent topical steroid preparations chosen for the specific body site involved. Very severe cases—with bulla formation, facial edema, or generalized discomfort—are best treated with oral prednisone in the absence of contraindications to its use. Initial doses should be in the range of 40 to 60 mg/day, tapered off to nothing over 2 weeks.

Lichen Simplex Chronicus

Also known as neurodermatitis circumscripta, lichen simplex chronicus (LSC) is the end result of habitual scratching or rubbing. Typical features include erythema, edema, hyperpigmentation, and lichenification (a coarsening of the skin surface markings). The central area becomes scaly and thickened. Since the ability to scratch or rub is a prerequisite for developing LSC, these lesions are most commonly found in areas that the patient can reach conveniently, such as the wrists, ankles, upper back, and sides of the neck. Solitary or multiple lesions may develop over months to years without any identifiable precipitant.

Treatment Successful management of LSC requires breaking the scratching habit. A short course of topical antibiotics may be indicated for superficial secondary infection, but in most cases a topical steroid preparation is the treatment of choice. A particularly useful product is an adhesive plastic film impregnated with a corticosteroid preparation (Cordran Tape). Applied daily after the bath or shower, this both reduces inflammation and provides a mechanical barrier to further manipulation. Saran Wrap occlusion of the site following application of a steroid preparation is an alternative. Relatively potent steroids are usually needed, and occasional lesions require treatment with intralesional triamcinolone injection.

Rosacea

Rosacea is a chronic idiopathic skin disorder frequently seen in the elderly. Typical lesions include erythema, easy flushing, telangiectasia, papules, and pustules, especially over the central face (Plate V). Comedones are absent. Alcohol, ingestion of hot beverages, sun exposure, and stress may exacerbate rosacea.[19]

The most common complications of rosacea are rhinophyma and ocular involvement. The former is a bulbous, irregular swelling of the distal nose with follicular prominence and sebaceous hyperplasia. Conjunctivitis is present in over half of rosacea patients.[20] Other ocular findings include blepharitis and corneal involvement, including keratitis.

Treatment Patients should be encouraged to avoid alcohol, hot beverages, spicy foods, and sun exposure. Stress management is sometimes helpful. Inflammatory lesions of rosacea respond very well to broad-spectrum oral antibiotics. Tetracycline 500 to 1000 mg/day usually eliminates pustules and papules within a few weeks. Up to one-third of patients have prolonged remissions after a 3-month course, but most require a low daily maintenance dose. Erythema and telangiectasia do not respond as well to antibiotics but may be treated with the argon or pulsed dye laser. The topical application of 1 percent metronidazole cream has been shown to have some beneficial effect on both the inflammatory and erythematous components of rosacea, but results are variable.[21] Rhinophyma is treated surgically, usually with dermabrasion or electrodesiccation. Topical corticosteroids are not indicated.[22]

Drug Eruptions

Drug eruptions can be the result of immunologic or nonimmunologic causes. Immunologic drug eruptions fall into several categories, including morbilliform eruptions, urticaria ("hives"), photoallergic reactions, fixed drug reactions, erythema multiforme and its more severe variant Stevens-Johnson syndrome, and drug-induced toxic epidermal necrolysis (TEN). Most occur within the first few days to weeks after initiating therapy. Allergic drug rashes theoretically have as a prerequisite prior exposure to the drug or a related compound, although this history is not always available. Sporadically used medications, self-prescribed over-the-counter medications, and food additives are agents that are frequently not elucidated by history and hence are particularly difficult to identify. At this time, unfortunately, there is no diagnostic laboratory test to identify the drug responsible for a specific eruption; causality must therefore be inferred from statistical probability, based on the available literature (Tables 37-3 and 37-4).

TABLE 37-3

Commonly Used Medications That Sometimes Cause Drug Eruptions

Acetaminophen	Epinephrine	Lidocaine
Amitryptyline	Erythromycin	Methyldopa
Colchicine	Ethacrynic acid	Milk of magnesia
Digoxin	Hydroxyzine	Prednisone
Docusate	Levothyroxine	Theophylline

SOURCE: Arnold HL, Odom RB, James WD: *Diseases of the Skin*, 8th ed. Philadelphia, Saunders, 1990.

Morbilliform drug eruptions are the most common. Generalized erythematous macules and papules with mild to moderate pruritus may involve the entire skin surface, including the palms, soles, and mucous membranes (Plate II). Fixed drug eruptions, in contrast, appear as one or a few sharply demarcated round to oval lesions (Plate VI). Within hours of drug ingestion, there is rapid appearance of intensely inflammatory, sometimes bullous, lesions that then slowly resolve, often leaving gray-brown hyperpigmentation that may persist for weeks to months. Lesions recur in the same exact spot with subsequent reexposure to the drug.

Urticarial eruptions account for nearly 25 percent of all drug rashes, and drugs in turn are probably the most frequent cause of urticaria. The lesions of acute urticaria are pruritic, erythematous, edematous papules or plaques that can achieve a diameter of 20 to 30 cm (Plate IX). Annular or arciform lesions are characteristic. Individual lesions typically last less than 24 hours. Severe urticaria may be associated with laryngeal or facial swelling and with anaphylaxis.

Sun-induced drug rashes have two distinct mechanisms. Phototoxic reactions are not immunologically mediated and theoretically occur in all persons exposed to sufficient doses of the drug and causative wavelengths of light, usually UV-A. Erythema identical to a sunburn reaction begins within a few hours and may worsen for several days before subsiding. Photoallergic reactions are immunologically mediated and are identical in their clinical features to other drug eruptions except that they appear only after sufficient sun exposure and are restricted to sun-exposed areas. Virtually all drugs that cause photoallergic reactions are also phototoxins. In general, they are polycyclic compounds capable of absorbing UV energy.

Erythema multiforme, Stevens-Johnson syndrome, and TEN represent a spectrum of reactions for which patients 65 years of age and older are more likely to require hospitalization than any other age group.[23] Erythema multiforme usually presents as

TABLE 37-4

Drug Eruptions and Their Common Etiologies

Morbilliform	Antibiotics, allopurinol, phenytoin, benzodiazepines, captopril, insulin, NSAID*
Urticarial	Penicillins, sulfonamides, codeine, morphine, NSAID, captopril
Fixed drug	Phenolphthalein, barbiturates, tetracyclines, NSAID, hydralazine
Phototoxic/Photoallergic	Sulfonamides, tetracyclines, phenothiazines, thiazides, oral hypoglycemics, griseofulvin, NSAID, furocoumarins
Erythema multiforme/Toxic epidermal necrolysis	Phenobarbitol, nitrofurantoin, trimethoprim/sulfamethoxazole, penicillins, phenytoin, NSAID, allopurinol

*Nonsteroidal anti-inflammatory drugs.
SOURCE: Arnold HL, Odom RB, James WD: *Diseases of the Skin*, 8th ed. Philadelphia, Saunders, 1990.

diffuse erythematous macules with, by definition, at least some characteristic target lesions; it resolves spontaneously in 2 to 3 weeks. Stevens-Johnson syndrome is regarded as a more severe form with abrupt onset, extensive mucosal involvement, and a longer course of 4 to 6 weeks, usually requiring hospitalization. Finally, TEN is characterized by a rapidly progressive necrosis and loss of the epidermis and hence the barrier layer (Plate VII).[24] The mortality rate for TEN in the elderly exceeds 50 percent, with death usually due to sepsis despite inpatient management, usually in burn units.

Treatment Treatment centers around discontinuation of the offending drug, based on the assumptions that eruptions will not resolve if the medication is continued and that a relatively mild eruption may evolve into a more severe one with continued antigenic exposure. If multiple drugs are potentially implicated, it is preferable to discontinue all and then reintroduce them one at a time, at intervals of at least several days, after the eruption has resolved. If practical considerations preclude this course, all nonessential drugs, particularly those commonly implicated in drug eruptions, should be discontinued. If it is necessary to substitute another drug in the same therapeutic class, care should be taken to avoid one known to cross-react with the suspected agent. For patients with Stevens-Johnson syndrome and TEN, in addition to discontinuation of the offending agent, hospitalization is advised for intravenous hydration and prevention of sepsis. Use of systemic corticosteroids is controversial in the absence of adequately controlled clinical trials, but current recommendations are to avoid them.[25]

Other measures are aimed primarily to symptomatic relief. Oatmeal baths and/or frequent applications of emollients are often all that is required. For those patients who experience significant pruritus, oral antihistamines can be used cautiously. The benefit of topical corticosteroids is usually minimal.

Vascular Lesions

Cherry Angiomas

Cherry angiomas are extremely common benign lesions occurring on the trunk as deep red, well-demarcated papules. They are of no known clinical or prognostic significance. Very small cherry angiomas may resemble petechiae or telangiectasia. No treatment is indicated, but lesions can be removed by electrodesiccation and curettage or pulsed tunable dye laser therapy.

Venous Lakes

Venous lakes are dark blue, compressible, slightly elevated 2- to 10-mm vascular lesions of no medical significance. They are found predominantly on the ear and vermilion border of the lip and are composed of dilated, blood-filled, thin-walled venules. Occasionally bleeding is noted following minor trauma. Lesions can be removed by excision, electrodesiccation, or laser therapy.

Spider Angiomas

Spider angiomas occur in as many as 15 percent of normal individuals but are also associated with liver disease and pregnancy. Based on these associations, a relationship to estrogens has been suggested. The central vessel of the spider angioma is an arteriole which is slightly raised above the skin surface, and blood flows out through radiating capillaries (spider legs). Once formed, lesions tend to persist except in pregnant women. They are most commonly found on the face, neck, and arms. Treatment consists of electrocautery or laser therapy of the central arteriole.

Angiokeratomas of Fordyce

Angiokeratomas of Fordyce are present on the scrotum in nearly 20 percent of men over 70 years of age.[26] Local venous hypertension may play an etiologic role.[27] They appear as 1- to 4-mm bright red to purple papules (Plate VIII). With advancing age, they become larger, darker, and more numerous. While these lesions are usually asymptomatic, patients occasionally complain of itching, pain, or bleeding. Identical lesions may also be present on the penis, upper thighs, and inguinal region. The most important differential diagnosis is angiokeratoma corporis diffusum (Fabry's disease), which occurs in younger men and is associated with renal failure.

Treatment Treatment is optional. Modalities include liquid nitrogen cryotherapy, electrodesiccation, and laser ablation.

Actinic Purpura

Also referred to as senile purpura due to its prevalence in the elderly, actinic purpura is due to weakening of perivenular connective tissue by chronic sun exposure.[28] The purpura occurs primarily on the sun-exposed surfaces of the forearms after minor trauma or without any recognized inciting event. The clinical appearance consists of one or more irregularly shaped, fairly well demarcated violaceous to red-brown macules varying in size from a few millimeters to several centimeters (Plate XI). Lesions are usually asymptomatic and may persist for many weeks. There is no effective treatment.

Infestations

Lice

Lice are wingless, six-legged obligate ectoparasites of mammals and birds. Humans are parasitized by two species: *Pediculus humanus* and *Pthirus pubic.* There are two subspecies of *P. humanus: P. humanus capitis,* the head louse, and *P. humanus humanus,* the body or clothing louse. *Pthirus pubis* is the pubic (crab) louse.

Lice obtain their nourishment directly from host blood vessels via percutaneous routes. Head and body lice tend to respect the geographic restrictions implied by their names. The crab louse will colonize axillary, eyelash, eyebrow, beard, trunk, and extremity hair in addition to pubic hairs. Head and body lice are 3 to 4 mm long, while pubic lice are much smaller. All forms of lice use leg claws to cling to the base of hairs, where the female lays her eggs. The ova, firmly attached to the base of the hair, hatch in approximately 7 to 9 days and mature in another week.

The prominent clinical feature of pediculosis is pruritus. The delay from infestation to pruritus is approximately 30 days, the time required for development of delayed hypersensitivity to the insects. Secondary complications from scratching include impetigo and furunculosis. Nits, which represent empty egg casings, are found on the hair shaft close to the skin surface and are usually far easier to detect than lice themselves. In pediculosis pubis, 1- to 2-mm bright red macules may be seen on the skin as a result of vascular cannulation by the louse. Maculae ceruleae, which are blue-gray vascular lesions less than 5 mm in diameter, are characteristic of body lice infestation but can also be seen on the skin of patients infested with pubic lice.

Head lice are predominantly seen in children but can infest any age group. Transmission is usually by direct head-to-head contact or shared clothing or brushes. Pediculosis corporis, also known as vagabond's disease, is relatively uncommon in developed countries and tends to appear where poverty and poor hygiene are common. Transmission is by direct bodily contact or sharing of infested clothing. The lice remain in clothing or bedding except when feeding, so they are rarely detected on the skin surface. Recognition of pediculosis corporis is essential because *P. humanus humanus* is the vector for the major louse-borne diseases in humans—epidemic typhus, trench fever, and relapsing fever. Pediculosis pubis is predominantly transmitted by close physical, usually sexual, contact. Detection of pubic lice should prompt a search of other hair-bearing areas as detailed above.

Treatment The goal of treatment is the destruction of both lice and ova. The mainstay has been gamma benzene hexachloride (lindane, Kwell). Due to the risk of neurotoxicity from lindane, especially in small children, pyrethrins are also widely used. Efficacy is comparable. The pyrethrins, such as Rid, are naturally occurring insecticides extracted from chrysanthemums. Synthetic pyrethrins, called permethrins, are available in varying concentrations from 1% (Nix) to 5% (Elemite).

For pediculosis capitis, only the scalp needs to be treated. Permethrin 1% Creme Rinse is the drug of choice and should be applied in the shower for 10 minutes and then washed off.[29] Nits can then be removed from hairs using a fine-toothed comb. Other conventional treatments include lindane (Kwell) shampoo, crotamiton (Eurax), and pyrethrins (Rid). Treatment of pediculosis corporis centers around elimination of lice and nits from the clothing and bedding. Dry cleaning destroys lice on wool clothing. Lice in clothing may also be killed by washing the clothes in hot water or boiling them and then ironing the seams. The patient need only wash with soap and water. Pediculosis pubis can be treated with lindane cream or lotion applied for 8 hours to all hair-bearing areas from the chin to the toes and then washed off. Lindane shampoo need be applied for only 4 minutes in the shower and washed off. Permethrin 1% Creme Rinse is equally effective applied to the same areas for 10 minutes and then washed off. Effective therapy for eyelash involvement is the application of petrolatum jelly to maintain a thick, continuous layer for 8 days, followed by mechanical removal of the nits. Clothing and fomites should be treated as described above.[30]

Pediculocides have varying degrees of ovacidal activity. Therefore one treatment may not completely eradicate the infestation, as the surviving eggs will hatch within 7 to 9 days. Patients should be carefully inspected for the presence of persistent eggs or lice, and retreatment is indicated in 7 to 10 days if there is any sign or doubt as to continued infestation. Sexual and close physical contacts should be treated at the same time as the patient. Treatment failures are uncommon if these guidelines are followed.[31]

Scabies

Scabies is caused by *Sarcoptes scabiei,* the itch mite. It is an oval, flattened 0.3- to 0.5-mm parasite with eight legs. After mating on the surface of the skin, the male dies and the female burrows into the skin to deposit her eggs. The female lays two to three eggs daily continuously for 4 to 6 weeks, after which she dies as well. The eggs hatch into larvae after 3 to 4 days, and these mature into adults in 10 to 14 days. The common sites for infestation are the digital web spaces and volar wrist. Other sites of predilection are the antecubital fossa, axillae, areolae, umbilicus, lower abdomen, genitals, and buttocks. The glans penis is often involved in men, and this is virtually pathognomonic (Plate XII). The face and scalp are not affected.

Scabies is usually contracted by close personal contact and is an underestimated problem among the elderly. Nursing home residents are especially at risk.[32] Sensitization to the mite begins 2 to 4 weeks after the female burrows into the skin, and this is the point at which pruritus begins. The pruritus will frequently wake the patient at night and cause him or her to scratch extensively. The clinical lesions are burrows, representing the path the female mite has taken, and excoriated papules. Definitive diagnosis is made by microscopic demonstration of the mite, eggs, or feces within lesional scrapings, although the clinical picture alone may be strongly suggestive.

An uncommon form of scabies is crusted or Norwegian scabies.[33] This is an overwhelming infestation of immunocompromised or institutionalized individuals with thousands of mites. It is highly transmissible. The lesions have a heavily scaled or crusted appearance, and the distal fingers, face, and scalp are frequently involved. Itching may be minimal. Treatment is essentially the same as for ordinary scabies. A short course of oral methotrexate may be effective.

Treatment Permethrin 5% cream (Elemite) is the safest, most effective treatment available.[34] It is applied from the chin to the toes, with careful attention to body folds, palms, soles, and the subungual areas. The cream is left on overnight and washed off thoroughly in the morning. This should be repeated in 1 week. All clothing, bed linen, towels, and personal articles in contact with the patient should be washed in hot water following each treatment period. Other topical preparations used in the treatment of scabies include lindane lotion, 5% precipitated sulfur in petrolatum, and crotamiton. Pruritus gradually diminishes over the ensuing week or two. During this time, patients must be reassured that their discomfort is due to a resolving hypersensitivity reaction, not to persistent infestation. Topical corticosteroid preparations and oral antihistamines may be useful in this resolution phase of scabies. Rarely, a tapering course of oral corticosteroids may be indicated. To prevent "back and forth" reinfestation, it is also necessary to treat all close personal contacts and sexual partners during the patient's illness because of the 2- to 4-week asymptomatic incubation period that precedes the recognized scabies infestation.

Infections

Tinea (Dermatophytes)

Tinea infections are very common in the elderly. The term *tinea* refers to a class of fungi, dermatophytes, that live in the dead outer layers of the stratum corneum or nail plates. They are not systemic pathogens. There are numerous forms (species) of dermatophytes that cause characteristic infections, named for the body site involved.

The feet are the most common site of dermatophyte infection. Tinea pedis is characterized by scaling of the sole in a "moccasin" distribution and/or toe web maceration (Plate XIII). The nails are frequently involved as well (onychomycosis). Web space fissures due to tinea may become secondarily infected by resident skin bacteria, including staphylococcal species or gram-negative pathogens.[35] Itching, burning, and an unpleasant odor may be prominent. Tinea pedis is usually chronic and very difficult to eradicate but warrants careful attention because of the risk of secondary infection and subsequent cellulitus. Another site frequently involved in the elderly is the groin (tinea cruris); the trunk and extremities (tinea corporis, "ringworm") are usually spared.

Diagnosis of tinea infections is best accomplished by demonstration of hyphae in potassium hydroxide (KOH) stains of the scale associated with these lesions. Cultures of lesional scrapings using Sabouraud's glucose agar or Dermatophyte Test Medium are also useful but require several weeks and are often falsely negative. It is important to differentiate dermatophyte infections from simple xerosis or other noninfectious eczematous lesions, particularly on the trunk or extremities. Candidal infections of the groin may also resemble tinea cruris. However, *Candida* tends to produce more intense inflammation, with erythema and satellite pustules (see next section). As well, the penis and scrotum are rarely involved in tinea cruris, another feature that helps to differentiate it from candidiasis.

Treatment Dermatophyte infections are best treated with a topical, broad-spectrum antifungal preparation containing an imidazole derivative, haloprogin, ciclopirox olamine, or naftifine. Imadozoles, which have antibacterial as well as antifungal activity, are particularly useful in the treatment of tinea pedis. A cream or solution should be applied twice daily until signs of infection have resolved and then continued for at least 2 weeks. Subsequent indefinite use of an antifungal powder may provide prophylaxis against reinfection by reducing the excessive moisture that often predisposes the individual to fungal infection. Topical corticosteroid preparations may appear to initially improve dermatophyte infections by reducing inflammation, but they should be used with caution because of the likelihood that the fungal infection will continue to spread with their use. Systemic antifungal therapy with griseofulvin or ketoconazole should be reserved for severe cases of dermatophytosis.

Candidiasis

Candida albicans (yeast) infections are also frequent in the elderly, particularly in diabetics. This opportunistic organism becomes invasive for the most part in the presence of excessive moisture or in the setting of impaired immunity. Therefore, *C. albicans* infections are commonly seen in body folds (intertriginous areas), where warmth, moisture, and maceration of the skin permit the organism to flourish. Frequently affected sites include the perianal and inguinal folds, inframammary folds, axillae, interdigital areas, and corners of the mouth. This latter condition, termed perlèche or angular cheilitis, appears in the elderly as ill-defined thickened areas with slight erythema in the oral commissures.

Involvement of the oral mucosa (thrush) typically occurs in the debilitated elderly patient, especially with the administration of broad-spectrum antibiotics. The buccal mucosa and the tongue are involved, with small erosions and characteristic small, white, tender plaques. The surface of the tongue may appear smooth and bright red. Thrush is also extremely common in patients with the acquired immunodeficiency syndrome (AIDS), and the observation of oral thrush in an adult with no known predisposing factors should prompt the clinician to consider this possibility.[36,37] Systemic candidiasis almost invariably occurs when there is underlying immunosuppression, as in patients with malignancies, AIDS, and those receiving immunosuppressive therapy. An in-depth discussion of this entity is beyond the scope of this chapter.

Intertriginous candidiasis typically presents as bright red, sharply demarcated, tender, sometimes pruritic areas with "satellite" papules and/or pustules. These infections should be differentiated from simple intertrigo (maceration of skin folds with erythema in the absence of infection) and tinea infections. With these disorders, the erythema tends to be less pronounced than with *C. albicans* infection.

Diagnosis can be made by KOH examination of lesional scrapings. Under the microscope, spores and budding yeasts (pseudohyphae) can be seen. The yeast forms can also be demonstrated as dense, gram-positive, ovoid bodies on gram-stained specimens. *Candida albicans* is also readily cultured on Sabouraud's agar.

Treatment Intertriginous candidiasis is effectively treated with broad-spectrum antifungal/antiyeast topical preparations. Available products include clotrimazole, micronazole, econazole, oxiconazole, sulconazole, and naftifine. Topical ketoconazole cream is also very effective. Care should be taken to improve the microenvironment of the treated area, specifically decreasing moisture and maceration. Improved ventillation of the area along with the frequent use of a nonmedicated, absorbent powder is usually satisfactory. Ointments, occlusive dressings, and cornstarch, which is metabolized by yeasts, should be avoided.

Oral candidiasis is rather easily treated with clotrimazole or nystatin rinses four times daily. The medication is held in the mouth for several minutes and then swallowed. The inflammation and fissuring associated with perlèche often responds well to the twice-daily application of one of the antiyeast creams mentioned above. Addition of a mild topical corticosteroid preparation for a few days may help to speed the resolution of these lesions. However, it should be stressed that topical corticosteroids predispose the skin to bacterial or fungal superinfection and therefore should be used sparingly. Oral ketoconazole should be reserved for those patients with severe, non-responsive candidiasis or those who are unable to cooperate with alternative therapies.

Bacterial Infections

The incidence of bacterial infections in the elderly is not known to differ substantially from that in young adults, but the clinical features of these infections may not be the same. Vascular compromise and an age-associated reduction in the cutaneous immune response may mute the clinical presentation of cellulitis or other cutaneous bacterial infections. In addition, once the diagnosis of bacterial infection is made, assessment of the clinical response to treatment can be difficult, since the initial lesion may not be very impressive. Furthermore, the elderly patient with diabetes, vascular insufficiency, or other disease may be prone to delayed wound healing and persistent infection and secondary ulceration.

Erysipelas (St. Anthony's fire) is an acute cellulitis caused by group A beta-hemolytic streptococci. The lesion typically begins on the face as an erythematous plaque and extends peripherally with a raised, sharply demarcated advancing edge. Intramuscular or intravenous penicillin (or ceftriaxone) should be effective within 48 hours. It is advisable to continue oral therapy for at least 10 days. Treatment for an uncomplicated community-acquired skin infection—such as cellulitis or herpes zoster which has become secondarily infected—should include coverage for streptococcal and staphylococcal species. Oral dicloxacillin is often sufficient, and erythromycin is an effective alternative where *Staphylococcus aureus* predominates or in patients with a penicillin allergy. The treatment of hospital-acquired cutaneous infections may be complicated by resistance to antibiotics and thus requires careful monitoring, with antibiotic selection based on culture-proven sensitivities. Evaluation and management of cutaneous ulcers is discussed elsewhere in this chapter.

Verrucae (Warts)

Warts are caused by the human papillomavirus (HPV), which is a member of the DNA-containing papovavirus group. There are currently over 50 types of HPV identified as pathogenic in humans, but the classification of these is largely of epidemiologic interest.[38] The most common clinical lesions caused by HPV are plantar warts, condyloma acuminatum (genital warts), and verruca vulgaris (common warts), all of which are less common in the elderly than in young adults.

The common wart occurs primarily on the hands and face as an elevated, rounded, flesh-colored lesion with a rough, papillated ("verrucous") surface. Renal transplant patients and those receiving immunosuppressive therapy are at increased risk for developing verruca vulgaris.[39] Plantar warts generally begin at pressure points on the bottom of the foot but may be anywhere on the plantar surface. These warts tend to be deep-seated, round, hyperkeratotic lesions with central "black dots," representing dilated capillary loops in the elongated dermal papilla. These can be seen most clearly after the lesion has been pared down with a scalpel blade. This helps to differentiate plantar warts clinically from corns or calluses. Condyloma acuminatum begin as small, flesh-colored papules on the penis, perineum, vulva, or anus but can become large, vegetating lesions if neglected. These lesions are sexually transmitted, with a significant rate of transmission from a single unprotected sexual contact.[40]

Treatment Treatment options include cryosurgery, electrodesiccation and curettage, podophyllin resin, salicylic acid, cantharadin, and CO_2 laser ablation, to name a few. The choice is determined by anatomic location, extent of the lesions to be treated, and the patients's general health.

Herpes Zoster

Herpes zoster or "shingles" is caused by the reactivation of latent varicella virus in one or more dorsal sensory ganglia. Prior infection with the DNA-containing varicella virus ("chickenpox") is a prerequisite to the development of zoster. Immunosuppression is not necessary for zoster to develop, but the severity of the disease in an immunosuppressed host is increased and the mild immunosuppression that accompanies normal aging is offered as an explanation for the high incidence of zoster among the elderly, exceeding 10 per 1000 annually at age 80 years.[41] The disease is frequently but not always accompanied by a prodrome of dysesthesia or paresthesia which may persist for a few days, but rarely more than a week. This is followed by the rapid appearance of clustered vesicles on an erythematous, edematous base in a dermatomal distribution. The initial lesion is a clear, fluid-filled vesicle, but such vesicles may become pustular or hemorrhagic within a few days. New lesions may continue to develop over several days, often extending along the affected dermatome. The diagnosis of herpes virus infection is confirmed by the presence of giant cells on a Tzanck preparation. Viral culture is difficult and rarely indicated.

The lesions of herpes zoster usually remain confined to a single unilateral dermatome. Bilateral or disseminated involvement suggests severe immunosuppression. Extensive cutaneous zoster may be accompanied by fever, headache, malaise, and signs of meningeal irritation. Hyperesthesia to light touch, itching, tenderness, and especially pain are prominent features of the acute infection. Lesions usually begin to crust in the second week and resolve within a month, although the course may be protracted in the elderly. Approximately 10 percent of all patients with herpes zoster experience intense, intractable pain for months following resolution of the clinical lesions, but 25 to 50 percent of patients over the age of 60 are affected by postherpetic neuralgia. The elderly in general are at an increased risk of developing this often debilitating complication. The severity of the acute phase symptoms does not accurately predict the risk or severity of postherpetic neuralgia, although certain clinical presentations, particularly herpes zoster ophthalmicus (involvement of the ophthalmic division of the fifth cranial nerve), place the patient at high risk (Plate X).[42] Moreover, on average, the elderly experience a longer and more severe course of postherpetic neuralgia than do younger individuals.

There is no increased risk of internal malignancy associated with herpes zoster infection. The earlier perception of this statistical association was due to the association of both disorders with advanced age.[43,44]

Treatment Initial management of herpes zoster centers around pain control, the prevention of bacterial superinfection, hastening resolution of the cutaneous lesions, and decreasing the risk of postherpetic neuralgia. Severe pain may require a short course of narcotic analgesics, although these drugs should be used with caution in the elderly. Application of hypertonic compresses such as Domeboro-soaked washcloths to the lesions for 15 to 20 minutes three to four times a day, followed by a topical antibiotic ointment, will decrease "weeping" and bacterial colonization of eroded areas.

The use of oral acyclovir for the treatment of herpes zoster in otherwise healthy older individuals is relatively recent, and uncomplicated zoster does not require the use of acyclovir. However, treated patients demonstrate reductions in the duration of viral shedding, new lesion formation, healing time, and pain severity if acyclovir is begun within 72 hours of the onset of the eruption. Moreover, 800 mg taken orally five times daily for 10 days has been shown to decrease the risk of postherpetic neuralgia in the elderly.[45,46]

A 2- to 3-week course of oral corticosteroids, tapered from an initial dose of 40 to 60 mg/day of prednisone or equivalent, has also been reported to decrease the risk of postherpetic neuralgia in the elderly.[47] No serious side effects were noted in the patients studied, but contraindications must be carefully considered. The risk of side effects with acyclovir appears significantly lower than with corticosteroids. The efficacies of oral corticosteroids and oral acyclovir in the prevention of postherpetic neuralgia are thought to be similar. Use of both agents in high-risk patients has been suggested, but data supporting additive efficacy are lacking.[48,49]

Once established, postherpetic neuralgia is extremely difficult to treat. The list of treatment options is extensive, and decisions should be tailored to the specific needs of the individual patient.[50]

Papulosquamous Disorders

Seborrheic Dermatitis

Seborrheic dermatitis is an extremely common chronic superficial inflammatory disorder of the skin characterized by erythema and scant, loose, "greasy" scale. Sites of predilection include the scalp, forehead, glabella, eyebrows, nasolabial folds, ears, presternal area, and groin. Involvement of the scalp is often referred to as "dandruff" by the patient. The etiology is unknown.

Treatment Seborrheic dermatitis responds very quickly to the application of low-potency topical corticosteroid preparations. Hydrocortisone cream is usually sufficient on the face and ears, while a medium-strength steroid (triamcinolone acetonide) may be required on the chest. Scalp involvement is best managed with tar or zinc pyrithionate–based shampoos used daily; severe cases may require the addition of a topical corticosteroid solution to the regimen for a short time. Improvement should be quite significant within the first few days. However, intermittent maintenance therapy is usually necessary indefinitely. A poor response to topical therapy should prompt the clinician to reevaluate the diagnosis.

An alternative treatment for those patients who respond poorly to corticosteroid preparations or who require protracted therapy is ketoconazole-based cream or shampoo.[51] The rationale for their use is the demonstration of increased numbers of the yeast *Pity-*

rosporum ovale in the lesions of seborrheic dermatitis.[52]

Psoriasis

Psoriasis affects approximately 1 to 2 percent of the population. There is often a family history of psoriasis, and onset in the latter decades of life is not uncommon.[53] Lesions are well-demarcated erythematous plaques with an adherent silvery scale, commonly involving the elbows, knees, scalp, and trunk (Plate XIX). Nail findings such as pitting, "oil-drops," and distal onycholysis (separation from the underlying nail bed) support the diagnosis.

Variants of psoriasis include inverse (intertriginous involvement), guttate, generalized pustular (von Zumbusch type), and palmoplantar psoriasis. Beta blockers and lithium can precipitate or exacerbate the disease.[54,55]

Treatment The mainstay of treatment for mild to moderate uncomplicated psoriasis is topical corticosteroids. Other effective topical treatments include anthralin, tar, and salicylic acid (to remove scale). Many patients benefit from casual sun exposure. Supervised phototherapy is often quite effective but typically requires the patient to travel to an office or hospital setting two or three times a week. Systemic therapy with methotrexate or etretinate is sometimes indicated, but in the elderly, these drugs should be employed with extreme caution due to their systemic toxicities. Numerous other therapeutic modalities and combination regimens are available, and referral to an experienced dermatologist is advised for severely affected patients.

Blistering Diseases

Bullous Pemphigoid

Bullous pemphigoid (BP) is an immunologically mediated idiopathic disease that has its peak incidence in the elderly, with males and females equally affected.[56] It is the most common blistering skin disease in the elderly. The classic lesions are large, tense bullae arising on either normal-appearing skin or erythematous, sometimes urticarial plaques (Plate XIV). Associated pruritus may be intense. Frequently affected sites include the trunk, groin, axillae, and flexor surfaces of the forearms. Oral involvement is present in one-third of patients but is rarely a presenting symptom. Large denuded areas are present where bullae rupture, and these may require extensive local care. Bullous pemphigoid is self-limited, lasting from several months to a few years. Most patients achieve a complete, lasting remission with treatment. However, 10 to 15 percent of patients experience a relapse after treatment is stopped.

Bullous pemphigoid is caused by circulating immunoglobulin G (IgG) antibodies directed against a 230-kilodalton protein, the bullous pemphigoid antigen (BPA), on the surface of the basal keratinocyte in contact with the basement membrane.[57,58] The binding of this IgG antibody to the BPA is thought to activate the complement cascade, and the subsequent inflammatory reaction causes separation of the dermis from the epidermis (subepidermal blister formation). Thus the full thickness of the epidermis forms the BP blister roof, accounting for the persistence of intact bullae. In contrast, in pemphigus vulgaris the split is within the epidermis and the blisters therefore tend to rupture easily.

The diagnosis of BP is confirmed by biopsy of an early bullous lesion for routine histochemical staining. A second biopsy may be taken from perilesional skin for immunofluorescence staining to demonstrate the diagnostic linear deposition of the third complement component (C3) and frequently IgG at the base of the epidermis. Indirect immunofluorescence studies using patient serum and monkey esophagus as the substrate demonstrate anti-BPA immunoglobulins (IgG subtype) in approximately two-thirds of patients. Referral to a dermatologist is recommended because special handling of the biopsy specimens for immunofluorescence is required. Like herpes zoster, BP is not a marker for internal malignancy, contrary to previous reports.[59,60]

Treatment In the presteroid era, BP was often a fatal disease, with death due to sepsis. High-dose systemic corticosteroids are extremely effective in bullous pemphigoid but are themselves hazardous in the elderly. In the absence of contraindications, oral prednisone should be started at doses of 60 to 100 mg/day. The dose should be tapered rapidly once new blisters have stopped forming and discontinued once a complete remission is obtained. Early, localized cases of BP may respond well to topical application of a potent corticosteroid preparation, but the majority of patients will require systemic corticosteroids. Adjuvant therapy with an immunosuppressive agent such as azathioprine may be instituted for its steroid-sparing effect, but 6 to 8 weeks are needed to obtain the full benefit. Other treatment options include sulfapyridine and dapsone. It is recommended that patients be managed in consultation with a dermatologist.

Pemphigus Vulgaris

Pemphigus vulgaris (PV) is an autoimmune, potentially life-threatening disease. It occurs with equal frequency in men and women, usually between 40 and 60 years of age, and is characterized by flaccid bullae and erosions on the neck, scalp, face, groin, and axillae. Mucous membrane lesions are common, and oral erosions are the presenting sign in 60 percent of patients. Firm, lateral pressure on the skin surface, especially at the margin of a lesion, may cause the epidermis to peel off, a phenomenon called the Nikolsky sign.

Pemphigus vulgaris is caused by an IgG antibody directed against a 210-kilodalton glycoprotein on the keratinocyte cell surface.[61] The result of this antigen-antibody interaction is the separation of keratinocytes from one another (acantholysis), leading to intraepidermal blister formation. Direct and indirect immunofluorescence staining exhibit intercellular IgG and C3 deposition throughout the epidermis.

Treatment The mortality rate for pemphigus vulgaris approached 100 percent prior to the availability of corticosteroids. The use of oral prednisone has greatly improved the prognosis, with death in only 5 to 10 percent of treated cases. Starting doses of at least 60 to 80 mg/day should be used, and far higher doses may be needed to suppress new blister formation, especially in extensive disease. For these reasons, early intervention is critical in PV. As with bullous pemphigoid, steroid-sparing agents such as azathioprine are sometimes indicated. Local measures—including Burow's solution soaks and silver sulfadiazine 1% cream—alleviate pain and risk of secondary infection. Other therapies for PV include methotrexate, cyclophosphamide, gold, dapsone, and plasmapheresis. Consultation with a dermatologist is strongly recommended.

Pruritus

Pruritus, or itching, is an unpleasant cutaneous sensation causing the patient to scratch or rub the affected area. It is a common problem in the elderly and can be localized or generalized.[62]

Most patients with significant pruritus will have excoriations or other evidence of scratching or rubbing. In addition, many have a primary cutaneous eruption (Table 37-5). In these cases, specific, usually quite effective therapy is available. Hence, a thorough history and physical examination should be performed, knowing that the elderly may have a muted inflammatory response and therefore often subtle physical findings. In the absence of primary skin lesions, underlying systemic diseases must be considered in the differential diagnosis of pruritus, although at least half and probably far more elderly patients with pruritus have no discernible etiology.

TABLE 37-5

Selected Causes of Pruritus in the Elderly

Cutaneous Disorders	Systemic Disorders
Contact dermatitis	Chronic renal failure
Atopic dermatitis	Polycythemia vera
Pediculosis	Lymphoma
Scabies	Obstructive biliary disease
Lichen planus	Cholestasis
Bullous pemphigoid	Hyperthyroidism
Urticaria	Hypothyroidism
Miliaria	Solid malignancy
Candida	Drug ingestion
Drug eruption	
Xerosis	

The frequency of occult systemic disease producing pruritus depends on the population studied, the criteria accepted for a causative relationship, and the character of pruritus included in the investigation. Severe pruritus of sudden onset is far more likely, for example, to be associated with significant underlying disease than is mild chronic itchiness. The most common metabolic cause of persistent generalized pruritus is chronic renal failure, but lesser degrees of renal insufficiency cannot be implicated.[63] Drugs that cause pruritus without also producing a rash may rarely do so by an allergic mechanism but more commonly by inducing cholestasis. Examples of the latter include phenothiazines, estrogens, and progestins.

An appropriate laboratory evaluation of the patient with generalized pruritus and no suggestive findings by history or physical examination should probably include a complete blood count with differential, free T3 and T4, liver function tests, electrolytes with BUN and creatinine, and a chest x-ray. However, this is a subject of controversy because the cost/benefit ratio of these surveys is unknown. A negative workup does not rule out an underlying cause of the pruritus, and the clinician should remain attentive to the course of the patient's symptoms.

Treatment Therapy of pruritus is ideally that of the underlying disease. Primary cutaneous disorders and underlying systemic diseases should be treated appropriately. However, symptomatic therapy must frequently be initiated in the absence of a specific diagnosis and then often fails to produce striking results. An initial measure that may provide significant relief is regular use of an emollient, even if xerosis is not detected, based on the fact that the elderly in particular are prone to have some measure of subclinical dryness that will exacerbate the sensation of itching. In addition, once scratching or rubbing begins, the integrity of the skin is compromised and symptoms may increase through a continuous cycle of itching and scratching. Emollients containing menthol or phenol, such as Sarna, are often especially effective in relieving the itching sensation. As noted elsewhere, all emollients are most effective if applied to moist skin, after the bath or shower. Topical anesthetics, although often transiently effective, expose the patients to the risk of allergic sensitization. Topical corticosteroids are effective in treating only certain dermatoses that cause pruritus; they should not be used routinely on normal-appearing skin. Oral antihistamines are prescribed frequently for pruritus, but their efficacy is often limited, and somnolence or paradoxical restlessness may preclude their use in some patients. Their major benefit is at bedtime in patients unable to sleep because of pruritus. Antihistamines may also exacerbate symptoms of prostatism, arrythmias, and gastrointestinal disorders.

Therapy for pruritus associated with uncorrectable systemic diseases is available in some instances, notably uremic pruritus and cholestasis, where insights into the pathophysiology of the disease has suggested specific therapies.[64–66]

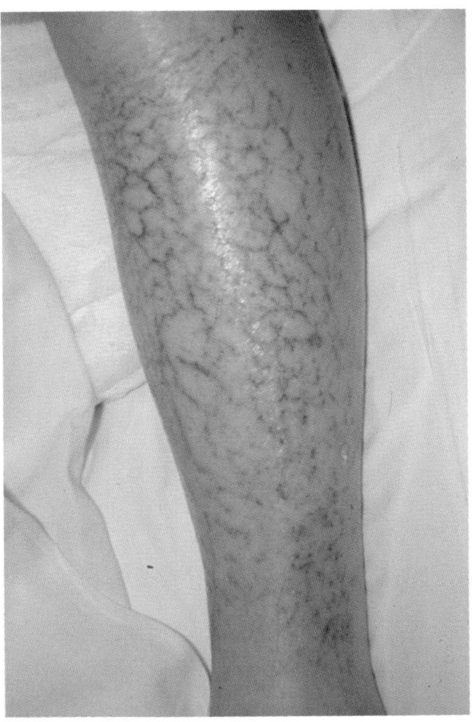

PLATE 1. **Asteatotic dermatitis with erythema craquelé.** Note the pattern of erythema between squamous islands, giving the appearance of "cracked porcelain."

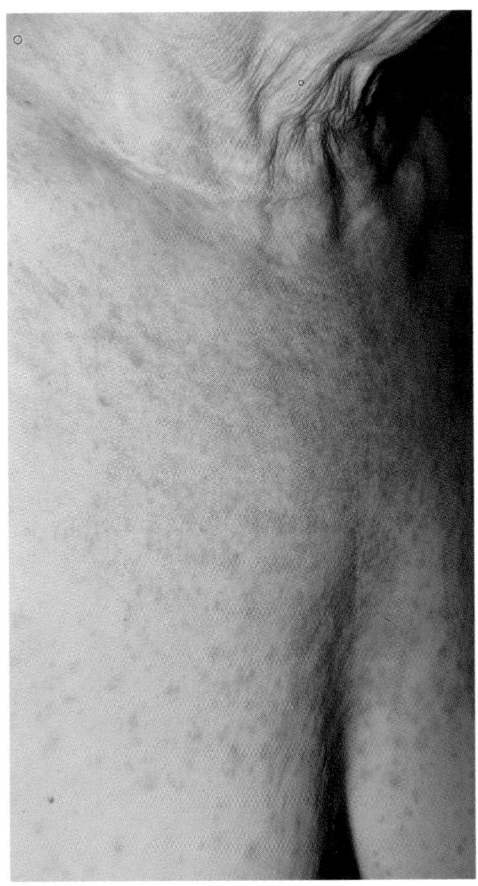

PLATE 2. **Morbilliform drug eruption.** Multiple erythematous macules and papules, nearly confluent in some areas. *(Photograph courtesy of Amal Kurban, M.D.)*

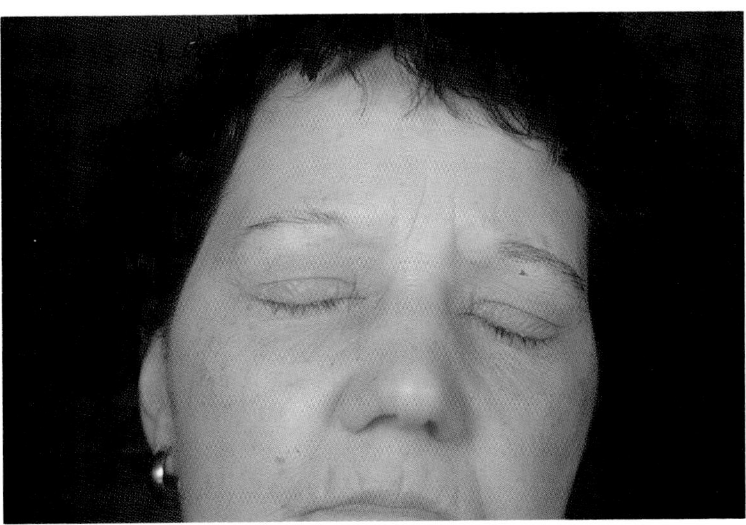

PLATE 3. **Contact dermatitis.** Edema and erythema involving the upper and lower lids. This lesion represents a localized reaction to cosmetic application.

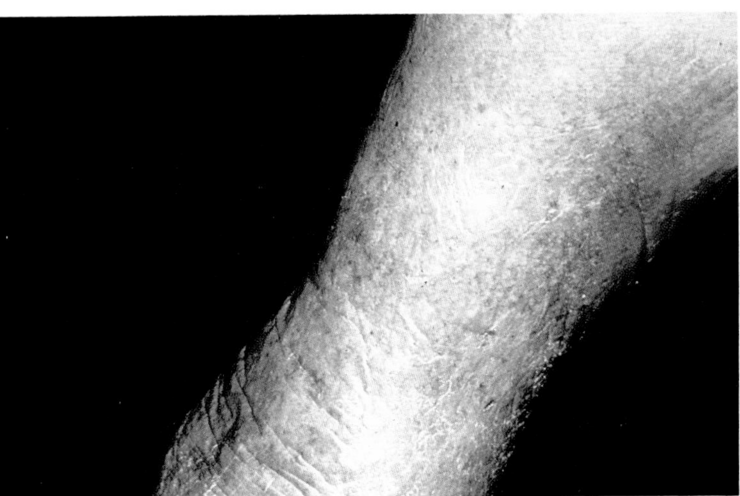

PLATE 4. **Stasis dermatitis.** Red-brown reticulated hyperpigmentation involving the distal lower extremity, with slight scale and epidermal atrophy indicated by increased light reflectance.

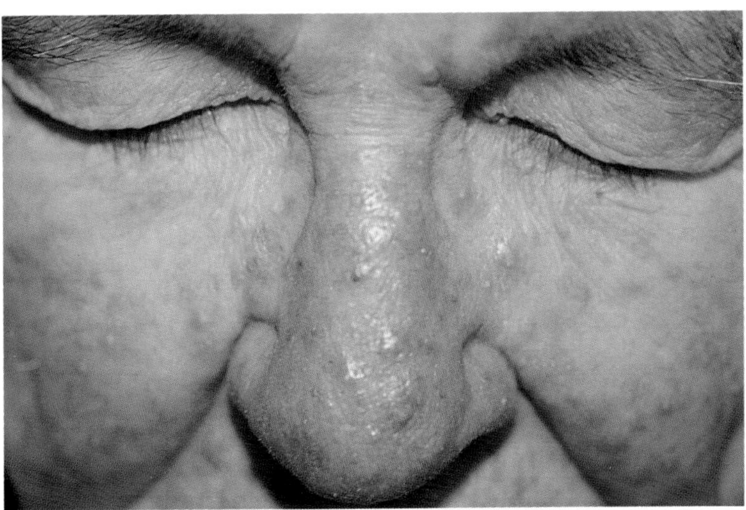

PLATE 5. **Rosacea.** Central facial erythema with telangiectasia, papules, and pustules. *(Photograph courtesy of Patricia Vitale, M.D.)*

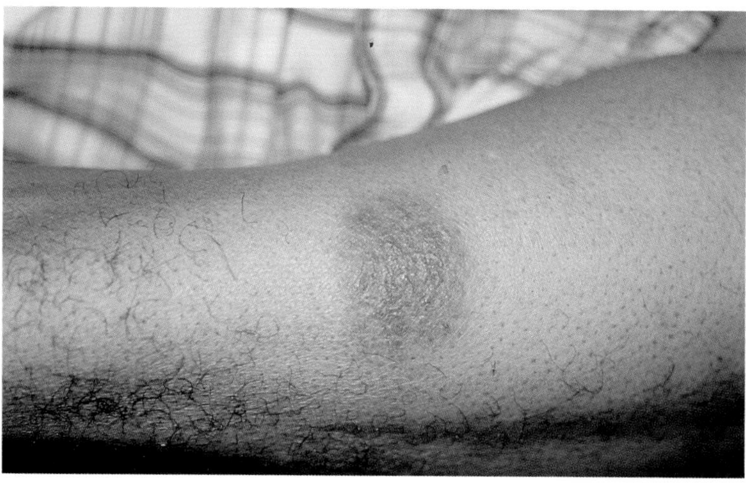

PLATE 6. Fixed drug eruption. Fairly well-demarcated erythematous plaque with central hyperpigmentation, arising on the forearm. *(Photograph courtesy of Patricia Vitale, M.D.)*

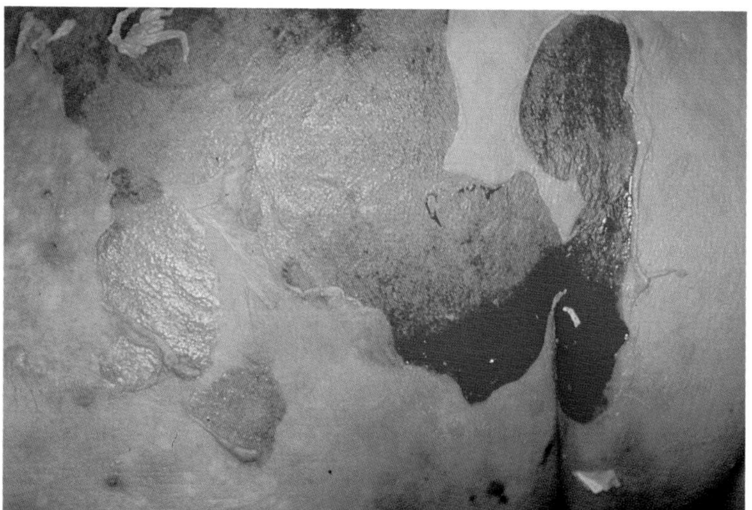

PLATE 7. Toxic epidermal necrolysis. Erosions with rolled necrotic epidermis visible at the margin. These lesions readily expand with gentle lateral pressure. *(Photograph courtesy of Amal Kurban, M.D.)*

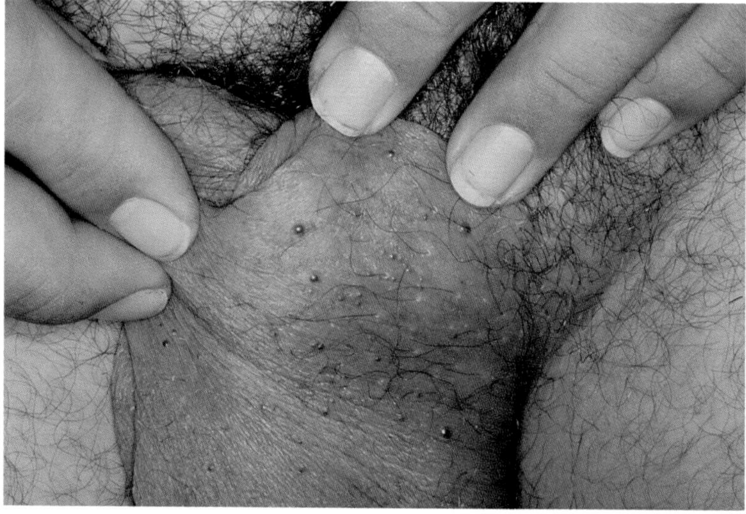

PLATE 8. Angiokeratomas of Fordyce. Multiple firm, violaceous, asymptomatic papules on the scrotum. *(Photograph courtesy of Amal Kurban, M.D.)*

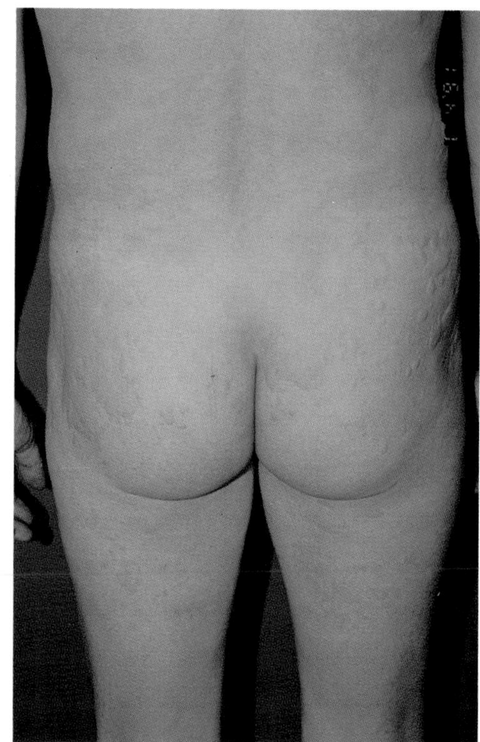

PLATE 9. Drug-induced urticaria. Multiple erythematous, pruritic plaques of various shapes widely distributed over the trunk, buttocks, and extremities. *(Photograph courtesy of Jeffrey Bakal, M.D.)*

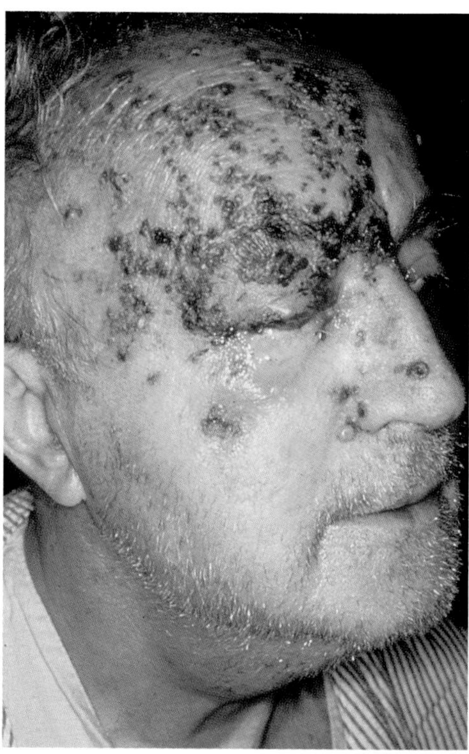

PLATE 10. Herpes zoster. Late phase with crusted and hemorrhagic lesions primarily in the distribution of the ophthalmic division of the trigeminal nerve. Eye involvement with corneal scarring is a potential complication. *(Photograph courtesy of Eva Balash, M.D.)*

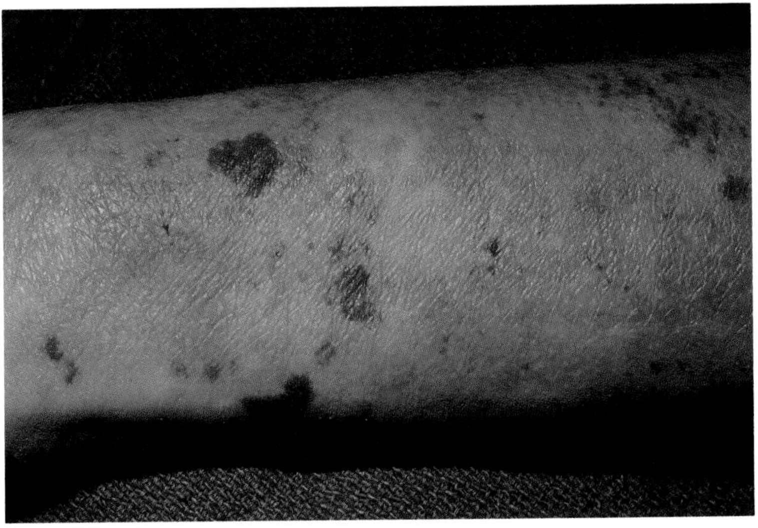

PLATE 11. Actinic purpura. Multiple well-demarcated persistent violaceous macules on the forearm, an area of habitual sun exposure. These lesions tend to arise after minimal trauma.

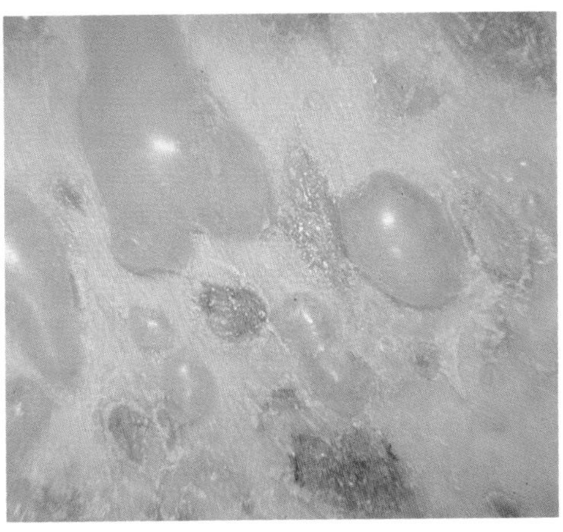

PLATE 14. Bullous pemphigoid. Tense bullae, some arising on an erythematous base, others on apparently normal skin. Lesions are in various stages of evolution, with erosions at the site of ruptured blisters. *(Photograph courtesy of Eva Balash, M.D.)*

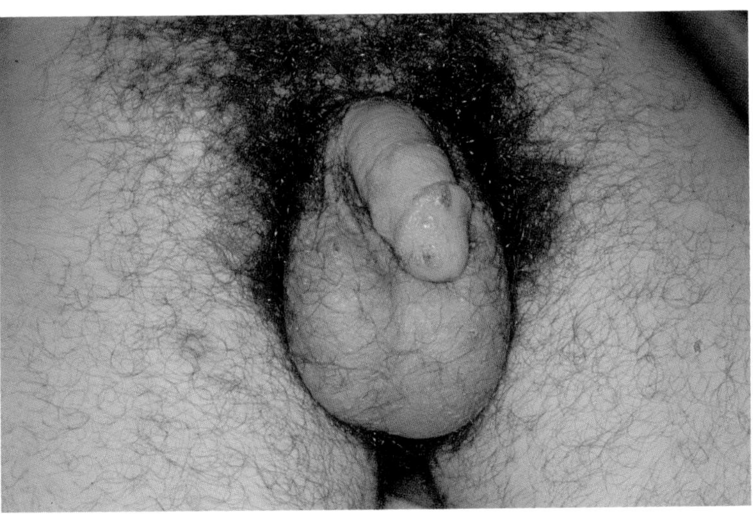

PLATE 12. Scabies infestation. Typical excoriated nodules on the glans penis and scrotum. *(Photograph courtesy of Eva Balash, M.D.)*

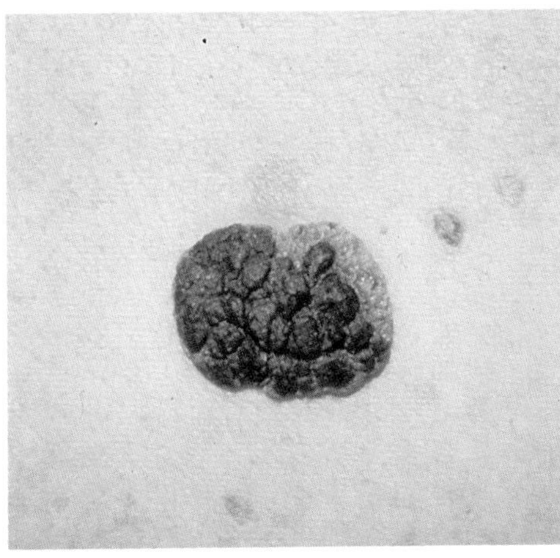

PLATE 15. Seborrheic keratosis. Dark-brown sharply demarcated plaque with a "verrucous" surface. *(Photograph courtesy of Eva Balash, M.D.)*

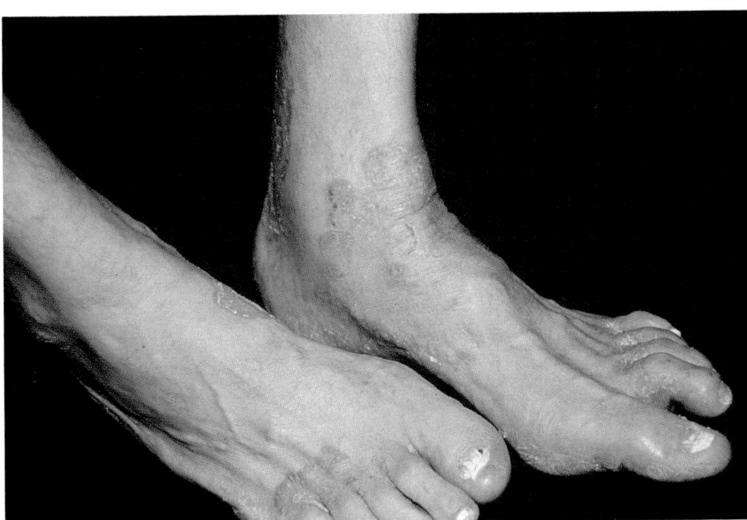

PLATE 13. Tinea pedis. "Moccasin" distribution of scaly erythematous plaques. Nail involvement is evident.

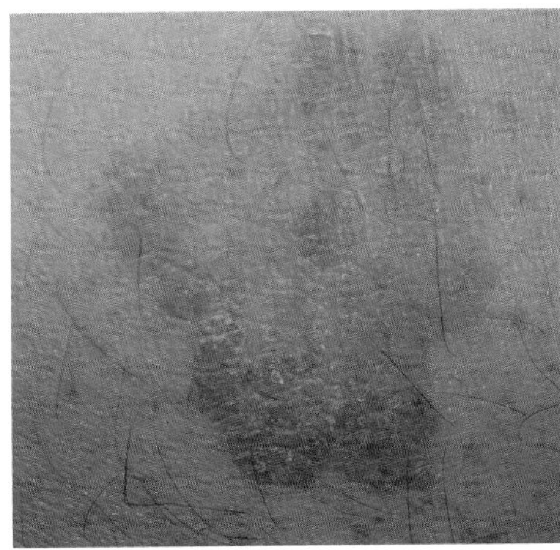

PLATE 16. Bowen's disease. Well-demarcated, asymmetric orange/red plaque with slight scale. *(Photograph courtesy of Patricia Vitale, M.D.)*

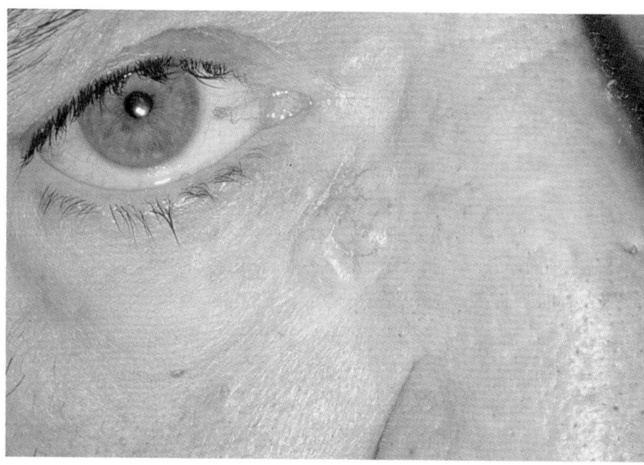

PLATE 17. Basal cell carcinoma. Firm, translucent plaque with prominent telangiectasia. *(Photograph courtesy of Amal Kurban, M.D.)*

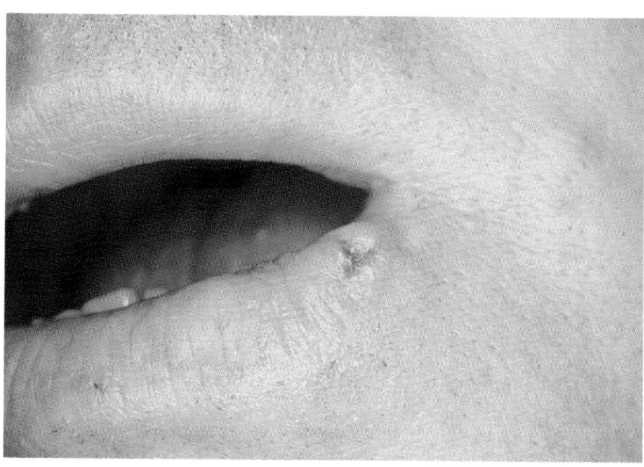

PLATE 20. Squamous cell carcinoma. Indurated nodule with central crusted erosion on the lower lip.

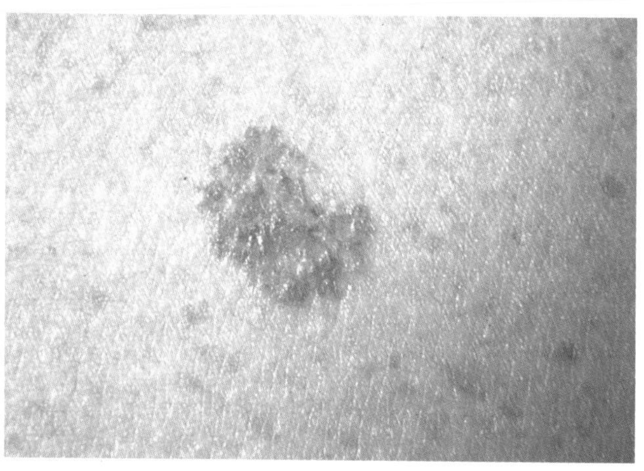

PLATE 18. Superficial spreading malignant melanoma. Irregularly pigmented thin plaque with an asymmetric border. Note the presence of a notched edge, which represents focal regression even in this early lesion.

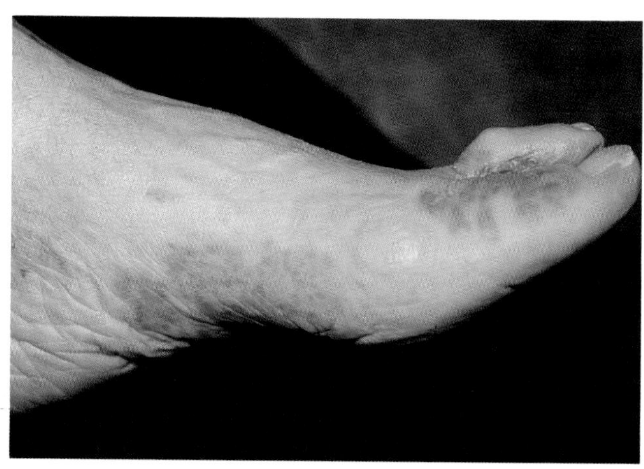

PLATE 21. Kaposi's sarcoma. Classical presentation of firm, violaceous plaques on the foot of an elderly male. *(Photograph courtesy of Patricia Vitale, M.D.)*

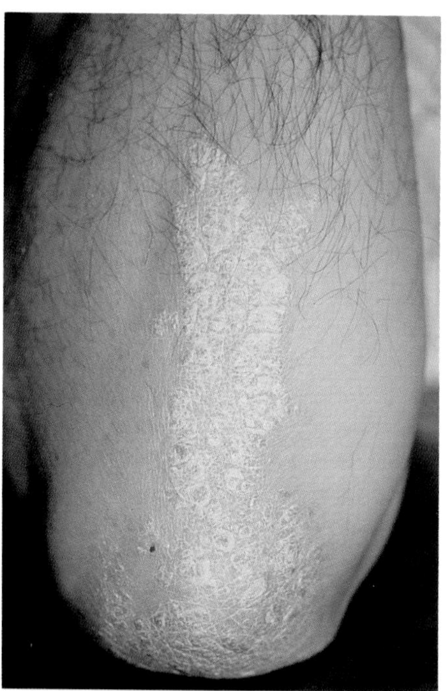

◀ **PLATE 19. Psoriasis.** Well-demarcated erythematous plaque with adherent silvery scale arising on the elbow. *(Photograph courtesy of Patricia Vitale, M.D.)*

▶ **PLATE 22. Lentigo maligna melanoma.** Well-demarcated, irregularly pigmented lesion with asymmetric, notched border arising on the cheek.

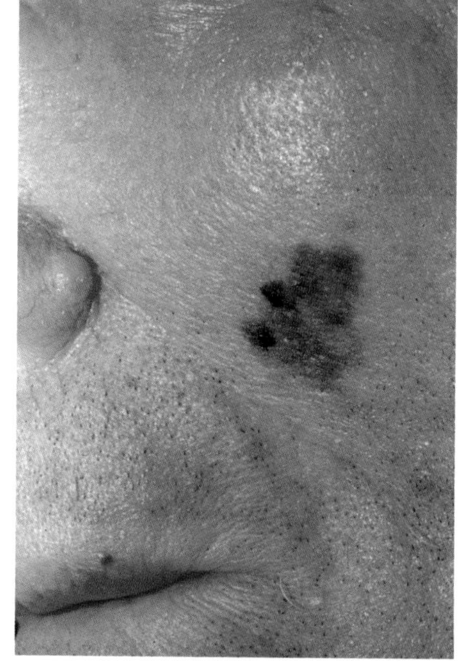

Benign Neoplasms

Seborrheic Keratoses

Seborrheic keratoses are benign lesions that are extremely common in the elderly. They usually begin insidiously in the fourth to fifth decade as multiple, oval, reddish brown to black, sharply demarcated papules or plaques with a rough, verrucous surface and give the appearance of having been "stuck-on" (Plate XV). The chest and back are the most frequently affected sites, but the scalp, face, neck, and extremities may also be involved. Seborrheic keratoses are usually asymptomatic but may become irritated by catching on clothing or infrequently from scratching secondary to pruritus.

The sudden appearance of numerous seborrheic keratoses, the sign of Leser-Trélat, has traditionally been classified as a marker for internal malignancy, most commonly adenocarcinomas of the stomach.[67] However, a review of the Swedish Cancer Registry involving 1752 cases of eruptive seborrheic keratosis from 1958 to 1983 failed to produce a statistically significant association with internal malignancy.[68]

The most important clinical aspect of seborrheic keratoses is the differentiation of these lesions from those of malignant melanoma. It is estimated that as many as 7 percent of malignant melanomas are misdiagnosed as seborrheic keratoses even by trained dermatologist.[69] Hence, all suspicious lesions should be referred to an experienced dermatologist for evaluation and possibly biopsy.

Treatment Liquid nitrogen cryotherapy is often a simple, effective method of removing seborrheic keratoses. An alternative is curettage under local anesthesia, especially for larger lesions. Scarring is usually minimal.

Lentigenes

Lentigenes are benign, sharply demarcated, oval or irregularly shaped hyperpigmented macules that occur on sun-exposed areas, especially the face, dorsal forearms, and hands.

Treatment Treatment is not necessary. Lesions can be lightened or removed with liquid nitrogen. Topical tretinoin applied daily for several months also appears to be effective.[70]

Malignant Neoplasms

Basal cell carcinoma

Basal cell carcinoma (BCC) is the most common malignancy in humans and accounts for approximately 75 percent of the 600,000 cases of skin cancer diagnosed annually in the United States.[71] More than 99 percent of patients are white, slightly more than half are men, and 95 percent are between the ages of 40 and 79. Sun (ultraviolet) exposure is the most important predisposing factor, with 85 percent of BCC occurring in the head and neck region and roughly a quarter of all BCC occurring on the nose alone.[72,73]

Typically, BCC are asymptomatic, firm, round to oval lesions with a rolled border of "pearly" papules and fine telangiectasias (Plate XVII). The center of the lesion may have a crust or ulceration, and lesions can be solitary or multiple, pigmented or cystic. BCC tend to be slow-growing tumors and often go unnoticed by the patient. Metastases are rare, but neglected lesions may produce extensive local tissue destruction.

Treatment Size and location of the tumor determines treatment selection. Many BCC can be effectively treated with electrodesiccation and curettage, with 5-year recurrence rates estimated at 4 to 6 percent. Central facial lesions and recurrent BCC are best treated with Mohs microscopically controlled surgery, which can produce cure rates as high as 99 percent. Other options include primary excision, cryotherapy, and ionizing radiation as well as more experimental treatments such as intralesional interferon or photodynamic therapy utilizing a hematoporphyrin derivative that localizes to the tumor and initiates a cytotoxic response after stimulation by light.

Approximately one-third of all patients with BCC will develop a second primary tumor.[74] This risk, in combination with the possibility of recurrence, warrants careful follow-up for at least 5 years after the initial lesion is removed. All patients should wear sunscreens on a daily basis to prevent further photodamage.

Squamous Cell Carcinoma

Squamous cell carcinoma (SCC) is the second most common form of human skin cancer after BCC. Over 100,000 new cases of SCC were diagnosed in 1990.[75] While ultraviolet light certainly plays a significant role in the pathogenesis of SCC, other predisposing factors include exposure to inorganic arsenic, chronic radiation dermatitis, human papillomavirus, sinus tracts, and chronic burn scars or leg ulcers. Squamous cell carcinomas are more common than BCC in black individuals and tend to occur at sites of scarring or chronic inflammation rather than in sun-exposed areas. Immunosuppression, particularly secondary to renal transplantation, is associated with an incidence of SCC that is 5 to 20 times higher than in the general population.

Several precursor lesions to invasive SCC have been described. The most common of these are actinic keratoses (AK), which are rough patches or scaly papules located on habitually sun-exposed skin. The malignant potential of these lesions is low, with an estimated annual rate of progression to SCC of 0.24 percent for each AK. However, the presence of these lesions indicates ample past sun exposure in an individual at high risk of developing either SCC or BCC. Bowen's disease is a form of SCC *in situ*. It appears as a sharply demarcated, slightly red-pink scaly plaque anywhere on the skin, and ranges in size from a few millimeters to several centimeters (Plate XVI). When present on the glans penis, SCC *in situ* is referred to as erythroplasia of Queyrat.

Invasive squamous cell carcinoma is an indurated, well-demarcated, erythematous, scaly plaque usually located on sun-exposed skin such as the face or the dorsum of the hands (in the absence of other predisposing factors). Squamous cell carcinoma of the lower lip accounts for more than 95 percent of all lip cancers (Plate XX). As SCC lesions enlarge, they may ulcerate and crust; eventually, they will become fixed to the underlying tissue. The risks of local recurrence and metastases vary depending on several factors.[76] The local recurrence rate for sun-induced SCC of the skin and lip approaches 10 percent; it is almost 20 percent for SCC of the ear. On average, 2 to 5 percent of sun-induced SCC metastasize, and SCC of the lower lip is 5 to 10 times more likely to do so. Squamous cell carcinomas arising in a chronic scar or ulcer tend to have a long latency period and metastasize in as many as 40 percent of cases. Recurrent SCC metastasize in approximately 30 percent of patients. The regional lymph nodes should be carefully inspected, as this is the primary route of metastatic spread.

Treatment Treatment of the primary lesion of SCC should be thorough, due to the significant potential for metastatic disease if there should be a recurrence. Mohs microscopically controlled surgery is an excellent treatment option, but high cure rates have also been achieved with electrodesiccation and curettage. Simple surgical excision, cryosurgery, systemic retinoids, and ionizing radiation can also be effective in the proper setting. Systemic chemotherapy or radiation therapy is indicated for metastatic disease.

Diligent follow-up is essential. The risk of recurrence and metastasis is greatest in the first 2 years after the primary tumor is removed, and patients should be examined regularly. Daily use of a sunscreen prevents further sun-induced tissue injury.

Melanoma

Malignant melanoma (MM) is a neoplasm of melanocytic origin. Positive risk factors for the development of MM include a family history of melanoma, white skin, atypical (dysplastic) nevi, advanced age, and intermittent exposure to the sun with blistering sunburns, especially early in life. Blacks are rarely affected. Over 32,000 Americans developed MM in 1991 (median age at diagnosis, 53 years), and 6700 died. Incidence rates have risen dramatically over the past four decades, and it is estimated that the lifetime risk for MM will reach 1 in 90 Americans by the year 2000. Although overall 5-year survival rates have improved over the past 40 years from 49 percent to a current projection of 81 percent[77] and age-adjusted death rates for men at or below age 55 and women at or below age 70 have remained constant at least since 1973, age-adjusted death rates in the elderly have actually increased. Between the mid-1970s and the mid-1980s, age-adjusted death rates in whites increased by nearly 50 percent in older women and 100 percent in older men. Men over 50 years of age currently account for nearly half of all melanoma deaths.[78]

Cutaneous melanoma is visible and therefore provides a unique opportunity for early diagnosis and intervention. *A*symmetry, *b*order irregularity, *c*olor variegation, or *d*iameter greater than 6 mm are the *ABCD* of melanoma (Plates XXII and XVIII). Ulceration and bleeding are late findings. Melanoma should be considered in any patient with a changing mole or a pigmented lesion that fulfills any one of the ABCD criteria. Unfortunately, MM is often asymptomatic and may occur in an area that the patient is unable to visualize. Approximately 50 percent of cutaneous melanoma lesions are self-discovered, with the remaining half roughly split evenly between medical personnel and family members.[79]

Seborrheic keratoses, pigmented basal cell carcinomas, and atypical nevi can all mimic cutaneous melanoma. When the diagnosis is in doubt or melanoma is suspected, a biopsy should be performed. An excisional biopsy is optimal because it allows for accurate staging; a punch biopsy through the most suspicious area of a larger lesion is also acceptable. Vertical tumor thickness is the most reliable prognostic indicator for localized, nonmetastatic disease (stage I). Overall 5-year survival rates are 85 to 90 percent, and lesions less than 0.75 mm in thickness have 5-year survival rates approaching 100 percent. The clinical subtype of MM (superficial spreading, nodular, acral-lentiginous, lentigo maligna) is not of major prognostic significance once tumor thickness has been considered. Stage II disease (nodal metastases) has a 36 percent 5-year survival rate. Stage III disease (distant metastases) has a median survival of just 6 months. Frequent sites of metastases include skin, lymph nodes, bone, lungs, liver, spleen, and brain.

Treatment Early detection and surgical excision of stage I melanoma remains the treatment of choice, but the size of tumor margins remains a subject of controversy. Regular follow-up is essential because of the risk of metastases and an increased risk of developing a second primary melanoma. Patients with stages II and III melanoma are best referred to regional centers, as management decisions are complex. Metastatic disease is generally incurable, and palliation is often the goal of treatment.

Kaposi's Sarcoma

Kaposi's sarcoma (KS) is a malignant vascular neoplasm. Originally described in 1872 in middle-aged or elderly men of southern and eastern European descent (classical form), other subtypes include immunosuppression-associated KS and KS that develops in up to 40 percent of homosexuals with AIDS.

Lesions of classical KS appear most often on the distal lower extremities as firm, violaceous or bluish-black coalescing macules and plaques (Plate XXI). The course is slowly progressive, with infrequent gastrointestinal tract or other internal involvement. Death usually occurs from unrelated causes.

Treatment All forms of KS are radiosensitive. Other options include systemic chemotherapy, cryosurgery, and laser ablation. A detailed discussion of these entities is beyond the scope of this chapter.

Cutaneous T-Cell Lymphoma

Originally termed mycosis fungoides by Bazin in 1851, cutaneous T-cell lymphoma (CTCL) is a malignancy of the T helper subset of lymphocytes. CTCL is rare, with a median age at onset of 66 years.[80] Men are affected twice as often as women and blacks twice as often as whites.[81] The prognosis is variable and depends on the extent of the cutaneous lesions as well as the presence of lymphatic or visceral disease. Advanced age is associated with a reduced 5-year survival rate.[82]

CTCL is generally divided into three clinical stages: patch, plaque, and tumor. Any region of the skin may be involved. The onset of the disease is often insidious, presenting as a nonspecific, pruritic dermatitis responsive to the application of topical steroids. With progression of the disease, the patch stage is characterized by erythematous and eczematous lesions that can simulate various primary skin diseases such as psoriasis or eczematous dermatitis. Biopsy of these lesions is often nondiagnostic. In the plaque stage, lesions become elevated as the dermal infiltrate of atypical lymphocytes increases. The tumor stage is characterized by nodules of various sizes which are made up of frankly neoplastic T helper cells. In sum, the clinician should be suspicious of any chronic, progressive, pruritic dermatosis that is not readily diagnosed.

Sézary syndrome is the leukemic phase of CTCL and is defined as having greater than 10 percent circulating malignant lymphocytes (Sézary cells). Clinically, there is generalized erythroderma and adenopathy.

Treatment At this time, no therapy has been shown to alter the natural disease course. In the early stages of CTCL, potent topical corticosteroids often eradicate lesions, at least temporarily. As the disease progresses, more aggressive therapies become necessary. Options include application of topical nitrogen mustard, radiation therapy, systemic chemotherapy, and PUVA (psoralens plus UVA). Extracorporeal photophoresis is a more recent therapy for the erythrodermic phase of CTCL, the Sézary syndrome.[83] Referral to a physician trained in the diagnosis and management of CTCL is recommended.

REFERENCES

1. Beauregard S. Gilchrest BA: A survey of skin problems and skin care regimens in the elderly. *Arch Dermatol* 123:1638, 1987.
2. Lavker RM, Sun TT: Heterogeneity in epidermal basal keratinocytes: Morphological and functional correlations. *Science* 215:1239, 1982.
3. Lavker RM et al: Morphology of aged skin. *Clin Geriatr Med.* 5:53, 1989.
4. Holick MF: Capacity of human skin to produce vitamin D_3, in Kligman AM, Takase Y (eds): *Cutaneous Aging.* Tokyo, University of Tokyo Press, chap IIIA, pp 223–248.
5. Prystowsky JH: Photoprotection and the vitamin D status of the elderly. *Arch Dermatol* 124:1844, 1988.
6. Lavker RM: Structural alterations in exposed and unexposed aged skin. *J Invest Dermatol* 73:59, 1979.
7. Montagna W, Carlisle K: Structural changes in aging human skin. *J Invest Dermatol* 73:47, 1979.
8. Cleaver J: DNA damage and repair in light-sensitive human skin. *J Invest Dermatol* 54:181, 1970.
9. Kligman LH et al: The contributions of UVA and UVB to connective tissue damage in hairless mice. *J Invest Dermatol* 84:272, 1985.
10. Gilchrest BA et al: Histologic changes associated with ultraviolet A–induced erythema in normal human skin. *J Am Acad Dermatol* 9:213, 1983.
11. Kligman LH: Photoaging, manifestations, prevention, and treatment. *Clin Geriatr Med* 5:235, 1989.
12. Gilchrest BA: Skin aging and photoaging. *Dermatol Nurs* 2:79, 1990.
13. Weinstein GD et al: Topical tretinoin for treatment of photodamaged skin: A multicenter study. *Arch Dermatol* 127:659, 1991.
14. Kligman AM: Perspectives and problems in cutaneous gerontology. *J Invest Dermatol* 73:39, 1979.
15. Phillips TJ, Dover JS: Let ulcers. *J Am Acad Dermatol* 25:965:87, 1991.
16. Phillips TJ et al: Nonhealing leg ulcers: A manifestation of basal cell carcinoma. *J Am Acad Dermatol* 25:47, 1991.
17. Leyden JJ, Kligman AM: Role of microorganisms in diaper dermatitis. *Arch Dermatol* 114:56, 1978.
18. Pegum JS: Diaper dermatitis. *Arch Dermatol* 114:1552, 1978.
19. Wilkins JK: Oral thermal-induced flushing in erythemato-telangiectatic rosacea. *J Invest Dermatol* 75:15, 1981.
20. Starr PAJ, McDonald A: Oculo-cutaneous aspects of rosacea. *Proc R Soc Med* 62:9, 1969.
21. Gamborg Nielson P: Treatment of rosacea with 1% metronidazole cream. *Br J Dermatol* 108:327, 1983.
22. Leyden JJ, Kligman AM: Steroid rosacea. *Arch Dermatol* 110:619, 1974.
23. Chan HL et al: The incidence of erythema multiforme, Stevens-Johnson syndrome, and toxic epidermal necrolysis: A population-based study with particular reference to reactions caused by drugs among outpatients. *Arch Dermatol* 126:43, 1990.
24. Avakian R et al: Toxic epidermal necrolysis: A review. *J Am Acad Dermatol* 25:69, 1991.

25. Ward DJ et al: Treatment of toxic epidermal necrolysis and a review of six cases. *Burns* 16:97, 1990.
26. Izaki M: Angiokeratoma of the scrotum (Fordyce type). *Keio J Med* 1:61, 1952.
27. Agger P, Osmundsen PE: Angiokeratoma of the scrotum (Fordyce). *Acta Derm Venereol* 50:221, 1970.
28. Feinstein RJ et al: Senile purpura. *Arch Dermatol* 108:229, 1973.
29. Bowerman JG et al: Comparative study of permethrin 1% creme rinse and lindane shampoo for the treatment of head lice. *Pediatr Infec Dis J* 6:252, 1987.
30. Kalter DC et al: Treatment of pediculosis pubis. *Arch Dermatol* 123:1315, 1987.
31. Taplin D et al: Permethrin 1% cream rinse for the treatment of *Pediculus humanus var capitis* infestation. *Pediatr Dermatol* 3:344, 1986.
32. Arlian LG et al: Prevalence of *Sarcoptes scabiei* in the homes and nursing homes of scabetic patients. *J Am Acad Dermatol* 19:806, 1988.
33. Hubler WR, Clabaugh W: Epidermic Norwegian scabies. *Arch Dermatol* 112:267, 1986.
34. Taplin D et al: Permethrin 5% dermal cream: A new treatment for scabies. *J Am Acad Dermatol* 15:995, 1986.
35. Kates SG et al: Microbial ecology of interdigital infections of toe web spaces. *J Am Acad Dermatol* 22:583, 1990.
36. Dover JS, Johnson RA: Cutaneous manifestations of human immunodeficiency virus infection: Part I. *Arch Dermatol* 127:1383, 1991.
37. Dover JS, Johnson RA: Cutaneous manifestations of human immunodeficiency virus infection: Part II. *Arch Dermatol* 127:1549, 1991.
38. Cobb MW: Human papilloma virus infection. *J Am Acad Dermatol* 22:547, 1990.
39. Rudlinger R et al: Human papillomavirus infections in a group of renal transplant recipients. *Br J Dermatol* 115:681, 1986.
40. Crum CP et al: Human papillomavirus type 16 and early cervical neoplasia. *N Engl J Med* 310:880, 1984.
41. Hope-Simpson RE: The nature of herpes zoster: A long-term study and a new hypothesis. *Proc R Soc Med* 58:9, 1965.
42. de Moragas JM, Kierland RR: The outcome of patients with herpes zoster. *Arch Dermatol* 75:193, 1957.
43. Fueyo MA, Lookingbill DP: Herpes zoster and occult malignancy. *J Am Acad Dermatol* 11:480, 1984.
44. Ragozzino MW et al: Risk of cancer after herpes zoster: A population-based study. *N Engl J Med* 307:393, 1982.
45. Balfour HH: Acyclovir halts progression of zoster in immunocompromised patients. *N Engl J Med* 308:1448, 1983.
46. McKendrick MW et al: Oral acyclovir in acute herpes zoster. *Br Med J* 293, 1529, 1986.
47. Keczkes K, Basheer AM: Do corticosteroids prevent post-herpetic neuralgia? *Br J Dermatol* 102:551, 1980.
48. Benoldi et al: Prevention of post herpetic neuralgia: Evaluation of treatment with oral prednisone, oral acyclovir, and radiotherapy. *Intl J Dermatol* 30:288, 1991.
49. Crooks RJ et al: Zoster associated chronic pain: An overview of clinical trials with acyclovir. *Scand J Infect Dis* 80(suppl):62, 1991.
50. Robertson DR, George CF: Treatment of post herpetic neuralgia in the elderly. *Br Med Bull* 46:113, 1990.
51. Green CA et al: Treatment of seborrheic dermatitis with ketoconazole. *Br J Dermatol* 116:217, 1987.
52. Faergemann J: Seborrheic dermatitis and *P orbiculare*. *Br J Dermatol* 114:695, 1986.
53. Melski JW, Stern RS: The separation of susceptibility of psoriasis from age at onset. *J Invest Dermatol* 77:474, 1981.
54. Gold MH et al: Beta blockers and psoriasis. *J Am Acad Dermatol* 19:837, 1988.
55. Skott A et al: Exacerbation of psoriasis during lithium treatment. *Br J Dermatol* 96:445, 1977.
56. Korman N: Bullous pemphigoid. *J Am Acad Dermatol* 16:907, 1987.
57. Mueller S et al: A 230 kD basic protein is the major bullous pemphigoid antigen. *J Invest Dermatol* 92:33, 1989.
58. Zhu XJ et al: Molecular identification of major and minor bullous pemphigoid antigens. *J Am Acad Dermatol* 23:876, 1990.
59. Lindelof B et al: Pemphigoid and cancer. *Arch Dermatol* 126:66, 1990.
60. Venning VA, Wojnarowska F: The association of bullous pemphigoid and malignant disease: A case control study. *Br J Dermatol* 123:439, 1990.
61. Eyre RW, Stanley JR: Identification of pemphigus vulgaris antigen extracted from normal human epidermis and comparison with pemphigus foliaceus antigen. *J Clin Invest* 81:807, 1988.
62. Denman ST: A review of pruritus. *J Am Acad Dermatol* 14:375, 1986.
63. Gilchrest BA et al: Clinical features of pruritus among patients undergoing maintenance hemodialysis. *Arch Dermatol* 118:154, 1982.
64. Bachs L et al: Comparison of rifampicin with phenobarbitone for treatment of pruritus in biliary cirrhosis. *Lancet* 1:574, 1989.
65. De Marchi S et al: Relief of pruritus and decreases in plasma histamine concentrations during erythropoietin therapy in patients with uremia. *N Engl J Med* 326:1016, 1992.
66. Jones EA, Bergasa NV: The pruritus of cholestasis: From bile acids to opiate agonists. *Hepatology* 11:884, 1990.
67. Holdiness MR: The sign of Leser-Trélat. *Int J Dermatol* 25:564, 1986.
68. Lindelöf B et al: Seborrheic keratoses and cancer. *J Am Acad Dermatol* 26:947, 1992.
69. Andersen WK, Silvers DN: "Melanoma? It can't be melanoma!" A subset of melanomas that defies clinical recognition. *JAMA* 266:3463, 1991.
70. Rafal ES et al: Topical tretinoin (retinoic acid) treatment for liver spots associated with photodamage. *N Engl J Med* 326:368, 1992.
71. Miller SJ: Biology of basal cell carcinoma: Part 1. *J Am Acad Dermatol* 24:1, 1990.
72. Dinehart SM et al: Basal cell carcinoma treated with Mohs surgery: A comparison of 54 younger patients with 1050 older patients. *J Dermatol Surg Oncol* 18:560, 1992.
73. Nahass GT et al: Basal cell carcinoma of the scrotum. *J Am Acad Dermatol* 26:574, 1992.
74. Robinson JK: Risk of developing another basal cell

carcinoma: A 5-year prospective study. *Cancer* 60:118, 1987.

75. Johnson TM et al: Squamous cell carcinoma of the skin (excluding lip and oral mucosa). *J Am Acad Dermatol* 26:467, 1992.
76. Rowe DE et al: Prognostic factors for local recurrence, metastasis, and survival rates in squamous cell carcinoma of the skin, ear, and lip. *J Am Acad Dermatol* 26:976, 1992.
77. Koh HK: Cutaneous melanoma. *N Engl J Med* 325:171, 1991.
78. Death rates of malignant melanoma among white man—United States, 1973–1988. *MMWR* 41:20, 1992.
79. Koh HK et al: Who discovers melanoma? Patterns from a population based survey. *J Am Acad Dermatol* 26:914, 1992.
80. Chuang TY et al: Incidence of cutaneous T-cell lymphoma and other rare skin cancers in a defined population. *J Am Acad Dermatol* 23:254, 1990.
81. Marti RM et al: Prognostic clinicopathologic factors in cutaneous T-cell lymphoma. *Arch Dermatol* 127:1511, 1991.
82. Epstein EH Jr et al: Mycosis fungoides: Survival, prognostic features, response to therapy, and autopsy findings. *Medicine* 15:61, 1972.
83. Edelson RL et al: Treatment of cutaneous T-cell lymphoma by extracorporeal photochemotherapy. *N Engl J Med* 316:297, 1987.

ADDITIONAL READINGS

Arnold HL et al: *Diseases of the Skin,* 8th ed. Philadelphia, Saunders, 1990.

Champion RH et al: *Textbook of Dermatology,* 5th ed. Boston, Blackwell, 1992.

Fitzpatrick TB et al: *Dermatology in General Medicine,* 4th ed. New York, McGraw-Hill, 1993.

Taylor CR et al: Photoaging/photodamage and photoprotection. *J Am Acad Dermatol* 22:1, 1990.

Chapter 38

THE ORAL CAVITY

Bruce J. Baum and Jonathan A. Ship

Studies on the status of the oral cavity in elderly populations have been infrequent and often limited in scope. In particular, there is a notable deficiency in the amount of epidemiological data available to describe oral tissues, in both health and disease, across the human life span. While information is available from national surveys on dental and periodontal status, it must be stressed that it is derived from cross-sectional, not longitudinal studies. Furthermore, almost no broad, descriptive population data exist on salivary gland function, oral mucosal status, chemosensory performance (taste, smell), and oral motor function. This is unfortunate, since many of the common stereotypes about aging and oral health status reflect on these functions. Most of these generalizations are unsubstantiated,[1] a situation which can cause considerable confusion for both patient and clinician.

The oral cavity serves two essential functions in human physiology: the production of speech and the initiation of alimentation. Discussion of the status of the oral cavity during aging must consider the impact of any disturbance of these functions on the elderly individual's life.

In order to speak and to process food, many specialized tissues have evolved in the mouth. The teeth, the periodontium, and the muscles of mastication exist to prepare food for deglutition. The tongue, besides occupying a central role in communication, is also a key participant in food bolus preparation and translocation. Salivary glands provide a secretion with multiple functions. Saliva, in addition to lubricating all oral mucosal tissues, keeping them intact and pliable, also moistens the developing food bolus, permitting it to be fashioned into a swallow-acceptable form. All of these tissue activities are finely coordinated, and a disturbance in any one tissue function can significantly compromise speech and/or alimentation and diminish the quality of a patient's life.

In addition, it is necessary to remember that the oral cavity is exposed to the external world and is potentially vulnerable to a limitless number of environmental insults. Exquisite mechanisms have evolved to protect the mouth and permit normal oral function. The oral cavity is richly endowed with sensory systems that contribute to our enjoyment of food and alert us to potential problems. These include mechanisms for taste (and its inextricable relationship with smell), thermal, textural, tactile, and pain discrimination. Also, saliva has an important protective role and contains a broad spectrum of antimicrobial proteins, which modulate oral bacterial and fungal colonization. Other proteins maintain the functional integrity of the teeth by keeping saliva supersaturated with calcium and phosphate salts and, in effect, repairing incipient caries (tooth decay) by a remineralization process.

This chapter will focus on specific oral tissues and their functions. It will attempt to present what is "normal" oral physiological status in the older adult, discuss how common systemic disease and its treatment may affect the oral tissues during aging, and briefly review the evaluation and management of oral disorders frequently encountered in the elderly. Additional information on the diagnosis and treatment of these oral disorders is available in several comprehensive reviews.[2–5]

DENTITION AND THE PERIODONTIUM

The loss of teeth has long been associated with aging. As noted in Table 38-1, recent national health surveys demonstrate that about 40 percent of Americans over the age of 65 are edentulous.[6] Although the prevalence of edentulous adults has dramatically decreased since the first National Health Survey in 1957–1958, the population above age 65 has an average of 11 missing teeth. Advances in dental treatment and disease prevention, increased availability of dental care, and improved awareness of dental needs have recently resulted in significant gains in dental health.

Tooth loss is attributed to two major etiologic processes: dental caries and periodontal disease. Caries affects the exposed dental surfaces, while periodontal disease is confined to the supporting bony and ligamentous dental structures. With current trends of increasing tooth retention in aging popula-

TABLE 38-1

Demographic Findings on the Dental Status of Adults in the United States*

A. Percent of edentulous adults

Ages	*1957–1958*	*1960–1962*	*1971–1974*	*1985–1986*
45–54	22.4	20.0	16.0	9.0
55–64	38.1	36.3	33.2	15.6
65–74	55.4	49.4	45.5	36.9

B. Percent of adults with 1 or more dental visits within a year of interview

Sample	*1963–1964*	*1969*	*1978–1979*	*1985–1986*	*%Change*†
Total U.S.A.	42.0	45.0	50.0	58.5	+39.3
65+	20.8	23.2	32.5	37.5	+80.3

C. Percent of adults with no dental visits within 5 years of interview

Sample	*1963–1964*	*1969*	*1978–1979*	*1985–1986*
Total U.S.A.	14.0	13.2	13.6	8.3
65+	51.7	46.9	44.0	26.5

D. Utilization of dental services by dentate and edentulous adults, aged 65+.‡

	Dentate Adults	*Edentulous Adults*
Adults with 1 or more dental visits within a year of interview	54.5%	13.0%
Adults with no dental visits within 5 years of interview	10.9%	49.1%

*Derived from National Health Surveys (year indicated) and the National Institute of Dental Research (NIDR) Survey of Oral Health in US Adults (1985–1986).
†Based on changes from 1963–1964 to 1985–1986.
‡Based on the NIDR Survey (1985–1986).

tions, there is a correspondingly greater risk for the development of both of these disease entities.

A tooth consists of several mineralized and nonmineralized components, supported by the periodontal ligament and alveolar bone. Enamel covers the coronal aspect of the tooth and is the first hard tissue exposed to caries-causing bacteria. Dentin constitutes the main portion of the tooth structure, extending almost the entire length of the tooth. The crown of the tooth (coronal portion) is covered by enamel, and the root (cervical portion) is covered by cementum. Cementum is most susceptible to caries-causing bacteria. The central, nonmineralized portion is the dental pulp, which houses the vascular, lymphatic, and neuronal supply to the tooth.

The periodontium consists of those tissues that invest and support the tooth. It is divided into the gingival unit (gums) and the attachment apparatus (cementum, periodontal ligament, and alveolar bony process). Gingivitis occurs when the gingival unit is inflamed. Periodontitis (or periodontal disease) exists when there is an inflammation and appreciable loss of the attachment apparatus due to the presence of pathogenic microorganisms.

Tooth loss in children and young adults is predominantly caused by dental caries, whereas in middle-aged and older adults periodontal disease plays a greater role in the loss of teeth. Longitudinal studies utilizing generally healthy adult males have found that the principal cause of tooth extraction is dental caries.[7] Furthermore, it must be stressed that caries activity continues throughout life and is not a phenomenon confined to any one period.[8]

There are two classifications of dental caries, depending on which surface of the tooth has been affected. Coronal caries, which is characteristic of caries in young adults and children, occurs when the enamel and dentin of the coronal portion of the tooth is affected. In older adults, if gingival recession or periodontal disease causes the root surfaces of the tooth to become exposed to the oral environment, root surface or cervical caries may occur.

The principal (though by no means exclusive) coronal caries-causing microorganism in humans is *Streptococcus mutans*,[9] and oral streptococci, actinomycetes, and lactobacilli are organisms commonly associated with cervical lesions.[10] The caries-causing bacteria reside on the tooth surface in what is commonly called dental plaque. Acid production by bacteria in plaque dissolves the mineral content of the enamel, dentin, or cementum. The exposed protein constituents are destroyed by hydrolytic enzymes, and caries results.[11] Dental plaque is considered to be a primary etiological factor in dental caries as well as a principal source of pathogenic organisms in periodontal disease. Microbial populations of plaque have been found to be qualitatively different in young and elderly subjects.[12]

The presence of a variety of oral microorganisms, through direct bacterial toxicity or via indirect mechanisms, results in the inflammatory responses and tissue destruction seen with periodontal disease.[13] The microbial species cross the gingival epithelium and enter subepithelial tissues, where they activate specific host-defense mechanisms. Eventually this causes tissue destruction, including bone loss and tooth morbidity.

As the dentulous individual ages, he or she is susceptible to coronal caries due to recurrent decay around existing restored surfaces, and the prevalence of root surface caries increases. There are many risk indicators for cervical caries. Increased age, decreased exposure to fluoride, coronal caries, loss of periodontal attachment, and several medical, behavioral, and social factors have been found to be associated with the incidence of root caries.[14]

Studies in the United States reveal an increase in the mean number of decayed and filled teeth among dentulous adults in the elder age cohorts over the last 30 years.[15] These trends (Table 38-1) are probably a reflection of the increased retention of the natural dentition and greater utilization of dental services by older adults; it is unlikely that they represent a true increase in dental caries activity.[16] However, epidemiological projections suggest that there will be significant increases in the prevalence of root surface caries in aging populations.[16]

Demographic studies have identified certain periodontal changes that occur in aging individuals. For example, cross-sectional studies have demonstrated that the prevalence of dental plaque, calculus (calcified dental plaque), and bleeding gingival tissues increases in older persons.[17] Older persons also experience greater gingival recession and loss of periodontal attachment.[17,18] Periodontitis is more prevalent and usually more extensive among blacks, subjects with less education, those who have not seen a dentist recently, and individuals with gingivitis.[18,19] Currently, it is believed that periodontal disease proceeds through a series of episodic attacks rather than as a slowly progressing, continuous process.[20] It is not known whether older age cohorts are more susceptible to periodontal destruction than younger populations. However, many systemic diseases and therapeutic regimens that are common to older individuals may adversely affect periodontal health.

For the older person with teeth, caries and periodontal disease are significant concerns and may be a source of pain and discomfort. Gross caries will appear as darkish lesions, frequently associated with dental plaque, on the coronal and/or cervical regions of a tooth. Long-standing caries ultimately results in the destruction of a tooth. Gingivitis may be detected by the presence of erythematous and/or edematous gingival tissues with occasional hemorrhage. When recession of the gingival tissues has occurred, exposing the roots of the tooth surface, periodontitis may be suspected. This will ultimately cause teeth to become mobile, a condition necessitating definitive treatment. The systemic health of an already compromised individual may be further threatened by bleeding and suppurating gingiva and coronal and cervical caries. Once teeth have been lost, mastication, phonation, and deglutition may be perturbed. Also, social contact and nutritional status can be affected in the substantially edentulous aging individual.

Although evidence exists that older age groups in the United States have dramatically increased their utilization of dental services in the past 25 years (Table 38-1), more than 25 percent of people above age 65 have not seen a dental professional in the past 5 years.[6] It is likely that dental caries and periodontal disease will remain substantial oral health concerns for older individuals. Adequate oral health care for the elderly should include preventive dental treatment and increased availability and utilization of dental health services. In addition, elderly persons with teeth are four times more likely to visit a dentist than those wearing complete dentures.[6] Persons with oral prostheses often experience multiple problems related to those appliances, including the development of oral candidiasis. If a white coating or an erythematous region is present beneath a removable prosthesis, it is likely that the prosthesis is infected with *candida* and/or is ill fitting.[21] Therefore individuals using such prostheses should be encouraged to have routine oral examinations and whatever treatment may be necessary to maintain the health of the prosthesis.

SALIVARY GLANDS

There are three major pairs of salivary glands (parotid, submandibular, sublingual) and several minor ones (e.g., labial, palatal, buccal) whose principal function is the exocrine production of saliva. Each gland type makes a unique secretion derived from either mucous or serous cell types, forming the fluid in the mouth termed whole saliva. Saliva includes many constituents that are critical to the maintenance of oral health (see Table 38-2). Saliva's most important functions are lubricating the oral mucosa, promoting remineralization of the teeth, and protecting against microbial infections. Although the role of saliva in digestion is limited, saliva helps prepare the food bolus for deglutition and is responsible for dissolving tastants and delivering them to taste buds.

Until recently, it was believed that saliva production diminished with aging. However, recent studies have revealed that in healthy older adults there is no general diminution in the volume of saliva produced.[22] The volume of fluid output from the parotid glands does not differ among nonmedicated healthy adults of different ages.[22,23] Similar investigations have been performed examining the fluid output from the submandibular and sublingual glands, but a consensus has not been reached. One report[24] suggested diminished submandibular/sublingual saliva production in older persons, while a more recent study[25] reported no age-related changes in this secretion among healthy nonmedicated adults. In the absence of complicating factors such as certain systemic

TABLE 38-2

Major Roles of Saliva in the Maintenance of Oral Health

Lubrication and repair of oral mucosa
Buffering acids produced by oral bacteria
Antibacterial and antifungal activities
Mechanical cleansing
Mediation of taste acuity
Remineralization of teeth

diseases and medication use, it can be assumed that there is no generalized age-related perturbation in salivary fluid production. In addition, there appear to be no significant alterations in the composition of saliva in older persons.[26]

These physiological findings contrast with the morphological changes seen in aging salivary glands. Human parotid and submandibular glands lose about 20 to 30 percent of their parenchymal tissue over the span of adult life.[27] The loss is primarily of acinar components, while proportional increases are seen in ductal cells and in fat as well as vascular and connective tissue. Since acinar components are primarily responsible for the secretion of saliva,[28] it is unclear why, with a significant reduction in the acinar volume of the gland, total fluid production does not diminish with increasing age. It has been suggested that salivary glands possess a functional reserve capacity,[25,29] enabling them to maintain fluid output throughout the span of human adult life.

The clinician must recognize that generalized significant changes in the physiology of the salivary glands do not normally occur with aging. Complaints of dry mouth (xerostomia) should not be considered to be normal sequelae of aging but rather as indicative of disease or its treatment. Xerostomia is a common condition linked with altered salivary gland performance. The most frequent etiology of salivary gland dysfunction is iatrogenic. Many medications taken by older persons reduce or alter salivary gland performance.[30,31] These include anticholinergic, antihypertensive, antidepressant, diuretic, and antihistaminic preparations. Additionally, common forms of oncologic therapy, such as radiation for head and neck neoplasms and cytotoxic chemotherapy, can have direct and dramatic deleterious effects on salivary glands.

The single most common disease affecting salivary glands is Sjögren's syndrome, an autoimmune exocrinopathy occurring mainly in postmenopausal women. Other systemic conditions have been associated with salivary gland dysfunction[31] and, although not frequently seen, many inflammatory and obstructive salivary gland disorders (e.g., bacterial infections, sialoliths, trauma, neoplasms) result in reduced gland function.

A clinician is likely to encounter many older patients with oral complaints related to salivary gland dysfunction. A brief clinical evaluation should include inspection of all major salivary gland orifices to ensure patent glands and application of a mild solution of citric acid or lemon juice to the tongue to determine if a patient's salivary glands can respond to a gustatory stimulus. Regardless of the etiology of salivary gland dysfunction, any of the major physiological roles influenced by saliva in the oral cavity (Table 38-2) may be adversely affected. With gland dysfunction, increased dental caries will ensue rapidly, accelerating the possibility of tooth loss. The oral mucosa can become desiccated and cracked, leaving the host more susceptible to microbial infection. Further, salivary gland dysfunction can lead to difficulty in swallowing or speaking at length, pain (which may arise from either the teeth or the oral soft tissues), and diminished enjoyment of food.

SENSORY FUNCTION

There are many reports suggesting that food enjoyment, recognition, and taste decline as a function of age.[32] Similarly, a number of studies imply that elderly individuals manifest significant nutritional deficits.[33] Recently it has been suggested that a true anorexia (loss of appetite) is associated with aging.[34] It is likely that this anorexia results from both behavioral and physiological factors.[35] Perturbations in taste and smell or other oral sensory modalities (Table 38-3), may occur with age and reduce the rewards of eating,[35] thus contributing to a diminished interest in food among the elderly.

The taste receptors of the human gustatory system are distributed throughout the oropharynx and are innervated by three cranial nerves: VII, IX, and X.[36] Recent reports indicate that, in both humans[37,38] and rodents,[39] the number of lingual taste buds do not diminish with age. The registration of a taste phenomenon is complicated, since—besides gustatory receptors—the olfactory apparatus and central integrative functions are involved. Clinically, the ability to taste is most often evaluated at two levels: (1) *threshold,* the most common measure, a "molecular level" event, which reflects the lowest concentrations of a tastant that an individual can recognize as being different than water; and (2) *suprathreshold,* a measure which is reflective of the ability to taste the intensity of substances at the functional concentrations encountered in daily life. Furthermore, other than detection, recognition and intensity, the normal sensation of taste involves a hedonic component, i.e., the degree of pleasantness.

Many earlier reports citing a higher frequency of taste complaints among older persons derived their data from the study of institutionalized persons, not the healthy elderly.[1] Recent studies evaluating subjec-

TABLE 38-3

Oral Sensory Functions in Healthy Human Aging

Function	Comparison of Older with Younger Persons
Olfaction	Diminished
Gustation	No change*
Temperature	No change
Viscosity	No change
Pressure	Diminished

*Quality-specific diminished function has been reported but is not generalizable for all tastants in both threshold and suprathreshold examinations.

tive reports of taste function among generally healthy, community-dwelling persons showed that only modest changes occur with increased age (in about 10 percent of those studied). However, among elderly persons taking prescription medications, there was a significant increase (threefold) in the frequency of subjective complaints of taste dysfunction.[40]

Several recent, carefully controlled studies have objectively evaluated gustatory function in generally healthy persons of different ages. Studies examining threshold[41,42] and suprathreshold[33,43,44] gustatory function have been reported for all four taste qualities (sweet, sour, salty, and bitter). In general, the decremental changes detected were modest and specific to taste quality. For example, the ability of older persons to detect salt decreased slightly with age, while no change in the detection threshold for sucrose (sweet) was noted. The importance of medication usage and place of residence in the evaluation of taste dysfunction was confirmed in threshold studies of institutionalized and noninstitutionalized elderly men.[42] Institutionalized men and men using more prescription medications had significantly elevated taste thresholds.

Other studies have evaluated the more complicated problems of flavor perception,[45] food recognition,[32] and food preference.[46] Although results are not uniform, older individuals do less well when performance is assessed in these tasks.[40] Murphy[47] has provided data to suggest that it is diminished olfactory performance that handicaps the assessment of complex stimuli (food analogs) by older individuals. There is considerable support for alterations in olfactory function becoming more prevalent with old age (see below).

A patient's oral hygiene and dental health may considerably influence taste judgments.[48] For example, inadequate removal of food particles can allow their breakdown or metabolic conversion by oral microorganisms to noxious, unpleasant substances. This may be exaggerated in patients with dental prostheses. Also, periodontal diseases can result in accumulations of putrefied acidic materials which may leak into the oral cavity and alter taste sensation. Similarly, periapical dental infections, with subsequent fistula formation, may contribute continuous, low levels of purulent matter to the mouth.

Olfactory receptor neurons are quite different from taste receptors. There has been little study of olfactory innervation with increased age in humans. Rodent studies suggest that the number of olfactory receptors decreases precipitously after 29 months,[49] although the biological significance of such change has not been determined.[39]

A number of objective studies have examined olfactory function across the life span. These include studies of thresholds, suprathreshold intensity judgments, and odor recognition. In aggregate, the available data suggest that olfactory performance declines with increased age. For example, Murphy[46] studied the threshold, intensity, and pleasantness of menthol in a healthy, ambulatory group of young adult and elderly persons. In comparison with younger subjects, elderly persons had higher average thresholds, their ability to perceive suprathreshold intensities was blunted, and their judgment of pleasantness was reduced. Other studies have examined the effects of age on odor recognition, and all are in general agreement that elderly individuals show reduced function.[50,51] Most older individuals showed a significant decline in their ability to identify the presented odors correctly.

In the real world, however, we typically do not ingest a single tastant in aqueous form, nor do we consume foods that contain only olfactory cues. While it is convenient and objective to use simple stimuli to assess chemosensory performance, foods are chemosensory mixtures, and the most relevant yet most difficult method of obtaining measures of gustatory and olfactory function will involve the use of complex food analogs. As noted earlier, several such studies have demonstrated the presence of age-related reductions in chemosensory performance.[32,45,47] In one study,[47] younger subjects were significantly better than their elders at recognizing stimuli in blended food. However, when younger persons repeated the test with their airways occluded, their performances declined to the level of the elderly subjects. An obvious conclusion to be drawn from this study is that, in daily life, the chemosensory functions of older individuals are compromised by diminished olfactory performance. Moreover, it has been suggested that, for many persons, the "anorexia of aging" can be reduced or reversed when flavor enhancers are added to foods.[52]

Many other sensory cues (temperature, texture, pressure) play a role in the experience of food enjoyment. One study demonstrated no age-related changes in the ability of subjects to distinguish fluids of varying temperatures and viscosities; however, a specific decline was observed in the perception of localized lingual pressure.[53]

In order to examine a patient's ability to identify some odorants, he or she can be given the University of Pennsylvania Smell Identification Test.[50] Impaired taste and other oral sensory deficits can be identified via patients' complaints, although these are not always reliable.[51] The etiologies of olfactory and gustatory dysfunction are diverse and occasionally difficult to diagnose. They include oral diseases (dental/alveolar abscess, salivary gland dysfunction, periodontal disease, candidiasis, the utilization of removable prostheses),[54] chronic upper respiratory infections, and diseases of the central nervous system. If complaints persist, referral to specialists may be warranted.

ORAL MUCOSA

The soft tissue lining the mouth is of three general types: (1) well-keratinized tissue, with a dense connective tissue layer and firm attachment to underlying bone (e.g., marginal gingiva, palatal mucosa); (2) slightly keratinized and freely movable tissue (e.g., labial and buccal mucosa, floor of the mouth); (3) specialized mucosa (e.g., dorsum of the tongue). The primary function of the oral mucosa is to act as a barrier that protects the underlying structures from desiccation, noxious chemicals, trauma, thermal stress, and infection. The oral mucosa plays a key role in the defense of the oral cavity.

Aging has frequently been associated with changes in the oral mucosa, similar to those seen in the skin, with the epithelium becoming thinner, less hydrated, and thus supposedly more susceptible to injury.[55] The reasons for such changes (if they are normally a sequela of aging) could be complex and may include alterations in protein synthesis, responsiveness to growth factors, and other regulatory mediators. Grossly, changes in the vascularity of oral mucosa (due to atherosclerosis)[56] probably contribute to an alteration in mucosal integrity because of reductions in cellular access to nutrients and oxygenation. Mucosal, alveolar, and gingival arteries show the effects of arteriosclerosis; clinically, varicosities on the floor of the mouth and lateral and ventral surfaces of the tongue (comparable to varicosities on the lower extremities) are apparent in geriatric patients.

The maintenance of mucosal integrity depends on the ability of the oral epithelium to respond to insult (i.e., physical compromise, exposure to chemical or microbiological toxins). Many studies have documented that the immune system undergoes a marked decline with age, and it is likely that this decline extends to mucosal immunity.[57] Therefore, the oral mucosa may be more susceptible to the transmission of infectious diseases as well as to delayed wound healing. Skin wounds in young and old subjects gain strength at a parallel rate, but in older individuals wounds cease to gain strength significantly earlier than in younger persons.[58] Similar findings have been reported in the healing of gingival tissues.[59]

It is also believed that cell renewal (i.e., mitotic rates) and the synthesis of proteins associated with keratinization of the mucosa occur at a slower rate in aging individuals. However, the normal tissue architecture and patterns of histodifferentiation, which are probably dependent upon complex interactions with the underlying connective tissue, do not display any changes with age.[60] Unfortunately, an adequate characterization of the status of the oral mucosa, particularly as regards cell proliferation and tissue renewal, does not exist.[61]

Recent studies have demonstrated that age per se has no effect on the clinical appearance of the oral mucosa.[62] However, there is considerable evidence to suggest that the utilization of removable prostheses has a potentially adverse effect on the health of oral mucosa.[62,63] The denture-bearing mucosa of aged maxillary and mandibular ridges shows significant morphologic changes.[56,64] Ill-fitting dentures can produce mechanical trauma to the oral tissues as well as mucosal hyperplasia. Oral candidiasis is frequently found on denture-bearing areas in the edentulous individual, often occurring with angular cheilitis (deep fissuring and ulceration of the epithelium at the commissures of the mouth). Therefore, the clinician should ask the patient to remove all removable prostheses in order to conduct an adequate oral examination.

Oral mucosal alterations in the older person are often a result of both local factors (dental state, condition of dentures, consumption of tobacco, secretion of saliva) as well as systemic disease.[65] Long-term utilization of antibiotics will frequently result in oral candidal infections, while drugs with xerostomic side effects (see above) will likewise increase the potential for mucosal injury. A complaint of a burning mouth is not uncommon among older adults, especially females, and can be caused by local factors (denture irritation and yeast infection), decreased salivary production, systemic factors (nutritional and estrogen deficiencies), psychogenic problems, and sensory neuropathies.[66] Most concerns about oral mucosal disease in older persons are similar to those for younger adults; the reader is referred to a comprehensive text dealing with these problems.[67]

Oral cancers comprise approximately 5 percent of all malignancies, and the incidence increases with age. Approximately 97 percent of all oral cancers occur in persons over 45 years of age; the incidence in males is almost three times that in females; and blacks have a higher rate than whites.[68] Neoplasms may arise in all oral soft and hard tissue, oropharyngeal, and salivary gland regions. The clinical appearance of oral carcinomas is quite diverse (ulcerative, erythematous, leukoplakic, papillary) and may be innocuous as well as asymptomatic.[69] If a patient presents with an unusual and suspicious lesion of no readily apparent etiology (as with a denture sore), the patient should be referred to a specialist more familiar with the appearance of the oral mucosa. Carcinoma should be considered as part of a differential diagnosis with any oral lesion.

MOTOR FUNCTION

The oral motor apparatus is involved in several routine yet intricate functions (speech, posture, mastication, and swallowing). Regulation of these activities may occur at three levels: the local neuromuscular unit, central neuronal pathways, and systemic influences. In general, aging is associated with changes in neuromuscular systems.[70,71] Animal studies[72] strongly suggest that age-associated deficiencies in motor function are not related to the composition and contractile function of skeletal muscles. Rather, these changes are probably related to such factors as neuromuscular transmission or propagation of nerve impulses.

Studies of oral motor function have shown that some alterations in performance (mastication, swallowing, oral muscular posture, and tone) can be expected with increased age.[73,74] These changes appear to be more common among predominantly edentulous persons than among those with a natural dentition. The most often reported oral motor disturbance in the elderly is related to altered mastication, and even fully dentate older persons are less able to prepare food adequately for swallowing than are younger individuals.[73,75] It has also been reported that older persons tend to swallow larger-sized food particles than do younger adults.[73] This suggests that there is a diminution in masticatory efficiency, which can be further exacerbated among individuals with a compromised dentition.

Following mastication, a food bolus is translocated to the pharynx. This phase of swallowing (the oral phase) requires well-coordinated neuromuscular processing, an intact mucosal barrier and adequate saliva production. Alterations in any of these components can disturb the oral phase.[76,77] Ultrasonic imaging provides a convenient way to visualize this swallowing phase. In healthy young adults, the oral phase takes about 1.5 to 2.0 seconds with only the endogenous salivary secretions in the mouth (dry swallow). When a 5-ml water bolus is present (wet swallow), the total time for the oral phase is reduced to about 1.0 to 1.5 seconds. In older persons, the duration of the oral phase of both dry and wet swallows is significantly increased (about 50 to 100 percent longer).[78] While these changes are statistically significant, patients with frank neuropathy may display oral swallow times four- to sixfold longer and may not even be able to produce the recognizable characteristics of an oral swallow.

The etiology of oropharyngeal dysphagia in the elderly is complex and can result in dramatically reduced nutritional intake.[74] During "normal aging," subclinical oral neuromotor changes occur in the swallowing mechanism; in the absence of other physiological alterations, these changes may not be of biological significance. However, when viewed in the context of the findings of Feldman et al.,[73] under unusual or stressful conditions, these perturbations may place older persons (especially those with dentures) at some risk of choking or aspiration. Individuals with a suggestive history of these possible problems should be counseled or referred for rehabilitative therapy.

The temporomandibular joint (TMJ) is located between the glenoid fossa and the condylar process of the mandible. The TMJ exhibits a functionally unique gliding and hingelike movement. It is of particular interest to clinicians, for it is the focus of a variety of craniofacial pain disorders. Using radiographic and postmortem evaluations, several investigators have reported that various components of this joint undergo degenerative alterations with increased age.[79] Recent work, however, does not confirm TMJ functional impairment as a "normal" age-associated event.[80] Conversely, many oral as well as systemic conditions commonly seen in the elderly are linked with temporomandibular disorders (TMD).[80] Orofacial pain in the elderly can frequently involve the TMJ complex and may be a concomitant to a number of chronic systemic diseases as well as to problems of the teeth and periodontium.[81] This presents a diagnostic problem to the clinician, but establishment of the source and cause of pain results in effective pain management.[81] Interestingly, there are data suggesting that older persons are more likely to seek or receive care for TMD pain.[82]

In general, two types of pathology are associated with the TMJ: *articular,* related to the joint itself, and *nonarticular,* pathology occurring in structures unrelated to the joint but causing similar or referred symptomatology.[83] Many types of articular abnormalities, common to all joints, affect the TMJ, including trauma, ankylosis, dislocation, and arthritis. Nonarticular disorders may result from a variety of clinical entities, including trigeminal neuralgia, dental pulpitis, and otitis. Nonarticular disorders include myofascial pain dysfunction and masticatory myalgia. Generally most such cases are felt to be psychophysiological in etiology and are associated with jaw clenching or tooth grinding, habits frequently associated with stress. Such actions can result in muscle fatigue and subsequent spasm. Clinically, the patient will present with pain in the TMJ, temporal, cervical or neck region, masticatory muscles, and oral cavity. Limited jaw opening (less than 40 mm from maxillary central incisor to mandibular central incisor) and pain upon mastication or during protrusive and lateral jaw movements may be indicative of TMD.

Several studies have evaluated aspects of speech production in the elderly and reported changes increasing with age.[84,85] These include alterations in such activities as tongue shape and function during specific phoneme production[84] and variability in frequency.[85] However, among older healthy persons, these changes do not compromise or alter speech in any perceptible way.[84] There are also age-associated alterations in intraoral and maxillofacial posture. Drooping of the lower face and lips in the elderly results not only from the loss of supporting hard tissues but also from a diminished tone of the circumoral muscles.[86] These latter changes may elicit esthetic concerns and can often lead to embarrassment from drooling or food spills due to the older individual's inability to close the lips competently while eating or speaking. Additionally, the drooling caused by reduced circumoral muscle tone can result in complaints of excess salivation by an elderly person.

It should be recognized that significant oral motor disorders may result from a number of therapeutic drug regimens; an example is the frequent association of tardive dyskinesia with phenothiazine therapy. These dyskinesias may include diminished performance and speech pathologies as well as frank alterations in movement (chorea, athetosis).

REFERENCES

1. Baum BJ: Research on aging and oral health: An assessment of current status and future needs. *Spec Care Dent* 1:156, 1981.
2. Berkey DB, Shay K: General dental care for the elderly. *Clin Geriatr Med* 8:579, 1992.
3. Baum BJ, Ship JA: Oral disorders, in Beck J (ed): *Geriatrics Review Syllabus—A Core Curriculum in Geriatric Medicine.* New York, American Geriatric Society. 1991, pp 332–336.
4. Papas AS, Niessen LC, Chauncey HH (eds): *Geriatric Dentistry.* St. Louis, Mosby, 1991.
5. Ship JA: Oral sequelae of common geriatric disorders. *Clin Geriatr Med* 8:483, 1992.
6. Miller AJ et al: The National Survey of Oral Health in U.S. Adults: 1985–1986. US Department of Health and Human Services, Public Health Service, National Institutes of Health. NIH Publication No. 87-2868. Washington DC, US Government Printing Office, 1987.
7. Chauncey HH et al: Dental caries—principal cause of tooth extraction in a sample of US male adults. *Caries Res* 23:200, 1989.
8. Manji F et al: Pattern of dental caries in an adult rural population. *Caries Res* 23:55, 1989.
9. Shaw JH: Causes and control of dental caries. *N Engl J Med* 317:996, 1987.
10. Bowden GHW: Microbiology of root surface caries in humans. *J Dent Res* 69:1205, 1990.
11. Menaker L: *The Biological Basis of Dental Caries.* Hagerstown, MD, Harper & Row, 1980.
12. Holm-Pedersen P et al: Composition and metabolic activity of dental plaque from healthy young and elderly individuals. *J Dent Res* 59:77, 1980.
13. Listgarten M: Nature of periodontal diseases: Pathogenic mechanisms. *J Periodont Res* 22:172, 1987.
14. Beck JD: The epidemiology of root surface caries. *J Dent Res* 69:1216, 1990.
15. Ship JA, Ship II: Trends in oral health in the aging population. *Dent Clin North Am* 33:33, 1989.
16. Banting DW: Dental caries in the elderly. *Gerodontology* 3:55, 1984.
17. Ship JA, Wolff A: Gingival and periodontal parameters in a population of healthy adults, 22–90 years of age. *Gerodontology* 7:55, 1988.
18. Oliver RC et al: Variations in the prevalence and extent of periodontitis. *J Am Dent Assoc* 122:43, 1991.
19. Beck JD et al: Prevalence and risk indicators for periodontal attachment loss in population of older community-dwelling blacks and whites. *J Periodontol* 61:521, 1990.
20. Haffajee AD, Socransky SS: Attachment level changes in destructive periodontal diseases. *J Clin Periodontol* 13:461, 1986.
21. Peterson DE: Oral candidiasis. *Clin Geriatr Med* 8:513, 1992.
22. Baum BJ: Salivary gland function during aging. *Gerodontics* 2:61, 1986.
23. Ship JA, Baum BJ: Is reduced salivary flow normal in old people? *Lancet* 336:1507, 1990.
24. Pedersen W et al: Age-dependent decreases in human submandibular gland flow rates as measured under resting and poststimulation conditions. *J Dent Res* 64:833, 1985.
25. Tylenda CA et al: Evaluation of submandibular salivary flow rate in different age groups. *J Dent Res* 67:1225, 1988.
26. Baum BJ: Saliva secretion and composition, in Ferguson DB (ed): *The Aging Mouth.* Basel, Karger, 1987, p 126.
27. Scott J: Structural age changes in salivary glands, in Ferguson DB (ed): *The Aging Mouth.* Basel, Karger, 1987, p 40.
28. Young JA, van Lennep EW: Transport in salivary and salt glands, in Giebisch G et al (eds): *Membrane Transport in Biology.* Berlin: Springer-Verlag, 1979, p 563.
29. Scott J: Structure and function in aging human salivary glands. *Gerodontology* 5:149, 1986.
30. Sreebny LM, Schwartz SS: A reference guide to drugs and dry mouth. *Gerodontology* 5:75, 1986.
31. Atkinson JC, Fox PC: Salivary gland dysfunction. *Clin Geriatr Med* 8:499, 1992.
32. Schiffman SS: Food recognition in the elderly. *J Gerontol* 32:586, 1977.
33. Murphy C, Withee J: Age and biochemical status predict preference for casein hydrolysate. *J Gerontol* 42:73, 1987.
34. Morley JE, Silver AJ: Anorexia in the elderly. *Neurobiol Aging* 9:9, 1988.
35. Shock NW: Commentary on anorexia in the elderly. *Neurobiol Aging* 9:17, 1988.
36. Mistretta CM: Aging effects on anatomy and neurophysiology of taste and smell. *Gerodontology* 3:131, 1984.
37. Arvidson K: Human taste: Response and taste bud number in fungiform papillae. *Science* 209:807, 1980.
38. Miller IJ Jr: Human taste bud density across adult age groups. *J Gerontol* 43:B26, 1988.
39. Mistretta CM, Baum BJ: Quantitative study of taste buds in fungiform and circumvallate papillae of young and aged rats. *J Anat* 138:323, 1984.
40. Weiffenbach JM: Taste and smell perception. *Gerodontology* 3:137, 1984.
41. Weiffenbach JM et al: Taste thresholds: Quality specific variation with human aging. *J Gerontol* 37:372, 1982.
42. Spitzer ME: Taste acuity in institutionalized and noninstitutionalized elderly men. *J Gerontol* 43:P71, 1988.
43. Bartoshuk LM et al: Taste and aging. *J Gerontol* 41:51, 1986.
44. Weiffenbach JM et al: Taste intensity perception in aging. *J Gerontol* 41:460, 1986.
45. Steven DA, Lawless HT: Age-related changes in flavor perception. *Appetite* 2:127, 1981.
46. Murphy C: Age-related effects on the threshold, psychophysical function and pleasantness of menthol. *J Gerontol* 38:217, 1983.
47. Murphy C: Taste and smell in the elderly, in Meiselman HL, Rivlin RS (eds): *Clinical Measurements of Taste and Smell.* New York: Macmillan, 1986, p 343.
48. Langan MJ, Yearick ES: The effects of improved oral hygiene on taste perception and nutrition of the elderly. *J Gerontol* 31:413, 1976.

49. Hinds JW, McNelly NA: Aging in the rat olfactory system: Correlation of changes in the olfactory epithelium and olfactory bulb. *J Comp Neurol* 203:441, 1981.
50. Doty RL et al: Development of the University of Pennsylvania smell identification test: A standardized microencapsulated test of olfactory function. *Physiol Behav* 32:489, 1984.
51. Ship JA, Weiffenbach JM: Age, gender, medical treatment, and medication effects on smell identification. *J Gerontol* 48:M26, 1993.
52. Schiffman SS, Warwick ZS: Flavor enhancement of foods for the elderly can reverse anorexia. *Neurobiol Aging* 9:24, 1988.
53. Weiffenbach JM et al: Oral sensory changes in aging. *J Gerontol* 45:M121, 1990.
54. Catalanotto F, Sweeney E: Oral conditions affecting chemosensory function, in Getchell T et al (eds): *Smell and Taste in Health and Disease.* New York, Raven Press, 1991, pp 643–649.
55. Miles AEW: Sans teeth: Changes in oral tissues with advancing age. *Proc Roy Soc Med* 65:801, 1972.
56. Nedelman CI, Bernick S: The significance of age changes in human alveolar mucosa and bone. *J Pros Dent* 39:495, 1978.
57. Schmucker DL, Daniels CK: Aging, gastrointestinal infections, and mucosal immunity. *J Am Geriatr Soc* 34:377, 1986.
58. Goodson WH, Hunt TK: Wound healing and aging. *J Invest Dermatol* 73:88, 1979.
59. Holm-Pedersen P, Loe H: Wound healing in the gingiva of young and old individuals. *Scand J Dent Res* 79:40, 1971.
60. Mackenzie IC, Hill MW: Connective tissue influences on patterns of epithelial architecture and keratinization in skin and oral mucosa of mouse. *Cell Tissue Res* 235:551, 1984.
61. Hill MW: The influence of aging on skin and oral mucosa. *Gerodontology* 3:35, 1984.
62. Wolff A et al: Oral mucosal appearance is unchanged in healthy, different-aged persons. *Oral Surg Oral Med Oral Pathol* 71:569, 1991.
63. Hand JS, Whitehill JM: The prevalence of oral mucosal lesions in an elderly population. *J Am Dent Assoc* 112:73, 1986.
64. Watson IB, MacDonald DG: Oral mucosa and complete dentures. *J Pros Dent* 47:133, 1982.
65. Osterberg T et al: The condition of the oral mucosa at age 70: A population study. *Gerodontology* 4:71, 1985.
66. Grushka M, Sessle BJ: Burning mouth syndrome. *Dent Clin North Am* 35:171, 1991.
67. McCarthy PL, Shklar G: *Diseases of the Oral Mucosa.* Philadelphia, Lea & Febiger, 1980.
68. US Department of Health and Human Services: *Cancers of the Oral Cavity and Pharynx: A Statistics Review Monograph 1973–1987.* Bethesda, MD, US Public Service, National Institutes of Health, 1991.
69. Silverman S: Precancerous lesions and oral cancer in the elderly. *Clin Geriatr Med* 8:529, 1992.
70. McCarter R: Effects of age on the contraction of mammalian skeletal muscle, in Kaldor G, DiBattista WJ (eds): *Aging in Muscles.* New York, Raven Press, 1978, p 1.
71. Pradhan SN: Central neurotransmitters and aging. *Life Sci* 26:1643, 1980.
72. McCarter R, McGee J: Influence of nutrition and aging on the composition and function of rat skeletal muscle. *J Gerontol* 42:432, 1987.
73. Feldman RS et al: Aging and mastication: Changes in performance and in the swallowing threshold with natural dentition. *J Am Geriatrics Soc* 28:97, 1980.
74. Sonies BC: Oropharyngeal dysphagia in the elderly. *Clin Geriatr Med* 8:569, 1992.
75. Heath MR: The effect of maximum biting force and bone loss upon masticatory function and dietary selection of the elderly. *Int Dent J* 32:345, 1982.
76. Sonies BC et al: Speech and swallowing in the elderly. *Gerodontology* 3:115, 1984.
77. Hughes CV et al: Oral-pharyngeal dysphagia: A common sequela of salivary gland dysfunction. *Dysphagia* 1:173, 1987.
78. Sonies BC et al: Durational aspects of the oral-pharyngeal phase of swallow in normal adults. *Dysphagia* 3:1, 1988.
79. Tonna EA: Aging of skeletal-dental systems and supporting tissues, in Finch CE, Hayflick L (eds): *Handbook of the Biology of Aging.* New York, Van Nostrand Reinhold, 1977, p 470.
80. Stohler CS: Temporomandibular disorders in the aged, in Carlson DS (ed): *Orthodontics in an Aged Society,* Monograph 22, Cranio-facial Growth Series. Ann Arbor, Center for Human Growth and Development, The University of Michigan, 1989, 137–158.
81. Heft MW: Orofacial pain. *Clin Geriatr Med* 8:557, 1992.
82. Von Korff M et al: Chronic pain and use of ambulatory health care. *Psychosom Med* 53:61, 1991.
83. Laskin DM: Dental and oral disorders, in Berkow R (ed): *The Merck Manual.* Rahway, NJ, Merck & Co. 1977, p 1654.
84. Sonies BC et al: Tongue motion in elderly adults: Initial in-situ observations. *J Gerontol* 39:279, 1984.
85. Benjamin BJ: Frequency variability in the aged voice. *J Gerontol* 36:722, 1981.
86. Baum BJ, Bodner L: Aging and oral motor function: Evidence for altered performance among older persons. *J Dent Res* 62:2, 1983.

Chapter 39

THE EYE

David D. Michaels

Each age has its virtues and its drawbacks, its duties and its delights. The drawbacks, unhappily, multiply disproportionately as we grow older. A dismal list of cumulative incapacities fills the geriatric literature. We are embalmed from birth, it seems, by the genetic limits of our protoplasm. If, however, little can be said for old age, even less can be asserted for the alternative. We cling to our universe for fear of finding something worse; however poor may be the start, few are anxious to depart.

THE AGING EYE

Senescence is inevitable but not identical for everyone; the strands of life unravel at different rates for the eye as well as other organ systems. Ocular morphologic changes are usually bilateral; often symmetrical; and, although not constant, fairly typical. Functional visual deficits exhibit a spectrum ranging from those that restrict daily activities to some that can be demonstrated only in the laboratory.[1] These changes place the ophthalmic diseases of later life in perspective.

The enophthalmos of aging is more apparent than real. Although orbital fat may shrink and fascial connections loosen, the primary factor is flaccidity of the lids. The increased flaccidity of the lower lid may result in an inward flip (senile entropion) or an outward sag (senile ectropion).

In older eyes, failure of the lacrimal pump coupled with displacement of the lacrimal punctum results in epiphora. Since tear production decreases with age, the older eye cries less but waters more.

The skin of the lids, like skin elsewhere, dries out from loss of oily secretions. The hair grays, and eyebrows and lashes thin out. Atrophy of subcutaneous fat leads to wrinkling and deepens the lid folds. Sagging skin may rest on the lashes to produce pseudoptosis. Freckles and lentigo are common, and the skin itself acquires a yellow tinge. Benign tumors such as papillomas, xanthelasma, and keratoses are common in the elderly.[2] Cosmetic surgery may be indicated in the eternal struggle to remain young or at least look young.

The aging conjunctiva becomes thinner and more friable, and it acquires a yellow color. Two common conjunctival lesions are pinguecula and pterygium. A pinguecula is a small, yellowish, elevated mass in the interpalpebral fissure and represents degenerated collagen fibers. Pterygium is a further progression to form the characteristic triangular fold of tissue that invades the cornea.

Aging changes in the cornea include stippling of Bowman's membrane (crocodile shagreen), excrescences on Descenet's membrane (Hassal-Henle bodies), and arcus senilis. When observed with the biomicroscope, Hassal-Henle bodies appear as dark holes in the endothelium. Annular accumulations of lipids in the peripheral cornea produce the arcus senilis, which may be complete or incomplete.

The sclera becomes more transparent and yellowish with age due to dehydration and lipid deposits. The yellow color should not be confused with jaundice. Local areas of excessive translucency (hyaline plaques) may be mistaken for tumors or inflammation. Intrascleral nerve loops are sometimes misdiagnosed as melanomas.

The anterior chamber becomes progressively shallower with age due to growth of the crystalline lens. The potential risks of angle closure following mydriatics therefore increase.

Atrophic changes in the iris are evident as depigmentation, pigment migration, and opacification of the supporting tissue.

Surface markings and crypts may be obliterated, resulting in partial color change. The pupil becomes more rigid and does not dilate readily.

Failure of the pupil to dilate well is one factor in the complaint of poor night vision among older people. Contributing to the pathophysiology are crystalline lens discoloration and opacification, increased light scatter, and slower dark adaptation. Increased reaction time and perceptual delays perhaps also play a role.

The ciliary muscle atrophies with age, but this does not appear to contribute to presbyopia. The ciliary processes become hyalinized and may contain granular calcium deposits. Aqueous secretion diminishes somewhat.

The crystalline lens continues its growth throughout life, although the rate slows with age.

Sclerosis of the lens substance and decreased elasticity of its capsule are the main factors causing loss of accommodation. Perhaps most remarkable is that these changes occur in all lens meridians symmetrically and in both eyes simultaneously.

Cataract is superimposed on the normal aging of the lens, and, indeed, differences may be imperceptible in early stages. Among well-established age changes are an increased proportion of insoluble proteins, yellow discoloration, and increased lens weight.

Age changes of the vitreous consist of liquefaction, cavitation, shrinkage, and detachment. Fibrillar aggregates may cast a shadow on the retina and become visible as muscae volitantes. Contraction of the vitreous gel with a separation of solid and liquid components is termed *syneresis*. This may occur 10 to 20 years earlier in myopic eyes. Vitreous detachment is responsible for "flashes."

The choroid is the vascular and pigmented tunic of the eye. Its thickness gradually diminishes with age due to arteriolar sclerosis, even in the absence of systemic vascular disease. Atrophic changes are particularly prominent around the optic disk (senile peripapillary atrophy). Diffuse attenuation of pigment occurs regularly with age and gives the senescent fundus its tessellated appearance.

The aging retina becomes thinner due to loss of neural cells. In the periphery, actual spaces appear, which may coalesce to form vacuoles (peripheral cystic degeneration). Lipofuscin, the degradation product of photoreceptor disks, accumulates in pigment epithelial cells and displaces melanin. The glistening ophthalmoscopic reflexes of the youthful fundus disappear, and the foveal reflex is lost. Degenerative changes in the optic nerve include corpora amylacea and arenacea, visible on histologic specimens; these have no clinical significance.

Our list of changes may suggest that the older eye does not see because nothing is as it used to be. In fact, in the absence of disease, acuity declines very little, visual fields remain full, ocular motility stays brisk, and night vision is only slightly impaired.[3] Of course, we must learn to put up with such minor annoyances as presbyopia and bifocals, color deficiencies under reduced illumination, spots and dots in our visual field, and assorted cosmetic blemishes.

CLINICAL EVALUATION OF THE AGED EYE

Examination of the aged eye takes more time, tact, and patience. It takes more time because older people frequently have many nonspecific complaints, poorly expressed and sequentially muddled. Some symptoms may go unreported because of memory loss, fear, or indifference. It takes more tact because some senescent diseases are not only chronic but irreparable. It takes more patience because the aged eye often suffers multiple defects. For example, reduced acuity may be caused by corneal endothelial changes, lens vacuoles, macular pigment dispersion, amblyopia, and misplaced spectacles. These factors must be considered in turn, since each can contribute to decreased vision, which, however, may not even be the chief complaint.

Much information can be obtained by simple observation—indeed, as soon as the patient walks into the room. Skin color and texture, posture and gait, cranial and facial features, ptosis and ectropion, head tilt and strabismus—all have diagnostic meaning. Old photographs sometimes separate acute from chronic afflictions.[4]

Of all the criteria of visual performance, acuity is the simplest, most widely used, and most clinically rewarding. The responses of patients with scotomas, hemianopia, amblyopia, latent nystagmus, ptosis, myopia, and presbyopia—although not diagnostic—are highly suggestive. Some lens opacities interfere with acuity more in dim light; some, more in bright light; some opacities tend to compromise near vision more than distance vision; other features may include metamorphopsia, halos, pain, or photophobia.

The absence of light perception is a serious diagnosis because it carries with it many therapeutic limitations. Patients may confabulate invisible targets, and surgical procedures to restore function will be disappointing for all concerned if light perception is absent. The diagnosis, therefore, should be made on the basis not only of subjective responses but also on objective evidence of an amaurotic pupil.

In contrast to tests for central acuity, perimetry measures the peripheral field of vision.[5] Ideally, every patient should have his or her fields recorded, but this is not always practical. Perimetry is indicated, however, in any elderly patient who gives headache as a primary complaint; who reports flashes, floaters, or curtains in the field of vision; who has episodes of transient visual loss or transient refractive changes; who exhibits personality and cognitive changes, diplopia, or other neuroophthalmic signs and symptoms; whose visual deficit cannot be explained by external or ophthalmoscopic findings; and whose intraocular tensions are outside the normal range.

The pupil is of signal importance[6] not only in diagnosing neuroophthalmic diseases but also in evaluating any eye with media opacities. If the fundus cannot be seen, one can still formulate an estimate of retinal integrity by noting whether the consensual reflex is present in the other eye. Anisocoria can be detected only if eyes are inspected in both dim and bright light. A spurious anisocoria results from a bound-down pupil following an old injury or uveitis. In Horner's syndrome, the abnormal pupil is miotic; in Adie's syndrome, the abnormal pupil is mydriatic. A blind eye still exhibits a near and consensual reflex. Light-near dissociation is not always luetic; other causes are pituitary lesions, myotonic dystrophy, Adie's syndrome, and aberrant regeneration of the third nerve. The afferent pupillary defect (Marcus Gunn pupil) is best elicited with the swinging flashlight test. Shining the light from one eye to the other, one sees the pupil dilating instead of constricting—an apparent paradoxical reaction. The significance of the Marcus Gunn pupil is that it practically always means a conduction defect in the optic nerve. Macular disease, medial opacities, and amblyopia do not cause afferent pupillary defects. A fixed, dilated pupil is usually caused by drugs, third nerve palsy, or compression. Myopathies never involve the pupil.

Intraocular tensions should be determined in every older patient at every routine examination.[7] Aplanation tonometry is preferred over Schietz, because it is not influenced by ocular rigidity. At any ocular pressure level, however, the risks of glaucomatous damage increase with age.

Biomicroscopy is a unique method of ophthalmic examination that is not duplicated by any other technique. It affords visibility of anatomic details not only magnified but also in depth and stereoscopically. The classification of senile cataracts is based on slit-lamp appearance. The location and fixation of intraocular implants can only be studied biomicroscopically.

Loss of corneal luster is common in older eyes. Sometimes this simply represents a deficiency of tears, but in many cases it reflects pathologic surface changes such as tumors, dystrophies, foreign deposits, and neovascularization. Simple flashlight inspection, therefore, can reveal a great deal about the state of corneal health.

The integrity of macular function is frequently compromised in the elderly, and the diagnosis may not be obvious from ophthalmoscopic inspection, even under high magnification. A simple test such as a grid can help localize disease to this area. The Amsler grid is a self-administered tangent screen test confined to the central 20°. A reasonably intelligent patient can be instructed to report any distortions in the grid.

In contrast to macular disease, optic neuritis causes a decrease in vision characterized by a central scotoma, sometimes a generalized field reduction, and defective color vision. Red-free ophthalmoscopy may also reveal nerve fiber dropout, atrophy of the disk, and fewer disk capillaries. If the retina is also involved (neuroretinitis), there may be papillitis and perifoveal exudates.

Gonioscopy is indicated in the initial workup of every glaucoma patient. It differentiates open- from closed-angle mechanisms, the treatment for each of which is fundamentally different. The most popular technique utilizes the biomicroscope and a contact lens applied to the topically anesthetized eye.

Refraction of the elderly patient proceeds at a more leisurely pace with more tolerance for indecision. Refractive errors are the most common cause of blurred vision, and their rehabilitation has probably added as much to the quality of life and extended its usefulness as any advance in biology.[8] But ametropia and presbyopia also occur in diseased eyes, and it is not unusual to confuse blurred vision with loss of vision. Even patients with cataract or macular disease can often have useful vision restored by proper refraction with or without low-vision aids. Examination of such combined disorders may require stronger light, higher contrast, and nearer test distances.

Transient refractive changes can be detected only by repeated examination. They may result from drugs used topically or systemically, lens swelling from electrolyte imbalances, and corneal edema from endothelial decompensation or with orbital masses and following ophthalmic surgical procedures.

AGE-RELATED OCULAR DISEASE: TOPICAL ASPECTS

Orbital Diseases

Cardinal features of orbital disease are proptosis, ptosis, pain, pulsation, and restricted ocular motility.[9] Neuropathies or myopathies cause diplopia. Trigeminal involvement produces corneal and periorbital anesthesia. Lacrimal complications lead to inadequate tear production. Pressure on the optic nerve may cause blindness; extension into the cranial cavity may cause death.

In evaluating orbital disorders, one notes rate of onset, progression, and systemic features of endocrine disease. In addition to inspection, palpation, compression, auscultation, visual fields, forced duction, plain x-ray, and biopsy, specialized diagnostic techniques include tomography, ultrasonography, venography, arteriography, pneumography, and contrast injections into orbital soft tissues. Computed tomography (CT) and magnetic resonance imaging (MRI) have revolutionized noninvasive methods of visualizing orbital tissues.

The most prominent presenting feature of orbital disease is proptosis (or exophthalmos). It may be unilateral or bilateral, and globe displacement may be axial or eccentric. Quantitative measurement with a Hertel-type exophthalmometer documents progression and helps rule out enophthalmos on the opposite side or an apparent proptosis due to lid retraction. The differential diagnosis usually centers around endocrine exophthalmos, inflammation, pseudotumor, vascular anomalies, true neoplasms, and trauma (for example, hematomas and foreign bodies). Since neoplasms may be primary or metastatic or may involve the orbit by extension from adjacent areas, neurologic, ear, nose, and throat, and general medical evaluations are often necessary. Laboratory tests for thyroid function, blood dyscrasias, sarcoidosis, diabetes, lues, and systemic infections are part of the workup.

Infection (cellulitis) causes rapidly developing proptosis with swelling, redness, pain, tenderness, lid edema, chemosis, fever, and leukocytosis. The source may be a foreign body, adjacent sinuses, the eye or its adnexa, or a systemic infection. Chronic cellulitis can occur with dacryoadenitis (Mikulicz syndrome), sarcoidosis, tuberculosis, or lues. An important cause to recognize (because it is potentially lethal) is mucormycosis. This fungus infection occurs in debilitated or diabetic patients or following cancer chemotherapy. The infection starts in the nose and spreads rapidly as a black, gangrenous mass through the soft tissue. Thrombophlebitis and cavernous sinus thrombosis may develop with alarming speed.

Pseudotumor is a nonspecific, chronic inflammatory process that mimics neoplasm. Unlike true tumors, the inflammation eventually involves both sides, some signs of inflammation may be found, there are usually no bone erosions, and the condition tends to respond to steroids. Indolent inflammation may involve the superior orbital fissure and produce a painful ophthalmoplegia (Tolosa-Hunt syndrome).

Vascular anomalies such as carotid-cavernous fistula or aneurysms exhibit pulsation, and the patient may complain of a bruit. Pulsations also occur because of defects in the orbital roof or angioma and may vary with head position.

Endocrine exophthalmos is considered in a subsequent section. It is important to point out, however, that although this is a systemic illness, the exophthalmos is often unilateral. Eye signs can occur in the absence of obvious thyroid dysfunction.

Orbital tumors in the elderly may include hemangiomas, lymphomas, neuromas, carcinomas, and meningiomas.[10] The diagnosis depends on clinical features and biopsy. X-ray changes in the optic canal may explain compressive optic neuropathy. A- and B-scan ultrasonography can identify size, location, configuration, and density of the lesion.

Trauma to the orbit can occur at any age. Deformity, muscle entrapment, persistent diplopia, neural involvement, and enophthalmos are major complications of blowout fractures of the orbital floor. Optic nerve function must be carefully monitored. Proper surgical repair, properly performed, can usually but not always restore normal function.

Diseases of the Lids

Patients with lid disorders may complain of pain, red eyes, itching, tearing, dryness, a sleepy sensation, swelling, tics, and cosmetic deformity. Common lid disorders in the elderly include inflammation, skin problems, ectropion and entropion, ptosis and pseudoptosis, anomalies of lid closure, trauma, and neoplasms.[11]

Infection of the lid margin (blepharitis) is common in the elderly and is usually associated with seborrhea of the eyebrows or skin of the nose, cheeks, and scalp. It is a chronic, annoying, sometimes disabling, and often disfiguring disorder. The lid margins are red and thickened; they may develop ectropion and are dusted by fine, dandrufflike flakes. Scarring may result from the rubbing of the lashes against the cornea. Secondary staphylococcal infections cause sties, ulceration, chalazia, and abscesses. The patient complains of itching, burning, scratching, and tearing and of intolerance to light, smoke, and dust. The wrinkled skin, especially at the canthi, predisposes to retention of moisture and tears, causing cracking and further irritation. All this is often complicated by allergic reactions to a variety of prescribed medications and assorted home remedies. These may include steroids used for long periods, causing iatrogenic glaucoma, cataract, superinfection, or reactivation of herpetic ulcers.

Clinical signs and symptoms of lid allergy are edema, redness, swelling, itching, eruptions, scaling, eczema, crusting, and lichenification. Of particular importance in the elderly is contact dermatitis caused by drugs, chemicals, cosmetics, and other substances applied to the skin surface. Atopic eczema is caused by pollens, dust, animal substances, and bacterial products in patients predisposed to hay fever and asthma. Some reactions are direct toxic effects of drugs such as atropine, eserine, phospholine iodide, and assorted antibiotics. Skin disorders frequently involve the lids of the elderly. Xanthelasma is a yellowish lipoidal degenerative condition typically presenting as a discrete, slightly elevated mass, often symmetrical, near the inner angle. It grows slowly and requires excision only for cosmetic reasons. Papillomas are elevated, localized, warty lesions that should not be confused with the infectious verrucae found in the young. Senile keratoses are flat, irregular, slightly brownish lesions, presumably due to long exposure to the sun; they are important because they are potentially malignant. Lentigines are senile freckles commonly known as liver spots, though they have nothing to do with liver function. Seborrheic keratoses are elevated, fleshy papules having a stuck-on appearance, with a characteristic greasy scale resembling candle-wax drippings. Small cysts or milia have an easily recognizable, pearly white appearance; clear cysts of occluded sweat glands disappear when punctured. The eyelids may also be involved in psoriasis, pseudoxanthoma elasticum, acne rosacea, and sebaceous adenomas of the face. Pruritus from dry, brittle skin is a common complaint that may persist despite local treatment.

Laxity of the lid margins may lead to eversion or ectropion. Chronic ectropion causes thickening of the lid margins, epiphora, excoriation of the skin, and exposure keratitis (Fig. 39-1). The degree of laxity can be estimated by the force required to pull the lower lid away from the globe. Senile flaccidity is the most common cause of ectropion. In contrast, loose tissue may cause the border of the tarsus to swing in, giving rise to senile (spastic) entropion. The chief symptoms are due to the constant rubbing of the lashes against the cornea, which produces a painful keratopathy. Both ectropion and entropion can be corrected by relatively simple surgical procedures.

Ptosis (blepharoptosis) may be congenital or acquired. The acquired forms can be neurogenic, myogenic, inflammatory, mechanical, or spurious (pseudoptosis). Neurogenic ptosis is seen in oculomotor nerve palsy and Horner's syndrome; myogenic ptosis

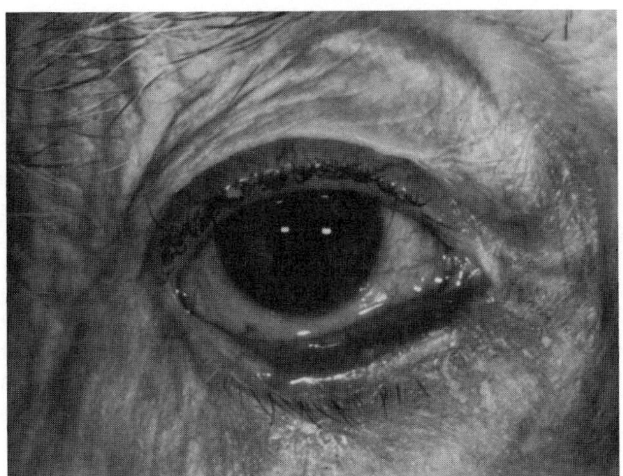

FIGURE 39-1
Ectropion. The lower lid is turned away from the eye. The conjunctiva and cornea are exposed. *(Courtesy of J. Dutton, M.D.)*

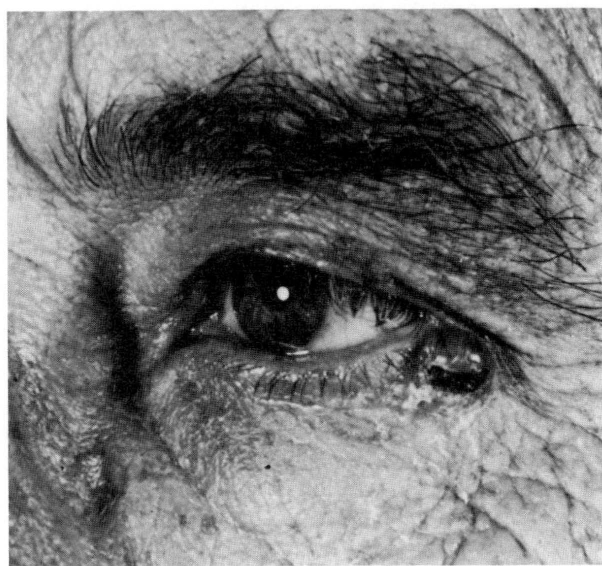

FIGURE 39-2
Basal cell carcinoma of the lower eyelid.

is associated with senile loss of levator tone, progressive external ophthalmoplegia, and myasthenia; inflammatory ptosis may accompany chronic lid edema; mechanical ptosis results from lid tumors and scarring; and pseudoptosis is seen in phthisis and dermatochalasia. In evaluating ptosis, measurements are obtained of the vertical diameter of the palpebral aperture in the primary position, and in up and down gaze. The presence of Bell's phenomenon should be noted. An edrophonium (Tensilon) test is indicated in any patient with ptosis and diplopia. Photographs are useful to document progression.

Anomalies of lid closure interfere with the tear film and may fail to protect the eye, particularly during sleep. A common cause in the aged is Bell's palsy. Although spontaneous resolution is the rule, tarsorrhaphy may be needed to protect the cornea. Orbicularis weakness associated with trigeminal anesthesia, hearing loss, and sixth nerve palsy should lead to intensive investigation for acoustic neuroma.

Blepharospasm is not unusual with a corneal foreign body, keratitis, uveitis, or any condition associated with intense photophobia. It is also a sequel to facial nerve palsy or stroke. It sometimes appears as an isolated, presumably psychogenic phenomenon for which no cause can be discovered. Some of these patients eventually manifest signs of parkinsonism.

Lid lacerations require prompt treatment if they are not to result in corneal exposure, deformity, and disfigurement. One should also check the eyeball for wounds or foreign bodies. Contusion injuries often cause massive hematomas, which may make examination of the globe difficult without special retractors. Orbital and skull fractures must always be considered. Thermal, radiation, and chemical injuries will require special attention.

The most common malignant lesion of the lid is basal cell carcinoma (Fig. 39-2). Other neoplasms such as squamous cell carcinoma, adenoacanthoma, cancerous melanosis, and melanoma are rare. The typical basal cell lesion occurs in the lower lid or inner canthus. It presents as a nodule with a central necrotic ulcer that has rolled, raised, pearly borders. Early lesions are nodular without ulcers; atypical lesions may be diffuse or multicentric. The diagnosis is confirmed by biopsy.

Diseases of the Conjunctiva

Many factors that normally protect the eye from infection and injury may be diminished in the elderly: the flushing action of sufficient tears, the bactericidal action of lysozyme, the mechanical barrier of normal blinking, and the presence of unimpaired immune mechanisms.

The causes of conjunctival disease are numerous: infectious, allergic, toxic, mechanical, traumatic, metabolic, degenerative, vascular, and neoplastic. Symptoms and signs might include hyperemia, exudates, scratchy or burning sensations, tearing, and chemosis. Symptoms may be out of proportion to apparent severity of disease. Pain, photophobia, and decreased vision occur if the cornea is involved; itching appears if there is an allergic component.

Evaluation should include a thorough history with respect to acute or chronic onset, the use of drugs or home remedies, predisposition to atopy and blephorrhea, and exposure to environmental toxins or allergens. Specific features of some types of conjunctivitis might include exudate, petechiae, membranes and pseudomembranes, granulomas, pigmentation, corneal staining, infiltrates, or neovascularization.[12] The type of conjunctival reaction—papillary or follicular—is also important. Finally, one evaluates the lacrimal sac as a source of infection. Scrapings, culture, and biopsy may be required for a definitive diagnosis.

The conjunctival response to infection may be categorized into two broad types; papillary and follicular. Papillae are tufts of new capillaries that rise perpendicularly in the tarsal conjunctiva. Follicles represent a lymphoid hyperplasia of the adenoid layer of the tarsal conjunctiva. Follicles are several times larger than papillae and appear as translucent, hemispheric protuberances. While both papillae and follicles are nonspecific and may occur together, the follicular response predominates in viral and toxic disorders.

A common cause of catarrhal conjunctivitis in the elderly is staphylococcal infection. The conjunctiva is edematous and hyperemic, and the papillary response gives it a velvety appearance. The usual symptoms are tearing, discharge, and irritation. Both eyes are generally involved. Lower corneal ulceration is common and may represent a reaction to exotoxins. Seborrhea predisposes the eye to chronic infection. Chronic irritation and maceration of the outer canthi may resemble angular conjunctivitis. Gram-negative infections occur in elderly debilitated individuals, not infrequently from chronic dacryocystitis or contaminated contact lenses.

In contrast to bacterial infections, viruses produce a follicular reaction and regional lymphadenopathy.[13] Corneal involvement is common and often characteristic. The most important viral infection from an epidemiologic viewpoint is adenoviral (epidemic) conjunctivitis. This disease is now endemic as well as intermittently epidemic. Symptoms and signs include marked hyperemia, a follicular reaction, lymphadenopathy, hemorrhages, lid edema, and, in severe cases, pseudomembranes. The clinical picture may resemble an injury. One week after onset, the cornea may show superficial punctate erosions, producing a foreign body sensation and photophobia. In about half the cases, this is followed by subepithelial, nonstaining corneal infiltrates that reduce vision and may last for months. The smear/scraping shows predominately lymphocytes. There is no satisfactory treatment for this infection. Recognizing it is important because it can be transmitted by fingers or instruments to the eye of the examiner and to the eyes of other patients.

Toxic follicular conjunctivitis is caused mainly by miotics such as eserine and antiviral agents such as idoxuridine. Occasionally, molluscum contagiosum may shed toxic material into the conjunctival sac and produce a follicular reaction. These conditions are chronic as long as the inducing agent persists.

Not every red eye is caused by infection. Conjunctival congestion can also result from air pollution, ultraviolet exposure, alcohol, and lack of sleep. Passive congestion may be caused by venous obstruction from orbital tumors or dysthyroid ophthalmopathy as well as by hyperviscosity syndromes such as multiple myeloma. Cavernous sinus fistulas and carotid stenosis produce active congestion. In uveal and scleral disease, the deeper vascular networks are involved; this may be mistaken for conjunctival injection.

Allergic conjunctivitis is generally characterized by itching, occasionally by burning, and by eosinophils in the smear. There is a watery discharge, redness, and papillary reaction, and this may be accompanied by an eczematous skin response.

Injuries to the conjunctiva are common and may be mechanical or chemical. Foreign bodies lodged in the fornix can easily be overlooked; even contact lenses have been "lost" in the upper fornix. It is most important to estimate the speed of a particle that has struck the eye. Drilling, nailing, and similar activities may allow perforation of the globe; this is not likely with something that "blows" into the eye. If, in addition, there is a conjunctival laceration, soft-tissue x-rays and exploration may be advisable.

Chemical burns can be industrial or agricultural; they may also result from the use of household agents. Alkali burns are especially dangerous because they do not delimit themselves. If the cornea is involved, hospitalization and intensive therapy may prevent permanent scarring. Finally, mild and often unrecognized injuries can cause subconjunctival hemorrhages that, though asymptomatic, greatly alarm the patient. The condition is benign and resolves within a few days. Repeated hemorrhages, however, should trigger an evaluation of hematologic disorders.

Diseases of the Cornea

The cardinal features of corneal disease are pain, photophobia, lacrimation, and impaired vision.[14] Pain from corneal disease may be described as sandy, scratchy, burning, or gritty. True photophobia is ocular pain, induced or exacerbated by light. It differs from dazzling or glare, in which discomfort results from excessive illumination. Lacrimation is a reflex response to trigeminal stimulation. Impaired vision follows excessive light scatter, clouding of the stroma, epithelial edema, and scarring. Corneal disease in the elderly may result from infections, toxins, metabolic changes, tear deficiency, exposure, trigeminal involvement, trauma, degenerations, and neoplasms.

Corneal ulcers are uncommon but may become an emergency in older patients who are diabetic or debilitated or whose immune system is suppressed. Failure to find and treat the cause may lead to corneal scarring at best or perforation and endophthalmitis at worst. Pyogenic ulcers are gray with poorly defined margins, and there may be iritis, hypopyon, and intense circumcorneal injection. Fungus ulcers have feathery edges and may have satellite lesions. Smears and cultures are mandatory.

Herpes simplex viruses are a leading cause of corneal disease. In adults, the ocular disease usually causes dendritic ulcers confined to the corneal epithelium. Attacks may be recurrent, so a history of prior eye or skin lesions is important. In early stages or as a recurrence variant, the infection may present as a superficial punctate keratitis or a localized stromal edema with or without epithelial involvement. The reason for the dendritic pattern is not known. A number of trigger mechanisms may lead to recurrence: fever, sunburn, mechanical trauma, contact lenses, emotional stress, and topical steroids. Stromal disease may be accompanied by iritis and elevated intraocular pressure. In some cases it results in a permanent discoid opacity.

Herpes zoster, when it involves the nasociliary nerve, can produce severe uveitis as well as keratitis; the corneal lesion may be confused with herpes simplex, and long after cutaneous lesions heal, neuralgic pains may persist and last for months and even years.

Toxic disorders of the cornea may follow the use of antimalarial drugs such as chloroquine, which produce a characteristic whorllike pattern; hyphema with elevated intraocular tension, which produces blood staining; the use of silver preparations, which cause argyrosis; and retained iron foreign bodies, which cause siderosis. Corneal changes also occur in disorders of fat, protein, copper, and calcium metabolism. Thus, the Kayser-Fleischer ring is pathognomonic of Wilson's disease.

Disorders of the mechanisms that maintain normal corneal detumescence alter optical homogeneity and therefore transparency. The marked affinity of the cornea for water is counteracted by an active metabolic pump within endothelial cells. Thus, endothelial disease (from dystrophy, trauma, or improper irrigating solutions during intraocular surgery), elevated intraocular pressure, or severe hypotony cause corneal edema. On the epithelial side, water may enter the stroma if the epithelial barrier is broken, the tear film loses its isotonicity, or there is chronic anoxia. Since the cornea swells perpendicular to its surface, edema can be quantified by measuring thickness (pachometry). An important example of endothelial disease is cornea guttata. This is an extension of the process of Hassall-Henle body formation on Descemet's membrane. As the endothelial cells are stretched over these excrescences, they become thinned and eventually disappear with endothelial pump decompensation. Water from the aqueous enters the stroma and percolates into and between epithelial cells. The swollen epithelial cells form vesicles, which burst to cause painful erosions, photophobia, and visual impairment. At this stage, the clinical picture resembles that of any other bullous keratopathy. Causes might include glaucoma, keratoconus, mechanical trauma, inflammation, vitreous touch syndromes, corneal graft failure, and contact lens overwear.

Dry-eye syndromes are an important cause of disability in the elderly. Tear volume is reduced, and so is the force and completeness of blinking. This is frequently complicated by lid-cornea incongruities (ectropion, trichiasis, pterygiums, contact lenses, lid margin hypertrophy), or orbicularis weakness. Finally, corneal sensitivity may be decreased. The problem, therefore, is not only a dry eye but the absence of a normal blink in response to the dryness. This results in dry spots (dellen), which may progress to erosion and ulceration. Symptoms include irritation, foreign-body sensation, intolerance to dust and smoke, and, occasionally, excessive tearing.

Exposure keratopathy is a variant of dry-eye syndromes in which, because of proptosis or lagophthalmos, the cornea is inadequately protected from tear evaporation. When exposure is coupled to loss of corneal sensitivity, trophic effects can quickly lead to disaster (neuroparalytic keratopathy).

Corneal injuries are common; some causes are abrasions, foreign bodies, chemicals, ultraviolet exposure, and excessive use of contact lenses. Most heal uneventfully and, if not too deep, without significant scarring. In some cases, however, the patient suffers recurrent erosions that present a clinical challenge. The epithelium repeatedly breaks down following some minor injury such as a fingernail scratch. Strangely, the recurrence is sometimes at a site different from that of the initial injury. The clinical picture is characteristic and the diagnosis can almost be made from the history. The patient, weeks or months after the original injury has healed, notes a sudden, sharp pain in the eye on awakening associated with all the other features of an abrasion. The pathology is not clearly understood but is apparently related to some defect in the synthesis of the basement membrane, which holds epithelial cells to the underlying Bowman's membrane.

Corneal neoplasms are rare. Important in the elderly are papillomas, Bowen's disease, and melanomas. Bowen's disease generally occurs at the limbus as an elevated, highly vascularized, gelatinous tissue. Diagnosis is confirmed by biopsy.

The normal cornea is avascular, and this protects it from immune mechanisms. Pathologic neovascularization diminishes this isolation and makes prognosis of keratoplasty less favorable. Indications for corneal grafting might include keratoconus, advanced corneal guttata, dense corneal scars, trauma, degenerative ulcers, and neoplasms. Grafts may be total or partial and are designed to achieve optical and/or therapeutic goals. The associated risks are warranted only when vision is considerably impaired.

Diseases of the Lens

Cataracts are naturally a major topic in any discussion of ocular disease in the aged.[15] The histopathology, despite varied clinical appearance, is remarkably uniform: degeneration and atrophy of epithelium, water clefts in the cortex, lens fiber fragmentation, and deposits of crystals such as calcium and cholesterol.

Whatever the means, the symptomatic end is equally simple: progressive visual impairment. The rate of progression can be months to years; patients should therefore be reassured that one or two opacities do not require immediate or even eventual surgery.

The causes of cataract can be congenital, toxic, metabolic, traumatic, or senescent. Although our discussion will be limited to the last, other causes should be kept in mind in the differential diagnosis. For example, diabetes may induce a specific type of cataract, but it also predisposes to ordinary senile cataracts at an earlier age.

Senile cataract is the most common disorder of the crystalline lens. The opacities may be classified as cortical, subcortical, and nuclear. In advanced stages, these coalesce. Cortical cataracts are characterized by translucent grayish spokes, flakes, and dots arranged radially. Subcapsular opacities usually involve the posterior poles and appear as irregular granules, vacuoles, and crystals of various colors. Nuclear cataracts are an exaggeration of the yellow aging change and may, by swelling, cause a myopic shift in refraction. Although senile cataract is a bilateral disorder, it is usually asymmetric; one eye may be involved months to years before the other.

In evaluating visual disability from cataract, distance acuity tests may be supplemented by other findings.[16] Some cataracts interfere more with far vision; others, with near vision. Glare may also be more incapacitating outdoors. A cleft or vacuole can cause monocular diplopia. Lens swelling produces transient refractive changes, and the patient may even be able to read without glasses. Sequential spectacle changes may restore useful vision for a time. A record of such refractive changes is helpful in choosing proper power for an intraocular lens implant.

The decision to operate for cataracts is based on three questions: What is the patient's disability? Will the operation reduce this disability? And what are the risks of adding to the disability? The primary indication is when patients can no longer carry out activities important to them. This will depend on age, occupation, driving, avocation, mental status, whether they must care for themselves, and so on. It follows that cataract surgery is sometimes necessary on an eye that is not in perfect health in patients who are not in the peak of condition. Balancing risks and rewards is, of course, the essence of surgical judgment. The choice between a visual result that may not be ideal versus a procedure that is never totally innocuous is always an individual matter. Results must be calculated not by what is taken but by what is left.

Several postoperative complications require immediate attention. These include loss of the anterior chamber; wound leakage, which sets the stage for ciliochoroidal detachment, hypotony, and potential infection; epithelial downgrowth; pupillary block glaucoma; vitreous touch syndromes; endothelial decompensation and corneal edema; implant dislocation; the "ugh" syndrome of pseudophakia (uveitis, glaucoma, and hyphema); ischemic optic neuropathy; endophthalmitis; cystoid macular edema; and retinal detachment. Retained lens material or posterior capsular opacification can be treated with lasers.

Cystoid macular edema is a condition of unknown etiology that is, unfortunately, a complication of cataract surgery. Typically, 1 to 3 months after surgery, acuity decreases several lines and the eye becomes irritable and photophobic with circumcorneal injection. Ophthalmoscopy may show little, or there may be some yellow deposits and cysts in the macula. The cystoid spaces are best seen with fluorescein angiography, which demonstrates the characteristic honeycomb leakage. Vitreous traction has been implicated but does not seem to be a major cause. Permanent macular degeneration may follow persistent edema.

Diseases of the Uveal Tract

Uveitis in the aged might be associated with surgical trauma, hypersensitivity to drugs or crystalline lens material, reactions to degeneration products in chronically sick eyes, intraocular tumors, systemic infections, severe ischemia, herpes zoster ophthalmicus, and intraocular foreign bodies.[17]

The signs and symptoms of anterior uveitis are rather typical. Pain results from irritation of the ciliary nerves and is referred to the eye or periorbital area. It is aggravated by light and pressure. Pain and photophobia are more severe in acute than in chronic iridocyclitis. Tearing is a minor feature and is secondary to reflex irritation of corneal and ciliary nerves. Circumcorneal injection differs from conjunctival hyperemia by its violet hue and the fact that the vessels do not blanch with topical vasoconstrictors. Blurred vision may be due to ciliary spasm, exudation into the anterior chamber, or macular edema. Prolonged inflammation may result in deposits of pigment and fibrous proliferation from the iris onto the lens capsule. This and an associated glaucoma with corneal edema further blurs vision. Keratitis can result from extension of inflammation into the peripheral cornea from the limbal circulation or through damaged endothelium. Persistent corneal edema is usually followed by pannus and neovascularization. Keratic precipitates are deposits of inflammatory cells on the corneal endothelium. Aqueous flare is a Tyndall phenomenon and represents disease activity. It is due to protein in the aqueous and is readily detected by the narrow slit of the biomicroscope in a dark room. Various cells may appear in the slit-lamp beam, including inflammatory cells, macrophages, pigment cells, and granules. Precipitates may be found in the chamber angle and on the surface of the iris. Aqueous containing fibrin may clot or, in some cases, an inflammatory exudate may form in the floor of the chamber (hypopyon).

Bleeding into the anterior chamber is not unusual in traumatic or herpetic uveitis. Iris atrophy results from prolonged inflammation. The loss of pigment is especially evident in heterochromic cyclitis. Synechiae in the chamber angle are detected by gonioscopy. Cataracts may result from the toxic effects of uveal inflammation (complicated cataract). Hypotony is characteristic of active uveitis; late glaucoma is a complication.

The signs and symptoms of posterior uveitis include vitreous opacities such as inflammatory cells, red blood cells, tissue cells, and debris, best seen with fundus biomicroscopy. Vitreous detachment is due to liquefaction and shrinkage. Retinal edema is common, and—if the macula is involved—causes reduced vision. Prolonged macular edema leads to cystic changes and permanent loss of central vision.

Disk edema is usually transitory and is the result of irritation when the inflammatory process is nearby. Active chorioretinal lesions appear gray or white and vary in size, shape, depth, and outline. Poorly defined edges indicate infiltration. Deeper lesions are often obscured by overlying tissue. Satellite lesions may appear in the vicinity of older, healed areas. Retinal detachment follows serous exudation, but holes are generally absent. Perivasculitis may occur from cellular infiltration or by retrograde inflammation into the perivascular spaces. Exudates, bleeding, and occlusion are secondary complications.

Serous choroidal detachment is a complication of intraocular and retinal detachment surgery. The combination of trauma and hypotony causes an abnormal aqueous flow into the space between the ciliochoroid and sclera. The result is a dramatic ophthalmoscopic picture of a large, dark bulge protruding into the vitreous that may be mistaken for a tumor or retinal detachment. The effusion tends to subside after 1 or 2 weeks. The most serious complication is a flat anterior chamber, which can become a surgical emergency.

Choroidal melanomas are the most important malignant intraocular tumors of the elderly. Approximately half of all uveal melanomas occur in the fifth and sixth decades of life. The chief symptom is a change in visual acuity, and this depends on tumor size, position, and associated retinal detachment. Macular edema may cause metamorphopsia. Pain and redness are uncommon. The chief sign is a mass in the fundus (Fig. 39-3). Appearance can vary from a small, flat lesion resembling a nevus to a large, protuberant mass that invades the vitreous. Retinal detachment invariably occurs, which may make visualization of the underlying solid tumor difficult. Pigmentation can vary greatly and may be absent. The differential diagnosis includes metastatic neoplasms, hemangiomas, and discoid degeneration. Since so much depends on a proper diagnosis, patients exhibiting a suspected mass in the fundus must be referred to an ophthalmologist who can promptly initiate ancillary diagnostic tests.

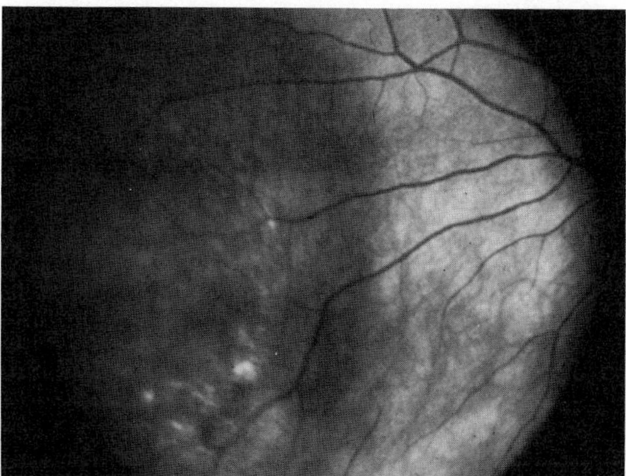

FIGURE 39-3
Malignant melanoma of the choroid.

Diseases of the Retina

Retinal disease is a dominant cause of visual disability in the elderly. One can usually relate visual impairment to the ophthalmoscopic picture.[18] Recent advances such as fluorescein angiography and electrophysiologic tests have clarified the basis for clinical findings. New therapeutic techniques such as photocoagulation, vitrectomy, and laser microsurgery have brought about exciting changes in prognosis.[19]

Despite its histologic and functional complexity, most diseases of the retina produce rather stereotyped changes. These include edema, infarcts, exudates, hemorrhages, dispersion of pigment, vascular changes, atrophy, deposits of foreign cells or material, cysts, holes, breaks, schisis, and detachments. In interpreting retinal lesions, one notes size, shape, location, color, border, depth, effect on adjacent tissue, translucency, and elevation.

Retinal edema may be localized or general, chronic or evanescent. The retina appears boggy, pale red or white, and more or less thickened. Color changes are most evident when contrasted to a normal area. The cherry-red macular spot of central retinal artery occlusion is a classic example. Macular edema is suggested by loss of transparency, thickening, and distortion of the narrow beam on fundus biomicroscopy. The patient may report metamorphopsia and decreased vision.

Infarcts, or cotton-wool spots, are sometimes called "soft exudates." They are white and fluffy, located mostly in the posterior pole, invariably superficial (that is, they cover retinal vessels), and do not stain with fluorescein. Histopathologically, infarcts represent focal swelling of nerve fibers (cytoid bodies).

Exudates (also called hard exudates)—yellow to white lesions with sharp margins—are most abundant in the posterior pole. Occasionally, they are arranged in a circinate or star-shaped pattern. They occur in the middle retinal layers and consist of fatty material. Hard exudates should be differentiated from drusen of Bruch's membrane. The latter are not associated with retinopathy and may fluoresce. Hemorrhages may be subretinal, intraretinal, or preretinal. Subretinal blood has a gray-green color. Intraretinal hemorrhages are punctate or rounded in the deeper layers and flame-shaped in the nerve fiber layer. Preretinal blood tends to form large masses and may have a fluid level. Extensive retinal hemorrhages are usually the result of venous congestion. Hemorrhages with a white center (Roth spots) occur in leukemia and endocarditis. Vitreous hemorrhage may result from breaks in proliferating vessels or from a retinal tear. Vitreous hemorrhage should be assumed to hide a retinal detachment until proved otherwise.

Pigment dispersion is a reaction to injury and may represent the loss or migration of pigmented epithelial cells, or phagocytosis. Although nonspecific, the distribution of pigment sometimes presents as a diagnostic pattern, as in retinitis pigmentosa. Vascular changes consist of alterations in the pattern, reflexes, diameters, and crossings of retinal arteries and veins. Narrowing, tortuosity, congestion, sheathing, obstruction, vascular shunts, and new vessels are adaptations to pressure changes, ischemia, and infection. Areas of atrophy are frequently surrounded by pigmented margins, which distinguish them from colobomas.

Foreign cells are exemplified by metastic tumors; foreign material is usually endogenous and might include cholesterol, hemosiderin, melanin, and lipoids. Bright, scintillating spots overlying an artery are atheromatous emboli. Breaks in Bruch's membrane take the form of angioid streaks, lacquer cracks, and traumatic ruptures. Schisis represents splitting within the retina, usually from the merging of cystic areas. Detachments represent a splitting between the neural and pigmented epithelial layers.

Intravenous injection of fluorescein allows observation of ocular circulation and adequacy of blood-aqueous barriers.[20] A permanent record is obtained by sequential photography. Normally, fluorescein does not stain the retina. Detachment of pigmented epithelium allows dye to puddle in the involved area. Blood and exudates in the retina obscure background fluorescence. Damaged retinal vessels leak dye into the retina proper. Fluorescein angiography might be indicated in diabetes, macular edema, nonrhegmatogenous detachments, discoid degeneration, vascular occlusion syndromes, sickle cell disease, presumed histoplasmosis, and whenever neovascularization is suspected.

Macular degeneration is by far the most important retinal disease in the aged (Fig. 39-4). The average age of onset is 65, and the second eye is generally involved within 4 years. Loss of central vision results from exudative detachment of pigmented epithelium, choroidal neovascularization, hemorrhage, and atrophy.[21] Thinning of the retina may result in a macular hole. In another form of this disease, there is an ingrowth of fibrovascular tissue from the choroid through breaks in Bruch's membrane. Rupture and bleeding of these new vessels causes sudden, total loss of central vision. Repair may be followed by a discoid atrophic scar that varies in color from white to brown or even black. Further hemorrhages may occur at the margins of the discoid lesion. Current interest centers around photocoagulating leaking vessels provided that the branches are sufficiently distant from the fovea.[22]

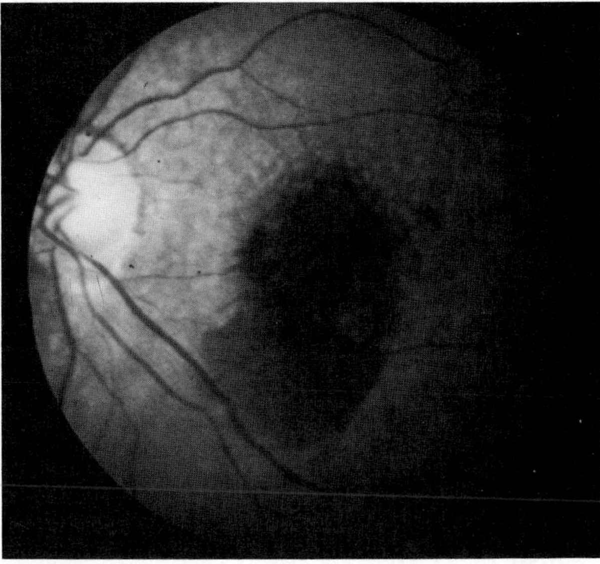

FIGURE 39-4
Age-related macular degeneration with a subretinal hemorrhage. Drusen is seen as yellow-white spots at the level of Bruch's membrane.

Occlusive disease of the retinal circulation may involve either arteries or veins. Central artery occlusion is the most dramatic, the most sudden, and the most catastrophic of all ocular diseases (Fig. 39-5). There may be a history of previous transient ischemic attacks. The cause can be thrombotic or embolic. Most but not all patients have accompanying systemic vascular disorders (carotid atheromas, giant cell arteritis, valvular heart disease, hypertension, or diabetes). Occlusion of branches of the retinal artery usually involves the temporal vessels, and visual loss depends on macular involvement. Obstruction of the central retinal vein also has a peak incidence in the sixth decade. The pathogenesis remains unknown, but concomitant arterial disease and local thrombotic factors are implicated. The clinical picture of massive hemorrhages with dilated vessels is characteristic. The most dreaded complication is neovascular glaucoma, which begins about 3 months later. The relation between preexisting glaucoma and vein obstruction dictates a careful workup in the opposite eye. Branch vein obstruction is much more common than central vein obstruction. The patient may describe loss of acuity or distorted vision. If the macula is not involved, there may be no symptoms. The ophthalmoscopic picture is a segmental area of hemorrhages and exudates.

Flashes and floaters are common complaints of the elderly. Floaters are usually vitreous opacities or

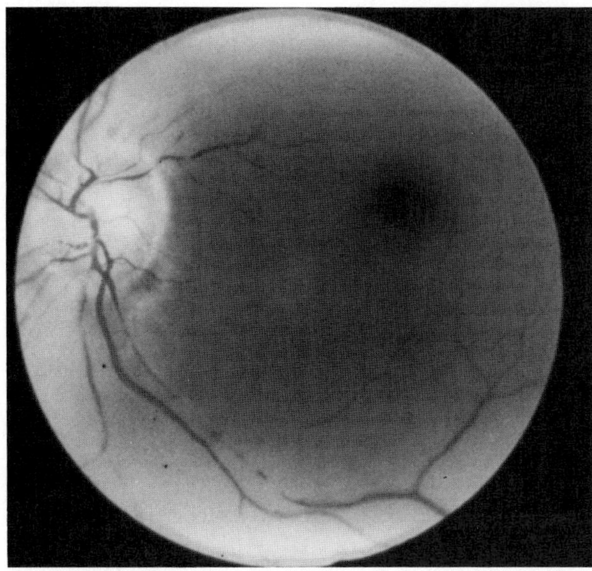

FIGURE 39-5
Central retinal artery occlusion. The blood column is interrupted in the retinal arterioles. Ischemic grayish-white edema involves the inner retina except in the fovea, where a cherry-red spot remains.

aggregates. The closer they are to the retina, the more obvious the shadow they cast. When the pupil is small, as in reading outdoors, the opacity is more likely to block the light and become visible. Movement depends on the fluidity of the vitreous. Traction on the retina or bumping of detached vitreous against the retina causes flashes, often compared to lightning streaks. They differ from the scintillating scotomas of migraine, which are uninfluenced by eye movements. The incidence of retinal complications in patients complaining of flashes and floaters is 10 to 15 percent. It follows that separating the innocuous from the pathologic requires meticulous examination with the indirect ophthalmoscope, fundus biomicroscope, and perimeter.

Retinal detachment is a complex disease that may occur with (rhegmatogenous) or without breaks. Most rhegmatogenous forms begin in the peripheral retina. Predisposing peripheral degenerations that may lead to holes are lattice degeneration, zonular traction tufts, and forms of retinal splitting. The retinal break connects the vitreous cavity to the subretinal space. Symptoms include blurred vision, flashes, floaters, and a curtain of visual loss corresponding to the detached area. Ophthalmoscopy reveals the typical gray membrane, with folds or bulla when highly elevated. Aphakia and myopia predispose to retinal detachment. The importance of identifying and localizing breaks is that these are surgically treatable lesions. An adhesive chorioretinitis surrounding the break is created by heat, laser, cold, or photocoagulation to reduce the risk of fluid undermining the retina.

Diseases of the Optic Nerve

Diseases of the optic nerve may be inflammatory, compressive, vascular, infiltrative, degenerative, toxic, or traumatic.[23]

Inflammation of the optic nerve, characterized by hyperemia, edema, and cells in the vitreous, may accompany any inflammatory process of the retina. When inflammation affects the nerve head, the term *papillitis* expresses the ophthalmoscope appearance. If the retroocular portion of the nerve is involved, the disk appears normal, and diagnosis depends on acuity, fields, pupil signs, and color or brightness comparison. The differential diagnosis of papillitis includes edema, high refractive errors, drusen, tilted-disk syndrome, myelinated nerve fibers, and preretinal gliosis. Although demyelinating diseases rarely start in later life, the residue of previous neuritis may be visible as optic atrophy.

Disk edema, as contrasted with papilledema, is the result of local ocular disease. There is progressive visual loss, an afferent pupillary sign, color defects, and field changes if conduction is compromised. Disk edema can be unilateral, whereas edema from raised intracranial pressure is always bilateral, although it may be asymmetric (for example, if there is prior optic atrophy on one side). Unilateral disk edema may be found in orbital disease, optic nerve tumors, uveitis, periphlebitis, intraocular tumors, papillitis, occlusive disease of retinal veins, hypotension following intraocular surgery, drusen, ischemic neuropathies, and accelerated hypertension. Fluorescein angiography and ultrasonography can help in the differential diagnosis. Papilledema is discussed under neuroophthalmic disorders.

Low-tension glaucoma is characterized by normal intraocular pressures yet complicated by progressive glaucomatous-type field loss and disk cupping. The mechanism apparently is some imbalance in ocular pulse volume and systemic blood pressure. The disease is difficult to treat and may involve central fixation much earlier than would be the case with ordinary open-angle glaucoma.

Ischemic optic neuropathy is primarily a disease of the elderly, with a peak incidence in the sixth decade. There is sudden loss of vision in one eye and practically no recovery. The ophthalmoscope reveals a pallid disk edema. Perimetry shows a typical altitudinal defect, although isolated central scotomas are also found. The nerve gradually becomes atrophic. A recurrent attack in the same eye is very rare, but months to years later a similar, often symmetrical attack occurs in the opposite eye. The second eye may be involved in one-third of cases, and in half of these within 6 months. Disk edema in the second eye, coupled with atrophy in the other, may be confused with a Foster-Kennedy syndrome. The pathology is an ischemic infarction of the prelaminar portion of the optic nerve. Associated diseases commonly found in these patients include hypertension, diabetes, arteriosclerotic heart disease, and cerebrovascular disease, but the relation, if any, remains unclear. There is no satisfactory treatment for this disorder. The differential diagnosis includes mainly two other entities: hypertensive optic neuropathy and temporal arteritis, both of which are treatable. These are discussed under systemic disorders.

Toxic optic neuropathies present as painless, bilateral, progressive loss of visual acuity. Visual fields may show a central or cecocentral scotoma with slopping margins. Among the causes implicated are malnutrition, pernicious anemia, tobacco or alcohol toxicity, heavy metals, chemicals such as methanol and benzene, and assorted drugs.

Optic atrophy in the elderly entails a difficult differential diagnosis. Care must be taken not to call every pale disk atrophic unless there is confirmatory acuity and visual field evidence. The most common cause is glaucoma, followed by vascular, demyelinating, compressive, and traumatic disorders. Drusen of the disk may give it a pale appearance.

Injuries to the optic nerve may occur at any age and can be direct or indirect. Direct injuries are caused by sharp instruments and missiles. Indirect avulsions and fractures are generally the result of head trauma. Visual loss is immediate and often complete. Pupillary signs are positive.

Glaucoma

Glaucoma is a leading cause of blindness throughout the world. Since the incidence of elevated intraocular pressure and susceptibility to optic nerve damage increases with age, early recognition is fundamental in the care of the elderly.

The term *glaucoma* refers to a group of diseases characterized by elevated intraocular pressure, which, if sustained, causes progressive damage to the optic nerve. Two broad categories are recognized, based on whether the angle of the anterior chamber is open or narrow. In addition, glaucoma may be classified as primary or secondary. Primary glaucomas are probably genetically influenced, although the exact cause is unknown. Secondary glaucomas are the result of some prior or concurrent ocular disease or trauma. Secondary glaucomas may have open angles (as in a steroid-induced pressure increase) or closed angles (for example, those induced by a swollen cataractous lens).

Patients with primary open-angle glaucoma have no symptoms; the condition is almost invariably discovered by checking intraocular tensions on routine examination. It is generally possible to distinguish three groups on the initial office visit: normal, glaucoma suspects, and those with definite glaucomatous disease. In the first group are those with normal disks, normal fields, and an intraocular tension under 21 mmHg. In the second group are those whose tension is above 21 mmHg and who will therefore require further investigation. In the third group are those whose tension is obviously abnormal (say, over 30 mmHg) or where the diagnosis is already established. The third group also includes those who have ophthalmoscopic or visual field changes consistent with glaucoma even though intraocular pressure appears to be within normal limits.

Angle-closure glaucoma occurs after pupil dilation in predisposed patients with shallow chambers. There is a sudden sharp rise in pressure associated with severe pain, corneal edema, a fixed pupil, decreased vision, and aqueous flare (Table 39-1). Treatment should be prompt instillation of a miotic followed by surgical iridectomy.

Several factors increase the risks of glaucoma: a family history of glaucoma, advanced age, myopia, previous retinal vein occlusion, increased pressure induced by steroids, diabetes, pseudoexfoliation of the lens capsule, evidence of prior uveitis, albinism, postoperative complications such as vitreous loss, and vascular crises such as changes in blood pressure or blood volume.

How does one detect early glaucomatous damage? The two primary techniques are examination of the optic disk and perimetry. While cupping of the

TABLE 39-1

Differential Diagnosis of Important Forms of Red Eyes

	Acute Conjunctivitis	Acute Iritis	Acute Glaucoma
Vision	Usually normal	Decreased somewhat	Severely decreased
Pain	Scratchy	Moderately severe	Very severe
Redness	Superficial injection	Circumcorneal	Circumcorneal
Pupil	Normal	Often irregular	Fixed—partially dilated
Cornea	Usually clear	Somewhat edematous	Steamy
Anterior chamber	Normal	Normal	Shallow
Tension	Normal	Normal or low	High

optic disk is highly correlated with field changes, the relation is by no means absolute. Older patients tend to demonstrate field loss before disk changes; hence, the two techniques complement each other.

Eyes that have suspicious pressures but no field or disk defect always present a challenge. One must balance potential visual damage months or years down the line with the inconvenience, side effects, and expense of lifelong treatment. Obviously, the higher the pressure, the greater the risk of eventual damage. In the context of this chapter, moreover, the older the patient, the greater the risk.

Table 39-2 lists a number of signs and symptoms which suggest referral for ophthalmologic evaluation. This list of "red flag" findings may also be useful in answering patients' questions over the phone.

AGE-RELATED OCULAR DISEASE: SYSTEMIC ASPECTS

Arteriosclerosis

The most significant effect of arteriosclerosis is narrowing of the vascular lumen, thus reducing blood flow. In addition to arteriosclerosis, narrowing or obstruction can result from thrombosis, embolism, spasm, inflammation, or mechanical compression.[24]

Normal retinal vessels are actually invisible; what is seen ophthalmoscopically are blood columns. When the walls become opacified, there is a change in color, and stripelike densities may appear along the vessel surface. The colors have been compared to copper or, in more advanced stages, to silver wire.

Occlusion of a branch of the retinal artery is usually the result of embolization. Cotton-wool spots appear in the region of nonperfusion and may last for days or weeks. In hypertension, occlusion may be due to focal arteriolar necrosis. The occlusions seen in collagen diseases probably stem from hypertension. Obstruction of the central retinal artery is usually due to atheromatous changes but may be caused by emboli or hemorrhages beneath the atheromas. Rarer causes are arteritis and trauma. The clinical picture is a white, edematous retina with a cherry-red macular spot and narrowed arteries.

TABLE 39-2

Important Signs and Symptoms

Decreased vision not explainable by refractive error
Diplopia of sudden onset
Red eye accompanied by decreased vision
Photophobia as primary symptom
Sudden onset of ptosis (lid droop)
Flashes and floaters (especially of sudden onset)
Unequal pupil size
Pain in eye or on eye movement
Distorted vision (metamorphopsia)
Curtain or blind area in field of vision
Transient or large changes in refraction
Transient episodes of visual loss (grayouts)
Foreign body in eye, especially if high-speed particle
Laceration of lids, conjunctiva, or cornea
Progressive proptosis
Blood or pus in anterior chamber
Fundus cannot be seen (black pupil)
Unilateral loss or decrease of brightness or color perception

Hypertension

The ophthalmic manifestations of hypertension can be classified in various ways, the most popular of which is Keith-Wagener. In fact, there is probably a qualitative change between early and later stages.

The diagnosis of hypertension is made with a blood pressure cuff, not an ophthalmoscope.[25] Nevertheless, fundus changes provide clues to severity and progression, particularly when the disease enters the accelerated stage. These include linear or flame-shaped hemorrhages, cotton-wool spots, hard exudates, and blot hemorrhages. Of course, exudates and hemorrhages are found in diseases other than hypertension; hence, the association between these and general medical features (for example, high blood pressure, dyspnea, proteinuria, and chest and cardiac findings) is crucial.

The malignant phase of hypertension is characterized by retinal and disk edema, in addition to exudates and hemorrhages. The pathology is fibrinoid necrosis of the arterioles. The patient may complain of headaches, shortness of breath, and blurred vision, and there may be signs and symptoms of renal failure. Papilledema is due to accumulated cotton wool spots at the disk rather than hypertensive encephalopathy, although axoplasmic transport block may occur in both. Prolonged disk edema may result in atrophy. Hypertensive optic neuropathy must be distinguished from ischemic neuropathy and the neuropathy associated with temporal arteritis.

Diabetes

Ophthalmic complications of diabetes are partly metabolic (crystalline lens swelling and cataract) but mostly vascular (diabetic retinopathy).[26] Although the vascular changes are evident mainly in the fundus, they also involve the conjunctiva, iris, choroid, ciliary body, and nerves (diabetic neuropathy). Diabetic fundus changes may be classified into background retinopathy (in which the pathology is essentially within the retina) and proliferative retinopathy (in which the changes extend over the retinal surface and into the vitreous).

Probably the earliest change in diabetic retinopathy is increased capillary permeability. This has been demonstrated by an elegant technique that measures small amounts of fluid in the vitreous. Leakage can be demonstrated within 6 months after onset, even in those without clinically recognizable retinopathy.

Although fundus changes in diabetes are not characteristic, they are generally so typical that the diagnosis can be suspected without difficulty (Fig. 39-6). Mild background retinopathy is characterized by microaneurysms and punctate hemorrhages in the posterior pole, particularly in the region temporal to the macula. The arrangement is haphazard, but occasionally they border an area of soft exudates. Cotton-wool spots gradually become more numerous but are less white and less opaque than those seen in hypertension.

Microaneurysms are much more numerous than one would suspect from ophthalmoscopic observation. This has been repeatedly demonstrated by fluorescein angiography. Microaneurysms are round, range in size from 15 to 50 μm, and may be the color of either venous or arterial blood. Aneurysms differ from blot hemorrhages in that the latter are absorbed and disappear. Capillary closure with areas of nonperfusion persists after the associated cotton-wool spot is absorbed. Shunt vessels connecting arterioles to venules appear. Venous changes include dilation, tortuosity, beading, and sheathing, and arteriosclerotic changes are accelerated. Hard exudates may coalesce or form a circinate or star pattern around the macula. The visual prognosis is poor if a ring is formed around the macula or hard exudates encroach on the fovea. Long-standing edema, macular hemorrhage, holes, or membranes signify a poor outlook for vision.

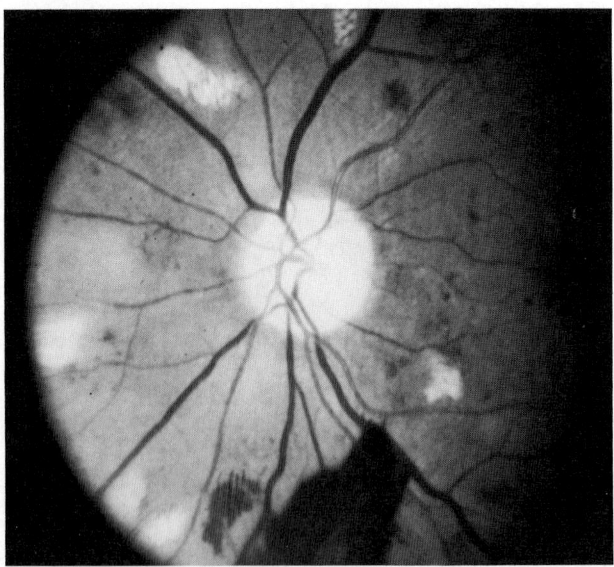

FIGURE 39-6
Diabetic retinopathy. Intraretinal point hemorrhages and flame-shaped nerve fiber layer hemorrhages are seen. A large subhyaloid hemorrhage originates from a retinal venule. White cotton-wool spots (soft exudates) are seen in all quadrants.

Proliferative diabetic retinopathy is characterized by the formation of new vessels, which may develop either on the disk or in the periphery. New disk vessels have a poorer prognosis because they tend to bleed into the vitreous. The vessels are accompanied by a thin film of fibrous tissue that runs across the retinal surface and through the internal limiting membrane. Hemorrhage and retinal detachment result from vitreous contracture.

Diabetic neuropathy may involve any of the ocular motor nerves (painful ophthalmoplegia); hence, diplopia may be the presenting symptom. Aberrant regeneration does not occur, and the pupil is spared. Differential diagnosis includes trauma, tumor, aneurysm, migraine, and increased intracranial pressure.

Giant Cell Arteritis

Giant cell arteritis (temporal arteritis, cranial arteritis, polymyalgia rheumatica) is an inflammatory disease of arteries in older people. The etiology is unknown, but both humoral and cellular immune reactions to elastic arterial tissue have been postulated. Any large- or medium-sized artery may be involved, and there is a predilection for extracranial vessels. The peak incidence is in the 60- to 75-year range.

The importance of recognizing this disease is that it is potentially blinding for both eyes consecutively, and treatment is available that may avoid these complications.

Ophthalmic findings include a sudden, transient loss of vision (amaurosis fugax) that may persist for minutes to hours.[27] This may be followed by unilateral blindness, either partial or complete. The pathology is an ischemic optic neuropathy. The opposite eye may be involved within a week or months later. If untreated, 65 percent of patients develop bilateral disease, and almost one-third of these are totally blind. Ophthalmoplegia with ptosis or other extraocular muscle palsy occurs in 5 percent of patients. More rarely, presenting findings are central artery occlusion or anterior segment ischemia with neovascular glaucoma. Ophthalmoscopy shows a pale, swollen disk.

The arterioles of the affected eye are narrowed and often show focal constrictions. The visual deficit is generally out of proportion to the disk changes. The optic nerve gradually becomes pale. The narrowed arteries persist, and no improvement in vision is to be expected.

The most significant laboratory findings are an elevated erythrocyte sedimentation rate (ESR)—usually exceeding 50 mm per hour by the Westergren method—and a positive temporal artery biopsy.[28] The histopathology shows the occluded lumen and multiple giant cells. Prompt recognition and initiation of steroid therapy may prevent loss of vision.

Transient Ischemic Attacks

Transient ischemic attacks (TIAs) are fleeting episodes of focal neurologic deficit lasting minutes to hours. An attack that lasts longer than 24 hours is treated as a completed stroke, and it is in the prevention of stroke that the recognition of TIAs is important.

Ophthalmic manifestations occur in 40 percent of patients with carotid disease and are the result of transient hypoxia of the retina rather than of the higher visual pathway. Monocular visual loss is therefore more common than transient episodes of hemianopia. Amaurosis fugax may be described by the patient as blurouts, grayouts, visual field contractions, a curtain or window-shade phenomenon, or a cloud or mist in the field of vision. During the attack, one may observe nonreactive pupils, narrowed retinal arteries, perhaps an embolus at the bifurcation of an artery, and occasionally a Horner syndrome. Cotton-wool spots and hemorrhages are features of retinal ischemia. Two types of emboli are commonly seen: orange, scintillating cholesterol plaques (Hollenhorst's plaques) and dull, white platelet emboli.

Ophthalmic signs of vertebrobasilar insufficiency may include transient visual loss, but this tends to be mild and is often unreported. Oculomotor palsies, including nystagmus, are important eye symptoms. Attacks may be precipitated by turning the head to one side or using one arm. Diplopia is uncommon with carotid insufficiency.[29]

Thyroid Ophthalmopathy

Ophthalmic features of Graves' disease include a characteristic frightened appearance because of proptosis and lid retraction, lid lag on down gaze, infrequent blinking, convergence insufficiency, and restriction of ocular movements (exophthalmic ophthalmoplegia). In rapidly progressive exophthalmos, these is chemosis, conjunctival injection, corneal exposure with ulceration, and optic nerve compression leading to atrophy. The proptosis is usually bilateral but may be unilateral. The differential diagnosis includes orbital masses, hemorrhage, vascular malfunctions, inflammation, uremia, and Cushing's syndrome. The most serious complication is optic nerve compression. Danger signals are a central scotoma, color defects, afferent pupil sign, and disk edema. Such findings require decompression to save vision.[30]

Neuroophthalmic Disorders

Headaches are probably universal, but the patient who presents with headache as the chief complaint deserves special attention. Since physical signs are usually absent, a meticulous history is essential. The key question is: In what way are these headaches different from those usually experienced? Any headache of sudden onset, incapacitating severity, or increasing frequency or duration that is not relieved by previously successful therapy or that is accompanied by focal neurologic signs or mood changes should have an ophthalmic workup, including pupil evaluation, intraocular tension, funduscopy, visual fields, blood pressure, carotid auscultation, temporal artery palpation, and whatever laboratory tests are indicated by the examination.[31]

About 60 percent of patients with brain tumors complain of headaches. The pain may be dull and intermittent; it may interrupt sleep. It is often made worse by factors that increase intracranial pressure (coughing, stooping, or straining). Mass lesions in the elderly may include abscess, aneurysm, and tumor. The tumors are frequently metastatic and may be symptomatic before the primary lesion.

The chief ophthalmoscopic sign of increased intracranial pressure is papilledema. Its features include hyperemia, blurring of the disk margin, venous congestion, peripapillary edema with concentric traction lines, and hemorrhages. Filling in of the physiologic cup is not a reliable sign, and an enlargement of the blind spot is of no help except in following the course of the disease. In contrast to optic neuritis, the vision is generally good, there are no signs of Marcus Gunn pupil, inflammatory cells in the vitreous, or pain upon eye movement. Color vision is not affected. Moreover, patients with increased intracranial pressure are generally ill, with nausea, vomiting, headaches, and even fluctuating levels of consciousness. In chronic papilledema, there may be rapid transient obscurations of vision.

Acquired diplopia is a serious, potentially life-threatening symptom in the elderly.[32] The causes may be traumatic, infectious, vascular, metabolic, or neoplastic. In a certain proportion of cases, no cause can be discovered. True diplopia can be distinguished from monocular diplopia by asking the patient to close one eye. Diagnosis is based on accompanying features, and in this way the disease can generally be traced to the orbit, the orbital apex, the cranial cavity, or the brainstem. For example, a painful sixth nerve palsy associated with a hearing loss on the same side may suggest Gradenigo syndrome or an angle tumor. Bilateral sixth nerve palsies with papilledema suggest intracranial pathology. Isolated fourth nerve palsies are often traumatic. Third nerve palsies may result from aneurysm, diabetes, migraine, and tumors. Aberrant regeneration is found after aneurysm and trauma, rarely with tumors, and never with infarcts or diabetes. Lesions of the base of the brain may show visual field defects or other signs of vascular insufficiency. Supranuclear palsies are characterized by disturbances of saccadic, pursuit, vergence, or vestibular eye movement systems; diplopia is rare. Brainstem lesions often involve adjacent nerves (facial, auditory, vestibular, or trigeminal), the pupils, and the medial longitudinal fasciculus.

Transient diplopia occurs in multiple sclerosis, vertebrobasilar insufficiency, epilepsy, myasthenia, parkinsonism, minor strokes, phoria decompensation, and intermittent squint. The presence of a head tilt means that fusion is present in some directions of gaze. Mechanical mechanisms of diplopia have no neural pattern. Peripheral neuropathies may involve any nerve branch.

Involvement of the extrapyramidal system—evident as rigidity, hypokinesia, flexed posture, and tremor—is common in the aged. Drug-induced parkinsonism should be ruled out. Disturbances of vertical gaze and lid movement, oculogyric crises, and blepharospasm are the usual ophthalmic findings.

Myasthenia gravis is a muscular disease that can occur at any age and in either sex. In males, the peak incidence is in the sixth and seventh decades. Bilateral ptosis or other extraocular muscle weakness occurs in 90 percent of cases. Weakness progresses with exercise or during the day. Pupils are never affected.

Joint and muscular disease in the elderly is frequently treated with corticosteroids. Steroid-induced glaucoma and cataracts, therefore, deserve special mention. Tonometry will reveal a rise in pressure, and funduscopy may show disk changes. The crystalline lens often exhibits posterior capsular opacities, and the patient may complain of glare, halos, monocular diplopia, and decreased vision.

This chapter has, of necessity, emphasized the constraints of age; little was said of its possibilities. But there is health as well as disease, pleasure as well as pain, growth as well as decay, life as well as death. The rules for caring for the old are also, it seems to me, good rules for growing old: to do what we can, the best we can, while we can.

REFERENCES

1. Sekuler R et al: *Aging and Human Visual Function.* New York, Liss, 1982.
2. Korting GW: *The Skin and the Eye.* Philadelphia, Saunders, 1973.
3. Coles WH: *Ophthalmology: A Diagnostic Text.* Baltimore, Williams & Wilkins, 1989.
4. Apple DJ: *Clinicopathologic Correlation of Ocular Disease.* St Louis, Mosby, 1978.
5. Walsh TJ: *Visual Fields.* San Francisco, American Academy of Ophthalmology, 1990.
6. Selhorst JB: The pupil and its disorders. *Neurol Clin* 1:859, 1983.
7. Vaughan D, Asbury T: *General Ophthalmology.* Los Altos, CA, Lange, 1980.
8. Michaels DD: *Visual Optics and Refraction,* 3d ed. St Louis, Mosby, 1985.
9. Jones IS: *Diseases of the Orbit.* New York, Harper & Row, 1979.
10. Reese AB: *Tumors of the Eye.* New York, Harper & Row, 1976.
11. Spalton DJ et al: *Atlas of Clinical Ophthalmology.* Philadelphia, Lippincott, 1984.
12. Fedukowicz HB: *External Infections of the Eye.* New York, Appleton-Century-Crofts, 1978.
13. Easty DL: *Virus Diseases of the Eye.* Chicago, Year Book, 1985.
14. Leibowitz HM (ed): *Corneal Disorders.* Philadelphia, Saunders, 1984.
15. Weinstock FJ (ed): *Management and Care of the Cataract Patient.* Boston, Blackwell, 1992.
16. Frisen L: *Clinical Tests of Vision.* New York, Raven Press, 1990.
17. Hedges TR: *Consultation in Ophthalmology.* Philadelphia, Decker, 1987.
18. Ryan SJ: *Retina.* St Louis, Mosby, 1989
19. Ai E, Freeman WR: New developments in retinal disease. *Ophthalmol Clin North Am,* 2: 1990.
20. Berkow, JW et al: *Fluorescein Angiography.* San Francisco, American Academy of Ophthalmology, 1991.
21. Gass JDM: *Stereoscopic Atlas of Macular Diseases.* St Louis, Mosby, 1987.
22. Bressler NM et al: Age related macular degeneration. *Surv Ophthalmol* 32:375, 1988.
23. Smith JL: *The Optic Nerve.* Miami, Neuro-ophthalmology Tapes, 1978.
24. Cogan DG: *Ophthalmic Manifestations of Systemic Vascular Disease.* Philadelphia, Saunders, 1974.
25. Gold DH (ed): Systemic associations of ocular disorders. *Int Ophthalmol Clin* 31:3, 1991.
26. American Academy Ophthalmology: Diabetic Retinopathy, Preferred Practice Pattern, 1989.
27. Slepyan DH et al: Amavrosis fugax: a clinical comparison. *Stroke* 6:493, 1975.
28. Karcioglu ZA: *Laboratory Diagnosis in Ophthalmology.* New York, Macmillan, 1987.
29. Gass JDM, Hupp SL: Retinal and optic nerve head disorders masquerading as diseases of the central nervous system. *Int Ophthalmol Clin* 31:83, 1991.
30. Sergott RC: Optic nerve sheath decompression: History, technique, and indication. *Int Ophthalmol Clin* 31:71, 1991.
31. Haik BG: Advanced imaging techniques in ophthalmology. *Int Ophthalmol Clin* 26: 1986.
32. Cogan DG: Neurology of Ocular Muscles. Ann Arbor, MI, Thomas Press, 1978.

Chapter 40

AUDITORY AND VESTIBULAR DYSFUNCTION

Thomas S. Rees, Larry G. Duckert, and Henry A. Milczuk

Hearing impairment is one of the most widespread sensory deficits associated with the normal aging process. Hearing loss is the third most commonly reported chronic problem in the over-65 age group, the most rapidly growing segment of the U.S. population.[1] It is certainly to be expected that the elderly are much more likely to have hearing impairment than younger persons. While only slightly more than 1 percent of people under the age of 17 have hearing loss, the prevalence rises to 12 percent between the ages of 45 and 64, to 24 percent between the ages of 65 and 74, and up to 39 percent for ages over 75.[2] This last statistic is especially pertinent, since the group above age 75, which has the highest prevalence of hearing loss, is growing at a faster rate than the elderly population as a whole. In the Framingham Heart Study cohort (ages 63 to 95), the prevalence of hearing loss for the most important frequencies was 42 percent.[3] While about 7 million persons over the age of 65 now have hearing impairment, continuation of the current trends suggests that this figure will rise to more than 11 million by the year 2000.

When one considers certain special populations of the aged, the prevalence of hearing loss is found to be even greater. People in nursing homes have a prevalence of hearing loss as high as 70 percent.[4] There is also an inverse relationship between income and hearing loss, as elderly people of low economic status have poorer hearing than elderly people with higher incomes.[5] Hearing loss in the elderly is the most common auditory disorder in the entire population.

GENERAL CONSIDERATIONS

While the insults of noise exposure and the biologic effects of diseases and ototoxic agents are major contributing factors in the etiology of hearing impairment, the term *presbycusis* ("old hearing") is used in this chapter to encompass the sum of all possible etiologies of age-related auditory dysfunction. The effect of the aging process on the human auditory system is manifested by deterioration in each of the two critical dimensions of hearing: namely, reduction in threshold sensitivity and reduction in the ability to understand speech. As early as 1891, Zwaardemaker[6] reported that the high-frequency ranges were the first ranges affected by advancing age. Since then, numerous studies have documented a characteristic pure tone finding associated with aging involving a symmetric bilateral high-frequency hearing loss.[7–9] Loss of high-frequency sensitivity due to biologic aging in the auditory system may, in fact, begin very early, as even infants lose hair cells in the basal end of the cochlea.[10,11]

The loss in threshold sensitivity is insidious in onset, involving the highest frequencies initially and slowly progressing to become clinically manifest in the fifth to sixth decades. Since most audiometers include only the frequency range up to 8000 Hz, threshold elevations that occur in the range of 8000 to 20,000 Hz are not detected in routine testing; therefore, hearing loss due to aging or other factors is not documented clinically until it reaches frequencies at or below 8000 Hz. Tinnitus is often an associated symptom of deteriorating hearing sensitivity, and its onset may even precede subjective recognition of a hearing loss. Males usually have poorer hearing than females at every age.[3,12]

Most often, the presbycusic patient does not complain of difficulty in hearing per se but is more likely to report difficulties in understanding speech. The common complaint of "I hear you but I can't understand you" can reflect not only the problem in hearing high-frequency consonant sounds due to the high-frequency threshold loss but also the effects of central nervous system (CNS) auditory deterioration. As early as 1948, Gaeth[13] observed that elderly patients have more difficulty with word-intelligibility tests than would be expected from younger patients with comparable sensitivity loss. This observation was subsequently substantiated by Jerger,[14] who investigated speech-understanding performance by age decade with the amount of pure tone sensitivity loss held constant. At any level of sensitivity loss, systematic decrement of speech intelligibility was demonstrated with increasing age. Central auditory processing disorder (CAPD) has been reported to have a prevalence of 50 percent in 51- to 91-year-old subjects and is relatively independent of cognitive decline.[15]

Whenever the speech message is degraded, the elderly listener's difficulties increase dramatically more than do the difficulties of younger listeners. That is, elderly persons have considerably greater problems than younger persons in understanding rapid speech, foreign accents, and speech transmitted via poor transmitting equipment or under unfavorable acoustic conditions.[16–18] These difficulties are accentuated when background noise or competing speech is present, as in group situations. Welsh and associates[19] have suggested that these decrements are due to a central integrative and synthesizing hearing disability which reflects a progressive deterioration of the CNS; they have called this phenomenon "central presbycusis." Such problems in the auditory processing of degraded speech by the aged have been shown to occur even when peripheral auditory function is clinically normal.

PSYCHOSOCIAL IMPLICATIONS OF HEARING LOSS

A major goal of medical practice is to help patients maintain function. The capacity for independent living requires maintenance of functional health. Functional health does not solely refer to physical health but also to emotional, cognitive, and social health. Physicians who provide care to elderly persons are in an excellent position to identify treatable conditions that may compromise their patients' functional performance. Unfortunately, many caregivers tend to view hearing loss in the elderly as a benign problem, not posing a threat to functional health. Far too often, when hearing loss is identified in an elderly person, the extent of the loss is documented, but the effects of the impairment are not clearly realized.

Although hearing impairment is most often not life-threatening and does not directly restrict physical activity, it is disabling, since it interferes with quality of life. The psychosocial impact of a hearing loss is poorly understood and poorly appreciated. Indeed, even people who live with a hearing-impaired person rarely fully grasp the all-pervasive effects of hearing impairment on daily living. The many ways in which we depend upon our hearing are simply not recognized until hearing loss is experienced directly or unless a very close acquaintance has impaired hearing. Few aspects of daily living are not affected by hearing loss in some way.

The primary impact of hearing loss is on communication, most notably free and easy communication. Due to the interference with communication caused by hearing loss, a sense of isolation is imposed on the hearing-impaired which can hinder opportunities for education, work, recreation, worship, entertainment, and so forth. A further sense of isolation can result from the inability to relate to the variety of sounds which keep us in contact with our environment, such as the sounds of nature (e.g., animals, wind, rain), the sounds of civilization (e.g., people, traffic, telephones), the sounds of warning or danger (e.g., sirens, alarms, smoke detectors), as well as the many sounds which provide important everyday information (e.g., running water, microwave buzzers, boiling water).

Misunderstanding, mistrust, and lack of sympathy for the hearing-impaired seem to be built into our cultural heritage. These attitudes are certainly quite different from our perceptions and treatment of blindness. Often the symptoms of hearing loss (for example, not answering when spoken to, answering inappropriately, or requiring repetition) encourage other people to talk to and treat the hearing-impaired as if their cognitive abilities were also diminished. This treatment seems to be applied especially often to the elderly hearing-impaired, since associations with senility are also construed.

The two most commonly reported consequences of hearing loss in the elderly are depression[20–22] and social isolation.[23–25] In addition, adverse effects on general well-being and on physical, cognitive, emotional, behavioral, and social function have been reported. Hearing loss can affect the elderly by producing or aggravating embarrassment, fatigue, increased irritability and tension, avoidance, and negativism.[26] Herbst[27] has reported the association of age-related hearing loss with poor general health, reduction in interpersonal interplay, and reduced enjoyment of life. Using a battery of disease-specific and generic measures, Mulrow and associates[25] found that significant social, emotional, and communication difficulties were associated with hearing loss in the elderly. Social and emotional handicaps were reported even in those with only mild to moderate hearing loss. The relationship of hearing loss in the elderly with the symptoms of paranoia has been reviewed by Zimbardo et al.[28] Since hearing loss is typically very gradual in onset and progression, the impaired individual and the individual's acquaintances may not be aware of the deficit. Not being able to hear may create frustration, anger, and suspiciousness that others are whispering and perhaps talking about the hearing-impaired person. Over time, social relationships may deteriorate, leaving the individual in isolation and with diminished quality of life. Bess et al.[29] analyzed the impact of hearing impairment in elderly patients by using the Sickness Impact Profile (SIP) to measure functional and psychosocial impairment. Poor hearing was associated with higher SIP scores (greater impairment) and increased dysfunction. Even mild amounts of hearing loss were related to poorer function. The data suggested that, when compared to other chronic conditions, hearing impairment is associated with a clinically significant level of functional impairment. Evidence has also been presented suggesting that hearing loss is associated with dementia and hearing impairment is correlated with the severity of cognitive dysfunction.[30]

Since progressive hearing loss in the elderly is associated with progressive physical and psychosocial dysfunction, it is of importance for the physician to identify and initiate remediation efforts for the hearing-impaired person. Efforts to improve the hearing of elderly persons can result in a significant and meaningful improvement in their functional health. At the least the psychosocial ramifications of hearing loss indicate the need for early identification and rehabilitation of the hearing-impaired elderly.

ANATOMIC AND PHYSIOLOGIC CORRELATES OF HEARING LOSS

External Ear

Aging affects the external ear and canal primarily by altering the nature of the skin and the cerumen glands contained therein. Cerumen glands are modified sweat glands and are found, in addition to apocrine and sebaceous glands, in the ear canal. The secretions from these glands, in addition to desquamated skin, combine to form cerumen. The aging process causes a reduction in the activity of the apocrine sweat glands and a decrease in the number of modified apocrine or cerumen glands. While there is no correlation between age and the amount of cerumen that is produced, the reduced activity and number of cerumen glands does correlate with the tendency for the cerumen of older individuals to become dryer. This may in part explain why cerumen impactions tend to be more common in the ear canals of older patients.

Atrophy of the epithelial sebaceous glands causes a decrease in epithelial oiliness and skin hydration. Dryness of the skin contributes to pruritus in the external auditory canal and is a common complaint in older patients. The skin itself is often atrophic and easily injured by the insertion of cotton-tip applicators, provoked by the pruritus. This irritation leads to further itching, and the scratch-itch cycle may provoke trauma and infection. Despite this, there does not appear to be a higher incidence of external ear infections in the older age group. It is important, however, that patients be discouraged from traumatizing the canal or further drying the skin with water or alcohol. In the absence of obvious infection or dermatitis, pruritus may be controlled by regular use of small amounts of baby oil.

Middle Ear

The effectiveness of the middle ear's sound conduction mechanism depends on the integrity of the ossicular chain and the dexterity of its joints. The aging process causes degenerative changes in the articular surfaces throughout the body, and, not surprisingly, those of the middle ear are not excluded. The incudomalleal and the incudostapedial joints are synovial in nature and are therefore lined by articular cartilages and surrounded by an elastic tissue capsule. Histologic studies have demonstrated degenerative changes within these joints which increase with age.[31] Calcification and even obliteration of portions of the joint space may occur. Despite these observations, the significance of the arthritic changes as they relate to sound transmission appears to be negligible. It would appear that the effects of aging on the ossicular chain have a minimal effect on middle ear function and are not clinically significant. Presbycusis is, therefore, exclusively a manifestation of inner ear degeneration.

Inner Ear

As with so many other organ systems in the body, the auditory system functions with decreasing efficiency after the fourth and fifth decades of life. Cells of the auditory pathways are unique, and because of their highly specialized function they cannot reproduce. In addition, they have very limited regenerative ability; therefore, the length of their cell life is determined by environmental influences and their ability to adjust and adapt.

Numerous variables contribute to the degeneration of the sensory and neural elements. These may include diet and nutrition, cholesterol metabolism, arteriosclerosis, and the organism's response to physical stress. It is likely that certain individuals are prone to develop presbycusis at an earlier age due to hereditary factors which may make their auditory system less durable and more exposed to both internal and external insult.

A variety of studies have been undertaken to assess the effects of environmental noise and serum cholesterol on the onset of presbycusis. While it appears that individuals with lower serum cholesterol and lower rates of coronary heart disease have better high-frequency hearing than age-matched controls, it is impossible to eliminate the multitude of other factors which may affect the onset of presbycusis. In general, it is impossible to define precisely the contributions of environmental and genetic factors to age-dependent hearing loss.

The clinical manifestations of presbycusis have been observed and categorized into four different types. Early efforts by Crowe et al.[32] and Saxon[33] described two types, one involving the organ of Corti and the other involving the cochlear neurons. These types have subsequently been termed *sensory presbycusis* and *neural presbycusis,* respectively, by Schuknecht,[34] who has also described two additional types, *strial presbycusis* and *cochlear conductive presbycusis.* The four types of presbycusis identified by Schuknecht, based on clinical manifestations and their histopathologic correlates, represent a more precise definition of the degenerative process.

1. *Sensory presbycusis.* Sensory presbycusis is characterized by a predominantly high-frequency, sensorineural hearing loss. The deterioration usually begins at middle age and is slowly progressive. The histologic correlate is degeneration of the organ of Corti at the basal end of the cochlea. Early in the course of the process, the organ of Corti may appear flattened and distorted. These changes are followed by degeneration of the supporting cells as well as the sensory cells and eventual dedifferentiation of the organ of Corti into an epithelial mound on the basilar membrane. That these changes are restricted to a few millimeters of the basilar turn explains the abrupt high-tone loss. Ganglion cell loss parallels in distribution and magnitude the degeneration of the organ of Corti.

2. *Neural presbycusis.* Neural presbycusis is characterized by a sensorineural hearing loss, and while the audiogram of the condition typically has a downward curve, the high-frequency deficit appears less abruptly than the deficit in sensory presbycusis. More importantly, the hearing loss is characterized by loss of speech discrimination which is in excess of what would be predicted for the amount of pure tone loss. The reduced discrimination scores are a reflection of the reduction in the number of cochlear neurons in the presence of a functional organ of Corti. Often there is an associated loss of neurons in the higher auditory pathways, and patients with progressive neural presbycusis may demonstrate other degenerative changes in the CNS manifested by incoordination, loss of memory, and central auditory processing disorders. Apparently the neuronal degeneration may occur at any age, but it does not become clinically manifest until the neuronal population falls below a critical level and interferes with transmission and processing.

3. *Strial (metabolic) presbycusis.* The stria vascularis is located on the lateral wall of the cochlear duct and is instrumental in maintaining the biochemical balance of the inner ear fluids and, therefore, the endolymphatic potential. The stria vascularis is also believed to be the source of endolymphatic fluid formation. Large amounts of oxidative enzymes necessary for glucose metabolism are also found within the stria. It is no wonder, then, that atrophy of the stria should result in a significant hearing loss. Degeneration of this tissue results in a progressive hearing loss which begins in the middle to older age groups. The audiometric pattern is usually flat, and speech discrimination is preserved. There may be patchy atrophy of the stria in the middle and apical turns of the cochlea, but more severe degeneration may occur. In general, the neuronal population is preserved, accounting for the excellent speech discrimination scores which may remain normal until the threshold elevation exceeds 50 decibels (dB).

4. *Cochlear conductive presbycusis.* This type of presbycusis is characterized by a straight-lined descending audiometric pattern. Speech discrimination scores are reduced in proportion to the degree of pure tone loss. A definite histopathologic correlate to cochlear conductive presbycusis has yet to be described. Whether or not this type of presbycusis actually exists is controversial; however, a number of degenerative patterns have been identified and offered as an explanation for the clinical condition. One such theory suggests as an explanation the stiffening of the basilar membrane, which interferes in cochlear motion mechanics. Another theory attributes the condition to hyalinization and deposition of calcium salts within the basilar membrane. Atrophic changes begin during childhood in the spiral ligament and progress through adulthood. The atrophy is distributed preferentially in the apical turns and is less severe in the basal turn. These atrophic changes may alter the configuration of the cochlear duct or may actually cause separation of the basilar membrane from the lateral wall.

It is unlikely that any one given individual with presbycusic hearing loss will fit exactly one of the four pure forms of presbycusis described. Certain aspects of the hearing loss may more closely approximate one of the four types described and implicate a specific histopathologic process which will help explain the audiometric pattern. In addition to changes in the pure tone thresholds and discrimination scores which may be explained on the basis of reduced ganglion cell populations, further disability may result from degeneration within more centrally located auditory pathways.

CLINICAL EVALUATION OF HEARING LOSS

The identification and evaluation of hearing disorders should be an integral component of geriatric medicine, although the subject is largely neglected by many providers of primary care. Despite the high prevalence of hearing loss in the elderly and the reported psychosocial ramifications of hearing loss, primary care physicians often fail to recognize the presence of hearing loss. Even when hearing loss is suspected or reported to the physician, more than half of such patients are not referred for further evaluation or treatment.[26] It has been suggested that often primary care physicians look upon hearing loss in the elderly in the same way that our society at large does; namely, that hearing loss is a common by-product of aging and there is little value in providing rehabilitation for these patients. This suggestion is consistent with a 1980 Gallup survey which reported that only 18 percent of those persons with hearing loss wear hearing aids. The U.S. Preventive Services Task Force has recommended that older persons be screened for hearing loss.[35] Auditory screening conducted in the offices of primary care physicians is attractive, since most elderly persons visit their physicians on an annual basis.

Identification of Hearing Loss

Physical diagnosis textbooks are confusing and contradictory in their recommended approaches to auditory evaluation. A survey of recent editions of nine physical examination textbooks showed that only two of the nine recommended audiograms. The number of textbooks in which specific auditory screening tests were recommended were as follows: whispered voice, seven; tuning forks, six; spoken voice, five; watch tick, four; and finger friction, one. In addition, the methods of test administration and interpretation varied considerably.[36]

Even though the elderly do not generally appear with medically manageable hearing loss, physical examination of the ears is necessary and important in order to rule out potentially treatable conductive hearing deficits. At times, cerumen impactions are noted; however, while the removal of occluding cerumen can indeed result in hearing improvement in some, all too often the locus of the hearing loss is in the sensorineural system. Attention should also be directed to the status and mobility of the tympanic membrane, as past ear disease or perforations can cause conductive hearing loss.

Typically, most hearing-impaired persons will seem to hear quite well in the confines of an office examination room; when asked about the presence of hearing loss, they will inevitably report they can hear the examiner quite well. One must be aware, however, that the office environment is generally quiet, without distracting background noises, and the patient is being afforded visual cues. Even persons with severe hearing loss can do rather well in such acoustically and visually ideal situations. Thus, communication with the physician is certainly quite different from communication in the patient's everyday world.

It is important for the physician to ask the aged patient carefully directed questions regarding specific hearing difficulties, such as problems hearing in groups, hearing soft voices, hearing voices at a distance, hearing on the telephone, and so forth. Not surprisingly, direct questions will often identify hearing loss undetected by the physical exam.

The most sensitive screening tool available in an office is a screening audiometer. Tuning forks are notoriously ineffective in hearing loss identification, since low-frequency tuning fork results usually do not indicate hearing difficulties because age-related hearing loss is predominantly high-frequency. Screening audiometers are simple and low-cost tools, easily utilized by office personnel and relatively easy to interpret.

An Audioscope is a portable screening audiometer housed within an otoscope and is readily suitable for use by primary care providers (Fig. 40-1). It includes four frequencies—500, 1000, 2000, and 4000 Hz—at one of three intensity levels—20, 25, and/or 40 dB hearing level (HL). Studies of the Audioscope's validity show that it can accurately differentiate among hearing-impaired and unimpaired adults and it has an overall accuracy for hearing screening of 75 to 80 percent.[37,38] Snyder[39] has provided a review of the technique and interpretation of office screening audiometry.

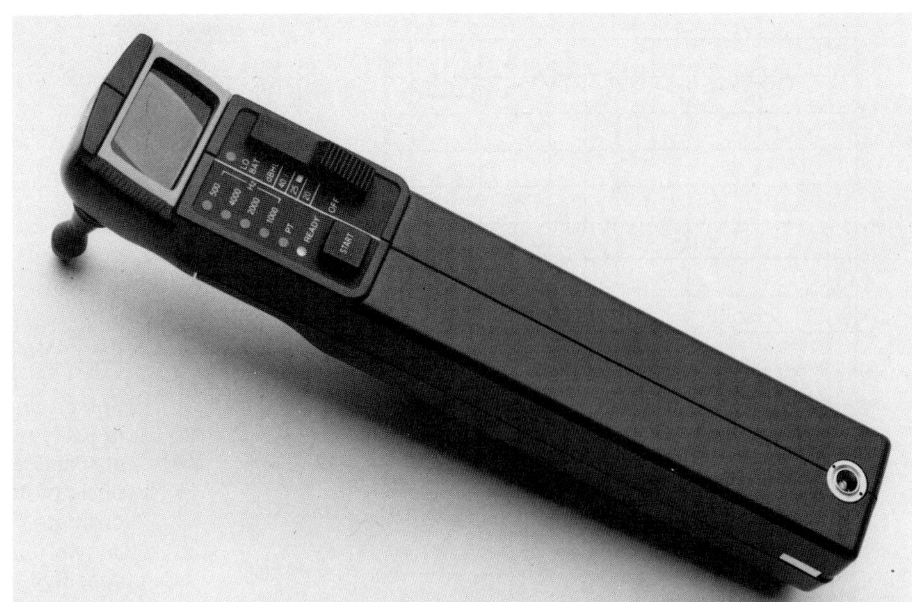

FIGURE 40-1
The Audioscope: A screening audiometer housed within an otoscope. Has four frequencies (500, 1000, 2000, and 4000 Hz) and three intensity levels (20, 25, and 40 dB HL). *(Photograph courtesy of Welch-Allyn, Inc., Skaneateles Falls, NY.)*

In order to evaluate hearing handicap, a number of self-assessment inventories have been developed.[40–42] These tests quantify hearing handicap by including questions about the self-perceived situational and psychosocial effects of decreased hearing on various aspects of daily function. One of these tests, the Hearing Handicap Inventory for the Elderly (HHIE), is specifically designed for use with noninstitutionalized elderly.[43] This 25-item questionnaire assesses the effects of hearing loss on emotional and social adjustment. A screening version of only 10 items is also available.[44] It has been shown to be a reliable and valid method for identifying handicapping hearing impairment among aged persons. The sensitivity and specificity rates of this tool are approximately 70 to 80 percent for identifying hearing losses of moderate or greater degree.[45,46] Information gained from such self-assessment tests helps provide insight as to the extent of the handicap caused by hearing loss.

Audiologic Evaluation of Hearing Loss

The clinical assessment of hearing loss includes the completion of an audiogram (Fig. 40-2). The frequency scale along the abscissa is measured for the octave frequencies of 250 through 8000 Hz. The most critical frequencies for speech reception and understanding are 500, 1000, 2000, and 3000 Hz; these frequencies are used in the AMA computation of hearing loss percentage.[47]

The intensity scale on the ordinate of the audiogram is measured in decibels ranging from a very faint −10 dB HL up to a very loud 110 dB HL. The 0 dB HL represents the average hearing sensitivity threshold for young adults. Sensitivity thresholds are obtained for each frequency for each ear separately, using earphones. Since air conduction testing measures the responsiveness of the entire auditory system, from the ear canal through the middle ear to the cochlea and associated neural pathways to the brain, any loss by air conduction may be due to a disorder anywhere in the entire auditory system.

The use of pure tone bone conduction audiometry defines the general anatomic location of the hearing disorder, since sound transmission by bone conduction bypasses the outer and middle ear. An oscillator is placed behind the ear to be tested and sensitivity thresholds are obtained for the frequencies from 250 to 4000 Hz.

In addition to establishing pure tone thresholds, the measurement of sensitivity for speech and the assessment of speech discrimination (intelligibility) are important. The Speech Reception Threshold (SRT) involves presenting two-syllable words through each earphone separately and finding the softest level at which 50 percent of the words can be identified. This level should agree with ±10 dB of the pure tone average (PTA) thresholds of 500, 1000, and 2000 Hz; it serves as a reliability check on the pure tone threshold levels.

Since age-related hearing loss is often manifested not only by sensitivity loss but also by a reduction in speech understanding, the assessment of speech intelligibility (clarity of speech) is an integral component of the audiologic assessment. The speech discrimination evaluation involves presentation of standardized lists of 25 to 50 monosyllabic words (i.e., darn, art, chief, etc.) to each ear at comfortably loud levels. Speech discrimination scores may range from 0 to 100 percent and scores of 90 to 100 percent are considered normal. The percentage of correct responses is

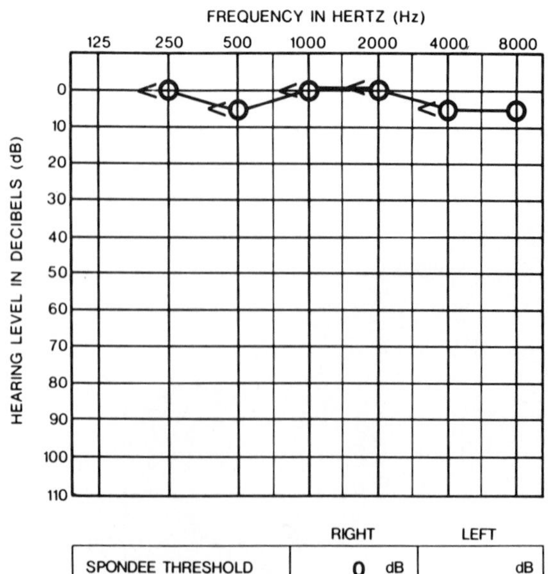

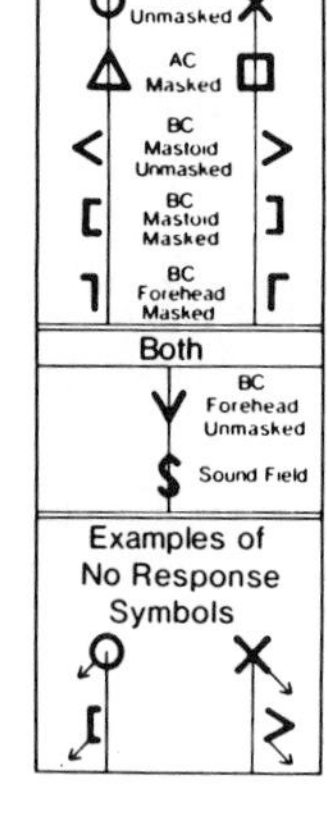

FIGURE 40-2

The Audiogram: Frequency in Hz is plotted on the abscissa and intensity in dB is plotted on the ordinate. This audiogram shows normal auditory sensitivity and 100 percent speech discrimination.

the speech discrimination score. This test is not a sensitivity test, as is the SRT or pure tone test, because the words are presented at levels well above the sensitivity threshold. Speech discrimination results provide information as to the extent of the communication handicap caused by the hearing loss.

Site-of-Lesion Evaluation

The basic audiologic test battery of pure tone air conduction, bone conduction, SRT, and speech discrimination assessment represents the minimum audiologic protocol for evaluating patients with hearing impairment. In the evaluation of asymmetric sensorineural hearing loss or clinical suspicion of eighth nerve or central auditory involvement, special audiologic procedures to define the site of impairment are available. The evaluation of the integrity of the stapedius (acoustic) reflex by immittance measurement is a helpful test in differentiating between cochlear and eighth nerve involvement. Electrophysiologic analysis using Brainstem Auditory Evoked Potentials (BAEPs) provides one of the most sensitive procedures in the diagnosis of acoustic tumors. Electrocochleography (ECoG) also is available for measuring the electrophysiologic activity originating within the cochlea and can supplement information provided by BAEP audiometry. The assessment of the patient who is suspected of manifesting functional (exaggerated) hearing loss requires the use of special audiologic test procedures developed specifically for this purpose.

Interpretation of Audiologic Tests

Degree of Hearing Loss The results obtained from the air conduction evaluation provide quantitative information as to the *amount* of hearing loss. Classification systems have been devised in an effort to relate the amount of air conduction hearing loss to the expected degree of handicap imposed by a hearing loss. Such systems typically use the PTA (average thresholds of 500, 1000, and 2000 Hz) to estimate various hearing loss categories and the expected impact of the loss on speech understanding. An example of such a classification system is shown in Table 40-1.

Classification systems have readily apparent drawbacks and limitations, since they do not consider such factors as etiology, age demands on hearing, or hearing loss configuration. For example, a 70-year-old in an institutionalized setting may not be "handicapped" by a hearing loss of 40 dB HL; however, a 70-year-old active adult may experience substantial disability and handicap with an identical amount of hearing loss.

There has been much discussion regarding recommended audiometric criteria to use in defining hearing handicap in the elderly. The use of both audiometry and self-assessment handicap scales is perhaps the preferred way to increase the overall accuracy of screening programs.[48]

Location of Auditory Impairment The general anatomic area of a particular case of hearing loss can be determined by comparing the air and bone conduction thresholds. A conductive hearing loss is present when air conduction results demonstrate a hearing loss but bone conduction results are within the normal range (Fig. 40-3). The difference between the air and bone conduction thresholds reflects the amount of conductive hearing impairment and is termed the *air-bone gap*. The etiology of the conductive loss cannot be determined by the audiogram alone, as any obstruction in the sound-conducting mechanism of the ear, from the external canal (e.g., cerumen impaction or foreign body) through the middle ear (e.g., middle ear effusion, otosclerosis, or ossicular disarticulation) may be the cause of the conductive hearing loss. Patients with pure conductive hearing loss have normal speech discrimination abilities (92 to 100 percent), since the sensorineural system is not impaired. Speech need only to be presented at louder-than-normal levels to compensate for the conductive deficit.

When a hearing loss is present by air conduction *and* by bone conduction, a sensorineural hearing loss is present (Fig. 40-4). The origin could be in the cochlea, in the associated neural pathways, or in both the sensory and neural auditory systems.

Speech discrimination test results in cases of sensorineural hearing loss often provide important diagnostic and rehabilitative signs. In general, pure cochlear lesions show speech discrimination scores that are compatible with the amount of hearing loss. On the other hand, retrocochlear disorders often demonstrate speech discrimination scores disproportionately poorer than would be expected from the pure tone

TABLE 40-1

Degree-of-Handicap Classification

Pure Tone Average	Classification	Effects on Speech Understanding
0–25 dB HL	Normal	No significant difficulty
25–40 dB HL	Mild	Difficulty with soft speech
40–55 dB HL	Moderate	Difficulty with normal speech
55–70 dB HL	Moderately severe	Difficulty with loud speech
70–90 dB HL	Severe	Can only understand shouted or amplified speech
90–110 dB HL	Profound	Usually cannot understand even amplified speech

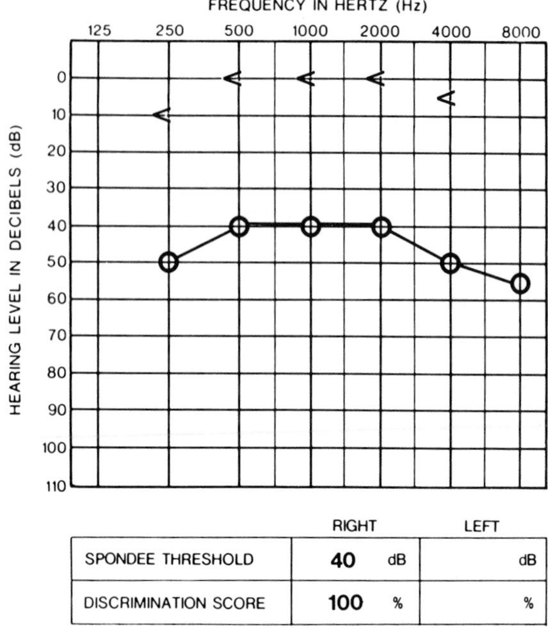

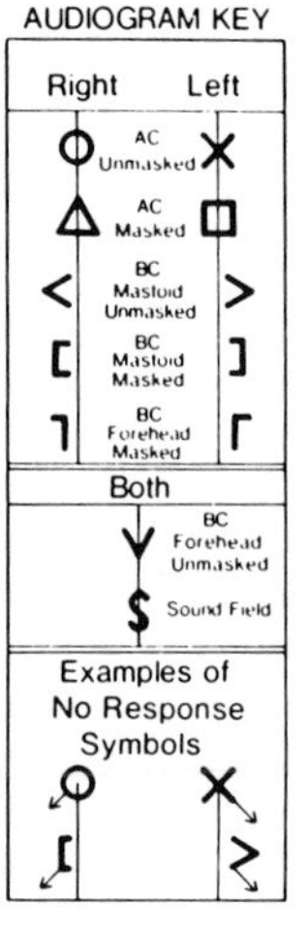

FIGURE 40-3
Conductive hearing loss: A hearing loss is present for air conduction but with normal hearing for bone conduction. Speech discrimination is normal since no sensorineural involvement is present.

audiometric results. For example, a sensorineural loss of 40 dB HL with a 72 percent speech discrimination score would be consistent with cochlear involvement, whereas a similar amount of hearing loss with only 10 percent speech discrimination would suggest the possibility of neural involvement. In addition, the better the speech discrimination results, the better the prognosis for the successful use of a hearing aid, since there is less distortion in the auditory system.

A loss in hearing sensitivity for bone conduction with a greater loss for air conduction represents a mixed hearing loss (Fig. 40-5). Speech discrimination performance reflects the amount and etiology of the sensorineural impairment. Correction of the conductive component by medical or surgical treatment should leave a sensorineural loss only, as reflected by the bone conduction thresholds.

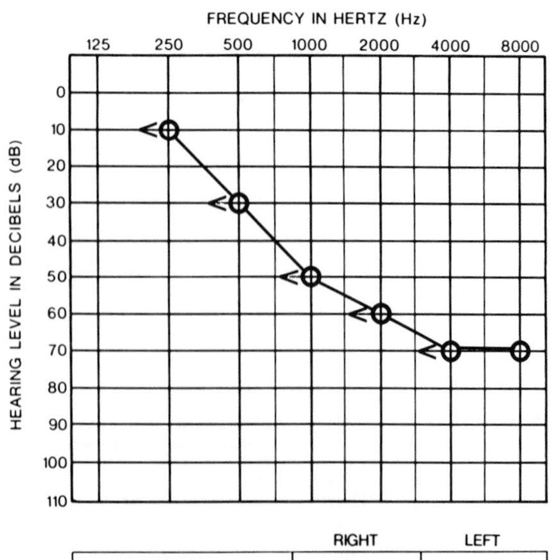

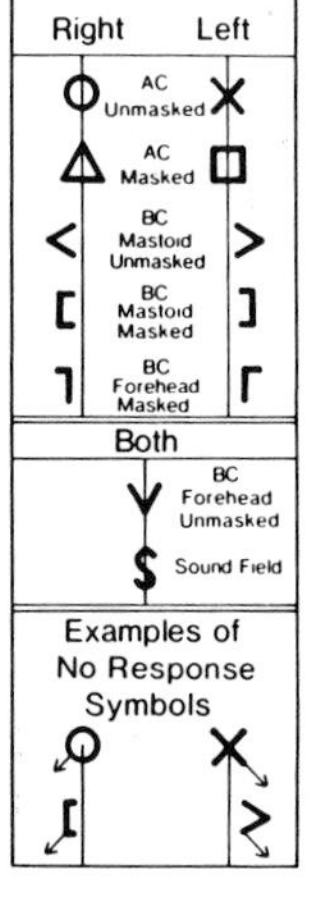

FIGURE 40-4
Sensorineural hearing loss: A similar amount of hearing loss is present for both air and bone conduction. This configuration is often found in age-related hearing loss, as hearing is normal for the low frequencies but shows impairment in the higher frequencies. Speech discrimination is relatively good (82 percent) but is reduced from normal.

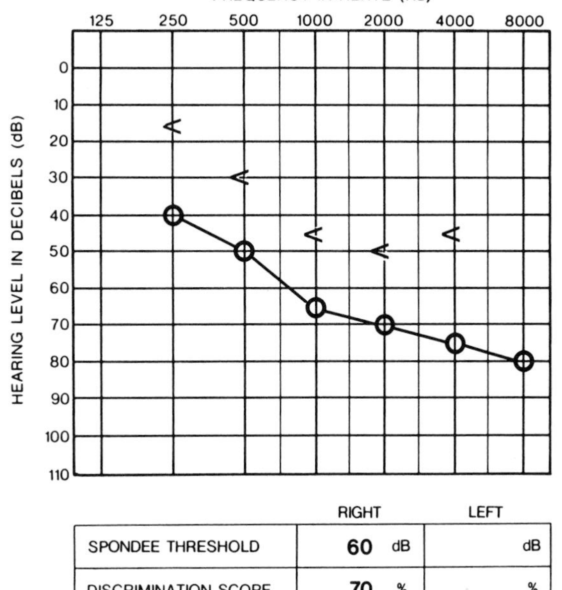

	RIGHT	LEFT
SPONDEE THRESHOLD	60 dB	dB
DISCRIMINATION SCORE	70 %	%

FIGURE 40-5
Mixed hearing loss: A hearing loss is present for bone conduction but with greater loss for air conduction. Speech discrimination is reduced (70 percent), reflecting the sensorineural component of the hearing loss.

REHABILITATION OF HEARING LOSS

Hearing Aid Amplification

It has been reported that of all persons with hearing loss, only 5 percent can be helped medically. This percentage would undoubtedly be even lower in the elderly population, due to the higher incidence of sensorineural impairment found in the elderly. Consequently, the most important rehabilitative approach for hearing-impaired elderly is the hearing aid. Hearing aids are the principal resource for improving communication and reducing hearing handicaps in persons with sensorineural hearing losses.

A hearing aid is simply a miniature, personal loudspeaker system designed to increase the intensity of sound and to deliver it to the ear with as little distortion as possible. While their physical appearance may vary considerably, all hearing aids have the following basic components and functions: (1) input microphone, which converts sound to electrical energy; (2) amplifier, which increases the strength of the electrical signal; (3) output receiver, which converts the amplified signal back into acoustic energy; (4) battery, which provides the power for the hearing aid; and (5) volume control, which permits the user to adjust the loudness of the amplified sound. Significant improvements in hearing aid design have made possible greater flexibility in selecting and fitting hearing aids for the typical hearing loss patterns associated with aging. Hearing aids can be modified to ease manipulation of volume controls, battery compartments, and switches, thereby improving hearing aid use for older persons with manual dexterity problems.

As shown in Fig. 40-6, several basic types of hearing aids are available for the hearing impaired:

1. *Behind-the-ear* (BTE). The components of the BTE aid fit into a curved case behind the ear, and sound is conducted via a tube to an ear mold in the ear canal. While many BTE aids are available, each model can provide varying amplification, as required by the hearing loss.
2. *Eyeglass hearing aid.* The components of this aid fit within the temple piece of an eyeglass frame and are connected via a tube to an ear mold. Eyeglass hearing aids are uncommon, since persons needing both eyeglasses and hearing aids find the combined use of both to be restricting.
3. *In-the-ear* (ITE). The ITE aid is a self-contained unit which fits into the bowl of the external ear. ITE aids are the preferred aids for many elderly patients, as they have the advantages of cosmetic appeal and ease of insertion and adjustment. They are custom-fitted to meet the anatomic and acoustic requirements of each patient.
4. *In-the-canal* (ITC). The ITC aid fits entirely within the external canal and thus possesses very desirable cosmetic appeal. Its amplification is similar to most ITE aids. The ITC's drawback relates to fitting persons with dexterity problems, who have difficulty in inserting and adjusting these very small aids.
5. *Body hearing aids.* The body or pocket hearing aid is the largest and most cumbersome type. These aids make up less than 2 percent of hearing aids, as they are needed only by those with severe-

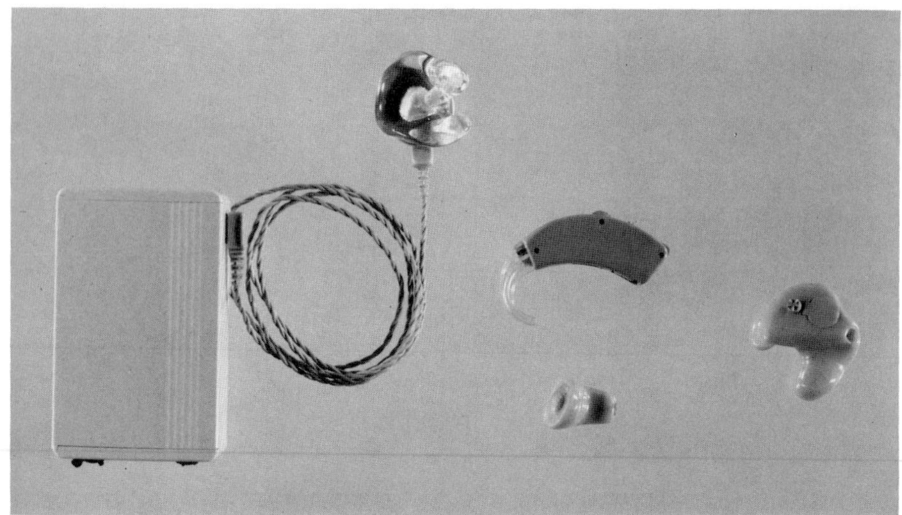

FIGURE 40-6
Hearing aid types (clockwise from left): Body aid, behind-the-ear aid, in-the-ear aid, and in-the-canal aid.

profound hearing loss and those who are unable to manipulate the other types of hearing aids.

Hearing Aid Candidacy Several misconceptions exist as to who should be considered as a candidate for the use of a hearing aid. While it was once popular to specify the amount of hearing loss necessary for hearing aid candidacy, such criteria no longer hold merit. The most important criteria relate to the patient's communicative difficulties, acceptance of the hearing loss, and motivation to try amplification. Whether regulated by state laws or local dispensing practices, most hearing aid dispensers offer at least a 30-day trial period prior to purchase. With this in mind, the hearing-impaired senior should be encouraged to pursue the use of amplification.

It is a disservice to the patient to discourage a hearing aid trial due to the outdated notion that a hearing aid does not help "nerve deafness." Whereas hearing aids were not very helpful for sensorineural deficits many years ago, this is simply not the case today, thanks to the substantial improvements in hearing aid technology. Also, some physicians merely tell their patients that they can probably "get by" without a hearing aid and should wait until the hearing loss progresses. Discouraging the trial of a hearing aid for an individual with communicative difficulties and a potentially remediable hearing loss serves only to invite isolation and frustration. Unless assurance and support is provided, hearing-impaired elderly patients may unfortunately postpone and avoid the use of amplification.

Once a hearing loss has been identified and it is clear that medical or surgical treatment is not indicated, referral to a certified clinical audiologist should be made. The clinical audiologist is a university-trained professional in the nonmedical management of hearing loss, whether with hearing aid amplification, rehabilitation therapies, assistive listening devices, or a combination of rehabilitative approaches. While some hearing aid dealers are relatively skilled in the evaluation of hearing impairment and the fitting of hearing aids, others possess only minimal training and are more oriented to sales. Many states, in fact, require that a hearing aid dealer meet only the minimal requirements of being 18 years old and passing a state licensing examination; there are typically no educational requirements. The clinical audiologist, on the other hand, holds at least a master's degree in the evaluation and rehabilitation of hearing loss. The audiologist is uniquely qualified to provide a full range of auditory assessment and rehabilitative services to elderly persons.[49]

After the necessary interview and evaluation, an audiologist/dispenser will recommend a type of hearing aid or aids, outline the acoustical requirements of the aids, and provide training in the use of amplification. The potential advantages and limitations of hearing aids are reviewed, and follow-up is provided during the initial trial as well as the postpurchase period.

Hearing Aid Prognostic Factors Adaptation to hearing aid use is at times difficult, and successful adjustment depends to a large degree on the personality dynamics of the individual. Often the senior adult is resistant to amplification because of the social stigma associated with hearing loss. Since our culture unfortunately views hearing loss as a consequence of aging, resistance to a hearing aid is inevitable. Kapteyn[50] reported that the variables most important to hearing aid satisfaction were psychosocial rather than auditory. Factors of motivation, personal adjustment, and family support were more related to hearing aid satisfaction than the adequacy of the hearing aid fit or auditory discrimination ability.

Rupp et al.[51] have summarized the important factors for successful hearing aid use in the elderly by offering a "Feasibility Scale for Predicting Hearing

Aid Use." Included in this scale are the following items for evaluation in determining potential hearing aid success:

1. Motivation and mode of referral (self versus family)
2. Self-assessment of listening difficulties (realistic versus denial)
3. Verbalization as to "fault" of communicative difficulties (self-caused versus projection on others)
4. Magnitude of hearing loss and difficulties in understanding (before and after amplification)
5. Informal verbalizations during initial hearing aid trial (positive versus negative)
6. Flexibility and adaptability of patient
7. Age (65 years versus 90 or more years)
8. Hand and finger dexterity and general mobility (good versus limited)
9. Visual ability (adequate versus limited)
10. Financial resources (adequate versus very limited)
11. Significant other person for assistance and support (available versus none)

After the hearing-impaired senior is assessed on each of the above factors, a score is obtained as to the anticipated prognosis for hearing aid acceptance and use. While the scale has not been without criticism, it does incorporate factors of importance in hearing aid success. Not infrequently, however, there are some hearing-impaired seniors who, although scoring poorly on the scale, do accept and utilize amplification effectively.

Aural Rehabilitation: Speech Reading/ Auditory Training

Speech reading is the use of visual cues to aid in speech understanding. The term *speech reading* is more accepted than the older term *lip reading,* for it encompasses not only the recognition of lip movements but also the interpretation of facial expressions, body movements, and gestures. All people, whether hearing-impaired or not, use speech reading to some extent, although perhaps they are not conscious of the importance of visual input in enhancing understanding. It is not surprising that many hearing-impaired persons, particularly those with a slowly progressive hearing loss, develop these skills through necessity and without formal training.

While of considerable help, the use of speech reading alone cannot provide complete understanding of speech. Only about one-third of English speech sounds are clearly visible. While certain sounds are relatively easy to see on the lips ("f" and "th"), others are not visible ("k" and "g"), and some are indistinguishable from each other ("b" and "p").

Speech reading is usually taught in conjunction with auditory training and hearing aid orientation. Auditory training teaches the listener to make the most effective use of the minimal auditory cues imposed by the hearing loss. The combination of visual input coupled with auditory input is superior to either one alone for the understanding of speech. Hearing aid orientation is often helpful for the senior hearing-impaired person, as it includes training in the effective use of amplification, including such basic skills as insertion and adjustment of the hearing aid, battery replacement, and manipulation of the hearing aid and the environment. Such programs are often held at senior citizen centers, community speech and hearing centers, and university audiology clinics. Aural rehabilitation strategies also try to teach the patient to be a more assertive listener. Those persons who quietly accept not understanding merely invite continued social isolation. Self-help groups are available; most notable is the Self Help for Hard of Hearing People (SHHH) organization, which offers local groups as well as an active national organization and a journal. The hearing-impaired listener should also inform others as to the most effective means of communication. Table 40-2 lists several considerations that are of importance to the listener and should be used by those who interact with hearing-impaired persons.

Assistive Listening Devices (ALDs)

Although substantial improvements have been achieved in hearing aid design and application, few of the hearing-impaired, if any, can ever come close to achieving normal auditory functioning with the use of a hearing aid alone. The inherent physiologic restrictions imposed by age-related hearing loss, coupled with the electronic limitations of hearing aids, render normal hearing impossible, especially considering the levels of noise and background interference found in most public places. The amplification of unwanted

TABLE 40-2

Guidelines for Communicating with the Hearing-Impaired

- Get listener's attention before speaking.
- Face listener directly to afford visual cues (do not cover mouth while talking or turn face away).
- Try to reduce background noise (turn down TV, radio, etc.).
- Use facial expressions and gestures.
- Speak slowly and clearly with more pauses than usual.
- Speak only slightly louder than normal; do not shout.
- Rephrase message if listener does not understand, rather than repeating it word for word.
- Alert listener to changes in topic before proceeding.
- Do not turn and walk away while talking.

sounds (e.g., others talking in a crowd, background noise, or ventilation) by a hearing aid often causes the desired message to be rendered unintelligible.

Assistive listening devices (ALDs) comprise a growing number of situation-specific amplification systems designed for use in difficult listening situations. ALDs generally use a microphone placed close to the desired sound source (e.g., a television, theater stage, or speaker's podium), and sound is directly transmitted to the listener; transmission methods include infrared, audio loop, FM radio, or direct audio input. Such direct transmission of sound to the listener improves the signal-to-noise ratio. That is, the desired message is enhanced while competing extraneous noises are decreased, thus permitting improved comprehension. These ALDs are becoming more available in churches, theaters, and classrooms, enabling hearing-impaired seniors to avoid the isolation imposed by the inability to hear a sermon, play, or public address.

Amplified telephones, low-frequency doorbells and telephone ringers, and closed-captioned TV decoders are just a few examples of a number of devices currently available for the hearing-impaired for everyday use. Flashing alarm clocks, alarm bed vibrators, and flashing smoke detectors provide valuable help for severely hearing-impaired individuals. Telephone communication is now possible for severely hearing-impaired people with the use of telephone devices for the deaf (TDDs). These instruments use a typed (written) message which is transmitted to a light-emitting diode (LED) display and/or printer.

While "treatment" of sensorineural hearing impairments with hearing aid amplification, assistive listening devices, and/or aural rehabilitation therapy does not "cure" the impairment or restore hearing and communicative efficiency to normal, such approaches do represent the best treatments available at this time. They will improve the ability of most older persons to communicate effectively and reduce the handicapping consequences of hearing loss.

VESTIBULAR DYSFUNCTION AND AGING

General Considerations

Vestibular dysfunction associated with aging may appear as a sensation of unsteadiness, disequilibrium, or true vertigo. Complaints of these sensations are very common in the older age group.[52]

Maintenance of balance is a complex function which depends not only upon the integrity of the vestibular system but also on visual cues and proprioceptive input. It is necessary, of course, that the more central pathways also be intact to integrate the signals from the periphery. Just as it affects other parts of the body, aging affects the visual and proprioceptive systems as well as central processing, all of which contribute to the patient's disequilibrium. Clearly, imbalance in the aged individual is not solely a result of vestibular degeneration but is, instead, multifactorial. As is true of the cochlea, the peripheral vestibular sensory cells have little or no capacity for regeneration. The peripheral and the more central portions of the vestibular system are also subject to the effects of vascular insufficiency, which may compound the problem.

Clinical Evaluation of Vestibular Problems

The evaluation of an elderly dizzy patient must be designed to consider multiple diagnostic possibilities. A thorough history will often indicate the diagnosis. A recent report on geriatric patients seen in a neuro-otology clinic indicates that nearly 70 percent of patients could be diagnosed by history.[53] An accurate description of the dizziness that the geriatric patient experiences is important when obtaining the history. "The sensation of dizziness" can mean a number of possibilities to the patient. Descriptions of dizziness that are important to differentiate are light-headedness, imbalance or disequilibrium, and vertigo—the perception of motion. This description of dizziness should then be quantified, thereby suggesting the site of lesion. Dizziness that results from a peripheral (vestibular) lesion is typically severe and disabling, with abrupt onset, and is often associated with nausea and vomiting. On the other hand, central lesions are less disabling and nausea with them is uncommon. Patients with systemic causes for their dizziness will frequently have other demonstrable neurologic or ophthalmologic deficits. Moreover, a history of cardiac or peripheral vascular disease would suggest that these problems are affecting the balance system. Finally, one should always inquire about medications that a patient is taking. A number of medications catalogued in the *Physicians' Desk Reference* list dizziness, light-headedness, imbalance, or vertigo among their adverse effects.

After a careful history is obtained, a directed physical exam will probably suggest or confirm the diagnosis. The gerontologist can perform otoscopy to rule out any middle ear disease that could be affecting the labyrinth. Basic audiometric evaluation should include tuning fork tests (Rinne and Weber) or testing with the three-frequency air conduction audiometer that can be found in many offices. Next, a routine cardiovascular exam should include auscultation for neck bruits. Cardiac tests that can be considered include an electrocardiogram, Holter monitoring, or echocardiography. The geriatrician should then perform a careful neurologic exam. Attention should be focused on visual acuity and visual fields by confrontation. In addition, testing for nystagmus should be performed. This should include gaze fixation, as spontaneous nystagmus may become apparent with gaze fixation. One type of nystagmus that should not be missed is vertical nystagmus, which is pathognomonic for central causes of dizziness. Also, complete cranial nerve examination may reveal intracranial pathology. The Romberg test, tandem gait, and past pointing are all tests of CNS integration for balance. These tests are nonspecific for peripheral vestibular lesions. The Hallpike maneuvers, though, can help establish a peripheral site of lesion.

With a little practice, the geriatrician can perform the Hallpike maneuvers to establish the diagnosis of benign positional vertigo (BPV). This is one of the most frequent causes of vestibular disorders in the elderly.[54] There is a classic history of BPV: episodic vertigo, episodes usually lasting less than 1 min, and episodes provoked by rapidly changing positions. Most BPV patients will display nystagmus during Hallpike testing, which is the diagnostic test of choice. This test can be performed in the office with a table. The patient is first sitting with his or her head at a 45-degree rotation and with eyes open. Then the examiner, holding the patient's head, quickly moves the patient supine, with the head hanging over the end of the examining table. The examiner then tells the patient to stare straight ahead. The patient's eyes are then observed for at least 20 sec. The patient is then returned to the sitting position and the same maneuver is performed with the head turned in the opposite direction.

Patients with BPV will demonstrate nystagmus with four characteristics when the affected ear is placed down. First, the nystagmus is delayed in onset and in direction (fast component) toward the downward ear. Second, the nystagmus is transient with a rapid crescendo, followed by a gradual decrease in intensity. Third, the patient experiences vertigo accompanying the nystagmus. Fourth, the nystagmus is fatigable. Other pathologies that produce dizziness can also produce nystagmus during the Hallpike maneuvers, but the observed nystagmus is invariably different in some manner than that just described for BPV.

Laboratory investigations are usually not helpful for peripheral lesions but may be of use for other potential etiologies of dizziness. Basic screening tests include complete blood count, sedimentation rate, and a metabolic profile. Suspected central lesions should be evaluated by computed tomography (CT), often with the use of intravenous contrast. More recently, magnetic resonance imaging (MRI) has supplanted CT as the imaging modality of choice for CNS lesions. For example, MRI is now considered the "gold standard" to diagnose acoustic neuroma.

Neurootologists are frequently asked to see elderly patients with dizziness complaints when the etiology is not apparent. The first task for the neurootologist is to exclude middle ear pathology by microotoscopy examination and then to do a complete audiometric evaluation. The configuration of the pure tone audiogram, asymmetry, and any air-bone gap may suggest the potential cause of dizziness. Probably the most objective test for vestibular lesions is electronystagmography (ENG). This test employs the corneoretinal potential as electrodes are placed around the eyes to measure eye movements. Several tasks are asked of the patient: visual pursuit, gaze fixation, tracking, and Hallpike maneuvers. There is also bithermal caloric testing of the horizontal semicircular canal. The Hallpike maneuver and caloric testing are most specific for peripheral lesions. However, in interpreting the results of ENG, it must be remembered that, in the elderly, there are variable changes in response to stimulation of the vestibular apparatus.[55] There are two other tests that may provide some useful information. The rotational chair test is an evaluation of bilateral stimulation to the horizontal semicircular canal and the vestibuloocular reflex. Posturography can assess the vestibulospinal system. Both of these tests lack specificity for determining unilateral lesions.[56]

The subjective sensation of dizziness is generally more difficult for an elderly patient to define than is an age-related hearing loss. Patients describe the sensation of dizziness in a variety of ways, according to their perceptions of the balance distortion. It is the responsibility of the clinician, therefore, to differentiate those conditions which produce nonvestibular dizziness from true vestibular dysfunction. In the elderly individual, conditions that produce true vestibular dysfunction are multiple and include central neurologic causes and metabolic imbalance, vascular insufficiency, and drug effects, among others. The reader is also referred to Chaps. 107 and 120 for discussions of syncope and gait disorders, respectively, both of which will affect the geriatric patient's perception of dizziness.

Anatomic and Physiologic Correlates of Vestibular Dysfunction

It is very likely that the vestibular labyrinth undergoes the same type of age-dependent degenerative changes as the cochlea. Sensory cell and ganglion cell degeneration occurs, and remaining cells have been shown to accumulate the lipoprotein lipofuscin. The distribution of this pigment within the sensory epithelium of the vestibular labyrinth carries the same implication as does its distribution in the cochlea. The presence of these granules probably indicates reduced protein synthesis as a consequence of aging.[57]

Sensory Degeneration

Age-related degeneration of sensory epithelium may result in a substantial reduction in the number of sensory cells in the cristae of the semicircular canals as well as in the maculas of both the saccule and utricle.[58] Cystic degeneration of the sensory epithelium has also been observed in these structures.[59] Vesiculation within the supporting cells and other degenerative changes of undetermined significance have also been observed.

The otoconia of the maculas are not spared by the aging process. Whereas in younger individuals the otoconia form a continuous layer over the new epithelium, large defects in this layer are apparent in older individuals.[60] Degeneration of the otoconia is a very slow and progressive process. Changes in the surface of the otoconia betray a slow process of dissolution, resulting in absorption of the crystal.

Neuronal Degeneration

Neuronal degeneration parallels the loss of sensory epithelium within the labyrinth. People over the age of 70 may demonstrate a loss of 40 to 50 percent of the number of myelinated nerve fibers present in a normal 30-year-old; this reduction begins slowly, shortly after the age of 40.[61] The myelinated fibers of the cristae appear to be more sensitive to the degenerative aging process and suffer the greatest loss. In addition to the loss of neural fibers, there is also a reduction in the number of Scarpa's ganglion cells after the age of 50.

Histologic Correlates

It is difficult to classify the vestibulopathies of aging, for most of which there are no pathologic and histopathologic correlates. Based on the clinical manifestations observed in patients with disequilibrium of aging, Schuknecht has described four types, one of which, cupulolithiasis of aging, is supported by pathologic documentation.[34]

Cupulolithiasis of Aging Cupulolithiasis of aging is defined by vertiginous attacks precipitated by head position. The onset is usually insidious in the older individual and the condition is chronic. The attacks may occur quite abruptly and cause the patient to fall to the ground. In most cases, because the vertigo is precipitated by head position, patients learn to avoid the precipitating head positions and to live with their disability. Histologic studies have revealed deposits of debris on the cupula of the posterior semicircular canal in patients with this disorder. It is believed that this debris is generated by breakdown and atrophy of the utricle and semicircular canals; the debris then settles in the more dependent part of the vestibular labyrinth and becomes fixed to the cupula of the posterior semicircular canal. These deposits then effect cupular deflections influenced by head position.

Ampullary Disequilibrium of Aging Patients with ampullary disequilibrium of aging describe vertigo which is precipitated by rotational head movement. A sense of rotation may persist after completion of the movement. Patients may complain of persistent disequilibrium after movements which repeatedly exercise the ampullary mechanism of the semicircular canals. This being the case, it is most likely that degenerative changes within the ampullated ends of the semicircular canals are responsible for the disequilibrium. A reduction in the response to caloric stimulation would support this diagnosis in the aging patient.

Macular Disequilibrium of Aging Changes in head position may also be responsible for evoking macular disequilibrium of aging. In contrast to ampullary disequilibrium, in which the inciting movement is rotatory, changes in position relative to the direction of gravity appear to be responsible in this condition. After the head has been held in given position for a length of time, patients may be disturbed by disequilibrium—which appears to be provoked by linear, as opposed to angular, movement. Sitting up in bed is a common provocative movement and may be confused with orthostatic hypotension. There may be no other evidence of vascular insufficiency, however, and the caloric response, in contrast to the condition of ampullary disequilibrium, will be normal.

Vestibular Ataxia of Aging Vestibular ataxia of aging is characterized by a constant sensation of disequilibrium and unsteadiness when walking. The patient's gait is broad-based, and there is a tendency to weave in an effort to maintain the center of gravity. If the patient remains stationary, there is no disequilibrium. Histologic documentation of this condition is lacking; however, it is Schuknecht's belief that more central lesions involving the vestibular nerve nuclei and the vestibular tracts may be responsible. This condition may be the vestibular counterpart of neural presbycusis.

The subjective sensation of dizziness is generally more difficult for an elderly patient to define than is an age-related hearing loss. Patients describe the sensation of dizziness in a variety of ways, according to their perceptions of the balance distortion. It is the responsibility of the clinician, therefore, to differentiate those conditions which produce nonvestibular dizziness from true vestibular dysfunction. In the elderly individual, conditions that produce true vestibular dysfunction are multiple and include central neurologic causes and metabolic imbalance, vascular insufficiency, and drug effects, among others.

REFERENCES

1. National Center for Health Statistics (NCHS): *Current Estimates from the National Health Interview Survey: United States, 1987*. Vital and Health Statistics, Series 10. Public Health Service. Washington, DC, U.S. Government Printing Office, 1987.
2. National Center for Health Statistics: *Health Interview Survey, 1981*, unpublished data.
3. Gates GA et al: Hearing in the elderly: The Framingham cohort, 1983–1985. *Ear Hear* 11:247, 1990.
4. Schow R, Nerbonne M: Hearing level in nursing home residents. *J Speech Hear Disord* 45:124, 1980.
5. Maurer JF, Rupp RR: *Hearing and Aging: Tactics for Intervention*. New York, Grune & Stratton, 1979.
6. Zwaardemaker H: Der Verlust an hohen Tonen mit

zunehmenden Alter; ein neues Gesetz. *Arch Ohrenh-kunde* 32:52, 1891.

7. Glorig A, Roberts J: Hearing levels of adults by age and sex, U.S., 1960–1962. *Vital Health Stat,* ser 11:11. Washington, DC, U.S. Dept of Health, Education and Welfare, 1965.
8. Spoor A, Passchier-Vermeer W: Spread in hearing levels of non-noise exposed people at various ages. *Int Audiol* 8:328, 1969.
9. Rowland M: *Basic Data on Hearing Levels of Adults 25–74 Years, U.S. 1970–75.* Washington, DC, U.S. Pub Health Service, U.S. Dept of Health, Education and Welfare, 11:215, 1980.
10. Johnsson LG, Hawkins JE: Sensory and neural degeneration with aging, as seen in microdissections of the human inner ear. *Ann Otol Rhinol Laryngol* 81:179, 1972.
11. Johnsson LG, Hawkins JE: Vascular changes in the human inner ear associated with aging. *Ann Otol Rhinol Laryngol* 81:364, 1972.
12. Arnst DJ: Presbycusis, in Katz J (ed): *Handbook of Clinical Audiology.* Baltimore, Williams & Wilkins, 1985, p 707.
13. Gaeth J: A Study of Phonemic Regression in Relation to Hearing Loss. Unpublished doctoral dissertation. Evanston, IL, Northwestern University, 1948.
14. Jerger J: Audiological findings in aging. *Adv Otorhinolaryngol* 20:115, 1973.
15. Jerger J et al: Speech understanding in the elderly. *Ear Hear* 10:79, 1989.
16. Bergman M: Central disorders of hearing in the elderly, in Hinchcliffe R (ed): *Hearing and Balance in the Elderly.* New York, Churchill-Livingstone, 1983, p 145.
17. Rousch J: Aging and binaural auditory processing. *Semin Hear* G:135, 1985.
18. Marshall L: Auditory processing in aging listeners. *J Speech Hear Disord* 46:226, 1981.
19. Welsh LW et al: Central presbycusis. *Laryngoscope* 95:128, 1985.
20. Ventry IM: Hearing and hearing impairment in the elderly, in Wilder CH, Weinstein BE (eds): *Aging and Communication Problems in Management.* New York, Haworth Press, 1984, p 7.
21. Herbst KG, Humphrey C: Hearing impairment and mental state in the elderly living at home. *Br Med J* 281:903, 1980.
22. Jones DA et al: Hearing difficulty and its psychological implications for the elderly. *J Epidemiol Commun Health* 38:75, 1984.
23. Weinstein BE, Ventry IM: Hearing impairment and social isolation in the elderly. *J Speech Hear Res* 25:593, 1982.
24. Norris ML, Cunningham DR: Social impact of hearing loss in the aged. *J Gerontol* 36:727, 1981.
25. Mulrow CD et al: Association between hearing impairment and the quality of life of elderly individuals. *J Am Geriatr Soc* 38:45, 1990.
26. Bess F: Changing hearing aid rehabilitation for the growing elderly (CHARGE), in Robinette MS, Bauch CD (eds): *Proceedings of a Symposium in Audiology.* Rochester, MN, Mayo Clinic-Mayo Foundation, 1987.
27. Herbst KG: Psycho-social consequences of disorders of hearing in the elderly, in Hinchcliffe R (ed): *Hearing and Balance in the Elderly.* New York, Churchill-Livingstone, 1983, p 174.
28. Zimbardo PG et al: Induced hearing deficit generates experimental paranoia. *Science* 212:1529, 1981.
29. Bess FH et al: Hearing impairment as a determinant of function in the elderly. *J Am Geriatr Soc* 37:123, 1989.
30. Uhlmann RF et al: Relationship of hearing impairment to dementia and cognitive dysfunction in older adults. *JAMA* 261:1916, 1989.
31. Ethalm B, Belal A: Senile changes in the middle ear joints. *Ann Otol Rhinol Laryngol* 83:49, 1974.
32. Crowe SJ et al: Observations in the pathology of hightone deafness. *Johns Hopkins Hosp Bull* 54:315, 1934.
33. Saxon A: Pathologic und Klinde der Altersschwerhoerigkeit. *Acta Otolaryngol* Suppl 23, 1937.
34. Schuknecht AF: *Pathology of the Ear.* Cambridge, MA, Harvard University Press, 1974.
35. U.S. Preventive Services Task Force: Screening for hearing impairment, in *Guide to Clinical Preventive Services: An Assessment of the Effectiveness of 169 Interventions.* Baltimore, Williams & Wilkins, 1989, p 193.
36. Uhlmann RF et al: Validity and reliability of auditory screening tests in demented and non-demented older adults. *J Gen Intern Med* 4:90, 1989.
37. Bienvenue GR et al: The Audioscope: A clinical tool for otoscopic and audiometric examination. *Ear Hear* 6:251, 1985.
38. Frank T, Petersen DR: Accuracy of a 40 dB HL Audioscope and audiometer screening for adults. *Ear Hear* 8:180, 1987.
39. Snyder JM: Office audiometry. *J Fam Pract* 19:535, 1984.
40. High W et al: Scale for self-assessment of handicap. *J Speech Hear Disord* 29:215, 1984.
41. Noble WG, Atherly GRC: The Hearing Measurement Scale: A questionnaire for the assessment of auditory disability. *J Aud Res* 10:229, 1970.
42. Giolas TG et al: Hearing performance inventory. *J Speech Hear Disord* 44:169, 1979.
43. Ventry IM, Weinstein BE: The Hearing Handicap Inventory for the Elderly: A new tool. *Ear Hear* 3:128, 1982.
44. Ventry I, Weinstein B: Identification of elderly people with hearing problems. *Am Speech Hear Assoc* 25:37, 1983.
45. Lichtenstein MJ et al: Diagnostic performance of the hearing handicap inventory for the elderly (screening version) against differing definitions of hearing loss. *Ear Hear* 9:208, 1988.
46. Mulrow CD et al: Discriminating and responsiveness abilities of two hearing handicap scales. *Ear Hear* 11: 176, 1990.
47. American Academy of Otolaryngology: Committee on Hearing and Equilibrium and the American Council of Otolaryngology Committee on the Medical Aspects of Noise: Guide for the evaluation of hearing handicap. *JAMA* 241:2055, 1979.
48. Lichtenstein MJ et al: Validation of screening tools for identifying hearing-impaired elderly in primary care. *JAMA* 259:2875, 1988.
49. Task Force on Hearing Impairment in Aged People: Position statement. *Audiol Today* 3:17, 1991.
50. Kapteyn T: Satisfaction with fitted hearing aids: II. An investigation into the influence of psychosocial factors. *Scand Audiol* 6:171, 1977.

51. Rupp R et al: A feasibility scale for predicting hearing aid use (FSPHAU) with older individuals. *J Acad Rehab Aud* 10:81, 1977.
52. Sloane P et al: Dizziness in a community elderly population. *J Am Geriatr Soc* 37:101, 1989.
53. Sloane PD, Baloh RW: Persistent dizziness in geriatric patients. *J Am Geriatr Soc* 37:1031, 1989.
54. McClure JA: Vertigo and imbalance in the elderly. *J Otolaryngol* 15:248, 1986.
55. Sloane PD et al: The vestibular system in the elderly: Clinical implications. *Am J Otolaryngol* 10:422, 1989.
56. Baloh RW, Furman JMR: Modern vestibular function testing. *West J Med* 150:59, 1989.
57. Mann DMA et al: The relationship between lipofuscin pigment and aging in the human nervous system. *J Neurol Sci* 37:83, 1978.
58. Engstrom H: Structural changes in the vestibular epithelia in elderly monkeys and humans. *Adv Otorhinolaryngol* 22:93, 1977.
59. Rosenthal U: Epithelial cysts in the human vestibular apparatus. *J Laryngol Otol* 88:105, 1974.
60. Ross MD: Observations in normal and degenerating human otoconia. *Ann Otol Rhinol Laryngol* 85:310, 1976.
61. Bergstrom B: Morphology of the vestibular nerve: II. The number of myelinated vestibular nerve fibers in man at various stages. *Acta Otolaryngol* 76:173, 1973.

Chapter 41

GERIATRIC GYNECOLOGY

Howard D. Homesley

Gynecologic care assumes increasing importance as women age in that minimal preventive care can be instrumental in averting catastrophic gynecologic illness. The morbidity and mortality of gynecologic malignancies can clearly be avoided. Gynecologic malignancies account for over 20,000 deaths in the United States each year.[1] Over half of these occur in elderly women. These cancers are detectable very early; yet, out of ignorance and neglect, women present in advanced stages. Except for ovarian cancer, these diseases can be detected in asymptomatic women by simple screening procedures. Elderly women may be more difficult to treat because of intercurrent medical illnesses; however, age usually has no independent clinical significance when they are treated aggressively.

By the same token, other gynecologic symptoms are largely disregarded out of fear of presumed ominous findings. Elderly women commonly first present with total uterovaginal prolapse. Yet age is no barrier to surgical repair, as vaginal surgery is well tolerated into the 80s and 90s.

GYNECOLOGIC HISTORY AND EXAM

The standard gynecologic history is applicable at any age. However, with elderly patients, it is especially important to ask probing questions about gynecologic symptoms, since these women may tend to overlook them or to be reticent in offering information about vaginal bleeding, discharge, burning, or pain—even of long duration.

Regardless of the presence of positive or negative findings by history, the vital opportunity to encourage a practice of regular pelvic examinations can be lost if its importance is not reinforced by the examining physician. Often, alleviation of a minor gynecologic complaint may develop rapport that will lead the patient to feel confidence in the physician and not reticent about seeing him or her promptly. As a result, possible malignancy may be detected sooner.

Vulva

A systematic examination of the vulva can be performed gently and quickly to make sure that no suspicious or gross lesions are present. Whether they are symptomatic or not, *all vulvar lesions must be biopsied* before any medications are prescribed. All too often, by the time patients with vulvar cancer present themselves to the physician, they have already been medicating themselves for months or have received topical treatment by physicians who failed to examine the vulva.

Vagina

Various sizes and types of vaginal speculums are available for individualized use as required. If present, the cervix should be visualized and the Pap smear obtained. As the speculum is removed, care should be taken to fully visualize the entire vagina.

Pelvic Exam

The bimanual and rectovaginal exam is then carefully performed to look for pelvic abnormalities. The more slowly this is done (while the patient is encouraged to relax), the more accurate will be the findings. Generous amounts of lubrication are helpful, with nearly all of the speculum pressure being directed posteriorly, toward the rectum.

Sexuality and the Gynecologic Exam

Older women may experience sexual dysfunction from many different causes.[2] At the time of the gynecologic exam, a helpful question might be: "Do you have any concerns about your sex life that you would like to discuss?" Simple problems such as vaginal dryness can easily be treated with topical estrogen. Other problems involve intricate interpersonal relations between the woman and her sexual partner and may require a combination of medical therapy and sex counseling.

Gynecologic cancer and cancer treatments are often accompanied by problems in sexual functioning. These may then lead to impaired relations and a damaged self-image, initiating a vicious circle of deteriorating sexual function. The clinician should maintain an attitude of openness to the possibility of sexual concerns among older women. Such concerns should be taken seriously and should not be dismissed as an inevitable part of aging (see Chap. 9).

Women who have undergone procedures that are highly likely to cause sexual dysfunction should be asked questions that might open the door to a discussion of sexuality. Sexual dysfunction should be recognized as a couple-oriented phenomenon. A woman's anxiety about her appearance, postoperative depression, or dyspareunia may be perceived by her partner as sexual rejection and may initiate a cycle of decreasing contact or even lead to erectile dysfunction. Sexual counseling should include both partners.

When a surgical procedure that will probably affect sexual function is contemplated, the couple should be counseled in advance. The description of surgery should not be confined to an outline of the contemplated procedures but should specifically address the anticipated sexual effects. Counseling should include a description of the basic anatomy and function of the genital organs. Illustrations and appropriate demonstrations during the physical examination should be used to ensure the patient's understanding. Descriptions should be accurate without being either frightening or falsely reassuring to the patient. The patient should be counseled about the benefits of including her partner in discussions.

VULVA

Dermatological Conditions

The approach to complex vulvar lesions can often involve the gynecologist, dermatologist, and pathologist.[3] Mixed findings of atrophy, inflammation, and neoplasia can go unrecognized. Biopsy is often needed to clarify the diagnosis. Chronic dermatological conditions may require systemic treatment similar to that for skin conditions at other sites.

Vulvar dystrophies range from atrophic to hyperplastic to ulcerated or cracking skin. The symptoms of pruritus, dryness, and pain can be disabling. Topical therapy should not be considered without a biopsy to exclude cancer. Vulvar dystrophies begin to present from age 40 up. The treatment of dystrophies is nonspecific and at times limited. A complete program of careful vulvar hygiene is instituted, using bland soaps, absorbent cotton underwear, and nonconstrictive clothing. The atrophic lesions quite often respond to topical 2% testosterone propionate in a petrolatum base. The testosterone can be used for years on an "as needed" basis. Steroid creams are also of some use for symptom relief. Often the patient is relieved of her symptoms while the vulvar lesions remain grossly unchanged.

There is no question that there is an interrelationship between the presence of vulvar dystrophy and vulvar cancer in that vulvar dystrophy is present in over 30 percent of vulvar cancer patients.[4] Typically the patient may suffer from vulvar dystrophy for many years before presenting with vulvar cancer. It is uncertain what the true incidence of squamous cell carcinoma in dystrophic patients might be, although it is probably quite low. Interestingly, patients who have radical vulvectomy for their cancer later often have a resumption of the dystrophic process in the areas of resection.

Surgical resection as well as laser vaporization of the involved areas of dystrophy are uniformly unsuccessful. Within 6 to 12 months of such ablative therapy, the dystrophic changes and earlier symptoms return.

Human Papillomavirus in Lesions of the Vulva

Since there has been a recognized epidemic of human papillomavirus (HPV) genital tract infections in younger women, the question has arisen as to what if any role HPV infection may play in the older woman. Increasingly, in many situations, abnormal vaginal cytology in patients over 60 to 70 years of age is attributed to the presence of HPV.

A clinical, pathologic, and molecular virologic analysis relating HPV to invasive squamous cell carcinoma of the vulva suggests a close correlation among the presence of HPV, subsets of invasive carcinoma, and age.[5] The presence of the virus was detected by the polymerase chain reaction and localized in the tumor and in the adjacent epithelium by in situ hybridization of paraffin sections of vulvectomy specimens. Specimens were examined for nucleic acid sequences. HPVs 6, 11, 16, and 18 were detected by in situ hybridization utilizing 35S-labeled antisense ribonucleic acid (RNA) probes and by the polymerase chain reaction using HPV type-specific primers for a segment of the E6 gene, followed by Southern hybridization of the amplified products. The mean age of women with HPV-negative tumors was 77 years, compared with 55 years for women with HPV-positive tumors. Basaloid and warty carcinomas had HPV detected nearly always, as opposed to less than 25 percent in squamous cell carcinomas.

Yet other investigators have reported squamous cell carcinoma arising in condyloma acuminatum of the vulva primarily in an elderly population with a mean age of 70 years.[6]

Vulvar Cancer

Vulvar carcinoma accounts for 3 to 4 percent of all female genital malignancies and occurs predominantly beyond age 65. The white, scaly, preinvasive lesions may be asymptomatic, but invasive lesions are almost uniformly ulcerative. Often odor rather than bleeding is the first complaint.

Lesion size and whether or not the patient presents with groin node metastases are the two prognostic determinants of survival.[4] The 5-year survivals for stages I through IV are 98 percent, 87 percent, 75 percent, and 29 percent. At low risk are patients with lesions less than 2 cm in diameter and no groin node metastases. Traditionally, all patients were treated with radical vulvectomy and bilateral groin node dissection. The radicality of the procedure now depends upon the size of the tumor, site of the lesion, depth of invasion, and presence or absence of vascular and lymphatic invasion.

VAGINAL DISEASE

Atrophic Vaginitis

Probably the most pervasive yet most easily treatable gynecologic disorders in elderly women is atrophic vaginitis. Long years of estrogen deprivation lead to atrophy of the vaginal epithelium. The woman who is not sexually active may be totally asymptomatic and need no therapy. At the other extreme are women who present with vigorous vaginal bleeding. In between are the majority of women, including a few who present with abnormal vaginal cytology at times suggestive of invasion.

Careful assessment is in order for the patient with abnormal cytology, as overtreatment could lead to multiple biopsies and possible cervical conization. The first step in management after a negative initial colposcopic examination is topical intravaginal estrogen. The patient is advised to insert the vaginal cream high into the vagina nightly at first and, within 2 to 3 weeks, no more than two to three times a week. The intravaginal estrogen then can be used intermittently as needed.

Vaginal Intraepithelial Neoplasia

Women with vaginal intraepithelial neoplasia (VAIN) are older than those with cervical intraepithelial neoplasia (CIN).[7] In the majority of cases, the diagnosis is made after cytologic testing. The lesions are nearly always (92.4 percent of them) in the upper third of the vagina. Vaginal intraepithelial neoplasia can be categorized into grades 1, 2, and 3, with most cases presenting as grade 2. The therapeutic modalities available are CO_2 laser, topical 5-fluorouracil, and surgical resection. The CO_2 laser is used most often, and failures are attributed mainly to the multifocal character of many lesions and difficulty in vaporizing areas such as the vaginal angles. Continued cytologic follow-up is mandatory and intravaginal estrogen cream is given the elderly to maintain a healthy vaginal epithelium.

Vaginal Cancer

Vaginal cancer is rare, comprising less than 1 percent of all genital cancers. Nearly 80 percent are found in patients over 60 years of age.[8] These women often present with heavy vaginal bleeding and a history of no pelvic examinations or any cytologic screening for many years. Survival is related to age, with a 50 percent survival for those below age 50 and survival near 30 percent for older patients. Stage of disease is the most significant prognostic factor (stage I = a 5-year survival of 76.7 percent versus a 5-year survival of 18 percent for stage IV). Younger age, location at the vaginal apex, and a well-differentiated tumor are more favorable factors. Therapy is usually by a combination of external pelvic irradiation and local application of radium.

Pelvic Relaxation

Some degree of relaxation of the pelvic floor occurs in practically all older parous women. Anatomic predisposition more than childbearing may account for this relaxation, as this condition is quite uncommon in African Americans. The bladder, uterus, and rectum are supported by an endopelvic fascia, which coalesces into the cardinal and uterosacral ligaments, and by the levator muscles, forming the pelvic sling. Ballooning downward of the anterior vaginal wall, especially if it protrudes through the introitus, is evidence of a cystocele, which can be accompanied by stress urinary incontinence, pressure, discomfort, backache, and/or ulceration. At times, unless a biopsy is obtained, ulceration of a prolapsing vaginal cancer can be mistaken for benign ulceration.

Protrusion of the posterior vaginal wall is a rectocele, which may be associated with herniation of the small or large bowel near the vaginal apex. Women with rectocele may have to strain a great deal to defecate.

Uterine prolapse can be partial or complete. Many women may prefer a pessary, but when the symptoms become debilitating (e.g., difficulty in walking, ulceration with pain, bleeding, or pelvic discomfort) surgical correction may be considered at any age.

The overall limitations imposed by symptoms of pelvic relaxation do affect the quality of life and pose the risk of social isolation. Surgical intervention should be offered for this non–life-threatening situation in spite of the risk of complications of surgery and anesthesia. However, very few women found to have pelvic relaxation need surgical repair. If they have no symptoms, it serves little purpose to stress these "incidental" findings of the pelvic examination.

GENITAL ORGAN CANCER

Based on rates from the National Cancer Institute Surveillance, Epidemiology, and End Results program from 1985 to 1987, 71,700 new cases of cancer of the uterine corpus, ovary, cervix, and other sites (Table 41-1) were estimated for 1991.[9] Although corpus or endometrial adenocarcinoma is the most common gynecologic malignancy, it arises less frequently in older women and often presents early in its course with vaginal bleeding. Ovarian cancer is slightly less common in the older woman, but it is devastating when detected late and is the most deadly. Cervical cancer is becoming less common with more widespread use of cervical cytologic screening. Nevertheless, elderly women may present with advanced disease.

Epidemiological Relationships

Epidemiological studies of the relationship between cigarette smoking and the risk of breast, endometrial, and ovarian cancers have revealed a reduction of risk for endometrial cancer among women aged 50 years and older who smoked cigarettes.[10] No association was observed among women with breast cancer and ovarian cancer.

Vulvar squamous precancers or vulvar intraepithelial neoplasia (VIN) are associated with cigarette smoking and human papillomaviruses.[11] However, epidemiological studies of invasive carcinoma of the vulva have produced conflicting evidence regarding these associations, in part because of a strong association with vulvar dystrophies. A history of cigarette smoking (88 percent versus 28 percent) was more often associated with vulvar cancer.

Surgery for Gynecologic Cancer in the Elderly

Radical, curative surgery may often not be considered in elderly patients with gynecologic cancer; yet the morbidity for this population from radiotherapy and cytotoxic agents may be high.[12] Older patients usually present with more advanced cancers and, as a group, have a significantly poorer presurgical performance status and more concurrent medical problems. Nevertheless, the planned radical surgical procedure can be carried out in 90 percent of elderly patients with a postoperative mortality of 1 to 2 percent. Chronological age alone is a weak index of surgical risk, and elderly patients withstand radical surgery almost as well as their younger counterparts. Vaginal hysterectomy may offer some advantage, especially in the morbidly obese patient; however, the morbidity can be high, depending upon underlying medical status.[13]

Aged patients can safely undergo major pelvic and abdominal surgery if one manages their associated medical conditions in a routine manner similar to that utilized in younger patients with similar problems.[14] The associated medical complications and not age per se should be the deciding factor. Same-day admission for surgery has not been noted to increase morbidity. Aged patients do well postoperatively with routine preoperative medical evaluation and postoperative care.

TABLE 41-1

Estimated New Genital Organ Cancer Cases in the United States—1991

Site	New Cases	Deaths
Corpus	33,000	5,500
Ovary	20,700	12,500
Cervix	13,000	4,500
Other	5,000	1,000

SOURCE: American Cancer Society: *Cancer Facts and Figures 1991*. Atlanta, GA, 1991.

Screening the Geriatric Population

Decreasing use of gynecologic examinations may explain the age-related decline in localized gynecologic cancers in the elderly.[15] In comparing the youngest women to the oldest women, the relative proportion of localized cervical, uterine, and ovarian cancer was lower for all sites in older women.

Screening for Cervical Cancer

Over half of women who present with invasive carcinoma of the uterine cervix have not received a Pap test within 3 years prior to diagnosis.[16] In one study, women who had not received a prior Pap smear tended to be older, less sexually active, less well educated, and to have more extensive disease at the time of diagnosis than women who had received cytologic examinations. Intensified efforts to ensure that all women have access to quality Pap screening services are needed. Older women need to be reached as much as or more than younger women. Physicians need to routinely offer older patients who present with nongynecologic conditions the opportunity to receive cytologic testing. As a public health issue, interventions to counteract the underrepresentation of elderly women in screened populations must be implemented.[17]

There is no reason to exclude women over 65 years of age from screening for cancer of the cervix.[18] Women of age 50 or above are less likely to have Pap smears (63 percent versus 89 percent) than those between 20 and 49.[19] The most positive associations with frequent Pap smears are a pattern of regular patient visits and lifetime of use of an obstetrician-gynecologist.[20] A study of the cost-effectiveness of cervical cancer screening for low-income elderly women indicates that the benefits from prevention programs for the elderly can offset the costs of these programs.[21]

Screening for Ovarian Cancer

Transvaginal sonography as a screening method for ovarian cancer is under evaluation, especially with reference to cost and the false-negative rate.[22] To meet the criteria of a screening test, the patient must be asymptomatic and have no history of ovarian cancer. The ovaries are measured and ovarian volumes calculated. The ovarian morphology is classified as hypoechogenic, cystic, solid, or complex. Vaginal sonography is a relatively simple test that can detect subtle changes in ovarian size and morphology.

Levels of serum CA 125, which is a tumor antigen marker, in patients with pelvic masses can help to distinguish between benign and malignant ovarian disease.[23] Patients with benign pelvic masses rarely have CA 125 levels greater than 65 units/ml (8 percent), whereas malignancies (75 percent) are usually associated with values greater than 65 units/ml. Greater sensitivity and specificity have been observed in postmenopausal than premenopausal women.

The potential value of combining vaginal ultrasound and serum CA 125 as a screening method for the early detection of ovarian cancer is under active study. Data from the United States on ovarian cancer incidence and survival have been used to estimate the potential reduction in ovarian cancer mortality from screening tests with various sensitivities.[24] A test with 80 percent sensitivity could reduce ovarian cancer mortality by 50 percent if all screening-detected cases were to experience current stage I survival rates. The benefit would be greatest among women aged 45 or older. For each cancer detected, there would be at least 50 false-positive screening tests unless test specificity were greater than 98 percent. Universal periodic screening of women aged 45 to 74 would result in about 5000 additional 5-year survivors of ovarian cancer annually.

ADENOCARCINOMA OF THE ENDOMETRIUM

Progestogens should be added to estrogen replacement therapy not only to prevent endometrial cancer in women with a uterus but also possibly to reduce the risk of breast cancer in some women.[25] Postmenopausal bleeding must be investigated for early diagnosis of endometrial cancer; when endometrial hyperplasia is found, it should be treated with progestogens to prevent adenocarcinoma. The progestogen challenge test is recommended for women with a uterus; if bleeding occurs, the progestogen should be continued for 13 days each month to prevent hyperplasia or cancer.

Current management of patients with endometrial cancer is based on clinical and surgicopathologic findings (surgical staging).[26] Approximately 70 to 80 percent of patients present in clinical stage I (cancer confined to the uterine fundus). Fractional uterine curettage or in-office endometrial sampling with endocervical curettage and pelvic examination are all that are required for staging.

Clinical stage I remains a heterogeneous mixture of patients at low, intermediate, and high risk for recurrence. The grading of the tumor is closely related to the depth of myometrial invasion. Grade 3 or anaplastic tumors are more likely to be deeply invasive into the myometrium and have associated lymph node metastasis with a poor prognosis. Preoperative radiation has the disadvantage of application of therapy without full knowledge of the true extent of the disease. On the other hand, with surgical staging, particularly of the patients at high risk for spread (anaplastic tumors), selective pelvic and periaortic node sampling can lead to the discovery of occult nodal metastasis.

Postoperative radiation can be individualized to treat either the pelvis, pelvis plus periaortic region, or even the whole abdomen. Adjunctive radiation has not been proven to be of benefit. Current clinical trials are comparing the value of whole abdominal radiation to chemotherapy. Doxorubicin is the most active single agent in endometrial cancer. Cisplatin has minimal activity.

Progesterone therapy has been used for several decades to treat patients with advanced and recurrent endometrial carcinoma.[27] Although the initial response rate may be as high as 30 to 40 percent, responses of long duration are less than 10 percent. Now chemotherapy is offered as first-line treatment in lieu of hormone therapy.

OVARIAN CANCER

Epithelial ovarian cancer is currently the most common gynecologic malignancy causing death in women in the United States (Table 41-1).[28] This cancer is usually detected in advanced stages and chemotherapy is necessary for successful management. First-line chemotherapy—platinum-based combination chemotherapy—has an anticipated high response rate (80 percent) and frequent complete clinical responses (50 percent). Unfortunately, only a small portion of patients ultimately achieve a surgically confirmed pathologic response documented by second-look laparotomy; even then, many "complete responders" progress.

The independent prognostic factors for patients with ovarian cancer are age and performance status of the patient, postoperative residual tumor burden, tumor grade, tumor ploidy, histologic type, and clonogenic assay data. The median survival rate for patients with suboptimal disease (residual largest tumor nodule larger than 3 cm) is 21 months. A more favorable optimal residual lesion group (less than 3 cm for largest tumor nodule) has a median survival of 53 months.

Intraperitoneal (IP) chemotherapy (antineoplastic drug delivered into the abdomen through an indwelling catheter) achieves higher concentrations of drug in the peritoneal cavity than systemic therapy. The toxicity of IP chemotherapy is still dependent on the agent given but is not necessarily less than that of systemic therapy. Intraperitoneal administration assures prolonged tumor exposure to the cytotoxic agent, but this form of chemotherapy may be applicable only in patients with minimal residual volumes of tumor (less than 5 mm in greatest diameter). There have been no prospective randomized trials showing IP chemotherapy to be superior to any other regimen for first-line therapy.

Once the patient has progressed after first-line platinum-based chemotherapy, there are a number of alternative approaches, none of which, however, offers a high response rate. The first-line platinum responders can be retreated with a different type of platinum such as carboplatinum, which has a different toxicity profile. High-intensity therapy for first- or second-line therapy has yet to be of any proven benefit. Phase II drugs are available and have the greatest likelihood of demonstrating activity in patients who have had the least pretreatment. Biologic response modifiers such as interferon may have some value in patients who are found at second-look laparotomy to have no residual site greater than 5 mm in diameter. The growth factors—such as G-CSF (granulocyte colony stimulating factor) and GM-CSF (granulocyte macrophage colony stimulating factor)—are now being used for treatment and prevention of neutropenia in ovarian cancer patients receiving myelotoxic chemotherapy.

Of 100 patients with stage III (confined to the abdomen) suboptimal (greater than 2 cm residual tumor after the first tumor debulking procedure) ovarian carcinoma treated with cisplatin-based chemotherapy, approximately half experience complete clinical remissions. However, at second-look laparotomy, only about 15 of the 50 clinical complete responders are negative for persistent disease. Unfortunately, about half of the 15 negative second-look patients will progress despite a negative second-look laparotomy.

CANCER OF THE CERVIX

Dysplasia of the cervix is a precancerous epithelial change that may precede invasive cancer by many years. Dysplastic cells noted on the Pap smear alert the clinician that colposcopic investigation is in order. The older patient normally has a stenotic cervical os. The cotton-tipped applicator has been most commonly used to obtain cells from the endocervix. A new type of endocervical brush (Cytobrush) has been introduced in recent years. This produces numerous groups and clusters of cervical columnar cells, in contrast to the much fewer number by the cotton swab smears.[29]

Although supracervical hysterectomy is becoming a vanishingly rare procedure, there are still many elderly women with a retained cervical stump.[30] The average time between the supracervical hysterectomy and the recognition of cervical cancer is nearly 27 years, with a median age at diagnosis of 63.5 years. The median age at diagnosis of cancer of the cervix in a patient with an intact uterus is 55 years of age. Survival after treatment of carcinoma of the cervical stump is equivalent to that seen in patients with an intact uterus.

Comparison of perioperative morbidity and mortality following radical hysterectomy in patients older than 65 years with a younger age group who underwent radical hysterectomy and pelvic lymphadenectomy for cervical carcinoma revealed that age alone should not be a contraindication to radical hysterectomy in the elderly patient with American Society of Anesthesiologists Physical Status I to III.[31]

Declining trends in cervical cancer appear related to the widespread use of cervical cytologic screening programs.[32] Incidence and mortality rates continue to decrease among both blacks and whites. Thus, in spite of the possible effects of increased sexual activity at an earlier age, increased cigarette smoking in women, and other risk factors such as HPV, cervical cancer screening programs may have counteracted anticipated increases in cancer incidence through detection and treatment of preinvasive lesions.

REFERENCES

1. Weintraub NT et al: Gynecologic malignancies of the elderly. *Clin Geriatr Med* 3(4):669, 1987.
2. Goldstein MK, Teng NN: Gynecologic factors in sexual dysfunction of the older woman. *Clin Geriatr Med* 7(1):41, 1991.
3. Ridley CM: Dermatological conditions of the vulva. *Baillieres Clin Obstet Gynaecol* 2(2):317, 1988.
4. Homesley HD et al: Assessment of current International Federation of Gynecology and Obstetrics staging of vulvar carcinoma relative to prognostic factors

for survival (A Gynecologic Oncology Group study). *Am J Obstet Gynecol* 164:997, 1991.
5. Toki T et al: Probable nonpapillomavirus etiology of squamous cell carcinoma of the vulva in older women: A clinicopathologic study using in situ hybridization and polymerase chain reaction. *Int J Gynecol Pathol* 10(2):107, 1991.
6. Downey GO et al: Condylomatous carcinoma of the vulva with special reference to human papillomavirus DNA. *Obstet Gynecol* 72(1):68, 1988.
7. Audet-Lapointe P et al: Vaginal intraepithelial neoplasia. *Gynecol Oncol* 36(2): 232, 1990.
8. Kucera H, Vavra N: Radiation management of primary carcinoma of the vagina: Clinical and histopathological variables associated with survival. *Gynecol Oncol* 40(1):12, 1991.
9. American Cancer Society: *Cancer Facts and Figures 1991.* Atlanta, GA, 1991.
10. Stockwell HG, Lyman GH: Cigarette smoking and the risk of female reproductive cancer. *Am J Obstet Gynecol* 157(1):35, 1987.
11. Andersen WA et al: Vulvar squamous cell carcinoma and papillomaviruses: Two separate entities? *Am J Obstet Gynecol* 165(2):329, 1991.
12. Lawton FG, Hacker NF: Surgery for invasive gynecologic cancer in the elderly female population. *Obstet Gynecol* 76(2):287, 1990.
13. Schneider J, Benito R: Extensive gynecologic surgical procedures upon patients more than 75 years of age. *Surg Gynecol Obstet* 167(6):497, 1988.
14. Nahhas WA, Brown M: Gynecologic surgery in the aged. *J Reprod Med* 35(5):550, 1990.
15. Grover AS et al: Delayed diagnosis of gynecologic tumors in elderly women: Relation to national medical practice patterns. *Am J Med* 86(2):151, 1989.
16. Nasca PC et al: An epidemiologic study of Pap screening histories in women with invasive carcinomas of the uterine cervix. *NY State J Med* 91(4):152, 1991.
17. Blesch KS, Prohaska TR: Cervical cancer screening in older women: Issues and interventions. *Cancer Nurs* 1493:141, 1991.
18. Fletcher A. Screening for cancer of the cervix in elderly women. *Lancet* 1:97, 1990.
19. Hayward RA et al: Who gets screened for cervical and breast cancer? Results from a new national survey. *Arch Intern Med* 148(5):1177, 1988.
20. Celentano DD et al: Cervical cancer screening practices among older women: Results from the Maryland Cervical Cancer Case-Control Study. *J Clin Epidemiol* 41(6):531, 1988.
21. Mandelblatt JS, Fahs MC: The cost-effectiveness of cervical cancer screening for low-income elderly women. *JAMA* 259(16):2409, 1988.
22. Higgins RV et al: Transvaginal sonography as a screening method for ovarian cancer. *Gynecol Oncol* 34(3):402, 1989.
23. Malkasian GD Jr et al: Preoperative evaluation of serum CA 125 levels in premenopausal and postmenopausal patients with pelvic masses: Discrimination of benign from malignant disease. *Am J Obstet Gynecol* 159(2):341, 1988.
24. Westholl C, Randall MC: Ovarian cancer screening: Potential effect on mortality. *Am J Obstet Gynecol* 165(3):502, 1991.
25. Gambrell RD Jr: Cancer in the older woman: Diagnosis and prevention. *Geriatrics* 43(9):27, 1988.
26. Homesley HD: Staging and current treatments for endometrial cancer. *Oncology* 1(7):53, 1987.
27. Reifenstein EC Jr: The treatment of advanced endometrial cancer with hydroxyprogesterone caproate. *Gynecol Oncol* 2:377, 1974.
28. Homesley HD: Cisplatin-based chemotherapy of epithelial ovarian cancer. *J Surg Oncol Suppl* 1:21, 1989.
29. Kawaguchi K et al: The value of the Cytobrush for obtaining cells from the uterine cervix. *Diagn Cytopathol* 3(3):262, 1987.
30. Kovalic JJ et al: Cervical stump carcinoma. *Int J Radiol Oncol Biol Phys* 20(5):993, 1991.
31. Fuchtner C et al: Radical hysterectomy in the elderly patient: Analysis of morbidity. *Am J Obstet Gynecol* 166(2):593, 1992.
32. Devesa SS et al: Recent trends in cervix uteri cancer. *Cancer* 64(10):2184, 1989.

Chapter 42

BREAST CANCER

Hyman B. Muss

The incidence of female breast cancer has been increasing for the last 30 years. In the United States, breast cancer is currently the most common cancer in women, accounting for 26 percent of all newly diagnosed malignancy, and also the second leading cause of death from cancer. In 1993, it is estimated there will be 183,000 new cases of breast cancer, resulting in 46,300 deaths.[1] Moreover, U.S. incidence and mortality data from the 1980s suggest that 12 percent of all women will be diagnosed with breast cancer and 3.5 percent will die from it.[2]

Although breast cancer has declined almost 13 percent among women less than 50 years of age, its incidence has increased 7 percent among older women. It is estimated that almost half the cases of breast cancer occur in women over age 65. In addition, incidence increases dramatically with age (Fig. 42-1), from a rate of 60 per 100,000 in women below age 65 to a rate of approximately 320 per 100,000 in women above age 65.[3] It is unclear whether increasing age is associated with poorer survival. In one major study, Adami et al.[4] found that increasing age was associated with higher mortality, but these data were not corrected for stage of disease at diagnosis. In contrast, data from the Surveillance, Epidemiology, and End Results Project (SEER) of the National Institutes of Health showed similar stage-adjusted 5-year survival for older and younger women.[3] It is unlikely that older age alone adversely influences survival.[5]

The above data indicate that breast cancer is a major health concern and will become even more important as the population ages. Although breast cancer is more frequent in older women, elderly patients are less likely to be appropriately screened, generally present for care at a more advanced stage, have inferior surgical and postoperative management, and are less likely to be entered onto clinical trials. Several excellent reviews have discussed in detail problems related to elderly patients with breast cancer[6,7] and excellent texts and monographs concerning breast cancer are available.[2,8]

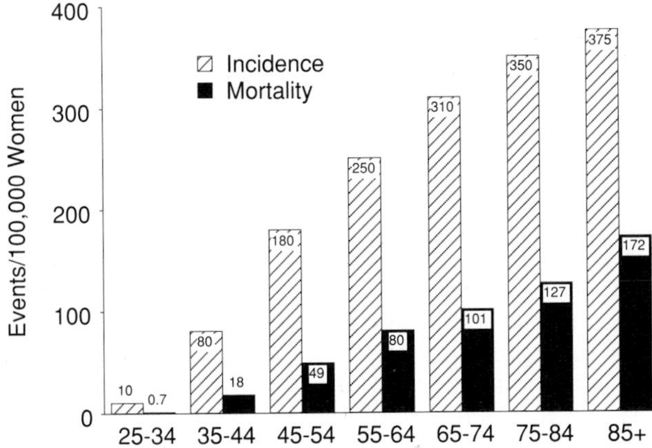

FIGURE 42-1

Breast cancer incidence and mortality by age. SEER data on 125,000 women from 1973 to 1984. (*Modified from Yancik et al.*[3])

RISK FACTORS, PATHOGENESIS, AND BIOLOGY

The cause of breast cancer is unknown. Geographic variability in incidence has long been recognized, with the highest incidence being found in affluent Caucasian populations. The reasons for differences in incidence are unknown but are probably related to genetic and environmental factors. Although breast cancer incidence differs among racial groups, such differences are minimized or lost when racial groups at low risk migrate to a high-risk environment.

Increasing age represents a major risk factor for the development of breast cancer. Furthermore, a strong family history of breast cancer (breast cancer in a first-degree relative), age above 30 at birth of first child, late menopause, benign breast disease (cysts, etc.), heavy radiation exposure, use of conjugated estrogens, obesity, and moderate to excessive alcohol use may increase the risk of breast cancer one to two times over that of a healthy age-matched control.[2,9] Patients with atypical hyperplasia (dysplasia), a lesion found in 5 to 10 percent of benign biopsy specimens, have a risk approximately four times normal. Although dietary fat intake has been implicated as a risk factor for colorectal cancer, its relationship to the development of breast cancer is less clear; studies currently under way should help resolve this issue.

Although a strong family history is associated with a higher risk of breast cancer, it is estimated that almost 80 percent of breast cancer cases are sporadic. Hereditary breast cancer, an autosomal dominant disease with almost complete penetrance, is uncommon and probably accounts for less than 5 percent of patients. Approximately 15 percent of women have a family history of breast cancer, but the distribution of involved relatives is not consistent enough to be considered hereditary. Women with either hereditary or familial breast cancer are usually diagnosed at younger ages and rarely present at an age above 65 years.

The physiologic changes that occur in breast tissue with aging are well recognized. After menopause, estrogen levels diminish, glandular and ductal tissue decrease, and fat tissue increases. In addition, postmenopausal patients have fewer cysts and fibroadenomas; therefore they face greater probability that any masses that are discovered will prove to be malignant.

Most breast cancers originate from ductal epithelium. Comparisons of older and younger patients with breast cancer reveal that infiltrating ductal carcinoma remains the most common histologic type in both groups, accounting for 75 to 80 percent of cases. Lobular, mucinous, and papillary carcinoma—histologic types that are associated with a somewhat lower risk of recurrence—are more common in older patients, while inflammatory carcinoma, an aggressive lesion with a poor prognosis, is extremely uncommon. Older patients are more likely to have well- and moderately differentiated lesions and to have malignancies that display both positive estrogen and progesterone receptors (60 to 70 percent of patients) when compared to their younger counterparts. Also, most investigators have found that measurements of tumor proliferation such as S-phase activity (the number of cells synthesizing DNA) and thymidine labeling index tend to be lower in older patients. These data suggest that breast cancer in older patients may be biologically less aggressive than it is in younger women.

PREVENTION AND SCREENING

Prevention

Except for draconian measures such as prophylactic mastectomy, there are no known effective means of breast cancer prevention. As the pathogenesis of breast cancer is likely to be related to interactions of estrogens, other hormones, and breast tissue, current research efforts in prevention are focused on the use of antiestrogens. Data from a recent metaanalysis involving 75,000 patients with early-stage breast cancer has suggested that the use of tamoxifen, an antiestrogen with weak estrogen agonist activities, may decrease breast cancer risk by 40 to 50 percent in postmenopausal patients. These data have stimulated the development of a national trial, currently under way, comparing tamoxifen with placebo in women at high risk for breast cancer. Of note, all women aged 60 or above are considered at high risk and are eligible to participate in this trial. Tamoxifen displays its major antiestrogenic effects on tumor tissue; in normal tissue, tamoxifen acts as a weak estrogen agonist, and several studies have suggested that the chronic use of tamoxifen decreases cardiovascular morbidity, lowers cholesterol and low-density lipoprotein levels, and increases or preserves vertebral bone density. Other research efforts in progress aimed at prevention include trials of dietary fat reduction and the use of retinoic acid.

Screening

Mammography and physical examination represent the cornerstones of effective breast cancer screening in the postmenopausal patient. Biologic changes in breast tissue with aging, especially the increased percentage of fat tissue, allows for improved contrast between small foci of malignancy and the surrounding breast tissue, resulting in fewer false-negative mammographic examinations. Several studies have conclusively shown that the routine use of screening mammography in women aged 50 through 70 has improved survival by detecting breast carcinoma at an earlier stage and before metastatic dissemination. It is estimated that a 25 to 30 percent reduction in breast cancer mortality could be achieved if all women in this age category received appropriate mammographic screening. Although data are sparse in women above age 70, a recent overview analysis has suggested that mammography is likely to be of major benefit in this group as well.[10] Since the life expectancy of a healthy woman in the 75- to 79-year-old age range is 10 years and for a woman 85 years of age 7 more years, screening in healthy women above age 75 appears prudent. As effective as mammography is, however, approximately 10 to 20 percent of all breast cancers detected by patients, physicians, and other health professionals are not visualized on the mammogram. Physical examination by health professionals and breast self-examination remain essential and complementary adjuncts to mammographic screening. Recent data have suggested that older women are less likely to be aware of screening and less likely to have participated in a screening program and that physician bias concerning the benefits of breast cancer screening in older women may be partly responsible for its underuse in this population. New programs focusing on both patient and physician education are likely to overcome these barriers. In addition, revisions in the Medicare law have provided for payment of screening mammography on a biannual basis. Since cost is frequently a major barrier to screening, this welcome change in Medicare regulations will further lower obstacles to this important procedure. Current recommendations for the screening of elderly women are presented in Table 42-1.

DIAGNOSIS AND STAGING

Diagnosis

The discovery of a breast mass in postmenopausal women demands prompt attention, as the majority of palpable masses in this age group are malignant. For lesions that are found on mammography but are not palpable, a needle-localization biopsy is usually required. This surgical technique allows for removal of the abnormal lesion for tissue diagnosis. Should the radiologist feel that the mammographic abnormality has a low probability of being malignant, the referring physician must carefully discuss with the patient the pros and cons of needle localization biopsy. For some patients, and with their informed consent, it is appropriate to reevaluate the patient in several months with physical examination and repeat mammography. For most patients, the fear of breast cancer and the possibility that even a low-risk lesion may prove to be malignant is usually a compelling motive for lesion excision.

For palpable lesions, fine needle aspiration (FNA) biopsy is a highly reliable method for making a tissue diagnosis. Although concerns have been expressed that needle biopsy may be associated with the tracking of malignant cells and a higher risk of local recurrence, such fears are unfounded. Should FNA be negative or inconclusive—that is, if the mass does *not* prove to be a cyst and does not resolve after aspiration—further biopsy, either repeat FNA or excision, is necessary. For patients who have a mass that is characteristic of malignancy on either physical examination or mammography, a treatment plan that includes complete excision of the lesion or mastectomy and axillary dissection may be preferable to a two-stage procedure involving an initial FNA or excisional biopsy followed by definitive surgery. In patients whose FNA is diagnostic of malignancy or in those who are scheduled for definitive surgery, preoperative evaluation should include a complete history and physical examination, a complete blood count and serum chemistry profile, and a chest x-ray. The latter studies are generally more helpful in determining the presence of comorbid illness than in finding metastases. Bilateral mammography should be performed on all patients to evaluate both the ipsilateral and contralateral breast for other nonpalpable lesions. Again, physicians should be aware that mammography may not image palpable lesions in as many as 20 percent of patients. A palpable lesion in a postmenopausal woman always requires biopsy; mammography in this setting is of value mainly for detecting other nonpalpable lesions in either the involved or the contralateral breast.

Management of Early Localized Lesions

It is now almost universally agreed that breast conservation procedures result in virtually identical relapse-free and overall survival outcomes when compared to more extensive surgical treatment, including simple, modified, and radical mastectomy.[2] Although older women who are in reasonable health tolerate simple or modified mastectomies almost as well as younger women, older women should have the right to decide if they wish to pursue breast-conserving surgical procedures. In general, breast-conservation procedures involve removing the tumor mass with a clear margin of several millimeters of surrounding normal breast tissue (lumpectomy, tylectomy, quadrantectomy, etc.) followed by local breast irradiation. Although breast

TABLE 42-1

Screening Guidelines for the Elderly

Test	Frequency	Comment
Breast self-examination	Monthly	Value uncertain, but most breast cancers will still be first detected by the patient.
Physical examination	Yearly	By physician or other health professional. Detects 15% of cancer *not* discovered on screening mammograms.
Mammography	Every 1 to 2 years	Value in improving survival in women above age 75 unproved, but extrapolation of data from studies in postmenopausal patients indicates it should be of benefit.

irradiation following removal of the tumor mass does not improve survival, it does reduce the likelihood of a recurrence in the affected breast from 40 percent to less than 10 percent.[11] Concurrent ipsilateral axillary node dissection is recommended by most medical, surgical, and radiation oncologists to provide essential prognostic data. Moreover, a carefully done axillary dissection that removes the nodes in the lower two axillary levels reduces the likelihood of axillary recurrence to less than 5 percent. Breast-conserving procedures require close cooperation between the surgeon, pathologist, and radiation oncologist and, prior to surgery, all patients should be seen in consultation by a radiation oncologist. The relative contraindications to breast-conserving surgery include large tumor masses (>5 cm), large breast size, and subareolar lesions. Age, however, is not a contraindication, and older patients have fared as well as younger patients with such treatment. Breast-conserving procedures, however, may be more costly than mastectomy, due to the cost of postoperative radiation therapy and the travel involved. Nevertheless, such treatment is preferred by many women irrespective of age, and the option of breast-conserving surgery provides further motivation for detecting early-stage lesions through screening. Moreover, patients who have had breast-conserving procedures have higher scores on self-appraisals of body image and sexuality than women who have had more extensive surgical intervention.

For older women who have had mastectomy, breast reconstruction represents another option capable of restoring body image. Many physicians, because of their personal bias, are unlikely to discuss reconstruction with older patients, but this procedure can be safely done in such patients, and they should be made aware of reconstructive procedures and be referred for consultation if they desire.[13] Recently several investigators have shown that for women with large breast cancers (greater than 4 cm), preoperative chemotherapy can result in substantial tumor shrinkage, allowing for breast-conserving procedures.[12] Such data indicate that breast-conserving procedures are now available for almost all women except those who present with extensive lesions.

The discovery of carcinoma in situ on breast biopsy has increased dramatically.[2] The more widespread use of screening mammography has led to a major increase in the diagnosis of ductal carcinoma in situ (DCIS). Previously, such lesions were usually detected on physical examination, were large, and had a cure rate exceeding 95 percent with mastectomy. Currently, most DCIS lesions are nonpalpable and small; they are suggested by microcalcifications found on screening mammography. Mastectomy can be expected to result in cure for almost all patients, but lesser procedures such as lumpectomy and breast irradiation are probably as effective for patients with lesions less than 2.5 cm in size. Axillary metastases are seen in less than 1 percent of patients; excision alone may be appropriate for some patients with lesions smaller than 1 cm that have a clear margin of normal tissue surrounding the in situ component. Lobular carcinoma in situ (LCIS) is more common in premenopausal patients, lacks clinical and mammographic signs, is bilateral in 25 to 35 percent of patients, and is usually an incidental finding after breast biopsy. Treatment ranges from observation to bilateral mastectomy. Of note, 20 to 40 percent of patients with LCIS subsequently develop invasive infiltrating ductal cancer, with both the ipsilateral and contralateral breast at similar risk. LCIS serves as a high-risk marker for subsequent invasive cancer, and treatment selection must rest on the desires of the patient.

In the past, postmastectomy "adjuvant" irradiation therapy to the chest wall and contiguous regional lymph nodes (internal mammary, supraclavicular, and upper axillary) was frequently employed. Numerous trials have now shown that such treatment does not improve survival but significantly reduces the risk of recurrence ("local recurrence") in the irradiated areas to less than 5 percent. Since the likelihood of local recurrence is directly proportional to the number of axillary nodes involved, postoperative adjuvant irradiation is still frequently recommended for patients with extensive (more than 4 positive nodes) nodal involvement. Postoperative irradiation can be delayed until the completion of adjuvant chemotherapy (see below) without increasing the risk of subsequent local recurrence.

Tamoxifen as Initial Treatment

For many older patients, especially those with advanced but localized lesions (T3 and T4 lesions, see below) and those with significant comorbidity or frailty, initial treatment with tamoxifen has been associated with tumor shrinkage in from 40 to 70 percent of patients. Although surgery is more likely to be effective (and potentially curative) in patients with small lesions, several randomized trials comparing surgery with tamoxifen for initial therapy have suggested that long-term survival is not changed by using tamoxifen as initial treatment and reserving surgical management for patients with tumor progression. Radiation therapy can also be used as "salvage" treatment after tamoxifen failure, but large tumor masses, especially those larger than 3 cm or those with extensive skin involvement, frequently respond only partially. For patients treated with tamoxifen, radiation therapy should be considered when tumor shrinkage is maximal to try and prolong the duration of local tumor control. In this author's opinion, older women with advanced breast cancer should be offered the same initial treatment options as younger patients; most patients treated initially with tamoxifen fail to achieve complete tumor regression and, over time, will likely need surgery or other treatment to control their primary lesion.

Staging

All patients with breast cancer should have accurate staging as described by American Joint Committee for Cancer (AJCC) guidelines (Fig. 42-2).[14] This system categorizes the extent of malignancy according to the size of the primary lesion (T), the extent of nodal involvement (N), and the occurrence of metastases (M). The AJCC breast cancer staging criteria are presented in Table 42-2. Tumor size and the extent of nodal involvement are best determined from pathologic examination of the specimen and should be required information in the pathology report. Less than 5 percent of the time, breast cancer presents as a diffuse infiltrating lesion and cannot be accurately measured. The number of axillary nodes removed and the number positive must also be reported. For the extent of nodal involvement to accurately reflect prognosis, a sample of at least 6 or more nodes should be removed during axillary dissection. Histologic type and tumor grade should be noted; although substantial interobserver variation exists in the grading of tumors, the use of a specific grading system by the pathologist will generally result in an accurate assessment. Other histologic factors that are of prognostic importance include an assessment of tumor necrosis, vascular invasion, lymphatic invasion, and skin involvement. The percentages of ductal carcinoma in situ and invasive carcinoma in the primary lesion should also be recorded. Unless the specimen is extremely small, it is mandatory that a sample of the primary lesion be assayed for estrogen and progesterone receptors. Previously, such receptor determinations have been done using biochemical methods that required 0.5 to 1.0 cm^3 of tumor tissue; current immunohistochemical methods allow accurate receptor assays on much smaller samples of freshly processed or paraffin-embedded tissue. Assays from fresh tumor samples provide the most accurate results. If feasible, a sample of tissue should be frozen for further analysis. Many potentially important prognostic factors are now being investigated which may be especially important in patients who have small, node-negative, primary lesions. These factors include measurement of tumor DNA content and S-phase activity by flow cytometry, oncogene expression such as c-erbB-2 (HER-2/neu), epidermal growth factor expression, and protease activity such as cathepsin-D. Several excellent reviews of prognostic factors are available.[15,16] Following initial treatment, asymptomatic patients who have had the preoperative evaluation described above require no further staging procedures. Tumor markers such as the carcinoembryonic antigen (CEA) and mucin antigen (CA 15-3), skeletal surveys, radionuclide bone scanning, and computed tomography (CT) of the brain, chest, abdomen, and pelvis are unnecessary in asymptomatic patients with normal physical findings.

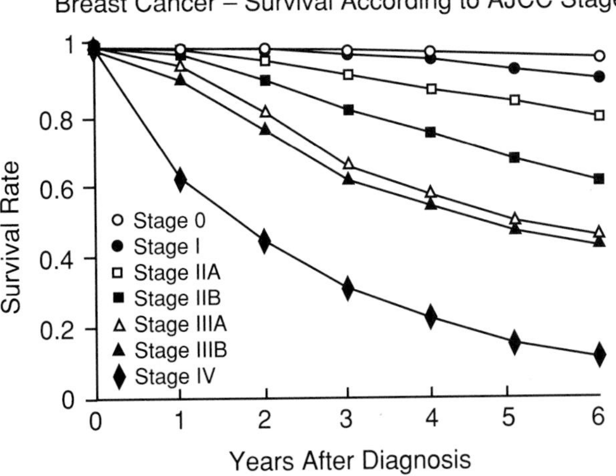

FIGURE 42-2

Breast cancer survival versus American Joint Committee (AJCC) stage. (*Modified from Manual for Staging of Cancer—1992.*[14] *Reproduced by permission.*)

Follow-up

After completion of primary treatment or adjuvant therapy (see below), follow-up is required to monitor patient progress. Although there is no evidence that close follow-up results in improved overall survival, the detection of early skin or lymph node (soft-tissue) recurrence may result in more effective palliation. Moreover, follow-up visits provide an opportunity for patients to express concerns and physicians to give reassurance. Extensive laboratory and radiologic procedures are now available for the detection of metastatic disease but numerous trials have indicated that a brief but focused history and a limited physical examination (skin, chest, breast, and abdominal examination) detects more than 75 percent of metastases.[17] The exception to the above is mammography, which should be performed yearly to detect new primary lesions in these high-risk patients. This author's suggestions for follow-up are presented in Table 42-3.

ADJUVANT SYSTEMIC THERAPY

Adjuvant systemic therapy involves preoperative or postoperative administration of endocrine therapy and/or chemotherapy to patients with localized breast cancer to reduce the risk of relapse or to delay its occurrence and thus improve survival. Such treatment is aimed at eradicating occult, clinically undetectable metastases that may have occurred before diagnosis and treatment of the primary lesion. Estimated improvements in relapse-free and overall survival for adjuvant systemic therapy are provided in

TABLE 42-2

Staging System for Cancer of the Breast—AJCC Criteria

Symbol in TNM system	Meaning
TX	Primary tumor cannot be assessed
T0	No evidence of primary tumor
Tis	Carcinoma in situ: intraductal carcinoma, lobular carcinoma in situ, or Paget's disease of the nipple with no tumor
T1	Tumor ≤2 cm in greatest dimension
T2	Tumor >2 cm but not >5 cm in greatest dimension
T3	Tumor >5 cm in greatest dimension
T4	Tumor of any size with direct extension to chest wall[a] or skin (includes inflammatory carcinoma)
NX	Regional lymph nodes cannot be assessed (e.g., previously removed, not removed)
N0	No regional lymph-node metastases
N1	Metastasis to movable ipsilateral axillary nodes
N2	Metastases to ipsilateral axillary nodes fixed to one another or to other structures
N3	Metastases to ipsilateral internal mammary lymph nodes
M0	No evidence of distant metastasis
M1	Distant metastases (including metastases to ipsilateral supraclavicular lymph nodes)

Stage	
0	Tis, N0, M0
I	T1, N0, M0
IIA	TO, N1, M0
	T1, N1, M0
	T2, N0, M0
IIB	T2, N1, M0
	T3, N0, M0
IIIA	T0 or T1, N2, M0
	T2, N2, M0
	T3, N1 or N2, M0
IIIB	T4, any N, M0
	Any T, N3, M0
IV	Any T, any N, M1

[a] The chest wall includes the ribs, intercostal muscles, and serratus anterior muscle but not the pectoral muscle.
SOURCE: American Joint Committee on Cancer: *Manual for Staging of Cancer.* Philadelphia, Lippincott, 1992.

TABLE 42-3

Follow-up after Diagnosis

	Frequency of Examination	
	Years 0–5	**5+ Years**
History/physical exam	Every 3–4 months	Every 6–12 months
CBC/blood profile	Every 6–12 months	Yearly
Mammogram[a]	Yearly	Yearly
Chest x-ray	Yearly	Yearly
Other[b]	PRN	PRN

[a] In patients treated with lumpectomy and breast irradiation, more frequent mammograms (every 4 to 6 months) are generally recommended for the first 3 years.
[b] Tumor marker studies, skeletal x-rays, radionuclide studies, and computed tomographic scans are not necessary in asymptomatic patients. Appropriate studies should be obtained for patients with signs or symptoms of recurrence.

the recent overview analysis of the Early Breast Cancer Trials Collaborative Group.[18] This landmark analysis calculated 10-year recurrence and mortality data from 75,000 women with early-stage breast cancer treated with systemic endocrine therapy, chemotherapy, and immunotherapy who were entered in randomized clinical trials that began before 1985. These data clearly confirmed the benefits of adjuvant endocrine therapy and chemotherapy, but not immunotherapy, in significantly reducing the risk of recurrence and death in women with early breast cancer. A summary of the overview results of adjuvant therapy for postmenopausal patients is presented in Table 42-4.

In postmenopausal women, most trials utilizing adjuvant endocrine therapy compared tamoxifen (Nolvadex), an antiestrogen, with either no treatment or chemotherapy. In women above age 71, there was a highly significant decrease in the annual odds of recurrence (28 percent) and death (21 percent) among those treated with tamoxifen. Longer treatment with tamoxifen was associated with superior results,[18,19] and current trials are evaluating its efficacy when given for periods of up to 10 years.[20–22] Doses of 20 mg per day orally appear optimal. Patients with positive estrogen receptors derive the greatest benefit from tamoxifen, but postmenopausal estrogen-receptor-negative patients also significantly benefit from tamoxifen treatment.[18,21,23,24] In addition, tamoxifen significantly decreased the annual odds of developing contralateral breast cancer by approximately 40 percent and was associated with a reduction in non–cancer-related deaths of 12 percent ($p = .05$), mostly due to a 25 percent decrease in vascular causes ($p = .06$).

The overview also found a significant decrease in the annual odds of recurrence and death for both node-negative and node-positive women 50 to 70 years old treated with combination chemotherapy (polychemotherapy); unfortunately, not enough data were available to estimate the results of chemotherapy in patients above age 70. Of note, the combination of tamoxifen and chemotherapy was superior to tamoxifen alone in prolonging relapse-free but not overall survival. Chemotherapy programs utilizing combinations of cyclophosphamide (C), methotrexate (M), doxorubicin (Adriamycin; A) and fluorouracil (F) were similar in efficacy and result in increased survival when compared to single-agent treatment,[18] with CMF, CAF, and CA being the most widely used regimens. A list of commonly used endocrine and cytotoxic agents is presented in Table 42-5. Much controversy exists concerning the optimal duration of adjuvant chemotherapy, but short treatment courses of 2 to 6 months appear as effective as treatment of longer duration. The dose intensity of chemotherapy

TABLE 42-4

Adjuvant Systemic Therapy in Women ≥ Age 50

Comparison	n[a]	*Percent Reduction in Annual odds of* Recurrence[b]	Death[b]
Tamoxifen			
Tamoxifen alone versus no adjuvant	13,114	30 (2)	19 (3)
Tamoxifen versus same without tamoxifen	21,262	29 (2)	20 (2)
Tamoxifen versus no tamoxifen in node-negative patients	9,473	28 (4)	16 (5)
Tamoxifen versus no tamoxifen in node-positive patients	11,807	33 (2)	22 (3)
Tamoxifen versus no tamoxifen in estrogen-receptor-negative (<10 fmol/mg) patients	3,311	16 (5)	16 (6)
Tamoxifen versus no tamoxifen in estrogen-receptor-positive (≥10 fmol/mg) patients	10,845	36 (3)	23 (4)
Chemotherapy			
Polychemotherapy[c] alone versus no adjuvant therapy	3,746	22 (4)	14 (5)
Chemotherapy versus no chemotherapy	12,300	17 (3)	9 (3)
Polychemotheraphy[c] versus monochemotherapy	1,792	14 (6)	17 (6)
Tamoxifen + Chemotherapy			
Tam + chemotherapy versus chemo alone	8,135	28 (3)	20 (4)
Polychemotherapy[c] + tam versus tam alone	3,392	26 (5)	10 (7)[d]

[a] Number of patients in analysis.
[b] Standard deviation in parentheses.
[c] Polychemotherapy given for 2 to 12 months.
[d] All odds reductions are significant ($p < .05$) except for this value.
SOURCE: Modified from Ref. 18.

TABLE 42-5

Endocrine and Cytotoxic Agents Used in the Treatment of Breast Cancer

Class/Agent	Common and Major Toxicities
Endocrine Therapy	
Tamoxifen (antiestrogen)	Hot flashes
Megestrol (progestin)	Weight gain
Aminoglutethimide (aromatase inhibitor)	Fatigue, nausea, rash
Stilbestrol (estrogen)	Nausea and vomiting (N+V), edema, fluid retention
Fluoxymestrone (androgen)	N+V, fluid retention, masculinization
Cytotoxic Agents	
Alkylating Agents	
Melphalan (L-PAM)	Myelosuppression (M)
Chlorambucil	Myelosuppression
Cyclophosphamide	M, N+V, cystitis
Antitumor Antibiotics	
Doxorubicin (Adriamycin)	M, N+V, mucositis (MS), alopecia, cardiomyopathy, vesication
Mitoxantrone	M, N+V, mild alopecia, cardiomyopathy
Mitomycin	M, N+V, MS, alopecia, vesication
Antimetabolites	
Methotrexate	M (uncommon), nephrotoxicity, MS
Fluorouracil	M (uncommon), N+V (uncommon), rash (rare)
Vincas	
Vincristine	Peripheral neuropathy, alopecia, M (rare), vesication
Vinblastine	M, neuropathy (uncommon), vesication

(the dose administered during a specific time period) may be a major factor in treatment outcome; one review showed a significant correlation between greater dose intensity and longer time to recurrence.[25] Adjuvant chemotherapy regimens that have shown a survival benefit for women between ages 50 and 70 are also well tolerated in the healthy elderly.[26] Even if newer experimental high-dose regimens prove to be superior to current polychemotherapy regimens such as CMF, CAF, or CA, these latter regimens may still prove to be of value in the older patient. Unlike tamoxifen however, chemotherapy had no effect on the risk of developing contralateral breast cancer in the overview analysis. The role of adjuvant chemotherapy in the management of elderly patients remains uncertain; too few patients have been studied to draw major conclusions and no major chemotherapy trials in postmenopausal women have included a large cohort of elderly patients.

In elderly patients, major factors in choosing treatment include the mental and physical status of the patient and the characteristics of the primary tumor. In general, patients with a short life expectancy (less than 5 years) should not be considered for adjuvant chemotherapy. Adjuvant endocrine therapy with tamoxifen significantly reduces breast cancer recurrence and mortality in older women with early-stage breast cancer irrespective of estrogen receptor status. Because of its minimal toxicity, tamoxifen represents an appropriate choice of adjuvant treatment in elderly patients with early-stage breast cancer who do not have other concurrent life-threatening illness. Chemotherapy is associated with higher cost and greater toxicity than endocrine therapy. Since it is unlikely that the biologic characteristics of breast cancer change substantially in women above age 70 years as compared to those between 50 and 70, chemotherapy will likely prove effective in significantly reducing relapse in elderly women who have a life expectancy of at least 5 years. Information that the gerontologist should have available when consulting the medical oncologist concerning adjuvant systemic therapy are presented in Table 42-6. Carefully designed trials of chemotherapy for elderly patients are needed and should include drug combinations that provide dose intensity similar to that of currently effective therapies.

TREATMENT OF METASTATIC DISEASE

Patients with metastatic breast cancer are currently incurable and have a median survival of approximately 2 years following the discovery of recurrence.

TABLE 42-6

Essential Information for the Management of Patients with Early Breast Cancer

Patient Characteristics
- Significant comorbidities
- Complete blood count
- Chemistry profile including liver and renal function
- Chest x-ray
- Mammographic report
- Clinical stage (TNM)

Type of Initial Treatment
- Mastectomy or lumpectomy
- Radiation therapy, type

Pathology
- Histologic type
- Tumor grade
- Presence of necrosis, vascular or lymphatic involvement
- Percent of invasive and intraductal cancer
- Tumor size (maximum diameter)
- Number axillary nodes removed
- Number axillary nodes positive
- Estrogen and progesterone receptors

Social Environment
- Physical and mental function
- Access to clinic (transportation)
- Family and social support
- Financial resources (coinsurance)

Nevertheless, patients may derive major palliative benefit from judiciously chosen palliative therapy. Bone, soft-tissue (skin and lymph nodes), pleural, and pulmonary metastases are the most common sites of breast cancer recurrence. Women with localized symptomatic lesions in brain, skin, lymph nodes, and bone should be considered for radiation therapy, which will reduce tumor size and relieve symptoms in the majority of patients.

Patients with disseminated metastases should be considered for palliative systemic treatment (Table 42-5). Several excellent reviews of this subject are available.[8,27–29] Endocrine therapy is usually associated with minimal toxicity, while the toxicity associated with chemotherapy is frequently substantial and, in a small percent of patients, life-threatening. Provided that metastases are not rapidly progressive or life-threatening, all women with metastases should have a trial of endocrine therapy irrespective of the estrogen and progesterone receptor status of their tumor. Even in receptor-negative patients, endocrine therapy results in complete and partial responses (50 percent shrinkage of the tumor mass) in approximately 20 percent of those treated. Chemotherapy may then be used when metastases become refractory to endocrine treatment; such a strategy has been shown to be safe[30] and most likely maintains the highest quality of life for the longest time period.

Tamoxifen represents the most commonly used endocrine agent for treatment of metastatic disease, with a response rate of approximately 30 percent in unselected patients. Responses to endocrine treatment generally last an average of about 1 year but may last many years in a small percentage of patients. Patients with receptor-positive tumors, time intervals of greater than 2 years from initial diagnosis to recurrence, soft-tissue or bone metastases, or a prior response to endocrine therapy are most likely to respond. For patients who have a recurrence while taking tamoxifen as adjuvant therapy, those who relapse on tamoxifen, or those few patients who cannot tolerate tamoxifen due to side effects, progestins, aromatase inhibitors, estrogens, and corticosteroids may be tried. Progestins, aromatase inhibitors, and estrogens are similar in efficacy to tamoxifen but are generally associated with greater toxicity. Patients who respond to one endocrine agent are likely to respond to another at time of progression; the use of successive endocrine agents in patients with minimally symptomatic metastases is an excellent treatment strategy for many patients.

Elderly patients with metastatic disease whose general health is otherwise satisfactory display similar response and toxicity profiles as their younger counterparts.[26,31] An excellent review of the principles of chemotherapy in the elderly is available.[32] Most cytotoxic drugs are metabolized in the liver, with only a select few dependent on renal excretion (methotrexate, carboplatin, and cisplatin); major liver dysfunction is probably required to significantly alter drug metabolism. Myelosuppression is more common in the elderly due to diminished bone marrow reserve with aging; nausea and vomiting is seen less frequently than in younger patients. Of importance, psychosocial adjustments to chemotherapy appear better for older than for younger patients.[33] Complete and partial responses to single-agent treatment range from 20 to 30 percent, while responses to combination chemotherapy average 50 to 60 percent. Responses generally last an average of 6 to 12 months; response rates to subsequent "salvage" regimens are generally low and last only a few months.

MALE BREAST CANCER

Male breast cancer is uncommon and accounts for less than 1 percent of incidence.[1] The natural history of male and female breast cancer is similar, but males usually present at a later stage, probably due to a delay in diagnosis.[34] Almost all cases are sporadic except for males with Klinefelter's syndrome (sex chromosomes XXY), in which the prevalence of breast cancer ranges from 3 to 6 percent. Mastectomy and axillary dissection represent the standard approach to treatment. Histologically, most lesions are infiltrating ductal carcinomas and the frequency of estrogen-receptor-positive lesions is approximately 70 to 80 percent. There are few data on the role of adjuvant systemic therapy. Because of the paucity of cases, it is unlikely that large randomized trials will be undertaken. Many oncologists use the same guidelines for adjuvant therapy in males as for women of similar stage and receptor status, but the value of such treatment is unresolved. Males with metastatic breast cancer are incurable but frequently respond to endocrine therapy including orchiectomy or tamoxifen; results with systemic chemotherapy are similar to those in females.

CONCLUSIONS

Breast cancer in the elderly represents a major gerontologic problem. Both physician and patient education concerning the screening, early diagnosis, and management of breast cancer in this age group is required. The available data indicate that optimal treatment of breast cancer in older patients results in similar outcome to that in younger women. Although significant comorbid illness is more frequently encountered in older patients and may confound breast cancer treatment, most patients can still be managed with judicious, "state-of-the-art" therapy. Barriers to the treatment of breast cancer in the elderly are generic to the treatment of all illness in this age group and include access to care, transportation, adequate family and social support, physician bias, and treatment costs. Changes in health care policy as well as focused research related to cancer in the elderly will be needed to help overcome these obstacles.

REFERENCES

1. Boring CC et al: Cancer statistics, 1992. *CA* 43:7, 1993.
2. Harris JR et al: Breast cancer. *N Engl J Med* 327:319, 390, 473, 1992.
3. Yancik R et al: Breast cancer in aging women: A population-based study of contrasts in stage, surgery, and survival. *Cancer* 63:976, 1989.
4. Adami HO et al: The relation between survival and age at diagnosis in breast cancer. *N Engl J Med* 315:559, 1986.
5. Mohle-Boetani J: Age at breast cancer diagnosis as a predictor of subsequent survival, in Macieira-Coehlo A, Nordenskjold B (eds): *Cancer and Aging.* Boca Raton, FL, CRC Press, p 245, 1990.
6. Stewart JA, Foster RS Jr: Breast cancer and aging (review). *Semin Oncol* 16:41, 1989.
7. Balducci L et al: Breast cancer of the older woman: An annotated review. *J Am Geriatr Soc* 39:1113, 1991.
8. Henderson IC: Chemotherapy for metastatic disease, in Harris JR, Hellman S, Henderson IC, Kinne DW (eds): *Breast Diseases.* Philadelphia, Lippincott, 1991, pp 604–665.
9. Love SM: Use of risk factors in counseling patients. *Hematol Oncol Clin North Am* 3:599, 1989.
10. Mandelblatt JS et al: Breast cancer screening for elderly women with and without comorbid conditions: A decision analysis model. *Ann Intern Med* 116:722, 1992.
11. Fisher B et al: Eight-year results of a randomized clinical trial comparing total mastectomy and lumpectomy with or without irradiation in the treatment of breast cancer. *N Engl J Med* 320:822, 1989.
12. Bonadonna G et al: Primary chemotherapy to avoid mastectomy in tumors with diameters of three centimeters or more. *J Natl Cancer Inst* 82:1539, 1991.
13. Handel N: Current status of breast reconstruction after mastectomy. *Oncology* 5:73, 1991.
14. American Joint Committee on Cancer: *Manual for Staging of Cancer.* Philadelphia, Lippincott, 1992.
15. McGuire WL et al: How to use prognostic factors in axillary node-negative breast cancer patients. *J Natl Cancer Inst* 82:1006, 1990.
16. Osborne CK: Prognostic factors in breast cancer: Principles and practice of oncology. *PPO Updates* 4:1, 1990.
17. Muss HB et al: Follow-up after stage II breast cancer: A comparative study of relapsed versus nonrelapsed patients. *Am J Clin Oncol* 11:451, 1988.
18. Early Breast Cancer Trialists' Collaborative Group: Systemic treatment of early breast cancer by hormonal, cytotoxic, or immune therapy: 133 randomised trials involving 31,000 recurrences and 24,000 deaths among 75,000 women. *Lancet* 339:1, 1992.
19. Fisher B et al: Prolonging tamoxifen therapy for primary breast cancer: Findings from the National Surgical Adjuvant Breast and Bowel Project clinical trial. *Ann Intern Med* 106:649, 1987.
20. Tormey DC, Jordan VC: Long-term tamoxifen adjuvant therapy in node-positive breast cancer: A metabolic and pilot clinical study. *Breast Cancer Res Treat* 4:297, 1984.
21. Anonymous: Breast Cancer Trials Committee, Scottish Cancer Trials Office: Adjuvant tamoxifen in the management of operable breast cancer: The Scottish Trial. *Lancet* 2:171, 1987.
22. Fisher B et al: A randomized clinical trial evaluating sequential methotrexate and fluorouracil in the treatment of patients with node-negative breast cancer who have estrogen-receptor-negative tumors. *N Engl J Med* 320:473, 1989.
23. Singh L et al: The relationship between histological grade, oestrogen receptor status, events and survival at 8 years in the NATO ("Nolvadex") trial. *Br J Cancer* 57:612, 1988.
24. "Nolvadex" Adjuvant Trial Organisation: Controlled trial of tamoxifen as a single adjuvant agent in the management of early breast cancer. *Br J Cancer* 57:608, 1988.

25. Hryniuk W, Levine MN: Analysis of dose intensity for adjuvant chemotherapy trials in stage II breast cancer. *J Clin Oncol* 4:1162, 1986.
26. Christman K et al: Chemotherapy of metastatic breast cancer in the elderly: The Piedmont Oncology Association experience. *JAMA* 268:57, 1992.
27. Henderson IC: Endocrine therapy of metastatic breast cancer in, Harris JR, Hellman S, Henderson IC, et al (eds): *Breast Diseases.* Philadelphia, Lippincott, 1991, pp 559–603.
28. Swain SE, Lippmann ME: Endocrine therapies of cancer, in Chabner BA, Collins JM (eds): *Cancer Chemotherapy: Principles and Practice.* Philadelphia, Lippincott, 1990, pp 59–109.
29. Ingle JN: Principles of therapy in advanced breast cancer. *Hematol Oncol Clin North Am* 3:743, 1989.
30. Taylor SG et al: Combination chemotherapy compared to tamoxifen as initial therapy for stage IV breast cancer in elderly women. *Ann Intern Med* 104:455, 1986.
31. Begg CB et al: A study of excess hematologic toxicity in elderly patients treated on chemotherapy protocols, in Yancik R (ed): *Cancer in the Elderly: Approaches to Early Detection and Management.* New York, Springer-Verlag, 1989.
32. Lewis CR et al: Principles of chemotherapy, in Caird FI, Brewin TB (eds): *Cancer in the Elderly.* London, Wright, 1990.
33. Nerenz DR et al: Psychosocial consequences of cancer chemotherapy for elderly patients. *Health Serv Res* 20:961, 1986.
34. Kinne DW, Hakes TB: Male breast cancer, in Harris JR, Hellman S, Henderson IC, et al (eds): *Breast Diseases.* Philadelphia, Lippincott, 1991, pp 782–790.

SECTION A The Cardiovascular System

Chapter 43

ALTERATIONS IN CIRCULATORY FUNCTION

Edward G. Lakatta

A review of the literature describing measured functional decline in various organ systems indicates that the rate of decline varies dramatically among organs within an individual subject and that within a given organ system there is substantial variation among individuals. This implies that multiple factors may be potent modulators of a "biological clock" or of genetic mechanisms that determine how we age.

One factor that modulates the "aging process" is the occurrence of specific processes that we have traditionally referred to as *disease* (Fig. 43-1). Quantitative information as to age-associated alterations in cardiovascular function is essential in attempting to differentiate the cardiovascular limitations of an elderly individual which are disease-related from those which may fall within expected normal limits. Much of cardiovascular disease identification and evaluation is made by the physician through assessment of the functional capacity of the heart as it pumps in relationship to the hemodynamic load placed upon it. For example, the severity of cardiac disease is most frequently graded in terms of left-ventricular (LV) hemodynamic measurements of pressure and/or volumes at rest or during exercise. Such values must be compared with those of normal individuals in the same age group.

Occult disease can be easily overlooked and can cause marked functional impairments. This consideration is especially pertinent to investigations of the effect of age on cardiovascular function in humans because coronary atherosclerosis, which increases exponentially with age, is present in an occult form in at least as great a number of elderly persons as the overt form of this disease.[1,2]

In addition to an increase in prevalence of disease, changes in lifestyle occur concomitantly with advancing age. These changes include habits of physical activity, eating, drinking, smoking, personality characteristics, etc. The impact of lifestyle variables on an aging process is presently not well defined. However, data are emerging to indicate that different nutritional habits may result in changes in arterial structure and function. The average daily physical activity level declines progressively with age.[3] Chronic exercise changes not only the function of the heart but also the heart size. Because the magnitude of the physical-conditioning effect can be so great,[3] studies which attempt to investigate to what extent a disease or an aging process alters cardiovascular function (particularly reserve function) must control for the physical activity status or at least consider it in the interpretation of the results.

CARDIOVASCULAR STRUCTURE AND FUNCTION AT REST

The overall control of cardiovascular function results from a complex interaction of modulating influences (Fig. 43-2). In some instances the changes in these variables that result from aging or disease are compensatory and enhance overall cardiovascular function, whereas in other instances the changes may compromise function. In assessing the capacity of the intact cardiovascular system, it is often difficult to quantify the contribution of each factor in Fig. 43-2. However, in attempting to define the mechanisms that are operative during failure of the system, each of these regulatory factors must be studied, to the ex-

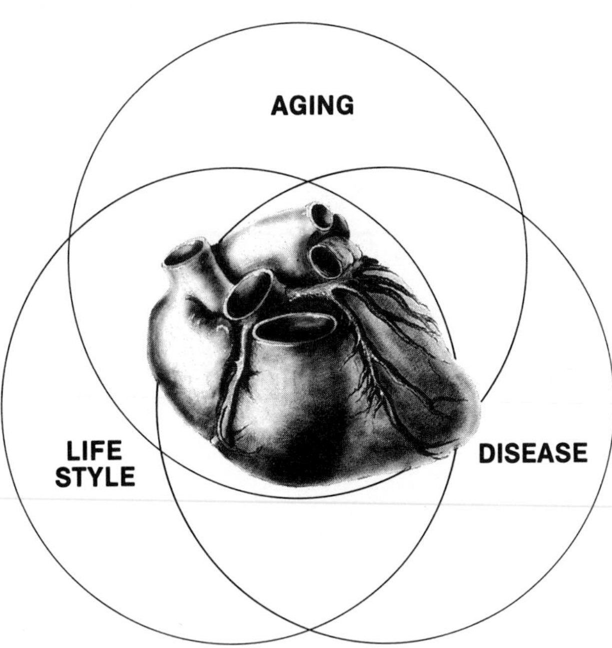

FIGURE 43-1

Diseases and changes in lifestyle occur with advancing age. Interactions among these and an "aging process" make it difficult to identify or characterize the effect of age on the heart. *(From Lakatta.[1])*

tent feasible, in isolation. "Failure" of the cardiovascular system is a relative concept; a limitation may be manifest at rest or may be detected only in response to graded stress. Therefore, studies conducted over a range of stressful conditions must be employed to detect and define evidence of any age-associated compromise in cardiovascular function.

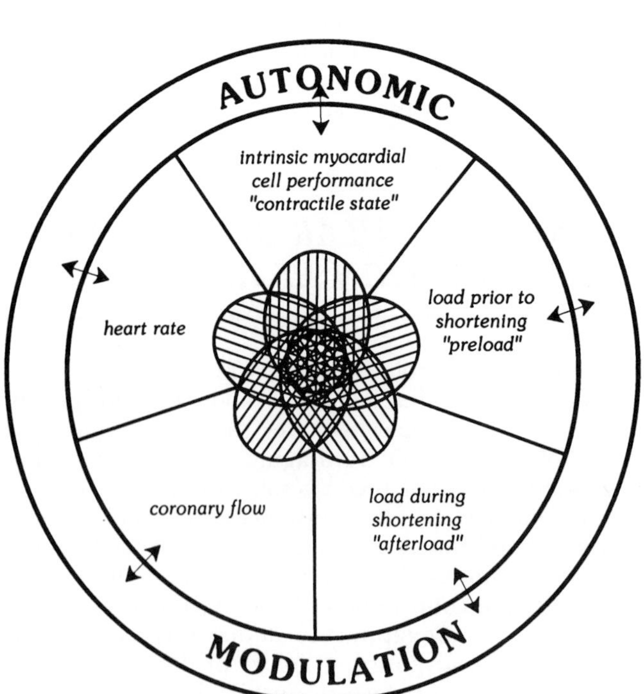

The cardiac output (or cardiac index, CI) at rest, as measured in different individuals of different ages (i.e., cross-sectional studies), has been found to remain unchanged, to decrease substantially, or even to increase slightly with age.[4,5] The variability likely stems from heterogeneity of selection criteria among the various studies. The resting peripheral vascular resistance (PVR), derived from cardiac output and mean arterial pressure, appears to increase with age in women but not in men.

HEART RATE AND RHYTHM

Most cross-sectional studies have indicated that the supine, basal heart rate does not differ among younger and older individuals.[6–8] Studies of a large number of rigorously screened, healthy individuals, however, indicate that in the sitting position, the heart rate decreases with age in both men and women.

The respiratory variation of the heart rate, which is determined largely by autonomic tone, becomes diminished with advancing age, as does the spontaneous variation in heart rate measured over a 24-hour period via Holter monitoring or via spectral analysis.[7–10] In the latter studies the decreased variation in heart rate is thought to be influenced by age-associated changes in both parasympathetic and sympathetic modulation. The intrinsic sinus rate, i.e., that measured in the presence of both sympathetic and parasympathetic blockade, is significantly diminished with age: at age 20 the average intrinsic heart rate is 104 beats per minute compared with 92 beats per minute in a 45- to 55-year age group.[11]

FIGURE 43-2

Factors that regulate cardiovascular performance. The ovals have been drawn to overlap each other in order to indicate the interaction among these parameters. The bidirectional arrows also indicate that each factor is not only modulated by, but also in part determines, the autonomic tone. *(From Lakatta.[4])*

With advancing age, there is an increase in elastic and collagenous tissue in all parts of the conduction system. Fat accumulates around the sinoatrial (SA) node, sometimes producing a partial or complete separation of the node from the atrial musculature. Beginning by age 60 there is a pronounced decrease in the number of pacemaker cells in the SA node, and by age 75 less than 10 percent of the cell numbers found in the young adult remains (see Fleg et al.[12] for review). A variable degree of calcification of the left side of the cardiac skeleton, which includes the aortic and mitral annuli, the central fibrous body, and the summit of the interventricular septum, occurs. Because of their proximity to these structures, the atrioventricular (AV) node, AV bundle, bifurcation, and proximal left and right bundle branches may be affected by this process, resulting in so-called primary or idiopathic heart block. A modest prolongation of the PR interval occurs with aging in healthy individuals and is localized to the proximal PR segment, probably reflecting delay within the AV junction.[6] An increase in both supraventricular and ventricular premature beats occurs in older healthy men and women compared to their younger counterparts.[13,14]

PRELOAD OR FILLING

LV pump function is dependent on preload, measured as the end-diastolic volume index (EDVI); the afterload, or impedance to the ejection of the blood from the ventricle; and the inotropic or contractile state of the ventricular muscle (Fig. 43-2). Resting LV end-diastolic dimension, area, and volume, as estimated by M-mode echocardiography, two-dimensional echocardiography, and gated blood pool scans, respectively, do not markedly change or may increase slightly with age in healthy adults.[5,15] The chest x-ray evaluation in longitudinal studies indicates that the cardiothoracic ratio increases over a mean period of 12 years because of a slightly increased cardiac and decreased thoracic diameter.[16,17] In men, a modest cardiac dilatation at end diastole occurs with aging at rest in the sitting position (Fig. 43-3*A*).[18] Although, as noted above, the resting heart rate decreases slightly,[4,13] in healthy older men the resting, sitting cardiac output is not reduced and stroke volume indexed to body surface area (SVI) is increased (Fig. 43-4*B*) due to the end-diastolic dilatation.[18] In contrast to cardiac output in men, cardiac output at rest in the sitting position slightly decreases in older versus younger healthy women, as neither the resting EDVI nor the SVI increases with age to compensate for the modest reduction in heart rate. These gender differences appear, in part, to be due to differences in body composition and in demand for blood flow in men and women. The PVR increases at rest with aging in women but not in men.

Early diastolic LV filling begins as ventricular pressure decreases below that in the atrium and continues during the cardiac diastole with a further evolution of the AV pressure gradient. Despite the popular notion that LV compliance decreases with aging, this parameter, in fact, has not been measured in healthy humans, as simultaneous measurements of pressure and volume have not been made. Whether

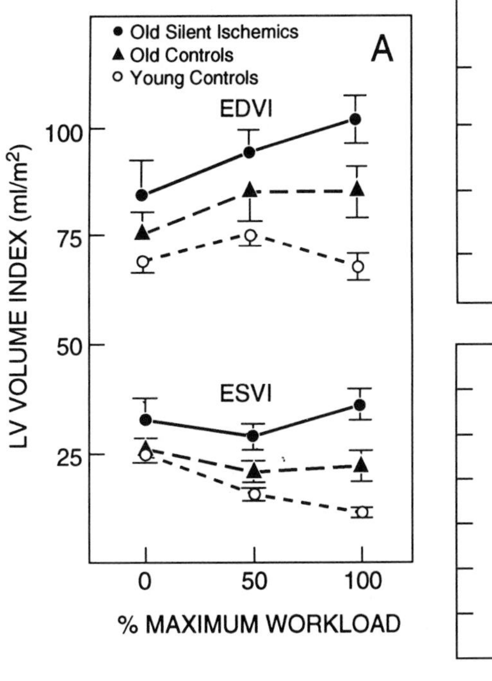

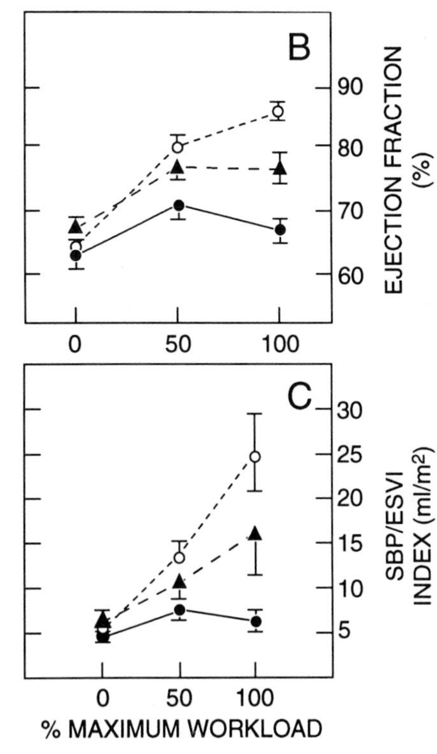

FIGURE 43-3
End-diastolic, end-systolic volumes (*A*) (ESVI = end-systolic volume index), ejection fraction (*B*), and LV contractility index (end-systolic volume divided by systolic blood pressure) (*C*) at rest and during vigorous exercise in healthy younger and older men and in older men with "silent" myocardial ischemia. *(From Fleg et al.[18])*

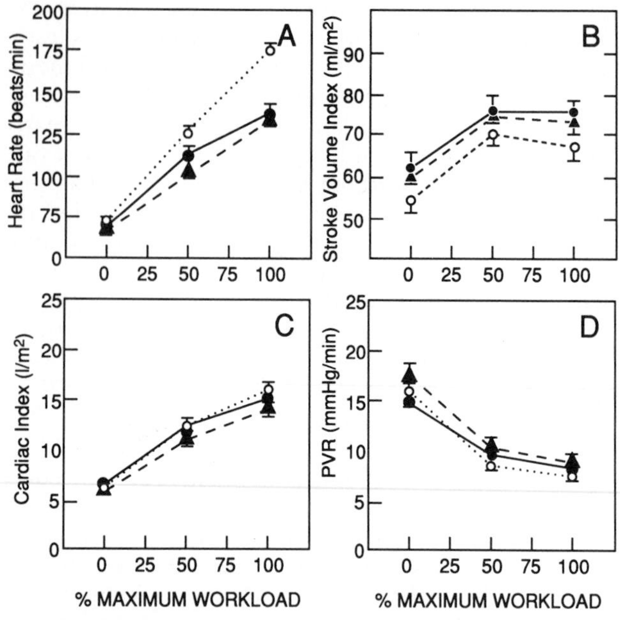

FIGURE 43-4

Heart rate (*A*), stroke volume index (SVI) (*B*), CI (*C*), and PVR (*D*) at rest and during exercise in subjects studied in Fig. 43-3. *(From Fleg et al.[18])*

the atrial or LV pressures during the early filling period or at end diastole differ in healthy younger and older individuals is also presently unknown. The time course of isovolumic myocardial relaxation, measured noninvasively as the time between aortic valve closure and mitral valve opening, becomes prolonged (40 percent increase) with aging in both men and women.[19] The peak rate at which the left ventricle (LV) fills with blood during early diastole is markedly (50 percent) reduced with aging between the ages of 20 and 80 in both healthy men and healthy women, as shown by multiple studies utilizing echocardiography, echo-Doppler (Fig. 43-5), or radionuclide techniques.[9,15,19–23] While this may be due in part to age-associated alterations in passive LV stiffness, it also likely reflects in part the age-associated prolonged relaxation phase of cardiac muscle contraction.[24,25] Asynchrony of relengthening among ventricular segments increases with aging and contributes to the reduction in filling rate.[21] In hypertensive persons, the decrease in the early ventricular filling rate varies directly with the isovolumic relaxation time.[26] Following Ca^{2+} channel blocker treatment in older hypertensive patients, increases in LV peak filling rate were accompanied by reductions in LV mass.[27] In a small study sample, in which neither systolic arterial pressure nor LV wall thickness increased with age, the pulmonary capillary wedge pressure, an index of the LV end-diastolic filling pressure, was still observed to increase with age, and a marked reduction in the early filling rate occurred in the older individuals.[22] This suggests that the early LV filling deficit that accompanies aging may not be directly related to an increase in LV wall thickness. Lifestyle variables, e.g., physical activity and ethanol, affect the LV filling rate measured via Doppler techniques in younger individuals.[23] However, the peak LV early filling rate measured by radionuclide imaging or by echo Doppler techniques does not differ between older endurance-trained athletes and age-matched, sedentary controls.[28,29]

Regardless of the uncertainties and the likely multifactorial nature of the reduction in the LV early diastolic filling rate with aging, the LV EDVI at rest is *not* reduced in older healthy individuals;[5,30] and in fact, as noted above, it increases with age in men (Fig. 43-3). The reduction in the early filling rate does not result in a reduced EDVI, in part because greater filling occurs later in diastole, particularly during the atrial contraction.[19,20,31] The enhanced atrial contribution to ventricular filling with advancing age (Fig. 43-5) is associated with left atrial enlargement[15] and is the basis of an audible fourth heart sound in most healthy older individuals.

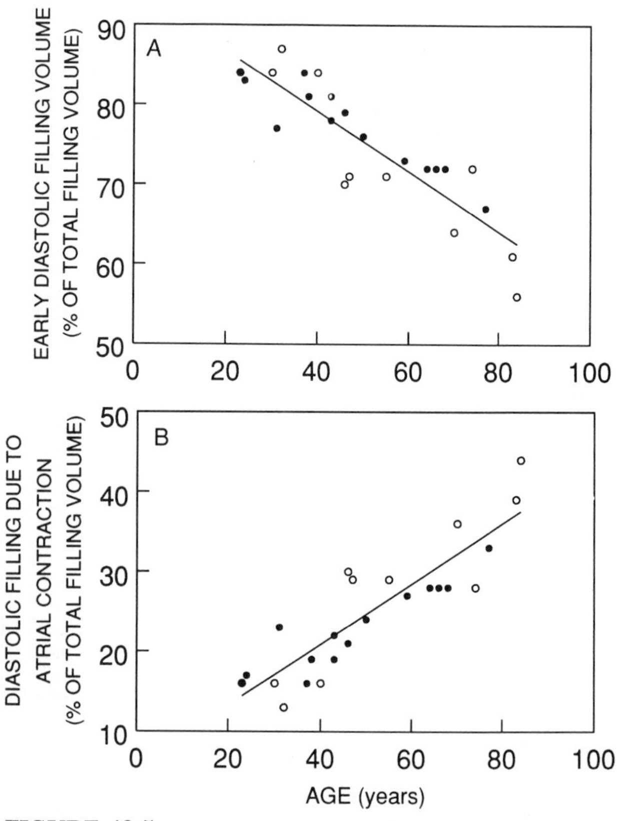

FIGURE 43-5

Comparison between the early diastolic (top) and atrial (bottom) contributions to LV filling assessed by each Doppler technique in healthy men (○) and women (●) of a broad age range. *(From Swinne et al.[20])*

VASCULAR STRUCTURE AND FUNCTION

Ventricular structure and function is in part regulated by the properties of the vasculature to which the heart is connected, i.e., by PVR, by arterial elastance, and by the amplitude and timing of reflected pulse waves, which are related to arterial stiffness.

Arterial stiffening occurs with aging even in the absence of clinical hypertension[32] (Fig. 43-6). This apparently results from changes within vascular media (among which are an age-associated change in the cross-linking of collagen, an increase in the amount of collagen, and changes in the nature of elastin). Even in the absence of clinical hypertension, systolic arterial pressure increases within the clinically "normal" range and is considered to result from the age-associated increase in arterial stiffness. In populations in which the increase in arterial stiffness with age is blunted, the arterial pressure increase with age is also blunted. The increased arterial stiffness with aging may not be related strictly to an age-associated change in vascular structure, but may also be due, in part, to increased arterial tonus. There is evidence that baroreceptor activity decreases with age, and this also has been implicated in the general age-associated increase in arterial pressure.

An increase in PVR accompanies aging in some, but not all, individuals and may, in part, be secondary to a reduction in skeletal muscle mass with aging with a concomitant reduction in capillary density. While the renal blood flow per gram of kidney weight decreases progressively after the fourth decade, this occurs in populations in which cardiac output remains unchanged with aging.[33] Thus, an increase in renal arterial resistance with aging is not secondary to reduced cardiac output and can occur in the presence of a normal total systemic vascular resistance.

Arterial stiffness is a major determinant of arterial impedance, which affects the pulsatile ejection of blood from the heart.[34] Abnormalities in aortic distensibility, such as those associated with advancing age, create a mismatch between ventricular ejection and aortic flow energies, causing the characteristic aortic impedance modulus to increase with age. The increased pulse wave velocity, due to increased vascular stiffness, causes wave reflection from peripheral sites to the ascending aorta to occur during the ventricular ejection period. This causes aortic and carotid pressures to continue to increase to a later time during ejection, resulting in an increase in systolic and pulse pressure and a change in the aortic pressure pulse contour of these arteries, which includes a late-occurring peak.[34] Pulse wave reflection, in addition to elevating aortic pressure, poses an additional component to the total vascular load on the LV. Thus, the total arterial load placed upon the LV can be characterized by PVR, characteristic aortic impedance, and pulse wave reflection. While each of these factors changes with age, the extent to which each changes varies dramatically among individuals.

There is mounting evidence that age-associated increases in arterial stiffness and pressure can be modified by lifestyle and diet. The NaCl dependence

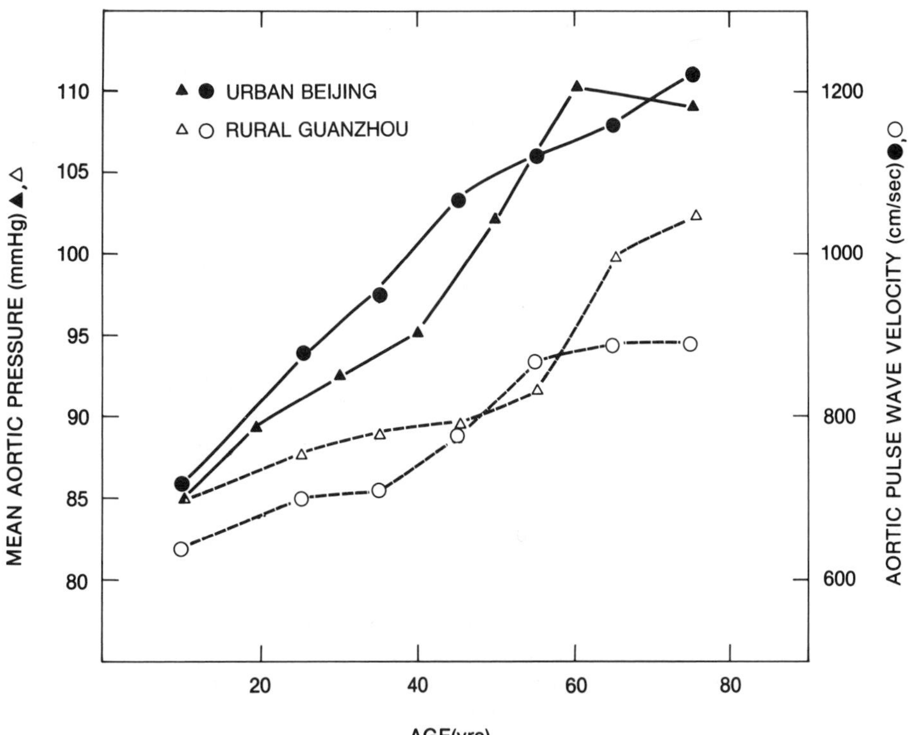

FIGURE 43-6
The mean aortic pressure and aortic pulse wave velocity as a function of age in two Chinese populations. *(Redrawn from Avolio et al.[32])*

of arterial pressure increases with age.[35,36] The rate at which the aorta stiffens with age, as manifest by the pulse wave velocity increase, has been found to differ in two Chinese populations that differ in exercise and dietary habits, particularly with reference to the amount of NaCl ingested (Fig. 43-6).[32] In a study population advised to ingest low quantities of NaCl (44 mmol/24 hours) for an average period of 2 years, the expected age-associated increases in aortic, arm, and leg pulse velocities did not occur.[37] It has been observed that age-associated increases in pulse wave velocity or carotid pressure pulse late augmentation are blunted in exercise-trained older athletes.[38] Additionally, in a healthy sedentary study population of a broad age range, arterial stiffness appears to vary inversely with aerobic capacity, independently of the effects of age to increase the former and decrease the latter.

CARDIAC STRUCTURE

The heart adapts to higher arterial stiffness, present in most older individuals, and to an increased PVR in some of these individuals, i.e., the LV wall thickens modestly with aging in healthy individuals (Fig. 43-7),[39] due, in large part, to an increase in myocyte size. The number of myocytes in the older heart may decrease, because of a dropout of some cells.[40] However, the increase in size of the remaining cells in most, but not all, instances compensates for the cell loss. An increase in the extent of interstitial collagen also occurs.

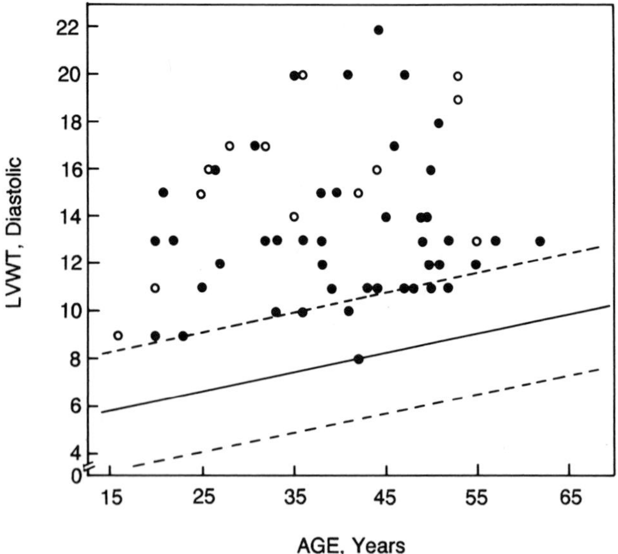

FIGURE 43-7

Least square linear regression of LV end diastolic wall thickness (LVWT) on age in healthy men and women as measured by echocardiography (solid line, mean; dotted lines, ±2 SD of the mean). Circles indicate the LVWT in patients with severe hypertension or aortic valve disease. *(From Sjogren.[39])*

CARDIAC PUMP AND MYOCARDIAL CONTRACTILE FUNCTION

The overall systolic function of the heart, *as a pump,* is best judged from the measurement of the ejection fraction [(EDV − ESV)/EDV, where EDV = end-diastolic volume and ESV = end-systolic volume]. The ejection fraction (Fig. 43-3*B*) is not altered with aging in healthy men or women at rest.[5] In the absence of clinical hypertension, the SVI at rest in the sitting position has been found not to decrease with age in many studies of highly screened subjects of a broad age range, in contrast to some prior studies (see Lakatta[1] for review). In fact, the resting SVI increases slightly with aging in men[18] (Fig. 43-4*B*), and this is attributable to the increase in EDVI with age (Fig. 43-3*A*), as EDVI and SVI are highly correlated with each other in healthy individuals.[41]

Because of the interaction of factors that regulate cardiac performance (Fig. 43-2), the intrinsic contractile behavior of myocardial fibers cannot satisfactorily be determined in situ. Several noninvasive indices that have been proposed to characterize myocardial "contractility" have essentially fallen by the wayside, due to their nonspecificity. The index of myocardial contractility that presently shares the limelight as being superior to others is the trajectory of ESV index (ESVI) versus mean arterial pressure, sometimes referred to as E_{max}, derived from a series of pressure-volume loops measured over a range of cardiac volumes.[42] In noninvasive studies in humans, a crude index of this trajectory, i.e., the ratio of the systolic arterial pressure to ESVI is not reduced at rest with age in either healthy men (Fig. 43-3*C*)[18] or healthy women.

Our present understanding of the effect of age on intrinsic cardiac muscle performance has come from studies of cardiac muscle isolated from the hearts of animals. While numerous studies have documented that the properties of muscle isolated from human hearts are very much like those of muscle isolated from hearts of most other mammals, it remains to be documented that the effect of age is similar in all species. Thus, some caution is advisable when extrapolating data from animal models. In some cases, however, similar age-associated phenomena have been observed across a wide range of species, including humans, and in these instances some degree of extrapolation to the human aging model may be justified.

With advancing adult age, characteristic changes in many aspects of cardiac muscle excitation-contraction coupling mechanisms have been noted to occur (see Lakatta[43] for review). In general, the kinetics of many of these steps discussed above are reduced in the senescent versus the younger adult muscle (see Table 43-1). The prolonged Ca_i transient is a cause of the prolonged relaxation of force of cardiac muscle of the older heart. Recall that the isovolumic relaxation period is prolonged in the human heart with aging; the basis for this prolongation could, in part, be prolonged contractile protein activation due to a prolonged Ca_i transient. While the rate of the reduction of cytosolic [Ca^{2+}] during contraction decreases with aging, there are no data to indicate that the diastolic cytosolic [Ca^{2+}] changes with age. In isotonic contractions, i.e., those in which one of the muscle ends is not fixed and in which macroscopic muscle shortening is permitted to occur, the speed and extent of shortening are less in cardiac muscle from senescent rats than they are in muscle from younger adult rats. The switching of myosin heavy chain gene expression with advancing adult age (see Table 43-1) may, in part, underlie the decline in the velocity of shortening in lightly loaded isotonic contractions with aging.[44,45] This change may also be related to the prolongation of the time to peak tension in isometric contractions and the prolonged time to peak shortening in isotonic contractions in cardiac muscle from adult versus older animals.

The multiple changes in cardiac excitation, myofilament activation, and contraction mechanisms that occur with aging are interrelated. Many of these changes can be interpreted as adaptive, as they also occur in the hypertrophied myocardium of younger animals that have adapted to experimentally induced chronic hypertension.[46,47] A similar pattern of altered expression of gene coding for myocardial proteins also occurs in both hypertension in young animals and aging in normotensive animals, and in neonatal heart cells exposed to growth factors. It is tempting to speculate that, because a nearly identical *pattern* of change in cell mechanisms occurs both in experimental pressure overload and in aging, and after exposure to growth factors in neonatal heart cells, this pattern may reflect a "logic" within the genome, i.e., that a common set of transcription factors regulates the expression of multiple genes resulting in cellular adaptation. This particular constellation of shifts in gene expression appears to be adaptive, in that it allows for an energy-efficient and prolonged contraction. In the hypertensive rodent heart it can be inferred that these changes in gene expression permit functional adaptations in response to an increased vascular "afterload."

TABLE 43-1

Aging Effects on Cardiac Muscle

I. Measures affected by aging
    - Prolonged isometric contraction
    - Decreased isotonic shortening velocity
        - ↓ Myosin Ca^{2+} activated ATPase activity
        - ↓ Myosin heavy chain (V_1 isoform) content and mRNA
        - ↑ Myosin heavy chain (V_3 isoform) content and mRNA
    - Prolonged transmembrane action potential
        - ↓ Transient outward K^+ current
        - ↑ Ca^{2+} current inactivation time
    - Prolonged Ca_i transient
        - ↓ Sarcoplasmic reticulum Ca^{2+} pumping rate
        - ↓ Sarcoplasmic reticulum Ca^{2+}-ATPase activity
        - ↓ Sarcoplasmic reticulum Ca^{2+}-ATPase protein and mRNA content
    - Increased atrial natriuretic factor mRNA
    - Decreased response to β_1-adrenergic receptor stimulation
    - Decreased threshold for cell Ca^{2+} overload and arrhythmias

II. Measures unaffected by aging
    - L-Type Ca^{2+} channel current amplitude
    - Inward rectifier K^+ current
    - Sarcoplasmic reticulum calsequestrin* mRNA
    - Actin mRNA

*A calcium-binding protein.

AN INTEGRATED VIEW OF CARDIOVASCULAR STRUCTURE AND FUNCTION AT REST WITH AGING

The age-associated changes, or lack thereof, in several aspects of cardiovascular function at rest in men are integrated in Fig. 43-8.[48] A unified interpretation of the cardiac changes observed in the figure suggests that these are adaptive, i.e., they occur in response to arterial changes that occur with aging. Arterial stiffening with aging (Fig. 43-6) leads to an enhanced pulse wave velocity which produces a late augmentation in systolic arterial pressure. The chronic augmentation in the pulse pressure causes aortic dilatation; cardiac hypertrophy (Fig. 43-7) results from an increased aortic impedance and reflected pressure waves. (Aortic dilatation which also occurs with aging may, to some extent, counteract the increase in arterial impedance due to arterial stiffening.) An increase in PVR may also contribute to an enhanced impedance to the ejection of blood from the heart in some but not all older individuals. SVI is preserved via ventricular dilatation at end diastole. The increase in LV wall thickness moderates the increase in LV wall tension occurring secondary to increased vascular loading (and the slight increase in LV EDVI). A prolonged myocardial contraction, which maintains a normal ejection time in the presence of the late augmentation of aortic impedance due to early reflected pulse waves, also contributes to the maintenance of the ejection fraction at rest; otherwise the increase of vascular loading of the myocardium in late systole would lead to premature closure of the aortic valve. Thus, systolic cardiac function at rest in clinically normotensive humans is not much altered by age (Figs. 43-3 and 43-4).

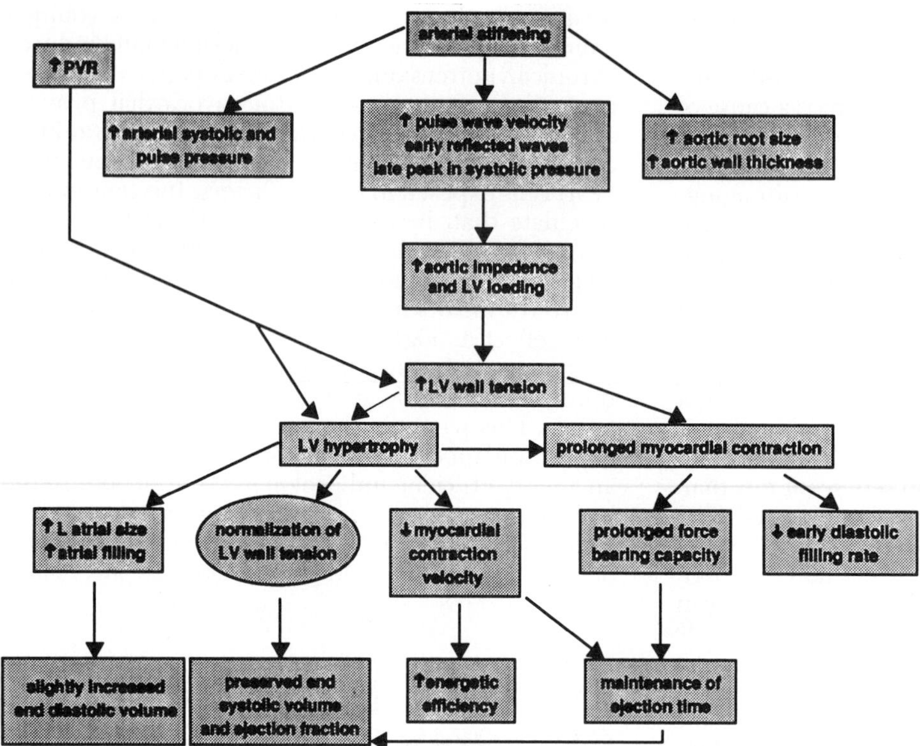

FIGURE 43-8
Arterial and cardiac changes that occur with aging in normotensive persons and at any age in hypertensive persons. One interpretation of the *constellation* (flow of arrows) is that vascular changes lead to cardiac structural and functional alterations that maintain cardiac function. *(Modified from Lakatta.[48])*

The disadvantage of prolonged contractile activation is that myocardial relaxation is relatively more incomplete in older than younger individuals at the time of the mitral valve opening. This is one factor that causes the early LV filling rate to be reduced in older individuals (Fig. 43-5). Structural changes and functional heterogeneity occurring within the LV with aging may also contribute to this reduction in peak LV filling rate. However, a concomitant adaptation—left atrial enlargement and an enhanced atrial contribution to ventricular filling (Fig. 43-5)—compensates for the reduced early filling and, in part, maintains an increased LV EDVI. The SVI is increased due to the slight increase in LV EDVI and normal LV ESVI.

In individuals with clinical hypertension, the same vascular and cardiac changes observed with aging in normotensive persons occur at a younger age and in some instances are exaggerated. The similarities between aging and hypertension are so striking that aging has been referred to as *muted hypertension,* or hypertension has been referred to as *accelerated aging.*[49,50] According to the perspectives depicted in Fig. 43-8, changes in the large arteries, cardiac mass, myocardial relaxation, and filling parameters in both normotensive persons with aging and hypertensive persons at any age form a continuum. In this regard a clinical distinction between normotensive and hypertensive persons may be somewhat artificial, but clinically useful, with regard to risk for cardiovascular morbidity and mortality. However, in hypertensive persons some changes occur with aging that are not observed in normotensives. In hypertensive men PVR increases substantially with aging, in contrast to the lack of change in PVR in normotensive men (Fig. 43-3). Thus, in hypertensive men an increase in PVR elevates diastolic and mean arterial pressures and plays a greater role in vascular loading of the heart than in normotensive men. In older hypertensive men, resting stroke volume and cardiac output are not maintained at the levels measured in younger hypertensive men.

While the cardiac changes in the scheme in Fig. 43-8 may be interpreted as resulting from increased vascular loading of the heart, a decrease in effective β-adrenergic stimulation of both the heart and the vasculature occurs with aging and in hypertension (see below) and may be implicated in the associated myocardial changes, in part via a reduction in the heart rate at rest in the sitting position and during stress, e.g., routine activities of daily life or exercise. In addition, potential age-associated changes in the level or activity of other growth factors that influence myocardial or vascular cells or their extracellular matrices may have a role in the schema depicted in Fig. 43-8.

CARDIOVASCULAR RESPONSE TO STRESS

The cardiovascular response to stress (e.g., to increases in arterial pressure or to physical exercise) in older individuals is of considerable interest in clinical medicine. First, as physicians we are called upon to provide advice and information concerning the broad aspects of cardiovascular potential of elderly persons, e.g., the effect or importance of conditioning on the maintenance of activity. Second, the cardiovascular response to stress is of importance in assessing the ability of older individuals to respond to disease states. Third, the cardiovascular response to stress has considerable value in terms of the diagnosis and management of patients with primary cardiovascular disease. Since the prevalence of cardiovascular disease is so high and progressive with age in the American population, it is of considerable importance to understand what the disease-free capabilities of the cardiovascular system are in response to exercise. Diagnostic tests that are designed to identify either the presence or the severity of cardiovascular disease frequently utilize exercise testing to enhance the ability of the testing procedure to either detect or quantitate the severity of cardiovascular disease. It is very clear that the value of such diagnostic tests and the validity of their interpretations are dependent upon rather precise information as to the normal limits of such stress-testing procedures relative to age.

ORTHOSTATIC STRESS

Cardiovascular reflex mechanisms become operative in response to perturbations from the supine, basal state and mediate the utilization of cardiovascular reserve functions. The end result of these reflex mechanisms is enhanced blood flow and preservation of arterial pressure within selected body organs. A change in blood flow from the heart depends upon the product of changes in heart rate and SVI, the latter being determined by the changes in EDVI and ESVI (Fig. 43-3). Changes in EDVI are determined, in part, by changes in venous return, which depends upon the ability of the blood to flow through the vascular system.

While there is no unanimity on the effect of aging on the response of PVR to orthostasis, several studies suggest a general tendency toward either maintenance or augmentation of PVR during orthostatic stress in subjects (mostly male) up to the ages of 60 to 70 years. In general, in healthy, community-dwelling older individuals, the arterial pressure change with posture is also maintained,[51–53] and postural hypotension or acute orthostatic intolerance, i.e., dizziness or fainting when assuming an upright from a supine position or during a passive tilt, thus does not occur.[53] In contrast to healthy, community-dwelling volunteer subjects, orthostatic intolerance is common in older (>70 years) debilitated, chronically institutionalized individuals.[54] The likelihood for orthostatic intolerance is increased in individuals who, prior to the orthostatic stress, exhibit marked reductions in peak LV filling rate, and in EDVI and SVI in the supine position.[55] In studies of this sort, however, the effects of advanced age cannot be dissociated from those of a sedentary lifestyle.

With age, the acute heart rate increase to orthostatic stress decreases in magnitude and takes longer to achieve. A decreased variability of heart rate observed in older versus younger individuals in the upright versus the supine position has been attributed to a diminished recruitment of baroreceptor activity with assumption of the upright position.[7,8] The baroreceptor sensitivity, i.e., the slope of the relationship of the change in heart rate versus the change in arterial pressure, is negatively correlated with increasing age and increased resting arterial pressure.[54] The low-pressure baroreceptor, or cardiopulmonary reflex, also decreases with age in normotensive but not in hypertensive persons.[56]

Although the heart rate increases to a lesser extent in older versus younger individuals during a postural stress, the SVI reduction tends to be less in healthy older than in younger individuals; thus, the postural change in cardiac output does not vary significantly with age because the lesser increase in heart rate in older individuals is balanced by a lesser reduction in SVI.[30] This leads to the profile of heart rate and SVI observed in healthy older men in the sitting position at rest discussed above. Even in studies that have found cardiac output to be reduced with aging in the supine position, on the basis of a reduced SVI in older versus younger men, this age effect was abolished in the sitting position, due to lesser reduction in SVI in the older men upon assumption of the upright position.[57] Responses to gradual tilt or to graded lower body negative pressure (LBNP) in elderly people are similar to responses to change in body position: SVI and cardiac output decrease *less* in older than in younger individuals,[58,59] although the heart rate increase is blunted in older individuals.[58,60] A lesser reduction in SVI in older versus younger individuals following a postural stress implies either a smaller reduction in EDVI or a greater reduction in ESVI in the older individuals. Cardiac volumes (measured by équilibrium gated cardiac blood pool scans) and heart rate have been measured in the steady state in supine and sitting positions in male volunteer subjects (aged 25 to 80 years) who had been rigorously screened to exclude cardiovascular disease.[30] In this study, a given change in cardiac output with posture in older versus younger individuals depended more upon changes in EDVI and SVI and less on heart rate change.

Although the cardiac filling rate during early diastole is less in older than in younger individuals, as noted above, and an apparent age-associated decrease in ventricular compliance is manifest during postural maneuvers,[61] filling volume deficits, in fact, do not occur in healthy older individuals either at rest or during an orthostatic stress. Rather, the LV EDVI and SVI in the sitting position at rest are preserved or even enhanced (Fig. 43-3*A*) in sedentary, healthy, older versus younger individuals.[5,30,62] A reduced venous compliance in older versus younger individuals, advanced as a mechanism to account for less of a peripheral fluid shift during orthostatic maneuvers,[58] could be a mechanism that preserves cardiac filling volume and maintains SV in the upright position in healthy, elderly individuals. A reduction in the venous response to β-adrenergic stimulation (relaxation) with preservation of the α-adrenergic (constrictor) response (see below), resulting in a greater relative venoconstriction in older individuals, may contribute to a reduced venous compliance with aging.

In contrast to the above observations, when old (74 ± 2 years) were compared with young (27 ± 3 years) individuals, the SVI decline with tilt was found to be greater in the former than in the latter and attributed not to differences in the EDVI response, but to a relative inability of older individuals to reduce their ESVI.[62] In this study, a substantial PVR increase in the older group occurred with tilt and was sufficient to maintain arterial pressure, whereas an increase in PVR did not occur in the younger group. Intriguingly, the age-associated differences in the ESVI response to postural stress were lessened after administration of a Ca^{2+} channel blocker,[62] perhaps associated with a reduction in Ca^{2+}-dependent determinants of arterial impedance (see above).

PRESSOR STRESS

The stress of sustained, isometric handgrip increases both arterial pressure and heart rate. The response varies in magnitude in proportion to the relative level and duration of effort. After 30 seconds of maximal handgrip, heart rate was observed to increase 50 beats per minute in younger (ages 23 to 31) versus 12 beats per minute in older (ages 54 to 78) healthy men.[63] During sustained isometric handgrip at 40 percent of maximum, held to fatigue, the heart rate increase in healthy men was found to diminish over a narrow (20 to 50 years of age) age range.[64]

The application of a pressor stress has also been used to assess the intrinsic myocardial reserve capacity. In response to a 30-mmHg increase in systolic blood pressure (SBP) induced by phenylephrine infusion (in the presence of β-adrenergic blockade), significant LV dilatation was noted in healthy older (60 to 68 years of age), but not in younger (18 to 34 years of age), men; the cardiac dilatation, measured via M-mode echocardiography, in older men occurred even in the presence of a smaller reduction of the heart rate in these men.[65] Thus, because of an apparent age-associated decrease in the intrinsic myocardial contractile reserve response to an increase in afterload, the senescent heart dilates and contracts from a greater preload than does the heart of younger adults. Age differences in response to α-adrenergic stimulation of the myocardial contractile state may, in part, account for the observation.

DYNAMIC EXERCISE STRESS

During dynamic exercise, changes in the mechanisms (Fig. 43-2) responsible for the augmentation of cardiac output during exercise are reasonably well understood from studies in experimental animals and in humans. As exercise begins, vagal tone decreases; cardiac output is initially augmented by an increase in venous return resulting from an increase in heart rate and sympathetic constriction of venous capacitance beds. Concomitantly, an increased workload is placed on the heart during the ejection of blood, reflected, in part, by an increase in SBP. The amount of blood ejected from the LV with each beat (i.e., the difference between ESVI and EDVI, or the SVI) increases, reflecting the fact that an increase in myocardial performance outweighs the increase in LV systolic load. These cardiac adaptations to exercise continue as moderately severe levels of exercise are encountered; the heart rate and performance of LV myocardium continue to increase as cardiac output and LV load are augmented as exercise proceeds. An additional factor, the Frank-Starling mechanism, also comes into play. Thus, during exercise there can be an increase in EDVI, and this can promote a large SVI with each heartbeat.

It might be expected that age-associated changes in the cardiovascular system might be initially manifest or most pronounced during exercise, when cardiovascular function must increase (up to as much as four- to fivefold) above the basal level. During high levels of physical exertion, the heart rate is substantially lower in healthy elderly versus younger individuals (Fig. 43-4*A*). The peak rate of LV filling increases in both younger and older individuals during exercise, but a diminished rate of filling of similar magnitude, i.e., about a 50 percent reduction, is still observed in older individuals during exercise, as at rest.[29] However, cardiac dilation at end diastole and end systole still occurs during vigorous exercise in older men (Fig. 43-3*A*). The resulting dilatation is more pronounced in those elderly individuals who have silent ischemia, i.e., who do not have signs or symptoms of coronary disease at rest but during exercise have both an abnormal ECG and thallium scan (Fig. 43-3*A*). Thus, healthy older individuals do not exhibit a compromised EDVI, due to a "stiff heart," either at rest or during exercise. However, end-diastolic pressure, which has not been measured in healthy older and younger individuals during exercise, may increase with age. During vigorous exercise the SVI, which depends upon the EDVI and ESVI, is not reduced in healthy elderly individuals (Fig. 43-4*B*). Thus, in these individuals the cardiac dilation end diastole outweighs the concomitant age-associated deficiency in ESVI reduction (Fig. 43-3*A*). The maximum CI is slightly decreased with age in healthy men (Fig. 43-4*C*) due to the heart rate deficit. In contrast, in older women, SVI during exercise is not maintained as well as it is in older men, due to a relatively smaller EDVI both at rest and during exercise in older women than in men. Thus, the maximum cardiac output during vigorous cycle exercise decreases in older women to a greater extent than it does in men due to the reduction in both heart rate and SVI in older versus younger women.

The change in ejection fraction between rest and exercise is used clinically as a diagnostic test for the detection and quantification of the severity of cardiac disease, particularly ischemic heart disease. Ejection fraction is thus of considerable clinical interest. The inability of healthy older individuals of both genders to reduce the LV ESVI during vigorous exercise accounts for a smaller increase in ejection fraction during exercise in these versus younger individuals (Fig. 43-3*C*). The failure to increase the LV ejection fraction during exercise is more severe in those older individuals who have silent ischemia than in those without evidence of coronary disease[18] and is due to a more pronounced inability to reduce the ESVI (Fig. 43-3*A*). The insufficiency in LV ESVI reduction during exercise in healthy older individuals can result from an age-associated (1) decrease in the myocardial contractile reserve or (2) failure of the ventricular afterload to decrease in older individuals to the extent that it does in younger ones. With respect to the latter, while the pulsatile determinants of ventricular afterload have not been characterized during exercise with respect to age, the PVR (Fig. 43-4*D*) during vigorous exercise declines to about the same extent in healthy older and healthy younger men.[5] The ESVI/SBP, an index of myocardial contractility (Fig. 43-3*C*), is not age-associated at rest but decreases with age during vigorous exercise.[18] The apparent decrease in LV contractility as manifest by this index is more severe in older individuals with silent ischemia than in healthy older individuals (Fig. 43-3*C*). The latter is a manifestation of the interaction of coronary artery disease and aging and must not be confused with an age-associated change in cardiac pump function.

β-ADRENERGIC STIMULATION

The hemodynamic profile of elderly individuals in Figs. 43-3 and 43-4 is strikingly similar to that of younger subjects who exercise in the presence of β-adrenergic blockade.[66] Recent observations suggest, in fact, that the age-associated differences in heart rate, LV EDVI, and SVI during exercise are abolished when this exercise is performed during β-adrenergic blockade.[67] β-Adrenergic blockade also abolishes the age-associated decrease in the peak filling rate in the sitting position, both at rest and during vigorous exercise.[29] These observations have led to the hypothesis that perhaps the most marked changes in cardiovascular response to stress that occur with aging in healthy subjects vigorously screened to exclude occult disease and highly motivated to perform exercise are due to a reduction in the efficacy of the β-adrenergic modulation of cardiovascular function.[66,68]

Catecholamines have a major modulatory influence on cardiovascular performance during acute stressful situations. Clinical evidence of an enhanced elaboration of catecholamines is found in the measurement of an increase in their levels within the plasma. The average basal level of norepinephrine has been found to increase with advancing age in many (but not all) studies. Virtually all studies have found that in response to stress the average level of norepinephrine increases to a greater extent in elderly than in younger individuals (Fig. 43-9).[10,69–71] It is noteworthy, however, that while the average plasma epinephrine and norepinephrine levels during perturbations from the basal state in elderly subjects are greater than those in younger ones, there is substantial heterogeneity among elderly individuals.

β-Adrenergic stimulation modulates the heart rate, arterial tone, and myocardial contractility. Both the β-adrenergic relaxation of arterial smooth muscle and the enhancement of myocardial performance (see below) facilitate the ejection of blood from the heart. Deficits in either with aging may be implicated in the alterations in the heart rate increase and in the ventricular ejection pattern in some elderly individuals, as shown in Fig. 43-3.

There is abundant evidence to indicate that both arterial and venous dilatation in response to β-adrenergic stimulation decline with age.[72–74] With aging a deficiency in arterial dilatation during exercise, in addition to structural changes that may occur within the large vessels, may contribute to an increase in vascular impedance during exercise[75] over and above the increase which may already be present at rest. In the presence of β-adrenergic blockade effected by propranolol, aortic impedance increases during exercise in younger dogs and the age-associated differences in impedance seen during exercise in the absence of propranolol are abolished.[75]

Age-associated changes in the effectiveness of β-adrenergic stimulation of the myocardium have also been demonstrated.[25] Isoproterenol infusion elicits less of an increase in ejection fraction in healthy older men compared with young men (Fig. 43-10*A*).[76] In isolated cardiac muscle, perfused myocardium, or cardiac cells from rats of advanced age, the β-adrenergic enhancement of the contraction amplitude is diminished compared with that in younger adult rat cardiac tissue or cells.[25,77]

The β-adrenergic modulation of pacemaker cells accounts, in part, for the increase in heart rate during exercise. The effect of bolus infusions of β-adrenergic agonists to increase heart rate (Fig. 43-10*B*) diminishes with advancing age in humans and experimental animals.[65,76–78] In contrast, the maximum heart rate

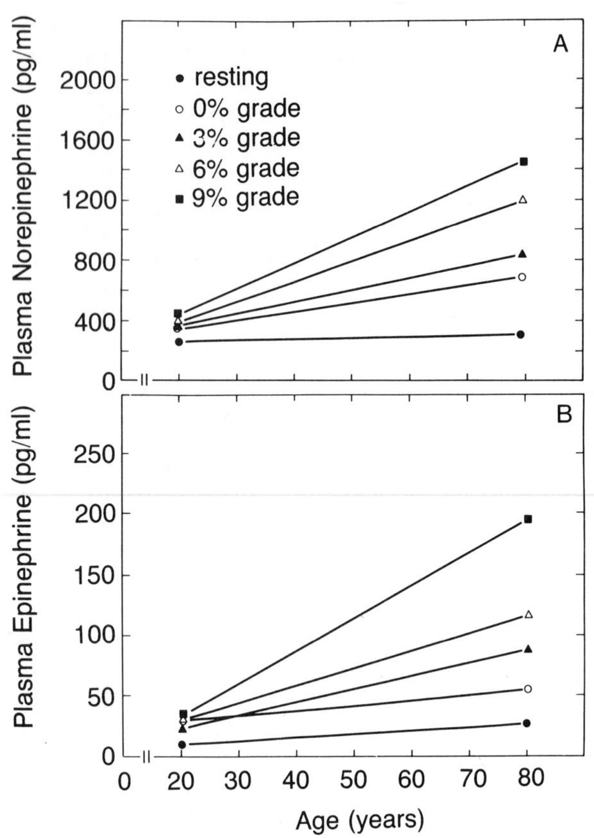

FIGURE 43-9
Norepinephrine (NE; *A*) and epinephrine (E; *B*) levels versus age at rest (●) and at common external submaximal treadmill work loads of 0 (○), 3 (▲), 6 (△), and 9 percent (■). The 9 percent grade represents maximal effort for three subjects, aged 54, 68, and 72, respectively. The NE level is unrelated to age at rest but increases with age at each workload. The slope of the NE–age regression increases progressively from 5.36 pg/year, $r = .44$, at 0 percent grade to 17.93 pg/year, $r = .64$, at 9 percent grade. The E level increases with age both at rest and at each common external workload. As with NE, the slope of the plasma E–age regression increases, from 0.67 pg/year, $r = .42$, at 0 percent grade to 2.82 pg/year, $r = .65$ at 9 percent grade. Both NE and E levels were also greater in older than in younger subjects at maximum exercise (not shown). All subjects were participants of the Baltimore Longitudinal Study of Aging who were judged to be free from occult coronary artery disease by a thorough examination that included prior stress testing with electrocardiographic monitoring. *(From Fleg.[69])*

that can be elicited by external electric pacing, which is far in excess of that elicited by isoproterenol infusion, is not age-associated.

PHYSICAL WORK CAPACITY AND AGING

The maximum oxygen consumption rate ($\dot{V}O_2$ max) achieved during stress can increase to greater than ninefold over the basal level. A ninefold increase in $\dot{V}O_2$ during exercise cannot be achieved by a four- to fivefold increase in cardiac output. Thus, in addition to an increase in cardiac output, O_2 extraction by working tissues increases and causes the arteriovenous O_2 difference to increase (up to twofold during strenuous exercise). This results, in part, from an increase (up to 15-fold) in the relative proportion of cardiac output delivered to work muscles. It has been well documented that $\dot{V}O_2$ max, adjusted for body weight, declines with age. The extent of the $\dot{V}O_2$ max decline with aging varies among studies, and this variation relates, in part, to uncontrolled population truncation due to cross-sectional sampling, differences in body weight and composition, and differences in the fitness levels among the individuals studied. Longitudinal studies report a more pronounced age-associated decline in $\dot{V}O_2$ max than do cross-sectional studies.[79]

Whether the same factors that regulate $\dot{V}O_2$ are limiting the $\dot{V}O_2$ max in individuals of different ages is not known with certainty.[3] Clearly, the maximum cardiac output is lower in older than in younger individuals due to the age-associated reduction in the maximum heart rate. However, during cycle exercise a reduction in SVI in healthy older men does not contribute to the reduction in CI because healthy sedentary older men exhibit a larger EDVI in the upright position both at rest and during exercise than do younger men, which under both conditions preserves SVI in older men, even though the reduction in ESVI during exercise is less in older than in younger men.

Whether, in fact, a measured reduction in cardiac output in older individuals (compared with younger individuals) at exhaustion actually *limits* treadmill exercise capacity and therefore $\dot{V}O_2$ max is difficult to sort out. Treadmill exercise is usually limited by dyspnea or leg fatigue. However, as the maximum minute ventilation is determined by respiratory muscle function (a peripheral determinant of $\dot{V}O_2$), and leg fatigue is influenced by muscle-conditioning status, dyspnea and leg fatigue during exercise may both relate to peripheral factors and to conditioning status. In other words, a reduction in respiratory or peripheral muscle reserve function in older individuals, due

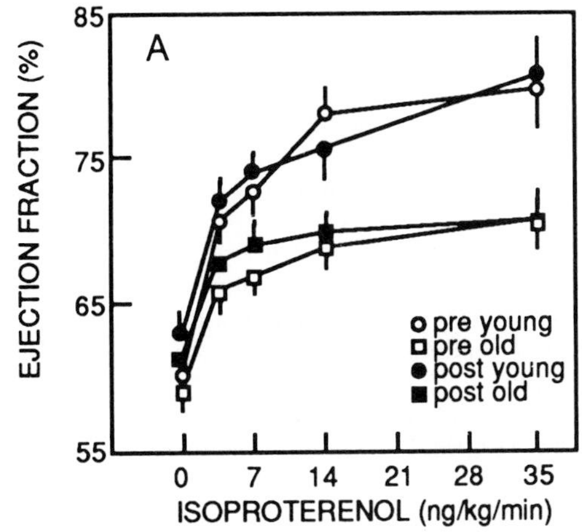

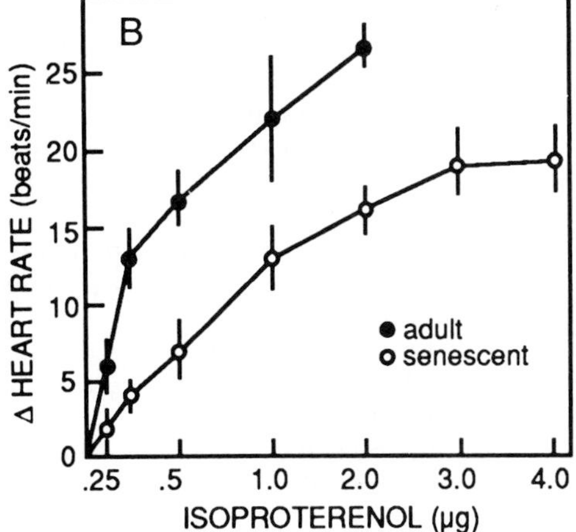

FIGURE 43-10

A. The effect of isoproterenol to increase the LV ejection fraction in younger and older healthy men in the supine position prior to (pre) and following (post) chronic endurance training. Endurance training had no effect on this index of cardiac pump function or on its response to isoproterenol. *(From Stratton et al.[76])*
B. The effect of bolus intravenous isoproterenol infusions to increase heart rate in healthy young and older men at rest. *(From Yin et al.[65])*

to an age-associated reduction in the number of muscle fibers or to a reduction in the muscle utilization of O_2 per muscle unit (due to aging or to a sedentary disposition), might contribute to the age-associated limitation of $\dot{V}O_2$ max. A concomitant reduction in cardiac output would be *expected* to accompany a reduced work capacity on this basis. Thus, a reduction in cardiac output measured at exhaustion does not mean it is the *cause* of the reduced work capacity and $\dot{V}O_2$ max. Indeed, some studies during graded upright cycle exercise have been interpreted to indicate that the cardiac response *for the work performed* ($\dot{V}O_2$ achieved) in older subjects is as adequate as that in younger subjects.[80] It is of note, however, that during cycle ergometry, the peak O_2 consumption in a given individual averages about 80 percent of that during treadmill exercise and the factor limiting the duration intensity of the exercise is usually exclusively leg fatigue. While this difference in peak O_2 consumption between the two modes of aerobic exercise is not age-related, it still may preclude extrapolation of the maximum cardiac output and $\dot{V}O_2$ measurements during cycle ergometry to cardiac output and $\dot{V}O_2$ achieved during maximum treadmill exercise in a given individual.

Noncardiac factors leading to a reduction in the peak arteriovenous $\dot{V}O_2$, e.g., age-associated changes in body composition and muscle mass,[81–85] also appear to be involved in the reduction in $\dot{V}O_2$ max with aging. In spite of a decline in the skeletal muscle mass with aging, total body mass remains constant because of an increase in body fat, not only subcutaneous but also intraperitoneal and intramuscular.[83,84] Normalization of peak $\dot{V}O_2$ to an index of muscle mass (creatinine excretion) markedly reduces the magnitude of the apparent "age-associated" decline in $\dot{V}O_2$ normalized for total body mass (weight in kilograms), i.e., the routine normalization procedure utilized in most studies.[81]

SUMMARY

Although aerobic capacity declines with advancing age in individuals without cardiac disease, the extent to which this can be attributed to a decrement in cardiac reserve is not certain. A substantial part of the age-associated decline in $\dot{V}O_2$ max appears to be due to peripheral factors and, in part at least, can be attributed to an increase in body fat and a decrease in muscle mass with age. While the heart rate is lower in healthy elderly versus younger individuals at high levels of dynamic exercise, cardiac dilation at end diastole and end systole occurs in older subjects. Thus, in health, older individuals do not exhibit a compromised EDVI, due to a "stiff heart" even during exercise. While the SVI during exercise in such individuals is preserved by the cardiac dilation, the increase in ejection fraction is blunted. This same hemodynamic pattern, i.e., a reduced exercise heart rate and greater cardiac dilation at end diastole and end systole, occurs in individuals of any age who exercise in the presence of β-adrenergic blockade. In fact, when perspectives from studies that range from measurements of the stress response in intact humans to measurements of subcellular biochemistry in animal models are integrated, a diminished responsiveness to β-adrenergic modulation is among the most notable changes that occur in the cardiovascular system with advancing age.

Alterations in cardiovascular function which exceed the identified limits for age-associated changes for healthy elderly individuals are most likely manifestations of interactions of aging per se with age-associated changes of severe physical deconditioning or the presence of cardiovascular disease, which are, unfortunately, so prevalent within our population.

REFERENCES

1. Lakatta EG: Cardiovascular function in later life. *Cardiovasc Med* 10:37, 1985.
2. Elveback L, Lie JT: Continued high incidence of coronary artery disease at autopsy in Olmsted County, Minnesota, 1950 to 1979. *Circulation* 70:345, 1984.
3. Raven PB, Mitchell J: The effect of aging on the cardiovascular response to dynamic and static exercise, in Weisfeldt ML (ed): *The Aging Heart.* New York: Raven, 1980, p 269.
4. Lakatta EG: Determinants of cardiovascular performance: Modification due to aging. *J Chronic Dis* 36:15, 1983.
5. Rodeheffer RJ et al: Exercise cardiac output is maintained with advancing age in healthy human subjects: Cardiac dilatation and increased stroke volume compensate for a diminished heart rate. *Circulation* 69:203, 1984.
6. Fleg JL et al: Age-associated changes in the components of atrioventricular conduction in apparently healthy volunteers. *J Gerontol* 45:M95, 1990.
7. Schwartz JB et al: Aging effects on heart rate variation. *J Gerontol* 46:M99, 1991.
8. Simpson DM, Wicks R: Spectral analysis of heart rate indicated reduced baroreceptor-related heart rate variability in elderly persons. *J Gerontol* 43:M21, 1988.
9. Kostis JB et al: The effect of age on heart rate in subjects free of heart disease: Studies by ambulatory electrocardiography and maximal exercise stress test. *Circulation* 65:141, 1982.
10. Pfeifer MA et al: Differential changes of autonomic nervous system function with age in man. *Am J Med* 75:249, 1983.
11. Jose AD: Effect of combined sympathetic and parasympathetic blockade on heart rate and cardiac function in man. *Am J Cardiol* 18:476, 1966.
12. Fleg JL et al: Pathophysiology of the aging heart and circulation, in Messerli FH (ed): *Cardiovascular Disease in the Elderly,* 2d ed. Boston, Nijhoff, 1988, p 9.
13. Fleg JL: Arrhythmias and conduction disorders, in Abrams WB, Berkow B (eds): *The Merck Manual of Geriatrics.* Rahway, NJ, Merck Sharp & Dohme Research Laboratories, 1990, p 370.
14. Fleg JL, Kennedy HL: Cardiac arrhythmias in healthy elderly population: Detection by 24-hour ambulatory electrocardiography. *Chest* 81:302, 1982.
15. Gerstenblith G et al: Echocardiographic assessment of a normal adult aging population. *Circulation* 56:273, 1977.
16. Potter JF et al: Effect of aging on the cardiothoracic ratio of men. *J Am Geriatr Soc* 30:404, 1982.
17. Ensor RE et al: Longitudinal chest x-ray changes in normal men. *J Gerontol* 38:307, 1983.
18. Fleg JL et al: Additive effects of age and silent myocardial ischemia on the left ventricular response to upright cycle exercise. *J Appl Physiol* 75:1993. in press.
19. Spirito P, Maron BJ: Influence of aging on Doppler echocardiographic indices on left ventricular diastolic function. *Br Heart J* 59:672, 1988.
20. Swinne CJ et al: Age-associated changes in left ventricular diastolic performance during isometric exercise in normal subjects. *Am J Cardiol* 69:823, 1992.
21. Bonow RO et al: Effects of aging on asynchronous left ventricular regional function and global ventricular filling in normal human subjects. *J Am Coll Cardiol* 11:50, 1988.
22. Kitzman DW et al: Age-related alterations of Doppler left ventricular filling indexes in normal subjects are independent of left ventricular mass, heart rate, contractility and loading conditions. *J Am Coll Cardiol* 18:1243, 1991.
23. Voutilainen S et al: Factors influencing Doppler indexes of left ventricular filling in healthy persons. *Am J Cardiol* 68:653, 1991.
24. Lakatta EG et al: Prolonged contraction duration in aged myocardium. *J Clin Invest* 55:61, 1975.
25. Lakatta EG, Yin FCP: Myocardial aging: Functional alterations and related cellular mechanisms. *Am J Physiol* 242:H927, 1982.
26. Smith VE et al: Echocardiographic assessment of left ventricular diastolic performance in hypertensive subjects: Correlation with changes in left ventricular mass. *Hypertension* 9(suppl 2):II81, 1987.
27. Schulman SP et al: The effects of antihypertensive therapy on left ventricular mass in elderly patients. *N Engl J Med* 322:1350, 1990.
28. Forman DE et al: Enhanced left ventricular diastolic filling associated with long-term endurance training *J Gerontol* R47:M56, 1992.
29. Schulman S et al: Age-related decline in left ventricular filling at rest and exercise: Another manifestation of decreased beta-adrenergic responsiveness in the elderly. *Am J Physiol,* in press.
30. Rodeheffer RJ et al: Postural changes in cardiac volumes in men in relation to adult age. *Exp Gerontol* 21:367, 1986.
31. Kuo LC et al: Quantification of atrial contribution to left ventricular filling by pulsed Doppler echocardiography and the effect of age in normal and diseased hearts. *Am J Cardiol* 59:1174, 1987.
32. Avolio AP et al: Effects of aging on arterial distensibility in populations with high and low prevalence of hypertension: Comparison between urban and rural communities in China. *Circulation* 71:202, 1985.
33. Danziger RS et al: The age-associated decline in glomerular filtration in healthy normotensive volunteers: Lack of relationship to cardiovascular performance. *J Am Geriatr Soc* 38:1127, 1990.
34. Nichols WW et al: Age-related changes in left ventricular/arterial coupling, in Yin FCP (ed): *Ventricular Vascular Coupling: Clinical Physiology, and Engineering Aspects.* New York, Springer-Verlag, 1987, p 79.
35. Khaw KT, Barrett-Connor E: The association between blood pressure, age, and dietary sodium and potassium: A population study. *Circulation* 77:53, 1988.
36. Luft FC et al: Salt sensitivity and resistance of blood pressure. Age and race as factors in physiological responses. *Hypertension* 17(suppl I):I102, 1991.
37. Avolio AP et al: Improved arterial distensibility in normotensive subjects on a low salt diet. *Arteriosclerosis* 6:166, 1986.
38. Haber P et al: Effects in elderly people 67–76 years of age of three-month endurance training on a bicycle ergometer. *Eur Heart J* 5(suppl E):37, 1985.

39. Sjogren AL: Left ventricular wall thickness in patients with circulatory overload of the left ventricle. Ultrasonic, physical, electrocardiographic and radiologic correlations. *Ann Clin Res* 4:310, 1972.
40. Olivetti G et al: Cardiomyopathy of the aging human heart. Myocyte loss and reactive cellular hypertrophy. *Circ Res* 68:1560, 1991.
41. Renlund DG: Interaction between left ventricular end-diastolic and end-systolic volumes in normal humans. *Am J Physiol* 258:H473, 1990.
42. Sagawa K: The pressure-volume relation of the ventricle: Definition, modifications and clinical use (editorial). *Circulation* 63:1223, 1981.
43. Lakatta EG: Cardiac muscle changes in senescence. *Annu Rev Physiol* 49:519, 1987.
44. Capasso JM et al: Myocardial biochemical, contractile and electrical performance after imposition of hypertension in young and old rats. *Circ Res* 58:445, 1986.
45. Alpert NR et al: The effect of age on contractile protein ATPase activity and the velocity of shortening, in Tanz RD et al (eds): *Factors Influencing Myocardial Contractility*. New York, Academic, 1967, p 127.
46. Lakatta EG: Do hypertension and aging have a similar effect on the myocardium? *Circulation* 75(suppl I):I69, 1987.
47. Lakatta EG: Regulation of cardiac muscle function in the hypertensive heart, in Cox RH (ed): *Cellular and Molecular Mechanisms of Hypertension*. New York, Plenum, 1991, p 149.
48. Lakatta EG: Normal changes of aging, in Abrams WB, Berkow R (eds): *Merck Manual of Geriatrics*. Rahway, NJ, Merck Sharp & Dohme Research Laboratory, 1990, p 310.
49. Pickering GW: *High Blood Pressure*. London, Churchill, 1955, p 154.
50. Wolinsky H: Long-term effects of hypertension on the rat aortic wall and their relation to concurrent aging changes. Morphological and chemical studies. *Circ Res* 30:301, 1972.
51. Jansen RW: The influence of age and blood pressure on the hemodynamic and humoral response to head-up tilt. *J Am Geriatr Soc* 37:528, 1989.
52. Shannon RP et al: The effect of age and sodium depletion on cardiovascular response to orthostasis. *Hypertension* 8:438, 1986.
53. Smith JJ, Porth CJM: Age and response to orthostatic stress, in Smith JJ (ed): *Circulatory Response to the Upright Posture*. Boca Raton, FL, CRC Press, 1990, p 1.
54. Lipsitz LA: Orthostatic hypotension in the elderly. *N Engl J Med* 321:952, 1989.
55. Lipsitz LA et al: Reduced supine cardiac volumes and diastolic filling rates in elderly patients with chronic medical conditions. *J Am Geriatr Soc* 38:103, 1990.
56. Cleroux J et al: Decreased cardiopulmonary reflexes with aging in normotensive humans. *Am J Physiol* 257:H961, 1989.
57. Fagard R, Staessen J: Relation of cardiac output at rest and during exercise to age in essential hypertension. *Am J Cardiol* 67:585, 1991.
58. Ebert TJ et al: Effect of age and coronary heart disease on the circulatory responses to graded lower body negative pressure. *Cardiovasc Res* 16:663, 1982.
59. Frey MAB, Hoffler GW: Association of sex and age with responses to lower-body negative pressure. *J Appl Physiol* 65:1752, 1988.
60. Astrand I et al: Reduction in maximal oxygen uptake with age. *J Appl Physiol* 35:649, 1973.
61. Nixon JV et al: Ventricular performance in human hearts aged 61 to 73 years. *Am J Cardiol* 56:932, 1985.
62. Shannon RP et al: Comparison of differences in the hemodynamic response to passive postural stress in healthy subjects >70 years and <30 years of age. *Am J Cardiol* 67:1110, 1991.
63. Kino M et al: Effects of age on responses to isometric exercise. Isometric handgrip in noninvasive screening for cardiovascular disease. *Am Heart J* 90:575, 1975.
64. Petrofsky JS, Lind AR: Isometric strength, endurance, and the blood pressure and heart rate responses during exercise in healthy men and women, with special reference to age and body fat content. *Pflugers Arch* 360:49, 1975.
65. Yin FCP et al: Age-associated decrease in ventricular response to haemodynamic stress during beta-adrenergic blockade. *Br Heart J* 40:1349, 1978.
66. Lakatta EG: Altered autonomic modulation of cardiovascular function with adult aging: Perspectives from studies ranging from man to cell, in Stone HL, Weglicki WB (eds): *Pathobiology of Cardiovascular Injury*. Boston, Nijhoff, 1985, p 441.
67. Fleg JL et al: Effect of propranolol on age-associated changes in left ventricular performance during exercise (abstract). *Circulation* 84:II–187, 1991.
68. Filburn CR, Lakatta EG: Aging alterations in beta-adrenergic modulation of cardiac cell function, in Johnson JE (ed): *Aging and Cell Function*. New York, Plenum, 1984, p 211.
69. Fleg JL et al: Age-related augmentation of plasma catecholamines during dynamic exercise in healthy males. *J Appl Physiol* 59:1033, 1985.
70. Rowe JW, Troen BR: Sympathetic nervous system and aging in man. *Endocrine Rev* 1:167, 1980.
71. Sowers JR et al: Plasma norepinephrine responses to posture and isometric exercise increase with age in the absence of obesity. *J Gerontol* 38:315, 1983.
72. Pan HY et al: Decline in beta adrenergic receptor-mediated vascular relaxation with aging in man. *J Pharmacol Exp Ther* 239:802, 1986.
73. O'Donnell SR, Wanstall JC: Beta-1 and beta-2 adrenoceptor-mediated responses in preparations of pulmonary artery and aorta from young and aged rats. *J Pharmacol Exp Ther* 228:733, 1984.
74. Tsujimoto G et al: Age-related decrease in beta adrenergic receptor-mediated vascular smooth muscle relaxation. *J Pharmacol Exp Ther* 239:411, 1986.
75. Yin FCP et al: Role of aortic input impedance in the decreased cardiovascular response to exercise with aging in dogs. *J Clin Invest* 68:28, 1981.
76. Stratton JR et al: Differences in cardiovascular responses to isoproterenol in relation to age and exercise training in healthy men. *Circulation* 86:504, 1992.
77. Sakai M et al: Contractile response of individual cardiac myocytes to norepinephrine declines with senescence. *Am J Physiol* 262:H184, 1992.
78. Vestal RE et al: Reduced beta-adrenoreceptor sensitivity in the elderly. *Clin Pharmacol Ther* 26:181, 1979.
79. Dehn MM, Bruce RA: Longitudinal variations in maximal oxygen intake with age and activity. *J Appl Physiol* 33:805, 1972.
80. Julius S et al: Influence of age on the hemodynamic response to exercise. *Circulation* 36:222, 1967.

81. Capasso JM et al: Differences in load dependence of relaxation between the left and right ventricular myocardium as a function of age in rats. *Circ Res* 65:1499, 1989.
82. Fleg JL, Lakatta EG: Role of muscle loss in the age-associated reduction in $\dot{V}O_2$ max. *J Appl Physiol* 65:1147, 1988.
83. Frontera WR et al: Strength training and determinants of $\dot{V}O_2$ max in older men. *J Appl Physiol* 68:329, 1990.
84. Frontera WR et al: Strength conditioning in older men: Skeletal muscle hypertrophy and improved function. *J Appl Physiol* 64:1038, 1988.
85. Lexell J et al: What is the cause of the ageing atrophy? Total number, size and proportion of different fiber types studied in whole vastus lateralis muscle from 15- to 83-year-old-men. *J Neurol Sci* 84:275, 1988.

Chapter 44

AGING AND ATHEROSCLEROSIS

Edwin L. Bierman

Atherosclerosis, a distinctly age-related disorder, is responsible for the majority of deaths in most westernized societies and is by far the leading cause of death in the United States above age 65.[1] It is the most common disorder included under the rubric of *arteriosclerosis,* a generic term for thickening and hardening of the arterial wall. Atherosclerosis is a disorder of the larger arteries that underlies most coronary artery disease and peripheral arterial disease of the lower extremities and also plays a major role in cerebrovascular disease. Nonatheromatous forms of arteriosclerosis include focal calcific arteriosclerosis (Mönckeberg's sclerosis) and arteriolosclerosis.

NATURAL HISTORY

Atherosclerosis in humans appears to begin very early in life and develops progressively over the years, resulting in an exponential increase in the incidence of clinical atherosclerotic events (myocardial infarction, angina pectoris, cerebrovascular accidents, gangrene) with age (Fig. 44-1). A high prevalence of atherosclerotic changes in the arteries of American males as early as the second and third decades of life has been documented from autopsies of casualties of war in Korea and Vietnam. Despite differences in prevalence rates of atherosclerosis among various countries, there is a progressively increasing mortality with age from atherosclerosis-related diseases.[2] In the United States, more than 80 percent of cases of atherosclerotic cardiovascular disease are found in individuals over age 65.

Thus, atherosclerosis is an almost universal age-related phenomenon in human populations and is therefore closely linked to aging. It is also apparent that atherosclerosis is a multifactorial disease. The hypothesis presented in this chapter and earlier reviews[3,4] is that both intrinsic aging processes and environmental factors (such as diet) operate over many years and are superimposed on unknown genetic factors to produce the disorder. Clearly, atherosclerosis is not simply the result of unmodified intrinsic biological aging processes, since most mammalian species age without spontaneously developing atherosclerosis. Furthermore, there are populations in the world that age to the life span appropriate to the human species without developing clinical evidence of atherosclerosis. Therefore, although there may be almost universal prevalence of atherosclerosis, there is considerable difference in the prevalence rate in various parts of the world, probably related to factors other than age per se.[1] The dramatically increased prevalence of atherosclerosis during the last century, albeit partly related to improved diagnosis, presumably largely reflects the marked increase in human life span.

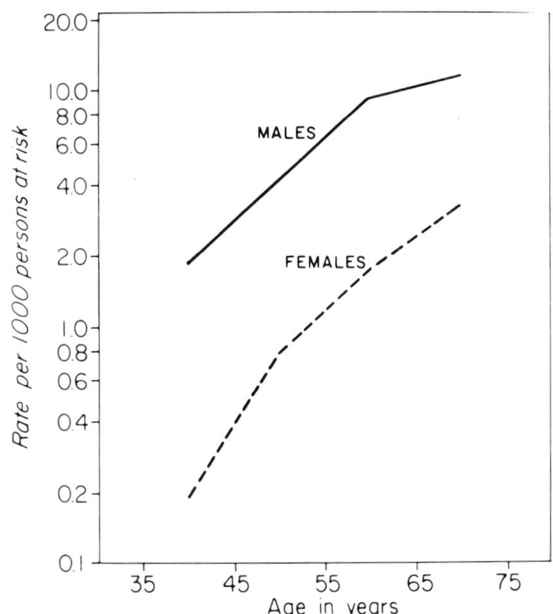

FIGURE 44-1

Average annual incidence rate of the first myocardial infarction in the Framingham population during a 16-year follow-up.

NONATHEROMATOUS ARTERIOSCLEROSIS

Focal calcific arteriosclerosis (Mönckeberg's sclerosis), a disorder of the medial layer of medium-sized muscular arteries, is also related to aging. It is rare in individuals below age 50 and affects both sexes indiscriminately. The process involves degeneration of medial smooth muscle cells followed by calcium deposition, which gives a characteristic radiological appearance consisting of regular concentric calcifications in cross section and a railroad track in longitudinal section, most often seen in arteries in the pelvis, legs, and feet. These changes are common in the elderly but alone do not narrow the arterial lumen, have little effect on the circulation, and may have little functional significance. However, in the lower extremities, medial sclerosis is often associated with atherosclerosis, contributing to arterial occlusion. In individuals with diabetes mellitus or who are receiving long-term corticosteroid drugs, focal calcification may be accelerated and severe. Focal calcification also is responsible for the arteriosclerotic aortic valve in the elderly which may progress to the severe calcific aortic stenosis of the aged.

Since little is known of the pathogenesis of either focal calcification or arteriolosclerosis (a degenerative disorder of arterioles in visceral organs related to hypertension) in relation to aging or otherwise, the remainder of the chapter will be devoted to a discussion of atherosclerosis, one of the scourges of modern industrialized civilizations.

RISK FACTORS FOR ATHEROSCLEROSIS IN RELATION TO AGING

A number of conditions and habits are present more frequently in individuals who develop atherosclerosis than in the general population ("risk factors"). Most people below age 65 with atherosclerosis have one or more identifiable risk factors other than aging per se (Table 44-1). The presence of multiple risk factors makes a person more likely to develop a clinical atherosclerotic event and to do so earlier than a person with no risk factors. Thus there is a lower prevalence of the major risk factors among the elderly afflicted with their first clinical manifestation.

Among the risk factors, age, male gender, and genetic factors are currently considered to be nonreversible, whereas there is continually emerging evidence that elimination of cigarette smoking, treatment of hypertension, reduction of hypercholesterolemia, and reduction of marked obesity reverse the high risk for atherosclerosis attributable to those factors. Potentially reversible factors currently under study include hyperglycemia and other forms of hyperlipidemia.

TABLE 44-1

Risk Factors for Atherosclerosis

Not Reversible
Aging
Male sex
Genetic traits—positive family history of premature atherosclerosis
Reversible
Cigarette smoking
Hypertension
Obesity
Hypercholesterolemia
Potentially or Partially Reversible
Hypertriglyceridemia and other forms of hyperlipidemia
Hyperglycemia and diabetes mellitus
Low levels of high-density lipoprotein (HDL)
Other Possible Factors
Physical inactivity
Emotional stress and/or personality type

These factors are not mutually exclusive since they clearly interact. For example, obesity appears to be causally associated with hypertension, hyperglycemia, hypercholesterolemia, hypertriglyceridemia, and low high-density lipoprotein (HDL) cholesterol. Genetic factors may play a role by exerting direct effects on arterial wall structure and metabolism, or they may act indirectly by imparting greater susceptibility to hypertension, hyperlipidemia, diabetes, and obesity. Aging appears to be one of the more complex factors associated with the development of atherosclerosis, since many of the risk factors in themselves are related to aging, e.g., elevated blood pressure, hyperglycemia, and hyperlipidemia. Thus, in addition to possible involvement of intrinsic aging in atherogenesis (perhaps through effects on arterial wall metabolism), a variety of associated metabolic factors are also age-dependent.

Obesity

There is both an inexorable and a preventable increase in adiposity with aging. Even if body weight remains constant throughout life, there are changes in body composition, with a decline in lean body mass (muscle and bone) and a reciprocal increase in the proportion of fat tissue, resulting in an increase in relative adiposity and a decrease in caloric requirements with age. Actually, in most westernized populations, body weight does not remain constant with age, perhaps because caloric intake is not decreased in harmony with reduced requirements, resulting in an absolute increase in adiposity as well. Obesity, defined as more than 30 percent above average weight, appears to be important in atherogenesis since, in general, morbidity and mortality from atherosclerotic heart disease are higher in direct relation to the degree of overweight, particularly apparent before age 50.[5] Recent studies have shown a close relationship between the regional distribution of obesity (i.e., abdominal) and coronary atherosclerosis.[6]

Hypertension

Blood pressure levels also appear to increase inexorably with age, and the risk of atherosclerosis appears to increase progressively with increasing blood pressure (and can be diminished by therapeutic reduction of blood pressure).[7] The nature of this age relation, however, varies among populations, since there are remote populations that appear to age without any changes in blood pressure levels, perhaps in relation to physical activity or salt intake. In contrast to other age-related risk factors, hypertension appears to increase the development of atherosclerosis throughout the life span[7] (see Chap. 47, "Hypertension"). It is an especially strong risk factor for cerebrovascular lesions resulting in stroke.

Hyperglycemia and Diabetes

Blood glucose levels increase progressively with age in most population studies, and hyperglycemia, in turn, appears to play a significant role in the development of atherosclerosis.[8] A high prevalence of diabetes and hyperglycemia is associated with clinically evident atherosclerosis. Increasing abdominal adiposity and decreasing physical activity probably play some role in the progressive increase in circulating glucose levels with age,[9] since there are primitive populations who remain active and thin and show minimal age-related changes. This suggests that intrinsic aging effects on glucose metabolism and glucoregulatory hormone homeostasis are present and contributory, but superimposed environmental factors, such as caloric excess, amplify the age-related effect. In known non–insulin-dependent diabetics (NIDDM), there is at least a twofold increase in incidence of myocardial infarction compared with the incidence in nondiabetics. However, the increased susceptibility for atherosclerosis among NIDDM cannot be accounted for merely by mechanisms associated with hyperglycemia, or, in fact, by increased prevalence of all of the common risk factors.[8] Additional candidate factors include accumulation of advanced glycosylated end product (AGE proteins) in the arterial wall[10] and accelerated oxidation of lipoproteins[11] in diabetes, both also concomitants of aging.

Hyperlipidemia

Both hypercholesterolemia and hypertriglyceridemia appear to be important age-related risk factors for the development of atherosclerosis. While genetic factors are important for emergence of premature atherosclerosis in affected individuals from families with one of the familial hyperlipidemias,[12] triglyceride and cholesterol levels in whole populations are also important, since they appear to increase with age.[13] Adiposity may play a critical role in the age-associated increase in triglyceride and cholesterol levels, since curves for the increase in plasma triglyceride with age and comparable curves for plasma cholesterol with age are superimposable on the obesity-age curve in populations.[3] Again, in primitive people who remain thin throughout adulthood, serum lipids do not increase with age. Metabolic mechanisms have been postulated whereby abdominal obesity, which is associated with insulin resistance and compensatory hyperinsulinemia, promotes enhanced production of triglyceride- and cholesterol-rich lipoproteins from the liver. Studies in humans have shown that overweight individuals have higher production rates of both triglyceride and cholesterol. Current concepts of plasma lipoprotein transport suggest that accumulation of cholesterol in the circulation may in part be secondary to excessive production of triglyceride-rich lipoproteins.[14] Furthermore, progressive accumulation of cholesterol in the bulk tissues of humans occurs during the lifetime, particularly in connective and adipose tissues. Thus, aging is associated with an expansion of both circulating and tissue pools of cholesterol.

The importance of hyperlipidemia as a risk factor for atherosclerosis varies in relation to age. Serum cholesterol levels appear to relate to the development of coronary heart disease in males, predominantly in young and middle-aged adults, and less so in older individuals.[15] Nevertheless, blood lipid levels, notably higher- and lower-density lipoprotein cholesterol levels, continue to predict coronary artery disease in the elderly. In a study in Seattle of the role of genetic forms of hyperlipidemia in clinical atherosclerosis in which 500 consecutive survivors of myocardial infarction were tested, hyperlipidemia was present in about one-third of the group. Approximately half of the males and two-thirds of the females below age 50 had either hypertriglyceridemia, hypercholesterolemia, or both. In contrast, in individuals over age 70, the prevalence of atherosclerotic coronary disease was very high, yet few males had hyperlipidemia and only about one-fourth of the females had elevated lipid levels. Thus there appeared to be a progressive decline with age in both sexes in the association of hyperlipidemia with this disorder.[16]

More than half of the hyperlipidemic-atherosclerotic survivors appeared to have simple, monogenic, familial disorders inherited as an autosomal dominant trait (familial combined hyperlipidemia, familial hypertriglyceridemia, and familial hypercholesterolemia, in descending order of frequency). These simply inherited hyperlipidemias (particularly familial hypercholesterolemia) were more frequent in myocardial infarction survivors below age 60 than in those who were older. In contrast, nonmonogenic forms of hyperlipidemia occurred with equal frequency above and below age 60.[4] Thus, it appears that genes associated with the simply inherited hyperlipidemias accelerate changes seen with age, leading to premature atherosclerosis.

Several lipoprotein fractions transport cholesterol (see Chap. 73). Low-density lipoproteins (LDLs) carry most of the plasma cholesterol; LDL cholesterol levels thus usually parallel plasma cholesterol concentrations and are directly related to the risk of atherosclerosis. In contrast, HDLs, which carry about 20 percent of the plasma cholesterol, are inversely related to the risk of atherosclerosis.[17] Thus, high HDL cholesterol levels are considered to be protective. HDL cholesterol levels do not appear to change with age after puberty, but other age-related factors, such as obesity and hypertriglyceridemia, are associated with low HDL cholesterol levels. Low HDL levels do appear to continue to predict the emergence of coronary heart disease over age 65.[18]

PATHOGENESIS OF ATHEROSCLEROSIS IN RELATION TO AGING

Cell Biology of Arterial Wall and Theories of Atherogenesis

One generally accepted theory for the pathogenesis of atherosclerosis consistent with a variety of experimental evidence is the *reaction to injury* hypothesis.[19] According to this theory, the endothelial cells lining the intima are exposed to repeated or continuing insults to their integrity. The injury to the endothelium may be subtle or gross, resulting in a loss of the cells' ability to function as a complete barrier. Examples of types of injury to the endothelium include chemical injury, as in chronic hypercholesterolemia; mechanical stress associated with hypertension; and immunological injury, as may be seen after cardiac or renal transplantation. Loss of endothelial cells at susceptible sites in the arterial tree would lead to exposure of the subendothelial tissue to increased concentrations of plasma constituents; the sequence of events that follows includes monocyte and platelet adherence, migration of monocytes into the arterial wall to become macrophages, platelet aggregation and formation of microthrombi, and release of platelet and macrophage secretory products, including potent mitogenic factors and cytokines (such as platelet-derived growth factor, colony stimulating factors, interleukins). These growth factors and cytokines in conjunction with other plasma constituents, including lipoproteins and hormones such as insulin, could stimulate both the migration of medial smooth muscle cells into the intima and their proliferation at these sites of injury. These proliferating smooth muscle cells would deposit a connective tissue matrix and accumulate lipid, a process that would be particularly enhanced with hyperlipidemia. Macrophages derived from circulating blood monocytes also accumulate lipid. Thus repeated or chronic injury could lead to a slowly progressing lesion involving a gradual increase in smooth muscle cells, macrophages, connective tissue, and lipid. Areas where the shearing stress on endothelial cells is increased, such as branch points or bifurcations of vessels, would be at greater risk. As the lesions progress and the intima becomes thicker, blood flow over the sites will be altered and potentially place the lining endothelial cells at even greater risk for further injury, leading to an inexorable cycle of events culminating in the complicated lesion. However, a single or a few injurious episodes may lead to a proliferative response that could regress, in contrast to continued or chronic injury. This reaction-to-injury hypothesis thus is consistent with the known intimal thickening observed during normal aging; it would explain how many of the etiological factors implicated in atherogenesis might enhance lesion formation, might explain how inhibitors of platelet aggression could interfere with lesion formation, and could help elucidate how therapy aimed at risk-factor reduction can interrupt progression or even produce regression of these lesions.

Potential Role of Aging Processes in Atherogenesis

Other theories of atherogenesis are not mutually exclusive and relate to aging processes as well. The *monoclonal hypothesis* suggests, on the basis of single isoenzyme types found in lesions,[20] that the intimal proliferative lesions result from the multiplication of single individual smooth muscle cells, as do benign tumors. In this manner, mitogenic and possibly mutagenic factors that might stimulate smooth muscle cell proliferation would act on single cells. Focal *clonal senescence* may explain how intrinsic aging processes contribute to atherosclerosis. According to this theory,[21] the intimal smooth muscle cells that proliferate to form an atheroma are normally under feedback control by diffusible agents (mitosis inhibitors) formed by the smooth muscle cells in the contiguous media, and this feedback control system tends to fail with age as these controlling cells die and are not adequately replaced. This is consistent with the observation that cultured human arterial smooth muscle cells, like fibroblasts, show a decline in their ability to replicate as a function of donor age.[22] If this loss of replicative potential applies to a controlling population of smooth muscle cells, then cells that are usually suppressed would be able to proliferate.

Intrinsic aging and loss of replicative potential, if it occurs in endothelial cells, could be critical, since it would lead to loss of integrity of the endothelial lining of the artery wall, the initial step leading to the progression of events in the "reaction to injury" hypothesis.

The *lysosomal theory* suggests that altered lysosomal function might contribute to atherogenesis. Since lysosomal enzymes can accomplish the generalized degradation of cellular components required for continuing renewal, this system has been implicated in cellular aging and the accumulation of lipofuscin, or "age pigment." It has been suggested that increased deposition of lipids in arterial smooth muscle cells may be related in part to a relative deficiency in the activity of lysosomal cholesterol ester hydrolase.[23] This would result in increased accumulation of cholesterol esters within the cells, perhaps accentuated by lipid overloading of lysosomes, eventually leading to cell death and extracellular lipid deposition. Consonant with this idea, impaired degradation of LDL by human arterial smooth muscle cells cultured from older donors has been observed.[24] Since LDL binding to the specific high-affinity receptors on arterial smooth muscle cells does not appear to decrease with donor age, smooth muscle cells are not protected from the increasing LDL concentrations associated with aging. These observations may be relevant to the enhanced accumulation of cellular cholesterol and LDL observed in atherosclerotic lesions in vivo.

AGE-ASSOCIATED RISK FACTORS AND THE PATHOBIOLOGY OF ATHEROSCLEROSIS

Obesity

Adiposity produces insulin resistance in peripheral tissues (mainly muscle and adipose), which leads to compensatory hyperinsulinemia. The liver is not resistant to some effects of insulin, and enhanced production of triglyceride-rich lipoproteins results, leading to elevated plasma triglyceride and cholesterol levels. Thus it has been demonstrated that body weight is related not only to triglyceride levels but also to cholesterol levels. Concomitantly, obesity is associated with increased total body cholesterol synthesis. Obesity, particularly the abdominal type, produces higher circulating levels of insulin, both in the basal state and after stimulation with glucose or other secretagogues. Since obesity is related to atherosclerosis—both directly and via hypertension, hypertriglyceridemia, hypercholesterolemia, and hyperglycemia—it is not surprising that many studies show a relationship between serum insulin levels, particularly after oral glucose intake, and atherosclerotic disease of the coronary and peripheral arteries.[8] A few studies, however, suggest that this association between insulin and atherosclerosis occurs independently of obesity. It has been postulated that insulin may directly affect arterial wall metabolism, leading to increased endogenous lipid synthesis and thus predisposing to atherosclerosis. Insulin has been shown in physiological concentrations to stimulate proliferation of arterial smooth muscle cells and enhance binding of LDL and very-low-density lipoproteins (VLDL) to fibroblasts; it therefore may be one of the plasma factors gaining increased access to the intima and media after endothelial injury and thus may be an additional factor in atheroma formation.

Hypertension

High mean arterial pressures may enhance atherogenesis by directly producing injury via mechanical stress on endothelial cells at specific high-pressure sites in the arterial tree. This would allow the sequence of events in the chronic injury hypothesis of atherogenesis to take place. In addition, hypertension might allow more lipoproteins to be transported through intact endothelial lining cells by altering permeability. Hypertension markedly increases lysosomal enzyme activity, presumably owing to stimulation of the cellular disposal system by the internalization of increased amounts of plasma substances. This might lead to increased cell degeneration and release of the highly destructive enzymes (within the lysosomes) into the arterial wall. Experimental hypertension also increases the thickness of the intimal smooth muscle layer in the arterial wall and increases connective tissue elements. It is possible that continued high pressure within the artery in vivo produces changes in the ability of smooth muscle cells or stem cells to proliferate. Studies using human aortic coarctation as a model have shown that smooth muscle cells cultured from tissue proximal to the site of coarctation had fewer population doublings and a slower replication rate than cells grown from a distal site.[25] Since the proximal cells presumably had been stimulated to divide excessively in vivo by chronic exposure to elevated intraarterial pressure, these results suggest that the number of prior smooth muscle cell divisions limits their further replicative potential. Thus characteristics of accelerated aging can be induced by chronic exposure to hypertension, which may be relevant to atherogenesis.

Diabetes and Hyperglycemia

Diabetes could provide a unique contribution to atherogenesis.[8] Although the fundamental genetic abnormalities in the varieties of human diabetes mellitus remain unknown, it has been suggested that one type of genetic diabetes in humans is associated with a primary cellular abnormality intrinsic to all cells, resulting in a decreased life span of individual cells, which in turn results in increased cell turnover in tissues. If arterial endothelial and smooth muscle cells are intrinsically defective in diabetes, accelerated atherogenesis can be readily postulated on the basis of any one of the current theories of pathogenesis. Platelet dysfunction in diabetes might also play a role.

The role of glucose in atheroma formation, if any, is poorly understood. Hyperglycemia is known to affect aortic wall metabolism. Sorbitol, a product of the insulin-independent aldose reductase pathway of glucose metabolism (the polyol pathway), accumulates in the arterial wall in the presence of high glucose concentrations, resulting in osmotic effects including increased cell water content and decreased oxygenation. Increased glucose also appears to stimulate proliferation of cultured arterial smooth muscle cells. Glycosylation of key proteins producing advanced glycosylated end products could impair their function and might also play a role by being deposited in the arterial wall and influencing function of arterial wall cells.[10] For example, glycosylated collagen has a great avidity for binding and trapping LDL. Further, glycosylated LDL may more readily deliver cholesterol to arterial cells.

Hyperlipidemia

The development of atherosclerosis accelerates in approximate quantitative relation to the degree of hyperlipidemia.[15] A long-established theory suggests that the higher the circulating levels of lipoprotein, the more likely they are to gain entry into the arterial wall. By an acceleration of the usual transendothelial transport, large concentrations of cholesterol-rich lipoproteins within the arterial wall could overwhelm the ability of smooth muscle cells and macrophages to metabolize them. Clonal senescence of arterial endothelial cells does not impair the processing of LDL and modified LDL. Low-density lipoproteins have been immunologically identified in atheromas, and in humans there is a direct relationship between plasma cholesterol and arterial lipoprotein cholesterol concentration. High-density lipoproteins may be protective by virtue of their ability to promote cholesterol removal from artery wall cells. Chemically modified or oxidized lipoproteins, possibly produced in hyperlipidemic disorders, could gain access to the scavenger arterial wall macrophages, leading to formation of foam cells, as in xanthomas. Macrophages accumulate lipid that has some of the characteristics of oxidized lipoproteins, and these cells themselves appear capable of modifying lipoproteins in vivo. The lipid that accumulates in the arterial wall with increasing age possibly results from infiltration of plasma cholesterol–rich lipoproteins which bind to matrix components. However, atheromatous lesions are associated with a more marked increase in arterial wall cell lipids than that associated with increasing age, which may result in part from injury to the endothelium, possibly produced by chronic hyperlipidemia, as demonstrated in cholesterol-fed monkeys. A further possible mechanism for accelerated atherogenesis in hyperlipidemia is related to the ability of LDL to stimulate proliferation of arterial smooth muscle cells.

Although not directly age-related, cigarette smoking is too powerful a risk factor to be overlooked. The effect of chronic smoke inhalation from cigarettes could result in repetitive injury to endothelial cells, thereby accelerating atherogenesis. Hypoxia stimulates proliferation of cultured human arterial smooth muscle cells; thus, since cigarette smoking is associated with high levels of carboxyhemoglobin and low oxygen delivery to tissues, another mechanism for atherogenesis is suggested. Hypoxia could produce diminished lysosomal enzyme degradative ability, as evidenced by impaired degradation of LDL by smooth muscle cells,[26] causing LDL to accumulate in the cells. Consistent with this suggestion is the fact that aortic lesions resembling atheromas have been produced in experimental animals by systemic hypoxia, and lipid accumulation in the arterial wall of cholesterol-fed rabbits and monkeys appears to be increased by hypoxia.

REVERSIBILITY AND REGRESSION IN RELATION TO AGING

Animal Models

In 1933, Anitschkow observed that lesions induced in cholesterol-fed rabbits appear to regress when the animals are placed on a normal diet. More recent extension of this type of study to cholesterol-fed nonhuman primates[27] has provided firm evidence for reversibility and regression. The usual protocol has been to induce lesions of varying severity by feeding the atherogenic diet to young monkeys for several years and then switching diets to a chow or low-fat diet, sacrificing the animals at intervals. Aortic and coronary lesions have been shown to decrease in size and in content of lipid, cells, and connective tissue. The relevance of these studies lasting a few years to the human lesions evolving over decades is open to some question, however. The mechanisms of regression are under study. In general, it appears that lower circulating levels of cholesterol and LDL lead to a healing endothelium, decreased ingress of LDL into the artery wall, less cell proliferation and collagen synthesis, and more egress of cholesterol from cells and wall. These studies have not yet approached the question of repeated insults (or repeated induction and regression cycles) which may be more relevant to the question of aging and atherosclerosis in humans.

Humans

Both retrospective and prospective human epidemiological studies support the concepts of reversibility and regression. Clinical and autopsy studies during the world wars showed less severe atherosclerosis in malnourished subjects, providing circumstantial evidence. Recent studies of plaque regression in living human subjects are providing some evidence of regression of advanced atherosclerosis based on functional effects and on evaluation of plaque size by sequential arteriographs taken before and after a period of treatment. Treatments that have been studied include drugs for hyperlipidemias; diet manipulation; combinations of diet, exercise, and drug therapy; and ileal bypass operations. Advanced atherosclerotic lesions appear to respond more favorably when serum cholesterol levels are reduced to the low levels that prevail in animals or humans consuming a low-fat, low-cholesterol diet. The effect of age has not been studied directly, since most of the subjects have been hyperlipidemic and below age 65. However, there is no reason to believe that older individuals would not respond similarly to dietary, drug, and lifestyle measures designed to limit progression or induce regression of atherosclerosis.

PREVENTION

The steps taken to delay or prevent atheroma formation ("primary prevention") must begin early in life, long before there is a suspicion of the existence of clinical disease. Steps taken to prevent recurrence of disease ("secondary prevention") later in life will not necessarily be the same. Although an effective program has not been defined with certainty, enough is known to guide both in identification of those individuals with a higher risk and in development of measures that probably will reduce that risk. Thus prevention currently is equated with risk-factor reduction.

Whole communities can be influenced to reduce smoking, change diet, and lower blood pressure levels by mass-media educational efforts.[28] There has been a trend toward lower consumption of cholesterol and saturated fat in the United States, coupled with increasing attention to reducing overweight and the use of exercise programs. Concomitantly, and perhaps causally, there has been a decline in mortality from atherosclerotic disease almost uniquely in the United States during the past 20 years.[1] Treatment of hyperlipidemia in some instances has been shown to reduce atherosclerotic involvement of peripheral and coronary arteries by both invasive and noninvasive measurement. Therefore, efforts to prevent atherogenesis and to interrupt progression by risk factor reduction at any age seem warranted.

The National Cholesterol Education Program has recommended screening, classification, and treatment of adults with "high-risk" cholesterol levels.[29] However, in the initial 1988 report, no specific recommendations were made for individuals over age 65, since the data to support interventions directed at lowering cholesterol levels in the elderly were sparse. In a recent revision, it was felt that data obtained from middle-aged persons and supporting intervention could be extrapolated across the age span, since it has been shown that elderly individuals above age 70 are responsive to cholesterol-lowering regimens and should not be excluded solely on the basis of age. As a first approach, attention to multiple risk factors and hygienic measures (diet and physical activity) appear appropriate. An atherosclerosis prevention trial involving the treatment of isolated systolic hypertension in otherwise healthy elderly has recently been completed. Reduction of hypertension substantially reduced atherosclerotic disease, both coronary heart disease and stroke.[30]

CONCLUSION

Atherosclerosis, the most prevalent form of arteriosclerosis, occurs so commonly with aging in industrialized populations that the disorder can be mistaken for a natural consequence of intrinsic aging rather than a superimposed disease. In this multifactorial disorder, environmental factors (such as diet) appear to operate over many years (age-related) in concert with intrinsic cellular aging processes and genetic determinants to generate the disease.

Since alteration of intrinsic aging processes and genetic manipulation remain only theoretical possibilities, efforts should be directed at understanding and reversing the age-related environmental factors that act over time and accelerate atherogenesis throughout the life span.

REFERENCES

1. Bierman EL: Atherosclerosis and other forms of arteriosclerosis, in Wilson JD et al (eds): *Harrison's Principles of Internal Medicine,* 12th ed. New York, McGraw-Hill, 1991, p 992.

2. Eggen DA, Solberg LA: Variation of atherosclerosis with age. *Lab Invest* 18:571, 1968.
3. Bierman EL: Ageing and atherosclerosis, in Stout R (ed): *Arterial Disease in the Elderly*. New York, Churchill Livingstone, 1984, p 17.
4. Bierman EL: Arteriosclerosis and aging, in Finch CE, Schneider EL (eds): *Handbook of the Biology of Aging*. New York, Van Nostrand Reinhold, 1985, p 842.
5. Hubert HB et al: Obesity as an independent risk factor for cardiovascular disease: A 26-year follow-up of participants in the Framingham Heart Study. *Circulation* 67:968, 1983.
6. Stern MP, Haffner SM: Body fat distribution and hyperinsulinemia as risk factors for diabetes and cardiovascular disease. *Arteriosclerosis* 6:123, 1986.
7. Kannel WB: Role of blood pressure in cardiovascular morbidity and mortality. *Prog Cardiovasc Dis* 17:5, 1974.
8. Bierman EL: Atherogenesis in diabetes. *Arterioscler Thromb* 12:647, 1992.
9. DeFronzo RA: Glucose intolerance and aging. *Diabetes Care* 4:493, 1981.
10. Kirstein M et al: Advanced protein glycosylation induces transendothelial human monocyte chemotaxis and secretion of platelet-derived growth factor: Role in vascular disease of diabetes and aging. *Proc Natl Acad Sci USA* 87:9010, 1990.
11. Steinberg D et al: Beyond cholesterol: Modifications of low-density lipoprotein that increase its atherogenicity. *N Engl J Med* 320:915, 1989.
12. Motulsky AG: The genetic hyperlipidemias. *N Engl J Med* 294:823, 1976.
13. U.S. Department of Health and Human Services: *The Lipid Research Clinics Population Studies Data Book*, vol I, *The Prevalence Study*. PHS NIH 80-1527, 1980.
14. Bierman EL, Glomset JA: Disorders of lipid metabolism, in Wilson JD, Foster DW (eds): *Williams Textbook of Endocrinology*, 8th ed. Philadelphia, Saunders, 1992, p 1367.
15. Wallace RB, Anderson RA: Blood lipids, lipid-related measures, and the risk of atherosclerotic cardiovascular disease. *Epidemiol Rev* 9:95, 1987.
16. Goldstein JL et al: Hyperlipidemia in coronary heart disease. *J Clin Invest* 52:1533, 1973.
17. Tyroler HA (ed): Epidemiology of plasma HDL cholesterol levels: The lipid research clinics program prevalence study. *Circulation* 62(suppl 4), 1980.
18. Gordon T et al: High density lipoprotein as a protective factor against coronary heart disease: The Framingham Study. *Am J Med* 62:707, 1977.
19. Ross R: The pathogenesis of atherosclerosis—An update. *N Engl J Med* 314:488, 1986.
20. Benditt EP, Benditt JM: Evidence for a monoclonal origin of human atherosclerotic plaques. *Proc Natl Acad Sci USA* 70:1753, 1973.
21. Martin GM: Clonal senescence of vascular smooth muscle and atherogenesis, in Bates SR, Gangloff EC (eds): *Atherogenesis and Aging*. New York, Springer-Verlag, 1987, p 135.
22. Bierman EL: The effect of donor age on the *in vitro* life-span of cultured human arterial smooth muscle cells. *In Vitro* 14:951, 1978.
23. Wolinsky H: The role of lysosomes in vascular disease: A unifying theme. *Ann NY Acad Sci* 275:238, 1976.
24. Bierman EL et al: Effect of donor age on the binding and degradation of low density lipoproteins by cultured human arterial smooth muscle cells. *J Gerontol* 34:483, 1979.
25. Bierman EL et al: Hypertension decreases replication potential of arterial smooth muscle cells: Aortic coarctation in humans as a model. *Proc Soc Exp Biol Med* 166:335, 1981.
26. Albers JJ, Bierman EL: The effect of hypoxia on uptake and degradation of low density lipoproteins by cultured human arterial smooth muscle cells. *Biochim Biophys Acta* 424:422, 1976.
27. Wissler RW: Current status of regression studies, in Paoletti R, Gotto AM Jr (eds): *Atherosclerosis Reviews*. New York, Raven Press, 1978, vol 3, p 213.
28. Farquhar JW et al: Effects of community wide education on cardiovascular disease risk factors. *JAMA* 264:359, 1990.
29. National Cholesterol Education Program: Report of the National Cholesterol Education Program Expert Panel on Detection. Evaluation and Treatment of High Blood Cholesterol in Adults (Adult Treatment Panel II). *JAMA* 269:3015, 1993.
30. SHEP Cooperative Research Group: Prevention of stroke by antihypertensive drug treatment in older persons with isolated systolic hypertension. Final results of the Systolic Hypertension in the Elderly Program (SHEP). *JAMA* 265:3255, 1991.

Chapter 45

DISORDERS OF THE HEART

Jeanne Y. Wei

EPIDEMIOLOGY OF HEART DISEASE IN THE ELDERLY POPULATION

Despite the recent decline in deaths due to cardiovascular disease, heart disease remains the single most common cause of death in older persons, accounting for a major portion of the health care costs in this age group.[1,2] Mortality due to heart disease continues to rise through very old age, from 41 percent in those 65 to 74 years old to 48 percent in the over-85 group. Between 80 and 85 percent of the cardiac deaths are attributed to ischemic heart disease.[1–3] Congestive heart failure accounts for about 6 percent of deaths in the 65- to 69-year-old group, but rises nearly threefold to approximately 16 percent in those over 85 years old.[4]

The prevalence of heart disease is nearly 50 percent in elderly persons. Each year at least half of all individuals aged 75 years and older who went to a doctor's office saw a physician for coronary artery disease. The yearly economic burden of cardiovascular disease in the United States totals over $135 billion.[5] Approximately 100 of the 135 billion is spent for coronary artery disease, of which about half is related to myocardial infarction (MI) and its prevention and treatment.[6,7] Nearly 750,000 elderly persons in the United States suffer from acute MI each year.[8]

Heart disease is a major contributor to disability in more than 20 percent of community-dwelling elderly persons who require some form of home assistance in order to avoid institutionalization.[1,2] Beginning in the fifth decade, the annual incidence of congestive heart failure rises nearly exponentially with increasing age, doubling every 10 years in men and every 7 in women.[1,4] Thus, heart diseases, particularly coronary heart disease and congestive heart failure, are diseases of the elderly population.

CORONARY ARTERY DISEASE

The severity of coronary atherosclerosis progresses with advancing age, with the disease in men typically leading that in women by approximately 15 years until after menopause; then the disease accelerates in women, and the severity becomes equal for women and men by age 75 years.[1,9] Angina pectoris shows a prevalence of about 10 percent in the elderly population and is often the first clinical sign of coronary artery disease.[1,2,9,10]

Angina Pectoris

In over 80 percent of elderly patients with coronary artery disease, angina pectoris is the presenting symptom.[9] In the Coronary Artery Surgery Study (CASS), 50 percent of elderly patients, and fewer than one-third of younger patients, presented with unstable angina pectoris.[2,11] The prevalence of prior MI and the serum cholesterol levels were similar in older and younger patients in this study, but more of the elderly patients had hypertension, cerebrovascular disease, congestive heart failure, and diabetes.[2,11] The elderly patients also had more multivessel coronary artery disease, left main coronary artery disease, and angiographic and hemodynamic evidence of left ventricular dysfunction.[11]

Clinical Presentation

Angina pectoris in elderly patients is often similar to that in younger patients.[2,11] Dyspnea rather than pain, however, may be the major complaint. In addition, syncope with exertion, sudden coughing during emotional stress, palpitations with effort, and sweating with exertion are also more commonly observed.

Atypical chest pain occurs less commonly in elderly persons.[2] Nonanginal causes of chest discomfort among elderly patients, which may be difficult to distinguish clinically from angina, include esophageal disease, chest wall pain, and episodic spells of anxiety. Other causes of severe chest pain which are usually easy to distinguish from angina include aortic dissection, pericarditis, pulmonary embolism, cervical spine disease, and abdominal emergencies.

Diagnosis

The patient's medical history is extremely important in making the diagnosis of angina.[2] The physical examination in elderly patients with angina pectoris is often nonspecific. Physical signs of peripheral vascular disease or evidence of predisposing factors such as hyperlipidemia, hypertension, or diabetes mellitus should heighten awareness of possible angina. The resting electrocardiogram may show ST-T wave changes that are nonspecific, especially when associated with increased QRS voltage compatible with left ventricular hypertrophy.[2,9,11] In those elderly patients who are able to exercise to increase heart rate to at least 60 percent of the predicted maximum, a standard exercise tolerance test may help to establish a diagnosis of coronary artery disease, particularly in patients with suggestive symptoms. Although more costly, the use of rest and exercise thallium 201 myocardial imaging may be helpful in delineating areas of decreased coronary perfusion during exercise-induced ischemia.[2] In those who are not able to exercise sufficiently, the administration of dipyridamole during thallium 201 myocardial imaging may yield important information.[12] Its use is limited by cost and accessibility, however.

Management

The management of angina can be considered in terms of two main approaches: (1) helping to change the patient's lifestyle to accommodate a reduced level of activity and (2) providing therapy—medical and surgical—to maintain the level of activity desired by the patient. Increasingly, elderly persons are remaining more active than their predecessors, so that aggressive medical and/or surgical therapy is now frequently considered.[2] For the past 10 years at Boston's Beth Israel Hospital, over 25 percent of the patients undergoing percutaneous transluminal coronary angioplasty (PTCA) or coronary artery bypass graft (CABG) surgery have been 65 years and older, and over 17 percent of all patients undergoing PTCA or cardiac surgery have been 70 years or older.

When considering the appropriate medical regimen, it is important to keep in mind that decreased renal function as well as decreased hepatic perfusion and drug metabolism may result in higher plasma drug levels in elderly patients, who are also often more prone to adverse drug effects (see Chap. 24). Nitrates are effective and are usually well tolerated. Hypotension and headaches may occur, however, and nitrate tolerance may develop.[2] In some instances, the calcium channel blocking agents may be preferred over certain beta blockers because calcium antagonists may exert less inotropic suppression at the usual clinical doses.[13] On the other hand, postural hypotension and impaired AV node conduction and/or heart block may occur following calcium antagonist administration.[13] Antianginal therapy should be accompanied by a treatment program to reduce cardiovascular risk factors. Such a program should emphasize discontinuation of cigarette smoking; management of hypertension; a low-fat, low-cholesterol diet supplemented with a lipid-lowering agent if hyperlipidemia is present; and a carefully planned exercise program, as appropriate.

It has been reported that with medical management of angina the 6-year survival of elderly patients with good ventricular function who have normal coronary arteries, one-vessel disease, or two-vessel disease is fairly good, at 86, 76, and 69 percent, respectively.[2,11]

Acute MI

Acute MI may occur in about 10 percent of patients with unstable angina. In patients aged 70 years and over with MI, the male/female ratio is nearly equal, while in younger MI patients, men outnumber women nearly 3:1.[2,14] Remote myocardial infarcts are common in elderly persons, occurring in 10 percent of men and 5 percent of women over age 65 years. The average annual incidence of acute MI in those over age 65 years is approximately 15 to 20 per 1000 individuals.[2]

Diagnosis

The elderly patient may present with symptoms other than classic chest pain or dyspnea, including confusion, syncope, stroke, vertigo, weakness, abdominal pain, persistent vomiting, and even cough. Sudden onset of intense dyspnea is often the dominant symptom of acute MI in advanced old age.[14] Syncope may be slightly more common. MI tends to occur at rest and during sleep more frequently in elderly patients.

In addition to differences in the clinical presentation of acute MI in elderly patients, the serum cardiac enzyme profile may also be altered with advancing age.[2,15,16] With an acute infarct, the finding of an elevated serum concentration of the myocardial fraction of creatine kinase (CK-MB isozyme) with a normal total plasma CK level occurs twice as often in patients aged 70 years and over than in younger patients.[15] These events likely represent nontransmural, non-Q-wave MI.[15,16] Whether a lower total CK level in the elderly patient represents a smaller infarct, decreased number of myocytes or myofibers in the myocardium, altered CK isozyme distribution (perhaps increased M fraction), or other changes (such as increased collateral blood supply or recanalization) in the older heart remains to be determined.[2,15–17] There may be an increased incidence of smaller, non-Q-wave infarcts in older patients.[2,17]

A higher percentage of elderly infarct patients have a history of systemic arterial hypertension.[2] Elevated systolic blood pressure (>160 mmHg) is associated with increased mortality and morbidity from ischemic heart disease.[2,14] In addition, elderly patients have a higher frequency of complications, including atrial arrhythmias, heart block, conduction defects, cardiogenic shock, pulmonary edema, cardiac rupture, hypovolemia, and right-sided heart failure during the acute infarct period.[2] The in-hospital mortality may be substantially higher (usually over 20 percent), and the length of hospital stay in those who survive the acute event may be longer.[2,16] The recovery-rehabilitation period also tends to be prolonged in older patients. In one study, patients aged 80 years and over had a 67 percent in-hospital mortality, compared with 15 percent in patients 79 years and younger.[16]

Management

The management of elderly patients with acute MI should be prompt and aggressive when indicated.[2,18] Complications associated with each of the procedures tend to increase with advancing age.[18] Therefore, although more aggressive therapeutic interventions have been performed with excellent results in patients in their 60s, 70s, 80s, and over,[2,19,20] and although advanced age should not be an absolute contraindication, one should be aware of the increased risks when treating older patients.

The incidence of failed insertion of intraaortic balloon counterpulsation catheters (due to tortuous vessels and atherosclerosis) and of associated complications from this procedure may be substantially higher in elderly patients.[2,11] In older patients with postinfarction cardiogenic shock with surgically remediable lesions such as ventricular septal defect, papillary muscle rupture, or pump failure, advanced age does not preclude a successful surgical result, and the long-term outcome may be excellent.[2,21–23]

Thrombolytic Therapy Thrombolytic therapy (intracoronary or intravenous) is being increasingly utilized to treat a greater number of elderly patients presenting within the first few hours after an acute MI.[2,19] Intravenous thrombolytic therapy has been reported to significantly reduce mortality in older persons, with the benefit being greater in patients 70 years and older compared with younger patients.[18] These recent studies have clearly defined the benefits of thrombolytic therapy in elderly patients.

Prophylactic Lidocaine The use of prophylactic lidocaine in elderly infarct patients is not clearly settled.[18] The incidence of primary ventricular fibrillation is lower in those over age 65.[2] Decreased hepatic perfusion and drug metabolism, together with increased CNS drug sensitivity, place the elderly patient at greater risk for developing lidocaine toxicity. Acute confusional state, lethargy, and seizures may occur more frequently in elderly patients receiving lidocaine. However, because it clearly reduces primary ventricular fibrillation and is more than 80 percent effective in treating ventricular arrhythmias during acute MI in younger patients, lidocaine prophylaxis may still be considered for the aged. To minimize the possibility of lidocaine toxicity, it is important to adjust for the reduced plasma volume (7 percent) and increased body fat (35 percent), as well as for the twofold prolongation of lidocaine's plasma half-life in elderly patients.[2] The loading dose should be reduced to one-half to two-thirds of the usual amount and the maintenance dose should be kept under 25 μg/kg per minute. Lidocaine prophylaxis against primary ventricular fibrillation should be discontinued within 24 hours after initial administration during the acute infarct. If high-grade ventricular ectopy is present, however, lidocaine therapy may be continued, at the lowest effective maintenance dose possible.

Antiarrhythmic Therapy During the acute MI period, lidocaine is the drug of choice for premature ventricular contractions.[18] Beta blockers may be successful against ventricular fibrillation and ectopic activity associated with increased sympathetic activation of myocardial ischemia. However, the negative inotropic effects and CNS side effects of some beta blockers may require lower doses and careful monitoring in elderly patients. Procainamide may accumulate in older patients owing to age-associated decreases in renal clearance and excretion.[2,24] The active metabolite of procainamide, *N*-acetylprocainamide (NAPA), has fewer associated untoward effects, such as the development of antinuclear antibodies, but it may accumulate to potentially toxic levels in patients who have poor kidney function.[24]

Other Medications Nitrates have been reported to be beneficial for older patients during MI.[18] It is not clear whether elderly patients may experience more negative side effects from nitrates. Calcium blockers are potentially beneficial for elderly MI patients and are generally well tolerated.[13] The efficacy of calcium blockers in elderly patients after MI, however, remains incompletely established. The use of angiotension-converting enzyme (ACE) inhibitors in MI patients has been shown to reduce mortality and improve cardiac function.[18] Therefore, the administration of ACE inhibitors is likely to be beneficial in older MI patients. The use of antiplatelet therapy in the form of low-dose aspirin has been shown to be efficacious in reducing mortality, as is the case for anticoagulation therapy in certain subsets of elderly MI patients.[18]

Cardiac Rehabilitation

Prolonged bed rest and inactivity, especially in elderly patients, contribute to the serious complications of thrombophlebitis, pulmonary embolism, cardiac and respiratory deconditioning, and negative nitrogen and potassium balance.[2] The physician should institute early, gradual ambulation, followed by progressive levels of activity during convalescence. In prescribing an exercise regimen for the elderly postinfarct patient, it is important to remember the following: Careful and gradual progression during training is imperative; warm-up must be slow and careful to ensure an appropriate increase in deep-muscle temperature and to help prevent muscle injuries; cool-down after exercise must be performed slowly. Elderly persons should continue some very light exercise, such as walking or unloaded pedaling, for a short time after active exercise. Static stretching techniques also are effective in preventing muscle injury.

Post-MI Medical Management

Beta-blockade therapy has been associated with a reduction in long-term mortality in elderly survivors of acute MI.[2,18,25] Metoprolol, propranolol, atenolol, and timolol have been shown to significantly decrease postinfarction mortality in older patients compared with age-matched patients who received placebo treatment. There was no major age difference in patient complaints, side effects, or withdrawal from the study.[25] The disparity between the number of old MI patients not receiving beta-blockade therapy and the prevalence of contraindications that would justify this therapeutic omission suggests that perhaps beta blockade should be considered for more elderly patients.[26] A careful regimen of selective beta blockade at low doses with adequate monitoring and follow-up may enable more elderly patients to benefit from this effective therapeutic intervention following acute MI.[26–28] Antiplatelet therapy in the form of low-dose aspirin should also be continued in the elderly post-MI patient, as should an ACE inhibitor, since both drugs have been shown to reduce mortality in older and younger MI patients.[18,29] The challenge is to balance the use of multiple drugs as preventive measures with other therapeutic agents needed by such patients, overall medication costs, and potential problems of noncompliance and adverse drug effects associated with a multidrug regimen.

Coronary Artery Bypass Surgery in Elderly Patients

The average age of patients in the United States undergoing CABG is rising each year.[2,30] However, data from the randomized trials for coronary artery disease involve a younger population, and there are no randomized trial data for patients aged 65 and older. Several possible explanations exist for the increased frequency of coronary bypass surgery in older patients: (1) older but active patients with angina are an expanding segment of our population, (2) many such patients have severely symptomatic coronary disease, and (3) techniques of CABG have steadily improved with successful application of this technique to subgroups of patients at higher risk, including elderly ones.

Compared with their younger counterparts, older patients undergoing revascularization tend to be sicker.[2,11,30] In one study, elderly patients were more symptomatic, with a higher incidence of unstable angina and a prior history of cardiac failure, and had a higher prevalence of associated medical diseases including diabetes, cerebrovascular disease, hypertension, peripheral vascular disease, and chronic lung disease. There was a higher incidence of left main coronary artery disease, triple vessel disease, and abnormal left ventricular function in older patients.[30]

Perioperative mortality is higher in elderly patients. However, even in the older population, the recent trend has been toward a reduction in perioperative mortality.[2,30] Clinical features of older patients at lower risk include the presence of stable angina, absence of heart failure, absence of current cigarette smoking, and, most important, absence of more than one associated medical disease. As with younger patients, surgical mortality is increased in the presence of left ventricular dysfunction and/or cardiomegaly and significant left main coronary artery disease.[2,30]

Perioperative morbidity is higher in elderly patients. In a series of patients aged 70 years and older, frequent nonfatal complications included stroke, psychoses, conduction disturbances, pulmonary emboli, and supraventricular arrhythmias. The older patients also had longer hospital stays.[30]

Long-Term Surgical Results

The cumulative long-term survival of patients in the CASS Registry aged 65 years and older was 83 percent compared with 91 percent in younger patients.[30] Major predictors of long-term mortality (in perioperative survivors) were indices of left ventricular dysfunction and the number of associated medical diseases. In older patients without LV dysfunction or other medical diseases, 5-year survival was almost 90 percent. Others have reported similar 5-year survival rates, ranging from 80 to 85 percent.[2,30] The older patients in the CASS Study experienced cessation of angina comparable to that of younger patients, although angina relief was more sustained in men than in women.[30] Therefore, the symptomatic benefits from coronary artery bypass surgery are similar in older and younger patients.

Medical Versus Surgical Therapy in Patients 65 Years or Older

The cumulative 6-year survival in the entire CASS Registry series (adjusted for the major differences in preoperative variables) was 79 percent in the surgical group and 64 percent in those treated medically ($P < .0001$). Among 234 "low-risk" patients with mild angina, relatively well preserved left ventricular function, and absence of left main coronary disease, survival was no different between surgically and medically treated patients, being 82 and 83 percent, respectively. Therefore, the current status of coronary artery surgery is such that the procedure can be effectively applied to the older population, with an increased but acceptable risk. In selected patient populations, excellent late survival and functional relief can be expected. Many elderly patients with symptomatic coronary disease constitute a "high risk" group who would likely benefit from bypass surgery, and their survival may be prolonged by this procedure, particularly since many may tolerate "maximal" medical therapy poorly.[2]

Percutaneous Transluminal Coronary Angioplasty

Each year an increasing number of patients aged 65 years or older with coronary artery disease are undergoing PTCA procedures.[20] Because of the higher morbidity and mortality as well as longer hospitalization in elderly patients undergoing revascularization surgery, PTCA has important potential applications in this age group. A number of studies have reported that PTCA success rates in elderly patients are very comparable to those in younger patients, and the procedure mortality, although higher, is not different from that seen with bypass surgery.[2,20,31–33] With increased experience and technical refinement, it is anticipated that multilesion PTCA may be performed in selected elderly patients with a high primary success rate and a relatively low procedural risk.

CONGENITAL HEART DISEASE

A number of congenital cardiac lesions do not preclude survival to old age. The classic diagnostic clinical findings associated with congenital heart lesions may be obscured or confounded in older patients by concomitant age-related changes or other diseases. Valvular lesions affecting the very old are either initially mild congenital lesions, lesions that develop in late life due to age-related processes, or a combination of these factors. As internists and cardiologists become increasingly aware of the safety, usefulness, and availability of recently developed noninvasive cardiac imaging techniques, the identification of congenital heart disease will probably increase in frequency in elderly patients.

Atrial Septal Defect

Elderly patients with intracardiac shunt lesions usually have minor defects. The major medical problem in most of them is one of differential diagnosis and antibiotic prophylaxis against infective endocarditis, with the exception being patients with atrial septal defects (ASDs).[34] Old patients with ASDs often present with congestive heart failure and atrial arrhythmias, and the diagnosis of ASD may be missed. When the atrial left-to-right shunt increases the volume of the pulmonary circulation by two or more times that of the systematic circulation, right ventricular hypertrophy together with pulmonary vascular prominence and plethora result. These features are usually considered to be the classic signs of ASD. Many elderly ASD survivors have modestly to moderately elevated pulmonary artery pressures because those who develop severe reactive pulmonary hypertension (about 15 percent of all patients with ASD) tend to do so in their 20s to 40s and often do not survive to old age.[34] Severe pulmonary hypertension (pulmonary artery pressures above 60 mmHg) with ASD, however, has been observed in older patients. In a study of patients aged 60 years or older, 18 of 56 (32 percent) had peak systolic pulmonary artery pressures of 60 mmHg or greater.[34] These patients tended to have a poorer functional class and an increased incidence of atrial fibrillation.

The clinical findings of ASD in elderly patients are usually not different from those in younger individuals (i.e., exaggerated precordial motion, a widely split and "fixed" second heart sound, a right-sided S_4, a pulmonic systolic ejection murmur, incomplete or complete right bundle branch block with first-degree AV block on electrocardiograms, and dilated main and pulmonary arterial branches with pulmonary plethora on chest x-ray films). The echocardiogram (M-mode and 2D) may reveal enlarged right ventricular chamber dimensions and paradoxical motion of the interventricular septum. Contrast echocardiography may demonstrate an intracardiac communication at the atrial level, and Doppler studies may reveal the presence of an interatrial flow signal.[2]

Older patients with ASD may be asymptomatic, or they may have some disability and present with symptoms of congestive heart failure. Dyspnea and heart failure may be precipitated by atrial arrhythmias (atrial flutter or fibrillation), which occur with increased likelihood in ASD patients. Heart failure typically involves the right ventricle, so that elevated central venous pressure, hepatomegaly, peripheral edema, and fatigue are often present.

For symptomatic ASD the treatment is usually surgical. The operative risk, although slightly higher in older persons, is very low, unless severe pulmonary hypertension is present. In a Mayo Clinic study of 66 older patients (mean age 65 years) who underwent surgical repair for ASD, postoperative death occurred in 4, all of whom also underwent other surgical procedures at the same operation.[34] Both early and late postoperative arrhythmias tend to be increased in elderly patients.[2,34] Abnormal right ventricular function may not revert to normal in old patients after ASD repair, but the long-term benefits of surgical repair of an atrial septal defect may otherwise be excellent.[2,34]

Coarctation of the Aorta

Coartation of the aorta usually manifests in early and mid adult life (90 percent of patients were under age 40 years in a recent report of 234 patients) but may be rarely diagnosed in very late life.[2,35,36] The diagnosis and treatment of this lesion in the elderly are similar to those for younger adults. Older patients with coarctation of the aorta frequently present with hypertension. In addition to congestive heart failure, other complications, including infective endocarditis, cerebrovascular accident, and aortic dissection, may occur. Coarctation is associated with a bicuspid aortic valve (which may cause valvular aortic stenosis in elderly patients) in 10 to 15 percent of patients.[2,35,36] Over half the patients who undergo surgical repair improve postoperatively.[35,36] Although the operative risk is higher in the older patient, surgery should be undertaken, if possible, because of the expected positive outcome following repair and the high likelihood of severe morbidity and/or premature mortality without corrective surgery. Management following coarctation repair should include exercise testing and monitoring for aortic valve disease.

Ventricular Septal Defect

Rarely do elderly patients present with unrepaired congenital ventricular septal defects (VSDs) of substantial size. This is because if the defect was significant and the left-to-right shunt was large, pulmonary vascular disease would usually have developed, making survival to old age unlikely. Therefore, a VSD in the elderly patient is usually tiny with a small left-to-right shunt; it does not require surgery, and prophylactic antibiotic therapy against infective endocarditis may be the only medical therapy needed. Management of older patients who develop acquired VSD following an acute MI was discussed in the section on coronary heart disease.

Patent Ductus Arteriosus

Patent ductus arteriosus (PDA) has been diagnosed in elderly patients. A continuous murmur at the base of the heart would be compatible with this diagnosis. Echocardiography and Doppler studies may be performed to evaluate possible causes of the continuous murmur.[2,37] Patients with a small PDA who are asymptomatic should simply be followed and provided with prophylactic antibiotic to prevent infective endocarditis. In the occasional symptomatic elderly patient with PDA and a large left-to-right shunt, surgical therapy (closure of PDA) should be recommended. In those symptomatic patients with smaller left-to-right shunts, or those with sizable left-to-right shunts without pulmonary vascular disease, the potential benefits of surgery must be weighed against the increased operative risk of dissection and hemorrhage at surgery in this age group (due to extensive atherosclerosis and markedly friable tissue around the ductus).

Cyanotic Heart Disease

In the elderly patient, cyanosis is usually due to pulmonary disease. However, diagnoses of pulmonary valve stenosis and, less frequently, tetralogy of Fallot, have been made in elderly patients. As more patients continue to survive into later years, mainly as a result of improved surgical repair techniques, more physicians will likely find unusual cases of congenital heart disease (primarily postoperative) in their geriatric patient population. In pulmonary valve stenosis, the diagnosis may be made noninvasively using echocardiography, and the valvular gradient may be estimated using Doppler techniques. Surgery should be recommended, if at all, for symptomatic patients only, since little information is available regarding surgical benefit versus risk for this age group.[2] Adult patients with unrepaired tetralogy of Fallot rarely survive beyond the third or fourth decade, but those with successful surgical correction will begin attaining the geriatric age range in the near future. The very late problems associated with surgical corrective procedures for these and other cardiac anomalies await definition in the elderly population.

Rarely Ebstein's disease may be diagnosed in an elderly patient. Supraventricular tachycardia and tricuspid insufficiency are the major complications. Tricuspid regurgitation may be quantified by two-dimensional Doppler echocardiography. If cyanosis with right-to-left shunt develops, surgical therapy should be considered.

VALVULAR HEART DISEASE

Aortic Stenosis

Diagnosis

Aortic stenosis may be difficult to diagnose in elderly patients because certain classic clinical features may be obscured or confounded by concomitant physiologic changes due to aging. Although systolic murmurs occur in 60 to 80 percent of elderly patients,[2,38] most are benign and are due to aortic valve sclerosis (thickening and calcification of the aortic leaflets as a result of long-term wear and tear). A small percentage of elderly patients with systolic murmurs have hemodynamically significant aortic stenosis. Uncorrected critical aortic stenosis carries a grave prognosis, but surgical aortic valve replacement or percutaneous aortic valvuloplasty can dramatically improve the long-term outlook, even in the very old. Although one should not overutilize diagnostic tests or subject patients with innocent murmurs to unnecessary evaluative procedures, it is important to correctly identify those patients with aortic stenosis who may significantly benefit from valvular surgery.

Medical History

Aortic stenosis in a person over 65 years old most frequently involves a tricuspid (rather than a congenital bicuspid) valve in which progressive sclerosis and calcification have markedly restricted leaflet mobility and critically narrowed the valve orifice.[2,38] Much less commonly, rheumatic and/or congenital valvular deformity may be the underlying pathologic lesion. A history of rheumatic or congenital heart disease or of the long-standing presence of a heart murmur may be helpful in establishing the diagnosis. The presence of exertional or postural syncope, progressive limitation of physical activity due to dyspnea on exertion, and/or angina pectoris are also important in the evaluation of the need for surgical therapy.[2] The problem with using symptoms as indicators of severe aortic stenosis in elderly patients is that they can be the result of coronary artery disease and/or cerebrovascular disease and are not as specific for aortic stenosis as in a younger patient. This is confounded by the coexistence in many elderly people of both aortic stenosis and coronary artery disease.[2,39]

Physical Findings

The "classic" signs of aortic stenosis may be less reliable and may be absent altogether in the elderly patient. For example, the location of the aortic ejection murmur may change so that instead of being most prominent at the base, it may be best heard at the apex.[2,38] The duration or the time of onset of the murmur may not be as reliable an indicator of the severity of aortic stenosis in the elderly patient, because left ventricular dysfunction may significantly alter these features.[2,38] One of the most reliable physical findings of hemodynamically significant aortic stenosis in young adults, that of the delay and diminished carotid upstroke, may be absent in the elderly patient because of noncompliant vasculature.[2] When the delayed carotid upstroke is present, however, it may be helpful in establishing the diagnosis of aortic stenosis, but it may also be confounded by the presence of severe carotid artery atherosclerosis. Although the aortic component of the second heart sound is frequently diminished with significant aortic stenosis, this is not a reliable sign either. Often with aortic stenosis, there is a sustained apical impulse and an S_4 gallop. However, these findings are also often found in elderly patients who do not have aortic stenosis.[2,38] A pale facial color is almost never helpful for diagnosing aortic stenosis in the elderly patient. When aortic stenosis becomes so severe that cardiac output is restricted, the systolic murmur may no longer be appreciated.[2] Thus, physical findings may be less reliable in the elderly patient.

Routine Laboratory Evaluation

The electrocardiogram may be helpful in supporting a suspicion of aortic stenosis. Findings compatible with left ventricular hypertrophy, especially in the absence of hypertension, suggest the possible presence of significant aortic stenosis. On the chest x-ray film, there may be evidence of left-sided cardiomegaly. However, because many elderly patients have a history of hypertension, these changes are less specific. In elderly kyphoscoliotic patients, chamber enlargement may be difficult to diagnose on the chest x-ray film.

Having noted all these limitations, one might ask whether the history, physical examination, and routine laboratory tests can ever reliably diagnose or exclude the presence of severe aortic stenosis in the elderly patient. The answer is that it is difficult but possible. As is the case with any diagnostic tool, the strength of the tool increases with the user's knowledge of its weaknesses. A late-peaking systolic ejection murmur and a diminished or absent A_2 suggest aortic stenosis, especially in the presence of electrocardiographic evidence of left ventricular hypertrophy in a patient without a history of hypertension. If the systolic murmur is accentuated after a premature ventricular beat and decreases with changing from a supine to a sitting or standing position, and if aortic regurgitation is also audible, significant aortic stenosis is likely. The patient should be referred for noninvasive cardiovascular evaluation when aortic stenosis is suspected.

Cardiologic Diagnostic Confirmation

Noninvasive studies can be very helpful in the diagnosis of severe aortic stenosis.[2,40] On the echocardiogram, thickening and diminished excursion of the aortic leaflets with left ventricular hypertrophy (usually concentric) are suggestive of aortic stenosis. If, in addition, the left atrium is enlarged in the absence of mitral valve disease, this would further point to the possibility of severe aortic stenosis.[2] Together with these findings, if the phonocardiogram reveals a late-peaking systolic ejection murmur, a delayed carotid upstroke with a prolonged time to one-half peak level, a prolonged left ventricular ejection time, and a prolonged time interval from the Q wave to the peak of the murmur, it is likely that critical aortic stenosis is present.[2] If, on the other hand, echocardiography (M-mode or 2D) demonstrates good systolic separation of the aortic leaflets ($\geq$1.3 cm), especially in the absence of concentric left ventricular hypertrophy, it is unlikely that severe aortic stenosis is present.[2] In patients with thickened aortic leaflets with markedly diminished excursion, continuous wave Doppler velocity estimation of the aortic valve gradient (both instantaneous and mean gradients) may be performed, and aortic valve area can be estimated noninvasively,[2,40] to quantify the severity of the aortic stenosis. Cardiac catheterization is often performed to confirm the presence of critical aortic stenosis prior to valve replacement.[40] In addition, because older patients have a high prevalence of coronary artery disease, coronary arteriography should be performed prior to valvular surgery, so that coronary bypass grafts, if needed, may be performed during the same operation.[39]

Aortic Valve Replacement

Once critical aortic stenosis has been diagnosed and if the patient is a surgical candidate, aortic valve replacement should follow. The operative survival for aortic valve replacement is lower in elderly patients (85 to 95 percent for those over 65 years versus 95 to 99 percent for younger patients). The choice of the valve, either a ball-cage, tilting disk, or biological tissue valve, depends on the circumstances of the specific case and a comparison between the durability of the valve, hemodynamic characteristics, and need for anticoagulation.[2] Because the porcine valve does not usually require long-term anticoagulation in the absence of atrial fibrillation, it is often the valve of choice for elderly patients, in whom anticoagulation may result in significant morbidity. On the other hand, physical size limitations may dictate the use of a ball-cage or a tilting disk prosthesis. A low-profile central-flow (St. Jude) prosthesis may be another alternative, but it does require anticoagulation. Elderly patients who undergo aortic valve replacement often also receive coincident coronary artery bypass grafts. These patients may have slightly higher operative mortality and morbidity.[2]

Postoperative Management

Frequent and thorough postoperative examination and treatment of problems, such as arrhythmias or heart failure, as they arise, are indicated. Antibiotic prophylaxis for dental work and other procedures likely to result in bacteremia, and chronic anticoagulation with warfarin and dipyridamole if the prosthetic valve is not porcine, or in the presence of atrial fibrillation even if it is porcine, are also required.[2] In addition, periodic evaluation of the patient's symptoms and physical examination findings should be performed to check for valvular dysfunction.

Nonsurgical Management of Critical Aortic Stenosis

Percutaneous balloon dilation of calcific aortic stenosis (aortic valvuloplasty) has been successfully performed in elderly patients with aortic stenosis, achieving a reduction of the aortic gradient with increases in cardiac index and aortic valve area.[2,41] This feasible, nonsurgical technique represents a major therapeutic advancement, which should find wide application especially for elderly patients with severe aortic stenosis for whom aortic valvular replacement is not an option.

When neither surgery nor valvuloplasty are elected, optimal medical management is directed at treating the symptoms. Specifically, this would include (1) maintenance of the hematocrit within the normal range to optimize oxygen delivery, (2) control of atrial and ventricular arrhythmias to ensure adequate atrial transport and ventricular filling, (3) treatment of left ventricular heart failure with digitalis and/or diuretics, (4) enhancement of diastolic coronary perfusion with carefully titrated doses of nitrates, and (5) supplementation of inspiratory oxygen if clinically indicated. Without surgery or valvuloplasty, the average life expectancy after the development of symptoms, especially of congestive heart failure, may be less than 2 years.

Despite the higher perioperative and long-term postoperative mortality rates for aortic valve replacement in elderly compared with younger patients with aortic stenosis,[2,39] the dismal prognosis on medical therapy alone, as well as the potentially excellent surgical or valvuloplasty results, justifies an aggressive approach to the diagnosis and treatment of debilitating aortic stenosis in an otherwise intact and healthy elderly patient. Patients with isolated aortic stenosis complicated by left ventricular heart failure often have excellent operative survival and postoperative left ventricular functional improvement.[2,42] In patients with cognitive impairment and/or serious multisystem problems, however, aortic valve replacement is not likely to significantly improve cognitive function and/or long-term prognosis.

Chronic Aortic Regurgitation

In elderly persons, chronic aortic regurgitation develops as a result of hypertension, atherosclerosis, valvular deformity (e.g., sclerosis, congenital, rheumatic, or postendocarditic), or root dilatation (e.g., atherosclerosis, myxomatous degeneration, or aortitis). The regurgitant lesion can be very well tolerated and is often associated with a long asymptomatic period. Development of effort intolerance is usually the first symptom to appear, followed by increasing symptoms of congestive heart failure. Diagnosis of chronic aortic regurgitation in elderly patients is similar to that in young ones (i.e., usually based on physical findings). Echocardiography and Doppler evaluation may be helpful in confirming the presence and estimating the severity of the lesion, as well as in diagnosing the underlying disease mechanisms. The issue of indication and timing for aortic valve replacement in chronic aortic regurgitation has been somewhat controversial.[2,43] In asymptomatic elderly persons, aortic valve replacement may not be necessary, while those who develop congestive heart failure secondary to aortic regurgitation should undergo prompt surgery. The presence of ventricular dilatation may complicate the surgical procedure and therefore needs careful consideration.

After valve replacement for symptomatic chronic aortic regurgitation (duration longer than 15 months), the postoperative improvement may not be as dramatic as that observed in patients with aortic stenosis. This may be due partly to irreversible muscle damage caused by left ventricular volume overload which occurred prior to the onset of severe clinical symptoms. One report suggested that surgery within 15 months of the onset of left ventricular dysfunction may result in significant clinical improvement and reversal of ventricular dysfunction.[43] In other series postoperative improvement has not been as dramatic in elderly patients, perhaps because of longer exposure time to the chronic regurgitant lesion.

Acute Aortic Regurgitation

Acute aortic regurgitation usually occurs as a result of either infective endocarditis (with valve perforation) or aortic dissection. In acute aortic regurgitation, no time has been allowed for compensatory left ventricular hypertrophy or dilatation to develop, so that cardiac failure may occur following the abrupt increase in volume overload. In this case, a more aggressive approach should be taken toward valve replacement, even in elderly persons. Emergency operations may have to be considered during an active infection, particularly if it is fungal or if hemodynamic compromise or aortic valve ring abscess develops. If the acute regurgitation is due to aortic dissection, surgery would require both repair of the dissection and replacement of the valve and would involve even higher operative risk. If indicated, such surgery should be performed on an urgent or emergency basis.

Mitral Stenosis

Mitral valvular stenosis in elderly persons usually results from rheumatic heart disease, which is almost always acquired before the age of 20 years, but which may not manifest clinical problems until several decades later.[2,44] The diagnosis and management of mitral stenosis in elderly persons is usually not different from that in younger individuals, except that "silent" mitral stenosis may occur more commonly in elderly persons and should be considered when dyspnea and/or atrial fibrillation are present. Occasionally, an elderly patient with no audible murmur may present with congestive heart failure and a small heart size on chest x-ray and be found to have mitral stenosis at echocardiography.

Noninvasive studies may be helpful in determining the severity of mitral stenosis as well as the pressure gradient and mitral valve area.[2,45] The secondary effect of the mitral stenotic lesion on the pulmonary circulation and right heart should also be assessed noninvasively to optimize the patient's management.[2,44] The natural history of mitral stenosis is related to several factors: the severity of the lesion, its rate of progression, and the presence of pulmonary hypertension, atrial arrhythmias, and/or systemic embolism. Patients often adapt well for some time and may not become symptomatic until the onset of atrial fibrillation in the sixth or seventh decade. The management of atrial fibrillation should be directed at controlling the rapid ventricular rate followed by chemical and/or electrical attempts at conversion to sinus rhythm. Maintaining sinus rhythm may allow postponement of valve replacement, repair, or balloon valvuloplasty and is associated with better long-term cognitive function.

Mitral Valve Prolapse

The syndrome of mitral valve prolapse in elderly patients continues to be defined and clarified.[2,46] Certain elderly patients may present with problems that are similar to those of young patients, having chest pain and arrhythmias most commonly, followed by progressive mitral regurgitation and congestive heart failure.[2,46,47] Severe congestive heart failure requiring valve replacement occurs in a limited number of elderly persons.

The medical management of elderly patients with mitral valve prolapse should consist of antibiotic prophylaxis against endocarditis for those with mitral regurgitation, symptomatic therapy including antiarrhythmic drugs for symptomatic arrhythmias, and antiplatelet therapy for those with prior cerebral emboli. Valve surgery should be considered only for severe mitral regurgitation.

Mitral Regurgitation

Inadequate valve closure could be due to dysfunction of the left ventricle, papillary muscle(s), chordae tendineae, mitral valve leaflets, mitral annulus, or atrioventricular contractile sequence. In elderly patients, the more common causes of mitral regurgitation include coronary artery disease and its complications, mitral valve prolapse, and mitral annular calcification. Mitral regurgitation is usually not difficult to diagnose and is similar for old and younger patients. Evaluation of the severity of the regurgitation, however, may be more challenging.

Myxomatous degeneration and/or long-term mitral regurgitation in patients with mitral valve prolapse could result in ruptured chordae tendineae. Chordal rupture may also be due to infective endocarditis or trauma or may be idiopathic. The diagnosis of ruptured chordae tendineae may be made clinically and confirmed with Doppler echocardiography. Prognosis depends partly on the severity of the mechanical overload and partly on the cardiac reserve of the patient. Surgery may be necessary, occasionally on an emergency basis. In some cases, valvuloplasty may be performed without prosthetic valve replacement.

Papillary muscle and/or ventricular wall dysfunction with postinfarction mitral regurgitation occurs commonly in elderly persons and usually does not require aggressive therapy. When the infarcted papillary muscle is ruptured, however, catastrophic hemodynamic compromise may ensue.[2,21] The development of cardiogenic shock may be abrupt and sometimes unheralded by prior development of a murmur. Whereas conservative medical management is associated with near-certain death, prompt medical and surgical treatment may be lifesaving and may yield dramatic improvements, especially in those patients with preserved left ventricular wall motion.[21–23] Elderly, like younger, patients can have excellent results, both short- and long-term, following prompt mitral valve surgery for postinfarction cardiogenic shock.[23]

Abrupt mitral regurgitation due to leaflet perforation of rupture of chordae tendineae may occur with infective endocarditis. These abrupt events dictate prompt medical and surgical therapy. Urgent surgery is indicated in the presence of hemodynamic compromise, fungal or *Staphylococcus aureus* infection, valve ring abscess, or new conduction block. If possible, surgery should be deferred until bacteriologic cure is attained or at least bacteremia is no longer present. Elderly patients should receive similar considerations as young individuals, but operative risk may be significantly higher in the aged.

Mitral Annular Calcification

Mitral annular calcification is common in elderly patients and is usually benign. Most elderly patients are asymptomatic and demonstrate no significant hemodynamic changes. A diastolic murmur may be appreciated, but it seldom implies mitral stenosis. While mitral valve replacement is generally not indicated, in rare instances the calcification is extensive, impeding mitral inflow and causing functional mitral stenosis.[2,48] Antibiotic prophylaxis should be instituted if there is significant mitral regurgitation.

Infective Endocarditis

Elderly people are among the most frequent victims of infective endocarditis.[2,49] The diagnosis and management are similar to those of younger patients, and emergency surgery is sometimes indicated. Prophylaxis with appropriate antibiotic coverage for known bacteremic procedures is important for those with valvular deformity and regurgitant lesions. In the elderly person with a regurgitant valve lesion who presents with an undiagnosed fever, prompt wide-spectrum antibiotic coverage during the initial evaluation may be lifesaving in some cases.

CONGESTIVE HEART FAILURE

In clinical geriatrics congestive heart failure is a common problem.[2,4,50] It may result from compromise of either systolic or diastolic function or both, resulting in elevated ventricular end-diastolic pressures.[51,52] Congestion of pulmonary or systemic veins and the organs they drain is the associated feature. Between 50 and 60 percent of older persons with congestive heart failure have normal or only slightly reduced ejection fractions.[2,53–55] Elderly patients with impaired diastolic function who are erroneously treated for systolic heart failure with digitalis and diuretics may experience further compromise.[51,56] It is important, therefore, to be aware of this possible problem and to administer the appropriate therapy with care.[2,52]

While coronary artery disease is common in elderly patients with congestive heart failure,[2,4,9,50] up to one-half of autopsy hearts of elderly persons dying in congestive heart failure have no significant coronary disease.[2,3,10] Therefore, congestive heart failure should not be equated with coronary artery disease.

Pathophysiology

Usually, the heart adapts to increased workload by one of the following mechanisms: (1) increased sympathetic nervous system stimulation, (2) myocardial hypertrophy, and (3) the Frank-Starling mechanism.[2,51,57] Responsiveness to beta-adrenergic stimulation is decreased with age.[2,58,59] Advanced age attenuates the hypertrophic response of the myocardium to acute pressure or volume overload.[2,57,60] The age-related prolongation in ventricular relaxation time,[61] together with increased myocardial stiffness of the aged heart,[56,62,63] results in increased left ventricular end diastolic pressure at rest and/or exercise such that pulmonary and systemic venous congestion may occur despite preserved systolic function.[2,51,64,65]

Diagnosis

Signs and symptoms of congestive heart failure are similar for old and young patients, but atypical presentations are more frequent in the elderly. Nonspecific signs of illness such as somnolence, confusion, disorientation, weakness, and fatigue may be the presenting features while dyspnea may be absent. Worsening of preexisting dementia is an important sign of congestive failure in some patients. Peripheral edema is not a reliable sign of heart failure, but jugular venous distension and hepatojugular reflux usually do indicate right heart failure. While an S_4 gallop does not necessarily signify heart disease, an S_3, or early diastolic, gallop usually indicates heart failure. Inspiratory rales in the lower half of the lung fields may or may not indicate heart failure.

It may be difficult to fully assess the extent of systolic versus diastolic dysfunction at the bedside. Noninvasive studies using Doppler echocardiography and radionuclide scintigraphic techniques may be helpful in clarifying these points.[2,54–56,66–68]

Management

For the patient with heart failure due to systolic dysfunction, the mainstays of therapy are rest, digitalis, diuretics, and reduction of afterload and preload. Because prolonged bedrest is dangerous, it is preferable to have the patient sit in a chair with his or her legs elevated. Chair rest enhances diuresis, as does oxygen supplementation. The value of long-term digitalis therapy in elderly patients has been questioned.[2,69] Digitalis is useful in managing acute and severe systolic dysfunction in patients with sinus rhythm or atrial fibrillation. However, its role in stable, compensated heart failure is less clear and should be considered in the context of its known toxicity. Vasodilator therapy may be preferred because it reduces afterload and thereby enhances myocardial shortening and increases stroke volume.[51,70]

The most frequently used vasodilators are the nitrates, which alone or in combination with hydralazine may be effective in reducing filling pressures, increasing cardiac output, increasing renal blood flow, and improving exercise tolerance.[2,70] Prazosin, an arterial and venous system vasodilator, reduces systemic and pulmonary venous pressure and may increase cardiac output,[73] but its effectiveness in elderly patients with heart failure has not been extensively investigated. While these agents can lead to symptomatic improvement in patients with heart failure, none have been shown to improve survival.

In contrast, angiotensin-converting enzyme (ACE) inhibitors such as captopril and enalapril are effective in treating heart failure[29,71] and reduce mortality. The ACE inhibitors appear to work predominantly on the peripheral vasculature.[72] Captopril has been shown to be effective in elderly patients who are refractory to digitalis, diuretics, and other vasodilators. It is possible that a combination of ACE inhibitors with other agents mentioned previously will result in additional synergistic effects.

For the patient with heart failure due to diastolic dysfunction but preserved systolic function, the goal is to enhance effective ventricular filling.[51,52] Calcium antagonist therapy, beta-adrenergic antagonist therapy, and ACE inhibitor therapy may prove beneficial for older patients with heart failure due to diastolic dysfunction.[13,27,51,71]

CARDIOMYOPATHY

Idiopathic cardiomyopathy is defined as a diffuse or generalized myocardial disorder without known underlying cause. All patients so diagnosed have idiopathic or primary involvement of the myocardium. However, valvular, hypertensive, or coronary artery disease often coexists with primary cardiomyopathy. Three broad types of ventricular dysfunction (which may overlap) are described. Dilated or congestive cardiomyopathy is characterized by impaired systolic function with dilatation (sometimes mild) of chambers and increased muscle mass without significant increase in wall thickness. Hypertrophic cardiomyopathy is characterized by normal or small chamber size, increased wall thickness, hyperdynamic systolic ejection, and impaired diastolic filling. In restrictive or infiltrative cardiomyopathy, the myocardium shows increased stiffness secondary to pathologic infiltrative lesions; systolic function is impaired and the atria are dilated in late stages.

Dilated or Congestive Cardiomyopathy

Dilated cardiomyopathy is often misdiagnosed as heart failure secondary to coronary artery disease. Although the condition is thought to be rare in elderly persons, approximately 10 percent of patients with this condition in several large studies were over age 65 years.[2] It is possible that its low incidence in elderly patients may represent a selection process such that few people with susceptibility to myocardial damage of this type survive beyond the seventh decade. The diagnosis of dilated cardiomyopathy is based upon exclusion of etiologic factors that may result in diffuse myocardial dysfunction [e.g., doxorubicin (Adriamycin) toxicity, postradiation damage, and chronic alcoholism] and is generally confirmed by echocardiography, which reveals four-chamber dilatation with depressed systolic pump function. The increased tendency for thrombus formation and subsequent systemic embolic events in these patients should be treated with anticoagulation therapy. Treatment for dilated cardiomyopathy is similar to that for heart failure and arrhythmias, with emphasis on the use of an ACE inhibitor and vasodilator therapy in addition to diuretics and antiarrhythmic agents. Digitalis may be particularly effective in the presence of atrial fibrillation or other atrial arrhythmias. Its use in elderly patients with heart failure was discussed earlier in the congestive heart failure section. Dosages of vasodilator drugs should be adjusted with caution, since excessive hypotension may prove hazardous.

Acute myocarditis occurs rarely in elderly persons and is difficult to diagnose clinically. Endomyocardial biopsy demonstrates conspicuous cellular infiltrates with cellular degeneration and necrosis. The common etiologic agents are viruses and rickettsiae, with coxsackie infection being probably the most frequent cause in the Western hemisphere. Immunosuppressive therapy has been proposed for the treatment of subacute and chronic myocarditis. However, diagnostic criteria and therapeutic efficacy are uncertain, and it remains to be determined whether such agents are well tolerated by elderly patients.

Hypertrophic Cardiomyopathy

Diagnosis

This condition was previously thought to be rare in older patients, but several studies have reported finding significant numbers of patients beyond the seventh decade.[2,74] Echocardiography is helpful in identifying asymptomatic or mildly symptomatic elderly patients with idiopathic cardiac hypertrophy.[2,74,75] The older patient often presents with symptoms similar to those of the younger patient (i.e., dizziness, syncope, dyspnea, chest pain, and palpitations). Despite the similarity in clinical presentation between old and young patients, the pathogenesis in elderly persons appears to differ from the genetic association in young persons with these clinical findings. Diagnosis is often delayed in elderly patients because symptoms of dizziness and syncope are incorrectly attributed to cerebrovascular causes, coronary artery disease, or pulmonary disease, with the proper diagnosis considered in only one-third of cases prior to referral.

The presence of left-ventricular outflow tract "obstruction" in the form of intraventricular pressure gradients may be observed with the characteristic physical signs. The typical bifid carotid pulse, however, may be absent in many elderly hypertrophic patients. Aortic regurgitation secondary to coexisting aortic valve calcification often coexists with hypertrophic "obstructive" cardiomyopathy.

The older patient with a hypertrophic heart appears similar to the younger patient, except that the hypertrophy in the old patient may be concentric, more pronounced, and with more severe free wall hypertrophy. Natural history studies emphasize the rarity of sudden death in elderly persons with this condition. This may indicate a different underlying mechanism for hypertrophic cardiomyopathy in old and young persons or may represent survival of a subgroup with a low propensity to sudden death. Fibrous endocardial thickening of the upper interventricular septum and of the anterior mitral leaflet may be observed. Associated abnormalities in elderly persons commonly include mitral annular calcification and degenerative calcific aortic valves, with coexistence of valvular and myocardial diseases.

Patients with a history of hypertension may present with chest pain or dyspnea and echocardiographically may have severe concentric left-ventricular hypertrophy with a small ventricular cavity and supernormal cardiac systolic function, with or without systolic anterior motion of the mitral valve and cavity obliteration, and may have hypertensive cardiomyopathy.[76] The reduced peak rate of increase in diastolic ventricular dimension likely accounts for the presenting symptoms of pulmonary congestion.

Management

Symptomatic patients are managed with beta-adrenergic blocking agents and/or calcium channel blocking agents. However, the elderly patient may be less tolerant to these drugs than the younger patient. Larger doses of calcium channel blockers may aggravate the clinical picture by causing significant hypotension and, therefore, need to be avoided. Surgery, namely myotomy and myectomy, may be performed with an acceptable low operative mortality in symptomatic patients having outflow gradients in whom medical therapy has failed. The use of amiodarone may be less indicated in elderly patients, due to apparently decreased frequency of sudden death in this population. Drugs such as digitalis, diuretics, and vasodilators are contraindicated because they may severely exacerbate the ventricular dysfunction in these patients.

Restrictive Cardiomyopathy

This disorder is characterized by small ventricles, dilated atria, elevated filling pressures, and thickened walls with a characteristic "sparkling" appearance on the echocardiogram. The electrocardiogram often shows low voltage with atrial fibrillation and conduction defects. Amyloidosis is one cause of restrictive cardiomyopathy. Senile cardiac amyloidosis is likely a separate pathologic condition that is usually observed after the age of 70 years.[77] The diagnosis may be confirmed by rectal, gingival, or endomyocardial biopsy. Amyloid deposition in the heart increases with age, reaching nearly 80 percent of the atria in persons over 90 years of age.[3,10] The macroscopic appearance, however, is often normal, and amyloid deposition may be largely limited to the atria.[3] Therefore, the term *restrictive cardiomyopathy* does not apply to all old hearts containing amyloid. Microscopically, the earliest deposits are seen in the atrial capillaries. In advanced cases, deposits may be present in the atrioventricular valves, while conduction tissue may be affected later. A restrictive type of physiology may occasionally result from radiation damage, which may not be observed until months or years after the radiation therapy. Restrictive cardiomyopathies rarely result in systolic heart failure. Treatment should be directed at optimizing filling and promoting diastolic relaxation.

ARRHYTHMIAS

Arrhythmias are common in elderly persons, including those without clinically apparent heart disease. The prevalence rate of frequent or complex arrhythmias is related to the presence and extent of underlying heart disease and reportedly ranges between 20 and 75 percent, with ventricular arrhythmias accounting for two-thirds and supraventricular arrhythmias for one-third of the cases.[78,79] The clinical significance of supraventricular arrhythmias varies from trivial to life-threatening, and proper management depends on accurate diagnosis of the rhythm disturbance and knowledge of the clinical circumstances.[2] Both benign and potentially malignant ventricular arrhythmias are common in asymptomatic and otherwise healthy elderly individuals. Although minor ventricular arrhythmias also occur frequently in symptomatic elderly persons, serious episodic arrhythmias are less common and often occur in relation to the onset of symptoms. The prognosis of a chronic arrhythmia is related to the severity of the underlying heart disease.

Management

Ventricular Arrhythmias

For post-MI patients, high-grade ectopic beats, especially in the presence of a low left ventricular ejection fraction, are associated with a poorer prognosis. This association provides a rationale for therapeutic trials to control such arrhythmias. However, antiarrhythmic regimens tested thus far have failed to improve prognosis in these patients. Furthermore, the multicenter cardiac arrhythmia suppression trial showed that certain agents are actually harmful.[80] Thus, management of potentially dangerous ventricular arrythmias in post-MI patients continues to present a therapeutic dilemma. In contrast, there is good evidence that the long-term use of beta blockade in elderly MI patients significantly reduces overall mortality, cardiac death, and reinfarction.[2,18,25]

If a decision is made to use an antiarrhythmic agent, the loading and maintenance doses should be adjusted for age and body weight (see previous discussion regarding lidocaine). Reduced clearance of quinidine and prolongation of its elimination half-life in elderly persons could predispose them to quinidine toxicity. The high incidence of such side effects as diarrhea also limits quinidine's usage. A major disadvantage of using disopyramide in elderly patients is its anticholinergic activity, which may result in urinary retention and visual blurring.[2,79,81] Age-related decreases in renal clearance and excretion result in higher serum levels of procainamide and its active metabolite NAPA in elderly persons.[24] The development of procainamide-induced lupus is common and is a major disadvantage of using this drug. It is clear that there is as yet no ideal antiarrhythmic agent that is effective, has a long dosing interval, and has few side effects. The physician must therefore weigh the benefits and risks of antiarrhythmic therapy and if needed select an appropriate agent carefully and empirically.[1,2,24,53,79,81] Electrophysiological testing, though invasive, may provide important information to guide such therapy.

Supraventricular Arrhythmias

The therapeutic approach to these arrhythmias should be similar in old and young patients. Atrial fibrillation may respond to drugs, electrocardioversion, or overdrive pacing. In patients with atrial fibrillation, anticoagulation should be considered if no major contraindications exist. Atrial flutter may be treated with electrocardioversion if there is hemodynamic compromise. For those with sick sinus syndrome who have periods of supraventricular arrhythmia as well as bradycardia, a permanent pacemaker is indicated only if the patient is symptomatic, since pacemaker implantation does not appear to affect life expectancy.[2,82]

CONDUCTION SYSTEM DISEASE

The sick sinus syndrome and trifascicular block are predominantly geriatric diseases.[2,82,83] In symptomatic elderly patients with conduction defects or heart block, a pacemaker may alleviate the symptoms. Although pacemakers increase survival of elderly patients who have complete heart block, they do not prolong life in cases of bifascicular or trifascicular block in the absence of symptoms.[2,82,83] Preservation of an atrial contribution to ventricular filling, which may be vital to some patients, can be accomplished by implanting an atrioventricular sequential pacemaker system. The prognosis of complete heart block—after permanent pacing is instituted—is related to the severity of the underlying heart disease.[83] Patients in their eighties who receive pacemakers for complete heart block can do very well with pacing and may survive as well as those without heart disease.

CONCLUSION

Disorders of the heart increase in prevalence, morbidity, and mortality with advancing age. As more of the older population continue to survive to older ages, our efforts at improving the prevention and treatment of heart disease in the elderly population become increasingly important. Education programs in health promotion and disease prevention will be ever more critical to these goals. Physical conditioning has received particular attention as a means of reducing the risk of age-related changes of cardiac function and cardiac disease.[84–89] An overall health promotion program emphasizing increased physical activity and increased dietary intake of fruits and vegetables together with cessation of smoking and decreased dietary intake of fat, excess calories, sugar, sodium, and alcohol may be vitally important to promoting healthful aging in older persons.

REFERENCES

1. Siegel JS: Recent and prospective demographic trends for the elderly population and some implications for health care, in Haynes SG, Feinleib M (eds): *Second Conference on the Epidemiology of Aging.* NIH Publication No. 80-969, Bethesda, MD. Washington, DC, US Department of Health and Human Services, 1980.
2. Wei JY, Gersh BJ: Heart disease in the elderly. *Curr Probl Cardiol* 12:1, 1987.
3. Pomerance A: Pathology of the myocardium and valves, in Caird FL et al (eds): *Cardiology in Old Age.* New York, Plenum, 1976, p 11.
4. McKee PA et al: The natural history of congestive heart failure: The Framingham study. *N Engl J Med* 285:1441, 1971.
5. Health Care Financing Administration Office of the Actuary: Expenditures and percent of gross national product for national health expenditures, by private and public funds, hospital care, and physician services; calendar years 1960–87. *Health Care Financ Rev* 10:2, 1988.
6. Wittels EH et al: Medical costs of coronary artery disease in the United States. *Am J Cardiol* 65:432, 1990.
7. Weinstein MC, Stason WB: Cost-effectiveness of interventions to prevent or treat coronary heart disease. *Annu Rev Public Health* 6:41, 1985.
8. American Heart Association: *1990 Heart Facts.* Dallas, American Heart Association National Center, 1991.
9. O'Rourke RA et al: Atherosclerotic coronary heart disease in the elderly. *J Am Coll Cardiol* 10:52A, 1987.
10. Lie JT, Hammond PI: Pathology of the senescent heart: Anatomic observations on 237 autopsy studies of patients 90 to 105 years old. *Mayo Clin Proc* 63:552, 1988.
11. Mock MB et al: Prognosis of coronary heart disease in the elderly patient: The CASS experience, in Coodley EL (ed): *Geriatric Heart Disease.* Littleton, MA, PSG, 1983, p 358.
12. Shaw L et al: Prognostic value of dipyridamole thallium-201 imaging in elderly patients. *J Am Coll Cardiol* 19:1390, 1992.
13. Wei JY: Use of calcium entry blockers in elderly patients. *Circulation* 80:IV171, 1989.
14. Krumholz HM, Wei JY: Acute myocardial infarction: Clinical presentations and diagnosis, in Gersh BJ, Rahimtoola SH (eds): *Acute Myocardial Infarction.* New York, Elsevier, 1991, p 101.
15. Heller GV et al: Implications of elevated myocardial isoenzymes in the presence of normal serum creatinine kinase activity. *Am J Cardiol* 85:24, 1983.
16. Hong RA et al: Elevated MB with normal total CK in suspected myocardial infarction: Associated clinical findings and prognosis. *Am Heart J* 111:1041, 1986.
17. Wei JY et al: Time course of serum cardiac enzymes after intracoronary thrombolytic therapy. *Arch Intern Med* 145:1596, 1985.
18. Forman DE et al: Management of acute myocardial infarction in the very elderly. *Am J Med* 93:315, 1992.
19. Fuentes F et al: Thrombolytic therapy in myocardial infarction of the elderly patient, in Coodley EL (ed): *Geriatric Heart Disease.* Littleton, MA, PSG, 1985, p 404.
20. Forman DE et al: PTCA in the elderly: The "young-old" versus the "old-old". *J Am Geriatr Soc* 40:19, 1992.
21. Wei JY et al: Papillary muscle rupture in fatal acute myocardial infarction: A potentially treatable form of cardiogenic shock. *Ann Intern Med* 90:149, 1979.
22. Weintraub RM et al: Repair of post-infarction VSD in the elderly: Early and long-term results. *J Thorac Cardiovasc Surg* 85:191, 1983.
23. Weintraub RM et al: Surgical repair of remediable post-infarction cardiogenic shock in the elderly: Early and long-term results. *J Am Geriatr Soc* 34:389, 1983.
24. Reidenberg MM et al: Aging and renal clearance of procainomide and acetylprocainamide. *Clin Pharmacol Ther* 28:732, 1980.
25. Gundersen T et al: Timolol-related reduction in mortality and reinfraction in patients ages 65–75 years surviving acute myocardial infarction. *Circulation* 66:1179, 1982.
26. Forman DE, Wei JY: Beta-blockade in older patients with myocardial infarction. *J Am Med Assoc* 266:2222, 1991.
27. Rodrigues EA et al: Improvement in left ventricular diastolic function in patients with stable angina after chronic treatment with verapamil and nicardipine. *Eur Heart J* 8:624, 1987.
28. Yusuf S et al: Changes in hypertension treatment and in congestive heart failure mortality in the United States. *Hypertension* 13:I74, 1989.
29. Pfeffer MA et al: Effect of Captopril on mortality and morbidity in patients with left ventricular dysfunction after myocardial infarction. *N Engl J Med* 327:669, 1992.
30. Gersh BJ et al: Coronary artery surgery in patients over 65 years of age, in Coodley EL (ed): *Geriatric Heart Disease.* Littleton, MA, PSG, 1985, p 411.
31. Holmes DR Jr.: Percutaneous transluminal coronary angioplasty, in Coodley EL (ed): *Geriatric Heart Disease.* Littleton, MA, PSG, 1985, p 439.
32. Hartzler GO et al: Late results of multiple lesion coro-

nary angioplasty in an aged population. *J Am Coll Cardiol* 7:21A, 1986.
33. Dorros G, Janke L: Percutaneous transluminal coronary angioplasty in patients over the age of 70 years. *Cathet Cardiovasc Diagn* 12:223, 1986.
34. St. John Sutton M et al: Atrial septal defect in patients ages 60 years or older: Operative results and long-term postoperative follow-up. *Circulation* 64:402, 1981.
35. Clarkson PM et al: Results after repair of coarctation of the aorta beyond infancy: A 10 to 28 year follow-up with particular reference to late systemic hypertension. *Am J Cardiol* 51:1481, 1983.
36. Liberthson RR et al: Coarctation of the aorta: Review of 234 patients and clarification of management problems. *Am J Cardiol* 43:835, 1979.
37. Stevenson JG et al: Noninvasive evaluation of Blalock-Taussig shunts: Determination of potency and differentiation from patent ductus arteriosus by Doppler echocardiography. *Am Heart J* 106:1121, 1983.
38. Roberts WC et al: Severe valvular aortic stenosis in patients over 65 years of age. *Am J Cardiol* 27:497, 1971.
39. Bonow RO et al: Aortic valve replacement without myocardial revascularization in patients with combined aortic valvular and coronary artery disease. *Circulation* 63:243, 1981.
40. Currie PJ et al: Continuous-wave Doppler echocardiographic assessment of severity of calcific aortic stenosis: A simultaneous Doppler-catheter correlative study in 100 adult patients. *Circulation* 71:1162, 1985.
41. McKay RG et al: Assessment of left ventricular and aortic valve function after aortic balloon valvuloplasty in adult patients with critical aortic stenosis. *Circulation* 75:192, 1987.
42. Henriksen L: Evidence suggestive of diffuse brain damage following cardiac operations. *Lancet* 1:816, 1984.
43. Bonow RO et al: Reversal of left ventricular dysfunction after aortic valve replacement for chronic aortic regurgitation: Influence of duration of preoperative left ventricular dysfunction. *Circulation* 70:570, 1984.
44. Selzer A, Cohn K: Natural history of mitral stenosis in review. *Circulation* 45:878, 1972.
45. Smith MD et al: Comparative accuracy of two-dimensional echocardiography and Doppler pressure half-time methods in assessing severity of mitral stenosis in patients with and without prior commissurotomy. *Circulation* 73:100, 1986.
46. Kolibash AJ et al: Mitral valve prolapse syndrome: Analysis of 62 patients aged 60 years and older. *Am J Cardiol* 52:534, 1983.
47. Wei JY et al: Mitral valve prolapse syndrome and recurrent ventricular tacharrythmias: A malignant variant refractory to conventional drug therapy. *Ann Intern Med* 88:6, 1978.
48. Osterberger LE et al: Functional mitral stenosis in patients with massive mitral annular calcification. *Circulation* 64:472, 1981.
49. Robbins N et al: Infective endocarditis in the elderly. *South Med J* 73:1335, 1980.
50. Kannel WB: Epidemiological aspects of heart failure. *Cardiol Clin* 7:1, 1989.
51. Wei JY: Congestive heart failure, in Abrams WB, Berkow R (eds): *Merck Manual of Geriatrics.* West Point, NY, Merck & Co, 1990, p 380.
52. Wei JY: Age and the cardiovascular system. *N Engl J Med* 327:1735, 1992.
53. Luchi RJ et al: Left ventricular function in hospitalized geriatric patients. *J Am Geriatr Soc* 30:700, 1982.
54. Dougherty AH et al: Congestive heart failure with normal systolic function. *Am J Cardiol* 54:778, 1984.
55. Soufer R et al: Intact systolic left ventricular function in clinical congestive heart failure. *Am J Cardiol* 55:1032, 1985.
56. Manning WJ et al: Reversal of changes in left ventricular diastolic filling associated with normal aging using diltiazem. *Am J Cardiol* 67:894, 1991.
57. Isoyama S et al: Effect of age on myocardial adaptation to volume overload in the rat. *J Clin Invest* 81:1850, 1988.
58. Raven PB, Mitchell J: The effect of aging on the cardiovascular response to dynamic and static exercise, in Weisfeldt ML (ed): *The Aging Heart.* New York, Raven, 1980, p 269.
59. Stratton JR et al: Differences in cardiovascular response to isoproterenol in relation to age and exercise training in healthy men. *Circulation* 86:504, 1992.
60. Takahashi T et al: Age-related differences in the expression of proto-oncogene and contractile protein genes in response to pressure overload in the rat myocardium. *J Clin Invest* 89:939, 1992.
61. Wei JY et al: Excitation-contraction in rat myocardium: Alterations with adult aging. *Am J Physiol* 246:H784, 1984.
62. Lipsitz LA et al: Reduced supine cardiac volumes and diastolic filling rates in advanced age: Implications for postural blood pressure homeostasis. *J Am Geriatr Soc* 38:103, 1990.
63. Nichols WW et al: Effects of age on ventricular-vascular coupling. *Am J Cardiol* 55:1179, 1985.
64. Ogawa T et al: Effects of aging, sex, and physical training on cardiovascular responses to exercise. *Circulation* 86:494, 1992.
65. Rodeheffer RJ et al: Exercise cardiac output is maintained with advancing age in healthy human subjects: Cardiac dilatation and increased stroke volume compensate for diminished heart rate. *Circulation* 69:203, 1984.
66. Sartori MP et al: Relation of Doppler-derived left ventricular filling parameters to age and radius/thickness ratio in normal and pathologic states. *Am J Cardiol* 59:1179, 1987.
67. White W et al: Effects of age and 24-hour ambulatory blood pressure on rapid left ventricular filling. *Am J Cardiol* 63:1343, 1989.
68. Aguirre FV et al: Usefulness of Doppler echocardiography in the diagnosis of congestive heart failure. *Am J Cardiol* 63:1098, 1989.
69. Lee DCS et al: Heart failure in outpatients: A randomized trial of digoxin versus placebo. *N Engl J Med* 306:699, 1982.
70. Chatterjee K, Parmley WW: Vasodilator therapy for acute myocardial infarction and chronic congestive heart failure. *J Am Coll Cardiol* 1:133, 1983.
71. The SOLVD Investigators: Effect of Enalapril on mor-

tality and the development of heart failure in asymptomatic patients with reduced left ventricular ejection fractions. *N Engl J Med* 237:685, 1992.

72. Massie B et al: Hemodynamic and radionuclide effects of acute captopril therapy for heart failure: Changes in left and right ventricular volumes and function at rest and during exercise. *Circulation* 65:1374, 1982.
73. Parmley WW et al: Hemodynamic effects of prazosin in chronic heart failure. *Am Heart J* 102(3 pt 2):622, 1981.
74. Shenoy MM et al: Hypertrophic cardiomyopathy in the elderly. *Arch Intern Med* 146:658, 1986.
75. Wei JY et al: The heterogeneity of hypertrophic cardiomyopathy: An autopsy and one-dimensional echocardiographic study. *Am J Cardiol* 45:24, 1980.
76. Topol EJ et al: Hypertensive hypertrophic cardiomyopathy of the elderly. *N Engl J Med* 312:277, 1985.
77. Wei JY: Coronary artery disease and congestive heart failure. *N Engl J Med* 327:1740, 1992.
78. Martin A et al: Five-year follow-up of 101 elderly subjects by means of long-term ambulatory cardiac monitoring. *Eur Heart J* 5:592, 1984.
79. Dreifus LS: Cardiac arrhythmias in the elderly: Clinical aspects. *Cardiol Clin* 4:273, 1986.
80. Greene HL et al: The cardiac arrhythmia suppression trial: First CAST, then CASTII. *J Am Coll Cardiol* 19:894, 1992.
81. Burk M, Peters U: Disopyramide kinetics in renal impairment. Determinants of interindividual variability. *Clin Pharmacol Ther* 34:331, 1983.
82. McAnulty JH et al: Natural history of "high risk" bundle-branch block: Final report of a prospective study. *N Engl J Med* 307:137, 1983.
83. Ginks W et al: Prognosis of patients paced for chronic atrioventricular block. *Br Heart J* 41:633, 1979.
84. Wei JY et al: Effect of exercise training on resting blood pressure and heart rate in adult and aged rats. *J Gerontol* 42:11, 1987.
85. Wei JY et al: Chronic exercise training protects aged cardiac muscle against hypoxia. *J Clin Invest* 83:778, 1989.
86. Forman DE et al: Enhanced left ventricular diastolic filling associated with long-term endurance training. *J Gerontol* 47:M56, 1992.
87. Larsson B et al: Health and aging characteristics of highly physically active 65 year old men. *Eur Heart J* 5:31, 1984.
88. Paffenbarger RS Jr et al: Physical activity as an index of heart attack risk in college alumni. *Am J Epidemiol* 108:161, 1978.
89. Larson EB, Bruce RA: Health benefits of exercise in an aging society. *Arch Intern Med* 147:353, 1987.

Chapter 46

PERIPHERAL VASCULAR DISEASE

Brian L. Thiele and D. Eugene Strandness, Jr.

Atherosclerosis is the most common condition affecting the arterial system in the elderly. Attempts to identify a single causative factor responsible for the development of atherosclerosis have so far been unsuccessful, but a number of predisposing factors, when present in isolation or in combination, are known to increase the risk of development of this disease. Foremost among these appear to be cigarette smoking, hypertension, lipoprotein abnormalities, the presence of diabetes mellitus, and a positive family history. While symptoms related to this disease most commonly appear in the fifth and sixth decades, a significant number of complications continue to occur with increasing age.

ARTERIOSCLEROSIS OBLITERANS

Pathogenesis and Disease Patterns

Current evidence suggests that the development of atherosclerosis is a continued response of the arterial wall to various types of endothelial injury.[1] Mechanical, chemical, and physical factors have been implicated in the initial damage to the lining of the arterial system and probably play a significant role in the continuing development of these lesions. There is also evidence to suggest that the arterial wall response to injury tends to vary and depends in part on the anatomic location of the vessel. Thus, it appears that arteries in different locations are either more susceptible to injury or respond to this insult in different ways.[2]

The early lesions of atherosclerosis commonly develop at the orifices of the intercostal and lumbar arteries, the distal portion of the superficial femoral artery, and the common iliac artery. Conduit arteries or those with no major branches throughout their course also appear to be susceptible to the early development of the atherosclerotic lesion. For as yet unknown reasons, diabetics have a peculiar predilection to the development of the disease at an early stage in the tibioperoneal arteries of the leg.[3]

The early plaques are usually flat with an intact or minimally denuded endothelial covering. Over time, the plaque undergoes significant changes: development of calcification, increase in size to encroach upon the lumen, hemorrhage within the plaque, and subsequent loss of surface covering with ulceration. It is the development of the complicated plaque that is usually associated with the development of symptoms.[4]

The majority of the clinical problems associated with atherosclerosis are the result of three phenomena: interference with the blood supply by the narrowing of the lumen, the sudden interruption of blood flow by thrombosis on a plaque, and the release of microemboli from ulcerated lesions.

Pathophysiology of Arterial Obstruction

The major causes of acute arterial occlusion include embolism, thrombosis, and trauma. The most common source of emboli is the heart, with the second being from an ulcerated atherosclerotic plaque at some point in the arterial system. Thrombosis does not occur in the normal arterial system. It develops when there has been some disruption of the endothelium exposing the subendothelial collagen to the flowing elements in blood.

Under resting flow conditions, the cross-sectional area of the artery in the region of the atherosclerotic plaque must be reduced by 80 percent before there is a decrease in pressure and flow.[5] Thus, flow is maintained at normal levels until the disease has reached a far advanced stage. It is now known that resting levels of blood flow can be maintained at normal levels even with total occlusion because of the development of collateral circulation. Most commonly, symptoms occur when the arterial system cannot meet the metabolic demands of the limb during exercise. Under these circumstances, the collateral arteries are unable to accommodate the increase in blood flow needed to maintain perfusion.

As noted earlier, embolization from atherosclerotic plaques may also be responsible for the development of symptoms.[6] The most common site for this to occur is the carotid bifurcation, but it can also occur at the limbs. These emboli may arise from any point in the artery where plaques occur. These emboli are usually small and result in the occlusion of small vessels, such as the digital arteries in the toes.[7] It is rare for emboli arising from atherosclerotic plaques to be large enough to occlude major vessels such as the superficial femoral artery. When embolic occlusion of large arteries occurs, it is usually secondary to mural thrombi in the cardiac chambers.[8]

While it is now well appreciated that thrombosis at the site of high-grade stenosis is often the terminal event leading to profound myocardial ischemia, it is not commonly recognized that this also occurs in the lower limb arteries and the carotid bifurcation. In the limbs, the event is usually not catastrophic because of the excellent collateral circulation and the relatively low metabolic requirements. Nonetheless, this condition is common and may be the cause of sudden worsening in a patient who is known to have chronic lower limb ischemia.

Clinical Features

Lower Limb Ischemia

The clinical manifestations with an acute occlusion depend entirely upon the size of the thrombus or embolus and the immediate availability of the collateral circulation. When the ischemia is serious enough to threaten the viability of the limb, time is of the essence, since irreversible tissue changes begin within 4 to 6 hours after the event. Recognition of the ischemia and its extent is best considered in terms of the six *P*'s, which include pain, pallor, paresthesia, pulselessness, and paralysis. The sixth *P*, which is the most important, is the physician, who must appreciate the importance of these symptoms and signs and seek immediate help from a vascular surgeon. Failure to do so will result in the needless loss of many limbs.

The most common presenting complaint in patients with chronic arterial occlusion of the lower limb arteries is intermittent claudication. This symptom is usually described as a dull ache that appears usually in the calf, is precipitated by exercise, and is relieved by rest. The most constant clinical feature of claudication is the walk-pain-rest cycle that is very consistent from day to day and is always aggravated by an increase in the exercise load, such as walking up an incline. This symptom never occurs in the absence of exercise and is not related to changes in posture.

The level of arterial occlusion may be surmised from a consideration of the muscle groups in which the symptoms appear. Obstruction of the superficial femoral artery results in calf claudication. When the iliac arteries are involved, the blood supply to both the calf and thigh muscles is impaired, and both muscle groups may be the site of symptoms. More proximal obstruction of the common iliac artery or the abdominal aorta will interfere with the blood supply of the musculature in the buttocks, thighs, and calves, any of which may be the site of pain. Obstruction at this level may also be responsible for the development of impotence in the male.

When more than one named artery of the arterial system is occluded or diffusely affected by atherosclerosis, the symptoms are usually more severe, with claudication developing even with minimal exercise. It is also under these circumstances that blood flow may be unable to meet resting requirements and lead to the development of rest pain. The rest pain is a severe, aching pain, usually located in the forefoot and digits, which is always aggravated by elevation and partially or totally relieved when the limb is dependent. Characteristically, patients first become aware of this symptom at night, with partial or complete relief obtained by suspending the leg over the side of the bed.

When blood flow to the foot is marginal, minor trauma frequently results in the development of a nonhealing ischemic ulceration. If something is not done to improve blood flow, tissue necrosis or gangrene may then develop. The severe ischemia seen in these circumstances also interferes with the ability of the tissues to resist or combat infection, which may also be responsible for rapid and marked additional tissue loss.

As noted earlier, atherosclerotic or thrombotic material from ulcerated plaques may embolize into the distal circulation and produce occlusion of the small arteries. This condition most commonly involves the plantar and digital arteries and is recognized clinically as the "blue-toes syndrome."[6–8]

Aneurysms

In some patients, atherosclerotic disease is not attended by a decrease in the cross-sectional area of the lumen of an artery but leads rather to weakening of the wall and local dilatation with the development of an aneurysm. This complication is predominantly a disease of males, with the peak incidence occurring in the sixth decade, or slightly later than that for the complications of arteriosclerosis obliterans. The most common sites for the development of atherosclerotic aneurysms are the abdominal aorta below the renal arteries, the popliteal artery, the iliac arteries, and the femoral arteries. Aneurysms of the abdominal aorta usually occur in isolation, but in a small proportion of patients they may be associated with aneurysms at one or more of these other sites.[9] When peripheral aneurysms are present, however, they are frequently bilateral and coexist at multiple sites.

Because of the weakening of the arterial wall in the region of the aneurysm, the most frequent complication is rupture. Factors that appear to predispose to this complication are the coexistence of hypertension and aneurysms of the abdominal aorta that are in excess of 6 cm in largest diameter.[10] While abdominal aneurysms are lined with a compacted layer of platelet-fibrin-thrombus, it is rare for emboli to occur from this site. By way of contrast, embolization and/or thrombosis of the aneurysms is the most common complication of popliteal aneurysms.[11] Because these aneurysms are in close proximity to major veins and nerves, the enlarging sac may compromise these structures, leading to symptoms that mimic deep venous thrombosis or peripheral neuropathy. Thrombosis of these aneurysms is attended with a high incidence of subsequent amputation because of severe ischemia.[12–14]

Clinical Features of Aneurysms Most arterial aneurysms, regardless of their location, enlarge slowly and will usually not produce symptoms until a relatively large size is obtained. When a patient develops symptoms in the presence of an abdominal aortic aneurysm, this is usually an ominous sign and should alert the physician that a true emergency exists. The classic triad of ruptured abdominal aneurysms is pain, the presence of a pulsatile mass, and hypotension. The pain associated with rupture of aneurysms is often severe and unremitting. Because of the urgency involved in the successful management of ruptured abdominal aortic aneurysms, any patient over 50 years old who presents with abdominal pain should be carefully evaluated for the presence of this lesion.

Iliac aneurysms are extremely difficult to diagnose, largely because of the difficulty of palpating them deep in the pelvis. In addition, rupture of these aneurysms is frequently associated with unusual pain syndromes, some of which may direct the physician's attention to the lower urinary tract, while others, caused by irritation of the femoral or obturator nerves, will result in hip, thigh, or knee pain as the primary presenting complaint.

Although the complication of rupture of abdominal aneurysms is largely size-related, a relationship between size and complications of peripheral arterial aneurysm is not as common. The classic presentation of popliteal aneurysms is thrombosis and/or distal embolization with acute ischemia of the leg and foot. Once this complication has occurred, the likelihood of amputation varies from 15 to 50 percent.[14] This high incidence of limb loss is the reason for the aggressive surgical approach to these lesions when diagnosed, even if they are asymptomatic.

Clinical Evaluation Intermittent claudication, while easily recognized when it occurs in its classic form, is frequently confused with leg pain during ambulation that is secondary to neurospinal causes, called pseudoclaudication. The two can usually be distinguished on the basis of the history. In true claudication, the walk-pain-rest cycle is constant from day to day; with pseudoclaudication, the patient has both good and bad days. In addition, neurospinal disorders frequently require the patient either to sit down or lie down for relief of pain.

The type 2 diabetic poses special problems because of several features that are unique to diabetes.[3] The major differences between vascular disease in diabetics and in nondiabetics are with regard to the following: (1) the more extensive involvement with atherosclerosis, particularly below the knee; (2) the frequent occurrence of a peripheral neuropathy (approximately 30 percent), which complicates healing; and (3) the lowered resistance to infection. All of these factors complicate the management of the patient's condition.

The presence of significant arterial disease can usually be suspected on the basis of the history. As noted previously, intermittent claudication is rarely confused with other problems as long as the history of walk-pain-rest cycle is consistent from day to day and pain is not present during periods of rest. Similar considerations apply in the evaluation of pain which occurs at rest. It cannot be stressed too much that a thorough history with attention to the details of the symptomatology as outlined above is necessary because, although atherosclerotic occlusive disease is frequently present in the elderly population, it may not be responsible for the patient's symptoms.

The important physical findings to be elicited include the presence of bruits at specific locations; namely, over the aorta, iliac vessels, and distal superficial femoral artery. In addition to auscultation for such bruits, the volume of pulses at the foot, popliteal, and femoral level should also be assessed. Pulses are absent distal to the sites or sites of occlusion and constitute the major physical findings. In addition to the evaluation for the presence or absence of pulses, the aorta, iliac, femoral, and popliteal should be specifically examined for undue prominence that may alert the examining physician to the fact that aneurysmal disease is present. In chronic ischemia, there may be loss of hair and an atrophy of the skin that produces the characteristic thin, shiny appearance. These changes are seen predominantly in the distal leg and foot. Nail growth is also disturbed in severe cases, with the resulting development of bizarre-shaped, hypertrophic nails. In severe cases, ulceration may be present, usually occurring over sites of frequent trauma and often precipitated by ill-fitting shoes.

In the diabetic patient, it is also important to evaluate the status of the peripheral nervous system to determine whether a peripheral neuropathy coexists with the arterial disease. Clinically, evaluation of all patients with vascular disease should include not only a detailed examination of the area in which symptoms are present but also a thorough examination of the whole of the vascular system, including that of the head and neck, the upper limbs, and the cardiac system. Bilateral arm pressures should be recorded, with a significant finding being a differential of 15 mmHg or greater between the two brachial pressures. The supraclavicular and neck areas should be auscultated for the presence of bruits.

At the conclusion of the history and physical examination, the examining physician should have decided whether the patient does have chronic occlusive vascular disease in the extremities, the site at which the occlusions or disease are present, and, finally, whether the symptomatology is consistent with the findings.

Ancillary Diagnostic Aids Since arterial occlusion always produces a pressure drop across the involved segment, its presence can be confirmed by measuring the systolic pressure at the ankle, using an ultrasonic velocity detector. This measurement is usually expressed as the ankle/arm index and normally should be greater than or equal to 1. When only one arterial segment is occluded, the index is usually greater than 0.5. When multiple levels of obstruction are present, it is often less than 0.5.[15] The absolute pressure level recorded is also of importance. If greater than 40 to 50 mmHg, the perfusion at rest is usually adequate to maintain tissue requirements. Pressures below this level are often associated with ischemic rest pain, and ulcers, when present, will usually not heal unless arterial inflow is improved.

While the diagnosis of intermittent claudication is usually not difficult to make, it is useful to establish the degree of walking disability and the physiological response to exercise. This is best done by a vascular laboratory and with a test that consists of walking on a treadmill at 2 mph on a 12 percent grade for 5 minutes, or until forced to stop by symptoms. Normally, in an individual without obstruction, the ankle systolic pressure after exercise will increase or remain unchanged. With arterial obstruction and claudication, the ankle pressure will fall to low levels and recover very slowly to the preexercise level.[16] If the pressure at the ankle falls to below 80 percent of the baseline and requires greater than 3 minutes to recover, the condition is considered abnormal.

Whenever an arterial aneurysm is suspected at any level of the limb or the abdominal aorta, an ultrasonic B-mode examination should be ordered, which provides an accurate estimation of arterial size, both in the longitudinal and transverse dimensions of the vessel.[17] This simple test has largely replaced conventional x rays of the abdomen for both establishing the diagnosis and estimating size. It also provides an excellent method of following the progress of the aneurysm with regard to changes in size.

Treatment

Chronic Ischemia

Most patients with arterial occlusive disease and intermittent claudication are treated conservatively and will never require operative correction.[18] It is important to attempt to control the associated risk factors, particularly cigarette smoking. Patients should be informed that if they continue to smoke, their arterial disease will continue to progress, and they may be placed in jeopardy for possible limb loss. In addition to discontinuing smoking, patients should optimize their weight and embark on a regular exercise program. Significant improvement can occur, particularly in patients with a recent history of the onset of claudication.

The only medication that has proved to be of any benefit for patients with claudication is pentoxifylline, which is an agent that lowers blood viscosity by making red blood cells more deformable. Patients who take this drug may in some instances obtain some mild improvement in their symptoms.[19]

If a patient is severely disabled and cannot work or carry out daily activities, then surgical correction may be considered. It is important at this stage to consult with an experienced vascular surgeon to assess the location of the problems and the feasibility of a surgical procedure. Arteriography to delineate the location and extent of involvement should be undertaken only if surgery is seriously contemplated. A variety of surgical options are available that can, in most instances, be tailored to the disease location and the patient's general physical condition.[20,21]

In selected cases, it may be feasible to dilate focal areas of stenosis with a balloon catheter. This method has the best chance of success in the common and external iliac artery segments. While the long-term results have not been documented as yet, the initial results for the proximal lesions are very good. The success rates are not as good for femoropopliteal stenoses or occlusions.[22] These procedures must always be performed as a joint venture between the vascular surgeon and the radiologist.

When the patient showers microemboli to one or both feet, we have been quite conservative, treating the patient with aspirin. While the dose is controversial, we have tended to give a total of 650 mg daily. If the microemboli are not controlled by this management, it may be necessary to perform arteriography to find the source and carry out direct arterial surgery.

The patient with ischemic rest pain and ulceration is an entirely different problem. In general, unless blood flow to the limb can be improved, tissue loss is inevitable, usually at the below-knee level. It is important to be aggressive at this stage, before tissue damage becomes irreversible and the patient is committed to an amputation.

In the context of arterial disease, the patient with diabetes mellitus presents special problems and requires more attention.[3,23] It is now well established that patients with diabetes have more extensive arterial involvement of the tibial and peroneal arteries, the same degree of disease in the superficial femoral artery, and less in the aortoiliac segment. The propensity to develop occlusive disease in the medium-sized arteries below the knee has a more profound effect on perfusion of the foot and also makes a surgical procedure less likely to succeed.

The other major factor that leads to the higher incidence of tissue necrosis in diabetics is the high incidence of neuropathy; up to 30 percent of diabetics will have this problem.[3] The inability to appreciate deep pain sensation often leads to the development of calluses and nonhealing ulcers over points of pressure or irritation such as might occur with a poorly fitting shoe. It must be emphasized that ulceration and secondary infection can occur with a neuropathy alone, independent of any arterial involvement. When the two problems coexist, the situation is often irretrievable. Thus, even improving the blood supply to a neuropathic foot will not ensure healing to the same degree it does in a nondiabetic with arterial disease. Since no effective method of treating the neuropathy is available, therapeutic measures require considerable patience and time.

If an ulcer develops secondary to a neuropathy alone, it is important to treat the lesion with limited surgical débridement and aggressive therapy of any secondary infection. When osteomyelitis or joint space involvement occurs, then amputation, which must be tailored to the location of the problem, becomes mandatory. If there is coexisting arterial disease that can be successfully bypassed, this should be done, provided there is some assurance that a limited foot amputation may be feasible.

Aneurysms

The patients with aortic aneurysms pose particularly difficult problems. If rupture occurs, operation is, of course, mandatory, but the mortality rate will be very high, ranging from 15 to 80 percent.[24] Because of the very high mortality associated with rupture, elective resection is recommended, for which the mortality rate will be much lower—in the 2 to 5 percent range. The difficult decision rests in selecting those patients who should be operated on when they are asymptomatic.

The best data available suggest that if an aneurysm is greater than 6 cm in diameter, the likelihood of rupture is at least 50 percent over the next 2 years.[10,24,25] In the elderly population, the decision to be aggressive is most dependent upon the degree of involvement in other major organ systems such as the heart, lung, and kidneys, because it is usually failure of one or more of these systems in the postoperative period that results in patient mortality. With improvements in surgical technique, anesthetic management, and postoperative care, it is possible to perform aneurysm resection in those considered at risk (defined as an aneurysm greater than 6 cm) with an acceptable mortality rate of 2 percent or less.

For patients in their late seventies and eighties in whom an aneurysm is relatively small (less than 6 cm), control of hypertension and regular follow-up at 3- to 6-month intervals with repeat B-mode scans are recommended. If the aneurysms show signs of enlarging, then the physician is justified in pursuing a more aggressive approach of surgical resection.

Peripheral aneurysms, particular in the popliteal segment, should be removed or bypassed unless there is a medical contraindication.[11] Thrombosis of a popliteal aneurysm is associated with a high incidence of limb loss. Also, the removal of a popliteal aneurysm is not associated with the same operative risk as a resection of an abdominal aneurysm with all its potential for cardiopulmonary complications.

Results of Therapy

In approaching the treatment of any patient with peripheral arterial disease, it is important to remember that the chance of limb loss, even if untreated, is relatively low. In the nondiabetic, the chance of limb loss is approximately 1 percent per year. However, when it is associated with diabetes, this figure will rise to about 5 percent per year, emphasizing the problems associated with this disease, as mentioned earlier.[23]

Surgical therapy for the treatment of intermittent claudication secondary to aortoiliac disease will give satisfactory results. Patency of the reconstructed segment will be maintained in 80 percent of the patients up to 5 years.[20] It must be remembered, however, that the operative mortality even in highly selected cases will approach 2 percent; thus, surgical therapy should not be undertaken lightly.

The operative management for the treatment of ischemia at rest and gangrene limited to the digits requires a great deal of judgment and evaluation to assess which form of therapy is most apt to give the best results. There is accumulating evidence that the appropriate use of long bypass grafts, even to the level of the ankle, is often able to provide both good early and long-term results. With better follow-up and attention devoted to the monitoring of the bypass vein grafts, long-term patency rates of 80 percent at 5 years are now feasible.

The results of aortic aneurysm resection in the long term are good. If the patient survives the operative procedure, the subsequent complications relate to the progression of occlusive disease if present, which is variable and unpredictable, and those complications that occur secondary to the prosthesis used to replace the aneurysms. The most feared complications are graft infection and aortoenteric fistulas. Fortunately, these occur in 1 percent or fewer of patients undergoing the procedures. Unfortunately, when they do occur, these complications are often lethal and tax the judgment and ingenuity of even the best vascular surgeons.

POSTTHROMBOTIC SYNDROME

When acute venous thrombosis develops, the involved vein is usually totally occluded, forcing the blood to follow alternative collateral pathways to the heart. The subsequent course of events depends upon several factors that include the extent of the residual occlusion and the development of valvular incompetence.[26] When the occlusion involves the iliofemoral segment, the major complaints include edema, heaviness, and thigh pain with exercise (venous claudication). This pain will only occur with vigorous exercise, so it is rarely a problem in the elderly, who usually cannot exercise enough to produce this complaint.

A more common problem comes with the development of valvular incompetence in the veins below the knee. When this occurs, there is reflux of blood with calf contraction, edema, pain, and the development of pigmentation along the medial side of the lower leg. If the reflux and edema are allowed to persist, the patient may develop an ulceration in the pigmented area that is difficult to heal. The most appropriate therapy is to apply a semirigid dressing from the base of the toes to below the knee; the dressing should be changed weekly. This therapy permits the patient to remain ambulatory and is successful in promoting healing in at least 90 percent of cases. After healing is accomplished, it is critical that the patient be fitted with a short leg-compression stocking to prevent swelling and recurrent ulceration. If this regimen does not work, it may be necessary to apply a skin graft, but this step is not usually required.

EXTRACRANIAL ARTERIAL DISEASE

Stroke is the third most common cause of death caused by arterial disease in the United States. While there is no doubt that it may be due to intracranial involvement, atherosclerosis of the extracranial arteries is now known to be a common and important factor in the pathogenesis of transient ischemic attacks and strokes.[27,28] Recognition of this fact is important, because there is increasing evidence that disease in this area can, in selected patients, be treated successfully with surgery or antiplatelet agents.

Pathogenesis of Transient Cerebral Ischemic Attacks and Strokes

For reasons poorly understood, atherosclerosis of the extracranial arteries tends to occur at branch points and bifurcations, sparing those arteries without branches and whose course is relatively straight. The most important site of involvement is the carotid bifurcation, where the atherosclerotic plaque will remain confined and be the source of problems.[27,29,30] Disease in this location produces problems by either a reduction in hemispheric blood flow or emboli to the brain.

The clinical outcome in any patient depends upon factors that are impossible to predict. In theory, at least, the brain would appear to be ideally protected against a total occlusion of one or more of its vessels of supply because of the circle of Willis. That the brain can in effect function well in the presence of significant disease is evidenced by patients who can survive unilateral or even bilateral occlusion of the internal carotid arteries. However, it is now well known that the circle of Willis is often incomplete and in some patients cannot function to preserve hemispheric or regional blood flow even if the occlusion occurs gradually.[30]

The realization that the surface of a plaque at the carotid bifurcation can ulcerate and be the source of microemboli to the brain represented a major advance in our understanding of the etiology of transient ischemic attacks and stroke.[27] Thus, it is currently accepted that up to 70 percent of patients in this category will have emboli as the basis for their cerebral ischemia and not a total reduction in hemispheric blood flow caused by a high-grade stenosis or a total occlusion of the internal carotid artery.

Clinical Presentation

For clinical purposes, it is convenient to subdivide patients into the following categories: (1) those with asymptomatic bruit, (2) those with focal symptoms, and (3) those with nonfocal symptoms.

The patient with a bruit in mid and high position of the neck must be considered as suspect for harboring a carotid bifurcation plaque. However, it is a nonspecific finding and does lead to a dilemma that will be addressed in the following sections.

Patients with focal symptoms are generally subdivided into the following categories: (1) those suffering transient ischemic attacks (TIAs), (2) those with reversible ischemic neurological deficit (RIND), and (3) those with a completed stroke. This classification is generally used to refer to problems that occur in the distribution of the internal carotid artery, and the symptoms produced are related to neurological dysfunction in the area of the brain supplied by that vessel. The most classic are disturbances of motor and sensory function and monocular visual disturbances.

The transient ischemic attacks are abrupt in onset and will resolve within a matter of minutes. For example, in the case of the eye, fleeting blindness (amaurosis fugax) may occur, which is described as a window shade being pulled across the field of vision. The duration of the deficit that one is willing to accept as signifying an ischemic event is somewhat variable, but if it persists in excess of 1 hour and then clears completely, it is probably more appropriately classified as a reversible ischemic neurologic deficit. The important fact to keep in mind is that the patient is neurologically normal after the attack has subsided.

Those with a completed stroke develop a deficit that remains fixed or at best shows improvement over days or weeks, but continued neurological impairment of some degree usually persists. The therapeutic implications in this group of patients are obviously different from those with reversible deficits.

Those patients with nonfocal and nonhemispheric symptoms are the most confusing and difficult to evaluate clinically. The potpourri of symptoms includes vertigo, ataxia, diplopia, drop attacks, dysarthria, syncope, dizziness, decreased mentation, and seizures. When these symptoms develop and are not related to some other definable etiology, the patients are often evaluated for the presence of vascular disease, particularly if they are elderly or have evidence of arterial disease in the neck or other locations. It should be stressed that a thorough neurological evaluation should be performed in these circumstances to exclude other causes before one is satisfied that the symptoms are related to extracranial vascular disease.

Diagnosis

The keystone of establishing a diagnosis is to discover a lesion or set of lesions that appear to be appropriate for the clinical picture. This may be relatively simple or complex, depending upon the presenting complaints.

The patient with an asymptomatic bruit presents a dilemma more with regard to management than workup. As already indicated, the bruit itself is nonspecific and does not predict with a high degree of accuracy the state of the carotid bifurcation. It has been shown that approximately one-third of the patients with such a finding will have a high-grade stenosis (50 to 90 percent diameter reduction), about 6 percent will be normal, and about 6 percent will have a total occlusion of the internal carotid artery. The remainder will have a disease of a lesser degree, narrowing the carotid artery by 10 to 49 percent.[29]

Of great importance is the relationship between the degree of narrowing and the occurrence of TIAs, strokes, and total occlusions of the internal carotid artery. It has been shown that patients with a greater than 80 percent diameter-reducing lesion of the internal carotid artery have a very high incidence of ischemic events within the first 6 to 9 months after discovery of the lesion.[29,30] The lesion is usually discovered by ultrasonic duplex scanning in asymptomatic patients who are found to have a cervical bruit. It should be noted that such high-grade or preocclusive lesions are found in about 6 percent of all asymptomatic patients with bruits.

With the availability of ultrasonic duplex scanning in most hospitals, it is not necessary to resort to arteriography to establish the presence and degree of carotid bifurcation involvement. The test is so accurate that it can be used for screening purposes and is an ideal method for following the natural history of the disease, regardless of how it is treated.[31]

There are specific situations in which a good cause-and-effect relationship may exist between nonspecific symptoms and vascular disease, such as the subclavian steal syndrome wherein blood may be siphoned away from the posterior circulation via the vertebral artery.[32] This syndrome occurs when there is a proximal stenosis or occlusion of the subclavian artery and can easily be detected by measuring the blood pressure in both arms. There should not be a differential of greater than 15 mmHg between the two arms.

It cannot be emphasized too strongly that the workup in all categories of patients with symptoms may have to include a computed tomography (CT) scan, electroencephalogram (EEG), and a complete neurological evaluation to avoid missing intracranial lesions such as tumors, which may be responsible for a patient's complaints.

Therapy

During the past few years, many of the controversies surrounding the treatment of patients with carotid artery disease have been resolved. The major concern was the lack of prospective, randomized trials documenting the role of medical therapy versus carotid endarterectomy. While the annual event rate for transient ischemic attacks and strokes for asymptomatic patients with carotid artery atherosclerosis is in the 4 percent range, these figures do not take into account the relationship between the degree of narrowing and outcome.[29,30]

The interim results of two major trials in asymptomatic patients are now available. The North American Symptomatic Carotid Endarterectomy Trial results showed that patients presenting with transient ischemic attacks and strokes (with partial or complete recovery) had a cumulative risk of stroke after 2 years of 26 percent for the medically treated patients, as compared to 9 percent for those who underwent carotid endarterectomy.[33] These results were obtained in 659 randomized patients who were found by arteriography to have a 70 to 99 percent diameter-reducing stenosis. Very similar results were reported by the European Carotid Surgery Trial.[34] No data are yet available for those symptomatic patients whose degree of diameter reduction of the carotid artery is in the 30 to 70 percent range.

The clinical trials examining the role of therapy for asymptomatic patients with carotid artery disease have not yet reported their results. While there remains some disagreement, the patients found most likely to benefit from carotid endarterectomy have a greater than 80 percent diameter reduction of the carotid bifurcation. It is this subset of patients who are likely to progress to total occlusion of the internal carotid artery. When this occurs, the likelihood of developing a completed stroke is in the range of 25 percent.

The patients with nonfocal symptoms continue to pose the greatest problems in management. While reversal of flow in the vertebral artery distal to an occlusion of the subclavian artery has been associated with the development of vertebrobasilar insufficiency, this is most often a clinically insignificant finding.[35]

Prior to the publication of the randomized trials, aspirin was the standard form of therapy for patients with carotid artery disease, be it symptomatic or asymptomatic. This is now in serious doubt, leaving the clinician with very little to use that is proven effective. With the release of ticlopidine (Ticlid), another antiplatelet agent has become available. In the Canadian American randomized trial of this drug against placebo in patients with thromboembolic stroke, it provided a risk reduction of 23.3 percent for stroke, myocardial infarction, or vascular death.[36] There are no data on its comparative effectiveness when matched against carotid endarterectomy.

REFERENCES

1. Ross T, Glomset JA: Pathogenesis of atherosclerosis. *N Engl J Med* 295:369, 1976.
2. Haimovici H et al: Fate of aortic homografts in experimental canine atherosclerosis: 1. Study of fresh thoracic implants into abdominal aorta. *Arch Surg* 76:282, 1958.
3. Strandness DE et al: Combined clinical and pathologic study of diabetic and non-diabetic peripheral arterial disease. *Diabetes* 13:366, 1964.
4. Haimovici H (ed): *Vascular Surgery: Principles and Techniques.* New York, McGraw-Hill, 1976, chap 15.
5. May AG et al: Hemodynamic effects of arterial stenosis. *Surgery* 53:513, 1964.
6. Wagner RB, Marin AS: Peripheral atheroembolism: Confirmation of a clinical concept with case report and review of the literature. *Surgery* 73:353, 1973.
7. Crane C: Atherothrombotic embolism to lower extremities in atherosclerosis. *Arch Surg* 94:96, 1967.
8. Hight DW et al: Changing clinical trends in patients with peripheral arterial emboli. *Surgery* 79:172, 1976.
9. Hirsch HJ et al: Aortic and lower extremity arterial aneurysms. *J Clin Ultrasound* 9:29, 1981.
10. Estes JE Jr: Abdominal aortic aneurysms: Study of 102 cases. *Circulation* 2:258, 1950.
11. Crawford ES, DeBakey ME: Popliteal artery arteriosclerotic aneurysms. *Circulation* 32:515, 1965.
12. Edmunds LH et al: Surgical management of popliteal aneurysms. *Circulation* 32:517, 1965.
13. Bouhoutsos J, Martin P: Popliteal aneurysms: A review of 116 cases. *Br J Surg* 61:469, 1974.
14. Gifford RW et al: An analysis and follow-up study of 100 popliteal aneurysms. *Surgery* 33:284, 1953.
15. Carter SA: Clinical measurement of systolic pressures in limbs with arterial occlusive disease. *JAMA* 207:1869, 1969.
16. Carter SA: Response of ankle systolic pressure to leg exercise in mild or questionable arterial disease. *N Engl J Med* 287:578, 1972.
17. Leopold G et al: Ultrasonic detection and evaluation of abdominal aortic aneurysms. *Surgery* 72:939, 1972.
18. Boyd AM: The natural cause of arteriosclerosis of the lower extremities. *Angiology* 61:10, 1960.
19. Porter JM et al: Pentoxifylline efficacy in the treatment of intermittent claudication: Multicenter controlled double-blind trial with objective assessment of chronic occlusive arterial disease patients. *Am Heart J* 2:66, 1982.
20. Nevelsteen AR et al: Aortofemoral grafting: Factors influencing late results. *Surgery* 88:642, 1980.
21. Sumner DS, Strandness DE Jr: Hemodynamic studies before and after extended bypass graft to the tibial and peroneal arteries. *Surgery* 86:442, 1979.
22. Rutherford RB et al: The current role of percutaneous transluminal angioplasty, in Greenhalgh RM, Jamieson CW, Nicolaides AN (eds): *Vascular Surgery: Issues in Current Practice.* New York, Grune & Stratton, 1986, chap 17.
23. Silbert S, Zazeela H: Prognosis in arteriosclerotic peripheral vascular disease. *JAMA* 166:1816, 1958.
24. Gore I, Hirst AE Jr: Arteriosclerotic aneurysms of the abdominal aorta: A review. *Prog Cardiovasc Dis* 16:113, 1973.
25. Bergan JJ et al: New findings in aortic aneurysm surgery, in Bergan JJ, Yao JST (eds): *Arterial Surgery.* New York, Grune & Stratton, 1988, pp 287–298.
26. Strandness DE Jr, Thiele BL: *Selected Topics in Venous Disorders.* Mt Kisco, NY, Futura, 1981, chap 5.
27. Imparato AM et al: The carotid bifurcation plaque: Pathological findings associated with cerebral ischemia. *Stroke* 10:238, 1979.
28. Thompson JE, Talkington CM: Carotid endarterectomy. *Ann Surg* 184:1, 1976.
29. Roederer GO et al: The natural history of carotid arterial disease in asymptomatic patients with cervical bruits. *Stroke* 15:605, 1984.
30. Moneta GL et al: Operative versus nonoperative management of asymptomatic high-grade internal carotid artery stenosis: Improved results with endarterectomy. *Stroke* 18:1005, 1987.
31. Langlois YE et al: Ultrasonic evaluation of the carotid bifurcation. *Echocardiography* 4:99, 1987.
32. Santschi DR et al: The subclavian steal syndrome: Clinical and angiographic considerations in 74 cases in adults. *J Thorac Cardiovasc Surg* 51:103, 1966.
33. North American symptomatic carotid endarterectomy trial collaborators: Beneficial effect of carotid endarterectomy in symptomatic patients with high-grade stenosis. *N Engl J Med* 325:445, 1991.
34. European carotid surgery trialists' collaborative group: Interim results for symptomatic patients with severe (70–99%) or with mild (0–29%) stenosis. *Lancet* 1:1235, 1991.
35. Bornstein NM, Norris JW: Subclavian steal: An harmless haemodynamic phenomenon? *Lancet* 2:303, 1986.
36. Gent M et al: The Canadian American Ticlopidine Study (CATS) in thromboembolic stroke. *Lancet* 1:1215, 1989.

Chapter 47

HYPERTENSION

William B. Applegate

In the last few years there has been an explosion of new knowledge on the epidemiology, pathophysiology, and treatment of hypertension in the elderly. Estimates of the prevalence of hypertension in the elderly vary greatly depending on the age and race of the population, the blood pressure cut points used for the definition of hypertension, and the numbers of measurements made.[1–3] Although hypertension is very prevalent in the elderly, most current prevalence figures are overestimates. The combination of data from clinical trials lending support to the notion that both isolated systolic and systolic-diastolic hypertension in the elderly should be treated[4–7] and the proliferation of new pharmacologic agents has stimulated the growing tendency to treat as many as 40 percent of elderly persons with some form of antihypertensive medication.[8]

Since the risk of future cardiovascular morbidity and mortality rises in a continuous fashion as either systolic blood pressure (SBP) or diastolic blood pressure (DBP) rises, there is really no threshold of either SBP or DBP which can definitively be described as "hypertensive."[9] Nonetheless, for the purposes of clarity, this chapter will use the following definitions based on clinical convention[2]:

Isolated Systolic Hypertension (ISH) = SBP greater than or equal to 160 mmHg and DBP less than 90 mmHg
Systolic-Diastolic Hypertension (SDH) = SBP greater than 140 to 160 mmHg and DBP greater than or equal to 90 mmHg

PHYSIOLOGY

The exact *causal* mechanisms for hypertension in the elderly and whether they are markedly different from the mechanisms involved in hypertension in younger persons remain to be fully elucidated. As will be pointed out below, much of the supposed rise in prevalence in hypertension in persons over age 65 is actually attributable to a rise in ISH rather than a rise in SDH. It has been presumed that structural changes in the large vessels play a predominant role in the rise in SBP levels with age. However, the degree to which vascular structural changes versus functional changes contribute to hypertension in the elderly is still not completely clear. Both a decrease in connective tissue elasticity and an increase in the prevalence of atherosclerosis result in an increase in peripheral vascular resistance and aortic impedance with age.[10–13] Vascular morphologic changes which occur in hypertension include hypertrophy and hyperplasia of the smooth muscle cells,[14,15] changes in collagen and elastin in the vessel wall,[16] and possible hyperplasia of the cells in the vascular endothelium.[16,17] The structural changes that occur with aging are qualitatively similar to but not as extreme as the changes observed with hypertension.[18] A study in laboratory rats indicates that blood pressure lowering in both normotensive and hypertensive rats could prevent the development of age-related changes in the vascular wall.[19] Simon et al.[20] have found a strong negative correlation between large-vessel compliance and systolic pressure in older patients. It has been shown that a decrease in aortic compliance results in greater resistance to systolic ejection and frequently in disproportionate elevations of SBP.[13]

In addition to undergoing structural changes, the vascular system also undergoes functional changes associated with hypertension and aging. Studies of age-related changes in alpha-adrenergic responsiveness of vascular smooth muscle have produced somewhat conflicting results.[21–25] However, the bulk of the evidence seems to indicate that alpha-adrenergic responsiveness of the vascular smooth muscle is not greatly changed with age.[26] It is more clear that the beta-adrenergic responsiveness of vascular smooth muscle declines with age,[27,28] with a consequent decrease in the relaxation of vascular smooth muscle.[29] This decrease may be specific to the beta-adrenergic system, since aging vessels continue to respond to other vasodilators, such as nitroglycerin.[18,28] It has been postulated that the increase in peripheral resistance in elderly hypertensives may in part be due to diminished beta-adrenergic–mediated vasodilation while alpha-adrenergic–mediated vasoconstriction continues unabated.[26]

It is possible that age-related vascular changes in responsiveness to vasoactive agents could be related to alterations in the handling of the calcium cation. Carrier et al.[21] reported that in aged rats, alterations in calcium concentration did not affect vascular smooth muscle responsiveness to norepinephrine. On the other hand, Cohen and Berkowitz[22] found that aortas from old rats were quite dependent on extracellular calcium for the extent of norepinephrine-induced contraction. Although the role of calcium in hypertension in the elderly has not been well defined, it should be noted that hypertension in the elderly responds well to treatment with calcium antagonists.[30] Lindner and colleagues[31] have reported a study in which young and middle-aged subjects were injected with plasma from patients with essential diastolic hypertension. This, it was found, increased the intracellular calcium in platelets taken from normal subjects, suggesting that certain factors in the plasma of patients with essential hypertension may increase the calcium content within vascular smooth muscle cells[31] and may play a role in increasing peripheral vascular resistance.

Whether the renin-angiotensin system or the renal management of electrolytes and water plays a central role in the pathogenesis of hypertension in the elderly is uncertain. It appears likely that both systems are involved to some extent but probably have a secondary role. It is clear that, on average, plasma renin levels decline with age.[32] Both basal plasma renin levels and the renin response to sodium depletion,[33,34] diuretic administration,[35] and upright posture decline with age.[36,37] However, neither the concentration of plasma renin substrate[33,34] nor levels of inactive renin decline in the elderly.[38] It is possible that the mechanisms responsible for converting inactive renin to active renin are primarily affected by age, but the exact reason for the decline in plasma renin levels with age is unknown.[36] Some studies of elderly hypertensive patients estimate that approximately 20 percent of elderly patients have relatively high renin values,[39] while other studies indicate that the proportion with high renin values is considerably lower than this.[40] Even though the prevalence of high renin levels may be low in elderly hypertensives, the renin-angiotensin system must play some role in the pathogenesis or maintenance of hypertension in a majority of elderly hypertensives, since most will experience significant blood pressure lowering when given an angiotensin converting enzyme inhibitor.[41] There is also a reduction in plasma aldosterone levels with age, but this decline is not as great as the decrease in renin levels.[36]

The role of the kidney in hypertension in the elderly is not well defined. Longitudinal studies indicate that there is a decline in glomerular filtration rate and creatinine clearance with age, even in the absence of renal or vascular disease.[42] Elderly persons are less able both to maximally retain and to excrete sodium. Studies indicate that it takes elderly subjects longer to excrete a given saline load, but the sodium is eventually excreted rather than retained.[35] Also, the ability of the kidney to respond maximally to antidiuretic hormone declines with age.[43] To date it does not appear that renal and adrenal mechanisms play a predominant role in the pathogenesis of hypertension in the elderly.

Studies of cardiovascular hemodynamics in elderly hypertensives have indicated that elderly patients with either ISH or SDH have increased peripheral vascular resistance.[40,44] Messerli and colleagues[40] found that elderly patients with SDH had lower resting cardiac output, heart rate, stroke volume, intravascular volume, renal blood flow, and plasma renin activity when compared to younger patients with SDH. Vardan and colleagues[44,45] reported that elderly patients with ISH had variable cardiac output and stroke volume.[44,45] Unfortunately, studies of cardiovascular hemodynamics in elderly hypertensives have been limited to date by small and possibly nonrepresentative samples. Few of the subjects have been over age 70, and the studies do not separate out the effects of aging versus increased blood pressure over time. It would be hazardous to make sweeping treatment recommendations based on such a limited data base. However, the most consistent cardiovascular physiologic change in elderly patients with either SDH or ISH is increased peripheral vascular resistance. The presumed pathophysiology of hypertension in the elderly is summarized in Table 47-1.

PREVALENCE AND RISK

As mentioned above, several epidemiologic studies have indicated that average SBP increases throughout the life span in most countries, while average DBP rises until age 55 to 60.[46] This increase in blood pressure occurs both in persons who have previously been classified as hypertensive plus those who have been normotensive. However, data from Framingham and other studies indicate that not all individuals experience this aging-related increase in blood pressure.[46] In addition, population studies from primitive societies indicate that average blood pressure does not tend to rise with age.[47] Such populations tend not to

TABLE 47-1

Physiology of Hypertension in the Elderly

Vascular systems
Decreased distensibility
Increased atherosclerosis
Normal alpha-adrenergic function
Decreased beta-adrenergic function
Renin-angiotensin system
Decreased renin levels
Probable secondary role
Cardiovascular hemodynamics
Increased peripheral resistance
Decreased cardiac output
Decreased renal blood flow
Decreased plasma volume

have the age-related weight gain usually seen in industrialized societies, have higher levels of habitual physical exercise, and consume diets low in sodium and rich in potassium.[47]

Unfortunately, the prevalence of SDH and ISH is considerable in the elderly. Since average DBP tends to level off around age 55, the prevalence of SDH tends to level off in persons over age 55 to 60.[46,48] Therefore, although some authors speak in general terms of the rise in the prevalence of hypertension with age, the prevalence of SDH rises little if at all with advanced age.[49,50] Actually, it is the rise in ISH which accounts for most of the overall increase in the prevalence of "hypertension" with advancing age.[48] Prevalence estimates of either SDH or ISH depend on the number of measurements taken (prevalence decreases to an extent with increasing numbers of measurement), the level of DBP or SBP used in the definition, and the population studied. When prevalence estimates for SDH and ISH are based on studies like the Hypertension Detection and Follow-up Program (HDFP) and the Systolic Hypertension in the Elderly Program (SHEP), which utilize measurements on more than one occasion, it appears that the prevalence of SDH in the elderly is about 15 percent in whites and 25 percent in blacks, while the prevalence of ISH varies with age from 10 to 20 percent.[49,50] Therefore, the total prevalence of hypertension in the elderly is not quite as high as the figure of 50 to 60 percent which is frequently reported.[1]

Although the clinical treatment of hypertension has classically focused on DBP levels, epidemiologic data indicate that for middle-aged and older adults, SBP is more predictive of future cardiovascular morbidity and mortality than is DBP.[51,52] For instance, analysis of the Framingham data indicates that DBP is somewhat more predictive of the development of coronary heart disease (CHD) in persons under age 45, but, as age continues to increase above 45 years, DBP declines somewhat in its ability to predict future CHD while SBP increases in its ability to predict CHD.[52] Above age 60, SBP is more predictive of CHD; in fact, a recent study by Taylor and colleagues[53] clearly demonstrated that elevations of SBP continue as a strong risk factor into advanced old age, while the importance of DBP wanes considerably. Both SBP and DBP are highly predictive of future cerebrovascular events. Analysis of Framingham data indicates that 42 percent of strokes in elderly men and 70 percent of strokes in elderly women are directly attributable to hypertension.[52] Again, SBP appears to be slightly more predictive than DBP, and the risk gradients for SBP do not wane with advancing age. Elevations of SBP are in part related to decreased arterial distensibility and increased rigidity of the major blood vessels, as measured by the depth of the dicrotic notch in pulse-wave recordings, which flattens with age.[11,54] However, when changes in the pulse wave are held constant, increased SBP is still predictive of future cardiovascular events.[11]

When all cardiovascular risk factors are taken into account in the elderly, it is clear that an increased level of SBP is the single greatest risk factor (other than age itself) for increased cardiovascular disease in this population.[46] It is also clear that increased blood pressure does interact with some of the other traditional cardiovascular risk factors to compound the risk.[46] For instance, although total serum cholesterol declines somewhat in predictive power as a cardiovascular risk factor in the elderly, it still confers some element of risk [especially when fractionated into the high-density lipoprotein/low-density lipoprotein (HDL/LDL) ratio] and compounds the risk for hypertensives.[46] Also, it has been known for some years that the development of left ventricular hypertrophy (LVH) is itself an independent cardiovascular risk factor.[55] Recent reports from the Framingham Study indicate that LVH is more prevalent in the elderly and is highly correlated with increased SBP.[56] It is also becoming more clear that LVH in hypertensives confers increased risk of ventricular arrythmias.[57]

RISK/BENEFIT RATIO OF THERAPY

Whether and how to treat hypertension in the elderly depends on a consideration of the risk/benefit ratio specific to old age.[3] Because treatment in the elderly has historically been cautious because of the concern about adverse side effects, these will be considered first. Although SDH and ISH have been shown to be associated with increased epidemiologic risk of subsequent cardiovascular disease, concerns about the toxicity from antihypertensive therapy in the elderly have led many authors to advise restraint or even therapeutic nihilism with regard to the treatment of hypertension in the elderly.[58] Theoretically, there are reasons why the risk/benefit ratio for the treatment of hypertension might increase with age. It is thought that the elderly are particularly susceptible to many of the side effects of antihypertensive medication.[59] For instance, it has been shown that elderly patients are more likely than younger patients to develop hyponatremia and hypokalemia when treated with standard doses of diuretics.[59,60] It is also thought that older patients are more likely to develop side effects such as depression and confusion when treated with antihypertensive medications that affect the central nervous system (medications such as beta blockers or drugs that affect the alpha-adrenergic nervous system).[61] As mentioned previously, there is good evidence that the baroreceptor reflex becomes less sensitive with age.[62,63] As a result, the elderly could be more sensitive to the postural hypotensive effects of antihypertensive medications, with a consequent propensity for falls and fractures.[64]

Although some investigators have argued that elderly persons with hypertension actually need the higher blood pressure to adequately perfuse vital organs such as the brain and kidney,[65] most studies have not shown that judicious use of antihypertensive medications in the elderly has a significant adverse effect on either renal or cerebral perfusion.[66–68] It is clear from the work of Strandgaard et al.[69] that in middle-aged patients with chronic essential hypertension the pressure–flow curve for cerebral autoregulation is reset to the right, so that the chronic hypertensive would be more susceptible to cerebral hypoperfusion if the mean arterial pressure were lowered substantially and acutely. It is quite possible that a similar situation might exist in an elderly patient who has been hypertensive for a number of years. Further work has indicated that cautious, slow lowering of blood pressure to normal levels in the chronic hypertensive, with continued control, results in a resetting of the cerebral pressure–flow autoregulation curve[68,70] to the left—that is, toward a more normal configuration. A few studies in middle-aged hypertensives suggest that acute initiation of antihypertensive drugs can lower cerebral perfusion modestly,[68,71,72] but chronic administration of appropriate doses of antihypertensive medications does not adversely affect cerebral blood flow.[66,68,70,73,74]

Actually there are surprisingly few data from large-scale clinical trials to definitively address the issue of the toxicity of antihypertensive medication in the elderly. A group of investigators from the Hypertension Detection and Follow-Up Program (HDFP) has reported that the total rate of adverse effects in this trial of the treatment of mild-to-moderate SDH was less for the subgroup aged 60 to 69 years at entry than for those under age 50.[75] While these data are helpful, it should be remembered that persons in the age range 60 to 69 would really be classified as "young old" and may not be as susceptible to side effects as the "old old" (aged 75 years and up). In addition, such trials tend to select the most "well" subjects and are not necessarily representative of elderly patients who have one or more serious comorbid diseases. The largest set of data available on the toxicity of antihypertensive therapy in the elderly comes from the European Working Party on Hypertension in the Elderly (EWPHE) randomized study of the efficacy of the treatment of SDH in a cohort of patients with a mean age at entry of 72 years.[6] Early reports from this trial indicate that treatment with a thiazide-triamterene combination (followed by alpha methyldopa as a second-step agent when needed) resulted in mild increases in glucose intolerance, serum creatinine, and uric acid and a mild decrease in serum potassium in the treatment group.[76] Treatment does not appear to have had a significant long-term effect on serum cholesterol levels.[77] To date only limited data on side effects have been reported. There was no significant difference between the treatment and control groups in the rate at which patients were dropped from the study because of presumed drug-related side effects. The biochemical side effects listed above were not thought to outweigh the benefits of treatment (described later). In addition, the recent SHEP study[7] demonstrated very modest side effects associated with active treatment.

Questions still remain about the possible degree of negative impact that antihypertensive therapy may have on the quality of life for elderly patients. Quality-of-life issues which are important to the elderly and which may be influenced by antihypertensive therapy (but which have not been well studied to date) include emotional state (depression, life satisfaction, anxiety), cognitive or intellectual processing (memory, psychomotor speed, problem solving), physical function (ability to perform self-care tasks, upper- and lower-extremity speed, gait and balance), and social interaction (social activities, contacts).[78] Several randomized controlled trials have evaluated the impact of various antihypertensive therapeutic regimens on quality of life in elderly people. The Treatment of Hypertension in the Elderly (THE) study conducted by the Veterans Affairs Cooperative Study Group enrolled 690 men over the age of 60 with a diastolic blood pressure of 90 to 114 mmHg and a systolic blood pressure of less than 240 mmHg. Participants were randomized to lower (25 mg) versus higher (50 mg) doses of hydrochlorothiazide. Those whose blood pressure was not controlled on the diuretic were then further randomized to one of four second-step drugs: hydralazine, methyldopa, metoprolol, or reserpine. Although methyldopa had significantly higher rates of intolerable side effects (16 percent) compared to the other three drugs (hydralazine, 2.9 percent; metoprolol, 4.6 percent; and reserpine, 4.6 percent), there were no differences between any of the second-step drugs in terms of effects on cognitive function, motor skills, memory, mood, or activities of daily living. In addition, there were no differences between the high- and low-dose diuretic regimens on any of these quality-of-life variables.[79] Applegate and colleagues[80] compared three newer medications in 240 older women with SDH to determine relative efficacy, side effects, and impact on quality of life. This trial randomized elderly women to titrated doses of atenolol (50 to 100 mg once a day), enalapril (5 to 20 mg once a day), and diltiazem SR (60 to 180 mg twice a day). Total rates of adverse events or side effects were equivalent across the three treatment arms. More patients on atenolol were classified as treatment failures (15 percent) than on diltiazem SR (2.5 percent) ($p = .009$). The treatment failure rate was intermediate on enalapril (8 percent). Despite use of an extensive quality-of-life battery, no significant differences were found on the scores of the participants in the three treatment arms. Therefore, there is little evidence to date to indicate that various antihypertensive regimens have any differential effect on quality of life in elderly persons.

EVIDENCE FOR EFFICACY OF ANTIHYPERTENSIVE THERAPY

Despite continued concern about the potential toxicity of antihypertensive therapy in the elderly, evidence exists that the benefits of treating SDH, at least for relatively healthy elderly persons up to the age of 85, outweigh the potential adverse effects.[3–5] For ISH, two recent trials have demonstrated that the drug treatment of either isolated[7] or predominant[5] systolic hypertension will reduce subsequent rates of stroke and other cardiovascular events. The current evidence that the treatment of SDH and ISH is beneficial is described below.

Systolic-Diastolic Hypertension

Since the Veterans Administration (VA) Cooperative Studies reported in 1967, 1970, and 1972, it has been generally accepted that treating adults under age 69 with a DBP greater than 104 mmHg would reduce subsequent morbidity and mortality from hypertension.[81] The results of the VA trial were indeterminate for adults with a DBP between 90 and 104 mmHg. As with most large trials of the efficacy of the drug treatment of SDH, the oldest persons enrolled in this trial were aged 69 on entry. The VA study collaborators did analyze their results for the cohort aged 60 to 69 years. There was a 32 percent lower rate of morbid events in this subgroup, but the numbers of subjects was small and the differences did not reach statistical significance.

Subsequent hypertension trials have tended to focus on the benefit of drug treatment of mild to moderate SDH (DBP 90 to 115 mmHg). In the HDFP multicenter trial, in randomized patients with SDH, the 5-year total mortality was 17 percent lower for the special care (SC) than for the referred care (RC) group, and cardiovascular mortality was 19 percent lower.[82] The SC group received individualized, intensive stepped-care treatment of high blood pressure at special clinics, while the RC group received usual care in the community. The HDFP included 2376 participants aged 60 to 69 years, and the SC group showed a significant 16.4 percent reduction in total mortality for this age cohort. A recent report from the HDFP study group reported on additional follow-up for over 8 years for most of the study cohort.[83] After 8 years, the oldest subgroup still showed mortality trends in favor of the SC group, although the magnitude of the differences had declined somewhat in the oldest cohort. The Australian Trial in Mild Hypertension randomized participants aged 40 to 69 years with a mean baseline DBP of 95 to 109 mmHg to medication treatment or placebo.[84] Although there was no significant difference between the two groups in total mortality, the treatment group did show a two-thirds reduction in cardiovascular deaths. Analyses of the frequency of total trial end points (both fatal and nonfatal) seemed to show a reduction in both cardiovascular and cerebrovascular events. For the subgroup aged 60 to 69 years at entry, there was a 39 percent reduction in trial end points in the treatment group.[85] Although the differences on the intention-to-treat analysis for the 60- to 69-year-old subgroup did not reach statistical significance, the magnitude of the apparent relative benefit in the older treatment subgroup was as great as that for the overall study cohort.

Since most major hypertension trials have only studied selected groups of "young old" persons, the EWPHE study was designed to investigate whether medication treatment of SDH in a wider age range of elderly subjects was effective. This trial enrolled persons over age 60 (mean age 72) and assigned them to treatment or placebo.[6] After an 8-year follow-up period, analyses revealed no effect on all-cause mortality but a significant 27 percent reduction in the cardiovascular mortality rate. There was a statistically significant 38 percent reduction in cardiac mortality as well as a 32 percent reduction in cerebrovascular mortality, which did not reach statistical significance. Further analysis of the EWPHE data indicates that the beneficial effects of treatment on cardiovascular mortality seemed to be limited to participants who were under age 80 at entry.[86] Treatment appeared to be effective for participants at all levels of entry SBP from 160 to 239 mmHg, but treatment did not appear to have an impact on participants with entry DBP in the range of 90 to 95 mmHg. The investigators in this study have concluded that treatment resulted in 29 fewer cardiovascular events and 14 fewer cardiovascular deaths per 1000 patient-years of treatment.

Because the EWPHE study left open the question whether treating SDH in persons over age 80 was beneficial, the Swedish Trial in Older Persons (STOP) hypertension study was conducted to assess the impact of treating very old persons (age 70 to 84) with SDH.[4] In this study, participants were eligible if their SBP was 180 to 230 mmHg with a DBP less than 90 mmHg or if the DBP was between 105 and 120 mmHg. In all, 1627 individuals were randomized to atenolol 50 mg, hydrochlorothiazide 25 mg, amiloride 2.5 mg, hydrochlorothiazide 50 mg, amiloride 5 mg, or placebo. If either the beta blocker or diuretic regimens failed to control the blood pressure after 2 months, the diuretic was added to the beta blocker arms or vice versa. After an average of 25 months of follow-up, compared to the placebo group, the combined active treatment groups demonstrated a significant 40 percent reduction in total cardiovascular morbidity and mortality, a significant 47 percent reduction in total fatal and nonfatal stroke, and a significant 43 percent reduction in total mortality (Table 47-2). There was also a 13 percent reduction in fatal

TABLE 47-2

Stop-H: Morbidity and Mortality by Treatment Group (rates per 1000)

	Active	Placebo	Relative Risk
Total stroke	16.8[b]	31.3	0.53
Total MI	14.4	16.5	0.87
Total CVD[a]	33.5[b]	55.5	0.60
Total mortality	20.2[b]	35.4	0.57

[a] CVD = cardiovascular disease.
[b] Significantly better than placebo.
SOURCE: Adapted from Ref. 4.

and nonfatal myocardial infarction and a 50 percent reduction in fatal MI plus sudden death, neither of which reached statistical significance. Results for the individual drug treatment arms have not been reported. However, the study appears to demonstrate the benefit of treating elevated SDH in patients at least up to 84 years of age.

It should also be noted from Table 47-3 that the estimated absolute benefit from the drug treatment of diastolic hypertension in persons over age 60 varied from 10 events prevented per 1000 person-years up to 100 events per 1000 person-years, depending on whether the initial level of diastolic hypertension was mild to moderate or severe. This level of benefit is significant and would account for the reduction of many thousands of morbid and mortal events if the entire population of elderly hypertensives in this country were treated. Nevertheless, the lower levels of absolute benefit for the treatment of mild SDH may or may not be sufficient for certain elderly *individuals* to want to undertake therapy, particularly if treatment has a substantial adverse effect on an individual's quality of life.

Isolated Systolic Hypertension

Recent data from the Systolic Hypertension in the Elderly Program (SHEP) trial[7] and the Medical Research Council Trial (MRC)[5] now indicate that the treatment of isolated and predominant systolic hypertension can lower subsequent cerebrovascular and cardiovascular morbidity and mortality. The results of these studies will very much revolutionize our understanding of the importance of focusing on SBP versus DBP elevations in older persons. The SHEP trial[7] was a 5-year, double-blind, placebo controlled trial with 4736 participants with ISH who were randomized to placebo or active treatment. The active treatment was a step-care regimen using chlorthalidone 12.5 to 25 mg (oral potassium supplement given if the serum potassium dropped below 3.5 meq/l) followed by the second-step drug atenolol (25 to 50 mg) or reserpine (0.05 to 0.1 mg) if atenolol was not tolerated. Overall the treatment group experienced a reduction of 30 cerebrovascular and 55 cardiovascular morbid and mortal events (over a 5-year period) per 1000 person-years of treatment (Table 47-4). The strong benefit of treatment of ISH indicates that all patients with a SBP in the range of the SHEP trial should be treated. In addition, as seen in Table 47-4, the diuretic-based regimen did produce an impressive and significant 25 percent reduction in combined fatal and nonfatal coronary heart disease events, with a 5-year absolute benefit of 16 events prevented per 1000 person-years. Also, there was a nonsignificant 13 percent reduction in total mortality. To date, subgroup analyses have indicated that benefit from treatment was seen in all age-race-gender subgroups, including persons over the age of 80 at entry. One interesting issue raised by the SHEP study is whether treatment of elevations of systolic blood pressure between 140 and 160 mmHg would also be beneficial. Because of regression to mean, throughout the SHEP trial the placebo group averaged a SBP of only 155 mmHg. It is clear from epidemiologic studies that an SBP of 140 to 160 mmHg confers a substantial risk on middle-aged and older persons.

Subsequent findings reported by the Medical Research Council (MRC) trial have tended to confirm the findings of the SHEP study. The MRC conducted a randomized antihypertensive trial involving 4396 men and women aged 65 to 74 with predominant systolic hypertension (SBP 160 to 209 mmHg and DBP of ≤ 115 mmHg).[5] Participants were randomized to atenolol 50 mg per day, hydrochlorothiazide 25 or 50 mg per day plus amiloride 2.5 or 5 mg per day, or placebo. The mean follow-up was 5.8 years. If the blood pressure was not controlled on the initial regi-

TABLE 47-3

Impact of Antihypertensive Therapy on Cardiovascular Morbidity and Mortality by Age Group

	Relative Reduction,[a] Percent		*Absolute Reduction[b] per 1000 Person-Years*	
Study	**<50 Years**	**>60 Years**	**<50 Years**	**>60 Years**
VA Cooperative (morbidity)	55	59	21	100
HDFP (mortality)	6	16	2	25
Australian (cardiovascular trial end points)	20	26	5	10

[a] Relative reduction is the percentage decline in the event rate in the intervention group as compared to the rate in the placebo group.
[b] Absolute reduction is the total number of events prevented in the treatment group versus the comparison group, per 1000 person-years of treatment.

TABLE 47-4

SHEP: Morbidity and Mortality by Treatment Group (rates per 1000)

	Active	Placebo	Relative Risk
Total stroke	4.1[a]	6.3	0.63
Total CHD	5.9[a]	7.8	0.75
Total CVD[b]	12.2[a]	17.5	0.68
Total mortality	9.0	10.2	0.87

[a] Significantly better than placebo.
[b] CVD = cardiovascular disease.
SOURCE: Adapted from Ref. 7.

men, the diuretic regimen could be added to the beta blocker and vice versa. Compared to the placebo group, actively treated subjects (diuretic and beta-blocker groups combined) had a 25 percent reduction in stroke ($p = .04$), a 19 percent reduction in coronary events ($p = .08$) and 17 percent reduction in all cardiovascular events ($p = .03$). Interestingly, the beta-blocker group when analyzed alone did not have a significant reduction of any of the cardiovascular end points when compared with the placebo group. However, the diuretic group did show significant reductions in stroke of 31 percent ($p = .004$), a 44 percent reduction in coronary events ($p = .009$), and a 35 percent reduction in all cardiovascular events ($p = .005$) compared to placebo. Although the poor results of the beta-blocker group are not compatible with other studies in the literature and may be due to a higher rate of dropouts in this group, the findings in the diuretic group tend to strongly confirm the SHEP finding with regard to the benefit of treating systolic or predominant systolic hypertension with a diuretic-based regimen.

Coronary Heart Disease

Clinical trials on the treatment of SDH have shown that treatment lowers the rate of strokes and heart failure but has little effect on rates of CHD.[3,87] Several theories have been offered to explain this. It is possible that too vigorous a lowering of DBP may actually result in impaired coronary artery blood flow, particularly to the subendocardial layer during diastole.[88] Three recent descriptive studies have shown that there may be a J-shaped relationship between treated DBP and mortality from myocardial infarction.[88–90] Two studies of middle-aged treated diastolic hypertensives[88,90] and one of elderly treated diastolic hypertensives[89] have shown that those individuals with the very lowest treated levels of DBP had higher rates of myocardial infarction. Some light has been shed on this issue by the studies of Coope and Warrender,[91,92] who performed a single-blind, randomized, placebo-controlled study of the treatment of SDH in elderly patients. Treatment apparently lowered the subsequent rate of strokes but not the rate of myocardial infarction. Further analysis of these data revealed a J-shaped relationship between entry DBP and subsequent rates of fatal and nonfatal myocardial infarction, but this relationship held for both the treatment and the placebo groups. Therefore, a likely explanation for these findings is that the subjects with the lowest levels of DBP may have had a higher prevalence of prior cardiovascular disease, with a reduction in the heart's ability to generate a higher DBP. Nonetheless, prudence would dictate that it is best not to treat SDH in elderly patients in an overly aggressive manner.

It is also possible that the diuretics used in many hypertension clinical trials partially offset the beneficial impact of blood pressure lowering by adversely affecting other risk factors, particularly lipid and glucose homeostasis. A recent prospective descriptive study by Samuelsson et al.[90] has shown that a reduction in SBP or DBP in middle-aged subjects which is not accompanied by a reduction in cholesterol (if elevated) has less impact unless both risk factors are improved. However, results from the EWPHE study and the recent SHEP pilot study trial indicate that diuretic treatment has only a transient adverse effect on serum lipids.[77,93] Further, the recent SHEP main study[7] indicates that at 1-year follow-up there was a difference of 6 mg/dl in total cholesterol in the treatment versus the placebo group. This narrowed to 3 mg/dl for the rest of the trial after 18 months of follow-up. This lack of effect on lipids in the elderly may be due to metabolic differences which occur with age or to the fact that these two trials used lower doses of diuretics. On balance, there are not enough negative data to proscribe use of diuretics in the elderly, but individual patients treated with diuretics who develop significant alterations of lipid or glucose levels should be placed on other agents.

In addition, the recent findings by the SHEP and MRC trials of low-dose diuretics used in combination with a potassium-sparing regimen now provide objective end-point data indicating that low-dose diuretics actually do lower the rates of CHD events about as would be expected from epidemiologic studies. Therefore, the rationale for not using diuretics, particularly in older persons, is very weak.

DIAGNOSTIC APPROACH

The basic approach to the evaluation of the elderly hypertensive patient involves accurately determining the baseline blood pressure, assessing any possible end-organ damage, and (in certain cases) ruling out any underlying conditions which might have caused the blood pressure to rise.[3] Since blood pressure is highly variable, it is important that the average of three readings on two or three occasions of measurement be used to define the baseline blood pressure.[1,94] High blood pressure readings show regression to the mean, so high initial blood pressure readings are often lower on the second and third follow-up visits. Evidence indicates that 40 percent of the elderly are being treated for hypertension at any point in time, many of whom may have been classified as normotensive if an adequate number of initial measurements had been taken.[8] Therefore, inadequate numbers of occasions of measurement of blood pressure have led to falsely high prevalence estimates in the literature and to overtreatment in practice. It should be noted that elderly hypertensive patients should have baseline (and periodic) evaluation of both supine and standing blood pressure, since the prevalence of postural hypotension increases with age and can be seriously aggravated by treatment with antihypertensive medications.[64,95]

Recently, several authors have written that pseudohypertension may be a fairly common problem in the elderly, frequently causing overestimation of the real blood pressure.[96–98] However, there are several scientific limitations to the studies of pseudohypertension which reduce the overall importance of this issue. First, some of the studies which initially described pseudohypertension in the elderly evaluated only selected patients already suspected of having the condition.[38,39] Also, most of these studies describe the measurement of intraarterial pressure in great detail, but none describe the indirect measurement using the blood pressure cuff in adequate detail to convince the reader that the indirect measures were done with precision and reliability.[38,39] Most of the studies to date indicate that, in these highly selected samples, indirect cuff measurement of blood pressure tends to significantly overestimate the intraarterial reading of diastolic pressure in some cases, but that direct and indirect measures of systolic blood pressure correlate fairly closely.[35,37] Recent studies indicate that pseudohypertension is not a very prevalent condition but does occur in some elderly patients with very rigid or calcified vessels. In fact, these are the very patients who are most likely to have ISH. Elderly patients with substantial elevations of SBP who have no evidence of hypertension-related end-organ damage are one group of patients in whom this entity should be suspected. The Osler maneuver has been touted as an aid to the clinician in determining if pseudohypertension might be a problem.[97] Unfortunately, recent studies have indicated that the Osler maneuver is neither sensitive nor specific. Although clinicians must be aware that pseudohypertension can occur in rare instances, no standard screening for this condition can be recommended. Instead the clinician should rely on signs of end-organ damage and on clinical symptoms (particularly lethargy and faintness in treated patients with apparently normal blood pressure).

The assessment for end-organ damage should include examination of the retina for hypertensive changes, examination of the peripheral pulses, and examination of the chest x-ray and the electrocardiogram (ECG) for signs of LVH. Recent studies indicate that LVH heightens the risk for cardiovascular morbidity and mortality.[55] In addition, it appears that adequate treatment of hypertension may result in regression of LVH.[99] Signs of end-organ damage should sway the clinician toward treatment in cases where the elevation of the blood pressure is borderline.

Most elderly patients with SDH or ISH have no underlying reversible disorder that, if treated, would result in reversal of their hypertension.[1] The diagnostic evaluation of the elderly hypertensive should include the same baseline tests recommended for the evaluation of younger hypertensives: thorough history and physical examination, hematocrit, serum potassium and creatinine, urinalysis for protein, chest x-ray, and ECG. Further evaluation for possible underlying causes of secondary hypertension should be undertaken in the elderly only if (1) there is a sudden onset of increased DBP greater than or equal to 105 mmHg in a person over the age of 55, (2) the DBP continues to average above 100 mmHg despite rational triple-drug therapy, (3) the elderly patient develops accelerated hypertension, or (4) the patient demonstrates spontaneous hypokalemia (not related to drug therapy) or symptoms highly suggestive of pheochromocytoma.[1] The presence of an abdominal bruit, especially if epigastric and radiating into the flank, is also an important physical sign suggesting the need for further evaluation.

TREATMENT

Once an elderly patient has been classified as having either SDH or ISH, there are basically two major types of therapy available. Nonpharmacologic therapy, including weight loss, sodium restriction, moderate consistent aerobic exercise, and relaxation therapy, may be helpful in some individual patients, particularly those with borderline elevations of blood pressure.[100,101] Previously, the only studies of the efficacy of nonpharmacologic interventions were conducted in young and middle-aged persons.[102,103] However, a recent study of the use of combined weight loss and sodium restriction in elderly women with mild diastolic hypertension indicates that such a regimen in overweight older persons can be effective in lowering both systolic and diastolic blood pressure.[104] Data currently available indicate that moderate weight loss (if a patient is overweight) is the most effective nonpharmacologic treatment of hypertension.[105] The only question regarding the efficacy of weight loss concerns the high rate at which the lost weight is regained over time. Studies of sodium restriction indicate that approximately one-third of hypertensive patients will respond to sodium restriction, especially if sodium intake can be decreased below 80 meq per day.[103] Many elderly persons tend to purchase substantial quantities of prepackaged or canned foods, which are high in sodium, and clinicians frequently find that their elderly patients would rather take a diuretic than severely restrict their salt. The limited data currently available on the impact of exercise and relaxation therapy on hypertension indicate that either intervention can have modest short-term beneficial effects on blood pressure.[101]

If nonpharmacologic therapy fails or is not appropriate, the clinician is left with pharmacologic therapy. The pathophysiology of hypertension in the elderly (as described earlier) may include high peripheral resistance, low renin levels, and a tendency to lower cardiac output.[40] In addition, it is known that as the cardiovascular system ages, it becomes less sensitive to both beta-adrenergic stimulation and beta blockade.[105] Based on these physiologic patterns, some experts have predicted that medications which work directly on peripheral resistance—such as diuretics, vasodilators, or calcium channel blockers—will prove to be the most effective antihypertensive agents in the elderly. However, treatment decisions based solely on pathophysiologic considerations have not always proved the most clinically useful in the field of hypertension. Elderly hypertensives are probably physiologically more heterogeneous than has been realized to date, and theoretically less favored drugs, such as beta blockers and angiotensin converting enzyme (ACE) inhibitors, do effectively lower blood pressure in the elderly.[106] There are currently only modest amounts of adequate clinical data comparing the efficacy of various antihypertensive regimens in the elderly. All of the large clinical trials which have shown some benefit of treating SDH and ISH in the elderly have used a diuretic as the first-step drug. Until studies are available indicating that other therapeutic regimens actually reduce subsequent cardiovascular morbidity and mortality, the drug of choice for first-step treatment of uncomplicated older hypertensives should be a low-dose diuretic. The clinician should be aware that many of the newer antihypertensive agents are frequently 10 to 30 times more expensive than a generically prescribed diuretic. Although these differences in cost may not be meaningful to some individuals, the aggregate impact of more expensive treatment strategies, if used in most elderly patients, may well be to add $500 million to $1 billion in charges to the nation's health care costs. For this reason, a few comments about specific classes of therapeutic agents are appropriate.[3]

Diuretics

There are ample data showing that thiazide diuretics and their equivalents are effective in lowering both systolic and diastolic pressure in the elderly. As a class, diuretics tend to lower peripheral vascular resistance and have minimal effect on cardiac output, but they may have adverse effects on serum lipids, potassium, and creatinine.[76,99] Both the EWPHE trial and the SHEP pilot study reported that diuretics are very effective in controlling SDH and ISH while causing minimal side effects. Both studies do confirm that diuretics tend to lower serum potassium and raise serum creatinine and glucose slightly. Now that both the SHEP[7] and MRC[5] studies have confirmed that low-dose diuretic associated with potassium sparing reduces CHD events, diuretics should be the first-choice antihypertensive treatment in uncomplicated older patients with high blood pressure.

Most of the controversy surrounding diuretics has resulted from some controversial findings from the Multiple Risk Factor Intervention Trial (MRFIT).[107] In this study, hypertensive males who had ECG abnormalities at baseline and were treated with a diuretic had a higher CHD death rate than did the comparable placebo group.[107] Certainly diuretics can induce hypokalemia, which can, in turn, lead to cardiac arrythmias.[108] However, analysis of the MRFIT data shows no relationship between either the participant's most recent potassium level or the presence of ventricular premature beats and CHD mortality.[109] Also, it is curious that the increased mortality attributed to diuretic treatment occurred only in the subset of participants treated with hydrochlorothiazide rather than those who were given chlorthalidone.[110] Further doubts about the significance of the MRFIT findings stem from the fact that they arose from a post hoc analysis and could well be due to chance alone.

Nonetheless, the issue of treatment-related CHD is still not easily dismissed. The HDFP group reanalyzed its data and concluded that there was no evidence that the treatment of hypertensives with baseline ECG abnormalities with a diuretic caused an adverse CHD death rate.[111] This conclusion is indeed warranted for the entire HDFP cohort, which included blacks and whites, males and females. When the recent HDFP data are closely scrutinized, however, it is clear that white males in HDFP who were hypertensive and had resting ECG abnormalities *did* have higher CHD death rates for the special-care group. Also, follow-up analysis of the Oslo trial on the treatment of mild hypertension (a study of middle-aged white males) indicated that participants with baseline ECG abnormalities had somewhat higher total CHD event rates.[112] Therefore, it is possible that, for some reason, white males are particularly likely to experience an adverse effect of diuretic treatment of hypertension *if* they have baseline ECG abnormalities. In order to examine this issue, the SHEP[7] study stratified participants at baseline according to those with and without baseline ECG abnormalities. The SHEP trial, using the low-dose diuretic regimen with potassium sparing, absolutely refuted the hypothesis that using diuretics in persons with baseline ECG abnormalities is harmful. In fact, the SHEP study[7] clearly indicates that older individuals with ISH who had baseline ECG abnormalities benefited from treatment and, when compared to the placebo group, had a reduction of all major types of cardiovascular events.

Beta Blockers

Because of the concern regarding the adverse effects of diuretics, many experts have recommended a beta blocker as the drug of first choice in the treatment of the elderly. As discussed previously, there are a number of theoretical reasons why beta blockers might not be as effective in lowering blood pressure in the elderly as they are in younger patients. However, two large randomized trials comparing a beta blocker with a diuretic as initial therapy of hypertension in the elderly have shown that the beta blocker and the diuretic were equivalent in efficacy and in side-effect rates.[113,114] While the beta blockers may not be physiologically ideal antihypertensives in the elderly, clinical trial data support the fact that they are generally safe and effective. However, the recent findings by Applegate and colleagues[80] that atenolol demonstrated more treatment failures in older hypertensive women than did diltiazem SR or enalapril and the curious findings of the MRC trial[5] still raise questions about whether beta blockers are the drug of choice for older persons. At present this is an unresolved issue.

Calcium Channel Blockers

Since calcium channel blockers decrease vascular resistance and have no significant effects on serum lipids or the central nervous system, they are theoretically ideal antihypertensive agents in the elderly.[99] Pool and colleagues[30] conducted a randomized, placebo-controlled trial of the efficacy of diltiazem as monotherapy for diastolic hypertension (DBP 95 to 110 mmHg); 77 participants were entered into the study (average age 58). The participants over age 60 had a significantly greater reduction in SBP and in standing blood pressure than did the subjects under age 60. There was no increase in orthostatic blood pressure drop in the diltiazem-treated group and no change in resting heart rate. The recent finding that calcium channel blockers were effective as monotherapy in treating SDH in older women and had a lower rate of treatment failures than did a beta blocker[80] indicate that calcium channel blockers are very effective in older persons.

Angiotensin Converting Enzyme (ACE) Inhibitors

For theoretical reasons, ACE inhibitors should be less effective in elderly hypertensives than in younger hypertensives. ACE inhibitors do lower peripheral resistance while having no adverse effects on serum lipids or cardiac output; however, the risk of inducing hyperkalemia must be kept in mind. As described earlier, most elderly hypertensives do not have elevated renin levels, so inhibition of the renin-angiotensin axis might have less effect. On the other hand, although the acute blood pressure response to ACE inhibitors is correlated with plasma renin levels, the chronic blood pressure response is not as highly correlated.[99] Moreover, ACE inhibitors also decrease kinin (vasodilators) clearance and may alter renal prostaglandin synthesis. Therefore, the ACE inhibitors are capable of lowering blood pressure in hypertensives who do not have high renin levels. Jenkins[41] has reported on a large surveillance study of captopril use with 975 patients over age 65. Overall, captopril appeared to be effective in lowering blood pressure in the elderly, but the authors report that only 15 percent of patients were treated with captopril alone, while 42 percent were treated with captopril plus a

TABLE 47-5

Guidelines for the Treatment of Hypertension in the Elderly

1. Treat with medication if the average blood pressure on at least two visits (three measurements per visit) is SBP > 160 mmHg and DBP > 100 mmHg.
2. Mild DH (SBP 140 to 160 mmHg and DBP 90 to 100 mmHg) should first be treated conservatively with nonpharmacologic interventions. If, over time, the average DBP remains above 95 mmHg, pharmacologic intervention should be initiated.
3. ISH (SBP ≥ 160 mmHg and DBP < 90 mmHg) should be treated. Both nonpharmacologic and pharmacologic approaches are appropriate.
4. Mild ISH (SBP 140 to 160 mmHg, DBP < 90 mmHg) is associated with as high an epidemiologic risk as a DBP of 95 to 105 mmHg. Nonpharmacologic therapy should certainly be considered. For persons with multiple cardiovascular risk factors or signs of hypertension-related end-organ damage, pharmacologic therapy should be considered. Since there is a lack of definitive data for persons with a BP in this range, the decision should be left up to the individual clinician and patient.
5. For elderly persons with mild DH (and probably mild ISH), the absolute benefit of drug treatment, in terms of mortal and morbid events reduced per 1000 person-years of treatment, is significant but possibly not so great that individual patients need always be treated in the face of disabling side effects from antihypertensive medications.
6. In using pharmacologic therapy, the initial daily dose should be half the recommended starting dose for middle-aged patients.
7. A diuretic is the drug of first choice for the treatment of hypertension in older patients. Diuretic dosages equivalent to 12.5 to 25 mg/day of chlorthalidone (or hydrochlorothiazide) appear to be most effective. The risks associated with toxicity outweigh efficacy once the dosage increases above the equivalent of 25 mg/day.
8. Mitigating factors such as comorbid disease or persistent lipoprotein disorders may mandate another first choice for monotherapy. Recent data indicate that calcium channel blockers are particularly effective in the long-term treatment of hypertension in older persons regardless of gender or race.
9. Pharmacologic therapy should not be continued for elderly patients with mild DH or ISH in whom significant side effects persist despite trials of a variety of pharmacologic agents.
10. After blood pressure has been controlled for 6 months, the dosage of the drug should be stepped down if possible.

SOURCE: From Applegate and Rutan.[117]

diuretic, 7 percent with captopril plus one other drug, and 36 percent with captopril plus two other drugs. These figures cast doubt on the efficacy of the ACE inhibitors as monotherapy for hypertension in the elderly.

Other Antihypertensive Agents

Insufficient data exist to support definitive statements about many other antihypertensive agents in the elderly. However, one recent study did indicate that reserpine in low doses was at least as effective as alpha methyldopa as a step-two agent for hypertension in the elderly.[115] Several experts have suggested that various vasodilators may also be effective in the treatment of hypertension in the elderly. Although definitive comparative data are lacking, it does appear that hydralazine is effective in the elderly, with less accompanying reflex tachycardia than is seen in younger patients.[116] Also, both the alpha beta blocker labetalol and the alpha blocker prazosin are probably effective, with a decreased risk of central nervous system side effects; but they can sometimes cause significant postural hypotension in the elderly.

In summary, the underlying pathophysiology and hemodynamics of hypertension in the elderly does cause the clinician, conceptually, to favor drugs which primarily lower peripheral vascular resistance and have relatively lower central nervous system side effects. However, ample studies are available indicating that some drugs which make less conceptual sense are also generally effective and well tolerated. The magnitude of benefit from treating ISH or SDH is substantial from a public health perspective, but some individual patients may refuse therapy for this level of predicted benefit, particularly if medication-related side effects which substantially impair quality of life cannot be avoided. Finally, data from the STOP study do indicate that the benefit from treating SDH may disappear for patients of advanced age (above 84 years old).[4] This does not mean that a biologically (rather than *chronologically*) young 80-year-old with SDH should not be treated.

RECOMMENDATIONS

Since diuretics need to be given only once a day, are relatively inexpensive, and have a large amount of data supporting their efficacy in lowering both blood pressure and subsequent morbidity and mortality, they are still considered the drugs of first choice for most elderly patients.[3] Diuretics should be used only in low doses, at the equivalent of 25 mg of hydrochlorothiazide or less per day. However, persons with lipid abnormalities or diabetes mellitus may be candidates for alternative therapy. Beta blockers, calcium channel blockers, and mild doses of vasodilators (in the absence of significant postural hypotension) are all acceptable alternatives, but these are usually more expensive than diuretics. The choice of a second-step antihypertensive agent if the blood pressure is not controlled with a first-step agent depends mostly on individual patient differences, since no data are available on the relative benefits of various second-step regimens in the elderly. See Table 47-5 for a summary of recommendations.[117]

REFERENCES

1. Statement on hypertension in the elderly: Report of the Working Group on Hypertension in the Elderly. *JAMA* 256:70, 1986.
2. The Final Report of the Subcommittee on Hypertension Definition and Prevalence of the 1984 Joint National Committee: Hypertension Prevalence and Status of Awareness, Treatment and Control in the United States. *Hypertension* 7:457, 1985.
3. Applegate WB: Hypertension in elderly patients. *Ann Intern Med* 110:901, 1989.
4. Dahlof B et al: Morbidity and mortality in the Swedish Trial in Old Patients with hypertension (STOP—hypertension). *Lancet* 338:1281–5, 1991.
5. MRC Working Party: Medical Research Council of trial treatment of hypertension in older adults: Principal results. *Br Med J* 304:405, 1992.
6. Amery A et al: Mortality and morbidity results from the European Working Party on High Blood Pressure in the Elderly Trial. *Lancet* 2:1349, 1985.
7. The Systolic Hypertension in the Elderly Program (SHEP) Cooperative Research Group: Prevention of stroke by antihypertensive drug treatment in older patients with isolated systolic hypertension: Final results of SHEP. *JAMA* 265:3255, 1991.
8. Furberg CD, and Black DM for the SHEP Research Group: The Systolic Hypertension in the Elderly Pilot Program: Methodological issues. *Eur Heart J* 9:223, 1988.
9. Kannel WB: Some lessons in cardiovascular epidemiology from Framingham. *Am J Cardiol* 37:269, 1976.
10. Hallock P, Benson IC: Studies of the elastic properties of human isolated aorta. *J Clin Invest* 16:595, 1937.
11. Kannel WB et al: Systolic blood pressure, arteriolar rigidity, and risks of stroke. *JAMA* 245:1225, 1981.
12. Chobanian AV: Pathophysiologic considerations in the treatment of the elderly hypertension patient. *Am J Cardiol* 52:49D, 1983.
13. Tarazi RC et al: The role of aortic distensibility in hypertension, in Milliez P, Sasar M (eds): *International Symposium on Hypertension.* Monaco, Boehringer Ingleheim, 1975, pp 143–145.

14. Rorive GL et al: Hyperplasia of smooth muscle cells associated with the development and reversal of renal hypertension. *Clin Sci* 59:335S, 1980.
15. Kanbe P et al: Studies of hypertension induced vascular high cultured smooth muscle cells from spontaneously hypertensive rats. *Hypertension* 5:887, 1983.
16. Wolinsky HA: Response of the rat aortic wall to hypertension: Morphological and chemical studies. *Circ Res* 26:507, 1970.
17. Haudenschild CC et al: Endothelial and subendothelial cells in experimental hypertension and aging. *Hypertension* 3(suppl 1):148, 1981.
18. Soltis EE et al: The vasculature in hypertension and aging, in Horan MJ, Steinberg GM, Dunbar JB, Hadley EC (eds): *Blood Pressure Regulation and Aging*. New York, Biomedical Information Corp, 1986.
19. Haudenschild CC, Chobanian AV: Blood pressure lowering age-related changes in the rat aortic intima. *Hypertension* 6:562, 1984.
20. Simon AC et al: Systolic hypertension: Hemodynamic mechanism and choice of antihypertensive treatment. *Am J Cardiol* 44:505, 1979.
21. Carrier GO et al: Influence of age on norepinephrine-induced vascular contractions as a function of extracellular calcium. *Res Commun Chem Pathol Pharmacol* 26:433, 1979.
22. Cohen ML, Berkowitz BA: Vascular contraction: Effective age and extracellular calcium. *Blood Vessels* 13:139, 1976.
23. Brink C et al: Decreased vascular sensitivity to histamine during aging. *Agents Actions* 14:8, 1984.
24. Elliott HL et al: Effect of age on vascular alpha adrenoreceptor responsiveness in man. *Clin Sci* 63:305S, 1982.
25. Scott PJ, Reid JL: The effect of age on the responses of human isolated arteries to noradrenalin. *Br J Clin Pharmacol* 13:237, 1982.
26. Abrass IB: Catecholamine levels and vascular responsiveness in aging, in Horan MJ, Steinberg GM, Dunbar JB, Hadley EC (eds): *Blood Pressure Regulation and Aging*. New York, Biomedical Information Corp, 1986.
27. Fleich JH et al: Beta-receptor activity in the aorta: Variations with age and species. *Circ Res* 26:151, 1970.
28. Fleich JH, Hooker CS: The relationship between age and relaxation of vascular smooth muscle in the rabbit and rat. *Circ Res* 38:243, 1976.
29. Van Brummelen P et al: Age-related increase in cardiac and peripheral vascular responses to isoproterenol: Studies in normal subjects. *Clin Sci* 60:571, 1981.
30. Pool PE et al: Diltiazem as a model therapy for systemic hypertension. *Am J Cardiol* 57:212, 1986.
31. Lindner A et al: Effects of a circulating factor in patients with essential hypertension on intracellular-free calcium in normal platelets. *N Engl J Med* 316:509, 1987.
32. Scott P, Giese J: Age and the renin-antiotensin system. *Acta Med Scand* 676(suppl):45, 1983.
33. Crane MG, Harris JJ: Effect of aging on renin activity and aldosterone excretion. *J Lab Clin Med* 87:947, 1976.
34. Noth RH et al: Age and the renin-aldosterone system. *Arch Intern Med* 137:1414, 1977.
35. Luft FC et al: Effects of volume expansion and contraction in normotensive whites, blacks, and subjects of different ages. *Circulation* 59:643, 1979.
36. Krakof LR: Renal and adrenal mechanisms pertinent to hypertension in an aging population, in Horan MJ, Steinberg GM, Dunbar JAB, Hadley EC (eds): *Blood Pressure Regulation and Aging*. New York, Biomedical Information Corp, 1986.
37. Weidmann P et al: Age versus urinary sodium for judging renin, aldosterone, and catecholamine levels. *Kidney Int* 14:619, 1978.
38. Nakamaru M et al: The effect of age on active and cryoactive plasma renin in normal subjects and patients with essential hypertension. *Jpn Circ J* 45:1231, 1981.
39. Niarchos AP, Laragh JH: Rein dependency in isolated systolic hypertension. *Am J Med* 77:407, 1984.
40. Messerli FH et al: Essential hypertension in the elderly: Hemodynamics, intravascular volume, plasma renin activity, and circulating catecholamine levels. *Lancet* 2:983, 1983.
41. Jenkins AC et al: Captopril in the treatment of elderly hypertensive patients. *Arch Intern Med* 145:2029, 1985.
42. Rowe JW et al: The effect of age on creatinine clearance in men: A cross-sectional and longitudinal study. *J Gerontol* 31:155, 1976.
43. Rowe JW et al: The influence of age on the renal response to water deprivation in man. *Nephron* 17:270, 1976.
44. Vardan S et al: Systolic hypertension in the elderly: Hemodynamic response to long term thiazide therapy. *JAMA* 250:2807, 1983.
45. Vardan S et al: Systemic systolic hypertension in the elderly: Correlation of hemodynamics, plasma volume, renin, aldosterone, urinary metanephrines, and response to thiazide therapy. *Am J Cardiol* 58:1030, 1986.
46. Kannel WB, Gordon T: Evaluation of cardiovascular risk in the elderly: The Framingham Study. *Bull NY Acad Med* 54:573, 1978.
47. Page LB, Friedlander J: Blood pressure, age, and cultural change, in Horan MJ, Steinberg GM, Dunbar JB, Hadley EC (eds): *Blood Pressure Regulation and Aging, Proceedings from an NIH Symposium*. New York, Biomedical Information Corp, 1986.
48. Drizd T et al: Blood pressure levels in persons 18–74 years of age in 1976–1980 and trends in blood pressure from 1960–1980 in the United States. Vital Health Statistics, no. 11. Washington, DC, US Government Printing Office, DHHS (PHS) 86-1684, 1986.
49. Hypertension Detection and Follow-up Program Cooperative Group: Blood pressure studies in 14 communities. *JAMA* 237:2385, 1977.
50. Vogt TM et al: Recruitment of elderly volunteers for multi-center clinical trial: The SHEP pilot study. *Controlled Clin Trials* 7:118, 1986.
51. *Build and Blood Pressure Study*. Chicago, Society of Actuaries, 1959.
52. Kannel WB et al: Systolic vs diastolic blood pressure and risk of coronary heart disease. *Am J Cardiol* 27:335, 1971.
53. Taylor JO et al: Blood pressure and mortality risk in the elderly. *Am J Epidemiol* 134:489, 1991.
54. Hickler RB: Aging and hypertension: Hemodynamic

implications of systolic pressure trends. *J Am Geriatr Soc* 31:421, 1983.
55. Kannel WB et al: Electro-cardiographic left ventricular hypertrophy and risk of coronary heart disease. *Ann Intern Med* 72:813, 1970.
56. Savage DD et al: The spectrum of left ventricular hypertrophy in a general population sample: The Framingham Study. *Circulation* 75(suppl 1):126, 1987.
57. McLenachan JM et al: Ventricular arrhythmia in patients with hypertensive left ventricular hypertrophy. *N Engl J Med* 317:787, 1987.
58. Williamson, J, Chopin JM: Adverse reactions to prescribed drugs in the elderly: A multicenter investigation. *Aging* 9:73, 1980.
59. Jackson G et al: Inappropriate antihypertensive therapy in the elderly. *Lancet* 2:1317, 1976.
60. Flanenbaun W: Diuretic use in the elderly: Potential for diuretic-induced hypokalemia. *Am J Cardiol* 57:38A, 1986.
61. Avorn J et al: Increased antidepressant use in patients prescribed beta-blockers. *JAMA* 255:357, 1986.
62. Gribbin B et al: Effect of age and high blood pressure on baroreflex sensitivity in man. *Cardiovasc Res* 29:424, 1971.
63. Lipsitz LA: Abnormalities in blood pressure hemostasis associated with aging and hypertension, in Horan MJ, Steinberg M, Dunbar JB, Hadley EC (eds): *Blood Pressure Regulation and Aging, Proceedings from an NIH Symposium.* New York, Biomedical Information Corp, 1986.
64. Caird FL et al: Effect of posture on blood pressure in the elderly. *Br Heart J* 35:527, 1973.
65. Jones JV, Graham DI: Hypertension and the cerebral circulation—Its relevance to the elderly. *Am Heart J* 96:270, 1978.
66. Strandgaard S: Cerebral blood flow and antihypertensive drugs in the elderly. *Acta Med Scand* 676(suppl):103, 1983.
67. Ram CBS et al: Antihypertensive therapy of the elderly: Effects on blood pressure and cerebral blood flow. *Am J Med* 82(suppl 1A):53, 1987.
68. Bertel O, Marx BE: Effects of antihypertensive treatment on cerebral perfusion. *Am J Med* 82(suppl 3B):29, 1987.
69. Strandgaard S et al: Autoregulation of brain circulation and severe arterial hypertension. *Br Med J* 3:507, 1973.
70. Strandgaard S: Auto-regulation of cerebral blood flow in hypertensive patients. *Circulation* 53:720, 1976.
71. Meyer JS et al: Effects of beta-adrenergic blockade on cerebral auto-regulation and chemical vasomotor control in patients with stroke. *Stroke* 5:167, 1974.
72. Aquayagi M et al: Effect of beta-adrenergic blockade with propranolol on cerebral blood flow, autoregulation, and CO_2 responsiveness. *Stroke* 7:219, 1976.
73. Griffith DNW et al: The effect of beta adrenergic receptor blocking drugs on cerebral blood flow. *Br J Clin Pharmacol* 7:491, 1979.
74. Barry I et al: The effect of chronic hypertension and antihypertensive drugs on the cerebral circulation space. *Acta Med Scand* 678(suppl):37, 1982.
75. Curb JD et al: Long-term surveillance for adverse effects of antihypertensive drugs. *JAMA* 253:3263, 1985.
76. Amery A et al: Antihypertensive therapy in patients above 60: Third interim report of the European Working Party on High Blood Pressure in the Elderly. *Acta Cardiol* 33:113, 1978.
77. Amery A et al: Influence of antihypertensive therapy on serum cholesterol in elderly hypertensive patients. *Acta Cardiol* 37:235, 1982.
78. Wenger NK, Matteson ME, Furberg CD, Elinson J: *Assessment of Quality of Life in Clinical Trials and Cardiovascular Therapies.* LeJacq Publishing, 1984.
79. Goldstein G et al: For the Department of Veterans Affairs Cooperative Study Group: Results of the Department of Veterans Affairs Cooperative Study. *Arch Intern Med* 151:1594, 1991.
80. Applegate WB et al: A randomized controlled trial of the effects of three antihypertensive agents on blood pressure control and quality of life. *Arch Intern Med* 151:1817, 1991.
81. Veterans Administration Cooperative Study Group: Effects of treatment in hypertension: Results in patients with diastolic blood pressure 90/114. *JAMA* 1213:1143, 1970.
82. Hypertension Detection Follow-up Cooperative Group: 5 Year Findings of the Hypertension Detection Follow-up Program. *JAMA* 242:2562, 1979.
83. Hypertension Detection and Follow-up Program Cooperative Group: Persistence of reduction in blood pressure and mortality participants in the Hypertension Detection and Follow-up Program. *JAMA* 259:2113, 1988.
84. Management Committee of the Australian National Blood Pressure Study: Prognostic factors in the treatment of mild hypertension. *Circulation* 69:668, 1984.
85. National Heart Foundation of Australia: Treatment of mild hypertension in the elderly. *Med J Aust* 247:633, 1981.
86. Amery A et al: Efficacy of antihypertensive drug treatment according to age, sex, blood pressure, and previous cardiovascular disease in patients over the age of 60. *Lancet* 1:589, 1986.
87. Culter JA, Furberg CD: Drug treatment trials in hypertension: A review. *Prev Med* 14:499, 1985.
88. Cruickshank JM et al: Benefits and potential harm of lowering high blood pressure. *Lancet* 1:581, 1987.
89. Applegate WB et al: Control systolic blood pressure in elderly black patients. *J Am Geriatr Soc* 30:391, 1982.
90. Samuelsson O et al: Cardiovascular morbidity in relation to change in blood pressure and serum cholesterol levels and treated hypertension. *JAMA* 258:1768, 1987.
91. Coope J, Warrender TS: Randomized trial of treatment of hypertension in elderly patients in primary care. *Br Med J* 293:1145, 1986.
92. Coope J, Warrender TS: Lowering blood pressure. *Lancet* 1:1380, 1987.
93. Hulley SB et al: Systolic hypertension in the elderly program: Antihypertensive efficacy of chlorthalidone. *Am J Cardiol* 56:913, 1985.
94. Joint National Committee in Detection: Treatment and Evaluation of High Blood Pressure, 1984 Report. NIH, Bethesda, MD, 84–1088, 1984.

95. Mader SL et al: Low prevalence of postural hypotension among community dwelling elderly. *JAMA* 258:1511, 1987.
96. Spence JD et al: Pseudohypertension in the elderly. *Clin Sci Mol Med* 55:399, 1978.
97. Messerli FH et al: Osler's maneuver and pseudohypertension. *N Engl J Med* 312:1548, 1985.
98. Vardan S et al: Systolic hypertension: Direct and indirect blood pressure measurements. *Arch Intern Med* 143:935, 1983.
99. Dzau BJ: Evolution of the clinical management of hypertension. *Am J Med* 82:36, 1987.
100. Kaplan NM: Non-drug treatment of hypertension. *Ann Intern Med* 102:359, 1985.
101. Final Report of the Subcommittee on Nonpharmacological Therapy of the 1984 Joint National Committee on Detection, Evaluation, and Treatment of High Blood Pressure: Nonpharmacological approaches to the control of high blood pressure. *Hypertension* 8:444, 1986.
102. Langford HG et al: Dietary therapy slows the return of hypertension after stopping prolonged medication. *JAMA* 253:657, 1987.
103. Stamler R et al: Nutritional therapy for high blood pressure. *JAMA* 257:1484, 1987.
104. Applegate WB, Miller ST, Elam JT: Nonpharmacologic intervention reduces blood pressure in older patients with mild hypertension. *Arch Intern Med* 152:1162, 1992.
105. Vestal RE et al: Reduced beta-adrenoceptor sensitivity in the elderly. *Clin Pharmacol Ther* 26:181, 1979.
106. Freis ED for the VA Cooperative Study Group: Age and antihypertensive drugs hydrochlorothiazide, bendroflumethiazide, nadolol and captopril. *Am J Cardiol* 61:17, 1988.
107. Multiple Risk Factor Intervention Trial Research Group: Multiple Risk Factor Intervention Trial. *JAMA* 248:1465, 1982.
108. Whelton PK, Watson AJ: Diuretic-induced hypokalemia and cardiac arrhythmias. *Am J Cardiol* 58:5A, 1986.
109. Kuller LH et al: Unexpected effects of treating hypertension in men with electrocardiographic abnormalities: A critical analysis. *Circulation* 73:114, 1987.
110. Moser M: Implications of the clinical trials on the management of hypertension. *Hypertension* 9(suppl III):80, 1987.
111. Hypertension Detection and Follow-up Program Cooperative Research Group: The effect of antihypertensive drug treatment on mortality in the presence of resting electrocardiographic abnormalities at baseline. *Circulation* 70:996, 1984.
112. Holme I et al: Treatment of mild hypertension with diuretics: The importance of ECG abnormalities in the Oslo Studies and in MRFIT. *JAMA* 251:1298, 1984.
113. Andersen GS: Atenolol vs bendroflumethiazide in middle aged and elderly hypertensives. *Acta Med Scand* 218:165, 1985.
114. Wikstrand J et al: Antihypertensive treatment with metoprolol or hydrochlorothiazide in patients aged 60–75 years. *JAMA* 255:1304, 1986.
115. Applegate WB et al: Comparisons of the use of reserpine vs alphamethyldopa for the second step treatment of hypertension in the elderly. *J Am Geriatr Soc* 33:109, 1985.
116. Veterans Administration Cooperative Study Group on Antihypertensive Agents: Efficacy of nadolol alone and combined with bendroflumethiazide and hydralazine for systemic hypertension. *Am J Cardiol* 52:1230, 1983.
117. Applegate WB, Rutan GH: Advances in management of hypertension in older persons. *J Am Geriatr Soc* 40:1164, 1992.

Chapter 48

AGING OF THE RESPIRATORY SYSTEM

Melvyn S. Tockman

PATHOPHYSIOLOGY OF THE AGING LUNG

Waning respiratory defenses and age-altered pulmonary physiology progressively impair the ability of the elderly lung to clear common infectious and environmental insults. With aging, older persons also lose important nonpulmonary defense mechanisms. Neurologic disorders and sedation lead to an increased tendency for aspiration through altered swallowing and impaired cough. Diminished activity of effector T cells, perhaps due to enhancement of suppressor cells or reduced capacity for functional differentiation, reduces the likelihood of containing a pulmonary infection.

The changes in pulmonary function with age are of fundamental importance, since impaired function (airways obstruction) is associated with increased rates of death from all causes (primarily cardiovascular disease and chronic obstructive pulmonary disease, COPD).[1] Further, ventilatory obstruction is associated with risk of subsequent lung cancer mortality.[2] Thus, impaired pulmonary function on spirometric testing can identify increased risk for three of the five leading causes of death in men and for three of the seven leading causes of death in women.[3] These observations, made after adjustment for other risk factors including cigarette smoking, provide compelling reasons to assess pulmonary function even in "normal" elderly individuals.

Following the end of adolescent growth and development, the age-related increase in lung volumes slows (after age 17 in females, after age 19 in males); forced expiratory airflows reach a maximum between 20 and 24 years of age in both sexes.[4] Further aging leads to a progressive decline in lung function, although until 40 years of age, the age-related decrease in forced vital capacity (FVC) and maximal expiratory flow rate are thought to be due to changes in body weight and strength rather than to attrition of tissues.[5]

This subsequent loss of lung function accelerates slightly as age increases[6] but is remarkably consistent across populations,[7] averaging for nonsmoking males 14 to 30 ml/year of FVC and 23 to 32 ml/year of 1-second forced expiratory volume (FEV_1). Nonsmoking females show slightly lesser rates of decline (FVC, 15 to 24 ml/year; FEV_1, 19 to 26 ml/year) (see Tables 48-1 and 48-2). The relatively constant rate of decline of lung function associated with aging suggests that (in the absence of additional respiratory insult) the most important factor determining whether individuals fall below the threshold of pulmonary impairment with advancing age is the level of forced expiration they reach at the completion of their growth.[8]

EFFECT OF AGING ON INTERACTION BETWEEN LUNG AND CHEST WALL

The volume of the resting lung (functional residual capacity, FRC) is determined by the equilibrium between the inward elastic tissue forces of the lung and the outward forces of the ribs and muscles of respiration. The loss of inward elastic recoil seen with increased age (especially after age 55) is usually evenly matched by a reduction of respiratory muscle strength and increased rib stiffness.[9] This balance is shown by the lack of change in total lung capacity (TLC) and the minimal increase of the FRC with increasing age (see Table 48-1 and Fig. 48-1).

During forced expiration, increasing contraction of chest wall voluntary muscles increases intrathoracic pressure and expiratory airflow until dynamic compression of the airways limits further expiratory flow (after approximately 25 percent of the vital capacity has been exhaled). Collapse of the airways (at the equal pressure point) is prevented only by intraalveolar (upstream) pressure, generated by elastic recoil within the lung.[10] The inward elastic recoil of the lung results from the combination of parenchymal elastic fibers and the surface forces generated at the

TABLE 48-1

Predicted Changes in Normal Pulmonary Function for Males (as determined by the age coefficient term from male reference value prediction equations)

Pulmonary Function	Equation[a]	95% Confidence Interval[b]	Loss of Function per Year of Age	Reference
TLC	0.0795 H + 0.0032 Age − 7.333	1.61	(increase) 3 ml	Morris et al.[25]
FRC	0.0472 H + 0.0090 Age − 5.290	1.46	(increase) 9 ml	Morris et al.[25]
RV	0.0216 H + 0.0207 Age − 2.840	0.76	(increase) 20 ml	Morris et al.[25]
FVC	0.0600 H − 0.0214 Age − 4.650	1.115	21 ml	Crapo et al.[7]
FEV_1	0.0414 H − 0.0244 Age − 2.190	0.842	24 ml	Crapo et al.[7]
FEV_1/FVC	−0.1300 H − 0.152 Age + 110.49	8.28	0.15%	Crapo et al.[7]
Pa_{O_2}	− 0.323 Age − 100.10		0.32 torr	Sorbini et al.[15]
$N_2 phase_{III}$	+ 0.010 Age + 0.710	0.84	(increase) 0.01% N_2/liter	Buist and Ross[13]
DL_{CO}, SB	0.4160 H − 0.219 Age − 26.34	8.20	0.2 ml CO/min/mmHg	Crapo and Morris[14]
Hgb corr. (Cotes[30])	0.4100 H − 0.210 Age − 26.31	8.20	0.2 ml CO/min/mmHg	Crapo and Morris[14]
$\dot{V}_{O_2max}$	− 0.032[a] Age + 4.2 (SD ± 0.4)		32 ml O_2/min	Jones et al.[21]
Expressed per kg	− 0.550 Age − 60 (SD ± 7.5)		0.55 ml/kg/min	Jones et al.[21]

[a] H = height in cm; Age = age at last birthday.
[b] Note lower boundary of normal determined by calculating predicted value from equation, then subtracting the 95 percent confidence interval.

air-fluid interface of the terminal respiratory units. The elastic fibers within alveolar walls are tethered to the respiratory and terminal bronchioles, helping to maintain the patency of these small conducting airways at low lung volumes. An age-associated disruption of elastic fiber attachments is more likely than an aging change in fiber length or diameter. The loss of these elastic attachments leads to increased compliance of affected alveoli, collapse of the small conducting airways, nonuniformity of alveolar ventilation, and air trapping. There is no evidence for an aging effect on either the inward-directed air–fluid surface forces or on the effectiveness of surfactant which mitigates these forces.[12]

The residual volume (RV) is the amount of air that remains in the lungs after a maximal exhalation. During younger years, while peripheral airways are patent, the RV is determined by the minimum size

TABLE 48-2

Predicted Changes in Normal Pulmonary Function for Females (as determined by the age coefficient term from female reference value prediction equation)

Pulmonary Function	Equation[a]	95% Confidence Interval[b]	Loss of Function per Year of Age	Reference
TLC	0.0590 H + 0.0000 Age − 4.537	1.08	(increase) 00 ml	Morris et al.[25]
FRC	0.0360 H + 0.0031 Age − 3.182	1.06	(increase) 3 ml	Morris et al.[25]
RV	0.0197 H + 0.0201 Age − 2.421	0.78	(increase) 3 ml	Morris et al.[25]
FVC	0.0491 H − 0.0216 Age − 3.590	0.676	22 ml	Crapo et al.[7]
FEV_1	0.0342 H − 0.0255 Age − 1.578	0.561	26 ml	Crapo et al.[7]
FEV_1/FVC	−0.2020 H − 0.252 Age + 126.58	9.06	0.25%	Crapo et al.[7]
Pa_{O2}	− 0.323 Age − 100.10		0.32 torr	Sorbini et al.[15]
N_2 $phase_{III}$ (<60 years old)	+ 0.009 Age + 1.036	1.12	(increase) 0.01% N_2/liter	Buist and Ross[13]
N_2 $phase_{III}$ (≥60 years old)	+ 0.058 Age + 1.777	2.55	(increase) 0.06% N_2/liter	Buist and Ross[13]
DL_{CO}, SB	0.256 H − 0.144 Age − 8.36	6.0	0.1 ml CO/min/mmHg	Crapo and Morris[14]
Hgb corr. (Cotes[30])	0.282 H − 0.157 Age − 10.89	6.1	0.1 ml CO/min/mmHg	Crapo and Morris[14]
$\dot{V}_{O_2max}$	− 0.014[a] Age + 2.6 (SD ± 0.4)		14 ml O_2/min	Jones et al.[21]
Expressed per kg	− 0.370 Age − 48 (SD ± 7.0)		0.37 ml/kg/min	Jones et al.[21]

[a] H = height in cm; Age = age at last birthday.
[b] Note lower boundary of normal determined by calculating predicted value from equation, then subtracting the 95 percent confidence interval.

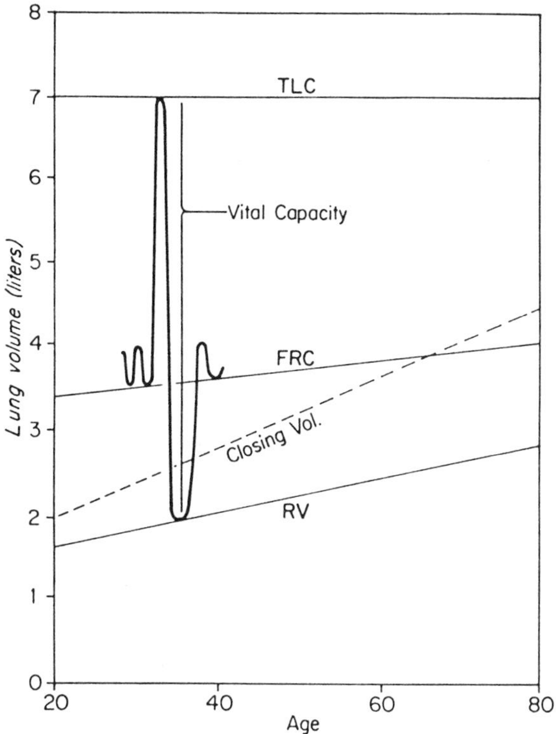

FIGURE 48-1

The effect of age on subdivisions of lung volume: TLC = total lung capacity, FRC = functional residual capacity, RV = residual volume. Values shown are for men of average height; the changes with age are similar for women.

reached by the bony thorax and the maximum ascent of the diaphragm. External compression of the young chest can, in fact, expel additional air from the lungs. The RV increases with age (Fig. 48-1), reflecting air trapped in peripheral airways following loss of the elastic fiber attachments described above. As the TLC remains constant with increasing age, the increase in RV comes at the expense of the vital capacity (VC), reducing the amount of air that can be blown from the lungs after a maximal inhalation (Fig. 48-1).

DISTRIBUTION OF VENTILATION

The distending force of the thoracic wall is modified by gravity. The erect individual has a declining gradient of distending (pleural) pressure from the apex to the base of the lung. As a result of this distending pressure gradient, airways at the apex of the lung are more widely patent than those at the base. As the lung empties from maximum to minimum distention during a normal expiration, the narrower airways at the base of the lung close first, and closure progresses from base to apex. The single breath nitrogen (SBN_2) washout technique has been used to determine the uniformity of alveolar ventilation and the lung volume at which small conducting airways collapse (the closing volume, or CV; see Fig. 48-1).[13] Nonuniformity of ventilation is shown by an increased slope of the SBN_2 phase III (alveolar plateau), while the volume at which the terminal respiratory units begin to close is demonstrated by elevations of the SBN_2 phase IV (closing volume). With advancing age, the slope of the N_2 $phase_{III}$ increases (see Tables 48-1 and 48-2) and the closing capacity (closing volume plus residual volume) may exceed the FRC, indicating that closure of terminal respiratory units occurs before the end of a normal tidal breath. Closing capacity begins to exceed the supine FRC at about 44 years of age and the sitting FRC at approximately 65 years of age.

DIFFUSING CAPACITY

Diffusion of gas from the alveoli into the blood depends upon two factors: the total area and thickness of the alveolar-capillary membrane and the ability of the blood elements to absorb the gas. Progressive age-related decreases in total pulmonary diffusing capacity are usually due to both morphologic changes (loss of surface area of the alveolar-capillary membrane) and increasing inhomogeneities in ventilation and/or blood flow.[5]

The single-breath carbon monoxide diffusing capacity (DL_{CO}) increases to a maximum in the early twenties and thereafter undergoes a gradual decline with age. This reduction has been estimated to be approximately 0.5 percent (0.2 ml CO/min per mmHg) per year (see Tables 48-1 and 48-2). The age-related decline in DL_{CO} is not linear, although linear prediction regressions are used.[14] Women are found to have 10 percent lower diffusion capacity values than men for the same age and height.

ARTERIAL O_2 TENSION

Although, at rest, airways and alveoli at the base are more nearly closed than are apical structures; at maximum inspiration, all alveolar units distend to approximately equal size. Thus, a greater proportion of the inhaled breath must go to the basal airways. In a fortunate arrangement, the greater proportion of blood circulates also to the bases of the lung, providing, in the normal individual, a ventilation-perfusion ratio of near unity. This matching of ventilation and perfusion leads to optimal gas exchange.

Inflammatory destruction or aging of alveolar structures leads to deterioration of the match of ventilation with perfusion. While collapse of peripheral airways decreases ventilation to alveoli, perfusion remains unaffected. These changes are accentuated by factors that reduce the FRC (e.g., the supine posture, obesity, small-airway closure from inflammation/edema). A ventilation-perfusion imbalance results in regional shunting of blood, impaired oxygen uptake, and arterial oxygen desaturation. Arterial O_2 tension follows a linear deterioration with age of approximately 0.3 percent Pa_{O_2} per year (see Tables 48-1 and 48-2).[15] Transfer of the more rapidly diffusible carbon dioxide is limited only by the rate of alveolar ventilation.

For the elderly individual, the consequences of a ventilation-perfusion mismatch are particularly harsh. The Pa_{O_2} (and thus O_2 delivery) may be further compromised by age-associated reductions in cardiac output.[16] When ventilation and perfusion are evenly matched, changing cardiac output has no effect on Pa_{O_2}. However, as ventilation-perfusion inequalities worsen, the Pa_{O_2} at any given cardiac output decreases; the further loss of cardiac output magnifies the reduction of O_2 delivery. It is possible, therefore, that the association (described above) between airway obstruction and mortality may be mediated by mechanical limitations of ventilation and a lowered arterial O_2 tension.

CONTROL OF BREATHING

Older persons who are otherwise healthy may be more vulnerable to transient reductions in levels of arterial oxygen tension (e.g., during pneumonia, exacerbation of COPD) due to age-related diminished responsiveness to hypoxia and hypercapnia.[17] However, more recent investigations question earlier evidence that the ventilatory hypoxic response is reduced by half in healthy older men (64 to 73 years of age) compared with young healthy men (22 to 30 years of age), while the ventilatory response to CO_2 is reduced by approximately 40 percent. The age-associated increase in ventilation rate (given work load) is attributed to a lower mechanical efficiency and deconditioning rather than an inappropriate CO_2 response.[18] Commenting on the results of a period of exercise training of sedentary subjects, a recent study concluded that "the increase in $VE/\dot{V}_{O_2}$ (ventilatory response for a given oxygen uptake) during sub maximal exercise observed with aging can be reversed by endurance training, and that after training, previously sedentary older individuals breathe at the same percentage of MVV during maximal exercise as highly trained (master) athletes of similar age."[19]

EXERCISE CAPACITY

Physical work capacity (fitness) is generally assessed by measurement of the ability to deliver O_2 to the tissues (maximal O_2 consumption, or $\dot{V}_{O_2max}$).[20] Three systems must interact to transport O_2 from the outside air to the working muscles: pulmonary ventilation, blood circulation, and muscle tissue. At any age, the $\dot{V}_{O_2max}$ is related to the physical dimensions of these three components: pulmonary (vital capacity, diffusing capacity), cardiovascular (heart stroke volume, blood volume, red blood cell mass), and skeletal muscle mass. The importance of body size to the measurement of $\dot{V}_{O_2max}$ is reflected by the inclusion of weight in the measurement (expressed as maximal O_2 uptake per kilogram of body weight, or $\dot{V}_{O_2max}$/kg). Cardiorespiratory performance is even more closely related to lean body mass than to weight (especially in obese subjects). Lean body mass may be obtained from body weight by correcting for body fat, as estimated from skin-fold measurements or underwater weighing.

The increase in work capacity ($\dot{V}_{O_2max}$) observed during childhood and adolescence is due to the growth of lungs, heart, and muscle. Following a plateau in the mid-twenties, the $\dot{V}_{O_2max}$ gradually declines due to reductions in two of these three components (cardiac output and muscle mass) seen with advancing years.[21] The gradual linear decline of O_2 delivery (32 ml/min per year in men and 14 ml/min per year in women) can be described by a prediction equation (see Tables 48-1 and 48-2) dependent only upon body size and age (which correlates with cardiac output and muscle mass).

Although ventilatory function also declines with age, reduced ventilation seldom limits exercise in healthy subjects. However, in patients with a ventilatory capacity reduced sufficiently to limit exercise performance, the FEV_1 is a reasonably accurate indicator of maximal ventilation in exercise. More typically, the reduced $\dot{V}_{O_2max}$ seen in elderly individuals with mild to moderate airway obstruction is due to cardiovascular deconditioning associated with lowered levels of habitual physical activity.

The differences in exercise performance between similarly aged men and women largely disappears when factors such as size (lean body mass), hemoglobin level, and levels of training are taken into account. Regular training can substantially slow the decline in maximal oxygen delivery due to age-related cardiovascular deconditioning.[5] Master atheletes who maintain training lose $\dot{V}_{O_2max}$ at half the rate of similarly aged sedentary controls.[22] Healthy 60- to 71-year-olds improve their $\dot{V}_{O_2max}$ in response to exercise to the same relative extent as younger people, independent of gender, age, and initial level of fitness.[23]

DEFENSE MECHANISMS

Clearance

An intact cough reflex is a necessary defense under conditions of dysphagia and impaired esophageal motility, which are more frequently encountered in old age. While cough is not essential for normal clearance of the respiratory tract, it is a powerful adjunct when normal mucociliary clearance is overloaded by foreign materials or secretions. Loss of an effective cough reflex (and subsequent aspiration) also contributes to an increased susceptibility to pneumonia in the elderly. While there seems to be an inverse relationship between age and the rate of mucociliary transport, the importance of mucus transport as a pulmonary defense mechanism has not yet been demonstrated experimentally. Nevertheless, clinical observations of patients with primary ciliary immotility of Kartagener's syndrome (situs inversus, chronic sinusitis, and bronchiectasis) demonstrate recurrent respiratory tract infections, chronic bronchitis, and bronchiectasis.[24]

Humoral Immunity

Humoral immune competence is only roughly predicted by immunoglobulin levels in the bloodstream. Despite the lack of age-related change in IgA and IgG concentrations, the antibody response to extrinsic antigens, such as pneumococcal and influenza vaccines, is reduced considerably in old age. It is possible that this diminished antibody response reflects age-related reductions in T-cell helper activity, increases in T-cell suppressor activity, or the reduced ability of B cells to produce normal high-affinity antibodies in response to antigen (all of which have been observed). The increased circulating immunoglobulin seen in older individuals may reflect increased production of antibody to various intrinsic antigens (i.e., autoantibodies), which replaces production of specific antibodies.[5]

Cellular Immunity

An age-related decline in functional ability has been seen most clearly in cell-mediated immunity. There is a reduced blastogenic response (to plant mitogens, phytohemagglutinin, and pokeweed mitogen) of lymphocytes from elderly adults (75 to 90 years old) compared with younger adults (25 to 50 years old). As measured by delayed hypersensitivity (the number of positive skin-test reactions to five common antigens), reduced cellular immunity among individuals over age 60 has been correlated with increased mortality over the subsequent 2 years. Finally, the decline of cell-mediated immunity with increasing age correlates with an increasing frequency of reactivation tuberculosis.

USE OF TESTS OF PULMONARY FUNCTION

Initial Assessment of Normality

A test such as spirometry should be obtained at baseline for every patient and at 5-year intervals thereafter (in the absence of occupational or environmental exposure) or more frequently if the patient is potentially exposed to inhaled toxins. A young, normal lung should be able to expel 80 percent of its vital capacity in the first second (a FEV_1/FVC ratio of 80 percent). Normalizing to the VC is an excellent way to standardize ventilatory function in healthy individuals. However, with the onset of pulmonary impairment, not only the 1-second forced expiratory volume but also the forced vital capacity are likely to deteriorate. In the absence of a constant VC, investigators have standardized their patients' results to spirometry from cross-sectional surveys of "normal" ("healthy," nonsmoking) individuals. These "normal" results are expressed as linear regression functions of age and height, expressed separately for males and for females (see Tables 48-1 and 48-2).

There are a variety of prediction equations in the literature and, until recently, their selection has been somewhat arbitrary. The research populations studied to develop these prediction equations are often quite different from the populations encountered in a chest clinic. The 1988 Snowbird Conference now recommends that directors of pulmonary function laboratories select the equation that best predicts as normal a sample of the clinically normal individuals tested in their laboratories. Since few of these prediction equations have included sufficient numbers of normal elderly individuals, it is advisable to inquire regarding the origin of the prediction equation used by the lab.

The prediction equation estimates the average function for individuals of similar sex, age, height, and race. The variation in normal pulmonary function is relatively constant across the range of adult ages and heights, so that the normal 95 percent of the population will fall within a fixed interval (confidence interval, CI) of the predicted range. The lower limit of normal can be calculated by subtracting a constant quantity from the predicted value for each test. Prediction equations and the appropriate subtraction constants for white males and females are given in Tables 48-1 and 48-2.

This method for determining the lower limit of normal replaces the commonly used 80 percent of predicted. If 80 percent of predicted were taken as the lower limit of normal, then as the predicted value got smaller with increasing age, the range of normal would become spuriously narrower. Several examples should clarify the point. From the FEV_1 prediction equation (Table 48-1), a 25-year-old man of 170 cm would be expected to have an FEV_1 of 4.2 liters. A male of similar age and height would still be considered to have a normal FEV_1 if he exhaled 4.2 minus 0.842 liters (95 percent confidence interval constant determined from table) or 3.4 liters. For a young man, this lower limit happens also to be 80 percent of the predicted value. Similarly, a 60-year-old man of 165 cm would be expected to have an FEV_1 of 3.2 liters. However, the lower limit of normal for this predicted value is 2.3 liters (3.2 minus 0.8842 liters), only 74 percent of predicted value. These considerations are particularly important for the elderly, where progressively smaller normal values would increase the likelihood of misclassification.

African-Americans have a similar pulmonary geometry to Caucasians, and their lungs have similar mechanical emptying characteristics. For any given standing height, however, African-Americans have a smaller trunk (smaller trunk/height ratio). A reduction of 12 percent from the Caucasian predicted value accommodates the racial difference in pulmonary function somewhat better than a regression based upon "sitting height."

Assessment of Risk for Morbidity and Mortality

The risks for heart disease, COPD, and lung cancer are not limited to the small proportion of the population with "abnormal" pulmonary function. Rather, there is a continuous increase in risk associated with progressively lower (although still normal) levels of ventilatory function. It is therefore of great importance to assess not only the initial pulmonary function but also the trend of pulmonary function with advancing age. Considerable pulmonary function may be lost before an individual crosses into the clinically abnormal range.

At the end of pulmonary growth and development, the ranking (percentile) of an individual's pulmonary function within the population might be ascertained in the same way that pediatric growth curves plot the percentile of height and weight for age.[27] Thereafter, at subsequent evaluations, it can be determined whether an individual's lung function is maintaining its expected ("normal") rate of decline or describes a more rapid rate of decline by crossing percentiles. Examples of these pulmonary function percentile curves (for FEV_1 and FVC for males and for females) are provided in Figs. 48-2 and 48-3. Elderly individuals with a more rapid rate of decline in pulmonary function may be correctly perceived to be at risk for mortality from several causes well in advance of developing "abnormal" pulmonary function.

Assessment of Type and Extent of Pulmonary Disorder

Finally, the common respiratory diseases—restrictive pattern, asthma, chronic bronchitis, and emphysema—can be distinguished by simple pulmonary function tests. Once a pulmonary function is recognized as abnormal (Tables 48-1 and 48-2), the abnormality may be quantified by the guidelines in Table 48-3.

The inability to inhale a normal volume of air is recognized as a "restrictive pattern" on the spirogram by the presence of a normal FEV_1/FVC and a reduced FVC. Restriction may be due to a scarring of the lung, to weakness or loss of neural stimuli to chest-wall muscles, or to changes in the shape of the bony thorax. Substantial obstruction with air trapping may produce a "mixed" pattern, but the underlying obstruction is often obvious if the forced expiration is carried out for at least 10 seconds. If the appearance of restriction persists, lung volume measurement is appropriate.

The obstructive diseases—asthma, chronic bronchitis, and emphysema—all demonstrate a reduction of the FEV_1/FVC on spirometry. Reversible obstruction is the hallmark of asthma (conventionally defined as an increase in FEV_1 equal to or greater than 15 percent of baseline). Bronchodilator reversibility may be absent when the pulmonary function is normal or severely abnormal. Incomplete reversibility suggests a component of "asthmatic bronchitis." The chronic (nonreversible) obstructive pulmonary diseases (chronic bronchitis and emphysema) both manifest a low FEV_1, but the destruction of the alveolar-capillary membrane associated with emphysema produces a lowered DL_{CO} in that condition.

APPROACH TO GERIATRIC PATIENTS WITH DISORDERS OF THE RESPIRATORY SYSTEM

Lung disease in the elderly has certain unique features. First, some importance must be attached to the setting in which the elderly patient is seen. Pneumonia is 50 times more frequent among residents of chronic care facilities than expected in the population at large. In contrast, elderly individuals residing in the community seem not to have an increased prevalence of pneumonia but do have a worse prognosis than younger individuals when pulmonary infections develop. Even with appropriate antibiotic therapy, elderly patients with pneumonia sustain a 15 to 20 percent mortality. Advanced age also modifies the organisms likely to be responsible for a pneumonic infiltrate.

Obviously, such factors as depressed level of consciousness and reduced level of self-care, which have been shown to contribute to the risk of pneumonia, also enhance the likelihood that such individuals will be institutionalized. Thus, the increased risk of pneumonia observed in institutionalized patients is certainly due in some part to the underlying reasons for which the individual remains in the institution. Yet the institutional setting itself adds to the risk of pulmonary infection in the elderly patient. In the closed populations of chronic care facilities, the attack rates among unvaccinated or immune-depressed elderly for both influenza and tuberculosis are striking.

It must be appreciated that the clinical presentation of elderly individuals may be different from that of younger adults. The blunted inflammatory response in the presence of infection is often a source of missed diagnoses in aged patients. The presentations

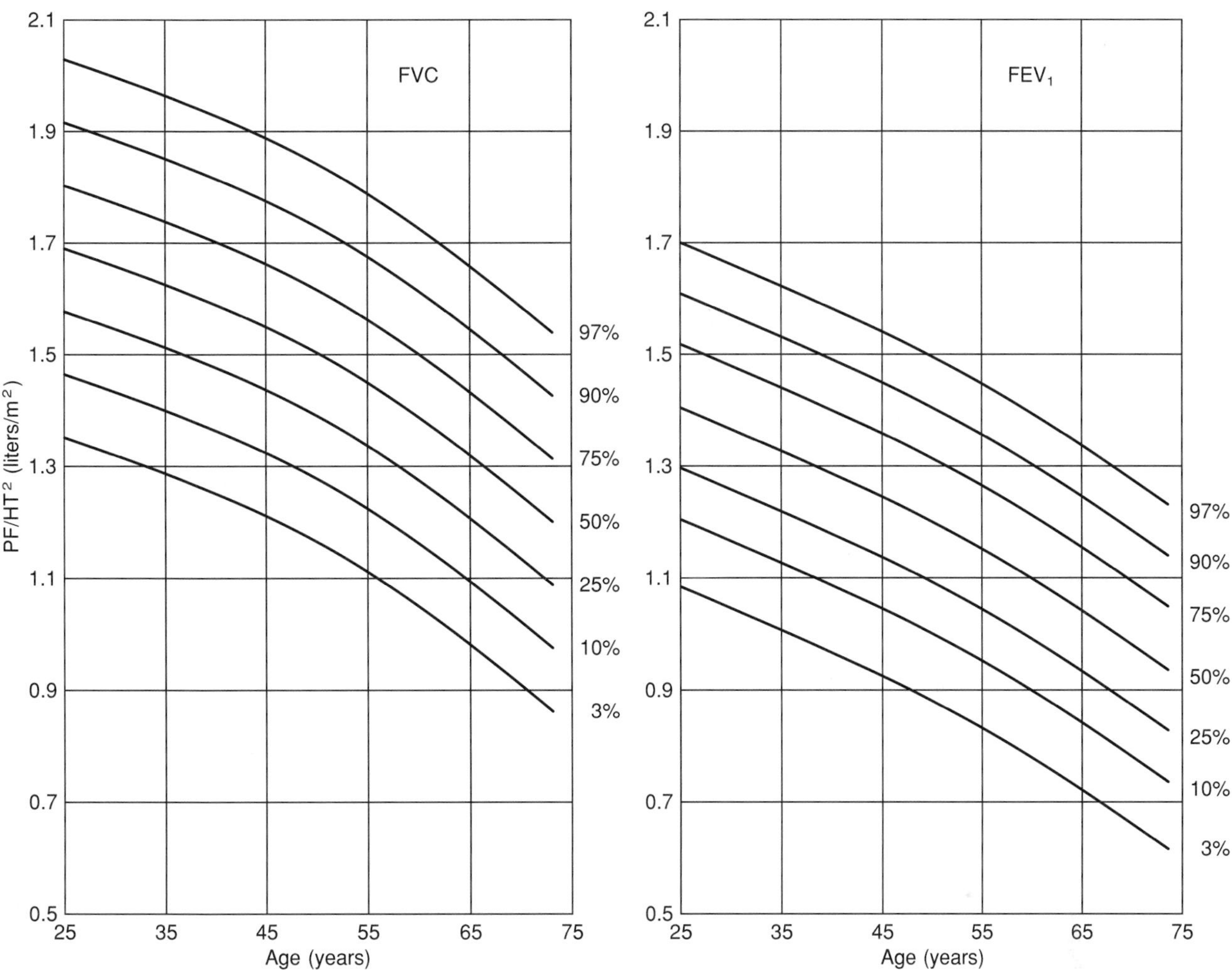

FIGURE 48-2
Percentile charts for height standardized pulmonary function of men. The "percentiles" of pulmonary function (liters) divided by height (meters) squared (PF/HT^2) presented here and in Figure 48-3 are based upon measurements of white nonsmokers who reported no respiratory symptoms, and who were drawn from a random sample of adults in six U.S. cities. *(Redrawn from Dockery DW et al: Distribution of forced expiratory volume in one second and forced vital capacity in healthy, white, adult never-smokers in six U.S. cities. Am Rev Respir Dis 131:511, 1985.)*

of pneumococcal pneumonia as a bronchopneumonia (instead of lobar consolidation) or tuberculosis as a miliary disease (instead of an apical infiltrate) are both more common in the elderly patient.

In contrast, the obstructive airway diseases have been so closely associated with advanced age that their presence often evokes little interest in the physician. Nevertheless since 1968 there has been a progressive increase in the age-adjusted death rate for COPD. In the United States, more than 4 million persons are estimated to have COPD, and recently more than $5 billion was spent for direct and indirect costs arising from COPD. The ease with which this condition can be detected by spirometry and the observation of slowing of ventilatory deterioration following smoking cessation strongly support the clinical recommendation that older smokers be routinely evaluated with this test.

One of the great challenges facing the physician responsible for the care of the elderly is ensuring that comprehensive medical care does not begin and end at the hospital door. This is especially true for chronic respiratory disease. The fluctuating respiratory impairment associated with seasonal change, episodic upper respiratory tract infections, and other intercurrent illness will require a variety of medical and nonmedical responses to maintain the health of the elderly respiratory patient. The physician must both recognize the need for respiratory outpatient support services and appreciate that other professionals—including a respiratory nurse, respiratory therapist, and social worker—will often be required to provide

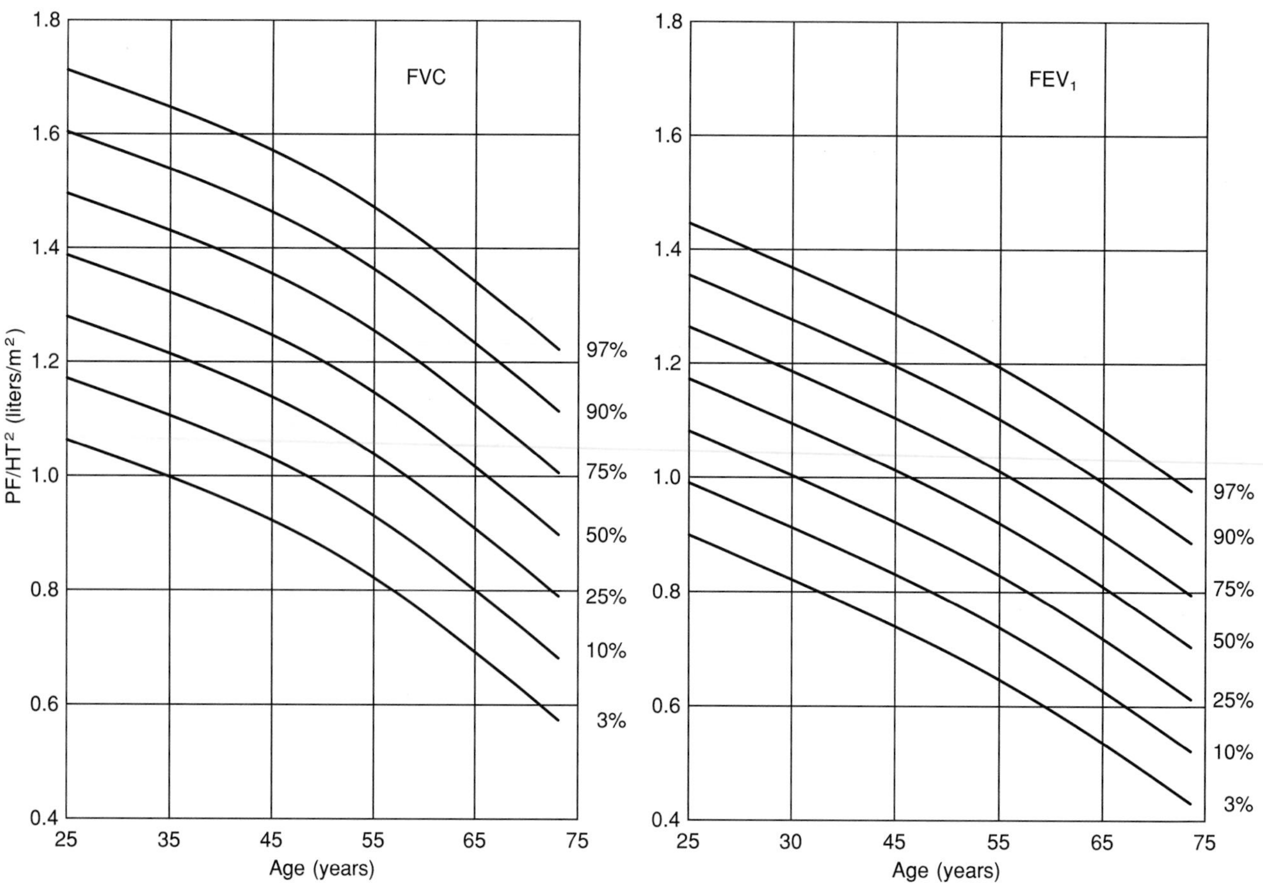

FIGURE 48-3
Percentile charts for height standardized pulmonary function of women. *(Redrawn from Dockery DW et al: Distribution of forced expiratory volume in one second and forced vital capacity in healthy, white, adult never-smokers in six U.S. cities. Am Rev Respir Dis 131:511, 1985.)*

them. There should be someone in the physician's office whom the patient can call regarding access to support services. A list of outpatient services which have been required by outpatients with chronic obstructive lung diseases is shown in Table 48-4. It is important that the physician's representative not only be knowledgeable about obtaining such services but also be able to recognize when such services are needed and make recommendations to both physician and patient.

The role of the patient in his or her own health care should not be neglected. A randomized study of 100 patients with COPD focused upon training patients in (1) knowledge of their disease; (2) knowledge of their medications, including effects and side effects; (3) knowledge of prophylaxis and precautions at times of exacerbations, including when to call the physician; (4) use of the peak flow meter; and (5) inhalation technique for medications.[28] Patients with COPD who received this training while in the hospital

TABLE 48-3

Quantitation of Impaired Pulmonary Function[a]

	FVC	FEV_1/FVC	TLC or RV	DL_{CO}
Normal	Within 1 CI	Within 1 CI	Within 1 CI	Within 1 CI
Slight (minimal)	1–1.75		±1–1.5	1–1.75
Moderate	>1.75–2.5	1–4	±>1.5–2.0	>1.75–2.5
Severe	>2.5	>4	±>2.0	>2.5

[a] Expressed as numbers of confidence intervals (CI) to be subtracted from predicted value.
SOURCE: Miller.[27]

TABLE 48-4

Services Needed for Comprehensive Respiratory Outpatient Care

1. Comprehensive evaluation
   a. Complete medical evaluation
   b. Evaluation of patient and family financial and emotional support
2. Interval medical attention
3. Pulmonary function studies
4. Chest radiography
5. General laboratory services
   a. Bacteriology
   b. Hematology
   c. Chemistry
   d. Cytology
6. Electrocardiography
7. Immunization services
8. Drugs, medical supplies, and equipment
9. Routine transportation and communication
10. Emergency services (mobile unit with expertise) to bring patient from remote area to intensive care facility
11. Bronchial hygiene
12. Breathing instruction
13. Physical conditioning
14. Nutrition
    a. Counseling
    b. Provision of adequate nourishment
15. Homemaker and housekeeping services
16. Personal hygiene services (bathing, shampooing, etc.)
17. Psychosocial counseling
18. Financial support and planning
19. Vocational counseling
    a. For patient, family, or both
    b. Job training and placement
20. Environmental control
    a. Occupational exposures
    b. Household exposures
21. Education
    a. Patient
    b. Family
    c. Professional
22. Patient interaction groups

reduced their outpatient consumption of health services, including fewer calls upon their physician and fewer readmissions to the hospital. Provision of home care services to patients with severe chronic respiratory disease by a hospital-based multidisciplinary home care program has reduced hospitalizations, hospital days, emergency room visits, and costs of home care.[29] Unfortunately, delivery of adequate outpatient education and supportive care to the aged respiratory patient has not kept pace with the improvements in diagnosis and therapy. The recognition of geriatric pulmonary disease and its appropriate treatment in the context of the diminished physiologic, emotional, and social reserves of the elderly make the practice of geriatric pulmonary medicine particularly challenging.

REFERENCES

1. Tockman MS, Comstock GW: Respiratory risk factors and mortality: Longitudinal studies in Washington County, Maryland. *Am Rev Respir Dis* 139(suppl):S56, 1989.
2. Tockman MS et al: Airways obstruction and the risk for lung cancer. *Ann Intern Med* 106:512, 1987.
3. *Cancer facts and figures—1992.* Pub 92-425M-No 5008 92-LE. ACS, Atlanta, GA, American Cancer Society, 1992.
4. Schwartz JD et al: Analysis of spirometric data from a national sample of healthy 6- to 24-years-olds (NHANES II). *Am Rev Respir Dis* 138:1405, 1988.
5. Murray JF: *Aging in the Normal Lung,* 2d ed. Philadelphia, Saunders, 1986, pp 339–360.
6. Ware JH et al: Longitudinal and cross-sectional estimates of pulmonary function decline in never-smoking adults. *Am J Epidemiol* 132:685, 1990.
7. Crapo RO et al: Reference spirometric values using techniques and equipment that meet ATS recommendations. *Am Rev Respir Dis* 123:659, 1981.
8. Dockery DW et al: Cumulative and reversible effects of lifetime smoking on simple tests of lung function in adults. *Am Rev Respir Dis* 137:286, 1988.
9. Turner JM et al: Elasticity of human lungs in relation to age. *J Appl Physiol* 25:664, 1968.
10. Mead J et al: Significance of the relationship between lung recoil and maximum expiratory flow. *J Appl Physiol* 22:95, 1967.

11. Niewoehner DE, Kleinerman J: Morphometric study of elastic fibers in normal and emphysematous human lungs. *Am Rev Respir Dis* 115:15, 1977.
12. Rooney SA: State of art. The surfactant system and lung phospholipid biochemistry. *Am Rev Respir Dis* 131:439, 1985.
13. Buist AS, Ross BB: Quantitative analysis of the alveolar plateau in the diagnosis of early airway obstruction. *Am Rev Respir Dis* 108:1078, 1973.
14. Crapo RO, Morris AH: Standardized single breath normal values for carbon monoxide diffusing capacity. *Am Rev Respir Dis* 123:185, 1981.
15. Sorbini CA et al: Arterial oxygen tension in relation to age in healthy subjects. *Respiration* 25:3, 1968.
16. West JB, Wagner PD: Pulmonary gas exchange, in West JB, Wagner PD (eds): *Bioengineering Aspects of the Lung*. New York, Dekker, 1977, pp 361–457.
17. Kronenberg RS, Drage CW: Attenuation of the ventilatory and heart rate responses to hypoxia and hypercapnia with aging in normal men. *J Clin Invest* 52:1812, 1973.
18. McConnell AK, Davies CTM: A comparison of the ventilatory responses to exercise of elderly and younger humans. *J Gerontol* 47:B137, 1992.
19. Yerg JE et al: Effect of endurance exercise training on ventilatory function in older individuals. *J Appl Physiol* 58:791, 1985.
20. Davies CTM: The oxygen-transporting system in relation to age. *Clin Sci* 42:1, 1972.
21. Jones NL et al: *Clinical Exercise Testing*. Philadelphia, Saunders, 1975.
22. Rogers MA et al: Decline in V_{O_2max} with aging in master athletes and sedentary men. *J Appl Physiol* 68(5):2195, 1990.
23. Kohrt WM et al: Effects of gender, age, and fitness level on response of V_{O_2max} to training in 60–71-yr-olds. *J Appl Physiol* 71(5):2004, 1991.
24. Wanner A: Pulmonary defense mechanisms: Mucociliary clearance, in Simmons DH (ed): *Current Pulmonology*, vol 2. Boston, Houghton Mifflin, 1980, pp 325–356.
25. Morris AM et al: *Clinical Pulmonary Function Testing: A Manual of Uniform Laboratory Procedures*, 2d ed. Salt Lake City, UT, Intermountain Thoracic Society, 1984.
26. Dockery DW et al: Distribution of forced expiratory volume in one second and forced vital capacity in healthy, white, adult never-smokers in six US Cities. *Am Rev Respir Dis* 131:511, 1985.
27. Miller A (ed): *Pulmonary Function Tests in Clinical and Occupational Lung Disease*. New York: Grune & Stratton, 1986.
28. Tougaard L et al: Economic benefits of teaching patients with chronic obstructive pulmonary disease about their illness. *Lancet* 339:1517, 1992.
29. Haggerty MC et al: Respi-Care: An innovative home care program for the patient with chronic obstructive pulmonary disease. *Chest* 100:607, 1991.
30. Cotes JE et al: Iron-deficiency anaemia: Its effects on transfer factor for the lung (diffusing capacity) and ventilation and cardiac frequency during sub-maximal exercise. *Clin Sci* 42:325, 1972.

Chapter 49

PNEUMONIA

John G. Bartlett

Pneumonia has long been recognized as a special problem for the elderly. Hourmann and Dechambre[1] published a series of papers entitled "Pneumonia in the Aged" in 1835, less than 20 years following Laennec's classic description of the disease. Osler referred to pneumonia as the "special enemy of old age" in the first edition of his textbook and as "the friend of the aged" in the third edition; he himself eventually succumbed to pneumonia, presumably caused by anaerobic bacteria.

There has obviously been a significant improvement in the prognosis for pneumonia since these early descriptions, and especially since antibiotics have become available. Nevertheless, infection of the lower respiratory tract remains the fifth leading category of disease responsible for death in the United States, and it is the most common lethal infection. Available data show that elderly patients continue to be at particular risk in terms of incidence, morbidity, and mortality. The major recognized predisposing factors include immunosenescence, a multiplicity of associated diseases, high rates of pharyngeal colonization with gram-negative bacilli, and the institutional setting. The predominant pathogens in these patients are pneumococci, gram-negative bacilli, anaerobic bacteria, *Haemophilus influenzae*, *Legionella*, and influenza. Recommendations for management should account for somewhat different bacteriologic patterns as compared to patterns in younger patients, a definite age-related mortality, and special considerations regarding therapeutic intervention.

INCIDENCE AND PROGNOSIS

A review of 44,684 cases of pneumonia in Massachusetts from 1921 to 1930 showed that the per capita incidence of pneumonia increased approximately fivefold for persons in the eighth decade of life as compared to those in the second decade of life.[2] Far more striking, however, was a nearly 100-fold increase in the mortality rate ascribed to pneumonia, an incidence which increased by approximately 10 percent for each decade of life beyond the age of 20. These studies in the preantibiotic era demonstrated an age-related susceptibility which is independent of modern chemotherapy. The availability of antibiotics has modified these statistics considerably. A more recent population-based survey in Houston showed that the annual rate of hospitalization for pneumonia (per 10,000 persons) was 30 to 60 cases during 3 years for persons over 65 years old, compared to a rate of about 5 to 15 cases during 3 years for all other age categories (by decade) for adults.[3] Lower respiratory tract infections are found in 25 to 60 percent of elderly patients at autopsy, and this kind of infection represents the most common cause of death in centenarians.

Nosocomial pneumonia is a well-recognized problem in acute care facilities, where it accounts for approximately 15 percent of all hospital-acquired infections and is the most frequent lethal nosocomial infection. Less readily apparent, however, is the comparable risk noted in chronic care facilities.[4–6] Surveys of residents in nursing homes and chronic care facilities show that the prevalence of pneumonia is similar to that noted in acute care hospitals, an incidence of approximately 100 cases per 1000 patient-years.[7] A review of 750 psychiatric patients over age 60 who were institutionalized showed that age-specific death rates were increased approximately sixfold over the anticipated rate during the first year following institutionalization and that pneumonia was the major cause of death in these patients.[8] The risk of fatal pneumonia was, in fact, approximately 50 times the rate noted for age-matched controls who were not institutionalized. The magnitude of this difference exceeded that for all other disease categories. These data account for the current concern regarding pneumonia in the elderly, with special attention to older individuals in acute or chronic care facilities.

PREDISPOSING FACTORS

There are numerous factors which contribute to the increased incidence and exaggerated mortality of pneumonia in the elderly. The most important has clearly been identified as influenza, based on a wealth of data showing that the rates for hospitalization and mortality ascribed to lower respiratory tract infections show a direct correlation with the seasonal and annual incidence of influenza.[3] Hospitalization or death is infrequently ascribed to influenza per se; instead, it is usually the result of a superimposed complication. Changes in pulmonary function which are part of the aging process and are believed to account for enhanced susceptibility are decreased effectiveness of cough, increased residual volume, increased compliance, increased closing volume, decreased diffusing capacity, and reduced oxygen saturation.[9] There is little evidence that these alterations in lung physiology associated with aging confer a substantial risk for pneumonia.[10–12] However, the compromise in pulmonary function appears to markedly increase susceptibility to morbid consequences with any further insult. A similar conclusion applies to chronic obstructive lung disease and chronic bronchitis, which are especially common in older individuals. A population-based study to assess risk factors associated with hospitalization for pneumonia showed that the highest risk rate was for persons over age 65 with chronic pulmonary conditions.[3] Thus, these patients may not only have a striking increase in prevalence rates of pneumonia, but they seem to do poorly when pulmonary infections develop. According to experimental animal studies, a number of conditions are associated with an increased incidence of and morbidity from bacterial pneumonia. The most important of these conditions is influenza; others include severe hypoxia, pulmonary edema, acidosis, alcohol intoxication, other forms of viral pneumonia, and azotemia. All of these conditions are frequently encountered among the elderly.

Lung defenses against invading microorganisms involve complex interrelated factors, including the mucociliary elevator, the alveolar macrophage, polymorphonuclear leukocytes, humoral defenses, and the cell-mediated immune system. Studies in healthy aged volunteers show that the functional capacity for most of these factors remains intact with age or is only mildly reduced. For example, humoral defenses as measured by serum antibody response to vaccination with tetanus or pneumococcal vaccine show a somewhat blunted response which is, nevertheless, generally adequate to provide "protective" levels in the elderly.[12] The functional capacity of leukocytes also appears to be maintained with advancing age. The most clearly defined and pronounced defect which occurs as a consequence of aging concerns T-lymphocyte function. This includes an intrinsic defect in effector T lymphocytes, enhanced activity of suppressor T lymphocytes, and an increase in committed precursors with reduced capacity for functional diversity.[10] The result of these deficiencies is readily demonstrable by the increased rate of anergy noted with common skin test antigens, which presumably accounts for the increased incidence of tuberculosis or possibly infections caused by other opportunistic pathogens including *Pneumocystis carinii* pneumonica on rare occasions.

Among the major contributing factors to increased susceptibility to pneumonia are the multiplicity of conditions which predispose to aspiration. These include sedative use, neurologic diseases, and other conditions associated with reduced consciousness or dysphagia. Compounding the problem is the loss of an effective cough reflex, which commonly accompanies reduced consciousness. The result is a reduction in the usual clearance mechanisms which protect the lower airways from abnormal entry of secretions originating in the oral cavity or stomach. These factors have been invoked to explain the high rates of pneumonia among elderly psychiatric patients, patients with senile dementia, and patients with chronic organic brain syndrome.

Another predisposing factor, recently recognized, is colonization of the oropharynx with gram-negative bacilli, which predisposes to gram-negative bacillary pneumonia. Early studies suggested that this mechanism was a major factor in the increased risk for pneumonia among hospitalized patients. Rates of colonization as well as the incidence of pneumonia correlated directly with the severity of the associated diseases. The relevance of this work to pneumonia in the elderly concerns the excessive colonization rate noted in patients of advanced age.[13] The prevalence of positive throat cultures for gram-negative bacilli appears to be directly related to the level of care required, suggesting that the patient's functional capacity for self-care is a critical factor.

ETIOLOGIC AGENTS

Available data suggest that the most important microbial pathogens in sporadic cases of pneumonia in the elderly are bacteria. However, information concerning the distribution of specific pathogens in these patients is sharply limited. The problem is that examination of expectorated sputum, the most frequently utilized specimen source for microbiological studies, is fraught with problems in interpretation due to contamination of the specimen, which occurs during passage through the upper airways. Most studies of pneumonia show that no likely pathogen is recovered in 30 to 50 percent of cases, and many of the organisms implicated in the remaining cases are identified largely because of arbitrary judgments.[14] Studies utilizing more readily acceptable diagnostic sources, such as cultures of transtracheal aspirates, blood cultures, and serologic studies, show that the following organisms account for most cases of pneumonia in the elderly: *Streptococcus pneumoniae*, gram-negative bacilli, anaerobic bacteria, *Legionella pneumophila*, and influenza virus.

Streptococcus Pneumoniae

S. pneumoniae is generally regarded as the major bacterial cause of community-acquired pneumonia in elderly patients as well as in younger individuals. The recovery rate of this organism in expectorated sputa ranges from 15 to 70 percent. Roentgenographic changes with pneumococcal pneumonia are somewhat different in elderly patients in that a bronchopneumonia pattern is far more common than lobar consolidation. The clinical presentation tends to be more subtle in that elderly patients often have minimal complaints and are frequently afebrile.[11] The outcome with pneumococcal pneumonia is also decidedly different in this group. Studies in the preantibiotic era showed a mortality rate of about 70 percent for those in the seventh decade, compared to 10 percent among patients 10 to 12 years old.[2] Even with appropriate antibiotic therapy, the mortality rate is 15 to 20 percent for all elderly patients, and is 30 to 50 percent for those with pneumococcal bacteremia.[2,7,11,12,15]

Gram-Negative Bacilli

Gram-negative bacilli play a relatively minor role in most cases of community-acquired pneumonia, even in elderly patients. This infection is far more common in patients who either are hospitalized or are residents of chronic care facilities. In such settings, coliforms and pseudomonads account for approximately 40 to 60 percent of all pneumonia cases.[13,16] The presumed source of the bacteria is the colonic flora, with subsequent oropharynx colonization in patients rendered susceptible by serious associated diseases or reduced capacity for self-care, as discussed above. An alternative source is gastric contents. Colonization of the stomach with large numbers of bacteria occurs with gastric achlorhydria, which is most common in elderly patients and those receiving antacids or H_2-receptor antagonists.[17] With the source of organisms in either the stomach or oropharyngeal secretions, the presumed mechanism of entry into the lower airways is by aspiration or "microaspiration"—that is, occult aspiration of small volumes, as distinguished from large-volume aspiration, which is traditionally referred to as "aspiration pneumonia." Risk factors associated with increased rates of nosocomial pneumonia due to aspiration in the elderly include neuromuscular disease, depressed alertness, and use of nasogastric tubes.[18] Another mechanism of exposure of the lower airways to gram-negative bacilli is with small-particle aerosols from reservoir nebulizers employed with ventilation equipment or introduced with instrumentation of the lower airways. The usual pathogens transferred in this fashion are bacteria which survive well in water, such as *Pseudomonas aeruginosa*, other pseudomonads, *Serratia marcescens, Achromobacter, Flavobacterium,* and *Acinetobacter.*

The predominant gram-negative bacilli causing pneumonia are *P. aeruginosa* and *Klebsiella pneumoniae*,[16] although different hospitals show distinctive epidemiologic patterns. Other gram-negative bacteria which are commonly encountered in pneumonia acquired in the institutional setting include *Enterobacter, Proteus, Escherichia coli, Acinetobacter,* and *S. marcescens.* Clinical features or gram-negative bacillary pneumonias are not unique, particularly in clinical or radiographic presentation.[16] However, one disturbing factor is the high mortality rate, which is generally reported at 25 to 50 percent.[16]

Anaerobic Bacteria

The role of anaerobic bacteria as pulmonary pathogens was well established at the turn of the century, but these organisms continue to represent elusive pathogens that are often unrecognized and seldom confirmed. The reason is that expectorated sputum is not valid for meaningful anaerobic culture. Thus, invasive diagnostic tests such as transtracheal aspiration, transthoracic needle aspiration, or fiberoptic bronchoscopy with a protected catheter and quantitative cultures must be performed in order to establish the etiologic diagnosis. Additional problems are the need to obtain specimens prior to antibiotic treatment and the need for meticulous anaerobic culture techniques in the laboratory.

Most patients with anaerobic pulmonary infections have aspiration pneumonia or its sequelae, including empyema, or lung abscess.[19] The usual clinical criteria for the diagnosis of aspiration pneumonia are clinical symptoms of a lower respiratory tract infection, roentgenographic evidence for pneumonia involving a dependent pulmonary segment, and an associated condition which predisposes to aspiration. The most common predisposing conditions are compromised consciousness due to alcoholism, general anesthesia, seizure disorder, sedative use, neurologic disorders, and other illnesses associated with altered consciousness. Dysphagia due to esophageal disease or neurologic disorder (such as Parkinson's disease) also predispose to aspiration. The usual source of the inoculum in these cases is secretions from the upper airway, especially the gingival crevice, which contain large concentrations of anaerobic bacteria.

The clinical presentation of anaerobic pulmonary infections shows considerable variation.[19] Some patients have acute symptoms which may resemble pulmonary infections due to other bacterial pathogens, such as pneumococci. Other patients have a much more indolent, chronically evolving course with few symptoms other than low-grade fever and cough, which may persist for weeks or months prior to the patient's seeking medical attention. Common sequelae include necrosis of tissue, resulting in a lung abscess or a bronchopleural fistula with empyema. It is in this advanced stage of the infection that sputum often has the putrid odor that is considered diagnostic of anaerobic infections. There are many patients, especially elderly individuals, who present with relatively subtle symptoms and a smoldering course, which may be referred to as "hypostatic pneumonia," "nursing home pneumonia," or "walking pneumonia," depending on the clinical setting. The etiologic agent for these infections is usually not discerned, but it is likely that anaerobic bacteria are involved in a major portion.

The mortality rate for anaerobic pulmonary infections is generally low if appropriate antimicrobial agents are used. Penicillin has traditionally been regarded as the preferred agent. Clindamycin is equally effective and may be preferred for patients with serious infections, patients with lung abscess, patients who have contraindications to penicillin, or patients who fail to respond to a therapeutic trial of penicillin.[19,20]

Staphylococcus Aureus

S. aureus is an important pulmonary pathogen, accounting for 10 to 30 percent of nosocomial pneumonias, including infections acquired in the nursing home setting.[14] It is also relatively common in bacterial infections superimposed on influenza. Clinical features of staphylococcal pneumonia include x-ray evidence of a bronchopneumonia (consolidation is rare) and a variable course, which may be acute and fulminant or relatively chronic and indolent.[21] Tissue necrosis with abscess formation is well documented in some cases, but it is far less common than is generally appreciated. Most strains produce β-lactamase and require drugs such as nafcillin or cephalosporins. A disturbing finding over the past decade is the increased prevalence of methicillin-resistant strains of *S. aureus*.[12] These strains now account for about 30 to 40 percent of nosocomial isolates of *S. aureus* and an increasing number of community-acquired strains as well.

Haemophilus Influenzae

H. influenzae is second only to pneumococcus as a potential pathogen recovered in expectorated sputum samples from elderly patients with community-acquired pneumonia. This organism also frequently colonizes the upper airways, making it difficult to interpret the significance of isolation in expectorated samples. This organism and the pneumococcus are also the two most frequent organisms implicated in exacerbations of chronic bronchitis. When *H. influenzae* causes pneumonia, there are no distinctive clinical features that set it apart from pneumonia caused by other common bacterial pathogens.

Legionella Pneumophila

Legionnaires' disease, caused by *L. pneumophila,* became the focus of national interest in 1976 with the epidemic in Philadelphia. A review of 182 cases at that convention showed that 75 percent of the patients were over the age of 40 and the risk of infection among those over age 60 was approximately twice that for younger individuals. Subsequent studies of this disease have continued to show a direct correlation between the attack rate and age.[23,24]

Legionnaires' disease may occur sporadically or in epidemics; the epidemics have most frequently occurred in buildings such as hotels or hospitals. The natural habitat of the putative agent is water, and the major source of the organism in outbreaks, when a source has been detected, is either the condensate of air conditioning cooling towers or potable water (resulting in contaminated showerheads). In either event, the organism is presumably inhaled following aerosolization. Common symptoms include high fever, cough which is usually nonproductive, pulmonary infiltrates, and certain extrapulmonary symptoms which are present with variable frequency. Many patients show systemic signs of infection that are far greater than the pulmonary complaints, a feature that makes this condition quite different from pneumococcal pneumonia. Another form of legionellosis is Pontiac fever, a flulike illness characterized by chills, fever, myalgias, and headache but showing no clinical or radiographic evidence for pneumonia. This form of the disease is associated with a favorable prognosis even in the absence of antibiotic treatment.

The organisms responsible for legionellosis include multiple species in the genus *Legionella,* but the most frequent pathogen is *L. pneumophila,* which accounts for 85 to 90 percent, followed by *L. medadei,* which accounts for 5 to 10 percent. Methods to detect legionellosis include cultivation of the organism from respiratory specimens such as expectorated sputum, direct fluorescent (DFA) staining of specimens, serology, or urinary antigen detection.[24,25] All of these are quite specific, but none are especially sensitive. Probably the most sensitive test for expeditious use when therapeutic decisions are required is the urinary antigen test. A point to emphasize is that negative standard tests for *Legionella* including DFA stain and culture of sputum will not exclude this diagnosis. The preferred treatment is erythromycin, with dose recommendations of 4 g/day given intravenously with or without rifampin for seriously ill individuals. The prognosis is relatively good for the patient with legionnaires' disease who is properly treated and does not have compromised immunologic defenses. As might be expected, advanced age is associated with a somewhat higher mortality rate. For example, in the original Philadelphia epidemic, it was noted that the mortality rate for victims over age 55 was 30 percent, approximately twice the rate noted for younger individuals.[26]

Chlamydia Pneumoniae

This organism has only recently been recognized as an agent of "atypical pneumonia." Initial studies suggested that the major clinical features were similar to *Mycoplasma pneumoniae* in the host at risk (healthy young adults) and course of infection (mild self-limited disease that does not require hospitalization). More recent studies suggest that *C. pneumoniae* may account for 5 to 10 percent of pneumonia cases in elderly patients who require hospitalization and 5 to 10 percent of nosocomial pneumonias as well.[27] A major limitation at present is the lack of any practical diagnostic test to establish the presence of this organism. *C. pneumoniae* is susceptible to erythromycin and tetracycline, which are the preferred drugs for most enigmatic pneumonias in adults.

Influenza

Viruses that play relatively important roles in lower respiratory tract infections among elderly patients are influenza, parainfluenza, and respiratory syncytial viruses.[28,29] The most important in terms of incidence and morbidity is clearly influenza.[28–32] Attack rates for influenza are highly variable, depending on antigenic patterns, strain virulence, and immunization status of the population. Attack rates are also age-related, so that persons over 70 years of age have an incidence of approximately four times that of persons under age 40. More impressive, however, is the increased morbidity and mortality associated with influenza in patients of advanced age or with debilitating associated diseases. One of the major complications is primary influenza pneumonia, which may follow a rapidly lethal course. Alternatively, influenza may be complicated by a bacterial superinfection, which often occurs 7 to 10 days after the onset of symptoms, at a time when there is a relatively small viral load but an apparent paralysis of alveolar macrophage activity as a sequela to the prior infection. The most frequently implicated bacterial agents responsible for superinfections in this setting are *S. pneumoniae* and *S. aureus*. Amantadine has established efficacy for the treatment of infections involving influenza A virus when given within 48 hours of the inception of symptoms. This drug is also advocated for prevention, particularly in closed populations such as those of nursing homes, where many in the residents have not received appropriate vaccines.[33] The drug has a relatively high rate of CNS complications in elderly patients, so that reduced doses (100 mg/day) and careful scrutiny are advocated.

MANAGEMENT

Recommendations for the diagnostic evaluation and therapy of pneumonia in the elderly utilize the basic principles which apply to pneumonia in general. The diagnosis is based on the usual clinical parameters, such as fever, leukocytosis, and, most importantly, the demonstration of an infiltrate on chest x-ray. It should be noted that the differential diagnosis in patients with these findings may include multiple noninfectious diseases such as atelectasis, pulmonary embolism with infarction, and congestive heart failure. The demonstration of a pulmonary infiltrate on chest x ray is usually required for the diagnosis of pneumonia. Similar symptoms consisting of cough, fever, and sputum production in the absence of an infiltrate usually indicate bronchitis or possibly sinusitis.

Many elderly patients present with rather subtle clinical findings and roentgenographic evidence of a pulmonary infiltrate in one or both lower lobes, a clinical pattern often referred to as "hypostatic pneumonia," "nursing home pneumonia," or "walking pneumonia."[11,34] These cases are usually due to bacterial infections and usually respond to antibiotic therapy directed against anaerobic bacteria or pneumococci. It should also be emphasized that some of the common associated findings in patients with acute pulmonary infections are less readily apparent in the elderly population. Elderly individuals are less likely to develop high fevers and, on some occasions, will have no demonstrable fever.[11] Similarly, elderly individuals are less likely to mount a vigorous leukocytic response, hence the peripheral white blood cell count, while elevated, does not usually reach levels comparable to those seen in acute bacterial pulmonary infections in younger patients. These factors may make the diagnosis less readily apparent in the elderly patient.

A major goal in management is identification of the etiologic agent so as to provide a guideline for the selection of antimicrobial agents. The time-honored specimen for diagnostic evaluation is expectorated sputum, although this specimen source is fraught with a considerable diagnostic inaccuracy due to contamination by the normal flora during passage through the upper airways. Nearly all studies of pneumonia which utilize expectorated sputa show that no clear etiologic agent can be identified in 30 to 50 percent of cases and that even those which do yield potential pulmonary pathogens must be interpreted with caution, since these organisms may simply reflect oropharyngeal colonization.[14] This especially applies to gram-negative bacilli, which, as noted above, are frequently present in the upper airways of elderly individuals. A commonly advocated method for improving the quality of expectorated sputum bacteriology is the use of cytologic screening with cultures restricted to specimens showing large numbers of polymorphonuclear leukocytes on microscopic examination. Gram stains of specimens may actually provide more useful information than culture. An additional advantage is that the results are immediately available and may be used at the time that therapeutic decisions are initially required.

The emphasis here regarding specimen sources concerns the usual bacterial causes of pneumonia. Different principles apply to the detection of other etiologic agents such as influenza, mycobacteria, pathogenic fungi, *Legionella, C. pneumoniae,* and most opportunistic pathogens. Numerous studies have shown that elderly individuals have compromised T-lymphocyte function, with suppressed cell-mediated immunity and age-related anergy to skin test antigens. Despite this defect, age per se does not appear to confer a major risk for the usual opportunistic pathogens which are encountered in other patients with similar defects, such as *Aspergillus, Mucor,* herpes simplex, toxoplasmosis, *Strongyloides,* and *Nocardia.* Thus, these organisms should not be highly suspect in patients of advanced age unless there are other associated risk factors, such as corticosteroid administration, lymphoproliferative disorders, cancer chemotherapy, or HIV infection.

Therapeutic agents recommended for the elderly do not differ from those recommended for younger people, with a few exceptions. Aminoglycosides must be used with particular caution in the elderly, including careful monitoring of serum levels and measurements of renal function. Even elderly patients with normal renal function by the usual laboratory standards have a considerable reduction in nephric reserve and are far more likely to develop nephrotoxicity than are their younger counterparts. Intravenous administration of fluids, electrolytes, and other forms of osmotic loading must often be done carefully as well, due to reduced cardiac reserve. Hypersensitivity reactions do not occur more frequently in elderly patients, although there is an age-associated risk for antibiotic-associated colitis. There are also multiple potential drug interactions between antibiotics and therapeutic agents commonly utilized by elderly patients, particularly sodium warfarin (Coumadin) and digitalis. These data suggest that the usual antibiotic options for the treatment of pneumonia apply to patients of advanced age, although therapeutic monitoring must often be done with greater care.

Recommendations for specific types of pneumonia are provided in Table 49-1. For seriously ill patients with community-acquired pneumonia and no defined etiologic agent, we recommend the combination of erythromycin and cefuroxime (or cefamandole) or erythromycin and trimethoprim-sulfamethoxazole. For empiric treatment of nosocomial pneumonia and the sepsis syndrome, common recommendations include an aminoglycoside plus an antipseudomonad penicillin, a third-generation cephalosporin, imipenem, ticarcillin plus clavulanate, or aztreonam.

The anticipated response of bacterial pneumonias to antibiotic therapy is variable, but a general rule is that changes in x-ray are delayed and often progress in the initial phases of appropriate treatment, so that other clinical parameters are more valuable for therapeutic monitoring early in the course. Considerations for patients with inadequate response include (1) wrong diagnosis; (2) inappropriate antibiotic; (3) inadequate drug dose (which is most common with aminoglycosides); (4) adverse drug reaction, usually in the form of drug fever; (5) superinfection; and (6) inadequate host. One of the more common explanations in elderly patients concerns inadequate response due to far advanced disease in a host who simply cannot respond. It must be remembered that the mortality rate for bacteremic pneumococcal pneumonia is 20 to 40 percent despite penicillin treatment. For the patient who fails to respond, continued and sometimes aggressive evaluation for alternative diagnoses is appropriate. This may include bronchoscopy, attempts to detect alternative etiologic agents, and studies for noninfectious or concurrent diseases. However, the common practice of repeated cultures of expectorated sputum samples with changes in the chemotherapeutic regimen on the basis of each new resistant isolate which is recovered cannot be justified. These specimens are expected to yield resistant organisms during the course of therapy, and a careful distinction must be made between superinfected sputum and superinfected patient. Follow-up x-rays after apparent recovery are necessary to ensure that pulmonary infiltrates have cleared and to exclude predisposing pulmonary lesions such as bronchogenic neoplasms.

PREVENTION

Nosocomial infections play a well-established role in acute care hospitals, and elderly patients are especially vulnerable in this setting. Less well recognized and controlled is the analogous problem in nursing homes, where several surveys have shown that the risk of nosocomial infection is about the same as it is for acute care hospitals, i.e., about 5 to 10 percent per year. The most celebrated pulmonary infections noted in this setting are influenza and tuberculosis and, to a lesser extent, gram-negative bacillary pneumonias, respiratory syncytial virus, and parainfluenza viruses. These experiences illustrate the need for standard infection control procedures, which are often not established or are not enforced. Immunization against influenza and pneumococci is commonly advocated for elderly patients as a potentially effective means of preventive care which is easily accomplished at little risk. The anticipated protection rate with influenza against strains included in the vaccine is approximately 70 percent for the general population when the epidemic and vaccine strains are well matched, but the rate appears to be lower for elderly persons.[32–34] Nevertheless, this vaccine is recommended for all persons over age 65 as well as other high-risk patients and health care personnel, and the highest priority is given to residents of nursing homes.[35] Amantidine may be used to prevent or to treat influenza, although caution is advised in elderly

TABLE 49-1

Recommendations for Treatment of Specific Types of Pneumonia

Organism	Agent*	Alternative (Comments)
Bacteria		
S. pneumoniae	Penicillin	Cephalosporins, erythromycin, clindamycin
S. aureus		
Methicillin-sensitive	Penicillinase-resistant penicillin*	Cephalosporins (1st or 2d generation), clindamycin, vancomycin
Methicillin-resistant	Vancomcyin	Sulfa-trimethoprim
Klebsiella†	Cephalosporin	Aminoglycoside, piperacillin, imipenem
Pseudomonas†	Aminoglycoside + antipseudomonad penicillin*	Aminoglycoside + imipenem, ceftazidime, cefoperazone, ciprofloxacin or aztreonam
Gram-negative bacilli (other)†	Aminoglycoside, cephalosporin, ampicillin, or antipseudomonad penicillin	
H. influenzae†	Ampicillin (ampicillin-sensitive strains) cefuroxime, third-generation cephalosporins	Tetracycline, chloramphenicol, sulfa-trimethoprim
Anaerobes	Penicillin or clindamycin	Tetracycline, chloramphenicol, antipseudoneonad penicillin, imipenem, metronidazole + penicillin, betalactam betalactamase inhibitor
Nocardia	Sulfonamides	Sulfa-trimethoprim, minocycline, doxycycline
Legionella	Erythromycin	Erythromycin + rifampin, sulfa-trimethoprim + rifampin
Mycoplasma	Erythromycin or tetracycline	
C. pneumoniae	Tetracycline	Erythromycin
Fungi		
Histoplasma, blastomycosis, coccidioidomycosis	Ketoconazole	Amphotericin B (histoplasmosis and coccidioidmycosis confined to the lung are usually not treated)
Candida, Aspergillus	Amphotericin B ± 5 fluorocytosine	
Phycomycetes (*Mucor*)	Amphotericin B	
Viruses		
Herpes simplex	Acyclovir	
Varicella-zoster	Acyclovir	
Influenza A	Amantadine	

*Antipseudomonad penicillins: Ticarcillin, piperacillin, and mezlocillin, usually considered equally effective; in vitro testing facilitates choice.
Penicillinase-resistant penicillins: Nafcillin, oxacillin, and methicillin.
Cephalosporins: In vitro testing determines choice.
Aminoglycosides: In vitro testing facilitates choice between tobramycin, gentamicin, and amikacin.
†GNB: In vitro testing required.

patients with respect to possible central nervous system toxicity.

Pneumococcal vaccine is advocated for persons over age 65. Reports of serologic response show that elderly patients generally develop "protective" titers following immunization with the polyvalent vaccine, which has antigens for 23 serotypes that account for 88 percent of all cases of bacteremic pneumococcal pneumonia. Clinical trials in outpatients over the age of 45 and residents of chronic care facilities have shown minimal reduction in the overall incidence of pneumonia or pneumococcal pneumonia,[7,12,36,37] although analysis by statistical methods appear to indicate vaccine efficacy of about 60 percent.[38]

Prophylactic use of antibiotics in the susceptible host may be theoretically attractive, especially in the patient who is prone to aspiration. However, utilization of this approach has not successfully reduced the incidence of pulmonary infections and, in fact, appears to enhance the risk of infection involving resistant strains.

Epidemics of pneumonia are likely to occur in institutions such as hospitals or nursing homes and may have devastating consequences. These epidemics are usually due to viral infections, particularly influenza, but may also be due to respiratory syncytial virus and parainfluenza.[28] Unlike bacterial infections, epidemics of viral infections tend to involve all exposed persons rather than just the debilitated hosts, acquisition is from an exogenous source rather than endogenous source, and the organisms responsible are usually implicated concurrently in community outbreaks. Attack rates of influenza with epidemics in nursing homes are often 25 to 65 percent, with case-fatality rates averaging 10 percent. Preventive measures include restriction of visitors and elective admissions, restriction of afflicted personnel, and respiratory isolation for patients with documented infections. These outbreaks may be blunted or prevented by immunization with influenza vaccine. Although the vaccine is not as effective in the elderly, the Advisory Committee on Immunization Practices has given nursing home residents the highest priority for influenza vaccination.[35] The vaccine is considered safe, is inexpensive ($2 to $3 per dose), and is reported to be both effective and cost-effective in this setting. Vaccine efficacy when the epidemic strain and the vaccine strain are identical varies between 40 and 95 percent for morbidity and mortality.[33] In several studies the vaccine proved to be not especially effective in preventing illness, but it showed a more impressive record for preventing severe disease resulting in hospitalization, pneumonia, or death.[34] As expected, efficacy for disease prevention and morbidity is less when the epidemic strain has drifted from the vaccine strain.

Amantadine also may be used for the prevention as well as the treatment of influenza A. Again, the Advisory Committee on Immunization Practices has given the highest priority to amantadine for the control of presumed influenza A outbreaks in institutions with high-risk patients.[31] In these cases, the drug should be given to all residents, regardless of vaccine status, as soon as possible after the outbreak is recognized and as long as there is influenza activity in the community. The recommended dose for prophylaxis for all adults and for treatment of patients over 65 years old is 100 mg/day; reduced doses are indicated in the presence of renal failure.

There has been recent interest in aggressive methods to prevent nosocomial pneumonia. Use of sucralfate in place of H_2 blocking agents or antacids appears useful in preserving the gastric barrier.[17,39] Aerosolized antibiotics or systemic antibiotics for the susceptible host are not favored.[39,40] Additionally, the use of oral antibiotics to interrupt the sequence of colonic colonization to pharyngeal colonization by gram-negative bacilli has not proven effective.[41]

REFERENCES

1. Hourmann and Dechambre: Recherches pour servir à l'histoire des maladies des vieillards, faites à la salpetrière. Maladies des organes de la respiration. *Arch Gen Med (Paris)* 8:405, 1835.
2. Heffron R: *Pneumonia.* Cambridge, MA, Harvard University Press, 1939, pp 304–308, 707–710.
3. Glezen WP et al: Survey of underlying conditions of persons hospitalized with acute respiratory disease during influenza epidemics in Houston, 1978–1981. *Am Rev Resp Dis* 136:550, 1987.
4. Haley RW et al: The nationwide nosocomial infection rate: A need for vital statistics. *Am J Epidemiol* 121:159, 1985.
5. Garibaldi RA et al: Infections among patients in nursing homes: Policies, prevalence and problems. *N Engl J Med* 305:731, 1981.
6. Setia U et al: Nosocomial infections among patients in a long term care facility: Spectrum, prevalence and risk factors. *Am J Infect Control* 13:57, 1985.
7. Bentley DW: Pneumococcal vaccine in the institutionalized elderly: Review of past and recent studies. *Rev Resp Dis* 3:561, 1981.
8. Craig TJ, Lin SP: Mortality among elderly psychiatric patients: Basis for preventive intervention. *J Am Geriatr Soc* 29:181, 1981.
9. Dhar S et al: Aging and the respiratory system. *Med Clin North Am* 60:1121, 1976.
10. Weksler ME: The senescence of the immune system. *Hosp Pract* 16:53, 1981.
11. Esposito AL: Community-acquired bacteremic pneumococcal pneumonia: Effect of age on manifestations and outcome. *Arch Intern Med* 144:945, 1984.
12. Forrester HL et al: Inefficacy of pneumococcal vaccine in a high-risk population. *Am J Med* 83:425, 1987.
13. Valenti WM et al: Factors predisposing to oropharyngeal colonization with gram-negative bacilli in the aged. *N Engl J Med* 298:1108, 1978.
14. Fang GD et al: New and emerging etiologies for community acquired pneumonia with implications for therapy. *Medicine* 69:307, 1990.
15. Austrian R: Pneumococcal pneumonia. *Chest* 90:738, 1986.
16. Bartlett JG et al: The bacteriology of hospital-acquired pneumonia. *Arch Intern Med* 146:868, 1986.
17. Driks MR et al: Nosocomial pneumonia in intubated patients given sucralfate as compared with antacids or histamine type 2 blockers. *N Engl J Med* 317:1376, 1987.
18. Hanson LC et al: Risk factors for nosocomial pneumonia in the elderly. *Am J Med* 92:161, 1992.
19. Bartlett JG: Anaerobic bacterial infections of the lung. *Chest* 91:901, 1987.
20. Levison ME et al: Clindamycin compared with penicillin for the treatment of anaerobic lung abscess. *Ann Intern Med* 98:466, 1983.
21. Kaye MG et al: The clinical spectrum of *Staphylococcal aureus* pulmonary infection. *Chest* 97:788, 1990.
22. Peacock JE et al: Methicillin-resistant *Staphylococcus aureus:* Microbiologic characteristics, antimicrobial susceptibilities, and assessment of virulence of an epidemic strain. *J Infect Dis* 144:575, 1981.
23. Tsai TF et al: Sporadic legionellosis in the United States: The first thousand cases. *Ann Intern Med* 31:219, 1980.

24. Edelstein PH, Meyer RD: Legionnaires' disease: A review. *Chest* 85:114, 1984.
25. Aguero-Rosenfeld ME, Edelstein PH: Retrospective evaluation of the DuPont radioimmunoassay kit for detection of *Legionella pneumophila* serogroup 1 antigenuria in humans. *J Clin Microbiol* 26:1775, 1988.
26. Fraser DW et al: Legionnaires' disease: Description of an epidemic of pneumonia. *N Engl J Med* 297:1189, 1977.
27. Grayston JT et al: A new respiratory tract pathogen: *Chlamydia pneumoniae* strain TWAR. *J Infect Dis* 161:618, 1990.
28. Gross PA et al: Epidemiology of acute respiratory illness during an influenza outbreak in a nursing home. *Arch Intern Med* 148:559, 1988.
29. Hall WN et al: An outbreak of influenza B in an elderly population. *J Infect Dis* 144:297, 1981.
30. Mathur U et al: Concurrent respiratory syncytial virus and influenza A infections in the institutionalized elderly and chronically ill. *Ann Intern Med* 3:49, 1980.
31. Centers for Disease Control: Outbreaks of influenza among nursing home residents. *MMWR* 34:478, 1985.
32. Patriarca PA et al: Efficacy of influenza vaccine in nursing homes. *JAMA* 253:1136, 1985.
33. Centers for Disease Control: Prevention and control of influenza. *Ann Intern Med* 107:521, 1987.
34. Gross PA et al: Association of influenza immunization with reduction in mortality in an elderly population. *Arch Intern Med* 148:562, 1988.
35. Centers for Disease Control: Update on adult immunization. *MMWR* 40 RR12:1, 1991.
36. Broome CV: Efficacy of pneumococcal polysaccharide vaccines. *Rev Infect Dis* 3:582, 1981.
37. Simberkoff MS et al: Efficacy of pneumococcal vaccine in high-risk patients: Results of a Veterans Administration Cooperative Study. *N Engl J Med* 315:1318, 1986.
38. Shapiro ED et al: The protective efficacy of polyvalent pneumococcal polysaccharide vaccine. *N Engl J Med* 21:1453, 1991.
39. Carven TD, Steger KA: Nosocomial pneumonia in the intubated patient: New concepts on pathogenesis and prevention. *Infect Dis Clin North Am* 3:843, 1989.
40. Flaherty JP, Weinstein RA: Infection control and pneumonia prophylaxis in the intensive care unit. *Semin Resp Infect* 5:191, 1990.
41. Gastinne H et al: A controlled trial in intensive care units of selective decontamination of the digestive tract with nonabsorbable antibiotics. *N Engl J Med* 326:594, 1992.

Chapter 50

TUBERCULOSIS: A SPECIAL PROBLEM IN THE ELDERLY

William W. Stead and Asim K. Dutt

The term *tuberculosis* means disease caused by *Mycobacterium tuberculosis,* although other mycobacteria can produce similar pathology in humans. The most common tuberculosis presentation is chronic fibrotic or cavitary disease of the lung, although extrapulmonary sites—such as kidney, bones, and the meninges—may be either the principal or the secondary site. In the elderly, the clinical course is most commonly a slowly progressive process marked by cough, low-grade fever, weakness, and loss of weight. However, the presentation may be much more acute, actually simulating bacterial pneumonia. Both courses may afford a great diagnostic challenge. Tuberculosis *always* warrants consideration in respiratory infections in older persons because of its frequency, its tendency to appear in persons not previously suspected of the infection, and its communicability and because it is the most easily treated serious infectious disease that is likely to occur in this age group.

ETIOLOGY, TRANSMISSION, AND PATHOGENESIS

Mycobacterium tuberculosis is a nonmotile slender rod, 0.2 to 0.4 μm in width and 1 to 4 μm in length, which grows so slowly on culture medium that 3 to 6 weeks are required for sufficient growth to permit identification. The bacillus is aerobic, but the presence of CO_2 in low concentration accelerates its growth. Owing to the waxy nature of the cell wall, most stains will not adhere to it.

Tuberculosis is transmitted almost exclusively in the form of droplet nuclei. Tiny droplets of respiratory secretions are aerosolized by coughing, singing, sneezing, and even talking. The droplets rapidly evaporate, leaving a droplet nucleus 1 to 5 μm in size, which may carry several viable bacilli. When inhaled, droplet nuclei of such size may reach the alveoli. Small numbers can be destroyed by alveolar macrophages. However, the waxy bacilli may penetrate the phospholipid (surfactant) coating and reach the alveolar wall. There, in the tuberculin-negative (nonimmune) person, they begin to multiply unimpeded, reaching the regional lymph nodes and even the bloodstream before being limited by sensitized T lymphocytes and responsive macrophages. Bacilli deposited in small numbers in organs with low oxygen tension (liver, spleen, bone marrow), where multiplication is not favored, are generally eliminated readily. Those which are deposited in organs with a high oxygen tension—e.g., at the apices of the lungs, kidney, and brain—may multiply fairly rapidly. Given normal immune function, specific immunity mediated by T lymphocytes develops within a few weeks and is usually effective in controlling the infection at both the primary and metastatic sites. However, in 5 percent of newly infected persons, the replication of the bacilli continues and may produce clinical tuberculosis within 3 to 12 months. Even in those in whom the infection is controlled, the bacilli may repropagate and the infection recrudesce years or decades later and produce disease. The determining factors for the recrudescence of ancient infection are not well understood, but general nutrition, adequate intake of vitamin D, and competence of T-cell function are almost surely involved. Immunosuppression, human immunodeficiency virus (HIV) infection, poor nutrition, and complicating diseases—e.g., silicosis, lymphoreticular diseases, and insulin dependent diabetes mellitus—all appear to reduce resistance and make it more likely for a dormant tuberculosis infection to reactivate and produce disease. The dominant cause of tuberculosis in elderly persons is recrudescence of an old infection acquired many years earlier.

Transmission is best checked by early detection and effective chemotherapy of each infectious person. Most infection in contacts is implanted before the discovery of the disease and initiation of chemotherapy in the index case. Cough and the number of bacilli in the sputum are both rapidly reduced by effective chemotherapy. The infectiousness of the patient drops rapidly within a week or two, even though the sputum may contain bacilli in the smear and/or culture. Patients are generally considered noninfectious after 10 to 14 days of effective chemotherapy.

Decontamination of a hospital room is best accomplished by ventilation with fresh air and beaming germicidal ultraviolet light across the top of the room. Tubercle bacilli in droplet nuclei which reach the upper air of such a room are quickly killed, and this largely decontaminates the room. Thus, when necessary, a patient may safely be admitted to a general hospital that has such a room. However, at present the majority are treated as outpatients from the start.

CLINICAL TUBERCULOSIS

Although adult tuberculosis may develop in any organ, it usually develops in the apex of one or both lungs as a fibrocaseous infiltrate. Hematogenous dissemination may occur at any stage of disease and produce miliary tuberculosis or meningitis. Infected persons generally develop a strong immunity. Reinfection with tubercle bacilli is a problem in the United States principally among persons with HIV infection and elderly persons whose infection is so remote and completely healed that the immune memory of the T cells has been lost (see below).

PRIMARY INFECTION

In normal persons, 95 percent of primary infections produce such a mild illness that they subside without therapy. However, in previously tuberculin-negative residents of a nursing home, 10 percent of primary infections may progress to produce chronic tuberculosis or even death (often ascribed to antibiotic-unresponsive pneumonia). The correct diagnosis of tuberculosis is rarely made unless the patient happens to be part of an outbreak of the disease, because determination of the cause of pneumonia in the elderly is not often pursued. There may be a tuberculous pleural effusion, but this is often mistakenly ascribed to congestive heart failure. Failure to recognize such an active case often results in a number of cases of progressive primary tuberculosis, as reported by one of us (W.W.S.).

CHRONIC PULMONARY TUBERCULOSIS

Tubercle bacilli which have lain dormant for years or decades in healed lesions may reactivate at any time. This is most common in the healed lesions at the apex of the lung, nodules often referred to as Simon foci. The characteristic of this form of disease is chronicity, cavitation, and production of a fibrous reaction (caseation). The bacilli are abundant in the caseum, which facilitates airborne transmission by droplet nuclei. The earliest complaints are malaise, weight loss, fatigue, depression, and cough. Sputum is usually yellow or green and may be blood-streaked. Dull chest ache or pleuritic pain may be present. Shortness of breath may occur with pleural effusion or from extensive damage of the lung due to a rapidly developing tuberculous pneumonia. Adult respiratory distress syndrome may develop if miliary spread occurs. A manifestation that is seen more commonly among the elderly than others is tuberculous bronchitis that leads to segmental atelectasis, most commonly in the anterior segment of an upper lobe or in the lingula or middle lobe. It is often assumed to be caused by a tumor unless bronchoscopy is performed with appropriate biopsy and bronchial washing for acid-fast bacillus (AFB) cultures.

PLEURAL DISEASE

Involvement of the pleura can occur either soon after initial infection or as a result of later reactivation of infection. In either case, the cause is usually rupture of a small peripheral lesion. The effusion is evoked by the T-cell response to the antigen released into the pleural space.

Diagnosis

Physical signs are of little help in detecting the presence of pulmonary tuberculosis in the great majority of cases. The chest roentgenogram is essential in recognizing the infiltrative process. Comparison of the present film with one taken 6 months to several years earlier further enhances its value, because minor changes in old fibrotic areas can be appreciated only by this means. Reticulonodular infiltration in the apicoposterior segments of one or both upper lobes, with or without cavitation, is the most common abnormality seen in reactivation tuberculosis. Bilateral distribution of a nodular infiltration in the upper zones of the lungs is highly suggestive of tuberculosis. Extensive consolidation of a lobe of the lung may occur due to tuberculous pneumonia. The lower lobe and opposite lung may become involved through bronchial spread. In progressive primary infection in elderly nursing home residents (see below), the infiltration most commonly involves the mid- and lower lung fields rather than the apical zones. Thus, a pleural effusion and almost any distribution of infiltration is compatible with tuberculosis. Miliary tuberculosis is more common in elderly persons today than in any other age group. It may be a result of either recent or recrudescent infection. In either case it is usually due to rupture of a caseous focus into the bloodstream.

Probably the best-known example is the death of Eleanor Roosevelt at age 76 from an infection she had acquired at age 19.

Skin testing with tuberculin is important among the elderly in two circumstances: (1) whenever a diagnosis of tuberculosis is suspected and (2) when patients have had close contact with a recently discovered case of tuberculosis. The intermediate strength of tuberculin (5 tuberculin units) should be used and injected intradermally. If initially negative, the test should be repeated in 1 to 3 weeks to see if a positive reaction can be elicited by recall of T-cell response. Contrary to common dogma, most elderly persons are tuberculin-negative, despite the fact that the majority had at one time been infected and were tuberculin-positive. Studies have shown that in only about 10 percent of instances is the failure to react actually due to anergy. Thus, the tuberculin test does have significance in the elderly when tuberculosis is suspected. If negative, the patient should be tested for anergy with other common delayed-hypersensitivity allergens, e.g., mumps, *Candida, Trichophyton,* or streptokinase, because anergy would render the negative tuberculin test uninformative. Conversion from negative tuberculin status (especially if negative on two occasions) to a positive reaction (especially if large, i.e., equal to or greater than 15 mm) signifies a new tuberculosis infection.

A stained smear of the sputum, pus, or tissue is helpful in identifying tubercle bacilli if present in large numbers. Early morning expectoration specimens, at least three in number, should be submitted for smear and culture. When sputum cannot be produced spontaneously, bronchoscopy may be necessary to obtain bronchial secretion. While low-power screening of a smear stained with auromine rhodomine stain is rapid, it produces many false positives. Thus, all suspicious slides must be confirmed by overstaining with the Ziehl-Neelsen or Kenyoun method.

The final proof of tuberculosis can only be the identification of *M. tuberculosis* from the body secretion, bronchial washing, or tissue. The most rapid and accurate way to do this is by polymerase chain reaction (PCR) techniques. Cultural growth may be apparent within 3 or 4 weeks, but cultures should be held for at least 6 to 8 weeks, because small inocula may take this long to produce visible growth. Laboratory methods are required to distinguish *M. tuberculosis* from other mycobacteria which may occasionally cause disease. The production of niacin by *M. tuberculosis* permits identification of this species. There are times when all efforts at finding tubercle bacilli fail, probably because the number of bacilli is small (as in progressive primary infection) or because the right material was not examined. The association of a positive tuberculin skin test, compatible clinical picture, and roentgenographic abnormalities/or a granulomatous tissue reaction is sufficient evidence on which to start antituberculosis chemotherapy pending culture results, even if the organisms cannot be found by microscopy.

In patients with pleural effusion, careful study of the pleural fluid and pleural biopsy is necessary. Tuberculous pleural fluid is an exudate. Cells are predominantly monocytic, and the pH is moderately reduced, i.e., 7.00 to 7.25. Bacilli are seldom seen in smear examinations of the fluid, and even the culture is positive in only about 20 percent of those who appear to have tuberculous effusion. Pleural tissue obtained by needle biopsy should be examined histologically by special stain for the bacilli and also cultured in liquid medium. This enhances the chance of positive bacteriology over the culture of pleural effusion alone. This PCR technology will soon be readily available to improve rapid diagnosis. In the absence of a definitive diagnosis, a presumptive diagnosis of tuberculous pleurisy is made from the finding of granuloma in the tissue associated with a positive reaction to purified protein derivative (PPD), even though culture of the fluid fails to grow the bacilli. This is also applicable to pericardial disease.

In tuberculous meningitis, lumbar puncture usually reveals elevated pressure, clear fluid with increased protein content, reduced glucose, and increased white blood cell count with predominance of lymphocytes. The fluid must be cultured, but therapy should be initiated on the basis of a clinical diagnosis without waiting for the culture report, because delay may lead to brain damage. A rapid and highly specific method of diagnosis is assay for tuberculostearic acid in the cerebrospinal fluid (CSF), which can be performed at the Centers for Disease Control (CDC) in Atlanta, Ga.

For early diagnosis of disseminated tuberculosis, biopsies of bone marrow, liver, and lymph nodes are helpful in the search for caseating granuloma containing acid-fast bacilli. Biopsy is also necessary for the diagnosis of bone and joint disease. Early morning specimens of urine should be examined for smear and culture in the diagnosis of genitourinary tuberculosis. Similarly, peritoneal fluid and tissue may aid in the diagnosis of abdominal tuberculosis.

In patients with lung infiltration, negative studies for fungal diseases, and positive PPD skin test in whom bacteriological confirmation cannot be obtained, it is acceptable to begin treatment for tuberculosis empirically to observe its effect on the illness. Such patients must be evaluated 10 to 12 weeks after initiation of therapy to establish whether therapy has been beneficial. If the disease has not shown response clinically and radiographically, aggressive diagnostic measures including an open-lung biopsy should be considered without delay. The availability of PCR technology should reduce the frequency with which this course of action is necessary.

Treatment

The treatment of tuberculosis is based on intensive and prolonged exposure of the organisms to more than one bactericidal drug. The overwhelming factor in recovery, irrespective of the site of involvement, is regular ingestion of adequate drugs for the necessary duration of therapy. Theoretically, the treatment should be effective in every case. In practice, however, occasional failures occur due to (1) failure of the physician to prescribe the proper drugs in adequate dosage, (2) failure of the drugs, or (3) failure of the patient to take them properly. Commonly used antituberculosis drugs—their dosages, side effects, and mode of action—are shown in Table 50-1.

Current Therapy

In recent years, with the addition of potent bactericidal drugs—isoniazid (INH), rifampin (RIF), and pyrazinamide (PZA)—it has become possible to treat even advanced cases of tuberculosis in half or one-third the time formerly required and with even greater effectiveness.

It is important to realize that bacilli are susceptible to the action of drugs *only* during replication. Tubercle bacilli exist in three different populations in the tuberculous host. The large population, about 1×10^7 to 1×10^9 in cavitary areas, is extracellular and replicates rapidly (about every 16 to 20 hours), owing to presence of high oxygen tension and a neutral or slightly alkaline medium. It is thus most rapidly eliminated by bactericidal therapy. The second population is small, about 1×10^4 to 1×10^5, and is located in the acid environment inside macrophages. These organisms divide infrequently, owing to low oxygen tension inside the cells. PZA is highly effective in this environment. The third population is also small and is located in the neutral medium in small, closed caseous nodules; these organisms divide infrequently. Elimination of slowly dividing organisms requires prolonged therapy. RIF is a particularly effective drug in eliminating these persisters.

Tubercle bacilli mutate naturally at known frequencies (about once in 1×10^5 to 1×10^6 divisions) to produce mutants resistant to any effective drug that is given singly. Resistance of the population develops through elimination of sensitive bacilli, leaving the resistant mutants. Mutants resistant to each drug occur independently. Thus, mutants resistant to two bactericidal drugs occur extremely rarely (once in 1×10^{10} to 1×10^{12} divisions).

The principle of modern chemotherapy is shown diagrammatically in Fig. 50-1. A combination of two bactericidal drugs, INH and RIF, is bactericidal for actively multiplying bacilli and also for organisms which are slowly or intermittently dividing in the lesion. Rapid eradication of actively multiplying large populations usually renders the sputum culture negative within 2 to 3 months. Prolonged taking of the drugs is required to kill the slowly or intermittently multiplying organisms so as to sterilize the lesion and prevent relapse after the chemotherapy is stopped.

Thus, in newly diagnosed elderly patients, the suggested regimen is still INH 300 mg and RIF 600 mg daily for 9 months. However, after initial therapy for 1 month with once-daily INH and RIF, the drugs can be given in doses of INH 900 mg and RIF 600 mg given together in a single dose twice weekly for another 8 months. The latter regimen has proved highly successful in over 95 percent of patients in Arkansas. The addition of ethambutol (EMB) or PZA to this regimen is generally recommended by the CDC. However, in the elderly, whose infection was acquired 40 to 70 years earlier, there can be little concern for drug-resistant organisms. Thus RIF and INH are adequate and the addition of a third drug only contributes to the chance of drug toxicity.

Bactericidal therapy with INH and RIF is well tolerated by most patients, even when elderly. Hepatic toxicity ranges from 3 to 4 percent, and even alcoholics tolerate the regimen well. Intermittent administration of the 600-mg dose of RIF gives rise to only an occasional hypersensitivity reaction manifest by a flulike syndrome or thrombocytopenia with or without purpura. Other minor side effects—e.g., gastrointestinal intolerance, rash, and fever—are encountered in less than 5 percent of patients.

The form in which the drugs are administered plays a major role in the development of drug resistance as well as in convenience for the patient. If they are given as two capsules of RIF and a single tablet of INH daily, it is common for the patient to reverse the number (two INH and one RIF) or to take only one drug or the other, thus inviting treatment failure and drug resistance. Both problems may be obviated by using two combination capsules, each of which contains half the daily dose of each drug. In addition, instead of a twice-weekly dose of two RIF capsules and three INH tablets, the equivalent dose of the combination capsules (Rifamate) is two capsules and two INH tablets twice weekly. Thus, both too much of one drug and not enough of the other and the invitation to drug resistance are avoided.

Treatment of Tuberculosis Due to INH-Resistant Bacilli

The use of only two drugs involves some risk that the organisms may be resistant to one of the drugs (usually INH). This would be equivalent to therapy with a single drug to which the organisms would soon become resistant. Drug resistance should be suspected in patients who have been treated before and have relapsed, who have acquired disease in countries or localities within the United States with a high prevalence of drug-resistant organisms, who had received INH preventive treatment in the past, or who are suspected to have acquired the disease from a patient with drug-resistant organisms. In such persons, therapy should be started with streptomycin (SM), 1 g daily 5 days/week (reduce by 50 percent if over age 60 or if renal function is impaired), INH 300 mg, RIF 600 mg, and PZA 25–30 mg/kg body weight daily for 8 weeks until the susceptibility test results are known. If the organisms show sensitivity to INH and RIF, therapy may then be completed with INH and RIF daily or twice weekly for a total period of 6 months. If the organisms prove to be resistant to INH, therapy is

TABLE 50-1

Antituberculosis Drugs: Mode of Action, Dosage, and Side Effects

Drug	Dosage: Daily	Dosage: Twice Weekly	Side Effects	Mode of Action
Bactericidal Drugs:				
Streptomycin	10–15 mg/kg (usually 0.5–1.0 g) 5 days/week IM*	20–25 mg/kg (usually 1.0–1.5 g) IM	Vestibular or auditory nerve (eighth cranial nerve) damage, dizziness, vertigo ataxia, nephrotoxicity, allergic fever, rash	Active against rapidly multiplying bacilli in neutral or slightly alkaline extracellular medium
Capreomycin	Same as above	Same as above	Same as above	Same as above
Isoniazid (INH)	5 mg/kg (usually 300 mg) PO† or IM	15 mg/kg (usually 900 mg) PO	Peripheral neuritis, hepatotoxicity, allergic fever and rash, lupus erythematosus phenomenon	Acts strongly on rapidly dividing extracellular bacilli and weakly on slowly multiplying intracellular bacilli
Rifampin (RIF)	10 mg/kg (usually 450–600 mg) PO	10 mg/kg (usually 450–600 mg) PO	Hepatotoxicity, nausea and vomiting, allergic fever and rash, flulike syndrome, petechiae with thrombocytopenia or acute renal failure during intermittent therapy	Acts on both rapidly and slowly multiplying bacilli either extracellular or intracellular, particularly on slowly multiplying "persisters"
(LM427 Rifabutin Ansamycin)	150–300 mg PO		Same as above	Same as above
Pyrazinamide (PZA)	25–30 mg/kg (usually 2.5 g) PO	45–50 mg/kg (usually 3.0–3.5 mg) PO	Hyperuricemia, hepatotoxicity, allergic fever and rash	Active in acid pH medium on intracellular bacilli
Bacteriostatic Drugs:				
Ethambutol (EMB)	15–25 mg/kg (usually 800–1600 mg) PO	50 mg/kg PO	Optic neuritis, skin rash	Weakly active against both extracellular and intracellular bacilli to inhibit the development of resistant bacilli
Ethionamide	10–15 mg/kg (usually 500–750 mg) in divided doses PO		Nausea, vomiting, anorexia, allergic fever and rash	Same as above
Cycloserine	15–20 mg/kg (usually 0.75–1.0 g) in divided doses with 100 mg of pyridoxine PO		Personality changes, psychosis, convulsions, rash	Same as above
Para-aminosalicylic acid (PAS; not available in the United States)	150 mg/kg (usually 12 g) in divided doses PO		Nausea, vomiting, diarrhea, hepatotoxicity, allergic rash and fever	Weak action on extracellular bacilli; inhibits development of drug-resistant organisms
Thiacetazone (not available in the United States)	150 mg daily PO		Allergic rash and fever, Stevens-Johnson syndrome, blood disorders, nausea and vomiting	Same as above
Clofazimine (antileprosy)	100 mg tid, PO		Pigmentation of skin, abdominal pain	Against *Mycobacterium intracellulare*

*IM = intramuscular.
†PO = oral.

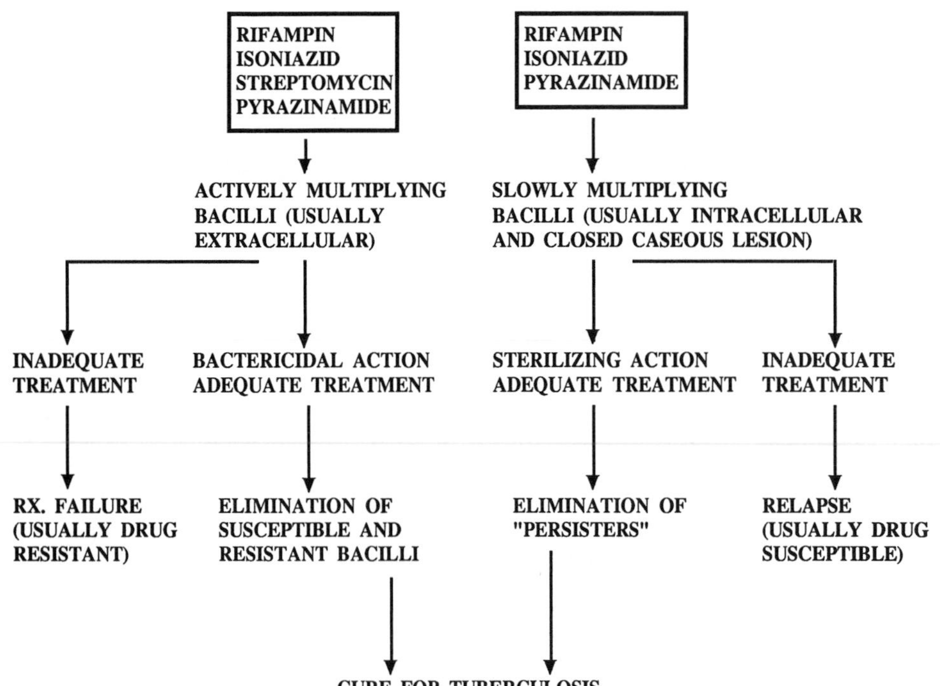

FIGURE 50-1
Schematic effects of drugs on tuberculosis in achieving a lasting cure of the disease and avoiding later relapse. Failure to eliminate large populations of organisms in the cavitary area results in drug resistance, while late relapse is due to regrowth of persisters, which are still totally sensitive to the medications.

completed with SM 2 days/week and RIF 600 mg and PZA 45 to 50 mg/kg body weight 2 days/week for a total of 9 months. INH may be included in the regimen for its probable action against the persistently sensitive bacilli which have escaped resistance by infrequent replication. EMB 25 mg/kg during daily or 50 mg/kg during twice-weekly therapy may replace SM in any of the above regimens. The regimen is well tolerated, with little increase in side effects over the standard two-drug regimen.

Noncompliance in taking oral medications may run as high as 25 percent, particularly among alcoholics, forgetful patients, and patients with psychiatric problems. In such patients, fully supervised short-course chemotherapy is recommended. Twice-weekly administration of the drugs facilitates direct supervision of their ingestion. Streptomycin, RIF, PZA, INH, and EMB are the drugs which can be used in twice-per-week therapy, while other antituberculosis drugs must be used on a daily basis.

EXTRAPULMONARY TUBERCULOSIS

The treatment of extrapulmonary tuberculosis is the same as described above for pulmonary tuberculosis. Generally the bacterial populations in extrapulmonary tuberculosis lesions are smaller than in cavitary pulmonary lesions. Thus, they do not require more prolonged chemotherapy or additional drugs. The surgical principle of draining an accumulation of pus must be observed, however.

Other Considerations

The treatment of tuberculosis coexisting with diabetes, malignancy, or corticosteroid therapy for a disease such as arthritis requires no additional drugs or prolongation of therapy beyond the usual 9 months. Treatment of tuberculosis in patients with concomitant HIV infection is the same, but it is prudent to prolong the duration of therapy to at least a year on INH thereafter for as long as it is tolerated.

Surgical intervention is rarely necessary in any form of tuberculosis provided that proper chemotherapy is administered. Rarely, lobectomy may be necessary in patients with massive hemoptysis. Empyema and bronchopleural fistula usually need proper surgical intervention for drainage and obliteration of the space.

Corticosteroid therapy is seldom indicated in tuberculosis. However, hydrocortisone or equivalent steroids may produce dramatic improvement in patients who are very ill with high fever and/or hypoxemia. After a response is established, the steroids should be tapered gradually over a period of 2 to 4 weeks to avoid the "rebound" phenomenon.

Surveillance of the patient for toxicity and bacteriological response is essential. The best way to detect the effect of therapy is to submit a sputum sample for AFB culture every 2 weeks until the culture is negative. Thereafter, the examination should be carried out every 2 months during chemotherapy and for 6 months after completion of therapy. Surveillance should be maintained monthly for side effects of the drugs or noncompliance by patients throughout the chemotherapy period. The patient should be told to watch for symptoms of toxicity, e.g., nausea, vomiting, anorexia, and jaundice. If toxicity is suspected, drugs should be stopped immediately and blood drawn for serum glutamic oxaloacetic transaminase (SGOT) estimation. If the SGOT rises three to five times above the baseline, hepatic toxicity from INH is the most likely offender. Unless the reaction is quite severe, the offending drug should be determined with sequential challenge with a half dose of each drug separately after the patient has recovered from the reaction and the SGOT has returned to normal. Often the reaction does not recur, and therapy may be completed as planned. If RIF is implicated, EMB may be substituted and treatment continued for 18 months. However, if INH cannot be resumed, EMB and PZA should be substituted.

Prognosis

With effective and adequate chemotherapy, 95 percent of patients who tolerate drugs are cured and may be expected to remain free from clinical tuberculosis. The risk of relapse in these patients is very small, and their follow-up need not be prolonged. Initial factors such as extent of disease, cavitation, age, sex, and surgical therapy are of little significance as indicators of failure or relapse.

SPECIAL PROBLEM OF TUBERCULOSIS IN THE ELDERLY

While it is true that a large proportion of elderly persons represent the survivors of heavy exposure and infection in early life, it is not true that most of them are tuberculin-positive today. It has long been accepted as conventional wisdom that "once tuberculin-positive, always so." From studies of the distribution of tuberculin reactions by age, it is known that in the 1930s and 1940s, when the present octogenarians were in their thirties and forties, they were about 80 to 90 percent tuberculin-positive. By 1961, when the people of this cohort were in their sixties, they were about 40 percent positive. Now, in Arkansas, they are consistently only about 10 to 20 percent positive. This is higher than the proportion of younger persons who are positive today but amazingly low by comparison with the same cohort in earlier years.

About 55 percent of the new cases of tuberculosis in Arkansas occur in persons who are 65 years of age or older, with men predominating 2 to 1. This shift to old age for tuberculosis cases is out of all proportion to the number of elderly persons in the population. This has led us to realize that elderly persons who still react to tuberculin are at a greater risk of developing tuberculosis than younger reactors. Indeed, the rate is three times as great for persons age 65 or older as for persons of 40 to 60 years of age. When one relates the risk of developing tuberculosis per 100,000 *tuberculin reactors,* it approaches 1 percent annually, which is about the same risk that tuberculin reactors have when there is radiographic evidence of healed scars of pulmonary tuberculosis. The practical implication of this fact is that tuberculosis must *always* be considered a possibility in any elderly person with a pulmonary infection, especially if the individual is known already to be tuberculin-positive or a recent skin test converter.

Another problem derives from this same set of facts: When elderly persons live in close quarters of a nursing home, anyone who develops active tuberculosis may endanger close associates who are nonreactors. It is in this way that an outbreak of tuberculosis may be set off in a nursing home. Persons who have lost their ability to react to tuberculin are again easy prey for the bacillus, while old reactors who are healthy appear to be at little risk of reinfection. Most of the other cases are of the primary (or new infection) type.

While the problem of anergy cannot be dismissed, it appears unlikely as the explanation of most of the reversion of reactors to negative even in old age. When newly infected, most older persons show a vigorous reaction to 5 tuberculin units of purified protein derivative (equal to or greater than 15 mm). Thus, it appears that their reactivity had simply waned with time after complete and natural eradication of the organisms from the earlier infection with a gradual loss of the memory of the T cells for the antigen.

PREVENTION OF TUBERCULOSIS IN THE ELDERLY

The guidelines for preventive therapy of tuberculin reactors published by the American Thoracic Society and the CDC recommend preventive therapy for reactors beyond the age of 35 only (1) if they are *converters,* close or household contacts of an active case; (2) if they are shown to have scars of postprimary tuberculosis; (3) if they are silicotic or diabetic; (4) if they have had a gastrectomy; or (5) if they are to be on prolonged corticosteroid therapy. Our experience in nursing homes has shown that the indication of tuberculin conversion is paramount. Not to treat demonstrable tuberculin converters is to invite development of clinical tuberculosis in 10 to 20 percent of converters, resulting in additional cases and further spread of the infection. Therefore, it is essential to establish the tuberculin status of elderly patients in nursing homes or other long-term care facilities at the time of admission. We require that the tuberculin status of each new resident admitted to a nursing home in Arkansas be determined (with two tests if the first is negative) and a record kept of the result. Positive reactions are noted on the front of the chart as a reminder to both physician and nurse to submit sputum for smear and culture for tuberculosis with any lower respiratory infection. If an active case is discovered, it is a simple matter to retest the previous nonreactors to determine which residents should be given preventive therapy with INH. By this means spread of tuberculosis among the residents and to visitors and employees can be eliminated. Residents who were already tuberculin-positive when the exposure occurred are at little risk of developing active disease and need not be treated.

Monitoring for toxic side effects of INH is largely clinical (observing for anorexia, nausea, or vomiting). If such symptoms develop, it should be determined whether hepatitis is present by appropriate tests of hepatic cell dysfunction. About 90 percent of elderly persons tolerate INH without difficulty, which is enough to curtail an incipient epidemic. Those who cannot tolerate the medication can be monitored clinically and radiographically for evidence of incipient disease.

ADDITIONAL READING

Comstock GW: Epidemiology of tuberculosis. *Am Rev Respir Dis* 125(suppl):8, 1982.

Dutt AK et al: Short course chemotherapy for tuberculosis with mainly twice weekly isoniazid and rifampin: Community physicians seven years experience with mainly outpatients: *Am J Med* 77:233, 1984.

Dutt AK et al: Nine month largely twice weekly INH and rifampin therapy for extrapulmonary tuberculosis: *Ann Intern Med* 104:7, 1986.

Fox W: Whither short course chemotherapy? *Br J Dis Chest* 75:331, 1981.

Grosset J: The sterilizing value of rifampicin and pyrazinamide in experimental short course chemotherapy. *Tubercle* 53:5, 1978.

Grosset J: Bacteriological basis of short course chemotherapy for tuberculosis. *Clin Chest Med* 1:231, 1980.

Houk UN et al: The epidemiology of tuberculosis infection in a close environment. *Arch Environ Health* 16:26, 1968.

Riley RL, O'Grady F: *Airborne Infection: Transmission and Control.* New York, Macmillan, 1961, p 26.

Stead WW: Pathogenesis of a first episode of chronic pulmonary tuberculosis in man: Recrudescence of residual of the primary infection or exotenous re-infection? *Am Rev Respir Dis* 95:729, 1967.

Stead WW, Lofgren JP: Tuberculosis as an endemic and nosocomial infection in nursing homes. *N Engl J Med* 312:1483, 1985.

Stead WW, To T: The significance of the tuberculin skin test in elderly persons. *Ann Intern Med* 107:837, 1987.

Stead WW: Undetected tuberculosis in prison: Source of infection of community at large. *JAMA* 260:2544, 1978.

Stead WW: Tuberculosis among elderly persons: An outbreak in nursing home. *Ann Intern Med* 94:666, 1981.

Stead WW, Dutt AK: What's new in tuberculosis? *Am J Med* 71:1, 1981.

Stead WW, Dutt AK: Tuberculosis in elderly persons. *Annu Rev Med* 42:267, 1991.

Stead WW, Lofgren JP: Does the risk of tuberculosis increase in old age? *J Infect Dis* 147:951, 1983.

Stead WW et al: Benefit-risk consideration in preventive treatment for tuberculosis in elderly persons. *Ann Intern Med* 107:843, 1987.

Chapter 51

CHRONIC AIRFLOW OBSTRUCTION AND RESPIRATORY FAILURE

Norman Adair

Obstructive lung diseases are the most common causes of respiratory impairment in older adults. Wheezing, cough, exertional dyspnea, and attacks of breathlessness are clinical features common to all of the obstructive airway diseases and may also occur in other cardiorespiratory disorders. The nonspecificity of these symptoms along with the interactive effects of age, environmental exposures, and genetics often make it difficult to define the specific cause of airflow obstruction in older adults. However, treatable elements are often present, regardless of the precise diagnosis, and a detailed clinical and laboratory evaluation can be beneficial. This chapter will review the pathogenesis, clinical presentation, and treatment of chronic obstructive pulmonary disease, asthma, and respiratory failure in older people.

CHRONIC OBSTRUCTIVE PULMONARY DISEASE

Chronic obstructive pulmonary disease (COPD) is defined as expiratory airflow limitation that is persistent over time and not acutely reversible to a significant degree after inhalation of a bronchodilator drug. Included in this "disease" are emphysema and chronic obstructive bronchitis or a combination of both.[1] Risk factors for COPD are cigarette smoking, age, occupational exposures, air pollution, male sex, and alpha-1-antiprotease deficiency. Possible contributing factors include airway hyperresponsiveness, atopy, childhood respiratory illness, diet, alcohol intake, and genetic influences. Except for patients with alpha-1-antiprotease deficiency, symptomatic COPD is largely confined to patients over age 50.

The physiologic hallmark of COPD is reduced expiratory airflow demonstrated by standard spirometry, a test which should be readily available to office-based physicians. Spirometry in the obstructive airway disorders characteristically shows the forced expired volume in 1 second (FEV_1) disproportionally reduced compared to the forced vital capacity (FVC; Table 51-1).

Natural History and Prognosis

Lung function declines with normal aging; the FEV_1 decreases through adult life and the decline accelerates somewhat past age 45 (See Chap. 48). The rate of decline in FEV_1 in longitudinal population studies of never-smoking adults is about 20 to 40 ml/year (Fig. 51-1). In smokers, the rate of decline in lung function is accelerated and the FEV_1 may decrease as much as 70 to 80 ml/year. Epidemiologic studies show a clear relationship between pack-years of smoking and loss of lung function, estimated at 7.4 ml per pack-year in men.[2] Generally, symptoms of exertional dyspnea become evident when the FEV_1 falls below 1.5 to 1.8 liters (approximately 60 percent predicted; Table 51-1). Exertional dyspnea becomes severe and the

TABLE 51-1

Grading and Definition[a] of Severity of Obstructive Ventilatory Defects[b]

Grade	Definition
Mild	$FEV_1 < 100\%$ and $\geq 70\%$ of reference value
Moderate	$FEV_1 < 70\%$ and $\geq 60\%$
Moderately severe	$FEV_1 < 60\%$ and $\geq 50\%$
Severe	$FEV_1 < 50\%$ and $\geq 34\%$
Very severe	$FEV_1 < 34\%$

[a] Definition: FEV_1/FVC ratio below normal range, generally < 70%.

[b] Criteria for reversibility after inhaled bronchodilator: $FEV_1 >$ 12% of prebronchodilator *and* an absolute change of 200 ml.

SOURCE: Lung function testing: Selection of reference values and interpretative strategies. *Am Rev Respir Dis* 144:1202, 1991.

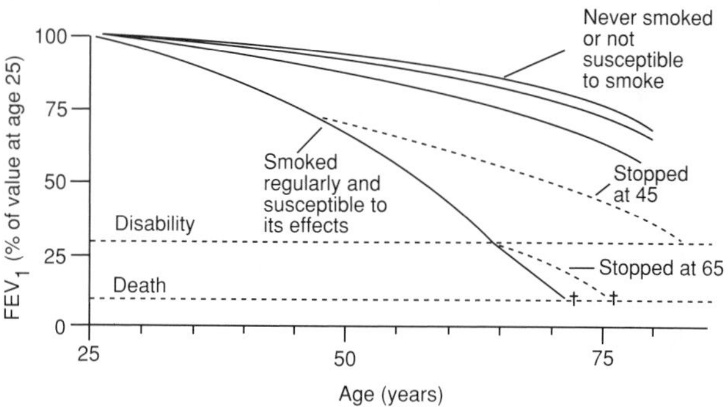

FIGURE 51-1

The effect of smoking on lung function in males: illustration of various outcomes based on continued smoking or stopping smoking. The onset of disability, rate of loss of lung function, and death can be altered by smoking cessation. *(From Fletcher C, Peto R: The natural history of chronic airflow obstruction. Br Med J 1:1645, 1977. Reproduced by permission.)*

patient is disabled when the FEV_1 falls below 30 percent. Death usually occurs within a few years once the FEV_1 falls below 500 ml (less than 20 percent predicted).

Chronic obstructive pulmonary disease is the fifth leading cause of death in the United States. It is estimated that the number of people over age 55 in the United States with COPD exceeded 5 million in 1985. Over 95 percent of the deaths from COPD occur past age 55. Mortality rates for COPD continued to increase in the 1980s, especially among women. An estimated 13 percent of adult hospitalizations are associated with COPD.[3] The annual total dollar costs (direct and indirect) of COPD in the United States are estimated to be in excess of $5 billion.

Emphysema

Most patients with respiratory impairment due to COPD have some degree of emphysema at autopsy. Emphysema is defined as abnormal airspace enlargement distal to the terminal bronchiole, accompanied by destructive changes of the alveolar wall.[1] Roentgenography may suggest advanced emphysema when there is overinflation, attenuation of pulmonary vascularity, hyperlucency, and bullous formation. However, the plain chest radiograph is insensitive to all but the most advanced stages of emphysema and radiographic changes often correlate poorly with the degree of airflow obstruction. High-resolution computed tomography (CT) has been used to more accurately identify and quantitate emphysema, but this technology is not currently considered clinically indicated for evaluation of COPD.

Certain physiologic abnormalities on pulmonary function testing suggest emphysema in patients with airflow obstruction. These include overinflation [elevated total lung capacity (TLC) greater than 120 percent predicted] and air trapping [elevated residual volume (RV) and RV/TLC ratio]. The diffusing capacity for carbon monoxide is typically reduced in emphysema and is the physiologic derangement that correlates best with the presence of anatomic emphysema. The combination of airflow obstruction (reduced FEV_1/FVC) and reduced carbon monoxide diffusion (DLCO) provides strong physiologic evidence for the presence of emphysema.

Emphysema causes a loss of lung compliance due to destruction of alveolar structures. This reduces the elastic recoil pressure of the lung that is needed to generate the force that drives expiratory airflow. Simultaneously, the loss of alveolar structures around intrapulmonary airways (loss of "tethering effect") allows these conduits to narrow and collapse prematurely during expiration. During inspiration, the emphysematous airspaces fill slowly and the incoming air is distributed unevenly, leading to mismatching of inspired gas with the pulmonary capillary blood. This produces impaired oxygen uptake and arterial hypoxemia. Inspiratory muscle function is impaired in severe emphysema due to overinflation of the thorax and subsequent flattening of the diaphragm, which shortens the muscle fibers and diminishes the inspiratory effort. The imbalance between the increased work of breathing and decreased inspiratory muscle efficiency may produce respiratory muscle fatigue and, consequently, hypercapnic respiratory failure.

Medical therapy in emphysema does not reverse the disease process. In fact, emphysema probably progresses in many instances, especially if tobacco smoking is not stopped. However, general fitness conditioning, assistance with secretion removal, elimination of resting bronchomotor tone with drugs, and smoking cessation can reduce symptoms and improve functional status.

Chronic Bronchitis

Chronic bronchitis is a clinical condition defined as chronic production of sputum for 3 months of each of 2 consecutive years in patients in whom other causes of mucus hypersecretion have been excluded.[1] Symptoms of chronic bronchitis are frequent in COPD. However, mucus hypersecretion as an isolated factor has not been shown to be independently associated with the development of airflow obstruction or to correlate with mortality in COPD after controlling for the level of FEV_1. Thus, the precise roles of cough and phlegm in the development and outcome of COPD are unclear.

The pathologic abnormalities associated with chronic bronchitis include airway fibrosis, mucous gland enlargement, excessive endobronchial secretions, and mucosal inflammation with edema. All of these except scarring are potentially reversible contributors to airflow obstruction. Despite uncertainties about the importance of mucus hypersecretion in the natural history of COPD, the potential for reversibility makes chronic bronchitis a clinically important subset in COPD.

Clinical Assessment of COPD

A complete history is important to define the extent of physical disability, clarify the diagnosis, and recognize significant comorbidity. Dyspnea in relation to daily activities (walking, stair climbing, bathing, etc.) should be determined. The smoking history is important. There may be certain features of the history which would suggest an alternative diagnosis, such as persistent asthma or bronchiectasis. Cardiac problems, including angina pectoris and rhythm disturbances, may be important in planning treatment.

Physical findings that are typical of advanced COPD are thoracic overinflation, signs of right heart failure with edema, pursed-lip breathing, accessory muscle recruitment, and markedly diminished breath sounds with or without wheezing. The diaphragm may be depressed and poorly mobile.

Pulmonary function testing is important during initial evaluation and should include spirometry before and after bronchodilator inhalation, carbon monoxide diffusing capacity, and an arterial blood gas on room air.

Management of COPD

An algorithm for management of patients with COPD is presented in Fig. 51-2. Smoking cessation is a high priority regardless of age. Stopping smoking, even after as much as 35 pack-years, can result in some improvement in ventilatory function. The physician should explicitly advise the patient to stop smoking. Showing patients their own spirometric values, to illustrate the current level of ventilatory capacity, and demonstrating graphically the effect of stopping smoking on the natural history of COPD may be useful (Fig. 51-1). The additional benefits of smoking cessation should be emphasized: reducing cancer and cardiovascular risks, reducing cough and phlegm production, saving money, and improving the patient's sense of well-being. Setting a date for stopping smoking and signing a "contract" between the patient and physician is a useful strategy. If available, referral to an established smoking cessation program should be considered. Nicotine replacement therapy, if well supervised, can be a helpful adjunct. However, nicotine replacement in the elderly may be associated in an increased risk of cardiovascular side effects. Nicotine replacement therapy is most effective when used in association with a formal smoking cessation program which incorporates group support and behavior modification. Selected patients may benefit from hypnosis or acupuncture; however, these techniques generally produce no greater long-term abstinence than more conventional approaches. Most smoking cessation programs have fairly disappointing results and no single technique for smoking cessation is consistently effective. The success rate at 12 months is less than 20 percent. Self-help materials and information on formal "stop smoking" programs are available through the local office of a national cancer, heart, or lung organization.

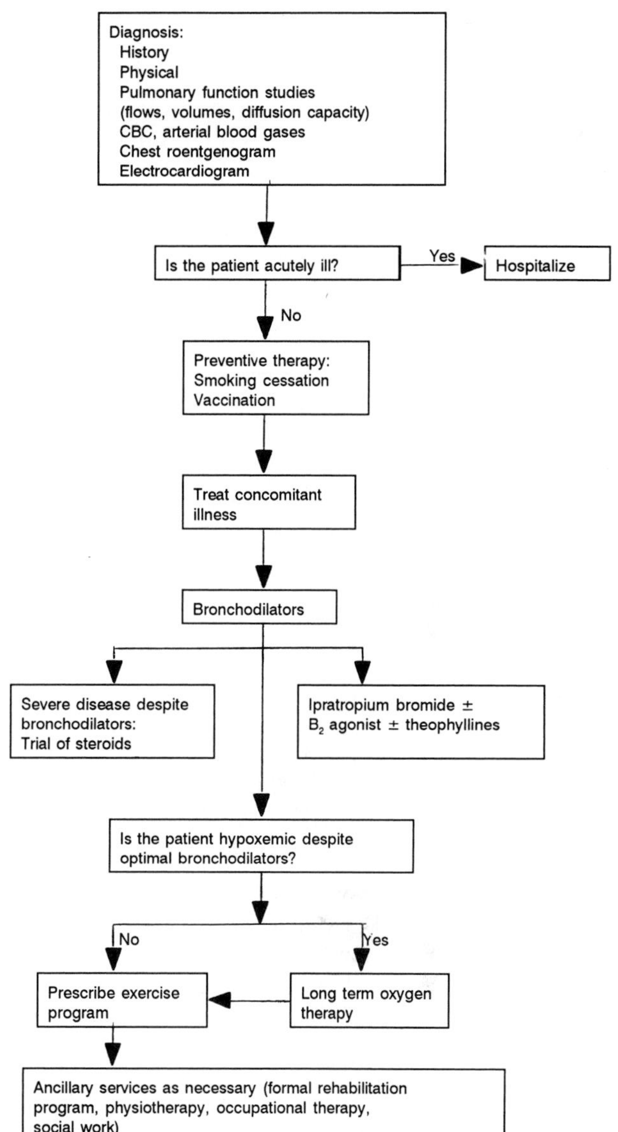

FIGURE 51-2
Management algorithm for COPD. *(From Kesten S, Rebuck AS: Management of chronic obstructive pulmonary disease. Drugs 38:160, 1989. Reproduced by permission.)*

Immunization

Lower respiratory tract infections are a major cause of morbidity and mortality in COPD. Pneumococcal multivalent vaccine should be administered once to all persons above age 65 and to patients with chronic cardiac and pulmonary disorders regardless of age. Annual influenza vaccine is recommended for patients with COPD.

Bronchodilator Therapy

The rationale for bronchodilator therapy in COPD is that reducing the airway resistance will produce decreases in dyspnea, respiratory work, and overinflation. Even though the degree of reduction in airway resistance after acute bronchodilator administration in COPD is often small, many patients do manifest physiologic as well as subjective benefit with long-term bronchodilator therapy. Sympathomimetic bronchodilators with beta-2 receptor selectivity are the preferred agents (Table 51-2). Inhalation is the best method of delivery; it causes fewer side effects (tremor, palpitations) and greater bronchodilation than oral sympathomimetics. The available agents for inhalation are of equal efficacy (albuterol, terbutaline, pirbuterol, and metaproterenol). Higher doses of inhaled beta sympathomimetics than those usually recommended may be needed in some patients with COPD. Supervised increases in dose can be monitored for heart rate and spirometric changes to arrive at the optimal prescription. The metered dose inhaler (MDI) is the most cost-effective method of inhalation therapy. However, proper technique is essential for benefit (Table 51-3). A variety of spacer devices are available for use with the MDI. These spacers reduce inertial impaction of the medication in the oropharynx and improve drug delivery to the bronchi. A spacer device should be routinely advised for patients

TABLE 51-3

Technique for Use of Metered-Dose Inhaler (MDI)

Shake the canister well prior to each activation.
Place the mouthpiece in front of opened lips.
Exhale fully.
Slowly inhale and activate MDI immediately.
Continue the slow inhalation until the lungs are completely full.
Hold the air in for 8 to 10 seconds, or as long as possible.
Relax and wait 1 to 2 minutes between additional doses.
Keep inhaler clean by removing canister and rinsing plastic actuator in water daily, then dry thoroughly.

TABLE 51-2

Commonly Used Bronchodilator Regimens

Beta-Sympathomimetic Drugs[a]

Metered-Dose Inhalers[b]	**Delivery, μg/puff**	**Usual Dose**
Albuterol	90 μg/puff	2 puffs q4–6h prn
Bitolterol	370 μg/puff	2–3 puffs q4–6h prn
Metaproterenol	650 μg/puff	2–3 puffs q3–4h prn
Terbutaline	200 μg/puff	2–3 puffs q4–6h prn
Pirbuterol	200 μg/puff	2 puffs q4–6h prn
Nebulizer Solutions	**Concentration**	**Usual Dose**
Albuterol	5 mg/ml	2.5 mg tid prn
Metaproterenol	unit dose 0.6%	1 unit dose tid or qid prn
	multidose 5%	0.3 ml in 2.5 ml saline tid or qid prn
Terbutaline[c]	1 mg/ml injection solution	2 mg tid or qid prn

Anticholinergic Drugs[a]

	Delivery, μg/puff	**Usual Dose**
Metered-dose inhaler,[b] ipratropium bromide	18 μg/puff	3 puffs q6h

[a] Dosage must be individualized; some patients may improve with high dosage but require close monitoring for benefit and toxicity.
[b] Spacer device recommended for optimal drug delivery.
[c] Not FDA-approved for this route of administration.

on bronchodilator therapy. Up to 55 percent of older COPD patients fail to master proper MDI inhalation technique and do not receive optimal benefit.[4] Consequently, time should be allotted during clinic visits to regularly check inhalation technique and correct any errors. Poor coordination or hand weakness may be circumvented by using a spacer device, switching to a breath-actuated dry powder inhaler, or obtaining a trigger aid (Vent-ease) to use with the MDI canister.

Compressor-driven nebulizer devices are no more effective than MDI therapy if proper MDI technique is used. Nebulizer devices are indicated for patients who are unable to use the MDI properly despite repeated instruction or when higher dosing than is achievable with the MDI is needed. Because nebulizer devices are expensive, documentation of benefit may be important for third-party reimbursement. A home trial of nebulizer treatment, administering the bronchodilator drug several times daily with weekly dose increases, could be monitored over several weeks based on subjective responses or, preferably, twice-daily peak expiratory flow (PEFR) measurements with a peak flowmeter.[5]

Anticholinergic drugs are also effective bronchodilators. However, the sympathomimetic drugs generally provide more rapid bronchodilation and subjective relief and thus are often preferred by patients. Ipratropium bromide is the only anticholinergic drug in a metered dose inhaler available in the United States. In single-dose studies, ipratropium bromide usually provides longer bronchodilation than the sympathomimetic drug albuterol, especially beyond the third and fourth hours. The magnitude of bronchodilation with either class of drug depends on the dose and the population studied. Most studies involving COPD patients have demonstrated little difference between an inhaled anticholinergic drug and a sympathomimetic drug in terms of peak improvement in FEV_1. It is reasonable to try ipratropium bromide if sympathomimetic drugs either fail despite adequate dose escalation or cause intolerable side effects. Combining the two bronchodilator agents is expensive and enhanced efficacy is controversial. Maximizing the dose and optimizing the delivery of a single agent should first be attempted.

Oral theophylline therapy in COPD has been the focus of numerous clinical trials with variable results. Some trials in COPD have reported theophylline therapy as effective in improving subjective dyspnea, minimally improving expiratory airflow, and increasing exercise tolerance. If used, theophylline should probably be administered only in conjunction with an inhaled bronchodilator. The principal advantage of theophylline therapy is oral administration. However, there are numerous drawbacks with theophylline therapy, including the narrow therapeutic range, the need for and expense of blood drug-level monitoring, the frequent intolerance (nausea, tremor, agitation), and the potential for cardiac rhythm disturbances. Finally, the pharmacokinetics of theophylline are extremely variable and influenced by a number of factors, including age, use of other drugs, and comorbid conditions (Tables 51-4 and 51-5). Thus, theophylline may be more difficult to use in older patients.

If theophylline is to be administered, the slow-release formulations are preferred because they may be given once or twice daily (Tables 51-4 and 51-5). Dyphylline is not effective. For adults, one may initiate oral theophylline therapy at 400 mg/day (use a lower dose if reduced hepatic clearance is anticipated). This initial dose may minimize side effects, such as tremor and nausea, and enhance compliance. After 3 to 5 days, the dose may be increased to 600 mg, then to 800 mg/day. The blood theophylline level in older patients should probably be maintained in the lower end of the commonly recommended range in order to reduce the potential for drug toxicity.

Nutritional Therapy

A significant number of COPD patients have abnormalities in body weight. The obese COPD patient suffers from the added respiratory burden imposed by

TABLE 51-4

Guidelines for Oral Theophylline Therapy

Sustained-release formulations are preferred.
Single daily or two divided doses.
Average target dose: 9 mg/kg/day
Start at low dose (e.g. 400 mg/day)
Increase to the target dose incrementally every 3 to 5 days.
Check theophylline blood level if symptoms of toxicity develop and when reaching the target dose.
Adjust maintenance dose to the lower end of generally recommended therapeutic range: 10–20 mg/dl (55–110 mol/liter).

TABLE 51-5

Factors Influencing Theophylline Clearance

Reduced Clearance—Increased Blood Concentration	
Physical Factors	**Drugs**
Older age	Cimetidine
Liver disease	Erythromycin
Congestive heart failure	Propranolol
	Allopurinol
	Influenza vaccine
	Ciprofloxacin
	Norfloxacin
Increased Clearance—Reduced Blood Concentration	
Physical Factors	**Drugs**
Young age	Phenytoin
Smoking	Phenobarbital

increased girth and chest-wall mass. Theoretically, weight reduction should improve dyspnea and ventilatory demands in such patients. About 25 percent of patients with COPD are underweight, presumably undernourished, and exhibit increased relative mortality. Caloric supplementation in short-term studies has improved limb and respiratory muscle strength in such patients. However, the long-term benefits of extra feeding are unclear, improving body weight in these patients is very difficult, and costs may be significant. Generally, undernourished COPD patients should try to achieve their estimated lean body weight for age by ingesting 30 to 35 kcal/kg through food and nutritional supplements. The distribution of the calories (fat, carbohydrate, protein) is probably not important.

Exercise Reconditioning

Regular exercise in patients with COPD can produce significant subjective benefit. Reconditioning the skeletal muscles does not improve lung function but can increase overall endurance with less associated dyspnea. The best method of achieving this desirable goal is unclear. Walking is probably the most natural activity for older patients, although some will prefer a stationary cycle. An outpatient exercise reconditioning program must be individualized and involve graded intensity. Until more precise guidelines are determined, patients should be encouraged to walk (or cycle) at their own pace for 10 to 15 minutes daily or every other day. Every week or two, the duration should be increased by 5 to 10 minutes, with a target of 45 to 60 minutes exercise time. Most patients should be evaluated for exercise-induced oxygen desaturation prior to starting the reconditioning program.

Comprehensive Rehabilitation Programs

Comprehensive pulmonary rehabilitation programs are designed to aid patients with COPD, as well as other chronic respiratory disorders, in adjusting physically and psychologically to their disability. These programs are often available at regional centers and supplement the office physician's medical evaluation and treatment plans. Standards for such programs have been established with the goals of improving exercise tolerance, increasing the ease of performing activities of daily living, maximizing patients' social integration, and reducing hospitalizations and cost of medical care.

The components of a comprehensive rehabilitation program include:

1. Review of medical condition and treatment plan
2. Patient and family education
3. Respiratory therapy techniques and education
4. Physical therapy assessment and planning
5. Psychosocial evaluation
6. Nutritional assessment and planning
7. Smoking cessation

Such programs typically are outpatient-directed and may extend over several weeks. Exercise reconditioning in these programs involves supervised exercise programs which serve to allay patient anxiety, emphasize regular compliance, and are individually tailored for intensity. The educational components help patients and their families accept the chronic aspects of COPD while improving motivation through knowledge and self-management guidelines. At the end of the program, a home exercise conditioning protocol is provided, and this is reinforced through telephone contacts to minimize the expected loss of enthusiasm and training effect. Patient motivation is crucial to the success of these programs, and the primary physician plays a key role in screening for and promoting self-motivation. In addition to poor compliance, other exclusionary criteria for such programs include severe cardiac disease, life-limiting malignancy, neurologic disability, and limited family or financial resources. Advanced pulmonary impairment should not exclude patients from participating in some aspects of these programs.

Oxygen Therapy

Long-term oxygen therapy in hypoxemic patients is the only treatment intervention in COPD that has been shown to reduce mortality; oxygen therapy may extend life by several years (Fig. 51-3). In order to achieve improvement in survival, however, hypoxemic patients with COPD must use oxygen at least 20 hours per day.[6] Continuous supplemental oxygen therapy is indicated for patients with COPD who have daytime hypoxemia [Pa_{O_2} 55 mmHg (7.3 kPa) or less]. The goal of oxygen therapy is to maintain the arterial P_{O_2} between 61 to 70 mmHg (8.1 to 9.3 kPa) or the arterial oxygen saturation between 91 and 94 percent. During sleep or exercise, the prescribed oxygen flow rate should be increased by 1 liter/min. Medicare will pay for long-term oxygen therapy in such patients.

Some patients recovering from an exacerbation of COPD may be hypoxemic at discharge from hospital and home oxygen should be prescribed prior to their discharge. However, many such patients will improve in the ensuing weeks and long-term oxygen therapy will not be required. Postdischarge follow-up at 3 to 6 weeks should include an assessment of room air arterial blood gas to identify those patients who may no longer require oxygen therapy. Long-term oxygen therapy should be prescribed for COPD patients who are hypoxemic while in a stable clinical state and on optimal medical treatment.

Continuous home oxygen therapy may also be indicated when the Pa_{O_2} is between 56 to 59 mmHg

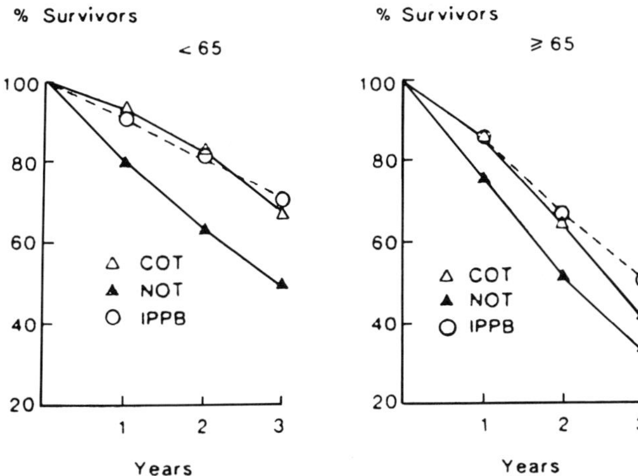

FIGURE 51-3

Survival in COPD relative to age and the influence of oxygen administration in hypoxemic COPD. All patients had $FEV_1 < 30$ percent predicted. Left panel: patients aged < 65 at onset of study. Right panel: patients aged > 65 at onset of study. COT = survival on continuous oxygen therapy (> 20 h/day). NOT = survival using only nocturnal oxygen. IPPB = survival in nonhypoxemic COPD patients from the NIH IPPB study. *(From Anthonisen NR, Weight EC, Hodgkin JE, and the IPPB Trial Group: Prognosis in chronic obstructive pulmonary disease. Am Rev Respir Dis 133:14, 1986. Reproduced by permission.)*

(7.4 to 7.8 kPa) and there is evidence for end-organ hypoxemia, such as clinical signs of cor pulmonale; or P pulmonale with P waves greater than 3 mm in leads II, III, or aVF; or secondary polycythemia with a packed cell volume greater than 0.56. Patients with Pa_{O_2} greater than 55 mmHg (7.3 kPa) accompanied by neuropsychiatric dysfunction, disabling dyspnea, or angina pectoris may theoretically benefit from home oxygen therapy, but effectiveness of supplemental oxygen in these circumstances has not been proven. Such special cases require written documentation and supportive information by the prescribing physician for consideration of payment by Medicare.

Hypoxemia during exercise is common in COPD. Patients who are normoxic at rest may have exercise-related oxygen desaturation, which can contribute to disabling dyspnea, aggravate pulmonary hypertension, and produce organ ischemia. Oxygen therapy during exercise can reduce these complications. A prescription for intermittent oxygen use during exercise will require documentation of exercise hypoxemia. This may conveniently be obtained during a walking exercise protocol using a pulse oximeter. More elaborate exercise testing is not usually indicated.

Patients with COPD may also experience sleep-related hypoxemia that is not associated with obstructive sleep apnea. Sleep hypoxemia in COPD occurs during rapid eye movement (REM) sleep. Generally, patients with the lowest Pa_{O_2} during wakefulness have the most severe REM-related oxygen desaturation. The adverse consequences of sleep hypoxemia in COPD include poor sleep quality, nocturnal myocardial ischemia, aggravation of pulmonary hypertension, and secondary polycythemia. Patients with COPD who are normoxic while awake but have pulmonary hypertension, elevated hematocrit, or sleep-related symptoms should be assessed with a nocturnal oximetric recording. Nighttime oxygen therapy may be advised when nocturnal hypoxemia complicates COPD and is associated with symptoms or adverse effects.

Oxygen sources for in-home use include compressed gas cylinders, oxygen concentrators/enrichers, and liquid oxygen reservoirs. Nasal cannulas are used to deliver the oxygen. The choice of oxygen source depends upon factors such as costs, availability, need for social integration, ambulation requirements, continuity of use, and flow rate. The algorithm in Fig. 51-4 suggests how the oxygen source may be selected for specific indications. The most economical and frequently prescribed oxygen sources are the concentrator/enricher device for in-home use and portable gas cylinders for exercise and out-of-home activities.

Patients with COPD who want to travel by air are at risk for hypoxic complications if their arterial oxygen tension is near the steep, linear portion of the oxyhemoglobin dissociation curve. Commercial aircraft are pressurized to approximately 8000 ft (2400 m), where the oxygen percentage is about 15 percent, not 21 percent. Patients whose Pa_{O_2} is around 70 mmHg (9.3 kPa) on the ground may have their oxygen tension fall below 55 mmHg (7.3 kPa) in flight. Patients already receiving oxygen therapy will require an increased concentration in flight. Those not receiving oxygen therapy but whose Pa_{O_2} is less than 70 mmHg on the ground will require further evaluation to determine if in-flight oxygen is recommended. Determination of the patient's needs well in advance of the anticipated travel is advisable, as prescribing in-flight oxygen can be a lengthy process.[7]

Corticosteroids

Systemic corticosteroid drugs are often employed in advanced COPD despite the controversial benefits of this practice and their known, frequent toxicity. A pooled analysis of controlled trials did not support long-term corticosteroid therapy in the outpatient management of most patients with COPD.[8] Nevertheless, occasional patients experience considerable improvement in FEV_1 while on corticosteroid treatment. In order to identify these exceptional responders, a trial of prednisone—20 to 40 mg daily for 2 weeks with pre- and posttreatment spirometry—can be undertaken. Subjective responses alone should not be used. An improvement in FEV_1 of 15 to 20 percent is a reasonable criterion for considering continued use

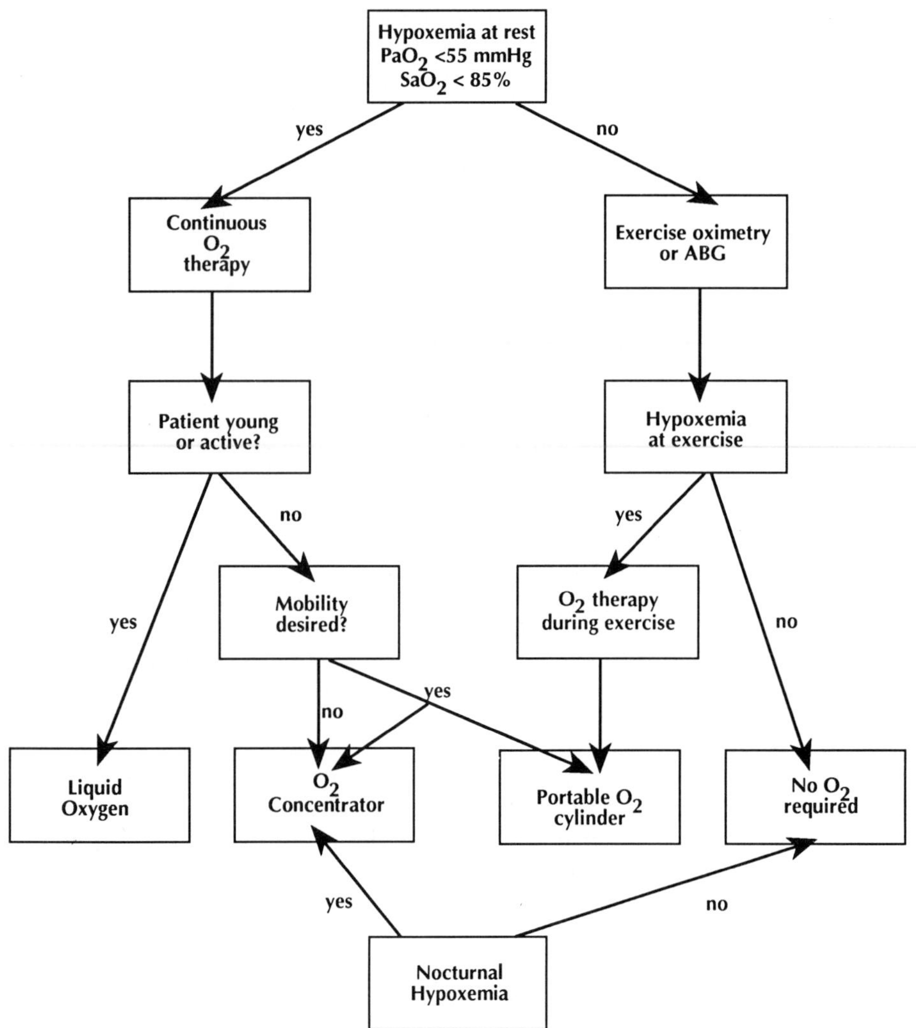

FIGURE 51-4
Selecting oxygen delivery options in hypoxemic COPD.

of corticosteroids. Inhaled corticosteroids in the management of COPD are not proven to be of value. Long-term oral corticosteroids should be prescribed in the lowest dose (for example, prednisone 10 mg or less daily) that maintains benefit. An alternate-day regimen will minimize adrenal suppression and should be attempted.

Exacerbation and Respiratory Failure in COPD

Worsening symptoms, primarily dyspnea and sputum production, characterize an exacerbation of COPD. Deterioration may be acute or subacute. Often the cause of an exacerbation is difficult to identify. Factors that may exacerbate symptoms in COPD include infection, air pollution, continued smoking, left ventricular failure, myocardial infarction, pulmonary thromboembolism, spontaneous pneumothorax, and medications such as beta blockers (including eyedrops) and sedatives.

Infection should be considered when the sputum changes color or its volume increases. Many patients with COPD harbor *Haemophilus influenzae* or *Streptococcus pneumoniae* in their sputum, and increased numbers of these bacteria may contribute to an exacerbation. Other infectious agents that have been suspected of inducing exacerbations in COPD are *Moraxella catarrhalis, Mycoplasma pneumoniae,* influenza viruses, and rhinoviruses. Antibiotics seem to reduce the duration of an exacerbation in COPD and may prevent deterioration leading to hospitalization.[9] Amoxicillin, trimethoprim-sulfamethoxazole, or a tetracycline are cost-effective options for the outpatient management of an exacerbation in COPD. Chronic use of antibiotics in COPD to suppress bacteria is not recommended due to unproven benefit.

Ambulatory care of an exacerbation includes intensification of inhaled bronchodilator therapy and oral antibiotics. Occasionally, a brief course of oral corticosteroids is useful. Expectorants may provide some adjunctive benefit.

Hospitalization for an exacerbation of COPD is indicated for (1) failure to respond to outpatient treatment, (2) development of respiratory failure, (3) presence of pneumonia, (4) worsening cor pulmonale, and (5) presence of comorbid conditions that complicate management. Intensive care is advised for patients with marked respiratory distress or respiratory failure, cardiac complications, and confusion/poor cooperation.

Oxygen therapy during an exacerbation of COPD should be carefully controlled in order to mitigate the possibility of a marked worsening in carbon dioxide retention. Oxygen therapy should be initiated at 1 to 2 liters/min via cannula or 24 to 28 percent oxygen via Venturi-type mask. An arterial blood gas should be obtained after 20 to 30 minutes. The level of oxygen should then be incrementally increased in an effort to obtain an arterial oxygen saturation of 90 percent or Pa_{O_2} greater than 55 mmHg (7.3 kPa). An oxygen tension greater than 70 mmHg (9.3 kPa) is not necessary and does not result in any significant increase in blood oxygen content. Controlled oxygen therapy will usually provide adequate arterial oxygen while maintaining the arterial pH above 7.25 to 7.3. This level of acidemia is generally well tolerated. Endotracheal intubation is indicated in the presence of worsening acidemia, cardiac complications, or significant deterioration in mental status.

Bronchodilator therapy during an exacerbation requiring hospitalization is more cost-effective when delivered using a MDI with a spacer device. The frequency of administration depends upon the severity of symptoms. Initial therapy may require 30-minute to hourly treatments of an inhaled beta-2 sympathomimetic drug. An anticholinergic drug may be added on a schedule of every 3 to 4 hours. Theophylline therapy is associated with potential toxicity and uncertain benefit, especially in the acute setting, and routine use of theophylline is becoming less popular.

Intravenous antibiotics are usually prescribed for severe exacerbations with purulent bronchitis or pneumonia. The presence of pneumonia warrants broad-spectrum antimicrobial therapy, which should be initiated pending the results of the cultures.

Pharmacologic doses of corticosteroids are generally considered beneficial in exacerbations of COPD. These agents may help lower airflow resistance by reducing mucus production and decreasing bronchial edema. The lowest effective dose is not known. A commonly employed regimen is methylprednisolone 0.5 to 1.0 mg/kg every 6 to 8 hours for 3 days. The treatment is then changed to oral prednisone, 40 to 60 mg, as a single daily dose that is tapered over the next 10 to 14 days. Complications of high-dose corticosteroid therapy include confusion and agitation, which may be particularly prominent in older patients. Hyperglycemia and hypokalemia may also complicate management. Corticosteroids may induce a metabolic alkalosis, especially during concomitant diuretic therapy, which can be managed with potassium and chloride replacement along with a judicious reduction in the corticosteroid dose.

Prognosis in COPD

The degree to which lung function is lost is a strong predictor of mortality in COPD and also correlates with all-cause mortality. However, there is considerable variability in survival for a given level of FEV_1, making prognostication difficult in an individual patient. Additional factors that are associated with increased mortality in COPD are advanced age, rate of decline in FEV_1, resting tachycardia, hypoxemia, pulmonary hypertension, continued smoking, and weight loss. The influence of age and hypoxemia on mortality are illustrated in Fig. 51-3 for patients with severe COPD ($FEV_1 < 30$ percent predicted). These data represent serial follow up of a large group (> 1000 patients) with COPD and provide insight into the natural history of the disorder. Note that continuous oxygen therapy improved the survival in hypoxemic patients comparable to that expected for nonhypoxemic patients with a similar degree of airflow obstruction.

The in-hospital mortality from acute respiratory failure (ARF) complicating COPD varies from 10 to 40 percent.[10] The 2-year survival after an episode of ARF in COPD may be as high as 50 percent.[11] The level of ventilatory function and overall functional status, along with the patient's nutritional state, are more important than age in determining survival during acute respiratory failure complicating COPD.

ASTHMA

Asthma is a syndrome defined by physiologic criteria that reflect variability in airflow obstruction. The airflow obstruction in asthma is due to hyperresponsiveness of the tracheobronchial tree to a variety of stimuli. An inflammatory response in the airways, either allergic or nonallergic, appears to be the basis for the bronchial hyperresponsiveness. Importantly, the airflow obstruction in asthma is considered to be completely or significantly reversible either spontaneously or after treatment.

Cough, wheeze, and dyspnea or chest tightness characterize asthma and are typically episodic. These symptoms are frequently worsened by factors such as cold air, tobacco smoke, other air pollution, exercise, strong odors, and weather changes. Upper respiratory infections seem to worsen asthmatic symptoms.

The underdiagnosis of asthma appears to be common, especially in older adults. Many older patients with asthma are diagnosed as having chronic bronchitis or emphysema. Asthma should be suspected as the cause of airflow obstruction if there is minimal tobacco smoke or other pollutant exposure, if symptoms are episodic, and if there is significant reversibility of obstruction after bronchodilator therapy. Symptoms, however, can be misleading. In a study of 120 adults aged 65 or older who reported episodic respiratory symptoms suggesting bronchial irritability, only 32 percent actually demonstrated variability in bronchial responses considered consistent with asthma when tested with either an inhaled bronchodilator or after a bronchial provocation challenge.[12] One useful diagnostic strategy for the patient with episodic respiratory symptoms but normal spirometry is in-home peak expiratory rate (PEFR) monitoring twice daily for several weeks. This may demonstrate variability in airflow obstruction. If this is not helpful, bronchial provocation challenge using histamine or methacholine can be obtained in the pulmonary function laboratory in order to document bronchial hyperresponsiveness. Bronchial hyperresponsiveness is typical of asthma but is not a specific diagnostic finding. False-positive bronchoprovocation challenges are possible, particularly after a recent viral respiratory infection. Patients suspected of being asthmatic but whose airflow obstruction has little acute bronchodilator reversibility should receive several weeks of treatment with an inhaled bronchodilator and an oral corticosteroid, followed by repeat spirometry. This may produce a dramatic improvement in the expiratory flow rates and supports the diagnosis of asthma. Finally, some patients with years of poorly controlled asthma will have fixed airflow obstruction, often severe, and appear indistinguishable from patients with COPD.[13]

Several features of the epidemiology and natural history of asthma are unique to older adults. Although population studies have indicated that symptomatic asthma past age 50 is more common in women, this may represent a public or physician "gender bias" in applying diagnostic terms. Asthma may have its onset past age 45, but most asthma probably develops prior to this age. Often older adults will claim recent onset of asthma, but careful history taking will indicate years of previous complaints suggesting "bronchial trouble." Allergy skin tests are typically negative in older asthmatics, whether their asthma is of recent or remote onset. Some studies have reported that older asthmatics demonstrate elevated levels of age-adjusted total IgE, despite nonreactive allergy skin tests. This observation is not consistent and its clinical significance is unclear. One study of 25 older asthmatics (above age 70) indicated that their total IgE levels were no different from those of age-matched nonasthmatics.[14] A large study of respiratory disease in older adults did demonstrate a close correlation between patient-reported presence of asthma and age-adjusted serum IgE levels.[15] The prevalence of asthma in the population over age 70 is around 3 to 6 percent, which is similar to that in other adult age groups. Asthma in the older adult has been characterized as being typically severe and frequently leading to steroid dependence, but the accuracy of this clinical impression has not been properly tested. However, asthma-related deaths are highest in the older population, and the utilization of hospital resources for asthma care is also highest in the elderly. Careful consideration of the diagnosis of asthma in older adults is important for identifying a group of patients who have a potentially manageable disorder that is associated with substantial morbidity and mortality.

Management

Management of asthma in the older adult is based on the severity of the condition and on identification of comorbidity. Heart disease, especially coronary insufficiency, may dictate the intensity of drug therapy. Theophylline and beta-agonist drugs increase myocardial oxygen consumption and may also aggravate cardiac dysrythmias. Of course, asthmatic patients should avoid beta blockers completely. Prostatism in an asthmatic may be worsened by theophylline. Systemic corticosteroids may contribute to cataract formation and complicate management of hypertension, diabetes, and lipid disorders. Poor coordination, musculoskeletal disorders, or cognitive dysfunction will compromise the effectiveness of MDI therapy. Poor hearing or vision can hinder efforts at patient education; consequently, treatment instructions should be written clearly in large letters. Outpatient regimens with multiple medications will not be effective if poverty, poor understanding, and social isolation prevent adequate compliance or supervision.

All asthmatics need to be evaluated for possible precipitating or aggravating factors. Avoidance measures are fundamental to any management plan. Allergy skin testing and historical features often do not indicate any apparent role for inhalant allergy in most cases of asthma in older adults. Some asthmatics may have nonallergic sensitivity to nonsteroidal anti-inflammatory drugs (aspirin sensitivity) or to sulfites. These should be avoided when a suggestive history is present. The role of gastroesophageal reflux as a factor in asthma is controversial. Generally, antireflux measures do not appear to be effective in reducing asthmatic symptoms. However, there may be a subset of patients whose asthma will improve with treatment for gastroesophageal reflux. Notably, it is common for reflux symptoms to abate when theophylline therapy is stopped or adjusted downward. Chronic sinusitis seems to aggravate asthmatic symptoms in some patients, and adequate medical or surgical treatment of sinus infection may produce a substantial remission in asthmatic symptoms. Indoor air pollution, such as sidestream tobacco smoke or household heating with poor exhaust (kerosene space heaters, wood stoves) will contribute to symptoms and should be avoided. Work, home, and recreational environments should be as free of respiratory irritants as possible.

The National Asthma Education Program has outlined a general management plan based on asthma severity with the goals of controlling asthmatic symptoms, preventing acute exacerbations, and maintaining as near normal as possible the levels of pulmonary function and general activity.[16] Mild asthma, characterized by episodic symptoms with near normal pulmonary function during baseline conditions, is managed by avoidance measures and use of an inhaled beta-2 sympathomimetic, as needed. Proper MDI inhalation technique cannot be overemphasized (Table 51-4) and should be serially assessed. Moderate asthma is characterized by more frequent symptoms, and the patient's spirometric tests are seldom normal. In this setting, an anti-inflammatory drug should be the primary pharmacologic intervention. An inhaled sympathomimetic is used, as needed, for symptom control. Inhaled corticosteroids are preferred for anti-inflammatory therapy (Table 51-6). Chromolyn sodium is an alternative but is usually not as effective as an inhaled corticosteroid. Sustained-release theophylline may also be added, following the guidelines in Table 51-4, when additional symptom control is required. Nocturnal symptoms, particularly, may dictate a trial of sustained-release theophylline therapy. Severe asthma is associated with frequent exacerbations and continuous symptoms, including awakenings due to smothering or wheezing, that affect most routine activities. Management of severe asthma requires higher-dose inhaled corticosteroids or oral systemic corticosteroids. While long-term oral corticosteroid treatment may be unavoidable in severe asthma, many patients may respond to higher doses of inhaled corticosteroids with substantially less risk of side effects.

In-home management of worsening asthma is best approached with a written crisis plan that entails patient-initiated increases in therapy as outlined by the physician. Home monitoring of PEFR can be especially useful in evaluating an exacerbation. Initially, inhaled bronchodilator therapy should be increased to as much as four puffs every 20 minutes for a hour or two. Inhaled steroids, if being used, should be doubled or tripled. If symptoms persist for 4 to 6 hours and/or the PEFR does not exceed 70 percent of baseline (which must be established for each patient), the patient should increase or initiate oral steroid therapy and the physician notified. Patients who fail to respond or worsen should go to the nearest emergency department.

In the emergency department, the degree of respiratory distress and PEFR reduction should be assessed. Very dyspneic or distressed patients require an arterial blood gas. Oxygen should be administered and an inhaled sympathomimetic drug given every 10 to 15 minutes for 1 to 1.5 hours, depending on response. Inhaled bronchodilator therapy should be used, since older patients are more likely to experience serious cardiovascular toxicity after subcutaneous epinephrine or terbutaline. Parenteral or oral corticosteroid therapy should be started. Theophylline (aminophylline) does not appreciably improve airflow obstruction in acute asthma and is not strongly indicated. An inhaled anticholinergic drug may provide some adjunctive benefit.

Hospitalization is indicated for respiratory failure, altered consciousness, or posttreatment PEFR or FEV_1 less than 25 percent predicted. Hospitalization should also be considered when the posttreatment PEFR or FEV_1 is less than 40 percent and there is significant comorbidity, a past history of intubation for asthma, chronic systemic steroid dependence, repeated health care contacts for asthma, or poor compliance with prior medical care. Most asthma patients requiring hospitalization should be initially in an intensive care nursing area where close observation of vital signs and PEFR measurements are available.

Discharge from hospital or emergency department is generally safe when the PEFR exceeds 60 percent (around 300 liters/min for men, 250 liters/min for women) and wheezing is mild, with no labored breathing at rest. A tapering dose of corticosteroids extending over 2 to 3 weeks after discharge is important in preventing early relapse. There should be medical follow-up within 1 to 2 weeks after discharge to adjust medications.

TABLE 51-6

Inhaled Corticosteroid Therapy

Drug	MDI Delivery, μg/puff	Usual Dose
Beclomethasone	42	2 puffs qid[a]
Triamcinolone	100	2 puffs qid[a]
Flunisolide	250	2–4 puffs bid[a]

[a] Use spacer device to optimize drug delivery. Higher doses, up to 20 puffs divided qid, may allow some patients to stop chronic oral steroid use.

RESPIRATORY FAILURE

Respiratory failure occurs when disorders of the respiratory system cause significant impairment in the regulation of arterial blood gas tensions. Respiratory failure may be classified into hypercapnic or hypoxemic failure. Although this classification is artificial, it is based on pathophysiology and may be useful for suggesting a differential diagnosis.

Hypercapnic Respiratory Failure

Hypercapnic respiratory failure can be defined by a Pa_{CO_2} greater than 50 mmHg (6.7 kPa) which is not due to respiratory compensation for a metabolic alkalosis. Hypercapnic respiratory failure may be due to global hypoventilation (e.g., neuromuscular diseases, upper airway obstruction) or to severe mismatching of regional ventilation and alveolar perfusion (e.g., COPD, life-threatening asthma). The degree of respiratory acidosis in hypercapnic respiratory failure depends on its duration, severity, and the extent of renal compensatory bicarbonate reabsorption, which requires several days for completion. In the acute setting, plasma buffering will raise the bicarbonate 1 mEq/liter for every 10 mmHg (1.33 kPa) rise in Pa_{CO_2}. After 3 to 4 days, renal compensation will raise the plasma bicarbonate 4 mEq/liter for the same elevation in Pa_{CO_2}.

The arterial oxygen tension is always reduced in hypercapnia unless supplemental oxygen is being used. In hypercapnic respiratory failure due to global hypoventilation, the alveolar-to-arterial oxygen tension difference ($a\text{-}AD_{O_2}$) will be normal. Of note, the $a\text{-}AD_{O_2}$ in the aged with otherwise normal lungs may be as high as 35 to 40 mmHg (4.7 to 5.3 kPa). In hypercapnic respiratory failure due to ventilation-perfusion mismatch, the $a\text{-}AD_{O_2}$ will be increased.

The management of hypercapnic respiratory failure involves identifying the cause, improving alveolar ventilation, and assuring adequate blood oxygenation. The management of neuromuscular disorders causing hypercapnic respiratory failure is often disease-specific, emphasizing the importance of an accurate diagnosis. Hypothyroidism, myasthenia gravis, and polymyositis, for example, are treatable causes of hypercapnic respiratory failure that require very different treatments. All patients with ventilatory weakness should be observed closely, probably in an intensive-care setting, and followed with serial measures of vital capacity, inspiratory force, and arterial blood gases. In neuromuscular disorders, a forced vital capacity of 1 liter or less is usually indicative of the need for mechanical ventilation, because progressive respiratory acidosis is likely. Hypercapnic respiratory failure complicating an exacerbation of COPD or during life-threatening asthma requires intensive care, including attention to associated medical problems, positive-pressure ventilator support, oxygen, and bronchodilator and corticosteroid drugs.

Hypoxemic Respiratory Failure

Hypoxemic respiratory failure may be defined by a Pa_{O_2} less than 60 mmHg (8 kPa). The Pa_{CO_2} may be normal or low. The pathophysiology involves ventilation-perfusion mismatching and right-to-left intrapulmonary shuntlike effect. These disturbances are usually due to alveolar filling or collapse caused by a variety of pathologic conditions. Examples of common diseases producing hypoxemic respiratory failure are pneumonia, cardiogenic pulmonary edema, noncardiogenic pulmonary edema (adult respiratory distress syndrome, or ARDS), pulmonary embolus, and pulmonary fibrosis. Only in advanced disease or at respiratory arrest will the Pa_{CO_2} rise in these disorders. The alveolar-arterial oxygen tension difference is always increased, often markedly so.

The management of hypoxemic respiratory failure involves maintaining arterial oxygenation and tissue oxygen delivery, identifying the cause and comorbidities, treating the underlying disease(s), and avoiding disease- or treatment-related complications. Maintaining adequate arterial oxygenation [$Sa_{O_2} >$ 90 percent, $Pa_{O_2} >$ 60 mmHg (8 kPa)] in hypoxemic respiratory failure can be difficult because there may be significant venoarterial shunting. Positive-pressure ventilation is indicated when the Pa_{O_2} is less than 60 mmHg (8 kPa) on greater than 60 percent mask oxygen. Positive-pressure ventilation may allow adequate blood oxygenation on less hyperoxic gas mixtures through the application of both inspiratory and expiratory positive pressures.

Survival in hypoxemic respiratory failure varies according to the underlying disease. Cardiogenic pulmonary edema requiring mechanical ventilation is associated with 15 to 30 percent mortality. However, there are subsets of patients with poor left ventricular function and congestive heart failure, such as recent myocardial infarction with associated hypotension, that have 80 percent mortality. The mortality accompanying respiratory failure in cancer patients or associated with bone marrow transplantation exceeds 90 percent. Survival in patients requiring mechanical ventilation for ARDS averages 40 to 50 percent. Advanced age is associated with increased mortality in hypoxemic respiratory failure.

Mechanical ventilation for respiratory failure places an extraordinary demand on limited health care resources. Furthermore, mechanical ventilation and other life-support interventions may serve only to forestall inevitable death, especially when provided to seriously ill patients with poor pre-existing health status. These issues are central to the dilemma of when and in whom life support should be withheld or withdrawn. Governmental and professional organizations are advocating that advance directives regarding medical care be established by patients. Such directives should arise from physician and patient discussions regarding individual prognosis, patient expectations for life, and the reported outcomes from life-support interventions. Advance directives do respect patient autonomy and may limit health care expenditures for unwanted life-prolonging care, but their actual impact on the legal, social, and ethical issues has yet to be determined. Regardless, the physician must continue to be the patient's advocate concerning appropriateness of care.

REFERENCES

1. Standards for the diagnosis and care of patients with chronic obstructive pulmonary disease (COPD) and asthma. *Am Rev Respir Dis* 136:225, 1987.
2. Dockery DW et al: The cumulative and reversible effects of lifetime smoking on simple tests of lung function in adults. *Am Rev Resp Dis* 137:286, 1988.
3. Feinleib M et al: Trends in COPD morbidity and mortality in the United States. *Am Rev Respir Dis* 140 (suppl):S9, 1989.
4. Armitage JM, Williams SJ: Inhaler technique in the elderly. *Age Ageing* 17:275, 1988.
5. Goldman JM et al: Simplifying the assessment of patients with chronic airflow limitation for home nebulizer therapy. *Respir Med* 86:33, 1992.
6. Nocturnal Oxygen Therapy Trial Group. Continuous or nocturnal oxygen therapy in hypoxemic obstructive lung disease. *Ann Intern Med* 93:391, 1980.
7. Gong H Jr: Air travel and oxygen therapy in cardiopulmonary patients. *Chest* 101:1104, 1992.
8. Callahan CM et al: Oral corticosteroid therapy for patients with stable chronic obstructive pulmonary disease. *Ann Intern Med* 44:216, 1991.
9. Anthonisen NR et al: Antibiotic therapy and exacerbations of chronic obstructive pulmonary disease. *Ann Intern Med* 106:196, 1987.
10. Derenne JP et al: Acute respiratory failure of chronic obstructive lung disease. *Am Rev Respir Dis* 130:1006, 1988.
11. Martin TR et al: The prognosis of patients with chronic obstructive pulmonary disease after hospitalization for acute respiratory failure. *Chest* 82:310, 1982.
12. Dow L et al: Respiratory symptoms as predictors of airways lability in an elderly population. *Respir Med* 86:27, 1992.
13. Brown PJ et al: Asthma and irreversible airflow obstruction. *Thorax* 39: 131, 1984.
14. Braman SS et al: Asthma in the elderly: A comparison between patients with recently acquired and longstanding disease. *Am Rev Respir Dis* 143:336, 1991.
15. Burrows B et al: Characteristics of asthma among elderly adults and a sample of the general population. *Chest* 100:934, 1991.
16. National Asthma Education Program: Guidelines for the diagnosis and management of asthma. Bethesda, MD, US Department of Health and Human Services, 1991.

Chapter 52

INTERSTITIAL LUNG DISEASE, HYPERSENSITIVITY PNEUMONITIS, AND PULMONARY VASCULAR DISEASE

Gary W. Hunninghake

INTERSTITIAL LUNG DISEASE

The interstitial lung diseases are a heterogeneous group of disorders characterized by inflammation (alveolitis) and destruction of the gas-exchange units (alveoli, capillaries, and small airways) and by interstitial fibrosis. Over 100 different disorders have been described. In some of these disorders, e.g., silicosis and asbestosis, the inciting agent which triggers the disease process is known; in others, such as idiopathic pulmonary fibrosis and sarcoidosis, the cause is unknown. Regardless of the etiology, each of these disorders can progress to end-stage lung disease and death of a patient if sufficient numbers of gas-exchange units are destroyed by the disease process.

Although there are no interstitial lung diseases which affect only the elderly, interstitial lung disease is common in this age group. The disease may be of recent onset or may be a long-standing disorder which began much earlier. In this discussion, no attempt will be made to evaluate all of the interstitial lung disorders, nor will the etiology and/or the mechanisms of lung parenchymal injury in these diseases be delineated except where this information is relevant to therapy; this information is readily available, however, in recent reviews. Instead, this chapter will focus on the clinical evaluation and care of elderly patients with interstitial lung disease.

Clinical Manifestations

The earliest symptoms of interstitial disease are usually nonspecific: fatigue, shortness of breath on exertion, vague loss of a sense of well-being, and often a chronic, nonproductive cough. These symptoms are sometimes first noted after a flulike illness. On physical examination, sharp, crackling rales may be heard throughout the chest, and clubbing of the fingers and toes may be present. As the disease progresses, the shortness of breath increases and becomes even more severe with minimal exertion. If the disorder evolves into an end-stage lung disease, there is a distressing dyspnea even at rest and, finally, death. Although patients may die in respiratory failure, the terminal event frequently is pneumonia, myocardial infarction, stroke, pulmonary embolus, arrhythmia, or acute right- or left-ventricular failure.

Pulmonary Function

When the patient is first seen, it is very important to obtain pulmonary function studies. Optimally, these studies should include spirometry and measurement of lung volumes, diffusing capacity, and arterial blood gases. The results of these studies will confirm the presence and determine the severity of the lung disease. In addition, these studies are extremely useful in providing baselines from which to determine whether there is a subsequent progression of the disorder.

In patients with interstitial lung disease, pulmonary function is characterized by (1) decreased lung volumes, such as the total lung capacity (TLC), residual volume (RV), and functional residual capacity (FRC; see Table 52-1); (2) decreased DL_{CO} (single breath diffusing capacity for carbon monoxide); and (3) decreased Pa_{O_2}, with an increased alveolar-arterial oxygen gradient. Both of the latter two abnormalities are magnified with exercise. In some patients, an obstruction to airflow may also be present. Although

TABLE 52-1

Effect of Interstitial Lung Diseases and Aging on Pulmonary Functions

Pulmonary Function*	Interstitial Lung Disease†	Aging
Lung Volumes		
TLC	↓	N
VC	↓	↓
FRC	↓	↑
RV	↓	↑
Spirometry		
FEV_1	↓	↓
FVC	↓	↓
FEF_{25-75}	↓	↓
Diffusing Capacity	↓	↓
Pa_{O_2}	↓	↓

*TLC, total lung capacity; VC, vital capacity; FRC, functional residual capacity; RV, residual volume; FEV_1, forced expiratory volume in 1 second; FVC, forced vital capacity; FEF_{25-75}, forced expiratory flow between 25 and 75 percent of vital capacity; Pa_{O_2}, partial pressure of oxygen in arterial blood.
†N = normal; ↓ = decreased; ↑ = increased. Data from normal populations allow an age adjustment on the predicted values for individual patients.

some of these alterations in pulmonary function may occur as a result of aging, it is usually not difficult to distinguish aging-associated alterations in lung function from those which occur as a result of the presence of an interstitial lung disease (Table 52-1). In this regard, the measurements of the TLC, RV, and FRC by body box plethysmography are especially useful, since these lung volumes do not normally decrease with aging alone. In addition, the Pa_{O_2} and the alveolar-arterial oxygen gradient do not worsen with exercise in older individuals unless an underlying disorder is present. Finally, an abnormal chest film and/or a high-resolution computed tomography (CT) scan of the chest often identifies interstitial lung disease as the cause of the altered pulmonary function.

Exercise studies may be associated with a higher risk of morbidity in the elderly and are therefore reserved for patients in relatively good clinical condition. The following examples demonstrate instances in which exercise studies may be useful in the evaluation of the elderly: (1) Since the Pa_{O_2} decreases and the alveolar-arterial oxygen gradient widens with exercise in the presence of even mild interstitial lung disease, exercise studies may be useful to detect or essentially rule out the presence of an underlying interstitial disorder in patients with relatively normal chest films and pulmonary functions. (2) Since the Pa_{O_2} of these patients decreases with exercise, these studies may be useful for monitoring the patients' need for oxygen therapy. (3) In patients with other causes for dyspnea, such as cardiovascular disease or poor muscle tone, exercise studies may be useful in determining the relative contribution of the lung disease versus the extrapulmonary disorders to the patients' shortness of breath.

Radiography

In interstitial lung disease, the radiograph usually shows a diffuse infiltrate which may be reticular, nodular, or reticulonodular in character (Fig. 52-1). In some disorders, such as idiopathic pulmonary fibrosis (IPF), the radiographic findings are nonspecific and may be mimicked by a number of other interstitial disorders. In others, like silicosis, the massive fibrotic lesions in the upper lung zones together with enlarged hilar lymph nodes surrounded by eggshell calcifications strongly suggest the correct diagnosis. The reader is referred to standard textbooks of pulmonary medicine for a complete discussion of the typical radiographic features of all the interstitial lung disorders. High-resolution CT scans of the chest may also be useful to evaluate patients with interstitial lung disease. In patients with IPF, there is a "honeycombing" pattern most prominent in the periphery of the lung and in the lung bases. In patients with sarcoidosis, by contrast, there are often nodular lung lesions and prominence of the bronchoalveolar bundles.

While the chest radiograph is very useful in establishing the presence of an interstitial lung disorder, the radiographic findings usually correlate poorly with the results of pulmonary function tests and with the patient's dyspnea. Serial radiographs are obtained periodically to evaluate the patient for the presence of congestive heart failure, pleural effusion, or new parenchymal infiltrates, which may or may not be related to the underlying interstitial disease.

Blood Tests

Analysis of blood tests provides only a limited amount of information regarding either the diagnosis or the progression of various interstitial lung diseases. For example, an elevated erythrocyte sedimentation rate does not necessarily indicate that the lung disease is active, nor does a normal erythrocyte sedimentation rate preclude progression of the disorder. In addition, increased titers of autoantibodies, such as antinuclear antibody and rheumatoid factor, are frequently present in interstitial lung disease; therefore, the presence of these autoantibodies may suggest but does not establish the presence of an interstitial lung disease associated with the collagen vascular disorders. Furthermore, the titers of these autoantibodies do not correlate with the progression of the lung disease in patients with collagen vascular diseases. Other tests which may suggest a specific diagnosis are precipitating antibodies to inhaled organic antigens in hypersensitivity pneumonitis and increased titers of angiotensin converting enzyme in sarcoidosis. Neither of these tests, however, can be used to determine the need for and/or adequacy of therapy in these disorders.

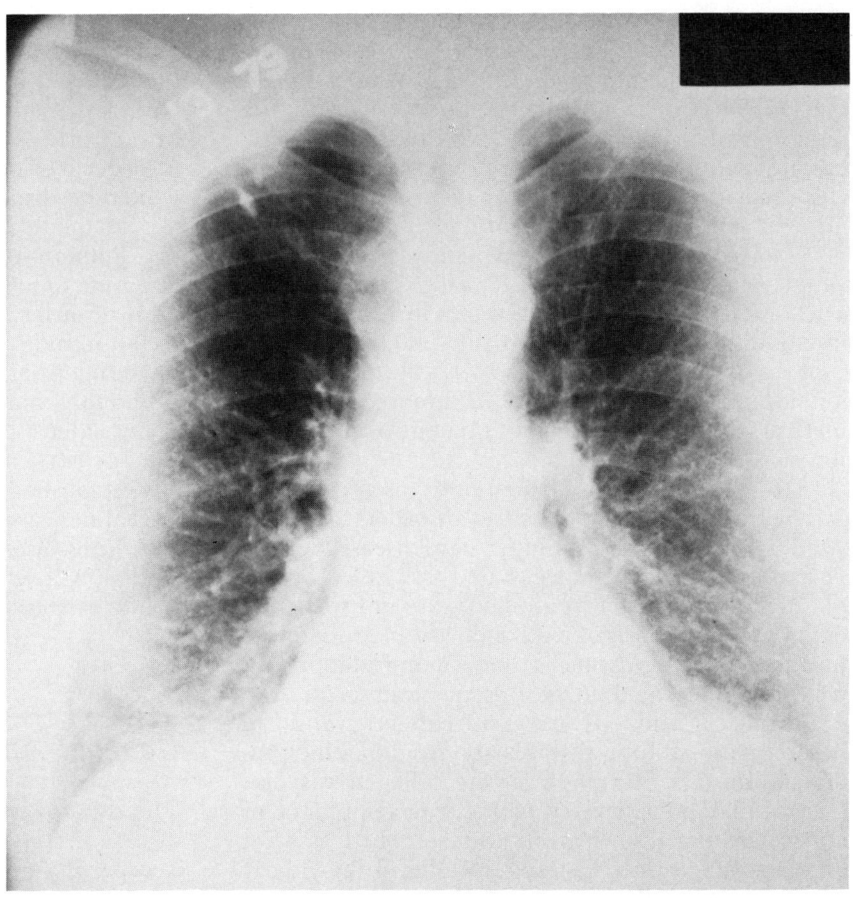

FIGURE 52-1
The chest x ray is of a 65-year-old male with interstitial lung disease associated with rheumatoid arthritis. The x ray shows a diffuse reticulonodular infiltrate which is more prominent in the lower lung zones.

Bronchoalveolar Lavage and Gallium 67 Lung Scans

As noted above, the interstitial lung diseases are characterized by alveolitis, destruction of gas-exchange units, and interstitial fibrosis. Two tests which have been used to obtain more specific information regarding the intensity of the alveolitis and, therefore, the need for therapy are bronchoalveolar lavage and gallium 67 lung scans. In spite of extensive studies, however, these tests have not been shown to provide clinical information any better than that obtained from chest x-rays and pulmonary function studies. Therefore these tests are not recommended for routine use.

General Approach to Elderly Patients with Interstitial Lung Disease

The presence of an interstitial lung disease is usually established with both a chest film and pulmonary function studies. It is imperative to evaluate the patient with a thorough history and physical examination. Although over 100 different types of interstitial lung disease have been described, the most common disorders in the elderly are idiopathic pulmonary fibrosis, interstitial lung diseases associated with the collagen vascular diseases, sarcoidosis, occupational lung diseases, hypersensitivity pneumonitis, and interstitial lung disease caused by drugs and irradiation.

A complete occupational history is especially important in the elderly because exposure at a much younger age to various inorganic dusts, such as silica or asbestos, may not result in a symptomatic lung disease until much later in life. Although a lung biopsy is sometimes required, the diagnosis of occupational lung disease can usually be established with a thorough history. There is no evidence that the natural history of these disorders is altered with the use of corticosteroid and/or cytotoxic therapy. Recurrent infections, especially episodes of bronchitis with production or purulent sputum, are very common in these patients and usually require antibiotic therapy. In addition, patients with silicosis have a high incidence of tuberculous infections; these must be treated, since such infections appear to accelerate the progression of the underlying interstitial disease. (Hypersensitivity pneumonitis in the elderly resulting from the inhalation of organic dust will be discussed in detail in the next section.)

Interstitial lung disease caused by drugs and irradiation may also be identified by a careful history. For example, interstitial lung disease may be caused by a variety of drugs administered to treat various malignancies. The antitumor agents associated with the highest incidence of interstitial lung disease are busulfan and bleomycin. Examples of other types of drugs which may cause interstitial lung disease include various antibiotics (especially nitrofurantoin), propranolol, gold salts, phenytoin, and methysergide. For a complete list, the reader is referred to recent review articles. Therapy of these disorders includes discontinuation of the offending drug and, frequently, a short course of corticosteroids. Local lung irradiation administered to treat various tumors is also routinely associated with the development of interstitial fibrosis.

Diagnosis of the interstitial lung diseases associated with the collagen vascular disorders must be based upon evidence of a multisystem disease. Serologic abnormalities, such as elevated titers of rheumatoid factor or antinuclear antibody, are not sufficient to make the diagnosis of a collagen vascular disease in the absence of compatible systemic manifestations. In this context, elevated titers of rheumatoid factor and/or antinuclear antibody are also frequently found in the occupational lung diseases and in idiopathic pulmonary fibrosis. Although all the collagen vascular diseases may be associated with the development of interstitial lung disorders, the disease which is most often associated with this lung disorder in the elderly is rheumatoid arthritis. In fact, this may be the most common interstitial lung disease in this age group. The interstitial lung disease associated with rheumatoid arthritis is frequently mild in the elderly and in some patients may require no specific therapy. In other patients, however, the untreated disorder may follow a malignant course and require aggressive therapy with corticosteroids and/or cytotoxic agents. The following general guidelines can be utilized to treat the interstitial lung diseases associated with the other collagen vascular disorders:

1. Disorders such as scleroderma and ankylosing spondylitis should not be treated, even in the presence of severe lung disease, since they do not routinely respond to therapy.
2. Disorders such as Wegener's granulomatosis and the polyarteritis nodosa group of vasculitides which are associated with vasculitis of large- or medium-size vessels should be treated with cyclophosphamide. Corticosteroids may also be necessary in these disorders for a short period of time until the disease stabilizes.
3. Corticosteroids are the initial therapy of choice in the other disorders; if the lung disease remains active and progresses in spite of corticosteroid therapy, the patient is then switched to cyclophosphamide.

Idiopathic pulmonary fibrosis is a chronic disorder of unknown etiology which frequently occurs in older individuals. The disorder is limited to the lung, and the diagnosis can be established only after all other causes of interstitial lung disease have been excluded. In most cases, this requires an open-lung biopsy. Corticosteroids are the drugs of choice in this disorder; cyclophosphamide may be used in cases in which the disease progresses while the patient is taking adequate amounts of corticosteroids.

Pulmonary sarcoidosis usually comes to clinical attention in younger patients. However, this is a common disorder, and it is not unusual for it to be detected in older individuals. In contrast to the disease in younger patients, the disease in the elderly is more frequently inactive or end-stage. For this reason, many elderly patients with sarcoidosis are not benefited by corticosteroid therapy. The diagnosis is usually established by transbronchial biopsy, which shows typical noncaseating granulomata. Other granulomatous lung disease (such as tuberculosis) must be excluded before the diagnosis of sarcoidosis can be firmly established.

General Approach to Therapy

The therapy of elderly patients with interstitial lung disease is complicated by the fact that these patients may be very fragile, may have other illnesses, and may be subject to a higher incidence of side effects from corticosteroid and/or cytotoxic therapy. Thus, it is important that therapy results in an improvement in the overall condition of the patient rather than just improvement in the interstitial lung disease. After the diagnosis is established and baseline pulmonary functions and chest radiographs are obtained, it is important to answer the following questions: (1) Is the patient's particular interstitial lung disease likely to respond to therapy? (2) Does the patient have a coexisting extrapulmonary disease which may be significantly aggravated by corticosteroid and/or cytotoxic therapy? (3) Would the patient's overall prognosis or sense of well-being improve were the lung disease to respond to therapy? (4) Is the lung disease sufficiently active to warrant therapy?

The purpose of the first question is to prevent exposure of the patient to corticosteroid and/or cytotoxic therapy for a lung disorder which is unlikely to respond to these agents. For example, the occupational lung diseases resulting from exposure to inorganic particulates and the lung diseases associated with scleroderma and ankylosing spondylitis rarely respond to immunosuppressive therapy, and frequently the overall clinical status of such patients is worsened by these agents.

The second question relates to the fact that there is a high prevalence of cardiovascular disease, systemic hypertension, diabetes mellitus, joint disease, and other disorders in elderly patients. Corticosteroids administered as therapy for an interstitial lung disease may significantly aggravate or accelerate these disease processes. For this reason, in a patient with an extrapulmonary disorder which might be significantly worsened by these agents, the physician might choose not to treat a mild interstitial lung disease with corticosteroids. In patients who require therapy for their lung disease, these considerations are only relative contraindications against therapy, since these complications can usually be managed with other medical therapies.

The third question is related to the prognosis of the patient, independent of the interstitial lung disease. For example, in some elderly patients, an extrapulmonary disorder may be present which will result in their demise in the near future; it would not be prudent to treat with immunosuppressive agents an interstitial lung disorder which will not cause a patient significant problems during his or her life span. In contrast, the patient's quality of life or the severity of the extrapulmonary disorders may be significantly improved by therapy of the lung disease. These are judgments which must be made on an individual basis.

The fourth question is pertinent to the therapy of interstitial lung disease in any patient population and is related to the likelihood that the disease will improve with therapy or progress without therapy.

It should be kept in mind that dyspnea in elderly patients with interstitial lung disease may also be due to pulmonary infections or to extrapulmonary disorders such as congestive heart failure. The sense of well-being of these patients is usually markedly improved by therapy of these associated conditions. In addition, dyspnea or fatigue with exertion commonly occurs in patients with interstitial lung disease because they have a relatively fixed cardiac output and the Pa_{O_2} declines with exercise. This may be ameliorated with supplemental oxygen therapy.

HYPERSENSITIVITY PNEUMONITIS

Hypersensitivity pneumonitis is characterized by an inflammation of the lung parenchyma following inhalation of an organic antigen. The response is limited to the alveoli and terminal airways. A variety of organic antigens have been implicated, including bacteria, saprophytic fungi, and animal danders, and proteins (Table 52-2).

Although most elderly patients will no longer be employed in occupations that would likely expose them to organic antigens found in the workplace, hypersensitivity pneumonitis is still a diagnosis that should be considered among elderly patients with respiratory disease. In addition to occupational sources, sensitizing antigens may be present in heating, air conditioning, or humidifying equipment that has been contaminated with microorganisms. Also, the excreta and proteinaceous material from pigeons, parakeets, parrots, and other domesticated birds can be a source of sensitizing antigen. Finally, elderly patients may suffer from chronic pulmonary symptoms resulting from occupational exposures which occurred many years earlier.

Clinical Features

In the acute form of the disease, respiratory and systemic symptoms develop within 4 to 6 hours of exposure and consist of dyspnea, cough, fevers, chills, malaise, and myalgias. The patient usually appears to be acutely ill, and the pulmonary exam reveals inspiratory crackles, predominantly in the lower lung fields.

TABLE 52-2

Examples of Hypersensitivity Pneumonitis

Disease	Source of Antigen	Antigen
Farmer's lung	Contaminated hay, grain, silage	Thermophilic actinomycetes*
Bird-fancier's or pigeon-breeder's lung	Avian excreta	Parrot, pigeon, parakeet, chicken, dove proteins
Bagassosis	Contaminated bagasse (sugar cane)	Thermophilic actinomycetes
Mushroom worker's lung	Mushroom compost	Thermophilic actinomycetes, other
Humidifier or air-conditioner lung	Contaminated water from humidifiers and air conditioners, others	Thermophilic actinomycetes, *Aureobasidium pullulans*, amoebae
Woodworker's lung	Pine and spruce pulp; oak, cedar, mahogany dusts	Wood dust, *Alternaria*
Sauna taker's lung	Contaminated sauna steam	*A. pullulans*, other
Malt worker's lung	Moldy barley	*Aspergillus fumigatus, Aspergillus clavatus*
Sequoisis	Redwood sawdust	*Aureobasidium, Graphium* sp
Maple bark disease	Maple bark	*Cryptostroma corticale*
Miller's lung	Infested wheat flour	*Sitophilus granarius* (wheat weevil)
Coffee worker's lung	Coffee beans	Coffee-bean dust

*Thermophilic actinomycetes include *Thermoactinomyces vulgaris, T. saccharri, T. viridis, T. candidus*, and *Micropolyspora faeni*.

A chest x ray taken during the acute phase may show a fine nodular, bilateral alveolar filling pattern. Routine laboratory data are nonspecific, although the white blood count may exceed 25,000 with a left shift. Eosinophilia is not usually seen. If measured at the time of the acute illness, pulmonary function studies will show a decreased forced vital capacity (FVC) and forced expiratory volume in 1 second (FEV_1), reduced lung volumes, a decreased diffusing capacity, and hypoxemia. These acute episodes will be followed by resolution of symptoms and normalization of chest x ray, pulmonary function tests, and laboratory abnormalities within 18 to 24 hours of removal from the offending agent. This classic acute form of the disease is rarely seen in elderly patients.

Most often, elderly patients present with the chronic form of hypersensitivity pneumonitis. This form of the disease is not characterized by acute exacerbations of symptoms with reexposure. Instead, these patients present with signs and symptoms similar to those seen in other interstitial lung diseases, including progressive shortness of breath, sputum production, chronic cough, weight loss, and malaise. Pulmonary function studies will show persistent restrictive physiology, and the chest x ray will be consistent with a diffuse interstitial process. Without a careful history and a high index of suspicion, chronic hypersensitivity pneumonitis may be difficult to distinguish from other interstitial lung disorders, especially idiopathic pulmonary fibrosis.

Diagnosis

More than 90 percent of patients with hypersensitivity pneumonitis will have precipitating antibodies directed against the offending agent. Serologic studies, however, have a low degree of specificity for disease. Up to 30 to 40 percent of exposed but asymptomatic individuals will also demonstrate precipitating antibodies. Therefore, a positive serologic study may raise the suspicion of hypersensitivity pneumonitis, but it does not confirm the diagnosis.

During the episodes of acute disease, leukocytosis without eosinophilia is frequently seen. Serum immunoglobulins may be mildly increased, and sometimes the rheumatoid factor may become transiently positive. Erythrocyte sedimentation rate may be normal or slightly increased. Studies of bronchoalveolar lavage fluid from patients with chronic hypersensitivity pneumonitis reveal an increase in total cell numbers and a significant elevation in the percentage of suppressor (OKT-8+) T lymphocytes.

Unfortunately, no single laboratory test or combination of tests is specific for the diagnosis of hypersensitivity pneumonitis. However, this diagnosis can usually be made with relative certainty when an appropriate history is confirmed by positive serology and characteristic chest x ray and pulmonary function abnormalities. If other diagnoses are strongly suspected, an open-lung biopsy may be necessary. This typically demonstrates an interstitial pneumonitis consisting primarily of lymphocytes and plasma cells that infiltrate alveolar walls. Interstitial fibrosis, granulomata, and bronchiolitis obliterans can also be seen.

Therapy and Prognosis

No specific therapy is required for mild forms of acute hypersensitivity pneumonitis. Avoidance of the offending antigen will usually result in resolution of symptoms within 24 hours. More severe attacks, however, may require prednisone as well as routine supportive care. The therapy of chronic hypersensitivity pneumonitis includes both avoidance of antigen and, in most instances, a trial of corticosteroids. Therapy of the chronic form of the disease usually improves symptoms and pulmonary function. Lung function may not return to normal, however, because of the pulmonary fibrosis which is frequently associated with this disorder.

PULMONARY VASCULAR DISEASE

A detailed review of the entire range of pulmonary vascular disease is beyond the scope of this chapter; therefore, the focus will be on two disorders which are commonly seen in the geriatric population, pulmonary embolism and pulmonary hypertension. These disorders are interrelated in that pulmonary embolism can cause both acute and chronic pulmonary hypertension, and pulmonary hypertension and its sequela, right heart failure, can predispose to recurrent thromboembolism.

Pulmonary Hypertension

The pressure in the pulmonary circulation is a result of both blood flow and vascular resistance. Blood flow through the lungs is almost identical to the output of the left ventricle of the heart; yet the mean pulmonary arterial pressure is only about one-seventh of the mean systemic arterial pressure. This implies that resistance in the pulmonary circulation is low in healthy individuals. In addition, when flow increases (as with exercise), pulmonary resistance may decrease further through vasodilatation as well as through recruitment of previously unperfused pulmonary vessels. In spite of this impressive ability to maintain a low pressure in the face of widely varying flow rates, the pressure in the pulmonary circulation can become abnormally elevated when the pulmonary artery systolic pressure exceeds 30 mmHg and the mean pulmonary artery pressure exceeds 20 mmHg.

Etiology

A number of cardiac abnormalities, such as atrial septal defect and ventricular septal defect, will result in pulmonary hypertension through an increase in pulmonary blood flow. These disorders usually become clinically manifest before old age and, therefore, are uncommon causes of newly diagnosed pulmonary hypertension in the geriatric population.

Disorders which result in a passive increase in pulmonary resistance by impeding pulmonary venous drainage also cause pulmonary hypertension. These include disorders such as mitral stenosis and left ventricular failure. Mitral stenosis has become an uncommon cause of pulmonary hypertension as a result of valvular surgery and a decreased incidence of rheumatic fever. For this reason, the most common cause of "passive" pulmonary hypertension in elderly patients is left ventricular failure, most commonly due to ischemic or hypertensive cardiomyopathy.

There are a number of other disorders which cause pulmonary hypertension by obstructing or obliterating the pulmonary vasculature. Pulmonary thromboembolism can result in both acute and chronic pulmonary hypertension. This will not occur, however, until 50 to 60 percent of the cross-sectional area of the circulation is obstructed in a previously normal lung. Obliterative vascular changes can occur in a number of other disorders associated with pulmonary vasculitis, interstitial lung disease, or emphysema.

Increased pulmonary resistance can also result from pulmonary vasoconstriction. Clearly, the most important pulmonary artery vasoconstrictor is alveolar hypoxemia. This response accounts for the majority, if not all, of the pulmonary hypertension seen with disorders such as sleep apnea syndrome and the obesity hypoventilation (pickwickian) syndrome. A number of disorders cause pulmonary hypertension through more than one mechanism. In diseases such as emphysema and pulmonary fibrosis, both hypoxemia vasoconstriction and destruction of the pulmonary vasculature may occur.

Clinical Findings

Dyspnea, especially with exertion, is usually the earliest symptom noted by patients with pulmonary hypertension. This dyspnea is often attributable to the underlying disorder which caused the pulmonary hypertension (e.g., emphysema, congestive heart failure, or interstitial lung disease). However, pulmonary hypertension per se can also cause dyspnea, although the exact mechanism for this is not known. Fatigue is also frequently present and is probably a consequence of the impaired cardiac output. Anginalike chest pain is sometimes noted and may occur as a result of right ventricular ischemia. Due to the high intercapillary pressures, microvascular aneurysms can form which protrude into the alveolar lumen. Rupture of these vessels can cause hemoptysis and/or pulmonary infiltrates. Finally, hoarseness is associated with severe, long-standing pulmonary hypertension. This is probably due to pressure on the left recurrent laryngeal nerve as it passes between the aorta and a dilated pulmonary artery.

The chronic load imposed on the right ventricle by prolonged pulmonary hypertension can lead to right ventricular hypertrophy and dilatation. Right ventricular failure may ensue if the degree of pulmonary hypertension is severe. Unfortunately, the findings of chronic pulmonary hypertension are frequently detected late in the course of the disease, after cardiac dysfunction has occurred. If right ventricular failure develops, there is usually evidence of tricuspid insufficiency, peripheral edema, and/or hepatic enlargement.

There are a number of tests which can support a clinical impression of pulmonary hypertension. An electrocardiogram may reveal changes consistent with right ventricular strain and/or hypertrophy. Right ventricular dilatation and an increased width of the descending branch of the right pulmonary artery may also be noted on chest x ray. The chest x ray may also reveal changes in the lung parenchyma which suggest a cause of the pulmonary hypertension (e.g., emphysema, interstitial lung disease, or congestive heart failure). There are no commonly used noninvasive tests, however, that allow for accurate quantitation of the degree of pulmonary hypertension. This requires right heart catheterization and direct measurement of pulmonary artery pressures.

Therapy

In all cases of pulmonary hypertension, the major therapeutic effort should be directed toward treating any underlying disease which contributes to the elevated pulmonary pressures. For example, recurrent pulmonary emboli should be treated with anticoagulation and/or vena caval interruption if indicated; patients with left ventricular dysfunction should receive appropriate therapy of their congestive heart failure; the pulmonary vasculitides usually improve with immunosuppressive therapy; mitral valve surgery may be indicated for those with mitral stenosis; morbidly obese patients often are helped by procedures designed for weight reduction; and patients with hypoxemia should receive supplemental oxygen.

Of the currently available pulmonary vasodilators, oxygen is clearly the most efficacious. It can not only decrease pulmonary vascular resistance through vasodilation but also decrease blood viscosity when the viscosity is caused by secondary polycythemia. Oxygen therapy has also been shown to improve neuropsychiatric symptoms and long-term survival. Therefore, it is essential that all hypoxemia patients receive adequate oxygen therapy. Although there have been many studies which have examined other potential pulmonary vasodilators, no agent has yet been shown to be consistently effective. In part this may be due to the fact that subsets of patients likely to benefit from vasodilator therapy have not been clearly identified. Although a trial of vasodilators may be warranted in selected individuals, these drugs are not without significant risks, and, initially, they require careful invasive monitoring to document both safety and efficacy.

Pulmonary Embolism

Pulmonary embolism is a major cause of morbidity and mortality in elderly patients. This is not primarily due to a lack of effective treatment but, in large part, stems from failure to consider the diagnosis and institute early therapy. In this regard, if a patient survives the first hour of a pulmonary embolism and appropriate therapy is instituted, the mortality rate is about 8 percent. Unfortunately, pulmonary embolism is not diagnosed in many patients, and in this undiagnosed group the mortality rate may be as high as 30 percent. An even more profound impact on mortality would be realized if patients at risk for the development of pulmonary embolism were identified and prophylactic therapy instituted before the development of venous thrombosis.

More than 90 percent of pulmonary emboli originate from the deep venous system of the pelvis and thighs. Rarely if ever do venous thrombi of the superficial venous system embolize. Calf vein thrombi, however, can propagate to the deep veins of the thigh in 5 to 20 percent of cases and may result in embolic disease of the lung. Three abnormalities commonly predispose patients to develop venous thrombosis: venous stasis, injury to vascular endothelium, and alterations in coagulability. Of these, venous stasis is, in most patients, the most important. As a group, elderly patients have a greater incidence of pulmonary emboli than do younger patients. Many predisposing factors are frequently present in the elderly, including congestive heart failure, chronic venous insufficiency, and immobility associated with various underlying disease states. Therefore, prophylaxis to prevent the development of venous thrombosis is especially important in the geriatric population.

Clinical Features

The classic presentation of pulmonary embolism includes the sudden onset of shortness of breath, apprehension, pleuritic chest pain, hemoptysis, and a pleural friction rub occurring in the setting of thrombophlebitis. With massive pulmonary emboli, signs of acute cor pulmonale may also be seen. More often, however, pulmonary embolism occurs with minimal signs and symptoms. The classic presentation of pulmonary embolism occurs in less than 20 percent of patients. Additionally, symptoms are usually nonspecific and can be confused with those of other disorders such as congestive heart failure, acute myocardial infarction, pneumonia, or atelectasis. One of the most common presentations is unexplained tachypnea and/or shortness of breath. Other findings which may be present are fever and bronchospasm.

Diagnosis

Pulmonary embolism can be difficult to diagnose with certainty. As noted, the signs and symptoms and physical findings may be nonspecific and frequently minimal. Although nonspecific, the following studies are frequently obtained as part of the evaluation for pulmonary embolism. The white blood cell count may be mildly elevated but rarely exceeds 15,000/mm^3. Characteristically, there is a decrease in Pa_{O_2}, although 10 to 15 percent of patients will have a normal Pa_{O_2}. Not infrequently, the Pa_{CO_2} will be decreased due to hyperventilation.

The chest x ray may reveal abnormalities; however, these are often subtle and nonspecific. They include platelike atelectases, an elevated diaphragm, pleural effusion, decreased vascular markings on the affected side (Westermark's sign), and infiltrates such as the classic Hampton's hump (a homogeneous, wedge-shaped, pleural-based density which extends toward the hilum and results from pulmonary infarction).

Nonspecific changes are usually present on the electrocardiogram, which may be abnormal, at least transiently, in most patients with acute pulmonary embolism. In the appropriate clinical setting, findings compatible with acute right ventricular strain are strongly suggestive of the presence of pulmonary emboli.

A more useful test is the perfusion lung scan. When multiple views of the lung are used, a negative perfusion scan virtually eliminates the diagnosis of pulmonary embolism. Frequently, however, some abnormality in perfusion exists in the elderly; therefore, this study must be supplemented with a ventilation scan. A high-probability ventilation/perfusion scan is said to occur when at least a segmental or larger perfusion defect occurs in an area of normal ventilation (a V/Q mismatch). A high-probability V/Q scan correctly diagnoses the presence of pulmonary embolism in more than 85 percent of patients with angiographically proven pulmonary emboli. In combination with a good clinical history for pulmonary embolus, a high-probability V/Q scan is frequently sufficient evidence upon which to base treatment. The role of a low-probability scan in establishing a diagnosis is less clear. If the clinical suspicion of pulmonary embolus is low, a low-probability scan may be sufficient to exclude pulmonary emboli. If the clinical suspicion is high, however, further diagnostic studies are needed to exclude or establish the diagnosis. These studies could include contrast venography or impedance plethysmography of the lower extremities. If these tests are normal, anticoagulation may be warranted.

Pulmonary angiography remains the gold standard for the diagnosis of pulmonary emboli. The serious nature of undiagnosed and untreated pulmonary emboli—as well as the risks of therapy—justify the use of pulmonary angiography in many circumstances. These include the following situations: (1) when the clinical impression is consistent with pulmonary embolism but the V/Q scan is of low or indeterminate probability; (2) when there is a probable pulmonary embolism based on V/Q scan and clinical history but either the risk of anticoagulation is great or vena caval interruption is being considered; (3) in the case of probable massive pulmonary embolism when surgical embolectomy or thrombolytic therapy is being considered; and (4) when there is a previous, unconfirmed diagnosis of "recurrent pulmonary emboli" and the V/Q scan is of a low or indeterminate probability.

Treatment

Once the diagnosis of pulmonary embolism is confirmed, the treatment is usually intravenous heparin followed by a course of oral anticoagulation. Heparin therapy is continued for 7 to 10 days, and the rate of infusion is adjusted to maintain an activated partial thromboplastin time at a value of 1½ to 2 times the normal laboratory control range. Oral anticoagulation is started 1 to 2 days after the initiation of heparin therapy. Recent studies have shown that, as compared with more intensive therapy, when oral anticoagulation therapy is monitored with a prothrombin time that uses rabbit brain thromboplastin (as is the case with most labs in the United States), adequate anticoagulation with fewer bleeding complications can be obtained when the prothrombin time is maintained between 1¼ and 1½ of control values. If the underlying problem which led to the initial venous thrombosis is corrected, 6 weeks of oral anticoagulation is probably sufficient; otherwise, at least 3 months of oral anticoagulation should be used. Exceptions are those individuals who have ongoing risk factors such as antithrombin III deficiency, protein C deficiency, underlying adenocarcinoma, or a history of two or more episodes of venous thrombosis and/or pulmonary embolism. Anticoagulation may need to be continued for an indefinite period of time in these individuals.

Other methods of therapy are used in certain instances. For the patient with massive pulmonary embolism that results in hemodynamic deterioration, thrombolytic agents such as streptokinase or urokinase may be warranted if there is no contraindication to their use. The role of the newer fibrin-specific agents, such as tissue plasminogen activator, is still being defined. Alternatively, pulmonary embolectomy may be considered in patients with massive pulmonary emboli which have caused a marked decrease in cardiac output and right heart failure. Additionally, vena caval devices, such as a Greenfield filter, are used in settings of recurrent pulmonary emboli while the patient is receiving adequate anticoagulation, development of bleeding or other complications referable to anticoagulation therapy, or following surgical pulmonary thrombectomy. The greatest impact on morbidity and mortality in elderly patients, however, could be achieved with the institution of timely prophylactic therapy to prevent venous thrombosis.

ADDITIONAL READING

Interstitial Lung Disease

Becklake MR: Asbestos-related diseases of the lung and other organs: Their epidemiology and implications for clinical practice. *Am Rev Respir Dis* 114:187, 1976.

Carrington CB, Gaensler EA: Clinical-pathologic approach to diffuse infiltrative lung disease, in Thurlbeck WM, Abell MR (eds): *The Lung: Structure, Function and Disease.* Baltimore, Williams & Wilkins, 1978, pp 58–87.

Carrington CB et al: Natural history and treated course of usual and desquamative interstitial pneumonia. *N Engl J Med* 298:801, 1978.

Crystal RG et al: Idiopathic pulmonary fibrosis: Clinical, histologic, radiographic, physiologic, scintigraphic, cytologic, and biochemical aspects. *Ann Intern Med* 85:769, 1976.

Crystal RG et al: Interstitial lung disease: Current concepts of pathogenesis, staging, and therapy. *Am J Med* 70:542, 1981.

Fishman AP: *Pulmonary Diseases and Disorders,* 2d ed. New York, McGraw-Hill, 1988.

Fraser RG, Pare JAP: *Diagnosis of Diseases of the Chest,* 2d ed, vol 3. Philadelphia, Saunders, 1979.

Hunninghake GW, Fauci AS: State of the art—Pulmonary disorders associated with the collagen vascular diseases. *Am Rev Respir Dis* 119:471, 1979.

Hunninghake GW et al: Inflammatory and immune processes in the human lung in health and disease: Evaluation by bronchoalveolar lavage. *Am J Pathol* 97:149, 1979.

Braunwald W et al (eds): *Harrison's Principles of Internal Medicine,* 12th ed. New York, McGraw-Hill, 1991.

Morgan WKC, Lapp NL: Respiratory disease in coal miners. *Am Rev Respir Dis* 113:531, 1976.

Spencer H: *Pathology of the Lung,* vols 1 and 2. Philadelphia, Saunders, 1977.

Wyngaarden JB, Smith LH (eds): *Textbook of Medicine,* vols 1 and 2. Philadelphia, Saunders, 1982.

Hypersensitivity Pneumonitis

Braun SR et al: Farmer's lung disease: Long-term clinical and physiologic outcome. *Am Rev Respir Dis* 119:185, 1979.

Emanuel DA, Kryda MJ: Farmer's lung disease. *Clin Rev Allergy* 1:509, 1983.

Richerson HB: Hypersensitivity pneumonitis—Pathology and pathogenesis. *Clin Rev Allergy* 1:469, 1983.

Stankus RP, Salvaggio JE: Hypersensitivity pneumonitis. *Clin Chest Med* 4:55, 1983.

Pulmonary Vascular Disease

Dalen JE, Hirsh J et al: ACCP-NHLBI National Conference on Antithrombotic Therapy. *Chest* 89(suppl):1S, 1986.

Hirsh J et al: Venous thromboembolism: Prevention, diagnosis and treatment. *Chest* 89(suppl):369S, 1986.

Keller CA et al: Pulmonary hypertension in chronic obstructive pulmonary disease: Multivariate analysis. *Chest* 90:185, 1986.

Matthay RA, Bergen HJ: Cardiovascular performance in chronic obstructive pulmonary disease. *Med Clin North Am* 65:489, 1981.

Nocturnal Oxygen Therapy Trial Group: Continuous nocturnal oxygen therapy in hypoxemic chronic obstructive lung disease. *Ann Intern Med* 93:391, 1980.

Rosenow EC et al: Pulmonary embolism. *Mayo Clin Proc* 56:161, 1981.

Rounds S, Hill NS: Pulmonary hypertensive disease. *Chest* 85:397, 1984.

Sharma GVRD, Sasalova AA: Diagnosis and treatment of pulmonary embolism. *Med Clin North Am* 63(1):239, 1979.

Chapter 53

LUNG CANCER

Michael C. Perry

EPIDEMIOLOGY/PATHOGENESIS

Lung cancer is now the most common cause of death due to cancer in both men and women. In 1993, 170,000 cases are anticipated; 100,000 in men and 70,000 in women.[1] The majority of these patients (93,000 men and 56,000 women, or a total of 88 percent) will die of their disease, since few are diagnosed early, when there is an opportunity for cure. Historically a male-dominated disease, the increased frequency of smoking among women has produced a predictable lung cancer increase in females.[2] The majority of cases occur in patients above age 50, with the greatest prevalence in the 65-and-older age group.[3]

Although some cases are attributable to other carcinogens—such as radon, nickel, chromium, and asbestos—85 to 90 percent of lung cancers are directly related to tobacco exposure via cigarette smoking. Even passive exposure to cigarette smoke increases the risk of lung cancer. The relative risk of death from lung cancer is directly related to the degree of cigarette abuse, and 15 or more years must elapse after a person stops smoking for the risk to approach that of nonsmokers.

SCREENING

Two methods are available for the early detection of lung cancer—pooled sputum cytology and chest x rays. To date, however, prospective randomized studies in high-risk populations (typically males over the age of 40 who were heavy smokers) using either or both techniques have not enhanced our ability to diagnose lung cancer at early, curable stages.[4] Consequently, neither the American Cancer Society nor the National Cancer Institute recommends routine screening for lung cancer.

CLINICAL PRESENTATION

In contrast to most other tumor sites, where a single histology is predominant, lung cancer is striking because of the diversity of tumor types (Table 53-1). Four histologic patterns—adenocarcinoma (including bronchoalveolar carcinoma), large cell, squamous cell (epidermoid), and small cell (formerly called oat cell)—comprise the majority of lung cancers. Because of its

TABLE 53-1

Lung Cancer Characteristics

	Adenocarcinoma	Large Cell	Squamous Cell	Small Cell
Frequency	25%	15%	35%	25%
Growth rate	Variable	Slow	Slow	Rapid
Location	Peripheral	Peripheral	Hilar/perihilar	Hilar/perihilar
Hormone production	Rare	Rare	PTH	Multiple
Optimal therapy	Surgery	Surgery	Surgery	Chemotherapy/radiotherapy

rapid growth, high frequency of distant metastases, and sensitivity to both chemotherapy and radiation therapy, small cell lung cancer (SCLC) is considered separately from the three other types. Collectively, the others are known as non-small cell lung cancers (NSCLC), and although there are many cases easily categorized as representing a specific histology, there are others where the distinction between the three types is not clear. Bronchoalveolar carcinoma is often detected in a setting of prior fibrotic lung disease, such as idiopathic pulmonary fibrosis, scleroderma, or asbestosis. Mixed histologies, most often the combination of large cell–small cell, are also seen.

Elderly patients seem to have more localized disease at diagnosis than middle-aged patients, and a distinct difference in the histologic types is seen. The proportion of squamous cell carcinoma rises and that of adenocarcinoma and SCLC falls with increasing age.[5] The combination of these two factors implies a greater likelihood that older patients will have more cases of resectable, and thus potentially curable, disease.

Local, Regional, and Metastatic Disease

Patients with lung cancer may present with either local, regional, or metastatic disease (Table 53-2). The symptoms and signs of local cancer depend upon the tumor's location—central or peripheral. Central tumors, which are often squamous or small cell in histology, may produce cough, hemoptysis, wheezing, stridor, dyspnea, and obstructive pneumonitis due to bronchial obstruction. Peripheral tumors, most often large cell or adenocarcinoma histologic types, also produce cough and dyspnea; they may also cause pain from pleural or chest wall involvement or may cavitate to form a lung abscess (although squamous cell carcinoma is the most common type to cavitate).

Depending upon their location, regional lung tumors may produce the superior vena cava syndrome, recurrent laryngeal nerve paralysis with resultant hoarseness, phrenic nerve paralysis with diaphragmatic elevation and dyspnea, Horner's syndrome, Pancoast's syndrome, obstruction of the trachea or esophagus, pericardial involvement with effusion and/or tamponade, pleural effusions, and lymphangitic metastases.

Metastases may occur in multiple sites, but bone, bone marrow, liver, lung, lymph nodes, and brain are most common. Paraneoplastic syndromes as a result of lung cancer include the production of ectopic parathyroid hormone (PTH) or adrenocorticotropic hormone (ACTH), the syndrome of inappropriate antidiuretic hormone (SIADH), the Eaton-Lambert syndrome, Trousseau's syndrome, and hypercalcemia. Hypercoagulable states and hypertrophic pulmonary osteoarthropathy occur most often with adenocarcinomas and hypercalcemia most commonly with squamous cell cancer.

DIAGNOSIS

A change in the usual symptoms of a chronic smoker is often an indication for a chest x ray, which, if abnormal, leads to further evaluation. Because both benign and other malignant diseases may mimic carcinoma of the lung, histologic or cytologic confirmation is essential. This can be accomplished by examination of sputum cytology or by fiberoptic bronchoscopy, which provides direct visualization of the bronchial tree, plus washings and brushings for pathologic examination. Fiberoptic bronchoscopy is well tolerated by elderly patients, and age alone should not exclude an appropriate diagnostic evaluation.[6,7]

Diagnostic tissue may also be obtained from other sites such as supraclavicular nodes, pleural effusions, or hepatomegaly. Transthoracic needle biopsy directed by computed tomography (CT) is also an option.

A sputum cytology specimen positive for malignancy can be relied upon with approximately 90 percent accuracy, but distinction of the individual histologic type is not as accurate, and discordant results are often seen between cytologic and histologic (obtained bronchoscopically or by needle biopsy) specimens.

TABLE 53-2

Signs and Symptoms of Lung Cancer

Local				
Central	**Peripheral**	**Regional**	**Distant**	**Paraneoplastic**
Cough	Cough	Superior vena cava obstruction	Bone pain	Ectopic PTH
Pain	Pain	Hoarseness (laryngeal nerve paralysis)	CNS changes	SIADH
Hemoptysis	Dyspnea	Elevated hemidiaphragm (phrenic nerve paralysis)		Ectopic ACTH
Dyspnea		Horner's syndrome		Clubbing
Wheezing		Pancoast's syndrome		Eaton-Lambert syndrome
Pneumonia				Trousseau's syndrome
				Pleural effusion
				Hypercalcemia

STAGING

The new international TNM (tumor, node, metastasis) staging system is usually used for NSCLC (Table 53-3). There are now five stages, 0 through IV, reflecting increasing extent/dissemination of disease.[8] To quote from the summary of that article:

> The new international proposal for staging lung cancer has five stages of disease, including a *Stage 0,* that provide for the classification of six groups of patients who have similar prognostic expectations and therapeutic options. *Stage I* includes only patients with the best prognostic expectations—those with T1 or T2 tumors and no evidence of metastases. *Stage II* disease includes those patients with a primary tumor classification of T1 or T2 and metastasis to the intrapulmonary (including hilar) lymph nodes. *Stage IIIa* disease designates those patients, usually within the realm of the surgical oncologist, with extrapulmonary extension of the primary tumor and/or ipsilateral mediastinal lymph node metastasis. *Stage IIIb* includes patients with more extensive extrapulmonary involvement than in the potentially operable group, those having malignant pleural effusion and those with metastasis to the contralateral mediastinum, hilum, or supraclavicular and scalene nodes. *Stage IV* is reserved for patients with metastasis to distant sites.

Stage 0 indicates an occult carcinoma with positive sputum cytology without evidence of a primary tumor, regional lymph node metastases, or distant metastases.

Although the TNM system is also appropriate for SCLC, it is usually replaced by a simpler designation of "limited" or "extensive" disease. Limited disease is defined by involvement of one lung, the mediastinum, and ipsilateral or contralateral supraclavicular lymph nodes or both (i.e., disease that could be encompassed in a single radiation therapy port). Spread beyond the lung, mediastinum, and supraclavicular lymph nodes—such as a positive pleural effusion, bone scan, bone marrow biopsy, liver scan, or brain scan—is considered extensive disease.

The NSCLC staging procedures are targeted at determining whether or not the tumor is potentially surgically resectable. The advent of chest CT scans has greatly enhanced this process by permitting better assessment of disease extent, particularly in the mediastinum. The presence of the superior vena cava syndrome, recurrent laryngeal nerve paralysis, Horner's syndrome, or pleural effusions usually (especially if cytologically positive) indicates advanced disease not suitable for surgery. If bronchoscopy indicates a lesion more than 2 cm distal to the carina and no other contraindication to surgery exists, mediastinoscopy is indicated for right-sided lesions and a Chamberlain procedure for left-sided lesions. The finding of positive mediastinal adenopathy by these procedures is usually indicative of a very low chance of cure with surgery. Other tests, such as radionuclide bone scans as well as abdominal and brain CT scans, are primarily reserved for patients with signs or symptoms referable to that area.

Since SCLC is considered to be disseminated at diagnosis, staging is aimed at the baseline determination of visible metastases for future follow-up and disease classification into limited or extensive categories. The workup includes a CT scan of the chest through the adrenal glands (thus including the liver), CT scan of the brain (looking for occult brain metastases), radionuclide bone scan, and bone marrow aspirate and bilateral biopsies. Serum chemistries to look for electrolyte abnormalities, evaluation of renal and hepatic function, and hematologic profiles are also routine, as is an electrocardiogram (ECG).

TREATMENT MODALITIES

Surgery

Of the three modalities currently in use for the therapy of lung cancer—surgery, radiation therapy, and chemotherapy—surgery remains the only consistently curative therapy and for NSCLC patients should be the primary consideration. Unfortunately, only a minority of patients are surgical candidates because of small cell histology, disseminated disease (stage IV) at presentation, locally advanced disease not permitting complete resection (typically stage IIIB), or complicating medical illnesses, such as chronic obstructive pulmonary disease or cardiac disease. Patients who remain potential candidates for curative surgery should have this alternative aggressively pursued.

Surgery for SCLC can be considered in two settings: peripheral nodules and as part of a multimodality approach. Peripheral nodules or "coin lesions" are often found to be SCLCs only after resection. Such patients should receive postoperative chemotherapy and/or radiotherapy. A minority of SCLC patients are candidates for surgery after chemotherapy (with or without radiotherapy) has produced a partial or complete response. The limitations of such surgery are similar to those outlined above for NSCLC, and only about 10 to 15 percent of patients are potentially resectable.

The ability of a patient to tolerate surgical resection can be assessed by pulmonary function tests, other physiologic parameters, and performance status. If the forced expiratory volume in 1 second (FEV_1) is greater than 2.5 liters, most patients can tolerate pneumonectomy; if it is less than 1 liter, the patient is usually inoperable. Between 1.1 and 2.4 liters, a lobectomy is usually tolerated. These factors are modified by the patient's cardiac status and other illnesses. The surgical goal is to leave the patient with an FEV_1 of at least 0.8 liters postoperatively. The use of preoperative FEV_1 and assessment of regional ventilation (by radionuclide lung scan) allows preopera-

TABLE 53-3

Revised TNM Definitions and Stage Groupings for Carcinomas of the Lung*

T	*Primary Tumor*
TX	Tumor proven by the presence of malignant cells in bronchopulmonary secretions, but not visualized roentgenographically or bronchoscopically; or any tumor that cannot be assessed as in a pretreatment staging.
T0	No evidence of primary tumor.
T1S	Carcinoma in situ.
T1	A tumor that is 3 cm in greatest dimension, surrounded by lung or visceral pleural, and without evidence of invasion proximal to a lobar bronchus at bronchoscopy.†
T2	A tumor more than 3 cm in greatest dimension, or a tumor of any size that either invades the visceral pleura or has associated atelectasis or obstructive pneumonitis extending to the hilar region. At bronchoscopy, the proximal extent of demonstrable tumor must be within a lobar bronchus or at least 2 cm distal to the carina. Any associated atelectasis or obstructive pneumonitis must involve less than an entire lung.
T3	A tumor of any size with direct extension into the chest wall (including superior sulcus tumors), diaphragm, or the mediastinal pleura or pericardium without involving the heart, great vessels, trachea, esophagus, or vertebral body; or a tumor in the main bronchus within 2 cm of the carina without involving the carina; or associated atelectasis or obstructive pneumonitis of the entire lung.
T4	A tumor of any size with direct invasion of the mediastinum or involving the heart, great vessels, trachea, esophagus, vertebral body or carina; or the presence of malignant pleural effusion.‡
N	*Nodal Involvement*
N0	No demonstrable metastasis to regional lymph nodes.
N1	Metastasis to lymph nodes in the peribronchial or the ipsilateral hilar region, or both, including direct extension.
N2	Metastasis to ipsilateral mediastinal lymph nodes and subcarinal lymph nodes.
N3	Metastasis to contralateral mediastinal lymph nodes, contralateral hilar lymph nodes, ipsilateral or contralateral scalene or supraclavicular lymph nodes.
M	*Distant Metastasis.*
M0	No known distant metastasis.
M1	Distant metastasis present—specify site(s).

Stage Groupings

TNM Classification			Stage
TX	N0	M0	Occult carcinoma
T1S	Carcinoma in situ		Stage 0
T1	N0	M0	Stage I
T2	N0	M0	
T1	N1	M0	Stage II
T2	N1	M0	
T3	N0	M0	Stage IIIA
T3	N1	M0	
T1–3	N2	M0	
T4	N (any)	M0	Stage IIIB
T (any)	N3	M0	
T (any)	N (any)	M1	Stage IV

*Modified from Mountain.[8]

†T1: The uncommon superficial tumor of any size with its invasive component limited to the bronchial wall which may extend proximal to the main bronchus is classified as T1.

‡T4: Most pleural effusions associated with lung cancer are due to tumor. There are, however, some few patients in whom cytopathological examination of pleural fluid (on more than one specimen) is negative for tumor, the fluid is not bloody and is not an exudate. In such cases where elements and clinical judgment dictate that the effusion is not related to the tumor, such patients should be staged T1, T2, or T3, excluding effusion as a staging element.

tive prediction of maximum resection, especially in high-risk patients such as the elderly.

A recent review quoted operative mortality rates of 6.2 percent for pneumonectomy, 2.9 percent for lobectomy, and 1.4 percent for lesser procedures such as segmentectomies.[9] In this review, older patients did have higher operative mortality rates, although others have reported that advanced age does not adversely affect prognosis following thoracotomy for lung cancer.[10]

Performance status is the single most important determinant of the patient's prognosis. Simply stated, ambulatory patients (Zubrod scores of 0, 1, or 2 or Karnofsky scores of 70 percent or greater) survive longer than nonambulatory patients. For NSCLC patients, advanced disease stage and weight loss (greater than 10 percent of body weight) are adverse prognostic factors. For SCLC patients, extensive stage, male sex, increased age, elevated serum lactate dehydrogenase (LDH), elevated serum alkaline phosphatase, and hyponatremia are significant adverse prognostic factors.

Radiation Therapy

Definitive radiation therapy in patients with regional NSCLC results in approximately a 5 percent cure rate, with most patients dying of disseminated disease.[11] Although it produces few long-term cures, radiation therapy is invaluable for the palliation of hemoptysis, obstructive pneumonia, and pain. Its use in stages II and IIIa is not yet established, although a case can be made for the inclusion of radiation therapy following surgery in a multimodal approach, perhaps with adjuvant chemotherapy.

SCLC, on the other hand, is quite sensitive to radiation therapy, which, in conjunction with chemotherapy, is now routinely administered to patients with limited disease.[12,13] The radiation therapy port or field includes the tumor, the mediastinal nodes, and often the supraclavicular lymph nodes. The role of prophylactic cranial radiation (PCI) is less clear. It is usually reserved for patients who have demonstrated a complete response to therapy. It may reduce the incidence of brain metastases but does not clearly improve survival.

Chemotherapy

Several generalizations can be made regarding lung cancer chemotherapy in the elderly: tumors are not necessarily more resistant in the elderly, physiologic age-related changes often necessitate changes in treatment to avoid toxicity, and there is increased toxicity due to some agents, such as doxorubicin, vincristine, and cisplatin.[14]

NSCLC is relatively insensitive to chemotherapy, with reported response rates of 25 to 40 percent (Table 53-4). Several agents are capable of producing response rates of 15 percent or greater, and in combination some studies reported response rates approaching 40 percent.[15] Some physicians regard such therapy as investigational, however, and opt for "best supportive care" (BSC). Nevertheless, several randomized trials of chemotherapy versus BSC have favored chemotherapy, although the difference was not great.[16] Since many patients either present with disseminated disease or develop it during their course, there are many candidates for such therapy. This is an area of active research.[17]

The situation is quite different in SCLC with multiple active agents and combinations. In limited disease, it is not uncommon to see response rates of greater than 80 percent; even in extensive disease, response rates of greater than 50 percent are common. With combination chemotherapy, complete response rates, a necessary requirement for cure, average 50 percent for limited disease and 30 percent for extensive disease. To date there is no single regimen that has proven to be superior to the others and also no clear evidence that alternating non–cross-resistant therapy adds to combination therapy. Combinations

TABLE 53-4

Single Agent and Combination Chemotherapy Activity in Lung Cancer

Non-Small Cell		*Small Cell*	
Single Agents	**Combinations**	**Single Agents**	**Combinations**
Carboplatin	CAP	Carboplatin	ACE
Cisplatin (P)	EP	Cisplatin (P)	CAV
Cyclophosphamide (C)	MVbP	Cyclophosphamide (C)	EP
Doxorubicin (Adriamycin)(A)		Doxorubicin (Adriamycin)(A)	MACC (Nu)
Etoposide (E)		Etoposide (E)	PACE
Ifosfamide (I)		Ifosfamide (I)	VdP
Mitomycin (M)		Lomustine (CCNU)	
Vinblastine (Vb)		Methotrexate (M)	
Vindesine (Vd)		Vincristine (V)	
		Vindesine (Vd)	

of doxorubicin (Adriamycin), cyclophosphamide, and etoposide (ACE); ACE plus cisplatin (PACE); vincristine, doxorubicin (Adriamycin), and cyclophosphamide (VAC); or etoposide and cisplatin (EP) are currently in common use.[18]

Because of fears of increased toxicity, many physicians elect not to treat elderly patients. Etoposide as a single agent orally appears to be both tolerable and effective in SCLC patients, with a complete response rate of 17 percent and an overall response rate of 79 percent in such patients.[19] Others have used lower doses with less toxicity.[20] Oral etoposide promises to become a standard in this setting.

TREATMENT BY STAGE AND HISTOLOGY

Non-Small Cell (Adenocarcinoma, Large Cell, and Squamous Cell)

Stage I These patients should be considered for surgery—ideally lobectomy rather than pneumonectomy if technically feasible—as the primary modality of therapy if their pulmonary status and coexistent illnesses permit.

Stage II Treatment recommendations are similar to those of stage I.

Stage IIIA These patients are usually considered borderline surgically resectable, and a recent study has suggested that the addition of chemotherapy to radiotherapy improves long-term survival.[21] Confirmatory studies are currently under way.

Stage IIIB Such patients are not resectable, and current research efforts are aimed at developing the best combinations of radiation therapy and chemotherapy to treat both local disease and distant metastases. Following such therapy, some patients may become candidates for surgical resection.

Stage IV Treatment choices are either best supportive care or chemotherapy, depending upon joint patient and physician decision. Radiotherapy may be useful for palliation of painful lesions, obstructive pneumonitis, or hemoptysis.

Current research strategies include the use of adjuvant chemotherapy for stages I through III; multimodal therapy (preoperative chemotherapy and/or radiotherapy) prior to surgery in stage III disease; and the development of new chemotherapeutic agents in stage IV disease.

Small Cell

Limited Disease Combination chemotherapy is the mainstay of therapy, and there is general agreement that radiotherapy to the primary tumor and mediastinum adds to disease control and survival.[12,13] Many oncologists utilize prophylactic cranial irradiation in patients who are complete responders.

Extensive Disease At this time, radiation therapy has a limited role in extensive SCLC, and combination chemotherapy is the best available therapy for most patients. Elderly patients may be candidates for single-agent oral etoposide.

SPECIAL PROBLEMS

Pancoast (Superior Sulcus) Tumors

These carcinomas develop peripherally in the apex of the lung and invade the superior pulmonary sulcus. Typically, they cause symptoms of pain in the shoulder, along the vertebral border of the scapula, and down the arm. As they extend into the thoracic inlet, they invade the sympathetic chain and stellate ganglion, causing Horner's syndrome. If the tumor is relatively confined and there is no evidence of distant spread, the current treatment is preoperative radiation therapy followed by en bloc resection of the upper lobe and involved ribs.

Superior Vena Cava Syndrome

About 80 percent of cases of the superior vena cava syndrome are caused by malignancy, and carcinoma of the lung—particularly small cell carcinoma—accounts for the majority of these. The syndrome consists of edema of the face and neck, with dilated veins in the neck and upper torso. Although considered by some to be a medical emergency, it is in fact only an "urgency." If the patient's condition permits, a rapid search for histologic confirmation of the diagnosis should be sought (as above), followed by appropriate treatment. If the patient is clearly deteriorating, emergency radiation therapy is appropriate, followed by diagnostic evaluation at a subsequent time.

SURVIVAL

Either clinical or the more rigorous surgical staging can be used to determine survival. For clinically staged NSCLC patients, stage I disease median survival ranges from over 60 months with small primary lesions (T1 N0 M0) to 26 months with larger (T2) lesions.[8] Patients with stage II disease have a median survival of 17 to 20 months, those with stage III lesions only 8 to 11 months, and those with stage IV disease only 6 months. In general, surgically staged patients (who have undergone resection) have better survivals.

For SCLC patients, median survival for limited disease is 14 to 18 months; it is 9 to 11 months for those with extensive disease. Approximately 15 to 25 percent of limited SCLC patients survive 2 years and are considered cured, although many develop second lung or other primary cancers.

THE FUTURE

To improve upon this dismal record, both local control (surgery and radiation therapy) and distant disease control (chemotherapy) must be improved. Prevention of second malignancies, particularly those of the upper aerodigestive tract, is a major problem in long-term survivors, who will also be prone to develop long-term complications of more intensive therapy. Most important, however, is the fact that this is a preventable malignancy with the cessation of smoking.[22]

REFERENCES

1. Boring CC et al: Cancer statistics, 1992. *CA* 42:19, 1992.
2. Humphrey EW et al: National survey of the pattern of care for carcinoma of the lung. *J Thorac Cardiovasc Surg* 100:837, 1990.
3. O'Rourke MA et al: Age trends of lung cancer stage at diagnosis: Implications for lung cancer screening in the elderly. *JAMA* 258:921, 1987.
4. Eddy DM: Screening for lung cancer. *Ann Intern Med* 111:232, 1989.
5. Teeter SM et al: Lung carcinoma in the elderly population: Influence of histology on the inverse relationship of stage to age. *Cancer* 60:1331, 1987.
6. Knox AJ et al: Fiberoptic bronchoscopy in the elderly: 4 years experience. *Br J Dis Chest* 82:290, 1988.
7. Lederle FA et al: Bronchoscopy to evaluate hemoptysis in older men with nonsuspicious chest roentgenograms. *Chest* 95:1043, 1989.
8. Mountain CF: A new international staging system for lung cancer. *Chest* 89(suppl 4):225S, 1986.
9. Ginsberg RJ et al: Modern thirty-day operative mortality for surgical resections in lung cancer. *J Thorac Cardiovasc Surg* 86:654, 1983.
10. Sherman S, Guidot CE: The feasibility of thoracotomy for lung cancer in the elderly. *JAMA* 258:927, 1987.
11. Mulshine JL et al: Treatment of non-small-cell lung cancer. *J Clin Oncol* 4:1704, 1986.
12. Perry MC et al: Chemotherapy with or without radiation therapy in limited small cell carcinoma of the lung. *N Engl J Med* 316:912, 1989.
13. Pignon JP et al: A meta-analysis of thoracic radiotherapy for small-cell lung cancer. *N Engl J Med* 327:1618, 1992.
14. Walsh SJ et al: Cancer chemotherapy in the elderly. *Semin Oncol* 16:66, 1989.
15. Idhe DC: Chemotherapy of lung cancer. *N Engl J Med* 327:1434, 1992.
16. Rapp E et al: Chemotherapy can prolong survival in patients with advanced non-small-cell lung cancer—Report of a Canadian multicenter randomized trial. *J Clin Oncol* 6:663, 1988.
17. Greco FA: Rationale for chemotherapy for patients with advanced non-small-cell lung cancer. *Semin Oncol* 13(suppl 3):92, 1986.
18. Bunn PA Jr: *Lung Cancer: Current Understanding of the Biology, Diagnosis, Staging, and Treatment* (monograph). Princeton, NJ, Bristol-Myers Squibb, 1992.
19. Carney DN et al: Single-agent oral etoposide for elderly small cell lung cancer patients. *Semin Oncol* 17(suppl 2):49, 1990.
20. Clark PI et al: Prolonged administration of single agent oral etoposide in patients with untreated small cell lung cancer (abstract). *Proc Am Soc Clin Oncol* 9:226, 1990.
21. Dillman RO et al: A randomized trial of induction chemotherapy plus high-dose radiation versus radiation alone in stage III non-small cell lung cancer. *N Engl J Med* 323:940, 1990.
22. Lin AY, Idhe DC: Recent developments in the treatment of lung cancer. *JAMA* 267:1661, 1992.

SECTION C

The Renal System and Urinary Tract

Chapter 54

AGING CHANGES IN RENAL FUNCTION

Laurence H. Beck

The kidneys of elderly individuals are smaller than those of younger individuals and have a lower blood flow and glomerular filtration rate. In addition, many of the homeostatic functions of the kidney are less robust in the elderly, leading to a greater likelihood of failure under stress. A healthy controversy continues about the genesis of these changes, i.e., whether the changes are age- or disease-associated. For the most part, data currently available have been derived from cross-sectional studies, usually of apparently healthy aged individuals. The relatively fewer longitudinal studies carried out on "clinically clean" aging cohorts have, in general, confirmed the conclusions of the cross-sectional studies, indicating aging per se as a major contributor to renal changes.

Despite the anatomic, histologic, and functional changes to be described herein, the aging kidney remains capable of maintaining body fluid and solute homeostasis remarkably well, even into the ninth and tenth decades of life, unless concurrent disease or severe stresses are imposed. In most elderly individuals, the loss of function is accompanied by no clinical signs or symptoms, and the internal environment is adequately maintained.

ANATOMIC CHANGES

The normal adult kidney weighs 150 to 200 g at age 30. There is a gradual decrease in mass with aging, so that by age 90 the average weight is 20 to 30 percent less, or 110 to 150 g.[1] Concomitantly, the renal size decreases. McLachlan and Wasserman[2] studied the length, area, and distensibility of kidneys from patients having intravenous urograms. They found that kidney length decreased by about 0.5 cm per decade after age 50; furthermore, they estimated that renal volume decreased 40 percent by age 90. Recently, a cross-sectional analysis of individuals aged 20 to 80, in which renal parenchymal thickness was measured using computed tomography (CT), has confirmed a decrease of about 10 percent per decade.[3]

Most of the tissue lost with aging is from the renal cortex[4] and represents parallel glomerular and tubular loss.[5] The total number of glomeruli falls by 30 to 40 percent by age 80,[6] and the glomerular surface area decreases progressively after age 40.[7] Equally important is the increasing number of totally sclerotic (and presumably nonfunctioning) glomeruli. Although fewer than 1 percent of glomeruli are sclerotic in the young adult, this percentage rises to 10 to 30 percent by age 80.[8,9] Within surviving glomeruli, numerous changes have been noted, including decreased size and number of glomerular tufts, increased basement membrane thickness, and expanded mesangium.[5,7,10]

Several vascular changes have been described in the aging kidney.[5,11,12] In the cortex, both the afferent and efferent arterioles tend to atrophy in a parallel manner, resulting in a bloodless glomerulus. In the juxtamedullary region, the atrophy is asymmetric, so that afferent-efferent arteriovenous fistulas (so-called continuous units) are formed. The result is that while cortical blood flow is reduced, juxtamedullary flow may be paradoxically increased (relative to overall renal blood flow). This increase probably contributes to the urinary concentrating deficit in the elderly patient by interfering with the countercurrent system balance of flows.[13]

The tubules also undergo changes. The number and length of proximal tubules decrease,[5] whereas tubular diverticula become common in the distal nephron.[7] Baert and Steg[14] have suggested that these diverticula may be the progenitors of the common simple cysts seen in the aged kidney.

The vascular and tubular changes in the aging kidney are often accompanied by mild interstitial fibrosis. Taken in concert, these vascular, tubular, and interstitial changes resemble those seen in several mild, chronic interstitial diseases. From a functional standpoint, therefore, it is useful to consider these changes as the "tubulointerstitial nephropathy of the elderly."

RENAL BLOOD FLOW

Numerous cross-sectional studies have documented a fall in total renal blood flow (RBF) of about 10 percent per decade after age 20, so that renal blood flow in the octogenarian averages only 300 ml/min, compared to 600 ml/min in the young adult.[15–17] Probably as a result of the anatomic changes described above, the major decrement in RBF occurs in the cortex. Hollenberg and colleagues,[17] using the xenon washout technique in healthy potential kidney donors, demonstrated that in the cortex there is a progressive decrease in RBF per renal mass with age, suggesting that the decreased RBF is not secondary to tissue loss but is probably primary in *causing* the parenchymal atrophy. Furthermore, they demonstrated less responsiveness of RBF to physiologic and pharmacologic maneuvers (saline infusion, acetylcholine) in older individuals than in younger individuals. The decrease in RBF probably results from the combination of decreased cardiac output and age-related changes in the larger hilar, arcuate, and interlobar arteries.

GLOMERULAR FILTRATION RATE

Given the fall in total RBF and the decrease in size and number of glomeruli, it is not surprising that the glomerular filtration rate (GFR) progressively decreases with age. Cross-sectional and longitudinal studies, using a variety of methodologies, have shown that GFR remains stable after adolescence through age 30 to 35 and then falls at the rate of about 8 to 10 ml/min per 1.73 m^2 per decade. In a large cross-sectional study of 548 normal men at the Gerontology Research Center of the National Institute of Aging, Rowe and colleagues[18] noted a mean creatinine clearance of 140 ml/min per 1.73 m^2 at age 30, with a progressive fall thereafter to 97 ml/min per 1.73 m^2 at age 80.

More recently, Lindeman and coworkers[19] reported the results of creatinine clearance measurements in a large number of normal volunteers followed for up to 23 years in the Baltimore Longitudinal Study of Aging. These men were carefully studied every 12 to 18 months; those with a minimum of five studies were reported. Of 446 normal volunteers who entered the study, a group of 254 was selected on the basis of absence of hypertension, urinary tract disease, or diuretic use. The mean decrease in creatinine clearance for this group was 0.75 ml/min per year. There was a normal distribution of values around the mean, including about 30 percent of subjects who showed no significant decrease in creatinine clearance over time.

The mechanism for the declining GFR over time is unknown. A number of theories have evolved which parallel the theories of aging per se. Recently, Anderson and Brenner,[20] drawing upon aging animal models, have suggested that the decrease in glomerular filtration rate that accompanies aging is a consequence of persistent glomerular hyperfiltration resulting from the usual high-protein diet of modern humans. Animal models have demonstrated that protein restriction can virtually eliminate the sclerotic glomerular changes that occur in normally aging rats fed an ad libitum diet.[21]

It has been demonstrated that the kidneys of elderly humans retain their acute responsiveness to a protein meal (GFR rises dramatically within 2 to 3 hours of a large protein load).[22] On the other hand, comparison of creatinine clearance in healthy vegetarians in Israel consuming less than 30 g of protein per day to nonvegetarians consuming 100 g of protein revealed no differences in any age group up to age 80.[23] Despite little direct support for the protein-aging kidney theory in humans, it has attracted widespread support.[21]

The fall in creatinine clearance with age is not accompanied by a rise in serum creatinine concentration, which remains essentially unchanged over the duration of adult life. Therefore, it follows that daily creatinine production (and urinary excretion of creatinine) must fall in parallel with the decrease in creatinine clearance. Such a decline was documented by Rowe and colleagues[18] and reflects the decreasing muscle mass with aging which parallels the fall in GFR. The important clinical consequences of these observations are that a normal serum creatinine concentration of 0.8 mg/dl in an 80-year-old reflects a GFR which is 40 to 50 percent less than the GFR of a 30-year-old of the same size with creatinine concentration of 0.8 mg/dl.

Several authors have sought to develop formulas or nomograms to predict the creatinine clearance in individuals from the steady-state serum creatinine concentration, taking into account the fall in GFR with age. The most widely used is that of Cockcroft and Gault[24]:

$$\text{Creatinine clearance} = \frac{(140 - \text{age, yr})(\text{weight, kg})}{72 \times (\text{serum creatinine concentration, mg/dl})}$$

Because of the time required and the logistical difficulties in collecting complete 24-hour urine specimens to calculate creatinine clearance, this formula is employed frequently, particularly for elderly individuals and for drug-dosing nomograms (see Chap. 24). Although such a formula is preferable to using the serum creatinine concentration alone, it must be recognized that the variability that characterizes the physiology of elderly individuals makes this and other formulas imprecise. Furthermore, the measured creatinine clearance overestimates the GFR (as measured by inulin clearance) to an increasing degree with increasing age.[22] Therefore, when dosages of potentially toxic renally cleared drugs are being calculated, direct measurement of GFR and/or appropriate serum drug levels is strongly recommended.

TUBULAR FUNCTIONS

With the exception of urinary concentration and dilution, tubular functions in the aged have not been well characterized or extensively studied. The available data do suggest, however, that, as with other renal functional parameters, the homeostatic limits are narrowed in the aging kidney for glucose transport, acid excretion, and sodium transport.

A series of studies carried out by Dontas and coworkers[25] and by Shock and his colleagues[26,27] addressed proximal tubular reabsorption and secretory capacity by measuring tubular transport of glucose, para-aminohippurate (PAH), and iodopyracet (Diodrast). Effective renal plasma flow (measured as PAH clearance) falls linearly from the fourth through the ninth decades. The filtration fraction remains constant throughout most of adult life and then shows a modest increase during the seventh, eighth, and ninth decades. Tubular transport maximums for PAH and Diodrast fall progressively with age but do so in parallel with the fall in GFR. These findings have been interpreted to indicate support for the intact nephron hypothesis, i.e., the hypothesis that there is not a specific age-associated defect in transport of these substances but that as nephrons atrophy with age, the total transport capacity decreases.

Glucose transport by the kidney was evaluated by Miller et al.[27] in individuals ranging in age from 20 to 90 years old. Maximum transport capacity for glucose (T_mG) was measured by standard clearance methods. The authors reported a fall in T_mG from 359 mg/min per liter per 1.73 m^2 at age 30 to 219 mg/min per liter per 1.73 m^2 at age 85. This decrease in T_mG closely paralleled the observed fall in GFR, so that the GFR:T_mG ratio remained constant across the decades. These findings also support the intact nephron hypothesis, suggesting that there is no specific defect in glucose transport per se but that the total capacity falls as the number of nephrons decreases with age.

In contrast to the diminished T_mG, the renal glucose threshold is increased with age.[28] This discrepancy has not been well explained but may be due to selective loss of nephrons with low individual thresholds, resulting in less splay in the titration curve.

Amino acid transport by the aging kidney has recently been evaluated by Nadvornikova and coworkers.[29] Serum concentrations of amino acids did not change with increasing age; however, GFR, and therefore the filtered load of amino acids, fell with age, but the fractional excretion of most amino acids rose in correlation with an increase in fractional excretion of sodium. The most likely explanation for these changes is that as functioning nephrons decrease in number, the decrease of sodium reabsorption per nephron is paralleled by a decrease in reabsorption of cotransported amino acids.

Although acid-base parameters are normal under basal conditions, the ability to respond to an acid load is impaired in the elderly. Adler and colleagues[30] administered 0.1 g/kg ammonium chloride (NH_4Cl) to 26 normal male volunteers, including nine aged 72 to 93. All subjects demonstrated a rapid increase in renal acid excretion, and minimum urinary pH was similar in young and old; however, the older men excreted only 19 percent of the acid load over 8 hours, compared to 35 percent excreted by the younger men. The decrease in net acid excretion was due to a decrease of both urinary NH_4 and phosphorus. Because the inulin clearance of the older men was markedly lower than that of the younger men, the authors concluded that the decrease in acid excretory capacity was proportional to the decrease in GFR and was the result of decreased nephron mass.

Agarwal and Cabebe[31] used ammonium chloride loading to assess acid excretion in 16 healthy male volunteers aged 29 to 86. Baseline net acid excretions were similar between young and old, as were ammonia excretion and titratable acid excretion when factored for GFR. After the short NH_4Cl load, despite an equivalent fall in plasma bicarbonate concentration, the older individuals, as compared with the younger men, showed significantly decreased net acid excretion in 6 hours. This defect was characterized by a slight difference in minimal urinary pH and a large decrease in NH_4 excretion, both absolute and when factored for GFR. Recently Schuck and colleagues,[32] using a similar protocol in individuals aged 18 to 70 years, demonstrated diminished titratable acid excretion in older subjects in addition to a limited NH_4 response.

SODIUM HANDLING

The limits of sodium excretion and sodium conservation have not been systematically addressed in the elderly, although it is probable that homeostatic flexibility is reduced, as with other solutes. It is usually stated that the aging kidney is sodium-wasting and that older individuals are more likely to become salt-depleted during periods of sodium deprivation. These presumptions are only weakly corroborated by experimental data. Epstein and Hollenberg[33] compared the time required to achieve sodium balance when healthy young (under 30) and older (over 60) adults were placed on a very low (10 meq) sodium diet. The half-time necessary for sodium balance was 17.6 hours in the younger individuals, compared with 31 hours in the elderly individuals. Although this difference was statistically significant, the clinical implication is uncertain. On the other hand, Weidmann and coworkers[34] found similar weight reduction (about 2.5 percent of body weight) in young (ages 20 to 30) versus older (ages 60 to 70) adults after 6 days of a 10-meq sodium diet, suggesting no serious impairment of sodium conservation in "young old" individuals.

If sodium conservation is limited, it may be due to defects in the renin-aldosterone axis that have been repeatedly demonstrated in older subjects. Tsunoda and colleagues,[35] for example, found that although total renin concentration remains stable with age, there is an age-dependent decline in *active* renin concentration as well as in plasma aldosterone concentration. Similarly, basal and stimulated plasma aldosterone concentration has been shown to decrease with age.[36] Weidmann and colleagues[34] evaluated the effect of sodium intake and posture on two groups of healthy volunteers of both sexes: 12 aged 20 to 30 and seven aged 62 to 70. Renin concentration, plasma renin activity (PRA), and serum aldosterone concentrations were measured on a low- (10 meq/day) and high- (120 meq/day) sodium diet and in the supine and upright positions. Despite comparable sodium and fluid balance between young and old, all measurements were lower in the older age group, and these changes were most pronounced in patients measured in the upright position while on the low-sodium diet. Interestingly, the aldosterone response to adrenocorticotropic hormone (ACTH) was similar between the two groups, suggesting that the diminished postural and volume-mediated aldosterone concentrations were due principally to the blunted renin response and not to any defect in the adrenal cortex.[34]

It is widely held that the elderly have diminished capacity to handle acute sodium loads. Although the decrease in GFR with age might well limit the rate of an acute response to volume expansion, systematic evaluation of the response to sodium loads has not been reported in older individuals. Of interest are recent studies[37–40] reporting that circulating levels of atrial natriuretic peptide (ANP) are higher in elderly individuals than in younger persons on the same sodium intake. Metabolic clearance of ANP is prolonged in the elderly,[39] and it has been suggested that there may be a diminished cellular response[37] to the peptide. It is uncertain whether these differences have physiologic importance in the maintenance of sodium homeostasis.

POTASSIUM HOMEOSTASIS

It is commonly believed that potassium homeostasis is impaired in old people and that, when stressed, they are more prone to develop hyperkalemia and hypokalemia than are their younger counterparts.[41] However, there are few systematic studies of the effect of age on potassium homeostasis. In one study,[42] the body compositions of 40 healthy elderly men and women (mean age 79) from a retirement community were compared with the body compositions of 20 healthy young medical students. Exchangeable potassium was 10 to 25 percent lower in the older subjects; this was correlated with, but out of proportion to, the lower lean body mass. Serum potassium concentration was not different between the two groups. These data suggest that potassium homeostasis is normal on standard dietary intakes.

Although several factors (decreased GFR, blunted renin-aldosterone axis, decreased tubular mass) predict that defense against hyperkalemia in the face of increased potassium loads may be impaired, such potassium-loading studies have not been reported. Similarly, the capacity for potassium conservation in the face of decreased intake or of nonrenal potassium loss has not been studied.

WATER HOMEOSTASIS

Age-associated changes in water metabolism are the best characterized of all the renal functional changes, in part because the clinical consequences can be so dramatic in the elderly.

Total body water, in both absolute and relative terms, decreases with age.[42] The proportion of body mass represented by water falls progressively with aging from about 55 to 60 percent at age 20 to 45 to 55 percent at age 80. This decrease is much more pronounced in women than in men, principally due to their proportionately decreased lean body mass and hence increased proportion of body fat. Because of the decrease in starting body water volume, losses and gains of water in women are reflected in more pronounced changes in body fluid osmolality.

In order to excrete a concentrated urine in the setting of fluid deprivation or hypertonicity of body fluids, a person needs an intact posterior pituitary capable of secreting vasopressin (antidiuretic hormone [ADH]), intact renal circulation and medullary solute gradient, and renal tubules that are responsive to ADH. Each of these components of the system has been evaluated in elderly subjects in an attempt to explain the well-described decrease in maximal urinary concentration.[43,44]

The pituitary response to osmotic and nonosmotic stimuli has been reported by several investigators. Although it has been suggested by some[13] that central ADH release is impaired, it is clear that this is not the case and that, in fact, elderly subjects have normal to *supra*normal responses to a variety of stimuli.

Helderman and colleagues[45] evaluated the pituitary ADH responses to ethanol and to hypertonic saline infusions in healthy elderly (aged 34 to 92, recruited from the Baltimore Longitudinal Study of Aging cohort) and compared them to those in younger individuals (aged 21 to 49). Baseline serum osmolality, plasma sodium concentration, and plasma immunoreactive arginine vasopressin (AVP) concentrations were similar. Both young and old demonstrated a prompt fall in AVP after an infusion of ethanol, a known inhibitor of pituitary vasopressin secretion. The suppression was much briefer in the older subjects, however, despite similar blood alcohol levels in the two groups. When hypertonic saline was infused to raise plasma osmolality, there was an increase in AVP in both groups, but the concentrations in the older subjects were almost double those in the younger subjects. For any given plasma osmolality change, the increase in AVP levels can be considered to represent the sensitivity of the hypothalamic-pituitary osmoreceptors; this sensitivity is clearly exaggerated in elderly subjects. Other investigators have found elevated *basal* AVP levels in healthy elderly as compared to levels in younger individuals.[46]

Despite the unimpaired AVP secretory capacity in elderly individuals, maximal urinary concentration after water deprivation is impaired. Over 50 years ago, Lewis and Alving[43] evaluated "normal men," aged 40 to 101, for their capacity to concentrate the urine after 24 hours of a "dry diet" (total fluid deprivation). Twenty men were studied in each age decade up to age 90. There was a progressive decrease in maximal specific gravity by decade after age 40, so that the average specific gravity at age 40 was 1.030, but by age 90 it had fallen to 1.023.

More recently, Rowe and coworkers[44] studied 98 active community-dwelling men from the Baltimore Longitudinal Study of Aging after 12 hours of water deprivation.[44] Mean urine osmolality was reported for men in age groups representing 20-year intervals. There was a fall in maximal osmolality from 1109 mOsm/kg for ages 20 to 39, to 1051 mOsm/kg for ages 40 to 59, and to 882 mOsm/kg for ages 60 to 79. Analysis of individual data indicated that the decrease in urinary osmolality was not correlated with the level of creatinine clearance (which also fell with increasing age).

Several investigators have evaluated the responsiveness of the kidney to vasopressin. Lindeman and colleagues[47] measured the response of normal men, aged 17 to 88 years, to submaximal vasopressin infusion (8 milliunits/h) administered during a water diuresis. Although their subjects had demonstrated an age-related decrease in maximal urinary osmolality (U_{max}) after 20 hours of water deprivation, the antidiuretic response to submaximal vasopressin during water diuresis was not different between younger and older men.

On the other hand, Miller and Shock,[48] using a similar protocol, gave large doses of vasopressin (0.5 milliunits/kg body weight) to healthy adult males aged 26 to 86 during a sustained water diuresis. Urine/plasma inulin ratio (U/P_{inulin}) was progressively lower with increasing age; mean value was 115 for the young men (mean age 35), 75 for the middle-aged men (mean age 55), and only 40 for the older men (mean age 73).

For humans, it is not known whether the age-related decrease in responsiveness to vasopressin is due to defective medullary circulation, altered medullary solute gradient, or a defect in the tubular cellular response to hormone. The relative increase in medullary blood flow and an increasing solute load to the intact remaining nephrons of the aging kidney could combine to decrease the medullary gradient.[49] On the other hand, studies in the aging rat, attempting to ascertain the mechanism of the age-related concentrating defect, have suggested a decrease in water permeability along the collecting duct.[50]

The decreasing maximal urinary concentrating ability with age, while real, should not be clinically significant unless water loss is severe or thirst, the other arm of the homeostatic system, is not intact. Unfortunately, for most elderly individuals thirst appears to be blunted. In an elegantly simply study, Phillips and colleagues[51] evaluated the pituitary and renal response as well as thirst response to 24 hours of water deprivation in two groups of healthy men, aged 20 to 31 and 67 to 75. Corroborating other studies, this study demonstrated increased plasma AVP levels and decreased urine osmolality in the older group after dehydration. Thirst, measured by a previously validated visual-analogue rating scale, revealed marked differences between young and old. Thirst ratings in younger individuals rose rapidly during deprivation and were significantly higher than during baseline. In contrast, the older subjects' ratings did not differ significantly before and after 24 hours of water deprivation. Even more striking was the spontaneous water intake after the end of the deprivation, when both groups were given free access to water. The younger men drank more water than the elderly men and quickly restored plasma osmolality to normal; the elderly had not corrected themselves after 2 hours, despite equal access to water. Other investigators have demonstrated this striking thirst deficit in healthy older individuals subjected to water deprivation,[52] thermal dehydration,[53] and hypertonicity without extracellular fluid volume depletion.[54]

The cause of age-related hypodipsia is unknown. There is some evidence that endogenous opioid release, an apparent stimulant of thirst, is reduced in the elderly.[55]

In summary, the water conservation defect and tendency to dehydration in the elderly is multifactorial in origin. Total body water is diminished as a proportion of weight. Despite normal to supranormal vasopressin release in the face of hyperosmolality, the elderly person's renal response to vasopressin is blunted, compared to the response of younger individuals, resulting in diminished urinary concentration. Superimposed upon these changes, the thirst response to dehydration is blunted or absent in normal aged persons.

The ability of elderly individuals' kidneys to dilute the urine and to excrete a water load have not been extensively evaluated. Healthy young adults excrete 80 percent or more of a standard oral water load (20 ml/kg) within 5 hours after ingestion, and they achieve a minimum urine osmolality of less than 100 mOsm/kg. Lindeman and colleagues[47] reported the minimal urine osmolality after such a load to be 52 mOsm/kg in a group of middle-aged men (mean age 31), 74 mOsm/kg in another group of middle-aged men (mean age 60), and 92 mOsm/kg in a group of older men (mean age 84). Free water clearance (C_{H_2O}), similarly, was lower in the older group, although when factored for GFR, the values were not different, suggesting that the difference in minimal urinary osmolality was due to the increased solute load per nephron in the elderly.[46]

Recently, Crowe and colleagues[52] carried out similar studies in a small number of healthy men (mean age 72) and came to a similar conclusion: there is a decrease in diluting capacity with age that is explained by the fall in GFR. Plasma AVP levels were measured and were found to be equally depressed after the water load in young and old groups, indicating that the decreased water excretion was not due to continuing inappropriate ADH secretion.

CLINICAL CONSEQUENCES OF PHYSIOLOGIC CHANGES

The functional changes of the aging kidney do not, of themselves, lead to clinical disease or disability. On the other hand, they leave the elderly individual much more vulnerable to a variety of environmental, disease-related, and drug-induced stresses. For example, the depressed GFR of the octogenarian, while not in a range to cause symptomatic retention of nitrogenous wastes, is much closer to the "uremic threshold" than the GFR of a younger person. Renal or nonrenal illnesses resulting in further depression of the GFR may lead to symptomatic renal failure with surprising rapidity in the elderly patient. Similarly, because the clearance of many potentially toxic drugs is primarily through glomerular filtration, the risk of such toxicity is markedly increased in normal elderly patients unless judicious dosage reduction is applied. This risk has been specifically demonstrated recently for gentamicin[56] and digoxin.[57] The principles of appropriate drug dose modification are found in Chap. 24.

Illness (and the management thereof) is a common setting for the occurrence of fluid and electrolyte disorders in elderly persons. Disorders of water metabolism in particular (hyponatremia and hypernatremia) are prevalent among elderly inpatients.[58–60] In the following sections, the common disorders of salt, water, and potassium homeostasis will be reviewed.

DISORDERS OF SALT (SODIUM) METABOLISM

The total body content of sodium is the principal determinant of extracellular and intravascular fluid volume. Deficiency of sodium results in hypovolemia with its attendant clinical signs: tachycardia, hypotension (notably postural), oliguria, and azotemia. Excess total body sodium results in edema with or without circulatory congestion.

Volume depletion is a common result of gastrointestinal disorders in the elderly. Primary salt losses occur through vomiting or diarrhea; anorexia, often accompanied by reduced mobility, frequently prevents adequate oral replenishment. Although younger individuals would rapidly reduce urinary excretion of sodium to zero in such situations, the older patient, because of the sluggish renin-angiotensin and aldosterone response described previously, may continue to excrete sodium inappropriately, contributing to further volume depletion. Since organ hypoperfusion is particularly dangerous to the elderly patient, it is imperative for the clinician to anticipate this tendency toward hypovolemia and take steps to counteract it, administering salt by the most appropriate route, both prophylactically and therapeutically. For patients with frank hypotension, the salt repletion should be rapid and parenteral, and it should always consist of physiologic ("normal") saline solution or colloid-containing fluid (plasma or blood). Only after circulatory stability has been achieved should the infusion be changed to a nonisotonic solution.

When dealing with salt loads, the low GFR of the elderly does not ordinarily prevent prompt sodium excretion unless large quantities are administered acutely. However, the frequent coincidence with heart disease may prevent the requisite increase in cardiac output and renal blood flow necessary to deliver that load to the nephron for excretion. Elderly patients are therefore more susceptible to pulmonary edema under conditions of such salt loads.

DISORDERS OF WATER METABOLISM

The serum sodium concentration is usually the best index of total body water balance: hyponatremia occurs whenever there is a relative excess of water (relative to sodium content) and almost always indicates a defect in or limitation upon water excretion. Hypernatremia, on the other hand, is virtually always the consequence of relative water lack.

Hyponatremia

The prevalence of hyponatremia increases with age, particularly in hospitalized patients.[58,61] In one study carried out in a geriatric inpatient unit, 11.3 percent of all patients had a serum sodium concentration less than 130 mmol/liter, and 4.5 percent were below 125 mmol/liter.[61] The prevalence of hyponatremia has been reported to be somewhat lower but still common (8 percent) in geriatric outpatients[62] and even higher (22 percent) in a chronic disease facility.[63] A recent study of prognosis in patients found to be hyponatremic on hospital admission indicated that this is a marker for serious illness: the likelihood of death in the hospital for someone with hyponatremia on admission was seven times the rate in nonhyponatremic-matched controls (8.7 versus 1.1 percent).[64]

Patients with hyponatremia are usually classified clinically into one of three general pathophysiologic groups: (1) patients who are truly volume-depleted, such as those with chronic diarrhea or diuretic-induced hypovolemia; (2) patients with edema states and excess total body sodium; and (3) patients who are normovolemic, most of whom fit the definition of the syndrome of inappropriate antidiuretic hormone secretion (SIADH). Treatment of patients in the first category is straightforward: repletion of intravascular and extracellular fluid volume with colloid or normal saline usually allows rapid excretion of the excess water and correction of the hyponatremia. Patients in the second group require management of the underlying edema-forming state (e.g., congestive heart failure or cirrhosis) as well as judicious restriction of free water.

Patients who fit into the third category are common among hyponatremic elderly because the diseases associated with SIADH are particularly prevalent (e.g., cancers, respiratory disorders, and central nervous system disease). In addition, a number of drugs used in the elderly can cause a drug-induced SIADH. Some of these drugs (such as chlorpropamide and indomethacin) appear to enhance the renal tubular action of ADH, while others (such as carbamazepine, narcotics, and tricyclic antidepressants) increase central ADH release. It has been suggested that normal aging itself can be a "cause" of SIADH.[65]

Diuretic-induced hyponatremia appears to be particularly common in elderly patients.[66] Although some of these patients, particularly those with marked potassium losses, are normovolemic and mimic idiopathic SIADH,[67] most cases are probably due to salt and volume depletion with volume-stimulated ADH secretion.[68] Correction is usually easily accomplished by discontinuation of diuretics and cautious salt administration.

Mild hyponatremia usually results in no appreciable clinical symptoms. However, hyponatremia that is severe (below 125 mmol/liter) or that develops rapidly is often accompanied by central nervous system symptoms, including lethargy, somnolence, seizures, and coma. These symptoms are all thought to be due to neuronal cell swelling in the brain, leading to increased intracranial pressure.

For mild hyponatremia unaccompanied by neurologic symptoms, management is simply to restrict free water intake. It must be remembered, however, that a patient with a persistently concentrated urine due to SIADH is dependent upon insensible loss for water excretion. Since, in the absence of fever, these losses rarely exceed 1000 ml/day, the restriction of intake must be below that level.

For more severe or symptomatic hyponatremia, more rapid correction is warranted. Although hypertonic (3%) sodium chloride solution can be used, the resultant volume expansion may overwhelm the circulatory system of an elderly patient and lead to pulmonary edema. Therefore, the well-described and effective technique of using a potent loop diuretic such as furosemide in combination with normal or hypertonic saline in an isovolemic "exchange" is safer.[69] There is controversy over the proper rate of correction of hyponatremia. A number of cases of a serious and potentially fatal central nervous system disorder, central pontine myelinolysis (CPM), have been described in patients who were severely hyponatremic and corrected rapidly. This disorder has not occurred in patients who were corrected rapidly but to less-than-normal values of serum sodium. Because the consequences of sustained severe hyponatremia are so dire, it is recommended that correction be made at the rate of about 2 mmol/liter until a concentration of 124 to 130 mmol/liter is reached; then the correction should be slowed. Regardless of the speed of correction, neurologic symptoms often require days following full correction for recovery in the elderly. Persistence of somnolence or other signs should not prompt an invasive neurologic workup unless additional suggestive signs are present.

Hypernatremia

The multiple defects in water conservation described previously make dehydration and hypernatremia an ever-present threat in sick or disabled elderly persons. Illness-induced water loss, lack of thirst, and lack of access to water (due to immobility or neurologic depression) combine to make hypernatremic dehydration a very common fluid-electrolyte disorder in older individuals. Hypernatremia has been used as a marker for a poor prognosis in hospitalized patients[70] and for neglect in nursing home populations.[71]

Hypernatremia occurs frequently in sick elderly patients. Snyder and colleagues[59] reviewed records at a general community teaching hospital over 2 years; of all hospital admissions for patients over the age of 60, 1.1 percent had confirmed hypernatremia (plasma sodium concentration greater than 148 mmol/liter). Half of the cases of hypernatremia were present on admission; the others developed during hospitalization. Whereas overall mortality of the elderly patients was 6 percent, mortality in the hypernatremic group was 42 percent! Mortality of hypernatremic patients was similarly high (48 percent) in another hospital series report by Mahowald and Himmelstein.[70]

The symptoms of hypernatremia are similar to those of hyponatremia; neurologic signs predominate, with obtundation, lethargy, and coma being the most common. These signs are thought to result from neuronal cell dehydration and brain shrinkage.

Management of hypernatremic dehydration consists of correcting intravascular hypovolemia first (with normal saline) and then correcting the hypertonicity by administering hypotonic fluids. Since many elderly patients with hypernatremia have suffered combined salt and water losses, this second phase of correction should be with hypotonic saline (one-half or one-quarter of normal). However, if the hypernatremia is the result of pure water loss (as may occur in unattended coma), then repletion can be with water alone (enteral water or intravenous dextrose and water).

The volume of free water required to restore body fluid tonicity to normal can be roughly estimated by the equation

$$\text{Water deficit} = \frac{[60\% \times \text{current body weight (kg)}]}{\times\ [(\text{PNa}/140) - 1]}$$

where PNa = current plasma sodium concentration (mmol/liter). In severe dehydration, one-half of the estimated deficit should be corrected over the first 24 hours, with the remaining correction occurring over the ensuing 48 to 72 hours. There is a danger in correcting the plasma sodium concentration to normal too rapidly—the paradoxical development of cerebral edema with worsening neurologic signs. This condition is thought to occur as the result of the production of "idiogenic osmols" in the brain during the period of dehydration. Because these osmotic particles cannot be rapidly inactivated, administered water is osmotically drawn into the intracellular space, resulting in cell swelling if the administration is too rapid. As in the case with the correction of hypotonicity, neurologic recovery may lag behind metabolic correction by several days.

DISORDERS OF POTASSIUM METABOLISM

Hyperkalemia

The combination of decreased GFR and sluggish renin-aldosterone system means that elderly persons are frequently operating near the upper limit of tolerance for potassium excretion even on a normal diet. Therefore, any large increase in load or further impairment in excretion can lead to serious hyperkalemia. Many acute illnesses are associated with rapid tissue catabolism, leading to release of potassium from lean body mass into the circulation. The same is true of internal bleeding into the gastrointestinal tract or into soft tissues, since red blood cells are a source of large quantities of potassium. Also, one must be aware that many older patients with hypertension or congestive heart failure who are placed on a low-sodium diet are unknowingly consuming a diet high in potassium, particularly if placed on a sodium-free salt substitute.

Probably the most common cause of hyperkalemia in elderly patients is the use of drugs that interfere with potassium excretion. Potassium-sparing diuretics (e.g., spironolactone, triamterene, and amiloride) are thought to be the major culprits.[58] These drugs, by interfering with distal renal tubular potassium secretion (the principal source of potassium excretion), can result in serious hyperkalemia by decreasing potassium clearance by the kidneys. Bender and colleagues[72] reported that 12 percent of a large group of elderly hypertensive individuals given a diuretic combination including triamterene became hyperkalemic. More recently, nonsteroidal anti-inflammatory drugs (NSAIDs) may be becoming the major source of drug-induced hyperkalemia in elderly patients,[73,74] since these drugs combine to block renin secretion and depress GFR. Because of the known physiologic effects of angiotensin converting enzyme (ACE) inhibitors, it is likely that these drugs also may predispose to hyperkalemia in the elderly. For these reasons, it is important to monitor serum potassium levels in elderly patients on potassium-sparing diuretics, especially if renal dysfunction exaggerating the propensity for hyperkalemia coexists.

The principles underlying the treatment of hyperkalemia are no different for older patients than for younger patients. Protocols can be found in standard textbooks.

Hypokalemia

Hypokalemia is also common in elderly patients,[58] and its clinical consequences can be serious. Although weakness and apathy may be the most common clinical manifestations of hypokalemia, gastrointestinal effects—including constipation, impaction, and ileus—

are causes of morbidity. The most serious side effect of hypokalemia is its predisposition to tachyarrhythmia, particularly in individuals taking digitalis glycosides.

The causes of hypokalemia in elderly patients are similar to causes in younger patients, the most prevalent being gastrointestinal loss or diuretic-induced renal loss. In addition, the average daily intake of dietary potassium is probably lower in the majority of older individuals than it was when they were younger.

Recent surveys show diuretics to be among the most commonly used drugs in the elderly.[73] Reviews of the incidence of hypokalemia in this population are sparse, but they range between 0 and 60 percent; this may be particularly common with longer-acting diuretics such as chlorthalidone.[75]

The management of hypokalemia in the elderly should follow the same management principles employed for younger patients. One of the most important tasks of the primary physician is to assess whether the risks of hypokalemia outweigh the risks of treatment.[76] Because of the tendency toward hyperkalemia in elderly individuals described above, the physician must be very cautious in prescribing potassium supplements or potassium-sparing diuretics on a chronic basis without close follow-up.

REFERENCES

1. McLachlan M: Anatomic structural and vascular changes in the aging kidney, in Nunez JFM, Cameron JS (eds): *Renal Function and Disease in the Elderly*. London, Butterworths, 1987, pp 3–26.
2. McLachlan M, Wasserman P: Changes in size and distensibility of the aging kidney. *Br J Radiol* 54:488, 1981.
3. Gourtsoyiannis N et al: The thickness of the renal parenchyma decreases with age: A CT study of 360 patients. *Am J Roentgenol* 155:541, 1990.
4. Dunnill MS, Halley W: Some observations on the quantitative anatomy of the kidney. *J Pathol* 110:113, 1973.
5. Goyal VK: Changes with age in the human kidney. *Exp Gerontol* 17:321, 1982.
6. McLachlan MSF et al: Vascular and glomerular changes in the aging kidney. *J Pathol* 121:65, 1977.
7. Darmady EM: The parameters of the aging kidney. *J Pathol* 109:195, 1973.
8. Kaplan C et al: Age-related incidence of sclerotic glomeruli in human kidneys. *Am J Pathol* 80:227, 1975.
9. Kappel B, Olsen S: Cortical interstitial tissue and sclerosed glomeruli in the normal human kidney, related to age and sex. *Virchows Arch [A]* 387:271, 1980.
10. Steffes MW et al: Quantitative glomerular morphology of the normal human kidney. *Lab Invest* 49:82, 1983.
11. Ljungqvist A, Lagergran C: Normal intrarenal arterial pattern in adult and aging human kidney. *J Anat* 96:285, 1962.
12. Takazakura E et al: Intrarenal vascular changes with age and disease. *Kidney Int* 2:224, 1972.
13. Brown W et al: Aging and the kidney. *Arch Intern Med* 146:1790, 1986.
14. Baert L, Steg A: Is the diverticulum of the distal and collecting tubules a preliminary stage of the simple cyst in the adult? *J Urol* 118:707, 1977.
15. Davies DF, Shock NW: Age changes in glomerular filtration rate, effective renal plasma flow, and tubular excretory capacity in adult males. *J Clin Invest* 29:496, 1950.
16. Papper S: The effects of age in reducing renal function. *Geriatrics* 28:83, 1973.
17. Hollenberg NK et al: Senescence and the renal vasculature in normal man. *Circ Res* 34:309, 1974.
18. Rowe JW et al: The effect of age on creatinine clearance in man: A cross-sectional and longitudinal study. *J Gerontol* 31:155, 1976.
19. Lindeman RD et al: Longitudinal studies on the rate of decline in renal function with age. *J Am Geriatr Soc* 33:278, 1985.
20. Anderson S, Brenner BM: Effects of aging on the renal glomerulus. *Am J Med* 80:435, 1986.
21. Rudman D, Cohan ME: Nutritional causes of renal impairment in old age. *Am J Kid Dis* 4:289, 1990.
22. DeSanto NG et al: Age-related changes in renal reserve and renal tubular function in healthy humans. *Child Nephrol Urol* 11:33, 1991.
23. Blum M et al: Protein intake and kidney function in humans: Its effect on "Normal Aging." *Arch Intern Med* 149:211, 1989.
24. Cockcroft DW, Gault MH: Prediction of creatinine clearance from serum creatinine. *Nephron* 16:31, 1976.
25. Dontas AS et al: Mechanisms of renal tubular defects in old age. *Postgrad Med J* 48:295, 1972.
26. Watkins DM, Shock NW: Agewise standard value for C_{in}, C_{PAH}, and T^{mPAH} in adult males. *J Clin Invest* 34:969, 1955.
27. Miller JH et al: Age changes in the maximal rate of renal tubular reabsorption of glucose. *J Gerontol* 7:196, 1952.
28. Butterfield WJH et al: Renal glucose threshold variations with age. *Br Med J* 4:505, 1967.
29. Nadvornikova H et al: Renal amino acid excretion and aging. *Physiol Res* 40:87, 1991.
30. Adler S et al: Effect of acute acid loading on urinary acid excretion by the aging human kidney. *J Lab Clin Med* 72:78, 1968.
31. Agarwal BN, Cabebe FG: Renal acidification in elderly subjects. *Nephron* 26:291, 1980.
32. Schuck O et al: Acidification capacity of the kidneys and aging. *Physiol Bohemosl* 38:117, 1989.
33. Epstein M, Hollenberg NK: Age as a determinant of renal sodium conservation in normal man. *J Lab Clin Med* 82:411, 1979.
34. Weidmann P et al: Effect of aging on plasma renin

and aldosterone in normal man. *Kidney Int* 8:325, 1975.
35. Tsunoda K et al: Effect of aging on the renin-angiotensin-aldosterone system in normal subjects: Simultaneous measurement of active and inactive renin, renin substrate, and aldosterone in plasma. *J Clin Endocrinol Metab* 62:384, 1986.
36. Hegstad R et al: Aging and aldosterone. *Am J Med* 74:442, 1983.
37. Ohashi M et al: High plasma concentrations of human atrial natriuretic polypeptide in aged man. *J Clin Endocrinol Metab* 64:81, 1987.
38. Haller BG et al: Effects of posture and aging on circulating atrial natriuretic peptide levels in man. *J Hypertens* 5:551, 1987.
39. Ohashi M et al: Pharmacokinetics of synthetic alpha-human atrial natriuretic polypeptide in normal men: Effect of aging. *Regul Pept* 19:265, 1987.
40. Hartter E et al: Circadian variation and age dependence of human atrial natriuretic peptide levels in hospitalized patients. *Horm Metab Res* 19:490, 1987.
41. Stern N, Tuck ML: Homeostatic fragility in the elderly. *Cardiol Clin* 4:201, 1986.
42. Fulop T et al: Body composition in elderly people. *Gerontology* 31:6, 1985.
43. Lewis WH, Alving AS: Changes with age in renal function in adult men. *Am J Physiol* 123:500, 1938.
44. Rowe JW et al: The influence of age on urinary concentrating ability in man. *Nephron* 17:270, 1976.
45. Helderman JH et al: The response of arginine vasopressin to intravenous ethanol and hypertonic saline in man: The impact of aging. *J Gerontol* 33:39, 1978.
46. Davis PJ, Davis FB: Water excretion in the elderly. *Endocrinol Metab Clin* 16:867, 1987.
47. Lindeman RD et al: Influence of age, renal disease, hypertension, diuretics, and calcium on the antidiuretic responses to suboptimal infusions of vasopressin. *J Lab Clin Med* 68:206, 1966.
48. Miller JH, Shock NW: Age differences in the renal tubular response to antidiuretic hormone. *J Gerontol* 8:446, 1953.
49. Bichet DG, Schrier RW: Renal function and diseases in the aged, in Schrier RW (ed): *Clinical Internal Medicine in the Aged.* Philadelphia, Saunders, 1982, pp 211–221.
50. Bengele HH et al: Urinary concentrating defect in the aging rat. *Am J Physiol* 240:F147, 1981.
51. Phillips RA et al: Reduced thirst after water deprivation in healthy elderly men. *N Engl J Med* 311:753, 1984.
52. Crowe MJ et al: Altered water excretion in healthy elderly men. *Age Aging* 16:285, 1987.
53. Miescher E, Fortney SM: Responses to dehydration and rehydration during heat exposure in young and older men. *Am J Physiol* 257:R1050, 1989.
54. Phillips PA et al: Reduced osmotic thirst in healthy elderly men. *Am J Physiol* 261:R166, 1991.
55. Silver AJ, Morley JE: Role of the opioid system in the hypodipsia associated with aging. *J Am Geriatr Soc* 40:556, 1992.
56. El-Sayed, Islam SI: Effect of age and renal function on gentamicin pharmacokinetic parameters. *Int J Clin Pharmacol Ther Toxicol* 27(10):503, 1989.
57. Algotsson A et al: Steady-state concentrations and dosage of digoxin in relation to kidney function in hospitalized patients over 70 years of age. *J Intern Med* 229(3):247, 1991.
58. Lye M: Electrolyte disorders in the elderly. *Clin Endocrin Metab* 13:377, 1984.
59. Snyder NA et al: Hypernatremia in elderly patients. *Ann Intern Med* 107:309, 1987.
60. Beck LH, Lavizzo-Mourey RJ: Geriatric hypernatremia. *Ann Intern Med* 107:768, 1987.
61. Sunderam SG, Mankikar GD: Hyponatremia in the elderly. *Age Aging* 12:77, 1983.
62. Miller M: Fluid and electrolyte balance in the elderly. *Geriatrics* 42:65, 1987.
63. Kleinfeld M et al: Hyponatremia as observed in a chronic disease facility. *J Am Geriatr Soc* 27:156, 1979.
64. Tierney WM et al: The prognosis of hyponatremia at hospital admission. *J Gen Intern Med* 1:380, 1986.
65. Goldstein CS et al: Idiopathic syndrome of inappropriate antidiuretic hormone secretion possibly related to advanced age. *Ann Intern Med* 99:185, 1983.
66. Ashouri OS: Severe diuretic-induced hyponatremia: A series of eight patients. *Arch Intern Med* 146:1295, 1986.
67. Fichman MP et al: Diuretic-induced hyponatremia. *Ann Intern Med* 75:853, 1971.
68. Ghose RR: Plasma arginine vasopressin in hyponatraemic patients receiving diuretics. *Postgrad Med J* 61:1043, 1985.
69. Hantman D et al: Rapid correction of hyponatremia in the syndrome of inappropriate secretion of antidiuretic hormone. *Ann Intern Med* 78:870, 1973.
70. Mahowald JM, Himmelstein DU: Hypernatremia in the elderly: Relation to infection and mortality. *J Am Geriatr Soc* 24:177, 1981.
71. Himmelstein DU et al: Hypernatremic dehydration in nursing home patients: An indicator of neglect. *J Am Geriatr Soc* 31:466, 1983.
72. Bender AD et al: Use of a diuretic combination of triamterene and hydrochlorothiazide in elderly patients. *J Am Geriatr Soc* 15:166, 1967.
73. Lamy PP: Renal effects of nonsteroidal antiinflammatory drugs: Heightened risk to the elderly? *J Am Geriatr Soc* 34:361, 1986.
74. Kleinfeld M, Corcoran AJ: Hyperkalemia in the elderly. *Comp Ther* 16(9):49, 1990.
75. Flamenbaum W: Diuretic use in the elderly: Potential for diuretic-induced hypokalemia. *Am J Cardiol* 57:38A, 1986.
76. Harrington JT et al: Our national obsession with potassium. *Am J Med* 73:155, 1982.

Chapter 55

URINARY TRACT INFECTIONS

Allan R. Tunkel and Donald Kaye

EPIDEMIOLOGY

The frequency of bacteriuria in the geriatric population is greater than in younger adults.[1] The prevalence of bacteriuria is below 5 percent among young to middle-aged women and below 1 percent among men. In people over the age of 65, however, bacteriuria is observed in at least 20 percent of women and 10 percent of men. In addition, the ratio of bacteriuric women to men decreases from approximately 30:1 to 2:1 or 3:1 in comparing a younger population to the elderly. Some studies[2,3] have also documented a substantial rise of bacteriuria among the elderly with advancing age; about 20 percent of women and 2 to 3 percent of men aged 65 to 70 will have bacteriuria found on a single survey, compared to 23 to 50 percent of women and 20 percent of men over the age of 80. This contrasts to other studies in which rates of bacteriuria were constant in patients above age 70 within the same living arrangements.[4,5]

A major factor in determining the prevalence of bacteriuria in the elderly is the place of residence. In single-survey studies, approximately 20 percent of elderly women and 10 percent of elderly men living at home had bacteriuria.[1–3,6,7] The prevalence is higher for patients living in extended care facilities or nursing homes, with bacteriuria there observed in 25 percent of women and 20 percent of men. These figures are even higher in hospitalized patients of both sexes, with a greater risk of developing bacteriuria being dependent upon the length of hospitalization. Among elderly women, the prevalence of bacteriuria was about 11 percent among those living in a life care community, about 18 percent among those living in a congregate living arrangement, and about 25 percent among those living in a nursing home.[1] Higher rates of bacteriuria among the nursing home residents were most likely related to the more debilitated state of the patients, with a higher incidence of perineal soiling, less complete bladder emptying, and bladder catheterization. Antecedent risk factors for the development of urinary tract infections that have been identified among nursing home residents include prior cerebrovascular accident, decreased functional status, decreased mental status, bladder catheterization, and prior antibiotic use; renal insufficiency, diabetes mellitus, anemia, malnutrition, age, and incontinence were not identified as risk factors.[8]

Several groups have examined the dynamic aspects of asymptomatic bacteriuria in elderly patients. One study examined patterns of bacteriuria on three surveys conducted at 6-month intervals in an ambulatory geriatric population of 184 women and 76 men over the age of 68.[4] On the initial survey, only 16 percent of women and 5 percent of men had bacteriuria, although the cumulative percentage of patients infected on at least one of the three surveys was 30 percent of women and 11 percent of men. Persistence of the same organism on all three surveys was found in only 6 percent of women and 1 percent of men. Extension of these 6-month surveys out to 6 years in a population of 865 women revealed a prevalence of about 11 percent in women in life care communities, with a cumulative positive incidence of 33 percent over 5 years.[5] Prevalences and cumulative positive incidences over the 5 years were about 18 and 52 percent, respectively, in women living in congregate housing arrangements, and about 25 and 57 percent, respectively, in women living in nursing homes. In another study from Finland of 101 women and 87 men over the age of 65,[9] bacteriuria was documented in 24 percent of women and 8 percent of men in one survey. The cumulative percentage of patients with bacteriuria after a second survey completed 5 years later was 38 percent of women and 15 percent of men. Similarly, a study from Greece of 231 women and 121 men over the age of 70 revealed that 27 percent of women and 19 percent of men had bacteriuria on initial survey.[10] After a second survey performed 1 year later, the cumulative percentage positive on at least one of the two surveys was 44 percent of women and 28 percent of men.

When these data are taken together, it appears that asymptomatic bacteriuria in the elderly is much more common than is apparent from performing a single survey. Additional surveys performed by the investigators would have undoubtedly increased the percentage of patients who had at least one episode of bacteriuria. Therefore, it seems likely that the majority of elderly women have episodes of asymptomatic bacteriuria at one time or another. Furthermore, these studies suggest that the geriatric population with bacteriuria is not a stable one. In one study, 17 percent of women and 6 percent of men with initially negative urine cultures had bacteriuria by the second or third survey, whereas 40 percent of women and 75 percent of men with initially positive urine cultures had no bacteriuria by the second or third survey.[4] Similar results were obtained in the studies from Finland[9] and Greece.[10] Thus, there is a high acquisition rate of bacteriuria among previously uninfected elderly women and men and a dramatic loss of bacteriuria in previously infected elderly patients. Therefore, the cumulative percentage of those patients infected at least once is much higher than the prevalence rate of bacteriuria, and persistence of bacteriuria occurs in only a minority of infected patients.

PATHOGENESIS

Routes of Infection

Urinary tract infection usually follows invasion of the urinary tract by the ascending route; the hematogenous and lymphatic routes are much less common.[11] The fact that urinary tract infections are more common in women than men supports the importance of the ascending route of infection; in women, the urethra is short and in close proximity to the vagina and perineum, making bacterial contamination likely. In men, the greater length of the urethra and the antibacterial properties of prostatic secretions are effective barriers to invasion by the ascending route.[12] For initiation of infection, bacteria must first colonize the anterior urethra.[1] Once bacteria gain access to the urinary bladder, colonization and multiplication can occur, followed by passage up the ureter to the kidney, a process that may be facilitated if vesicoureteral reflux is present.

Passage of bacteria into the bladder may be facilitated by several factors. In women, massage of the urethra or sexual intercourse can force bacteria into the bladder.[13,14] In addition, bladder catheterization has been shown to produce urinary tract infection in 1 to 2 percent of ambulatory patients following one catheterization and within 3 or 4 days in essentially all patients with indwelling bladder catheters and open drainage systems.[11] This high infection rate has led to development of closed catheter systems (i.e., an indwelling bladder catheter inserted into a collection tube that is fused to a collection bag on its distal end) to decrease the risk of bacteriuria. However, bacteriuria also occurs with the closed catheter system as a result of several factors[15,16]: (1) enhanced uropathogen colonization of the urethra; (2) the catheter serving as a conduit for movement of bacteria into the bladder via the catheter lumen (when the collection bag becomes contaminated) or its external surface; (3) the catheter surface offering a niche for bacteria to develop a microenvironment within a biofilm layer, and these bacteria appearing to be well protected from the mechanical flow of urine and possibly even antibiotics; (4) the greater numbers of bacteria adhering to the uroepithelial cells of catheterized patients; and (5) the blunting of adequate polymorphonuclear neutrophil function by the catheter.

Bacterial Virulence Factors

The likelihood of bacterial colonization of the urinary tract depends upon the virulence characteristics and inoculum size of the infecting microorganism and the status of host defense mechanisms. The most important organism virulence factor in the pathogenesis of urinary tract infection is thought to be adherence to vaginal and uroepithelium.[17] The presence of fimbriae, or pili, has been demonstrated to be important for the attachment of *Escherichia coli* to urinary tract epithelium. P and S fimbriae are most commonly and specifically expressed by pyelonephritic strains of *E. coli,* whereas type 1 fimbriae appear to play a more important role in colonization of the vagina, perineum, and bladder. Although the prevalence of urinary tract infections is increased in elderly women, no increased adherence of *E. coli* to the uroepithelial cells of elderly women as compared to young women was demonstrated.[18] However, increased adherence of organisms to the uroepithelium of elderly men as compared to young men was demonstrated, which may contribute to the increased frequency of bacteriuria among elderly men.

Bacterial lipopolysaccharide likely plays an important role in induction of the local inflammatory response and in the production of constitutional symptoms and signs during cystitis and pyelonephritis.[17] In addition, *E. coli* organisms possessing high quantities of capsular K antigens (K1, K2, K5, and K13 or K51) appear to be more virulent than other *E. coli* strains, since they are more likely to infect the kidney. Bacterial urease production has been shown to increase the risk of pyelonephritis in experimental animals. Production of urease, together with the presence of bacterial motility and fimbriae, may favor the production of upper-tract infection by organisms such as *Proteus.*

Host Defense Mechanisms

The host possesses several defense mechanisms to prevent the development of urinary tract infection, and these mechanisms may be deficient in the elderly.[1] Low vaginal pH is the most important factor in preventing colonization by uropathogens. Estrogen therapy may be effective in maintaining a low vaginal pH, although it is not clear that vaginal pH changes in elderly women. Vaginal and periurethral antibodies probably also act to prevent bacterial adherence, but it is unknown if these antibodies are deficient in the geriatric population. Although urine itself is considered to be a good culture medium for bacteria, it often possesses some antibacterial activity, including low pH, extremes of osmolality, high urea, high organic acid concentration, and—in males—bactericidal prostatic secretions. These urinary defense mechanisms may be decreased or absent in elderly patients. The decline of renal function that occurs with aging may diminish the ability to acidify the urine and reach extremes of osmolality. Dietary or renal changes may result in decreases in urea concentrations in the urine. The presence of glucosuria, secondary to a higher frequency of diabetes in elderly patients, also provides a better culture medium for bacteria. Prostatic secretions in urine may be decreased in elderly men as well. Tamm-Horsfall protein, which adheres to and covers type 1 fimbriae on gram-negative bacteria, thus reducing bacterial attachment to the mucosal surface of the urinary tract, is also decreased in the urine of elderly patients.[19] Micturition with complete bladder emptying is probably the most important defense mechanism in preventing urinary tract infection. Urine flow first dilutes the bacterial inoculum, then voiding flushes it from the bladder. This defense is likely to be impaired in the elderly secondary to prostatic disease in men, bladder prolapse in women, and neurogenic bladder in both sexes.[9,20]

MICROBIOLOGY

The most common causative organisms of urinary tract infection in young adults are *E. coli* and *Staphylococcus saprophyticus,* being responsible for about 80 to 90 percent of cases.[1,21] *Escherichia coli* is also the most common infecting microorganism among the elderly,[4,22] although these patients are more likely than younger patients to have infection with *Proteus, Klebsiella, Enterobacter, Serratia, Pseudomonas,* other gram-negative bacilli, and the *Enterococcus.* In one study of asymptomatic bacteriuria in a geriatric population,[4] the Enterobacteriaceae were predominantly isolated in women and gram-positive organisms predominantly in men; 93 percent of isolates from women but only 44 percent of isolates from men were Enterobacteriaceae. In another report of cultures of bladder urine from a heterogeneous group of men with a mean age of 66, 39 percent of infections were caused by gram-positive organisms.[23] The reason for this high rate of gram-positive organisms among elderly men with bacteriuria is unknown. Multiple organisms may also be more common among elderly patients, reported in 14 to 30 percent of urinary tract infections from one center.[22,24,25] However, in less impaired patients, multiple organism infection is rare.

The increased prevalence of organisms other than *E. coli* among the elderly with bacteriuria may be due, in part, to the greater frequency of hospitalization of this patient population. The hospital environment is an important factor in determination of the bacterial flora that colonizes the anterior urethra, and organisms such as *Proteus, Klebsiella, Enterobacter, Serratia, Pseudomonas,* and *Enterococcus* are more often isolated from hospitalized patients than from outpatients with bacteriuria.[26] Other possible reasons for this altered microbiology of bacteriuria in the geriatric population include urinary tract obstruction (i.e., related to neurogenic bladder, prostatic enlargement in men, bladder prolapse in women), increased frequency of urethral catheterization and/or instrumentation, and increased use of antimicrobial agents which may select for urethral colonization by antibiotic-resistant microorganisms.

CLINICAL FEATURES

The clinical presentation of lower urinary tract infection in the elderly may include dysuria, urgency, and frequency, which occur as a result of inflammation and irritation of the urethral and bladder mucosa. Occasionally the urine is blood-tinged or grossly bloody, reflecting damage to the superficial blood vessels in the bladder mucosa. The classical clinical manifestations of typical upper tract disease include fever, chills, flank pain, and tenderness; however, these symptoms may be altered or absent in elderly patients.[27] Gastrointestinal or respiratory symptoms or signs may dominate the clinical picture; in addition, there may be a diminished mental status. Elderly patients with upper tract disease or bacteremia may be unable to mount a febrile response or may even present with hypothermia. Peripheral leukocytosis is commonly absent. In a survey of acute pyelonephritis in elderly uncatheterized patients, the diagnosis was missed in 21 percent owing to the presence of gastrointestinal or pulmonary signs or symptoms, which are common in the elderly with or without pyelonephritis. Bacteremia and shock were present in 61 and 26 percent of the elderly patients, respectively, much higher than would be seen in a younger population with acute pyelonephritis.

The urinary tract is a frequent site of origin of bacteremia in the geriatric population. Although the bacteremia may be transient and self-limited, it may also be symptomatic, not infrequently leading to shock and death. The chances that an elderly patient will develop bacteremia increases in several clinical situations: instrumentation of the genitourinary tract, renal abscess, acute pyelonephritis, infection in the face of urinary tract obstruction or diminished host defenses, and catheter-associated bacteriuria with obstruction or impaired host defenses.[28] One study[29] in predominantly male nursing home patients found the presence of an indwelling urinary catheter to be the leading risk factor for development of bacteremia. Patients with catheters were 39 times more likely to be bacteremic than those without catheters. Of 27 patients catheterized at the beginning of the 1-year study, 16 (59 percent) had become bacteremic by year's end; in all cases, a urinary source was the cause of the bacteremia.

The large majority of elderly patients with bacteriuria are without urinary symptoms.[1] In addition, even when urinary symptoms are present, they can be difficult to interpret, because the symptoms of urgency, frequency, and incontinence are commonly experienced in uninfected elderly persons. To determine whether asymptomatic bacteriuria is really asymptomatic, 72 patients (mean age 85 years) without dysuria were questioned about urinary symptoms (urgency, frequency, incontinence) and about symptoms that would indicate a lack of well-being, both during and when episodes of bacteriuria were absent.[30] Although symptoms indicating lack of well-being were commonly reported and urinary symptoms were occasionally noted, no differences were found in either the frequency or severity of symptoms when subjects had or did not have bacteriuria. Therefore, asymptomatic bacteriuria (i.e., absence of dysuria) in the elderly is indeed asymptomatic.

DIAGNOSIS

Urinalysis

A carefully performed urinalysis with microscopic examination should be performed on all patients with suspected urinary tract infection.[31] Detection of pyuria is one of the most important aspects of urine examination. Pyuria is present in almost all symptomatic urinary tract infections, and its absence should suggest another diagnosis. Virtually all symptomatic patients with bacterial urine cultures revealing $\geq 10^5$ bacteria/ml have pyuria (defined as ≥ 10 leukocytes/mm^3 of urine). Pyuria has been reported to be present in only 36 to 79 percent of elderly patients with bacteriuria,[1,3] although one study utilizing quantitative methods found pyuria in 93.5 percent of elderly women with asymptomatic bacteriuria.[32] However, pyuria is not useful as a marker of bacteriuria among asymptomatic elderly women because of its frequency among those without infection. Of 133 women with pyuria, 39.1 percent had bacteriuria, whereas in 184 women without pyuria, only 4.3 percent had bacteriuria, indicating that the presence of pyuria was an imperfect predictor of the presence of bacteriuria.[32] However, the absence of pyuria was a very good predictor for the absence of bacteriuria, demonstrating that a quantitative leukocyte count in urine may be useful to screen for the absence of bacteriuria.

Microscopic examination of the urine should also be performed to look for the presence of bacteria. The presence of at least one bacterium per oil immersion field in a properly collected midstream clean-catch, gram-stained, uncentrifuged urine specimen correlates with $\geq 10^5$ bacteria/ml of urine (i.e., significant bacteriuria) with a sensitivity and specificity of almost 90 percent.[31] The absence of bacteria in several microscopic fields of a stained sedimented specimen indicates the probability of $<10^4$ bacteria/ml of urine and is evidence against bacteriuria.

Urine Culture

The microbiologic criteria for the diagnosis of urinary tract infection in the elderly is generally the same as in younger populations.[1] If there are $\geq 10^5$ bacteria/ml in a clean-catch midstream urine specimen from an asymptomatic female, there is an 80 percent probability that this represents true infection. If two different specimens demonstrate $\geq 10^5$ of the same bacteria/ml of urine, the probability increases to 95 percent. However, the situation has become more confusing with the observation that certain patient populations (e.g., sexually active young women) with acute symptomatic coliform urinary tract infection may have 10^2 to 10^5 bacteria/ml isolated from midstream clean-catch urine specimens.[31] It is undoubtedly also true that symptomatic elderly women and symptomatic men of any age have urinary tract infection with $<10^5$ bacteria/ml of urine, although this needs confirmation by cultures of suprapubic aspirates or bladder catheterization specimens. The current concept is that $\geq 10^5$ bacteria/ml in midstream urine on two confirmatory cultures should remain the standard for diagnosis of asymptomatic bacteriuria in women and $\geq 10^4$ bacteria/ml should remain the standard for men. In patients with urinary tract symptoms, $\geq 10^2$ Enterobacteriaceae/ml of urine usually indicates infection.

The validity of midstream clean-catch urine cultures in elderly women has been challenged. One study[33] in elderly women compared cultures of midstream clean-catch urine to suprapubic aspiration and found a false-positive rate of 57 percent, indicating only a 43 percent probability of a positive culture representing infection. However, lower false-positive rates have been reported for midstream clean-catch urine samples in this patient population,[34] and the specificity of various studies is undoubtedly related to proper technique and effort in obtaining the specimen. In contrast, other authors have suggested that occult upper tract foci of infection are more common than currently believed and can be missed by routine midstream clean-catch urine cultures. One study[35] found bacteriuria (defined as 3.2×10^3 to 8.8×10^5 organisms/ml) in catheterized urine samples after forced diureses in 16 of 34 (47 percent) elderly women who had sterile urine before diuresis. Of the 13 women who were tested for antibody-coated bacteria, 11 were positive, suggesting an upper-tract localization of infection.

In another study[36] examining a "representative" sample of elderly women and men ages 72 and 79 years, bacteriuric patients were followed by monthly urine cultures to determine the persistence of bacteriuria. In nine of 10 *E. coli* infections and 22 of 22 non-*E. coli* infections with $<10^6$ organisms/ml of urine, infections resolved spontaneously, whereas when *E. coli* bacteriuria with $\geq 10^6$ organisms/ml was present, infections persisted for at least 3 months (17 of 20 persisting infections were present for 3 months or more). High-titer bacteriuria ($\geq 10^6$ organisms/ml) and the isolation of *E. coli* were significantly associated with persistent bacteriuria in this study, and because of the greater likelihood of contaminated specimens from elderly patients, 10^6 organisms/ml may be a better standard for bacteriuria, challenging the usual standard of $\geq 10^5$ organisms/ml of urine.

Localization of Infection

The differentiation of upper-tract from lower-tract infection can sometimes be difficult. One method (Fairley washout technique) involves insertion of an indwelling catheter and sterilizing the bladder by washing it out with an antibiotic solution (neomycin) to eliminate free-floating and loosely attached bacteria.[37] Serial quantitative urine cultures are then taken through the catheter at frequent intervals. Since, theoretically, all bacteria previously present in the bladder have been killed, organisms in early specimens will have collected in the bladder from the ureter, localizing infection to the upper tract. Another method involves direct catheterization of the ureters for quantitative cultures; the right and left systems may be evaluated separately. However, despite the availability of these two methods, they are too invasive for practical use. In elderly, institutionalized women with asymptomatic bacteriuria, one group attempted to correlate the site of infection with the degree of pyuria.[25] Using the Fairley washout technique, they determined that two-thirds of the 51 infections involved the upper urinary tract. Utilizing a cutoff of ≥ 20 leukocytes/mm^3 of urine, the positive predictive value was 80 percent for the presence of upper urinary tract infection and the negative predictive value was 88 percent for the absence of upper-tract infection. Despite these good predictive values, the usefulness of this test in clinical situations is doubtful.

The detection of antibody-coated bacteria in urine has been used epidemiologically to differentiate upper- from lower-tract infection primarily in younger populations.[38] Fluorescein-conjugated antihuman globulin is added to bacteriuric urine and the urine is then examined under a fluorescent microscope. Fluorescence indicates the presence of antibody-coated bacteria and usually correlates with upper-tract infection. However, many false-positive and false-negative results have relegated testing for antibody-coated bacteria to use in clinical research situations, and this test does not play a significant role in the management of patients with urinary tract infection.

MANAGEMENT

Upper-Tract Infection

Hospitalization is more often required in the elderly patient with acute pyelonephritis than in younger populations because elderly patients are more likely to have bacteremia and hypotension,[27] necessitating use of parenteral antimicrobial agents. Empiric therapy for the hospitalized patient with acute pyelonephritis should be guided by the urine Gram's stain. When gram-positive cocci in chains are seen, suggesting infection with *Enterococcus,* therapy with parenteral ampicillin or a ureidopenicillin (e.g., mezlocillin, piperacillin) should be instituted. Vancomycin should be used in the penicillin-allergic patient. If gram-negative bacilli are seen, initial parenteral antimicrobial therapy can be a third-generation cephalosporin (e.g., cefotaxime, ceftizoxime, ceftriaxone), a ureidopenicillin (e.g., mezlocillin, piperacillin), aztreonam, trimethoprim-sulfamethoxazole, ampicillin-sulbactam, an aminoglycoside (e.g., gentamicin), or a fluoroquinolone (e.g., ciprofloxacin, ofloxacin). In patients who acquire gram-negative bacillary pyelonephritis in the hospital or nursing home, infection is more likely to be caused by multiple antibiotic resistant organisms, such as *Pseudomonas aeruginosa.* Empiric antimicrobial therapy should be directed against this pathogen with agents such as ceftazidime, aztreonam, ciprofloxacin, or a ureidopenicillin (e.g., mezlocillin, piperacillin) with or without an aminoglycoside. Because of the risks of aminoglycoside-induced ototoxicity and/or nephrotoxicity, aminoglycosides should be used with caution in the elderly, with dosages adjusted for diminished renal function. We prefer to avoid aminoglycosides in the elderly if at all possible, although patients with bacteremia caused by organisms such as *P. aeruginosa* may require combined beta-lactam plus aminoglycoside therapy. Dosages of intravenous antimicrobial agents for use in upper urinary tract infection are shown in Tzble 55-1.

Once the infecting microorganism has been identified and antibiotic susceptibilities are determined, antimicrobial therapy can be adjusted to use the safest, least expensive agent to which the organism is susceptible. In the elderly, the penicillins and cephalosporins are generally the agents least likely to cause adverse reactions. Once the patient has a clinical response, the regimen can be changed from parenteral to oral therapy to complete a 14-day course of treatment.[39]

In patients who fail to respond by 72 hours despite administration of an appropriate antimicrobial agent in adequate dosages, the possibility of urinary

TABLE 55-1

Dosages of Selected Intravenous Antimicrobial Agents for Use in Hospitalized Patients with Upper Urinary Tract Infections*

Antimicrobial Agent	Dosage and Dosing Interval
Ampicillin	1–2 g q4h
Ampicillin-sulbactam	1.5–3 g q6h
Aztreonam	1–2 g q8h
Cefotaxime	1–2 g q6h
Ceftizoxime	1–2 g q8h
Ceftriaxone	1–2 g q24h
Ciprofloxacin	200–400 mg q12h
Gentamicin†	1–1.7 mg/kg q8h
Mezlocillin	3 g q4h
Piperacillin	3 g q4h
Trimethoprim-sulfamethoxazole	4–5 mg/kg q12h§
Vancomycin†	1 g q12h

*Patients with normal renal and hepatic function. Dosage adjustment may be needed in the elderly due to deterioration of renal function.

§Dosage based on trimethoprim component.

†Need to monitor serum peak and trough concentrations.

tract obstruction or intrarenal or perinephric abscess should be considered. In men with obstruction due to prostatic enlargement, bladder catheterization will usually be required. Percutaneous nephrostomy placement is needed for infection behind a ureter obstructed by a calculus, followed by removal of the stone. Perinephric abscesses usually require percutaneous[40] or open surgical drainage; intrarenal abscesses can usually be treated successfully with prolonged antimicrobial therapy,[41,42] although drainage may occasionally be needed.

Patients with upper-tract infection who do not require hospitalization can be treated with oral antimicrobial therapy (e.g., trimethoprim-sulfamethoxazole or a fluoroquinolone) for a 14-day course; appropriate dosages of these agents are shown in Table 55-2.

TABLE 55-2

Dosages of Selected Oral Antimicrobial Agents for Use in Urinary Tract Infections*

Antimicrobial Agent	Dosage and Dosing Interval
Amoxicillin-clavulanate	250–500 mg q8h
Amoxicillin	250–500 mg q8h
Cephalexin	250–500 mg q6h
Ciprofloxacin	250–500 mg q12h
Norfloxacin	400 mg q12h
Ofloxacin	200–300 mg q12h
Trimethoprim	100 mg q12h
Trimethoprim-sulfamethoxazole	160 mg/800 mg q12h

*Patients with normal renal and hepatic function. Dosage adjustment may be needed in the elderly due to deterioration of renal function.

Lower-Tract Infection

For elderly women with typical symptoms of lower urinary tract infection, empiric therapy should be initiated if pyuria is present; urine culture at the first presentation is not mandatory.[1] If there is no response to therapy, however, urine culture should be obtained to guide further treatment. If there is an initial clinical response but symptoms recur upon discontinuation of therapy, upper-tract infection may be present and urine culture should be taken to guide therapy. A urine culture should always be obtained in men to evaluate lower urinary tract symptoms.

In women with urinary tract infections restricted to the bladder, there is now substantial evidence that short-course antimicrobial therapy (i.e., 3 days or even a single dose) gives results comparable to courses of 7 to 14 days.[43,44] Short-course therapy has the advantages of high compliance rate, low cost, and fewer adverse reactions. Three days of therapy may be more advantageous than single-dose therapy because there is a lower reinfection rate due to a higher eradication rate of Enterobacteriaceae from the vagina and feces.[39] Antimicrobial agents that can be utilized include trimethoprim-sulfamethoxazole, trimethoprim, norfloxacin, ciprofloxacin, ofloxacin, cephalexin, and amoxicillin-clavulanate. Because of the increasing resistance of many *E. coli* isolates, neither the sulfonamides nor ampicillin should be used as empiric therapy. Our preference is trimethoprim-sulfamethoxazole, trimethoprim, or a fluoroquinolone (e.g., norfloxacin, ciprofloxacin, ofloxacin) because of their high degree of in vitro activity against most uropathogens and their low toxicity. Elderly male patients with symptoms of urinary tract infection should be treated with 7 to 10 days of appropriate antimicrobial therapy[1,12]; evaluation of the urinary tract for a structural abnormality is also usually indicated. Dosages of oral antimicrobial agents for use for three days in lower urinary tract infection are shown in Table 55-2.

Eradication of bacteria from the urinary tract of elderly patients on a long-term basis is a controversial issue. Very high rates of reinfection and relapse have been documented among the institutionalized elderly, suggesting that antimicrobial therapy is not very efficacious in this patient population.[22,24,45,46] In one study of therapy versus no therapy in elderly ambulatory women treated with a single oral dose or 3 days' therapy,[47] a cure rate of 68 percent was achieved at 2 weeks and 64 percent at a 6-month follow-up, compared to a 35 percent spontaneous cure at 6 months in the no-therapy group. It appears that the ability to eradicate bacteriuria from the elderly on a long-term basis is much more dependent upon patient characteristics (e.g., place of residence, functional status, underlying diseases) than the choice of antimicrobial agent or the infecting organisms, a concept supported by numerous investigators.[22,24,46,47] Elderly patients with a higher functional status are more likely to remain free of bacteriuria after completing a course of antimicrobial therapy.

Relapse

There are several likely explanations for patients to relapse after appropriate antimicrobial therapy for urinary tract infection, including renal involvement, structural abnormality of the urinary tract (e.g., stone or obstruction), and chronic bacterial prostatitis. In all patients who have a relapse, an investigation for structural abnormalities should be considered (see below) and, in males, an attempt should be made to diagnose chronic bacterial prostatitis by the quantitative bacterial localization technique.[48] In this technique, quantitative cultures of midstream urine are obtained after a course of an antimicrobial agent that does not penetrate into prostatic secretions (e.g., ampicillin, cephalexin, or nitrofurantoin). These cultures are compared to cultures of expressed prostatic secretions or an ejaculate. A 10-fold higher titer of organisms in the secretions or ejaculate compared to the midstream specimen is diagnostic of a prostatic focus.

Cure is difficult in patients with chronic bacterial prostatitis because few antimicrobial agents penetrate well into the noninflamed prostate.[48] In addition, the focus of infection may be small prostatic calculi or abscesses which may be difficult to sterilize. Therapy with 4 to 12 weeks of trimethoprim-sulfamethoxazole or a fluoroquinolone is indicated, and longer durations of therapy may be indicated if symptomatic episodes continue to occur.

Asymptomatic relapses probably do not require treatment.[1] Symptomatic relapses may require a longer duration of antimicrobial therapy (i.e., 2 weeks if the previous course was shorter). In a woman who has a relapse after a 2-week course of an antimicrobial agent and who has no structural abnormalities, a more prolonged course (e.g., 3 to 6 weeks) should be considered. Long-term suppressive therapy with low doses of antimicrobial agents (e.g., trimethoprim-sulfamethoxazole or a fluoroquinolone in half the usual dosages) may also be utilized in patients who have repeated symptomatic relapses after initial therapy has been discontinued.

Reinfection

Patients with symptomatic reinfection of the urinary tract following successful cure can be classified as to whether the reinfections occur relatively infrequently (i.e., up to several reinfections per year) or frequently (i.e., reinfection develops shortly after therapy is discontinued).[1] If symptomatic reinfections are infrequent, each new episode should be treated with short-course antimicrobial therapy; asymptomatic reinfections should not be treated. In the elderly patient who develops symptomatic urinary tract infection so frequently so as to be incapacitated, long-term prophylactic therapy may be indicated to reduce the number of reinfections. Low-dose trimethoprim-sulfamethoxazole (e.g., one-half single-strength tablet nightly) or trimethoprim alone has been shown to be useful for this role in younger patients[49]; the newer fluoroquinolones may also be effective. Patients receiving long-term prophylaxis should be followed with urine cultures every 1 to 2 months. The same antimicrobial agent is continued as long as the patient remains nonbacteriuric. A new agent is chosen if bacteriuria persists or recurs. Most authorities recommend a 6-month trial of prophylaxis, after which the regimen is discontinued and the patient observed for further infection. Others have advocated a longer prophylaxis period of 2 years or more in women who continue to have symptomatic reinfection; use of trimethoprim, trimethoprim-sulfamethoxazole, or nitrofurantoin for as long as 5 years has been reported to be effective and well tolerated.[50]

Catheter-Associated Bacteriuria

Hospitalized elderly patients often receive placement of urinary tract catheters, and once the urethral catheter is in place, the incidence of bacteriuria is 3 to 10 percent per day.[15,16] Prevention of bacteriuria in the catheterized patient depends upon maintaining the catheter system closed and minimizing the duration of catheterization. Breaking the integrity of this system, most commonly for the collection of urine specimens, will increase the incidence of bacteriuria. Such specimens should be obtained without opening the catheter–collection tube junction but rather utilizing a needle and syringe and puncturing either the distal catheter or a port designed for this purpose. Other methods attempted include irrigation of the catheter with antibacterial solutions as well as use of antibacterial substances in the collection bag. However, these methods of irrigation offer additional opportunities for entry of bacteria and are more expensive. Silver-coated catheters have also been evaluated, with conflicting results.[15,16,51] Trials of antimicrobial prophylaxis in the presence of a closed catheter system have demonstrated lower instances of bacteriuria than in controls, but resistant organisms usually begin to appear in the urine after several days of therapy. A recent study found that ciprofloxacin prophylaxis was effective and safe in the prevention of catheter-associated urinary tract infections in postoperative patients requiring 3 to 14 days of bladder drainage[52]; ciprofloxacin-resistant mutants of normally sensitive gram-negative bacteria were not observed. However, because of the possibility of emergence of resistant organisms, relative lack of effectiveness, and cost, we do not advocate prophylaxis in this circumstance. Furthermore, asymptomatic bacteriuria should not be treated as long as the catheter remains in place. It is reasonable, however, to treat asymptomatic bacteriuria in catheterized patients just before the catheter is to be removed, although bacteriuria will disappear in many patients with catheter removal whether or not antimicrobial therapy is administered. In one study[53] it was noted that asymptomatic bacteriuria after short-term catheter placement frequently became symptomatic, thereby necessitating treatment. These authors recommended treatment of asymptomatic bacteriuria in this situation if the bacteriuria persisted more than 48 hours; they found that single-dose trimethoprim-sulfamethoxazole was effective in resolution of infection in 30 of 37 patients (81 percent).

For catheterized patients who develop symptoms or signs of pyelonephritis or bacteremia, an evaluation for catheter obstruction and periurethral infection (especially in men) should be performed. Parenteral antibiotics should be administered based on results of urine Gram's stain (see above).

Several alternatives to long-term urethral catheterization should be considered in patients who are unable to void on their own.[15,16] One is intermittent catheterization with insertion of a sterile or clean catheter every 3 to 6 hours.[54] Although bacteriuria develops in most of these patients, it likely occurs at lower rates than in those patients with indwelling catheters. Suprapubic catheterizations can also be utilized to decrease the incidence of bacteriuria; the lower density of bacteria on the anterior abdominal skin should yield lower rates of bacteriuria than that associated with urethral catheterization. External collection devices (i.e., condom catheters) can be used in male patients, and these appear to be associated with a lower but by no means zero incidence of bacteriuria.

Adjunctive Therapy

Several nonspecific therapies have been advocated in the treatment of urinary tract infection.[1] Forcing fluids has been suggested, on the theory that hydration results in a rapid reduction of bacterial counts in urine and flushes bacteria from the bladder. Renal medullary hypertonicity may also be reduced, thus enhancing leukocyte migration to the area. However, forcing fluids may also hinder therapy by increasing urinary output, thereby lowering urinary concentrations of antimicrobial agents. Since there is no evidence that hydration improves the result of appropriate antimicrobial therapy, its routine use is not recommended. However, dehydration is frequently present in patients with urinary tract infection and must be appropriately treated.

Changing the urinary pH has also been recommended as an adjunct to antimicrobial therapy in the treatment of urinary tract infection.[1] A lower urinary pH enhances the antibacterial activity of urine by increasing the concentration of undissociated molecules of organic acids normally found in the urine; these undissociated molecules probably penetrate better into bacterial cells. In addition, certain antibacterial agents (e.g., methenamine mandelate or methenamine hippurate) require a low urine pH (<5.5) for activity. Acidification of the urine can be achieved by the use of ascorbic acid or methionine and by diet modification (e.g., restricting milk, sodium bicarbonate, and fruit juices). One exception to these restrictions is cranberry juice, which increases the urinary concentration of hippuric acid, a compound that has antibacterial activity at low urine pH. However, with the current spectrum of antimicrobial agents available for the treatment of urinary tract infections, acidification of the urine is now rarely, if ever, utilized.

Recently several reports have documented the usefulness of low-dose oral or intravaginal estrogens in the management of recurrent urinary tract infections in postmenopausal women. Estrogen is needed to maintain adequate glycogen stores in the vaginal epithelium, thereby supporting the growth of lactobacilli and maintaining normal vaginal pH at or below 4.5. Loss of the estrogen effect is associated with atrophic vaginitis, with subsequent elevation of vaginal pH and local overgrowth by fecal flora. One study[55] found that in five patients in whom vaginal pH was at or above 5.2, reduction to 4.6 or less with intravaginal estrogens led to elimination of further attacks of cystitis. Another study[56] demonstrated a dramatic decrease in the frequency of recurrent urinary tract infections in 12 patients after use of oral or intravaginal estrogens. These studies suggest that use of estrogens as an adjunct to standard antimicrobial therapy may be useful in elderly women with frequent or recurrent urinary tract infections. However, it must be emphasized that the role of an estrogen effect (or lack thereof) in the pathogenesis of urinary tract infection remains unclear. Although estrogens help to maintain a normal vaginal flora,[57] there is evidence in experimental animal models and in humans that estrogens enhance bacterial adherence.[1] Therefore, the role of estrogens in the pathogenesis and prevention of urinary tract infections in women requires further study.

Radiologic Imaging

Radiologic imaging (i.e., ultrasonography, intravenous urography, computed tomography) is often important in the diagnosis and management of patients with urinary tract infection.[58] Evaluation should be considered in elderly patients who have bacteremia secondary to urinary tract infection or pyelonephritis that does not respond well to antimicrobial therapy. Urinary tract obstruction, intrarenal abscess, or perinephric abscess should be considered in these patients. Urinary tract infection in elderly men suggests the possibility of obstructive uropathy from prostatic enlargement or urethral stricture, and evaluation in these patients should include measurement of postvoid residual urine by bladder catheterization, intravenous urography with postvoiding films of the bladder, or, preferably, a bladder ultrasound which may demonstrate the presence or absence of prostatic obstruction. Computed tomography is of particular value in the diagnosis of intrarenal or perinephric abscesses.[40] The large majority of women with urinary tract infection do not require radiologic imaging, but evaluation may be indicated in female patients with multiple symptomatic episodes.

Asymptomatic Bacteriuria

Symptomatic urinary tract infection should be treated in patients of any age for symptom relief, but the significance of asymptomatic bacteriuria in the elderly is unclear. Some investigators have found evidence of decreased renal function or development of hypertension in elderly patients with bacteriuria, although this has not been substantiated by others.[1,59] Currently, since no clear causal relationship has been found between uncomplicated urinary tract infection and development of renal insufficiency, treatment of asymptomatic urinary tract infection in the elderly to prevent worsening renal function is not justified. This principle extends to patients with indwelling catheters, in whom prophylactic treatment is not indicated (but prompt treatment of clinically significant infections is clearly appropriate).

A more important concern relates to the possibility of an increased mortality rate among elderly patients with bacteriuria. Two studies[9,59] have demonstrated decreased survival in bacteriuric patients in comparison to nonbacteriuric patients. However, it is unclear whether this decreased survival is causally related to the bacteriuria. Increased susceptibility of the elderly to bacteriuria is related to immobility, dementia, cerebrovascular disease, and/or other debilitating diseases that may result from fecal soiling of the perineum from incontinence and incomplete bladder emptying.[8,45] Therefore, if increased mortality does occur, it may be secondary to various underlying diseases that predispose to bacteriuria. However, bacteriuria may be a cause of undetected bacteremia and subsequent death in elderly patients, or it may lead to decreased survival by some other mechanism. More recent studies have failed to confirm an increase in mortality rate among elderly patients with bacteriuria.[22,24,34]

Patterns of bacteriuria among the elderly may also have implications for survival. In previous studies, subjects were categorized as bacteriuric or nonbacteriuric based on results of initial urine cultures. Therefore, despite subsequent acquisition or loss of bacteriuria (which is very common among the elderly), the subject's category was not changed. A recent study revealed different patterns of bacteriuria on three surveys in elderly patients performed at 6-month intervals: occasional episodes of bacteriuria, persistent bacteriuria, and frequent reinfections.[4] Each of these patterns may have different implications for survival. For example, persistent bacteriuria may correlate more with decreased survival than occasional episodes of bacteriuria, and frequent reinfections may possibly have the worst prognosis, because subjects with serious underlying disease may be more prone to frequent reinfection than persistent bacteriuria. Frequent reinfection may also be more likely to cause bacteremia than persistent bacteriuria, in which protective antibody is more likely to be present. However, in a recent study in which patients received a 6-year follow-up,[60] no differences in survival between groups of elderly patients who were nonbacteriuric, intermittently bacteriuric, or continuously bacteriuric were documented.

It appears that more information is needed to determine whether bacteriuria is associated with excess mortality. Several studies have examined the effect of treatment on survival in elderly patients with bacteriuria. In one study,[22] 36 institutionalized elderly men with bacteriuria were randomly assigned to therapy or no therapy and followed monthly for 2 years. Although relapse and reinfection were very common, there were no significant differences in morbidity or mortality between the two groups. A second study[24] that used a similar design but studied 50 elderly institutionalized women over a 1-year period yielded similar results.

These data demonstrate that in the absence of urologic obstruction, asymptomatic bacteriuria in the elderly does not require treatment. Because of the high prevalence and recurrence rates in the elderly, it is not possible to eradicate all bacteriuria. In addition, because the elderly have higher rates of adverse effects related to antimicrobial therapy and the rate of emergence of resistance among organisms is increased, it seems best to avoid a vigorous approach to the treatment of asymptomatic bacteriuria in the elderly; the risk-benefit and cost-effectiveness ratios are unfavorable.[1]

REFERENCES

1. Baldassarre JS, Kaye D: Special problems of urinary tract infection in the elderly. *Med Clin North Am* 75:375, 1991.
2. Brocklehurst JC et al: The prevalence and symptomatology of urinary tract infection in an aged population. *Gerontol Clin* 10:242, 1968.
3. Sourander LB: Urinary tract infection in the aged—An epidemiologic study. *Ann Intern Med Fenn* 55(suppl 45):7, 1966.
4. Boscia JA et al: Epidemiology of bacteriuria in an elderly ambulatory population. *Am J Med* 80:208, 1986.
5. Abrutyn E et al: Epidemiology of asymptomatic bacteriuria in elderly women. *J Am Geriatr Soc* 39:388, 1991.
6. Gladstone JL, Recco R: Host factors and infectious

diseases in the elderly. *Med Clin North Am* 60:1225, 1976.
7. Lye M: Defining and treating urinary tract infections. *Geriatrics* 33:71, 1978.
8. Powers JS et al: Antecedent factors in urinary tract infection among nursing home patients. *South Med J* 81:734, 1988.
9. Sourander LB, Kasanen A: A 5-year follow-up of bacteriuria in the aged. *Gerontol Clin* 14:274, 1972.
10. Kasviki-Charvati P et al: Turnover of bacteriuria in old age. *Age Aging* 11:169, 1982.
11. Measley RE Jr, Levison ME: Host defense mechanisms in the pathogenesis of urinary tract infection. *Med Clin North Am* 75:275, 1991.
12. Lipsky BA: Urinary tract infections in men: Epidemiology, pathophysiology, diagnosis, and treatment. *Ann Intern Med* 110:138, 1989.
13. Bran JL et al: Entrance of bacteria into the female urinary bladder. *N Engl J Med* 286:626, 1972.
14. Nicolle LE et al: The association of urinary tract infection with sexual intercourse. *J Infect Dis* 146:579, 1982.
15. Warren JW: The catheter and urinary tract infection. *Med Clin North Am* 75:481, 1991.
16. Stamm WE: Catheter-associated urinary tract infections: Epidemiology, pathogenesis, and prevention. *Am J Med* 91(suppl 3B):65S, 1991.
17. Sobel JD: Bacterial etiologic agents in the pathogenesis of urinary tract infection. *Med Clin North Am* 75:253, 1991.
18. Sobel JD, Kaye D: The role of bacterial adherence in urinary tract infection in elderly adults. *J Gerontol* 42:29, 1987.
19. Sobel JD, Kaye D: Reduced uromucoid excretion in the elderly. *J Infect Dis* 152:653, 1985.
20. Sobel JD, Kaye D: Host factors in the pathogenesis of urinary tract infection. *Am J Med* 76(suppl 5A):122, 1984.
21. Sobel JD, Kaye D: Urinary tract infections, in Mandell GL, Douglas RG Jr, Bennett JE (eds): *Principles and Practice of Infectious Diseases,* 3rd ed. New York, Churchill Livingstone, pp 582–611.
22. Nicolle LE et al: Bacteriuria in elderly institutionalized men. *N Engl J Med* 309:1420, 1983.
23. Lipsky BA et al: Diagnosis of bacteriuria in men: Specimen collection and culture interpretation. *J Infect Dis* 155:847, 1987.
24. Nicolle LE et al: Prospective, randomized comparison of therapy and no therapy for asymptomatic bacteriuria in institutionalized elderly women. *Am J Med* 83:27, 1987.
25. Nicolle LE et al: Localization of urinary tract infection in elderly, institutionalized women with asymptomatic bacteriuria. *J Infect Dis* 157:65, 1988.
26. Turck M, Stamm WE: Nosocomial infection of the urinary tract. *Am J Med* 70:651, 1981.
27. Gleckman R et al: Acute pyelonephritis in the elderly. *South Med J* 75:551, 1982.
28. Johnson CC: Definitions, classification, and clinical presentation of urinary tract infections. *Med Clin North Am* 75:241, 1991.
29. Rudman D et al: Clinical correlates of bacteremia in a Veterans Administration extended care facility. *J Am Geriatr Soc* 36:726, 1988.
30. Boscia JA et al: Lack of association between bacteriuria and symptoms in the elderly. *Am J Med* 81:979, 1986.
31. Pappas PG: Laboratory in the diagnosis and management of urinary tract infections. *Med Clin North Am* 75:313, 1991.
32. Boscia JA et al: Pyuria and asymptomatic bacteriuria in elderly ambulatory women. *Ann Intern Med* 110:404, 1989.
33. Moore-Smith B: Bacteriuria in elderly women. *Lancet* 2:827, 1972.
34. Nordenstam GR et al: Bacteriuria and mortality in an elderly population. *N Engl J Med* 314:1152, 1986.
35. Dontas AS et al: Diuresis bacteriuria in physically dependent elderly women. *Age Aging* 16:215, 1987.
36. Norderstam GR et al: Bacteriuria in representative population samples of persons aged 72–79 years. *Am J Epidemiol* 130:1176, 1989.
37. Fairley KF et al: Simple test to determine the site of urinary tract infection. *Lancet* 2:715, 1967.
38. Jones SR et al: Localization of urinary tract infections by detection of antibody-coated bacteria in urine sediment. *N Engl J Med* 290:591, 1974.
39. Johnson JR, Stamm WE: Urinary tract infections in women: Diagnosis and treatment. *Ann Intern Med* 111:906, 1989.
40. Gerzof SG, Gale ME: Computed tomography and ultrasonography for diagnosis and treatment of renal and retroperitoneal abscesses. *Urol Clin North Am* 9:185, 1982.
41. Hoverman IV et al: Intrarenal abscess: Report of 14 cases. *Arch Intern Med* 140:914, 1980.
42. Schiff M Jr et al: Antibiotic treatment of renal carbuncle. *Ann Intern Med* 87:305, 1977.
43. Kunin CM: Duration of treatment of urinary tract infections. *Am J Med* 71:849, 1981.
44. Souney P, Polk BF: Single-dose antimicrobial therapy for urinary tract infections in women. *Rev Infect Dis* 4:29, 1982.
45. Brocklehurst JC et al: Bacteriuria in geriatric hospital patients: Its correlates and management. *Age Aging* 6:240, 1977.
46. Nicolle LE et al: Outcome following antimicrobial therapy for asymptomatic bacteriuria in elderly women residents in an institution. *Age Aging* 17:187, 1988.
47. Boscia JA et al: Therapy vs no therapy for bacteriuria in elderly ambulatory nonhospitalized women. *JAMA* 257:1067, 1987.
48. Meares EM Jr: Prostatitis. *Med Clin North Am* 75:405, 1991.
49. Stamm WE et al: Antimicrobial prophylaxis of recurrent urinary tract infection: A double-blind, placebo-controlled trial. *Ann Intern Med* 92:770, 1980.
50. Stamm WE et al: Natural history of recurrent urinary tract infections in women. *Rev Infect Dis* 13:77, 1991.
51. Johnson JR et al: Prevention of catheter-associated urinary tract infection with a silver oxide-coated urinary catheter: Clinical and microbiologic correlates. *J Infect Dis* 162:1145, 1990.
52. Van der Wall E et al: Prophylactic ciprofloxacin for catheter-associated urinary-tract infection. *Lancet* 339:946, 1992.
53. Harding GKM et al: How long should catheter-acquired urinary tract infection in women be treated?

A randomized controlled study. *Ann Intern Med* 114: 713, 1991.
54. Bakke A, Digranes A: Bacteriuria in patients treated with clean intermittent catheterization. *Scand J Infect Dis* 23:577, 1991.
55. Parsons CL, Schmidt JD: Control of recurrent lower urinary tract infection in the postmenopausal woman. *J Urol* 128:1224, 1982.
56. Privette M et al: Prevention of recurrent urinary tract infections in postmenopausal women. *Nephron* 50:24, 1988.
57. Brandenberg A et al: Low dose oral estriol treatment in elderly women with urogenital infections. *Acta Obstet Gynecol Scand Suppl* 140:33, 1987.
58. Merenich WM, Popky GL: Radiology of renal infection. *Med Clin North Am* 75:425, 1991.
59. Dontas AS et al: Bacteriuria and survival in old age. *N Engl J Med* 304:939, 1981.
60. Nicolle LE et al: The association of bacteriuria with resident characteristics and survival in elderly institutionalized men. *Ann Intern Med* 106:682, 1987.

Chapter 56

RENAL DISEASE

John M. Burkart and Vincent J. Canzanello

Virtually every disease or condition that affects the kidneys of children or young adults can occur as well in patients above the age of 65. In general, the presentation and manifestations in the elderly are similar to those in younger patients, although the underlying intrinsic age-related changes in renal function described in Chap. 54 may alter the expression or course of the disease. Some diseases of the kidney become increasingly prevalent with age, while others are found exclusively in elderly individuals.

The presence of concurrent disease is more often the rule than the exception in the very old. Chronic conditions involving the cardiopulmonary, skeletal, and gastrointestinal systems may modify the presentation or expression of renal disease, giving support to the familiar observation that common diseases may present uncommonly in the elderly. An example is the onset of acute glomerulonephritis in the older patient: congestive heart failure may dominate the clinical picture, whereas oliguria and smoky urine is the more classic presentation in the younger patient.

The diagnostic approach must be modified in evaluating an elderly person with suspected or manifest kidney disease. Reference has already been made in Chap. 54 to the need to recognize the lower rate of creatinine production in the elderly and the reflection of this change in serum creatinine concentration and estimated creatinine clearance. In addition, the increased susceptibility to acute renal failure demands particular caution in the use of radioiodinated contrast agents. For many evaluations, if not most, the information obtained from a renal sonogram and/or nuclear scan will be adequate and will avoid the risk of dye-induced nephrotoxicity. Similarly, underlying vascular disease and decreased renal size makes renal biopsy a higher-risk procedure in the very old patient than it is in the younger patient. The clinician must carefully weigh the benefit against this increased risk of complication.

The following chapter reviews the major clinical renal syndromes: vascular disease, vasculitis, glomerular disease, tubulointerstitial disease, acute renal failure, chronic renal failure, and end-stage renal disease (ESRD). The discussion will highlight prevalence patterns, when available, and the characteristics of the syndromes which require particular attention in the elderly patient.

VASCULAR DISEASES OF THE KIDNEY

Renovascular Disease

Renovascular disease, by definition an anatomic narrowing of a main renal artery or its branches, is particularly common in the elderly population. In most cases the obstruction is due to atherosclerosis, though fibromuscular disease can also occur in elderly patients.[1]

Renovascular disease typically results in varying degrees of hypertension and/or renal insufficiency though some degree of renal artery stenosis may be present in 32 to 40 percent of normotensive patients.[2] In a prospective study of 1302 consecutive patients undergoing diagnostic cardiac catheterization at Duke University, Harding and coworkers[3] found a 15 percent prevalence of hemodynamically significant renal artery stenosis (luminal diameter narrowing equal to or greater than 50 percent). Multivariate analysis of this population revealed older age, severity of coronary artery disease, and the presence of peripheral vascular disease (but not hypertension) to be significant clinical predictors of renovascular disease. Nonetheless, hypertension remains the most important clinical clue to the presence of underlying renovascular disease. While the prevalence of associated renovascular disease in the general hypertensive population is 1 to 4 percent, this figure approaches 45 percent in elderly patients with accelerated hypertension, grade 3 or 4 hypertensive retinopathy, and progressive renal insufficiency.[4]

Deterioration of renal function following the initiation of angiotensin converting enzyme (ACE) inhibitor therapy is an important diagnostic clue to the presence of extensive underlying renovascular disease,[5] though this phenomenon can occur in patients with essential hypertension. In general, however, the diagnosis of renovascular disease should be considered in an elderly patient who suddenly develops hypertension, escapes previously satisfactory blood pressure control, develops acute renal failure following ACE inhibitor therapy, or has unexplained chronic renal insufficiency in the presence of known atherosclerotic vascular disease. The importance of this consideration rests in the potential for improvement in blood pressure control and/or renal function following successful renal revascularization.

The selective renal arteriogram with oblique views, if necessary, remains the gold-standard test for the diagnosis of renal artery stenosis. Intraarterial digital subtraction angiography also provides excellent images of the renal artery, is less invasive, and requires a smaller dose of contrast material.[6] Nevertheless, the risks (contrast nephropathy, atheroembolism, local vascular trauma), patient discomfort, and cost of arteriography continue to limit its use in many elderly patients who often have varying degrees of renal insufficiency. This dilemma has prompted a continuously evolving search for accurate low-risk screening tests. The rapid-sequence intravenous pyelogram (with tomography) and the isotope renogram are considerably less accurate than arteriography, having sensitivities and specificities in the range of 75 to 80 percent and 75 to 88 percent, respectively.[4] The captopril challenge test, which involves measurement of the plasma renin activity at baseline and one hour following an oral dose of captopril, has not proven very accurate in the presence of bilateral renal artery stenosis and/or azotemia, both of which are common in elderly patients with renovascular disease.[7] Renal artery duplex sonography (combining B-mode ultrasonography with Doppler analysis of renal blood flow)[8] and captopril renography using ^{99m}Tc-DTPA with or without ^{131}I-orthohippurate[9] appeared to be more accurate than intravenous pyelography and standard isotope renography. Their accuracy is not significantly reduced in the presence of azotemia and, in the case of captopril renography,[10] may have considerable predictive power with respect to blood pressure outcome following renal revascularization. However, renal arteriography is still required despite a negative or equivocal noninvasive study in those patients with a high clinical suspicion of renovascular disease who are acceptable candidates for renal revascularization.

The natural history of atherosclerotic renovascular disease is one of slow progression, which can result in worsening blood pressure control, chronic renal insufficiency, and, possibly, ESRD.[1,11] Chronic medical therapy may control hypertension but does not consistently prevent further renal parenchymal loss.[1,12] Percutaneous transluminal renal angioplasty (PTRA) and surgical revascularization are effective both in improving blood pressure control and improving or stabilizing renal function.[13] In general, PTRA is a reasonable first choice in patients with stenotic lesions of the proximal renal artery and can usually be performed at the time of diagnostic arteriography. Surgical revascularization has been particularly successful in those patients with ostial stenoses. Both procedures have been successfully employed in elderly patients.[13,14] If conservative (i.e., medical) therapy is chosen for a patient with confirmed or suspected renovascular disease, renal function should be closely monitored.

Thromboembolic Disorders

Sudden occlusion of the main renal artery or its major branches results from either embolism to these vessels or in situ thrombosis. Hypertension and azotemia can result, depending upon the extent of renal ischemia or infarction. Embolism from the heart is the most common cause of renal artery occlusion. Cardiac conditions associated with an increased risk of renal artery embolism include rheumatic heart disease, congestive heart failure, myocardial infarction, atrial fibrillation, and infective endocarditis. The aortic arch and thoracic aorta have recently been described as occult sources of systemic embolization.[15] Additional sources include tumor, fat, and paradoxical venous emboli. In situ thrombus formation is less common than renal artery embolism and is usually associated with blunt abdominal trauma, vascular surgery, angiographic catheters, or a hypercoagulable state.[16]

The clinical manifestations of renal thromboembolism are quite variable and the diagnosis is frequently missed, being attributed to, for example, nephrolithiasis, pyelonephritis, myocardial infarction, or acute cholecystitis.[17] Suggestive findings in one of the above clinical settings include abdominal or flank pain, nausea, vomiting, fever, the sudden onset of hypertension, or exacerbation of previously controlled hypertension. Renal function depends upon the degree of ischemic damage and can range from normal in cases of segmental infarction to acute oliguric renal failure in patients with bilateral renal artery occlusions or occlusion of a single functioning kidney. Nonnephrotic proteinuria and microscopic hematuria are common, although the urinalysis may be normal. Elevations in serum enzymes abundant within renal tissue depend upon the extent of renal infarction and follow a predictable time course, with the serum glutamic-oxaloacetic transaminase (SGOT) level increasing within 24 hours of infarction and decreasing by day 4, the lactate dehydrogenase (LDH) level increasing by day 1 or 2 and remaining elevated for up to 2 weeks, and the alkaline phosphatase level increasing by days 3 to 5 and remaining increased for 3 to 4 weeks. Increasing urinary concentrations of LDH and alkaline phosphatase may allow differentiation from infarction of other organs. Definitive diagnosis of renal artery thromboembolism requires either standard or intraarterial digital subtraction arteriography. Nonvisualization or the absence of function by intravenous pyelography or isotope renography, respectively, suggests the diagnosis of renal artery thromboembolism (particularly if renal ultrasonography confirms the presence of a nonobstructive kidney) but does not obviate the need for renal arteriography. In patients with preexisting cardiac conditions, echocardiography may identify a potential embolic source. In this regard, transesophageal ultrasonography has been particularly useful.[15]

Management is directed towards control of hypertension and restoration of renal blood flow. In general, recovery of renal function is greater following medical or surgical therapy in elderly as opposed to younger patients, probably because of greater collateral blood flow in the former.[18] Unilateral thromboembolic disease has been successfully treated with systemic anticoagulation (heparin/warfarin)[17] and systemic or intraarterial thrombolytic therapy using streptokinase[19] or urokinase.[20] Systemic anticoagulation with warfarin should be continued indefinitely if the risk of thromboembolism persists (for example, in patients with chronic atrial fibrillation).

Surgical thrombectomy/embolectomy should be reserved for those cases where anticoagulation or thrombolytic therapy is contraindicated or has been unsuccessful after several hours.[16] Additional indications for surgery include bilateral renal artery occlusions (particularly in younger patients), uncontrollable hypertension, or retroperitoneal hemorrhage from infarcted renal tissue. In general, however, hypertension due to the ischemic kidney can be controlled with standard antihypertensive regimens, particularly those including a converting enzyme inhibitor.

Atheroembolic Renal Disease

Atheroembolic renal disease is typically seen in elderly patients with diffuse atherosclerotic vascular disease. The increasing use of aggressive medical, radiologic, and surgical interventions in these patients has led to a heightened recognition of this disorder, particularly as a cause of ESRD in the elderly.[11] Dislodgement of atheromatous material during catheterization or surgical manipulation of the aorta or renal arteries is the most common cause of renal atheroembolism.[18] Additional precipitating events include systemic anticoagulation, cardiopulmonary resuscitation, intraaortic balloon counterpulsation, and the intravenous administration of streptokinase or tissue plasminogen activator. Rarely, the disease occurs spontaneously in an elderly patient with underlying diffuse atherosclerotic vascular disease.

The clinical presentation of atheroembolic renal disease can range from the new onset of hypertension, acceleration of previously controlled hypertension, and insidious but progressive renal insufficiency to a more explosive syndrome of acute oliguric renal failure with embolism to multiple organ systems such as the retina, brain, pancreas, gallbladder, bowel, and bone marrow. Fever and abdominal pain are common. The lower extremities are a frequent site of distal embolization. The development of livedo reticularis, painful papules, or digital ischemic changes in the presence of intact pulses is very suggestive of the diagnosis in the proper clinical setting. Biopsy of clinically involved skin, histologic examination of amputated necrotic digits, or renal biopsy will usually demonstrate the presence of cholesterol emboli.

Renal insufficiency results from obstruction of the interlobular renal arteries by atheromatous debris, with a subsequent foreign body-type reaction around this material. Since this process is preglomerular in nature, the urinalysis is often benign, though eosinophiluria[21] or proteinuria, even to a nephrotic range,[22] may occur. An elevated erythrocyte sedimentation rate, transient hypocomplementemia,[23] and nonspecific increases in the SGOT and LDH may also be present. We have found an otherwise unexplained eosinophilia in an appropriate clinic setting to be the most consistent laboratory abnormality.

Acute renal failure following arteriography or major vascular surgery is a common occurrence. In addition to atheroembolic renal disease, other causes such as acute tubular necrosis (due to contrast material or ischemia), thromboembolic disease of the renal arteries, acute interstitial nephritis, or obstructive uropathy must be considered in the differential diagnosis. These disorders are discussed elsewhere in this chapter. The clinical presentation of systemic atheroembolic disease and the constellation of laboratory abnormalities described above may also be confused with systemic necrotizing vasculitis, infective endocarditis, cryoglobulinemia, or atrial myxoma.

The management of atheroembolic renal diseases is supportive. Treatment with glucocorticoids, dextran infusions, sympathetic block, and intraarterial infusions of vasodilators has not been effective.[18] Anticoagulants should be avoided in view of their association with this disorder. Relentless progression of renal insufficiency is the rule, although improvement may occur in sporadic instances.[24] If renal replacement therapy becomes necessary, peritoneal dialysis, in contrast to hemodialysis, has the theoretical advantage of avoiding the need for systemic albeit transient heparinization. In those patients demonstrating persistent systemic embolization, endarterectomy of the suspected source, if feasible, should be considered.

SYSTEMIC NECROTIZING VASCULITIS

The systemic vasculitides are a heterogeneous group of disorders characterized by inflammation and necrosis of blood vessels. The clinical manifestations are myriad and include vague constitutional symptoms, fever, purpura, arthritis, mononeuritis multiplex, central nervous system dysfunction, and infarction of various organs. Depending on the criteria used, some degree of renal involvement occurs in 70 to 90 percent of patients.[25]

The necrotizing vasculitides are probably immunopathogenic in nature. The prevailing theory is that injury occurs from the deposition of immune complexes in blood vessel walls,[26] although cell-mediated mechanisms may also be involved.[27] Because of the broad spectrum of clinical manifestations involved, it is difficult to subclassify these diseases succinctly. The diagnosis is often evasive because of the nonspecific clinical features at presentation and an occasional paucity of pathologic findings. To be sure, there is no pathognomonic glomerular lesion of vasculitis. However, renal biopsy is useful, as the presence of a focal segmental necrotizing glomerulonephritis with minimal endocapillary proliferation or basement membrane abnormalities is presumptive evidence for a systemic vasculitis.[28]

Early diagnosis and treatment of systemic vasculitis is important to prevent complications and end-organ damage. A recent review by Weiss and Crissman[29] showed that 57 to 78 percent of patients with various types of necrotizing vasculitis involving the kidney progressed to ESRD. The development of ESRD appeared to be related to both the timing of the diagnosis and the promptness with which therapy was initiated.

Polyarteritis Nodosa

The vasculitic syndrome of polyarteritis nodosa consists of a variable mix of signs and symptoms which include fever, weight loss, anemia, arthritis, dermatitis, myopathy, neuropathy, hypertension, and both gastrointestinal and renal disease. Mononeuritis multiplex is a typical feature of peripheral nerve involvement, and testicular pain is fairly common. The peak incidence occurs in the sixth decade of life, and males are affected twice as often as females. The urinary sediment typically is very active, and protein, white blood cells, red blood cells, and red blood cell casts are usually seen. Nephrotic syndrome is unusual, and progressive renal failure is usually a late manifestation of the disease.[25] Diagnosis is based on biopsy findings of an involved organ or arteriographic evidence of multiple aneurysm formation.[30] The classic form of polyarteritis nodosa involves segmental inflammation of small and medium-sized muscular arteries. "Microscopic polyarteritis nodosa" is an overlap syndrome caused by disease involving small arterioles and capillaries of major visceral organs.

The typical course of polyarteritis nodosa is highly variable, but 50 percent of patients follow a low-grade remitting course. Deaths due to the vasculitis itself occur early in the disease course, whereas later deaths are due to organ failure from vascular compromise or from a complication of treatment.[31] Although the treatment of polyarteritis nodosa is controversial, a consensus exists about the beneficial effect from use of corticosteroids. The controversy is based on various reports on the efficacy of cytotoxic drugs. Major reviews by Balow[28] and Fauci[27] favor the use of cyclophosphamine in conjunction with maintenance steroids.

Other Forms of Systemic Vasculitis

Other forms of systemic necrotizing vasculitis also occur in elderly populations, but with much less frequency. Examples include cutaneous hypersensitivity vasculitis, Wegener's granulomatosis, and the vasculitides associated with systemic disease processes such as systemic lupus erythematosus. In recent years the prognosis for all of these conditions has shown improvement coincidental with more aggressive therapy using both cyclophosphamine and prednisone. Treatments for these specific disorders are outlined in previous publications.[29,32]

GLOMERULAR DISEASES

In the elderly population, the renal glomerulus is subject to a variety of insults which may result in clinical disease. The resulting glomerular lesions are associated with a high degree of morbidity and mortality. Increasing numbers of elderly patients are now being accepted into ESRD programs, often due to an undiagnosed glomerulonephritis. Recent reports have shown that efficacious treatment exists for some glomerular diseases; therefore any elderly patient with presumptive evidence for a glomerular lesion should be evaluated appropriately to rule out a reversible lesion.

Prevalence

The actual incidence and prevalence rates of glomerular diseases in the elderly are unknown for several reasons. First, glomerular disease often mimics other, more common medical diseases of the elderly, making the diagnosis difficult. Most nephrologists can recall diagnosing nephrotic syndrome in a patient first treated for heart failure or finding a pulmonary renal syndrome in a patient initially treated for pneumonia. This difficulty of diagnosis is supported by a recent literature review of 46 patients over 50 years of age who presented with classic signs and symptoms of acute glomerulonephritis, of whom only 5 were initially diagnosed correctly.[33] Second, previous literature would suggest that the prevalence of glomerulonephritis in the elderly is rare.[34,35] In one review of 173 cases of glomerulonephritis, none of the patients was over the age of 60.[34] Consequently, there appears to be a low index of clinical suspicion for glomerular disease in the elderly patient, and the disease often goes undiagnosed ante mortem.[36] However, recent literature dealing specifically with either acute glomerulonephritis[37] or nephrotic syndrome[38] in the elderly concludes that these diseases are more prevalent than was initially believed. Newer data like these should help physicians become more aware of these disease possibilities in the elderly patient so that appropriate therapy can be initiated.

Clinical Presentation

The major clinical syndromes associated with glomerular disease in the elderly are (1) acute glomerulonephritis, (2) rapidly progressive glomerulonephritis, (3) chronic glomerulonephritis, (4) persistent urinary abnormalities with few or no symptoms, and (5) nephrotic syndrome with or without renal insufficiency. Although these presentations can mimic other common medical illnesses, these presentations should certainly make the physician consider the presence of underlying glomerular pathology. Occasionally the clinical manifestations of the disease are obvious enough to lead one to a specific diagnosis, i.e., type I crescentic glomerulonephritis in a patient with pulmonary hemorrhage, oligoanuria, a nephritic sediment, and a positive circulating antiglomerular basement membrane antibody (Goodpasture's disease). In patients who have only asymptomatic urinary abnormalities, a high index of suspicion and consideration of a renal biopsy may be needed to correctly diagnose an underlying glomerular disease. The physician can seldom predict the actual renal pathology from clinical signs and symptoms alone, although an important diagnostic clue is the rate of reduction, if any, of the glomerular filtration rate (GFR).

Acute Glomerulonephritis

Acute glomerulonephritis is a syndrome characterized by the abrupt onset of hematuria and proteinuria, often accompanied by edema, hypertension, and a reduction in the GFR. With few exceptions, the underlying disease process is immunologic in nature and can be subdivided into the following categories: (1) diseases mediated by antibodies directed at specific antigens native to the glomerulus itself, (2) damage from immune complex deposition (circulating immune complexes or those formed in situ), or (3) damage due to cell-mediated processes. Organ involvement may be systemic or localized to the kidney. Although all types of acute glomerulonephritis have been reported in the elderly (Table 56-1), most are infrequent except for rapidly progressive glomerulonephritis with crescent formation without immunoglobulin deposition.[39] Some of these disease states are potentially treatable; therefore recognition is important in order to prevent progression to ESRD.

Clinical Manifestations

In most cases the clinical manifestations of acute glomerulonephritis are fairly fulminant and consist of edema, hypertension, oligoanuria, a decline in GFR,

TABLE 56-1

Comparative Prevalence of the Different Glomerular Diseases Found on Renal Biopsy in Elderly Patients and in Younger Patients

Diagnosis	Elderly Adults >60 Years Old, %	Other Patients <60 Years Old, %
Primary glomerular disease	69.0	56.0
Idiopathic crescentic nephritis	11.0	4.0
Membranous nephropathy	15.0	6.0
Minimal change disease	4.0	7.0
Focal proliferative/mesangial glomerulonephritis	13.0	10.0
Diffuse proliferative glomerulonephritis	3.5	2.0
Chronic glomerulonephritis	5.0	7.0
Membranoproliferative glomerulonephritis	1.0	9.0
Glomerulosclerosis	10.0	8.0
Focal sclerosis	1.0	3.0
Secondary renal disease	23.0	29.0
Vasculitis	6.0	3.0
Amyloidosis	9.0	1.0
Other systemic disease	8.0	15.0
Miscellaneous	8.0	15.0

hematuria, proteinuria, and red blood cell casts. Not all patients have a classic presentation and some may have only asymptomatic urinary abnormalities. Patients may also complain of or present with symptoms related to any associated systemic disease causing the acute glomerulonephritis, such as pulmonary hemorrhage (Wegener's granulomatosis), heart failure (endocarditis), or arthritis (systemic lupus).

Rapidly progressive glomerulonephritis with crescent formation is the most common discrete glomerular disease found in elderly populations in association with acute glomerulonephritis. Most of these cases have negative immunofluorescent microscopy findings, suggesting that the process is not immunoglobulin-mediated and is probably a forme fruste of vasculitis,[39] hence the term "pauci-immune crescentic glomerulonephritis." The pathogenic mechanisms are unknown, but they are thought to be cell-mediated.[40] This is of interest because of the well-described decline in cell-mediated immunity associated with aging.[41] At the present time there is no explanation for this apparent paradox. Recently it has been found that 70 to 80 percent of these patients have circulating antineutrophil cytoplasmic antibodies (ANCA) similar to those found with Wegener's granulomatosis and in systemic necrotizing vasculitis.[42] Constitutional symptoms and other findings of systemic disease involvement are also occasionally found. The historical prognosis is poor, but recent data suggests that "pulse" methylprednisolone[43] may be helpful in preventing progression to ESRD. The combination of prednisone and intravenous cyclophosphamide has also been used with success, but controlled studies are still lacking.

Other causes of acute glomerulonephritis in the elderly are poststreptococcal glomerulonephritis, drug-induced glomerulonephritis (as with nonsteroidals), glomerulonephritis associated with systemic lupus erythematosus (SLE), chronic infection (endocarditis), and cancer.

Pathologic Findings

For definitive pathologic diagnosis, it is important to obtain light microscopy, immunofluorescence (IF), and electron microscopic (EM) analysis of the biopsy material in all cases. Renal biopsy or autopsy material from an elderly patient with acute glomerulonephritis most often shows a crescentic glomerulonephritis (40 to 66 percent) with no evidence of immunoglobulin deposition on EM or IF studies or, less commonly, a postinfective glomerulonephritis (16 to 20 percent).[44,45] Other types of glomerular pathology are also seen, especially those associated with a systemic vasculitis or collagen vascular disease, but with much less frequency.

Prognosis

Acute glomerulonephritis in the elderly as opposed to younger patients has a poor prognosis.[45] The reasons for this are multifactorial but are mostly due to the patient's older age, other associated illnesses, a higher incidence of oligoanuria necessitating dialysis, and, if present, the underlying systemic diseases that cause the glomerulonephritis itself.

Diagnosis

Clinical signs and symptoms are usually present that allow the physician to make the diagnosis. However, the cardiovascular manifestations of the disease may predominate; therefore cardiac disease is more often considered than renal disease.[46] Throat culture and antistreptolysin O (ASO) titers should be obtained, but in elderly patients they occasionally do not rise, necessitating other serologic tests, such as ADNAase B or antihyaluronidase levels.[47] Other tests should include rheumatologic studies such as antinuclear antibodies (ANA), ANCA and rheumatoid factor, complement levels,[48] cryoglobulin level, hepatitis B surface antigen, blood cultures to rule out endocarditis, and a protein immunoelectrophoresis. Renal biopsy should be considered despite its slight increased risk in an elderly patient.

Treatment

The treatment of acute glomerulonephritis in the elderly is based not only on the underlying disease state and renal biopsy findings but also on the patient's other associated underlying diseases, his or her physical condition, and the likelihood of response to treatment. Most therapeutic interventions would include corticosteroids, alone or in combination with cytotoxic drugs such as cyclophosphamide or azothioprine. Because of the potential for side effects, the patient's overall medical history must be considered very closely. If the acute glomerulonephritis is associated with a systemic disease process, the treatment of the glomerular lesion usually involves treatment of the systemic disease or chronic infection. Specific treatments exist for some of the idiopathic types of glomerulonephritis found in the elderly patient and are guided by renal biopsy findings.[47] At least 50 percent of patients with rapidly progressive forms of glomerulonephritis stabilize or improve after treatment with high-dose oral or intravenous "pulse" corticosteroids[43] if therapy is initiated "early" in the course of the disease. Conservative treatment alone is all that is usually needed for acute poststreptococcal glomerulonephritis.

Conservative therapy alone can often control many of the manifestations of acute glomerulonephritis but may not alter the underlying disease process. The physician should carefully monitor intake/output and weight to prevent acceleration of hypertension and volume overload. Hyperkalemia should be avoided, and the total CO_2 should be kept greater than or equal to 15 meq/liter. Hyperphosphatemia should be minimized by strategies outlined in the section on chronic renal failure. Protein restriction may also be helpful, but caloric intake must be maintained.[49]

Nephrotic Syndrome

The nephrotic syndrome consists of urinary protein losses in excess of 3.5 g/1.73 m^2 of body surface area per day in association with hypoalbuminemia, hyperlipidemia, a hypercoagulable state, and peripheral edema. The onset is usually insidious and, because the major clinical manifestation of the disease is generalized edema, elderly patients are frequently thought to have congestive heart failure. The etiologies of nephrotic syndrome are diverse and include such disease states as primary glomerular diseases, infiltrative diseases, and glomerular disease secondary to drugs, neoplasia, chronic infections, or other systemic diseases.

Incidence in the Elderly

About one in four cases of nephrotic syndrome in adults occurs in patients over the age of 60.[50] However, the exact incidence and prevalence rates for nephrotic syndrome in the elderly are unknown because of the frequency of its misdiagnosis.

Clinical Manifestations

Patients usually present with generalized edema, hypertension (33 percent), and renal failure (30 percent).[51] If a systemic disease is the cause of the nephrotic syndrome, there may be associated extrarenal manifestations of that disease. The urine contains protein and oval fat bodies and may occasionally have some nephritic elements.

Pathologic Findings

In a recent review of five published series of nephrotic syndrome in patients over 60 years of age, the most common light-microscopic finding was membranous nephropathy.[33] Minimal change disease and amyloidosis were the next most common findings. Other primary glomerular diseases are occasionally seen, as are lesions associated with systemic disease processes such as diabetes.

Diagnosis

Nephrotic syndrome is often masked by other concomitant medical diseases, so a high index of clinical suspicion must be maintained. Hematuria and red blood cell (RBC) casts are unusual. Evaluation should include serologic studies such as an ANA; rheumatoid factor; complement studies; hepatitis B antigen studies; blood cultures; serum and urine protein immunoelectrophoresis; if applicable, human immune deficiency virus studies; and an initial search for neoplasia. The most common types of nephrotic syndrome in the elderly adult are likely to show a negative serologic workup. Therefore, renal biopsy is important from a diagnostic, treatment, and prognostic standpoint.

Prognosis

Membranous glomerulonephritis is thought to have a favorable prognosis. Johnson and Couser[52] have reported that 50 percent of patients progress to ESRD; 25 percent have stable renal function but persistent urinary abnormalities, and the remaining 25 percent have a spontaneous remission. Membranous glomerulonephritis has been associated with cancer in approximately 20 percent of cases in patients over the age of 60.[53] For patients with a cancer causing the glomerulonephropathy, the prognosis usually depends on that of the associated neoplasm. Therefore, adults with a renal biopsy diagnosis of membranous glomerulonephritis should always have a complete physical and other appropriate laboratory studies done to detect a treatable cancer, not only at the time of presentation but also during subsequent years of follow-up. Because of the indolent nature of the disorder and the tendency for spontaneous remissions, many nephrologists would not treat patients with normal renal function and asymptomatic urinary abnormalities. However, for those patients with membranous glomerulonephritis who seem to have progressive disease, there is some evidence that medical intervention is helpful. The National Collaborative Study of the Adult Idiopathic Nephrotic Syndrome showed increased remissions and decreased progression to ESRD independent of age with the use of high-dose alternate-day prednisone.[54] Other treatment modalities using prednisone and chlorambucil[55] or cyclophosphamide[56] may also be efficacious.

Minimal change glomerulonephritis is a disease characterized by remitting and relapsing symptoms and a therapeutic susceptibility to corticosteroid therapy. It is felt to have a good prognosis in adults, including the elderly. In a review of 50 patients, 80 percent responded to glucocorticoid treatment,[33] although they tended to respond more slowly than did children. Some may require as much as 16 to 20 weeks of therapy (as opposed to 4 weeks for most children).[57] Progression to ESRD is unusual.

Amyloidosis causes 9 to 20 percent of cases of nephrotic syndrome in elderly patients. It is usually primary in origin but also occurs in a secondary form. It is characterized by heavy proteinuria, a serum or urinary monoclonal gamma globulin spike, and, usually, progressive renal insufficiency. Unfortunately, there is no known effective treatment for primary amyloidosis, although melphalan and prednisone have been used with some success.[58] Three-year survival in patients with nephrotic syndrome from amyloidsis is less than 10 percent.[59]

Treatment

The treatment of nephrotic syndrome should first be directed toward patient symptomatology and should include sodium restriction and judicious use of diuretics. Any underlying systemic disease that may be causing the glomerular lesion should then be treated. Treatment of the idiopathic forms of glomerulonephritis, such as membranous and minimal change glomerulonephritis, usually consists of corticosteroids and/or cytotoxic drugs, as already described.[47,54,55] Because of the potential side effects of these treatments, the physician must always consider the patient's overall condition, the natural history of the disease, and the risk/benefit ratio of using these drugs in the individual patient. Concomitant tuberculosis or other chronic infections should always be excluded.

TUBULOINTERSTITIAL NEPHRITIS

Tubulointerstitial nephritis and *interstitial nephritis* are terms used interchangeably to describe processes that prinicipally damage the renal interstitium. The etiologies of these diseases are diverse and include infectious, physical, chemical, immunologic, hereditary, drug, and unknown causes. As a group, tubulointerstitial nephritides are important disease states because they are common, and some are amenable to prevention and treatment. The elderly are especially predisposed to develop these because older people are more prone to infection, may have other acute or chronic medical illnesses, and are frequently on medication that may damage the renal interstitium.

Aging itself is associated with a progressive decrease in the kidneys' ability to defend the internal environment (see Chap. 54). These changes are associated with the presence of histologic changes in the interstitium and therefore can be considered the tubulointerstitial nephropathy of the elderly. However, interstitial disease in the geriatric patient is not limited to the aging process per se. As mentioned, there are systemic diseases to which the elderly are also predisposed that can cause interstitial damage. Therefore, careful consideration of these diagnoses must be given before ascribing the chronic renal insufficiency and urinary findings to aging alone.

Functional Defects

Despite the heterogeneous group of etiologies causing tubulointerstitial nephritis, the functional abnormalities induced are similar. These include (1) impaired ability to concentrate the urine, (2) impaired ability to excrete an acid load, (3) impaired ability to conserve salt, and (4) impaired ability to excrete potassium. Clinically, these abnormalities manifest themselves as polyuria, nocturia, metabolic acidosis, salt wasting, and hyperkalemia out of proportion to the patient's impairment in GFR. While these abnormalities can occur with any type of renal disease that is near the end stage, in tubulointerstitial nephritis they occur early in the disease course.

In addition to functional abnormalities, a number of other clinical features are suggestive of tubulointerstitial nephritis. In contrast to glomerular disease, patients, with tubulointerstitial nephritis usually present with less than 2 g of protein per 24 hours. The urinary sediment is characterized by the presence of white blood cells and occasionally white blood cell casts. Red blood cells are less frequent, and oval fat bodies and red blood cell casts are distinctly unusual. Eosinophiluria, best demonstrated by Wright's stain, may be seen in the setting of drug-induced tubulointerstitial nephritis. Clincially and to some degree pathologically, these diseases can be divided into acute and chronic forms.

Acute Tubulointerstitial Nephritis

The two most common and well-recognized forms of acute tubulointerstitial nephritis are acute bacterial pyelonephritis and acute drug-induced hypersensitivity reactions.

Acute Bacterial Pyelonephritis

Acute bacterial pyelonephritis is a disabling infection in the elderly that is usually due to gram-negative infections. It occurs in both sexes and is the most common form of renal disease in the aged. One autopsy series of patients aged 50 to 101 reported a 20 percent prevalence rate of pyelonephritis.[60] As with other renal diseases of the elderly, the disease is often a diagnostic challenge, for affected patients do not always present with the classic findings found in a younger population. Costovertebral angle tenderness, irritative voiding symptoms, and leukocytosis are unusual, whereas bacteremia, central nervous system changes, tachypnea, and hypotension are common.[61] The diagnostic evaluation should include urinalysis and blood and urine cultures. Blood cultures are positive in more than 50 percent of elderly patients with pyelonephritis,[62] so that—despite absence of clinical symptoms—a positive blood culture in a septic elderly patient with an organism identical to one recovered from the urine provides strong presumptive evidence for pyelonephritis.

Therapy is aimed at treating any systemic manifestations of the disease and at eradication of the infection. Septic shock may necessitate monitoring of central venous pressure to guide fluid replacement, especially in patients with heart failure. Other medical complications, such as disseminated intravascular coagulation and adult respiratory distress syndrome, may occur and require respiratory support and further supportive care. Initial treatment in a septic patient should include broad-spectrum intravenous antibiotics. Once the etiologic agent has been identified and susceptibility tests completed, a more specific agent that is less nephrotoxic can be substituted. Patients with uncomplicated pyelonephritis should show improvement within 48 to 72 hours after initiation of antibiotics. If the expected improvement has not occurred, the physician should obtain an ultrasound examination of the collecting system and kidneys to rule out an impediment to urinary flow such as a renal calculus, a sloughed renal papilla, or any other anatomic form of obstruction (such as prostatic disease). In these cases, perinephric abscess must also be excluded, for its treatment would most often include aggressive surgical intervention. In uncomplicated cases, the usual course of treatment is 10 days to avoid side effects from the antibiotic, such as pseudomembranous colitis.[63] Patients with complicated conditions may require longer therapy. Patients with anatomic abnormalities require urologic evaluation.

Drug Hypersensitivity

Acute interstitial nephritis due to hypersensivity to drugs is a well-recognized and increasingly common cause of acute renal failure.[64] Most reported cases have been due to methicillin or other beta-lactam derivatives[65]; however, this reaction has been reported in association with over 40 drugs[66] and therefore must always be considered in a patient on medications who develops acute renal failure.

The clinical presentation is variable and seldom classic in an elderly patient. Fever is present in 81 to 100 percent of patients, with microscopic hematuria in about 90 percent. Eighty percent of patients develop eosinophilia, but this is usually transient, lasting 1 or 2 days. A maculopapular rash is seen in less than half of the patients.[67] Sterile pyuria, eosinophiluria, and proteinuria may also be seen. The classical clinical triad of rash, fever, and eosinophilia is seen in only one-third of cases, so a high index of suspicion of the syndrome is imperative.[66]

The mainstay of therapy for acute allergic interstitial nephritis is to discontinue the offending agent. Supportive care and dialysis, if needed, are also indicated. Further therapy is controversial, and there are no good prospective randomized studies in the literature to support the use of corticosteroids in the treatment of all patients with allergic interstitial nephritis; however, this has been suggested by some authors[68–70] for selected patients. Galpin et al.[68] compared outcomes in treated and untreated adults. The numbers in the two groups were small, but the serum creatinine returned to baseline more often and faster in the treated versus the untreated group. Certainly, once an individual has developed known allergic interstitial nephritis in response to a certain drug, this class of drug should be avoided in the future.

Other Forms of Acute Interstitial Nephritis

Acute interstitial nephritis occasionally occurs in other settings. It rarely occurs in association with nephrotic syndrome in patients using nonsteroidal anti-inflammatory drugs (NSAIDs). Cimetidine has been reported to cause allergic interstitial nephritis due to an alteration in cell-mediated immunity. Through unknown mechanisms, it has occasionally developed in association with systemic infection. An idiopathic form of allergic interstitial nephritis also exists. Discussion and treatment of these diseases can be found in most textbooks of nephrology.

Chronic Interstitial Nephritis

The interstitium of the kidney is especially susceptible to toxic injury for a multitude of reasons. Normal physiologic processes that metabolize drugs can cause toxic metabolic products to concentrate in the medulla, predisposing it to injury. Systemic diseases may also cause chronic injury to the interstitium. Immunologic mechanisms can cause chronic damage to the interstititum and renal tubules. Finally, subtle, chronic damage to the renal microcirculation can cause ischemic injury. The end result of these types of chronic injury is renal insufficiency which may ultimately progress to ESRD.

Analgesic Nephropathy

Chronic consumption of compound analgesics can cause chronic renal insufficiency which may lead to ESRD.[71] Renal tubular acidosis, nephrocalcinosis, and chronic renal insufficiency are also common. Although most patients present in their forties, older patients can also present with the disease. The classic patient is female and has a history of peptic ulcer disease, headache, anemia, and sterile pyuria. The patients typically have ingested large quantities of analgesic mixtures. The cause of the renal damage is unknown, and early literature seemed to implicate phenacetin. Removal of phenacetin from compound analgesics in Canada has resulted in a significant reduction in new cases of analgesic nephropathy,[72] although the Australian experience has not been as rewarding. Discontinuation of analgesic consumption usually results in stabilization or slight improvement of renal function, although in some patients continued deterioration occurs. An increased risk for the development of uroepithelial carcinomas has also been reported.[73] Induction time for development of these carcinomas in a Swedish series was 22 years, with range of 9 to 42 years. Therefore, even though analgesic consumption may have halted, complications of the disease may occur in older patients.

Hypercalcemic Nephropathy

Chronic hypercalcemia—whether it occurs in primary hyperparathyroidism, multiple myeloma, sarcoidosis, vitamin D intoxication, or from metastatic bone disease—can produce both functional and structural damage to the renal interstitium. The most common functional defect is a concentrating defect associated with hypercalcemia. Renal tubular acidosis, salt-losing nephropathy, and chronic renal insufficiency are also seen. Clinically, hypercalcemia is initially characterized by an acute reversible prerenal type of acute renal failure. This is primarily due to marked polyuria and solute loss as well as to vasoconstriction of efferent arterioles. Hypercalcemia can also cause slow, progressive damage which may lead to chronic renal insufficiency. Treatment is directed at normalizing the hypercalcemia, replacing volume deficits, and correcting any underlying systemic disease processes.

Neoplastic Diseases Associated with Interstitial Nephritis

Neoplastic diseases may damage the renal interstitium in a multitude of ways. Direct renal invasion of the kidneys may occur with leukemia or lymphoma or by metastatic spread from other organ primaries. As mentioned, hypercalcemia due to cancer can cause interstitial disease, as can hyperuricemia, amyloidosis, or excessive radiation therapy.

Multiple myeloma is associated with multiple types of renal dysfunction. These include proteinuria, acute renal failure, progressive renal insufficiency, isolated renal tubular defects, amyloidosis, and pyelonephritis. By far the most important pathogenic factor in the development of chronic renal insufficiency of multiple myeloma is light-chain proteinuria, which may precipitate within the tubules and cause intrarenal obstruction or direct toxic damage.[74] Multiple myeloma is predominantly a disease of the elderly (median age at diagnosis is 60) and therefore must be considered in all elderly patients with proteinuria. Proteinuria is present in virtually all patients, and acute renal failure is common. Factors which can precipitate acute renal failure in these patients are hypercalcemia, dehydration, and certain nephrotoxic drugs. These factors seem to facilitate intrarenal precipitation of proteinaceous casts in these patients.[75] Progressive renal insufficiency in patients with multiple myeloma is far more common than acute renal failure and is most common in patients with immunoglobulin D myeloma or those with kappa light chains in their urine. In patients presenting with acute or chronic renal failure, survival is on the average less than 2 years.[76]

To make the diagnosis, the physician should obtain a protein immunoelectrophoresis on both the serum and urine along with urine for Bence Jones proteins. Other studies include a bone marrow aspirate and appropriate radiologic exams.

The main principle in the management of renal complications of myeloma is prevention. It is important to maintain adequate hydration, avoid use of nephrotoxic drugs, minimize use of intravenous contrast usage, and vigorously treat hypercalcemia and hyperuricemia.[77] Treatment of the myeloma itself usually involves prednisone and other cytotoxic drugs.

Aging-Associated Interstitial Disease

Aging itself is associated with a progressive decrease in the ability of the kidney to withstand major challenges to the patient's overall fluid and electrolyte balance. This decreased ability is due primarily to age-related renal tubular dysfunction which is termed *tubulointerstitial nephropathy of the elderly.* Although there are also age-related decreases in GFR, as mentioned in Chap. 54, these do not account for all the observed changes in renal function. There are histologic changes in the renal interstitium associated with aging,[78] hence the term *tubulointerstitial nephropathy of the elderly* is warranted. The major clinical manifestations of these age-related changes are no different than those from any other form of interstitial nephritis and can be accentuated by the known age-related decrease in aldosterone production[79] and renin[80] secretion. Pyuria (present in up to one-third of patients over age 70), is the typical urinary finding of tubulointerstitial nephropathy in the elderly. It is important to realize that asymptomatic hematuria or proteinuria are not normal changes associated with aging of the kidney and that these are signs of pathology involving the kidney, ureter, or bladder.

ACUTE RENAL FAILURE

Acute renal failure is an abrupt decrease in renal function sufficient to cause an increase in serum blood urea nitrogen (BUN) and creatinine concentrations. The etiologies of acute renal failure in the elderly are myriad and, as in younger age groups, can be divided into one of six major syndromes: prerenal azotemia, acute intrinsic renal failure (acute tubular necrosis), acute glomerulonephritis or vasculitis, acute interstitial nephritis, acute renovascular disease, and obstructive uropathy. The elderly population is especially prone to develop acute renal failure, which accounts for a significant amount of morbidity in these patients. A recent study found that 20 percent of all patients admitted to a geriatric unit had significant renal impairment[81]; therefore anyone taking care of elderly patients must be acquainted with the differential diagnosis and evaluation of acute renal failure.

Prerenal Azotemia

Prerenal azotemia due to dehydration is especially common in elderly patients because of both the age-related decrease in renal function and the inability of the kidney in the elderly to defend maximally against changes in the internal environment (see Chap. 54).

Causes of prerenal azotemia include volume depletion from both extrarenal and renal losses (vomiting, nasogastric suction, diarrhea, mineralocorticoid deficiency, osmotic diuresis as with hyperglycemia, and congestive heart failure). The treatment of these conditions is to first replace any volume losses and then to treat the underlying disease leading to the decreased perfusion of the kidney.

Acute Tubular Necrosis

Decreases in GFR resulting from prolonged renal ischemia or from a nephrotoxin that are not immediately reversed upon discontinuation of the insult are classified as causing acute tubular necrosis (ATN). Pathologically, the kidneys do not always demonstrate specific changes, and there does not appear to be an absolute structural/functional correlation. Physiologically, there is a prolonged cellular insult, which then results in sustained vasoconstriction, tubular obstruction, and decreased glomerular permeability. Clinically, one finds azotemia, and examination of the urinary sediment reveals granular casts, occasional white blood cells, and renal tubular cells. The patients may or may not be oliguric.

The causes of ATN are multifactorial and can be divided into two general etiologic groups: ischemic and nephrotoxic. Renal hypoperfusion is the most frequently recognized single insult leading to ATN.[82] Renal hypoperfusion can occur in the setting of intravascular volume depletion, decreased cardiac output, increased renovascular resistance, or renovascular obstruction; it can also occur postsurgically for unknown causes or by interference in renal autoregulation. Major surgery is implicated in 30 percent of cases. Interestingly, systemic hypotension does not have to occur. Hypotension was documented in only 50 percent of cases of postsurgical acute renal failure in a recent review by Hou and colleagues.[83] The most critical factor in the development of ATN is an actual decrease in renal blood flow with subsequent decrease in GFR. This decrease in renal blood flow can then cause graded renal parenchymal damage, manifested clinically by (1) mild reduction in GFR (prerenal azotemia), (2) frank ischemic damage (acute tubular necrosis), or (3) bilateral renal cortical necrosis. Elderly populations are likely to have multiple predisposing factors for the development of renal hypoperfusion, partially explaining the high incidence of ATN in these groups.

Antibiotics, particularly aminoglycosides,[84] are among the most common causes of nephrotoxic ATN. Inappropriate use and overdosage of aminoglycosides are important risk factors. Many physicians erroneously estimate a normal GFR in an elderly patient based on the serum creatinine concentration and fail to recognize that this serum creatinine concentration is "normal" only because of a decrease in muscle mass associated with aging. The GFR may actually be lower than expected despite the normal serum creatinine (see Chap. 54). A creatinine clearance should always be estimated when ordering dosages of an aminoglycoside and the total dose reduced by either increasing the interval between doses or decreasing the amount of drug given per dose. Other common causes of nephrotoxic ATN include the use of radioiodinated contrast agents, pigment nephropathy (myoglobin), amphotericin B, and some chemotherapeutic agents (e.g., *cis*-platinum).

Treatment is directed toward discontinuation of the offending agent (if possible) and general supportive care. Supportive care should include a close determination of volume status and treatment of any volume deficiencies, if present, watching for signs or symptoms of electrolyte imbalance, monitoring patients' acid-base status, and prescribing dialysis (if indicated). In most cases the renal dysfunction is reversible, but not always back to baseline levels. Anuria and a prolonged course are poor prognostic signs.

Interference with Renal Autoregulation

The increased use of two new classes of drugs, ACE inhibitors and prostaglandin synthetase inhibitors, has resulted in increasing reports of acute renal failure associated with their use. In general, the acute renal failure occurs under conditions where renal autoregulation of the afferent and efferent arteriolar tone is important for maintenance of GFRs.

Nonsteroidal anti-inflammatories such as propionic acid derivatives (ibuprofen, naproxen, and fenoprofen) and indoleacetic acid derivatives [tolmetin sodium (Tolectin) and indomethacin] have been reported to cause acute renal failure in selected patients. These patients have tended to have a reduction in the actual, or "effective," renal perfusion associated with states such as congestive heart failure, cirrhosis, nephrotic syndrome, sepsis, and preexisting renal disease.[85] In these disease states, the renin-angiotensin cascade is activated. This angiotensin II-induced vasoconstriction of afferent and efferent arterioles could further decrease renal perfusion and GFRs. Normally, renal prostaglandins are also produced in this circumstance, including an important compensatory vasodilatation to counterbalance the vasoconstriction and thereby maintain the GFR through intrinsic renal autoregulation. However, since NSAIDs decrease prostaglandin synthesis, this can leave the angiotensin II-induced vasoconstriction unopposed, causing acute renal failure.[86] Discontinuation of the drug usually results in improvement of the condition of renal dysfunction.

Angiotensin converting enzyme inhibitors (captopril, enalapril, and lisinopril) have been reported to produce a severe deterioration in renal function in patients with renal artery disease.[87] In patients with a critical degree of renal artery stenosis, a low perfusion pressure exists, so maintenance of the GFR depends on the crucial balance of afferent and efferent arteriolar resistance. These resistant arterioles are regulated primarily by the renin-angiotensin system.[88] Inhibition of angiotensin II production by use of an ACE inhibitor then blocks this renal autoregulation, resulting in a decreasing GFR and subsequent acute renal failure. As in NSAID-induced disease, the renal dysfunction usually reverses with discontinuation of the drug; this reversal reaction is the mainstay of treatment. In patients in whom this dysfunction has been demonstrated, the physician must consider that the patient may have underlying atherosclerotic renovascular disease.

Obstructive Uropathy

Obstruction to urinary flow can cause acute or chronic renal failure. Urinary flow obstruction can be due to extra- or intraureteral problems, bladder outlet obstruction, or urethral obstruction. Elderly patients are predisposed to prostatic, pelvic, or other abdominal cancers such as lymphoma, all of which may obstruct urinary flow; therefore it is of utmost importance that a renal ultrasound or other radiologic study be obtained to rule out obstruction in all causes of acute renal failure in an elderly patient. Many of these causes of obstruction are amenable to medical treatment or surgical therapy, with resulting reversal of renal dysfunction.

CHRONIC RENAL FAILURE

Chronic renal failure and the signs and symptoms thereof are the net result of irreversible damage to renal parenchymal mass. The clinical manifestations are similar no matter what disease process caused the initial damage. Chronic glomerular, interstitial, renovascular, metabolic, immunologic, or obstructive disease states can all cause chronic renal failure and may progress to ESRD.

A brief overview of treatable causes of ESRD was recently published.[89] Of utmost importance in any patient with newly diagnosed renal failure is to attempt to find a reversible cause for the disease and remedy it. If no specific treatment exists, an attempt to prevent progression should be initiated, which includes controlling any coexisting diabetes, hypertension,[90] and perhaps protein intake. This empiric treatment is based on studies such as those by Meyer et al.[91] They have suggested that excessive protein intake in the setting of chronic renal insufficiency may hasten the progression to ESRD by causing progressive glomerular sclerosis or capillary hypertension and glomerular hyperfiltration.

In an individual patient, renal disease tends to progress at a constant rate. A plot of 1/serum creatinine versus time for each patient tends to form a linear rate of progression.[92] Chronic follow-up of these patients should show the expected rate of decline of renal function. Although an accelerated decline may be part of the natural history of the disease, if the rate of decline is found to be faster than expected, the physician must suspect development of another intercurrent medical illness. Such compounding problems may include urinary tract infection, uncontrolled hypertension, renal artery disease, de novo glomerulonephritis, de novo interstitial nephritis, drug-induced renal dysfunction, or anatomic obstruction to urinary outflow. Treatment is then aimed at attempting to reverse the acute renal failure resulting from the superimposed illness.

Sodium and Water

As the GFR declines, the remaining nephrons must be able to excrete an ever-increasing percentage of the filtered load of sodium. In some patients, sodium intake overwhelms the remaining kidney's ability to excrete the daily ingested load. These patients may need sodium restriction to prevent volume overload. An occasional elderly patient will be misdiagnosed as developing heart failure and unnecessarily placed on digoxin when the actual problem is excessive sodium intake (more appropriate treatment would be salt restriction and diuretics). When diuretics are needed to maintain volume status in a patient with chronic renal insufficiency, loop diuretics, such as furosemide or ethacrinic acid, are preferable. To determine the amount of sodium intake needed per day, a 24-hour urine collection for sodium excretion should be obtained. In most patients, a 2- to 4-g sodium-restricted diet is sufficient to maintain sodium balance. However, sodium conservation is impaired in a few patients, such as those with adult polycystic kidney disease, chronic interstitial nephritis, or medullary cystic disease; it is also impaired in some patients just as a result of aging. In these patients with impaired conservation, 24-hour urine sodium losses may be as much as 10 to 20 g/day.[93] These patients would then need sodium supplementation rather than restriction to maintain a normal extracellular fliud volume.

Patients with chronic renal failure tend to have a decreased ability to excrete a water load. For these patients the amount of daily water intake can be estimated by measuring daily urine output and adding about 500 ml for insensible losses to that total.

Potassium Homeostasis

Potassium is freely filtered by the glomerulus, reabsorbed proximally, and secreted distally. Most of the potassium excreted in the urine comes from distal secretion. This distal secretion is facilitated by aldosterone. Unless hyporeninemia or hypoaldosteronism is present, it is unusual for a patient with chronic renal insufficiency to become hyperkalemic unless the GFR is below 10 ml/min. Selective hypoaldosteronism is common in elderly patients, especially those with diabetes. In that circumstance, an elderly patient may become hyperkalemic sooner than expected as evidenced by measured creatinine clearance alone.[94] To maintain potassium homeostasis, patients with chronic renal insufficiency have increased colonic potassium losses, presumably due to aldosterone-dependent mechanisms. Constipation is a common problem for the elderly, and treatment of hyperphosphatemia in patients with chronic renal failure with aluminum-containing phosphate binders can aggravate both constipation and the tendency toward hyperkalemia.

Treatment of hyperkalemia is tailored toward the severity of its elevation. In mild cases, prevention is the goal and is achieved by restricting dietary potassium intake or by facilitating potassium exchange by the distal renal tubule. Dietary intake should be restricted to 2 to 4 g/day. The use of oral sodium bicarbonate and/or mineralocorticoids can facilitate potassium secretion distally. If medical therapy is attempted, the physician must watch for salt and water overload from the increased sodium intake. Symptomatic hyperkalemia requires acute intervention. Intravenous glucose, insulin, sodium bicarbonate, and/or calcium chloride may temporarily reverse the cardiac manifestations of hyperkalemia by facilitating movement into the cells.[95] However, these therapies do not reduce the total body stores of potassium and so must be followed by oral or rectal administration of sodium polystyrene sulfonate (Kayexalate), by forced renal losses through diuresis, or by dialysis, all of which reduce total body potassium.

Acid-Base Status

Patients with chronic renal failure tend to develop a metabolic acidosis due to the kidneys' decreased ability to excrete the normal daily acid production. Respiratory compensation is usually adequate to maintain a nearly normal systemic pH. However, it may be necessary to treat the acidosis when the serum bicarbonate level falls to less than 18 meq/liter. This is especially true for an elderly patient who may have concomitant respiratory disease and not be able to compensate adequately for the acidosis, or for those patients with ischemic cardiac disease in which systemic acidosis may predispose to arrhythmias. Appropriate treatment involves the use of oral sodium bicarbonate or calcium carbonate to buffer the acid load. Calcium carbonate may be preferable in that it reduces the sodium load and may help prevent development of renal osteodystrophy by binding dietary phosphorus.

Calcium and Phosphorus Metabolism

Progressive renal insufficiency results in major alterations in calcium and phosphorus metabolism. These alterations are due to the combined effects of phosphate retention, decreased production of 1,25-dihydroxy vitamin D, and increased parathyroid hormone levels. The decreased availability of 1,25-dihydroxy vitamin D causes decreased intestinal absorption of calcium and also decreases the effect of the action of parathyroid hormone on bone. These decreases, along with the phosphorus retention, tend to cause a decrease in the serum ionized calcium, which leads to a secondary increase in parathyroid hormone levels. Consequently, early in chronic renal insufficiency, normocalcemia is maintained at the expense of an ever-increasing level of parathyroid hormone.[96] This secondary hyperparathyroidism can lead to renal osteodystrophy, characterized clinically by bone pain, proximal muscle weakness, and occasionally hypercalcemia. Hypercalcemia in the face of hyperphosphatemia can result in metastatic calcification of arteries, bones, and heart as well as deposition of calcium-phosphorus in the skin, which may cause pruritus.

Initial treatment is aimed at preventing progressive hyperparathyroidism. Of primary importance is the restriction of dietary phosphorus intake. Unfortunately, this usually results in a concomitant restriction of calcium intake, so supplemental calcium must also be provided. If the hyperphosphatemia persists despite dietary restriction, phosphate binders should be added. Aluminum hydroxide, calcium carbonate, or calcium acetate is given with meals to bind phosphorus in the gut and prevent its absorption. Aluminum hydroxide–containing binders have been associated with the development of a disabling form of osteomalacia, dementia, and anemia in patients with chronic renal insufficiency and ESRD[97]; consequently, excessive doses should be avoided and calcium-containing binders are preferred. Calcium carbonate has the added advantages not only of binding phosphate and providing calcium supplementation but also of avoiding possible aluminum accumulation. Supplemental vitamin D should be considered when hypocalcemia persists despite normal phosphate levels or when there is a progressive rise in serum alkaline phosphatase. Serum alkaline phosphatase levels can be used as a marker for prevailing parathyroid hormone activity. A slowly increasing level suggests that the present serum calcium level is being maintained at the expense of calcium loss from bone. The various forms of vitamin D should facilitate calcium absorption from the gut, raising the serum calcium and tending to decrease parathyroid hormone levels. Dosage adjustment is often needed to avoid hypercalcemia, for hypercalcemia has been reported to accelerate the progression to ESRD.[98]

Dietary Protein Intake

Nitrogen balance is important in patients with chronic renal insufficiency. Excessive protein intake by such patients may both hasten onset of uremic symptoms and accelerate the progression to ESRD.[91] Conversely, symptoms of uremia may be decreased and, in some cases, dialysis avoided by restricting protein intake. Of therapeutic importance are preliminary studies which suggest that protein restriction may slow or prevent the progression to ESRD.[99] A multicenter trial investigating the role of modification of diet in the progression of renal disease is presently in progress. To achieve optimal nitrogen balance, patients with chronic renal failure should ingest between 0.5 to 1.0 g protein/kg body weight per day, predominantly protein of high biological value.

Diet and Vitamins

Patients with chronic renal failure develop folate, vitamin C, and pyridoxine deficiencies. Therefore, a multivitamin supplying these vitamins is usually prescribed. Vitamin D deficiency due to loss of renal parenchymal mass has already been discussed. Vitamins A and E should be avoided, for their stores normally increase in association with chronic renal failure.

Anemia of Chronic Renal Failure

Anemia is associated with chronic renal failure and is due to multiple factors: erythropoietin levels are decreased as renal parenchymal mass falls, vitamin deficiencies may predispose to anemia, RBC life is shortened in uremic plasma, repeated phlebotomies may tend to deplete iron stores, there may be associated gastrointestinal blood loss, and drugs such as nonsteroidal anti-inflammatory agents and beta blockers may decrease the effect of circulating levels of erythropoietin on the uremic bone marrow. Normally transfusion is not indicated for hemoglobins in the range of 7 g/100 ml or above unless the patient is symptomatic. For older patients with underlying atherosclerotic heart disease, maintenance of a hemoglobin level of 10 g/100 ml or greater would be a reasonable goal of therapy to prevent congestive heart failure or angina. Use of recombinant human erythropoietin has resulted in the reversal of the anemia and its accompanying symptoms.[100]

Drug Dosages

Many drugs are metabolized and/or excreted by the kidney. As GFRs drop, lower doses of these drugs are needed. One important example of this principle is insulin, which is usually filtered and then metabolized by the proximal tubules. It is common for a diabetic patient with chronic renal insufficiency to need less insulin as the disease progresses. Many elderly patients develop concomitant heart disease, such as congestive heart failure. It is important to remember to reduce the dose of digoxin in these patients, with a recommended starting dose of 0.125 mg every other day. Serum levels should be monitored. Some drugs, such as aminoglycosides, are nephrotoxic, and their use is clearly more risky in patients with impaired renal function. Their doses must be carefully adjusted as the GFR changes and alternative drugs should always be considered.

As mentioned previously, the physiologic decline in GFR seen in the elderly is not accompanied by a parallel rise in serum creatinine. Hence actual creatinine clearance, rather than serum creatinine concentrations, should be used to guide drug dosages for renally excreted drugs. Twenty-four-hour urine collection is the best way to determine creatinine clearance, which is only an estimate of GFR. Nomograms and formulas may also be used to estimate creatinine clearance but may overpredict actual clearances in the geriatric population (see Chap. 54).

Drugs must always be considered as a cause of renal dysfunction. Of particular relevance to geriatrics is the occurrence of drug-induced renal dysfunction in patients using NSAIDs. They can cause nephrotic syndrome, renal papillary necrosis, hyponatremia, hyperkalemia, water intoxication, or "resistant hypertension."

Indications for Dialysis

There are no absolute levels of BUN or creatinine above which dialysis is always indicated. A serum creatinine of 4 mg/dl in a 90-year-old female may represent a worse GFR than a serum creatinine of 7 mg/dl in a 20-year-old male. In general, the patient should begin chronic dialysis once the first symptoms of uremia occur. These include symptoms such as anorexia, weight loss, or a decrease in the patient's overall exercise tolerance. Absolute indications for dialysis include severe acid-base disturbances, intractable hyperkalemia, volume overload unresponsive to medical therapy, encephalopathy, pericarditis, and progressive peripheral neuropathy. The patient's overall functional status, personal preferences, and the appropriateness of instituting such life-supportive therapy should be addressed before either acute or chronic dialysis therapy is begun.

END-STAGE RENAL DISEASE

Since the advent of chronic renal replacement therapy in the early 1960s, the ESRD population in the United States has grown to over 163,000.[101] Of these,

30,568 patients were age 65 to 74 and 15,222 were age 75 or older in 1991. Along with this growth in the total ESRD population there has been a marked increase in the incidence of ESRD in patients of age 65 and older. It is estimated that over 60 percent of the ESRD patients in the United States will be above 65 years of age by the year 2000, and only this age group is expected to continue to grow in size. This increase is not so much due to a change in various disease spectrums as it is to the estension of medical coverage to most patients with ESRD and to older patients, including those with illnesses such as diabetes (Social Security Amendment of 1972—Public Law #92-603, Section 2991). In Michigan, for example, the yearly number of patients aged 0 to 54 who entered ESRD programs changed very little from 1974 to 1983, whereas there was a marked increase in the number of patients entering the program aged 55 and older.[102] Recent Department of Health and Human Services data, reporting on total case loads for ESRD patients, showed that 15 percent of all patients seen were over the age of 70.[103] This is supported by data from the 1991 United States Renal Data Systems (USRDS) annual report, which showed that the unadjusted incidence of treated ESRD in patients aged 65 to 74 increased from about 290 cases per million population in 1982 to about 590 cases per million population by 1989. During that same time period, the incidence rates for treated ESRD in patients aged 20 to 44 changed very little.[101] Consequently, the median age of new dialysis patients in the United States has increased to 60 years of age.[101]

Elderly patients with ESRD present a number of unique problems. They not only have ESRD but they are likely to have other comorbid medical illnesses. They have to adjust to the aging of their peers, families, and, in some, the progressive loss of their support systems. Equally important is the fact that the cost of ESRD can be a considerable financial burden for many patients. Close attention must be paid to their special needs by counseling, discussing the various therapeutic modalities available to them, and, importantly, explaining the expected benefits and possible ramifications of treatment on quality of life. This kind of discussion certainly should be undertaken before initiating long-term-maintenance dialysis therapy.

Because of their older age and the likelihood of other comorbid medical problems, the life expectancy of older dialysis patients' is less than that of younger patients. According to data from the USRDS,[101] the 2-year survival rate for all treated Medicare patients (1984–1988 cohort) was 65 percent, whereas the 2-year survival rates were 53 and 38 percent, respectively, for patients aged 65 to 74 and those aged 75 and older. Despite this lower life expectancy, most nephrologists are not averse to offering maintenance dialysis therapy to elderly patients.

One reason for offering this therapy is based on the quality-of-life issues. A patient's personal quality of life is best judged by the individual patient and family, not by those providing care. Studies by Westlie et al.[104] and Chester et al.[105] suggest that the majority of older patients in their dialysis populations did not consider themselves worse off than their peers. Bailey et al.[106] looked at rehabilitation in old and young dialysis patients and concluded that elderly patients had comparable levels of rehabilitation when compared to younger patients. These reports strongly support providing ESRD therapy to all patients without age restriction but do not eliminate the need for assessing each individual's potential benefits from dialysis and approaching the patient with a multidisciplinary effort when explaining dialysis options.

Elderly patients with ESRD, like younger patients, have multiple therapeutic options available to them. These include hemodialysis, chronic ambulatory peritoneal dialysis, renal transplantation, conservative medical therapy, or acceptance of death from uremia.

Hemodialysis

Hemodialysis is the most common therapeutic choice for ESRD therapy in the elderly. The basic principle of this therapy is to remove unwanted solute and water from the patient by movement across an artificial membrane into dialysate by diffusion using an extracorporeal system. The patient typically receives a 3- to 5-hour treatment three times a week. Chester et al.[105] analyzed data from their hemodialysis patients aged 80 or above and found that hemodialysis provided them with an average of 22 months of additional life versus patients in the comparison group (mean age 42), who had an average survival of 39 months. Although survival for elderly hemodialysis patients is statistically less than that of younger patients, quality-of-life issues such as those reported by Westlie et al.,[104] Chester et al.,[105] and Bailey et al.[106] should be considered and would suggest that in most elderly patients maintenance dialysis would be indicated.

The increased mortality rate in the elderly is due to multiple associated risk factors. Among these are age, which in itself increases the risk of dying by 1.2 for each added decade of life,[107] and any comorbid medical diseases. The increased prevalence of coronary artery disease in elderly patients increases the risk for dialysis-induced angina, arrhythmias, hypotension, and cerebrovascular accidents. The presence of coronary artery disease and its associated conditions does not preclude treatment of ESRD but at times may make the patient's individual treatment somewhat more difficult. Use of recombinant human erythropoietin can treat the anemia and help to alleviate these problems.[100] Cardiovascular drugs used to treat underlying arrythmias, angina, or hypertension require close attention to dosing. Mental status changes are common and may be due to concurrent drug use, underlying central nervous system pathology, or complications of uremia and dialysis itself. "Dialysis dementia,"[108] which may be due to the accumulation of aluminum, must always be considered in elderly patients with faltering mental status or syndromes of failure to thrive.

Special care must be taken when considering the creation of access for hemodialysis. Some data suggest that the construction of autogenous arteriovenous fistulas in elderly patients is less feasible than in the general population[109] and should be considered only in selected patients. Prognostic factors which collectively argue against autogenous reconstruction are diabetes, prolonged incidence of secondary hyperparathyroidism, diffuse atherosclerotic disease, previous stroke with paresis or paralysis of the extremity, repeated venipuncture, or history of intravenous cannulation of the vein. If autogenous construction is not possible, Gore-tex grafts are an acceptable alternative.[109]

Peritoneal Dialysis

Continuous ambulatory peritoneal dialysis (CAPD) was first described in 1976[110] but not widely used until 1978. This technique uses a sterile, closed system composed primarily of the peritoneal cavity, a chronic indwelling catheter, connecting tubing, and a collapsible plastic bag containing the dialysate. Dialysate dwells in the peritoneal cavity for 4- to 8-hour periods, during which "dialysis" occurs. After each such period, the dialysate is drained, a new bag is connected, and the peritoneal cavity is refilled by gravity. Forms of automated peritoneal dialysis (APD) are modifications of CAPD. These techniques involve 4 to 12 rapid exchanges of dialysate, usually during the night, with the help of an automated cycling machine. Some of these patients will also need a daytime dwell.

By 1983 the segment of the total dialysis population dialyzing at home had increased to 15 percent, of which 62.5 percent were using CAPD.[101] Along with the increase in number of patients on CAPD, the percentage of these patients over the age of 60 has increased from an estimated 31 percent in 1981[111] to 48 percent by 1986.[112] Elderly patients therefore presently account for at least one-third of CAPD populations, and as CAPD becomes a more accepted technique, the absolute number of elderly patients on this form of ESRD therapy is expected to grow.

Reasons for choosing CAPD include the convenience of dialyzing at home, the stability of serum chemistries, the reduction of stress on the cardiovascular system, patient preference, and physician selection bias. A large body of literature now exists comparing hemodialysis to peritoneal dialysis in elderly patients. Few differences in morbidity and mortality have been reported in many studies. The Canadian Renal Failure Registry[113] showed no difference in the survival of elderly patients on hemodialysis versus peritoneal dialysis, although peritoneal dialysis had a higher rate of technique failure. A recent Italian study[114] reported better patient survival for those aged 66 and older with peritoneal dialysis after adjustment for comorbid conditions. At the present time there appears to be no reason to systematically exclude the elderly from peritoneal dialysis.

Potential medical advantages of peritoneal dialysis versus hemodialysis in the elderly include better control of hypertension, preservation of renal function, lack of need for vascular access, avoidance of rapid changes in volume status, and avoidance of treatment-induced cardiac arrhythmias. Morbidity associated with peritoneal dialysis includes peritonitis, catheter tunnel and exit site infections, and failure of the technique. Peritonitis rates, catheter function, and catheter longevity are reported to be the same or better in older versus younger populations,[115] while overall morbidity, technique survival, and biochemical control are similar between groups of young versus old CAPD populations.

Transplantation

It has generally been thought that older patients had a high mortality risk after undergoing renal transplantation. However, recent studies have suggested that there is no statistically significant difference in survival rates over a 4-year period of follow-up for transplant recipients below age 40, between ages 40 and 50, and above 50 years of age[116] (few such recipients were truly elderly, however). As with all groups, the greatest attrition rates for the elderly recipients occurred during the first year after transplantation. The use of newer, more specific immunosuppressive drugs, such as cyclosporine A and the generalized decline in T-cell function associated with aging[40] may facilitate graft survival in elderly patients. However, this generalized decline in T-cell function may also be responsible for the increased predisposition to infectious complications, which in fact has been reported for transplant patients over the age of 50.[117]

While recipient survival rates have improved over those from the 1960s, the main causes of death and their rank order have remained fairly constant. Infections, cardiovascular diseases, and stroke continue to be the principal causes of death in older transplant populations. Despite the increased risk associated with infections and the potential cardiovascular risks associated with surgery and immunosuppressive drugs, reported 3-year survival rates for transplant patients of age 50 or above was 84 percent.[118] This is in contrast to reported 1- and 3-year survival rates for almost 36,000 dialysis patients over the age of 50 of 77 percent and 48 percent, respectively. While this difference may be due in part to the rigorous patient selection for transplantation, it suggests that transplantation is a viable mode of therapy for selected older patients with ESRD.

REFERENCES

1. Schreiber MJ et al: The natural history of atherosclerotic and fibrous renal artery disease. *Urol Clin North Am* 11:383, 1984.
2. Eyler WR et al: Angiography of the renal areas including a comparative study of renal arterial stenoses in patients with and without hypertension. *Radiology* 78:879, 1962.
3. Harding MB et al: Renal artery stenosis: Prevalence and associated risk factors in patients undergoing routine cardiac catheterization. *J Am Soc Nephrol* 2:1608, 1992.
4. Madias NE: Renovascular hypertension. *AKF Nephrol Lett* 3:27, 1986.
5. Hricik DE, Dunn MJ: Angiotensin-converting enzyme inhibitor-induced renal failure: Causes, consequences, and diagnostic uses. *J Am Soc Nephrol* 1:845, 1990.
6. Kaplan NM: Renal vascular hypertension, in Kaplan NM (ed): *Clinical Hypertension*, 5th ed. Baltimore, William & Wilkins, 1990, p 318.
7. Muller FB et al: The captopril test for identifying renovascular disease in hypertensive patients. *Am J Med* 80:633, 1986.
8. Hansen KJ et al: Renal duplex sonography: Evaluation of clinical utility. *J Vasc Surg* 12:227, 1990.
9. Davidson R, Wilcox CS: Diagnostic usefulness of renal scanning after angiotensin converting enzyme inhibitors. *Hypertension* 18:299, 1991.
10. Setaro JF et al: Simplified captopril renography in the diagnosis and treatment of renal artery stenosis. *Hypertension* 18:289, 1991.
11. Meyrier A et al: Atheromatous renal disease. *Am J Med* 85:139, 1988.
12. Dean RH: Comparison of medical and surgical treatment of renovascular hypertension. *Nephron* 44(suppl 1):101, 1986.
13. Canzanello VJ et al: Percutaneous transluminal renal angioplasty in management of atherosclerotic renovascular hypertension: Results in 100 patients. *Hypertension* 13:163, 1989.
14. Olin JW et al: Renovascular disease in the elderly: An analysis of 50 patients. *J Am Coll Cardiol* 5:1232, 1985.
15. Tunick PA et al: Atheromatosis of the aortic arch as an occult source of multiple systemic emboli. *Ann Intern Med* 114:391, 1991.
16. Canzanello VJ, Harrington JT: Renal artery embolism and thrombosis, in Hurst JW (ed): *Medicine for the Practicing Physician*, 2d ed. Boston, Butterworths, 1988, pp 1169–1170.
17. Lessman RK et al: Renal artery embolism—Clinical features and long-term follow-up of 17 cases. *Ann Intern Med* 89:477, 1978.
18. Ives HE, Daniel TO: Vascular diseases of the kidney, in Brenner BM, Rector FC Jr (eds): *The Kidney*, 4th ed. Philadelphia, Saunders, 1991, pp 1502–1505.
19. Fischer CP et al: Renal artery embolism: Therapy with intra-arterial streptokinase infusion. *J Urol* 125:402, 1981.
20. Kennedy JS et al: Simultaneous renal arterial and venous thrombosis associated with idiopathic nephrotic syndrome: Treatment with intra-arterial urokinase. *Am J Med* 90:124, 1991.
21. Wilson DM et al: Eosinophiluria in atheroembolic renal disease. *Am J Med* 91:186, 1991.
22. Fine MJ et al: Cholesterol crystal embolization: A review of 221 cases in the English literature. *Angiology* 38:769, 1987.
23. Cosio FA et al: Atheroembolic renal disease causes hypocomplementaemia. *Lancet* 2:118, 1985.
24. Smith MC et al: The clinical spectrum of renal cholesterol embolization. *Am J Med* 71:174, 1981.
25. Davson J et al: The kidney in periarteritis nodosa. *Am J Med* 17:175, 1948.
26. Cochrane CG, Dixon FJ: Antigen-antibody complex induced disease, in Meischer PA, Muller-Eberhard HJ (eds): *Textbook of Immunopathology*, 2d ed, vol 1. New York, Grune & Stratton, 1976, p 137.
27. Fauci AS et al: The spectrum of vasculitis: Clinical, pathologic, immunologic, and therapeutic considerations. *Ann Intern Med* 89:660, 1978.
28. Balow JE: Renal vasculitis. *Kidney Int* 27:954, 1985.
29. Weiss MA, Crissman JD: Segmental necrotizing glomerulonephritis: Diagnostic, prognostic, and therapeutic significance. *Am J Kidney Dis* 6:199, 1985.
30. Travers RL et al: Polyarteritis nodosa: A clinical and angiographic analysis of 17 cases. *Semin Arth Rheum* 8:184, 1979.
31. Cupps TR, Fauci AS: *The Vasculitides*. Philadelphia, Saunders, 1981.
32. Balow JE, Austin HA: Vasculitic diseases of the kidney, in Suki WN, Massry SG (eds): *Therapy of Renal Diseases* and *Related Disorders*. Boston, Nijhoff, 1984, p 273.
33. Brown WW: Glomerulonephritis in the elderly, in Michelis MF et al (eds): *Geriatric Nephrology*. New York, Field, Rich, 1986, p 90.
34. Ellis A, Toronto MD: Natural history of Bright's disease: Clinical, histological and experimental observations. *Lancet* 1:1, 1942.
35. Fishberg AM: *Hypertension and Nephritis*, 5th ed. Philadelphia, Lea & Febiger, 1954, p 529.
36. Nesson HR, Robbins SL: Glomerulonephritis in older age groups. *Arch Intern Med* 105:23, 1960.
37. Montoliu J et al: Acute and rapidly progressive forms of glomerulonephritis in the elderly. *J Am Geriatr Soc* 29:108, 1981.
38. Zech P et al: The nephrotic syndrome in adults aged over 60: Etiology, evaluation and treatment of 76 cases. *Clin Nephrol* 18:232, 1982.
39. Stilmant MM et al: Crescentic glomerulonephritis without immune deposits: Clinicopathologic features. *Kidney Int* 15:184, 1979.
40. Abrass CK: Glomerulonephritis in the elderly. *Am J Nephrol* 5:409, 1985.
41. Roberts-Thompson IC et al: Aging, immune response and mortality. *Lancet* 2:368, 1974.
42. Falk RJ et al: Antineutrophil cytoplasmic autoantibodies with specificity and/or myeloperoxidase in patients with systemic vasculitis and idiopathic necrotizing and crescentic glomerulonephritis. *N Engl J Med* 318:1651, 1988.

43. Bolton WK: Crescentic glomerulonephritis, in Glassock RJ (ed): *Current Therapy in Nephrology and Hypertension*. Philadelphia, Decker, 1984, p 213.
44. Arieff AI et al: Acute glomerulonephritis in the elderly. *Geriatrics* 26:74, 1971.
45. Potviliege PR et al: Necropsy study on glomerulonephritis in the elderly. *J Clin Pathol* 28:891, 1975.
46. Samiy AH et al: Acute glomerulonephritis in elderly patients: Report of seven cases over sixty years of age. *Ann Intern Med* 54:603, 1961.
47. Glassock RJ et al: Primary glomerular disease, in Brenner BM, Rector FC (eds): *The Kidney*. Philadelphia, Saunders, 1981, p 929.
48. Madaio MP, Harrington JT: The diagnosis of acute glomerulonephritis. *N Engl J Med* 309:1299, 1983.
49. Schrimsow NS: An analysis of past and present recommended dietary allowances in health and disease. *N Engl J Med* 294:136, 1976.
50. Fawcett LW et al: Nephrotic syndrome in the elderly. *Br Med J* 2:387, 1971.
51. Lustig S et al: Nephrotic syndrome in the elderly. *Isr J Med Sci* 18:1010, 1982.
52. Johnson RJ, Couser WG: Membranous nephropathy, in Glassock RJ (ed): *Current Therapy and Nephrology and Hypertension*. Philadelphia, Decker, 1984, p 207.
53. Zech P et al: The nephrotic syndrome in adults aged over 60: Etiology, evolution, and treatment of 76 cases. *Clin Nephrol* 18:232, 1982.
54. Collaborative Study of the Adult Idiopathic Nephrotic Syndrome: A controlled study of short-term prednisone treatment in adults with membranous nephropathy. *N Engl J Med* 301:1301, 1979.
55. Ponticelli C et al: Controlled trial of methylprednisolone and chlorambucil in idiopathic membranous nephropathy. *N Engl J Med* 310:946, 1984.
56. West et al: A controlled trial of cyclophosphamide in patients with membranous glomerulonephritis. *Kidney Int* 32:579, 1987.
57. Korbet SM et al: Minimal-change glomerulopathy of adulthood. *Am J Nephrol* 8:29, 1988.
58. Kyle RA et al: Primary systemic amyloidosis: Resolution of the nephrotic syndrome with melphalan and prednisone. *Arch Intern Med* 142:1445, 1982.
59. Cohen AS et al: Survival of patients with primary (AZ) amyloidosis: Colchicine-treated patients compared with cases seen in previous years (1961–1978). *Am J Med* 82:1182, 1987.
60. Brocklehurst JC: *Textbook of Geriatric Medicine and Gerontology*. Edinburgh, Scotland, Churchill Livingstone, 1973, p 296.
61. Gleckman R et al: Acute pyelonephritis in the elderly. *South Med J* 75:551, 1982.
62. Gleckman RA et al: Urosepsis: A phenomenon unique to elderly women. *J Urol* 133:176, 1985.
63. Gleckman RA: Infectious problems in the geriatric nephrology patient, in Michelis MF et al (eds): *Geriatric Nephrology*, New York, Field, Rich, 1986, p 58.
64. Kleinknecht D et al: Acute interstitial nephritis due to drug hypersensitivity: An up to date review with a report of 19 cases. *Adv Nephrol* 13:271, 1983.
65. Appel GB, Neu HG: Acute interstitial nephritis induced by B lactam antibiotics, in Fillastre JH et al (eds): *Antibiotic Nephrotoxicity*. Paris, INSERM, 1984.
66. Appel GB, Kunis CL: Acute tubulointerstitial nephritis, in Cotran RS (ed): *Tubulo-interstitial Nephropathies: Contemporary Issues in Nephrology*, vol 10. New York, Churchill Livingstone, 1982, p 151.
67. Cotran RS et al: Tubulointerstitial diseases, in Brenner BM, Rector FC (eds): *The Kidney*. Philadelphia, Saunders, 1986, p 1143.
68. Galpin JE et al: Acute interstitial nephritis due to methicillin. *Am J Med* 65:756, 1978.
69. Linton AL: Acute interstitial nephritis due to drugs. *Ann Intern Med* 93:735, 1980.
70. Laberke HG, Bohle A: Acute interstitial nephritis: Correlations between clinical and morphological findings. *Clin Nephrol* 14:263, 1980.
71. Buckalew VM Jr, Schey HM: Renal diseases from habitual antipyretic analgesic consumption: An assessment of the epidemiologic evidence. *Medicine* 11(1):291, 1986.
72. Wilson DR, Gault MM: Declining incidence of analgesic nephropathy in Canada. *Can Med Assoc J* 127:500, 1982.
73. Gonwa TA et al: Analgesic associated nephropathy and transitional cell carcinoma of the urinary tract. *Kidney Int* 93:249, 1980.
74. Hill GS et al: Renal lesions in multiple myeloma: Their relationship to associated protein abnormalities. *Am J Kidney Dis* 2:423, 1983.
75. Hoyer JR, Seiler MW: Pathophysiology of Tamm-Horsfall protein. *Kidney Int* 16:999, 1979.
76. Alexanian R et al: Prognostic factors in multiple myeloma. *Cancer* 36:1192, 1975.
77. Cohen HJ, Rundles W: Managing the complications of multiple myeloma. *Arch Intern Med* 135:177, 1975.
78. Anderson S, Brenner BM: The aging kidney: Structure, function, mechanisms, and therapeutic implications. *J Am Geriatr Soc* 35:590, 1987.
79. DeFronzo RA: Hyperkalemia and hyporreninemic hypoaldosteronism. *Kidney Int* 17:118, 1980.
80. Noth RH et al: Age and the renin-aldosterone system. *Arch Intern Med* 137:1414, 1977.
81. Kafetz K, Hodkinson H: Uraemia in the elderly. *J Clin Exper Geriatr* 4:63, 1982.
82. Rasmussen HH, Ibels LS: Acute renal failure: Multivariate analysis of causes and risk factors. *Am J Med* 73:211, 1982.
83. Hou SH et al: Hospital-acquired renal insufficiency: A prospective study. *Am J Med* 74:243, 1983.
84. Humes DH: Aminoglycoside nephrotoxicity. *Kidney Int* 33:900, 1988.
85. Henrich WL, Blachley JD: Acute renal failure with prostaglandin inhibitors. *Semin Nephrol* 1:57, 1981.
86. Carmichael J, Shankel SW: Effects of nonsteroidal anti-inflammatory drugs on prostaglandins and renal function. *Am J Med* 78:992, 1985.
87. Hricik DE et al: Captopril-induced functional renal insufficiency in patients with bilateral renal artery stenosis or renal artery stenosis. *N Engl J Med* 308:373, 1983.
88. Blythe WB: Captopril and renal autoregulation. *N Engl J Med* 308:390, 1983.
89. Burkart JM et al: Prevention of renal failure, in Maher JR (ed): *Replacement of Renal Function by Dialysis*, 3rd ed. Boston, Kluwer Academic, 1989.
90. Baldwin DS, Neugarten J: Blood pressure control

and progression of renal insufficiency, in Mitch WE et al (eds): *The Progressive Nature of Renal Disease*. New York, Churchill Livingstone, 1986, p 81.

91. Meyer TW et al: Dietary protein intake and progressive glomerular sclerosis: The role of capillary hypertension and hyperfusion in the progression of renal disease. *Ann Intern Med* 98:832, 1983.
92. Mitch WE: A simple method of estimating progression of chronic renal failure. *Lancet* 2:1326, 1976.
93. Stanbury SW, Mahler RF: Salt-wasting renal disease: Metabolic observations on a patient with "salt-losing nephritis." *Q J Med* 28:425, 1959.
94. Michelis MF, Murdaugh HV: Selective hypoaldosteronism. *Am J Med* 59:1, 1975.
95. Tannen RL: The patient with hypokalemia or hyperkalemia, in Schrier RW (ed): *Manual of Nephrology, Diagnosis and Therapy*, 2d ed. Boston: Little, Brown, 1985, p 31.
96. Slatopolsky ER et al: On the pathogenesis of hyperparathyroidism in chronic experimental renal insufficiency in the dog. *J Clin Invest* 50:492, 1971.
97. Benno I et al: Aluminum associated bone disease: Clinico-pathologic correlation. *Am J Kidney Dis* 2:255, 1982.
98. Johnson WJ: Use of vitamin D analogs in renal osteodystrophy. *Semin Nephrol* 6:31, 1986.
99. Maschio G et al: Effects of dietary protein and phosphorus restriction on the progression of early renal failure. *Kidney Int* 22:371, 1982.
100. Eschback JW et al: Correction of the anemia of end-stage renal disease with recombinant human erythropoietin. *N Engl J Med* 316:73, 1987.
101. US Renal Data System: *USRDS 1991 Annual Data Report*. Bethesda, MD, National Institutes of Health, National Institute of Diabetes and Digestive and Kidney Diseases, August 1991.
102. Port FK et al: Outcome of treatment modalities for geriatric end stage renal disease: The Michigan kidney registry, in Michelis MF et al (eds): *Geriatric Nephrology*. New York, Field, Rich, 1986, p 149.
103. End-Stage Renal Disease Program Medical Information System: *Facility Survey Tables, 1982*. Washington, DC, Health Care Financing Administration, Bureau of Support Services, 1982.
104. Westlie L et al: Mortality, morbidity, and life satisfaction in the very old dialysis patient. *Trans Am Soc Artif Intern Organs* 30:21, 1984.
105. Chester AC et al: Hemodialysis in the eighth and ninth decades of life. *Arch Intern Med* 139:1001, 1979.
106. Bailey GL et al: Hemodialysis and renal transplantation in patients of the 50–80 age group. *J Am Geriatr Soc* 20:421, 1972.
107. Capelli JP et al: Comparative analysis of survival on home hemodialysis, in-center hemodialysis, and chronic peritoneal dialysis (CAPD-IPD) therapies. *Dial Transplant* 14:38, 1977.
108. Alfrey AC: Dialysis encephalopathy. *Kidney Int* 29:S53, 1986.
109. Hinsdale JG et al: Vascular access for hemodialysis in the elderly: Results and perspectives in a geriatric population. *Dial Transplant* 14:560, 1985.
110. Popovich RP et al: The definition of a novel portable/wearable equilibrium peritoneal dialysis technique. *Abstr Am Soc Artif Intern Organs* 5:64, 1976.
111. Steinberg SM et al: A comprehensive report on the experience of patients on continuous ambulatory peritoneal dialysis for the treatment of end-stage renal disease. *Am J Kidney Dis* 4:233, 1984.
112. Nolph KD et al: Special Studies from the NIH Registry. *Periton Dial Bull* 6:28, 1986.
113. Posen GA et al: The Canadian experience with peritoneal dialysis in the elderly. *Adv Periton Dial* 6:47, 1990.
114. Maiorca R et al: A multicenter, selection-adjusted comparison of patient and technique survivals on CAPD and hemodialysis. *Periton Dial Int* 11:118, 1991.
115. Nissensen AR et al: CAPD in the elderly—Regional experience, in Maher JF, Einchester JF (eds): *International Peritoneal Congress Proceedings*. New York, Field, Rich, 1985, p 312.
116. Riggio RR et al: Transplantation in the elderly, in Michelis MF et al (eds): *Geriatric Nephrology*. New York, Field, Rich, 1986, p 141.
117. Lee PG, Terasaki PI: Effect of age on kidney transplants, in Terasaki PI (ed): *Clinical Kidney Transplants*. Los Angeles, UCLA Tissue Typing Laboratory, 1985, p 123.
118. Sommer BG et al: Renal Transplantation in patients over 50 years of age. *Trans Proc* 13:33,1981.

Chapter 57

DISORDERS OF THE PROSTATE

Charles B. Brendler

This chapter discusses two disorders of the prostate that are common in elderly men: benign prostatic hyperplasia (BPH) and adenocarcinoma of the prostate.

THE NORMAL PROSTATE

Anatomy

The normal adult prostate is a firm, elastic organ weighing about 20 g. It is located caudad to the base of the bladder and is traversed by the first portion of the urethra. It is bordered anteriorly by the symphysis pubis and posteriorly by the rectum. The paired seminal vesicles are attached to the prostate and are located posterior to the bladder (Fig. 57-1).

A cross section of the human prostate reveals two concentric anatomic regions: the inner periurethral zone composed of short glands and the outer peripheral zone composed of longer, branched glands. These regions are separated by a thin layer of fibroelastic tissue, the so-called surgical capsule (Fig. 57-2). BPH arises within the inner periurethral zone in a specific region near the verumontanum called the transition zone.[1] In contrast, prostatic carcinoma usually arises in the outer peripheral zone.[2]

BENIGN PROSTATIC HYPERPLASIA

Incidence

BPH is a disease of advancing age. Histologically, BPH is rarely identified before age 40; subsequently, however, the incidence progressively increases to about 90 percent by age 80. Clinically, BPH begins to produce symptoms of urethral obstruction at about age 50. Thereafter, the incidence and severity of symptoms cumulatively increases with age as both the incidence of BPH and average prostate weight simultaneously increase. As a result, the probability that a 50-year-old man will ultimately require treatment for BPH is about 25 percent.[3]

Etiology

Although the exact etiology of BPH is unknown, it is closely related to both aging and age-associated changes in circulating hormones. Circulating androgens and dihydrotestosterone (DHT), the active androgen in the prostate, play a key role in the genesis of BPH. BPH does not develop in men who are castrated or lose testicular function before puberty.[4] In men with established BPH, castration causes atrophy of the prostatic epithelium.[5]

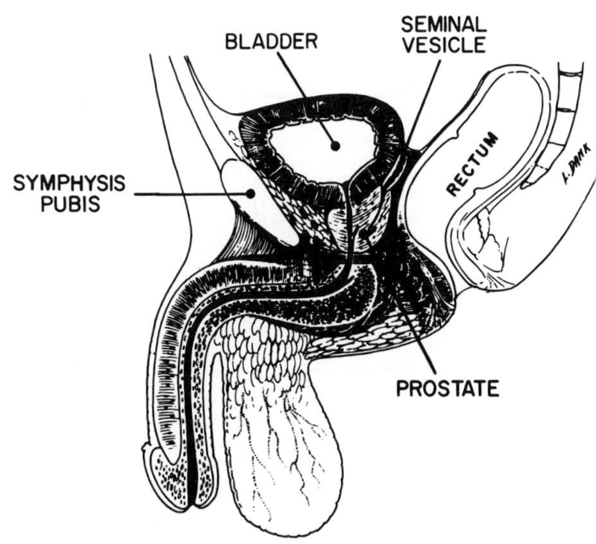

FIGURE 57-1
The anatomic relationship of the prostate to adjacent structures. *[After Brendler H, in Glenn JF (ed): Urologic Survey, 3d ed. Philadelphia, Lippincott, 1983.]*

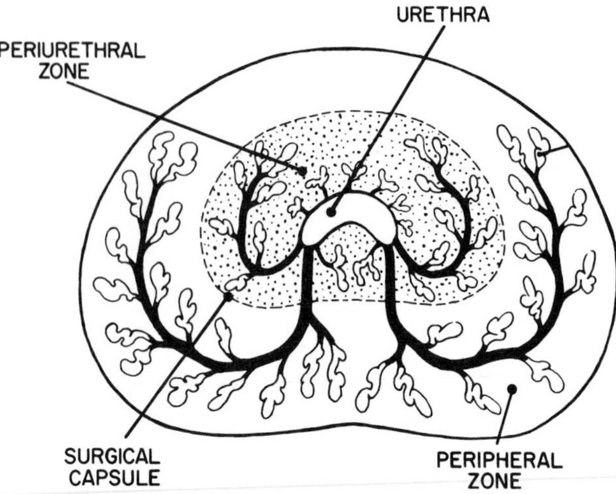

FIGURE 57-2
A coronal section through the prostate demonstrating the anatomic relationships between the urethra, periurethral tissue, surgical capsule, and the peripheral tissue. *[After Brendler H, in Glenn JF (ed): Urologic Surgery, 3d ed. Philadelphia, Lippincott, 1983.]*

Pathogenesis

As the hyperplastic prostate enlarges, it compresses the urethra, producing symptoms of urinary obstruction that ultimately may progress to urinary retention. Urethral obstruction may cause incomplete emptying of the bladder, giving rise to urinary stasis, urinary tract infection, and bladder calculi. Furthermore, increased intravesical pressure can lead to hypertrophy of the bladder muscle, hydronephrosis, and bladder diverticula. Bladder neoplasms are more likely to arise in bladder diverticula, especially if the diverticula drain poorly and are chronically infected.

Symptoms

Symptoms due to BPH can be categorized as either obstructive or irritative. Obstructive symptoms include hesitancy to initiate voiding, straining to void, decreased force and caliber of the urinary stream, prolonged dribbling after micturition, a sensation of incomplete bladder emptying, and urinary retention. These symptoms result directly from narrowing of the bladder neck and prostatic urethra by the hyperplastic prostate.

Irritative symptoms include urinary frequency, nocturia, dysuria, urgency, and urge incontinence. These symptoms may result from incomplete emptying of the bladder with voiding or may be due to urinary tract infection secondary to prostatic obstruction. More commonly, irritative symptoms result from reduced bladder compliance as a result of prostatic obstruction.[6]

It is important to recognize and distinguish patients who present mainly with irritative symptoms, since these symptoms may be caused by other conditions unrelated to prostatic obstruction, such as bladder carcinoma, neurogenic bladder, and urinary tract infection. All too frequently, patients with irritative urinary tract symptoms are presumed to have prostatic obstruction without receiving an adequate diagnostic evaluation, resulting in delayed and sometimes inappropriate therapy.

Physical Examination

Other than a distended bladder, the usual physical findings in BPH are confined to the prostate. Examination of the prostate should be performed with the patient either in the knee-chest position or bent over the bed with his chest touching his elbows. The examining glove should be well lubricated, and the index finger should be inserted slowly into the rectum to allow the anal sphincter time to relax. A helpful maneuver is for the physician to place his or her other hand against the patient's lower abdomen, which helps steady the patient and allows gentle counterpressure as the examining finger is advanced into the rectum.

The normal prostate is the size of a walnut and has the consistency of a pencil eraser. The hyperplastic prostate is variably enlarged, usually no more than two or three times normal size but occasionally exceeding the size of a lemon. The consistency remains rubbery but is somewhat more fleshy than normal, particularly in the larger glands. It should be noted that rectal examination affords only a rough estimate of prostatic size and should never be relied upon to rule out prostatic obstruction. A much more accurate appraisal of prostatic size can be obtained with ultrasonography and cystourethroscopy.

The rectal examination is, however, a valuable screening test for prostatic carcinoma. The entire posterior surface of the gland should be examined for areas of induration suggestive of malignancy. After examination of the prostate, the full length of the index finger should be advanced into the rectum and a careful circumferential examination performed to rule out carcinoma of the rectum. A stool guaiac also should be obtained.

Diagnostic Tests

The most valuable test for documenting urinary obstruction is measurement of the urinary flow rate.[7] Inexpensive flowmeters are available that allow an accurate determination of the patient's voided volume and peak urinary flow rate. These values are plotted along with the patient's age on a nomogram. It must be emphasized that a decreased flow rate per se is never an indication for prostatectomy, but uroflometry, when used and interpreted correctly, is an excellent physiologic test for prostatic obstruction.

An abdominal ultrasound examination is useful to rule out pathology of the upper urinary tract, such as hydronephrosis, stones, or renal masses. Furthermore, with this technique an accurate measurement of postvoid residual urine volume and prostatic size can be made.

Cystourethroscopy is often employed as a screening test for prostatic obstruction, but its value in this regard is limited because the anatomic appearance of the bladder neck and prostatic urethra during cystourethroscopy may be misleading. An anatomically small prostate may produce significant obstruction during voiding, while an anatomically large prostate may produce little or no obstruction. The place for cystourethroscopy is in the operating room after the decision to perform a prostatectomy has been made. With the patient under anesthesia, a full evaluation of the prostatic urethra can be made and also a decision as to whether the prostate is small enough to be resected transurethrally or is sufficiently large to require open surgical removal. Before proceeding to prostatectomy, a careful inspection of the bladder is made to rule out bladder diverticula, stones, and, most importantly, tumors.

Other tests that may be helpful in evaluating patients with symptoms of BPH include a retrograde urethrogram when a urethral stricture is suspected and formal urodynamic testing, including a cystometrogram in patients with complex voiding symptomatology or a suspected neurogenic bladder.

Treatment

The indications for treating BPH are (1) voiding symptoms that are troublesome to the patient, (2) urinary retention, (3) recurrent urinary tract infections caused by postvoid residual urine, (4) compromised renal function due to hydronephrosis from prostatic obstruction, (5) recurrent gross hematuria with no other explanation, and (6) urge incontinence due to prostatic obstruction.

Until recently, the most common treatment for BPH was a partial prostatectomy, in which the obstructing hyperplastic periurethral tissue is removed surgically. The surgical objective of a partial prostatectomy done for BPH is to reestablish a wide open bladder neck and prostatic urethra by removing all the hyperplastic prostatic tissue. Surgical removal of this tissue is facilitated by the presence of the surgical capsule, a layer of fibroelastic tissue separating the periurethral adenoma from the peripheral prostate.

Prostatectomy for benign hyperplasia can be accomplished either by transurethral resection or by open surgical enucleation of the adenoma. The decision as to whether a transurethral or an open prostatectomy is done is usually based on the size of the gland, adenomas of less than 70 g usually being approached transurethrally. Regardless of the surgical approach employed, the surgical objective is the same, i.e., to removal all the hyperplastic tissue down to the surgical capsule, leaving the peripheral prostate intact.

In recent years, several medical and minimally invasive treatments for BPH have been developed. These include (1) the use of alpha-adrenergic blocking agents to reduce smooth muscle tone in the bladder neck and prostate[8]; (2) hormonal therapy to decrease the size of the prostate[9]; (3) laser prostatectomy[10]; (4) balloon dilatation of the prostatic urethra[11]; and (5) placement of an indwelling metal stent within the prostatic urethra.[12]

Alpha-adrenergic blocking agents, originally marketed for the treatment of hypertension, reduce smooth muscle tone in the bladder neck and prostatic urethra and significantly improve voiding function in many men with BPH. The agent most commonly used is terazosin (Hytrin), 2 to 5 mg at bedtime. Terazosin is started at a dose of 1 mg and administered before sleep to minimize the risk of symptomatic orthostatic hypotension.[8]

Finasteride (Proscar) is a recently marketed hormonal agent that reduces androgen action in the prostate and thus causes a decrease in prostatic size. Finasteride is a competitive inhibitor of the enzyme 5 alpha-reductase, which converts testosterone to dihydrotestosterone, the active androgen in the prostate. Finasteride is administered in a dose of 5 mg daily and appears not to have any significant side effects. Because it does not decrease serum testosterone, no other antiandrogenic side effects are observed, and, most importantly, libido and sexual function are preserved. Because of its efficacy and apparently limited toxicity, finasteride may become the preferred initial treatment for BPH in the near future.[9]

Transurethral laser prostatectomy is currently being evaluated as another alternative to transurethral prostatectomy using electrocautery. Lasers are currently being used to both incise and coagulate prostatic tissue. Initial studies in dogs have demonstrated that the laser can be used safely and effectively to ablate prostatic tissue.[10] Trials are currently under way in humans to further test this modality.

Balloon dilatation of the prostatic urethra is performed by placing an inflatable balloon cystoscopically within the prostatic urethra and inflating it to between 3 and 5 atmospheres of pressure for 10 to 30 minutes. This results in compression of the prostate with less bleeding than that associated with transurethral prostatectomy. Initial reports were encouraging, but a recent randomized trial demonstrated no significant benefit in patients undergoing balloon dilatation compared with a control group who underwent cystoscopy alone.[11] Further studies are required to determine whether balloon dilatation is truly effective in the treatment of BPH.

Indwelling metal stents have also been evaluated in the treatment of BPH. Intraurethral stents have been used most often in men who are poor surgical risks. Although the follow-up period is short, 80 to 90 percent of men in urinary retention have been able to void spontaneously following placement of a stent. Although most men experience irritative urinary symptoms for several weeks after placement of a stent, these symptoms usually subside spontaneously.

CARCINOMA OF THE PROSTATE

Incidence

Carcinoma of the prostate is rare before age 50, but the incidence subsequently increases steadily with age. Overall, it is the second most common malignancy in American men and the third most common cause of cancer deaths in men over age 55 (behind lung cancer and colorectal cancer). Carcinoma of the prostate is more common as a cause of death among black Americans (22 deaths per 100,000 men) than white Americans (14 deaths per 100,000 men).

Etiology

The etiology of prostatic carcinoma is unknown. Although the disease does not occur in men castrated before puberty and regresses following castration or estrogen therapy, a precise hormonal etiology has not been established. BPH does not appear to be causally related.[13] Environmental factors may be involved, since men migrating from areas where prostatic cancer is uncommon to areas where it is more common develop the disease with increased frequency. Oncogenic viruses have been detected within prostatic cancer cells, but a direct etiologic relationship has not been established. Recent evidence has shown a familial pattern of inheritance in some men with prostatic carcinoma.[14]

Pathogenesis

Ninety-five percent of prostatic cancers are adenocarcinomas, with the remainder being transitional cell carcinomas, squamous cell carcinomas, and sarcomas. Adenocarcinoma of the prostate usually arises in the peripheral region of the prostate, although it commonly invades the periurethral tissue where BPH originates, subsequently producing urethral obstruction. Prostate cancer may produce ureteral obstruction either by direct extension into the bladder or by spreading behind the bladder through the seminal vesicles. Distant spread occurs through lymphatic and hematogenous routes. The pelvic lymph nodes and skeleton are the most frequent sites of metastatic disease, and the pelvis and lumbar spine are the bones most commonly involved. Visceral metastases occur later and less commonly; the lungs, liver, and adrenals are the organs most frequently involved.

The natural history of prostatic cancer is unpredictable and seems to vary considerably among individual patients. In some men the disease progresses very slowly, and patients may do well for many years without treatment. However, in other patients the disease pursues an extremely fulminant course with rapid metastatic spread and early death. In general, we lack the ability to predict which patients can be followed conservatively and which patients deserve prompt treatment. Until we develop this prognostic ability, we are obliged to treat patients with prostatic cancer aggressively, to the extent that an individual's age and general health permit.

Symptoms

Early carcinoma of the prostate is asymptomatic. As the disease spreads into the urethra, it may cause symptoms of urinary obstruction indistinguishable from those produced by BPH. If the tumor has progressed to obstruct the ureters, the patient may present with uremia. Skeletal pain and pathologic fractures caused by metastatic disease may be the initial symptoms of advanced disease.

Physical Examination

The patient may present with lymphadenopathy, signs of uremia and congestive heart failure, or urinary retention with a distended bladder. More commonly, the pathologic physical findings are confined to the prostate. On rectal examination, the prostate feels harder than the normal or hyperplastic prostate, and the normal boundaries of the gland may be obscured. Approximately 50 percent of localized indurated areas within the prostate will prove to be malignant, with the remainder being due to prostatic calculi, inflammation, prostatic infarction, or postsurgical change in a patient having previously undergone a partial prostatectomy for BPH. If induration is detected that is suggestive of carcinoma, the examiner should determine whether it is focal or diffuse in nature and whether it seems to extend beyond the border of the prostate.

Diagnosis

The diagnosis of prostatic cancer is made most often by performing a needle biopsy of the prostate through the rectum or perineum. Both transrectal and transperineal techniques are accurate, with reported false-negative rates of about 10 percent. Transrectal biopsy is somewhat easier to perform, since the needle is advanced over a finger within the rectum directly into the prostate, and therefore may be more accurate for those inexperienced with the transperineal technique. However, because the needle is advanced through the rectal wall, transrectal biopsy with the 14-gauge Tru-Cut needle that was previously used was associated with a significant risk of sepsis. The recently introduced Biopty-Gun, which uses a spring-loaded smaller 18-gauge needle, is very easy to use and has a much lower risk of sepsis. Nevertheless, patients undergoing transrectal biopsy should be given a cleansing enema and prophylactic antibiotics.

Transperineal biopsy, while more difficult to master, is nearly as accurate as the transrectal approach and somewhat safer, since rectal contamination is avoided. Prophylactic antibiotics are not required with transperineal biopsy unless the rectal wall is violated.[15]

Fine-needle aspiration of the prostate is performed using a 22-gauge needle that is advanced through the rectum into the prostate. The needle is moved back and forth within the prostate and suction is applied; the aspirated cells are then smeared on a microscopic slide, fixed with either air or alcohol, and stained for subsequent cytologic examination. Fine-needle aspiration in experienced hands is very accurate, with false-positive and false-negative rates of about 10 percent.[16] Since fine-needle aspiration requires the expertise of a trained cytopathologist, its popularity has declined in recent years, particularly with the introduction of the Biopty-Gun, which has made core-needle biopsy of the prostate a much easier and more accurate technique.

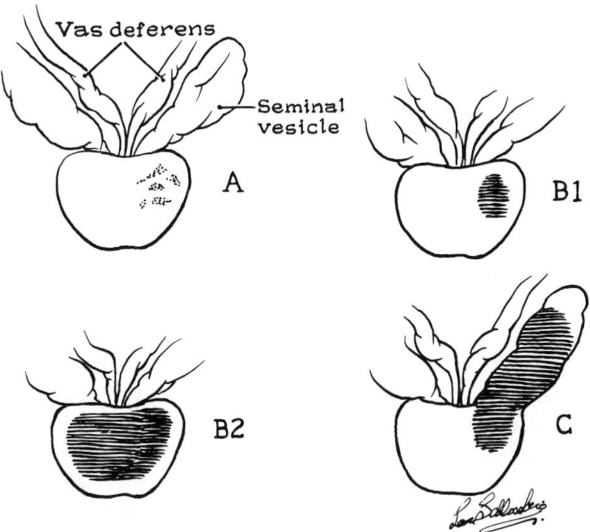

FIGURE 57-3
Whitmore staging classification of prostatic carcinoma. A, microscopic disease in a clinically benign gland; B-1, nodule involving less than one posterior lobe; B-2, nodule involving one entire lobe or both posterior lobes; C, extension beyond the peripheral capsule of the prostate; stage D (not pictured), metastatic disease.

Staging Classification

The treatment of prostatic carcinoma depends primarily on the stage of the disease. In the United States the most widely used staging system is that proposed by Whitmore,[17] which includes four staging categories: A, B, C, and D. Alternative staging systems include the use of the Roman numerals I, II, III, and IV instead of letters and the TNM (tumor, nodes, metastases) system devised by the International Union Against Cancer (UICC).[18] The Whitmore staging system will be used in the following discussion and is summarized in Fig. 57-3.

Stage A prostatic carcinoma refers to tumors that are discovered incidentally on histologic examination of prostatic tissue that has been removed for presumed BPH. Stage A tumors are subdivided into *stage A-1* lesions, which are well-differentiated or moderately well-differentiated tumors involving less than 5 percent of the removed tissue, and *stage A-2* lesions, which are either poorly differentiated or involve more than 5 percent of the removed tissue.

Stage B refers to tumors that are palpable on rectal examination and that are confined within the boundaries of the prostate. *Stage B-1* includes tumors involving less than one posterior lobe, and *stage B-2* includes tumors that involve one whole or both posterior lobes.

Stage C includes tumors that extend beyond the boundaries of the prostate but are confined within the pelvis. These tumors have penetrated the peripheral capsule of the prostate and may extend cephalad into the seminal vesicles or laterally toward the bony pelvic side walls.

Stage D includes metastatic tumors. Stage D-1 includes tumors which have spread to the pelvic lymph nodes, while Stage D-2 implies distant metastatic disease.

Staging Evaluation

Since the treatment of prostatic carcinoma is predicated largely on the stage of the tumor, accurate staging is essential in order to manage this disease properly. The digital rectal examination is invaluable in assessing the local extent of tumor, but in recent years our ability to stage prostatic carcinoma has been greatly enhanced by new serologic and radiographic tests.

Prostate-specific antigen (PSA) is a glycoprotein that is produced exclusively by prostatic epithelial cells. Precise radioimmunologic assays have been developed to measure serum levels of PSA accurately. Mean serum PSA levels in men with clinically localized prostate cancer are not significantly different from those in men with BPH.[19] Therefore, PSA alone is of limited value in screening men for early prostatic carcinoma. The combination of PSA and digital rectal examination, however, is more accurate than either test alone in detecting early prostatic carcinoma, and it has currently been recommended that all men over 50 have an annual PSA and digital rectal examination.[20]

Serum PSA levels rise with advancing stages of prostatic carcinoma; therefore PSA is very helpful in staging this disease. Two-thirds of men with prostatic carcinoma and PSA levels above 20 ng/ml will have disease extending through the prostatic capsule and two-thirds with PSA values above 40 ng/ml will have metastatic disease.[21] Nevertheless, PSA alone should not be used to determine stage of disease and to exclude patients from radical prostatectomy who are otherwise surgical candidates. There have been several cases of men with pathologically confined prostatic carcinoma whose preoperative PSA levels were above 100 ng/ml.

Since the discovery of PSA in 1978, PSA has largely replaced prostatic acid phosphatase (PAP) in staging men with prostatic carcinoma. Although an elevated enzymatic prostatic acid phosphatase in men with prostatic carcinoma is virtually pathognomonic of metastatic disease, the sensitivity of prostatic acid phosphatase in detecting metastatic disease is quite low. Indeed, it is very unusual for an elevated prostatic acid phosphatase to be the only evidence of advanced prostatic carcinoma, and most patients with an elevated PAP will have an abnormal digital rectal examination, PSA, or bone scan.[22]

Transrectal ultrasonography (TRUS) is currently being used extensively in the diagnosis and staging of prostatic carcinoma. Although more sensitive than digital rectal examination in detecting prostatic carcinoma, TRUS has a specificity of only 30 percent. In other words, more than two-thirds of the lesions detected by TRUS as suspicious for carcinoma will be benign on biopsy.[23] This is due to the markedly variable ultrasonographic appearance of prostatic carcinoma. Therefore, TRUS should not be used to screen men for prostatic carcinoma. TRUS is valuable, however, in biopsying the prostate, and TRUS-guided needle biopsies are more accurate than digitally guided biopsies, particularly for small palpable or nonpalpable lesions.[24]

Extensive evaluation thus far has shown that TRUS is of limited value in staging prostatic carcinoma. This is due to the inability of TRUS to detect microscopic capsular penetration and seminal vesicle involvement.[25] Pelvic computed tomography (CT) and magnetic resonance imaging (MRI) with body coils have similar limitations and are not widely used in the staging of prostatic carcinoma.[26]

MRI using endorectal coils is a relatively new technique that appears very promising in staging prostatic carcinoma. This technique appears much more sensitive than other forms of radiography in detecting microscopic invasion of the prostatic capsule and extension of disease into the seminal vesicles.[27]

A radionuclide bone scan is the most accurate test to detect skeletal metastases in men with prostatic carcinoma and is still routinely obtained. A recent study, however, demonstrated that no patient with prostatic carcinoma and a serum PSA below 10 ng/ml had a positive bone scan.[28] It may, therefore, be unnecessary to obtain a bone scan in men with serum PSA levels below 10 ng/ml.

In men with otherwise clinically localized disease, it is important to assess the pelvic lymph nodes for metastatic disease prior to treatment. Unfortunately, radiologic assessment of the pelvic lymph nodes has proved difficult. Lymphangiography is unreliable, mainly because this technique does not consistently demonstrate the primary sites of lymphatic drainage from the prostate, which are the obturator and hypogastric lymphatic chains. Pelvic CT is similarly unreliable, and, in addition, has a low sensitivity in detecting microscopic lymph node metastases. Therefore, in patients with otherwise localized disease, a staging pelvic lymphadenectomy usually is done prior to performing a radical prostatectomy.[29] Until recently, pelvic lymphadenectomy was performed in conjunction with radical prostatectomy, relying on a frozen-section evaluation of the lymph nodes. There has been recent interest in laparoscopic pelvic lymphadenectomy, which is done several days prior to a planned radical prostatectomy. This technique, although time-consuming, appears to have little morbidity and allows for a complete pathologic assessment of the pelvic lymph nodes prior to radical prostatectomy.[30] Laparoscopic pelvic lymphadenectomy is probably not indicated in men with low-stage and low-grade prostatic carcinoma, since the incidence of positive pelvic lymph nodes is less than 10 percent. However, in order to spare these patients the morbidity of an open surgical procedure, it may have application in men with a higher stage or grade of disease who have a much greater chance of having positive pelvic lymph nodes.

Treatment

Until recently, patients with stage A-1 prostatic carcinoma have not usually been treated, since the disease was thought to be latent and of no clinical significance. Recent data, however, have shown that 10 to 20 percent of untreated patients with A-1 disease will develop disease progression within 10 years.[31] Thus, it may be advisable to aggressively treat healthy men under age 65 who have stage A-1 disease.

Patients with stages A-2 and B disease require further therapy since, untreated, many will progress to develop metastatic disease. The treatment options for these clinical stages include radical prostatectomy and radiation therapy. Radical prostatectomy involves

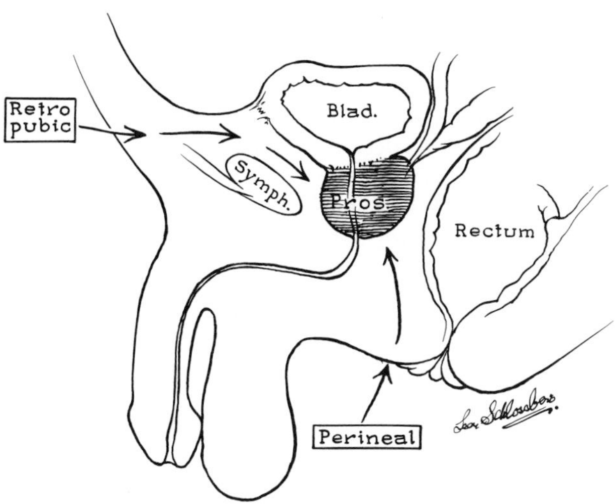

FIGURE 57-4
Anatomic drawing depicting the retropubic and perineal approaches to the prostate.

the surgical removal of the entire prostate and seminal vesicles and is accomplished either through a perineal or retropubic approach (Fig. 57-4). The cure rate for patients undergoing radical prostatectomy for localized disease is excellent, with the 15-year survival rate for patients with pathologically confined disease equaling that of age-matched men without prostatic cancer.[32]

The major complications of radical prostatectomy include urinary incontinence and impotence. However, with recent advances in surgical technique, the risk of significant urinary incontinence currently is less than 2 percent.[33] Furthermore, recent understanding of pelvic anatomy has allowed identification and preservation of the nerves to the corpora cavernosa of the penis, allowing preservation of potency in many patients.[34]

Radiation therapy is administered via either external beam or interstitial radioactive seeds that are implanted surgically into the prostate. Although in some series the success rates with radiation therapy approach those achieved with radical prostatectomy,[35] in other series the results are not nearly as favorable.[36] Although the issue remains controversial, radiation therapy seems most appropriate in patients with localized disease who either are unwilling to undergo radical prostatectomy or are not surgical candidates for reasons of age and health. Radiation therapy is also the treatment of choice for patients with clinical stage C disease that has extended beyond the borders of the prostate and is therefore not curable surgically.

Hormonal therapy remains the only effective treatment for patients with stage D disease. The objective of endocrine therapy is to deprive prostatic tumors of circulating androgens and thereby produce regression of both primary and metastatic lesions. Hormonal ablation can be achieved either by castration or by administration of exogenous hormones. Diethylstilbestrol (DES) administered at a dose of 3 mg/day lowers plasma testosterone to castrate levels, but DES, the most commonly used agent previously, is no longer used today because other agents with equal efficacy and lower cardiovascular toxicity have been introduced.

Hormonal androgen ablation is currently accomplished with luteinizing hormone-releasing hormone (LH-RH) analogs.[37] There is some evidence that the addition of an antiandrogen such as flutamide may provide additional palliation beyond that achieved with an LH-RH analog alone,[38] but the evidence is not compelling. Although as effective as castration, medical hormonal therapy does not provide additional therapeutic benefit. This is because prostatic cancer is composed of a heterogeneous cell population, some cells being hormone-sensitive and others hormone-resistant. Relapse following hormonal therapy is due to continued growth of hormone-resistant cells, and further attempts to lower serum testosterone provide no additional palliation.

Patient response to hormonal therapy varies considerably: 10 percent of patients live less than 6 months, 50 percent survive less than 3 years, and only 10 percent live longer than 10 years.[39] The timing of endocrine therapy also appears to make little difference clinically in the course of the disease. Initiation of treatment at the time of diagnosis may provide a longer symptom-free interval but little in the way of effective palliation once relapse has occurred. For this reason, in the hope of providing increased long-term palliation, it may be preferable to delay hormonal therapy until the patient has become symptomatic.

Unfortunately, there has never been any effective chemotherapy for relapsing, hormone-resistant prostatic carcinoma. Traditional cytotoxic agents have been ineffective, due in part to the slow growth of prostatic carcinoma, with only a small percentage of the cell population undergoing mitosis at a given time. Suramin, a drug that was originally used to treat African sleeping sickness, appears to inhibit prostatic growth factors and does provide additional palliation in some patients. However, suramin has considerable toxicity, against which its limited efficacy must be considered.[40] Clearly, a major goal for the future is to develop new forms of therapy that will be effective against hormone-resistant prostatic cancer; the development of such therapy will represent a major advance in the treatment of this disease.

REFERENCES

1. McNeal JE: Origin and evolution of benign prostatic enlargement. *Invest Urol* 15:340, 1978.
2. McNeal JE: Origin and development of carcinoma in the prostate. *Cancer* 23:24, 1969.
3. Birkhoff JD: Natural history of benign prostatic hypertrophy, in Hinman F (ed): *Benign Prostatic Hypertrophy.* New York, Springer-Verlag, 1983, p 5.
4. Wilson JD: The pathogenesis of benign prostatic hyperplasia. *Am J Med* 68:745, 1980.
5. Wendel EF et al: The effect of orchiectomy and estrogens on benign prostatic hyperplasia. *J Urol* 108:116, 1972.
6. Turner-Warwick R: Observations on the function and dysfunction of the sphincter and detrusor mechanisms. *Urol Clin North Am* 6:11, 1979.
7. Abrams P, Torrens M: Urine flow studies. *Urol Clin North Am* 6:71, 1979.
8. Lepor H et al: The efficacy and safety of terazosin for the treatment of BPH. *Prostate* 18:345, 1991.
9. MK-906 (Finasteride) Study Group: One-year experience in the treatment of benign prostatic hyperplasia with finasteride. *J Androl* 12:372, 1991.
10. Assimos D et al: Canine transurethral laser-induced prostatectomy. *J Endourol* 5:145, 1991.
11. Lepor H et al: Randomized, double-blind study comparing the effectiveness of balloon dilation of the prostate and cytoscopy for the treatment of symptomatic benign prostatic hyperplasia. *J Urol* 147:639, 1992.
12. McLoughlin J et al: The use of prostatic stents in patients with urinary retention who are unfit for surgery: An interim report. *Br J Urol* 66:66, 1990.
13. Armenian HK et al: Relation between benign prostatic hyperplasia and cancer of the prostate: A prospective and retrospective study. *Lancet* 2:115, 1974.
14. Steinberg GD et al: Family history and the risk of prostate cancer. *Prostate* 17:337, 1990.
15. Packer MG et al: Prophylactic antibiotics and Foley catheter usage in transperineal needle biopsy of the prostate. *J Urol* 131:687, 1984.
16. Melograna F et al: Prospective controlled assessment of fine-needle prostatic aspiration. *Urology* 19:47, 1982.
17. Whitmore WF Jr: Symposium on hormones and cancer therapy: Hormone therapy in prostatic cancer. *Am J Med* 21:697, 1956.
18. *UICC TNM Klassifikation der malignen Tumoren,* ed 3. Berlin, Springer-Verlag, 1979, p 114.
19. Bhatti PG et al: An evaluation of prostate specific antigen in prostatic cancer. *J Urol* 137:686, 1987.
20. Catalona WJ et al: Measurement of prostate specific antigen in serum as a screening test for prostate cancer. *N Engl J Med* 324:1156, 1991.
21. Stamey TA et al: Prostate-specific antigen as a serum marker for adenocarcinoma of the prostate. *N Engl J Med* 317:909, 1987.
22. Burnett AL et al: The value of serum enzymatic acid phosphatase in the staging of localized prostate cancer. *J Urol* 148:1832, 1992.
23. Carter HB et al: Evaluation of transrectal ultrasound in the early detection of prostate cancer. *J Urol* 142:1008, 1989.
24. Rifkin MD et al: Palpable masses in the prostate: Superior accuracy of US-guided biopsy compared with accuracy of digitally guided biopsy. *Radiology* 179:41, 1991.
25. Hamper UM et al: Capsular transgression of prostatic carcinoma: Evaluation with transrectal US with pathologic correlation. *Radiology* 178:791, 1991.
26. Rifkin MD et al: Comparison of magnetic resonance imaging and ultrasonography in staging early prostate cancer: Results of a multi-institutional cooperative trial. *N Engl J Med* 323:621, 1990.
27. Schnall MD et al: Prostate cancer: Local staging with endorectal surface coil MR imaging. *Radiology,* 178:797, 1991.
28. Oesterling JE: Prostate specific antigen: A critical assessment of the most useful tumor marker for adenocarcinoma of the prostate. *J Urol* 145:907, 1991.
29. Epstein JI et al: Frozen section detection of lymph node metastases in prostatic carcinoma: Accuracy in grossly uninvolved pelvic lymphadenectomy specimens. *J Urol* 136:1234, 1986.
30. Schuessler WW et al: Transperitoneal endosurgical lymphadenectomy in patients with localized prostate cancer. *J Urol* 145:988, 1991.
31. Zhang G et al: Long-term follow-up results after expectant management of stage A_1 prostatic cancer. *J Urol* 146:99, 1991.
32. Lepor H et al: Cause-specific actuarial survival analysis: A useful method for reporting survival data in men with clinically localized carcinoma of the prostate. *J Urol* 141:82, 1989.
33. Steiner MS et al: Impact of anatomical radical prostatectomy on urinary continence. *J Urol* 145:512, 1991.
34. Quinlan DM et al: Sexual function following radical prostatectomy: Influence of preservation of neurovascular bundles. *J Urol* 145:998, 1991.
35. Bagshaw MA: The role of radiation therapy in the management of prostatic carcinoma. *Prob Urol* 1:181, 1987.
36. Paulson DF et al: The Uro-Oncology Research Group: Radical surgery versus radiotherapy for adenocarcinoma of the prostate. *J Urol* 128;502, 1982.
37. The Leuprolide Study Group: Leuprolide versus DES in the initial therapy of advanced prostatic cancer: A randomized prospective trial. *N Engl J Med* 311:1281, 1984.
38. Crawford ED et al: A controlled trial of leuprolide with and without flutamide in prostatic carcinoma. *N Engl J Med* 321:419, 1989.
39. Blackard CE et al: Orchiectomy for advanced prostatic carcinoma. A reevaluation. *Urology* 1:553, 1973.
40. LaRocca RV et al: Use of suramin in treatment of prostatic carcinoma refractory to conventional hormonal manipulations. *Urol Clin North Am* 18:123, 1991.

Chapter 58

AGING OF THE GASTROINTESTINAL SYSTEM

Michael J. Baime, James B. Nelson and Donald O. Castell

The gastrointestinal tract, on the whole, retains normal physiologic function during the aging process, in large part due to the inherent redundancy incorporated into this multiorgan system. Still, changes with increasing age in both animal and human digestive systems have been reported, and these are likely to lead to alterations in function, especially during times of stress. On the other hand, some of these age-associated changes may be adaptive, helping to maintain homeostasis over time. Moreover, it may be difficult to extrapolate animal studies of aging to humans because of individual species variation.

It is the purpose of this chapter to review alterations in the structure and function of the gastrointestinal tract with increasing age and to relate this information to possible pathologic consequences. More detailed information regarding specific disease states associated with aging in the gastrointestinal tract will be discussed in the chapters which follow. Table 58-1 summarizes the changes in digestive function that develop with age.

AGING AND PHARYNGOESOPHAGEAL FUNCTION

The act of swallowing can be subdivided into three distinct stages: the voluntary or oral stage, the involuntary or pharyngeal phase, and the esophageal stage.[1] The oral and pharyngeal stages are regulated by cortical input to medullary swallowing centers with output to skeletal muscle groups. The proximal esophagus also contains skeletal muscle, but the distal esophageal musculature consists of smooth muscle regulated by its own intrinsic innervation.

The reduction in lean muscle mass which accompanies aging may result in dysfunction of the oral and pharyngeal phase of swallowing as well as mastication. In a study evaluating skeletal muscle fiber changes from the pharyngeal constrictor from 50 necropsies (subject ages 1 to 93), there was an age-associated decrease in the smaller fraction of type I fibers. In addition, the standard deviation of fiber diameters was significantly larger in the older group (over age 50) and there was a general trend toward hypertrophy of individual muscle fibers with decreased fiber density.[2] These findings may cause functional changes during the oropharyngeal phase of swallowing. One study of 100 asymptomatic individuals over 65 found that 22 subjects had pharyngeal muscle weakness and abnormal cricopharyngeal relaxation with puddling of barium in the valleculae and pyriform sinuses. A few also demonstrated tracheal aspiration of barium, possibly due to cricopharyngeal muscle weakness.[3]

Morphologic changes associated with the aging process can also be demonstrated in both the smooth muscle of the esophagus and its intrinsic innervation. In elderly individuals there is a decrease in the number of myenteric ganglion cells per unit area as well as thickening of the smooth muscle layer.[4,5] Similar to what occurs in pharynx and skeletal muscle portion of the esophagus, the standard deviation of smooth muscle fiber diameters is greater in the elderly, with hypertrophy exceeding atrophy. An overall decrease in slow-acting, type I fibers also develops in the aging distal esophagus, and there is a corresponding decrease in the density of fibers per unit area.[2]

TABLE 58-1

Age-Related Changes in Digestive Function

Oral cavity		Colon	
Mastication	↓	Mucosa	↓
Mandibular bone	↓	Musculature	↓
Salivary flow	↓(−)	Transit	↓
Taste sensation	↓	Diverticular disease	↑
Pharynx/esophagus		Anus/rectum	
Pharyngeal muscles	↓	Muscle wall elasticity	↓
Esophageal motility	?	Continence	↓
Gastroesophageal reflux	(−)	Innervation	↓?
Stomach		Pancreas	
Gastric emptying	?	Weight/size	(−)
Acid production	↓	Ductal size	↑
Pepsin production	?	Acinar glands	↓
Gastrin production	↑	Secretion	(−)?
Gastric mucosa	↓(−)	Bile ducts/gallbladder	
Small intestine		Bile duct size	↑
Transit time	(−)	Gallbladder emptying	(−)
Motility/smooth muscle	↑	Gallstones	↑
Innervation	↓	Liver	
Mucosa	?	Size	↓
Absorption/enzyme activity		Blood flow	↓
Water/electrolytes	↓	Hepatocyte number	↓
Disaccharidases (lactase)	↓(−)	Metabolic functions	
Fat	(−)	Bromsulphalein (BSP) clearance	↓
Fat-soluble vitamins	↑	Microsomal oxidation (antipyrine)	↓
Water-soluble vitamins	(−)	Nonmicrosomal oxidation (alcohol)	(−)
Vitamin D	↓	Demethylation (benzodiazapines)	↓
Folate/vitamin B_{12}	(−)	Conjugation (INH)	(−)
Protein	(−)	Superoxide dismutase/catalase	↓
Calcium	↓	Protein synthesis (vitamin K)	↓
Iron	↓	Albumin synthesis	?↓

Key: ↓, Impaired or altered structure/function; ↑, increased or improved structure/ function; (−), no change; ?, uncertain.

Controversy remains about whether aging itself leads to disordered esophageal function. An early study by Soergel et al.[6] evaluated esophageal function in a group of 15 nonagenarians by means of intraluminal manometry and barium radiography. The only exclusive criteria were the presence of gastric disease, esophageal disease, or central nervous system disease other than senile dementia. Cineradiographic findings included frequent nonpropulsive, tertiary contractions coupled with delayed esophageal emptying and moderate uniform dilatation. These findings were associated with a high incidence of nonpropulsive contractions after swallows, decreased lower esophageal sphincter (LES) relaxations, and a greater incidence of intrathoracic sphincters. Secondary peristalsis initiated by intraluminal balloon distension was less often impaired. The conclusion was that a "presbyesophagus" developed in older individuals with a motility pattern that resembled diffuse esophageal spasm.

Ten years later a similar study was conducted by Hollis and Castell,[7] who compared esophageal motility using intraluminal pressure transducers in a group of elderly men (70 to 87 years old) with a young adult control group (19 to 27 years old). This study differed from the earlier one by excluding subjects with a history of diabetes or neuropathy. In contrast to the previous report, there was no increase in abnormal motility in the group of elderly men; they had a normal frequency of peristaltic contractions and LES relaxations after a swallow. The number of spontaneous contractions also did not differ between the two groups. An age-related reduction in amplitude of esophageal contractions was seen, however, in a subgroup of 80-year-olds, implying a functionally intact neural system with a weakening of the smooth muscle.[8]

In a group of healthy individuals over age 60, Khan et al.[9] found an increased frequency of abnormal LES responses to deglutition, including a reduced amplitude of the aftercontraction, as compared to that of a group under age 40. The older group also showed a reduced amplitude of peristaltic contraction in the upper and lower esophagus, reduced peristaltic velocity, and an increased frequency of simultaneous contractions. Basal LES pressures were comparable between the two groups. In contrast, Csendes et al.[10]

found no differences in amplitude or duration of waves in the distal esophagus, but resting LES pressure did tend to decrease after the age of 65. A decrease in the percentage of peristaltic waves was also observed.

Finally, a more recent study found an increase in distal esophageal amplitude and duration with age until the sixth decade, with individuals over the age of 60 showing decreased values.[11] In this study, age had no effect on peristaltic velocity, basal LES pressures, or frequency of "abnormal" double- and triple-peaked wave forms.

One can conclude, therefore, that in normal, healthy individuals, the physiologic function of the esophagus is well-preserved with increasing age, save for, perhaps, in very old age. Further support for this conclusion includes a study in which the frequency of spontaneous gastroesophageal reflux, as measured by an ambulatory pH system, was no different between a group of normal volunteers with a mean age of 49 years and a group with a mean age of 22 years.[12] Whether the same finding holds at more advanced ages has yet to be determined. Age-associated changes of the esophageal mucosa have not been extensively studied.

AGING AND GASTRODUODENAL FUNCTION

Because of the stomach's accessibility, the effect of aging on the secretory and motor aspects of gastric function has been well studied. Conflicting reports, however, have emerged regarding the effect of age on gastric emptying, in part because varied modalities are used to study emptying.

Gastric emptying involves the complex interaction of multiple physiologic events which are influenced by dietary composition, physical activity, and central nervous system (CNS) input.[13,14] Gastric motility varies in fasting and fed states. During fasting, there is cyclic contractile activity which is determined by the interdigestive migrating motor complex (MMC). This is the primary means of emptying nondigestible solids. During the fed state, "receptive relaxation" occurs in the fundus to accommodate the food bolus. This reservoir function is mediated by noncholinergic, nonadrenergic inhibition. An increase in antral peristalsis is associated with receptive relaxation of the fundus; this allows solids to be ground into liquified chyme against the closed pylorus. Finally, metered emptying of food into the duodenum is controlled with neurohumoral regulatory mechanisms which permit more rapid emptying of liquids and suspended particles less than 2 mm in size.

It is not surprising that aging may adversely affect these precise gastric regulatory mechanisms. Conflicting data, however, have been reported. Some early fluoroscopic studies of hunger-associated gastric activity in dogs found that older animals had a longer fasting pattern and shorter hunger-associated activity than their younger counterparts.[15] Early human investigations utilizing gross fluoroscopic techniques found no difference in gastric emptying between a group of elderly men and a group of young adults.[16] Unfortunately, interpretation of these early studies was hampered by the use of nonphysiologic ingestants like barium or micropaque.[17] A more recent study, using radiolabeled orange juice, found that gastric emptying half-times were significantly prolonged in a group of 11 older individuals (ages 72 to 86) compared with those of 7 healthy young volunteers (ages 22 to 31). More definite conclusions cannot be extrapolated from these data due to the limited sample size and the fact that the elderly group also suffered from systemic diseases.[18] Using a dual-isotope technique, Moore et al.[19] studied gastric emptying of solid and liquid meals in young males, mean age 31, and an older group of men with a mean age of 76. Both groups were comparable in that no participant had a history of diabetes or gastrointestinal diseases. This study, too, found a delay in liquid emptying in the aged group while solid food emptying was unaffected. A loss of the differential emptying of liquids and solids was also observed (Figs. 58-1 and 58-2).

Stability of solid-food emptying during aging has been demonstrated in other studies in both man and rat.[19–22] The mechanism behind the loss of differential emptying of solids and liquids with age remains unclear; diminished fundal contractility due to changes in the oblique muscle layer is one possible explanation.[19] There are animal data which indicate that aging may result in a decrease in cholinergic gastric smooth muscle receptors.[23] Alternatively, there may be an impairment in adaptive relaxation in the elderly.[24] Further complicating the picture is a study

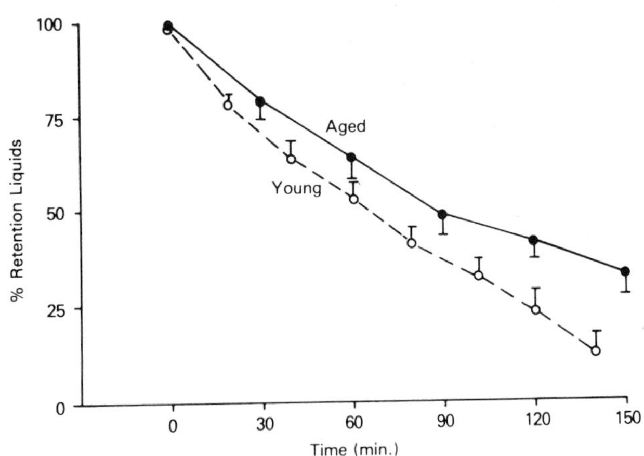

FIGURE 58-1

Percent liquid tracer in young ○----○ and aged ●——● study groups. Each counting interval represents a mean of the normalized counts ± SEM (brackets). (*From Moore et al, Dig Dis Sci 28:340, 1983.*)

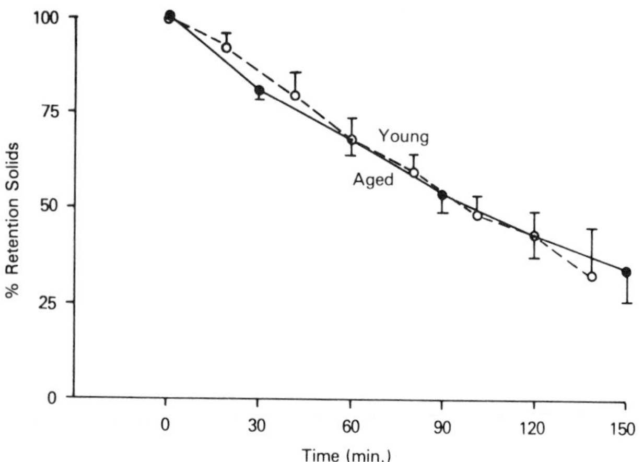

FIGURE 58-2

Percent solid tracer retention in young o----o and aged •——• study groups. Each counting interval represents a mean of the normalized counts ± SEM (brackets). (*From Moore et al, Dig Dis Sci 28:340, 1983.*)

showing that in patients with gastric achlorhydria, gastric emptying of solids is delayed but can be improved with intragastric instillation of acid or treatment with the dopamine-receptor antagonist metoclopramide.[25]

The clinical impact of these observed changes in gastric emptying on elderly patients remains uncertain, since most are asymptomatic. The increased variability in drug pharmacokinetics in the elderly may be, in part, due to changes in gastric emptying.[26] In addition, asymptomatic reductions in gastric emptying may increase the risk of drug-induced gastritis from agents like NSAIDs if their exposure to the mucosa is prolonged.

It has generally been accepted that aging results in an overall decline in gastric acid output, probably due to a reduction in parietal cell mass. One of the earliest studies found a significant decline with age in both basal and histamine-augmented acid secretion in humans, especially in women.[27] In fact, it was estimated that in women, peak acid output declines by approximately 5 meq/h per decade over the age of 30. This original report studied a relatively small number of individuals, and few were over the age of 60. A larger study conducted by Grossman et al.,[28] however, confirmed the findings. Using betazole (Histalog), basal and stimulated acid output decreased after the age of 50 with a greater decline in males. Histalog-fast achlorhydria was present in 21 percent of the men and 10 percent of the women.

In a later study, Andrews et al.[29] were able to correlate diminished histamine-stimulated gastric acid secretion with both gastric mucosal atrophy and decreases in the number of parietal cells. Another recent study, however, failed to demonstrate a significant decrease in peak acid output using pentagastrin, despite declines in parietal cell mass.[30] Since parietal cells are stimulated by histamine, gastrin, and acetylcholine via three separate receptor systems, accommodations may be made when dysfunction develops in one agonist-receptor system. More definite declines in acid output tend to be associated with more severe atrophic mucosal changes.[31]

A recently proposed hypothesis states that the age-related decline in gastric secretory reserve may be associated with *Helicobacter pylori* infection, which is more common among the elderly.[32,33] An interesting 1991 study documented that healthy volunteers between the ages of 44 to 71 actually had higher basal, meal-stimulated, and gastrin-stimulated acid secretory rates than did subjects aged 23 to 42. The increased secretion with age was only statistically significant in male subjects. The presence of *H. pylori* infection, however, was associated with diminished basal acid secretion.[34] It is possible that studies which have suggested a diminished gastric acid secretion in the elderly may have included more subjects with atrophic gastritis or *H. pylori* infection. This controversial and clinically relevant topic will need clarification from additional research.

The development of relative achlorhydria with aging theoretically may decrease absorption of weakly acidic drugs, since formation of less lipophilic, and, therefore, less permeable compounds occurs at higher pH. To date there have been no studies which have documented this phenomenon. One study found no difference in absorption of the antibiotic tetracycline between achlorhydric elderly and young, normal subjects.[35]

There are inconsistencies in the literature with regard to pepsin secretion over age. In one study using pepsinogen as an indicator of pepsin secretion, age appeared to have no significant effect on pepsin secretion.[36] A more recent report utilizing a radioimmunoassay (RIA) for serum pepsinogen I found that 40 percent of tested individuals over age 70 had values less than 50 ng/dl, compared to only 5 percent of subjects below 40.[37] Goldschmeidt's[34] 1991 study, however, also found an increase in serum pepsinogen I and II levels in subjects over the age of 42.

Serum gastrin levels, determined by RIA in humans, have been more clearly shown to increase with age, an effect believed to be secondary to achlorhydria from long-standing type A gastritis which spares the antrum.[38] In the absence of inhibition by acid, the increase in functional G (gastrin) cell mass is reflected by age-related increases in basal- and protein-stimulated gastrin secretion.[39]

Gastric mucosal changes represent a balance between cellular death and cellular renewal, with mucosal atrophy developing due to accelerated cellular death or decreased renewal. Several studies have reported that atrophy of the gastric mucosa occurs with increasing age. The reported incidence of age-related gastric mucosal changes, however, varies widely depending on whether histologic or biochemical data were evaluated and on the methodologies employed. An early study of vacuum-tube gastric mucosal biopsies from 30 subjects over age 60 found no evidence of mucosal atrophy.[40] Supporting this finding, in part, is a recent report which found an actual increase in the total number of gastric cells per milligram tissue weight, with no change in the number of parietal cells per milligram mucosa with age.[41] However, the number of nonparietal cells was increased, indicating a change in mucosal composition, in part due to atrophy.

The weight of evidence favors an increased incidence of gastric mucosal atrophy with age. Andrews et al.[29] found some degree of atrophic gastritis in 23 of 24 asymptomatic subjects over age 60. In a larger study, Kekki et al.[31] found a concomitant increase in the incidence and severity of atrophic changes in the gastric body mucosa which correlated with a reduction of acid output with increasing age. However, the finding by Bird et al.[42] of a near-normal histology in up to one-third of achlorhydric patients over 80, as well as the lack of correlation between age and the degree of atrophic changes, underlines the fact that age is not the sole determinant of gastric atrophy. As noted, recent data suggest an increase in the incidence of infection with *H. pylori*, a potential pathogen causing gastritis, with age.[33]

Recent research has also addressed the effect of aging on gastric and duodenal mucosal prostaglandin content. A 1991 study examined biopsy specimens of gastric mucosa from 10 healthy young (ages 19 to 30 years) and 10 elderly (ages 60 to 74) volunteers and found no difference in the tissue 6-keto prostaglandin $F_{1\alpha}$ content.[43] Another study examined a larger number of subjects and documented significant decreases in tissue prostaglandin $F_{2\alpha}$ and E_2 content in biopsies of the fundus, antrum, and postbulbar duodenum. This group also confirmed their earlier findings of increased gastric acid secretion in the elderly group and noted that these findings may be linked by the suppression of parietal cell acid secretion by prostaglandins.[44]

Additional factors which complicate the interpretation of gastric mucosal changes with age include studies showing a greater progression of atrophic gastritis proximally along the lesser curvature[45]; progression of atrophic and metaplastic changes in the antrum as compared to the fundus[46]; and actual improvement in superficial body gastritis in 18 percent of patients followed over 20 years.[47]

Aside from affecting secretory function, an important feature associated with atrophic gastritis is the development of intestinal metaplasia, a possible precursor for gastric carcinoma. A study from Japan showed an increase in diffuse-type metaplasia with age which correlated with the degree of atrophic changes.[48] What mechanism underlies these mucosal changes remains unclear; however, recent data suggest a role for sulfated glycosaminoglycans, which may vary in composition and amount with age.[49]

Finally, duodenal bicarbonate secretion and aging were studied in a rat model.[50] These investigations disclosed that while basal bicarbonate secretion did not change with age, acid-stimulated bicarbonate secretion was reduced significantly in older animals. The significance of this finding for human pathology is unknown, but it has been used to explain, in part, the increasing incidence of peptic ulcer disease among the elderly.

AGING AND SMALL-INTESTINAL FUNCTION

Age-related alterations in small-intestinal motility have been evaluated in animals and humans, with studies of both in vivo transit and in vitro smooth-muscle activity. In a study using ^{85}Sr-labeled microspheres as a nonabsorbable marker of small intestinal transit in Wistar rats, total transit time did not vary across the life span.[21] This finding is supported by another animal study using the well-accepted aging model, the Fischer 344 rat. Small-intestinal transit did not change between a group of young, postpubertal animals (5 to 12 months old) and a senescent group (26 to 28 months old) using ^{51}Cr-marker and geometric-mean analysis.[51] Lin and Hayton, however, found that the transit rates in 31-month-old senescent rats were higher in the proximal small intestine but significantly lower in the distal small intestine as compared to the rates in a group of mature, 16-month-old animals.[52]

Human studies have also corroborated relative stability of small-intestinal transit over age. Early studies using liquid barium movement during small-bowel studies to estimate transit time showed no change in transit time over several age groups.[53] Two more recent reports utilizing breath-hydrogen measurements to estimate small-bowel transit found no differences in transit times between younger and elderly individuals.[24,54] Anuras and Sutherland[55] examined small-intestinal motility using jejunal manometry in a group of 10 healthy older subjects, mean age 72, and 10 younger adults, mean age 25. While the motility pattern during the fasting period was no different between the two groups, the motility index during the fed state was significantly reduced in elderly subjects, suggesting age-related alterations in the neurohumoral response to food.

In contrast to the relatively stable pattern of small-intestinal motility in vivo, a variety of in vitro studies have demonstrated dynamic changes with age. In a 1985 report by Kobashi et al.,[56] a decrease in sensitivity to the smooth-muscle agonist acetylcholine (ACh) was observed at mid-age in Wistar rat jejunal muscle strips, followed by an increase during senescence. This decrease corresponded to increases in acetylcholinesterase activity in the mid-age and aged groups, suggesting a form of adaptive supersensitivity developing in senescence. A form of supersensitivity was also observed by Bortoff et al.,[57] who found that both maximal tension and sensitivity of cat jejunal circular smooth-muscle strips to ACh was higher in older animals than in younger ones. We have also demonstrated increases in sensitivity of Fischer 344 rat ileal circular smooth muscle with age in depolarizing concentrations of potassium chloride, possibly due to changes in calcium utilization and/or the contractile mechanism.[58] Therefore, the reported stability of small-intestinal motility over age may, in part, be due to ongoing changes at the neuromuscular level.

There is a paucity of information regarding the morphometric changes in the enteric nerves and muscularis externa of the small intestine with age. What little information is available suggests a decrease in neuron number along with an increase in thickness and cross-sectional area of the muscle coat with age.[59,60] Possible age-related changes in specific receptors and neurotransmitters await further investigation.

Much more detailed information is available on age-associated changes in small-intestinal size, weight, and villus morphology. Moog[61] reported an age-related increase in the absolute and relative weights of mice small intestine from 6 to 24 months of age, especially in the terminal ileal region where amyloid-like material accumulated in the lamina propria. Penzes,[62] on the other hand, found no significant age differences in small-intestinal total carbon and nitrogen content per fat-free dry weight of the female rat. Small-intestinal length has been shown to increase with age in male Wistar rats but to stay the same with age in the female Wistar rats.[21,63] Comparable human data are, however, lacking.

Studies also differ regarding aging effects on mucosal architecture. An age-associated increase in jejunal villus height, as well as villus atrophy and irregular architecture, have been reported in rats.[64,65] Regional differences seem to exist, since the changes appear to be confined primarily to the proximal and distal small intestine.[65,66] Animal studies have also indicated stability in the number of villi over age, although in the proximal rat small intestine, fusion of villi becomes more frequent with age.[67] Ultrastructural changes with age have also been noted in the microvilli, which shorten and become more disoriented.[68] Although one might anticipate a concomitant reduction in mucosal absorptive area, such a reduction has not been borne out by additional animal studies.[69]

Complicating interpretation of animal data is the lack of consistency in nutrition and the presence or absence of infections, all of which can influence mucosal architecture. In a recent study using the Fischer 344 rat, a barrier-reared animal kept on a constant nutritional regimen, aged animals demonstrated no change in villus crypt length or villus height in the proximal small intestine and showed an actual increase in ileal villus height.[70]

More limited data are available on the aging human small intestine. Warren et al.[71] analyzed peroral jejunal biopsies from 10 young individuals and 10 older individuals ages 60 to 73. The average villus height and height of the individual enterocyte did not vary between the two groups. Mucosal surface area was reduced over age using a template method. However, when postmortem specimens from younger adults were compared with biopsy specimens from older individuals, a mean reduction in villus height was found.[72] Scanning electron microscopy analysis has shown that proximal jejunal villi are shorter and broader in young adults than they are in children.[73] Species differences in this area make definitive conclusions difficult. It is also difficult to equate structure with function because studies have demonstrated age-related alterations in epithelial enzyme expression despite an unchanged villus structure.[74]

Studies of age-related differences in mucosal cellular kinetics have also reached inconsistent conclusions. The small-intestinal mucosa is a highly prolific tissue and renews itself continuously by migration of crypt cells to the villus tip, where they are sloughed. In the classic studies of Lesher,[75] a prolonged crypt-to-villus transit time was observed in the upper intestine of aging mice, with the villus becoming populated with more mature cells. A compensatory increase in crypt-to-villus ratio has also been reported, balancing the reduction in proliferation.[76] Once again, regional differences exist with no changes in proliferative rates in the ileum.[77] A report using the more standardized Fischer rat model, however, found no differences in crypt-cell migration between young and old animals. Further clouding the picture is evidence suggesting only modest changes in protein synthesis in the mouse small intestine, with ribosomal synthetic capacity increasing despite decreased ribosomal activity.[78]

The absorptive capacity of the small intestine is influenced by a host of factors, including the number and integrity of absorbing cells, the mucosal surface, the ingested material, intestinal motility and blood flow, gastric emptying, and the status of the unstirred water layer.[8] Interestingly, the absorption of vitamin A, a compound with a high lipid solubility, is faster in elderly subjects, reflecting a possible change in the composition of the unstirred layer.[79] Water and electrolyte transport may also vary with age, and have been shown to decrease in the jejunum and ileum of rats.[80]

Brush-border enzyme activity has been evaluated primarily in animal models. Levels of the marker enzymes alkaline phosphatase and acid phosphatase are decreased in aged rats, possibly due to a reduction in the number of enterocytes.[67] Human jejunal alkaline phosphatase activity is also decreased in older individuals, although the mechanism of this alteration is unclear.[81] The disaccharidases (maltase, sucrase, and lactase) also demonstrate reduced activity in aged rats.[82] Holt[83] has recently found a similar decrease in the specific activities of sucrase, maltase, lactase, and adenosine deaminase in the upper intestines of old Fischer 344 rats, in part due to a delay in enzyme differentiation resulting in an increase in the proportion of undifferentiated villus epithelial cells. Human jejunal lactase activity also decreases with age, with the other disaccharidases remaining relatively stable until the seventh decade and then declining.[81]

How do these morphologic and biochemical

changes in the small intestine translate into functional changes in absorption? Of the carbohydrates, D-xylose is the best-studied. Because this pentose is passively absorbed by the small bowel, its urinary excretion after ingestion is widely used to assess the integrity of the small intestine. Early investigations indicated an age-related decline in xylose absorption. More recently, however, Kendall[84] used both oral and intravenous administration to show that the presumed decline in absorption was actually caused by reduced excretion due to renal impairment developing with age. A subsequent study found a 26 percent prevalence of impaired D-xylose absorption in a group of subjects over age 63, though only urinary measurements were performed.[85] When corrected serum levels are evaluated, D-xylose malabsorption does not appear to develop with age except perhaps beyond 80 years.[86] A more recent report, using a pharmacokinetic approach, did demonstrate declines in the absorption rate constant for D-xylose, indicating some minor reductions in absorption with advancing age.[87] Similarly, the affinity constant for D-glucose absorption increases with age in rats, indicating a decline in carrier affinity.[88] This effect, however, may be counterbalanced by resistance changes in the unstirred water layer so that glucose uptake remains stable.[89]

Human data on the subject of carbohydrate absorption are scant, although one study measuring postprandial breath-hydrogen appearance from meals containing varying amounts of carbohydrates found excess breath-hydrogen excretion in one-third of subjects over age 65.[90] It is likely, however, that significant changes in carbohydrate absorption with age reflect a combination of factors, including changes in gastric emptying, intestinal transit, and the bacterial flora.

Studies on fat malabsorption are fraught with technical problems, and results vary with the methodology used. When micronephelometry was used to measure the light-scattering index in the plasma of individuals after consuming a 100-g fat meal, fat absorption was impaired in a group of elderly subjects and could be partially corrected with pancreatic supplement.[91] Animal (rat) data also suggest an impairment in fat absorption with age when assessed using labeled triolein.[92] However, human studies using [^{14}C]triolein have found no significant differences in fat absorption between healthy young and old subjects.[93] An interesting finding of some studies is a variable pattern of fat absorption with aging. While triglyceride absorption may be reduced, cholesterol absorption may increase with age.[94,95] Thus, while fat absorption may be altered with age, other changes, including pancreatic function and gastric emptying, could have a greater impact than the mucosal integrity alone. In addition, the clinical importance of this finding may only become apparent with consumption of a high-fat diet.[96]

The absorption of fat-soluble vitamins, notably vitamins A and K, is increased in the elderly.[79,97] Data derived from rats, on the other hand, suggest a mucosal defect in vitamin D absorption with age when [^{14}C] vitamin D_3 is perfused intraduodenally.[92] In elderly humans, impaired intestinal absorption of ^{3}H-cholecalciferol and lower serum levels of the active metabolite 1,25-dihydroxyvitamin D_3 have been described.[98,99] The overall importance of age-related changes in vitamin D absorption remains unclear, but one cannot exclude vitamin D malabsorption as a contributing factor to the development of osteoporosis.

In general, increasing malabsorption of water-soluble vitamins does not appear to develop with age. Vitamin B_1 (thiamine) absorption, when assessed by measurement of urinary thiamine excretion, decreased in senescent rats.[100] However, Thompson[101] found no significant differences in thiamine excretion between groups of young and 80-year-old human subjects. Low plasma levels of vitamin C (ascorbic acid) are present in many elderly individuals and are likely due to reduced intake rather than malabsorption.[102] Reduced levels of erythrocyte folate in many older individuals was proposed to be due to impaired absorption of dietary folate in one study.[103] However, this finding was refuted in another report which documented no differences in folate absorption up to the age of 70 as estimated by measurement of urinary ^{3}H-folate.[104]

Malabsorption can also result from vitamin B_{12} (cyanocobalamin) deficiency, but age does not appear to affect ileal absorption of the vitamin.[105] Fleming and Barrows[106] observed no difference in radiolabeled-B_{12} absorption in three age groups of rats. McEvoy,[107] studying whole-body retention of ^{58}Co-B_{12} in 51 healthy adults, found no correlation between B_{12} absorption and age. Other conditions—including gastric achlorhydria, pernicious anemia, pancreatic insufficiency, and ileal disease—have a greater impact on B_{12} absorption than age alone.

The process of protein digestion and assimilation remains intact throughout the life span. One animal study indicated that neutral amino acids were absorbed with a lower affinity than basic amino acids in old age; human studies, however, are lacking.[88]

Finally, with regard to mineral absorption, much information has been gathered indicating that calcium absorption declines with age.[108–113] It is unclear whether the age-associated defect in calcium absorption is due to associated vitamin D deficiency or a decline in the content or responsiveness of calcium-binding proteins in the intestinal mucosa.

Serum levels of both iron and transferrin have been reported to fall with advanced age, although iron absorption appears to remain intact. Marx[114] used a double-isotope technique to compare iron absorption in 40 active elderly individuals over age 65 with iron absorption in 25 young, healthy subjects. While mucosal iron uptake and transfer were not decreased in the aged group, red-cell iron uptake was, suggesting ineffective erythropoiesis. Nonetheless, some degree of food-iron malabsorption may occur in the elderly because the increased prevalence of gastric achlorhydria would reduce the absorption of non-heme iron.[115]

AGING AND COLONIC FUNCTION

The colon executes a variety of functions, including absorption, secretion, and motility, as well as functioning as a storage organ. There is surprisingly little data on the structural alterations in the colon with aging. Yamajata[116] compared biopsy specimens from healthy subjects with autopsy specimens. Age-related changes included mucosal atrophy, abnormalities of the mucosal glands, cellular infiltration of the mucosa and lamina propria, hypertrophy of the muscularis mucosa, and arteriolar sclerosis. In contrast to the absence of atrophic changes in small intestinal smooth muscle, atrophy of the muscularis externa develops and there is an increase in the connective tissue component. Evaluation of colonic epithelial cells using an electron microscope has shown vacuolization and nuclear abnormalities and an increase in electron density within the cytoplasm and nucleus.[8]

A more recent study examined the effect of aging on the proliferation of colonic epithelial cells. Microautoradiography was used to measure the incorporation of labeled thymidine into biopsy specimens to determine the amount and localization of cellular proliferation. Subjects more than 66 years of age had significantly more proliferating cells, and proliferation was increased most at the more superficial portions of the colonic crypts.[117] Similar changes of cellular proliferation are found in individuals with adenomatous colon polyps, and it is possible that these changes are associated with the increased incidence of colon cancer with age.

Information regarding age-associated changes in colonic transit comes largely from animal studies. Varga[21] used ^{85}Sr-labeled microspheres to measure intestinal transit in rats and found an age-related delay in transit through the cecum and large intestine. A more recent study by McDougal et al.[102] confirmed this finding. Using the Fischer 344 rat model and calculating the geometric mean of a radioactive tracer, the study found colonic transit to be significantly slower in senescent animals than postpubertal animals. This slowing correlated with an increase in diameter of the senescent colons and decreases in maximum response in vitro to both electrical and cholinergic stimulation. No age-related differences in the water content of the feces were found. The overall conclusion was that decreased colonic transit was due to decreased responsiveness to neurotransmitters as well as a deficit in innervation. Decreased transit has also been observed in aged humans, but constipation has been associated with a decrease in fecal water content, which contrasts with the animal data.[118,119] A recent study using a liquid formula diet found no age-related changes in intestinal transit times.[54]

Preliminary data suggest additional mechanisms underlying derangements in colonic activity with aging. An age-associated decline in the amplitude of inhibitory junctional potentials has been described and may correspond to a decrease in either the release of inhibitory neurotransmitters or the number of binding sites.[120,121] This decrease may result in a form of functional obstruction as segmentation predominates over mass movement. There also may be increases in opioid receptor subtypes, possibly resulting in a greater sensitivity to the inhibitory effects of endogenous opioids with age.[122]

It has long been known that diverticular disease increases in incidence with age, affecting up to 30 percent of individuals over age 60, and perhaps 60 percent of people over age 80.[123] Speculation as to the genesis of diverticula includes age-associated alterations in connective tissue elements and/or changes in colonic pressures.[124] In fact, as previously noted, there is an increase with age in the amount of fibrosis and elastin in both muscle layers in the normal sigmoid colon, but no such changes in elastin content develop in the muscular layer with diverticular disease. What is found is an increase in the number of fine and coarse elastin fibers in the taeniae coli, with an increase in thickness of taenia and circular smooth muscle. One theory, therefore, would be that an age-associated shortening of the colon, secondary to changes in the taenia, creates higher intraluminal pressures.[125] Indeed, others have shown that the colon in diverticular disease does become more distensible.[126] Age alone, however, must not be the only factor influencing the development of diverticular disease. Repeat barium enema examinations have demonstrated stabilized disease in 70 percent of patients with diverticula after 5 years,[127] and environmental factors, especially dietary fiber, probably play an equally important role.[128]

AGING AND ANORECTAL FUNCTION

Normal defecation and continence are the result of programmed activation or inhibition of pelvic and anorectal muscles. Several studies have now established that aging is associated with alterations in anorectal structure and activity.

A recent histologic study evaluated the development of sclerosis of the anal sphincter with aging. Collagenous connective tissue was found to increase with age and to replace sphincter smooth muscle in specimens from elderly subjects. This would explain the manometric findings of increased resting sphincter tone with decreased maximum contractile pressure that have been found with aging in some studies.[129] In a study comparing healthy elderly subjects with younger subjects using anorectal manometry, loss of muscle elasticity with aging was suggested since the elderly group experienced lower maximum tolerance and higher rectal pressures at similar volumes.[130] The rectal distending balloon also elicited internal sphincter relaxation at smaller volumes, but, interestingly, the subjective perception of rectal distension was unchanged with age.

Additional studies have come to somewhat different conclusions, depending on the sex distribution, the health of the subjects, and the methodology employed. A recent report evaluated anorectal function with intraluminal transducers in 18 healthy elderly subjects (mean age 72) and 18 healthy young volunteers (mean age 29). Age did not significantly affect anal length, highest anal resting zone, pull-through pressures at rest and during voluntary squeeze, threshold or amplitude of the rectosphincteric reflex, threshold of sensation, critical volume, or rectal wall elasticity.[131] When these data were analyzed by gender, females had a significantly lower maximum anal resting zone, lower anal pull-through pressures during rest and voluntary squeeze, and a lower threshold of rectal sensation than the corresponding group of males. This observation emphasizes the need for adequate sex matching when assessing the results of such studies. In a larger study of 88 continent subjects separated by sex into three age groups (younger than 40, 40 to 60, and over 60), aging was associated with decreased anal pressure at rest, along with reduced maximum anal squeeze pressure and pressure in the rectal ampulla, especially after the age of 60 in both sexes.[132]

These findings were corroborated by a 1991 study which recorded anal sphincter competence in 49 healthy women ranging from 20 to 79 years of age. Closing pressure—the difference between the maximum resting anal pressure and rectal pressure—diminished more with age than the maximum resting pressure; the authors hypothesized that this may play a role in the development of fecal incontinence with aging.[133] Another recent study found no significant changes in anal manometry with aging but did document considerable variation among different measurements of the same subject, demonstrating the difficulty of studies of this topic.[134]

Bannister et al.[135] compared anorectal function in a group of 37 elderly subjects, all with concomitant medical illnesses and on various medications, with anorectal function in a group of 48 young, healthy volunteers. The older group had significantly lower mean basal and squeeze anal pressures, the differences being greater in the females. Higher rectal pressures in response to distension, along with reduced maximum-tolerated volumes and slower stimulated defecation, also were seen in the elderly group. More importantly, elderly females also required less rectal distension to produce a sustained relaxation of the anal sphincter, produced a less obtuse anorectal angle when straining, and had greater perianal descent than their younger counterparts. Hence, the risk of fecal incontinence is accentuated in the elderly and especially in elderly females, owing to intrinsic musculature weakness compounded by birth trauma and postmenopausal changes in connective tissue elasticity.

While no systematic study of age-related alterations in myoneural elements involved in anorectal function has been performed, electrophysiologic studies of the external anal sphincter in patients with

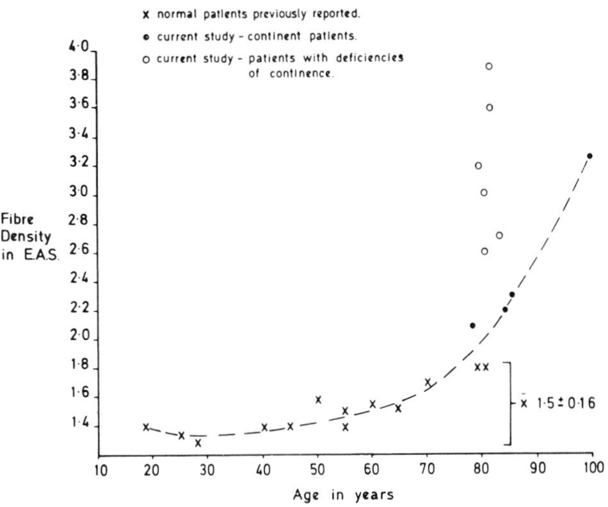

FIGURE 58-3
The relation between fiber density in the external anal sphincter and age in 23 patients. The data from 13 normal patients previously reported have also been recorded. The fiber densities in the 6 patients with varying degrees of incontinence segregate above the projected curve of fiber densities in normal subjects (EAS = external anal sphincter). (*From Percy et al, Age Aging 11:175, 1982.)*

and without fecal incontinence indicate that aging is associated with an increase in motor-unit fiber density. The studies were performed using single-fiber electromyography (Fig. 58-3). The associated increase suggests that denervation, followed by renervation of muscle fibers from undamaged axons, develops with age.[136] A more recent study also examined the function of the pudendal nerve (which supplies the external anal sphincter muscle) and found that latencies were increased, suggesting that the nerve was damaged.[137] When denervation is more severe, as demonstrated histologically, higher motor-unit fiber densities develop with resulting fecal incontinence.[138] The correlation between denervation and incontinence is, however, not that close, so that other factors, such as looseness of the stool and diminished cerebral function, often coexist before incontinence develops.

AGING AND PANCREATIC FUNCTION

The pancreas has many functions, which include secreting proteolytic and lipolytic enzymes, neutralizing gastric acid secretion, and maintaining glucose homeostasis. Roughly 20 percent of the dry weight of the pancreas is enzyme protein.[8] Perhaps one of the pancreas's most striking characteristics is its large functional reserve capacity; 90 percent of function can be lost before signs of insufficiency, such as steatorrhea, develop.

Autopsy series have found little change in the weight of the pancreas with age expressed as either absolute average weight or percent of total body weight.[139] Also, Zimmerman et al.[140] found no change in the overall size of the gland in people 15 to 90 years old. Postmortem studies, however, have shown an age-associated dilatation of the main pancreatic ducts and ectasia of branched ducts.[141] Sahel[142] evaluated endoscopic retrograde cholangiopancreatography (ERCP) studies in 125 subjects over age 70 and found an age-associated increase in the caliber of the main pancreatic duct. In addition, 5.8 percent of subjects demonstrated incomplete stenosis of the pancreatic ducts without other pathologic changes.

Morphometric and ultrastructural studies of the exocrine pancreas have shown an increased amount of intralobular fibrous material along with some focal fatty deposition in the normal pancreas over the age of 70.[140] Acinar atrophy due to shrinkage of individual acini, acinar cell vacuolization, absence of zymogen granules, and dilatation of ductal structures containing inspissated PAS-positive material are additional age-related phenomena that develop in both humans and rats.[143–145] Squamous metaplasia of intralobular and interlobular ducts, proliferation of ductal cells, and alterations in the amount of nuclear material have also been demonstrated. Slavin[146] has shown a large quantity of perivascular lipofuscin-containing cells and an increase in the amount of lysosomes in acinar cells of aging rats.

Age-related vascular lesions include fibrotic thickening of the walls of small and medium-sized arteries, necrosis of the intima, and infiltration by mononuclear cells and eosinophils in rats.[145] In a human series of 423 autopsies of individuals aged 0 to 92 years, minor focal changes of arteriosclerosis were detected.[147]

As one might anticipate in an organ with such a large reserve capacity, the aforementioned changes in structure do not necessarily correlate with physiologic changes in secretion. Part of the difficulty in interpreting the data again lies in the variety of methodologies used to assess pancreatic secretory function. In favor of the stability of pancreatic function over the age span is a study by Rosenberg et al.,[148] who assessed pancreatic fluid and bicarbonate output in response to intravenous secretin and found no differences in 59 subjects above and 44 below the age of 50. Supporting this study are the studies of Gullo et al.,[149] who initially evaluated pancreatic bicarbonate secretion and output of trypsin, chymotrypsin, and lipase in response to continuous IV infusion of secretin and cerulein in 25 elderly and 30 young subjects. Only mild decreases in enzyme output were observed in three of the elderly subjects, with no age-associated changes in the volume of the duodenal aspirate or bicarbonate output. A more recent study by the same group using the fluorescein dilaurate test found no differences in pancreatic function between the patients under 80 years and those over 80.[150]

In contrast, three other studies indicate an age-related decline in pancreatic function. Fikry[151] performed the secretin test in 23 subjects aged 60 to 72 and found a decrease in the volume of the duodenal aspirate, with a selective reduction in amylase and trypsin levels and no change in lipase output. Bartos and Groh[152] found decreases in bicarbonate and amylase output only after repeated injections of secretin and cholecystokinin (CCK) in 10 subjects between ages 61 and 73, suggesting a decline in reserve capacity.[152] Both studies have been criticized because of methodological problems, including the use of one stimulant and possible incomplete recovery of the duodenal juice. However, a study by Laugier,[153] who performed duodenal aspirates across a wide age range (15 to 75 years), found pancreatic volume and bicarbonate concentration peaking in the fourth decade, then declining. By contrast, outputs of lipase, phospholipase, and trypsin declined linearly with age. In addition, decreased outputs of volume and protein (or lipase) in response to secretin or CCK were observed, especially after age 65.

Assessment of serum levels of pancreatic enzymes has also yielded conflicting information. Both unchanged and increased serum immunoreactive trypsin levels have been noted over age, the latter attributed to impaired renal function.[154,155] Carrere et al.[156] also observed no difference in serum trypsin 1 levels or serum lipase levels and activity between 35 elderly and 51 young subjects. By contrast, Mohiuddin et al.[157] reported significant increases in serum trypsin and lipase levels over age; the increase was attributed to an age-associated "leakage" of enzymes out of acinar cells.

AGING AND HEPATOBILIARY FUNCTION

The common bile duct undergoes changes with age similar to those that occur in the main pancreatic duct. In a study using IV cholangiography in 84 healthy Japanese individuals, the common bile duct dilated progressively with age.[158] The mean diameter at age 20 was 6.8 mm, while at age 70 it was 9.2 mm. Distally, however, the preampullary portion progressively narrows with age.[159] How these changes are related to the increasing incidence of cholelithiasis and choledocholithiasis with age remains unclear.[160,161]

The gallbladder serves several functions, including concentration and delivery of bile to the small intestine. The effect of age on the concentrating ability of the gallbladder has not been investigated. Cholecystographic examinations have demonstrated stability of gallbladder emptying with increasing age.[162] Part of the pathogenesis of gallstones relates to the lithogenicity of bile. A numerical value, the lithogenic index, has been developed to describe the relative solubility of cholesterol in bile, with higher values reflecting more saturated bile. Valdivieso et al.[163] addressed the effect of age on bile saturation by comparing biliary lipid composition in a group of Chilean women under 25 to that of an older group over 50. The proportions of phospholipids and cholesterol increased significantly in the older group, which corresponded to an increased lithogenic index. Supersaturated bile was found in only 8.3 percent of the young women, whereas it was found in 41.7 percent of the older women (Fig. 58-4). Since there was no change in total bile acid and cholic acid pools, it was speculated that aging resulted in an increase in canalicular lipid secretion, resembling that which is seen in obesity. Trash et al.[164] also found the lithogenic index to rise with age. It therefore seems likely that gallstone occurrence in the aged is related to alterations in biliary lipid composition.

A variety of morphologic and functional changes have been demonstrated in the aging liver. The liver gradually decreases in size with increasing age, accounting for 2.5 percent of total body weight before age 50 but only 1.6 percent at age 90.[139] In addition, with age the liver gradually conforms to the shape of adjoining structures. One study showed that the livers of Japanese women were markedly domed, probably due to tight belts worn as part of traditional dress.[165] Hepatic regeneration with aging was recently studied in rats following partial hepatectomy. These studies found that age did not influence the rate of regeneration, but because older rats had larger livers prior to resection, it took them longer to fully replace the resected hepatic mass. The clinical significance of this study is unclear because, in humans, hepatic mass does not increase with age, but the more frequent use of hepatic resection in cancer surgery makes it a topical subject.[166]

Liver blood flow also appears to decrease with age. Estimated declines of 0.3 to 1.5 percent per year have been reported.[167–169] A more recent study used gray-scale B ultrasound to document liver volume and plasma clearance of indocyanine green to indirectly estimate liver blood flow in 65 subjects ranging from 24 to 91 years of age. When linear regression analysis was used to extrapolate to values that would be expected at ages 24 and 91, the older subjects would have a 41 percent decrease in liver volume/kg total body weight and a 47 percent decrease in weight-adjusted hepatic blood flow.[170] The potential clinical importance of the change in hepatic blood flow with advancing age is obvious when one realizes the importance of the liver in drug metabolism.

Microscopically, the liver undergoes numerous alterations with age. An early study listed the following as the most common histologic alterations in biopsies of normal subjects over age 70: mild ductular proliferation, especially around portal tracts; mixed periportal inflammatory infiltrate; single or small areas of liver cell necrosis; and increased amounts of lipofuscin pigment in Kupffer's cells in over one-third

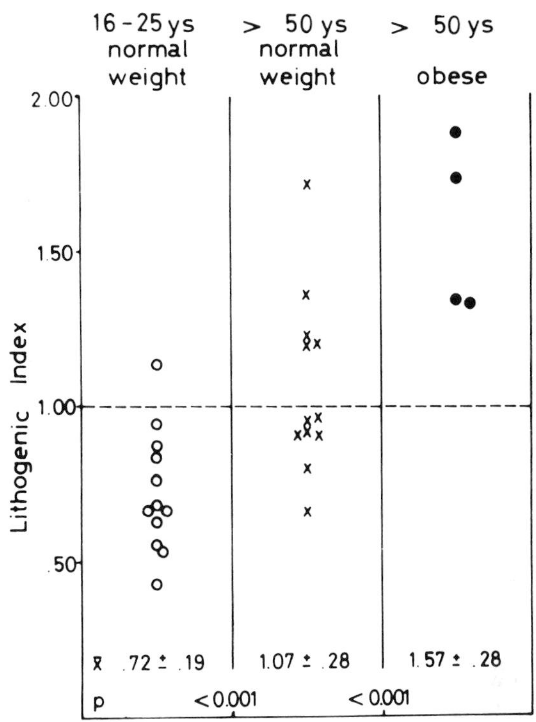

FIGURE 58-4
Lithogenic indexes of fasting gallbladder bile in young normal, older normal, and older obese Chilean women. (*From Valdivieso et al, Gastroenterology 74:871, 1978.*)

of the subjects.[171] More recent work by Watanabe and Tanaka[172] defines additional changes in hepatocyte morphology, including a decrease in the number of hepatocytes accompanied by increases in mean cell volume and variance in cell size, variation in nuclear size and volume of nuclear DNA, and an increase in aneuploidy and binucleate cells. These findings, along with the finding of a decreased number but increased volume of mitochondria and lysosomes, seem to indicate that the remaining hepatocytes are hyperfunctioning, possibly to compensate for their reduced numbers. Supporting this indication is the study of Schmucker,[173] who found a decrease in the surface area of the Golgi apparatus but an increase in the amount of rough and smooth endoplasmic reticulum. Hypertrophy and hyperplasia are the mechanisms by which liver regrowth occurs following partial resection as well; it seems that the compensatory response to cell loss from both aging and resection is similar.[174]

Functional changes in the liver with age have been defined in a variety of ways. Standard liver function tests—including serum concentrations of bilirubin, aminotransaminases, and alkaline phosphatase—do not vary significantly with age.[175] Albumin and transferrin levels have been reported to either decrease or remain stable.[169,176] These standard liver function tests, however, do not measure dynamic functions.

The clearance of anionic dyes such as sulfobromophthalein (Bromsulphalein, or BSP) by the liver is one such dynamic test. After IV administration, sulfobromophthalein is extracted from blood, stored in hepatocytes, and finally excreted unchanged in bile. An early report, using constant IV infusion of BSP, demonstrated that while the storage capacity declined with age, the secretory transport maximum did not.[177] Using simultaneous cytofluorometric measurements of BSP retention and nuclear DNA in rat hepatocytes, Nakanishi[178] further defined the nature of the storage defect by showing a selective decrease in the storage capacity of polyploid cells which increase in number with age.

Microsomal oxidation and hydroxylation has been evaluated using clearance of the drug antipyrine, but the results have been controversial. In a study of 307 healthy males, ages 18 to 92, a decline of 18.5 percent in antipyrine clearance was seen in the older subjects.[179] However, when looked at using multiple regression analysis, other environmental factors, specifically caffeine and cigarette use, were highly correlated with enhanced antipyrine metabolism and were considerably lower in prevalence in the older males. In fact, smoking alone accounted for 12 percent of the changes in metabolism, with age accounting for only 3 percent. Nonetheless, Swift[180] found lower antipyrine clearances in a group of elderly, otherwise healthy nonsmokers (ages 75 to 86) as compared to the clearances of a younger group (ages 20 to 29). Greenblatt et al.,[181] who studied antipyrine kinetics in 51 smoking and nonsmoking adults, also concluded that age was the most significant variable affecting clearance rates. In addition, Salem et al.[182] reported that liver enzymes of older individuals are less "inducible," which may compound the effects of age on mixed oxidase function.

The nutritional status of an older patient has also been shown to affect microsomal oxidative metabolism. Reduced antipyrine clearance was observed in a group of elderly patients found to be ascorbic-acid deficient. Following correction of the deficiency with a 2-week course of multivitamins, antipyrine metabolism normalized.[183]

Acetanilid is an alternative drug used to assess hepatic microsomal oxidation. Impaired oxidation was suggested in a group of 23 subjects over 65 as the half-life of acetanilid was increased in this group.[26] Nonmicrosomal oxidation via alcohol dehydrogenase appears to be unaffected by age, as the rate of elimination of ethanol administered intravenously was constant in 50 healthy subjects ages 21 to 81.[184] On the other hand, the maximum ethanol level attained with a fixed infusion correlated strongly with age, presumably because the elderly have a decreased lean body mass and therefore a smaller volume of distribution for ethanol. The likelihood of deleterious interactions between alcohol and medications is also increased in the elderly.[185]

Demethylation is another means of drug metabolism by the liver. Specifically, the benzodiazepines, chlordiazepine, and diazepam are eliminated by this process, as is the drug aminopyrine. Jori et al.[186] found the half-life of aminopyrine was increased to 8.1 hours in 40 elderly subjects (over age 65), compared to 3.3 hours in 25- to 30-year-olds. Likewise, plasma clearance of chlordiazepoxide and diazepam is reduced with increasing age, necessitating dosing adjustments in older patients[187,188] (Chap. 24).

While a number of animal studies have shown an absolute reduction with age in microsomal enzyme activity, such as that of NADH-cytochrome C reductase and cytochrome P-450, human studies have not.[189] James et al.[190] found no age-related changes in the activities of the microsomal enzymes aldrin epoxidase and 7-ethoxycoumarin-0-diethylase in humans, and no alterations in microsomal protein content per unit wet weight of liver. The nonmicrosomal system, utilizing glutathione, which assists in metabolizing such drugs as acetaminophen, was also not reduced over age in noncirrhotic patients.

Hepatic conjugation reactions, such as acetylation in the case of isoniazid or glucuronidation, the primary mode of metabolism of oxazepam or lorazepam, are not altered by age.[191,192] Drugs which undergo high hepatic first-pass metabolism by extraction from the blood may have altered clearance with age due to the age-related reductions in hepatic blood flow previously mentioned.[193] This effect was demonstrated with propranolol.[194]

Total body-protein synthesis as measured by ^{15}N-glycine was lower by 37 percent in a group of 69- to 91-year olds than in a group of subjects in their early twenties.[195] This finding was attributed to impaired hepatic production and is supported by numerous animal studies. Indeed, while the metabolism of warfarin is unaffected by age, the amount of the drug necessary to achieve therapeutic anticoagulation is decreased in older individuals, presumably due to decreased synthesis of vitamin K-dependent factors.[196]

An interesting recent finding is that the decline in hepatic synthetic function with aging in rats is diminished by food restriction, which is the only experimental manipulation that has been shown to consistently increase the survival of mammals.[197] A review by Ward and Richardson[198] summarizes these current findings and notes that the augmentation of hepatic protein synthesis with dietary restriction may play a role in the prolonged survival seen in these animal models.

Data regarding the synthesis and breakdown of albumin in humans have been conflicting, despite evidence suggesting a reduction in serum levels with increasing age.[199] One study showed that while a decreased plasma albumin concentration developed in a group of older subjects (64 to 78 years old) on a low-protein diet, the rate of albumin synthesis was comparable to that of a group of younger subjects (19 to 24 years old), suggesting that albumin synthesis is controlled at a lower set point in the elderly.[200] In addition, a number of drugs highly bound to albumin, including diazepam and phenytoin, have reduced binding with age, permitting more free drug in the serum.[189,201]

A final point should be made regarding the activity of "protective" hepatic enzymes, such as superoxide dismutase (SOD) and catalase, which, respectively, protect against oxygen free radicals and prevent peroxidation. Studies have demonstrated a 50 percent reduction in the specific activity of these enzymes in aged animals.[202] The importance of protecting the organism from environmental toxins is obvious; however, the relevance of this finding as it applies to aging humans remains uncertain.

In summary, the liver undergoes several changes with advancing age including a decrease in size, a decrease in blood flow, alterations in hepatocyte size and ultrastructural features including increased aneuploidy, ductular proliferation and liver cell necrosis, reduced protein synthesis, and a reduction in metabolism of a number of drugs which may contribute to the increased frequency of adverse drug reactions found in the elderly.

REFERENCES

1. Nelson JB, Castell DO: Esophageal motility disorders. *Dis Mon* 34:299, 1988.
2. Leese G, Hopwood D: Muscle fibre typing in the human pharyngeal constrictors and oesophagus: The effect of aging. *Acta Anat* 127:77, 1986.
3. Piaget F, Fouillet J: Le pharynx et l'oesuphage seniles: Etude clinique radiologique et radiocinematographique. *J Med Lyon* 40:951, 1959.
4. Almy TP: Factors leading to digestive disorders in the elderly. *Bull NY Acad Med* 57:709, 1981.
5. Eckhardt VF, Le Compte PM: Esophageal ganglia and smooth muscle in the elderly. *Dig Dis* 23:443, 1978.
6. Soergel KH et al: Presbyesophagus: Esophageal motility in nonagenerians. *J Clin Invest* 43:1472, 1964.
7. Hollis JB, Castell DO: Esophageal function in elderly men. A new look at "presbyesophagus." *Ann Intern Med* 80:371, 1974.
8. Geokas MC et al: The aging gastrointestinal tract, liver, and pancreas. *Clin Geriatr Med* 1:177, 1985.
9. Khan TA et al: Esophageal motility in the elderly. *Dig Dis Sci* 22:1049, 1977.
10. Csendes A et al: Relation of gastroesophageal sphincter pressure and esophageal contractile waves to age in man. *Scand J Gastroenterol* 13:443, 1978.
11. Richter JE et al: Esophageal manometry in 95 healthy adult volunteers: Variability of pressures with age and frequency of "abnormal" contractions. *Dig Dis Sci* 32:583, 1987.
12. Spence RAJ et al: Does age influence normal gastrooesophageal reflux? *Gut* 26:794, 1985.
13. Castell DO, Dubois A: *Esophageal and Gastric Emptying*. Boca Raton, FL, CRC Press, 1984.
14. Minami H: The physiology and pathophysiology of gastric emptying in humans. *Gastroenterology* 86: 1592, 1984.
15. Carlson AJ: *The Control of Hunger in Health and Disease*. Chicago, University of Chicago Press, 1916, p 56.
16. Van Liere EJ, Northup DW: The emptying time of the stomach of old people. *Am J Physiol* 134:719, 1941.
17. Webster SGP, Leeming JT: Assessment of small bowel function in the elderly using a modified xylose tolerance test. *Gut* 16:109, 1975.
18. Evans MA et al: Gastric emptying rate in the elderly: Implications for drug therapy. *J Am Geriatr Soc* 29:201, 1981.
19. Moore JG et al: Effect of age on gastric emptying of liquid-solid meals in man. *Dig Dis Sci* 28:340, 1983.
20. Davies WT et al: Gastric emptying in atrophic gastritis and carcinoma of the stomach. *Scand J Gastroenterol* 6:297, 1971.
21. Varga F: Transit time changes with age in the gastrointestinal tract of the rat. *Digestion* 14:319, 1976.
22. McDougal JW et al: Intestinal transit and gastric emptying in young and senescent rats. *Dig Dis Sci* 25:A-15, 1980.
23. Goldberg PB, Roberts J: Effect of age on rat smooth muscle cholinergic receptors. *Gerontologist* 20:111, 1980.
24. Kupfer RM et al: Gastric emptying and small bowel transit rate in the elderly. *J Am Geriatr Soc* 33:340, 1985.
25. Frank EB et al: Abnormal gastric emptying in patients with atrophic gastritis with or without pernicious anemia. *Gastroenterology* 80:1151, 1981.
26. James OFW: Gastrointestinal and liver function in old age. *Clin Gastroenterol* 12:671, 1983.
27. Baron JH: Studies of basal and peak acid output with an augmented histamine test. *Gut* 4:136, 1963.
28. Grossman MI et al: Basal and histolog-stimulated gastric secretion in control subjects and in patients with peptic ulcer or gastric ulcer. *Gastroenterology* 45:14, 1963.
29. Andrews GR et al: Atrophic gastritis in the aged. *Aust Ann Med* 16:230, 1967.
30. Gialosa A, Cheli R: Correlations anatomosecretoires gastriques en fonction de l'age chez des sujets ayant une muguegues fundique normale. *Gastroenterol Clin* 3:647, 1979.
31. Kekki M et al: Age- and sex-related behavior of gastric acid secretion at the population level. *Scand J Gastroenterol* 17:737, 1982.
32. Dooley CP et al: Prevalence of *Helicobacter pylori* infection and histologic gastritis in asymptomatic persons. *N Engl J Med* 321:1562, 1989.
33. Perez-Perez GJ et al: *Campylobacter pylori* antibodies in humans. *Ann Intern Med* 109:11, 1988.
34. Goldschmeidt M et al: Effect of age on gastric acid secretion and serum gastrin concentrations in healthy men and women. *Gastroenterology* 101:977, 1991.
35. Kramer PA et al: Tetracycline absorption in elderly patients with achlorhydria. *Clin Pharmacol Ther* 23:467, 1978.

36. Bock OAA et al: The serum pepsinogen level with special reference to the histology of the gastric mucosa. *Gut* 4:106, 1963.
37. Samloff JM et al: Serum group I pepsinogens by radioimmunoassay in control subjects and patients with peptic ulcer. *Gastroenterology* 69:83, 1975.
38. McGuigan JE, Trudeau WL: Serum gastrin concentrations in pernicious anemia. *N Engl J Med* 282:358, 1970.
39. Korman MG et al: Progressive increase in the functional G cell mass with age in atrophic gastritis. *Gut* 14:549, 1973.
40. Palmer ED: The stage of the gastric mucosa of elderly persons without upper gastrointestinal symptoms. *J Am Geriatr Soc* 2: 171, 1954.
41. Ruoff HJ et al: Morphologically different biopsy specimens of the human gastric mucosa: I. The use of enzymatic cell isolation for quantitative determination of parietal cells. *Pharmacology* 33:121, 1986.
42. Bird T et al: Gastric histology and its relation to anemia in the elderly. *Gerontology* 23:309, 1977.
43. Moore JG et al: Age does not influence acute aspirin-induced gastric mucosal damage. *Gastroenterology* 100:1626, 1991.
44. Cryer B et al: Effect of aging on gastric and duodenal mucosal prostaglandin concentrations in humans. *Gastroenterology* 102:1118, 1992.
45. Kimura K: Chronological transition of the fundipyloric border determined by stepwise biopsy of the lesser and greater curvatures of the stomach. *Gastroenterology* 63:584, 1972.
46. Ormiston MC et al: Five year follow-up study of gastritis. *J Clin Pathol* 35:757, 1982.
47. Ihamäki T et al: Long-term observation of subjects with normal mucosa and with superficial gastritis: Results of 23–27 years' follow-up examinations. *Scand J Gastroenterol* 13:771, 1978.
48. Nakano G, Nakamura T: Histopathological study of intestinal metaplasia of postmortem stomachs in the aged Japanese. *Cancer Detect Prev* 4:361, 1981.
49. Geocze S et al: Sulfated glycosaminoglycan composition of human gastric mucosa: Effect of aging, chronic superficial gastritis and adenocarcinoma. *Braz J Med Biol Res* 18:487, 1985.
50. Kim SW et al: Effects of aging on duodenal bicarbonate secretion. *Ann Surg* 212:332, 1990.
51. McDougal JN et al: Age-related changes in colonic function in rats. *Am J Physiol* 247:G542, 1984.
52. Lin CF, Hayton WL: GI motility and subepithelial blood flow in mature and senescent rats. *Age Ageing* 6:46, 1983.
53. Kim SK: Small intestine transit time in the normal small bowel study. *Am J Roentgenol* 104:522, 1968.
54. Nobles LB et al: No effect of fiber and age on oral cecum transit time of liquid formula diets in women. *J Am Diet Assoc* 91:600, 1991.
55. Anuras S, Sutherland J: Small intestinal manometry in healthy elderly subjects. *J Am Geriatr Soc* 32:581, 1984.
56. Kobashi YL et al: Age-related changes in the reactivity of the rat jejunum to cholinoceptor agonists. *Eur J Pharmacol* 115:133, 1985.
57. Bortoff A et al: Age-related changes in mechanical properties of cat circular intestinal muscle, in Christensen J (ed): *Gastrointestinal Motility*. New York, Raven Press, 1980, p 161.
58. Nelson JB et al: Evaluating age-related changes in rat ileal smooth muscle activity using KCl and chemical skinning. *Gastroenterology* 92:1551, 1987.
59. Nelson JB et al: Histologic changes associated with aging in rat ileal smooth muscle: Correlation with physiologic data. *Gastroenterology* 92:1551, 1987.
60. Gabella G: Unpublished data, 1988.
61. Moog F: The small intestine in old mice: Growth, alkaline phosphatase, and disaccharidase activities, and deposition of amyloid. *Exp Gerontol* 12:223, 1977.
62. Penzes L: Data on the chemical composition of the aging intestine. *Digestion* 3:174, 1970.
63. Penzes L: Letter to the editor. *Exp Gerontol* 17:243, 1982.
64. Ecknauer R et al: Intestinal morphology and cell production rate in aging rats. *J Gerontol* 37:151, 1982.
65. Hohn P et al: Differentiation and aging of the rat intestinal mucosa: II. Morphological, enzyme, histochemical and disc electrophoretic aspects of the aging of the small intestine mucosa. *Mech Ageing Dev* 7:217, 1978.
66. Jakab L, Penzes L: Relationship between glucose absorption and villus height in aging. *Experientia* 37:740, 1981.
67. Penzes L: Intestinal response in aging: Changes in reserve capacity. *Acta Med Hung* 41:263, 1984.
68. Rowlatt C: Cell aging in the intestinal tract, in Cristofalo V, Holeckova E (eds): *Cell Impairment in Aging and Development*, vol 53, *Advances in Experimental Medicine and Biology*. New York, Plenum Press, 1975, p 215.
69. Meshkinpour H et al: Influence of aging on the surface area of the small intestine in the rat. *Exp Gerontol* 16:399, 1981.
70. Holt PR et al: Effect of aging upon small intestinal structure in the Fischer rat. *J Gerontol* 39:642, 1984.
71. Warren PM et al: Age changes in small intestinal mucosa. *Lancet* 2:849, 1978.
72. Webster SGP, Leeming JT: The appearance of the small bowel mucosa in old age. *Age Ageing* 4:168, 1975.
73. Stenling R et al: Surface ultrastructure of the small intestine mucosa in healthy children and adults: A scanning electron microscopic study with some methodological aspects. *Ultrastruct Pathol* 6:131, 1984.
74. Holt PR: Effects of aging upon intestinal absorption, in Moment G (ed): *Nutritional Approaches to Aging*, Research Uniscience Series, Methods in Aging Research. Boca Raton, FL, CRC Press, 1982, p 157.
75. Lesher S et al: Influence of age on transit time of cells of mouse intestinal epithelium: I. Duodenum. *J Lab Invest* 10:291, 1962.
76. Clarke WJL, Anderson JW: The effects of age on mucosal morphology and epithelial cell production in rat small intestine. *J Anat* 123:805, 1977.
77. Fry RJM et al: Influence of age on transit time of cells of mouse intestinal epithelium: III. Ileum. *J Lab Invest* 11:289, 1962.
78. Goldspink DF et al: Protein synthesis during the developmental growth of the small and large intestine of the rat. *Biochem J* 217:527, 1984.

79. Krazinski SD et al: Aging changes vitamin A absorption characteristics. *Gastroenterology* 88:1715, 1985.
80. Esposito G et al: Age-related changes in rat intestinal transport of D-glucose, sodium, and water. *Am J Physiol* 249:G328, 1985.
81. Welsh JD et al: Intestinal disaccharidase activities in relation to age, race, and mucosal damage. *Gastroenterology* 75:847, 1978.
82. Rommel K, Böhmer R: Beziehungen zwishchen Lebensalter, intestinal en Disaccharidasen und Monosaccharidabsorption der Ratte. *Ärztl Forschg* 26:453, 1972.
83. Holt PR et al: Delayed enzyme expression: A defect of aging rat gut. *Gastroenterology* 89:1026, 1985.
84. Kendall MJ: The influence of age on the xylose absorption test. *Gut* 11:498, 1970.
85. Webster SGP, Leeming JT: Assessment of small bowel function using a modified xylose absorption test. *Gut* 16:109, 1975.
86. Montgomery RD et al: The aging gut: A study of intestinal absorption in relation to nutrition in the elderly. *Q J Med* 47:197, 1978.
87. Laue R et al: Age-dependent alterations of intestinal absorption: I. Theoretical aspects. *Arch Gerontol Geriatr* 3:87, 1984.
88. Penzes L: Intestinal absorption in the aged. *Acta Med Acad Sci Hung* 37:203, 1980.
89. Thomson ABR: Unstirred water layer and age-dependent changes in rabbit jejunal D-glucose transport. *Am J Physiol* 236:E685, 1979.
90. Feibusch J, Holt PR: Impaired absorption capacity for carbohydrates in the elderly. *Am J Clin Nutr* 32:942, 1979.
91. Webster SGP et al: A comparison of fat absorption in young and old subjects. *Age Ageing* 6:113, 1977.
92. Holt PR, Dominguez AA: Intestinal absorption of triglyceride and vitamin D_3 in aged and young rats. *Dig Dis Sci* 26:1109, 1981.
93. McEvoy A: Investigation of intestinal malabsorption in the elderly, in Evans JG, Laird FI (eds): *Advanced Geriatric Medicine*. London: Pitman, 1982, p 100.
94. Becker GH et al: Fat absorption in young and old age. *Gastroenterology* 14:80, 1950.
95. Hollander D et al: Does essential fatty acid absorption change with age? *J Lipid Res* 25:129, 1984.
96. Werner I, Hambraeus L: The digestive capacity of elderly people, in Carlson LA (ed): *Nutrition in Old Age*. Uppsala, Sweden, Almquist and Wiksell, 1978, p 55.
97. Hollander D, Morgan D: Aging: Its influence on vitamin A intestinal absorption in vivo by the rat. *Exp Gerontol* 14:301, 1979.
98. Barragry JM et al: Intestinal cholecalciferol absorption in the elderly and in younger adults. *Clin Sci Mol Med* 55:213, 1978.
99. Gallagher JC et al: Intestinal calcium absorption and serum vitamin D metabolites in normal subjects and osteoporotic patients. *J Clin Invest* 64:729, 1979.
100. Rafsky HA, Newman B: Vitamin B_1 excretion in the aged. *Gastroenterology* 1:737, 1943.
101. Thomson AD: Thiamine absorption in old age. *Gerontol Clin* 8:354, 1966.
102. Booth JB, Todd GB: Subclinical scurvy-hypovitaminosis C. *Geriatrics* 27:130, 1972.
103. Baker H et al: Severe impairment of dietary folate utilization in the elderly. *J Am Geriatr Soc* 26:218, 1978.
104. Elsborg L: Reversible malabsorption of folic acid in the elderly with nutritional folate deficiency. *Acta Haematol* 55:140, 1976.
105. Hyams DE: The absorption of vitamin B_{12} in the elderly. *Gerontol Clin* 6:193, 1964.
106. Fleming BB, Barrows CH: The influence of aging on intestinal absorption of vitamin B_{12} and niacin in rats. *Exp Gerontol* 17:121, 1982.
107. McEvoy AW et al: Vitamin B_{12} absorption from the gut does not decline with age in normal elderly humans. *Age Ageing* 11:180, 1982.
108. Schachter D et al: Accumulation of ^{45}Ca by slices of the small intestine. *Am J Physiol* 198:275, 1960.
109. Ambrecht HJ et al: Effect of age on intestinal calcium absorption and adaption to dietary calcium. *Am J Physiol* 236:E769, 1979.
110. Avioli LV et al: The influence of age on the absorption of ^{47}Ca in women and its relation to ^{47}Ca absorption in post-menopausal osteoporosis. *J Clin Inves* 44:1960, 1965.
111. Bullamore MR et al: Effect of age on calcium absorption. *Lancet* 2:535, 1970.
112. Ireland P, Fordtran JS: Effect of dietary calcium and age on jejunal calcium absorption in humans studied by intestinal perfusion. *J Clin Invest* 52:2672, 1973.
113. Nordin BEC et al: Calcium absorption in the elderly. *Cell Tissue Res* 21:442, 1976.
114. Marx JJM: Normal iron absorption and decreased red cell iron uptake in the aged. *Blood* 53:204, 1979.
115. Jacobs P et al: Role of hydrochloric acid in iron absorption. *J Appl Physiol* 19:187, 1964.
116. Yamajata A: Histopathological studies of the colon due to age. *Jpn J Gastroenterol* 62:224, 1965.
117. Roncucci L et al: The influence of age on colonic epithelial cell proliferation. *Cancer* 62:2373, 1988.
118. Broclehurst JC, Kahn MY: Study of fecal stasis in old age and in the use of "Dorbanex" in its prevention. *Gerontol Clin* 11:293, 1969.
119. Burkitt DP et al: Dietary fiber and disease. *JAMA* 229:1068, 1974.
120. Koch TR et al: Changes in some electrophysiological properties of circular muscle from normal sigmoid colon of aging patient. *Gastroenterology* 90:1497, 1986.
121. Koch TR et al: Inhibitory neuropeptides and intrinsic inhibitory innervation of descending human colon. *Dig Dis Sci* 36:712, 1991.
122. Culpepper-Morgan J et al: Increased mu and kappa opiate receptors in guinea pig colon. *Gastroenterology* 94:A82, 1988.
123. Whiteway J, Morson BC: Pathology of ageing-diverticular disease. *Clin Gastroenterol* 14:829, 1985.
124. Watters DA et al: Strength of the colon wall in diverticular disease. *Br J Surg* 77:257, 1990.
125. Parks TG: Natural history of diverticular disease of the colon. *Clin Gastroenterol* 4:53, 1975.
126. Smith AN, Shepherd J: The strength of the colon wall in diverticular disease. *Br J Surg* 63:666A, 1976.
127. Homer JL: Natural history of diverticulosis of the colon. *Am J Dig Dis* 3:343, 1958.
128. Painter NS, Burkitt DP: Diverticular disease of the

sigmoid colon, a 20th century problem. *Clin Gastroenterol* 4:3, 1975.
129. Klosterhalfen B et al: Sclerosis of the internal anal sphincter—A process of aging. *Dis Col Rect* 33:606, 1990.
130. Ihre T: Studies on anal function in continent and incontinent patients. *Scand J Gastroenterol* 9(suppl):1, 1974.
131. Leoning-Baucke V, Anuras S: Effects of age and sex on anorectal manometry. *Am J Gastroenterol* 80:50, 1985.
132. Poos RJ et al: Influence of age and sex on anal sphincters: Manometric evaluation of anorectal continence. *Eur Surg Res* 18:343, 1986.
133. Haadem K et al: Anal sphincter competence in healthy women: Clinical implications of age and other factors. *Obstet Gynecol* 78:823, 1991.
134. Krough Pedersen I, Christiansen J: A study of the physiological variation in anal manometry. *Br J Surg* 76:69, 1989.
135. Bannister JJ et al: Effect of ageing on anorectal function. *Gut* 28:353, 1987.
136. Percy JP et al: A neurogenic factor in fecal incontinence in the elderly. *Age Ageing* 11:175, 1982.
137. Lauaraberg S, Swash M: Effects of aging on the anorectal sphincters and their innervation. *Dis Col Rect* 32:737, 1989.
138. Parks AG et al: Sphincter denervation in anorectal incontinence and rectal prolapse. *Gut* 18:656, 1977.
139. Calloway NC et al: Uncertainties in geriatric data: II. Organ size. *J Am Geriatr Soc* 13:20, 1965.
140. Zimmerman W et al: Das normale pankreas Darstellung im Sonogramm in Abhängigkent zum Lebenstalter. *Fortschr Med* 99:1178, 1981.
141. Kreel L, Sandin B: Changes in pancreatic morphology in association with aging. *Gut* 14:962, 1973.
142. Sahel J et al: Morphometrique de la pancreatographie endoscopique normale du sujet age. *Gastroenterol Hepatol* 15:574, 1979.
143. Andrew W: Senile changes in the pancreas of Wistar Institute rats and of man with special regard to the similarity of locule and cavity formation. *Am J Anat* 74:97, 1944.
144. Martin ED: Different pathomorphological aspects of pancreatic fibrosis, correlated with etiology: Anatomical study of 300 cases, in Gyr KE (ed): *Pancreatitis: Concepts and Classification*. New York, Elsevier, 1984, p 77.
145. Kendrey G, Roe FJC: Histopatholgical changes in the pancreas of laboratory rats. *Lab Anim* 3:207, 1969.
146. Slavin BG et al: Morphological changes in the ageing mammalian pancreas, in John JE Jr (ed): *Ageing Cell Structure*, vol 2. New York, Plenum Press, 1984.
147. Aoyama S et al: Histopathological study on aging of the pancreas from 423 autopsy cases. *Jpn J Geriatr* 16:574, 1979.
148. Rosenberg IR et al: The effect of age and sex upon human pancreatic secretion of fluid and bicarbonate. *Gastroenterology* 50:191, 1966.
149. Gullo L et al: Exocrine pancreatic function in the elderly. *Gerontology* 29:407, 1983.
150. Gullo L et al: Aging and exocrine pancreatic function. *J Am Geriatr Soc* 134:790, 1986.
151. Fikry ME: Exocrine pancreatic functions in the aged. *J Am Geriatr Soc* 16:463, 1968.
152. Bartos V, Groh J: The effect of repeated stimulation of the pancreas on the pancreatic secretion in young and aged men. *Gerontol Clin* 11:56, 1969.
153. Laugier R, Sarles H: The pancreas. *Clin Gastroenterol* 14:749, 1985.
154. Ventrucci M et al: Comparative study of serum pancreatic isoamylase, lipase, and trypsin-like immunoreactivity in pancreatic disease. *Digestion* 28:114, 1983.
155. Koehn HD, Mostbeck A: Age-dependence of immunoreactive trypsin concentrations in serum. *Clin Chem* 27:502, 1981.
156. Carrere J et al: Human serum pancreatic lipase and trypsin 1 in aging: Enzymatic and immunoenzymatic assays. *J Gerontol* 42:315, 1987.
157. Mohiuddin J et al: Serum pancreatic enzymes in the elderly. *Ann Clin Biochem* 21:102, 1984.
158. Nagase M et al: Surgical significance of dilation of the common bile duct with special reference to choledocholithiasis. *Jpn J Surg* 10:296, 1980.
159. Nakadi I: Changes in morphology of the distal common bile duct associated with aging. *Gastroenterol Jpn* 16:54, 1981.
160. Bateson MC: Gallbladder disease and cholecystectomy rates are independently variable. *Lancet* 2:621, 1984.
161. Glenn F, McSherry CK: Calculous biliary tract disease, in *Current Problems in Surgery*. Chicago, Yearbook, 1975, p 1.
162. Boyden EA, Grantham SA Jr: Evacuation of the gallbladder in old age. *Surg Gynecol Obstet* 62:34, 1936.
163. Valdivieso V et al: Effect of aging on biliary lipid composition and bile acid metabolism in normal Chilean women. *Gastroenterology* 74:871, 1978.
164. Trash DB et al: The influence of age on cholesterol saturation of bile. *Gut* 17:394, 1976.
165. Okuda K et al: Ageing and gross anatomical alterations of the liver, in Kitani K (ed): *Liver and Ageing*. Amsterdam, Elsevier, 1978, p 159.
166. Beyer HS et al: Aging associated with reduced liver regeneration and diminished thymidine kinase mRNA content and enzyme activity in the rat. *J Lab Clin Med* 117:101, 1991.
167. Sherlock S et al: Splanchnic blood flow in man by the bromsulphthalein method. *J Lab Clin Med* 35:823, 1950.
168. Koff RS et al: Absence of an age effect of sulfobromophthalein retention in healthy men. *Gastroenterology* 65:300, 1973.
169. Mooney H et al: Alterations in the liver with ageing. *Clin Gastroenterol* 14:757, 1985.
170. Wynne HA et al: The effect of age upon liver volume and apparent liver blood flow in healthy man. *Hepatology* 9:297, 1989.
171. Schaffner F, Popper H: Nonspecific reactive hepatitis in aged and infirm people. *Am J Dig Dis* 4:389, 1959.
172. Watanabe T, Tanaka Y: Age-related alterations in the size of human hepatocytes. *Virchows Arch* 39:9, 1982.
173. Schmucker DL: Age-related changes in hepatic fine structure: A quantitative analysis. *J Gerontol* 31:135, 1976.

174. Smanik EJ et al: "Old" livers don't regenerate in a week. *J Lab Clin Med* 117:89, 1991.
175. Kampmann JP et al: Effect of age on liver function. *Geriatrics* 30:91, 1975.
176. McEvoy AW, James OFW: Anthropometric indices in normal elderly subjects. *Age Ageing* 11:97, 1982.
177. Thompson EN, Williams R: Effect of age on liver function with particular reference to bromsulphthalein excretion. *Gut* 6:26, 1965.
178. Nakanishi K et al: Decline of bromosulfophthalein storage capacity in polyploid hepatocytes demonstrated by cytofluorometry. *J Exp Gerontol* 15:103, 1980.
179. Vestal RE et al: Antipyrine metabolism in man: Influence of age, alcohol, caffeine, and smoking. *Clin Pharmacol Ther* 18:425, 1975.
180. Swift CG et al: Antipyrine disposition and liver size in the elderly. *Eur J Clin Pharmacol* 14:149, 1978.
181. Greenblatt DJ et al: Antipyrine kinetics in the elderly: Prediction of age-related changes in benzodiazepine oxidizing capacity. *J Pharmacol Exp Ther* 20:120, 1982.
182. Salem SAM et al: Reduced induction of drug metabolism in the elderly. *Age Ageing* 7:68, 1978.
183. Smithard DJ, Langman MJS: The effect of vitamin supplementation upon antipyrine metabolism in the elderly. *Br J Clin Pharmacol* 5:181, 1978.
184. Vestal RE et al: Ageing and ethanol metabolism. *Clin Pharmacol Ther* 21:343, 1977.
185. Scott RB, Mitchell MC: Aging, alcohol and the liver. *J Am Geriatr Soc* 36:255, 1988.
186. Jori A et al: Rate of aminopyrine disappearance in young and aged humans. *Pharmacology* 8:273, 1972.
187. Roberts RK et al: Effect of age and parenchymal liver disease on the disposition and elimination of chlordiazepoxide. *Gastroenterology* 75:479, 1978.
188. Macklon AF et al: The effect of age on the pharmacokinetics of diazepam. *Clin Sci* 59:479, 1980.
189. Kato R: Hepatic microsomal drug metabolising enzymes in aged rats—history and future problems, in Kitani K (ed): *Liver and Ageing*. Amsterdam, Elsevier, 1978, p 287.
190. James OFW et al: Lack of ageing effect on human microsomal mono-oxygenase enzyme activities, in Kitani K (ed): *Liver and Ageing*. Amsterdam, Elsevier, 1982, p 395.
191. Farah F et al: Hepatic drug acetylation and oxidation—effects in man. *Br Med J* 2:155, 1977.
192. Wilkinson CR: The effects of liver disease and ageing on the disposition of diazepam, chlorodiazepoxide, oxazepam, and lorazepam in man. *Acta Psychiatr Scand* 274(suppl):56, 1978.
193. Vestal RE: Aging and determinants of hepatic drug clearance. *Hepatology* 9:331, 1989.
194. Castleden CM, George C: The effect of ageing on hepatic clearance of propranolol. *Br J Clin Pharmacol* 7:49, 1979.
195. Young VR et al: Total human body protein synthesis in relation to protein requirements at various ages. *Nature* 253:192, 1975.
196. Shepherd AMM et al: Age as a determinant of sensitivity to warfarin. *Br J Clin Pharmacol* 4:315, 1977.
197. Ward WF: Enhancement by food restriction of liver protein synthesis in the aging Fischer 344 rat. *J Gerontol* 43:B50, 1988.
198. Ward W: Effect of age on liver protein synthesis and degradation. *Hepatology* 14:935, 1991.
199. Greenblatt DJ: Reduced serum albumin concentration in the elderly: A report from the Boston Collaborative Drug Surveillance Program. *J Am Geriatr Soc* 27:20, 1979.
200. Gersovitz M et al: Albumin synthesis in young and elderly subjects using a new stable isotope methodology: Responses to level of protein intake. *Metabolism* 29:1075, 1980.
201. Hayes MJ et al: Changes in drug metabolism with increasing age. *Br J Clin Pharmacol* 2:73, 1975.
202. Gershon H, Gershon D: Inactive enzyme molecules in aging mice. *Proc Natl Acad Sci USA* 70:909, 1973.

Chapter 59

DISORDERS OF THE ESOPHAGUS

Wallace C. Wu

Esophageal symptoms in the elderly are more similar than dissimilar to those in younger adults. However, the disease pattern may be somewhat different. Congenital lesions are rare, while some diseases such as motor disorders, esophageal strictures of various causes, and pill-induced esophagitis may be more common in the elderly population. These and other esophageal lesions will be discussed in this chapter. Dysphagia from lesions proximal to the esophagus is called *oropharyngeal dysphagia.* This can be caused by local lesions of the mouth, tongue, and pharynx and also by a variety of neurologic and neuromuscular disorders. Oropharyngeal dysphagia is covered in Chap. 115 and will not be discussed here.

GASTROESOPHAGEAL REFLUX DISEASE

Gastroesophageal reflux is an extremely common problem in our population. A recent Gallup survey found that 20 percent of the American population suffered from heartburn more than three times a month and an additional 25 percent had experienced monthly heartburn. Heartburn is the major indication for antacid consumption in the United States.[1] Several studies have shown that the prevalence of heartburn as well as endoscopic esophagitis increases after age 50.[2,3]

Pathophysiology

Prolonged pH recordings have shown that many healthy subjects have daily episodes of acid reflux without symptoms—"physiologic reflux." These episodes occur after meals and are short-lived; they almost never occur at night.[4] The gradation from "physiologic" to "pathologic" reflux is a multifactorial process. The major antireflux barrier is the lower esophageal sphincter. However, other contributing factors include esophageal acid clearance, irritating effects of the gastric contents, delayed gastric emptying, and the intrinsic resistance of the esophageal mucosa.

Symptoms

The classic symptoms of gastroesophageal reflux disease include heartburn, acid regurgitation, water brash, and dysphagia. *Heartburn* (pyrosis) is a substernal burning sensation with a typical upward-moving character. When the refluxed material flows into the mouth, it is called *regurgitation.* Both heartburn and regurgitation occur particularly after meals and with postural changes, such as lying down or stooping over. *Water brash* is the sudden appearance of a slightly sour fluid in the mouth. Dysphagia is a frequent complaint of reflux patients. Persistent or slowly progressive dysphagia for solids is often due to fibrosis and stricture formation. It can be caused by inflammation alone or by concomitant motility disturbances. However, severe esophagitis and its complications in the elderly can be entirely asymptomatic.

Gastroesophageal reflux disease may also be present with symptoms not immediately referable to the gastrointestinal tract. The development of chest pain in an adult patient raises the possibility of ischemic heart disease. However, 10 to 30 percent of patients undergoing coronary angiography have normal studies. Recent investigations suggest that acid reflux is the cause of noncardiac chest pain in 20 to 46 percent of these patients.[5] Aspiration into the airways of reflux material may lead to laryngeal and bronchopulmonary symptoms. Persistent hoarseness, laryngeal granulomas, and subglottic stenosis may result from intermittent acid reflux. Chronic persistent cough and recurring aspiration pneumonitis may be due to gastroesophageal reflux disease. There is also mounting evidence of an association between reflux disease and asthma, either by microaspiration of acid or via vagally mediated bronchospasm triggered by intraesophageal acid exposure.[6]

Diagnosis

Tests for gastroesophageal reflux disease evaluate different variables in the disease spectrum.[7] Unfortunately, no single test has been accepted as the "gold standard" for diagnosis. In addition, the ease of administration, the need for technical training, special equipment, expense, and discomfort to the patient are important factors in determining the priority with which diagnostic tests are administered and the decision to have the test done by generalists or specialists. Based on these variables, the following diagnostic and therapeutic approaches to the patient with gastroesophageal reflux disease are suggested (Fig. 59-1).

Barium Esophagram

Multiphasic views of the esophagus permit good visualization of mucosal detail and excellent definition of hiatal hernias, ulcers, rings, and strictures. Although insensitive to mild inflammatory changes, radiologic sensitivity and specificity approaches 100 percent in more severe grades of esophagitis.[8] Radiographic evidence of reflux may be demonstrated in up to 40 percent of symptomatic patients, but this is a nonspecific finding, as it can also be induced in approximately 25 percent of asymptomatic individuals. Hiatal hernias are more commonly observed in reflux patients and may impair esophageal acid clearance. The barium swallow with upper GI series is used primarily as a screening test to exclude other diagnoses, such as esophageal motility disorders and peptic ulcer disease, and to identify possible complications of reflux.

Acid Perfusion (Bernstein) Test

This is a simple test whose reported sensitivity and specificity approaches 80 percent.[7] It demonstrates sensitivity of the distal esophagus to acid. If the patient's symptoms (heartburn or chest pain) can be reproduced by acid instillation, a working diagnosis of reflux disease is confirmed and the patient treated accordingly. The test can be performed in the office, as it requires only a nasogastric tube and bottles of saline and 0.1N HCl.

Endoscopy with Biopsies

Endoscopic findings of esophagitis provide the most definitive diagnosis of gastroesophageal reflux disease, but these may be absent in up to 50 percent of symptomatic patients.[7] The presence of erosions, friability, exudate, ulcers, strictures, or Barrett's epithelium allows a definitive diagnosis of reflux injury (specificity 95 percent).[7] Mucosal biopsies may improve the diagnostic yield but are unnecessary with clear-cut endoscopic changes of esophagitis. One exception would be patients with suspected Barrett's

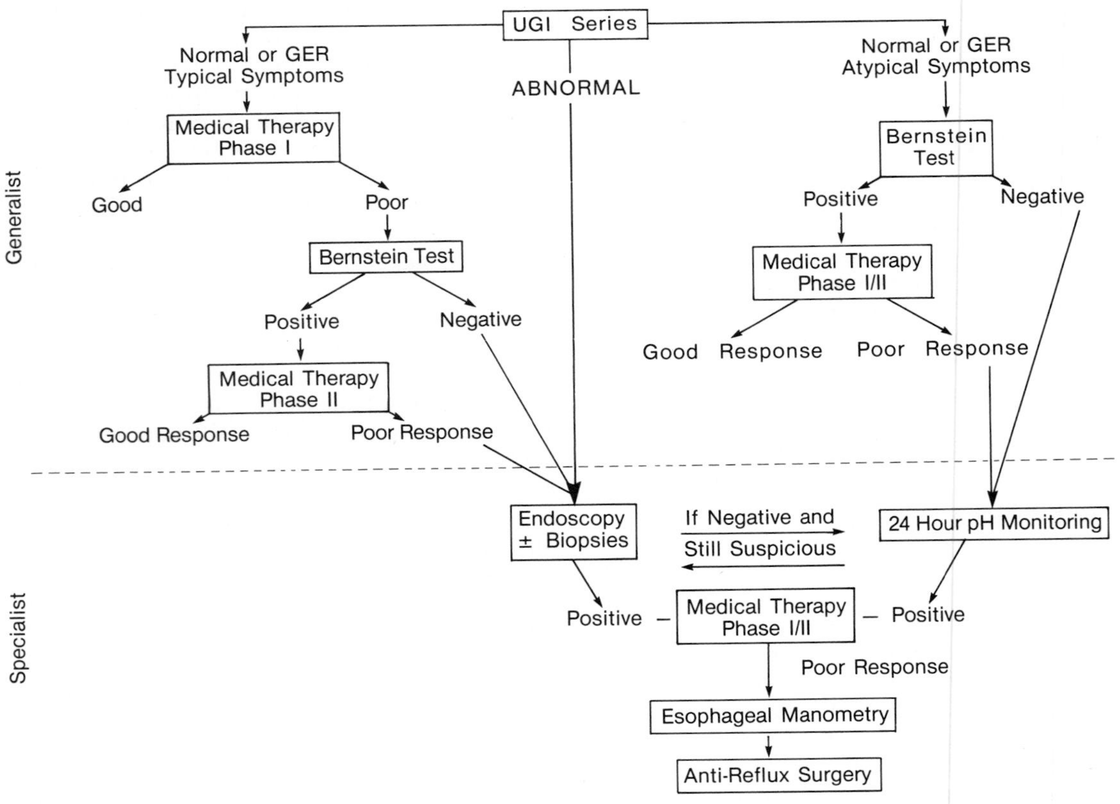

FIGURE 59-1
Symptoms suggestive of gastroesophageal reflux.

esophagus, where mucosal biopsies are important to identify the abnormal columnar epithelium.

Esophageal Manometry

Although lower esophageal sphincter pressure is a major determinant of gastroesophageal reflux, an *isolated* measurement is not an important diagnostic discriminator. Therefore, manometry should be reserved for patients in whom another diagnosis is suspected (esophageal motility disorder) or prior to antireflux surgery. For patients with severe reflux disease having either weak peristaltic pressures or severely disordered peristalsis, fundoplication may result in severe postoperative dysphagia due to poor esophageal clearance. If this abnormality is noted before surgery, it may provide a warning to the surgeon to do a "loose" plication.

24-Hour pH Monitoring

A pH probe placed 5 cm above the lower esophageal sphincter permits monitoring of esophageal acid exposure time. It provides the most physiologic measurements of acid reflux, incorporating information obtained over an extended time period.[9] A 24-hour ambulatory pH monitoring is now done with the patient in a work or home environment.[10] It is difficult to assess the sensitivity of this test, since it is generally accepted as the standard to which other diagnostic tests are compared. Although ambulatory pH systems are readily available, the expense and discomfort of such monitoring makes it appropriate only for the more difficult cases. It may be most helpful in patients with atypical symptoms or those who have clear-cut reflux symptoms in whom other tests have been negative, and it may also provide a correlation between pulmonary, ear-nose-throat, or chest pain symptoms and reflux episodes.

Treatment

Patients with symptomatic gastroesophageal reflux disease should be approached from the point of view that this is usually a long-standing, chronic disease. An overall medical and surgical approach may be structured by dividing current therapies into three phases (Table 59-1).

TABLE 59-1

Treatment of Gastroesophageal Reflux Disease

I. Phase I therapy
    A. Lifestyle modification
        1. Elevation of head of bed (6 in)
        2. Dietary modification
        3. Weight loss
        4. Decrease or stop smoking
        5. Avoid potentially harmful medications
    B. Antacids or alginic acid
II. Phase II therapy
    A. Inhibit gastric acid output; cimetidine, ranitidine, famotidine, nizatidine
    B. Omeprazole
    C. Others
III. Phase III therapy
    Antireflux surgery

Lifestyle Modifications

An underemphasized aspect of medical therapy is lifestyle modifications. Elevation of the head of the bed on 6-in blocks significantly decreases nocturnal esophageal acid exposure. Recent studies suggest that this maneuver alone is nearly as effective as an H_2 blocker without head elevation.[11] There are at least two potential benefits of diet modification. Certain foods—including fats, chocolates, excessive alcohol, and carminatives—impair lower esophageal sphincter function, while other foods—including citrus juices, tomato products, and coffee—are direct irritants.[12] In addition, many patients have more symptoms after large meals, particularly if such meals are taken less than 3 hours prior to retiring. Cigarette smoking produces a marked reduction in lower esophageal sphincter pressure and should be avoided. Weight reduction is a traditional component of the treatment of obese patients. Loss of a few critical pounds may be sufficient to control symptoms. Finally, drugs that lower sphincter pressure or interfere with esophageal or gastric emptying may facilitate gastroesophageal reflux. This category includes the anticholinergics, calcium channel blockers, theophylline, diazepam, and beta-adrenergic agonists. If possible, these drugs should be avoided in patients with gastroesophageal reflux disease.

Antacids and Alginic Acid

Antacids are widely used for their acid neutralizing effect and also because they increase lower esophageal sphincter pressure. In uncontrolled studies, antacids seem to be effective in controlling symptoms in 60 to 70 percent of patients. However, a recent study suggests that antacids may be no more effective than placebo therapy.[13] Nevertheless, in clinical practice, antacids (one dose 30 minutes after meals and at bedtime) and lifestyle modification appear to be effective in the control of intermittent mild-to-moderate symptoms of reflux disease. Alginic acids combined with antacids (Gaviscon) form a viscous foam which floats on the surface of gastric contents, acting as a mechanical barrier. The usual dose is two tablets chewed 30 minutes after meals and at bedtime. Clinical studies suggest that Gaviscon may be effective in the relief of reflux symptoms, but it is probably no better than antacid therapy.

Histamine Receptor Antagonists

Histamine receptor antagonists markedly decrease acid production and are the most popular agents available for the treatment of gastroesophageal reflux disease. Cimetidine (400 mg bid), ranitidine (150 mg bid), famotidine (20 mg bid), and nizatidine (150 mg bid) have consistently been shown to relieve reflux symptoms and decrease the use of antacids compared to placebo. All drugs also allow some degree of endoscopic and histologic healing of esophagitis.[14] The H_2 blockers should be initial therapy for patients with mild to moderate reflux symptoms with or without mild endoscopic esophagitis. Unlike their application in treating ulcer disease, H_2 blockers should be administered in divided doses. Recently it has been shown that doubling the usual dosage of these agents will be more effective in relieving symptoms and healing esophagitis than the standard dose.[14] Unfortunately, doubling the dose will increase cost significantly and should be reserved for patients who are not responding or who have severe esophagitis. Over 50 percent of patients with reflux esophagitis will relapse when medical therapy is discontinued.[15] Therefore, maintenance H_2 blocker therapy may be indicated in these patients. Preliminary studies suggest that divided dosages also will be required for prevention of relapses.

Proton Pump Inhibitors

Omeprazole is the only agent currently available in this category of drugs. Since it inactivates the enzyme that is the final common pathway for acid secretion, it is more effective than any agent in abolishing gastric acid secretion. When used in a dose of 20 mg/day, omeprazole has been shown to be the most effective agent in medical therapy of patients with reflux disease.[14,15] It should now be the agent of choice in patients with severe endoscopic esophagitis with or without refractory symptoms. Since the drug produces carcinoid-like tumor in rats, the Food and Drug Administration has recommended that it should not be used for more than 2 to 3 months. However, these tumors have not been reported so far in patients who have received omeprazole on a long-term basis. At this time it is recommended that after acute therapy on omeprazole, patients should then be maintained on H_2 blockers.

Other Drugs

With the introduction of histamine receptor antagonists and the proton pump inhibitor, other agents such as promotility agents and sucralfate are now relegated to secondary roles in the therapy of reflux disease. Bethanechol is a cholinergic agent that increases lower esophageal sphincter pressure and improves esophageal acid clearance. Metoclopramide, a dopamine antagonist, increases lower esophageal sphincter pressure and improves gastric emptying. Both drugs decrease reflux symptoms and antacid use, but only bethanechol has been convincingly shown to heal the esophagitis. Promotility drugs may be effective alone, but they are more commonly used in conjunction with H_2 blockers in patients with more recalcitrant reflux symptoms. The development of newer promotility drugs such as domperidone and cisapride may produce more effective agents with fewer side effects.

Sucralfate binds to ulcerated mucosa, protecting it from acid, pepsin, and bile and thus providing an alternative approach to treatment of acid-peptic disease. European studies found sucralfate as effective as antacids, Gaviscon, or H_2 blockers in the treatment of reflux esophagitis. However, studies from the United States suggest that it may not be as effective. Sucralfate is given in a dose of 1 g 30 minutes before meals and bedtime. In the elderly patient, the large tablet may produce some difficulty with swallowing. This can be avoided by dissolving the tablet in water for 1 or 2 minutes.

Surgery

An estimated 10 percent of patients may require surgery because of intractable reflux symptoms or complications. In fact, a recent study shows that surgery is more effective than standard medical therapy in the treatment of reflux disease. However, except for patients with Barrett's esophagus, surgical interventions are seldom necessary in the elderly. The antireflux procedures improve lower esophageal sphincter pressure and decrease reflux episodes. Surgery initially improves symptoms in over 90 percent of patients, but the competency of the surgical repair appears to deteriorate with time.[16]

Complications

Complications of reflux disease generally result from long-standing chronic acid exposure of the distal esophagus.

Peptic Strictures

Strictures result from fibrous scarring of the distal esophagus. Patients with such strictures usually complain of solid-food dysphagia but may or may not have heartburn. Strictures can usually be managed by medical therapy combined with intermittent bougie dilatation as needed to maintain an adequate degree of swallowing.[17] The use of proton pump inhibitors may decrease the frequency of esophageal dilatations. The procedure of dilatation is well tolerated even in the elderly and has a low complication rate.

Barrett's Esophagus

In some patients with long-standing reflux esophagitis, the normal squamous epithelium undergoes metaplastic changes to specialized columnar epithelium, i.e., Barrett's esophagus. The prevalence of this lesion varies. Barrett's esophagus is reported in 11 to 36 percent of patients with endoscopic esophagitis and 44 percent of patients with chronic peptic esophageal strictures.[18] It is usually diagnosed in middle or late life. There is a strong male predominance (65 to 80 percent), and the disease is rare in blacks. Of great concern, up to one-third of patients presenting with adenocarcinoma associated with Barrett's epithelium describe no prior symptoms of reflux disease. The prevalence of adenocarcinoma in Barrett's esophagus is about 10 percent. Subsequent development of malignancy in a previously defined Barrett's esophagus, however, is much less frequent (1 in 81 to 1 in 441 cases person/years). The presence of specialized columnar epithelium, or a long segment of Barrett's esophagus, increases the likelihood of developing an adenocarcinoma. Effective long-term prevention of gastroesophageal reflux is required, but whether this can best be achieved with combination medical therapy or surgery needs to be established. The increased incidence of adenocarcinoma suggests that these patients should be placed in an endoscopic surveillance program, though the rate and frequency of its development is uncertain at this time.

ESOPHAGEAL MOTOR DISORDERS

Recent advances in investigative methods have enabled the classification of esophageal motor disorders in a more logical manner, based on manometric and radiologic studies (Table 59-2). These are the only methods that actually assess abnormalities in esophageal peristalsis. Endoscopy contributes little in the evaluations of these diseases since its main role is to rule out mucosal lesions. It has been thought that aging may cause abnormalities in primary peristalsis (presbyesophagus). However, the initial study describing this phenomenon[19] included subjects with a variety of medical disorders such as peripheral neuropathies and diabetes mellitus. When a group of healthy elderly subjects was studied,[20] no defects in peristalsis were seen, although contraction amplitudes were diminished in the very elderly. At present the definition of presbyesophagus remains unclear.

TABLE 59-2

Esophageal Motor Disorders

1. Achalasia: aperistalsis in esophageal body, high lower esophageal sphincter (LES) pressure with incomplete relaxation
2. Diffuse esophageal spasm: nonperistaltic contractions with intermittent normal peristalsis
3. Nutcracker esophagus: normal peristalsis with high peristaltic amplitude
4. Hypertensive LES: mean LES pressure >50 mmHg with normal relaxation and normal peristalsis
5. Nonspecific esophageal motor disorders

Secondary Esophageal Motor Disorders

1. Collagen-vascular diseases: progressive systemic sclerosis, systemic lupus erythematosus, etc.
2. Endocrine and metabolic disorders: diabetes mellitus, hyper- and hypothyroidism, amyloidosis
3. Neuromuscular diseases: myotonic dystrophy, myasthenia gravis, multiple sclerosis, Parkinson's disease, cerebrovascular diseases, amyotrophic lateral sclerosis
4. Chronic idiopathic intestinal pseudoobstruction
5. Chagas' disease
6. Possibly aging (presbyesophagus)

Achalasia

Achalasia is the best recognized of all the esophageal motor disorders. It is characterized by the absence of normal peristalsis in the smooth muscle portion of the esophagus. Lower esophageal sphincter pressure is generally elevated, and the sphincter does not relax completely on deglutition.[21] These abnormalities are secondary to the absence of ganglion cells in Auerbach's plexuses, resulting in a functional obstruction at the level of the lower esophageal sphincter.

Achalasia is not uncommon in the elderly. Patients usually present with either esophageal or respiratory symptoms. Dysphagia for both solids and liquids is the main esophageal symptom. Postural maneuvers resulting in increase in intrathoracic pressure may facilitate passage of the bolus. Odynophagia is uncommon, but chest pain, presumably secondary to esophageal dysmotility, is not. Heartburn can be present, owing to esophageal stasis rather than reflux. Regurgitation of retained material, resulting in aspiration, may occur. Weight loss and malnutrition may also be significant.

Diagnosis is confirmed by radiology and esophageal manometry. Occasionally the diagnosis may be made by a chest film showing a markedly dilated and tortuous esophagus with retained food and fluid. An esophagram will show the absence of normal peristaltic activity with or without esophageal dilatation, and the hypertensive lower esophageal sphincter will fail to relax, giving a characteristic "bird beak" appearance. However, these abnormalities may be missed on routine esophagraphy. Esophageal manometry, therefore, is the diagnostic procedure of choice. Radionuclide testing with both solids and liquids will also demonstrate esophageal retention. Endoscopy is not necessary in establishing the diagnosis of achalasia. However, it is extremely useful in differentiating achalasia from peptic strictures or from a carcinoma at the gastroesophageal junction. Hence, it should be performed in all cases.

The major differential diagnoses are peptic stricture caused by gastroesophageal reflux disease or infiltrating carcinoma arising from the gastroesophageal junction[22] and other types of motor disorders. Esophagram, endoscopy, and manometry would permit differentiation. Patients with a markedly dilated esophagus from long-standing achalasia are also at an increased risk of developing squamous cell carcinoma of the esophagus.

Pharmacologic therapy with nitrates and calcium channel blockers[23,24] may be tried. By relaxing the smooth muscle, they decrease the lower esophageal sphincter pressure and hopefully improve esophageal emptying. Short-term studies suggest that some patients may benefit from these two medications, but long-term drug efficacy data are not available. Mechanical disruption of the lower esophageal sphincter with a balloon dilator (pneumatic dilatation)[25] or surgery[26] are the two therapeutic options. The former is performed by placing a specially constructed balloon across the gastroesophageal junction. The balloon is then inflated to mechanically disrupt the lower esophageal sphincter. The major complication is esophageal perforation, which occurs 5 percent of the time. Heller myotomy is a surgical procedure in which the muscle at the gastroesophageal junction is cut. Severe gastroesophageal reflux disease is the major complication. Controversy surrounds the initial choice of therapy for patients with achalasia. We recommend performing a pneumatic dilatation first and, if unsuccessful, repeating it once, after which surgery should be performed.

Diffuse Esophageal Spasm

Diffuse esophageal spasm is characterized by dysphagia and chest pain.[21,27] Esophageal manometry shows normal peristalsis interrupted by simultaneous (nonperistaltic) contractions. As shown in Table 59-2, other abnormalities may also coexist. The pathogenesis is uncertain. Thickening of the esophageal muscular wall has been reported, but ganglion cell loss has not been observed.

Clinically, patients can have chest pain, which may be indistinguishable from cardiac pain. Intermittent and nonprogressive dysphagia for solids and liquids may also occur. Diagnosis is made by esophagram and manometry. Esophagram reveals nonperistaltic contractions with to-and-fro movement and segmentation. Therapy has thus far been disappointing. Short- and long-acting nitrates, anticholinergics, or calcium channel blockers can be tried. Pneumatic dilatations may be performed in patients with documented lower esophageal sphincter dysfunction. In patients with intractable symptoms, a long myotomy may provide some relief.[28]

Other Esophageal Motor Disorders

"Nutcracker esophagus" is characterized by the presence of high-amplitude peristaltic contractions in the distal esophagus with or without increased peristaltic duration. Because this condition is found in a large number of patients who present initially with noncardiac chest pain, it is thought that the increased peristaltic pressure may be the source of the pain. However, evidence suggests that many patients may have underlying psychologic disorders, and the elevated pressure may just be a footprint of these emotional disturbances.[29] Therapeutic trials with calcium channel blockers and antidepressants have shown some promise in treating this ailment.

A variety of other abnormalities are also seen on manometry which cannot be categorized as achalasia, diffuse esophageal spasm, or nutcracker esophagus. They are collectively known as *nonspecific esophageal motor disorders.* Patients may or may not be symptomatic, and quite often the motor disorder may be secondary to a variety of medical illnesses (Table 59-2). In general, no therapy is needed.

Noncardiac Chest Pain

At least 20 percent of patients with chest pain undergoing coronary arteriogram will be found to have normal or insignificant coronary artery disease. In at least half of these patients, the esophagus may be the potential cause of discomfort.[30] Nutcracker esophagus is the most common manometric finding. Provocative tests using acid infusion, endrophonium, and balloon distension may also indict the esophagus as the primary cause of chest pain. 24-hour intraesophageal pH monitoring has recently shown that reflux disease is the most common esophageal abnormality in this group of patients.[31]

ESOPHAGEAL RINGS AND WEBS

Esophageal rings and webs are thin, diaphragmlike membranes interrupting the lumen of the esophagus. They are called *rings* if they are situated at the squamocolumnar junction and *webs* if they are located anywhere else along the body of the esophagus.[32] They are common and are often incidental findings at esophagraphy and endoscopy. The two most common varieties are the cervical esophageal web and the lower esophageal (Schatzki) ring.

Cervical Esophageal Webs

A cervical esophageal web is located in the immediate postcricoid area. Women are predominantly affected and may have iron-deficiency anemia. This is called the Patterson-Kelly or Plummer-Vision syndrome. Cervical web may be an incidental finding, but 15 percent of such patients complain of dysphagia. The pathogenesis of this entity is unknown. The diagnosis is made by cineradiography. Endoscopy may miss this lesion unless the instrument is passed under direct vision. The major differential diagnosis includes inflammatory stricture, postcricoid impression due to venous plexus distension and, most importantly, postcricoid carcinoma. Treatment consists of rupturing the web either with the endoscope or with esophageal bougies.

Lower Esophageal (Schatzki) Ring

Lower esophageal (Schatzki) rings are extremely common, being found with a frequency of 6 to 14 percent in routine barium examinations of the esophagus. Symptomatic rings, however, are far less common, occurring in approximately 0.5 percent of such examinations.[32,33] Lower esophageal rings are found to lie at the squamocolumnar junction. The pathogenesis of the lower esophageal ring is unknown. Although the association is widely cited, there is no evidence that the lower esophageal ring is related to gastroesophageal reflux disease.

The lower esophageal ring is probably the most common cause of intermittent solid-food dysphagia. The patient may also present with acute obstruction. The caliber of the ring is the main factor in determining symptoms. In general, rings less than 13 mm in diameter are always symptomatic, whereas rings larger than 20 mm rarely produce symptoms.[34] The absence of an effective propulsive force, i.e., abnormal peristalsis, may also contribute to symptoms in some patients.

Rings are best demonstrated by esophagraphy. However, the lower esophagus must be adequately distended for the ring to be visualized. A marshmallow or barium tablet may help distend the lower esophagus and confirm the diagnosis. Upper gastrointestinal (GI) endoscopy may miss these rings if the lower esophagus has not been fully distended. Treatment[32,34] consists of esophageal dilatation with a single large-size bougie.

ESOPHAGEAL DIVERTICULA

Esophageal diverticula are divided into three categories: Zenker's diverticulum, arising just above the upper esophageal sphincter; traction or midthoracic diverticulum; and epiphrenic diverticulum, located just above the lower esophageal sphincter. Zenker's and epiphrenic diverticula are thought to result from discoordinated motility at the cricopharyngeus and lower esophagus respectively.[35,36] Traction diverticulum was initially thought to be due to scarring and traction on the esophagus by external inflammatory processes in the mediastinum. Recently it has been shown that up to half of these patients have associated esophageal motor disorders.[37]

Patients may complain of dysphagia. This may result from either the associated motor disturbances or because the diverticula become filled with food. In the case of Zenker's, the sac may become noticeable in the neck. These patients may also complain of gurgling and regurgitation of ingested food. These diverticula can become so large that they distort the normal anatomy of the esophagus.

Radiology is the diagnostic approach of choice, since endoscopy can be difficult and even dangerous. Manometry may be helpful in ruling out associated motor disorders. The treatment is surgical. Diverticulectomy is usually done together with therapy directed at the underlying motor disorder. This may include a cervical myotomy in patients with Zenker's and cricopharyngeal discoordination or esophageal myotomy for patients with associated diffuse esophageal spasm or achalasia.[36,38]

MALLORY-WEISS SYNDROME

The Mallory-Weiss syndrome involves longitudinal mucosal tears 1 to 5 cm in length along the lower esophagus or gastric fundus. Such tears often straddle the gastroesophageal junction. This is one of the most common causes of upper gastrointestinal bleeding.[39] Two associated clinical events frequently occur. Almost half of the patients give a history of excessive alcohol intake. Many will also have retching and vomiting prior to hematemesis. Such tears may also be iatrogenic, having been reported after endoscopy and placement of nasogastric tubes. The tear presumably occurs because of sudden changes in intraabdominal pressure due to retching or vomiting. Whether this lesion is related to hiatal hernia remains to be proven. Bleeding is usually mild but may be of sufficient volume to produce shock. An upper GI series is not helpful and diagnosis is made by endoscopy.

Management is supportive, as most Mallory-Weiss tears will stop bleeding spontaneously. Healing is nearly complete in 3 days. However, up to one-third of patients have continued hemorrhage requiring intervention. Results of nonsurgical intervention, including balloon tamponade, vasopressin infusion, selective embolization, and various endoscopic methods have been inconsistent at best. Surgical intervention may be required.

INFECTIONS OF THE ESOPHAGUS

Infections of the esophagus were once thought to be rare. However, the advent of the barium esophagram and endoscopy with biopsy and cytology have increased the diagnostic yield, particularly in susceptible patients.[40] Esophageal infections occur primarily in patients with underlying disorders such as malignancy (especially leukemia and lymphoma); diabetes mellitus and other endocrine disorders (hypothyroidism, hypoparathyroidism, and hypoadrenalism); or a history of using antibiotics, cytotoxic agents, immunosuppressives, and corticosteroids; they also occur in those who are immunodeficient or malnourished. However, these infections are also found in healthy individuals. The two most frequent infections of the esophagus are caused by *Candida albicans* and herpes simplex virus. Symptoms usually consist of dysphagia, odynophagia, substernal burning, and awareness of the food bolus passing down the esophagus, but patients may also be asymptomatic. Examination of the oral cavity for lesions can be helpful when these are present. Absence of oral herpetic or monilial lesions does not rule out esophageal involvement.

Candidiasis

Candida albicans may account for up to 75 percent of esophageal infections. Many of these patients may have no predisposing diseases. The presence of swallowing difficulties in patients with predisposing factors should alert the clinician to the diagnosis of esophageal candidiasis.[41,42] The diagnosis can be suggested by barium esophagraphy. However, definitive diagnosis requires endoscopy, biopsy, and cytology. The major differential diagnoses are other infectious causes of esophagitis and severe gastroesophageal reflux disease. Treatment consists of correcting the underlying predisposing factors together with the institution of nystatin, ketoconazole, fluconazole, or amphotericin B.[43]

Herpes Simplex

Herpes simplex infection of the esophagus is less common than candidiasis. Clinical presentation is similar in both diseases. Radiographically and endoscopically, herpes is characterized by clean, punched-out ulcerations which are quite distinct from candidiasis.[44] However, the two diseases can coexist, particularly in severely immunosuppressed patients. Endoscopy, biopsies with cultures, and cytology are, in general, diagnostic. Acyclovir, both intravenous and oral, is now the treatment of choice.

MEDICATION-INDUCED ESOPHAGEAL INJURY

Esophageal injury as a result of oral medications was first reported in 1970. Since then many cases have been reported.[45] It is now clear that medication-induced esophageal injury may be a commonly overlooked cause of esophageal disease, particularly in the elderly.[46] Doxycycline and other tetracycline preparations are the most common culprits reported in this country. Other potential offending medications included potassium chloride, quinidine, clindamycin, lincomycin, ferrous sulfate, alprenolol, ascorbic acid, phenobarbital, theophylline, cromolyn, aspirin, and a variety of nonsteroidal anti-inflammatory agents.

Esophageal damage is caused by direct injury to the mucosa from prolonged contact with the causative agent. This usually results in a localized inflammatory reaction, culminating in an ulceration and, rarely, in stricture formation.[47] The most common sites of injury are near the level of the aortic arch and the distal esophagus. The former site may be predisposed to injury because of impingement of the great vessels or because of the transition from skeletal to smooth muscle; it may also be especially vulnerable in patients with low peristaltic amplitude. Pills and capsules have been shown to remain in the esophagus of supine healthy subjects, particularly the elderly, for a significant period of time.[46]

Most patients give a characteristic history of dysphagia for the particular offending medication taken at bedtime, followed by the acute onset of odynophagia. A barium examination and/or endoscopy will show the discrete esophageal ulceration, usually in the proximal two-thirds of the esophagus. Treatment consists of withdrawing the offending medication if possible. Viscous lidocaine may be helpful, and it seems reasonable to institute antireflux therapy to minimize further injury. Patients should be instructed to take their medications in the upright position with an ample quantity of liquid and to avoid immediately returning to bed.

TUMORS OF THE ESOPHAGUS

Benign neoplasms of the esophagus such as leiomyoma, lipoma, squamous papilloma, and inflammatory polyps are quite rare. They are usually discovered incidentally during radiologic or endoscopic examination performed for nonesophageal complaints. Rarely, they can be symptomatic, requiring surgical or endoscopic removal.

Squamous Cell Carcinoma

In the United States, black males tend to have the highest risk of developing squamous cell carcinoma of the esophagus. Their incidence is four times that of the white male (15.6 per 100,000 versus 4 per 100,000). The two major identifiable environmental factors that predispose to squamous cell carcinoma of the esophagus are alcohol and smoking. Other predisposing factors include a history of lye stricture and chronic stasis as a result of achalasia.

Progressive dysphagia first for solids and then for liquids is the cardinal symptom. This may be accompanied by pain. Anorexia and significant weight loss are also usually present. The occasional patient may present with complications such as aspiration pneumonia and fistula formation. Diagnosis is made by esophagraphy and endoscopy. Direct biopsies plus cytology will provide histologic confirmation in almost all cases. Benign stricture, particularly as a result of gastroesophageal reflux disease, is a major item in the differential diagnosis. The extent of tumor involvement outside of the esophageal lumen can be assessed by computed tomography of the chest. Recently, endoscopic ultrasonography has been shown to be of some value in staging the disease.

The esophagus is in direct contact with most mediastinal structures. This, together with the absence of a serosa, leads to early spread of esophageal cancer. Hence, the results of therapy are rather dismal. There is still no general agreement on the best therapy for patients with squamous cell carcinoma of the esophagus.[48–50] In Western countries the 5-year survival is less than 10 percent. However, in the Orient, survival rates of about 25 percent have been achieved by performing aggressive surgery[51] and early screening with brush cytology. At this time most patients with localized disease should have surgery as primary therapy. The presence of metastasis will make the patient a candidate for radiation therapy combined with chemotherapy.[50,52] All squamous cell carcinomas are initially radiosensitive. Most tumors will shrink, and some patients may even achieve a cure.

Since results of treatment are so poor, many palliative methods have been devised. The aim is to alleviate dysphagia so the patient can avoid aspiration and maintain nutrition. This can be achieved by several methods, including periodic esophageal bougie dilatation, placement of an esophageal stent to maintain luminal patency, or application of laser or electrocautery to relieve the obstruction temporarily.[53,54] Tracheoesophageal fistulas can also be temporarily occluded by placement of a stent.

Adenocarcinoma

Adenocarcinoma represents 3 to 7 percent of the malignant carcinomas of the esophagus. It most commonly arises in Barrett's epithelium of the esophagus but occasionally develops from mucous glands deep in the esophagus. The major differentiation is an adenocarcinoma of the gastric fundus with extension into the esophagus. The clinical presentation is similar to that of squamous cell carcinoma. Diagnosis is confirmed by endoscopy with biopsies and cytology. Unlike squamous cell carcinoma, this lesion is not radiosensitive. Therefore, primary therapy is surgical removal. Unfortunately, because of early metastasis, results are poor and 5-year survival is less than 10 percent.

OTHER DISEASES

The esophagus may be involved in a variety of systemic ailments. Progressive systemic sclerosis is classically associated with esophageal aperistalsis and decreased lower esophageal sphincter pressure. This combination may result in troubling gastroesophageal reflux.[54] Patients with diabetes mellitus and neuropathy can also have esophageal motor disturbance. Fortunately, these patients are usually asymptomatic. Chronic alcoholism together with peripheral neuropathy may also be associated with the loss of primary and secondary peristalsis. Pemphigoid and epidermolysis bullosa can affect the esophagus just as they affect the skin, in the form of bullous lesions. The esophagus can also be affected with deep ulcerations in Behçet's disease. In patients with bone marrow transplant, the esophagus may be involved in graft-versus-host disease. This is characterized by severe inflammation with mucosal fibrosis. Endoscopy and x-ray may reveal esophageal webs, strictures, and aperistalsis.

Since many elderly patients are edentulous and also have esophageal diseases, food impaction is relatively common. Most of these patients can be treated expectantly. However, if the bolus has been impacted in the esophagus for a significant period of time, endoscopic removal may be required.[55] It is imperative that these patients should have an esophageal workup to rule out an underlying esophageal ailment.

REFERENCES

1. Graham DY et al: Why do apparently healthy people use antacid tablets? *Am J Gastroenterol* 78:257, 1983.
2. Thompson WG, Keaton KW: Heartburn and globus in apparently healthy people. *Can Med Assoc J* 126:46, 1982.
3. Brunner PL et al: Severe peptic esophagitis. *Gut* 10:831, 1969.
4. DeMeester TR et al: Patterns of gastroesophageal reflux in health and disease. *Ann Surg* 184:459, 1976.
5. DeMeester TR et al: Esophageal function in patients with angina-type chest pain and normal coronary angiogram. *Ann Surg* 196:488, 1982.
6. Barish CF et al: Respiratory complications of gastroesophageal reflux. *Arch Intern Med* 145:1882, 1985.
7. Richter JE, Castell DO: Gastroesophageal reflux: Pathogenesis, diagnosis, and therapy. *Ann Intern Med* 97:93, 1982.
8. Ott DJ et al: Reflux esophagitis revisited. *Gastrointest Radiol* 6:1, 1981.
9. Johnson LF, DeMeester TR: Twenty-four hour pH monitoring of the distal esophagus: A quantitative measure of esophageal reflux. *Am J Gastroenterol* 62:325, 1974.
10. Ward BW et al: Ambulatory 24 hour esophageal pH monitoring: Technology searching for a clinical application. *J Clin Gastroenterol* 8(Suppl):59, 1986.
11. Harvey RF et al: Effects of sleeping with the bed head raised and of randitidine in patients with severe peptic esophagitis. *Lancet* 2:1200, 1987.
12. Richter JE, Castell DO: Drugs, foods and other substances in the cause and treatment of reflux esophagitis. *Med Clin North Am* 65:1223, 1981.
13. Graham DL, Patterson DJ: Double-blind comparison of liquid antacid and placebo in the treatment of symptomatic reflux esophagitis. *Dig Dis Sci* 559, 1983.
14. Sontag SJ: The medical management of reflux esophagitis. *Gastroenterol Clin North Am* 19:683, 1990.
15. Sontag SJ et al: Two doses of omeprazole versus placebo in symptomatic erosive esophagitis: The US multicenter study. *Gastroenterology* 102:109, 1992.
16. Spechler SJ: Comparison of medical and surgical therapy for complicated gastroesophageal reflux disease in veterans. *N Engl J Med* 326:786, 1992.
17. Patterson DJ et al: Natural history of benign esophageal stricture treated by dilatation. *Gastroenterology* 85:346, 1979.
18. Spechler SJ, Goyal RK: Barrett's esophagus. *N Engl J Med* 315:362, 1986.

19. Soergel KH et al: Presbyesophagus: Esophageal motility in nonagenarians. *J Clin Invest* 43:1472, 1964.
20. Hollis JB, Castell DO: Esophageal function in elderly men: A new look at presbyesophagus. *Ann Intern Med* 80:371, 1974.
21. Castell DO: Achalasia and diffuse esophageal spasm. *Arch Intern Med* 136:571, 1976.
22. Tucker HJ et al: Achalasia secondary to carcinoma: Manometric and clinical features. *Ann Intern Med* 89:315, 1978.
23. Gelfond M et al: Effect of nitrates on LOS pressure in achalasia: A potential therapeutic aid. *Gut* 22:312, 1981.
24. Bokrtolotti M, Labo G: Clinical and manometric effects of nifedipine in patients with esophageal achalasia. *Gastroenterology* 80:39, 1981.
25. Vantrappen G, Hellemans J: Treatment of achalasia and related motor disorders. *Gastroenterology* 79:144, 1980.
26. Csendes A et al: A prospective randomized study comparing forceful dilatation and esophagomyotomy in patients with achalasia of the esophagus. *Gastroenterology* 80:789, 1981.
27. Richter JE, Castell DO: Diffuse esophageal spasm: A reappraisal. *Ann Intern Med* 100:242, 1984.
28. Ellis FH et al: Surgical treatment of esophageal hypermotility disturbances. *JAMA* 188:862, 1964.
29. Richter JE et al: Psychological similarities between patients with the nutcracker esophagus and the irritable bowel syndrome. *Dig Dis Sci* 31:131, 1986.
30. Katz PO et al: Esophageal testing of patients with noncardiac chest pain or dysphagia. *Ann Intern Med* 106:593, 1987.
31. Hewson EG et al: Twenty-four hour esophageal pH monitoring: The most useful test for evaluating noncardiac chest pain. *Am J Med* 90:576, 1991.
32. Wu WC: Esophageal rings and webs, in Castell DO (ed): *The Esophagus.* Boston, Little Brown, 1992, p 343.
33. Goyal RK et al: The nature and location of lower esophageal ring. *N Engl J Med* 284:1775, 1971.
34. Eckardt VF et al: Single dilation of symptomatic Schatzki rings. *Dig Dis Sci* 37:577, 1992.
35. Debas HT et al: Physiopathology of lower esophageal diverticulum and its implications for treatment. *Surg Gynecol Obstet* 151:593, 1980.
36. Borrie J, Wilson RL: Esophageal diverticula: Principles of management and appraisal of classification. *Thorax* 35:759, 1980.
37. Kaye MD: Oesophageal motor dysfunction in patients with diverticula of the mid-thoracic oesophagus. *Thorax* 29:666, 1974.
38. Ellis FH et al: Cricopharyngeal myotomy for pharyngo-esophageal diverticulum. *Ann Surg* 170:340, 1969.
39. Graham DY, Schwartz SJ: The spectrum of the Mallory-Weiss tear. *Medicine* 57:307, 1978.
40. Wheeler RR et al: Esophagitis in the immunocomprised host: Role of esophagoscopy in diagnosis. *Rev Infect Dis* 9:88, 1987.
41. Kodsi BE et al: Candida esophagitis: A prospective study of 27 cases. *Gastroenterology* 71:715, 1976.
42. Scott BB, Jenkins D: Gastro-oesophageal candidiasis. *Gut* 23:137, 1982.
43. Laine L et al: Fluconazole compared with ketoconazole for the treatment of candida esophagitis in AIDS. *Ann Intern Med* 117:655, 1992.
44. Howiler W, Goldberg HI: Oesophageal involvement in herpes simplex. *Gastroenterology* 70:775, 1976.
45. Kikendall JW et al: Pill-induced esophageal injury: Case reports and review of the medical literature. *Dig Dis Sci* 28:174, 1983.
46. Eypasch EP et al: Age influences capsule entrapment in the esophagus. *Gastroenterology* 94:A120, 1988.
47. Bonavina L et al: Drug-induced esophageal strictures. *Ann Surg* 206:173, 1987.
48. Parker EF, Moertel CG: Carcinoma of the esophagus: Is there a role for surgery? *Dig Dis Sci* 23:730, 1978.
49. Earlam R, Cunha-Melo JR: Oesophageal squamous cell carcinoma: I. A critical review of surgery. *Br J Surg* 67:31, 1980.
50. Earlam R, Cunha-Melo JR: Oesophageal squamous cell carcinoma: II. A critical review of radiotherapy. *Br J Surg* 67:457, 1980.
51. Wong J: Esophageal resection for cancer: The rationale of current practice. *Am J Surg* 153:18, 1987.
52. Herskovic A et al: Combined chemotherapy and radiotherapy compared with radiotherapy alone in patients with cancer of the esophagus. *N Engl J Med* 326:1593, 1992.
53. Puera D et al: Esophageal prothesis in cancer. *Am J Dig Dis* 23:796, 1978.
54. Turner R et al: Esophageal dysfunction in collagen disease. *Am J Med Sci* 265:191, 1973.
55. Webb WA: Management of foreign bodies of the upper gastrointestinal tract. *Gastroenterology* 94:204, 1988.

Chapter 60

DISORDERS OF THE STOMACH AND DUODENUM

Robert M. Kerr

The stomach of the elderly person reflects changes associated with long years of use (physiological aging) and sometimes abuse (pathological aging). It is well established that most tissues are constantly being destroyed and replaced by a regenerative process at a rate more or less sufficient to maintain the status quo. If regeneration is not quite perfect, over many years, gradual changes can be expected, culminating in obvious histological and physiological modifications. As these alterations are slow to occur and physiological reserves are substantial, it is likely that fairly gross deviations from the original condition are necessary before an individual becomes aware that something is amiss. *Helicobacter* (formerly *Campylobacter*) *pylori*, an organism recently identified as a source of chronic gastric infection, contributes to this process. Furthermore, as organ systems become less efficient, medications are used to bolster their lagging function. However, a chemical that improves one organ system may injure another system directly or adversely affect its physiological function [as is the case with nonsteroidal anti-inflammatory drugs (NSAIDs)]. The following topics relating to the stomach and duodenum have been selected for discussion because of their importance and common occurrence in the elderly population: the effect of *H. pylori* and NSAIDs on the stomach and duodenum; gastritis; peptic ulcer disease; motility disorders; bleeding; and neoplasia.

HELICOBACTER PYLORI

Helicobacter pylori was identified in gastric mucosa in 1982 and since then has become recognized as an important human pathogen associated with chronic gastritis, peptic ulcer disease, and gastric cancer.[1] This organism causes continuous inflammation in the stomach and may remain for many years. The infection clusters in families, particularly those of low socioeconomic status. In many developing countries with poor sanitary practices, most of the population is infected by the age of 10. By contrast, only 50 percent of 60-year-olds in the United States harbor the organism. *H. pylori* is not invasive, resides under the mucous layer, and releases a host of soluble factors. It is thought that its proximity to the epithelium and the products of its metabolism cause the inflammatory response and trigger the host to mount an immune response. This reaction is sufficient to cause inflammation and the development of antibodies, but for reasons not evident, the organism is usually not eradicated by these natural defenses. Major diagnostic techniques for the detection of *H. pylori* infection include culture,[2] histology,[3] urease testing,[4] [^{13}C]urea breath test,[5] and serology,[6,7,8] all of which are more than 95 percent accurate.[1] The urea breath test and the serologic tests have the advantage of not requiring a gastric biopsy. The serologic tests change slowly after treatment and are of limited use for follow-up.

Triple therapy with bismuth, metronidazole, and amoxicillin or tetracycline is recommended for treatment of *H. pylori* infection. An eradication rate of 80 percent can be expected with such therapy as initial treatment; however, even remote prior exposure to metronidazole can cause the *H. pylori* to be resistant to this drug, making the successful elimination of *H. pylori* less than 20 percent. Although the usual regimen is 2 weeks, a recent report suggests that 1 week is adequate if the organisms are susceptible.[9] In a recent study, compliance in taking the prescribed treatment seemed most important in ensuring a cure.[10] *H. pylori* is not affected by H_2 blockers but is susceptible to proton pump inhibitors (omeprazole). Thus, amoxicillin plus omeprazole can be considered an alternative treatment regimen. However, at the time of this writing there are numerous ongoing therapeutic trials, and undoubtedly better treatment regimens will evolve. Current consensus suggests that treatment be limited to those patients who have documented *H. pylori* infection and (1) symptomatic gastritis, (2) refractory peptic ulcer disease or frequent ulcer recurrences, or (3) refractory ulcer disease, and in whom conventional treatment has failed.

NSAIDs

NSAIDs decrease prostaglandin synthesis, thereby interfering with normal mucosal defense mechanisms. Over 3 million people in the United States take daily NSAIDs, and about 10 percent have active gastric ulcers.[11] Duodenal ulcers are also increased among chronic NSAID users.[12] Moreover, the incidence of peptic ulcer disease is greater with higher NSAID dosage.[13] The overall risk of an adverse GI event in NSAID users is two to five times greater than for nonusers.[14,15,16] *H. pylori* infection is not associated with NSAID intolerance[17] or increased risk for mucosal injury from NSAIDs.[18] NSAIDs also interfere with platelet aggregation. With aspirin this inhibition lasts for the life of the platelet. Thus, it is not surprising that NSAIDs have increasingly been linked to GI bleeding and perforation in elderly persons.[11,19,20] Individuals at high risk for complications are older and often have a prior history of NSAID intolerance.

Many elderly patients with endoscopically demonstrated ulcer report no pain.[21] Their paucity of symptoms may be due to altered pain perception, underlying CNS disease impairing their ability to communicate, or the inherent analgesic effect of NSAIDs. These features, coupled with the high cost of ulcer screening tests and the serious morbidity and mortality from ulcer disease in elderly persons, make a good case for prophylactic ulcer therapy in selected NSAID users. Although the prostaglandin E_1 analogue misoprostol reduces the chance of developing gastric ulcers and erosions during NSAID treatment, this drug has not been shown to heal ulcers during continued NSAID therapy[22] and is not helpful for preventing or treating duodenal ulcers. In contrast H_2 antagonists are effective in preventing duodenal ulcers,[11,12,23] and 90 percent of small gastric or duodenal ulcers will heal on standard H_2 blocker treatment.[24] Although K^+-H^+ pump inhibitors heal ulcers faster,[25] there has been no evidence to date that the rate of complications is decreased. Indiscriminant prophylaxis in all NSAID users is not recommended.[26] However, it is reasonable to consider for prophylactic ulcer therapy NSAID-using patients over 60 with a past history of recurrent ulcers, patients with severe rheumatic disease requiring concomitant corticosteroids, and patients at risk for serious morbidity or mortality from ulcer complications.

GASTRITIS

The diagnosis of *gastritis* implies that there is either active inflammation of the gastric mucosa or changes suggestive of prior inflammation. Although it has been a recognized entity for over 100 years, it is only recently that modern endoscopic and biopsy techniques have allowed convenient study. Based on histochemical, immunological, and other studies, gastritis may be classified as in Table 60-1.[27]

Acute Gastritis

Mucosal damage can be seen after the ingestion of any number of locally toxic substances.[28] Elderly persons may be more prone to such damage. Not only can one expect aging to diminish their normal defenses, but they have a general need for more medications, some of which directly injure the mucosa. In other words, insults that a younger stomach can absorb with equanimity are more likely to result in more profound damage in the elderly person. Alcohol and NSAIDs are the primary agents causing acute injury. Although bacterial toxins may affect the stomach, little is known about this subject. In any event, the use of the term *acute* implies a transient process.

Symptoms are either absent or nonspecific (e.g., anorexia, epigastric distress, nausea, and sometimes bleeding). Routine tests are unremarkable, and the diagnosis is usually made by the history and endoscopic findings. Generally, the disease is relatively short-lived and heals spontaneously; therefore, treatment is supportive. The physician should discontinue NSAIDs when possible and add antinauseants if necessary.

Chronic Gastritis

Chronic gastritis is common in the general population; random biopsy samples show that it increases with age with perhaps a preponderance of males.[29,30] The gastritis can predominantly involve either the fundus (type A) or the antrum (type B).

Fundal Gastritis (Type A)

The antrum is usually normal in a patient with fundal gastritis. Histological changes in the fundus have one of three possible appearances: (1) superficial gastritis, (2) chronic gastritis, and (3) gastric atrophy. With superficial gastritis, an uncommon condition, an infiltrate of lymphocytes and plasma cells is limited to the outer third of the mucosa and the fundal glands appear normal. This picture contrasts with that

TABLE 60-1

Classification of Gastritis

Acute gastritis
Chronic gastritis
Fundal gastritis (type A)
Antral gastritis (type B)
Hypertrophic gastritis

of atrophic gastritis, in which the full thickness of the mucosa is involved. In this circumstance, gland tubules show varying degrees of atrophy and some appear to be absent. Chief and parietal cells are decreased. Spaces left by disappearing structures are replaced by mucous-secreting glands, and scattered goblet cells are seen. Gastric atrophy is distinguished by the *absence* of fundal glands. Epithelium and crypts have been replaced by goblet cells. Inflammatory changes are minimal or entirely absent. These changes are considered *intestinal metaplasia* because the tissue takes on the appearance of intestinal epithelium; absorptive function and histochemical changes compatible with intestinal epithelium have also been described. There are two types of intestinalization. One has the appearance of small bowel with Paneth's and endocrine cells; the other, with increased goblet cells and no Paneth's cells, is more reminiscent of the colon.[31]

The loss of parietal cells causes reduced or absent acid production. Because the antrum is normal in cases of fundal gastritis, serum gastrin levels can be remarkably elevated.[32,33] Antibodies to the parietal cell as well as binding and blocking antibodies to intrinsic factor are often detected, and when these antibodies are present, vitamin B_{12} malabsorption is common. Thyroid antibodies are present in greater than 50 percent of patients with pernicious anemia, while parietal cell antibodies are more commonly identified with Hashimoto's thyroiditis, thyrotoxicosis, and hypothyroidism. Genetic factors have been implicated in the development of type A gastritis.[27]

Pernicious anemia (PA) develops insidiously and may be found 6 to 18 years after the initial diagnosis of gastritis.[34] The classic triad of sore tongue, weakness, and paresthesias is often not appreciated in the elderly patient, who may present with a profound anemia. Recently it has been shown that B_{12} deficiency (even borderline reduction) is accompanied by increased serum methylmalonic acid and homocystine levels.[35] Measurement of these metabolites is more sensitive than determination of serum or red cell B_{12} levels in identifying B_{12}-deficient individuals. The diagnosis of PA is established by demonstrating a lack of gastric acid production and an abnormal Schilling test.

Antral Gastritis (Type B)

In antral gastritis, primarily the antrum is involved, with variable changes in the fundus. Antral histology is hard to evaluate because the mucosa is thick and normally has some cellular infiltrate. The degree of infiltration, whether the pyloric glands are obliterated, and the extent of intestinal metaplasia are subjective attributes used to grade antral gastritis. Serum gastrin levels are often reduced. Parietal cell antibodies are absent, and impairment of acid secretion is generally mild. Associated lesions include gastric ulcer and gastric cancer. The genesis of type B gastritis is thought to involve local damage from "environmental" factors such as alcohol, NSAIDs, malnutrition, stress, and bile reflux.[27] Type B gastritis can be further divided into a hypersecretory variety (accompanied by duodenal ulcer) and an atrophic type (associated with intestinal metaplasia).[36] Both these types of gastritis have a high association with *H. pylori*.[27,37]

Clinical Concerns

Clinical manifestations of chronic gastritis are nonspecific and include early satiety, weight loss, and bloating after meals. Some patients with antral gastritis paradoxically complain of heartburn (rarely with nocturnal awakening). As many as 60 percent of patients have no complaints. Endoscopy with biopsy is considered the diagnostic procedure of choice. While gastric secretory testing is not routinely practiced, the demonstration of achlorhydria is helpful if PA is suspected.

Treatment

In the treatment of chronic type A gastritis, the dyspeptic symptoms of some patients with achlorhydria (paradoxically) respond to antacids. Likewise, the empirical use of 2 teaspoons of a mixture of equal parts of elixir of Benadryl (diphenhydramine hydrochloride), liquid Donnatal, and a liquid antacid taken half an hour before meals may also relieve symptoms in some patients. With type B gastritis, if *H. pylori* is identified, treatment of the infection may be helpful. Anemia can occur with either variety of gastritis. It is important to correctly classify and treat the underlying cause.

Complications

Several recent studies suggest that long-term *H. pylori* infection is a risk factor for gastric adenocarcinoma.[38–40] The decline in incidence of gastric cancer and increased incidence of duodenal ulcer in developed countries parallels the delay in acquisition of *H. pylori*. Gastritis can interfere with gastric acid production and allow bacteria other than *H. pylori* to colonize the stomach. It is these other organisms that can convert nitrogenous compounds into carcinogens. Fortunately, malignancies are slow to develop and seem related to the duration of the gastritis. The progression from superficial to atrophic gastritis may take up to 20 years.[41] Among those with chronic gastritis, some will develop cancer in the evolution of these changes, but it is not possible to identify the patient who is especially at risk. Of 116 patients with atrophic gastritis followed for 22 to 26 years, approximately 10 percent developed cancer.[30] Other studies have shown a similar incidence, but these studies were of shorter duration (6 to 20 years), and it was not clear how long the gastritis had actually been present before the diagnosis was made.[42] On the negative side, one recent study failed to document an increased cancer risk for the patient with pernicious anemia.[43] Carcinoid tumors of the stomach have been associated with type A gastritis. Many of these patients have a markedly elevated serum gastrin level. Gastrin is known to be trophic for the enterochromaffin-like cells. Perhaps this explains why there is an increased prevalence of carcinoid in the stomachs of patients with atrophy. A small proportion of such patients (20 percent) have metastases when the carcinoid is first identified, confirming its malignant potential.[44]

How should the clinician manage those patients who may have an increased chance for developing cancer? On the one hand, it would seem that early detection of gastric cancer should be lifesaving, and if the technology to provide screening is available, it should be used regardless of cost. On the other hand, to endorse such an approach would expose the majority of these patients to the expense and hazard of endoscopy and biopsy with little chance of finding a significant lesion. Furthermore, there is little to indicate that early diagnosis of these cancers makes the patient more comfortable or prolongs life. Thus, a reasonable approach is to offer a screening examination every 5 years or as needed should there be a change in symptoms. Obviously, other health factors weigh heavily as to when and whether screening should be undertaken.

Hypertrophic Gastritis

P. Ménétrier described diffuse thickening of the gastric wall by excessive proliferation of the mucosa about 100 years ago. In this circumstance the weight of the stomach is increased and the folds are often greater than 1 cm wide and 3 cm high. Increased polymorphonuclear leukocytes are present in dilated crypts while increased lymphocytes occur in the muscularis mucosa and lamina propria. Symptoms are nonspecific and include anorexia, nausea, occasionally vomiting, postprandial aching epigastric pain, and in some cases profound weight loss. Protein loss may occur through the enlarged gastric folds, causing hypoproteinemia with its associated symptoms. The major difference between patients with and patients without protein loss is that the former have a greater incidence of weight loss, edema, diarrhea, and skin rash. The differential diagnosis of hyperrugosity of the stomach includes the Zollinger-Ellison syndrome, lymphoma, histoplasmosis, and even secondary syphilis. Endoscopic snare biopsy is most useful in establishing the diagnosis. The use of H_2 blockers is the initial treatment of choice, although improvement is often transient with their use. There have been anecdotal reports of therapeutic success with corticosteroids, anticholinergics, and tranexamic acid. Surgery may be necessary for unremitting pain that does not yield to other treatment attempts.[45]

PEPTIC ULCER

Approximately 4.5 million ulcers are diagnosed each year in the United States.[14] Although mortality due to ulcer disease has declined in recent years, hospitalization rates for ulcer in the elderly population has risen dramatically. Elderly patients suffer increased complications, and about 80 percent of those who die from ulcer disease are greater than 65 years of age.[21] Although the majority of complications occur from gastric ulcer, increased complications from duodenal ulcers have also been noted. A recent study reported 15 percent mortality in patients over 60 years compared with 2 percent in younger patients.[22] Surgical mortality for ulcer complications in patients over 60 years was 29 percent.[46]

A number of factors, whether acting alone or in various combinations, are thought to be responsible for the genesis of gastric and duodenal ulcers. The gastrointestinal mucosa is constantly exposed to substances capable of causing injury (acid, pepsin, and various ingested substances), but the potential for significant damage is normally balanced by a remarkable defensive armament (mucus, mucosal blood flow, epithelial cell proliferation, and so on). Thus, minor insults are steadily delivered to the mucosa, but ordinarily the extent of injury is limited and repair is prompt. An extraordinary insult in the face of a normal defense mechanism or else a routine attack against decreased defenses can upset this process and cause more extensive mucosal injury. Ordinarily, it is neither purely one circumstance nor another but rather some combination of circumstances that results in ulceration. When the results of an attack are sufficiently great, the patient is often aware of symptoms and the clinician is likely to observe inflammation and/or ulceration in the mucosa on radiologic or endoscopic examination.

The fundamental ability to produce acid and pepsin and the characteristics that offer mucosal protection are genetically determined. With advancing age, all these factors are altered, but not always simultaneously or to the same degree. Moreover, the less robust mucosa of the elderly person may also be exposed to various toxic insults (e.g., tobacco, ethanol, or NSAIDs) which tilt the delicate balance of damage and repair toward destruction. The fact that ulcers occur in small areas illustrates the importance of local factors; if local factors did not matter, the entire mucosal surface would tend to slough. There are remarkable similarities in the pathogenesis of gastric and duodenal ulcers; the fact that different portions of the upper gut are affected reflects discrepancies in the way the stomach and duodenum defend themselves against acid, pepsin, and other insults. Gastric and duodenal ulcers share a strong association with *H.*

pylori,[1] and its elimination leads to ulcer healing and a low recurrence rate. Although ulcers can be healed by acid-reducing treatment, with cessation of therapy the recurrence rate is 70 to 80 percent within 1 year. Recent clinical trials have demonstrated that eradicating *H. pylori* in conjunction with healing either duodenal or gastric ulcer reduces the chance of recurrence to 10 percent or less.[1,47]

The majority of patients with duodenal ulcers do not have excessive acid output. Moreover, there is a gradual decrease in gastric acid production with advancing age. Thus, a less robust defense against acid and pepsin is thought to be central in the genesis of ulcers in elderly persons and would account for the fact that there is no reduction in the incidence of duodenal ulcers with advancing age.[48] In contrast, the incidence of gastric ulcer rises with age.[49] Gastric ulcers are generally located on the lesser curvature on the border between antral and acid-secreting mucosa. The migration of this junction toward the gastric fundus with aging accounts for the high lesser curvature location of many gastric ulcers in the elderly patient.[29]

Clinical Manifestations

Symptoms accompanying either gastric ulcer or duodenal ulcer are variable. Gnawing epigastric discomfort occurring an hour or so after meals and relieved by food is common to both ailments. Pain immediately increased by eating is more usual with gastric ulcer. Nocturnal wakening for either ulcer suggests a more aggressive process. Back pain, more common with duodenal ulcer, can be the patient's presenting symptom and may cloud the issue by suggesting an orthopedic or pancreatic problem. Many patients complain of anorexia, bloating, and a change in bowel habits. Both gastric and duodenal ulcers may be accompanied by chronic blood loss to the extent that cardiac and/or nervous system symptoms overshadow those of the gut. Acute hemorrhage can be the presenting manifestation of either type of ulcer. Patients in this group are generally older (>65), have a prior history of complications, and often are taking NSAIDs. Giant ulcers (>3 cm in the stomach, and >2 cm in the duodenum) are prone to occur in elderly persons and are accompanied by anorexia, weight loss, constantly feeling bad, fever, increased erythrocyte sedimentation rate, and leukocytosis.[50]

Diagnosis

The possibility of an ulcer is suggested by a history of ulcer symptoms spanning many years. The development of nausea and vomiting suggests gastric outlet obstruction from scarring of the duodenum. Observing undigested food in the vomitus or eliciting a succession splash are important diagnostic clues suggesting such obstruction. Positive identification of an ulcer requires visualization of the stomach and duodenum. Endoscopy is more accurate than x-ray examination and for this reason is preferred. Although either method is ordinarily satisfactory, a confusing radiographic appearance may require endoscopic clarification. The major endoscopic hazard is respiratory depression from overzealous premedication. Most elderly patients require very little sedative, and the endoscopic procedure is generally well tolerated. Giant duodenal ulcers are uncommon but are important to diagnose.[51,52] These are ulcers greater than 2 cm in diameter, involve a substantial portion of the duodenal bulb, are more common in men (generally in their seventies), and often appear without antecedent symptoms. The pain of giant duodenal ulcer may mimic that of pancreatic or biliary disease. Weight loss is common because food ingestion aggravates the pain. The most frequent complication is bleeding (often massive), while perforation occasionally occurs. Duodenal obstruction can be present but usually develops late in the evolution of giant duodenal ulcers. Low albumin levels have been reported and reflect poor nutrition as well as protein loss through the large ulcer bed.

Complications

With increasing age, the frequency of complications also rises. About one-half of patients over age 70 with ulcers can be expected to suffer significant complications.[53] Gastric ulcers tend to be large and deeply penetrating and are prone to increased complications (inadequate healing, performation, or bleeding).[54] Of patients requiring surgery for such ulcers, 63 percent had emergency procedures with nearly a 25 percent postoperative mortality. Bleeding is a major problem and often occurs without prior symptoms. The mortality of the older patient with upper gastrointestinal bleeding is 4 to 10 times that of a younger person.[21] The "geriatric ulcer" found high on the posterior wall of the stomach is not usually associated with excessive gastrointestinal bleeding.[55] Perforation is the second most common peptic ulcer disease complication in the elderly patient. Despite the catastrophic events, the subdued atypical presentation and lack of prior history of peptic ulcer disease (30 percent) in the older patient conspire to delay treatment for up to 24 hours in 50 percent.[56]

Gastric outlet obstruction, when it occurs, is usually due to duodenal scarring from long-standing ulcer disease. Cancer of the stomach is not a true complication of gastric ulcers. Chronic irritation caused by the ulcer does not lead to a malignant change; rather, malignancies ulcerate and then masquerade as benign ulcers. At least 5 percent of all gastric ulcers may be malignant at diagnosis.[57,58] The majority of giant gastric ulcers are benign. Duodenal ulcers are seldom confused with malignancy because cancer of the duodenum is extremely rare.

Treatment

The dictum "no acid, no ulcer" remains true for both gastric and duodenal ulcers. Accordingly, treatment for either variety traditionally remains that of modifying acid production and bolstering defenses. Dietary manipulation is useful only insofar as it may alleviate symptoms. The patient is advised to eat at least three small nutritious meals per day, avoiding foods known to aggravate symptoms, and to discontinue the use of any exogenous ulcer-promoting substances such as NSAIDs, ethanol, and tobacco. Once these issues are addressed, other options which may accelerate ulcer healing include (1) neutralizing acid, (2) interfering with acid production, and (3) protecting the damaged mucosa. In prospective controlled studies, there was no significant difference among these options regarding short-term treatment. The choice among the options depends primarily on the clinical situation but is also influenced to some extent by patient and physician preferences and economics.

A small uncomplicated ulcer causing only daytime symptoms is best treated with intermittent antacids. (Be aware that antacids vary considerably in their sodium content.) With nocturnal awakening, an H_2 blocker taken at bedtime for 6 to 8 weeks is advisable. Side effects are infrequent, dose-dependent, and easily reversed upon stopping medication, and differences among the various H_2 blockers are small.[59] The occasional patient who has headache secondary to famotidine or ranitidine or gynecomastia from cimetidine can be switched to another product. There is too little information at this time to evaluate side effects from nizatadine. Acid suppression at night is sensible because this is the time when intragastric pH is normally low, and there is no other convenient way of dealing with this phenomenon. It is acceptable to add daytime antacids if necessary. If the ulcer is due to NSAIDs, recurrence is not usual if the NSAID is stopped. Gastric and duodenal ulcers not due to NSAIDs are prone to recur, but the average time is in the range of 4 months or so.[60] For this reason, it is acceptable to discontinue initial treatment after an initial response and reinstitute as needed.

Treatment of *H. pylori* infection is not recommended except for patients who present a serious management problem requiring either continuous medication or consideration for surgery. If therapy is undertaken, the most efficacious combination should be employed, i.e., bismuth subsalicylate 262 mg (Pepto Bismol) one tablet qid plus tetracycline 500 mg qid and metronidazole 400 tid, all given for 2 weeks. Amoxacillin can be substituted for metronidazole but has more side effects. About a 90 percent "cure" rate can be expected.[61]

Sucralfate does not affect hydrogen ion secretion or neutralize acid but offers the same increase in the rate of healing produced by H_2 blockers. This effect is considered a reflection of several of sucralfate's properties.[62] One is that the disassociated sucralfate molecule adheres to the base of the ulcer and protects it from the action of acid-activated pepsin. This protective effect allows maximum epithelial growth from the ulcer margin. Also, sucralfate apparently stimulates endogenous prostaglandin formation, stimulates mucosal bicarbonate formation, and binds to pepsin and bile.

If the patient has had a giant ulcer healed medically or has suffered a serious complication (bleeding or perforation), then long-term H_2 blocker use is recommended. This should be continued for at least 1 year; indefinite treatment is recommended for very old and/or infirm patients who have had major hemorrhage not related to NSAID use. In the case of a "silent bleed," there are no specific guidelines, but it would seem appropriate to continue H_2 blockers longer and make sure that other factors promoting ulcers have been eliminated. As for pyloric and duodenal obstruction, balloon dilation may be considered depending on the clinical situation.

The follow-up treatment of duodenal and gastric ulcers differs. Usually duodenal ulcers, once diagnosed, can be treated with confidence as long as the patient feels better. Subsequent assessment of healing is not necessary. In contrast, because a small percentage of gastric ulcers are actually malignant, following the patient to complete healing is prudent. If the ulcer was initially well seen radiographically, subsequent x-ray examination should suffice. If the ulcer was missed initially, the x-ray film was equivocal, or the ulcer fails to heal in a reasonable period of time, endoscopic follow-up is required. A persistently nonhealing ulcer always raises the question of patient compliance versus malignancy. Especially given the cost of some medications, patient compliance may be a significant problem.

Surgery is generally reserved for treatment of serious complications, when prompt surgery is usually advocated, but a mortality rate of up to 50 percent can be expected.[63] Nonoperative treatment (NG suction, IV fluids, antibiotics, and H_2 antagonists) has been successful in some patients. Surgery is mandatory if there is no improvement within 12 hours of treatment. Patients over 70 do not do well with this approach.[64]

GASTRIC-EMPTYING DISORDERS

During and after a meal, the fundus of the stomach functions as a reservoir, while the antrum is a grinding, mixing, and pumping station. It is well known that fluids empty from the stomach more rapidly than solids and that solids will not empty until their size is reduced to less than 2 mm in diameter. How the stomach distinguishes between fluid and solid is unknown. Between meals, vigorous contractile activity begins in the stomach, sweeps down the antrum, across the pylorus, and down the small bowel to the colon. These contractions are so vigorous that the stomach is purged except for debris retained because of insufficient size reduction. The mechanisms controlling these complex processes have not been thoroughly explained, but they clearly involve a delicate coordination of neural and hormonal events. It is probable that a single lapse in any one or a combination of these processes will result in a gastric-emptying disorder. Undoubtedly, the aging process exacts a toll in this regard, but it is uncertain to what degree. Crucial factors would be the patient's medical condition as well as medical requirements. In any event, it is well known that many puzzling symptoms can be explained by defects in gastric motility. Several recent reviews discuss various aspects of gastric motility and its disorders.[65–68]

Clinical Concerns

Rapid gastric emptying is usually a result of gastric surgery. Postgastrectomy symptoms include gastrointestinal symptoms (nausea, vomiting, pain, and diarrhea) and vasomotor symptoms (sweating, tachycardia, flushing, etc.). This is not a special problem of aging and will not be discussed further. In contrast, impaired gastric emptying, while found at any age, is perhaps more common in the elderly population. Many possible causes contribute to poor emptying of the stomach and are easily confused with other medical problems. Conditions resulting in slowed gastric emptying are *gastric stasis syndromes*, while the result is identified as *gastroparesis*.

Historical features are often vague. Frequent complaints include early satiety, bloating, chronic nausea, and weight loss. Vomiting, if present, is often late in the day and vomitus may contain food eaten a number of hours before. A succussion splash observed 4 hours after last ingesting food or fluid is a characteristic physical finding. Because the symptoms are vague, the first test performed is often an upper GI x-ray examination. This will not yield useful information unless food in a large atonic stomach is observed when the patient is known to have fasted for many hours prior to the examination. To eliminate the possibility of a remediable mechanical outlet obstruction, endoscopy is advisable. Although there are numerous marker techniques and considerable day-to-day variation within single subjects,[69] the best diagnostic method to confirm the clinical impression is that of a solid-phase gastric-emptying study. This need not be done on every patient but is helpful for a patient who has bothersome symptoms otherwise unexplained.

The most common cause for impaired gastric emptying is anatomic obstruction. Such an obstruction is usually the result of duodenal or pyloric scarring from chronic peptic ulcer, but antral carcinoma must be considered, especially in the elderly patient.

In the absence of outlet obstruction, there are a number of potential causes for gastroparesis, including disorders of the CNS, drugs (particularly those with anticholinergic properties, and pain medications), diabetes (autonomic dysfunction), muscular disorders (myopathies, scleroderma), and a small number of causes that remain "idiopathic" for lack of some other clinical association. The condition may be transient (as is medication-induced gastroparesis) or permanent.

Treatment

Therapy is not always satisfactory. First the physician must identify causes such as drugs that impair gastric emptying; diabetes; or remedial CNS problems. Those patients who do not respond to such simple measures as drug discontinuation may benefit from dietary modification because the stomach handles liquids differently than solids. Small, frequent feedings of a liquid or blenderized diet is sometimes useful. The patient who is still symptomatic may benefit from the addition of pharmacological agents. Two readily available options are bethanechol and metoclopramide. Bethanechol, a cholinergic agent, can be tried in doses of 10 to 20 mg before meals, though response to treatment is inconsistent.[70] Side effects are generally infrequent and mild; if there is no response at these levels, it is unlikely that larger doses will improve the results. Metoclopramide acts both centrally and peripherally. The central effect is to suppress dopamine receptors in the chemoreceptor trigger zone and vomiting center, while its peripheral effect may be related to local release of acetylcholine from cholinergic neurons. At a dose of 10 mg taken before meals, metoclopramide may cause a significant number of patients to experience symptoms of irritability, excitation, and sometimes disorientation and hallucinations. Dystonic reactions can also occur and are related to metoclopramide's central antidopaminergic properties. Elderly patients are particularly prone to have adverse reactions. Because the drug elevates prolactin levels, galactorrhea, breast enlargement, and menstrual disorders have been reported in nonelderly individuals. Patients experiencing side effects can sometimes tolerate a small dose of metoclopramide in combination with bethanechol. Cisapride (Janssen Pharmaceutica, Inc.) is a recent addition to the list of gastrointestinal "prokinetic" agents. In contrast to metoclopramide and domperidone, Cisapride has no antidopaminergic properties and acts mainly to release acetylcholine from enteric neurons. Cisapride has been shown to accelerate gastric emptying in most syndromes associated with gastroparesis (progressive systemic sclerosis, diabetes, and idiopathic gastroparesis). Erythromycin (a macrolide compound) at less than the antibiotic dose stimulates the onset of a migrating motor complex.[71] It is thought to act through motalin receptors. Although erythromycin has been shown to improve gastric emptying in a few patients with diabetic gastroparesis,[72] further studies are necessary to demonstrate its effectiveness in idiopathic gastroparesis. A number of other drugs in several classes that are under investigation have recently been reviewed.[73]

GI BLEEDING

Upper GI bleeding is a major problem in elderly patients. Many have no preceding symptoms,[74] and their mortality is significantly greater than that of younger bleeding patients.[55] Predictors of a poor outcome include transfusions of more than 5 units of blood, taking concurrent NSAIDs, and serious coexisting disease.[74,75] Elderly persons tolerate hypotension poorly, and azotemia, peripheral vascular failure, and dehydration can develop quickly. These complications are challenging to manage in a fragile patient who may have marginal cardiac reserve. Thus, an important objective in dealing with bleeding patients is to recognize early those who have massive bleeds which are unlikely to respond to medical management or those are likely to have recurrent bleeds. In this special group, avoiding needless delay in surgical intervention should avoid complications and improve overall survival.

Important causes of bleeding from the stomach and duodenum in elderly patients are (1) Mallory-Weiss tear, (2) hiatal hernia,[76] (3) gastritis, (4) gastric or duodenal ulcer, (5) malignancy, (6) vascular malformations,[77] and (7) the Deiulafoy lesion,[78] which represents a defect of 2 to 5 mm in an unusually large submucosal artery, usually within 5 cm of the cardioesophageal junction. The Dieulafoy lesion is important because of massive and often recurrent bleeding, and it will only be identified if carefully looked for.[79]

Historical features are important in properly evaluating the bleeding patient. Was hematemesis, melena, or hematochezia first noted? The vomiting of blood leaves no doubt that the hemorrhage is from the upper gut. Occasionally a patient with upper GI bleeding does not vomit blood but instead produces maroon-colored stools. Maroon-colored stools indicate that the blood was not greatly altered by passing through the intestine. One possibility in this circumstance is that bleeding originated low in the gut and, due to the proximity of the rectum, was retained only long enough to cause minor changes in appearance. Alternatively, an upper GI source may produce a similar result; however, this takes a massive hemorrhage, and it is likely the patient will have a history of syncope and/or shock. A more leisurely bleed is more likely to be accompanied by shortness of breath, weakness, melena, and sometimes syncope. If there is some doubt that the bleeding is upper gut in origin, then an abruptly rising blood urea nitrogen test may provide a useful clue, as this is not expected if bleeding comes from the lower gut. A Mallory-Weiss tear is suggested by hematemesis after severe retching. Other specific inquiries are directed toward a past history of ulcer disease, prior bleeds, gastric surgery, alcohol use, known bleeding disorders, and current medications (particularly NSAIDs and anticoagulants). If the patient has a prosthetic heart valve or artificial joint, antibiotic prophylaxis may be necessary prior to endoscopy.

During the history and physical examination, venous access with one or more large-bore IVs should be established, and blood components administered as required. It is important to avoid fluid overload in elderly patients with a marginal cardiorespiratory reserve; thus, it is prudent to monitor central venous pressure. Despite the lack of evidence that H_2 blockers are useful in the treatment of active GI bleeding,[80] most centers continue to use acid-reducing and/or neutralizing therapy. Their only justification is their ability to speed ulcer healing as an issue separate from the hemorrhage.[81] Although they are relatively safe, some side effects and drug interactions can be a problem with H_2 blockers.[22] At least initially a nasogastric (NG) tube is useful until a better grasp of the source and extent of bleeding is established. Gross blood from an NG tube guarantees an active upper GI source; however, bleeding can be intermittent, so a negative aspirate does not rule out an upper GI source. In the presence of *active* bleeding, almost all clinicians would agree that maintaining an NG tube in place is appropriate, as this may give an early clue to accelerating blood loss. Water or saline lavage may also be helpful in evaluating the extent of the bleeding. In the elderly patient, it is better to use water so as to avoid an inadvertent excessive salt load. Room temperature water interferes less with blood coagulation.[82] The question of whether all upper GI bleeders should have an NG tube also remains controversial. For example, in a patient who has stopped bleeding, an NG tube may give an early warning of recurrent bleeding before a change in the central venous pressure is observed, but in some cases the presence of the tube may actually promote recurrent bleeding. In the event that an upper GI source of bleeding has been identified from which there is neither active bleeding nor a significant risk of rebleeding, then it is best to leave the NG tube out. Finally, with large clots in the stomach, lavage through a large-bore tube is helpful prior to endoscopy.

While some studies suggest that transfusion requirements and mortality are not significantly altered by early endoscopy, most accept the notion that it is more comfortable for the physician to manage bleeding when its source and nature are known. Elderly patients tolerate endoscopy with little discomfort and no appreciable risk of increased morbidity.[83,84] Moreover, the severity of the bleed can be assessed, and certain patients suitable for early surgery can be singled out. About 85 percent of all upper GI bleeding episodes can be expected to stop spontaneously. Can those who are going to keep bleeding be identified early? Endoscopic as well as clinical clues may help in this regard. The majority of cases in which there is an active spurting of blood on initial endoscopy require surgery; in this instance it is best not to delay. In the case of oozing, probably half need urgent surgery. In this case, if the patient is stable and has tolerated the bleed well, it is reasonable to closely monitor the evolution of the bleeding episode, but to be poised to proceed directly to surgery should the need arise. If the bleeding has stopped and there is an adherent clot (either fresh or old) or visible vessel, there is a significant chance for rebleeding, although the incidence varies.[55] Attempts to stop active bleeding or avoid recurrent bleeding by therapeutic endoscopic techniques (heater probe, bicap) to postpone or eliminate the need for surgery are attractive, and recent data are encouraging.[85] The medical management of upper GI bleeding demands careful monitoring. In general, gastric ulcers are more likely to rebleed than duodenal ulcers, but the presence of an ooze or clot in conjunction with either variety may have mortal consequences.[86] Specific lesions prone to rebleeding include giant ulcers, Dieulafoy lesions, malignancies, and vascular ectasias. Clean gastric and duodenal ulcers, Mallory-Weiss tears, and gastritis are less likely to bleed again, and conservative management can be continued with reasonable confidence.

Clinical presentation is also extremely useful in predicting outcome. For example, a patient who presents with a sudden hemorrhage culminating in shock and endoscopy revealing an ulcer with visible vessel or clot has an 80 percent chance of rebleeding.[87] Clearly, fibrin plugs in a large vascular defect are likely to be unstable, and recurrent bleeding is common. The severity of the bleed is also reflected in the transfusion requirements. At the time of admission approximately one-third of the patients do not require transfusion, approximately one-third require less than 4 units of blood, and the remaining one-third have bleeding that is heavy and recurrent. The majority needing surgery are from this last group (requiring greater than 6 units of blood).[88] If there is a reasonable indication for surgery and a major medical complication does not coexist, elderly patients tolerate the surgery surprisingly well. An occasional severe bleeder has such an overwhelming surgical risk that laser, heater probe, bipolar electrocautery, injecting the bleeding site with 1/10,000 epinephrine, or even radiologic intervention is considered.[89] Generally, patients in such desperate straits have a dismal outcome regardless of treatment efforts, and they are probably best served by offering meticulous supportive care. Clearly, the medical-surgical management of the fragile, unstable, elderly bleeding patient with multiple medical problems remains a major challenge.

GASTRIC NEOPLASMS

Adenocarcinoma

Gastric cancer has for unknown reasons been decreasing in prevalence in this country. Several decades ago it was the most common type of cancer in the United States, but it now ranks third in frequency among GI neoplasms. In this country, the incidence remains in the range of 25,000 new cases per year, the majority of which occur in the population aged over 60.[90] A 2:1 male preponderance persists. Dietary factors traditionally have been suspected to play an important role. Much effort has been devoted to the identification of carcinogens that might be responsible. Some of these are food contaminant (polycyclic hydrocarbons) while others (nitrosamines) may be produced in the stomach in vivo. Genetics may play a role, but this has been hard to prove. In addition to *H. pylori* infection and gastric atrophy (discussed earlier), subtotal gastrectomy and polyps are also preexisting conditions that may lead to malignant change. Surgery that decreases acid production is associated with an increased incidence of cancer in the remaining gastric pouch.[91] Such cancers are found about 20 years after the stomach surgery. Because the incidence of postgastrectomy cancer in the United States is low, surveillance endoscopy in these patients is not warranted.[14] Gastric polyps are found incidentally in up to 3 percent of gastric examinations. Most gastric polyps (80 percent) are hyperplastic, occur in multiples, are less than 1 cm in diameter, and have no serious malignant potential. Of the remainder, most are adenomatous lesions, of which about 40 percent will, with time, develop carcinomatous changes. Thus, it is best to remove by snare cautery polyps greater than 1 cm in diameter. The selection and timing of follow-up endoscopies for cancer surveillance remain controversial.[92]

Gastric neoplasms vary widely in appearance. The possibilities range from polypoid lesions growing into the lumen of the stomach to diffuse infiltrating neoplasms that can come to involve the entire stomach wall (either of which may be ulcerated), or any variation between these extremes. Early gastric cancer, first reported by the Japanese in the early 1960s, was originally thought to be confined to Japan. In recent years it has been identified in most other areas of the world, albeit less commonly. By definition, early gastric cancer neoplasms are superficial and, at the time of detection, show no evidence of spread; thus, their early recognition is important to ensure a favorable outcome. Screening for early gastric cancer is routinely practiced in Japan, where 95 percent 5-year survivals are reported. In the United States the tumor is relatively unusual (4 to 13 percent of all GI cancers,[93,94] making routine evaluation of asymptomatic patients impractical. The majority of gastric neoplasms that are ulcerated begin in the antrum and metastasize early, while the polypoid tumors are more likely to be located in the proximal stomach. Direct invasion of adjacent organs, and blood and lymphatic metastases, are common.

Most gastric cancer in the United States is detected at a time when it has already spread. Partially contributing to this feature is an average delay of 6 to 12 months between the time symptoms first appear and the establishment of the diagnosis. A loss of taste for meats, as well as early satiety and nausea, is probably responsible for the weight loss noted in 70 to 80 percent of patients with gastric cancer. The associated decreased food intake contributes to the common complaint of constipation. Pain is reported in about 70 percent of the patients, but there is nothing very characteristic in its description, and the location varies widely. Some patients may experience a fullness relieved with belching, while others will have nonspecific dyspeptic complaints simulating peptic ulcer disease. Chronic blood loss is common, but hematemesis is unusual. The location of the tumor may dictate the presenting complaint. For example, tumors involving the fundus often cause dysphagia, while antral tumors may give gastric outlet obstruction. Metastases cause symptoms based on the location and may contribute to the formation of ascites and jaundice and cause neurological symptoms. When the symptoms of patients with "early gastric cancer" are compared with those of patients harboring advanced disease, it turns out that most individuals in both groups were studied because of "indigestion." Thus, the hope of identifying early gastric cancer by history is remote; by the time symptoms occur, the disease is well established. The physical examination is equally unrewarding other than the fact that the patient looks indisposed, has evidence of weight loss, and may demonstrate evidence of complications due to metastatic disease.

Routine laboratory examinations are appropriate in patients with gastric cancer. However, sophisticated tests such as those for pepsinogen I, carcinoma enbryonic antigen, and gastrins; gastric analysis; etc.; while of some academic interest, have little practical value in clearly establishing the diagnosis. Upper GI x-ray films when properly performed are reasonably accurate in identifying the nature of the problem, but endoscopy with biopsy and cytologic examination is more accurate and yields a tissue diagnosis. The differentiation of a benign gastric ulcer from a malignant lesion is important. For this reason, following an ulcer to complete healing (by either endoscopy or x-ray examination) is indicated and identifies the majority of patients harboring a malignancy. To delay the diagnosis of gastric cancer by 8 weeks or so has no effect on treatment or outcome.

Treatment by chemotherapy, radiation, and immunotherapy is not satisfactory. The best hope for a modest improvement in survival is by surgery. Roughly 80 percent of all patients with gastric cancer are considered suitable candidates for laparotomy. Of this group, fewer than half are found at the time of surgery to be candidates for curative resection.[95] Despite these "encouraging" statistics, only 15 to 25 percent who undergo "curative resection" survive for 5 years.[96] However, compared with doing no surgery (1-year survival, 5 percent), surgery for those who can tolerate it has a somewhat better outlook. A heavy penalty is paid for this modest improvement in survival, however. In some instances, the patients are subjected to a procedure with high morbidity without achieving any improvement, while in other instances, their demise is hastened. Age should not be a criterion for determining whether to operate or not; more important factors include a patient's general medical status and whether (or what) other medical conditions coexist, as well as patient preference. There are no absolute right answers, but careful thought and considerable judgment are required to advise for or against surgery. Patients not suitable for surgical treatment may be considered for palliation with radiation, chemotherapy, and various local modalities applied via endoscope.

Benign Tumors

A number of benign tumors occur in the stomach, and these are found more frequently in the elderly population. A general idea of the relative frequency of the most important tumors follows: (1) hyperplastic polyps, 38 percent, (2) adenomatous polys, 10 percent, and (3) leiomyoma, 24 percent. The remainder are obscure tumors such as fibromas, lipomas, leiomyoblastomas, and ectopic pancreatic tumors, each of which can occur up to 5 percent of the time.[97] Leiomyomas are the most common smooth muscle tumor. Other mesenchymal tumors such as fibromas and neural tumors are occasionally encountered.

Lymphomas

Lymphoma is much less common than adenocarcinoma. Of the extranodal lymphomas, gastric lymphoma is the most common. Symptoms and roentgenographic signs are very similar to those of adenocarcinoma in as many as 60 percent of patients. The presence of large, irregular gastric folds, large ulcerated masses, and antral narrowing are more in keeping with lymphoma.[98,99] Endoscopic biopsy is important, because the treatment of lymphoma and that of adenocarcinoma are markedly different. However, definitive endoscopic diagnosis can be elusive and may require repeat examination and mucosal snare biopsy.[100] Treatment of lymphomas can be quite complex. Most patients with early gastric lymphoma who undergo surgery may expect a 5-year survival of up to 80 percent.[101] However, it is not possible to extrapolate such aggressive treatment to the elderly population because other afflictions often alter the long-term outlook. The sagacious physician understands that most elderly patients are best served by avoiding surgery and proceeding directly with radiation and/or chemotherapy. Overall, the expected 5-year survival is approximately 50 percent.

Other rare malignancies include gastric myosarcomas and carcinoid tumors. With regard to carcinoid, it is of interest that gastrin is known to be trophic for enterochromaffin-like cells and that there is an increased number of gastric carcinoids in patients known to be achlorhydric and with elevated gastrin levels. What effect long-term treatment with potassium-hydrogen ATPase inhibitors may have on this phenomenon remains to be seen.

REFERENCES

1. Blaser MJ: *Helicobacter pylori*: Its role in disease. *Clin Infect Dis* 15:386, 1992.
2. McKinlay AW et al: *Helicobacter pylori*: Bridging the credibility gap. *Gut* 31:940, 1990.
3. Montgomery EA et al: Rapid diagnosis of *Campylobacter pylori* by Gram's stain. *Am J Clin Path* 90:606, 1988.
4. McNulty CA et al: Detection of *Campylobacter pylori* by the biopsy urease test: An assessment of 1445 patients. *Gut* 30:1058, 1989.
5. Graham DY et al: *Campylobacter pylori* detected noninvasively by the ^{13}C-urea breath test. *Lancet* 1:1174, 1987.
6. Truesdale RA et al: Serology predicts treatment eradication of *Helicobacter pylori*. *Gastroenterology* 100:A176, 1991.
7. Glassman MS et al: *Helicobacter pylori*–related gastroduodenal disease in children. Diagnostic utility of enzyme-linked immunosorbent assay. *Dig Dis Sci* 35:993, 1990.
8. Drumm B et al: Intrafamilial clustering of *Helicobacter pylori* infection. *N Engl J Med* 322:359, 1990.
9. Logan RP et al: One week eradication regimen for *Helicobacter pylori*. *Lancet* 338:1249, 1991.
10. Graham DY et al: Factors influencing the eradication of *Helicobacter pylori* with triple therapy. *Gastroenterology* 102:493, 1992.
11. Graham DY: Prevention of gastroduodenal injury induced by chronic nonsteroidal anti-inflammatory drug therapy. *Gastroenterology* 96(2 pt 2 suppl):675, 1989.
12. McCarthy DM: Nonsteroidal anti-inflammatory drug-induced ulcers: Management by traditional therapies. *Gastroenterology* 96:662, 1989.
13. Griffin MR et al: Non-steroidal anti-inflammatory drug use and increased risk for peptic ulcer disease in elderly persons. *Ann Intern Med* 114:257, 1991.
14. Isenberg JI et al: Acid-peptic disorders, in Yamada T (ed): *Textbook of Gastroenterology*. Philadelphia, Lippincott, 1991, p 1241.
15. Gabriel SE, Bombardier C: NSAID induced ulcers. An emerging epidemic? *J Rheumatol* 17:1, 1990.
16. Fries JF et al: Toward and epidemiology of gastropathy associated with nonsteroidal anti-inflammatory drug use. *Gastroenterology* 96(2 pt 2 suppl):647, 1989.
17. Gubbins GP et al: *Helicobacter pylori* seroprevalence in patients with rheumatoid arthritis: Effect of nonsteroidal anti-inflammatory drugs and gold compounds. *Am J Med* 93:412, 1992.
18. Graham DY et al: Long-term nonsteroidal antiinflammatory drug use and *Helicobacter pylori* infection. *Gastroenterology* 100:1653, 1991.
19. Graham DY: The relationship between non-steroidal anti-inflammatory drug user and peptic ulcer disease. *Gastroenterol Clin North Am* 19:171, 1990.
20. Connelly CS, Panush RS: Should nonsteroidal anti-inflammatory drugs be stopped before elective surgery: *Arch Intern Med* 151:1963, 1991.
21. Gilinsky NH: Peptic ulcer disease in the elderly. *Gastroenterol Clin North Am* 19:255, 1990.
22. McCarthy DM: Acid peptic disease in the elderly. *Clin Geriatr Med* 7:231, 1991.
23. Ehsauollah RSB et al: Prevention of gastroduodenal damage induced by nonsteroidal antiinflammatory drugs. Controlled trial of ranitidine. *Br Med J* 297:1017, 1988.
24. McCarthy DM: NSAID-induced gastrointestinal damage. A critical review of prophylaxis and therapy. *J Glin Gastroenterol* 12(suppl 2):s13, 1990.
25. Walan A et al: Effect of omeprazole and ranitidine on ulcer healing and relapse rates in patients with benign gastric ulcer. *N Engl J Med* 320:69, 1989.
26. Barrier CH, Hirschowitz BI: Controversies in the detection and management of nonsteroidal antiinflammatory drug induced side effects of the upper gastrointestinal tract. *Arthritis Rheum* 32:926, 1989.
27. Green LK, Graham DY: Gastritis in the elderly. *Gastroenterol Clin North Am* 19:273, 1990.
28. Rotterdam H, Sommers SC: *Biopsy Diagnosis of the Digestive Tract*. New York, Raven, 1981, p 59.
29. Katz K, Jablonowski H: Functional and histological gastric changes with age, in Hellmans J, Vantappen G (eds): *Gastrointestinal Tract Disorders in the Elderly*. Edinburgh, Churchill Livingstone, 1984, p. 62.
30. Sirula M, Varis K: Gastritis, in Sircus W, Smith AN (eds): *Scientific Foundations of Gastroenterology*. Philadelphia, Saunders, 1980, p. 357.
31. Barwick KW: Chronic gastritis. The pathologist's role. *Pathol Ann* 22:223, 1987.
32. Stockbrugger R et al: Serum gastrin and atrophic gastritis in achlorhydric patients with and without pernicious anemia. *Scand J Gastroenterol* 11:713, 1976.
33. Stockbrugger R et al: Antral gastritis cells and serum gastrin in achlorhydria. *Scand J Gastroenterol* 12:209, 1977.
34. Strickland R, MacKay I: A reappraisal of the nature and significance of chronic atrophic gastritis. *Am J Dig Dis* 18:426, 1973.
35. Holt PR et al: Causes and consequences of hypochlorhydria in the elderly. *Dig Dis Sci* 34:933, 1989.
36. Correa P: Chronic gastritis: A clinico-pathological classification. *Am J Gastroenterol* 83:504, 1988.
37. Graham DY: *Campylobacter pylori* and peptic ulcer disease. *Gastroenterology* 96(2 pt 2 suppl):615, 1989.
38. Parsonnet J et al: *Helicobacter pylori* infection and the risk of gastric carcinoma. *N Engl J Med* 325:1127, 1991.
39. Nomura A et al: *Helicobacter pylori* infection and gastric carcinoma among Japanese-Americans in Hawaii. *N Engl J Med* 325:1132, 1991.
40. Talley NJ et al: Gastric adenocarcinoma and *Helicobacter pylori* infection. *J Natl Cancer Inst* 83:1734, 1991.
41. Siurala M et al: Prevalence of gastritis in the rural population. *Scand J Gastroenterol* 3:211, 1968.
42. Svendsen JH et al: Gastric cancer risk in achlorhydric patients. A long term follow-up study. *Scand J Gastroenterol* 1:16, 1986.
43. Schafer LW et al: Risk of development of gastric carcinoma in patients with pernicious anemia. A population based study in Rochester, Minnesota. *Mayo Clin Proc* 60:444, 1985.
44. Broch K et al: Endocrine cell proliferation and carci-

noid development: A review of new aspects of hypergastrinemic atrophic gastritis. *Digestion* 35 (suppl I):106, 1986.
45. Cooper BT: Ménétrier's disease. *Dig Dis Sci* 5:33, 1987.
46. Kulber DA et al: The current spectrum of peptic ulcer disease in the older age group. *Am Surg* 56:737, 1990.
47. Graham DY et al: Effect of treatment of *Helicobacter pylori* infection on the long-term recurrence of gastric or duodenal ulcer. A randomized controlled study. *Ann Intern Med* 116:705, 1992.
48. Permutt RP, Cello JP: Duodenal ulcer disease in the hospitalized elderly patient. *Dig Dis Sci* 27:1, 1982.
49. Mowat NAD et al: The natural history of gastric ulcer in a community: A 4 year study. *Q J Med* 44:45, 1975.
50. Brandt LJ: *Gastrointestinal Disorders of the Elderly*. New York, Raven, 1984, p 120.
51. Mistilis SP et al: Giant duodenal ulcer. *Ann Intern Med* 59:155, 1963.
52. Klamer TW, Mahr MM: Giant duodenal ulcer: A dangerous variant of a common illness. *Am J Surg* 135:760, 1978.
53. Steinhaber FU: Ageing and the stomach. *Clin Gastroenterol* 14:657, 1985.
54. Jenses HE et al: High gastric ulcers. *World J Surg* 11:325, 1987.
55. Reinus JF, Brandt LJ: Upper and lower gastrointestinal bleeding in the elderly. *Gastroenterol Clin North Am* 19:293, 1990.
56. Steinheber FU: Acute abdomen, in Hellemans J, Vantrappen G (eds): *Gastrointestinal Disorders in the Elderly*. Edinburgh, Churchill Livingstone, 1984, p 195.
57. Tragardh B, Haglund U: Endoscopic diagnosis of gastric ulcer. Evaluation of benefits of endoscopic follow-up observation for malignancy. *Acta Chir Scand* 151:37, 1985.
58. Bytzer P: Endoscopic follow-up study of gastric ulcer to detect malignancy: Is it worthwhile? *Scand J Gastroenterol* 26:1193, 1991.
59. Lipsy RJ et al: Clinical review of histamine$_2$ receptor antagonists. *Arch Intern Med* 150:745, 1990.
60. Dawson J et al: Effect of Ranitidine on gastric ulcer healing and recurrence. *Scand J Gastroenterol* 19:665, 1984.
61. Heatley RV: Review article: The treatment of *Helicobacter pylori* infection. *Aliment Pharmacol Ther* 6:291, 1992.
62. Colin-Jones DG: There is more to healing ulcers than suppressing acid. *Gut* 27:475, 1986.
63. Coleman JA, Denham MJ: Perforation of peptic ulcer in the elderly. *Age Aging* 9:257, 1980.
64. Crofts TJ et al: A randomized trial of nonoperative treatment for perforated peptic ulcer. *N Engl J Med* 320:970, 1989.
65. Vantrappern G et al: Gastrointestinal motility disorders. *Dig Dis Sci* 31(Sept suppl):55, 1986.
66. Kim CH, Malagelada JR: Electrical activity of the stomach: Clinical implications. *Mayo Clin Proc* 61:205, 1986.
67. Funch-Jensen P: Basal upper gastrointestinal motility in healthy people. *Scand J Gastroenterol* 128(suppl):52, 1987.
68. Minami H, McCallum RW: The physiology and pathophysiology of gastric emptying in humans. *Gastroenterology* 86:1592, 1984.
69. Brophy CM et al: Variability of gastric emptying measurements in man employing standardized radiolabeled meals. *Dig Dis Sci* 31:799, 1986.
70. Sheiner HJ, Catchpole BN: Drug therapy for post gastrectomy gastric stasis. *Br J Surg* 69:608, 1976.
71. Otterson MF, Sarna SK: Gastrointestinal motor effects of erythromycin. *Am J Physiol* 259(3 pt 1):G355, 1990.
72. Janssens J et al: Improvement of gastric emptying in diabetic gastroparesis by erythromycin. Preliminary studies. *N Engl J Med* 322:1028, 1990.
73. Reynolds JC, Putnam PE: Prokinetic agents. *Gastroenterol Clin North Am* 21:567, 1992.
74. Cooper BT et al: Acute upper gastrointestinal haemorrhage in patients aged 80 years or more. *Q J Med* 69(258):765, 1988.
75. Booker JA et al: Prognostic factors for continued or rebleeding and death from gastrointestinal hemorrhage in the elderly. *Age Aging* 16:208, 1987.
76. Cameron AJ, Higgins JA: Liniar gastric erosion. A lesion associated with large diaphragmatic hernia and chronic blood loss. *Gastroenterology* 91:338, 1986.
77. Quintero E et al: Upper gastrointestinal bleeding caused by gastroduodenal vascular malformations. Incidence, diagnosis and treatment. *Dig Dis Sci* 31:897, 1986.
78. Veldhugzen Van Zanten SJO et al: Recurrent massive hemetemesis from Dieulafoy vascular malformations—A review of 101 cases. *Gut* 27:213, 1986.
79. Reilly HF, al-Kawas FH: Dieulafoy's lesion: Diagnosis and management. *Dig Dis Sci* 36:1702, 1991.
80. Papp JP: Management of upper gastrointestinal bleeding. *Clin Geriatr Med* 7:255, 1991.
81. Collins R, Langman M: Treatment with histamine H_2 antagonists in acute upper gastrointestinal hemorrhage. Implications of randomized trials. *N Engl J Med* 313:660, 1985.
82. Ponsky JL et al: Saline irrigation in gastric hemorrhage: Effect of temperature. *J Surg Res* 28:204, 1980.
83. Brussaard CC, Vandewoude MFJ: A prospective analysis of elective upper gastrointestinal endoscopy in the elderly. *Gastrointest Endosc* 34:1118, 1988.
84. Fleisher D: Monitoring the patient receiving conscious sedation for gastrointestinal endoscopy: Issues and guidelines. *Gastrointest Endosc* 35:262, 1989.
85. Laine L: Multipolar electrocoagulation in the treatment of peptic ulcers with nonbleeding visible vessels. A prospective, controlled trial. *Ann Intern Med* 110:510, 1989.
86. Chang-Chien CS et al: Different implications of stigmata of recent hemorrhage in gastric and duodenal ulcer. *Dig Dis Sci* 33:400, 1988.
87. Bornman PC et al: Importance of hypovolemic shock and endoscopic signs of predicting recurrent hemorrhage from peptic ulcer. A prospective evaluation. *Br Med J* 291:245, 1985.
88. Peterson WL et al: Routine early endoscopy in upper gastrointestinal bleeding. A randomized controlled trial. *N Engl J Med* 304:925, 1981.
89. Kovacs TUG, Jensen DM: Endoscopic control of gastrointestinal hemorrhage. *Annu Rev Med* 38:267, 1987.

90. Keppen M: Upper gastrointestinal malignancies in the elderly. *Clin Geriatr Med* 3:637, 1987.
91. Lundeqardh G et al: Stomach cancer after partial gastrectomy for benign ulcer disease. *N Engl J Med* 319:195, 1988.
92. DeKker W, op den Orth JO: Polyps of the stomach and duodenum. Significance and management. *Dig Dis* 10:199, 1992.
93. Bringaze WL et al: Early gastric cancer: 21 year experience. *Ann Surg* 204:103, 1986.
94. Green PHR et al: Early gastric cancer. *Gastroenterology* 81:247, 1981.
95. Dupont BJ et al: Adenocarcinoma of the stomach. Review of 1,497 cases. *Cancer* 41:941, 1978.
96. Myers WC et al: Adenocarcinoma of the stomach. Changing pattern over the last four decades. *Ann Surg* 205:1, 1987.
97. Nelson RS, Lanza FL: Benign and malignant tumors of the stomach (other than carcinoma), in Berk JE et al (eds): *Bockus Gastroenterology*. Philadelphia, Saunders, 1985, vol 2, p 1255.
98. Loehr WJ et al: Primary lymphoma of the gastrointestinal tract. A review of 100 cases. *Ann Surg* 170:232, 1969.
99. Lewin KJ et al: Lymphoma of the gastrointestinal tract. The study of 117 cases presenting with gastrointestinal disease. *Cancer* 42:693, 1978.
100. Spinelli P et al: Endoscopic diagnosis of gastric lymphoma. *Endoscopy* 12:211, 1980.
101. Weingrad DN et al: Primary gastrointestinal lymphoma: A 30 year review. *Cancer* 49:1258, 1982.

Chapter 61

HEPATOBILIARY DISORDERS

John H. Gilliam

THE EFFECT OF AGING ON THE LIVER

With aging, morphologic derangements in the liver are comparatively slight. With age there is a decline in weight of the entire liver and of each of its respective lobules. Grossly the liver is characterized by brown atrophy. The color change is due to the accumulation of lipofuscin granules in lysosomes, possibly due to food contaminants that the hepatocytes cannot clear. Similar changes occur in younger patients with severe malnutrition; therefore, brown atrophy is not specific to aging. However, hepatocytes are decreased in number and are larger with aging, while in malnutrition they are smaller but of normal number. The intake of higher levels of dietary protein may accelerate aging changes seen at autopsy.[1,2] The ability of the aged liver to regenerate after injury or partial resection is slightly delayed. Protein synthesis remains intact, but catabolism of synthesized proteins may be impaired. There is an increase in extrahepatocytic space and in intralobular collagen with aging, but collagen synthesis is reduced, and no functional impairment results.[1]

Functional derangements in the liver of an aged person in good health also are slight. Liver blood chemistry tests remain normal in elderly persons; when they are abnormal, liver disease is indicated. Data on changes in specific biochemical functions in aged hepatocytes are very conflicting but suggest no consistent alterations. There is reduced mitochondrial mass which, coupled with the reduced liver mass and mild alterations in hepatic blood flow, may result in altered drug metabolism.[1,3]

Jaundice in Elderly Persons

The majority of elderly patients with jaundice have biliary tract obstruction; malignant obstruction is more common than choledocholithiasis. Hepatitis is less common in elderly persons and when present is more likely to be drug-induced.[4–6]

Obstructive jaundice is to be suspected when there is a history of biliary colic, pruritis, and acholic stools, or if there is recurrent fluctuation in severity, stable deep jaundice, or progressive jaundice.[4] Helpful findings are a palpable gallbladder and a cholestatic liver blood test pattern, which suggest extrahepatic obstruction, most often pancreatic cancer in this instance. A history of epigastric and back pain exacerbated by eating might also lead the physician to suspect pancreatic cancer. It should be noted that marked elevation in aminotransferase levels is not specific for hepatocellular disease and may occur with extrahepatic biliary tract obstruction.[7,8] An unusual manifestation of severe obstructive jaundice is sinus node dysfunction. If significant sinus bradycardia develops in a patient with obstructive jaundice, electrocardiographic monitoring is necessary.[9]

Should the spleen be enlarged, an underlying myeloproliferative disorder, cirrhosis, hemolysis, or splenic vein thrombosis (from pancreatic cancer or pancreatitis) should be suspected. A spongy feel to an enlarged liver may indicate congestive heart failure. A pulsatile liver is indicative of tricuspid insufficiency. The presence of unconjugated hyperbilirubinemia is seen when pulmonary infarction is superimposed on congestive heart failure. Other causes of jaundice include hemolytic anemias, septicemia, lymphoreticular malignancies, transfusion reactions, and hypotension.

Evaluation of the elderly patient with jaundice should include an imaging study to exclude extrahepatic biliary obstruction. The most convenient and cost-effective approach is ultrasonic evaluation of the gallbladder, biliary tree, liver, and pancreas. Computed tomography (CT) is also an excellent diagnostic test. Endoscopic retrograde cholangiopancreatography (ERCP) or percutaneous cholangiography may be necessary. The reader is referred to several excellent reviews on the diagnostic approach in obstructive jaundice.[11–14] It is important to remember that imaging studies do not diagnose *all* cases correctly, since obstructive jaundice can present with normal-sized ducts and dilated ducts are not always pathologic. If cholestasis is present but there is no evidence of dilated bile ducts, a good medication history should be obtained and intrahepatic cholestasis considered. A liver biopsy then is warranted.

Drug-Induced Liver Injury

Since elderly patients have many medical diseases and drugs frequently are prescribed for them, it is surprising that adverse reactions to drugs are not more common among such patients. Still, adverse reactions of all types occur in approximately 15 percent of elderly patients over age 60, 20 percent over age 70,[15] and 24 percent over age 80.[16] Up to 20 percent of jaundice in elderly patients may be drug-induced.[17] It remains unclear whether liver aging alone explains this finding, since elderly patients are prescribed drugs more frequently than younger patients are and possess altered pharmacokinetics in extrahepatic drug metabolism as well.[18,19]

As classified by Zimmerman, drug reactions fall into three general types: hepatocellular, mixed hepatocellular, and cholestatic.[20] Hepatotoxicity occurs through varied mechanisms. Toxins which are cytotoxic are *direct* and those which cause subcellular organelle damage are *indirect* hepatotoxins. Some agents affect only certain hosts and are idiosyncratic, acting by allergic mechanisms or by formation of toxic metabolites. The reader is referred to Zimmerman's comprehensive textbook for a thorough review of this subject and could consult this reference when confronted with a patient with toxic liver injury.[20]

Whatever the drug responsible, it appears to be well documented that liver toxicity becomes more severe with advancing age. In one large series,[21] halothane hepatotoxicity was fatal in 3 of 14 patients (21 percent) under age 30 and in 27 of 37 (73 percent) over age 70. It is considered rare to recover from fulminant hepatic failure from any cause after age 50, although the mortality below this age remains distressingly high. Susceptibility to isoniasid hepatitis increases from 0.3 percent under age 34 to 2.3 percent at age 50 or older.[22]

Many commonly used drugs are potential liver toxins: antihypertensives (alpha methyldopa), antibiotics (nitrofurantoin, sulfonamides, ketoconazole, penicillin, erythromycin, and tetracycline), anticonvulsants (diphenylhydantoin), psychotropic drugs (chlorpromazine and imipramine), hormones (estrogens and anabolic steroids), oral hypoglycemics, nonsteroidal anti-inflammatory drugs, and anesthetic agents. The list of hepatotoxic drugs is extensive and has been tabulated.[23]

In most cases, drug toxicity stops upon recognition and withdrawal of the offending agent. Usually, drug hepatotoxicity is not severe, and survival depends on the nature and severity of the underlying lesion at the time the drug is stopped. Cholestasis can persist for months after phenothiazine[24] or imipramine[25] injury, however. Several drugs can cause chronic hepatitis and should be considered in the differential diagnosis in the elderly patient.[26]

Alcohol-Induced Liver Injury

Alcoholic hepatitis is an uncommon disease in elderly persons, but it does occur in occasional patients over age 60. The symptoms of anorexia, nausea, abdominal pain, and weight loss are similar to those of viral hepatitis. Physical finding of hepatomegaly, depleted nutritional stores, jaundice, and ascites are common.[27] The level of alanine aminotransferase (abbreviated ALT; formerly SGPT) in alcoholic hepatitis is one-half or less of the level of aspartate aminotransferase (abbreviated AST; formerly SGOT), in contrast to the respective levels of these enzymes in viral hepatitis. In severe cases fever and leukocytosis are more common. Specific markers associated with a poor survival include encephalopathy, azotemia, prolongation of prothrombin time, and leukocytosis.[28] Alcoholic hepatitis can occur with or without cirrhosis. Liver biopsy is diagnostic but is not necessary for diagnosis when the illness is severe and can be diagnosed clinically. Abstinence and attention to caloric intake are recommended for treatment.[29]

Particular mention should be made about acetaminophen use in alcoholic patients. Acetaminophen-induced hepatotoxicity can occur without overdose at therapeutic levels in alcoholic patients. At initial evaluation, a careful history should be obtained for any use of over-the-counter products that contain acetaminophen. However, the history can be notoriously unreliable, and an immediate acetaminophen blood level test should be obtained routinely at admission when the cause for acute liver deterioration in an alcoholic patient is unclear. Marked elevation of the levels of AST and lactate dehydrogenase discriminates acetaminophen-induced hepatitis from alcoholic hepatitis, and this finding at admission should lead to early oral treatment with acetylcysteine. As long as substantial blood levels of acetaminophen remain, therapy with acetylcysteine can be effective, since alcoholic patients frequently have more of a subacute than an acute overdose from this medicine.[30,31]

Viral Hepatitis

The older literature suggested that viral hepatitis is more common in elderly persons, and in one series acute fulminant hepatitis was more common in an elderly population.[32] However, these series preceded the current improvements in serodiagnostic testing. A recent report of 159 patients with viral hepatitis found 74 (47 percent) to be type B and 85 (53 percent) to be non-B; many of the latter had hepatitis A. Of interest, only 4 of the 159 (2.5 percent) were aged 65 or older.[33] This report suggests that viral hepatitis is infrequent in the elderly population.

Hepatitis B can cause severe acute hepatitis, particularly if delta agent hepatitis is superimposed. Elderly patients are more likely to have an acute fulminant course and to be sicker if chronic hepatitis ensues.[34]

Non-A, non-B (typically type C) hepatitis is most frequently transfusion- or hospital-acquired in the elderly patient. The identification of clones from the viral RNA genome of this parenterally transmitted agent has been a landmark.[35] Subsequent work from many laboratories has established that nearly all parenterally transmitted non-A, non-B viral hepatitis is due to this agent, now known as hepatitis C. This virus is a single-stranded RNA virus of approximately 10,000 base pairs, akin to the flaviviruses and pestiviruses. About 90 percent of the genome has been mapped, with molecular techniques, but the virus at this writing has not been identified conclusively with electron microscopy. Only 20 percent of the patients are icteric, and 50 percent of the patients develop chronic hepatitis after initial infection. Typically hepatitis C has low acute virulence, although fulminant hepatitis can occur. Most cases of hepatitis C are mildly asymptomatic and are discovered only by blood chemistry screening. Hepatitis C can progress to cirrhosis and, like hepatitis B, can cause hepatocellular carcinoma.[34]

Serologic diagnosis of acute hepatitis C is not possible, since it takes an average of 12 weeks for the standard antibody assay to become positive. In acute form, hepatitis C remains a diagnosis of exclusion. There is evidence now that the incidence of posttransfusion hepatitis *has* been reduced by the routine screening for and exclusion of blood donor products which are positive for hepatitis C antibody (and by autologous operative transfusion). One report estimates the risk of posttransfusion hepatitis as 3 per 10,000 units transfused.[36] The first-generation enzyme-linked immunosorbent assay (ELISA) antibody is being replaced with newer-generation assays that test for four regions on the genome. Presumably these newer assays will allow better and more specific blood screening. To date no report indicates clear efficacy of the use of alpha interferon in the setting of acute hepatitis C, although interferon has been investigated in this setting [in contrast to chronic hepatitis C infection (see below)].[37]

Chronic Hepatitis

As in younger patients, in older patients autoimmune chronic active hepatitis (CAH) must be distinguished from chronic viral hepatitis (B or C), chronic drug-induced hepatitis, and other chronic liver diseases. Primary biliary cirrhosis (PBC) and choledocholithiasis must be excluded. Serologic testing is useful. Characteristic findings in autoimmune CAH are elevated levels of globulins (polyclonal on protein electrophoresis and type IgG on immunoglobulin quantitation), a positive antinuclear antibody test, and a positive anti–smooth muscle antibody (antiactin antibody test).[38] Antimitochondrial antibody tests may be positive, but typically the antibody is of lower titer than that of antismooth muscle antibody. Also typical is elevation of transaminase levels to 5 to 15 times normal, and rouleaux may be seen on peripheral blood smear. Liver biopsy is diagnostic, revealing a lymphoplasmocytic portal infiltrate with piecemeal or bridging necrosis. Cirrhosis may be present. The intralobular bile ducts are normal.

Some patients present with an acute course; in these cases a 6-month history is not necessary for the diagnosis. Up to 20 percent of autoimmune CAH may present after age 60. Treatment may be more difficult in the elderly patient. Prednisone (or prednisolone) with or without azathioprine is considered standard therapy.[39]

Chronic hepatitis C is characterized by mild symptoms and aminotransferase levels that fluctuate from less than 10 times elevated to within the normal range. Often it is necessary to test liver enzymes on several occasions to assess hepatitis activity. When therapy is considered, liver biopsy must be done.

A major recent advance is proof of the efficacy of treating chronic hepatitis C with alpha interferon. A well-done prospective trial demonstrated that 3 million units subcutaneously, 3 days per week for 24 weeks, led to normalization of blood tests and suppression of hepatitis on biopsy in 46 percent of the patients treated.[40] However, the relapse rate is approximately 50 percent after therapy is withdrawn. Several reports suggest that longer therapy and the use of higher doses improve the remission rate and lower the relapse rate. This is an area of intense research interest and rapid change. It remains to be shown that therapy with alpha interferon can change the long-term outlook in hepatitis C, but early experience with antiviral therapy is quite encouraging.

Cirrhosis

Cirrhosis is a prevalent disease in the elderly population, being the fifth leading cause of death in men and the sixth in women ages 55 to 74.[28] It is not unusual for patients in this age group to present with complications of cirrhosis such as variceal bleeding, ascites, or encephalopathy. An evaluation to determine the cause of cirrhosis is indicated, and laboratory evaluation coupled with liver biopsy can be diagnostic. A few pertinent causes are discussed below.

Hemochromatosis becomes symptomatic in the fifth decade for men and often in the sixth decade for women. Patients classically present with lassitude, a metallic gray skin color, cirrhosis, diabetes, arthritis, impotence, and congestive heart failure. The serum ferritin level is markedly elevated, and transferrin saturation is high. Liver biopsy for routine stains and tissue iron quantitation is diagnostic. Aggressive phlebotomies yield dramatic therapeutic results, improving survival and the quality of life.[41] If the diagnosis can be established and treatment begun before cirrhosis develops, survival is normal. If cirrhosis is present at diagnosis, survival with treatment is diminished compared with patients without cirrhosis, and there is a late risk of developing hepatocellular carcinoma.[42]

PBC has 6:1 to 10:1 female preponderance and a mean age of onset of 50 to 55 years. Usually the onset is insidious. The most common symptom is pruritus, followed by fatigability, jaundice, osteopenia with vertebral fractures, xanthomas, and other features of advanced cirrhosis. Up to 50 percent of patients with PBC are asymptomatic, but development of jaundice is an ominous sign.[43] Antimitochondrial antibody is present in about 95 percent during the course of the disease, and IgM and IgG immunoglobulin levels are elevated. Plasmacytic portal infiltration and destruction of intralobular ductules are found. Cirrhosis may be absent or present in PBC, and granulomas may imply a more benign prognosis. Other autoimmune diseases may be present, including Sjögren's syndrome, thyroiditis, rheumatoid arthritis, and systemic lupus erythematosus. Treatment is supportive with supplemental calcium and vitamins A, D, E, and K. Cholestyramine may help the pruritus.[44] D-Penicillamine is now known not to be helpful,[45] but early reports show an effect from colchicine[46] or ursodiol.

Alpha-1-antitrypsin deficiency may present late in life and is a cause of "cryptogenic" cirrhosis.[47] Diagnosis is by confirmation of reduced blood levels of alpha-1 antitrypsin or by blood Pi typing. Paraaminosalicylic acid–positive diastase-resistant intracytoplasmic globules are seen in periportal hepatocytes on biopsy. No specific treatment is available.

The Liver in Circulatory Failure

In shock from any cause, ischemic liver injury can result. This may be mild, with marked elevation of levels of transaminases and lactic dehydrogenase, or may be severe with frank liver infarction, centrizonal necrosis, and subsequent death.[48] As with any organ system, the severity of the injury depends on the duration and degree of hypotension.

Postoperative jaundice may have many causes and is a true diagnostic challenge.[49] There is a very high incidence of jaundice (23 percent) after open heart surgery, classified as moderate or severe in 7 percent in one recent prospective report from Taiwan.[50]

Chronic congestive heart failure is well known to cause mild jaundice frequently, the level of bilirubin being greater than 2 mg/dl in one-third of cases; however, jaundice may be severe in heart failure when cardiac cirrhosis develops.[51,52] Occasionally, ischemic hepatitis from left heart failure alone may mimic viral hepatitis.[53] Treatment is directed at the underlying heart disease.

Pyogenic Liver Abscess and Sepsis

Most commonly, pyogenic liver abscess develops from biliary tract disease with ascending cholangitis.[54] In these cases, treatment is directed at relief of the biliary tract obstruction and coverage with broad-spectrum antibiotics. Solitary pyogenic abscesses develop from septicemia or intraabdominal infections. Treatment is by surgical or percutaneous drainage, combined with appropriate antibiotic coverage.[55] Patients present with right upper quadrant pain, fever, and jaundice. The diagnosis can be made with any imaging study, and liver abscess should be looked for aggressively when these symptoms are present.

Jaundice due to septicemia without liver abscess is uncommon. Hepatomegaly may be present. When liver biopsy is done, cholestasis is seen. Successful treatment of the underlying septicemia corrects the hepatic functional abnormalities.[56]

THE EFFECT OF AGING ON THE GALLBLADDER AND BILIARY TRACT

There are minimal effects of aging on the anatomy of the biliary tract. The common bile duct enlarges slightly, in association with narrowing of the sphincter of Oddi. There is little effect of aging on gallbladder size or contractility. However, gallstone disease is far more common in elderly patients, presumably attributable to the duration of bile supersaturation in older persons. Surgery has been the mainstay of treatment and remains so for gallbladder disease. However, many advances in endoscopic therapy, percutaneous therapy, lithotripsy, and dissolution therapy have revolutionized the current management of biliary tract stones. Further, benign and malignant strictures often can be managed without surgery. These newer techniques are appealing for older patients and will be discussed briefly below.

Cholelithiasis

The commonest abdominal operation performed in the geriatric population is cholecystectomy, and the total number of cholecystectomies performed annually in the United States has been estimated at 500,000. Most gallbladder diseases are due to gallstones. Gallstones are composed of cholesterol, calcium, bile salts, and protein, in various proportions. By gross appearance gallstones are commonly classified as cholesterol, black pigment, or brown pigment in type. The principal component of gallbladder stones is cholesterol, which is insoluble in water. Cholesterol is solubilized in bile by micelles, which are formed by phospholipids (mainly lecithin) and primary bile salts. The formation of gallstones is complex, but it is believed that cholesterol gallstones form after bile becomes supersaturated with cholesterol. Then nucleation factors lead to the coalescence of cholesterol crystals, followed by gallstone growth. When the gallbladder is healthy, it acidifies and concentrates gallbladder bile, and it contracts vigorously in response to meals. In the presence of gallbladder disease, these functions are impaired. Cholesterol gallstones are generally radiolucent and (calcified) pigment stones are radioopaque, but many stones are of mixed composition.[57]

Diagnosis of cholethiasis is by oral cholecystogram or abdominal ultrasound. Oral cholecystography is better in evaluating stone size and number and in evaluating gallbladder function (cystic duct patency and contractility of the gallbladder fundus). Abdominal ultrasound is better when patients are acutely ill and in some patients may detect disease missed on oral cholecystograms. In current practice, ultrasound has replaced oral cholecystography for all practical purposes. One comparative study estimates the sensitivity of ultrasound at 93 percent and of oral cholecystogram at 65 percent in detecting gallstones in patients coming to elective cholecystectomy. However, when adenomyosis and cholesterolosis are considered, the oral cholecystogram correctly diagnosed 87 percent of patients with gallbladder disease.[58]

Many patients have gallstones without abdominal pain. Gracie and Ransohoff studied a healthy population, predominantly men, and found the cumulative probability of developing biliary colic to be 10 percent by 5 years, 15 percent by 10 years, and 18 percent by 15 and 20 years, after initial detection by oral cholecystogram in asymptomatic persons.[59] There were no deaths from biliary tract disease. Later, they used decision analysis to argue against prophylactic cholecystectomy,[60] but their study has been criticized because it examines the course in a predominantly male nondiabetic population. The management of silent gallstones remains controversial, but prophylactic cholecystectomy in the elderly population is riskier than that in a younger population. Simple observation is not bad practice in elderly patients with asymptomatic gallstones.

Nonsurgical treatment of gallbladder stones in elderly patients with asymptomatic gallbladder stones is not recommended. In symptomatic patients with functioning gallbladders and solitary stones, extracorporeal shock wave lithotripsy fragmentation, combined with low-dose oral dissolution therapy, was investigated in the United States in the 1980s,[61] but there has not been a success in the United States to date. Immediate chemical dissolution with methyl *tert*-butyl ether remains experimental.[62]

Dissolution of gallstones by the administration of oral bile acids has been investigated thoroughly. After initial enthusiasm the National Cooperative Gallstone Study's final report on chenodeoxycholic acid therapy was disappointing. Complete dissolution occurred in only 13.5 percent of patients given "high-dose" chenodeoxycholic acid (750 mg/day) at 2 years. Chenodeoxycholic acid has the disadvantages of causing diarrhea in about 30 percent of patients; costliness; and causing some patients to develop lithocholate-induced hepatotoxicity. After several years of general disinterest, enthusiasm rose again for oral bile acid therapy after the release of ursodiol. Ursodiol does not cause diarrhea or lithocholate-induced hepatotoxicity.[63] Its maximum effectiveness is at 8 to 10 mg/kg, instead of 13 to 15 mg/kg (for chenodiol).[64] The two drugs may be used in low-dose combination.[65] However, the maximum complete stone dissolution from oral bile acid therapy likely will not exceed 29 percent at 1 year.[64] Oral bile acid therapy thus appears to have only a limited role, and it is not recommended currently except in unusual situations.

In summary, while promising, these recent developments in the nonsurgical management of silent gallstones have not been highly effective. Cholecystectomy remains the most effective treatment. As interest in alternative treatments waned, laparoscopic cholecystectomy was developed and appears to have earned a permanent place in gallstone management. The improved patient tolerance, acceptance, and shorter hospital stay have resulted in rapid popularity. Enthusiasm for laparoscopic cholecystectomy is a major reason for the decline in interest in nonsurgical alternatives. The procedure is not without risk, however, and the incidence of common duct injury is at least four times higher than with standard cholecystectomy. Because of the increased morbidity and higher degree of difficulty, the procedure is under some criticism; but it is here to stay, in the author's opinion.

Acute Cholecystitis

In contrast to silent gallstones, acute cholecystitis is a serious and often subtle disease in elderly patients. The mechanism in acute calculous cholecystitis is obstruction of the cystic duct by calculi. Following this, lipids permeate the gallbladder wall, the gallbladder dilates, mucosal blood flow decreases as pressure increases, and infection develops. It has been emphasized that the physical findings are subtle, peritoneal signs are seen in fewer than half, the temperature is frequently low-grade, and some patients have no abdominal tenderness. It is not uncommon for patients to present with a toxic appearance and disorientation, but without abdominal signs.[66] Leukocytosis is seen in only about two-thirds of this group. About 40 percent of patients felt to be acutely ill with cholecystitis have empyema, gangrene, or perforation, and 15 percent have subphrenic, subhepatic, or liver abscesses.[66] Although *Escherichia coli* and *Klebsiella* are the most common organisms, anaerobic infection is not uncommon, and cephalosporins alone provide inadequate coverage.

The mortality from surgery for acute cholecystitis in elderly patients is high. One large series reported a mortality of 9.8 percent in patients 65 or older.[67] Obviously, this reflects the severity of the disease and the associated diseases of this age group. There is no effective therapy other than surgery. In patients who are acutely ill, successful medical therapy usually is not possible. Stabilization efforts should be as expedient as possible, and surgery should not be delayed. The diagnosis is readily made if acute emphysematous cholecystitis is present[68] or if classic abdominal findings are present. If this is not the case, abdominal ultrasound and radionuclide scanning are the procedures of choice.

Acalculous cholecystitis is similar to acute calculous cholecystitis in clinical presentation but is most prevalent after surgery, trauma, or repeated transfusions. It may also occur after burns and prolonged total parenteral nutrition or in patients with cancer. Gangrenous gallbladders are found in 40 percent, and perforation is common.[69,70] The diagnosis may be difficult but should be suspected in the appropriate setting.

Choledocholithiasis

Typically, choledocholithiasis presents with obstructive jaundice as its principal manifestation. In elderly patients with intact gallbladders, one series found presenting symptoms to be pain and jaundice in 75.5 percent, pain alone in 18 percent, and jaundice alone in 6.5 percent.[71] Of this group, 27 percent had acute cholangitis and 18 percent had acute pancreatitis at presentation. In patients with acute cholecystitis, 10 to 30 percent may have choledocholithiasis. In one large endoscopic series, 53 percent of the patients with choledocholithiasis had intact gallbladders.[72] Surgical series have a greater proportion of patients with intact gallbladders, as would be expected.

The most common duct stones in patients with in situ gallbladders are cholesterol stones, but ductular pigment stones are quite common. In the elderly patient, the presence of periampullary duodenal diverticula is thought to be of pathogenic importance in the development of biliary calculi. Once patients have had cholecystectomy the incidence of recurrent choledocholithiasis is lower. However, if symptoms of pancreatobiliary disease later develop, calculi will be found in 87.5 percent of patients with periampullary diverticula but in only 39 percent of patients without periampullary diverticula.[73] It is also known that bile cultures for *E. coli* are more likely to be positive if duodenal diverticula are closer to the ampulla than if they are remotely located. This may be due to excessive beta glucuronidase in the bile of these patients, allowing easier formation of pigment stones.[74] The incidence of duodenal diverticula increases with age, though the explanation for this finding is not clear. It has not been possible to attribute specific manometric abnormalities of the sphincter of Oddi to the presence of diverticula.

The preferred treatment of choledocholithiasis in patients age 70 or older, or in patients of any age who are unfit for surgery, is endoscopic sphincterotomy (ES). Extensive worldwide experience with ES has changed management for many patients who previously required surgery. ES with complete clearance of all ductular stones, by Dormia basket or balloon catheters, can be achieved in at least 74 percent of all cases attempted; and ES alone can be achieved in almost all cases.[71,74] Complications occur in 5 to 10 percent of cases, and most frequently include cholangitis. Bleeding, pancreatitis, and perforation occur less frequently. Numerous series have shown mortality from ES to be less than 1.5 percent.[72,75–77] In the setting of acute suppurative cholangitis, the mortality is higher, but the mortality from ES remains significantly lower than surgery.[74] For patients with in situ gallbladders, the likelihood of subsequent need for cholecystectomy in long-term follow-up is on the order of 5 percent. An early risk of inducing acute cholecystitis with empyema of the gallbladder exists, particularly if clinically evident cholangitis is present at the time of ES.[71,72]

If ductular clearance is not achieved, surgical risk should be reappraised and the patient treated surgically. Surgery is warranted if acute cholecystitis is present. Mortality rates from operative common duct exploration vary but in patients over age 60 are reported to be 6 to 12 percent, and the rates are higher in emergency surgery.[78–81] Most operative deaths are cardiovascular in origin and reflect the significant associated diseases in the elderly population. Postoperative morbidity is higher in all series than that reported with successful endoscopic management. However, some elderly patients with unextractable ductular stones are quite fit for surgery and tolerate it well. Obviously, clinical judgment is extremely important in these decisions, as is surgical consultation.

Newer modalities are developing for those who cannot tolerate surgery. Percutaneous assistance for endoscopic procedures is a major advance. Extracorporeal shock wave lithotripsy and direct laser or electrohydraulic lithotripsy by choledochoscopy are exciting advances. It is becoming unusual in specialized centers for endoscopic, or at least nonsurgical, ductular stone clearance to fail in nonoperative candidates. Experience is still limited, and these specialized treatments are not available widely.

Adenocarcinoma of the Gallbladder

Although its incidence is low, adenocarcinoma of the gallbladder is seen in about 1 percent of cholecystectomy specimens and is more common in autopsy series. It is rare under age 50, and the peak incidence is in women in the sixth and seventh decades. The majority of cases (60 to 90 percent) are associated with gallstones, but a causal relationship has not been established. The tumor usually is not detected by imaging techniques and is diagnosed surgically. Western countries have reduced the mortality significantly, owing to widespread cholecystectomy in this age group. Since the tumor invades early, it is often diagnosed after obstructive jaundice develops from metastases to the porta hepatis.[82]

The best management of gallbladder cancer is surgical, unless obstructive jaundice is present. Then endoscopic or transhepatic palliation can be beneficial. Endoscopic stent placement can palliate the jaundice, reduce the frequency of cholangitis, and prolong survival.[83] If endoscopic stent placement cannot be achieved, or if cholangitis is not controlled after endoscopic therapy, percutaneous drain placement is necessary to prevent cholangitis. Percutaneous drains can be converted to internal-external drains or used to assist endoscopic stent placement. Regardless of the techniques used, palliative drainage is worthwhile and prolongs survival. Adenocarcinomas are not radiosensitive and respond poorly to chemotherapy. The overall 5-year survival for carcinoma of the gallbladder is 1 to 3 percent when unresectable and 10.6 percent when all disease is resectable.[84]

Adenocarcinoma of the Bile Ducts

Usually, malignant tumors of the bile ducts are adenocarcinomas. They occur with a peak incidence in patients in their early seventh decade, occur more commonly in men, and are less common than gallbladder carcinoma. These tumors are more commonly scirrhous, less commonly bulky, and may be multicentric in origin. Bile duct carcinomas are known to be associated with parasitic bile duct infestation in the Orient, and with thorotrast infusion, sclerosing cholangitis, and choledochal cysts. In the West bile duct carcinomas generally occur without a known predisposing cause. Biliary lithiasis is associated with this tumor, but a causal relationship is not established.

The prognosis is poor. The best treatment is surgical resection, and this is best achieved when the tumor involves the extrahepatic biliary tree and is resectable. Some tumors can be resected at the bifurcation, and stents can be placed surgically to decompress the intrahepatic biliary tree.[85] Palliation usually requires generous excision of the extrahepatic biliary tree and a choledochoenteric or hepaticodochoenteric anastomosis. Distal cholangiolar carcinomas can be managed by a pylorus-sparing Whipple procedure.

Secondary problems with bile duct obstruction and cholangitis are substantial and contribute to the morbidity and mortality from bile duct carcinomas. These tumors respond poorly to radiation therapy or chemotherapy. Unresectable bile duct carcinomas are treated by placement of endoscopic or percutaneous stents.[83,86]

REFERENCES

1. Popper H: Aging and the liver, in Popper H, Schaffner F (eds): *Progress in Liver Diseases.* New York, Grune & Stratton, 1986, vol 8, p 659.
2. Tauchi H, Sato T: Hepatic cells of the aged, in Kitani K (ed): *Liver and Aging.* Amsterdam, Elsevier/North Holland, 1978, p 3.
3. Greenblatt DJ et al: Drug disposition in old age. *N Engl J Med* 306:1081, 1982.
4. O'Brien GF, Tan CV: Jaundice in the geriatric patient. *Geriatrics* 25:114, 1970.
5. Huete-Armijo A, Exton-Smith AN: Causes and diagnosis of jaundice in the elderly. *Br Med J* 1:1113, 1962.
6. Naso F, Thompson CM: Hyperbilirubinemia in the patient past 50. *Geriatrics* 22:206, March 1967.
7. Patwardhan RV et al: Serum transaminase levels and cholescintigraphic abnormalities in acute biliary tract obstruction. *Arch Intern Med* 147:1249, 1987.
8. Ginsberg AL: Very high levels of SGOT and LDL in patients with extrahepatic biliary tract obstruction. *Am J Dig Dis* 15:803, 1970.
9. Bashour TT et al: Severe sinus node dysfunction in obstructive jaundice. *Ann Intern Med* 103:384, 1985.
10. Tandon BN et al: Bedside ultrasonography: A low-cost definitive diagnostic procedure in obstructive jaundice. *J Clin Gastroenterol* 9:353, 1987.
11. O'Connor KW et al: A blinded prospective study comparing four current noninvasive approaches in the differential diagnosis of medical versus surgical jaundice. *Gastroenterology* 94:1498, 1983.
12. Vennes JA, Bond JH: Approach to the jaundiced patient. *Gastroenterology* 84:1615, 1983.
13. Richter JM et al: Suspected obstructive jaundice: A decision analysis of diagnostic strategies. *Ann Intern Med* 99:46, 1983.
14. Scharschmidt BF et al: Current concepts in diagnosis: Approach to the patient with cholestatic jaundice. *N Engl J Med* 308:1515, 1983.
15. Hurwitz N: Predisposing factors in adverse reactions to drugs. *Br Med J* 1:536, 1969.
16. Seidl LG et al: Studies on the epidemiology of adverse drug reactions: III. Reactions in patients on a general medical service. *Bull Johns Hopkins Hospital* 119:299, 1966.
17. Eastwood HDH: Causes of jaundice in the elderly. *Gerontol Clin* 13:69, 1971.
18. Roberts J, Turner N: Pharmacodynamic basis for altered drug action in the elderly. *Clin Geriatr Med* 4(1):127, 1988.
19. Vestal RE: Drug use in the elderly: A review of problems and special considerations. *Drugs* 16:358, 1978.
20. Zimmerman HJ: *Hepatotoxicity: The Adverse Effects of Drugs and Other Chemicals on the Liver.* New York, Appleton-Century-Crofts, 1978.
21. Inman WHW, Mushin WW: Jaundice after repeated exposure to halothane. *Br Med J* 2:1455, 1978.
22. Mitchell JR et al: Isoniazid liver injury: Clinical spectrum, pathology, and probable pathogenesis. *Ann Intern Med* 84:181, 1976.
23. Ludwig J, Axelsen R: Drug effects on the liver: An updated tabular compilation of drugs and drug-related hepatic diseases. *Dig Dis Sci* 28:651, 1983.
24. Ishak KG, Irey NS: Hepatic injury associated with phenothiazines: Clinicopathologic and follow-up study of 36 patients. *Arch Pathol* 93:283, 1972.

25. Horst DA et al: Prolonged cholestasis and progressive hepatic fibrosis following imipramine therapy. *Gastroenterology* 79:550, 1980.
26. Maddrey WC, Boitnott JK: Drug-induced chronic liver disease. *Gastroenterology* 72:1348, 1977.
27. Lischner MW et al: Natural history of alcoholic hepatitis: I. The acute disease. *Am J Dig Dis* 16:481, 1971.
28. Galambos JT: *Cirrhosis.* Philadelphia, Saunders, 1979, Major Problems in Internal Medicine, vol 17.
29. Saunders JB: Alcoholic liver disease in the 1980's. *Br Med J* 287:1819, 1983.
30. Kaysen GA et al: Combined hepatic and renal injury in alcoholics during therapeutic use of acetaminophen. *Arch Intern Med* 145:2019, 1985.
31. Hall AH, Rumack BH: The treatment of acute acetaminophen poisoning. *J Intensive Care Med* 1:29, 1986.
32. Fenster LF: Viral hepatitis in the elderly: An analysis of 23 patients over 65 years of age. *Gastroenterology* 78:535, 1965.
33. Osmon DR et al: Viral hepatitis: A population-based study in Rochester, Minn, 1971–1980. *Arch Intern Med* 147:1235, 1987.
34. Koff RS, Galambos JT: Viral hepatitis, in Schiff L, Schiff ER (eds): *Diseases of the Liver,* 6th ed., Philadelphia, Lippincott, 1987, p 457.
35. Choo QL et al: Isolation of a cDNA clone derived from a blood-borne non-A, non-B viral hepatitis genome. *Science* 244:359, 1989.
36. Donahue JG et al: The declining risk of post-transfusion hepatitis C virus infection. *N Engl J Med* 327:369, 1992.
37. Viladomiu L et al: Interferon-alpha in acute posttransfusion hepatitis C: A randomized controlled trial. *Hepatology* 15:767, 1992.
38. Maddrey WC: Subdivisions of idiopathic autoimmune chronic active hepatitis. *Hepatology* 7:1372, 1987.
39. Sherlock S: *Diseases of the Liver and Biliary System,* 7th ed. Boston, Blackwell, 1985.
40. Davis GL et al: Treatment of chronic hepatitis C with recombinant interferon alfa: A multicenter randomized, controlled trial. *N Engl J Med* 321:1501, 1989.
41. Williams R et al: Venesection therapy in idiopathic hemochromatosis. *Q J Med* 38:1, 1969.
42. Niederan C et al: Survival and causes of death in cirrhotic and noncirrhotic patients with primary hemochromatosis. *N Engl J Med* 313:1256, 1985.
43. Kapelman B, Schaffner F: The natural history of primary biliary cirrhosis. *Semin Liver Dis* 1:273, 1981.
44. Kaplan MM: Primary biliary cirrhosis. *N Engl J Med* 316:521, 1987.
45. Dickson ER et al: Trial of penicillamine in advanced primary biliary cirrhosis. *N Engl J Med* 312:1011, 1985.
46. Kaplan MM et al: A prospective trial of colchicine for primary biliary cirrhosis. *N Engl J Med* 315:1448, 1986.
47. Rakela J et al: Late manifestation of chronic liver disease in adults with alpha-1-antitrypsin deficiency. *Dis Dig Sci* 32:1358, 1987.
48. de la Monte SM et al: Midzonal necrosis as a pattern of hepatocellular injury after shock. *Gastroenterology* 86:627, 1984.
49. Lamont JT, Isselbacher KJ: Current concepts: Postoperative jaundice. *N Engl J Med* 288:305, 1973.
50. Chu CM et al: Jaundice after open heart surgery: A prospective study. *Thorax* 39:52, 1984.
51. Sherlock S: The liver in heart failure: Relation of anatomical, functional and circulatory changes. *Br Heart J* 13:273, 1951.
52. Sherlock S: The liver in circulatory failure, in Schiff L, Schiff ER (eds): *Diseases of the Liver,* 6th ed. Philadelphia, Lippincott, 1987, p 1051.
53. Cohen JA, Kaplan MM: Left-sided heart failure presenting as hepatitis. *Gastroenterology* 74:583, 1978.
54. Rubin RH et al: Hepatic abscess: Changes in clinical, bacteriologic and therapeutic aspects. *Am J Med* 57:601, 1974.
55. McDonald MI et al: Single and multiple pyogenic liver abscesses: Natural history, diagnosis and treatment with emphasis on percutaneous drainage. *Medicine* 63:291, 1984.
56. Zimmerman HJ et al: Jaundice due to bacterial infection. *Gastroenterology* 77:362, 1979.
57. Schoenfield LJ, Marks JW: Formation and treatment of gallstones, in Schiff L, Schiff ER (eds): *Diseases of the Liver,* 6th ed. Philadelphia, Lippincott, 1987, p 1267.
58. Gelfand DW et al: Oral cholecystography vs. gallbladder sonography: A prospective, blinded reappraisal. *Am J Roentgenol* 151:69, 1988.
59. Gracie WA, Ransohoff DF: The natural history of silent gallstones. The innocent gallstone is not a myth. *N Engl J Med* 307:798, 1982.
60. Ransohoff DF et al: Prophylactic cholecystectomy or expectant management for silent gallstones. A decision analysis to assess survival. *Ann Intern Med* 99:199, 1983.
61. Sauerbruch T et al: Fragmentation of gallstones by extracorporeal shock waves. *N Engl J Med* 314:818, 1986.
62. Allen MJ et al: Rapid dissolution of gallstones by methyl tert-butyl ether. Preliminary observations. *N Engl J Med* 312:217, 1985.
63. Schoenfield LJ et al: Chenodiol (chenodeoxycholic acid) for dissolution of gallstones: the National Cooperative Gallstone Study. A controlled trial of efficacy and safety. *Ann Intern Med* 95:257, 1981.
64. Erlinger S et al: Franco-Belgian cooperative study of ursodeoxycholic acid in the medical dissolution of gallstones: A double-blind, randomized, dose-response study, and comparison with chenodeoxycholic acid. *Hepatology* 4:308, 1984.
65. Podda M et al: A combination of chenodeoxycholic acid and ursodeoxycholic acid is more effective than either alone in reducing biliary cholesterol saturation. *Hepatology* 2:334, 1982.
66. Morrow DJ et al: Acute cholecystitis in the elderly: A surgical emergency. *Arch Surg* 113:1149, 1978.
67. Glenn F: Surgical management of acute cholecystitis in patients 65 years of age or older. *Ann Surg* 193:56, 1981.
68. May RE, Strong R: Acute emphysematous cholecystitis. *Br J Surg* 58:453, 1971.
69. Glenn F, Becker CG: Acute acalculous cholecystitis: An increasing entity. *Ann Surg* 195:131, 1982.
70. Howard RJ: Acute acalculous cholecystitis. *Am J Surg* 141:194, 1981.
71. Davidson BR et al: Endoscopic sphincterotomy for common bile duct calculi in patients with gallbladder in situ considered unfit for surgery. *Gut* 29:114, 1988.

72. Escourrou J et al: Early and late complications after endoscopic sphincterotomy for biliary lithiasis with and without the gallbladder "in situ." *Gut* 25:598, 1984.
73. Lotveit T et al: Recurrent biliary calculi: Duodenal diverticula as a predisposing factor. *Ann Surg* 196:30, 1982.
74. Wurbs DFW: Calculus disease of the bile ducts, in MV Sivak Jr (ed): *Gastroenterologic Endoscopy*. Philadelphia, Saunders, 1987, p 652.
75. Safrany L: Duodenoscopic sphincterotomy and gallstone removal. *Gastroenterology* 72:338, 1977.
76. Siegel JH: Endoscopic papillotomy in the treatment of biliary tract disease. 258 procedures and results. *Dig Dis Sci* 26:1057, 1981.
77. Wurbs D: Endoscopic papillotomy. *Scand J Gastroenterol* 17(suppl 77):107, 1982.
78. Cotton PB: Endoscopic management of bile duct stones; (apples and oranges). *Gut* 25:587, 1984.
79. Sheridan WG et al: Morbidity and mortality of common bile duct exploration. *Br J Surg* 74:1095, 1987.
80. McSherry CK, Glenn F: The incidence and causes of death following surgery for nonmalignant biliary tract disease. *Ann Surg* 191:271, 1980.
81. Pitt HA et al: Factors affecting mortality in biliary tract surgery. *Am J Surg* 141:66, 1981.
82. Warren KW et al: Diseases of the gallbladder and bile ducts, in Schiff L, Schiff ER (eds): *Diseases of the Liver*, 6th ed. Philadelphia, Lippincott, 1987, p 1289.
83. Deviere J et al: Long-term follow-up of patients with hilar malignant stricture treated by endoscopic internal biliary drainage. *Gastrointest Endosc* 34:95, 1988.
84. Appelman RM et al: Long-term survival in carcinoma of the gallbladder. *Surg Gynecol Obstet* 117:459, 1963.
85. Cameron JL et al: Proximal bile duct tumors: Surgical management with silastic transhepatic biliary stents. *Ann Surg* 196:412, 1982.
86. Huibregtse K, Tytgat GN: Palliative treatment of obstructive jaundice by transpapillary introduction of large bore bile duct endoprosthesis: Experience in 45 patients. *Gut* 23:371, 1982.

ADDITIONAL READING

Brandt LJ: Pancreas, liver and gallbladder, in Rossman I (ed): *Clinical Geriatrics*. Philadelphia, Lippincott, 1986, p 302.

Chapter 62

PANCREATIC DISORDERS

John H. Gilliam

AGING AND THE PANCREAS

Healthy, elderly patients without pancreatic disease have normal pancreatic exocrine function. Gullo and coworkers found that 60 nonhospitalized elderly persons (mean age 78 years) had normal pancreatic exocrine function, as measured by the fluorescein dilaurate (pancreolauryl) test.[1] There was no difference in pancreatic function compared with a healthy control population (mean age 36 years). The study population was normal nutritionally, had no recognizable digestive diseases, and had no history of diabetes or alcoholism.[1] Secretin testing previously has shown no change in bicarbonate output with age, although men under 50 have a higher peak volume output than men over 50.[2] A further study, using continuous IV infusion of secretin and cerulein found elderly subjects able to secrete normal volumes of pancreatic juice, containing normal amounts of bicarbonate, trypsin, and chymotrypsin.[3] Although the literature is limited on this subject, these studies confirm the clinical impression that age per se does not affect pancreatic function.

However, there are some impressive morphologic alterations in the pancreas that occur with aging. Of patients over age 49, 79 percent were found at autopsy to have "adipose tissue invasion."[4] The degree of adipose tissue present correlated also with obesity, but not with sex. Atherosclerosis affecting the pancreatic vasculature is common, although pancreatic infarction is quite rare.[5] Dilation of acini and ductules is common in elderly persons and may be focal or quite diffuse.[4,6] In some elderly patients, ductular ectasia becomes cystic. Associated with these findings, periductular, intralobular, and perilobular fibrosis frequently occur.[7] The width of the main pancreatic duct on necropsy ductograms increased about 8 percent per decade in one study,[6] but others have had difficulty confirming this. With advanced age there is a tendency for the pancreas to lie in a lower craniocaudal position. Calcifications in surrounding arteries are common.

The era of endoscopic retrograde cholangiopancreatography (ERCP) has allowed extensive worldwide experience with pancreatic ductograms. It is clear that there is a wide range of normal in the size of the main pancreatic duct. The length of the pancreatic duct does not change with age.[8] However, there is variation in the degree of opacification of branches, the ease of acinar filling, and the course of the ducts. This variability of the normal pancreatic ductogram has caused endoscopists to have difficulties in avoiding false-positive diagnoses. Cotton found no correlation between duct width and age,[9] and he considered the cystic changes described by Kreel and Sandin to be rare.[6] More recently, the difficulty of interpreting pancreatic ductograms in elderly patients was reevaluated in an autopsy series. Six endoscopists were asked independently to grade ductograms obtained at autopsy without knowledge of the histologic findings. Of 69 human pancreata, none of which had pancreatitis, 81 percent were interpreted as showing chronic pancreatitis (37 percent minimal, 33 percent moderate, and 11 percent severe[7]). By correlating the ductograms with histologic findings and gross inspection, it was learned that the ductular changes seen were due to perilobular fibrosis. It was speculated that this developed because of intraductal epithelial hyperplasia. In summary, the morphologic pancreatic changes from aging may be striking. Experienced endoscopists must be aware of the difficulties in interpretations of ERCP findings and be cautious in diagnosing chronic pancreatitis in elderly patients.

ACUTE PANCREATITIS

In most patients independent of age, acute pancreatitis presents with abdominal pain, hyperamylasemia, abdominal tenderness, and nausea and/or vomiting. The pain is steady, lasts for hours, and often bores through to the back. Flexing the back in various positions may ease the pain somewhat. Acute pancreatitis may manifest as a very mild illness, with pain as the predominant symptom and with few abdominal signs. Alternatively, it can present as a fulminant illness, with shock, respiratory distress, renal failure, pericarditis, myoclonus or coma, hypocalcemia, leukocytosis, and fever. Most patients with acute pancreatitis fall between these two extremes.[10]

Often, the diagnosis is difficult. While hyperamylasemia is the rule, it is well known that hyperamylasemia is not specific for pancreatitis, since it may be present in burns, diabetic ketoacidosis, small bowel ischemia or obstruction, ovarian carcinomas, tubal pregnancy, macroamylasemia, and severe renal failure. Distinguishing acute pancreatitis from macroamylasemia is not problematic, since urine excretion of amylase is marked in acute pancreatitis and minimal in macroamylasemia. However, several of the other conditions listed above can cause an elevated amylase/creatinine clearance ratio. The early enthusiasm for the amylase/creatinine clearance ratio[11] as a specific diagnostic test has waned, after extensive experience has shown that the specificity is low.[12]

Much attention has been given to the development of other serodiagnostic tests which might be more specific than the serum amylase test. Lipase measurement is more specific than amylase measurement and is a useful, rapidly obtainable, ancillary test. Pancreatic isoamylase and trypsinogen assays have been employed, but they are not available in most emergency labs. Measurement of pancreatic isoamylase levels can be valuable in subacute situations, because elevation of the salivary amylase level can be excluding.[13] All these blood tests have been studied critically in an excellent study by Steinberg and coworkers.[14] Using confirmation by ultrasound, computed tomography, and/or laparotomy as the gold standard, the following data were obtained from a series of 39 patients. In diagnosing pancreatitis, sensitivities were as follows: amylase (Beckman), 94.9 percent; amylase (Phadebas), 94.9 percent; trypsinogen radioimmunoassay (RIA), 97.4 percent; lipase, 86.5 percent; and pancreatic isoamylase, 92.3 percent. Specificities were as follows: amylase (Beckman), 88.9 percent; amylase (Phadebas), 86.0 percent; trypsinogen RIA, 82.8 percent; lipase, 99.0 percent; and pancreatic isoamylase, 85.1 percent.[14] This is the best critical evaluation of these tests to date.

Imaging studies are important ancillary tests. Abdominal ultrasound can be very helpful and diagnostic. Its usefulness, however, can be impaired by ileus or obesity. Computed tomography is an excellent diagnostic test and obviates these problems. However, critically ill patients may not be able to withstand the procedure. An imaging study is indicated during treatment in acute pancreatitis to look for pseudocyst formation when resolution is delayed. Imaging may both underestimate and overestimate the diagnosis, and there remains no perfect gold standard.[15]

Criteria for evaluating the severity of acute pancreatitis have been established in several reports.[16–20] Age over 55 years is an independent variable associated with a higher mortality. Although there is no study of pancreatitis restricted to a geriatric population, it is clear that alcoholic pancreatitis occurs less frequently in an elderly than in a younger population, particularly de novo. Gallstones are found in 60 percent of nonalcoholic patients with pancreatitis.[20] Therefore, this is the major root cause of pancreatitis in the elderly population. Other important causes are drugs, hyperlipidemia, trauma, and pancreatic cancer.

Gallstone Pancreatitis

Commonly, gallstone passage into the common bile duct causes temporary obstruction at the papilla of Vater. When pancreatic secretions are blocked, pancreatitis results. Patients may present with mild or fulminant pancreatitis. Debate has been active regarding the appropriate timing of surgery for biliary pancreatitis, and the issue is controversial.[21] Kelly has recommended surgery within 72 hours, if the pancreatitis worsens, but found the best outcome with surgery delayed 5 to 7 days from onset.[22] There has been a shift to endoscopic sphincterotomy as recommended treatment, where available, after several centers have shown that ERCP does not worsen the pancreatitis. Sometimes, duodenoscopy confirms stone impaction at the ampulla. The first large series of patients treated by endoscopic sphincterotomy was by Classen and colleagues.[23] A later series by Safrany and Cotton confirmed the safety of endoscopic sphincterotomy in acute stone impaction with severe pancreatitis and found that improvement after successful treatment was often dramatic.[24] Endoscopic treatment of gallstone pancreatitis has not replaced surgery but has some definite advantages in very ill elderly patients. The risk of subsequent pancreatitis is diminished after endoscopic sphincterotomy. All experts in this area recommend definitive treatment, because recurrent pancreatitis occurs in over 30 percent if surgery or adequate endoscopic sphincterotomy is not performed.[21]

Hyperlipidemia and Pancreatitis

It is well recognized that chylomicronemia and hypertriglyceridemia are associated with recurrent acute pancreatitis. A low-fat diet can prevent further attacks of pancreatitis in this group.[25] Strict adherence to a low-fat diet and avoidance of nonselective beta-adrenergic blockers (which inhibit lipoprotein lipase) are mandatory. This unusual type of pancreatitis can be quite severe. More commonly, type IV hyperlipoproteinemia (hypertriglyceridemia without chylomicronemia) is seen transiently with attacks of acute pancreatitis, typically in alcoholic patients.[26] If serum is not obtained at admission, chylomicronemia can be missed, and patients may be misclassified as type IV.[27] It is best to restudy lipid profiles after resolution of the symptoms, if hyperlipoproteinemia is found. This form of pancreatitis is uncommon in elderly patients, particularly first-episode chylomicronemic pancreatitis, given the declining prevalence of alcohol abuse among older persons and the high probability of first episodes' having occurred earlier in those with genetically determined hypertriglyceridemia. However, such episodes can occur de novo among elderly patients with poorly controlled diabetes or among women with familial hypertriglyceridemia treated with estrogens (see Chap. 73).

Drugs and Pancreatitis

Pancreatitis appears to be definitely associated with the use of azathioprine, thiazides, sulfonamides, furosemide, estrogens (via hyperlipemia), and tetracycline.[28] A probable association exists with corticosteroid use (also possibly via secondary hypertriglyceridemia). Other possible associations exist but are suspect because the information is based largely on case reports. The reader is advised to consider drugs as a source of pancreatitis in the elderly patient, but the incidence is low. This subject has been well reviewed.[28,29]

General Considerations

The differential diagnosis of acute pancreatitis in the elderly patient certainly includes pancreatic carcinoma, which may present as pancreatitis. This is discussed in a later section.

Management of the acute attack is well standardized, regardless of cause. Patients are given intravenous fluids aggressively and are kept fasting, or are given nasogastric suction if the illness is severe. Attention to levels of serum electrolytes, calcium, and magnesium is mandatory. Pulmonary, renal, and central nervous system complications need additional attention. Antibiotics (unless infection is clearly present), aprotonin, and somatostatin are not helpful. Surgery is to be avoided, except in gallstone pancreatitis.[10,30,31]

CHRONIC PANCREATITIS

Most often, chronic pancreatitis is due to alcoholism. Therefore, the incidence of chronic pancreatitis in the elderly population is low, since most alcoholic patients do not live to reach geriatric age. Only celiac disease is a commoner cause of steatorrhea in patients aged over 65.[32] Gallstones cause acute, relapsing pancreatitis, but chronic pancreatitis can result from traumatic, idiopathic, and familial pancreatitis.

Steatorrhea is a hallmark symptom but does not occur unless pancreatic lipase excretion is 10 percent or less of normal output.[33] Steatorrhea *can* develop acutely, along with pain, from pancreatic cancer. Therefore, one should use caution in ascribing steatorrhea to chronic pancreatitis in the elderly patient, when the diagnosis is not of long standing or is not clear cut. Pain is a typical symptom of chronic pancreatitis, particularly in alcoholic patients, but certainly is not a required symptom for the diagnosis. Often diabetes due to chronic pancreatitis is brittle, because there is a failure also of glucagon secretion, rendering patients more susceptible to recurrent hypoglycemic attacks when treated with insulin. Nevertheless, insulin is the preferred treatment for diabetes due to chronic pancreatitis, and oral hypoglycemics generally are ineffective.

Pancreatic exocrine function can be evaluated by several methods. The standard test is the 72-hour stool fat collection, which should be obtained on an outpatient basis with the patient eating regular meals. While this test is not popular with patients or physicians, it remains the gold standard for defining steatorrhea. Considerable effort has been made to find other, more acceptable tests. Promising results are reported from the measurement of serum trypsin–like immunoreactivity[34] and the bentiromide test,[35] but these are used infrequently.

Pancreatic enzyme replacement is the treatment for steatorrhea due to pancreatic insufficiency. Several preparations are available, and the most potent ones are especially effective. Their effectiveness can be enhanced by the simultaneous administration of sodium bicarbonate or cimetidine, since lipase can be permanently inactivated below pH 4. There are variations in patient tolerance, and the "best" preparation to use is the one each individual patient will tolerate.[10,36]

PANCREATIC CANCER

There is no doubt that pancreatic cancer is common, and the incidence is increasing. In men, this is the fourth commonest cause of cancer deaths, and in women, the fifth most common. Three percent of cancers and 5 percent of deaths from cancer in the United States are due to this devastating malignancy.[37] Carcinoma of the pancreas accounts for 22 percent of deaths from gastrointestinal cancers in the United States.[38] Most patients die within 6 months of the diagnosis of pancreatic cancer, the 1-year survival is less than 20 percent, and the 5-year survival is 3 percent.[38,39] There is some new information about the epidemiology and risk factors. There is a male/female ratio of 1.3 : 1, with a higher incidence in black men compared with white men. Cigarette smoking (relative risk ≥ 1.5), prior peptic ulcer surgery (relative risk increased 15 to 20 times), a high-fat and/or high-protein diet, diabetes, and exposure to toxins such as gasoline derivatives all increase the risk of pancreatic cancer. The earlier concern about coffee consumption as a risk factor has not been confirmed by other investigators.[40]

Despite intense interest in aggressive therapies, we have altered the course of this disease but little in the last several decades. Pancreatic cancer remains a devastating malignancy. One problem is the failure to diagnose the disease at an early, resectable stage. Although two-thirds of these malignancies are in the head of the pancreas, obstructive jaundice develops when the disease is not curable. There are no early symptoms. Aggressive use of abdominal ultrasound and computed tomography has not led to earlier diagnosis. The population developing pancreatic cancer is not being diagnosed any earlier than they were before the era of imaging studies.

Frequently patients present with painless obstructive jaundice, often with a palpable gallbladder (Courvoisier's sign). It is not uncommon for a patient to present with constant, boring, epigastric pain, exacerbated by meals, which may radiate straight through to the back. Anorexia, weight loss, and depression are frequent presenting symptoms. Depression is such a well-known presenting finding that unexplained depression in an elderly patient without an antecedent history mandates a search for pancreatic cancer. A previously stable diabetic patient whose diabetes becomes brittle without explanation may have developed pancreatic cancer.

There are numerous ways to diagnose pancreatic cancer. Perhaps the best initial study is computerized axial tomography, which has a sensitivity of 94 percent, but a specificity of only 60 percent.[41] Other useful modalities include celiac angiography, ERCP, ultrasound, and exploratory laparotomy.[41,42] A major advance in diagnosis is the development of Chiba needle aspiration biopsy, guided by ultrasound or computerized axial tomography, which has improved the specificity of imaging techniques. Despite concern about contamination of the needle tract with tumor cells, this procedure definitely is an advance.[40] Also, there is interest in the blood test CA 19-9,[43] which appears to have very good sensitivity and specificity for the diagnosis of pancreatic cancer. However, CA 19-9 may be normal in early pancreatic cancer, and its role as a screening test is quite limited. The ratio of plasma testosterone to dihydrotestosterone, normally around 10, falls below 5 in 70 percent of men with pancreatic cancer, and this ratio has been shown to be more specific for pancreatic cancer than CA 19-9.[40] Unfortunately, we remain far from having a reliable blood test for early diagnosis of this malignancy.

Therapy of pancreatic cancer remains problematic and ineffective. Surgery does not prolong survival, but as a palliative measure it is considerably more effective if the disease is ampullary carcinoma rather than pancreatic carcinoma. ERCP provides a definite advance in staging, should the disease appear to be localized by CT scanning. Direct visualization of the ampulla with biopsy and brush cytology of the pancreatic duct can help differentiate ampullary cancer from pancreatic cancer. Survival after resection of ampullary cancer is more favorable. Surgery can be useful to perform choledochoenterostomy, gastroenterostomy, and occasionally a diverting pancreaticojejunostomy. Only occasionally is surgery needed these days to establish the diagnosis. Increasingly, it is possible to place endoscopic or percutaneous stents to alleviate obstructive jaundice when the disease is deemed unresectable. One modification worthy of more experience is the practice of using laparoscopy prior to planned resection to look for liver, peritoneal, or omental metastases missed on preoperative evaluation. Despite the dismal general prognosis, there is evidence of improved survival after resection in carefully selected patients.[40] Chemotherapy and radiotherapy have been disappointing in this disease.

REFERENCES

1. Gullo L et al: Aging and exocrine pancreatic function. *J Am Geriatr Soc* 34:790, 1986.
2. Rosenberg IR et al: The effect of age and sex upon human pancreatic secretion of fluid and bicarbonate. *Gastroenterology* 50:191, 1966.
3. Gullo L et al: Exocrine pancreatic function in the elderly. *Gerontology* 29:407, 1983.
4. Wallace SA, Ashworth CT: Early degenerative lesions of the pancreas. *Tex St J Med* 37:584, 1942.
5. McKay JW et al: Infarcts of the pancreas. *Gastroenterology* 35:256, 1958.
6. Kreel L, Sandin B: Changes in pancreatic morphology associated with aging. *Gut* 14:962, 1973.
7. Schmitz-Moormann P et al: Comparative radiological and morphological study of human pancreas. Pancreatitis-like changes in post-mortem ductograms and their morphological pattern. Possible implication for ERCP. *Gut* 26:406, 1985.
8. Kasugai T et al: Endoscopic pancreatography: I. The normal endoscopic pancreatocholangiogram. *Gastroenterology* 63:217, 1972.
9. Cotton PB: The normal endoscopic pancreatogram. *Endoscopy* 6:65, 1974.
10. Banks PA: *Pancreatitis*. New York, Plenum, 1979.
11. Warshaw AI, Fuller AF: Specificity of increased renal clearance of amylase in diagnosis of acute pancreatitis. *N Engl J Med* 292:325, 1975.
12. Levitt MD, Johnson SG: Is the C_{am}/C_{cr} ratio of value for the diagnosis of pancreatitis? *Gastroenterology* 75:118, 1978.
13. Moossa AR: Diagnostic tests and procedures in acute pancreatitis. *N Engl J Med* 311:639, 1984.
14. Steinberg WM et al: Diagnostic assays in acute pancreatitis: A study of sensitivity and specificity. *Ann Intern Med* 102:576, 1985.
15. Spechler SJ: How much can we know about acute pancreatitis? *Ann Intern Med* 102:704, 1985.
16. Ranson JHC et al: Prognostic signs and the role of operative management in acute pancreatitis. *Surg Gynecol Obstet* 139:69, 1974.
17. Blamey SL et al: Prognostic factors in acute pancreatitis. *Gut* 25:1340, 1984.

18. Williamson RCN: Early assessment of severity in acute pancreatitis. *Gut* 25:1331, 1984.
19. Corfield AP et al: Prediction of severity in acute pancreatitis: Prospective comparison of three prognostic indices. *Lancet* 2:403, 1985.
20. Ranson JHC: Etiological and prognostic factors in human acute pancreatitis: A review. *Am J Gastroenterol* 77:633, 1982.
21. Ranson JHC: The timing of biliary surgery in acute pancreatitis. *Ann Surg* 189:654, 1979.
22. Kelly TR: Gallstone pancreatitis: The timing of surgery. *Surgery* 88:345, 1980.
23. Classen M et al: Pancreatitis—An indication for endoscopic papillotomy? *Endoscopy* 10:223, 1978.
24. Safrany L, Cotton PB: A preliminary report: Urgent duodenoscopic sphincterotomy for acute gallstone pancreatitis. *Surgery* 89:424, 1981.
25. Farmer RG et al: Hyperlipoproteinemia and pancreatitis. *Am J Med* 54:161, 1973.
26. Buck A et al: Hyperlipidemia and pancreatitis. *World J Surg* 4:307, 1980.
27. Cameron JL, Margolis S: Invited commentary. *World J Surg* 4:312, 1980.
28. Mallory A, Kern F Jr: Drug-induced pancreatitis: A critical review. *Gastroenterology* 78:813, 1980.
29. Nakashima Y, Howard JM: Drug-induced acute pancreatitis. *Surg Gynecol Obstet* 145:105, 1977.
30. Geokas MC et al: Acute pancreatitis. *Ann Intern Med* 103:86, 1985.
31. Soergel KH: Medical treatment of acute pancreatitis: What is the evidence? *Gastroenterology* 74:620, 1978.
32. Price HL et al: Steatorrhea in the elderly. *Br Med J* 1:1582, 1977.
33. DiMagno EP et al: Relations between pancreatic enzyme outputs and malabsorption in severe pancreatic insufficiency. *N Engl J Med* 288:813, 1973.
34. Jacobsen DG et al: Trypsin-like immunoreactivity as a test for pancreatic insufficiency. *N Engl J Med* 310:1307, 1984.
35. Toskes PP: Bentiromide as a test of exocrine pancreatic function in adult patients with pancreatic exocrine insufficiency: Determination of appropriate dose and urinary collection interval. *Gastroenterology* 85:565, 1983.
36. Regan PT et al: Comparative effects of antacids, cimetidine and enteric coating on the therapeutic response to oral enzymes in severe pancreatic insufficiency. *N Engl J Med* 297:854, 1977.
37. Hermann RE, Cooperman AM: Current concepts in cancer: Cancer of the pancreas. *N Engl J Med* 301:482, 1979.
38. American Cancer Society: *Cancer Facts and Figures 1991*. Atlanta, American Cancer Society, 1991.
39. National Cancer Institute: *Annual Cancer Statistics Review 1973–1988*. NIH publication 91-2789. Bethesda, MD, Department of Health and Human Services, 1991.
40. Warshaw AL, Castillo CF: Pancreatic carcinoma. *N Engl J Med* 326:455, 1992.
41. Fitzgerald PJ et al: The value of diagnostic aids in detecting pancreas cancer. *Cancer* 41:868, 1978.
42. DiMagno EP et al: A prospective comparison of current diagnostic tests for pancreatic cancer. *N Engl J Med* 297:737, 1977.
43. Steinberg W: The clinical utility of the CA 19-9 tumor-associated antigen. *Am J Gastroenterol* 85:350, 1990.

Chapter 63

COLONIC DISORDERS

Lawrence J. Cheskin and Marvin M. Schuster

A number of colonic disorders are of particular importance in the elderly patient because of both marked age-associated increases in prevalence and differences in presentation and prognosis between young and old patients with the same disease. Some of these disorders are discussed elsewhere, i.e., fecal incontinence (Chap. 113), constipation (Chap. 116), and diarrhea and inflammatory bowel disease (Chap. 117).

This chapter will focus on two diseases of major importance in developed countries: diverticular disease and carcinoma of the colorectum. While these are obviously quite different disorders which happen to affect the same organ, they are epidemiologically linked. In addition, both diseases show an age-associated increase in prevalence, most strikingly for diverticular disease. Both are more common in Westernized countries, and there is some evidence that this is because of dietary differences, in particular intake of dietary fiber, which is low in areas with a high incidence of these diseases.

DIVERTICULAR DISEASE

The terminology used for related conditions is widely misunderstood. *Diverticular disease* refers to the entire spectrum of manifestations described in this condition. *Diverticulosis* refers simply to the anatomic presence of colonic diverticula, without presuming that there are any symptoms associated with this finding. *Diverticulitis* refers to an inflammatory condition which involves one or more colonic diverticula and is almost always symptomatic. *Painful diverticular disease* refers to symptomatic diverticulosis in the absence of evidence of diverticular inflammation.

Epidemiology and Pathogenesis

The prevalence of colonic diverticula is strongly correlated with advancing age and is about equally prevalent in men and women of a given age. Diverticula are uncommon before the age of 40 (less than 5 to 10 percent prevalence) and increase to over 50 percent prevalence after the age of 70.[1] It has also been found that the number of diverticula per patient is greater in older patients.[2]

As noted, diverticular disease is seen almost exclusively in Westernized countries. It has been postulated that differences in diet, in particular intake of dietary fiber, contribute to these differences in prevalence.[3,4] Evidence in support of this hypothesis includes the following:

1. Diverticular disease was virtually unknown before 1900; its initial description was coincident with the start of milling, which removes two-thirds of the fiber content of flour. In the United States, crude fiber intake fell by 28 percent from 1909 to 1975.[5]
2. Vegetarians have a much lower prevalence of diverticular disease than nonvegetarians.[6]
3. Dietary fiber is lower among both vegetarians and nonvegetarians who have diverticular disease than among those who do not have diverticular disease.[7]
4. Animal studies show that a lifelong low-fiber diet, but not a high-fiber diet, is associated with the formation of diverticula.[8]

While the association of low dietary fiber and diverticular disease is well established, the mechanism is less clear. It is known that there are higher levels of motility and intraluminal pressure in colonic segments which bear diverticula than in normal segments, particularly in response to meals or cholinergic stimuli.[9] These areas of high pressure are associated with hypertrophy of circular muscle (myochosis) and possibly the formation of diverticula, since biophysical law dictates that narrowing of the lumen of a closed tube will result in an inversely proportional increase in intraluminal pressure. It is not known why abnormalities in colonic motility and muscle hypertrophy exist in diverticular disease or why there is such a striking correlation with increasing age. The increase in collagen[10] or elastin[11] seen in the aging colon may play a role here, leading to shortening and narrowing of the colon and higher intraluminal pressures.

Diverticular disease is usually seen with multiple rather than single diverticula. In fact, diverticular lesions are herniations of the mucosa through gaps in the muscular layers, often at points of entry of blood vessels. Two areas are most susceptible to herniation. The first is between the taenia coli, longitudinal gatherings of muscle which are present throughout the colon but not in the rectum or appendix (locations which almost never develop diverticula). The second area of susceptibility is in the narrow bands of connective tissue between rings of circular muscle. Seventy-five percent of all patients with diverticula have them exclusively in the sigmoid colon, and the sigmoid bears diverticula in over 90 percent of all cases of diverticulosis. It is thought that the narrow caliber of the sigmoid results in higher intraluminal pressure and hence a greater risk of herniation. Diverticula occur with decreasing frequency as one moves proximally in the colon, though they occur more frequently in the right colon in Asian populations.[12]

Clinical Features

As noted, there is a wide range of clinical presentation. Perhaps 80 to 85 percent of diverticulosis never presents clinically, either because it is entirely asymptomatic or because the symptoms are mild and infrequent and insufficient to cause the patient to seek medical attention. Symptomatic disease presents either as painful diverticular disease (75 percent) or as diverticulitis or hemorrhage (25 percent). In most cases which become symptomatic, the anatomic abnormality of diverticulosis is present several years before the onset of symptoms. There are some cases, however, in which characteristic symptoms (left lower quadrant pain, often in the setting of constipation) precede anatomic disease.[13] In these cases barium enema examination will often reveal saw-toothed spasm and thickening of the muscular wall of the colon, called myochosis. This is considered a prediverticular condition.

Symptomatic Diverticular Disease

Painful or symptomatic diverticular disease presents as attacks of colicky or steady left-lower-quadrant abdominal pain, usually exacerbated after meals and improved by bowel movement or passage of flatus. Alteration in bowel habit, more often constipation than diarrhea or alternating constipation and diarrhea, is seen in 46 to 63 percent of cases.[2,14] Physical examination of the abdomen may reveal a tender loop of sigmoid colon in the left lower quadrant, but the exam is often unremarkable. The presence of a fever or elevated blood leukocyte count or signs of peritonitis point toward an attack not of painful diverticular disease but to the more serious inflammatory condition, diverticulitis. Although it is tempting to conclude that the elderly patient with symptoms consistent with painful diverticular disease and radiographic or endoscopic proof of the presence of diverticula is indeed suffering from painful diverticular disease, this conclusion is not necessarily warranted. The extraordinarily high prevalence of diverticular anatomy means that discovering diverticula adds little to your diagnostic certainty. Of special note, more than half of the elderly patients with abdominal pain due to advanced carcinoma of the colon also have diverticula.

Diverticulitis

Diverticulitis, inflammation of one or more diverticula and pericolic tissues, is thought to develop when perforation of one or more diverticula occurs. These perforations may be microscopic or macroscopic. The perforation is the result of persistent high pressures intraluminally with or without a superimposed process of any etiology which weakens the wall of the diverticula. Diverticulitis is the most common complication of diverticulosis. It increases in incidence with age and the duration of the prerequisite diverticulosis. This complication of diverticulosis is also more common in those individuals with the highest number of diverticula. Recent retrospective studies have also found an increased incidence of complications of diverticular disease in patients chronically taking nonsteroidal anti-inflammatory drugs.[15–17] The perforated diverticula of diverticulitis are almost always located in the sigmoid colon. When macroscopic perforations occur, abscesses form between the colon and neighboring tissues, with accompanying scarring and granulation tissue as healing occurs. Thus, fistulas may form to the bladder, vagina (especially posthysterectomy), small bowel, or skin. Rarely, free perforation into the peritoneal cavity occurs, and the patient presents with a surgical abdomen.[14] Diverticular abscesses have a variable natural history: they may resolve spontaneously, either by draining back into the colonic lumen or by becoming walled off and healing, or they may enlarge, sometimes to the point of requiring surgical intervention.

Classically, the pain of acute diverticulitis is severe, persistent, and abrupt in onset; it increases in severity with time, with localization to the left lower quadrant; and it is accompanied by a variable amount of anorexia, nausea, and/or vomiting. Altered bowel function is common, more often constipation than diarrhea, and sometimes alternating constipation and diarrhea. Urinary frequency, dysuria, or abdominal pain aggravated by micturition may indicate involvement of the bladder in the inflammatory process or simply diverticulitis contiguous to the urinary tract. This may lead to the development of a colovesical fistula, often marked by symptoms of pneumaturia or fecaluria. Fever with or without chills is usually present and is sometimes the presenting complaint.

On physical examination, localized tenderness is usually present in the left lower quadrant, although occasionally suprapubic or right-lower-quadrant signs predominate and may be mistaken for acute appendicitis.

The abdomen is often distended, tympanitic to percussion, with the bowel sounds diminished. A localized tender mass may be felt at the site of inflammation. Signs of generalized peritonitis are rare unless free perforation has occurred, though the psoas and/or obturator signs may be positive and there may be some rebound tenderness locally. About a quarter of patients with diverticulitis will have rectal bleeding, usually occult. Thus carcinoma of the rectum or colon should be ruled out as well as inflammatory or ischemic bowel disease. A leukocytosis is almost invariably present, frequently with a shift to more primitive forms. The urine sediment may reveal white or red blood cells when the bladder or ureter is involved in the inflammatory process.

One must be aware that the classical presentation of acute diverticulitis described above may be altered in the elderly patient. In particular, the symptoms and signs are often less striking. For example, fever may be absent, the abdominal examination may not show impressive tenderness, there may be no mass felt, and the pain may not be very severe. None of these negative findings should lead one to strike diverticulitis from the differential diagnosis of the elderly patient with an acute abdominal or pelvic complaint, especially when colonic diverticula are known to be present. Even when the presentation is more typical of acute diverticulitis, the severity of the attack should not be underestimated when the symptoms are mild or the leukocytosis unimpressive. In older patients, the total picture may be muted even when the disease is quite severe. It is prudent to examine such patients carefully over a period of days so that a sudden worsening of the patient's condition is detected early.

The diagnosis is made largely on clinical grounds, but some auxiliary testing is helpful. Flat and upright (or lateral decubitus) abdominal radiographs may show evidence of adynamic ileus or, less commonly, mechanical obstruction. The location and extent of the inflammatory mass may be revealed by its effect on adjoining organs. Occasionally, air in the bladder or free in the abdomen will point to colovesical fistula or free perforation, respectively. Because diverticulitis is usually a clinical diagnosis and shares presenting features with several other diseases of the colorectum—notably carcinoma, inflammatory bowel disease, and ischemic colitis—we recommend that a sigmoidoscopy be performed early. A flexible sigmoidoscopy performed without vigorous bowel preparation will help rule out these other diseases, as well as show whether there are diverticula present in the sigmoid. Air insufflation during the procedure is kept to a minimum to avoid worsening or causing perforation. It is probably best not to advance the instrument into diverticula-containing areas until the patient's condition has improved and several weeks have passed to allow for healing of the acute inflammation. At that point, either a barium enema or a full colonoscopy should be performed to examine the remainder of the colon, in particular to rule out carcinoma proximal to the rectosigmoid region. Radiographic findings in diverticulitis, besides diverticula, may include confined extravasation of contrast material outside of the bowel through a perforated diverticulum, intraluminal abscess cavities, fistulas, or a mass effect on the outline of the bowel from an inflammatory focus. Local colonic spasm or thickening of the wall may be seen, but, as an isolated finding, is not evidence for diverticulitis. Computed tomography (CT) of the abdomen can be very useful in making a diagnosis of diverticulitis, since it is excellent at imaging the pericolonic structures where diverticular abcesses reside.[18] It is rapidly replacing other radiographic and endoscopic studies for the tentative diagnosis of diverticulitis in the acute setting and can be especially useful in following patients who are not responding to conservative medical management and who may require operative intervention.[19]

Treatment in most cases of suspected acute diverticulitis requires hospitalization, especially in the elderly patient who has multiple medical problems or is debilitated. Conservative therapy should be tried first. The bowel and the patient should be put to rest, with intravenous hydration and broad-spectrum antibiotics to cover gram-positive cocci and both aerobic and anaerobic gram-negative gut flora. A common antibiotic regimen is ampicillin and metronidazole or gentamicin. In selected mild cases, outpatient treatment with an oral agent like tetracycline can be tried if there is minimal or no fever or leukocytosis. Although at least three-quarters of patients will respond to conservative medical management, it is prudent to obtain a surgical consultation on admission to the hospital so that, should it become necessary, surgery can be performed expeditiously. The patient should be followed closely, and signs of worsening inflammation or lack of response to treatment should be considered as indications for excision of the inflamed segment of the colon. Analgesics may be used, but they should be administered cautiously and with frequent clinical monitoring, as they may further mask the symptoms of deterioration in the elderly patient. Clinical improvement is usually seen in 3 to 10 days if the patient is going to respond to medical treatment. If the response is favorable, the diet can be advanced over a few days to a normal diet. In fact, it is probably safe to allow a clear liquid diet from the start of treatment if there are no signs of obstruction, such as abdominal distension or nausea. For those patients who respond to medical treatment, a recurrence rate of 25 percent can be expected, most of which will occur in the first 5 years.[20] There is probably no role for prophylactic hemicolectomy after recovery from an attack of acute diverticulitis which has responded to medical management. A fiber supplement and/or a high-fiber diet is usually recommended for patients who have recovered from an attack of acute diverticulitis. For those patients who do not respond to medical treatment, especially with spreading peritonitis, urgent resection is indicated. In younger patients in whom peritoneal contamination is slight or contained in a small abscess, resection with primary anastomosis is feasible. For most elderly patients, however, a two-stage procedure is necessary: the first a resection with diverting colostomy proximal to the resection; the second a takedown of the colostomy with reestablishment of intestinal continuity. In selected cases, preoperative percutaneous drainage of an isolated diverticular abscess may allow sufficient healing for a one-stage operation to become feasible, resulting in lower operative mortality.[21,22]

Bleeding

Bleeding from diverticula is the most common cause of major lower gastrointestinal tract hemorrhage in the elderly,[23] followed closely by bleeding from angiodysplasias. Some 10 to 25 percent of patients with diverticular disease will at some point have bleeding through the rectum; 3 to 5 percent will have severe hemorrhage requiring transfusions[24] rather than occult bleeding. It must be borne in mind that rectal bleeding in a patient with known diverticular disease is not necessarily related to the diverticula. Such patients may be bleeding from angiodysplastic or neoplastic lesions, hemorrhoids, or inflammatory or ischemic bowel disease rather than a diverticulum. In one study, colonoscopy performed right after hemorrhage in patients with diverticular disease revealed a 30 percent prevalence of second lesions which might have caused the hemorrhage.[25] Diverticular bleeding, in contrast to diverticulitis, involves the right rather than the left colon in two-thirds of cases. A single diverticulum is usually the source of bleeding and results when the media of one of the small arteries which penetrates the muscular wall next to a diverticulum becomes thinned and ruptures. The cause of this thinning is not clear, but it does not appear to be related to an inflammatory process.

Classically, diverticular hemorrhage occurs in an elderly patient with previously undiagnosed, or at least previously asymptomatic, diverticular disease. The patient presents suddenly with mild lower abdominal discomfort and urgency and subsequently passes a large, dark-red, maroon, or melenic stool. More bloody bowel movements often occur over the next few days, but some 70 to 80 percent of patients stop bleeding spontaneously with conservative treatment. The recurrence rate is 20 to 25 percent and increases with each subsequent episode of bleeding.[24]

The diagnostic certainty can be increased in a patient presenting with classical features by a series of studies. First, a nasogastric tube should be passed and gastric or duodenal fluid aspirated and checked for blood. If blood is absent, this will essentially rule out a rapid upper gastrointestinal tract bleeding site. Next, proctoscopy can be performed to rule out a diffuse inflammatory process and hemorrhoidal bleeding. If the rate of bleeding appears to be high and continuing, selective mesenteric arteriography may be performed to localize a site of extravasation and often will distinguish a diverticulum from an angiodysplasia or a tumor. If the rate of bleeding is felt to be less than 1 ml/min, arteriography is unlikely to demonstrate extravasation, though it may still identify possible bleeding sites, especially an anatomic vascular anomaly. For slower rates of bleeding, a ^{99m}Tc-tagged red blood cell scan is much more sensitive than arteriography, but it can only define the approximate site of bleeding, not determine the type of lesion responsible for the bleeding. Nevertheless, this anatomic information can be very useful, especially if surgical resection is ultimately required. Colonoscopy is difficult to perform when massive bleeding is occurring but is very useful in defining possible bleeding sites when bleeding has slowed or ceased.

Treatment of diverticular bleeding, like diverticulitis, should be conservative, with hospitalization, bed rest, bowel rest, blood transfusions, and correction of any coagulopathy, since most patients stop bleeding spontaneously. When active bleeding continues and has been identified by selective mesenteric arteriography as being diverticular (or angiodysplastic) in origin, vasoconstriction with intraarterial vasopressin or local embolization can be attempted.[26–28] Though these procedures entail a risk of precipitating bowel wall infarction, they are worth trying, particularly in elderly patients who are poor surgical risks. Massive or persistent hemorrhage which does not respond to conservative treatment or interventional radiologic procedures is a surgical emergency. Surgical resection should also be considered on an elective basis after recurrent hemorrhages if the risk of recurrence appears to outweigh the risk of surgery. The choice of operation is controversial and beyond the scope of this discussion; but, in general, partial colectomy is recommended when the site of bleeding has been well established, while subtotal colectomy is necessary when the patient is exsanguinating and the site is uncertain.

COLORECTAL CANCER

Epidemiology and Pathogenesis

In the United States in 1992, cancers of the colon and rectum accounted for 14 percent of all cancers in men and women, and, after lung and breast cancers, were the third leading cause of cancer deaths overall and the first in women over age 75.[29] Men have about a 6 percent lifetime chance of developing a colorectal cancer; women have about the same. The incidence is 4 to 5 times higher in people aged 65 and older than in the 45- to 64-year-old age group.[30] For women, this ratio is higher for colorectal cancers than it is for cancer in general. The incidence of colorectal cancer continues to rise throughout life, approximately doubling with each decade over age 50, to age 75 and older. More than two-thirds of colorectal cancers occur in people aged 65 or older. The death rate from colorectal cancer has not changed significantly in the past 50 years. Overall 5-year survival is 57 percent and is somewhat worse in geriatric groups, even after adjusting for increases in other causes of death in the elderly.

It is now well established that there is a gradual continuum of changes in the colonic epithelium which lead to an invasive cancer. The earliest macroscopically identifiable of these precursor lesions is the adenomatous polyp. Hyperplastic polyps, which are similar in gross appearance to adenomatous polyps, are thought to have no malignant potential, but adenomatous polyps do. It is not clear exactly what proportion of these premalignant lesions will progress to frank carcinoma (certainly less than 10 percent),[31] but it is clear that virtually all cancers of the colorectum arise from these precursors.[32] The chance of an individual polyp containing invasive cancer rises with its size (>2 cm = 40 percent), degree of cellular atypia, and histologic type. A minimum of approximately 5 years is needed for an early polyp to become an invasive cancer. This is reflected in the fact that the incidence curve for adenomatous polyps parallels that for colorectal cancer, shifted to the left by 5 to 10 years.[33]

The stage at which a cancer of the colorectum is detected has a marked effect on the patient's outcome. Cancers confined to the mucosal layers (Dukes' stage A) are associated with about an 80 to 90 percent 5-year survival, compared to about 5 percent for metastatic cancers (Dukes' stage D).[34,35] Currently, only about one-third of colorectal cancers are diagnosed at local stages (Dukes' A or B), and it has been estimated that it takes 4 years on average for tumors to progress from Dukes' A to Dukes' D.[36] Over 85 percent of tumors detected while asymptomatic are still at Dukes' stages A or B. Thus, early detection of tumors can have a potentially major impact on the death rate from this important form of cancer. Fortunately, colorectal polyps are directly accessible to the physician via fiberoptic endoscopy and can be safely removed with a wire snare and electrocautery, avoiding surgery in most cases. The most complete and most accurate form of screening for colorectal lesions involves examining the entire organ with a colonoscope. Since this procedure is costly, requires extensive bowel preparation, and is technically fairly difficult, lack of unlimited resources dictates that full colonoscopy be reserved for those patients with known disease or symptoms and those at higher than average risk for colorectal cancer. Although some shift to the proximal colon has occurred in the past decade, the distribution of colorectal cancer is still weighted to the distal portion of the colon and the rectum. About 60 percent of cancers and 70 percent of polyps are in the left colon, within reach of a 60-cm flexible sigmoidoscope. Thus, screening of people at average risk can be accomplished fairly effectively with a far lesser degree of resource utilization. Flexible sigmoidoscopy technique can be learned by nonspecialists in a short time, takes an average of 10 minutes to complete,[37] and has a very low incidence of complications when performed in the elderly for screening purposes.[38] Who should be screened and by which methods are critical and still controversial questions. Although much is known about certain high-risk groups, such as patients with long-standing ulcerative colitis or the autosomal dominant familial polyposis syndrome, much less is known about screening in the far larger population at average or moderately increased risk of colorectal polyps and carcinomas. Besides familial polyposis, there are several other syndromes with strong genetic components—including Gardner's syndrome, site-specific colorectal cancer, and cancer family syndrome. These patients may develop early-onset and often multiple cancers with a proximal colon site predominance.[39–41]

Factors which cause more modest increases in the risk of colorectal cancer include personal or family history of colorectal, breast, or endometrial carcinoma; age; and the presence of adenomatous polyps. The degree of cancer risk rises with the number of adenomas present. Diet, in particular a diet low in fiber and high in fat, probably is a risk factor as well.[42,43]

Primary prevention is an attractive method of reducing the mortality from colorectal cancer, although the etiology and risk factors are not as clear-cut as in lung cancer, for example. Epidemiologic studies reveal that there is a broad range of colorectal cancer incidence across geographic boundaries around the world. In general, third-world countries have far lower age-adjusted incidences than industrialized areas, although there are notable differences even among industrialized nations (for example, Japan is low, whereas the United States is high). These epidemiologic studies have correlated the incidence of large-bowel cancer with various dietary constituents, notably fats, meats, sugar, and total caloric intake.[44–46] At least 14 case-control studies have also been done, with conflicting results. Inconsistent findings in part arise from methodologic differences, but it also seems true that the specific factors which influence the risk of large-bowel cancer depend on the general dietary pattern in the population under study.[47]

One popular hypothesis relates increased risk of colorectal cancer to a high-fat, low-fiber diet.[48,49] The rate of degradation of cholesterol and primary bile acids to secondary bile acids by bacterial 7-α-dehydroxylases is increased in populations at high risk for,[50] and patients with, colorectal cancer.[51] Some of these bacterially degraded bile acid products are known carcinogens[52] and are cocarcinogens[53–56] and comutagens[57] in animal models.

Bacterial 7-α-dehydroxylation is inhibited at a pH of less than 6.5.[58,59] Acidification of the stool results from increasing the fiber content of the diet,[60] probably because of degradation of fiber constituents to short-chain fatty acids by colonic anaerobes.[61,62] Indeed, bran consumption results in a reduced proportion of degraded bile acids in bile.[63,64] The ingestion of the nonabsorbed sugar lactulose, or ingestion of milk in lactose-intolerant individuals, would also be expected to acidify the stool[65] and thus inhibit 7-α-dehydroxylation of bile acids. Increased consumption of fats did not alter fecal pH in one study[60] but does raise fecal bile acid excretion,[66] since 7-α-dehydroxylases are inducible[58] with increased substrate. This induction would only occur, however, if the pH were conducive, raising the possibility that an acidified colonic environment would negate the effect of a high-fat, low-fiber diet on fecal bile acid metabolism.[67]

There is evidence in the rat dimethylhydrazine colon carcinogenesis model that acidification of stool reduces the risk of this experimental cancer.[68] In humans, fecal pH correlated with the population risk of colon cancer in one study,[69] although fecal pH could not be correlated with fiber intake. This may be because fecal pH does not accurately reflect intracolonic pH.[70]

Recently, the chromosomal basis for the progression from normal colonic mucosa to adenoma and carcinoma has been elucidated;[71–74] this may provide the means to detect early colon carcinomas through identification of abnormal genetic constituents in blood or stool.

Thus, there is considerable experimental evidence to suggest that a complex interaction between dietary substrate, bacterial metabolism, and colonic pH influences the production of potentially carcinogenic substances. This, coupled with mechanical factors such as intestinal motility (duration of exposure to carcinogenic conditions) and genetic factors, may determine the individual's risk of developing colorectal polyps and cancer.

Clinical Features

Although the prognosis becomes significantly worse in symptomatic patients, many patients do not seek medical care until worrisome symptoms occur. The most common presenting symptoms of colorectal cancer are bleeding through the rectum and changes in bowel habits. The site of the lesion influences which presenting features are most common. Left-sided colonic lesions tend to cause narrowing of the colonic lumen as they grow, so that obstructive symptoms may occur. A change in bowel habits is reported, usually constipation, sometimes with pencil-thin stools and occasionally diarrhea. Bleeding from rectal and left-sided lesions is commonly visible in the stool. Right-sided colonic tumors grow in a wider-bore environment and one in which the stool traffic is liquid rather than semisolid, as in the left colon. Thus, right-sided tumors rarely present with obstructive symptoms. Instead, they cause bleeding, which is usually slow and not visible in the stool; thus the patient is more likely to present with symptoms of anemia than hematochezia. Occasionally, right-sided tumors cause abdominal discomfort in the right lower quadrant. Premalignant adenomatous lesions are usually asymptomatic, though they often bleed, usually in an intermittent fashion, which is detectable upon testing the stool for occult blood. A specific pathologic type of polyp, the villous adenoma, can present with profuse watery diarrhea. Villous adenomas are particularly likely to progress to malignancy or already to contain it.

The physical examination of the patient with a noncancerous polyp or an early-stage carcinoma is usually unrevealing unless the lesion happens to be within reach of the examining finger in the rectum or there are signs of anemia. With a larger but potentially still resectable tumor, a mass may be felt in the abdomen. Patients with more advanced lesions may show signs of weight loss, liver enlargement or ascites from metastases, or a Virchow's node. The examination of an elderly patient should include a digital rectal examination and testing of the stool that adheres to the glove for occult blood. If the specimen is negative for blood, three additional specimens should be obtained on consecutive days.

In older patients with suggestive symptoms or blood in the stools, the diagnosis of colorectal adenoma or carcinoma is best made by colonoscopy with biopsy or excision of suspicious lesions. Many clinicians begin with a rigid or flexible sigmoidoscopy. If this reveals a polyp or tumor, biopsy specimens are taken and the rest of the colon is examined with a colonoscope to rule out synchronous lesions. If sigmoidoscopy has been negative, the remainder of the colon can be examined by air-contrast barium enema. The barium enema is more likely than colonoscopy to miss small lesions, and it must be followed by a colonoscopy to obtain biopsy specimens if an abnormality is found. It is, however, less costly than colonoscopy. The alternative is to proceed directly from symptoms or rectal bleeding to full colonoscopy. This is rapidly becoming the standard approach where colonoscopy is readily available and cost is not a limiting consideration. It should be emphasized that discovery of hemorrhoids on rectal examination or sigmoidoscopy is not adequate assurance that the source of rectal bleeding or cause of a change in bowel habits has been discovered. This is especially true in elderly patients because of the rising incidence of adenomas and carcinomas of the colorectum with advancing age.

Treatment

When polyps have been found, all should be removed during colonoscopy by electrocautery unless they are too large to remove safely by this technique. Biopsy specimens of large lesions can be obtained to confirm that they are cancerous, and they can then be removed surgically. Pathologic examination of polyps excised during colonoscopy will define the type of polyp, whether there is evidence of a malignant focus, and whether there are malignant cells invading the submucosa or stalk of the polyp. Hyperplastic-type polyps, unlike tubular or villous adenomas, are generally believed to have no malignant potential and do not place the patient in a high-risk category for screening purposes.

Initial laboratory tests which may be helpful in the workup of patients with colorectal adenoma or carcinoma are a complete blood count with red cell indices, serum transaminases, γ-glutamyltranspeptidase, bilirubin, and alkaline phosphatase.

Further treatment is required for frank carcinomas of the colorectum or polyps, which, upon colonoscopic excision, prove to have a focus of malignancy which invades the submucosa or involves only the mucosa but is not excised in its entirety. Surgical excision, the extent of which is determined by the depth of invasion of the tumor and other findings at laparotomy, is the only potentially curative treatment available. In advanced lesions involving lymph nodes but without distant metastases, adjuvant chemotherapy or radiotherapy may have a slight benefit, but there is no accepted standard of treatment of such lesions. The 5-year survival ranges from 13 to 40 percent. Patients with metastatic lesions noted at the time of diagnosis or at laparotomy have a dismal prognosis. Palliative treatment is then indicated. Removal of the tumor mass is not recommended routinely but only when a specific indication exists, such as bleeding or obstruction by the mass.

In patients who will have potentially curative surgery, the level of serum carcinoembryonic antigen (CEA) may be useful in postoperative follow-up. Often this antigen will be elevated preoperatively, return to normal postoperatively, and give early warning of tumor recurrence if a rise in level is noted at a later time. Its sensitivity, however, ranges from only 30 percent in Dukes' A to 83 percent in Dukes' stage D tumors.[75,76] Smokers[77] and patients with liver disease, peptic ulcer, pancreatitis, diverticulitis, and inflammatory bowel disease have a higher false-positive rate than other controls.[78] Older patients also have slightly higher levels of CEA on average than younger persons, more than can be accounted for by a greater prevalence of the benign conditions associated with elevated CEA levels in the elderly.[79] As a result of these limitations, CEA has come to be viewed as a more effective tool for assessing patients with known colorectal tumors for recurrence and response to treatment than as a screening tool for the presence of tumor.

The risk of recurrence is high following curative resection. Over half of the recurrences are local.[80] Follow-up of patients with resected colorectal carcinoma should include periodic history and physical examinations, including stools for occult blood, a CEA level every 3 months for at least 5 years, and colonoscopy every 6 months to 1 year for the first 5 years, and every 3 years thereafter if earlier colonoscopies are negative.

Screening

Because of the high incidence of colorectal cancer in the United States and the real potential for decreasing mortality and morbidity by secondary prevention (i.e., removing precancerous adenomas), the American Cancer Society, the American College of Physicians, and other organizations have made recommendations for screening the population at large over the age of 50. The recommendations include periodic stool testing for occult blood, digital rectal examinations, and sigmoidoscopy.

Occult blood testing is based on a chemical reaction usually involving a guaiac-hemoglobin-peroxidase reaction. Stools are collected on 3 different days and, depending on the specific commercial product, may be tested by the patient or returned to the laboratory. Since colonic lesions often bleed only intermittently, sensitivity is improved when more specimens are taken. It is also improved by rehydration of the stool smear before testing, but specificity then falls.[81] True false-positive tests may result from taking iron supplements, ascorbic acid, cimetidine, iodine or large portions of rare red meat, raw broccoli, turnips, radishes, parsnips, or cauliflower.[82] Other false-positives for cancer reflect other sources of internal bleeding, such as peptic ulcers, erosions from nonsteroidal anti-inflammatory compounds, menses, or hemorrhoids, but not from cancer or polyps.

Mass screening programs have yielded a rate of positive tests from 1 to 8 percent.[83–86] Of these positives, 8 to 15 percent prove to have cancer and 9 to 36 percent adenomas.[87] The rest have no lesion that is found. A recent study[88] concluded that if testing stools for occult blood is the only screening method used in asymptomatic people over 45 years old, 50–60 percent of cancers will not be detected because of a sensitivity of around 50 percent.

One reasonable approach to screening average-risk elderly patients for colorectal adenomas and carcinoma is to perform a rectal examination and test stools for occult blood at least yearly and preferably more frequently if the patient is being seen anyway for other reasons. A flexible sigmoidoscopy should be done even if the history and rectal exam is normal and the stools show no occult blood. If the sigmoidoscopy is normal, it should be repeated once every 5 years unless symptoms develop or a stool specimen shows occult blood. If any sigmoidoscopy reveals an adenomatous polyp, a full colonoscopy should be performed, since the presence of an adenoma in the rectosigmoid is associated with a 25 to 34 percent prevalence of more proximal colonic adenomas.[89] One very recent study,[90] however, found that when only a small (<1 cm) adenoma or even more than one small adenoma was found on screening by rigid sigmoidoscopy, the risk of colon cancer developing subsequently was not increased unless there was also a family history of colon cancer. The risk was increased if screening sigmoidoscopy revealed even a single larger (>1 cm) adenoma or any size adenoma of tubulovillous or villous architecture. Also, if the stools are ever found to contain occult blood, a full colonoscopy (or a barium enema plus proctoscopy) is the minimum advisable workup unless there is a known upper gastrointestinal tract source of blood loss, such as peptic ulcer, and the stools are no longer occult-blood–positive after the known lesion has been treated.

Once a polyp with malignant potential has been discovered, the patient is considered at high risk for recurrence for the indefinite future and should be screened with semiannual tests of stools for occult blood and annual to biannual colonoscopy. If two annual colonoscopies reveal no further adenomas, it is reasonable to stretch out the time between screenings to as long as every 5 years.

A recent case-control study[91] strongly supports the use of endoscopic screening methods to reduce mortality from colorectal cancer. Patients who had died of distal colonic or rectal cancer were far less likely to have had screening sigmoidoscopy in the 10 years prior to diagnosis than age- and sex-matched controls. Patients who had died of colon cancers located above the reach of the sigmoidoscope used for screening were just as likely to have had screening sigmoidoscopy as controls. There was a 60 to 70 percent reduction in the risk of death from rectal or distal colon cancer in those who had undergone screening rigid sigmoidoscopy compared to those who had not. Furthermore, the risk of death was reduced for 10 years after a single sigmoidoscopy.

A recent analysis by members of the U.S. Congress's Office of Technology Assessment of the cost-effectiveness of screening for colorectal cancer in the elderly[92] has conservatively estimated that annual fecal occult blood testing in the elderly would detect at least 17 percent of the expected cases of cancer and cost $35,000 per year of life saved. Screening which also included periodic (every 3 to 5 years) sigmoidoscopy should detect at least one-quarter of expected cases but would cost about $43,000 per year of life saved. Currently, Medicare does not cover the cost of the above test when done solely for the purpose of screening for colorectal cancer.

REFERENCES

1. Whiteway J, Morson BC: Pathology of ageing: Diverticular disease. *Clin Gastroenterol* 14:829, 1985.
2. Parks TG: Natural history of diverticular disease of the colon. *Br Med J* 4:639, 1969.
3. Painter NS, Burkitt DP: Diverticular disease of the colon: A deficiency disease of western civilization. *Br Med J* 2:440, 1971.
4. Burkitt DP et al: Effect of dietary fiber on stools and the transit time and its role in the causation of disease. *Lancet* 2:1048, 1972.
5. Heller SN, Hackler LR: Changes in the crude fiber content of the American diet. *Am J Clin Nutr* 31:1510, 1978.
6. Painter NS, Burkitt DP: Diverticular disease of the colon: A deficiency disease of Western civilization. *Br Med J* 2:450, 1971.
7. Gear JSS et al: Symptomless diverticular disease and intake of dietary fibre. *Lancet* 1:511, 1979.
8. Hodgson WJB: An interim report on the production of colonic diverticulosis in the rabbit. *Gut* 13:802, 1972.
9. Painter NS, Truelove SC: The intraluminal pressure patterns in diverticulosis of the colon. *Gut* 5(201):365, 1964.
10. Boranstein P: Disorders of connective tissue function and the ageing process. *Mech Ageing Dev* 5:305, 1976.
11. Whiteway J, Morson BC: Elastosis in diverticular disease of the sigmoid colon. *Gut* 26:258, 1985.
12. Perry PM, Morson BC: Right-sided diverticulosis of the colon. *Br J Surg* 58(12):902, 1971.
13. Havia T: Diverticulosis of the colon: A clinical and histologic study. *Acta Chir Scand* 137:415S, 1971.
14. Parks TG: Natural history of diverticular disease of the colon. *Clin Gastroenterol* 4:53, 1975.
15. Corder A: Steroids, non-steroidal anti-inflammatory drugs and serious septic complications of diverticular disease. *Br Med J* 295:1238, 1987.
16. Campbell K, Steele RJC: Non-steroidal anti-inflammatory drugs and complicated diverticular disease: A case-control study. *Br J Surg* 78:190, 1991.
17. Coutrot S et al: Acute perforation of colonic diverticula associated with short-term indomethacin. *Lancet* 2:1055, 1978.
18. Labs JD et al: Complications of acute diverticulitis of the colon: Improved early diagnosis with computerized tomography. *Am J Surg* 155:331, 1988.
19. Welch CE: Computerized tomography scans for all patients with diverticulitis. *Am J Surg* 155:366, 1988.
20. Larson DM et al: Medical and surgical therapy in diverticular disease. *Gastroenterology* 71:734, 1976.
21. Neff CC et al: Abdominal-gastrointestinal/interventional radiology. *Radiology* 163:15, 1987.
22. Mueller PR et al: Sigmoid diverticular abscesses: Percutaneous drainage as an adjunct to surgical resection in 24 cases. *Radiology* 164:321, 1987.
23. Boley SJ et al: Lower intestinal bleeding in the elderly. *Am J Surg* 137:57, 1979.
24. McGuire HH, Haynes W: Massive hemorrhage from diverticulosis of the colon: Guidelines for therapy based on bleeding patterns observed in fifty cases. *Ann Surg* 175(6):847, 1972.
25. Tedesco F et al: Colonoscopic evaluation of rectal bleeding: A study of 304 patients. *Ann Intern Med* 89:907.
26. Goldberger LE, Bookstein JL: Transcatheter embolization treatment of diverticular hemorrhage. *Diagn Radiol* 122:613, 1977.
27. Athanasoulis CA et al: Mesenteric arterial infusions of vasopressin for hemorrhage from colonic diverticulosis. *Am J Surg* 129:213, 1975.
28. Baum S et al: Selective mesenteric arterial infusions in the management of massive diverticular hemorrhage. *N Engl J Med* 288(24):1269, 1973.
29. Cancer statistics, 1992. *CA* 42(1):9, 1992.
30. Baranovsky A, Myers MH: Cancer incidence and survival in patients 65 years of age and older. *CA* 36(1):26, 1986.
31. Winawer SJ et al: National polyp study, abstract. *Gastroenterology* 80:1316, 1981.
32. Morson BC: Genesis of colorectal cancer. *Clin Gastroenterol* 5:505, 1976.
33. Bernstein MA et al: Distribution of colonic polyps:

Increased incidence of proximal lesions in older patients. *Radiology* 155:35, 1985.
34. Turvnen MJ, Peltokallio P: Surgical results in 657 patients with colorectal cancer. *Dis Colon Rectum* 26:606, 1983.
35. Jarvinsen HJ, Turvnen MJ: Colorectal carcinoma before 40 years of age: Prognosis and predisposing conditions. *Scand J Gastroenterol* 104:99, 1984.
36. Eddy DM et al: Screening for colorectal cancer in a high-risk population: Results of a mathematical model. *Gastroenterology* 92:682, 1987.
37. Winawer SJ et al: Comparison of flexible sigmoidoscopy with other diagnostic techniques in the diagnosis of rectocolon neoplasia. *Dig Dis Sci* 24:277, 1979.
38. Helzberg JH, McCallum RW: Flexible sigmoidoscopy—Safety and usefulness in the geriatric patient. *Geriatrics* 40(5):105, 1985.
39. Love RR, Morrissey JF: Colonoscopy in asymptomatic individuals with a family history of colorectal cancer. *Arch Intern Med* 144:2209, 1984.
40. Mecklin JP, Jarvinen HJ: Clinical features of colorectal carcinoma in cancer family syndrome. *Dis Colon Rectum* 29:160, 1986.
41. Lynch HT et al: Hereditary nonpolyposis colorectal cancer (Lynch syndromes I and II). *Cancer* 56:934, 1985.
42. Kritchevsky D: Diet, nutrition and cancer: The role of fiber. *Cancer* 58:1830, 1986.
43. McKeown-Eyssenge GE: Fiber intake in different populations and colon cancer risk. *Prev Med* 16:532, 1987.
44. Wynder EL: The epidemiology of large bowel cancer. *Cancer Res* 35:3388, 1975.
45. Drasar BS, Irving D: Environmental factors and cancer of the colon and breast. *Br J Cancer* 27:167, 1973.
46. Armstrong B, Doll R: Environmental factors and cancer incidence and mortality in different countries with special reference to dietary practices. *Int J Cancer* 15:617, 1975.
47. Macquart-Moulin G et al: Case-control study on colorectal cancer and diet in Marseilles. *Int J Cancer* 38:183, 1986.
48. Haenszel W et al: Large bowel cancer in Hawaiian Japanese. *J Natl Cancer Inst* 51:1765, 1973.
49. Wynder EL, Reddy BS: Diet and cancer of the colon. *Curr Concepts Nutr* 6:55, 1977.
50. Hill MJ et al: Bacteria and aetiology of cancer of large bowel. *Lancet* 1:95, 1971.
51. Mastromarino AJ et al: Fecal profiles of anaerobic microflora of large bowel cancer patients and patients with nonhereditary large bowel polyps. *Cancer Res* 38:4458, 1978.
52. Hill MJ: Bacteria and the etiology of colonic cancer. *Cancer* 34:815, 1974.
53. Narisawa T et al: Promoting effect of bile acids on colon carcinogenesis after intrarectal instillation of *N*-methyl-*N*-nitrosoguanidine in rats. *J Natl Cancer Inst* 53:1093, 1974.
54. Reddy BS et al: Promoting effect of bile acids on colon carcinogenesis in germ-free and conventional F344 rats. *Cancer Res* 32:3238, 1977.
55. Cohen BI et al: Effect of cholic acid feeding on *N*-methyl-*N*-nitrosourea induced colon tumours and cell kinetics in rats. *J Natl Cancer Inst* 64:573, 1980.
56. Martin MS et al: Effect of dietary chenodeoxycholic acid on intestinal carcinogenesis induced by 1,2-dimethylhydrazine in mice. *Br J Cancer* 43:884, 1981.
57. Wilpart M et al: Mutagenicity of 1,2-dimethyl hydrazine towards *Salmonella typhimurium;* co-mutagenic effect of secondary bile acids. *Carcinogenesis* 4:45, 1983.
58. Aries V, Hill MJ: Degradation of steroids by intestinal bacteria II. *Biochim Biophys Acta* 202:535, 1970.
59. Thornton JR, Heaton KW: Do colonic bacteria contribute to cholesterol gallstone formation? Effects of lactulose on bile. *Br Med J* 1:1018, 1981.
60. Walker ARP et al: Fecal pH value and its modification by dietary means in South African black and white school children. *S Afr Med J* 33:495, 1979.
61. Cummings JH et al: Changes in fecal composition and colonic function due to cereal fiber. *Am J Clin Nutr* 28:1468, 1976.
62. Hellendoorn EW: Fermentation as the principal cause of the physiologic activity of indigestible food residue, in Spiller GA, Amen RJ (eds): *Topics in Dietary Fiber Research.* New York, Plenum Press, 1978.
63. Pomare EW et al: The effect of wheat bran upon bile salt metabolism and lipid composition of bile in gallstone patients. *Am J Dig Dis* 21:521, 1976.
64. McDougall RM et al: Effect of wheat bran on serum lipoproteins and biliary lipids. *Can J Surg* 21:433, 1978.
65. Bowen RL et al: Effects of lactulose and other laxatives on ileal and colonic pH as measured by a radiotelemetry device. *Gut* 15:999, 1974.
66. Cummings JH et al: Influence of diets high and low in animal fat on bowel habit, gastrointestinal transit, fecal microflora, bile acid and fat excretion. *J Clin Invest* 61:953, 1978.
67. Thornton JR: High colonic pH promotes colorectal cancer. *Lancet* 1:1081, 1981.
68. Samuelson SL et al: Protective role of faecal pH in experimental colon carcinogenesis. *J R Soc Med* 78: 230, 1985.
69. Walker ARP et al: Faecal pH, dietary fiber intake, and proneness to colon cancer in four South African populations. *Br J Cancer* 53:4898, 1986.
70. Lupton JR et al: Influence of luminal pH on rat large bowel epithelial cell cycle. *Am J Physiol* 249:G382, 1985.
71. Vogelstein B et al: Allelotype of colorectal carcinomas. *Science* 244(4901):207, 1989.
72. Baker SJ et al: Chromosome 17 deletions + p53 gene mutations in colorectal carcinomas. *Science* 244(4901): 217, 1989.
73. Fearon ER et al: Identification of a chromosome 18q gene that is altered in colorectal cancers. *Science* 247(4938):49, 1990.
74. Kinzler KW et al: Identification of a gene located at chromosome 5q 21 that is mutated in colorectal cancers. *Science* 251(4999):1366, 1991.
75. Wanebo HJ et al: Pre-operative CEA as a prognostic indicator in colorectal cancer. *N Engl J Med* 299:448, 1978.
76. Herbeth B, Bagrel A: A study of factors influencing plasma CEA levels in an unselected population. *Oncodeo Biol Med* 1:191, 1980.
77. Clarke C et al: CEA and smoking. *J R Coll Physicians Lond* 14:227, 1980.
78. Fletcher RH: Carcinoembryonic antigen. *Ann Intern Med* 104:66, 1986.
79. Toniton Y et al: Cumulative effects of age and pathology on plasma CEA in an unselected elderly population. *Eur J Cancer Clin Oncol* 20:369, 1984.

80. Rao AR et al: Patterns of recurrence following curative resection alone for adenocarcinoma of the rectum and sigmoid colon. *Cancer* 48:1492, 1981.
81. Simon JB: The pros and cons of fecal occult blood testing for colorectal neoplasms. *Cancer Metastasis Rev* 6:397, 1987.
82. Norfleet RG: Effect of diet on fecal occult blood testing in patients with colorectal polyps. *Dig Dis Sci* 31:498, 1986.
83. Johnson MG, Jolly PC: Analysis of a mass colorectal cancer screening program for cost-effectiveness. *Am J Surg* 154(3):261, 1987.
84. Kronborg O et al: Initial mass screening for colorectal cancer with fecal occult blood test: A prospective randomized study at Funen in Denmark. *Scand J Gastroenterol* 22(6):677, 1987.
85. Hardcastle JD et al: Fecal occult blood screening for colorectal cancer in the general population: Results of a controlled trial. *Cancer* 58(2):397, 1986.
86. Norfleet RG et al: Hemoccult screening for colorectal neoplasms: Report of a mail-out project without dietary restriction in a prepaid health plan. *Wis Med J* 82(4):23, 1983.
87. Winawer SJ et al: Screening for colorectal cancer. *Bull WHO* 65(1):105, 1987.
88. Allison JE et al: Hemoccult screening in detecting colorectal neoplasm: Sensitivity, specificity, and predictive value. *Ann Intern Med* 112:328, 1990.
89. Warden MG et al: The role of colonoscopy and flexible sigmoidoscopy in screening for colorectal carcinoma. *Dis Colon Rectum* 30:52, 1987.
90. Atkins WS et al: Long-term risk of colorectal cancer after excision of rectosigmoid adenomas. *N Engl J Med* 326:658, 1992.
91. Selby JV et al: A case-control study of screening sigmoidoscopy and mortality from colorectal cancer. *N Engl J Med* 326:653, 1992.
92. Wagner JL et al: Cost-effectiveness of colorectal cancer screening in the elderly. *Ann Intern Med* 115:807, 1991.

Chapter 64

AGING OF THE HEMATOPOIETIC SYSTEM

D. A. Lipschitz

NORMAL BONE MARROW FUNCTION

Hematopoiesis is regulated by a complex series of interactions between hematopoietic cells, their stromal microenvironment, and diffusible regulatory molecules that affect cellular proliferation. The orderly development of the hematopoietic system in vivo and the maintenance of homeostasis require that a strict balance be maintained between self-renewal, differentiation, maturation, and cell loss. Within the hematopoietic system, populations of terminally differentiated cells are continually entering the peripheral blood, to be replaced by cells from a transit or amplification compartment.

The earliest morphologically recognizable (differentiated) cells of the myeloid and erythroid series are the myeloblasts and proerythroblasts (Fig. 64-1). These cells are derived from the morphologically unrecognizable progenitor or stem cells that can only be identified by appropriate in vitro culture techniques. There are two forms of erythroid stem cells. A more primitive precursor, which forms large colonies in cultures containing high concentrations of erythropoietin, is referred to as a burst forming unit–erythroid (BFU-E). This precursor is thought to give rise to a more mature stem cell, which develops colonies in culture at shorter intervals and requires lower erythropoietin concentrations. It is the immediate precursor of the proerythroblast and is referred to as the colony forming unit–erythroid (CFU-E). A committed myeloid stem cell, or colony forming unit–culture (CFU-C), also known as colony forming unit–granulocyte/macrophage (CFU-GM), is the immediate precursor of the myeloblast. The committed progenitor cell compartments are supplied, in turn, by a common pluripotent stem cell, which is derived from totipotential stem cells that have the capacity to differentiate into either hematopoietic or lymphoid cells.[1]

The hierarchy of cellular proliferation and differentiation through this pathway is shown in Fig. 64-1. The pluripotent hematpoietic stem cell shown in Fig. 64-1 is also called a colony forming unit–spleen (CFU-S) by virtue of its ability to produce colonies in spleens of lethally irradiated mice. CFU-S is also capable of repopulating the marrow of irradiated recipients and preventing marrow failure.[2] A unique feature of the CFU-S compartment is the ability to divide and give rise to an identical multipotential daughter cell and a progenitor cell that is committed to specific hematopoietic development. It is the self-renewal capacity that allows a small CFU-S compartment to amplify into large numbers of differentiated hematopoietic cells. The CFU-S is the earliest hematopoietic cell that can be satisfactorily assayed and constitutes a powerful research tool for studying differentiation and growth control.[2] There is very little information on factors regulating these cells. There is evidence that the number of CFU-S in cell cycle is minimal but that cycling can be greatly increased if demands for regeneration are increased.[3] Most evidence suggests that regulation of proliferative control is local and is presumably mediated by the environmental milieu.[4] Furthermore, studies have shown that the cellular milieu can also influence cell production and differentiation.[5] If commitment is defined as a loss of pluripotentiality, there is some evidence that committed cells, restricted to one or two of the hematopoietic cell lines, can undergo extensive (but not indefinite) self-renewal in vivo.[6]

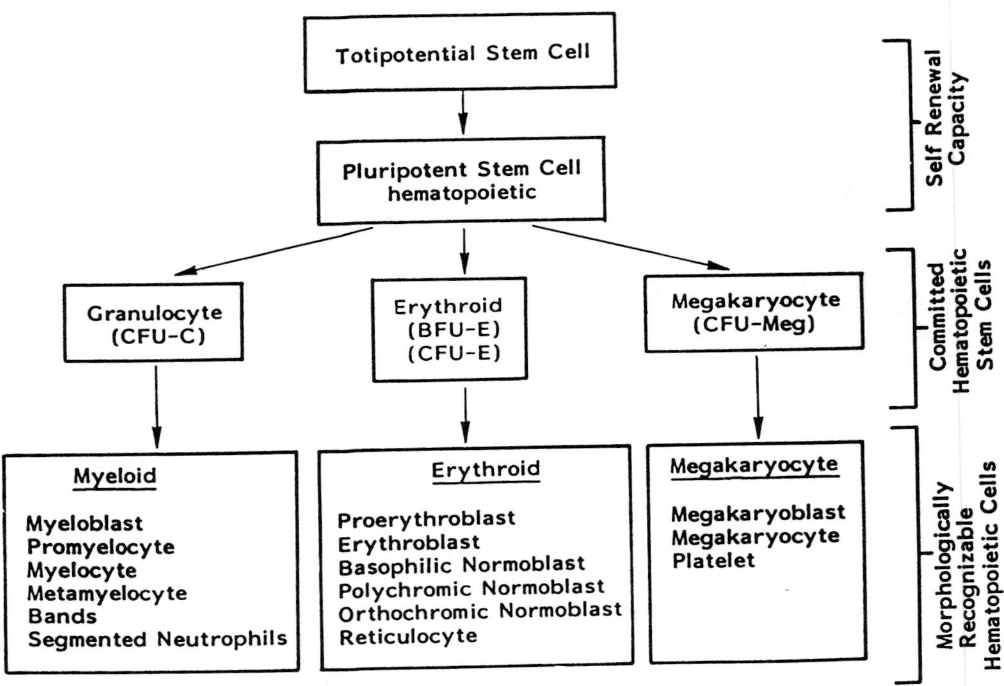

FIGURE 64-1
The hierarchy and production of hematopoietic precursors from primitive pluripotent stem cells.

EFFECT OF AGE ON CFU-S

One of the major questions with regard to the aging hematopoietic system is whether or not the pluripotent hematopoietic stem cell has a finite replicative capacity. There is evidence that CFU-S has a heterogeneous self-renewal capacity and an age structure in which young CFU-S with high self-renewal capacity produce older CFU-S with decreasing self-renewal capacity and increasing differentiation potential.[7,8] This hypothesis has been strengthened by studies of long-term bone marrow culture, which showed that CFU-S with a high replicative history are likely to be recruited into committed progenitor cells more readily than CFU-S that have divided a fewer number of times.[9] We have shown that maintenance of hematopoiesis in long-term bone marrow culture varies inversely with the age of the donor from which the culture was initiated.[10] Additional evidence for a finite replicative capacity for stem cells has been obtained in a series of elegant studies in which stem cell kinetics and myeloid cell production was examined in long-term bone marrow cultures subjected to varying doses of irradiation.[11–13]

Studies using serial transplantation to assess finite replicative capacity have yielded conflicting results. When cells are subjected to in vivo serial transfer by repeated injection into lethally irradiated recipients, they gradually lose their ability to self-replicate.[8,14] There is evidence that CFU-S from young donors are better able to repopulate the marrow of irradiated mice than stem cells obtained from old donors. The growth capacity of old stem cells remains characteristically old, even after prolonged self-replication in the bone marrow of young recipients. This fact suggests an intrinsic characteristic of the CFU-S which cannot readily be altered. However, the spleen colony growth capacity of young stem cells can be reduced by allowing them to self-replicate in old recipients. Thus, the rate at which young cells age can be accelerated by allowing them to replicate in old recipients. Other host factors affect the rate of colonization. An inadequate architectural milieu in the old spleen may retard the seeding of transplanted stem cells.[5] There are also data that CFU-S decline minimally or not at all with age.[15] Ogden and Micklem[16] have simultaneously transplanted two bone marrow cell populations with different chromosome markers into lethally irradiated syngeneic recipients. One marrow population was obtained from young and one from old donors. No consistent difference in the rates of spleen colonization was noted. More recent evidence suggests that results of earlier serial transplant studies were related to methodologic artifact.[17,18] Even if its life span is finite, it is clear that the CFU-S has a reserve capacity to produce adequate numbers of hematopoietic cells for periods that far exceed the maximum life expectancy of the animal.[19]

EFFECT OF NORMAL AGING ON BONE MARROW FUNCTION

The effect of age on committed hematopoietic stem cell number and on the number of differentiated hematopoietic bone marrow cells has also been examined.[20] In mice no age-related reduction in the number of erythroid (BFU-E, CFU-E) or myeloid/macrophage (CFU-C) progenitor cells occurs. In addition, the number of differentiated erythroid and myeloid precursors in the bone marrow is unaffected by age in normal animals. Erythrokinetic studies show that red blood cell survival is unchanged with aging, the plasma iron turnover and erythron iron turnover are unchanged, and the red blood cell mass is normal. The apparent anemia frequently observed in aged mice appears to be due to an expansion of plasma volume.

These findings and those of others[21,22] indicate that no change in basal hematopoiesis occurs with aging. However, the ability of the aged hematopoietic system to respond to increased demands appears to be compromised. For example, older mice recover their hemoglobin values more slowly after phlebotomy than do young mice.[23,24] Furthermore, when aged animals are placed in a high-altitude chamber, the expected increase in hemoglobin level is more variable and tends to be lower in older as compared with younger animals.[25] Interpretation of data with phlebotomy or exposure to high altitude is difficult because many other physiologic variables determine the measured hematopoietic response. For example, alterations in cardiorespiratory or renal function may compromise the ability of the bone marrow from old animals to respond to increased stimulation.

One approach that allows the study of hematopoiesis while minimizing other variables is to create polycythemia in mice by the injection of homologous red cells.[25] This results in a predictable switching off of erythropoiesis that is characterized by marked decreases in bone marrow differentiated erythroid cell and CFU-E number. When erythropoietin is injected into these animals, a predictable and measurable wave of erythropoiesis occurs. Twenty-four hours after injection, bone marrow CFU-E and proerythroblasts are significantly increased. After 48 hours, polychromic and orthochromic normoblasts are elevated. Between 48 and 72 hours, these cells leave the bone marrow and appear in the blood as reticulocytes. Studies using this model demonstrate that old polycythemic mice develop a smaller wave of erythropoiesis after erythropoietin injection than do young animals. The number of new red blood cells appearing in the circulation after injection of erythropoietin is significantly less in the aged. The decrease in response does not, however, universally affect all erythroid precursors. Thus, the increase in proerythroblast and normoblast (differentiated cell) number after the injection of erythropoietin is significantly less in old as compared with young animals. In contrast, the increase in the committed erythroid progenitor cell number (CFU-E) after erythropoietin injection was identical in both young and old animals, suggesting that a uniform defect in the proliferative response of all cells does not occur with aging. The mechanism for the reduced responsiveness of differentiated cells in the aged remains to be determined.

Erythropoietin is the most important stimulator of erythropoiesis. In vitro culture methods are available that allow the examination of the responsiveness to erythropoietin of the erythroid stem cells (BFU-E and CFU-E) and of differentiated erythroid cells that have the capacity to divide. The number of colonies that develop from erythroid stem cells increases in direct proportion to the concentration of erythropoietin in the cultures. In addition, the level of differentiated erythroid cell proliferation varies in direct proportion to the erythropoietin concentration. These methods are ideally suited to the study of the effect of age on erythropoiesis.[26] Results found when young and old bone marrow is studied using this in vitro approach confirm the in vivo findings described. Thus, when differentiated cells from aged animals are cultured in the presence of erythropoietin, the proliferative response to the increased stimulation is significantly lower than when bone marrow from young animals is studied. Proliferation is, however, identical when the effect of increasing concentrations of erythropoietin on CFU-E and BFU-E cultures from the marrow of old or young mice is examined.

The fragility of the aged hematopoietic system is further highlighted by studies on mice approaching their maximal life expectancy.[20] The median life span of C57BL/6 mice is 24 months, but the maximum reported life expectancy is 48 months. Provided that 48-month-old mice are housed in individual cages (one animal per cage), no change in hematopoiesis is seen. If, however, they are housed in groups of five animals per cage, a significant alteration on bone marrow function occurs. The animals become more anemic and the number of stem cells in their bone marrow decreases. Significant decreases also occur in the morphologically recognizable erythroid precursors. These findings are identical to hematopoietic changes described with overcrowding. The effects of overcrowding, however, are seen only when young or even 24-month-old animals are housed in groups of ten mice per cage. This finding indicates that a minor stress, which does not affect hematopoiesis in young animals, causes significant abnormalities in aged animals.

THE EFFECT OF AGE ON HEMATOPOIESIS IN HUMANS

The evaluation of hematopoiesis in older humans is made virtually impossible by the complex interaction of environmental variables with the host over extended periods of time. This applies particularly to

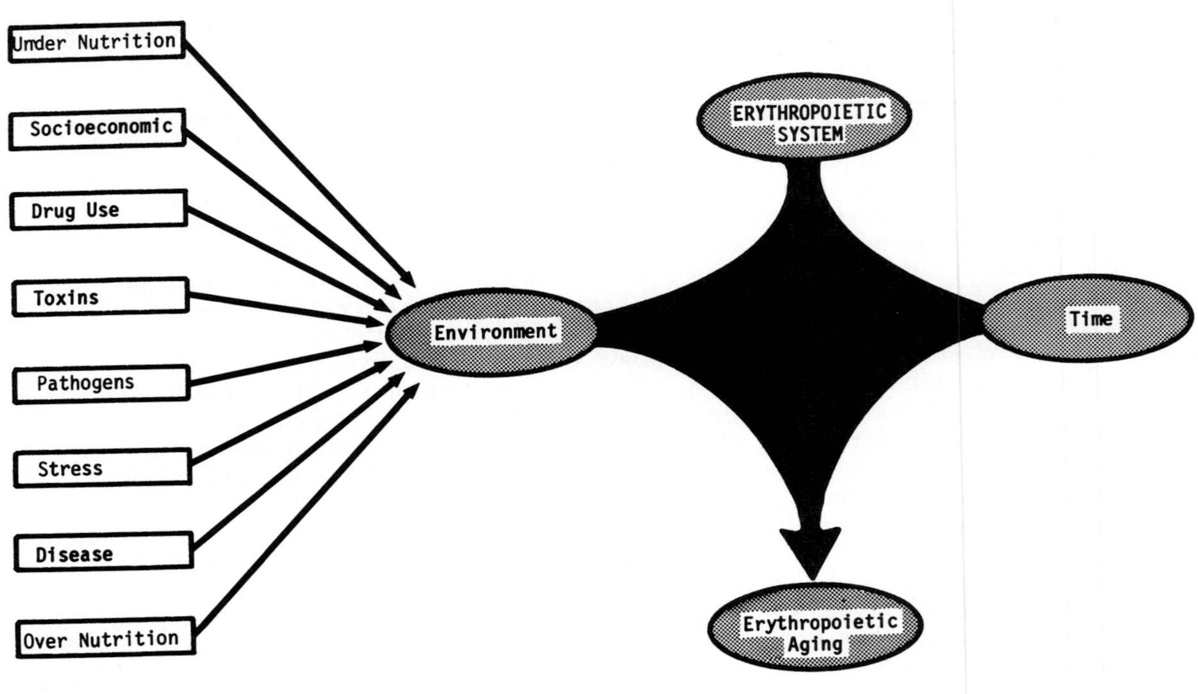

FIGURE 64-2
External variables likely to modify age-related decrements in erythropoiesis.

hematopoiesis, which is very sensitive to a large series of extraneous variables. For example, Fig. 64-2 illustrates the large number of factors which may modulate erythropoietic function in elderly subjects. Controlling for these external variables is extremely difficult and makes it somewhat hard to determine whether any decrements occur in hematopoietic function as a consequence of age alone. An extensive study has been performed on a group of carefully selected, healthy young and elderly subjects who were clearly hematologically normal (Table 64-1).[27] When hematopoiesis was evaluated in these individuals, no significant differences in peripheral blood or ferrokinetic data could be demonstrated. Furthermore, quantitation of bone marrow, hematopoietic stem cells, and differentiated precursors demonstrated no significant differences between the young and the elderly group. A series of longitudinal studies of hematologic parameters on a group of affluent subjects examined in New Mexico demonstrated no obvious hematologic problem, and no abnormalities developed during a 3-year follow-up.[28] Based upon these observations and the animal studies described above, it is highly likely that no change in basal hematopoiesis occurs with aging. It is also highly likely that elderly humans have a compromised reserve capacity that will result in a diminished ability—as compared with a younger subject—of an elderly subject's marrow to compensate for a given degree of acute or chronic disease, thus making the elderly more prone to the development of disease-induced hematologic abnormalities. As will be discussed in Chap. 65, anemia that is not due to the commonly recognized causes is extremely prevalent in apparently healthy elderly subjects.[29] Evidence is presented that the anemia is not a consequence of normal aging but reflects

TABLE 64-1

Hematologic Profile in Young and Elderly Hematologically Normal Subjects

	Young	Elderly
Age (years)	34.0 ± 2.0[a]	78.0 ± 2.0
Hemoglobin (g/dl)	15.4 ± 0.3	15.0 ± 0.2
Mean corpuscular volume (fl)	89.0 ± 0.9	90.7 ± 1.8
Serum iron (μg/dl)	107.0 ± 8.1	93.0 ± 5.0
TIBC (μg/dl)	297.0 ± 10.0	307.0 ± 13.0
Saturation (%)	36.0 ± 3.0	30.1 ± 2.2
Serum ferritin (ng/ml)	126.0 ± 17.0	219.0 ± 26.0
Proto:heme (μmol/mol)	24.4 ± 1.4	22.0 ± 1.8
Vitamin B_{12} (μg/ml)	476.0 ± 34.0	451.0 ± 34.0
Serum folate (ng/ml)	5.6 ± 0.8	4.8 ± 0.5
Retic index	1.1 ± 0.3	1.0 ± 0.2
Leukocyte ($\times 10^3/\mu$l)	8.8 ± 0.4	7.6 ± 0.5
Neutrophils ($\times 10^3/\mu$l)	5.9 ± 0.3	4.5 ± 0.6
Lymphocyte ($\times 10^3/\mu$l)	1.9 ± 0.8	1.9 ± 0.3
Platelet ($\times 10^3/\mu$l)	361.0 ± 38.0	277.0 ± 2.1
EIT[b]	0.5 ± 0.1	0.5 ± 0.1
Total myeloid precursors ($\times 10^9$ cells/kg)	38.0 ± 16.0	40.0 ± 15.0
CFU-C (-10^6/kg)	0.9 ± 0.3	0.7 ± 0.2

[a] Mean ± SE.
[b] Erythron iron turnover (mg/dl whole blood per day).

a response to a stress that would be unlikely to cause a hematologic problem in younger individuals.

THE EFFECT OF AGE ON NEUTROPHIL FUNCTION

The most important function of neutrophils is to phagocytose and kill bacteria. For this to occur, the neutrophil must be able to adhere to endothelial surfaces, migrate to the site of inflammation (chemotaxis), engulf the ingested bacteria, and then kill them. Killing is achieved by the generation of a series of toxic radicals and microbicidal halogens and by the release of a series of enzymes located in neutrophil granules. The process of bacterial killing is associated with a 100-fold increase in neutrophil metabolism and oxygen uptake. This reaction is referred to as the respiratory burst.[30,31] The neutrophil also plays an important role in the inflammatory response.

Neutrophil function can be assessed by measuring the ability of the neutrophils to phagocytose and kill bacteria. Alternatively, neutrophils can be exposed to a series of chemotactic peptides or other reagents which stimulate the respiratory burst and cause the secretion of enzymes from neutrophil granules. The burst can be evaluated by assessing oxygen metabolism in the cells. Alternatively, the end products of the burst—namely, the generation of superoxide, which is the first step in the generation of toxic radicals—can be measured.

Utilizing these approaches, a series of studies have examined the effects of aging on neutrophil function. In response to a wide variety of stimuli, respiratory burst activity of neutrophils from elderly individuals is decreased and the level of various neutrophil enzymes secreted during degranulation is reduced.[32–35] A typical response of a neutrophil from the elderly is shown in Fig. 64-3. In this study, secretion of the enzyme lysozyme was determined both in the basal state and following challenge of the cell by the chemotactic peptide formyl-methyl-leucine-phenylalanine (FMLP). In neutrophils from the young and the old, secretion in the basal state is very similar. Following stimulation, however, the rate and total amount of enzyme released is clearly reduced in the old. This response in a single cell bears remarkable similarity to the effects of age on the decrements in response of many organ systems. Because function can be measured in the basal state and following stimulation, in which metabolic function is markedly amplified, the neutrophil offers a unique opportunity to examine the effects of aging on cellular function.

Utilizing the neutrophil, studies have examined the effects of age on signal transduction.[35] Employing FMLP, we demonstrated an impaired ability of neutrophils from elderly volunteers to release the second messengers, inositol triphosphate (IP_3) and diacylglycerol (DAG), and to mobilize calcium to the cytosol. These second messengers play a central role in the response of cells to stimulation. The defect occurred at a point distal to the FMLP membrane receptor, which was unaffected by aging.[36] We further localized the lesion to a point proximal to the generation of IP_3 and DAG, as function could be corrected if the cells were activated by a mechanism that bypassed the membrane receptor or if the concentrations of cytosolic calcium or DAG were increased prior to activation of the cell by FMLP. Further studies demonstrated the prime defect with age to be a decline in the concentration of the metabolically active phosphoinositide precursors of IP_3 and DAG. This, in turn, leads to a reduced ability to generate second messengers. These data indicate that aging is associated with an alteration in the composition of membrane lipids that leads to an impaired ability of the cell to respond to maximal stimulation. Alteration in membrane lipids also decreases membrane viscosity and impairs transport ability. Of most importance are the observations that the age-related decline in neutrophil function and the alterations in the composition of membrane lipids occur as a consequence of a defect that is extrinsic to the cell and reversible.[37] This implies that strategies may eventually be available to correct the declines in cellular function that occur with age. This may have important implications for age-related declines in function or manifestations of age-depended diseases.

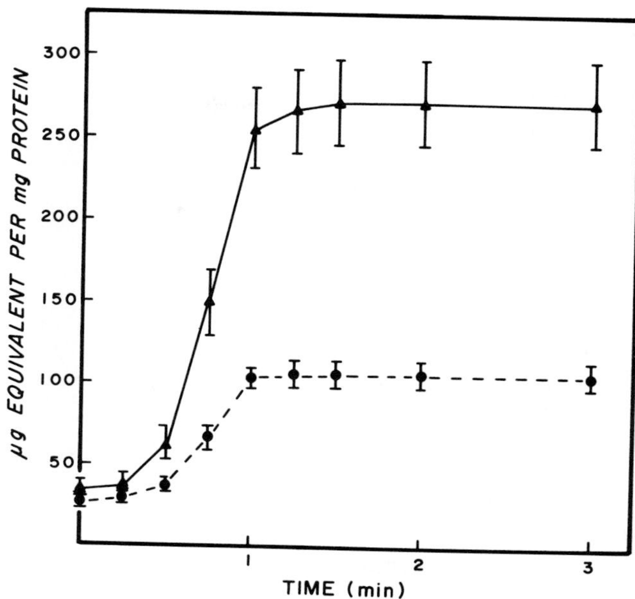

FIGURE 64-3
Secretion of the enzyme lysozyme in the basal state and at various times following activation of the neutrophil by FMLP. The mean ± SEM is shown for neutrophils obtained from six young volunteers (▲ —— ▲) and six elderly volunteers (● —— ●).

These findings provide useful insights into the fundamental mechanisms accounting for the diminished ability of aged cells to respond to stimulation.

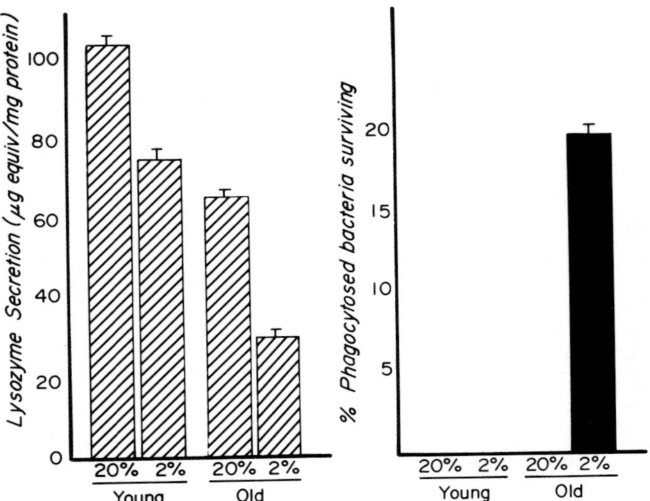

FIGURE 64-4

Secretion of the enzyme lysozyme (left-hand panel) following activation of neutrophils from young (6-month-old) or old (24-month-old) mice fed a 20 percent (normal) or 2 percent protein diet for 3 weeks prior to sacrifice. The right-hand panel shows the percentage of phagocytosed bacteria not killed by neutrophils from young and old mice fed a 2 percent or 20 percent protein diet. The results clearly demonstrate that neutrophils obtained from old mice fed a 2 percent protein diet are unable to kill all phagocytosed bacteria.

The key question is whether the decline in neutrophil function, described as a consequence of aging, has any clinical relevance. Although neutrophil function is diminished with aging, the defect is not large enough to interfere with the ability of neutrophils from the elderly to phagocytose or to kill bacteria. However, the diminished neutrophil reserve capacity does have relevance. When mice are made protein-deficient, a modest reduction in neutrophil function occurs which is very similar to that seen with aging.[38] In old mice, the effects of protein deficiency and aging are additive, so that in this circumstance neutrophil function decreases to a level where the ability of the cell to undertake its most critically important role of phagocytosis and bacterial killing is severely compromised (Fig. 64-4). This finding is of particular importance, as it may help to explain the high prevalence of serious bacterial infection in hospitalized and older individuals who are frequently malnourished. It also demonstrates the relevance of diminished reserve capacity resulting in increased susceptibility of disease.

SUMMARY

Evaluation of the effect of age on hematopoiesis at the organ or cellular level demonstrates evidence of a diminished reserve capacity. Abnormalities in function, not evidenced in the basal state, become apparent when function is amplified by appropriate stimulation. In addition to being lower, the aged response tends to be more variable. Given a comparable stress, hematologic abnormalities are likely to occur earlier and to be of greater severity in the old as compared to the young.

REFERENCES

1. Schofield R: The pluripotent stem cell. *Clin Haematol* 8:221, 1979.
2. Till JE, McCulloch EA: A direct measurement of the radiation sensitivity of normal mouse bone marrow cells. *Rad Res* 14:213, 1961.
3. Becker AJ et al: The effect of differing demands for blood cell production on DNA synthesis by hemopoietic colony-forming cells of mice. *Blood* 26:296, 1965.
4. Gidali J, Lajtha LG: Regulation of haemopoietic stem cell turnover in partially irradiated mice. *Cell Tissue Kinet* 5:147, 1972.
5. Wolf NS: The haemopoietic microenvironment. *Clin Haematol* 8:469, 1979.
6. Phillips RA: Stem cell heterogeneity: Pluripotent and committed stem cells of the myeloid and lymphoid lineages, in Clarkson B et al (eds): *Differentiation of Normal and Neoplastic Hematopoietic Cells.* Cold Spring Harbor, NY, Cold Spring Harbor Conference on Cell Proliferation, 1978, p 109.
7. Schofield R, Lajtha LG: Effect of isopropyl methane sulphonate (MS) on haemopoietic colony-forming cells. *Br J Haematol* 25:195, 1974.
8. Schofield R et al: Self maintenance capacity of CFU-s. *J Cell Physiol* 103:355, 1980.
9. Mauch P et al: Evidence of structured variation in self-renewal capacity within long-term bone marrow cultures. *Proc Natl Acad Sci USA* 77:2927, 1980.
10. Lipschitz DA et al: The use of long term marrow culture as a model for the aging process. *Age* 6:122, 1983.
11. Hellman S et al: Proliferative capacity of murine hematopoietic stem cells. *Proc Natl Acad Sci USA* 75:490, 1978.
12. Reincke U et al: Proliferative capacity of murine hematopoietic stem cells in vitro. *Science* 215:1619, 1982.

13. Mauch P et al: Decline in bone marrow proliferative capacity as a function of age. *Blood* 60:245, 1982.
14. Albright JA, Makinodan T: Decline in the growth potential of spleen-colonizing bone marrow stem cells of long lived aging mice. *J Exp Med* 144:1204, 1976.
15. Chen MG: Age related changes in hematopoietic stem cell population of a long lived hybrid mouse. *J Cell Physiol* 78:225, 1971.
16. Ogden DA, Micklem HS: The fate of serially transplanted bone marrow cell populations from young and old donors. *Transplantation* 22:287, 1976.
17. Harrison DE et al: Loss of proliferative capacity in immunohemopoietic stem cells caused by serial transplantation rather than aging. *J Exp Med* 147:1526, 1978.
18. Ross EAM et al: Serial depletion and regeneration of the murine hematopoietic system: Implication for hematopoietic organization and the study of cellular aging. *J Exp Med* 155:432, 1982.
19. Harrison DE: Normal production of erythrocytes by mouse bone marrow continuous for 73 months. *Proc Natl Acad Sci USA* 70:3184, 1972.
20. Williams LH et al: An evaluation of the effect of age on hematopoiesis in C57BL/6 mouse. *Exp Hematol* 14:827, 1986.
21. Everitt AV, Webb C: The blood picture of the aging male rat. *J Gerontol* 13:255, 1958.
22. Coggle JE, Proukakis C: The effect of age on the bone marrow cellularity of the mouse. *Gerontologia* 16:25, 1970.
23. Boggs DR, Patrene KD: Hematopoiesis and aging: III. Anemia and a blunted erythropoietic response to hemorrhage in aged mice. *Am J Hematol* 19:327, 1985.
24. Tyan ML: Old mice: Marrow response to bleeding and endotoxin. *Proc Soc Exp Biol Med* 169:295, 1982.
25. Udupa KB, Lipschitz DA: Erythropoiesis in the aged mouse: I. Response to stimulation in vivo. *J Lab Clin Med* 103:574, 1984.
26. Udupa KB, Lipschitz DA: Erythropoiesis in the aged mouse: II. Response to stimulation in vivo. *J Lab Clin Med* 103:581, 1984.
27. Lipschitz DA et al: Effect of age on hematopoiesis in man. *Blood* 63:502, 1984.
28. Garry PJ et al: Iron status and anemia in the elderly. *J Am Geriatr Soc* 31:389, 1983.
29. Lipschitz DA et al: The anemia of senescence. *Am J Hematol* 11:47, 1981.
30. Babior BM, Cohen HJ: Measurement of neutrophil function: Phagocytosis, degranulation, the respiratory burst and bacterial killing, in Cline MJ (ed): *Leukocyte Function.* New York, Churchill Livingstone, 1981.
31. Babior BM et al: Biological defense mechanisms: The production by leukocytes of superoxide, a potential bactericidal agent. *J Clin Invest* 52:741, 1973.
32. McLaughlin B et al: Age-related differences in granulocyte chemotaxis and degranulation. *Clin Sci* 70:59, 1986.
33. Nagel JE et al: Oxidative metabolism and bactericidal capacity of polymorphonuclear leukocyte from young and aged adults. *J Gerontol* 37:529, 1982.
34. Suzuki K et al: Age-related decline in lysosomal enzyme release from polymorphonuclear leukocytes after *N*-formyl-methionylleucyl-phenylalanine stimulation. *Exp Hematol* 11:1005, 1982.
35. Lipschitz DA et al: The role of calcium in the age-related decline of neutrophil function. *Blood* 71:659, 1988.
36. Lipschitz DA et al: Effect of age on second messenger generation in the neutrophil. *Blood* 78:1347, 1991.
37. Lipschitz DA et al: Evidence that microenvironmental factors account for the age-related decline in neutrophil function. *Blood* 70:1131, 1987.
38. Lipschitz DA, Udupa KB: Influence of aging and protein deficiency on neutrophil function. *J Gerontol* 41:690, 1986.

Chapter 65

ANEMIA

D. A. Lipschitz

It is generally recognized that anemia is a common clinical problem in the elderly. Studies have shown a high prevalence in hospitalized older subjects, patients attending geriatric clinics, and institutionalized older individuals. However, if stringent criteria are employed for the selection of apparently normal subjects, the elderly should have minimal if any decline in hemoglobin values. This chapter will review the etiology of anemia and present evidence that declines in hemoglobin levels with advancing age are not a consequence of the normal aging process. A rational approach to the clinical evaluation of subjects with anemia will be presented.

PREVALENCE OF ANEMIA

A series of epidemiologic studies from the United States, Canada, and Europe[1–5] demonstrated a high prevalence of anemia in the elderly. In women above age 59, anemia occurs as frequently as in women of childbearing age. In men, a definite increase in the prevalence of anemia is found in older age groups. Studies from Great Britain are important, as they have determined the incidence of anemia in large numbers of subjects above age 60. In both men and women, the prevalence of anemia increased significantly with each successive decade. An analysis of the second National Health and Nutrition Education Survey (NHANES II) demonstrated a significant reduction in hemoglobin levels with advancing age in apparently healthy males and a minimal although significant decrease in elderly females.[6] Based upon a lower normal limit of 14 g/dl for hemoglobin concentration, a very large percentage of elderly males would be found to be anemic. This study proposed that the reduction for males was a consequence of aging and suggested that age-specific reference standards for hemoglobin concentration be adopted.

An evaluation of apparently healthy elderly subjects with mild anemia has revealed that the cause is not usually obvious.[7] A careful assessment of hematopoiesis in these individuals revealed mild marrow failure, as evidenced by reductions in bone marrow differentiated and stem cell number and modest decreases in peripheral leukocyte counts.[8]

A major unanswered question is whether this decline in hemoglobin with advancing age is a consequence of the normal aging process or reflects some yet to be defined abnormality. Of particular importance in this regard is the finding that anemia is extremely rare in an affluent, healthy elderly population examined in New Mexico.[9] None of the elderly males and females in this group were anemic. Furthermore, longitudinal monitoring of these subjects over a 5-year period failed to demonstrate an increased prevalence of anemia. Based upon this observation and the animal studies of hematopoiesis (see Chap. 64), it seems highly likely that the decrease in hemoglobin seen commonly with advancing age is not a consequence of the normal aging process and is related to some extrinsic variable that remains to be determine.

Inflammation or chronic disease is one likely etiology of apparent age-related anemia (see below for a discussion of this type of anemia).[10] A second possibility is that the anemia has a nutritional basis. This is suggested by a closer examination of data obtained in epidemiologic surveys in which anemia has been shown to be most prevalent in populations that are at a low socioeconomic level, where the prevalence of nutritional deficiencies is high.

We have performed a comprehensive nutritional and hematologic evaluation of a group of 73 elderly veterans living in a domiciliary facility. A high prevalence of anemia was present in this population. A close evaluation demonstrated that iron deficiency, folate deficiency, and other commonly described causes of anemia were rare. We then performed a multivariate analysis of the data using age, hematopoietic, and nutritional factors as covariants. We demonstrated that while age appeared to be the major variable accounting for the decline in immunologic measurements observed in this elderly population, age did not appear to be an important factor in the prevalence of anemia. In contrast, serum albumin, transferrin, and prealbumin, which assess nutritional status, appeared to be excellent predictors of anemia. This information provides indirect evidence that a nutritional variable may contribute to the anemia seen in these elderly populations. Further evidence suggesting that a nutritional factor may contribute to the anemia comes from the observation that there is a marked similarity between the alterations in immunologic and hematopoietic function that occur with aging and those that occur with protein deprivation (Table 65-1). This raises the possibility that protein deprivation in some form may contribute to the hematopoietic changes normally ascribed to aging.

There is evidence that correction of protein-energy malnutrition in the hospitalized elderly can markedly improve hematopoietic function.[11] In these subjects, interpretation of improvements in hematologic status is extremely difficult. Any hospitalized elderly individual has coexisting diseases that can affect hematopoietic function. Thus the overall improvement seen with nutritional rehabilitation may reflect an overall improvement of the patient's medical status. The effect of increased feeding on hematopoietic status has been examined in relatively healthy elderly individuals who lived at home, who were ambulatory but were underweight and had marginal evidence of protein-energy deprivation. By providing polymeric dietary supplements to these subjects between meals, it was possible to correct nutritional deficiencies and obtain weight gain. Despite a positive impact on nutritional status, however, the anemia, invariably present in this population, did not improve.[12]

Some conclusions can be drawn from these observations. It is clear that significant nutritional deficiencies reversibly aggravate the hematologic abnormalities in the elderly. Even in apparently healthy older individuals, it is possible that nutritional factors contribute to hematopoietic changes, but alternative mechanisms other than simple nutritional deficiency must be considered. Marginal reductions of one or more nutrients acting alone or in combination over a prolonged period of time may modulate hematopoietic change usually ascribed to aging. Alternatively, nutrient delivery to the target organ may be altered with aging or changes in nutrient target interaction may occur. These possibilities could account for the higher prevalence of anemia reported in epidemiologic studies. They remain no more than potential hypotheses that will require further research.

In contrast to healthy older persons, in whom the prevalence of anemia is relatively low, the disorder is extremely common in hospitalized patients in both acute and chronic care settings. In a recent survey of hospitalized patients in a Veterans Affairs hospital, 56 percent of patients over the age of 75 had a significant anemia.[13]

TABLE 65-1

Similarities Between Changes in Immune and Hematopoietic Function Caused by Aging or Protein-Energy Malnutrition

	Aging	Protein-Energy Malnutrition
Cell mediated immunity		
Delayed cutaneous hypersensitivity	Decreased	Decreased
T-cell number	Decreased	Decreased
Percentage of T-suppressor cells	Increased	Increased
Blastogenic response to mitogen	Decreased	Decreased
Humoral immunity		
B-cell number	Unchanged	Unchanged
Antibody production	Moderately decreased	Moderately decreased
Erythropoiesis		
Hemoglobin	Decreased	Decreased
Marrow erythroid cells	Decreased	Decreased
CFU-E number	Decreased	Decreased
BFU-E number	Normal	Normal
Myelopoiesis		
Granulocyte number	Reduced	Reduced
Granulocytosis after endotoxin administration	Decreased	Decreased
CFU-C number	Decreased	Decreased

EVALUATION OF ANEMIA IN THE ELDERLY

For practical purposes we recommend 12 g/dl as a lower limit of normal for hemoglobin for both elderly men and elderly women. Attempting to define the cause of anemia when the hemoglobin concentration is between 12 and 14 g/dl in elderly men only rarely yields an etiology. Even at a level of 12 g/dl, a decision as to how aggressively to evaluate a patient with borderline low hematocrit must rest on clinical judgment. The complex nature of the problems that present in older individuals, together with the high risk of multiple pathologies occurring simultaneously, makes this decision much more critical. On the other hand, once a decision has been made to investigate a low hemoglobin in an older person, the principles involved in assessment and evaluation are very similar to those that would be used in subjects of any age group. The etiologies of the various anemias seen in the elderly are summarized in Table 65-2.

The initial approach to the patient with anemia must include a complete history and physical examination, as well as a complete blood count (CBC) in order to evaluate the size and production rate of red blood cells. Microcytosis, defined as a mean corpuscular volume (MCV) of less than 84 (Coulter counter), indicates an impairment of hemoglobin synthesis. Macrocytosis, defined as an MCV of over 100, may be caused by reticulocytes or more frequently by an ab-

TABLE 65-2

Physiologic Classification of Anemia

Hypoproliferative	Ineffective	Hemolytic
1. Iron-deficient erythropoiesis a. Iron deficiency b. Chronic disease c. Inflammation	1. Megaloblastic a. Vitamin B_{12} b. Folate c. Refractory	1. Immunologic a. Idiopathic b. Secondary to drug, tumor, or disease
2. Erythropoietin lack a. Renal b. Nutritional c. Endocrine	2. Microcytic a. Thalassemia b. Sideroblastic	2. Intrinsic a. Metabolic b. Abnormal hemoglobin
3. Stem cell dysfunction a. Aplastic anemia b. Red blood cell aplasia	3. Normocytic a. Stromal disease b. Dimorphic	3. Extrinsic a. Mechanical b. Lytic substance

normality in nuclear maturation. Red cell production is estimated from the reticulocyte production index. Hemolytic anemia usually has a reticulocyte index greater than 3, whereas a failure of production is indicated by a reticulocyte index of less than 2. Decreased production is caused by the hypoproliferative anemias or by ineffective erythropoiesis. The latter disorder is characterized by significant increases in erythroid cell proliferation. Due to abnormalities in maturation, these cells are unable to exit the bone marrow and are destroyed by marrow reticuloendothelial cells in a process referred to as intramedullary hemolysis. The disorder may be associated with either macrocytosis or microcytosis. An elevated lactate dehydrogenase (LDH) level and indirect hyperbilirubinemia result from the increased destruction of red cell precursors in the marrow and may be used to distinguish ineffective erythropoiesis from hypoproliferative anemia.

Observation may be reasonable for those older individuals who have a mild decrease in hemoglobin (10.5 to 12 g/dl), a normal reticulocyte index, normochromic normocytic indices, no leukocyte or platelet abnormalities, and no occult blood in the stool. Further investigation is indicated if the anemia worsens or a change in the peripheral blood pattern occurs. For individuals with mild anemia and hypochromic microcytic indices or more severe anemia with normochromic normocytic indices, a more extensive workup is required. Similarly the presence of macrocytosis warrants additional investigation. A rational approach to the laboratory workup of anemia is illustrated in Figs. 65-1 and 65-2. A significantly elevated reticulocyte count, indirect hyperbilirubinemia, and elevated LDH are diagnostic of hemolytic anemia. A low reticulocyte count, elevated indirect biluribin, and elevated LDH suggest ineffective erythropoiesis. In older persons with ineffective erythropoiesis, macrocytosis strongly suggests vitamin B_{12} or folate deficiency and microcytosis should suggest sideroblastic anemia (Fig. 65-1).

THE HYPOPROLIFERATIVE ANEMIAS

Figure 65-2 illustrates an approach to the workup of hypoproliferative anemia, which accounts for the majority of anemias in the elderly. Iron is the only nutrient that limits the rate of erythropoiesis. Thus inadequate iron supply for erythropoiesis, the commonest cause of anemia in older persons, results in a hypoproliferative anemia. This is diagnosed by the presence of a decreased serum iron and a reduced transferrin saturation (serum iron divided by the total iron binding capacity, or TIBC, expressed as a percent). Absolute iron deficiency (blood loss) is the commonest cause of iron deficient erythropoiesis in younger subjects. In the elderly, the etiology is more likely to be the "anemia of chronic disease" or anemia associated with inflammation. Iron-deficient erythropoiesis in these disorders results from a defective ability of the reticuloendothelial system to reutilize iron derived from senescent red cells. Thus tissue iron stores are normal or increased, resulting in a serum ferritin concentration above 50 ng/ml and reduction in the TIBC. This contrasts with a low serum ferritin and high TIBC, which reflect absent iron stores in blood-loss anemia.

Blood loss, the anemia of inflammation, and chronic disease and that associated with protein-energy malnutrition are the most prevalent anemias in elderly populations. In younger individuals, iron deficiency anemia is usually due to either blood loss or nutritional iron deficiency. In both men and women, a progressive increase in iron stores occurs with advancing age. In older men, tissue iron stores average 1200 mg; in women, iron stores increase from a mean of 300 mg to approximately 800 mg over the decade following menopause. Thus nutritional iron deficiency is very rare in the elderly despite the prominence of other nutritional problems. When unex-

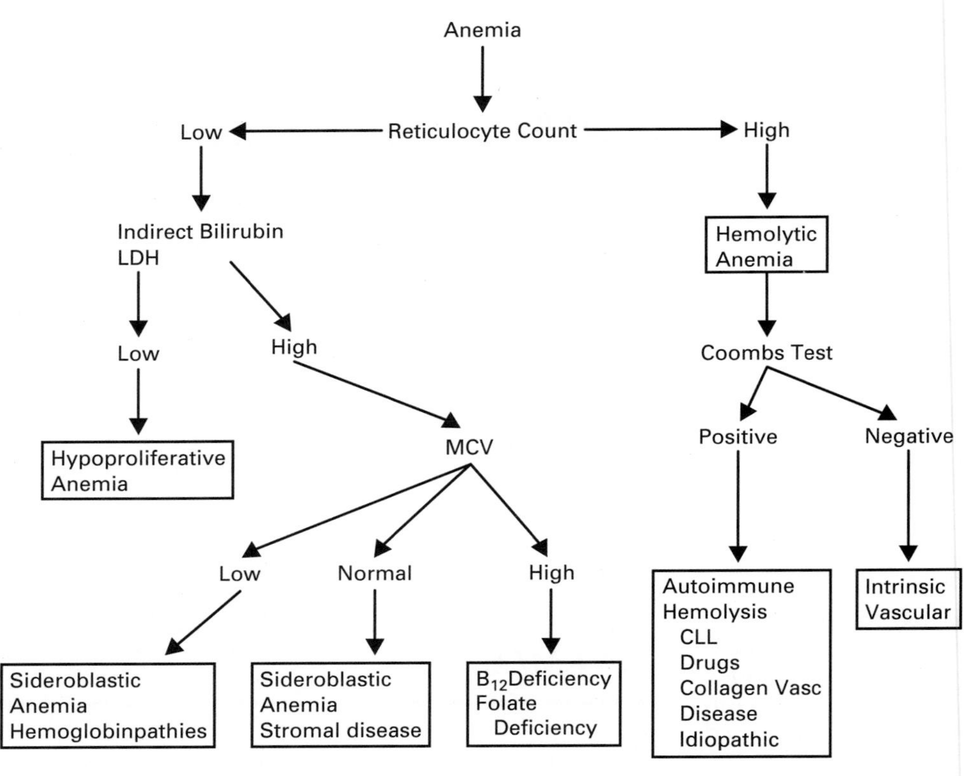

FIGURE 65-1
A rational strategy for the workup of anemia in the elderly. The initial approach is to exclude hemolysis and ineffective erythropoiesis.

plained iron deficiency does occur, it is almost exclusively due to blood loss from the intestinal tract, even if bleeding is not detected by repeated stool guaiac determinations. Other routes of bleeding may occur but are easily recognizable (epistaxis, abnormal bleeding from the uterus, hematuria). The causes of blood loss in the elderly include drugs (aspirin) and bleeding due to a neoplasm. Angiodysplasia of the large bowel and diverticular disease are frequent causes but should only be considered once a neoplasm

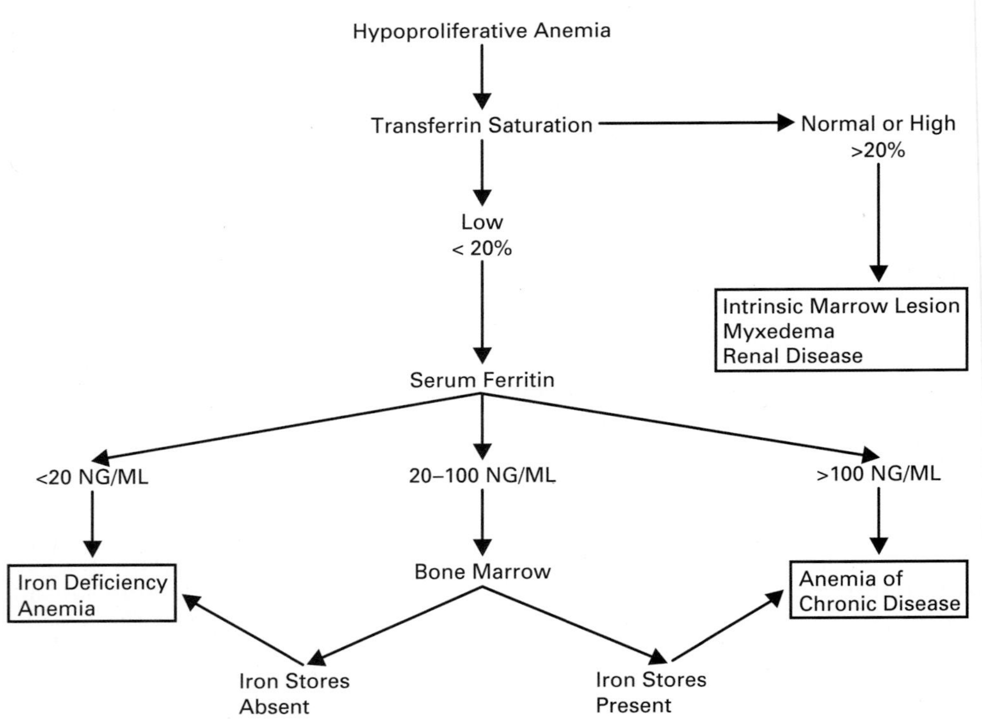

FIGURE 65-2
The workup of hypoproliferative anemia in the elderly.

has been excluded. Rarely, iron deficiency can result from malabsorption or urinary losses of iron which occur in the face of intravascular hemolysis.

Inflammation is a second important cause of anemia in the elderly and is perhaps the more frequent. Inflammation may be the result of bacterial infection, immune reaction, tissue necrosis, or neoplasm. Usually the decrease in hematocrit is moderate. Hematologic findings differ from iron deficiency in that the iron block is less severe and microcytosis is usually minimal. In some instances, these hematologic findings may be present with little or no evidence of inflammation. Inadequate food intake and increased tissue breakdown may contribute to the severity of the anemia through decreased erythropoietin stimulation. Treatment is that of the underlying disease. Only rarely is anemia severe enough to require transfusion. Iron therapy is usually ineffective owing to the limited absorption of iron in the presence of inflammation and the trapping of parenteral iron in the macrophage.

The term *anemia of chronic disease* is often used to explain an anemia associated with some other major disease process. Examples include cancer, collagen vascular disorders, rheumatoid arthritis, and inflammatory bowel disease. Occasionally the anemia may be the initial manifestation of an occult disease. It is critical for the clinician to be aware of this possibility and to assure a rational and appropriate workup. Management of the anemia associated with inflammation or chronic disease consists of ensuring adequate nutrition and treating the underlying disease process.

Nutritional deprivation in the aged generally results in a normocytic normochromic anemia with an essentially normal peripheral smear. In the hospitalized patient, evidence of iron-deficient erythropoiesis (low transferrin saturation) is common and the serum ferritin is elevated. There is usually a history of weight loss, and laboratory studies indicate a reduced serum albumin and a decreased TIBC (<240 g/dl). This disorder is particularly important, as there is evidence that correction of the nutritional deficiency and its underlying cause can result in significant improvement in the hemoglobin level and other hematopoietic parameters.

Marrow failure due to interference with the proliferation of hematopoietic cells occurs in the elderly. The disorder is generally associated with suppression of all marrow elements and is suggested by the presence of peripheral pancytopenia. Common causes include drugs, immune damage to the stem-cell population, intrinsic marrow lesions, and marrow replacement by malignant cells or fibrous tissue. The latter is usually associated with a myelophthisic blood picture (nucleated red cells, giant platelets, and metamyelocytes on smear) as a reflection of the disruption of marrow stromal architecture. The presence of pancytopenia and the absence of iron-deficient erythropoiesis is an indication for bone marrow aspiration and biopsy. Occasionally isolated suppression of erythropoiesis occurs, which is referred to as pure red cell aplasia. This disorder may be drug-related or may be caused by benign or malignant abnormalities of lymphocytes, including thymoma. These subjects present with isolated anemia, an elevated serum iron, and absent erythroid precursors on bone marrow examination.

INEFFECTIVE ERYTHROPOIESIS

Macrocytic anemias in the elderly result from vitamin B_{12} and folate deficiency. The prevalence of pernicious anemia increases significantly with advancing age. The disorder results from malabsorption of vitamin B_{12} as a consequence of antibodies against gastric parietal cells and intrinsic factor. Atrophic gastritis and decreased secretion of extrinsic factor occur, resulting in failure of vitamin B_{12} absorption. Pernicious anemia occurs most frequently in subjects over the age of 60 and is more common in women. The anemia may be very severe, presenting with weakness and a lemon-yellow discoloration, although occasionally anemia is absent.[14] Neurologic abnormalities—including peripheral neuropathy, ataxia, loss of position sense, and upper motor neuron signs—are frequent. Behavioral abnormalities and dementia are well described and may occur in the absence of anemia or macrocytosis.[15] Occasionally there is evidence of a more generalized immunologic disorder, manifesting with myxedema, hypoadrenalism, and vitiligo.

The presence of pancytopenia, macrocytosis, hypersegmented polymorphonuclear leukocytes in the peripheral smear, a decreased reticulocyte index, an increased LDH, and indirect hypobilirubinemia suggests a diagnosis of megaloblastic anemia. The bone marrow classically shows giant metamyelocytes, hypersegmented polymorphonuclear leukocytes, and enlarged erythroid precursors with more hemoglobin than would be expected from the immaturity of their nuclei (nuclear cytoplasmic dissociation). The diagnosis is made by demonstrating serum vitamin B_{12} concentration of less than 100 pg/ml. However, one study reported that one-third of patients with pernicious anemia had a value >100 pg/ml.[14] Vitamin B_{12} deficiency may also be caused by diseases of the ileum. The Schilling test is able to distinguish a deficiency of intrinsic factor (malabsorption corrected by ingested vitamin B_{12} and intrinsic factor) from an abnormality in the ability of the ileum to absorb the vitamin B_{12} intrinsic factor complex (absorption still impaired with intrinsic factor plus vitamin B_{12}). Treatment consists of weekly or biweekly injection of 100 g of vitamin B_{12} until stores are replenished. A maintenance dose at monthly intervals is then adequate.

Epidemiologic studies have generally shown an adequate folate nutriture in the elderly. Folate deficiency of sufficient severity to cause anemia in the elderly is most frequently found in association with protein-energy malnutrition and excessive alcohol consumption. Alcohol and various other drugs are also known to interfere with folate absorption and internal metabolism. Vulnerability to deficiency is significantly greater when folate requirements are increased as a result of inflammation, neoplastic disease, or hemolytic anemia. The hematologic profile is identical to that described for vitamin B_{12} deficiency. The diagnosis is made by the demonstration of significant reductions in the serum (<2 ng/ml) or red cell (<100 ng/ml) folate concentration. Prior to commencement of therapy with folate, it is important to exclude vitamin B_{12} deficiency, as treatment with folate can aggravate the neurologic abnormalities in the latter disorder.

The major causes of ineffective erythropoiesis and microcytosis are thalassemia and the sideroblastic anemias. Although thalassemia is generally diagnosed at an earlier age, there are reports of its initial detection in older people. On the other hand, acquired sideroblastic anemia is primarily a disease of the elderly. It is a heterogenous group of disorders characterized by the presence of iron deposits in the mitochondria of normoblasts. The disorder is a consequence of impaired heat synthesis. It usually reflects an intrinsic marrow lesion (idiopathic) but may be secondary to inflammation, neoplasia, or drug ingestion. The common finding is the presence of a dimorphic red cell population, in part markedly hypochromic and in part well filled with hemoglobin. The diagnosis is made by the demonstration of ringed sideroblasts in the bone marrow as well as the presence of maturation abnormalities of myeloid and erythroid precursors. A fraction of elderly patients with sideroblastic anemia show some response to pharmacologic doses of pyridoxine (200 mg three times daily). This dose should be given to all patients until it becomes apparent that a rise in hemoglobin concentration will not occur. For patients who are unresponsive to pyridoxine, the anemia must be treated symptomatically.

Di Guglielmo's syndrome is more common in older people presenting with megaloblastic erythroid precursors. Frequently, abnormal sideroblasts will also be seen. The peripheral smear usually demonstrates pancytopenia with occasional nucleated red cells or immature myeloid and megakaryocytic precursors. The bone marrow is markedly hyperplastic. It is essential to exclude vitamin B_{12} and folate deficiency, and a trial of pyridoxine may be indicated. Treatment is usually supportive. There is some evidence that these disorders are premalignant, evolving rarely into a subacute or acute myelogenous leukemia.

HEMOLYTIC ANEMIAS

The causes of hemolytic anemia in the elderly are somewhat different than those found in younger subjects. Although most patients with congenital disorders will previously have been identified, an occasional patient with congenital hemolytic anemia may present for the first time with symptoms related to cholelithiasis. Autoimmune hemolytic anemia is the commonest cause in the elderly; the diagnosis is made by the presence of a positive Coombs' test. In younger subjects, an etiology of the autoimmune hemolysis is only rarely identified. In the elderly, on the other hand, the anemia is more likely to be associated with a lymphoproliferative disorder (non-Hodgkin's lymphoma or chronic lymphocytic leukemia), collagen vascular disease, or drug ingestion. Steroids and splenectomy are usually effective in patients with red cell antibodies of the IgG type. Patients with red cell antibodies of the IgM variety are more likely to be refractory to such treatment.

A disorder of some importance in the aged is microangiopathic hemolytic anemia. This is usually associated with severe infections or disseminated neoplasm and presents with not only hemolytic anemia but also a consumptive coagulopathy. The presence of red cell fragmentation, thrombocytopenia, a prolonged partial thromboplastin time, and hemosiderinuria should suggest this diagnosis.

COMPLEX PRESENTATION OF ANEMIA IN THE ELDERLY

The presence of multiple pathologies frequently makes the evaluation of anemia difficult in older persons. As illustrated in Table 65-3, an investigation of hospitalized patients indicated that multiple diagnoses contributed to the anemia in 53 percent. A classic example is a patient with active rheumatoid disease who has lost blood from aspirin ingestion. Similarly protein-energy malnutrition or blood loss will markedly aggravate the anemia associated with neoplasia. Iron deficiency and vitamin B_{12} deficiency may coexist, presenting confusing red blood cell indices. The possibility of a multifactorial etiology—including blood loss, malnutrition, folate deficiency, or hemo-

TABLE 65-3

The Diagnosis of Anemia in Patients over Age 75 in an Acute Care Veterans' Hospital

Diagnosis	Percentage
Multiple diagnoses	53
No diagnosis	17
Single diagnosis	30
Anemia of chronic disease	10
Malnutrition	9
Infection	4
Post-op bleeding	3
Alcohol	1
Iron deficiency	1

lytic disease—should always be considered when the anemia of chronic disease or inflammation is associated with a hemoglobin below 10 g/dl. In this circumstance, laboratory investigations frequently give equivocal results; hence a bone marrow examination may be required. In this circumstance, clinical judgment is critically important in deciding how aggressive the workup for anemia should be.

REFERENCES

1. Hill RD: The prevalence of anemia in the over-65s in a rural practice. *Practitioner* 217:963, 1967.
2. McLennan WJ et al: Anaemia in the elderly. *Q J Med* 52:1, 1973.
3. Myers MA et al: The hemoglobin level of fit elderly people. *Lancet* 2:261, 1968.
4. *Nutrition Canada: National Survey.* Ottawa, Canada, Information Canada, 1973.
5. Parson PL et al: The prevalence of anemia in the elderly. *Practitioner* 195:656, 1965.
6. Yip R et al: Age-related changes in laboratory values used in the diagnosis of anemia and iron deficiency. *Am J Clin Nutr* 39:427, 1984.
7. Lipschitz DA et al: The anemia of senescence. *Am J Hematol* 11:47, 1981.
8. Lipschitz DA et al: Effect of age on hematopoiesis in man. *Blood* 63:502, 1984.
9. Garry PJ et al: Iron status and anemia in the elderly. *J Am Geriatr Soc* 31:389, 1983.
10. Dallman PR et al: Prevalence and causes of anemia in the United States, 1976 to 1980. *Am J Clin Nutr* 39:437, 1984.
11. Lipschitz DA, Mitchell CO: The correctability of the nutritional, immune and hematopoietic manifestations of protein calorie malnutrition in the elderly. *J Am Coll Nutr* 1:17, 1982.
12. Lipschitz DA et al: Nutritional evaluation and supplementation of elderly subjects participating in a "meals on wheels" program. *J Parenter Enter Nutr* 9:343, 1984.
13. Rothstein G: Personal communication.
14. Carmel R: Pernicious anemia. The expected findings of very low serum cobalamin levels, anemia, and macrocytosis are often lacking. *Arch Intern Med* 148:1712, 1988.
15. Lindenbaum J et al: Neuropsychiatric disorders caused by cobalamin deficiency in the absence of anemia or macrocytosis. *N Engl J Med* 318:1720, 1988.

Chapter 66

WHITE CELL DISORDERS

Gerald Rothstein

Elderly people experience many of the disorders and alterations in circulating white cells which occur in younger adults. However, the white cell system of the elderly differs from that of younger people in significant ways. For example, some diseases—such as chronic lymphocytic leukemia, polycythemia vera, and atypical chronic myelocytic leukemia—are so common in the aged population that they could be considered diseases of the elderly. In addition, in elderly people the marrow regenerates slowly, and this likely underlies the observation that elderly people have greater difficulty in regenerating marrow after chemotherapy. To recognize and respond effectively to disorders of the white cells in the elderly patient, it is necessary to have a fundamental knowledge of the physiology of the white cell system and the strategies for its evaluation.

FUNCTIONS OF THE WHITE CELLS

The principal functions of the white cell system are the same in elderly as in young adults: maintenance of host resistance to infection and immune surveillance. The white cells are a multicomponent system which is essential for adequate antimicrobial defense and immune function. The cells which constitute this system are the neutrophils, lymphocytes, monocytes/macrophages, eosinophils, and basophils (Table 66-1). The *neutrophils* have the ability to migrate to tissues, where they ingest and kill invading microorganisms. When the supply of neutrophils is severely diminished, the incidence of life-threatening bacterial infection rises dramatically.[1] The *lymphocytes* contribute to host resistance by interacting with one another to generate antibodies, maintaining the ability to mount delayed hypersensitivity reactions, and producing cytokines which regulate the immune system.[2] These cytokines are also regulators of blood cell production and they participate in maintaining cellular and humoral immunity. *Monocytes* and *macrophages* play important roles in resistance to intracellular pathogens such as mycobacteria,[3] and they also participate in the regulation of iron metabolism, red cell destruction, and tumor surveillance.[4] *Eosinophils* provide a line of defense against parasitic organisms, and they modulate hypersensitivity reactions.[5] The function of *basophils* is poorly understood, but these cells may serve as a source of secreted histamine.[6]

FUNCTIONAL CHANGES IN THE WHITE CELLS DURING AGING

There are no consistently demonstrated changes in the function of neutrophils during aging. However, monocytes from aged rodents are diminished in their ability to kill intracellular pathogens. Similar monocyte defects have not been demonstrated in aged humans. If such defects do exist, they might underlie the unusual susceptibility of elderly people to infection with intracellular pathogens as well as the increased incidence of malignant disorders in elderly persons. The function of the T lymphocytes of the elderly is also impaired in vitro and may contribute to the age-associated reduction in the antibody response to immunizations.

STRATEGIES FOR EVALUATING THE WHITE CELLS

The white cells can be evaluated in several ways: assessment of their function, quantification of their numbers, evaluation of their morphology, and determination of their karyotypic characteristics.

Functional Evaluation

The function of the white cell system can be most directly assessed by obtaining a history of the frequency and severity of infection. In an elderly patient, re-

TABLE 66-1

Cells of the Leukocyte System

Cell Type	Anatomic Location	Actions
Neutrophils	Blood, marrow, tissues	Microbial killing
B lymphocytes	Blood, marrow, lymph nodes, tissues	Antibody production
T lymphocytes	Blood, thymus, lymph nodes	Antigen processing Cytokine production Immune suppression Delayed hypersensitivity
Monocytes	Blood, marrow, lymph nodes	Killing of intracellular pathogens Cytokine production
Eosinophils	Blood, marrow, tissues	Resistance to parasitic infestation, modulation of hypersensitivity reactions
Basophils	Blood, marrow, tissues	Unknown; a source of histamine

peated acute bacterial infection or severe infection with only a trivial insult most often indicates a reduced neutrophil supply (e.g., in postchemotherapy neutropenia or leukemia) and/or an insufficient supply of immunoglobulin antibodies (e.g., in chronic lymphocytic leukemia). Infection with organisms of low virulence (*Pneumocystis, Candida, Serratia,* or atypical acid-fast organisms) suggests defective lymphocyte-mediated cellular immunity, which can occur during the course of certain lymphomas or in subjects with acquired immunodeficiency syndrome (AIDS). If there is no evidence of an increase in infections, this should be taken as evidence against a functionally significant disorder of the leukocytes, even if the white cell count is depressed. Physical examination is useful in determining the site, extent, and type of infection. In addition, physical findings may point to the underlying etiology of a white cell disorder.

Numerical and Morphologic Evaluation

The white cells are counted and their morphologic types are identified in the course of a complete blood count (CBC). The information in the CBC report includes the "white blood cell count" (WBC) and the differential count. It should be realized, however, that current technology for the WBC registers *all* nucleated cells, not only the white cells. Furthermore, the WBC alone does not specify the various types of white cells. Consequently, when the question of disorders of white cells arises, a differential count should be performed. The term *total white cell count* refers to all of the leukocytes regardless of their morphologic type. In addition, using the WBC and differential count, *absolute counts* can be calculated. The absolute count is calculated by multiplying the percentage of a cell type, such as neutrophils, by the total WBC. For example, if the WBC is $10 \times 10^3/\mu l$ and the percentage of neutrophils (by differential count) is 5 percent, then the absolute neutrophil count is $0.5 \times 10^3/\mu l$. From this example, it can be seen that neither the WBC nor the differential alone is completely informative. At the present time, differential counts are routinely performed electronically using special stains and analyses that depend on color scanning and determination of cellular size. When reports are returned from these automated differential counts, the term *granulocytes* includes both fully segmented neutrophils and the nonsegmented band forms. In some cases, this information is not sufficient, and microscopic examination can be of considerable importance. For example, the presence of band forms ("bands") can be useful support for the diagnosis of an active bacterial infection, even when the WBC is normal or reduced. In adults, the normal values for bands have not been established, but differential percentages of >3 percent bands should be considered as consistent with but not definitive for a diagnosis of active bacterial infection or other inflammatory process. Also, increased counts for large unstained cells (LUC) may signal the presence of circulating neoplastic cells, such as blasts or lymphoma cells, and should prompt a microscopic examination of the blood smear.

The normal ranges for the WBC, electronically determined differential count, and absolute leukocyte counts do not differ between healthy elderly and young adults. Reference values are shown in Table 66-2.

THE SIGNIFICANCE OF INCREASED LEUKOCYTE COUNTS

Increases in the counts for neutrophils, lymphocytes, eosinophils, monocytes, and basophils can be found in both nonmalignant and malignant disease. An in-

TABLE 66-2

Total and Absolute Leukocyte Counts for Adults*

Test	Mean $\times 10^3/\mu l$	Range $\times 10^3/\mu l$
White blood count		
Men		3.8–10.6
Women		3.6–11.0
Lymphocytes	2.06	0.9–3.22
Monocytes	0.37	0.12–0.62
Neutrophils	4.01	1.4–6.71
Eosinophils	0.13	0.00–0.30
Basophils	0.05	0.01–0.09
Large unstained cells	0.12	0.00–0.31

*The data for absolute neutrophils are based on measurements made with 64 male medical students, ages 23 to 31.
SOURCE: From Wintrobe.[7]

crease in the total WBC to above $11 \times 10^3/\mu l$ is referred to as *leukocytosis* and, taken by itself, is a nonspecific finding. To determine the significance of leukocytosis, the counts for the individual types of white cells must be determined by calculating absolute counts for neutrophils, lymphocytes, monocytes, basophils, and eosinophils. The disease associations for increases in these various white cells are shown in Table 66-3.

TABLE 66-3

Conditions Associated with Increased Leukocyte Counts

Increased Neutrophil Counts
1. Nonmalignant
   - Acute infections
   - Noninfectious inflammation (e.g., burns, gout, myocardial infarction)
   - Acute hemorrhage
   - Acute hemolysis
   - Physiologic neutrophilia (exercise, epinephrine administration)
   - Steroids
   - Leukemoid reactions
2. Clonal or malignant disorders
   - Secondary to metastatic cancer
   - Chronic myelocytic leukemia
   - Polycythemia vera

Increased Lymphocyte Counts
1. Nonmalignant
   - Viral infections (e.g., cytomegalovirus, hepatitis)
2. Malignant
   - Chronic lymphocytic leukemia
   - Lymphomas

Increased Eosinophil Counts
1. Allergic conditions
   - Medicines
   - Asthma
2. Skin diseases
3. Parasitic infection
4. Hypereosinophilic syndrome

Increased Monocyte Counts
1. Intracellular pathogens (e.g., tuberculosis, listeriosis)
2. Other infections
3. Malignancies
4. Chronic steroid use

Increased Basophil Counts
1. Chronic myelocytic leukemia
2. Polycythemia vera
3. Lymphomas
4. Hypothyroidism

Increases in Large Unstained Cells
1. Hematologic malignancy

Increased Neutrophil Counts

When the absolute number of neutrophils is greater than $6.7 \times 10^3/\mu l$, *neutrophilia* is said to be present. Neutrophilia can be a manifestation of either a nonmalignant or a malignant process.

Nonmalignant Neutrophilias

Neutrophilia due to nonmalignant causes rarely exceeds 40×10^3 neutrophils/μl. Causes of nonmalignant neutrophilia (Table 66-3) include acute infections, particularly coccal infections. During bacterial infection, there is frequently a "left shift" of the WBC differential; i.e., there are increased numbers of band neutrophils in the blood because the marrow has dispatched immature neutrophils into the circulation.[8] A left shift also occurs during inflammatory processes such as burns, myocardial infarction, and gout[9] as well as following acute hemorrhage or hemolysis.[10] Another type of neutrophilia is *physiologic neutrophilia,* which occurs after exercise or after the administration of epinephrine.[11] Physiologic neutrophilia is usually modest (less than $15 \times 10^3/\mu l$), and since epinephrine and exercise elevate the neutrophil count by redistributing intravascular neutrophils, this neutrophilia is not associated with a left shift. Neutrophilia is also caused by glucocorticoids[12] and may occur during the endogenous steroid release due to infection or other stressful illness or treatment with corticosteroids. When neutrophilia is due to chronic steroid administration, the mechanism for the increased count is a delayed migration of neutrophils from the blood. Thus, a left shift is not expected. A usual characteristic of nonmalignant neutrophilias is that leukocytes more immature than myelocytes are rarely seen in the blood. Consequently, when very immature neutrophils are found in the blood (particularly blasts or promyelocytes), this should raise the question of leukemia. The exception to this is that some patients may have *leukemoid reactions* in response to such nonmalignant conditions as tuberculosis, meningitis, and severe hemorrhage.[13]

Leukemoid reactions are usually associated with total WBCs above $50 \times 10^3/\mu l$, and some of the circulating cells may be very immature. In some cases, it may be difficult to distinguish a true leukemia from a leukemoid reaction. Hematologic consultation may be necessary to make this distinction.

Neutrophilia and Malignancy

Neutrophilia may also be a marker for *malignant disease* (Table 66-3), such as metastatic cancer, particularly when marrow or liver are involved. Neutrophilia also occurs in certain malignant or clonally proliferative hematologic disorders, such as *chronic myelocytic leukemia* (CML)[14–21] and *polycythemia vera* (PV)[22–28] (see below for a discussion of these disorders). In the early stages of CML and in PV, the neutrophilia is composed primarily of mature neutrophils. Both of these disorders are of clonal origin, and the clone responsible for the disease is derived from a primitive hematopoietic precursor. Since these primitive clones produce more than one type of differentiated cell, elevations in the platelet and/or red cell count may accompany the neutrophilia in either PV or CML.

Increased Lymphocyte Counts

Lymphocytosis, defined as an absolute lymphocyte count of $>3.22 \times 10^3/\mu l$, accompanies certain infectious or hematopoietic diseases.

Nonmalignant Lymphocytosis

Lymphocytosis may follow transfusion, which is likely to be due to cytomegalovirus infection. Lymphocytosis can also occur during the course of infectious hepatitis. Increased lymphocyte counts have also been described in subjects with thyrotoxicosis; this is most likely to be a *relative lymphocytosis* (increased percentage of lymphocytes in the differential count) rather than a true increase in the absolute lymphocyte count.

Malignant Lymphocytosis

Lymphocytosis may be the hallmark of hematologic disease. For example, an increased lymphocyte count is an invariable finding in chronic lymphocytic leukemia (CLL),[30–35] where it is usually $>15 \times 10^3/\mu l$ (see below).[29] Indeed, in elderly persons, the most frequent explanation for sustained lymphocytosis of $>15 \times 10^3/\mu l$ is CLL. In addition to CLL, lymphocytosis is observed in T-cell lymphoma/leukemia, prolymphocytic leukemia, cutaneous T-cell lymphoma, and hairy cell leukemia.

Increases in Eosinophil Counts

Eosinophilia is present when the absolute eosinophil count exceeds $0.7 \times 10^3/\mu l$.[7] Allergic conditions, such as reactions to medicines (e.g., sulfonamides, nitrofurantoin[36]), angioneurotic edema, and bronchial asthma are associated with eosinophilia, and counts as high as 30×10^3 eosinophils/μl have been recorded.[37] Eosinophilia is also found in a variety of allergic and nonallergic skin disorders, including psoriasis, eczema, and scabies. In certain geographic areas, parasitic infestation should be considered as a cause of eosinophilia. The association of eosinophilia with *Trichinella spiralis* infestation is well documented[38] and, in fact, challenge with *T. spiralis* remains a standard for inducing experimental eosinophilia in animals. Echinococcal infection may also induce eosinophilia,[39] as may *Ascaris* infection.[40] In some patients, sustained eosinophilia of marked degree is associated with a hypereosinophilic syndrome,[41] with extensive infiltration and potentially life-threatening damage of the lungs, myocardium, and pericardium. Eosinophilia may also occur as a secondary manifestation of malignancies, including CML and AML.[42]

Increases in Monocyte Counts

Monocytosis is defined as an absolute monocyte count[7] of $>0.95 \times 10^3/\mu l$ and may be associated with listeriosis[43] or tuberculosis,[44] both of which are caused by pathogens which intracellularly infect monocytes and macrophages. Increases in circulating monocytes have also been observed in patients with bacterial endocarditis, malignancies, lymphomas, collagen vascular disease, and sarcoidosis as well as during the chronic use of steroids.[7]

Increases in Basophil Counts

Basophilia is present when the absolute basophil count exceeds $0.09 \times 10^3/\mu l$.[7] Increases in the basophil count frequently accompany CML and PV[45] and may be observed in Hodgkin's disease, systemic mastocytosis, and during active hemolysis. Basophilia also occurs in patients with hypothyroidism.[46]

Increases in Large Unstained Cells (LUC)

Sustained increases in LUC ($>0.31 \times 10^3/\mu l$)[7] usually signify an increase in circulating large lymphocytes or very immature nucleated blood cells. Morphologic examination of the blood cells should be carried out, particularly to consider the diagnosis of acute leukemia or lymphoma. Certain viral infections, such as those due to cytomegalovirus, may also be associated with large atypical lymphocytes which appear as LUC in the electronic differential count.

THE SIGNIFICANCE OF DECREASED WHITE CELL COUNTS

Decreases in the Neutrophil Count

Neutropenia is defined as an absolute blood neutrophil count of $<1.4 \times 10^3/\mu l$.[7] A reduced neutrophil count can occur because of an inadequate supply of neutrophils, because of altered distribution of neutrophils in the circulation, because of sequestration of neutrophils outside the circulation, or because of increased destruction of neutrophils.

The Production, Kinetics, and Distribution of Neutrophils

An understanding of the production, survival, and intravascular distribution of neutrophils is valuable in determining the significance of neutropenic states. In Fig. 66-1, a schematic representation of normal neutrophil production, survival and distribution are shown. In this dynamic system, the critical factors are neutrophil production (the rate of cellular input), the maintenance of a stored supply of neutrophils, the distribution of neutrophils in the blood, and the rate of egress of neutrophils from the blood. Neutrophils remain in the blood for a half-life ($T_{1/2}$) of only 4 to 10 hours,[47] so that even in normal persons, the bone marrow is required to replace (produce) between 62 and 400 × 10^7 neutrophils/kg body weight/day.[48] As neutrophils mature within the marrow, they are stored in the *neutrophil storage pool* (NSP), which is a ready reserve of 10 to 14 times more mature neutrophils than are normally in the entire circulating peripheral blood[48] (Fig. 66-1). Thus, the NSP is a ready supply source for already mature neutrophils and permits rapid neutrophil responses to infectious challenges. In the healthy steady state, the size of the NSP remains constant because neutrophil production and utilization are equal and balanced. However, disruption of that balance can lead to neutropenia. For example, when utilization of neutrophils (e.g., during infection[49]) exceeds the production of neutrophils, the NSP can become completely depleted[50]; then neutropenia will occur. Reduced production of neutrophils (e.g., during cytotoxic chemotherapy) is also a cause of depletion of the NSP because cellular input to the NSP is impaired. This may lead to neutropenia even when subjects are not under increased demand for neutrophils.[1] The neutropenias due to diminished marrow supply are diminished-supply neutropenias. When neutrophil supply is severely diminished, there is a greatly increased risk of life-threatening infection.

Another type of neutropenia is related to *maldistribution* of neutrophils in the blood. The circulating blood neutrophils are distributed within two populations, the circulating and marginal neutrophil pools (Fig. 66-1).[51] The *circulating neutrophil pool* (CNP) consists of cells freely distributed in the flowing blood; therefore, the CNP is freely accessible to the sampling venipuncture needle when blood is drawn for a CBC. In contrast, the *marginal neutrophil pool* (MNP) consists of cells which are believed to be distributed along the walls of postcapillary venules and are therefore not accessible to the venipuncture needle. Therefore, the WBC and differential reflect only cells in the CNP and not those in the MNP. The *total blood neutrophil pool* (TBNP) is the sum of the CNP and MNP. All of the neutrophils of the TBNP can migrate to sites of inflammation and resist infection, so the size of the TBNP and its turnover are the most reliable determinants of the functional circulating neutrophil mass.

Usually, the distribution of cells in the CNP and MNP is such that measurements of the WBC and differential do correlate with the size of the TBNP. However, a major shift of neutrophils to the MNP can reduce the CNP (and consequently reduce the absolute neutrophil count) even though the TBNP remains normal. This redistribution of circulating neutrophils is known as *pseudoneutropenia*.[51] Because the TBNP is normal in pseudoneutropenia, there is no increased

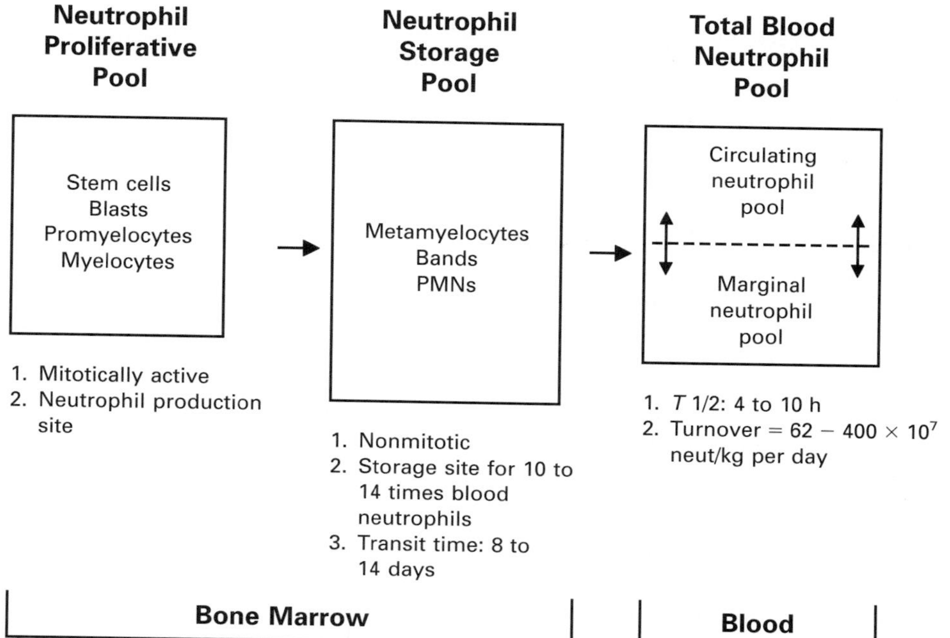

FIGURE 66-1
Schematic diagram of the normal human neutrophil system.

risk for infection. Pseudoneutropenia occurs during exposure to bacterial endotoxin and is one of the mechanisms for the neutropenia of rheumatoid arthritis (Felty's syndrome). Although the CNP and MNP can be quantified experimentally, the techniques for such measurements are not generally available or practical. Thus, pseudoneutropenia usually remains a postulated rather than a proven diagnosis. However, it is pertinent that leukokinetic studies have demonstrated that most chronically neutropenic subjects do have low TBNP values.[47] Neutropenia can also occur in subjects with splenomegaly, and distribution of neutrophils to this site of sequestration has been proposed as a mechanism for reduced neutrophil counts.

A General Approach to Neutropenia

When neutropenia has been identified, repeat counts may be useful to confirm the finding. In cases of sustained neutropenia, one of the earliest steps in the workup should be to determine whether the patient is unusually susceptible to infection. This can only be determined by a careful history to identify frequent or unexplained episodes of serious infection. Additional history should be obtained to identify any ongoing infection. Physical examination is equally important to identify specific sites of infection and to examine for bone tenderness, splenomegaly, or adenopathy. It should be recalled that in elderly persons, bacterial infection frequently occurs without fever.[52] Indeed, hypothermia may be a sign of infection in aged patients. In elderly persons with neutropenia and fever, hypotension, shock, or hypothermia, the presumptive diagnosis should be infection until proven otherwise. Prior to empiric antibiotic treatment, blood and appropriate body fluids should be cultured. When neutropenia is not associated with a history, signs, or symptoms of infection, empiric antibiotics have not proven to be of benefit and they may promote the development of resistant strains. Additional laboratory studies should be performed to determine whether the neutropenia is the only count which is reduced or whether it is accompanied by reduced numbers of platelets or by anemia.

Diminished-Supply Neutropenia

These neutropenias may be associated with vitamin and nutritional deficiency states, certain infections, and hematopoietic disorders; they may also occur as a side effect of certain medicines (Table 66-4). Neutropenia may occur as a consequence of the megaloblastic states caused by vitamin B_{12} deficiency (pernicious anemia) or folic acid deficiency. Neutropenia may also occur in cachectic patients. Clues to the presence of vitamin B_{12} deficiency (*pernicious anemia*) or *folic acid deficiency* are anemia, macrocytic red cell indices (mean corpuscular volume above 100/fl) and hypersegmented neutrophils. The diagnosis can be confirmed by finding reduced blood levels of B_{12} and/or folate and by morphologic examination of the marrow. Because untreated PA is progressively disabling and ultimately fatal, patients with this disorder should receive vitamin B_{12} parenterally for life. PA is particularly prevalent in elderly people, and over one-third of all cases occur in individuals above age 65.[53] The neutropenia of folate deficiency is particularly important when it occurs in the presence of alcoholism because of the additive effect of alcohol in blocking the action of folic acid.[54,55] Indeed, in individuals with alcoholism, neutropenia, and acute infection, the prognosis is poor and prompt institution of antibiotics and folate supplementation is indicated.

Diminished-supply neutropenia occurs during some infections if the increased use of neutrophils outstrips the marrow's ability to supply more cells. When this occurs, the infection is frequently overwhelming and immediately life-threatening, such as occurs in elderly subjects with pneumococcal sepsis[56] and in some cases of miliary tuberculosis.[57] These neutropenias are particularly prevalent in patients with already limited hematopoiesis due to factors such

TABLE 66-4

Conditions Associated with Decreased Leukocyte Counts

Decreased Neutrophil Counts
1. Diminished-supply neutropenias
    - Deficiency states
        - B_{12}, folate
        - Cachexia
        - Alcoholism, in conjunction with nutritional deficiency
    - Infections
        - Overwhelming bacterial infection
        - Viral infections
    - Medicines
        - Antimetabolites, cytotoxic agents
        - Analgesics, phenothiazines, gold salts, etc.
    - Hematologic disorders
        - Leukemias
        - Myeloproliferative disorders
        - Aplastic anemia
2. Pseudoneutropenias
    - Endotoxinemia
    - Felty's syndrome (selected cases)
    - Idiopathic

Decreased Lymphocyte Counts
1. Malnutrition
2. Tuberculosis
3. Lymphomas
4. Acquired immunodeficiency syndrome
5. Heart failure
6. Bacterial infection
7. Corticosteroids

Decreased Monocyte or Basophil Counts
1. No reliable association with disease

Decreased Eosinophil Counts
1. Bacterial infection
2. Endogenous corticosteroid release
3. Corticosteroid administration

as B_{12} or folate deficiency or in association with chemotherapy or marrow irradiation. Certain viral infections such as hepatitis can also deplete the marrow of neutrophils. When the marrow neutrophils are depleted during infection, examination of the blood usually discloses a shift to the left of the neutrophils ("bandemia"). The finding of increased percentages of band forms in the blood of elderly individuals with neutropenia, even in the absence of fever, should raise suspicion that there is a serious infection.

Elderly people with hematopoietic disorders frequently exhibit diminished-supply neutropenia. Among these disorders are myelodysplastic syndrome, the acute leukemias (see below), aplastic anemia, the lymphomas, and myelofibrosis.

Myelodysplastic Syndrome

Because of its increased incidence in older persons, myelodysplastic syndrome (MDS) should be considered a disease of the elderly. Indeed, over 50 percent of cases occur in people above age 70, and MDS is rare in individuals under age 50.[58] The clinical presentation of MDS is nonspecific and is usually attributable to anemia. On physical examination, the liver and spleen are frequently palpable.[59] Anemia is almost always present, and one-half of patients are pancytopenic at the time of diagnosis. Abnormal neutrophil morphology may be seen, immature blasts may be in the circulation, and the circulating red cells are frequently misshapen. The marrow is usually hypercellular and characteristic "megaloblastoid" red cell changes are seen. Another frequent marrow finding is that of distinctive "ringed sideroblast" forms with stainable cytoplasmic inclusions of iron. Karyotypic abnormalities are seen in over one-half of the patients. Interestingly, many patients with MDS never need treatment and die of diseases unrelated to the hematopoietic disorder. Chemotherapy has not been conclusively shown to be of value, and when treatment is given, it usually consists of transfusion with red cells or platelets. The median survival in MDS ranges from 5 to 49 months; in one-fourth of patients, the disease terminates in acute leukemia.[60]

The diagnoses of *acute leukemia, aplastic anemia,* and *lymphoma* should be entertained when neutropenia is accompanied by other cytopenias, by the presence of immature nucleated cells in the blood, and by physical findings of bone tenderness (particularly of the lower sternum), and by splenomegaly, which may reach very large proportions in myelofibrosis. A definitive diagnosis is usually aided by expert examination of the blood smear, special staining of abnormal or immature cells, karyotypic analysis, and examination of the marrow. Marrow examination is usually best carried out with biopsy, smeared cells from aspiration, and examination of sections of the clot obtained at the time of marrow aspiration. It is best to anticipate the need for simultaneous morphologic examination, special staining, and karyotypic analysis of the marrow, so that all of these essentials can be completed with a single invasive procedure.

Drug-Induced Neutropenia

Medicines should also be considered as causes of neutropenia (Table 66-5), particularly in elderly persons whose use of medicines is much greater than that of young adults. Certain of the agents used for chemotherapy of malignancy routinely cause neutropenia if given in sufficient quantity. These include alkylating agents, antimetabolites, colchicine, and agents which interfere with the synthesis of RNA or DNA. Because these drugs interfere with cellular replication, they affect only those marrow cells which are capable of cell division. Therefore, the neutropenia does not occur when the drugs are first given because of the buffering effect of already formed mature cells held in reserve in the NSP (Fig. 66-1). For this reason, there is usually a delay of one to two weeks before the neutropenia following chemotherapy occurs. Elderly people appear to be particularly sensitive to cytotoxic therapy and usually require reductions in cytotoxic drug doses to avoid toxicity.[1] The mechanism for this increase in toxic potential is not clear, but animal studies have revealed a decrease in the ability of the neutrophils of aged animals to regenerate.[61] Recent studies demonstrate that the ability of otherwise healthy elderly people to express hematostimulatory cytokines is diminished,[62] and this may be the underlying defect. However, elderly patients do appear to be responsive to therapeutically administered cytokines, and these may ameliorate the toxicity of chemotherapy.

A wide range of other medicines are less regularly but significantly associated with neutropenia[63] (Table 66-5). These agents are usually associated with hypoproductive neutropenia, and evaluation of the marrow (including biopsy) should be included in the

TABLE 66-5

Agents That Cause Neutropenia

Agents That Uniformly Cause Neutropenia*
1. Ionizing radiation
2. Alkylating agents
3. Antimetabolites
4. Colchicine
5. Anthracycline derivatives

Agents That Sometimes Cause Neutropenia
1. Analgesics
2. H_2 blockers
3. Antihistamines
4. Antimicrobial agents
5. Anticonvulsants
6. Antithyroid agents
7. Phenothiazines, other tranquilizers
8. Sulfonamides
   - Antibacterial agents
   - Diuretic agents
   - Hypoglycemic agents

*These agents regularly cause neutropenia if given in sufficient dose.

workup, along with cessation of all likely offending medicines. The kinetic basis for some drug-induced neutropenias appears to be a shortened survival of immunoglobulin-coated neutrophils.

Decreases in the Lymphocyte Count

Lymphopenia is defined as an absolute lymphocyte count of less than $0.9 \times 10^3/\mu l$. The causes of lymphopenia are varied and have not been categorized kinetically in the manner applied to neutrophils. However, reduced lymphocyte counts do accompany a number of conditions which are frequently found in elderly persons. For example, lymphopenia is one of the markers for the diagnosis of undernutrition, along with a history of greater than 15 percent weight loss, reduced transferrin (iron-binding capacity) in the serum, reduced prealbumin, and reduced serum cholesterol.[64] Lymphopenia is also found in subjects with tuberculosis,[65] lymphomas,[66] AIDS,[67] and in some subjects with heart failure.[68] Lymphocyte counts are usually also reduced during acute bacterial infection,[65] presumably due to the endogenous increase in corticosteroid production. The administration of corticosteroid medicines also induces lymphopenia.[69] When lymphopenia is associated with an increased susceptibility to unusual pathogens, the diagnoses of lymphoma (particularly Hodgkin's disease) and AIDS should be entertained.

Decreases in the Basophil, Eosinophil, or Monocyte Count

The absolute basophil count may approach zero in otherwise healthy individuals, and the persistent absence of these cells on differential counting is not known to be clinically significant. Reductions in circulating monocytes are also not reliably associated with disease.

In contrast, the persistent absence of circulating eosinophils is usually associated with identifiable disease.[70] For example, during bacterial infection or even some noninfectious inflammatory processes, the number of circulating eosinophils decreases markedly or falls to zero, rising again during the recovery phase.[71] The kinetic bases of eosinopenia are redistribution of eosinophils within or outside of the circulation, an inhibition of the release of eosinophils from the marrow, or inhibition of eosinophil production. The physiologic factors which are known to induce eosinophilia by these mechanisms are C5a and corticosteroids.[71,72]

MALIGNANT AND CLONAL DISORDERS OF THE HEMATOPOIETIC CELLS

Increased Incidence of Hematologic Malignancies in Elderly People

A number of malignant and nonmalignant clonal disorders of the white cells have their greatest incidence in elderly people. For example, the peak incidences of CLL, AML, CML, and multiple myeloma (MM) all occur in individuals over age 60, and the peak incidence of polycythemia vera is age 65. Indeed, the incidences of CLL, AML, myeloma, and CML range from 10 to 40/100,000 in individuals over the age of 80.[73,74] Because the rather nonspecific initial symptoms of these disorders are common among elderly people, a high index of suspicion for hematologic malignancy may facilitate an early diagnosis.

During their symptomatic phases, the hematologic malignancies produce symptoms and physiologic impairment which amplify many of the physical and social problems of elderly persons. For example, in a patient with compromised coronary and cerebral circulation, anemia may worsen angina and/or cardiac function and accentuate cognitive disorders. These physiologic consequences may act as barriers to physical activity, resulting in deconditioning and inability to perform activities of daily living which were previously possible. These and other problems should be anticipated and interventions devised to strengthen social and health care support systems, particularly those which can be carried out in the patient's place of residence.

Chronic Myelocytic Leukemia (CML)

CML (also referred to as chronic granulocytic leukemia) has a peak incidence of >20/100,000 in individuals over the age of 75. CML may present with fatigue and weight loss as early symptoms. However, physical examination and examination of the blood point clearly to CML when it is present. CML invariably begins with an elevated total leukocyte count and neutrophilia. Total leukocyte counts at the time of diagnosis range from 27 to $1076 \times 10^3/\mu l$, and sometimes the disease is discovered as an incidental finding on routine CBC.[15] The physical examination is helpful because, in contrast to benign causes of neutrophilia, CML is usually associated with splenomegaly, pallor, and sternal tenderness.[14] Other features of the blood picture differ from most nonmalignant neutrophilias in that 84 percent of subjects are anemic at the time of diagnosis and very immature neutrophil precursors (myeloblasts and promyelocytes) are frequently seen on the blood smear.[16] At the time of diagnosis, the absolute number of basophils is increased, and the number of eosinophils and monocytes is also usually increased.[16] A useful diagnostic feature of CML is its frequent association with the Philadelphia (Ph^1) chromosome. This distinctive chromosome is produced by a reciprocal exchange of DNA between chromosomes 9 and 22. Karyotypic analysis is usually possible with cells taken from the blood, and the Ph^1 chromosome is demonstrated in a major subset of patients.[17]

Ph^1-positive (Ph^1+) CML occurs in a group with a mean age of 42 years, but another Ph^1-negative (Ph^1-) form of CML is found in individuals with a much greater mean age of 60. Patients with the Ph^1- form tend to exhibit lower leukocyte and platelet counts early in the disease than in typical CML.[18] The mainstays of treatment for CML are alkylating agents, such as busulfan[19]; in young patients, allogeneic bone marrow transplantation has been used with some success. However, marrow transplantation has not been established as an acceptable option in geriatric patients. In patients without symptoms, treatment may be delayed until a benefit in symptoms or functional status would be expected. When remission is induced in symptomatic patients, functional status and general well-being improve. However, even when remission is induced in the chronic phase of the disease, survival is not increased, and the ultimate course of CML remains unaffected. The Ph^1+ variety of CML carries a median survival of 40 months, whereas patients with the age-associated Ph^1- variety have a median survival of only 8 months.[18] The usual cause of death is infection or hemorrhage.[20] In 60 to 90 percent of patients, the terminal phase of CML is characterized by an acute leukemialike picture with a predominance of blast cells in the blood.[21] This acute phase is frequently resistant even to aggressive therapy.

Polycythemia Vera (PV)

PV is a consequence of a clonal proliferation of primitive precursors or stem cells from which the granulocytes, erythrocytes, and platelet-producing megakaryocytes are derived.[22] PV occurs well into the geriatric age group: the peak age of onset is age 65 (18 percent of cases), with about 40 percent occurring in individuals age 65 or older and one-third in individuals over age 70.[23] Symptoms of PV include headache, weakness, pruritus, visual disturbances, and dizziness, at least one of which occurs in over one-third of subjects.[24] Again, these are frequent symptoms in elderly patients, and a diagnosis of PV will depend on a knowledge that it belongs among the differential diagnostic considerations. Itching after bathing is a more distinctive symptom of PV. On physical examination, ruddiness of the face is common, and over 75 percent of patients exhibit splenomegaly.[25] The disease is associated with an increase in the circulating red cell mass and an increased hematocrit value; there is usually an increase in the leukocyte and/or platelet count. Sometimes, iron deficiency prevents the increase in red cell mass, but when this occurs, it is accompanied by a reduction in the mean red cell volume (MCV). Measurements of arterial oxygen aid in differentiating PV from polycythemia secondary to hypoxemia. In PV, oxygen saturations greater than 92 percent are expected, although PV can coexist with diseases which cause hypoxemia. Elevations of the total WBC to $>12 \times 10^3/\mu l$ occur in up to 87 percent of patients,[25] and the WBC can exceed $50 \times 10^3/\mu l$. There is usually an increase in the absolute neutrophil concentration and a shift to the left. Increases in the circulating eosinophils, basophils, and monocytes are also observed. The Ph^1 chromosome is absent in PV, and measurements of the leukocyte alkaline phosphatase are usually elevated.[25]

The course of PV is a chronic one, and it is common practice to reduce hematocrits of over 55 to 58 percent because of the risk of vascular sludging or occlusion. The principal interventions are phlebotomy, ^{32}P, and various forms of chemotherapy, most usually alkylating agents. When hematocrits are elevated, particularly in elderly individuals with compromised circulation of the coronaries or cerebral vessels, phlebotomy is a first line of treatment. Particular care must be exercised in performing phlebotomy to avoid abruptly reducing the intravascular volume in elderly subjects with impaired homeostatic mechanisms for adjusting vascular tone and blood flow. The volume of the initial phlebotomy should not exceed 200 ml, and inquiry should be made as to the presence of symptoms such as chest discomfort, shortness of breath, or signs of cerebral ischemia. In addition, the blood pressure (including postural changes) should be carefully monitored. In selected patients with cardiovascular instability, it may be necessary to replace withdrawn blood volume for volume with normal saline.

In subjects with elevated platelet counts, existing cerebrovascular disease, or coronary disease, the coincident use of alkylating agents or radioactive phosphorus may be indicated to reduce platelet counts and prevent vascular-occlusive episodes. These occlusive episodes occur in 47 percent of subjects treated with phlebotomy alone.[26] With modern therapy, the mean survival of patients with PV is approximately 12 years.[27] The disease frequently terminates in myelofibrosis, sometimes with marked splenomegaly requiring splenectomy or splenic irradiation.[28] Less frequently, PV terminates with acute leukemia.

Chronic Lymphocytic Leukemia (CLL)

In any patient with a persistent lymphocyte count $>5.0 \times 10^3/\mu l$, the diagnosis of CLL should be entertained. Although the vast majority of CLL occurs as a consequence of malignant clonal proliferation of B lymphocytes,[30] a number of subtypes exist for the disease, including proliferation of early B cells, plasma cells, and "hairy cell leukemias."[31,32] CLL is largely a disease of the geriatric population, with the median incidence for the most prevalent types occurring at age 65.[31] The diagnostic criteria for CLL are a sustained blood lymphocyte count of $>10 \times 10^3/\mu l$, a marrow aspirate showing >30 percent lymphocytes, and a majority of peripheral blood lymphocytes with B-cell markers.[33] About one-fourth of patients are asymptomatic at the time of diagnosis of CLL[32] and, initially, fever is quite rare.[34] Fatigue is a common presenting complaint, and some patients report masses corresponding to enlarged lymph nodes. The most common presenting physical findings are lymphadenopathy, splenomegaly, and hepatomegaly.

Treatment of CLL is usually conducted with alkylating agents, such as chlorambucil and cyclophosphamide, although corticosteroids and radiotherapy may be employed. The mean survival from the time of diagnosis is approximately 6 years, although a subgroup experiences a shorter mean survival of about 3 years. When the only signs of CLL are lymphocytosis in the blood and bone marrow, patients usually experience a longer survival. In contrast, the presence of lymphadenopathy, splenomegaly, anemia, and thrombocytopenia carry progressively poorer prognoses. When lymphocytosis and thrombocytopenia are present in CLL, the mean survival is only 30 months.[35]

Hairy Cell Leukemia (HCL)

Hairy cell leukemia is a relatively rare variant of CLL. The disease is characterized by abnormal lymphocytes in the blood and marrow, enlargement of the spleen, pancytopenia, and the absence of enlarged lymph nodes. In most series the median age of incidence is about 50 years, and males outnumber females by 4 to 1.[75] The hairy cells themselves are distinctive in morphology and stain positively for tartrate-resistant alkaline phosphatase (TRAP) in almost all cases. In addition, the hairy cells possess B-cell markers. Bone marrow biopsy and aspiration are useful for judging the degree of marrow replacement by this tumor. The course of the disease is a long one, and a variety of treatments have proven value. For example, splenectomy induces a partial or complete remission in over 90 percent of patients and substantially improves survival.[76] However, some authors suggest that splenectomy is of less benefit when the marrow is extensively involved or if the platelet count is below 60×10^3.[77] Alpha-interferon has also been used as therapy, and with it, some patients have survived as long as 22 years in a study that is still ongoing.[77,78] Other agents have excellent efficacy in HCL, and these include 2′deoxycoformycin (Pentostatin), which induces remission in at least three-fourths of those who fail alpha-interferon.[79]

Acute Myeloblastic Leukemia (AML)

The incidence of AML rises steadily from a rate of 2/100,000 among people aged 40 to more than 20/100,000 in individuals above age 75. In addition, elderly patients have a poor prognosis as compared with younger adults.[80] When AML is preceded by a myelodysplastic syndrome or by CML, the prognosis is particularly poor, and both of these conditions have their highest incidence in elderly people. The clinical presentation of AML is attributable to the cytopenias which occur as normal blood cell production disappears in the presence of the leukemia. Patients are typically anemic, thrombocytopenic, and neutropenic at the time of diagnosis. Pallor is the rule, and petechiae, ecchymoses, and epistaxis occur in about one-half of patients. Fever is a common presenting symptom and should be considered to be a symptom of infection requiring antibiotic therapy until proven otherwise if severe neutropenia is present. By the time of diagnosis, 50 percent of patients have also experienced weight loss. Leukemic elderly patients with bowel complaints should raise the consideration of perirectal abscess or necrotizing colitis because of leukemic involvement of the colon itself.[81]

Even when absolute neutropenia is present, the total leukocyte count is elevated in over 50 percent of patients, although it exceeds $100 \times 10^3/\mu l$ in only 20 percent of subjects.[82] Microscopic examination of the blood smear usually reveals blast cells; the morphology of these immature cells can be classified using a schema known as the French-American-British (FAB) classification.[83] In the FAB classification, the varieties M1, M2, and M3 are granulocytic in morphology; M4 contains at least 20 percent monocytic cells; M5 has more than 89 percent monocytic cells; and M6 displays megaloblastoid erythroid differentiation. M7 is a variety with megakaryocytic differentiation. Some aspects of AML in elderly people are distinctive when compared to AML in young adults. For example, in elderly patients, AML appears to arise from a cell which is more primitive than that found in young adults.[84] The AML cells of elderly patients as opposed to those of young adults are also less likely to contain Auer rod inclusions, and in elderly people the leukemia is more frequently preceded by a myelodysplastic syndrome.

Treatment of AML is intensive and employs multiple chemotherapeutic agents in an attempt to eradicate the leukemic population. In the process, any normal marrow is also eradicated, and during the postchemotherapy period, patients are extremely cytopenic and at serious risk for death due to infection or bleeding. Although elderly patients are more sensitive to the toxicity of chemotherapy[1] and the prognosis for AML in an elderly patient is poor, chemotherapy still induces a remission in approximately 50 to 60 percent of elderly people with AML, although this figure is lower than the 75 percent remission rate seen in some groups of young adults.[85–87] The mechanism for the reduced responsiveness of elderly AML patients to treatment has not been identified. One hypothesis is that the reduced tolerance of elderly people to chemotherapy precludes use of aggressive treatment regimens which might be more effective. There may also be important factors which are intrinsic to AML as it occurs in elderly people. Indeed, cytokinetic characteristics predict a favorable outcome in adults with AML below age 50, particularly when the leukemic cells have an aneuploid karyotype.[87]

The decision to treat elderly patients with AML aggressively should be individualized. In all cases, those considered for treatment must be well informed regarding the morbidity, expense, and risk. Elderly patients may be at increased risk for toxicity due to agents such as the anthracycline derivatives (e.g., adriamycin, daunomycin), which affect the heart or the gastrointestinal tract; when the doses of these drugs are reduced to avoid toxicity, the likelihood of a remission is also reduced. In any case, in an elderly patient, impaired cardiac function, impaired hepatic function, or a significantly reduced performance status should be considered factors weighing against aggressive chemotherapy. Very little experience has been accumulated with marrow transplantation in elderly people, and it cannot now be considered a therapeutic alternative for AML.

Acute Lymphoblastic Leukemia (ALL)

The presentation of ALL is variable but can be similar to that of other acute leukemias in adults. Early symptoms include fatigue, petechiae, ecchymoses, and fever; transfusion with red cells and platelets may be indicated in response to symptomatic anemia or thrombocytopenia. Most cases of ALL occur in children. However, the disease is also seen in adults, with a median age of onset of between ages 30 and 40. The diagnosis is suggested by the presence of cytopenias and circulating blasts or by increased numbers of blasts in the marrow. Studies of cell surface markers reveal that in approximately two-thirds of adult cases of ALL, the blasts are early pre-B cells. This type is associated with the most favorable responses to treatment and the longest survival.[88] T-cell ALL accounts for about 20 percent of adult cases; it is associated with higher initial WBC and an increased risk for central nervous system involvement. In addition, mediastinal masses are found in approximately 60 percent of patients with T-cell ALL. Childhood ALL is the most responsive of the acute leukemias to treatment, with complete remission occurring in over 95 percent of patients and a predicted cure rate of 70 percent.[88,89] However, the prognosis is not as favorable in adults. In patients over age 50 with ALL, only 50 percent are disease-free after 5 years.[90] Indeed, the median duration of remission in adults is approximately 2 years.[91] When complete remission is obtained, treatment is usually continued for a maintenance period, during which more aggressive therapy is given periodically. As is the practice in children, radiotherapy to the central nervous system and intrathecal methotrexate are given, even if evaluation of the spinal fluid is negative for malignant cells. Although the optimum duration of therapy is not defined in adults, treatment is usually continued for 3 years or more. As with AML, marrow transplantation is not presently an alternative for the treatment of ALL in elderly people.

REFERENCES

1. Bodey GP et al: Quantitative relationships between circulating leukocytes and infection in patients with acute leukemia. *Ann Intern Med* 64:328, 1966.
2. Paraskevas F, Foerster J: The lymphocytes, in *Wintrobe's Clinical Hematology,* 9th ed. Philadelphia, Lea & Febiger, 1992, p 354.
3. Krahenbuhl JL et al: Cytototoxic and microbicidal properties of macrophages, in van Furth R (ed): *Mononuclear Phagocytes: Functional Aspects.* The Hague, Martinus Nijhoff, 1980.
4. Hibbs JB Jr et al: The macrophage as an antineoplastic surveillance cell: Biological perspectives. *J Reticuloendothel Soc* 24:549, 1979.
5. Butterworth AE, David JR: Eosinophil function. *N Engl J Med* 304:154, 1981.
6. Dvorak HF, Dvorak AM: Basophilic leucocytes: Structure, function and role in disease. *Clin Haematol* 4:651, 1975.
7. *Wintrobe's Clinical Hematology,* 9th ed. Philidelphia, Lea & Febiger, 1992, pp 2298, 2302.
8. Boggs DR: Kinetics of neutrophilic leukocytes in acute infection. *Rev Med* 17:2325, 1976.
9. Rosseff R et al: The acute phase response in gout. *J Rheumatol* 14:974, 1987.
10. Musser JH Jr: The leukocytes after hemorrhages. *Am J Med Sci* 162:40, 1921.
11. Athens JW et al: Leukokinetic studies: III. The distribution of granulocytes in the blood of normal subjects. *J Clin Invest* 40:159, 1961.
12. Bishop CR et al: Leukokinetic studies: XIII. A nonsteady-state kinetic evaluation of the mechanism of cortisone-induced granulocytosis. *J Clin Invest* 47:249, 1968.
13. Hilts SV, Shaw CC: Leukemoid blood reactions. *N Engl J Med* 249:434, 1953.
14. Marsh JC: Analysis of 106 patients with chronic myelocytic leukemia examined in the University of Utah Hematology Clinic, 1944 to 1963. Unpublished.
15. Witts LJ et al: Chronic granulocytic leukaemia: Comparison of radiotherapy and busulphan therapy. Report of the Medical Research Council's Working Party for Therapeutic Trials in Leukaemia. *Br Med J* 1:201, 1968.
16. Spiers ASD et al: The peripheral blood in chronic

granulocytic leukaemia: Study of 50 untreated Philadelphia-positive cases. *Scand J Haematol* 18:25, 1977.
17. Nigam R, Dosik H: Chronic myelogenous leukemia presenting in the blastic phase and its association with a 45 XO Ph[1] karyotype. *Blood* 47:223, 1976.
18. Canellos GP et al: Chronic granulocytic leukemia without the Philadelphia chromosome. *Am J Clin Pathol* 65:467, 1976.
19. Gordon MY, Douglas IDC: The effects of busulphan, hydroxyurea and cytosine arabinoside on the colony forming cells in chronic granulocyte leukaemic and non-leukemic marrow. *Leuk Res* 1:71, 1977.
20. Vodopick H et al: Spontaneous cyclic leukocytosis and thrombocytosis in chronic granulocytic leukemia. *N Engl J Med* 286:285, 1972.
21. Karanas A, Silver RT: Characteristics of the terminal phase of chronic granulocytic leukemia. *Blood* 32:293, 1985.
22. Adamson JW et al: Polycythemia vera: Stem cell and probable clonal origin of the disease. *N Engl J Med* 295:913, 1976.
23. Berlin NI: Diagnosis and classification of the polycythemias. *Semin Hematol* 12:339, 1975.
24. Szur L et al: Polycythaemia vera and its treatment with radioactive phosphorus. *Q J Med* 28:397, 1959.
25. Perkins J et al: Polycythaemia vera: Clinical studies on a series of 127 patients managed without radiation therapy. *Q J Med* 33:499, 1964.
26. Orlowitz HL, Broksky I: Busulphan treatment of polycythaemia vera. *Br J Haematol* 52:1, 1982.
27. Berk PD et al: Therapeutic recommendations in polycythemia vera based on Polycythemia Vera Study Group protocols. *Semin Hematol* 23:132, 1986.
28. Glasser RM, Walker RI: Transitions among the myeloproliferative disorders. *Ann Intern Med* 71:285, 1969.
29. Binet JL et al: Clinical staging system for chronic lymphocytic leukemia derived from multivariate survival analysis. *Cancer* 48:198, 1981.
30. Solanki DL et al: Chronic lymphocytic leukemia: A monoclonal disease. *Am J Hematol* 13:159, 1982.
31. Catovsky D et al: The Medical Research Council CLL trials 1 and 2. *Nouv Rev Fr Hematol* 7230:423, 1988.
32. Foon KA et al: Chronic lymphocytic leukemia: New insights into biology and therapy. *Ann Intern Med* 133:525, 1990.
33. Cheson BD et al: Guidelines for clinical protocols for chronic lymphocytic leukemia: Recommendations of the NCI sponsored working groups. *Am J Hematol* 29:152, 1988.
34. Boggs DR et al: Factors influencing the duration of survival of patients with chronic lymphocytic leukemia. *Am J Med* 40:243, 1966.
35. Binet JL et al: Chronic lymphocytic leukemia: Recommendations for diagnosis, staging and response criteria. *Ann Intern Med* 110:236, 1989.
36. Beeson PB, Bass DA: *The Eosinophil.* Philadelphia: Saunders, 1977.
37. Knott FA, Pearson RSB: Extreme eosinophilia and leukocytosis in connection with bronchial asthma. *Acta Med Scand* 144:119, 1952.
38. Reifenstein EC et al: Trichiniasis. *Am J Med Sci* 183:688, 1932.
39. Katz AM, Pan CT: Echinococcus disease in the United States. *Am J Med* 25:759, 1958.
40. Beaver PC, Danaraj TJ: Pulmonary ascariasis resembling eosinophilic lung. *Am J Trop Med Hyg* 7:100, 1958.
41. Chusid MJ et al: The hypereosinophilic syndrome. *Medicine* 54:1, 1975.
42. Isaacson NH, Rapoport P: Eosinophilia in malignant tumors: Its significance. *Ann Intern Med* 25:893, 1946.
43. Hoeprich PD: Infection due to *Listeria monocytogenes. Medicine* 37:143, 1958.
44. Doan CA, Wiseman BK: The monocyte, monocytosis and monocytic leukosis: A clinical and pathological study. *Ann Intern Med* 8:383, 1934.
45. May ME, Waddell CC: Basophils in peripheral blood and bone marrow. *Am J Med* 76:509, 1984.
46. Thonnard-Neumann E: The influence of hormones on the basophilic leukocytes. *Acta Haematol (Basel)* 25:261, 1963.
47. Bishop CR et al: Leukokinetic studies: XIV. Blood neutrophil kinetics in chronic steady-state neutropenia. *J Clin Invest* 50:1678, 1971.
48. Cartwright GE et al: The kinetics of granulopoiesis in normal man. *Blood* 24:780, 1964.
49. Marsh JC et al: Neutrophil kinetics in acute infection. *J Clin Invest* 46:1943, 1967.
50. Christensen RD et al: Blood and marrow neutrophils during group B streptococcal sepsis: Quantification of storage proliferative and circulating pools. *Pediatr Res* 16:549, 1982.
51. Athens JW et al: Neutrophilic granulocyte kinetics and granulocytopoiesis, in Gordon AS (ed): *Regulation of Hematopoiesis.* New York, Appleton-Century-Crofts, 1970.
52. Weksler ME: Age-associated changes in the immune response. *J Am Geriatr Soc* 30:718, 1982.
53. Chanarin I: *The Megaloblastic Anemias.* London, Blackwell Scientific, 1979.
54. Herbert V et al: Correlation of folate deficiency with alcoholism and associated macrocytosis, anemia and liver disease. *Ann Intern Med* 58:977, 1963.
55. MacFarland W, Libre EP: Abnormal leukocyte response in alcoholism. *Ann Intern Med* 59:865, 1963.
56. Murphy TF, Fine BC: Bacteremic pneumococcal pneumonia in the elderly. *Am J Med Sci* 288:114, 1984.
57. Ball K et al: Acute tuberculous septicemia with leucopenia. *Br Med J* 2:869, 1967.
58. Beris P: Primary clonal myelodysplastic syndromes. *Semin Hematol* 26:216, 1989.
59. Koeffler HP: Myelodysplastic syndromes (preleukemia). *Semin Hematol* 23:284, 1986.
60. Sanz GF, Sanz MA: Prognostic factors in myelodysplastic syndromes. *Leuk Res* 16:77, 1992.
61. Rothstein G et al: Kinetic evaluation of the pool sizes and proliferative response of neutrophils in bacterially challenged aging mice. *Blood* 70(6):1836, 1987.
62. Buchanan JP et al: Disordered hematopoiesis and reduced production of hematopoietic growth factors in aged mice and humans. *Clin Res* 38:150a, 1990.
63. Athens JW: Neutropenia, in *Wintrobe's Clinical Hematology,* 9th ed. Philadelphia, Lea & Febiger, 1992.
64. Rudman D et al: Antecedents of death in the men of a Veterans Administration nursing home. *J Am Geriatr Soc* 35:496, 1987.
65. Shillitoe AJ: The common causes of lymphopenia. *J Clin Pathol* 3:321, 1950.

66. Zacharski LR, Linman JW: Lymphocytopenia: Its causes and significance. *Mayo Clin Proc* 46:168, 1971.
67. Fauci AS et al: Acquired immunodeficiency syndrome: Epidemiologic, clinical, immunologic and therapeutic considerations. *Ann Intern Med* 100:92, 1984.
68. Hurdle ADF et al: Occurrence of lymphopenia in heart failure. *J Clin Pathol* 19:60, 1966.
69. Schoenfeld Y et al: Prednisone-induced leukocytosis. *Am J Med* 71:773, 1981.
70. Krause JR, Boggs DR: Search for eosinopenia in hospitalized patients with normal blood leukocyte concentrations. *Am J Hematol* 24:55, 1987.
71. Bass DA: Eosinophil behavior during host defense reactions, in *Advances in Host Defense Mechanisms,* vol 1. New York, Raven Press, 1982.
72. Bass DA et al: Eosinopenia of acute infection. *J Clin Invest* 65:1265, 1980.
73. Young JL, Percy CL, Asire SJ (eds): Cancer Morbidity and Mortality in the United States, 1973–77. *Natl Cancer Inst Monogr* 57:73, 1981.
74. Kyle RA: Multiple myeloma: Review of 869 cases. *Mayo Clin Proc* 50:29, 1975.
75. Golomb HM et al: Hairy cell leukemia: A clinical review based on 71 cases. *Ann Intern Med* 89:677, 1978.
76. Jansen J, Hermans J: Splenectomy in hairy cell leukemia: A retrospective multicenter analysis. *Cancer* 47:2066, 1981.
77. Ratain MJ et al: Prognostic variables in hairy cell leukemia after splenectomy as initial therapy. *Cancer* 62:2420, 1988.
78. Ratain MJU et al: Durability of responses to interferon alfa-2b in advanced hairy cell leukemia. *Blood* 69:872, 1985.
79. Ho AD et al: Response to Pentostatin in hairy cell leukemia refractory to interferon-alpha. *J Clin Oncol* 7:1533, 1989.
80. Brincker H: Estimate of overall treatment results in acute non-lymphocytic leukemia based on age-specific rates of incidence and of complete remission. *Cancer Treat Rep* 69:5, 1985.
81. Keidan R et al: Recurrent typhlitis. *Dis Colon Rectum* 32:206, 1989.
82. Boggs DR et al: The acute leukemias. *Medicine* 41:163, 1962.
83. Bennett JM et al: Proposals for the classification of the acute leukemias. *Br J Haematol* 33:451, 1976.
84. Fialkow PJ et al: Clonal development, stem-cell differentiation, and clinical remissions in acute nonlymphocytic leukemia. *N Engl J Med* 317:468, 1987.
85. Beguin Y et al: Treatment of acute nonlymphocytic leukemia in young and elderly patients. *Cancer* 56:2587, 1985.
86. Peterson BA, Bloomfield CD: Treatment of acute nonlymphocytic leukemia in elderly patients. *Cancer* 40:647, 1977.
87. Kantarjian HM et al: Pretreatment cytokinetics in acute myelogenous leukemia. *J Clin Invest* 76:319, 1985.
88. Radford JE et al: Adult acute lymphoblastic leukemia: Results of the Iowa HOP-L protocol. *J Clin Oncol* 7:58, 1989.
89. Rivera GK et al: Improved outcome in childhood acute lymphoblastic leukaemia with reinforced early treatment and rotational combination chemotherapy. *Lancet* 1:61, 1991.
90. Jacobs AD, Gale RP: Recent advances in the biology and treatment of acute lymphoblastic leukemia in adults. *N Engl J Med* 311:1219, 1984.
91. Hoelzer D, Gale RP: Acute lymphoblastic leukemia in adults: Recent progress, future direction. *Semin Hematol* 24:27, 1987.

Chapter 67

MALIGNANT LYMPHOMA, HODGKIN'S DISEASE, AND MULTIPLE MYELOMA

William B. Ershler

THE NON-HODGKIN'S LYMPHOMAS

The non-Hodgkin's lymphomas (NHL) are a varied group of proliferative disorders that have in common the clonal expansion of cells of lymphoid origin. There is a wide clinical spectrum of NHL and there is controversy with regard to appropriate therapy for elderly patients. Recent advances in research have provided important leads to our better understanding of the mechanisms of pathogenesis and also to the development of curative treatment strategies.

Classification

Since the first description in the early nineteenth century of the conditions we now know as Hodgkin's disease and non-Hodgkin's lymphoma, there have been several distinct classification systems. This has resulted in difficulty in comparing clinical features and assessing treatment outcomes. To remedy this situation, a National Cancer Institute panel of experts representing all of the modern classification schemes proposed a working formulation (Table 67-1) which divides NHL into four basic groups (low-grade, intermediate, high-grade, and miscellaneous).[1] The classification highlights an intriguing paradox, present for lymphoma at all ages but nowhere more clearly evident than in the elderly. In general, low-grade lymphomas frequently present with few symptoms but with widespread disease and are generally not curable with present modalities. Intermediate- and high-grade lymphomas present at earlier stages with more systemic symptoms and are, in some cases, curable even at an advanced stage. It is the challenge for those treating lymphomas in elderly patients to assess the likelihood of meaningful treatment response and weigh it against the enhanced rate and severity of treatment toxicity.

Epidemiology

The American Cancer Society estimates that 35,600 new patients with NHL were detected in 1990 and that 18,200 deaths were so attributed.[2] This 25 percent increase since 1950 reflects at least two phenomena. The first is that NHL is one of a few AIDS-associated malignancies; accordingly, there has been a rise in incidence, especially in young and middle-aged males. However, the median age for NHL is over 60 years, and more than two-thirds of newly diagnosed patients are over 65 (one-third are over 70).[2] With the demographic changes in our population, it is not surprising that NHL is observed with increasing frequency.

Evaluation/Staging

In contrast to Hodgkin's disease (see below), the precise pathologic staging (Table 67-2) of NHL is not as important. This is because prior clinical experience has indicated that clinical stage (extent of anatomic distribution) has not correlated as well with survival as it does for Hodgkin's disease. For example, in the low-grade lymphomas, the disease may be at stage IV without much change in prognosis compared to earlier stages; in the higher-grade lymphomas, systemic treatment is necessary even for disease confined to one anatomic region. Staging laparotomies are rarely indicated for NHL. Systemic symptoms do not have the same dire prognostic significance as in Hodgkin's disease but still indicate a poorer prognosis. High-grade lymphomas may require evaluation of the cen-

TABLE 67-1

Classification of Non-Hodgkin's Lymphoma

Grade	Working Formulation	Rappaport Classification
Low grade (favorable)	Small lymphocytic	Diffuse, lymphocytic, well differentiated
	Follicular, predominantly small cleaved cell (FSC)	Nodular, lymphocytic, poorly differentiated
	Follicular, mixed small cleaved, large-cell (FM)	Nodular, mixed, lymphocytic and histiocytic
Intermediate grade	Follicular, predominantly large	Nodular histiocytic
	Diffuse, small cleaved cell (DSC)	Diffuse, lymphocytic
	Diffuse, small and large cell (DM)	Diffuse, mixed, lympho- and histiocytic
	Diffuse, large cell (DL): Cleaved or noncleaved cell	Diffuse histiocytic
High grade (unfavorable)	Immunoblastic (IBL)	Diffuse histiocytic
	Lymphoblastic (LL) convoluted or nonconvoluted cell	Diffuse, lymphoblastic
	Small, noncleaved cell (SNC): Burkitt's or non-Burkitt's	Diffuse, undifferentiated
Miscellaneous	Mycosis fungoides	
	Extramedullary plasmacytoma	
	Composite	
	Unclassifiable	

tral nervous system (CNS), especially in those patients with diffuse histology and bulky abdominal lymphadenopathy. Finally, there is a much greater likelihood that NHL will arise in extranodal tissue, such as gastric, intestinal, cutaneous, pulmonary, or CNS tissues. Alternate staging systems using largest tumor mass and LDH greater than 500 IU/l as indicators of tumor bulk may turn out to be more accurate indicators of prognosis.

TABLE 67-2

Staging for Hodgkin's and Non-Hodgkin's Lymphoma—Ann Arbor Classification

Stage	*Description*
Stage I	Single node region
IE[a]	Single extralymphatic site
Stage II	Two or more node regions on the same side of the diaphragm
IIE	Single node region + localized single extralymphatic site
Stage III	Node regions on both sides of the diaphragm
IIIE	+ Localized single extralymphatic site
IIIS[b]	+ Spleen involvement
IIISE	+ Localized single extralymphatic site and spleen involvement
Stage IV	Diffuse involvement, extralymphatic organ/site node regions
All stages A	Without weight loss/fever/sweats
B	With weight loss/fever/sweats

[a] E = Extranodal
[b] S = Spleen involved

Clinical Features and Therapy

Low-Grade Lymphomas

The low-grade lymphomas (well-differentiated lymphocytic lymphoma and nodular poorly differentiated lymphocytic lymphoma according to the Rappaport classification) are the most common lymphomas in older persons. These lymphomas are usually of B-cell origin. Most commonly, older patients present with advanced disease—with multiple lymph nodes in the neck, axillae, inguinal area, mediastinum, and paraaortic area. Often splenomegaly is also present. Bone marrow biopsy will reveal the presence of lymphoma in the majority of cases.

The median age of patients with these tumors is over 55 years; both types of low-grade lymphomas are rare before age 40. Diffuse, well-differentiated lymphocytic lymphoma occurs in patients who are well into their eighties, whereas nodular, poorly differentiated lymphocytic lymphoma occurs rarely after age 70. Initially, the small-cell lymphomas produce few symptoms. Fevers, sweats, and weight loss (the typical "B" symptoms) are uncommon and should prompt the physician to evaluate other potential causes, such as infections, histologic conversions (see below), or second malignancies.

These tumors are not curable by current therapeutic maneuvers except in the very select case in which a stage I tumor may be cured by radiation therapy. Many investigators would consider even these tumors to be incurable. However, disease progression is often slow even for older, frail patients and median survival with advanced disease is 5 to 8 years.

These tumors convert to more aggressive large-cell lymphomas in 1 to 10 percent of cases, often after 5 to 8 years of fairly indolent disease (Richter's conversion). These converted tumors are more resistant to treatment, and prognosis is adversely affected (median survival of less than 6 months). Commonly, one finds a single node or group of nodes growing out of proportion to other nodes. Biopsy of these nodes reveals the large-cell lymphoma, with small-cell lymphoma still being present in other nodes or in the bone marrow.

Clinically quantifiable immunologic abnormalities are rare in most histologic types of low-grade lymphomas except the well-differentiated lymphocytic lymphoma, which is similar in nature to chronic lymphocytic leukemia (CLL). In this disorder, hypogammaglobulinemia is common and is associated with a propensity to infection, primarily with encapsulated bacterial organisms but also with common viruses. Monoclonal gammopathies are sometimes seen and, if examined by very sensitive techniques, are common. Circulating tumor cells can be detected by immunoglobulin gene-rearrangement studies even when peripheral lymphocyte counts are not elevated. Hemolytic anemias, especially cold-agglutinin disease (1.7 percent) and immune thrombocytopenia (0.4 percent), are uncommon but well-known complications of lymphomas.[3]

A simplified staging evaluation is sufficient for the low-grade lymphomas. Precise staging is much less important than in Hodgkin's disease, since curative radiotherapy is not an option. Therefore, staging by physical exam, routine laboratory tests (complete blood count, chemistry panel) chest x-ray, computed tomography (CT) of the abdomen, and bone marrow biopsy is generally sufficient to plan treatment and offer prognostic information. Only in rare circumstances would such tests as liver biopsy, lymphangiography, gallium-67 scanning, or staging laparotomy be indicated. Since the stage of the disease is most often III or IV (Table 67-2) and since curative therapy is not an option regardless of stage, further investigations should be based only on localizing symptoms or concerns for local complications. Because CNS invasion by low-grade lymphomas is rare, routine evaluation of the CNS (by CT scan or spinal fluid analysis) is not warranted. However, Richter's conversion lymphomas do invade the CNS, and evaluation should be as described below for the high-grade lymphomas.

The treatment of indolent lymphomas, although safe and effective, remains controversial. The major question is whether early therapy prior to the development of clinical symptoms prolongs survival or whether it is sufficient to wait until organ dysfunction or symptoms mandate treatment. Furthermore, it is also not known whether aggressive treatment (regimens used for high-grade lymphomas), less aggressive multiagent chemotherapy such as cytoxan-vincristine-prednisone (CVP), or single-agent therapy is the treatment of choice. One study comparing chlorambucil with CVP showed a higher complete response rate with CVP. However, by 4 years, disease status and survival were equivalent.[4] Other studies have confirmed these findings.[5,6]

Patients who had no symptoms and slowly enlarging nodes over a period of months were selected in another study for initial observation only.[7] Therapy was initiated if symptoms developed, low blood counts occurred from marrow involvement, or the function of a vital organ was threatened. Often, therapy was initiated only after a prolonged period of time, although a number of patients required therapy within 1 to 2 months of initial evaluation. It appeared that long-term control and survival were unaffected by this approach.

In young, otherwise healthy patients, investigations into very aggressive treatment have been disappointing because permanent remissions seem not to occur. Therefore, it appears that such treatment is inappropriate for the patient who does not have significant symptomatology or rapidly progressive disease. On the other hand, for those who do have more rapidly progressive tumors, more intensive therapy appears to be beneficial. The regimen comprising cyclophosphamide, Oncovin (vincristine), procarbazine, and prednisone (COPP) was shown in an Eastern Cooperative Oncology Group (ECOG) study to achieve a 56 percent remission rate, and 57 percent survived more than 5 years.[8] Whether this regimen improves survival is difficult to evaluate because of the already lengthening median survival for patients with these indolent lymphomas. Our experience with this regimen is that it is relatively well tolerated by older patients, in contrast to regimens containing doxorubicin (e.g., Adriamycin), although vincristine bowel toxicity remains a problem.

Intermediate-Grade Lymphomas

The intermediate-grade lymphomas (diffuse mixed lymphoma, diffuse histiocytic lymphoma, and immunoblastic lymphoma) often present with diffuse adenopathy without marrow or other organ parenchymal involvement. Patients with marrow, CNS, liver, or pulmonary involvement along with adenopathy have a poorer prognosis. Also common are lymphomas primary to extranodal sites, such as Waldeyer's ring, stomach, liver, spleen, and the CNS. These diseases must be considered separately from primary nodal disease.

Diffuse large-cell (histiocytic) lymphoma, originally thought to be a tumor of histiocytes, is now known to be either of B- or T-cell origin. In fact, some of these tumors are true histiocytic lymphomas, but they are quite rare (approximately 1 percent). Prognosis seems to be independent of the cell of origin. The median age of patients is in the late fifties, but there is a wide age distribution. The other intermediate-grade lymphomas are all of B-cell origin. Immunoblastic lymphomas occur in an age distribution similar to diffuse large-cell lymphoma, whereas diffuse mixed-cell lymphoma is rare after age 80.

These intermediate-grade lymphomas are now generally considered curable by modern chemotherapy. There remains controversy over whether the diffuse mixed-cell histology is curable, but long-term remissions are achieved in about 30 percent of patients. In contrast with the indolent lymphomas, these tumors often present with a rapid increase in nodal masses accompanied by systemic constitutional symptoms, such as fever or weight loss; untreated, they are often rapidly fatal. For example, untreated diffuse large-cell lymphoma has a median survival of 2 to 3 months. With treatment, median survival is now in the range of 3 to 5 years, with some subgroups having greater than 50 percent cure rates.

Several studies show that advanced age is a negative prognostic factor in large-cell lymphomas. In one study of 73 patients, 39 under the age of 60 years and 34 over age 60, the only negative prognostic feature was age. The older patients survived a median of 18 months, whereas the median survival was 48 months for younger patients.[9] The difference did not appear to be related to the intensity of treatment or its tolerance.

The Nebraska Lymphoma Study Group[10] used the CAP/BOP regimen (cyclophosphamide, Adriamycin, procarbazine, bleomycin, Oncovin, and prednisone) to treat all patients with diffuse mixed- or large-cell lymphoma. They found a similar overall complete remission rate of 65 percent in patients over and under the age of 60. However, patients younger than 60 had a 62 percent 5-year survival, whereas those over 60 had a 35 percent 5-year survival. The investigators found that treatment toxicity was similar and that deaths from apparently unrelated causes accounted for most of the survival difference. Duration of complete remission (CR) was similar in older and younger groups as opposed to the prior study, in which duration of CR was poor in the older populations.[9]

The Southwest Oncology Group (SWOG)[11] studied cyclophosphamide, Adriamycin, vincristine, and prednisone (CHOP) chemotherapy with or without bleomycin or immunotherapy in patients of all ages, with an initial dose reduction required for patients over the age of 65. They found that complete remission rates declined with age, from 65 percent under the age of 40 years to 37 percent over the age of 65 years. Survival also declined from 101 + months under the age of 40 to 16 months over age 65. When full-dose initial chemotherapy was given to the older patients in violation of the protocol, the differences in CR and death rates declined among the different age groups, suggesting that the dose reduction may have accounted for some of the survival difference. Toxicity was similar in all age groups. The addition of bleomycin had an adverse effect in older patients. Several other recent studies of other intensive chemotherapy regimens (M-BACOD,[12] ProMACE-MOPP,[13] and MACOP-B[14]) have shown poorer survival and increased toxicity in older age groups.

Aggressive Lymphomas

The aggressive lymphomas are Burkitt's (and the similar undifferentiated non-Burkitt's lymphoma) and lymphoblastic lymphoma. Since lymphoblastic lymphoma is almost completely a disease of adolescence and young adulthood, it is not considered here.

In the United States, the Burkitt's-like lymphomas usually present with rapidly expanding abdominal masses, high lactate dehydrogenase (LDH) and uric acid levels, and systemic symptoms. Untreated, the median survival is 1 to 2 months, and treatment is often an emergency. Although Epstein-Barr virus is associated with the endemic (African) form, its role in the pathogenesis of Burkitt's lymphoma in the United States is unclear. These tumors arise from relatively mature B cells, as evidenced by expression of surface immunoglobulin (SIg) and B4 (CD19), B1 (CD20), and B3 (CD22) antigens. Immunophenotypic differences between the two clinical subtypes of Burkitt's lymphoma (endemic and sporadic) have been reported. The tumor can be identified karyotypically by one of three characteristic chromosomal translocations [t(8:14), t(8:22), or t(2:8)], all of which result in juxataposition of the c-myc proto-oncogene (chromosome 8) to one of the three immunoglobulin heavy-chain genes.

Prognosis is poor in older patients because of the need for extremely aggressive treatment. Often, the bone marrow is involved, which makes the condition essentially incurable in the older patient. Treatment requires prophylaxis against tumor lysis syndrome (IV fluids, alkalinization of the urine, and allopurinol), intensive doses of chemotherapy for several months, and CNS prophylaxis with intrathecal chemotherapy and whole-brain irradiation.

HODGKIN'S DISEASE

Epidemiology

Hodgkin's disease (HD) in the United States has a bimodal age-specific incidence.[15] The early peak is between the ages of 20 and 30; the later peak occurs between 70 and 80, with the incidence starting to increase around age 50. Men far outnumber women in the later peak. It has been thought that two different etiologic processes may explain the bimodal distribution. MacMahon[16] proposed an infectious etiology for HD in the younger population (ages 15 to 34). The epidemiologic finding of increased risk in higher socioeconomic classes (similar to paralytic polio) suggests that HD in this age group is the rare result of a common (probably viral) infection that occurs later in life than is usual in the lower socioeconomic classes.[17] This effect of socioeconomic class persisted in persons aged 40 to 54 at the time of diagnosis but was absent in persons older than 54. Although a specific etiologic factor has not been found for either younger or older presentations of HD, these data, as well as the shift in pathologic subtypes outlined below, suggest the possibility of different etiologic mechanisms for younger and older persons developing Hodgkin's disease.

Presentation and Staging

Adenopathy is the most common presenting sign of Hodgkin's disease in all age groups. In one study, adenopathy was a more common presentation in younger patients (80 percent) than in patients over the age of 60 years (50 percent), whereas 25 percent of older patients had systemic symptoms, in contrast to only 2 percent of younger patients.[18] Abdominal disease was more prevalent in older patients. Another study found older patients to be more likely to have bulk abdominal disease, whereas younger patients were more likely to have thoracic and nodal disease independent of histology.[19]

Unexplained adenopathy was found to be the most common presentation (65 percent) in patients over 60 years old, and "B" symptoms were the presenting complaint in 29 percent.[20] Forty-two percent of these patients had significant intercurrent disease, including coronary artery disease or peripheral vascular disease, chronic obstructive pulmonary disease (COPD), diabetes mellitus, and hypertension. Staging laparotomy was performed in 48 percent of patients, including 45 percent of patients with intercurrent disease. Seventy-five percent of patients over 60 years old were considered to be adequately staged, and 64 percent were considered to be adequately treated by standards of that time. The experience from this group and others is that elderly patients who present with localized HD should have a full staging evaluation, including staging laparotomy.

These studies suggest that the presentation of HD in older patients is different than in younger patients. Although some of this difference is accounted for by different histology (nodular sclerosis is more likely in the thorax, mixed cellularity in the abdomen), other differences are not related to histology and may relate to altered etiology or host response.

Histologies

The diagnostic cell for HD is the Reed-Sternberg (RS) cell, which is a large, binucleated cell with prominent nucleoli. Strict criteria require the presence of an RS cell to diagnose HD. However, on occasion HD may be diagnosed if the mononuclear form—the "Hodgkin's cell"—is prominent. The RS cell can occasionally be found in other disorders but is considered to be the malignant cell in HD.

Hodgkin's disease has four histologic types: lymphocyte predominant, nodular sclerosis, mixed cellularity, and lymphocyte depleted.[21] Of these, lymphocyte predominant and nodular sclerosis (NS) are generally considered to have a better prognosis than the other two; however, this advantage largely disappears when pathologic stage is considered. The malignant cell in HD is thought to be the RS cell, whereas infiltrating lymphocytes, eosinophils, and neutrophils are thought to be reactive phenomena. Although the aggressive histologies of HD contain abundant RS cells, the indolent forms have few.

It is generally thought that histologic subtypes of HD occur in different frequencies in older than in younger patients. According to Hellman et al.,[22] the NS histology occurs most frequently in adolescents and young adults and is unusual in patients over age 50. Studies comparing histologic patterns in older and younger patients are somewhat contradictory but support a decline in the incidence of NS compared to mixed cellularity (Table 67-3).[19,20,23]

However, the Specht and Nissen[19] study of 506 unselected patients found that in those over age 60, NS, although less prevalent than in younger patients, was still the most common subtype, found in 44 percent of patients, whereas 37 percent had mixed cellularity. Lymphocyte-depleted histologies were notably uncommon in this study.

Investigators at Stanford University found that 65 percent of their older patients had NS histologies.[24] However, only 52 of 1169 patients were over the age of 60 in that study, suggesting a possible referral bias. The Cancer and Acute Leukemia Group B (CALGB)[25] reported that 73 of 385 patients who were over age 60 were on protocols for advanced HD. Only 7 percent had NS histology, compared to 30 percent of patients under age 40 with NS. The low percentage is explained by the small likelihood of this histology presenting with advanced disease.

These studies suggest that there is a shift toward mixed cellularity and away from NS histologies with advancing age. They also reveal that this histology is not uncommon in older persons, nor is mixed cellularity uncommon in younger populations. Whether

TABLE 67-3

Influence of Age on Histologic Patterns of Hodgkin's Disease

	Specht & Nissen[19]		*Peterson et al.*[20]		*Wedelin et al.*[23]	
Histology	**Age <40**	**Age >60**	**Age <40**	**Age >60**	**Age <50**	**Age >50**
Lymphocyte predominant	12%	12%	7%	11%	12%	17%
Nodular sclerosing	61	44	30	7	49	21
Mixed cellularity	25	37	42	52	29	46
Lymphocyte depleted	<1	2	14	20	7	13
Unclassified	2	4	7	11	4	4

these moderate shifts in histologic subtypes with age are indicative of a differing etiology (as mentioned above), biology of the malignancy, or differing host responses to the malignancy remains unclear.

Other histologic changes occurring with HD in older patients include decreased infiltration of eosinophils.[25] This may be due to different histologies or different immunologic reactions.

Therapy

The therapy for HD has become better defined as a result of clinical trials (Table 67-4). For younger patients, there remain few areas of substantial controversy. Stage IA or B and Stage IIA patients with supradiaphragmatic disease may be cured with involved field irradiation. Stage IIIA patients with nonbulky disease have good relapse-free survival rates with total nodal irradiation, and many who relapse may ultimately be cured with chemotherapy. Treatment of Stage IIB patients is an area of controversy, as the relapse rate with radiation is higher than with chemotherapy, and it is unclear if salvage rates with chemotherapy make this plan as helpful as up-front chemotherapy. Stage IIIA patients with bulky disease and stages IIIB, IVA, and IVB require chemotherapy. Patients with early-stage disease with large mediastinal masses (greater than 50 percent of pleural cavity diameter by chest x-ray) have a high relapse rate with radiation therapy alone; therefore combined modality therapy is recommended.

Many regimens have been used to treat advanced HD, including MOPP (nitrogen mustard, Oncovin, procarbazine, and prednisone),[26] ABVD (Adriamycin, bleomycin, vinblastine, and DTIC),[27] BCVPP (BCNU, cyclophosphamide, vinblastine, procarbazine, and prednisone),[28] and alternating regimens (MOPP-ABVD)[29] and hybrids (MOPP/ABV).[30] The best regimens are yet to be determined. However, alternating MOPP-ABVD or the hybrid for 8 to 12 cycles (at least 4 beyond documented complete remission) is an aggressive, reasonable approach. Although BCVPP is better tolerated than MOPP, there are concerns that BCNU is more leukemogenic; therefore it is now less commonly used.

Toxicity from both radiotherapy and chemotherapy increases with age. Typical side effects of radiation therapy for HD include acute and transient anorexia with occasional nausea, vomiting, diarrhea, transient and occasionally permanent drying of salivary secretions, transient pharyngitis and esophagitis, fatigue, and cytopenias. Long-term side effects include hypothyroidism (common), pneumonitis, constrictive pericarditis, rare endocardial or myocardial fibrosis, skin pigmentation and breakdown, and leukemias.[22] Long-term follow-up of patients who have received radiation therapy to upper mantle areas should include periodic thyroid evaluations.

Side effects of chemotherapy also tend to be worse in older patients. However, many tolerate intensive chemotherapy surprisingly well. Certain drugs were found by the Eastern Cooperative Oncology Group (ECOG) to cause more severe toxicity in older patients,[31] including vinblastine, methotrexate (possibly because of decreased renal function in older patients, the sole mode of clearance of the drug), VP-16, and Adriamycin. Liver metabolism of other drugs is probably slowed in older persons.[32]

Despite the possibility of enhanced toxicity, the older person with HD may still be safely treated with curative intent. Even for those in whom curative treatment is not indicated, significant palliation and prolongation of life can be achieved with localized radiation and single or multiagent chemotherapy.

Response to Treatment and Survival

Many studies report poorer survival in older patients with HD.[19,20,23,24,32–35] These studies, however, are difficult to interpret because modern staging and treatment were not applied consistently, and it is now understood that age bias may influence cancer therapy outcomes.

The Stanford study described earlier[20] reported decreasing freedom from relapse with increasing age in patients treated from 1968 to 1981. The 5-year freedom-from-relapse rate was 81 percent for those younger than age 17, 70 percent for ages 17 to 49, 63 percent for ages 50 to 59, and 38 percent for those aged 60 and older. Multivariate analysis revealed that

TABLE 67-4

Recommended Therapy for Hodgkin's Disease

Stage	Therapy
I, II (A or B, negative laparotomy)	Subtotal lymphoid irradiation
I, II (A or B with mediastinal mass >1/3 diameter of chest wall)	Combination chemotherapy followed by irradiation of involved field
$IIIA_1$ (minimal abdominal disease)	Total lymphoid irradiation
$IIIA_2$ (extensive abdominal disease)	Combination chemotherapy with irradiation of involved sites
III B	Combination chemotherapy
IV (A or B)	Combination chemotherapy

age was the most important factor in determining freedom from relapse.

In the Stockholm studies,[23] patients above age 65 were treated similarly to younger patients. However, 5-year survival was only 28 percent in patients over age 50, compared to 74 percent for younger patients. Stage had no influence on prognosis in the older group. However, because staging laparotomy and lymphangiography were used much less often, understaging probably occurred. The Finsen Institute study[19] did not demonstrate age to be an independent predictor of poorer disease-free survival but did find it to be a strong predictor of death from HD.

MULTIPLE MYELOMA AND OTHER PLASMA CELL DYSCRASIAS

The autonomous proliferation of plasma cells, unlike most other immune cells, is associated with the elaboration of a monoclonal protein—either an intact immunoglobulin or a fragment thereof (usually the light-chain component). Plasma-cell malignancies are classified according to the type of monoclonal immunoglobulin produced (see Table 67-5). The unusual clinical features of the plasma-cell malignancies in general and multiple myeloma in particular can be explained by:

1. The pathophysiologic effects of the abnormal protein
2. The production of an osteoclast-activating factor by plasma cells resulting in bone resorption
3. The "crowding out" of normal marrow, with resulting cytopenias

Epidemiology

Although multiple myeloma is still a rare disease, the incidence is gradually increasing, for reasons that are unclear. In the United States, there are two or three new cases per 100,000 population per year, which is similar to the incidence of HD or chronic lymphocytic leukemia. Myeloma accounts for 1 percent of all malignancies. Although the age range is wide, it is considered a disease of older adults. Cases are rare before the age of 30, and the peak incidence is in the seventh decade. Males are affected slightly more frequently than females, and it is more common among African Americans than other races.

TABLE 67-5

Plasma-Cell Disorders

Disease		Frequency	Prognosis, Months
Multiple myeloma	IgG	52%	29–35
	IgA	21%	19–22
	IgD	2%	9
	IgE	<0.01%	—
	Light chains only	11%	10–28
Waldenström's macroglobulinemia	IgM	12%	50

Etiology

Radiation or other carcinogen exposure and antigenic stimulation are involved in the cause of this disease. Japanese survivors of the atomic bomb have had a fivefold relative risk. In mice, the spontaneous development of plasma-cell tumors is less in animals maintained in a germ-free environment. Additionally, intraperitoneal deposition of mineral oil will produce a granulomatous inflammatory response, frequently followed by activation or overexpression of certain oncogenes (most notably c-myc and H-ras) and intra-abdominal plasma-cell tumors which produce monoclonal immunoglobulin. Chronic antigenic stimulation, therefore, is considered a probable etiologic feature in the mouse, but the association in humans is less apparent.

Because of the low fraction of cells actively involved in DNA synthesis, few mitoses are usually available to define karyotypic abnormalities in multiple myeloma. Therefore, unlike leukemia and lymphoma, myeloma-specific anomalies have not been identified. Analysis of nuclear DNA content by flow cytometry (that does not depend on mitoses) has demonstrated aneuploidy in 80 percent of patients.[36] Chromosomal translocations were found in 10 percent of cases and, interestingly, t(8:14) abnormalities were associated with an IgA type myeloma.

Kishimoto and colleagues[37] have described a three-signal model for the activation, proliferation, and differentiation of normal B cells by the cytokines interleukin-4 (IL-4), IL-5, and IL-6. It is now believed that these molecules are also important in the pathogenesis of myeloma. For example, receptors for IL-6 have been found on the surface of myeloma cells, and these same cells have been shown to actively secrete IL-6. Additionally, this molecule is a potent stimulator of osteoclasts, implying its role in the erosive bone disease characteristic of the disorder.

Pathogenesis of Clinical Features

Hyperviscosity and Other Defects Due to High Circulating Protein

Many of the features of myeloma are due to the high concentration of serum protein. Hyperglobulinemia, whether it is polyclonal or monoclonal, produces similar effects. Plasma becomes viscous when the IgM exceeds 2 gm/dl (as seen in Waldenström's macroglobulinemia), but also in IgA myeloma if IgA polymerization occurs, and occasionally with high levels of IgG. Hyperviscosity decreases cerebral blood flow, producing headache, nausea, visual impairment, and mental clouding. Decreased renal blood flow may contribute to the renal failure so common in multiple myeloma (Table 67-6). The blood volume expands and congestive heart failure may develop. The high concentrations of serum protein interact with erythrocyte membranes and cause a coinlike stacking of red cells known as rouleaux formation. Coating of platelets results in diminished aggregation and purpura. The high protein level may also interfere with coagulation factors by inhibiting fibrin polymerization, and bleeding may result.

In the absence of glomerular kidney disease, the intact immunoglobulin molecule is too large to be filtered and is therefore not found in the urine. However, immunoglobulin light chains are filtered and then to a variable extent reabsorbed by the proximal tubule and secreted by the distal tubule. Crystals of light-chain protein have been demonstrated in the tubular cells, and protein casts often are seen in tubular lumens. These findings are associated with renal tubular dysfunction and overt renal failure in many patients. Monoclonal lambda light chains are more likely to produce tubular injury than kappa. Renal injury may explain the poorer prognosis of lambda (median survival 11 months) versus kappa (28 to 30 months) in patients with light-chain disease.

Bone Erosion Due to Osteoclast Activating Factors (IL-1β and IL-6) and Plasma Cell Tumor

Approximately 70 percent of patients with myeloma initially complain of bone pain. X-rays reveal either localized punched-out lytic lesions or diffuse osteoporosis, usually in bones with active hematopoietic tissue. In fact, the myeloma patient without radiographic evidence of bone disease is uncommon.

The discrete lytic lesions are characterized by large and numerous osteoclasts on the bone-reabsorbing surface. Myeloma cells grown in culture secrete IL-1β and IL-6, both of which are potent stimulators of osteoclast activity. Thus, bone destruction in myeloma appears to be an exaggeration of the normal bone remodeling process that is mediated by these cytokines.

With bone demineralization due to osteoclast activation and decreased activity because of pain, hypercalcemia may be expected. The symptoms of hypercalcemia (drowsiness, confusion, nausea, and thirst) are nonspecific, but their occurrence should alert the physician to investigate this possibility. Cardiac arrhythmias, renal insufficiency, and profound CNS depression can develop as hypercalcemia progresses.

Tumor Expansion

In the early stages of multiple myeloma, as many as 10^{11} malignant plasma cells may occur in clusters in the marrow. A single bone-marrow sample may not reveal the abnormal cells despite positive serum or urine tests. As the disease evolves, however, a random marrow aspirate characteristically will reveal large numbers of plasma cells (as the total approaches 10^{12}). The normal hematopoietic tissue disappears and, in most cases, a normochromic, normocytic anemia develops with moderate neutropenia and thrombocytopenia. Plasma cells may also form a tumor mass that erodes and destroys vertebrae, causing collapse. Extrusion of the mass into the epidural space can lead to spinal cord compression. Infiltration in the liver, spleen, lung, and other vital organs can occur but usually does not compromise their function. Occasionally plasma cells will be found in the peripheral blood. IgE myeloma presents a distinct clinical entity—plasma-cell leukemia—which, in contrast to multiple myeloma, is characterized by greater tissue and organ involvement, less bone destruction, and a more fulminant course. It resembles acute leukemia more than myeloma.

Clinical Presentation

Multiple myeloma occurs primarily in older patients. In a large series, only 2 percent were less than 40 years of age, and the greatest incidence was in the seventh decade.[38] Bone pain is the most frequent symptom, reported by 70 percent at presentation. However, fatigue, weakness, or recurrent infections may also cause the patient to seek medical attention. Occasionally, a patient will, when being examined for other medical problems, be found to have an incidental myeloma. These patients generally develop overt myeloma, although this presymptomatic period may last a decade or longer (their condition is not to be confused with benign monoclonal gammopathy, as described below). Death from infection, renal failure, or hypercalcemia occurs when the tumor burden reaches approximately 3×10^{12} cells. The bone-marrow aspirate or biopsy characteristically reveals more than 20 percent plasma cells, many of which are

TABLE 67-6

Causes of Renal Failure in Myeloma

Causes of Renal Failure in Myeloma
Light-chain deposition in tubules ("myeloma kidney")
Hyperviscosity
Hypercalcemia
Hyperuricemia
Infection
Dehydration (especially after intravenous pyelogram)
Associated amyloidosis

large, immature, and multinucleated. The prognosis varies somewhat by the type of myeloma present (Table 67-5).

Therapy

Effective treatment for myeloma patients includes chemotherapy, radiotherapy, and aggressive use of supportive measures. The current standard chemotherapy is intermittent oral melphalan (phenylalanine mustard) and prednisone. Cyclophosphamide, nitrosoureas (BCNU), doxorubicin, and vincristine have all been used either alone or in combination with variable success. More than 90 percent reduction in myeloma cells is unusual and cures do not occur. Focal radiotherapy is used for pain relief and to decrease the risk of fracture.

Measures designed to maintain activity and hydration are also important. Analgesics, orthopedic surgery, and supports facilitate mobilization. With adequate mobilization and fluid intake, the symptom complex of hypercalcemia, dehydration, and renal failure can often be avoided. Objective responses to chemotherapy currently approach 70 percent, and the median survival for new patients is approximately 36 months. This is a marked improvement over the survival of myeloma patients prior to the use of chemotherapy and aggressive medical management (less than 12 months).

Other Plasma Cell Dyscrasias Seen in Geriatric Populations

Waldenström's Macroglobulinemia

This disorder is due to a proliferation of a neoplastic clone of IgM-producing cells called lymphocytoid plasma cells. Bone destruction is not a feature. In many respects, macroglobulinemia resembles a well-differentiated lymphocytic lymphoma (low grade) with infiltration of the marrow by lymphocytes or lymphocytoid plasma cells, lymphadenopathy, and splenomegaly.

The circulating monoclonal IgM (macroglobulin) appears to explain much of the clinical picture. The macroglobulin coats platelets and interferes with clotting. The oncotic expansion of the plasma volume because of the macroglobulin leads to spurious anemia and may result in congestive heart failure. The hyperviscosity syndrome is common.

Therapy is directed at both the proliferating malignant clone of cells and the abnormal circulating protein. Agents such as chlorambucil have proven effective in prolonging survival. If hyperviscosity causes symptoms, plasmapheresis can produce dramatic, albeit temporary, relief.

Heavy Chain Disease

These rare malignancies are characterized by the proliferation of plasma cells, which produce an abnormal monoclonal heavy chain without associated light-chain synthesis. Like macroglobulinemia, these disorders resemble lymphoma more than myeloma. Bone disease does not occur, but lymphadenopathy and hepatosplenomegaly are common. Gamma, alpha, and mu heavy-chain diseases have been described. Alpha-chain disease is usually associated with lymphoma involving the gastrointestinal tract, often with malabsorption, whereas the mu heavy-chain disease is associated with long-standing chronic lymphocytic leukemia. Gamma heavy-chain disease can present as a lymphoma that histologically resembles HD.

Amyloidosis

Amyloidosis is a heterogeneous group of disorders characterized by the deposition of insoluble protein in tissues with eventual compromise in function of the involved organs. Several different proteins have been identified in deposits, but two are common. In type I amyloid, the principal protein is immunoglobulin light chains, whereas in type II, a nonimmunoglobulin protein (protein A) is found. In both types, the proteins form noncovalent polymers in a fibrillar pattern which can be recognized by electron microscopy. Different patterns of tissue distribution are associated with the types of protein deposited.

When amyloidosis is associated with plasma cell dyscrasia (type I), amyloid deposits are found primarily in the muscles (including heart and tongue), gastrointestinal tract, and skin. In conditions associated with protein A deposition (such as chronic infections and familial Mediterranean fever), amyloid deposition is in the kidney, spleen, liver, and adrenals. Mixed patterns, however, are frequent, and the presenting site of involvement is not sufficient to classify the type of amyloid involved.

Benign Monoclonal Gammopathy

Not all patients with monoclonal serum immunoglobulins have a malignant disease. Three percent of individuals over the age of 60 and 10 percent of those over 80 have a monoclonal immunoglobulin that is either stable or transient. Contrasting features between early myeloma and benign monoclonal gammopathy are presented in Table 67-7. Indeed, some cases will be early myeloma whereas others reflect a completely different pathogenesis and do not result in clinically important disease. Early myeloma will show signs of disease progression over the first year or two, whereas benign gammopathy will have stable protein readings, no bone disease, and a marrow that may or may not show a mild to moderate plasmacytosis but will have normal-appearing plasma cell morphology. It is important to make this distinction, because benign gammopathy is common and does not require therapy.

TABLE 67-7

Early Myeloma versus Benign Monoclonal Gammopathy (BMG)

	Early Myeloma	BMG
Pathogenesis	Neoplastic plasma cell disorder (malignant)	Disordered immunoregulation (most common) or benign B-cell neoplasm (less common)
Bone marrow	Frequently >10% plasma cells with many bizzare multinucleated forms	Usually less than 10% plasma cells, and these appear normal
Bone	Majority will have bone erosions or diffuse osteoporosis (even early)	Usually no bone disease
Symptoms	Bone pain, fatigue, weight loss, or those associated with kidney failure	Usually no symptoms
Serum spike	Progressively rising	Stable level IgG <3.5 g/dl IgA <2.0 g/dl BJ <1.0 g/24 h (urine)

TABLE 67-8

Summary Points for the Practicing Geriatrician

General
- Older patients will present with more advanced disease.
- Published cooperative trials on which standard therapy is based include disproportionately few elderly patients.
- Older patients are not, a priori, more resistant to chemotherapy. However, end-organ toxicity, especially heart, lung, and bone marrow, may be greater.

Non-Hodgkin's lymphoma
- Increases in frequency with advancing age, especially the "low grade" histologies.
- High-grade lymphomas need to be treated aggressively or survival will be short.

Hodgkin's disease
- Older patients have relatively more "unfavorable" histologies (i.e., mixed cellularity or lymphocyte depletion.)
- Chemotherapy has been less successful in achieving cures in older patients, perhaps because of comorbidity.

Multiple myeloma
- It is important to differentiate early myeloma from benign monoclonal gammopathy (see Table 67-7).
- Myeloma should be a consideration for all older patients with persistent bone (especially low back) pain. The average delay in diagnosis from first presentation is 6 months or more.

REFERENCES

1. The Non-Hodgkin's Lymphoma Pathologic Classification Project: National Cancer Institute sponsored study of classifications on Non-Hodgkin's lymphomas: Summary and description of a working formulation for clinical use. *Cancer* 49:2112, 1982.
2. Silverberg E et al: Cancer statistics, 1990. *CA* 40:7, 1990.
3. Jones SE: Autoimmune disorders and malignant lymphoma. *Cancer* 31:1092, 1973.
4. Portlock CS et al: Treatment of advanced non-Hodg-

kin's lymphomas with favorable histologies: Preliminary results of a prospective trial. *Blood* 47:747, 1976.
5. Lister TA et al: Comparison of combined and single-agent chemotherapy in non-Hodgkin's lymphoma of favorable histological type. *Br Med J* 1:533, 1978.
6. Kennedy BJ et al: Combinations versus successive single agent chemotherapy in lymphocytic lymphoma. *Cancer* 41:23, 1978.
7. Rosenberg SA: The low-grade non-Hodgkin's lymphomas: Challenges and opportunities. *J Clin Oncol* 3:299, 1985.
8. Ezdinli EA et al: Moderate versus aggressive chemotherapy of nodular lymphocytic poorly differentiated lymphoma. *J Clin Oncol* 3:769, 1985.
9. Solal-Celigny P et al: Age as the main prognostic factor in adult aggressive non-Hodgkin's lymphoma. *Am J Med* 83:1075, 1987.
10. Vose JM et al: The importance of age in survival of patients treated with chemotherapy for aggressive non-Hodgkin's lymphoma. *J Clin Oncol* 6:1838, 1988.
11. Dixon DO et al: Effect of age on therapeutic outcome in advanced diffuse histiocytic lymphoma: The Southwest Oncology Group experience. *J Clin Oncol* 4:295, 1986.
12. Skarin AT et al: Improved prognosis of diffuse histiocytic and undifferentiated lymphoma by use of high-dose methotrexate alternating with standard agents (M-BACOD). *J Clin Oncol* 1:91, 1983.
13. Fisher RI et al: Diffuse aggressive lymphoma: Increased survival after alternating flexible sequences of ProMACE and MOPP chemotherapy. *Ann Intern Med* 98:304, 1983.
14. Klimo P, Conners JM: MACOP-B chemotherapy for the treatment of diffuse large-cell lymphoma. *Ann Intern Med* 102:596, 1985.
15. Young J et al: *Surveillance, Epidemiology, and End Result: Incidence and Mortality*. Bethesda, MD, National Cancer Institute, 1981.
16. MacMahon B: Epidemiology of Hodgkin's disease. *Cancer Res* 26:1189, 1966.
17. Gutensohn N: Social class and age at diagnosis of Hodgkin's disease: New epidemiologic evidence for the "two-disease hypothesis." *Cancer Treat Rep* 66:689, 1982.
18. Lokich JJ et al: Hodgkin's disease in the elderly. *Oncology* 29:484, 1974.
19. Specht L, Nissen HI: Hodgkin's disease and age. *Eur J Haematol* 43:127, 1989.
20. Peterson B et al: Effect of age on therapeutic response and survival in advanced Hodgkin's disease. *Cancer Treat Rep* 66:889, 1982.
21. Lukes RT et al: Report of the nomenclature committee. *Cancer Res* 26:1311, 1966.
22. Hellman S et al: Hodgkin's disease, in Devita V, Hellman S, Rosenberg S (eds): *Cancer: Principles and Practice of Oncology*. Philadelphia, Lippincott, 1989, p 1698.
23. Wedelin C et al: Prognostic factors in Hodgkin's disease with special reference to age. *Cancer* 53:1202, 1984.
24. Austin-Seymour M et al: Hodgkin's disease in patients over 60 years old. *Ann Intern Med* 100:13, 1984.
25. Newell GR et al: Age differences in the histology of Hodgkin's disease. *J Natl Cancer Inst* 45:311, 1970.
26. DeVita VT et al: Combination chemotherapy in the treatment of advanced Hodgkin's disease. *Ann Intern Med* 73:891, 1970.
27. Santoro A, Bonadonna G: Prolonged disease-free survival in MOPP-resistant Hodgkin's disease after treatment with ABVD. *Cancer Chemother Pharmacol* 2:101, 1979.
28. Durant JR et al: BCNU, velban, cyclophosphamide, procarbazine and prednisone (BCVPP) in advanced Hodgkin's disease. *Cancer* 42:2101, 1978.
29. Santor A et al: Alternating drug combinations in the treatment of Hodgkin's disease. *N Engl J Med* 306:770, 1982.
30. Klimo P, Connors JM: MOPP/ABU hybrid program: Combination chemotherapy based on early introduction of seven effective drugs for advanced Hodgkin's disease. *J Clin Oncol* 3:1174, 1985.
31. Begg CB et al: A study of excess hematologic toxicity in elderly patients treated on cancer chemotherapy protocols, in Yancik R, Yates JW (eds): *Cancer in the Elderly*. New York, Springer-Verlag, 1989, p 149.
32. Robert J, Hoerni B: Age dependence on the early-phase pharmacokinetics of doxorubicin. *Cancer Res* 43:4467, 1983.
33. Lokich JJ et al: Hodgkin's disease in the elderly. *Oncology* 29:484, 1974.
34. Axtell LM et al: Prognostic indicators of Hodgkin's disease. *Cancer* 29:1481, 1972.
35. Patchefsky AS et al: A clinical and pathologic study of 235 cases. *Cancer* 32:150, 1973.
36. Gould J et al: Plasma cell karyotype in multiple myeloma. *Blood* 71:453, 1988.
37. Kishimoto T: Factors affecting B-cell growth and differentiation. *Annu Rev Immunol* 3:133, 1985.
38. Kyle RA: Multiple myeloma: Review of 869 cases. *Mayo Clin Proc* 50:29, 1975.

Chapter 68

THROMBOTIC AND HEMORRHAGIC DISORDERS IN THE ELDERLY

John Owen

OVERVIEW OF THE HEMOSTATIC SYSTEM

The influence of age on disorders of hemostasis is at best poorly understood. Certainly and properly, age is an important variable in assigning probabilities to specific diagnoses, and age enters into the equation for determining appropriate therapy. But age as an independent risk factor for thrombotic or hemorrhagic disease is weak at best. In the context of diagnosis, age may well be a surrogate for other factors. The risk of malignancy increases with age, as does the extent of atherosclerosis. On the other hand, congenital severe bleeding disorders are unlikely first to become manifest in old age. The situation with the congenital disorders which predispose to thrombosis is somewhat different. In these disorders the first thrombotic episode can occur in the older patient. The pathophysiology of bleeding and of thrombosis is usually viewed in disparate terms. The underlying biochemistry is, however, the same. It is the same hemostatic system which is implicated in venous thrombosis, arterial thromboembolism, and spontaneous hemorrhage. It should thus not be surprising that bleeding and thrombosis can and do occur simultaneously. Nor should it be surprising that "correction" of a bleeding diathesis can predispose to thrombosis. We are all aware that treatment of thrombosis with anticoagulants predisposes to bleeding. This chapter will address thrombotic and hemorrhagic disorders by focusing on common mechanisms. As far as possible, clinical observations and basic science will be reconciled. A limited number of references have been included which can serve as starting points for more extensive search of the primary literature. For most purposes, a specialized text in hematology will give adequate further detail; but for the more arcane issues, appeal to specialized texts in thrombosis and hemostasis might be necessary.

Procoagulant Functions

These are the reactions which directly lead to the formation of either the hemostatic plug or to a thrombus. Note that these systems are dominated by positive feedback and would be expected to proceed to completion if unopposed.

The Coagulation Cascade

This biochemical construct has served us well as a model of the reactions involved in hemostasis. Superficially the cascade has changed little over the past twenty years. In fact a great many changes have been wrought, and perhaps of equal importance, many details have withstood the test of time. The basic cascade is shown below in Fig. 68-1. Note that factor VIIa is shown activating factor IX to IXa and not factor X to Xa. This change reconciles the biochemical pathway with the clinical observation of the severity of the hemophilias (factor VIII or factor IX deficiency). The backbone of this system is composed of the serine proteases, which are converted from inactive zymogens to active enzymes, signified by the addition of the suffix "a." Factors V and VIII act differently. These are cofactors which serve to accelerate the proteolytic activity of factors Xa and IXa, respectively. The cofactor activity of factors V and of VIII is markedly increased by limited proteolysis by thrombin or by factor Xa. More extensive proteolysis by either enzyme leads to progressive loss of cofactor function, but it is the action of activated protein C which is the major control agent for the accelerators. Proteolytic cleavage of either factor V or of factor VIII by activated protein C results in complete loss of procoagulant function. Factor VIIa is inactivated by the tissue factor pathway inhibitor in a complex reaction requiring the formation of a complex between factor VIIa, factor Xa, tissue factor, and the inhibitor. The inactivation of the central axis serine proteases is accom-

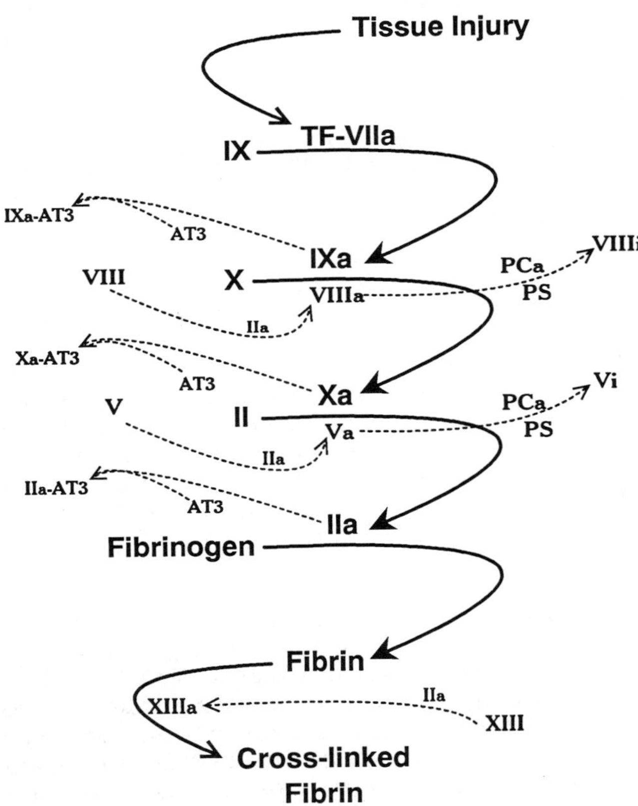

FIGURE 68-1

The coagulation cascade is shown complete with the major checks and balances.

plished by complex formation with antithrombin III (AT3 of Fig. 68-1). These complexes show no procoagulant activity. The mode of inactivation of factor XIIIa is uncertain.[1–6]

Platelets

Platelets are important in both hemostasis and in thrombosis. The property of platelets to adhere and the ability to promote coagulation are particularly important. The view of platelets as providing bulk, like stones in concrete, is probably overly simplistic. Activated platelets bind to fibrin and form a focus of coagulant activity.[7,8] More fibrin is laid down over the platelet and another activated platelet is attracted to adhere. The platelet-fibrin mass grows, resisting the effects of blood flow. Hemostasis is secured or thrombus is formed; only the location differs. White clots and red clots have achieved some level of individual recognition. The distinction has much in common with the perennial discussion of brown eggs versus white eggs: a superficial distinction. Thrombi formed in flowing blood, particularly in regions of high shear, will contain many platelets and few red cells. The platelets adhere to the growing platelet-fibrin mass, the red cells are swept away. In nonflowing blood there is no opportunity for nonadherent cells to be swept away, and red cells outnumber platelets 20 to 1. It is hardly surprising that venous thrombi are mostly red. The critical biochemistry, however, remains the same: fibrin formation is the central event in hemostasis and in thrombogenesis in both the arterial and venous circulations.

Anticoagulant Functions

The anticoagulant functions are essential in that they provide the only means of limiting the activity of the procoagulant functions. This function is carried out by the serpin antithrombin III and by the natural anticoagulant system.

Antithrombin III

A major problem with the cascade as classically described is that there is no obvious way to turn the system off. It has been suggested that, with the first significant trauma to our vasculature, we should convert all blood to clot. This dilemma has been resolved by integration into the system of the inhibitors and negative regulators of the cascade. The principal inhibitor is antithrombin III. This serine protease inhibitor, a member of the serpin family, acts to irreversibly inhibit the activated forms of coagulation factors II (prothrombin), IX, and X. This is achieved by covalent binding to the active center of the serine protease, creating an inactive protease-inhibitor complex. Heparin, which has no intrinsic anticoagulant activity, functions to accelerate the inhibitory action of antithrombin III against factor IIa (thrombin) and against factor Xa. So while in the coagulation lexicon antithrombin III is also known as heparin cofactor, mechanistically it is probably more correct to consider heparin as the antithrombin III cofactor.[9]

Natural Anticoagulant System

The second major regulatory system involves protein C.[10,11] This has been referred to as the natural anticoagulant system. Protein C is a serine protease with marked homology to the procoagulant serine proteases. It, like factors II, VII, IX, and X, undergoes vitamin K–dependent posttranslational modification of specific glutamic acid residues. Protein C (PC in Fig. 68-2) is activated by a compound enzyme composed of a bimolecular complex of thrombin with thrombomodulin (TM in Fig. 68-2). Thrombomodulin is an integral membrane protein found on all endothelial cells. When thrombin is bound to thrombomodulin, thrombin loses its ability to convert fibrinogen to fibrin and acquires the capacity to activate protein C. The resulting activated protein C converts factors V and VIII to inactive forms. The activated forms of factors V and VIII are preferred substrates for PCa, but preactivation of factors V and VIII is not required for action by PCa. Following the common theme, protein Ca activity is dependent on the presence of a cofactor, protein S (PS in Fig. 68-2); PS is also a member

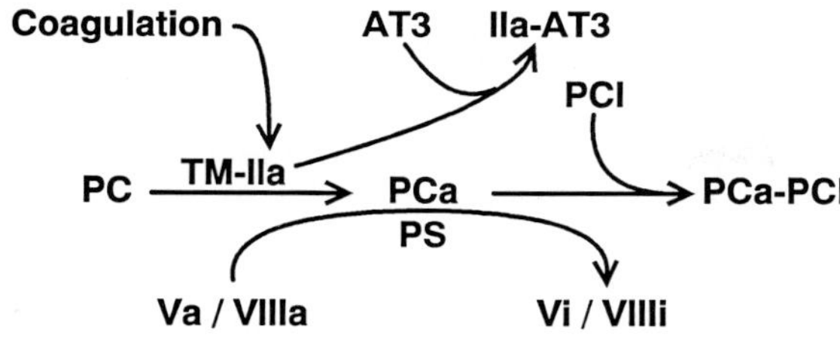

FIGURE 68-2
The principal reactions of the natural anticoagulant systems.

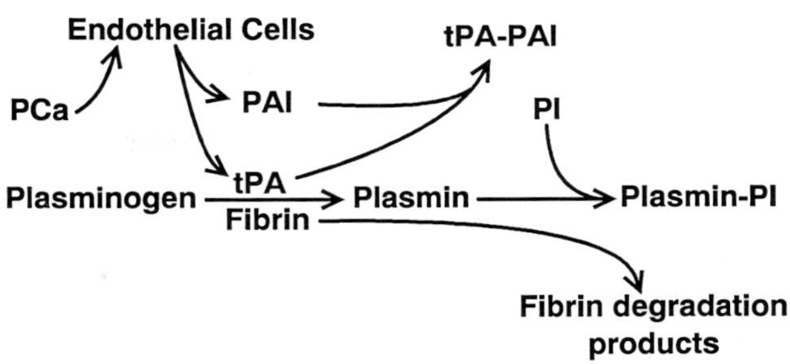

FIGURE 68-3
Principal components of the fibrinolytic system.

of the vitamin K–dependent protein family. Protein S shows marked sequence homology with the vitamin K–dependent serine proteases, but protein S shows no enzymatic activity. An important part of this system is the means of inactivation. Thrombin (IIa) is inactivated by complexing with antithrombin III, while PCa is inactivated by forming a complex with the protein C inhibitor.

Resolution

While plasmin is usually thought of as the central effector in this phase of hemostasis, it must be remembered that there are other systems which are also activated. The inflammatory response is one of these, and the neutral proteases released from granulocytes are potent fibrinolytic agents. Local infection is sometimes seen as the cause of bleeding due to dissolution of hemostatic plugs. Unfortunately for some patients with venous thrombosis, these proteases do not show the same degree of substrate specificity as does plasmin. The result in such patients is destruction of vascular valves in addition to resolution of the thrombotic obstruction. The resulting valvular insufficiency is the dominant long-term consequence of venous thrombosis.

Fibrinolysis

If protein C, protein S, and antithrombin III are thought of as checks of the coagulation cascade, then the fibrinolytic system should be thought of as its balance. The interplay between coagulation and fibrinolysis is central to hemostasis and to thrombogenesis. Plasmin is to fibrinolysis what thrombin is to coagulation. Plasmin is formed from plasminogen by the action of a plasminogen activator. Most commonly this is the tissue type plasminogen activator (t-PA in Fig. 68-3), but urokinase plays both a physiologic as well as a pharmacologic role. t-PA is released from endothelial cells along with its principal inhibitor, type 1 plasminogen activator inhibitor (PAI-1). In this setting it is the balance between activator and inhibitor which determines the net activity of the fibrinolytic system. Supranormal activation of the fibrinolytic system follows activation of coagulation; the balance is maintained with fibrinolysis responding. Homeostasis is thus driven by the relative activity of the two systems, but complications occur when the difference in activity of the two systems exceeds some threshold value. Excess thrombin activity predisposes to thrombosis, while excess plasmin activity leads to a bleeding diathesis.[12–14]

BLEEDING DISORDERS

Assessment of a bleeding diathesis demands the integration of laboratory investigation and traditional history and physical examination. A complete history and physical examination is essential and forms the basis for the selection of appropriate laboratory studies. Certain features in the history and physical examination are of particular importance and should be explicitly addressed, in a focused fashion if necessary. Any history of bleeding beyond that expected must be considered significant. Examples would be any transfusion given after a simple procedure like tonsillectomy. Judgment is required, however. Many elderly patients may have undergone such procedures in circumstances that precluded transfusion. So the absence of a history of transfusion does not necessarily imply the absence of a bleeding diathesis. In the elderly it is often more useful to inquire about bleeding following tooth extraction. In general there is little significance to the reported rate of blood loss. The critical features are the time from onset to cessation of bleeding, whether some form of intervention was required to stop the bleeding, and whether bleeding recurred after completely stopping. There is some diagnostic value to knowing the site(s) of bleeding. Recurrent bleeding at a single site is usually due to some anatomic defect. Spontaneous bleeding into joints is always significant, as is spontaneous bleeding into muscles. Gum bleeding is often unhelpful unless it is profound and of recent onset. Epistaxes, gum bleeding, bruising, and petechiae are usually associated with thrombocytopenia or dysfunctional platelets. Deep muscle hemorrhage and intraarticular bleeding is more commonly seen in disorders of the coagulation system. Neither constellation is sufficiently reliable to use as the sole means of making a diagnosis of the cause of hemorrhage but can be useful in directing the course of initial laboratory investigation.

Presurgical Assessment of Bleeding Risk

We are often presented with the need to certify a patient's fitness to withstand surgery. Without doubt, the medical history is the most useful and reliable index of bleeding risk. The elderly are more likely to need surgery, but fortunately they are also more likely to have undergone a surgical procedure in the past. While prior experience does not perfectly forecast the future, history does tend to repeat itself—at least in hemostatic terms. The patient who had major hemostatic problems at two previous operations is likely to have problems again. One who has undergone multiple procedures without problem will likely have little trouble in the future. These generalizations hold provided no major change occurs in the patient's overall condition. When there is no prior exposure, risk is much more difficult to assess. The standard laboratory tests offer more comfort than assurance. The bleeding time is probably the most widely used screening test, and it derives an aura of credibility from the fact that it is inflicted directly upon the patient by means of a sharp instrument. But even this has proved unreliable in predicting clinically significant surgical bleeding.[15] How much faith can we place in the activated partial thromboplastin time (aPTT), a test performed on cell-free plasma using reagents made from a chloroform extract of brain and incorporating ground glass as an accelerator? The distance from in vivo hemostasis to these artificial systems is such that it is not at all difficult to see why they perform poorly as global tests of the efficacy of the hemostatic system.

It is now generally accepted, though less widely practiced, that patients without a history of abnormal bleeding are at low risk of significant bleeding at surgery provided that they have been placed at risk in the past. The individual who has not had prior surgery, a tooth extracted, significant trauma, or been delivered of a child must be considered an unknown quantity. Such people are the most likely to benefit from some screening tests of hemostatic function. But it is in this very situation that the standard tests are least informative. It has become the norm in many centers to do a battery of tests as a preoperative screen for occult bleeding disorders. The combination of prothrombin time (PT) and partial thromboplastin time (PTT), with or without a bleeding time, is particularly popular. We remain skeptical that this approach efficiently or effectively identifies individuals at risk. Individuals with a clear history of abnormal bleeding should be investigated as thoroughly as possible. The greatest risk in this setting is to ascribe the bleeding to the first abnormality uncovered, failing to uncover the presence of a second, more significant abnormality. Once the abnormality is known, risk assessment and appropriate management can be based on a broad body of experience, taking into account the details of the proposed surgical procedure. This approach does not guarantee the outcome for any single patient, but overall it maximizes the benefit to be obtained from screening and from prophylaxis. In general the approach of using screening tests of coagulation and hemostasis is not a substitute for history and reasoned judgment.

Approach to the Bleeding Patient

There are a number of critical questions to answer at the outset. How did the bleeding start? When did the bleeding start? Has the bleeding ceased at any time, only to restart? What maneuvers have been tried to stem the bleeding, and with what success? Has this ever happened before? Is the patient known to have a hemostatic defect, and what is it? This is only a partial list of the significant variables, and it is immediately obvious that they can be combined in very many ways, too many to treat each combination as a distinct entity. Some simplification is essential, and the mode of presentation forms a useful starting point. In most circumstances all of these questions will be addressed in the initial evaluation, as will an assessment of the urgency of the situation. A lifelong problem or a clear positive family history suggests an inherited disorder; recent onset suggests an acquired disorder. It is not uncommon, though, for a mild congenital deficiency of factor VIII or of factor IX to become evident in later life, a possibility easily overlooked when the aPTT is only slightly abnormal. Such individuals nonetheless can experience profound hemorrhage in response to surgical trauma. As automation enters the coagulation laboratory, screening tests are becoming more sophisticated and, most important, more available. Some form of mixing study which tests the ability of added normal plasma to correct an abnormal PT or aPTT is widely available. This test is very useful to distinguish coagulation factor deficiency from inhibitor. The test, however, may not detect the presence of a mild but clinically significant deficiency of either factor VIII or factor IX. Nor will a simple mixing study distinguish a lupus inhibitor with attendant risk of thrombosis from anti–factor VIII producing acquired hemophilia. An appreciation of the limitations of these tests is crucial to making appropriate decisions regarding diagnosis and intervention.

Petechiae or Minor Bruising

In general this presentation is associated with defects in the platelet–vessel wall interaction. Thus thrombocytopenia must be ruled out before embarking on a costly effort to determine the functional capacity of platelets. Older individuals develop friable skin and seem to have increased capillary fragility. This often manifests as ecchymoses on the forearms, but the problem is not confined to this area. Recent onset of thrombocytopenia can be due to an autoimmune problem but can also be the first sign of a myelodysplastic syndrome or of acute leukemia. The template bleeding time is useful in this setting. A normal result is strong evidence that platelet function is intact provided that the patient does not have a myelodysplastic syndrome. The bleeding time in patients with a myelodysplastic syndrome is an unreliable and potentially misleading guide to in vivo platelet function.[16] Mild von Willebrand's disease is the most common diagnosis in this group, but the diagnosis is far from simple. The plasma level of von Willebrand factor behaves as an acute-phase reactant, leading to considerable variability in test results.

Major Bruising

This presentation is most often seen in patients with deficiencies of one or more coagulation factors. An acquired inhibitor of factor VIII, vitamin K deficiency, warfarin overdose, liver disease, and disseminated intravascular coagulation are all possible. Distinction among them requires the use of the laboratory, but the clinical setting can give some clues to the most likely diagnosis. The PT and aPTT are the most useful tests in this setting, though some type of mixing study coupled with specific factor assays may be necessary for precise diagnosis.

Epistaxis or Gum Bleeding

Platelet disorders predominate here, though other possibilities must be kept in mind. In addition to primary disorders of the oropharynx, primary hematologic malignancy must be entertained.

Hemorrhage

It is critically important to distinguish generalized from localized breakdown of the hemostatic system. Localized bleeding almost always is the result of some anatomic defect. Peptic ulcer, tumor, laceration, surgery, and trauma are common. Defects in the hemostatic system which under normal circumstances are clinically silent can now become major factors. Often, however, correction of the mild hemostatic defect is not practicable, and correction of the anatomic defect is required. Thrombocytopenia or platelet dysfunction can also be contributing hemostatic system abnormalities. In general, multiple abnormalities are the rule rather than the exception. Bleeding from multiple sites almost always signifies a profound disturbance of the hemostatic system. Rebleeding at old puncture sites suggests excess fibrinolytic system activity, a common scenario in a patient with fulminant disseminated intravascular coagulation. Coagulation factor deficiencies more typically are manifest in failure of primary hemostasis or in rebleeding shortly after bleeding appears controlled. As with those patients who present with major bruising, the PT and aPTT are most important tests, but now the level of fibrinogen and fibrin(ogen) degradation products become important. Thrombocytopenia is frequently seen in this setting, so a platelet count is essential.

DIAGNOSIS AND TREATMENT OF SPECIFIC DISORDERS OF HEMOSTASIS

Von Willebrand's Disease

The majority of patients with von Willebrand's disease have the mild variety. This mild disorder is sometimes referred to as heterozygous, but the precise genetics of this condition are uncertain at best. The bleeding time is usually prolonged; factor VIIIc is about 50 percent of normal; ristocetin-induced platelet agglutination is decreased; ristocetin cofactor level is about 50 percent of normal; and immunologic measurement shows the von Willebrand protein to be about 50 percent of the normal level. The bleeding diathesis is usually mild and characteristically variable. This diagnosis is often difficult to make with assurance and is not infrequently made in error. This is not a diagnosis of exclusion. Only very rarely is some form of prophylaxis required for these patients on a day-to-day basis. If surgery is needed, then the aim is to raise the von Willebrand protein level to normal before the operation. The mainstay of treatment has been the infusion of cryoprecipitate, and this remains a viable option. The best choice today is to administer the vasopressin analogue DDAVP.[17] DDAVP stimulates the release of von Willebrand factor from endothelial cells, achieving much the same result as infusing cryoprecipitate. There is clear evidence that DDAVP administration will shorten the bleeding time and adequate evidence that it improves hemostasis. The usual dose is 0.4 μg/kg immediately before surgery. The same dose can be repeated every 12 hours until the patient is safely beyond risk of bleeding. A larger dose of DDAVP does not produce a higher level of von Willebrand factor, and more frequent administration leads to tachyphylaxis. Occasional patients have one of the variant forms of von Willebrand's disease, including a severe disorder which appears much like hemophilia. The diagnosis and treatment of these patients is beyond the scope of this text, and such patients should be referred to a coagulation specialist.

Vitamin K Deficiency

The dietary requirement for vitamin K is about 100 μg/day, and frank deficiency of vitamin K due solely to an inadequate diet is extremely rare. A borderline intake of vitamin K, however, can easily be unmasked by any intercurrent illness. Most commonly the problem manifests in an acute care setting when appetite is diminished or feeding withheld and antibiotics are being administered. A presumptive diagnosis can often be made based on the clinical situation and confirmation obtained by the response to vitamin K administration. Oral administration is almost always adequate, even in the face of all but the most profound fat malabsorption. More commonly in the acute setting, vitamin K is administered subcutaneously. Intravenous administration is also feasible: not more than 10 mg, infused over at least 30 minutes in at least 100 ml of saline. Significant shortening of the PT and the aPTT is usually evident within 12 hours, and virtually complete normalization occurs in 24 to 36 hours. The laboratory can be most helpful in confirming the diagnosis by comparing the plasma concentration of the vitamin K–dependent factors II, VII, IX, and X. The different levels of the factors allows a recreation of the time frame of development of the deficiency. Comparison with the level of factor V controls for the possibility that the patient suffers from liver dysfunction leading to decreased protein synthesis.

Warfarin Overdose

Once again the setting here suggests the diagnosis, and the same maneuvers can be tried as outlined for vitamin K deficiency. In the elderly it is not uncommon to find patients who appear to be exquisitely sensitive to warfarin. It has been suggested that this is a feature of aging, but the "hypersensitivity" disappears when the dietary intake is supplemented with 80 to 100 μg of vitamin K daily. With this steady supplementation, dietary intake of vitamin K becomes a minor component of the equation and sensitivity to warfarin returns to normal. The patient with warfarin overdose who is thought to need continuous anticoagulation presents a special problem. The usual pharmacologic dose of vitamin K (10 mg subcutaneously) often makes it difficult to reestablish controlled therapeutic anticoagulation. Consideration must be given to instituting some other form of prophylaxis as an interim measure, and subcutaneous heparin offers a reasonable choice. When administered by the subcutaneous route, heparin takes many hours to reach full effect, approximating the time taken for vitamin K to reverse the effect of warfarin. Alternatively, infusion of plasma at a dose of 10 ml/kg body weight will rapidly bring the prothrombin time down to the usual therapeutic range, avoiding the overcorrection effect. As noted above, borderline vitamin K depletion leads to warfarin hypersensitivity. Some patients, particularly among the elderly, develop marked prolongation of the prothrombin time not as a result of warfarin overdose but because of the development of vitamin K deficiency. These individuals can easily be controlled by the daily oral administration of 80 to 100 μg of vitamin K. A special case is worthy of note. The rat poison warfarin has been reformulated to contain a different coumarin. When ingested by humans, the anticoagulant effect lasts for weeks. Accidental poisonings have been reported, and prolonged administration of pharmacologic doses of vitamin K is necessary before the effect disappears.

Disseminated Intravascular Coagulation (DIC)

There is no single test which can be used to make a diagnosis of DIC; rather, it is a diagnosis based on a constellation of clinical and laboratory findings. At the pathophysiologic center is thrombin activity in the fluid phase of blood. The complications and clinical manifestations can be grouped, giving three rather different syndromes or stages (Tables 68-1 and 68-2). Without being quantitative, consider the consequences of generating different amounts of thrombin in the circulation. At the lowest pathologic rate of generation of thrombin the principal biochemical effects are to activate components of the coagulation cascade. Factor VIII in particular, but also factor V, becomes activated and behaves as though the plasma concentration had been markedly increased. This increased coagulant potential is promoted by platelets, which also become activated by thrombin. This constellation is prothrombotic and is sometimes referred to as a hypercoagulable state. Such patients benefit from the administration of heparin in low dose, about 500 U/h intravenously. While this condition is generally prothrombotic, thrombocytopenia is a frequent finding. Occasional patients are seen in whom the thrombocytopenia is the dominant feature, and such patients are often refractory to platelet transfusion. Responsiveness to platelet transfusion can be restored in some patients by the administration of low-dose heparin, even though the patient's own platelets may take days to weeks to return to normal numbers.

If the amount of thrombin in the circulation is somewhat higher, the situation changes to one in which there is defective primary hemostasis. Protein C activation occurs and, in turn, factors V and VIII undergo proteolytic degradation. The resulting low levels of factors V and VIII are characteristic of "classic" DIC. The PT and the aPTT are prolonged, thrombocytopenia is almost always present, and the fibrinogen level is low. Plasma levels of degradation products of fibrin(ogen) are significantly increased, whether measured as crude nonclottable material or as neoantigenic monomeric fibrin. More commonly today some form of D-dimer measurement is the test offered. While there is considerable controversy regarding the nature and mechanism of generation of the moiety being measured, the tests have proven useful in the clinical arena. Treatment of this variant of DIC centers on replacement of the depleted clotting factors. Fresh frozen plasma has been the mainstay of treatment and remains popular today. Platelet

TABLE 68-1

Idealized Classification of the Stages of DIC

Stage	Prothrombin Time	Partial Thromboplastin Time	Fibrinogen	D-dimer	Platelets
I	Normal	Short	Normal	Weak pos.	Decreased
II	Prolonged	Prolonged	Low	Positive	Low
III	Prolonged	Prolonged	Low	Strong pos.	Low

TABLE 68-2

Other Features in DIC

Stage	Dominant Pathophysiology	Typical Clinical Manifestation	Principal Treatment Modality
I	Thrombin activation of factors V and VIII and of platelets	Increased risk of thrombosis	Low-dose heparin
II	Activated protein C–mediated consumption of factors V and VIII	Bleeding from new wounds	Coagulation factor and platelet replacement; consider low-dose heparin after replacement
III	Activation of the fibrinolytic system	Spontaneous rebleeding from old wounds	Platelet and coagulation factor replacement; consider using a fibrinolytic inhibitor, but only after giving heparin

transfusions are indicated, certainly if the patient is bleeding. There is a mounting body of data suggesting that replacement of antithrombin III may be particularly beneficial, but this still requires rigorous testing. Once clotting factors have been replaced, consideration should be given to administering low-dose heparin. Data are unclear in this area, though there seems to be sufficient experience to contraindicate full anticoagulation. Well-reasoned attempts to use full anticoagulation have produced more than an occasional catastrophe.

Yet higher levels of thrombin and/or more time leads to a state in which there is activation of the fibrinolytic system and plasminemia. This plasmin serves to digest the fibrin hemostatic plugs in old wounds. The clinical picture is that of spontaneous bleeding from wounds in which hemostasis had initially been secured. This occurs in addition to failure of primary hemostasis. The PT and aPTT are prolonged, fibrinogen levels are frequently below 50 mg/dl, and profound thrombocytopenia is almost invariant. Adequate therapy must be able to contain the fibrinolytic response, and it is both rational and appropriate to use an inhibitor of plasmin. Before introducing a plasmin inhibitor, it is essential that the excess thrombin activity be controlled by the administration of heparin. Again, only a low dose of heparin is required, but in this setting even a low dose might well significantly contribute to the bleeding diathesis. It is therefore essential that missing coagulation factors be replaced first, then low-dose heparin, and finally a plasmin inhibitor. Around the world there are a number of plasmin inhibitors in use or under development; in the United States, epsilon aminocaproic acid (EACA, Amicar) and tranexamic acid (Cyklocapron) are available for intravenous use. There is only limited experience using tranexamic acid in this setting. The usual dose of EACA is 1 g/h by constant intravenous infusion. Some practitioners have given a loading dose of some 4 to 6 g before beginning the constant infusion. There are no data showing the need for a loading dose, but it makes good theoretical sense and certainly produces a therapeutic level much more quickly.

Liver Dysfunction

The major problem here stems from failure of the liver to synthesize the components of the hemostatic system. This failure extends far beyond the coagulation factors to include the inhibitors and regulators of the hemostatic system. In general, the parallel reduction in the levels of all components allows a patient with only marginal liver function to suffer only minimal hemorrhagic complications. However, there is little room to maneuver, and minor stress can lead to major consequence. It had been thought that the majority of patients with severe liver disease had ongoing activation of the coagulation system, the strongest evidence being the frequent finding of fibrin(ogen) degradation products in the plasma of such patients. It is now clear that most such patients have dysfibrinogenemia, and it is this nonclottable molecule which had been mistaken for a degradation product.[18] A small number of patients with liver disease do indeed have an ongoing DIC-like syndrome, but they are the exception and not the rule. A common problem is the need to correct the abnormal PT and aPTT prior to some invasive procedure in a patient with liver disease. The usual procedure is to transfuse 2 units of fresh frozen plasma. This rote formula is convenient but hardly optimal. Patients with only slightly abnormal tests are usually treated this way, though whether the plasma actually reduces the risk of bleeding is not at all clear. The amount of clotting factor in 2 units of fresh frozen plasma would at best raise the circulating levels by about 15 percent. So the success of this regimen may be more a reflection of the careful selection of patients who undergo invasive procedures than of the prophylactic effect of 2 units of fresh frozen plasma. At the other extreme is the patient with severe liver disease and markedly low levels of all coagulation factors produced in the liver. In the acute setting in this circumstance, if the abnormality must be corrected, infusion of coagulation factor concentrates is needed. Prothrombin complex concentrate contains all of the vitamin K–dependent factors; cryoprecipitate is a good source of fibrinogen; and platelets provide factor V. Each of these must be used to give full replacement doses of each factor, an added benefit being the transfusion of the regulators protein C and protein S. For the average patient, 3000 units of prothrombin complex, 10 units (bags) of cryoprecipitate, and 8 units of platelets will be proper doses. Now that prothrombin complex concentrates are heat-treated, there is only a small risk of transmitting hepatitis B and HIV; however, transmission of hepatitis C is still possible. A significant risk is that of induction of thrombosis—a risk that must be balanced against the need to normalize the levels of the coagulation factors.

THROMBOTIC DISORDERS

Thrombogenesis remains something of a mystery, principally because it is so difficult to observe the initial event. The seminal observation, made by Virchow, was that venous thrombogenesis required a change in the vessel, a change in the blood, and stasis to occur at the same time. The change in the vessel was originally described as inflammatory. We now believe that some change occurs in the endothelial cells lining the vessel.[19] This change alters the nature of the endothelial cell from antithrombotic to prothrombotic. Indeed, under some conditions the endothelial cell appears to behave much like the platelet. Prostacyclin, a potent platelet inhibitor, is produced by the endothelial cell; von Willebrand factor is synthesized and secreted; plasminogen activator and the inhibitor of plasminogen activator are produced and secreted. There are binding sites for coagulation factors, and the surface promotes coagulation; the whole of the pathway from factor XIa action on factor IX to fibrin formation is supported on the surface of the endothelial cell. Thrombomodulin, the cofactor which alters the specificity of thrombin to become the protein C activator, is an integral membrane protein of the endothelial cell. Knowledge of the variety and complexity of endothelial cell function increases daily. It is clear that the endothelial cell can no longer be considered as passive in coagulation.

The change in the blood is best seen as a shift in the balance of coagulation and fibrinolysis. This concept was first put forward by Astrup in the 1940s.[12] He suggested that in normal individuals there is constant and ongoing activity of both systems. In recent years this has become generally accepted, though it has not yet become dogma. This paradigm of balanced thrombin and plasmin activity predicts that either increased thrombin action or decreased plasmin action will predispose to thrombosis.[20] Both situations are well recognized in clinical practice. Increased thrombin action occurs when there is exposure of the blood to tissue factor or elaboration of tissue factor activity on circulating monocytes. Malignant tissue has been shown to produce a procoagulant, and severely hypoxic endothelial cells produce an activator of factor X.[21] Increased thrombin activity also occurs when there is a deficiency of any of the natural anticoagulants, protein C, protein S, or antithrombin III. Decreased plasmin activity occurs when there is decreased activity of plasminogen activator or increased plasminogen activator inhibitor activity. Similarly deficiencies of activatable plasminogen predispose to thrombosis, as do antibody inhibitors of the fibrinolytic system. It is worth noting that in patients developing thrombosis after surgery, changes are evident in the blood as much as 3 days before the thrombus becomes evident by fibrinogen scanning. This opens a window of opportunity both for detection of the impending thrombus and for intervention to prevent the actual formation of a thrombus.

The role of venous stasis in the genesis of thrombosis is far from clear. As noted above, it has recently been shown that hypoxic endothelial cells produce an activator of factor X. For some time it has been recognized that intermittent pneumatic compression of the legs reduces the risk of thrombosis. The simple explanation of preventing stasis is called into question by the data of Knight and Dawson,[22] who demonstrated that compressing one leg has a protective effect on the contralateral side. In similar fashion, intermittent pneumatic compression has been shown to alter the balance of thrombin and plasmin activity, particularly in the 2 days following surgery.[23]

Venous Thromboembolic Disorders

Risk Factors for the Development of Venous Thrombosis

In assessing risk factors for venous thrombosis, it is useful to consider three time frames: immediate, short-term, and long-term. The immediate category includes trauma, surgery, and temporary immobility. The short term includes those listed under immediate risk factors and is extended to include malignancy, pregnancy, and severe illness. Factors predicting long-term risk include an empiric group based on multiple prior episodes of thrombosis, and a better understood group made up of acquired and congenital thrombophilic disorders. The congenital disorders include deficiency of protein C, protein S, antithrombin III, plasminogen, plasminogen activator, and some dysfibrinogenemias. The acquired disorders in this group include autoantibodies that inhibit some step in the fibrinolytic cascade. The lupus anticoagulant, an antibody directed against phospholipid, is between empiric and understood. There are many proposed mechanisms for the prothrombotic effect; one of them may well prove correct. At this time it is not known which of many competing explanations will survive. Investigation of an individual with a history of recurrent thrombosis and a clear family history of thrombosis will yield a clear diagnosis in but 10 to 15 percent of cases. Deficiency of free protein S is the most common disorder, but this explains only a small fraction of the patients with strong evidence of congenital thrombophilia. The age-related risk of thrombosis is still being defined for the thrombophilias. An approximate rule for the heterozygotes for proteins C and S and for antithrombin III is that there is low risk of thrombosis until age 15 to 20, then about half will develop thrombosis by age 50, and about one-quarter will not develop thrombosis by age 80. Inverting these numbers, one can see that some 25 percent of these deficient patients will present with their first episode of thrombosis between the ages of 50 and 80. Thus, even in the geriatric population, these congenital deficiencies must be considered.

Presurgical Assessment of Thromboembolic Risk

This question can be better answered than the question of risk of bleeding. There are a number of studies that have identified significant risk factors for the development of postoperative venous thrombosis. These risk factors have been elaborated into scoring schemes which allow the probable risk of thrombosis to be assessed. The major impetus for such schemes is the notion that prophylaxis is indicated for those at highest risk while being unnecessary or even contraindicated for those at lowest risk.

The major risk factor is the procedure itself. Some operations carry low risk of thrombosis, others a very high risk. Second, the condition of the patient exerts a powerful effect; the old adage that sick patients do poorly applies in this setting. The presence of intercurrent illness is significant, particularly malignancy. And any laboratory evidence of activation of the coagulation system is associated with increased risk. The independent influence of age on the risk of thrombosis is not clear. Older hospitalized patients are more likely to have venous thrombosis than young hospitalized patients. But the frequency of other risk factors is much higher in the older patients; heart failure, malignancy, and immobility in particular. Older patients also, in general, have a lower tolerance for pulmonary embolism. Furthermore, the diagnosis of pulmonary embolism may be missed by ascribing increasing shortness of breath to worsening heart failure. A high level of suspicion is warranted at all times, particularly in the geriatric population.

Diagnosis of Venous Thrombosis and Pulmonary Embolism

It is clearly impracticable to screen all patients all the time and equally clear that we need to identify patients with venous thromboembolism in order to institute therapy promptly. The appropriate diagnostic test depends on the situation, particularly on the mode of presentation and on any intercurrent conditions. The intercurrent conditions can be reduced to one issue, the strength of the contraindication to using heparin anticoagulation. The patient with high probability of venous thromboembolism in whom the use of heparin is strongly contraindicated must have the diagnosis of thrombosis established beyond reasonable doubt before beginning anticoagulation. It is important to recognize that, in general, a contraindication does not mean interdiction, nor does the presence of thrombosis mandate full anticoagulation. Judgment is essential, and there is no formula to balance the competing risks.

The gold standard for establishing the presence of venous thrombosis remains contrast venography, but sonography is now a realistic alternative. Color Doppler sonography can demonstrate the presence of thrombus with high precision and sensitivity, but only in accessible veins. The abdomen and pelvis remain difficult to probe with noninvasive tools. The patient with low probability of thrombosis should be approached with noninvasive testing.[24] The use of serial impedance plethysmography has been well established. This approach is possible because a negative study is a reliable way to rule out the presence of significant proximal venous thrombosis in the lower limb. The negative study does not rule out the development of significant thrombosis, so serial studies are needed to be confident of the outcome. This approach avoids invasive tests but does so at the cost of the inconvenience of repeated testing and significant monetary cost to the patient. Efforts have been made to develop blood tests for the diagnosis of venous thrombosis. Most of the proposed tests have been impractical for routine clinical use but have shown promise in that negative tests reliably predict those without thrombosis.[25]

Recently the application of a monoclonal antibody technology has allowed the development of assays which are facile and fast. These new tests for specific degradation products of fibrinogen show promise as clinical tools in the diagnosis of patients with thrombosis. The principal problem with making the diagnosis of pulmonary embolism is one of vision. The young patient "looks too young to have a PE," while the older patient does not "look like the typical case of PE"; too young meaning they should be older, atypical in that they do not fit the classic description of a young person with PE. The second problem to be overcome is the use of the arterial Po_2 as a screening test. It is true that most patients with massive pulmonary embolism have low arterial Po_2, but these are not the difficult diagnostic dilemmas. It is the atypical patient we seek to identify. Once clinical suspicion has been raised, it is appropriate, when possible, to proceed to a radionuclide ventilation and perfusion lung scan. A negative result essentially rules out pulmonary embolism, and for most purposes a scan interpreted as high probability of pulmonary embolus can usually be taken as adequate evidence to begin therapy. In those cases where stronger evidence, positive or negative, is needed, then pulmonary arteriography is the next step. This procedure should be reserved for the few patients in which the answer is of paramount importance, but in that small group it should be pursued aggressively. In the elderly, the dye load is often of concern. The load can be lessened by using the radionuclide lung scan to select the most appropriate areas of the lung for selective visualization, the selection depending on the question of whether to rule in or to rule out thromboembolism.

Treatment of Venous Thromboembolism

In selecting a course of therapy, it is important to keep in mind the objective of that treatment. In general terms, these can be considered in three time frames. The first is to gain immediate control of the thrombotic process and to overcome the hemodynamic consequences of any embolus. The second is to minimize the short-term risk of new pulmonary embolism. The third is to minimize long-term risk of further thromboembolism and to reduce the likelihood of the development of the postphlebitic syndrome.

Immediate Therapy For the majority of patients, immediate therapy will consist of the administration of intravenous heparin. There are both theoretical and practical arguments that favor the rapid establishment of an effective level of anticoagulation. At the theoretical level, we recognize that the coagulation system operates under positive feedback. Thus it is critically important to interrupt this process with an adequate dose of heparin before real control can be established. This phenomenon is in large part responsible for the apparent heparin resistance which is seen at the time of initiating treatment. At the practical level there is evidence that patients who achieve a therapeutic level of anticoagulation within the first 24 hours have a better outcome. It is not clear, however, whether this is a consequence of more aggressive anticoagulation or a reflection of the underlying disorder. This issue cannot be resolved without a randomized trial, but the implication is that we should try to achieve therapeutic levels of heparin as quickly as is practicable without placing the patient at major risk of hemorrhage from heparin overdose.

Reducing the Risk of New Pulmonary Embolism For a short time after heparin treatment is started, new embolization is common, but there is only a small risk of further significant pulmonary embolism. In general, no other treatment is required. Exceptionally, the consequence of further embolism becomes significant. The presence of severe hemodynamic compromise is perhaps most common and is particularly seen in older patients. Prevention of embolization by mechanical means then assumes a greater importance, particularly the placement of filters in the vena cava. Transvenous placement of filters has brought this tool to the forefront, and the ease of placement has certainly had a major impact on the frequency with which this option is exercised. Caval filters have proved to be associated with surprisingly few side effects, and this—coupled with the ease of insertion—has led to the notion that the caval filter is a substitute for anticoagulation. This rationale is ill founded. Hemodynamic status determines the consequences of embolization; control of coagulation determines the probability of embolization. Taken together, they define the risk of pulmonary embolism. The determinants of the development of the postphlebitic syndrome are unclear, but extent of thrombosis is a significant factor. Anticoagulation effectively limits the further growth of thrombus and is singly the most effective means of preventing this devastating complication of thrombosis. The substitution of a caval filter for anticoagulation, while effective in the short term, is likely to predispose to long-term complications. In patients with thrombophilia, a foreign body in the vasculature may well act as a focus for further thrombus formation, mandating rather than obviating the need for anticoagulant therapy.

Long-Term Prophylaxis Some period of anticoagulation with warfarin is usually appropriate. Initial studies suggested some 3 months following acute thrombosis as being the high-risk period. These data form the basis for the typical recommendation of 3 to 6 months of anticoagulation following an acute thrombosis. This period is frequently doubled after a second episode and may be extended indefinitely after a third episode. These figures are somewhat arbitrary but nonetheless useful guidelines for duration of warfarin therapy.

Intensity of therapy has received considerable attention, and the current recommendations are summarized in Table 68-3.[26] Note that the recommended intensities are given as International Normalized Ratios (INR).

The INR has been introduced in response to the

TABLE 68-3

Current Recommendations for Anticoagulation Therapy

Condition	**Recommended INR**	**Prothrombin Time Ratio if ISI = 2.3**
Deep venous thrombosis	2.0–3.0	1.35–1.61
Atrial fibrillation	2.0–3.0	1.35–1.61
Postmyocardial infarction	3.0–4.5	1.61–1.92
Mechanical, replacement cardiac valves	3.0–4.5	1.61–1.92
Tissue, replacement cardiac valves	2.0–3.0	1.35–1.61

observation that different preparations of the reagent used to perform PT measurement give different degrees of prolongation at the same intensity of warfarin therapy. The INR corrects for the differences in the reagents and allows direct comparison of data obtained from different laboratories, even from different countries. This comparability has little impact on the week-to-week management of anticoagulation dose. Rather, it allows a degree of confidence in the choice of target values. It should also be remembered that these recommendations are no substitute for clinical judgment.[27] They are meant to give a starting point for the otherwise undifferentiated patient. The patient who has developed thrombosis with an INR of 2.0 may best be served by increased anticoagulant dose to achieve an INR of 3.0. The patient with a history of bleeding may be better served with a lower INR. In all cases it is important to recognize that it is the balance of risks which is being manipulated, greater protection from thrombosis can be bought at the expense of increased risk of bleeding.

Specific Disorders

Renal Vein Thrombosis This is usually seen in the patient with protein-losing nephropathy, and the role of urinary loss of antithrombin III has been suggested to be central.[28] While there is no doubting the attractiveness of this notion, there is no compelling reason to assume causation. Deficiency of plasma albumin is just as good as a marker of the risk of thrombosis in patients with nephrotic syndrome.

Hepatic Vein Thrombosis This is a devastating condition which carries a generally miserable prognosis. The principal risk factors appear to be hematologic, myeloproliferative and myelodysplastic disorders in particular. Intrahepatic microvascular thrombosis is a well-recognized complication of bone marrow transplantation and has been associated with the use of the birth control pill. Anticoagulation is appropriate in most patients, but all too often the process cannot be reversed and surgical intervention is required. Shunt procedures to reduce portal pressure are appropriate when there is adequate residual liver function. In cases where there is no adequate residual function, liver transplantation offers the only hope.

Superior Vena Caval Syndrome External compression, often by mediastinal malignant tissue or the presence of an indwelling central catheter, are potent inducers of this syndrome. Since the clinical syndrome is produced by the obstruction to blood flow, appropriate therapy requires adequate diagnosis. Patients with thrombotic occlusion of the superior vena cava have a significant incidence of pulmonary thromboembolism, and for this reason anticoagulation is indicated. A few patients have been treated with thrombolytic agents, and at least some patients have experienced dramatic improvement. There is insufficient information at this time to recommend one course of action, but anticoagulation is usually valid, and thrombolytics should at least be considered.

Arterial Thromboembolic Disorders

Risk Factors for the Development of Arterial Thrombosis

Many, but not all risk factors for venous thrombosis are also risk factors for arterial thrombosis. Antithrombin III deficiency and protein C deficiency have been most commonly associated with venous thrombosis. To some extent this is biased by early studies of these deficiencies which examined stored plasma samples from patients with venous thrombosis. It is now clear that arterial thrombosis is also a problem.[29] Defects in the fibrinolytic system seem to predispose to arterial thrombosis more than venous thrombosis. Atherosclerosis is a particularly potent risk factor, so much so that many would consider a causal relationship to have been established.

Specific Arterial Thrombotic Disorders

Acute arterial occlusion generally produces immediate and often devastating downstream effects. The slow development of occlusion is usually accompanied by the development of a collateral circulation which minimizes the immediate problems but may still leave significant dysfunction. This is best appreciated by contrasting acute myocardial infarction with chronic stable angina. In general, we need to consider the problems of arterial thrombosis and embolism in separate time frames and with due regard for the site of the actual or impending occlusion. In contrast to thrombosis in the venous system, lysis of the offending thrombus is a major goal of therapy in patients with acute arterial occlusion. Restoration of blood flow is seen as an important and urgent factor in the viability of the organ or limb at risk.

Acute Myocardial Infarction This disorder has been the subject of a great deal of research, both formal and informal. The notion that coronary artery thrombosis causes acute myocardial infarction has been around for a long time, but it was the work of DeWood and colleagues[30] that proved the point. It is now accepted that atherosclerosis sets the stage and thrombosis changes stable coronary artery disease into acute myocardial infarction. Further support for this construct is the spectacular success of thrombolytic therapy in reversing the changes of acute myocardial infarction.

Risk Factors Risk factors for the development of coronary artery disease are well known. Hyperlipidemia, hypertension, obesity, smoking, and lack of exercise are but a sampling of the more than 200 identified risk factors. Less clear are risk factors which relate to the development of thrombotic occlusion in an atherosclerotic vessel. In this category it is tempting to place plasma fibrinogen and factor VII but also to invoke the old saw that "correlation doth not causation make." Attempts to demonstrate increased baseline activity of the coagulation system in patients at high risk have largely been unsuccessful. On the other hand, coagulation clearly is central to thrombogenesis. These observations are best reconciled by the postulate that thrombosis is the result of episodic activation of the coagulation cascade. Such a construct is strengthened by data obtained in patients with unstable angina. This condition appears to be a drawn out version of the transition state. The coagulation system is active and thrombus is continuously being laid down and removed from the coronary arteries.[31]

Thrombolytic Therapy Thrombolytic agents have not assumed a central role in the treatment of patients with acute myocardial infarction. The fear of inducing an intracranial bleed has been placed in perspective and the initial wild enthusiasm for tissue plasminogen activator significantly tempered. The GISSI study has forever changed the way we approach such patients.[31a] This study clearly demonstrated the benefit of early thrombolytic therapy in the treatment of the patient with acute myocardial infarction. It is, however, the observation that concurrent aspirin administration added benefit which will make the greatest long-term contribution. This finding is the best evidence to date that platelets are actively involved in thrombogenesis and that control of procoagulant forces is essential for full thrombolytic efficacy.

Full discussion of the relative merits of the three best-known thrombolytic agents is beyond the scope of this chapter. There are pros and cons to each. Streptokinase is relatively inexpensive, but there is a concern over the effect of antistreptokinase antibodies. Tissue plasminogen activator offers some degree of thrombus selectivity and preservation of fibrinogen, but it is expensive and must be given by continuous infusion over a number of hours. Urokinase is a direct activator of plasminogen, but it is also somewhat expensive and offers little or no thrombus selectivity. Single-chain plasminogen activator does offer some selectivity and may act synergistically with tissue plasminogen activator, but the combination is expensive and thus far has not been shown to offer any clinical advantage. The move now is to develop adjunct therapies to achieve even better results than those obtained with streptokinase plus aspirin. The concern, of course, is that greater efficacy will be gained only at the expense of increased risk of hemorrhage.

Prevention It is sometimes thought that the biochemistry of arterial thrombosis is profoundly different from that of venous thrombosis. Specific thrombin inhibitors are potent agents in preventing arterial thrombosis and patients with deficiencies of antithrombin III are at increased risk for arterial thrombosis. These observations suggest that the underlying biochemistry is the same; it is the situation which is different. Platelets appear to be more important in arterial thrombogenesis[32] than in venous thrombogenesis. This likely relates to the ability of the platelet to adhere and to focus the activity of the coagulation system. This view is supported by experience with monoclonal antibodies, which block the adherence function and which are effective in blocking arterial thrombogenesis.[32] It is not yet at all clear which approaches will prove most effective against the thrombotic component of acute myocardial infarction.

Stroke and Reversible Ischemic Neurologic Deficits Patients with stroke can be divided into three roughly equal groups according to etiology. One group has intracranial hemorrhage, a diagnosis which is now easy to make with the use of computed tomography (CT). A second group has clear evidence of embolism with a plausible source such as a carotid artery or intracardiac lesion. The third group has no evidence of intracranial bleeding and clinically the presentation is that of an embolic event. The interest lies in the absence of an identifiable lesion which could be the source of the embolus.

Risk Factors The majority of cerebrovascular accidents occur in the context of abnormal vasculature. Aneurysms and arteriovenous malformations predispose to hemorrhage while arteriosclerosis predisposes to vascular occlusion. Identifiable risk factors for thrombus development have been difficult to ascertain. Deficiency of the natural anticoagulant proteins, particularly of protein S, has been noted in patients presenting with nonhemorrhagic stroke, and individuals congenitally deficient in these factors are at increased risk of stroke. However, there are no adequate data which address the question of the predictive value of routine measurements of such factors in the general population.

Treatment It is important to search for and correct hemostatic abnormalities in patients with hemorrhagic stroke. In the elderly there is an increased frequency of vitamin K deficiency, a condition easily treated once recognized. As mentioned earlier, the appropriate intervention depends on the urgency with which correction is desired. Parenteral vitamin K is appropriate, but if even faster correction is needed, infusion of a commercial prothrombin complex concentrate should be considered. Such concentrates contain all of the vitamin K–dependent factors, and they can be used to obtain virtually instant complete correction of the defect induced either by deficiency of vitamin K or by warfarin ingestion.

There is considerable support for the use of anticoagulation in treating thrombotic stroke in evolution. Recently there has developed a renewed interest in the use of thrombolytic agents to effect removal of the offending thrombotic occlusion.[33] It is too early to form a conclusion regarding the efficacy and safety of this approach, but the paucity of therapeutic options make this an attractive possibility.

Prevention In this setting the best preventive measures are those directed toward reducing the risk of atherosclerosis. Prevention of hemorrhagic stroke in individuals with no known defect in hemostasis is beyond current knowledge. Prevention of thrombotic stroke by interfering with the hemostatic system has been attempted but has enjoyed only limited success. Given the central role of platelets in arterial thrombosis, these cells form a logical target for therapy. Aspirin appears to confer some protection but is ineffective in a significant number of patients. This has led to a reconsideration of warfarin anticoagulation, a drug which can be used with greater assurance now that intracranial bleeding can be ruled out with confidence by CT scanning. This approach has yet to be fully tested in clinical trials, but pathophysiology supports the possibility.

Peripheral Artery Embolism and Thrombosis There is little challenge to making the diagnosis of acute peripheral artery obstruction. Chronic obstruction is somewhat more insidious in onset, but even in this setting the diagnosis is usually evident. Therapeutic options are limited to the use of heparin to minimize thrombus extension and thrombolytic agents to restore patency.

Surgical removal of the thrombus is usually the first approach to the patient with acute peripheral artery obstruction. Not infrequently the distal vessel is found to be occluded by thrombus which cannot be removed effectively by the use of a Fogarty catheter. If the procedure has succeeded in restoring some blood flow, then the natural fibrinolytic system may be adequate to dissolve the remaining thrombus. This may require the use of heparin anticoagulation to prevent further thrombus generation. Some patients will require pharmacologic intervention to adequately resolve the residual thrombus. Such patients respond well to protracted intraarterial infusion of a thrombolytic agent.[34] A small-bore catheter is so placed that the tip is just proximal to the residual thrombus and a constant infusion of thrombolytic agent, usually urokinase, is begun. The rate of infusion is typically 50,000 to 100,000 U/h, at which rate there is only minimal systemic activation of the fibrinolytic system. The infusion is continued for as long as 48 hours. Progress can be monitored by x ray with contrast medium injected through the catheter. This approach is highly successful in some patients but has been singularly unsuccessful in others. At this time there is no good way to select appropriate candidates for the procedure. In general terms, fresh thrombus is more amenable to lysis than old thrombus, but this has not proved as strong a factor as it is for coronary artery thrombus.

Purple Toe Syndrome This term has been used for two apparently different conditions, both associated with warfarin therapy. A few patients taking warfarin develop a dusky discoloration of the toes. This is not accompanied by any pain, tenderness, or sensory changes and appears to be benign. An entirely different condition is the onset, usually sudden, of profound discoloration resembling gangrene.[35] The distinction from gangrene is usually straightforward in that sensation is well preserved. Where there is differential involvement of the toes, there may be sparing of the great and fifth toes. This syndrome appears to be due to cholesterol embolization, presumably from an atherosclerotic lesion in a proximal vessel. The emboli induce both spastic and thrombotic changes in the blood vessels. Anticoagulation is useful in minimizing the thrombotic complications while the vasospastic response resolves. There is limited experience with the use of thrombolytic agents delivered via catheter to the affected limb; in some patients there has been dramatic resolution of the occlusion with restoration of near normal blood flow.

Microvascular Thrombosis

General Considerations

This is a heterogeneous group of disorders in which organ failure is the predominant feature. Histologically and pathophysiologically they are characterized by microvascular occlusion. Not infrequently there are multiple organs involved, though some conditions have characteristic patterns of involvement.

Specific Conditions

Disseminated Intravascular Coagulation In this disorder the occlusions are platelet-fibrin thrombi. The typical picture of purpura fulminans is striking and is often followed or even accompanied by breakdown in hemostasis. This two-faced and protean picture can confound the treatment, and the conflicting issues are difficult to resolve. In the absence of life-threatening hemorrhage, treatment of thrombosis takes precedence over treatment of bleeding. Heparin administration is at the heart of such treatment, and suitable attention must be paid to restoring hemostatic function. Fortunately, the thrombotic tendency is usually controlled by administration of only a small amount of heparin. Unfortunately, even this small amount may induce a significant breakdown in hemostasis in a compromised patient. The use of heparin in this setting is extremely valuable but should not be undertaken without a clear understanding of the potential complications.

Thrombotic Thrombocytopenic Purpura (TTP) TTP is a mysterious disease. The widespread organ dysfunction is clearly the result of microvascular occlusion by platelet-fibrin thrombi, but there is no evidence of generalized activation of the coagulation system. Most workers in the field will agree that the endothelial cell is involved in pathogenesis, but the nature of that involvement remains the subject of debate. Without treatment, the mortality rate is in excess of 90 percent; with the best available treatment, the mortality rate is less than 20 percent. This marked difference underscores the importance of making the diagnosis and instituting appropriate therapy. The paradigm for this disease is the patient with the pentad of thrombocytopenia, microangiopathic hemolytic anemia, renal dysfunction, fever, and fluctuating neurologic dysfunction. In daily practice the paradigm must be replaced by a set of minimum criteria. Thrombocytopenia and microangiopathic hemolysis with normal coagulation studies are reasonable minimum criteria. Elevation in the plasma level of LDH is universal in this disease, though typically not to the degree which can be seen in megaloblastic states. Once the diagnosis is made, treatment should begin as soon as possible. Patients with TTP can suffer cardiac arrest without warning, and such patients are extremely difficult if not impossible to resuscitate. On the other hand the neurologic dysfunction of TTP is essentially completely reversible. This dissociation of clinical condition from prognosis is nowhere more extreme than in TTP and is the most cogent argument for seeking expert assistance with such patients.

The most important treatment modality is the infusion of plasma. Most centers now use plasmapheresis rather than simple infusion, and this choice is supported by the results of a randomized clinical trial.[36] A great deal of therapy has not been formally tested, and agents in use include aspirin, dipyridamole, prednisone, and vincristine. Splenectomy was once the principal mode of treatment, but this has been eclipsed by plasmapheresis in recent years. It is not clear whether splenectomy would be appropriate for those patients who fail to respond to plasma infusion.

Hemolytic Uremic Syndrome (HUS) This disorder bears some similarities to TTP, and some contend that both diseases are part of the same spectrum. Since the etiology of both diseases remains unknown, the issue is moot. It is clear that the presentation of HUS is usually different than TTP. In HUS there is always marked renal dysfunction, coagulation abnormalities are common, neurologic defects tend to be global rather than focal, and fever is less common. Optimum treatment has not been defined for HUS, but the combination of plasma infusion with an antiplatelet agent seems to produce good results in the majority of patients. In a few patients the coagulation abnormalities overshadow the thrombocytopenia and microangiopathy and treatment for DIC will need to be instituted.

Warfarin-induced Skin Necrosis This condition is recognized by the sudden onset of patchy skin necrosis, usually at the time of starting warfarin anticoagulation. The pathophysiology is thought to be related to the short half-life of protein C in the circulation. The level of this anticoagulant falls rapidly after beginning warfarin, rendering the individual temporarily in prothrombotic imbalance. If there is concomitant activation of the coagulation system, the risk of thrombosis is significant. There is no satisfactory explanation for the predilection for microvascular thrombosis. This pathophysiology predicts that individuals congenitally deficient in protein C would be at particular risk, a prediction borne out in practice. Protein S deficiency also appears to increase the risk of this disorder, presumably by its role as cofactor to activated protein C. Patients with known deficiency of protein C and previous skin necrosis have been successfully reanticoagulated with warfarin by gradual increase in dose or by the use of heparin anticoagulation until full warfarin effect has developed.

Multiple Organ System Failure and the Sepsis Syndrome These conditions are the scourge of the intensive care unit, being responsible for the majority of late deaths in a wide variety of primary disorders. The organ dysfunction appears to be due to microvascular occlusion, in most cases by platelet-fibrin thrombi. The morbidity and mortality associated with these conditions is high, and thus far treatment has been largely ineffective. It is fatuous to note that prevention is the best remedy, since these syndromes occur in the face of the best that medical science has to offer. Perhaps the next round of biologic modifiers will offer better control.

Cryoproteinemia and Cold Agglutinin Disease These are included for completeness. In most cases the vascular occlusion involves the extremities and is transient, induced by cold exposure, and resolved by warming. Occasionally, a thrombotic component supervenes and the occlusion does not reverse with warming. These patients may benefit from heparin infusion to limit progression of the thrombosis, but loss of tissue often occurs in this setting. The use of thrombolytic agents is attractive but not proven by clinical studies.

REFERENCES

1. Furie B, Furie BC: The molecular basis of blood coagulation. *Cell* 53:505, 1988.
2. Esmon CT: The protein C anticoagulant pathway. *Arterioscler Thromb* 12:135, 1992.

3. Bauer KA et al: Factor IX is activated in vivo by the tissue factor mechanism. *Blood* 76:731, 1990.
4. Nemerson Y: The tissue factor pathway of blood coagulation. *Semin Hematol* 29:170, 1992.
5. Davie EW, Ratnoff OD: Waterfall sequence for intrinsic blood clotting. *Science* 145:1310, 1964.
6. MacFarlane RG: An enzyme cascade in the blood clotting mechanism, and its function as a biochemical amplifier. *Nature* 202:498, 1964.
7. Hantgan RR et al: Platelets interact with fibrin only after activation. *Blood* 65:1299, 1985.
8. Tracy PB et al: Human prothrombinase complex assembly and function on isolated peripheral blood cell populations. *J Biol Chem* 260:2119, 1985.
9. Rosenberg RD et al: Protease inhibitors of human plasma. Antithrombin-III. "The heparin-antithrombin system." *J Med* 16:351, 1985.
10. Hartzler GO et al: Percutaneous transluminal coronary angioplasty with and without thrombolytic therapy for treatment of acute myocardial infarction. *Am Heart J* 106:965, 1983.
11. Walker FJ: Protein S and the regulation of activated protein C. *Semin Thrombos Hemostas* 10:131, 1984.
12. Astrup T, Permin PM: Fibrinolysis in the animal organism. *Nature* 159:681, 1947.
13. Nossel HL: Relative proteolysis of the fibrinogen B beta chain by thrombin and plasmin as a determinant of thrombosis. *Nature* 291:165, 1981.
14. Francis CW, Marder VJ: Physiologic regulation and pathologic disorders of fibrinolysis. *Hum Pathol* 18:263, 1987.
15. Lind SE: The bleeding time does not predict surgical bleeding. *Blood* 77:2547, 1991.
16. Rasi V, Lintula R: Platelet function in the myelodysplastic syndromes. *Scand J Haematol Suppl* 45:71, 1986.
17. Rodeghiero F et al: Clinical indications for desmopressin (DDAVP) in congenital and acquired von Willebrand disease. *Blood Rev* 5:155, 1991.
18. Van DeWater L et al: Analysis of fibrin(ogen) degradation product levels in patients with liver disease. *Blood* 67:1468, 1986.
19. Gerlach H et al: Modulation of endothelial hemostatic properties: An active role in the host response. *Annu Rev Med* 41:15, 1990.
20. Owen J et al: Thrombin and plasmin activity and platelet activation in the development of venous thrombosis. *Blood* 61:476, 1983.
21. Ogawa S et al: Modulation of endothelial function by hypoxia: Perturbation of barrier and anticoagulant function, and induction of a novel factor X activator. *Adv Exp Med Biol* 281:303, 1990.
22. Knight MTN, Dawson R: Effect of intermittent compression of the arms on deep thrombosis in the legs. *Lancet* 2:1265, 1976.
23. Weitz J et al: Effects of intermittent pneumatic calf compression on postoperative thrombin and plasmin activity. *Thromb Haemost* 56:198, 1986.
24. Hull R et al: Cost effectiveness of clinical diagnosis, venography, and noninvasive testing in patients with symptomatic deep-vein thrombosis. *N Engl J Med* 304:1561, 1981.
25. Kaplan KL, Owen J: Blood tests in the diagnosis of venous thrombosis, in Hirsh J (eds): *Methods in the Diagnosis of Thrombosis and Pulmonary Embolism.* Edinburgh, Scotland, Churchill Livingstone, 1987, p 77.
26. Hirsh J: Oral anticoagulant drugs. *N Engl J Med* 324:1865, 1991.
27. Loeliger EA: Therapeutic target values in oral anticoagulation—Justification of Dutch policy and a warning against the so-called moderate-intensity regimens. *Ann Hematol* 64:60, 1992.
28. Ellis D: Recurrent renal vein thrombosis and renal failure associated with antithrombin-III deficiency. *Pediatr Nephrol* 6:131, 1992.
29. Coller BS et al: Deficiency of plasma protein S, protein C, or antithrombin III and arterial thrombosis. *Arteriosclerosis* 7:456, 1987.
30. DeWood MA et al: Prevalence of total coronary artery occlusion during the early hours of transmural myocardial infarction. *N Engl J Med* 303:897, 1980.
31. Mizuno K et al: Angioscopic evaluation of coronary-artery thrombi in acute coronary syndromes. *N Engl J Med* 326:287, 1992.
31a. Maggioni AP et al: GISSI trials in acute myocardial infarction. Rationale, design and results. *Chest* 97:146, 1990.
32. Coller BS: Antiplatelet agents in the prevention and therapy of thrombosis. *Annu Rev Med* 43:171, 1992.
33. Mannucci PM, Vigano S: Deficiencies of protein C, an inhibitor of blood coagulation. *Lancet* 2:463, 1982.
34. Martin M: Thrombolytic therapy in arterial thromboembolism. *Prog Cardiovasc Dis* 21:351, 1979.
35. Lebsack CS, Weibert RT: "Purple toes" syndrome. *Postgrad Med* 71:81, 1982.
36. Rock GA et al: Comparison of plasma exchange with plasma infusion in the treatment of thrombotic thrombocytopenic purpura. *N Engl J Med* 325:393, 1991.

SECTION F

The Endocrine System and Metabolism

Chapter 69

AGING OF THE ENDOCRINE SYSTEM

L. Cass Terry and Jeffrey B. Halter

Central nervous system (CNS) control of anterior pituitary hormone secretion is mediated by episodic release of neuropeptides (releasing or release-inhibiting hormones) and neurotransmitters (biogenic amines) into the hypothalamic-adenohypophyseal (hypophyseal) portal circulation from hypothalamic tuberoinfundibular neurons and neurosecretory axons from other brain regions (Fig. 69-1). On a higher order, the activity of these tuberoinfundibular neurons is influenced by a complex neural network of biogenic aminergic and peptidergic neurons from the brainstem, limbic system, diencephalon, and neocortex. These systems are autoregulated by inhibitory feedback mechanisms at several levels, including hypothalamic (ultrashort), pituitary (short), and end-organ (long) loops and multiple metabolic factors (i.e., blood glucose, thyroid hormone) that act on brain and pituitary. These intricate and sensitive neuroendocrine systems are influenced by internal oscillators or biologic clocks as well as several higher cortical functions such as sleep, stress, exercise, and depression.

The aging process can alter neuroendocrine function at multiple levels (i.e., through its effects on biogenic aminergic and peptidergic neurons, anterior pituitary cells, and end organs) (Fig. 69-1). In this chapter we will describe age-related disturbances in growth hormone (GH), adrenocorticotropin (ACTH), and male gonadotropin (LH/FSH) secretion and review clinical disorders of the neuroendocrine system relevant to the elderly.

NEUROTRANSMITTER REGULATION

There is abundant evidence that biogenic aminergic and peptidergic neurons strongly influence the secretion of hypothalamic hormones.[1,2] Those most studied are the "classic" neurotransmitters dopamine, norepinephrine, epinephrine, and serotonin and the opioids. Other bioamines and peptides have been studied less extensively, and the data are somewhat confounding and inconclusive.[2]

Dopamine

The predominant dopaminergic innervation of the hypothalamus is by the tuberoinfundibular, tuberohypophyseal, and incertohypothalamic systems.[1] Most information on aging attends to the tuberoinfundibular system. Although histochemical studies have shown that the number of dopamine cell bodies do not change with age in rats, there is a marked decrease in the steady-state concentration of dopamine and its rate-limiting biosynthetic enzyme tyrosine hydroxylase and a decline in dopamine turnover, a more reliable index of dopaminergic activity, in the hypothalamus.[1] Also, the processing of dopamine by

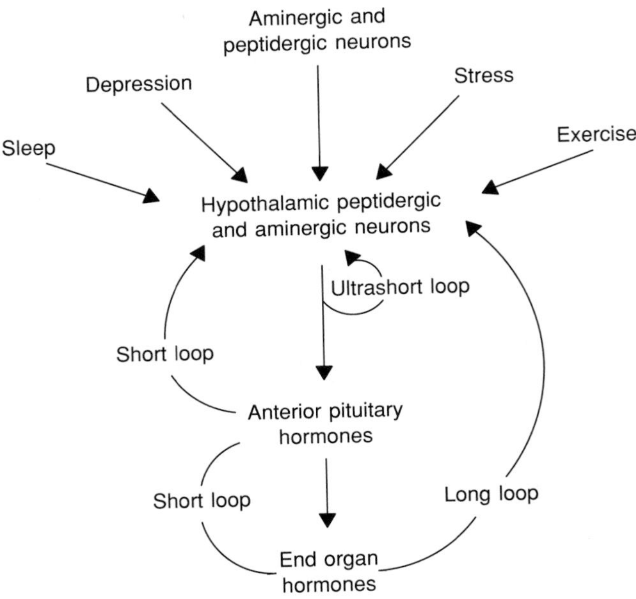

FIGURE 69-1
The hypothalamic-pituitary unit and factors that affect its activity, including inputs from other brain regions and feedback regulatory systems at several levels.

the anterior pituitary decreases in aged animals, and these changes are not observed in longer-living strains of animals.[1] Thus, with aging the amount of dopamine delivered to the pituitary is decreased. Since dopamine exerts a tonic inhibitory action on prolactin, this may explain the association of high plasma prolactin levels in aged animals.[2]

Norepinephrine

The hypothalamus is innervated by the dorsal and ventral noradrenergic bundles that originate from brainstem nuclei and send axons to several hypothalamic regions. Numerous studies have shown that norepinephrine levels and turnover and its biosynthetic enzyme (dopamine-β-hydroxylase) decline with age in rodents and other animal species.[1] Also, in aged female rats there is a decreased ability of noradrenergic neurons to respond to ovarian signals.[1] The noradrenergic system exerts a stimulatory influence on secretion of several pituitary hormones (i.e., growth hormone, luteinizing hormone, and thyrotropin),[2] and its age-associated decline may be directly related to hyposecretion of these hormones.

Serotonin

The indoleamine serotonin has a purported role in neuroendocrine regulation.[1,2] Serotoninergic neurons in the ventral and dorsal raphe nuclei of the brainstem project axons to hypothalamic structures.[1,2] Although tyrosine hydroxylase, the rate-limiting enzyme for serotonin synthesis, declines with age, the data on brain serotonin levels are conflicting.[1] Thus, to date, there is no consistent age-related effect on serotonin.

Opioids

There is evidence that the steady-state levels of proopiomelanocortin-derived peptides (ACTH, β-endorphin, β-lipotropin, and a 16 kDa fragment) decline with age.[1,2] Also, the posttranslational processing of β-endorphin is decreased in old rats.[1] Because decreased brain concentrations could reflect diminished synthesis or enhanced release, Simpkins and Millard[1] have hypothesized that old rats may be "hypo- or hyperopioid." It remains to be determined which, if either, condition occurs with aging. Both states could provide an explanation for some of the neuroendocrine manifestations of aging, including disruption of autonomic nervous system function.[1,2]

THE HYPOTHALAMIC-PITUITARY-ADRENAL AXIS

The hypothalamic-pituitary-adrenal (HPA) system (Fig. 69-2) consists of three elements: (1) corticotropin-releasing hormone (CRH or CRF), which is synthesized by hypothalamic neurons and released from their nerve terminals into capillaries of the hy-

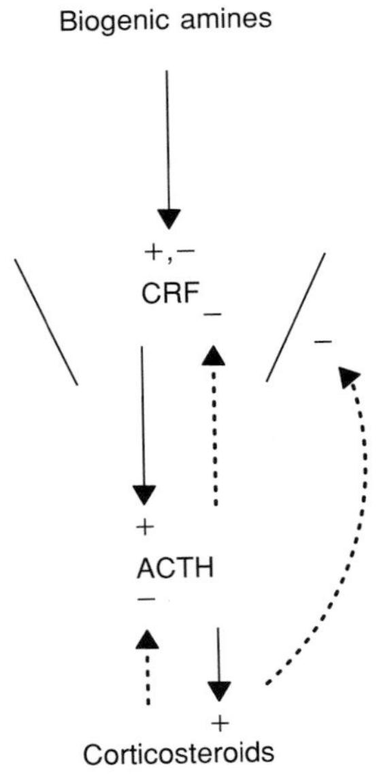

FIGURE 69-2
The hypothalamic-pituitary-adrenal axis. Inhibitory feedback pathways are represented by broken lines.

pophyseal portal system; (2) corticotropin (ACTH, adrenocorticotropic hormone), secreted by anterior pituitary corticotropes into the circulation; and (3) adrenal hormones, primarily glucocorticoids, from the adrenal cortex.

The HPA is considered by many[2] to be the "quintessential" neuroendocrine system because it most clearly portrays complex interactions between the brain and the endocrine system to (1) maintain homeostasis and control the response to exogenous and endogenous stimuli (i.e., stress response) and (2) generate hormonal secretory rhythms.

Corticotropin-Releasing Hormone

Human CRH, a 41-amino-acid peptide hormone, causes ACTH secretion by stimulation of 3′-5′-cyclic-AMP after binding to specific receptors on pituitary cell membranes.[2,3] Its action is calcium-dependent, and it enhances phospholipid methylation. ACTH and cortisol levels remain elevated for 2 to 3 hours after an intravenous CRH bolus. CRH has been measured in pituitary portal blood of rats and cerebrospinal fluid of humans.[2] Although CRH stimulates β-endorphin and other proopiomelanocortin-derived peptides, it has little, if any, physiologic action on other pituitary hormones.

The neurohypophyseal hormone vasopressin also has an effect on corticotropic cells to cause ACTH release, although vasopressin is on the order of 1000 times less potent than CRH. However, vasopressin, as well as epinephrine and norepinephrine, have marked synergistic actions with CRH to facilitate pituitary ACTH secretion.[2]

In addition to its pituitary effects, CRH stimulates the sympathetic nervous system to cause release of adrenal epinephrine and norepinephrine and increase blood pressure and heart rate.[2] These actions are accompanied by behavioral changes manifested primarily by increased locomotor activity and arousal, signs indicative of the stress response. These effects may be mediated by CRH systems outside the hypothalamus.

ACTH

Human ACTH is a peptide that contains 39 amino acids, of which the first 19 are essential for its action on the adrenal cortex.[2] Adrenocorticotropic hormone is derived from the prohormone proopiomelanocortin (POMC). The peptides derived from processing of POMC include ACTH, β-lipotropin, β-endorphin, and a 16-kDa fragment. In addition to the anterior pituitary, discrete brain regions are known to synthesize and secrete POMC-derived ACTH and β-endorphin, and the POMC gene has been found in many other tissues.[2]

ACTH acts on the adrenal cortex to stimulate glucocorticoid and androcorticoid (sex hormone) secretion by binding to specific receptors and activation of a "second messenger system." Its effect on mineralocorticoids (i.e., aldosterone) is relatively minor compared to that of the renin-angiotensin system.

Physiologic Secretion

ACTH is secreted in episodic bursts averaging two per hour in humans.[3] There is an underlying diurnal pattern: the highest plasma levels are seen in the morning (4 to 9 a.m.), and the lowest before midnight. This rhythm is generated by the hypothalamus and its connections through the release of CRH. The diurnal pattern is a result of a greater amplitude of ACTH secretion per burst rather than an increase of burst frequency.[4] Extrahypothalamic brain regions have differential effects on hypothalamic CRH neurons. For example, within the limbic system the amygdala appears to facilitate and the hippocampus to attenuate ACTH secretion, whereas midbrain structures have both effects on the pituitary-adrenal axis.[2]

The effects of pharmacologic agents on ACTH are believed to be mediated by their actions on CRH. The literature is confusing because of the variability of responses of different laboratory animals to different aminergic agonists and antagonists. In humans, α-adrenergic activation and β-adrenergic blockade facilitate the ACTH response to insulin-induced hypoglycemic stress. Also, there is evidence that serotonin and acetylcholine enhance ACTH and GABA is inhibitory. The opioids β-endorphin and met-enkephalin decrease plasma ACTH levels, and the opiate receptor blocker naloxone has the opposite effect.[2] Because CRH stimulates β-endorphin, opioid suppression of ACTH secretion may represent a feedback inhibitory mechanism.

Glucocorticoids provide primary feedback inhibition of CRH and ACTH section. Receptors for glucocorticoids have been demonstrated in the pituitary and several brain regions, including hypothalamic nuclei that contain CRH.[2] The hippocampus contains the highest density of neurons with glucocorticoid receptors,[2] and, as mentioned previously, stimulation of this region inhibits ACTH secretion. Although a short loop feedback pathway for ACTH has been proposed,[2] the data are contradictory and inconclusive.

Adrenal Hormones

Cortisol is the principal glucocorticoid secreted in humans. ACTH has a direct effect on glucocorticoid-containing cells to cause immediate release of cortisol. The half-life of cortisol in plasma is 60 to 90 minutes, and approximately 10 percent circulates in the free form, which is available to cells.[2] Cortisol has effects on cell membranes and the genes that code for enzymes that regulate lipid, carbohydrate, and protein metabolism and stimulate cell differentiation.[2] ACTH also stimulates androcorticoids (dehydroepiandrosterone) and the mineralocorticoid aldosterone. Adrenal androgens are converted to testosterone in peripheral tissues, and aldosterone is primarily under control of the renin-angiotensin system.

Effects of Aging on the HPA

Normal Aging

Tissue concentrations of POMC-derived peptides in the basal hypothalamus are decreased up to 50 percent in aged female rats compared to young rats.[5] However, no release or turnover studies have been performed to determine if this effect is due to decreased synthesis or increased release or degradation.

Adrenal cortical cells show ultrastructural changes in mitochondria with age,[6] and biochemical alterations as well. Popplewell et al.[7,8] have shown that aging is associated with a decreased ability of adrenals to acquire, synthesize, and process cholesterol needed for steroidogenesis. However, the importance of these activity changes in steroidogenic enzymes on corticosterone production capacity is unknown.

Age-related changes in ACTH and cortisol secretion appear to be subtle and variable. ACTH levels are either decreased or unchanged with aging in experimental animals[1,9] and increased or unchanged with age in healthy humans.[10,11] However, this previous work has not taken into account the complexity of pulsatile ACTH secretion.[12] A significant age-related phase advance of the cortisol rhythm, similar to that found in depressed patients, has been reported.[13] Although there is a suggestion that the adrenal responsiveness to ACTH may be decreased in aging,[14] this capability is maintained to a high degree.[11]

The age-related disruption of the HPA most consistently demonstrated is the response to and recovery from situations that increase plasma levels of ACTH and glucocorticoids (i.e., stress). Animal studies have shown that the HPA response to stress is age dependent, and aging of the HPA system is influenced by environmental factors.[15] Following HPA activation, elderly people excrete large amounts of cortisol and both hormones may remain elevated for a longer period of time compared to younger adults.[1,2] Also, dexamethasone causes less suppression of cortisol in older patients.[16,17] a factor to consider when performing dexamethasone suppression tests for depression in elderly patients. This appears to be due to a defect in feedback inhibition by glucocorticoids, and it may represent a diminution in hippocampal glucocorticoid receptors, the activation of which is believed to inhibit CRH release . In fact, it has been hypothesized that a decrease in hippocampal glucocorticoid receptors may explain the impaired ability of older animals to terminate the adrenocortical response to stress.[18]

Alzheimer's Disease

Numerous investigations provide evidence that brain CRH systems are affected by Alzheimer's disease. CRH levels in brain regions and cerebrospinal fluid are decreased in this disorder.[3,19] This diminution in CRH correlates with a reduction in choline acetyl transferase,[20] the enzyme responsible for acetylcholine biosynthesis. There is a decrease in CRH receptor binding in brain and blood lymphocytes,[21,22] which may be accompanied by an "upregulation" of cerebral cortical CRH receptors.[21] The ACTH response to CRH may be blunted in patients with Alzheimer's disease.[11] The increase in plasma cortisol normally observed after opiate receptor blockade with naltrexone is not seen in these patients.[23] The clinical significance of these findings remains to be determined.

Conclusions

The bulk of evidence indicates that of the alterations in the HPA that develop with aging, the one most clearly demonstrable is a diminution in feedback inhibition of ACTH and/or CRH systems by glucocorticoids. Thus, there appears to be a prolonged response to HPA activation by stressful stimuli, suggesting an imbalance in the recovery phase of HPA-mediated homeostasis. The significance of decreased brain CRH levels in the pathogenesis and treatment of Alzheimer's disease requires further investigation.

THE GROWTH HORMONE AXIS

Growth Hormone Secretion

Growth hormone (GH) is synthesized and secreted by anterior pituitary somatotropes. The gene for human GH is located on chromosome 17. Human GH is secreted as a 199 amino acid polypeptide. Although secretory patterns vary with species, GH is released episodically in experimental animals and humans.[2] The control and generation of this endogenous rhythm is mediated by the episodic release of GH-releasing hormone (GHRH) and somatostatin (GH-release-inhibiting hormone) from hypothalamic tuberoinfundibular neurons into the hypophyseal portal circulation (Fig. 69-3). The disconnected hypothalamus can maintain pulsatile GH in rats, but the rhythm and plasma concentrations are altered, suggesting that hypothalamic afferent connections influence the timing and generation of GH release through their effects on GHRH and somatostatin neurons. GH secretion in humans is particularly associated with sleep, especially slow-wave sleep, which tends to occur early after sleep onset.

Stimulation of GH secretion is believed to be mediated by activation of specific brain neurotrans-

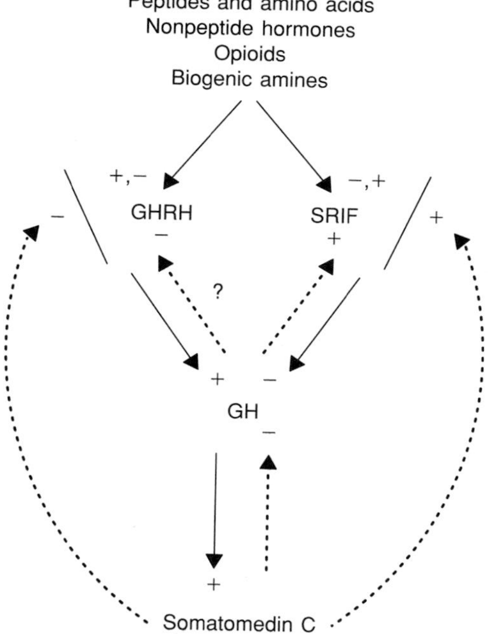

FIGURE 69-3

The hypothalamic-pituitary-somatomedin axis. Multiple factors affect hypothalamic release of growth hormone-releasing hormone (GHRH) and the GH-inhibiting hormone somatostatin (SRIF). Inhibitory feedback pathways are represented by broken lines. Somatomedin C is equivalent to insulin-like growth factor I.

mitter systems that project to the hypothalamus.[2] In general, α-adrenergic and dopaminergic receptor activation facilitates GH secretion, and β-adrenergic receptor stimulation inhibits it. For example, α-adrenergic blockade inhibits GH release induced by exercise and hypoglycemia in humans. There is also evidence in experimental animals that GH release by activation of "extrahypothalamic" regions or opiate receptors is mediated by catecholamines.[2] Sleep-associated GH secretion may involve both serotoninergic and cholinergic neurotransmission.

Morphine and endogenous opioids and their analogs increase plasma GH concentrations in humans and animals.[1,2] Although GH release induced by severe physical exercise is blocked by opiate receptor blockade with naloxone, this agent has little effect, if any, on stress-induced or basal GH secretion.[1,2] Thus, except for drastic stress, there is no indication that endogenous opioids are involved in GH release.

GH secretion is also under feedback control (Fig. 69-3). GH can inhibit its own secretion in animals by several demonstrated feedback control mechanisms, but more investigation is needed to show GH feedback in humans. Both GH and somatomedin C stimulate somatostatin release from the rat hypothalamus. Also, somatomedin C acts directly on the pituitary to inhibit the action of GHRH.[2] Somatomedin C and GH may also have direct hypothalamic actions to inhibit GHRH release.

Growth Hormone Action

Circulating human GH is unbound, has an estimated half-life of 17 to 45 minutes, and acts at several tissues rather than a specific target organ.[2,24] Actions attributed to GH include stimulation of skeletal and muscle growth, enhancement of amino acid uptake, and regulation of lipolysis. Whereas its growth-promoting actions are similar to those of insulin, GH has opposite effects to insulin on carbohydrate and fat metabolism. GH can act directly on some tissues. However, most of the actions of GH are believed to be mediated by its ability to stimulate synthesis and/or release of a number of growth-promoting peptides, known collectively as the somatomedins.

The best understood of these peptides is somatomedin C (SM-C), also known as insulinlike growth factor I (IGF I).[24] SM-C/IGF I is a 70-amino-acid polypeptide that has considerable homology with human proinsulin. Most of the SM-C/IGF I in the circulation is a result of secretion by the liver in response to GH. Circulating levels of SM-C/IGF I are substantially influenced by a number of specific binding proteins. However, the physiologic significance of these binding proteins is not known. Because of these binding proteins, total SM-C/IGF I levels in the circulation are relatively high. However, most of the effects of GH on tissue growth and metabolism mediated by SM-C/IGF I appears to be due to SM-C/IGF I production at the local tissue level.[24]

Effects of Aging

GH Secretion

Amplitude and frequency of GH secretory episodes in humans vary considerably with age.[1,2,24] For humans entering puberty, there is a marked increase in the magnitude and frequency of GH bursts. Those bursts that occur early in sleep are the highest. As early adulthood is approached, the amount of GH secreted declines, especially during sleep. GH secretion clearly declines progressively in aging males[24] and falls in females after menopause.[25] These declines are also most evident during sleep.[26,27]

In the aged male rat there is a marked decrease in the total amount of GH secreted,[24] and a decrease in GH mRNA in pituitary tissue of old rodents has been observed.[28,29] Analysis of GH secretory profiles indicates a marked decline in the GH secretory peaks, whereas the frequency and nadir levels are relatively unaffected.[1,25] Aged females exhibit lower peak amplitudes and higher interpeak basal GH levels.[1]

Similar findings have been observed in monkeys, baboons, and sheep.[1] This age-related decrease in GH secretion is accompanied by lower plasma levels of SM-C/IGF I.[24]

Sites of Involvement

There are several sites at which the hypothalamic-pituitary axis could be affected by aging. Because catecholaminergic neurotransmission declines with aging, the amount of dopamine, norepinephrine, and epinephrine delivered to GHRH and somatostatin nerve terminals may be reduced, resulting in either decreased GHRH or increased somatostatin release. Sonntag et al.[30] have shown that L-dopa restores GH pulse amplitudes to levels found in young adult rats, and clonidine-induced GH release is diminished in old male rats. Also, there is a diminution of catecholamine-dependent morphine-induced GH in aged male rodents.[1] Nevertheless, replenishment of catecholamine stores is reported not to restore the GH response to GHRH,[31] whereas pyridostigmine does.[32,33] Although the increase in GH response to GHRH is diminished with age, the response to arginine and GHRH is not.[34] Thus, the age-associated decline in noradrenergic tone, as well as decreased GH synthesis and transcription, may contribute to hyposomatotropinism in senescent animals and humans.

Hypothalamus: Growth Hormone-Releasing Hormone (GHRH) Recent studies have shown that GHRH content, gene expression, and binding sites are altered with aging, whereas GHRH release from hypothalamic tissue remains constant.[24,35–37] Morimoto et al.[38] have demonstrated a decrease in median eminence GHRH terminals of aged male rats, but there was no change in the number of GHRH cell bodies. Thus, a decrease in GHRH terminals, synthesis, release, or binding to pituitary somatotropes could contribute to the decline in the GH pulse amplitude with aging.

Hypothalamus: Somatostatin A body of evidence supports the theory that somatostatin secretion increases with age in male rats.[24,35] In vivo and in vitro experiments in aged male rats have shown that (1) immunoneutralization of circulating somatostatin increases plasma GH levels and the pituitary response to GHRH when compared to young adults[1] and (2) potassium-induced somatostatin release from hypothalami is enhanced along with an increase in the proportion of somatostatin-28 compared to somatostatin-14.[1] Somatostatin-28 is more potent in its ability to inhibit GH secretion, and it has a longer half-life than the 14 amino acid molecule.[2] Data regarding somatostatin activity in female rats[1] is conflicting and inconclusive at present. Recent studies have shown there are age-related alterations in somatostatin gene expression and receptors.[39–41]

Further support for the hypothesis of age-induced facilitation of somatostatin release derives from studies on stress-related GH changes in the rat and human. In the rat, stress causes suppression of pulsatile secretion, a phenomenon that is believed to be mediated by somatostatin.[2] It has been shown that stress-induced GH inhibition is greater in mature versus postnatal female rats.[42] In humans, hypoglycemic stress induced by insulin facilitates GH release.[2] Wakabayashi et al.[43] observed that hypoglycemia-induced GH release is greater than GHRH-induced GH release in middle-aged males, whereas in children, both provocative stimuli release equal amounts of GH, suggesting that basal somatostatin release is greater in older men. Thus, aging appears to be associated with enhanced somatostatin secretion.

Pituitary Responsiveness to GHRH In addition to age-related alterations in aminergic and peptidergic factors that regulate GH secretion, there is increasing evidence of changes in pituitary somatotrope responsiveness to GHRH and somatostatin.[44–46] There is general agreement from in vivo studies that GHRH-stimulated GH release declines in aged rats and humans.[24,47–49] In contrast, repetitive GHRH administration[50] and co-administration with Growth Hormone Releasing Peptide[51] or theophylline[52] have been reported to restore the age-related decrease of GH response to GHRH.

In vitro studies on the isolated pituitary are in conflict. Ceda et al.[47] found the GH releasing ability of GHRH was partially impaired in cultured pituitary cells from old male rats, whereas basal GH release was unaffected. On the other hand, Sonntag and Gough[30] observed similar GHRH-induced GH release from pituitary slices of old, middle-aged, and young rats, but basal release was reduced by 50 percent in old compared to young rats. These variations may be due to different methodologies (i.e., tissue preparations) and age and strain differences. They demonstrate that the variability in experimental results may increase significantly in aged animals.

Pituitary studies on the age-related cAMP response to GHRH demonstrate less variability than the GH response to this peptide. Two laboratories have shown that GHRH-facilitated cAMP accumulation is decreased in the pituitaries of aged animals.[47,53] Also, Robberecht et al.[54] have shown that the efficacy of GHRH to stimulate adenylate cyclase activity was decreased by approximately 50 percent, with no change in the potency of GHRH, in old and senescent rats. They concluded that aging induces a selective loss of functional GHRH receptors. These results must be interpreted with the caveat that the diminished GH response to GHRH in the aged may be due to a concomitant decrease in pituitary GH content.[1]

Pituitary Responsiveness to Somatostatin Developmental studies on pituitary sensitivity to somatostatin clearly show an age-related effect. Khorram et al.[55] observed that early postnatal pituitary cells are relatively resistant to GH inhibition by somatostatin. These results were confirmed by Cutler et al.[56] when they demonstrated that the inhibitory effect of somatostatin on basal, GHRH-, and cAMP-stimulated GH from pituitary cell cultures is age-dependent. Thus, it appears that pituitary somatotropes become more sensitive to somatostatin inhibition with age. An enhanced inhibitory effect of somatostatin with age has also been observed in pancreatic tissue, suggesting that this may be a uniform phenomenon in tissues subject to its inhibitory action.[57]

Feedback Inhibition

Data are scant in regard to age-related disturbances in the feedback regulation of GH. It is possible that the ultrashort loop feedback inhibition of somatostatin upon itself is defective. Also, there may be altered responsiveness of the hypothalamic-pituitary axis to gonadal and adrenal steroids. In particular, estrogen deficiency contributes to decreased GH secretion in postmenopausal women.[24,25] Increased clearance or decreased responsiveness to GH at the peripheral level is not likely because (1) the plasma half-life of circulating GH is not changed with age,[58] and (2) old rats respond to GH administration by an increase in growth[59] and regeneration of thymic tissue,[60] which is normally lost with aging.

Effects on SM-C/IGF I

The age-related decline in GH secretion is associated with lower levels of SM-C/IGF I in experimental animals and humans,[24,61,62] although the magnitude of this decline may vary with the physical activity status of the population.[63] This effect is not a result of diminished responsiveness to GH in aging, because GH administration leads to a brisk increase in SM-C/IGF I levels.[62] It is possible that diminished GH and SM-C/IGF I contribute to a number of biomarkers of aging. Studies of GH or SM-C/IGF I replacement have demonstrated prolongation of life expectancy in mice,[64] reversal of age-related changes in immune system function,[65] and reversal of age-related changes in elastin gene expression in rat aortic tissue.[66] Initial studies in elderly humans using recombinant human GH have demonstrated enhancement of lean body mass, a slight increase in lumbar vertebral bone density, and normalization of plasma IGF I levels.[61] These findings suggest the possible use of GH replacement to achieve anabolic effects in debilitated elderly patients.[67,68] Future studies will demonstrate whether potential beneficial effects of GH replacement in such patients outweigh potential adverse effects such as impaired glucose tolerance, hypertension, or the reported effect of GH to contribute to the development of nephrosclerosis in rats.[69]

Conclusions

Investigations of the age-related decline in episodic GH secretion point to several sites in the hypothalamic-pituitary axis where there may be disruption of regulatory mechanisms. At the extrahypothalamic level, there is evidence for diminished catecholamine neurotransmission that could cause decreased stimulation of GHRH or enhanced suppression of somatostatin release. At the hypothalamic level, there is evidence that somatostatin release is increased in aged animals, and the proportion of the more potent and longer lasting form, somatostatin-28, increases with age. It appears as if the synthesis and/or release of GHRH decline with age. At the pituitary level, some studies suggest that the pituitary responsiveness to GHRH is decreased, possibly due to a loss of functional GHRH receptors. However, this may be due to the age-associated decline in pituitary GH content. Evidence from developmental studies indicates that the inhibitory influence of somatostatin on pituitary somatotropes is facilitated during the aging process. At present, there is no evidence to indicate that feedback inhibition, plasma clearance, or the peripheral actions of GH are significantly altered in aging.

There is a consistent decline in SM-C/IGF I with age that can be reversed with GH administration. Low-dose GH replacement therapy may be able to slow or reverse some aspects associated with aging. The potential therapeutic use of GH replacement in debilitated elderly people requires further investigation.

THE HYPOTHALAMIC-PITUITARY-TESTICULAR AXIS

The hypothalamic-pituitary-ovarian axis is the subject of another chapter, and the actions and characterizations of gonadotropin-releasing hormone (GnRH) and the gonadotropins, luteinizing hormone (LH) and follicle-stimulating hormone (FSH), are described therein. This section will focus on the hypothalamic-pituitary-testicular axis (HPT) (Fig. 69-4) and the effects of aging upon it.

Gonadotropin-Releasing Hormone

The hypothalamus controls LH and FSH secretion by the episodic release of GnRH into the capillaries of the hypophyseal portal system (Fig. 69-4). GnRH is secreted in bursts approximately every 60 to 90 minutes. This secretory pattern is suppressed if GnRH is infused continuously; it must be administered episodically at a similar frequency to sustain high levels of FSH and LH.[2] Also, evidence indicates that the frequency of GnRH pulses determines the ratio of FSH/LH secreted (e.g., infrequent pulses increase this ratio).[2] Hypothalamic GnRH neurons in males control the onset of puberty, generation of basal episodic secretion, and the integration of sexual behavior and performance.[2]

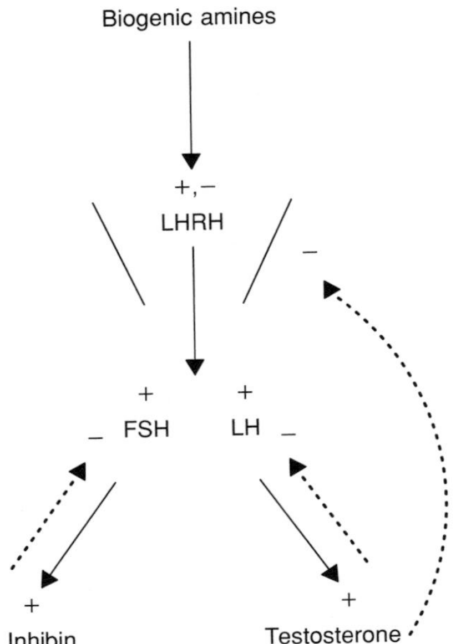

FIGURE 69-4
The hypothalamic-pituitary-testicular axis. Luteinizing hormone-releasing hormone (LHRH or GnRH) stimulates release of LH and FSH. Inhibitory feedback pathways are represented by dotted lines.

Gonadotropins and Gonadal Hormones

LH stimulates the secretion of testosterone from testicular interstitial Leydig cells. Follicle-stimulating hormone facilitates the secretion of the peptide inhibin by the testicular Sertoli cells. Inhibin feeds back to regulate FSH secretion. FSH also stimulates the secretion of androgen-binding protein by the Sertoli cells.[2] Testosterone is the cardinal androgenic steroid in humans. It is synthesized from cholesterol in the mitochondria and cytosol of the Leydig cells of the testis. A similar biosynthesis occurs at a much lower level in the adrenal cortex.[2] Testosterone is reduced by target tissues to its active form, 5-α-dihydrotestosterone, which binds to cytoplasmic androgen receptors. Because approximately 80 percent of circulating 5-α-dihydrotestosterone derives from these tissues, levels of this steroid are thought to be a reliable index of the amount of available testosterone.

Neurotransmitter Control

Numerous experiments have been performed to determine which neurotransmitters have a function as regulators of the HPT.[1,2] The bulk of evidence indicates that norepinephrine stimulates LH release, and activation of opioid receptors is inhibitors. Also, α-melanocyte-stimulating hormone and substance P facilitate and CRH and neuropeptide Y inhibit LH secretion.[2] Literature concerning other aminergic and peptidergic transmitters is extensive and inconclusive.

Feedback Inhibition

Pathways involved in feedback regulation of gonadotropin and androgen secretion are illustrated in Fig. 69-4. Abnormally low plasma levels of testosterone cause an increase in FSH and LH release, and high androgen concentrations inhibit gonadotropin secretion. Also, testosterone administration causes suppression of FSH and LH by actions believed to occur at a hypothalamic site.[2] Finally, there is evidence to indicate that inhibin suppresses FSH, whereas testosterone has a greater feedback inhibitory effect on LH.[2]

Effects of Aging on the HPT

Testicular Function

There is considerable evidence from both human and animal studies suggesting that primary testicular failure is a manifestation of aging.[70] While aging-related declines of testicular function may be accentuated by primary testicular disease or other systemic factors including acute and chronic illness, alterations of testicular function can be demonstrated even in otherwise healthy individuals. There is a decrease in testicular size in men, which is associated with a decrease in the number of both the Leydig cells which make testosterone[71] and the Sertoli cells which produce sperm.[71] The decline in Sertoli cell number is functionally significant, as it is associated with decreased sperm production. There is also evidence for a decrease in production of inhibin in human aging.[72] Similarly, the decline of Leydig cell number is associated with a decrease in serum testosterone levels. While the age-related decline of testosterone levels is modest in magnitude and somewhat variable, it has been documented in multiple studies.[70] There appears to be a greater and more consistent age-related fall of bioavailable free testosterone due to increased levels of sex hormone binding globulin in older men. The age-related increase of FSH and LH, which has also been observed in multiple studies, suggests that the age-related decline of testicular function is primarily due to a testicular problem.[73]

Pituitary and Feedback Regulation

FSH and LH levels increase with age in response to the age-related decline of testosterone and inhibin. However, there is evidence suggesting that these increases may not represent a fully normal pituitary response. The LH secretory response to LHRH stimulation has been reported to decline somewhat with age, although this effect is variable.[73,74] In addition, there is evidence that some elderly individuals secrete relatively less bioactive LH, particularly in response to LHRH stimulation.[75] However, these findings are subtle and there is not uniform agreement.[73] Because testosterone and inhibin levels are critical to interpretation of pituitary responses, subtle defects may be missed when comparisons are made between groups of individuals with differing testosterone or inhibin levels.

Hypothalamic Factors: GnRH

There is general agreement that hypothalamic GnRH declines with age in male rats.[1] Recent work indicates that GnRH gene expression and tissue levels in brain decline with age and are dependent upon testicular feedback.[76] In humans the characteristics of LH pulse frequency and amplitude have been used as indirect markers of GnRH secretion. Although some aspects of LH pulse patterns have been reported to be unchanged with age, recent work suggests an age-related decrease of LH pulse amplitude, which may be compensated for by increased LH pulse frequency.[77] Similar FSH and LH responses to clomiphene (a substance that blocks hypothalamic estrogen receptors and therefore feedback inhibition) have been reported in young and elderly humans.[78] However, a diminished LH response to another antiestrogen, tamoxifen, has also been reported.[75] Again, differences in testosterone and inhibin levels between young and old may interfere with the ability to pick up subtle defects in hypothalamic regulation.

Hypothalamic Factors: Opioids

The role of opioids in age-related changes in the HPT axis is unclear. The opioid β-endorphin inhibits GnRH release.[79] Thus increased opioid activity could contribute to diminished GnRH release with age. However, opioid blockade with naltrexone results in a smaller LH response in older men, not reversal of the age effect on LH secretion.[80]

Hypothalamic Factors: Prolactin

There is evidence of a minor age-related increase in the basal prolactin level and a modest increase of the prolactin response to thyrotropin-releasing hormone.[81] However, it is unlikely that these small changes with age contribute much to the age effect on the HPT axis, particularly in view of the finding that prolactin bioactivity decreases with age.[82]

Conclusion

There is considerable evidence that normal aging is accompanied by primary testicular failure that is modest in degree in most individuals. This age-related testicular failure results in diminished availability of testosterone and inhibin as well as a decrease in sperm production. While there is a gonadotropin response to this testicular failure, there is growing evidence for subtle defects in hypothalamic-pituitary regulation that may contribute to the age-related decline in testicular function. Because of the role that the central neurotransmitter norepinephrine and opioids play in regulation of the hypothalamic pituitary axis, alterations in these central neurotransmitters with aging may contribute to the hypothalamic-pituitary alterations observed.

DISORDERS OF THE NEUROENDOCRINE SYSTEM

Disorders of the neuroendocrine system have clinical features related to hormone excess, hormone deficiency, or local physical effects from endocrine tumors. Clinical recognition of hormone deficiency states may be particularly challenging in an elderly patient population. Symptoms of adrenal, testicular, or pituitary insufficiency can be nonspecific and may include weight loss, fatigue, loss of appetite, muscle wasting, and impaired sexual function. As any of these findings may be manifestations of chronic illness in an older person, it is understandable that an endocrine cause for such symptoms, which would be relatively rare, can be overlooked. The diagnostic challenge is further compounded by age-related changes in neuroendocrine function, as detailed previously, since decreased growth hormone and testosterone production occur with age in the absence of neuroendocrine disease.

Hypothalamic-Pituitary Disorders

Hypopituitarism

Pituitary failure is a relatively rare condition, but it can clearly occur in older people. Major causes include autoimmune destruction, infarction, infection (particularly tuberculosis), metastatic tumor, and infiltrating diseases such as amyloidosis or hemochromatosis. Hypopituitarism can also result from the presence of a large pituitary tumor secreting growth hormone, ACTH, or prolactin. Although symptoms may be nonspecific, a diagnosis of hypopituitarism should be considered seriously in any male with a decline in sexual function and other evidence of hypogonadism. The finding of testosterone levels lower than what would be expected for age, associated with a lack of increase of gonadotropins, provides the basis for further investigation. Such further investigation should include provocative testing of the HPA axis, thyroid function tests, and imaging studies of the sella turcica. The lack of elevation of gonadotropins in a postmenopausal woman is also suggestive of pituitary failure. Since the pituitary-gonadal axis is particularly sensitive to interruption by pituitary disease, it is unusual to find significant pituitary dysfunction in the absence of abnormalities of the pituitary-gonadal system. As hormone replacement therapy can completely reverse the widespread functional deterioration that usually accompanies pituitary failure, it is a diagnosis worthy of consideration even though it is relatively uncommon.

Acromegaly

The clinical syndrome of acromegaly is due to chronic excessive secretion of GH as a result of a GH secreting tumor. The clinical syndrome is recognized by thickening of the skin and soft tissues, which is the predominant cause of the characteristic enlargement of extremities and coarsening of facial features. An increase in the diameter of bones and excessive growth of the mandible leading to protrusion of the jaw are also characteristic. Mass effects of the pituitary tumor can also be present, resulting in headaches and visual field defects. However, these findings are relatively uncommon. The diagnosis of acromegaly can generally be confirmed quite easily with measurement of circulating GH, although the levels may be highly variable and in some patients difficult to differentiate from the normal range. Serum levels of IGF I are elevated in acromegaly and can confirm the diagnosis. Acromegaly can contribute to age-related conditions including hypertension, heart disease, diabetes mellitus, and osteoarthritis. For these reasons, treatment should be seriously considered, while recognizing that reversal of bony enlargement or joint disease may not be feasible. Pituitary surgery via the transsphenoidal route or external radiation may be helpful to control the disease, but it is not often curative. More recently, use of a long-acting analog of somatostatin has shown promise as an approach to long-term management of this problem.[83,84] Not only are GH levels suppressed, but tumor shrinkage also often occurs with this intervention.

Hyperprolactinemia

Elevated production of prolactin resulting in hyperprolactinemia is a relatively common endocrine problem that can result in hypogonadism and contribute to age-related changes in sexual function. Thus measurement of serum prolactin is an important part of the workup of any many with sexual dysfunction. There is also evidence that the hypogonadism associated with elevated prolactin levels can result in accentuation of age-related bone loss in men and may contribute to the development of osteoporosis.[85] Thus prolactin measurement should also be part of the workup for osteoporosis in a male.

Elevated prolactin levels may result from disease of the hypothalamus interfering with inhibitory dopaminergic pathways that regulate prolactin production or can result from a prolactin-secreting tumor of the pituitary (prolactinoma). Drugs that inhibit the dopamine system, such as phenothiazines, cimetidine, and others, can also cause elevations of serum prolactin. Hypothryoidism also generally results in an increased prolactin level because TRH is a stimulus for prolactin secretion. Since hypothalamic disorders generally cause alterations of multiple hormone systems, it is usually not difficult to differentiate between hypothalamic versus pituitary causes of elevated prolactin levels. Once interfering drugs are eliminated as a cause of elevated prolactin, the focus for further workup should be on the pituitary. Modern computed tomographic scans or magnetic resonance imaging can allow demonstration of both large pituitary tumors as well as very small ones (microadenomas) which can be the source of increased prolactin production.

When considering treatment for hyperprolactinemia, there are many options available. These include surgery, radiotherapy, drugs, and no intervention. As the natural history of microadenomas is not established, particularly among the elderly, simple observation may be the most appropriate course to take. However, given the potential adverse effects of elevated prolactin production on gonadal function in men and on bone metabolism, it may make sense to be more aggressive with intervention. Large tumors may require intervention because of mass effect and generally can be approached surgically by the transsphenoidal route. Dopaminergic agonists are available and can be used effectively to lower prolactin levels and also to reduce tumor size during long-term treatment.[86]

Gynecomastia

Enlargement of breast gland tissue in males is a common finding that may be due to multiple alterations in the hormone milieu. The prevalence of gynecomastia appears to increase with age.[87] Asymptomatic gynecomastia of modest size and not associated with other evidence of endocrine disease is generally not clinically significant. In contrast, the presence of tenderness on physical examination and/or a history of recent breast tenderness associated with the finding of gynecomastia requires further workup. Important factors to consider in the differential diagnosis of gynecomastia include states of increased estrogen production, such as chronic liver disease and during the early recovery phase of malnutrition (refeeding gynecomastia); states associated with elevated gonadotropins, including primary hypogonadism and ectopic gonadotropin production by tumors; and multiple drugs that can influence breast gland tissue. These include estrogens, digitalis, cimetidine, spironolactone, and a host of others. Drugs and the combination of drugs and other illness were the causes of nearly two-thirds of all cases of symptomatic gynecomastia in a male veteran population.[87] It should be kept in mind that carcinoma of the breast can occur in male patients and should receive appropriate workup if suspicious signs are present. Gynecomastia can be quite uncomfortable and may require treatment. Surgical removal is one consideration, but antiestrogens such as tamoxifen may be preferable for short-term management. Identification of contributing medications and their removal is the preferred treatment when possible.

Testicular Disorders

As indicated previously, normal aging is accompanied by a somewhat variable decline in testicular function which appears to be due to primary changes in the testis. The question that has been difficult to answer is when does this age-related decline in testicular function reach the point at which a clinically important androgen deficiency exists. As discussed in more detail in Chap. 9, there is a concomitant decline in sexual function with age in men. However, it is clear that this decline in sexual function and the increased rate of impotence in men with age has a complex origin, one component of which may be the age-related decline in gonadal function. Similarly, declines in muscle strength, muscle mass, and bone mass with aging in males may be the result of multiple factors including chronic illness, disability, nutritional problems, and others. The role of the age-related decline in androgen levels as a contributing factor to these problems has not been defined.

On the one hand, there is no doubt that overt gonadal failure with clinical androgen deficiency can occur in elderly men. Surveys of populations of elderly men with sexual dysfunction suggest that a small percentage of such individuals have clearly subnormal testosterone levels, even compared to age-matched controls. While the prevalence of overt hypogonadism is probably less than 10 percent of elderly males with sexual dysfunction,[88] such individuals are candidates for testosterone replacement therapy. Clear-cut guidelines for determining which patients are candidates for hormone replacement therapy have not been established. However, it seems reasonable to consider treating patients with a serum testosterone level below 300 ng/dl (usual lower limit of normal is 400 ng/dl).

In general, patients with long-standing gonadal failure do not complain of sexual dysfunction or provide a history of poor sexual function in the past unless questioned specifically about this topic. The diagnosis is often made at the time of physical examination when very small testes are observed, often accompanied by significant gynecomastia. Laboratory findings will confirm a very low testosterone level associated with elevated gonadotropins when there is primary testicular failure. The finding of low- or normal-range gonadotropin levels in this setting should focus attention on the pituitary for further workup. Because such patients may be unconcerned about their lack of sexual function and interest, it could be argued that hormone replacement therapy is not appropriate for some individuals. However, the important anabolic effects of androgens on muscle and bone provide a rationale for treatment even if sexual function is not an important issue.

Although oral androgens are widely available, most carry a risk of hepatic toxicity. Thus intramuscular injection of testosterone remains the treatment of choice. Patients can either be taught to self-administer the testosterone or other arrangements can often be made for injections at home. Long-acting preparations are available which require an injection once every 2 to 4 weeks. A more short-acting preparation should be used to initiate therapy, although injections every other day will be required. This approach allows rapid discontinuation if adverse effects appear. It should be remembered that testosterone can be metabolized to estrogen. Thus, during the initial phases of treatment, gynecomastia may actually worsen. However, with longer-term treatment gonadotropin levels will be suppressed and gynecomastia generally resolves.

Disorders of the Adrenal Gland

Clinical problems of the adrenal gland that may occur in elderly patients result from overproduction of adrenal steroids, underproduction of adrenal steroids, or adrenal neoplasms. There is no evidence that older people are particularly prone to the development of these relatively rare adrenal problems. However, many of the clinical problems seen in elderly people could be manifestations of adrenal disease. These range from hypertension and diabetes mellitus associated with overproduction of glucocorticoids or mineralocorticoids to weight loss, fatigue, and hypotension that are manifestations of adrenal insufficiency. Thus, it is important to keep adrenal disorders in mind when evaluating elderly patients who present with these problems. This by no means implies that all elderly patients with hypertension, diabetes, or weight loss should be worked up extensively for adrenal disease. The physical examination for signs of cortisol excess or deficiency and routine laboratory assessment for electrolyte abnormalities are particularly important means for screening of such patients. Benign adrenal neoplasia is increasingly recognized in older individuals who are subjected to abdominal imaging procedures for workup of a variety of clinical findings. Because benign adrenal neoplasms are common, incidental findings on abdominal imaging studies do not merit extensive further workup unless there is a specific clinical indication.

Glucocorticoid Excess

Cushing's syndrome due to excessive secretion of cortisol can result from primary diseases of the adrenal gland (either a benign or malignant neoplasm), from overproduction of ACTH by the pituitary (a condition usually referred to as Cushing's disease), or from ectopic secretion of ACTH or CRH from a malignant tumor. All of these are rare conditions that are recognized clinically by the classic features of Cushing's syndrome in the absence of an exogenous source of steroids. The workup involves documentation of excessive production of cortisol. This is usually done by showing failure of normal suppression after overnight treatment with dexamethasone and/or by measuring urinary excretion of free cortisol. Once excessive cortisol production is documented, the patient should be referred to an endocrinologist for further workup to establish the primary cause of the syndrome. Treatment is then targeted at the primary cause.

By far the most common cause of glucocorticoid excess in the elderly population is iatrogenic: the therapeutic use of glucocorticoids for a variety of clinical conditions. Elderly patients may be particularly at risk for adverse effects of therapeutic use of glucocorticoids, since glucocorticoid excess will exacerbate a substantial number of conditions that already occur with high prevalence in this population. These include diabetes mellitus, hypertension, osteoporosis, impaired wound healing, and diminished host responses to infection. Thus every effort should be made to minimize the use of glucocorticoids in elderly patients. It must be remembered that withdrawal of glucocorticoid therapy may be associated with an extended period of diminished responsiveness of the HPA axis due to the suppressive effects of glucocorticoid excess on the hypothalamus and pituitary. This is an important consideration when weaning elderly patients off of glucocorticoids or if discontinuation of glucocorticoids is possible. Under these circumstances, patients should be instructed to use glucocorticoids in moderate doses (e.g., 10 to 15 mg/day of prednisone) to cover themselves during major illnesses or stressful events such as a major surgical procedure. The cosyntropin (synthetic ACTH) stimulation test can be used to help to determine if such coverage is necessary. A normal increase of plasma cortisol in response to cosyntropin provides indirect evidence that HPA axis recovery has occurred. There is currently little evidence available about whether older people are more susceptible to long-term HPA axis suppression by glucocorticoid therapy than younger people.

Mineralocorticoid Excess

Overproduction of mineralocorticoid by the adrenal gland (Conn's syndrome) is an uncommon cause of hypertension due to an adrenal tumor or hyperplasia. Workup for this syndrome is indicated in patients with hypertension who have hypokalemia in the absence of diuretic therapy. Although suppressed plasma renin is a characteristic of this syndrome, the age-related decline in renin levels interferes with the use of renin measurement to help in screening. The key is to document elevated aldosterone levels. Because the conditions for making such measurements are critical and the results can help to distinguish between an adrenal adenoma and hyperplasia, this workup should be carried out by an endocrinologist.

Adrenal Insufficiency

Bilateral adrenal cortical failure (Addison's disease) is a dramatic clinical syndrome that is life-threatening. Weakness, fatigue, and weight loss are virtually pathognomonic findings. They are associated with hyperpigmentation of the skin due to increased ACTH, hypotension, and electrolyte abnormalities including hyponatremia and hyperkalemia. Adrenal insufficiency can be due to autoimmune destruction, infection (such as tuberculosis), hemorrhage from anticoagulant therapy, adrenal infiltration as in amyloidosis, or metastatic tumor. The diagnosis can be established by a simple cosyntropin stimulation test documenting low cortisol levels and failure of those levels to increase after injection. Treatment is straightforward and life saving. It involves replacement doses of a glucocorticoid with appropriate increases of the dose during times of stressful illness. Patients with primary adrenal failure often can be managed with cortisone alone, although a mineralocorticoid may also be necessary in some patients.

REFERENCES

1. Simpkins JW, Millard WJ: Influence of age on neurotransmitter function. *Endocrinol Metab Clin North Am* 16:893,1987.
2. Martin JB, Reichlin S: *Clinical Neuroendocrinology,* 2d ed. Philadelphia, Davis, 1987.
3. Owens MJ, Nemeroff CB: Physiology and pharmacology of corticotropin-releasing factor. *Pharmacol Rev* 43:425, 1991.
4. Veldhuis JD et al: Amplitude, but not frequency, modulation of adrenocorticotropin secretory bursts gives rise to the nyctohumeral rhythm of the corticotropic axis in man. *J Clin Endocrinol Metab* 71:452, 1990.
5. Barnea A et al: A reduction in the concentration of immunoreactive corticotropin, melanotropin and lipotropin in the brain of the aging rat. *Brain Res* 232:345, 1982.
6. Murakoshi M et al: Mitochondrial alterations in aged rat adrenal cortical cells. *Tokai J Exp Clin Med* 10:531, 1985.
7. Popplewell PY, Azhar S: Effects of aging on cholesterol content and cholesterol-metabolizing enzymes in the rat adrenal gland. *Endocrinology* 121:64, 1987.
8. Popplewell PY et al: The influence of age on steroidogenic enzyme activities of the rat adrenal gland: Enhanced expression of cholesterol side-chain cleavage activity. *Endocrinology* 120:2521, 1987.
9. Sonntag WE et al: Diminished diurnal secretion of adrenocorticotropin (ACTH), but not corticosterone,

in old male rats: Possible relation to increased adrenal sensitivity to ACTH in vivo. *Endocrinology* 120:2308, 1987.

10. Waltman C et al: Spontaneous and glucocorticoid-inhibited adrenocorticotropic hormone and cortisol secretion are similar in healthy young and old men. *J Clin Endocrinol Metab* 73:495, 1991.
11. Dodt C et al: Different regulation of adrenocorticotropin and cortisol secretion in young, mentally healthy elderly and patients with senile dementia of Alzheimer's type. *J Clin Endocrinol Metab* 72:272, 1991.
12. Carnes M et al: Pulsatile ACTH secretion in rhesus monkeys: Variation with time of day and relationship to cortisol. *Peptides* 8:325, 1988.
13. Sherman B et al: Age-related changes in the circadian rhythm of plasma cortisol in man. *J Clin Endocrinol Metab* 61:439, 1985.
14. Potter CL et al: Aldosterone production and hormone responsiveness in adrenal glomerulosa cells from cows of different ages. *Gerontology* 33:77, 1987.
15. Brodish A, Odio M: Age-dependent effects of chronic stress on ACTH and corticosterone responses to an acute novel stress. *Neuroendocrinology* 49:496, 1989.
16. Stuck AE et al: Kinetics of prednisolone and endogenous cortisol suppression in the elderly. *Clin Pharmacol Ther* 43:354, 1988.
17. Weiner MF et al: Influence of age and relative weight on cortisol suppression in normal subjects. *Am J Psychiatry* 144:646, 1987.
18. Sapolky R et al: The neuroendocrinology of stress and aging: The glucocorticoid cascade hypothesis. *Endocrine Rev* 7:284, 1986.
19. Bissette G et al: Corticotropin-releasing factor-like immunoreactivity in senile dementia of the Alzheimer type: Reduced cortical and striatal concentrations. *JAMA* 254:3067, 1985.
20. Whitehouse PJ et al: Reduction sin corticotropin releasing factor-like immunoreactivity in cerebral cortex in Alzheimer's disease, Parkinson's disease, and progressive supranuclear palsy. *Neurology* 37:905, 1987.
21. de Souza EB et al: CRH defects in Alzheimer's and other neurologic diseases. *Hosp Pract [Off]* 23:59, 1988.
22. Singh VK et al: Binding of [125l] corticotropin releasing factor to blood immunocytes and its reduction in Alzheimer's disease. *Immunol Lett* 18:5, 1988.
23. Pomara N et al: Loss of the cortisol response to naltrexone in Alzheimer's disease. *Biol Psychiatry* 23:726, 1988.
24. Kelijman M: Age-related alterations of the growth hormone/insulin-like-growth-factor I axis. *J Am Geriatr Soc* 39:295, 1991.
25. Ho KY et al: Effects of sex and age on the 24-hour profile of growth hormone secretion in man: Importance of endogenous estradiol concentrations. *J Clin Endocrinol Metab* 64:51, 1987.
26. Terry LC et al: Physiologic secretion of growth hormone and prolactin in male and female rats. *Clin Endocrinol* 6:19S, 1977.
27. Prinz P et al: Plasma growth hormone during sleep in young and aged men. *J Gerontol* 38:519, 1983.
28. Crew MD et al: Age-related decreases of growth hormone and prolactin gene expression in the mouse pituitary. *Endocrinology* 121:1251, 1987.
29. Martinoli MG et al: Growth hormone and somatostatin gene expression in adult and aging rats as measured by quantitative in situ hybridization. *Neuroendocrinology* 54:607, 1991.
30. Sonntag WE, Gough MA: Growth hormone releasing hormone induced release of growth hormone in aging male rats: Dependence on pharmacological manipulation and endogenous somatostatin release. *Neuroendocrinology* 47:482, 1988.
31. Lima L et al: Replenishment of brain catecholamine stores does not restore the impaired growth hormone (GH) responsiveness to GHRH in aged rats. *Pharmacol Res* 21:87, 1989.
32. Ghigo E et al: Pyridostigmine partially restores the GH responsiveness to GHRH in normal aging. *Acta Endocrinol* 123:169, 1990.
33. Panzeri G et al: Age-related modulatory activity by a cholinergic agonist on the growth hormone response to GH-releasing hormone in the rat. *Proc Soc Exp Biol Med* 193:301, 1990.
34. Ghigo E et al: Growth hormone (GH) responsiveness to combined administration of arginine and GH-releasing hormone does not vary with age in man. *J Clin Endocrinol Metab* 71:1481, 1990.
35. Ge F et al: Relationship between growth hormone-releasing hormone and somatostatin in the rat: Effects of age and sex on content and in-vitro release from hypothalamic explants. *J Endocrinol* 123:53, 1989.
36. Abribat T et al: Alterations of pituitary growth hormone-releasing factor binding sites in aging rats. *Endocrinology* 128:633, 1991.
37. DeGennaro Colonna V et al: Reduced growth hormone releasing factor (GHRF)-like immunoreactivity and GHRF gene expression in the hypothalamus of aged rats. *Peptides* 10:705, 1989.
38. Morimoto N et al: Age-related changes in growth hormone releasing factor and somatostatin in the rat hypothalamus. *Neuroendocrinology* 47:459, 1988.
39. Florio T et al: Age-related alterations of somatostatin gene expression in different rat brain areas. *Brain Res* 557:64, 1991.
40. Sonntag WE et al: Somatostatin gene expression in hypothalamus and cortex of aging male rats. *Neurobiol Aging* 11:409, 1990.
41. Sonntag WE: Increased pituitary response to somatostatin in aging male rats: Relationship to somatostatin receptor number and affinity. *Neuroendocrinology* 50:489, 1989.
42. Strbak V et al: Maturation of the inhibitory response of growth hormone secretion to ether stress in postnatal rat. *Neuroendocrinology* 40:377, 1985.
43. Wakabayashi I et al: A divergence of plasma growth hormone response between growth hormone-releasing factor and insulin-induced hypoglycaemia among middle-aged healthy male subjects. *Clin Endocrinol (Oxf)* 24:279, 1986.
44. Parenti M et al: Age-related changes of growth hormone secretory mechanisms in the rat pituitary gland. *J Endocrinol* 131:251, 1991.
45. Millard WJ et al: Growth hormone and thyrotropin secretory profiles and provocative testing in aged rats. *Neurobiol Aging* 11:229, 1990.
46. Deslauriers N et al: Dynamics of growth hormone responsiveness to growth hormone releasing factor in aging rats: Peripheral and central influences. *Neuroendocrinology* 53:439, 1991.

47. Ceda GP et al: Diminished pituitary responsiveness to growth hormone-releasing factor in aging male rats. *Endocrinology* 118:2109, 1986.
48. Lang I et al: Effects of sex and age on growth hormone response to growth hormone-releasing hormone in healthy individuals. *J Clin Endocrinol Metab* 65:535, 1987.
49. Pavlov E et al: Responses of growth hormone (GH) and somatomedin-C to GH-releasing hormone in healthy aging men. *J Clin Endocrinol Metab* 62:595, 1986.
50. Iovino M et al: Repetitive growth hormone-releasing hormone administration restores the attenuated growth (GH) response to GH-releasing hormone testing in normal aging. *J Clin Endo Metab* 69:910, 1989.
51. Walker RF et al: Robust growth hormone (GH) secretion in aged female rats co-administered GH-releasing hexapeptide (GHRP-6) and GH-releasing hormone (GHRH). *Life Sci* 49:1499, 1991.
52. Davoli C et al: Restoration of normal growth hormone responsiveness to GHRH in normal aged men by infusion of low amounts of theophylline. *J Gerontol* 46:155, 1991.
53. Parenti M et al: Different regulation of growth hormone-releasing factor-sensitive adenylate cyclase in the anterior pituitary of young and aged rats. *Endocrinology* 121:1649, 1987.
54. Robberecht P et al: Decreased stimulation of adenylate cyclase by growth hormone-releasing factor in the anterior pituitary of old rats. *Neuroendocrinology* 44:429, 1986.
55. Khorram O et al: Development of hypothalamic control of growth hormone secretion in the rat. *Endocrinology* 113:720, 1983.
56. Cutler L et al: The effect of age on somatostatin suppression of basal, growth hormone (GH)-releasing factor-stimulated, and dibutyryl adenosine 3′,5′-monophosphate-stimulated GH release from rat pituitary cells in monolayer culture. *Endocrinology* 119:152, 1986.
57. Casad RC, Adelman RC: Aging enhances inhibitory action of somatostatin in rat pancreas. *Endocrinology* 130:2420, 1992.
58. Goya RG et al: Half-life of plasma growth hormone in young and old conscious female rats. *Exp Gerontol* 22:27, 1987.
59. Turner JD et al: Interaction between hypersomatotropism and age in the Wistar-Furth rat. *Growth* 50:402, 1986.
60. Kelley KW et al: GH3 pituitary adenoma cells can reverse thymic aging in rats. *Proc Natl Acad Sci USA* 83:5663, 1986.
61. Rudman D et al: Effects of human growth hormone in men over 60 years old. *N Engl J Med* 323:1, 1990.
62. Marcus R et al: Effects of short term administration of recombinant human growth hormone to elderly people. *J Clin Endocrinol Metab* 70:519, 1990.
63. Poehlman ET, Copeland KC: Influence of physical activity on insulin-like growth factor-I in healthy younger and older men. *J Clin Endocrinol Metab* 71:1468, 1990.
64. Khansari DN, Gustad T: Effects of long-term, low-dose growth hormone therapy on immune function and life expectancy of mice. *Mech Ageing Develop* 57:87, 1991.
65. Weidermann CJ et al: In vitro activation of neutrophils of the aged by recombinant human growth hormone. *J Infect Dis* 164:1017, 1991.
66. Foster JA et al: Effect of age and IGF-1 administration on eleastin gene expression in rat aorta. *J Gerontol* 45:B113, 1990.
67. Binnerts A et al: The effects of human growth hormone administration in elderly adults with recent weight loss. *J Clin Endocrinol Metab* 67:1312, 1988.
68. Kaiser FE et al: The effect of recombinant human growth hormone on malnourished older individuals. *J Am Geriatr Soc* 39:235, 1991.
69. Goya RG et al: Plasma levels of growth hormone correlate with the severity of pathologic changes in the renal structure of aging rats. *J Lab Invest* 64:29, 1991.
70. Vermeulen A: Androgens in the aging male. *J Clin Endocrinol Metab* 73:221, 1991.
71. Neaves W et al: Leydig cell numbers, daily sperm production, and serum gonadotropin levels in aging men. *J Clin Endocrinol Metab* 59:756, 1984.
72. Tenover JS, Bremner WJ: Circadian rhythm of serum immunoreactive inhibin in young and elderly men. *J Gerontol Med Sci* 46:M181, 1991.
73. Vermeulen A, Kaufman JM: Role of the hypothalamo-pituitary function in the hypoandrogenism of healthy aging (editorial). *J Clin Endocrinol Metab* 74:1226A, 1992.
74. Kaufman JM et al: Influence of age on the responsiveness of the gonadotrophs to luteinizing hormone-releasing hormone in males. *J Clin Endocrinol Metab* 72:1255, 1991.
75. Urban R et al: Attenuated release of biologically active luteinizing hormone in healthy aging men. *J Clin Invest* 81:1020, 1988.
76. Gruenewald DA, Matsumoto AM: Age-related decreases in serum gonadotropin levels and gonadotropin-releasing hormone gene expression in the medial preoptic area of the male rat are dependent upon testicular feedback. *Endocrinology* 129:2442, 1991.
77. Veldhuis JD et al: Attenuation of luteinizing hormone secretory burst amplitude as a proximate basis for the hypoandrogenism of healthy aging men. *J Clin Endocrinol Metab* 75:52, 1992.
78. Tenover J et al: The effects of aging in normal men on bioavailable testosterone and luteinizing hormone secretion: Response to clomiphene citrate. *J Clin Endocrinol Metab* 65:1118, 1987.
79. Morley J: Neuropeptides, behavior, and aging. *J Am Geriatr Soc* 34:52, 1986.
80. Vermeulen A et al: Influence of antiopioids on luteinizing hormone pulsatility in aging men. *J Clin Endocrinol Metab* 68:68, 1989.
81. Blackman MR et al: Basal serum prolactin levels and prolactin responses to constant infusions of thyrotropin releasing hormone in healthy aging men. *J Gerontol* 41:699, 1986.
82. Briski KP, Sylvester PW: Comparative effects of various stressors on immunoreactive versus bioactive prolactin release in old and young male rats. *Neuroendocrinology* 51:625, 1990.
83. Steven WJ et al: Long-term treatment of acromegaly with the somatostatin analogue. *N Engl J Med* 313:1576, 1985.
84. Barnard L et al: Treatment of resistant acromegaly

with a long-acting somatostatin analogue. *Ann Intern Med* 105:856, 1986.
85. Greenspan S et al: Osteoporosis in men with hyperprolactinemic hypogonadism. *Ann Intern Med* 104:777, 1986.
86. Liuzzi A et al: Low doses of dopamine agonists in the long-term treatment of macroprolactinomas. *N Engl J Med* 313:656, 1985.
87. Carlson H: Gynecomastia. *N Engl J Med* 303:795, 1980.
88. Kaiser F et al: Impotence and aging: Clinical and hormonal factors. *J Am Geriatr Soc* 36:511, 1988.

Chapter 70

THYROID DISEASES

Robert I. Gregerman and Michael S. Katz

The diagnosis of thyroid diseases in the elderly can be difficult. A number of features considered in the young to be "typical" of thyroid diseases are encountered less often or are less apparent at advanced age. Hence, the patient presents fewer diagnostic cues to the physician. Another factor contributing to difficulty of diagnosis is the frequent coexistence or suspected presence in the elderly of other diseases, to which symptoms and findings may be erroneously ascribed. Young patients are less likely to carry such diagnostic diversions. The remaining difficulty is that the ordinary laboratory tests for hyper- and hypothyroidism are often misleading or can fail to be diagnostic in some elderly individuals.

LABORATORY TESTS IN THE DIAGNOSIS OF THYROID DISEASE

The effect of age on thyroid function tests has been extensively studied. Age per se has little effect on the usual parameters of thyroid function (see below). On the other hand, the effects of nonthyroidal illness—which occurs so frequently in the elderly—can have marked effects on these measurements and can obscure correct diagnosis. Detailed descriptions of thyroid function tests and nomenclature are given elsewhere.[1–3] The standard blood tests of thyroid function are serum thyroxine (T_4); serum triiodothyronine (T_3); triiodothyronine resin uptake (T_3U) or thyroid hormone–binding ratio (THBR); free thyroxine index (FT_4 index), an estimate of the unbound or "free" T_4 (FT_4); the free T_4; and thyrotropin (TSH).

The T_3 resin uptake (T_3U) test is a simple but indirect measure of thyroxine-binding globulin (TBG), the major protein carrier for T_4 in plasma. The T_3U was long reported as the percentage of T_3 taken up by a nonspecific absorbent (resin), but it is preferably normalized and expressed as a ratio of the patient's test sample to a standard reference serum. In this form it has been given a new name, thyroid hormone-binding ratio (THBR).[2] Because of the varied forms of reporting, the clinician must be certain which values represent a high or low TBG.

In the initial evaluation of a patient, the serum T_4 must always be assessed in conjunction with an estimate of the plasma TBG. A high or low T_4 can be interpreted as reflecting thyroid function and T_4 secretion only if the plasma binding of T_4 is normal—that is, only if the TBG (T_3U or THBR) is normal. For convenience, the T_4 and THBR are often combined to give a free T_4 index (FT_4 index) by simply multiplying one number by the other. This procedure "compensates" for the high or low T_4 which results from an abnormality of TBG concentration, and with the THBR provides an estimate of the unbound or "free" T_4, the concentration of which correlates better with the physiologic (thyroid) status than does the serum T_4 (total). The FT_4 index is also confusingly reported by some laboratories as the "T_7" or "T_{12}."

Another test is the "free T_4 (FT_4)," the small fraction of the T_4 that is not bound to protein. The free T_4 must not be confused with FT_4 index, although in most cases the FT_4 parallels the FT_4 index. In the simple example of the high TBG state that accompanies estrogen excess, both will be normal, even though the T_4 is elevated. Although the FT_4 has long been thought to be a sensitive indicator of thyroid function, problems of interpretation arise in many seriously ill patients, since a variety of nonthyroidal diseases—ranging from acute infections to liver disease—can result in elevation of the FT_4 even without an abnormality of the TBG. The probable explanation for this phenomenon is the appearance in the plasma during nonthyroidal illness of an inhibitor of protein binding of T_4. In this situation the serum T_4 is normal or low but the FT_4 can be high. Thus, an elevated FT_4 is *not* a specific finding related solely to thyroid status, and in complex situations the FT_4 has no diagnostic advantage over the FT_4 index. This consideration is important, since many elderly patients suspected of having hyperthyroidism will, in fact, have other nonthyroidal illness that may elevate the FT_4. The diagnosis of hyperthyroidism should be made with great caution if only the FT_4 is elevated. None of the available methods for measuring the FT_4 circumvents the problems of using this measurement to estimate thyroid function during nonthyroidal illness. Most measurements of FT_4 are little more than an approximation of the free hormone concentration.

The serum T_3 is measured by radioimmunoassay. In order to avoid confusion with the T_3U test or its variants, the serum T_3 is often termed "serum total T_3" or "T_3 by RIA" (radioimmunoassay). The serum T_3 in young persons is almost always elevated in hyperthyroidism, and the T_3 has been said to be the single most *specific* indicator of hyperthyroidism; its *sensitivity* for this diagnosis approaches that of the TSH. A small but diagnostically important proportion of hyperthyroid patients of any age, regardless of cause, show an elevation *only* of the T_3 ("T_3 toxicosis").

Only a small proportion of very elderly patients have a minimally low T_3 due to age per se. However, many nonspecific illnesses, drugs, and even decreased food intake depress the T_3 in the elderly and young alike. Such mechanisms presumably contribute to the finding that the T_3 may occasionally not be increased during hyperthyroidism in the elderly (see below).

TSH assays were originally conventional radioimmunoassays (RIAs). These have been largely replaced by assays variably and confusingly referred to as new, sensitive, ultrasensitive, radioimmunoenzymatic, immunofluorescent, chemiluminescent, and so on.[4–6] The most recent classification is simply "second generation" and "third generation," 10- and 100-fold more sensitive respectively than the original generation of clinically useful TSH assays.

The conventional TSH assays (RIAs) in use during the 1970s and through the mid-1980s could easily detect elevations of TSH above normal but were too insensitive to read the low-normal range and thereby identify the suppressed values that are seen in hyperthyroidism. Currently, physicians, in interpreting TSH results, need know only whether the assay being used can identify low values (second-generation) and whether it is sensitive enough (third-generation) to distinguish hyperthyroidism from other causes of low TSH (normal aging, euthyroid sick syndrome).

The TSH is elevated in hypothyroidism. However, second-generation assays add nothing here; their increased sensitivity is not needed. Moreover, an elevation of TSH is *not* specific. TSH may be elevated in the nonacute phase of nonthyroidal illness, especially during recovery. Minor elevations (5 to 15 μU/ml) are very common in the sick and elderly and must not be overinterpreted. In hospitalized (sick) patients, major elevations (>20 μU/ml) must be distinguished from hypothyroidism by serial measurements, clinical considerations, and measurements of T_4. The TSH, however it is measured, is not the "single best test" in a complex medical situation, and it is unlikely that a single test will ever be adequate. A combination of function tests must still be used to define thyroid status. Moreover, all test values may change with the evolution of the illness. At best, a single, static test can give a high probability of identifying a thyroid disorder, and none comes close to perfection.[5]

Determination of serum TSH after intravenous administration of thyrotropin-releasing hormone (TRH test) was useful in diagnosing suspected cases of hyperthyroidism prior to the development of newer TSH assays but has largely been supplanted by the latter. The normal increase of TSH that follows TRH administration is abolished by the excessive amounts of thyroid hormones that are produced in hyperthyroidism. The TRH test remains occasionally useful in the diagnosis of hypothyroidism because the TSH response to TRH is exaggerated above normal even when the unstimulated TSH value is borderline elevated.

Thyroidal radioiodide uptake (RaIU) tests are now much less often used—or needed—than in the past. These tests are far more expensive and time-consuming than measurements of blood hormones. Test values may be depressed by contamination from iodide-containing compounds, usually contrast media, especially in hospitalized patients. Moreover, studies of the utility of RaIU tests in elderly persons with hyperthyroidism show that these tests have lost much of their earlier diagnostic value, presumably due to increased dietary intake of iodide. In young persons the RaIU is still diagnostic in nearly 90 percent of cases, but in the elderly only 50 percent have diagnostic values. Diagnostic values are, moreover, seen in only 30 percent of elderly hyperthyroid patients with multinodular goiter, despite adjustment of the normal range downward in recent years.

SCREENING FOR THYROID DISEASE

Populations of Healthy Persons versus the Individual Patient (Case Finding)

Because of the relative frequency of thyroid diseases and the difficulties of clinical diagnosis, a rational argument can be made in favor of attempting to detect clinically inapparent thyroid disease by laboratory tests in individuals without overt symptoms.[7,8] Experienced clinicians have long held that modest degrees of hypo- or hyperthyroidism are essentially impossible to detect by routine clinical means, and several careful studies have recently confirmed this impression.[4] However, the screening of asymptomatic populations by laboratory testing has been shown to be not cost-effective. Most investigators favor a case-finding approach—that is, testing only patients who are seeing a physician for symptoms. In patients who exhibit any clinical findings that could conceivably be attributable to thyroid disease, laboratory testing should be done, but this approach should probably not be termed screening.

Use of Second-Generation TSH Assays

In recent years most of the studies that have been attempted to detect thyroid disease during screening (or case finding) have focused on evaluation of the "sensitive" ("second-generation") assays for TSH (see above) and their use as a single screening test. These are 10 times more sensitive than earlier RIAs (now termed "first-generation") and, unlike the earlier assays, can recognize low (suppressed) values—those which are below the lower limit of the normal range (0.3 to 5 μU/ml). In these assays, the TSH is undetectable in patients with hyperthyroidism. Unfortunately, this finding is sensitive but not specific; many sick persons and even normal elderly patients are found to have low levels of TSH.[6,9,10] Thus, used alone, second-generation assays *cannot establish* a diagnosis of hyperthyroidism, whether in community populations or in sick patients at any age. A normal TSH *can* be useful in *excluding* a diagnosis of hyperthyroidism, but so can a normal T_4 (or FT_4 index), at lower cost. Second-generation assays, like first-generation assays, can facilitate a diagnosis of hypothyroidism.

The results of screening for thyroid disease, using second-generation TSH tests and appropriate follow-up of abnormal values, are remarkably consistent in various populations.[4,8,11,12] About 1 percent of apparently healthy individuals, all ages included, are found to be hypothyroid. Many fewer individuals are shown to be hyperthyroid (0.1 to 0.2 percent). Women over 40 have the most thyroid disease; young men have virtually none. In hospitalized patients, 3 to 5 percent will have low TSH but less than 1 percent will prove to be hyperthyroid. The yield in geriatric units is much higher (2 to 5 percent). Screening in such units, to be distinguished from general hospitals and intensive care units, is probably worthwhile. Screening in nursing homes and homes for the elderly will yield 1 to 3 percent of patients that will be newly found to be hypothyroid.[13] Routine screening of *hospitalized* patients using TSH is to be avoided; far too many will have false-positive (low) results.[8,11,14,15]

Laboratory-Driven Screening and Case Finding

The authors believe that screening and case finding procedures should be laboratory-driven and not dependent on a physician to follow up an initial abnormal result. The laboratory should routinely proceed from one test to the next. The least expensive approach uses a serum T_4 as the initial test. If the result is abnormal, the laboratory obtains a T_3 uptake to calculate an FT_4 index on the same specimen. Low values are followed with a TSH, elevated values with a T_3 (RIA) and/or TSH. The approximate cost of this approach in screening populations for each case detected is $2000 when T_4 is the first test compared to $5000 when a second-generation TSH is used first.

Third-Generation TSH Assays

Only within the past 1 to 2 years have "third-generation" assays been introduced (10 times more sensitive than second-generation assays; 100 times more sensitive than the original, first-generation assays, or RIAs). These assays are only now becoming widely available in commercial and hospital laboratories. At their best, third-generation assays should make possible a distinction between the nondetectable levels seen in hyperthyroidism and the low but generally detectable TSH of the low T_4 state of severe nonthyroidal illness (euthyroid sick syndrome; see below). For the present and until more experience with their use has been gained, the results of third-generation assays should be interpreted with great caution, especially in the elderly.

HYPERTHYROIDISM

Incidence of Hyperthyroidism in the Elderly

Contrary to the usual belief that hyperthyroidism is more common in the young than in the old, studies of the occurrence of the disease in persons over age 60 show a sevenfold greater incidence than in persons below this age. This statistical fact has led to the rather startling conclusion that hyperthyroidism should be considered a disease of old age.[16]

Symptoms and Signs of Hyperthyroidism in the Elderly

Constitutional Findings

Nonspecific systemic or constitutional symptoms are common and may prompt the presentation. In addition to lack of energy, easy fatigability, and lassitude, the patient may be merely aware of feeling unwell and unable to articulate the complaints. About 50 percent of young patients have these symptoms; fewer than 25 percent of the elderly admit to such problems.[17,18] Weight loss, nearly as frequent a symptom in hyperthyroidism as is "nervousness," is seen in 60 to 70 percent of hyperthyroid patients of all ages. Those elderly patients who experience marked weight loss often become severely debilitated or develop apathetic hyperthyroidism (see below). Heat intolerance, a classic symptom of hyperthyroidism, is certainly seen in the elderly but probably less frequently than in young patients, at least in some series (25 percent of the elderly versus 50 percent of the young).

Neuromuscular Findings

Patients with hyperthyroidism may complain of feeling "nervous," a vague term which includes such symptoms as restlessness (hyperkinesis), irritability, and tremor. This complaint is the most common manifestation of hyperthyroidism and is seen in most young patients but in less than 50 percent of the elderly. Tremor—present in 50 percent of the elderly—may be erroneously ascribed to "aging." Other central nervous symptoms such as depression and withdrawal are seen occasionally.[17,18] A variety of less common neurologic manifestations of thyroid disease have been reviewed.[19] Muscle weakness, contrary to expectation, is not usually a spontaneous complaint of elderly hyperthyroid patients. Muscle weakness has been reported in only about 5 percent of elderly patients as compared with 20 percent of young ones. When present, severe muscle weakness usually affects the proximal musculature predominantly. Rheumatic complaints, although quite common in elderly patients, do not appear to be increased in hyperthyroidism.

Gastrointestinal Findings

In young patients, a classic symptom of hyperthyroidism is increased appetite, while anorexia is only occasionally encountered. In elderly patients, increased appetite is seen in only about 10 percent, while in some 30 percent of cases, anorexia is a major feature. When anorexia occurs, weight loss may be striking. Such "unexplained" weight loss in the elderly may trigger a search for a "hidden malignancy." It is not generally appreciated that some elderly hyperthyroid patients may also have nausea, vomiting, abdominal pain, or diarrhea. Less common features are dry mouth and dysphagia. Occasionally, constipation rather than increased frequency of stools or diarrhea may occur, but this variation is not unique to the elderly. As many as 15 percent of elderly patients with hyperthyroidism show a combination of anorexia, constipation, and weight loss, a triad strongly suggestive of gastrointestinal tract carcinoma.

Cardiac Findings

Palpitations are common in young patients (75 percent) and are also seen in the elderly (50 percent). On the other hand, tachycardia—generally thought to be an almost invariable finding in hyperthyroidism—is actually seen in no more than 50 percent of patients, whether young or old. Atrial fibrillation is a classic cardiac manifestation of hyperthyroidism and occurs almost exclusively in older patients. The effects of hyperthyroidism upon cardiac function have recently been reviewed.[20]

Congestive heart failure occurs in more than 50 percent of elderly patients with hyperthyroidism. A significant number of patients present initially in acute pulmonary edema. While congestive failure due to hyperthyroidism can occur in young persons, it does so infrequently and only in patients with severe, long-standing disease. Angina may be precipitated in the elderly by hyperthyroidism, or preexistent angina may be exacerbated. In occasional young persons, hyperthyroidism may produce angina pectoris and even myocardial infarction in the absence of angiographic evidence of ischemic heart disease.[21]

Ocular Findings

An important difference between the hyperthyroidism of the young and that of the elderly is the striking lack of ocular findings in old persons, due in large measure to the fact that at least 50 percent of elderly patients have nodular goiter rather than Graves' disease as the cause of their hyperthyroidism. Although hyperthyroidism of any cause can produce minor eye findings—such as lid retraction, lid lag, or stare—only Graves' disease produces major eye problems (infiltrative ophthalmopathy). Severe exophthalmos is relatively rare in the young, but it seems to be even less common in elderly patients with Graves' disease.

Thyroid Enlargement

Almost all young persons with hyperthyroidism have a visibly or palpably enlarged thyroid, while about 30 percent of the elderly do not have even a palpably enlarged gland; in a few (10 to 15 percent), no thyroid enlargement can be discerned even by scanning or sonography. The important clinical point is that lack of thyroid enlargement in the elderly does not exclude a diagnosis of hyperthyroidism.

Laboratory Tests in Hyperthyroid Elderly Patients

TSH values, measured with newer TSH assays, are invariably suppressed in hyperthyroidism, although suppression of TSH is not specific (see prior discussion). Almost all elderly patients with hyperthyroidism have an elevated T_4 and FT_4 index; only a small number (2 percent) will have normal values. In these, the serum T_3 is elevated. Elevation of the serum T_3 is considered by some—at least in young patients—to be the single most specific indicator of hyperthyroidism, since an elevated T_3 excludes the possibility of misdiagnosis based on only an elevation of T_4 (and FT_4 index) due to nonthyroidal illness, with the exception perhaps of acute psychiatric disease (see below). However, although the T_3 is elevated in more than 95 percent of young hyperthyroid patients, it has been reported normal in up to 30 to 40 percent of those that are elderly. The explanation for the failure of T_3 to be elevated in some elderly patients with hyperthyroidism is not entirely clear. Determination of T_3 as part of the *initial* evaluation process is still useful in the elderly when expeditious evaluation is essential or T_3 toxicosis must be excluded. An elevated T_3 helps to differentiate true hyperthyroidism from elevation of T_4 (and FT_4I) due to nonspecific illness (see below). It should also be noted that high-dose radiocontrast agents can elevate the T_4 (and FT_4 index) and decrease the T_3, as may occur for up to 3 weeks following cholecystography. When considerations of cost are important or screening (case finding) is the goal, measurement of the T_3 test may be deferred until the serum T_4 (and FT_4 index) are known.

Nonhyperthyroid Elevation of T_4 (and FT_4 index) in the Elderly: Hyperthyroxinemia of Nonspecific Illness

It is now generally appreciated that severe nonthyroidal illnesses can depress the T_4 (and FT_4 index). This phenomenon has been termed the *euthyroid sick syndrome* and is discussed elsewhere (see Hypothyroidism, below). Nonthyroidal illness can also produce a different type of euthyroid sick syndrome in which the T_4 is elevated rather than reduced. The term *euthyroid hyperthyroxinemia* has been used for such cases. The problem is not unique to the elderly population, because it can be encountered in young persons, especially those newly admitted to a hospital with an acute psychiatric diagnosis.[22,23]

Special Variants of Hyperthyroidism in the Elderly Patient

Masked and Apathetic Hyperthyroidism

These terms have been used to describe clinical types of hyperthyroidism which are seen mainly in elderly patients.[24] The term *masked* was originally used to denote patients who presented with thyrotoxic cardiac disease, where focus on this single system involvement obscured (masked) the underlying problem. Hyperthyroidism in the elderly patient is so frequently masked and this situation is so common that the term has probably outlived its usefulness. *Apathetic hyperthyroidism*—a term originally used a half-century ago—defines a form of thyrotoxicosis in which the usual hyperkinesis of the typical young hyperthyroid patient is replaced by "nonactivation."[24]

Iodide-Induced Thyrotoxicosis (IIT) in the Elderly Patient

Iodide, iodine-containing x-ray contrast agents, and iodine-containing drugs can induce hyperthyroidism in patients without previous thyroid disease as well as in individuals with previous hyperthyroidism or Graves' disease and in those with preexisting nodular or nonnodular goiter. In regions where goiter is still endemic or iodide intake is very low because iodization of salt was never introduced (e.g., Germany), the occurrence of this phenomenon seems to be higher than in the United States.[25]

A number of reports suggests that the risk of IIT is greatest in the elderly population. Subjects with nodular goiters of long standing seem to be at greatest risk. In cases of nonendemic goiter, women are more often affected by IIT than are men. In the absence of preexisting thyroid disease, men more often develop IIT. Evidence of Graves' disease is absent in IIT. The thyroid may not be enlarged and it is not tender. When enlargement is present, it may resolve with resolution of the disease. The RaIU is low. Characteristically, the disease is self-limited (1 to 6 months).

Elderly people are more likely than young people to undergo radiographic examinations that employ iodine-containing contrast media (gallbladder examinations, pyelograms, angiograms, computed tomography using "enhancement"), and these procedures may contribute to increased risk of developing IIT. The physician should be especially alert to the subsequent development of IIT in elderly patients who have undergone radiographic examinations 6 months to several years earlier. Another issue is that of iodide-containing drugs. Amiodarone has been widely used in Europe for the treatment of angina pectoris and arrhythmias and is now available in the United States. About 2 percent of patients receiving this drug have developed IIT. In addition, this agent, like some compounds used to visualize the gallbladder, can inhibit the conversion of T_4 to T_3 and produce a mild increase of the T_4 *and* TSH. Elevation of T_4 alone should not be taken as evidence of hyperthyroidism in this situation.[25] The therapy of IIT is symptomatic and similar to that of hyperthyroidism due to painless thyroiditis (see below).

Hyperthyroidism Due to Lymphocytic "Silent" (or "Painless") Thyroiditis

A variant of thyroiditis has been found to be responsible for an increasing number of cases of hyperthyroidism. The syndrome is associated with lymphocyte infiltration of the thyroid, minimal to modest painless and nontender thyroid enlargement, depression of RaIU, a relatively mild degree of hyperthyroidism, and a self-limited course of several months. Blood levels of both T_4 and T_3 are elevated. Most cases have been described in young women, often in the postpartum state, but cases in elderly persons have been recognized.[26] The disease can be suspected if the RaIU—often the only clue to a specific diagnosis—is obtained and found to be very low (less than 5 percent). Definitive diagnosis can, of course, be made only by needle biopsy of the thyroid. Symptomatic therapy with propranolol is appropriate. RaI therapy is neither appropriate nor possible in view of the low RaIU, and there is no clear rationale for the use of antithyroid drugs.

Therapy of Hyperthyroidism in the Elderly Patient

Radioactive Iodide

For most elderly patients with hyperthyroidism, whether due to Graves' disease or nodular goiter, radioactive iodide (^{131}I, RaI) is the therapy of choice. Surgery is rarely, if ever, indicated for hyperthyroidism in the elderly patient. Moreover, the conventional approach used for young persons—in which a low initial RaI dose is used in an attempt to avoid hypothyroidism—should be modified for the elderly patient. The conventional approach for young people often requires multiple doses of RaI, thus delaying and prolonging the time required for restoration of the euthyroid state. For a variety of obvious medical reasons, such delay is not acceptable in the elderly patient. If serious consequences of hyperthyroidism are not already present, they may develop before therapy is completed; some therapeutic urgency is thus always present in older patients. The use of a large dose of RaI—which could raise concerns about possible long-term adverse effects of radiation in young patients—is not a concern in the older age group.

The large doses of RaI used to eliminate the hyperthyroid state rapidly are quite likely to produce hypothyroidism. Such therapy has been termed *deliberate thyroid ablation.* It is the authors' preferred method of administering RaI to elderly patients. In most cases, hyperthyroidism is eliminated within 4 to 6 weeks; complications are not seen. Even when ablative doses of RaI are used, a second dose may occasionally be necessary. Concern over clinical exacerbation of the hyperthyroidism by RaI is essentially anecdotal. Serial observations of the T_4 and T_3 following ablative RaI therapy have given no evidence for more than minimal and transiently increased hormone levels; usually, T_4 and T_3 fall progressively, beginning almost immediately following the RaI.

Ablative doses of RaI are in the range of 12 to 15 mCi for small to moderately enlarged thyroid glands; doses of up to 30 mCi may be used for large glands or multinodular goiters. Determination of RaIU is helpful to the therapist in selection of the dose. Adjunctive therapy is often appropriate (see below).

For hyperthyroidism due to toxic adenoma, a large, ablative dose of 30 to 50 mCi of ^{131}I (delivering 10 to 15 mCi to the adenoma) should be used. If the surrounding normal tissue—which is suppressed—survives the therapy, the patient may become euthyroid; hypothyroidism, if it ensues, should be treated in the usual way. Surgery may occasionally have a place in the treatment of an elderly patient with a toxic adenoma. The procedure may be performed as a simple nodulectomy under regional-block anesthesia.[27]

Antithyroid Drugs

A place remains for the use of propylthiouracil, methimazole, or other antithyroid drugs in the elderly patient. In order to ensure that the time needed to reach the euthyroid state will be as short as possible, an antithyroid drug may be administered following the RaI. If the physician is concerned—despite the assurances offered above—about the possibility of RaI-induced exacerbation of the hyperthyroidism, the patient may be made euthyroid with an antithyroid drug prior to definitive treatment with RaI. In this case, the therapeutic dose of RaI is given while the antithyroid drug is briefly withheld, and the drug may be readministered afterward. Details of antithyroid drug dosage and monitoring of the patient following RaI are given in standard texts.[3] It is important to recall that in the elderly—as in the young—the use of a prolonged course of antithyroid drugs alone in an attempt to allow a remission in Graves' disease is attended by less than a 50 percent chance of success. Furthermore, a remission following drug therapy will not occur in hyperthyroidism due to nodular goiter. Since at least half of the cases of hyperthyroidism in the elderly population are due to nodular goiter and no more than half of those due to Graves' disease will go into remission, RaI becomes the definitive therapy for 75 percent or more of all cases of hyperthyroidism in elderly patients.

Adjunctive Therapy with Beta Blockers, Iodide, and Contrast Media

Propranolol is useful for symptomatic relief of tachycardia, restlessness, and tremor. In young persons, large doses may be necessary in hyperthyroidism (frequently 120 to 240 mg/day, rarely up to 640 mg/day). Theoretically, at least, the use of large doses in elderly individuals could precipitate or worsen heart failure by depressing already compromised myocardial contractility. However, if rapid heart rate is thought to contribute to the failure, propranolol should be tried judiciously. The propranolol-like drug practolol, withdrawn from use in Europe because of noncardiac toxicity and never available in the United States, was successfully used in the treatment of cardiac failure associated with hyperthyroidism.

The beta blockers atenolol and timolol have had limited use in the treatment of hyperthyroidism. While undoubtedly effective, their advantages over propranolol remain to be proved. Pindolol, a beta blocker with intrinsic sympathomimetic activity, is not only less effective than propranolol in reducing heart rate in hyperthyroid patients but also may accelerate tachycardia, although other manifestations of hyperthyroidism may be ameliorated.

Iodide therapy (inorganic, nonradioactive) probably offers the most rapid control of hyperthyroidism due to Graves' disease or toxic goiter and should be used in patients with severe disease. Iodide should not be given immediately prior to therapy with RaI but may follow, either alone or in combination with an antithyroid drug. The dose is 1 drop (50 mg) of a saturated solution of potassium iodide (KI) given daily. Larger doses are unnecessary and may lead to iodide toxicity.[25] As soon as the T_4 has returned to the normal range, iodide can be discontinued. Iodine-containing contrast media have recently been advocated as adjunctive therapy. Part of their actions may be due to their release of iodide, but these agents also inhibit the conversion of T_4 to T_3, at least theoretically a benefit. Glucocorticoids and propranolol have similar actions.

Follow-up post-RaI and Treatment of Ablation-Related Hypothyroidism

If RaI is the sole therapy and an antithyroid drug is not used, the T_4 monitors residual but decreasing thyroid function quite well. The T_4 should fall significantly within a few weeks. If the T_4 fails to reach normal levels within 8 weeks, additional RaI should be given without delay. As soon as the T_4 falls below the normal range or the patient develops symptoms of hypothyroidism, thyroxine can be added to avoid the development of severe hypothyroidism. If the patient is very old or has had major complications, especially ischemic or dysrhythmic cardiac disease, the initial dose of thyroxine can be 0.025 mg daily by mouth; otherwise 0.075 mg can be given from the onset (see Therapy of Hypothyroidism in the Elderly, below). Further adjustment of dosage upward or downward at several monthly intervals can then be made as necessary.

HYPOTHYROIDISM

The problem of hypothyroidism in the elderly population deserves special attention for several reasons. Not only is hypothyroidism commonly encountered at advanced age, but in the elderly patient the diagnosis can easily be overlooked. The cause of the diagnostic difficulty in elderly persons has long been recognized.[28]

> It is precisely at this time of life that gradual degenerative processes are usually expected and are tolerated—if reluctantly. All well and good—unless the true diagnosis is myxedema. How easy it is to attribute to age rather than to myxedema such conditions as mental slowing, lack of energy, neurotic or psychotic behavior, loss of . . . hearing, odd paresthesias, gain in weight, musculoskeletal discomfort, unsteady gait, change in facial appearance, and dry skin. The changes are often so subtle and gradual that the patient, his family, and his physician have almost continuously observed them and are thrown off guard. . . .[28]

The most difficult step in diagnosis is the simple clinical appreciation of the possibility that the patient may be hypothyroid. Once the thought occurs to the physician, aspects of the history and physical examination will fall into place and the laboratory will easily confirm the diagnosis. Many aspects of hypothyroidism and age-related changes of thyroid function have been reviewed in detail.[29]

Much was written in the past of the notion that aging is due to hypothyroidism or of age-related alteration of thyroid hormone action on peripheral tissues. Although aging is accompanied by a decreased metabolic rate and a decreased rate of thyroid hormone secretion, these changes find their causes in changes of body composition with age and in the mechanisms for metabolic disposal of thyroid hormones. No evidence exists in the human for any gross alteration of thyroid hormone action during aging.

Causes of Hypothyroidism

While the same causes can produce hypothyroidism in elderly as in young persons, most cases in the elderly are idiopathic and nongoitrous. Pathologically one sees atrophic destruction of the thyroid. Most cases are undoubtedly autoimmune; the vast majority (90 percent) show elevations of thyroid autoantibodies in the serum. Elevated titers of antimicrosomal antibodies are more common than those directed to thyroglobulin. An ever-increasing number of cases are iatrogenic—that is, the result of previous therapy of hyperthyroidism with radioiodide or surgery.

As populations grow older, an increasing proportion of persons have elevations of serum thyrotropin (TSH) while their serum thyroxine (T_4) is still normal. These individuals are thought to have autoimmune thyroiditis which has produced hypothyroidism of a degree that provokes increased secretion of TSH and elevation of blood TSH—a sensitive indicator of hypothyroidism—but has not yet produced clinically obvious manifestations (see below, Interpretation of Elevation of TSH in the Elderly). They represent a subset of elderly patients who are victims of an age-related autoimmune disease process, but they do not represent the fate of all persons as they age.

Clinical Presentation of Hypothyroidism

There has long been a tendency to describe the symptoms of hypothyroidism as either "classic" or conversely, uncommon or unusual. The latter symptoms are in fact not nearly as unusual as once believed and are now being more widely recognized.[28,30] Relative frequencies of occurrence of various signs and symptoms vary widely in different reports.

The so-called classic symptoms and signs of hypothyroidism are slowness of speech, thought, and movement; hoarse voice; cold intolerance; facial puffiness (myxedema); thickening and scaling of skin with an acquired yellowish tint (carotenemia); dryness and coarseness of hair; nonpitting peripheral edema; bradycardia; slowed gastrointestinal function with constipation; and delay of relaxation phase of deep tendon reflexes. These and other less common findings are described in more detail below and elsewhere.[30] Only about one-third of all cases present with such findings; two-thirds present with nothing more than debilitation and apathy or may be entirely "asymptomatic." Thus, the clinical recognition of hypothyroidism in the elderly can be very difficult. A strong argument for screening by laboratory means can be made.[31] Other aspects of screening are discussed above.

Hypothyroidism versus Myxedema

The deposition of mucopolysaccharides in subcutaneous and other tissues and the development of fluid accumulations in body cavities and joints constitute the clinical state known as *myxedema.* However, symptomatic hypothyroidism may occur in the absence of overt myxedema. Thus, the terms *hypothyroidism* and *myxedema* are not truly interchangeable and should not be used as such. Hypothyroidism in the elderly patient—because it is more likely to remain unappreciated for a long period and because even severe cases may escape diagnosis—is more likely to be associated with true myxedema than is hypothyroidism in young persons.

Clinical Features in Young versus Elderly Individuals

Psychiatric Manifestations and Dementia

Lethargy and increased sleep requirement are common with hypothyroidism at all ages but may be erroneously attributed to aging when encountered in the elderly patient. Hypothyroid patients are classically placid and torporous, showing sluggish mental function with exceedingly slow patterns of thought and speech. It has been believed that, in the elderly person, hypothyroidism may be a reversible type of dementia characterized by confusion and disorientation. Other commonly encountered mental changes include impaired cognitive function, a decreased level of awareness, irritability, and paranoia. Occasionally psychosis—colorfully described as myxedema madness—may occur. An important study of newly diagnosed cases of hypothyroidism in elderly patients presents a different concept.[32] About one-quarter of the patients were found to have a depressive illness and a much smaller number paranoia or delirium. The number of depressed patients was several times greater than in a control group. Hypothyroidism in the elderly person appears to predispose to the development of these disturbances. In contrast, no excess number of cases of dementia was seen. Response to thyroxine therapy of the depressed and paranoid patients was excellent, while the demented patients did not respond. These results notwithstanding, it is certainly true that occasional hypothyroid patients with dementia do recover with thyroxine therapy; unfortunately, they appear to be disappointingly exceptional.

It is true that dementia in the elderly patient is not infrequently accompanied by hypothyroidism. However, coincidental association would not be unexpected in view of the frequency of both sets of disorders. While many have held the view that dementia may be *caused* by hypothyroidism (myxedema), this conclusion is not statistically established.[32] Furthermore, only rarely does a truly demented hypothyroid individual return to normal psychiatric function following restoration of the euthyroid state.

Central Nervous System

Cold intolerance due to temperature malregulation is a common phenomenon in the very old, even when the individual is euthyroid, and may result in hypothermia on minimal exposure to modest reductions of environmental temperature. Hypothyroidism is accompanied by impairment of thermogenesis and may also cause hypothermia and blunted febrile responses to stress (surgery, infection). Whether age and the hypothyroid state interact in this regard is not known, but frank hypothermia occasionally becomes the presenting manifestation in hypothyroid elderly persons. A clue in the differential diagnosis is the occasional occurrence of pink to red skin color resulting from peripheral vasodilation in nonhypothyroid elderly patients who are hypothermic. One does not encounter such skin changes in hypothyroidism.

Impairment of eighth-nerve function seems to be a special feature of the hypothyroid state. Both auditory and vestibular branches can be affected, although the auditory manifestations are more common and more generally recognized. Decreased auditory acuity is, of course, an invariable accompaniment of aging (presbycusis), but hypothyroidism can also produce hearing loss and tinnitus. Again, these problems—when they develop—are often attributed to aging. Fluid accumulations in the middle ear and/or endolymph have been blamed for the hearing loss of hypothyroidism. The deafness associated with hypothyroidism is frequently reversible with treatment. Ataxia and vertigo may also be seen, presumably related to a similar mechanism. Improvement is said to occur when the hypothyroid state is treated.[19]

Cerebellar Function

Cerebellar function may also be affected in elderly patients with hypothyroidism. Ataxia can occur and is often mistakenly attributed to aging. Patients may offer as their presenting complaints unsteadiness, loss of equilibrium, poor balance, and even incoordination of their extremities.[19] Reversibility with therapy is usual, but coexistence of hypothyroidism with other neurologic problems which occur in elderly patients may result in a disappointing outcome.

Other Neuromuscular Problems

Complex disturbances of respiratory function can occur in severe hypothyroidism. These include impaired chest-wall mechanics and complicated disturbances of upper airway function. An increased prevalence of hypothyroidism has been noted in patients with the sleep apnea syndrome. Such problems may contribute to the pathophysiology of myxedema coma, but—aside from the likelihood that this dreaded complication is more likely to occur in old persons—no special relationship to aging is clear.

Peripheral Nervous System

Many elderly patients with hypothyroidism complain of paresthesias in their extremities. The most common of such problems in hypothyroid patients of all ages is a nerve entrapment syndrome in which the median nerve is compressed in the carpal tunnel. However, the carpal tunnel syndrome is also seen in association with many other clinical states and does not seem to be especially associated with advanced age.

Skin

Classic skin changes in hypothyroidism include dryness, scaling, and subcutaneous thickening ("doughy" consistency), the latter due to mucopolysaccharide deposition. In the elderly patient, in whom epidermal atrophy is common, the superimposition of the changes of hypothyroidism may produce a combination of changes which result in a stiff, translucent appearance described as "parchmentlike." These changes are especially easy to appreciate over the backs of the hands and on the forearms. While many hypothyroid persons develop puffiness or fullness around the eyes, elderly patients are especially prone to develop fluid- (lymph-) filled sacs ("bags of water") beneath the lower eyelids. This sign is not pathognomonic, but its presence should be a strong clue to the possible presence of hypothyroidism in an elderly person.

Diffuse loss of scalp hair is common in the elderly hypothyroid patient. Clinical anecdote has it that the loss of the outer third of eyebrows—well described in younger patients—occurs infrequently in elderly patients.

Musculoskeletal and Rheumatic Disorders

One of the most common accompaniments of aging is the development of musculoskeletal disease, especially osteoarthritis. Furthermore, arthritislike symptoms are very common in hypothyroid patients. The problem of differential diagnosis may be compounded by the development in hypothyroidism of joint swelling with synovial effusions containing calcium pyrophosphate crystals, but signs of active joint inflammation will be lacking. These findings can easily and erroneously be attributed to minor degrees of osteoarthritis shown on x-ray. Other possible misdiagnoses include seronegative rheumatoid arthritis and fibrositis.

Although painful extremities, back pain, stiffness, cramps, and other symptoms are all too readily ascribed to "arthritis," careful history taking can provide the first clue to the nonarthritic nature of these symptoms in hypothyroidism which are, in fact, due to myopathy rather than skeletal changes. Patients usually complain of muscle weakness or easy fatigability and have difficulty with repetitive movements. The myopathy is accompanied by elevated concentrations of muscle enzymes in the plasma. Creatine phosphokinase (CPK) is especially likely to be increased, but serum glutamic oxaloacetic transaminase (SGOT), aldolase, and lactic dehydrogenase (LDH) are also increased in up to 80 percent of hypothyroid patients and in all with significant muscular symptoms. Response to therapy is gratifying, but worsening of symptoms may occur during the first few weeks following the institution of therapy. Hypertrophy of muscle and pseudomyotonia are rare in hypothyroidism and are not age-related.

Gastrointestinal Disorders

Constipation is such a common complaint in the elderly population that it is not likely to alert the physician to the possibility of this frequent accompaniment of hypothyroidism. A diagnosis of hypothyroidism may be suggested by the radiologist who discovers megacolon during barium examination of the colon. Hypothyroidism should also be suspected in elderly patients presenting with clinical findings of intestinal pseudo-obstruction.

Cardiovascular Conditions

Hypercholesterolemia and hyperlipidemia are accompaniments of the hypothyroid state. The experimental induction of hypothyroidism contributes to diet-induced atherosclerosis in experimental animals, and women with Hashimoto's thyroiditis have an increased frequency of ischemic heart disease. Thus, while this issue has been debated for many years, evidence suggests that severe hypothyroidism may predispose to atherosclerotic disease.

Hypothyroidism appears to impair myocardial function and can result in cardiomegaly. In addition, pericardial effusion is not infrequent and may produce the appearance of cardiomegaly, sometimes in association with pleural effusions. Whether overt congestive heart failure can occur as a result of hypothyroid cardiomyopathy is not clear. Occasionally ascites may be a presenting feature of hypothyroidism, Usually, but not always, other manifestations of the disease are readily apparent by this point of severity. Given these circumstances, congestive heart failure may be incorrectly diagnosed in elderly patients and a digitalis glycoside administered. Clinical digitalis toxicity may then result from the increased sensitivity to digitalis and decreased metabolic clearance that are both present in hypothyroidism.

Hypertension, like hypothyroidism, is positively correlated with age, and their coexistence is not remarkable. However, hypothyroidism appears to predispose to the development of hypertension. Perhaps related is the magnified age-related increase of plasma norepinephrine in hypothyroid persons. Some 30 to 50 percent of hypothyroid hypertensive patients can be expected to become normotensive when treated with thyroid hormone. A short duration of hypothyroidism seems to be associated with reversibility of the hypertensive state.

Renal and Electrolyte Abnormalities

Abnormalities of water metabolism occur in many hypothyroid patients, although it is only a minority who show hyponatremia, the ultimate expression of an inability to excrete water normally. Underlying these abnormalities are several factors, including altered renal hemodynamics and excessive secretion of antidiuretic hormone (ADH). Overtly hyponatremic patients with hypothyroidism are nearly always elderly. Whether this in some way relates to the known effect of age on water metabolism and the enhanced secretion of ADH or is merely a reflection of the association of hypothyroidism with advanced age is not clear. Nonetheless, hypothyroidism must be included in the differential diagnosis of the syndrome of inappropriate secretion of antidiuretic hormone (SIADH) and chronic hyponatremia in the elderly.

Hematologic Changes

Elderly individuals who develop a macrocytic anemia come under investigation for deficiency of vitamin B_{12} (pernicious anemia) or folate deficiency (dietary); another possibility is hypothyroidism. Clues to the differential diagnosis can be found in the morphology of the polymorphonuclear leukocytes (multilobed) and platelets (enlarged) in vitamin B_{12} or folate deficiency; these changes do not occur in hypothyroidism, in which only the red blood cells are affected. Macrocytosis in a hypothyroid patient may occasionally be due to true vitamin B_{12} deficiency, since there is a 20-fold increased incidence of pernicious anemia in patients with autoimmune thyroid disease. Rarely, in an old person with hypothyroidism and macrocytosis, the red-cell abnormality may not disappear with replacement hormone therapy, since very elderly patients may have a mild macrocytosis (mean corpuscular volume $\pm$ 100 μm^3), which is apparently related to aging per se.

Drug Effects and Surgery

Elderly patients may be sensitive to the toxic pharmacologic effects of drugs. Similar drug sensitivity can be seen in hypothyroid patients. When hypothyroidism occurs in the elderly patient, the effect appears to be additive. The usual doses of sedative drugs may produce somnolence or coma, while ordinary anesthesia may result in paralysis of the respiratory center. Prolonged periods may be required to recover from ordinary general anesthesia. These phenomena constitute a cogent argument against elective surgery for elderly patients known to have clinically overt hypothyroidism, although data on this issue are not available. In contrast, recent studies in middle-aged persons (35 to 67 years) have clearly shown that elective surgery (cholecystectomy; coronary artery bypass) may be performed without appreciable risk of increased morbidity or mortality in patients with only mild to moderate hypothyroidism.[33] These studies should not be extrapolated to severely hypothyroid persons and certainly not to the severely hypothyroid elderly patient. The blunted ventilatory responsiveness of hypothyroidism improves fairly rapidly with replacement therapy in middle-aged persons; again, elderly patients were not studied.[34] A study of middle-aged hypothyroid persons indicates that percutaneous transluminal coronary angioplasty (PTCA) is tolerated without increased morbidity or mortality and has suggested that PTCA may be preferred to coronary revascularization in patients intolerant of full thyroid hormone replacement.[35] Again, no comparable data are available in elderly patients.

Coma as a Complication in the Elderly Patient

Myxedema coma only rarely occurs in young individuals and seems to be mainly a complication of the hypothyroid state in elderly persons. Coma can be precipitated by such factors as hypothermia on exposure to cold (even that which can be encountered in a home that is not well heated), trauma, infectious illness (e.g., pneumonia), drugs (hypnotics, sedatives, analgesics, anesthetics, or the psychotropic agents so commonly used in elderly patients), and nonspecific stress (trauma). Some have suggested that coma results from "immediate" causes such as electrolyte disturbances (hyponatremia, hypokalemia), hypoglycemia, and respiratory failure with hypoxia and hypercapnia. In most patients some of these features are present but not to a degree that would ordinarily be expected to result in coma. Not well appreciated is the prodrome of severe frontal or occipital headache and new onset of grand mal seizures ending in coma.[36] In some of these patients the use of anticonvulsants in conventional dosage may contribute to prolongation of the duration of the coma. There is agreement among most experts that thyroid hormone therapy should be promptly and vigorously instituted as soon as the diagnosis of coma due to hypothyroidism is made or even seriously considered. Differentiation of myxedema coma from the "euthyroid sick syndrome" is discussed below.

Laboratory Diagnosis

Ordinarily, in the ambulatory patient the diagnosis of hypothyroidism will be confirmed by the combination of a low T_4 (and FT_4 index) and a high TSH. Provided the elderly individual under consideration is not acutely or seriously chronically ill with another illness, this combination of test results is diagnostic of at least biochemical hypothyroidism.

Determinations of serum T_3 are not useful in the diagnosis of hypothyroidism in the elderly. The T_3 is minimally—if at all—reduced in *normal* elderly persons, and can be normal in hypothyroidism at any age. Furthermore, the T_3 is nonspecifically depressed by all manner of pathophysiologic states, including such common situations as reduced intake of food.

Interpretation of Elevation of TSH in Elderly People

An increased TSH is considered the most sensitive indicator of hypothyroidism in patients of all ages. Increased frequency of TSH elevation in association with increasing age has been reported and is considered to reflect an increasing frequency of early thyroid gland failure due to autoimmune thyroiditis.

A frequently encountered clinical situation is that in which an apparently euthyroid patient is found to have a T_4 within the normal range and a TSH that is modestly elevated above the upper limits of normal but is below 15 to 20 μU/ml. Depending on the cutoff point for the elevation of TSH, some 15 percent of patients over age 60 show such findings. Women are several times more likely than men to show such elevations. The significance of this situation is not completely clear. In one study, serial determinations of T_4 over a period of 4 years in elderly patients with elevated TSH values showed that overt thyroid failure with T_4 falling below the normal range occurred in one-third.[37] All those with initial TSH levels above 20 μU/ml and 80 percent of those with high titers of thyroid antimicrosomal antibodies became hypothyroid. Conversely, none of the patients with low titers of thyroid autoantibodies developed thyroid gland failure. The levels of TSH elevation and the presence of thyroid autoantibodies are therefore prognostically important and help identify those patients who should receive prophylactic therapy with thyroxine.

The status of those patients who have minimal elevations of TSH and no demonstrable thyroid autoantibodies is less clear. However, several studies question the heretofore accepted absolute specificity of clinical TSH measurements using antibodies. The serum of some individuals has been shown to contain heterotypic antibodies (cross-reacting antibodies to one of the anti-TSH antibodies used in radioimmunoassay). These antibodies can produce spurious elevations of TSH in first-generation radioimmunoassays and may interfere in second-generation assays as well.[9]

Yet another—albeit speculative—explanation for the frequent occurrence in elderly patients of elevation of TSH in the presence of normal T_4 is that the TSH secreted by some elderly persons may not contain full biological activity. In two other clinical situations, evidence for abnormal glycosylation of TSH has been obtained; first, in some persons with the low T_4 state of severe nonthyroidal illness, and, second, in hypothyroidism due to pituitary or hypothalamic disease. Until the issue of TSH assay specificity is settled, an elevation of TSH in an elderly person with serum T_4 still well within the normal range should be interpreted cautiously, since a diagnosis of hypothyroidism may not always be justified. The issue is also relevant to the use of TSH alone in monitoring replacement therapy (see below). High titers of thyroid autoantibodies (antithyroglobulin, antimicrosomal) in association with elevated TSH favors both diagnoses, autoimmune thyroiditis and hypothyroidism.

Low T_4 State of Severe Nonthyroidal Illness (Euthyroid Sick Syndrome) versus Hypothyroidism

The diagnosis of hypothyroidism is frequently considered in severely ill elderly patients such as those encountered in a hospital's intensive care unit. The possibility of hypothyroidism is usually raised by some aspect of the gross appearance of the patient or a finding such as hypothermia, often in association with sepsis. The serum T_4 and FT_4 index may be well into the hypothyroid range. However, a diagnosis of hypothyroidism cannot be made on the basis of these results alone. The FT_4—as opposed to the FT_4 index—may be elevated, normal, or low; if low, the value will often not be reduced in proportion to the T_4 and FT_4 index. In most such cases the TSH—rather than being elevated as it is in hypothyroidism—is normal or suppressed, a finding which rules out primary hypothyroidism but does not exclude the rare possibility of secondary (pituitary) hypothyroidism. The mortality rate associated with a low T_4 in this setting is very high. When clinical recovery ensues, the T_4 returns to normal. The TSH may actually be somewhat or even grossly increased during the recovery phase, so that both the T_4 and TSH lie within the hypothyroid range at this point in the patient's course. When this is the case, only serial measurements will distinguish the situation from that of hypothyroidism. Prudence dictates that if the clinical findings are suggestive of hypothyroidism, treatment with thyroid hormone be instituted. In the absence of pressing clinical findings, serial measurements may be in order and hormone therapy can be deferred.

To date, the euthyroid sick syndrome has been recognized predominantly in severely ill patients, but it also occurs in chronically ill, nonhospitalized individuals. This phenomenon must be considered to avoid an incorrect diagnosis of hypothyroidism in these elderly patients. TSH secretion is suppressed and serum TSH is greatly reduced during this syndrome, but this is demonstrable only with a sufficiently sensitive assay for TSH.[38] Thus, it is possible that the syndrome is in fact a functional form of secondary hypothyroidism. The mechanism of suppression of TSH may be an increase of the cytokines interleukin 1-β and tumor necrosis factor α/cachectin, mediators of inflammation which have been shown to inhibit secretion of TSH in both the rat and human. At the present time, the limited information available concerning the possible efficacy of replacement therapy with thyroid hormone (T_4 and/or T_3) under these circumstances does not suggest any benefit. Some have ascribed a homeostatic, protective effect to the low T_3 state. This complex syndrome has been reviewed and discussed elsewhere.[38,39]

Therapy of Hypothyroidism in Elderly Patients

Several principles should be observed. First, the maintenance dose of thyroxine tends to be lower in elderly than in young patients. Second, therapy should be instituted slowly and cautiously in the old. Third, adequate therapy should not be unduly delayed or denied because of medical considerations which may seem reasonable (e.g., congestive heart failure, chronic lung disease) but are in fact inappropriate. Fourth, the goal of therapy in the elderly patient is to eliminate as many of the clinical manifestations of hypothyroidism as possible without introducing adverse clinical symptoms. Last, therapy of hypothyroidism, at any age but especially in the elderly patient, should be with thyroxine, administered as a preparation which can be relied upon to be of accurate dosage and predictable bioavailability.

Direct demonstration of a decreased thyroid hormone secretion rate with increasing age suggested 30 years ago that the clinically suspected decreased thyroid hormone replacement of elderly patients was in fact correct. Studies of the replacement dose of thyroxine in elderly patients using restoration of a normal serum TSH as the end point indicate a considerable reduction from the usual dose in young patients.[40–42] Whereas most young persons need from 0.1 to 0.125 mg of thyroxine daily, some old persons need as little as 0.05 mg. The variability is very great, however; therefore a maintenance level must be found for each individual and may have to be reduced as the patient grows older.

In young adults without known preexistent cardiac disease, replacement therapy can be safely initiated with the maintenance dose of 0.1 to 0.125 mg of thyroxine given daily. In elderly patients, the major reason for initiating replacement therapy at a low dose is concern for the possibility of inducing cardiac events such as myocardial infarction or arrhythmias. These concerns are, in turn, based on anecdotal experience but seem to be valid. Accordingly, therapy can be initiated at a dose of thyroxine of 0.025 to 0.05 mg with—in the absence of untoward clinical consequences—incremental increases of 0.025 mg at 2- to 4-week intervals until the full maintenance dose is reached. Complications with such a conservative approach seem to be rare, but several months may be required to produce a significant clinical response. The physician should offer strong reassurance and encouragement during this time.

When an elderly patient has known cardiac disease, especially preexistent angina, therapy must be initiated even more cautiously. Physicians are often reluctant to initiate therapy at all in such patients, since usual clinical teaching states that thyroxine therapy will exacerbate angina. Such is not always the case. Cautious initiation of therapy should be attempted using 0.025 mg of thyroxine—or even less—with increments as tolerated at 4-week intervals. Restoration of the euthyroid state—or at least relief of myxedema—may actually be accompanied by improvement in anginal symptoms. Furthermore, it is important to realize that in such circumstances the patient may be much improved even by a dose of thyroxine that is less than optimal. For example, some tolerable degree of angina may develop at a dose of thyroxine that is sufficient to eliminate grossly symptomatic myxedema even while some clinical or laboratory evidence of hypothyroidism persists. In such a situation the patient will undoubtedly have been markedly improved from an overall symptomatic standpoint. Some of these patients will be responsive to intensive therapy of angina by the usual means. The precise indications for the use of antianginal drugs (beta blockers, calcium channel blockers) in such patients is not clear, but they should probably be judiciously employed with special attention to dosage, since this might possibly be affected by the hypothyroid state. To discontinue or deny hormone therapy out of fear of dire consequences is, however, a common mistake. Therapy should also not be withheld on the assumption that other coexistent disease (e.g., chronic lung disease) contraindicates initiation of thyroxine therapy. The issues of thyroid status, replacement therapy, angina, and the problems related to coronary angiography, coronary angioplasty, and coronary bypass surgery continue to receive attention.[33–35,43]

The objective of replacement therapy with thyroxine in the elderly patient is to restore the euthyroid state, if possible, or at least to eliminate the clinical manifestations of hypothyroidism. Monitoring of thyroxine therapy in the elderly patient is therefore first and foremost clinical; the laboratory is important *but* adjunctive. The authors recommend that thyroxine be given to elderly patients until the T_4 is within the normal range. The plasma thyrotropin (TSH) may then be determined and the dose of thyroxine further increased until the elevated TSH is returned to or near normal. This approach should be modified in an elderly patient to the extent that a return of the T_4 to the normal range may be sufficient. However, no compelling need exists to restore the TSH to normal, since this may occur at a level of T_4 that is unacceptably high from the point of view of clinical symptoms (e.g., angina pectoris). Moreover, the possibility of artifactual elevation of TSH should be borne in mind. Obviously, if both T_4 and TSH can be normalized, so much the better. In monitoring the response of the serum T_4, attention should be given to the timing of the replacement dose of thyroxine. Administration of thyroxine by mouth is followed by an increase of serum T_4 lasting for at least 6 hours; thus, the blood sample should be obtained prior to the daily dose rather than soon afterward.

Much has been written concerning variability of the potency of thyroxine preparations.[44] In the elderly patient especially, in whom inappropriate dosage of hormone during replacement therapy may have adverse effects, this issue is of special concern. Several major brands of thyroxine in current use in the United States appear to be reliable and predictable. Generic preparations are less expensive and may be equally efficacious but remain suspect. Whenever the relatively small difference of cost is not important, the physician should avoid the risk of introducing a possible element of error into replacement therapy with thyroxine by choosing a reputable name brand.

The absorption of thyroxine (and other pharmacologic agents) may be decreased by bile-salt sequestering agents (colestipol, cholestyramine) now widely used to treat hypercholesterolemia. This problem may require judicious timing of the medications or an increase of the dose of T_4.

GOITER

Goiter—an enlarged thyroid gland—is the most common thyroid abnormality at any age. The term implies nothing about the thyroid's functional state, although thyroid enlargement may be the first clue to detection of abnormal thyroid function. The presence of a goiter demands careful clinical and laboratory evaluation, especially in an elderly patient, in whom the assessment of clinical thyroid status may be particularly difficult.

Diffuse goiter, also termed *simple goiter,* denotes a thyroid which is uniformly and more or less symmetrically enlarged without apparent palpable irregularity. (Some use the term *simple goiter* to denote any nontoxic or nonhyperfunctioning gland regardless of its anatomy.) Diffuse goiter in elderly patients should suggest Graves' disease, thyroiditis, drug-induced goiter, or such rarities as lymphoma or amyloid infiltration of the thyroid.

Sporadic goiter occurs in a small percentage of the population and increases in frequency with age. Goiter in elderly people is most often multinodular and of unknown cause. The thyroid—if examined pathologically—typically shows proliferative and degenerative changes, multiple adenomatous nodules of varying size, areas of fibrosis, and cyst formation.

Recognition of Goiter

A visible mass may be noted by the patient or physician or is detected by palpation during routine physical examination. A sonogram is the best test for evaluation of the anatomy (size, nodularity) of an enlarged thyroid. In an elderly person, an enlarged thyroid is often neither visible nor readily palpable but is an incidental finding when x-ray examination of the chest or esophagus is performed. In these cases, a mass in the superior mediastinum or retrosternal space is noted by the radiologist, who may suggest the diagnosis. Asymptomatic displacement (deviation) of the trachea or esophagus is common in such cases. Confirmation of the functional nature of the mass can best be obtained by radionuclide scanning, while computed tomography can help delineate its location. A Valsalva maneuver may bring the gland into the neck where it becomes visible or palpable.

Goiters large enough to compress—as opposed to merely displace—the trachea are uncommon. However, the possibility of tracheal narrowing should be considered in any elderly patient with a goiter or tracheal deviation who has symptoms of respiratory distress. Sudden development or worsening of this symptom or acute pain suggests rapid enlargement of the goiter, usually due to intrathyroidal hemorrhage in an area of cystic degeneration. Tracheal narrowing can be evaluated by plain films, CT scan, or ventilation flow-loop study, the latter being the most sensitive, since the compressed trachea may collapse only during exhalation.

Differential Diagnosis

Clinical and laboratory assessment of thyroid function, plus testing for thyroid autoantibodies, should be made in all cases of goiter. The clinician must recognize that the functional state of a goiter may change with time, sometimes rather rapidly, and hence the precise diagnosis may not be possible on a single examination. Elderly patients may be found to have normal thyroid function by clinical and laboratory examinations, only to develop hyperthyroidism over the subsequent year or more. An argument can be made for periodic reevaluation of such individuals by routine laboratory testing at intervals of 1 to 2 years.

Goiter in association with hyperthyroidism suggests Graves' disease, toxic nodular goiter, or a hyperfunctioning ("hot") nodule. Hypofunction in association with goiter is likely to represent Hashimoto's thyroiditis, but other possibilities such as drug ingestion may have to be excluded. Thyroid autoantibodies are elevated to diagnostic levels in 90 percent of cases of Hashimoto's thyroiditis. Determination of such antibodies (antithyroglobulin and antimicrosomal) should be routine in the evaluation of goiter.

If the clinical and laboratory assessments indicate normal thyroid function, the diagnosis of nontoxic or euthyroid goiter is made. Multinodular enlargement almost always indicates a process of many years' standing. Differentiation of diffuse enlargement from nodular enlargement may require scintiscanning or sonography, since small nodules may be missed on physical examination. When only small, nonpalpable nodules are present, an optimally performed scan may show irregular ("patchy") uptake of tracer, but even the best scintiscanning techniques can delineate nodules of only about 1 cm in size. A goiter composed of many such small nodules may appear to represent a nonnodular thyroid on both physical examination and scan. Sonography is a useful complement or alternative to scintiscanning. Micronodules as small as 0.5 cm can be delineated and precise assessment of overall size and nodularity of the gland can be made.

A proper history will point to the possibility that the goiter may be drug-induced. Rapid enlargement or pain, such as that which occurs with hemorrhage into a cyst or inflammatory thyroiditis, suggests benign rather than malignant lesions.

Treatment of Nontoxic Goiter

In patients up to about age 40 to 50, suppression therapy of goiter is often properly undertaken for cosmetic reasons. Suppression therapy is also clearly indicated for relatively young individuals with many years of life ahead of them, during which time mechanical problems can be anticipated if further thyroid enlargement occurs.

In many elderly patients, the duration of the goiter will not be known to the physician at the time of discovery, but the goiter can generally be presumed to have been present for many years. Such goiters—if they have not already produced the mechanical problems of tracheal narrowing or interference with esophageal function—are not likely to do so in the future. Accordingly, suppression therapy is not recommended for such patients, although such therapy may prevent further thyroid enlargement. If suppression is undertaken in an elderly patient, the dose of thyroid hormone should be reduced. Some 20 to 50 percent of nontoxic nodular goiters are nonsuppressible;[45] that is, they remain functional (autonomous) despite suppression of TSH secretion by exogenous thyroid hormone. Attempts at suppression therapy in such patients can, if not carefully monitored, lead to iatrogenic hyperthyroidism. Monitoring is facilitated by use of a second-generation TSH assay. The TSH should be lowered to below the lower limit of normal; concomitantly the serum T_4 should not be elevated above normal. Obviously, if nonsuppressibility is demonstrated, the therapy should be terminated. Details of monitoring of suppression therapy are given elsewhere.[3]

Goiter so large as to produce not merely a deviation but significant tracheal compression, as assessed above, or to interfere with swallowing has become a rarity in areas where iodide deficiency has been eliminated. Dysphagia attributable to goiter does occur, but only with severe symptoms confirmed by radiographic studies of swallowing should surgery be undertaken and then only with reluctance. Surgical removal of a goiter producing significant airway obstruction, although attended by significant morbidity, may have to be considered in an elderly patient, since suppression therapy is unlikely to be effective in reducing the size of a large, long-standing, invariably multinodular goiter. If surgery is to be undertaken, the fact must be borne in mind that the procedure may be technically difficult and should be performed only by an experienced surgical team. Radioiodide therapy can be considered for such cases, especially in elderly people with other serious medical problems that add to surgical morbidity or mortality. While the response is slow and multiple doses may be required, a useful reduction in size of the goiter may be achieved. Concern may be expressed that, in any patient with a severely compromised airway, the transient swelling that sometimes occurs following radioiodide treatment could further narrow the trachea and is at least a theoretical hazard of this form of therapy. A recent series of such patients were, however, successfully treated in this fashion.[46]

Issue of Carcinoma in Multinodular Goiter

The occurrence of carcinoma in multinodular goiter has been debated for years. Although a significant proportion of thyroids from older persons harbor microscopic carcinomas, these are of no clinical significance. In elderly people, multinodular goiter should be considered to be a benign disease; surgical excision is rarely—if ever—warranted out of concern for carcinoma. Rapid, often painful enlargement of a dominant nodule in an elderly patient with multinodular goiter prompts concern over the possibility of development of an anaplastic carcinoma but is almost always due to hemorrhage or cyst formation.

THYROID NEOPLASMS

Thyroid Nodules

As shown in the classic community survey in Framingham, thyroid nodules are common and were found in 3 percent of adults between the ages of 30 and 60. New nodules appeared at the rate of 1 case per 1000 people per year. Other studies suggest that about 5 percent of all women over age 50 have a thyroid nodule.[47] These nodules—regardless of their histopathology—are almost all clinically nonaggressive. In the Framingham Study, follow-up of up to 15 years showed not one nodule behaving in a clinically aggressive manner; that is, not a single *clinical* case of thyroid cancer was seen to develop. In another smaller study in which all patients with nodules were treated with thyroid hormone suppression, no cancers developed in follow-ups of 5 to 15 years, while two-thirds of the nodules regressed or disappeared. The frequency of new nodule appearance after age 50 falls off rapidly, so that by age 80 very few new nodules will be encountered.

Clinical Approach to the Elderly Patient with a Solitary Thyroid Nodule

In encountering an apparently solitary thyroid nodule in an elderly person, several issues must be considered. Is the nodule new? Is it solitary or is it part of a nodular goiter? If it is truly solitary, what is its functional status? What should be done about it?

In establishing whether the patient has only a single nodule, palpation by an experienced examiner is essential. Frequently the "solitary" nodule, especially in the elderly patient, turns out to be one of several in a nodular goiter. An apparently single nodule in a clearly enlarged thyroid is probably one of several, since an enlarged gland is likely to be harboring many small, nondiscrete nodules. Sonography (ultrasound echogram) is very useful in delineating the anatomy of the nodule and, importantly, whether the remainder of the thyroid is enlarged and/or nodular. This noninvasive procedure also usually provides an objective determination of nodule size as a basis for follow-up. Cysts, usually resulting from degenerative changes in benign adenomas, can be best and readily identified by ultrasound.

The functional state of the solitary nodule can be surmised from the results of the T_4 (FT_4 index) and T_3. Elevated values may be associated with hyperthyroidism, the presence of which may not have been previously appreciated. The nodule may be hyperfunctioning relative to the remainder of the gland ("hot" nodule), even though it may not produce amounts of thyroid hormone sufficient to elevate the T_4 or T_3 above the normal range, and produce a TSH (second-generation assay) that is low. If the nodule is clearly hyperfunctioning as shown by the serum T_4 or T_3, a radionuclide scan should be performed to confirm that it is hot, followed by RaI therapy (or surgical removal), as discussed under Hyperthyroidism, above. Only about 5 percent of hyperthyroidism is due to hot nodules. These lesions are always benign. Clinical hyperthyroidism, if it is to develop from a hot nodule, will do so over 3 to 4 years; such lesions are invariably at least 3 to 4 cm in diameter. About 30 percent of hot nodules go on to produce hyperthyroidism; the remainder remain functionally stable or eventually involute. All hot nodules should be followed up by means of laboratory testing every 2 years.

Most nodules are "cold"—that is, functionally hypoactive relative to the remainder of the gland. The diagnostic workup and therapeutic approach to these lesions will be determined by a number of clinical considerations which are related to age of the patient and the biological potential of the nodule. In the elderly even more than in the young, a conservative approach is necessary.

The major concern with most cold nodules is, of course, malignancy. How much of a risk does this hold for the patient over age 50 or 60? In general, the older the patient, the less likely the nodule is to be cancerous. The incidence of cancerous nodules peaks at age 50 and falls off rapidly thereafter. Most nodules represent benign lesions; 75 to 90 percent are adenomas or cysts. Thus, the overall risk is small if nothing further is done. The risk is smaller still when one recalls that the remaining lesions—if they were excised—would prove to be clinically if not pathologically relatively benign papillary or follicular carcinomas. These lesions are almost always nonlethal and slow-growing, so that a conservative course is always feasible. This view is taken despite the recent realization that papillary or follicular carcinomas occurring in women over age 50 or men over age 40 are those most likely to be associated with a poor prognosis.[48–50] However, it should still be recalled that the vast majority of carcinomas, even in these older groups, follow a clinically benign course. Anaplastic carcinoma is a malignancy found only in the elderly population, but it is not likely to present as a single small nodule of a few centimeters' size (see below).

Given this sanguine set of considerations of the likelihood of carcinoma in nodules and the behavior of those lesions that are carcinomas, should one then pursue the diagnostic workup at all? In the authors' opinion, observation alone or suppression therapy with follow-up by clinical examination (preferably with sonogram) at 3 to 6 months is a safe approach especially applicable in an elderly patient. However, until recently, many physicians proceeded to immediate surgical excision of all nodules. Currently, many medical experts recommend needle biopsy using fine-needle aspiration for cytologic examinations or aspiration with small-bore needle for histologic examination. These procedures are safe, direct, and useful, but their limitations are several and go beyond the ability of the operator (endocrinologist or surgeon) to obtain a satisfactory specimen. Although it is probably possible to make an accurate diagnosis in about 90 percent of cases biopsied, it must be strongly stressed that the most important consideration in the use of needle biopsy is the expertise of the pathologist examining the biopsy material. If a specially trained cytopathologist is not available or if the patient is reluctant to have an invasive procedure, needle biopsy should be avoided and a conservative course adopted (below). It is important to realize that the clinical outcome will be unaffected by the choice of any of these available approaches: immediate excision; biopsy followed by excision; or treatment by suppression of TSH. Suppression therapy must not be equated with procrastination or no therapy.[51]

Thyroid Carcinomas

In the United States only about 1500 persons die of thyroid carcinoma each year. It is the least common cause of death due to cancer. More than half of these deaths are due to anaplastic carcinoma. The remainder are due to aggressive or metastatic follicular carcinoma or, rarely, papillary carcinoma. Anaplastic carcinoma is almost unknown below age 35, but by age 50 about 10 percent and by age 80 nearly half of the small number of cases of thyroid carcinoma encountered at these ages are of the anaplastic type. These lesions appear to arise in preexistent nodular goiters, but this consideration should not lead to the routine excision of such glands, since the risk of developing an anaplastic carcinoma is very low.

The clinical presentation of anaplastic carcinoma is usually that of a new, rapidly enlarging mass. Symptoms develop early and are likely to involve pain, hoarseness, dysphagia, or hemoptysis. Presentation as a small, discrete nodule is rare. Clinical reexamination at monthly intervals for several months will delineate the situation; rapid enlargement will alert the physician to the need for further evaluation. Needle biopsy is useful in selecting patients for early surgery, although no evidence exists to suggest that early extirpation is more likely to result in a cure. If an anaplastic lesion is found and the lesion is not already inoperable, surgery should be attempted, since resectable disease without evidence of metastases can be associated with long-term survival in 20 to 30 percent of patients, even when extension outside the thyroid capsule has occurred. Anaplastic carcinomas of the small-cell type may be confused—even by expert pathologists—with the rare case of lymphoma arising in the thyroid. Lymphoma, unlike anaplastic carcinoma, is radiosensitive and amenable to radiotherapy and/or chemotherapy. Medullary carcinoma, accounting for no more than 1 to 2 percent of thyroid cancer, is not likely to be encountered in elderly patients.

Surgical Removal versus Suppression Therapy of Cancerous Nodules

In elderly people all thyroid carcinomas diagnosed by needle biopsy need not be surgically removed. Conservative therapy alone (TSH suppression as described above) may well be indicated for a very elderly patient with an established diagnosis of papillary or even follicular thyroid carcinoma. Having excluded anaplastic carcinoma, one must consider the indolent, clinically benign course of most thyroid cancers against the expected longevity of the elderly person. The use of needle biopsy was introduced to reduce the frequency of unnecessary surgical procedures in an area of the United States where common practice dictated—by the fear of carcinoma—that all nodules should promptly be surgically excised. Since fine needle aspiration results in nearly 25 percent of specimens being labeled as "suspicious," it would be unfortunate if the introduction of this technique resulted in an increased number of operations for suspected or even real thyroid carcinoma in the elderly population.

REFERENCES

1. Stockigt JR: Serum thyrotropin and thyroid hormone measurements and assessment of thyroid hormone transport, in Braverman LE, Utiger RD (eds): *Werner and Ingbar's the Thyroid,* 6th ed. Philadelphia, Lippincott, 1991, chap 19, pp 463–485.
2. Larsen PR et al: Revised nomenclature for tests of thyroid hormone and thyroid-related proteins in serum. *J Clin Endocrinol Metab* 64:1089, 1987.
3. Gregerman RI: Thyroid disorders, in Barker LR, Burton JR, Zieve PD (eds): *Principles of Ambulatory Medicine.* Baltimore, Williams & Wilkins, 1991, pp 952–976.
4. Eggertsen R et al: Screening for thyroid disease in a primary care unit with a thyroid stimulating hormone assay with a low detection limit. *Br Med J* 297:1586, 1988.
5. Ross DS et al: The use and limitations of a chemiluminescent thyrotropin assay as a single thyroid function test in an outpatient endocrine clinic. *J Clin Endocrinol Metab* 71:764, 1990.
6. Spencer C et al: Specificity of sensitive assays of thyrotropin (TSH) used to screen for thyroid disease in hospitalized patients. *Clin Chem* 33:1391, 1987.
7. Bagchi N et al: Thyroid dysfunction in adults over age 55 years: A study in an urban U.S. community. *Arch Intern Med* 150:785, 1990.
8. Helfand M, Crapo IM: Screening for thyroid disease. *Ann Intern Med* 112:840, 1990.
9. Ehrmann DA, Sarne DH: Serum thyrotropin and the assessment of thyroid status. *Ann Intern Med* 110:179, 1989.
10. Sawin CT et al: Low serum thyrotropin (thyroid-stimulating hormone) in older persons without hyperthyroidism. *Arch Intern Med* 151:165, 1991.
11. Finucane P et al: Thyroid function tests in elderly patients with and without an acute illness. *Age Aging* 18:398, 1989.
12. Parle JV et al: Prevalence and follow-up of abnormal thyrotropin (TSH) concentrations in the elderly in the United Kingdom. *Clin Endocrinol (Oxf)* 34:77, 1991.
13. Drinka PJ, Nolten WE: Prevalence of previously undiagnosed hypothyroidism in residents in a midwestern nursing home. *South Med J* 83:1259, 1990.
14. Hennemann G, Krenning EP: Pitfalls in the interpretation of thyroid function tests in old age and nonthyroidal illness. *Hormone Res* 26:100, 1987.
15. Small M et al: Value of screening thyroid function in acute medical admission to hospital. *Clin Endocrinol (Oxf)* 32:185, 1990.
16. Rønnov V, Kirkegaard C: Hyperthyroidism—A disease of old age? *Br Med J* 1:41, 1973.
17. Stiel JN et al: Thyrotoxicosis in an elderly population. *Med J Aust* 2:986, 1972.
18. Davis PJ, Davis FB: Hyperthyroidism in patients over the age of 60 years. *Medicine* 53:161, 1974.
19. Swanson JW et al: Neurologic aspects of thyroid dysfunction. *Mayo Clinic Proc* 56:504, 1981.
20. Woeber KA: Thyrotoxicosis and the heart. *N Engl J Med* 327:94, 1992.
21. Resnekov L, Falicov RE: Thyrotoxicosis and lactate-producing angina pectoris with normal coronary arteries. *Br Heart J* 39:1051, 1977.
22. Borst GC et al: Euthyroid hyperthyroxinemia. *Ann Intern Med* 98:366, 1983.
23. Roca RP et al: Thyroid hormone elevations during acute psychiatric illness: Relationship to severity and distinction from hyperthyroidism. *Endocr Res* 16:415, 1990.

24. Thomas FB et al: Apathetic thyrotoxicosis: A distinctive clinical and laboratory entity. *Ann Intern Med* 72:679, 1970.
25. Fradkin JE, Wolff J: Iodide-induced thyrotoxicosis. *Medicine* 62:1, 1983.
26. Gordon M, Gryfe CI: Hyperthyroidism with painless subacute thyroiditis in the elderly. *JAMA* 246:2354, 1981.
27. Hamburger J: The autonomously functioning thyroid adenoma (editorial). *N Engl J Med* 309:1512, 1983.
28. Zellman HE: Unusual aspects of myxedema. *Geriatrics* 23:140, 1968.
29. Robuschi G et al: Hypothyroidism in the elderly. *Endocr Rev* 8:142, 1987.
30. Klein I, Levey GS: Unusual manifestations of hypothyroidism. *Arch Intern Med* 144:123, 1984.
31. Livingston EH et al: Prevalence of thyroid disease and abnormal thyroid tests in older hospitalized and ambulatory persons. *J Am Geriatr Soc* 35:109, 1987.
32. Bahemuka M, Hodkinson HM: Screening for hypothyroidism in elderly inpatients. *Br Med J* 2:601, 1975.
33. Ladenson PW et al: Complications of surgery in hypothyroid patients. *Am J Med* 77:261, 1984.
34. Ladenson PW et al: Prediction and reversal of blunted ventilatory responsiveness in patients with hypothyroidism. *Am J Med* 84:877, 1984.
35. Sherman SI, Ladenson PW: Percutaneous transluminal coronary angioplasty in hypothyroidism. *Am J Med* 90:367, 1991.
36. Impallomeni MG: Unusual presentation of myxoedema coma in the elderly. *Age Aging* 6:71, 1977.
37. Rosenthal MJ et al: Thyroid failure in the elderly: Microsomal antibodies as discriminant for therapy. *JAMA* 258:209, 1987.
38. Wehmann RE et al: Suppression of thyrotropin in the low thyroxine state of severe nonthyroidal illness. *N Engl J Med* 312:546, 1985.
39. Wartofsky L, Burman KD: Alterations in thyroid function in patients with systemic illness: The euthyroid sick syndrome. *Endocr Rev* 3:164, 1982.
40. Rosenbaum RL, Barzel US: Levothyroxine replacement dose for primary hypothyroidism decreases with age. *Ann Intern Med* 96:53, 1982.
41. Sawin CT et al: Aging and the thyroid. *Am J Med* 75:206, 1983.
42. Davis FB et al: Estimation of physiologic thyroxine replacement dose in hypothyroid patients. *Arch Intern Med* 144:1752, 1984.
43. Klein I, Levey GS: Thyroxine therapy, hypothyroid patients, and coronary revascularization. *Ann Intern Med* 96:250, 1982.
44. Fish LH et al: Replacement dose, metabolism and bioavailability of levothyroxine in the treatment of hypothyroidism: Role of triiodothyronine in pituitary feedback in human. *N Engl J Med* 316:764, 1987.
45. Smeulers J et al: Response to thyrotropin-releasing hormone and triiodothyronine suppressibility in euthyroid multinodular goiter. *Clin Endocrinol (Oxf)* 7:389, 1977.
46. Kay TWH et al: Treatment of non-toxic multinodular goiter with radioactive iodine. *Am J Med* 84:19, 1988.
47. Brander A et al: Thyroid gland: Ultrasonography screening in middle aged women with no previous thyroid disease. *Radiology* 173:507, 1989.
48. Cady B et al: Changing clinical, pathologic, therapeutic and survival patterns in differentiated thyroid carcinoma. *Ann Surg* 184:541, 1976.
49. Samaan NA et al: Impact of therapy for differentiated carcinoma of the thyroid: An analysis of 706 cases. *J Clin Endocrinol Metab* 56:1131, 1983.
50. Høie J et al: Distant metastases in papillary thyroid cancer: A review of 91 patients. *Cancer* 61:1, 1988.
51. Molitch ME et al: The cold thyroid nodule: An analysis of diagnostic and therapeutic options. *Endocr Rev* 5:185, 1984.

Chapter 71

DIABETES MELLITUS AND GLUCOSE METABOLISM IN THE ELDERLY

Andrew P. Goldberg and Patricia J. Coon

Diabetes mellitus is a disease recognized by the presence of high blood glucose levels. However, it is a more complex condition than simply an abnormality in glucose regulation due to an inadequate amount of insulin and should be viewed as a syndrome characterized by generalized metabolic dysfunction and various clinical disorders. Although diabetes mellitus is primarily characterized by abnormal glucose metabolism, it is also associated with abnormal regulation of lipid and protein metabolism and with the development of vascular and nervous system disease.

Elderly people appear to be more susceptible to the development of hyperglycemia than younger people. The presence of comorbidity and polypharmacy in elderly diabetic patients makes the treatment of hyperglycemia more challenging. These patients are also at risk for hypoglycemia in response to therapy with oral hypoglycemic agents and insulin. The effects of treating hyperglycemia or other risk factors for atherosclerosis on the incidence of cardiovascular complications in older people with diabetes mellitus are currently unknown.

Many of the clinical manifestations and consequences of diabetes mellitus in older people may resemble age-related pathophysiologic changes. Declines in organ function commonly associated with aging occur more frequently and at an accelerated rate in diabetic patients. The development of cataracts; the onset of symptoms and signs of atherosclerotic cardiovascular disease (CVD); a decline in peripheral sensory and motor neural function; a deterioration in renal function; retinopathy; or an infection may already be evident at the time of diabetes diagnosis in elderly people. Rarely are presenting symptoms acute, as in insulin-dependent ketosis-prone diabetes mellitus (IDDM); rather, the slow, gradual onset and progression of complications characterizes non-insulin-dependent diabetes mellitus (NIDDM) in elderly people. This chapter focuses on the pathophysiology, diagnosis, clinical management, and complications of NIDDM, or type II diabetes, the most common disorder of impaired glucoregulation in older people.

GLUCOSE METABOLISM IN HEALTHY ELDERLY PERSONS

The majority of human studies show that aging is associated with a progressive decline in glucose tolerance.[1–3] Major abnormalities in glucose homeostasis can occur in older people in the absence of the characteristic clinical complications of diabetes mellitus and are often associated with a variety of medical conditions which commonly occur in older people. These include obesity, physical inactivity, reduced muscle mass, improper diet, and the development of coexistent diseases which require the use of multiple medications which can affect glucose tolerance and insulin action. There may not be any detectable primary defect in insulin action or pancreatic beta cell function, and there may not be any changes in capillary basement membrane structure or the vessel wall in older people with glucose intolerance. Whether or not this is a disease, and whether the older patient with glucose intolerance alone is at heightened risk for the development of diabetic complications, excessive morbidity, and the rapid progression to death if untreated, is not known. A rational approach to this conundrum is central to understanding the pathophysiology and formulating the appropriate treatment for the older diabetic patient.

There is an age-related increase in the prevalence of diabetes mellitus, undiagnosed diabetes, and impaired glucose tolerance (Table 71-1). The ability to dispose of an oral glucose load is reduced in more than 40 percent of individuals older than 60 years of age.[4] If the criteria of the National Diabetes Data Group (NDDG) for normal glucose tolerance are ap-

TABLE 71-1

OGTT Results in the National Health and Nutrition Examination Survey II (1976–1980)

	Age in years			
	20–44	**45–54**	**55–64**	**65–74**
1. Diabetes known prior to testing	1.1%	4.3%	6.6%	9.3%
2. Diabetes revealed through testing	1.0%	4.4%	6.5%	8.6%
Total prevalence of diabetes	2.1%	8.7%	13.1%	17.9%
3. Impaired glucose tolerance	6.5%	14.9%	15.2%	22.9%
Total diabetes and impaired glucose tolerance	8.6%	23.6%	28.3%	40.8%

plied to older populations, nearly 50 percent of individuals over 60 years would have an abnormal oral glucose tolerance test (OGTT). However, most of these people are without overt symptoms or disease and would not meet criteria for diabetes by NDDG standards.[5] Such a decline in glucose tolerance in the absence of systemic disease could well be considered a physiologic sequela of the aging process, not a disease per se.

Numerous studies indicate an average 1 mg/dl per decade age-related increase in fasting plasma glucose levels in healthy normal individuals after maturity.[3] This small age-related increase in fasting glucose levels is accompanied, however, by a striking 9 to 10 mg/dl per decade increase in plasma glucose levels 2 hours after an oral glucose challenge.[1–3] These higher postprandial glucose levels may cause slight increases in hemoglobin A_{1c} levels with age.[6] This decline in glucose tolerance with aging is often associated with elevated plasma insulin concentrations, possibly caused by a blunting of the action of insulin on the uptake of glucose by peripheral tissues.[7–11] This suggests that the deterioration in glucose tolerance and the hyperinsulinemia associated with aging are due, at least in part, to the development of insulin resistance. The association of numerous conditions which often covary with aging, such as obesity and physical inactivity, with insulin resistance and hyperinsulinemia has led some to propose that the glucose intolerance of aging is not a primary consequence of biological aging processes. However, when the effects of obesity, an upper body fat distribution, and physical conditioning status on glucose tolerance were considered in a carefully selected healthy population screened for disease and medications, age remained a significant determinant of the decline in glucose tolerance after age 60.[3] From the early adult to middle-aged years, however, the secondary aging processes of physical deconditioning and abdominal obesity entirely accounted for the decline in glucose tolerance in both men and women.

The OGTT is inadequate for determining the mechanism for the deterioration in glucose tolerance and the hyperinsulinemia with aging because (1) plasma glucose levels are not maintained constant because of variable gastrointestinal absorption, (2) the glycemic stimulus to the pancreatic beta cell differs during the test, making comparisons of plasma insulin levels and the extrapolation to secretion among individuals impossible, and (3) the rate of peripheral glucose disposal differs among individuals of different physical conditioning status, adiposity, and health status, additional factors which affect insulin secretion and action. Furthermore, gut hormones, sympathoadrenal responses, and cellular mechanisms affect glucose metabolism and insulin secretion and action; the effects of aging on these responses during the OGTT are unknown.

Some of the problems inherent to the OGTT in the study of the effects of aging on glucose metabolism and insulin secretion are obviated by the glucose clamp. In this technique the glucose stimulus can be controlled to permit the measurement of endogenous insulin secretion and action at a sustained, elevated plasma glucose level (hyperglycemic clamp), or a known concentration of insulin can be infused during euglycemia to increase glucose utilization (euglycemic hyperinsulinemic clamp).[12] When insulin is infused sequentially at various concentrations and the plasma glucose concentration maintained constant by the simultaneous infusion of glucose (multidose hyperinsulinemic, euglycemic clamp), whole-body insulin sensitivity can be determined and insulin–glucose dose response curves constructed (Fig. 71-1). Several studies report an impaired effect of insulin on glucose utilization in healthy nondiabetic older people compared with younger controls.[7–10] The dose–response curves of older persons with normal glucose tolerance tend to be shifted to the right (Fig. 71-2), but maximal glucose utilization in response to very high doses of insulin is normal.[8,9] This defect in insulin action has been attributed to a receptor defect in some studies,[13,14] and to an abnormality distal to the receptor by investigators who found normal receptor binding in the presence of impaired glucose utilization.[8,15,16] The finding by Menielly et al.[17] that the suppression of hepatic glucose production by insulin is normal in older subjects with reduced glucose disposal suggests that the defect in insulin action is primarily in muscle.

Recent evidence suggests that the decrease in glucose utilization with aging is related to an age-associated reduction in physical conditioning status

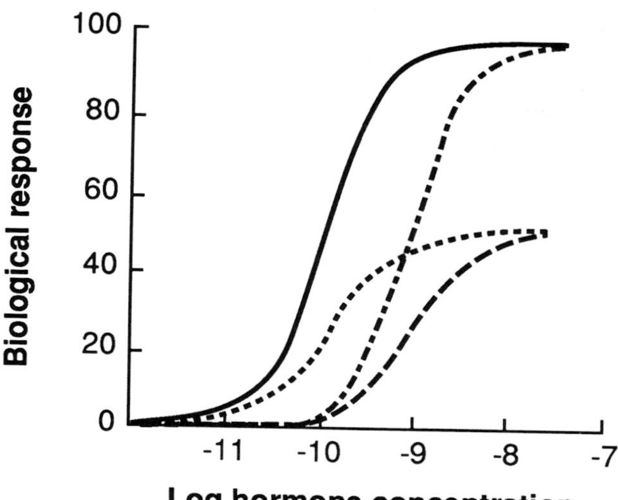

FIGURE 71-1

Insulin resistance involves three forms of altered biological response to insulin compared with normal (——): decreased sensitivity (– – – –); decreased responsiveness (- - - -); and decreased sensitivity and responsiveness (— — —).

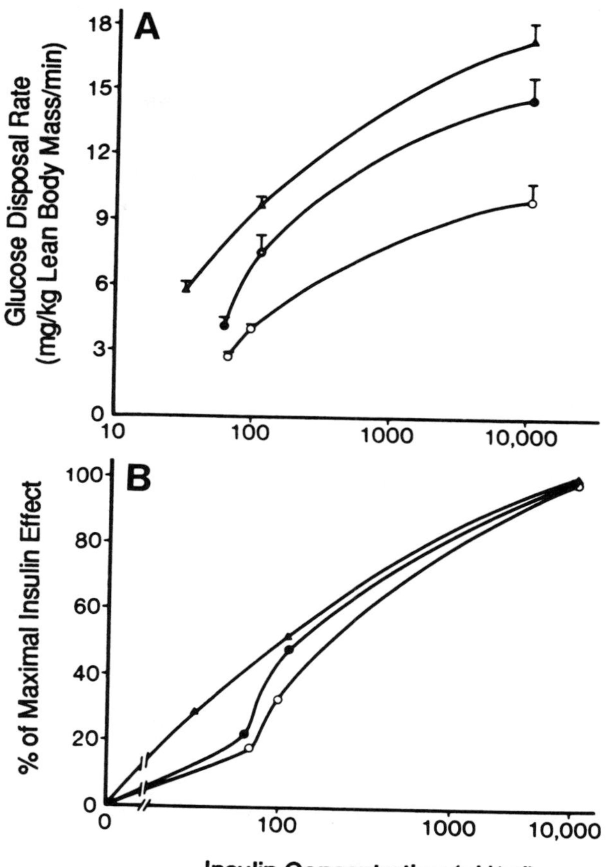

FIGURE 71-2

A. Mean dose–response glucose utilization curves in response to different insulin doses for nonelderly patients (▲), elderly patients with normal glucose tolerance tests (●), and elderly patients with nondiagnostic glucose tolerance tests (°). *B.* Mean dose–response curves for the three groups in *A* plotted as the percentage of maximal glucose utilization at each insulin concentration infused. (*Reprinted by permission from Fink et al.*[8])

and alterations in body composition. In healthy older men up to the age of 75 years, insulin sensitivity and glucose tolerance are affected primarily by the regional distribution of body fat, and physical deconditioning and obesity contribute to the decline in glucose metabolism independent of age.[18] Glucose disposal rates and insulin sensitivity were comparable over a wide range of insulin levels in older and young men matched for waist/hip ratio, percentage body fat, or maximal aerobic capacity ($\dot{V}O_2$ max). This supports the hypothesis that in the absence of disease, the decline in insulin sensitivity at least into the eighth decade of life is due primarily to changes in body composition and physical fitness, not biological aging processes.[18,19] However, further investigation is necessary to determine whether other mechanisms or age-associated processes are responsible for the independent effect of age on glucose tolerance in the very old.[3]

There have been several reports of impaired insulin secretion and clearance accompanying impaired glucose utilization in older subjects. These studies showed appropriate insulin responses to mixed meals and intravenous glucose administration for the degree of glycemia and insulin resistance under physiologic conditions;[20] however, under hyperglycemic conditions the insulin secretion response in older subjects was lower than that of younger controls despite a greater degree of insulin resistance in the older subjects. To control for the effect of insulin resistance on insulin secretion, Kahn et al.[21] matched older subjects with young controls for insulin sensitivity index. In that study, insulin secretion was reduced in the elderly subjects. However, in a larger study of the effects of aging and obesity on glucose and insulin dynamics, the decline in glucose tolerance with age was related primarily to decreased insulin sensitivity, not decreased insulin secretion.[22,23] Studies of the effects of physical conditioning, dietary modification, and weight loss on glucose and insulin homeostasis will be important for determining the pathogenesis of glucose intolerance in elderly persons and mechanisms by which diabetes can be prevented in older, high-risk populations.

Despite the prevalence of apparent defects in glucose metabolism and insulin action and secretion with aging, many older individuals exhibit glucose tolerance with insulin responses comparable to those of young normal individuals.[24] In selected healthy older men, screened for disease and matched as closely as possible with younger men for percentage body fat, maximal aerobic capacity, and regional distribution of body fat, measurement of insulin sensitivity during euglycemic hyperinsulinemic clamps was comparable to that of younger controls.[25] The improved glucose tolerance and insulin sensitivity seen in older people after 3 days of high-carbohydrate feeding suggests that dietary factors also play a significant role in the regulation of carbohydrate metabolism in the elderly population.[10,26]

Thus, independent processes influence the decline in glucose tolerance associated with aging. In the first, the so-called lifestyle habits of overeating, consumption of a low-carbohydrate high-fat diet, and physical inactivity have profound effects on glucose tolerance; modification of diet, body weight, and exercise capacity have the potential to improve glucose tolerance.[27–31] A large population study showed that less than 10 percent of the variance in the total plasma glucose response could be attributed to differences in age.[32] Results of other investigations suggest that when the variables of body composition (percentage body fat and waist/hip ratio) and physical conditioning status (indexed as $\dot{V}O_2$ max) are taken into account, the decline in glucose tolerance and insulin sensitivity with aging is reduced.[18,19] This suggests that in the design of studies examining the pathogenesis of the decline in glucose tolerance with aging, older and younger subjects should be matched for obesity, maximal aerobic capacity, body fat distribution, and health, and that pretest diets and activity should be controlled prior to the performance of metabolic tests.

TABLE 71-2

Clinical Symptoms and Signs of Diabetes Mellitus in the Elderly Patient

Common

1. Unexplained weight loss, fatigue, slow wound healing, mental status
2. Cataracts, microaneurysms, and retinal detachment
3. Recurrent bacterial or fungal infections of skin (pruritus vulvae in women), intertriginous areas, and urinary tract
4. Neurologic dysfunction, including paresthesias, dysesthesias, and hypoesthesias, muscle weakness and pain (amyotrophy), cranial nerve palsies (mononeuropathy), and autonomic dysfunction of the gastrointestinal tract (diarrhea), cardiovascular system (postural hypotension), reproductive system (impotence), and bladder (atony, overflow incontinence)
5. Arterial disease (macroangiopathy) involving the cardiovascular system (silent ischemia, angina, and myocardial infarction), cerebral vasculature (transient ischemia, and stroke), or peripheral vasculature (diabetic foot, gangrene)
6. Small-vessel disease (microangiopathy) involving the eyes (macular disease, hemorrhages, exudates), kidneys (proteinuria, glomerulopathy, uremia), and nervous system (mononeuropathy)
7. Comorbid endocrine-metabolic abnormalities, including obesity, hyperlipidemia, and osteoporosis.
8. A family history of NIDDM or IDDM and a history of gestational diabetes or large babies

Rare

1. Classical polyuria, polydipsia, and polyphagia as in young persons with IDDM
2. Lesions of the skin, such as diabetic dermopathy, Dupuytren's contractures, and facial rubeosis

DIABETES MELLITUS

The primary metabolic defect in diabetes mellitus is a disturbance in glucose homeostasis. This disturbance may be the result of one or more functional abnormalities in three major organ systems: muscle, the major tissue utilizing glucose in the body; the endocrine pancreas, which secretes insulin and glucagon necessary for glucose utilization by tissues and regulation of hepatic glucose production; and the liver, which as the sole producer of glucose in the fasted state is critical or glucoregulation. In NIDDM, there may be impaired insulin secretion by the pancreatic beta cell, ineffective insulin action at tissues and cells, overproduction of glucose by the liver, or a combination of defects in all these processes that limits the maintenance of glucose homeostasis.[33–36] The disease NIDDM in older individuals is characterized by a variety of nonspecific clinical manifestations (Table 71-2) plus the diagnostic biochemical abnormalities of fasting and postprandial hyperglycemia and glucosuria. Diabetes coexists with obesity in most older people and is for the most part ketosis-resistant. However, under stressful conditions such as infection or surgery, insulin resistance may exceed endogenous insulin secretory capacity and frank hypoinsulinemia may ensue, necessitating insulin therapy to avoid ketoacidosis. Although over 90 percent of patients with NIDDM have a positive family history of diabetes, the linkage between genetic mechanisms and disease is not as evident as with insulin-dependent diabetes. The high concordance rate for NIDDM in monozygotic twins after age 40 suggests that genetic factors are operative in the disease process.[37,38]

Although glucose intolerance and insulin resistance frequently occur with aging, further deterioration might be avoided in older patients who remain healthy, lean, and physically active. Thus, all older individuals should be counseled to change imprudent habits of overeating the wrong foods, physical inactivity, and cigarette smoking to attempt to reduce the risk of progression to disease. There is evidence that at all ages, morbidity and mortality increase in individuals with impaired glucose tolerance, as well as diabetes mellitus.[39–41] In these individuals, macrovascular disease develops at an accelerated rate causing atherosclerosis of the coronary, cerebral, and peripheral vessels while microvascular angiopathy progresses in the kidney, retina, and nervous system. The macroangiopathic complications cause the major morbidity and mortality in older diabetic persons; hence, vigorous treatment of diabetes seems prudent to prevent macroangiopathy.[39–42] However, the effects of vigorous therapy to control hyperglycemia and reduce other risk factors for atherosclerosis, such as hyperlipidemia, cigarette smoking, and hypertension, on the progression of macro- and microangiopathic vascular complications in older diabetic patients are not known because elderly and diabetic persons are often excluded from clinical trials.

Epidemiology of Diabetes

NIDDM is the more prevalent form of diabetes in the elderly population, and in Western societies it affects approximately 1 out of every 10 whites over 65 years of age and 1 out of every 4 people who are over 85 years of age.[43,44] A few studies have examined racial differences in glucose tolerance among people living in the same environment. In Evans County, Georgia, the prevalence of diabetes among individuals in the fifth decade of life was twofold higher in black women than among either white women, white men, or black men.[45] A National Health Survey found a 60 percent higher age-adjusted prevalence of diabetes in blacks than whites between the ages 18 and 79 years, and a greater proportion of blacks than whites with plasma glucose levels exceeding 200 mg/dl 1 hour after the ingestion of 50 g of glucose.[46]

The incidence rate of NIDDM in older individuals increases from 5 to 6 per 1000 persons per year to as high as 8 to 10 per 1000 persons in surveys of individuals aged 70 to 79. However, extremely high rates are observed in populations where there is a heightened prevalence of obesity, specifically Nauruans and Pima Indians. Among these people the incidence of diabetes in men age 50 to 59 years is 40 to 50 per 1000 people per year.[47–49] Perhaps the best estimates of the prevalence of diagnosed and undiagnosed diabetes in the United States are available from the 1976 Health Interview Survey and the National Health and Nutrition Examination Survey II.[4] Using OGTT criteria proposed by the NDDG, the results of these surveys indicate that the total prevalence of NIDDM increases from 2.1 percent in the age group 20 to 44 years to 17.9 percent among 65- to 74-year-olds (Table 71-1). In the older group, the prevalence of undiagnosed diabetes equaled the estimate of diagnosed NIDDM, and an additional 23 percent of these older individuals were found to have impaired glucose tolerance. These data probably underestimate the prevalence of diabetes among older populations, since nearly 15 percent of institutionalized nursing home patients have the disease[50] and are usually excluded from "free living" representative statistics.

While differences in dietary practice and physical activity status have been considered possible explanations for the divergent incidence of diabetes among older and younger people as well as among blacks and whites, the prevalence of obesity, reduced muscle mass, and socioeconomic and environmental factors also must be considered. Accurate age-, gender-, and race-adjusted guidelines for the diagnosis of diabetes are needed to determine the most appropriate guidelines for treatment to prevent complications. For example, should the criteria for diagnosis and treatment of a hyperglycemic 35-year-old be the same as for a hyperglycemic 80-year-old? Will the outcomes be the same? Are the risks of aggressive therapy comparable? Should these be modified based on race or gender? In the absence of specific markers for NIDDM and its evolution, it is impossible to determine who is at risk for complications and whether the risk factors for complications are similar or different among young and older patients. Moreover, it is not known whether the development of NIDDM in older persons can be substantially modified by interventions other then drug therapy. The geriatrician's ability to treat diabetes optimally will require resolutions of these issues and the accurate quantification of the prevalence and consequences of diabetes in the elderly population. This will depend on the quality of the techniques used to determine that diabetes is present, the criteria for its diagnosis, the accurate assessment of the natural history and evolution of complications in diabetes, and the determination of the effects of different modes of treatment on patient outcome.

Diagnostic Criteria for Diabetes

The results of glucose tolerance testing in older individuals and the expression of age-specific criteria for diagnosis of diabetes are based on studies which are poorly standardized with respect to the administered dose of glucose, the uniformity of the pretest diet, the activity of the subjects during testing, the timing and method of blood sampling, and the techniques used to measure plasma glucose levels. In older individuals, the clinical signs and symptoms of diabetes may be subtle, and some individuals may require an OGTT when there is a strong clinical suspicion of diabetes, even in the presence of a normal fasting plasma glucose level (Table 71-2). In the older patient with hyperglycemia and clinical symptoms and signs of diabetes, the diagnosis can be made easily and treatment initiated without fear of a false-positive diagnosis. Although undiagnosed diabetes exists in about 3 percent of the American population, the prevalence of undiagnosed and diagnosed diabetes increases with aging.[4]

The current recommended diagnostic tests for diabetes are neither 100 percent specific nor 100 percent sensitive. Rather, there is considerable overlap between test results in normal persons and those with diabetes because the sensitivity and specificity of the diagnostic test frequently vary inversely. Highly sensitive tests detect all individuals with diabetes (there are no false negatives) but misdiagnose some normal persons, whereas highly specific tests correctly identify all normal persons (no false positives occur) and miss some individuals with diabetes by classifying them as normal. Considering these facts, the risk to the patient of inappropriate diagnosis of NIDDM outweighs the benefits gained by the indiscriminate screening for diabetes in older individuals and the initiation of therapy before thorough evaluation to ensure a proper diagnosis. Yet, testing for diabetes is somewhat analogous to screening for hypertension and hyperlipidemia, since hyperglycemia, hypertension, and hypercholesterolemia are major risk factors for atherosclerotic disease, frequently coexist, and warrant medical evaluation and treatment.

When should the physician be concerned about making a diagnosis of diabetes mellitus in an older individual? Should all older individuals be screened for diabetes mellitus, or should evaluation be limited to those with a high risk in whom the disease is present or likely to develop?[51] In the absence of a definitive marker for diabetes independent of the fasting plasma glucose concentration, the physician must balance finding asymptomatic diabetes versus the potential dangers of making a diagnosis of diabetes in a person who does not have the disease and is not likely to develop it. The social, medical, and economic implications of a false-positive diagnosis must be carefully weighed against the dangers inherent in making a false-negative diagnosis of normality. The authors believe that testing for diabetes should be part of the routine annual physical examination of all older patients.

The NDDG standards for the diagnosis of diabetes emphasize the importance of measuring the fasting plasma glucose concentration rather than performing a full OGTT.[5] However, although the NDDG standards for the OGTT are not age-adjusted, they are endorsed because they err on the side of specificity rather than sensitivity and avoid a false-positive diagnosis of diabetes. The NDDG report is comprehensive in its description of the exact techniques for the performance of the OGTT for diabetes in adults and in its definition of diagnostic standards and specific criteria for interpreting the test and diagnosing the disease. It provides a detailed scheme for the clinical classification of diabetes, as well as other diseases associated with hyperglycemia which are not regarded as diabetes in themselves. As new epidemiologic and experimental longitudinal information emerges on the natural history of diabetes, the standards of the NDDG undoubtedly will be modified.

Measurement of Fasting Plasma Glucose Level

Measuring the fasting plasma glucose concentration is advantageous because of the relative consistency and day-to-day reproducibility of the concentration in people whose reading lies in either the normal or abnormal range (>140 mg/dl). An individual is rarely diabetic at one time and normal at another, and the fasting plasma glucose level is relatively unaltered by age. The plasma glucose measurement is easy to standardize since an overnight fast can commonly be achieved with little excess burden to the patient or physician. Furthermore, the measurement is performed rapidly, cheaply, and conveniently, and it is rarely (and, if so, minimally) affected by the caloric intake, the composition of the diet, or physical activity prior to the test.

For a firm diagnosis of diabetes, the NDDG recommends a cutoff point for the fasting plasma glucose level at 140 mg/dl, even though some investigators propose that the upper limit of normal be 115 mg/dl. The higher value maximizes test specificity, since the OGTT shows a diabetic response in all individuals with fasting plasma glucose levels ≥140 mg/dl. The NDDG report states that people with fasting plasma glucose concentrations between 120 and 139 mg/dl probably will have abnormal OGTTs, and even levels between 115 and 120 mg/dl must be viewed with suspicion. This borderline zone might even extend down a bit further, but age-adjusted standards and epidemiologic information are needed to relate them to the development of diabetes. If a fasting glucose value above 140 mg/dl is confirmed by second test, it is indicative of diabetes, and an OGTT is not required. However, below the level of 140 mg/dl, an OGTT should be performed if the clinical suspicion for diabetes is high.

Oral Glucose Tolerance Test

Prior to making a decision to perform an OGTT, it is important to consider the possible consequences of a false-positive as well as a false-negative diagnosis of diabetes. For the false-positive test, these consequences include inappropriate treatment with hypoglycemic drugs and the potential risk of life-threatening hypoglycemia; unnecessary lifestyle changes affecting social behavior including food choices, alcohol consumption, prolonged exercise, and stress; increased medical and insurance costs related to a "diabetic label"; inappropriate labeling of family members as being at risk for diabetes; and potential bias in employment. On the other hand, failure to diagnose diabetes may lead to inadequate preparation at the time of stressful events such as surgery, infection, trauma, burns, heart attack, or exercise; lack of awareness of the need for appropriate health care habits—such as changing diet, losing weight, regular exercise, and stopping cigarette smoking—to prevent the chronic vascular and neuropathic complications of the disease; and the failure to inform family members who might be at high risk. The authors believe that the risk/benefit ratio favors making an accurate diagnosis of diabetes mellitus in older individuals at high risk for other comorbidity which further increases their risk of complications from borderline or asymptomatic NIDDM.

Symptoms and signs of diabetes may be present in some older people who do not have fasting hyperglycemia. Under these conditions, the performance of an OGTT represents the most sensitive way to detect the diabetic state. The OGTT should always be performed in the morning after an overnight 10- to 16-hour fast under resting conditions without cigarette smoking. After a fasting blood sample is drawn, sampling should be made at 30-minute intervals for 2 hours after the oral administration of a 75-g dose of glucose. Measurement of glucose should be done on venous plasma by a glucose oxidase method. The interpretation of the OGTT depends first upon the fasting plasma glucose level, second on the glucose value at 2 hours, and third upon the highest glucose level of the three intermediate time points, 30, 60, and 90 minutes. There is one cutoff point for intermediate time points and two cutoff points for the 2-hour value, at 140 and 200 mg/dl (Fig. 71-3*A*).

Thus, there are six test possibilities (Fig. 71-3*B*). The terminology for these test results includes *diabetic* (glucose ≥ 200 mg/dl at both intermediate and 2-hour time points), *normal* (glucose below 200 mg/dl and below 140 mg/dl at these two time points), *impaired glucose tolerance* (glucose ≥200 and between 140 and 199 mg/dl at the intermediate time points), and *nondiagnostic* for the other three categories of results. Prior to the report of the NDDG, a value greater than 140 mg/dl was considered abnormal at 2 hours of the OGTT. Hence, moving the 2-hour criterion

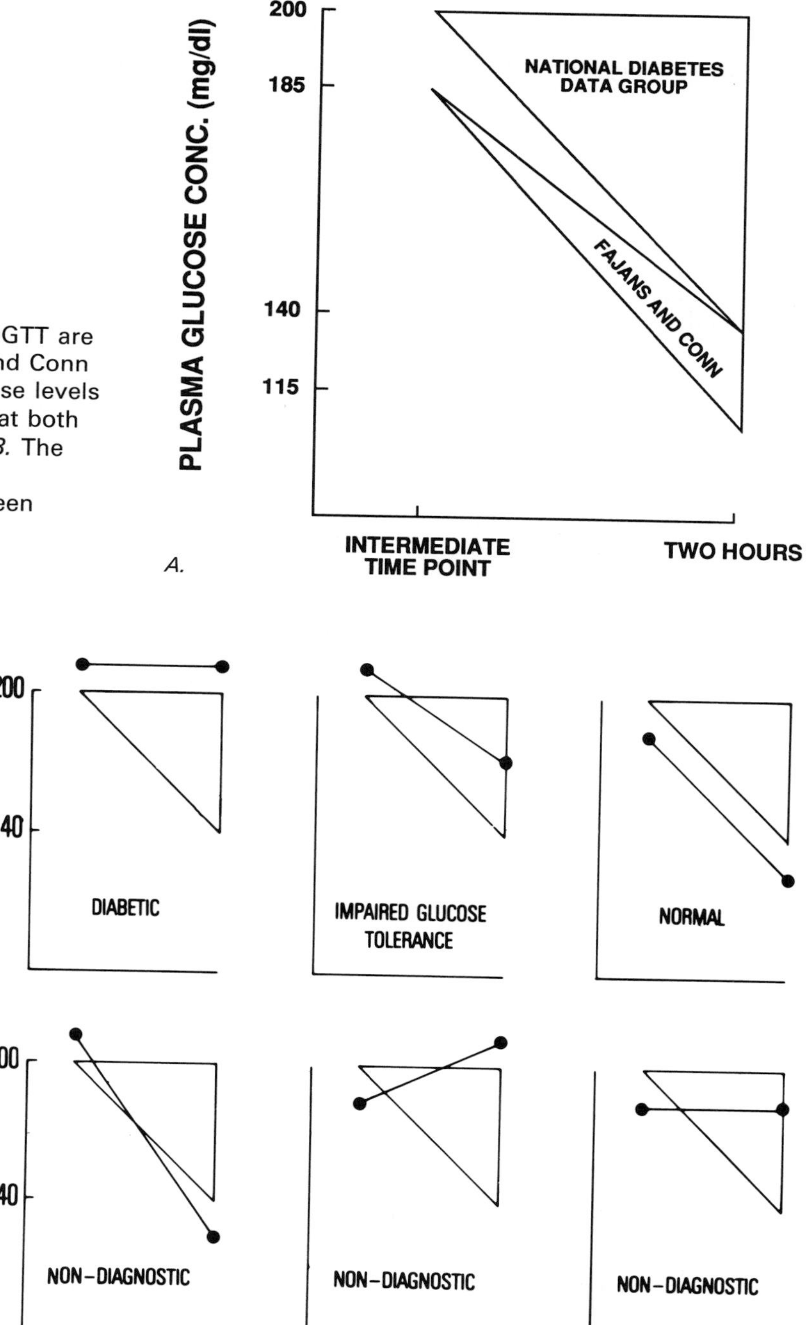

FIGURE 71-3

A. The NDDG standards for interpreting the OGTT are depicted in comparison with the old Fajans and Conn criteria. The shift upward toward higher glucose levels in the new versus the old criteria is apparent at both the intermediate and the 2-hour time points. *B.* The diagnostic categories for results of the OGTT according to the NDDG criteria. These have been related to the actual cutoff points defining the diagnostic triangle in *A.*

from 140 to 200 mg/dl has, in effect, greatly reduced the percentage of OGTT results in a diabetic range, especially in middle-aged and older individuals. A relatively high percentage of older individuals are classified as impaired, and some unreported fraction of older people are in the nondiagnostic range. According to these criteria, perhaps only about half of all people 70 years or older might receive a completely normal label using the OGTT as a routine diagnostic tool for diabetes.

A major problem in the use of the OGTT is difficulty with its interpretation and its lack of reproducibility. Glucose tolerance differing by greater than 50 mg/dl has been demonstrated on retesting. A large number of acute and chronic medical conditions, the administration of certain drugs (Table 71-3), physical inactivity, dietary intake of carbohydrate and caloric amount prior to testing, and age affect the OGTT. Even when these factors are controlled, there is a significant degree of test-retest variability in the results of the OGTT. Because of this, an absolutely certain diagnosis of diabetes mellitus should not be made solely on the basis of OGTT. The OGTT should be abnormal on 2 occasions and conditions known to affect the validity of the OGTT are absent or strictly controlled.

Other Diagnostic Tests

Measurement of glycosylated hemoglobin (HbA_{1c}) is a possible test which might offer advantages over the fasting plasma glucose level and OGTT in making a diagnosis of diabetes in older individuals. This is because its measurement theoretically reflects the time-integrated blood glucose level of the 120-day life span of the erythrocyte. The positive relationship between age and HbA_{1c}, and the finding of a large number of false-positive results in normal people, limits the usefulness of the HbA_{1c} level as a single diagnostic test for diabetes mellitus.[6]

The intravenous glucose tolerance test (IVGTT) has been used most frequently, especially in research studies, to diagnose diabetes. Whereas values above 1.0 percent/minute are considered normal, a decrease in the glucose disappearance rate of approximately 0.2 percent/minute per decade has been reported with aging. While the impact of age on glucose metabolism is demonstrated by the IVGTT, recommendations for establishing criteria for the test are limited by the relatively few studies which have utilized this technique to diagnose diabetes mellitus. The cortisone oral glucose tolerance test and the intravenous tolbutamide response test serve primarily as research tools but also have demonstrated an age-related decline in glucose tolerance. Thus, except for the OGTT there are limited reference data for other diagnostic tests for diabetes.

Classification of Diabetes

There are four mutually exclusive clinically relevant subclasses of diabetes mellitus:

1. *Type I, or insulin-dependent, diabetes mellitus* is caused by an autoimmune destructive process in the beta cells of pancreatic islets. It accounts for 10 to 20 percent of known cases of diabetes occurring primarily in patients under 45 years of age, but a very small percentage of older diabetic per-

TABLE 71-3

Commonly Used Drugs Affecting Glucose Tolerance in Older Persons

Worsen Hyperglycemia	Potentiate Hypoglycemia
1. Intrinsic Hyperglycemic Action • Diuretic (thiazide, chlorthalidone, furosemide) • Glucocorticoids • Estrogens • Nicotinic acid • Phenothiazines • Phenytoins • Sympathomimetic agents • Lithium • Growth hormone • Sugar-containing medications (cough syrup) • Isoniazid 2. Increased Sulfonylurea Metabolism • Alcohol • Rifampin	1. Intrinsic Hypoglycemic Action • Insulin • Alcohol • Salicylates • Monoamine oxidase inhibitors 2. Affect Sulfonylurea Pharmacology • Interfere with metabolism: bishydroxycoumarin, pyrazolone derivatives (phenylbutazone, etc.), chloramphenicol, monoamine oxidase inhibitors • Decrease renal excretion: salicylates, cimetidene, probenecid, allopurinol, phenylbutazone, sulfonamides • Displace from albumin binding site: salicylates, clofibrate, pyrazolone derivatives, sulfonamides 3. Impede glucoregulation • Beta blockers • Alcohol • Guanethidine

sons have IDDM. Patients with IDDM present with a rapid acceleration of glucosuria, weight loss, and anorexia, often for fewer than 2 months. They are thin and usually have symptoms of ketoacidosis, the primary mode of presentation. Although greater than 90 percent of older diabetic persons are ketosis-resistant and have NIDDM, or type II diabetes mellitus, under stressful acute medical conditions such as surgery, infections, or acute myocardial infarction, the older patient with NIDDM may become ketosis-prone and require insulin. With resolution of the acute medical condition, the metabolic state of these patients usually returns to NIDDM and no longer requires insulin therapy.

2. *Idiopathic type II diabetes mellitus (NIDDM)* defines a group of patients generally over the age of 50 years who are either obese at presentation or who have been obese in the past. Among older people, it is the most common form of diabetes. There is usually significant glucose intolerance for a number of years before the detection of the syndrome. Rarely is there an acute precipitating metabolic event in NIDDM; these patients are often first seen for complications of the disease, either in a coronary care unit or by an ophthalmologist, neurologist, nephrologist, or gynecologist. Genetic factors seem to be operative in NIDDM, as up to 25 percent of parents and 40 percent of siblings of these patients have an impaired or diabetic OGTT. To date, no specific associated HLA serotypes have been identified as in IDDM. Typically 80 percent of patients with NIDDM are or have been obese and 20 percent are of normal weight; however, obesity itself is not the primary cause of this disease. Studies among the Pima Indians support the likelihood that the presence of obesity is one factor which hastens the transition from impaired glucose tolerance to the actual development of NIDDM.[48] The coexistence of obesity with NIDDM worsens the degree of hyperglycemia and the severity of the syndrome; dietary adherence and weight reduction improves the OGTT and reduces symptoms and complications in many obese patients with NIDDM.

   In some patients with NIDDM, especially those who are at ideal body weight, increasing hyperglycemia may require treatment with insulin despite therapy with a proper diet and exercise regimen. Some of these patients may develop progressive hypoinsulinemia as the disease progresses, while others may develop another disease that worsens glucose metabolism. In most cases, however, worsening of hyperglycemia in older patients with NIDDM suggests that there is an acute underlying infection or stress. Treatment of the acute condition usually returns glucose metabolism to baseline and allows insulin therapy to be discontinued.

3. *A history of gestational diabetes* is of particular importance in older women. Of the 2 percent of pregnant women who exhibit glucose intolerance of sufficient magnitude to qualify for the diagnosis of gestational diabetes, half may be expected to become diabetic within 15 to 20 years. Gestational diabetes most resembles NIDDM, and although clinically mild, it is worsened by increased body weight, especially in the upper body distribution.[52] Older women with a history of gestational diabetes often develop hypertension, which increases morbidity and mortality. The treatment of hypertension in these women with thiazide diuretics or beta blockers, or the administration of estrogen-containing compounds to relieve menopausal symptoms, may worsen the diabetic state.[53,54] Therefore, older women with a history of gestational diabetes or large babies should be monitored periodically for the emergence of NIDDM.

4. *Diabetes mellitus can be secondary to other diseases or drugs* that promote the development of insulin resistance and hyperglycemia in older individuals in a manner similar to that seen in NIDDM. To control hypertension, arthritis, seizures, depression, or postmenopausal symptoms, older people often are treated with various drugs which also will worsen glucose tolerance (Table 71-3). Progressive pancreatic disease due to chronic pancreatitis, alcoholism, or carcinoma may lead to pancreatectomy and the need for insulin replacement. Other diseases such as Cushing's syndrome, glucagonoma, acromegaly, hemochromatosis, pheochromocytoma, and primary aldosteronism should be considered as possible, but rare, causes of hyperglycemia in the elderly patient.

Implications of Diabetes

What are the implications of a diagnosis of diabetes in older individuals? For normal and diabetic categories of glucose tolerance, the clinical implications are clear. Age-specific mortality rates are consistently higher in overt diabetes from complications of atherosclerosis, especially myocardial infarction and stroke.[55–57] Age, the level of hyperglycemia, and the severity and duration of obesity are major predictors of the natural history of diabetes in most people; however, the morbidity and mortality from CVD in diabetic persons are significantly affected by the coexistence of other risk factors, especially systolic hypertension, hyperlipidemia, cigarette smoking, male gender, and a family history of diabetes.[41,55–57] Since NIDDM is as potent a risk factor for CVD in older women as it is in men, other factors such as sex steroid hormone metabolism, the regional distribution of body fat, physical conditioning status, diet, and insulin resistance require consideration in studies of the pathogenesis of the complications of diabetes in women.[52,58,59]

Whether one is dealing with the disease NIDDM or a condition which is a natural sequela of the aging process, hyperglycemia creates a therapeutic dilemma for the geriatrician. In the absence of complications of atherosclerotic CVD, neuropathy, renal disease, cataracts, or retinopathy in the hyperglycemic older patient at the time of initial evaluation, initially other disorders or drugs should be considered as the cause of hyperglycemia. The most prominent one is obesity, but obese and mildly overweight individuals are often sedentary, and physical inactivity may be equally important in the pathogenesis of hyperglycemia in older people. Obese, older, sedentary individuals often have hypertension requiring treatment with diuretics which may worsen glucose homeostasis and reduce renal perfusion. As renal blood flow declines, renin and angiotensin levels increase, leading to renal hypertension and ultimately a deterioration in renal function. These individuals present with diabetes and nephropathy, yet the natural history of the disease may be due solely to diabetes. Although NIDDM usually does not present in a standard fashion in older patients (Table 71-2), the presence of subtle signs of diabetes such as weight loss or fatigue, impaired vision, nocturia, urinary incontinence, nonspecific dysesthesias and paresthesias, diarrhea, postural hypotension, a recurrent poorly healing peripheral vascular foot lesion, and increased susceptibility to infection usually confirm the diagnosis in the older individual with suspected diabetes. However, this clinical pattern does not occur in all older individuals with hyperglycemia.

If the progressive deterioration in glucose tolerance that accompanies aging represents a stage in the evolution of the diabetic syndrome and the potential for subsequent deleterious complications, then treatment is indicated. Although it is not yet known whether the microvascular complications of neuropathy and retinopathy can be prevented with vigorous treatment of hyperglycemia, the macrovascular complications of NIDDM have a multifactorial origin and tend to progress unless (1) preventive measures are instituted to normalize blood pressure, lipid levels, and body weight; (2) cigarette smoking is eliminated; and (3) hyperglycemia is properly controlled. If the natural history of the diabetic syndrome in older individuals were known (i.e., whether or not the decline in glucose tolerance with advancing age is a disease or a physiologic benign consequence of the aging process), properly designed therapeutic interventions could be initiated to reduce risk for the development of complications from the diabetes. When the appropriate diagnosis is made and therapy initiated, however, the risk of hypoglycemia also increases in older people.

Complications of Diabetes

The economic burden of diabetes in the United States is estimated as requiring between 25 and 30 million hospital days with direct medical costs of $10 billion a year and nearly the same costs for disability and premature death related to the vascular complications of diabetes.[60] The prevalence of diabetes increases with advancing age, and morbidity and mortality from CVD complications are increased in older diabetic patients as well as in borderline diabetic patients when compared with normal older people. The clinical appearance of diabetic complications is related to the duration of the disease; hence most older diabetic patients have many complications. There are three major clinical complications of diabetes in the elderly patient: the most common involves accelerated atherosclerosis of large vessels; the second, microvascular disease of capillary basement membranes in the kidney and retina; and the third, neuropathy causing peripheral sensorimotor defects and autonomic nervous system dysfunction. In the older diabetic patient, these complications increase the incidence of vascular insufficiency and gangrene by 20-fold; hypertension by 3-fold; myocardial infarction by 2.5-fold; and stroke, renal disease, and blindness by 2-fold.[61–65] The pathogeneses of these complications are multifactorial, but they often occur at the same time or shortly after diabetes is diagnosed. This suggests that early detection and treatment of diabetes are probably the best preventive measures.

Chronic Vascular Complications

Vascular complications in diabetes are related to the duration of blood vessel exposure to hyperglycemia and hyperinsulinemia, as well as the coexistent effects of hyperlipidemia, hypertension, obesity, and cigarette smoking, and risk factors for accelerated atherosclerosis. The macrovascular complications of diabetes primarily affect mortality, while the microvascular complications are responsible for chronic morbidity associated with retinopathy, nephropathy, and neuropathy.

Microangiopathy The high incidence of renal disease, retinopathy, and neuropathy in older diabetic patients is likely the result of microvascular disease due to the long duration of untreated diabetes prior to detection. The risk for the development of renal failure and need for life-sustaining dialysis is high in older diabetic patients. These patients tend to do poorly and have many complications, including cardiovascular events, infections, and susceptibility to hypoglycemia. This is because of the long duration of untreated, poorly controlled diabetes, polypharmacy, and the synergistic effects of uremia on atherosclerosis.

Diabetic retinopathy increases in prevalence and severity with the duration of diabetes and poor control of hyperglycemia. Significant retinopathy, especially macular edema, central angiopathy, and neovascularization, may be entirely asymptomatic at the time of diagnosis of diabetes, but shortly thereafter reduced vision or blindness may develop suddenly. Cataracts, glaucoma, and retinal detachment are also common in older diabetic patients and may be difficult to detect on routine examination (see Chap. 39). Regular eye examinations by an ophthalmologist are essential for early diagnosis and treatment to prevent blindness in the older diabetic patient.

Peripheral neuropathy occurs often in older diabetic persons and can be disabling because of severe pain. Sensory involvement is more common than motor, and when combined with severe peripheral vascular disease increases the risk for injury to lower extremities. Older diabetic persons with this combination are prone to diabetic foot ulcers and sepsis. Diabetic patients should check their feet daily, wear comfortable shoes, avoid going barefoot, cut toenails horizontally, and immediately notify their physician of a change in skin color, break in the skin, or drainage from the foot. Pain and muscle atrophy in the hip girdle and lower extremities suggests the presence of diabetic amyotrophy, a painful complication of diabetes that responds poorly to treatment but usually resolves spontaneously in 1 to 2 years. Diabetic autonomic neuropathy also is disabling and affects numerous organ systems. The loss of cardiovascular reflexes is associated with postural hypotension, syncope, arrhythmias, and silent myocardial infarction. The presence of autonomic neuropathy and vascular disease increases risk for impotence, incontinence, and susceptibility to urinary tract infections in older diabetic persons. Gastrointestinal involvement in autonomic neuropathy manifests itself as incapacitating nighttime diarrhea, fecal incontinence, and occasionally constipation with the development of bezoars. Prevention of diabetic neuropathy through early detection of diabetes and aggressive treatment of hyperglycemia and its toxicity on nerve metabolism seems the best treatment, since neuropathic complications respond poorly to drugs.

Macroangiopathy The high incidence of atherosclerosis and vascular compromise which occurs with advancing age in Western societies makes diabetes the prototypic disease for studying accelerated atherosclerosis in aging humans.[41] Data from the Framingham study suggest that with increasing age and duration of diabetes, both the hypertensive and the hyperlipidemic diabetic person is at heightened risk for CVD complications and early mortality from myocardial infarction and stroke.[41] Every manifestation of CVD occurs with increased frequency and severity in the diabetic person, and almost 75 percent of deaths in diabetic persons are attributable to coronary artery disease (CAD). NIDDM is characterized by high levels of plasma triglycerides, cholesterol, and apoprotein B and reduced levels of high-density lipoprotein cholesterol (HDL-C) and apoprotein A-I levels.[66] The heightened prevalence of these lipid abnormalities, coupled with hyperglycemia, obesity, hyperinsulinemia, and hypertension, common in NIDDM, promotes the development of atherosclerosis (see also Chap. 44).[41,66–68]

Obesity and hypertension, the most common risk factors of CVD in older diabetic persons, profoundly worsen the severity of atherosclerotic vascular disease to raise morbidity and mortality from macro- and microvascular complications in the older diabetic person. Hyperinsulinemia and insulin resistance promote atherogenesis in these persons through direct effects on the vessel wall to increase smooth muscle cell proliferation, and indirectly through effects on lipoprotein metabolism and intracellular cholesterol accumulation.[41] The development of arteriosclerotic complications in NIDDM also is related to genetic factors. The prevalence of impaired glucose tolerance, NIDDM, and risk factors for CVD are increased in family members of patients with NIDDM.[56] In diabetic persons, atherogenesis is accelerated by various cellular processes which interact with platelets, macrophages, lipoproteins, and cholesterol esters within arterial walls to form atheroma. These processes include nonenzymatic glycosylation of proteins to advanced glycosylation end products;[69] autoxidative glycosylation,[70] and increased production of free radicals and lipid peroxidation;[71] increased secretion of hormones (insulin, insulinlike growth factor, growth hormone), intrinsic growth factors (platelet-derived and macrophage-derived growth factors, cytokines) which increase platelet aggregation, smooth muscle cell proliferation, and connective tissue synthesis;[41,72] and reduced antioxidant defense systems[73] (see also Chap. 44). In addition, in diabetes the insoluble collagen fraction and matrix of the vessel wall become resistant to digestion by collagenase and enriched in glycosaminoglycan complexes and glycosylated protein products.[69] Coexistent hyperinsulinemia and hyperlipidemia promote atherosclerosis in this environment, narrowing blood vessels and leading to cardiovascular, cerebrovascular, and peripheral vascular disease with the resultant complications of heart attack, stroke, ulcers, and gangrene.

Risk for CVD is even more pronounced in women with NIDDM than in men; hence, diabetes seems to eliminate the protective advantage in relation to atherosclerotic complications afforded aging women over aging men. This may be related to the upper body fat distribution and hyperinsulinemia characteristic of older women with NIDDM. The CVD syndromes of silent ischemia and silent myocardial infarction are more common in diabetic than in nondiabetic persons, and their complications are greater.[74] This is because of the nature of the neuropathic disease associated with diabetes. Pain perception is reduced in older diabetic persons, and functional abnormalities in contractile properties of the myocardium lead to the development of microaneurysms, interstitial fibrosis, and myocardial degeneration. This results in myopathy and causes diabetic persons to have more congestive heart failure, arrhythmias, and conduction defects during ischemic episodes and more myocardial infarctions than nondiabetic persons. All these factors increase mortality during myocardial infarction 2-fold in the diabetic man and 4.5-fold in the diabetic woman when compared with nondiabetic controls.[42]

The multifactorial etiology of atherosclerotic complications in older diabetic persons makes understanding the pathogenesis of atherogenesis in this chronic disease of paramount importance to reduce the high morbidity, mortality, and medical costs of diabetes.[41] Whether or not the heightened incidence of vascular complications in older diabetic patients can be prevented or delayed by early detection of diabetes and by aggressive medical and/or surgical intervention in patients with atherosclerotic vascular disease to ultimately reduce morbidity and prolong survival needs to be determined.

Acute Metabolic Emergencies

Hypoglycemia Regardless of the therapy required to control hyperglycemia or manage other medical conditions in the older diabetic patient, caution must be exercised because older patients may be sensitive to glucose-lowering drugs and at risk for hypoglycemia. Hypoglycemia is the most frequent acute emergency in older diabetic patients and is extremely serious because these episodes may be associated with and may precipitate cerebrovascular accidents, myocardial infarction, coma, and death. Thus, in the elderly diabetic person hypoglycemia may be even more serious than the symptoms and consequences of diabetes itself. This is because older diabetic persons often have preexistent CVD; often have autonomic neuropathic dysfunction with impaired counterregulatory adrenergic hormone responses to hypoglycemia ("hypoglycemic unawareness"); and often live alone, which when accompanied by limited mobility compromises their ability to access lifesaving therapy. The clinical manifestations of hypoglycemia in the elderly patient may be more nonspecific than in younger individuals. Symptoms related to activation of the sympathetic nervous system (neurogenic) may be blunted, while those caused by neuronal dysfunction secondary to glucose deprivation (neuroglycopenic) are generally nonspecific and may be difficult to distinguish from already-existent manifestations of central nervous system and neuropsychiatric dysfunction (Table 71-4).

The major causes of hypoglycemia in elderly patients (Table 71-5) are the same as in younger patients, except the threshold for hypoglycemia may be lower, symptoms may be more protean, and morbidity and mortality may be higher in some older diabetic patients. Drugs are the major cause of hypoglycemia in the elderly diabetic patient because diabetes-related complications can affect renal and hepatic drug metabolism, reduce blood flow to organs, alter gastrointestinal absorption, and change drug pharmacokinetics to increase blood levels of the drug. The decline of renal function due to microangiopathy (diabetic nephropathy) and atherosclerotic disease reduces renal metabolism and excretion of sulfonylureas and insulin, often by as much as 50 percent.

TABLE 71-4

Clinical Manifestations of Hypoglycemia

Neuroglycopenic	Neurogenic
Fatigue or listlessness	Palpitations
Inappropriate behavior	Diaphoresis
Cognitive impairment	Anxiety or agitation
Fatigue or dizziness or faintness	Tremor
Focal neurologic defect	Pallor
Hunger	Hypertension
Paresthesias	
Seizures	
Loss of consciousness or coma	
Death	

TABLE 71-5

Causes of Hypoglycemia

1. Drugs: insulin, sulfonylureas, alcohol, other polypharmacy
2. Organ dysfunction: renal, liver, cardiovascular, central and autonomic nervous system, sepsis, gastrointestinal, immobility (musculoskeletal)
3. Poor and irregularly scheduled nutrition, anorexia, social factors (poverty, living alone)
4. Hormonal deficiency: glucagon, epinephrine, growth hormone, cortisol
5. Non-beta cell or beta cell tumors

Overmedication with insulin and oral hypoglycemic agents can occur in the older diabetic patient because of poor vision, memory impairment, and difficulty with drug administration due to arthritis and reduced flexibility. Whatever the medical condition requiring drug therapy, the incidence of adverse side effects and drug interactions is increased in the elderly patient (see Chap. 24). Older diabetic patients frequently have other medical conditions, like hypertension and arthritis, which require treatment with drugs which independently may cause hypoglycemia through drug interactions with sulfonylureas, or by blunting counterregulatory responses necessary for recovery from hypoglycemia (Table 71-3). The surreptitious use of alcohol should be considered when the cause of hypoglycemia is unclear and depression, sleep disturbances, dementia, unexplained trauma, and neurologic disturbances are present. Many social factors affect the management of older diabetic patients and may increase the risk of hypoglycemia. Poor and irregular nutrition, immobility, cognitive impairment, living alone with inadequate social supports, poverty, and lack of appropriate diabetes education regarding prevention of complications are all contributing factors.

The treatment of hypoglycemia involves the provision of exogenous glucose by mouth in mild cases, or intravenously (IV) in more severe cases in which the mental status of the patient is compromised. The stimulation of endogenous glucose production with substantaneous (SC) or intramuscular (IM) 1-mg glucagon therapy is less optimal in the elderly patient in whom liver glycogen stores may be reduced, but such therapy should be available for use by family members when oral therapy is not feasible and emergency medical care has not yet arrived. Ideally, the plasma glucose concentration should be documented prior to treatment, but in patients who think they are hypoglycemic or are semi- or unconscious when the suspicion of hypoglycemia is high, the dangers of untreated hypoglycemia outweigh that of unnecessary glucose administration.

Mild hypoglycemia, with limited symptoms and neurologic impairment, can be treated with 10 to 20 g of available carbohydrate in a drink that contains complex carbohydrates, such as milk. In more severe hypoglycemia, oral carbohydrate may still suffice, but orange juice, liquid glucose (syrups), or glucose tablets are preferred because of their higher glucose content and more rapid absorption. Complex carbohydrates then should be administered because of their longer duration of action. In patients who cannot take oral feedings because of impaired sensorium, neurologic deficits, or coma, IV glucose injection (25 g initially) followed by continuous infusion of a glucose solution (5 or 10% based on the severity of the hypoglycemia) should be given with the 25-g bolus repeated in 10 minutes if the patient is still unconscious. Once the patient is conscious, a 5 to 10% glucose solution should be infused continuously to keep the blood glucose level within the normal range until the cause of the hypoglycemia is determined and the patient is eating normally. This treatment may need to be continued for 48 to 72 hours in cases of overmedication with sulfonylureas, drug interactions, sepsis, or suspicion of tumor-producing hypoglycemia. Once the patient is stable, short- and long-term measures must be instituted to prevent hypoglycemia by correction of the inciting causes.

Hyperosmolar Hyperglycemic Nonketotic Coma (HHNC) HHNC affects older patients more frequently than ketoacidosis and is characterized by the insidious onset of drowsiness, ultimately resulting in frank coma.[75,76] The average age of patients with this syndrome is 65 years, and the condition is associated with a 40 to 70 percent mortality rate. HHNC may develop insidiously over a period of days in patients without previously diagnosed diabetes. A very high index of suspicion is essential, since early diagnosis and aggressive therapy reduce mortality. Unfortunately, misdiagnosis is common. The typical patient gradually becomes sleepy, confused, or semicomatose; appears dehydrated; and may have localizing neurologic signs that can be mistaken for a stroke. There may be a family history of diabetes, and about half the patients are known to have mild NIDDM. In most cases there is a history of several days of increasing polyuria and thirst, acute or chronic treatment with certain precipitating drugs, or a history of a recent medical procedure known to be associated with HHNC (Table 71-6).

A critical feature of HHNC is that thirst becomes impaired (possibly due to effects of severe hyperosmolarity, hyperglycemia, or concomitant drug therapy on the hypothalamic thirst center), resulting in a cycle of progressive dehydration, volume depletion, and hyperosmolarity. Reduced renal function and an inability to respond to hyperglycemic hyperosmolarity may predispose patients to progress to a hyperosmolar state. The reason for the absence of ketosis in the presence of severe hyperglycemia and insulin deficiency remains mysterious. Insulin must be administered to normalize glucose metabolism in the presence of a severe osmotic diuresis and dehydration.

Clinical features of HHNC include severe hyperglycemia (plasma glucose level usually greater than 600 mg/dl) in the absence of ketoacidosis, profound dehydration, and variable neurologic signs ranging from confusion to coma. The severity of the depressed sensorium is directly related to the degree of hyperosmolarity mediated by intracellular dehydration of the brain. Serum osmolarity often exceeds 350 osmol/kg water, and hemoconcentration may be followed by both arterial and venous thrombosis, which are frequent complications of HHNC. A massive osmotic diuresis due to prolonged, severe hyperglycemia results in a greater loss of water than of electrolytes. Serum sodium and potassium concentrations are usually high but may be normal or low depending on the balance between the intravascular and extravascular volume and the history of previous therapy with diuretics.

The goal of therapy for HHNC is to correct the severe volume depletion (up to one-fourth of body water may be lost) and the hyperosmolar state. A careful search must be made for correctable underlying precipitating factors (infections, inflammatory processes, vascular accidents, and diuretics). Fluid

TABLE 71-6

Precipitating Factors for HHNC

Drugs	Procedures
Diuretics (thiazides, furosemide, diazoxide, chlorthalidone, ethacrynic acid)	Hemodialysis and peritoneal dialysis
Immunosuppressive agents (glucocorticoids)	Intravenous hyperalimentation
Propranolol	Intravenous dye injection (pyelogram, cardiac catheterization, etc.)
Phenytoin	
Cimetidine	
CNS-active drugs (chlorpromazine)	

replacement is the cornerstone of treatment, and early insulin administration is needed to reduce the osmotic diuresis caused by hyperglycemia. Insulin should be given regularly IM or IV; 25 units is recommended as an initial dose, and this should be repeated in 2 hours if the blood glucose level does not fall more than 100 mg/ml. Often no additional insulin is required after the initial dose. If hypotension is present, isotonic saline should be infused initially to prevent shock. This should be followed by several liters of half-normal saline with added potassium to restore intravascular volume. In older patients with CVD, central venous pressure, cardiac hemodynamics, and urine output must be monitored to avoid congestive heart failure and acute renal failure. A total of 6 to 18 liters of fluid in 24 to 36 hours may be necessary, with 8 to 10 liters being the average. Urine output, electrolytes, the electrocardiogram, and central venous pressure require constant monitoring. Five percent glucose should be added to solutions when the plasma glucose level falls below 250 mg/dl. Following recovery from this metabolic disorder, the older patient rarely needs insulin to manage what is usually a mild diabetic state.

Diabetic Ketoacidosis (DKA) Worsening of hyperglycemia despite adherence to treatment may occur due to an increase in the severity of diabetes, causing insulinopenia and the development of ketoacidosis. Older patients who are prone to DKA often have coexistent disease and are lean or cachectic. These patients not only require insulin to prevent serious ketoacidosis, coma, and death, but also need aggressive treatment of any coexistent disease.

The incidence of DKA in older diabetic patients is lower than that in younger diabetic patients, but the fatality rate is higher. The heightened mortality reflects the serious nature of the underlying diseases that may precipitate ketoacidosis in older diabetic patients (e.g., sepsis, surgical emergency, and acute vascular occlusion) and the possibility that DKA may present in an atypical fashion with stroke or confusion, causing a delay in diagnosis and therapy.

DKA in older patients must be distinguished from septic shock, since hyperventilation, hypotension, oliguria, peripheral vascular collapse, central nervous system disturbances, and low plasma bicarbonate levels are common to both conditions. Infection is a leading cause of DKA in older patients[77] and may be present in as many as 40 percent of patients, with septicemia in about 6 percent. Diabetic persons are particularly susceptible to urinary tract infections, candidiasis, cholecystitis, pneumoccal pneumonia, influenza, and staphylococcal skin infections. Pseudomonas infection may cause malignant otitis externa or necrotizing fasciitis in older diabetic persons. All infections are more common in diabetic persons, and when established, run a more florid course. Mortality from DKA is much higher when associated with infection than with other precipitating causes. As in HHNC, it is imperative that a thorough search for the site of infection be instituted and appropriate therapy started promptly if infection is suspected as the underlying cause of ketoacidosis.

Major factors responsible for death in ketoacidosis are infection, arterial thrombosis, and shock.[78] Older diabetic persons are more likely to have preexisting atherosclerosis resulting in compromised circulatory dynamics, aggravated by reduced cardiac output and autonomic neuropathy. Hyperviscosity, dehydration, a procoagulant state with increased platelet aggregation, and reduced oxygen delivery to tissues increase risk for arterial occlusion in the older diabetic patient, even for several days after successful treatment of ketoacidosis. Hypovolemic shock is also responsible for a large proportion of fatalities from DKA in elderly patients. The degree of the initial intravascular volume depletion appears to be a major prognostic index for the subsequent therapeutic outcome. In conditions in which blood volume is reduced, transfusion may be necessary to restore tissue perfusion and oxygen transport. Commonly, patients may have lost 10 percent of their body weight as fluid; volume replacement with half-normal saline is less effective than with isotonic saline. Aggressive insulin therapy during DKA often transiently lowers an already-depleted intravascular volume; thus, fluids must be aggressively replaced during treatment as rapidly as required to restore intravascular volume promptly and to prevent shock and oliguria. As in HHNC, it is necessary to monitor central venous pressure, cardiac hemodynamics, and urine output during rapid hydration to prevent congestive heart failure and renal failure. Cerebral edema, a complication caused by rapid correction of hyperosmolarity in children with DKA, occurs rarely in the elderly patient but is of concern if acidosis is severe and large doses of insulin and fluid are required.

In the treatment of DKA, normal circulating effective insulin levels can be achieved by low-dose IM or IV administration of regular insulin, e.g., 5 to 10 units IM every hour or 0.15 U/kg normal body weight as a bolus IV, followed by a continuous IV infusion of 0.15 U/kg per hour. These are the most effective, simplest routes of insulin delivery and minimize the development of late-onset hypoglycemia. Frequent monitoring of physiologic responses is required (glucose, potassium, and bicarbonate levels, and urine output), and insulin dosage, fluids, and electrolytes should be increased when the glucose-lowering response and correction of acidosis is inadequate. In the patient who did not require insulin prior to the episode of DKA, treatment of the underlying, precipitating disease may cause a rapid fall in insulin requirements and increased susceptibility to hypoglycemia.

Management of Diabetes

General Considerations

The goals of treatment of older patients with NIDDM are to achieve good control of hyperglycemia in the hope of minimizing long-term organ complications and to provide good medical care while simultaneously avoiding the risks of vigorous treatment—the most serious of which is hypoglycemia. It is estimated that treatment with insulin or oral sulfonylureas is needed for only one-half of older diabetic patients; hence, the geriatrician must select carefully those older diabetic patients for whom drug therapy is required. Many elderly patients already have macrovascular and microvascular complications at the time diabetes is discovered, and it is important to prevent these conditions from worsening by attempting to achieve euglycemia. Persistent hyperglycemia results in glycosuria, which may cause an osmotic diuresis leading to fluid and electrolyte depletion. The polyuria initially may become symptomatic as incontinence, but the development of dehydration and sodium depletion due to osmotic diuresis requires treatment to prevent hypotension, weakness, hyperosmolarity, and their complications. The persistent loss of calories in the urine and worsening hyperglycemia due to insulin deficiency will lead to increased fatty acid mobilization, lipid oxidation, and protein catabolism resulting in muscle wasting and cachexia. The loss of weight, weakness, and instability impair motor function leading to immobility, susceptibility to infection, restriction to bed, development of pressure ulcers, and other complications. Correction of insulin deficiency, refeeding, and maintenance of euglycemia reverse the cycle of metabolic imbalance.

The NIH Consensus Conference on Diet and Exercise in Non-insulin Dependent Diabetes Mellitus[27] concluded that achievement and maintenance of normal weight is the cornerstone of therapy for NIDDM. Oral agents should be added only as necessary to maintain blood glucose levels near normal. Exercise training, on the other hand, in the obese patient with NIDDM (80 percent of NIDDM patients are obese) has variable effects on metabolic control, and in some patients these may be small. Despite the minimal impact of physical exercise alone in the treatment of the obese patient with NIDDM, regular aerobic exercise was recommended as a useful adjunct to dietary therapy in some patients. The efficacy of smoking cessation, dietary changes, physical conditioning, aggressive treatment of hypertension and hyperlipidemia, or combinations thereof in preventing the macrovascular and microvascular complications of diabetes are unfortunately unknown, especially in the elderly patient, in whom the socioeconomic costs and morbidity and mortality from atherosclerotic complications related to diabetes are the highest. Diagnostic criteria and specific therapeutic guidelines for the management of hyperglycemia and other metabolic consequences of diabetes are needed if the conundrum—whether or not to treat NIDDM in the asymptomatic older individual—is to be resolved and the heightened prevalence of vascular complications and increased morbidity and mortality from diabetes mellitus is to be reduced in older people.

Older diabetic patients frequently have other diseases which require additional therapy, and there are special conditions associated with the aging process that may affect the treatment of diabetes (Table 71-7).

TABLE 71-7

Special Issues in Care of Older Diabetic Patients

General

Activity level: gait, coordination, flexibility, strength, agility
Special senses: vision, taste, smell, hearing, position, hunger, thirst
Diet: appetite, food preferences, dentition and salivation, ability to prepare food, feed self, and eat (tremor, arthritis), body weight
Drugs: other medications and their potential for adverse interactions (toxicity), drug excretion and dose adjustment, alcohol, caffeine, allergy
Social factors: living alone, poverty, hygiene, resistance to change in habits, education
General (chronic): weight loss, fever, neoplasia, abscess, tuberculosis

Diseases (by system)

Cardiovascular: hypertension, postural hypotension, ischemia (silent), previous infarction, arrhythmias, peripheral vascular insufficiency, cardiomyopathy
Pulmonary: smoking, bronchitis, hypoxia, asthma, chronic obstructive lung disease
Central nervous: mental status, memory, sensory perception, motor and autonomic function, tremor, stroke
Renal: uremia, nephrotic syndrome, papillitis, pyelonephritis
Gastrointestinal: motility, constipation, diarrhea, nutrient absorption, blood loss
Hepatobiliary: obstruction, inflammation, gallstones
Hematologic: anemia, bleeding, bruisability
Musculoskeletal: arthritis, deformity, weakness, wasting
Integumentary: infections, rashes, poor healing
Neuropsychiatric: cognitive and affective disorders, need for supervision, dementia, sleep behavior
Infections: pruritus, urinary tract, otitis, foot ulcers, cholecystitis, fasciitis

These special conditions should be understood so that optimal therapy can be provided. First, a complete assessment of the patient with a full history, physical examination, and laboratory evaluation is necessary. Attention should focus on general (chronic) conditions such as dietary habits, weight loss, chills, fever, inactivity, gastrointestinal function, and special senses, i.e., vision, etc.; coexistent disease of the cardiovascular, pulmonary, renal, hepatobiliary, and central nervous systems; the use of other drugs, especially ones that affect glycemic control (Table 71-3); integrity of the musculoskeletal and integumentary systems, especially the feet; mental status and cognitive function; and the social situation. The laboratory evaluation should include an electrocardiogram, measurement of the functional status of the major organ systems and plasma lipids, urinalysis, and a 24-hour urine collection for the measurement of glucose levels, protein levels, and creatinine clearance.

Treatment goals should focus initially on the presence of coexistent medical and social factors, other than diabetes itself, which may affect metabolic control. Coexistent diseases should be treated when possible with medications which do not alter glucose homeostasis (Table 71-3). Hypertension is common in older diabetic persons and acts additively with diabetes to accelerate vascular disease and cardiovascular complications. Therefore, early intervention is important; however, antihypertensive therapy brings new risks to older diabetic persons. As recommended in the treatment of hyperglycemia, nonpharmacologic therapy of diet (low salt, hypocaloric if weight reduction is goal) and exercise is the first step. Diuretic therapy is the next choice, but in the older diabetic patient thiazides are associated with worsening glycemic control, hyperlipidemia, hyperuricemia, hypokalemia, and risk of HHNC. Low doses may avoid these side effects, but if metabolic abnormalities develop, a potassium-sparing diuretic can be tried in patients with normal renal function. Serum potassium levels should be monitored, as the risk for hyperkalemia is higher in elderly persons. Angiotensin-converting enzyme (ACE) inhibitors should be considered as the first-line antihypertensive agent in diabetic patients because of their efficacy in lowering blood pressure, and in reducing intraglomerular pressure and proteinuria without a deterioration in glomerular filtration or metabolic function.[79] Calcium channel blockers are also effective in lowering blood pressure without major side effects, but beta blockers, alpha blockers, reserpine, alpha methyldopa, and clonidine are less effective because of side effects and worsening hyperglycemia, reduced hypoglycemic awareness, and postural hypotension.[80]

The next treatment goals involve counseling in diet and physical activity habits. It is often essential to involve family and other professionals (dietitian, nurse, and exercise physiologist) in this aspect of care, so that the patient can readily agree to the dietary and activity changes built around already-established patterns of life. This is of particular importance in the older patient with central nervous system dysfunction, limitations in activity, or impairments in special senses. Social factors, such as living alone without social supports, low socioeconomic and financial status, immobility, and lower educational level affect the older individual's ability to cope with diabetes management and influence compliance. Therefore, an interdisciplinary team evaluation (geriatrician, nurse, social worker, dietitian, and psychologist) is recommended, with the individualization of the treatment regimen.

Dietary Guidelines

The diet program should address factors such as dentition, salivation, and altered taste which may affect food preference in older patients. The diet should fulfill the principles of the American Diabetes Association Diet[81] for proper nutrition. These principles include, in addition to the restriction of calories in overweight patients to promote weight loss of 1/2 to 1 lb/week, a diet whose composition is enriched in complex carbohydrates and fiber to 55 to 60 percent of daily caloric intake. For most patients the diet should contain <30 percent of calories as fat (<10 percent as saturated fat) and not more than 300 mg/day cholesterol; but the diet may need adjustment to treat hyperlipidemia according to the guidelines of the American Heart Association.[82]

Weight reduction and its maintenance are the cornerstone of therapy for the obese, older patient with NIDDM.[27] In addition to improving glucose tolerance and insulin sensitivity, weight loss also lowers blood pressure as well as plasma cholesterol and triglyceride levels, and raises HDL-C levels in most obese diabetic patients. Once sufficient weight is lost, a weight-maintaining diet should be determined. The diet plan should be written out for the patient and for those who prepare the food. Regular follow-up sessions with the patient and caretaker are recommended for continuing education and to monitor body weight and compliance.[83] The ratio of low risk to high benefit makes dietary therapy attractive for many older diabetic patients.

Exercise Program

In view of the reported increase in insulin sensitivity, improvement of glucose tolerance, reduction in body weight, and improvement in plasma lipid levels and blood pressure achieved by exercise training in some diabetic patients, regular physical exercise is advocated as an adjunct to diet in the treatment of NIDDM (see Chap. 7). In the treated patient with NIDDM, exercise training often results in the reduction in dosage or discontinuation of oral sulfonylurea agents. However, most of the benefits of exercise training are based on results from high-intensity training programs in young and middle-aged individuals and cannot be readily extrapolated to diabetic patients over 65 years of age. Since atherosclerotic complications, renal disease, retinopathy, and musculoskeletal and neurologic dysfunction are common in older diabetic patients, involvement in programs of physical activity should be preceded by a thorough physical examination with special attention to the vascular system, extremities, and eyes. Functional capacity should be determined during a physician-administered exercise treadmill stress test with electrocardiographic, blood pressure, and symptom monitoring to identify patients with silent ischemia, exercise-induced arrhythmias, hypertension, or autonomic dysfunction causing vascular and central nervous system instability during exercise. All risks for adverse physiologic (cardiovascular, pulmonary, neurologic, metabolic, and musculoskeletal) responses during exercise are best determined during this test. Patients with abnormal exercise tests should be referred for further evaluation by a specialist in the area of dysfunction.

The exercise prescription should be based on the patient's functional capacity, as determined by physical examination and the results of an exercise treadmill test. If oxygen consumption can be measured during the exercise test, functional capacity can be expressed in ml(kg^{-1})(min^{-1}) oxygen consumed and related to heart rate. The intensity of activity can then be defined, with the peak and average intensity of exercise estimated by determining 60 and 85 percent of the functional capacity. This can be easily related to heart rate, and the target heart rate during exercise can be calculated as the training intensity or percentage of functional capacity × (maximal exercise heart rate − resting heart rate) + resting heart rate. The energy expenditure for most physical activities is calculated in METs [1 MET − resting oxygen consumption = 3.5 ml$(kg^{-1})(min^{-1})$, or 1 kcal $(kg^{-1})(h^{-1})$] and extrapolated to a safe range of exercise intensity (4 to 8 METs) for most older individuals who display no cardiovascular limitations during maximal exercise testing. Target heart rate is then monitored during exercise sessions as an index of training intensity. It is also worthwhile to monitor perceived exertion during exercise testing in older individuals using a visual analogue scale, where 6 is the least and 20 is the most intense, to monitor subjective responses during training.

Initial physical activity should be supervised and undertaken in a slow, progressive manner to ensure that the patient's capabilities are not exceeded, injury is prevented, and cardiovascular (blood pressure, pulse) responses are safe and appropriate. Aerobic conditioning (walking, swimming, stationary bicycling, and jogging) is the preferred type of exercise because it involves movement of major muscle groups and the energy expenditure (METs) is usually known; these aerobic activities tend to enhance glucose utilization to the greatest extent. Attention should be given to proper foot care and avoidance of injury during exercise. Exercises associated with straining and breath holding, such as low-repetition weight lifting and strength-training isometric exercises, are high tension and may raise blood pressure and increase risk of retinal detachment, vitreous hemorrhage, stroke, and albuminuria. Thus, strength or resistive training should be high repetition, low tension and supervised by an exercise physiologist. The duration, frequency, and progression of exercise should be under frequent monitoring with reassessment of exercise capacity on the treadmill with electrocardiographic monitoring if hemodynamic instability develops.

Compliance with Diet and Exercise Regimen

Compliance is the major problem in maintaining diet and the optimal body weight to control hyperglycemia in diabetic patients. Recidivism is high, and few obese patients successfully maintain good eating habits and weight loss after completion of structured programs. Physical activity may be an effective adjunct to diet therapy because it enhances weight loss by increasing utilization of ingested calories and may improve the patient's psychosocial state even during periods of caloric restriction. Regular physical exercise, by increasing energy expenditure, may permit fewer dietary restrictions during weight loss. Guidelines are needed for the most effective treatment and maintenance programs for obese older patients with NIDDM.

Older people fear injury during exercise, and caution is recommended to avoid this complication by prescribing a slow progression of exercise intensity, frequency, and duration. Rarely does an older person return to a program following an injury precipitated during exercise. The use of behavior modification techniques in conjunction with the weight loss or exercise program may improve the treatment outcome, but prolonged maintenance varies directly with the success of the follow-up program. Peer interaction, frequent telephone contact by the therapist, and frequent maintenance meetings seem to produce the best success. When the patient is unable to comply and hyperglycemia persists, drug therapy is indicated to improve metabolic control and avoid complications.

Drug Therapy

In addition to the treatment of hyperglycemia in the older patient with NIDDM, other measures of management include the treatment of systolic and diastolic hypertension and hyperlipidemia, and the cessation of cigarette smoking. The successful management of these conditions is of utmost importance because of their heightened prevalence and impact on the progression of atherosclerosis in diabetic persons; their control has the potential to reduce the incidence of cardiovascular complications in diabetic patients.

Treatment with oral sulfonylureas or insulin should be considered in the older diabetic patient with persistent symptomatic hyperglycemia (polyuria, polyphagia, polydipsia) causing weight loss, fatigue, weakness, and recurrent infection. This type of patient usually responds to therapy with oral sulfonylureas, provided that there is concurrent adherence to diet and exercise regimens. Twenty percent of older diabetic patients are lean and may not respond to oral sulfonylureas because they are insulinopenic. Older diabetic patients with multiple risk factors for metabolic and vascular complications which are worsened by persistent hyperglycemia require aggressive treatment. These patients are prone to infections, have deteriorating renal function and retinopathy, and are at risk for life-threatening acidosis during stress.[84] In general, these patients tend to do poorly owing to the coexistence of multiple vascular complications from NIDDM, but better control of hyperglycemia and risk factors for atherosclerosis may be achieved in some patients with strict adherence to diet, physical activity, sulfonylurea or insulin therapy, and the addition of a lipid-lowering drug.

Several sulfonylurea drugs of differing potency and duration of action are available for use as oral hypoglycemic agents (Table 71-8).[85] The use of these drugs to control hyperglycemia; prevent neurologic, renal, and ophthalmologic complications; and retard the progression of vascular disease in patients of any age with NIDDM remains uncertain as a result of the controversial findings of the University Group Diabetes Program study. The metabolic advantages of oral

TABLE 71-8

Oral Sulfonylurea Drugs

Sulfonylurea	Dosage (day^{-1}), mg	Onset of Action, h	Duration of Action, h	Route of Excretion/Activity of Metabolite
1. First-generation				
Tolbutamide	500–3000	0.5–1.0	6–12	Urine/inactive
Tolazamide	100–1000	4–6	12–24	Urine/inactive
Chlorpropamide	100–500	1–2	24–90	Urine/active or unchanged
2. Second-generation				
Glipizide	2.5–40	1–3	12–18	Urine/inactive
Glyburide	1.25–20	0.5–1	16–24	50% urine/active 50% bile/active

sulfonylureas over adequate doses of insulin are not clear,[86] even though their mode of action affects the major underlying metabolic abnormalities in NIDDM, i.e., peripheral insulin resistance, increased hepatic glucose production, and impaired insulin secretion. Benefits of oral sulfonylurea therapy in older patients, other than the convenience of oral medication, include a reduction in the risk of HHNC and DKA, a high degree of efficacy, and a relative ease of acceptance without need of the major behavioral changes required by insulin therapy.[87] However, these drugs have no place in the acute management of IDDM, DKA, or HHNC.

There are several problems associated with the use of sulfonylureas to control hyperglycemia, and these seem to occur more often and may be more severe in the elderly population. The most serious is prolonged hypoglycemia, probably related to irregular and reduced caloric intake and the decrease in drug metabolism common in the elderly patient. Older people receiving these agents must eat regularly, as they may be less likely to recognize hypoglycemic symptoms or mount an adequate counterregulatory hormone response (catecholamines, glucagon, and growth hormone) to maintain glucose homeostasis.

Treatment with oral sulfonylureas should begin at a low dose in older patients because they may be exquisitely sensitive to these drugs. We advise the use of second-generation sulfonylureas because the risk for hypoglycemia may be lower than with the longer-acting first-generation oral sulfonylureas. Second-generation oral sulfonylureas bind nonionically to albumin and have a lower risk for displacement by anionic drugs, as was seen with the first-generation oral agent chlorpropamide. There is virtually no evidence of an antidiuretic effect resulting in hyponatremia with the second-generation drugs, although rare cases have occurred in patients with renal disease on diuretic therapy. Both glyburide and glipizide are usually administered once a day and are of comparable efficacy in lowering glucose levels in older patients with NIDDM. Although the half-life of glyburide is longer than that of glipizide and its metabolites are active, an advantage of glyburide over glipizide is its dual clearance by the liver and kidney, which may reduce the risk of hypoglycemia in patients with impaired renal or hepatic function.[85]

There are three types of secondary failure with oral sulfonylurea agents, all of which occur often in older people. In the first, there is progression of disease, and glycemic control is inadequate despite maximal doses of oral sulfonylureas and adherence to diet and exercise regimens. This type of failure occurs most often in lean older people, in whom combined therapy with oral agents and insulin may be successful. This should be used only in patients capable of home blood glucose monitoring, as the risk of nocturnal hypoglycemia may be increased in older patients, and evening insulin should be administered with caution. The results of combined therapy are highly variable, and controlled studies are needed to determine the characteristics of patients most likely to respond favorably. In the second type of failure, there is a temporary and usually reversible deterioration in glycemic control during periods of illness, infection, or stress. Insulin treatment is needed at these times, and oral therapy usually can be reinstated when the acute problem resolves. The third and most common failure associated with oral sulfonylurea therapy is dietary noncompliance. In such cases insulin therapy transiently improves hyperglycemia, but side fluctuations in glucose levels and the metabolic effects of increasing doses of insulin can promote overeating and weight gain. Intensive dietary counseling, behavioral therapy, and caretaker education may help some of these patients. In the more obese noncompliant patient, hospitalization for very low caloric feeding may be considered.

Regimens for insulin administration in older diabetic patients do not differ from those routinely used for younger diabetic patients, but the goals of management should be modified. Attempts to "normalize" blood glucose levels completely by intensive insulinization carry the risk of hypoglycemia and precipitation of vascular accidents in an already compromised vascular system and should therefore be avoided. It is almost always possible to reduce plasma glucose levels to the desired level with insulin. The critical decision is to determine what glucose level is desired and whether there is risk of severe hypoglycemia. It may be appropriate to involve the patient and family in this decision. Urine glucose testing is an inadequate way to monitor therapeutic response, not only because of the usual poor correlation of glucosuria with blood glucose levels, but also because of the elevated and variable renal threshold for glucose excretion with aging. Home blood glucose monitoring in the initial stages of insulin therapy, with measurement of glycosylated hemoglobin levels for assessment of control in the more stable patient, are useful approaches to long-term management. Impairment of vision may require the use of premixed insulin in a supply of disposable syringes, or devices that permit the accurate withdrawal of insulin from the vial. Such patients also may be candidates for therapy with oral agents and should be enrolled in a visiting nurse program.

In summary, the treatment of overweight older diabetic patients may not require insulin or oral sulfonylureas; compliance with diet and increased physical activity regimens usually improves insulin sensitivity and lowers blood glucose levels. However, many elderly patients have persistent hyperglycemia (despite attempts to adhere to diet and exercise regimens). Such patients can be treated initially with an oral sulfonylurea. The use of a second-generation agent, glipizide or glyburide, is recommended over the first-generation agents chlorpropamide, tolazamide, or tolbutamide because of their more rapid absorption and metabolism, and possibly lower risk of drug interactions, hyponatremia, and hypoglycemia. The risks of treatment with either oral sulfonylurea or insulin, particularly hypoglycemia, need to be considered in the older diabetic patient. In the absence of evidence that tight control of glycemia in the normal range reduces the risk of diabetic complications in older individuals, it seems prudent to manage the older diabetic patient conservatively by limiting the risk of hypoglycemia and balancing the control of hyperglycemia, hyperlipidemia, and hypertension at levels to prevent the progression of vascular disease and maintain an optimal lifestyle.

CONCLUDING REMARKS

Aging and diabetes express their morbidity through common mechanisms leading to the development of micro- and macrovascular complications involving the heart, eyes, kidneys, and nervous system. Macrovascular disease (atherosclerosis) is the most common feature of diabetes in the elderly population, the age group most susceptible to the clinical consequences of atherosclerosis. Diabetes accelerates the atherosclerotic process, primarily through direct effects on the vascular wall, but also due to coexistent hyperlipidemia, hyperinsulinemia, and abnormal cellular function common to the disease, and the high prevalence of comorbid diseases, especially hypertension and renal disease.

Interactions among the social (lifestyle) and biological changes that accompany aging can lead to a pathophysiologic condition resembling diabetes, but the clinical presentation is often subtle and may not include fasting hyperglycemia or clinical complications of diabetes. This condition often improves after weight loss, modification of the diet, and an increase in physical activity, suggesting that lifestyle habits are important risk factors for glucose intolerance and hyperglycemia in some older individuals. Similar lifestyle changes will benefit the health of older people with NIDDM and its clinical complications, yet often drug therapy is needed to control hyperglycemia and reduce the risk of CVD in these patients.

The major complications of diabetes in the elderly population are related to vascular disease and seem to covary with the duration of the disease, severity of hyperglycemia, and coexistence of hypertension, obesity, hyperlipidemia, and hyperinsulinemia. Acute emergencies occur most often in older diabetic patients who live alone, take several drugs for comorbid medical conditions, and have impaired cognitive function and limited mobility. These patients are at increased risk for hypoglycemia due to drug interactions and may develop HHNC due to infection, misuse of diuretics, and inability to obtain fluids because of limited mobility and social factors. Ketoacidosis is less frequent in the elderly diabetic person but must be considered in the differential diagnosis of septic shock since severe acidosis and circulatory collapse are common to both medical emergencies. The mortality rate from HHNC and DKA rises to over 40 percent in patients over 70 years. Prevention is the key to managing the chronic vascular and acute metabolic complications of older diabetic patients. Changes in dietary and activity habits are the cornerstone of therapy in older diabetic patients. Drug therapy with oral sulfonylureas or insulin should be instituted slowly and monitored carefully to avoid hypoglycemia and interactions with drugs used to treat coexistent medical diseases.

REFERENCES

1. Andres R: Aging and diabetes. *Med Clin North Am* 55:835, 1971.
2. Davidson MB: The effect of aging on carbohydrate metabolism: A review of the English literature and a practical approach to the diagnosis of diabetes mellitus in the elderly. *Metabolism* 28:688, 1978.
3. Shimokata H et al: Age as independent determinant of glucose tolerance. *Diabetes* 40:44, 1991.

4. Harris M: The prevalence of diabetes, undiagnosed diabetes and impaired glucose tolerance in the United States, in Melish JS et al (eds): *Genetic Environmental Interaction in Diabetes Mellitus.* Amsterdam, Excerpta Medica, 1982, p 70.
5. National Diabetes Data Group: Classification and diagnosis of diabetes mellitus and other categories of glucose intolerance. *Diabetes* 28:1039, 1979.
6. Graf RJ et al: Glucosylated hemoglobin in normal subjects and subjects with maturity onset diabetes: Evidence for a saturable system in man. *Diabetes* 27:834, 1978.
7. DeFronzo RA: Glucose intolerance and aging: Evidence for tissue insensitivity to insulin. *Diabetes* 28:1095, 1979.
8. Fink RI et al: Mechanism of insulin resistance in aging. *J Clin Invest* 71:1523, 1983.
9. Rowe JW et al: Characterization of the insulin resistance of aging. *J Clin Invest* 71:1581, 1983.
10. Chen M et al: Pathogenesis of age-related glucose intolerance in man: Insulin resistance and decreased beta-cell function. *J Clin Endocrinol Metab* 60:13, 1985.
11. Jackson RA et al: Influence of aging on hepatic and peripheral glucose metabolism in humans. *Diabetes* 37:119, 1988.
12. DeFronzo RA et al: Glucose clamp technique: A method for quantifying insulin secretion and resistance. *Am J Physiol* 237:E214, 1979.
13. Pagano G et al: Insulin resistance in the aged: The role of peripheral insulin receptors. *Metabolism* 30:46, 1981.
14. Lonnroth P, Smith U: Aging enhances the insulin resistance in obesity through both receptor and postreceptor alterations. *J Clin Endocrinol Metab* 62:433, 1986.
15. Fink RI et al: The role of the glucose transport system in the postreceptor defect in insulin action associated with human aging. *J Clin Endocrinol Metab* 58:721, 1984.
16. Fink RI et al: The effects of aging on glucose mediated glucose disposal and glucose transport. *J Clin Invest* 77:2034, 1986.
17. Menielly GS et al: Insulin action in aging man: Evidence of tissue-specific differences at low physiologic insulin levels. *J Gerontol* 42:196, 1987.
18. Coon PJ et al: Role of body fat distribution in the decline of insulin sensitivity and glucose tolerance with aging. *J Clin Endocrinol Metab* 75:1125, 1992.
19. Rosenthal M et al: Demonstration of a relationship between level of physical training and insulin-stimulated glucose utilization in normal hormones. *Diabetes* 32:408, 1983.
20. Gumbiner B et al: Effects of aging on insulin secretion. *Diabetes* 38:1549, 1989.
21. Kahn SE et al: Exercise training delineates the importance of B-cell dysfunction to the glucose intolerance of human aging. *J Clin Endocrinol Metab* 74:1336, 1992.
22. Walton C et al: Evaluation of four mathematical models of glucose and insulin dynamics with analysis of effects of age and obesity. *Am J Physiol* 262:E755, 1992.
23. Bergman RN et al: Quantitative estimation of insulin sensitivity. *Am J Physiol* 77:E667, 1979.
24. Seals D et al: Glucose tolerance in young and older athletes and sedentary men. *J Appl Physiol* 56:1521, 1984.
25. Coon P et al: Increased physical fitness attenuates the age-related decline in insulin sensitivity. *Gerontologist* 28:233A, 1988.
26. Chen M et al: The role of dietary carbohydrate in the decreased glucose tolerance of the elderly. *J Am Geriatr Soc* 35:417, 1987.
27. National Institutes of Health: Consensus development conference on diet and exercise in non-insulin dependent diabetes mellitus. *Diabetes Care* 10:639, 1987.
28. Schneider SH et al: Studies on the mechanisms of improved glucose control during regular exercise in type 2 (non-insulin dependent) diabetes. *Diabetologia* 26:355, 1984.
29. Goldberg AP: Health promotion and aging: "Physical exercise," in Abdellah FG, Moor SR (eds): *Surgeon General's Workshop, Health Promotion and Aging.* Washington, DC, 1988, p C1.
30. Tonino RP: Effect of physical training on the insulin resistance of aging. *Am J Physiol* 256:E352, 1989.
31. Kahn SE et al: Effect of exercise on insulin action, glucose tolerance, and insulin secretion in aging. *Am J Physiol* 258:E937, 1990.
32. Zavaroni I et al: Effect of age and environment factors on glucose tolerance and insulin secretion in a worker population. *J Am Geriatr Soc* 34:271, 1986.
33. Olefsky JO, Kolterman OG: Mechanisms of insulin resistance in obesity and noninsulin dependent (type II) diabetes. *Am J Med* 70:151, 1981.
34. Kolterman OG et al: Receptor and postreceptor defects contribute to insulin resistance in noninsulin dependent diabetes mellitus. *J Clin Invest* 68:957, 1981.
35. Ward WK et al: Pathophysiology of insulin secretion in noninsulin dependent diabetes mellitus. *Diabetes Care* 7:491, 1984.
36. Kahn CR: Insulin resistance, insulin insensitivity, insulin unresponsiveness: A necessary distinction. *Metabolism* 27:1893, 1978.
37. Tattersall RB, Pyke DA: Diabetes in identical twins. *Lancet* 2:1120, 1972.
38. Albin J, Rifkin H: Etiologies of diabetes mellitus. *Med Clin North Am* 66:1209, 1982.
39. Fuller J et al: Coronary heart disease risk and impaired glucose tolerance: The Whitehall study. *Lancet* 1:1373, 1980.
40. Nathan DM et al: Non-insulin dependent diabetes in older patients: Complications and risk factors. *Am J Med* 81:837, 1986.
41. Bierman EL: Atherogenesis in diabetes. *Arterioscler Thrombo* 12:647, 1992.
42. Kannel WB: Lipids and diabetes in coronary heart disease: Insights from the Framingham study. *Am Heart J* 110:1100, 1985.
43. Wilson PNF et al: Epidemiology of diabetes in the elderly: The Framingham study. *Am J Med* 80 (suppl 15A):3, 1982.
44. Bennett PH: Diabetes in the elderly: Diagnosis and epidemiology. *Geriatrics* 39:37, 1984.
45. Deubner DC et al: Logistic model estimation of death attributable to risk factors for cardiovascular disease in Evans County, Georgia. *Am J Epidemiol* 112:135, 1980.
46. National Center for Health Statistics: *Glucose Levels in Adults: United States 1960–1962.* Vital Health Statistics,

ser 11, no 18. Washington, DC, Government Printing Office, 1966.

47. Zimmet P et al: The high incidence of diabetes mellitus in the Micronesian population of Nauru. *Acta Diabetol Lat* 19:75, 1982.
48. Knowler WC et al: Diabetes incidence and prevalence in Pima Indians. A 19-fold-greater incidence than in Rochester, Minnesota. *Am J Epidemiol* 108:497, 1978.
49. Knowler WC et al: Diabetes incidence in Pima Indians: Contributions of obesity and parental diabetes. *Am J Epidemiol* 113:144, 1981.
50. Moorandian AD et al: Diabetes in elderly nursing home patients. A survey of clinical characteristics and management. *J Am Geriatr Soc* 36:391, 1988.
51. Singer DE et al: Screening for diabetes mellitus. *Ann Intern Med* 109:639, 1988.
52. Lapidus L et al: Distribution of adipose tissue and risk of cardiovascular disease and death: A 12 year follow-up of participants in the population study of women in Gothenburg, Sweden. *Br Med J* 289:1257, 1984.
53. Tuck M: Treatment of hypertensive diabetic patients. *Diabetes Care* 10:828, 1988.
54. Houston MC: The effects of antihypertensive drugs on glucose intolerance in hypertensive nondiabetics and diabetics. *Am Heart J* 115:640, 1988.
55. Pyorala K et al: Diabetes and atherosclerosis: An epidemiological view. *Diabetes/Metab Rev* 3(2):463, 1987.
56. Sarlund H et al: Early abnormalities in coronary heart disease risk factors in relatives of subjects with non-insulin dependent diabetes. *Arterioscl and Thrombosis* 12:657, 1992.
57. Jarrett RJ et al: The Bedford survey: 10 year mortality rates in newly diagnosed diabetics, borderline diabetics, and normal glycemic controls, and risk indices for coronary artery disease in borderline diabetics. *Diabetologia* 22:79, 1983.
58. Stern MP, Haffner SM: Body fat distribution and hyperinsulinemia as risk factors for diabetes and cardiovascular disease. *Arteriosclerosis* 6:123, 1986.
59. Larsson B et al: Abdominal adipose tissue distribution, obesity and risk of cardiovascular disease and death: 13 year follow-up of participants in the study of men born in 1913. *Br Med J* 288:1401, 1984.
60. Conference Summary: Financing the care of diabetes mellitus in the 1990's. *Diabetes Care* 13:1021, 1990.
61. Barrett-Conner E, Orchard T: Diabetes and heart disease, in *Diabetes in America.* DHHS (NIH)85-1468. Bethesda, MD, National Diabetes Data Group, 1985, p 1.
62. Palumbo PJ, Melton LJ III: Peripheral vascular disease and diabetes, in *Diabetes in America.* DHHS(NIH)85-1468. Bethesda, MD, National Diabetes Data Group, 1985, p 1.
63. Green DR: Acute and chronic complications of diabetes mellitus in older patients. *Am J Med* 80(suppl C):39, 1986.
64. Ewing W, Clarke BF: Diabetic autonomic neuropathy: Present insight in future prospects. *Diabetes Care* 9:648, 1986.
65. Rosenstalk J, Raskin T: Early diabetic nephropathy assessment and potential therapeutic interventions. *Diabetes Care* 9:529, 1986.
66. Schonfeld G: Diabetes, lipoproteins, and atherosclerosis. *Metabolism* 34(suppl 1):45, 1985.
67. Stolar MN: Atherosclerosis in diabetes: The role of hyperinsulinemia. *Metabolism* 37:1, 1988.
68. DeFronzo Ra, Ferrannini E: Insulin resistance: A multifaceted syndrome responsible for NIDDM, obesity, hypertension, dyslipidemia and atherosclerotic cardiovascular disease. *Diabetes Care* 14:173, 1991.
69. Cerami A et al: Protein glycosylation and the pathogenesis of atherosclerosis. *Metabolism* 34(suppl 1):37, 1985.
70. Baynes JW: Role of exudative stress in the development of complications in diabetes. *Diabetes* 40:405, 1991.
71. Hunt JV et al: Hydroxyl radical production and autooxidative glycosylation. *Biochem J* 256:205, 1988.
72. Steinberg D et al: Beyond cholesterol: Modifications of low density lipoprotein that increase its atherogenicity. *N Engl J Med* 320:915, 1989.
73. Stankova L et al: Plasma ascorbate concentrations and blood cell dehydroascorbate transport in patients with diabetes mellitus. *Metabolism* 33:347, 1984.
74. Nesto RW, Phillips RT: Asymptomatic myocardial ischemia in diabetic patients. *Am J Med* 80(suppl C):40, 1986.
75. Podolsky S: Hyperosmolar nonketotic coma in the elderly diabetic. *Med Clin North Am* 62:815, 1978.
76. Wachtel TJ et al: Prognostic factors in the diabetic hyperosmolar state. *J Am Geriatr Soc* 35:737, 1987.
77. Smith IM: Common infections in the elderly diabetic. *Geriatrics* 35:55, 1980.
78. Clements RS, Vourganti B: Fatal diabetic ketoacidosis: Major causes and approaches to their prevention. *Diabetes Care* 1:314, 1978.
79. Parving HH et al: Effect of captopril on blood pressure and kidney function in normotensive insulin dependent diabetics with nephropathy. *Br Med J* 299:533, 1989.
80. Christlieb AR: Treatment selection considerations for the hypertensive diabetic patient. *Arch Intern Med* 150:1167, 1990.
81. Special report: Principles of nutrition and dietary recommendations for individuals with diabetes mellitus. *Diabetes* 20:633, 1971; 28:1027, 1979.
82. AHA Nutrition Committee and Council on Arteriosclerosis: Joint statement. Recommendations for the treatment of hyperlipidemia in adults. *Arteriosclerosis* 4:445A, 1984.
83. Wing RR et al: Behavioral change, weight loss, and physiological improvements in type II diabetic patients. *J Consult Clin Psychol* 53:111, 1985.
84. Watkins PJ: ABC of diabetes: Diabetic emergencies. *Br Med J* 285:360, 1982.
85. Lebovitz HE: A look at sulfonylurea drugs. *Diabetes Spectrum* 4:314, 1991.
86. Nathan DM et al: Glyburide or insulin for metabolic control in noninsulin-dependent diabetes mellitus. *Ann Intern Med* 109:334, 1988.
87. Halter JB, Morrow LA: Use of sulfonylurea drugs in elderly patients. *Diabetes Care* 13(suppl):86, 1990.

Chapter 72

MORTALITY AND OBESITY: THE RATIONALE FOR AGE-SPECIFIC HEIGHT-WEIGHT TABLES

Reubin Andres

It is generally recognized that both extremely high and extremely low degrees of fat accumulation have serious health consequences. In economically advanced societies, a large fraction of the adult population is frequently within the dangerously overweight range, while a smaller fraction is in the seriously underweight range. To quantify those fractions accurately requires the definition of the "normal" weight range. This effort has, especially in recent years, become very controversial.

STANDARDS OF NORMAL WEIGHT

Attempts at defining normal weight have sometimes been based upon statistical analysis of height and weight distributions in populations, but the selections of the weight ranges judged to be abnormal have been entirely arbitrary. The notion that the average weight of 20- to 25-year-old subjects is ideal for all subsequent ages has been widely accepted, but this seemingly reasonable assumption is, as will be shown, incorrect.

The setting of normal weight standards is more properly accomplished by analyzing the association of weight with other risk factors present in those subjects or, better, by long-term follow-up studies of populations in which the independent variable is an index of obesity and the dependent variables are such outcomes as specific diseases (heart disease, diabetes, cancer, stroke) or, indeed, mortality itself. In fact with a variable such as adiposity, a multidimensional interplay of beneficial and harmful effects would be anticipated. Harm might be expected to exceed benefit at both extremes of the adiposity distribution curves within populations.

It is remarkable that, until the 1960s, a variable as easily measured as weight-for-height was examined as a risk factor for mortality only by the pioneering efforts of the life insurance industry. Periodic analyses of their conclusions have been presented for the past 70 years—in 1913, 1932, 1942–1943, 1959, and most recently in 1983. The last three sets of height-weight tables have had identical formats: separate tables for men and women, heights in inches, and three overlapping ranges of weight for each of three body frame categories (small, medium, and large). These sets of tables were devised by actuaries of the Metropolitan Life Insurance Company. Weight ranges in the 1942–1943 tables were identified as "ideal," the 1959 weights were downgraded to "desirable," and the 1983 tables are identified simply as "1983 height-weight tables."[1]

The insurance industry studies that provide the primary data from which these tables were constructed have been criticized on a number of grounds: (1) subjects seeking insurance do not represent a random sample of the general population; (2) those who are granted policies represent a further selection of elite subjects (from a health standpoint); (3) some subjects are represented more than once, since individual policies (rather than subjects) are tabulated; (4) heights and weights have not been invariably measured (some are simply statements made by the subjects); furthermore, (5) height and weight measurements alone are poor estimates of body fatness; (6) no anthropometric measurements of body frame were made: and (7) the possible confound of cigarette smoking with body weight and with mortality was not considered.

Data are, however, now available from a large number of other populations which provide estimates of obesity and its relationship to mortality. These populations are all selective in one respect or another, but, as in all epidemiological studies of this sort, the search for patterns of consistency may provide cumulative evidence of some biological principles which are generalizable to all human beings or at least to the ones living in developed societies. (There are no data from economically underdeveloped areas of the world.) The basic design of each consisted of an assessment of height and weight (and, rarely, of other anthropometric indices of obesity) of each member of a selected population at one moment in the life span. From these measurements an index of obesity was assigned to each subject. Generally, one or another of the available weight tables was selected as the reference standard; the 1959 Desirable Weight Table has been most commonly chosen, although recently even the 1913 version was used. When the 1959 table has been used, the middle of the weight range for the medium frame was selected as the single weight goal. A *relative weight* (RW) or *obesity index* was then computed for each subject by dividing the subject's actual weight by the weight goal for his or her height. Thus a man 69 inches tall whose actual weight was 149 pounds and whose weight goal was also 149 pounds would have an RW of 1.00; another of the same height whose actual weight was 179 pounds would have an RW of 1.20 and would generally be described as 20 percent overweight. The actual RW value obtained by such calculations obviously depends upon the particular reference base selected. Consequently subjects described as being 20 percent overweight in two studies may indeed not be comparably obese if different reference bases were used to classify them.

COMPUTATION OF BODY MASS INDEX

To avoid the problem of different reference bases, the computation of a *body mass index* (BMI) or *Quetelet index* has been gaining favor as a technique for combining height and weight into a single index of relative obesity. In most populations, weight increases directly with the height squared. Thus weight divided by height squared (wt/ht^2) may be used to "correct" for height, and this quotient defines the BMI. It is important to realize that the midweights for the medium frame in the 1959 Desirable Weight Table divided by their respective heights squared give values for the BMI which average 21.6 for men and to 21.2 for women provided the weight and heights squared are expressed in metric units (kilograms per square meter) and that suitable corrections are made for clothing weight and shoe height. (It has been recommended that for men and for women, respectively, 7 and 5 pounds should be subtracted for weight of clothes and that 1 and 2 inches should be subtracted for height of shoes from the values given in the Metropolitan tables.) In other words, BMIs of 21.6 and 21.2 in the 1959 tables are equivalent to an RW of 1.00 for men and women. This equivalency conversion is a useful aid in the interpretation of the BMI for those unfamiliar with its use as an index of relative obesity. In the 1983 tables, the recommended adjustments for the weight of clothing are 5 and 3 pounds for men and women, respectively, and 1 inch for both for the height of shoes.

The use of height and weight as the sole measurements upon which to assess obesity is subject to overt error in some individuals. The weight standards used in the selection of recruits during World War I seemed reasonable until it became obvious that young men who were burly and muscular (but not fat) were being excluded from service. A number of techniques are available for estimating body fatness,[2] but these have generally not been applied to population studies, since their complexity precludes their use for measuring large numbers of individuals. Despite this limitation, in population groups it is the "overweight" who tend overwhelmingly to be the "overfat"; conclusions based upon analyses in which height and weight have been measured agree remarkably well with analyses based, for example, upon skinfold thickness measurements, a more direct index of true fatness.[3]

If relative obesity is defined as the percentage of total body weight composed of fat, then young adults and elderly subjects of the same height and weight are not comparably obese. There is an inexorable loss of lean body mass (or cellular mass) with advancing age. This loss is primarily skeletal muscle. Thus, if body weight is maintained without change during aging, this can be accomplished only by replacing skeletal muscle to some extent by connective tissue but predominantly by fat. This biological fact would not, in itself, introduce an error into recommendations which might be made concerning body weight, provided that the studies upon which the recommendations are based have taken age into account.

EFFECT OF BODY WEIGHT ON MORTALITY

In this chapter consideration will be given mainly to the effect of body weight on total mortality in different age segments of populations. In one sense, this is a very limited approach, since other deleterious effects of obesity could also be considered. Mortality is, however, the quintessential "end point," and it is mortality which has been used in the construction of the height-weight tables. It is conceivable, indeed nearly certain, that recommended weights based upon mortality will be higher than those which, for example, would be associated with the lowest prevalence of diabetes mellitus, hypertension, and hyperlipidemia. Weight tables based upon the mortality of healthy populations are applicable only to individuals of comparable health status, not to persons who are hypertensive, hyperlipidemic, or diabetic. This fact is rarely appreciated.

There are now some 50 other populations which have undergone study in a manner comparable with that performed by the insurance industry. The technical quality of these studies varies greatly, and comparisons among them are difficult for a number of reasons: (1) no standardized techniques for assessing the independent variable (obesity) have been proposed or followed; (2) the techniques used for selecting and sampling the population vary (some samples represent "captive" populations such as employees, others are recruited as community volunteers and the response rates vary, others are self-selected, etc.); (3) follow-up periods sometimes cover only a small fraction of the human life span; (4) eligibility for inclusion in the original sample differs widely, since some studies apply no exclusionary health criteria while in others initial health examinations may be very thorough; (5) variables which interact with obesity and which also influence mortality (cigarette smoking is the prime example) have rarely been analyzed and reported; and (6) sample sizes vary from several dozen to several million subjects. The wide diversity in the types of populations selected for study is, of course, an advantage even if differences in results among them can rarely be explained adequately.

Results from a number of these studies have been summarized recently.[4,5] Several of the more important ones will be summarized here. Ancel Keys[3] reported 10-year follow-up studies in some 12,000 men from seven countries (the United States, Japan, Yugoslavia, Italy, Greece, the Netherlands, and Finland) aged 40 to 59 years at entry. Relative weight was determined from height and weight, and in six of the countries an index of obesity also was derived from skinfold measurements. Croatians and Serbians in Yugoslavia were analyzed separately; thus eight populations were reported. Mortality data were presented for deciles of relative weight in each population, but the number of deaths in some groups was so small that the data have been collapsed into quintiles. In seven of the eight populations, the highest mortality occurred in the leanest quintile. Lowest mortality was in the heaviest quintile in three populations, in next to the heaviest in two, in the middle quintile in two, and in the lightest quintile in one population. Furthermore in the seven populations which had skinfold measurements, the highest mortality occurred in either the leanest or next to the leanest quintile in five groups, and the lowest mortality occurred either in the middle quintile or the most obese quintile in six of the seven groups.

The American Cancer Society[6] enrolled about 750,000 apparently healthy men and women from 26 states and followed them for 12 years. Heights and weights were obtained by means of a questionnaire. Subjects were assigned relative weights based upon age-sex group averages from this population. However, the men aged 30 to 70 years in this study were on average 14 to 16 percent heavier than the midweights for the medium frame from the 1959 Desirable Weight Table, while women in the study averaged 8 to 18 percent above their "desirable" weights. The lowest mortality occurred in men of average weight, i.e., distinctly above desirable, and in women generally in the 80 to 89 relative weight category, i.e., essentially at their desirable weight. However, the 80- to 89-year-old men and women with lowest mortality were distinctly on the overweight side at enrollment, albeit there was little weight effect on mortality across the entire weight spectrum.

A report from the Framingham Heart Study[7] analyzed the mortality experience of nonsmoking male and female survivors after they reached age 65. The follow-up period averaged 9.5 years. Subjects were divided into four unequal-sized BMI groups and the relative risk of dying was computed for each group. In men, lowest mortality occurred in the 23.0- to 25.2-BMI group, and in women, in the 24.1- to 26.1-BMI group. Mortality in the next higher BMI group (up to about 28.5 in men and women) was higher, but the increase was not statistically significant. These values may be compared to the Metropolitan 1959 recommendations (about 19.7 to 24.7 in men and 18.8 to 24.2 in women) and to the Metropolitan 1983 tables (about 20.5 to 25.8 in men and 19.6 to 26.1 in women). The Gerontology Research Center (GRC) table recommends values for 65-year-old men and women ranging from 23.9 to 29.7. Thus, the lowest mortality in Framingham older men and women falls within the upper one-third or so of the Metropolitan 1983 weights and within the lower one-third or so of the GRC weights.

An impressive, comprehensively analyzed study has been reported by Waaler.[8] All persons over age 15 in Norway (but excluding Oslo) were invited to participate. In all, over 1.7 million persons were enrolled and followed for 16 years. The report is a model of clarity of analysis and presentation. It clearly demonstrates U-shaped BMI:mortality curves from ages 20 to 24 years into the very oldest groups, but with a progressive flattening of the curves. BMI becomes less and less associated with mortality as aging progresses. In general, minimal mortality occurred at BMIs of about 25 in the later years in both men and women.

Several arguments have been raised in criticism of studies relating body weight to mortality.[9] These include (1) failure to take cigarette smoking into account; (2) failure to exclude subjects at entry into the study who were already ill, had been losing weight, and were destined to die early, (3) inappropriate multiple regression analyses; and (4) relatively short follow-up periods. The theoretical basis of the smoking argument is that, in most populations, smokers weigh less than nonsmokers and certainly have higher mortality rates. Thus curves relating body weight to mortality will be distorted because of "contamination" of the true weight effect by the associated smoking effect. This confound can be tested by examining the weight–mortality association separately in smokers and in nonsmokers. When this has been done, the BMI:mortality U-shaped curves have been found to be very similar in shape. Minimal mortality occurs at about the same body weights in smokers as in nonsmokers, and the nadirs for both groups are about the same as that for all subjects. For example, in an analysis not yet published of the National Health and Nutrition Survey I Follow-up Study (NHFUS) of 15 years duration (Zonderman, Costa, and Andres), minimal mortality in 55- to 74-year-old white men occurred at BMIs of 27.7 in smokers, 26.7 in nonsmokers, and 27.4 in the combined group—values all far in excess of the Metropolitan 1959 and 1983 standards but quite in agreement with the GRC table. A review of other studies shows similar results—for example, the 30-year Framingham report by Feinleib.[10]

The objection that weight-losing ill patients might have been included in some studies has been met in various ways by different investigators: (1) clinical evaluation at the time of recruitment allows the identification (and subsequent exclusion) of subjects with significant illnesses; (2) subjects who die in the earlier years of the study have been excluded; and (3) subjects who report significant unexplained weight loss in the preenrollment period have been excluded. There are no convincing data, however, that failure to "clean up" the population makes a significant impact on the shape of the weight:mortality curve. In the NHFUS referred to above, the BMI of 55- to 74-year-old white men was 27.9 in the total population and 27.4 after 28 percent of the total enrollees were excluded either because of the presence of identifiable diseases or because they died within the first 2 years of follow-up. In white women, comparable values were 27.5 and 27.2 (22 percent excluded).

Relatively short follow-up periods probably distort results, primarily in studies with relatively small initial enrollment and therefore with relatively few deaths. This problem is obviously more serious in studies of younger populations who manifest low mortality rates to begin with. Waaler,[11] in a summary of the remarkable study of 1.7 million Norwegians, noted that "in studies with few observations there might be difficulties in demonstrating any correlation at all between BMI and mortality. As the size of the material is increasing, the first observation will be some linear positive correlation. This will be partly obscured by the U-shape, which will be visible only in rather big study populations . . . " In his study, Waaler showed that the excess mortality of very lean and very obese individuals can be seen clearly at 1 or 2 years of follow-up and at all annual analyses up to the end of his study at 16 years. In the NHFUS analysis, the 15-year follow-up of individuals enrolled for study at ages 55 to 75 years results in the deaths of one-third of the women and one-half of the men by the time their status is determined at ages 70 to 90 years. Thus 15 years is, in fact, a long follow-up period for older individuals provided that a sample of at least several hundred men and an equal or greater number of women has been initially enrolled.

AN ANALYSIS OF ACTUARIAL DATA

The weight standards for Americans in this century have clearly been those produced by actuaries of the Metropolitan Life Insurance Company. A National Institutes of Health Consensus Development Conference on Health Implications of Obesity[12] did not show preference for either the 1983 version of the tables[1] or the 1959 version,[13] but it clearly did favor their use. The tables were recognized as being deficient in that age was not included as a variable, but no age recommendations were offered. The 1983 version provided some liberalization of the weight ranges previously recommended. Because of this, criticism has been raised by those who believe that the public should be advised to remain distinctly lean. Since actuarially derived tables have become the generally accepted weight standards since the 1942-1943 version was published, it is surprising that updated tables based upon the most recent experience of the insurance industry should be criticized and that the 1959 version based, in essence, on data collected from 1935 to 1953 should be supported. Therefore, it is necessary to consider the source of the data from which the height-weight tables are derived. The mortality experience of 25 companies was pooled and has been reported in great detail in book form as the *Build Study 1979*.[14] Mortality data were presented on nearly 4,200,000 policies taken out between 1954 and 1972 on men and women 15 to 69 years of age. Data on ages 15 to 19 are sparse and will not be considered further. The total experience includes some 106,000 deaths, an unparalleled number. The mortality ratio (actual/expected number of deaths) was presented separately for each age decade from 20 to 29 through 60 to 69 years for men and for women. Subjects were divided into one of five height groups, from very short to very tall; for each height group, subjects were placed into one of eighteen weight groups, from very light to very heavy. Theoretically, there could be as many as 90 height-weight groups for each age decade for each sex. Actually, data were not available on some of the more extreme groups—for example, very short subjects of the highest weight.

We have taken advantage of this comprehensive compilation of data to carry out an independent analysis of the insurance experience. The data from the large number of height-weight groups can be combined and analyzed for each sex-age group by computing the mean body mass index for each category. An example of such data demonstrates that the mortality ratios follow a U-shaped distribution (Fig. 72-1), with high mortality at both the very low and very high BMIs and with lowest mortality at an intermediate zone. A quadratic equation defines a curve which fits the actual data points very well:

$$\text{Mortality ratio} = a + b\ (\text{body mass index}) + c\ (\text{body mass index})^2$$

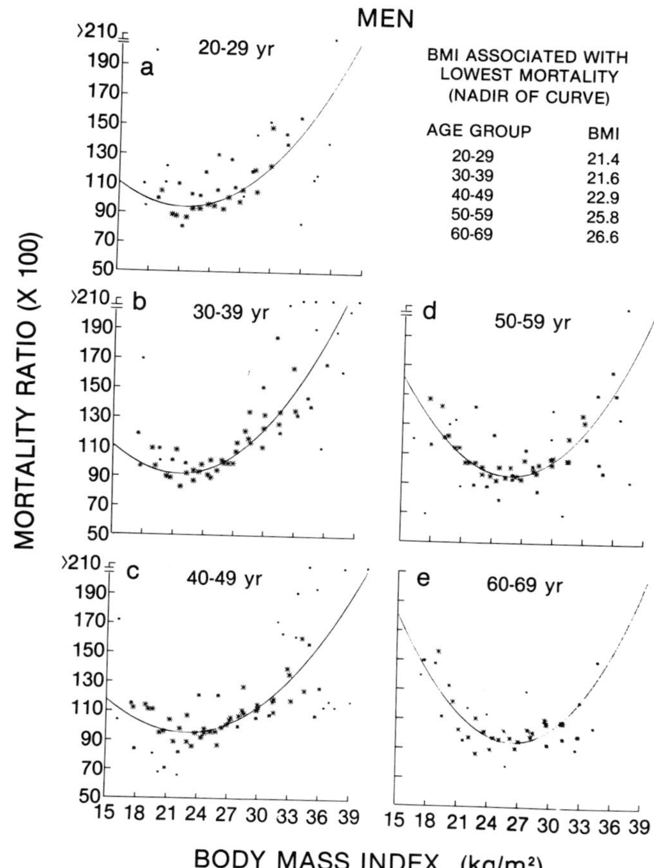

FIGURE 72-1

The U-shaped relationships between body mass index (BMI) and mortality ratio. Data are derived from the *Build Study 1979*.[14] The curves were constructed from the quadratic relationship between the two variables. A mortality ratio of 100 represents the average or expected mortality for the specific age-sex group. The nadirs of the curves represent that BMI associated with minimal mortality. The two points at which the curves intersect the 100 mortality ratio line represent those BMIs associated with mortality ratios less than the average; those BMIs can, therefore, be used to define a recommended weight range.

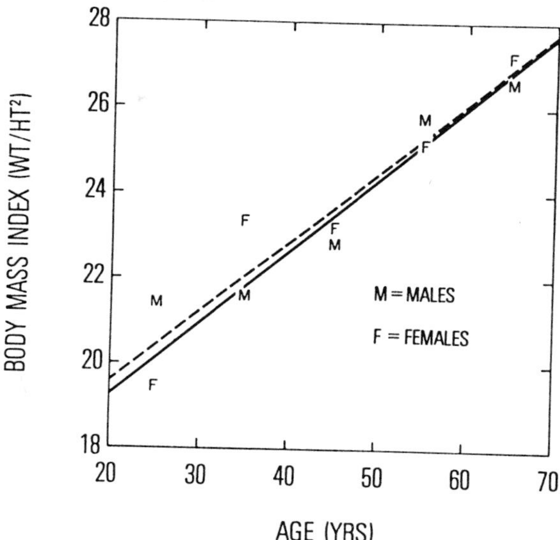

FIGURE 72-2

The effect of age on the BMI associated with lowest mortality. Minimal mortality points were computed for each age-sex group as indicated in Fig. 72-1. The regression lines were computed separately for men (——) and for women (– – –). Note that there is a strong effect of age on the BMI associated with lowest mortality and that the regression lines for men and women are nearly identical. (Based upon data reported in the *Build Study 1979*.[13])

From the equations derived for each of the five age decades for both men and women, the nadir of each curve can be computed. The nadir represents that body mass index associated with the lowest mortality. The plot of these nadirs (Fig. 72-2) shows that there is a progressive increase in the "best" BMI with age in both sexes and that there is no consistent difference across the age span of five decades between men and women.

Since a useful table of recommended weights must provide a *range* of weights rather than a single point, we made an empirical decision based on the fact that the quadratic curve intersects the 100 percent mortality line at two points (Fig. 72-1). The BMI values at those two points represent the upper and lower BMI limits for mortality ratios which are less than the average. Since these BMI limits are very similar in men and women, the weight goals do not need to be adjusted for gender. Women, who are, on average, fatter than men across the age spectrum, evidently benefit from this adiposity.

A recommended height-weight table has been constructed (Table 72-1), which presents the computed weight ranges for each age decade 20 to 29 through 60 to 69 years. For comparison, the corresponding weight ranges from the 1983 Metropolitan Life Insurance Company tables are also shown. Since no anthropometric data were available on the insured subjects other than height and weight, the individual weight ranges for each of the three body frames represent only a conjecture of the weight adjustment that should be permitted for frame size. It would seem preferable to provide an age-adjusted table (for which data are available) and to avoid a frame-adjusted table (for which data are not available).

Over the major portion of the height spectrum, the 1983 Metropolitan Life Insurance Company weight range for men and women[1] falls near the weights in the age-adjusted table for individuals in their thirties or forties. Thus, the 1983 Metropolitan Life Insurance Company tables provide weights that are higher than the primary insurance data would justify for young adults and lower than the insurance

TABLE 72-1

Comparison of the Weight-for-Height Tables from Actuarial Data: Non-Age-Corrected Metropolitan Life Insurance Company and Age-Specific Gerontology Research Center Recommendations

	Metropolitan 1983 Weights (25–59 yr)*		*Gerontology Research Center* (Age-Specific Weight Range for Men and Women)*				
Height (ft and in)	**Men**	**Women**	**20–29 yr**	**30–39 yr**	**40–49 yr**	**50–59 yr**	**60–69 yr**
4 10		100–131	84–111	92–119	99–127	107–135	115–142
4 11		101–134	87–115	95–123	103–131	111–139	119–147
5 0		103–137	90–119	98–127	106–135	114–143	123–152
5 1	123–145	105–140	93–123	101–131	110–140	118–148	127–157
5 2	125–148	108–144	96–127	105–136	113–144	122–153	131–163
5 3	127–151	111–148	99–131	108–140	117–149	126–158	135–168
5 4	129–155	114–152	102–135	112–145	121–154	130–163	140–173
5 5	131–159	117–156	106–140	115–149	125–159	134–168	144–179
5 6	133–163	120–160	109–144	119–154	129–164	138–174	148–184
5 7	135–167	123–164	112–148	122–159	133–169	143–179	153–190
5 8	137–171	126–167	116–153	126–163	137–174	147–184	158–196
5 9	139–175	129–170	119–157	130–168	141–179	151–190	162–201
5 10	141–179	132–173	122–162	134–173	145–184	156–195	167–207
5 11	144–183	135–176	126–167	137–178	149–190	160–201	172–213
6 0	147–187		129–171	141–183	153–195	165–207	177–219
6 1	150–192		133–176	145–188	157–200	169–213	182–225
6 2	153–197		137–181	149–194	162–206	174–219	187–232
6 3	157–202		141–186	153–199	166–212	179–225	192–238
6 4			144–191	157–205	171–218	184–231	197–244

*Values in this table are for height without shoes and weight without clothes. The Metropolitan Life Insurance Company[1] presented a table for nude heights and weights (Table 4) as well as a table for heights and weights clothed (Table 1).

data would dictate for older adults. The increased weight allowance in our age-specific table is close to 10 pounds per decade of life or 1 pound per year, somewhat in excess of the actual mean weight increase that occurs in American men and women across the adult age span.

It must be stressed that tables of recommended weight are applicable only to subjects who do not have medical conditions which, in themselves, are affected by or which affect body weight. Furthermore, it is difficult to recommend weights for individuals over the age of 70. Data from the American Cancer Society Study[6] for men and women in their seventies and eighties suggest that the weight gain permitted with increasing age should be maintained into very old age. A number of other studies of elderly populations also suggest that the weights associated with lowest mortality remain on the relatively high side.

IMPORTANCE OF DISTRIBUTION OF BODY FAT

There are several recent studies which may cause a total reconsideration of recommendations for body weight.[15,16] These concern not only weight itself but also the epidemiological implications of the distribution of body fat—"where fat?" in addition to "how fat?", as it were. The suggestion has been made that when fat is distributed primarily in the lower part of the body (hips, buttocks, and thighs), the obesity is relatively benign: associated abnormalities of blood pressure, glucose tolerance, and serum lipid levels may not occur. In contrast, when the fat is distributed intraabdominally or in the neck, shoulder, and arm areas, the obesity takes on a more "malignant" metabolic prognosis. A simple measure of fat distribution may be the ratio of waist circumference to hip circumference. These few studies are intriguing and of potentially great importance. It is an area which should develop rapidly in the next few years.

In summary, it would appear that for healthy individuals, the weights associated with minimal mortality increase with age and that therefore the old saw that one's best weight is that achieved at age 20 or 25 needs to be discarded. There appears to be a rather broad range of weights associated with low mortality; weights both below and above those limits become increasingly harmful. More refined weight prescriptions modified for body habitus and age will have to await the compilation of evidence that is not available at the present time. Rapid advances in adipocyte physiology, including studies of regional differences in the adipocytes and carefully designed longitudinal obesity-mortality studies, will cause major revisions in our current thoughts concerning age-specific ranges of desirable body weight.

REFERENCES

1. *1983 Metropolitan Height and Weight Tables. Stat Bull Metropol Life Ins Co* 64(Jan–Jun):2, 1983.
2. Grande F: Assessment of body fat in man, in Bray GA (ed): *Obesity in Perspective.* U.S. Department of Health, Education, and Welfare Publication (NIH) 75–708, 1975, p 189.
3. Keys A: *Seven Countries: A Multivariate Analysis of Death and Coronary Heart Disease.* Cambridge, MA, Harvard, 1980.
4. Andres R: Effect of obesity on total mortality. *Int J Obes* 4:381, 1980.
5. Andres R: Aging, diabetes, and obesity: Standards of normality. *Mt Sinai J Med (NY)* 48:489, 1981.
6. Lew EA, Garfinkel L: Variations in mortality by weight among 750,000 men and women. *J Chronic Dis* 32:563, 1979.
7. Harris T et al: Body mass index and mortality among nonsmoking older persons: The Framingham Heart Study. *JAMA* 259:1520, 1988.
8. Waaler HT: Height, weight and mortality: The Norwegian experience. *Acta Med Scand* 215(suppl 679):1, 1984.
9. Manson J et al: Body weight and longevity: A reassessment. *JAMA* 257:353, 1987.
10. Feinleib J: Epidemiology of obesity in relation to health hazards. *Ann Intern Med* 103:1019, 1985.
11. Waaler HT: Hazard of obesity—The Norwegian experience. *Acta Med Scand [suppl]* 223(suppl 723):17, 1988.
12. Foster WR, Burton BT (eds): Health implications of obesity. *Ann Intern Med* 103 (number 6, part 2):979, 1985.
13. New weight standards for men and women. *Stat Bull* 40 (Nov–Dec):1, 1959.
14. *Build Study 1979.* Chicago, Society of Actuaries and Association of Life Insurance Medical Directors of America, 1980.
15. Björntorp P, Smith U, Lönnroth P (eds): Health implications of obesity. *Acta Med Scand* 223 (suppl 723):1, 1988.
16. Shimokata H et al: Studies in the distribution of body fat: I. Effects of age, sex, and obesity. *J Gerontol* 44:M66, 1989.

Chapter 73

DYSLIPOPROTEINEMIA

William R. Hazzard

Dyslipoproteinemia is a generic term that describes patterns of lipoprotein distributions and levels associated with dysfunction and disease. It is to be preferred over the more historical term *hyperlipoproteinemia* or *hyperlipidemia* because it is increasingly clear that certain forms of dyslipoproteinemia are associated either with normal plasma lipid levels [e.g., a low high-density lipoprotein (HDL) level in the presence of a normal total cholesterol level] or, especially relevant to gerontology and geriatrics, with *hypo*cholesterolemia. Moreover, because the association between lipid levels and disease is continuous and graded ("seamless"), dyslipoproteinemia is a relative more than an absolute concept, and the maintenance of optimal lipid patterns regardless of age may involve approaches, notably nutritional (a diet restricted in total cholesterol and fat, specifically saturated fat), that are as appropriate for the entire population as for those at the extremes of the distributions. Both population and individualized approaches to prevention and treatment are appropriate, and the former is being implemented widely through mechanisms such as the Adult Treatment Panel of the National Cholesterol Education Program, which relied heavily on the media to disseminate its recommendations. This has practical implications for physicians who care for elderly persons, who, especially while in good health and for good reasons, usually have great interest in such issues as heart disease. Thus it is becoming commonplace for patients to initiate investigation of their cardiovascular risk status and hence for physicians to be responding to such initiative rather than raising the issue in the first place. Here up-to-date information is clearly at a premium.

Plasma lipoprotein disorders are highly relevant to aging and geriatrics because of their common association with chronic disease processes that pass the clinical horizon in middle, and, increasingly, old age, especially atherosclerosis and its clinical sequelae (see especially Chaps. 12, 15, 45, and 46), pancreatitis (see Chap. 62), and failure to thrive in the elderly population (Chap. 110). Modulation of plasma lipoprotein levels is also heavily influenced by age-related physiological (and pharmacological) alterations in body mass and composition and hormone levels, both (most obviously the latter) reflected in the strong influence of gender upon the atherogenic process (see especially Chaps. 3 and 74). In this chapter information will be synthesized from those other chapters, minimizing redundancy and devolving into a focus upon (1) physiological regulation of human lipoprotein metabolism, (2) genetic determinants of abnormal lipoprotein metabolism, (3) the interaction among the hereditary basis of lipoprotein disorders, lifestyle (notably diet and nutrition), physiological and body composition changes across the lifespan (notably adiposity and sex hormone changes), and the aging process in determining lipoprotein patterns with advancing age, (4) a physiological, pathophysiological, and pharmacological rationale for the management of lipoprotein disorders, (5) the relationship between lipoprotein levels and clinical (especially atherosclerotic) disease across the adult lifespan, with special emphasis upon lipoprotein lipid levels and disease risk in old age; (6) the relationship between *hypo*cholesterolemia and failure to thrive, and associated diseases which are concentrated in the elderly, and (7) considerations that frame the present dilemma whether or not (and how) to treat dyslipoproteinemia in elderly patients.

THE REGULATION OF HUMAN LIPOPROTEIN METABOLISM

A cartoon summarizing contemporary understanding of the regulation of human lipoprotein metabolism is given in Fig. 73-1 (with its detailed legend). The translation of this scheme to patterns of lipoprotein levels, pathophysiological bases, hereditary and secondary forms, aging- and lifestyle-related forces, and management (both dietary and pharmacological) is summarized in Table 73-1.

A gerontological principle central to the understanding of this complex scheme is the following: The earlier in the lifespan that a disease passes the clinical horizon, the more likely it is to be unifactorial in origin and that, in turn, to be of hereditary cause. Conversely, the later a disease presents (and hence the closer to the upper limit of the human life span), the

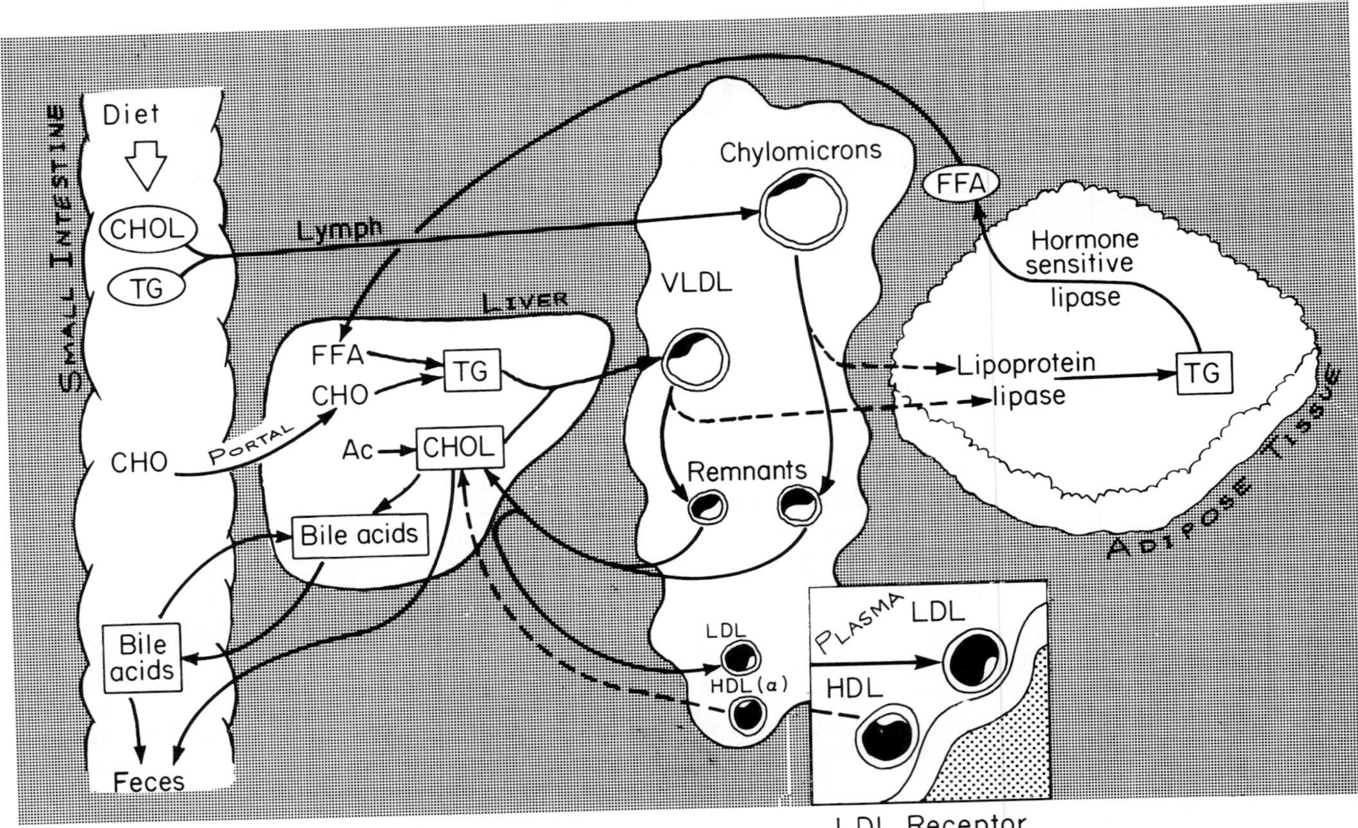

FIGURE 73-1

Cartoon of the physiological regulation of human lipoprotein metabolism highlighting the principal points of normal and abnormal regulation. Lipids in the diet are partially hydrolyzed, absorbed across the small intestinal mucosa (point 1), secreted into intestinal lymph as triglyceride-rich chylomicrons (triglyceride indicated in white, cholesterol in black), bypassing the liver to enter the plasma via the thoracic duct. Very low density lipoproteins (VLDLs) are secreted principally by the liver, their triglyceride having been synthesized intrahepatically from carbohydrate (CHO) and free fatty acid (FFA) precursors (fatty acids derived principally in turn from peripheral triglyceride hydrolysis mediated by hormone-sensitive lipase, which is coordinately regulated with lipoprotein lipase in diametrically opposite fashion); triglyceride synthesis and VLDL secretion are labeled control point 2. Both chylomicrons and VLDL serve as substrates for lipoprotein lipase in the extraction and hydrolysis of their constituent triglyceride (control point 3); this enzyme is up-regulated by insulin, while insulin suppresses hormone-sensitive lipase. The extraction of triglyceride via lipoprotein lipase generates surplus surface free cholesterol and phospholipids on chylomicrons and VLDL; these serve as the substrate for lecithin cholesterol acyltransferase (LCAT), HDL serving as the acceptor of the generated esterified cholesterol [and its apolipoprotein A-1 (apo A-1) is the principal activator of LCAT]. The successive actions of lipoprotein lipase and LCAT generate chylomicron and VLDL remnants; chylomicron remnants are taken up via specific hepatic receptors (apo E is thought to be the key signal for this process), while VLDL remnants are either removed irreversibly (if they contain apo E) (point 4) or are further hydrolyzed (perhaps by hepatic triglyceride lipase) to LDL, which is taken up by specific hepatic and extrahepatic apo E,B receptors (step 5, see inset). HDL accepts cholesterol from peripheral tissues and delivers it to the liver either directly or after transfer to VLDL remnants (via cholesterol ester transfer protein) for uptake via the apo E,B receptor (step 6). Cholesterol is also synthesized endogenously from acetate (Ac) precursors, regulated principally by the enzyme HMG CoA reductase (step 7). Cholesterol may then be resecreted into plasma on VLDL, excreted directly into bile, or converted via 7-alpha hydroxylase to bile acids (step 8), which in turn are excreted in bile and the feces or, principally, reabsorbed in the enterohepatic circulation (step 9). Abnormalities at these regulatory steps account for the major disorders of lipoprotein metabolism, and strategies of dietary and pharmacological management of dyslipoproteinemia can be rationalized by their effects at these control points.

more likely it is to be multifactorial, reflecting interaction among the genetic "set point," lifestyle (nutritional habits), and the passage of time, which in turn is perforce highly correlated with aging. Thus, for example, the monogenic disorder familial hypercholesterolemia, when inherited in homozygous form (approximately 1 in 1 million), is based upon a total absence of functioning low-density lipoprotein (LDL receptors) and causes a quadrupling of LDL cholesterol levels regardless of dietary intake. It is associated with vastly premature atherosclerosis, rarely permitting survival beyond age 20. The same disorder inherited in heterozygous fashion (approximately 1 in 500) is associated with a doubling of LDL cholesterol levels and the development of clinical coronary heart disease in the midforties in men and midfifties in women; few affected individuals survive past age 70 without clinical atherosclerosis. Not surprisingly, familial hypercholesterolemia both heterozygous and homozygous can be diagnosed in cord blood and is clearly manifest in elevated LDL cholesterol levels in childhood in a manner consistent with a simple pattern of inheritance, in which vertical transmission from affected parent to child is clearly evident. By the same token, this disorder is rarely first encountered in elderly persons. When this does occur, countervailing, antiatherogenic forces can usually be identified, such as a high HDL level (predictably more common in women with this disorder)

More subtle are disorders that, though also simply inherited, are influenced by age-related changes as well as by diet and other lifestyle influences. Thus familial combined hyperlipidemia (probably synonymous with familial hyperapobetalipoproteinemia and present in as many as 1 in 200 to 300 of the population) is not clearly diagnosable until adulthood (but is nearly universally expressed by age 30). Here the age-associated influences producing phenotypic penetrance of this autosomal dominant disorder are speculative but most likely are related to the nearly universal (and hence "normal" and arguably physiological) accretion of adipose tissue, which begins beyond adolescence and progresses throughout the remainder of life, but most clearly accumulates in the "first half of adult life" (my term, ages ~ 25 to 50). During this interval plasma cholesterol and triglyceride levels increase on average in all adults in parallel with increasing relative body weight (Fig. 3-7). However, this is exaggerated in those with genetically determined familial lipid disorders associated with a high endogenous very low density lipoprotein (VLDL) secretion rate, be it large VLDL disproportionately enriched in triglyceride (as in familial hypertriglyceridemia) or smaller, denser, more-cholesterol-rich VLDL (as in familial combined hyperlipidemia). From a pathophysiological perspective, the latter is clearly the more ominous, generating a more atherogenic VLDL remnant, which appears to proceed catabolically to a triglyceride- and protein-enriched, especially dense LDL particle that, together with an elevated total plasma apolipoprotein B level, defines this disorder. The average age of onset of associated coronary disease in men with familial combined hyperlipidemia (51 years in the Seattle-based study which first defined it)[1] is beyond the typical age of presentation of those with heterozygous hypercholesterolemia (averaging 46 years in the Seattle study); nevertheless, because of its prevalence, this is the familial lipid disorder most commonly associated with coronary heart disease, representing a full 10 percent of those presenting with myocardial infarction prior to age 60 in the Seattle study (as opposed to 3 percent with familial hypercholesterolemia).

Whether or not such age-associated increases in body adiposity confer net risk or benefit to overall health remains the subject of lively debate (see especially Chaps. 12 and 72). What experts agree upon, however, is that adult weight gain in the upper-body, central, "apple-shaped," typically male "android" pattern carries more ominous pathophysiological implications than the lower-body, typically female ("gynoid"), pear-shaped pattern of adipose mass accretion. Paradoxically, this adverse effect of upper-body weight gain during adulthood is most apparent when it occurs atypically in women, in whom risk of premature atherosclerosis and, notoriously, diabetes mellitus is greatly enhanced (most clearly demonstrated as fat deposited within the abdominal cavity by CT or other imaging techniques but indicated clinically and epidemiologically by a waist/hip ratio exceeding 0.9 in women and 1.0 in men). Such upper-body weight gain is especially highly correlated with decreased insulin sensitivity and compensatory hyperinsulinism. The phenomenon of hyperinsulinism is part of the insulin resistance syndrome,[2] which is characterized not only by insulin resistance and compensatory hyperinsulinism but also by obesity, hypertension, and hypoalphalipoproteinemia (low HDL levels, which appear to be based in accelerated HDL catabolism). Family studies of patients with coronary disease have clearly identified a familial basis for this syndrome, sometimes referred to as *familial dyslipidemic hypertension*,[3] probably the basis of the common finding of a low HDL cholesterol level in persons at increased risk of coronary heart disease across the entire adult life span. Once again, it appears to be an interaction between a genetic predisposition and an aging-related physiological alteration in adipose mass (and its distribution) that results in the dyslipoproteinemia which accelerates atherogenesis and causes vascular disease to pass the clinical horizon in middle age or beyond.

Age-related physiological changes in sex hormones also clearly influence plasma lipoprotein metabolism at several points in the scheme presented in Fig. 73-1. In general, estrogens and androgens appear to exert opposing (and offsetting) influences upon the regulation of human lipoprotein metabolism: estrogens, for instance, appear to (1) increase VLDL (and especially triglyceride) secretion, (2) increase VLDL removal [probably via enhanced apolipoprotein E (apo E) recognition yet still within the

TABLE 73-1

Aging and Dyslipoproteinemia: Patterns, Mechanisms, and Treatment*

Lipids		*Lipoproteins*											
C	**TG**	**VLDL**	**LDL**	**HDL**	**Other**	**Pathophysiology**	**Familial Cause(s)**	**Secondary or Aggravating Cause**	**Relation with Aging**	**Relation with Disease**	**Dietary Treatment**	**Drug Treatment**	**Remarks**
⇆	↑	↑	⇆ or ↓	↓	+Fasting chylomicrons when severe	↑ VLDL production	Familial hypertriglyceridemia (FHTG) (ca. 1 in 200) (autosomal dominant)	1. Hyperinsulinism secondary to weight gain, obesity 2. Alcohol 3. Estrogen 4. ?Thiazides, β-blockers	1. ↑ with weight gain (esp. central adiposity)	1. Chylomicronemic (hyperlipidemic) pancreatitis (when severe, usually precipitated by second cause) 2. ?Associated with CHD	1. Caloric restriction 2. AHA step 1 diet[†]	1. Nicotinic acid 2. Fibric acid derivatives 3. HMG CoA reductase inhibitors 4. Androgenic progestins or anabolic steroids	1. Avoid estrogens 2. Avoid bile acid sequestrants (can ↑ TG)
⇆ or ↑	↑ ↑ ↑	↑–↑ ↑ ↑	↓ ↓	↓ ↓	Fasting chylomicrons	↓ TG removal [lipoprotein lipase (LPL) deficiency]	Homozygously inherited LPL deficiency (autosomal recessive)	1. Uncontrolled diabetes 2. ↑ VLDL production (as with hyperinsulinism, weight gain)	1. Usually presents in childhood 2. May present in adulthood with weight gain, drugs	1. Chylomicronemia syndrome (pancreatitis, eruptive xanthoms)	1. Very low fat diet (<20%)	1. Omega-3 fatty acids 2. Fibric acid derivatives 3. Androgenic progestins or anabolic steroids	Rare in old age
↑–↑ ↑	⇆ or ↑–↑ ↑	↑ or ⇆	↑ or ⇆	⇆ or ↓	TG-rich, C-poor, apo B-rich, dense LDL	↑ apo-B production with varying G production	Familial combined hyperlipidemia (FCHL) (hyperapobetalipoproteinemia) (ca. 1 in 200–300) (autosomal dominant)	1. Nephrotic syndrome 2. Hypothyroidism 3. β-blockers, thiazides 4. Corticosteroids 5. Anabolic steroids, androgenic progestins (also ↓ HDL)	1. Aggravated by estrogen deficiency 2. Aggravated by weight gain	1. Strongly associated wtih premature CHD	1. Caloric restriction when overweight 2. AHA Step I–II diet,[†,‡]	1. Nicotinic acid 2. Fibric acid derivatives 3. HMG CoA reductase inhibitors (or combinations)	1. Use bile acid sequestrant with care (can ↑ ↑ TG) 2. Some are heterozygous for LPL deficiency

↑–↑↑	↑–↑↑↑	↑	↓	↓	Fasting chylomicron + VLDL remnants (β-VLDL); apo $E_{2,2}$ phenotype	↑ VLDL production (usually FCHL), plus ↓ chylo + VLDL removal due to nonrecognition of apo E_2 by E,B (LDL) receptor	Familial dysbetalipoproteinemia (type III hyperlipoproteinemia) (ca. 1 in 10,000) (coinheritance of FCHL plus apo $E_{2,2}$)	1. Hyperinsulinism secondary to obesity 2. Hypothyroidism 3. Uncontrolled diabetes	1. Aggravated by weight gain 2. Aggravated by estrogen deficiency	1. Palmar planar + tuberous xanthomas 2. Premature CHD & PVD	1. AHA Step I–II diet†,‡	1. Estrogen in women 2. Fibric acid derivatives 3. Nicotinic acid 4. HMG CoA reductase inhibitors	1. Coexists with FCHL in most kindreds
↑ or ⇋	↑ or ⇋	↑ or ⇋	↑ or ⇋	↓↓		↑ VLDL production, ↑ HDL removal, ? ↓ HDL production	Familial dyslipidemic hypertension (probably autosomal dominant)	1. Aggravated by weight gain—very common in obesity, esp. central	1. Weight gain esp. adult and central 2. May be unmasked in old age as part of non-insulin-dependent diabetes	1. Insulin resistance syndrome—hypertension, obesity, diabetes 2. Strongly associated with CHD	1. Weight reduction 2. Salt restriction (when hypertensive) 3. AHA Step I–II†,‡	1. Unclear relation with FHTG, FCHL, and familial hypoalphalipoproteinemia	
↑↑	⇋ or slt. ↑	⇋ or slt. ↑	↑↑	⇋–↓		1. Functioning LDL receptors or 2. Defective apo B (Arg 3500 → Gln)	1. Familial hypercholesterolemia (FH) (ca. 1 in 500) (autosomal dominant) 2. Familial defective apo B-100 (ca. 1 in 600) (autosomal dominant)	Hypothyroidism Cyclosporine	Usually presents with CHD in middle age and limits longevity	1. Tendon xanthomas, premature arcus corneae 2. Very strongly associated with premature CHD	1. AHA Step II diet‡	1. Estrogen in postmenopausal women 2. Bile acid sequestrants 3. HMG CoA reductase inhibitors 4. Nicotinic acid 5. Combinations of above	HDL level modulates rate of atherogenesis and important in regression in secondary prevention
⇋	↑ or ⇋	↑ or ⇋	⇋	↓↓		(?) ↓ HDL production, ↑ HDL removal	Familial hypoalphalipoproteinemia (?autosomal dominant)	1. Anabolic steroids 2. Thiazides, β-blockers	1. Low HDL remains strong risk factor with aging	1. CHD	1. AHA Step I–II diet,†,‡	1. Nicotinic acid 2. Fibric acid derivatives	1. Overlaps with dyslipidemic hypertension

*Abbreviations: TG = triglyceride; C = cholesterol; VLDL = very low density lipoproteins; LDL = low-density lipoproteins; HDL = high-density lipoproteins; ↑ = increased; ↓ = decreased; and ⇋ = normal.
†AHA (American Heart Association) step I: ≤30% fat calories (≤10% sat., 10–15% monounsat., ≤10% polyunsat., <300 mg cholesterol).
‡AHA (American Heart Association) step II: ≤30% fat calories (<7% sat., 10–15% monounsat., ≤10% polyunsat., <249 mg cholesterol).

VLDL or the more buoyant intermediate-density lipoprotein (IDL) range], (3) increase apo-E,B receptor activity, (4) decrease formation of LDL by virtue of irreversible hepatic VLDL remnant uptake prior to its conversion to LDL (perhaps also inhibited via decreased hepatic triglyceride lipase activity, a clear-cut effect of estrogens[4]), (5) increase HDL (and specifically apo A-I) synthesis, and (6) possibly decrease HDL catabolism as well [also perhaps mediated via decreased hepatic triglyceride (and phospholipase) activity[5]]. The net effects of all these changes are the age-associated trends in average lipoprotein lipid levels depicted in Fig. 3-1 and summarized in Chap. 3. Moreover, exogenous sex hormone replacement (notably estrogen supplementation in the premenopausal era in combination oral contraceptives, and postmenopausal estrogen replacement therapy given alone or in combination with such progestational agents as medroxyprogesterone [Provera]) fully restores and, indeed, when given orally, exaggerates the effects associated with endogenous estrogen secretion in the premenopausal era. These influences are further summarized in Chaps. 3, 12, and 74.

Most germane to this chapter is the potential therapeutic value of exogenous estrogens given to women with dyslipoproteinemia: estrogens reduce LDL cholesterol levels in women with familial hypercholesterolemia[6] (presumably via up-regulating the remaining LDL receptor activity) and cause a net reduction in the LDL cholesterol levels without exaggerating hypertriglyceridemia in women with familial combined hyperlipidemia (Hazzard et al., unpublished), but may aggravate hypertriglyceridemia in those with familial hypertriglyceridemia to the point of risking hyperlipemic pancreatitis.[7] A special role for estrogen has been identified in patients with familial dysbetalipoproteinemia (type III hyperlipoproteinemia) (present in ~1 in 10,000), who most often have the independently coinherited combination of familial combined hyperlipidemia (hyperapobetalipoproteinemia) (present in ~1 to 2 percent of the population) and the homozygous apo E-2 allele (which occurs in ~ 1 percent of the general population). Such women demonstrate remarkable, paradoxical reductions in triglyceride (as well as cholesterol) levels when treated with estrogen,[8] suggesting that it has a special additional effect in enhancing non-apo-E-2-dependent chylomicron- and VLDL-remnant removal.

The age at which the clinical horizon for the atherosclerotic cardiovascular disease associated with dyslipoproteinemia is crossed is heavily dependent upon the magnitude and duration of that dyslipoproteinemia.[9] As a result, given that hereditary, especially monogenic, dyslipoproteinemias are particularly severe and chronic compared with sporadic or polygenic dyslipoproteinemias, CHD occurs earlier in those with hereditary disorders, and such disorders are highly prevalent in those with premature CHD (generally defined as having onset before age 55 in men and 65 in women).[2] The rate of atherogenesis is also clearly influenced by other elements in the coexisting cardiovascular risk profile, notably the presence or absence of cigarette smoking and/or hypertension. For example, studies of pedigrees with familial combined hyperlipidemia have clearly identified earlier-onset CHD in affected members with other risk factors than in those lacking such risk factor even at equivalent lipoprotein lipid levels: e.g., a male smoker with familial combined hyperlipidemia may suffer a myocardial infarction 1 to 2 decades earlier than his nonsmoking sibling with the same disorder. In similar fashion, brothers from pedigrees with familial combined hyperlipidemia (and notably those with dysbetalipoproteinemia) typically experience onset of their clinical coronary disease a decade earlier than their sisters with the same disorder (though here the lipoprotein patterns of men are clearly more adverse than those of their sisters, who are protected by endogenous estrogens until the menopause). Thus the *rate* of atherogenesis is clearly multifactorially determined, the age of onset of clinical disease being determined by that rate. As a result, whereas cardiovascular disease incidence increases exponentially across the adult life span in both men and women, women enjoy an 8- to 10-year relative immunity to CHD (e.g., 55-year-old women have the same average risk as 45-year-old men, 65-year-old women as 55-year-old men, etc.) (Fig. 73-2). Thus, though women (who outlive men) come ultimately to have a lifetime probability of CHD nearly equivalent to that of men, it is typically of

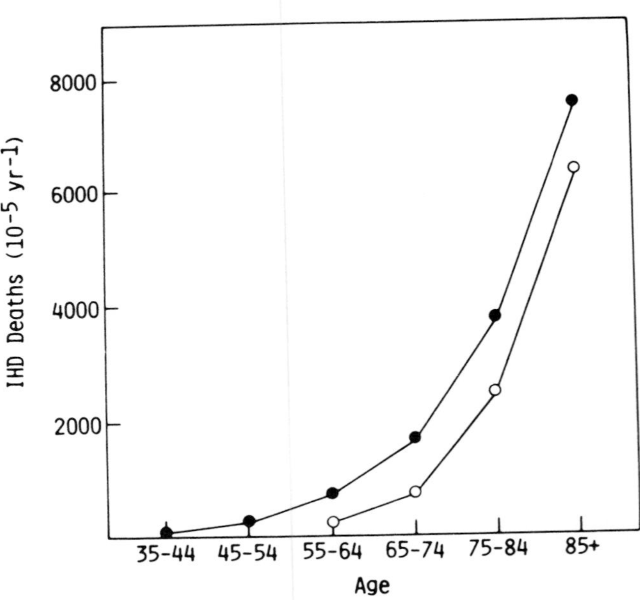

FIGURE 73-2

Death rates per 100,000 population for ischemic heart disease by age in years in men (closed circles) and women (open circles) in the United States in 1976. *(From Sullivan JL:* The sex differential in ischemic heart disease. *Perspect Biol Med 26:658, 1983, with permission.)*

later onset and commonly first occurs in old age. Another principle proceeds from appreciation of this rate phenomenon: reduction of associated risk factors (e.g., cigarette smoking cessation, effective hypertension treatment) may result in later onset of CHD even in those with genetically determined forms of dyslipoproteinemia (and deserves first priority in reducing CHD risk in such persons). It can therefore be predicted that as cigarette smoking declines in the population, the presence of a positive family history for *premature* CHD may be less relevant in determining a patient's cardiovascular risk profile, and in the future even hereditary dyslipoproteinemia may present with new-onset CHD in old age. For the present, however, most CHD in the elderly will occur in persons with mild dyslipoproteinemia or even normal lipid levels.

LIPOPROTEIN METABOLISM IN OLD AGE

Direct, primary effects of aging upon the regulation of lipoprotein metabolism have been difficult to identify other than those related to alterations in adiposity and sex hormone physiology described earlier. Certain studies have suggested decreasing LDL receptor activity with advancing age in humans,[10] but these results are confounded by the chronically high burden of elevated LDL cholesterol levels that is typical in Western societies (attributable in turn to a diet high in saturated fat and cholesterol).[11] Through time the accumulation of intrahepatic free cholesterol may downregulate the LDL receptor (as well as HMG CoA reductase). Therefore, the chronic cholesterolemic burden, rather than aging per se, may be the force down-regulating LDL receptor activity with time (and perforce with aging). Other studies have implied decreased VLDL clearance with advancing age, possibly attributable to diminished lipoprotein lipase activity, but this remains to be clearly established.[12]

More relevant to aging, perhaps, is the plateau in average cholesterol levels reached in midlife (beyond ~ age 50 in men and ~ age 60 in women) in parallel with the plateau in relative body weight observed in both genders (Figs. 3-7 and 3-8). Relevant to old age, moreover, are the parallel declines in plasma cholesterol and triglyceride levels and relative body weight in the final phase of life. These declines, evident in Fig. 3-7, have not been universally observed (e.g., Fig. 3-8). The explanation for the clear decline in plasma lipid levels in some studies and its absence even at advanced ages in others may relate to subject selection: some may be epidemiological studies of community-dwelling older volunteers, selectively examining healthier older persons, while other studies that include, for example, institutionalized older persons may selectively overrepresent dependent, frail, and failing persons, a critical distinction, as emphasized below.

HYPOCHOLESTEROLEMIA IN THE ELDERLY POPULATION

What is more clear in geriatrics is the other side of the coin of hyperlipidemia, namely, *hypo*cholesterolemia and its adverse and ominous implications. Just as has been increasingly appreciated for relative body weight (Chap. 72) and blood pressure (Chap. 47), the relationship between cholesterol levels and total mortality risk appears to be J-shaped,[13] i.e., increased at the lower as well as the upper ranges of cholesterol levels, minimum mortality being in between (generally ~160 to 200 mg/dl in Western populations). While still subject to lively debate, this association of low cholesterol levels with increased mortality risk is clearly present in populations with other, principally nonatherosclerotic, mortality risks [cancer, diabetes mellitus in males, accidents, infections, hemorrhagic stroke, and multisystem failure (Fig. 73-3)]. Careful studies of institutionalized populations have identified hypocholesterolemia and its association with increased mortality risk in the nursing home[14] and in the hospital, the latter notably in those with hypocholesterolemia *acquired* in the hospital setting.[15] Among these patients, hypocholesterolemia was associated with not only increased risk of mortality but also increased rates of several kinds of complications (especially infection), clear biochemical evidence of malnutrition, and higher duration and cost of hospitalization. The mechanism of such, often terminal, hypocholesterolemia is clearly complex, involving decreased nutritional intake as well as enhanced catabolism (and decreased production of visceral proteins), issues dealt with in detail in Chap. 111. Suffice it to say here that falling cholesterol levels, especially among older persons, may portend disease onset in the near and sometimes even relatively remote future: e.g., a low cholesterol level appears to be associated with increased cancer risk even well (up to 5 to 10 years) before the onset of clinical disease,[13,16] as well as providing a marker for adverse clinical status among those already ill (e.g., suggesting the presence of infection or malignancy).

Suffice it also to interject that this phenomenon of acquired hypocholesterolemia has confused the debate as to whether or not and how aggressively to treat hypercholesterolemia in the elderly patient. Here the distinction between long-standing, chronic hypocholesterolemia and that of relatively recent origin seems crucial. On the one hand among those with *lifelong* hypocholesterolemia, the risk of cardiovascular disease is actually diminished across the entire adult lifespan; indeed, genetically determined hypobetalipoproteinemia appears to represent a "longevity syndrome"[17] (as does familial hyperalphalipoproteinemia).[18] This is in contrast to acquired hypocholesterolemia, attributable to associated inflammatory and other disease processes, which occurs in patients in whom the risk of impending demise is clearly en-

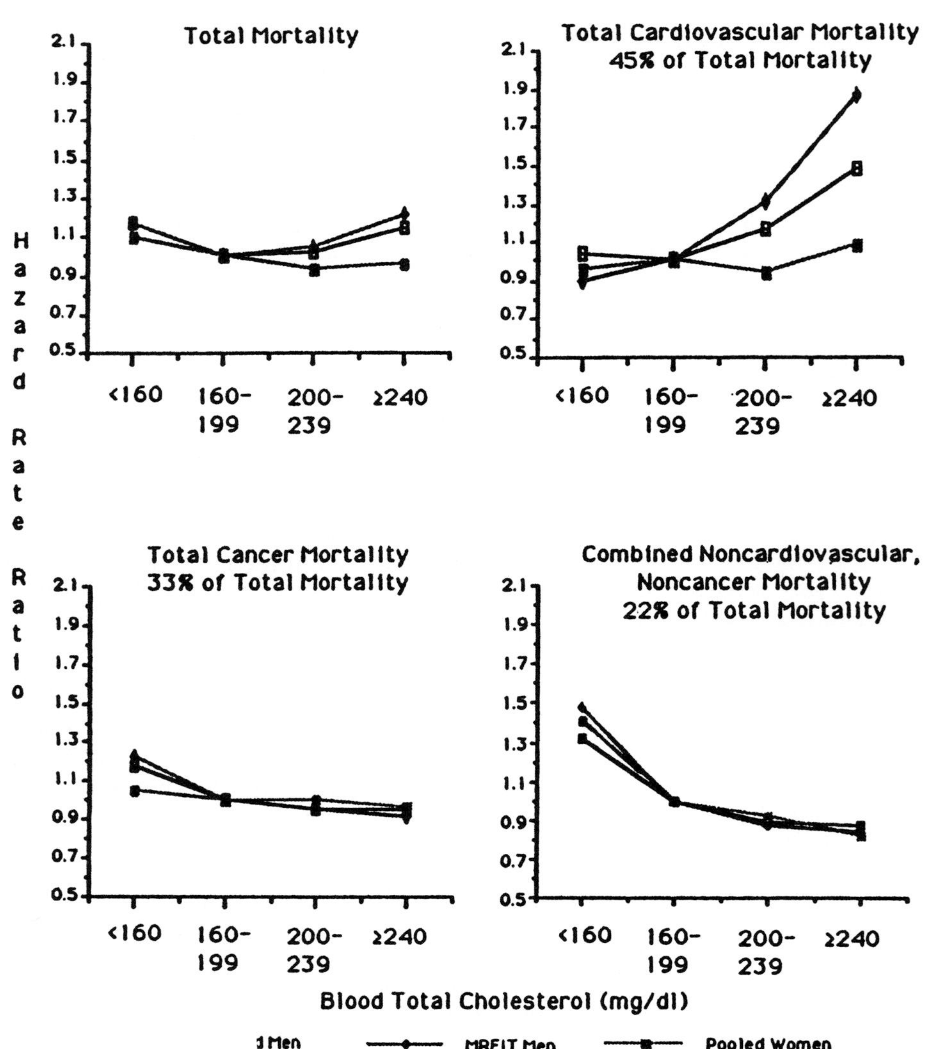

FIGURE 73-3
Graphs of pooled and Multiple Risk Factor Intervention Trial estimates of adjusted hazard rate rations in deaths occurring at least 5 years after baseline in men and women aged 35 to 69 years without CHD at baseline. *(Reprinted with permission from Jacobs et al.[13])*

hanced. Those in stable health with established CHD (but without debilitating congestive failure) appear not to fall into this latter category. Indeed, their antecedent dyslipoproteinemia very likely accelerated their underlying atherogenesis, and thus, lipid reduction (specifically LDL-lowering therapy) appears to be strongly indicated, even to a target LDL level of 100 mg/dl. In such persons the net benefit of lipid lowering would clearly outweigh the theoretical risk of hypocholesterolemia per se (in the absence of associated inflammation or malignancy), given their more proximate risk of recurrent or progressive atherosclerosis. Moreover, it is the unusual patient with CHD in whom even the most aggressive lipid-lowering therapy results in lowering LDL cholesterol levels to much below 100 mg/dl, (and total cholesterol levels to below 140 mg/dl, which appears to represent the threshold below which total mortality risk rises abruptly). Thus the fear of increasing overall mortality risk through aggressive lipid-lowering therapy in those with established coronary disease appears unfounded, a distinction that was made clear in the latest Adult Treatment Panel II recommendations as part of the revised National Cholesterol Education Program (NCEP) published in 1993.[19] These guidelines stress the importance of secondary versus primary prevention in directing the approach to and defining the goals of the management of dyslipoproteinemia (specifically undesirably elevated LDL levels), with age being only a tangential consideration, as reflected below.

HYPERLIPIDEMIA IN THE ELDERLY PATIENT—SHOULD IT BE TREATED?

Atherosclerotic cardiovascular disease is by far the leading cause of death in the elderly population. The process of atherogenesis is clearly time- and perforce age-related. Hence death from its complications accelerates at an exponential rate throughout adult life, culminating in mortality rates that far outstrip all other causes in the ninth and tenth decades.

The multifactorial basis of CHD is well known. Of all the factors, age is the most powerful correlate, but most presentations of CHD risk adjust for age, masking its importance in the minds of many practitioners and public health experts. However, as the impact of the favorable outcome of the Coronary Primary Prevention Trial of the Lipid Research Clinics in 1984[20] was amplified through the Cholesterol Consensus Conference the following year,[21] the subsequent dissemination efforts of the Adult Treatment Panel of the Cholesterol Education Program[19] and related public education campaigns, and widespread media attention, a central question of enormous public health significance has emerged as the most pressing unresolved controversy in preventive medicine in the geriatric arena—should hypocholesterolemia in the elderly patient be treated?

A clear majority of those in the fraternity of lipid experts argue persuasively that hyperlipidemia should be managed at least as aggressively in older patients as in those not yet old, who have been shown to benefit from such therapy. The key points in this argument are as follows:

1. Atherosclerosis appears to be identical in those dying of the disorder in the ninth and tenth decades as in those succumbing far earlier.
2. Dyslipoproteinemia remains a powerful predictive risk index in the elderly. [Even though the slope of the line describing the risk of CHD to the *individual* as a function of cholesterol level is gentler with advancing age (Fig. 73-4), the aggregate ("population-attributable") risk of hypocholesterolemia is even greater in old age because of the exponential rise in CHD rates with age.[19]]
3. Primary prevention by reducing (LDL) cholesterol levels in younger persons clearly works, and there is no compelling reason to postulate that intervention would be any less effective in elderly persons. Perhaps even more germane, the efficacy of secondary prevention through very aggressive lowering of LDL levels (and increasing HDL levels) in those with established coronary disease is being demonstrated in a growing number of studies.[22,23]
4. Drugs that correct lipid disorders in younger persons appear to work equally as well and are perhaps even more powerful, dose for dose (and hence potentially less costly), in elderly persons. This also appears to be achieved without apparent increased toxicity or side effects, though certain agents require special consideration in older persons, such as constipation from bile acid–binding resins, the formation of gallstones in those on fibric acid derivatives or estrogen, gout from hyperuricemia aggravated by nicotinic acid as well as pruritus and dry eyes from the same agent, and risk of myopathy in those with limited renal function precipitated by HMG CoA reductase inhibitors.
5. Given the vulnerability of very old persons to a catastrophic cascade of multisystem failure triggered by the onset of disease in one system, prevention of myocardial infarction or another such complication of atherosclerosis assumes paramount importance in the maintenance of independence, functional integrity, and the quality of life in the elderly person. If such catastrophes can be deferred until just before death in very old

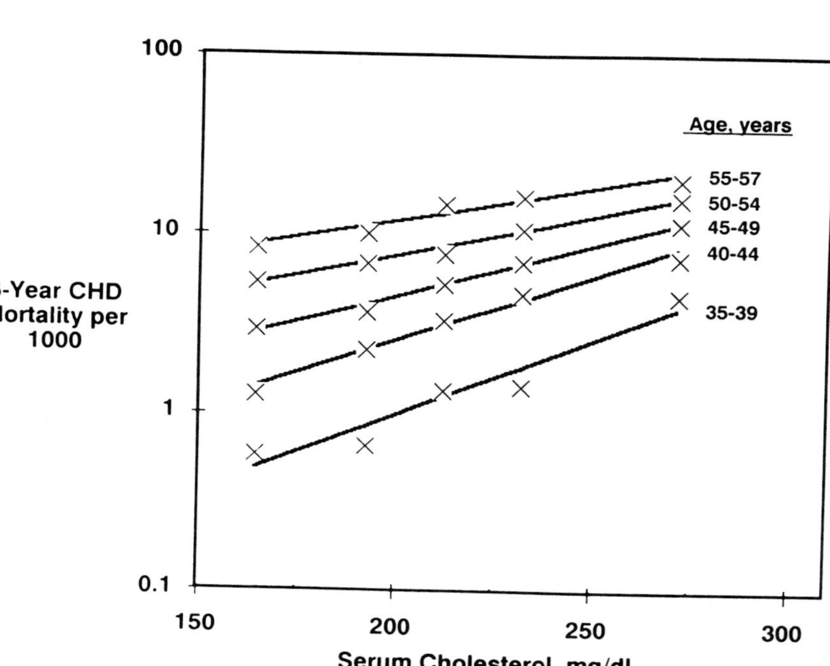

FIGURE 73-4

Relationship of age, cholesterol, and CHD mortality in 356,222 Multiple Risk Factor Intervention Trial screenees. For each age group shown, the odds for CHD death in 6 years of follow-up in each quintile of serum cholesterol is plotted (on a log scale) versus the mean cholesterol level of men in that quintile. The log coefficient for the cholesterol-CHD relationship within each age group was estimated as the slope of the corresponding least-squares regression line. *(Reprinted from Gordon DJ, Rifkind BM,* Treating high blood cholesterol in the older patient. *Am J Cardiol 63:49H, 1989, with permission.)*

age, the dream of "compression of morbidity" will have been realized.[24,25]

However, the reluctance of geriatricians to treat lipid disorders in their elderly patients is widespread, and we must examine that conservatism with respect. My encounters in discussing this issue with many such practitioners suggest the following rational elements in their reluctance:

1. On the one hand, the most robust older people have demonstrated their resilience in the face of time and the aging process (perhaps tolerating a high total cholesterol level because of a concomitant high HDL level, an especially common combination in older women).[26,27] To tamper with that favorable record of homeostatic balance is to invite iatrogenic disaster, a phenomenon with which geriatricians are all too familiar. Even a change in diet may alter that balance for the worse.

   Of note, the failure of total cholesterol levels to continue to correlate with CHD and total mortality above age 65 in women (while continuing to do so in men)[13] probably reflects the higher average HDL levels in women, reinforcing the logic of devoting special attention to HDL levels (or LDL/HDL or total/HDL cholesterol ratios) in individualizing lipid-lowering therapy in older women.[19]
2. On the other hand, *frail* elderly persons have too many other, more urgent problems to contend with to justify aggressive lipid-lowering therapy regardless of cholesterol level. They in particular may be vulnerable to the adverse effects of a diet limited in fat and calories.
3. No trial has *demonstrated* conclusively that CHD prevention through lipid lowering in elderly persons (those over 65) has a favorable risk/benefit ratio. Absent such proof, conservatism should hold sway.
4. Given that no study has shown a reduction in total mortality through lipid lowering at any age [though the long-term follow-up of those (nonelderly) treated with niacin in the Coronary Drug Project was suggestive[27]], only in those with substantial predicted remaining longevity should lipid lowering be contemplated. Since studies of CHD prevention through lipid lowering have suggested that at least 2 years must pass before clear-cut benefit in CHD reduction can be demonstrated,[20] clinical assessment that estimates survival beyond 2 years would seem an essential element in the decision to treat with lipid-lowering agents in the elderly patient.
5. Cost, especially of expensive newer drugs, is of great importance in the decision to treat with such agents in older people, most of whom subsist on fixed incomes (full-dose HMG CoA reductase inhibitor therapy may cost well over $1000 per year). And from the standpoints of cost-effectiveness, therapy with high-cost agents is especially difficult to justify in elderly patients.[9,28]

So for the time being at least, we are left with a clinical conundrum, and carefully considered clinical judgment must prevail as we deal with this decision in each of our individual elderly patients. Unfortunately, the absence of experimental data on this crucial issue appears unlikely to be rectified in the near future. The Cholesterol Reduction in Seniors Program, recently initiated in pilot form, was designed specifically to test the efficacy and safety of HMG CoA reductase–inhibitor–mediated LDL cholesterol reduction in generally healthy older persons (including both men and women, with and without CHD, over 65 and well into their 70s). However, funding considerations prevented its expansion into a full-scale, definitive study. Thus, it is likely that we shall enter the twenty-first century with at best but a partial solution to the void in clear information on this pivotal geriatric problem.

Pending such information, I tend to trust the clinical experience of those I have informally polled at the end of at least two dozen presentations on this issue in the past several years. This exercise is conducted as follows: I pose the clinical vignette of an asymptomatic, robust, 92-year-old woman with a cholesterol level of 320 mg/dl and ask, "Who would treat this woman?" To date only one evangelical enthusiast (a nongeriatrician) has raised his hand at this point. "What if she were 85?" Still no one. "80?" Here several have ventured, "If she requested it" (pointing to the central role of patient initiative in the decision-making process), or, "Maybe with diet," highlighting the aversion to the cost and risk of drugs in elderly persons but perhaps naively assuming that diet therapy is free of such burdens (or thinking of diet as a harmless placebo that would indicate care and concern, clearly of substantial value to many patients). "How about 75?" Here a few more hands go up. "70?"—lots more. "65?"—here the clear majority have their hands in the air, and by "60?" all but a few curmudgeonly skeptics have indicated their eagerness to treat. All in all I would estimate the center of the distribution at about age 70 [interestingly, the age beyond which extrapolation of cholesterol reduction versus estimates of associated CHD reduction intersects the null point in certain primary prevention and population studies such as the Multiple Risk Factor Intervention Trial (MRFIT) and Framingham] (Fig. 73-5).

So far, older patients and their physicians are proving even more conservative in action than in their good intentions on this issue. Whereas various estimates of the prevalence of hyperlipidemia warranting intervention, according to 1987 NCEP guidelines, among community-dwelling adults over 65 are as high as 36 percent, fewer than 5 percent are being treated pharmacologically. However, short of persuasive evidence that such treatment affords substantial benefit at acceptable risk and cost, physicians treating elderly patients are likely to hold to their present, largely expectant treatment patterns. And no expert is likely to prove them wrong until at least the turn of the century.

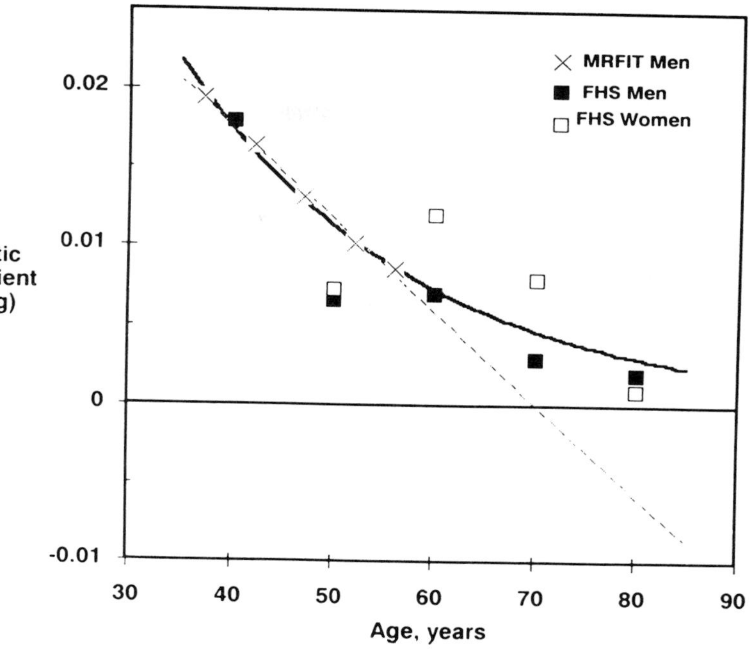

FIGURE 73-5

The age-specific logistic regression coefficients relating cholesterol levels and CHD mortality in 356,222 MRFIT screenees and in men and women in the Framingham Heart Study are plotted versus the midpoint of the corresponding age range. Two alternative extrapolations of the MRFIT coefficients, a linear (dashed line) and an exponential decay (solid line) curve, are shown. *(Reprinted from Gordon DJ, Rifkind BM,* Treating high blood cholesterol in the older patient. *Am J Cardiol 63:51H, 1989, with permission.)*

REFERENCES

1. Goldstein JL et al: Hyperlipidemia in coronary heart disease: II. Genetic analysis of lipid levels in families and delineation of a new inherited disorder, combined hyperlipidemia. *J Clin Invest* 52:154, 1973.
2. Reaven GM: Role of insulin resistance in human disease. *Diabetes* 37:1595, 1988.
3. Williams RR et al: Familial dyslipidemic hypertension: Evidence from 58 Utah families for a syndrome present in approximately 12 percent of patients with essential hypertension. *JAMA* 259:3579, 1988.
4. Applebaum DM et al: Effect of estrogen on post-heparin lipolytic activity: Selective decline in hepatic triglyceride lipase. *J Clin Invest* 59:601, 1977.
5. Hazzard WR et al: Preliminary report: Kinetic studies on the modulation of high-density lipoprotein, apolipoprotein, and subfraction metabolism by sex steroids in a postmenopausal woman. *Metabolism* 33:779, 1984.
6. Tikhanen JJ et al: Natural estrogen as an effective treatment for type II hyperlipoproteinemia in postmenopausal women. *Lancet* 1:490, 1978.
7. Glueck CJ et al: Estrogen-induced pancreatitis in patients with previously covert familial type V hyperlipoproteinemia. *Metabolism* 21:756, 1972.
8. Kushwaha RS et al: Type III hyperlipoproteinemia: Paradoxical hypolipidemic response to estrogen. *Ann Intern Med* 87:517, 1977.
9. Goldstein JL et al: Hyperlipidemia in coronary heart disease: I. Lipid levels in 500 survivors of myocardial infarction. *J Clin Invest* 52:1533, 1973.
10. Miller NE: Why does plasma low density lipoprotein concentration in adults increase with age? *Lancet* 1:263, 1984.
11. Miller NE: Aging and plasma lipoproteins, in Hazzard WR et al (eds): *Principles of Geriatric Medicine and Gerontology,* 2d ed. New York, McGraw-Hill, 1990, p 767.
12. Huttunen JK et al: Post-heparin plasma lipoprotein lipase and hepatic lipase in normal subjects and in patients with hypertriglyceridemia: Correlations to sex, age, and various parameters of triglyceride metabolism. *Clin Sci Mol Med* 50:249, 1976.
13. Jacobs D et al: Report of the conference on low blood cholesterol: Mortality associations. *Circulation* 86:1046, 1992.
14. Rudman D et al: Prognostic significance of serum cholesterol in nursing home men. *J Parenter Enter Nutr* 12:155, 1988.
15. Noel MA et al: Characteristics and outcomes of hospitalized older patients who develop hypocholesterolemia. *J Am Geriatr Soc* 39:455, 1991.
16. Kritchevsky SB et al: Changes in plasma lipid and lipoprotein cholesterol and weight prior to the diagnosis of cancer. *Cancer Res* 51:3198, 1991.
17. Glueck CL et al: Hyperalpha- and hypobeta-lipoproteinemia in octogenarian kindreds. *Atherosclerosis* 27:387, 1977.
18. Glueck CL et al: Familial hyperalphalipoproteinemia: Studies in 18 kindreds. *Metabolism* 24:1243, 1975.
19. Summary of the second report of the National Cholesterol Education Program (NCEP) Expert Panel on Detection, Evaluation, and Treatment of High Blood Cholesterol in Adults (Adult Treatment Panel II). *JAMA* 209:3015, 1993.
20. Lipid Research Clinics Program: The Lipid Research Clinics Coronary Primary Prevention Trial results: I. Reduction in incidence of coronary heart disease. *JAMA* 251:365, 1989.
21. Consensus Conference: Lowering blood cholesterol to prevent heart disease. *JAMA* 253:2080, 1985.
22. Blankenhorn DH et al: Beneficial effects of combined colestipol-niacin therapy on coronary atherosclerosis

and coronary venous bypass grafts. *JAMA* 257:323, 1987.
23. Brown G et al: Regression of coronary artery disease as a result of intensive lipid-lowering therapy in men with high levels of apolipoprotein B. *N Engl J Med* 323:1289, 1990.
24. Fries J: Aging, natural death, and the compression of morbidity. *N Engl J Med* 303:130, 1980.
25. Fries JF et al: Health promotion and the compression of mortality. *Lancet* 1:481, 1989.
26. Applebaum-Bowden D et al: Lipoprotein, apolipoprotein, and lipolytic enzyme changes following estrogen administration in postmenopausal women. *J Lipid Res* 30:1895, 1989.
27. Canner PL et al: Fifteen year mortality in Coronary Drug Project patients: Long-term benefit with niacin. *Am J Cardiol* 8:1245, 1986.
28. Oster G, Epstein A: Cost-effectiveness of antihyperlipidemic therapy in the prevention of coronary heart disease. *JAMA* 258:2381, 1987.

Chapter 74

THE MENOPAUSE AND HORMONE REPLACEMENT THERAPY

Paul B. Marshburn and Bruce R. Carr

The term *menopause* refers to the cessation of menses, the transitional period in a woman's life in which there is progressive loss of ovarian function. During this time, a woman usually experiences various endocrine, somatic, and psychological changes. The median age of menopause in the United States is about 51 years[1] (Fig. 74-1). The average age of menopause has remained constant and does not appear to be related to the age of onset of menarche, social/economic conditions, race, parity, height, or weight. Environmental influences, however, may affect the age of menopause in that cigarette smokers experience an earlier spontaneous menopause than do nonsmokers.[2,3] Because U.S. women have an average life expectancy of 79 years, approximately one-third of a woman's life is spent after the menopause. Furthermore, it is estimated that by the year 2000, the life expectancy of women will extend more than 30 years after the menopause.[1] Thus, a large proportion of the primary care physician's time is spent in the medical management of postmenopausal women.

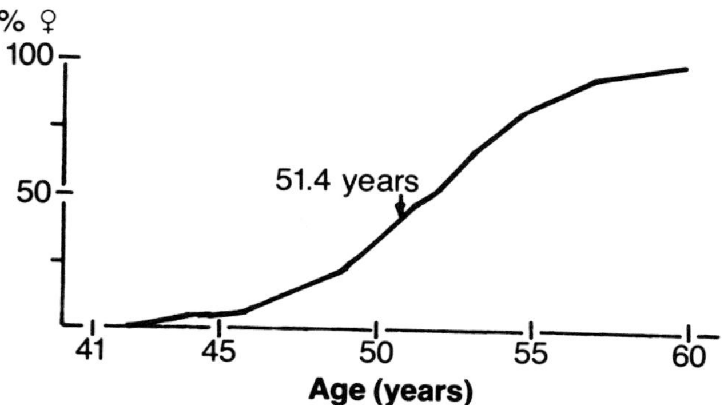

FIGURE 74-1

Frequency distribution of age at menopause. *(Reproduced with permission from Jaszmann LJB: Epidemiology of the climacteric, in Campbell S (ed): Management of the Menopause and Postmenopausal Years. Lancaster, England, MTP Press, 1976, p 12.)*

With an increase in the total number of women living to the age of menopause and beyond, it is important that the physiological changes of the female climacteric be understood and women's health problems be addressed. Because the menopause is a clearly recognized physiological milestone, it is an excellent opportunity for physicians to educate their patients about preventive care, disease screening, and hormone replacement therapy. In this chapter, we will review the changes associated with the female climacteric as well as present our current understanding of the benefits and risks of hormone replacement therapy during the postmenopausal years.

ENDOCRINE CHANGES DURING THE FEMALE CLIMACTERIC

The principal endocrine changes that are characteristic of the female climacteric are caused primarily by decreased ovarian estrogen secretion. This cessation of ovarian estrogen secretion is caused, in turn, by a loss of ova and associated follicles, mainly by atresia, a process that begins before birth (at 20 weeks of gestation) and continues until menopause. The ovary contains a maximum number of follicles during fetal life at midgestation (approximately 7 million); thereafter, however, the number decreases and, by the time of birth, approximately 1 million remain (Fig. 74-2). At menarche, the number of ova has decreased to 400,000; by the time of menopause, only a few follicles can be demonstrated.[4] However, relatively few ova—on average, fewer than 500—are lost by ovulation.

There is evidence in support of the view that the ovary becomes less responsive to gonadotropins a few years prior to the time of menopause.[5] First, in

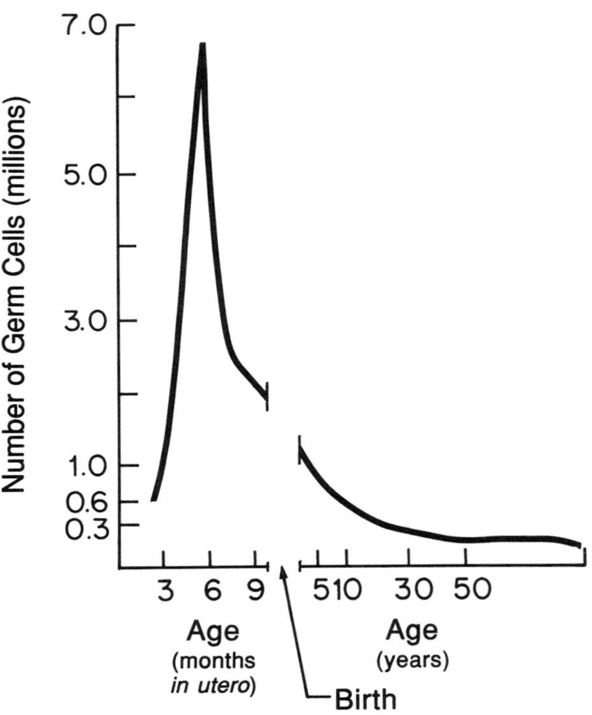

FIGURE 74-2
Changes in germ cell number in the human ovary with increasing age. *(Adapted from Baker TG: Oogenesis and ovulation, in Austin CR, Short RV (eds): Reproduction in Mammals: I. Germ Cells and Fertilization. London: Cambridge University Press, 1972, p 14).*

women over 45, the length of the ovarian cycle is often shortened, primarily because of a decrease in the length of the follicular phase; after ovulation, the length of the luteal phase remains unaffected. Second, associated with a shortened follicular phase, the plasma levels of 17β-estradiol are lower during the follicular and luteal phases of the cycle.[6] The decreased levels of 17β-estradiol probably are caused by a diminished capacity for (or resistance of) the remaining follicles to be stimulated to secrete estrogen, because the metabolic clearance rate of 17β-estradiol is not increased in postmenopausal women.[7] Presumably in response to decreasing levels of 17β-estradiol and inhibin, a decrease in negative feedback to the hypothalamic-pituitary axis occurs. Consequently, follicle stimulating hormone (FSH) levels are greater in perimenopausal women during the ovarian cycle. Later as the time of menopause nears, the interval between menses lengthens, anovulatory cycles are common, and finally menstruation ceases as the capacity of the few remaining ovarian follicles to respond to gonadotropins diminishes to zero.

After menopause, the levels of plasma gonadotropins and the concentrations of the major circulating C_{19}-steroids and estrogens are altered compared with values found in premenopausal women during the early follicular phase of the cycle. The cessation of follicular development that leads to a decline in the production of 17β-estradiol and other hormones causes further loss of negative feedback to the hypothalamic-pituitary centers (Fig. 74-3). In turn, the levels of gonadotropins increase, with levels of FSH rising to a greater extent than those of luteinizing hormone (LH). The higher concentration of FSH than of LH in postmenopausal women is believed to be due to loss of suppression of FSH by follicular inhibin or due to the fact that FSH is cleared less rapidly than LH because of the higher sialic acid content of FSH. Gonadotropin-releasing hormone (GnRH) administered to postmenopausal women causes a pronounced increase in the secretion of both LH and FSH, similar to the enhanced hypothalamic-pituitary secretion of GnRH that occurs in other forms of ovarian failure.[8] Some investigators find that the concentration of both gonadotropins remain fairly constant after the age of 60,[8] but others report the finding of a downward trend during later decades of life.[9]

Estrogen and C_{19}-steroid levels in postmenopausal women are reduced significantly compared with

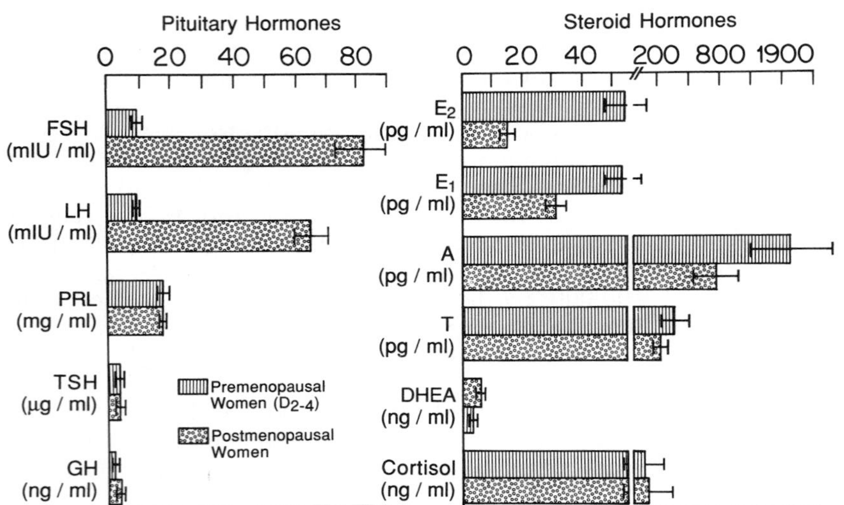

FIGURE 74-3
Levels of pituitary and steroid hormones in premenopausal women compared to postmenopausal women during days 2 to 4 of the menstrual cycle. *(Reproduced with permission from Yen SSC: J Reprod Med 18:287, 1977.)*

those in women during reproductive life. Estrogen production in postmenopausal women is diminished but not totally absent. Estrogen secretion by the postmenopausal ovary is minimal, however, and oophorectomy does not cause any further decline in estrogen levels.[9] Plasma levels of 17β-estradiol, the principal estrogen secreted during reproductive life, are lower than levels of estrone in postmenopausal women. Furthermore, the adrenal cortex does not secrete significant quantities of estrogen in pre- or postmenopausal women.[10] As neither the ovary nor the adrenal gland of postmenopausal women secretes significant quantities of estrogens, what then is the source of the estrogen produced in such women? Pioneering work by Siiteri and MacDonald[11] demonstrated that the extraglandular conversion of adrenal androstenedione to estrone provided the predominant source of postmenopausal estrogen production. The principal sites of extraglandular aromatization of androstenedione are adipose tissue, bone, muscle, skin, and brain. Thus, total estrogen production may be considerable in obese postmenopausal women.

Prior to menopause, plasma androstenedione is derived almost equally from the adrenal and the ovary; after menopause, however, the ovarian secretion of androstenedione is minimal and the plasma levels of androstenedione fall by 50 percent (Table 74-1). The menopausal ovary does continue to secrete testosterone, which is believed to be formed in the stromal cells, the principal structural component of the ovary of postmenopausal women.[10]

STRUCTURAL AND PHYSIOLOGICAL CHANGES ASSOCIATED WITH THE MENOPAUSE

The ovary of the postmenopausal women is reduced in size, weighing less than 2.5 g, and is wrinkled or prunelike in appearance. The cortical area is reduced in size because of loss of ova and follicular cells; thus the stromal cells predominate. As a result of decreased 17β-estradiol secretion in postmenopausal women, there is a progressive decrease in weight and size of the organs of the female genitourinary tract and the breasts. The endometrium becomes thin and atrophic in most postmenopausal women, although cystic hyperplasia may be present in up to 20 percent of such women. As a consequence of estrogen deficiency, the vaginal mucosa and urethra also become thin and atrophic. The mild degrees of hirsutism noted by many postmenopausal women may be due to diminished estrogen production and unopposed testosterone action at the hair follicle unit. There is, however, a general decrease in scalp, pubic, and axillary hair and a decrease in skinfold thickness, with a thinning of the epidermis in particular.

Certain symptoms or disorders believed to be characteristic of the postmenopausal woman are caused primarily by the decrease in ovarian secretion of estrogen, and some of these disorders are of such magnitude to cause significant physical, emotional, and economic hardships. The term *menopausal syndrome* is used to describe a spectrum of symptoms that may occur at or about the time of the menopause. These symptoms include the hot flush (vasomotor instability), dryness and atrophy of the urogenital epithelium and vagina, and probably other related disorders that include osteoporosis, psychological symptoms including insomnia, mood changes, irritability, and nervousness. The vasomotor symptoms and urogenital atrophy are related more clearly to the early estrogen deficiency of the menopause (Figure 74-4). Longer-term and more serious consequences of postmenopausal hypoestrogenism involve the accelerated development of osteoporosis and cardiovascular disease.

VASOMOTOR SYMPTOMS AND GENITOURINARY CHANGES

The initial symptoms indicating the need for estrogen use often involve vasomotor instability and atrophy of the urogenital epithelium. Approximately 30 to 80 percent of all women in the menopausal age group

TABLE 74-1

Comparison of Plasma Sex Hormone Concentrations in Pre- and Postmenopausal Women

Hormone Concentration	Premenopausal		Postmenopausal
	Min	Max	
Estradiol, pg/ml	50–60	300–500	5–25
Estrone, pg/ml	30–40	150–300	20–60
Progesterone, ng/ml	0.5–1.0	10–20	0.5
Androstenedione, ng/ml		1.0–2.0	0.3–1.0
Testosterone, ng/ml		0.3–0.8	0.1–0.5

SOURCE: From Mishell DR: *Menopause—Physiology and Pharmacology*. Chicago, Year Book, 1987, p 48. Reproduced with permission.

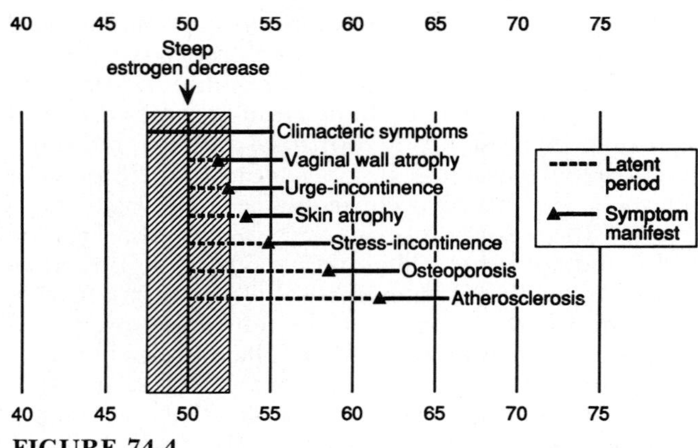

FIGURE 74-4

Time course of menopausal symptomatology. *(Adapted from Van Keep PA, Kellerhals J: Front Horm Res 2:160, 1973 with permission of the authors.)*

experience hot flushes. Of these, 80 percent will experience hot flushes for more than 1 year.[12] Rarely, though, do hot flushes continue for more than 5 years after menopause.

The pathogenesis of the hot flush is unclear, although it does appear to involve alterations in the thermoregulatory center of the hypothalamus secondary to estrogen withdrawal. Early studies noted a relationship between pulses of LH and the hot flush[13,14]; however, because hot flushes are not abolished in women treated with GnRH analogs or following hypophysectomy, these LH pulses do not appear necessary for vasomotor symptoms.[15] Current hypotheses on the etiology of the hot flush support the concept that the decrement in estrogen at menopause may cause an "opioid withdrawal"[16] or a decrease in noradrenergic neuronal function in the hypothalamus.[17] This latter hypothesis is supported by the finding that $alpha_2$-agonists, such as clonidine, are effective in reducing hot flushes.[18]

In a very detailed description of the hot flush, Hannan[19] noted that the first symptom was a pressure sensation in the head that progressed in intensity until the flush occurred.[19] Occasionally, heart palpitations were experienced. The hot flush itself, which is a sensation of heat or burning, began in the head and neck and spread over the entire body. After this, the women experienced total body sweating, especially in the head, upper chest, back, and neck. The entire episode lasted from seconds to as long as 30 minutes. A change in skin conductance, as measured by perspiration, is the first quantifiable sign of a hot flush.[20] This is followed by a change in skin temperature, indicating cutaneous dilation and subsequently a drop in core temperature by an average of 0.2°C. Subjective sensations of the hot flush are usually gone when physiological changes can still be detected. Vasomotor instability occurs in women in whom there is a fairly sudden loss of ovarian estrogen secretion (either by surgical or natural processes) or sudden discontinuation of estrogen therapy.[21,22] Women with Turner's syndrome, who have low levels of estrogen, experience hot flushes only if they are first treated with estrogens and the estrogen therapy is then discontinued.[23] Circulating estrogen levels have not been found to change before or after a hot flush, although adrenal steroids (cortisol, androstenedione, and dehydroepiandrosterone) are noted to be significantly increased.[22] Not all women experience complete relief of vasomotor symptoms after estrogen replacement; therefore some of these symptoms may not be due singularly to estrogen deficiency.

Diminished estrogen production also leads to atrophy of the vagina and symptoms of atrophic vaginitis. Atrophic vaginitis is characterized by itching, discomfort, burning, dyspareunia, and sometimes vaginal bleeding as the epithelium thins. Estrogen deficiency can also lead to loss of uterine support, with subsequent uterine descensus. Other symptoms of estrogen deficiency include urinary urgency and stress incontinence, dysuria, and urinary frequency. Estrogen treatment is effective in relieving the symptoms of atrophic vaginitis and other symptoms of estrogen deficiency of the lower urinary tract.[24] Of interest is that estrogen therapy has been reported to increase skin collagen in postmenopausal women.[25] Clinical evidence of urinary tract infection, vaginal neoplasia, and infectious vaginitis may produce symptoms similar to those of atrophic vaginitis and should always be sought prior to estrogen therapy.

OTHER SYMPTOMS

The menopause is not associated with an increase in major psychiatric disorders. The appearance of somatic and psychological symptoms, however, does occur, although these symptoms could be secondary to other physiological changes related to hypoestrogenism, such as sleep disturbance.[26] Nonetheless, randomized, prospective, double-blinded, placebo-controlled trials have demonstrated improvement in cognitive and affective function with estrogen use, especially with regard to improvement in memory, insomnia, anxiety, and irritability.[27]

ESTROGEN THERAPY AND OSTEOPOROSIS

Osteoporosis (see Chap. 76) is defined as the loss of structural support in trabecular bone, predominantly of the axial skeleton. Bone loss after the menopause appears to proceed at a rate of 1 to 2 percent per year.[28] By the age of 80, there is an estimated loss of 50 percent of bone mass in Caucasian women. Thus, if left untreated, osteoporosis is one of the most dev-

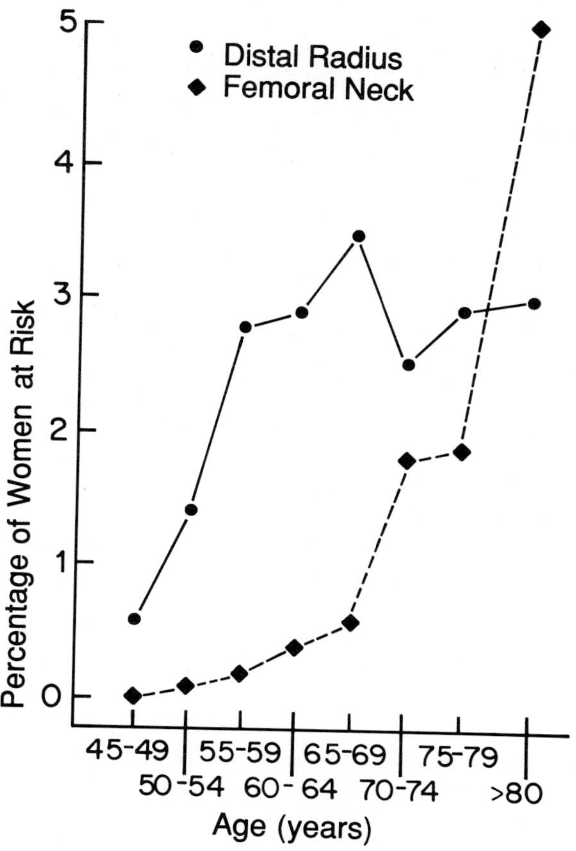

FIGURE 74-5

Relationship of the incidence of fractures of the distal radius and femoral neck with the age of women. *(Reproduced with permission from Aitken JM: Bone metabolism in postmenopausal women, in Beard RJ (ed): The Menopause: A Guide to Current Research and Practice. Lancaster, England, MTP Press, 1976, p 99.)*

astating diseases of aged women. It has been estimated that 25 percent of all women over the age of 60 have radiological evidence of vertebral crush fractures.[29] Such fractures in the elderly (and the complications thereof) are a major cause of death as well as disability and morbidity (Fig. 74-5).

Estrogen deficiency is believed to be a major cause of bone loss in women. An action of estrogen directly on bones in humans has not been definitively proven. Recent studies, however, have identified estrogen receptors on cultured osteoblasts,[30] and in animal studies estrogen deficiency results in an interleukin-6–mediated stimulation of osteoclastogenesis.[31] Hypoestrogenism may also lead to an increased sensitivity to parathyroid hormone (PTH) in bone, whereas the sensitivity in other organs such as the kidney and intestine remains the same. The end result would be increased bone resorption and mobilization of calcium without increased urinary or intestinal excretion of calcium. Studies on calcitonin metabolism, however, found no difference in calcitonin levels in pre- and postmenopausal women or before and after oral estrogen therapy.[32]

Estrogen treatment attenuates height loss, improves calcium balance, maintains bone density, and reduces the number of vertebral, wrist, and hip fractures in young castrated and postmenopausal women.[33,34] Many earlier clinical studies focused on measurements of the peripheral skeleton and not the axial skeleton. These techniques included radiogrammetry (measuring cortical thickness and its area in the metacarpals) and single-photon absorptiometry (measuring the amount of cortical bone in the distal radius).[35,36] Unfortunately, these radiographic tests do not address the axial skeleton, where the devastating effects of osteoporosis on trabecular bone are most severe. Dual-photon absorptiometry and computed tomography (CT) techniques are used most commonly to evaluate vertebral bone mass.[37,38] Improved modalities for assessing vertebral bone mineral content have been developed. Quantitative digital radiography (QDR) and dual-energy x-ray absorptiometry (DEXA) utilize less radiation than the gadalidium radioactive source of dual-photon absorptiometry and are fast, precise, and accurate.

The major factors known to increase the risk of osteoporosis include white or Asian heritage; low body weight; hypoestrogenism; early menopause; positive family history for osteoporosis; diet low in calcium and vitamin D and high in caffeine, phosphate, alcohol, and protein; cigarette smoking; and a sedentary lifestyle (Table 74-2).[39] Importantly, uncommon medical conditions including glucocorticoid use, renal failure, hyperthyroidism, primary hyperparathyroidism, and hyperadrenalism are associated with osteoporosis and should be identified. Persons who are immobilized for long periods of time lose bone mass and bone fragility develops, i.e., increased bone resorption with normal rates of bone formation.[40]

Studies indicate that early and long-term estrogen replacement in women undergoing surgical or natural menopause is beneficial for skeletal maintenance. If estrogen replacement is to be of most benefit, it should be initiated before serious loss of bone density has occurred. Bone loss, as measured by bone biopsy or by indirect techniques, is attenuated by estrogen (Fig. 74-6), and a decreased rate of develop-

TABLE 74-2

Major Risk Factors for Osteoporosis

Hypoestrogenism
Low body weight
White or oriental race
Early menopause
Positive family history for osteoporosis
Diet low in calcium and vitamin D
Diet high in caffeine, phosphate, and protein
Alcoholism
Cigarette smoking
Sedentary lifestyle

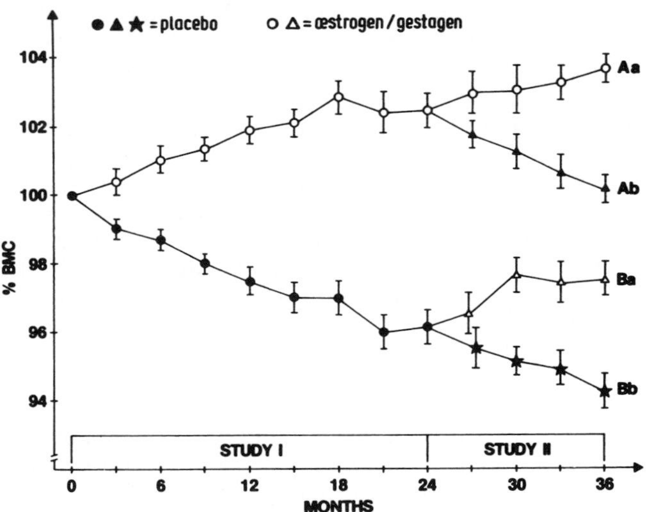

FIGURE 74-6

Bone mineral content as a function of time and treatment in 94 (study I) and 77 (study II) women soon after menopause. (*Reproduced with permission from Christiansen et al.*[43])

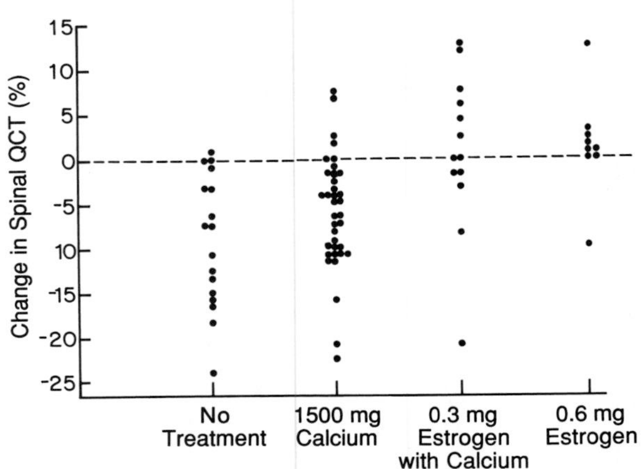

FIGURE 74-7

Change in spinal quantitative computed axial tomography after 1 year in untreated menopausal women compared to menopausal women treated with 1500 mg calcium only, 0.3 mg conjugated estrogen plus calcium, or only 0.6 mg conjugated estrogen daily. (*Reproduced with permission from Genast et al.)*

ment of fractures was reported in women who ingested estrogens.[41–43] In addition, women receiving 1500 mg of calcium each day in combination with 0.3 mg of conjugated estrogen were found to have no evidence of bone loss or decreased bone mass in comparison with subjects who were untreated or treated with calcium alone (Fig. 74-7).[44] Postmenopausal women require a daily intake of 1500 mg of elemental calcium to keep up with bone loss. This requirement is usually not met in the average U.S. diet. Therefore, for the greatest protection from osteoporosis, estrogen therapy should be combined with calcium supplementation and prudent lifestyle measures, along with minimization of smoking and ethanol intake.

Nonsteroidal medical therapies have been evaluated and preliminary evidence suggest that they may serve as potential alternatives to women who cannot receive hormone therapy. Bisphosphonates (etidronate) plus calcium are effective in the treatment of osteoporosis,[45] and salmon calcitonin is approved for use in women with established osteoporosis who cannot tolerate estrogens.[46] Sodium fluoride is a potent stimulator of bone formation and, in one properly controlled study, decreased spinal fractures.[47] The prominent gastrointestinal side effects of sodium fluoride with most current regimens limit its usefulness, however.

THE CARDIOPROTECTIVE EFFECTS OF POSTMENOPAUSAL ESTROGEN THERAPY

Diseases of the heart and circulatory system are the leading cause of death among women in the United States. Estrogens exert a cardioprotective effect in part attributable to an associated favorable impact on lipid metabolism (Table 74-3). Serum cholesterol was

TABLE 74-3

Concentrations of Lipids and Lipoproteins in Users and Nonusers of Estrogen

	Mean ± SD (Median)	
Lipid Profile	**Nonuser**	**Equine Estrogen**
Cholesterol	230 ± 44.3 (226)	219 ± 33.9 (218)*
Triglyceride	174 ± 66.9 (100)	141 ± 71.5 (126)*
HDL cholesterol	61 ± 15.6 (61)	69 ± 17.7 (67)*
LDL cholesterol	154 ± 43.8 (147)	133 ± 33.9 (131)*
VLDL cholesterol	16 ± 13.8 (13)	18 ± 12.5 (16)

*$p < 0.05$.
SOURCE: Reproduced with permission from Wahl P et al: Effect of estrogen/progestin potency on lipid/lipoprotein cholesterol. *N Engl J Med* 308:802, 1983.

TABLE 74-4

Risk of Coronary Heart Disease in Prospective Studies of Hormone Replacement Therapy

Investigator	*N*	Endpoint	Relative Risk
Burch et al., 1974	737	CHD	0.4
Hammond et al., 1974	610	CHD	0.3
Petitti et al., 1979	1,675	MI	1.2
Petitti et al., 1986	1,675	MI	0.5*
Wilson et al., 1985	1,234	CHD	1.9
Stampfer et al., 1985	32,317	CHD	0.5
Bush et al., 1987	2,270	Fatal CHD	0.37

*Study addressed total mortality.

4 percent lower in women on estrogen, although serum triglycerides were 26 percent higher. Median high-density lipoprotein (HDL) cholesterol levels were 10 percent higher and median low-density lipoprotein (LDL) cholesterol levels 11 percent lower.[48] Both increased levels of LDL and decreased levels of HDL correlate positively with risk for coronary heart disease, the opposite of what is seen in estrogen users. Other studies have shown even greater decreases in LDL cholesterol and greater increaes in HDL.

Epidemiological studies reveal clear evidence for a reduced risk of cardiovascular disease (CVD) in women receiving hormone replacement therapy (Table 74-4). These reports and others indicate an approximately 50 percent reduction in CVD in women who received postmenopausal estrogens.[49–53] Cardiac catheterization studies demonstrate that women on hormone replacement develop less severe coronary atherosclerosis, and women with more severe CVD at the time of initial catheterization derived the greatest protective benefit from estrogen therapy (Fig. 74-8).[49,51] Not only is the patient with previous myocardial infarction not at increased risk of developing complications from hormone replacement therapy, but these women obtain the greatest CV benefit from estrogen replacement therapy (ERT).[54] Doses of

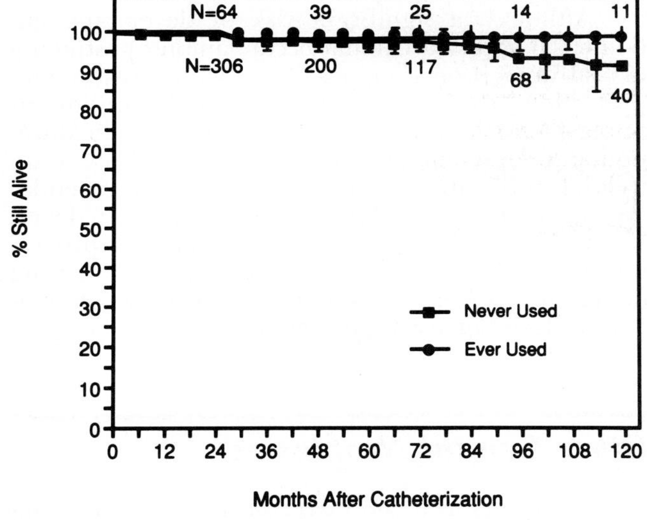

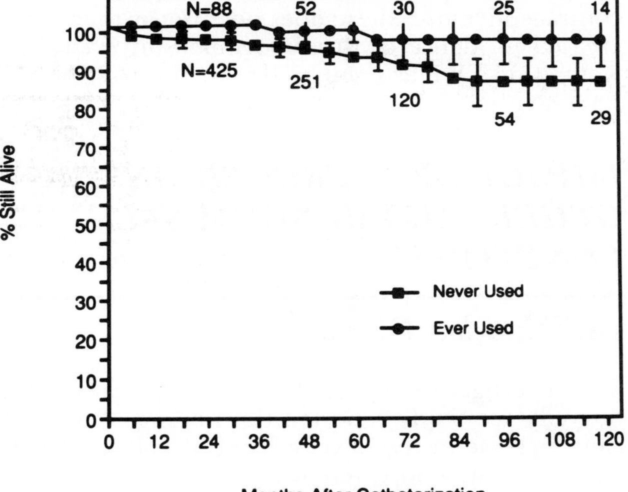

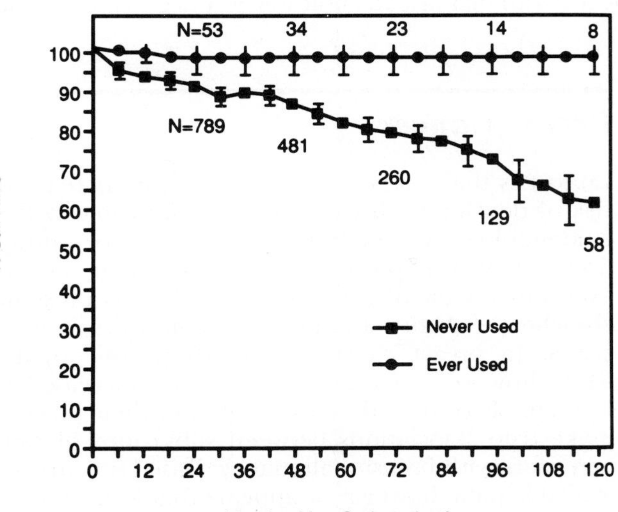

FIGURE 74-8

Effect of estrogen on 10-year survival after cardiac catheterization of patients who had (a) initially normal coronary arteriograms, (b) coronary stenosis varying between detectable and 69 percent, and (c) left main coronary stenosis 50 percent or greater or other stenosis 70 percent or greater. *(Adapted with permission from Sullivan et al.)*

estrogens administered for postmenopausal therapy can be safely used in women who smoke, have well-controlled diabetes mellitus, or are hypertensive. As mentioned, the most favorable health outcome is achieved with attention to modifications of correctable cardiovascular risk factors along with estrogen therapy

HYPERTENSION AND THROMBOEMBOLISM

In prospective randomized trials that examined possible associations between postmenopausal estrogen therapy and hypertension, no significant increase in blood pressure was found.[54,55] In fact, some evidence suggests that postmenopausal estrogen therapy may slightly decrease blood pressure.[56] Therefore, the occasional relationship between elevated blood pressure and estrogen in oral contraceptive formulations is not observed in doses of estrogen used for postmenopausal therapy. Furthermore, in contrast to oral contraceptive use, there does not appear to be an increased incidence of thromboembolism or stroke in women on ERT as compared with controls.[57,58]

IMPACT OF ESTROGEN ON OTHER POSTMENOPAUSAL CONDITIONS

Gallbladder Disease

The investigators of the Boston Collaborative Drug Surveillance Study reported the finding of a significant increase in the development of gallbladder disease in postmenopausal women taking conjugated estrogens,[59] presumably because estrogen therapy causes an increase in cholesterol concentration in bile.

Breast Cancer

Concerns that exogenous estrogen may increase the risk of developing breast cancer stem primarily from epidemiological data linking the extent of endogenous estrogen exposure with breast malignancy. An excellent review of this important issue is presented elsewhere.[60] Many studies have demonstrated no increase in breast cancer risk with postmenopausal ERT; however, two have reported an increase.[61–69] Epidemiological studies are limited in their power to make true associations between subgroups of estrogen users with breast malignancy. Based on currently available data, however, it appears that long-term use of conjugated estrogens in small doses does not substantially increase the risk of breast cancer. Women with benign breast disease remain a controversial group, but estrogen should not be withheld until definitive data indicate otherwise. The minimal theoretical increased risk of breast malignancy with estrogen certainly appears justified with the clear benefit in protection from accelerated osteoporosis and CVD. Despite evidence that women on estrogen who develop breast cancer have improved survival,[70] carcinoma of the breast remains a contraindication to estrogen replacement therapy.

Endometrial Cancer

Unopposed estrogen treatment (i.e., without progestational therapy) and increased amounts of endogenously produced estrogen in postmenopausal women are associated with an increased incidence of endometrial adenocarcinoma.[71–74] It is now known that those postmenopausal women with features commonly associated with endometrial cancer, notably, obesity, are the women who produce the most estrogen in extraglandular sites.

Although a significant risk of developing endometrial adenocarcinoma occurs among postmenopausal women on unopposed estrogen replacement, protection can be achieved with cyclic or continuous progestational therapy. Studies suggest that the duration and dosage of combined estrogen and progestin treatment is important for protection against endometrial carcinoma.[27] Most patients are protected with 12 to 15 days of a 10-mg dosage of medroxyprogesterone (MPA) acetate in cyclic regimen or a 2.5-mg dosage of MPA in continuous treatment (see Therapeutic Recommendations, below).

Other Genital Neoplasias

There appears to be no increased risk of developing cancer of the ovary, cervix, fallopian tubes, vagina, or vulva in women on long-term postmenopausal ERT.

Contraindications and Precautions for Hormone Replacement Therapy

Table 74-5 lists the conditions that may constitute relative contraindications to hormone replacement therapy.[75]

Therapeutic Recommendations

Before beginning ERT, all patients should be thoroughly screened to determine their candidacy. Along with a complete history and physical examination oriented toward identification of specific contraindications for ERT, patients should undergo baseline laboratory tests including blood pressure, urinalysis,

TABLE 74-5

Contraindications and Precautions to Postmenopausal Hormone Therapy

Contraindications to hormone replacement therapy include:
- Unexplained vaginal bleeding
- Active liver disease
- Chronic impaired liver function
- Recent vascular thrombosis (with or without emboli)
- Carcinoma of the breast
- Endometrial carcinoma, except in certain circumstances[38]

Conditions that may constitute relative contraindications include:
- Seizure disorders
- Hypertension
- Uterine leiomyomas
- Familial hyperlipidemia*
- Migraine headaches
- Thrombophlebitis
- Endometriosis
- Gallbladder disease

*Specifically, familial hypertriglyceridemia.
SOURCE: Reproduced with permission from American College of Obstetrics and Gynecology.[75]

complete blood count, and determination of serum lipids. Perimenopausal or postmenopausal women with abnormal uterine bleeding should have an endometrial biopsy. Hormone replacement therapy does not mimic the natural or physiological hormone production that occurs during reproductive life and is, in fact, treatment rather than replacement therapy. In most studies where attempts were made to investigate optimum dosage, various therapeutic agents with diverse dosages and treatment periods were commonly used. It has therefore been difficult to interpret the clinical and laboratory effects of the various estrogens and progestins used.

Currently, hormone therapy is widely recommended in all estrogen-deficient women in whom there is no contraindication. A commonly used treatment regimen in the United States is 0.625 mg of conjugated equine estrogen or estrone sulfate for the first 25 days of each month. Most clinicians currently administer estrogens continuously on a daily basis and also give progestins for 15 continuous days each month in women with an intact uterus. The addition of progestins to both continuous and cyclic ERT regimens is associated with a decreased incidence of endometrial hyperplasia and endometrial cancer.[76–79] Studies have indicated that 0.625 mg of conjugated equine estrogen will optimally protect against accelerated bone resorption and still favorably affect the serum lipid profile.[80] Another popular route of administration is transdermal delivery of estradiol (E_2). (Of note, however: Transdermal estrogen does not alter lipid levels, presumably due to a lack of "first-pass" effect on hepatic metabolism that is characteristic of orally administered sex steroids.) A 4-cm patch (containing 0.05 mg) can produce constant levels of E_2 of approximately 72 pg/ml and of E_1 of 37 pg/ml.[81] With this route of administration, hepatic effects are limited and the patch must be replaced every 3 to 4 days. Subcutaneous implants or injections of hormone, while effective, do not provide for easy discontinuance of treatment if complications develop. Various estrogen-containing vaginal creams offer an alternative to oral replacement therapy; however, an appropriate dose that provides the long-term benefits on bone and the cardiovascular system are unknown.

In cases where progestins are administered alone, bone mineral content will be maintained better than with placebo, but this will not be as effective as ERT. Of at least theoretical concern, progestin treatment may also lead to increased LDL and decreased HDL, risk indices for coronary heart disease.[82] However, this effect appears to be dependent upon the potency, dose, and length of therapy of the progestin. Cyclic administration of medroxyprogesterone acetate (5 to 10 mg) appears to have fewer adverse effects on serum lipids and lipoproteins than effective doses of progestins of the 19-nortestosterone family (e.g., levonorgestrel, norethindrone). Addition of oral micronized natural progesterone at 200 to 400 mg/day for 10 days of each treatment cycle does not appear to influence HDL cholesterol or its subtractions. Natural progesterone, however, must be given in divided doses to maintain effective serum levels, and it can induce drowsiness. Therefore, compliance with micronized progesterone would be difficult and therefore would not be a good alternative to the synthetic progestins used currently. Continuous daily treatment with both an estrogen and progestin has also been advocated by some, although the alterations in lipids need to be addressed more closely. In women without a uterus, estrogens used alone are sufficient and progestins are not recommended. Recommended dosages and regimens for various oral estrogens and progestins are presented in Table 74-6.

A variety of other medications are somewhat effective in relieving vasomotor symptoms but do not ameliorate urogenital tract atrophy, osteoporosis, or cardiovascular disease. Among these agents are progestins (medroxyprogesterone acetate, 20 mg/day orally or 150 mg IM monthly, and megestrol 40 mg/day); somewhat less effective results have been obtained with clonidine, propranolol, naloxone, and sedatives in some women in whom estrogens are contraindicated.

TABLE 74-6

Regimens for Hormone Replacement Therapy

Cyclic Estrogen/Progestin Therapy

	Dose	**Days**
Oral conjugated estrogen	0.625 mg	Continuously
Medroxyprogesterone acetate	5–10 mg	1–15 per month

Continuous Combined Therapy

Daily estrogen	0.625 mg conjugated estrogen or 1.0 mg micronized estradiol
Daily progestin	2.5 mg medroxyprogesterone acetate

CONCLUSION

After the menopause, the rate of estrogen production decreases, but the postmenopausal state is not one of absolute estrogen deprivation. There is a transfer from 17β-estradiol predominance to one of estrone dominance; most if not all estrone is formed in extraglandular sites. Low-dose estrogen is effective for treatment of vasomotor symptoms and urogenital atrophy. Estrogen is beneficial in preventing symptoms of osteoporosis in young castrated women and is effective in preventing fractures in older women when treatment is started early. All women who are treated with estrogen must be evaluated carefully at semiannual visits for blood pressure elevation, breast masses, and the development of endometrial hyperplasia. Most gynecologists recommend endometrial biopsy prior to ERT and yearly thereafter for women on ERT alone.

In the future, considerable research effort must be directed to define the pathophysiology of vasomotor symptoms, alternatives to steroid hormone replacement for such symptoms, the mechanism of development and prevention of osteoporosis, the lipid changes associated with various treatment modalities, and the role of estrogens in the pathogenesis of endometrial carcinoma. As the number of women who live beyond the menopause increases, evaluation and treatment of menopausal disorders will continue to be of major concern in the health care of women, and issues focusing on the appropriate duration of estrogen/progestogen replacement therapy and its efficacy in the elderly (notably those over 75 years of age) will assume increasing importance.

REFERENCES

1. Bureau of the Census: *A Statistical Portrait of Women in the U.S.* Publication 58, Current Population Reports, Special Studies Series. Washington, DC, US Department of Commerce, 1976, p 23.
2. Utian WH: *Menopause in Modern Perspective.* New York, Appleton-Century-Crofts, 1980.
3. Linquist O, Bengtsson C: Menopausal age in relation to smoking. *Acta Med Scand* 205:73, 1979.
4. Baker TG: A quantitative and cytological study of sperm cells in human ovaries. *Proc R Soc (Biol)* 158:417, 1963.
5. Sherman BM et al: The menopausal transition: Analysis of LH, FSH, estradiol, and progesterone concentrations during menstrual cycles of older women. *J Clin Endocrinol Metab* 42:629, 1976.
6. Sherman BM, Korenman SG: Hormonal characteristics of the human menstrual cycle throughout reproductive life. *J Clin Invest* 55:699, 1975.
7. Longcope C: Metabolic clearance and blood production rates of estrogens in postmenopausal women. *Am J Obstet Gynecol* 111:778, 1971.
8. Scaglin HM et al: Pituitary LH and FSH secretion and responsiveness in women of old age. *Acta Endocrinol (Kbh)* 81:673, 1976.
9. Chakravarti S et al: Hormonal profiles after the menopause. *Br Med J* 2:784, 1976.
10. Judd HL: Hormonal dynamics associated with the menopause. *Clin Obstet Gynecol* 19:775, 1976.
11. Siiteri PK, MacDonald PC: Role of extraglandular estrogen in human endocrinology, in Greep RO, Astwood E (eds): *Handbook of Physiology: Endocrinology,* vol 2, pt 1. Washington, DC, American Physiological Society, 1973, p 615.
12. Jaszmann LJB et al: The menopausal symptoms. *Med Gynecol Sociol* 4:268, 1969.
13. Tataryn IV et al: LH, FSH and skin temperature during the menopausal hot flash. *J Clin Endocrinol Metab* 49:152, 1979.
14. Casper RF et al: Menopausal flushes: A neuroendocrine link with pulsatile luteinizing hormone secretion. *Science* 205:823, 1979.
15. Mulley G et al: Hot flushes after hypophysectomy. *Br Med J* 2:1062, 1977.
16. D'Amico JF et al: Induction of hypothalamic opioid activity with transdermal estradiol administration in postmenopausal women. *Fertil Steril* 55:754, 1991.
17. Foul SM et al: Estrogen-induced efflux of endogenous catecholamines from the hypothalamus *in vitro. Brain Res* 178:499, 1979.
18. Clayden JR et al: Menopausal flushing: Double-blind trial of a nonhormonal medication. *Br Med J* 1:409, 1974.
19. Hannan JH: In Tindall and Cox (eds): *The Flushings of the Menopause.* London, Baill'ere, 1927, p. 1.
20. Tataryn I et al: Postmenopausal hot flushes: A disorder of thermoregulation. *Maturitas* 2:101, 1980.
21. Ausel S et al: Vasomotor symptoms, serum estrogens and gonadotropin levels in surgical menopause. *Am J Obstet Gynecol* 126:165, 1976.
22. Meldrum D et al: Gonadotropins, estrogens, and adrenal steroids during the menopausal hot flush. *J Clin Endocrinol Metab* 50:685, 1980.
23. Yen SSC: The biology of menopause. *J Reprod Med* 18:287, 1977.
24. Bergman A, Brenner PF: Beneficial effects of pharmacologic agents—genitourinary, in Mishell DR Jr (ed): *Menopause.* Chicago, IL, Year Book, 1987, pp 151–164.
25. Brincat M et al: The long term effects of the menopause and administration of sex hormones on skin collagen and skin thickness. *Br J Obstet Gynaecol* 92:256, 1985.
26. Schiff I et al: Effects of estrogens on sleep and psychological state of hypogonadal women. *JAMA* 242:2405, 1979.
27. Campbell S, Whitehead M: Oestrogen therapy and

the menopause syndrome. *Clin Obstet Gynecol* 4:31, 1977.
28. Gordon G et al: Prevention of age related bone loss: Proceedings of the Arnold O. Beckman Conference. *Clin Chem* 3:1, 1980.
29. Heanly RP: Estrogens and postmenopausal osteoporosis. *Clin Obstet Gynecol* 19:791, 1976.
30. Komm BS et al: Estrogen binding, receptor mRNA, and biologic response in osteoblast-like osteosarcoma cells. *Science* 141:81, 1988.
31. Jilka RL et al: Increased osteoclast development after estrogen loss: Mediation by interleukin-6. *Science* 257:88–91, 1992.
32. Lobo RA et al: Estrogen and progestin effects on urinary calcium and calcitrophic hormones surgically induced post-menopausal women. *Horm Metab Res* 17:369, 1985.
33. Gordon GS: Postmenopausal osteoporosis: Cause, prevention and treatment. *Clin Obstet Gynecol* 4:169, 1977.
34. Horsman A et al: Prospective trial of oestrogen and calcium on postmenopausal women. *Br Med J* 2:789, 1977.
35. Garn SM: *The Earlier Gain and Later Loss of Cortical Bone, in Nutritional Perspective.* Springfield, IL, Charles C Thomas, 1970, p 146.
36. Cameron JR et al: Measurement of bone mineral in vivo: An improved method. *Science* 142:230, 1963.
37. Madsen M et al: Vertebral and total body mineral content by dual absorptiometry, in Pors-Nielsen S, Hjorting-Hansen E (eds): *Calcified Tissues, 1975.* Copenhagen, FAPL Publishing, 1976, p 361.
38. Cann CE et al: Spinal mineral loss in oophorectomized women: Determination of quantitative computed tomography. *JAMA* 244:2056, 1980.
39. Shoemaker ES et al: Estrogen treatment of postmenopausal women: Benefits and risks. *JAMA* 238:1524, 1977.
40. Trotter M et al: Densities of bones of white and negro skeletons. *J Bone Joint Surg* 42A:50, 1960.
41. Hutchinson TA et al: Post-menopausal oestrogens protect against fractures of hip and distal radius: A case-control study. *Lancet* 2(8245):705, 1979.
42. Weiss NS et al: Decreased risk of fractures of the hip and lower forearm with postmenopausal use of estrogen. *N Engl J Med* 303:1195, 1980.
43. Christiansen C, Christensen MS, Transboi I: Bone mass in postmenopausal women after withdrawal of oestrogen/gestagen replacement therapy. *Lancet* 1:459, 1981.
44. Genast HK et al: Quantitative computed tomography for spinal mineral assessment in osteoporosis. *Proceedings of the Copenhagen International Symposium on Osteoporosis,* Marion Laboratories, p 69, 1984.
45. Watts NB et al: Intermittent cyclic etidronate treatment of postmenopausal osteoporosis. *N Engl J Med* 323:73, 1990.
46. MacIntyre I et al: Calcitonin for prevention of postmenopausal bone loss. *Lancet* 1:900, 1988.
47. Pak CYC et al: Safe and effective treatment of osteoporosis with intermittent slow release sodium fluoride: Augmentation of vertebral bone mass and inhibition of fractures. *J Clin Endocrinol Metab* 68:150, 1989.
48. Wallentin L, Larsson-Cohn U: Metabolic and hormonal effects of postmenopausal oestrogen replacement treatment: II. Plasma lipids. *Acta Endocrinol [Copenh]* 86:597, 1977.
49. Sullivan JM et al: Estrogen replacement and coronary artery disease: Effect on survival in postmenopausal women. *Arch Intern Med* 150:2557, 1990.
50. Rosenberg L et al: Myocardial infarction and estrogen therapy in post-menopausal women. *N Engl J Med* 294:1256, 1976.
51. Gruchow HW et al: Postmenopausal use of estrogen and occlusion of the coronary arteries. *Am Heart J* 115:954, 1988.
52. Bush TL et al: Cardiovascular mortality and noncontraceptive use of estrogen in women: Results from the lipid research clinics program follow-up. *Circulation* 75:1102, 1987.
53. Bush TL, Barrett-Connor E: Noncontraceptive estrogen use and cardiovascular disease. *Epidemiol Rev* 7:80, 1985.
54. Mashchak CA, Lobo RA: Estrogen replacement therapy and hypertension. *J Reprod Med* 30(10 suppl):805, 1985.
55. Hazzard WR: Estrogen replacement and cardiovascular disease: Serum lipids and blood pressure effects. *Am J Obstet Gynecol* 161:1847, 1989.
56. Wren BG, Routledge AD: The effect of type and dose of oestrogen on the blood pressure of post-menopausal women. *Maturitas* 5:135, 1983.
57. Barrett-Conner E et al: Heart disease risk factors and hormone use in postmenopausal women. *JAMA* 241:2167, 1979.
58. Pfeffer RI et al: Estrogen use and blood pressure in later life. *Am J Epidemiol* 110:469, 1979.
59. Boston Collaborative Drug Surveillance Program: Surgically confirmed gallbladder disease, venous thromboembolism, and breast tumors in relation to postmenopausal estrogen therapy. *N Engl J Med* 290:15, 1974.
60. Thorneycroft IH, Koulianos G: Hormonal treatment of menopausal women: Risks and benefits, in Carr BR, Blackwell R (eds): *Reproductive Medicine.* Norwalk, CT, Appleton Press, 1992, pp 601–618.
61. Ross RK et al: A case-control study of menopausal estrogen therapy and breast cancer. *JAMA* 243:1635, 1980.
62. Jick H et al: Replacement estrogens and breast cancer. *Am J Epidemiol* 112:586, 1980.
63. Brinton LA et al: Menopausal estrogen use and breast cancer. *Cancer* 47:2577, 1981.
64. Hoover R et al: Conjugated estrogens and breast cancer risk. *J Natl Cancer Inst* 67:815, 1981.
65. Hiatt RA et al: Exogenous estrogen and breast cancer after oophorectomy. *Cancer* 54:139, 1984.
66. Kaufman DW et al: Noncontraceptive estrogen use and the risk of breast cancer. *JAMA* 252:63, 1984.
67. Kelsey JL et al: Exogenous estrogens and other factors in the epidemiology of breast cancer. *J Natl Cancer Inst* 67:327, 1981.
68. Hulka BS et al: Breast cancer and estrogen replacement therapy. *Am J Obstet Gynecol* 143:638, 1982.
69. La Vecchia C et al: Noncontraceptive estrogens and the risk of breast cancer. *Int J Cancer* 38:638, 1982.
70. Bergkvist L et al: Prognosis after breast cancer diagnosis in women exposed to estrogen and estrogen-progestogen therapy. *Am J Epidemiol* 130:221, 1989.
71. Smith DC et al: Association of exogenous estrogen

and endometrial carcinoma. *N Engl J Med* 293:1167, 1975.

72. Ziel HK, Finkle WD: Increased risk of endometrial carcinoma among users of conjugated estrogens. *N Engl J Med* 293:1167, 1975.
73. Weiss NS et al: Endometrial cancer in relation to patterns of menopausal estrogen use. *JAMA* 242:261, 1979.
74. Walker AM, Jick DH: Declining rates of endometrial cancer. *Obstet Gynecol* 56:733, 1980.
75. American College of Obstetrics and Gynecology: Technical Bulletin: *Hormone Replacement Therapy.* (166):1, 1992.
76. Hammond CB et al: Effects of long-term estrogen replacement therapy: II. Neoplasia. *Am J Obstet Gynecol* 133:531, 1979.
77. Gambrell RD: The prevention of endometrial carcinoma in postmenopausal women with progestins. *Maturitas* 1:107, 1978.
78. Thorn MH et al: Prevention and treatment of endometrial disease in climacteric women receiving oestrogen therapy. *Lancet* 2:455, 1979.
79. Paterson MEL et al: Endometrial disease after treatment with oestrogens and progestogens in the climacteric. *Br Med J* 1:822, 1980.
80. Lindsay R et al: The minimum effective dose of estrogen for prevention of postmenopausal bone loss. *Obstet Gynecol* 63:759, 1984.
81. Laufer LR et al: Estrogen replacement therapy by transdermal estradiol administration. *Am J Obstet Gynecol* 146:533, 1983.
82. Burkman RT: Lipid and lipoprotein changes in relation to oral contraception and hormonal replacement therapy. *Fertil Steril* 49 (suppl) (5):39S, 1988.

SECTION G

Disorders of Bone and Mineral Metabolism

Chapter 75

CALCIUM AND BONE HOMEOSTASIS AND CHANGES WITH AGING

David J. Baylink and John C. Jennings

This chapter deals with calcium (Ca) metabolism, bone metabolism, and the interaction between these two systems in adults. The function of Ca metabolism is to ensure a normal serum Ca level, whereas the function of bone metabolism is not only to participate in serum Ca regulation but also to provide adequate mechanical support. Because bone constitutes a depot of Ca to be utilized during Ca stresses, one would anticipate that the two systems of Ca metabolism and bone metabolism would be highly integrated, and this is certainly the case. Both the Ca and bone metabolism systems are perturbed by aging. However, in terms of function, it is only the bone metabolism system that is disrupted and as a result bone volume* is lost, leading to inadequate mechanical support. For example, during aging Ca is malabsorbed, which one might expect to cause hypocalcemia, but instead, the Ca reservoir property of bone functions well, and as a result, a normal serum Ca level is maintained, but at the expense of bone loss, which leads to osteoporosis.

*Bone volume and bone density are two terms which are used, in essence, interchangeably in this chapter. When using the term *bone density,* we are usually referring to the density obtained from a bone densitometer (viz. a quantitative CT scan). When using the term *bone volume,* we are referring to quantitative morphological data by which one can measure the volume of the bone (excluding marrow spaces), but not its density. In osteoporosis, some patients have a fraction of bone that is slightly less dense than that seen in normal individuals. However, the maximum effect of this "Ca-deficient bone" is to reduce the bone density by less than 10 percent. Consequently, one can adequately describe the amount of bone as bone volume or bone density.

Thus, during aging, despite abnormalities of Ca metabolism, it is not the serum Ca level but the bone volume that is adversely affected.

In this chapter, we describe the anatomical and functional components of the Ca metabolism and the bone metabolism systems; subsequently, we present concepts and models of the behavior of these two highly integrated systems under conditions of health, menopause, and aging.

CALCIUM METABOLISM AND SERUM CALCIUM REGULATION

In normal persons during aging, the extracellular fluid concentration of Ca remains in the normal range in spite of extensive exchanges of Ca between extracellular fluid, the intestine, the skeleton, and the kidney.[1] This remarkable regulation of the extracellular concentration of Ca is achieved by the actions and interactions of parathyroid hormone (PTH), vitamin D, and calcitonin on these organs. Figure 75-1 is a schematic overview of the three organs involved in normal serum Ca regulation: the small intestine, the kidney, and bone. In this section, we will describe the mechanisms by which each of these organs and hormones regulates Ca levels and emphasize how specific aspects of this system change with age.

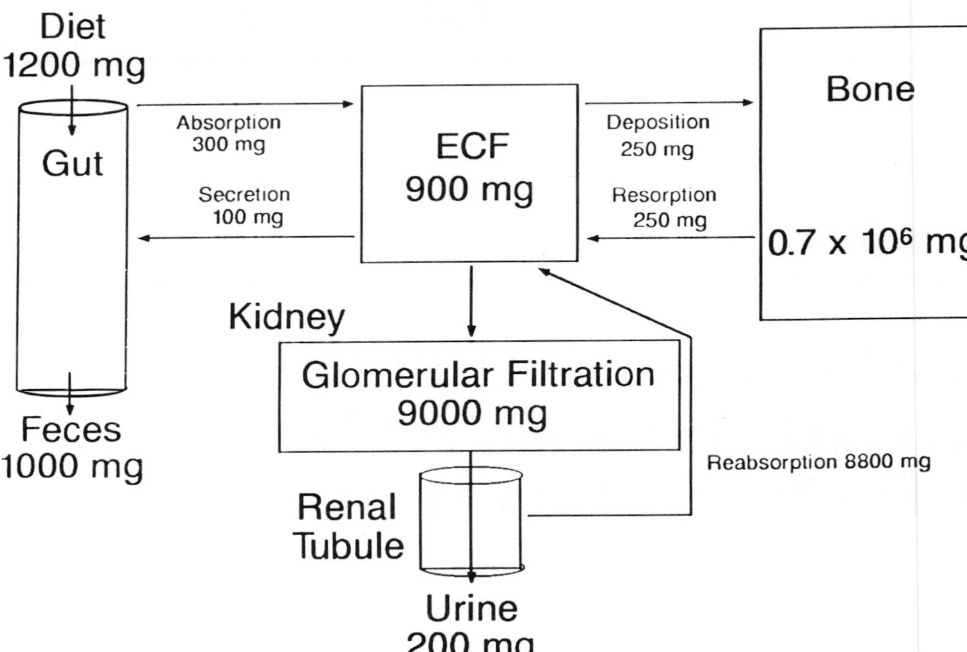

FIGURE 75-1
Model of Ca metabolism. The principal organs (small intestine, kidney, and bone) involved in mass calcium transport and the approximate daily flux rates of calcium between the compartments in young normal women. The sizes of the compartments are given in milligrams, and the daily flux rates are indicated next to the corresponding arrows.

Organs Involved in Calcium Metabolism

Small Intestine

The small intestine regulates serum Ca homeostasis through the absorption of dietary Ca. Normal dietary Ca intake is approximately 800 to 1200 mg/day, of which 15 to 40 percent is absorbed in the proximal small intestine by both active transport and passive diffusion. Vitamin D, after conversion to its active metabolite 1,25-dihydroxyvitamin D (1,25D), is the major hormone controlling the active component of the intestinal absorption of Ca, such that when the levels of 1,25D rise, intestinal Ca absorption increases, and when levels of 1,25D decrease, intestinal Ca absorption also decreases.[2–4]

Normally, intestinal Ca absorption is carefully regulated to meet the body's need to regulate serum Ca levels. However, there is a progressive decline in Ca absorption efficiency (absorption efficiency is the percentage of the oral Ca load that is absorbed) after about 60 years of age. This age-related decline in Ca absorption can be in part attributed to both decreased serum concentrations of 1,25D and to an age-related decrease in 1,25D intestinal receptors.[5] This decreased Ca absorption may be further aggravated in some elderly persons by (1) diminished gastric acid production (gastric acid is required for solubilizing Ca and for maintaining Ca in an ionized state, the only state of the element which is absorbed), (2) development of acquired lactase deficiency with aging with consequent avoidance of dairy products, and (3) a lower overall dietary Ca intake compared with that of young individuals.[6,7]

The age-related decrease in Ca absorption efficiency leads to a slight decrease in serum Ca concentrations (within the normal range), which subsequently leads to an increase in PTH secretion. This increase in PTH in turn stimulates bone resorption in order to maintain normal serum Ca levels.

Another abnormality in Ca absorption in elderly persons is decreased ability to adapt to a low Ca intake by increasing the efficiency of Ca absorption. Ordinarily, variation in dietary calcium intake is compensated for by changes in the efficiency of calcium absorption (i.e., the efficiency of calcium absorption increases as the amount of dietary calcium is reduced, and vice-versa). However, in elderly persons, compared with young normal persons, adaptation to a low-calcium diet is less efficient, such that in the elderly person, an inadequate dietary Ca intake is more likely to produce a negative Ca balance.

Kidney

The second major organ involved in mass Ca transport is the kidney, which both filters and reabsorbs Ca. About 9 g of Ca is filtered per 24 hours by the glomeruli; 90 percent of the filtered Ca is reabsorbed in the proximal tubule. Ca reabsorption in the proximal tubule is not controlled by Ca-regulating hormones but is coupled to sodium reabsorption. About 10 percent of the filtered Ca is delivered to the distal tubules, where Ca reabsorption is tightly controlled by PTH, which acts to increase Ca reabsorption. This response to PTH occurs within minutes and thus provides a mechanism for acute maintenance of normocalcemia.[1] Only about 1 to 2 percent of filtered Ca is excreted in urine (Fig. 75-1).

Although the glomerular filtration rate decreases with aging in both men and women, there is no direct evidence for impairment in renal tubular Ca handling with aging. If there were impaired tubular functions during aging, urine Ca levels would increase, but such a change is not seen.

Bone

The third organ system involved in serum Ca regulation is bone, which is the major Ca reservoir in the body. In normal adults, bone resorption delivers approximately 200 to 600 mg/day of Ca into the extracellular fluid. In young normal adults, the amount of osteoclastic bone resorption is balanced by an equivalent amount of bone formation (200 to 600 mg/day),[1] and bone density is stable. In elderly persons, the overall Ca balance varies from 0 to about minus 30 mg/day. In women, given a total peak skeletal Ca amount of 700 g, 30 mg/day is a small loss rate. However, over a period of 30 years, the accumulated loss would be almost one-half the total skeletal Ca. Thus, even a modest negative Ca balance can eventually lead to significant bone loss.

Hormones Involved in Serum Calcium Regulation

Parathyroid Hormone

PTH, an 84–amino acid peptide, plays a predominant role in the maintenance of Ca homeostasis, as evidenced by the life-threatening hypocalcemia that may occur after parathyroidectomy. PTH increases serum Ca levels by the following mechanisms: (1) stimulation of renal tubular Ca reabsorption, (2) stimulation of the renal 1α-hydroxylase activity, which increases conversion of 25(OH)-vitamin D (25D) to 1,25D, and (3) mobilization of Ca from bone by stimulation of osteoclastic bone resorption.[1] The effect of PTH to increase 1,25D not only increases Ca absorption but also bone resorption since PTH and 1,25D act synergistically to increase bone resorption.

Because PTH increases serum Ca levels, the only manner in which PTH could function in a negative feedback mechanism would be for PTH to be secreted in response to a decrease in the serum Ca level. Indeed, PTH synthesis and secretion are regulated by the concentration of ionized Ca in extracellular fluids. For example, when serum Ca levels fall, PTH is released, whereas increased serum Ca levels inhibit PTH secretion. The secreted peptide is metabolized in the serum, liver, and kidney, which results in several circulating fragments.[8] The biologically active amino-terminal fragments and the intact molecule, which represent approximately 5 to 10 percent of the measurable immunoreactive plasma PTH, have short serum half-lives (minutes). The biologically inactive carboxy-terminal (C-terminal) fragments, which represent approximately 80 percent of the measurable serum PTH, have long serum half-lives (hours). The amino-terminal fragments are taken up by bone and, to a lesser extent, filtered and degraded in the kidney. The C-terminal fragments are eliminated by glomerular filtration. The clinical significance of these features of PTH metabolism is that with the decrease in glomerular filtration rate during aging, there is an accumulation of inactive C-terminal fragments in serum such that a radioimmunoassay (RIA) based on a C-terminal epitope could lead to overestimation of the true PTH status of the individual.[9] Current immunoradiometric assays (IRMAs) for PTH (which measure intact PTH) provide a biologically accurate assessment of PTH status.

Most studies have shown an increase in circulating PTH levels with age.[9–15] The increase in serum PTH during aging could reflect a reduced glomerular clearance of PTH by the kidney (see above), an increase in PTH secretion, altered peripheral metabolism of PTH, or a combination of these variables. Because there is an age-related increase in nephrogenous adenosine 3′,5′-cyclic phosphate (cyclic AMP) and an age-related decrease in tubular maximum phosphate reabsorption (two changes that are suggestive of increased PTH action), it seems likely that there is a true increase in circulating biologically active PTH with aging.[12,13] This rise in PTH activity with aging is clearly not an indication of primary hyperparathyroidism, since serum Ca levels tend to decline slightly during aging. It seems likely that the age-related decline in the efficiency of intestinal Ca absorption coupled with the decrease in dietary Ca intake contributes to this secondary hyperparathyroidism.

Vitamin D

The normal metabolism of vitamin D is schematically represented in Chap. 76. The production of vitamin D_3 by ultraviolet photoconversion of 7-dehydrocholesterol to vitamin D_3 in the skin is one of the two major sources of circulating vitamin D. In the United States, supplementation of the diet with vitamin D_2 (primarily in milk and other processed dairy products) is the other major source of vitamin D.[16,17] Vitamin D_2 and vitamin D_3 are metabolized identically, and their active metabolites are similar in potency. Thus, further distinction between vitamins D_2 and D_3 will not be made in the following discussion of vitamin D metabolism.

Vitamin D is synthesized in the skin; released into the bloodstream, where it binds to a carrier protein; and then transported to sites of critical metabolism, namely, liver and kidney. (Since vitamin D fulfills the criteria of a hormone, skin is analogous to an endocrine organ.) The first step in vitamin D metabolism is the hydroxylation of vitamin D to 25D by the hepatic enzyme vitamin D 25–hydroxylase. This initial hydroxylation of vitamin D is closely dependent upon substrate (vitamin D) concentration and does not appear to be regulated by hormones. The biologically active form of vitamin D, 1,25D, is produced by a second hydroxylation, which is mediated by the 1α-hydroxylase in the kidney.[16,17] The activity of the renal 1α-hydroxylase is directly regulated by serum PTH, serum Ca, and serum phosphorus concentrations and possibly by other factors such as estradiol and other steroid hormones.[17] Unlike the hepatic 25D hydroxylation, 1,25D hydroxylation is largely independent of substrate concentration except at very low and very high concentrations of 25D. Vitamin D is the hormone precursor, 25D is the circulating storage form of the hormone (though at supraphysiologic concentrations it has activities identical to those of 1,25D), and 1,25D is the active hormone which (like 25D) is transported in serum (associated with a carrier protein) to its major target organs: intestine, bone, and parathyroid glands.

With respect to its action on bone, 1,25D promotes the mineralization of newly formed bone by providing an adequate supply of Ca and phosphate in serum.[18] In addition, 1,25D directly promotes bone resorption by acting synergistically with PTH to increase the proliferation and differentiation of osteoclasts and thus the number of osteoclasts.[19]

Regarding the age-related changes in the vitamin D endocrine system, there is a linear decrease of plasma 25D and 1,25D levels between the ages of 65 and 90.[20,21] Serum 25D levels must decrease to less than 8 ng/ml to alter Ca metabolism. Such levels may occur in elderly persons by any one or a combination of the causes listed in Table 75-1. Causes 1 to 5 in Table 75-1 lead first to a decrease in serum 25D levels. Decrements of serum 25D levels due to inadequate exposure to sunlight may be seen particularly in housebound elderly persons. Only cause 6 (i.e., production of 1,25D by the kidney) involves a direct impairment of the mechanism whereby 25D is converted to 1,25D. This impairment involves a diminished ability of the kidney to increase 1α-hydroxylase activity in response to PTH, as evidenced by the finding that in elderly persons prolonged infusion of PTH results in an impaired serum 1,25D response compared with that of young normal individuals under the same conditions.[22] This abnormality could lead to less Ca absorption and more bone resorption (compared with young individuals), and thus net bone loss.

TABLE 75-1

Causes of Vitamin D Deficiency in Elderly Persons

1. Deprivation of sunlight (e.g., subjects living in northern latitudes)
2. Diminished capacity of the skin to convert cholesterol to vitamin D
3. Intestinal malabsorption of the fat-soluble vitamin D
4. Diminished dietary vitamin D intake by avoidance of vitamin D–supplemented dairy products
5. Drug-induced increase in 25D degradation in the liver (e.g., diphenylhydantoin, phenobarbital)
6. Diminished production of 1,25D by the kidney (selective partial resistance to PTH)

Interestingly, hormones can be autocrine-paracrine agents as well as hormones [for example, insulin-like growth factor I (IGF-I) is a circulating hormone, but it also acts locally at sites of synthesis as an autocrine-paracrine agent], and 1,25D appears to have these dual functions.[23,24] Regarding its autocrine-paracrine functions, 1,25D is produced in many different tissues, including osteoblasts, and appears to act locally as an autocrine-paracrine agent. While it is difficult to ascribe a specific function to the role of 1,25D as an autocrine-paracrine agent, it appears to act in many tissues as an agent to promote differentiation, an action which is certainly true in osteoblasts, where it increases alkaline phosphatase activity and other differentiated cell functions.[25]

Despite the fact that 1,25D is made at multiple sites throughout the body, when the kidneys are removed there is very little circulating 1,25D, indicating that the major circulating level of this hormone is the domain of renal tissue. The decline in functional renal tissue as a consequence of aging is associated with a decrease in 1,25D production by this organ. This probably contributes to the reduction in the efficiency of Ca absorption that attends aging. Thus, aging is associated with a decline in the hormonal level of 1,25D.

In addition, 1,25D acts on the parathyroid glands to inhibit PTH secretion. Thus, the age-related increase in PTH could be caused not only by the decreased efficiency of Ca absorption but also by a decreased serum 1,25D level and/or action to inhibit PTH secretion directly.

Calcitonin

Calcitonin is a 32–amino acid peptide which is produced by the parafollicular C cells within the thyroid gland.[26] Physiologic doses of calcitonin decrease bone resorption by a direct action on the osteoclast. Calcitonin is secreted in response to increases in serum Ca levels and may also be secreted in response to a Ca-containing meal via stimulation of gastrin release. This acute action of calcitonin may prevent the potential rise in serum Ca levels in the immediate postprandial state and in so doing conserve bone. Accordingly, in the absence of calcitonin, the serum Ca level would tend to rise after an oral calcium load; however, in the presence of calcitonin, the amount of Ca absorbed is counterbalanced by the effect of calcitonin to decrease bone resorption equivalently, thus providing stable serum calcium levels and also a reduction in bone resorption, and therefore, a conservation of bone. It seems unlikely, however, that calcitonin plays a significant role in chronic serum Ca regulation in the human since in states of extreme calcitonin deficiency (e.g., total thyroidectomy), there do not appear to be major abnormalities in the regulation of serum Ca levels.[26]

With aging there is a decrease in serum total calcitonin concentrations which appears to represent a decrease in the inactive fragments rather than the biologically active intact calcitonin.[27]

BONE METABOLISM AND BONE VOLUME REGULATION

Bone metabolism is regulated both by systemic hormones, such as 1,25D and PTH, which direct bone's participation in serum Ca homeostasis, and by local mechanisms intrinsic to bone which are involved in adapting bone density to mechanical needs. Before discussing the regulation of bone metabolism, we will describe the structure and the cells of bone.

Bone Structure

Skeletal tissue consists of cortical and trabecular bone. These two types of bone are sufficiently different in structure so as to behave differently in response to aging; therefore, they will be considered separately.

Cortical Bone

Cortical bone accounts for three-fourths of the weight of the skeleton. Cortical bone forms the outer wall of all bones but is found primarily in the long bones of the appendicular skeleton. Cortical bone consists of tightly packed osteons or haversian systems. It has a low surface-to-volume ratio (i.e., low porosity), and, since bone formation and bone resorption occur on surfaces, accounts for only one-third of the total remodeling surface.

Two important structural changes occur in cortical bone with aging: (1) a reduction in cortical thickness, and (2) an increase in cortical porosity. Progressive cortical thinning occurs mainly by removal of bone from the inner or endosteal surface and results from increased bone resorption which is not entirely compensated by an increase in bone formation. The increase in the porosity occurs by erosion of the haversian systems, a process which is more pronounced near the endosteal surface (Fig. 75-2),[28] perhaps because of the continuity between the endosteum and nearby haversian systems.

Trabecular Bone

Trabecular bone accounts for the remaining 25 percent of the skeletal weight and is found largely in the axial skeleton, the flat bones, and the ends of long bones. Trabecular bone has a high surface-to-volume ratio (i.e., high porosity) due to its three-dimensional branching network, is surrounded by active or fatty hematopoietic tissue, and is contained within a cortical shell. It accounts for two-thirds of the total skeletal remodeling surface. The configuration and orientation of the trabeculae in the three-dimensional network are determined by the mechanical stresses in the corresponding bone structure. This configuration provides maximum tensile and compressive strength with minimum weight.

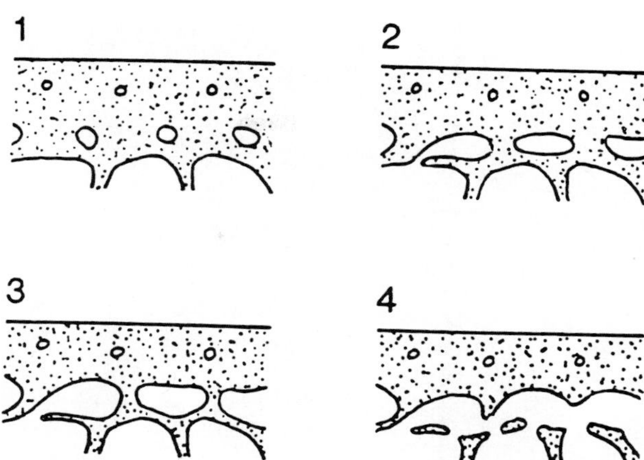

FIGURE 75-2
Microscopic structural stages of cortical bone loss. Illustrated are the few successive stages in osteoclast-dependent thinning of cortical bone: 1 shows normal adult cortex; 2 shows enlargement of the subendosteal spaces and communication of these spaces with the marrow cavity; 3 shows further enlargement of these spaces and conversion of the inner third of the cortex to a structure that topographically resembles trabecular bone, with an attending expansion of the marrow cavity; 4 shows perforation and disconnection of the new trabecular structures. (*Adapted with permission from Parfitt AM, Calcif Tissue Int 36(suppl):S123, 1984.*)

With aging, trabecular bone loss occurs as a result of thinning of normal trabeculae and of destruction of entire trabeculae.[29,30] This latter mechanism accounts for two-thirds of trabecular bone loss and leads to a change in the network arrangement (Fig. 75-3).[28] Current dogma suggests that these lost trabeculae cannot be replaced. This emphasizes the importance of the prevention of bone loss (see Chap. 76). During aging, in the absence of therapy to prevent bone loss, some trabeculae are removed and the remaining trabeculae become thinner.[29] The possible mechanisms underlying the loss of trabecular and cortical bone are discussed later in this chapter.

Bone Cells

There are two types of mature cells in bone: osteoblasts and osteoclasts. The function of the mature forms of these cell types is relatively clear; the osteoblast produces (deposits) bone matrix, and the os-

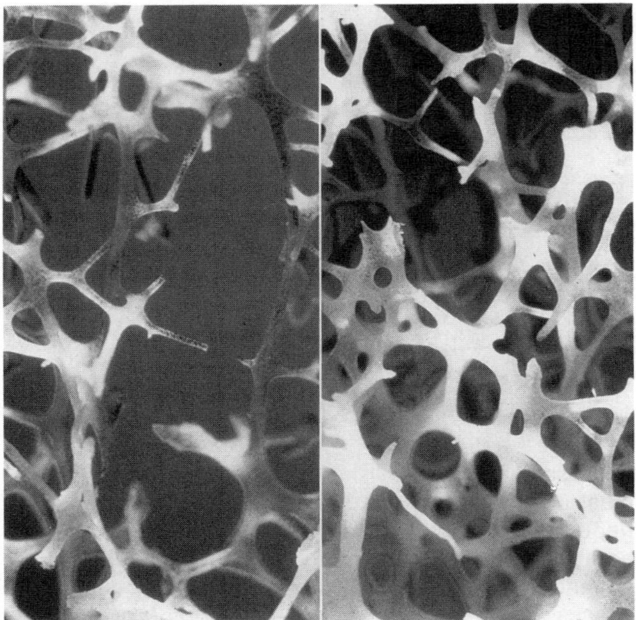

FIGURE 75-3
Three-dimensional views of trabecular bone architecture from individuals at (*A*) skeletal maturity and (*B*) old age. These photographs show the conversion of an inner-connected continuous network of trabeculae present at skeletal maturity to a discontinuous network seen at old age. The loss of trabecular connections leads to a greater loss in strength than would be predicted by the corresponding loss in bone volume.

teoclast removes (resorbs) bone. The mechanisms by which these differentiated cells arise from their putative stem cell precursors are less well understood and are addressed briefly below. Osteocytes, which are osteoblasts that have become entrapped in bone matrix, are considered separately from osteoblasts because their function is probably different from that of osteoblasts.

Osteoblasts

The presumed stem cell for the osteoblast is mesenchymal in origin (Fig. 75-4). Under the influence of growth factors and perhaps unknown factors, progeny of the osteoblast stem cell differentiate into "preosteoblasts" and then to mature osteoblasts. Mature osteoblasts synthesize bone matrix, which contains proteins such as type I collagen, proteoglycans, phosphoproteins, and osteocalcin and also several growth factors which may act as regulators of bone cell function (Fig. 75-4).[31–35] The mature osteoblast is identified by a high concentration of alkaline phosphatase in its plasma membrane and by osteocalcin synthesis. There is evidence that bone formation by osteoblasts decreases with aging.[36] It seems likely that this age-related decline in matrix synthesis is due more to a decrease in the number of osteoblasts than to a decrease in synthetic activity per osteoblast.

Osteocytes

Once osteoblasts become entrapped in bone matrix, they are referred to as osteocytes. We believe that osteocytes sense increases or decreases in mechanical strain relative to the prevailing bone density and then send chemical messages to surface-lining cells (i.e., resting osteoblasts), which then elaborate growth factors or cytokines to effect an increase or decrease in bone density through changes in bone formation or bone resorption, thereby providing a means for bone density to adapt appropriately to changes in mechanical stress. Similarly, osteocytes could detect microdamage (originating from excess local bone stress) and subsequently send a chemical message to surface-lining cells, which could respond by elaborating cytokine messages to stimulate proliferation of osteoclast precursors and, ultimately, bone resorption.

This model responds to mechanical stress, but not to all mechanical stress in a stereotypical manner. In vivo, different types of mechanical stress lead to different bone cell activities. Compressive forces lead to increased bone formation, whereas tensional forces lead to increased bone resorption. Thus, osteocytes and lining cells must have the ability to send out appropriate signals (to increase or decrease osteoblast proliferation or to increase or decrease osteoclast proliferation), depending on the type of stress manifested.

Osteoclasts

A number of lines of evidence suggest that the osteoclast stem cell is a mononuclear cell of the hematopoietic lineage. The mononuclear stem cell progeny, under the influence of 1,25D and certain cytokines, fuse and form multinucleated osteoclasts which resorb bone (Fig. 75-5).[37] There is currently no evidence that there are deficiencies in osteoclast function with aging. Indeed, for age-related bone loss to occur, osteoclastic bone resorption must exceed osteoblastic bone formation.

Interaction between Osteoblasts and Osteoclasts

There is considerable evidence that osteoclast metabolism is controlled in part by the osteoblast. Osteoblasts produce cytokines and other factors that increase osteoclast production (such as 1,25D, interleukin-1, granulocyte-macrophage colony-stimulating factor, macrophage colony-stimulating factor, interleukin-6)[38] and at least one factor, transforming growth factor β, which decreases osteoclast production.[39,40] These factors regulate osteoclast precursor proliferation and differentiation. If osteoblasts regulate osteoclasts, what regulates osteoblasts? Apparently, osteoblasts process the information derived from interaction with systemic hormones such as estrogen or PTH and then send cytokine messages to

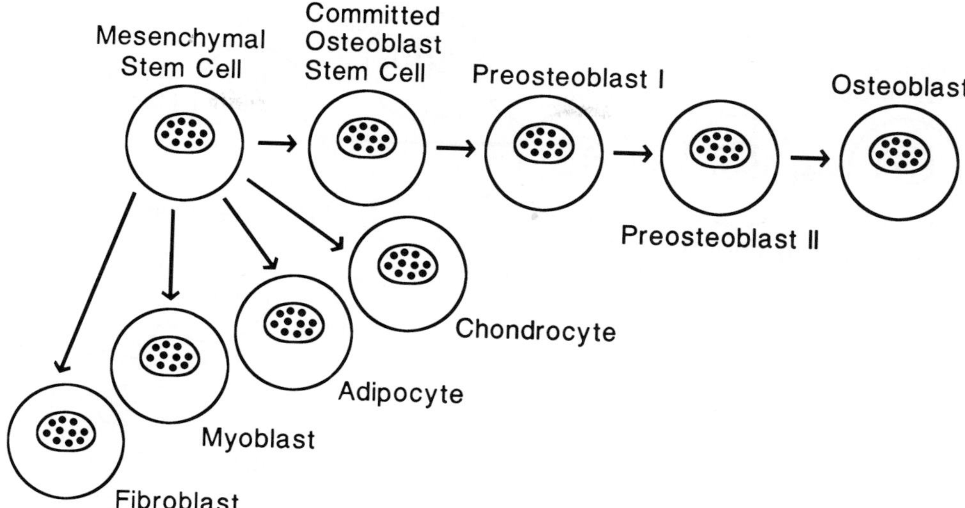

FIGURE 75-4

The osteoblast lineage. Mesenchymal stem cells give rise to (1) osteoblasts, (2) chondrocytes, (3) fibroblasts, (4) adipocytes, and (5) myoblasts. (We do not mean to imply that each mesenchymal stem cell differentiates through each of the depicted stages. Instead, each of these stages represents a population of cells.) The growth factors that regulate the progression from stem cells through the various differentiation stages to osteoblasts include insulin-like growth factors I and II (IGF-I, IGF-II), platelet-derived growth factor (PDGF), fibroblast growth factor (FGF), and transforming growth factor β (TGF-β), and bone morphogenetic proteins (BMPs). All these growth factors probably act on one or more of the differentiation stages depicted, though the importance of each of these growth factors for a given stage is not yet known. Some growth factors are particularly important for proliferation; these include PDGF and FGF, whereas others stimulate proliferation and also increase differentiation as indicated by increased alkaline phosphatase activity in cells; these include the IGFs, the BMPs, and TGF-β. Bone morphogenetic proteins are unique in their action on bone cells since only the BMPs can act alone on stem cells to produce progeny which differentiate to osteoblasts. The number of stages depicted between the stem cell and the osteoblast is arbitrary, based on in vitro observations.

osteoclasts (and probably their precursors) to regulate bone resorption.[41] Local factors may also act on the osteoblast to regulate bone resorption. Accordingly, osteoblasts (because of their communication with osteocytes) are in an excellent geographic position to detect microdamage and variations in bone strain as described earlier.

Regulation of Bone Remodeling and Volume

In contrast to certain other tissues such as brain tissue, bone continues to be remodeled throughout the entire life span of the individual. After cessation of growth at skeletal maturity, both trabecular and cortical bone are subject to continuous replacement, a process called remodeling. Remodeling does not occur uniformly throughout the bone surface but rather takes place in microscopically discrete local sites.[28,42,43] In cortical bone, it has been shown that formation of new bone within the cortex occurs only at sites where bone has been resorbed. In cortical bone, the resorptive phase lasts for 30 days, the bone-forming phase lasts about 130 days, and a further 3 to 6 months may be required for the bone to become fully mineralized.[43] Under certain conditions, trabecular bone sites may exhibit bone formation without prior resorption.[28]

There are three quantitative variables that characterize bone remodeling and volume.

The Sites Where Remodeling Occurs

While we do not have a comprehensive knowledge of the factors which determine where remodeling occurs, we do know that mechanical factors are an important determinant, and perhaps *the* most important determinant, of where remodeling occurs. Mechanical factors include microdamage and mechanical

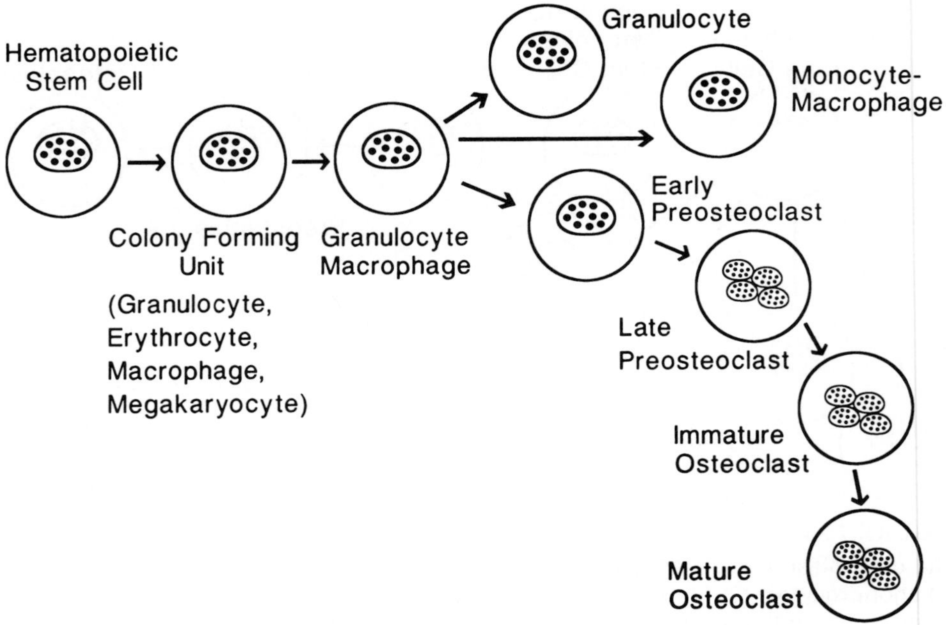

FIGURE 75-5
The osteoclast lineage. Osteoclasts arise from the hematopoietic stem cell. The hematopoietic stem cells give rise to different colony-forming units (CFUs), each of which then gives rise to the corresponding mature cell type; the cell types include erythrocytes, megakaryocytes, granulocytes, macrophages, eosinophils, and basophils. Osteoclasts arise from the granulocyte-macrophage CFUs. (We do not mean to imply that each hematopoietic stem cell differentiates through each of the depicted stages. Instead, each of these stages represents a population of cells.) Several cytokines and other local factors promote the production of osteoclasts from hematopoietic stem cells. These include granulocyte-macrophage colony-stimulating factor (GM-CSF), macrophage CSF, interleukin-1, interleukin-3, and interleukin-6. 1,25D also increases osteoclast formation. Prostaglandin E_2 promotes osteoclast formation. TGF-β is thought to inhibit osteoclast production. Osteoblasts produce all these factors and are a likely source for the osteoclast. Precursor marrow cells also produce many of these factors.

strain. A localized increase in strain results in a corresponding local increase in bone formation. This mechanism could explain the increase in bone density in the dominant (but not the nondominant) arm of a tennis player. Conversely, the localized decrease in strain that occurs in immobilization or in the weightlessness of space flight is accompanied by decreased bone formation and thus leads to bone loss.[44,45]

The Rate of Bone Remodeling

The remodeling rate is the quantity of bone remodeled (resorbed and formed) per unit of time, expressed as a fraction of the bone volume. Systemic factors are important determinants of the rate of bone remodeling. Local factors such as cytokines and growth factors frequently mediate the actions of systemic hormones at the cell level and as such also influence the rate of bone remodeling. Systemic factors that affect the rate of bone remodeling include PTH, calcitonin, thyroid hormone, growth hormone, estrogen, and testosterone. For example, patients with hyperthyroidism or with primary hyperparathyroidism typically have increased bone remodeling, whereas those with hypoparathyroidism typically have very low levels of bone remodeling.[46,47]

The significance of the remodeling rate in terms of bone loss (at least in postmenopausal subjects) is that, in general, the higher the remodeling rate (or the bone resorption rate) the greater the absolute loss of bone density (Fig. 75-6). Conversely, inhibition of bone resorption leads to a decrease in the absolute bone loss rate. This would explain why elderly patients with long-standing hypoparathyroidism have substantially higher bone density levels than euparathyroid subjects of a similar age. Moreover, the major basis for the reduction in bone loss in response to antiresorptive drugs such as estrogen, calcitonin, and the bisphosphonates is that the remodeling rate is lowered to the extent that the absolute bone loss is reduced, as would be predicted from Fig. 75-6.

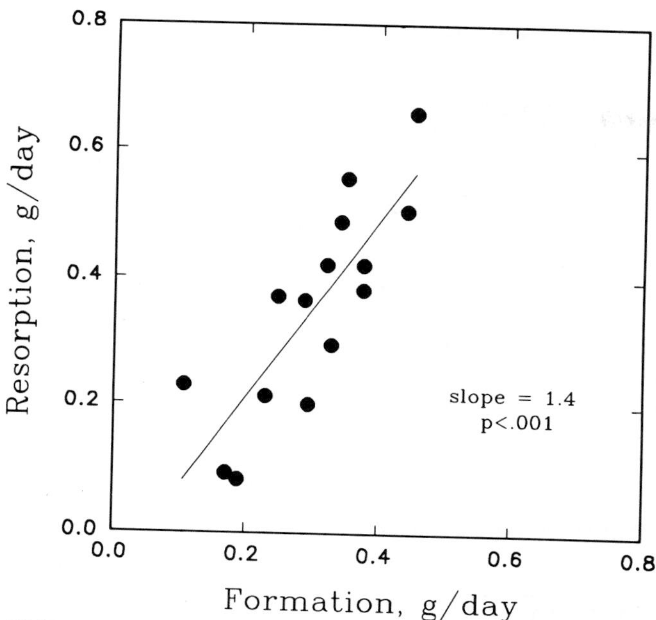

FIGURE 75-6

Relationship between bone formation and bone resorption in postmenopausal osteoporosis. The slope of 1.4 indicates poor coupling. (Appropriate coupling would give a slope of 1.0.) The coupling defect tends to be a fixed percentage of the bone resorption rate such that as the bone resorption rate increases, the amount of absolute bone loss also increases.

The Balance between the Volume of Bone Resorbed and Formed at a Given Site: Coupling of Bone Formation to Bone Resorption

The coupling of bone formation to bone resorption (the extent of resorption cavity fill-in, i.e., complete fill-in indicates normal coupling) is a major regulator of bone volume.[48–50] Our hypothetical model of coupling is depicted in Fig. 75-7 and described below. Growth factors stored in matrix are released during the initial stage of bone resorption and subsequently stimulate the proliferation and differentiation of nearby osteoblast precursors.[31–34,51] When the osteoclastic resorptive phase is completed, this expanded pool of osteoblast then attaches to the walls of the resorptive cavity and produces bone to fill in the resorption cavity. The final extent of filling-in of the resorption cavity is determined by the number of osteoblasts created. The number of osteoblasts created is determined by the amount of growth factors released by bone resorption and, subsequently, by the amount of growth factor released from those contemporary osteoblasts involved in filling in the resorption cavity. For example, exercise-induced local increases in mechanical strain could enhance growth factor production by contemporary osteoblasts and result in an actual overfill of the surface cavity. If the strain rates are unchanged, the fill-in would be normal as depicted in stage E. In contrast, during Ca deficiency or glucocorticoid excess, the amount of resorption cavity fill-in is impaired (stage F).[52] Thus, it is apparent that the final amount of cavity fill-in is dependent upon regulatory cues originating from outside the osteoblast, some from bone mechanical factors, and others from systemic hormones.

The extent of fill-in is not the only determinant of bone volume, since the number of these sites in the skeleton (which is reflected by the remodeling rate) also determine the overall bone volume. Accordingly, bone loss during a pathological process or the correction of a bone volume deficit by a drug is determined by three factors: (1) the size of the resorptive cavity, (2) the extent of the subsequent fill-in (factors 1 and 2 together determine local bone balance), and (3) the total number of these remodeling sites throughout the skeleton. Figure 75-7 illustrates the balance at a given remodeling site, whereas it does not illustrate that the overall skeletal balance is also importantly influenced by the number of these sites. (Those factors that influence the rate of remodeling, which reflects the number of remodeling sites, are presented above.)

When coupling is effective such that bone formation and bone resorption are equal, bone volume is stable. However, when coupling is impaired (bone resorption > bone formation), bone is lost. Impaired coupling is a prerequisite for the development of osteoporosis.

There are situations in which so-called impaired coupling is physiologically appropriate, namely during Ca deficiency. If this were not the case, bone could not serve one of its most important functions (to provide a reservoir of Ca during times of Ca deficiency). Thus, during Ca deficiency there is a deliberate attempt by Ca-regulating hormones to cause impaired coupling and in so doing release Ca from bone stores. Ca deficiency is an example of impaired coupling mediated by systemic factors (i.e., increased PTH and 1,25D levels, together with a decreased serum Ca level). A molecular model illustrating a potential mechanism for the bone loss that occurs with Ca deficiency is shown in Fig. 75-8.[53]

Physiologically appropriate impaired coupling can also originate from bone itself (i.e., the bone loss that occurs with immobilization). (To lose bone with immobilization and to gain bone with exercise is physiologically appropriate in the same sense that it is physiologically appropriate for muscle mass to vary with the level of exercise.) This impaired coupling is locally mediated, as evidenced by the fact that only the immobilized limb is affected.[54] During immobilization, the key mechanistic finding is that as bone resorption increases, bone formation fails to increase correspondingly.[44,45] The exact mechanism for this inadequate increase in bone formation in response to bone resorption is unknown. However, pertinent to this issue is that physical loading of the skeleton leads to an increase in streaming potentials (i.e., electric fields) in the bone.[55] Because in vitro and in vivo studies with electric fields have shown a stimulation of bone formation, such endogenously produced electric fields could be responsible for the stimulation of bone

A. INITIATION OF BONE RESORPTION **B. RESORPTION CAVITY DEVELOPS**

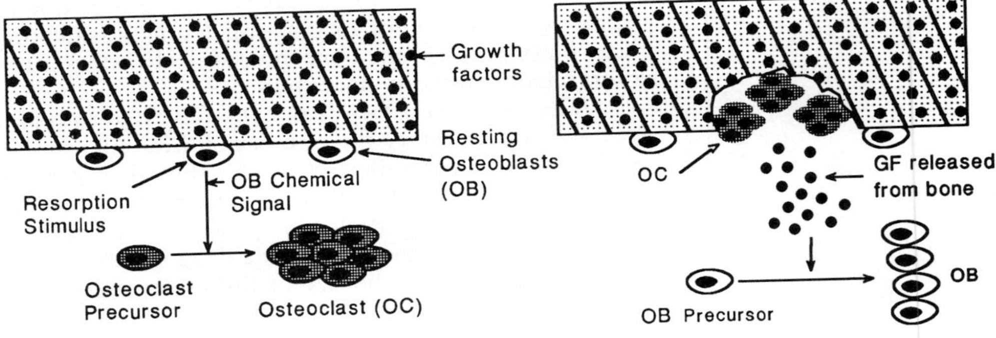

C. RESORPTION COMPLETE **D. OB LINE RESORPTION CAVITY**

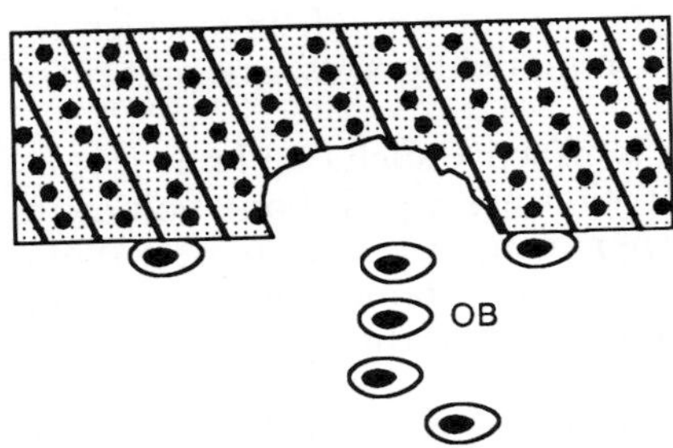

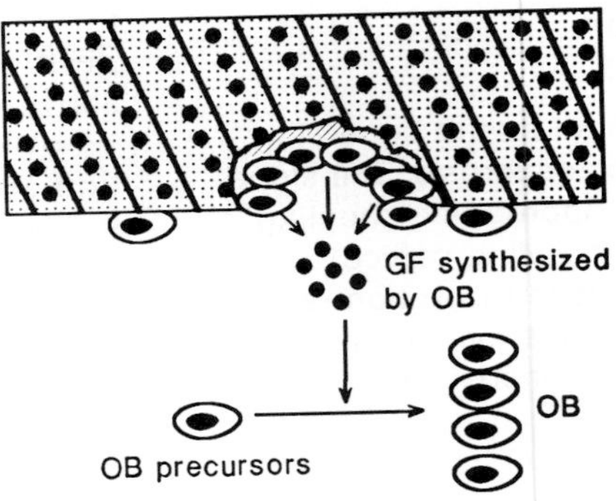

E. BONE FORMED = BONE RESORBED **F. BONE FORMED < BONE RESORBED**

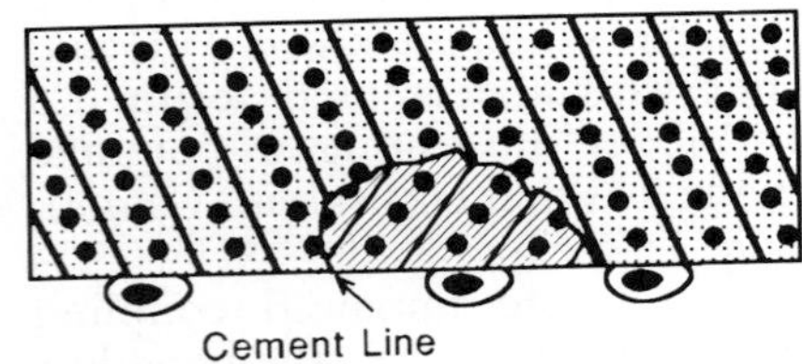

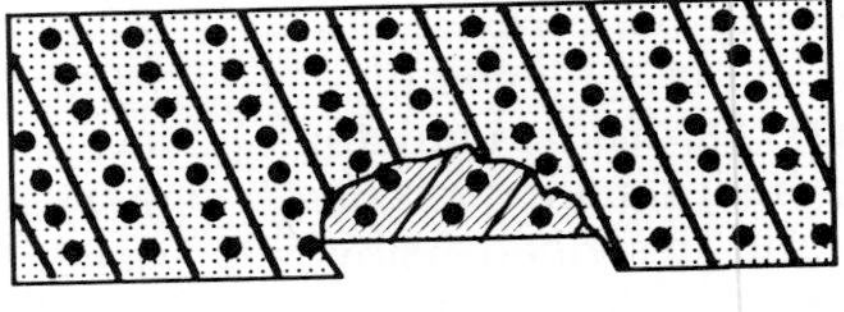

FIGURE 75-7
Models of successive stages of the coupling of bone formation to bone resorption. *A.* Bone resorption is initiated by a systemic stimulus such as PTH which acts on resting osteoblasts (OBs) to produce a chemical signal which in turn acts on osteoclast (OC) precursors to produce more OCs and on OCs to increase their resorption activity. *B.* OCs excavate bone and in so doing release growth factors (GFs) from bone substance (see Fig. 75-4). These GFs act on OB precursors to produce OBs. *C.* Resorptive phase is complete and OCs disappear from the surface of the resorptive cavity. *D.* Mature OBs formed during the resorptive phase now line up on the cavity surface and begin to fill in cavity with new bone. These contemporary OBs produce GFs which act on OB precursors to produce more OBs. The extent of resorptive cavity fill-in is determined by the amount of GF produced by contemporary OBs. The amount of GFs produced is determined by either local or systemic signals acting on OBs. *E.* The amount of new bone formed in normal individuals is equal to the amount of bone resorbed (i.e., bone formation and bone resorption are coupled). *F.* The amount of new bone formed is less than the amount resorbed, as would be the case during menopausal bone loss (Fig. 75-10) or calcium deficiency (Fig. 75-12).

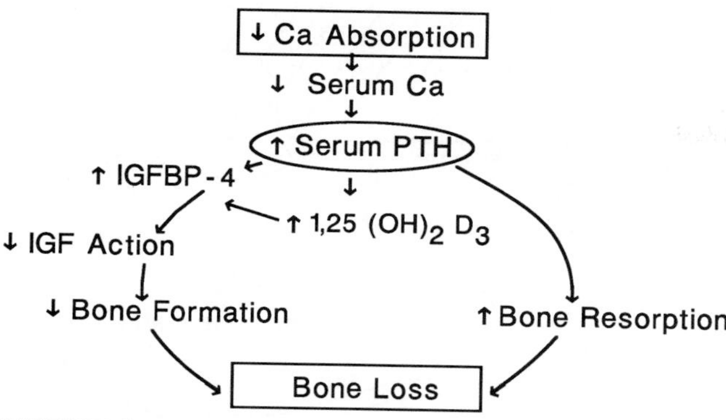

FIGURE 75-8

Model of the mechanisms of bone loss during calcium deficiency. Inadequate calcium intake evokes mechanisms which allow the organism to tap the calcium reservoir in bone. To do this, bone resorption must exceed bone formation. The mechanism for this is as follows: Low calcium intake leads to a decrease in serum calcium levels, and this in turn stimulates serum PTH synthesis. Increased serum PTH levels increase bone resorption directly and also by stimulating 1,25D synthesis. Increased serum PTH levels also decrease bone formation (when attended by hypocalcemia, i.e., by secondary hyperparathyroidism). This model incorporates a potential mechanism to explain this decrease in bone formation: Increased serum PTH levels increase 1,25D levels, and together these two hormonal changes increase the serum concentration of IGF binding protein 4 (IGFBP-4), which, in turn, inhibits the anabolic actions of IGF-I and IGF-II on bone cells. Because the IGFs appear to be important determinants of bone formation, this mechanism could contribute to the observed decrease in bone formation seen with calcium deficiency.

formation that occurs with mechanical loading. Thus, the lack of an increase in bone formation in response to bone resorption may be the result of a decrease in the production of streaming potentials from the immobilized bone. In vitro electromagnetic field studies show that the increased bone formation is associated with increased growth factor production.[56] Thus, it is possible that immobilization leads to a reduction in growth factor production by contemporary osteoblasts (stage D in Fig. 75-7) and ultimately bone loss. Apart from these two examples, Ca deficiency and immobilization, most other types of impaired coupling are pathological.

Major Determinants of Bone Volume in Women

The four major determinants of bone volume in women are estrogen deficiency, Ca malabsorption, lifestyle factors, and the genetic effects to achieve peak bone density.[57] These four determinants influence bone density at different times during the life span. Estrogen deficiency is an important factor for the first 8 to 10 years after the menopause. Calcium malabsorption usually occurs after about 70 years of age. Lifestyle factors such as calcium intake and physical activity can influence bone density throughout the entire life span. Genetic effects predominantly determine peak bone density, and thus these effects are less obvious after about 18 to 20 years of age. The cellular and also the physiological aspects of these four factors are considered below.

Estrogen Deficiency at the Menopause: Impaired Coupling of Bone Formation and Bone Resorption

Estrogen deficiency is a major determinant of postmenopausal, or type I osteoporosis. According to our model, the negative Ca balance is the result, not the cause, of bone loss (i.e., the loss of Ca from the body results because of the lack of direct effect of estrogen on bone cells, which results in increased bone resorption). The excess bone resorption leads to Ca homeostatic adjustments which serve to eliminate the excess Ca released via increased bone resorption (Fig. 75-9).

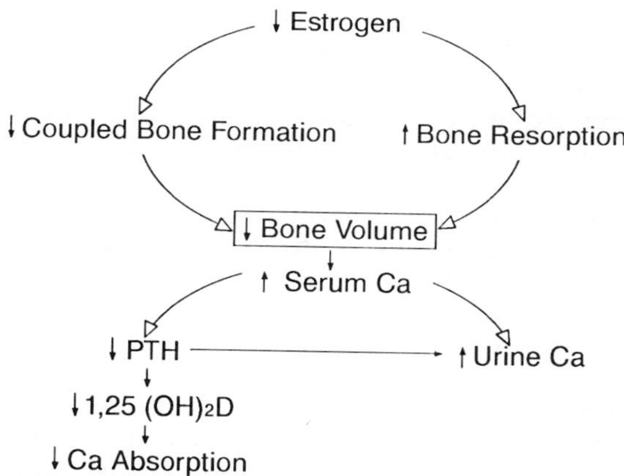

FIGURE 75-9

Model of mechanisms of bone loss and consequent counterregulatory effects in estrogen deficiency. Estrogen deficiency increases bone resorption (BR), and estrogen therapy decreases BR. The molecular mechanisms for the effect of estrogen on BR are illustrated in Fig. 75-11. Estrogen deficiency, in addition to increasing BR, also leads to decreased coupled bone formation (BF). The cause for this effect of estrogen deficiency is not clear; however, it is known that estrogen stimulates the secretion of TGF-β, which is an anabolic growth factor for osteoblasts. This action could be related to the poor coupling seen in estrogen deficiency and illustrated in Fig. 75-6. The increase in BR with impaired coupling of BF to BR leads to bone loss, which in turn invokes serum calcium counterregulatory mechanisms (decreased calcium absorption; increased urine calcium levels) to prevent the enhanced calcium release from bone to increase serum calcium levels.

In sharp contrast, in type II osteoporosis associated with Ca malabsorption, the negative Ca balance is not the result but the cause of the bone loss. In this regard, there is an obligatory loss of about 200 mg of calcium per day in sweat, feces, and urine, such that, when calcium absorption falls below 200 mg/day, the deficit must be made up by parathyroid hormone–mediated bone resorption in order to prevent hypocalcemia.

That it is estrogen deficiency rather than some other factor attending the menopause that causes bone loss is substantiated by the fact that this bone loss can be completely abrogated by estrogen replacement therapy.[58] The effect of estrogen deficiency to cause bone loss occurs predominantly for about 8 to 10 years after the menopause.[59] Why bone loss rate decreases markedly after about 10 years is not clear. Perhaps estrogen controls a specific fraction of the total skeleton, and once that fraction is gone, estrogen deficiency is without further effects. Alternatively, the mechanical consequences of the rapid bone loss may invoke compensatory bone changes which retard further bone loss.

While we do not know why bone resorption slows 10 years after the menopause, we do know that the acute effects of estrogen deficiency on the bone loss are due to impaired coupling of bone formation to bone resorption. The cellular mechanisms involved in the impaired coupling are considered in the model shown in Fig. 75-10. This model incorporates two mechanisms:

Increased Bone Resorption From a morphometric standpoint, there are two bone resorption changes brought about by estrogen deficiency that account for the increase in bone resorption: (1) there is an increase in resorption cavity depth and (2) there is an increase in the number of sites where resorption is occurring (the increase in resorption depth may reflect increased osteoclast activity, and the increase in the number of bone-resorbing sites may reflect increased osteoclastogenesis). The potential molecular basis for these two changes in bone resorption is described below. Recently, estrogen receptors have been found on osteoblasts.[60,61] This is pertinent because, as mentioned earlier, there is now considerable evidence that the regulation of osteoclastic resorption is at least in part due to signals arising from osteoblasts.[62,63] Thus, estrogen may modulate the action of osteoblasts to regulate bone resorption (by perturbation of the osteoblast chemical resorptive signals to osteoclasts and their precursors) such that a deficiency of estrogen could alter this regulation in such a manner as to accelerate bone resorption (Fig. 75-10). Regarding potential resorptive signals from osteoblasts, one of the actions of estradiol on osteoblasts is to inhibit the production of the cytokine interleukin-1. Interleukin-1 probably acts on osteoblasts in an autocrine and paracrine manner to increase interleukin-6 levels. Interleukin-6 then acts on osteoclasts to regulate their activity. Thus, interleukin-6 is one of the mediators whereby osteoblasts regulate osteoclast activity. In addition, both interleukin-1 and interleukin-6 act on

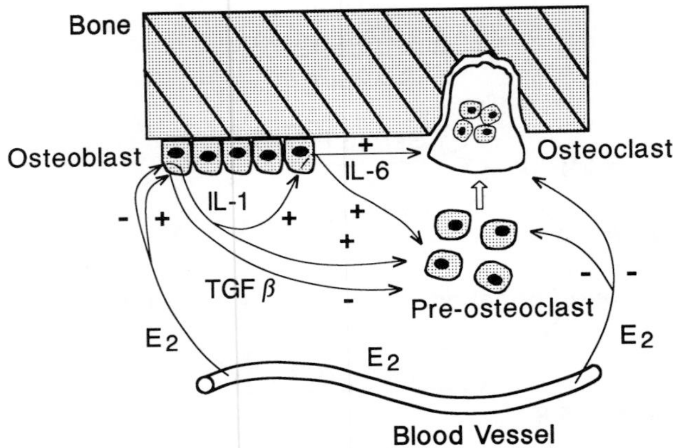

FIGURE 75-10
Model of how estrogen regulates bone resorption at the molecular level. In this model of bone, a systemic hormone, estrogen (E2), alters the production of the cytokine interleukin-1 (IL-1) and the growth factor TGF-β, and in so doing, influences the rate of osteoclastic bone resorption. E2 acts in two cell types to alter bone resorption by osteoclasts:
(1) osteoblasts: it acts on osteoblasts to decrease IL-1 production. Normally, IL-1 acts in an autocrine and paracrine manner to increase IL-6 production by osteoblasts. IL-6 then acts directly on the osteoclast to increase osteoclast resorptive activity. IL-6 directly and IL-1 directly increase the proliferation of preosteoclasts and thereby produce more osteoclasts. E2 also increases the synthesis of TGF-β, which inhibits the proliferation of preosteoclasts. Thus, with E2 deficiency, there is an increase in IL-1 and IL-6 levels and a decrease in TGF-β levels, all of which promote BR. (2) Osteoclasts: recent evidence suggests that E2 may act directly on osteoclast precursors and on osteoclasts to inhibit bone resorption. Thus, E2 causes bone loss at the menopause by direct action on bone cells.

osteoclast precursors to enhance the osteoclast pool. Thus, the increased interleukin-1 and interleukin-6 levels lead to an increase in osteoclast number as well as osteoclast activity.[64,65]

In addition, transforming growth factor β (TGF-β), which has an inhibitory effect on osteoclastogenesis,[39,40] increases in response to estrogen[66] and presumably decreases in response to estrogen deficiency. Thus, with estrogen deficiency, one would predict an increase in osteoclastogenesis due to the reduction in TGF-β (Fig. 75-10). There is also the possibility that estrogen has direct effects on osteoclast precursors. Finally, there is preliminary evidence to suggest that estrogen may act directly on osteoclasts themselves to decrease their activity.[67]

Impaired Coupling of Bone Formation to the Increased Bone Resorption Estrogens are now known to stimulate growth factor production, particularly transforming growth factor β, by osteoblasts[66] such that a deficiency of estrogen could impair growth factor production and thereby lead to impaired coupling.

Efficiency of Ca Absorption in Elderly Women

In elderly women, compared with early menopausal women, bone continues to be lost but at a slower rate. It seems probable that in a population of elderly women, there are several factors contributing to this late bone loss. One important factor is the Ca deficiency that arises as a result of a low Ca intake and/or decreased efficiency of Ca absorption (Fig. 75-11). In this type of bone loss, the PTH level is high, consistent with a Ca deficiency state (i.e., secondary hyperparathyroidism, as shown in Fig. 75-11), whereas, by way of comparison, in estrogen deficiency the serum PTH level is low (Fig. 75-9) because the increased bone resorption is non-PTH-mediated.

Pertinent to the issue of aging and Ca metabolism is that the response of bone, kidney, and small intestine to Ca deficiency is more efficient in conserving bone Ca in young than in aged individuals. Accordingly, in young adults, there are three reasons why Ca deficiency results in minimal bone loss: (1) PTH also causes Ca conservation by the kidney, (2) PTH, by increasing 1,25D production, increases the efficiency of enteral Ca absorption, and (3) the increase in bone resorption produced by PTH is attended by an efficient coupling of resorption to formation. Thus, in this way bone loss is minimized. However, during aging there is a defect in the ability of PTH to increase

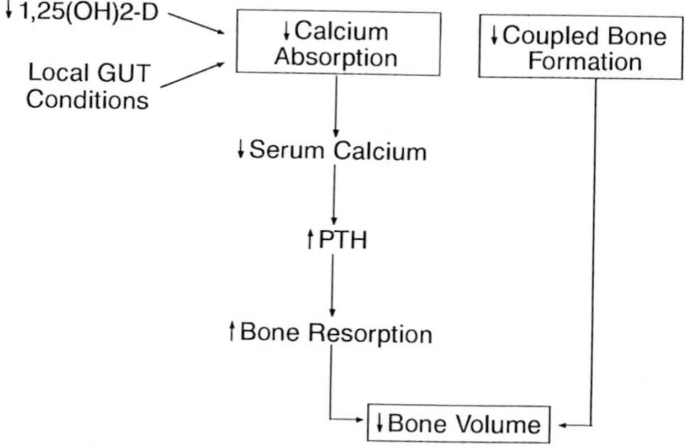

FIGURE 75-11

Model of mechanisms of bone loss due to Ca deficiency in both sexes after about 65 years of age. Variable degrees of Ca malabsorption occur with aging and lead to increased PTH-mediated bone resorption. In addition, there may be an age-related impairment of the coupling of bone formation to bone resorption. For example, in elderly men, testosterone deficiency could lead to poor coupling of bone formation and bone resorption together. These two defects lead to decreased bone density. (See text for further discussion.)

serum 1,25D, a change which during even a mild Ca stress would limit the participation of intestine and enhance the participation of bone in serum Ca regulation. Moreover, the coupling mechanism is probably less effective in maintaining bone balance in aged persons (see below). Thus, a low Ca stress probably is more likely to cause bone loss in aged than in young persons.

In terms of the cause of bone loss in postmenopausal women, calcium deficiency is not nearly as prevalent as is estrogen deficiency. Thus, all postmenopausal women experience estrogen deficiency, and bone loss occurs in all estrogen-deficient women. On the other hand, only a fraction of the total population of postmenopausal osteoporotic patients has typical calcium deficiency with elevated bone resorption and elevated serum PTH levels. Nonetheless, even though calcium deficiency is less prevalent than estrogen deficiency in the postmenopausal women, both problems are readily correctable with specific therapies.

In addition to Ca malabsorption, during aging there could be other causes of impaired coupling, including age-related defects in the coupling mechanism. Accordingly, while it is not known whether osteoblast synthesis of growth factors or bone matrix concentration of growth factor decreases with aging, there is evidence that serum IGF-I levels (a growth factor produced by bone as well as other tissues) decrease with aging.[68,69] Moreover, there is preliminary evidence that bone IGF concentrations decrease with age.[70] This evidence raises the possibility that production of local growth factors by bone cells is decreased during aging. It is also possible that cell responsiveness to growth factor decreases with aging.[70a] Such changes could result in defective coupling and thus produce bone loss with aging.

Lifestyle Factors

In contrast to factors such as the menopause, which influences bone volume over a decade, lifestyle factors can influence bone volume over the entire life span of the individual. Several lifestyle factors have been shown to influence bone volume. Two of the most important so far identified are Ca intake and exercise. Regarding Ca intake, although intuitively one might think that a higher-Ca diet should promote bone formation, as pointed out earlier, the only evidence that we have for the effect of Ca intake on bone volume is to decrease bone resorption. The epidemiological and clinical aspects of this issue are discussed in Chap. 76.

With respect to exercise, this lifestyle factor is uniquely important because one of the dual functions of bone is to maintain mechanical support, and because bone is an adaptive organ, there is a proportionality between mechanical strain and bone volume. Thus, with inactivity to the point of immobilization, there is a progressive loss of bone volume to such an extent that fractures may occur.[44,45] On the other hand, the bone volume of weight lifters is much greater than that of nonexercising cohorts.[71] Another reason why exercise is considered to have a unique influence on bone is because the orientation of trabeculae are always reflective of the normal stresses and strains on the bone. Thus, not only the overall bone volume, but also the distribution of the supporting bony struts within the bone volume are influenced by exercise.

With respect to the cellular and molecular mechanisms involved in mediating mechanical influences on bone, we are concerned about two issues: (1) how bone loss occurs in response to immobilization, and (2) how bone volume increases in response to exercise. It seems likely that bone loss in response to immobilization is largely due to mechanisms and mediators inherent within bone itself. It seems doubtful that a hormone or other systemic mediator might be involved, because the mechanical effects on bone are not necessarily a generalized phenomenon throughout the skeleton, but rather are localized to that portion of the skeleton that is being mechanically loaded or unloaded. We do not know just what osteolytic cytokines are involved in mediating this increased resorptive response from mechanical unloading of the bones. As previously mentioned, we postulate that osteocytes detect the amount of loading and unloading because of their strategic position within bone, and that they then communicate signals through their cell processes via canaliculae to the surface cells, namely osteoblasts and osteoclasts. Thus, with decreased loading, there would be signals that ultimately would lead to increased bone resorption.

Regarding the cellular and molecular mechanisms leading to increased bone formation, with increased loading, signals elaborated by the osteocytes would ultimately lead to an increase in bone formation. The increase in bone formation might take the form of overfilling the resorptive cavity (Fig. 75-7). Thus, with progressive overfilling of each resorptive cavity, there would be an increase in bone volume. In addition, it is conceivable that there could be increased bone formation on previously neutral surfaces which could also contribute to the effects of increased mechanical loading.

Our model of the increase in bone formation in response to increased mechanical loading is shown in Fig. 75-12. Accordingly, exercise is associated with increased growth hormone secretion, which in turn would be expected to increase the elaboration of IGF-I, a potent bone cell mitogen. In addition to this systemic effect, there also may be a local osseous elaboration of growth factors in response to mechanical stress (Fig. 75-12).

There is circumstantial evidence to suggest that there is a deficiency of bone formation relative to the mechanical stress and strain in the aging osteoporotic skeleton. Accordingly, patients with osteoporosis undoubtedly have very high stresses and strains on their osteoporotic skeleton because there is a greater reduction in bone density than there is in physical activity in these patients. Moreover, some patients undergo spontaneous fracture, implying that there are considerable stresses and strains on the corresponding osteoporotic bones. If bone formation is proportional to strain, then one would expect to see an increase in bone formation in osteoporotic bones, whereas the bone formation in osteoporosis remains in the same range as in younger individuals with normal skeletal density. This suggests that there is some abnormality in the bone formation mediated by mechanical stresses and strains, or that there is a basic general defect in bone formation in osteoporosis.

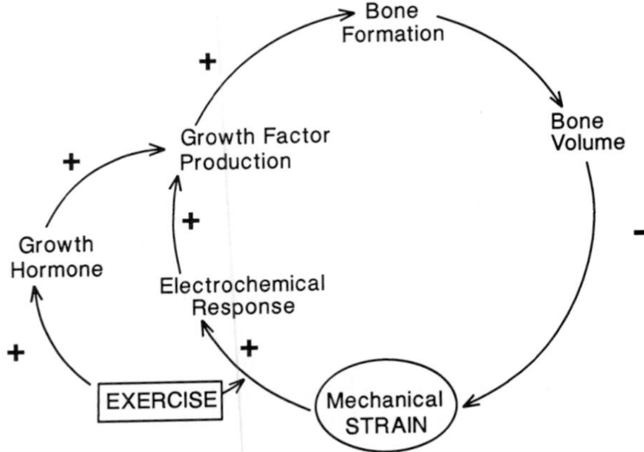

FIGURE 75-12
Model of the effect of exercise to increase bone formation and bone volume. Exercise alters bone formation via both systemic and local factors. There are two components to this model, systemic and local. Systemically, exercise increases growth hormone secretion, which in turn would be expected to increase systemic levels of IGF-I, which then increases bone formation, and thus bone volume. Locally, exercise increases mechanical strain, which produces an electrochemical response, which in turn increases the production of the IGFs by bone cells, and thus bone formation and bone volume. The increase in bone volume occurring through this mechanism decreases the mechanical strain and thus closes the feedback loop.

For more detailed consideration of the clinical aspects of lifestyle factors on the development of osteoporosis, see Chap. 76.

Genetic Factors

According to twin studies, genetic factors appear to determine from 50 to 70 percent of peak bone volume, which is achieved at about 35 years of age.[72] Apparently genetic factors have much less influence on bone loss associated with aging than on the development of peak bone density.[73–76] The significance of peak bone density is that the greater the peak bone density, the greater the amount of bone that must be lost to arrive at the fracture threshold (i.e., the bone density level below which there is an increased risk for fracture) (Fig. 75-13). Interestingly, those twins with the highest peak bone density had the lowest bone remodeling rates. As mentioned earlier, if there is impaired coupling, the lower the remodeling rate, the lower the absolute amount of bone lost.

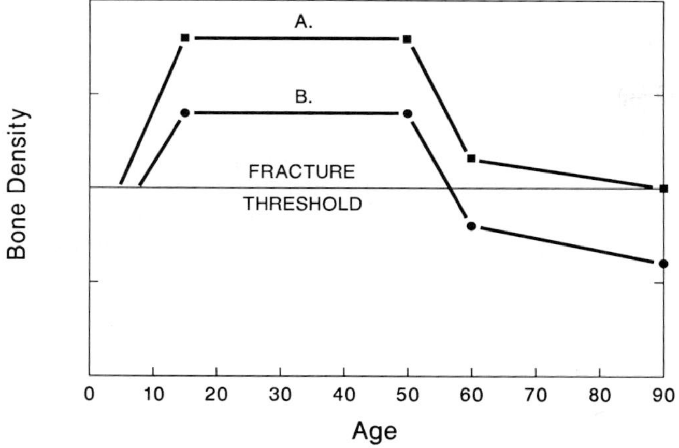

FIGURE 75-13

The relationship between peak bone density and fracture risk. This model illustrates how peak bone density will determine the age at which the patient arrives at that density considered to be the fracture threshold (i.e., the density below which the incidence of fracture frequency increases). Individual B with a lower peak bone density than that of A, but with a rate of bone loss at menopause similar to that of A, would reach the fracture threshold at 55, while individual A would not reach the fracture threshold until age 90. Thus, the higher the peak bone density, the less the likelihood of developing osteoporosis and fractures.

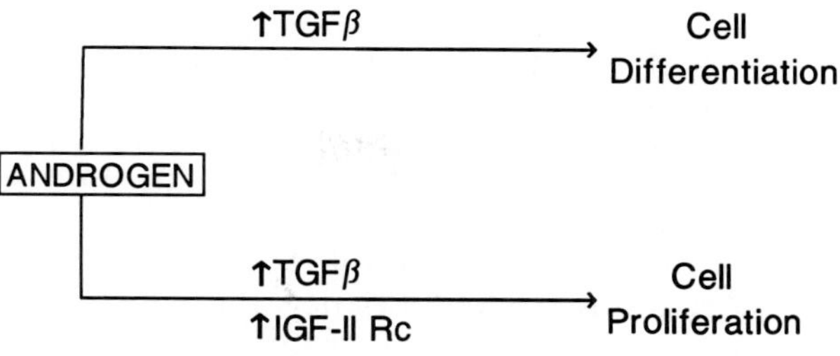

FIGURE 75-14

Model of the anabolic actions of androgens on bone cells. Androgens have been shown to have strong anabolic actions on both bone cell proliferation and bone cell differentiation. The increase in proliferation may be mediated in part by an increased production of TGF-β and by an increased number of IGF-II receptors. The increase in differentiation could also be in part a consequence of the increase in TGF-β.

Major Determinants of Bone Volume in Men

Less is known about bone volume regulation in males than in females. However, the same four determinants of female bone volume (sex hormone deficiency; Ca malabsorption; lifestyle factors; and genetics, which largely determines peak bone density) are probably operational in men as well as in women. In regard to these four factors, men compared with women have a lower incidence of osteoporosis for the following reasons: (1) peak bone density is greater in men than in women, and it seems likely that the higher circulating levels of testosterone contribute to this, but this issue has not yet been settled. Testosterone is clearly a more anabolic hormone than estrogen. For example, in vitro studies indicate that testosterone is directly anabolic to osteoblasts (Fig. 75-14). (2) Males tend to be more physically active than females. (3) The decline in sex hormone with aging is much more abrupt and much larger in magnitude in women than in men. Ca malabsorption is a problem that is prevalent in both men and women.

Thus, the two major determinants of bone loss in the elderly man appear to be testosterone deficiency and Ca deficiency. In men, bone loss begins at about 65 years of age. This bone loss appears to be in part a consequence of testosterone deficiency and/or Ca deficiency. Men begin to show a decrease in serum free testosterone (the biologically active fraction) levels at about 65 years of age. This gonadal hormone deficiency in men differs in three ways from that seen in women: (1) not all men have a decrease in serum testosterone levels, (2) in those men who exhibit a decrease in serum testosterone levels, the decrease is gradual, extending over a period of years, and (3) those men who do develop serum testosterone level reductions express variable degrees of reductions, and there is seldom a complete cessation of testicular testosterone production. Although it is now well established that testosterone deficiency is a risk factor for bone loss,[77–79] much less is known about the specific pathophysiological effects of testosterone than those of estrogen on skeletal tissue.

There is evidence that testosterone deficiency, like estrogen deficiency, is associated with an increase in bone resorption.[77] Moreover, because testosterone appears to be more anabolic for bone cells than estrogen, testosterone deficiency would be expected to impair bone formation.[39] This could explain how testosterone deficiency impairs the coupled bone formation in response to bone resorption. Two findings at the growth factor level could be relevant to the increased bone resorption and the impaired coupling attending that deficiency: (1) transforming growth factor β production by bone cells is clearly increased by testosterone treatment in vitro,[80] and (2) testosterone treatment of bone cells in vitro leads to increased proliferation and differentiation in association with increased IGF-II receptor number (Fig. 75-14).[81] Thus, testosterone deficiency would tend to increase bone resorption* (i.e., decreased transforming growth factor β production) and decrease bone for-

*It is likely that testosterone, like estrogen, has effects on bone-resorbing cytokines, viz. interleukin-1 and interleukin-6, but this has not yet been studied.

mation (i.e., decreased transforming growth factor β and decreased IGF-II receptor number). In summary, testosterone deficiency clearly causes bone loss, and the information available about the actions of testosterone suggests that testosterone deficiency, like estrogen deficiency, is associated with increased bone resorption and decreased coupled bone formation.

Besides testosterone deficiency, the other major known risk factor for bone loss with aging in men is Ca deficiency. The model of the effect of Ca deficiency to impair coupling of bone formation to bone resorption is applicable to men as well as women (Figs. 75-8 and 75-12). The causes of Ca deficiency in elderly men have not been as well defined as the causes of Ca deficiency in elderly women; however, it has been established that in men, as in women, the efficacy of Ca absorption decreases with age. Serum PTH levels increase with aging in men, and it seems likely that Ca malabsorption strongly contributes to this change.

REFERENCES

1. Stewart AF: Calcium metabolism without anguish. *Postgrad Med* 77:2831, 1985.
2. Gallagher JC et al: Intestinal calcium absorption and serum vitamin D metabolites in normal subjects and osteoporotic patients. *J Clin Invest* 64:729, 1979.
3. Heaney RP et al: Calcium nutrition and bone health in the elderly. *Am J Clin Nutr* 36:986, 1982.
4. Sheikh MS et al: Role of vitamin D–dependent and vitamin D–independent mechanisms in absorption of food calcium. *J Clin Invest* 81:126, 1988.
5. Ebeling PR et al: Evidence of an age-related decrease in intestinal responsiveness to vitamin D: Relationship between serum 1,25-dihydroxyvitamin D_3 and intestinal vitamin D receptor concentrations in normal women. *J Clin Endocrinol Metab* 75:176, 1992.
6. Recker RR: Calcium absorption and achlorhydria. *N Engl J Med* 313:70, 1985.
7. Newcomer AD et al: Lactase deficiency: Prevalence in osteoporosis. *Ann Intern Med* 89:218, 1978.
8. Martin KJ et al: The peripheral metabolism of parathyroid hormone. *N Engl J Med* 301:1092, 1979.
9. Arnaud CD et al: Influence of immunoheterogeneity of circulating parathyroid hormone results of radioimmunoassays of serum in man. *Am J Med* 56:785, 1974.
10. Gallagher JC et al: The effect of age on serum immuno-reactive parathyroid hormone in normal and osteoporotic women. *J Lab Clin Med* 95:373, 1980.
11. Insogna KL et al: Effect of age on serum immunoreactive parathyroid hormone and its biological effects. *J Clin Endocrinol Metab* 53:1072, 1981.
12. Young G et al: Age-related rise in parathyroid hormone in man: The use of intact and midmolecule antisera to distinguish hormone secretion from retention. *J Bone Min Res* 2:367, 1987.
13. Forero MS et al: Effect of age on circulating immunoreactive and bioactive parathyroid hormone levels in women. *J Bone Min Res* 2:363, 1987.
14. Epstein S et al: The influence of age on bone mineral regulating hormones. *Bone* 7:421, 1986.
15. Queseda JM et al: Influence of vitamin D on parathyroid function in the elderly. *J Clin Endocrinol Metab* 75:494, 1992.
16. DeLuca HF: The vitamin D story: A collaborative effort of basic science and clinical medicine. *FASEB J* 2:224, 1988.
17. Bell NH: Vitamin D–endocrine system. *J Clin Invest* 76:1, 1985.
18. Baylink DJ et al: Vitamin D and bone formation in mineralization, in Norman AW et al (eds): *Chemical, Biochemical and Clinical Endocrinology of Calcium Metabolism.* Berlin, Walter de Gruyter, 1982, p 363.
19. Maierhofer WJ et al: Bone resorption stimulated by elevated serum 1:25-$(OH)_2$-vitamin D concentrations in healthy men. *Kidney Int* 24:555, 1983.
20. Lamberg-Allardt C: The relationship between serum 25-hydroxyvitamin D levels and other variables related to calcium and phosphorus metabolism in the elderly. *Acta Endocrinol* 105:139, 1984.
21. Fujisawa Y et al: Role of change in vitamin D metabolism with age in calcium and phosphorus metabolism in normal human subjects. *J Clin Endocrinol Metab* 59:719, 1984.
22. Slovik DM et al: Deficient production of 1,25-dihydroxyvitamin D in elderly osteoporotic patients. *N Engl J Med* 305:372, 1981.
23. Howard GA et al: Human bone cells in culture metabolize $25(OH)D_3$ to $1,25(OH)_2D_3$. *J Biol Chem* 256:7738, 1981.
24. Manglesdorf DJ et al: 1,25-dihydroxyvitamin D_3–induced differentiation in a human peomyelocytic leukemia cell line (HLCO): Receptor mediated maturation to macrophage-like cells. *Cell Biol* 98:391, 1984.
25. Kyeyune-Nyombi E et al: 1,25-dihydroxyvitamin D_3 stimulates both alkaline phosphatase gene transcription and mRNA stability in human bone cells. *Arch Biochem Biophys* 291:316, 1991.
26. Austin LA, Heath H III: Calcitonin—Physiology and pathophysiology. *N Engl J Med* 304:269, 1981.
27. Tiegs RD et al: Calcitonin secretion in postmenopausal osteoporosis. *N Engl J Med* 312:1097, 1985.
28. Parfitt AM: Bone remodeling and bone loss: Understanding the pathophysiology of osteoporosis. *Clin Obstet Gynecol* 30:789, 1987.
29. Weinstein RS, Hutson MS: Decreased trabecular width and increased trabecular spacing contribute to bone loss with age. *Bone* 8:137, 1987.
30. Bergot C et al: Measurement of anisotropic vertebral trabecular bone loss during aging by quantitative image analysis. *Calcif Tissue Int* 43:143, 1988.
31. Hauschka PV et al: Growth factors in bone matrix. *J Bone Chem* 261:12665, 1986.
32. Linkhart TA et al: Characterization of mitogenic activities extracted from bovine bone matrix. *Bone* 7:479, 1986.

33. Mohan S et al: Identification and quantification of four distinct growth factors stored in human bone matrix (abstract). *J Bone Min Res* 2(suppl 1):44, 1987.
34. Seyedin SM et al: Purification and characterization of two cartilage inducing factors from bovine demineralized bone. *Proc Natl Acad Sci USA* 82:2267, 1985.
35. Termine JD: Noncollagen proteins in bone, in Evered D, Hartnett S (eds): *Cell and Molecular Biology of Vertebral Hard Tissues.* Ciba Foundation Symposium 136. Chichester, John Wiley, 1988, p 178.
36. Rubin CT et al: Suppression of the osteogenic response in the aging skeleton.
37. Roodman GD et al: 1,25(OH)2 vitamin D3 causes formation of multinucleated cells with osteoclast characteristics in cultures of primate marrow. *Proc Natl Acad Sci USA* 82:8213, 1985.
38. Felix et al: Production of hemopoietic growth factors by bone tissue and bone cells in culture. *J Bone Min Res* 3:27, 1988.
39. Pfeilschifter J et al: Transforming growth factor beta inhibits bone resorption in fetal rat long bone culture. *J Clin Invest* 82:680, 1988.
40. Chenu C et al: Transforming growth factor beta inhibits formation of osteoclast-like cells in long-term human marrow culture. *Proc Natl Acad Sci USA* 85:5683, 1988.
41. McSheehy PMJ, Chambers TJ: Osteoblast-like cells in the presence of parathyroid hormone release soluble factor that stimulates osteoclastic bone resorption. *Endocrinology* 119:1654, 1986.
42. Frost HM: *Bone Remodeling Dynamics.* Springfield, IL, Charles C Thomas, 1963.
43. Eriksen EF: Normal and pathological remodeling of human trabecular bone: Three dimensional reconstruction of remodeling sequence in normals and in metabolic bone disease. *Endocr Rev* 7:379, 1986.
44. Globus RK et al: The temporal response of bone to unloading. *Endocrinology* 118:733, 1986.
45. Minaire P et al: Quantitative histological data on disuse osteoporosis. *Calcif Tissue Res* 17:57, 1974.
46. Potts JTJ: Management of asymptomatic hyperparathyroidism. *J Clin Endocrinol Metab* 70:1489, 1990.
47. Wartofsky L: Osteoporosis: A growing concern for the thyroidologist. *Thyroid Today* 11:1, 1988.
48. Harris WH, Heaney RP: Skeletal renewal and metabolic bone disease. *N Engl J Med* 280:193, 1969.
49. Frost HM: *Bone Biodynamics.* Boston, Little, Brown, 1964.
50. Howard GA et al: Parathyroid hormone stimulates bone formation and resorption in organ culture: Evidence for a coupling mechanism. *Proc Natl Acad Sci USA* 78:3204, 1981.
51. Farley JR et al: In vitro evidence that bone formation may be coupled to resorption by release of mitogen(s) from resorbing bone. *Metabolism* 36:314, 1987.
52. Lukert BP, Raisz LG: Glucocorticoid-induced osteoporosis: Pathogenesis and management. *Annals Intern Med* 112:352, 1990.
53. Rosen C et al: The 24/25-kDa serum insulin-like growth factor binding protein is increased in elderly women with hip and spine fractures. *J Clin Endocrinol Metab* 74:24, 1992.
54. Huddleston AL et al: Bone mass in lifetime tennis athletes. *JAMA* 244:1107, 1980.
55. Basset CAL, Becker RO: Generation of electric potentials by bone in response to mechanical stress. *Science* 137:1063, 1962.
56. Fitzsimmons RJ et al: Low-amplitude, low-frequency electric field-stimulated bone cell proliferation may in part be mediated by increase IGF-II release. *J Cell Physiol* 150:84, 1992.
57. Jennings J et al: Osteoporosis, in Calkins E et al (eds): *Practice of Geriatrics.* Philadelphia, Saunders, 1992, p 363.
58. Grady D et al: Hormone therapy to prevent disease and prolong life in postmenopausal women. *Ann Intern Med* 117:1016, 1992.
59. Stepan JJ et al: Bone loss and biochemical indices of bone remodeling in surgically induced postmenopausal women. *Bone* 8:279, 1987.
60. Eriksen EF et al: Evidence of estrogen receptors in normal human osteoblast-like cells. *Science* 241:84, 1988.
61. Komm BS et al: Estrogen blinding, receptor mRNA, and biologic response in osteoblast-like osteosarcoma cells. *Science* 241:81, 1988.
62. Rodan GA, Martin TJ: Role of osteoblasts in hormonal control of bone resorption—A hypothesis. *Calcif Tissue Int* 33:349, 1981.
63. McSheehy PMJ, Chambers TJ: Osteoblastic cells mediate osteoclastic responsiveness to parathyroid hormone. *Endocrinology* 118:824, 1986.
64. Roodman GD: Interleukin 6: An osteotropic factor? *J Bone Min Res* 7:475, 1992.
65. Girasole G et al: 17β Estradiol inhibits interleukin-6 production by bone marrow derived stromal cells and osteoblasts in vitro: A potential mechanism for the antiosteoporotic effect of estrogens. *J Clin Invest* 89:883, 1992.
66. Oursler MJ et al: Modulation of transforming growth factor β production in normal human osteoblasts by 17β-estradiol and parathyroid hormone. *Endocrinology* 129:3313, 1991.
67. Oursler MJ et al: Avian osteoclasts as estrogen target cells. *Proc Natl Acad Sci USA* 88:6613, 1991.
68. Bennett AE et al: Insulin-like growth factors I and II: Aging and bone density in women. *J Clin Endocrinol Metab* 59:701, 1984.
69. Hammerman MR: Insulin-like growth factors and aging. *Endocrinol Metab Clin North Am* 16:995, 1987.
70. Nicolas V et al: Evidence for a progressive decline in IGF-I in human bone in both males and females as a function of age (abstract). *J Bone Min Res* 7(suppl 1): S255, 1992.
70a. Pfeilschifter J et al: Mitogenic responsiveness of human bone cells in vitro to hormones and growth factor decreases with age. *J Bone Min Res* 6:707, 1993.
71. Colletti LA et al: The effects of muscle-building exercise on bone mineral density of the radius, spine, and hip in young men. *Calcif Tissue Int* 45:12, 1989.
72. Ott SM: Attainment of peak bone mass. *J Clin Endocrinol Metab* 71:1082, 1990.
73. Smith DM et al: Genetic factors in determining bone mass. *J Clin Invest* 52:2800, 1973.
74. Dequeker J et al: Genetic determinants of bone mineral content at the spine and radius: A twin study. *Bone* 8:207, 1987.
75. Seeman E et al: Reduced bone mass in daughters of women with osteoporosis. *N Engl J Med* 320:554, 1989.

76. Evans RA et al: Bone mass is low in relatives of osteoporotic patients. *Ann Intern Med* 109:870, 1988.
77. Foresta C et al: Osteoporosis and decline of gonadal function in the elderly male. *Horm Res* 19:18, 1984.
78. Finkelstein JS et al: Increases in bone density during treatment of men with idiopathic hypogonadotropic hypogonadism. *J Clin Endocrinol Metab* 69:776, 1989.
79. Stepan JJ et al: Castrated men exhibit bone loss: Effect of calcitonin treatment on biochemical indices of bone remodeling. *J Clin Endocrinol Metab* 69:523, 1987.
80. Kasperk CH et al: Androgens directly stimulate proliferation of bone cells in vitro. *Endocrinology* 124:1576, 1989.
81. Kasperk C et al: Studies of mechanism by which androgens enhance mitogenesis and differentiation in bone cells. *J Clin Endocrinol Metab* 71:1322, 1990.

Chapter 76

OSTEOPOROSIS

Charles H. Chesnut III

Primary osteoporosis, which is postmenopausal in the female and senile in the male, and secondary osteoporosis, which is associated with other diseases or medications (Cushing's disease, corticosteroids, etc.), are the most common of the metabolic bone diseases in the elderly. A classification of such osteoporoses is noted in Table 76-1.

DEFINITION

Common to all osteoporotic conditions is a reduction of bone mass and bone mass per unit volume to a level leading to fracture, especially of the vertebrae, distal radius, and proximal femur. *Skeletal osteopenia* generally refers to bone mass reduction, while *osteoporosis* usually refers to bone mass reduction to a point of fracture, although it is obvious that a fall or other appropriate trauma may obliterate the distinction between these two conditions. While bone mass is reduced in osteoporosis, current data suggest that the bone composition which is present is essentially normal,[1] although bone microarchitecture may be compromised[2] in terms of thinner and more easily perforated trabecular struts.[3]

EPIDEMIOLOGY

Osteoporosis is a public health problem of epidemic proportions, particularly for the elderly. An estimated 1.5 million fractures per year are attributable to osteoporosis in the United States alone.[4,5] In 1985, 247,000 hip fractures occurred in the United States; such fractures carry a 5 to 20 percent excess mortality during the year after the fracture. Eight percent of women currently 35 years old will experience a hip fracture in later life. Economically, the expenses of osteoporotic fractures are overwhelming; direct and indirect costs of osteoporosis (including lost productivity, long-term nursing care, etc.) are estimated to be in excess of $10 billion annually. The morbidity of the osteoporotic fracture, particularly of the hip, is considerable for the elderly individual as well as for society, as the deterioration in the quality of life following fracture may be catastrophic.

PATHOGENESIS

Osteoporosis is a heterogeneous disease of multiple etiologies. In secondary osteoporosis, the pathogenesis of bone mass loss and fractures may be readily apparent (e.g., corticosteroid excess in Cushing's disease); in primary osteoporosis, the exact pathogenesis may be more difficult to define. The pathogenesis of primary osteoporosis, however, may be approached from the standpoint of osteopenia and osteoporosis as defined previously. Osteopenia may be due to multiple causes, including inadequate bone mass at skeletal maturity (age 12 to 21 for females), and/or to subsequent age-related and post-menopausal bone loss. Regardless of the pathogenesis of the osteopenia, osteoporosis with fracture is *principally* due to low bone mass; it should, however, be noted that other determinants of fracture include bone quality (trabecular architecture and the ability to heal microfractures) and propensity to fall (see Fig. 76-1). The latter determinant is most important for the elderly, since decreased neuromuscular coordination, as well as such environmental factors as medication-induced confusion/dizziness and the use of throw rugs, will increase the occurrence of falls. As a fracture determinant, the increased number and traumatic severity of falls in the elderly population may be of equal importance to bone quantity and quality.

The pathogenetic basis of inadequate bone mass, particularly in the elderly, may also be considered from the standpoint of *tissue, hormonal,* and *cellular abnormalities*. The basic abnormality in all types of osteoporosis is a disturbance of the normal bone remodeling sequences at the *tissue* level. To fully understand the pathogenesis of osteoporosis, therefore, a knowledge of bone remodeling is necessary (Fig. 76-2).

Bone is constantly turning over (remodeling); the skeleton acts as a reservoir for calcium, and the re-

TABLE 76-1

Classification of the Osteoporoses

Primary Osteoporosis (basic etiology unknown, no associated disease)
- Postmenopausal osteoporosis (elderly females)
- Senile osteoporosis (elderly males)

Secondary Osteoporosis (secondary to heritable or acquired abnormalities/diseases, or to physiological abnormality)
- Hyperparathyroidism
- Cushing's disease
- Multiple myeloma
- Hyperthyroidism, endogenous and iatrogenic
- Idiopathic hypercalciuria:
  - Due to renal calcium leak
  - Due to renal phosphate leak
- Malabsorption (including partial gastrectomy)
- 25-(OH)D deficiency:
  - Due to chronic liver disease
  - Due to chronic anticonvulsant therapy (diphenylhydantoin, barbiturates)
- 1,25-$(OH)_2$D deficiency due to lack of renal synthesis, associated with chronic renal failure
- Adult hypophosphatasia
- Chronic renal failure (renal osteodystrophy)
- Chronic hepatic failure (hepatic osteodystrophy)
- Osteogenesis imperfecta tarda
- Male hypogonadism (Klinefelter's syndrome)
- Female hypogonadism (Turner's syndrome)
- Conditions consistent with hypoestrogenism secondary to anorexia and/or exercise:
  - Anorexia nervosa, bulimia
  - Exercise-induced amenorrhea
- Conditions associated with disuse:
  - Paraplegia/hemiplegia
  - Immobilization
  - Prolonged bed rest
- Alcoholism
- Diabetes mellitus (?)
- Rheumatoid arthritis
- Chronic obstructive pulmonary disease
- Systemic mastocytosis
- Associated with the usage of the following medications:
  - Corticosteroids
  - Heparin
  - Anticonvulsants (as noted above)
  - Excess thyroid hormone replacement (as noted above)
  - Prolonged exposure to GnRH agonist
  - Hemochromatosis
  - Malignancy

SOURCE: Adapted from Chesnut CH: Osteoporosis, in DeLisa J (ed): *Rehabilitation Medicine: Principles and Practice.* Philadelphia, Lippincott, 1988, pp 865–875.

modeling process provides calcium to the organism without sacrificing the skeleton. As noted in Fig. 76-2*B*, an increase in bone resorption as mediated by the osteoclast (the bone cell primarily responsible for bone resorption) is the initial event in normal bone remodeling. This event is typically followed within 40 to 60 days by an increase in bone formation as mediated by the osteoblast (the bone cell primarily responsible for bone formation). Bone resorption and formation are normally and homeostatically coupled: an increase or decrease in resorption produces a corresponding increase or decrease in formation, with no net change in bone mass. However, in postmenopausal and probably senile osteoporosis, as noted in Fig. 76-2*C*, bone resorption is increased over normal resorption levels without a corresponding increase in bone formation, leading to a net loss in bone mass. In other forms of osteoporosis, such as corticosteroid-induced osteoporosis, a primary decrease in bone formation may occur as noted in Fig. 76-2*D*, with a similar result in either situation (Fig. 76-2*C* or 76-2*D*) of a loss of bone mass leading to an increased risk of fracture. Such abnormalities of bone remodeling at the tissue level may therefore contribute to the pathogenesis of the disease.

The etiology of such an increase in bone resorption in osteoporosis is unclear, but it is undoubtedly related to *hormonal* alterations. Changes in a number of hormonal modalities (estrogen, parathyroid hormone, calcitonin, and the D metabolites) affect bone cell function and bone mass. While there are numerous age- and menopause-related alterations in the physiology of such hormones, a pathogenetic hor-

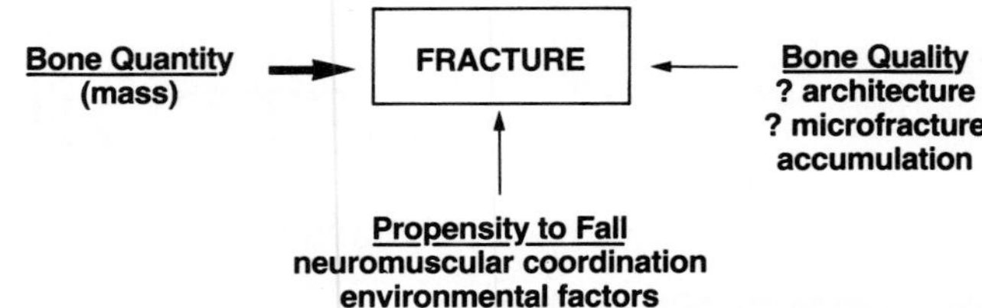

FIGURE 76-1

Determinants of osteoporotic fracture, including bone quality and propensity to fall. *(From Chesnut CH: Osteoporosis, in DeLisa J (ed): Rehabilitation Medicine: Principles and Practice. Philadelphia, Lippincott, 1988, p 866. Reproduced by permission.)*

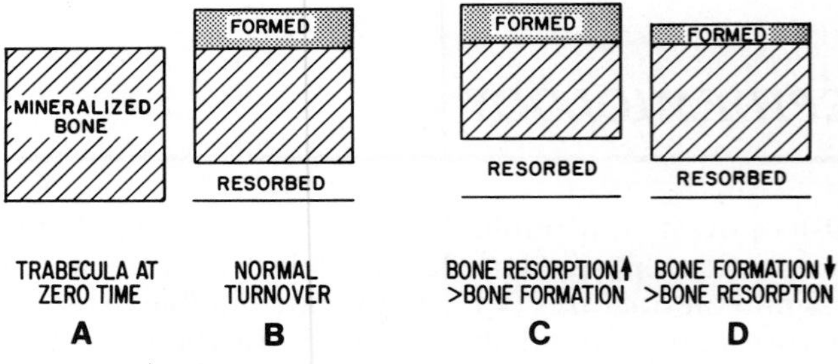

FIGURE 76-2

Pathogenesis of osteoporosis at the tissue level. A disruption of normal bone-remodeling sequences: *A* and *B* denote a bone trabecula at 0 time and with normal bone turnover, respectively; *C* and *D* denote two possible mechanisms of abnormal bone remodeling. *(From Chesnut CH, Kribbs PJ: Osteoporosis: Some aspects of pathophysiology and therapy. J Prosthet Dent 48:407, 1982. Reproduced by permission.)*

monal abnormality specific for osteoporosis (excluding the osteopenias associated with hypercorticism) has rarely been defined. Estrogen deficiency is, however, most frequently incriminated in the pathogenesis of postmenopausal osteoporosis; indeed, estrogen deficiency of any etiology, including early oophorectomy,[6] exercise- or anorexia-induced amenorrhea,[7] and the postmenopausal state is associated with bone mass loss. The specific mechanism of estrogen's effect on bone is unclear, although estrogen receptors have been noted in osteoblast-like cells.[8,9] A reasonable hypothesis for estrogen's effect is its apparent ability to decrease bone resorption, possibly by decreasing the responsiveness of the osteoclast to endogenous circulating immunoreactive parathyroid hormone (iPTH).[10] Such a decreased responsiveness of the osteoclast may be mediated through signals from the osteoblast (with its postulated estrogen receptors). Estrogen deficiency from any cause would then result in increased skeletal responsiveness to PTH, increased bone resorption, a subsequent transient increase in serum calcium, and a resultant decrease in iPTH secretion. With such a decrease in iPTH, a reduction in formation of the active form of vitamin D, 1,25-$(OH)_2$ cholecalciferol would be expected (the renal 1 α-hydroxylase enzyme requires PTH for its action), and a consequent decrease in calcium absorption would then occur.[11] A number of such hormonal perturbations are indeed documented in osteoporotic populations; however, all postmenopausal females are relatively estrogen-deficient but not all develop osteoporosis. Menopause and its subsequent estrogen deficiency is therefore an incomplete pathogenetic explanation for postmenopausal osteoporosis; it also does not explain senile osteoporosis.

In approximately 10 percent of osteoporotic women, iPTH levels are increased, and in these patients PTH may be related causally to bone loss through an increase in bone resorption. In the majority of postmenopausal osteoporotic females, however, PTH levels are normal or low compared to those of normal elderly females; as noted previously, a low serum PTH may have a permissive or sustaining pathogenetic role in maintaining bone mass loss (through decreased 1,25$(OH)_2$D production). However, the overall contribution of PTH to the pathogenesis of osteoporosis is unclear.

A number of abnormalities of two additional calciotrophic hormones, vitamin D and calcitonin, also occur with aging. Decreased serum levels of 1,25-$(OH)_2$D and impaired conversion of 25-(OH)D to 1,25-$(OH)_2$D have been noted in the aged; however, a vitamin D abnormality specific for osteoporosis (rather than simply for aging) has not been fully defined. A postulated defect is osteoporosis of the renal 1 α-hydroxylation of 25-(OH)D in response to PTH has been proposed[12] but not conclusively proved.[13] Nevertheless, calcium absorption does decrease with aging and is even lower in patients with postmenopausal osteoporosis.[14] A deficiency of the hormone calcitonin could also contribute to ongoing bone loss; calcitonin inhibits osteoclast activity and may thus decrease osteoclastic bone resorption. While serum levels of immunoreactive calcitonin are indeed lower in women than in men and decrease with age, a decreased calcitonin secretion in osteoporotic women, as compared to secretion in normal aged women, has not been conclusively proved.[15,16] The pathogenetic roles in osteoporosis of the D metabolites and calcitonin are unclear.

Conclusive evidence of *cellular* abnormalities contributing to the pathogenesis of osteoporosis is also lacking, principally due to an inability to define bone cell (osteoblast, osteoclast, or osteocyte) abnormalities which are specific for osteoporosis and separate from bone cell abnormalities which may occur with aging alone. As noted previously in the discussion of bone remodeling, it may be that failure of the osteoblast, due to either decreased cell number or decreased cell activity, may accompany advancing age, but such failure is not specific of osteoporosis.

In conclusion, the specific pathogenesis of osteoporosis is quite possibly a combination of heretofore undefined cellular, hormonal, and tissue abnormalities; such abnormalities, however, all contribute to a deficiency of bone mass, which, in combination with other previously noted determinants, may result in bone loss and subsequent osteoporotic fractures.

RISK FACTORS

Multiple risk factors (Table 76-2) may act independently or in combination to produce diminished bone mass in an individual patient. Presumably the pres-

TABLE 76-2

Factors Contributing to the Risk of Osteopenia/Osteoporosis in the Elderly

Estrogen depletion (in the female):
  Postmenopausal state (natural or artificial)
  History of athletic amenorrhea, anorexia nervosa, oligomenorrhea, etc.
Calcium deficiency
Diminished peak bone mass at skeletal maturity; varies with sex, race, and heredity
Diminished physical activity
Positive family history of osteoporosis
Testosterone depletion (in males)
Aging
Leanness (adipose tissue is the major source of postmenopausal extragonadal estrogen production)
Alcoholism
Smoking
Excessive dietary protein intake (resulting in increased loss of calcium in the urine)
Medications (corticosteroids, excessive thyroid hormone, prolonged heparin usage)

SOURCE: Adapted from Chesnut CH: Osteoporosis, in DeLisa J (ed): *Rehabilitation Medicine: Principles and Practice.* Philadelphia, Lippincott, 1988, pp 865–875.

ence of one or more of these risk factors in the elderly increases the risk of accelerated bone loss and subsequent fracture; the weighting of each of these risk factors in terms of relative etiological importance in osteoporosis is undefined, although presumably in the elderly female estrogen, depletion, calcium deficiency (either decreased calcium intake or decreased efficiency of calcium absorption), diminished peak bone mass in adolescence, and diminished physical activity are the most important.

In senile osteoporosis in males, alcoholism and testosterone depletion must be considered as significant risk factors; in the elderly male, however, the specific etiology of osteopenia and osteoporosis may be difficult to define.[17]

CLINICAL PRESENTATION

A fracture of the proximal femur, the distal forearm, the ribs, and especially the vertebrae—associated typically with minimal trauma—is usually the first clinical indication of osteoporosis, both primary and secondary. While hip, rib, and forearm fractures present with obvious pain symptoms, in some patients vertebral fractures may occur asymptomatically. More frequently, however, there will be acute onset of pain in the area of the affected vertebra, with lateral pain radiation, paravertebral muscle spasm, and tenderness to percussion over the vertebra. Such pain may persist for 6 to 8 weeks and then subside until the next fracture occurs. The persistence of pain beyond 6 months at the site of previous vertebral fractures suggests etiologies other than osteoporosis for the pain complex (e.g., psychiatric, medical/legal, or pathologic-metastatic etiologies). In some individuals, typically those who are postmenopausal, the disease may relentlessly progress, with 4 to 6 spinal fractures occurring; the etiology of this progressive form of osteoporosis is unclear, but it seems to occur in younger women (age 50 to 60) and may be associated with an accelerated trabecular bone loss. It is unlikely that osteoporosis produces pain in the absence of fracture, although it is possible that painful vertebral microfractures may develop; such microfractures may not be seen on x-ray but may be detected on radionuclide bone scan.

Kyphosis ("dowager's hump" deformity), loss of height, and chronic back pain (midthoracic or lumbosacral) presumably secondary to mechanical deformity and paraspinous muscle spasm, may result from collapsed or severely wedged vertebrae. In addition, with progressive spinal deformity and height loss, abdominal protuberance and gastrointestinal discomfort (constipation) may occur, as well as a degree of pulmonary insufficiency secondary to thoracic cage deformity. In some severely affected individuals, the spinal deformity is sufficient to produce a painful rubbing of the lower ribs on the iliac crest.

DIAGNOSIS

Osteoporosis is diagnosed absolutely only in the presence of an atraumatic fracture of spine, femur, and/or distal radius. However, it is obviously of value from the standpoint of patient management to evaluate the patient at risk for fracture prior to the occurrence of the fracture, as well as to determine the cause of the fracture in patients in whom a fracture has occurred. Prior to describing such a diagnostic evaluation, a brief outline of techniques available for invasively and noninvasively measuring the quantity and quality of bone mass is indicated, as such techniques are currently an integral part of the diagnostic osteoporosis workup.

Principles of the Measurement of Bone Mass Quantity and Quality

As noted previously, bone mass is the primary, although not the sole, determinant of fracture; theoretically, therefore, measurements of bone mass quantity and quality would be of value in patients with bone-wasting diseases such as osteoporosis in predicting the risk of fracture, assessing the severity of bone wasting, and assessing the response of bone to treatment.[18] There are now definitive data confirming the ability of bone mass quantitation to predict future fracture risk.[19,20] Procedures currently available for quantitation of bone mass include single- and dual-photon absorptiometry (SPA and DPA), dual-energy x-ray absorptiometry (DEXA), and computed tomography (CT). Measurement of ultrasound (US) velocity/speed can theoretically both quantitate bone mass and measure its quality.[21] Usage of SPA, DPA, DEXA, and CT provides quantitations of bone mass at the axial and appendicular sites which are the principal areas usually involved in osteoporosis (e.g., the spine, wrist, and hip); in addition, it is also possible to quantitate bone mass at the os calcis (using SPA or US) and throughout the entire skeleton (using DPA or DEXA), and possibly to qualitate and quantitate bone mass at the patella (using US). The technique of radiographic absorptiometry of the phalanges requires further study as a possible low-cost assessment of cortical bone.[22]

The invasive technique of iliac crest bone biopsy (BX) may quantitate bone mass at this site; in addition, some aspects of bone quality can be assessed. It should be kept in mind that x-rays of the spine are quite insensitive for quantitating bone mass, since 30 to 35 percent of bone mass must be lost before radiographic demineralization is detected. On the other hand, the x-ray is obviously the primary discriminant of the presence of osteoporosis (e.g., presence of a fracture) and in this sense provides the final diagnostic information regarding the presence or absence of osteoporotic disease. Anterior and posterior vertebral height loss is also presumably a precursor of an absolute spinal compression fracture, and its presence would indicate some risk for osteoporosis that the practitioner, without access to bone mass quantitating and qualitating techniques, may use in diagnostic deliberations.

The ideal noninvasive and invasive techniques would be those quantitating and possibly qualitating primarily trabecular bone, which is metabolically more active than cortical bone and may be preferentially altered in osteoporosis and by osteoporosis therapy. The spine and hip would be the sites targeted for measurement, as they are the sites most associated with osteoporosis morbidity, although obviously Colles' fracture of the wrist is a component of the osteoporosis disease spectrum. The ideal technique would also be one capable of identifying individuals at risk for fracture. Acceptable precision and accuracy, low radiation exposure, a reasonable cost, acceptability to patients, and applicability to assessing therapeutic response would be other features of the ideal noninvasive and invasive techniques.

Specific Techniques

The techniques described previously satisfy the ideal criteria to varying degrees (see Table 76-3). For instance, SPA possesses a reasonable cost, precision, and low radiation exposure but utilizes primarily a quantitation of cortical bone mass at the wrist, which is neither the site nor the type of bone usually involved in osteoporosis. No definitive evidence[23] exists that measurement of wrist bone mass significantly predicts hip or spine bone mass or bone mass change.[24] The DPA, DEXA, and CT techniques are therefore currently the most utilized methodologies, since they quantitate bone mass at the two principal target sites of osteoporosis, the spine and the hip. Measurement of the total skeleton with DPA and DEXA is available but is used primarily in research studies. The cost of DPA, DEXA, and CT is higher than that of SPA; radiation dose is high with CT, although quite acceptable with DPA and DEXA; and quality control and patient logistics are acceptable with each of these techniques. Precision and accuracy are quite reasonable with DPA and DEXA, although in both accuracy may be compromised in the elderly by the presence of extraskeletal calcification, such as osteophytes and aortic calcification. Marrow fat provides a significant accuracy error for single-energy CT; such an error may be corrected with dual-energy CT but with a subsequent decrease in precision and an increased radiation dose.

With DPA, DEXA, and CT, difficulties may arise in accuracy owing to previously compressed vertebral bodies, kyphosis, and vertebral sclerosis. While the lateral DEXA scan may provide some improvement in accuracy, this may be at the expense of precision. DPA and DEXA quantitate both trabecular and cortical bone mass of the entire vertebral body, including the spinous and transverse processes, the posterior elements, and also calcification within surrounding tissues. CT measures almost exclusively trabecular bone within the vertebral body; in terms of fracture risk, such a measurement may provide a biologically more important quantitation of bone mass than a measurement of the entire vertebral body. Femoral bone mass may be measured at multiple sites with DPA and DEXA; precision and radiation exposure

TABLE 76-3

Noninvasive and Invasive Techniques for Quantitating/Qualitating Bone Mass

Technique	Site Measured	Cortical/ Trabecular %	Precision/ Accuracy	Risk Prediction	Response to Therapy	Radiation	Cost	Remarks
	Radius/ulna:							
	(a)distal	80–95/20–25	±2–4%/±3–4%	+	±*			
SPA	(b)ultradistal	25/75	±2–4%/?	?	?	10 mrem	$75–125	*estrogens
	Os calcis	20/80	±2–4%/?	+	?			
	Spine:L1–L4*	35/65	±2–5%@/±2–4%	+	+	10 mrem	$125–200	**total* vertebral
DPA-DEXA	Femur:neck	75/25	±3–5%/?	?	+	10 mrem	$50–75	body including
	:trochanter	50/50	±3–5%/?	?	+	10 mrem		spinous process @ DEXA 1%
CT	Single-energy spine:T12–L4*	5/95	±3–5%/±6–30%**	+	+	500–750 mrem	$125–175	*area of interest *within* vertebral body**? due to marrow fat
	Dual-energy spine:T12–L4*	5/95	±5–10%/±5%	?	?	750 mrem	?	
US	Total Patella, os calcis	?5/95	3–5%/?	+	?	—	$25–50	5-minute test
BX	Iliac crest	1° trabecular	15–25%/?	±	±	—	$500–600	invasive

SOURCE: Adapted from Chesnut CH: Measurement of bone mass. Triangle, *Sandoz J Med Sci* 27:37, 1988. (Copyright Sandoz Ltd., Basel, Switzerland, with permission.)

are acceptable. However, the contribution of bone mass quantity to the risk of subsequent hip fracture is unknown.[25] DEXA provides improved precision, decreased scanning time, improved resolution, and possibly a lower procedure cost; it is currently the clinical technique of choice for quantitating bone mass. Although SPA, DPA, DEXA, and CT lack the ability to definitively discriminate between normal populations and populations with osteoporotic fractures,[26] all can be used to follow the response of bone mass to therapy and to predict risk of fracture.

US provides a measurement of bone quantity and, presumably, bone quality in the patella and os calcis. At both these sites, the bone is primarily trabecular, and the precision of US is acceptable (although accuracy is as yet undefined). In studies to date,[21] the discrimination of US between normal and osteoporotic populations and its ability to predict risk of fracture is equivalent to that of SPA, DPA, and CT. An improved scanning time (3 to 5 minutes), a presumed lower cost, and a lack of radiation exposure are US's putative assets.

BX quantitates primarily trabecular bone at the iliac crest. While useful information in terms of bone remodeling may be obtained about the mechanism of drug action on bone mass, BX would obviously not be utilized in the individual patient to follow response to treatment. Its poor precision and its cost, as well as the occasional side effects associated with its invasive nature, would prevent its widespread usage for quantitation of bone mass or for assessing treatment response. Indeed, its primary value in the individual patient is to exclude other diseases of bone wasting, such as osteomalacia, multiple myeloma, and hyperparathyroidism.

Indications for the Noninvasive Techniques

When used appropriately, the noninvasive techniques (particularly DPA, DEXA, and CT) are of definite value in the clinical evaluation of the osteopenic or osteoporotic patient. The clinical situations in which they may be used are as follows (adapted from Johnston et al.[26]):

1. In selected perimenopausal and postmenopausal patients in defining their risk for subsequent fracture, when combined with the assessment and presence of historical risk factors (see Table 76-2)
2. In defining the need for prophylactic estrogen therapy
3. In screening for significant bone loss and conditions in which osteopenia is an accompanying manifestation, such as exercise-induced amenorrhea and steroid-induced osteopenia
4. In following response to treatment
5. In research endeavors, such as epidemiologic and clinical therapy studies

At the present time, there appears to be little justification for the use of noninvasive bone-mass quantitating techniques in mass screening of all perimenopausal women[27,28] or in quantitating the severity and/or progression (exclusive of therapy) of disease in the osteoporotic patient.[29]

Diagnostic Evaluation of the Patient at Risk for Osteoporosis

The at-risk patient (most frequently the immediately postmenopausal woman) requires a relatively brief evaluation:

1. A brief history to determine the absence of the medical conditions noted in Table 76-1 which result in secondary osteoporoses and to determine the presence of the risk factors noted in Table 76-2.
2. A brief physical examination to exclude the secondary osteoporoses (hyperthyroidism, Cushing's disease, etc.).
3. A minimal laboratory evaluation to include a determination of serum calcium, phosphorus, and alkaline phosphatase levels, as well as a 24-hour urine calcium/creatinine determination; however, the overall cost-benefit ratio of even these minimal procedures is unproven. In primary osteoporosis, laboratory tests typically are normal; such tests are utilized primarily to exclude other diseases (with the exception of urinary calcium, as noted below), and frequently such exclusion can be accomplished by the history and physical examination alone.
4. A measurement, noninvasively, of bone mass quantity (and, in the future, possibly bone mass quality as well), usually at the spine (using DPA, DEXA, or CT), in the individual patient with positive risk factors. If such a bone mass measurement is low, more aggressive prophylactic therapy (e.g., estrogen) may be indicated; if the measurement is normal, activity and increased calcium intake may be sufficient.

Diagnostic Evaluation of the Patient with Osteoporosis (Fractures)

The patient with osteoporosis, most frequently a female in her late fifties, sixties, or seventies, may present with one to six vertebral fractures and requires a more thorough evaluation:

1. A complete history, again to determine the presence of risk factors and, specifically, to exclude medical conditions resulting in the secondary osteoporoses. In this elderly age group, the search

for other diseases is most important, since multiple myeloma, hyperparathyroidism, and hyperthyroidism are not uncommon.

2. A more thorough physical examination is performed, but again its primary purpose is to exclude the secondary osteoporoses. In addition to the physical findings noted in the previous evaluation, alveolar ridge resorption resulting in dental osteopenia with missing teeth and dentures, as well as proximal muscle weakness and discomfort in osteomalacia, should be kept in mind.
3. A maximal laboratory evaluation in this group may be indicated: serum ionized and total calcium, PTH (intact molecule), phosphorus, protein electrophoresis, complete blood count (CBC), and vitamin D congeners. A 24-hour urine collection for calcium/creatinine remains a mainstay of the evaluation of the osteoporotic patient; assessment of dietary calcium adequacy and dietary calcium gut absorption and the absence of idiopathic hypercalciuria (either due to a renal leak of calcium or to hyperabsorption of calcium at the gut level) can be obtained. If the urinary calcium level is low, either inadequate calcium intake or absorption or a vitamin D abnormality must be considered; if the value is high, either dietary calcium excess or idiopathic hypercalciuria is a possibility. A 24-hour urinary hydroxyproline sample and serum GLA protein (gamma-carboxyglutamic acid or osteocalcin, a noncollagenous bone protein measurable in serum) can also be obtained; they can monitor possible states of high bone remodeling, which may respond particularly to antiresorptive therapeutic agents. In addition, the collagen cross-link pyridinoline is a most sensitive and specific urinary marker for bone resorption. A low serum GLA protein, a low 24-hour urine hydroxyproline, and a low urinary pyridinoline may indicate low remodeling and an inactive and senescent bone. Such a condition may respond more favorably to bone-forming therapies. Last, BX may be used primarily to exclude osteomalacia or other metabolic bone disease.
4. A noninvasive measurement of spinal bone mass will be of value as a baseline measurement to monitor response to treatment over time; such a measurement may also quantitate the severity of the disease, but such a quantitation should not be the primary indication for such a procedure. Last, such a measurement may also be used to define the risk for future fracture.

Diagnostic Evaluation of the Osteoporotic Patient with Back Pain

Acute and/or chronic back pain in the osteoporotic patient may be related to recent compression fractures, mechanical derangement of the spine (such as kyphosis), and/or paraspinous muscle spasm. As noted previously, the radionuclide bone scan can be used in the evaluation of back pain. Increased radionuclide accretion at the site of a recent fracture (usually a vertebral body but also the hip) generally indicates ongoing bone formation and bone healing, although a fracture nonunion will also demonstrate increased radionuclide uptake. Normal radionuclide accretion indicates that healing is complete and that the metabolic activity at that site is normal. A positive scan correlates well with the presence of acute pain and indicates the need for continued aggressive therapies such as a back brace, analgesia, and so on. A normal scan reflects reasonable healing and a subsequent lesser need for aggressive therapy; a bone scan typically returns to normal within 6 months after fracture. Continued back or hip pain in the presence of a normal bone scan suggests a nonskeletal origin of the pain, such as paraspinous muscle spasm. However, a positive bone scan with a negative x ray of the same spinal site, in the absence of metastatic disease, is a combination which may indicate a microfracture (stress fracture) of a vertebral body or proximal femur; such a microfracture may progress in time to a radiographically demonstrable macrofracture. Aggressive therapy, including short-term immobilization, may prevent completion of such an incipient fracture.

TREATMENT

Osteoporosis therapy may be divided into symptomatic treatment and treatment of the underlying disease (skeletal osteopenia/bone mass loss).

Symptomatic Treatment

Spinal compression fractures, due to either primary or secondary osteoporosis, may result in significant pain, necessitating analgesia, limitation of activity, and a back support capable of reducing spinal movement and resultant pain. Such limitation of activity may involve short-term bed rest (3 to 5 days). It is imperative that extensive and prolonged bed rest with associated spinal immobilization (a situation in which bone resorption may exceed bone formation at the tissue level) be avoided so as to prevent increased bone wasting. In addition, should a back support be utilized, a flexible back brace is indicated; a rigid back brace with near-total spinal immobilization, while decreasing pain, may increase bone loss if used over an extensive period of time (months) and thus would be counterproductive.

The acute pain phase of spinal osteoporosis may last for 1 to 2 months; then the pain eventually lessens and the fractured vertebral body heals. In a number of patients, however, the acute pain phase may be replaced within 2 to 4 months following fracture by a particularly debilitating, chronic, and frequently severe lumbosacral discomfort.[30] Such discomfort may be secondary to lumbosacral muscle spasm, in turn produced by an accentuated lumbar lordosis compensating for the thoracic kyphosis resulting from fracture. Such a chronic pain phase may last for months; mild analgesia, muscle relaxants, heat, and rest periods in a reclining position will alleviate muscle spasm. A flexible lumbar back support (and time) will also be of value in managing this condition.

Concomitant with this period of acute and/or chronic back pain, a number of the specific pharmacologic therapies noted below may be prescribed; it should be noted that such therapies (with the possible exception of calcitonin) are not expected to alleviate pain symptomatology but rather to treat the underlying bone loss associated with osteoporosis. However, if such therapy can increase bone mass or slow bone mass loss, further fracture may not occur; in the absence of fractures, pain symptomatology will usually, but not always, improve.

Symptomatic treatment of hip and wrist fractures is described in standard orthopedic texts.

TABLE 76-4

Therapeutic Agents for Osteoporosis to Slow Bone Loss and/or to Increase Bone Formation

Decreased Bone Resorption (Anti–bone-resorbers)
Calcium
Estrogen
Calcitonin
Bisphosphonates[a]
Vitamin D (by increasing gut calcium absorption)
Increased Bone Formation (Positive bone formers)
Sodium fluoride[a]
Testosterone[a]
Anabolic steroids[a]
? Vitamin D metabolites (calcitriol)[a]
Exercise

[a] Experimental.

SOURCE: Adapted from Chesnut CH: Osteoporosis, in DeLisa J (ed): *Rehabilitation Medicine: Principles and Practice.* Philadelphia, Lippincott, 1988, pp 865–875.

Treatment of Bone Mass Deficiency (Skeletal Osteopenia/Osteoporosis)

Treatment of secondary osteoporoses may be accomplished by treatment of the underlying disease (e.g., alleviation of the hyperthyroid state). However, the ideal goal of treatment in any form of osteoporosis and osteopenia would be either prophylactic or restorative, depending on the patient's bone mass and fracture history. An inadequate skeletal mass is the primary determinant of fracture risk in the osteopenic or osteoporotic patient. Therefore, in an aging subject with relatively normal bone mass and no previous fracture, the therapeutic goal involves a slowing of age-related bone loss and maintenance of current bone mass. On the other hand, in subjects with a low bone mass and previous fracture, therapy should involve not only a slowing of age-related bone loss but also restoration of bone previously lost.

Bone loss may be prevented by a decrease in bone resorption if the process of bone formation is maintained at its normal level. A similar prevention of bone loss will occur if bone formation decreases to the same degree as bone resorption, as no *net* change in bone mass will result. Restoration of previously lost bone mass, however, ideally requires both an increase in formation and a decrease in resorption, although an increase in resorption with a greater increase in formation or a decrease in resorption with a lesser decrease in formation will also result in the desired *net* positive bone mass change.

As noted in Table 76-4, several therapeutic agents slow the loss of bone mass by decreasing bone resorption ("anti–bone resorbers"). The primary efficacy of such therapeutic modalities may be prophylactic, in that they prevent significant bone loss. Such anti–bone-resorbing agents, such as estrogen, would have their greatest therapeutic rationale in patients in whom bone mass has not decreased below a hypothetical fracture threshold, as is often seen immediately after the menopause (Fig. 76-3). In such a clinical situation, bone mass would be maintained above a fracture threshold and presumably would be sufficient to prevent fractures.

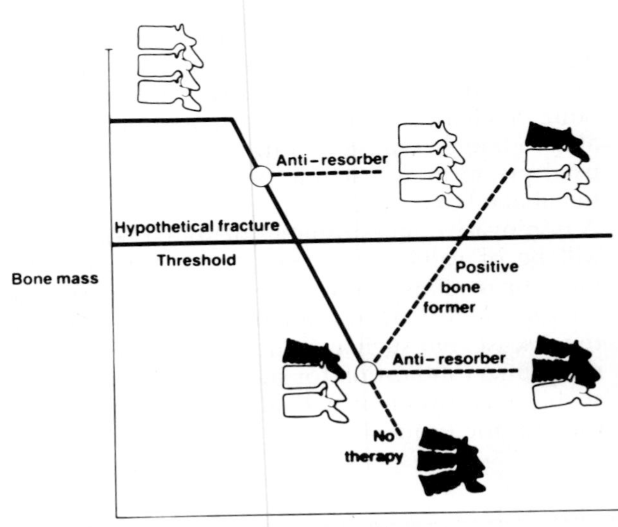

FIGURE 76-3
Therapy of osteoporosis based on bone mass; darker vertebrae represent compression fractures. *(From Chesnut CH: Treatment of postmenopausal osteoporosis. Comp Ther 7:41, 1984. Courtesy of the Laux Co., Maynard, MA. Reproduced by permission.)*

As also noted in Table 76-4, a number of therapeutic agents are capable of increasing bone formation ("positive bone formers"); such agents would restore previously lost bone mass and theoretically prevent further fractures. As shown in Fig. 76-3, such positive bone formers would increase bone mass and possibly elevate skeletal mass above the hypothetical fracture threshold, thus again decreasing the occurrence of future fractures. Theoretically, a combination of a positive bone-forming agent with an anti–bone-resorbing agent would be of particular value for the patient with osteoporotic fractures and low bone mass, as, according to this therapeutic rationale, it would both prevent further loss and replace previously lost bone.

TABLE 76-5

Specific Therapies

Medication	Usual Dosage[a]	Side Effects
Calcium	1000–1500 mg qd	Increased urinary calcium
Multivitamin with D_2 or D_3	400 IU qd	None known
Estrogen	.625 mg qd (Premarin or equivalent) cycled 21/30 days with/without progesterone	Endometrial carcinoma, breast cancer
Calcitonin (salmon)	50–100 IU units qd/qod IM/sub Q (Calcimar or miacalcin)	Flushing, local skin irritation
Bisphosphonates (EHDP)[b]	400 mg qd 2 weeks/3 months	Mild diarrhea—mineralization defect?
Sodium fluoride[b]	44–88 mg qd	Gastric upset, tendonitis, arthritis, plantar fasciitis, possibly increased risk of fractures
Anabolic steroids (stanozolol[b]—Winstrol or equivalent)	2 mg tid cycled 3/4 weeks	Decreased HDL, liver toxicity, masculinization

[a] Oral unless otherwise specified.
[b] Experimental therapy; not approved for usage by the FDA.
SOURCE: Adapted from Chesnut CH: Osteoporosis, in DeLisa J (ed): *Rehabilitation Medicine: Principles and Practice.* Philadelphia, Lippincott, 1988, pp 865–875.

Specific Therapies (see Tables 76-4 and 76-5)

Calcium

A therapeutic rationale for calcium therapy in osteoporosis exists: calcium, which is a major component of hydroxyapatite crystal, presumably can decrease PTH-mediated bone resorption via a slight and transient elevation in serum calcium and therefore may function as an anti–bone resorber. Calcium absorption is low in osteoporotic women as compared to absorption levels in age-matched normal women; calcium intake is deficient in teenage, perimenopausal, and postmenopausal women in the United States. However, whether calcium is of value in preventing bone loss in all individuals over an extended period of time is unproven. Current data do support a decrease in hip fractures in patients with high intakes of calcium[31–33] and an improvement in bone density at the iliac crest in patients who were previously calcium-deficient.[34] Other evidence, however, suggests that up to 2000 mg of calcium daily is not effective in preventing either cortical or trabecular bone loss[35] in the immediately menopausal woman.

It does appear that a significant proportion of the population, perhaps those individuals with chronically low calcium intakes, respond to increasing calcium intake with bone-mass stabilization for a significant period of time; at the present time, however, it is impossible to identify these patients. It seems reasonable to ensure a calcium intake of a minimum of 1000 to 1500 mg per day in all perimenopausal and postmenopausal women.[36] Calcium is generally safe (in the absence of previous nephrolithiasis or idiopathic hypercalciuria), comparatively inexpensive, and logistically simple to ingest. Milk and dairy products and calcium supplements are reasonable sources of calcium; calcium carbonate is currently perhaps the most efficacious calcium supplement, since 40 percent of this preparation is elemental calcium. Calcium citrate, however, has the postulated advantages of increased solubility in the urine and, possibly, increased bioavailability. The practitioner should remember that excessive calcium intake may result in elevated urinary calcium levels and, rarely, a predisposition to kidney stones and nephrocalcinosis; however, urinary calcium excretions of up to 250 mg per 24 hours are acceptable in persons without a history of nephrolithiasis.

Intermittent intravenous calcium infusion and thiazide diuretics have not proven to be efficacious in improving bone mass status. The putative rationale for thiazide usage would be a reduction in urinary calcium and a subsequent improvement in calcium balance.

Vitamin D

A multivitamin with 400 to 800 IU of vitamin D is a logical part of the prophylaxis and therapy of postmenopausal osteoporosis; a mild dietary vitamin D deficiency may exist in the elderly. Vitamin D (D_2 or D_3) dosages greater than 1000 IU/day are contraindicated for the treatment of postmenopausal or senile osteoporosis; PTH-mediated bone resorption may occur due to a permissive effect of vitamin D on PTH action. Currently, usage of such active forms of vitamin D as 1,25-$(OH)_2D_3$ (calcitriol) in osteoporosis remains controversial and experimental.[37,38]

Estrogens

The estrogen compounds are primarily anti–bone resorbers and they prevent the loss of bone mass by decreasing the responsiveness of bone to PTH; a direct or mediated action on bone cells remains a possibility, as receptors for estrogen are present on osteoblasts. Estrogens maintain bone mass, but restoration of bone mass previously lost may be minimal. Their use as sole therapeutic modalities in women with low bone mass and spinal compression fractures is therefore questionable (Fig. 76-3), although recent data do suggest potential benefit in established osteoporosis disease.[39] The primary value of estrogens in osteoporosis would appear to be prophylactic or in combination with agents that stimulate bone formation. A daily dosage of 0.625 mg of conjugated equine estrogen (Premarin) or its equivalent is indicated to prevent bone loss; transdermal estrogen is also an approved preparation for the treatment of osteoporosis.

Side effects of estrogen administration include endometrial carcinoma, thromboembolic disease, and/or a possible association with gallbladder disease and breast carcinoma. Endometrial cancer can be prevented by cycling estrogen with a progestational agent, but this is done at the expense of recurrent episodes of uterine bleeding after the menopause. In addition, a possibly beneficial effect of estrogens on lipids may be circumvented by its combination with certain progestational agents. Such a beneficial estrogen effect on lipids may be associated with a decreased risk of cardiovascular disease; in addition, estrogens may have a protective effect on heart disease through a direct effect on blood vessel walls. In the woman with an intact uterus who does elect to receive "unopposed" estrogen therapy (without progesterone), a pelvic examination and (possibly) endometrial biopsies are indicated at yearly intervals.

As primarily an anti–bone-resorbing agent, estrogen should be given for maximal benefit as soon as possible after the menopause and continued (if there are no contraindications) through perhaps age 65 to 70. Treating osteoporosis with estrogens alone after the age of 70 would appear to be of unproven value if an effect on bone mass is the primary indication for estrogen administration; however, the putative cardioprotective effect of estrogens should be kept in mind when their usage in the elderly is being considered.

Calcitonin

Calcitonin is an inhibitor of osteoclast activity; as such, it has a reasonable therapeutic rationale as an anti–bone-resorbing agent. Studies[40] indicate short-term efficacy (26 months) of synthetic salmon calcitonin (Calcimar or miacalcin) in slowing bone loss and in transiently increasing bone mass by an inhibition of bone resorption without a simultaneous inhibition of bone formation mechanisms. Efficacy beyond 3 to 5 years is unconfirmed; an apparent "resistance" to drug action (possibly due to a downregulation of receptor sites) may occur after 16 months of use. Alteration of drug dosage may alleviate this apparent loss of drug effect (e.g., 50 IU of synthetic salmon calcitonin every other day may be superior to 100 IU every day). The expense and route of administration (subcutaneously or intramuscularly) of calcitonin may prevent its extensive use in the osteoporotic patient. Calcitonin is, however, quite safe, and as such it may be a reasonable prophylactic alternative to estrogen therapy if a more suitable route of administration can be found. In this light, studies with nasal spray calcitonin[41] suggest that this formulation to be a suitable therapeutic agent. In the future, calcitonin via nasal spray may be indicated for prophylaxis in patients unable or unwilling to utilize estrogen therapy and via injection either alone or in combination with positive bone formers for patients with osteoporosis. In addition, calcitonin may have an analgesic effect in osteoporotic women; such an effect may be mediated by a stimulation of endorphins or by prostaglandin inhibition. In the pain associated with acute spinal fracture, a dosage of 50 to 100 IU every day or every other day for 1 to 2 weeks may be of value.

Bisphosphonates

The bisphosphonates (originally "diphosphonates") are potentially beneficial anti–bone-resorbers which chemisorb to bone crystal, decreasing bone resorption and overall bone remodeling. These agents are currently experimental and are under evaluation for the treatment of osteoporosis; EHDP [ethane-1-hydroxy-1,1-diphosphonate acid (Didronel)] has proven effectiveness over 2 years in the treatment of elderly women with osteoporotic fractures. When given in intermittent fashion, the medication is quite safe at a dosage of 400 mg daily for 2 weeks of every 3 months.[42]

Sodium Fluoride

Sodium fluoride is a proven positive bone former; with its use, an increase in bone mass occurs by stimulation of the osteoblast. With fluoride administration, a new bone crystal (fluorapatite) is produced; with formation of such a new bone crystal, some concern has arisen regarding structural integrity of bone and a possibly greater fracture potential. Indeed, current data do suggest a compromise of skeletal strength and integrity in individuals treated with sodium fluoride.[43] Its usage remains experimental.

Side effects of sodium fluoride are significant and include gastric symptoms, peptic ulcer disease, tendonitis/fasciitis, and exacerbation of arthritic symptoms. Perhaps 35 percent of patients are unable to tolerate sodium fluoride due to its side effects; in addition, about 25 to 35 percent of osteoporotic patients will show a limited response to such therapy.

Anabolic Steroids

A primary increase in bone formation, probably due to osteoblastic stimulation without a corresponding increase in bone resorption, was noted following treatment of postmenopausal osteoporotic women with the anabolic steroid stanozolol over 2 years.[44] It would therefore appear that this group of agents would be of value in both slowing bone loss and restoring bone previously lost. Side effects—including elevation of hepatic enzymes, fluid retention, androgenic effects, and high-density lipoprotein (HDL) reduction—prevent these agents' widespread use in osteoporosis, and they are not currently approved for therapy by the Food and Drug Administration. Although such side effects appear to be dose-related, the physician using these agents should be aware of their negative potential and should balance the need for an effective treatment accordingly.

Testosterone may be of value in the treatment of elderly males, particularly those who are hypogonadal. However, prostate and cholesterol status should be checked prior to usage, and it should be kept in mind that testosterone is an experimental medication for osteoporosis.

Exercise

A reasonable exercise program should be an integral part of any osteoporosis treatment regimen; exercise is presumably of value because it increases bone formation to a greater extent than bone resorption, with a subsequent increase in bone mass. Weight-bearing exercise, such as walking and aerobics, is usually recommended. In general, exercise should be performed up to and possibly slightly beyond the point of bone pain, although it is frequently important to reduce exercise in a patient who suffers an acute spinal fracture. A flexion exercise program may be contraindicated; extension or isometric exercises seem to be more appropriate for patients with postmenopausal osteoporosis.[45]

OSTEOPOROSIS THERAPY: GENERAL RECOMMENDATIONS

In patients with essentially normal bone mass and without fractures (typically patients who are immediately postmenopausal) who are nevertheless at high risk for development of significant osteopenia and bone loss, a therapy of increased calcium intake, a multivitamin with vitamin D, an exercise program, and avoidance of such risk factors as the ingestion of alcohol and cigarette smoking should be recommended. Estrogen should be strongly considered in the absence of contraindications to this medication. The rationale of this therapeutic regimen is prevention of significant bone loss.

On the other hand, for patients with low bone mass and fractures, a therapy of calcium, vitamin D supplements, exercise, avoidance of risk factors, and consideration of estrogen or calcitonin is reasonable.

THERAPY FOR SECONDARY OSTEOPOROSIS

In secondary osteoporosis, the principal aim may be discontinuation of the osteopenia-producing entities (e.g., corticosteroids, heparin, or thyroid medication) or treatment of the underlying pathologic process (e.g., hyperthyroidism or Cushing's disease). Whether the therapies for primary osteoporosis are of equal value in the treatment of secondary osteoporoses is unclear; the treatment of corticosteroid-induced osteopenia and osteoporosis is particularly disappointing. While such therapeutic regimens as calcium, vitamin D replacement (400 to 800 IU of vitamin D orally daily), calcitonin, bisphosphonates, and possibly thiazides may be of value, definitive data establishing efficacy of such therapeutic regimens are lacking in these conditions.

MONITORING RESPONSE TO TREATMENT

Obviously, the ultimate determinant of therapeutic success is the absence of new spine, wrist, and hip fractures; the occurrence of new fractures, particularly at the spine, after 12 months of treatment suggests therapeutic failure and necessitates reevaluation of therapy. Monitoring bone mass at different skeletal sites, such as the spine and hip, by currently available techniques may be advantageous in defining trends in bone mass change; presumably, a stabilization of bone mass or an increase in bone mass over time would indicate a beneficial therapeutic response.

CONCLUSIONS

Osteoporosis is a major disease in the elderly population in terms of both morbidity (and possible mortality) and economics. Definite advances have been possible over the last decade in the diagnosis and treatment of this disease, and, with increasing attention to the health care needs of the elderly, it is likely that such diagnostic and therapeutic advances will continue. It is imperative that the geriatrician be cognizant of these developments.

REFERENCES

1. Burnell JM et al: Bone matrix and mineral abnormalities in postmenopausal osteoporosis. *Metabolism* 31:1113, 1982.
2. Parfitt AM et al: Relationships between surface, volume and thickness of iliac trabecular bone in aging and in osteoporosis. *J Clin Invest* 72:1396, 1983.
3. Dempster DW et al: A simple method for correlative light and scanning electron microscopy of human iliac crest bone biopsies: Qualitative observations in normal and osteoporotic subjects. *J Bone Mineral Res* 1:15, 1986.
4. Riggs BL, Melton LJ III: Involutional osteoporosis. *N Engl J Med* 314:1676, 1986.
5. Osteoporosis, in Berg RL, Cassells JS (eds): *The Second Fifty Years: Promoting Health and Preventing Disability.* Washington, DC, National Academy Press, 1990, p 76.
6. Richelson LS et al: Relative contributions of aging and estrogen deficiency to postmenopausal bone loss. *N Engl J Med* 311:1273, 1984.
7. Drinkwater BL et al: Bone mineral content of amenorrheic and eumenorrheic athletes. *N Engl J Med* 311:277, 1984.
8. Erickson EF et al: Evidence of estrogen receptors in normal human osteoblast-like cells. *Science* 241:84, 1988.
9. Komm BS et al: Estrogen binding, receptor mRNA, and biologic response to osteoblast-like osteosarcoma cells. *Science* 241:81, 1988.
10. Heaney RF: A unified concept of osteoporosis. *Am J Med* 39:377, 1965.
11. Gallagher JC et al: Effect of estrogen on calcium absorption and vitamin D metabolism in postmenopausal osteoporosis. *J Clin Endocrinol Metab* 51:1359, 1980.
12. Slovik DM et al: Deficient production of 1,25-dihydroxyvitamin D in elderly osteoporotic patients. *N Engl J Med* 305:372, 1981.
13. Riggs BL et al: Assessment of 25-hydroxy vitamin D 1-α-hydroxylase reserve in postmenopausal osteoporosis by administration of parathyroid extract. *J Clin Endocrinol Metab* 53:833, 1981.
14. Gallagher JC et al: Intestinal calcium absorption and serum vitamin D metabolites in normal subjects and osteoporotic subjects: Effects of age and dietary calcium. *J Clin Invest* 64:729, 1979.
15. Taggart HM et al: Deficient calcitonin response to calcium stimulation in postmenopausal osteoporosis. *Lancet* 2:475, 1982.
16. Tiegs RD et al: Calcitonin secretion in postmenopausal osteoporosis. *N Engl J Med* 312:1097, 1985.
17. Seeman E et al: Risk factors for spinal osteoporosis in men. *Am J Med* 75:997, 1983.
18. Chesnut CH: Noninvasive methods of measuring bone mass, in Avioli LV (ed): *The Osteoporotic Syndrome,* 3d ed. Orlando, FL, Grune & Stratton, 1993, p 77.
19. Riggs BL, Wahner HW: Bone densitometry and clinical decision making in osteoporosis. *Ann Intern Med* 108:293, 1988.
20. Ross PD et al: Detection of prefracture spinal osteoporosis using bone mineral absorptiometry. *J Bone Mineral Res* 3:1, 1988.
21. Heaney RP et al: Osteoporotic bone fragility: Detection by ultrasound transmission velocity. *JAMA* 261:2986, 1989.
22. Cosman F et al: Radiographic absorptiometry: A simple method for determination of bone mass. *Osteop Int* 2:34, 1991.
23. Ott SM et al: Comparisons among methods of measuring bone mass and relationship to severity of vertebral fracture in osteoporosis. *J Clin Endocrinol Metab* 66:501, 1987.
24. Ott SM et al: Longitudinal changes in bone mass after one year as measured by different techniques in patients with osteoporosis. *Calcif Tissue Int* 39:139, 1986.
25. Cummings SR et al: Bone density at various sites for prediction of hip fracture. *Lancet* 1:72, 1993.
26. Johnston CC et al: Clinical indications for bone mass measurements. *J Bone Mineral Res* 4(suppl):1, 1989.
27. Melton LJ et al: Screening for osteoporosis. *Ann Intern Med* 112:516, 1990.
28. Tosteson ANA et al: Cost-effectiveness of screening perimenopausal white women for osteoporosis: Bone densitometry and hormone replacement therapy. *Ann Intern Med* 113:594, 1990.
29. Ott SM et al: Ability of four different techniques of measuring bone mass to diagnose vertebral fractures in postmenopausal women. *J Bone Mineral Res* 2:201, 1987.
30. Frost HM: Managing the skeletal pain and disability of osteoporosis. *Orthop Clin North Am* 3:561, 1972.
31. Matkovic V et al: Bone status and fracture rates in two regions of Yugoslavia. *Am J Clin Nutr* 32:540, 1979.
32. Holbrook TL et al: Dietary calcium and risk of hip fracture: 14-year prospective population study. *Lancet* 2:1046, 1988.
33. Chapuy MC et al: Vitamin D_3 and calcium to prevent hip fractures in elderly women. *N Engl J Med* 327:1637, 1992.
34. Burnell JM et al: The role of calcium deficiency in postmenopausal osteoporosis. *Calcif Tissue Int* 38:187, 1986.
35. Riis BL et al: Does calcium supplementation prevent postmenopausal bone loss? *N Engl J Med* 316:173, 1987.
36. *Physicians Resource Manual on Osteoporosis: A Decision Making Guide,* 2d ed. Washington, DC, National Osteoporosis Foundation, 1991.
37. Tilyard MW et al: Treatment of postmenopausal osteoporosis with calcitriol or calcium. *N Engl J Med* 326:357, 1992.
38. Chesnut CH: Osteoporosis and its treatment (editorial) *N Engl J Med* 326:406, 1992.
39. Lufkin EG et al: Treatment of postmenopausal osteoporosis with transdermal estrogen. *Ann Intern Med* 117:1, 1992.
40. Gruber HE et al: Long-term calcitonin therapy in postmenopausal osteoporosis. *Metabolism* 33:295, 1984.
41. Overgaard K et al: Effect of salcatonin given intranasally on bone mass and fracture rates in established osteoporosis: A close-response study. *Brit Med J* 305:556, 1992.
42. Watts NB et al: Intermittent cyclical etidronate treat-

ment of postmenopausal osteoporosis. *N Engl J Med* 323:73, 1990.

43. Riggs BL et al: Effect of fluoride treatment on the fracture rate in postmenopausal women with osteoporosis. *N Engl J Med* 322:802, 1990.
44. Chesnut CH et al: Stanozolol in postmenopausal osteoporosis: Therapeutic efficacy and possible mechanisms of action. *Metabolism* 32:571, 1983.
45. Sinaki M, Mikkelsen BA: Postmenopausal spinal osteoporosis: Flexion versus extension exercises. *Arch Phys Med Rehabil* 65:593, 1984.

ADDITIONAL READING

Avioli LV (ed): *The Osteoporotic Syndrome,* 3d ed. Orlando, FL, Grune & Stratton, 1993.

Riggs BL, Melton LJ: Involutional osteoporosis. *N Engl J Med* 314:1676, 1986.

Riggs BL, Melton JL (eds): *Osteoporosis: Etiology, Diagnosis and Management.* New York, Raven Press, 1988.

Riggs BL, Melton LJ: The prevention and treatment of osteoporosis. *N Engl J Med* 327:620, 1992.

Physicians Resource Manual on Osteoporosis: A Decision Making Guide, 2d ed. Washington, DC, National Osteoporosis Foundation, 1991.

Chapter 77

OSTEOMALACIA

David J. Baylink

GENERAL CONSIDERATIONS

The term *osteomalacia* denotes a group of diseases in adults characterized by a mineralization defect. Clinically, this leads to skeletal deformity and pain. Osteomalacia, however, is an uncommon disease. In patients presenting with spontaneous spinal compression fractures, less than 2 percent will have histological evidence of osteomalacia, the remainder showing osteoporosis. A higher fraction of patients will show osteomalacia in such clinics as gastrointestinal and renal, inasmuch as small-bowel diseases and renal disease can result in osteomalacia (Table 77-1). The importance of making the diagnosis of osteomalacia lies in the fact that this condition is, in general, readily cured by treatment. Therefore, nowadays, one rarely sees severe osteomalacia and severe bone pain (i.e., most osteomalacia patients are treated and cured before severe osteomalacia evolves).

Suggested additional readings on osteomalacia are provided at the end of this chapter.

ETIOLOGY AND PATHOGENESIS

Osteomalacia can be caused by disorders that reduce serum calcium (including vitamin D deficiency and calcium deficiency), disorders that produce hypophosphatemia, and certain types of drugs for which the mechanism provoking the osteomalacic response is unknown. The etiologies of different types of osteomalacia are shown in Table 77-1.

Etiology of Vitamin D–Deficiency Osteomalacia

Special emphasis is placed on vitamin D metabolism because vitamin D deficiency is the most common cause of osteomalacia in the elderly (Table 77-1). A schema of normal vitamin D metabolism is shown in Fig. 77-1. Actually, vitamin D is not a vitamin but a hormone, and the generalities that apply to steroid hormones also apply to vitamin D. Thus, the active metabolite of vitamin D, $1,25(OH)_2D$, is bound to a carrier protein in serum, acts on cells via binding to a receptor (nuclear acceptor) molecule, has precursors metabolized in different tissues, and has a serum level which is under tight physiological regulation through negative feedback mechanisms. The hormonal changes attending calcium deficiency illustrate this negative feedback regulation of serum $1,25(OH)_2D$: A deficiency of calcium from any cause leads toward a decrease in serum calcium, which in turn acts on the

TABLE 77-1

The Etiology of the Different Types of Osteomalacia in the Elderly

- I. Vitamin D deficiency
  - A. Insufficient parent compounds
    - 1. Inadequate sunlight exposure*: vitamin D_3 deficiency
    - 2. Inadequate gut absorption*: vitamin D_2 deficiency
      - *a.* Dietary deficiency
      - *b.* Small intestinal diseases with malabsorption
      - *c.* Partial gastrectomy
  - B. Impaired metabolite conversion
    - 1. Liver disease: 25-OHD deficiency
    - 2. Anticonvulsant therapy: 25-OHD deficiency
    - 3. Chronic renal failure: $1,25(OH)_2D$ deficiency
- II. Phosphate deficiency
  - A. Ingestion of phosphate binders (e.g., aluminum hydroxide)
  - B. Renal phosphate leak
    - 1. Idiopathic
    - 2. Neoplasms (soft tissue tumors, prostate cancer)
    - 3. Hereditary
      - *a.* X-linked
      - *b.* Idiopathic hypercalciuria
- III. Drug and chemical inhibition of mineralization
  - A. Fluoride therapy
  - B. Diphosphonate therapy
  - C. Aluminum toxicity in renal failure patients

*Both of these factors (i.e., inadequate sunlight exposure and inadequate vitamin D_2 absorption) must be inadequate to cause a deficiency of parent compounds.

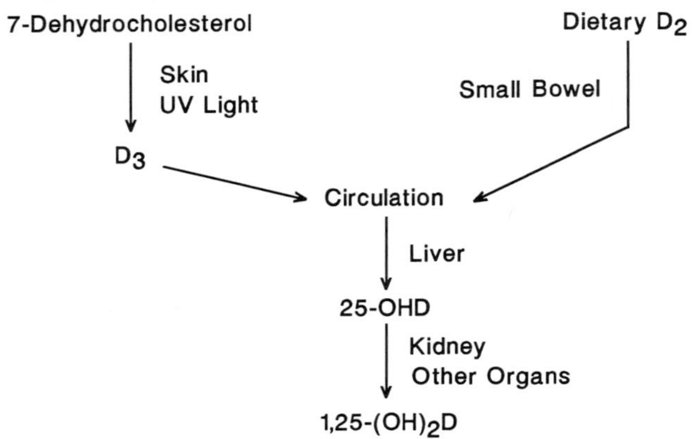

FIGURE 77-1
Schema of normal vitamin D metabolism.

parathyroid glands to stimulate parathyroid hormone (PTH) secretion. PTH acts on its target organs, kidney and bone, to increase serum calcium in a negative feedback manner. PTH also accomplishes this increment in serum calcium by enhancing the production of 1,25$(OH)_2D$ which, in turn, acts on its target organs, gut and bone, to increase serum calcium. Thus, the level of 1,25$(OH)_2D$ is dependent upon the level of serum PTH; and 1,25$(OH)_2D$ functions with PTH to maintain serum calcium in a negative feedback mechanism.

Because vitamin D is metabolized in several tissues (Fig. 77-1), there are several metabolic sites that may produce vitamin D deficiency. Vitamin D_3 (cholecalciferol) is synthesized in skin from 7-dihydrocholesterol in response to ultraviolet (UV) irradiation (Fig. 77-1). If there is inadequate exposure to sunlight, vitamin D deficiency may result. Inadequate exposure will not invariably result in vitamin D deficiency because there is another source of vitamin D: milk is supplemented with vitamin D_2 (ergocalciferol which is produced by ultraviolet irradiation of the plant sterol, ergosterol); vitamins D_2 and D_3 are chemically distinct but biologically quite similar. Thus, to become vitamin D–deficient because of insufficient parent compounds (vitamins D_2 and D_3), one must have inadequate sun exposure and also inadequate absorption of vitamin D_2 from gut. It is noteworthy that subjects over 70 years of age are at risk for this combined deficiency state, apparently because skin production and gut absorption of the vitamin tend to decline in the elderly. This combined deficiency could ultimately lead to osteomalacia.

Vitamin D deficiency can also result from diseases that affect the liver, intestine, and kidney. Diseases of the intestine and liver can lead to vitamin D deficiency because these organs are concerned with acquisition and metabolism of vitamin D respectively. Diseases of the small intestine can cause impairment of fat and vitamin D_2 absorption and thus a deficiency of vitamin D_2 (Fig. 77-1, Table 77-1), but again the patient will not become vitamin D–deficient unless skin production of vitamin D_3 is also diminished. Because optimum fat absorption also requires adequate bile secretion, malabsorption of vitamin D_2 may be seen in biliary diseases.

Vitamins D_2 and D_3 are converted in the liver to 25-OHD_2 and 25-OHD_3, respectively (Fig. 77-1). In hepatocellular diseases, this conversion can be impaired with a resultant decrease in serum 25-OHD (25-OHD_2 plus 25-OHD_3).* Certain drugs (namely anticonvulsants) increase liver activity of drug-metabolizing enzymes which indiscriminately destroy 25-OHD and thereby cause low serum levels of 25-OHD. During the evolution of vitamin D deficiency from a deficiency of parent compounds or from liver disease, the consequent deficiency of 25-OHD results in a compensatory increase in the 1α-hydroxylase activity in kidney, mediated in part by an increase in serum PTH; as a result, a normal serum level of 1,25$(OH)_2D$ is maintained until a substantial decrease in 25-OHD occurs, at which time serum 1,25$(OH)_2$ begins to decline.

The final organ which, when diseased, may result in vitamin D deficiency is the kidney, which acts to convert 25-OHD to 1,25$(OH)_2D$ in response to physiological cues (Fig. 77-1). A deficiency of 1,25$(OH)_2D$ is commonly seen in renal failure, probably as a result of decreased renal mass. Thus, in renal failure, there is a progressive decline in renal mass, which leads to a decrease in 1,25$(OH)_2D$ production, which in turn leads to hypocalcemia and ultimately to osteomalacia.

There are two additional causes of a deficiency of 1,25$(OH)_2D$ at the kidney level, neither of which is common. First, there is idiopathic impairment of 1,25$(OH)_2D$ production without renal failure, which seems to occur at any age and has been documented to occur after 50 years of age. Second, there is a soft-tissue tumor that is associated with severe hypophosphatemia, decreased serum 1,25$(OH)_2D$ levels, and resistance to vitamin D. In both of these situations one sees osteomalacia.

In addition to a deficiency of vitamin D per se, there are two changes in 1,25$(OH)_2D$ status which are age-related and thus pertinent to the issue of osteomalacia in the elderly: (1) With aging, there is a decrease in serum 1,25$(OH)_2D$, which may be in part a consequence of the age-related decline in renal mass. (2) In addition, there is an age-related decrease in intestinal 1,25$(OH)_2D$ receptors, which could in part explain the age-related decrease in enteral calcium absorption. Neither of these two changes in vitamin D metabolism is sufficient to cause osteomalacia in itself. However, these changes, in combination with certain other changes (see below) in calcium metabolism, could together eventuate in osteomalacia. For exam-

*A decrease in serum 25-OHD is not invariably associated with osteomalacia; in mild vitamin D deficiency (i.e., without hypocalcemia) osteomalacia may not occur. Instead, osteoporosis due to secondary hyperparathyroidism occurs. With only a modest decrease in serum 25-OHD, there is an increase in serum 1,25$(OH)_2D$, but at the expense of increased PTH, which leads to increased bone resorption and thus bone loss. With vitamin D deficiency sufficient to cause hypocalcemia, osteomalacia occurs.

ple, an institutionalized elderly patient not on vitamin D supplementation and housebound, and thus not exposed to sunlight, could develop a decrease in serum 25-OHD. In young adults, a decrease in serum 25-OHD does not necessarily lead to a decrease in serum $1{,}25(OH)_2D$ because, as serum 25-OHD decreases, there is an increase in PTH, which appropriately increases the serum level of $1{,}25(OH)_2D$. In the elderly, however, the ability of an elevated PTH to increase the production of $1{,}25(OH)_2D$ is impaired. Consequently, in the elderly a modest decrease in 25-OHD may lead to a decrease in serum $1{,}25(OH)_2D$. This, together with an age-related decrease in $1{,}25(OH)_2D$ receptors, could lead to a decrease in serum calcium and, consequently, osteomalacia.

Etiology of Phosphate-Deficiency Osteomalacia

The second most common cause of osteomalacia in the elderly is hypophosphatemia. Mild hypophosphatemia usually results in osteoporosis, whereas moderate to severe cases produce osteomalacia. A schema of normal phosphate metabolism is shown in Fig. 77-2. Three organs are involved in mass transfer of phosphate: bone, kidney, and gut (Fig. 77-2); in practice, however, only an abnormal function of the kidney (i.e., renal tubular dysfunction) or phosphate binder antacid therapy results in a chronically decreased serum phosphate in the elderly. Because phosphate is ubiquitous in nature and is so well absorbed (Fig. 77-2), a selective dietary deficiency of phosphate does not occur naturally. A deficient absorption of phosphate may occur, however, when phosphate binders (antacids) are used to treat gastrointestinal disorders, and long-term ingestion of these antacids may result in hypophosphatemia and osteomalacia. As can be seen in Fig. 77-2, bone resorption contributes only modestly to the extracellular pool of phosphate, which is one reason why changes in bone resorption have little effect on the serum phosphate.

Another cause of hypophosphatemia is an impaired renal tubular maximum phosphate (TmP) reabsorption. In adults, serum phosphate is largely regulated by TmP. A chronically depressed TmP and the corresponding hypophosphatemia can be due to either an acquired or a hereditary abnormality. Patients with severe hereditary hypophosphatemia will exhibit signs of childhood rickets, such as short stature and bone deformities. The causes of acquired forms of impaired TmP are poorly understood, with the exception that there is a soft-tissue tumor which produces severe hypophosphatemia by depression of TmP and which also produces impaired renal 1α-hydroxylase activity, resulting in a concomitant deficiency of $1{,}25(OH)_2D$. Both metabolic abnormalities are rapidly corrected by removal of the tumor. Severe hypophosphatemia associated with such tumors results in marked muscle weakness, a complication not

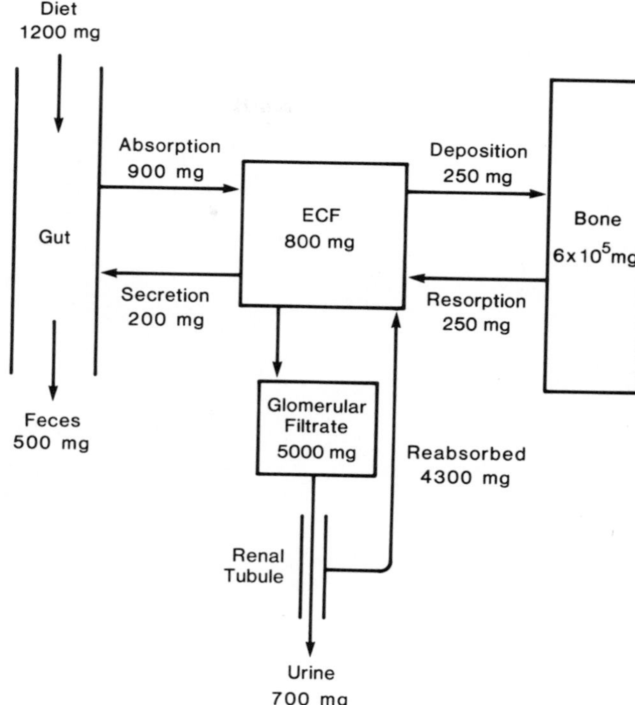

FIGURE 77-2

Schema of normal phosphate metabolism. All values associated with fluxes are in milligrams per day. For example, dietary phosphorus intake is 1200 mg/day. The values for ECF and bone represent phosphate content in milligrams.

experienced by hereditary X-linked hypophosphatemic patients.

Because physiological hypophosphatemia is seen after ingestion of glucose or other rapidly metabolizable substrates, a correct diagnosis of hypophosphatemia must be made from analysis of *fasting* serum samples. Hypophosphatemia in the elderly is not as common as vitamin D deficiency, but since it can be effectively treated, *fasting* serum phosphate levels should routinely be determined in all patients presenting with metabolic bone disease.

Pathogenesis of Vitamin D–Deficiency and Phosphate Deficiency Osteomalacia

The characteristic feature of osteomalacia is excess osteoid tissue (Fig. 77-3). This excess of osteoid tissue results because (1) there is an increase in osteoid width (osteoid is bone matrix which has not yet begun to mineralize); and (2) there is an increase in the bone surface lined by osteoid. The reason for the increase in osteoid width is shown in Fig. 77-4. In essence, in osteomalacia the osteoblasts are capable of synthesiz-

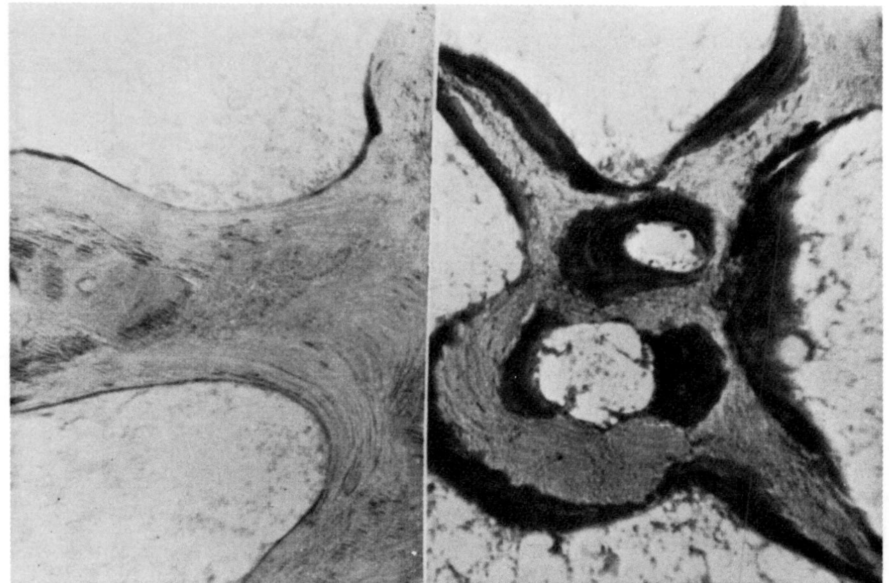

FIGURE 77-3
Goldner's stained mineralized sections of bone from a normal subject (left) and from a patient with severe osteomalacia (right). Osteoid appears black and mineralized bone gray. In the biopsy from the patient with osteomalacia, there is an increased amount of surface covered with osteoid and an increase in osteoid width.

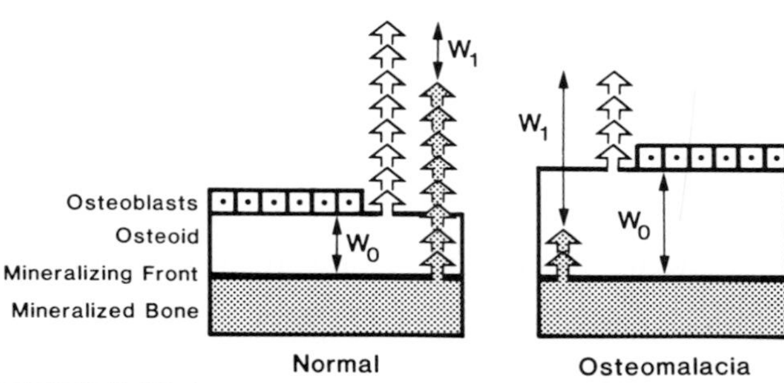

FIGURE 77-4
Schema of the pathogenesis of osteomalacia. Osteoblasts form osteoid matrix, which undergoes a maturation process before mineralization is initiated at the mineralizing front. W_0 = osteoid width at 0 time, W_1 = osteoid width at a later time. The open arrows indicate the linear rate at which the osteoid front advances. (The greater the number of arrows, the greater the rate of advancement.) The speckled arrows indicate linear rate of advancement of the mineralizing front. Under normal conditions, the production and the maturation of osteoid are proceeding at identical rates; therefore advancement of the osteoid and mineralizing fronts are traveling at identical rates, such that osteoid width at time W_1 is identical to that seen at time W_0. In osteomalacia, the following three important changes are illustrated: (1) both of the above rates are depressed; (2) osteoid width is increased at W_0 because, during the development of osteomalacia, the rate of advancement of the mineralizing front is less than the rate of advancement of the osteoid front; and (3) osteoid width is greater at W_1 than at W_0 because of this continuing disparity.

ing and depositing osteoid matrix, but because of insufficient calcium and/or phosphate in the circulation, this osteoid cannot be mineralized at the same rate that it is produced; as a result, osteoid width increases. Thus mineralization is impaired because of the low concentration of calcium and phosphate in serum. In addition, there may be effects of decreased serum calcium and/or phosphate on osteoblast function, which impairs matrix maturation and thus mineralization. An increase in osteoid width, as assessed by bone biopsy, usually indicates osteomalacia, but there are exceptions to this interpretation. Therefore, a more specific measure for osteomalacia has been devised, namely, the mineralization lag time, which is the time between the deposition of matrix and the subsequent initiation of mineralization of this matrix. This parameter is assessed morphometrically from bone biopsies.

The cause of the increase in forming surface in osteomalacia is not established. One explanation is that because the half-life of osteoid is prolonged, there will be an accumulation of osteoid-covered surface. Alternatively, the hormonal changes attending osteomalacia may actually result in stimulation of production of new osteoblasts. Because different types of osteomalacia exhibit different hormonal changes yet all types have increased forming surface, it follows that of the two, the prolonged half-life of osteoid is the more likely explanation for the accumulation of forming surface.

DIAGNOSIS

For the diagnosis of osteomalacia, one may utilize bone biopsy, x-ray, bone density, bone scintigraphy, clinical laboratory, and clinical approaches, all of which are discussed below. Severe osteomalacia will be evident from each of the above approaches, whereas mild osteomalacia is usually difficult to diagnose. The most common form of mild osteomalacia in the elderly is vitamin D–deficiency osteomalacia. Vitamin D deficiency is simple to diagnose. The serum 25-OHD will be low; however, whether the low 25-OHD is attended by osteoporosis or osteomalacia is frequently difficult to determine. In any case, from a practical standpoint, the patient should be treated with vitamin D, in which case the cause of the skeletal disease will be abrogated.

Bone Biopsy Findings

Normal morphometric values for osteoid width, osteoid length, and mineralization lag time (all of which are characteristically increased in osteomalacia) are available for two biopsy sites: anterior iliac crest and transilial. Osteoid parameters can be measured only on undemineralized sections (Fig. 77-3). The major disadvantage of the bone biopsy approach to the diagnosis of osteomalacia is the lack of sensitivity of this method—a deficiency which is largely due to the poor ability to reproducibly sample a given bone site. Because of this inherent problem, it is difficult to detect mild degrees of osteomalacia by this method.

The other pitfall of this method results in false-positive conclusions and occurs when excessive osteoid width or osteoid area (both of which can occur with high bone formation rates) is equated with evidence of osteomalacia. This problem is not encountered when the mineralization lag time is used. To measure this latter parameter, however, there is a requirement for visualization of tetracycline fluorescent time markers.

A bone biopsy can be definitive in making a diagnosis of osteomalacia, but it does not usually provide diagnostic information regarding its cause. Bone biopsy approaches are generally reserved for difficult diagnostic problems.

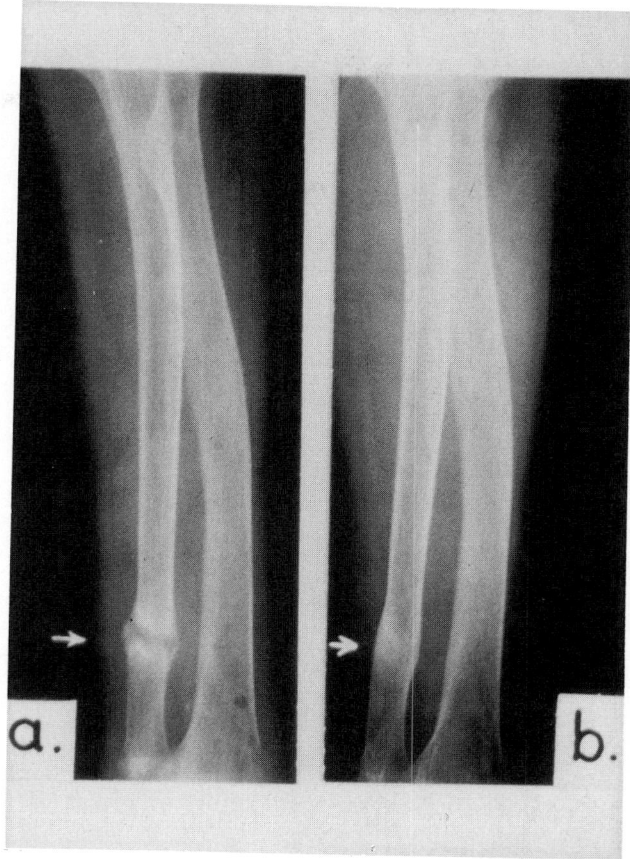

FIGURE 77-5
X rays of pseudofracture of the ulna in the patient with severe osteomalacia shown in Fig. 77-8. The pseudofracture before treatment is shown in panel a and the pseudofracture after 3 months of vitamin D therapy is shown in panel b.

X-Ray Findings

Three x-ray features are relatively specific for osteomalacia, but none of them occurs early during the evolution of this disease. First, in trabecular bone regions, such as the vertebral body, the trabecular architecture appears blurred and fuzzy. Second, pseudofractures are characteristic of osteomalacia but, again, are usually seen only with severe disease (Fig. 77-5). These appear as radiolucent bands usually flanked on either side by radiopaque bands, representing abundant callous formations. Pseudofractures are frequently bilateral, and commonly affected bones include the ulna (Fig. 77-5), scapula, pelvis, inner aspect of the femur near the femoral neck, metatarsals, and ribs. Inability to repair microdamage (because of the mineralization defect) is thought to be involved in the pathogenesis of pseudofractures. In untreated patients such fractures may be present for years. Third, patients with severe osteomalacia combined with osteoporosis may exhibit skeletal deformities (Fig. 77-6). This complication is usually seen in patients who are 70 years of age or older and who have severe vitamin D deficiency.

Despite this lack of sensitivity, x rays of painful skeletal sites should always be obtained when osteomalacia is suspected.

Bone Density and Bone Scintigraphic Findings

The bone density of patients with osteomalacia may vary from normal to low and can be measured by several methods: single-photon absorptometry (which is usually applied to measure the radius), dual energy

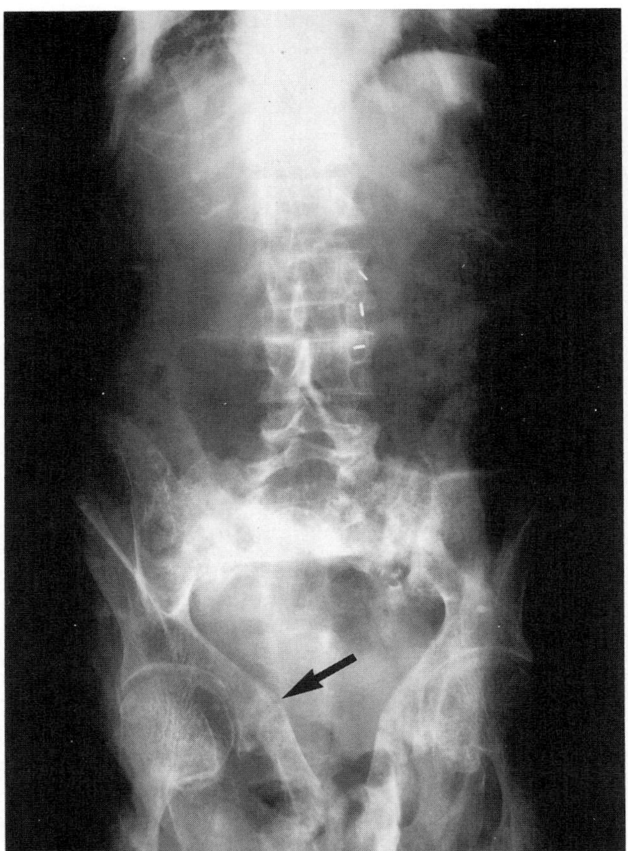

FIGURE 77-6
X-ray showing severely deformed pelvis in an elderly female with vitamin D–deficiency osteomalacia [i.e., severe deformity of the pelvic bones (trifold deformity) due to slow fracture healing.] The arrow indicates one of the several slow-healing fractures of the pelvis.

x-ray densitometry (which is applied to measure both the spine and peripheral skeleton), and quantitative computed tomography (which is applied to measure spinal bone density). In elderly patients with vitamin D–deficiency osteomalacia, there is usually an element of osteoporosis (because of the attendant secondary hyperparathyroidism); as a result, bone density is usually low. A patient with a low bone density could have osteoporosis or osteoporosis plus osteomalacia, and thus a low bone density is not a diagnostic criterion for osteomalacia.

Bone scintigraphy is one procedure with the potential to discriminate osteomalacia from osteoporosis. A bone scintigraph demonstrates normal generalized skeletal uptake of the bone-seeking radionuclide in osteoporosis but increased generalized skeletal uptake of radionuclide (predominantly in trabecular bone) in osteomalacia. Microscopically, the increased radionuclide uptake is due to the increased length of the mineralizing front (i.e., the low mineral-content bone adjacent to osteoid) which contains the reactive bone mineral that fixes the radionuclide. Unfortunately, like many other discriminatory tests, the bone scan is positive for osteomalacia only when the disease is moderate to severe. To diagnose patients with suspected osteomalacia, we would obtain a bone scintigraph before obtaining a bone biopsy (because the bone biopsy is invasive).

Clinical Laboratory Findings

A bone biopsy (excess osteoid) or an x-ray (pseudofracture) can provide definitive evidence of osteomalacia. However, such techniques do not detect mild osteomalacia, nor do they distinguish between osteomalacia due to such causes as vitamin D deficiency, renal failure, or phosphate deficiency. Serum and urine chemistries, however, are helpful for these situations.

Clinical Laboratory Findings in Mild Vitamin D–Deficiency Osteomalacia

By far the most common cause of mild osteomalacia in the elderly is vitamin D deficiency, which is typically seen in elderly housebound patients or elderly patients living at northerly latitudes where dermal vitamin D production is not efficient. In such patients, the serum calcium and phosphate tend to be low, alkaline phosphatase high, the urine calcium low (i.e., 50 mg/24 h or less), and the serum PTH high. Patients with severe osteomalacia usually exhibit all of these changes (Table 77-2; Fig. 77-7). Unfortunately,

TABLE 77-2

Serum and Urine Chemistries in Different Types of Osteomalacia*

	S Ca†	SP	AlP	25-OHD	$1,25(OH)_2D$	PTH	U Ca	TmP	U Dpyr
Vitamin D deficiency	↓	↓	↑	↓	↓	↑	↓	↓	↑
Phosphate deficiency, low $1,25(OH)_2D$	N	↓	↑	N	↓	N	N	↓	?
Phosphate deficiency, high $1,25(OH)_2D$	N	↓	↑	N	↑	↓	↑	↓	↑
Renal failure	↓	↑	↑	N	↓	↑	↓	NA	NA

*These changes pertain to *severe* osteomalacia from the corresponding cause.
†Key: S Ca = serum calcium; SP = serum phosphate; AlP = alkaline phosphatase; PTH = parathyroid hormone; U Ca = urine calcium; TmP = tubular maximum phosphate; U Dpyr = urine deoxypyridinoline; NA = not applicable; N = normal.

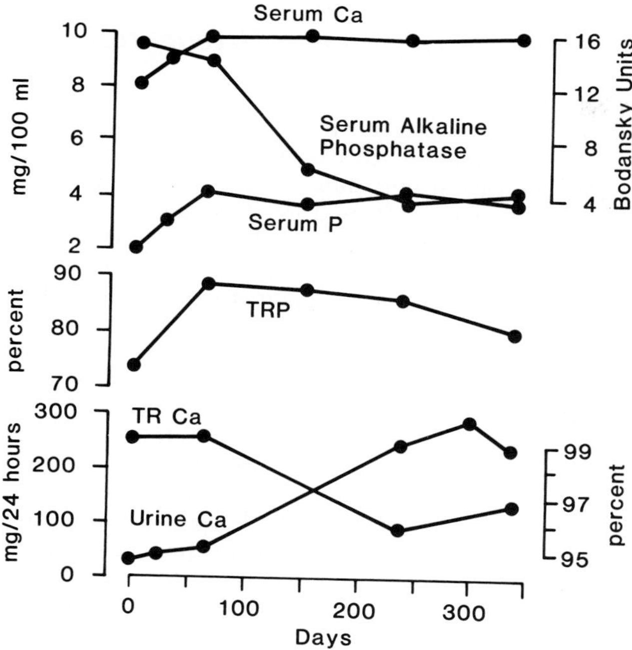

FIGURE 77-7

Serum and urine chemical data, before and during 1 year of vitamin D treatment in the patient with severe osteomalacia shown in Fig. 77-8. At 0 time, therapy with vitamin D, 100,000 IU/day, and oral calcium supplements of 2 g/day was initiated. Because of the urine calcium of approximately 250 mg/24 h at 240 days of treatment, the dose of vitamin D was decreased to 50,000 IU/day. However, the urine calcium continued to rise to the abnormally high value of 300 mg/day, and at this point vitamin D was discontinued. In retrospect, the vitamin D should have been discontinued at 240 days, when the urine calcium was 250 mg/24 h, which is the upper limit of normal for females. Serum calcium, serum phosphate, and tubular reabsorption of phosphate (TRP) were all depressed initially and were all corrected after approximately 2 months of therapy. In contrast, the serum alkaline phosphate, which reflects the bone status, was not corrected until after approximately 240 days of therapy. Before therapy, urine calcium was low, less than 50 mg/24 h, as is typical in vitamin D–deficiency osteomalacia. The percentage of tubular reabsorption of calcium (TRCa) was high before treatment, contributing to the low urine calcium, and decreased as urine calcium subsequently increased. Presumably, before therapy, serum PTH was high and serum $1,25(OH)_2D$ was low; during therapy, they both normalized.

not all patients with mild osteomalacia due to vitamin D deficiency will exhibit all of these findings. Indeed, many patients will only exhibit one or two of these typical changes (namely high alkaline phosphatase and/or low urine calcium). Patients with even mild osteomalacia will have elevated serum alkaline phosphatase, and the diagnosis cannot be sustained without this change. Other diseases in the elderly, however, can be attended by high serum alkaline phosphatase (Paget's disease and calcium deficiency without osteomalacia). Thus, a high alkaline phosphatase is necessary for the diagnosis but is not definitive. A high alkaline phosphatase attended by a low serum 25-OHD (i.e., <8 ng/ml) indicates for certain that the patient is vitamin D–deficient, but since mild vitamin deficiency can lead to osteoporosis rather than osteomalacia, these changes do not constitute a definitive diagnosis of osteomalacia. However, from a practical standpoint, the patient needs vitamin D therapy and will exhibit correction of these laboratory changes regardless of whether or not he or she has proven osteomalacia. Thus, the patient will receive the correct treatment even if the skeletal pathology is not entirely clear.

Clinical Laboratory Findings in Early Renal Failure Osteomalacia

The typical serum and urine chemistry changes seen with severe vitamin D deficiency are described in Table 77-2. In patients with osteomalacia due to renal failure, the patients exhibit two key laboratory changes (reflecting the role of the kidney in mineral metabolism): (1) decreased serum $1,25(OH)_2D$ and (2) high serum phosphate. Therapy is directed at these two abnormalities.

Clinical Laboratory Findings in Mild Osteomalacia Due to Hypophosphatemia

There are two syndromes of hypophosphatemia, and while both result in osteomalacia, it is important to distinguish between them because their treatment is different (Table 77-2).

In the first syndrome, the patient will manifest hypophosphatemia and a high urine calcium. Hypercalciuria results from an increased calcium absorption, which is a consequence of a high serum $1,25(OH)_2D$ level—which, in turn, occurs in response to the hypophosphatemia. The effect of a low serum phosphate in increasing the serum $1,25(OH)_2D$ is part of a normal regulatory mechanism whereby $1,25(OH)_2D$ acts to increase serum phosphate. $1,25(OH)_2D$ increases serum phosphate by (1) increasing enteral calcium absorption, which, in turn, increases serum phosphate by decreasing serum PTH; (2) increasing enteral phosphate absorption; and (3) increasing bone resorption. Because $1,25(OH)_2D$ stimulates bone resorption, there tends to be a high urine hydroxyproline and a high urine pyridinoline in patients with a high serum $1,25(OH)_2D$ but not in those with a normal serum $1,25(OH)_2D$.

In the second syndrome, the patient will have hypophosphatemia without a high urine calcium. Such patients have a 1α-hydroxylase abnormality as well as a renal tubular phosphate transport abnormality, such that the low serum phosphate cannot increase the 1α-hydroxylase activity. Serum alkaline phosphatase is consistently elevated in both forms of hypophosphatemia when osteomalacia is present.

Clinical Findings

The patient with osteomalacia due to either vitamin D or phosphate deficiency may complain of diffuse bone pain and tenderness, bony deformities, muscle weakness, increased fatigability, and emotional depression. During the evolution of vitamin D deficiency, muscle weakness, increased fatigability, and emotional depression appear before bone pain and tenderness. Although these earlier symptoms are not specific for vitamin D deficiency, only vitamin D treatment abolishes them.

Regarding skeletal pain, some pseudofractures are painful and some are not, and not all skeletal pain is limited to sites of pseudofractures. Skeletal pain at sites which appear normal by x-ray is probably a consequence of stress fractures, which are usually evident by bone scintigraphy. In hypophosphatemia, as in vitamin D deficiency, muscle weakness and general debilitation may be more prominent than skeletal symptoms early in the evolution of the disease. For both vitamin D deficiency and hypophosphatemia, the proximal muscles are predominantly involved. Patients with severe osteomalacia may have a wide-based, cautious shuffle—wide-based because of muscle weakness and a shuffle (i.e., scooting the sole along the ground) because any jarring motion precipitates pain in pseudofractures and stress fractures.

The most likely but as yet unproven mechanism for the development of pseudofractures (one of the characteristic skeletal lesions leading to symptomatology in adults with osteomalacia) is that the impaired mineralization results in a slower healing of the normal microdamage that occurs in the skeleton from routine use. As a result of this slow healing, the microdamage tends to accumulate and to propagate. This weakens the bone at the corresponding site, stimulating further callous formation, which is unable to mineralize properly because of the impaired mineralization. This leads to an abundant callous formation with incomplete healing. Thus, a pseudofracture is a fracture which can be only partially healed.

In less severe forms of osteomalacia and where there is an attendant calcium deficiency, as in the osteomalacia that is a consequence of partial gastrectomy or that seen in housebound institutionalized patients, there tends to be osteoporosis together with a mild mineralization defect, two changes which can lead to skeletal lesions characteristic of stress fractures. These are spontaneous, atraumatic fractures which generally appear as very thin radiolucent lines on x-rays. Frequently, a stress fracture is most evident radiologically after healing has begun, at which time (2 to 3 weeks) one sees a thin radiopaque callus.

TREATMENT OF OSTEOMALACIA

The three major causes of osteomalacia—vitamin D deficiency, renal failure, and hypophosphatemia–can all be effectively treated.

Vitamin D–Deficiency Osteomalacia

In vitamin D deficiency, the objective of vitamin D therapy is correction of the low serum 25-OHD without overcorrection to the extent that hypercalcemia or hypercalciuria supervenes. The serum 25-OHD should be increased from a low level (i.e., <8 ng/ml) to not more than 100 ng/ml. (When 25-OHD is >100 ng/ml, it begins to act on the $1,25(OH)_2D$ receptors, so that it can cause hypercalcemia.) In nutritional vitamin D deficiency, a supplement of 1000 U/day is adequate. Total treatment time can be reduced by giving 50,000 IU/day for 1 to 2 months instead of 1000 IU/day for 6 or more months. In severe osteomalacia, the serum calcium will be corrected before the bones are healed (Fig. 77-7; compare serum alkaline phosphatase curve with serum calcium curve). Once the serum calcium is corrected, the bones will eventually heal. When renal failure is not present, 24-h urine calcium can be used as an end point to establish the proper dose of vitamin D. For example, in nutritional vitamin D deficiency, an increase in urine calcium from 50 to 150 mg/day suggests adequate vitamin D therapy. When urine calcium exceeds 200 mg/day, vitamin D therapy should be withdrawn for two reasons: First, a urine calcium of >250 mg/day in females and >300 mg/day in males can result in renal stone formation; second, hypercalciuria heralds hypercalcemia, which is the most serious complication of vitamin D therapy. Serum and urine calcium should be monitored every 1 to 3 months during vitamin D therapy. Monitoring is needed because, even before the bones are healed, the patient can develop hypercalcemia, and because one needs evidence of an effective dose, which varies considerably from patient to patient.

One might reason that it would be physiologically most rational to use $25\text{-}OHD_3$ therapy for the low serum 25-OHD seen in liver cirrhosis. However, if given a high dose of vitamin D (e.g., 50,000 to 100,000 IU/week), patients with liver cirrhosis can produce normal amounts of 25-OHD. Thus, $25\text{-}OHD_3$ itself is seldom needed for treatment of vitamin D deficiency associated with liver disease.

All patients with vitamin D–deficiency osteomalacia should receive adequate amounts of calcium during vitamin D treatment. The normal recommended allowance in a young adult of either sex is 800 mg/day of calcium, whereas in postmenopausal women the requirement increases to 1500 mg/day. Patients with vitamin D–deficiency osteomalacia should receive at least 1500 mg/day of calcium, and healing may occur faster if the patient receives an amount in excess of the recommended allowance, such as 2 g daily. The most commonly prescribed forms of calcium are calcium carbonate salts. These include Tums, which contain 200 mg or 300 mg of calcium per tablet, and Os-Cal, which contains 250 mg or 500 mg of calcium per tablet. Calcium citrate preparations are also available and are probably more readily absorbed by elderly patients than calcium carbonate.

Renal Failure Osteomalacia

The objective of $1,25(OH)_2D$ therapy in renal failure is to increase calcium absorption (which cannot be measured routinely) and to decrease serum PTH (which can be measured), and to do so without producing hypercalcemia. During the evolution of renal failure, $1,25(OH)_2D$ therapy should be started early (i.e., when the serum PTH begins to increase). One starts with the lowest dose of $1,25(OH)_2D$—0.25 μg/day—monitoring serum calcium and serum PTH every 1 to 2 weeks (serum $1,25(OH)_2D$ is not useful to monitor). After 1 to 2 weeks of treatment, if the serum calcium is not above normal, the dose is increased to .5 μg/day. The approach is repeated until the serum calcium rises to the upper normal limit (at which time the corresponding dose is maintained) or until the serum PTH (i.e., IRMA intact) becomes normal (at which time the dose which produced the normal serum PTH is maintained). The amount of calcium carbonate supplement used in renal failure is large because calcium carbonate is used not only as a supply of calcium but also as a phosphate binder to control serum phosphate.

The advantages of $1,25(OH)_2D$ over 25-OHD or vitamin D in renal failure are that $1,25(OH)_2D$ acts more quickly and its action dissipates more quickly. Thus, when hypercalcemia is a complication of treatment, the hypercalcemia spontaneously resolves more quickly after $1,25(OH)_2D$ than after vitamin D therapy. The reason for the more rapid action of $1,25(OH)_2D$ over vitamin D is that $1,25(OH)_2D$ is biologically active without further metabolism, whereas, under physiological conditions, vitamin D must be metabolized to 25-OHD and then to $1,25(OH)_2D$ before it is biologically active. The reasons for the differential duration of action of vitamin D and its metabolites are as follows: First, because vitamin D is stored in body fat, this storage depot must be depleted before the action of vitamin D dissipates. Second, 25-OHD, which in high concentrations acts directly on target tissues without further metabolism, has a longer duration of action than does $1,25(OH)_2D$ because its affinity for vitamin D–binding protein in blood is much greater than that of $1,25(OH)_2D$. Accordingly, the serum half-life of 25-OHD is 10 days and that of $1,25(OH)_2D$ less than 1 day. (See Chap. 56 for further information on the treatment of renal failure.)

Hypophosphatemia Osteomalacia

For treatment of osteomalacia due to hypophosphatemia, one uses neutral phosphate salts. A solution of neutral phosphate salt can be made up at a local pharmacy or is commercially available in capsule form as Neutrophos, which is a sodium- and potassium-containing neutral phosphate salt, or as Neutrophos K, which contains no sodium. Patients requiring phosphate therapy for osteomalacia usually have a renal phosphate leak, i.e., a depressed tubular maximum for phosphate reabsorption. Thus, after phosphate salt ingestion, the postabsorptive increase in serum phosphorus is only transient. Nevertheless, by administering 500 mg of phosphate four times a day it is usually possible to correct the serum phosphate levels for sufficient time to allow normal or at least improved bone mineralization.

Some patients may require more than 2 g/day of phosphate for correction of the osteomalacia. However, adults who take more than 2 g/day frequently have an unacceptable amount of diarrhea. Gastrointestinal symptoms are the main complication of neutral phosphate salts taken orally. The effect of phosphate treatment on bone mineralization can be monitored by serial measurement of serum alkaline phosphatase, which will decrease to normal as the osteomalacia heals.

In those patients with osteomalacia due to phosphate deficiency who do not have hypercalciuria [i.e., have depressed serum levels of $1,25(OH)_2D$], it is important to add $1,25(OH)_2D$ to the therapeutic program. If this is not done, the serum calcium will tend to fall, which will lead to a rise in the serum PTH, which in turn will further depress the TmP and thereby lead to a drop in the basal serum phosphate level. Thus, by administering $1,25(OH)_2D$ to maintain a normal or high normal serum calcium, one can maintain or even increase the TmP. Because of this indirect effect of $1,25(OH)_2D$ (via depression of PTH) to increase TmP, it is important to use the highest dose of $1,25(OH)_2D$ that does not produce hypercalciuria (defined as a urine calcium of >250 mg/day in females and >300 mg/day in males).

ILLUSTRATIVE CASE HISTORY

A 70-year-old female presented with muscular weakness, symptoms of emotional depression, weight loss, and generalized skeletal pains (Fig. 77-8). The patient was experiencing severe skeletal pain and was depressed to the extent that she wished to be left alone to die. On physical examination she was emaciated; she had a wide-based, cautious gait, dorsal kyphosis, several thoracic vertebral compression fractures, and weak and flaccid muscles. She complained of tenderness over the right scapula.* X rays revealed a total of

*As mentioned at the opening of this chapter, patients with osteoporosis rarely have osteomalacia as well. This patient is an exception in that she had spontaneous vertebral compression fractures indicative of osteoporosis as well as osteomalacia, which was diagnosed by bone biopsy. The reason for the combined skeletal diseases in this patient probably relates to her primary disease: gastrointestinal malabsorption. It seems possible that during the evolution of her skeletal disease, she first developed calcium malabsorption, which led to secondary hyperparathyroidism and osteoporosis. As her stores of vitamin D diminished, she became mildly vitamin D deficient, an abnormality that also tends to lead to osteoporosis. Ultimately, the patient became severely vitamin D deficient and, as a result, osteomalacia ensued. Thus, because the disease went unrecognized for several years, it probably evolved through osteoporosis to a combination of osteoporosis and osteomalacia.

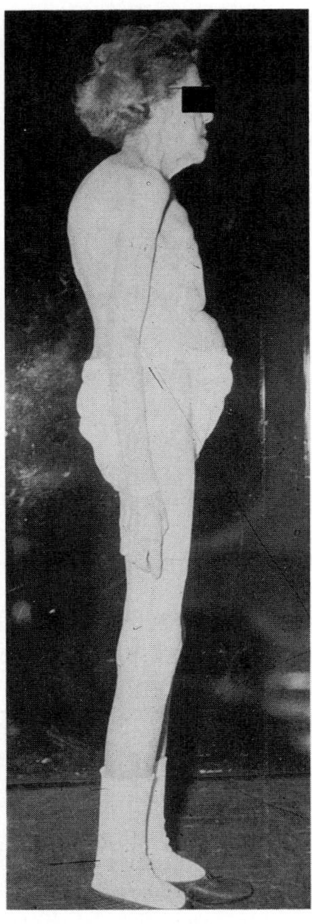

FIGURE 77-8
Photograph of patient with severe osteomalacia as a consequence of malabsorption syndrome. This patient exhibits severe dorsal kyphosis, flaccid abdominal muscles, and emaciation.

23 pseudofractures, one of which was located in the tender site in the right scapula. The most obvious pseudofracture was in the ulna (Fig. 77-5). A bone biopsy of the iliac crest revealed severe osteomalacia characterized by increased osteoid width and length (mineralized sections were prepared, since osteoid cannot be visualized on demineralized sections). A small-bowel biopsy showed the typical changes of gluten enteropathy, and the serum changes were consistent with osteomalacia as a consequence of vitamin D deficiency: serum calcium and phosphate and urine calcium were decreased, and serum alkaline phosphatase was elevated (Fig. 77-7). Most of her symptoms had been present and progressive over the previous 2 years with the exception of weight loss, which began approximately 5 years before admission.

The mechanisms responsible for the chemical changes shown in Fig. 77-7 were as follows: Fat malabsorption led to a decreased serum vitamin D_2 level which, in turn, resulted in a decreased serum 25-OHD. When the latter became severe, the $1,25(OH)_2D$ level dropped, and this resulted in two independent changes: (1) decreased calcium absorption and (2) an impaired ability of PTH to liberate bone mineral, which together acted to decrease serum calcium and thus to increase serum PTH. The secondary hyperparathyroidism increased the tubular reabsorption of calcium in an attempt to rectify the hypocalcemia and also decreased the tubular reabsorption of phosphate which contributed to the hypophosphatemia.

The patient was placed on a gluten-free diet and given 100,000 IU of vitamin D_2 and 2 g calcium daily. Within 3 months the pseudofracture of the ulna was almost healed (Fig. 77-5), and within 6 to 9 months the patient was completely free of skeletal pain, had gained weight, and was without any symptoms of depression and increased fatigability. After approximately 8 months of therapy, the urine calcium was found to be in excess of 200 mg/day (Fig. 77-7); therefore, the vitamin D_2 dose was reduced to 50,000 IU daily. However, on the next examination, the urine calcium had continued to increase; vitamin D_2 was thus discontinued. A biopsy at the end of the 1-year treatment period revealed complete healing of the osteomalacia.

ADDITIONAL READINGS

General

Fourman P et al: Calcium metabolism and the bone, 2d ed. Oxford, England, Blackwell, 1968, p 656.

Campbell GA: Osteomalacia: diagnosis and management. *Br J Hosp Med,* 44:332, 1990.

Pitt MJ: Rickets and osteomalacia are still around. *Radiol Clin North Am,* 29:97, 1991.

Dent DE, Stamp TCP: Vitamin D, rickets, and osteomalacia, in Avioli LV, Krane SM (eds): *Metabolic Bone Disease.* New York, Academic, 1977, pp 237–305.

The Production and the Actions of $1,25(OH)_2D$

Chertow BS et al: Decrease in serum immunoreactive parathyroid hormone in rats and in PTH secretion in vitro by 1,25-dihydroxycholecalciferol. *J Clin Invest* 56:668, 1975.

Hughes MR et al: Regulation of serum 1α,25-dihydroxyvitamin D_3 by calcium and phosphate in the rat. *Science* 190:578, 1975.

Kumar R: Metabolism of 1,25-dihydroxyvitamin D_3. *Physiol Rev* 64:478, 1984.

Baylink DJ et al: Vitamin D and bone, in Norman AW (ed): *Vitamin D: Molecular Biology and Clinical Nutrition.* New York, Dekker, 1980, pp 387–453.

Radiology of Osteomalacia

Greenfield GB: Osteomalacia, in *Radiology of Bone Diseases,* 4th ed. Philadelphia, Lippincott, 1986, pp 30–40.

Osteomalacia Due to Gastrointestinal Disease

Herlong HF et al: Bone disease in primary biliary cirrhosis: Histologic features and response to 25-hydroxyvitamin D. *Gastroenterology,* 83:103, 1982.

Matloff DS et al: Osteoporosis in primary biliary cirrhosis: Effects of 25-hydroxyvitamin D_3 treatment. *Gastroenterology* 83:97, 1982.

Morgan DB, Hunt G, Paterson CR: The osteomalacia syndrome after stomach operations. *Q J Med* 39:395, 1970.

Hajjar ET, Vincenti F, Salti IS: Gluten-induced enteropathy: Osteomalacia as its principal manifestation. *Arch Intern Med* 134:565, 1974.

Compston JE, Thompson RPH: Intestinal absorption of 25-hydroxyvitamin D and osteomalacia in primary biliary cirrhosis. *Lancet* 1:721, 1977.

Compston JE, Creamer B: Plasma levels and intestinal absorption of 25-hydroxyvitamin D in patients with small bowel resection. *Gut* 18:171, 1977.

Gertner JM et al: 25-hydroxycholecalciferol absorption in steatorrhea and postgastrectomy osteomalacia. *Br Med J* 1:1310, 1977.

Parfitt AM et al: Metabolic bone disease with and without osteomalacia after intestinal bypass surgery: A bone histomorphometric study. *Bone* 6:211, 1985.

Bisballe S et al: Osteopenia and osteomalacia after gastrectomy: Interrelations between biochemical markers of bone remodeling, vitamin D metabolites, and bone histomorphometry. *Gut* 32:1303, 1991.

Compston JE et al: Osteomalacia after small-intestinal resection. *Lancet* 1:9, 1978.

Osteomalacia Due to Vitamin D Deficiency

Baylink DJ et al: Formation, mineralization, and resorption of bone in vitamin D-deficient rats. *J Clin Invest* 49:1122, 1970.

Howard G, Baylink DJ: Matrix formation and osteoid maturation in vitamin D-deficient rats made normocalcemic by dietary means. *Miner Electrolyte Metab* 2:131, 1980.

Osteomalacia Due to Hypophosphatemia

Carmichael KA et al: Osteomalacia and osteitis fibrosa in a man ingesting aluminum hydroxide antacid. *Am J Med* 76:1137, 1984.

Sherrard DJ et al: Pseudohyperparathyroidism: Syndrome associated with aluminum intoxication in patients with renal failure. *Am J Med* 79:127, 1985.

Drezner MK et al: Evaluation of a role for 1,25-dihydroxyvitamin D_3 in the pathogenesis and treatment of x-linked hypophosphatemic rickets and osteomalacia. *J Clin Invest* 66:1020, 1980.

Weinstein RS, Whyte MP: Heterogeneity of adult hypophosphatasia: Report of severe and mild cases. *Arch Intern Med* 141:727, 1981.

Baylink DJ et al: Formation, mineralization, and resorption of bone in hypophosphatemic rats. *J Clin Invest* 50:2519, 1971.

Chines A, Pacifici R: Antacid and sucralfate-induced hypophosphatemic osteomalacia: A case report and review of the literature. *Calcif Tissue Int* 47:291, 1990.

Kassem M et al: Antacid-induced osteomalacia: A case report with a histomorphometric analysis. *J Int Med* 229:275, 1991.

Cooke N et al: Antacid-induced osteomalacia and nephrolithiasis. *Arch Intern Med.* 138:1007, 1978.

Osteomalacia Due to Calcium Deficiency

Stauffer M et al: Decreased bone formation and mineralization and enhanced resorption in calcium-deficient rats. *Am J Physiol* 225:269, 1973.

Osteomalacia Due to Renal Failure

Goodman WG et al: Renal osteodystrophy in adults and children, in Fauvus MJ (ed): *Primer on the Metabolic Bone Diseases and Disorders of Mineral Metabolism.* Kelseyville, American Society for Bone and Mineral Research, 1990, pp 200–212.

Coburn JW et al: Osteomalacia and bone disease arising from aluminum. *Semin Nephrol* 6:68, 1986.

Slatopolsky E et al: Marked suppression of secondary hyperparathyroidism by intravenous administration of 1,25-dihydroxycholecalciferol in uremic patients. *J Clin Invest* 74:2136, 1984.

Sherrard DJ et al: Quantitative histological studies on the pathogenesis of uremic bone disease. *J Clin Endocrinol Metab* 39:119, 1974.

Coburn JW et al: Clinical efficacy of 1,25-dihydroxyvitamin D_3 in renal osteodystrophy, in Norman AW (ed): *Vitamin D: Biochemical, Chemical, & Clinical Aspects Related to Calcium Metabolism.* Proceedings of the third workshop on vitamin D. New York, DeGruyter, 1977, p 973.

Oncogenic Osteomalacia

McClure J, Smith PS: Oncogenic osteomalacia. *J Clin Pathol* 40:446, 1987.

Taylor HC, et al: Oncogenic osteomalacia and inappropriate antidiuretic hormone secretion due to oat-cell carcinoma. *Ann Intern Med* 101:786, 1984.

Drezner MK, Feinglos MN: Osteomalacia due to 1α,25-dihydroxycholecalciferol deficiency—Association with a giant cell tumor of bone. *J Clin Invest* 60:1046, 1977.

Ryan EA, Reiss E: Oncogenous osteomalacia—Review of the world literature of 42 cases and report of two new cases. *Am J Med* 77:501, 1984.

Drezner MK: Disorders of vitamin D metabolism: Rickets and osteomalacia, in Manolagas SC, Olefsky JM (eds): *Metabolic Bone and Mineral Disorders,* vol 5. New York, Churchill Livingstone, 1988, pp 103–129.

Osteomalacia Due to Renal Tubular Acidoses

Ohashi K et al: "Superscan" appearance in distal renal tubular acidosis. *Clin Nuclear Med* 16(3):318, 1991.

Gaucher A et al: Osteomalacia, pseudosacroiliitis and necrosis of the femoral heads in fanconi syndrome in an adult. *J Rheumatol* 8:512, 1981.

Drug-Induced Osteomalacia

Davie MWJ et al: Low plasma 25-hydroxyvitamin D and serum calcium levels in institutionalized epileptic subjects: Associated risk factors, consequences and response to treatment with vitamin D. *Q J Med* 205:79, 1983.

Boyce BF et al: Focal osteomalacia due to low-dose diphosphonate therapy in Paget's disease. *Lancet* 1:821, 1984.

Collins N et al: A prospective study to evaluate the dose of vitamin D required to correct low 25-hydroxyvitamin D levels, calcium, and alkaline phosphatase in patients at risk of developing antiepileptic drug-induced osteomalacia. *Q J Med, New Series,* 78:113, 1991.

Briancon D, Meunier PJ: Treatment of osteoporosis with fluoride, calcium, and vitamin D. *Orthop Clin North Am* 12:629, 1981.

Chapter 78

HYPERPARATHYROIDISM

Kenneth W. Lyles

BACKGROUND

Hyperparathyroidism is a common disorder of calcium, phosphorus, and bone metabolism caused by increased circulating levels of parathyroid hormone (PTH). This disease is important to geriatricians because it occurs with increasing frequency in older patients. Over the past three decades the diagnosis of primary hyperparathyroidism has become more common with the introduction of routine multiphasic serum chemistry studies. Currently, the disease occurs twice as frequently in women as in men; current incidence rates are 2 cases per 1000 women over 60 years of age and 1 case per 1000 men over 60 years.[1] Indeed, most of these cases are asymptomatic at presentation.

In hyperparathyroidism, PTH is inappropriately secreted by single or multiple glands in the presence of increased serum calcium levels. The disease is considered primary when autonomous hypersecretion of PTH is due to a single adenoma, diffuse hyperplasia, multiple adenomas, or, rarely, a parathyroid carcinoma. Secondary hyperparathyroidism occurs when there is a prolonged hypocalcemic stimulus, as in cases of vitamin D deficiency or chronic renal failure. Tertiary hyperparathyroidism occurs in patients with chronic secondary hyperparathyroidism who develop autonomous hypersecretion of PTH and hypercalcemia, e.g., patients who undergo successful kidney transplants. This chapter will focus on primary hyperparathyroidism only.

ETIOLOGY AND PATHOLOGY

The etiology of primary hyperparathyroidism is unknown. When calcium is infused into hypercalcemic hyperparathyroid patients, there is a failure to suppress the PTH levels. Furthermore, when cells from hyperparathyroid glands are incubated in vitro, higher levels of ionized calcium in the medium are required to suppress PTH release than are required to suppress PTH release from cells from normal glands.[2] These data suggest that in part the abnormality occurring in the parathyroid gland is an elevation of the set point at which ionized calcium levels suppress PTH release.

In most cases of hyperparathyroidism, no etiologic agent can be identified; these represent sporadic cases. Recent work suggests that previous neck exposure to ionizing radiation is associated with an increased incidence of hyperparathyroidism.[3] Lithium, when used for therapy of bipolar disorders, is associated with hypercalcemia and increased PTH levels in up to 10 percent of patients. A few causes of hyperparathyroidism, usually parathyroid hyperplasia, are familial disorders which have an autosomal dominant mode of transmission: (1) familial hyperparathyroidism; (2) multiple endocrine neoplasia type I (Wermer's syndrome: hyperparathyroidism, islet cell tumors, and pituitary tumors); (3) multiple endocrine neoplasia type II (Sipple's syndrome: medullary carcinoma of the thyroid, pheochromocytoma, and hyperparathyroidism).[4,5] Only rarely does hyperparathyroidism occur in multiple endocrine neoplasia type IIB or III (medullary carcinoma of the thyroid, pheochromocytoma, mucosal neuromas, and marfanoid body habitus).[6]

The pathological abnormality in the parathyroid gland(s) may be an adenoma, four-gland hyperplasia, multiple adenomas, or carcinoma. Single adenomas cause 80 percent of cases of hyperparathyroidism. Hyperplasia of all four glands is found in 15 percent of cases; parathyroid carcinomas and multiple adenomas comprise the remainder. Frequently, determining whether a single gland is an adenoma or chief cell hyperplasia is difficult to do by histological features alone. Often it is necessary to consider the gross pathology seen at operation to classify the disease. An adenoma is diagnosed when only one abnormal gland is found (all other glands are normal). Chief cell hyperplasia is diagnosed when more than one abnormal gland is found. Controversy currently exists regarding whether it is possible to have multiple adenomas. In several studies, enlargement of only two glands was documented, with the remaining two being normal.[7] A rarer form of parathyroid hyperplasia is called "water–clear cell" hyperplasia, in which large, membrane-lined vesicles fill the cytoplasm. Finally, parathyroid carcinoma is diagnosed by finding mitotic figures in the gland or finding capsular or vascular invasion in pathological specimens obtained during surgery.

SIGNS AND SYMPTOMS

Patients with primary hyperparathyroidism can present with a varying spectrum of signs and symptoms ranging from a total lack of symptoms to acute hypercalcemic crisis. Currently, diagnosis is most frequently made by routine calcium measurements with multichannel screening chemistries in a patient with either no symptoms or only weakness or easy fatigability; acute hypercalcemic crisis is now a rare form of presentation.[8] Most of the specific signs and symptoms of hyperparathyroidism involve the skeleton or the kidneys.

Patients with hyperparathyroidism show evidence of increased bone remodeling on bone biopsy, with increased amounts of osteoid surface and eroded surface when compared to normal subjects. However, dynamic parameters of bone remodeling show that the mineral apposition rate is unchanged.[9] The classic bone biopsy lesion of osteitis fibrosa cystica with increased areas of resorption and peritrabecular fibrosis is much less common. Although radiographic evidence of hyperparathyroid bone disease in hand films—with subperiosteal resorption, and loss of the distal tuft of the phalanges—is rare in cases of primary hyperparathyroidism now, it is found in patients with secondary hyperparathyroidism from chronic renal failure.

Other skeletal abnormalities include diffuse osteopenia or osteosclerosis which when present in the skull gives a mottled "salt and pepper" appearance. In more severe cases, brown tumors or bone cysts made up of collections of osteoclasts and fibrous tissue are found in hands, feet, ribs, long bones, jaws, or pelvic bones. These lesions can produce pain, or they may result in fracture. Patients with radiographic evidence of hyperparathyroidism have elevations of the skeletal isoenzyme alkaline phosphate in serum, and in the urine there are increased amounts of hydroxyproline reflecting increased bone resorption.

Because osteoporosis is such a major health problem in older patients, attention has been directed at determining PTH's effect upon bone mass. With improved techniques to measure bone mass, it is possible to assess changes in both trabecular and cortical bone envelopes. Several early cross-sectional studies have suggested that hyperparathyroid subjects have decreased amounts of trabecular bone in the vertebrae.[10,11] More recent work shows that cortical bone as measured in the forearm or femur is reduced in affected patients.[12,13] Thus, elevated levels of PTH seem to have different effects upon cortical bone. Two studies suggest that patients with hyperparathyroidism have an increase in vertebral compression fractures,[14,15] but a third study found no evidence of an increased incidence of vertebral fractures.[16] At present, no data are available on hip or wrist fractures. Epidemiological studies will be necessary to determine whether the reduction in bone mass seen with this disease leads to increased fracture rates.

Nephrolithiasis occurs in 20 to 25 percent of hyperparathyroid patients. Of patients with kidney stones, approximately 5 percent have hyperparathyroidism. PTH causes a proximal renal tubular acidosis, increasing bicarbonate loss and decreasing hydrogen ion excretion as well as lowering the phosphate reabsorption threshold. These changes cause a hyperchloremic metabolic acidosis, and up to 50 percent of patients will be hypophosphatemic. Hyperparathyroidism can cause nephrocalcinosis and a subsequent decline in the glomerular filtration rate. Hypercalcemia can lead to nephrogenic diabetes insipidus when the renal tubule becomes unresponsive to the action of antidiuretic hormone. A recent study has shown that many asymptomatic patients with primary hyperparathyroidism have defects in their ability to concentrate their urine.[17]

Most other signs and symptoms of hyperparathyroidism can be attributed to the resultant hypercalcemia or, more specifically, the elevated ionized calcium level. *Gastrointestinal* disorders include anorexia, nausea, vomiting, and constipation. Peptic ulcer disease occurs with increased frequency, and, rarely, it may be the first clue to a multiple endocrine neoplasia type I syndrome (hyperparathyroidism; islet cell tumors, especially gastroma; and, finally, pituitary tumors). Pancreatitis can also occur or be exacerbated by the hypercalcemia. *Central nervous system* disorders include impaired cognition, recent memory loss, anosmia, depression, lethargy, and coma. Thus, hypercalcemia and hyperparathyroidism are rare but important considerations in the differential diagnosis of depression and dementia in the elderly. *Neuromuscular* disturbances include a proximal weakness, more prominent in lower than in upper extremities. Many patients complain of malaise and fatigue. Rarely, pruritus can be caused by metastic calcification in the skin. *Articular* disturbances include pseudogout from calcium pyrophosphate crystal deposition in articular cartilage, calcific tendonitis, and chondrocalcinosis. The main *cardiovascular* disturbance is an increased frequency of hypertension; however, this may be an occurrence of two common diseases in the same patient.

Physical signs are unusual in hyperparathyroidism. Soft-tissue calcification can cause pseudogout or cutaneous calcification. When present in the eye, deposits of calcium phosphate crystals can cause conjunctivitis. In the cornea, band keratopathy (a vertical line of calcium phosphate deposition parallel to and within the ocular limbus) is best appreciated with a slit-lamp examination. Enlarged parathyroid glands are difficult to palpate in the neck; generally when a nodule is found in the neck of a suspected hyperparathyroid patient, it represents thyroid rather than parathyroid tissue.

DIAGNOSIS

Primary hyperparathyroidism is diagnosed by elevated serum calcium levels and, frequently, associated hypophosphatemia, without any other apparent disease or drug causing the abnormalities. The serum calcium should be measured fasting on several occasions with minimal or no venous stasis. Over the last 25 years techniques for measuring PTH have improved significantly, making it possible to diagnose hyperparathyroidism directly, rather than by exclusion as had been done previously. Thus, to prove hyperparathyroidism, serum PTH levels should be measured directly. Early assays measured the carboxy-terminal portion of PTH.[18] Since this fragment is cleared by the kidney, the diagnosis of hypercalcemia in patients with renal insufficiency was confounded. With improvement in assay techniques and development of amino-terminal and especially midmolecule and intact assays,[19,20] it is now easier to discriminate between parathyroid and nonparathyroid causes of elevations in serum calcium levels. Most clinical PTH assays have been validated so that the laboratory provides a range reflecting previous experience with the assay and showing where the patient's PTH and serum calcium levels fall in relation to the laboratory's other cases of hyperparathyroidism. In most nonparathyroid causes of hypercalcemia, PTH levels will be suppressed, except in the unusual case of a malignant neoplasm that produces PTH. As will be discussed below, malignancy-associated hypercalcemia is always a concern in the differential diagnosis of hypercalcemia, but neoplasms that are actually proven to produce active PTH are unusual, most such cases being renal, pancreatic, ovarian, or hepatic carcinomas.[20] In such instances the PTH-related peptide secreted by the tumor does not usually cross-react with PTH of parathyroid origin in the immunoassays employed in most laboratories.

Serum phosphate levels may be low in hyperparathyroidism, but they can be normal, especially if there is renal impairment. Although PTH does cause phosphaturia, other factors such as dietary intake and time of day may affect renal phosphate handling. Furthermore, patients with malignancy-associated hypercalcemia can have a decrease in the renal phosphate reabsorption threshold from hypercalcemia per se or from the tumor-derived peptides which produce the hypercalcemia.[21] Other serum electrolyte abnormalities, such as elevated chloride, low bicarbonate, and low magnesium levels, are not specific enough to be of diagnostic value. Both an elevated serum alkaline phosphatase level and increased urinary hydroxyproline level suggest significant skeletal involvement from hyperparathyroidism.

Patients who are being evaluated for hyperparathyroidism should have a 24-hour urine calcium and creatinine excretion measured. Patients with a calcium/creatinine ratio of 0.1 may have familial hypercalcemic hypocalciuria, a disorder with normal PTH levels which does not require surgery.[22] Determination of nephrogenous cyclic AMP with serum and urine cyclic AMP is utilized less frequently to diagnose primary hyperparathyroidism, since patients with malignancy-associated hypercalcemia also have elevated levels.

Routine use of preoperative localization of abnormal parathyroid tissue in hyperparathyroidism should not be part of the diagnostic evaluation, since noninvasive imaging techniques require further development before being valid for such application. Arteriography and selective venous catheterization looking for "stepped-up" levels is a technically difficult procedure and should be performed by experienced hands only when hyperparathyroidism persists after a failed neck exploration.

DIFFERENTIAL DIAGNOSIS

The differential diagnosis of hyperparathyroidism is that of hypercalcemia, which can be caused by a diverse group of diseases and drugs (Table 78-1). A major concern when hypercalcemia is encountered is whether it is due to a neoplasm. The clinical setting must be considered. Most patients with malignancy-associated hypercalcemia have obvious neoplastic disease on thorough examination and routine diagnostic workup.[23] Thus, a chest x ray, a mammogram, and a serum and urine protein electrophoresis should be ordered when evaluating hypercalcemia. Since primary hyperparathyroidism is a common disease in older women, an elderly female with hypercalcemia without obvious evidence of malignant disease will be more likely to have primary hyperparathyroidism than occult malignancy.[23]

Familial hypocalciuria hypercalcemia (FHH) should be considered in an evaluation of hypercalcemia. Although uncommon, FHH can present with hypercalcemia, but there is usually a family history reflecting an autosomal dominant mode of inheritance, and 24-hour urinary calcium/creatinine excretion ratio of 0.1 is highly suggestive. At present no adverse effects of the hypercalcemia have been reported from affected kindreds under supervision,[24] and parathyroidectomy does not alter the hypercalcemia.

Drugs that cause hypercalcemia, such as thiazide diuretics and calcium supplements, can be excluded by withdrawing them for 4 weeks and making sure that serum calcium levels return to normal. Hypercalcemia caused by vitamin D intoxication can be diagnosed by measuring 25-hydroxyvitamin D levels and finding a level above 120 ng/ml. Hypercalcemia can be found in sarcoidosis, tuberculosis, and chronic fun-

TABLE 78-1

Differential Diagnosis of Hypercalcemia

Increased parathyroid hormone levels
- Primary hyperparathyroidism
- Secondary hyperparathyroidism
- Tertiary hyperparathyroidism
- Malignancy-associated hypercalcemia (rare)

Normal-to-low parathyroid hormone levels
- Malignancy-associated hypercalcemia
  - Hematological malignancies
  - Nonhematological malignancies
- Familial hypocalciuric hypercalcemia
- Hyperthyroidism/Hypothyroidism
- Adrenal insufficiency
- Pheochromocytoma
- Vipoma
- Calcium supplementation
- Thiazide diuretics
- Vitamin D intoxication
- Vitamin A intoxication
- Retinoic acid derivative usage
- Lithium
- Beryllium
- Theophylline
- Chronic granulomatous diseases
  - Sarcoidosis
  - Tuberculosis
  - Leprosy
  - Fungal infections
- Immobilization
- Milk-alkali syndrome
- Disseminated cytomegalovirus infection in AIDS

gal infections. The mechanism in all these diseases is believed to be increased production of 1,25-dihydroxyvitamin D by the granulomatous tissue, which causes increased calcium absorption from the gastrointestinal tract. Other diseases causing hypercalcemia, such as hyperthyroidism, adrenal insufficiency, and vitamin D intoxication, should be diagnosed by their historical or clinical features.

THERAPY

Treatment of hyperparathyroidism depends upon the way in which the patient presents to the physician. Since most cases are asymptomatic at presentation, no immediate therapy is usually necessary, and a thorough diagnostic evaluation can be undertaken. When the patient presents with a hypercalcemic crisis (e.g., obtunded with serum calcium levels of greater than 12 mg/dl), management of the hypercalcemia must take precedence over diagnostic studies. Most hypercalcemic patients are dehydrated and may require several liters of parenteral fluids to lower the serum calcium into the 11.0 mg/dl range. Once hydration has been reestablished and the patient is stable, further decisions about therapy can be made.

At this time there is no effective medical therapy for primary hyperparathyroidism. Beta blockers, estrogen therapy in postmenopausal women, phosphate supplementation with potassium phosphate (Neutra-Phos-K), etidronate disodium (Didronel), or oral cellulose phosphate with dietary calcium restriction may lower serum calcium levels, while other aspects of the disease may progress.[25] Therefore, long-term management of hyperparathyroidism must involve a decision about whether to intervene surgically or to follow the patient until there is an indication for surgery.

Since many cases of hyperparathyroidism are asymptomatic and without any potential complications of the disease at diagnosis, immediate surgery is not necessary, and some patients may never need an operation. A recent NIH consensus conference points out that since surgery is the only effective therapy for this disorder, the patient and the physician must realize that meticulous, long-term follow-up is necessary.[26] Understanding of long-term complications is incomplete, and no study has randomized asymptomatic patients to surgery or medical follow-up.

There are certain indications for surgery in asymptomatic patients with primary hyperparathyroidism: (1) markedly elevated serum calcium (above 12.0 mg/dl); (2) history of life-threatening hypercalcemia; (3) reduced creatinine clearance (above 30 percent for age-matched normals); (4) nephrolithiasis; (5) markedly elevated 24-hour urinary calcium excretion (above 400 mg); and (6) substantially reduced bone mass as measured by direct measurement (more than 2 standard deviations below age-matched normals). Surgery should be considered strongly in the following circumstances: (1) the patient desires surgery; (2) meticulous, long-term follow-ups are unlikely; (3) coexistent illness complicates management; and (4) the patient is young (below age 50).

Patients with serum calcium levels below 11.0 mg/dl and no other evidence of disease may be safely followed. There is agreement that malaise and fatigue are associated with hyperparathyroidism, but no prospective studies are available to show that these complaints improve with surgery. This is also true for neuropsychiatric disturbances in patients with serum calcium levels below 11.0 mg/dl. At present, no markers are available in lieu of direct measurements to suggest who will lose bone, develop nephrolithiasis, or have a decline in glomerular filtration rate. Therefore, patients with asymptomatic hyperparathyroidism require close follow-up; in addition, they should be educated about the signs and symptoms of hypercalcemia. These patients should have yearly serum measurements of calcium and creatinine, determination of creatinine clearance, and yearly kidney-ureter-bladder x-ray searching for nephrolithiasis. Most experts believe that bone mass measurements (spine, hip, and possibly radius) should be followed annually for 2 to 3 years until stable. Thus, if physician and patient decide not to operate for hyperparathyroidism, education and long-term follow-up are necessary.

For patients who require surgery, the most important aspect is referral to a surgeon who is experienced in neck dissections and identification of parathyroid glands. With an experienced surgeon, parathyroidectomy is usually not a major procedure unless the sternum must be split to find a substernal gland. All four glands should be identified and biopsied for histological confirmation. Since 80 percent of the cases of hyperparathyroidism are caused by a single adenoma, removal of the offending gland is curative. When hyperplasia is identified, most surgeons remove three and one-half glands, marking the remaining portion of gland so it can be identified if necessary in the future. Transplantation of parathyroid tissue into the forearm after removal of all of the glands from the neck is used by some surgeons, especially when they anticipate removing more tissue should hyperplasia become a problem at a later time (e.g., with chronic renal failure).

Postoperatively, patients should be watched closely for 72 hours for signs of hypocalcemia. Nervousness, tingling, and a positive Chvostek or Trousseau sign may indicate hypocalcemia, which should be confirmed by total or ionized serum calcium levels. Many patients have transient hypocalcemia, and additional calcium should be given only if the level is below 8.0 mg/dl. Intravenous calcium as the chloride or gluconate salt may be given for several days, but persistent hypocalcemia will require oral calcium in a dose of 1000 to 1200 mg daily. If hypocalcemia is severe, 1,25-dihydroxyvitamin D (calcitriol) can be added at 0.5 to 1.0 μg/day in doses divided every 12 hours. Calcitriol can cause hypercalcemia and hypercalciuria; therefore, serum and urine levels must be monitored. Patients who have developed hypocalcemia from skeletal uptake of calcium and phosphorus with healing of osteitis fibrosa cystica ("hungry bones") have normal or low serum phosphorus levels. This complication is currently rare because of early detection of the disease; treatment with calcium supplements and calcitriol can be necessary for up to 3 months. Permanent hyperparathyroidism is a rare complication of parathyroidectomy (when performed by experienced surgeons), but it can occur. Hypocalcemia with persistent hyperphosphatemia postoperatively suggests hyperparathyroidism. This can occur transiently from bruising of the glands as they are identified and biopsied at surgery, so follow-up is required to determine whether parathyroid function returns over time. Finally, hyperparathyroid patients can have low serum magnesium levels, another cause of hypocalcemia. Thus, the serum magnesium level should be checked if hypocalcemia develops postoperatively. Since serum magnesium levels may not reflect tissue stores, patients should receive parenteral magnesium if a low normal level is found.

REFERENCES

1. Heath H III et al: Primary hyperparathyroidism incidence, morbidity, and potential impact in a community. *N Engl J Med* 302:189, 1980.
2. Brown EM et al: Dispersed cells prepared from human parathyroid glands: Distinct calcium sensitivity of adenoma vs primary hyperplasia. *J Clin Endocrinol Metab* 46:267, 1978.
3. Katz A, Braunstein GD: Clinical, biochemical, and pathologic features of radiation-associated hyperparathyroidism. *Arch Intern Med* 143:79, 1983.
4. Wermer P: Genetic aspects of adenomatosis of endocrine glands. *Am J Med* 16:363, 1954.
5. Sipple JH: The association of pheochromocytoma with carcinoma of the thyroid gland. *JAMA* 31:163, 1961.
6. Marx SJ et al: Familial hyperparathyroidism: Mild hypercalcemia in at least nine members of a kindred. *Ann Intern Med* 78:371, 1973.
7. Verdonk CA, Edis AJ: Parathyroid double adenomas: Fact or fiction? *Surgery* 90:523, 1981.
8. Fitzpatrick LA, Bilezikian JP: Acute primary hyperparathyroidism. *Am J Med* 82:275, 1987.
9. Bilezikian JP et al: Characterization and evaluation of asymptomatic primary hyperparathyroidism. *J Bone Mineral Res* 6(suppl 2):585, 1991.
10. Richardson ML et al: Bone mineral changes in primary hyperparathyroidism. *Skeletal Radiol* 15:85, 1986.
11. Pak CYC et al: Photon absorptiometric analysis of bone density in primary hyperparathyroidism. *Lancet* 2:7, 1975.
12. Heath H: Clinical spectrum of primary hyperparathyroidism: Evolution with changes in medical practice and technology. *J Bone Mineral Res* 6(suppl 2):563, 1991.
13. Peacock M: Interpretation of bone mass determinations as they relate to fracture: Implications for asymptomatic primary hyperparathyroidism. *J Bone Mineral Res* 6(suppl 2):577, 1991.
14. Dauphine RT et al: Back pain and vertebral crush fractures: An unexplained mode of presentation from primary hyperparathyroidism. *Ann Intern Med* 831:365, 1975.
15. Kochersberger GG et al: What is the clinical significance of bone loss in primary hyperparathyroidism? *Arch Intern Med* 147:1951, 1987.
16. Wilson RJ et al: Asymptomatic primary hyperparathyroidism is not a risk factor for vertebral fractures. *Ann Intern Med* 109:959, 1988.
17. Mitlak BH et al: Asymptomatic primary hyperparathyroidism. *J Bone Mineral Res* 6(suppl 2):S103, 1991.
18. Mallette LE et al: Radioimmunoassay for the middle region of human parathyroid hormone using an homologous antiserum with a carboxy-terminal fragment of bovine parathyroid hormone as radioligand. *J Clin Endocrinol Metab* 54:1017, 1982.

19. Potts JT Jr et al: *Current Clinical Concepts: Assessment of Parathyroid Function with an N-Terminal Specific Radioimmunoassay for Intact Parathyroid Hormone.* San Juan Capistrano, CA, Nichols Institute Reference Laboratories, 1987.
20. Kochersberger GG, Lyes KW: Skeletal disorders in malignant disease. *Clin Geriatr Med* 3:561, 1987.
21. Broadus AE et al: Humoral hypercalcemia of cancer identification of a novel parathyroid hormone-like peptide. *N Engl J Med* 319:556, 1988.
22. Mary SJ et al: Familial hypocalciuric hypercalcemia: The relation to primary parathyroid hyperplasia. *N Engl J Med* 307:416, 1982.
23. Mundy GR, Martin TJ: The hypercalcemia of malignancy: Pathogenesis and management. *Metabolism* 31:1247, 1982.
24. Law WM Jr, Heath H III: Familial benign hypercalcemia (hypocalciuric hypercalcemia): Clinical and pathogenetic studies in 21 families. *Ann Intern Med* 102:511, 1985.
25. Shane E: Medical management of asymptomatic primary hyperparathyroidism. *J Bone Mineral Res* 6(Suppl 2):S131, 1991.
26. Consensus Development Panel: Diagnosis and management of asymptomatic primary hyperparathyroidism: Consensus Development Conference Statement. *Ann Intern Med* 114:593, 1991.

Chapter 79

PAGET'S DISEASE OF BONE

Frederick R. Singer

EPIDEMIOLOGY

Paget's disease of bone is a common disorder of the elderly in England, Australia, New Zealand, North America, and continental Europe. In these areas the disease may affect 3 percent or more of the population over 40 years of age.[1] In contrast, this condition is rarely diagnosed in Scandinavian countries, Japan, China, or India.

In most studies the disease has been reported to affect males slightly more often than females. It is also now more widely appreciated that multiple members of a family may manifest Paget's disease. As many as 25 percent of patients have at least one family member with the disease. In most instances the patterns of familial aggregation suggest an autosomal dominant transmission of the disease. In a number of families genetic susceptibility is also suggested by the finding of linkage between the HLA haplotype and the clinical manifestations of the disease.

PATHOLOGY

The pathogenesis of Paget's disease involves several stages. In the earliest phase a proliferation of osteoclasts produces a localized loss of bone which is followed by an influx of undifferentiated mesenchymal cells into the marrow spaces and by proliferation of blood vessels in marrow spaces filled with fibrous connective tissue.[2] The osteoclasts often are much larger than normal and as many as 100 nuclei may be seen in a cross-section of a single cell.[3] These bone-resorbing cells often contain nuclear and cytoplasmic inclusions which resemble viral nucleocapsids of the Paramyxoviridae family of viruses. These inclusions have not been observed in other bone or bone marrow cells.

In most lesions of Paget's disease osteoclastic activity is accompanied by equally intense osteoblastic activity. Numerous plump osteoblasts overlie previously resorbed bone surfaces and studies utilizing tetracycline labeling of bone indicate that the rate of bone formation is increased.

The bone in Paget's disease is usually lamellar in character and normally mineralized, although in very active lesions woven bone may be present as well as regions of poorly mineralized osteoid. A characteristic mosaic pattern of the bone matrix features irregularly shaped pieces of lamellar bone with an erratic pattern of cement lines, undoubtedly a consequence of disorderly and accelerated bone resorption and formation. Despite the fact that Paget's disease is initiated by a localized increase in bone resorption, most fully developed lesions actually exhibit increased bone mass.

Occasionally the disease may reach a "burned out" stage in which the sclerotic lesion may remain in the absence of excessive bone cell activity. The adjacent marrow usually consists mainly of fat cells with few areas of hematopoietic or fibrovascular elements.

ETIOLOGY

A variety of hypotheses have been proposed to explain the genesis of Paget's disease (Table 79-1). No convincing data have been accumulated indicating that Paget's disease is a disorder of hormonal imbalance, vascular disorder, neoplasm, autoimmune disorder, or inborn error of connective tissue.

TABLE 79-1

Proposed Causes of Paget's Disease

- Hormonal imbalance
  - Hyperparathyroidism
  - Excess growth hormone secretion
  - Adrenal insufficiency
  - Calcitonin deficiency
- Vascular disorder
- Neoplasm
- Autoimmune disorder
- Inborn error of connective tissue
- Slow-virus infection

A viral cause of Paget's disease appears to be a reasonable possibility at present.[4] Patients with Paget's disease and slow-virus infections of the nervous system such as subacute sclerosing panencephalitis share a number of clinical and pathologic characteristics. These include a long subclinical course, the absence of fever, localization of the disease to a single organ, the absence of polymorphonuclear leukocytes in pathologic lesions, the presence of characteristic giant cells in these lesions, and the presence of intracellular viral nucleocapsid-like structures in all patients.

There has been partial success in identifying the nuclear and cytoplasmic inclusions found in the osteoclasts of Paget's disease. Immunohistologic studies of bone biopsies or surgical specimens have revealed the antigens of a number of Paramyxoviridae viruses, particularly measles and respiratory syncytial virus, in the osteoclasts of Paget's disease.[5,6] In addition mRNA of the nucleocapsid proteins of measles[7] and canine distemper virus[8] has been identified in pathologic material. However, as yet, an infectious virus has not been isolated from long-term cultures of pagetic bone cells.

CLINICAL MANIFESTATIONS AND COMPLICATIONS

The disease may affect any part of the skeleton and may be unifocal or multifocal.[9] Thus, there is a wide spectrum of clinical presentations which depend on the sites and severity of the lesions. However, it should be emphasized that many individuals with Paget's disease are asymptomatic and may not require treatment.

The symptoms and signs of Paget's disease are outlined in Table 79-2.

TABLE 79-2

Clinical Manifestations of Paget's Disease

Musculoskeletal
Pain (bone or joint)
Deformity (including skeletal enlargement)
Neurologic
Hearing loss and, less commonly, other cranial nerve deficits
Pain from spinal stenosis
Muscle weakness
Bladder and/or bowel dysfunction
Cardiovascular
High cardiac output
Congestive heart failure
Increased skin temperature over affected extremities
Metabolic
Symptoms of hypercalcemia in immobilized patients
Hypercalciuria and renal stones
Angioid streaks of retina

Bone pain in Paget's disease is generally mild to moderate. Severe pain usually indicates a neurologic complication or more frequently degenerative arthritis. Paget's disease involving the pelvis, femur, and tibia is not infrequently associated with symptomatic degenerative arthritis of the hip and knee joints, probably due to abnormal biomechanics brought on by alterations in bone structure. Acute pain also develops as a consequence of pathologic fractures of affected vertebral bodies, long bones, and, less commonly, the pelvis.

The most serious complication in patients with Paget's disease is the development of a malignant bone tumor.[10] Osteosarcomas, chondrosarcomas, fibrosarcomas, or tumors of mixed histology may develop, almost always in a preexisting pagetic lesion. Therefore, these tumors are very difficult to detect at an early stage. Rapid worsening of bone pain and/or deformity should indicate the need for radiologic evaluation followed by bone biopsy if suspicion of a tumor remains. Despite recent advances in the therapy of malignant bone tumors, the prognosis remains poor in patients with Paget's disease. Fortunately, these tumors develop in fewer than 1 percent of patients.

Benign bone tumors may also arise in pagetic lesions; giant cell tumors are most common. These tumors are often locally aggressive and tend to recur after surgery.

LABORATORY EVALUATION

Radiology

The diagnosis of Paget's disease is almost always established by the characteristic roentgenographic appearance of the lesions. As in the case of the pathologic evolution of the disease, there are distinct stages of Paget's disease detected radiologically.[11]

The earliest detectable lesions of Paget's disease are osteolytic and are usually most readily observed in the skull and long bones. In the skull, discrete oval or round areas of osteopenia have been termed *osteoporosis circumscripta* (Fig. 79-1). In lower-extremity long bones the disease usually begins as a localized lesion in the subchondral region of the epiphyses. The lesion usually has a V or arrowhead shape at its advancing edge. These lesions have been observed to progress toward the opposite end of the affected long bone at an average rate of approximately 1 cm/year in untreated patients.

As the osteolytic process slowly progresses to involve much of the long bone or skull, the more familiar osteosclerotic (or "osteoblastic") lesions of Paget's disease replace the osteolytic regions. Over a period of many years the bone becomes chaotic in structure and thickened. The overall bone size may increase considerably. In the skull a "cotton-wool" appearance may develop (Fig. 79-2). Bowing of the weight-bear-

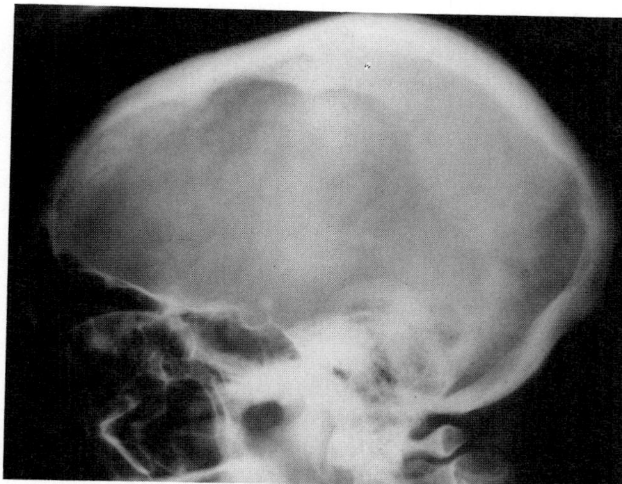

FIGURE 79-1
Extensive osteolytic lesion in the skull of a 62-year-old man with Paget's disease.

ing long bones is common when the disease involves most of the bone. In some cases incomplete small transverse fissures are found in the cortex along the convex side of the bowed long bone. These lesions may precede pathologic fractures.

In the final stage of a pagetic lesion involving an entire bone, there is predominance of osteosclerosis, although secondary osteolytic fronts may be present.

The development of a neoplasm in lesions of Paget's disease is particularly difficult to detect in an early stage since the chaotic underlying structure obscures the presence of the neoplastic lesions. In the case of a malignant lesion the suspicion is often raised when the tumor finally erodes through the cortex into the surrounding soft tissue.

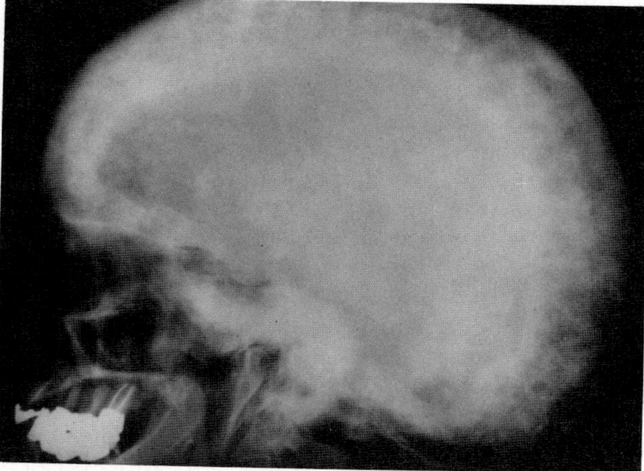

FIGURE 79-2
Skull of a 70-year-old man with Paget's disease exhibiting marked calvarial thickening and generalized patchy sclerosis.

Computed tomography (CT) and magnetic resonance imaging (MRI) are newer modalities of diagnostic imaging whose full role has not been established in the care of patients with Paget's disease. However, in patients with back pain, CT has been particularly useful in defining whether degenerative arthritis, spinal stenosis, or nerve root impingement are likely to be responsible for the symptoms.

A variety of radioisotopes can be used to assess the metabolic activity of pagetic lesions. Most commonly technetium 99m–labeled bisphosphonates are used.[12] These are bone-seeking agents whose localization in bone appears dependent both upon relative vascularity and on the extent of hydroxyapatite crystal surface available for binding of the bisphosphonate. Bone scans utilizing the radiolabeled bisphosphonates have been extensively demonstrated to be far more sensitive in detecting asymptomatic lesions of Paget's disease than roentgenograms, although "burned-out" sclerotic lesions may be missed. Bone scans should be done when there is a question of the activity of a particular lesion of Paget's disease or when it is desirable to document the full extent of the disease.

Gallium 67 uptake, reflecting cellular activity, can also localize pagetic lesions and is a reasonably sensitive means of following the response to calcitonin therapy.[13]

Biochemistry

The measurement of alkaline phosphatase activity in the circulation is the most frequently used test in the biochemical assessment of Paget's disease. The activity of this enzyme, which is located in the plasma membrane of osteoblasts, is believed to reflect the number and functional state of osteoblasts in patients with bone disease who are not pregnant and who have no other disease which might produce a rise in other isoenzymes of alkaline phosphatase. In Paget's disease the level of alkaline phosphatase activity has been found to correlate with the extent of the skeleton affected by the disease as established by roentgenographic survey.[14] In untreated patients serial alkaline phosphatase determinations generally reveal a constant or slowly rising level of activity over a period of years. It should also be appreciated that normal levels of alkaline phosphatase activity in patients with small regions of skeletal involvement do not necessarily indicate burned-out disease since intense activity in these lesions often can be demonstrated by bone scan.

Urinary hydroxyproline excretion is a biochemical index of bone matrix resorption. It is usually measured in a 24-hour urine specimen while the patient is on a low-gelatin diet, although a fasting urinary hydroxyproline/creatinine measurement provides equally relevant information. As with serum alkaline phosphatase activity, hydroxyproline excretion correlates well with the extent of Paget's disease.[14] This test should not be considered a routine test in Paget's disease, but it is indicated when a patient has a complicating disorder which produces elevation of extraskeletal alkaline phosphatase activity. As in the case of total serum alkaline phosphatase activity, measurement of urinary hydroxyproline excretion is not specific for metabolic activity of bone. Excretion of this amino acid may be increased in patients with extensive burns or skin diseases such as psoriasis. More specific tests for determining the rate of bone resorption have recently been developed. Estimates of urinary collagen pyridinoline cross-links appear to have more specificity than hydroxyproline.[15]

TREATMENT

General Considerations and Indications

In evaluating a symptomatic patient with Paget's disease, it is important to consider whether the main complaints are, in fact, due to Paget's disease. In many cases the symptoms that cause the patient to seek care are not a direct consequence of Paget's disease. This is particularly true in patients who have degenerative arthritis.[14] Close attention to the nature of the symptoms, the physical examination, and the roentgenograms should allow the clinician to determine whether treatment of Paget's disease is indicated.

Table 79-3 lists indications for drug therapy of Paget's disease. Since safe and effective drug therapy has been available for less than 20 years, the indications for treatment continue to evolve as experience with the available drugs expands.

Drug Therapy

At present, three drugs have been approved for treating Paget's disease in the United States: salmon calcitonin, human calcitonin, and disodium etidronate. The treatment schedules and special characteristics of each agent are indicated in Table 79-4. Biochemical indices are decreased by 50 percent during chronic treatment. The clinical benefits of long-term calcitonin therapy include relief of bone pain, reduction of increased cardiac output, reversal of some neurologic deficits, stabilization of hearing deficit, healing of osteolytic lesions, and reduction in complications of orthopedic surgery.

Side effects (usually minor) occur in about 20 percent of patients treated with salmon calcitonin and in a higher percentage treated with human calcitonin. These include nausea, vomiting, facial flushing, perioral paresthesias, metallic taste sensation, chills, and polyuria. Tetany is extremely rare, and allergic reactions induced by salmon calcitonin are also rare.

Resistance to chronic salmon calcitonin therapy develops in more than 20 percent of patients after a successful initial treatment period.[16] This is usually associated with high titers of anti–salmon calcitonin antibodies in the circulation. These patients are responsive to treatment with human calcitonin. A small number of patients have become resistant to either salmon or human calcitonin in the absence of any circulating antibodies.

Questions about calcitonin therapy which still need to be answered include should the dosage be based on the extent and activity of the patient's disease and how long the hormone should be administered. Patients with rapidly progressive osteolytic disease may require higher doses to produce healing of the lesions. If long-term treatment with calcitonin is discontinued, exacerbation of biochemical abnormalities and symptoms usually occurs within 1 year.

Preliminary studies using a nasal spray form of salmon calcitonin suggest that this mode of administration may replace injections in the future.[17]

The bisphosphonates (formerly diphosphonates) are pyrophosphate (P-O-P) analogues whose pharmacologic effects are to inhibit both bone resorption and formation.[18] They bind to hydroxyapatite crystals and may remain in bone for a prolonged time after treatment is discontinued.

Disodium etidronate is currently the only bisphosphonate approved for use in the United States. The advantage of this agent is that it can be used orally, although absorption is poor and rather variable. After absorption it localizes to bone and to sites of ectopic calcification, or it is excreted unchanged in the urine. A standard recommended dose of disodium etidronate (5 mg/kg body weight daily for 6 months) produces suppression of disease activity and symptoms in a similar manner as calcitonin, with several exceptions. Although bone pain is usually relieved, there is a paradoxical increase in pain in 10 percent of patients. However, pain lessens if the drug is discontinued. Another surprising difference is that the drug seldom heals osteolytic lesions despite improvement of biochemical indices.[11,19] Therefore it is preferable to use calcitonin in patients with osteolytic lesions. Side effects are less common than with calcitonin; loose bowel movements and nausea are uncommon. Hyperphosphatemia commonly occurs, particularly if higher than recommended doses are given. High doses also produce a mineralization defect and may predispose to pathologic fractures.

TABLE 79-3

Indications for Drug Therapy of Paget's Disease

- Bone pain
- Preparation for orthopedic surgery
- Prevention or treatment of medical complications such as hypercalcemia and high-output congestive heart failure
- Prevention or treatment of neurologic complications including hearing loss and spinal cord or nerve dysfunction
- Prevention of fracture or skeletal deformity in patients with rapidly progressive osteolytic lesions or in young patients

TABLE 79-4

Drug Therapy of Paget's Disease

Drug	Effective Regimen	Special Characteristics
Salmon calcitonin	50–100 MRC units subcutaneously daily or three times weekly	Anti-salmon calcitonin antibodies develop in 60%; clinical resistance in >20%.
Human calcitonin	0.5 mg subcutaneously daily	Effective in patients with high antibody titers who are resistant to salmon calcitonin. Nausea is common side effect.
Disodium etidronate	5 mg/kg body weight orally for 6 months	Effective orally. Sometimes a remission of years occurs after 6 months therapy. Some patients have transiently increased bone pain. Osteolytic lesions do not heal. Osteomalacia occurs at high doses.

After the recommended 6-month treatment course, biochemical and symptomatic remissions may persist for months or, occasionally, years. In most patients biochemical indices return toward pretreatment levels within a year. When symptoms recur, the 6-month treatment can be given again.

Second- and third-generation bisphosphonates have been developed which do not produce a mineralization defect at the doses used. Intravenous pamidronate, which is approved only for treatment of malignant hypercalcemia, is quite effective in treatment of Paget's disease.[20]

Plicamycin (mithramycin) is a toxic cancer drug which can be used to treat severe Paget's disease but should probably be limited to patients who fail to respond adequately to other drugs.[21] A combination of oral calcium supplementation and chlorthalidone has been reported to reduce bone pain and partially suppress biochemical indexes in patients with Paget's disease.[22] It is the least expensive means of treatment.

Surgery

Surgical intervention in Paget's disease is most often needed when degenerative arthritis of the hip or knee produces severe pain on weight bearing and impairs mobility. Often anti-inflammatory agents produce little relief of symptoms in such patients. Total hip replacement is highly effective in relieving hip pain and restoring mobility of patients with hip disease[23] (Fig. 79-3*A* and *B*), and tibial osteotomy is similarly effec-

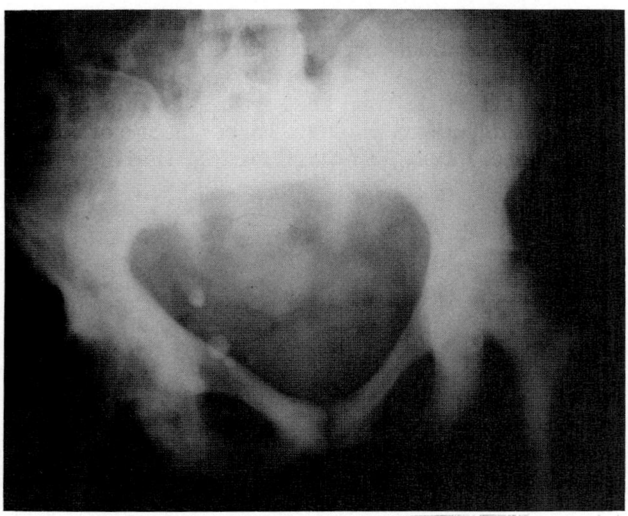

A.

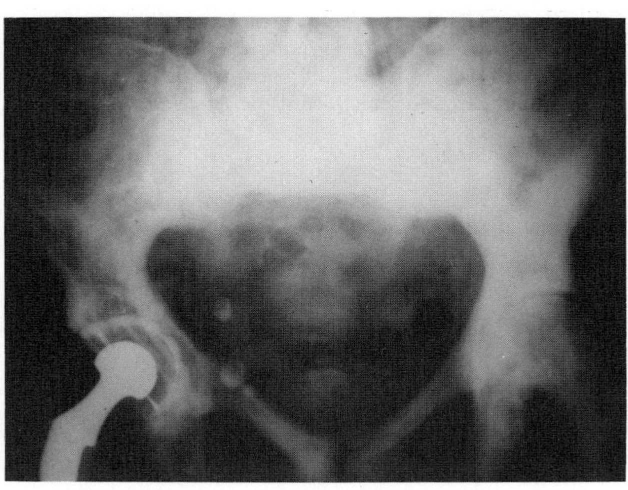

B.

FIGURE 79-3

A. Pelvis of a 64-year-old woman revealing extensive Paget's disease with loss of the right hip joint space. The patient had marked pain on weight bearing. *B.* After total hip replacement the patient could ambulate without pain.

tive in relieving knee pain in patients with severe tibial bowing.[24] Total knee replacement is occasionally required for relief of pain due to severe deterioration of cartilage.[25] Surgery may also be required in patients with neurologic symptoms related to basilar impression, spinal stenosis, or nerve root compression. Prior to any surgery it is desirable, if possible, to reduce disease activity by drug therapy in order to prevent excessive blood loss during orthopedic procedures. A reduction in serum alkaline phosphatase activity approaching 50 percent of pretreatment levels is probably adequate preoperative control.

REFERENCES

1. Singer FR: Paget's disease of bone, in Martin TJ, Raisz LG (eds): *Clinical Endocrinology of Calcium Metabolism.* New York, Dekker, 1987, p 369.
2. Schmorl G: Uber Ostitis Deformans Paget. *Virchows Arch Pathol Anat Physiol* 283:694, 1932.
3. Rubinstein MA et al: Osteoblasts and osteoclasts in bone marrow aspiration. *Arch Intern Med* 92:684, 1953.
4. Singer FR, Mills BG: Evidence for a viral etiology of Paget's disease of bone. *Clin Orthop Relat Res* 178:245, 1983.
5. Rebel A et al: Viral antigens in osteoclasts from Paget's disease of bone. *Lancet* 2:344, 1980.
6. Mills BG et al: Evidence for both respiratory syncytial virus and measles virus antigens in the osteoclasts of patients with Paget's disease of bone. *Clin Orthop Relat Res* 183:303, 1984.
7. Basle MF et al: Measles virus RNA detected in Paget's disease bone tissue by in situ hybridization. *J Gen Virol* 67:907, 1986.
8. Gordon MT et al: Canine distemper virus localised in bone cells of patients with Paget's disease. *Bone* 12:195, 1991.
9. Ziegler R et al: Paget's disease of bone in West Germany. Prevalence and distribution. *Clin Orthop Relat Res* 194:199, 1985.
10. Barry HC: *Paget's Disease of Bone.* Baltimore, Williams & Wilkins, 1969.
11. Maldague B, Malghem J: Dynamic radiologic patterns of Paget's disease of bone. *Clin Orthop Relat Res* 217:126, 1987.
12. Vellenga CJLR et al: Untreated Paget disease of bone studied by scintigraphy. *Radiology* 153:799, 1984.
13. Waxman AD et al: Gallium scanning in Paget's disease of bone. Effect of calcitonin. *Am J Roentgenol* 134:303, 1980.
14. Franck WA et al: Rheumatic manifestations of Paget's disease of bone. *Am J Med* 56:592, 1974.
15. Uebelhart D et al: Urinary excretion of pyridinium crosslinks: A new marker of bone resorption in metabolic bone disease. *Bone Mineral* 8:87, 1990.
16. Singer FR et al: Salmon calcitonin therapy for Paget's disease of bone: The problem of acquired clinical resistance. *Arthritis Rheum* 23:1148, 1980.
17. Nagant de Deuxchaisnes C et al: New modes of administration of salmon calcitonin in Paget's disease. *Clin Orthop Rel Res* 217:56, 1987.
18. Fleisch H: Bisphosphonates: Mechanisms of action and clinical applications, in Peck WA (ed): *Bone and Mineral Research Annual 1.* Amsterdam, Excerpta Medica, 1983, p 319.
19. Nagant de Deuxchaisnes C et al: The action of the main therapeutic regimens on Paget's disease of bone, with a note on the effect of vitamin D deficiency. *Arthritis Rheum* 23:1215, 1980.
20. Stone MD: Treatment of Paget's disease with intermittent low-dose infusions of disodium pamidronate. *J Bone Min Res* 5:1231, 1990.
21. Lebbin D et al: Outpatient treatment of Paget's disease of bone with mithramycin. *JAMA* 213:1153, 1970.
22. Evans RA et al: Long-term experience with a calcium-thiazide treatment for Paget's disease of bone. *Miner Electrolyte Metab* 8:325, 1982.
23. McDonald DJ et al: Total hip arthroplasty in Paget's disease. *J Bone Joint Surg* 69A:766, 1987.
24. Myers M, Singer FR: Osteotomy for tibia vara in Paget's disease under cover of calcitonin. *J Bone Joint Surg* 60A:810, 1978.
25. Gabel GT et al: Total knee arthroplasty for osteoarthrosis in patients who have Paget's disease of bone at the knee. *J Bone Joint Surg* 73A:739, 1991.

SECTION H

The Musculoskeletal and Joint Systems

Chapter 80

AGING AND THE MUSCULOSKELETAL SYSTEM

David Hamerman

This chapter reviews biochemical aspects of connective tissue components that constitute the musculoskeletal system. The focus is on age-related changes in this system. There is a more detailed consideration of diarthrodial joints, particularly in relation to the pathophysiology of osteoarthritis (OA). The clinical aspects of OA are discussed in Chap. 85. Aging changes in bone relate fundamentally to those seen in osteoporosis, a subject reviewed in Chap. 76.

DIARTHRODIAL JOINTS

Articular Cartilage

Overview

The articular surface of diarthrodial joints is composed of hyaline cartilage. Three special features of this cartilage need to be considered in relation to the maintenance of its integrity for articulation and the alterations that occur in OA, the most common disease which affects diarthrodial joints in older people. The first feature is that articular cartilage is avascular and must derive nutrients from the synovial fluid and the subchondral spaces to sustain metabolic functions of the chondrocytes.[1] The factors that contribute to the maintenance of the normal avascular state of articular cartilage are not well understood but may be due in part to the presence of protease inhibitors.[2] The avascular state of articular cartilage is violated in OA by invasion of vascular and cellular elements derived from the subchondral marrow, with endochondral formation of new cartilage and bone in the form of osteophytes.

The second consideration relating to articular cartilage is that the chondrocytes are responsible for the production of the extracellular matrix. Maintenance of the mechanical properties of the cartilage during articulation depends on the integrity of the macromolecules in this matrix.[34] The matrix, in turn, plays a key role in modulating the metabolic functions of the chondrocytes.[35] Matrix depletion in OA seems to be a key factor in promoting proliferation of cells which normally have a very low mitotic rate. The proliferating chondrocytes form clones or clusters and, at least early, synthesize more matrix proteoglycans and even some collagen types, such as type X, more traditionally observed in hypertrophic chondrocytes.[5]

The third important aspect of cartilage is compositional heterogeneity; i.e., the appearance of the cells and the macromolecular composition of the matrix change from the surface to the base.[6] Cells at the surface are more flattened, while those in the more basal parts are oval. The collagen meshwork is more dense at the surface, and the proteoglycans (PG; see Fig. 80-1) are of smaller molecular size and generally not linked with hyaluronic acid (HA) because of the absence of link protein. Chondrocytes at the surface make less keratan sulfate (KS) than they do in the more basal parts of the cartilage.

Studies examining the biochemical changes in cartilage utilize several approaches: (1) extraction and biochemical analysis of matrix components from the cartilage itself; (2) organ cultures, in which plugs or slices of cartilage are maintained in medium in vitro for days to weeks; (3) culture of cells dispersed from cartilage and studied initially or in subsequent passages. Systems (2) and (3) are more conducive to manipulation of the experimental conditions. General approaches used in all systems include radiolabeling of newly synthesized macromolecular components:

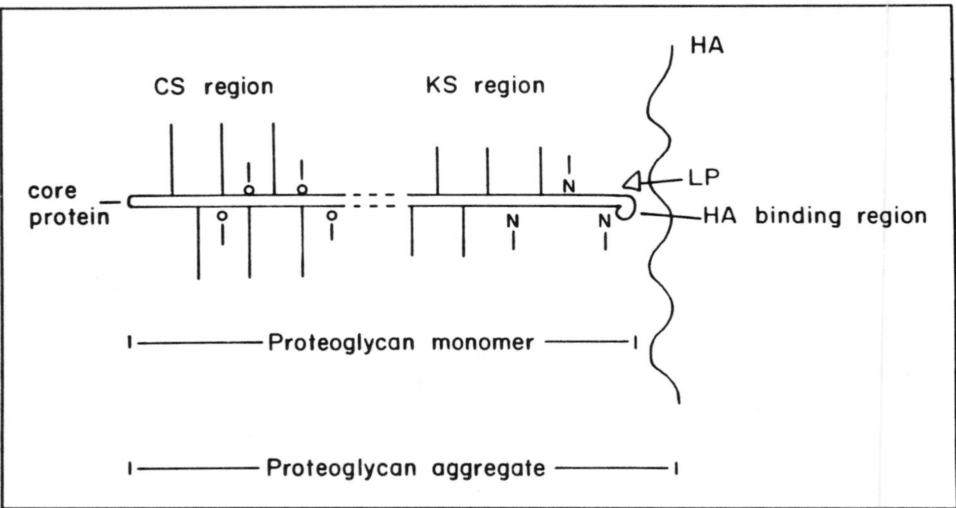

FIGURE 80-1
This is a diagram of the proteoglycan aggregate. The proteoglycan subunit or monomer has a hyaluronic acid-binding (HA-binding) region at the N-terminal part of the core protein, and the linkage to HA is further stabilized by link protein (LP). Attached to the core protein are side chains of glycosaminoglycans with regions enriched in chondroitin sulfate (CS) or keratan sulfate (KS). Short chains of oligosaccharides are also attached to the protein core by N-linkage through asparagine or O-linkage through serine or threonine. (*Adapted from Hunziker and Schenk.*[10])

with leucine for noncollagen proteins, sulfate for PG, glucosamine for PG and HA, and proline for collagen. Labelled components can then be extracted and subjected to further isolation, purification, and identification by density gradient centrifugation or column chromatography. Newer modalities to identify components in cells and cartilage include use of monoclonal antibodies for PG localization in cartilage,[7] and in situ hybridization[5] techniques for measuring messenger ribonucleic acids (mRNA) of collagens and PG.

Biochemistry

Cartilage is composed of water (over 70 percent), chondrocytes, and macromolecular components that constitute the matrix. A detailed description of the macromolecular composition of articular cartilage is beyond the scope of this chapter, and extensive reviews may be consulted in relation to the proteoglycans[8–11] and collagens.[12] The basic concepts are these:

1. PG (Fig. 80-1) contain sulfated polysaccharide chains called glycosaminoglycans (GAG) covalently linked to a protein core. The most abundant PG in cartilage is called aggrecan, which consists of an extended protein core to which many chondroitin sulfate (CS) and KS chains are attached. This PG is immobilized in the cartilage matrix by specific binding to HA through link protein to form a proteoglycan aggregate. Other PG present in cartilage, particularly at its surface, are called dermatan sulfate proteoglycans and exist in two forms, biglycan (DSPG I) and decorin (DSPG II).
2. The predominant (95 percent) collagen of articular cartilage is type II. Three chains designated $[\alpha 1(11)]_3$ form a triple helix, with nonhelical ends. Some "minor" collagens also exist in cartilage, particularly types XI and IX, both of which contribute to the organizational and mechanical stability of the collagen type II network.

The interactions between the chondrocyte, pericellular PG, and type II collagen may be promoted by a collagen-binding glycoprotein called anchorin CII, isolated from chondrocyte membranes. Matrix proteins and PG in cartilage[9] appear able to modify chondrocyte synthetic functions through signals transduced by the chondrocyte cytoskeleton,[3,13] as discussed below.

Mechanical Properties

The negatively charged GAG chains attached to the protein core of the PG are constrained from full expansion by the dense collagen network and create a large osmotic pressure that draws water into the cartilage, expands the collagen network, and provides the compressive and elastic properties that are key to the articular functions of cartilage. It is as if there were innumerable coiled springs, compressed by loading and extruding water onto the surface of cartilage ("weeping lubrication"), and then regaining a more extended domain when the compressive force is relaxed, increasing the swelling pressure, and imbibing water and nutrients from the surface of the cartilage. The integrity of the macromolecules of the matrix is thus the key to the mechanical properties of the intact articular cartilage, as noted; to the extent that the matrix molecules are altered in aging and in OA, normal joint function is impaired.

Aging in Cartilage

Maturation may be a more appropriate term than *aging* for the changes in articular cartilage over time. In fetal cartilage, the PG monomers are large in size, more uniform in length (less polydisperse), and contain virtually no KS. In postfetal maturation, the CS chains decrease both in number and in size, and the content of KS increases.[14] These changes in PG monomers could be due to a number of factors[15]: (1) modifications in the activity of the various enzymes in the chondrocyte responsible for the synthesis of GAG chains; (2) proteolytic cleavage between the CS and KS portion of the protein core, which would produce shortened protein cores with CS chains and enrichment in both protein and KS in those fragments containing the HA-binding region retained within the tissues; and (3) altered stresses across the joint that could modify chondrocyte function, leading to enrichment in KS. Increased sulfated GAG synthesis was observed in chondrocyte cultures subjected to intermittent compressive force.[16]

Although reduced PG content itself may not be a factor in age-related decrease in tensile strength of articular cartilage, aging cartilage does have impaired mechanical properties attributable to altered structure of the PG and collagens in the matrix. An age-related factor seems to contribute to "fatigue life" of cartilage: the projections for how long it takes for cartilage to fatigue are much longer in a 50-year-old than in a 60-year-old.[17]

Articular Cartilage in Osteoarthritis

Cartilage Biochemistry

Epidemiologic studies relate OA to aging; biochemical studies however, distinguish changes in aging cartilage from those in osteoarthritic cartilage (Table 80-1).[4,18] Yet, as Solursh[19] has pointed out, "from the perspective of the developmental biologist, OA, like aging, can be considered a developmentally related process." The hydration of cartilage appears to be a critical factor in the inception of OA. The increase in water content of cartilage is likely due to an altered collagen fiber network, particularly collagen type IX,[12] which loses its tight "weave" and promotes water imbibation and swelling. This change in collagen, along with dilution of PG, leads to functional deterioration of the mechanical properties of the cartilage and reduced content of PG, due in part to diffusion out of the matrix components into the joint fluid.

TABLE 80-1

Comparison of Articular Cartilage Changes in Aging and Osteoarthritis

Criteria	Aging	Osteoarthritis
Water content	Decreased	Increased
GAG*		
CS	Normal or slightly less	Decreased
Ratio CS 4/6	Decreased	Increased
KS	Increased	Decreased
HA	Increased	Decreased
PG		
Aggregation	Normal	Diminished
Monomer size	Decreased	Decreased
Link protein	Fragmented	Normal
Proteases	"Normal"	Increased

*GAG = glycosaminoglycans; CS = chondroitin sulfate 4 or 6; KS = keratan sulfate; HA = hyaluronic acid; PG = proteoglycan.
SOURCE: Based on information from Muir[4] and Brandt.[18]

Pressure loading produces more deformation, less elastic return, with increased contact pressure on subchondral bone.[20] Whatever the inherent "program" of the chondrocyte in OA, an altered intercellular environment and mechanical impact modify chondrocyte synthetic patterns and indeed may promote abnormal ones, such as release of hydrolytic enzymes capable of degrading matrix constituents.[21]

Problems in studying the biochemistry of cartilage in OA are, the nonuniformity of cartilage involvement in different parts of the articular surface, the duration of the condition over years, and the mix of degradative and reparative changes.[3] It is agreed that KS is decreased, the 4-sulfate form of CS is increased with respect to the 6-sulfate form, and HA is decreased. Articular cartilage obtained from autopsy specimens showed increased neutral metalloprotease activity accompanying fibrillation primarily in the superficial layer.[21] Among the metalloproteinases are stromelysin-1, capable of degrading PG; link protein; and cartilage collagens.[12] Rampant hydrolytic action in the affected cartilage is unlikely, however, because many studies show no change in PG monomer size or in the potential for PG to aggregate with HA.

Organ Cultures

Several model systems are available for studying the changes in cartilage that occur due to osteoarthritis. Intact cartilage samples maintained in nutrient medium in vitro constitute an organ culture. In this system the influence of changes in culture conditions on the biosynthetic properties of the chondrocyte can be studied in the intact cartilage. PG content, as revealed by direct chemical analysis in the cartilage or more quantitatively by isotopic labeling of the sulfate moiety of the GAG, reflects changes in matrix turnover of the PG. The culture conditions that can be modified include (1) deleting or adding serum or growth factors to the nutrient medium, (2) adding peptide mediators that affect chondrocyte metabolism, and (3) adding hydrolytic enzymes that directly degrade the matrix PG. These modifications of the culture medium demonstrate the capacity for dynamic responses of the chondrocyte that may be relevant to basic mechanisms in OA.

The presence of serum in the medium of the organ culture is necessary to promote chondrocyte synthesis of PG and to prevent chondrocyte release of matrix-degrading hydrolases.[22,23] If serum is omitted from the medium, PG content in the cartilage sample falls sharply. Chondrocyte-mediated PG loss can be accelerated by adding to the medium a peptide of about 17,000 molecular weight called interleukin-1 (IL-1). This peptide, a member of a group of polypeptide mediators called cytokines,[24,25] mimics the results of serum depletion: chondrocyte PG synthesis is inhibited; chondrocyte release of proteases, prostaglandins (PGE_2), and collagenases is enhanced; and a switch in collagen synthesis from type II to types I and III is induced.[24] Knowledge about the functions of IL-1 began not in connective tissue research but in immunology, when this peptide was identified as a major immunoregulator of T-cell function. Relevance to arthritis occurred when it was shown that blood monocytes/macrophages, or other activators, could release IL-1 directly from synovial membrane lining cells.[24] The interaction of cells in various joint components is reflected by a cycle: synovial cells release IL-1, perhaps in response to partially degraded cartilage products in the joint fluid; the IL-1 then gains access to cartilage and activates chondrocytes to release matrix-degrading hydrolases, thus increasing cartilage breakdown products entering the joint fluid. Such a cycle may be operative in the osteoarthritic joint.[26] This possibility gains support from the demonstration of IL-1 in osteoarthritic joint fluid, but levels have not been shown to correlate with disease activity.[27] Other cytokines such as interleukin-6 and tumor necrosis factor alpha also may be important mediators of cartilage degradation.

If there are many ways to induce degradation in organ cultures, there are also ways to promote matrix synthesis.This can be achieved by adding to the culture medium a class of peptides called growth factors. Indeed, in what appears to be a basic mechanism of action, growth factors such as the fibroblast growth factors are present in the interface between the extracellular matrix—where they are bound on the one hand to proteoglycans containing heparan sulfate and on the other hand to the cytoskeleton of the cell membrane of chondrocytes—and are able to transduce (activate) signals that in turn influence nuclear DNA expression.[28,29] The growth factors and some of their key effects on cells that constitute the musculoskeletal system are shown in Table 80-2, where they are also defined.

When IGF-I[23] or TGF-β[30] was added to cartilage organ cultures, biosynthesis of PG was increased and breakdown of PG decreased. Stimulation of synthesis and depression of catabolism of PG were comparable to the effects of calf serum alone in the nutrient medium and, indeed, it is IGF-1 which is thought to mediate the effects of calf serum itself.[23] FGF stimulated a marked increase in tritiated thymidine incorporation indicating actual cell replication.[31]

The relevance of experiments which use cartilage organ cultures to OA is that they suggest cartilage homeostasis likely depends on the interactive effects of cytokines, such as IL-1, promoting matrix degradation (turnover), and a variety of growth factors, known to be present in cartilage and bone, which promote chondrocyte replication and/or synthetic activity. Articular cartilage abrasions produced experimentally in the rabbit joint failed to heal, but infusion of bFGF into the joint promoted healing.[32] Thus, these data suggest future directions for research, which—although theoretical at this time—may have therapeutic implications: on the one hand, means to promote IL-1 (or other cytokine) receptor antagonists[33] which may block cellular effects of IL-1, and, on the other hand, means to introduce growth factors into the joint itself,[32] where chondrocyte replication, migration, and new matrix formation could repair superficial defects in the cartilage.

Chondrocyte Cultures

When samples of cartilage are enzymatically digested, the chondrocytes, liberated from the matrix in which they are embedded in the intact cartilage, can be grown on dishes maintained in the laboratory. At confluence, the chondrocytes are trypsinized and subcultured, resulting in successive passages up to a finite life span, when the cells no longer replicate.

Cell culture is another system in which to study the behavior of chondrocytes when their environment is modified. The information may complement studies on chondrocyte behavior in intact organ cultures but more often may be divergent and more difficult to interpret, particularly if the chondrocyte phenotype changes due to the culture conditions. The primary reason for this discrepancy is that with successive passages in culture, chondrocytes undergo a modification in their metabolic properties so that now these properties are no longer those that occur in the intact tissue. Properties such as oval cell shape, synthesis of type II collagen, and cartilage-specific PG identify the chondrocyte phenotype. Repeated passage of chondrocytes in culture alters the phenotype: the cells modulate or dedifferentiate and show more stellate shape; they synthesize type I or type III collagen and fibronectin.[5,34] These changes are not related to cell senescence, for they can be reversed when culture conditions—particularly the substrate on which the cells are grown—are modified.

Thus, means to preserve chondrocyte phenotype in culture become critical in studies of these cells in vitro, because when the phenotype is altered, the investigator cannot feel confident that the "chondrocyte" is displaying the traits these cells would show if they were still phenotypically stable or if they were in the intact cartilage.

TABLE 80-2

Growth Factors with Relevance to the Musculoskeletal System*

Growth Factor	Structure	Source	Actions
PDGF	PDGF-A 31 kDa PDGF-B 28 kDa 51% homology B chain 93% homology with c-sis-oncogene	Mononuclear cells Macrophages Platelets	Mitogen for fibroblasts and smooth muscle cells but *not* endothelial cells Promotes collagenase, PGE_2 release Promotes wound healing Competence factor in cell division
EGF	5.8 kDa	Submaxillary glands Biological fluids (urine, milk, saliva)	Promotes skeletal growth
FGF	Acidic FGF 15.5 kDa Basic FGF 16.5 kDa 53% homology Family of related proteins	Neural tissue Bone Above, and cells of many other tissues	Angiogenesis Mitogen Angiogenesis Mitogen Wound healing
TGF	α 7.8 kDa	Transformed cells	Transforming factor Binds to EGF receptor Angiogenesis
	β-1 25 kDa β-2 25 kDa 70% homology Multiple forms of TGF-β	Platelets Bone Soft tissues Cartilage Kidney	Angiogenesis in vivo Growth inhibiting in most cell types in vitro Promotes myochondrogenesis Macrophage and fibroblast chemotaxis Wound healing Bone formation
IGF-I	7.6 kDa	Somatomedins in plasma and tissues, related to insulin	Regulated by growth hormone Cartilage and bone growth
IGF-II	7.4 kDa		

*PDGF = platelet-derived growth factor; EGF = epidermal growth factor; FGF = fibroblast growth factor; TGF = transforming growth factor; IGF = insulin-like growth factor. Not included in this table are hemopoietic growth factors, nerve growth factor, and the cytokine mediators—the interleukins (IL), tumor necrosis factors (TNF), and interferons (IFN).
SOURCE: Based primarily on Sporn MB, Roberts AB (eds): *Peptide Growth Factors and their Receptors* (*Handb Exp Pharm*). New York, Springer-Verlag, 1990, 95:I, II.

One way to preserve the chondrocyte phenotype in vitro is to maintain its rounded shape.[34,35] This has been done by coating the tissue culture dish on which the cells adhere with methacrylate to prevent cell adhesivity and flattening on the usual plastic surface, or by suspending the cells in a more viscous medium (collagen gels, agar, or agarose). Again, these "mechanical" aspects of in vitro cell culture systems have their counterpart in vivo, or in organ culture, where the cartilage matrix stabilizes and maintains the cellular phenotype.[5]

In chondrocyte culture systems, the effects of growth factors on chondrocytes have been tested. bFGF[36,37] has been shown to enhance chondrocyte DNA synthesis, promote replication, and preserve phenotypic properties. The role of TGF-β is less clear, since it may be more dependent on dose and the culture system: in organ cultures of cartilage, TGF-β promoted cartilage matrix synthesis;[30] in chondrocyte cultures, TGF-β appeared to destabilize the chondrocyte phenotype, modifying the oval shape to stellate, and promoting synthesis of type I collagen.[38] There also are inductive or bone morphogenetic proteins present in cartilage and bone, with the capacity to produce new bone under the appropriate conditions.[39,40] Some of these proteins are related to TGF-β in what has been called the TGF-β superfamily. One of the bone morphogenetic proteins, called osteogenin—in synergism with EGF, PDGF, and bFGF—provided optimal conditions for reexpression of cartilage phenotype in dedifferentiated chondrocytes.[41]

Whether chondrocytes dispersed from human osteoarthritic cartilage can be used as a "model" to study the disease in vitro is not entirely clear, but studies along these lines have been done.[42,43] Several molecular sizes of PG can be isolated from the culture medium, which may reflect the functional heterogeneity of the cells cultured from osteoarthritic cartilage.[44] Chondrocyte cultures from cartilage lesions of moderate grade appeared to synthesize more PG and to produce more proteoglycanases than chondrocytes derived from normal cartilage.[45]

One final point of interest that chondrocyte cultures have revealed is the complexity of the interactions between cytokines and growth factors. The surprising finding is that substimulatory concentrations of IL-1, which barely induce metalloproteinase and PGE_2 production by chondrocytes, may actually do so strongly after the addition of PDGF, aFGF, or bFGF.[46–48] Thus, these growth factors potentiate IL-1 cell release or increase chondrocyte receptor sensitivity. The implications of these cytokine–growth factor interactions observed in cell cultures for the larger scope of events that occurs in the osteoarthritic joint are not clear at this time. An attempt to depict some of the complex interactions involved in cartilage breakdown and repair in the pathogenesis of OA are shown in Fig. 80-2.

Synovial Membrane

In the diarthrodial joint, the synovial membrane forms the inner lining of the capsule enclosing the joint cavity. The structure of the synovial membrane in human joints, unaffected by trauma or arthritis (as revealed by light microscopy), shows a surface layer of lining cells, capillaries close to the surface within a fibrous and/or fatty stroma, and virtually no inflammatory cells. Few studies appear to have been done on aged joints, although fibrotic changes in the synovial membrane may occur with aging. The extent and significance of inflammation in OA has been the subject of controversy, but many studies reveal evidence for at least modest inflammatory changes in the synovium, including vascular proliferation and engorgement, lining cell proliferation, and foci of round cell infiltrates within the stroma.

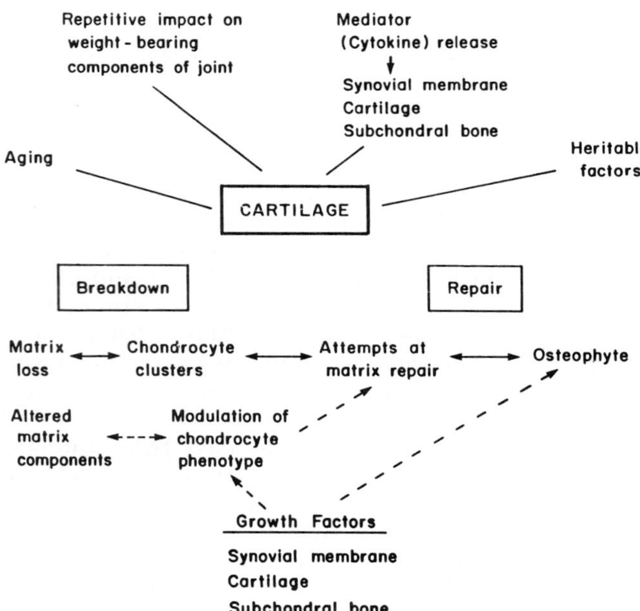

FIGURE 80-2

Factors contributing to the evolution of osteoarthritis. Solid lines denote generally accepted predisposing conditions and observed histologic changes. Interrupted lines represent speculations discussed in the text. (*Reprinted from Ref. 3 with permission of* The New England Journal of Medicine.)

On the basis of studies using the electron microscope,[49] the lining cells were classified into type A, macrophage-like, and type B, fibroblast-like. An "intermediate" cell, type C, has been described, and may be more prevalent in rheumatoid arthritis.

Synovial cells can be dispersed from the membrane by enzymatic digestion with hyaluronidase and collagenase and maintained in culture.[50,51] A functionally and morphologically heterogeneous cell population is revealed, and HA and CS proteoglycans are synthesized and secreted by the synovial cells into the culture medium. Whether the same lining cells are responsible for the synthesis of HA and sulfated PG is not known.

In the past few years several laboratories have attempted to characterize the synovial cells in culture based on morphology, immunologic properties, and secretory functions.[51,52] In general, three types of cells have been identified: a round or rhombic-shaped macrophage-like cell; an elongated, spindle-shaped fibroblast-like cell; and a novel cell with a stellate or dendritic appearance and long cytoplasmic processes. The macrophage-like cell is probably equivalent to the type A cell and is phagocytic in vitro. The fibroblast-like cell is similar in appearance to type B cells and is only slightly phagocytic. The dendritic cells are not phagocytic; they secrete collagenase and their cell surface membrane stains for Ia antigen—a marker for tissue macrophages. The Ia-positive cells are in a lineage similar to epidermal Langerhans cells and may be the principal accessory cell for antigen presentation to lymphocytes. Reversion between synovial cell types is possible in vitro, since addition of prostaglandins (PGE_2) converts a fibroblast-like cell to a stellate (dendritic) cell, and removal of PGE_2 from the medium reverts the cell back.[51]

The dendritic cells appear mainly responsible for IL-1 secretion,[51] but the other cell types can do so as well, to a lesser extent. The fact that silica particles induce IL-1 secretion to a greater degree than that which occurs in resting cells is strong support for the role of a variety of cartilage-derived degradation products present in the joint fluid which could be taken up by the lining cells and provoke an ongoing or intermittent secretion of IL-1, PGE_2, collagenase, and other proteases.[26] Synovial cells appear to synthesize bFGF and express receptors for this growth factor.[53]

Synovial lining cells are very likely the source of HA in the synovial fluid,[54] and staining of sections of synovial membrane using a hyaluronic acid–binding region protein revealed localization in the loose connective tissue and perivascular tissue.[55] The mediators TNF α, IL-1, and the growth factors TGF-β and PDGF seemed to promote connective tissue cell proliferation and local release of HA. These features may prevail to a greater extent in rheumatoid arthritis synovium.[55]

Synovial membrane microvascular endothelial cells were isolated for the first time and grown to confluence on gelatin-coated tissue culture dishes. Compared to umbilical vein endothelial cells, synovial-derived endothelial cells showed enhanced responsiveness to IL-1 with respect to a neutrophil-specific adhesive molecule called ELAM-1 and an intercellular adhesion molecule called ICAM-1.[56]

Synovial Fluid

So-called normal synovial fluid has been obtained from human cadaver knees[57] or aspirated from the knees of volunteers.[58] Usually less than 1 ml of highly viscous fluid is obtained and the components of the fluid can be divided into those derived from the lining cells of the synovial membrane (such as HA and traces of sulfated GAG) and those derived from plasma (cells, proteins, glucose, and electrolytes). Lower levels of HA were found in synovial fluid from the knee joints of older deceased subjects than from younger subjects,[57] but there does not seem to be any systematic study of HA levels in synovial fluid from aging joints.

The viscosity of the fluid is due to the presence of high-molecular-weight HA. Whether the lubricating function of the fluid is due to the polymerized HA or to a glycoprotein ("lubricin")[59] is not clear. Lubricating properties of synovial fluid in OA generally do not seem to be impaired.[60]

In the osteoarthritic joint, inflammation and cell proliferation in the synovial membrane, and degradation and repair in the articular cartilage, may be reflected by components ("markers") associated with these processes in the synovial fluid (Table 80-3).[27,61–66] In particular, because protein core-KS fragments were first readily measured in synovial fluid and serum,[66] attempts have been made to correlate levels of this "marker" of cartilage matrix breakdown with fluctuations in the clinical course of OA. This has generally not reflected the course of OA, and Brandt[67] has offered a "pessimistic view" at the present time of serologic markers as indicators of the clinical state of the articular cartilage in OA.

TABLE 80-3

"Markers" in Synovial Fluid That May Reflect Underlying Responses in the Synovial Membrane or Articular Cartilage in the Osteoarthritic Joint

	Reference
Cytokines	
IL-1*	27,61
TNF-α	61
IFN	61
Growth Factors	
TGF-β	62
PDGF	63
aFGF	63
NGF	64
Proteoglycans	
Core protein–CS-rich fragments	65
HA binding fragments	65
Core protein–KS-rich fragments	66

*See Tables 80-1 and 80-2 for abbreviations.

Meniscus

The menisci are fibrocartilages on the opposing surfaces of the femur and tibia in the knee. This brief discussion is drawn largely from the comprehensive review by Ghosh and colleagues.[68] The functions of the menisci are to increase joint congruency, stabilize the joint, improve articular cartilage nutrition and lubrication, and facilitate the rotation of opposing articular surfaces of the joint during the "lock home" movement. Collagen types I and II, rather than PG, appear to contribute most significantly to the tensile properties of the menisci. The PG are similar to those in articular cartilage, but with more dermatan sulfate.

Aging changes reveal a decline in noncollageneous matrix proteins between the ages of 30 to 70, but the significance of this in functional terms is not clear. Studies suggest that, as observed with articular cartilage chondrocytes, the "fibrochondrocytes" of the menisci respond to IL-1 and release collagenase and proteoglycanases. The inner and central regions of the meniscus are most susceptible to horizontal tears, perhaps secondary to degeneration of the meniscus core, with serious consequences for joint function and the potential for the development of OA.

SKELETAL MUSCLE

Mesenchymal cells in the limb bud evolve as primitive myoblasts or chondroblasts.[69] The view that such primitive cells follow a predestined pattern constitutes the so-called lineage hypothesis of differentiation, in contrast to the view that there exists in the limb bud a population of uncommitted multi-potential cells that, under specific environmental conditions, can be induced to differentiate into muscle, cartilage, or other connective tissues. Studies with a monoclonal antibody (designated CSAT) support the lineage theory.[69] In cultures of the limb bud, CSAT induced selective detachment of those cells destined to be myogenic and left attached to the plate those cells destined to be chondrocytes.

The fine structure of muscle cells and the biochemical and anatomic basis for contraction are discussed elsewhere.[70,71] In postnatal life, fiber hypertrophy has been thought to occur, rather than new fiber formation, yet there is actually enhanced DNA and protein synthesis in muscle of the maturing rat from day 20 to day 140.[71] The cell type that appears to make the greatest contribution to such synthetic activities in the muscle is the satellite cell. In adult life, satellite cells are inactive and actually decline in number with aging. They can be activated by injury. Growth factors can modulate the action of satellite cells in vitro.[71] IGF stimulated satellite cell proliferation and differentiation; pituitary- or brain-derived FGF (with insulin) stimulated proliferation but suppressed differentiation of a muscle cell line; TGF-β appeared to inhibit differentiation of myoblasts and satellite cells.

Three types of skeletal muscle fibers can be identified in adults: type I (slow-twitch, high oxidative fiber), type IIA (fast-twitch, high oxidative fiber), and type IIB (fast-twitch, slow oxidative fiber).[72] A decline in fiber number contributing to a reduced muscle mass—the major component of lean body mass—does occur with aging;[73–75] however, decrease in the cross-sectional area of individual fibers—but with no loss of fibers—is a reversible condition associated with decrease in physical activity.[76] There is some controversy as to which muscle fiber type declines with age, and some attribute this decline to a selective loss of type II fibers; others report an increase in the proportion of tension developed by the type I fiber. The decline in fiber number is not uniform in all muscles and may be less in those muscles in constant use (e.g., the diaphragm) than in those where use is more intermittent (e.g., the lower extremities). Perhaps the most critical issue is whether the decrease in muscle mass with aging is associated with loss of muscle strength. There is a high correlation between the size of a muscle and its ability to apply force, i.e., its strength-producing characteristics.[74] The apparent diminution of muscle strength with aging may be a feature of the muscle group tested, the exercise and nutritional history of the individual, motivation, and general state of health. Hand grip strength has been most widely assessed. A study of muscles in the ankle joint revealed only a modest decrease in strength up to age 75 among those who remained active. It was not until age 90, which is certainly at the extreme end of the spectrum of aging at the present time, that muscle strength was reduced by half. Loss of muscle strength does not appear to be due to failure of muscle activation[75] and may be due to a population of denervated fibers.[76] It has been noted that "maintenance or initiation of a physically active life style in old age can reduce the degree of muscle weakness and fatigue."[77] The apparent benefits of exercise[77,78] are also associated with a sense of well-being in our health-conscious society; more specific metabolic effects include enhanced insulin sensitivity and glucose tolerance, increased rate of maximum oxygen uptake, decreased blood pressure, and lower levels of triglycerides and cholesterol in plasma.[79] Nevertheless, according to Masoro and McCarter,[79] restricted caloric intake in rats is effective in extending life span, while lifelong wheel running did *not* affect length of life and "did not greatly influence the rate of aging."

The strength of muscles is of great importance to the aging individual in order to diminish the risk of functional decline. Means to preserve muscle strength are part of the growing interest in aging well or "successfully."[80] Since bone is part of the overall lean body mass and bone density decreases with aging, exercise programs are important both to strengthen muscles and to retard so-called inevitable bone loss. There is a physiologic adaptation to training and improvement in performance at any age. Quadriceps strength of men aged 69 to 74 increased after a training program;[78] this was not necessarily related to a change in muscle mass but possibly to recruitment of additional muscle units. "It is apparent that the human biological system has a substantial reserve capacity than can overcome measured degenerative changes that occur with aging."[81]

An experimental study in healthy men age 61 to 81 was undertaken to test whether the administration of biosynthetic human growth hormone could reverse in a relatively short time (6 months) some of the so-called age-related body-compositional decline. The premise on which the study was undertaken was that the reduced availability of growth hormone in late adulthood may contribute to the contraction in lean body mass reflected in "atrophic processes" in skeletal muscle, in a number of organs, and in skin and bone. Indeed, the administration of growth hormone to the men was accompanied by an 8.8 percent increase in lean body mass, a 14.4 percent decrease in adipose tissue mass, and a 1.6 percent increase in average lumbar vertebral bone density.[82] In an editorial accompanying the study and in a brief literature review, Vance[83,84] noted the potential adverse effects of long-term administration of growth hormone on carbohydrate metabolism (glucose intolerance) and the cardiovascular system (hypertension and edema). However, the potential benefits of growth hormone in improving muscle function and exercise capacity in late adult life certainly warrant further study.

TENDON

Tendon is a dense connective tissue made up of cells and macromolecules. Polarized light studies revealed rows of cells that transmit forces between muscle and bone.[85] Type I collagen makes up 70 percent of the dry weight of tendon, with other collagen types also present, including III and VI; the PG includes DS and CS. Stiffness of the tendon increases with age as does nonregainable deformation in cyclic loading.[86] This may increase the tendency for injuries in the event of violent stresses, especially when the tendon or ligament is attached to osteoporotic bone.

Age-related loss in water content of dense connective tissues may reflect decline in GAG. In tendons of aging male rats, reduction in the galactosamine-containing moiety (i.e., CS or DS) occurred, with unchanged HA.[86] Exercise appeared to retard age-related loss of tendon GAG. The biosynthesis and/or molecular assembly of PG are affected by variations in mechanical stimuli on the tendon.

While the PG and type II collagen fibers in which they are enmeshed are the components that provide for the mechanical properties of articular cartilage, the tensile strength that characterizes tendons, ligaments, and the menisci is due to their content of collagen and elastin (fibrous proteins).[87] The particular arrangement of the collagen and elastin chains that has relevance to aging relates to cross-linking based on aldehyde formation from lysine of hydroxylysine side chains. The only enzyme required, lysyl oxidase, serves both collagen and elastin. In elastin, desmosine and isodesmosine are the main cross-linking residues derived from lysine. Inhibited cross-linking is part of the underlying pathology in several inborn diseases of collagen. The relation of cross-linking to aging is not clear, but enhanced cross-linking of the fibrous proteins may contribute to strength of the tendons, while in bone, cross links seem to decrease with age, contributing to mechanical weakness.

THE SPINE: FACET JOINTS AND INTERVERTEBRAL DISCS

The intervertebral disc and facet joints constitute the weight-bearing components of the spine and serve as a three-joint complex that forms a motion segment,[88] allowing for flexibility and resisting compression. The facet joints are synovial or diarthrodial joints, as discussed in the first section of this chapter, and are maximally involved when the disc is compressed and the spine is in extension. Facet osteoarthritis, which will not be further considered here, is "largely if not completely dependent on previous development of changes in the mechanics or height of the intervertebral disc as a result of degeneration."[88]

The intervertebral disc acts as a shock absorber and a weight-bearing element of the spine. The end plates that cover the vertebral bodies are hyaline cartilage, to which the disc is attached by collagen fibers. The collagenous outer portion of the disc is known as the annulus fibrosus; the inner part, a relatively gelatinous central core, is called the nucleus pulposus. Like the articular cartilage, the cells of the annulus and nucleus maintain an extensive extracellular matrix.

The shock-absorbing function occurs when the end plates take the vertical stresses on the spine and transmit them to the elastic annulus by way of the gelatinous nucleus. As in articular cartilage, chondrocytes in the disc produce a highly hydrated PG gel restrained within a network of collagen fibers. Once again, the mechanical properties of a structure undergoing compressive forces are dependent on the interplay between the PG and collagen. The disc PG components are, on average, considerably smaller than those from cartilage. With respect to collagen, the outer annulus contains mostly type I, while chiefly type II collagen is present in the inner annulus and in the nucleus pulposus.[89]

With aging, the water content of the nucleus pulposus drops from over 85 percent to somewhere in the range of 70 to 75 percent; the PG units decrease in size and fewer aggregate with HA. These changes appear to occur at about age 40, when the nucleus pulposus becomes increasingly fibrillar and loses its gel form and capacity for shock absorbance.[89] This places stress on the wall of the annulus. At a weak point, a fissure may occur, with extension of semisolid nuclear gel through the annular wall. However, while disc degeneration increases with old age, this is not invariable; in a study of lumbar discs,[90] 72 percent of the discs from elderly subjects did not show "pathologic disc degeneration." Since weight bearing is concentrated on the lower two lumbar disc spaces (L4–5), disc degeneration and thinning are more prone to occur at these sites.

REFERENCES

1. Poole AR: Physiology of cartilage: Formation, function, and destruction, in Cruess RL (ed): *Musculoskeletal System: Embryology, Biochemistry, and Physiology.* New York, Churchill Livingstone, 1982, p 289.
2. Kuettner KE et al: Protease inhibitors in cartilage. *Arthritis Rheum* 20(suppl 6):124S, 1977.
3. Hamerman D: Mechanisms of disease: The biology of osteoarthritis. *N Engl J Med* 320:1322, 1989.
4. Muir H: Heberden Oration, 1976: Molecular approach to the understanding of osteoarthrosis. *Ann Rheum Dis* 36:199, 1977.
5. von der Mark K et al: The fate of chondrocytes in osteoarthric cartilage: Regeneration, differentiation, or hypertrophy? in Kuettner KE et al (eds): *Articular Cartilage and Osteoarthritis.* New York, Raven Press, 1992, p 221.
6. Aydelotte MB et al: Heterogeneity of articular chondrocytes, in Kuettner KE et al (eds): *Articular Cartilage and Osteoarthritis.* New York, Raven Press, 1992, p 237.
7. Caterson B et al: Modulation of native chondroitin sulfate structure in tissue development and in disease. *J Cell Sci* 97:441, 1990.
8. Hardingham TE et al: Aggrecan, the chondroitin sulfate proteoglycan from cartilage, in Kuettner KE et al

(eds): *Articular Cartilage and Osteoarthritis.* New York, Raven Press, 1992, p 5.
9. Heinegård D, Oldberg A: Structure and biology of cartilage and bone matrix non-collagenous macromolecules. *FASEB J* 3:2042, 1989.
10. Hunziker EB, Schenk RK: Structural organization of proteoglycans in cartilage, in Wight TN, Mechan RP (eds): *Biology of the Proteoglycans.* New York, Academic Press, 1987, p 155.
11. Rosenberg LC: Structure and function of dermatan sulfate proteoglycans in cartilage, in Kuettner KE et al (eds): *Articular Cartilage and Osteoarthritis.* New York, Raven Press,1992, p 45.
12. Eyre DR: The collagens of articular cartilage. *Semin Arthritis Rheum* 21:2, 1991.
13. Daniels K, Solursh M: Modulation of chondrogenesis by the cytoskeleton and extracellular matrix. *J Cell Sci* 100:249, 1991.
14. Thonar EJ-MA, Kuettner KE: Biochemical basis of age-related changes in proteoglycans, in Wight TN, Mecham RP (eds): *Biology of Proteoglycans.* New York, Academic Press, 1987, p 211.
15. Roughley PJ: Changes in cartilage proteoglycan structure during ageing: Origin and effects—A review. *Agents Actions Suppl* 18:19, 1986.
16. Van Kampen GPJ et al: Cartilage response to mechanical force in high-density chondrocyte cultures. *Arthritis Rheum* 28:419, 1985.
17. Unsworth A: Some biomechanical factors in osteoarthritis. *Br J Rheumatol* 23:173, 1984.
18. Brandt KD: Osteoarthritis: Relation to aging. *Clin Geriatr Med* 4:279, 1988.
19. Solursh M: Environmental regulation of limb chondrogenesis, in Kuettner KE, Schlayerbach R, Hascall VC (eds): *Articular Cartilage Biochemistry.* New York, Raven Press, 1986, p 145.
20. Radin EL et al: Mechanical determinants of osteoarthritis. *Semin Arthritis Rheum* 21:12, 1991.
21. Martel-Pelletier J, Pelletier JP: Neutral metalloproteases and age-related changes in human articular cartilage. *Ann Rheum Dis* 46:363, 1987.
22. Morales TI, Hascall VC: Factors involved in the regulation of proteoglycan metabolism in articular cartilage. *Arthritis Rheum* 32:1197, 1989.
23. McQuillan DJ et al: Stimulation of proteoglycan biosynthesis by serum and insulin-like growth factor-I in cultured bovine articular cartilage. *Biochem J* 240:423, 1986.
24. Goldring MB, Goldring SR: Skeletal tissue responses to cytokines. *Clin Orthop* 258:245, 1990.
25. Nathan C, Sporn M: Cytokines in context. *J Cell Biol* 113:981, 1991.
26. Hamerman D, Klagsbrun M: Osteoarthritis: Emerging evidence for cell interactions in the breakdown and remodelling of cartilage. *Am J Med* 78:495, 1985.
27. Wood DD et al: Isolation of an interleukin-1-like factor from human joint effusions. *Arthritis Rheum* 26:975, 1983.
28. Rouslahti E: Proteoglycans in cell regulation. *J Cell Chem* 264:13369, 1989.
29. Rifkin DB, Moscatelli D: Recent developments in the cell biology of basic fibroblast growth factor. *J Cell Biol* 109:1, 1989.
30. Morales TI, Roberts AB: Transforming growth factor β regulates the metabolism of proteoglycans in bovine cartilage organ cultures. *J Biol Chem* 263:12828, 1988.
31. Osborn KD et al: Growth factor stimulation of adult articular cartilage. *J Orthop Res* 7:35, 1989.
32. Cuevas P et al: Basic fibroblast growth factor (FGF) promotes cartilage repair *in vivo. Biochem Biophys Res Commun* 156:611, 1988.
33. Arend WP: Interleukin-1 receptor antagonist: A new member of the interleukin-1 family. *J Clin Invest* 88:1445, 1991.
34. Aulthouse AL et al: Expression of the human chondrocyte phenotype in vitro. *In Vitro Cell Dev Biol* 25:659, 1989.
35. Solursh M: Extracellular matrix and cell surface as determinants of connective tissue differentiation. *Am J Med Genet* 34:30, 1989.
36. Hamerman D et al: A cartilage derived growth factor enhances hyaluronate synthesis and diminishes sulfated glycosaminoglycan synthesis in chondrocytes. *J Cell Physiol* 127:317, 1986.
37. Hill DJ, Han VK: Paracrinology of growth regulation. *J Dev Physiol* 15:91, 1991.
38. Rosen DM et al: Transforming growth factor-β modulates the expression of osteoblasts and chondrocyte phenotypes in vitro. *J Cell Physiol* 134:337, 1988.
39. Wozney JM et al: Growth factors influencing bone development. *J Cell Sci Suppl* 13:149, 1990.
40. Sampath TK et al: Bovine osteogenic protein is composed of dimers of OP-1 and BMP-2A, two members of the transforming growth factor-β superfamily. *J Biol Chem* 265:13198, 1990.
41. Carrington JL et al: Osteogenin (bone morphogenetic protein-3) stimulates cartilage formation by chick limb bud cells in vitro. *Dev Biol* 146:406, 1991.
42. Harmond MF et al: Proteoglycan synthesis in chondrocyte cultures from osteoarthrotic and normal articular cartilage. *Biochim Biophys Acta* 717:190, 1982.
43. Oegema TR Jr, Thompson RC Jr: Metabolism of chondrocytes derived from normal and osteoarthritic human cartilage, in Kuettner KE et al (eds): *Articular Cartilage Biochemistry.* New York, Raven Press, 1986, p 257.
44. Malemud CJ: Biosynthesis of sulfated proteoglycans in vitro by cells derived from human osteochondrophytic spurs of the femoral head. *Connect Tissue Res* 12:319, 1984.
45. Nojima T et al: Secretion of higher level of active proteoglycanases from human osteoarthritic chondrocytes. *Arthritis Rheum* 29:292, 1986.
46. Smith RJ et al: Platelet-derived growth factor potentiates cellular responses of articular chondrocytes to interleukin-1. *Arthritis Rheum* 34:697, 1991.
47. Stevens P, Shatzen EM: Synergism of basic fibroblast growth factor and interleukin-1 β to induce articular cartilage degradation in the rabbit. *Agents Actions* 34:216, 1991.
48. Chandrasekhar S, Harvey AK: Induction of interleukin-1 receptors on chondrocytes by fibroblast growth factor: A possible mechanism for modulation of interleukin-1 activity. *J Cell Physiol* 138:236, 1989.
49. Barland P et al: Electron microscopy of the human synovial membrane. *J Cell Biol* 14:207, 1962.
50. Hamerman D et al: Glycosaminoglycans produced by human synovial cell cultures. *Coll Relat Res* 2:313, 1982.

51. Goto M et al: Spontaneous production of an interleukin-1-like factor by cloned rheumatoid synovial cells in long-term culture. *J Clin Invest* 80:786, 1987.
52. Winchester RJ, Burmester GR: Demonstration of Ia antigens on certain dendritic cells and on a novel elongate cell found in human synovial tissue. *Scand J Immunol* 14:439, 1981.
53. Melnyk VO et al: Synoviocytes synthesize, bind, and respond to basic fibroblast growth factor. *Arthritis Rheum* 33:493, 1990.
54. Hamerman D, Wood DD: Interleukin-1 enhances synovial cell hyaluronate synthesis. *Proc Soc Exp Biol Med* 177:205, 1984.
55. Wells AF et al: Correlation between increased hyaluronan localized in arthritic synovium and the presence of proliferating cells: A role for macrophage-derived factors. *Arthritis Rheum* 35:391, 1992.
56. Abbot SE et al: Isolation and culture of synovial microvascular endothelial cells. *Arthritis Rheum* 35:401, 1992.
57. Hamerman D, Schuster H: Hyaluronate in normal human synovial fluid. *J Clin Invest* 37:56, 1958.
58. Fawthrop F et al: A comparison of normal and pathological synovial fluid. *Br J Rheumatol* 24:61, 1985.
59. Swan D et al: The lubricating activity of human synovial fluids. *Arthritis Rheum* 27:552, 1984.
60. Davis WH Jr et al: Boundary lubricating ability of synovial fluid in degenerative joint disease. *Arthritis Rheum* 28:1367, 1985.
61. Westacott CI et al: Synovial fluid concentration of five different cytokines in rheumatic diseases. *Ann Rheum Dis* 49:676, 1990.
62. Fava R et al: Active and latent forms of transforming growth factor β activity in synovial effusions. *J Exp Med* 169:291, 1989.
63. Hamerman D et al: Growth factors with heparin binding affinity in human synovial fluid. *Proc Soc Exp Biol Med* 186:384, 1987.
64. Aloe L et al: Nerve growth factor in the synovial fluid of patients with chronic arthritis. *Arthritis Rheum* 35:351, 1992.
65. Saxne T, Heinegård D: Synovial fluid analysis of two groups of proteoglycan epitopes distinguishes early and late cartilage lesions. *Arthritis Rheum* 35:385, 1992.
66. Campion GV et al: Levels of keratan sulfate in the serum and synovial fluid of patients with osteoarthritis of the knee. *Arthritis Rheum* 34:1254, 1991.
67. Brandt KD: A pessimistic view of serologic markers for diagnosis and management of osteoarthritis: Biochemical, immunologic and clinicopathologic barriers. *J Rheum* 16(suppl 18):39, 1989.
68. Ghosh P et al: The knee joint meniscus: A fibrocartilage of some distinction. *Clin Orthop* 224:52, 1987.
69. Sasse J et al: Separation of precursor myogenic and chondrogenic cells in early limb bud mesenchyme by a monoclonal antibody. *J Cell Biol* 99:1856, 1984.
70. Karpate G: Muscle: Structure, organization and healing, in Cruess L (ed): *The Musculoskeletal System: Embryology, Biochemistry, and Physiology.* New York, Churchill Livingston, 1982, p 323.
71. Allen RE, Boxhorn LK: Inhibition of skeletal muscle satellite cell differentiation by transforming growth factor-beta. *J Cell Physiol* 133:567, 1987.
72. Kalu DN, Masoro EJ: The biology of aging with particular reference to the musculoskeletal system. *Clin Geriatr Med* 4:257, 1988.
73. Reed RL et al: The relationship between muscle mass and muscle strength in the elderly. *J Am Geriatr Soc* 39:555, 1991.
74. Wilmore JH: The aging of bone and muscle. *Clin Sports Med* 10:231, 1991.
75. Phillips SK et al: The weakness of old age is not due to failure of muscle activation. *J Gerontol* 47:M45, 1992.
76. Faulkner JA et al: Skeletal muscle weakness and fatigue in old age: underlying mechanisms. *Annu Rev Gerontol Geriatr* 10:147, 1990.
77. Montoye HJ: Health, exercise, and athletics: A millenium of observations—A century of research. *Am J Hum Biol* 4:69, 1991.
78. Seto JL, Brewster CE: Musculoskeletal conditioning in the older athlete. *Clin Sports Med* 10:401, 1991.
79. Masoro EJ, McCarter RJM: Aging as a consequence of fuel utilization. *Aging* 3:117, 1991.
80. Rowe JW, Kahn RL: Human aging: Usual and successful. *Science* 237:143, 1987.
81. Jokl P: The biology of aging muscle—Quantitative versus qualitative findings of performance capacity and age, in Nelson CL, Dwyer AP (eds): *The Aging Musculoskeletal System: Physiological and Pathological Problems.* Lexington, MA, Collamore Press, 1984, p 49.
82. Rudman D et al: Effects of human growth hormone in men over 60 years old. *N Engl J Med* 323:1, 1990.
83. Vance ML: Growth hormone for the elderly? *N Engl J Med* 323:52, 1990.
84. Vance ML: Growth hormone therapy in adults. *Trends Endocrinol Metab* 3:46, 1992.
85. Silver FH: *Biological Materials: Structure, Mechanical Properties, and Modeling of Soft Tissues.* New York, New York University Press, 1987.
86. Vailas AC et al: Patella tendon matrix changes associated with aging and voluntary exercise. *J Appl Physiol* 58:1572, 1985.
87. Eyre DR et al: Cross-lining in collagen and elastin. *Annu Rev Biochem* 53:717, 1984.
88. Oegema TR, Bradford DS: The inter-relationship of facet joint osteoarthritis and degenerative disc disease. *Br J Rheum* 30(suppl 1):16, 1991.
89. Urban J, Maroudas A: The chemistry of the intervertebral disc in relation to its physiological function and requirements. *Clin Rheum Dis* 6:51, 1980.
90. Twomey LT, Taylor JR: Age changes in lumbar vertebra and intervertebral discs. *Clin Orthop* 224:97, 1987.

Chapter 81

NONSTEROIDAL ANTI-INFLAMMATORY DRUGS

Jeffrey L. Carson and Brian L. Strom

Nonsteroidal anti-inflammatory drugs (NSAIDs) are the most frequently prescribed class of drugs in the world.[1] The use of these drugs has been steadily rising. It was estimated that in 1985, 30 million patients were taking these drugs worldwide. NSAIDs account for 4 percent of all prescriptions written in the United States and elderly patients are the group that use these drugs most often. NSAIDs are used by over 20 percent of the U.S. population aged 60 or older. Therefore, it is essential that physicians caring for older persons are knowledgeable about the use of these drugs. In this chapter, we provide an overview of the use of NSAIDs in the elderly.

PHARMACOLOGY

NSAIDs are a divergent group of chemical entities that share the property of inhibiting prostaglandin production (Table 81-1). Most NSAIDs are weak organic acids which are absorbed completely from the gastrointestinal tract, tightly bound to albumin, and metabolized by the liver. These drugs inhibit the enzyme cyclooxygenase, which blocks the production of prostaglandins (PG) by suppressing the conversion of arachidonic acid to PGG_2.[2] The in vitro inhibition of prostaglandin synthesis correlates with in vivo anti-inflammatory activity. These drugs also inhibit lipoxygenase production, affect white cell function, unmask T-cell suppressor activity, and block lysosomal enzyme release, superoxide generation, and lymphocyte production. However, the clinical importance of these divergent activities is unknown at the present time.

Aging has an inconsistent effect on the metabolism of NSAIDs.[3] The metabolism of aspirin, ibuprofen, indomethacin, etodolac, and piroxicam are not altered by age. However, the half-lives of ketoprofen, sulindac, diclofenac, and naproxen have been demonstrated to be longer in the elderly in some studies. It has been suggested that the dose of naproxen should be reduced by half in the elderly.[4] In general, however, there is marked variation in clearance of these drugs among individual patients; therefore the plasma half-lives may vary up to fivefold. As with most drugs in the elderly, the lowest effective dose should be used and careful monitoring for side effects should be undertaken.

The clinically most important drug interactions with NSAIDs are displayed in Table 81-2.[5] Drug interactions occur by either of two mechanisms: pharmacokinetic alteration (in which one drug affects the absorption, distribution, or elimination of another drug), and pharmacodynamic interaction (in which one drug affects the sensitivity to the effect of another drug).[4] It is important to emphasize that many potential interactions have not been examined. Furthermore, even when one NSAID has been demonstrated to lead to an interaction, it is not possible to extrapolate the effect to other drugs of the class. Thus, it is important to be very cautious when one is prescribing these drugs in settings where drug interactions may occur.

Several drug interactions deserve emphasis. NSAIDs may increase the risk of bleeding from oral anticoagulants by altering the metabolism of warfarin (Coumadin). NSAIDs also inhibit the antihypertensive effect of beta blockers, diuretics, and angiotensin converting enzyme (ACE) inhibitors by causing water retention and vasoconstriction.[6] If blood pressure rises, discontinuation of an NSAID should be considered. Finally, antacids and cholestyramine may block the absorption of all NSAIDs. If both drugs are needed, they should be taken at different times of the day.

Doses of NSAIDs should be reduced in patients with either cirrhosis or renal disease. Since most NSAIDs are metabolized by the liver and some NSAIDs have been demonstrated to accumulate in patients with liver disease, lower doses should be prescribed. The rationale for lower doses in patients with

TABLE 81-1

Characteristics of the NSAIDs Prescribed in the United States

Generic name	United States Trade Name	Chemical Classification	Dose Range, mg/d	Doses per day	Half-life, hours	Cost,* dollars
Diclofenac	Voltaren	Acetic acid	75–200	2–4	1.25	60.65
Diflunisal	Dolobid	Nonacetated aspirin	500–1000	2	15	51.84
Etodolac	Lodine	Acetic acid	600–1200	2–4	6.7	57.75
Fenoprofen	Nalfon	Propionic acid	600–2400	3–4	2.7	28.75–48.41
Flurbiprofen	Ansaid	Propionic acid	200–300	2–4	5	65.99
Ibuprofen	Motrin Rufen Advil Medipren	Propionic acid	800–3600	3–4	1.7	12.94–23.78
Indomethacin	Indocin	Acetic acid	75–200	3	4.5	10.55–43.63
Ketoprofen	Orudis	Priopionic acid	150–300	3–4	1.7	85.36
Meclofenamate	Meclomen	Fenamic acid	200–400	3–4	3.3	38.74
Nabumetone	Relafen	Nonacetic compound	1000–2000	1	24	54
Naproxen	Naprosyn Anaprox	Propionic acid	500–1500	2	13	40.53
Piroxicam	Feldene	Enolic acid	10–20	1	38	59.38†–68.61
Sulindac	Clinoril	Acetic acid	300–400	2	16	44.83†–51.67
Tolmetin	Tolectin	Acetic acid	600–2000	3–4	2	49.60

*Wholesale cost based on lowest usual dose for rheumatoid arthritis, based on average wholesale price listing in the *Drug Topics Red Book 1992* and *April Update*. Adapted with permission from Medical Letter, 1992.

†Lower cost is for generic price.

renal disease is that they are more susceptible to acute renal toxicity. This is likely due to the role of prostaglandins in maintaining maximal renal blood flow and glomular filtration rate in people with renal disease or injury.

INDICATIONS FOR AND EFFICACY OF NSAIDS

NSAIDs are effective for the treatment of rheumatoid arthritis and osteoarthritis.[2] However, while NSAIDs were developed to treat inflammatory arthritis, they are widely used for other indications including bursitis, tendonitis, and other types of nonarticular rheumatism. They are also effective analgesic and antipyretic agents. NSAIDs reduce the signs of inflammation: heat, erythema, swelling, and pain. However, they have no effect on the basic course of rheumatoid or osteoarthritis and do not protect against tissue or joint injury. Concerns have been raised that NSAIDs may lead to chondrocyte injury and/or accelerate osteoarthritis,[7] but this finding has not been consistently demonstrated and requires a definitive clinical trial.[8]

There are no large clinical trials that have consistently demonstrated that one NSAID drug is consistently more efficacious than other agents. For the most part, all of the NSAIDs can be used interchangeably. However, there is marked variation in the response of individual patients to individual drugs.[9] Patients may have individual preferences for specific drugs and may dramatically improve with one agent but not another. Drugs should be given for approximately 1 to 2 weeks to establish efficacy before changing to another agent.[10] Despite the fact that different indications are emphasized for different drugs, the pharmacologic properties of these drugs are similar. The more recently marketed NSAIDs offer no important clinical advantages over older agents, and—like all new drugs—should be used cautiously until the full side-effects profile is known.

ALTERNATIVE THERAPY

NSAIDs are indicated for patients with inflammatory arthritis, such as rheumatoid arthritis. However, most uses of NSAIDs are osteoarthritis, soft-tissue injuries, or acute and chronic pain. Therefore, this discussion is confined to these latter indications.

Bradley et al.[11] conducted a randomized clinical trial comparing acetaminophen (4000 mg/day), low-dose ibuprofen (1200 mg/day), and high-dose ibuprofen (2400 mg/day) in patients with degenerative joint disease of the knee. After 4 weeks, 40 percent of each group improved. However, the amount of improvement in overall pain, rest pain, and walking pain was generally small (2 to 15 percent). Several other studies have found similar results. Thus, acetometophin may

TABLE 81-2

Drug Interactions with NSAIDs

Drug	NSAID	Effect
Pharmacokinetic interactions		
NSAID affecting other drug		
Oral anticoagulants	Phenylbutazone Oxyphenbutazone	Inhibition of metabolism, increasing anticoagulant effect
Lithium	Probably all (except possibly sulindac and aspirin)	Inhibition of renal excretion, increasing concentrations, and risk of toxicity
Oral hypoglycemic agents	Phenylbutazone Oxyphenbutazone Apazone	Inhibition of metabolism of sulfonylurea drugs, prolonging their half-life and increasing the risk of hypoglycemia
Phenytoin	Phenylbutazone Oxyphenbutazone	Inhibition of metabolism of phenytoin, increasing plasma phenytoin concentration and risk of toxicity
Methotrexate (high nonrheumatologic dose)	Others	Displacement of phenytoin from plasma protein, reducing total concentration for the same unbound (active) concentration
Digoxin	All	Potential reduction in renal function (particularly in very young and very old patients), reducing digoxin clearance and increasing plasma digoxin concentration and risk of toxicity (no interaction if renal function normal)
Aminoglycosides	All	Reduction in renal function in susceptible persons, lowering aminoglycoside clearance and increasing plasma aminoglycoside concentration
Antacids	Indomethacin Others	Variable effects of different preparations: rate and extent of absorption of indomethacin reduced by aluminum-containing antacids
Probenecid	Probably all	Reduction in metabolism and renal clearance of NSAIDs and acyl glucuronide metabolites, which are hydrolyzed back to parent drug
Barbiturates	Phenylbutazone, possibly others	Increased metabolic clearance of NSAID
Cholestyramine	Naproxen and probably others	Anion-exchange resin binding of NSAIDs in gut, reducing rate (and possibly extent) of absorption
Metoclopramide	Aspirin and others	Increased rate and extent of absorption of aspirin in patients with migraine
Pharmacodynamic interactions		
NSAID affecting other drug		
Antihypertensive agents Beta blockers Diuretics Angiotensin converting enzyme inhibitors	Indomethacin Others (possibly except sulindac)	Reduction in hypotensive effect, probably related to inhibition of prostaglandin synthesis in kidneys (producing retention of salt and water) and blood vessels (producing increased vasoconstriction)
Diuretics	Indomethacin Others (possibly except sulindac)	Reduction in natriuretic and diuretic effects; may exacerbate congestive cardiac failure
Anticoagulants	All	Damage to mucosa of gastrointestinal tract and inhibition of platelet aggregation, both increasing risk of gastrointestinal bleeding in patients taking anticoagulants
Combination of NSAIDS with increased risk of toxicity	All	Combination associated with increased risk of hemodynamic renal failure
General		
Triamterene	Indomethacin	Potentiation of nephrotoxicity, even in subjects with normal renal function
Potassium-sparing	All	Potassium retention and hyperkalemia

SOURCE: Modified with permission from Brooks PM, Day RO: Nonsteroidal anti-inflammatory drugs—differences and similarities. *N Engl J Med* 324:1716, 1991.

be as effective as NSAIDs, but acetometophin has a much lower incidence of serious side effects.

More limited data also suggest that supervised isometric and isotonic exercises increase function and decrease pain.[12] Kovar et al.[13] evaluated the effect of supervised walking and patient education in 102 patients with osteoarthritis of the knee in a randomized controlled trial. Patients randomized to the walking program increased their functional status by 39 percent, had 27 percent less arthritis pain, and used less medication ($p = .08$). In addition, physical conditioning can improve aerobic capacity, endurance, ability to walk, and sense of well-being. Whether these forms of therapy add anything to pharmacological therapy is unknown.

ADVERSE EFFECTS

Gastrointestinal

The most common adverse drug reactions from NSAIDs are listed in Table 81-3. The gastrointestinal system is the most frequent site of adverse drug reactions. Gastrointestinal symptoms have been reported to occur in 10 to 61 percent of exposed patients. The spectrum of these reactions ranges from mild symptoms, such as indigestion, to ulcer formation and life-threatening gastrointestinal hemorrhage.

The association between NSAIDs and gastrointestinal toxicity has been documented through multiple pharmacoepidemiologic studies. These studies were recently summarized using metaanalysis.[14] Data summarized from 9 case-control studies and 7 cohort studies found that the overall risk of developing serious gastrointestinal complications was 2.7 times greater (95 percent confidence interval, 2.5 to 3.0) in patients exposed to NSAIDs than in unexposed patients. The risk was higher (odds ratio 5.5; 95 percent confidence interval 4.6 to 6.6) in patients 60 years of age or older than in patients less than 60 years of age (odds ratio 1.6; 95 percent confidence interval, 1.1 to 2.5). These and other data[15,16] also suggested that the risk was highest during the initial months of exposure, in patients with concomitant corticosteroid and oral anticoagulant exposure, and in heavy alcohol users. A dose-response relationship has been demonstrated in several studies.[15,16] Some but not all studies suggest a higher risk of gastrointestinal toxicity with piroxicam. However, like all drugs for the elderly, piroxicam should be prescribed at the lowest dose possible.

NSAIDs are thought to cause serious gastrointestinal side effects through the inhibition of prostaglandins.[17] Prostaglandins support the defense mechanisms of the gastric mucosa by stimulating the production of mucous and bicarbonate secretion and by inhibiting gastric acid and gastrin secretion. In addition, direct mucosal contact by some NSAIDs leads to mucosal injury.

Both gastric and duodenal ulcers from NSAIDs may be prevented with prophylactic use of misoprostol, a prostaglandin analog.[18,19] H_2 receptor blockers have been demonstrated to prevent duodenal but not gastric ulcers.[20] Omeprazole reduces the risk of gastric ulcer.[21] However, each of these prophylactic trials were short-term studies, and the long-term efficacy of these drugs is unknown. Furthermore, it is unclear how long prophylactic therapy should be continued. Misoprostol is indicated only in patients with prior peptic ulcer disease in whom use of NSAID is absolutely necessary. The most common side effect of misoprostol is diarrhea.

TABLE 81-3

Common Adverse Drug Reactions from Nonsteroidal Anti-inflammatory Drugs

Site	**Adverse reaction**
Gastrointestinal tract	Gastric ulcer Duodenal ulcer Upper gastrointestinal bleeding Gastritis Intestinal perforation
Kidney	Acute renal failure Chronic renal failure Interstitial nephritis Nephrotic syndrome Hyperkalemia Hyponatremia Acute flank pain syndrome
Liver	Acute hepatitis Fulminant hepatitis Chronic hepatitis
Hematologic	Neutropenia Aplastic anemia
Other	Anaphylactoid reactions Skin reactions

Hepatic

Nearly every NSAID has been associated with liver disease in case reports.[22] The clinical spectrum of liver disease thought to be due to NSAIDs ranges from mild elevation of liver enzyme tests to severe hepatocellular injury resulting in death. Both hepatitic and cholestatic patterns of injury have been seen. Benoxaprofen is the NSAID best documented to cause acute liver disease. A series of reports of fatal liver disease in the early 1980s led to the worldwide withdrawal of this drug from the market.[23] Many of the patients affected were elderly. Many cases of serious liver disease have been reported in patients taking NSAIDs other than benoxaprofen, but no controlled studies have demonstrated an association.

The most compelling evidence to support a causal relationship between NSAIDs and hepatitis are case reports of recurrent hepatitis on inadvertent rechallenge with the offending drug. Sulindac has repeatedly been reported to lead to hepatitis on rechallenge.[22] Numerous case reports suggesting an association between diclofenac and hepatitis have recently been published, including positive rechallenges.[24]

However, two epidemiologic studies have not found an association between NSAIDs and liver disease. Johnson et al.[25] evaluated the frequency of hospitalization 3 months after ibuprofen exposure in 13,230 members of a health maintenance organization. Although there were no hospitalizations for liver disease, all the patients were less than 65 years of age, and ibuprofen was mostly used for short periods of time. Carson and colleagues[26] assessed the incidence of hospitalization for acute symptomatic hepatitis in a case-control study. The incidence of hepatitis was 2.2 cases per 100,000 people per year and the odds ratio for NSAID use was 1.2 (95 percent confidence interval, 0.5 to 2.8). These results suggest that liver disease from NSAIDs is an infrequent clinical problem.

Renal

Acute renal disease has been reported to be associated with nearly all NSAIDs in case reports. While early reports suggested that sulindac was renal sparing,[27] others have failed to reproduce these findings.[28] Many of the renal adverse reactions, acute renal failure, water retention, hyponatremia and hyperkalemia, can be explained by the physiologic role of renal prostaglandins in patients with altered hemodynamics and renal disease.[29] The mechanism of the acute flank pain syndrome with reversible acute renal failure is thought to involve the crystallization of uric acid in the renal tubules.[30]

Prostaglandins have little effect on renal function under normal circumstances. However, prostaglandins are very important for the maintenance of renal hemodynamics in patients with congestive heart failure, volume contraction, and cirrhosis. These three conditions reduce renal blood flow and lead to increased production of vasoconstriction mediators: norepinephrine, renin, and angiotensin. Renal prostaglandins produce vasodilation and block the vasoconstriction effect of norepinephrine and angiotensin. If NSAIDs block the production of renal prostaglandin, renal failure may result from unopposed vasoconstriction. Thus patients with effective volume depletion are at special risk for acute renal failure when given NSAIDs.

Prostaglandins also serve an important function in patients with renal disease. Patients with chronic parenchymal disease require the maximum vasodilatory effect that prostaglandins mediate. When prostaglandin production is blocked, the glomerular filtration rate may fall.

NSAIDs also influence fluid and electrolyte balance. NSAIDs enhance sensitivity of renal tubular cells to antidiuretic hormone and may lead to hyponatremia and fluid retention. Up to 10 percent of patients using NSAIDs have been reported to develop edema. Hyperkalemia also may develop by an NSAID-induced hypoaldosterone, hyporenin state which blocks the renal excretion of potassium.

There are inconsistent epidemiologic data linking NSAIDs with chronic renal failure. Beard et al.,[31] in a case-control study of patients with acute renal failure undergoing renal biopsy, found no overall risk (odds ratio 1.6; 95 percent confidence interval 0.9 to 3.0) associated with NSAIDs, although in patients over 53 years of age the odds ratio for NSAID use was 3.9 (95 percent confidence interval, 1.4 to 11.5). Sandler et al.[32] also performed a case-control study composed of cases defined as patients admitted to the hospital with a creatinine persistently elevated above 1.5 mg/dl. While an overall risk from NSAIDs was evident (odds ratio 2.1; 95 percent confidence interval 1.1 to 4.1), the risk was isolated to men above age 65, in whom the risk was 10.0. Morans et al.,[33] in a case-control study of patients with end-stage renal disease, identified a risk of 2.5 (95 percent confidence interval, 1.2 to 5.2) with aspirin. Gurwitz and colleagues monitored renal function after initiation of treatment with a NSAID in 114 patients (mean age 87) living in a long-term-care facility.[34] Renal function declined by 50 percent in 13 percent of patients. The two factors associated with the reduced renal function was concomitant use of loop diuretics and use of high-dose NSAIDs. However, Fox and Jick[35] found no risk of renal disease associated with NSAIDs, and their data suggested a much lower incidence of clinically important renal disease. Thus, further data are needed to clarify the risk of NSAID-induced renal failure.

Hypersensitivity Reactions

Numerous isolated case reports indicate that nonsteroidal anti-inflammatory drugs cause allergic and/or hypersensitivity reactions. In March 1983, zomepirac was recalled by its manufacturer because of reports of five deaths that were possibly related to allergic or hypersensitivity reactions. Two studies have confirmed the presence of the risk of hypersensitivity reactions from NSAIDs and demonstrated that the risk is highest when the drugs are used intermittently.[36,37] Hypersensitivity reactions probably occur with all NSAIDs.

Hematologic

Since the recognition of phenylbutazone-induced agranulocytosis,[38] there has been concern whether other NSAIDs may cause the same problem. Multiple case reports of agranulocytosis have been reported in patients taking other NSAIDs. Two case-control studies have been performed to address this question. The

International Agranulocytosis and Aplastic Anemia Study found an increased risk of these two conditions with phenylbutazone and indomethacin.[39] The study was too small to examine other NSAIDs. However, the incidence rate for agranulocytosis absent other risk factors for the disease was very small. A second study using a Medicaid data base found that neutropenia was associated with the use of NSAIDs as a class, but there were inadequate data to examine most individual NSAIDs.[40]

PRINCIPLES OF NSAID USE IN THE ELDERLY

The most frequent indications for NSAIDs in the elderly are osteoarthritis and acute pain syndromes. Prior to prescribing an NSAID, the physician should consider other forms of therapy. For example, acetaminophen has been demonstrated to be effective in 40 percent of patients with osteoarthritis, and might be tried first in their treatment. It has the advantages of being inexpensive and safe, with minimal short-term side effects. Alternatively, physical therapy, supervised exercise, and/or weight loss in patients with hip and lower-extremity osteoarthritis may be effective. These other forms of therapy should definitely be offered to patients at high risk of developing an adverse reaction from NSAIDs.

If an NSAID is to be used, then low-dose ibuprofen (200 mg qid) might be considered first. Ibuprofen is the least expensive NSAID and is one of the safest of the available drugs. Studies which have compared the gastrointestinal toxicity of these drugs, their most frequent adverse reaction, have generally found ibuprofen among the safest of the NSAIDs. In addition, the adverse drug reactions are dose-related, and this drug is available in the lowest dose on the market.

There is little evidence to suggest that there are important clinical differences in the efficacy of or adverse reactions from the remaining NSAIDs. The patient should be started with the lowest dose and the drug can be increased as needed until the maximum dose is reached, relief of symptoms is achieved, or side effects develop. There are large differences in individual patient responses and preferences to these agents which cannot be predicted prior to beginning therapy. If the initial agents are ineffective, several other drugs should be tried.

To avoid the expense and side effects of these drugs, the physician should avoid long, open-ended courses of treatment. Short courses (1 to 2 weeks) of these drugs should be tried first. The natural history of osteoarthritis includes exacerbations and remissions. Treatment may be required only during times when symptoms are at their worst. Some patients' symptoms may be controlled by administering the drug on an "as needed" basis or with only an evening dose to allow for sleep.[2] Symptoms from osteoarthritis often result from mechanisms other than inflammation. However, in patients with significant inflammation, therapy with higher doses for longer periods of time may be required. Progress should be monitored frequently, particularly during the first several weeks. Besides determining the clinical response, laboratory studies should be performed to evaluate patients for side effects (renal, liver, and blood), and blood pressures must be checked. There is no evidence that a combination of two NSAIDs is more effective than one drug alone, and the side effects of two drugs are additive. Thus, only one of these drugs should be used at a time.

These drugs should not be used in patients at high risk for adverse drug reactions; these drugs are rarely if ever lifesaving. Patients with a prior history of peptic ulcer disease or those receiving oral anticoagulants should avoid these drugs. If an NSAID must be used in a patient with a prior history of peptic ulcer disease, misoprostol should be considered, and with such a patient it is even more important than usual to use the lowest possible dose of NSAID for the shortest period of time. In patients at risk for side effects, if one drug is not effective, the physician should try another agent before increasing the dose. Care must be taken in prescribing these drugs for patients with volume depletion, congestive heart failure, or cirrhosis. Renal function should be monitored early, since these side effects may develop within days and with low doses.

REFERENCES

1. *The National Disease and Therapeutic Index, 1981–84.* Ambler, PA, IMS America.
2. Paulis HE: Nonsteroidal antiinflammatory drugs, in Kelley WN et al (eds): *Textbook of Rheumatology,* 3rd ed. Philadelphia, Saunders, 1991, chap 46, pp 765–789.
3. Johnson AG, Day RO: The problems and pitfalls of NSAID therapy in the elderly, part 1. *Drugs Aging* 2:130, 1991.
4. Brater DC: Drug-drug and drug-disease interactions with nonsteroidal antiinflammatory drugs. *Am J Med* 80(suppl 1A):62, 1986.
5. Brooks PM, Day RO: Nonsteroidal antiinflammatory drugs—differences and similarities. *N Engl J Med* 324:1716, 1991.
6. Radack K, Deck C: Do nonsteroidal anti-inflammatory drugs interfere with blood pressure control in hypertensive patients? *J Gen Intern Med* 2:108, 1987.
7. Rashad S et al: Effect of nonsteroidal anti-inflamma-

tory drugs on the course of osteoarthritis. *Lancet* 2:519, 1989.

8. Pelletier JP, Martel-Pelletier J: The therapeutic effects of NSAIDs and corticosteroids in osteoarthritis: To be or not to be. *J Rheumatol* 16:266, 1989.
9. Huskinson EC et al: Four new anti-inflammatory drugs: Responses and variations. *Br Med J* 1:1048, 1976.
10. Greene JM, Winickoff RN: Cost-conscious prescribing of nonsteroidal anti-inflammatory drugs for adults with arthritis. *Arch Intern Med* 152:1995, 1992.
11. Bradley JD et al: Comparison of an antiinflammatory dose of ibuprofen, an analgesic dose of ibuprofen, and acetaminophen in the treatment of patients with osteoarthritis of the knee. *N Engl J Med* 325:87, 1991.
12. Liang MH, Fortin P: Management of osteoarthritis of the hip and knee. *N Engl J Med* 325:125, 1991.
13. Kovar PA et al: Supervised fitness walking in patients with osteoarthritis of the knee: A randomized controlled trial. *Ann Intern Med* 116:529, 1992.
14. Gabriel SE et al: Risk of serious gastrointestinal complications related to use of nonsteroidal anti-inflammatory drugs: A meta-analysis. *Ann Intern Med* 115:787, 1991.
15. Carson JL et al: The association of nonsteroidal anti-inflammatory drugs with upper GI bleeding. *Arch Intern Med* 147:85, 1987.
16. Griffin MR et al: Nonsteroidal anti-inflammatory drug use and increased risk for peptic ulcer disease in elderly persons. *Ann Intern Med* 114:257, 1991.
17. Soll AH: The pathogenesis of ulcers caused by nonsteroidal anti-inflammatory drugs, in Soll AH (moderator): Nonsteroidal anti-inflammatory drugs and peptic ulcer disease. *Ann Intern Med* 114:307, 1991.
18. Graham DY et al: Prevention of NSAID-induced gastric ulcer with misoprostol: Multicentre, double-blind, placebo-controlled trial. *Lancet* 2:1277, 1988.
19. Roth S et al: Misoprostol heals gastroduodenal injury in patients with rheumatoid arthritis receiving aspirin. *Arch Intern Med* 149:775, 1989.
20. Ehsanullah RSB et al: Prevention of gastroduodenal damage induced by non-steroidal anti-inflammatory drugs: controlled trial of ranitidine. *Br Med J* 297:1017, 1988.
21. Walan A et al: Effect of omeprazole and ranitidine on ulcer healing and relapse rates in patients with benign gastric ulcer. *N Engl J Med* 320:69, 1989.
22. Zimmerman HJ: Update of hepatotoxicity due to classes of drugs in common clinical use: Non-steroidal drugs, anti-inflammatory drugs, antibiotics, antihypertensives, and cardiac and psychotropic agents. *Semin Liver Dis* 10:322, 1990.
23. Taggert HM, Alderice JM: Fatal cholestatic jaundice in elderly patients taking benoxaprofen. *Br Med J* 284:1372, 1982.
24. Helfgott SM et al: Diclofenac-associated hepatotoxicity. *JAMA* 264:2660, 1990.
25. Johnson JH et al: A follow-up study of ibuprofen users. *J Rheumatol* 12:549, 1985.
26. Carson JL et al: Safety of NSAIDs with respect to acute liver disease. *Arch Intern Med* (in press).
27. Ciabattoni G et al: Effects of sulindac and ibuprofen in patients with chronic glomerular disease: Evidence for the dependence of renal function on prostacyclin. *N Engl J Med* 310:279, 1984.
28. Roberts DG et al: Sulindac is not renal sparing in man. *Clin Pharmacol Ther* 38:258, 1985.
29. Clive DM, Stoff JS: Renal syndromes associated with nonsteroidal antiinflammatory drugs. *N Engl J Med* 310:563, 1984.
30. Strom BL et al: The epidemiology of the acute flank pain syndrome from suprofen. *Clin Pharmacol Ther* 46:693, 1989.
31. Beard K et al: Nonsteroidal anti-inflammatory drugs and acute renal disease: A case control study. Pharmacoepidemiol Drug Safety 1:3, 1992.
32. Sandler DP et al: Nonsteroidal anti-inflammatory drugs and the risk for chronic renal disease. *Ann Intern Med* 115:165, 1991.
33. Morans M et al: End-stage renal disease and non-narcotic analgesics: A case-control study. *Br J Clin Pharmacol* 30:717, 1990.
34. Gurwitz JH et al: Nonsteroidal anti-inflammatory drug-associated azotemia in the very old. *JAMA* 264:471, 1990.
35. Fox DA, Jick H: Nonsteroidal anti-inflammatory drugs and renal disease. *JAMA* 251:1299, 1984.
36. Strom BL et al: The effect of indication on hypersensitivity reactions associated with zomepirac sodium and other nonsteroidal antiinflammatory drugs. *Arth Rheum* 30:1142, 1987.
37. Strom BL et al: The effect of indication on the risk of hypersensitivity reactions associated with tolmetin sodium vs. other nonsteroidal antiinflammatory drugs. *J Rheumatol* 15:695, 1988.
38. Inman WHW: Study of fatal bone marrow depression with special reference to phenylbutazone and oxyphenbutazone. *Br Med J* 1:1500, 1977.
39. International Agranulocytosis and Aplastic Anemia Study. Risks of agranulocytosis and aplastic anemia: A first report of their relation to drug use with special reference to analgesics. *JAMA* 256:1749, 1986.
40. Strom BL et al: Nonsteroidal anti-inflammatory drugs and neutropenia. *Arch Intern Med* (in press).

Chapter 82

POLYMYALGIA RHEUMATICA AND GIANT CELL ARTERITIS

Gerald M. Eisenberg

Of all musculoskeletal conditions, none are so closely identified with the geriatric population as polymyalgia rheumatica (PMR) and giant cell arteritis (GCA). Because these entities may present with a myriad of signs and symptoms, an index of suspicion must be maintained to consider these diagnoses when the presentation is not typical. Often a patient may have vague symptoms, have seen a variety of physicians, and have experienced a protracted course. The patient and/or physician may mistakenly believe that these are merely symptoms of growing older or that depression may be taking a toll. However, the appropriate diagnosis and therapy will not only relieve the patient's symptoms but also avert potentially catastrophic sequelae.

PMR and GCA are separate but closely related entities that have been recognized for the past 100 years.[1] Symptoms of PMR are noted in up to 60 percent of patients with GCA, while a smaller percentage of patients with PMR has histologic evidence of GCA.[2] Although an elevated sedimentation rate is considered the laboratory hallmark of these conditions, there are numerous reports documenting both PMR and histologically proven GCA in patients with normal sedimentation rates.[3] A trial of steroids should, therefore, be considered in the appropriate patient despite a normal or modestly elevated sedimentation rate. Of major importance is the awareness that both PMR and GCA may present atypically, suggesting an infectious, metabolic, or malignant syndrome.

PATHOGENESIS AND ETIOLOGY

The etiology of PMR and GCA is unknown. The fact that GCA involves only those arteries with elastic laminae suggests an autoimmune process directed against elastic tissue. Since GCA and PMR occur only in the elderly, senescense of immune surveillance may be implicated as the cause of abnormal immune hyperactivity. Immune complex levels in serum have been correlated with disease activity by some investigators but not others.[4] Others have demonstrated a higher incidence of anticardiolipin antibody in patients with GCA than in those with "pure" PMR or no disease.[5] They suggest that IgG-type cardiolipin antibody may serve as a marker for GCA complicating PMR and that antiphospholipid antibodies may play a role in the vasculopathy associated with GCA. Another interpretation of the same data, however, would suggest that these antibodies arise as the result of endothelial injury.

Familial aggregation of both PMR and GCA has been described, despite the lack of association of HLA-A, B, and C antigens with these syndromes. There is, however, an increased prevalence of HLA-DR3 and/or HLA-DR4 in patients with PMR associated with GCA. Interestingly, the same finding was not seen in PMR or GCA alone.[6]

Epidemiologic evidence suggests that the incidence of PMR and GCA varies with ethnicity and, perhaps, geography as well. The highest incidence of both syndromes is seen in northern Europeans and in Americans of Scandinavian ancestry. A prevalence rate of 17 cases/100,000 persons over age 50 has been noted by investigators from the Mayo Clinic, while the prevalence is 1.6/100,000 in Shelby County, Tennessee, and only 0.5/100,000 in Israel.[7–9] Although it is now clear that both PMR and GCA occur in blacks, the Shelby County study demonstrated a sevenfold increase in prevalence in whites as compared to blacks. Some argue that this racial disparity may be related to poorer surveillance and underdiagnosis in black communities.

Autopsy studies demonstrated a 1 percent overall prevalence of GCA, suggesting that PMR and GCA remain underdiagnosed during life. Consideration of these diseases in patients with a broader range of signs and symptoms may result in more accurate diagnoses and improved patient outcome.

CLINICAL PRESENTATION

The diagnosis of PMR and GCA rests with the recognition of characteristic signs and symptoms, very frequently accompanied by evidence of systemic inflammatory reaction. PMR is characterized by aching and stiffness in the shoulder and hip girdles. Profound morning stiffness is especially suggestive and should be specifically sought out during the history. It is quite common for an affected individual to require help in getting out of bed in the morning. The condition is seldom seen before the age of 50, and its mean age of onset is 70 years.[10] The onset may be either very abrupt or gradual. The stiffness about the hips and shoulders may become generalized, involving the neck and knees and even extending into the wrists and fingers. Prominent constitutional complaints include malaise, weight loss, low-grade fever, and depression. Indeed, constitutional complaints may be the predominant presenting symptom.[11]

The physical examination may demonstrate difficulty with movement of the proximal joints. Arising from a chair or moving the arms above the head may be difficult or impossible. Although the patient will describe weakness, objective muscle testing demonstrates good strength unless general inanition has resulted in disuse atrophy and weakness. Findings are likely to be more impressive if the patient is examined in the morning. Despite the patient's subjective discomfort, the painful areas are not usually tender. Visible inflammatory features are generally not present, although swelling and effusions have occasionally been noted in the knees or small joints of the wrists and fingers.

Taken as a separate entity, the classic features of GCA are a reflection of inflammation with resulting ischemia in the distribution of the temporal artery (i.e., temporal arteritis). These features include temporal headache, generally unilateral, accompanied by temporal artery swelling and tenderness. However, if one were to limit the possibility of this diagnosis solely to those who present with this picture, many patients would remain undiagnosed, as they may present with other symptoms (Table 82-1). It is important to remember that symptoms of PMR occur in up to 60 percent of GCA patients and actually may be the initial manifestations in one-third of GCA patients.[2] Fever, malaise, and weight loss may predominate, suggesting a picture of "failure to thrive" in the older adult. Although fever is usually low-grade, the fever curve is occasionally hectic and high, suggesting a septic picture.

Symptoms of visual compromise occur in one-third of patients and are a harbinger of the most feared consequence of GCA, permanent visual loss. Fortunately, increased recognition of this problem and aggressive steroid therapy have resulted in a rate of permanent visual loss of no greater than 10 to 15 percent.[11] Transient visual symptoms include brief visual loss (amaurosis fugax) related to ischemia of the posterior ciliary artery or diplopia because of compromised blood flow to the nerves of the extraocular muscles. In patients with transient symptoms, the funduscopic examination is generally normal. Half of patients with permanent visual loss experience monocular blindness, with the other half experiencing binocular loss.[11] Most often, permanent loss is preceded by transient symptoms for days or weeks. In patients with bilateral loss, the second eye is often involved within days of the first. Thus, recognition of GCA as a cause of monocular blindness is of critical importance in preventing total blindness. Since visual loss is related to local ischemia, the funduscopic exam will demonstrate optic ischemia.

Recently, neurologic complications involving both the central and peripheral nervous systems have been recognized as sequelae of GCA (Table 82-2).[12] GCA should be considered in patients presenting with mononeuritis, stroke, or progressive dementia. In patients with documented GCA, all of these ischemic neurologic sequelae have been described.[13]

Intermittent claudication may occur in multiple muscle groups, especially in the muscles of mastication. In fact, jaw claudication strongly suggests the diagnosis of GCA if mechanical dental factors are eliminated as a cause of symptoms.[14] Ischemia of the vocal musculature may result in onset of hoarseness

TABLE 82-1

Presenting Signs and Symptoms in Giant Cell Arteritis

Temporal headache with tender temporal artery (temporal arteritis)
Shoulder/hip girdle stiffness and pain (PMR picture)
"Failure to thrive" in the elderly
Fever
Weight loss
Malaise
Nonspecific headache
Jaw claudication
Transient visual complaints and occasionally irreversible blindness
Extremity claudication
Aortic arch syndrome (aortic aneurysm)

TABLE 82-2

Neurologic Manifestations in GCA

Depression	Neuropathies
Deafness	Tinnitus
Diabetes insipidus	Vertigo
Diplopia	Headache
Paralysis	Tremor
Stroke	Dementia
Seizures	Psychosis
TIA	Confusion
Syncope	Aseptic meningitis
Ataxia	Transverse myelopathy

SOURCE: Adapted from Reich et al.[12]

or cough, representing the presenting complaints in up to 5 percent of GCA patients.[15] Claudication may involve the arms or legs, due to vasculitis in the aorta or its branches. Examination of these patients reveals bruits in the neck or proximal extremities and asymmetrical pulse deficits.[16]

PATHOLOGY AND LABORATORY FEATURES

The only characteristic laboratory abnormality seen in PMR and GCA is an elevation of the Westergren sedimentation rate usually above 50 mm/h. Elevations greater than 100 mm/h may be seen in either disease. Other markers of the acute-phase response, such as elevated C-reactive protein, are seen also. However, a normal sedimentation rate should not dissuade the physician from considering a temporal artery biopsy or a trial of steroids in patients with typical signs and symptoms. The sedimentation rate is normal in up to 15 percent of patients.

Both PMR and GCA are considered to be "serologically silent," that is, not associated with antinuclear antibody (ANA), rheumatoid factor, or other autoantibodies. Senescence of the immune system, however, will result in an increase in levels of ANA or rheumatoid factor in the elderly, thus occasionally confusing the clinical picture. Von Willebrand factor antigen is synthesized in the vascular endothelium. Thus, elevated levels of this antigen represent a sensitive measurement of disease activity in patients with GCA, reflecting endothelial inflammation and destruction.[17] Liver enzymes may be mildly elevated in either PMR or GCA, although significant liver dysfunction is unusual. Mild anemia may result from chronic inflammation. Unfortunately, none of these laboratory measurements is specific for GCA or PMR or predictive of serious sequelae, such as visual involvement.

Nuclear imaging of bone with technetium 99m pertechnatate demonstrates inflammatory uptake in the shoulders, suggesting a low-grade synovitis as the source of proximal myalgia in PMR patients.[18] Several arthroscopic studies confirm nonspecific synovitis in the shoulder.[19]

The definitive diagnosis of GCA rests with a careful histologic examination of a sizable section of temporal artery. GCA is characterized by alternating areas of involved and noninvolved segments of the arteries. Thus, it is imperative to obtain a biopsy segment of temporal artery measuring no less than 2.5 cm in length. Of equal importance is the detailed examination of multiple sections by the pathologist. While somewhat inconvenient, temporal artery biopsy is generally well tolerated and quite safe. The biopsy can be performed in the outpatient setting with local anesthesia. Some centers have demonstrated a 10 to 15 percent increase in positive yield if contralateral biopsy is performed following a negative biopsy on one side.[11]

Temporal artery biopsy should be undertaken as soon as the diagnosis of GCA is considered. Any delay between institution of steroid therapy and biopsy will result in a predictable decrease in positive findings. In one study, the percentage of positive biopsies in untreated patients was 82 percent. This percentage fell to 10 percent in patients receiving 1 week or more of steroid therapy.[20]

Histologically, GCA causes inflammatory changes within the media of all arteries containing internal elastic membrane. In fact, the relationship between inflammation and the internal elastic membrane suggests a pathologic process specific for this structure. The internal elastic membrane may be disrupted by a mononuclear cell infiltrate. In full-blown cases, mononuclear infiltration throughout the entire vessel wall is noted, along with granulomas containing multinucleated giant cells.

Any patient suspected of GCA should undergo biopsy, as the morbidity associated with high-dose steroid therapy demands as accurate a diagnosis as possible. The question of temporal artery biopsy in patients with PMR but without specific symptoms of GCA is more difficult to answer. While the presence of GCA is noted in a variable percentage of PMR patients, it is clear that the majority of PMR patients will respond completely to low-dose steroids. Biopsy should, therefore, be considered only in those PMR patients with incomplete response to low-dose steroids or persistent elevation of sedimentation rate despite treatment.

DIFFERENTIAL DIAGNOSIS

The variety of presentations of PMR and GCA make the differential diagnosis quite extensive. Depression, early dementia, and fibromyalgia are all conditions associated with malaise, weight loss, and muscle aches. However, all are marked by a normal sedimentation rate and a lack of significant response to low-dose steroids. Fever, with increased acute-phase reactants, appetite loss, and aching may represent an infectious process, but localizing signs should suggest a specific nidus of infection. Chronic sinusitis, urinary tract infection, or subacute infectious endocarditis may be difficult to diagnose by symptomatology alone.

The relationship between malignancy and PMR has been repeatedly evaluated. Certainly, both of these disorders are seen much more frequently in the elderly, but there is not a greater incidence of malignancy in the people with PMR. However, certain malignancies may present with PMR-like symptoms, especially diffuse hematologic malignancies or metastatic disease. Patients with these diseases will not respond to low-dose steroids.

Endocrinopathies, especially hypothyroidism, "apathetic" hyperthyroidism, and hyperparathyroidism should all be considered in the differential diagnosis, as each may be associated with prominent constitutional and musculoskeletal complaints. Sedimentation rate will be normal in these settings and appropriate hormonal testing diagnostic.

Other rheumatic diseases should be considered in many patients presenting with constitutional and musculoskeletal symptoms. Systemic lupus erythematosus (SLE) will be marked by a positive ANA, low complement levels, and some evidence of other organ system involvement. Polymyositis will cause true weakness on examination and will be accompanied by elevated muscle enzymes such as creatine kinase. Special mention should be made of rheumatoid arthritis (RA), as synovitis, the hallmark of RA, may be evident in some patients with PMR. Many investigators have called attention to the overlap between PMR and RA in that both may arise in the elderly, produce synovitis, and be accompanied by profound stiffness and aching.[21] However, PMR is seronegative, involves the proximal musculature, and never produces erosive changes in the joints. Although a period of observation may be necessary, a clear-cut distinction can ultimately be made in most cases.

The differential diagnosis of GCA is considerably smaller than for PMR. It is important to remember that temporal arteries are frequently more prominent in the elderly. Atherosclerotic disease in patients with an elevation of the sedimentation rate for other reasons may call attention to this vessel prominence. Rarely, metastatic cancer to the scalp may produce localized tenderness accompanied by an increased sedimentation rate.

TREATMENT AND COURSE

The relationship between PMR and GCA extends to the beneficial effect on both conditions of corticosteroid therapy. The response to corticosteroids in both settings is generally so dramatic and complete as to constitute a diagnostic response. Indeed, the lack of response to low doses of prednisone in a patient with PMR should cast doubt on that diagnosis and suggest either GCA or a totally unrelated diagnosis.

The dosage of prednisone sufficient to suppress PMR is generally inadequate for GCA. A dosage of 20 mg, or less, of prednisone daily will generally suppress all symptoms and signs of PMR within 4 or 5 days, frequently overnight. The dosage of prednisone for GCA is considerably higher. Dosages of 60 mg daily, divided through the day, should be used initially until all signs and symptoms have resolved and the sedimentation rate has normalized. In rare instances, higher dosages may be necessary for disease control. It is rare for visual or other complications to occur once adequate steroid therapy is begun. Although a significant decrease in biopsy positivity is seen within days of institution of therapy, steroids should never be withheld while awaiting biopsy for fear of intervening visual loss or other complications.

Alternate-day steroids are to be avoided as they cause wide swings in day-to-day symptomatology. In addition, one study has demonstrated that alternate-day therapy for GCA is accompanied by an unacceptable incidence of blindness, despite therapy.[22] Good practice suggests that the initial dose of steroids sufficient to induce remission of symptoms and normalization of the sedimentation rate should be continued for at least 1 month. At that point, the dosage may gradually be reduced by no more than 10 percent every 2 to 4 weeks. The maintenance dose of corticosteroids is guided by symptoms as well as changes in the sedimentation rate. Most patients require 1 to 2 years of therapy. Although remission is the rule, several investigators emphasize the need for follow-up because of recurrent symptoms and signs. Some investigators report success with nonsteroidal anti-inflammatory drugs in suppressing symptoms of PMR.[10] However, nonsteroidal drugs are not sufficient for treatment of GCA.

REFERENCES

1. Bruce W: Senile rheumatic gout. *Br Med J* 2:811, 1888.
2. Hunder GG, Allen GL: Giant cell arteritis: A review. *Bull Rheum Dis* 29:980, 1978–1979.
3. Wong RL, Korn JH: Temporal arteritis without an elevated erythrocyte sedimentation rate. *Am J Med* 80:959, 1986.
4. Papaionnou CC et al: Circulating immune complexes in giant cell arteritis and polymyalgia rheumatica. *Arth Rheum* 23:1021, 1980.
5. Espinosa L et al: Anticardiolipin antibodies in polymyalgia rheumatica giant cell arteritis: Association with severe vascular complications. *Am J Med* 90:474, 1991.
6. Richardson J et al: HLA-DR4 in giant cell arteritis: Association with polymyalgia rheumatica syndrome. *Arth Rheum* 30:11, 1987.
7. Machado E et al: Trends in incidence and clinical presentation of temporal arteritis in Olmstead County, Minnesota, 1950–1985. *Arth Rheum* 31:6, 1988.
8. Smith CA et al: The epidemiology of giant cell arteritis: Report of a 10 year study in Shelby County, Tennessee. *Arth Rheum* 26:1214, 1983.

9. Friedman G et al: Epidemiology of temporal arteritis in Israel. *Isr J Med Sci* 18:241, 1983.
10. Chuang TY et al: Polymyalgia rheumatica: A 10 year epidemiologic and clinical study. *Ann Intern Med* 97:672, 1982.
11. Calamia KT, Hunder GG: Clinical manifestations of giant cell (temporal) arteritis. *Clin Rheum Dis* 6:389, 1980.
12. Reich KA et al: Neurologic manifestations of giant cell arteritis. *Am J Med* 89:67, 1990.
13. Caselli RJ et al: Neurologic disease in biopsy-proven giant cell (temporal) arteritis. *Neurology* 38:352, 1988.
14. Goodman BW: Temporal arteritis. *Am J Med* 67:839, 1979.
15. Larson TS et al: Respiratory tract symptoms as a clue to giant cell arteritis. *Ann Intern Med* 101:594, 1984.
16. Klein RG et al: Large artery involvement in giant cell (temporal) arteritis. *Ann Intern Med* 83:806, 1975.
17. Federici AB et al: Elevation of von Willebrand factor is independent of ESR and persists after glucocorticoid therapy in giant cell arteritis. *Arth Rheum* 27:1046, 1984.
18. O'Duffy JD et al: Joint imaging in polymyalgia rheumatica. *Mayo Clin Proc* 55:515, 1976.
19. Douglas WA et al: Polymyalgia rheumatica: An arthroscopic study of the shoulder joint. *Ann Rheum Dis* 42:311, 1983.
20. Allison M, Gallagher P: Temporal artery biopsy and corticosteroid treatment. *Ann Rheum Dis* 43:416, 1984.
21. Healey LA, Sheets PK: The relation of polymyalgia rheumatica to rheumatoid arthritis. *J Rheum* 15:5, 1988.
22. Hunder GG et al: Daily and alternate-day corticosteroid regimens in the treatment of giant cell arteritis. *Ann Intern Med* 82:613, 1975.

Chapter 83

POLYMYOSITIS, DERMATOMYOSITIS, AND INCLUSION BODY MYOSITIS

Gerald M. Eisenberg

The inflammatory myopathies are systemic illnesses characterized by muscle weakness and associated to variable degrees with dermatitis, vasculitis, malignancy, and other rheumatic diseases. Previously dermatomyositis (DM) and polymyositis (PM) have been viewed as pathogenetically similar and have been differentiated primarily by clinical expression. More recent advancements in histologic and immunopathologic techniques, along with the recognition of inclusion body myositis (IBM) as a separate entity, allow a typology of this group of myopathies and their outcomes.[1] The clinical classification of myopathies, originally proposed by Bohan and Peter, is being revised as basic pathologic mechanisms of the diseases are elucidated.[2]

PATHOGENESIS

Although DM and PM are associated with other autoimmune diseases, accompanied by various autoantibodies and are responsive to immune suppressive therapy, no specific muscle or capillary antigens have, as yet, been identified that are involved in the pathogenesis of these diseases.

In DM, the earliest pathologic changes are seen in the intramuscular vasculature.[3] It appears that complement-dependent vasculitic ischemia in these vessels eventually leads to muscle necrosis from microinfarcts. In PM and IBM, there is no evidence of humoral-mediated vasculitis, but, rather, direct muscle injury mediated by cytotoxic T cells.[4]

Up to 30 percent of patients with inflammatory myositis (primarily PM and DM) demonstrate a variety of circulating autoantibodies. Most are not specific. Of greatest interest is the presence of an autoantibody against cytoplasmic ribonucleoprotein, anti-Jo-1, which is correlated with the presence of interstitial lung disease.[5]

Numerous lines of evidence implicate viruses as triggering factors in myositis, although clear-cut proof remains lacking. Reports indicate the presence of myxovirus-like or picornavirus-like particles on election microscopic examination of some biopsy specimens. This is of particular interest because some animal picornaviruses have regions of homology with the Jo-1 antigen, offering a tantalizing hint of a viral infection with a cross-reactive autoimmune response.[6]

CLINICAL MANIFESTATIONS

Although PM and DM are the most commonly occurring acquired myopathies, they are still uncommon. With the addition of IBM, the prevalence is 1/100,000 people.[7] PM and DM occur more frequently in women (3:1) and in blacks. DM affects all age groups, whereas PM is rare in children. IBM occurs more frequently in males, whites, and people over 50 years of age. Seasonal variation in the onset of PM and DM suggests that environmental factors may influence the development of the diseases.[8]

All three forms of myopathy share clinical features including proximal and symmetrical weakness with variable muscle pain and tenderness. For PM and DM the weakness develops over a period of weeks to months, while the course in IBM is even more insidious. Routine activities of daily living gradually become more difficult, and climbing steps, arising from a chair, or combing one's hair all are affected as proximal weakness progresses. Distal musculature may be involved relatively early in IBM and may also be a feature of well-established PM and DM. Involvement of the ocular and facial muscles is very unusual in all three myopathies; however, pharyngeal and neck extensor muscle involvement may manifest as dysphagia and the inability to hold up one's head.

Proximal weakness is always greater than distal weakness, in contrast to the findings in neuropathic disease. Additionally, sensation remains normal in the inflammatory myopathies. Deep tendon reflexes are preserved unless there is supervening muscle atrophy with profound muscle weakness.

Cutaneous manifestations differentiate DM from PM.[9] The rash of DM may precede the muscle weakness. The pathognomonic lesions include heliotrope (purple-red) discoloration over the upper eyelids and raised, violaceous eruptions over the knuckles (Gottron's sign). A less specific erythematous, scaly rash may occur over the knees, elbows, chest, or shoulders. Nail fold microscopy will demonstrate dilated nail fold capillaries. Aside from Gottron's sign, fissuring of the palmar surface of the hands has been referred to as *mechanic's hand.* In children, DM is accompanied by more systemic features, but the cutaneous features are similar. DM in adults appears to be associated with an increased incidence of malignancy,[10] and it can also be seen in conjunction with rheumatic diseases, especially systemic sclerosis or mixed connective tissue disease.

PM is not characterized by rash, and this may result in some delay in diagnosis. PM occurs more frequently in the setting of other rheumatic diseases than DM does. Aside from idiopathic muscle inflammation, parasites, bacteria, and viral infections may produce focal or diffuse inflammatory myopathy and need to be considered in the differential diagnosis (Table 83-1).

IBM should be considered when a patient with presumed PM does not respond to therapy.[11] The increased frequency in males, as opposed to the female preponderance in PM and DM, along with distal involvement may also suggest the diagnosis. Quadriceps involvement is prominently mentioned in descriptions of IBM and may be accompanied by early loss of the patellar reflex.[12] Muscle biopsy is always necessary for this diagnosis.

TABLE 83-1

Differential Diagnosis of Idiopathic Inflammatory Myopathies

Polymyalgia rheumatica
Endocrinopathies (especially hypothyroidism)
Non-Hodgkin's lymphoma (may cause ↑ CK)
HIV myopathy (with or without zidovudine therapy)
Glycogen storage diseases
Fibromyalgia
Trichinosis
Systemic lupus erythematosus
Rheumatoid arthritis
Scleroderma
Viral (influenza, Coxsackie)
Toxic (alcohol, glucocorticoid)
Muscular dystrophy (limb-girdle)
Necrotizing carcinomatosis myopathy

ASSOCIATED CLINICAL FEATURES

The most common gastrointestinal disorder is dysphagia. One-third of DM patients and somewhat fewer PM patients have weakness of the striated crycopharyngeal musculature.[13] Along with proximal esophageal involvement, this may lead to recurrent aspiration. Decreased gastric and intestinal motility are occasionally seen, but not as frequently as in scleroderma. Cardiac abnormalities are seen in up to 40 percent of patients, almost all of whom have DM. Conduction defects, decreased ejection fraction, and dilated cardiomyopathy have all been described.[14] Some investigators suggest that cardiac involvement is an indicator of poor survival in PM and DM.[15] Arthralgias occur in DM and in PM associated with other rheumatic diseases. Joint pain in PM is associated with interstitial lung disease.

The most important systemic manifestation of inflammatory myopathies is pulmonary disease. Contributing factors to the development of lung disease include primary weakness of the thoracic musculature, recurrent aspiration, medications, interstitial inflammatory infiltrates, and opportunistic infection. Hypoxemia may result.[16] Primary interstitial lung disease develops in 10 percent of PM and DM patients, of whom one-half demonstrate antibodies to Jo-1.

The incidence of malignancy appears to be increased only in older patients with DM. However, a recent review from one center demonstrates a disturbingly high incidence of malignancy in younger as well as older patients with PM as well as DM.[17] Although most studies suggest that malignancy can be diagnosed on the basis of a thorough history and physical examination along with "routine" studies such as a complete blood count, blood chemistry tests, urinalysis, and chest x-ray films, others propose more comprehensive evaluation including mammography, sigmoidoscopy, and upper and lower GI examination. Abdominal and pelvic CT scanning also have been advocated. A practical approach is to perform a comprehensive history and physical examination accompanied by surveillance methods appropriate to a particular patient, as determined by age and gender.

Myositis occurs concomitantly with other rheumatic diseases in up to 20 percent of cases. DM, particularly, may overlap with systemic sclerosis or mixed connective tissue disease.[18] Mild PM may be seen in association with Sjögren's syndrome, systemic lupus erythematosus, or rheumatoid arthritis.

LABORATORY FEATURES

The diagnosis of myositis requires a history of muscle weakness, physical findings of weakness, and, perhaps, cutaneous involvement accompanied by abnormalities in levels of serum muscle enzymes, electromyography, and muscle biopsy. Muscle enzymes are released into the serum when myositis causes muscle inflammation and damage. The most sensitive enzyme is creatine kinase (CK), which almost invariably shows elevated levels with active disease. CK levels may be elevated 50-fold in PM and DM. In IBM, elevations in CK levels are somewhat less, up to 10-fold greater than normal. CK levels may occasionally be normal in PM and DM as well as IBM. Levels of aldolase, myoglobin, and creatine may also be elevated, and myoglobinuria may be present. It is very important to remember that hypothyroidism as well as non-Hodgkin's lymphoma may cause elevations of CK levels. However, the CK levels do not respond to corticosteroid therapy in these instances.

Electromyography (EMG) demonstrates a nonspecific pattern of short-duration, low-amplitude polyphasic action potentials along with fibrillations, spontaneous discharges, and positive sharp waves. In addition, 30 percent of patients with IBM may show EMG signs of axonal neuropathy.

Muscle biopsy will not only confirm the presence of inflammatory myositis but will frequently pinpoint the specific form as well (Table 83-2). Proliferation of lymphocytes, phagocytosis, necrosis and regeneration of muscle fibers, muscle atrophy, and capillary obliteration are all seen in various degrees in DM, PM, and IBM.[1] In DM, the infiltrates are predominately perivascular or in the interfascicular septa around the muscle fascicles. In PM and IBM the infiltrate is mostly within the fascicles, involving individual muscle fibers. Capillary involvement is also noted only in DM, with endothelial hyperplasia.[19] Likewise, perifascicular atrophy is specific for DM. IBM is characterized by the presence of basophilic inclusions rimming vacuoles within individual muscle fibers. Electron microscopy demonstrates filamentous inclusions in the cytoplasm about the rimmed vacuoles. The basophilic inclusions confirm the diagnosis of IBM.[20]

TREATMENT AND PROGNOSIS

Prognosis depends on the form of inflammatory myositis. DM may be more acute and aggressive but is also more responsive to therapy. Symptoms tend to wax and wane with gradual diminution in severity over the years. Occasionally, only skin disease may exacerbate without evidence of muscle inflammation. PM, while more insidious, responds more slowly and incompletely to therapy. IBM is unresponsive to treatment. In patients with IBM, the morbidity associated with steroids and other immunosuppressives can be avoided upon definite diagnosis.

Prednisone is the drug most frequently used in the treatment of DM and PM. The degree of residual weakness is determined by the aggressiveness of therapy at onset. For this reason, high doses of prednisone, 1 to 2 mg/kg per day, are used initially until levels of muscle enzymes have normalized and the patient's strength has returned.[21] When this state is reached, generally within 1 to 2 months, the prednisone may be tapered by 5 to 10 percent every 2 to 4 weeks while muscle enzyme levels and objective muscle strength are monitored. Up to 75 percent of patients can ultimately discontinue prednisone, while the remainder may require small doses of daily or alternate-day prednisone to suppress symptoms.

If prednisone in high doses provides no objective benefit after 3 months, the disease is steroid-resistant and additional immunosuppressive medications may prove useful. Treatment with azathioprine or methotrexate may be beneficial in this setting. There is no evidence that one of these is superior to the other, although both methotrexate and azathioprine are used more frequently than other agents such as cyclophosphamide or cyclosporine. Azathioprine doses up to 3 mg/kg per day or methotrexate up to 25 mg/week orally may be tried in steroid-resistant patients or

TABLE 83-2

Distinctive Features of DM, PM, and IBM

	DM	PM	IBM
Earliest age at onset	Any age	18 yr	50 yr
Associated connective tissue disease	Yes (esp. scleroderma)	Yes	Yes, up to 15%
Associated malignancy	Yes	No	No
Associated HIV	No	Yes	No
Familial	No	No	Occasionally
Pathologic features			
Perifascicular atrophy and Capillary damage	Yes	No	No
Complement-mediated	Yes	No	No
Predominant infiltrating cell	B	T	T
Rimmed vacuoles	No	No	Yes
Filamentous inclusions on EM	No	No	Yes

where "steroid sparing" is desirable because of steroid-induced morbidity. Physical therapy, initially to preserve range of motion and later to rebuild strength, is an important adjunct in therapy of PM and DM and represents the only current therapy for IBM.

When treatment of PM is unsuccessful, the patient should be carefully reevaluated and repeat muscle biopsy considered. The long-term use of prednisone may cause a noninflammatory atrophy of type-II muscle fibers associated with weakness. Other diagnoses should also be considered, including IBM, limb-girdle muscular dystrophy, metabolic myopathy, endocrinopathy (especially hypothyroidism), and neurogenic myopathies.

Survival statistics for PM and DM have improved with the availability of steroid therapy. Survival of 83 percent at 8 years has been documented. Of interest is the fact that mortality correlated with older age in this study, independent of the frequency of malignancy.[15] Additional studies confirm that cardiac involvement is the most important clinical factor associated with poor prognosis.

REFERENCES

1. Dalakis MC: Polymyositis, dermatomyositis, and inclusion body myositis. *N Engl J Med* 325:21, 1991.
2. Bohan A, Peter JB: Polymyositis and dermatomyositis. *N Engl J Med* 292:344, 403, 1975.
3. Kissell JT et al: Microvascular deposition of complement membrane attack complex in dermatomyositis. *N Engl J Med* 314:329, 1986.
4. Engel AG, Arahata K: Monoclonal antibody analysis of mononuclear cells in myopathies: II. Phenotypes of autoinvasive cells in polymyositis and inclusion body myositis. *Ann Neurol* 16:209, 1984.
5. Hochberg ML et al: Antibody to Jo-1 in polymyositis/dermatomyositis: Association with interstitial pulmonary disease. *J Rheumatol* 11:663, 1984.
6. Targoff IN: Immunologic aspects of myositis. *Curr Opin Rheumatol* 1:432, 1989.
7. Medsger TA et al: The epidemiology of polymyositis. *Am J Med* 48:715, 1979.
8. Manta P et al: Evidence for seasonal variation in polymyositis. *Neuroepidemiology* 8:262, 1989.
9. Ansell BM (ed): Inflammatory diseases of muscle. *Clin Rheum Dis* 10:1, 1984.
10. Callen JP: Malignancy in polymyositis/dermatomyositis. *Clin Dermatol* 2:55, 1988.
11. Carpenter S et al: Inclusion body myositis: A distinct variety of idiopathic inflammatory myopathy. *Neurology* 28:8, 1978.
12. Eisen A et al: Inclusion body myositis: Myopathy or neuropathy? *Neurology* 33:1109, 1983.
13. Dietz F et al: Cricopharyngeal muscle dysfunction in the differential diagnosis of dysphagia in polymyositis. *Arth Rheum* 23:491, 1980.
14. Askari AD: Cardiac abnormalities. *Clin Rheum Dis* 10:131, 1984.
15. Hochberg MC et al: Adult onset polymyositis/dermatomyositis: An analysis of clinical and laboratory features and survival in 76 patients with a review of the literature. *Semin Arthritis Rheum* 15:168, 1986.
16. Lakhanpal S et al: Pulmonary disease in polymyositis/dermatomyositis: A clinicopathological analysis of 65 autopsy cases. *Ann Rheum Dis* 46:23, 1987.
17. Schulman P et al: A reexamination of the relationship between myositis and malignancy. *J Rheumatol* 18(11):1689, 1991.
18. Mimori T: Scleroderma-polymyositis overlap syndrome: Clinical and serologic aspects. *Int J Dermatol* 26:419, 1987.
19. Emslie-Smith A, Engel AG: Microvascular changes in early and advanced dermatomyositis: A qualitative study. *Ann Neurol* 27:343, 1990.
20. Lotz BP et al: Inclusion body myositis. *Brain* 112:727, 1989.
21. Oddis CV, Medsger TA. Current management of polymyositis and dermatomyositis. *Drugs* 37:382, 1989.

Chapter 84

RHEUMATOID ARTHRITIS AND THE AUTOIMMUNE RHEUMATIC DISEASES IN THE OLDER PATIENT

Evan Calkins, John D. Reinhard, and Adrian O. Vladutiu

Although autoimmune rheumatic disorders do not emerge among the more frequent entities afflicting the elderly, frequent difficulties in diagnosis and important implications regarding therapy result in concern and perplexity among physicians caring for older patients.

This chapter is divided into two sections. The first addresses the most common of these entities, rheumatoid arthritis (RA). Special emphasis is placed on the differential diagnosis of osteoarthritis (OA) and polymyalgia rheumatica and on management. In the second section, we will describe briefly several other members of this group of diseases, including Sjögren's syndrome, systemic lupus erythematosus, drug-induced lupuslike syndromes, and progressive systemic sclerosis. This section is introduced by a review of the serologic reactions frequently utilized in the diagnosis of these disorders. Polymyalgia rheumatica, one of the most common rheumatic disorders in older people, is reviewed in detail in Chap. 82.

RHEUMATOID ARTHRITIS

Several excellent epidemiologic studies show that the frequency of RA increases with advancing age, at least until age 70.[1,2] In the National Health Examination Survey of 1960–1962, "definite" RA, according to American Rheumatoid Association criteria, was found in 1.8 percent of men and 4.9 percent of women age 65 and older.[3]

From the clinician's point of view, it is helpful to think of these patients as falling into two groups: first, those with new-onset disease and second, persons with long-standing RA who have "grown old with their disease." Approximately three-fourths of older patients with new-onset disease exhibit a gradual onset, occurring over the course of weeks or months, accompanied by relatively mild constitutional manifestations.[4,5]

In the remainder, the disease arises in a more acute and flamboyant fashion, with onset occurring over the course of days.[6] These patients often experience constitutional manifestations, including fever and, occasionally, night sweats. Patients in this latter group appear to have a somewhat greater chance for spontaneous remission than patients with gradual-onset disease. Taken together, the frequency of remission in older-onset RA is somewhat less than in younger persons, probably not exceeding 50 percent. There is little indication that any of the modes of therapy for this disorder, at any age, significantly influence this spontaneous remission rate.

The clinical features of RA are well known. The disease is heralded by pain, stiffness, limited motion, swelling, and tenderness, usually starting in the proximal interphalangeal and metacarpophalangeal joints and/or corresponding joints of the feet. The symptoms then spread, in a varying pattern and degree, to the hips, knees, wrists, shoulders, elbows, and spine. Although a large joint is occasionally the first to be involved, this is unusual in elderly persons. Almost all patients exhibit morning stiffness lasting for an hour or more, occasionally extending throughout the day. It should be stressed that RA is not confined to the joints and periarticular tissues but may involve the peripheral nerves, muscle, bone, pericardium, pleura, lung, eye, spleen, and blood.

Radiologic findings depend on the stage of the disease. Early changes are especially evident in the hands and feet. Initially, x-ray examination is normal or, if one looks carefully, one can often see the line of demarcation of the engorged synovium. This will be accompanied by fairly localized subchondral osteoporosis and tiny erosions at the point of insertion of the synovium with the distal metaphasis. The course of the disease may be characterized by continuing activity or by periods of activity separated by intervals of disease inactivity. However, each interval of active disease leads to a certain amount of joint destruction.

The erythrocyte sedimentation rate is almost always elevated, usually in the range of 20 to 60 mm/h. Rheumatoid factor (RF), present in approximately one-third of the cases, is of little value diagnostically if the titer is low. As presently determined, the RF may be present in unrelated chronic inflammatory diseases and, in low titer, in many normal older persons. However, titers of RF above 1:256 are more likely diagnostic of RA. Conversely, the factor may be absent in many patients with RA. Synovial fluid examination will often help in differentiating rheumatoid arthritis from osteoarthritis (OA), gout, calcium pyrophosphate deposition disease, and infection. In RA, the fluid is typically slightly cloudy and less viscous than normal, with a white cell count in the range of 3000 to 25,000/ml. Occasionally it will be as high as 50,000/ml. Synovial fluid glucose levels are moderately reduced in comparison with simultaneously obtained blood glucose concentration, with a differential rarely greater than 40 mg/ml. Urate and calcium pyrophosphate crystals are not seen.

Differential diagnosis of RA from other forms of rheumatic disease is often more difficult among older people than younger ones. This is partly because, in this age group, several forms of arthritis may be present in the same person. In addition, two disorders, frequent among the elderly but rarely seen in younger persons, emerge as "great imitators"—OA and polymyalgia rheumatica.

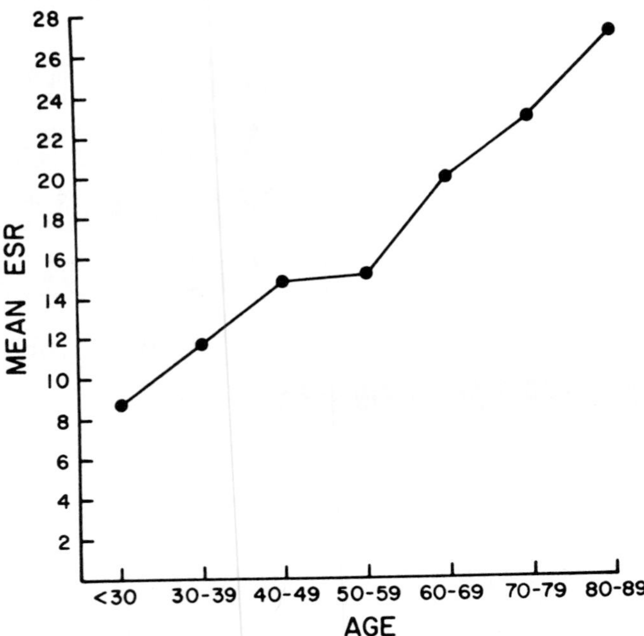

FIGURE 84-1
Mean erythrocyte sedimentation rate by age. (From Hayes and Stinson,[7] reproduced by permission.)

Differential Diagnosis of RA

The differentiation between RA and OA proves to be much more complex in older persons than one would like. While OA is usually regarded as a disorder of gradual onset, many patients with OA develop their symptoms in a subacute fashion, resembling the onset of RA. Osteoarthritis, in its active stage, may exhibit many of the characteristics of an inflammatory disorder, including synovial thickening often accompanied by warmth, tenderness, and effusion. Osteoarthritis is present, coincidentally, in many patients with RA and may be a result of the rheumatoid process. Thus, some patients will exhibit radiologic changes of OA as well as those of RA. Finally, the classic laboratory manifestations that help to differentiate these disorders in the younger patient are less helpful in the elderly. Many older patients exhibit elevations in erythrocyte sedimentation rate to values in the range of 30 to 35 mm/h, even in the absence of any demonstrable inflammatory disorder[7] (see Fig. 84-1). As mentioned, rheumatoid factor is present in many older adults who are entirely free of rheumatic disease.

Given the problems outlined above, how is one to differentiate these two entities? More important, is it all that essential to do so? The answer to the latter question is definitely yes. With increasing evidence showing the effectiveness of methotrexate in the treatment of RA and an appreciation of the effectiveness of low-dose prednisone therapy in many older patients with this disorder, correct resolution of this differential diagnosis provides an essential basis for management.

Table 84-1 lists symptoms and signs which, if carefully assessed and evaluated, help to differentiate RA from OA. Morning stiffness is evidenced by essentially all patients with rheumatoid arthritis. Its duration, which ranges between 1 hour and the entire day, can almost always be established accurately following careful questioning and provides a fairly reliable indication of the activity of the rheumatoid process. Morning stiffness is not diagnostic of RA, however, since it occurs in other autoimmune rheumatic diseases, especially polymyalgia rheumatica and systemic lupus erythematosus. While patients with OA often experience morning stiffness, it almost always subsides within 30 or 40 minutes. "Gelling" following prolonged sitting in a chair is a characteristic of both disorders.

The pattern of joint involvement is another important differential point between these two entities. Both disorders frequently involve the small joints of the hands. In RA, the proximal interphalangeal and metacarpophalangeal joints are most frequently involved, while in OA involvement is usually more evident in the distal interphalangeal joints, the proximal interphalangeal joints, and the carpometacarpal of the thumb. A small percentage of patients with OA, however, will also exhibit swelling, tenderness, and

TABLE 84-1

Features Helpful in Differentiation RA and OA

	RA	OA
Morning stiffness	An hour or more; often lasts 3–4 hours	Usually limited to 3/4 hour or less or all day.
Time of day when symptoms are worst	Mornings	On first arising from bed and after prolonged use. End of day.
Pattern of joint involvement	Interphalangeal joints and metacarpophalangeal joints are almost always involved. Wrists, shoulder, knees, hips may also be involved, almost always in a symmetrical pattern.	Involvement usually focused in a small number of joints—knees, hips, metacarpophalangeal joint of the thumb, distal interphalangeal joints, or shoulders, but rarely are they all involved at once. May be asymmetrical.
Systemic or constitutional manifestations	Fatigue, weight loss, vasomotor instability often seen.	Fatigue may be present due to persistent pain but is less striking than in RA.
Synovial fluid	Decreased viscosity WBC count 3000–25,000 (rarely 50,000) Blood-fluid glucose differential <40 mg/ml.	Viscosity normal, WBC count <3000. May be bloody. Calcium pyrophosphate crystals may be seen.

warmth of the metacarpophalangeal joints of the other fingers, resembling that seen in RA and, in some cases, accompanied by an ulnar drift.[8]

While OA is generally localized to articular cartilage and periarticular structures, RA, by contrast, is a *constitutional* disease that affects many organ systems. When active, it is almost always accompanied by significant constitutional manifestations. These are rarely present to a significant degree in patients with OA except in the presence of a simultaneous systemic illness.

Despite the points noted above, clear differentiation of these two entities may still be difficult to achieve during an initial examination. In these patients it is well to initiate therapy with simple measures that would be appropriate for either condition and to watch for differential points as time passes. Despite the inflammatory component that frequently accompanies OA and the short-term relief that often follows intraarticular corticoid administration, the use of systemic prednisone therapy in this disorder is not recommended. Similarly, use of other second-line antirheumatic agents, such as methotrexate, is not justified in OA.

Increasing appreciation of the close relationship of RA and polymyalgia rheumatica (PMR)[9] does not lessen the importance of differentiating them on clinical grounds for two reasons. The first is the important and frequent association of PMR with temporal arteritis, with its attendant risk of blindness[10] (see Chap. 82). Second, initiation of systemic corticoid therapy in patients with seronegative RA, in the mistaken idea that they may suffer from PMR, can lead to dependence on corticoids, leaving the patient with an unintended commitment to long-term corticoid use. Although prolonged use of low-dose prednisone therapy is indicated in certain patients with RA who are unresponsive to other forms of therapy, this decision should be based on its own merits and not made accidentally as the result of an erroneous diagnosis of PMR.

The clinical characteristics of both disorders are similar. While the onset of PMR is typically rather abrupt, often occurring a few weeks after a mild infection,[12] this is also the experience of many patients with seronegative RA. Systemic manifestations and marked morning stiffness are characteristic of both entities. Both disorders are usually accompanied by an increased erythrocyte sedimentation rate (ESR). Although the increase in ESR is typically greater in patients with PMR than in those with RA, there is considerable overlap. Although PMR is not accompanied by actual joint deformities, such as ulnar deviation or flexion deformity, these are also seen only rarely in the early course of rheumatoid arthritis. Mild thickening of the synovium of wrists, knees, and, to a lesser extent, finger joints may occur in both conditions.

The clues to the diagnosis of PMR are subtle; they include marked stiffness of the muscles of the back and thighs, often resulting in great difficulty in rolling over in bed. However, in patients exhibiting synovial involvement in the peripheral joints, differential diagnosis with seronegative RA and other autoimmune rheumatic disease becomes increasingly difficult. As Dixon[13] has noted, the rapidity of response to a short trial of therapy with prednisone, 15 mg/day, may be helpful in differential diagnosis. In PMR, the symptomatic response usually occurs immediately, within hours or by the next day, while in RA improvement is characteristically not noted until the second day after initiating therapy. This differential point is not infallible, however. We have seen several patients with systemic lupus erythematosus, systemic sclerosis, and even amyloidosis whose initial clinical manifestations resembled those of PMR and who exhibited immediate symptomatic improvement following initiation of 15 mg of prednisone.

Management of New-Onset RA in the Older Patient

As with many chronic diseases, the goals of therapy for RA in an older person are significantly different from those in persons who are young or middle-aged. The goals also vary depending on whether the person has new-onset disease or has "grown old with his or her disease."

For the young adult, who faces the likelihood of a lifetime encounter with what may be a devastating chronic illness, the chief objective is to do everything possible to enhance the likelihood of a true remission.[14] While the evidence that we can, in fact, achieve this goal is marginal at best, the means that have been advocated include bed rest early in the disease, appropriate active exercises, salicylates, and, in unresponsive cases, use of one of the so-called remittive agents (now believed to exhibit an anti-inflammatory rather than a truly remittive action).

The use of many of these measures in older people is fraught with hazard. Extensive bed rest, to the extent one might use it in the younger person, constitutes a major risk for older people, in whom periods of markedly reduced physical activity may lead to an inability to regain the full pace of normal life. In addition, prolonged periods of bed rest in persons of advanced age increase the risk of pressure sores, thrombophlebitis, and pulmonary embolism. The use of almost any pharmacologic intervention carries a significantly greater risk in older patients. Also, the benefit of suppressing joint damage, if indeed that is possible, is much more important in younger patients with a long life expectancy than in older individuals with fewer years ahead of them. Even when the goal of management is directed toward symptomatic benefit, the nonsteroidal antirheumatic agents pose a greater risk in older patients than in younger individuals, due primarily to gastropathy and the accompanying hazard of gastrointestinal bleeding[15] (see Chap. 81).

Given these constraints, how is a physician to design a pharmacologic regimen for an older person with very active symptomatic RA? The use of NSAID therapy is probably justified in such patients, but at dosage levels lower than one would employ in a younger person. If the patient has additional risk factors for gastropathy—including previously demonstrated peptic ulcer disease, previous or present prednisone therapy, or coincidental chronic diseases—the physician should consider reducing the risk of gastropathy by concomitant administration of a prostaglandin antagonists such as misoprostol.[16]

One approach to this dilemma in patients with markedly active disease who are unresponsive to limited periods of rest, hot soaks and other local measures, and safe doses of NSAIDs is to weigh the risks of toxicity and effectiveness of continued NSAID therapy against the benefits and risks of long-term low-dose prednisone therapy.[17,18] Experience has shown that most of the serious complications of corticosteroid therapy occur with doses in the range of 10 mg/day or higher. If the daily dose is maintained at 8 mg or less for a man or 7 mg or less for a woman, the likelihood of serious adverse effects, even following a decade of therapy, is relatively low. The onset of the most feared complication, severe osteoporosis, appears to depend on total accumulated dose of corticosteroid over time, usually requiring a total dose of 30 g or more.[19] At a dosage of 7 mg/day, this would require 11.5 years of continuous treatment. For a patient 80 years of age, for example, the provision of greater comfort and capacity for independence over the years immediately ahead would almost always be regarded as more important than the hazard of osteoporosis 8 or 10 years later. Unfortunately, many older patients, especially women, already have osteopenia. Therefore, careful weighing of the risks and benefits for the individual patient is always indicated.

An alternative approach involves usage of a "second-line" drug, of which methotrexate is now by far the most widely used.[20–22] Given in a dose of 7.5 mg per week, methotrexate has been shown to exhibit a powerful anti-inflammatory effect in most patients, usually starting 3 to 5 weeks after onset of treatment. The medication may be given as three 2.5 mg tablets all at once or in three doses, separated by 12-hour intervals. Initially, one should obtain a complete blood cell count and liver function tests, urinalysis and serum creatinine, and a chest x-ray examination. Cell count should be repeated at monthly intervals and liver and renal function tests at intervals of 3 months. However, changes are very infrequently seen and will almost always subside promptly when the medication is stopped. Occasionally patients will develop a macrocytic anemia, for which they should be given 1 mg of folic acid by mouth daily.

A small percentage of patients on methotrexate therapy will develop hepatic fibrosis. Although this is usually nonprogressive and clinically unimportant, progression to cirrhosis remains a concern. Unfortunately, this hepatic fibrosis is not usually accompanied by symptoms or, uniformly, by transaminase elevations. It can be detected by percutaneous liver biopsy, but it is unclear whether periodic liver biopsies or hepatic fibrosis poses a greater threat. Occasionally, long-term use of methotrexate will be accompanied by pulmonary inflammation or fibrosis, which may be irreversible. One should be alert to the development of pulmonary symptoms such as a dry, nonproductive cough and nonspecific pneumonitis. Chest x-ray examination and pulmonary function tests should probably be performed at intervals of approximately 2 years in patients receiving long-term methotrexate therapy, and the drug should be discontinued if changes occur.

There is considerable doubt whether methotrexate actually induces a remission or prevents or even retards progressive joint damage. Nevertheless, the goal of management in older patients is not necessarily to induce remission—it is to enhance function. Methotrexate appears to be effective in most patients in this regard. Indeed, in view of the frequency of use of nonsteroidal antirheumatic agents in the older population and considering their potentially lethal consequences as compared with methotrexate, there is at least a reasonable argument that methotrexate may be as safe as well as more effective.

Hydroxychloroquine appears to be an effective agent in some patients with RA.[23] Ocular toxicity is a concern, and regular follow-up by an ophthalmologist is mandatory.[24] The role of sulfasalazine, gold, penicillamine, and immunosuppressive drugs in the treatment of RA, systemic lupus erythematosus (SLE), Sjögren's syndrome, scleroderma, and the other collagen vascular diseases is the subject of three recent reviews.[25–27] Although we occasionally use sulfasalazine, we rarely use the other agents in the treatment of older patients with RA.

Nonpharmacologic Treatments

In all patients with RA, pharmacotherapy is only one of a number of components of comprehensive management.[14] This is especially true for older persons, in whom the likelihood of toxic drug effects and pharmacologic interaction is markedly increased. Three important aspects of nonpharmacologic management include exercise and other modalities of physical therapy, orthopedic management, and psychosocial support.

Exercise has an important place in the management of all forms of arthritis. In OA, for example, progressive anaerobic muscle-strengthening exercises, performed against resistance, especially with muscles stretched to maximal length, have been shown to be highly effective in combating the muscle shortening which accompanies aging (and is accentuated by arthritis), in restoring strength, and in decreasing pain and functional limitation.[28] In patients with active RA with swollen, tender, painful joints, the objectives of physical therapy are different and include preservation of range of motion and lessening of deformities as well as an effort to maintain muscle strength. The exercises, which should be performed every day, should always be carried out *within* limits of pain. As a general rule, although a given exercise may be accompanied by some joint discomfort, this should subside within 3 or 5 minutes following completion of the exercise; if it exists for a longer period of time, the exercise was probably more intensive than appropriate for the patient at that stage of his or her disease. In later stages, when acute symptoms have subsided, more intensive exercises should be introduced, including the same type that are effective in OA, but they should be considerably less intensive and, again, always undertaken within the limits of pain.

Dr. Walter Bauer, one of the early leaders of rheumatology in this country, often emphasized that effective treatment does not "come out of a bottle." It involves the commitment, by the patient, to carry out the exercise program, maintain mobility, and learn to live a full life despite the disease. To dramatize this concept, it is important that the exercises be carried out *by the patient*, preferably at home, and not by the therapist in the physical therapy department. Even with procedures that can most effectively be carried out within the physical therapy department, it is important to place responsibility for *doing* the exercise on the patient's shoulders.

In patients with acutely inflamed joints, use of casts or splints, worn for part of the day or during the night, will often help decrease the extent of inflammation and joint deformity. Heat, applied through hot soaks or moist hot packs, for periods of 20 minutes three times a day, may also help control symptoms. Safe and effective moist packs that can be plugged in at home can now be obtained at most medical supply houses.

Orthopedic Surgery

The extraordinary developments in the field of orthopedic surgery, especially in the area of joint replacement, are among the most important innovations in the field of rheumatology in the past 40 years.[29] Particularly appropriate in patients with long-standing rheumatoid or osteoarthritis, orthopedic procedures are also important in patients with relatively early or at least midstage disease. The goal here is to repair, early in the game, structural damage which, if left unattended, will result in significant disability over the long term. An excellent example is the need to reconstruct extensor tendons of the fingers in the event that they become interrupted through erosion by hypertrophic synovium or tendon sheaths over the dorsum of the wrist or hand. This complication can be identified by the sudden onset of "drop fingers," that is, the inability to extend a finger. The procedure is highly effective. Another example of an important orthopedic procedure is incision of wrist tendons of a patient with carpal tunnel syndrome, which may accompany RA as well as OA. Tendon transplantation and other aspects of reconstructive surgery of the hand, carried out in relatively early stages of joint deformity, will contribute substantially to maintaining both function and appearance.

Occasionally patients in any age group may suffer from markedly destructive forms of RA leading to major damage within a few years of the onset of the disease. When this occurs in the hips or knees of older patients, even at the age of 80 or above, the patient should not be denied the benefits of joint replacement if it is likely to result in improved physical functioning. Insertion of joint prostheses may be particularly appropriate in elderly persons, who have much to gain through restoration of function and tend to put less mechanical stress on their prostheses. For these reasons, the threat of breakdown of the prosthesis which, even now, tends to occur after a period of about 15 years, is less of a problem in older patients than in younger individuals.

Psychosocial Support

Social and psychological support is important in all patients with chronic illness. This is especially true of older patients, whose social support systems may have become attenuated. People with chronic arthritis often become discouraged, particularly as a result of pain and functional loss, and may become convinced that they have fallen into the grip of an "awful illness" they do not thoroughly understand.[30] Clear explanation of the nature of the disease, the prognosis (even if it is for continuation of the disease process), and the nature and purpose of treatment contributes greatly to the patient's sense of confidence and often enables him or her to adapt to the disease and decrease reliance on medication.[31]

Older patients with RA frequently suffer one or more other chronic conditions which have an additive impact on their health, comfort, and functional status. Furthermore, the spouse or other care provider may have health problems or diminished functional status. Under these circumstances, rheumatoid arthritis can destabilize a fragile homeostasis and threaten independent living arrangements. Medical, psychological, and social support must all be maximized to preserve autonomy.

Management of the Patients with RA Who Have "Grown Old with Their Disease"

Many of the principles outlined above for the older patient with new-onset disease apply also to the management of patients who enter the older age group having experienced RA for a considerable portion of their lives. There are several additional aspects to management that become particularly important in this age group. The first is the need to remain alert to the possibility that, even in instances of well-established deforming arthritis, the symptoms that brought the patient to the physician may not be related to the arthritis but rather to a concomitant unrelated disorder. We have seen a number of patients with what was initially presumed to be reactivation of or acute sequelae to RA, unresponsive to therapy, in whom the correct diagnosis was an unrelated disorder such as Hodgkin's disease, carcinoma of the prostate, or pernicious anemia. Failure to recognize the correct diagnosis has resulted in fruitless exposure to the toxic effects of antirheumatic agents and loss of the opportunity for prompt treatment of the intercurrent entity.

A second major goal for many of these patients involves a coordinated effort to maintain or restore functional capacity. Here, proper reintroduction of an appropriate exercise program and relatively early reliance on joint replacement emerge as important theraputic considerations. Before undertaking any intensive orthopedic and rehabilitative program, it is essential to assess the status and function of all relevant joints. For example, to correct a knee deformity in a person who also has extensive and possibly irreversible damage to hips, ankles, and/or feet will prove frustrating and disappointing and may represent a waste of medical resources.

There are two complications of long-term RA to which the physician should always remain alert. The first is the sudden development of serious neurologic sequelae due either to atlantoaxial subluxation or to subluxation of the cervical vertebrae themselves.[31–33] Although radiologic examination will frequently show features indicative of these two conditions, only a minority of cases develop serious complications. When this happens, however, it may occur rapidly and lead to serious, even life-threatening neurologic sequelae. Clues to potentially serious involvement include very severe neck or occipital pain, inability to touch the chin to the sternum, numbness and tingling of hands or feet, a sense of limb heaviness, and urinary retention. Repeat x-ray examination may show progression of the spinal deformity. Examination by magnetic resonance imaging (MRI) will confirm the extent of the lesion. Surgical reduction and fusion should be done as an emergency procedure.

The second complication is the development of sudden laryngeal obstruction due to rheumatoid synovitis of the cricoapophyseal joints.[34] This condition—frequently leading to voice change, dysphagia, and pain—may be exacerbated by a superimposed infection or during induction of anesthesia. The possibility of both cervical cord involvement and laryngeal obstruction should be brought to the attention of the anesthesiologist prior to surgery on any patient with long-standing RA.

Patients who have "grown old with their disease" do not, in our experience, require or demand pharmacologic treatment for relief of pain due to their arthritis to the same extent as do patients with new-onset disease. Although the chronic inflammatory processes in the joints can become less painful over the years, it is more likely that the survivors of prolonged active arthritis learn to accept and adapt to their discomforts without relying on medication to the extent that they may have done in former years. Indeed, it is hard to avoid the conclusion that this ability to accept the disease without reliance on extensive pharmacologic treatment has contributed substantially to these patients' ability to survive, perhaps due, at least to some degree, to avoidance of the serious toxic effects that accompany most anti-inflammatory or remittive medications.[35,36]

The development of a comprehensive program of management for patients with severe RA is a team effort, involving imaginative, thoughtful input from physicians, nurses, physical and/or occupational therapists, orthopedists, podiatrists, and others as may be needed for special problems.[37] This is a situation in which the patient and family should be regarded as "members of the team." Skillful care of these patients presents a challenge which can be as rewarding to the care providers as it is helpful to and appreciated by the patients and their families.

OTHER AUTOIMMUNE RHEUMATIC DISEASES IN OLDER PERSONS

It is increasingly apparent that the characteristics of each of the autoimmune rheumatic diseases differ to some degree in older as opposed to younger individuals. To an increasing degree, as patients grow older, the manifestations of one disease resemble those of another. From the point of view of the primary care physician, these changes result in an understandable confusion, both in sorting out the patient's individual clinical features and in interpreting the ever larger number of immunologic tests currently available. The following section begins with a summary of the immunologic tests currently in widest use and how they can be utilized to help clarify a diagnosis.

Serologic Tests in Autoimmune Rheumatic Disease of Older Persons

These diseases are characterized by the presence of one or more autoantibodies that react with components of the nucleus, cytoplasm, or surface of cells. Many of these autoantigens are well characterized and even cloned, but their pathogenic role, if any, is still not understood. Newer assays that use these pure autoantigens are more sensitive than previously used assays. Therefore, the prevalence of some autoantibodies in various systemic rheumatic diseases is higher than has been previously reported (Table 84-2).

Antinuclear Autoantibodies (ANA)

The most commonly measured antibodies are antinuclear antibodies (ANA), usually determined by the immunofluorescence (IF) method of Coons. This has led to the designation IF-ANA. The ANA reaction reflects the presence of any one or several of scores of antibodies to specific nuclear components. Thus, the IF-ANA assay is an excellent starting point for the confirmation of the presence of an autoimmune rheumatic disease in patients whose symptomatology strongly suggests this possibility. Since low-titer ANAs will also occur in many normal individuals, especially those of advanced age, only titers of 1:160 or above are considered to be clinically significant.[38] With human cell line substrates, which are now commonly used, the test is positive in more than 95 percent of patients with untreated SLE. The test is also positive in a smaller percentage of patients with Sjögren's syndrome, systemic sclerosis, polymyositis/dermatomyositis, and rheumatoid arthritis[39–41] (see Table 84-2).

Recently developed techniques, especially immunoblotting and molecular cloning, have made it possi-

TABLE 84-2

Prevalence of the Most Commonly Tested Antibodies Associated with Systemic Rheumatic Diseases

Antibody	RA[a]	SLE	Drug-Induced Lupus	PSS	CREST Syndrome	MCTD	PM/DM	Sjögren's Syndrome
IF-ANA	30–40%	>95%	>95%	80–90%	80–90%	95%	30–40%	70–90%
Anti-dsDNA	—	50–60%[b]	<1%	—	—	—	—	—
Anti-Histone	—	50–70%	>90%[b]	—	—	—	—	—
Anti-Sm[c]	—	15–30%[b]	—	—	—	—	—	—
Anti-U1-RNP	—	35–40%	—	15–20%	5–20%	>95%[b]	5%	<5%
Anti-SS-A/Ro	5–10%	30–50%	—	—	—	—	<5%	80–95%
Anti-SS-B/La	—	15–20%	—	—	—	—	—	70–95%[b]
Anti-Scl-70	—	—	—	30–60%[b]	15–20%	—	—	—
Anti-Centromere	—	—	—	15–25%	70–85%[b]	—	—	—
Anti-PM-1 & Jo-1	—	—	—	—	—	—	30–60%[b]	—

[a] Abbreviations: RA, rheumatoid arthritis; SLE, systemic lupus erythematosus; PSS, progressive systemic sclerosis; CREST, variant of scleroderma; MCTD, mixed connective tissue disease; PM/DM, polymyositis/dermatomyositis; IF-ANA, immunofluorescent antinuclear antibodies.

[b] High diagnostic value of the antibodies.

[c] As measured with immunodiffusion. In ELISA, IgG is more important for SLE (positive in 50 percent of patients) whether IgA anti-Sm is also found in drug-induced lupus.

ble to detect a large number of nuclear antigens, and clinical-serologic associations continue to emerge. Antibodies to some of these antigens have a specificity for certain rheumatic diseases. For example, anti-Sm are most specific for SLE, anti-DNA toposomerase 1 (anti-Scl-70) for systemic sclerosis, and anti-centromere antibodies for its CREST variant. While the finding in the serum of autoantibodies that react with one of these antigens does not, by itself, prove the presence of the disease entity, it should provide a high index of suspicion or confirm the presence of the disease in a person exhibiting appropriate signs or symptoms. Conversely, although a negative ANA test does not exclude the diagnosis of a rheumatic disease, it makes the diagnosis unlikely. In the case of SLE, the revised (1982) ARA criteria for classification of this disease include IF-ANA (they were not included in the older, 1971 criteria).[42] The nuclear staining patterns in the IF-ANA test (e.g., homogenous, speckled, nuclear rim) are of relatively little importance at the present time. The antibodies to ssDNA are not specific for SLE and are not commonly measured.

The *Crithidia lucilliae* trypanosome is presently used as a cellular substrate for the demonstration of anti-dsDNA by indirect immunofluorescence. Sixty percent of patients with SLE will have a positive test for dsDNA antibodies at some time during the course of their disease. These antibodies are not seen in normal persons or in patients with drug-induced lupus.

Antibodies to Sm and RNP

Anti-Sm (Smith) and anti-RNP react with complexes of proteins and small nuclear RNA (snRNP) rich in uridine (named U1, U4-U6) and are found in 25 percent of patients with SLE. Detection of anti-Sm has a high diagnostic value for SLE. Anti-Sm antibodies will also exhibit anti-RNP (also named U1-RNP) antibodies, but the latter may also be found without anti-Sm antibodies. The clinical and diagnostic relevance of anti-U1 RNP remains to be established.

The SS-A/Ro antigen is a small RNA protein complex present in both the cytoplasm and the nucleus. With the laboratory procedure currently in clinical use (enzyme immunoassay with cloned antigen), anti-SS-A/Ro are exhibited in the serum of about 85 percent of patients with Sjögren's syndrome and 33 percent of patients with SLE.[43] They are also present in a smaller percentage (5 to 10 percent) of persons with other rheumatic diseases. Anti-SS-A/Ro, accompanied by anti-SS-B/La, are more frequently seen in patients with late-onset SLE (after age 50) than in patients with early onset disease.[44] The presence of these autoantibodies in patients with SLE indicates that there is a greater likelihood that the patients will also have Sjögren's syndrome—accompanied by vasculitis, lymphadenopathy, and leukopenia—but a decreased likelihood for the development of nephritis.[43] Anti-SS-B/La can be used as a diagnostic tool for Sjögren's syndrome, and this condition is sometimes suspected only after finding the antibodies.[46]

Antibodies to ribosomal nucleoprotein (rRNP) have been detected in about 10 percent of patients with SLE, and about half of these patients have psychiatric symptoms.[47] Antibodies to Ki antigen have been found in 20 percent of patients with SLE, and these patients also had a higher prevalence of central nervous system (CNS) involvement.[46] About 50 percent of patients with SLE and a third of patients with polymyositis will also exhibit antibodies to Hsp-90, a mammalian heat shock protein. Antibodies to proliferating cell nuclear antigen (PCNA, or cyclin) have been detected in a very small percentage (less than 5 percent) of patients with SLE.[39] Antibodies Scl-70, to a 70-kDa nuclear topoisomerase 1, are important for the diagnosis of systemic sclerosis. Patients with these antibodies (anti-Scl-70) tend to have a more severe disease course, more internal involvement, and diffuse rather than limited skin involvement.[48] Anti-Jo-1 antibodies are seen in many patients with myositis. The presence of these antibodies can precede and predict the development of myositis, their level varying with disease activity. Anti-centromere antibodies are closely associated with the CREST variant of systemic sclerosis.[49]

Most of these serologic reactions (see Table 84-2) are carried out in the laboratories of many tertiary care medical centers and are also available commercially. They are expensive—in the range of $20 to $60 per test—and they should be used only for specific clinical indications. For example:

1. In patients presenting symptoms suggestive of one of the autoimmune rheumatic diseases (i.e., seronegative RA, PMR, Raynaud's phenomenon, or keratoconjunctivitis sicca). IF-ANA is a good starting point. If ANA are present (titer ≥ 1:160), or in the presence of strongly suggestive clinical symptoms (even in the absence of IF-ANA), one should request one or more of the other tests, as suggested below.
2. In patients with a clinical syndrome characteristic of SLE and a positive IF-ANA test, the presence of anti-dsDNA will provide confirmation of the diagnosis of SLE and may be of assistance in following the patient's course. A positive anti-Sm test will provide additional confirmation but is not necessary. In patients with proven SLE, tests for anti-SS-A/Ro and anti-SS-B/La can be useful in detecting the possible coexistence of Sjögren's syndrome.
3. IF-ANA are present in both SLE and drug-induced lupus. However, antibodies to Sm, if present, and anti-dsDNA are specific for SLE.
4. In patients with Raynaud's phenomena in whom one wants to rule out systemic sclerosis or SLE, the IF-ANA is a good starting point. If it is negative, the diagnosis of SLE is unlikely. Anti-dsDNA and anti-Sm will also be negative and should not be requested. In patients with symptoms suggestive of systemic sclerosis, this diagnosis can be supported by an anti-Scl test.

5. In patients with symptoms suggestive of keratoconjunctivitis sicca, confirmed by positive Schirmer's and rose Bengal tests, it is appropriate to obtain an anti-SSA/Ro and anti-B/La.

It is rarely necessary or indicated to obtain a full battery of serologic tests or to order them repeatedly. Careful selection of tests that are appropriate for the condition suspected on clinical grounds avoids unnecessary confusion and cost. Except for assistance in following patients with SLE, it is seldom necessary or helpful to repeat the tests at frequent intervals in hopes that one of them will "turn positive." Usually, the results obtained when the disease has become clinically manifest will provide as much information as one is apt to derive from this approach.

Systemic Lupus Erythematosus

Most rheumatologists and immunologists define late-onset SLE as occurring at or after age 50. However, this demarcation deemphasizes the fact that SLE is a rare entity among persons aged 70 and older[44] (see Fig. 84-2). Nevertheless, it has been reported in a number of very old persons, including one woman aged 90.[50]

In the medical literature, considerable attention has been devoted to the question: Are the manifestations of "late onset" SLE significantly different from those in patients with onset in early or midlife? Although there are some areas of agreement among these studies, there are also striking areas of disagreement. Recently, Ward and Pollison[51] conducted a meta-analysis of studies from the world literature which utilized recognized criteria for the diagnosis of SLE and preset criteria for the presence or absence of specific organ involvement. Nine studies were identified. Definition of the age "cut point" for late-onset disease ranged between 45 and 60 years. The authors concluded that patients with late-onset disease exhibited greater frequency of interstitial pulmonary disease, serositis, and a constellation of features suggestive of secondary Sjögren's syndrome than did patients whose disease commenced in early or midlife. Those with early-onset disease exhibited greater frequency of fever, Raynaud's phenomenon, lymphadenopathy, and neuropsychiatric illness. In contrast to the widely accepted view, no difference was noted in the frequency of nephritis. The two groups were also essentially identical with regard to the frequency of photosensitivity, myalgia, leukopenia, and thrombocytopenia. No significant difference was noted with regard to the frequency of arthritis or cutaneous manifestations. Serologic tests showed greater frequency of anti-La in the older onset group, while hypocomplementemia, rheumatoid factor, and anti-nDNA were more frequently exhibited by patients with early-onset disease. There was no statistically significant difference between the two groups with regard to anti-Ro, anti-Sm, or anti-RNP. Both clinical and serologic differences are probably more a reflection of a continuum of disease than of two specific syndromes.[52]

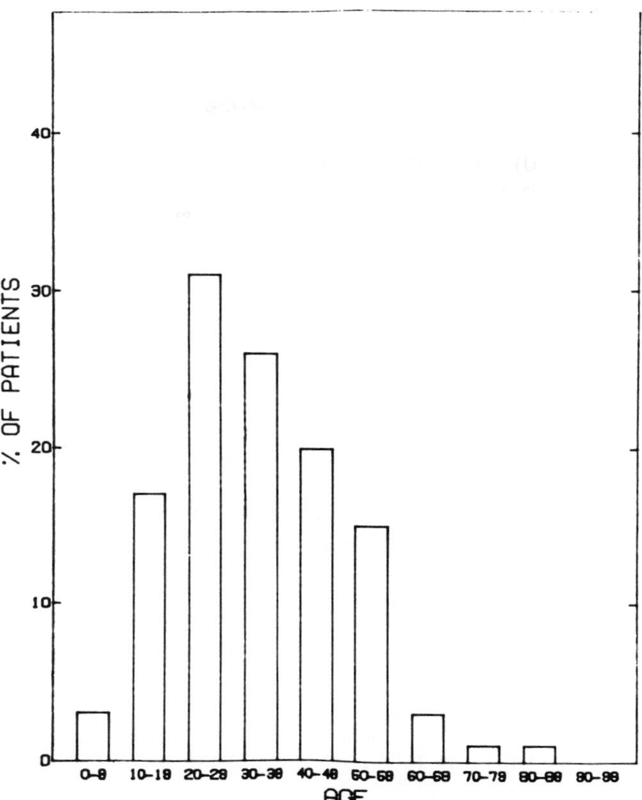

FIGURE 84-2
Prevalence of systemic lupus erythematosus by age. (From Hochberg et al,[44] reproduced by permission.)

Especially in the older patient, SLE may be initiated by a nonspecific constellation of symptoms including fever, polyarthralgia, fatigue, and weight loss.[53,54] The diagnosis of SLE is frequently overlooked during this initial phase, in which the patient may be regarded as having seronegative rheumatoid arthritis or PMR.[55] In one study, the duration of illness in older patients, from its time of onset to diagnosis, averaged 4 years.[52]

In view of the infrequency of SLE in patients over age 65, it is not surprising that little information is available concerning the indications and risks of various forms of treatment in this age group. In view of the already reduced immune responsiveness that accompanies advanced age, it does not seem reasonable to subject older patients to immunosuppressive drugs and, in our view, treatment with oral prednisone alone is probably appropriate.[56] For patients unresponsive to this regimen, methotrexate, 7.5 mg/week orally, may be added.[57] Patients with less severe manifestations of SLE, such as arthritis, pleuritic pain, and easy fatigability, especially those who exhibit photosensitivity, may be treated with chloroquine, one or two 250 mg tablets daily, or hydroxychloroquine, one or two 200 mg tablets daily.[58,59] As with patients with RA treated with this drug, the patient should receive an ophthalmologic examination initially and thereafter at 6-month intervals. Whether the administration of antimalarials will permit maintenance of the patient on a lower dose of prednisone has not been proven.

Drug-Induced Lupus

The multiplicity of drugs consumed by many elderly patients places them at increased risk for drug-induced lupus. The symptoms can suggest to the physician, unaware of the nature of the problem, a variety of diagnostic possibilities that are both serious in their own right and common among the elderly. Table 84-3 lists the clinical features of lupus erythematosus induced by procainamide, one of the drugs most often implicated as a cause of drug-induced lupus.[60] Arthralgia, which can be migratory, may affect many joints: fingers, wrists, shoulders, elbows and, to a lesser extent, knees, ankles, and temporomandibular joints. Although few patients exhibit true arthritis, diffuse myalgia is common, often accompanied by severe morning stiffness, a combination of symptoms not unlike those seen in PMR. Pleuropulmonary involvement, usually manifested by pleuritic pain, pleural effusion, basilar infiltrates, and, occasionally, hemoptysis, yields a syndrome resembling pulmonary infarction. In contrast to SLE, one rarely sees renal disease, vasculitis, or CNS involvement in drug-induced lupus.

TABLE 84-3

Signs and Symptoms in Procainamide-Induced Lupus-like Syndrome

	Percent, n = 44
Rheumatic symptoms	
Arthralgia	77
Arteritis	18
Myalgia	47
Pleuropulmonic involvement	52
Fever	46
Hepatomegaly	20
Lymphadenopathy	10
Abdominal pain	10
Pericarditis	12
Splenomegaly	5
Raynaud's phenomenon	5
Rash	5
Central nervous system symptoms	2
History of drug reaction	23

SOURCE: From Blomgren et al.,[60] modified to show percentage frequency (in 44 cases).

The manifestations of drug-induced lupus may not appear until after the inciting drug has been taken for many years. In the study by Blomgren et al.,[60] the duration of therapy before the onset of drug-induced lupus ranged from 1 month to 8 years. In most instances, the manifestations subside following discontinuation of the drug. A moderate dose of prednisone (10 to 15 mg/day) will almost always lead to prompt resolution of symptoms. If symptoms do not resolve on their own or if they recur after a short course of prednisone, one must consider the possibility that the drug has proved an inciting agent for the development of SLE. Essentially all patients with this syndrome exhibit positive IF-ANA, with titers of 1:640 or higher. Antibodies to histones occur frequently, but antibodies to dsDNA, RNP, Sm, SS-A/Ro, and SS-B/La are rarely seen.

Drugs that have been implicated in causing this syndrome are listed in Table 84-4. Procainamide is the agent most widely implicated, with hydralazine a close second.[61,62] Antinuclear antibodies develop in between 50 and 75 percent of patients who receive either of these drugs over a 9- to 12-month period, and between 20 and 50 percent of these develop a lupus-like syndrome.[61] Recent studies of patients with hydralazine-induced lupus have shown a high predilection for recurrence of the disorder in persons with two genetic characteristics. The first is a deficiency in the activity of the enzyme *N*-acetyl transferase, and, with this, a decrease in the ability to acetylate foreign substances or drugs ("slow acetylators"). The second is the presence of the HLA DR4 antigen.[62] Gender distribution varies among the individual drugs. The preponderance of persons with procainamide-induced lupus are males, whereas the majority of those with hydralazine-induced lupus are females.

Sjögren's Syndrome

Sjögren's syndrome (SS) is a cell-mediated autoimmune disease resulting in intense inflammation and, ultimately, dysfunction of the exocrine glands. The condition invariably involves the major and minor salivary glands, resulting in the classic sicca syndromes of xerophthalmia and xerostomia. Although the con-

TABLE 84-4

Drugs Implicated in Induction of a Lupus-like Syndrome

Procainamide	Ethosuximide
Hydralazine	Penicillin
Isoniazid	Phenylbutazone
Sulfonamides	Tetracycline
Diphenylhydantoin	Streptomycin
Mephenytoin	Para aminosalicylic acid
Primethadione	Griseofulvin

SOURCE: From Blomgren et al.[60]

dition is seldom listed among the major musculoskeletal or rheumatic diseases affecting the elderly, it clearly deserves much greater attention for a number of reasons.[63] First, the symptoms of SS are both bothersome, and, in some instances, serious. Second, the manifestations of Sjögren's syndrome closely parallel those exhibited by many older persons without known rheumatologic disease. Examples include severe fatigue, depression, migraine headaches, chronic pulmonary insufficiency, digestive problems, and a range of neurologic disorders, including peripheral neuropathy and stroke. The fact that an older patient with one or several of these conditions may be suffering from SS is frequently overlooked. Finally, SS is a very frequent problem in older individuals.

Epidemiologic studies suggest that 15 to 25 percent of normal older people—more commonly women—suffer symptoms of xerostomia and xerophthalmia. The large majority have atrophy of the mucus-producing cells, with preserved lacrimal function. This must be differentiated from true SS, the incidence of which is unknown. However, the prevalence of this disorder, among the autoimmune rheumatic diseases appears to be second only to that of rheumatoid arthritis.[63,64]

In the majority of cases, SS develops in association with one of the other rheumatic diseases. Between 10 and 20 percent of patients with rheumatoid arthritis will exhibit symptoms of SS and an even higher percentage, if biopsied, display histologic changes consistent with the disorder.[65] Catoggio et al.[54] detected SS in 38 percent of their cases of late-onset SLE, as compared with 21 percent of those with younger-onset disease. In the study by Hochberg et al.,[44] the figures were 36.9 percent for late-onset disease, 21 percent in those with onset at ages 23 to 49, and 11.1 percent for those with onset at or under age 22. Sjögren's syndrome has also been described in a small percentage of patients with progressive systemic sclerosis and mixed connective tissue disease.

In approximately one-third of cases, the syndrome occurs in the absence of any of the other rheumatic diseases. In one of the few studies attempting to document the incidence of so-called "primary Sjögren's syndrome" among the older population, the frequency was estimated at just under 5 percent.[64] In another study, of unselected elderly women living in a nursing home, 39 percent were found to have sicca symptoms, and the incidence of SS was established at between 2 and 14 percent, depending on diagnostic criteria used.[65] In most of these patients, the disorder was unrecognized.

Clinical Manifestations

The most conspicuous clinical manifestations of SS are xerophthalmia and xerostomia due, respectively, to serious dysfunction of the lacrimal or salivary glands. As a result of loss of adequate tearing, patients experience a "foreign-body sensation" or sense of dryness or grittiness in the eyes. In severe cases, patients develop superficial erosions of the cornea, a condition known as keratoconjunctivitis sicca. This may be accompanied by a loss of visual acuity and a sense of "film" across the visual field.

Xerostomia, due to inadequate salivary secretion, results in "dry mouth." Patients with this disorder may need to drink copious fluids to assist in mastication and swallowing, and they frequently complain of a sore mouth. They may lose their sense of taste and smell, and dental caries become a serious problem. The salivary glands may become swollen and occasionally tender.

While the cardinal clinical manifestations of SS relate to the effect of the syndrome on exocrine glands, the condition is frequently accompanied by marked inflammation of the small blood vessels of many organs, leading to a variety of systemic manifestations.[65–67] These include Raynaud's syndrome, symmetrical distal polyarthralgia, interstitial pneumonitis, loss of normal esophageal mobility, decreased pancreatic exocrine function, hypo- or achlorhydria, vasculitic skin eruptions, and a wide range of important neurologic and psychiatric manifestations.[68–70] The latter may include migraine and, occasionally, Bell's palsy, stroke, and epilepsy. An excellent review of the clinical features of peripheral neuropathy in patients with SS has recently been published.[71] In some instances, neurologic manifestations precede the development of xerophthalmia or xerostomia. The kidneys can also be the target of autoimmune attacks, leading to renal tubular dysfunction.

The lacrimal, salivary, pulmonary, renal, vascular, and neurologic manifestations of SS are associated with an intense infiltration of inflammatory cells. This infiltration is often predominantly lymphocytic and can become quite extensive. In its extreme form, it is called pseudolymphoma. Between 5 and 10 percent of patients with long-standing disease eventually develop a B-cell lymphoma.

It is our impression that many of these systemic manifestations are more frequent in younger patients, often occurring in the context of a systemic autoimmune disease. When symptoms occur in older individuals, it is much more difficult to tell whether they are due to primary SS, to an associated comorbidity, or to the effects of normal aging. A comparison of signs and symptoms of older SS patients with age-matched controls is badly needed.

Diagnosis

Schirmer's test provides a useful preliminary screening procedure. A piece of Whatman no. 41 filter paper, ¼ cm wide and 3 cm long, is folded and the upper edge is placed within the lower eyelid. Normally, tears will rapidly moisten the filter paper so that, within 5 min, at least 15 mm^2 will be saturated. In patients with keratoconjunctivitis sicca, less than 5 mm^2 of the paper is moistened within 5 min. It should be stressed, however, that many older persons will exhibit a deficiency of tears and of salivary secretions associated with age-related atrophy of the lacrimal and salivary glands. Additional support to the diagnosis of SS will be provided by examining the eye with a slit lamp, following intraocular installation of rose Bengal dye, and through use of several techniques for measuring of parotid salivary flow, visualization of the salivary glands, and estimation of their function by determining uptake, concentration, and secretion of radiolabeled pertechnetate.

Definitive confirmation of the diagnosis of SS can be obtained through biopsy of the lacrimal or salivary glands. The preferred site of biopsy is now the minor salivary glands of the lip[72]; the specimen is obtained through making a small incision on the inner aspect of the lip. The procedure is easily accomplished and not particularly bothersome to patients, although it is occasionally followed by persistent loss of sensation in the area of the biopsy. Persons with SS will characteristically exhibit either focal or diffuse lymphocytic infiltration of these glands. However, these changes must be differentiated from the fibrosis of fatty infiltration, which will be exhibited by many older patients in the absence of SS. AntiSS-A/Ro and antiSS-B/La antibodies are helpful in the evaluation of patients with suspected SS, but they cannot be used, in and of themselves, to confirm the diagnosis.

Standardization of techniques for the establishment of the presence of SS in a clinical practice is still in the process of evolution. The specific techniques for determining salivary flow and function, while useful in a research setting, are not readily available in most clinical offices, and the lip biopsy is not welcomed by most patients. In our clinical practice, we currently rely on the overall clinical picture, buttressed by the Schirmer and rose Bengal tests, with added support from antiSS-A/La and antiSS-B/Ro if positive.

Treatment

Treatment of SS is symptomatic. Artificial tears and, where appropriate, lemon-and-glycerine mouth rinse are the backbone of therapy. Corticosteroid-containing eye medication should not be used because of the likelihood of further damage to the cornea. In patients with prominent enlargement or painful infiltration of the salivary glands, systemic corticosteroids in relatively low doses can be helpful. Constitutional symptoms are also ameliorated by corticosteroids. The effect of corticosteroids on the other manifestations of SS has not been adequately studied.

Progressive Systemic Sclerosis (Scleroderma)

Progressive systemic sclerosis (scleroderma) occurs primarily in persons of late middle age.[73] It is seen in an occasional patient aged 65 or older, either as a new entity or an instance of "growing old with the disease." In a general medical or geriatric practice, the key point to bear in mind is that a number of clinical manifestations of scleroderma so closely mimic changes exhibited by many normal older persons that the presence of scleroderma is apt to be overlooked.[74]

The key clinical features of scleroderma are thickening of the skin, especially in the area proximal to the interphalangeal joints, accompanied by sclerodactyly, pitting of the fingertips, and diffuse pulmonary fibrosis.[75] Decreases in esophageal motility are frequently encountered, and many patients will also have clinical symptoms related to progressive fibrosis or vascular changes in the gastrointestinal tract, heart, and kidneys.[76] Most patients also exhibit Raynaud's phenomenon.

Two other syndromes, CREST (calcinosis, Raynaud's phenomenon, esophageal dysmotility, sclerodactyly, and telangiectasias)[77] and the so-called mixed connective tissue disease are either closely related to or variants of scleroderma. In the CREST variant, skin changes largely limited to the fingers and Raynaud's phenomenon are prominent. Small telangiectasias appear on the hands, face, and upper trunk. Esophageal changes are similar to those encountered in diffuse scleroderma. Other gastrointestinal manifestations are unusual. Involvement of the kidneys and lungs is rare, but pulmonary hypertension occurs in up to 20 percent of patients. Although pulmonary hypertension carries a poor prognosis, the disease is otherwise relatively benign.

Mixed connective tissue disease is characterized by edema of the hands, arthralgia, Raynaud's phenomenon, dysphagia, and, at times, pulmonary changes or myositis.[78] Up to two-thirds of the cases will eventually evolve to more classic scleroderma. Unfortunately, little information is available concerning the frequency of these manifestations in an elderly population.

Course and Treatment

The course of scleroderma tends to be progressive, but the rate of progression is highly variable. Long periods of stability may occur and skin changes may regress. Three stages have been recognized.[79] In stage I, involvement is localized to the skin and esophagus, frequently accompanied by Raynaud's phenomenon. In stage II, the disorder has progressed to involve the lungs and additional regions of the gastrointestinal tract. Stage III disease is characterized by cardiovascular and renal involvement, frequently accompanied by hypertension.

Treatment of stage I disease involves supportive measures such as use of heated gloves or socks, down-insulated slippers or boots, emollients for the skin, and avoidance of physical damage. Patients should be instructed to stop smoking. In the presence of severe Raynaud's phenomenon, several therapeutic options are available. These include treatment with calcium channel blocking agents, alpha-adrenergic blocking agents, or drugs that deplete catecholamines or their formation, such as reserpine.[79]

For active stage II disease, penicillamine is

thought to be helpful, although its efficacy has never been established in controlled trials. This drug should be instituted in a dose of 250 to 500 mg/day and continued for a period of 2 to 4 years. In hopes of achieving the best results, the drug should be started early. Adverse reactions of the sort that have been described in the treatment of rheumatoid arthritis or SLE are rarely seen with the doses indicated, and this program can usually be continued, without adverse affect over a period of many years. Immunization against influenza and pneumococcal pneumonia should be given. Occasionally, treatment with prednisone 20 to 60 mg a day will be indicated, although some investigators worry that this may increase the risk of renal crisis.

In past years, stage III disease, especially if accompanied by hypertensive crisis with renal failure, was uniformly fatal.[80] More recently, it has been shown that this development can often be averted through use of potent antihypertensive drugs, especially an angiotensin converting enzyme inhibitor. Renal dialysis may be necessary.

With improvement in the treatment of renal crisis due to scleroderma, pulmonary disease has become the major cause of death in this condition[81]. The most common manifestation is diffuse pulmonary fibrosis, characterized by a nonproductive cough, dyspnea on exertion, and dry, crackling rales at the lung bases. X-ray reveals fine interstitial markings at the bases, or, occasionally, a honeycomb pattern. Pulmonary function tests are consistent with a restrictive pattern. Clubbing is uncommon, possibly due to the frequent presence of sclerodactyly. Although these patients usually exhibit the characteristic sclerodermatous involvement of the skin, this is not always the case. Therefore, other manifestations associated with scleroderma—such as Raynaud's phenomenon, esophageal dysmotility, and a positive IF-ANA reaction, possibly accompanied by anti-Scl—should be looked for in patients with pulmonary fibrosis of unknown cause. Although adrenal corticosteroids and d-penicillamine have been tried in scleroderma-related pulmonary fibrosis, there is little evidence of benefit. However, in the small group of patients in whom pulmonary fibrosis is accompanied by active alveolitis, as demonstrated by pulmonary lavage, encouraging results have been obtained from treatment with cyclophosphamide.[83] Detailed information concerning the management of systemic sclerosis and related disorders is provided in the excellent article by Oliver and Winkelmann.[79]

SUMMARY

The diagnosis and management of older patients with RA and the autoimmune rheumatic diseases presents a fascinating challenge to physicians, whether they be rheumatologists, geriatricians, primary care physicians, physiatrists, or orthopedists. Careful application of classic clinical skills and reliance on support from professionals in a range of disciplines usually yield results which are satisfying both to the patient and their families and to care providers.

REFERENCES

1. Linos A et al: The epidemiology of rheumatoid arthritis in Rochester, Minnesota: A study of incidence, prevalence, and mortality. *Am J Epidemiol* 111:87, 1980.
2. Mikkelsen WM et al: Estimates of the prevalence of rheumatic diseases in the population of Tecumseh, Michigan, 1959–60. *J Chronic Dis* 20:351, 1967.
3. Lawrence RC et al: Estimates of the prevalence of selected arthritic and musculoskeletal disease in the United States. *J Rheumatol* 16:427, 1989.
4. Brown JW, Sones DA: The onset of rheumatoid arthritis in the aged. *J Am Geriat Soc* 15:873, 1967.
5. Deal CL et al: The clinical features of elderly-onset rheumatoid arthritis: A comparison with younger-onset disease of similar duration. *Arthritis Rheum* 28:987, 1985.
6. Corrigan AB et al: Benign rheumatoid arthritis in the aged. *Br Med J* 1:444, 1974.
7. Hayes GS, Stinson IN: Erythrocyte sedimentation rate and age. *Arch Ophthalmol* 94:939, 1976.
8. MacFarlane DG, Dieppe PA: Pseudo-rheumatoid deformity in elderly osteoarthritic hands. *J Rheumatol* 10:489, 1983.
9. Healey LA, Sheets PK: The relation of polymyalgia rheumatica to rheumatoid arthritis. *J Rheumatol* 15:750, 1988.
10. Desmet GD et al: Temporal arteritis: The silent presentation and delay in diagnosis. *J Intern Med* 227:237, 1990.
11. Kyle V, Hazelman BL: Stopping steroids in polymyalgia rheumatica and giant cell arteritis. *Br Med J* 300:344, 1990.
12. Chuang TY et al: Polymyalgia rheumatica: A ten year epidemiologic and clinical study. *Ann Intern Med* 97:672, 1982.
13. Dixon ASJ: Polymyalgia rheumatica. *Rep Rheum Dis* 86:1983.
14. Podgorski M, Edmonds J: Non-pharmacological treatment of patients with rheumatoid arthritis. *Med J Aust* 143:511, 1985.

15. Griffin MR et al: Nonsteroidal anti-inflammatory drug use and increased risk for peptic ulcer disease in elderly persons. *Ann Intern Med* 114:257, 1991.
16. Roth SH: Prevention of NSAID-induced gastric mucosal damage and gastric ulcer: A review of clinical studies. *J Drug Devel* 1:255, 1989.
17. Lockie LM et al: Low dose adrenocorticosteroids in the management of elderly patients with rheumatoid arthritis: Selected examples and summary of efficacy in the long term management of 97 patients. *Semin Arthritis Rheum* 12:373, 1983.
18. Harris ED Jr, et al: Low dose prednisone therapy in rheumatoid arthritis: A double blind study. *J Rheumatol* 10:713, 1983.
19. Dykman TR et al: Evaluation of factors associated with glucocorticoid-induced osteopenia in patients with rheumatic diseases. *Arthritis Rheum* 28:361, 1985.
20. Weinblatt ME et al: Efficacy of low dose methotrexate in rheumatoid arthritis. *N Engl J Med* 312:818, 1985.
21. Tugwell P: Methotrexate in rheumatoid arthritis: Feedback on American College of Physicians Guidelines. *Ann Intern Med* 110:581, 1989.
22. Gispen JG et al: Toxicity of methotrexate in rheumatoid arthritis. *J Rheumatol* 14:74, 1987.
23. Paulus H: Antimalarial agents compared with or in combination with other disease modifying antirheumatic drugs. *Am J Med* 1985:45, 1988.
24. Easterbrook M: Ocular effects and safety of antimalarial agents. *Am J Med* 1985:23, 1988.
25. Smith MD: Disease-modifying antirheumatic drugs: Gold, penicillamine, antimalarials, and sulfasalazone. *Curr Opinion Rheum* 2:489, 1990.
26. DeJesus A, Talal H: Practical use of immunosuppressive drugs in autoimmune rheumatic diseases. *Crit Care Med* 18(suppl):132, 1990.
27. Melnyk V: Geriatric rheumatology: Safe and potentially toxic antirheumatics. *Geriatrics* 43:83, 1988.
28. Fisher NM et al: Muscle rehabilitation: Its effect on muscular and functional performance of patients with osteoarthritis. *Arch Phys Med Rehabil* 72:367, 1991.
29. Bentley G, Dowd GSE: Surgical treatment of arthritis in the elderly. *Clin Rheum Dis* 12:291, 1986.
30. Anderson KO et al: Rheumatoid arthritis: Review of psychological factors related to etiology effect and treatment. *Psychol Bul* 98:358, 1985.
31. Winfield JB: Arthritis patient education: Efficacy, implementation and financing. The ACR/AHPA/AF/NAAB Task Force on Arthritis Patient Education. *Arthritis Rheum* 32:1330, 1989.
32. Morizono Y et al: Upper cervical involvement in rheumatoid arthritis. *Spine* 12:721, 1987.
33. Moncur C, Williams HJ: Cervical spine management in patients with rheumatoid arthritis: Review of the literature. *Phys Ther* 68:509, 1988.
34. Polisar IA et al: Bilateral midline fixation of cricoarytenoid joints as a serious medical emergency. *JAMA* 172:901, 1960.
35. Girdwood RH: Death after taking medicaments. *Br Med J* 1:501, 1974.
36. Pincus T, Callahan F: Taking mortality in rheumatoid arthritis seriously—Predictive markers, socioeconomic status and co-morbidity. *J Rheumatol* 13:841, 1986.
37. Halstead LS: Team care in chronic illness: A critical review of the literature of the past 25 years. *Arch Phys Med Rehab* 57:507, 1976.
38. James K, Meek G: Evaluation of commercial enzyme immunoassays compared to immunofluorescence and double diffusion for autoantibodies associated with autoimmune diseases. *Am J Clin Pathol* 97:559, 1992.
39. Nakamura RM, Tan EM: Update on autoantibodies to intracellular antigens in systemic rheumatic disease. *Clin Lab Med* 12:1, 1992.
40. Sturgess A: Recently characterized autoantibodies and their clinical significance. *Aust NZ J Med* 22:279, 1992.
41. Tan EM: Antinuclear antibodies: Diagnostic markers for autoimmune disease and probes for cell biology. *Adv Immunol* 44:93, 1989.
42. Tan EM et al: The 1982 revised criteria for the classification of systemic lupus erythematosus. *Arthritis Rheum* 25:1271, 1982.
43. Bylund DJ, Nakamura RM: Importance of detection of SS-A/Ro autoantibody in screening immunofluorescence tests for autoantibodies to nuclear antigens. *J Clin Lab Anal* 5:212, 1991.
44. Hochberg MC et al: Systemic lupus erythematosus: A review of clinical laboratory features and immunogenetic markers in 150 patients with emphasis in demographic subsets. *Medicine* 64:285, 1985.
45. Weiss RA et al: Diagnostic tests and clinical subsets in systemic lupus erythematosus: Update 1983. *Ann Allergy* 516:135, 1983.
46. Venables PJW et al: Anti-La(SS-B): A diagnostic criterion for Sjögren's syndrome? *Clin Exp Rheumatol* 7:181, 1989.
47. Miyachi K, Tan EM: Antibodies reacting with ribosomal ribonucleoproteins in connective tissue disease. *Arthritis Rheum* 22:87, 1979.
48. Jarzabek-Chorzelska M et al: Scl-70 antibody—A specific marker of systemic sclerosis. *Br J Dermatol* 115:393, 1986.
49. Sakamoto M et al: Purification and characterization of Ki antigen and detection of anti-Ki antibody by enzyme linked immunosorbent assay in patients with systemic lupus erythematosus. *Arthritis Rheum* 32:1554, 1989.
50. Wallace DJ: Active idiopathic systemic lupus erythematosus in a 90 year old woman requiring corticosteroid therapy. *J Rheumatol* 18:1611, 1991.
51. Ward MM, Pollison RP: A meta-analysis of the clinical manifestations of older-onset systemic lupus erythematosus. *Arthritis Rheum* 32:1226, 1989.
52. Maddison PJ: Systemic lupus erythematosus in the elderly. *J Rheumatol* 14(Supl 13):182, 1987.
53. Baer AN, Pincus T: Occult systemic lupus erythematosus in elderly men. *JAMA* 249:3350, 1983.
54. Catoggio LJ et al: Systemic lupus erythematosus in the elderly: Clinical and serologic characteristics. *J Rheumatol* 11:175, 1984.
55. Hutton CW, Madisson PJ: Systemic lupus erythematosus presenting as polymyalgia rheumatica in the elderly. *Ann Rheumat Dis* 45:641, 1986.
56. Kimberly RP: Systemic lupus erythematosus treatment: Corticosteroids and anti-inflammatory drugs. *Rheum Dis Clin North Am* 14:203, 1988.
57. Rothenberg RJ et al: The use of methotrexate in steroid-resistant systemic lupus erythematosus. *Arthritis Rheum* 31:612, 1988.
58. Rothfield N: Efficacy of antimalarials in systemic lupus erythematosus. *Am J Med* 85:53, 1988.
59. The Canadian Hydroxychloroquine Study Group: A

randomized study of the effect of withdrawing hydroxychloroquine sulfate in systemic lupus erythematosus. *N Engl J Med* 324:150, 1991.

60. Blomgren SE et al: Procainamide-induced lupus erythematosus. *Am J Med* 52:338, 1972.
61. Alarcon-Segovia D et al: Clinical and experimental studies on the hydralazine syndrome and its relationship to systemic lupus erythematosus. *Medicine* 46:1, 1967.
62. Batchelor JR et al: Hydralazine-induced systemic lupus erythematosus: Influence of HLADR and sex on susceptibility. *Lancet* 1:1107, 1980.
63. Sreebny LM, Valdini A: Xerostomia: A neglected symptom. *Arch Intern Med* 147:1333, 1987.
64. Drosos AA et al: Prevalence of primary Sjögren's syndrome in an elderly population. *Br J Rheumatol* 27:123, 1988.
65. Strand V, Talal N: Advances in the diagnosis and concept of Sjögren's syndrome (autoimmune exocrinopathy). *Bull Rheum Dis* 30:1046, 1979–80.
66. Alexander EL et al: Sjögren's syndrome: Association of anti-Ro/SSA antibodies with vasculitis, hematologic abnormalities, and serologic hyperactivity. *Ann Intern Med* 98:155, 1983.
67. Kelly CA et al: Primary Sjögren's syndrome in North East England—A longitudinal study. *Br J Rheumatol* 30:437, 1991.
68. Alexander EL et al: Neurologic complications of primary Sjögren's syndrome. *Medicine* 61:247, 1982.
69. Molina R et al: Peripheral inflammatory vascular disease in Sjögren's syndrome: Association with nervous system complications. *Arthritis Rheum* 28:1341, 1985.
70. Malinow KL et al: Neuropsychiatric dysfunction in primary Sjögren's syndrome. *Ann Intern Med* 103:344, 1985.
71. Kaplan JG et al: Invited review: Peripheral neuropathy in Sjögren's syndrome. *Muscle Nerve* 13:570, 1990.
72. Greenspan JS et al: The histopathology of Sjögren's syndrome in labial salivary gland biopsies. *Oral Surg* 37:217, 1974.
73. Medsger TA, Masi AT: Epidemiology of systemic sclerosis (scleroderma). *Ann Intern Med* 74:714, 1971.
74. Barnett AJ: The neck sign in scleroderma. *Arthritis Rheum* 32:209, 1989.
75. Silver RM: Lung involvement in systemic sclerosis. *Bull Rheum Dis* 41(2):3, 1992.
76. Botstein GR, LeRoy C: Primary heart disease in systemic sclerosis (scleroderma): Advances in clinical and pathologic features, pathogenesis and new therapeutic approaches. *Am Heart J* 102:913, 1981.
77. Hodkinson HM: Scleroderma in the elderly, with special reference to the CREST syndrome. *J Am Geriat Soc* 19:224, 1971.
78. Alarcon-Segovia D, Cardiel MH: Comparison between three diagnostic criteria for mixed connective tissue disease: Study of 593 patients. *J Rheum* 16:328, 1989.
79. Oliver GF, Winkelmann RK: The current treatment of scleroderma. *Drugs* 37:87, 1989.
80. Traub YM: Hypertension and renal failure (scleroderma renal crisis) in progressive systemic sclerosis: Review of a 25 year experience with 68 cases. *Medicine* 62:335, 1983.
81. Silver RM et al: Evaluation and management of scleroderma lung disease using bronchoalveolar lavage. *Am J Med* 88:470, 1990.

Chapter 85

OSTEOARTHRITIS

Rose S. Fife

Osteoarthritis (OA) is the most common form of arthritis in humans. It affects approximately 40 million Americans[1] and is the second most common cause of disability in this country.[2] The incidence of OA increases with aging.[3–5] In studies of large numbers of individuals whose knee radiographs were available for evaluation, approximately 30 to 60 percent of those over the age of 65 had changes consistent with OA.[6–8] Indeed, OA was often considered as merely a normal variant of aging and not as a true disease, but there is now much data indicating that this is not the case.[3,5] As discussed below, significant differences exist between the biochemistry and appearance of cartilage from normal aged and osteoarthritic joints.[5] Thus, OA is not merely a final common pathway of aging but is truly a disease process, the incidence of which increases with aging.

One may wonder why OA should be considered separately in a textbook of gerontology, since it is such a widespread problem and its manifestations may not seem to be very different in individuals of different ages. However, some of the manifestations and consequences of the disease and possible therapeutic modalities can be altered by the aging process. This chapter will not address the pharmacologic treatment of OA, since that will be considered elsewhere in this book (see Chap. 81), but other types of therapy will be discussed here.

BIOCHEMICAL CHANGES OF CARTILAGE IN OA AND AGING

As indicated above, OA was previously considered to be a normal variant of aging by some, but this is no longer the case. As can be seen in Table 85-1, major differences are found between the biochemistry of normal aged articular cartilage and that of osteoarthritic cartilage.[5] OA is characterized by an increase in tissue water content[9,10] and a progressive decrease in glycosaminoglycans, including chondroitin sulfate, keratan sulfate, and hyaluronic acid.[11–13] The extractability of proteoglycans and collagen is increased in osteoarthritic cartilage.[14–16] This is thought to be due to the abnormal hydration of cartilage that occurs in OA, with resultant disruption of the collagen network.[5,6] Aggregation of proteoglycans with hyaluronic acid, which is stabilized by link proteins, is markedly diminished in OA, so that few aggregates are found and those that do exist are much smaller than normal.[17,18] The increased activity of various degradative enzymes, including the matrix metalloproteinases, has been well documented in OA.[19,20] These enzymes are believed to be responsible for much of the destruction that occurs in OA.

OA is characterized biochemically by an initial increase in proteoglycan synthesis,[21] which ultimately diminishes to levels that are below normal.[22] Alterations occur in the ratio of glycosaminoglycan chains synthesized by osteoarthritic cartilage. A relative increase in chondroitin 4-sulfate compared with chondroitin 6-sulfate is observed, along with a decrease in keratan sulfate.[23,24]

In contrast, the tissue water content of normal aged cartilage is decreased,[5] and the quantity of some of the glycosaminoglycans, including keratan sulfate and hyaluronic acid, is increased.[25] The ratio of chondroitin 6-sulfate to chondroitin 4-sulfate also increases with age.[26] Dermatan sulfate proteoglycans are enriched in cartilage from older individuals.[27] Proteoglycan extractability decreases with age.[26]

Obviously, normal articular cartilage from elderly individuals is not biochemically identical to that from younger individuals. Furthermore, biomechanical alterations occur over time and probably contribute to the changes found in aged cartilage. Increased incongruity of the joint surfaces occurs with aging, probably as a result of alterations in blood flow as well as in the load distribution across the joint.[5,28,29] The subchondral bone changes with age, possibly as a result of long-term weight-bearing, and this can alter the overlying cartilage.[29,30] Extensive discussions of the comparisons between aging and OA cartilage have been presented elsewhere.[3,5,13] Also see Chap. 80.

TABLE 85-1

Comparison between Normal Aged Articular Cartilage and Osteoarthritic Cartilage

Measurement	Aging	Osteoarthritis
Tissue water content	Decreased	Increased
Gycosaminoglycans		
Chondroitin sulfate content	Normal or slightly decreased	Progressively decreased
Chondroitin sulfate chain length	Decreased	Increased early; decreased with progression of disease
Ratio of chondroitin 4-sulfate:chondroitin 6-sulfate	Decreased	Increased
Keratan sulfate content	Increased	Decreased
Hyaluronic acid content	Increased	Decreased
Proteoglycans		
Extractability	Decreased	Increased
Aggregation	Normal	Diminished
Size of monomers	Decreased	Decreased
Rate of maturation of hyaluronate-binding region	Decreased	Increased
Tissue content of free hyaluronate-binding region	Increased	Unknown
Link protein	Fragmented	Normal
Degradative enzyme activity		
Neutral proteoglycanase	Normal	Increased
Acid protease	Normal	Increased
Collagenase	Normal	Increased

(From Brandt and Fife,[5] reproduced with permission.)

PATHOLOGY OF OSTEOARTHRITIC CARTILAGE

Macroscopically, OA cartilage becomes ulcerated.[31] Eventually, later in the disease, the subchondral bone is exposed and rubs upon the adjacent bone with each movement of the joint, in the absence of normal cushioning by intervening cartilage. This leads to increased joint destruction.[32,33]

At the microscopic level, there is initially some hypercellularity of chondrocytes in OA.[34] However, as time passes, the number of cells diminishes. In contrast, cell density in normal articular cartilage remains relatively constant with age.[5]

RISK FACTORS FOR OA

While the cause of OA remains unknown, a number of factors have been identified which can put an individual at risk for the disease. The mechanism by which a particular risk factor leads to the development of OA is not always obvious.

One such risk factor is obesity, which correlates best with knee OA.[35–39] Obesity results in abnormal loading across the joint, altering the stresses to which it is normally exposed. This may produce OA, especially if some degree of joint incongruity exists.[2]

An inverse correlation has been described between bone density and OA, especially in postmenopausal women.[2,40] The explanation for this association is unknown, but one possibility that has been suggested is that osteopenic bone can absorb some of the stress that normally falls upon the joint cartilage.[2]

The relationship between repetitive mechanical overuse of a joint, as the result of vocational or avocational activities, and the development of OA in that joint has been recognized for a long time. Examples include shoulder OA in baseball pitchers, elbow OA in ditch diggers, and knee OA in individuals engaged in activities associated with repetitive bending.[31,41] Again, as with obesity, mechanical stresses are thought to be responsible for the development of OA in these joints. Previous trauma or inflammatory arthritis (e.g., rheumatoid arthritis, gout, chondrocalcinosis) also can predispose a given joint to OA.

A role for heredity in at least some forms of OA has long been suspected. Stecher[42] identified a familial tendency to inflammatory OA of the hands in women. Recent studies have demonstrated point mutations in collagen in individuals from kindreds with syndromes resembling OA.[43–45] While these individuals did not have true classic OA, the identification of such mutations raises the possibility that future studies might reveal mutations associated with typical OA.

CLINICAL MANIFESTATIONS OF OA IN THE ELDERLY

Osteoarthritis is a chronic degenerative disease of diarthrodial joints, which results in thinning and ultimate loss of cartilage.[46] The clinical characteristics of OA are joint pain and swelling, decreased range of motion of the joint, and crepitus with movement.[31,47] Osteoarthritis typically involves large weight-bearing joints, such as the hips and knees, as well as the distal interphalangeal (DIP) joints and proximal interphalangeal (PIP) joints of the hands.[31,47] Other joints, including the first carpometacarpal joints of the thumbs, are also commonly involved.[47] Elbows, shoulders, ankles, and toes are less commonly affected by OA unless there has been preexisting trauma to or repetitive usage of these joints, as noted earlier. Radiographically, OA is characterized by joint space narrowing, bony sclerosis along the joint margins, and osteophytes, which are outgrowths of bone at the edges of the joints.[48]

Several subsets of OA have been described. The most common is the oligoarticular form, which involves one or two of the large weight-bearing joints of the lower extremities. This disease tends to occur fairly equally in both sexes and is more prevalent with age.[47] Another subset is erosive or generalized OA, which was originally described by Kellgren and Moore.[49] Women are more likely to develop this inflammatory form of OA of the DIPs and PIPs, often as early as the age of 30. Inflammatory OA has a tendency to run in families, especially in women, as discussed above. Its activity often ceases spontaneously by the age of 50 or so, leaving the patient with deformities of the hands, but the hands are usually fairly functional and pain-free. Another major form of OA appears to occur as a result of preexisting trauma or other damage to a joint, such as long-standing rheumatoid arthritis or gouty arthritis.[31] The prevalence of this form of OA increases with age.

The symptoms of OA in the elderly are very similar to those in younger individuals. Elderly patients have joint pain, swelling, and decreased range of motion. There is bony prominence of particular joints, such as the DIPs, called Heberden's nodes, and the PIPs, called Bouchard's nodes.[47] The elderly may become debilitated faster than younger individuals as a result of progressive OA because of their greater frailty. A painful hip in an older person, which alters his or her gait, obviously puts that individual at greater risk for a fall which, in turn, is likely to produce a fractured bone, which can be very devastating in the elderly. To that extent, the potential risks of OA in older individuals are greater than in younger people.

The joints that are involved in the elderly are usually the same as described above—that is, the large weight-bearing joints of the lower extremities, the PIPs and DIPs of the hands, whether the disease is inflammatory or not, and joints that have been previously damaged. Physical examination usually will reveal tenderness along the joint line, Heberden's nodes, Bouchard's nodes, synovial effusions, and loss of range of motion, initially due to effusions and subsequently to bony deformities.

When an elderly person presents with a joint effusion, the joint should be aspirated, just as in younger patients. The fluid of an OA joint is typically noninflammatory, usually with fewer than 1000 white cells/mm^3.[50] If the fluid is inflammatory, another cause of arthritis must be sought. It should be borne in mind that even though a joint may show radiographic changes of OA, other forms of arthritis still can occur in such a joint and can cause inflammatory effusions. Such diseases include septic arthritis, gout, pseudogout, hydroxyapatite crystal–induced arthritis, and other forms of inflammatory arthritis, including rheumatoid arthritis. As will be discussed elsewhere in this text, gout and pseudogout occur more commonly in the elderly (Chap. 86).

Radiographs should be obtained in individuals who complain of joint pain. In elderly people, as indicated above, one expects to see some changes of OA even in joints that are asymptomatic. The absence of such changes would argue against the presence of severe OA, but the presence of such changes is not very sensitive and only means that the patient has OA; it does not, however, permit a determination of the severity of the disease. This has been demonstrated by the lack of correlation between radiographic grades and arthroscopic findings in joints with respect to OA.[51]

MANAGEMENT OF OA IN THE ELDERLY

Pharmacologic treatment with the nonsteroidal anti-inflammatory drugs (NSAIDs) is discussed in Chap. 81 However, it should be pointed out that the elderly are more susceptible to adverse effects from these agents, particularly reactions involving the liver and kidneys, than are younger individuals.[52] Therefore, the minimum effective dosage of these medicines should be used in the elderly. Since OA is not typically an inflammatory disease except in its earliest stages and in the erosive form, NSAIDs may not be more useful in its treatment than are analgesics, such as acetaminophen, which tend to be safer.[53] The judicious use of intraarticular steroid injections can provide relief in some patients with knee OA but is especially helpful in those with inflammatory OA of the hands. A given joint should not be injected more often than three times a year at the most.

One of the mainstays of treatment for OA in the elderly is early management by physical and occupational therapists. Maintaining muscle tone and posture and teaching joint protection are keys to keeping an elderly individual able to function on his or her own.[41] The therapeutic application of superficial heat can decrease local discomfort due to OA in an affected joint.[41] Ultrasound can be used to provide deeper penetration of heat and can decrease joint pain.[54] Cold also has been used successfully in some individuals as a therapeutic modality to reduce pain.[41]

Regular programs of low-impact or no-impact exercise are excellent ways to improve muscle strength and tone. A set of water exercises, which avoids the effects of gravity on joints and does not require the ability to swim, has been developed through the Arthritis Foundation.

The transcutaneous electrical nerve stimulator, or TENS unit, has been used to reduce joint pain. It is probably most commonly used for back disease, but its success for pain relief in knee OA has been reported.[55] However, a more recent report indicated that the TENS unit may not be superior to placebo.[56]

Orthotic devices for shoes and splinting of the hands can provide significant benefits in patients with OA.[41] A number of assistive devices are available to help the individual with most of the activities of daily living, including jar openers, key holders, and so on. Such simple tools can dramatically improve an individual's ability to maintain his or her independence. The use of a cane or a walker to give the individual more stability and to protect him or her from falling should be encouraged when appropriate.

Arthroscopy sometimes can produce beneficial results in patients with knee OA. Debridement of cartilage, removal of loose bodies and osteophytes, and even repair of meniscal tears can be performed and can result in decreased pain and disability in selected individuals. Some studies have suggested that joint lavage with irrigating solutions through the arthroscope can be beneficial in OA, perhaps by removing loose fragments and macromolecules, such as the matrix metalloproteinases which are thought to be involved in the pathogenesis of OA.[57] However, more work needs to be done to evaluate the efficacy of lavage.

Orthopedists also have a lot to offer many elderly patients with OA, particularly involving the hips or knees. Osteotomy and debridement are sometimes quite successful in reducing knee pain. Prostheses for hips and knees are very successful in restoring mobility and alleviating pain. These procedures are typically reserved for individuals with severe pain, including pain at night, and with severe limitation in ambulation. Numerous types of prostheses are available and their longevity in the patient is considerably greater than that of their earlier counterparts. Joint function and range of motion can be restored dramatically. However, a patient must be able to cooperate with and participate in the intensive rehabilitation required postoperatively. An otherwise healthy elderly person—that is, someone without major cardiac or pulmonary disease, obesity, or diabetes, for example—is an excellent candidate for a total hip or knee replacement and usually receives a great deal of benefit from such a procedure. Obviously, individuals with major medical problems are poor surgical risks and often cannot be offered surgical intervention. Arthroscopy might be considered as an alternative in such patients.

SUMMARY

Osteoarthritis is not a normal variant of aging. It is a disease process that increases in incidence as individuals age. Osteoarthritis can cause a great deal of disability and discomfort and can be managed appropriately in elderly patients with a combination of modalities that should include analgesia, rehabilitation and joint protection, and surgery when indicated.

REFERENCES

1. Bland JH, Cooper SM: Osteoarthritis: A review of the cell biology involved and evidence for reversibility. *Semin Arthritis Rheum* 14:106, 1984.
2. Peyron JG, Altman RD: The epidemiology of osteoarthritis, in Moskowitz RW, Howell DS, Goldberg VM, Mankin HJ (eds): *Osteoarthritis: Diagnosis and Medical/Surgical Management,* 2d ed. Philadelphia, Saunders, 1992, pp 15–37.
3. Hough AJ Jr, Webber RJ: Aging phenomena and osteoarthritis: Cause or coincidence? *Ann Clin Lab Sci* 16:502, 1986.
4. Davis MA: Epidemiology of osteoarthritis. *Clin Geriatric Med* 4:241, 1988.
5. Brandt KD, Fife RS: Ageing in relation to the pathogenesis of osteoarthritis. *Clin Rheum Dis* 12:117, 1986.
6. Lawrance JS et al: Osteoarthrosis: Prevalence in the population and relationship between symptoms and x-ray changes. *Ann Rheum Dis* 25:1, 1966.
7. Lawrance JS: *Rheumatism in Populations.* London, Heinemann Medical, 1977.
8. Peyron JG: Epidemiologic and etiologic approach to osteoarthritis. *Semin Arthritis Rheum* 8:288, 1979.

9. Venn MF, Maroudas A: Chemical composition and swelling of normal and osteoarthrotic femoral head cartilage: I. Chemical composition. *Ann Rheum Dis* 36:121, 1977.
10. Maroudas A, Venn M: Chemical composition and swelling of normal and osteoarthrotic femoral head cartilage: II. Swelling. *Ann Rheum Dis* 36:399, 1977.
11. Inerot S et al: Articular-cartilage proteoglycans in aging and osteoarthritis. *Biochem J* 169:143, 1978.
12. Thonar EJ-MA et al: Hyaluronate in articular cartilage: Age-related changes. *Calcif Tiss Res* 26:19, 1978.
13. Brandt KD: Osteoarthritis. *Clin Geriatric Med* 4:279, 1988.
14. Brandt KD: Enhanced extractability of articular cartilage proteoglycans in osteoarthritis. *Biochem J* 143: 475, 1974.
15. Eyre DR et al: Biosynthesis of collagen and other matrix proteins by articular cartilage in experimental osteoarthritis. *Biochem J* 188:823, 1980.
16. Ronziere MC et al: Comparative analysis of collagens solubilized by human foetal, and normal and osteoarthritic adult articular cartilage, with emphasis on type VI collagen. *Biochim Biophys Acta* 1038:222, 1990.
17. Brandt KD et al: Aggregation of cartilage proteoglycans: I. Evidence for the presence of a hyaluronate binding region in proteoglycans from osteoarthritic cartilage. *Arthritis Rheum* 19:1308, 1976.
18. Moskowitz RW et al: Cartilage proteoglycan alterations in an experimentally induced model of rabbit osteoarthritis. *Arthritis Rheum* 22:155, 1979.
19. Sapolsky A et al: Metalloproteases of human articular cartilage that digest cartilage proteoglycan at neutral and acid pH. *J Clin Invest* 58:1030, 1976.
20. Pelletier J-P et al: Collagenase and collagenolytic activity in human osteoarthritic cartilage. *Arthritis Rheum* 26:63, 1983.
21. Bollet AJ et al: Chondroitin sulfate concentration and protein-polysaccharide composition of articular cartilage in osteoarthritis. *J Clin Invest* 42:853, 1963.
22. Thompson RC Jr, Oegema, TR Jr: Metabolic activity of articular cartilage in osteoarthritis: An *in vitro* study. *J Bone Joint Surg* 61A: 407, 1979.
23. Mankin HJ, Lippiello L: The glycosaminoglycans of normal and arthritic cartilage. *J Clin Invest* 45:1103, 1966.
24. Bollet AJ, Nance JL: Biochemical findings in normal and osteoarthritic articular cartilage: II. Chondroitin sulfate concentration and chain length, water and ash content. *J Clin Invest* 45:1170, 1966.
25. Elliot RJ, Gardner DL: Changes with age in the glycosaminoglycans of human articular cartilage. *Ann Rheum Dis* 38:371, 1979.
26. Roughley PJ, White RJ: Age-related changes in the structure of the proteoglycan subunits from human articular cartilage. *J Biol Chem* 255:217, 1980.
27. Rosenberg LC et al: Structural changes in proteoglycans in aging cartilages, in Peyron JG (ed): *Osteoarthritis: Current Clinical and Fundamental Problems.* Paris: Ciba-Geigy, 1985, pp 179–191.
28. Bullough PG: The geometry of diarthrodial joints, its physiologic maintenance, and the possible significance of age-related changes in geometry-to-load distribution and the development of osteoarthritis. *Clin Orthop* 156:61, 1980.
29. Lane LB et al: The vascularity and remodelling of subchondral bone and calcified cartilage in adult human femoral and humeral heads. *J Bone Joint Surg* 59B:272, 1977.
30. Radin EL et al: Subchondral bone changes in patients with early degenerative joint disease. *Arthritis Rheum* 13:400, 1970.
31. Brandt KD: Osteoarthritis: Clinical patterns and pathology, in Kelley WN, Harris ED Jr, Ruddy S, Sledge CB (eds): *Textbook of Rheumatology,* 2d ed, vol 2. Philadelphia, Saunders, 1985, pp 1432–1448.
32. Radin EL et al: Role of mechanical factors in pathogenesis of primary osteoarthrosis. *Lancet* 1:519, 1972.
33. Radin EL et al: Mechanical factors in the aetiology of osteoarthrosis. *Ann Rheum Dis* 34 (suppl):132, 1975.
34. Weiss C, Mirow S: An ultrastructural study of osteoarthritic changes in articular cartilage of human knees. *J Bone Joint Surg* 54A:954, 1971.
35. Davis MA et al: Obesity and osteoarthritis of the knee: Evidence from the National Health and Nutrition Examination Survey (NHANES I). *Semin Arthritis Rheum* 20 (suppl):34, 1991.
36. Anderson JJ, Felson DT: Factors associated with osteoarthritis of the knee in the first national Health and Nutrition Examination survey (NHANES I): Evidence for an association with overweight, race and physical demands of work. *Am J Epidemiol* 127:179, 1988.
37. Felson DT et al: Obesity and knee osteoarthritis: The Framingham Study. *Ann Intern Med* 109:18, 1988.
38. Felson, DT: The epidemiology of knee osteoarthritis: Results from the Framingham Study. *Semin Arthritis Rheum* 20:42, 1990.
39. Kohatsu ND, Schurman DJ: Risk factors for the development of osteoarthritis of the knee. *Clin Orthop* 261:242, 1990.
40. Cooper C et al: Osteoarthritis of the hip and osteoporosis of the proximal femur. *Ann Rheum Dis* 50:540, 1991.
41. Hicks JE, Gerber LH: Rehabilitation in the management of patients with osteoarthritis, in Moskowitz RW, Howell DS, Goldberg VM, Mankin HJ (eds): *Osteoarthritis: Diagnosis and Medical/Surgical Management,* 2d ed. Philadelphia, Saunders, 1992, pp 427–464.
42. Stecher RM: Heberden's nodes: A clinical description of osteoarthritis of the finger joints. *Ann Rheum Dis* 14:1, 1955.
43. Knowlton RG et al: Genetic linkage of a polymorphism in the type II procollagen gene (COL2A1) to primary osteoarthritis associated with mild chondrodysplasia. *N Engl J Med* 322:526, 1990.
44. Ala-Kokko L et al: Single base mutation in the type II procollagen gene (COL2A1) as a cause of primary osteoarthritis associated with a mild chondrodysplasia. *Proc Natl Acad Sci USA* 87:6565, 1990.
45. Eyre DR et al: Cartilage expression of a type II collagen mutation in an inherited form of osteoarthritis associated with a mild chondrodysplasia. *J Clin Invest* 87:357, 1991.
46. Mankin HJ et al: Workshop on etiopathogenesis of osteoarthritis: Proceedings and recommendations. *J Rheumatol* 13:1127, 1986.
47. Moskowitz RW: Osteoarthritis—Signs and symptoms, in Moskowitz RW, Howell DS, Goldberg VM, Mankin HJ (eds): *Osteoarthritis: Diagnosis and Medical/Surgical*

Management, 2d ed. Philadelphia, Saunders, 1992, pp 255–261.
48. Resnick D, Niwayama G: *Diagnosis of Bone and Joint Disorders.* Philadelphia, Saunders, 1988.
49. Kellgren JH, Moore R: Generalized osteoarthritis and Heberden's nodes. *Br Med J* 1:181, 1952.
50. Ropes MW, Bauer W: *Synovial Fluid Changes in Joint Disease.* Cambridge, MA: Harvard University Press, 1953.
51. Fife RS et al: Relationship between arthroscopic evidence of cartilage damage and radiographic evidence of joint space narrowing in early osteoarthritis of the knee. *Arthritis Rheum* 34:377, 1991.
52. Schlegel S, Paulus H: Uptake on NSAID use in rheumatic diseases. *Bull Rheum Dis* 36:1, 1986.
53. Bradley JD et al: Comparison of an antiinflammatory dose of ibuprofen, an analgesic dose of ibuprofen, and acetaminophen in the treatment of patients with osteoarthritis of the knee. *N Engl J Med* 325:87, 1991.
54. Lehmann JF: Diathermy, in Krusen FH et al, *Handbook of Physical Medicine and Rehabilitation,* 2d ed. Philadelphia, Saunders, 1971, pp 273–345.
55. Taylor T et al: Treatment of osteoarthritis of the knee with transcutaneous electrical stimulation. *Pain* 11:233, 1981.
56. Lewis D et al: Transcutaneous electrical stimulation in osteoarthritis: A therapeutic alternative. *Ann Rheum Dis* 43:47, 1984.
57. Arnold WJ et al: Tidal irrigation versus medical management in patients with osteoarthritis of the knee: Results of a single blind randomized multicenter study. *Arthritis Rheum* 32 (suppl):S138, 1989.

Chapter 86

GOUT AND PYROPHOSPHATE GOUT (CHONDROCALCINOSIS)

J. Edwin Seegmiller

Both gout[1] and pyrophosphate gout (chondrocalcinosis)[2] are examples of crystal-induced arthritis. They differ, however, in the type of crystal responsible, the mechanism of the crystal formation, the sites of crystal deposition, and, to some degree, the clinical presentation, age profile, and sex of patients affected. They also differ historically. The clinical features of acute gouty arthritis are so distinctive that it was readily recognized and described by Hippocrates in the fourth century B.C. The needle-shaped crystals of tophaceous deposits were described by Leeuwenhoek in the seventeenth century and identified as a salt of uric acid in the eighteenth century.[1,2] By contrast, pyrophosphate gout was first described in 1960 in Czechoslovakia as a distinctive radiographic pattern of calcium deposition in and about joints by Zitnan and Sitaj, who named it chondrocalcinosis.[3] The crystals in synovial fluid responsible for the acute inflammatory reaction were first identified as calcium pyrophosphate dihydrate by McCarty et al. in 1962.[4] Gouty arthritis is predominantly a disease of young adult men, with presentation usually as a monoarticular involvement of a peripheral joint. Women seldom have gout before the menopause. On the other hand, pyrophosphate gout affects both men and women, in a ratio of 1.5:1, and is seldom seen below age 50; the prevalence increases remarkably with increasing age beyond the fifth decade. In an over-90 age group admitted to a British nursing home, fully one-half of the individuals showed x-ray evidence of chondrocalcinosis.[5] In both gout and pyrophosphate gout deposits of aggregated crystals can accumulate in and about some joints without necessarily producing an attack of acute arthritis; in both disorders this accumulation is associated with dispersion of crystals in the synovial fluid, where they undergo phagocytosis and elicit an intense inflammatory response. Gout is very seldom seen in association with rheumatoid arthritis, while pyrophosphate gout is quite frequently found in association with osteoarthritis. Furthermore, the clinical presentation of pyrophosphate gout can mimic a wide range of rheumatological syndromes, including septic arthritis, gout (whence the term *pseudogout*[4]), osteoarthritis, traumatic arthritis, neuropathic joint disease, and ankylosing spondylitis. In both disorders enzyme abnormalities of purine metabolism have been described in some but not all patients.[1,6]

GOUT

Gouty arthritis results from the deposition of needle-shaped crystals of monosodium urate monohydrate in and about the joints from supersaturated hyperuricemic extracellular body fluids. Both the degree and the duration of hyperuricemia appear to be determinants for the chance formation of the first seed crystal, which then leads to further crystal deposition. Once sufficient crystals accumulate in the joint space to pass a critical threshold, the body initiates an attack on the crystals by phagocytic cells, thus treating the crystals as the equivalent of invading microorganisms. The resulting intense inflammatory response, with its sudden onset usually in a single joint of the extremity, produces clinical symptoms of intense pain, exquisite tenderness, redness, swelling, and warmth, which together constitute the clinical presentation of the acute attack of gout. Even if untreated the acute attack gradually subsides over a 1- or 2-week period, and the patient may go many months or even years before experiencing a second acute attack in the same or a different joint. The course with time varies greatly from one patient to another. Some patients experience acute attacks only rarely. In others the disease can progress over the years if untreated, with the intervals between attacks becoming shorter and a chronic stage eventually developing with progressive and permanent destruction of joints and subchondral bone; a concurrent progressive renal impairment due to urate nephropathy and concomitant hypertension may accelerate the progress of the disease and can become life-threatening. Precipitating factors for developing the acute attack include environmental events, such as emotional upset, minor trauma, surgery, unusual exertions or exercise, and ingestion of certain drugs, foods, or alcoholic drinks.

Hyperuricemia

Hyperuricemia is a condition defined by a serum urate value above 7.0 mg/dl. This value is also approximately the limit of solubility for monosodium urate in plasma.[1] The hyperuricemia responsible for the development of gout results from a heterogeneous group of biochemical and physiological abnormalities of function. In up to 10 percent of patients a genetically determined excessive synthesis of the purine precursors of uric acid is responsible, but in the majority of patients purine synthesis is normal and a diminished renal excretion of uric acid is the cause of the hyperuricemia. In still other patients both mechanisms contribute in various degrees to the hyperuricemia. Hyperuricemia can also result from the side effects of a number of drugs, such as salicylates at doses less than 3 g/day, pyrazinamide, and thiazide diuretics. Hyperuricemia and gout can also result from chronic alcohol ingestion or from toxic effects of beryllium poisoning or of low-level lead poisoning.

Initially hyperuricemia is entirely without clinical symptoms and may remain so throughout a person's life, especially in patients who show only a modest degree of hyperuricemia. However, up to 25 percent of hyperuricemic subjects eventually experience the deposition of crystals composed of monosodium urate monohydrate in and about the joint, with the resulting intermittent attacks of acute gouty arthritis. The likelihood of depositing the crystals is undoubtedly increased in older patients with higher serum urate levels from the longer duration of exposure to the supersaturated body fluids. As deposits accumulate they can lead to clinically palpable nodules called tophi, which, in an advanced state of development, can produce a progressive permanent erosive damage to joint cartilage and bone. When tophaceous deposits are near the surface, the overlying skin shows a light pink coloring; from time to time the tophus may break through the skin and discharge a white, chalky material which, under the microscope, shows myriads of tiny needle-shaped crystals of monosodium urate. Although rare, similar deposits in the parenchyma of the kidney can lead to the deterioration of renal function. Kidneys can be further compromised by the frequent development of renal calculi composed of uric acid or calcium oxalate.

Associated Disorders

Gouty arthritis can be associated with a wide range of other clinical disorders. This possibility of associated disease mandates a complete examination, especially when the patient presents with the first attack. The associated disorders include hemolytic anemia; a wide range of myeloproliferative diseases; psoriasis; endocrine abnormalities, including hypothyroidism, hypoparathyroidism, and hyperparathyroidism; vascular disease, including hypertension and myocardial infarction; renal disease; and glomerulonephritis.

In addition, gout can result from a number of hereditary diseases. Among those associated with an excessive rate of purine synthesis are certain X-linked enzyme defects, for which a family history can be of particular value in showing maternal inheritance characteristic of X-linked disorders. Virtually complete deficiency of the enzyme hypoxanthine guanine phosphoribosyltransferase (HPRT) results in Lesch-Nyhan disease,[7] with its choreoathetosis, spasticity, and compulsive self-mutilation, as well as a four- to sixfold increase in uric acid production which leads to early onset of gouty arthritis, uric acid kidney stones, and progressive damage to kidneys.[1,8] Patients with a less severe enzyme deficit show a marked attenuation of the clinical expression of the syndrome, with less severe expression of the neurological symptoms. Other patients with more residual HPRT enzyme activity show no neurological symptoms and show only a two- to threefold increase over normal in uric acid production, but they still have the uric acid kidney stones and gouty arthritis that result from higher-than-normal uric acid levels. The latter two features are also found in another X-linked enzyme abnormality, in which they are caused by a genetically determined increase in activity of the enzyme phosphoribosylpyrophosphate synthetase.[9] In at least three families this enzyme abnormality has been associated with hereditary deafness and other neurological abnormalities.[10] Other hereditary diseases associated with excessive uric acid production and gout include glycogen storage disease (type I)[11] and symmetric adenolipomatosis.[12]

The following hereditary disorders show a normal rate of purine synthesis with a diminished renal clearance of uric acid to account for the hyperuricemia: hereditary nephritis, polycystic kidney disease, vasopressin-resistant nephrogenic diabetes insipidus, and branched-chain ketoaciduria (maple syrup urine disease). In addition, glycogen storage disease type I shows both excessive production and diminished renal excretion of uric acid.[10] Hyperuricemia also is found in patients with hereditary fructose intolerance from homozygosity for aldolase B deficiency. Ingestion of fructose results in severe adverse clinical reactions that can be fatal along with an accumulation of the substrate for the missing enzyme, fructose 1-phosphate, a marked depletion of ATP, and a decrease in levels of inorganic phosphate.[13] Phosphorus 31 magnetic resonance spectroscopy was used before and after 50 g of oral fructose to identify heterozygotes in families of patients with hereditary fructose intolerance. Of the nine heterozygotes identified, three had gouty arthritis.[14] The same procedure used to study 11 patients with familial gout identified 2 patients as heterozygotes.[15] The calculated incidence of the heterozygotes in the European population (1/80 in Switzerland and 1/250 in England) is of sufficient frequency to account for a significant portion of gout patients, thus providing the first indication of a relatively common genetic basis for garden-variety familial gout.[15]

The following miscellaneous conditions can be associated with development of a hyperuricemia: obesity, starvation, exercise, psoriasis, respiratory acidosis, diabetic ketoacidosis, beryllium disease and lead poisoning, hyperoxaluria, cystinuria, Down's syndrome, idiopathic hypercalciuria, sarcoidosis, Paget's disease of bone, Bartter's syndrome, postadrenalectomy, and alcoholism.

Diagnosis

The clinical features of the acute gouty attack are usually sufficiently characteristic to permit a presumptive diagnosis to be made at the bedside. The acute attack characteristically comes on suddenly and usually involves a single peripheral joint in an otherwise healthy, middle-aged man or postmenopausal woman. However, two or more peripheral joints are involved in approximately 5 percent of patients with gout. Approximately half of the patients show involvement of the first metatarsophalangeal joint in the first attack, and this involvement is seen at some time in the course of the disease in around 90 percent of patients. The pain progresses within a few hours of its onset to an intense severity that is often incapacitating. The affected joint shows marked swelling, exquisite pain, and tenderness, with varying degrees of erythema and warmth. The pain can be either throbbing or constant, but it is often worse at night and is usually so severe that the patient cannot bear any weight on the joint. These symptoms at the peak presentation suggest inflammation from a septic joint or cellulitis with the overlying skin being red, tense, and shiny. Furthermore, systemic symptoms of chilliness, fever, and leukocytosis are also commonly found. As a consequence, patients may receive inappropriate and unsuccessful treatment with antibiotics. In general, the swelling involved in a septic process of a joint is associated with a more doughy consistency of the area and a more pronounced pitting edema than is noted with the acute gouty attack. In addition, lymphangitis and lymphadenopathy are present in the nodes draining the septic joint but are seldom seen in the acute gouty process. A very careful examination for skin abrasion or other port of entry for the invading organism in septic arthritis is often helpful in making the correct diagnosis.

With progression of the acute gouty attack, the skin overlying the joint develops a characteristic violaceous hue and reveals dilated veins. During subsidence of the attack the skin often develops a scaling desquamation with a moderate pruritus and appears somewhat wrinkled and thin. For many years a prompt therapeutic response of the pain to the administration of the ancient drug colchicine has been used as a diagnostic test for gout. In the early years of the disease, even an untreated acute attack will regress spontaneously, over a variable period ranging from days to weeks, leaving no residual symptoms whatsoever, although more slowly than when treated. The presence of a family history of gout or renal calculi and a personal history of recurrent monoarticular arthritis are additional clinical features supporting the presumptive diagnosis. An intense search should be made for the presence of tophi, which are found most often around previously affected joints, over tendinous insertions in peripheral joints, or at sites of previous trauma. The presence of tophi on the helix of the ear, although not commonly present, can be especially helpful in the diagnosis.

It is important, particularly in patients presenting for the first time, to distinguish the acute attack from a septic process. In addition to the clues on physical examination noted above, this is best done by aspirating joint fluid using sterile precautions, then culturing a portion of it, centrifuging the remainder, and preparing a Gram's stain on a portion of the sediment for detection of bacteria. The remainder of the concentrated sediment is transferred into a hemocytometer chamber for microscopic examination for detection of the characteristic needle-shaped crystals of monosodium urate monohydrate. The crystals are most readily seen by examining the fluid under cross-polarizing filters with one polarizing filter placed on the light source of the microscope and the other in the eyepiece. The rotation of polarized light by the crystals allows them to be readily seen as bright needles against a black background. In sediment from joint fluid aspirated during an acute attack, over 90 percent of the crystals are found to be engulfed in phagocytes. By inserting a first-order red compensator (retardation plate) filter into the optical system, the negatively birefringent needle-shaped crystals of monosodium urate monohydrate can readily be distinguished from the positively birefringent rhomboid-shaped crystals of calcium pyrophosphate dihydrate characteristic of pyrophosphate gout. Under these conditions the crystals of monosodium urate located at right angles to the plane of polarization show a yellow color, whereas crystals of calcium pyrophosphate when viewed at this same angle show a lavender or blue color. (A few patients show both types of crystals.) This procedure is especially helpful in distinguishing gouty tophi from Darwinian tubercles on the ear and from subcutaneous lipomatous nodules or the subcutaneous nodules of rheumatoid arthritis. Tophi about the elbow are often difficult to distinguish from rheumatoid nodules. A biopsy of such a nodule with a frozen section or fixation in alcohol with examination of unstained sections using polarizing filters should reveal the presence of urate crystals. While staining procedures usually remove the crystals, the surrounding granulomatous changes characteristic of gouty arthritis are distinctive.

The typical radiologic lesion in gout results from tophus formation and consists of a "punched out" area in the subchondral bone, most frequently in the first metatarsophalangeal joint. In some cases this lesion may appear before any other evidence of tophaceous gout. With progression of the disease, subchondral tophi can enlarge, and they may appear in and about other joints with resulting destruction of the phalangeal joints in more advanced stages of the disease.

Treatment

As a result of improvements in therapy over the past four decades, virtually all patients with gouty arthritis can now enjoy a full and productive life without serious disability from their arthritis, provided they are diagnosed early and are maintained under continuous therapy with adequate supervision. As a result the emphasis has shifted from simple treatment of the recurring acute attacks to a preventive program aimed at management of the disease by correcting the underlying chemical disorder of hyperuricemia.

This therapeutic objective can be achieved by relatively simply procedures: (1) termination of the acute attack with one of a variety of anti-inflammatory drugs now available; (2) daily use of colchicine, usually 0.6 mg one to three times daily as tolerated, as prophylaxis against recurrence of the acute attack, especially during recovery from an attack and throughout the first few months of therapy with a drug for controlling the hyperuricemia; (3) evaluation of uric acid production in the 24-hour urine after equilibration on a diet virtually free of purines as a guide to selection of the drug most appropriate for maintenance therapy; and (4) initiation of treatment with a drug for lowering the serum urate level to the normal range. Such treatment must be initiated during a quiescent stage of the disease; experience shows that institution of such drugs *during* an acute attack delays recovery and exacerbates the attack. Maintenance of serum urate values between 5 and 6 mg/dl permits unsaturated body fluids to dissolve away all crystals of monosodium urate, thus removing the cause of the acute attacks and preventing the development of tophaceous gout, with its attendant potential for permanent joint and renal damage.

The severity of pain and disability usually seen in the patient with acute gouty arthritis demands intervention, even though the attacks are self-limited and show spontaneous recovery in 1 to 2 weeks. General measures for control of the acute attack include complete rest of the affected joint, a high fluid intake of 2 to 3 liters per day, a diet low in purines, and avoidance of alcohol. The intense pain frequently requires use of an analgesic or even a narcotic drug such as meperidine (Demerol). Usually 50 to 100 mg is required to control the severe pain. The attack can be readily terminated by the highly specific traditional drug colchicine, at 0.6 mg given hourly until the relief of pain or the appearance of nausea or diarrhea, at which point the colchicine is stopped. After recovery from gastrointestinal disturbance, 0.6 mg colchicine daily to tid can help to speed recovery and to suppress the tendency for recurrence of an attack upon beginning a drug for lowering serum urate levels. Intravenously administered colchicine, 2 mg in 20 ml of saline, produces a more rapid response and usually avoids the gastrointestinal side effects. Colchicine must not be administered by this route to patients with impaired renal function, however, and extravasation must be avoided. The use of nonsteroidal anti-inflammatory drugs has largely replaced the use of oral colchicine. These medications can be used at the maximum dosage for 2 to 3 days and then in a tapering dose over 1 week (see Chap. 81). Intraarticular corticosteroids are useful for gouty attacks of the large joints such as the knee or wrist.

Classification

Since lowering the serum urate level to the normal range requires a patient's lifetime commitment to a specific therapy, it is worthwhile to take extra time to obtain the basal daily uric acid production, which is then used to select the urate-lowering drug that will meet the patient's specific needs. This is best done as the acute attack is subsiding, while the patient is taking prophylactic daily colchicine (0.6 mg one to three times daily as tolerated) to prevent exacerbation or recurrence. This is a convenient time to evaluate the patient's 24-hour excretion of uric acid and creatinine while compliance in following instructions for this test is likely to be optimal. During this period, alcoholic drinks, as well as drugs such as aspirin, allopurinol, or uricosuric drugs or x-ray contrast drugs which are known to alter uric acid production or excretion, are to be avoided. The patient is usually sufficiently motivated by his or her recent experiences with the acute attack to follow a diet virtually free of purines for a 6-day period. This requires elimination of meat, fish, chicken, beans, peas, fermented beverages, and caffeine-containing drinks from the diet. Although caffeine does not produce uric acid, its end product, methylated uric acid, can register as uric acid in the colorimetric assays in general use. Dairy products are used as the major source of protein during the test period. During the last 3 days of the diet, each 24-hour urine sample is collected in a large bottle containing 3 ml of toluene or 0.25 g of thymol crystals as preservative to allow assessment of the degree of uric acid production. The urine should be stored at room temperature to minimize the amount of sediment formed. After any sediment present in each bottle of the urine is completely dissolved by warming and agitation, the total volume of each day's urine is measured and an aliquot sent to the laboratory for analysis of uric acid and creatinine levels, along with a blood sample for analysis of serum urate and creatinine levels. The upper range of normal excretion for an adult male patient is 600 mg of uric acid/24 hours. A normal serum urate level at the end of the collection period is evidence of the magnitude of the contribution of dietary habits, particularly excessive alcohol ingestion, as a major factor in generation of hyperuricemia. In occasional patients mere avoidance of alcohol is sufficient to maintain the serum urate level in the normal range. In an obese patient a modest degree of hyperuricemia can be corrected by weight loss, which can be presented as a possible valid alternative to drug treatment if the patient wishes to explore it. However, starvation diets without adequate carbohydrate and protein intake should be avoided, as they exacerbate the hyperuricemia and can induce an attack of gout.

Patients should be warned of the increased risk of developing an acute attack during the first few months after initiation of treatment with any drug given to lower the serum urate concentration to the normal range. This tendency is greatly diminished by prophylactic colchicine, 0.6 mg one to three times daily. The patient should be advised to reduce the dose of colchicine if gastrointestinal symptoms develop and to take an extra dose at the very first sign of an impending attack.

Patients who show no evidence of renal calculi or impaired renal function and who are excreting less than 600 mg of uric acid per day are producing normal amounts of uric acid; their hyperuricemia thus results from a decreased renal efficiency in uric acid excretion. Their primary deficit in renal excretion of uric acid can be corrected by administration of the uricosuric drug probenecid, initially at a dosage of 0.25 g ($\frac{1}{2}$ tablet) daily with a gradual increase over the course of a week to a maintenance dosage of 0.5 g twice daily; additional increases in dosage to as high as 1.0 g three times daily may be used as needed to maintain the serum urate concentration below 6.0 mg/dl. Sulfinpyrazone is an alternative uricosuric drug of greater potency (than probenecid) which may be needed in some patients. It is started at a dosage of 50 mg ($\frac{1}{2}$ tablet) once daily and increased gradually over a 2-day period to 100 mg three or four times daily. If necessary, up to twice this amount can be used, but this further increase is very seldom required. Benzbromarone is an even more potent uricosuric drug that has been in use in Europe for several years. It is administered in a divided dose of up to 300 mg/day.

Because patients with gout have an increased risk of developing renal calculi, they should develop the habit of drinking 3 liters of fluid (mostly water) per day to counter this tendency; this increased fluid intake can be presented as a very inexpensive and real form of health insurance against the risk of renal calculi development. Since salicylates block the action of uricosuric drugs, they must be avoided and can be replaced by acetaminophen (Tylenol), which does not have the blocking effect and provides comparable analgesia. The most frequent adverse reactions to uricosuric drugs are gastrointestinal symptoms and skin rash; hepatic necrosis or bone marrow depression are rare occurrences.

Patients excreting greater than 600 mg of uric acid per day are producing excessive amounts of uric acid and should be started on allopurinol, 100 mg daily as a single daily dose, after full recovery from the acute attack. The slow excretion of allopurinol makes divided doses unnecessary. Allopurinol not only blocks uric acid production by inhibiting the enzyme xanthine oxidase responsible for its synthesis but also diminishes the excessive purine synthesis in most patients, except those with Lesch-Nyhan disease or its variants.[1] Other indications for using allopurinol are intolerance of the uricosuric drug, evidence of impaired renal function, or the presence of uric acid calculi of the urinary tract. The latter will eventually undergo dissolution with continued allopurinol therapy. For each patient, follow-up examinations of serum urate levels should be done initially at monthly intervals until the proper dose of allopurinol (usually 300 mg daily) is found to reduce the serum urate level to between 5 and 6 mg/dl; then the examinations should be performed at 6-month intervals, along with routine checks on renal and hematological function, to prevent recurrence of the disease. The objective of this approach is to maintain the serum urate level in the normal range throughout life. The results are most gratifying to the patient, who thereby can live an essentially normal life without incapacitation from gouty arthritis. If the serum urate level is maintained in the normal range, eventually even the most severe deposits of tophaceous gout will be resolved, and most joints, with the exception of those permanently damaged by erosive action of the tophi, will be restored to essentially normal function.

PYROPHOSPHATE GOUT (CHONDROCALCINOSIS)

Pseudogout was the term first used to describe the clinical syndrome of acute gout-like arthritis associated with the presence of crystals of calcium pyrophosphate dihydrate in synovial fluid.[4] Subsequent studies showed this gout-like presentation to be just one aspect of the far larger range of clinical presentations of patients showing radiologic evidence of a characteristic pattern of calcification within the joints, which is called *chondrocalcinosis*[3] and more precisely designated as *calcium pyrophosphate dihydrate crystal deposition disease.*[2] Since these multiple names for the same basic pathological process are confusing to both students and professionals, a subcommittee of the American College of Rheumatology is recommending the name *pyrophosphate gout* as being a more specific and simple designation for naming a whole family of pathological states that would include apatite gout, cholesterol gout, and oxalate gout, with the prototype, urate gout, being referred to simply as *gout.*[16]

Pyrophosphate gout shows similarities to gouty arthritis in that it is a crystal-induced arthritis with intermittent acute attacks associated with appearance of crystals within phagocytes in the joint fluid and a consequent acute inflammatory reaction.[2,4] The overall incidence is also comparable with that of gout.

Pyrophosphate gout differs from gouty arthritis in a number of important ways. It shows a far wider range of clinical presentations. Instead of needle-shaped crystals of monosodium urate monohydrate deposited in and about the joint as seen in gouty arthritis, the deposits of crystals in pyrophosphate gout consist of rhombic or broad-shaped crystals of calcium pyrophosphate dihydrate that are typically found as a punctate or lamellar layer in the midzone of the cartilage. This is most often seen on x-ray films of the knee in meniscal fibrocartilage, as well as in the articular cartilage of the knee, in the articular disk of the distal radioulnar joint of the wrist, and, less frequently, in and about other major joints.[17]

The mechanism of formation of the crystals in pyrophosphate gout is entirely different from that responsible for the formation of crystals in gout. The plasma and other extracellular body fluids, with the exception of synovial fluid, show no elevation of either pyrophosphate or calcium levels in most patients with pyrophosphate gout.[2,18] Likewise, the calculated mean concentration of calcium and pyrophosphate in the cytoplasm of cells does not exceed the theoretical solubility product constant for this crystal.[19] This has led to the view that crystals may arise in a matrix vesicle rather than within the intracellular or extracellular space. It has been proposed that a possible role for calcium pyrophosphate may be as an intermediate source of the calcium and orthophosphate used for the formation of hydroxyapatite in the growth plate of the bone and possibly in bone remodeling. Excised cartilage from affected patients readily releases pyrophosphate into the surrounding medium.[20] Furthermore, chondrocytes cultured from affected patients show a two- to threefold increase over normal in intracellular pyrophosphate content,[21] as do fibroblasts or lymphoblasts cultured from the same patients,[22] thus providing evidence of a generalized metabolic abnormality with clinical pathological lesions limited to the cartilage.[23] Increased activity of the ectoenzyme nucleoside triphosphate pyrophosphohydrolase has been found both in cartilage extracts and in fibroblasts cultured from patients with sporadic but not familial forms of the disease.[23,24]

Several large pedigrees of hereditary pyrophosphate gout have been reported, most of which show evidence of a dominant pattern of inheritance.[10,26–28] The close association of osteoarthritis and pyrophosphate gout[5] has been recently confirmed by autopsy studies showing a frequency of concurrence of these diseases sixfold greater than would be expected from the chance association represented by the respective frequencies of both individual diseases in the population.[5,29] The discovery of modest elevations of pyrophosphate levels in synovial fluid of patients with more severe osteoarthritis suggests a possible metabolic link between the two diseases.[1] The greater-than-expected association of the pseudogout form of this disease with osteoarthritis in later years of life has suggested that it might result from clefts generated by the cartilage degeneration of osteoarthritis opening up passages by which crystals are more readily deposited into articular space to produce acute or subacute inflammation of one or more joints. Of particular interest is the fact that radiologic evidence of pyrophosphate gout is seldom found below age 50, while in the age group over 90 some 50 percent of patients show such evidence.[5] An exception is the appearance of pyrophosphate gout in adolescents in an inbred population of the Chiloé Island off the coast of southern Peru.[26] In pyrophosphate gout the distribution of affected joints differs from that found in gouty arthritis.[2] The joint most frequently involved with pyrophosphate gout is the knee, followed by the wrist and shoulders. Unlike gouty arthritis, pyrophosphate gout affects both men and women in the older age group.

Associated Disorders

A rational basis for the association of pyrophosphate gout with metabolic disorders such as hyperparathyroidism exists in the accompanying increase in the serum calcium concentration; in hereditary hypophosphatemia from a hereditary deficiency of alkaline phosphatase, the rational basis for association exists in the elevated concentration of pyrophosphate in serum and urine that occurs in this disorder. The associated impairment of bone mineral formation in this disorder provides strong evidence for pyrophosphate's being the major precursor of the orthophosphate used in the formation of the hydroxyapatite of bone since alkaline phosphatase has pyrophosphatase activity.[30] Less rational associations have been reported with hemochromatosis, hypophosphaturia, hypothyroidism, ochronotic arthritis, Wilson's disease, and even gout. In fact, some 20 percent of patients with pyrophosphate gout show hyperuricemia. The sporadic form of pyrophosphate gout is the most common form, but in some cases this may in fact represent a late-onset hereditary form.

Clinical Presentation

Pyrophosphate gout shows a wide range of clinical presentation that can resemble infectious arthritis, gout, rheumatoid arthritis, osteoarthritis, traumatic arthritis, neuropathic joint disease, or ankylosing spondylitis. Ryan and McCarty have described five clinical patterns based on a clinical analysis of 80 cases.[2]

Pseudogout

In approximately one-third of patients with pyrophosphate gout, presentation consists of acute attacks similar to those of gout, lasting from 1 day to several weeks. These most commonly present in the knees, wrists, and shoulders, with only occasional presentation in the first metatarsophalangeal joint. Fever may be present, especially in older patients, suggesting a septic arthritis. Joint aspiration and crystal identification are necessary for proper diagnosis. The attacks can be precipitated by trauma, severe illness, or initiation of diuretic therapy.

Pseudo–Rheumatoid Arthritis

Multiple joint involvement mimicking rheumatoid arthritis occurs in less than 10 percent of the patients, but unlike patients with rheumatoid arthritis, pyrophosphate gout patients with pseudo–rheumatoid arthritis usually show one to several joints that are more intensely inflamed than others. However, the differential diagnosis can be very difficult since both diseases may coexist in the same individual. Nonspecific symptoms of inflammation, such as morning stiffness and fatigue, are common, as are such signs as synovial thickening, localized pitting edema, and limitation of joint motion. Erythrocyte sedimentation rates may also be elevated. A variant has been described that can cause substantial clinical confusion: the patient, usually elderly, has multiple acutely inflamed joints, marked leukocytosis, fever of 39 to 40°C (102 to 104°F), and mental confusion or disorientation. A systemic septic process is usually suspected by the physician, and antibiotics are prescribed without benefit. The entire clinical picture in such patients responds promptly to anti-inflammatory therapy.

Pseudo-Arthritis

The pseudo-arthritis presentation characterizes approximately one-half of the patients. The preponderance of such cases is in women. They show a progressive degeneration of multiple joints, with the knees most commonly affected, followed in decreasing frequency by the wrists, metacarpophalangeal joints, hips, spine, shoulders, elbows, and ankles. Involvement is most often symmetric bilaterally, and flexion contractures of involved joints are common. Pseudo-arthritis frequently involves joints not usually involved in primary osteoarthritis, including the wrists, elbows, shoulders, and metacarpophalangeal joints. Indeed, such aberrant involvement should raise suspicion of this possible variant. Approximately one-half of the patients with this type of presentation also have a history of episodes of superimposed acute attacks. Calcium pyrophosphate crystals are often found in synovial fluid, even in joints that show no radiologic evidence typical of this disease.

Lanthanic (Asymptomatic) Pyrophosphate Gout

Lanthanic pyrophosphate gout is the most common presentation of all, in which most of the joints showing calcium pyrophosphate dihydrate deposits are asymptomatic, even in patients with acute or chronic symptoms in other joints. This presentation is most commonly associated with relatively mild wrist complaints and genu varus deformities.

Pseudoneuropathic Pyrophosphate Gout

Pseudoneuropathic pyrophosphate gout is the least common form of presentation, in which severe degeneration of the neuropathic type (Charcot-like joint) has been found in the absence of neurological abnormalities. It is also found in patients with tabes dorsalis.

Diagnosis

The diagnosis is based on one of the above clinical presentations along with x-ray demonstration of chondrocalcinosis, as well as the demonstration in joint fluid of the characteristic weakly positive birefringent rhomboid or rodlike crystals by compensated polarized light microscopy (see description above). Synovial fluid may contain a few leukocytes or as many as 100,000/mm^3 in the acutely inflamed joints, but the usual range is between 2000 and 20,000 leukocytes/mm^3.

Prognosis and Management

As in gouty arthritis, acute attacks are usually self-limited and joint function preserved. More severe destructive changes are seen in patients showing the pseudorheumatoid, pseudo-osteoarthritic, and pseudoneuropathic type of presentation associated with loss of joint function. Intravenous colchicine at a dose of 2 mg may be quite effective in the management of some acute attacks. As in gout, oral colchicine 0.6 mg one to three times daily gives a suppressive effect on the inflammatory symptoms in many patients. Nonsteroidal anti-inflammatory agents are also useful in the management of either acute or chronic forms of inflammation. Other nonpharmacological modalities of treatment useful in other forms of joint inflammation have a similar role in the treatment of symptomatic pyrophosphate gout. As yet no rational approach is known for correction of the underlying metabolic abnormality responsible for crystal formation and the resulting development of the disease. Patients with this disease should be screened for detection of the associated metabolic diseases mentioned above.

REFERENCES

1. Seegmiller JE: Disease of purine and pyrimidine metabolism, in Bondy PK, Rosenberg LE (eds): *Metabolic Control and Disease,* 8th ed. Philadelphia, Saunders, 1980, p 777.
2. Ryan LM, McCarty DJ: Calcium pyrophosphate crystal deposition disease; pseudogout; articular chondrocalcinosis, in McCarty DJ (ed): *Arthritis and Allied Conditions: A Textbook of Rheumatology,* 10th ed. Philadelphia, Lea & Febiger, 1985, p 1515.
3. Zitnan D, Sitaj D: Chondrocalcinosis polyarticularis (familiaris). *Cesk Radiol* 14:27, 1960.
4. McCarty DJ et al: The significance of calcium phosphate crystals in the synovial fluid of arthritis patients: The "pseudogout syndrome." I. Clinical aspects. *Ann Intern Med* 56:711, 1962.
5. Wilkins E et al: Osteoarthritis and articular chondrocalcinosis in the elderly. *Ann Rheum Dis* 42:280, 1983.
6. Tenenbaum J et al: Comparison of phosphohydrolase activities from articular cartilage in calcium pyrophosphate deposition disease and primary osteoarthritis. *Arthritis Rheum* 24:492, 1981.
7. Seegmiller JE et al: Enzyme defect associated with a sex-linked human neurological disorder and excessive purine synthesis. *Science* 155:1682, 1967.
8. Lesch M, Nyhan WL: A familial disorder of uric acid metabolism and central nervous system function. *Am J Med* 36:561, 1964.
9. Becker MA et al: Purine overproduction in man associated with increased phosphoribosylpyrophosphate synthetase activity. *Science* 179:1123, 1973.
10. Seegmiller JE: Disorders of purine and pyrimidine metabolism, in Emery A, Rimoin D (eds): *The Principles and Practices of Medical Genetics,* 2d ed. New York, Churchill Livingstone, 1990, p 1697.
11. Alepa FP et al: Relationships between glycogen storage disease and tophaceous gout. *Am J Med* 42:58, 1967.
12. Greene ML et al: Benign symmetric lipomatosis (Launois-Bensaude adenolipomatosis) with gout and hyperlipoproteinemia. *Am J Med* 48:239, 1970.
13. Gitzelmann R et al: Essential fructosuria, hereditary fructose intolerance, and fructose-1,6-diphosphatase deficiency, in Scriver CR et al (eds): *The Metabolic Basis of Inherited Disease,* 6th ed. New York, McGraw-Hill, 1989, p 399.
14. Oberhaensli RD et al: Study of hereditary fructose intolerance by use of ^{31}P magnetic resonance spectroscopy. *Lancet* 2:931, 1987.
15. Seegmiller JE et al: Fructose-induced aberrations of metabolism in familial gout identified by ^{31}P magnetic resonance spectroscopy. *Proc Natl Acad Sci USA* 87:8326, 1990.
16. Simkin PA: Articular oxalate crystals and the taxonomy of gout (editorial). *JAMA* 260:1285, 1988.
17. Resnick D: Crystal-induced arthropathy: Gout and pseudogout. *JAMA* 242:2440, 1979.
18. Russell RGG et al: Inorganic pyrophosphate in plasma, urine and synovial fluid of patients with pyrophosphate arthropathy (chondrocalcinosis, or pseudogout). *Lancet* 2:899, 1970.
19. Dieppe P, Watt I: Crystal deposition in osteoarthritis: An opportunistic event? *Clin Rheum Dis* 11:367, 1985.
20. Howell DS et al: Pyrophosphate release by osteoarthritis cartilage incubates. *Arthritis Rheum* 19:488, 1976.
21. Lust G et al: Inorganic pyrophosphate and proteoglycan metabolism in cultured human articular chondrocytes and fibroblasts. *Arthritis Rheum* 19:479, 1976.
22. Lust G et al: Increased pyrophosphate in fibroblasts and lymphoblasts from patients with hereditary diffuse articular chondrocalcinosis. *Science* 214:809, 1981.
23. Ryan LM et al: Elevated intracellular pyrophosphate (PPi) and ecto-nucleoside triphosphate pyrophosphohydrolase activity (NTPPH) in fibroblasts of patients with calcium pyrophosphate dihydrate (CPPD) crystal deposition disease (abstract). *Clin Res* 32:792A, 1984.
24. Tenenbaum J et al: Comparison of phosphohydrolase activities from articular cartilage in calcium pyrophosphate deposition disease and primary osteoarthritis. *Arthritis Rheum* 24:492, 1981.
25. Ryan LM et al: Pyrophosphohydrolase activity and inorganic pyrophosphate content of cultured human skin fibroblasts: Elevated levels in some patients with calcium pyrophosphate dihydrate deposition disease. *J Clin Invest* 77:1689, 1986.
26. Van der Korst JK, Gerard J: Articular chondrocalcinosis in a Dutch pedigree. *Arthritis Rheum* 19:405, 1976.
27. Reginato AJ: Articular chondrocalcinosis in the Chiloé Islanders. *Arthritis Rheum* 19:395, 1976.
28. McKusick V: *Mendelian Inheritance in Man,* 7th ed. The Johns Hopkins University Press, 1986.
29. Sokoloff L, Varma AA: Chondrocalcinosis in surgically resected joints. *Arthritis Rheum* 31:750, 1988.
30. Rasmussen H: Hypophosphatasia, in Stanbury JB et al (eds): *The Metabolic Basis of Inherited Disease,* 5th ed. New York, McGraw-Hill, 1983, p 1497.

Chapter 87

BURSITIS, TENDINITIS, AND RELATED DISORDERS

Elliott L. Semble

Bursitis, tendinitis, and other related soft-tissue rheumatic disorders represent a large group of musculoskeletal conditions seen frequently in the geriatric population. These entities result in varying degrees of pain and functional loss. This review will provide a general description of the major types of these disorders and summarize their diagnosis and management.

BURSITIS

Bursae are fluid-filled sacs located between tendons and bone. They are lined by a thin layer of synovial cells and serve to reduce friction where two muscles cross each other in opposite directions or where tendons and muscles merge. Some bursae are constant and present at birth (e.g., subacromial, olecranon) while others are formed in response to abnormal stress (e.g., bunion).[1]

Acute and chronic trauma are the most common causes of bursitis.[2] Bursal inflammation may also be due to crystal precipitation, as in gout, pseudogout, or hydroxyapatite deposition disease. Bursal infections are usually caused by *Staphylococcus aureus* or other gram-positive organisms. Bursitis may also occur in rheumatoid arthritis, and nodules may form in the olecranon bursae of rheumatoid patients with long-standing disease.

Subacromial Bursitis

The subacromial (subdeltoid) bursa is located between the deltoid muscle and the shoulder capsule and extends up under the acromion and coracoacromial ligament. The onset of subacromial bursitis may be acute or chronic. It is often secondary to trauma or inflammation of the supraspinatus or biceps tendon.

Pain may be severe and is often exacerbated by shoulder movements in abduction and flexion. Activities such as combing the hair and dressing become painful. Pain commonly radiates down the upper arm in a C5 dermatomal distribution. Physical examination reveals tenderness over the rotator cuff, especially at the lateral aspect of the shoulder and subacromial space. Shoulder abduction may exacerbate the pain, but in chronic bursitis pain may occur with internal and external rotation as well as adduction and flexion. Radiographs are usually normal in the acute stage, but calcific deposits may be seen in chronic subacromial bursitis. The calcific material is noted within the bursa or at the insertion of the supraspinatus tendon; it is best detected on x-ray films taken in the anterior-posterior view with the shoulder held in external rotation.

Calcific or traumatic subacromial bursitis is managed using rest, nonsteroidal anti-inflammatory drugs (NSAIDs), and the intrabursal injection of corticosteroid–local anesthetic mixtures. Seventy percent of patients seen in a rheumatology clinic improved following such injections.[3] Adjunctive therapy includes ultrasound or applications of heat or cold. Surgical excision of a chronically inflamed bursa is rarely indicated, after intensive medical therapy has failed.

Olecranon Bursitis

The olecranon bursa separates the skin and the olecranon process. Bursal inflammation occurs with trauma, gout, rheumatoid arthritis, or infection. Olecranon bursitis is characterized by bursal swelling, tenderness, minimal pain, and normal elbow motion. Peribursal edema and pain on motion, however, may be seen in septic olecranon bursitis.[4] Traumatic olecranon bursitis is usually caused by mechanical pressure. Patients should be told not to rest their elbows on the arms of chairs or arm rests of automobiles. Hospitalized patients should be provided with foam rubber protectors to prevent shear injury to the elbows.

A swollen olecranon bursa should be aspirated to exclude infection or crystal deposition disease. Serosanguineous or hemorrhagic fluid with white blood cell counts below 200/mm^3 usually indicates trauma. Bursal fluid white blood cell counts above 1000/mm^3 are typical of crystal-induced or infectious bursitis. Inflammatory fluids must be cultured to rule out infection and examined using the polarizing microscope for the presence of crystals.

Traumatic olecranon bursitis may be treated with steroid injections. Resolution of complaints is usually seen within 1 to 2 weeks.[5] Septic bursitis is most frequently caused by *S. aureus*.[6] Dicloxacillin or methicillin are the drugs of choice in patients who are not allergic to penicillin and should be continued for 3 to 4 weeks. Both agents produce adequate bursal fluid levels. Frequent needle aspiration of the bursa may shorten the duration of infection.[6]

Trochanteric Bursitis

The deep trochanteric bursa lies between the tendon of the gluteus maximus and the posterolateral aspect of the greater trochanter, while a more superficial bursa lies directly over the greater trochanter. Trochanteric bursitis may present acutely, but it most often occurs in a subacute or chronic form perhaps related to repetitive trauma to aging tendons and muscles. The condition is more common in individuals over 40 years of age, with females predominating over males.[7]

Patients usually complain of a dull ache, occasionally with a burning quality, along the lateral aspect of the hip. The pain may radiate down the lateral aspect of the thigh to the knee. It is worse with activity and exacerbated by sitting with legs crossed. Since patients may not be able to lie on their involved side without pain, sleep may be affected. Tenderness on palpation approximately 1 inch posterior and superior to the greater trochanter suggests the diagnosis. Acute trochanteric bursitis may be associated with some limitation of hip motion; in chronic bursitis, however, normal motion is found. External rotation in combination with abduction of the affected hip is painful, while flexion and extension are usually painless.

Normal radiographs are seen in younger patients. Roentgenograms in older patients may demonstrate sclerosis of the greater trochanter and/or supratochanteric calcifications. Calcium deposits may be detected by radiographs taken in internal or external rotation or in the frog-leg position.

Trochanteric bursitis may occur as a primary condition, but it is often related to other diseases such as osteoarthritis of the hip or lumbar spine or injury to the low back, hips, or lower extremities.[3,8] Obesity, chronic muscle strain, and weakness of the abdominal or back muscles may precipitate an attack. Hip pain in the elderly may be due to osteoarthritis, but if night pain becomes a prominent complaint, trochanteric bursitis should be considered.

The treatment of trochanteric bursitis includes steroid-injections into the bursa, NSAIDs, and weight loss in the obese patient. Sleeping with a small pillow under the affected buttock aids in keeping the body weight off the tender bursa. Knee-chest exercises to stretch the gluteal muscles, pelvic tilt exercises to correct lumbar lordosis, and strengthening of the gluteus medius muscle may also be helpful.

Ischiogluteal Bursitis

The ischiogluteal bursa lies between the ischial tuberosity and the gluteus maximus muscle. The bursa may become inflamed as a result of acute or chronic irritation. Pain is noted in the buttock and posterior thigh. Prolonged sitting on hard surfaces may exacerbate the pain.

Ischiogluteal bursitis is suggested by tenderness over the ischial tuberosity. Forward bending may result in severe buttock pain. The Valsalva maneuver and coughing exacerbate symptoms. A bulging or painful resistance is often felt on the affected side during rectal examination.

Therapy of ischiogluteal bursitis includes NSAIDs and the use of a cushion or padding if prolonged sitting is anticipated. Steroid injection(s) into the bursa are helpful but should be done carefully to avoid injuring the sciatic nerve.[9]

Anserine Bursitis

The anserine bursa is located between the tendons of the sartorius, gracilis, and semitendinosus muscles and the tibial collateral ligament approximately 2 inches below the joint margin at the medial aspect of the knee.[10] The majority of patients are overweight, middle-aged to elderly women with osteoarthritis of the knees. Pain, noted over the medial region of the knee, is exacerbated by climbing stairs. Night pain may become a major complaint. Tenderness is found on physical examination on the medial aspect of the knee just below the joint margin at the tibial collateral ligament.

The differential diagnosis of anserine bursitis includes spontaneous osteonecrosis of the knee, which is a cause of knee pain in the elderly. Osteonecrosis of the knee may be excluded by radionuclide scanning, as routine radiographs are often unremarkable.[11] Management of anserine bursitis consists of rest and steroid injections.

Retrocalcaneal Bursitis

The retrocalcaneal bursa is located between the calcaneus and the posterior surface of the Achilles tendon. Findings include pain in the posterior aspect of the heel with ankle dorsiflexion and exquisite tenderness anterior to the Achilles tendon.[12] Swelling of the bursa results in bulging on the medial and lateral aspects of the tendon. Retrocalcaneal bursitis may be difficult to distinguish from Achilles tendinitis, and the two conditions may coexist. Therapy for retrocalcaneal bursitis consists of rest, NSAIDs, and steroid injections carefully directed into the bursa, avoiding the Achilles tendon.

TENDINITIS

Tendinitis is characterized by localized pain and dysfunction. Tendons may be damaged by trauma, systemic inflammatory diseases, degenerative processes, and crystal deposition. Tendinitis is commonly due to overuse as a result of performing repetitive motion at work or during leisure activities. Impingement of tendons between bone and ligaments may occur, leading to tendon inflammation. This happens most often at the shoulder, where the rotator cuff is compressed between the humeral head and the acromion and coracoacromial ligament during overhead activity.

Rotator Cuff Tendinitis

The rotator cuff is formed by the tendons of the supraspinatus, infraspinatus, and teres minor muscles, which insert into the greater tuberosity of the humerus, and the subscapularis, which inserts into the less tuberosity. The major functions of the rotator cuff are humeral head rotation and dynamic stabilization of the glenohumeral joint. External and internal rotation of the humerus are also mediated by rotator cuff muscles. Age-associated degenerative changes affect the rotator cuff tendons, predisposing them to injury following stressful shoulder activities.

Rotator cuff tendinitis may present acutely with severe shoulder pain. Patients complain of painful motion between 60 and 120° of abduction with elevation and lowering of the affected arm. Chronic rotator cuff tendinitis is characterized by aching of the shoulder, which exacerbated during certain movements, especially on abduction or internal rotation. Nocturnal pain is common usually as a result of difficulty in positioning the involved shoulder. A painful catching sensation may be noted, and patients may have trouble dressing or performing activities requiring overhead elevation of the arm, such as reaching into kitchen cabinets, changing a lightbulb in a ceiling fixture, or combing the hair.

Physical examination may reveal tenderness over the greater tuberosity of the humerus, with painful or restricted shoulder motion. Pain is elicited on active abduction and exacerbated by resistance provided by the examiner. Passive abduction is associated with less pain than active abduction. The impingement sign is occasionally present in rotator cuff tendinitis. The examiner elicits this sign by raising the patient's arm in maximum forward flexion with one hand while holding down the scapula with the other. The arm is internally rotated at maximum elevation. If pain develops by or before 180° of forward flexion, the test is positive. This suggests that the rotator cuff is being impinged between the greater tuberosity of the humerus and the acromion (Fig. 87-1).[13]

Radiographs are usually normal in acute rotator cuff tendinitis, while sclerosis of the greater tuberosity of the humerus or calcifications may be detected in chronic disease. Calcific densities occur most often at the insertion of the supraspinatus tendons on the greater tuberosity and are best seen on roentgenograms of the shoulder done in external rotation. Calcifications appear round or oval and may be several centimeters in length. Calcium deposits may resolve over time and correlate poorly with shoulder complaints.

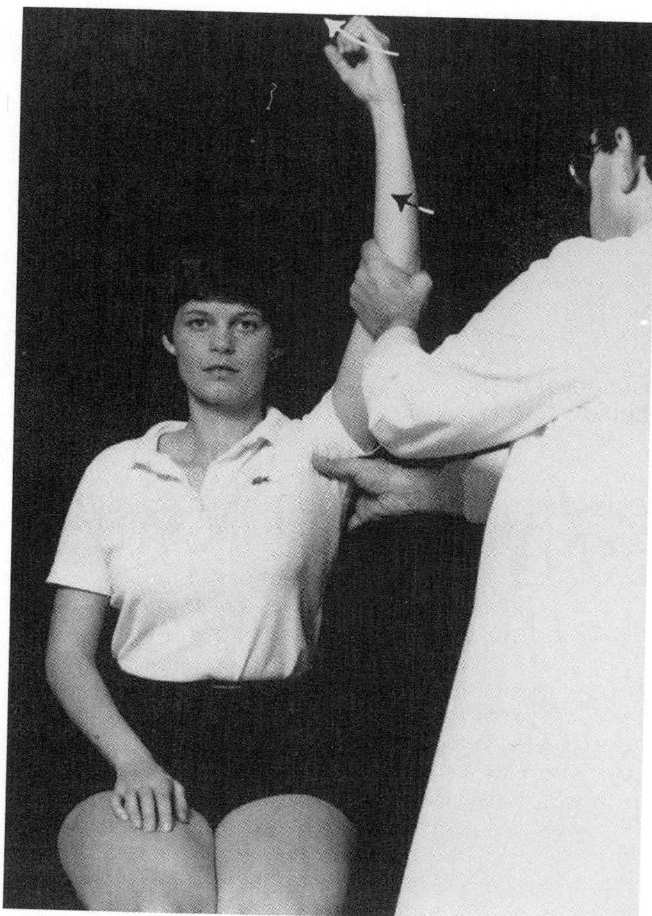

FIGURE 87-1

Test for impingement in rotator cuff tendinitis. Note that arm is internally rotated at maximum elevation. *(Reprinted with permission from Sheon RP et al: Soft Tissue Rheumatic Pain: Recognition, Management, Prevention, 2nd ed. Philadelphia, Lea & Febiger, 1987, p 71.)*

Rotator cuff tendinitis has multiple causes. Patients over 45 years of age may overuse their shoulders during occupational or avocational activities, especially with repetitive overhead movements. Aging and decreased use of shoulder muscles result in weakness of the rotator cuff. Osteoarthritis of the acromioclavicular joint, inflammatory arthritis (e.g., rheumatoid arthritis), and trauma may also cause rotator cuff tendinitis.

Trauma is not only associated with rotator cuff tendinitis, but may result in tears in the rotator cuff (Fig. 87-2).[14] Elderly patients may sustain an injury to the rotator cuff following a fall on the affected shoulder or on an outstretched arm. Rotator cuff tears may be complete, resulting in a communication between the glenohumeral joint and subacromial bursa; or they may be partial, in which case at least one layer of tissue separates the two cavities. Degeneration of the rotator cuff is seen with aging, and mild trauma or strain in an older patient may cause a smaller or partial tear to become complete.

Pain from a rotator cuff tear is usually worse at night. It is exacerbated by activities necessitating shoulder abduction. Physical examination reveals limited active abduction but normal passive abduction. A large rotator cuff tear is suggested by the presence of the drop-arm sign. This sign is positive when the affected arm is passively elevated to at least 90° but falls to the side when support is withdrawn.

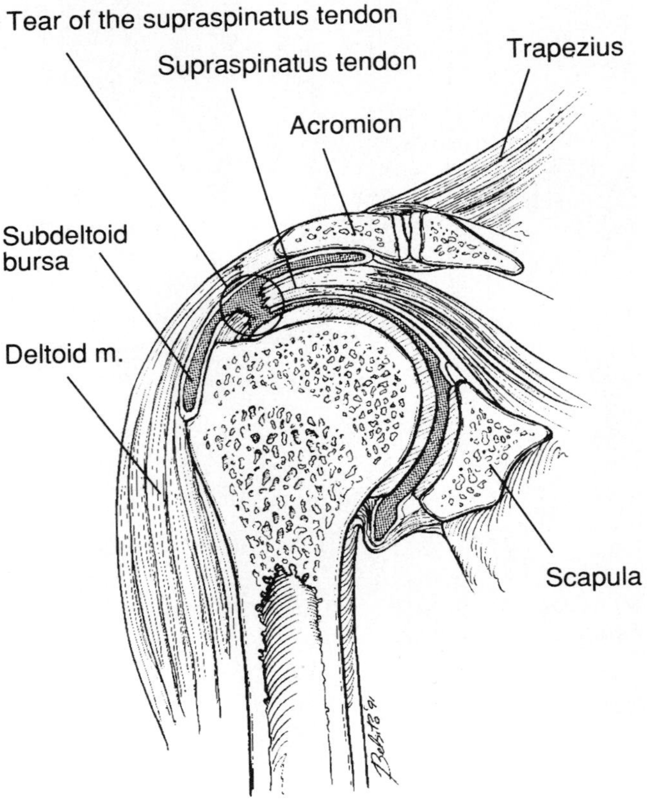

Radiographic assessment is necessary to exclude fractures or other pathology and to provide supporting evidence for chronic rotator cuff disease. A complete rotator cuff tear is suggested by a reduced acromiohumeral distance of 5 mm or less (normal distance is 6 to 14 mm). Although routine radiographs may be helpful in diagnosing rotator cuff tears, confirmation requires contrast arthrography. If a complete tear has occurred, dye enters the subacromial space from the glenohumeral joint.

Rotator cuff tears may be associated with the presence of hydroxyapatite crystals. In 1981, McCarthy et al.[15] described this entity and labeled it the Milwaukee shoulder syndrome. This condition occurs primarily in elderly women and is characterized by varying degrees of shoulder pain, limited motion, and joint instability.

FIGURE 87-2
Rotator cuff tear (tear in the supraspinatus tendon). *(Reprinted with permission from Biundo JJ Jr, Torres-Ramos FM: Common shoulder problems. Primary Care Rheum 1:7, 1991.)*

Management of Rotator Cuff Tendinitis

General Principles

The initial phase of therapy consists of the recognition that the patient's signs and symptoms represent rotator cuff disease. Systemic inflammatory illnesses (e.g., polymyalgia rheumatica), localized neurologic disorders (e.g., thoracic outlet syndrome), tumors (Pancoast's syndrome), or referred pain from diaphragmatic irritation must be excluded.

Decreased pain and improved function are the major goals of therapy. Restoration of function is critical because of the importance of the shoulder in performing activities of daily living. Rotator cuff tendinitis is usually caused by chronic overuse or repetitive trauma and has a tendency to reoccur. Patient education is important in preventing recurrent disease. Activities or aggravating factors which contribute to shoulder dysfunction need to be identified and modified. The height of shelves may have to be adjusted and overhead arm use minimized. Strenuous activities may need to be restricted.

The performance of activities of daily living may precipitate rotator cuff disease in the poorly conditioned elderly. Exercises or physical therapy directed at improving shoulder muscle function is helpful in preventing chronic shoulder problems.

Specific Therapeutic Modalities

The treatment of rotator cuff tendinitis includes steroid injections, NSAIDs, and exercises. Pain relief is rapid when steroids are injected into appropriate sites in the shoulder, permitting patients to resume their activities of daily living and improving sleep. Kessel and Watson[16] noted good results with injections of methylprednisolone and local anesthetics in 66 of 68 patients with rotator cuff tendinitis.

NSAIDs may be used alone or in conjunction with steroid injections for rotator cuff tendinitis. A prospective study done by Petri et al.[17] in patients with rotator cuff disease showed that both a steroid–local anesthetic injection and naproxen were superior to placebo. The steroid–local anesthetic injection was slightly more efficacious than naproxen when the treatments were used separately. NSAIDs, however, need to be taken judiciously by the elderly due to their potential for side effects.

Home exercise programs should be designed for patients with rotator cuff tendinitis. Pendulum or Codman's exercises are used to mobilize the affected shoulder. These exercises involve grasping a 2- to 5-pound weight and swinging the affected arm in a 12-inch-diameter circle while leaning slightly to the side (Fig. 87-3).[18] Other mobilizing exercises for the shoulder include wall walking and shoulder capsule stretching. Exercises should be performed twice daily and continued for several weeks after the pain has resolved. Strengthening exercises of the shoulder girdle muscles may be started after tenderness and range of motion have improved.

The prognosis of rotator cuff tendinitis is generally good. A positive outcome is seen in about 90 percent of patients within 3 to 6 weeks.[19–20] Patients who do not respond to intensive medical therapy in 6 to 8 months should have an orthopedic evaluation.

Therapy for Rotator Cuff Tear

The treatment of a rotator cuff tear depends on the activity level of the patient prior to the onset of pain or injury and the extent of disability. Elderly patients should be managed initially with mild analgesics or NSAIDs. Steroid injections may be utilized, but multiple injections can cause degeneration of tendons. Assisted range-of-motion exercises are necessary to maintain shoulder mobility. Surgical intervention should be restricted to those individuals who do not respond to 6 months of conservative therapy. Functional improvement following surgery, however, remains unpredictable.

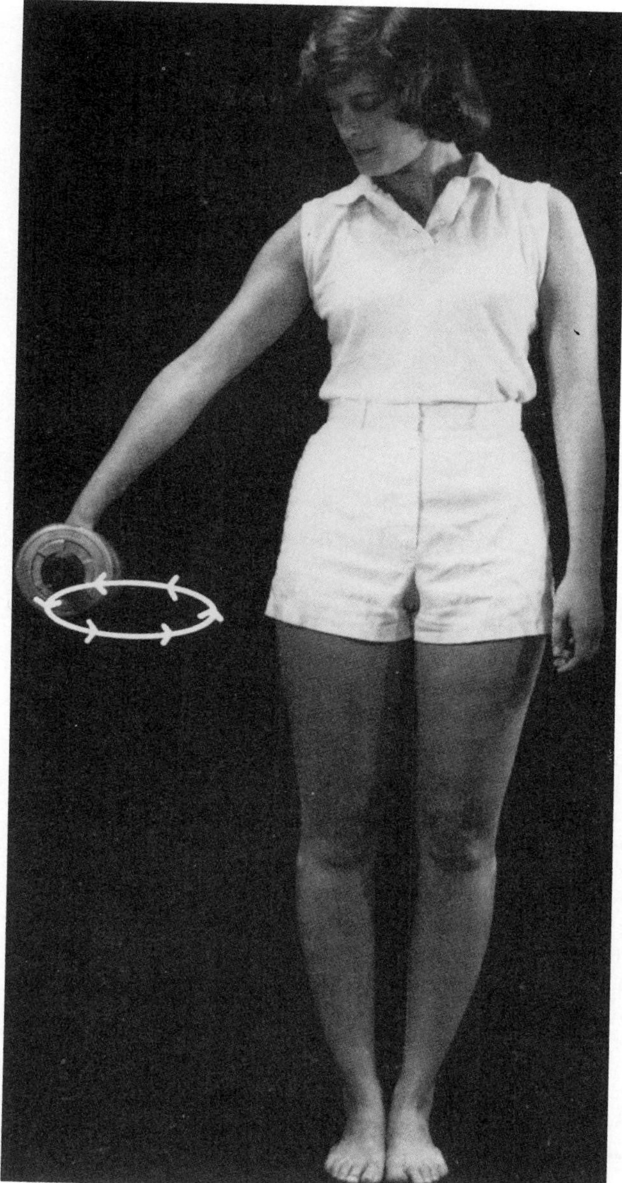

FIGURE 87-3
Pendulum or Codman's exercise for shoulder mobilization. Using a 2- to 5-pound weight, the patient rotates the arm in a 12-inch-diameter circle while leaning to the side. This is carried out for a minute in each direction. *(Reprinted with permission from Sheon RP et al: Soft Tissue Rheumatic Pain: Recognition, Management, Prevention, 2nd ed. Philadelphia, Lea & Febiger, 1987, p 82.)*

Bicipital Tendinitis

Bicipital tendinitis may occur in association with rotator cuff tendinitis or as a primary condition. Anterior shoulder pain is the major complaint with this disorder. Tenderness on physical examination is noted on palpation of the bicipital tendon in the bicipital groove. Yergason's sign is frequently present in bicipital tendinitis. The maneuver involves asking patients to forcefully turn the palmar aspect of the hand upward (supination) against resistance while the elbow is held in a flexed position. Pain is elicited in the bicipital groove in bicipital tendinitis (Fig. 87-4).[21]

Repetitive motion, as in tightening the lids on jars or working overhead, may cause bicipital tendinitis. It is often a chronic condition and may be related to impingement of the bicipital tendon by the acromion. Chronic tenosynovitis of the long head of the biceps may result in degeneration and fibrosis of the tendon.

The therapy of bicipital tendinitis includes rest, heat, steroid injections, NSAIDs, and range-of-mo-

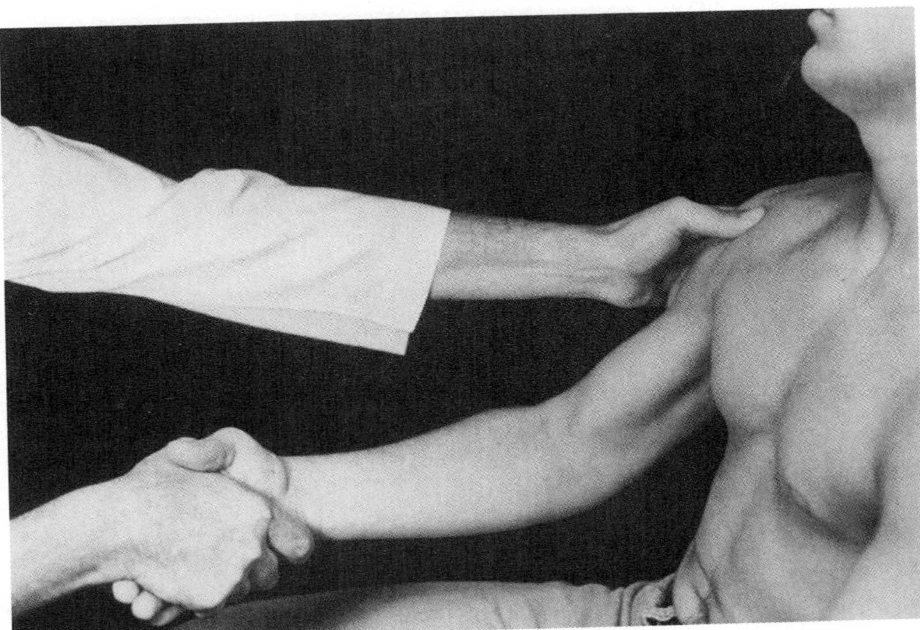

FIGURE 87-4
Yergason's sign for bicipital tendinitis. Patient forcefully supinates the forearm against resistance while the elbow is held in a flexed position. Supination is carried out against the examiner's resistance. Pain is felt in the bicipital groove in the presence of bicipital tendinitis. *(Reprinted with permission from Sheon RP et al: Soft Tissue Rheumatic Pain: Recognition, Management, Prevention, 2nd ed. Philadelphia, Lea & Febiger, 1987, p 73.)*

tion exercises. Steroid injections must be carefully done to avoid rupture of the biceps tendon. After puncturing the skin, the needle is directed parallel to the course of the tendon in the tendon sheath. Wand exercises in which the unaffected arm gently forces the involved arm into extension are useful to stretch the biceps tendon and regain lost motion. A good result is expected if aggressive therapy is instituted early in the course of the disorder, before chronic shoulder pain and disability have developed.

ADHESIVE CAPSULITIS

Adhesive capsulitis (frozen shoulder) is a common soft-tissue rheumatic pain syndrome affecting the shoulder which is characterized by generalized pain, severe loss of motion in all planes, and muscle atrophy.[14,22] The entity occurs most frequently in individuals 40 years of age or older, and females are affected more often than males. Adhesive capsulitis results from many diverse conditions including trauma, myocardial infarction, diabetes mellitus, cervical disk disease, cerebrovascular accidents, lung cancer, etc. Patients whose upper extremities are immobilized are at increased risk for this disorder. Other factors which may be contributory include a low pain threshold, depression, or improper management of the primary problem.

The condition starts insidiously in one shoulder. Pain at night occurs, with loss of shoulder motion. Patients have difficulty in reaching backward to fasten a brassiere or slip arms into a coat. The pain is localized to the anterolateral aspect of the shoulder, anterolateral arm, and flexor aspect of the forearm. Physical examination reveals a loss of active and passive motion of the affected shoulder. Tenderness is detected on palpation of the rotator cuff. Shoulder girdle muscle atrophy is noted with long-standing disease. Arthrography is useful in confirming the diagnosis of adhesive capsulitis. It shows a decrease in volume of the shoulder joint, with loss of size of the subscapular and auxillary recesses. Pathologic changes include thickening and contraction of the shoulder capsule, with either chronic inflammation or fibroplasia.

The management of adhesive capsulitis must be comprehensive. NSAIDs and steroid injections directed into multiple sites around the shoulder (e.g., glenohumeral joint, subacromial bursa, bicipital tendon sheath, posterior joint capsule) are helpful in alleviating pain. An exercise program should start with gentle range-of-motion exercises such as pendulum exercises and progress to wand and wall-walking exercises. Adjunctive therapy includes ice packs, ultrasound, or transcutaneous electrical nerve stimulation (TENS).

Pain usually decreases over time with appropriate therapy. Range of motion improves, but elderly patients may have residual loss of motion.[23–24] Resistant cases may be treated with manipulation under anesthesia, but this procedure is used as a last resort, since capsular tears may result.

ENTRAPMENT NEUROPATHIES

The entrapment neuropathies are soft-tissue rheumatic pain syndromes due to focal peripheral nerve damage. Nerve compression may be caused by trauma, structural abnormalities such as thoracic outlet syndrome (e.g., cervical rib or scalene anticus syndrome) or cervical or lumbar spinal stenosis; it may also be associated with peripheral nerve disease such as diabetes mellitus or Guillain-Barré syndrome.

Carpal Tunnel Syndrome

Median nerve impingement, causing the carpal tunnel syndrome, is the most common entrapment neuropathy.[25–26] At the wrist, the median nerve and extrinsic flexor tendons pass through a common osteofibrous canal which is bordered dorsolaterally by the carpal bones and volarly by the transverse carpal ligament. Any pathology which encroaches on the carpal tunnel may compress the median nerve. Women are affected more often than men, and aging has been associated with narrowing of the bony carpal tunnel.

The condition is usually seen as an isolated syndrome in menopausal women. Carpal tunnel syndrome, however, may result from trauma or be associated with osteophytes, ganglion cysts, or pregnancy. Rheumatoid arthritis affecting the tenosynovial sheathes of the wrist, gout, pseudogout, or other nonspecific synovitis of the extrinsic flexor tendons may also cause the syndrome. Other diseases associated with this condition include myxedema, amyloidosis, multiple myeloma, and acromegaly.

The most common complaints associated with carpal tunnel syndrome are numbness, tingling, or burning pain in a median nerve distribution (i.e., thumb, index finger, middle finger, and radial half of the ring finger). Pain may occasionally radiate up the arm or even to the shoulder. Patients awake in the early morning with numbness and shake or run water over their hands in an attempt to alleviate symptoms. Activities which require repetitive use of the hands—such as sewing, knitting, wringing out clothes, or driving—may provoke pain. Patients may note that their hands feel clumsy and that they drop objects. Physical signs are late manifestations of the disease. Thenar flattening or atrophy may occur. Tests for median nerve compression at the wrist include Tinel's sign, which consists of tingling of the affected fingers following tapping over the nerve at the wrist (Fig. 87-5),[26] and Phalen's sign, which produces paraesthesias of the digits with prolonged palmer flexion of the wrists (Fig. 87-6).[26] Electrodiagnostic studies may support the diagnosis of carpal tunnel syndrome. Findings include slowed median nerve conduction velocity and an increased terminal motor latency of the evoked response potential. Up to 10 percent of patients with this condition may have normal test results.

Management of this syndrome includes splinting the wrists in neutral position or in 30° of dorsiflexion, steroid injections into the carpal tunnel, and avoidance of repetitive motion in using the hands. Medical therapy controls symptoms in about two-thirds of patients. Exercises which involve stretching the volar carpal ligament have been recommended for this disorder.

If medical treatment fails or thenar atrophy is present, decompression of the carpal tunnel by surgical release of the volar carpal ligament is performed. Older patients and those with a longer duration of symptoms have a worse outcome. Motor functional loss is usually not markedly improved by surgery, but nocturnal pain resolves and progressive motor dysfunction is prevented.[27]

Tarsal Tunnel Syndrome

The tarsal tunnel syndrome is an entrapment neuropathy of the posterior tibial nerve as it crosses

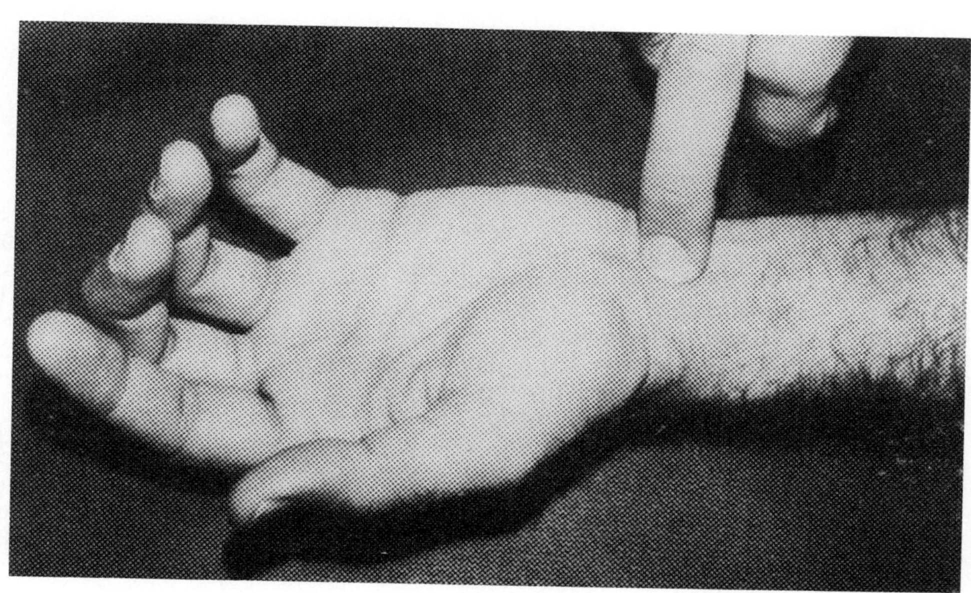

FIGURE 87-5
Tinel's sign: Tapping over the compressed median nerve at the wrist reproduces pain and parasthesias distally in the affected digits. *(Reprinted with permission from the Minnesota Medical Association and Tountas CP et al: Carpal tunnel syndrome: A review of 507 patients. Minn Med 66:279, 1983.)*

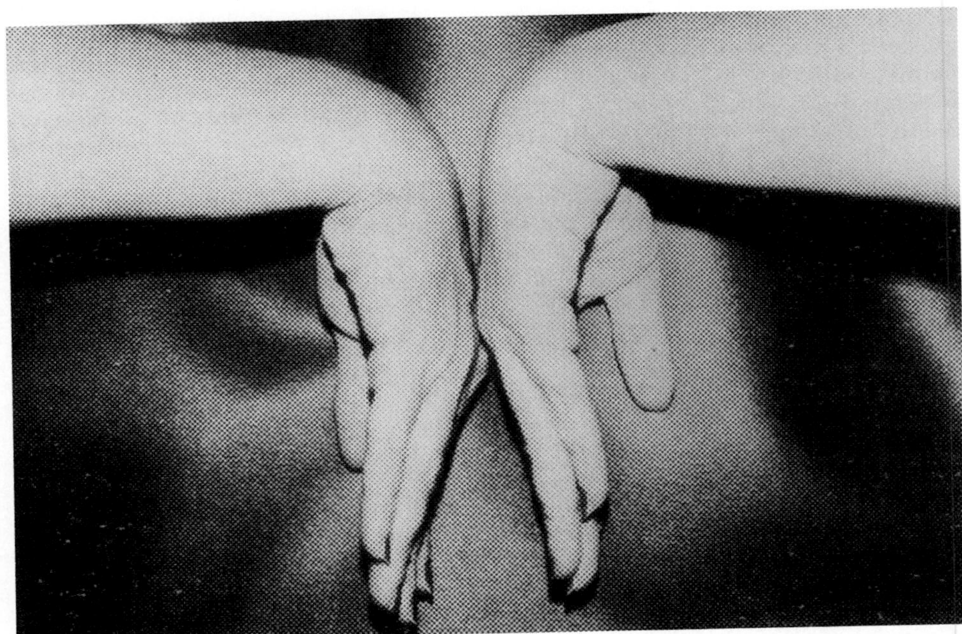

FIGURE 87-6
Phalen's sign: Wrist flexion for 30 to 60 seconds reproduces parasthesias in patients with carpal tunnel syndrome. *(Reprinted with permission from the Minnesota Medical Association and Tountas CP et al: Carpal tunnel syndrome. A review of 507 patients. Minn Med 66:479, 1983.)*

through the tunnel underneath the flexor retinaculum on the medial aspect of the ankle.[28,29] The tarsal tunnel contains the tendon of the flexor digitorum longus and flexor hallucis longus, and the posterior tibial nerve and its two branches, the medial and lateral plantar nerves. Women are most often affected by this syndrome, and individuals with valgus foot deformities or hypermobility may be at greater risk.[30]

Patients complain of burning or aching pain and paresthesias in the sole of the foot and toes. Pain is frequently nocturnal and relief may be achieved by moving the leg, ankle, or foot. Standing and walking may also exacerbate the pain. Physical examination reveals loss of pinprick and two-point discrimination in the posterior tibial nerve distribution, but rarely is swelling or atrophy noted. Patients may report tingling or numbness when the nerve is tapped posteroinferior to the medial malleolus. The diagnosis of tarsal tunnel syndrome is confirmed by electrodiagnostic studies. Prolonged latency and abnormal sensory nerve conduction is indicative of disease. Normal values, however, do not exclude the condition.

The syndrome often results from tenosynovitis of the tendons passing through the canal. This usually occurs after trauma and may be associated with rheumatoid arthritis. Therapy of this disorder includes steroid injections into the tarsal tunnel and shoe modification. Response to injections is often inadequate, and surgical decompression should be considered in resistant cases.

REFERENCES

1. Bywaters EGL: Lesions of bursae, tendons and tendon sheaths. *Clin Rheum Dis* 5:883, 1979.
2. Ellman MH: Diagnosis and management of bursitis. *Comp Ther* 10:14, 1984.
3. Larsson LG, Baum J: The syndromes of bursitis. *Bul Rheum Dis* 36:1, 1986.
4. Ho G Jr, Miklich DJ: Bacterial infection of the superficial subcutaneous bursae. *Clin Rheum Dis* 12:437, 1986.
5. Weinstein PS et al: Long-term follow-up of corticosteroid injection for traumatic olecranon bursitis. *Ann Rheum Dis* 43:44, 1984.
6. Ho G Jr, Su EY: Antibiotic therapy of septic bursitis: Its implication in the treatment of septic arthritis. *Arthritis Rheum* 24:905, 1981.
7. Gordon EJ: Trochanteric bursitis and tendinitis. *Clin Orthop* 20:193, 1961.
8. Hartzog CW, Boulware DW: A clinical approach to hip pain. *Primary Care Rheum* 2:1, 1992.
9. Swartout R, Compere EL: Ischiogluteal bursitis. *JAMA* 227:551, 1974.
10. Larsson LG, Baum J: The syndrome of anserine bursitis. *Arthritis Rheum* 28:1062, 1985.
11. Houpt JB et al: Natural history of spontaneous osteonecrosis of the knee (SONK): A review. *Semin Arthritis Rheum* 13:212, 1983.

12. Canoso JJ et al: Aspiration of the retrocalcaneal bursa. *Ann Rheum Dis* 43:308, 1984.
13. Sheon RP et al: *Soft Tissue Rheumatic Pain: Recognition, Management, Prevention,* 2nd ed. Philadelphia, Lea & Febiger, 1987, p 71.
14. Biundo JJ Jr, Torres-Ramos FM: Common shoulder problems. *Primary Care Rheum* 1:1, 1991.
15. McCarty DJ et al: "Milwaukee shoulder"—Association of microspheroids containing hydroxyapatite crystals, active collagenase, and neutral protease with rotator cuff defects: I. Clinical aspects. *Arthritis Rheum* 24:464, 1981.
16. Kessel L, Watson M: The painful arc syndrome: Clinical classification as a guide to management. *J Bone Joint Surg* 59-B:166, 1977.
17. Petri M et al: Randomized, double-blind, placebo-controlled study of the treatment of the painful shoulder. *Arthritis Rheum* 30:1040, 1987.
18. Sheon RP et al: *Soft Tissue Rheumatic Pain: Recognition, Management, Prevention,* 2nd ed. Philadelphia, Lea & Febiger, 1987, p 82.
19. Bland JH et al: The painful shoulder. *Semin Arthritis Rheum* 7:21, 1977.
20. Simon WH: Soft tissue disorders of the shoulder: Frozen shoulder, calcific tendinitis, and bicipital tendinitis. *Ortho Clin North Am* 6:521, 1975.
21. Sheon RP et al: *Soft Tissue Rheumatic Pain: Recognition, Management, Prevention,* 2nd ed. Philadelphia, Lea & Febiger, 1987, p 73.
22. Murnaghan JP: Adhesive capsulitis of the shoulder: Current concepts and treatment. *Orthopedics* 11:153, 1988.
23. Clarke GR et al: Preliminary studies in measuring range of motion in normal and painful stiff shoulders. *Rheumatol Rehab* 14:39, 1975.
24. Reeves B: The natural history of the frozen shoulder syndrome. *Scand J Rheum* 4:193, 1975.
25. Wakefield G: The entrapment neuropathies. *Clin Rheum Dis* 5:941, 1979.
26. Tountas CP et al: Carpal tunnel syndrome: A review of 507 patients. *Minn Med* 66:479, 1983.
27. Harris CM et al: The surgical treatment of carpal tunnel syndrome correlated with preoperative nerve conduction studies *J Bone Joint Surg* 61A:93, 1979.
28. Keck C: The tarsal tunnel syndrome. *J Bone Joint Surg* 44:180, 1962.
29. Goodgold J et al: The tarsal tunnel syndrome. *N Engl J Med* 273:742, 1965.
30. Francis H et al: Benign joint hypermobility with neuropathy: II. Documentation and mechanism of the tarsal tunnel syndrome. *J Rheumatol* 14:577, 1987.

SECTION I

The Nervous System

Chapter 88

NEUROCHEMISTRY OF THE AGING HUMAN BRAIN

Judes Poirier and Caleb E. Finch

Aging of the human central nervous system has often been associated with an irreversible loss of functions and a decline of its global abilities. This oversimplified picture is far from a true reflection of the plastic nature of the adult brain, which has a remarkable ability to compensate functionally for neuronal loss or atrophy. There is some significant age-related loss of neurons, loss of dendritic arborization, and loss of enzymes and receptors involved in the neurotransmission function of the brain, but, as we discuss later, these losses should not be considered as *general* or even necessary phenomena. On the contrary, the loss of function is usually associated with *specific* areas of the brain. We also emphasize that the reported changes described in the biochemistry and structure of the aging human brain do not necessarily affect the ordinary activities of living or occupational performance until 75 years of age. Even at later ages, a fortunate subgroup of us will remain remarkably intact.[1]

Studies of age-related diseases like Alzheimer's, Parkinson's, and Huntington's have helped us to understand how the aging brain copes with selective, but severe, dysfunctions. For example, in Parkinson's disease the striatum must lose more than 70 percent of its endogenous dopamine content before abnormal motor symptoms appear. This ability of the brain to function despite a severe loss of neurons is only one demonstration of its impressive plastic ability. It is thus important to keep in mind that the different types of loss (or gain) that we will describe later may not necessarily have immediate functional correlates in the view of the brain's plastic ability. Limited space precludes discussion of animal data except nonhuman primates. For more complete reviews, see Rogers and Bloom,[2] Morgan et al.,[3] Finch and Morgan,[4] and Finch.[5,6]

USUAL AGING IN HUMAN BRAIN

Morphological Considerations

The brain undergoes an early period of growth, remains relatively stable during adulthood, and then slowly declines during senescence. A major distinction must, however, be drawn between aging in neurons as opposed to aging in other cell types. Peripheral cells in some tissues retain mitogenic capacity throughout the human life span (hematopoiesis), whereas proliferation is lost in others during differentiation (myocardium). In general, differentiated neurons cannot go through cell division, whereas glia can. Neurons, therefore, are not replaced when they die, whereas glia may proliferate. However, compensatory dendrite proliferation with age, as observed in several labs, was proposed as a means by which selected neuronal pathways are able to maintain contact with their target despite neuronal losses.[7,7a] Homologous as well as heterologous synaptic replacement is quite common in mature brain. The view that human brain usually undergoes general, major atrophy[8] has been challenged by CT scan longitudinal studies showing highly selective atrophy in restricted areas.[9,10] It is accompanied by a net 10 to 15 percent reduction in the blood flow while the capillary network of the cerebral cortex appears to increase in diameter, volume, and length, explaining why the cerebral blood flow is reduced.[11] Interestingly, in 40 healthy subjects (aged 20 to 80 years) who showed unaltered cognitive function and absence of brain disease, the oxidative metabolism in 25 distinct brain regions remained relatively unchanged with advancing age,[12] suggesting the possibility that a decline in oxidative cerebral functions may not be an inevitable part of human aging in the absence of specific pathological lesions.

The extent of neuronal loss is presently quite controversial, mostly because of diverse technical considerations.[1,4,21] However, most evidence indicates some neuronal loss (10 to 60 percent) with normal aging in the human and primate neocortex, cerebellum, and hippocampus, whereas cell loss may be less dramatic in subcortical structures (except for the locus ceruleus).[7] Loss of neurons in cortical structures varies greatly between regions. The superior temporal gyrus loses as much as 55 percent of its neuronal content, whereas the inferior temporal gyrus and the tip of the temporal lobe show only a 10 to 35 percent loss.[7] Readers may note that decrease in neuronal volume with age may exaggerate apparent neuronal loss.[21] Current data indicate that the age-related cortical neuronal loss is most prominent in large neurons, whereas in the subcortical pigmented structures like the substantia nigra and the locus ceruleus, cells with the most neuromelanin appear to be more vulnerable.[13] The nucleus basalis of Maynert also suffers little or no neuronal loss with aging. These discrepancies might be related to unrecognized senile dementia or other neurological diseases. Small cortical neurons are difficult to evaluate since the loss of large neurons will generally induce the proliferation of glial cells, which are small like some cortical neurons. Primates also show age-related, region-specific loss of cortical neurons.

On the other hand, there is an increased dendritic growth in some neurons of the cerebral cortex and hippocampus of aging humans and nonhuman primates.[7,7a,14] Thus, it is not surprising to observe some neurochemical compensatory mechanisms in the areas affected by neuronal loss. Before describing in detail the neurochemical alterations of the aging, we will review age changes in the brain bulk constituents.

Chemical Constituents of the Aging Brain

Proteins

The decrease in weight observed in human brain with aging is associated with a concomitant loss of proteins that appears to be proportional to the gain of water.[15] The protein content may be reduced with aging, but not all proteins are affected. For example, abnormal proteins contained in intraneuronal neurofibrillary tangles and neuritic plaques with extracellular amyloid increase gradually with age. During Alzheimer's disease, plaques and tangles accumulate markedly in the hippocampus, some cortical regions, and the nucleus basalis of Maynert, while other regions remain relatively free of changes, e.g., primary sensory cortex. On the other hand, some enzymes not related to neurotransmission show marked decreases of activity or amount. Among others, these include fructose-6-phosphate dehydrogenase, glucose-6-phosphate dehydrogenase, and glycerol-3-phosphate dehydrogenase, which are involved in glucose catabolism. Carbonic anhydrase, a key enzyme in CO_2 detoxification, is also reduced. For more complete lists of enzymes and proteins modified by the aging process, see Refs. 2, 6, 16, and 17.

Nucleic Acids

Neurons of the central nervous system contain the same amount of DNA as any other somatic cells, and little or no change of the DNA content is reported in the brain. However, the story is noticeably different with RNA content. Because messenger RNA populations are thought to vary widely between types of neurons because of selective transcription, it is no surprise that the RNA changes with age vary between brain regions. In the neurons of the hypoglossal nucleus, the total RNA content increases in the first two decades of life and then decreases through the ninth decade.[18] Similar biphasic changes occur in the motor neurons of the ventrolateral nucleus, with decreases after 50 to 60 years,[19] and in the basal nucleus of Meynert.[20,21] In the subicular region of the hippocampus, the concentration of bulk neuron RNA in nondemented individuals increases by more than 50 percent at advanced ages, whereas neurons in the cortex of the same individuals have less RNA.[22] The relation of changes in RNA to protein synthesis is presently unknown.

A remarkable new phenomenon was recently described, in which a genetic defect becomes spontaneously cured during aging because of somatic mutations in brain neurons. The Brattleboro rat strain has well-known deficiencies of vasopressin, which result from a frame shift mutation that prevents intracellular processing through the translated, but abnormal COOH-terminal glycoprotein. However, from birth onward, the Brattleboro rat hypothalamus shows an increased number of solitary neurons with normal vasopressin and COOH-terminal glycoprotein;[23] these cells are hemizygous for the mutant and revertant protein. cDNA cloned by polymerase chain reaction (PCR) from older Brattleboro rats showed clusters of frame shift revertant cells (van Leewen et al., unpublished). These remarkable findings imply the reverse process through which normal genes could become damaged at a slow rate to yield hemizygous mutant neurons or glia.

Lipids

Lipids account for more than half of the dry weight of the brain. A loss in total lipids occurs after 50 years of age.[24,25] However, the relative lipid content may be increased or unchanged during the same period because of the global loss of brain weight.[26] The loss of myelin lipids may be at a fairly constant rate between 60 and 90 years of age. The loss is most pronounced in the white matter but is also evident in cerebral cortex. There is also a correlation between the loss of myelin and the brain content of cerebroside and ethanolamine plasmalogen,[24] the latter two major components being constituents of myelin. Other lipids like ganglioside, choline phosphoglyceride, ethanolamine phosphoglyceride, cerebroside, sulfatide, sphingomyelin, and cholesterol are also reduced in the aging human brain.[24,26] Although little is known about the changes in lipid turnover in the human brain, aging rodents show a decreased lipid turnover rate and a decreased lipid concentration that parallels a decrease in lipid catabolism and synthesis.[26]

Biochemical Aspects of Conduction and Neurotransmission

Principles of Neurotransmitter Biology

The transmission of neuronal information can be subdivided into two distinct mechanisms: an *electrical* counterpart that carries the information from the cell body along the axon to the terminals and a *chemical* counterpart that is activated by the arriving action potential, which triggers the release of neurotransmitters at the terminal level. The chemical cascade is initiated by the entry of Ca^{2+} into the terminals, which promotes the fusion of the neurotransmitter-containing vesicles with the plasma membrane. The transmission between two neurons involves the synthesis, storage, and release of one or more different neurotransmitters in response to nerve-ending depolarization. These neurotransmitters have been classified as inhibitory, excitatory, or modulatory. Modulatory neurotransmitters have certain effects on the other neurotransmitters. Once released, a neurotransmitter diffuses to the postsynaptic membrane, where it binds transiently with highly specific receptor proteins. The complex formed by the transmitter and its receptor then modulates the electrical excitability of the postsynaptic cell and promotes inhibition, stimulation, and modulation (or a combination of all three) of an electrical impulse through modification of the polarization state of the cell. Once the signal is transmitted, the receptor releases its neurotransmitter into the synaptic cleft, where it is deactivated by specific catabolic enzymes or sequestered by presynaptic surfaces.

Pre- and Postmortem Considerations

Study of the biochemical and neurochemical changes in aging human brain is complicated by the variability of postmortem intervals until the specimen is fixed or frozen. Agonal states strongly influence the structure and the chemistry of the brain and often differ widely among individuals. The handling of postmortem tissues has not yet been set by common conventions, and protocols for freezing tend to vary greatly among institutions. One has also to consider that an underlying disease might be present in some of the so-called control brains. A careful neuropathological investigation is needed for each specimen to distinguish age-related from pathologic non-age-related changes. Contrary to common belief, human brain tissues processed biochemically retain many types of undegraded macromolecules for up to 24 hours postmortem, including active enzymes and messenger RNAs.[27,28]

Catecholamines and Serotonin

The catecholamine neurotransmitter family is composed of three distinct neurotransmitters: dopamine, norepinephrine, and epinephrine. Although dopamine is a precursor of norepinephrine and epinephrine, and norepinephrine a precursor of epinephrine, each of the three has a separate brain localization and relatively distinct functions. These neurotransmitters are mostly involved in the control and modulation of visceral functions and of emotions and attention. Serotonin, whose amino acid precursor is tryptophan, is known to be involved in many central regulatory processes, including drinking, respiration, heart beat, thermoregulation, sleep, and memory.

During aging in apparently normal individuals, several investigators have showed a significant loss of synthetic capability of certain catecholaminergic and serotonergic neurons. Tyrosine hydroxylase (TH), the enzyme that converts tyrosine into dihydroxyphenylalanine (dopa), becomes somewhat reduced with age in the caudate nucleus, putamen, and amygdala but not in the hypothalamus.[29,30] However, most of the decline of TH activity occurs before 20 years of age. Under such circumstances, it seems more appropriate to talk of relative changes. The extent of changes in dopa decarboxylase (DCC), which converts dopa into dopamine, varies tremendously among regions, and no conclusion is yet possible.[31] The dopamine content is particularly reduced in the striatum, up to 50 percent by 75 years, as well as in mesencephalic structures. Dopamine beta-hydroxylase activity, which converts dopamine to norepinephrine, is not notably affected by aging.[2,32] The loss of TH, DCC, dopamine, and norepinephrine closely parallels the loss of dopaminergic and noradrenergic neurons described in the substantia nigra and the locus ceruleus. Two enzymes degrade dopamine and noradrenaline: monoamine oxidase (MAO), mainly the MAO-B subtype, and catechol-*o*-methyltransferase (COMT). They appear to be differentially altered with aging. MAO activity is consistently elevated with aging in the frontal cortex, striatum, globus pallidus, and substantia nigra in humans, whereas COMT activity remains unchanged except in the hippocampus, where it is increased.[33,34] However, COMT activity in rodent brains changes differentially than in humans; it tends to parallel MAO increases with age. The increase in MAO (and perhaps COMT) with age is consistent with the apparent increases of monoamine catabolites observed in the cerebrospinal fluid of elderly patients.[2,33,35]

At least two types of dopaminergic receptors have been investigated in the human aging striatum, the D1 receptor, which is positively linked to adenylate cyclase activity, and the D2 receptor, which appears to be negatively coupled with adenylate cyclase. The human striatum loses approximately 2 percent of its D2 receptors per decade, whereas little or no change in D1 receptor content has been reported with aging in the striatum.[36,37] These observations strengthen the results obtained by positron emission tomography (PET) scan studies in vivo.[38,39] As for noradrenergic receptors, the beta subtypes appear to decrease in the cerebellum with aging. This is corroborated by rodent studies, where most of the brain regions studied (including the cerebellum) present a 20 to 30 percent loss.[40] Finally, serotonin receptors are reduced in the cerebral cortex, but not in the striatum of aging humans.[40,41]

Acetylcholine

Cholinergic neurons synthesize acetylcholine from choline and acetyl coenzyme A (acetyl-CoA). The enzymes responsible for the degradation and synthesis of acetylcholine are synthesized in the soma and are transported to the terminals. Acetyl-CoA, which comes from pyruvate metabolism, is combined with choline via the activity of choline acetyltransferase (CAT). The choline can be taken up directly through synaptic membranes, or it may be formed from the catabolism of phosphatidylcholine. Once released from its vesicular form, acetylcholine can interact pre- and postsynaptically with two types of receptors, namely the nicotinic and muscarinic receptors. Finally, the neurotransmitter is inactivated by acetylcholinesterase (AChE), while free choline is released from the process. CAT and AChE activity change little with normal aging in human brain. CAT activity appears to be prominently reduced in the cerebral cortex but remains unchanged in the striatum.[29] The loss of CAT activity is accompanied by a significant reduction (20 to 85 percent) of AChE activity and choline uptake in the human cortex with aging. Studies in rhesus monkeys show a similar loss of AChE after 20 years of age.[20,42] Loss of cholinergic function with age is, however, still controversial; inclusion of unrecognized Alzheimer's disease specimens might be responsible for the trend. Acetylcholine, like tryptophan hydroxylase, is too labile to be accurately measured in human postmortem tissues.

Muscarinic receptors are significantly reduced in the cerebral cortex and hippocampus with age, but not in the basal ganglia.[41] Rodents show consistent age-related decrease in the M_2 cholinergic receptor control in the striatum and hippocampus, and in the regulation of acetylcholine release.[5,43] Nicotinic receptors, on the other hand, are reduced only in cortical structures.

GABA and Glutamic Acid

Gamma aminobutyric acid (GABA) and glutamate are both metabolic intermediates and neurotransmitters. Their respective metabolisms are strongly interrelated. Glutamic acid decarboxylase (GAD) catalyzes the conversion of glutamate into GABA in neurons, whereas the conversion of GABA into glutamine in glial cells is mediated by glutamine synthetase. Subsequently, glutamine is taken up by the neurons and transformed into glutamate via glutaminase activity. There appears to be no specific storage of glutamate and GABA in the terminals, in contrast to catecholaminergic and acetylcholine neurotransmitters. GABA release is known to have mostly inhibitory actions at the postsynaptic level, whereas glutamate promotes a postsynaptic stimulatory response. Since little is known about the neurobiology of glutamate in the aging human brain, this discussion will focus on GABA metabolism. GAD activity falls (20 to 30 percent) with age in human cortical areas and in the thalamus.[31] GAD activity is also reduced in the basal ganglia.[31] GABA uptake in decreased in the neocortex with age, but the receptor binding of muscimol, a GABA agonist, increases in the temporal lobe with age in humans.[2] Similar changes were observed in the frontal cortex when investigated using a GABA-binding assay. The increased sensitivity of elderly patients to benzodiazepines has prompted several investigators to study the interaction of GABA with benzodiazepine binding sites. However, neither benzodiazepine binding nor GABA interaction with benzodiazepine receptors appears affected by the aging process in humans.[2]

Caution is needed in interpreting studies of amino acid neurotransmitter metabolism, since it is difficult for the moment to distinguish the neurotransmitter-related functions from those of intermediary metabolism. Some of the changes might simply reflect altered metabolism and not altered neurotransmission. It should also be noted that GAD is affected by preterminal coma conditions and certain antibiotics.

Neuropeptides

The synthesis of neuropeptides can occur from two different pathways. For short peptides, like carnosine and glutathione, enzymes called *synthetases* catalyze the synthesis from amino acid components. But for most of the larger peptides found in the central nervous system—like nerve growth factor or the endorphins—a prohormone is synthesized via the usual translation of messenger RNA. The prohormone is processed in the secretory granules during the axonal transport, and the mature peptides are secreted. Fortunately for neurochemists, most neuropeptides are quite stable post mortem. There is no loss of substance P with aging in the frontal cortex, caudate nucleus, globus pallidus, thalamus, or hypothalamus, whereas an important decrease has been observed in the putamen.[44] No changes have been noted in somatostatin levels in the striatum, frontal cortex, globus pallidus, or substantia nigra in normal human subjects.[44] In contrast, Alzheimer's disease patients show a severe loss of somatostatin (approximately 60 percent) in the hippocampus[45,46] and in cortex.[47]

Neurotensin levels in the human frontal cortex, caudate nucleus, putamen, nucleus accumbens, olfactory tubercles, septum, and globus pallidus remain unchanged during the life span.[44] However, a loss of neurotensin (approximately 40 percent) was found in the substantia nigra with aging in humans, but not in rats. The vasoactive intestinal peptide (VIP) content of the human temporal lobe increases between the sixth and the ninth decade.[48] Little is known about the role of these peptides, their metabolism, or the effects of a loss (or a gain) in the aging human brain.

The dynamics of secretion of pituitary hormones show age-related changes in humans which represent the altered secretion of neuropeptide-releasing hormones by the hypothalamus. Both sexes tend to have fewer nocturnal episodes of growth hormone secretion.[6] The wide differences between individuals may reflect the undefined effects of exercise, diet, or adiposity. The pulsatile secretions of luteinizing hormone also decrease in frequency and amplitude in elderly men, again with wide individual differences. These changes also occur in aging rodents and may be linked in future studies to altered neurotransmitter regulation.[49]

AGE-RELATED DISEASES OF THE AGING BRAIN

Any description of the neurochemical alterations of the brain due to aging requires mention of the most important late-age-onset neurological diseases, namely Parkinson's disease (PD) and Alzheimer's disease (AD). In patients who die in "preclinical" phases of these diseases and who are therefore classified as "neurologically intact controls," changes due to early phases of these diseases may be attributed to "normal" aging. As the average age of the population in industrialized countries has persistently increased over the last decades, more and more individuals have become at risk to develop one of these terrible age-related diseases of the central nervous system. By the end of the century, more than 15 percent of the total population of the United States will be over 65, and at progressively increased risk for AD and PD.

Parkinson's Disease

The clinical features,[50,51] pathology,[52] and treatment[53] of PD are discussed in detail in Chap. 93.

Biochemical Abnormalities

Although the etiology of PD still remains unknown, the 90 percent (or more) loss of dopamine in the substantia nigra-striatum axis is almost certainly responsible for most symptoms. Moreover, PD symptoms can be induced by means of specific dopamine antagonists, by the virus which caused the epidemic of Encephalitis lethargica earlier this century, or by chemical compounds such as carbon monoxide, manganese, or *n*-methyl-4-phenyl-1,2,3,6-tetrahydropyridine (MPTP). The genetic risk factors in PD have not been generally established. The abnormal neurochemical parameters observed in PD are summarized in Table 88-1.

TABLE 88-1

Neurochemical Parameters in Parkinson's Disease

	Areas												
	SNA	CAU	PUT	PAL	FCx	VTA	HIP	HYP	ACC	A25	SIN	LC	OLF
Dopamine	–	–	–		–	–	–	–	–	–			–
D1 receptor			0										
D2 receptor		+	+										
TH	–	–	–	–									
DCC	–	–	–	–									
Homovanillic acid	–	–	–										
Noradrenalin	–	–	–					–	–			–	
Serotonin		–						–					
CAT					–						–		
GAD	0	0	0		0			0	0		0		
Peptides													
Met-enkephalin	–	0	–	–	0	–	0	0					
Leu-enkephalin	0	0	–	–	0	0	0	0					
Substance P	–	0	–	0	0	0	0	0					
CCK-8	–	0	0	0	0	0	0	0					
Somatostatin	0	0	0	0	–*	0	–*	0					
TRH	0	0	0	0	0	0	0	0					
Bombesin	0	–	0	–	0	0	0	0					
Neurotensin	0	0	0	0	0	0	–						

Key: SNA: substantia nigra, CAU: caudate, PUT: putamen, PAL: globus pallidus, FCx: frontal cortex, VTA: ventral tegmental area, HIP: hippocampus, HYP: hypothalamus, ACC: nucleus accumbens, A25: Broca's area 25, SIN: substantia innominata, LC: locus ceruleus, OLF: olfactory tubercules, CCK-8: cholecystokinen, TRH: thyrotropin releasing hormone, –: Decreased, 0: not changed, +: increased in Parkinson's disease versus age-matched controls, –*: decrease in demented patients.
SOURCE: Adapted from Barbeau[50] and Jellinger.[52]

Alzheimer's Disease

The clinical features,[55–58] structural neuropathology,[55,59] and treatment of Alzheimer's disease are discussed in detail in Chap. 92.

Biochemical Characteristics

Four different ascending projection pathways are involved in Alzheimer's disease: (1) the cholinergic system, which arises from the nuclear basalis of Maynert; (2) the noradrenergic system, which arises from the locus ceruleus; (3) the serotoninergic pathway, which arises from the raphe nucleus and the dorsal tegmentum; and (4) the reticular projection, which arises from the paramedian reticular nucleus. There is also evidence for a progressive disconnection of the hippocampus from the rest of the brain and a loss of connections between different cortical areas.[7a,59,61] In AD there is a significant loss of neurons in the locus ceruleus and in the nuclear basalis of Maynert. Plaques and tangles which are common markers of aging are more numerous in AD, particularly in early-onset AD (see Chap. 92).

Table 88-2 summarizes the neurotransmitter changes in AD. The loss of cholinergic function is one of the most important neurotransmitter alterations reported in AD. CAT as well as AChE are severely reduced in the cerebral cortex and hippocampus of Alzheimer's patients. The cholinergic loss occurs as early as the first year of the disease, but varies widely among subjects. Muscarinic (postsynaptic) receptors appear unchanged. Somatostatin, a neuropeptide present in medium-size and large neurons, also decreases in the hippocampus and cerebral cortex.

CONCLUSION

It is no longer possible to associate the aging of the brain with loss of function and structure without taking into consideration the plastic nature of the central nervous system. Although there is an age-related loss

TABLE 88-2

Neurochemical Parameters in Alzheimer's Disease

	Areas																				
	SNA	CAU	PUT	PAL	LC	PONS	THAL	HYP	MAM	AMYG	CING	HIP	CER	NA	CCNE	MIDB	SIN	TCx	OCx	PCx	FCx
Acetylcholine																					
CAT	–	–				–	–	–	–	–	–	–	–	–	–	–		–	–	–	–
AChE	–	–				–	–	–	–	–	–	–	–	–	–	–		–	–	–	–
Muscarinic receptor		0	0				0					0						0		0	0
GABA	0	0	0	0						0/–		–						–	0	0	0
GAD	0	0				0	0	0	0	0	0	–	0	0	–	–		–	–	–	0
GABA receptor		–	0									0						+/–	0		0
Glutamate receptor		+/–	0				0			0											
Noradrenaline		–	–	–				–			–#	–#						–#			0
Dopamine beta hydroxylase												–						–			
Alpha- and beta-3 adrenergic dopamine receptor		0	0									0 0						0	0	0	0 0
Serotonin		–						–			–	–									–
Serotoninergic receptor										–	0	–						–		–	–
Somatostatin								+				–						–		–	–
Substance P											–	–						–	–		–
Oxytocin	0	0		0	0		0					–						–	0	0	0
Cholecystokinin	0	0		0								0						0	0	0	0
VIP		0		0								0						0	0	0	0
Corticotropin-releasing factor		–						0		0		0	0					0	–	0	–

Key: SNA: substantia nigra, CAU: caudate, PUT: putamen, PAL: pallidum, LC: locus ceruleus, THAL: thalamus, HYP: hypothalamus, MAM: mamillary bodies, AMYG: amygdala, CING: cingulate cortex, HIP: hippocampus, CER: cerebellum, NA: nucleus accumbens, CCNE: calcarine cortex, MIDB: mid brain, SIN: substantia innominata, TCx: temporal cortex, OCx: occipital cortex, PCx: parietal cortex, FCx: frontal cortex. #: young patients (age < 79), –: Decreased, 0: not changed, +: increased in Alzheimer's disease versus age-matched controls.
SOURCE: Adapted from Terry and Katzman[57] and Morgan et al.[41]

of neurons, this loss remains restricted to specific areas of the brain and is often associated with compensatory dendritic proliferation. On the other hand, there are still uncertainties concerning which, if any, of the age-related changes are physiological consequences of aging and which might be of unrecognized disease origin. The new techniques of molecular biology have great potential in resolving these unknowns.

REFERENCES

1. Katzman R, Terry R: Normal aging of the nervous system, in Katzman R, Terry R (eds): *The Neurobiology of Aging*. Philadelphia, Davis, 1983, p 15.
2. Rogers J, Bloom FE: Neurotransmitter metabolism and function in the aging nervous system, in Finch CE, Schneider EL (eds): *Handbook of the Biology of Aging*. New York, Van Nostrand Reinhold, 1985, p 645.
3. Morgan DG et al: Dopamine and serotonin system in human and rodent brain. Effects of age and neurodegenerative disease. *J Am Geriatr Soc* 35:334, 1987.
4. Finch CE, Morgan DE: RNA and protein metabolism in the aging brain. *Ann Rev Neurosci* 13:75.
5. Finch CE: Aging in the nervous system, in Siegel G et al. (eds): *Basic Neurochemistry*, 5th ed, New York, Raven, in press.
6. Finch CE: *Longevity, Senescence, and the Genome*. Chicago, University of Chicago Press, 1990.
7. Coleman PD, Flood DG: Neuron numbers and dendritic extent in normal aging and Alzheimer's disease. *Neurobiol Aging* 8:521, 1987.
7a. Cotman CW et al: Molecular cascades in adaptive versus pathological plasticity, in A Gorio (ed): *Neuroregeneration*. New York, Raven Press, p 217.
8. DeKaban AS, Sadowsky BS: Changes in brain weight during the life span of human life: Relation of brain weight to body heights and body weights. *Ann Neurol* 4:345, 1978.
9. Duara R et al: Human brain glucose utilization and cognitive function in relation to age. *Ann Neurol* 16:702, 1984.
10. Stafford JL et al: Age-related differences in CT scan measurements. *Adv Neurol* 45:409, 1988.
11. Meier-Ruge W et al: Effect of age on morphological and biochemical parameters of the human brain, in Stein D (ed): *The Psychobiology of Aging*. New York, Elsevier, 1980, p 297.
12. Duara R et al: Human brain glucose utilization and cognitive function in relation to age. *Ann Neurol* 16:702, 1984.
13. Mann DMA, Yates PO: Pathogenesis of Parkinson's disease. *Arch Neurol* 39:545, 1982.
14. Cotman CW, Anderson KJ: Synaptic plasticity and functional stabilization in the hippocampal formation: Possible role in Alzheimer's disease. *Adv Neurol* 47:313, 1988.
15. Davis JM, Himwich WA: Neurochemistry of the developing and aging mammalian brain, in Ordy JM, Brizzee KR (eds): *Neurobiology of Aging*. New York, Plenum, 1975, p 329.
16. Finch CE: Enzyme activities, gene function and ageing in mammals. *Exp Gerontol* 7:53, 1972.
17. Wilson PD: Enzyme levels in animals of various ages, in Florini JR et al (eds): *CRC Handbook of Biochemistry in Aging*. Boca Raton, FL, CRC Press, 1981, p 163.
18. Uemura F, Hartmann HA: Age-related changes in RNA content and volume of the human hypoglossal neuron. *Brain Res Bull* 3:207, 1978.
19. Hyden H: Biochemical and molecular aspects of learning and memory, in *Biological and Clinical Aspects of the Central Nervous System*. Basel, Sandoz Symposium, 1967, p 17.
20. de Lacalle S et al: Differential changes in cell size and number in topographic subdivisions of human basal nucleus in normal aging. *Neuroscience* 43:445, 1991.
21. Finch CE: Neuron atrophy during aging: Programmed or sporadic? *Trends Neurosci*, 16:104, 1993.
22. Uemura F, Hartmann HA: RNA content and volume of nerve cell bodies in human brain. *Exp Neurol* 65:107, 1079.
23. van Leeuwen F et al: Age-related development of a heterozygous phenotype in solitary neurons of the homozygous Brattleboro rat. *Proc Nat Acad Sci USA* 86:6417, 1989.
24. Rouser G et al: Lipids in the nervous system of different species as a function of age, in Paoletti R, Kritchevsky K (eds): *Advances in Lipid Research*. New York, Academic, 1972, p 261.
25. Svennerholm L et al: Membrane lipids in the aging human brain. *J Neurochem* 56:2051, 1991.
26. Horrock LA et al: Changes in brain during aging, in Ordy JM, Brizzee KR (eds): *Neurobiology of Aging*. New York, Plenum, 1975, p 359.
27. Hardy JA, Dodd PR: Metabolic and functional studies on postmortem human brain, in Osborne NN (ed): *Selected Topics from Neurochemistry*. New York, Pergamon, 1985, p 25.
28. Johnson SA et al: Extensive postmortem stability of RNA from rat and human brain. *J Neurosci Res* 16:267, 1986.
29. McGeer EG, McGeer PL: Neurotransmitter metabolism and the aging brain, in Terry RD, Gershon S (eds): *Neurobiology of Aging*. New York, Raven, 1976, vol 3, p 389.
30. Pradhan SN: Central neurotransmitters and aging. *Life Sci* 26:1643, 1980.
31. McGeer EG: Aging and the neurotransmitter metabolism in the brain, in Katzman R, Terry RD, Bick KL (eds): *Alzheimer's Disease: Senile Dementia and Related Disorders*. New York, Raven, 1978, p 427.
32. Grote SS et al: Study of selected catecholamine metabolizing enzymes: A comparison of depressive suicides and alcoholic suicides with controls. *J Neurochem* 23:791, 1974.
33. Robinson DS et al: Aging, monoamines and monoamine oxidases. *Lancet* 1:290, 1972.
34. Robinson DS: Changes in monoamines oxidase and monoamines in human development and aging. *Fed Proc* 34:103, 1975.
35. Stahl SM et al: CSF monoamine metabolites in move-

ment disorders and normal aging. *Arch Neurol* 42:166, 1985.
36. Seeman P et al: Human brain dopamine receptors in children and aging adults. *Synapse* 1:399, 1987.
37. Morgan DG et al: Divergent changes in D-1 and D-2 dopamine binding sites in human brain during aging. *Neurobiol Aging* 8:195, 1987.
38. Baron JC et al: Loss of striatal ($^{76}Br^-$) bromospiperone binding sites demonstrated by positron tomography in progressive supranuclear palsy. *J Cereb Blood Flow Metab* 6:131, 1986.
39. Wong D et al: Effect of age on dopamine and serotonin receptors measured by positron tomography in the living human brain. *Science* 226:1393, 1984.
40. Hess GD, Roth GS: Receptors and aging, in Johnson JE (ed): *Aging and Cell Function*. New York, Plenum, 1984, p 149.
41. Morgan DG et al: Neurotransmitter receptors in normal human aging and Alzheimer's disease, in Sen AK, Lee TY (eds): *Receptors and Ligands in Neurological Disorders*. London, Cambridge University Press, 1988, p 120.
42. Ordy JM et al: Life-span neurochemical changes in the human and non human primate brain, in Brody H et al (eds): *Clinical, Morphological and Neurochemical Aspects in the Central Nervous System*. New York, Raven, 1975, p 133.
43. Araujo DM et al: Effects of aging on nicotinic and muscarinic autoreceptor function in the rat brain: Relationship to presynaptic cholinergic markers and binding sites. *J Neurosci* 10:3069, 1990.
44. Buck SH et al: Survey of substance P, somatostatin and neurotensin levels in aging in the rat and human central nervous system. *Neurobiol Aging* 2:257, 1981.
45. Davies P et al: Reduced somatostatin-like immunoreactivity in the cerebral cortex form cases from Alzheimer's disease and Alzheimer senile dementia. *Nature* 288:279, 1980.
46. Morrison JH et al: Somatostatin immunoreactivity in neuritic plaques of Alzheimer's patients. *Nature* 314:90, 1985.
47. Rossor MN et al: Neurochemical characteristics of early and late onset types of Alzheimer's disease. *Br Med J* 288:961, 1984.
48. Perry EK et al: Neurochemical activities in human temporal lobe related to aging and Alzheimer-type changes. *Neurobiol Aging* 2:251, 1981.
49. Finch CE: Neural and endocrine determinants of senescence: Investigation of causality and reversibility by laboratory and clinical interventions, in Warner HR et al (eds): *Modern Biological Theories of Aging*. New York, Raven, 1987, p 261.
50. Barbeau A: Parkinson's disease: Clinical features and etiopathology, in Vinken PJ et al (eds): *Handbook of Clinical Neurology*. New York, Elsevier, 1986, p 87.
51. Schoenberg BS et al: Prevalence of Parkinson's disease in the biracial population of Copiah county, Mississippi. *Neurology* 35:841, 1985.
52. Jellinger K: Pathology of Parkinson's disease, in Fahn S et al (eds): *Recent Developments in Parkinson's Disease*. New York, Raven, 1986, p 33.
53. Campanella G et al: Drugs affecting movement disorders. *Ann Rev Pharmacol Toxicol* 27:113, 1986.
54. Poirier J et al: Environment, genetics and idiopathic Parkinson's disease. *Can J Neurol Sci* 18:70, 1991.
55. Katzman R: Alzheimer's disease. *N Engl J Med* 314:964, 1986.
56. Eslinger PJ, Damasio AR: Preserved motor learning in Alzheimer's disease: Implications for anatomy and behavior. *J Neurosci* 6:3006, 1986.
57. Terry RD, Katzman R: Senile dementia of Alzheimer type. *Ann Neurol* 14:497, 1983.
58. Bird TD et al: Familial Alzheimer's disease in American descendants of the Volga Germans: Probable genetic founder effect. *Ann Neurol* 23:25, 1988.
59. Morrisson JH et al: Anatomic and molecular characteristics of vulnerable neocortical neurons in Alzheimer's disease, in Finch CE, Davies P (eds): *Bambury Report: Alzheimer's Disease*. Cold Spring Harbor, NY, Cold Spring Harbor Laboratory, 1989.

Chapter 89

COGNITION AND AGING

Marilyn S. Albert

Significant changes in cognitive function develop with age. These changes are evident in several major aspects of mental ability. However, declines do not develop uniformly, either within or across cognitive domains. The nature of the changes that occur, the points at which changes become apparent, and the magnitudes and rates of changes vary, depending upon the cognitive function in question. This chapter will discuss general methodological issues pertaining to the assessment of cognitive changes with age and review recent findings concerning six major areas of cognitive ability: attention, language, memory, visuospatial ability, conceptualization, and general intelligence.

GENERAL METHODOLOGICAL ISSUES

One of the most important methodological difficulties relevant to the study of cognitive change with age concerns subject sampling and generational change. Cross-sectional testing tends to maximize differences between age groups, whereas longitudinal testing minimizes these differences.[1]

Schaie and his associates[2] developed a testing procedure called a *cohort-sequential design* in which age changes are studied while time of measurement is controlled. However, since the cost of such an undertaking is considerable, most investigators continue to employ cross-sectional study techniques. When reviewing the results of these cross-sectional data, one therefore needs to consider how well cohort differences have been controlled and how much they are likely to have contributed to the study results.

The other general issue that should be pointed out with regard to measures of cognition with age is the increasing variability that is evident among individuals in the older age ranges. This is, in fact, not only true for cognition but is also true for physiologic measurements in the elderly. There is both increasing intraindividual and interindividual variability with age. The intraindividual variability is reflected by the fact that within the same individual some functions change and others do not. An individual whose verbal IQ remains relatively stable into the eighth or ninth decade may still show a significant decline in performance IQ. Similarly, an individual whose nerve conduction velocity undergoes little significant change may well have considerable reductions in cardiac output.

Perhaps more striking is the interindividual variability that one observes among people as they age. While the mean value of a particular variable may decline substantially with age, one can find many elderly subjects whose scores fall within the range of individuals 20 or 30 years younger than themselves. Gerontological research has consistently demonstrated that many older persons show little cognitive, physiologic, or functional loss when compared with their younger counterparts, even though the mean for their age group may have declined. Since they have escaped the "usual" aging pattern, these persons have recently been said to represent "successful aging."[3] Although previous research has focused almost entirely on general trends among elderly subjects, it has been argued that more attention should be focused on these "unusual" individuals.[3] The study of successful aging is not merely the obverse of looking for age-related declines. One must ask not only what is maintained with age and why, but what factors enable some individuals to maintain high function even when the average individual is showing declines. If future studies suggest that the factors that contribute to successful aging are under external control, then there is the possibility that gerontologists can contribute to the expansion of the number of people who age successfully in future generations.

ATTENTION

The concept of attention is presently thought to encompass at least two interrelated aspects: sustained attention, or vigilance; and selective attention, or the ability to extract relevant from irrelevant information (see Refs. 4 and 5 for reviews). A third aspect of attention, attentional capacity (or the total attentional resources available to an individual), is being increasingly incorporated into theories that attempt to explain age-related changes in memory, concept formation, etc., and is therefore incorporated into the discussion below.

Tests that evaluate sustained attention assess an individual's ability to focus on a simple task and perform it without losing track of the object of the task. Memory demands are minimized in tests of sustained attention by limiting the information that needs to be remembered to material that falls within a person's immediate memory span (i.e., 5 ± 2). Digit span forward is the most commonly used test of attention since it is included on both the Wechsler Adult Intelligence Scale (WAIS)[6] and the Wechsler Memory Scale (WMS).[7] Visual and auditory continuous performance tasks that require the individual to identify a repeating letter (e.g., *A*) or a repeated letter sequence (e.g., *I before X*) are another common means of evaluating sustained attention.[8]

Numerous studies have demonstrated that tests of sustained attention are performed extremely well into old age. These studies indicate that there is less than 1 standard deviation of change between ages 20 and 80.

Selective attention is generally assessed by paradigms that require the subject to ignore irrelevant information. For example, a subject may be asked to detect a target as the number of nontargets increases. Earlier studies indicated that older individuals have difficulty in performing tasks that require them to ignore irrelevant stimuli.[9] However, recent studies have demonstrated that this is not the case.[10–12] It seems likely that previous results were related to the perceptual difficulties of older individuals in discriminating targets, rather than attentional difficulties in ignoring irrelevant information.

LANGUAGE

Linguistic ability is thought to encompass at least four domains: phonologic, lexical, syntactic, and semantic. Until recently, it was assumed that all linguistic abilities were preserved into very old age, primarily because performance on the vocabulary subtest of the WAIS, the best general estimate of verbal intelligence, is well maintained until individuals are in their eighties.[13] However, within the last decade, a number of studies have shown that although most aspects of linguistic ability are preserved in elderly persons, at least one aspect, semantic knowledge, declines with age.

Phonologic knowledge refers to the use of the sounds of language and the rules for their combination. Phonologic capabilities are well preserved with age.[14]

Lexical knowledge refers to both the lexical representation of a word (i.e., the name of an item) and its semantic representation (i.e., the meaning of a word). The lexicon of healthy older individuals appears to be intact, as are the semantic relationships of the lexicon.[15–17]

Syntactic knowledge refers to the ability to meaningfully combine words. A large number of studies have shown that age has little effect on syntax.[18–22]

The one area of language function that appears to change significantly with age is *semantic knowledge.* One way of assessing the semantic aspects of word retrieval is by testing naming. The most commonly used naming tests entail showing a person a picture of a common object and asking the person to produce the name. Several groups of investigators have reported that scores on naming tests such as these decrease with age.[23–26] However, as shown in Fig. 89-1, declines in naming ability do not become statistically significant until subjects are in their seventies.[26]

Verbal fluency also assesses semantic ability. In a verbal fluency task, a subject is asked to name as many examples of a category (e.g., *animals* or *vegetables*) as possible in a specified period of time (e.g., 1 minute) or as many words beginning with a particular letter (e.g., *F*) within a specified period of time. Several studies report a decline in verbal fluency with age.[26–28] These changes also occur relatively late in the life span (>70 years). Thus, semantic linguistic ability appears to change with advancing age, while other aspects of linguistic ability are relatively well preserved.

MEMORY

Age-related alterations in memory have been more widely studied than alterations in any other aspect of cognition, apart from overall IQ. This is most likely related to the fact that numerous theoretical models

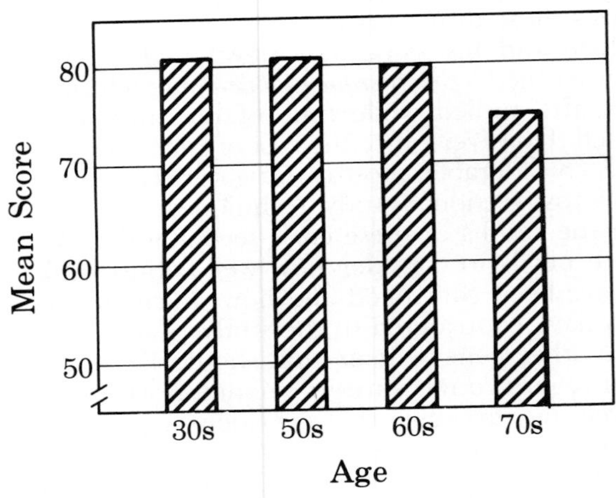

FIGURE 89-1
Performance on the Boston Naming Test by subjects age 30 to 80 years. There is a significant decline in accuracy by subjects in their seventies.

have been proposed to explain normal memory function, thus offering investigators a variety of models to test.

The most widely accepted model of memory conceptualizes memory as a series of specific, yet interactive, stores.

Sensory memory represents the earliest stage of information processing. It concerns perceiving and attending to information. It is modality-specific (i.e., visual, auditory, haptic), highly unstable, and characterized by rapid decay (i.e., losses occur after 1/3 second). There is a considerable amount of information to indicate that changes in sensory memory are minimal with age.[29–31] For example, the time necessary to identify a single letter does not change with age.[29]

Primary memory, once called short-term memory, pertains to the ability to retain a small amount of information over a brief period of time. Information must be actively rehearsed to be retained in primary memory. Numerous studies also indicate that primary memory shows few, if any, losses with age. For example, most studies have found no significant age differences in digit span forward,[32,33] no age differences in word span,[34] and moderate differences in letter span.[35]

Secondary, or long-term, memory is viewed as a memory store that can contain an unlimited amount of information for an indefinite period of time (e.g., hours, days, years). In contrast to the minimal age changes in sensory and primary memory, there are substantial changes in secondary memory. The degree of loss is related to the type of material to be remembered and the method of assessment. Large age differences are found in free recall.[35–38] When given a large amount of new information to retain over a relatively long delay, individuals show declines in memory at a relatively early age. Figure 89-2 shows the performance of a group of optimally healthy subjects on the delayed recall of two paragraphs from the WMS. As can be seen, declines in memory are evident on this task by 50.[39] Age decrements are, however, greater when subjects are asked to recall information than when they are asked to recognize which of several stimuli they were previously exposed to. This is true whether words, line drawings, or pictures are used.

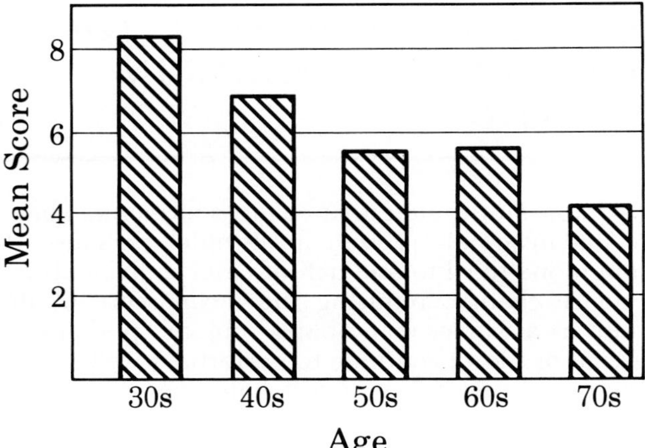

FIGURE 89-2

Delayed recall of paragraphs from the Wechsler Memory Scale by subjects 30 to 80 years old. There is a significant decline in performance by age 50.

Recently it has been argued that a *working memory,* or the simultaneous processing and storing of information,[40] may serve an important integrative function between primary and secondary memory; in tests of primary memory, a small amount of information is typically learned, held passively, and reproduced in an untransformed fashion, whereas in tests of working memory, though the amount of information to be remembered is small, active processing and manipulation of information must take place. Tests of working memory also show age-related decline.[41]

All the above aspects of memory have been traditionally evaluated by explicit memory tasks that require subjects to study target materials and then consciously retrieve the target information through recall or recognition tasks. Recent research, however, indicates that implicit memory tasks that evaluate memory indirectly, i.e., that do not require conscious or intentional recollection, produce results that are often substantially different from explicit memory tasks. The outcome of studies of implicit memory are variable; some demonstrate similar levels of performance across the age range (see Ref. 42 for a review) while others show significant, but small, age-related declines.[43]

VISUOSPATIAL ABILITY

Visuospatial ability, the ability to perceive and function in the spatial domain, is generally assessed by both the production and the recognition of figures. Complex visual tasks, such as the ability to identify incomplete figures,[44] the ability to recognize embedded figures,[45] and the ability to arrange blocks into a design,[46,47] show declines in elderly persons. Perhaps more importantly, the perception and production of relatively simple three-dimensional drawings are altered with age. For example, Plude et al.[48] asked groups of young and old adults (whose mean ages were 21 and 67, respectively, and who were equated for static visual acuity) to draw a cube to command. The drawings of the young adults were rated as significantly better than those of the elderly ones. In addition, the older subjects were less accurate than the young ones in judging the adequacy of drawings of cubes that were distorted to various degrees. The elderly subjects were also less accurate than the young ones in discriminating between distorted and undistorted cubes. Thus, both the ability to perceive and the ability to reproduce figures in three dimension are apparently altered with age.

CONCEPTUALIZATION

Conceptualization refers to the ability to form concepts, switch from one concept or category to another, generalize from a single instance, and apply rules or principles. Therefore, tests of conceptualization generally assess abstraction capacities and/or mental flexibility.

A large variety of tests have been developed to examine conceptualization. They include tests of proverb interpretation, reasoning, sorting, and set shifting. Some of these tasks make substantive memory demands and therefore show significant changes with age. However, conceptualization tasks that do not make substantive memory demands also demonstrate age differences. For example, series completion tasks that require the subject to examine a series of letters or numbers and determine the rule that governs the sequencing of the items show significant age-related change.[49–53] Some investigators developed specially constructed series completion problems in order to determine whether declines are related to alterations in the ability to appreciate abstract concepts or to declines in the ability to detect cyclic periodicity.[53] They concluded that age-related alterations on series completion tasks are the result of progressive problems in abstraction and flexibility rather than an inability to detect cyclic periodicity. Consistent with these findings are the results of proverb interpretation tasks which also show substantial age-related change.[54,55] The greatest age differences appear among subjects in their seventies (see Fig. 89-3).

GENERAL INTELLIGENCE

Intelligence tests examine many of the abilities previously discussed, but they do so in a complex manner.

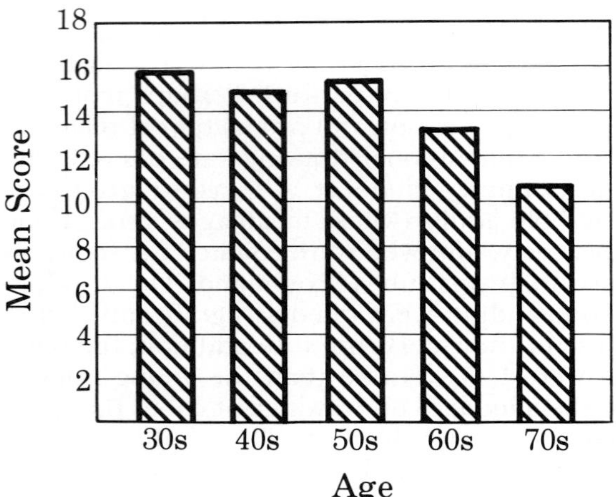

FIGURE 89-3

Performance on Gorham's Proverb Test by subjects 30 to 80 years old. There is a significant decline among subjects in their seventies.

This is because intelligence tests were designed to predict with a reasonable degree of certainty how a person would function in an academic environment. They were not designed as a complete assessment of cognitive function. Thus, intelligence tests do not assess all aspects of cognitive ability. For example, the WAIS does not include an evaluation of memory. In addition, IQ tests do not assess cognitive abilities in relative isolation from one another. Many of the tests require a complex interaction of cognitive abilities to be performed well, and they often depend on speed for an adequate level of performance. Nevertheless, intelligence testing has been one of the most widely explored topics in the field of the psychology of aging.

There is widespread agreement that there are changes in intelligence test performance with age. There has, however, been considerable debate concerning both the point at which declines occur and the magnitude of the declines. The age at which decrements are observed appears to be determined by the methodology employed. There is some consensus that relatively little decline in performance occurs until people are about 50.[3,56–59] After this age, results differ depending upon whether cross-sectional or longitudinal methods were employed. The cross-sectional method shows declines of 1 standard deviation or more beginning about 60.[46,60,61] Over the age of 70, scores drop sharply.[46] The longitudinal method shows declines among subjects beginning in the late sixties. Both methodologies find substantial declines after individuals are in their midseventies. Thus the major difference between the results of cross-sectional and longitudinal investigations is observed between subjects in their early fifties to late sixties. In this age range, the cross-sectional method shows greater age declines than the longitudinal method. Figure 89-4 shows the results of a cohort-sequential study of intelligence conducted by Schaie and his colleagues.[52]

POTENTIAL MECHANISMS FOR AGE-RELATED CHANGES IN COGNITION

It is important to note that changes in mental ability are not invariably present in all older persons. Although one-third to one-half of older individuals experience change, reducing the mean score of the group as a whole, many older subjects (perhaps 50 percent or more) continue to perform as well as subjects many decades younger than themselves. The cause of this variability is unclear. However, it is unlikely to be entirely the result of the presence of clinical disease, since declines are present even among optimally healthy older individuals.

The most likely explanation for changes in cognitive function with age pertains to alterations in the brain. Within the last decade it has been demon-

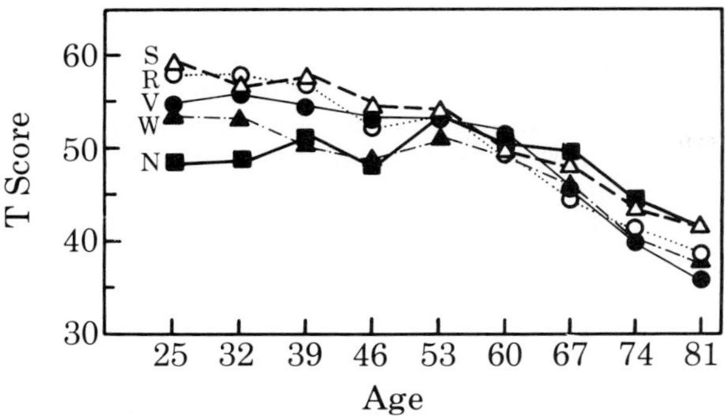

FIGURE 89-4

Factor score changes with age on the Primary Mental Abilities Test derived from a sequential design methodology. The within-subjects analysis showed significant age decrement on all subtests after approximately age 60. The factors on the Primary Mental Abilities Test are: S = space, R = reasoning, V = verbal, W = word fluency, N = number. (*From Schaie KW: The Seattle Longitudinal Study: A 21-year exploration of psychometric intelligence in adulthood, in Schaie KW (ed): Longitudinal Studies of Adult Psychological Development. New York, Guilford, 1983. Copyright 1983 by the Guilford Press. Reprinted with permission.*)

strated quite conclusively that there are structural and functional alterations in the brains of optimally healthy individuals, as reflected by measures of computed tomography (CT) scans, quantified electroencephalography (qEEG), magnetic resonance imaging (MRI), etc. This suggests that age-related changes in cognitive function may be at least partially related to age-related changes in the brain.

For example, there is increased atrophy (i.e., larger ventricles, increased sulcal widening, etc.) and increased EEG fast activity (i.e., increased beta and decreased delta and theta) with advancing age.[62,63] Moreover, structural relations modeling, a statistical procedure that assesses the "causal" relationships among domains, has demonstrated that there is a strong statistical relationship between these structural and functional changes in the brain and declines in memory, executive function, etc.[64] However, there is surprisingly little information regarding the specific brain regions and neurotransmitter systems that are responsible for age-related alterations in memory and other cognitive abilities, primarily due to the technological limitations in imaging procedures that have, until recently, prevented such investigations.

However, recent autopsy data in humans and in nonhuman primates indicate that, contrary to previously published reports, there appears to be minimal cortical neuronal loss with age.[65,66] On the other hand, there appear to be profound alterations at the subcortical level. For example, there is significant age-related neuronal loss in the nucleus basalis in nonhuman primates[67] and MRI evidence of shrinkage in white matter, but not gray matter, with age in humans.[68] This suggests that structural or functional alterations in the brain, apart from cortical neuronal loss, are likely to be primarily responsible for the significant age-related changes in cognitive function that are observed. For example, neurotransmitter alterations and/or degeneration in intracortical and subcortical white matter and the cortical neuropil may produce alterations in reciprocal modulation among brain regions or changes in synaptic connections that lead to altered cognition.

These alterations are, however, likely to be highly selective since those aspects of cognitive function that show age-related declines are very specific (e.g., secondary memory ability, executive function, and three-dimensional representation, confrontation naming), and many abilities are preserved. This selectivity is yet to be explored.

Moreover, recent data also suggest that numerous external factors may modify the development or expression of age-related changes in cognition. Craik et al. compared young subjects with three groups of older individuals (ages 65 to 88) who differed in levels of daily activity, verbal intelligence, and socioeconomic status.[69] They found that the elderly group with the greatest amount of education and highest socioeconomic status differed from the young on only one of six memory tests (free recall with no cues at either encoding or retrieval). Similarly, Arbuckle et al., who examined the memory performance of subjects aged 65 to 88, found that performance on a variety of memory tasks depended strongly on social and personality factors, such as educational level, intellectual activity, and introversion.[70] Clarkson-Smith and Hartley compared persons who were sedentary with those who exercised vigorously and found that performance on verbal and nonverbal reasoning tasks best differentiated the groups, with tests of working memory and reaction time showing less striking relationships with level of activity.[71] This is consistent with several studies that have used reaction time as the primary dependent measure of cognition, before and after a program of aerobic exercise, and have varied in outcome; some showed changes in speed following the exercise program[72,73] and others did not.[74] There is clearly much that remains to be learned about the neurobiologic underpinnings of age-related changes in cognition and the degree to which they can be modified.

SUMMARY

In summary, several aspects of cognitive ability are altered with age. Cross-sectional studies indicate that the earliest change is in secondary memory function: the ability to recall relatively large amounts of information over long periods of time. Subjects in their midfifties are significantly different from younger individuals. Proficiency at constructional tasks, divided-attention capabilities, and general intelligence show alterations in the midsixties. Abstraction and naming ability are significantly different when subjects are in their seventies. Longitudinal findings, where they exist, are comparable, although—as is generally the case with longitudinal studies—declines occur slightly later in the life span.

There is, however, great variability in the degree of cognitive change shown by older individuals. Whereas a sufficient number of older individuals experience change so that the mean of the group is reduced, many older subjects continue to perform as well as subjects many decades younger than themselves. The cause of this variability may be related to age-related alterations in brain function and their interaction with external factors that modify their expression.

REFERENCES

1. Kleemier RW: Intellectual change in the senium. *Proceedings of the Social Statistics Section of the American Statistical Association,* 1962, p 290.
2. Schaie KW et al: Generational and cohort-specific differences in adult cognitive function: A fourteen-year study of independent samples. *Dev Psychol* 9:151, 1973.
3. Rowe JW, Kahn R: Human aging: Usual versus successful. *Science* 237:143, 1987.
4. Parasuraman R, Davies R: *Varieties of Attention.* New York, Academic, 1984.
5. Hasher L, Zacks RT: Automatic and effortful processes in memory. *J Exp Psychol* 108:356, 1979.
6. Wechsler D: *The Assessment and Appraisal of Adult Intelligence.* Baltimore, Williams & Wilkins, 1958.
7. Wechsler D: A standardized memory scale for clinical use. *J Psychol* 19:87, 1945.
8. Mirsky A: Attention: A neuropsychological perspective, in *Education and the Brain.* Chicago, National Society for the Study of Education, 1978.
9. Rabbit PMA: An age decrement in the ability to ignore irrelevant information. *J Gerontol* 20:233, 1965.
10. Gilmore GC et al: Aging and similarity grouping in visual search. *J Gerontol* 40:586, 1985.
11. Nissen MJ, Corkin S: Effectiveness of attentional cueing in older and younger adults. *J Gerontol* 40:185, 1985.
12. Nebes RD, Madden DJ: The use of focused attention in visual search by young and old adults. *Exp Aging Res* 9:139, 1983.
13. Owens NA: Age and mental abilities: A longitudinal study. *Genet Psychol Monog* 48:3, 1953.
14. Bayles KA, Kaszniak AW: Communication and cognition, in *Normal Aging and Dementia.* Boston, Little, Brown, 1987.
15. Howard DV et al: Semantic priming of lexical decisions in young and old adults. *J Gerontol* 36:707, 1981.
16. Cerella J, Fozard JL: Lexical access and age. *Dev Psychol* 20:235, 1984.
17. Bowles NL, Poon LW: Aging and retrieval of words in semantic memory. *J Gerontol* 40:71, 1985.
18. Obler LK et al: On comprehension across the adult life span. *Cortex* 21:273, 1985.
19. Nebes RD, Andrews-Kulis MS: The effect of age on the speed of sentence formation and incidental learning. *Exp Aging Res* 2:315, 1976.
20. DeRenzi E: A shortened version of the Token Test, in Boller F, Dennis M (eds): *Auditory Comprehension: Clinical and Experimental Studies with the Token Test.* New York, Academic, 1979, p 33.
21. Orgass B, Poeck K: Clinical validation of a new test for aphasia: An experimental study of the Token Test. *Cortex* 2:222, 1966.
22. Noll JD, Randolph SR: Auditory semantic, syntactic, and retention errors made by aphasic subjects on the Token Test. *J Commun Disorders* 11:543, 1978.
23. Borod J et al: Normative data on the Boston Diagnostic Aphasia Examination, parietal lobe battery, and Boston Naming Test. *J Clin Neuropsychol* 2:209, 1980.
24. Goodglass H: Naming disorders in aphasia and aging, in Obler LK, Albert ML (eds): *Language and Communication in the Elderly: Clinical, Therapeutic, and Experimental Issues.* Lexington, MA, Lexington Books, 1980, p 37.
25. LaBarge E et al: Performance of normal elderly on the Boston Naming Test. *Brain Lang* 27:380, 1986.
26. Albert MS et al: Changes in naming ability with age. *Psychol Aging* 3:173, 1988.
27. Obler LK, Albert ML: Language and aging: A neurobehavioral analysis, in Beasley DS, Davis GA (eds): *Aging: Communication Processes and Disorders.* New York, Grune & Stratton, 1981, p 107.
28. Spreen O, Benton A: *Neurosensory Center Comprehensive Examination for Aphasia.* Victoria, BC, Neuropsychology Laboratory, Department of Psychology, University of Victoria, 1969.
29. Walsh DA et al: Age differences in peripheral perceptual processing: A monoptic backward masking investigation. *J Exp Psychol (Hum Percept)* 4:232, 1978.
30. Cerella J et al: Age and iconic read-out. *J Gerontol* 37:197, 1982.
31. Cerella J, Poon LW: Age and parafoveal sensitivity (abstract). *Gerontologist* 76, 1981.
32. Drachman DA, Leavitt J: Memory impairment in the aged: Storage versus retrieval deficit. *J Exp Psychol* 93:302, 1972.
33. Kriauciunas R: The relationship of age and retention interval activity in short term memory. *J Gerontol* 23:169, 1968.
34. Talland GA: Three estimates of the word span and their stability over the adult years. *Q J Exp Psychol* 17:301, 1965.
35. Botwinick J, Storandt M: *Memory, Related Functions and Age.* Springfield, IL, Charles C Thomas, 1974.
36. Kausler DH, Lair CV: Associative strength and paired-associated learning in elderly subjects. *J Gerontol* 21:278, 1966.
37. Gilbert JG, Levee RF: Patterns of declining memory. *J Gerontol* 26:70, 1971.
38. Craik FIM: Age differences in human memory, in Bir-

ren JE, Schaie KW (eds): *Handbook of the Psychology of Aging.* New York, Van Nostrand Reinhold, 1977, p 384.

39. Albert MS et al: Nonlinear changes in cognition and their neurophysiologic correlates. *Can J Psychol* 41:141, 1987.
40. Baddeley A: *Working Memory.* Oxford, Clarendon Press, 1986.
41. Morris R et al: Age differences in working memory tasks: The role of secondary memory and the central executive system. *Q J Exp Psychol* 42A:67, 1990.
42. Light L: Memory and aging: Four hypotheses in search of data. *Annu Rev Psychol* 42:333, 1991.
43. Hultsch DF et al: Adult age-differences in direct and indirect tests of memory. *Psychol Sci* 46:22, 1991.
44. Danziger WL, Salthouse TA: Age and the perception of incomplete figures. *Exp Aging Res* 4:67, 1978.
45. Axelrod S, Cohen LD: Senescence and embedded-figure performance in vision and touch. *Perspect Mot Skills* 12:283, 1961.
46. Doppelt JE, Wallace WL: Standardization of the Wechsler Adult Intelligence Scale for older persons. *J Abnorm Soc Psychol* 51:312, 1955.
47. Klodin VM: "Verbal Facilitation of Perceptual-Integrative Performance in Relation to Age." Doctoral dissertation, St. Louis, Washington University, 1975.
48. Plude DJ et al: Age differences in depicting and perceiving tridimensionality in simple line drawings. *Exp Aging Res* 12:221, 1986.
49. Cornelius SW: Classic pattern of intellectual aging: Test familiarity, difficulty and performance. *J Gerontol* 39:201, 1984.
50. Hooper FH et al: *Personality and Memory Correlates of Intellectual Functioning: Young Adulthood to Old Age.* Basel, Karger, 1984.
51. Lachman ME, Jelalian E: Self-efficacy and attributions for intellectual performance in young and elderly adults. *J Gerontol* 39:577, 1984.
52. Schaie KW: The Seattle Longitudinal Study: A 21-year exploration of psychometric intelligence in adulthood, in Schaie K (ed): *Longitudinal Studies of Adult Psychological Development.* New York, Guilford, 1983, p 64.
53. Salthouse TA, Prill K: Inferences about age impairments in inferential reasoning. *Psychol Aging* 2:43, 1987.
54. Bromley D: Effects of age on intellectual output. *J Gerontol* 12:318, 1957.
55. Albert MS: Cognitive function, in Albert MS, Moss MB (eds): *Geriatric Neuropsychology.* New York, Guilford, 1988, p 33.
56. Owens WA: Age and mental abilities: A second adult follow-up. *J Educ Psychol* 57:311, 1966.
57. Riegel KF et al: Socio-psychological factors of aging: A cohort-sequential analysis. *Human Dev* 10:27, 1967.
58. Eisdorfer C, Wilkie F: Intellectual changes with advancing age, in Jarvik LF et al (eds): *Intellectual Functioning in Adults.* New York, Springer, 1973, p 21.
59. Blum JE et al: The New York State Psychiatric Institute study of aging twins, in Jarvik et al (eds): *Intellectual Functioning in Adults.* New York, Springer, 1973, p 13.
60. Green RF: Age-intelligence relationship between ages sixteen and sixty-four: A rising trend. *Dev Psychol* 1:618, 1969.
61. Schaie KW: Rigidity-flexibility and intelligence: A cross-sectional study of the adult life-span from 20 to 70. *Psychol Monogr* 72:462, 1958.
62. Stafford JL et al: Age-related differences in CT scan measurements. *Arch Neurol* 45:409, 1998.
63. Duffy FH et al: Age-related differences in brain electrical activity of healthy subjects. *Ann Neurol* 16:430, 1984.
64. Jones K et al: Modeling age using cognitive, physiological and psychosocial variables. *Exp Aging Research* 17:227, 1991.
65. Terry RD et al: Neocortical cell counts in normal adult aging. *Ann Neurol* 21:530, 1987.
66. Vincent S et al: Effects of aging on the neurons within Area 17 of rhesus monkey cerebral cortex. *Anat Rec* 223:329, 1989.
67. Rosene D, Moss M: Age-related loss of cholinergic neurons in the basal forebrain of the rhesus monkey. *Primate Rep,* in press.
68. Albert M et al: Measurement of age-related differences in gray matter, white matter and CSF. Unpublished.
69. Craik FIM et al: Patterns of memory loss in three elderly samples. *Psychol Aging* 2:79, 1987.
70. Arbuckle TY et al: Cognitive functioning of older people in relation to social and personality variables. *Psychol Aging* 1:55, 1986.
71. Clarkson-Smith L, Hartley A: Structural equation models of relationships between exercise and cognitive abilities. *Psychol Aging* 5:437, 1990.
72. Elsayed M et al: Intellectual differences of adult men related to age and physical fitness before and after an exercise program. *J Gerontol* 35:383, 1980.
73. Dustman R et al: Aerobic exercise training and improved neuropsychological function of older individuals. *Neurobiol Aging* 5:35, 1984.
74. Blumenthal J, Madden D: Effects of aerobic exercise training, age, and physical fitness on memory-search performance. *Psychol Aging* 3:280, 1988.

Chapter 90

DELIRIUM (ACUTE CONFUSIONAL STATES)

Zbigniew J. Lipowski

Delirium, also referred to as *acute confusional states,* represents one of the most common mental disorders encountered in hospitalized elderly patients. Despite its frequency and clinical importance, however, this syndrome is often misdiagnosed and had been relatively little investigated until recently. Formulation of explicit diagnostic criteria for delirium and introduction of uniform terminology have helped to stimulate research on this common syndrome.[1] Two recently published books provide a comprehensive review of the available knowledge about delirium.[2,3]

DELIRIUM DEFINED

Delirium is an organic mental syndrome featuring global cognitive impairment, disturbances of attention, reduced level of consciousness, increased or reduced psychomotor activity, and disorganized sleep-wake cycle.[3,4] Its onset is acute, a matter of hours or a few days, and its duration seldom exceeds 1 month. The severity of its symptoms tends to fluctuate unpredictably over the course of a day and be most marked during a sleepless night. Delirium can occur at any age but is by far most common in elderly persons, those 65 years old and older.

FREQUENCY AND IMPORTANCE

Few epidemiological studies of delirium in elderly persons have been carried out to date, and the reported incidence and prevalence vary widely.[3,5–7] Its reported frequency is likely to be different in a geriatric unit or a psychiatric or a general medical or surgical ward. A geriatric multicenter British study found that 35 percent of patients aged 65 years and older had delirium at some point during the index hospitalization.[8] About 15 percent of elderly patients admitted to general medical wards are delirious on admission,[3,5] while 5 to 10 percent of those found to be nondelirious on initial examination develop delirium during their hospital stay.[9] Of 2000 patients aged 55 years and older admitted to a department of medicine in a university hospital, 9 percent were demented on admission, and 41.4 percent of them were also found to be delirious, while 25 percent of all delirious patients were demented.[10] These findings highlight the frequent concurrence of dementia and delirium in the elderly general hospital patients.

Delirium in the elderly is clinically important not only because it is highly prevalent but also on account of the fact that it often constitutes a presenting feature of a physical illness or drug intoxication.[2,3,5,8,11] If its diagnosis is missed, as is often the case, the patient's underlying medical condition could also remain undiagnosed and untreated, with potentially lethal consequences for him or her. In an elderly patient, the syndrome may be the most conspicuous presenting feature of a myocardial infarction, pneumonia, or subacute bacterial endocarditis, for example.[3,11] Delirium in a demented patient may be mistaken for an exacerbation of the dementia, with consequent failure to diagnose and treat the underlying pathological condition. Delirium has a relatively high mortality.[3,5] Moreover, an agitated, disoriented, and fearful delirious patient is at high risk of sustaining an injury, such as a fracture following a fall, resulting from frantic attempts at escape. Such a patient may pull out intravenous catheters or tear off sutures. Measures often taken to control the patient's agitation may involve parenteral injection of a neuroleptic drug and application of physical restraints. The former may cause serious hypotension, while the latter may result in deep vein thrombophlebitis and pulmonary embolism.[12] For all these reasons, prevention and early diagnosis of delirium should be aimed at.

CLINICAL FEATURES

The clinical picture of delirium is often protean, and this may result in failure to diagnose it.[3] In fact, its diagnosis is often missed.[13,14]

Type of Onset

Delirium comes on acutely, usually over hours or a few days. An elderly patient may develop it more insidiously than a younger one. Prodromal symptoms may herald its onset over the course of several days. They include restlessness, anxiety, difficulty in thinking coherently, insomnia, disturbing dreams, and even fleeting hallucinations.[3]

Global Disorder of Cognition

This constitutes one of the essential features of delirium. *Global* in this context implies that the main cognitive functions, i.e., thinking, memory, and perception, are all impaired or abnormal to some extent. Acquisition, processing, retention, retrieval, and utilization of information are all impaired, and this results in difficulties in problem solving, learning new material, goal-directed behavior, and ability to make sense of what is going on in the immediate environment. Consequently, a delirious patient is more or less helpless and in need of protective care.

Thinking is disorganized and incoherent, and the patient has difficulty in directing it at will. In some patients it is dreamlike (oneiric) and rich in imagery and fantasy, while in others it is just impoverished. The ability to think logically and sequentially, to solve problems, to use abstract concepts, and to plan action is invariably compromised to some extent. As a result, the patient's grasp of the situation, judgment, and spatiotemporal orientation are impaired. As a rule, he or she is disoriented for time, that is, unable to state correctly the date, day of the week, and time of the day. Such temporal disorientation may fluctuate in degree over the course of the day and tends to be most marked at night. It is the first form of disorientation to be exhibited by the patient and the last to clear up. A more severely delirious patient is also disoriented for place and persons. Typically, such a patient tends to mistake an unfamiliar place or person for a familiar one. In the most severe cases, the patients are totally disoriented for time and unaware of their whereabouts; they may even fail to recognize their family members.

A form of pathological thought displayed by some, but not by all, delirious patients is the expression of false beliefs, that is, delusions. They are most often persecutory, poorly systematized, and readily influenced by environmental stimuli. The most common type of delusion in delirium is the belief in the veridical nature of one's hallucinations. Confabulations may also be present and are difficult to tell apart from delusions.

Memory is impaired in its key aspects: registration, retention, and recall. Immediate recall, or short-term memory, is impaired probably as a consequence of reduced attention span. Both retrograde and anterograde amnesia of some degree are present. Recent memory is usually more impaired than remote memory. The patient has diminished capacity to acquire and retain new information. Some degree of amnesia for the experience of delirium after its resolution is the rule.

Perception is marked by reduced ability to discriminate and integrate percepts. Perceptual disturbances in delirium may involve illusions, that is, mislabeling of sensory stimuli, and hallucinations, that is, experiences of perceptual vividness that occur in the absence of proper sensory stimuli. About 40 to 70 percent of delirious patients hallucinate.[3] The illusions and hallucinations may involve any sensory modality but are most often visual or visual and auditory. Their presence is not necessary for the diagnosis of delirium. Most patients accept their hallucinations as real perceptions and, since the hallucinations tend to be vivid and are often threatening, respond to them with fear or anger and attempts at fight or flight. Some patients hallucinate only at night and may have difficulty in telling apart their hallucinations from dreams. This form of confusion, if present, is quite typical of delirium. The hallucinations may range in complexity from flashes of light to complex scenes, involving humans or animals in motion.[3]

The above cognitive deficits and abnormalities constitute an essential diagnostic feature of delirium.[4] They tend to fluctuate in severity over the course of a day and be most marked during the night. At any time the patient may be more lucid for a varying period, only to become more severely impaired again. Such irregular and unpredictable fluctuations of the cognitive impairment in the course of just 1 day, with nocturnal exacerbation, are strongly suggestive of delirium and are seldom exhibited in any other mental disorder.

Global Disorder of Attention

Disturbances of the major aspects of attention are invariably present. Alertness (vigilance), i.e., readiness to respond to sensory stimuli, as well as the ability to mobilize, shift, sustain, and direct attention at will, are always disturbed to some extent. Alertness may be either abnormally increased or decreased, but in either case the selectiveness and directiveness of attention are impaired.[3,4,11] Whether predominantly hypoalert or hyperalert, the patient shows a reduced attention span, that is, is distractible. Just as cognitive impairment tends to fluctuate unpredictably over the course of a day, so do the attentional disturbances. Consequently, the patient is more or less accessible and able to respond to attempts to communicate with him or her. Some writers refer to delirium as *global disorders of attention,* implying that attentional deficits and abnormalities are its basic psychopathological features.[15] Basic or not, they constitute one of its diagnostic criteria and help distinguish it from dementia, another global cognitive disorder.

Reduced Level of Consciousness

For over a century delirium has been regarded as a disorder of consciousness.[3] More specifically, the syndrome has been considered to be characterized by, or to be a manifestation of, the so-called clouding of consciousness. This vague concept implies no more than the presence of global cognitive-attentional deficits and the limited accessibility of the patient to meaningful communication. The concept has been removed from the latest edition of the official classification of mental disorders.[4] This latest edition includes, however, a reduced level of consciousness as one of the characteristic features of delirium.[4] This concept implies a diminished ability to be aware of one's self and one's surroundings, to respond to sensory inputs in a selective and sustained manner, and to be able to relate the incoming information to previously acquired knowledge and hence to grasp its meaning.

Disordered Sleep-Wake Cycle

Disorganization of the sleep-wake cycle is one of the essential features of delirium.[3,4] Wakefulness is either abnormally increased and the patient sleeps little or not at all, or is reduced during the day but excessive during the night. Typically, but not invariably, the patient suffers from insomnia at night and displays drowsiness and periods of sleep during the day. The sleep-wake cycle is reversed in some cases. Night sleep is usually fragmented and reduced, and the patient tends to be restless, agitated, and hallucinating while awake during the night.

Disorder of Psychomotor Behavior

A disturbance of both verbal and nonverbal psychomotor activity is the last essential feature of delirium. A delirious patient may be predominantly either hyperactive or hypoactive. Some patients shift unpredictably from abnormally increased psychomotor activity to lethargy and vice versa.[3] This feature of delirium has been described since antiquity[3] and has led some more recent writers to propose that two distinct syndromes may be distinguished on the basis of the predominant form of psychomotor behavior displayed by the patient.[16] According to this viewpoint, alcohol withdrawal delirium (delirium tremens) represents the prototype of delirium and features hyperactivity, while the hypoactive behavior indicates that the patient suffers not from delirium but from an acute confusional state.[16] By contrast, other writers, including the present one, hold a unitary view of delirium and distinguish its two subtypes, i.e., a hyperactive and a hypoactive one.[3,11,17] A psychomotorically hyperactive patient is typically hyperalert, agitated, and hallucinating. By contrast, a hypoactive one tends to be hypoalert, drowsy, and less likely to experience hallucinations. Such a patient's delirium is readily missed by the medical staff, and he or she may be diagnosed as being depressed. Many elderly patients, notably those suffering from a metabolic encephalopathy, are predominantly hypoactive and hypoalert. Some patients display involuntary movements such as a coarse tremor or asterixis.

Associated Features

Delirious patients may experience and display a variety of emotions, such as fear, anger, apathy, depression, and euphoria. One of these emotions tends to predominate. Fear or anger are particularly common and are accompanied by sympathetic nervous system hyperarousal, manifested by flushed face, dilated pupils, tachycardia, sweating, and elevated blood pressure. Elderly delirious patients tend to be apathetic. Incontinence of urine and feces is quite common in the delirious elderly patient.

Course and Outcome

By definition, delirium is a transient disorder, one that seldom lasts more than a month. In an elderly patient it tends to last longer than in a younger one. In the majority of cases the outcome is favorable and the patient returns to his or her premorbid level of functioning. In many elderly patients, however, delirium results from a terminal illness, one followed by death. Recent studies indicate that delirium in the elderly tends to identify those at risk for increased length of hospital stay, mortality, and institutionalization.[6,18] More studies are clearly needed to establish the outcome of the syndrome in elderly patients. It is still unknown in what proportion of cases delirium is followed by dementia, for example.

ETIOLOGY

Delirium is caused by one or more organic factors that bring about widespread cerebral dysfunction.[3,4,11] One may distinguish predisposing, facilitating, and precipitating (organic) causal factors.[3] Age over 65 years, brain damage, and chronic cerebral disease such as Alzheimer's disease constitute the main predisposing factors.[3,11] Psychological stress, sleep loss, and sensory deprivation and overload may be regarded as factors that facilitate the development of delirium and also help maintain it.[3,11] The precipitating (organic) causal factors fall into four main classes[3]: (1) primary cerebral diseases, (2) systemic diseases affecting the brain secondarily, notably metabolic encephalopathies, neoplasms, infections, and cardiovascular and collagen diseases, (3) intoxication with exogenous substances, including medical and recreational drugs, and poisons of plant, animal, and industrial origin, and (4) withdrawal from substances of abuse in a person addicted to them, mostly alcohol and sedative-hypnotic drugs. In elderly patients more than one organic factor is often implicated. Intoxication with medical, especially anticholinergic, drugs is probably one of the most common causes of delirium in an elderly person. Other common causes of the syndrome in the elderly include congestive heart failure, pneumonia, urinary tract infection, cancer, uremia, hypokalemia, dehydration and/or sodium depletion, epilepsy, and cerebral infarction involving the right hemisphere.[2,3,5,11]

Some recent studies have attempted to identify risk factors for delirium in hospitalized elderly persons.[19,20] In one study such factors included urinary tract infection, low serum albumin levels, elevated white blood cell count, and proteinuria.[19] In the other study the risk factors involved prior cognitive impairment, fracture on admission, symptomatic infection, and the use of neuroleptic and narcotic drugs.[20] It is surprising that the authors of this study found that the use of anticholinergic drugs was not associated with delirium.[20] This finding runs counter to many previously reported observations.[3]

PATHOGENESIS

This aspect of delirium has not yet been fully elucidated. The best-documented hypothesis postulates that the syndrome results from a widespread reduction of cerebral oxidative metabolism and imbalance of neurotransmission.[3] Engel and Romano[17] have postulated that a reduction of brain metabolism underlies all cases of delirium and accounts for the associated generalized showing of the electroencephalogram (EEG) background activity. The syndrome may be considered to be a disorder of cortical function.[21] Impairment of cerebral oxidative metabolism results in reduced synthesis of neurotransmitters, notably acetylcholine, whose relative deficiency in the brain is a common denominator in metabolic-toxic encephalopathies.[22] Hypoxia and hypoglycemia impair acetylcholine synthesis and bring about changes in mental function.[23] The inhibition of acetylcholine metabolism may be due to calcium-dependent release of this neurotransmitter.[23] It appears that the cholinergic deficit is currently the most convincing pathogenetic hypothesis of delirium.[3,5,23] Numerous experimental studies have shown that the syndrome can be readily induced by anticholinergic agents.[24] The central cholinergic system is affected by aging, and even more so by degenerative brain disease, notably Alzheimer's disease, with resulting reduction in the synthesis of acetylcholine.[3] An adequate supply of this neurotransmitter is necessary for normal cognitive functioning, attention, and sleep-wake cycle. Its deficiency is postulated to play a key pathogenetic role in the development of many, if not all, cases of delirium, and seems to make patients with Alzheimer's disease particularly prone to develop the syndrome.[3,23] Changes in the levels of other neurotransmitters, such as glutamate and dopamine, may also be involved.[23]

DIAGNOSIS AND DIFFERENTIAL DIAGNOSIS

Diagnosis of delirium involves two crucial steps: first, its recognition on the basis of history and the essential clinical features; and second, identification of its cause (or causes).[3,11] An attempt has been made recently to operationalize the diagnostic criteria for delirium.[25] A number of screening instruments for the diagnosis of the syndrome have been developed and used for research purposes as well as clinically.[26,27] Guidelines have been published for nurses to help them identify delirium.[28] The diagnosis of the syndrome is still made on clinical grounds. Acute onset of global cognitive-attentional deficits and abnormalities, whose severity tends to fluctuate during the day and be highest at night, is practically diagnostic. The cognitive-attentional impairment is observed at the bedside and in the course of a diagnostic interview with the patient. One of the developed screening devices may be used to help establish the diagnosis.[26,27]

The EEG is a helpful tool in the diagnosis of delirium.[3,17,29,30] Engel and Romano carried out classic studies of the EEG in delirium in the 1940s.[17] All their patients showed bilateral, diffuse slowing of the EEG background activity, which was positively correlated with the degree of cognitive impairment: the more severe the impairment, the slower the EEG background activity was found to be. Recent studies have largely confirmed those early findings.[29,30] Quantitative EEG methods have been recommended as a clinically useful supplement to the conventional EEG in the assessment of delirium in the elderly.[30] In alcohol or sedative-hypnotic withdrawal delirium, the background rhythms may be normal or show excessive low-amplitude fast activity.[29] A patient with dementia may have slowing of the dominant background activity, and this may make differential diagnosis from delirium difficult.[31] Serial EEG recordings may be needed in some cases to establish whether the slowing of the background activity subsides as the patient's cognitive functioning improves, since such a change would tend to confirm the diagnosis of delirium.[32]

Delirium needs to be distinguished from dementia, functional psychosis (schizophrenia, mania), and a psychogenic dissociative state.[3] A history of cognitive impairment present for months or years; a relatively stable course over the course of a day; relatively normal attention and level of consciousness; and a lack of concurrent physical illness or drug intoxication suggest the diagnosis of dementia.[3,11] An acutely schizophrenic or manic patient may appear to be confused but, on close inquiry, fails to show cognitive impairment and is more likely to have predominantly auditory hallucinations and systematized delusions.[3] An EEG may help in that in a functional psychosis it is likely to be normal.

MANAGEMENT

Management of delirium involves two key aspects: first, treatment of the underlying pathological condition causing cerebral cortical dysfunction, and second, symptomatic and supportive therapy.[3] In an elderly patient, all drugs, notably those with anticholinergic activity, are suspect and need to be withdrawn or their dosage be reduced. Polypharmacy is contraindicated. The cause of delirium needs to be established by physical, including neurological, examination and selected laboratory tests.[3]

Symptomatic treatment involves treating agitation with haloperidol orally or parenterally, in a dose of 0.5 to 5 mg twice daily.[3,33] General supportive measures imply ensuring water and electrolyte balance, adequate nutrition, and vitamin supply. The patient is best cared for in a quiet, well-lit room. Good nursing care is essential and should involve reorientation, reassurance, and emotional support. Psychiatric consultation is often indicated to help with the diagnosis, management, and medicolegal issues (consent for treatment).[34] Prevention of severe delirium should be aimed at in all cases and has been achieved in some cases of the syndrome in patients with hip fracture, a condition associated with an incidence of delirium as high as 50 percent.[35]

REFERENCES

1. Miller NE, Lipowski ZJ (eds): Delirium. Advances in research and clinical practice. *Int Psychogeriatrics* (special issue) 3:97, 1991.
2. Lindesay J et al: *Delirium in the Elderly*. Oxford, England, Oxford University Press, 1990.
3. Lipowski ZJ: *Delirium: Acute Confusional States*. New York, Oxford University Press, 1990.
4. *Diagnostic and Statistical Manual of Mental Disorders*, 3d ed revised. Washington DC, American Psychiatric Association, 1987.
5. Francis J, Kapoor WN: Delirium in hospitalized elderly. *J Gen Intern Med* 5:65, 1990.
6. Francis J et al: A prospective study of delirium in hospitalized elderly. *JAMA* 263:1097, 1990.
7. Johnson JC et al: Using DSM-III criteria to diagnose delirium in elderly general medical patients. *J Gerontol* 45:M113, 1990.
8. Hodkinson HM: Mental impairment in the elderly. *J R Coll Physicians London* 7:305, 1973.
9. Levkoff S et al: Epidemiology of delirium: An overview of research issues and findings. *Int Psychogeriatrics* 3:149, 1991.
10. Erkinjuntti T et al: Dementia among medical inpatients. *Arch Intern Med* 146:1923, 1986.
11. Lipowski ZJ: Delirium in the elderly patient. *N Engl J Med* 320:578, 1989.
12. Gillick MR et al: Adverse consequences of hospitalization in the elderly. *Soc Sci Med* 16:1033, 1982.
13. Perez EL, Silverman M: Delirium: The often overlooked diagnosis. *Int J Psychiatry Med* 14:181, 1984.
14. Lyness JM: Delirium: Masquerades and misdiagnosis in elderly patients. *J Am Geriatr Soc* 38:1235, 1990.
15. Geschwind N: Disorders of attention. *Philos Trans R Soc Lond Biol* 298:173, 1982.
16. Adams RD, Victor M: *Principles of Neurology*, 2d ed. New York, McGraw-Hill, 1981.
17. Engel GL, Romano J: Delirium, a syndrome of cerebral insufficiency. *J Chronic Dis* 9:260, 959.
18. Levkoff SE et al: Delirium. The occurrence and persistence of symptoms among elderly hospitalized patients. *Arch Intern Med* 152:334, 1992.
19. Levkoff SE et al: Identification of factors associated with the diagnosis of delirium in elderly hospitalized patients. *J Am Geriatr Soc* 36:1099, 1988.
20. Schor JD et al: Risk factors for delirium in hospitalized elderly. *JAMA* 267:827, 1992.
21. Blass JP et al: Delirium: Phenomenology and diagnosis—A neurobiologic view. *Int Psychogeriatrics* 3:121, 1991.
22. Blass JP et al: Cholinergic dysfunction: A common denominator in metabolic encephalopathies, in Pepew G, Ladinsky H (eds): *Cholinergic Mechanisms*. New York, Plenum, 1981, p 921.
23. Gibson GE et al: The cellular basis of delirium and its relevance to age-related disorders including Alzheimer's disease. *Int Psychogeriatrics* 3:373, 1991.
24. Itil T, Fink M: Anticholinergic drug-induced delirium: Experimental modification, quantitative EEG and behavioral correlations. *J Nerv Ment Dis* 143:492, 1966.
25. Gottlieb GL et al: Delirium in the medically ill elderly: Operationalizing the DSM-III criteria. *Int Psychogeriatrics* 3:181, 1991.
26. Levkoff S et al: Review of research instruments and techniques used to detect delirium. *Int Psychogeriatrics* 3:253, 1991.
27. Inouye SK et al: Clarifying confusion: The confusion assessment method. *Ann Intern Med* 113:941, 1990.
28. Inaba-Roland KE, Maricle RA: Assessing delirium in the acute care setting. *Heart Lung* 21:48, 1992.
29. Brenner RP: Utility of EEG in delirium: Past views and current practice. *Int Psychogeriatrics* 3:211, 1991.
30. Leuchter AF, Jacobson SA: Quantitative measurement

of brain electrical activity in delirium. *Int Psychogeriatrics* 3:231, 1991.

31. Rae-Grant A et al: The electroencephalogram in Alzheimer-type dementia. *Arch Neurol* 44:50, 1987.
32. Pro JD, Wells CE: The use of electroencephalogram in the diagnosis of delirium. *Dis Nerv Syst* 38:804, 1977.
33. Steinhart MJ: The use of haloperidol in geriatric patients with organic mental disorder. *Curr Ther Res* 33:132, 1983.
34. Fogel BS et al: Legal aspects of the treatment of delirium. *Hosp Community Psychiatry* 37:154, 1986.
35. Gustafson Y et al: A geriatric-anesthesiologic program to reduce acute confusional states in elderly patients treated for femoral neck fractures. *J Am Geriatr Soc* 39:655, 1991.

Chapter 91

STROKE

John C. M. Brust

Systematic discussions of stroke—epidemiology, anatomy, physiology, symptoms, signs, diagnosis, treatment, and prognosis—are available in textbooks small[1,2] and large.[3–5] I will focus here on aspects of stroke especially pertinent to elderly patients.

Symptomatic cerebrovascular disease affects about 5 percent of people over age 65[6]; conversely, about 85 percent of stroke victims are in that age group.[7] Unlike many other afflictions of the aged such as congestive heart failure or prostate cancer, stroke—often literally overnight—affects a person's very identity. Whether one is rendered hemiparetic, ataxic, aphasic, or demented, a vital part of one's self—in the most ontological sense—is suddenly cut away. Moreover, while a stroke can be catastrophic at any age—indeed, it could be argued that the younger the patient the greater the tragedy—elderly victims confront their illness with considerably less physical or psychological reserve. Mild hemiparesis might result in a circumducting gait in a middle-aged patient; in an elderly patient already unsteady or arthritic, the same degree of weakness might mean never walking again. Similarly, a young person might recover without apparent cognitive impairment from a stroke that would render an older person demented—even if there was no evident intellectual decline beforehand. Motivation for rehabilitation is also likely to be less in the elderly, particularly if they are depressed. Stroke frequently leads to depression, and depression is a common affliction of the elderly, with or without strokes.

DIAGNOSTIC PROBLEMS: TIAs

A transient ischemic attack (TIA) is a neurological impairment of presumed ischemic origin that by definition lasts less than 24 hours. (In fact, most last closer to 24 minutes than 24 hours; a definition limiting symptoms to 1 hour might be more practical.) At any age the differential diagnosis includes seizures and migraine. TIAs portend permanent infarction in roughly a quarter of affected patients,[8,9] and scientifically accredited treatment includes antiplatelet agents (aspirin, ticlopidine) or surgical correction of severe carotid stenosis. Much thus depends on a correct diagnosis, which, regrettably, can be especially difficult in an elderly person.

When TIAs consist of hemiparesis or aphasia, the diagnosis is usually straightforward. When symptoms are limited to one body part (e.g., weakness or numbness of only the face, an arm, or a leg), matters are less clear. In elderly patients, five symptoms produce special diagnostic difficulty.

1. *Drop attacks* consist of sudden loss of tone or strength causing the subject to fall abruptly to the ground. Injury can occur, but recovery is otherwise rapid. Consciousness is preserved. In young people, drop attacks often have an identifiable cause (e.g., astatic seizures or colloid cyst of the third ventricle); in the elderly, in whom they are a good deal more common, they are usually cryptogenic and except for the hazard of hip fracture carry a favorable prognosis.[10] Some, however, probably signify vertebrobasilar ischemia. A patient seen at Harlem Hospital Center had several drop attacks and then permanent quadriplegia. At autopsy there was infarction of both pyramidal tracts at the pontomedullary junction.[11]

   Further confounding the problem of drop attacks are other causes of falling. The annual incidence of falls is about 25 percent at age 70 and 35 percent above age 75; half of elderly persons who fall do so repeatedly.[12] The great majority of falls are neither drop attacks nor TIAs but rather result from such diverse conditions as impaired vision and hearing, proprioceptive loss or peripheral neuropathy, musculoskeletal disorders, Parkinson's disease, postural hypotension, syncope, and medications, especially sedatives.[12,13]

2. *Syncope*—defined as sudden spontaneous loss of consciousness with rapid spontaneous recovery—is a common symptom at any age. In young people the usual causes are benign—vasovagal (emotional reflexic) attacks and postural hypotension

of adolescence. In elderly people more serious diagnoses emerge—cardiac arrhythmia and sometimes disabling postural hypotension (either drug-induced or spontaneous). Syncope is considered a rare manifestation of vertebrobasilar insufficiency, but there is no reason why basilar artery ischemia could not affect the reticular activating system along with other brainstem structures.

3. *Transient monocular blindness* (amaurosis fugax) refers to transient ischemia of the retina, supplied by the central retinal artery, which arises from the ophthalmic artery, which in turn arises from the internal carotid artery. Such visual loss is often experienced as if a curtain were drawn over the eye. The basis is sometimes embolic; cholesterol, platelet, or calcium emboli (*Hollenhorst plaques*) temporarily lodge at bifurcations of retinal arterioles, breaking up and moving distally as vision improves.[14] Difficulties arise when the diagnosis depends entirely on the history, especially in elderly subjects unable to describe symptoms precisely or having other reasons for visual impairment. Symptoms associated with cataracts, glaucoma, diabetic retinopathy, and so-called senile macular degeneration are not always as static as one might expect.
4. *Vertigo*—defined as hallucinated motion, most often rotatory—often occurs episodically in elderly persons. Usually benign and unaccompanied by other brainstem symptoms, it tends to have features more suggestive of peripheral than central nervous system disease, and its origin is more often cryptogenic than defined (e.g., Ménière's disease or neoplasm). Episodic vertigo alone is unlikely to signify transient ischemia.[15] Vertiginous TIAs do occur, however, either intraparenchymally or peripherally. The inner ear is supplied by the internal auditory artery, which arises from either the basilar or the anterior inferior cerebellar artery. A TIA consisting of combinations of vertigo, tinnitus, and deafness thus could affect the sensory organ itself, analogous to transient monocular blindness.
5. *Transient global amnesia* (TGA) consists of sudden loss of recent memory. There is retrograde amnesia for events hours, days, or weeks before the attack and anterograde amnesia—inability to remember new information—during the several hours that most attacks last. The subject remains alert and attentive and is usually acutely aware that something is wrong. ("Where am I? What's happening?") Recovery is spontaneous; retrograde loss clears and ability to memorize returns, but there is permanent amnesia for the episode. TGA is overdiagnosed; a definite diagnosis should require that the patient be examined by a physician during an attack.[16] Even if the diagnosis is confidently made, its basis remains obscure. Etiologic candidates include epilepsy, migraine, and transient ischemia bilaterally affecting the hippocampus or the dorsomedial thalamus.

HEMORRHAGIC STROKE IN THE ELDERLY PATIENT

In young and middle-aged people the commonest causes of hemorrhagic stroke are hypertensive intraparenchymal bleeding, subarachnoid hemorrhage from a ruptured saccular (*berry*) aneurysm, and bleeding from a congenital vascular malformation. Less common causes include rupture of a septic (*mycotic*) aneurysm, hematological disorders, bleeding into a neoplasm, and anticoagulant or bone marrow suppressant therapy. Hypertensive intraparenchymal hemorrhage most often occurs deep in the cerebral hemispheres (affecting the basal ganglia, the internal capsule, or the thalamus), as well as the pons and the cerebellum. Saccular aneurysms, which can rupture into the parenchyma as well as into the subarachnoid space, are most often located at the junction of the anterior communicating and anterior cerebral arteries, the junction of the posterior communicating and internal carotid arteries, the main bifurcation of the middle cerebral artery, and, in the posterior fossa, at the top of the basilar artery and the origin of the posterior inferior cerebellar artery. Vascular malformations can occur anywhere in the central nervous system.

Thus, symptoms, signs, and computed tomography (CT) not only indicate the location of spontaneous intracranial hemorrhage but offer clues to the underlying lesion. An infrequent exception to this statement is subarachnoid hemorrhage; if the CT examination is negative, a lumbar puncture is necessary to rule the diagnosis in or out.

The surgical management of ruptured saccular aneurysm raises special questions in elderly patients. Until recently, surgical clipping of aneurysms was usually delayed for a week or two after rupture because cerebral vasospasm produced unacceptable surgical morbidity and mortality. After 2 weeks the risk of rebleeding declines and eventually reaches a steady rate of about 3 percent per year.[17] Surgical risk increases with age—in fact until recently it probably exceeded the risk of rebleeding in many elderly patients. That situation has now changed. Improved surgical technique and the demonstrated value of the calcium channel blocker nimodipine in reducing the morbidity associated with vasospasm (as well as the possible value of postsurgical hypervolemia) have led to increased popularity of early surgery—within 3 days of rupture—before vasospasm has made an appearance.[18] Elderly patients remain poorer surgical risks than middle-aged patients, but older calculations of risk based on operative mortality and likelihood of late rebleeding no longer apply.

In patients over age 65 another cause for hemorrhagic stroke assumes increasing importance, namely amyloid (*congophilic*) angiopathy.[19] Clues to this diagnosis are a lobar rather than a deep cerebral hemorrhage and multiple hemorrhages, especially bilaterally. Such patients are frequently demented, and the relationship of amyloid angiopathy to Alzheimer's disease, in which vascular amyloid deposits are also seen, is uncertain. Lobar hematomas in amyloid angiopathy, especially those in the nonlanguage hemisphere, are accessible to surgical decompression in deteriorating patients. On the other hand, the underlying pathological lesion increases the risk of further bleeding during surgery. Furthermore, because of the possibility that a vascular malformation lies within a hematoma, magnetic resonance imaging (MRI) should precede surgical intervention.

CEREBRAL INFARCTION: PHARMACOTHERAPY, SURGERY, AND ELDERLY PATIENTS

Pharmacotherapy for cerebral infarction is complicated and controversial and will soon become more so. Specific treatments include the following.

1. *Antiplatelet Agents* Aspirin is of demonstrable benefit in reducing the likelihood of stroke, myocardial infarction, and death in patients with TIA or mild cerebral infarction.[20,21] The optimal dosage, however, is controversial. While controlled studies have reported benefit from 300,[22] 75,[23] or 30 mg daily,[24] such recommendations have been challenged on methodological grounds.[25] In the Physicians' Health Study, in which doctors without known cardiovascular or cerebrovascular disease received aspirin 325 mg or placebo every other day, the incidence of myocardial infarction was less in the aspirin group, but the incidence of stroke was actually somewhat increased; the number of strokes in both groups, however, was much less than predicted.[26]

   Side effects of aspirin are dose-related and of particular concern in elderly patients, who are at risk not only for gastrointestinal bleeding but for aspirin-related renal damage. In persons with normal renal function, aspirin's effects on the kidney are a minor worry, but in those with preexisting renal compromise—far likelier in elderly patients—aspirin could be hazardous.[27]

   Ticlopidine impairs platelet function by a mechanism different from aspirin's. In a trial comparing its efficacy with aspirin in patients with TIA or mild cerebral infarct, ticlopidine was somewhat more effective in reducing the incidence of stroke and death. Side effects were commoner, however, including diarrhea, rash, and marked (but reversible) neutropenia.[28] Because of ticlopidine's marginal added risk reduction, more frequent side effects, and high cost, aspirin remains the preferred treatment in most patients with TIA or mild cerebral infarction. On the other hand, aspirin was shown in a controlled study to be no better than placebo in preventing recurrence in survivors of major cerebral infarction,[29] whereas ticlopidine, in a comparable study, was shown to reduce the risk of stroke recurrence, myocardial infarction, or vascular death.[30] Whether ticlopidine will turn out to have special problems or advantages in elderly patients remains to be seen.

   Dipyridamole, which inhibits platelet function by still another mechanism, is one of the most widely prescribed medications in the world, yet no evidence supports its use in cerebrovascular disease. It confers no additional benefit when added to aspirin in patients with TIA or cerebral infarction, and it has never been tested alone against placebo.[20] (Such a study is under way.) On theoretical grounds, dipyridamole might benefit certain patients unable to take aspirin or ticlopidine. It does not appear to offer any advantages or disadvantages in the elderly.
2. *Anticoagulants* Four decades after their introduction, the role of heparin and warfarin in cerebrovascular disease remains uncertain. In three well-designed trials warfarin prevented stroke in selected patients with nonvalvular atrial fibrillation.[28] Methodological flaws make it impossible to interpret studies attesting to the benefit of anticoagulants in TIA, stroke in evolution, or fixed infarction.[8,32,33] Although never systematically compared with placebo in patients with cerebral infarction associated with myocardial infarction, valvular disease, or cardiac arrhythmia (e.g., atrial fibrillation or tachy-bradyarrythmia syndrome), their use is accepted in such patients, and the major controversy involves timing; both the risk of recurrent embolic stroke and the risk of hemorrhagic transformation are greatest during the first week or two after a cardioembolic stroke. The usual current practice is to give heparin early if CT excludes hemorrhage and if the infarct, by clinical and CT criteria, is deemed small. When the infarct is large, CT is repeated after 5 days, and if it does not show hemorrhagic transformation, warfarin can be started.[33] The potential for catastrophe in either case is obvious.

   Anticoagulants pose special dangers in the elderly, particularly those with hypertension or other illness, those with a propensity to falling, and those with cognitive impairment. Adding to the dilemma is the likelihood that embolic stroke is underdiagnosed and frequently classified as "cerebral infarction of uncertain cause."[34] Moreover, ulcerated plaques in the aortic arch and mitral annular calcification have each been identified as risk factors for stroke in elderly persons.[35,36] Until their value in noncardioembolic cerebrovascular disease is better defined, however—a warfarin study is in progress—anticoagulants are best avoided unless an embolic source is clearly identified.

3. *"Hyperacute Therapy"* Studies are currently assessing pharmacotherapies that require early intervention—within a few hours of symptom onset. These include calcium channel blockers (e.g., nimodipine), thrombolysins (e.g., streptokinase and recombinant tissue plasminogen activator), and inhibitors of excitatory neurotransmitters [e.g., *N*-methyl-D-aspartate (NMDA) receptor blockers]. The benefit of calcium channel blockers would be either from vasodilatation or, as suggested by studies on vasospasm after subarachnoid hemorrhage, from reduced calcium entry into ischemic cells.[37] The benefit of thrombolysins would depend on restoration of blood flow into an ischemic area before the development of irreversible infarction (and an attendant risk of hemorrhagic transformation).[38] The benefit of NMDA receptor blockers would be from reduced calcium conductance through the receptor channels.[39]

   The elderly will pose special problems if these treatments become scientifically accredited. Whereas patients with symptomatic myocardial infarction do tend to rush to hospitals, making thrombolytic and other emergency therapies practical, patients with stroke often do not, particularly elderly ones. For hyperacute therapy to have an impact in this age group, there will have to be considerable education not only of potential patients but of physicians, family members, and nursing home staffs.

4. *Surgery* After decades of uncertainty, several studies have finally begun to clarify the role of surgery in occlusive cerebrovascular disease. Extracranial-intracranial (EC-IC) bypass surgery was based on reasonable hypotheses yet unexpectedly turned out to be of no value in all identified subgroups.[40] If there are still potential candidates for this procedure, the burden of proof is on those who presume benefit. By contrast, carotid endarterectomy was shown to be of considerably greater benefit than aspirin in patients with TIAs or mild infarcts and severe carotid artery stenosis.[41] For patients with lesser degrees of stenosis, trials are still running. At the time of this writing, a comparable study is in progress to determine the value, if any, of endarterectomy in patients with asymptomatic carotid artery disease.[42]

   The North American Symptomatic Carotid Endarterectomy Trial included patients up to the age of 80; age per se is not a contraindication to carotid endarterectomy.

GENERAL MANAGEMENT OF STROKE IN ELDERLY PATIENTS

The less glamorous aspects of stroke management include prevention of pneumonia, decubiti, contractures, thrombophlebitis, and fecal impaction; each of these complications is especially likely in the elderly. Pneumonia is sometimes apparent on admission; dysphagia, the supine position, delayed mobilization, and insertion of nasogastric or endotracheal tubes each set the stage for aspiration. Decubiti—which can require surgical grafts or progress to osteomyelitis and fatal sepsis—are preventable by frequent turning, skin care, and special mattresses or beds; in patients with urinary incontinence, intermittent straight catheterization is preferable to an indwelling Foley catheter, which practically ensures urinary tract infection. Contractures are probably unavoidable with lasting hemiplegia but can be prevented in those destined to improve by frequent passive movement and splints. Thrombophlebitis is also preventable by frequent passive movement as well as early mobilization, elastic stockings (it is unclear if they help, but they do no harm), and low-dose heparin. As for fecal impaction, prevention is preferable to treatment.

As noted, depression is a common aftermath of stroke, especially in an elderly patient who previously had little to look forward to. It can be difficult to determine whether depression is a psychic reaction to devastating illness or a consequence of the cerebral lesion itself, and there is controversy as to whether particular lesions are specifically associated with depression.[43] In any case, tearfulness more often signifies depression than "pseudobulbar palsy," and while psychiatric consultation and pharmacotherapy are sometimes necessary, most depressed patients can be reasonably managed by a caring neurologist, internist, or geriatrician.

VASCULAR DEMENTIA

Twenty years ago it was widely believed that "senile dementia" is the result of cerebral "hardening of the arteries." Although such a view is today obsolete—Alzheimer's disease does not have a vascular basis, and the reduced cerebral blood flow encountered in such patients is secondary to reduced cerebral metabolism, not its cause—cerebrovascular disease is today considered the second commonest cause of dementia in people over age 65. Three different mechanisms of cerebrovascular dementia have been proposed, some poorly understood and controversial.[44–46]

The first mechanism is destruction of brain regions critical for particular mental activities. Consistent with a vascular basis for TGA, memory loss follows bilateral hippocampal or medial thalamic infarction, supplied by branches of the posterior cerebral and posterior communicating arteries. Decreased initiative, psychomotor slowing, or frank abulia follows infarction of medial frontal and orbitofrontal structures supplied by the anterior cerebral arteries. When aphasia is mixed or severe, there is nearly always additional nonlanguage cognitive difficulty—i.e., the patient does not resemble an otherwise normal person who speaks only a foreign language; such impairment is hardly surprising, for sufficient damage to the circuits subserving language would be expected to disrupt other cognitive skills as well. Finally, damage to the non-language-dominant hemisphere not only impairs spacial perception and manipulation (including, sometimes, striking hemineglect, anosognosia, and asomatognosia), but sometimes causes, either transiently or more lastingly, inattentiveness, agitation, and incoherent thinking.

The second mechanism of vascular dementia involves multiple infarcts (*multiinfarct dementia*). Here the crucial determinant is not so much the exact location of damage as its overall extent. Controversial is how great that extent—volumetrically—must be. A classic pathological study of the brains of demented elderly people found that when infarction was the only abnormality present (i.e., there were no significant Alzheimer changes), at least 60 ml of brain softening was present, and the amount of tissue loss seemed more important than its location. In that study some brains had evidence of both infarction and Alzheimer's disease, and several of these had volumes of infarction or numbers of senile plaques found in controls, suggesting that each disease lowered the threshold for expression of the other.[48] Other clinicopathological studies have associated dementia with considerably smaller volumes of infarction,[49] and many investigators have diagnosed multiinfarct dementia on the basis simply of clinical stroke (often inferred from an *ischemic score*), regardless of extent and without pathological exclusion of coexisting Alzheimer's disease. It cannot be overstressed that clinical—or even pathological—evidence of a stroke does not necessarily mean that the stroke had anything to do with a patient's dementia. This point holds particularly true for so-called multiple lacunes—small deep cerebral infarcts often resulting from hypertensive damage to small penetrating arteries supplying the diencephalon, basal ganglia, and deep white matter. Lacunes are seldom numerous enough to cause dementia, and when they do ("l'état lacunaire") there is likely to be gait disturbance and pseudobulbar palsy.[50] Nonetheless, considerable literature on alleged multiinfarct dementia—including psychometric and cerebral blood flow studies—has been based on fallacious assumptions of cause and effect.[51]

The third proposed mechanism of vascular dementia is diffuse small vessel disease. Such a mechanism invokes the concepts of so-called Rip Van Winkle syndrome and of Binswanger's disease. The former refers to decreased regional cerebral blood flow sufficient to impair intellectual functioning without causing frank infarction. Although proponents of such a condition have offered evidence based on cerebral blood flow studies—in particular increased oxygen extraction preceding dementia, followed by cognitive impairment when this compensatory mechanism fails[45,52]—most current investigators reject the concept. Binswanger's disease refers to diffuse ischemic lesions of the cerebral periventricular white matter, frequently in the presence of hypertension and presumably related to the similar vascular pathological condition that leads to more discrete small deep infarcts.[53] Binswanger's disease was until recently considered rare, but CT and MRI findings suggest it may be underdiagnosed. Periventricular abnormalities possibly associated with Binswanger changes—lucency on CT and increased signal on MRI—turn out to be very common in elderly people (*leukoaraiosis*).[54–56] Unanswered, however, is how often such changes actually correlate with either dementia or pathological evidence of ischemia.

Thus, vascular dementia is probably overdiagnosed when the criteria are simply evidence of preceding stroke. On the other hand, a form of vascular dementia of Binswanger's type or resulting from diffusely decreased cerebral perfusion may be underdiagnosed. Such uncertainty has led to attempts to establish diagnostic criteria for vascular dementia, but consensus has been elusive.[57–61] What we can surely agree on is that even if vascular dementia is often difficult to diagnose in individual patients, it is not rare. Indeed, when Alzheimer's disease is already present, stroke may contribute more to cognitive impairment than when it strikes alone.[62] As Sokoloff observed, "Even if the brain ages independently of the circulation, when vascular disease develops, it becomes the pacemaker of the aging process within the brain."[63]

REFERENCES

1. Rowland LP (ed): *Merritt's Textbook of Neurology,* 8th ed. Philadelphia, Lea & Febiger, 1989.
2. Adams RD, Victor M: *Principles of Neurology,* 4th ed. New York, McGraw-Hill, 1989.
3. Joynt RJ (ed): *Clinical Neurology,* rev ed. Philadelphia, JB Lippincott, 1992, vols 1–4.
4. Barnett HJM et al: *Stroke: Pathophysiology, Diagnosis, and Management,* 2d ed. New York, Churchill Livingstone, 1993.
5. Toole JF et al (eds): *Handbook of Clinical Neurology, Cerebrovascular Diseases.* Amsterdam, Elsevier Science, 1989, vols 53, 54, and 55.
6. Whisnant JP: The decline of stroke. *Stroke* 15:160, 1984.
7. Baum HM, Robins M: Survival and prevalence: The national survey of stroke. *Stroke* 12(suppl 1):159, 1981.
8. Brust JCM: Transient ischemic attacks: Natural history and anticoagulation. *Neurology* 12:701, 1977.
9. North American Symptomatic Carotid Endarterectomy Trial Collaborators: Beneficial effect of carotid endarterectomy in symptomatic patients with high-grade carotid stenosis. *N Engl J Med* 325:446, 1991.
10. Meissner I et al: The natural history of drop attacks. *Neurology* 36:1029, 1986.

11. Brust JCM et al: The pathology of drop attacks: A case report. *Neurology* 29:786, 1979.
12. Tinetti ME, Speechley M: Prevention of falls among the elderly. *N Engl J Med* 320:1055, 1989.
13. Sudarsky L: Gait disorders in the elderly. *N Engl J Med* 322:1441, 1990.
14. Hollenhorst RW: Significance of bright plaques in the retinal arterioles. *JAMA* 178:23, 1961.
15. Fisher CM: Vertigo in cerebrovascular disease. *Arch Otolaryngol* 85:529, 1967.
16. Caplan LB: Transient global amnesia, in Vinken P, Bruyn G, Klawans H (eds): *Handbook of Clinical Neurology*. Amsterdam, Elsevier Science, 1985, p 205, vol 45, part 1.
17. Salomon RA, Fink ME: Current strategies for the management of aneurysmal subarachnoid hemorrhage. *Arch Neurol* 44:769, 1987.
18. Haley EC et al: The International Cooperative Study on the Timing of Aneurysm Surgery. The North American experience. *Stroke* 23:205, 1992.
19. Gilbert JJ, Vinters HV: Cerebral amyloid angiopathy: Incidence and complications in the aging brain: I. Cerebral hemorrhage. *Stroke* 14:915, 1983.
20. Easton JD: Antiplatelet therapy for the prevention of stroke. *Cerebrovasc Dis* 2(suppl 1):6, 1992.
21. Antiplatelet Trialists Collaboration: Secondary prevention of vascular disease by prolonged antiplatelet treatment. *Br Med J* 296:320, 1988.
22. UK-TIA Study Group: United Kingdom transient ischemic attack trial: Interim results. *Br Med J* 296:316, 1988.
23. The SALT Collaborative Group: Swedish aspirin low-dose trial (SALT) of 75 mg aspirin as secondary prophylaxis after cerebrovascular ischaemic events. *Lancet* 338:1345, 1991.
24. The Dutch TIA Trial Study Group: A comparison of two doses of aspirin (30 mg vs. 283 mg a day) in patients after a transient ischemic attack or minor ischemic stroke. *N Engl J Med* 325:1262, 1991.
25. Dyken ML et al: Low-dose aspirin and stroke: "It ain't necessarily so." *Stroke* 23:1395, 1992.
26. Steering Committee of the Physicians' Health Study Research Group: Final report on the aspirin component of the ongoing physicians' health study. *N Engl J Med* 321:129, 1989.
27. Clive DM, Stoff JS: Renal syndromes associated with nonsteroidal anti-inflammatory drugs. *N Engl J Med* 310:563, 1984.
28. Hass WK et al: A randomized trial comparing ticlopidine hydrochloride with aspirin for the prevention of stroke in high-risk patients. *N Engl J Med* 321:501, 1989.
29. Swedish Cooperative Study: High dose acetylsalicylic acid after cerebral infarction. *Stroke* 18:325, 1987.
30. Gent M et al: The Canadian-American Ticlopidine Study in thromboembolic stroke. *Lancet* 1:1215, 1989.
31. Albers GW et al: Stroke prevention in non-valvular atrial fibrillation: A review of prospective randomized trials. *Ann Neurol* 30:511, 1991.
32. Duke RJ et al: Intravenous heparin for the prevention of stroke progression in acute partial stable stroke: A randomized controlled trial. *Ann Intern Med* 105:825, 1986.
33. Rothrock JF, Hart RG: Antithrombotic therapy in cerebrovascular disease. *Ann Intern Med* 115:886, 1991.
34. Yatsu FM et al: Anticoagulation of embolic strokes of cardiac origin: An update. *Neurology* 38:314, 1988.
35. Foulkes MA et al: The Stroke Data Bank: Design, methods, and baseline characteristics. *Stroke* 19:547, 1988.
36. Amarenco P et al: The prevalence of ulcerated plaques in the aortic arch in patients with stroke. *N Engl J Med* 326:221, 1992.
37. Benjamin EJ et al: Mitral annular calcification and the risk of stroke in an elderly cohort. *N Engl J Med* 327:374, 1992.
38. Robinson MJ, Teasdale GM: Calcium antagonists in the management of subarachnoid hemorrhage. *Cerebrovasc Brain Metab Rev* 2:205, 1990.
39. Levine SR, Brott TG: Thrombolytic therapy in cerebrovascular disorders. *Prog Cardiovasc Dis* 34:235, 1992.
40. Zivin JA, Choi DW: Stroke therapy. *Sci Am* 265:56, 1991.
41. The EC/IC Bypass Study Group: Failure of extracranial-intracranial arterial bypass to reduce the risk of ischemic stroke: Results of an international randomized trial. *N Engl J Med* 313:1191, 1985.
42. Toole JF et al: Nearing the finish line? The asymptomatic carotid atherosclerosis study. *Stroke* 23:1054, 1992.
43. House A et al: Mood disorders after stroke and their relation to lesion location. A CT scan study. *Brain* 113:1113, 1990.
44. Brust JCM: Dementia and cerebrovascular disease, in Mayeux R, Rosen WG (eds): *The Dementias*. New York, Raven, 1983, p 131.
45. Scheinberg P: Dementia due to vascular disease: A multifactorial disorder. *Stroke* 19:1291, 1988.
46. Tatemichi TK: How brain failure becomes chronic: A view of the mechanisms of dementia related to stroke. *Neurology* 40:1652, 1990.
47. Hachinski VC et al: Multi-infarct dementia. A cause of mental deterioration in the elderly. *Lancet* 2:207, 1974.
48. Tomlinson BE et al: Observations on the brains of demented old people. *J Neurol Sci* 11:205, 1970.
49. del Ser T et al: Vascular dementia. A clinicopathological study. *J Neurol Sci* 96:1, 1990.
50. Fisher CM: Lacunar strokes and infarcts: A review. *Neurology* 32:871, 1982.
51. Brust JCM: Vascular dementia is overdiagnosed. *Arch Neurol* 45:799, 1988.
52. O'Brien MD: Vascular disease and dementia in the elderly, in Smith WL, Kinsbourne M (eds): *Aging and Dementia*. New York, Spectrum, 1977, p 77.
53. Roman GC: Senile dementia of the Binswanger type. A vascular form of dementia in the elderly. *JAMA* 258:1782, 1987.
54. Hachinski VC et al: Leuko-araiosis. *Arch Neurol* 44:21, 1987.
55. Hershey LA et al: Magnetic resonance imaging in vascular dementia. *Neurology* 37:29, 1987.
56. Steingert A et al: Cognitive and neurologic findings in subjects with diffuse white matter lucencies on computed tomographic scan (leuko-araiosis). *Arch Neurol* 44:32, 1987.

57. Loeb C: Vascular dementia. *Dementia* 1:175, 1990.
58. Roman GC et al: Vascular dementia: Diagnostic criteria for research studies. Report of the NINDS-AIREN International Workshop. *Neurology* 43:250, 1993.
59. Erkinjuntti T, Hachinski VC: Rethinking vascular dementia. *Cerebrovasc Dis* 3:3, 1993.
60. Brust JCM: Vascular dementia reconsidered. *Cerebrovasc Dis* 3:26, 1993.
61. Chui HC et al: Criteria for the diagnosis of ischemic vascular dementia proposed by the State of California Alzheimer's Disease Diagnostic and Treatment Centers. *Neurology* 42:473, 1992.
62. O'Brien MD: Vascular dementia is underdiagnosed. *Arch Neurol* 45:797, 1988.
63. Sokoloff L: Cerebral circulatory and metabolic changes associated with aging. *Res Proc Assoc Res Nerv Ment Dis* 41:237, 1966.

Chapter 92

ALZHEIMER'S DISEASE

Richard Mayeux and Peter W. Schofield

Alzheimer's disease is the most common cause of dementia in the elderly and is consistently the most frequent postmortem diagnosis for those entering a hospital with dementia.[1] This progressive disabling degenerative process accounted for the dementia in the majority of those persons found to be demented in a small Midwestern community over a 4-year period.[2]

Alois Alzheimer described this illness as a specific disease over 80 years ago,[3] but many of its pathological features had been recognized before that time. Although the disease was originally considered primarily as a cause of presenile dementia, in 1964 pioneering investigations by Terry and associates[4] indicated that Alzheimer's disease is also the cause of senile dementia. Roth and associates[5,6] observed a relationship between the severity of dementia during life and the quantity of the defining pathological changes at death in elderly psychiatric patients. In 1975, Katzman brought the "malignancy" of the conditions to the attention of clinicians,[7] and he and others warned of an impending epidemic in the future.[8] This prediction was based on two parallel observations: Alzheimer's disease rapidly increases in frequency after the age of 60, and in most industrialized countries life expectancy is increasing.

Most clinicians are aware of the devastating effects of Alzheimer's disease. Currently, it has been proposed that the remaining life expectancy is halved,[9] that the quality of life is reduced for the patient and family,[10] and that the cost of health care is exorbitantly high.[11] However, basic and clinical research in Alzheimer's disease has increased significantly, resulting in a proliferation of information regarding early manifestations and the natural history of the disorder, improved diagnostic methods and management, as well as insight into the pathogenesis of what Lewis Thomas has referred to as the "disease of the century."

CLINICAL DIAGNOSIS

The most consistent symptom and finding in patients with Alzheimer's disease is memory loss. However, memory loss is seldom the only feature. A gradual decline in intellectual function that is also progressive is the hallmark and an essential component of the criteria for primary degenerative dementia in the revised third edition of the *Diagnostic and Statistical Manual of Mental Disorders* (Table 92-1).[12] Other features include impairment in orientation, judgment, problem solving, language, and perception. A joint work group of the National Institute of Communicative Disorders and Stroke and the Alzheimer's Disease and Related Disorders Association (NINCDS-ADRDA)[13] extended these criteria to enable clinicians to have a range of certainty in the diagnosis of Alzheimer's disease: probable, possible, and definite (Table 92-2). Postmortem studies have validated these criteria.[14]

A diagnosis of probable Alzheimer's disease is suggested for patients between ages 40 and 90 who, in the absence of systemic diseases or other brain disorders which might cause dementia or altered consciousness, are found to have intellectual decline that can be documented by neuropsychological tests. Memory and at least one of the following higher brain functions—judgment, language, perception, or cognition—must be defective. In patients whose laboratory studies are generally normal, lack of the ability to be independent in activities of daily living, and associated symptoms such as depression, hallucinations, and outbursts of irrational verbal or physical behavior, also support the diagnosis. A diagnosis of possible Alzheimer's disease is used when a second condition is present that might contribute to the dementia but is not considered to be a causal factor.[13] A diagnosis of definite Alzheimer's disease is reserved for patients in whom the clinical criteria are met and for whom there is confirmation of the diagnosis by pathological evidence found at autopsy or with brain biopsy.

These clinical criteria and other similar criteria[15] used for research are remarkably accurate during life at predicting those patients who will have the characteristic pathological changes in the brain at death. Because of the ease with which these criteria can be adapted to the examination of the patients with dementia, the clinician can develop a routine examination that will ensure an accurate diagnosis of Alzheimer's disease in demented patients over 85 percent of the time.

TABLE 92-1

Characteristics of Dementia

A. Demonstrable evidence of impairment in short- and long-term memory. Impairment in short-term memory (inability to learn new information) may be indicated by inability to remember three objects after 5 minutes. Long-term memory impairment (inability to remember information that was known in the past) may be indicated by inability to remember past personal information (e.g., what happened yesterday, birthplace, occupation) or facts of common knowledge (e.g., past Presidents, well-known dates).

B. At least one of the following:
   1. Impairment in abstract thinking, as indicated by inability to find similarities and differences between related words, difficulty in defining words and concepts, and other similar tasks
   2. Impaired judgment, as indicated by inability to make reasonable plans to deal with interpersonal, family, and job-related problems and issues
   3. Other disturbances of higher cortical function, such as aphasia (disorder of language), apraxia (inability to carry out motor activities despite intact comprehension and motor function), agnosia (failure to recognize or identify objects despite intact sensory function), and "constructional difficulty" (e.g., inability to copy three-dimensional figures, assemble blocks, or arrange sticks in specific designs)
   4. Personality change, i.e., alteration or accentuation of premorbid traits

C. The disturbance in A and B significantly interferes with work or usual social activities or relationships with others.

D. The condition does not occur exclusively during the course of delirium.

E. Either 1 or 2:
   1. There is evidence from the history, physical examination, or laboratory tests of a specific organic factor (or factors) judged to be etiologically related to the disturbance.
   2. In the absence of such evidence, an etiologic organic factor can be presumed if the disturbance cannot be accounted for by any nonorganic mental disorder, e.g., major depression accounting for cognitive impairment.

SOURCE: Reprinted from American Psychiatric Association,[12] with permission.

COGNITIVE AND BEHAVIORAL MANIFESTATIONS

Memory loss is the most common presenting feature of Alzheimer's disease, but a change in personality or an impairment in the ability to perform demanding intellectual tasks such as calculations may herald the onset. Nonetheless, memory for recent events and the ability to learn new information are affected and deteriorate over time. Recall of past events and previously acquired information may also be defective. Orientation to time and place may become a problem near or at the time of disease onset. On examination, the patient may have difficulty learning a name and address or a list of words. Recall of memorable events may be spotty and even grossly impaired.

Language impairment is also prevalent among patients with Alzheimer's disease.[16,17] Anomia, or word-finding difficulty, often begins with the onset of dementia. Cummings and associates have reported a progression to a transcortical, sensory-like aphasia in most patients.[16] Severe language disturbance has been associated with a poor prognosis[18,19] and is often present in familial Alzheimer's disease.[20] Some consider the aphasia of Alzheimer's disease to be rather specific, distinguishing it from dementia associated with stroke or with Parkinson's disease.[21] It is also critical to separate the syndrome of progressive aphasia without dementia[22,23] from aphasia associated with dementia because of the better prognosis of the former. This rare disorder has a pattern of impairment that does not include memory loss; brain imaging and pathological findings support the focal nature of this disorder.[23]

Patients with Alzheimer's disease manifest a visuospatial disturbance often characterized by difficulty getting around the neighborhood or house. Simple constructional tasks can be disturbed, such as drawing the face of a clock, as illustrated in Fig. 92-1.[24] "Dressing apraxia," difficulty following directions, and getting lost in a familiar place are each a type of visuospatial disorder that occurs with Alzheimer's disease.

The loss of interest in activities such as personal habits or community affairs parallels the intellectual decline. This may be a result of the dementia, but many patients become apathetic before dementia is severe. When apathy with depression is present, the diagnosis can be confusing because of the resemblance to dementia. However, depression occurs in about one-third of patients with clinically diagnosed Alzheimer's disease.[26]

Delusions and hallucinations are prevalent in patients with Alzheimer's disease and may be associated with a more rapid decline in function.[27] The delusions are usually simple in content and may or may not be of a paranoid type.[28] Abusive or belligerent behavior can accompany delusions, occur independently or in tandem, and pose serious management problems.[28]

Atypical presentations of Alzheimer's disease occur in up to 10 percent of patients.[29] For example, some patients who initially present with a pure aphasic syndrome may after several years show signs of other cognitive deficits which then progress to give rise to the clinical picture of dementia. The pathological condition in such cases is heterogeneous but appears to include patients with Alzheimer's disease.[30] Other atypical, focal presentations of Alzheimer's disease include patients who initially present with prominent visual symptoms,[31] patients with disproportionate visuospatial deficits (i.e., a "parietal lobe syndrome"),[25] or patients who present with promi-

TABLE 92-2

Criteria for Clinical Diagnosis of Alzheimer's Disease

I. The criteria for the clinical diagnosis of *probable* Alzheimer's disease include
   - Dementia established by clinical examination and documented by the Mini-Mental Test,[33] Blessed Dementia Scale,[6] or some similar examination, and confirmed by neuropsychological tests
   - Deficits in two or more areas of cognition
   - Progressive worsening of memory and other cognitive functions
   - No disturbance of consciousness
   - Onset between ages 40 and 90, most often after age 65
   - Absence of systemic disorders or other brain diseases that in and of themselves could account for the progressive deficits in memory and cognition.

II. The diagnosis of *probable* Alzheimer's disease is supported by
   - Progressive deterioration of specific cognitive functions such as language (aphasia), motor skills (apraxia), and perception (agnosia)
   - Impaired activities of daily living and altered patterns of behavior
   - Family history of similar disorders, particularly if confirmed neuropathologically
   - Laboratory results of
     - Normal lumbar puncture as evaluated by standard techniques
     - Normal pattern or nonspecific changes in EEG, such as increased slow-wave activity
     - Evidence of progressive cerebral atrophy documented with serial CT scans

III. Other clinical features consistent with the diagnosis of *probable* Alzheimer's disease, after exclusion of causes of dementia other than Alzheimer's disease, include
   - Plateaus in the course of progression of the illness
   - Associated symptoms of depression; insomnia; incontinence; delusions; illusions; hallucinations; catastrophic verbal, emotional, or physical outbursts; sexual disorders; and weight loss.

IV. Features that make the diagnosis of *probable* Alzheimer's disease uncertain or unlikely include
   - Sudden, apoplectic onset
   - Focal neurological findings such as hemiparesis, sensory loss, visual field deficits, and incoordination early in the course of the illness
   - Seizures or gait disturbances at the onset or very early in the course of the illness.

V. Clinical diagnosis of *possible* Alzheimer's disease
   - May be made on the basis of the dementia syndrome, in the absence of other neurological, psychiatric, or systemic disorders sufficient to cause dementia, and in the presence of variations in the onset, in the presentation, or in the clinical course
   - May be made in the presence of a second systemic or brain disorder sufficient to produce dementia, which is not considered to be *the* cause of the dementia
   - Should be used in research studies when a single, gradually progressive, severe cognitive deficit is identified in the absence of other identifiable cause

VI. Criteria for diagnosis of *definite* Alzheimer's disease are
   - The clinical criteria for probable Alzheimer's disease
   - Histopathological evidence obtained from a biopsy or autopsy

VII. Classification of Alzheimer's disease for research purposes should specify features that may differentiate subtypes of the disorder, such as
   - Familial occurrence
   - Onset before age of 65
   - Presence of trisomy-21
   - Coexistence of other relevant conditions such as Parkinson's disease.

SOURCE: Reprinted from McKhann et al[13] with permission.

nent "frontal lobe" features.[32] Such atypical cases appear to reflect predominant dysfunction in several areas of the brain not usually affected early in Alzheimer's disease.

Most of the cognitive and behavioral manifestations can be observed during a routine office visit or bedside examination, but the clinical history should be obtained from the patient's spouse, a relative, or a companion. A few brief scales are available and are useful guides for the assessment of cognition, but most do not include the neurological or medical examinations or methods necessary to identify depression and psychosis. Excellent brief cognitive scales include the Mini-Mental State Examination,[33] the Blessed Dementia Rating Scale,[6] and the Orientation-Memory-Concentration test.[34] The Alzheimer's Disease Rating Scale[35] has the advantage of including some questions regarding behavior. In general, these scales are quite valid measures and are reliable for clinical use. The Clinical Dementia Rating Scale is also a good measure of severity in patients with Alzheimer's disease.[36]

PHYSICAL MANIFESTATIONS

Research criteria for the diagnosis of *probable Alzheimer's disease* require the absence of coexistent metabolic or structural brain lesions (e.g., stroke) that may themselves be associated with cognitive impairment. Clearly, however, patients with Alzheimer's disease are not protected from such conditions, and the possi-

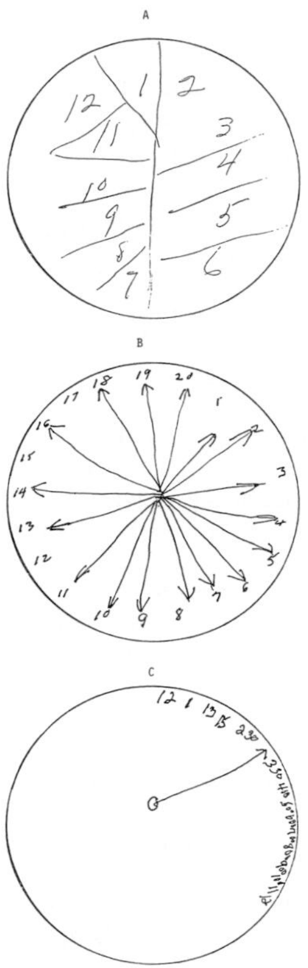

FIGURE 92-1
Examples of clocks drawn by three patients with Alzheimer's disease. There is a general disorganization and tendency to perseverate numbers and "hands." Spatial neglect is suggested in clock C. (*Clock samples provided by Gerald Dal Pan, M.D., Hospital of University of Pennsylvania.*[24])

bility for interaction, or synergy, of effect exists in such cases. Patients with stroke[37] and those with Parkinson's disease[38] can also develop Alzheimer's disease. In the NINCDS-ADRDA classification,[13] patients with coexisting or possibly contributing disorders are classified as having possible Alzheimer's disease. Patients with Alzheimer's disease may be more at risk of developing a delirium[39] or acute confusional state as a consequence of a wide variety of intercurrent acute illnesses, or due to inappropriate medications, and an accurate assessment of the severity of the dementia presupposes the absence of a coexistent confusional state.

Provided additional illnesses are not present, however, the neurological examination changes very little as Alzheimer's disease continues its devastating effect on the intellectual functions of the brain.[40] The cranial nerves, sensation, and gross motor functions remain intact, but primitive reflexes or "frontal release" signs and some higher sensory functions, such as smell, may be impaired. Muscle tone may be increased, resulting in rigidity, a plastic-like resistance to passive movement.[41] This type of rigidity may or may not be accompanied by a stooped posture resembling parkinsonism. This feature occurs in about one-third of patients and may be associated with a greater severity of illness.[42] There are accompanying changes in the substantia nigra in these patients which suggest an overlap between Parkinson's disease and Alzheimer's disease.[43]

Myoclonus (rapid, brief, irregular muscle jerks) occur in 10 to 15 percent of patients, and these movements are also associated with greater severity of disease.[41] Myoclonus can vary from random simple movements of a muscle to gross regular movements of limbs and trunk.[44] Seizures, both myoclonic and generalized may occur in as many as 20 percent of patients and may coexist in the same person.[45]

Some of the physical signs mentioned above have pathological and biochemical correlates in the brain which will be described later, but, more importantly, may have predictive power with regard to prognosis. Stern and associates[42] and others[43,46] have found that patients diagnosed as having probable Alzheimer's disease who have these signs progress more rapidly in terms of cognitive and functional disability than patients in whom these signs do not appear.

LABORATORY STUDIES

There have been several attempts to identify a consistent peripheral marker for Alzheimer's disease;[47–49] so far, no marker is available. Analysis of blood chemistry analyses and the hematological profile are performed as screens to eliminate metabolic diseases associated with dementia, such as hypothyroidism and combined systems disorder.

The cerebrospinal fluid obtained by lumbar puncture is normal in Alzheimer's disease, and some have advocated eliminating it from the routine clinical assessment of dementia.[50,51] However, this might conceal the condition of the rare patient with cryptococcal or other fungal meningitis or of the patient with an occult malignancy.

Standard brain imaging, such as skull radiographs, computed tomography (CT), or magnetic resonance, offers little specific information in the diagnosis of Alzheimer's disease. However, these studies are part of a standard workup intended to exclude stroke or tumor as a cause of dementia.

Experimental brain imaging techniques, such as positron emission tomography (PET)[52] and single photon emission computed tomography (SPECT),[53] use labeled compounds such as glucose to determine the metabolic activity in the brains of living patients with Alzheimer's disease. With these techniques, investigators have identified an area of reduced metabolic activity at the junction of the temporal, parietal, and occipital areas of both cerebral hemispheres.[52,53] The pathogenesis of this metabolic defect is unknown, but it is consistently identified. The expense and technology required to use these instruments may limit their wide-scale use for diagnosis. Furthermore, to be of value in this regard, the technique must offer benefits over current standards of clinical evaluation, supported by the usual investigations which seek to exclude alternative pathological conditions. Several recent studies have sought to address this issue.[54,55] In contrast, a regional cerebral blood flow study, which uses radioactive xenon to measure cortical perfusion and, indirectly, metabolic activity, is less expensive and requires less technical expertise. The same focal defect described above as being found with PET and SPECT is identifiable by regional cerebral blood flow measurement in confirmed cases of Alzheimer's disease.[56] More recently, measuring regional cerebral blood flow has been suggested in the early stage of the diagnostic process.[37]

The electroencephalogram (EEG) measures cortical function, but its usefulness in the diagnosis and management of dementia is questionable. The EEG changes during the aging process. For example, the mean alpha rhythm for young adults is approximately 10 to 10.5 Hz, but for an older person (70 to 80 years of age) it averages between 8.5 and 9 Hz.[58] Conversely, beta activity, which occurs at a rate of about 18 to 30 Hz in young and elderly subjects, persists with age. Activities normally infrequent in the EEG of the young adult, such as theta and delta rhythm, are commonly reported over temporal regions, particularly on the left, in people over the age of 60.[58] The EEG in Alzheimer's disease shows a reduction in the posterior dominant alpha rhythm in proportion to the severity of the dementia and may have some predictive utility.[59] As the severity of dementia increases, mild and intermittent reduction in the posterior rhythm to 7 Hz and then to theta and delta rhythms occurs. Generalized slowing of all cerebral activity occurs with progression. Other neurophysiologic measures, such as contingent negative variation, P-300 waves, evoked potentials, and computerized electroencephalography, may prove to be useful in the diagnosis of dementia, but the application of these techniques in the diagnosis is still under investigation.[60]

EPIDEMIOLOGY

The prevalence of clinically diagnosed Alzheimer's disease has been reviewed by Rocca et al.[61] and is summarized in Table 92-3. For people 65 years of age and older the prevalence ranged from 971 per 100,000 in Turku, Finland,[62] to 5800 per 100,000 in Great Britain.[63] A still higher figure was found by Evans et al. in a recent community study in East Boston with an estimated prevalence of 10,300 per 100,000 among those over 65 years.[64] This wide variation in rates probably reflects differences in diagnostic criteria and case ascertainment. Nonetheless, the age-specific prevalence of clinically diagnosed Alzheimer's disease increases with each decade. In nearly all the studies mentioned in Table 92-3, the prevalence rate more than doubles between the sixth and eighth decades of life. Because of the increase in the population over 65 years of age, a dramatic increase in the prevalence of Alzheimer's disease is anticipated over the next several years in developed countries. In France, for example, a 9 percent increase in the prevalence is expected by the year 2000, while in Japan a 76.6 percent increase is projected. The United States falls in the middle, at 42 percent.[61]

The incidence of clinically diagnosed Alzheimer's disease also rises acutely with advanced age.[61] Table 92-4 summarizes six major studies of the incidence of Alzheimer's disease. The age-specific incidence rates for all people over 60 again varied but were alarmingly high, ranging from about 127 new cases of Alzheimer's disease per 100,000 annually in Sweden[64a] to 260 cases per 100,000 annually in the United States. The differences in rates have been attributed to the inclusion of other diagnoses, such as senile psychosis and multi-infarct dementia. The use of strict diagnostic criteria for dementia indicate an incidence rate of 123.2 per 100,000 annually in Rochester, Minnesota, for people over 30 years of age,[2] and in a 5-year longitudinal cohort study of volunteers aged 75 to 85, nondemented at intake, Katzman et al.

TABLE 92-3

Prevalence of Clinically Diagnosed Alzheimer's Disease

Location	Year(s)	Population	Age (Years)	Prevalence Ratio (per 100,000)
Great Britain	1960–64	Urban (rs)*	>65	4200
Sweden	1964	Rural (cs)	>60	740
Japan	1965	Urban (rs)	>65	1900
Great Britain	1970	Urban (rs)	>65	5800
Finland	1976	Urban (pb)	>65	971
Finland	1977–80	Population	>30	900
		representative	>65	3600
United States	1978	Rural population	>40	500
United States	1986	Urban	>65	10,300

*rs means random sample, cs means complete survey, and pb means population-based.
SOURCE: This table was adapted from Rocca et al: Epidemiology of clinically diagnosed Alzheimer's disease. *Ann Neurol* 19:415, 1986.

TABLE 92-4

Incidence Rates of Clinically Diagnosed Alzheimer's Disease

Location	Year(s)	Population	Age Range (Years)	Incidence Rates (per 100,000 person-years)
Sweden	1964	Rural (complete survey)	>60	127
United States	1958–78	Cohort	>60	260*
Finland	1973–76	Urban population	>65	192
Israel	1974–78	Hospital population†	40–60	2.4
United States	1960–64	Urban	>30	123
United States	1985	Cohort	75–90	2000

*Calculated from Table 8-2 in Ref. 68.
†Refers to a hospital-based study in Israel using the National Disease Registry.

found an incidence of 2.0 per 100 person-years of risk of Alzheimer's disease.[65]

There may be cultural or ethnic differences in the prevalence and incidence rates of Alzheimer's disease. Treves et al. found higher rates of Alzheimer's disease occurring before age 60 among European Jews than among the Afro-Asian-born Jews in Israel.[66] In Copiah county, the prevalence of severe dementia was slightly higher for blacks and for women than for whites or men.[67] Neither study has been replicated.

RISK FACTORS

The analytic studies examining risk factors for Alzheimer's disease are complicated by the potential misdiagnosis of patients, as well as the difficulty in obtaining historical information because informants other than the patient need to be interviewed. In spite of these complications, a few putative risk factors have consistently emerged and are listed in Table 92-5. Family history of dementia is an important risk factor, but the relationship between head injury and thyroid disease has not been confirmed.[68,69] There is an increased frequency of Down's syndrome in the families of patients with Alzheimer's disease,[70,71] and the majority of Down's syndrome patients develop clinical and pathological Alzheimer's disease.[72]

TABLE 92-5

Putative Risk Factors for Alzheimer's Disease

1. Family history of dementia (OR* = 2.6 to 11)
2. Down's syndrome (OR = 4)
3. Maternal age (OR = 0.4 to 4.7†)
4. Head injury (OR = 4.5 to 5.3†)
5. Thyroid disease (OR = 2.3 to 3.5†)

†OR indicates the odds ratio or the odds risk ratio. This is the odds of Alzheimer's disease given the risk factor. The † implies that the confidence of this calculation is not always statistically significant.
SOURCE: This table was adapted from Table 4 of Rocca et al.[61]

An important risk factor is family history of dementia, particularly in a sibling. For many years it was recognized that Alzheimer's disease occurs in an autosomal dominant pattern in some families, but this was considered unusual. In some families with early-onset Alzheimer's disease, 50 percent of their relatives are affected in subsequent generations. Breitner and colleagues[73] have suggested that the "morbid risk" (the likelihood of developing Alzheimer's disease) by a given age can be as high as 50 percent if all family members are followed long enough, as noted in the graph in Fig. 92-2. Because the cumulative incidence of clinically diagnosed Alzheimer's disease increases

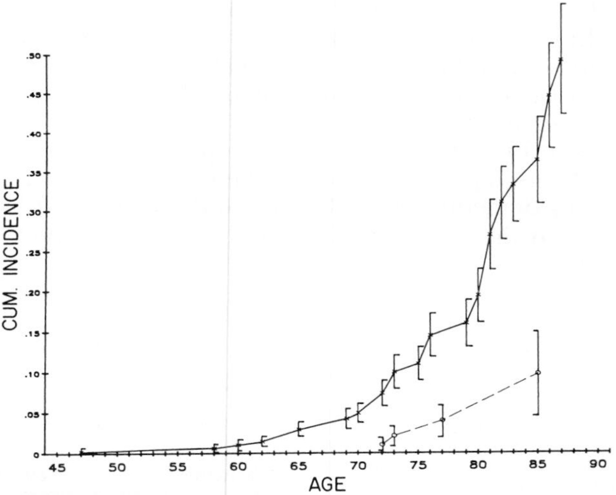

FIGURE 92-2

The cumulative incidence of an Alzheimer-type dementia in first-degree relatives of probands with Alzheimer's disease compared to elderly controls. The authors conclude that there may be a 50 percent morbid risk by age 90 for first-degree relatives. (*Reprinted with permission from Breitner JCS et al: Familial aggregation in Alzheimer's disease: Comparison of risk among relatives of early- and late-onset cases, and among male and female relatives in successive generations. Neurology 38:207, 1988.*)

to about 50 percent by age 87, even in the more typical late-onset form of the disease, genetic transmission is implied

Genetic linkage studies of separate kindreds with familial Alzheimer's disease have suggested at least four different chromosomal locations that may play a role in the disease.[74–77] Such studies commonly employ the technique of identifying *restriction fragment length polymorphisms* (RFLPs). These consist of short polymorphic fragments of DNA which are inherited in a simple Mendelian fashion, can be located within the genome, and can thus be used as markers. The proximity of a marker to a particular gene determines the likelihood that the gene and marker will become separated when crossing over of genetic material takes place at meiosis: the closer they lie, the more likely they will be inherited together, or *linked*. The logarithm of odds score (LOD score) is an estimate of the likelihood that the association between an identified RFLP and the occurrence of disease (postulated to be due to an inherited gene) could happen by chance. By convention, an LOD score of 3 or greater is regarded as evidence for linkage, that is, there is a probability of less than 1 in a 1000 that the linkage could occur by chance alone.

Studies of this kind have identified two separate loci on chromosome 21 wherein abnormalities may segregate with the trait. In several families with Alzheimer's disease of early onset, a point mutation causing a single amino acid substitution in the amyloid precursor protein (APP) molecule of probands has been found.[75,78,79] In other families, the locus is some distance from the APP gene.[79,80,81] Several different groups have identified families in which there is linkage with a locus on chromosome 14.[76] There is thus good evidence for genetic heterogenity. In yet other families, with late-onset Alzheimer's, the disease colocalizes with a defect on chromosome 19.[77] The gene for apolipoprotein E is located on chromosome 19q13.2 near the site of linkage to late-onset familial Alzheimer's disease.[77a] Apolipoprotein E binds to the β-amyloid peptide, is present in senile neuritic plaques, and the ε4 allele has been strongly associated with both sporadic and familial late-onset Alzheimer's disease.[77b] The question of the extent to which genetic factors have a role in the etiology of Alzheimer's disease is controversial. The apparent lack of complete concordance of Alzheimer's disease in homozygotic twin pairs[82] argues strongly against an entirely genetic etiology, and a striking difference in the age of onset of disease,[83] even in concordant twins, points to the likelihood that, even in such cases, environmental factors are of importance and probably interact with genetic factors in the pathogenesis. Methodological problems constrain linkage studies to a considerable extent. If patients included in the analyses are incorrectly diagnosed as having Alzheimer's disease, or have a sporadic form of the disease (a real possibility in those families where onset is characteristically late), the analysis may be compromised.[84]

The effect of education on the risk of Alzheimer's disease has recently received attention. In a study of 5055 elderly individuals in Shanghai, Zhang et al.[85] showed an inverse relationship between years of education and the prevalence of dementia. One interpretation of this finding is that it may represent an artifact of testing: the less-educated perform poorly in a testing situation, simply out of unfamiliarity with such tasks. An alternative interpretation, namely that higher levels of education may in some way provide a "cognitive buffer" and delay the clinical manifestations of underlying pathological lesions of Alzheimer's disease, has been advanced by Stern et al.[86] For a given level of dementia on cognitive testing, they observed an inverse relationship between education and parietotemporal perfusion deficits on regional cortical blood flow studies. This suggested more advanced disease pathologically, at a given level of cognitive performance, among the better educated. A study by Beard et al., by contrast, did not find any association between education and Alzheimer's disease.[87]

PATHOLOGY

The histologic criteria for Alzheimer's disease consist primarily of an abundance of senile plaques (neuritic plaques) and neurofibrillary tangles in the neocortex and hippocampus. Specific diagnostic criteria suggested by a work group at the National Institute on Aging include quantities of senile plaques and neurofibrillary tangles for different age groups.[88] These criteria have been validated to some extent in at least one clinicopathological study.[14] Alternative neuropathological criteria in which plaque counts take precedence have more recently been proposed.[89] Alzheimer's disease is pathologically, qualitatively, and quantitatively distinct from normal aging of the brain. Most patients with Alzheimer's disease have a slight reduction in brain weight, with the majority ranging from 900 to 1100 g. Mild to moderate cerebral cortical atrophy can be present, although many patients show little or no atrophy. The subcortical areas, including the centrum semiovale (white matter), also diminish in size, which results in the enlargement of the lateral ventricles.

Senile or neuritic plaques, neurofibrillary tangles (NFTs), amyloid deposition, neuronal loss, granulovacuolar degeneration, and Hirano bodies are the major microscopic elements seen in Alzheimer's disease. Senile plaques (SPs) are microscopic lesions, the key component of which is amyloid.[90] These are best demonstrated by silver impregnation (Bielshowsky or Bodian stains), with the amyloid component being well displayed by periodic acid–Schiff, Congo red, or thioflavin S.[91] Several subcategories of SP have been identified, according to the composition of the amyloid material and the presence and nature of the surrounding cellular or structural elements. Thus, diffuse plaques contain nonfibrillary amyloid precursor protein.[92] Primitive plaques have in addition surrounding neuritic structures. Mature plaques comprise fibrillary amyloid surrounded by neuritic structures, microglia, and astrocytes. Burnt out plaques consist primarily of a core of amyloid.[91] Though this terminology implies that senile plaques may individually evolve from primitive to burnt out, the evidence for such a progression is clearly hard to obtain (Fig. 92-3). Senile plaques are present in large numbers in the amygdala, hippocampus, and cerebral cortex, and rarely in the brainstem and basal ganglia. There is a quantitative relationship between the number of senile plaques and the severity of dementia,[6] as well as a reduction in choline acetyltransferase activity, a biochemical marker for acetylcholine.[93]

The source of the amyloid which is deposited in the SPs is a source of ongoing controversy, and there is circumstantial evidence pointing to either neuronal cell or vascular (blood or vessel) origin.[94]

A β-amyloid peptide of 28 to 43 amino acids (β/A4) is the principal component of SPs[95] and accounts for the fibrillary structure of the deposits. This peptide derives from a larger glycoprotein, APP. APP exists as a transmembrane protein which is synthesized in at least four different forms by alternative splicing of messenger RNA. Of the four—695, 714, 751, and 770 amino acid residues long, respectively—the last three contain a conserved sequence found in the family of Kunitz protease inhibitors.[96–99] APP is widely distributed in the brain, in both neural and nonneural cells.[100] The gene coding for APP maps to the long arm of chromosome 21.[101] Neuronal APP is delivered to axons via the fast anterograde axonal transport system,[102] and may play a role in synaptic adhesion and efficiency.[103] The APP is inserted into the cell membrane, and in subsequent processing, cleavage takes place outside the membrane, releasing a large portion of the amino terminus of the protein.[104] The site of this cleavage, determined by the distance from the plasma membrane, lies within the β/A4 domain,[105] and consequently the formation of β/A4 cannot arise by this process. There is evidence, in addition, for intracellular, endosomal-lysosomal processing of APP within neurons,[106,107] and intermediate peptide sequences that do include the β/A4 domain have been identified as arising during metabolism in a number of neuronal cell models.[107–109] Intermediate, potentially amyloidogenic peptides have been found in association with brain microvessels, consistent with a vascular or hematogenous origin.[109] The β/A4 itself may be a normal product of cellular metabolism.[110,111] These observations raise the possibility that in Alzheimer's disease normal metabolic pathways of APP are for some reason enhanced, causing the formation of excess β/A4, which becomes deposited in SPs. In support of this model, Citron et al. recently showed that cultured cells bearing a double mutation in the APP gene—as found in a Swedish familial Alzheimer's disease family—produced six- to eightfold more β/A4 than cells expressing normal APP.[112]

Neurofibrillary tangles (NFTs), initially described by Alois Alzheimer in 1907, are neuronal cytoplasmic collections of tangled filaments present in abundance in the neocortex, hippocampus, amygdala, basal forebrain, substantia nigra, locus ceruleus, and other brainstem nuclei. They are also frequently present in the cortex and, in particular, the hippocampus. NFTs consist of a neurofilament protein which is normally not found in the neuronal perikaryon.[113] The NFT consists in large part of paired helical filaments which contain epitopes reacting with antibodies for tau proteins that are abnormally phosphorylated,[114] with microtubule-associated protein,[115] and with neurofilaments and gangliosides.[116,117] Phosphorylation of tau may represent a critical step, accounting for the aggregation of the neurofilaments and ultimately leading to the formation of the NFTs.[118] The NFT may contain some of the same peptides as the plaque,[119] and the amyloid-

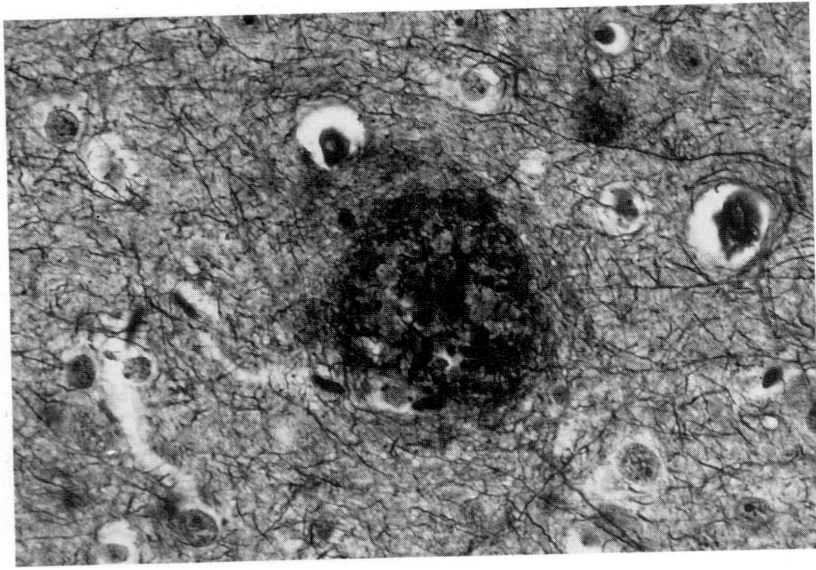

FIGURE 92-3
A senile plaque with a dense core of amyloid protein. It is surrounded by a ring of filamentous material. These structures are present in the brains of normal elderly but are increased in quantity in patients with Alzheimer's disease. The number of senile plaques also correlates with the severity of dementia. (*Photograph provided by James Goldman, M.D., Ph.D. of Columbia University and the New York State Psychiatric Institute.*)

core protein contains a 100-kDa protein bearing a sequence homologous to tau.[120] Paired helical filaments may also be found individually in the bodies or processes of neurons, where they are referred to as *neuropil threads.*[121] NFTs are found in Down's syndrome, dementia associated with boxing (dementia pugilistica), and the parkinsonian dementia complex of Guam. They are also present in the brains of normal elderly persons and may represent a nonspecific response to a variety of insults.

Amyloid β-protein deposition occurs not only in senile plaques but also in the walls of capillaries, arterioles, and small arteries in the brain in subarachnoid spaces. Almost all patients with Alzheimer's disease have these changes.[122] The protein is very similar to the amyloid proteins previously described for the senile plaque.

Neuronal loss is one of the major histologic features of Alzheimer's disease and is greatest in the neocortex, particularly the temporal lobe hippocampus, subiculum, and superior and inferior parietal lobes. To a lesser extent the amygdala shows a reduction of overall volume as well as neuron number. Neuronal loss is a striking feature of the cholinergic basal forebrain nucleus of Meynert[123] and the septal nuclei; losses in both correlate with the changes seen in the cholinergic system.[124] There are substantial losses of neurons from other brainstem nuclear centers, such as the locus ceruleus, substantia nigra, and raphe.[125–128]

Granulovacuolar degeneration consists of cytoplasmic structures composed of a central argyrophilic granule surrounded by a vacuole. These can be multiple and may be found in the pyramidal layer of the hippocampus. They are composed of electron-dense granular filaments surrounded by a membrane-bound clear zone. They contain tubulin-like immunoreactivity and occur in a number of diseases, as well as in normal aging.

The Hirano body is a small filament which is an eosinophilic ovoid or spherical intracytoplasmic inclusion commonly seen in the pyramidal layer of the hippocampus in Alzheimer's disease. It contains actin and is seen in other diseases and in normal aging.

The role of the cytoskeletal abnormalities (NFTs and neuropil threads) and amyloid deposition in the pathogenesis of the dementia is unclear. Clinicopathological studies have variously suggested correlations between density counts of NFTs or SPs and the severity of dementia, although the strongest morphological correlate of dementia appears to be synaptic loss.[129] There is evidence that amyloid is itself neurotoxic,[130–132] and this offers a plausible link between the morphological findings and dementia, but the issue remains controversial.

A remarkable overlap between the pathological as well as clinical features of Alzheimer's disease and Parkinson's disease was alluded to earlier. Numerous studies indicate that patients with Parkinson's disease become demented, and when they do, it is usually the result of coexistent Alzheimer's disease.[38,133–135] Similarly, patients with Alzheimer's disease develop parkinsonian features[41,46] with an associated loss of pigmented neurons in the substantia nigra, primarily from the pars compacta and locus ceruleus.[43] Lewy bodies (round eosinophilic hyalin cytoplasmic inclusions) are present in some remaining neurons in the substantia nigra. Often Lewy bodies are found in the basal forebrain in patients with either disease and in patients with both problems.

BIOCHEMISTRY

Neurotransmitter alterations were recognized approximately 10 years ago in Alzheimer's disease.[136] Most studies have described cortical neurochemical abnormalities such as the loss of presynaptic cholinergic, noradrenergic, and serotonergic markers; these abnormalities are thought to be due to neuronal dysfunction in afferent connections from subcortical neuronal sites.[137] However, the changes in the cholinergic system occur very early in the disease and in newly diagnosed patients can be seen by brain biopsy.[138] Reductions in levels of certain peptides such as somatostatin-like reactivity and corticotropin-releasing factor probably reflect the loss of intrinsic cortical neurons.[139–144] Other neuropeptides have also been implicated, such as vasopressin,[145] substance P, and neuropeptide Y.[146–148] Alterations in gamma aminobutyric acid and its related receptors are also probably due to the loss of intrinsic neurons and afferent projections as well.[149–151].

A relationship between the loss of neurotransmitter markers and NFTs and senile plaques exists.[93,124] The cholinergic markers previously mentioned have the most striking correlation to the presence of senile plaques, as well as NFTs, but somatostatin, glutamine, and other neurotransmitters also relate to these morphological features.

A consistent abnormality which has opened the way for treatment is the loss of cortical presynaptic cholinergic markers, such as choline acetyltransferase, the rate-limiting enzyme for the production of acetylcholine. Remarkably, muscarinic receptors appear to be normal,[138] but Whitehouse and others[152–154] have described a reduction in the numbers of nicotinic receptors. More variable losses for noradrenergic and serotonergic markers in the brainstem occur because of loss of cells in both the locus ceruleus and the raphe nuclei.[155] The magnitude of these losses and their behavioral correlations have not been forthcoming but are currently under investigation. Most of these neurochemical abnormalities involve classic neurotransmitters found in subcortical nuclei which project to the cortex.

It is quite unlikely that a single neurotransmitter deficiency can account for the numerous manifestations related to Alzheimer's disease. Numerous transmitters and neuropeptides may be related to the pathogenesis of this disorder. The specific relationships between diseased neuronal populations, chemical losses or changes, and behavior have yet to be determined. In the simplest sequence, the cholinergic system appears to be related to memory, but, as yet, enhancing cholinergic metabolism has not reversed the course of Alzheimer's disease.

The primary cause of cholinergic neuron loss is not established, and there is little evidence that this loss in the basal forebrain is caused by a mechanism distinct from that leading to the loss of other neurotransmitter systems. It can be assumed, however, that the loss of various neurotransmitters is secondary to neuronal loss and cytopathological lesions found in Alzheimer's disease rather than their cause. It is suspected that macromolecular changes that accompany neuronal degeneration occurring with normal brain aging, and in Alzheimer's disease, play a role in progressive cell death, loss, or change in neurotransmitter systems, and in the subsequent abnormalities of behavior.

MANAGEMENT

Experimental Therapies

The *cholinergic hypothesis*[156] has provided a rationale for specific treatment strategies in Alzheimer's disease. Several observations suggested that impaired function in cholinergic pathways within the brain may be of singular importance with regard to the cognitive deficits which are characteristically seen. Significant cell loss occurs in the basal forebrain cholinergic complex in Alzheimer's disease,[124] and a relationship between the severity of the dementia and the degree of choline acetyltransferase reduction exists.[93] Furthermore, the anticholinergic scopolamine, when given to normal young people, causes transitory memory and cognitive deficits bearing some resemblance to those seen in patients with Alzheimer's disease.[156] In the light of these observations, numerous drugs have been investigated in an effort to enhance cholinergic transmission within the brain, in the hope that significant clinical improvement might follow. The pharmacological strategies have included loading patients with precursor substances necessary for acetycholine synthesis,[157–160] the administration of acetylcholinesterase inhibitors, and the use of muscarinic receptor agonists.[161–163]

Precursor loading with phosphatidylcholine (lecithin) has not proved to be of benefit and has been associated with a variety of side effects, predominantly gastrointestinal.[158–160] Physostigmine, an anticholinesterase, has been associated with slight improvements in memory in some patients, but no overall improvement in the activities of daily living have accompanied these benefits.[164–171.]

The cholinesterase inhibitor tetraaminoacridine (THA) has been the subject of numerous studies.[172,173] Some of the early studies appeared promising.[172] Recently, a large multicenter study of THA has been concluded.[174] The study population was "enriched" by inclusion of only those patients who appeared to respond to THA during an initial dose titration phase. The double-blind phase, involving 215 patients, lasted only 6 weeks. The group taking THA showed smaller declines in performance on a cognitive subscale of the Alzheimer's disease assessment scale, and in activities of daily living. The differences, although statistically significant, were small. There were no statistically significant changes in minimental score. The authors concluded that the effects were very modest, and that "enhancement of acetylcholine transmission is inadequate to reverse the signs and symptoms of Alzheimer's disease."

A variety of other compounds have been assessed in clinical trials, all without demonstrable benefit. Pramiracetam, one of the class of so-called nootropic drugs that enhance learning acquisition and reverse learning impairment in experimental animals, proved without benefit in a small study.[175] The vasopressin-related peptide DGAVP citrate caused no improvement in patients receiving once-daily intranasal treatment over 84 days.[176]

Because the efficacy of neurotransmitter replacement therapy is limited, there is growing interest in the possibility of enhancing the survival and function of neurons that are prone to degeneration. Acetyl levocarnitine hydrochloride, an agent which may stimulate natural scavenger functions to reduce oxidized radicals, was associated with slowed deterioration on some cognitive measures in a recent double-blind study.[177] So-called neurotrophic factors, proteins which have a role in neuronal growth and survival, have been the focus of increasing attention.[178] The first and best characterized of these trophic factors is nerve growth factor (NGF). Intraventricular administration of NGF has been shown to prevent the degeneration of basal forebrain cholinergic neurons following section of their axons in primates.[179] This finding is of considerable relevance, in view of the special vulnerability of cholinergic neurons in Alzheimer's disease. Intraventricular administration of NGF to a 69-year-old woman with dementia was recently reported to be accompanied by several measures of improvement, including verbal episodic memory.[180] NGF and related neurotrophic factors[178,181] are candidates for future clinical studies in patients with Alzheimer's disease.

The search for therapies which might halt the pathological changes of Alzheimer's disease parallels similar efforts in Parkinson's disease, where, on the other hand, neurotransmitter replacement strategies have been spectacularly successful, although ultimately limited. Indeed the monoamine oxidase B inhibitor deprenyl, which has recently been reported to slow the progression of Parkinson's disease, possibly by reducing the oxidative stresses on at-risk cells,[182] is currently under investigation in patients with Alzheimer's disease.

Practical Management

Psychiatric manifestations listed as "other clinical features" consistent with the diagnosis of probable Alzheimer's disease by the NINCDS-ADRDA criteria[13] include depression; insomnia; incontinence; delusions; hallucinations; illusions; catastrophic verbal, emotional, or physical outbursts; sexual disorders; and weight loss. Numerous studies suggest that antipsychotics used for hallucinations are effective and can also be used to control paranoid or disturbing behaviors.[28]

Controlled studies of neuroleptics have been equivocal. There is limited evidence to suggest that neuroleptics may be effective in relatively low doses in some patients. A recent meta-analysis of published placebo-controlled trials of neuroleptics in agitated dementia patients indicated a modest improvement with neuroleptics compared with placebo.[183] Because no neuroleptic has been shown to be consistently better than any other, it may be best to withdraw them periodically to reaffirm the need for their use. Most studies have focused on inpatients rather than outpatients, and it is unclear how effective these medications would be in an outpatient setting. In a recent study by Devanand et al.,[184] low-dose haloperidol was effective in reducing delusions, but side effects occurred, including parkinsonism and worsening of intellectual function.

Several studies have compared haloperidol, a high-potency drug with low anticholinergic properties, to thioridazine, a low-potency drug with high anticholinergic effects. No difference has been observed, and, if anything, a marginal advantage for thioridazine was noted. It would be expected that a medication with high anticholinergic properties would increase the chances of adverse effects, but this was not observed.[185–188.]

Some clinicians consider benzodiazepines to be better than thioridazine in the management of symptoms such as anxiety, insomnia, and agitation in patients without hallucinations or delusions. However, in a double-blind study in which thioridazine was compared with diazepam on measures of anxiety and global psychopathology, thioridazine was better.[185] More recently in a study comparing haloperidol to oxazepam, no differences were found in efficacy, with both drugs producing modest decreases in targeted aberrant behavior.[189]

Side effects are certainly to be expected with neuroleptics and include sedation, extrapyramidal syndrome, orthostatic hypotension, and anticholinergic effects including dry mouth, blurred vision, and urinary retention. For this reason, neuroleptics should be started at extremely low doses and raised gradually while monitoring closely for adverse effects. Orthostatic hypotension has profound implications in the elderly but appears to be relatively uncommon if low dosages of neuroleptics are maintained. It is best to use a noctural dosing schedule so that hypotension is not a problem. Psychomotor retardation and extrapyramidal side effects are much more common in medications such as haloperidol and increase the disability associated with dementia. There is some evidence to suggest that elderly demented patients may be at increased risk for developing tardive dyskinesia with consequent severe movement and feeding difficulties.

Conclusions

Fortunately, interest in Alzheimer's disease and related disorders has increased at a time when answers are sorely needed. The establishment of Alzheimer's Disease Research Centers on a state and federal level signifies the extent to which the public is willing to support research efforts concerned with this disease. Because of the growing numbers of individuals reaching the age of greatest risk, this effort will have to be sustained until the etiology, the pathogenesis, and a treatment of Alzheimer's disease are found.

REFERENCES

1. Wells CE: Diagnostic evaluation and treatment in dementia, in Wells CE (ed): *Dementia,* 2d ed. Philadelphia, Davis, 1977, p 247.
2. Schoenberg BS et al: Alzheimer's disease and other dementing illnesses in a defined United States population: Incidence rates and clinical features. *Ann Neurol* 22:724, 1987.
3. Alzheimer A: Uber eine eigenartige Erkrankung der Hirnrinde. *All Z Psychiatr* 64:146, 1907.
4. Terry RD et al: Ultrastructural studies in Alzheimer's presenile dementia. *Am J Pathol* 44:269, 1964.
5. Roth M: The natural history of mental disorder in old age. *J Ment Sci* 101:281, 1955.
6. Blessed G et al: The association between quantitative measures of dementia and of senile change in the cerebral gray matter of elderly subjects. *Br J Psychiatry* 114:797, 1968.
7. Katzman R: The prevalence and malignancy of Alzheimer disease: A major killer. *Arch Neurol* 33:217, 1976.
8. Plum F: Dementia: An approaching epidemic. *Nature* 279:372, 1979.
9. Neilsen J et al: Follow-up 15 years after a gerontopsychiatric prevalence study. Conditions concerning death, cause of death, and life expectancy in relation to psychiatric diagnosis. *J Gerontol* 32:554, 1977.

10. Pfeffer RI et al: Prevalence of Alzheimer's disease in a retirement community. *Am J Epidemiol* 125:420, 1987.
11. Kay DWK et al: Mental illness and hospital usage in the elderly: A random sample follow-up. *Compr Psychiatry* 11:26, 1970.
12. *Diagnostic and Statistical Manual of Mental Disorders,* 3d ed. Washington, American Psychiatric Association, 1987.
13. McKhann G et al: Clinical diagnosis of Alzheimer's disease: Report of the NINCDS-ADRDA work group under the auspices of the Department of Health and Human Services Task Force on Alzheimer's disease. *Neurology* 34:939, 1984.
14. Tierney MC et al: The NINCDS-ADRDA Work Group criteria for the clinical diagnosis of probable Alzheimer's disease: A clinico-pathologic study of 57 cases. *Neurology* 38:359, 1988.
15. Morris JC et al: Validation of clinical diagnostic criteria for Alzheimer's disease. *Ann Neurol* 24:17, 1988.
16. Cummings JL et al: Aphasia in dementia of the Alzheimer type. *Neurology* 35:394, 1985.
17. Kirshner HS et al: Language disturbance: An initial symptom of cortical degenerations and dementia. *Arch Neurol* 41:491, 1984.
18. Kaszniak AW et al: Predictors of mortality in presenile and senile dementia. *Ann Neurol* 3:246, 1978.
19. Faber-Langendoen K et al: Aphasia in senile dementia of the Alzheimer type. *Ann Neurol* 23:365, 1988.
20. Folstein MF, Breitner JCS: Language disorder predicts familial Alzheimer's disease. *Johns Hopkins Med J* 149:145, 1981.
21. Powell AL et al: Speech and language alterations in multi-infarct dementia. *Neurology* 38:717, 1988.
22. Mesulam M-M: Slowly progressive aphasia without generalized dementia. *Ann Neurol* 11:592, 1982.
23. Chawluk JB et al: Slowly progressive aphasia without generalized dementia: Studies with positron emission tomography. *Ann Neurol* 19:68, 1986.
24. Dal Pan G et al: Clock-drawing in neurological disorders. *Behav Neurol* 2:39, 1989.
25. Crystal HA et al: Biopsy-proved Alzheimer's disease presenting as a right parietal syndrome. *Ann Neurol* 12:186, 1982.
26. Reifler BV et al: Coexistence of cognitive impairment and depression in geriatric outpatients. *Am J Psychiatry* 139:623, 1982.
27. Stern Y et al: Measurement and prediction of functional capacity in Alzheimer's disease. *Ann Neurol* 38:248, 1988.
28. Devanand DP et al: Psychosis, behavioral disturbance, and the use of neuroleptics in dementia. *Compr Psychiatry* 29:387, 1988.
29. Katzman R: Alzheimer's disease. *N Engl J Med* 314:964, 1986.
30. Pogacar S, Williams RS: Alzheimer's disease presenting as slowly progressive aphasia. *RI Med J* 67:181, 1984.
31. Kiyosawa M et al: Alzheimer's disease with prominent visual symptoms. Clinical and metabolic evaluation. *Ophthalmology* 96:1077, 1989.
32. Montaldi D et al: Measurements of rCBF and cognitive performance in Alzheimer's disease. *J Neurol Neurosurg Psychiatry* 53:33, 1990.
33. Folstein MF et al: "Mini-mental state": A practical method for grading the cognitive state of patients for the clinician. *J Psychiatr Res* 12:189, 1975.
34. Katzman R et al:Validation of a short Orientation-Memory-Concentration test of cognitive impairment. *Am J Psychiatry* 140:734, 1983.
35. Rosen WG et al: A new rating scale for Alzheimer's disease. *Am J Psychiatry* 141:1356, 1984.
36. Hughes CP et al: A new clinical scale for the staging of dementia. *Br J Psychiatry* 140:566, 1982.
37. Wade JPH et al: The clinical diagnosis of Alzheimer's disease. *Arch Neurol* 44:24, 1987.
38. Boller F et al: Parkinson's disease, dementia, Alzheimer's disease: Clinicopathological correlations. *Ann Neurol* 1:329, 1980.
39. Levkoff SE et al: Delirium. The occurrence and persistence of symptoms among elderly hospitalized patients. *Arch Intern Med* 152:334, 1992.
40. Huff FJ et al: The neurologic examination in patients with probable Alzheimer's disease. *Arch Neurol* 44:924, 1987.
41. Mayeux R et al: Heterogeneity in dementia of the Alzheimer type: Evidence of subgroups. *Neurology* 35:453, 1985.
42. Stern Y et al: Predictors of disease course in patients with probable Alzheimer's disease. *Neurology* 37:1649, 1987.
43. Ditter SM, Mirra SS: Neuropathologic and clinical features of Parkinson's disease in Alzheimer's disease patients. *Neurology* 37:754, 1987.
44. Jacob H: Muscular twitchings in Alzheimer's disease, in Wolstenholme GEW, O'Connor M (eds): *Alzheimer's Disease and Related Conditions.* London, Churchill, 1970, p 75.
45. Hauser WA et al: Seizures and myoclonus in patients with Alzheimer's disease. *Neurology* 36:1226, 1986.
46. Chui HC et al: Clinical subtypes of dementia of the Alzheimer type. *Neurology* 35:1544, 1985.
47. Nerl C et al: HLA-linked complement markers in Alzheimer's and Parkinson's disease: C4 variant (C4B2) a possible marker for senile dementia of the Alzheimer type. *Neurology* 34:310, 1984.
48. Blass JP, Zemcov A: Alzheimer's disease: A metabolic systems degeneration? *Neurochem Pathol* 2:103, 1984.
49. Zubenko GZ et al: Platelet membrane abnormality in Alzheimer's disease. *Ann Neurol* 22:237, 1987.
50. Hammerstrom DC, Zimmer B: The role of lumbar puncture in the evaluation of dementia: The University of Pittsburgh Study. *J Am Geriatr Soc* 33:397, 1985.
51. Larson EB et al: Diagnostic tests in the evaluation of dementia: A prospective study of 200 elderly outpatients. *Arch Intern Med* 146:1917, 1986.
52. Duara R et al: Positron emission tomography in Alzheimer's disease. *Neurology* 36:876, 1986.
53. DeKosky ST et al: Role of single photon emission computed tomography (SPECT) in the diagnosis of Alzheimer's disease. *Neurology* 37:159, 1987.
54. Powers WJ et al: Blinded clinical evaluation of positron emission tomography for probable Alzheimer's disease. *Neurology* 42:765, 1992.
55. Herholz K et al: Criteria for the diagnosis of Alzheimer's disease with positron emission tomography. *Dementia* 1:156, 1990.
56. Hagberg B, Ingvar DH: Cognitive reduction in presenile dementia related to regional abnormali-

ties of the cerebral blood flow. *Br J Psychiatry* 128:209, 1976.
57. Prohovnik I et al: Cerebral perfusion as a diagnostic marker of early Alzheimer's disease. *Neurology* 38:931, 1988.
58. Pedley TA, Miller JA: Clinical neurophysiology of aging and dementia, in Mayeux R, Rosen W (eds): *The Dementias*. New York, Raven, 1983, p 31.
59. Rae-Grant A et al: The electroencephalogram in Alzheimer-type dementia. *Arch Neurol* 44:50, 1987.
60. Duffy FH et al: Brain electrical activity in patients with presenile and senile dementia of the Alzheimer's type. *Ann Neurol* 16:439, 1984.
61. Rocca WA et al: Epidemiology of clinically diagnosed Alzheimer's disease. *Ann Neurol* 19:415, 1986.
62. Molsa PK et al: Epidemiology of dementia in a Finnish population. *Acta Neurol Scand* 65:541, 1982.
63. Broe GA et al: Neurological disorders in the elderly at home. *J Neurol Neurosurg Psychiatry* 39:362, 1976.
64. Evans DA et al: Prevalence of Alzheimer's disease in a community population of older persons. Higher than previously reported. *JAMA* 262:2551, 1989.
64a. Åkesson HO: A population study of senile and arteriosclerotic psychoses. *Human Hered* 19:546, 1969.
65. Katzman R et al: Development of dementing illnesses in an 80-year-old volunteer cohort. *Ann Neurol* 25:317, 1989.
66. Treves T et al: Presenile dementia in Israel. *Arch Neurol* 43:26, 1986.
67. Schoenberg BS et al: Severe dementia, prevalence and clinical features in a bi-racial U.S. population. *Arch Neurol* 42:740, 1985.
68. Sluss TK et al: The use of longitudinal studies in the investigation of risk factors for senile dementia—Alzheimer type, in Mortimer JA, Schuman IM (eds): *Epidemiology of Dementia*. New York, Oxford, 1984, p 132.
69. Henderson AS: The epidemiology of Alzheimer's disease. *Br Med Bull* 42:3, 1986.
70. Heston LL et al: Dementia of the Alzheimer type: Clinical genetics, natural history, and associated conditions. *Arch Gen Psychiatry 38:1085, 1981.*
71. Heyman A et al: Alzheimer's disease: A study of epidemiological aspects. *Ann Neurol* 34:335, 1984.
72. Wisnieski KE et al: Occurrence of neuropathological changes and dementia of Alzheimer's disease in Down's syndrome. *Ann Neurol* 17:278, 1985.
73. Breitner JCS et al: Familial aggregation in Alzheimer's disease: Comparison of risk among relatives of early- and late-onset cases, and among male and female relatives in successive generations. *Neurology* 38:207, 1988.
74. St. George-Hyslop PH et al: The genetic defect causing familial Alzheimer's disease maps to chromosome 21. *Science* 235:885, 1987.
75. Goate AM et al: Segregation of a missense mutation in the amyloid precursor protein gene with familial Alzheimer's disease. *Nature* 349:704, 1991.
76. Schellenberg GD et al: Genetic linkage evidence for a familial Alzheimer's disease locus on chromosome 14. *Science* 258:668, 1992.
77. Pericak-Vance MA et al: Linkage studies in familial Alzheimer's disease: Evidence for chromosome 19 linkage. *Am J Hum Genet* 48:1034, 1991.
77a. Myklebost O, Rogne S: A physical map of the apolipoprotein gene cluster on human chromosome 19. *Hum Genet* 78:244, 1988.
77b. Strittmatter WJ et al: Apolipoprotein E: High affinity binding to beta-amyloid and increased frequency of type 4 allele in late-onset familial Alzheimer's disease. *Proc Nat Acad Sci* 90(5):1977, 1993.
78. Chartier-Harlin M et al: Early onset Alzheimer's disease caused by mutations at codon 717 of the β-amyloid precursor protein gene. *Nature* 353:844, 1991.
79. Murrell J et al: A mutation in the amyloid precursor protein associated with hereditary Alzheimer's disease. *Science* 254:97, 1991.
80. Tanzi RE et al: The genetic defect in familial Alzheimer's disease is not tightly linked to the amyloid B-protein gene. *Nature* 329:156, 1987.
81. Van Broeckhoven C et al: Failure of familial Alzheimer's disease to segregate with the A-4 amyloid gene in several European families. *Nature* 329:153, 1987.
82. Kumar A et al: Anatomic, metabolic, neuropsychological, and molecular genetic studies of three pairs of identical twins discordant for dementia of the Alzheimer's type. *Arch Neurol* 48:160, 1991.
83. Cook RH et al: Twins with Alzheimer's disease. *Arch Neurol* 38:300, 1981.
84. St George-Hyslop PH et al: Familial Alzheimer's disease: Progress and problems. *Neurobiol Aging* 10: 417, 1989.
85. Zhang M et al: The prevalence of dementia and Alzheimer's disease in Shanghai, China: Impact of age, gender and education. *Ann Neurol* 27:428, 1990.
86. Stern Y et al: Inverse relationship between education and parietotemporal perfusion deficit in Alzheimer's disease. *Ann Neurol* 32:371, 1992.
87. Beard CM et al: Lack of association between Alzheimer's disease and education, occupation, marital status, or living arrangement. *Neurology* 42:2063, 1992.
88. Khachaturian ZS: Diagnosis of Alzheimer's disease. *Arch Neurol* 42:1097, 1985.
89. Mira SS et al: The consortium to establish a registry for Alzheimer's disease: II. Standardization of the neuropathological assessment of Alzheimer's disease. *Neurology* 41:479, 1991.
90. Masters CL et al: Amyloid plaque core protein in Alzheimer disease and Down syndrome. *Proc Natl Acad Sci USA* 82:4245, 1985.
91. Tomlinson BE: Ageing and the dementias, in Adams JH et al (eds): *Greenfields Neuropathology*. New York, Oxford University Press, 1992, p 1289.
92. Yamaguchi H et al: Diffuse type of senile plaques in the brains of Alzheimer-type dementia. *Acta Neuropathol* 77:113, 1988.
93. Perry EK et al: Correlation of cholinergic abnormalities with senile plaques and mental test scores in senile dementia. *Br Med J* 2:1457, 1978.
94. Selkoe DJ: Molecular pathology of amyloidogenic proteins and the role of vascular amyloidosis in Alzheimer's disease. *Neurobiol Aging* 10:387, 1989.
95. Masters CL et al: Neuronal origin of a cerebral amyloid: Neurofibrillary tangles of Alzheimer's disease contain the same protein as the amyloid of plaque cores and blood vessels. *EMBO J* 4:2757, 1985.
96. Ponte P et al: A new A4 amyloid mRNA contains a domain homologous to serine proteinase inhibitors. *Nature* 331:528, 1988.

97. Tanzi RE et al: Protease inhibitor domain encoded by an amyloid protein precursor mRNA associated with Alzheimer's disease. *Nature* 331:528, 1988.
98. Kang J, Muller-Hill B: Differential splicing of Alzheimer's disease amyloid A4 precursor RNA in rat tissues: PreA4 695 mRNA is predominantly produced in rat and human brain. *Biochem Biophys Res Commun* 166:1192, 1990.
99. Kitaguchi N et al: Novel precursor of amyloid protein shows protease inhibitor activity. *Nature* 311:530, 1988.
100. Coria F et al: Distribution of Alzheimer's disease amyloid protein precursor in normal human and rat nervous system. *Neuropathol Appl Neurobiol* 18:27, 1992.
101. Tanzi R et al: Amyloid B protein gene: cDNA, mRNA distribution and genetic linkage near the Alzheimer locus. *Science* 235:880, 1987.
102. Koo EH et al: Precursor of amyloid protein in Alzheimer disease undergoes fast anterograde axonal transport. *Proc Natl Acad Sci USA* 87:1561, 1990.
103. Schubert D. The possible role of adhesion in synaptic modification. *Trends Neurosci* 14:127, 1991.
104. Weideman A et al: Identification, biogenesis, and localization of precursors of Alzheimer's disease A4 amyloid protein. *Cell* 57:115, 1989.
105. Sisodia SS et al: Evidence that β amyloid protein in Alzheimer's disease is not derived by normal processing. *Science* 248:492, 1990.
106. Benowitz LI et al: The amyloid precursor protein is concentrated in neuronal lysosomes in normal and Alzheimer disease subjects. *Expl Neurol* 106:237, 1989.
107. Haas C et al: Targeting of cell-surface β-amyloid precursor protein to lysosomes: Alternative processing into amyloid-bearing fragments. *Nature* 357:500, 1992.
108. Estus S et al: Potentially amyloidogenic, carboxyl-terminal derivatives of the amyloid protein precursor. *Science* 255:726, 1992.
109. Tamaoka A et al: Identification of a stable fragment of the Alzheimer amyloid precursor containing the β-protein in brain microvessels. *Proc Natl Acad Sci USA* 89:1345, 1992.
110. Shoji M et al: Production of the Alzheimer amyloid β-protein by normal proteolytic processing. *Science* 258:126, 1992.
111. Haas C et al: Amyloid β-peptide is produced by cultured cells during normal metabolism. *Nature* 359:322, 1992.
112. Citron M et al: Mutation of the β-amyloid precursor protein in familial Alzheimer's disease increases β-protein production. *Nature* 360:672, 1992.
113. Cork LC et al: Phosphorylated neurofilament antigens to neurofibrillary tangles in Alzheimer's disease. *J Neuropathol Exp Neurol* 45:56, 1986.
114. Kosik KS et al: Microtubule-associated protein tau is a major antigenic component of paired helical filaments in Alzheimer's disease. *Proc Natl Acad Sci USA* 83:4044, 1986.
115. Dammerman M et al: Isolation and characterization of cDNA clones encoding epitopes shared with Alzheimer neurofibrillary tangles. *J Neurosci Res* 19:43, 1988.
116. Sternberger NH et al: Aberrant neurofilament phosphorylation in Alzheimer's disease. *Proc Natl Acad Sci USA* 82:4274, 1985.
117. Emory CR et al: Gangioside monoclonal antibody (A2B5) labels Alzheimer's neurofibrillary tangles. *Neurology* 37:768, 1987.
118. Yankner BA, Mesulam M-M: β-amyloid and the pathogenesis of Alzheimer's disease. *N Engl J Med* 325:1849, 1991.
119. Masters CL et al: Tau protein. *Eur Mol Biol Org* 4:2757, 1987.
120. Goedert M et al: Cloning and sequencing of the cDNA encoding a core protein of the paired helical filament of Alzheimer's disease: Identification as the microtubule-associated protein, tau. *Proc Natl Acad Sci USA* 85:4051, 1988.
121. Masliah E et al: Three-dimensional analysis of the relationship between synaptic pathology and neuropil threads in Alzheimer's disease. *J Neuropath Exp Neurol* 51:404, 1992.
122. Wong CW et al: Neuritic plaques and cerebrovascular amyloid in Alzheimer's disease are antigenically related. *Proc Natl Acad Sci USA* 82:8729, 1985.
123. Whitehouse PJ et al: Alzheimer's disease and senile dementia: Loss of neurons in the basal forebrain. *Science* 215:12379, 1982.
124. Whitehouse PJ et al: Alzheimer's disease: Evidence for selective loss of cholinergic neurons in the nucleus basalis. *Ann Neurol* 10:122, 1981.
125. Marcyniuk B et al: Loss of cells from locus ceruleus in Alzheimer's disease is topographically arranged. *Neurosci Lett* 64:247, 1986.
126. Mann DMA et al: Dopaminergic neurotransmitter systems in Alzheimer's disease and in Down's syndrome at middle age. *J Neurol Neurosurg Psychiatry* 50:341, 1987.
127. Mann DMA et al: Alzheimer's presenile dementia, senile dementia of Alzheimer type and Down's syndrome in middle age form an age-related continuum of pathological changes. *Neuropathol Appl Neurobiol* 10:185, 1984.
128. Carcio CA Kemper T: Nucleus raphe dorsalis in dementia of the Alzheimer type: Neurofibrillary changes and neuronal packing density. *J Neuropathol Exp Neurol* 43:359, 1984.
129. Terry RD et al: Physical basis of cognitive alterations in Alzheimer's disease: Synaptic loss is the major correlate of cognitive impairment. *Ann Neurol* 30:572, 1991.
130. Yankner BA et al: Neurotoxicity of a fragment of the amyloid precursor associated with Alzheimer's disease. *Science* 245:417, 1989.
131. Yankner BA et al: Neurotrophic and neurotoxic effects of amyloid β protein: Reversal by tachykinin neuropeptides. *Science* 250:279, 1990.
132. Yankner BA et al: Nerve growth factor potentiates the neurotoxicity of β-amyloid. *Proc Natl Acad Sci USA* 87:9020, 1990.
133. Price DL et al: Cellular pathology in Alzheimer's and Parkinson's disease. *Trends Neurosci* 29, 1986.
134. Whitehouse P et al: Basal forebrain neurons in the dementia of Parkinson's disease. *Ann Neurol* 13:243, 1983.
135. Ruberg M et al: Muscarinic binding and choline ace-

tyltransferase activity in Parkinsonism subjects with reference to dementia. *Brain Res* 232:129, 1982.

136. Bartus RT et al: The cholinergic hypothesis of geriatric memory dysfunction. *Science* 217:408, 1982.
137. Price DL et al: Alzheimer's disease. *Annu Rev Med* 36:349, 1985.
138. Francis PT et al: Neurochemical studies of early-onset Alzheimer's disease. *N Engl J Med* 313:7, 1985.
139. Davies P et al: Reduced somatostatin-like immunoreactivity in cerebral cortex from cases of Alzheimer's disease and Alzheimer senile dementia. *Nature* 288:279, 1980.
140. Davies P, Terry RD: Cortical somatostatin-like immunoreactivity in cases of Alzheimer's disease and senile dementia of the Alzheimer type. *Neurobiol Aging* 2:9, 1981.
141. Rossor MN et al: Reduced amounts of immunoreactive somatostatin in the temporal cortex in senile dementia of Alzheimer type. *Neurosci Lett* 20:373, 1980.
142. Taminga CA et al: Reduced brain somatostatin levels in Alzheimer's disease. *N Engl J Med* 313:1294, 1985.
143. Bissette G et al: Corticotropin-releasing factor-like immunoreactivity in senile dementia of the Alzheimer type. *JAMA* 254:3067, 1985.
144. De Sousa EB et al: Reciprocal changes in corticotropin-releasing factor (CRF)-like immunoreactivity and CRF receptors in cerebral cortex of Alzheimer's disease. *Nature* 319:593, 1986.
145. Rossor MN et al: Arginine vasopressin and choline acetyltransferase in brains of patients with Alzheimer type senile dementia. *Lancet* 2:1367, 1980.
146. Beal MF et al: Neuropeptide Y immunoreactivity is reduced in cerebral cortex in Alzheimer's disease. *Ann Neurol* 20:489, 1986.
147. Crystal HA, Davies P: Cortical substance P-like immunoreactivity in cases of Alzheimer's disease and senile dementia of the Alzheimer type. *J Neurochem* 38:1782, 1982.
148. Beal MF, Martin JB: Neuropeptides in neurological disease. *Ann Neurol* 20:547, 1986.
149. Chu DCM et al: Cortical $GABA_B$ and $GABA_A$ receptors in Alzheimer's disease: A quantitative autoradiographic study. *Neurology* 37:1454, 1987.
150. Sasaki H et al: Regional distribution of amino acid transmitters in postmortem brains of presenile dementia of the Alzheimer-type dementia. *Ann Neurol* 19:263, 1986.
151. Greenamyre JT et al: Alterations in L-glutamate binding in Alzheimer's and Huntington's diseases. *Science* 227:1496, 1985.
152. Whitehouse PJ et al: Nicotinic acetylcholine binding sites in Alzheimer's disease. *Brain Res* 371:146, 1986.
153. Nordberg A et al: Reduced number of [^{3}H]nicotine and [^{3}H]acetylcholine binding sites in frontal cortex of Alzheimer brains. *Neurosci Lett* 72:15, 1986.
154. Shimohama S et al: Changes in nicotinic and muscarinic cholinergic receptors in Alzheimer-type dementia. *J Neurochem* 46:28, 1986.
155. D'Amato RJ et al: Aminergic systems in Alzheimer's disease and Parkinson's disease. *Ann Neurol* 22:229, 1987.
156. Drachman DA, Leavitt J: Human memory and the cholinergic system: A relationship to aging? *Arch Neurol* 30:113, 1974.
157. Cohen EL, Wurtman RJ: Brain acetylcholine: Control by dietary choline. *Science* 191:561, 1976.
158. Wurtman RJ et al: Lecithin consumption raises serum-free-choline levels. *Lancet* 2:68, 1977.
159. Canter NL et al: Lecithin does not affect EEG spectral analysis or P300 in Alzheimer's disease. *Neurology* 32:1260, 1982.
160. Smith RC et al: Comparison of therapeutic response to long-term treatment with lecithin versus piracetam plus lecithin in patients with Alzheimer's disease. *Psychoparmacol Bull* 20:542, 1984.
161. Davous P, Lamour Y: Bethenechol decreases reaction time in senile dementia of the Alzheimer type. *J Neurol Neurosurg Psychiatry* 48:1297, 1985.
162. Harbaugh RE et al: Preliminary report: Intracranial cholinergic drug infusion in patients with Alzheimer's disease. *Neurosurgery* 15:514, 1984.
163. Penn RD et al: Intraventricular bethanechol infusion for Alzheimer's disease: Results of double-blind and escalating-dose trials. *Neurology* 38:219, 1988.
164. Harrell LE et al: The effect of long-term physostigmine administration in Alzheimer's disease. *Neurology* 40:1350, 1990.
165. Thal LJ et al: Oral physostigmine and lecithin improve memory in Alzheimer's disease. *Ann Neurol* 13:491, 1983.
166. Mohs RC et al: Oral physostigmine treatment of patients with Alzheimer's disease. *Am J Psychiatry* 142:28, 1985.
167. Peters BH, Levin HS: Memory enhancement after physostigmine treatment in the amnestic syndrome. *Arch Neurol* 34:215, 1977.
168. Davis KL, Mohs RC: Enhancement of memory processes in Alzheimer's disease with multiple-dose intravenous physostigmine. *Am J Psychiatry* 139:1421, 1982.
169. Beller SA et al: Efficacy of oral physostigmine in primary degenerative dementia. *Psychopharmacology* 87:147, 1985.
170. Caltagirone C et al: Oral administration of chronic physostigmine does not improve cognitive or amnestic performances in Alzheimer's presenile dementia. *Int J Neurosci* 16:247, 1982.
171. Stern Y et al: Effects of oral physostigmine in Alzheimer's disease. *Ann Neurol* 22:306, 1987.
172. Summers WK et al: Oral tetrahydroaminoacridine in long-term treatment of senile dementia Alzheimer's disease. *N Engl J Med* 315:1241, 1986.,
173. Summers WK et al: Use of THA in the treatment of Alzheimer-like dementia: Pilot study in twelve patients. *Biol Psychol* 16:145, 1981.
174. Davis KL et al: A double-blind, placebo-controlled multicenter study of tacrine for Alzheimer's disease. *N Eng J Med* 327:1253, 1992.
175. Claus JJ et al: Nootropic drugs in Alzheimer's disease: Symptomatic treatment with pramiracetam. *Neurology* 41:570, 1991.
176. Wolters EC et al: DGAVP (Org 5667) in early Alzheimer's disease patients: An international double-blind placebo-controlled, multicenter trial. *Neurology* 40:1099, 1990.
177. Sano M et al: Double-blind pilot study of acetyl

levocarnitine in patients with Alzheimer's disease. *Arch Neurol* 49:1137, 1992.
178. Hefti F et al: Function of neurotrophic factors in the adult and aging brain and their possible use in the treatment of neurodegenerative diseases. *Neurobiol. Aging* 10:515, 1989.
179. Koliatsos VE et al: Human nerve growth factor prevents degeneration of basal forebrain cholinergic neurons in primates. *Ann Neurol* 30:831, 1991.
180. Olson L et al: Nerve growth factor affects 11C-nicotine binding, blood flow, EEG, and verbal episodic memory in an Alzheimer patient (case report). *J Neural Transm Park Dis Dement Sect* 4(1):79, 1992.
181. Kordower JH, Mufson EJ: NGF and Alzheimer's disease: Unfulfilled promise and untapped potential. *Neurobiol Aging* 10:543, 1989.
182. The Parkinson Study Group. Effect of deprenyl on the progression of disability in early Parkinson's disease. *N Engl J Med* 321: 1364, 1989.
183. Schneider LS et al: A metaanalysis of controlled trials of neuroleptic treatment in dementia. *J Am Geriatr Soc* 38:553, 1992.
184. Devanand DP et al: A pilot study of haloperidol treatment of psychosis and behavioral disturbance in Alzheimer's disease. *Arch Neurol* 46:854, 1989.
185. Risse SC, Barnes R: Pharmacologic treatment of agitation associated with dementia. *J Am Geriatr Soc* 34:368, 1986.
186. Gilleard CJ et al: Patterns of neuroleptic use among the institutionalized elderly. *Acta Psychiatr Scand* 68:419, 1983.
187. Prien Y et al: The use of psychoactive drugs in elderly patients with psychiatric disorders: Survey conducted in twelve Veterans Administration hospitals. *J Am Geriatr Soc* 23:104, 1975.
188. Helms PM: Efficacy of antipsychotics in the treatment of the behavioral complications of dementia. *J Am Geriatr Soc* 33:206, 1985.
189. Burgio LD et al: A behavioral microanalysis of the effects of haloperidol and oxazepam in demented psychogeriatric inpatients. *Int J Geriatr Psychiatry* 7:253, 1992.

Chapter 93

PARKINSON'S DISEASE AND RELATED DISORDERS

Fletcher H. McDowell

Although the disorder was not formally given its eponym until 1817, when James Parkinson described six individuals with shaking palsy, the condition existed long before his observation. In writings from Egyptian, Greek, Medieval, and Renaissance physicians, references are found which suggest that shaking palsy, or paralysis agitans, was a known disorder before Parkinson wrote his now-famous essay.[1] His description of "involuntary, tremulous motion with lessened muscular power in parts not in action and even when supported with the propensity to bend the trunk forward and to pass from a walking to a running pace, the senses and intellect being uninjured," still serves as a fairly adequate description of the condition.[2] Parkinson did not observe the existence of rigidity or the commonly encountered postural instability or the almost inevitable loss of intellect that are now clearly part of the disorder.

Parkinson's disease is characterized by fairly obvious clinical phenomena and is essentially a diagnosis based on visual observation. The most obvious symptoms of Parkinson's disease are a rapid rhythmic tremor at rest; a decrease in automatic reflex movement with slowing of voluntary movement, resulting in changes in facial expression; reduced or absent arm swing when walking and moving, which causes difficulty walking; and impaired postural reflexes with imbalance and falling.

CLASSIFICATION

Many of these symptoms and signs are encountered in combination with other conditions, which often causes some confusion in clinical diagnosis when a patient develops some of the signs and symptoms of Parkinson's disease along with evidence of other disturbances in nervous system and body function. Such conditions are generally referred to as *parkinsonian syndromes*. The classic description of Parkinson's disease is now reserved for idiopathic Parkinson's disease.

Table 93-1 gives a classification of parkinsonism dividing the condition into primary and secondary diagnoses. The most common among the primary category is idiopathic Parkinson's disease. The others consist of a variety of syndromes with parkinsonian symptoms which have been described in the past three or four decades. These conditions include some manifestations of parkinsonism but have other phenomena which indicate pathologic lesions in several areas of the brain. They are generally referred to as Parkinson-plus syndromes. Included in this group are progressive supranuclear palsy, the Shy-Drager syndrome, olivopontocerebellar degeneration, and a group of geographically localized disorders, such as the Guamanian Parkinson–amyotrophic lateral sclerosis (ALS)–dementia complex, and the Azorean motor system degeneration.

Parkinsonian symptoms can be found in a variety of other conditions and are generally classified under secondary parkinsonism. These can have metabolic,

TABLE 93-1

Parkinson's Disease Classification

Primary (parkinsonian symptoms present initially)

1. Idiopathic Parkinson's disease
2. Progressive supranuclear palsy
3. Olivopontocerebellar degeneration
4. Shy-Drager syndrome
5. Striatonigral degeneration
6. Parkinson–amyotrophic lateral sclerosis–dementia complex of Guam
7. Azorean motor system degeneration

Secondary (parkinsonian symptoms may be present during course of illness)

1. Metabolic: Wilson's disease, Hallervorden-Spatz syndrome, Fahr's syndrome
2. Infectious: postencephalitic Parkinson's disease
3. Toxic: carbon monoxide poisoning; cerebral anoxia; manganese poisoning; meperidine analogue poisoning; reserpine, phenothiazine, and butyrophenone intoxication
4. Vascular: arteriosclerotic parkinsonism

infectious, or toxic causes. Under these headings are included Wilson's disease, Hallervorden-Spatz disease, postencephalitic Parkinson's disease, carbon monoxide poisoning, manganese poisoning, meperidine analogue *n*-methyl-4-phenyl-1,2,3,6-tetrahydropyridine (MPTP) poisoning,[3] toxic reactions to medications such as reserpine and phenothiazines, and, rarely, arteriosclerotic vascular disease and brain tumor.

When the clinical diagnosis of Parkinson's disease is checked with findings at autopsy, the clinical diagnosis is found to be inaccurate over 25 percent of the time.[3] The standard for a pathologic diagnosis of Parkinson's disease at autopsy is loss of cells in the substantia nigra with Lewy bodies in those cells remaining. The most common causes of error in the clinical diagnosis of idiopathic Parkinson's disease are progressive supranuclear palsy and strionigral degeneration. Idiopathic Parkinson's disease can be diagnosed with confidence when there is evidence either from the history of symptoms or findings on examination of tremor, usually unilateral; bradykinesia with micrographia; slow performance of daily activities; impaired balance; muscle rigidity on examination; and a positive response to treatment with levodopa[3] (Table 93-2).

The most common diagnostic error clinically is confusion of essential tremor or drug-induced parkinsonism with idiopathic Parkinson's disease. Repeated examination may be required over several months to be certain that the clinical diagnosis is correct.

EPIDEMIOLOGY

After stroke and Alzheimer's disease, Parkinson's disease is the most commonly encountered neurological disorder in the elderly population. The incidence of Parkinson's disease is extremely difficult to determine, as the diagnosis is often not made until the symptoms are quite obvious. Unless very careful studies are done on a specific population with a careful neurological evaluation, incidence figures are generally inadequate. One study of incidence has been done in Rochester, Minnesota, and found a rate of 20 new cases per 100,000 population per year. Prevalence studies have been more common and are probably more accurate. An early study from New Zealand found 90 to 100 individuals with Parkinson's disease per 100,000 population in New Zealand.[4] Prevalence in Rochester, Minnesota, is reported to be 157 per 100,000 population. Careful house-to-house ascertainment of prevalence in other studies has yielded slightly higher figures of 347 per 100,000 population in individuals age 40 and older.[6] Using this data it is possible to calculate the prevalence and number of new cases occurring each year in the United States. Assuming the current population statistics, there would be somewhere between 600,000 and 650,000 persons with Parkinson's disease in the United States, with approximately 40,000 new cases occurring every year.

Parkinson's disease has been encountered in all countries where adequate statistics have been gathered about disease. The disorder is slightly more prevalent in males than in females. There have been no apparent differences in ethnic or socioeconomic status related to its occurrence. It is relatively common to encounter patients who give a family history of a relative who was believed to have Parkinson's disease. Generally, it is accepted that somewhere between 5 and 10 percent of the patients with Parkinson's disease report that they have a relative with a disorder suggestive of the condition. This is often very difficult to determine with certainty, as a number of other causes of tremor exist, and generally the most obvious thing patients remember about a relative who may have had Parkinson's disease is the existence of tremor.

In the initial studies of identical twins there was little clinical evidence of a high level of concordance in developing Parkinson's disease in the twin of a patient with Parkinson's disease. Subsequent follow-up studies have shown more concordance, and position emission tomography (PET) studies have shown decreased uptake of [^{18}F]dopa in the putamen of unaffected monozygotic twins.[7] This suggests that genetic factors are more of an element in the etiology of the condition than previously suspected.

Parkinson's disease most commonly begins in the age period 50 to 69, when about two-thirds of the patients first note onset of symptoms, with a mean age of onset of 55 to 60. Twenty-five percent note onset of symptoms between age 30 and 50, and about 10 percent after age 70.[8] Onset in adolescence and young adulthood occurs, but onset in this age period should always prompt investigation for other disorders with parkinsonian symptoms.

TABLE 93-2

Diagnosis of Idiopathic Parkinson's Disease Symptoms and Signs Which Make Diagnosis Highly Accurate

1. Unilateral onset of tremor and bradykinesia
2. Slowed performance of daily activities
3. Impaired balance
4. Muscle rigidity on examination
5. Relief of symptoms by levodopa

PATHOLOGY

The most consistent gross anatomical change found in the brains of patients with Parkinson's disease has been depigmentation of the substantia nigra. When this area is examined microscopically, there is also a major loss of neurons, most obvious in the compact zone or lateral portion of the substantia nigra. In addition, loss of other neurons has been observed in the locus ceruleus, the dorsal vagus nucleus, and the basal nucleus of Mynert.

Microscopic examination reveals considerable loss of the large pigmented cells in the substantia nigra. Those substantia nigra neurons which remain may have inclusion bodies which stain with eosin and were originally described by Lewy. These inclusion bodies are most commonly found in the substantia nigra of individuals with idiopathic Parkinson's disease, but they can be found in other cells in the brain and have been observed in the brains of individuals without Parkinson's disease. Decline in the number of neurons in the substantia nigra in normal persons and in patients with Parkinson's disease is a life-long process. The number of cells declines with increasing age, with the greatest decrement occurring during adolescence.

It is generally believed that symptoms of Parkinson's disease begin when the number of neurons in the zona compacta of the substantia nigra is reduced by 70 to 80 percent. Usually other areas of the brain are intact, but some patients have diffuse cortical atrophy. When the cerebral hemispheres are examined, the cell changes are similar to those seen in Alzheimer's disease. Senile plaques and neurofibrillary tangles have been consistently observed in the brains of patients who died with Parkinson's disease.[9]

BIOCHEMICAL PATHOLOGY

New insights into the pathology of Parkinson's disease came about with the demonstration that dopamine is a neurotransmitter, and that this substance is greatly decreased in the brains of patients with Parkinson's disease. It was later demonstrated that the cells in the compact zone of the substantia nigra are a main source of dopamine production. Those parts of the basal ganglia which receive nigral input, such as the caudate nucleus, putamen, and globus pallidus, have considerable decreases in dopamine concentrations, especially the putamen and the caudate nucleus.

Postmortem examinations of brains of patients with Parkinson's disease have demonstrated that the substantia nigra contains only 15 percent of the expected levels of dopamine, the putamen 5 percent, and the caudate nucleus 13 percent. Noradrenaline and serotonin levels have been found to be decreased in the same areas. The metabolic pathway in the production of dopamine requires the conversion of tyrosine to levodopa by tyrosine hydroxylase and the conversion of levodopa to dopamine by dopa decarboxylase. In neurons dopamine is metabolized to noradrenaline by dopamine β-hydroxylase or to methylated metabolites by monoamine oxidase or catecholamine methyltransferase. The main metabolite of dopamine, homovanillic acid, has also been found to be decreased in the brain and spinal fluid of patients with Parkinson's disease. The enzymes necessary for the metabolic conversion of tyrosine to dopa and of dopa to dopamine—tyrosine hydroxylase and dopa decarboxylase—are reduced in brains of patients who have died with Parkinson's disease.

These observations led to more definitive therapy for Parkinson's disease with increased production of dopamine in the brain following a marked increase in substrate availability of dopa, when dopa is given orally.

In patients with Parkinson's disease there is also a decrease in dopamine and tyrosine hydroxylase activity in the ventral tegmental and cortical limbic systems. Reduced quantities of dopamine have been demonstrated in the hypothalamic dopaminergic system but not in other dopaminergic systems.

Agid et al. have described the course of events which help explain the development of the various stages of Parkinson's disease.[10] The number of dopamine-producing neurons and the amount of dopamine deficiency varies considerably from patient to patient as the disease begins and nigral cells die. The remaining dopaminergic neurons are capable of increased dopamine turnover and have the ability to maintain adequate dopaminergic activity in the striatum despite the continued loss of cells. This occurs when degeneration of dopaminergic cells in the substantia is not marked, probably by less than 70 percent.

With further cellular degeneration in the substantia nigra zona compacta, dopamine levels fall to 20 percent of normal or less. Then there is insufficient maintenance of dopaminergic transmission and the symptoms of Parkinson's disease begin. It is in this stage of the disease that replacement therapy with levodopa is most effective. When there is more than a 90 percent decrease in neurons in the dopaminergic system, increased cellular production of dopamine is no longer able to compensate. In this phase the symptoms of Parkinson's disease are most marked and patients who are getting supplemental therapy with levodopa begin to show major fluctuations in response to treatment.

Studies of function at the dopaminergic synapse have shown that it is possible by manipulation to alter activity at this synapse. This is usually done by either increasing availability of the precursor substance, levodopa, by direct stimulation of the receptors by dopamine agonists, or by decreasing dopamine metabolic enzyme activity. Development of dopamine agonists which bypass the metabolic process necessary for dopamine production and stimulate the postsynaptic neuron receptor directly has been a major pharmacologic advance. Agents have been found to increase dopaminergic activity by blocking dopamine β-hydroxylase activity, which reduces the degradation of dopamine in the synaptic cleft. All these methods have been used in the treatment of patients with Parkinson's disease.

Investigation has found that there is more than one dopamine receptor. The two best characterized are D_1 and D_2. D_1 receptors are linked to an adenylate cyclase system which is sensitive to stimulation by dopamine. D_2 receptors do not have an adenylate cyclase system but have a high binding affinity for neuroleptic drugs and are the site of action of the newly developed dopaminergic drugs. These terminals may exist in more than one form, so it is possible there may actually be four dopamine receptors.

The importance of recognizing the dopamine receptor systems has been the development of agents which act directly at these sites, bypassing the metabolic pathways required to produce dopamine. Identification of the receptors and the development of specific agents for their stimulation has improved Parkinson's disease pharmacologic therapy.

CLINICAL FEATURES AND CLINICAL COURSE[1,9]

It is often extremely difficult for patients to recall when symptoms of Parkinson's disease began and which were the first ones to be noticed. Initially patients may report discomfort in the back, neck, and limbs with sensations of muscle tightness and stiffness. These are nonspecific symptoms, and it is not until tremor begins or bradykinesia becomes obvious that the patient realizes that something is wrong. Patients who develop Parkinson's disease usually report excellent health before symptoms begin.

Tremor, being the most obvious symptom, is usually reported first and begins unilaterally, usually in the upper extremity. Although tremor is the most obvious symptom in Parkinson's disease, it does not occur in up to 30 percent of patients who have classic disease. Tremor is characteristically rapid and rhythmic at a rate of 4 to 10 cycles per second. It is absent during sleep and is reduced by sedation. When questioned, patients report that tremor is not constant and that it is worse under some circumstances than others. When patients are upset, tense, or angry, tremor is more marked. When they are at rest and content, they may not have tremor. Being embarrassed by having tremor and having it noticed by others always makes it worse. Tremor tends to become more marked with time and may spread to other parts of the body and involve the lower extremities, face, jaw, and tongue. Patients report that they mainly have tremor when their arms are at rest and do not have it when carrying out a skilled act. Tremor can become so marked that it interferes with the performance of daily activities, but in general it is the most benign of the manifestations of Parkinson's disease.

Almost invariably when patients recall the onset of tremor, if questioned, they will report some difficulties with skilled movement and slowing in performance of daily activities. Slowing of motor function will cause changes in facial expression, resulting in a masklike face, and a decrease in associated movements of the hands and body when talking or sitting, resulting in a wooden look. Slowing of movement, or bradykinesia, causes a decrease in or an absence of the usual automatic movements that accompany walking with a noticeable decrease in arm swing and loss of postural reflexes needed for balance. Changes in gait are usually obvious and are noticed by the patient or family. Absence of or a decrease in the normal reciprocal arm swing when walking, or dragging a foot on one side, are noticed early in the course of the disease.

Further slowing of movement causes increasing difficulty with performing many daily activities. Patients report difficulty dressing, especially with buttons; difficulty using their knife and fork when cutting food; problems with bathing; and difficulty getting in and out of bed or chairs. Speech may be affected, with a decline in voice volume and the development of impaired articulation with a rapid, clipped form of speech.

If bradykinesia develops first on the dominant side, handwriting is affected, with a decline in the size of their script, or miocrographia. Writing becomes smaller and smaller as patients write, and often they become unable to write or to read what they themselves write. All skilled movements become less dextrous and more difficult to perform. These problems become worse with progression of the disorder, and patients may become unable to care for themselves and need help in performance of all daily activities.

Posture changes. Patients tend to be bent forward with flexion at the neck and trunk. This may later become so marked that patients can be markedly bent forward all the time and are unable to straighten up. Postural stability is affected. Patients report that they do not feel safe on their feet. They tend to get off balance and fall, especially when backing up, getting out of chairs, or changing direction while walking in tight spaces. Postural instability can easily be demonstrated at this time by pushing the patient, while the patient is standing, forward or backward and noting whether they are able to use automatic balancing reflexes to avoid getting off balance. In these situations their gait changes, and patients may be unable to take anything but small short steps (festination) and appear as if glued to the ground (freezing), or they may find themselves running forward (propulsive gait) or backward (retropulsion) until they fall or run into something which stops them. They may become unable to move and be unable to resume walking for several moments. Curiously, patients may report hesitating or freezing when crossing thresholds or when entering automatic elevators but have no trouble walking up or down stairs. As the usual postural reflexes decrease or become absent, postural instability becomes more marked and falling more frequent. Injuries and fractures are common. Postural instability can become the most disabling problem in the late stages of the disease. Postural instability is especially serious in female patients who have osteoporosis. Hip fracture is common in these patients.

Other reflex activities are affected. Patients tend to blink less, giving them a staring expression. Swallowing becomes less automatic, and saliva accumulates in the mouth. It tends to run forward to the lips because of head flexion and then drools from the corners of the mouth.

Patients often report that despite severe difficulty walking or performing daily activities, they may suddenly be relieved of all symptoms of Parkinson's disease and function normally for very brief periods. Such episodes are unpredictable. It is also generally observed that when patients with Parkinson's disease must function better, they somehow can rise to the occasion and do so, but such changes are rarely sustained for long periods.

Declining intellectual ability occurs in most patients with Parkinson's disease if they live long enough. In the Cornell Medical College study when patients were followed for 15 to 18 years after entering a levodopa treatment program, 80 percent were moderately or severely demented before they died.[11] A decline in intellect begins early after the onset of Parkinson's disease. In studies of early Parkinson's disease, patients performed generally less well on standard tests of intellect than did controls. A decline in intellectual ability usually begins with reports from the patient or family that the patient is not as quick intellectually and that recent memory is not as good. This is generally at first attributed to age, but it progresses. Patients' families report that the usual work of household responsibilities become difficult for the patient and that often the patient is asked to take early retirement if still working. Household tasks such as balancing checkbooks, paying bills, preparing income tax data, and planning social activities are taken over by the marital partner. These activities may become impossible for the patient to perform or are done slowly or inaccurately. Patients become less and less intellectualy active, sitting much of the day and sleeping too much. They rarely initiate conversation or activity. At this stage, hallucinations and delusions about spouse and money may occur. Hallucinations are almost always visual and generally nonthreatening for the patient. Patients may not report hallucinations unless specifically asked about them. When they occur, a review of medication intake should be made to be sure that drug intake is not at fault, as all antiparkinsonian medications and other drugs which have an action on the nervous system can cause or aggravate the problem. Even after all antiparkinsonian medication is reduced or stopped, hallucinations may continue. Psychological testing at this stage reveals abnormalities in new learning, recent memory, and vocabulary. Patients are often confused when awakened at night and in new environments become confused and anxious. Sleep-wake cycles are often reversed, causing considerable difficulty for the caregiver.

Patients with Parkinson's disease who show declining intellect are very sensitive to the effects of a general anesthetic. When surgery is necessary, local or spinal anesthesia should be used as a general anesthetic may increase confusion and cause serious delirium which may take several days to clear. Thereafter some patients are left with a considerable decline in intellectual function which may be permanent.

Changing the environment by vacations often increases confusion and disorientation and is best avoided unless the vacation home or hotel is very familiar.

The decline in intellectual capacity continues to become worse, and the patients may become unaware of their environment or of individuals in it. It is at this stage that a nursing home is seriously considered. The character of the behavior of the persons losing their intellect is heavily modified by previous behavior patterns. When intellectual decline becomes apparent, great care should taken to avoid use of any medication which has central nervous system effects, especially narcotic analgesics, tranquilizers, sedatives, and dopamine agonists. All these agents tend to increase confusion and may cause delirium.

A variety of other problems occur with the progression of Parkinson's disease. Constipation is common in patients, and treatments for the Parkinson's disease tend to make the constipation worse. Anticholinergic medications are especially likely to increase constipation, and unless they are clearly needed, they should be decreased or stopped when constipation becomes a problem. A bowel program should be established, with increased fluid intake (at least 2 quarts per day), increased fiber content in the diet, and a regular mild laxative. This should be started to be sure that the patient has a bowel movement at least every other day. Patients should not go longer than 2 to 3 days without a movement, to avoid fecal impaction. When mild laxatives are no longer effective, stronger ones should be used.

Patients who have had Parkinson's disease for several years—usually 5 to 10 years—often report urinary urgency and frequency. This may increase and become a problem because of incontinence. The concern of patients about the embarrassment of possible incontinence in social situations may prevent them from going out, which results in decreasing social and intellectual stimulation. Anticholinergic medications may reduce the sensation of urgency and give patients a sense of security that they will not become incontinent. As the disease progresses, incontinence, especially at night, can become frequent. This can be due to inability to get out of bed in time to urinate or unawareness of being incontinent during sleep. Incontinence becomes a serious problem for a caregiver and is often the cause of transfer to a nursing home. Incontinence in male patients should be evaluated carefully and prostatectomy avoided unless urethral obstruction is clearly demonstrated. Unnecessary prostate surgery often makes incontinence worse.

EXAMINATION[1,9]

Examination of patients with obvious or suspected Parkinson's disease begins by observing the patient walk, looking for absent or reduced arm swing on one or both sides and a hesitant or shuffling gait. While the patients are standing, they should be checked for postural instability by gently pushing them forward or backward and noting the presence or absence of postural reflexes. When these reflexes are absent or reduced, patients may take a few steps forward or backward before checking their balance or they may fall in either direction. While the patients are standing, posture is observed; patients may be bent forward at the neck, trunk, and legs. They should be asked to straighten up, which is usually possible, and the erect posture is maintained for a few minutes.

The range of ocular movements should be carefully checked. Parkinson's disease does not limit the range of eye movement but progressive supranuclear palsy does, and any impairment of upward or downward gaze should raise the possibility of this diagnosis.

Strength may be slightly reduced in the upper and lower extremities, but this is rarely marked. Passive movement of the arms and legs may reveal rigidity. If rigidity is intermittent (usually on the side of tremor), it may give a cogwheel sensation, i.e., "cogwheel rigidity." If there is no increased resistance to passive movement, this may be brought out by having the patient make a fist with the opposite hand, which may increase the resistance to passive movement on the tested side. Skilled hand movement is almost always impaired. This is tested by having the patient rapidly pronate and supinate the hands or rapidly move fingers as if typing or playing the piano. Slowed rapid movements are usually obvious on one or both sides. Slight intention tremor may be present, but if it is marked, the diagnosis of essential tremor should be considered. Tendon reflexes are usually normal but may be somewhat increased on the involved side. Some slowing of rapid foot movements are usual on the involved side or both sides. Resistance to passive movement may be found when the examiner passively flexes and extends the leg or internally and externally rotates the foot at the ankle. Tendon reflexes are usually normal, and plantar responses are flexor. Extensor plantar responses should prompt consideration of additional diagnoses. Sensory perception is not affected.

Findings on examination may be slight in early-onset disease but can be marked in the late stages when patients may be unable to walk, unable to stand without support, or unable to perform any of these tests. Changes in the physical examination parallel the report of increasing difficulty in function and in performance of daily activities.

The general physical examination is usually quite normal, but some patients may have a mild degree of orthostatic hypotension, which is usually not symptomatic.

Laboratory examination is generally not helpful. Imaging of the brain by CT scans or MRI is usually normal, but in the advanced stages of the disease, MRI or CT scan may show some evidence of cortical atrophy. If there is any question that the diagnosis of idiopathic Parkinson's disease is not correct, then brain imaging should be done to eliminate treatable disorders. Examination of the cerebrospinal fluid is rarely if ever indicated.

PROGNOSIS

There is usually evidence of progression of all the symptoms of Parkinson's disease, although the rate of progression is extremely variable. Patients may go for long periods without any apparent evidence of progression or may rapidly become worse. There is no accurate way to predict the rate of progression, but in general the rate of progression in the past predicts the rate in the future. Progession is inevitable, and eventually all manifestations of Parkinson's disease become worse. Those problems which cause the most impairment of the ability for patients to remain independent are increasing bradykinesia, fluctuation of response to treatment, postural instability, and declining intellect. In the period before levodopa became available for treatment, three-quarters of patients who survived 10 years were severely disabled. With current treatment this outlook has changed, and the observed:expected mortality ratio has dropped from 2.9 in the pre-dopa era to 1.5 at 5 years of treatment but rises to 1.9 after 16 years of treatment.[8]

DIFFERENTIAL DIAGNOSIS[1,9]

There are several conditions that are commonly confused with idiopathic Parkinson's disease. The most common one is essential tremor, which is more common than idiopathic Parkinson's disease.

Essential tremor has definite characteristics which include tremor with skilled activity and no tremor when at rest. The tremor is worse when patients are stressed or embarassed. There is usually a family history of similar tremor, and often reports that the tremor is reduced or abolished by alcohol. Essential tremor never occurs with slowness of movement, increased resistance to passive movement, or impaired balance. It most commonly involves the hands and head, and at times an individual's voice may have a tremulous quality. Testing handwriting or asking the patient to draw spirals often demonstrates the tremor by irregular lines, as does asking the patient to drink from a full glass of water, which commonly results in spilling. Essential tremor and Parkinson's disease may coexist, and patients with essential tremor may develop Parkinson's disease.

Progressive supranuclear palsy is often confused with Parkinson's disease because of the frequent onset with symptoms of bradykinesia, rigidity, and tremor. In the majority of cases there is an impaired range of eye movement for upward or downward gaze, which when present makes the diagnosis. Patients with supranuclear palsy respond minimally or not at all to levodopa, and the course of the disease progresses to increasing disability more rapidly.

Occasionally patients with *multiinfarct dementia* or *Alzheimer's disease* develop symptoms suggesting Parkinson's disease. These occur when dementia is already quite evident and rarely cause confusion in diagnosis. Patients with this combination of symptoms rarely have much response to levodopa. Patients with *striatonigral degeneration* and *olivopontocerebellar degeneration* have either additional evidence of corticospinal tract dysfunction or evidence of cerebellar dysfunction (see Chap. 94). If these signs are not present when patients are first examined, they may be found on follow-up examination and should be suspected when patients do not have a good response to levodopa.

When symptoms of Parkinson's disease occur with orthostatic hypotension, which at times is symptomatic, the differential diagnosis should include the *Shy-Drager syndrome* (see Chap. 94). In this condition, orthostatic hypotension can become increasingly severe and can be so marked that patients are unable to stand without syncope. Treatment to raise the blood pressure is rarely successful.

TREATMENT[1,9]

There is no known cure for Parkinson's disease. Treatment is directed toward relief of symptoms and recently to slow or stop progression. Treatment is not usually started until symptoms begin to interfere with the performance of daily activities or work. If there is no impairment of work or daily activities, patients should be encouraged to remain at work, continue to be active socially, physically, and intellectually, and return for examination if there is any increase in symptoms or impairment of function.

Table 93-3 lists the medications used in the treatment of Parkinson's disease. Some are used as initial treatment when symptoms are mild and others are used when symptoms interfere with daily activities.

Agents with an anticholinergic action have been used as treatment for Parkinson's disease since belladonna was found to have symptom-depressing effects in the nineteenth century. The mechanism of action is believed to be correction of relative cholinergic overaction as the inhibitory action of dopamine declines. None of these agents have been conspicuously effective as treatment, and symptomatic improvement of about 20 percent is usually reported. Side effects are common, including dry mouth, constipation, urinary retention, and blurred vision. These agents are often used as initial treatment to reduce tremor and bradykinesia. With disease progression, their effect becomes less evident. When patients have been taking anticholinergic medications for long periods, the indications should not be abruptly stopped, as this may cause marked worsening of the symptoms of the disease. The medications are often responsible for impairment of thinking, and when mentation problems arise in patients taking the medications, they should be gradually stopped and the patient observed for improved mentation.

It is now common to begin treatment with either amantadine or selegiline. Amantadine is moderately effective in reducing tremor and alleviating rigidity and bradykinesia. Its beneficial effects can wear off, and a brief vacation from the medication may restore a good response. Side effects are usually not a prob-

TABLE 93-3

Medications Commonly Used in Treating Parkinson's Disease

Drug	Dose per Day, mg
1. Drugs with anticholinergic effects	
a. Trihexyphenidyl (Artane)	2–20
b. Procyclidine (Kemadrin)	5–40
c. Benztropine (Cogentin)	0.5–7
d. Biperiden (Akineton)	2–6
2. Drugs with antihistamine action	
a. Diphenhydramine (Benadryl)	50–150
b. Orphenadrine (Norflex)	100–200
3. Drugs as dopamine precursors	
a. Levodopa (dihydroxyphenylalanine)	2000–4000
b. Levodopa with carbidopa, a dopa decarboxylase inhibitor (Sinemet)	75/300–250/2500
4. Dopamine agonists	
a. Bromocriptine (Parlodel)	2.5–100
b. Pergolide (Permax)	0.05–7
c. Apomorphine (subcutaneous)	2–7
5. Antidepressants	
a. Amitriptyline (Elavil)	25–150
b. Imipramine (Tofranil)	25–150
6. Inhibitors of monoamine oxidase B	
a. Selegiline (Eldepryl, Deprenyl)	5–10
7. Drugs with unknown mechanism of action	
a. Amantadine (Symmetrel)	100–200

lem, but some patients develop discoloration of the skin of the legs (lividoreticularis) or ankle edema. A rare patient may complain of nervousness and insomnia. The action of the medication is not known, but it has some anticholinergic effects and may enhance the effect of levodopa. Its main use has been as an antiviral agent.

Selegiline blocks the conversion of dopamine to noradrenaline in nerve cells by inhibiting monoamine oxidase B. This inhibitor does not increase blood pressure, as do the A forms of monoamine oxidase inhibitors, which are used in the treatment of depression. Selegiline has been used for several years to potentiate the effects of levodopa and to reduce or eliminate the fluctuating response that frequently occurs after long-term treatment with levodopa. Its effect on this problem has not been remarkable, but it has been helpful in some patients.

When it was shown that pretreatment of an experimental animal with this monoamine oxidase inhibitor could prevent the development of Parkinson's disease caused by the meperidine analogue MPTP, the question arose as to whether it could prevent the occurrence or progression of Parkinson's disease. Treatment trials were started and showed that for patients with newly diagnosed Parkinson's disease, not yet treated with levodopa, the use of levodopa or Sinemet was delayed by 6 months to 1 years. This was not observed in controls, and the study concluded that selegiline could slow or prevent progression.[12] It is now used extensively for that purpose, but for the individual patient it is impossible to ensure that progression will not occur. Selegiline has some mild antiparkinsonian effects, probably because of its effect in inhibiting the metabolic conversion of dopamine, which results in retaining dopamine in the synaptic cleft longer. It is also used to enhance the effect of levodopa and carbidopa (Sinemet).

Shortly after it was found that levodopa can reverse the effects of reserpine, which produces a parkinsonian state in rats, and that dopamine lack is the cause of the state, experiments began with humans who had Parkinson's disease. Early trials were not impressive, and it was not until 1969 when Cotzias et al. reported that a high intake of levodopa can relieve many if not all the symptoms of Parkinson's disease that it was clear that an important advance in treatment had been made.[13] Treatment programs with levodopa required a slow increase in the intake of levodopa over many weeks from a few milligrams per day to an average of 4000 mg, which produced remarkable improvement, with one-half to three-quarters of patients being relieved of most if not all evidence of Parkinson's disease.[14] This program of treatment was difficult because of the nausea and vomiting caused by high blood levels of dopamine, which were the result of the rapid metabolism of dopa to dopamine in peripheral blood, because of the large amount of dopa decarboxylase in the body. High blood levels of dopamine stimulate the vomiting center in the brainstem, which is outside the blood-brain barrier. Patients eventually became adapted to high dopamine blood levels, but some were unable to take enough levodopa to give relief of symptoms. The introduction of an inhibitor of dopa decarboxylase which did not cross the blood-brain barrier made a major advance in treatment. Because of this, a much lower dose of levodopa could be given, which avoided most of the side effects of nausea and vomiting, as dopamine blood levels never reached high enough levels to produce these symptoms. The combination of the decarboxylase inhibitor with levodopa has become the standard treatment for the disease. The combination of carbidopa and levodopa (Sinemet) is the most widely used treatment. Sinemet is usually prescribed when patients develop difficulty performing daily activities and have had a decline in response to amantadine or anticholinergic medication. Sinemet is available in three dose combinations with various amounts of carbidopa and levodopa. They are 10/100, 25/100, and 25/250; the first figure indicates the amount of carbidopa and the second the amount of levodopa. Sinemet is started usually with 25/100 tablets given one to three times per day. The dose is gradually increased by raising the total daily dose one tablet every 3 to 4 days. Patients who develop some nausea may be managed by starting with lower doses, such as one-half tablet once or twice a day and gradually increasing the dose. At each dose increase, patients are asked to note whether they have noticed improvement or not. The dose is increased until there is no further evidence of improvement or until there are side effects which indicate that a maximum dose of medication has been reached. The side effect which provides this endpoint is the development of involuntary movements. The involuntary movements usually consist of facial grimacing, restless movements of the arms, head, neck, and legs. These may be slight at first and be noticed only by family or friends, as the patient may be unaware of their occurrence. Such movements can be asymptomatic at first, but later they may become uncomfortable and distressing. They can become so frequent that they add to the already present disability of Parkinson's disease. Involuntary movements can be painful, especially dystonic foot cramps, which are a frequent form of involuntary movements. Initially they are dose-related, and a decrease in the dose of Sinemet eliminates them.

Initially a patient's response to Sinemet is quite even throughout the day, and this pattern of response can continue for several years. Eventually patients begin to notice some wearing off of the effect of the medication at the end of the interval between doses, when some of their initial symptoms of Parkinson's disease return. The good effects are regained with the next dose, but the period of good effects may become shorter. Patients may notice that involuntary movements follow a dose of Sinemet in about 30 to 40 minutes and last for several minutes. When they stop, patients may report functioning normally. Some patients report involuntary movements occurring at the end of a dose period and relief by the next dose. Involuntary movements tend to appear with either a rising or a falling blood level of dopa. Fluctuations in response to treatment become marked in patients treated with dopa for long periods and can become as disabling as the more severe symptoms of Parkinson's disease. Wearing off of the beneficial effects of treatment and the occurrence of involuntary movements are almost an invariable part of the progression of dopa-treated disease.

Some patients report that they at times have an abrupt return of parkinsonian symptoms unrelated to their dose schedule, lasting for a few minutes to an hour, followed by an abrupt return of the drug's good effects on symptoms. This phenomenon has been called the *on-off* response and is believed to be due to receptor block and hypersensitivity at the dopamine synapse. These fluctuations in response to treatment, wearing off and on-off, become more and more difficult to manage with disease progression. A number of strategies to overcome fluctuation in response have been tried with differing results. More frequent and smaller doses of Sinemet have been used to produce a more stable dopa blood level. This program was suggested when it was observed that dopa given as a constant-rate intravenous infusion can stop fluctuations. Infusion of dopa is not practical, and other means to provide a more constant dopa blood level have been used. Slow-release Sinemet is slow in the onset of its effect, and blood levels of dopa tend to rise toward the end of the day and often cause increased dyskinesia at that time. Usually an initial first dose of regular Sinemet is needed to rapidly produce relief of symptoms. Slow-release preparations help in reducing the number of tablets that a patient must take during the day and are at times useful in smoothing the response to therapy.

Levodopa is absorbed in the small intestine, and the absorption is considerably affected by gastric emptying. Diets high in carbohydrate speed gastric emptying, while diets high in protein slow it. The makeup of the diet can thus affect the action of levodopa. It is best taken before meals as it is then more rapidly and completely absorbed. Protein in the diet decreases the intestinal absorption of dopa and its passage from the blood into the brain, because of competition with other amino acids for intestinal absorption and passage through the blood-brain barrier. A meal high in protein may greatly decrease the effects of dopa. Decreasing the daily intake of protein has been used to reduce fluctuations in response to treatment. In an effort to provide a more stable response to dopa during the day, diets without protein are given during the day, and the need for protein is made up at the evening meal. This program has smoothed the course of treatment during the day, but it has not been successful in more than one-half of the patients trying it.

In an effort to prolong the good effects of dopa and to reduce the chance of fluctuations, limiting the amount of dopa given to a patient or delaying its use until symptoms are marked have been used. Studies show that limiting the intake of dopa can reduce the chances of developing involuntary movements or dyskinesias later, but this occurred at the expense of suboptimal treatment and has not been confirmed in other studies.[15] Delaying use of Sinemet has not produced any changes in mortality, and the delay results in long periods of impaired function, which has no advantages.[16]

To be effective dopa must be first metabolized to dopamine in nerve cells and released into the synaptic cleft and they must bind to the dopamine receptor of the connecting cell. With the decline in the number of cells able to produce dopamine, response to increased availability of dopa steadily declines. To bypass this problem, agents which have a direct dopaminergic agonist effect were identified and developed. Two of these are available in the United States and are used in the treatment of Parkinson's disease. The advantages of both agents are that they have a longer half-life than the 2 hours of levodopa, and that they are more potent activators at the dopamine synapse, milligram for milligram, than levodopa is. The available agents are bromocriptine (Parlodel) and pergolide (Permax). Both these drugs are useful in reducing the fluctuations due to the wearing-off effect that becomes common with long-term treatment with levodopa.

Bromocriptine is available in 5-mg capsules and 2.5-mg tablets. Initial doses begin at 2.5 mg once or twice per day, and the doses are then increased gradually. A total dose of up to 60 mg or more may at times be needed to produce the desired benefit. Because bromocriptine acts as an agonist at the D_2 receptor and as a dopamine antagonist at the D_1 receptor, better effects are gained when it is given with levodopa. This may allow lower doses of levodopa, which are believed to lessen the chances of developing involuntary movements and wearing-off effects. Side effects occur with bromocriptine. The most common are nausea, vomiting, orthostatic hypotension, and delirium. Delirium with increasing confusion is most common in the elderly patient with Parkinson's disease who is beginning to show some evidence of intellectual decline. In this situation bromocriptine should be used only if fluctuations in response to levodopa are disabling and then should be used with caution.

Pergolide is more potent than bromocriptine and is available in tablet form in doses of 0.05, 0.25, and 1 mg. Patients are started on the smallest dose one to two times per day, and this dosage is continued for a week to determine if orthostatic hypotension develops, which may occur early. If this is not a problem, the dose can be raised by giving 0.25 mg and raising the dose by adding one 0.25-mg tablet every 3 days. A therapeutic dose is usually 2 to 4 mg/day. Side effects include nausea and vomiting, constipation, orthostatic hypotension, pain, dyskinesias, and delirium. Pergolide used alone tends to lose its effect and is better given in combination with small amounts of levodopa. The most serious side effect in the elderly patient with Parkinson's disease is disturbance of mentation, with confusion, hallucinations, and delusions. Both bromocriptine and pergolide are much more likely to cause these problems than levodopa is.

Patients with Parkinson's disease who take these medications should be carefully monitored for any evidence of increasing confusion, decline in memory, and appearance of hallucinations.

Apomorphine is a potent dopaminergic agonist which was tried as a treatment for Parkinson's disease but because of the marked side effect of nausea was abandoned. Recently subcutaneous injections of apomorphine in amounts of 2 to 7 mg have been reported to abruptly end off responses to levodopa treatment.[17] This has been found useful in keeping patients functional or making them easier to be cared for when they have become completely dependent. The medication is not yet available in the United States.

The tremor of Parkinson's disease is difficult to control as it is affected greatly by the emotional state of the patient. Situations in which the patient is under pressure, angry, tense, anxious, or embarrassed increase tremor. When first introduced for treatment of allergies, antihistaminic drugs were found to reduce tremor, probably because of their sedative action. Diphenhydramine or (Benadryl) and orphenadrine (Norflex) have been used extensively to reduce tremor. Diphenhydramine is most commonly used. It is usually given in doses of 50 mg once or twice a day. Patients may note sedation early, but this effect wears off, usually with remaining evidence of antitremor effect. Orphenadrine comes in extended-release tablets and may often be useful in reducing tremor when diphenhydramine is not. Patients should be advised that tremor cannot be completely suppressed unless they are heavily sedated, and that their emotional state will always have a profound influence on the occurrence of tremor.

Surgical treatment of Parkinson's disease was used extensively in the predopa era. It was effective in stopping or reducing tremor but had no influence on the progression of the disease or the attendant bradykinesia and rigidity. The original operation was thalamotomy. The recent renewed interest in surgical treatment involves highly accurately placed lesions in the globus pallidus. The procedure is for the relief of tremor and is reserved for young patients with unilateral tremor which is the disabling symptom.

Transplantation of cells with dopaminergic production potential has been tried with adrenal medullary cortical cells and with fetal substantia nigra cells. Use of adrenal medulla cell transplants has been abandoned, and fetal tissue transplantation is being extensively evaluated.[18] It has been reported as being somewhat effective in reducing the need for levodopa intake, but it is generally believed that it is not possible from one or even two fetal substantia nigra to obtain enough cells to replace the large numbers of cells lost before symptoms of the disease begin. There is also considerable doubt about the survival of transplanted cells. However, PET scans of patients who have had fetal transplants have shown metabolic activity with [^{18}F]dopa, which suggests survival. Current techniques are being directed toward genetically altering cells to make them able to produce dopamine, growing them in cell culture, and obtaining large enough quantities to replace lost substantia nigra cells and be sure of their survival.

Depression is a common problem for patients with Parkinson's disease. When depression occurs, the symptoms of the disease worsen and patients often believe that they have suddenly become worse. Depression is not only associated with changes in mood, but often its main features are difficulty sleeping, loss of weight, and decreasing activity. It should be treated with antidepressants. Usually either amitriptyline or imipramine are satisfactory. Amitriptyline has the advantage of sedative action and helps with sleep if given at night. Doses should be small beginning with 25 mg before going to bed. The dose can be raised, but generally small doses are effective. For patients who have agitated depression and who do not respond to antidepressants, electroshock therapy has been effective in relieving the depression and improving the response to anti-parkinsonian medication.

Physical Therapy and Physical Activity

Patients with Parkinson's disease, especially elderly patients, tend to become increasingly physically inactive and with this quickly become physically deconditioned. Increasing bradykinesia and rigidity with progression of the illness contribute to more and more inactivity. The result is that any physical activity is reported to cause fatigue, and patients then become less active. This can become a downward cycle which leads to dependence on others for all daily activities and the attendant complications of inactivity such as contractures, edema of the lower extremities, and pulmonary emboli. With mild disease most patients will not need physical therapy except for instruction for exercises, but those with moderate or severe disease benefit from instruction from therapists about gait, posture, and a program of exercises. It is usually difficult to persuade patients to continue an exercise program at home, so group exercise programs in hospitals or with Parkinson's disease support groups are useful in keeping patients in better physical condition. They also serve as a social activity. Therapy programs designed to instruct patients to have better patterns of gait when they develop festination, freezing, and postural instability are usually advised but rarely produce long-term benefit. Even intense instruction about proper gait with normal reciprocal arm swing and increased stride length rarely has evident carryover to function at home, even when patients are well aware of the benefits of such instruction. Regular group exercise programs are probably the best method to maintain any degree of adequate physical conditioning.

Speech therapy is often suggested for patients who develop speech with low volume and impaired articulation. This can produce some immediate benefit but rarely is associated with long-term improvement.

The elderly patient with Parkinson's disease presents special problems, most often when there is evidence of intellectual decline. In this situation medications which improve motor function may also worsen mentation, causing hallucinations, delusions, and disorientation. When this occurs it is usually necessary to settle for less mobility and ability to perform daily activities in favor of improved mentation, which always calls for a reduction in antiparkinsonian medication. First anticholinergic medications are decreased and stopped, followed by dopamine agonists (bromocriptine or pergolide) and selegeline. If mentation is not improved, Sinemet must be reduced and possibly stopped. Even with this program of eliminating medications, patients may remain confused, delusional, and hallucinating. This is most common when there has been growing evidence of intellectual decline or dementia. Medications are gradually stopped over several days, as abrupt changes in medication may cause sudden worsening of the symptoms of Parkinson's disease.

REFERENCES

1. Stern G: *Parkinson's Disease.* Baltimore, Johns Hopkins University Press, 1990.
2. Parkinson J: *An Essay on the Shaking Palsy.* London, Sherwood, Heely, and Jones, 1817.
3. Ballard PA et al: Permanent human Parkinsonism due to 1-methyl-4-phenyl-1,2,3,6-tetrahydropyridine (MTPT): Seven cases. *Neurology* 35:949, 1985.
4. Hughes AJ et al: Accuracy of clinical diagnosis of idiopathic Parkinson's disease: A clinico-pathological study of 100 cases. *J Neurol Neurosurg Psychiatry* 55:181, 1992.
5. Pollock M, Hornabrook RW: The prevalence, natural history and dementia of Parkinson's disease. *Brain* 89:866, 1966.
6. Schoenberg BS et al: Prevalence of Parkinson's disease in the biracial population of Copiah County, Mississippi. *Neurology* 35:841, 1985.
7. Mark MH et al: Parkinson's disease and twins: An 18F-Dopa PET Study. *Neurology* 41(suppl 1):255, 1991.
8. Hoehn MM, Yahr MD: Parkinsonism: Onset progression and mortality. *Neurology* 12:427, 1967.
9. McDowell FH, Cedarbaum JM: The extrapyramidal system and disorders of movement, in Joynt RJ (ed): *Clinical Neurology.* Philadelphia, JB Lippincott, 1991, p 19.
10. Agid Y et al: The biochemistry of Parkinson's disease, in Stern G (ed): *Parkinson's Disease.* Baltimore, Johns Hopkins University Press, 1990, p 99.
11. McDowell FH, Cedarbaum JM: Natural history of dopa treated Parkinson's disease 18 years follow-up in Rose FC (ed): *Parkinson's Disease Clinical and Experimental Advances.* London, John Libby, 1987, p 119.
12. Parkinson Study Group: Effects of deprenyl on the progression of disability in early Parkinson's disease. *N Engl J Med* 321:1364, 1989.
13. Cotzias GC et al: Modification of Parkinsonism chronic treatment with L-dopa. *N Engl J Med* 280:337, 1969.
14. McDowell FH et al: Treatment of Parkinson's disease with dihydroxyphenylalanine levodopa. *Ann Intern Med* 72:29, 1970.
15. Cedarbaum JM et al: "Early" initiation of levodopa treatment does not produce the development of motor response fluctuations, dyskinesias, or dementia in Parkinson's disease. *Neurology* 41:622, 1991.
16. Diamond SG et al: Multi-center study of Parkinson mortality with early versus later treatment. *Ann Neurol* 22:8, 1986.
17. Stibe CMH et al: Subcutaneous apomorphine in parkinsonian on-off oscillations. *Lancet* 1:403, 1988.
18. Lindvall O et al: Grafts of fetal dopamine neurons survive and improve motor function in Parkinson's disease. *Science* 247:574, 1990.

Chapter 94

OTHER DEGENERATIVE DISORDERS OF THE NERVOUS SYSTEM

Samuel E. Gandy

The "other degenerative disorders of the nervous system" are less frequently encountered than, for example, the more common entities of Alzheimer's disease and Parkinson's disease. These rarer diseases include Pick's disease, Lewy body disease, progressive supranuclear palsy (or Steele-Richardson-Olszewski syndrome), the primary autonomic failure–multiple system atrophy–Shy-Drager syndrome–spinocerebellar degeneration spectrum of disease(s), and motor neuron diseases (including Lou Gehrig's disease). In general, this group of illnesses can be conceptualized as diseases in which failure of one or another neuroanatomic region or system is associated with neuronal loss pathologically and clinically with appropriate symptoms and signs referable to the region or system in failure. Because of the lower prevalence and the specialized information required for the proper diagnosis of these disorders, the care of patients with the rarer diseases is almost always provided in consultation with a neurologist or neurological subspecialist. Nonetheless, the gerontologist should be familiar with the existence of these disorders within the spectrum of neurological illness of late life and with the evolving issues regarding their nosology, genetics, molecular neuropathology, and, in some cases, experimental therapy.

PICK'S DISEASE

Pick's disease, described by Arnold Pick and Alois Alzheimer at the turn of the century, is a dementing disorder characterized by prominent focal lobar atrophy which typically affects the gray and white matter of the frontal or temporal lobes (or both).[1] The differential diagnosis of Pick's disease includes primarily Alzheimer's disease, either disease being distinguished from secondary dementias by application of the principles used in the diagnosis of any primary dementia (see, e.g., Alzheimer's disease, Chapter 92). However, Pick's disease is often virtually impossible to distinguish from Alzheimer's disease on the basis of routine clinical examination, except in instances of Pick's disease in which language disturbances (typically aphasia and/or perseveration) are prominent early features. Otherwise, the onset of Pick's disease, like that of Alzheimer's disease, is characterized by an amnestic syndrome which is accompanied by a loss of intellectual function and personality change. Physical and neurological examinations are otherwise inconclusive in Pick's disease: as frontal lobar dysfunction progresses, pathological grasp and suck reflexes become prominent. Neuroimaging studies with computed tomography (CT) or magnetic resonance imaging (MRI) may disclose relatively circumscribed lobar or polar atrophy of the frontal and/or temporal lobes, but a more diffuse distribution of volume loss is also consistent with the diagnosis of Pick's disease. Preliminary studies suggest that positron emission tomography (PET) might provide a pattern sufficiently distinctive from Alzheimer's disease to improve premortem diagnosis.[2]

The most characteristic change of Pick's disease, the Pick bodies, can only be detected upon neuropathological examination. These structures are argentophilic and filamentous; they distend the cytoplasm of neurons, giving the cells a chromatolytic appearance. Recent advances in the understanding of the etiology and pathogenesis of Pick's disease include immunochemical investigation of Pick bodies which suggests that their composition is related to that of the "standard" neurofibrillary change which accompanies Alzheimer's disease. Specifically, Pick bodies are immunoreactive with the same phospho-state-specific antibodies which identify phosphorylated forms of the cytoskeletal proteins tau and neurofilament as they are typically incorporated into the neurofibrillary tangles (NFTs) of Alzheimer's disease.[3–5] While these shared components suggest a molecular relationship among these various abnormal structures, other factors must determine their differential disease-specific laminar and lobar distribution and the heterogeneous morphologies of the inclusions. It is also possible that the cytoskeletal structural and biochemical pathological lesions are not disease-specific but rather represent the limited repertoire of neuronal responses to injuries of various sorts and are superimposed upon more specific components (analogous to the way that morphologically and histochemically indistinguishable NFTs characterize the brain affected by etiologically disparate entities such as Alzheimer's disease and certain pedigrees of Gerstmann-Straussler-Scheinker disease).[6] Other structural features of Pick's disease, in addition to Pick bodies, include amyloid plaques and granulovacuolar degeneration (in both cases less than that observed in Alzheimer's disease), and neuronal loss which is apparent in the outer three cortical layers of affected regions. No heritable form of Pick's disease has been recognized in any species, and no candidate genes have yet been implicated. However, recent studies of the neurochemistry of Pick's disease suggest that a defect in lipid metabolism may play a role in the cause or pathogenesis of the neurodegeneration.[7]

Care is supportive.

LEWY BODY DISEASE

Recently, attention has been drawn to a complex spectrum of clinicopathological changes known as the Lewy body diseases (LBDs). These illnesses are degenerative diseases which are typically characterized by prominent clinical components of both dementia and parkinsonism (i.e., bradykinesia, tremor, and rigidity; for details, see Parkinson's disease, Chap. 93), which occur in association with the neuropathological development of classic concentric hyaline eosinophilic cytoplasmic inclusions (i.e., Lewy bodies) in various populations of neurons. Thus, the clinical diagnosis of LBD may be appropriately entertained in the differential diagnosis of either dementia or parkinsonism. However, as in Pick's disease (see above), definitive diagnosis may be difficult or impossible to establish ante mortem. Patients with clinical Alzheimer-type dementia or clinically typical parkinsonism may be discovered to have extensive "diffuse" Lewy bodies (i.e., cortical and diencephalic, in addition to the mesencephalic Lewy bodies of typical idiopathic Parkinson's disease), and the movement disorder may be responsive to levodopa.[8] A syndrome mimicking progressive supranuclear palsy (see below) has also been described.[9] Some authors suggest that in addition to dementia, the presence of prominent hallucinosis and delusions early in their course may distinguish LBD patients from Alzheimer's disease patients,[10] but the specificity and reliability of these features are not yet established. Of note, Lewy bodies have been estimated to be present in low abundance in up to 5 percent of the asymptomatic elderly population.[11]

Detailed molecular analysis of the Lewy body, like that of the Pick body, is lacking because of the unavailability of a pure preparation. Histochemical and immunocytochemical analyses of the Lewy body, like those described for the Pick body above, have revealed kinship to the NFTs typically associated with Alzheimer's disease. Components which are consistently identified as being common to Lewy bodies and Alzheimer NFTs include neurofilament and ubiquitin.*[12–19] In fact, antiubiquitin immunohistochemistry is considered to be the most sensitive method of detecting Lewy bodies. Unlike the nerve processes surrounding amyloid plaques, the neuropil surrounding Lewy bodies lacks ubiquitin immunoreactivity.[20]

Another important feature distinguishing Lewy bodies from Alzheimer NFTs is the Lewy body's apparent absence of consistent immunoreactivity for the microtubule-associated protein tau,[15,16,19] the major antigenic component of the paired helical filament constituent of NFTs. Aberrant tau is not detected by standard antibodies either as a component of the Lewy bodies themselves or in the neuropil surrounding them.[19,20]

Lewy bodies have also been reported to be immunoreactive with antibodies specific for APP (the Alzheimer amyloid precursor protein),[21] for gelsolin (the precursor of the amyloid molecule in familial amyloidosis, Finnish type),[22] and for tropomyosin.[23] Of note, the brainstem Lewy body of idiopathic Parkinson's disease apparently lacks the immunoreactivity for tropomyosin.[22] Thus, morphologically distinct structural changes (Pick bodies, Lewy bodies, paired helical filaments) may be derived from molecular constituents which may be conformed or assembled in varied fashion in different diseases or in different neuronal subtypes. This tendency toward incorporation into various pathological structural bodies perhaps reflects the inherent "structure" (e.g., fibrillogenicity or rigidity) of certain domains of abundant neuronal molecules. In other instances (e.g., cortical versus brainstem Lewy bodies), morphologically indistinguishable structures may contain certain common "core" components but perhaps contain some other disparate components which may be specified by either the pathophysiology of the disease or the "host" cell type. The overall result is that neuropathological structures may be generally considered to be composites of some relatively disease-specific constituents (which may be unknown or may be a novel constituent of a "standard" structure) in addition to other nonspecific constituents, usually cytoskeletal proteins which are inherently structure-forming.

Neurochemically, LBD is similar to Alzheimer's disease. No animal model or candidate gene has been

*Ubiquitination is a posttranslational covalent biochemical reaction which links the short ubiquitin peptide to another protein and targets that protein for proteolytic degradation within the cytoplasm. Ubiquitination is typical of many pathological cytoplasmic structures and probably marks the cell's effort at scavenging intracellular debris.

identified. Evidence for a possible genetic component of LBD is currently unavailable.

Levodopa is the chief pharmacotherapeutic agent for management of the movement disorder, as is the case for idiopathic Parkinson's disease (Chap. 93).

PROGRESSIVE SUPRANUCLEAR PALSY

Progressive supranuclear palsy (PSP; Steele-Richardson-Olszewski syndrome) is the descriptive clinical phenotype applied to the "parkinsonism-plus" syndrome of branchial dystonia and ocular disturbance which was described in the early 1960s by Steele, Richardson, and Olszewski.[1] Visuomotor abnormality is initially restricted to vertical gaze (especially down gaze) but progresses to include horizontal eye movement as well. Pseudobulbar palsy is usually present and is accompanied by progressive neck rigidity and extension. The parkinsonian-like masked facies develops as the disease progresses, and the rigidity eventually includes the limbs as well. Cognitive changes are typically present but are not as prominent as in Alzheimer's and other dementias.[24] Differential diagnosis of PSP involves the distinction of this disease from idiopathic Parkinson's disease and other parkinsonian syndromes (see Chap. 93): the absence of tremor and the prominence of the extraocular abnormality in PSP provide the chief clinical criteria for its distinction. No reliable MRI changes have been identified as useful adjuncts to clinical diagnosis[25,26]; PET consistently demonstrates hypometabolism in the frontal lobes of affected individuals.[27–31]

Neuropathologically, PSP is notable for brainstem neuronal loss and gliosis, accompanied by striking neurofibrillary changes in affected neurons. These NFTs tend to be thicker and more "globose" in morphology than those of Alzheimer's disease.[32] In addition, the NFTs of PSP are formed in a population of brainstem neurons distinct from those involved in Alzheimer NFTs. While both Alzheimer and PSP NFTs are argyrophilic and immunoreactive with standard antibodies which recognize phosphorylated tau,[32,33] PSP NFTs are not entirely immunochemically identical to Alzheimer NFTs as demonstrated in studies performed with specialized monoclonal reagents.[34] This provides evidence that in some instances, NFTs may be morphologically similar structures which differ in their molecular constituents or modification depending upon whether the NFTs are formed in distinct cell populations or in the course of different diseases.

Like Parkinson's disease, PSP is characterized neurochemically by loss of brainstem cholinergic neurons. Unlike Parkinson's disease, PSP appears to preserve somatostatin and choline acetyltransferase levels in the neocortex,[35] and there is widespread preservation of various opioid and other neuropeptides.[36] Also distinguishing PSP from Parkinson's disease is the level of the redox marker glutathione in the substantia nigra; glutathione is diminished in Parkinson's disease but increased in PSP.[37]

No definitive familial or environmental component has been recognized to contribute to the predisposition to PSP.[38] Unlike Parkinson's disease, PSP is typically unresponsive to dopaminergic or anticholinergic pharmacotherapy, although therapy with these compounds is usually attempted, particularly early in the course of the illness. Supportive nursing care is a mainstay in the management of PSP.

PRIMARY AUTONOMIC FAILURE, MULTIPLE SYSTEM ATROPHY, SHY-DRAGER SYNDROME, AND SPINOCEREBELLAR ATROPHY

The degenerative diseases represented within the spectrum of primary autonomic failure, multiple system atrophy, Shy-Drager syndrome, and spinocerebellar atrophy are an enormously varied and poorly understood group of illnesses. This group, perhaps more than those in the foregoing sections, is associated with the atrophy of particular neuroanatomically or neurophysiologically related systems in the absence of conspicuous structural features such as those associated with Alzheimer's, Parkinson's, Pick's, and Lewy body diseases.

The designation *primary autonomic failure* (PAF) replaces the previous term *idiopathic orthostatic hypotension* and refers to a primary disorder of autonomic function in the absence of evidence of involvement of other neurological systems. The symptoms which are most common include orthostatic hypotension; heat intolerance due to decreased sweating; impotence; and urinary incontinence.[39] Among these, orthostatic hypotension is by far the most common complaint and is typically manifested as light-headedness associated with rising from a sitting or recumbent position, with exercise, upon exposure to heat, or following a meal. A complete bedside examination in the assessment of these complaints should include the recording of pulse and blood pressure with the patient in the supine, sitting, and standing positions, and may serve to demonstrate the pressure drop. Syncope is a complication which may be attended by traumatic injuries and obviously should be prevented if possible.

The neuropathological basis of PAF is degeneration of postganglionic sympathetic neurons, with sparing of the parasympathetic system.[1]

Management consists of advising slow, careful postural changes and, if symptoms are severe and cause falls, pharmacotherapy with fludrocortisone or adrenergics.[40]

When autonomic failure is associated with signs of basal ganglia disease (typically parkinsonian-like rigidity and/or tremor) or cerebellar disease (typically truncal and appendicular ataxia), the designation Shy-Drager syndrome (SDS) or multiple system atrophy (MSA) is usually applied. Physiologically, the adrenergic response to orthostatic changes is absent.[41] The neuropathological basis of SDS includes degeneration of the preganglionic lateral horn neurons of the thoracic spinal cord in addition to loss of neurons in the substantia nigra, striatum, or cerebellum, paralleling the parkinsonism and ataxia, respectively. A recent report describes the presence of tubular structures in neurons and oligodendrocytes, which are immunolabeled by antibodies to ubiquitin but not by antibodies to cytoskeletal components,[42] providing preliminary evidence for structural neuropathological changes in this spectrum of disease.

When the clinical picture is dominated by cerebellar dysfunction, MSA may be more specifically described as spinocerebellar atrophy (SCA) or olivopontocerebellar atrophy (OPCA). The chronic onset of truncal and appendicular ataxia is characteristic of MSA-SCA-OPCA, and the differential diagnosis most commonly includes demyelinating diseases and alcoholic cerebellar degeneration.

Advances in neuroimaging and molecular genetics have contributed to the current approach to this subgroup and to the understanding of them. MRI may demonstrate prominent cerebellar atrophy as well as abnormal signal from the pontocerebellar region.[43] PET may contribute additional sensitivity to the neuroimaging armamentarium, demonstrating in some instances pontocerebellar hypometabolism in excess of the tissue loss.[44]

Glutamate dehydrogenase activity has been reported to be diminished in some series but normal in others.[45–48] Of substantial promise in the outlook for a molecular basis of these diseases is this report of a murine mutant model[49] and the identification on chromosome 6 of a genetic locus for autosomal dominant familial MSA-SCA-OPCA.[50–56]

The prognosis of these disorders is poor, and adequate rehabilitative nursing care and nutritional support constitute the primary avenues of therapy.

MOTOR NEURON DISEASES (INCLUDING LOU GEHRIG'S DISEASE)

The motor neuron diseases (MNDs) are a group of disorders which are characterized by dysfunction of either upper motor neurons, lower motor neurons, or both, but without apparent abnormality of other neuronal systems. The syndromes included form a spectrum of clinical and pathological entities, analogous to the continuum of PAF-MSA-SDS-SCA described above. Perhaps the best recognized among the MNDs is that designated *amyotrophic lateral sclerosis*, or Lou Gehrig's disease, the features of which include a combination of upper and lower motor neuronal symptoms and signs, exemplified by spasticity, hyperreflexia, atrophy, and fasciculations. When upper motor neuron dysfunction predominates (spasticity, hyperreflexia, extensor plantar responses), the designation is usually *primary lateral sclerosis*, while *spinal muscular atrophy* is used to describe the situation of predominant lower motor neuronal abnormality (weakness, atrophy, fasciculations). Demonstration of fasciculations of the tongue is often a useful clinical sign of MND. The motor signs are often asymmetrical at presentation but become generalized as disease progresses.

The bedside examination of MND is complemented by testing in the neurophysiological laboratory, where the electromyogram typically demonstrates evidence of muscle denervation in the presence of nerve conduction velocities which tend to be relatively preserved. The differential diagnosis of the MNDs tends to focus most commonly on the exclusion of polyneuropathic and/or myelopathic diseases and intoxications, particularly by heavy metals. In young adults, GM2-gangliosidosis, a hereditary lysosomal disorder of lipid catabolism, may be a specific diagnosable cause of MND.[57] Contemporary magnetic resonance neuroimaging technology is typically utilized primarily for the exclusion of compressive causes of myelopathy but may reveal brain changes which support the diagnosis of MND.[58] Changes in regional cerebral cortical blood flow and glucose utilization have also been observed.[59,60]

The neuropathology of the MNDs is characterized by the initial formation of structural lesions within motor neurons, which, over the course of the illness, progressively become more shrunken and eventually die. Curiously, certain cranial nerve nuclei (III, IV, VI) are spared. Some of the structural lesions, like those in some other neurodegenerations discussed above, are apparently derived from normal phosphorylated cytoskeletal components and ubiquitin.[61] Other structural changes include the accumulation of intraneuronal lipofuscin and less well characterized cytoplasmic Lewy body-like inclusions and eosinophilic intranuclear inclusions known as Bunina bodies. These latter structures are apparently ubiquitinated but are not immunoreactive with antibodies for cytoskeletal proteins.[61]

Perhaps in association with the affliction of several popular and visible celebrities with MND (Lou Gehrig, Senator Jacob Javits, physics professor Stephen Hawking), awareness of these diseases has improved of late, and attempts to advance the understanding of their basis (or bases) are receiving substantial attention. Viral causes have been suspected, perhaps because of the clinical kinship of spinal muscular atrophy with poliomyelitis, but have not been proved. Some evidence has been presented for familial clustering[62] and genetic linkage.[63] A mutation in the coding sequence of the superoxide dismutase gene has recently been discovered to be the cause of certain forms of familial MND.[63a] Immunological abnormalities[64,65] and alterations in excitotoxic neurotransmitters[66] have received considerable attention in their association with MNDs, but neither has yet progressed as of this writing to permit a definitive statement about primary MNDs, although a subtype of secondary MND has been identified which appears to be associated with lymphoproliferative disorders.[67,68]

The prognosis in the MNDs is poor, with death occurring within 2 to 5 years after diagnosis in most cases. Bulbocervical involvement, compromising maintenance of nutrition and pumonary toilet, are often directly responsible for demise.

Like other neurodegenerations, the therapy of MND has historically focused on adequate nursing support. Thyrotropin-releasing hormone, once a popularly attempted mode of therapy, appears not to be generally beneficial.[69] Very recently, however, two groups have independently reported success in the therapeutic use of a recombinant form of the neurotrophic growth factor *ciliary neurotrophic factor* (CNTF) to prevent or slow motor neuron dysfunction in two distinct murine models of MND.[70,71] This work has sparked enthusiasm that such an application might mark an important milestone in clinical neuroscience: namely, the first successful application of a neurotrophic factor to a previously untreatable neurodegenerative disease. Further, such success would suggest that elucidating the etiology of such diseases need not necessarily be a prerequisite for the development of useful therapy. Extension of this work to human MNDs represents an obvious next step and is eagerly anticipated.

REFERENCES

1. Adams RD, Victor M: *Principles of Neurology*, 3d ed. New York, McGraw-Hill, 1985.
2. Kamo H et al: Positron emission tomography and histopathology in Pick's disease. *Neurology* 37:439, 1987.
3. Case Records of the Massachusetts General Hospital. *N Engl J Med* 326:397, 1992.
4. Pollock NJ et al: Filamentous aggregates in Pick's disease, progressive supranuclear palsy, and Alzheimer's disease share antigenic determinants with microtubule-associated protein, tau. *Lancet* 2:1211, 1986.
5. Perry G et al: Filaments of Pick's bodies contain altered cytoskeletal elements. *Am J Pathol* 127:559, 1987.
6. Hsaio K et al: Mutant prion proteins in Gerstmann-Straussler-Scheinker disease with neurofibrillary tangles. *Nature Genet* 1:68, 1992.
7. Scicutella A, Davies P: Marked loss of cerebral galactolipids in Pick's disease. *Ann Neurol* 22:606, 1987.
8. Mark MH et al: Levodopa-nonresponsive Lewy body parkinsonism: Clinicopathologic study of two cases. *Neurology* 42:1323, 1992.
9. Fearnley JM et al: Diffuse Lewy body disease presenting with a supranuclear gaze palsy. *J Neurol Neurosurg Psychiatry* 54:159, 1991.
10. Hansen L et al: The Lewy body variant of Alzheimer's disease: A clinical and pathologic entity. *Neurology* 40:1, 1990.
11. Gibb WRG et al: Clinical and pathological features of diffuse cortical Lewy body disease(Lewy body dementia). *Brain* 110:1131, 1987.
12. Goldman JE et al: Lewy bodies of Parkinson's disease contain neurofilament antigens. *Science* 221:1082, 1983.
13. Forno LS et al: Reaction of Lewy bodies with antibodies to phosphorylated and non-phosphorylated neurofilaments. *Neurosci Lett* 64:253, 1986.
14. Love S et al: Alz-50, ubiquitin and tau immunoreactivity of neurofibrillary tangles, Pick bodies and Lewy bodies. *J Neuropathol Exper Neurol* 47:393, 1988.
15. Galloway PG et al: Lewy bodies contain epitopes both shared and distinct from Alzheimer neurofibrillary tangles. *J Neuropathol Exper Neurol* 47:654, 1988.
16. Bancher C et al: An antigenic profile of Lewy bodies: Immunocytochemical indication for protein phosphorylation and ubiquitination. *J Neuropathol Exper Neurol* 48:81, 1989.
17. Kuzuhara S et al: Lewy bodies are ubiquitinated: A light and electron microscopic immunocytochemical study. *Acta Neuropathol* 75:345, 1988.
18. Schmidt ML et al: Epitope map of neurofilament protein domains in cortical and peripheral nervous system Lewy bodies. *Am J Pathol* 139:53, 1991.
19. Pollanen MS et al: Detergent-insoluble cortical Lewy body fibrils share epitopes with neurofilament and tau. *J Neurochem* 58:1953, 1992.
20. Dickson DW et al: Diffuse Lewy body disease: Light and electron microscopic immunocytochemistry of senile plaques. *Acta Neuropathol* 78:572, 1989.
21. Arai H et al: Lewy bodies contain beta-amyloid precursor proteins of Alzheimer's disease. *Brain Res* 585:386, 1992.
22. Wisniewski T et al: Lewy bodies are immunoreactive with antibodies raised to gelsolin related amyloid-Finnish type. *Am J Pathol* 138:1077, 1991.
23. Galloway PG, Perry G: Tropomyosin distinguishes Lewy bodies of Parkinson disease from other neurofibrillary pathology. *Brain Res* 541:347, 1991.
24. Dubois B et al: Slowing of cognitive processing in progressive supranuclear palsy: A comparison with Parkinson's disease. *Arch Neurol* 45:1194, 1988.
25. Savoiardo M et al: MR imaging in progressive supranuclear palsy and Shy-Drager syndrome. *J Comput Assist Tomogr* 13:555, 1989.
26. Stern MB et al: Magnetic imaging in Parkinson's disease and parkinsonian syndromes. *Neurology* 39:1524, 1989.
27. Leendsers KL et al: Steele-Richardson-Olszewski syn-

drome: Brain energy metabolism, blood flow and fluorodopa uptake measured by positron emission tomography. *Brain* 111:615, 1988.
28. Foster NL et al: Cerebral hypometabolism in progressive supranuclear palsy studied with positron emission tomography. *Ann Neurol* 24:399, 1988.
29. Goffinet AM et al: Positron tomography demonstrates frontal lobe hypometabolism in progressive supranuclear palsy. *Ann Neurol* 25:131, 1989.
30. Blin J et al: Positron emission tomography study in progressive supranuclear palsy: Brain hypometabolic pattern and clinicometabolic correlations. *Arch Neurol* 47:747, 1990.
31. Bhatt MH et al: Positron emission tomography in progressive supranuclear palsy. *Arch Neurol* 48:389, 1991.
32. Gibb WR: Neuropathology of Parkinson's disease and related syndromes. *Neurol Clin* 10:361, 1992.
33. Tabaton M et al: Alz 50 recognizes abnormal filaments in Alzheimer's disease and progressive supranuclear palsy. *Ann Neurol* 24:407, 1988.
34. Schmidt ML et al: Properties of antigenic determinants that distinguish neurofibrillary tangles in progressive supranuclear palsy and Alzheimer disease. *Lab Invest* 59:460, 1988.
35. Epelbaum J et al: Brain somatostatin concentrations do not decrease in progressive supranuclear palsy. *J Neurol Neurosurg Psychiatry* 50:1526, 1987.
36. Taquet H et al: Brain neuropeptides in progressive supranuclear palsy. *Brain Res* 411:178, 1987.
37. Perry TL et al: Brain amino acids and glutathione in progressive supranuclear palsy. *Neurology* 38:943, 1988.
38. Davis PH et al: Risk factors for progressive supranuclear palsy. *Neurology* 38:1546, 1988.
39. Bannister R (ed): *Autonomic Failure*, 2d ed. New York, Oxford University Press, 1988.
40. Matsubara S et al: Shy-Drager syndrome: Effect of fludrocortisone and L-threo-3,4-dihydroxylphenylserine on blood pressure and regional cerebral blood flow. *J Neurol Neurosurg Psychiatry* 53:994, 1990.
41. Fahn S: Parkinson's disease and other basal ganglion disorders, in Asbury AK et al (eds): *Diseases of the Nervous System*. Philadelphia, Saunders, 1986.
42. Papp MI, Lantos PL: Accumulation of tubular structures in oligodendroglial and neuronal cells as the basic alteration in multiple system atrophy. *J Neurol Sci* 107:172, 1992.
43. Savoiardo M et al: Olivopontocerebellar atrophy: MR diagnosis and relationship to multisystem atrophy. *Radiology* 174:693, 1990.
44. Gilman S et al: Cerebellar and brainstem hypometabolism in olivopontocerebellar atrophy detected with positron emission tomography. *Ann Neurol* 23:223, 1988.
45. Plaitakis A et al: Abnormal glutamate metabolism in an adult-onset degenerative neurological disorder. *Science* 216:193, 1982.
46. Kajiyama K et al: Decreased glutamate dehydrogenase protein in spinocerebellar degeneration. *J Neurol Neurosurg Psychiatry* 51:1078, 1988.
47. Aubby D et al: Leukocyte glutamate dehydrogenase activity in patients with degenerative neurological disorders. *J Neurol Neurosurg Psychiatry* 51:893, 1988.
48. Rosenberg R, Banner C: Normal glutamate dehydrogenase protein in spinocerebellar degeneration. *J Neurol Neurosurg Psychiatry* 52:666, 1989.
49. Sotelo C, Guenet JL: Pathologic changes in the CNS of dystonia musculorum mutant mouse: An animal model for human spinocerebellar ataxia. *Neuroscience* 27:403, 1988.
50. Rich SS et al: Spinocerebellar ataxia: Localization of an autosomal dominant locus between two markers on human chromosome 6. *Am J Hum Genet* 41:524, 1987.
51. Zoghbi HY et al: Spinocerebellar ataxia: Variable age of onset and linkage to human leukocyte antigen in a large kindred. *Ann Neurol* 23:580, 1988.
52. Zoghbi HY et al: Assignment of autosomal dominant spinocerebellar ataxia centromeric to the HLA region on the short arm of chromosome 6 using multilocus linkage analysis. *Am J Hum Genet* 44:255, 1989.
53. Wilkie PJ et al: Spinocerebellar ataxia: Multipoint linkage analysis of genes associated with the disease locus. *Hum Genet* 87:405, 1991.
54. Ranum LP et al: Localization of the autosomal dominant HLA-linked spinocerebellar ataxia locus, in two kindreds, within an 8 cM subregion of chromosome 6p. *Am J Hum Genet* 49:31, 1991.
55. Ranum LP et al: Autosomal dominant spinocerebellar ataxia: Locus heterogeneity in a Nebraska kindred. *Neurology* 42:344, 1992.
56. Volz A et al: Regional mapping of the gene for autosomal dominant spinocerebellar ataxia by localizing the closely linked D6S89 locus to 6p24.2-p23.05. *Cytogenet Cell Genet* 60:37, 1992.
57. Kolodny EH, Raghavan SS: GM2-gangliosidosis hexosamindase mutations not of the Tay-Sachs type produce unusual clinical variants. *Trends Neurosci* 6:16, 1983.
58. Goodin DS et al: Magnetic resonance imaging in amyotrophic lateral sclerosis. *Ann Neurol* 23:418, 1988.
59. Waldemar G et al: Focal reductions of cerebral blood flow in amyotrophic lateral sclerosis: A [99mTc]-D,L-HMPAO SPECT study. *J Neurol Sci* 107:19, 1992.
60. Hoffman JM et al: Cerebral glucose utilization in motor neuron disease. *Arch Neurol* 49:849, 1992.
61. Murayama S et al: Immunocytochemical and ultrastructural studies of lower motor neurons in amyotrophic lateral sclerosis. *Ann Neurol* 27:137, 1990.
62. Strong MJ et al: Familial amyotrophic lateral sclerosis, 1850–1989: A statistical analysis of the world literature. *Can J Neurol Sci* 18:45, 1991.
63. Siddique T et al: Linkage of a gene causing familial amyotrophic lateral sclerosis to chromosome 21 and evidence of genetic locus heterogeneity. *N Engl J Med* 324:1381, 1991.
63a. Rosen DR et al: Mutations in Cu/Zn superoxide dismutase are associated with familial amyotrophic lateral sclerosis. *Nature* 362:59, 1993.
64. Delbono O et al: IgG from amyotrophic lateral sclerosis affects tubular calcium channels of skeletal muscle. *Am J Physiol* 260:1347, 1991.
65. Appel SH et al: Immunoglobulins from animal models of motor neuron disease and from human amyotrophic lateral sclerosis patients passively transfer physiological abnormalities to the neuromuscular junction. *Proc Natl Acad Sci USA* 88:647, 1991.

66. Rothstein JD et al: Decreased glutamate transport by the brain and spinal cord in amyotrophic lateral sclerosis. *N Engl J Med* 326:1464, 1992.
67. Shy Me et al: Motor neuron disease and plasma cell dyscrasia. *Neurology* 36:1429, 1986.
68. Younger DS et al: Lymphoma, motor neuron diseases and amyotrophic lateral sclerosis. *Ann Neurol* 29:78, 1991.
69. Munsat TL et al: Intrathecal thyrotropin-releasing hormone does not alter the progressive course of ALS: Experience with an intrathecal drug delivery system. *Neurology* 42:1049, 1992.
70. Sendtner M et al: Ciliary neurotrophic factor prevents degeneration of motor neurons in mouse mutant progressive motor neuronopathy. *Nature* 358:502, 1992.
71. Helgren ME et al: Ciliary neurotrophic factor slows the progression of motor dysfunction in the Mnd mouse. *Neurology* 42:1426, 1992.

Chapter 95

INFECTIONS OF THE CENTRAL NERVOUS SYSTEM

Suzanne F. Bradley and Carol A. Kauffman

Microorganisms may invade the subarachnoid space and cause meningitis following dissemination from a distant source of infection or a site of asymptomatic colonization, or they may enter directly through extension from a contiguous focus of infection. Upon entry into the central nervous system (CNS), pathogens multiply rapidly since the subarachnoid space has limited native host defenses. Complement and immunoglobins are generally absent in the cerebrospinal fluid (CSF), and phagocytes must be recruited from the systemic circulation. If the infection is acute and severe and treatment is not initiated, death ensues rapidly even in a healthy host.

Common pyogenic bacteria are clearly the pathogens which most frequently cause CNS infections in aged persons, with viral, fungal, tuberculous, and spirochetal infections occurring much less often. Why elderly persons appear to acquire some kinds of CNS infection more often and have an even poorer outcome than younger persons is not clear. Defects in T-lymphocyte function and cell-mediated immunity seen in aged persons may explain some of their propensity to reactivate tuberculosis, cryptococcus, or herpes infections and to acquire *Listeria* infection. On the other hand, no specific defects in phagocytes, complement, or immunoglobulins have been found in aged persons to explain their propensity to develop meningitis due to common bacterial pathogens. Chronic illnesses that lead to debility, malnutrition, hospitalization, and medical intervention probably are more closely associated with the development of meningitis in elderly persons than specific age-related defects in the immune system.

MENINGOENCEPHALITIS

Bacterial Meningitis

The incidence of bacterial meningitis appears to have increased in the elderly population in the last several decades, perhaps due to improved recognition of atypical presentations in this age group, as well as an actual increase in the number of cases. In elderly patients, mortality rates range from 35 to 84 percent, much higher than that noted in other age groups, with the exception of neonates. Although the mortality rate varies depending on the pathogen, delay in diagnosis and treatment, and underlying risk factors, almost all series show increasing age to be a significant risk factor for death from meningitis.

The most common cause of bacterial meningitis in the elderly is *Streptococcus pneumoniae,* accounting for roughly 50 percent of all cases. *Haemophilus influenzae,* the most common cause of meningitis in children, and *Neisseria meningitidis,* another major pathogen in the young, are uncommon in the elderly. In contrast to children and younger adults, the elderly are at increased risk for meningitis due to *Listeria monocytogenes, Staphylococcus aureus,* and aerobic gram-negative bacilli, such as *Escherichia coli, Klebsiella pneumoniae,* and *Pseudomonas aeruginosa*.

Predisposing factors for the development of bacterial meningitis in the elderly include alcoholism, diabetes mellitus, cancer, and other debilitating diseases. Meningitis may follow trauma causing a subdural tear, sinusitis, or otitis, which increase the likelihood of contiguous spread of bacteria to the CNS.

Elderly patients with meningitis due to *S. pneumoniae* and *H. influenzae* frequently have concomitant pneumonia, otitis, or sinusitis. The diagnosis of endocarditis should always be suspected in elderly patients who develop *S. aureus* meningitis without preceding head trauma or a neurosurgical procedure. While most gram-negative bacillary meningitis occurs following cranial or head and neck surgical procedures, in the elderly several studies have noted an association with hematogenous spread following urinary tract or other focal infections.

The presenting symptoms of bacterial meningitis occur acutely; most patients have fever, headache, and mental status changes, which vary from confusion and lethargy to coma. Patients with meningitis following a surgical procedure may have a longer duration and fewer symptoms than those with community-acquired meningitis. In the elderly, fever and confusion may be the only symptoms present early in the course of meningitis. Although very nonspecific, the diagnosis of meningitis must always be entertained when an elderly patient presents with these symptoms.

Signs manifested by elderly patients with bacterial meningitis include fever, changes in mental status, and nuchal rigidity. Nuchal rigidity may be difficult to evaluate in an elderly individual who has preexisting Parkinson's disease or cervical osteoarthritis; on the other hand, this sign may be absent in the elderly, often portending a poor outcome. Neurologic findings which are present less frequently include paresis, cranial nerve palsies, Babinski's sign, and seizures.

The diagnosis of meningitis is made by examination of CSF. Lumbar puncture must be performed *immediately*, and treatment should be initiated as soon as CSF is obtained. Typical findings in the CSF are shown in Table 95-1. Almost always, leukocytosis with a predominance of neutrophils, hypoglycorrhachia, and elevated protein levels are present. Gram's stain is very useful and should be performed immediately on centrifuged CSF. Culture of CSF, blood, and other body fluids, if indicated, should be done. When culture of CSF does not yield a pathogen, antigen detection for pathogens such as *S. pneumoniae* can be very useful. CT scan, sinus films, chest x-ray films, and other diagnostic tests should be obtained when indicated, but only after the patient has received initial antibiotic therapy and is stable.

Initial treatment of bacterial meningitis is empiric while awaiting the results of Gram's stain and culture. Therapy should be directed toward the most likely pathogen in a given clinical situations. In general, it is essential to use bactericidal antimicrobial agents, only those types of agents which achieve adequate concentrations in the CSF, and high enough doses of drug to ensure bactericidal levels in the CSF.

For elderly patients with community-acquired bacterial meningitis, most likely due to *S. pneumoniae* and less likely due to *Listeria*, *Haemophilus*, or *Neisseria*, initial treatment should be ampicillin. For those patients with meningitis acquired after surgery or as a nosocomial infection, initial treatment should be ceftriaxone to cover gram-negative bacilli and either vancomycin or nafcillin for staphylococcal coverage. Specific therapy, as detailed in Table 95-2, should be used after the microorganism is identified.

Treatment should be continued for 2 weeks for most cases of community-acquired meningitis. Since *Listeria* is an intracellular pathogen and frequently causes brain abscesses in addition to meningitis, treatment should be continued longer and a CT scan should be done to determine if abscesses are present. In the usual case of meningitis, repeat lumbar puncture is not necessary unless the patient has not responded clinically or has recrudescence of symptoms. This is most likely to occur with meningitis due to gram-negative bacilli, which are often resistant to many antibiotics and may require prolonged therapy. The entire course of antibiotic therapy should be given intravenously. As the infection resolves, inflammation decreases and the concentration of antibiotic diffusing into the CSF decreases. Thus, it is important to achieve high concentrations of antibiotics in serum with intravenous administration to ensure that adequate levels diffuse into the CSF throughout the entire course of treatment.

Although encouraging data have been reported on the use of corticosteroids at initial presentation of *H. influenzae* meningitis in children, corticosteroid use

TABLE 95-1.

Typical Findings in CSF of Patients with Various Types of CNS Infections

Infection	WBC (no./μl)	Major Cell Type (%)	Protein (mg/dl)	Glucose (mg/dl)
Meningoencephalitis				
Bacterial	↑ (500–10^4)	PMN (90–100)	↑ (100–500)	↓ (0–40)
Viral	↑ (5–100)	mono (80–100)*	↑ (50–100)	nl†
Herpes simplex	↑ (5–100)	mono (60–100)*	↑ (50–200)	nl†
Tuberculous	↑ (50–500)	mono (60–100)*	↑ (100–300)	↓ (10–40)
Fungal	↑ (50–500)	mono (60–100)*	↑ (100–300)	↓ (10–40)
Syphilitic				
Meningitis	↑ (10–1000)	mono (90–100)	↑ (100–400)	↓ (10–40)
Paresis	↑ (5–100)	mono (90–100)	↑ (50–100)	nl
Focal Infections				
Brain abscess	↑ (5–1000)‡	PMN (40–90)	↑ (50–200)	nl
Subdural empyema and epidural abscess	↑ (5–1000)	PMN (60–100)	↑ (50–200)	nl

Key: wbc = white blood cells; mono = monocytes; nl = normal; pmn = polymorphonuclear cells.
*Early in the course of infection, CSF pleocytosis may be predominantly neutrophilic.
†Rarely, CSF glucose levels may be low in herpes simplex meningitis and in meningitis from mumps and lymphocytic choriomeningitis viruses.
‡The CSF cell count and predominant cell type vary widely. If the abscess breaks through into the subarachnoid space, the CSF findings are those of bacterial meningitis.

TABLE 95-2.

Suggested Treatment Regimens for Bacterial Meningitis*

Organisms	Treatment of Choice	Alternative in Allergic Patient†
S. pneumoniae	Penicillin, 24 million units or Ampicillin, 12 g	Chloramphenicol, 4 g or Ceftriaxone, 4 g
H. influenzae	Ceftriaxone, 4 g‡ or Ampicillin, 12 g	Chloramphenicol, 4 g
N. meningitidis	Penicillin, 24 million units or Ampicillin, 12 g	Chloramphenicol, 4 g or Ceftriaxone, 4 g
6xl,16*S. aureus*	Vancomycin, 2 g§ Nafcillin, 12 g	Vancomycin, 2 g
L. monocytogenes	Ampicillin, 12 g	TMP-SMX, 15 mg/kg (TMP component)
P. aeruginosa¶	Ceftazidime, 8 g	Aztreonam, 8 g
Other gram-negative bacilli¶	Ceftriaxone, 4 g	Aztreonam, 8 g TMP-SMX, 15 mg/kg (TMP component)

*Total daily doses for adults with normal renal function. For elderly patients, dosage requires adjustment per creatinine clearance.
†In patients with anaphylaxis to penicillin, avoid cephalosporins.
‡If ampicillin-resistant [β-lactamase (+)], use ceftriaxone.
§If methicillin-resistant *S. aureus,* vancomycin required; otherwise use nafcillin.
¶Initial therapy; final therapy per antibiotic susceptibilities.

in adults is controversial and cannot be recommended at this time.

Any patient with a second episode of meningitis, especially due to *S. pneumoniae,* or any patient with the onset of meningitis following a history of trauma to the head, should be investigated for a possible dural tear, which is often secondary to a fracture of the cribiform plate.

Viral Meningoencephalitis

Viral infections of the CNS are infrequent in the elderly. However, during outbreaks of arthropod-borne infections, such as St. Louis encephalitis or Western equine encephalitis, elderly persons have been noted to have a higher rate of symptomatic disease than younger individuals. Although uncommon in the elderly, meningoencephalitis due to herpesviruses is very important because the infection can be severe and treatment options do exist.

Viral or aseptic meningoencephalitis usually occurs in the late spring or early fall, presenting with headache, fever, mental status changes, and sometimes seizures. Patients do not appear as ill as those with bacterial meningitis. Physical examination almost always reveals no focal neurologic deficit, and nuchal rigidity is often absent. Typical CSF findings are listed in Table 95-1. Although the CSF should always be cultured for the full range of pathogens, especially since the fluid findings may be similar to those shown in fungal and tuberculous meningitis, viral cultures of CSF are rarely positive.

There is no treatment for viral meningoencephalitis due to enteroviruses or arthropod-borne viruses; the disease usually runs a benign course. However, in the elderly, St. Louis encephalitis, in particular, has been associated with a poor outcome.

Encephalitis due to herpes simplex presents a very different picture from that found in meningoencephalitis due to other viruses. Patients have an abrupt onset of fever, headaches, and mental status changes, progressing rapidly over a few days to seizures, obtundation, and coma. The virus causes a necrotizing process with prominent temporal lobe involvement. Without treatment, death or severe neurologic dysfunction is the rule.

CSF findings are not diagnostic (Table 95-1). The EEG usually shows abnormal wave activity localized to the temporal lobe. CT scan of the head shows an area of decreased attenuation in the temporal lobe, which usually occurs by day 6 of the illness. MRI scan is preferred as a diagnostic tool since it is more sensitive, showing inflammatory changes in the temporal lobe 2 to 3 days earlier than the CT scan. Although brain biopsy is definitive, this procedure has become less common. A compatible clinical picture, abnormal

EEG, CT or MRI scan showing involvement of one or both temporal lobes, and the absence of another pathogen have become the typical criteria for diagnosis.

Treatment with acyclovir should be initiated as soon as the possibility of herpes simplex encephalitis is entertained even though the diagnosis has not been confirmed, since the outcome is dismal unless therapy is begun early. Even when therapy is initiated early, morbidity is high and mortality remains approximately 30 percent.

Varicella-zoster virus can cause meningoencephalitis in elderly patients with shingles. Although the course is usually benign, this manifestation of infection can be severe, causing seizures, mental obtundation, and residual neurologic deficits. Even more uncommon is the occurrence of contralateral hemiplegia following herpes zoster ophthalmicus. When this occurs, it is almost always in elderly individuals, may happen weeks to months after the zoster eruption has subsided, and presents as a stroke syndrome. The reason for the occurrence of granulomatous angiitis in the distribution of the ipsilateral middle cerebral artery following varicella-zoster infection is unknown. Whether acyclovir has a role in treatment of this complication has not been established.

Tuberculous Meningitis

Although previously a disease of childhood, tuberculous meningitis is now seen most often in the elderly. It is usually due to reactivation of an existing focus of tuberculosis next to the meninges and usually runs a subacute to chronic course. Most elderly patients have meningitis only; less commonly, an individual may have meningitis as one manifestation of disseminated infection.

Symptoms and signs include headache, fever, malaise, and mental status changes progressing over several weeks to obtundation or stupor, nuchal rigidity, cranial nerve palsies, papilledema, and seizures. Increased intracranial pressure is common. The meningitis is primarily a basilar granulomatous process with hydrocephalus a frequent complication.

The diagnosis of tuberculous meningitis is often difficult. Typically a lymphocytic pleocytosis in CSF is found (Table 95-1). A low level of serum sodium due to inappropriate antidiuretic hormone secretion should make one think of tuberculous meningitis, but this is not specific. Tuberculin skin tests are often negative in an ill patient with meningitis and are of little diagnostic help. Chest roentgenogram may show active tuberculosis but most often shows only nonspecific changes or old granulomatous disease.

The most specific assays, i.e., visualization of mycobacteria using an acid-fast stain and growth of *Mycobacterium tuberculosis* in culture of CSF, are not very sensitive. Acid-fast bacilli are seen in only 10 to 40 percent of specimens although the yield can increase to 85 to 91 percent if multiple smears are assiduously reviewed by a trained observer. Culture is positive in only 45 to 90 percent, and may take 6 to 8 weeks to show growth. Repeated lumbar punctures for CSF analysis and culture are important to help establish the diagnosis.

Treatment must be begun prior to proof of mycobacterial infection in most cases. Treatment should be with bactericidal drugs which attain adequate concentrations in the CSF. The best treatment regimen is probably isoniazid and rifampin continued for 1 year. It may also be prudent to add a third drug, such as pyrazinamide, for the first several months. There is too little experience with short-course therapy to recommend its use for meningitis. The use of corticosteroids is debatable, but if increased intracranial pressure is present, they may be beneficial. Whether corticosteroids prevent hydrocephalus by decreasing inflammation is still open to question. The mortality of tuberculous meningitis remains at 20 to 30 percent.

Fungal Meningitis

The fungus most often encountered as a cause of meningitis is *Cryptococcus neoformans,* an encapsulated yeast with worldwide distribution. However, in the southwestern United States, *Coccidioides immitis* also is an important cause of meningitis. Less commonly, other fungi, such as *Candida albicans, Histoplasma capsulatum,* and *Blastomyces dermatitidis* cause meningitis.

Almost always, the initial infection is pulmonary, with subsequent spread to the CNS. Although many elderly patients have predisposing illnesses leading to a decrease in cell-mediated immunity (i.e., lymphoma, corticosteroid use), others have no obvious immunosuppression other than increased age. Diabetes mellitus may be a risk factor for both cryptococcal and coccidioides meningitis.

Fungal meningitis is usually subacute to chronic in its course. Over several weeks, patients have gradually increasing headache, visual changes, personality changes, nausea, and vomiting. Focal findings and seizures may occur but are not common. Fever is usually present, but may be low-grade or absent. Many patients have signs of increased intracranial pressure (papilledema, sixth nerve palsy) by the time they are seen. Occasionally, an elderly person with cryptococcal meningitis will present only with dementia, without headache or fever.

The major differential diagnoses in a patient with fungal meningitis is tuberculous meningitis, although sarcoidosis, Lyme disease, and tumors may present a similar clinical picture. The most important diagnostic procedure is lumbar puncture. However, if the patient has focal signs and/or signs of increased intracranial pressure, CT scan should be performed first to rule out a mass lesion.

CSF findings usually show a lymphocytic pleocytosis (Table 95-1). It is very important that the laboratory be alerted to the possibility of fungal meningitis. Although *C. neoformans* grows readily in most cases, only a small number of organisms may be present, requiring that large amounts of CSF (as much as 10 ml) be obtained. India ink preparation of CSF is helpful to highlight the encapsulated yeasts, but a more sensitive assay is the latex agglutination test for cryptococcal antigen, which should be performed on both CSF and blood in all patients with chronic meningitis. The yield of *C. immitis* from CSF is very low, and generally diagnosis requires special serologic tests on CSF.

The initial treatment of cryptococcal meningitis is amphotericin B and flucytosine. Therapy is given for at least 6 weeks and many times longer. Alternatively, amphotericin B and flucytosine can be given for a few weeks until the patient is stable and then fluconazole used for the remainder of therapy, which should probably extend at least 6 months. Even with optimal therapy, the relapse rate is approximately 10 to 15 percent and the mortality rate is as high as 20 to 30 percent.

Treatment of coccidioidal meningitis is difficult. Fluconazole has become the treatment of choice but probably requires lifelong therapy. The alternative is intrathecal administration of amphotericin B.

Neurosyphilis

The spirochete *Treponema pallidum* causes many different clinical syndromes affecting the CNS. Syphilitic invasion of the CNS has been noted even with primary infection. Some patients may clear their CSF of spirochetes without sequelae, while others may develop acute aseptic meningitis after several weeks, and still others may harbor spirochetes without symptoms for years. Of these asymptomatic patients with active, persistent CNS inflammation, 4 to 8 percent will develop neurosyphilis over a 5- to 30-year period.

Most studies of the epidemiology of syphilis have not included the aged within their cohort, even though it has been shown that 3 to 4 percent of hospitalized elderly patients have serologic evidence of exposure to syphilis. Many clinicians do not consider early syphilis in an elderly person based on the assumption that the aged are no longer sexually active. An aged person may have any of the manifestations of syphilis from primary chancre to neurosyphilis, including aseptic meningitis, meningovascular disease, tabes dorsalis, and generalized paresis.

The CNS manifestations of secondary syphilis are similar to those described for other kinds of acute meningitis. Symptoms of meningitis usually occur either shortly after or up to a year following the appearance of a chancre, but rarely they may occur years later. Because the spirochete invades the basilar meninges, involvement of the optic and auditory cranial nerves is common. Other ocular findings such as iritis, uveitis, and conjunctivitis have also been described. Following 5 to 10 years of asymptomatic infection, neurologic signs and symptoms may develop as inflammatory responses occur in cerebral arteries previously invaded by spirochetes. In this case, patients present with cerebral infarction rather than aseptic meningitis.

Chronic inflammatory changes may also slowly develop within the parenchyma of the brain or spinal cord resulting in generalized paresis or tabes dorsalis. Generalized paresis usually presents as a slow, progressive decline in cognition over 10 to 30 years. In tabes dorsalis, involvement of the posterior column of the spinal cord results in diminished vibratory and positional senses with resulting wide-based slapping (tabetic) gait, ataxia, and positive Romberg sign. The dorsal ganglia and their roots are also altered, resulting in shooting pains, particularly in the lower extremities. Another manifestation of neurosyphilis is the Argyll-Robertson pupil, which accommodates but is unable to react.

The early diagnosis of neurosyphilis is essential since the disease is debilitating, progressive, and irreversible. Unfortunately, the initial nontreponemal flocculation screening tests, such as the Venereal Disease Research Laboratory (VDRL) and the rapid plasma reagin (RPR), become negative over time in 25 to 30 percent of patients with active infection. Patients strongly suspected of having neurosyphilis should have a more specific serologic test for treponemes [fluorescent treponemal antibody absorption (FTA-ABS) or microhemagglutination (MHA-TP) test] whether or not their serum VDRL or RPR test is positive. A positive FTA-ABS or MHA-TP test suggests that the patient has had exposure to syphilis but unfortunately does not reflect the activity of the disease.

A lumbar puncture should be performed in any patient with a positive specific treponemal test and symptoms that suggest CNS syphilis. Lymphocytosis and elevation of CSF protein levels are present in 30 to 70 percent of patients with secondary syphilis and 10 to 30 percent of patients with tertiary syphilis (Table 95-1). While CSF pleocytosis and protein levels tend to decrease over the course of the disease, the likelihood that the CSF VDRL will be positive increases with time. However, in 10 to 20 percent of patients, the CSF VDRL may be negative, so its absence does not exclude neurosyphilis. Some have advocated the use of CSF MHA-TP and FTA-ABS tests as more specific tests when the CSF VDRL is negative, but their use in CSF is controversial.

For neurosyphilis, the goal of treatment is to halt further damage to the CNS. The only effective treatment is intravenous benzyl penicillin G; intramuscular benzathine penicillin G does not achieve adequate spirochetocidal levels in the CNS. Failures have occurred even with intravenous penicillin therapy, and alternative regimens for penicillin-allergic patients are being evaluated. With treatment, CSF pleocytosis, protein levels, and VDRL elevated titers will slowly decline over time, although the VDRL test may remain positive for years.

FOCAL INFECTIONS

Brain Abscess

In the elderly, as in patients in other age groups, brain abscess is usually secondary to a contiguous focus of infection, such as sinusitis or otitis, and less often is acquired hematogenously from a distant focus, such as endocarditis. Rarer predisposing factors include pulmonary arteriovenous fistula, lung abscess, and meningitis with organisms such as *Listeria*.

The presentation of brain abscess is usually subacute and may be subtle, especially in the elderly. Systemic complaints and signs are uncommon unless brain abscess is a manifestation of endocarditis. Both fever and leukocytosis are present in only about half of the patients. Focal neurologic signs, hemiparesis, cranial nerve palsies, and seizures may occur. When the abscess is in the frontal lobes, nonspecific findings, such as confusion, inattentiveness, and personality changes may be the only manifestations. With increased intracranial pressure, headache, vomiting, sixth nerve palsy, and papilledema occur.

The microorganisms responsible for causing brain abscess vary with the location of the abscess. Those associated with sinusitis usually occur in the frontal lobes and are most often caused by aerobic and anaerobic streptococci. In addition, *Bacteroides* and *Fusobacterium* species, and less often *S. aureus* and other flora of the upper airways, may be present. Abscesses associated with otic foci are found in the temporoparietal lobes or posterior fossa and frequently contain, in addition to streptococci and *Bacteroides* species, gram-negative bacilli, such as *Proteus mirabilis*. Abscesses associated with endocarditis are usually due to *S. aureus* and often are multiple. Less common causes of brain abscess include *Actinomyces* and *Nocardia*.

The diagnosis of brain abscess is almost always made by contrast CT scan. Single or multiple lesions with central hypodense areas surrounded by an area of contrast enhancement and edema are usually noted. MRI scan may be more sensitive for diagnosing an early abscess when the CT scan is negative but adds little information if the CT scan shows an abscess.

Lumbar puncture should *not* be performed. The yield for determining the microbial cause of the abscess is low (<10 percent), the CSF findings are nonspecific (Table 95-1), and the procedure is very risky when an abscess causing edema and mass effect is present. Aspiration of the abscess cavity is required to determine the cause unless the patient has endocarditis with positive cultures obtained from blood.

Treatment of brain abscess varies with the microorganisms isolated. Before culture data are available, one should begin therapy with broad-spectrum antibiotics based on the most likely cause of an abscess for a given location. Antibiotics that will penetrate the blood-brain barrier and achieve bactericidal levels inside the abscess should be used. For frontal lobe abscesses and those associated with sinusitis, empiric therapy with intravenous benzyl penicillin G and metronidazole will cover streptococci and anaerobes. For abscesses associated with an otic focus and for temporoparietal or posterior fossa abscesses, therapy should cover aerobic gram-negative bacilli as well as anaerobes and streptococci. The addition of intravenous ceftriaxone or trimethoprim-sulfamethoxazole (TMP-SMX) to the previous regimen is appropriate. When the pathogens are identified, antibiotics should be switched to the most efficacious drug.

In the patient with edema surrounding the abscess and increased intracranial pressure, measures to reduce intracranial pressure may be life-saving. Corticosteroids usually are used and are rapidly tapered following response to antibiotic and/or surgical therapy.

Surgical drainage of the abscess is preferred but may not be possible when multiple abscesses are present. In this case, cures with long-term antibiotic therapy have been reported. The progress of therapy should be monitored with CT scans until the lesions have resolved.

Subdural Empyema–Epidural Abscess

Abscesses in the subdural or epidural space are less common than brain abscesses. Subdural empyema usually occurs in the area of the frontal or temporal lobes, rarely over the spinal cord. Predisposing factors include sinusitis, prior surgical procedure, and trauma. Microorganisms associated with subdural empyema include streptococci and anaerobes as in brain abscess, but also *S. aureus* and aerobic gram-negative bacilli.

The clinical symptoms and signs are very similar to those seen with brain abscess. Diagnosis is made by CT scan, and surgical drainage is almost always necessary. Initial empiric therapy should include an antistaphylococcal drug, either nafcillin or vancomycin, a drug such as ceftriaxone to cover gram-negative bacilli, and metronidazole for anaerobes.

Epidural abscesses usually occur within the spinal canal, rather than within the cranium. The most common cause of infection is *S. aureus*, followed by aerobic gram-negative bacilli. Patients with spinal epidural abscess may give a history of back trauma. They present with fever and back pain and progress insidiously to flaccid paralysis secondary to spinal cord compression. Elderly patients, in particular, may have evidence of vertebral osteomyelitis on spine roentgenogram. A prior history of bacteremia with *S. aureus* or a history of a urinary tract infection or urologic procedure may be elicited.

MRI scan is the diagnostic procedure of choice if available, but CT or myelogram also may be diagnostic. Lumbar puncture should be avoided in a febrile patient with back pain and suspected epidural abscess since the needle may actually introduce organisms into the cerebrospinal fluid, causing meningitis. Initial antimicrobial therapy should include nafcillin or vancomycin plus ceftriaxone or TMP-SMX until results of Gram's stain and cultures are known. If signs of cord compression develop, emergent laminectomy must be carried out.

BIBLIOGRAPHY

Bacterial Meningitis

Behrman RE et al: Central nervous system infections in the elderly. *Arch Intern Med* 149:1596, 1989.

Gorse GJ et al: Bacterial meningitis in the elderly. *Arch Intern Med* 144:1603, 1984.

Cherubin CE et al: Listeria and gram-negative bacillary meningitis in New York City, 1972-1979. *Am J Med* 71:199, 1981.

Berk SL: Bacterial meningitis, in Gleckman RA, Gantz NM (eds): *Infections in the Elderly.* Boston, Little, Brown, 1983, p 235.

Spagnuolo PJ et al: *Haemophilus influenzae* meningitis: The spectrum of disease in adults. *Medicine* 61:74, 1983.

Geiseler PJ et al: Community-acquired purulent meningitis: A review of 1316 cases during the antibiotic era, 1954–1976. *Rev Infect Dis* 2:725, 1980.

Tunkel AR et al: Bacterial meningitis: Recent advances in pathophysiology and treatment. *Ann Intern Med* 112:610, 1990.

Tauber MG, Sande MA: Principles in the treatment of bacterial meningitis. *Am J Med* 74:224, 1984.

Gray LD, Fedorko BP: Laboratory diagnosis of bacterial meningitis. *Clin Microbiol Rev* 5:130, 1992.

LeFrock JL et al: Gram-negative bacillary meningitis. *Med Clin North Am* 69:243, 1985.

Talan DA et al: Role of empiric parenteral antibiotics prior to lumbar puncture in suspected bacterial meningitis: State of the art. *Rev Infect Dis* 10:365, 1988.

Sen P, Louria DB: Central nervous system infections, in Cunha BA (ed): *Infectious Disease in the Elderly.* Littleton, MA, PSG, 1988, p 25.

Viral Meningitis

Whitley RJ et al: Vidarabine versus acyclovir therapy in herpes simplex encephalitis. *N Engl J Med* 314:144, 1986.

Ho DD, Hirsch MS: Acute viral encephalitis. *Med Clin North Am* 69:415, 1985.

Powell KE, Blakely DL: St. Louis encephalitis. The 1975 epidemic in Mississippi. *JAMA* 237:2294, 1977.

Whitley RJ: Viral encephalitis. *N Engl J Med* 323:242, 1990.

Verghese A, Sugar AM: Herpes zoster ophthalmicus and granulomatous angiitis. An ill-appreciated cause of stroke. *J Am Geriatrics Soc* 34:309, 1986.

Tuberculous Meningitis

Molavi A, LeFrock JL: Tuberculous meningitis. *Med Clin North Am* 69:315, 1985.

Ogawa SK et al: Tuberculous meningitis in an urban medical center. *Medicine* 66:317, 1987.

Fungal Meningitis

Lewis JL, Rabinovich S: The wide spectrum of cryptococcal infections. *Am J Med* 53:315, 1972.

Stockstill MT, Kauffman CA: A comparison of cryptococcal and tuberculous meningitis. *Arch Neurol* 40:81, 1983.

Neurosyphilis

Hook EW, Marra CM: Acquired syphilis in adults. *N Engl J Med* 326:1060, 1992.

Corrado OJ et al: The prevalence of positive serological tests for syphilis among elderly hospital patients. *Age Ageing* 18:407, 1989.

Berinstein D, DeHertogh D: Recently acquired syphilis in the elderly population. *Arch Intern Med* 152:330, 1992.

Brain Abscess

Britt RH, Enzmann DR: Clinical stages of human brain abscesses on serial CT scans after contrast infusion. *J Neurosurg* 59:972, 1983.

Garvey G: Current concepts of bacterial infections of the central nervous system. *J Neurosurg* 59:735, 1983.

Subdural Empyema–Epidural Abscess

Kaufman DM et al: Sinusitis-induced subdural empyema. *Neurology* 33:123, 1983.

Hlavin ML et al: Spinal epidural abscess: A ten-year perspective. *Neurosurgery* 27:177, 1990.

Chapter 96

HEAD INJURY

Dennis G. Vollmer and Marc E. Eichler

Because trauma is the leading cause of death of individuals less than 45 years of age,[1–3] it is generally considered to be an affliction of young people. It should be remembered, however, that injuries rank fifth among causes of death for adults 65 years of age or older; 25 percent of all trauma fatalities occur in this age group, which constitutes only about 11 percent of the population.[4–6] Furthermore, the cost of trauma is substantial, with nearly one-third of the annual health care resources available for the treatment of trauma consumed by the elderly.[7,8] Serious trauma is not more frequent in the geriatric population, but when it occurs, it has a greater likelihood of producing a fatal outcome.[6] Within this context, traumatic brain injury is particularly important because of its high toll in mortality and serious morbidity. It has been increasingly well appreciated that even a relatively mild head injury may produce prolonged sequelae.[9–14] Survivors of more severe brain trauma often suffer significant disability. Many such patients have severe neuropsychological deficits despite the absence of gross neurologic or physical sequelae.[14–17] In the geriatric age group, mortality rates following severe brain trauma approach 90 percent.[18–26] Elderly survivors tend to have more prolonged hospitalizations and are left with more severe sequelae.[18] Elderly patients also appear to have a lesser ability to recover from neurologic insult so that milder injuries are less well tolerated.[9,19,27,28] Despite the serious implications of head injury in the older adult, relatively few studies have concentrated primarily on the problem of head injury in this age group.[19,29–31] It is clear, however, that with the aging of the population in most developed countries and with the rapidly escalating cost of medical care, the issue of traumatic brain injury in the geriatric patient will be of ever-increasing interest and importance. In this chapter, we will focus upon head injury in the elderly patient, examining epidemiology, pathophysiology, and treatment.

EPIDEMIOLOGIC CONSIDERATIONS

The overall incidence of head injury in the United States is estimated to be in the range of 200 per 100,000 per year.[3] Considerable differences are observed, however, when age-specific incidence rates are examined (Fig. 96-1). Most studies have demonstrated a peak incidence for young adults in the 15- to 25-year age range with a secondary rise in incidence rates in the elderly population.[1,3,18,32] For individuals age 65 or over, the incidence has been estimated to approximate the overall national rate.[3]

In most studies a gender effect is observed into the extremes of old age (Fig. 96-2). For example, Cooper et al. have shown a twofold or greater incidence of head injury in men older than 65 compared with women in this same age group.[32] The causes for male predominance in geriatric head injury are less clear than for younger age groups. Many of the factors usually blamed for injuries in elderly persons would appear to affect both sexes equally. According to census data from 1982, there are 1.5 women for each man in the population 65 and older.[4] This changing sex ratio observed in the population over age 65 acts to obscure somewhat the sex-related dif-

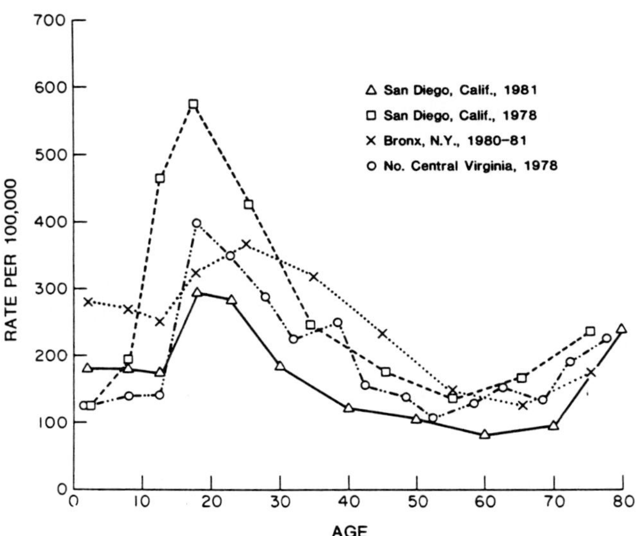

FIGURE 96-1
Age-specific incidence rates for head injury. Note the rise in incidence after age 60. (*From Kraus,[3] with permission.*)

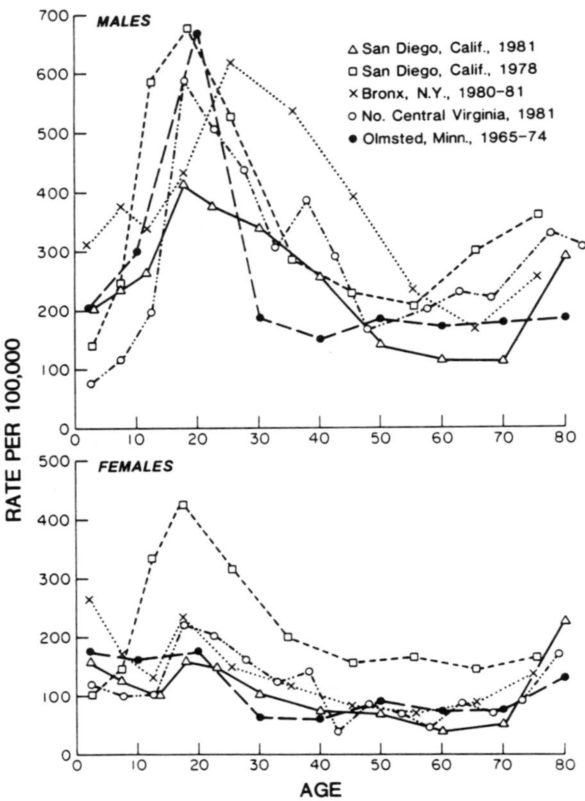

FIGURE 96-2

Age-specific incidence rates of head injury for males (upper) and females (lower). The incidence rate for males is approximately twice that for females for all age groups. (*From Kraus,*[3] *with permission.*)

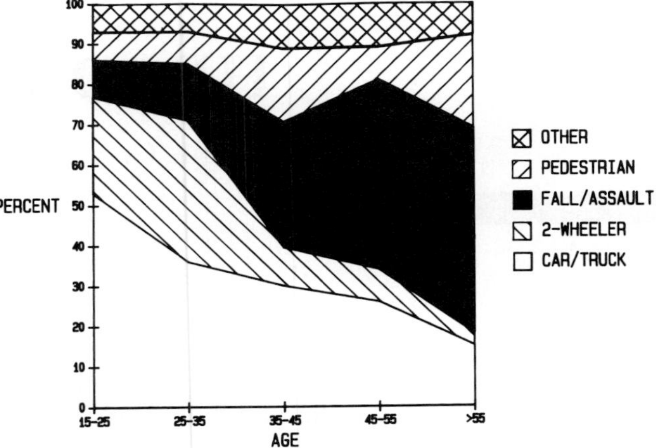

FIGURE 96-3

Mechanism of injury according to age for 540 patients analyzed in the National Institutes of Health—Traumatic Coma Data Bank. Note the increase in the percentage of injuries due to falls and assaults in the older patients with the reciprocal decline in the percentage due to vehicular accidents.

ferences in incidence. For this reason many hospital-based studies of head injury may report equal numbers of elderly men and women treated.[30]

The distribution of causes observed for head injuries varies depending upon numerous factors. The characteristics of the population under study—e.g., urban versus rural, higher versus lower socioeconomic status, differences in racial composition—all influence the relative frequency of the different causes observed.[3] In addition, the cause of an injury varies with the severity of the injury, i.e., studies of severe injuries have higher frequencies of vehicular accidents, whereas falls are more common in studies of minor injuries. Age is also a key determinant of the cause of head trauma. In a preliminary analysis of data on severe head injury from the National Institutes of Health—Traumatic Coma Data Bank,[33] the cause of injury was clearly associated with the age of the patient (Fig. 96-3).[34] Older adults tended to have much higher rates of falls and assaults, whereas the percentage of individuals injured in vehicular accidents decreased with age. Pedestrian injuries were more common in older age groups as well.

The significance of fall injuries in the elderly person is well known.[35–37] It has been noted that 35 to 40 percent of all individuals over age 65 suffer at least one fall each year and that the risk increases sharply with advancing age.[38] It is not surprising then that older patients with head injuries are more likely to have had a fall as the causative event. The reasons for the greater risk of falling in the elderly, including postural hypotension, cardiac dysrhythmias, degenerative joint disease, and polypharmacy, are also well described.[35,39–41] Further, decreases in visual acuity, coordination, balance, proprioception, and muscle strength have also been cited as contributing to higher rates of falling in the elderly population.[41] Many of these same factors increase the risk for pedestrian injury as well.

CLINICAL PATHOLOGY

The age of a patient appears to influence the frequency with which specific brain disease is encountered after head injury. For example, it is recognized that patients with subdural hematomas are older on average than patients with other disease processes.[42,43] The reasons for this observation are clearly multiple. It has been well documented by both laboratory and clinical study that a fall injury is more likely to result in biomechanical forces which favor the production of an acute subdural hematoma.[44] On the other hand, the biomechanics of motor vehicle accidents appear more likely to result in a so-called diffuse axonal shearing injury. In a clinical series, Gennarelli et al. noted that falls and assaults caused a disproportionate number of acute subdural hematomas (72 percent), whereas the cause of diffuse axonal shearing injury was vehicular in 89 percent of cases.[45] It therefore stands to reason that elderly persons, who have a higher incidence of falling, would also have a greater chance of sustaining an acute subdural hematoma. Other factors also appear to predispose elderly patients to the development of acute subdural hematomas. Brain atrophy, which occurs with age, places the parasagittal bridging veins on a greater degree of stretch, making them more prone to rupture after an impact. Similarly, in the setting of brain atrophy, a given degree of angular acceleration is likely to produce more brain movement because there is more space. Changes in the viscoelastic properties of the brain parenchyma and the vascular elements brought on by the aging process may also play a role.[44,46]

The acute subdural hematoma is the most lethal of the mass lesions and of all abnormalities is associated with the greatest risk of dying. Mortality rates above 60 percent are frequently reported.[24,45,47,48] In rapidly expanding subdural hematomas, signs of increased intracranial pressure may appear soon after trauma. However, in the elderly person with cerebral atrophy, there is increased intracranial capacity available to accommodate the hematoma. The onset of symptoms, therefore, is usually more insidious, and changes in mentation and focal findings tend to predominate as opposed to signs of increased intracranial pressure. In the National Institutes of Health—Traumatic Coma Data Bank there was a strong association between age and dying in those patients with severe injuries and subdural hematoma, so that patients younger than 40 years had less than a 40 percent chance of dying (the lowest rate yet reported in large series), whereas those older than 40 years had a 70 percent chance (unpublished data). These data are supported by more recent studies in which older patients were more often seen with acute subdural hematomas and large hemorrhagic lesions resulting in a significantly worse outcome.[49,50]

In contrast to acute subdural hematoma, the incidence of epidural hematoma appears to decrease with age, although skull fractures seem to be just as common in elderly as in younger patients.[34,51] The greater adherence of the dura to the inner table of the skull in older individuals likely impedes the development of an extradural collection.

The syndrome of delayed traumatic intracerebral hematoma, however, does appear to occur more frequently in older patients.[52] The clinical hallmark of this entity is the relatively abrupt neurologic deterioration of a patient several days after a head injury which often was only of mild or moderate severity. The lesions in delayed traumatic intracerebral hematoma tend to develop in areas of contusion.[52] Neurologic deterioration may not be readily apparent in patients who are initially comatose, however; thus a low threshold for repeat computed tomographic (CT) scanning particularly in patients who have elevated intracranial pressure must be maintained.

CHRONIC SUBDURAL HEMATOMA

Chronic subdural hematoma is a distinct clinicopathologic entity which differs significantly in its manner of presentation, treatment, and prognosis from acute subdural hematoma, discussed previously.[31,53–55] This entity largely affects patients who are middle-aged or older with increasing incidence associated with advancing age. It is generally felt that brain atrophy with the associated tethering of the parasagittal bridging veins results in a propensity for the formation of chronic subdural hematomas. Further, the decreased cerebral volume in this situation allows larger hematomas to accumulate without significant symptoms. Although the injury may be mild, trauma is generally thought to be the precipitating factor in the formation of these lesions. However, a clear history of head injury may be absent in 20 to 50 percent of patients.[42,53] Patients with chronic subdural hematomas, by definition, present 3 or more weeks after injury.[42] Hematomas presenting earlier after trauma have been traditionally termed subacute subdural hematomas. This distinction is somewhat arbitrary. From a practical point of view, patients who present with slowly progressive signs and symptoms, with a liquid clot in the subdural space, are comparable regardless of the exact history of trauma.[4]

The presentation of chronic subdural hematoma is quite variable.[31,42,53] Signs and symptoms tend to be insidious and slowly progressive. Although focal neurologic deficits may prompt a search for an intracranial mass lesion, patients with chronic subdural hematoma often present with nonspecific signs and symptoms such as headache, nausea and vomiting, apathy, alteration in level of consciousness, personality changes, or overt dementia. The lack of a clear relationship of this deterioration with antecedent trauma further complicates the diagnosis. Because chronic subdural hematoma commonly affects elderly persons, who are at risk for a great many other neurologic and systemic disorders, the diagnosis is often delayed.

CT scanning is presently the diagnostic method of choice for patients suspected of harboring a chronic subdural hematoma.[54] In the majority of cases, the lesions are hypodense crescentic collections over the convexity of the cerebral hemispheres. There is frequently associated mass effect with shift of compression of the ventricular system. Occasionally the CT scan appearance is less straightforward, with the lesions demonstrating multiple densities within the collection or with layering of hyperdense material posteriorly. In some cases, the hematomas may be isodense with normal brain, and in these cases the radiographic signs of an intracranial mass, as well as the obliteration of the cortical sulci, should raise the question of a chronic subdural hematoma. When there is doubt, contrast enhancement can help establish the diagnosis. Magnetic resonance imaging (MRI) scans also demonstrate these lesions adeptly.[38,41] MRI has certain advantages over CT. MRI clearly demonstrates the subdural hematoma that is in the isodense and hypodense phase on CT. MRI also better depicts small subdural collections at the vertex, at the base of the skull, and in the posterior fossa.[56,57] While MRI has shown advantages in the demonstration of nonacute subdural hematomas, CT remains the procedure of choice in the acute setting.

Chronic subdural hematomas, being largely liquid, are often amenable to a much less extensive surgical treatment than acute subdural hematomas. Although numerous variations in treatment have been advocated, drainage of the collection using burr holes and a small twist drill craniostomy with closed system drainage appear to be the methods most commonly employed (Fig. 96-4*A* and *B*).[31,53–55,58,59]

The prognosis for chronic subdural hematoma is significantly better than for acute subdural hematoma. Mortality rates in most series have generally been lower than 15 percent.[55] Higher mortality and morbidity seem to occur in patients whose level of neurologic function is more severely impaired prior to treatment. In addition, elderly or debilitated patients tend to fare worse, in terms of both mortality and morbidity.[31] Recurrence of the collection requiring further treatment is not uncommon and may occur in as many as 20 percent of patients.[55]

MINOR HEAD INJURY

A head injury is considered minor when it produces a transient loss of consciousness, usually 20 minutes or

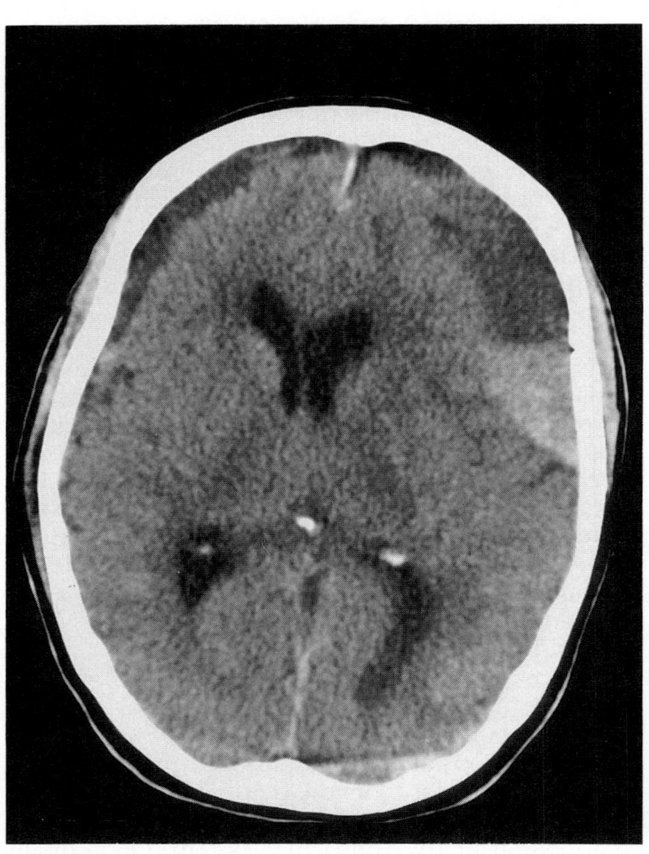

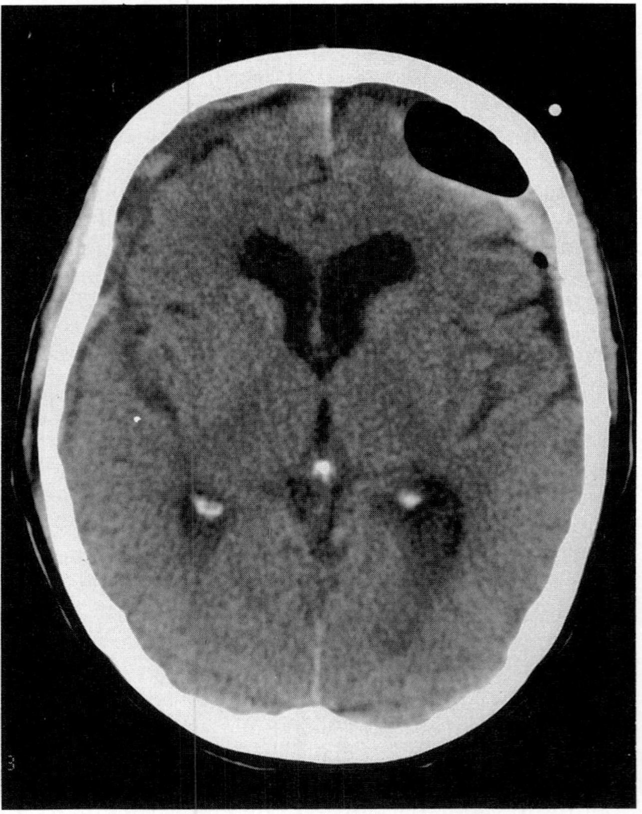

FIGURE 96-4

CT scan of a 90-year-old woman with a history of falling 1 week previously. The patient was comatose at the time of the scan shown in *A*. *A*. CT scan demonstrating a chronic and subacute subdural hematoma over the left frontoparietal region. A smaller extraaxial fluid collection is noted over the right frontal region. A remarkable midline shift to the right side is also noted. *B*. CT scan 24 hours after the initiation of subdural drainage through a twist drill craniostomy and closed system drainage reveals definite reduction in the volume of the subdural hematoma. Although some subdural fluid remains, the midline shift has resolved. The patient is fully alert and oriented without focal neurologic signs.

less in duration, with a relatively rapid return to full alertness. Patients present for evaluation with a Glasgow Coma Scale (GCS) score of 13 or better. In a series of 1248 consecutive head injury patients seen at the University of Virginia, such minor head injuries accounted for 55 percent of the total.[13] Patients age 60 years or older accounted for 4 percent of this series. In a subsequent series of minor head injuries studies at the same institution, 81 of 1216 patients (6.7 percent) were 60 years of age or older.[9,10] In these studies it does not appear that the geriatric population is predisposed to head injuries of this severity. However, these data are not population-based, so strict conclusions about the epidemiology of minor head injury in the elderly population cannot be made.

In recent years, it has become more apparent that minor head injuries can and do result in sequelae which persist for a considerable length of time.[60] Rimel et al. reported a series of patients examined 3 months after minor head injury.[13] While only 2 percent manifested positive findings on neurologic examination, the majority of patients tested (n = 69) showed substandard scores on a battery of neuropsychological tests. Furthermore, 34 percent of patients gainfully employed prior to a mild head injury remained unemployed 3 months after the injury. Other studies have described similar results.[12,16,61,62] Although the duration of subsequent impairment continues to be debated, most investigators agree that minor head injury produces significant, objective neuropsychological deficits. None of the studies alluded to have specifically examined the effects of minor head injury on the elderly patient. It seems logical to assume that similar sequelae might be seen in aged persons, but the question as to whether these effects are more severe cannot be answered with confidence. However, in a recent study, older age did correlate significantly with the likelihood of an abnormal CT scan after minor head injury.[63] Further, Colohan et al. performed a linear multiple regression analysis of factors associated with hospital stay and return to normal social activity after minor head injury.[9] In each instance, advanced age proved to be a highly significant, independent predictor of a poorer outcome.

OUTCOME

It is well known that the prognosis following a closed head injury worsens significantly with increasing age.[2,18,20,26,27,34,49,64] Figure 96-5 shows outcome data according to age for patients entered into the National Institutes of Health—Traumatic Coma Data Bank between January 1984 and September 1986. Mortality increases with age for all levels of severity of injury studied. Vegetative survival, however, appears to be relatively constant in all age groups, approximating 5 percent.

Although a relatively large number of patients were studied in the National Institutes of Health—

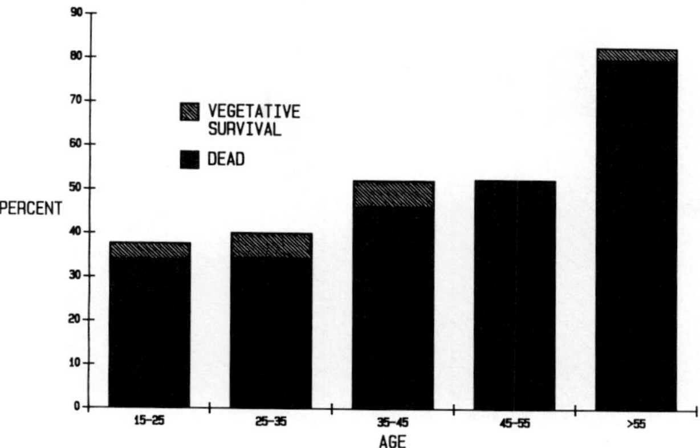

FIGURE 96-5
Outcome after severe head injury according to age. Percentage dead or surviving in a vegetative state for 540 patients entered into the National Institute of Health—Traumatic Coma Data.

Traumatic Coma Data Bank, it is not possible to assess accurately whether the age-related risk of mortality after head injury increases in a linear fashion or whether there are increments of risk at various age thresholds. In the International Data Bank, a continuous relationship was found between age and outcome,[25] whereas other studies have suggested that inflections in the age–outcome curve may occur at 20, 40, and 60 years of age.[18,64]

The causes of the adverse effect of age on the outcome in head injury are also unclear. Several authors have attributed the higher rates of mortality to the greater frequency of prior systemic illness or secondary medical complications seen in elderly patients.[27,65] Others have suggested that events primary to the central nervous system may be involved.[10,34] Furthermore, the greater frequency of intracranial hematomas in elderly patients may play a role since the mortality associated with these lesions remains high. Interestingly, in the International Data Bank, older patients who did not have an intracranial hematoma did not fare any better than the cohort of those who did.[20]

In the National Institutes of Health—Traumatic Coma Data Bank, the primary cause of death was determined for 236 patients (Fig. 96-6). No age-related increase in extracerebral causes of death were noted.[34] These findings contrast sharply with those of Carlsson et al., who attributed excess mortality associated with increasing age to extracranial complications.[27] Interestingly, however, in Carlsson's series, patients with "surgically oriented complications such as intracranial hematoma, depressed fracture, lacerations of the brain, and localized space-occupying cerebral confusion" were not included. In the National Institutes of Health—Traumatic Coma Data Bank in which CT scans were utilized, elderly patients demonstrating none of these complications constituted a very small minority (5 percent). Hypotension or hypoxemia are well known to increase the chances

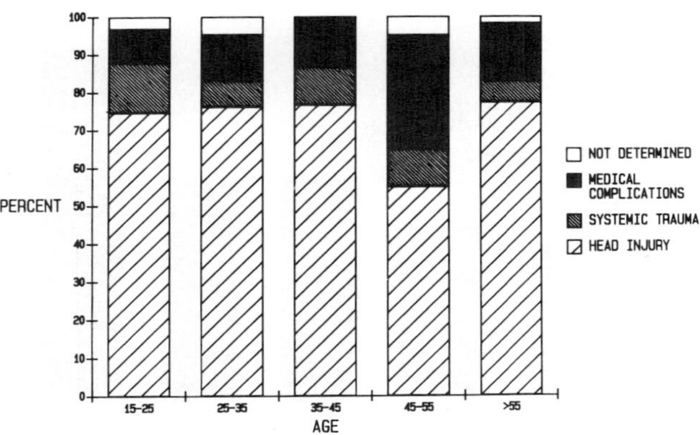

FIGURE 96-6

Primary cause of death as determined by the medical team caring for 236 patients. No significant differences or trends are observed according to age. (*From National Institutes of Health—Traumatic Coma Data Bank.*)

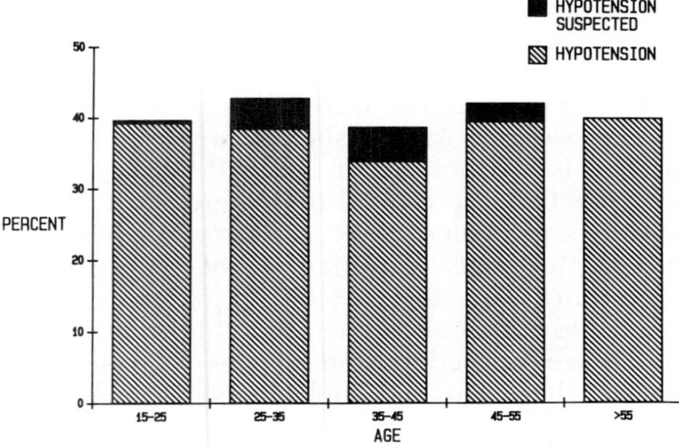

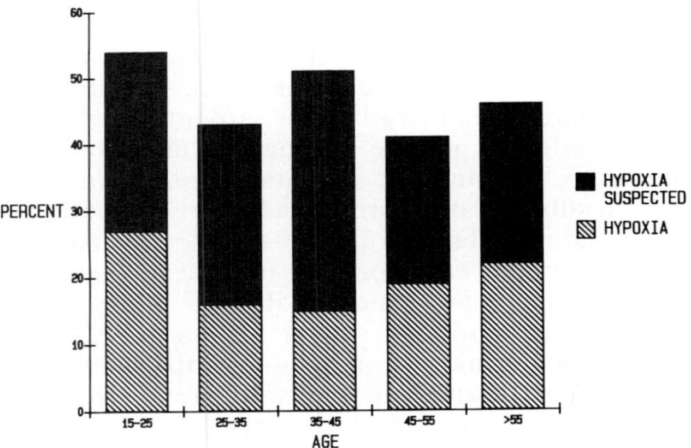

FIGURE 96-7

Hypotension and hypoxia in severe injury. *A.* Percentage of 539 patients with hypotension, defined as systolic blood pressure lower than 100 mmHg (upper). *B.* Percentage of 524 patients exhibiting hypoxia defined as PaO_2 less than 60 mmHg. No significant differences were observed for the various age groups. (*From National Institutes of Health—Traumatic Coma Data Bank.*)

of death after head injury.[66] In the National Institutes of Health—Traumatic Coma Data Bank, neither of these abnormalities was more common in the older groups of patients (Fig. 96-7), but multiple injuries were less frequent in older patients (Fig. 96-8). This is not surprising when the cause of injury is taken into account, since multiple injuries are more common after vehicular trauma. Multiple injuries in elderly patients, however, result in particularly poor outcomes.

In addition to having a higher overall mortality rate after head injury, geriatric patients also continue to die further along in their hospital course (Fig. 96-9). Of patients admitted to the hospital who ultimately die of their injuries, 60 percent age 55 years or older die later than 48 hours after injury. In contrast, 61 percent of patients younger than 55 who ultimately die do so within 48 hours of injury.[34] The implication is that older patients may be dying from different causes than their younger counterparts. Further study is required to determine these causes as well as to possibly define subsets within the elderly head-injured population whose prognosis is substantially better (or worse) than the age group as a whole.

Age has also been shown to be a powerful predictor of outcome in statistical models that considered multiple variables and their interactions. Jennett, Tesdale, and their coworkers[67–69] demonstrated that an accurate prediction of outcome with a high level of confidence can be made using information from the International Data Bank in models employing a sequential Bayes method. Using this technique and data from 305 patients admitted to the Netherland centers, Braakman and his associates ranked the order of variables that best fitted the model. On admission, the rank order of best predictors were age, pupillary responses, and the eye and motor score (from the GCS). At different times after injury, the relative importance of these variables changed within the model, but age always ranked highly.[64] Narayan, Stablein, and their coworkers[70,71] applied a logistic regression model to analyze their data from patients admitted in acute traumatic coma. The rank order of the 12 most important variables is shown in Table 96-1.

Lesion appearance on CT scans has been used to predict neuropsychological outcome from brain injury in patients of all age groups.[49,72] More recently, additional studies have demonstrated neurologic deficits in association with trauma evident on MRI such as diffuse axonal injury.[73,74] Eventually, lesion location and severity as identified by acute-phase MRI may be associated with specific types of neurobehavioral deficits after head injury. Presently, however, there is a relative paucity of information regarding the functional outlook for elderly survivors of head injury. Pazzaglia et al. showed a decreasing quality of survival with increasing age for patients after coma-producing

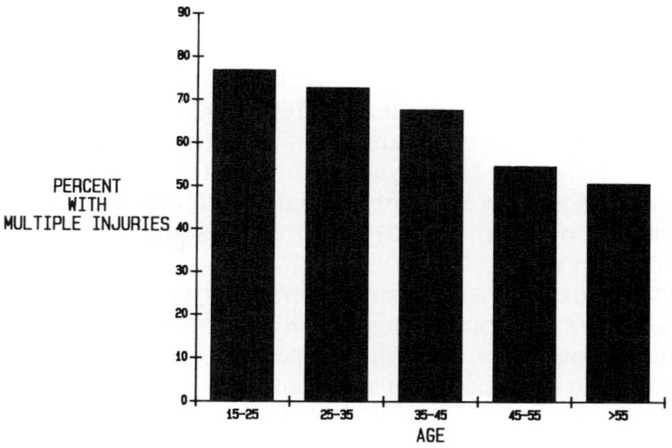

FIGURE 96-8

Percentage of 540 patients with severe head injury who have multiple injuries, defined as an associated injury scale greater than 1. The decline in multiple injuries in older age groups was statistically significant. (*From National Institutes of Health—Traumatic Coma Data Bank.*)

TABLE 96-1

Statistical Importance of 12 Variables*

Ranking of Factors in Order of Prognostic Importance	Regression Coefficients (Mean ± SEM)	Asymptomatic Z Test
1. Requirement for surgical decompression	−2.55 ± 0.98	−2.60
2. Age	−0.06 ± 0.02	−2.56
3. $P_{O_2} \leq 65$; $P_{CO_2} > 45$; systolic blood pressure ≤ 90; hematocrit ≤ 30	−2.72 ± 1.18	−2.32
4. Motor response	−3.57 ± 1.59	−2.24
5. Pupil light response	−2.59 ± 1.31	−1.97
6. Interaction between motor response and presence of mass lesion	3.23 ± 1.71	1.89
7. Mass lesion presence on CT scan	−1.81 ± 1.01	−1.80
8. Eye opening to pain	−1.63 ± 1.01	−1.62
9. Pupil size	−1.75 ± 1.24	−1.41
10. Sex	1.18 ± 0.91	1.29
11. Oculocephalic response	1.46 ± 1.26	1.16
12. Verbal response	0.785 ± 0.99	0.80

*The regression coefficient for the intercept term is $a = 6.23 \pm 1.54$.

SOURCE: From Stablein et al.[71]

head injury.[24] Similarly, the study of mild head injury reported by Colohan et al. demonstrated that age is an independent predictor both for longer hospital stay and for later return to baseline social functioning.[9] On the other hand, in a series of 26 head-injured elderly patients admitted to a rehabilitation unit, 85 percent were noted to return to a home setting, with over half being independent in activities of daily living.[29] Thus, a uniformly pessimistic attitude does not appear to be justified.

Many studies have demonstrated an association between head trauma and Alzheimer's disease.[75–78] The hypothesis of a "threshold" of neuronal loss and damage to the blood-brain barrier offers the most plausible mechanism by which head trauma could be of etiologic importance in the development of Alzheimer's disease.[79] Neuronal loss increases with age, and it is possible that this loss may be accelerated by a head injury. Further, aging has also been implicated in the ability of neuronal systems to recover from structural damage.[80] Therefore, the brain's ability for regrowth and reorganization may diminish with age, resulting in an even higher association of head trauma and Alzheimer's disease in the elderly population.[76]

EVALUATION AND TREATMENT

In principle, the evaluation and treatment of the elderly, head-injured patient differs little from that of

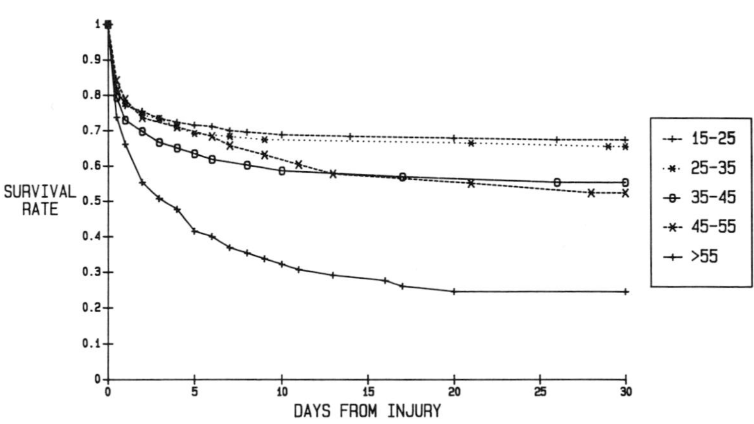

FIGURE 96-9

Survival rates according to age for severely head-injured patients. Note that survival rates within the first 24 hours are similar for all age groups. Older patients continue to die later in their hospital course. (*From National Institutes of Health—Traumatic Coma Data Bank.*)

the younger adult[81]; the primary goal is the prevention of secondary brain damage. Initial attention, as in all trauma patients, should be directed to the airway, respiratory function, and hemodynamic status. Because the injured brain is more susceptible to the effects of hypoxia and ischemia, intubation and ventilatory support should be considered early in the management of severe head injury. It has been shown that longer times from injury to intubation correlate with poorer outcomes.[11] Furthermore, hypoxia is common in head injuries even in the absence of apparent respiratory difficulty.[82] Aggressive fluid resuscitation may be necessary to maintain adequate cerebral perfusion, especially when there are associated extracranial injuries.

Associated cervical spine injuries should be assumed to be present until ruled out by appropriate radiographic examination. The patient should therefore be immobilized. Degenerative and inflammatory arthritides and osteopenia, more common in the elderly population, may increase the risk of associated spine fractures in this age group. One should be cognizant of both a retropharyngeal hematoma causing upper airway obstruction after hyperextension injury in an elderly patient[83] and central cord syndrome following a hyperextension injury in patients with congenital or spondylotic cervical spinal stenosis. This central cord syndrome is most commonly observed in an elderly male patient who has suffered a fall and is immediately rendered quadriparetic, most severely in the upper extremities, often with significant preservation of lower-extremity function.

The baseline neurologic assessment is performed during the initial resuscitation. This evaluation should not be exhaustive and time-consuming but should rather focus upon the patient's level of consciousness, the presence of lateralizing deficits, and the status of brainstem reflex function. The specific aspects of the examination must be tailored to the patient's status.

The GCS provides a reproducible means of objectively quantifying the level of consciousness by examining verbal, eye-opening, and motor responses. It has been shown to correlate well with outcome and has become a standard means for quantifying the severity of injury in head trauma literature. While the GCS[20,23,69] is a useful tool for the evaluation of head-injured patients, there are limitations to its use. The GCS may overestimate brain injuries in patients who are hypoxemic, postictal, or intoxicated or who are in shock.[81] Several studies have examined the importance of assessing brainstem function in severe head injury and have found that this assessment adds significantly to prognostic accuracy.[64,67,70,84] This part of the examination should assess the pupillary light reflex, spontaneous eye movements, oculocephalic or oculovestibular responses, the response to corneal stimulation, the presence of gag and cough reflexes, and the respiratory rate and pattern. The motor examination is incorporated in part in the GCS, but attention should also be directed to the presence of lateralizing findings such as a hemiparesis or hemiplegia. These abnormalities often indicate the presence of an expanding intracranial mass lesion particularly when coupled with a fixed or dilated pupil. When present, a unilaterally dilated pupil is ipsilateral to a mass lesion in more than 95 percent of cases. Although it is usually contralateral to a mass, hemiplegia is occasionally ipsilateral to a lesion. This seems to occur most often in mass lesions which develop rapidly.

In the assessment of elderly patients following head injury, one must be careful to consider the possibility of other confounding diseases. For example, a head injury sustained in a fall may have been precipitated by a syncopal episode or cerebral ischemia. Similarly, a motor vehicle accident may be the cause, or the result, of an intracerebral hemorrhage in an elderly motorist. While these scenarios may occur in patients of any age, they are most apt to occur in the geriatric patient with the greater incidence of underlying disease.

SUMMARY AND CONCLUSIONS

Head injury in the elderly adult is not uncommon and may affect more than 200 per 100,000 population per year in the United States. The magnitude of the problem is further compounded when the excessive rates of mortality and morbidity for patients in this age group are examined. The mortality rate after severe head injury rises continuously with increasing age and exceeds 75 percent in the older age groups. Morbidity in terms of both neurologic and nonneurologic complications also appears to increase with advancing age.

Falls are the leading cause of head injury in the geriatric age group. Older individuals are also at greater risk for pedestrian injury. Age-related differences in the incidence of intracranial mass lesions are also observed. The elderly have higher rates of acute and chronic subdural hematomas and delayed traumatic intracerebral hemorrhage. Epidural hematoma is less frequently seen in elderly head-injured patients.

Further study of clinical head injury in the elderly as well as of the basic neurobiology of aging is required to fully understand the age-related differences in outcome. An improved understanding of the pathophysiology involved may lead to more effective treatment.

The excessive incidence of adverse outcome in the head-injured elderly patient remains a difficult challenge for modern health care. For the present, it would appear that the greatest reductions in mortality and morbidity might be achieved through efforts directed at the prevention of injury. As suggested by the data on causes of injury in the elderly population, measures which can reduce the likelihood of falling or the likelihood of sustaining a head injury if a fall occurs should receive a high priority.

REFERENCES

1. Annegers JF et al: The incidence, causes, and secular trends of head trauma in Olmsted County, Minnesota, 1935–1974. *Neurology* 30:912, 1980.
2. Conroy C, Kraus JF: Survival after brain injury; cause of death, length of survival and prognostic variables in a cohort of brain-injured people. *Neuroepidemiology* 7:13, 1988.
3. Kraus JF: Epidemiology of head injury, in Cooper PR (ed): *Head Injury,* 2nd ed. Baltimore, Williams & Wilkins, 1987.
4. Brody JA et al: Trends in the health of the elderly population. *Annu Rev Public Health* 8:211, 1987.
5. Lauer AR: Age and sex in relation to accidents. *Traffic Safety Res Rev* 3:21, 1959.
6. Oreskovich MR et al: Geriatric trauma: Injury patterns and outcome. *J Trauma* 24:565, 1984.
7. Mueller MS, Gibson RM: Age difference in health care spending. *Soc Secur Bull* 39:18, 1976.
8. Saywell RM et al: The value of age and severity as predictors of costs in geriatric head trauma patients. *J Am Geriatr Soc* 37:625, 1989.
9. Colohan ART et al: Factors influencing outcome after mild head injury. Paper presented at the Congress of Neurological Surgeons Meeting, Hawaii, September 1985.
10. Farmer JP et al: Less than severe head injury—An overview. *Acta Anaesthesiol Belg* 38:427, 1987.
11. Gildenberg PL, Makela M: Effect of early intubation and ventilation on outcome following head trauma, in Dacey RG Jr et al (eds): *Trauma of the Central Nervous System.* New York, Raven, 1985, p 79.
12. O'Shaughnessy EJ et al: Sequence of mild closed head injuries. *J Fam Pract* 18:391, 1984.
13. Rimel RW et al: Disability caused by minor head injury. *Neurosurgery* 9:221, 1981.
14. Rimel RW et al: Moderate head injury: Completing the clinical spectrum of brain trauma. *Neurosurgery* 11:344, 1982.
15. Jennett B, Teasdale G: *Management of Head-Injuries.* Philadelphia, Davis, 1981.
16. McLean A Jr et al: Psychosocial functioning at one month after head injury. *Neurosurgery* 14:393, 1984.
17. Tabaddor K et al: Cognitive sequelae and recovery course after moderate and severe head injury. *Neurosurgery* 14:701, 1984.
18. Heiskanen O, Sipponen P: Prognosis of severe brain injury. *Acta Neurol Scand* 46:343, 1970.
19. Hernesniemi J: Outcome following head injury in the aged. *Acta Neurochir* 49:67, 1979.
20. Jennett B et al: Prognosis of patients with severe head injury. *Neurosurgery* 4:283, 1979.
21. Klun B, Fettich M: Factors determining prognosis in acute subdural hematoma. *Acta Neurochir* 28 (suppl):134, 1979.
22. Orosz E: Factors influencing the outcome of coma in severely injured patients. *Acta Neurochir* 28 (suppl):137, 1979.
23. Overgaard J et al: Prognosis after head injury based on early clinical examination. *Lancet* 2:631, 1973.
24. Pazzaglia P et al: Clinical course and prognosis of acute post-traumatic coma. *J Neurol Neurosurg Psychiatry* 38:149, 1975.
25. Teasdale G et al: Age and outcome of severe head injury. *Acta Neurochir* 28(suppl):140, 1979.
26. Teasdale G et al: Age, severity and outcome of head injury, in Grossman RG, Gildenberg PL (eds): *Head Injury: Basic and Clinical Aspects.* New York, Raven, 1982, p 213.
27. Carlsson CA et al: Factors affecting the clinical course of patients with severe head injuries: 1. Influence of biological factors. 2. Significance of post-traumatic coma. *J Neurosurg* 29:242, 1968.
28. Russell WR: Cerebral involvement in head injury: A study based on the examination of two hundred cases. *Brain* 55:549, 1932.
29. Davis CS, Acton P: Treatment of the elderly brain-injured patient; experience in a traumatic brain injury unit. *J Am Geriatr Soc* 36:225, 1988.
30. Pentland B et al: Head injury in the elderly. *Age Ageing* 15:193, 1986.
31. Raskind R et al: Chronic subdural hematoma in the elderly: A challenge in diagnosis and treatment. *J Am Geriatr Soc* 20:330, 1972.
32. Cooper KD et al: The epidemiology of head injury in the Bronx. *Neuroepidemiology* 2:70, 1983.
33. Marshall LF et al: The National Traumatic Coma Data Bank: I. Design, purpose, goals and results. *J Neurosurg* 59:279, 1983.
34. Vollmer DG et al: Age and outcome following traumatic coma: Why do older patients fare worse? *J Neurosurg* 75(suppl):37, 1991.
35. Baker SP, Harvey AH: Fall injuries in the elderly. *Clin Geriatr Med* 1:501, 1985.
36. Hadley E et al: Falls and gait disorders among the elderly: A challenge for research. *Clin Geriatr Med* 1:497, 1985.
37. Morse JM: Computerized evaluation of a scale to identify the fall-prone patient. *Can J Public Health* 77 (suppl 1):21, 1986.
38. Sipponen JT et al: Chronic subdural hematoma: Demonstration by magnetic resonance. *Radiology* 150:79, 1984.
39. Degutis LC, Baker CC: Trauma in the elderly: A statewide perspective. *Conn Med* 51:161, 1987.
40. Rubenstein LZ et al: Falls and instability in the elderly. *J Am Geriatr Soc* 36:266, 1988.
41. Ellis GL: Subdural hematoma in the elderly. *Emerg Med Clin North Am* 8:281, 1990.
42. McKissock W et al: Subdural hematoma: A review of 389 cases. *Lancet* 1:1365, 1960.
43. Seelig JM et al: Traumatic acute subdural hematoma; major mortality reduction in comatose patients treated within four hours. *N Engl J Med* 304:1511, 1981.
44. Gennarelli TA, Thibault LB: Biomechanics of acute subdural hematoma. *J Trauma* 22:680, 1982.
45. Gennarelli TA et al: Influence of the type of intracranial lesion on outcome from severe head injury. *J Neurosurg* 56:26, 1982.
46. Gennarelli TA: Head injury in brain and experimental animals: Clinical aspects. *Acta Neurochir* 32(suppl):1, 1983.

47. Bowers SA, Marshall LF: Outcome in 200 consecutive cases of severe head injury treated in San Diego County: A prospective analysis. *Neurosurgery* 6:237, 1980.
48. Fell DA et al: Acute subdural hematomas. Review of 144 cases. *J Neurosurg* 42:37, 1975.
49. Yamaura A et al: CT findings and outcome in head injuries—Effects of aging. *Neurosurgical Rev* 12 (suppl):178, 1989.
50. Jamjoom A et al: Outcome following surgical evacuation of traumatic intracranial haematomas in the elderly. *Br J Neurosurg* 6:27, 1992.
51. Jamieson KG, Yelland JDN: Extradural hematoma. Report of 167 cases. *J Neurosurg* 29:13, 1968.
52. Young HA et al: Delayed traumatic intracerebral hematoma: Report of 15 cases operatively treated. *Neurosurgery* 14:22, 1984.
53. Cameron MM: Chronic subdural haematoma: A review of 114 cases. *J Neurol Neurosurg Psychiatry* 41:834, 1978.
54. Markwalder TM: Chronic subdural hematomas: A review. *J Neurosurg* 54:637, 1981.
55. Weir BKA: Results of burr hole and open or closed suction drainage for chronic subdural hematomas in adults. *Can J Neurol Sci* 10:22, 1983.
56. Kelly AB et al: Head trauma: Comparison of MR and CT experience in 100 patients. *AJNR* 9:699, 1988.
57. Snow RB et al: Comparison of magnetic resonance imaging and computed tomography in the evaluation of head injury. *Neurosurgery* 18:45, 1986.
58. Oku Y et al: Trial of a new operative method for recurrent chronic subdural hematoma. *J Neurosurg* 61:269, 1984.
59. Robinson RG: Chronic subdural hematoma: Surgical management in 133 patients. *J Neurosurg* 61:263, 1984.
60. Dacey RG et al: Neurosurgical complications after apparently minor head injury. *J Neurosurg* 65:203, 1986.
61. Dikmen S et al: Neuropsychological and psychosocial consequences of minor head injury. *J Neurol Neurosurg Psychiatry* 49:1227, 1986.
62. Gronwall D, Wrightson P: Delayed recovery of intellectual function after minor head injury. *Lancet* 2:605, 1974.
63. Jaret JS et al: Clinical predictors of abnormality disclosed by computed tomography after mild head injury. *Neurosurgery* 32:9, 1993.
64. Braakman et al: Systemic selection of prognostic features in patients with severe head injury. *Neurosurgery* 6:362, 1980.
65. Becker DP et al: The outcome from severe head injury with early diagnosis and intensive management. *J Neurosurg* 47:491, 1977.
66. Eisenberg H et al: The effects of three potentially preventable complications on outcome after severe closed head injury, in Ishii S et al (eds): *Intracranial Pressure V.* New York, Springer-Verlag, 1983, p 549.
67. Born JD et al: Relative prognostic value of best motor response and brain stem reflexes in patients with severe head injury. *Neurosurgery* 16:595, 1985.
68. Jennett B et al: Predicting outcome in individual patients after severe head injury. *Lancet* 1:1031, 1976.
69. Teasdale G, Jennett B: Assessment and prognosis of coma after head injury. *Acta Neurochir* 34:45, 1976.
70. Narayan RK et al: Improved confidence of outcome prediction in severe head injury. *J Neurosurg* 54:751, 1981.
71. Stablein DM et al: Statistical methods for determining prognosis in severe head injury. *Neurosurgery* 6:243, 1980.
72. Uzell BP et al: Influence of lesions detected by computed tomography on outcome and neuropsychological recovery after severe head injury. *Neurosurgery* 20:396, 1987.
73. Godersky JC et al: Magnetic resonance imaging and neurobehavioural outcome in traumatic brain injury. *Acta Neurochir* 51(suppl):311, 1990.
74. Wilson JTL et al: Early and late magnetic resonance imaging and neuropsychological outcome after head injury. *J Neurol Neurosurg Psychiatry* 51:391, 1988.
75. Chandra V et al: Case control study of late onset "probable Alzheimer's disease." *Neurology* 37:1295, 1987.
76. Graves AB et al: The association between head trauma and Alzheimer's disease. *Am J Epidemiol* 131:491, 1990.
77. Mortimer JA et al: Head injury as a risk for Alzheimer's disease. *Neurology* 35:264, 1985.
78. Shalat SL et al: Risk factors for Alzheimer's disease: A case-control study. *Neurology* 37:1630, 1987.
79. Mortimer JA, Pirozzolo FJ: Remote effects of head trauma. *Dev Neuropsychol* 1:215, 1985.
80. Giannotta SL et al: Prognosis and outcome in severe head injury, in Cooper PR (ed): *Head Injury.* Baltimore, Williams & Wilkins, 1982.
81. Eisenberg HM et al: Emergency care: Initial evaluation, in Cooper PR (ed): *Head Injury,* 2d ed. Baltimore, Williams & Wilkins, 1987, p 20.
82. Frost EAM et al: Pulmonary shunt as a prognostic indicator in head injury. *J Neurosurg* 50:768, 1979.
83. Smith JP et al: Retropharyngeal hematomas. *J Trauma* 28:553, 1988.
84. Levati A et al: Prognosis of severe head injuries. *J Neurosurg* 57:779, 1982.

Chapter 97

SEIZURES AND EPILEPSY

John W. Miller and James A. Ferrendelli

Seizures are the clinical manifestation of sudden abnormal and excessive discharges of electrical activity in populations of neurons in the brain. *Epilepsy* is the condition in which seizures recur chronically. Seizures are common, with an annual incidence of 75 per 100,000 in an American urban population, and epilepsy has an incidence of 48 per 100,000 and a prevalence of 5.5 per 1000.[1] The incidence of epilepsy is greatest in infancy, somewhat lower in childhood, and lowest in adolescence and during most of adult life.[1] However, it increases greatly in those over 60 with a rate of 82 per 100,000 per year.[1] This chapter will review the clinical assessment and treatment of geriatric patients with seizures, including their differentiation from other phenomena which cause transient neurological disturbance, and the investigation, definition, and treatment of underlying causes.

CLASSIFICATION OF SEIZURE TYPES

Accurate classification is an essential prerequisite for correct decisions in evaluation and management. Modern classification is based on both clinical and electroencephalographic criteria.[2] The major distinction is between *partial* seizures, which clinically and electrographically originate focally in a specific region of the cerebral cortex, and *generalized* seizures, which involve the cerebral hemispheres bilaterally and symmetrically at onset.

Partial Seizures

Partial seizures are subdivided into *simple partial seizures,* when consciousness is not impaired; *complex partial seizures,* when it is; and *secondarily generalized tonic-clonic seizures,* when a partial seizure spreads to generate a generalized convulsion. Simple partial seizures have diverse manifestations, including motor, sensory, affective, autonomic, or elaborate psychic symptoms. The signs or symptoms of these seizures reflect the normal function of the area of the cortex in which the seizure occurs.[3,4] Complex partial seizures most commonly arise in the temporal or frontal lobes. Many of their symptoms are assumed to result from incorporation of deeper limbic and diencephalic structures in the seizure. In most cases of complex partial seizures, loss of awareness is accompanied by amnesia for at least a portion of the clinical event. Clinical evidence of focal onset for a secondarily generalized tonic-clonic convulsion is not always available from the history or even from its direct observation. In many cases a focal onset for generalized convulsions may be deduced from the presence of focal abnormalities on neurological examination, imaging studies, or the EEG.

Generalized Seizures

These include a variety of convulsive and nonconvulsive seizures with the first clinical and electrographic changes indicating involvement of both cerebral hemispheres simultaneously.[2] Usual nonconvulsive seizures are *absence seizures,* which are brief periods of unawareness and staring without loss of posture or postictal symptoms. Absence seizures are associated with trains of generalized spike-and-wave or multispike-and-wave EEG discharges. Generalized tonic-clonic convulsions may also have a bilaterally symmetric electrographic onset consisting of low-voltage fast activity or rapid generalized spiking.[2,3] It is occasionally difficult to distinguish absence from complex partial seizures and primary from secondarily generalized convulsions on clinical grounds alone. The EEG is then the most useful test for making this distinction.

ETIOLOGY OF SEIZURES

Definition of the cause is essential for rational and successful treatment. Seizures may occur acutely as a result of some transient cerebral dysfunction caused by metabolic or toxic disturbances including hyponatremia, hypoglycemia, rapid withdrawal from sedative-hypnotic drugs, and intoxication with agents such as theophylline or penicillin. Cerebral infarction and intracranial infections or bleeding may also produce transient seizures. Epilepsy, i.e., chronic recurrent seizures, is usually a consequence of some chronic cerebral abnormality which may be static or progressive. Epilepsy may be a result of idiopathic or genetic factors, *primary epilepsy,* or of an acquired cerebral abnormality, *secondary epilepsy.* It is assumed that most individuals with primary epilepsy have some abnormality of neurotransmission mechanisms which lowers seizure threshold. Most secondary epilepsies are a consequence of some injury to cerebral cortex, most often from cerebral infarctions, intracranial infections, brain tumors, or head trauma. Patients with primary epilepsy most often suffer from nonconvulsive or convulsive generalized seizures. Partial seizures or secondarily generalized convulsions are the usual clinical manifestations of patients with secondary epilepsies.

Newly diagnosed epilepsy in an elderly patient should always be considered to be secondary, since essentially all patients with primary epilepsy begin having seizures during childhood or adolescence. However, some patients with primary epilepsy infrequently may continue to have seizures into old age. Since most elderly patients have secondary epilepsy, it is not surprising that the cause of their seizures can often be defined. For example, in a study of a geriatric Scandinavian population,[5] 75 percent of patients had an identifiable cause for their seizures, with previous cerebral infarct the cause in 32 percent and tumors the cause in 14 percent. Other causes included prior severe head trauma, alcohol and drug abuse, dementing illnesses, and metabolic disorders including hypoglycemia and hyponatremia. These results are confirmed by other recent studies of geriatric patients.[6–8]

EVALUATION OF SEIZURES

The first step in the assessment of a patient with new spells is to confirm that they are actually seizures rather than some other type of transient disturbance of neurological function such as syncope, migraine, or transient ischemic attack or if they have a psychiatric cause. If the patient indeed has epileptic seizures, the next step is to classify them using the history and laboratory evaluation. The final step is to determine, if possible, their cause, taking care to exclude reversible causes.

The history should reconstruct, moment by moment, experiences during typical episodes and include interviews with witnesses. It should be noted whether there is any apparent precipitating factor or postictal confusion, memory disturbance, or dysphasia. With complex partial or generalized tonic-clonic seizures, one should also inquire whether the patient also has simple partial seizures preceding those seizures or whether simple partial seizures occur at other times. It should be inquired whether there is a history of seizures during childhood or in other family members and whether the patient had severe head trauma, has risk factors for neoplasm or cerebrovascular disease, or has a history of any other neurological symptoms or diseases.

A careful neurological examination should be performed. A focal deficit may indicate an underlying structural lesion, or it may be a postictal deficit from a recent partial seizure. If the patient is on antiepileptic drugs, it should be noted whether there is evidence of toxicity. The general physical examination should look for clues of underlying cause such as evidence of cardiac, cerebrovascular, or neoplastic disease.

Especially in the elderly, a cranial CT scan with contrast material or a magnetic resonance imaging study, and an EEG are essential. With appropriate activation techniques such as hyperventilation, photic stimulation, and sleep, abnormalities with a specific association with seizures such as spikes, sharp waves, or generalized spike-and-wave complexes may be seen in about 50 percent of initial EEG studies and in up to 90 percent of patients after multiple EEGs.[9] The finding of interictal epileptiform activity confirms that a patient's spells are seizures and helps to distinguish between partial seizures and seizures that are generalized from onset. If the nature of the spells is unclear after careful clinical and laboratory evaluation, the most useful diagnostic test is an extended EEG which records typical spells, preferably with videotaping of behavior.

TREATMENT OF SEIZURES

General Principles

Treatment should be directed at both controlling seizures and, if possible, correcting the underlying disease or disorder producing them. For those patients with a single or a few seizures from some transient disorder such as drug intoxication; withdrawal from alcohol or sedative-hypnotic drugs; hyponatremia; or hypoglycemia, antiepileptic drugs may be unnecessary or may be necessary only briefly. Patients who have recurrent seizures secondary to a treatable neurological disease such as brain tumor or intracranial infection should be treated with antiepileptic drugs and should also receive treatment for the underlying problem. In many patients the cause of seizures is undefined or is a static process such as completed cerebral infarction or brain contusion secondary to head injury. In these patients treatment with antiepileptic drugs is the only possible therapy.

Regardless of the cause, patients with chronic recurrent seizures should be treated with antiepileptic drugs. There is controversy, however, as to whether antiepileptic drug treatment should be begun after a single first seizure. It has been argued[10] that since many of these patients will not have a second seizure in several years of follow-up, there is no justification in beginning antiepileptic drugs and subjecting the patients to possible side effects. For example, in one retrospective study,[11] only 60 percent of patients had a second seizure in 5 years. However, this view has been challenged[12] primarily because, overall, patients with recurrent seizures are far more common than those with single seizures,[13] and the majority of the patients in retrospective studies of the prognosis of a single seizure[11] were in fact treated with antiepileptic drugs. In any case, antiepileptic drug treatment should be considered in at least some patients after a first seizure, especially when further seizures may be especially dangerous, because of individual circumstances. It should also be noted that the risk of seizure recurrence is higher in patients with generalized spike-and-wave EEG activity, but relatively low in patients who have been seizure-free 6 months or more after the first seizure.[11]

Treatment with antiepileptic drugs should follow certain basic principles. Therapy should be started with a single suitable agent. For partial and secondarily generalized seizures, appropriate drugs are carbamazepine, phenytoin, primidone, or phenobarbital; the first two are more desirable because of the sedating and behavioral side effects[14] of phenobarbital and primidone. For primary generalized tonic-clonic seizures, valproate, phenytoin, and carbamazepine are the most appropriate agents. Absence seizures are best treated with valproate or ethosuximide. A fundamental principle of antiepileptic drug treatment is that seizure control should be achieved, if possible, by increasing the dosage of the single initial agent rather than by adding a second one. Dosage changes should be guided by the patient's clinical response rather than by drug levels, with inadequate seizure control indicating the need for raising the dose, unless toxicity has appeared. Drug levels are usually not needed in patients with good seizure control on a well-tolerated medication. Knowing the drug levels can be useful under some circumstances—for example, when inadequate seizure control or toxicity is present, especially in a patient on more than one medication. Knowing the levels may also be useful in understanding drug interactions, when the level of one drug is altered by concomitant administration of another antiepileptic drug or other agent. This is usually due to competition for, or induction of, enzymatic systems for drug metabolism or to altered binding to plasma proteins.

If seizure control cannot be achieved with the first medication, a second agent should be considered. Two or more antiepileptic drugs used in combination should be avoided whenever possible, usually being appropriate only in patients in whom monotherapy with several agents fails. It should be recognized that simultaneous treatment with several antiepileptic drugs is more likely to cause toxicity and often does not produce better control than a single agent.[15] With chronically intractable seizures, it is usually counterproductive to continually add new antiepileptic drugs. A better approach is to reevaluate the patient to be sure that the spells are indeed epileptic seizures and that the initial impressions regarding seizure type and cause are correct. For a select subgroup of patients with intractable, disabling partial seizures, evaluation for epilepsy surgery may be considered.[16] Surgical excision of an epileptic focus requires careful electrographic recording of the patient's typical seizures, usually with subdural, epidural, or depth electrodes, to document a consistent site of seizure origin which is accessible to removal without unacceptable risk of significant neurological deficits.

Therapy with antiepileptic drugs is often compromised by adverse drug effects. All the antiepileptic drugs produce dose-related neurotoxicity, most commonly sedation and incoordination or impairment of cognition. All may be particularly disabling in the elderly and should be avoided by using the lowest effective dosage and the fewest drugs possible. Idiosyncratic reactions usually occur within the first 6 weeks to 6 months of therapy and include allergic reactions, severe leukopenia, aplastic anemia, and hepatotoxicity. All can be serious or even fatal, but fortunately occur very infrequently. An idiosyncratic reaction requires immediate cessation of the offending drug. Several side effects occur with each of the anticonvulsant drugs and include gingival hyperplasia, changes in appetite and weight, reversible leukopenia, and elevation of liver enzyme levels. Treatment of side effects may or may not require lowering the dose or discontinuation of the drug, depending on the side effect and the drug involved.

Status Epilepticus

Convulsive status epilepticus is a condition in which repeated generalized convulsions occur for at least 30 minutes without recovery of consciousness.[17] This is a medical emergency. Without prompt treatment it leads to irreversible neurological damage, progressive metabolic disturbance, and death. The causes of status epilepticus are diverse but include abrupt withdrawal of antiepileptic drugs; withdrawal of alcohol, barbiturates, or benzodiazepines; trauma; cerebrovascular disease; CNS infection; and hypoxia.[18]

In treating status epilepticus, the initial and most important step is to support vital functions.[17–20] The airway should be protected as needed, and oxygenation should be maintained. As intravenous access is obtained, blood should be sent for determination of glucose, electrolytes, and antiepileptic drug levels. At that time 50 ml of 50% glucose and 100 mg of thiamine should be given. If the blood pH is less than 7.2, bicarbonate should be given and fluid and electrolyte disturbances corrected.

There are various acceptable approaches to anticonvulsant administration in status epilepticus.[17,19,20] Whatever approach is chosen, it should be initiated promptly, adequate loading doses should be administered, and preparations should be made to support respirations if they are depressed by these medications.

A reasonable way to initiate therapy is with intravenous benzodiazepines, either 10 mg of diazepam over 2 minutes or 4 mg of lorazepam, monitoring for respiratory depression and hypotension. Immediately afterward an intravenous phenytoin infusion of 15 to 25 mg/kg should be given, no faster than 50 mg/min to reduce the risk of hypotension and bradycardia. Phenytoin cannot be mixed with dextrose, and intramuscular administration should be avoided. Since phenytoin is rapidly acting, an additional medication should be given if seizures do not stop by the end of the infusion. Phenobarbital may be given at a rate of 100 mg/min to a loading dose of 5 to 10 mg/kg.[17,19] Ventilatory support may be needed by this point.

If seizures are not controlled, care should be taken to ensure that possible metabolic or structural causes have been addressed. Additional infusions of diazepam or lorazepam are usually used in intractable status epilepticus. If seizures persist, one may administer general anesthesia with a short-acting barbiturate such as pentobarbital.[19] The efficacy of such treatment has been demonstrated using a loading dose of 15 mg/kg of pentobarbital over 1 hour, a maintenance infusion of 1 to 2 mg/h, and use of dopamine as needed for hypotension.[21] This requires EEG monitoring to maintain a state of burst suppression, intubation, ventilation, and monitoring of hemodynamics with an arterial line and a central venous pressure or Swan-Ganz catheter.

Antiepileptic Drugs[17,22]

Barbiturates

Phenobarbital and primidone are inexpensive, safe, and effective for partial and generalized tonic-clonic seizures, but have substantial undesirable sedative and behavioral effects. Phenobarbital has an oral half-life of 3 to 5 days; 1 to 4 mg/kg can be given as a single daily dose, preferably at bedtime. Primidone has a half-life of 3 to 12 hours and can be given in 2 or 3 doses per day for a total of 10 to 20 mg/kg. Since primidone is metabolized partially to phenobarbital, these two drugs should not be given together.

Phenytoin

Phenytoin is effective for partial and generalized tonic-clonic seizures. Typical adult doses are 200 to 400 mg in one or two divided doses per day. At lower serum concentrations, the half-life is 15 to 24 hours; however, at high concentrations, saturation of elimination mechanisms occurs, leading to a longer half-life. For this reason large increases in doses should be avoided. Dose-related neurotoxicity usually begins at levels of 20 to 30 mg/ml and includes nystagmus, ataxia, and lethargy as the concentration increases. Possible chronic side effects include osteomalacia, gum hypertrophy, and mild peripheral neuropathy.

Carbamazepine

Carbamazepine is also used for generalized tonic-clonic convulsions and partial seizures, particularly complex partial seizures. The dose is 7 to 15 mg/kg per day in three divided doses, and the half-life is 8 to 36 hours. Dose-dependent neutropenia is not uncommon, but idiosyncratic aplastic anemia is very rare. With a neutrophil count of 1200 or less, carbamazepine should be discontinued or the dose reduced. Hyponatremia is another potentially serious side effect, especially in the elderly. Diplopia and ataxia are the most common neurotoxic symptoms with high doses.

Valproate

Valproate is effective for seizures that are generalized from onset. Recently valproate monotherapy has been shown to be less useful for partial seizures than carbamazepine,[23] but nonetheless valproate has been used successfully as an adjunct medication for this seizure type. It should be administered in the enteric-coated slow-release form, sodium divalproex, in a dose of 10 to 60 mg/kg in three or four divided doses. It has a half-life of 8 to 12 hours. Neurological toxicity is usually minor, with tremor being the most common. Other common side effects include gastrointestinal upset and increased appetite and weight gain. The most serious adverse effect is idiosyncratic hepatic failure, which is rare and usually occurs in children who are also taking other antiepileptic drugs.[24]

REFERENCES

1. Hauser WA, Kurland LT: The epidemiology of epilepsy in Rochester Minnesota 1935 through 1967. *Epilepsia* 16:1, 1975.
2. Commission on Classification and Terminology of the International League Against Epilepsy: Proposal for revised clinical and electroencephalographic classification of epileptic seizures. *Epilepsia* 22:489, 1981.
3. Miller JW et al: Clinical electroencephalography and related techniques, in Joynt R (ed): *Clinical Neurology*. Philadelphia, JB Lippincott, 1992.
4. Penfield W, Jasper H: *Epilepsy and the Functional Anatomy of the Human Brain*. Boston, Little, Brown, 1954.
5. Luhdorf K et al: Etiology of seizures in the elderly. *Epilepsia* 27:458, 1986.
6. Roberts MA et al: Epileptic seizures in the elderly: Etiology and type of seizure. *Aging* 11:24, 1982.

7. Lopez JLP et al: Late onset epileptic seizures: A retrospective study of 250 patients. *Acta Neurol Scand* 72:380, 1985.
8. Dam AM et al: Late onset epilepsy: Etiologies, type of seizure, and value of clinical investigations, EEG and computerized tomography scan. *Epilepsia* 26:227, 1985.
9. Salinski M et al: Effectiveness of multiple EEGs in supporting the diagnosis of epilepsy: An operational curve. *Epilepsia* 28:231, 1987.
10. Hauser WA: Should people be treated after a first seizure? *Arch Neurol* 43:1287, 1986.
11. Annegers JF et al: Risk of recurrence after an initial unprovoked seizure. *Epilepsia* 27:45, 1986.
12. Hart RG, Easton JD: Seizure recurrence after a first, unprovoked seizure. *Arch Neurol* 43:1289, 1986.
13. Goodridge DM, Shorvon SD: Epileptic seizures in a population of 6000: II. Treatment and prognosis. *Br Med J* 287:645, 1983.
14. Mattson RH et al: Comparison of carbamazepine, phenobarbital, phenytoin and primidone in partial and secondarily generalized tonic-clonic seizures. *N Engl J Med* 313:145, 1985.
15. Schmidt D: Medical intractability in partial epilepsies, in Lüders HO (ed): *Epilepsy Surgery.* New York, Raven, 1992, p 83.
16. Bourgeois BDF: General concepts of medical intractability, in Lüders HO (ed): *Epilepsy Surgery.* New York, Raven, 1992, p 77.
17. Dodson WE, Ferrendelli JA: Convulsive disorders and their management, in Wirth FP, Ratcheson RA (eds): *Neurosurgical Critical Care,* vol 1: *Concepts in Neurosurgery.* New York, Williams & Wilkins, 1987, p 169.
18. Aminoff MJ, Simon RP: Status epilepticus. Causes, clinical features and consequences in 98 patients. *Am J Med* 69:657, 1980.
19. Simon RP: Management of status epilepticus, in Pedley TA, Meldrum BS (eds): *Recent Advances in Epilepsy,* no. 2. New York, Churchill Livingstone, 1985.
20. Delgado-Escueta AV et al: Management of status epilepticus. *N Engl J Med* 306:1537, 1982.
21. Lowenstein DH et al: Barbiturate anesthesia in the treatment of status epilepticus: Clinical experience with 14 patients. *Neurology* 38:395, 1988.
22. Woodbury DM et al: *Antiepileptic Drugs,* 2d ed. New York, Raven, 1982.
23. Mattson RH et al: Comparison between carbamazepine and valproate for complex partial and secondarily generalized tonic clonic seizures. *Epilepsia* 32 (suppl 3):18, 1991.
24. Dreifuss FE et al: Valproic acid hepatic fatalities. A retrospective review. *Neurology* 37:379, 1987.

Chapter 98

BRAIN TUMORS IN THE ELDERLY

Charisse D. Litchman and Jerome B. Posner

Intracranial tumors affect all ages. Brain tumors are second only to leukemia as causes of childhood cancer and are as common as Hodgkin's disease in adults.[1] However, their incidence increases with increasing age.[2] There is now evidence that intracranial malignancies are actually increasing in frequency, especially in the elderly.[3–7] Only a portion of the measured increase in incidence of brain tumor can be accounted for by the better ascertainment resulting from advances in brain imaging.[3] In general, the same types of intracranial tumors occur throughout adult life, but those in the elderly are more likely to be malignant.[8] The elderly also differ from their younger counterparts in that some of the classic symptoms and signs of brain tumor (i.e., headache and papilledema) occur less frequently; instead, elderly patients often present with cognitive dysfunction suggesting dementia rather that tumor. Even when the diagnosis is made, the treatment may be more complicated in elderly than in younger patients. The patient may suffer from a second disorder which makes brain tumor surgery dangerous. The elderly brain tolerates radiation and chemotherapy less well than the younger brain does. Thus, even if treatment of the tumor is successful, the patient may suffer long-term side effects of the treatment which may cause disability equal to that of the tumor itself.

This chapter discusses the classification and epidemiology of intracranial tumors, diagnostic considerations, and treatment. Additional reviews are found elsewhere.[9–11]

CLASSIFICATION AND EPIDEMIOLOGY

Table 98-1 classifies the major intracranial tumors encountered in the elderly population (over 65) and gives very approximate percentages of each. The data are similar to those of a national survey of discharges from acute care hospitals conducted in 1973 and 1974.[12] The major findings of that study are that both primary and metastatic intracranial neoplasms increase in incidence throughout adulthood until approximately age 60, when they level off. There is a decline in incidence after age 75. The same decline is also apparent in another epidemiological study from Rochester, Minnesota,[2] only when those intracranial neoplasms diagnosed prior to death are considered. However, if autopsy data are included, the incidence of intracranial tumors increases throughout the lifespan. Some of the tumors undiagnosed in the elderly before death are asymptomatic meningiomas, but others are gliomas in which an incorrect diagnosis of cerebral vascular disease or dementia was made. "Inapparent" brain tumors were found in approximately 1 percent of elderly patients at autopsy. With the advent of noninvasive brain scans such as computed tomography (CT) and magnetic resonance imaging

TABLE 98-1

Major Intracranial Tumors in Adults

Metastatic	**50%**
Lung	40
Breast	20
Melanoma	20
Miscellaneous	20
Primary	**50%**
Brain Parenchyma	70
Glioblastoma	40
Anaplastic astrocytoma	20
Astrocytoma	15
Lymphoma	10
Oligodendroglioma	5
Miscellaneous	10
Intracranial	30
Meningioma	80
Acoustic neuroma	10
Pituitary adenoma	5
Miscellaneous	5

(MRI), more diagnoses are being made before death in the elderly. Better diagnoses account for some but not all of the reported increases in brain tumors.[3]

One study examining U.S. mortality data from 1968 to 1983 indicates an 8 percent annual rise in primary brain malignancy mortality of white men in the 65- to 84-year-old age group and women in the 75- to 84-year-old age group.[7] The increased incidence began in the late 1960s and has continued to the present time. Most of the data were collected before widespread use of the CT scan, making it unlikely that the increased incidence is simply due to better diagnosis.[7] These same dramatic increases in incidence do not appear in the younger age group. With increasing age, low-grade astrocytomas become less common and more malignant gliomas, particularly glioblastoma multiforme, become more common.[8,12] Malignant gliomas also appear to be more malignant in the elderly.[12] Anaplastic astrocytomas constitute 46 percent of malignant gliomas encountered in patients under the age of 40, 14 percent in patients age 40 to 60, and only 7 percent in those over the age of 60.[12] Median survivals in the elderly are shorter even when controlled for the histological type of glioma. Meningiomas and probable pituitary adenomas also increase in incidence with increasing age. Primary lymphomas of the nervous system, which are thought to represent less than 1 percent of primary brain tumors, occur most often in the sixth and seventh decades[13] and also appear to be increasing in frequency, particularly in the elderly, even in those patients who are not obviously immunosuppressed.[14,15]

In the elderly, metastatic brain tumors are more common than primary tumors.[12] Clinical evidence suggests that two-thirds to three-quarters of metastatic brain tumors are symptomatic during life,[16] but they generally occur in patients already known to have cancer and usually do not represent a major diagnostic problem.

DIAGNOSIS

Clinical Presentation

Table 98-2 lists some of the symptoms of brain tumor and compares symptoms in patients over and under 60 years of age.[17] The differences in symptoms between older and younger people probably result from the loss of normal brain substance which occurs with aging. This allows tumors to grow larger in the elderly without raising intracranial pressure. As a result, headache is less common and papilledema is rare. The absence of papilledema probably results only in part from lower intracranial pressure, but also in part from the fact that intracranial pressure, even when elevated, is less likely to be transmitted to the optic nerve head because of obliteration of the perioptic subarachnoid space by fibrosis.

TABLE 98-2

Some Significant Differences in Symptoms of Intracranial Tumor by Age

	Over 60 years (%)	Under 60 years (%)
Headaches	48.9	63.1
Disturbances of gait	28.3	21.5
Personality changes	25.2	18.4
Disturbances of memory	19.3	15.1
Confusion	15.5	7.4
Speech disorders	21.0	12.2
Epileptic attacks	17.9	25.0

Mental changes, including personality change (often mimicking depression),[18] disturbance of memory, and confusion are more common in the elderly than in the young. Seizures are less common. Focal findings such as hemiparesis and visual field defects are not significantly different.

Symptoms of brain tumor usually present and progress insidiously. However, in some patients either an apoplectic onset or paroxysmal symptoms may dominate the clinical picture. As many as 10 percent of patients with malignant glioma may have a sudden or paroxysmal onset of their symptoms. An apoplectic onset may be caused by hemorrhage or vascular obstruction, but in most instances the cause is not known. Paroxysmal symptoms appear to result from seizures originating from the cerebral cortex surrounding the tumor. Unlike typical epileptic focal or generalized seizures, in which positive symptoms (e.g., tonic and clonic movement of extremities) are common, paroxysmal symptoms in patients with brain tumors are often negative[19] (e.g., aphasia, paralysis, episodic confusion) and may last hours rather than the usual few minutes of a focal seizure.

Thus, the diagnosis of brain tumor in the elderly may be difficult. When the symptoms begin insidiously as confusion or personality change, but without headache or papilledema, the physician may suspect psychiatric disease (e.g., depression) or a degenerative disorder (e.g., Alzheimer's disease). If a careful neurological examination yields focal motor or sensory changes, one should suspect a brain tumor, but, particularly when the tumor is in the frontal lobe, there may be no such changes. When the symptoms are apoplectic, the physician is more likely to suspect cerebrovascular disease, which is usually apoplectic in onset and much more common than brain tumor. Progression of neurological symptoms after apoplectic onset suggests tumor and warrants careful imaging studies. Paroxysmal neurological symptoms mimic transient ischemic attacks and also suggest vascular disease. However, paroxysmal symptoms in brain tumors tend to last longer[20] and present more complex symptoms (i.e., apraxia and confusion in addition to the usual hemiparesis and aphasia of transient ischemic attacks). Despite these clinical clues, the presence of a brain tumor can often be differentiated from the more common dementing illnesses or vascular diseases of the elderly only if the physician suspects the presence of a tumor and does appropriate diagnostic testing.

Brain Imaging

The diagnosis of intracranial tumors in all age groups has been revolutionized first by CT and more recently by MRI and magnetic resonance spectroscopy (MRS). While clinical suspicion of cerebral neoplasm has a specificity of 78 percent with correct localization in 63 percent, the CT has a diagnostic specificity of 86 percent.[21] MRI is even more sensitive in detecting neoplasms than CT. Further, the addition of the paramagnetic substance gadolinium, which is used as contrast enhancement with MRI, has increased the sensitivity of this technique. In one study, postcontrast images revealed lesions not seen on precontrast scans in 20 percent of patients and helped to better characterize and approximate size in previously detected lesions.[22] Small meningiomas, which, because of their isodensity with brain are hard to distinguish from normal brain on noncontrast CT or MRI, become obvious by intense homogeneous contrast enhancement; neither CT nor MRI is believed to be superior to the other in diagnosing intracranial meningiomas.[23] Elderly patients suspected of harboring a brain tumor should have an MRI scan both without and with contrast material. If a lesion is found, the MRI scan should be done in sagittal, coronal, and axial planes to help determine if surgery is feasible by giving the neurosurgeon a three-dimensional image. Only cardiac pacemakers, cerebral aneurysm clips, and one particular kind of artificial heart valve are contraindications to MRI (CT must be done instead). Claustrophobia can usually be controlled by a small dose of an anxiolytic agent. The MRI contrast material gadolinium has many fewer side effects than does the CT contrast material iodine.

Although extremely sensitive for detection of brain lesions, neither CT nor MRI specifically proves that an abnormality is a neoplasm or, if it is a neoplasm, its type. In the appropriate clinical context, lesions identified by CT or MRI that occupy space and are surrounded by edema are likely to be tumors rather than infarct, abscesses, or inflammatory lesions. Certain other clues help identify the nature of the tumor. Multiple lesions within the substance of the brain, particularly if they possess contrast-enhancing rings on CT or MRI scan or are each surrounded by extensive edema, suggest metastatic disease. Even single lesions in the cerebellum in the elderly suggest metastatic disease since primary tumors of the cerebellum are uncommon in older patients. A single lesion with a contrast-enhancing ring of irregular size and shape suggests a malignant glioma. A glioma can also appear as an area of hypodensity in the white matter which does not contrast-enhance and is sometimes confused with a cerebral infarct. Such an appearance suggests a low-grade glioma, but high-grade tumors may also fail to contrast-enhance (although such tumors appear to have a poorer prognosis than low-grade tumors that do not contrast-enhance).[24] A densely and uniformly contrast-enhancing lesion deep in the white matter surrounding the ventricular system suggests primary lymphoma.[15] Primary lymphomas are often multicentric (about 30 percent), whereas primary gliomas are monocentric (95 percent); exceptions exist. Primary lymphoma has a distinct appearance in AIDS and in non-AIDS patients. In the former, 82 percent are multiple lesions less than 2 cm in size and located primarily in the temporal lobes and basal ganglia, while in the latter, 75 percent are solitary lesions greater than 2 cm and located primarily in the deep parietal lobe.[25] Lesions on the surface of the brain (attached to the dura) that uniformly contrast-enhance suggest meningioma, although dural-based metastases from carcinomas of the breast, prostate, and other tumors may appear similar.

Recently, the potential of MRS as a noninvasive diagnostic tool is gaining appreciation. Using carbon 13, proton, and phosphorus 31, a metabolic map of the brain can be produced. MRS seems useful in differentiating between different grades of astrocytomas and in confirming the diagnosis of meningiomas.[26] Another technique which images the distribution of biologically relevant radiolabeled compounds is positron emission tomography (PET). When fluorodeoxyglucose (FDG) PET scans are used, the overall rate of glucose utilization in different tissues can be estimated. One important application is the differentiation between radiation necrosis and tumor recurrence.[27] CT and MRI are often unhelpful in making this distinction. Some groups suggest that the magnitude of FDG uptake can be correlated with patient survival,[28] can detect malignant degeneration of low-grade glioma,[29] and can follow tumor response to therapy.[30–32]

Metastatic brain tumors are more common than primary brain tumors in the elderly.[1] Metastases are single lesions in only 50 percent of patients, so that an elderly patient with more than one brain lesion should be considered to harbor a metastasis until proved otherwise. However, evaluation looking for a primary tumor is often not revealing.[33] If CT examination of the chest or the kidneys is negative and if the patient's general physical examination (including rectal examination, stool guaiac, and breast examination) is negative, it is unlikely that a more extensive search will identify a primary lesion. One should consider going directly to brain biopsy, which will both establish that the tumor is metastatic and point toward a likely primary source. Furthermore, for most single metastatic lesions, surgical removal is probably the best treatment (see below).

Other Diagnostic Tests

Examination of the CSF may reveal malignant cells, particularly in primary lymphomas of the nervous system or metastatic tumors that have invaded the leptomeninges.[15] Lumbar puncture should not be performed until MRI or CT rules out a large space-occupying lesion which might cause herniation after an inappropriate lumbar puncture. Tumor markers in both blood and spinal fluid may give clues as to the presence of a systemic cancer and whether or not it has invaded the CNS.[34]

Arteriography can help differentiate vascular disease from tumor. If the external carotid artery is injected, the arteriogram will determine if a tumor is fed by the external carotid circulation, a characteristic feature of meningiomas and dural-based metastases. In both meningiomas and highly malignant gliomas, the vasculature is often abnormal (tumor blush). However, despite the fact that they sometimes aid in diagnosis, cerebral angiograms are invasive. In most instances, when a brain tumor is suspected on the basis of CT or MR, arteriography does not add substantially to the diagnostic information and is not worth the risk. Recently, magnetic resonance angiography (MRA) has been used to gain much of the information afforded by conventional arteriography with none of the associated risk.

Biopsy

If CT or MRI reveals a space-occupying lesion suspected of being a tumor, surgical resection or biopsy is the next step. A patient with known cancer and typical metastatic lesions of the brain on scan need not be biopsied, but one must remember that other brain lesions (e.g., meningiomas) can coexist with systemic cancer. Generally speaking, tumors that can be, should be surgically resected; a craniotomy with removal of the tumor both establishes the diagnosis and treats the disease. This approach holds true for most meningiomas, pituitary adenomas, neurinomas, and gliomas. However, there is no evidence that malignant lymphomas benefit by surgical removal,[15] and often a patient's neurological symptoms are worsened by attempted removal. The same is true of patients with multiple metastatic tumors or surgically inaccessible gliomas. In those instances, because the CT or MRI lesion may not be a tumor and both the treatment of tumor and its prognosis depend in part on histological type, an attempt should be made to establish a histological diagnosis. This can usually be done by stereotactic needle biopsy under CT or MRI control.[35] The procedure can be done under either local or general anesthesia and carries a morbidity of under 2 percent, the primary complication being hemorrhage into the tumor site. A definitive diagnosis can be made in most instances, distinguishing primary from metastatic tumors and both of those from infectious, inflammatory, or demyelinating processes that may mimic tumors.

TREATMENT

General Considerations

For the most part, treatment of intracranial tumors is dictated by the tumor type and not the age of the patient. With some qualification, this holds true in the elderly. One study shows a slightly lower perioperative mortality in patients over 60 years of age than in those under, and a slightly lower incidence of worsened neurological condition on discharge in the older patients.[17] However, at any age, the overall health of the patient is a consideration in determining specific treatment. This is especially true in the elderly since coincident coronary artery disease, hypertension, diabetes, chronic obstructive pulmonary disease, venous insufficiency, and other common general medical problems may limit the therapeutic options. With those caveats the usual brain tumor treatments of adrenal corticosteroids (steroids), surgical extirpation, radiation therapy, chemotherapy, and immunotherapy are available to both the young and the elderly.

Adrenal Corticosteroids (Steroids)

Steroids have been used in the treatment of brain tumors for over 30 years. Their beneficial effects result from decreasing the edema which invariably surrounds malignant glial tumors, metastatic brain tumors, and rapidly growing meningiomas. The salutary effect on edema appears to be a result of "closing" the blood-brain barrier which has broken down both within and immediately surrounding the tumor.[36] Some symptomatic improvement is observed in the majority of patients, usually within 24 to 48 hours of beginning treatment. The symptoms most likely to respond are those which reflect generalized brain dysfunctions (headache, confusion, gait difficulty) due to cerebral edema, increased intracranial pressure, and brain shifts.

Focal signs and symptoms (hemiparesis, aphasia) generally respond less favorably but are improved in many instances. The most widely used steroid preparation, because of its minimal mineralocorticoid activity, is dexamethasone; it also appears less likely to cause mental changes than other steroids. The standard starting dose is 16 mg of dexamethasone a day in divided doses with increasing doses being used if patients do not respond to the lower dose. Elderly patients respond as well to steroids as the younger ones.[37] Only 5 percent of elderly patients suffer major side effects, which include psychosis, hyperglycemia, and bowel perforation.[32] However, prolonged use of steroids leads to osteoporosis, myopathy, and hypertension, and we have observed severe oral candidiasis, pneumocystis pneumonia, and herpes zoster as complications of steroid therapy in the elderly as well. Thus, although steroids are effective in ameliorating the symptoms of brain tumor, they should be used at the lowest possible dose and tapered as soon as definitive therapy permits.

Surgery

Surgical extirpation is the treatment of choice for most intracranial neoplasms. The goal is either to remove the tumor completely, thus obviating recurrence (meningiomas, pituitary adenomas, single metastases), or to remove as much of the lesion as possible (debulk) in order to allow additional therapy (i.e., radiation and chemotherapy) to be more effective. When a surgical procedure is undertaken, the surgeon should attempt to remove as much of the tumor as possible. There is no increase in postoperative morbidity in patients who undergo major resections compared with those who undergo small resections or biopsies.[38] In fact, the incidence of postoperative herniation is higher in those patients who have had small resections. Furthermore, survival is substantially better in those patients with malignant gliomas who have little or no residual tumor identifiable on CT scan after surgery when compared with those patients in whom substantial residual tumor remains.[39]

Not all elderly patients in whom a brain tumor is identified require surgery. A small meningioma found either incidentally or after a seizure can be followed or treated with anticonvulsants. The growth rate may be so slow as not to require surgery before the patient lives out his or her natural life span. Small single metastatic lesions in elderly patients with widespread cancer are probably best treated by radiation therapy (see below), since it is often possible to control these tumors beyond the time that the systemic tumor incapacitates or kills the patient.

Radiation Therapy

External beam radiation therapy is a primary treatment for lymphomas of the brain (but radiation therapy should probably be preceded by chemotherapy),[40] multiple metastatic brain tumors, and some pituitary adenomas. Radiation therapy is indicated following surgery in patients with malignant gliomas and meningiomas that cannot be totally resected, and probably after resection of a single intracerebral metastasis.[41,42] However, radiation therapy is not without its complications, and there is some evidence that chronic radiation damage to the nervous system is more severe in the older age groups than in patients of younger age who have received similar radiation therapy.[43] Smaller daily fractions (e.g., 200 cGy) (hyperfractionation) are safer to the normal brain than are larger fractions (e.g., 300 cGy); however, small fractions take more time, and in patients with systemic cancer who have a very limited life span, larger fractions may be more appropriate.

Side effects of radiation therapy are classified as immediate (acute), early delayed, and late delayed. (1) Acute complications include headache, fever, lethargy, and increase in preexisting neurological signs; they respond to steroids. (2) Early delayed complications occur after a delay of weeks with exacerbation of preexisting symptoms and lethargy often responding to steroids or resolving spontaneously. (3) Late side effects appear months to a few years after treatment and are characterized by dementia with or without focal signs[44]; they are usually irreversible; steroids may provide transient symptomatic improvement or none at all.

When radiation is prescribed for an elderly patient, the physician and the radiation oncologist should work together to identify the smallest total dose to the smallest brain volume which will control the tumor effectively.

Brachytherapy, or stereotactic interstitial implantation into the tumor bed with ^{125}I, is used in some cases of malignant gliomas as an adjunct to traditional external beam radiation. Some centers have reported up to 50 percent improvement in survival.[45–48] Others have shown a shift in the recurrence pattern following brachytherapy. After external beam radiation therapy, 90 percent of the tumors recur within 2 cm of the original tumor edge,[49] while after combined external beam radiation therapy and implantation, 82 percent recur at the margins of the implant volume or at distant sites, including the contralateral hemisphere and spinal axis.[50,51] Use of brachytherapy has been extended to other well-circumscribed tumors, such as brain metastases.

A number of centers are performing stereotactic radiosurgery for the treatment of brain metastasis.[52] The technique allows a high dose of radiation therapy to be delivered to a localized area in one or two treatments, sparing the remainder of the brain. It may be used alone or combined with some whole-brain radiation therapy (to eliminate micrometastases). Its exact role in the treatment of brain metastases or primary intracranial tumors is still uncertain.[52,53]

Chemotherapy

Chemotherapy is an important treatment for patients with primary lymphomas of the brain.[40] Many centers now utilize systemic chemotherapy prior to radiation therapy to treat CNS lymphomas. There is some evidence that metastatic brain tumors may also respond to chemotherapy independent of their response to radiation therapy.[54,55] Chemotherapy added to surgery and radiation therapy appears to prolong the survival of some patients with malignant brain tumors.[56] The elderly tend to tolerate chemotherapy somewhat less well than younger people do, and doses may have to be adjusted to decrease toxicity.

TREATMENT AND PROGNOSIS OF SPECIFIC TUMORS

Malignant Gliomas

The current conventional treatment of malignant gliomas, whether in the young or the elderly, is a maximally feasible resection of the tumor, followed by radiation, with the tumor receiving approximately 60 Gy.[56,57] Concomitant chemotherapy with carmustine (BCNU) in a dose of 200 mg/m^2 every 8 weeks does not appear to significantly increase median survival in elderly patients, but does increase the long-term survival in about 25 to 30 percent of patients. The new Brain Tumor Cooperative Group chemotherapy phase III trial is comparing intravenous BCNU, a combination of intravenous BCNU and intraarterial cisplatin, or 10-ethyl-10-deazaaminopterin. Brachytherapy with ^{125}I implantation and interstitial hyperthermia are becoming more widely utilized.

Age is the major prognostic factor in malignant gliomas. The median survival of patients aged 60 to 70 years with grade IV astrocytoma was 6 months with a 23 percent 1-year survival rate, according to the Radiation Therapy Oncology Group report.[58] The poorer prognosis associated with advanced age may be in part due to the predilection toward higher-grade astrocytomas,[59] though there is an age effect independent of histological type.[60] Better prognosis is associated with better functional state at presentation, tumor location in temporal lobes, and the use of more than one treatment modality.[59] Recent reports of patients not controlled for age cite a median survival of 54 weeks with brachytherapy[61] and 67 weeks with hyperthermia treatment.[62]

Low-Grade Gliomas

Low-grade gliomas are uncommon in the elderly. When the tumors are symptomatic, conventional treatment involves maximally feasible resection followed by radiation therapy, approximately 55 Gy to the tumor. Whole-brain radiation is not given, and there is no evidence that chemotherapy helps.

Even low-grade astrocytomas carry a 5-year survival rate of only 12 percent for those over the age of 50 compared with a 35 percent 5-year survival rate for those of ages 20 to 49 and an 83 percent 5-year survival rate for those of ages less than 19 years.[63] The most significant prognostic factor with low-grade astrocytomas is age.[64]

Metastatic Tumors

Single metastasis in patients who are either free of systemic disease as a result of treatment or whose disease appears to be under control respond better if the brain tumor is extirpated than if they receive radiation therapy alone.[42,65] Radiation therapy after the tumor is removed appears to increase the time to recurrence and thus is probably indicated.[41] For multiple metastatic tumors, radiation therapy is the treatment of choice. If the cancer is widespread, radiation should be delivered in large fractions over a short period of time (e.g., 3 Gy × 10 days). However, if the patient's systemic disease is under control and it is likely that he or she will live longer than 6 months to a year, smaller fractions (e.g., 2 Gy × 20 days) will decrease some of the late delayed effects of radiation therapy. In those patients whose tumors are chemosensitive (e.g., carcinoma of the breast) one might consider the use of chemotherapy either in addition to or independent of radiation therapy. Stereotactic radiosurgery may substitute for craniotomy if the surgical risk is high or the tumor inaccessible.[66]

Median survival for patients with multiple brain metastases is 1 month without treatment and 3 to 6 months after whole-brain radiation therapy and steroid therapy.[67,68] Surgical resection of solitary brain metastases increases survival further.[42]

Lymphoma

Primary CNS lymphoma is sensitive to both radiation and chemotherapy. A significant number of tumors disappear when they are treated with corticosteroids alone, so the surgeon cannot perform a biopsy and the oncologist cannot obtain diagnostic information that would be valuable in determining therapy on recurrence. Despite this sensitivity, the tumors almost invariably recur, usually within a year to 14 months, and are fatal. Most current protocols now call for the use of chemotherapy followed by whole-brain radiation, 45 to 50 Gy.[40] Some investigators believe that intrathecal methotrexate is also indicated to eradicate leptomeningeal tumor, which is detected along with parenchymal lesions in 30 percent of patients at diagnosis.[13] Postradiation chemotherapy with another drug, such as cytarabine, is also utilized.

Mean survival with supportive care alone is 1.8 to 3.3 months,[68,69] with surgery alone is 3.3 to 5 months,[68,70] and with combined radiation therapy and chemotherapy (intravenous methotrexate plus intrathecal methotrexate and postradiation high-dose cytarabine) is 42 months.[40]

Meningiomas

Surgical resection is the treatment of choice for meningiomas. When surgical resection is complete, no further therapy is necessary. If the surgical resection is incomplete, or if the tumor recurs despite an apparent complete resection, radiation therapy is indicated at the time of recurrence.[71] The radiation should be delivered in doses of about 50 Gy to a focal port encompassing the tumor. There is at present no effective chemotherapy for this neoplasm. Rates of recurrence and progression do not increase in older age groups.[72]

Neurinomas

The commonest neurinoma in both the young and the elderly is the acoustic nerve neurinoma. The treatment is surgical resection. With modern techniques of surgery and particularly with early detection of acoustic neurinomas, removal may allow preservation of both facial muscle function and hearing. Only large tumors are associated with morbidity involving the CNS. Radiosurgery has also been reported to be effective.

Pituitary Adenomas

Symptomatic adenoma of the pituitary can be treated with a high cure rate and low morbidity by transsphenoidal resection of the tumor.[73] If the tumor cannot be completely resected or is invasive, postoperative radiation therapy is indicated. Bromocriptine may be the treatment of choice in patients with prolactin-secreting tumors, particularly if the patient is a poor surgical or radiation therapy candidate.[57] Asymptomatic pituitary tumors can be followed.

REFERENCES

1. Boring CC et al: Cancer statistics, 1991. *Cancer* 41:19, 1991.
2. Codd MB, Kurland LT: Descriptive epidemiology of primary intracranial neoplasms. *Prog Exp Tumor Res* 29:1, 1985.
3. Desmeules M et al: Increasing incidence of primary malignant brain tumors: Influence of diagnostic methods. *J Natl Cancer Inst* 84:442, 1992.
4. Boyle P et al: Is the increased incidence of primary malignant brain tumors in the elderly real? *NAH Cancer Inst* 82:1594, 1990.
5. Davis DL, Schwartz J: Trends in cancer mortality: US white males and females, 1968–83. *Lancet* 1:633, 1988.
6. Riggs JE: Longitudinal gompertzian analysis of primary malignant brain tumor mortality in the US, 1962–1987: Rising mortality in the elderly is the natural consequence of competitive deterministic dynamics. *Mechanisms Ageing Develop* 60:225, 1991.
7. Davis DL et al: Epidemiology. International trends in cancer mortality in France, West Germany, Italy, Japan, England and Wales, and the USA. *Lancet* 2:474, 1990.
8. Chang CH et al: Comparison of postoperative radiotherapy and combined postoperative radiotherapy and chemotherapy in the multidisciplinary management of malignant gliomas. *Cancer* 52:997, 1983.
9. Cairncross JG, Posner JB: Brain tumors in the elderly, in Albert ML (ed): *Clinical Neurology of Aging*. New York, Oxford University Press, 1984, p 445.
10. Werner MH, Schold SC: Primary intracranial neoplasms in the elderly. *Clin Geriatr Med* 3:765, 1987.
11. Caird FI: Intracranial tumours in the elderly: Diagnosis and treatment. *Age Ageing* 13:152, 1984.
12. Walker EA et al: Epidemiology of brain tumors. *Neurology* 35:219, 1985.
13. Murray K et al: Primary malignant lymphomas of the central nervous system. *J Neurosurg* 65:600, 1986.
14. Eby NL et al: Increasing incidence of primary brain lymphoma in the US. *Cancer* 62:2461, 1988.
15. DeAngelis L et al: Primary CNS lymphoma: Combined treatment with chemotherapy and radiotherapy. *Neurology* 40:80, 1990.
16. Cairncross JG et al: Radiation therapy of brain metastases. *Ann Neurol* 7:29, 1980.
17. Schirmer M, Bock WJ: Intracranial tumors in advanced age. *Adv Neurosurg* 12:145, 1984.
18. Meyers BS: Increased intracranial pressure and depression in the elderly. *J Am Geriatr Soc* 32:936, 1984.
19. Fisher CM: Transient paralytic attacks of obscure nature: The question of nonconvulsive seizure paralysis. *Can J Neurol Sci* 5:267, 1978.
20. Levy DE: How transient are transient ischemic attacks? *Neurology* 38(suppl 1):108, 1988.
21. Sotaniemi KA et al: Clinical and CT correlates in the diagnosis of intracranial tumors. *J Neurol Neurosurg Psychiat* 54:645, 1991.
22. Hesselink JR et al: Benefits of Gd-DTPA for MR imaging of intracranial abnormalities. *J Comput Assist Tomogr* 12 (2):266, 1988.
23. Schubeus P et al: Intracranial meningiomas: How frequent are indicative findings in CT and MRI? *Neuroradiology* 32(6):467, 1990.
24. Piepmeier JM: Observations on the current treatment of low-grade astrocytic tumors of the cerebral hemispheres. *J Neurosurg* 67:177, 1987.
25. Schwaighofer BW et al: Primary intracranial CNS lymphoma: MR manifestations. *AJNR* 10 (4):725, 1989.
26. Gill SS et al: Proton MR spectroscopy of intracranial tumours: In vivo and in vitro studies. *J Comput Assist Tomogr* 14 (4):497, 1990.
27. Doyle WK et al: Differentiation of cerebral radiation necrosis from tumor recurrence by (18F)FDG and 82Rb positron emission tomography. *J Comput Assist Tomogr* 11(4):563, 1987.
28. Alavi JB et al: Positron emission tomography in patients with glioma. A predictor of prognosis. *Cancer* 62(6):1074, 1988.
29. Francavilla TL et al: Positron emission tomography in the detection of malignant degeneration of low-grade gliomas. *Neurosurgery* 24(1):1, 1989.
30. Minuera K et al: Early and late stage positron emission tomography (PET) studies on the haemocirculation and metabolism of seemingly normal brain tissue in

patients with gliomas following radiochemotherapy. *Acta Neurochir* 93(3-4):110, 1988.
31. Ogawa T et al: Changes of cerebral blood flow and oxygen and glucose metabolism following radiochemotherapy of gliomas: A PET study. *J Comput Assist Tomogr* 12(2):290, 1988.
32. Rozental JM et al: Glucose uptake by gliomas after treatment. A positron emission tomographic study. *Arch Neurol* 46(12):1302, 1989.
33. Voorhies RM et al: The single supratentorial lesion. *J Neurosurg* 53:364, 1980.
34. Malkin MG, Posner JB: Cerebrospinal fluid tumor markers for the diagnosis and management of leptomeningeal metastases. A review. *Eur J Cancer Clin Oncol* 23(1):1, 1987.
35. Bullard DE: Role of stereotaxic biopsy in the management of patients with intracranial lesions. *Neurol Clin* 3:817, 1985.
36. Delattre J-Y et al: High dose versus low dose dexamethasone in experimental epidural spinal cord compression. *Neurosurgery* 22:1005, 1988.
37. Graham K, Caird FI: High-dose steroid therapy of intracranial tumour in the elderly. *Age Ageing* 7:146, 1978.
38. Fadul C et al: Morbidity and mortality of craniotomy for excision of supratentorial gliomas. *Neurology* 38:1374, 1988.
39. Wood JR et al: The prognostic importance of tumor size in malignant gliomas: A computed tomographic scan study by the Brain Tumor Cooperative Group. *J Clin Oncol* 6:338, 1988.
40. DeAngelis LM et al: Combined modality therapy for primary CNS lymphoma. *J Clin Oncol* 10:635, 1992.
41. DeAngelis LM et al: The role of post-operative radiotherapy after resection of single brain metastases. *Neurosurgery* 24:798, 1989.
42. Patchell RA et al: A randomized trial of surgery in the treatment of single metastases to the brain. *N Engl J Med* 322:494, 1990.
43. Stylopoulos LA et al: Longitudinal CT study of parenchymal brain changes in glioma survivors. *Am J Neuroradiol* 9:517, 1988.
44a. Delattre J-Y, Posner JB: Neurological complications of chemotherapy and radiation therapy, in Aminoff MJ (ed): *Neurology and General Medicine*. New York, Churchill Livingstone, 1989.
44b. Gutin PH et al: *Radiation Injury to the Nervous System*. New York, Raven Press, 1991.
45. Gutin PH et al: Recurrent malignant gliomas: Survival following interstitial brachytherapy with high-activity iodine-125 sources. *J Neurosurg* 67:864, 1987.
46. Gutin PH et al: Brachytherapy of recurrent malignant brain tumors with removable high activity iodine-125 sources. *J Neurosurg* 60:61, 1984.
47. Munninger F, Weigel K: Long-term results of stereotactic interstitial curietherapy. *Acta Neurochir* (suppl 33):367, 1984.
48. Szilka G et al: Interstitial and combined irradiation of supratentorial gliomas. Results in 61 cases treated 1973–1981. *Acta Neurochir* (suppl 33):355, 1984.
49. Hochberg FG, Pruitt A: Assumptions in the radiotherapy of glioblastoma. *Neurology* 30:90, 1980.
50. Loeffler JS et al: Clinical patterns of failure following stereotactic interstitial irradiation for malignant gliomas. *Int J Radiat Oncol Biol Phys* 19:1455, 1990.
51. Wallner KE et al: Patterns of failure following treatment for glioblastoma multiforme and anaplastic astrocytoma. *Int J Radiat Oncol Biol Phys* 16:1405, 1989.
52. Adler JR et al: Stereotactic radiosurgical treatment of brain metastases. *J Neurosurg* 76:444, 1992.
53. Loeffler JS et al: Radiosurgery for brain metastases. *Princip Pract Oncol* 5:1, 1991.
54. Buckner JC: The role of chemotherapy in the treatment of patients with brain metastases from solid tumors. *Cancer Metastasis Rev* 10:335, 1991.
55. Ushio Y et al: Chemotherapy of brain metastases from lung carcinoma: A controlled randomized study. *Neurosurgery* 28:201, 1991.
56. Shapiro WR: Therapy of adult malignant brain tumors: What have the clinical trials taught us? *Semin Oncol* 13:38, 1986.
57. Malkin MG et al: Brain tumors, in Porter RJ, Schoenberg BS (eds): *Controlled Clinical Trials in Neurological Disease*. The Hague, Netherlands, Kluwer Academic, 1990, p 343.
58. Nelson DF et al: Survival and prognosis of patients with astrocytoma with atypical and anaplastic features. *J Neuro-Oncol* 3:99, 1985.
59. Ampil F et al: Intracranial astrocytoma in elderly patients. *J Neuro-Oncol* 12:125, 1992.
60. Burger PC, Green SB: Patient age, histologic features and length of survival in patients with glioblastoma multiforme. *Cancer* 59:1617, 1987.
61. Leibel SA et al: Survival and quality of life after interstitial implantation of removable high-activity iodine-125 sources for treatment of patients with recurrent malignant gliomas. *Int J Radiat Oncol Biol Phys* 17:1129, 1989.
62. Marchovsky JA et al: Hyperthermia treatment of brain tumors. *Missouri Med* 87:29, 1990.
63. Laws ER et al: Neurosurgical management of low-grade astrocytoma of the cerebral hemispheres. *J Neurosurg* 61:665, 1984.
64. Medbery CA et al: Low-grade astrocytomas: Treatment results and prognostic variables. *J Radiat Oncol Biol Phys* 15:837, 1988.
65. Mandell L et al: The treatment of single brain metastases from non-oat cell lung carcinomas. Surgery and radiation versus radiation therapy alone. *Cancer* 58:641, 1986.
66. Coffey RJ et al: Radiosurgery for solitary brain metastases using the cobalt-60 gamma unit: Methods and results in 24 patients. *Int J Radiat Oncol Biol Phys* 20:1287, 1991.
67. Patchell RA et al: Single brain metastases: Surgery plus radiation or radiation alone. *Neurology* 36:447, 1986.
68. Henry JM et al: Primary malignant lymphomas of the central nervous system. *Cancer* 34:1293, 1974.
69. Jellinger K et al: Primary malignant lymphomas of the central nervous system in man. *Acta Neuropathol (Berl)* 6:95, 1975.
70. Woodman R et al: Primary non-Hodgkin's lymphoma of the brain. A Review. *Medicine* 64:425, 1985.
71. Barbaro NM et al: Radiation therapy in the treatment of partially resected meningiomas. *Neurosurgery* 20:525, 1987.
72. Mirimanoff RO et al: Meningioma: Analysis of recurrence and progression following neurosurgical resection. *J Neurosurg* 62:18, 1985.
73. Ciric I: Pituitary tumors. *Neurol Clin* 3:751, 1985.

Chapter 99

DEPRESSION

Dan G. Blazer

The themes of aging and depression often coalesce. Simone de Beauvoir, in her book *The Coming of Age,* tells of Prince Siddhartha on one of his frequent visits from his protected palace.[1] On this particular day he encounters a tottering, wrinkled, white-haired, decrepit old man who is stooped and mumbling incomprehensibly while making his way along a road with a stick to improve his balance. The sight of the old man disturbs the young prince, and Siddhartha informs his charioteer, "It is the world's pity that we as ignorant beings, drunk with the vanity of youth, do not behold old age. Let us hurry back to the palace. What is the use of pleasures . . . since I myself am the future dwelling-place of old age?" It is tempting to perceive mood disturbances as being on a continuum, with mood declining as age increases owing to the inevitable physical disabilities and mental incapacitation associated with aging.

Such a perception, however, is of little value in the clinical management of the depressed older adult. Precise boundaries cannot be identified between a normal depressed mood and the extremes of depressive illness.[2] Nevertheless, most clinical investigators do not perceive depression as phenomenologically homogeneous. For this reason, the *Diagnostic and Statistical Manual of Mental Disorders* categorizes the depressive disorders as a group of distinct entities or independent syndromes presenting with a depressed mood, analogous to the different disease entities that might contribute to the symptoms and signs of an anemia.[3] Therapy of depression can therefore be selected based upon a thorough diagnostic workup, differential diagnosis, and selection of diagnostic-specific therapeutic modalities. Given the availability of excellent, but at times expensive and potentially dangerous, biological therapies, the categorical approach is accepted by most geriatric psychiatrists.

EPIDEMIOLOGY

Mood disorders are among the most common psychiatric disorders of adulthood. Nevertheless, the prevalence of major depression is lower in late life than in midlife.[4–6] The prevalence of major depression in community populations of older adults from the Epidemiologic Catchment Area (ECA) project ranges from less than 1 to 3 percent.

In contrast, the prevalence of depressive symptoms in the elderly remains relatively high. For example, Blazer and Williams reported significant dysphoria in almost 15 percent of a community-based sample of older adults.[4] Gurland et al. found 13 percent of the 65-and-over age group to have "pervasive depression."[7] In a recent study, 27 percent of older adults in the community reported depressive symptoms, with 8 percent suffering from clinically significant depressive symptoms associated predominantly with physical problems.[5]

Depression is more common in institutional settings. Folks and Ford diagnosed major depression in 26 percent of subjects in a medical-surgical inpatient unit.[8] Meador et al. found major depression in 11 percent and clinically significant depressive symptoms in an additional 20 percent of 130 consecutive men 70 years of age and over admitted to a medical and neurologic service of a large teaching hospital.[9] Parmelee et al., in a survey of a long-term care facility, found depressive neurosis in 12 percent of the sample, and clinically significant depressive symptoms in an additional 20 percent.[10] Depressive symptoms are therefore common among older adults, and major depression is a frequent problem encountered in acute and chronic care facilities. The prevalence of major or clinical depression in community populations, however, is not as great as has been previously described.

Despite the relatively lower prevalence of severe depression in community-dwelling elders, suicide rates are positively correlated with age. This correlation is exclusively explained by the higher suicide rates among white men over the age of 60.[11] No adequate explanation is forthcoming for this trend that has been recognized throughout the twentieth century in most Western countries. Nevertheless, the association of suicide with medical illness, decreased impulse control (which is occasionally associated with decreased cognitive functioning), social isolation, and loss of a loved one may contribute to the elevated risk of suicide among a group of older adults who may be more alienated emotionally—namely, the widowed white man who has survived his friends and grown apart from his family.

ETIOLOGY

Etiologic theories of mood disorders include biological, psychological, and psychosocial theories. No single causal agent has been identified for any mood disorder, and therefore the onset of depression in late life undoubtedly involves a web of causation, with contributions from each of these domains intermixed in unique ways in each individual experiencing a depressive disorder.

Structural brain changes, disregulation of chemical messengers, hormonal feedback mechanisms, and circadian rhythms are most often implicated in the pathophysiology of mood disorders. These abnormalities derive in part from a genetic predisposition, but the association of the majority of mood disorders in late life with a clear mode of inheritance has not been demonstrated. Structural brain changes have been observed with increased frequency in both normal older adults and depressed older adults compared with persons of middle age. These changes include patchy white matter lesions (probably secondary to vascular insufficiency) in the subcortical areas of the brain and relatively smaller nuclei in the limbic system, especially the hippocampus. These changes are more common in depressed elders than in nondepressed elders and are not inevitably associated with cognitive impairment.

Norepinephrine and serotonin are the neurotransmitters most often thought to contribute to the pathophysiology of mood disorders. In the early 1970s Robinson et al. found the concentrations of both these neurotransmitters to decrease with age; but levels of the metabolic product of serotonin, 5-hydroxyindoleacetic acid (5-HIAA), and the enzyme monoamine oxidase (MAO) were found to increase with age.[12] More recent studies have been equivocal. No convincing evidence exists that significant neurotransmitter abnormalities increase with advancing age. Nevertheless, changes in receptor sensitivity, such as a dysfunction of the imipramine receptors (which naturally occur in both brain tissue and in platelets in the blood), have been associated with both depression and increased age.

Disregulation of the hypothalamic-pituitary-adrenal (HPA) axis has also been implicated as associated with depression. The finding of increased secretion of cortisol in many depressed patients led to the adaptation of the dexamethasone suppression test (DST) as a laboratory marker of melancholic depression.[13,14] Rosenbaum et al., in a study of the DST across the life cycle, found a positive relationship between age and cortisol levels after administration of dexamethasone.[15] For example, 4 percent of subjects under 65 years of age had a cortisol level of 5 μg/dl after the test, whereas 12.5 percent of those subjects over the age of 65 were nonsuppressors. Each was physically healthy and not depressed. In general, however, there has been no overwhelming evidence of a propensity for older persons to suffer disregulation of the HPA axis significantly greater than persons in midlife, at least up until the age of 75.

Desynchronization of circadian rhythms has also been implicated in the onset of major depression. Abnormalities of sleep architecture are among the most robust biological markers of depression. The major abnormality identified is a decrease in rapid eye movement (REM) latency (the time between falling asleep and the first REM period).[16] Disruption of normal sleep with increasing age suggests the possibility of circadian abnormalities contributing to the etiology of late-life depression. As age increases, there is a gradual diminution in overall sleep time, a decrease in sleep continuity, and a decreased REM latency.[17]

The psychological contribution to depression includes at least three predisposing factors. The first, and most intuitive, is loss of a valued object. Older persons generally experience fewer stressful life events, but the majority of these events are *exit events*. Freud postulated that the ambivalent introjection of the lost object into the ego leads to typical depressive symptoms derived from a lack of energy available to the ego. Guilt ensues when the individual cannot express anger externally toward the lost object, and the depressed person then internalizes this anger. Though older persons experience loss frequently, the loss is generally an "on-time" experience. For example, the older married woman anticipates that she will outlive her husband and has rehearsed widowhood. Therefore, adaptation to the death of her spouse is more easily facilitated.

According to cognitive theories, depression results from negative distortions of life experiences, negative self-evaluation, pessimism, and hopelessness. For example, automatic thoughts resulting from an event lead to depressive symptoms. Depressed older adults may view the absence of a phone call from a child as an overt statement devaluing the parent for past failures. In reality, the reasons for not contacting the parent may relate to an overbooked schedule or even the inability to contact the parent because of the parent's busy schedule. Older persons are just as susceptible to cognitive distortions as younger persons in the midst of a severe depression or when depression is associated with cognitive dysfunction.

The third putative theory for the cause of depression in late life derives from Erikson's eighth stage of development, i.e., integrity versus despair. Late life is a time for "the acceptance of one's one and only life cycle and of the people who have become significant to it as something that had to be and that, by necessity, permitted of no substitutions."[18] If one fails to integrate one's life, to link one's life to both past heritage and future generations, then despair ensues. "Time is short, too short for the attempt to start another life and to try out alternative roads to integrity."[18] The acquisition of integrity, which is roughly analogous to cumulative wisdom, may protect the older adult psychologically from the development of the cognitive distortions resulting from mild to moderate depressed mood.

Social factors may also contribute to the onset of depression in the elderly. Pfifer and Murrell found that health and social support played both an additive and an interactive role in the onset of depressive symptoms.[19] Life events themselves had only weak effects, and sociodemographic factors, overall, did not contribute to depression onset. However, a weak support network and the presence of poor physical health placed older persons at especial risk for the onset of depression.

DIAGNOSIS AND DIFFERENTIAL DIAGNOSIS

The diagnostic criteria for major depression are listed in Table 99-1. Older persons suffering from major depression do not differ significantly from persons at earlier stages of the life cycle in the distribution of these symptoms, except that they are less likely to express feelings of worthlessness or guilt overtly and more likely to suffer from weight loss.[20] Though the older adult may be reticent to report a depressed mood or dysphoria spontaneously, once asked about depression, he or she is no less likely to report such a mood than persons at earlier stages of the life cycle. Though older persons do not report more difficulty concentrating (contrary to traditional beliefs about the frequency of self-reported cognitive dysfunction in late life when compared with persons in midlife), they do suffer more overt symptoms of cognitive impairment. The association of depression and dementia is far more common than the masking of depression as dementia, i.e., pseudodementia.[21]

The determination that an individual is suffering from a major or clinical depression (compared with a less severe presentation of depressive symptoms) is the important first step in the diagnostic process. Regardless of cause, major depression deserves careful evaluation by the clinician, for it must be disaggregated from other disorders, both physical and psychiatric, in order to prescribe the most appropriate therapy.

To assist in disaggregating major depression in the elderly, a series of diagnostic distinctions are important (Table 99-1). First, melancholic depression must be distinguished from nonmelancholic depression. Melancholic depression is more responsive to biological intervention, and nonmelancholic depression more responsive to psychosocial intervention. Persons suffering from a melancholic depression should be prescribed trial on a pharmacotherapeutic agent. The second distinction of importance is psychotic versus nonpsychotic depression. Psychotic depression is more common in late life than in midlife and is more resistant to pharmacologic intervention than nonpsychotic major depression, but is responsive to electroconvulsive therapy (ECT).[22]

TABLE 99-1

The Diagnosis of Major or Clinical Depression in Late Life

Diagnostic Criteria

Depressed mood and/or loss of interest or pleasure, plus four of the following (three if both depressed mood and loss of interest or pleasure):

- Weight loss or weight gain (more common)
- Insomnia or hypersomnia
- Psychomotor agitation or retardation
- Fatigue or loss of energy
- Feelings of worthlessness or of guilt (less common)
- Difficulty concentrating
- Recurrent thoughts of death or suicidal ideation

Diagnostic Distinctions of Importance

Melancholic-endogenous (at least five of the following) versus nonmelancholic:

- Loss of interest or pleasure
- Lack of reactivity to pleasurable stimuli
- Worse symptoms in morning
- Psychomotor agitation or retardation
- Significant weight loss
- Previous response to somatic therapies
- Previous episodes with remission
- Psychotic (delusions and/or hallucinations) versus nonpsychotic: Psychotic depression is relatively more prevalent in late life
- Single episode versus recurrent (especially rapid cycling)
- Seasonal (recurrence in winter months with full remission in summer months; atypical symptoms such as excessive sleep and weight gain) versus sporadic
- Pseudodementia versus mixed depression and dementia: Pseudodementia is not common
- Retarded depression versus agitated depression (mixed depression-anxiety)
- Pure major depression versus double depression (major depression plus dysthymia)
- Treatment-sensitive versus treatment-resistant: Elders more likely to be resistant to tricyclic antidepressants

SOURCE: Adapted from *Diagnostic and Statistical Manual of Mental Disorders*, 3d ed (rev). (*DSM*-III-R) Washington, American Psychiatric Association, 1987.

Psychiatrists have become more aware in recent years of the problem of recurrent depressions. In fact, most episodes of major depression tend to recur. Fortunately, these recurrences are usually separated by many years. In some cases, however, depression in late life recurs frequently, i.e., *rapid cycling*. This rapid-cycling variant may reflect an underlying bipolar disorder but may never manifest itself in overt manic episodes. Rapid-cycling depression usually requires intervention with lithium or carbamazepine along with an antidepressant medication. At times, discontinuation of the antidepressant drug decreases the propensity to cycle. Older persons may also suffer seasonal affective disorders, a variant of rapid-cycling depression, with recurrence of depression meeting criteria for major depression during the winter months and a full remission in the summer. Most persons suffering from a seasonal affective disorder report atypical symptoms of depression, such as excessive sleep and weight gain.

Depression is often associated with symptoms of agitation. Phenomenologically, depression may therefore be divided into a retarded depression versus an agitated depression. Closely associated with agitated depression is the mixed anxiety-depression syndrome. Anxious depression is associated with a poor prognosis and often requires the use of multiple pharmacologic agents, such as the combined prescription of an antianxiety medication along with an antidepressant medication. Though the symptoms of depression usually remit over time, the symptoms of anxiety are often chronic.

The differential diagnosis of depression is complex and is presented in Table 99-2. Within the mood disorders, an episode of major depression may reflect unipolar depression (single episode or recurrent), a bipolar depressive episode, or an atypical bipolar disorder—now classified as a mood disorder NOS (not otherwise specified). Older persons may experience the first onset of a manic episode in late life. Even if this episode meets the *Diagnostic and Statistical Manual of Mental Disorders,* third edition, revised (*DSM*-III-R) criteria for a manic episode, it is often atypical. Clinicians who have treated elderly bipolar patients often observe a "dysphoric" manic episode. Agitation, decreased sleep, increased energy, increased irritability, angry outbursts, and paranoid ideation predominate

TABLE 99-2

The Differential Diagnosis of Depressive Symptoms in Late Life (*DSM*-III-R)

Mood Disorders
- Major depression (single episode or recurrent)
- Dysthymia (or depressive neurosis)
- Bipolar disorder, depressed
- Depressive disorder NOS (i.e., atypical depression or mild biogenic depression)

Adjustment Disorders
- Adjustment disorder with depressed mood
- Uncomplicated bereavement

Organic Mental Disorders
- Primary degenerative dementia with associated major depression
- Organic mood disorder, depressed
- Secondary to physical illness (e.g., hypothyroidism, stroke, carcinoma of the pancreas)
- Secondary to pharmacologic agents (e.g., methyldopa, propranolol)

Psychoactive Substance-Use Disorders
- Alcohol abuse and/or dependence
- Sedative, hypnotic, or anxiolytic abuse and/or dependence

Somatoform Disorders
- Hypochondriasis
- Somatization disorder

the clinical picture. In other situations, older adults may experience periodic and definitive episodes of major depression that are intermixed with episodes of hypomania. During these latter episodes, the older person exhibits increased activity, some decreased sleep, and an exaggerated sense of well-being, and may profusely praise the clinician for his or her miraculous cure. Such patients must be monitored carefully, for these hypomanic symptoms can lead to behaviors that are potentially damaging, though the elder may not manifest overt psychotic behavior. The antidepressant medications, especially the MAO inhibitors, can precipitate hypomanic and even overt manic episodes in a previously depressed older adult.

Adjustment disorders account for many of the depressive symptoms exhibited by older adults. As noted above, depressive symptoms frequently ensue as a reaction to a chronic or painful physical illness, especially an illness that decreases functional capacity. Other stressors for older adults include retirement, marital problems (which can derive from increased contact), difficulty with children, loss of a social role, or an ill-advised change of residence. The most frequent stressor, however, is a physical illness.

In the study by Reiffler and colleagues, approximately 20 percent of all subjects suffering from primary degenerative dementia were concurrently experiencing a major depressive episode.[21] When they were treated with antidepressant medications, the depressive symptoms remitted but the dementia persisted. This combined clinical presentation is much more common than pseudodementia, i.e., a pure depressive episode which masks as a cognitive dysfunction.

Several physical illnesses and pharmacologic agents can induce a depressed mood. The association between depression and hypothyroidism has been well established. Symptoms of myxedema include constipation, cold intolerance, psychomotor retardation, decreased exercise tolerance, and cognitive changes along with the depressed affect. A low tetraiodothyroxine (T_4) level and elevated serum thyroid-stimulating hormone (TSH) level usually confirm the diagnosis. Left-sided stroke is also associated with depression and catastrophic responses manifested by episodes of profuse crying, feelings of despair, hopelessness, anger, and self-depreciation. A number of medications have been implicated in the etiology of depression, including frequently used antihypertensive agents and sedative-hypnotic or anxiolytic agents. Alcohol dependence often is disguised as a depressive episode or is comorbid with major depression.

Hypochondriasis is another confounder of the differential diagnosis of the depressed older adult. Depressed mood is common in hypochondriacal elders, though the essential feature of hypochondriasis is an unrealistic interpretation of physical signs or sensations as abnormal, which in turn leads to a preoccupation with fear or to the belief that one is suffering from a serious illness.[3] The prevalence of hypochrondriacal symptoms is increased among the depressed elderly, though the course of the disorder and response to usual therapeutic intervention should differentiate the two conditions. Concurrence of depressive symptoms and hypochondrical symptoms may increase the risk for suicide.

DIAGNOSTIC EVALUATION

The clinical interview is fundamental to the diagnostic evaluation of depressed elders. Both the older adult patient and family members should be included in this interview process. The length of the current depressive episode, a history of previous episodes, a history of drug and alcohol abuse, the response to previous therapeutic interventions for depressive illness, a family history of depression, suicidal ideations or attempts, and the level of physical functioning of the depressed elder can be determined by eliciting and comparing information from both patient and family. The severity of the depressive symptoms, including risk for suicide, should be established regardless of the differential diagnosis in order to decode whether the depressed elder is to be hospitalized. A number of clinical rating scales are available to assist the clinician, including the Hamilton Depression Rating Scale, the Montgomery-Asberg Depression Rating Scale, and the Global Assessment Scale. Scores on these operationalized ratings of severity also provide the clinician with a tool for tracking improvement during therapy.

The mental status examination of a patient assists in determining the quality of mood and affect, perceptual distortions that may result from depression (such as delusions and hallucinations), and psychomotor agitation or retardation. A thorough evaluation of cognitive status assists the clinician in distinguishing depression from a mixed depression-dementia syndrome. Orientation, memory, judgment, insight, and ability to abstract are key components of the cognitive assessment. A number of cognitive function screening scales are available to the clinician, such as the Mini-Mental State Examination and the Blessed Dementia Rating Scale.

Physical examination should include a neurologic evaluation to determine the presence of soft neurologic signs, such as frontal release signs or laterality. Weight loss and psychomotor retardation may precipitate peroneal palsy because of sitting with crossed legs. Both lying and standing blood pressures should be recorded, for postural hypotension frequently is caused by antidepressant medication.

The laboratory diagnostic workup of the depressed older adult is outlined in Table 99-3. Though no definitive laboratory test for depression has emerged, the pattern of laboratory findings across a number of diagnostic tests not only rules out physical illness as the cause of depressive symptoms but also delineates depressive illness that is in part biologically determined. Baseline laboratory values, such as the electrocardiogram, are important in monitoring the impact of medication. The (DST) has been extensively described as a diagnostic procedure, but its value is debated frequently. Cortisol levels greater than 5 μg/dl at 3 and 10 P.M. on the day following nighttime administration of 1 mg of dexamethasone are abnormal. Such levels are found in 50 to 70 percent of depressed patients and are no different for older adults, at least to the age of 75. The DST is not specific for depression, and the reading may be abnormal in patients with severe organic mental disorders. The greatest value of the test, may be in tracking the progress of treatment. If a positive value returns to a normal value and remains normal, this bodes well for short-term outcome.

TABLE 99-3

The Laboratory Diagnostic Workup of the Depressed Older Adult

Routine Laboratory Studies
- Clinical blood count and differential (B_{12} and/or folate deficiency)
- Urinalysis
- Chest x-ray film (to rule out cancer of lung)
- Electrocardiogram (baseline before beginning antidepressant therapy)
- Blood chemistry tests (to screen for dehydration secondary to severe depression or hypokalemia)

Endocrinologic Studies
- DST (may be most valuable in predicting outcome)
- Thyroid panel and TSH (adequate for assessment of thyroid status)

Polysomnography
- Sleep EEG, ECG, EMG, etc. (diagnostic test that complements the DST; patient must be drug-free if the test is to be effective; screens for sleep apnea syndrome)

Experimental or Less Frequently Used Diagnostic Studies
- MRI (depressed elderly exhibit increased leukoencephalopathy)
- Tritiated imipramine binding in platelets (may be more specific for melancholic depression in late life than in midlife)
- Urinary 3-methoxy-4-hydroxyphenyl glycol (MHPG) and 5-hydroxyindoleacetic acid (5-HIAA) (of questionable value in differential diagnosis or selection of pharmacologic agents)
- Platelet MAO inhibition (if tested before and after prescription of MAO inhibitor, provides evidence of peripheral effectiveness of the drug)

Psychological Tests and Rating Scales
- Standardized diagnostic interviews: Schedule for Affective Disorders and Schizophrenia (SADS), Diagnostic Interview Schedule (DIS), Geriatric Mental Status (GMS)
- Personality inventories: Structured Interview for DSM-III—Personality Disorders (SID-P), Millon, Dysfunctional Attitude Scale, Attributional Style Questionnaire
- Clinical assessment scales of severity: Hamilton Rating Scale for Depression, Montgomery-Asberg Depression Scale, Global Assessment Scale
- Self-rated assessment scales of severity: Center for Epidemiologic Studies—Depression Scale (CES-D), Zung SDS, Beck Depression Inventory, Geriatric Depression Scale

COURSE AND PROGNOSIS

The risk for suicide in the depressed older adult has been described above. Depression, however, may lead to other adverse outcomes. The all-cause mortality among depressed older adults evaluated in psychiatric facilities has been shown to be higher when compared with general population groups of the same age.[23,24] Though these depressed elders, at baseline, often experience poor physical health, poor health alone does not explain the increased mortality rate. Older persons are thought to experience loss of meaningful roles and emotional support through retirement, widowhood, death of friends, low economic status, and increased isolation. These factors are known to contribute to increased mortality in the elderly and may in turn interact with depressive symptoms. In addition, depressed elders may be less willing to care for themselves physically, and poor health practices contribute to increased mortality.

There is no evidence to support the impression that older adults are less likely to recover from a major depressive episode than middle-aged adults. Combined results from a number of outcome studies suggest that approximately one-third of depressed elders recover from an index episode of depression within 1 year and maintain recovery. One-third do not recover from the episode, and an additional one-third recover but experience a relapse.[25–27] These results are based on both inpatient and outpatient studies of uncomplicated depressive episodes. If elders experience comorbid major depression and significant physical illness, outcome is poorer and mortality rates are higher during the year of follow-up. Many of those individuals who recover suffer symptoms at follow-up.[25] That is, many older adults who recover from an episode do not recover entirely but experience some residual depressive symptoms.

Approximately 2 percent of depressed elders suffer from a dysthymic disorder (depressive neurosis). By definition, these individuals must experience mild to moderate depressive symptoms (but symptoms not meeting criteria for a major depressive episode) for at least 2 years. Some of these persons will suffer intermittent episodes of major depression. Therefore, when they are treated with pharmacologic agents (or even electroconvulsive therapy), they exhibit recovery from the major depression yet remain dysthymic. Some studies suggest that persons with dysthmic disorder with concurrent major depression (i.e., double depression) have a poorer prognosis for major depression, but this finding has not been validated for older adults.[28]

CLINICAL MANAGEMENT

The clinical management of depression in late life is four-pronged: psychotherapy, pharmacotherapy, electroconvulsive therapy, and family therapy. Cognitive-behavioral psychotherapy, along with interpersonal therapy (a cognitive-behavioral orientation to improving interpersonal relationships), has been developed specifically to treat depressive illness.[29,30] Cognitive-behavioral therapy has been used in treating depressed older adults and has been demonstrated to be effective.[31,32] These therapies are based upon cognitive theories of depression, with a goal of changing behavior and modes of thinking. Change is accomplished through behavioral interventions such as weekly activity schedules, graded task assignments, and logs of mastery or pleasure. Negative cognitions are restructured and automatic thoughts are challenged by testing empirical reality, examining distortions such as overgeneralizations, and generating new ways of viewing one's life. Such therapies are especially attractive to clinicians treating the depressed elder, for they are directive (and therefore culturally more suited to older adults), time-limited (usually requiring between 10 and 25 sessions), and educational. The depressed elder who views self as inadequate and defective (and therefore interprets experiences as being caused by problems with self) is challenged to rethink the course of events that has led to the negative cognition. When negative or disturbing events occur, the elder can mobilize new means of interpreting these events that preclude the onset of feelings of worthlessness, helplessness, and hopelessness.

Pharmacotherapy of the depressed elder is indicated in cases where depressive symptoms are at least moderately severe and/or where clear symptoms of a melancholic or endogenous depression are evident. Tricyclic antidepressants (TCAs) remain the agents of choice, despite the marketing of new antidepressants in recent years. A list of pharmacologic agents used in the treatment of depression in late life and characteristics of these agents appears in Table 99-4. Medications which are relatively free of side effects (especially cardiovascular side effects) and yet effective are preferred. Among the TCAs, nortriptyline, desipramine, and doxepin are the most popular agents for treating major depression in the elderly.

Dosing TCAs must be case-specific. The daily dose will usually be less for elders than for persons in midlife. For example, 25 to 50 mg of nortriptyline PO qhs or 25 mg of desipramine bid are commonly prescribed doses for relieving depressive symptoms in older adults. The new-generation agents have been less used. Nevertheless, in some circumstances these agents are preferred. Trazodone is virtually free of anticholinergic effects and would appear to be an ideal agent for treating depressed elders. Unfortunately, the drug is not free of side effects, especially sedative effects and occasional priapism. Fluoxetine is relatively free of anticholinergic effects and may be especially valuable in treating less severe but previously pharmacologically resistant episodes in late life. Agitation is a frequently troublesome side effect of fluoxetine. The drug also has a very long half-life, and therefore side effects may persist for days following discontinuation of the drug.

TABLE 99-4

Characteristics of Pharmacologic Agents Used in the Treatment of Depression in Late Life

Generic Name	Starting Daily Dose	Sedative Effect	Relative Anticholinergic Effect	Therapeutic Blood Level
Tricyclic tertiary amines				
Doxepin (Sinequan, Adapin)	50–75 mg	+++	+++	>100 ng/dl
Tricyclic secondary amines				
Nortriptyline (Pamelor, Aventyl)	25–50 mg	++	++	50–150 ng/dl
Desipramine (Norpramin)	25–50 mg	+	+	>125 ng/dl
New agents				
Buproprion (Wellbutrin)	75–225 mg	+	+	NA
Trazodone (Desyrel)	100–150 mg	+++	0	NA
Fluoxetine (Prozac)	10 mg	0	+	NA
MAO inhibitors				
Tranylcypromine (Parnate)	20 mg	+	++	≥80% reduction of MAO activity in platelets
Lithium				
Lithium carbonate	150–300 mg	++	0	0.4–0.7 mmol/liter
Psychostimulants				
Methylphenidate	5–10 mg	0	0	NA
Potentiating agents				
T_3 (Cytomel)	25 μg	0	0	NA

SOURCE: Adapted in part from Jenike MA: *Handbook of Geriatric Psychopharmacology*. Littleton, MA, PSG, 1985.

MAO inhibitors are not tolerated better than TCAs. When symptoms are atypical, however, such as increased sleep and increased appetite along with associated significant symptoms of anxiety, an MAO inhibitor may be indicated. Jenike recommends the less-used MAO inhibitor tranylcypromine.[33] When a depressive episode is severe, patients fail to respond to an antidepressant medication, and ECT is considered to be a viable treatment, the clinician must remember that use of an MAO inhibitor precludes initiation of ECT until 10 days to 2 weeks following discontinuance of the drug. Such a delay, coupled with Medicare constraints upon psychiatric hospital days, renders the use of an MAO inhibitor in the hospital less desirable.

The administration of low-dose stimulants, such as methylphenidate in the morning, or augmentation of TCAs with T_3 (Cytomel) may improve mood in the apathetic older adult. The effect of these augmentating medications, however, has yet to be conclusively demonstrated among the depressed elderly. Stimulants are generally safe in low dosages, and rarely does withdrawal lead to significant side effects. In some patients suffering from rapid-cycling depression, even if no manic episodes emerge in the clinical picture, the use of lithium carbonate is indicated. If lithium is not effective, other agents that are used include carbamazepine and clonazepam.

For the severe and pharmacologically resistant major depressive episodes in late life, ECT is the treatment of choice. Despite the adverse publicity that has been associated with ECT, the number of persons being treated has increased in recent years across the life cycle, especially among the elderly. In most general psychiatric units, nearly 50 percent of subjects who receive ECT are over the age of 60. Reasons for the frequent use of ECT in late life include the probable (though not documented) increased number of pharmacologically resistant cases, the effectiveness of ECT in pharmacologically resistant patients, and the relative lack of side effects. Even persons suffering from moderately severe cardiovascular disease can undergo ECT, usually at less risk than taking antidepressant medications.

ECT is not without problems. Even the use of unilateral, nondominant electrode placement does not eliminate the transient memory loss that accompanies treatment. Though recent and remote memory generally return to normal, the amnestic period during treatment is disturbing to the depressed elder. Older adults in the midst of a depressive episode who express concern regarding their cognitive capacities are especially at risk for agitation and worry about the memory loss that accompanies ECT. Persons who are suffering combined depression and dementia, a syndrome that is not always readily identified during an index episode of depression requiring ECT, may exhibit sustained confusion and memory difficulties for several weeks following ECT. If the depression recurs (ECT does not prevent the recurrence of depression but only relieves an existing episode), the clinician will have difficulty disaggregating the memory impairment secondary to depression from the memory impairment secondary to ECT. Six to 10 treatments are usually required for effective therapy and should be performed in the hospital under the care of a psychiatrist experienced in the administration of ECT.

The depressed older adult cannot be treated in isolation. Family members usually initiate the depressed elder's visit to the clinician's office or to the hospital. Severely depressed elders are often incapable of making decisions regarding treatment, yet will listen to family members who advise hospitalization. Clinicians should make an effort to ally with family members from at least two generations, usually the spouse and a child. In some situations, a sibling or a grandchild may also provide significant support and assistance during the course of treating severe depression. Most depressed elders do not resist ongoing interaction between the clinician and family members. Not only can valuable information be derived from diagnostic interviews with family members, but families should be instructed as to the nature of depressive illness, its course, and the potential for adverse outcomes—especially suicide. Such preventive measures early in the care of the depressed elder render care much more effective.

REFERENCES

1. de Beauvoir S: *The Coming of Age*. Paris, Editions Gallimard, 1970.
2. Blazer D et al: Depressive symptoms and depressive diagnoses in a community population: Use of a new procedure for analysis of psychiatric classification. *Arch Gen Psychiatry* 45:1078–1084, 1988.
3. *Diagnostic and Statistical Manual of Mental Disorders,* 3d ed (rev). Washington, American Psychiatric Association, 1987.
4. Blazer D, Williams CD: Epidemiology of dysphoria and depression in an elderly population. *Am J Psychiatry* 137:439, 1980.
5. Blazer D et al: The epidemiology of depression in an elderly community population. *Gerontologist* 27:281, 1987.
6. Myers JK et al: Six-month prevalence of psychiatric disorders in three communities: 1980 to 1982. *Arch Gen Psychiatry* 41:959, 1984.
7. Gurland BJ et al: The epidemiology of depression and dementia in the elderly: The use of multiple indicators of these conditions, in Coles JO, Barrett JE (eds): *Psychopathology of the Aged*. New York, Raven, 1980.
8. Folks DG, Ford CV: Psychiatric disorders in geriatric medical/surgical patients. *South Med J* 78:239, 1985.
9. Meador KG: Detection and treatment of major depression in older medically ill hospitalized patients. *Int J Psychiatry Med* 18:17, 1988.
10. Parmelee PA et al: Depression among institutionalized aging: Assessment and prevalence estimation. *J Gerontol* 44:M22, 1989.
11. Blazer DG et al: Suicide in late life: Review and commentary. *J Am Geriatr Soc* 34:519, 1986.
12. Robinson DS et al: Relation of sex and aging to monoamine oxidase activity of human plasma and platelets. *Arch Gen Psychiatry* 24:536, 1971.
13. Sachar EJ: Neuroendocrine abnormalities in depressive illness, in Sachar EJ (ed): *Topics in Psychoendocrinology*. New York, Grune & Stratton, 1975.
14. Carroll BJ et al: A specific laboratory test for the diagnosis of melancholia: Standardization, validity, and clinical utility. *Arch Gen Psychiatry* 38:15, 1981.
15. Rosenbaum AH et al: The DST in normal control subjects: A comparison of two assays and the effects of age. *Am J Psychiatry* 141:1550, 1984.
16. Kupfer DJ et al: Sleep EEG and motor activity as indicators in affective states. *Neuropsychobiology* 1:296, 1975.
17. Kupfer DJ: Neuropsychological markers: EEG sleep measures. *J Psychiatr Res* 18:467, 1984.
18. Erikson EH: *Identity, Youth, and Crisis*. New York, Norton, 1968.
19. Pfifer JF, Murrell SA: Etiologic factors in the onset of depressive symptoms in older adults. *J Abnorm Psychol* 95:282, 1986.
20. Blazer D et al: Major depression with melancholia: A comparison of middle-aged and elderly adults. *J Am Geriatr Soc* 35:927, 1987.
21. Reiffler BV et al: Coexistence of cognitive impairment and depression in geriatric outpatients. *Am J Psychiatry* 39:623, 1982.
22. Meyers BS et al: Late-onset delusional depression: A distinct clinical entity? *J Clin Psychiatry* 45:347, 1984.
23. Murphy E et al: Increased mortality rates in late-life depression. *Br J Psychiatry* 152:347, 1988.
24. Rabins PV et al: High fatality rates of late-life depression associated with cardiovascular disease. *J Affective Disord* 9:165, 1985.
25. Blazer D et al: Age and impaired subjective support: Predictors of depressive symptoms at one-year follow-up. *J Nerv Ment Dis* 180(3)172–178, 1992.
26. Murphy E: The prognosis of depression in old age. *Br J Psychiatry* 142:111, 1983.
27. Post F: The management and nature of depressive illness in late life: A follow-through study. *Br J Psychiatry* 121:393, 1972.
28. Keller MB, Shapiro RW: Major depressive disorder: Initial results from a one-year prospective naturalistic follow-up study. *J Nerv Ment Dis* 169:761, 1981.
29. Beck AT et al: *Cognitive Therapy of Depression*. New York, Guilford, 1979.
30. Klerman GL et al: *Interpersonal Psychotherapy of Depression*. New York, Basic Books, 1984.
31. Gallagher D, Thompson LW: Differential effectiveness of psychotherapies for the treatment of major depressive disorder in older adults. *Psychother Theor Res Pract* 19:42, 1982.
32. Steuer JL et al: Cognitive-behavioral and psychodynamic group psychotherapy in treatment of geriatric depression. *J Consult Clin Psychol* 52:180, 1984.
33. Jenike MA: *Handbook of Geriatric Psychopharmacology*. Littleton, MA, PSG, 1985.

Chapter 100

PARAPHRENIAS AND OTHER PSYCHOSES

Leila B. Laitman and Kenneth L. Davis

Paraphrenia and other late-onset psychoses are poorly understood; nonetheless, as many as 15 to 33 percent of schizophrenic patients have an onset after age 40, and 5 to 14 percent after age 50.[1] The prevalence of primary psychoses in psychiatric patients with onset of illness at 60 years of age or older has been reported as anywhere from 2 to 3 percent[2,3] to 10 percent.[4,5] In a general population sample of subjects aged 65 or older, 0.1 percent were found to have some form of late-onset psychosis.[6] As high as these figures are, they do not include psychoses which are secondary to other illnesses, such as dementia, delirium, or affective disorders. Yet very little systematic research has been done on this group of late-life psychotic states.

One obstacle to the rigorous investigation of paraphrenia and related conditions is that the terminology has changed continually for more than 100 years. The terms *paranoia, paraphrenia,*[7] *late paraphrenia,*[4] *senile schizophrenia,*[3] *paranoid disorder,*[8] *delusional disorder,*[9] *paranoid hallucinosis,*[10] *schizophreniform psychosis,*[10,11] *schizophrenic syndrome,*[10] *reactive psychosis,*[11] *paranoid psychosis, paranoiac psychosis,*[12] and *late-onset paranoid schizophrenia*[9] have all been used to describe late-onset psychoses. Many diagnostic categories overlap, and there are no universally accepted diagnostic criteria for the late-onset psychoses. Indeed, the term *paraphrenia* does not even appear in the *Diagnostic and Statistical Manual of Mental Disorders, third ed, revised (DSM* III-R), the major American diagnostic resource which revised and replaced *DSM* III. The intent of this chapter is (1) to discuss these nosologic issues in an attempt to clarify the terminology which has confounded research and treatment efforts for so long and (2) to raise a few implications for future research.

DEFINITION OF TERMS

The two primary paranoid psychoses found in the elderly—paraphrenia and delusional (paranoid) disorder—will be the focus of this chapter. In the early twentieth century, Kraepelin defined *paranoia* as a state in which there are completely systematized delusions of a jealous or persecutory nature, without the presence of hallucinations.[7] He devised the term *paraphrenia* for the state characterized by paranoia and hallucinations. In both conditions, he said the patients' symptoms remain essentially unchanged over the course of the illness. The later onset of symptoms and nondeteriorating course set paraphrenic patients apart from those with "dementia praecox," which is now called *schizophrenia.*[7]

In the 1930s, doubt was cast on the unchanging nature of Kraepelin's patients. Kolle and Mayer-Gross followed Kraepelin's paraphrenic group and learned that in the majority the diagnosis had been changed to schizophrenia.[13,14] Thus, whether paraphrenia was a true diagnostic entity or was simply a variant of schizophrenia or some other diagnosis in the elderly remained unclear. As a consequence, the term was discarded by the psychiatric community, and elderly patients with paranoid symptoms were considered to have arteriosclerosis, senile dementia, or an "involutional" diagnosis.

In 1955, the term *paraphrenia* was reintroduced by Roth[4] to describe schizophrenia of late onset. Roth found that about 10 percent of all first-admission elderly psychiatric patients were schizophrenic and usually paranoid. These patients had no evidence of dementia or serious affective illness. He called them "late paraphrenics" because they fit the clinical picture of paraphrenia described by Kraepelin but had an even later onset of illness. Subsequently, Kay and Roth described late paraphrenia more fully as a psychiatric disorder of late onset (usually after age 60) involving paranoid delusions and possibly hallucinations (including auditory, visual, tactile, and olfactory) without evidence of dementia or primary affective disorder.[15] The patient's overall personality does not change in late paraphrenia as it does in schizophrenia. There is little, if any, looseness of association, affective incongruity, blunting, loss of volition, or other classic negative symptoms of schizophrenia.

In essence, paraphrenia is somewhat of an intermediate state between paranoia, as Kraepelin described it, and paranoid schizophrenia, as defined by

DSM III-R.[9] In paranoia as described by Kraepelin, hallucinations could not accompany the paranoid delusions, whereas in paraphrenia they could. Paranoid schizophrenia, too, is characterized by both paranoid delusions and hallucinations; however, the course is one of deterioration in level of functioning and change in overall personality. So paraphrenia develops later in life and is unassociated with many symptoms frequently found in paranoid schizophrenia, yet meets *DSM* III-R criteria for schizophrenia, late onset.

Paraphrenia is a primary paranoid psychosis of late onset by its very definition. Delusional (paranoid) disorder, however, is a primary paranoid psychosis that can appear for the first time in late life, although it more frequently appears in younger patients. Paranoia as Kraepelin described it was considered by *DSM* III to be one of the "paranoid disorders," the others being "shared paranoid disorder" and "acute paranoid disorder." The paranoid disorders were defined by *DSM* III as states in which there was an insidiously developing delusional system in the presence of otherwise clear and orderly thinking. The delusions were of a persecutory or jealous nature. Paraphrenia differed from paranoid disorder in two ways: (1) hallucinations could be present in paraphrenia but not in paranoid disorders, and (2) age of onset of paraphrenia was generally over age 60, whereas there was no minimum age of onset for paranoid disorder.

In the revision of *DSM* III (*DSM* III-R), the paranoid disorders were named as delusional (paranoid) disorders. In this diagnostic category, delusions are not confined to those of persecution and jealousy, as in *DSM* III, but now include the following subtypes: erotomanic, grandiose, jealous, persecutory, somatic, and unspecified.[9] Thus many more patients can be classified as having this diagnosis, and, as a consequence, far fewer patients with late-life psychoses are classified as "atypical" cases. The former subtypes of paranoid disorder in *DSM* III, "paranoia," "shared paranoid disorder," and "acute paranoid disorder," were eliminated in *DSM* III-R and subsumed in other categories. In the new category of delusional (paranoid) disorders, patients may have hallucinations if the hallucinations are not prominent. It is thus conceivable that some patients with late paraphrenia as described by Roth can now be classified according to *DSM* III-R as having delusional (paranoid) disorder. Indeed, paraphrenia does not appear as a diagnostic category in *DSM* III-R. It may not appear in ICD 10 in order to achieve uniformity with *DSM* III-R.[16,17] If delusions are very bizarre or if hallucinations are quite prominent, *DSM* III-R provides for a late-onset schizophrenia which develops after age 45.

VALIDATORS OF *DSM* III

DSM III-R has chosen to avoid the term *paraphrenia,* but includes later-life-onset schizophrenia. Therefore, the patient who has onset of primary psychosis in old age can be diagnosed as having either delusional (paranoid) disorder or paranoid schizophrenia, late onset. However, the question that must be asked is whether this nosologic system is correct. Is paraphrenia a separate entity from delusional disorder or late-life schizophrenia? Is it even possible that paraphrenia or delusional disorder in the elderly is a subtype of affective illness? These and similar queries speak to the issue of diagnostic validity.

To address the validity of these diagnostic categories, the available data will be organized into three categories: (1) antecedent validators, (2) concurrent validators, and (3) predictive validators. Antecedent validators include family history, premorbid personality, demographic factors, and precipitating events. Concurrent validators are symptoms and biological markers. Predictive validators encompass diagnostic consistency over time, outcome data, and therapeutic response. These data must be viewed with some reservation, as the terminology and methodology are not consistent across studies from which information on validity was extracted. For example, the data on delusional (paranoid) disorder derives from patients below age 60, and the nature of delusions has been redefined.

Antecedent Validators

Family History

Europeans view late paraphrenia as being part of a spectrum of schizophrenia-like disorders. Data from family history studies have indicated increased incidence of schizophrenia in the first-degree relatives of late-onset paranoid patients, compared with incidence of schizophrenia in the general population.[7,10,18] However, the expectancy rate of 2.5 percent for schizophrenia in the siblings of paraphrenic patients is significantly less than the 7.4 percent expectancy rate for schizophrenia among the siblings of younger schizophrenic patients.[18]

Other data indicate that relatives of elderly paranoid patients have an increased overall expectancy for any psychosis of the same magnitude as that found in first-degree relatives of schizophrenic and manic-depressive patients.[15,18] There is mildly increased expectancy for personality disorders, compared with expectancy for the community at large.[19] Thus, paraphrenia differs in genetic pattern from schizophrenia. Familial linkage does seem to exist, but any more specificity than linkage to psychoses is difficult to establish.

The familial relationship between delusional (paranoid) disorder and schizophrenia is also rather weak. When compared with controls, some data have shown an increased prevalence of schizophrenia (but not significantly increased) in relatives of patients with paranoid psychoses similar to Kraepelin's concept of "paranoia." Most reports, however, have found no increased risk of schizophrenia in the first-degree relatives of paranoid psychotic probands.[18,21,22] Affective disorder, as well, seems to be unrelated to delusional disorder from family history data.[18,23]

The family history of the delusional disorder patient shows major chronic psychiatric illness in excess of normal expectations, if anything. The illness is similar in kind to the illness in the proband. This suggests a qualitative difference from nonparanoid schizophrenia in that the delusional disorder "breeds true."[24] Still, family studies do not demonstrate that delusional disorder clusters strongly in families.[25]

Thus, paraphrenia has been compared with schizophrenia and with affective illness through family history studies. A direct comparison with delusional disorder has not been done, nor has delusional disorder been studied in the elderly. The family history data point to paraphrenias' being a condition distinct from schizophrenia and affective illness. The data tentatively suggest that delusional disorder is a separate entity from schizophrenia and affective disorder, and from paraphrenia as well.

Premorbid Personality

The retrospective determination of premorbid personality carries with it many methodological difficulties and must be viewed with caution. The premorbid personality of paraphrenia seems to be predominantly paranoid and schizoid in type. Common traits are jealousy, suspiciousness, arrogance, egocentricity, emotional coldness, and extreme solitariness.[15,19]

A particular type of premorbid personality has not been established for delusional disorder patients. Compared with schizophrenic patients, they are less likely to be schizoid, introverted, or submissive, and more likely to have inferiority feelings[25] and to be hypersensitive.[12]

The premorbid personality data add little to the validity of the diagnosis of paraphrenia. The specific familial link to marked inferiority feelings in delusional disorder patients can be interpreted to mean that the personality prone to delusional disorder is different from that prone to schizophrenia. Beyond that, premorbid personality has not been a helpful validator for the diagnosis of delusional disorder.

Demographic and Precipitating Factors

In paraphrenia, women predominate over men in the ratio of about 7:1. Paraphrenic patients of both sexes are unlikely to be married or to have children. Compared with affective disorder patients, significantly more paraphrenic patients were living alone and were socially isolated at the time they became ill (40 percent of paraphrenic versus 12 percent of affective disorder patients).[15] Interestingly, deafness seems to play a large part in the isolation. An association between acquired deafness and paranoid illness in the elderly has been demonstrated.[2,15,26] Paraphrenic patients also have significantly more cataracts and far-vision problems than do affective disorder patients.[27]

Age-at-onset data suggest that paraphrenia is separate from schizophrenia but may be part of a continuum in late life.[1,4,12,28] Most schizophrenic patients emerge as such before age 30. While catatonic and hebephrenic conditions generally emerge in the twenties, paranoid schizophrenic conditions invariably emerge later. Data has shown that most schizophrenic patients with onset after 40 are paranoid and that patients with the older age-of-onset and late-onset psychoses are for the most part paranoid. Some data indicate that 13 percent of all schizophrenic patients had onset of symptoms in the fifth decade, 7 percent in the sixth decade, and 3 percent thereafter.[23]

It is not clear whether delusional disorder patients are more likely to be male or female.[12,30] Marriage rates were found to be significantly higher in delusional disorder patients than in schizophrenic ones.[12,31] Delusional disorder patients have been reported to be more socially isolated and to have more "conflicts of conscience" than schizophrenic patients. They are more likely to have a precipitating factor, such as immigration, than are schizophrenic patients, who often have none.[32] Age-at-onset data show delusional disorder patients to be older than schizophrenic patients at time of onset of illness.[12,13,25,30,31]

So, paraphrenia has later age of onset than schizophrenia, but not distinctly so. Delusional disorder patients have onset at older ages than typical schizophrenic patients. Social isolation and sensory loss are strong premorbid factors in both delusional disorder and paraphrenia compared with schizophrenia and affective disorder. The distinctness of the diagnoses of paraphrenia and delusional disorder is supported weakly by these data.

Concurrent Validators

Symptoms

The typical paraphrenic patient is similar to the schizophrenic patient, except for the absence of thought disorder and the fact that personality remains basically unchanged from the premorbid state.[15] Paranoid delusions and hallucinations (including auditory, visual, tactile, and olfactory) may be present together, or the delusions may occur alone. Delusions may be as bizarre as they are in schizophrenia, including delusions of influence and passivity. Frequent themes involve sexual molestation, poisoning, or other bodily harm. Paraphrenics may believe that lethal gases are being pumped into their homes or that their food and water are poisoned. They complain of being stabbed, cut, irradiated, or otherwise bodily manipulated by persons in distant settings. They feel controlled by demonic instruments or machines. Hallucinations may be voices communicating about the patient in the third person. While incoherence of speech and even neologisms occur, they are unusual except in cases of long duration. In general there is initially no looseness of association and only mild affective incongruity, affective blunting, or loss of volition.[15,19] Studies that examined diagnostic criteria for late paraphrenia found them compatible with *DSM* III criteria for paranoid schizophrenia except that age of onset is over age 45.[33,34] In *DSM* III-R, the age-45 cutoff for onset has been removed from paranoid schizophrenia, and a late-onset subcategory now exists. Late paraphrenia as a diagnosis is now compatible with a late-onset schizophrenia from the symptomatic point of view.

Delusional disorder commonly manifests itself by delusions concerning marriage, plots, and being unfairly treated. Delusions of reference, jealousy, and persecution are common. Delusions in schizophrenia and in paraphrenia are typically more bizarre than in delusional disorder. The symptomatology of delusional (paranoid) disorder in *DSM* III-R has been expanded to include persecutory, jealous, erotomanic, somatic, grandiose, and other types of delusions. Hallucinations may be present if they are not prominent. No thought disorder is present. Some paraphrenic patients might meet these criteria as well. Thus, diagnostic criteria for paraphrenia continue to overlap with both late-onset schizophrenia, paranoid type, and delusional (paranoid) disorder in *DSM* III-R. From a symptomatic point of view, delusional disorder is distinct from schizophrenia but not from paraphrenia.

Biological Markers

There have been few biological data using techniques of modern biological psychiatry to validate the diagnosis of either paraphrenia or delusional disorder. Some work on investigation of brain lesions through CT scan[35–37] and MRI[38] suggests that "occult" vascular disease may be more of a factor than once thought in late-onset psychosis, but a direct connection is far from clear. A larger ventricular brain ratio (VBR) may be present in paraphrenic patients compared with age-matched normal persons, but VBR did not vary directly with the severity of symptoms.

One study on genetic markers in late paraphrenia suggested increased frequency of HLA-B and HLA-C antigens in late paraphrenic patients compared with controls, and no HLA-A antigens as are found in paranoid schizophrenia. This suggests that paraphrenic patients might be genetically distinct from schizophrenic patients.[39] More work in this area needs to be done.

Predictive Validators

Diagnostic Consistency over Time

Kraepelin originally believed that paraphrenia was a chronic, unremitting condition that did not progress to a state in which patients could no longer function, think clearly, or take care of themselves.[7] Follow-up of his paraphrenic group, however, showed that in most cases the diagnosis had been changed to schizophrenia. Most data agree that the clinical changes seen over time in patients diagnosed with paraphrenia are the same as those seen in schizophrenia. At least 40 percent of paraphrenic patients progress to paranoid schizophrenia. However, the pronounced deterioration of intellect, personality, and habits that occurs in some chronic schizophrenic patients is not usual in paraphrenic patients. Paraphrenic patients, for the most part, remain clean, tidy, and generally well-conducted.[13–15] Paraphrenic patients are often able to survive well in noninstitutional settings because they can carry on the activities of daily living quite adeptly. Younger schizophrenic patients, however, more often require some kind of institutionalization even after active symptoms have subsided as they have a marked disintegration of previous personality and ability to care for themselves.[10,23]

In delusional disorder, there seems to be longitudinal diagnostic consistency.[18,39] Only a small portion (3 to 22 percent) of patients eventually develop schizophrenia. No more than 6 percent of delusional disorder patients evolve into affective disorder patients.[25] Thus, on this parameter, the validity of the delusional disorder diagnosis is established. The paraphrenia diagnosis is not as durable over time. It is not consistently possible to separate paraphrenia from schizophrenia based on these data.

Outcome Data

The outcome of paraphrenia was originally regarded as poor. This may have been because data existed only on hospitalized patients. Many paraphrenic persons, however, never require hospitalization and never come to medical attention. Another factor implicating poor outcome for paraphrenia was that much of the original data was collected before the advent of the use of neuroleptics. Efforts at psychological therapy are usually unrewarding, although situational or environmental manipulation can sometimes produce symptomatic response.[40] Electroconvulsive therapy (ECT) has been tried, but it is usually helpful only in cases in which there are significant affective symptoms.[29,41] Outcome, however, is not as poor as it once seemed. Neuroleptics and community-based therapeutic programs have allowed many paraphrenic persons to lead independent lives, free from hospitalization.

In general, the outcome of delusional disorder patients is good in that most are discharged from hospitals back to the community, with fewer rehospitalizations than occur with schizophrenic patients.[12,24] Paraphrenic and delusional disorder patients are equally able to function occupationally and socially despite their symptoms, whereas schizophrenic patients are not. Thus, a distinction from schizophrenia is apparent.

Therapeutic Response

Clinical management of paraphrenic patients after an appropriate organic workup has been done relies almost totally on neuroleptic drugs. No one medication has been shown to be specifically efficacious.[16,29] ECT is not deemed particularly helpful in effecting long-lasting remission. There is no evidence that psychotherapy is beneficial except in helping maintain a patient on neuroleptics for a longer period of time. Factors such as the type of neuroleptic, dosage, blood levels, side effects, and degree of improvement in specific symptoms have not been adequately studied.[29]

Treatment of paraphrenic symptoms with adequate initial and maintenance neuroleptic therapy has been shown to lead to the disappearance or attenuation of symptoms. There is striking improvement in the long-term outcome of paraphrenia with neuroleptic treatment. Factors predicting a good outcome for patients were (1) immediate response to treatment, (2) insight gained secondary to treatment, (3) success in maintaining a longer period of drug treatment, (4) marriage, (5) younger age, and (6) good premorbid relationships predicting cooperation during maintenance treatment.[10] Outpatients often have poor compliance with taking oral medication. It has been found that giving an extremely low dose of a long-acting depot intramuscular neuroleptic preparation can be an effective and safe treatment when "crisis intervention" for the paraphrenic patient is necessary.[42]

Delusional disorder is most often treated with neuroleptics as well. No placebo control studies have been done. Neuroleptics seem helpful initially, but results are not dramatic. Patients remain symptomatic but able to function socially. Psychotherapy has similar effects. The effect of ECT is not delineated.[24,25] Neuroleptics are nonspecific treatments, and thus the validity of neither paraphrenia nor delusional disorders can be established on this parameter. Nonetheless, some similarity with schizophrenia is suggested by the parallel in responsivity to the same class of drugs.

SUMMARY

Let us now attempt to answer a series of critical questions regarding the paraphrenias and other late-life psychoses.

Are the DSM III-R diagnostic categories of delusional (paranoid) disorder and paranoid schizophrenia, late onset, sufficient to give a diagnosis to all patients who have onset of primary psychosis in old age that is not a nosologic afterthought?

The answer is a qualified yes. Looking purely at the majority of concurrent validating data on symptoms, there is a consensus that the illness called *late paraphrenia* in Europe is compatible with a late-onset schizophrenia. The problem with *DSM*-III was that there was an age-45 cutoff for schizophrenia. Now that a subcategory of late-onset type exists in *DSM* III-R, the diagnosis should no longer be classified as "atypical" psychosis. The elderly-onset psychotic patient can also be diagnosed as having delusional (paranoid) disorder if hallucinations are not prominent and there is no thought disorder. According to *DSM* III-R criteria, delusions can be persecutory, jealous, erotomanic, somatic, grandiose, or "other."

Is paraphrenia a separate entity from delusional (paranoid) disorder and schizophrenia?

This question of diagnostic validity is still difficult to answer. Paraphrenia has been compared with schizophrenia and with affective illness. A direct comparison with delusional disorder has not been done, nor has delusional disorder been studied in the elderly. The antecedent validator of family history points to paraphrenia's being distinct from schizophrenia. Family studies suggest that delusional disorder is not closely related to schizophrenia but does have a familial link to inferiority feelings. Thus, there are tentative data that paraphrenia seems to be a separate entity from schizophrenia and delusional disorder.

Premorbid personality does not conclusively separate paraphrenia from schizophrenia, although paraphrenic patients seem to be more hypersensitive premorbidly. The typical paraphrenic patient has a schizoid or paranoid premorbid personality. Delusional disorder patients differ from schizophrenic patients in that they have more inferiority feelings than schizophrenic patients do and are less schizoid, submissive, and introverted. The question of delineation of paraphrenia from delusional disorder cannot be answered from these data.

Paraphrenia has later age of onset than schizophrenia, but the older the age of onset of schizophrenia, the more likely it is to be of a paranoid variety. So it is not clear from available data whether paraphrenia is merely a very late onset schizophrenia or a distinct entity. Delusional disorder patients have onset at older ages than typical schizophrenic patients do.

Social isolation and sensory loss seem to be strong premorbid factors in both delusional disorder and paraphrenia, compared with schizophrenia and affective illness. Thus, paraphrenia and delusional disorder can be separated from schizophrenia on these parameters but not from each other.

The symptoms of paraphrenia overlap with both delusional disorder and schizophrenia. No consistent diagnostic criteria exist for paraphrenia. It is not possible to differentiate paraphrenia from delusional disorder or schizophrenia based on symptomatology.

There have been virtually no biological investigations of the molecular or cellular basis for paraphrenia or delusional disorder as there have been for schizophrenia and affective illness. Whether these illnesses can be differentiated on biological measures from each other or from illnesses which display early onset of symptoms demands investigation.

The predictive validator of longitudinal diagnostic consistency points to paraphrenia's being some type of schizophrenia. Delusional disorder seems to remain diagnostically consistent over time. Outcome, however, is better for both paraphrenic and delusional disorder patients than it is for schizophrenic ones. Paraphrenic and delusional disorder patients also are less likely to be chronically institutionalized than schizophrenic patients are. Although paraphrenic patients respond to treatment as schizophrenic patients do, neuroleptics are nonspecific treatments. The symptoms of delusional disorder patients do not seem to respond as well to treatment, but the patients can still function. Thus, the parameter of treatment response does not separate paraphrenia from delusional disorder or schizophrenia.

Could paraphrenia or delusional disorder in the elderly be subtypes of affective illness?

Neither illness seems to be related to affective disorder. This is borne out by all validators, although delusional disorder has not been studied in the elderly.

Until *DSM* III-R, American psychiatry had been lumping too many diagnoses together into "atypical" categories. The addition of a late-onset category in schizophrenia and the acceptance of the Kraepelinian description of paranoia, with subtypes of persecutory, jealous, erotomanic, somatic, grandiose, and "other" for delusional (paranoid) disorder, are major steps in recognizing diagnostic realities that have been evident for years in European literature.

FINAL THOUGHTS

Now that a clearer nosology exists, it would be useful to launch an epidemiological study to determine the incidence and prevalence of these late-life paranoid states. Additional family studies must be done to clarify the genetic relationship, if any, to schizophrenia or affective disorder, and to determine if these conditions "breed true." Modern biological methodology must be applied to these patients. The areas of personality integration, sensory loss, and life expectancy are also underinvestigated and might yield a great deal of data on the process of schizophrenia and of aging. Finally, rigorous psychopharmacological treatment studies need to be conducted. Until these kinds of data are collected, it will not be possible to know conclusively if late-onset psychoses are merely subtypes of illnesses that appear in the young or are unique entities in themselves.

REFERENCES

1. Larson C, Nyman G: Age of onset in schizophrenia. *Hum Hered* 20:241, 1970.
2. Leuchter AF, Spar JE: The late-onset psychoses: Clinical and diagnostic features. *J Nerv Ment Dis* 173:488, 1985.
3. Fish F: Senile schizophrenia. *J Ment Sci* 106:938, 1960.
4. Roth M: The natural history of mental disorder in old age. *J Ment Sci* 101:281, 1955.
5. Blessed G, Wilson ID: The contemporary natural history of mental disorder in old age. *Br J Psychiatry* 141:59, 1982.
6. Kay DWK et al: Old age mental disorders in Newcastle-upon-Tyne. *Br J Psychiatry* 110:146, 1964.
7. Kraepelin E: *Dementia Praecox and Paraphrenia*, reprint of 1919 ed. New York, Krieger, 1971.
8. American Psychiatric Association: *Diagnostic and Statistical Manual of Mental Disorders,* 3d ed. Washington, American Psychiatric Association, 1980.
9. American Psychiatric Association: *Diagnostic and Statistical Manual of Mental Disorders,* 3d ed (rev) Washington, American Psychiatric Association, 1987.
10. Post F: *Persistent Persecutory States of the Elderly.* Oxford, Pergamon, 1966.
11. Langfeldt G: The prognosis in schizophrenia and the factors influencing the course of the disease. *Acta Psychiatr Neurol Scand* (suppl 13):1, 1937.
12. Retterstol N: *Paranoid and Paranoiac Psychoses*. Springfield, IL, Charles C Thomas, 1966.
13. Kolle K: *Die Primare Verrucktheit*. Leipzig, Thieme, 1931.
14. Mayer-Gross W: *Die Schizophrenie*. Berlin, Springer, 1932.
15. Kay DWK, Roth M: Environmental and hereditary factors in the schizophrenia of old age ("late paraphrenia") and their bearing on the general problem of causation in schizophrenia. *J Ment Sci* 107:649, 1961.
16. Munro A: A plea for paraphrenia. *Can J Psychiatry* 36:667,1991.
17. Quintal M et al: Late paraphrenia and ICD 10. *Int J Geriatr Psychiatry* 6:111, 1991.
18. Funding T: Genetics of paranoid psychoses of later life. *Acta Psychiatr Scand* 37:267, 1961.
19. Herbert ME, Jacobson S: Late paraphrenia. *Br J Psychiatry* 113:461, 1967.
20. Debray Q: A genetic study of chronic delusions. *Neuropsychobiology* 1:313, 1975.
21. Watt JAG et al: Paranoid states of middle life: Familial occurence and relationship to schizophrenia. *Acta Psychiatr Scand* 61:413, 1980.
22. Kendler K, Hays P: Paranoid psychoses (delusional disorder) and schizophrenia: A family history study. *Arch Gen Psychiatry* 38:547, 1981.
23. Bridge TP, Wyatt JW: Paraphrenia: Paranoid states of late life: II. American research. *J Am Geriatr Soc* 28:201, 1980.
24. Winokur G: Delusional disorder (paranoia). *Compr Psychiatry* 18:511, 1977.
25. Kendler K: The nosologic validity of paranoia (simple delusional disorder). *Arch Gen Psychiatry* 37:699, 1980.

26. Cooper AF et al: Hearing loss in paranoid and affective psychoses of the elderly. *Lancet* 1:851, 1974.
27. Cooper AF, Porter R: Visual acuity and ocular pathology in the paranoid and affective psychoses of later life. *J Psychosom Res* 20:107, 1976.
28. Astrup C et al: *Prognosis in Functional Psychoses.* Springfield, IL, Charles C Thomas, 1962.
29. Harris MJ, Jeste DV: Late onset schizophrenia: An overview. *Schizophr Bull* 14:39, 1988.
30. Rimón R et al.: A sociopsychiatric study of paranoid psychoses. *Acta Psychiatr Scand* 40(suppl 180):335, 1964.
31. Bonner H: The problem of diagnosis in paranoiac disorder. *Am J Psychiatry* 107:677, 1951.
32. Eitinger L: The symptomatology of mental disease among refugees in Norway. *J Ment Sci* 106:947, 1960.
33. Grahame PS: Schizophrenia in old age (late paraphrenia) *Br J Psychiatry* 145:493, 1984.
34. Craig TJ, Bregman Z: Late onset schizophrenia-like illness. *J Am Geriatr Soc* 36:104, 1988.
35. Miller BL, et al: Late-life paraphrenia: An organic delusional syndrome. *J Clin Psychiatry* 47:204, 1986.
36. Naguib M, Levy R: Late paraphrenia: Neuropsychological impairment and structural brain abnormalities on computed tomography. *Int J Geriatr Psychiatry* 2:83, 1987.
37. Flint AJ et al: Late-onset paranoia: Distinct from paraphrenia? *Int J Geriatr Psychiatry* 6:103, 1991.
38. Breitner JCS et al: Cerebral white matter disease in late-onset paranoid psychosis. *Biol Psychiatry* 28:266, 1990.
39. Naguib M et al: Genetic markers in late paraphrenia: A study of HLA antigens. *Br J Psychiatry* 150:124, 1987.
40. Retterstol N: Jealousy-paranoiac psychoses. *Acta Psychiatr Scand* 43:75, 1968.
41. Raskind M: Paranoid syndromes in the elderly, in Eisdorfer C, Fann WE (eds): *Treatment of Psychopathology in the Aging*. New York, Springer, 1982, p 184.
42. Bridge TP, Wyatt JW. Paraphrenia: Paranoid states of late life: I. European research. *J Am Geriatr Soc* 28:193, 1980.
43. Raskind M: Fluphenazine enanthate in the outpatient treatment of late paraphrenia. *J Am Geriatr Soc* 27:459, 1979.

Chapter 101

AGING OF THE CHRONICALLY NEUROPSYCHOLOGICALLY IMPAIRED

Steven R. Gambert

DEFINING THE PROBLEM

Despite a decline in the incidence of birth defects over the past few decades, many persons are alive today who were born with disabilities affecting proper growth and development and lifelong functioning. Although both inherited and congenital disabilities may affect numerous aspects of functioning, this chapter will focus only on those persons with chronic neuropsychological impairments (CNI), often referred to as mental retardation.

CNI has been defined by any one or combination of the following: IQ test score, social adaptability, neurological functioning, and behavioral competence. The most widely accepted classification refers to a general intellectual functioning that is significantly below average and exists concurrently with deficits in adaptive behavior; changes must have manifested during the developmental period. While some prefer four categories of CNI (mild, moderate, severe, and profound) others use only two (mild and severe). Mild CNI is defined as an IQ of less than 70 or 2 standard deviations below the mean with a concurrent impairment in adaptive behavior; severe CNI is defined as an IQ below 50. Modern medicine has improved our capacity to provide preventive health care and treat problems early in their course. Even those limited by some genetic defect are living longer than ever before, and the life span for many persons with CNI approaches that of the general population.

Those with CNI are often grouped epidemiologically with persons with other developmental disabilities, including chronic epilepsy, autism, and cerebral palsy. Although each has its own set of distinct problems, many similarities exist. Full independence throughout life is often difficult in all groups especially during later life after a decline in primary family support. Because of considerable overlap between these disorders, there is great difficulty in ensuring exactly how many persons exist in each category.

Based on data from the 1990 census, there are approximately 175,000 persons over the age of 60 with a lifelong neuropsychological impairment. Most agree that this number greatly underestimates those with CNI. Lubin reported the prevalence of older adults with CNI to be 4.5 per 1000 general population or 1.5 million persons over the age of 60.[1] As an overall estimate of persons with CNI, the Association for Retarded Citizens has historically used 3 percent of the general population. This is in contrast to 0.4 percent of the population with chronic epilepsy and 0.3 percent with cerebral palsy. Stratification of data by age, however, is less certain. Although data regarding the prevalence of persons with severe mental retardation is easier to find and reports range from 3 to 5 per 1000 general population, identifying persons with mild CNI is more difficult. Many escape recognition until later in life when aged parents can no longer provide the structured environment necessary to meet daily needs. Many persons with mild CNI perform minor tasks in order to maintain financial independence. This may become increasingly more difficult as age-related disorders couple with underlying CNI to prevent continued employment; economic loss may force them to seek public assistance or even institutional living.

LIFE EXPECTANCY

Recent decades have seen a dramatic rise in the average life expectancy of the general population. Although those with CNI share in this increase, they continue to have higher age-specific mortality rates. As a group, average life expectancy for persons with

CNI is 59.1 years. Those with Down's syndrome, or trisomy 21, can expect to live, on average, 54.0 years. This is not a small achievement, since Down's syndrome babies could expect to live only 9 years in 1929, 12 to 15 years in 1947, and 18.3 years in 1961. While most of this change has been attributed to the decline in childhood mortality resulting from improved preventive health care, immunization programs, and a philosophy of active intervention, changes have also been noted after maturity. While genetic defects may be difficult to resolve, i.e., increased amyloid deposits in the brains of persons with Down's syndrome, persons with CNI resulting from problems such as cerebral anoxia should not be expected to live any less than the general population. Unfortunately, CNI is not a pure entity, and coexisting problems are common. These include nutritional abnormalities and increased risk of infections, especially in those living in institutional settings. Crowding and closed environments may lead to a high exposure to infectious diseases, including *Neisseria* meningitis, influenza, tuberculosis, and hepatitis. Diets may be less than optimal, especially for those with limited attention spans requiring individualized feeding programs. Mass cooking practices may also result in suboptimal nutrition. Efforts to deinstitutionalize those persons with CNI have already realized benefits and should continue to increase life spans. Although many factors have historically been associated with the decision to institutionalize a given person, including severity of disability, gender, ethnicity, associated handicaps, and availability of community services, current trends favor deinstitutionalization whenever possible.

DOWN'S SYNDROME

The most commonly identified genetic abnormality is Down's syndrome, or trisomy 21. Despite the fact that few persons with Down's syndrome live beyond their 50s, this entity has long fascinated gerontologists. It has been reported that nearly all individuals with Down's syndrome over the age of 40 have neuropathological changes consistent with Alzheimer's disease, i.e., neurofibrillary tangles, plaques, and nucleovacuolar degeneration.[2,3] Recent data identifying a genetic defect on chromosome 21 in familial cases of Alzheimer's disease lend further support to the hypothesis linking these two disorders.[4] Despite neuropathological findings suggestive of an Alzheimer-type dementia in almost all persons over 40 with Down's syndrome, however, a diagnosis of clinical dementia cannot be made to the same degree of certainty in this population. The patient's limited attention span may interfere with the physician's ability to properly assess mental status. When a change in cognition is identified, however, coexisting dementia must be considered. Changes in behavior, increased regressive tendencies, or loss of learned behavior may be suggestive of degenerative changes. It is equally as important, however, not to blame all changes on a presumed diagnosis of Alzheimer's disease. As with all cases of dementia, all treatable causes must be considered, especially in a population at risk for trauma, infections, drug toxicities, nutritional abnormalities, and so forth.

COEXISTING MEDICAL CONDITIONS

Persons with CNI often have coexisting medical problems and physical disabilities. This is particularly pronounced during later life. Poor health screening and lack of preventive measures may result in an accelerated aging process; diseases may occur at an earlier age than in the general population. Table 101-1 lists problems more commonly noted in adult persons with CNI compared with the general population.

Scoliosis may progress and result in frequent muscular strain and backaches. Advanced disease may eventually compromise normal respiratory function, leading to decreased pulmonary reserve and infection. Down's syndrome patients frequently have poor ligamentous support for the cervical spine. This can result in a subluxation of the cervical spine that may lead to paraplegia and even quadriplegia. Radiological monitoring of this problem is advised; cervical collars and even cervical spine fusion are well-recognized preventive measures.

Untreated hip dislocation can lead to loss of mobility; this may greatly hamper a person's ability to be independent and may accelerate other changes including demineralization of the bones and reduced muscular and cardiovascular fitness.

One of the most common findings in adult persons with Down's syndrome is poor dentition and gingival disease. This often leads to loss of teeth, discomfort, and difficulty chewing. When coupled with poor attention span, nutritional problems may become significant. Dentures are rarely accepted by persons with

TABLE 101-1

Problems More Commonly Found in Persons with CNI

Scoliosis
Cervical spine subluxation
Hip dislocation
Dental caries and gingivitis
Nutritional deficiency states
Obesity
Visual abnormalities
Hearing deficits
Seizure disorders
Medication toxicity
Emotional disorders (including "institutional behavior")
Dementia

CNI and few dentists are willing to take the extra time and effort needed to fit them properly. Lifelong attention to good dental hygiene is the best way to prevent dental and gingival disease in this population. A program ensuring proper brushing and flossing prior to bedtime is a minimal necessity when twice-daily oral care is not possible. Regular visits to the dentist and fluoride treatments during early life also help maintain a healthy oral environment.

As stated above, nutritional problems are frequently encountered. In certain cases diets may contain excessive quantities of calories, salt, and fats, especially for those living within institutional settings. This increases the risk of developing atherosclerotic cardiovascular disease, hypertension, obesity, and even cancer late in life. Obesity, further exacerbated by diminished physical activity, may accelerate articular changes in weight-bearing joints as well as increase the risk of developing type II diabetes. Dietary deficiencies in calcium, minerals, and vitamins may also be noted. The use of dietary supplements may be necessary if certain nutrients are not being consumed on a regular basis. Multiple small, but well-balanced, meals are often better tolerated. An adequate intake of protein (0.8 g/kg body weight) is essential.

Regular screening to detect changes in hearing is advised. Congenital hearing deficits are not uncommon in this population, and age-related changes may result in a functional disturbance earlier than otherwise expected. Isolation, apathy, declining cognition, and impaired communication may be the only signs of hearing impairment. Any change in daily care pattern or ability to interact with others must be explored and hearing deficits carefully evaluated. Although newer hearing aids are capable of selectively increasing certain frequency sounds, thus improving functional hearing, many persons with CNI lack the interest or capacity to wear an assistive device. For this reason, care providers and health professionals must speak slowly and use amplifying devices whenever a hearing problem exists. Since neurosensory hearing loss may make discrimination of sounds more difficult, extraneous sounds should be reduced as much as possible or attempts made to use an FM amplifier with individual headsets to improve direct communication.

Although congenital vision problems are common, age-related changes and age-prevalent diseases affecting vision may further compromise function. Keratoconus, glaucoma, and cataracts usually present at a more advanced stage due to difficulty in ascertaining vision changes in this population. Screening programs that hopefully detect and treat problems early are encouraged.

Regardless of the severity of mental retardation, emotional disorders must be anticipated and recognized. Loss of loved ones, family, roommates, and care providers may precipitate an emotional crisis; an atypical presentation may be the only warning. All attempts should be made to limit changes in environmental surroundings and anticipate stressful situations. An impaired judgment in social situations may require that help be given to form new friendships despite an advanced age. Once formed, however, bonding is usually strong even in those with severe mental retardation. Social interactions are important in promoting self-esteem and avoiding feelings of isolation. Institutionalization is thought to decrease feelings of self-reliance. The least restrictive yet safe environment should be chosen.

Much like the general aging population, persons with CNI have feelings of loss, loneliness, and depression. While emotional disorders may be reactive to specific handicaps, at times no specific cause can be found. In either case, a careful medication review and assessment of physical well-being is advised in order that treatable problems be dealt with as early as possible. Changes in the ability to conduct activities of daily living, changes in interest in attending group activities and workshops, changes in sleep-wake cycles, or changes in sexual behavior may indicate a deeper emotional disorder in need of investigation and treatment. Persons with a CNI are nearly twice as likely as the general population to develop several behavioral disorders. This may result from the retarded person's difficulty in processing information, handicaps, cultural-familial factors, and/or society's nonacceptance. It is of note, however, that despite equivalent degrees of CNI and controlled living conditions, young and middle-aged adults received a statistically greater amount of psychotropic medications to manage behavioral problems than children, adolescents, or the elderly. No apparent reason could be found for this based on over 35,000 subject observations.[5]

A decline in cognition, or "dementia," is often difficult to detect until gross changes have been noted. Depending on underlying pathological conditions and baseline functioning, subtle changes in behavior may be the only warning sign that a dementia exists. Although persons with Down's syndrome have a greater chance of developing dementia of the Alzheimer type after age 40, other causes of dementia should be considered and ruled out prior to making a definitive diagnosis. Antiseizure medications should be continually evaluated and monitored and attempts made to discontinue therapy under close supervision as indicated. These medications have a significant potential for interacting with other medications, and toxicities must be carefully watched for. The long-term use of phenytoin, for example, has been associated with osteomalacia, ataxia, and gingival hyperplasia; early recognition of these problems may reduce morbidity.

With advancing age and decreased reserve capability, falls from seizures may increase the risk of fractures from direct trauma and cerebral, cardiac, and renal damage from transient hypotension and cerebral anoxia. Care providers should be advised what precautions are necessary. In those instances in which seizures do not respond to pharmacological therapy, protective head gear and joint padding may be essential.

The prevalence of medical conditions in elderly persons with CNI is somewhat different from age-

TABLE 101-2

Prevalence of Medical Conditions Noted in Elderly Persons with CNI Following Geriatric Assessment

Condition	Percent
Hearing deficit	80
Dental problem	70
Cardiovascular disease	60
Gerontourinary problem	50
Infectious disease	50
Visual impairment	40
Gastrointestinal disorder	40
Endocrine disorder	40
Rheumatological problem	30
Obesity	30
Cerebrovascular disease	20
Dermatological condition	10

matched cognitively intact individuals. While many of the problems listed in Table 101-1 occur more frequently in persons with CNI than in the general population, they do not necessarily represent the most commonly noted problems. Table 101-2 lists in order those conditions found most commonly in a geriatric assessment program of persons with CNI.[6]

In a study of elderly Down's syndrome (aged 32 to 56 years) and non-Down's syndrome (aged 52 to 79 years) persons living in the community, very few required assistance in their activities of daily living and were able to bathe, dress, toilet, transfer, feed, and ambulate with minimal assistance. The more complex instrumental activities of daily living, however, such as shopping, preparing meals, using money, using the telephone, and so forth, posed significant problems for almost 80 percent. While 70 percent could answer a telephone, only 10 percent could look up a number in the telephone book.[7]

AGING AND CNI

While Down's syndrome is the most frequent genetic cause of CNI, it is responsible for less than 30 percent of cases of CNI in those over 50 years of age and less than 5 percent of cases in those over 65. Cerebral anoxia at birth appears to be the major cause of CNI in this elderly population. A variety of other genetic and environmental causes may also be responsible.

Elderly persons with CNI are indeed at double jeopardy. Advanced age and mental retardation may result in problems not encountered in either population when considered separately. Health professionals must consider not only those conditions associated with normal aging and age-prevalent disease, but also problems related to circumstances surrounding the CNI. In many cases, elderly persons with CNI have spent time within an institutional setting. Although recent decades have seen major changes in the ability to care for the disabled, and although individual rights and freedoms are protected, the elderly person with CNI has lived in less illustrious times and can often bear witness to societal and family abandonment. Despite advances, many problems still exist. In an attempt to provide persons with CNI with structured activities, those living in federally funded homes must continue to attend "workshop" activities comparable to going to work regardless of advanced age. There is no option to "retire" unless physical ailments preclude activities. Even then, group homes find it increasingly difficult to keep those persons who do not leave the residence during the day—budgets simply do not allow for increased staffing requirements. Many elderly persons with CNI, therefore, are facing premature dismissal from community residences to more restricted settings including nursing homes.

Although future generations of persons with CNI will most likely be living longer and leading more functional lives thanks to preventive health measures, the present cohort of elderly persons with CNI must still be considered at great risk of developing premature functional impairment. Deinstitutionalization throughout life, regular screening by a team of health professionals, and active intervention when necessary, including updating immunizations, can help maintain function throughout life.[6]

A comprehensive geriatric assessment program should be integrated with ongoing care. Despite little change in function, community-dwelling elderly persons with CNI are often thought to be in need of nursing home placement earlier than is necessary.[8] The perception of caregivers may be clouded by their inability to recognize and even care for many age-prevalent disorders. IQ and social adaptive age have not been shown to correlate with functional status, and ongoing individual assessment is necessary. An evaluation team combining individuals with expertise in both geriatric health care and CNI can greatly affect clinical outcome and help maintain the older person with CNI in the community.

REFERENCES

1. Lubin RA et al: Projected impact of the functional definition of developmental disabilities: The categorically disabled population and service eligibility. *Am J Ment Defic* 87:73, 1982.
2. Malanuid N, Stevens HA, Heba R (eds): *Neuropathology in Mental Retardation.* Chicago, University of Chicago Press, 1964, p 429.

3. Mozar HN et al: Perspectives on the etiology of Alzheimer's disease. *JAMA* 257:1503, 1987.
4. St. George-Hyslop PH et al: The genetic defect causing familial Alzheimer's disease maps on chromosome 21. *Science* 235:885, 1987.
5. Jacobson JW: Problem behavior and psychiatric impairment within a developmentally disabled population. *Psychotrop Medication Res Dev Disabil* 9:23, 1988.
6. Gambert SR et al: Lifelong preventive health care for elderly persons with disabilities. *J Assoc Persons Severe Handicap* 12:292, 1987.
7. Hawkins BA et al: Research identifies age-related changes in people with DD. *Advantage* 4:1, 1992.
8. Gambert SR et al: A geriatric assessment program for the mentally retarded elderly. *NY Med Q* 8:132, 1988.

Chapter 102

CHEMICAL DEPENDENCY

Patricia P. Barry

DEFINITIONS AND DIAGNOSTIC CRITERIA

This chapter addresses the problem of chemical dependence (substance abuse) by the elderly. As defined by the American College of Physicians,[1] chemical dependence encompasses both alcohol and drug addiction and includes dependence upon social drugs, such as alcohol; licit drugs, both prescription and nonprescription; and illicit drugs. Additionally, in the absence of dependence, problem use may occur, including abuse, misuse, and overuse.

The most commonly used diagnostic criteria are those of the revised third edition of the *Diagnostic and Statistical Manual of Mental Disorders* of the American Psychiatric Association, known as the *DSM* III-R.[2] The diagnosis of psychoactive substance *abuse* includes a maladaptive pattern of use, and symptoms that persist for longer than 1 month, or occur repeatedly, but do not meet the criteria for dependence. Criteria for psychoactive substance *dependence* include at least three of the following: (1) substance taken in greater amounts or for longer than intended, (2) persistent desire or inability to control use, (3) considerable time spent obtaining, taking, or recovering from the drug, (4) frequent intoxication or withdrawal symptoms when expected to fulfill major obligations, (5) reduced social, occupational, or recreational activities, (6) continued use despite persistent problems, (7) marked tolerance, (8) characteristic withdrawal symptoms, and (9) substance taken to avoid withdrawal. In addition, dependence requires some symptoms persisting for at least 1 month or occurring repeatedly. The *DSM* III-R also states that psychoactive substance abuse and dependence often involve more than one substance. Atkinson notes that *DSM* III-R criteria numbers 3, 4, and 5 may not be appropriate for the elderly alcoholic patient, and he points out that coexisting substance abuse in the elderly person is usually of legally prescribed drugs.[3] Miller and colleagues also criticize the *DSM* III-R's emphasis on the consequences of abuse, which are often very different in elderly persons and consist primarily of psychiatric and medical problems.[4] Blazer and Pennybacker have found that studies of alcoholism in the elderly use such diverse diagnostic criteria as quantity and frequency of consumption, social problems or problems in role performance, tolerance and withdrawal, and physical health problems.[5] Since different criteria have been used, many descriptive studies and evaluations of treatment programs may not be truly comparable.

CHARACTERISTICS

Although some observers have noted a decreasing prevalence of alcoholism with increasing age, this finding is debatable. Drew reviewed cross-sectional studies and concluded that alcoholism appears to be a self-limited disease which tends to "disappear with increasing age."[6] He proposed three possible explanations: morbidity and mortality resulting in death or chronic institutionalization, beneficial effects of treatment (probably unlikely), and "spontaneous recovery." Barnes's 1979 report of alcohol use in 1041 adults in the general population also showed decreased consumption in the cohort over age 60, when compared with cohorts aged 50 to 59 or 18 to 49.[7] He speculated that many chronic alcohol abusers are dead or institutionalized by old age and thus may not be found in the general population.

A 1981 cross-sectional study of 928 older Bostonians also found that those over 75 were less likely to drink than those 60 to 75.[8] However, the "very old" reported different lifelong drinking habits, parental drinking habits, and attitudes about alcohol and health, suggesting that there may be significant cohort differences. Recent results from the Normative Aging Study support the hypothesis that cohort differences confound cross-sectional studies.[9] Longitudinal assessment of the effects of birth cohort and aging on mean alcohol consumption level, prevalence of drinking problems, and frequency of alcohol consumption indicated that there was no tendency for these 1700 men to reduce their consumption over time, or to have fewer drinking problems. The authors concluded that generational or attitudinal factors may be more important than age as determinants of drinking behavior. However, Adams and her colleagues recently found a decline over 7 years in the proportion of drinkers among a cohort of 270 healthy elderly persons, aged 61 to 86 at entry.[10]

If the prevalence of alcohol problems is related to cohort factors, then a future increase may occur in the proportion of elderly persons who are alcoholic, as cohorts with a higher alcohol consumption grow older. Although premature morbidity and mortality might remove some of these elderly alcoholic persons from the general population by institutionalization or death, a significant number would no doubt remain in the community and require the attention of health care providers. Gurnack and Thomas point out five major reasons for heightened concern about problem drinking in later life[11]: (1) the projected increase in numbers of older persons, (2) the changing characteristics of older cohorts, which make them more likely to use psychiatric services, (3) the aging of cohorts with more heavy drinkers, (4) the likelihood of misdiagnosis by physicians, and (5) the high institutional and treatment costs of alcohol abuse.

Physiologic factors may contribute to a decrease in consumption of alcohol by the elderly. A cross-sectional study by Vestal and his associates, using standard ethanol infusions in 21- to 81-year old (nonalcoholic) volunteers, demonstrated a significant increase in peak blood ethanol concentration with age; the authors proposed that a smaller volume of distribution and reduced lean body mass affected drug distribution.[12] A 1984 study of social drinkers aged 19 to 63, consuming high doses of alcohol, reported higher blood alcohol levels in older subjects compared with younger ones.[13] Impairment of task performance also increased significantly with age, suggesting that behavioral effects might cause older persons to decrease their alcohol intake in social situations. If the results of these studies in nonalcoholic persons can be extrapolated to alcoholic persons, the frequency and quantity of consumption may be reduced in elderly alcoholic persons as well, and using these parameters as identification criteria would underestimate the prevalence of alcoholism in the elderly.

Two elderly alcoholic populations have been proposed by Rosin and Glatt[14]: those with long-standing alcohol problems who have simply grown old, and those with emerging alcohol abuse exacerbated by the stresses of aging, such as retirement, bereavement, and loneliness. Gaitz and Baer described most of the 100 elderly alcoholic patients admitted to their psychiatry screening ward as having begun abuse in early adulthood.[15] However, Schuckit concluded that alcoholic persons in the elderly population include a substantial proportion who began abuse late in life, with a resulting increase in their medical problems.[16] He estimated the prevalence of alcoholism in the general elderly population as 2 to 10 percent, with 10 percent of all alcoholic persons being over the age of 60.

A 1981 Swedish study of over 400 70-year-old men, examined at 5-year intervals, found a 10 percent prevalence of alcohol abuse or heavy consumption in this group, as well as in a comparison group of 489 men in a cohort 5 years younger.[17] Brody estimates the prevalence at 1 to 5 percent in the general population over age 65, with a prevalence of 10 to 15 percent in those seeking medical attention.[18] Solomon has stated that alcoholism is the second leading cause for admission of elderly persons to psychiatric institutions and is a major factor in 15 to 20 percent of nursing home admissions, 5 to 15 percent of medical outpatient visits, and 10 percent of hospital admissions of elderly persons.[19] He estimates that approximately 1.5 million alcoholic persons are aged 65 and older in the United States. Thus, the prevalence of alcoholism in the elderly population is not exactly known but probably lies between 5 and 10 percent. Most experts also agree that the prevalence of alcoholism is higher in the "young-old," between 60 and 70 years of age, compared with the "old-old," and is higher in older men than in older women.

Simon and associates reported a 28 percent prevalence of alcoholism in their study of 534 first-admission psychiatry patients over age 60,[20] and Gaitz and Baer found that 44 percent of 100 elderly psychiatric patients were alcoholics.[15] These studies, as well as those cited previously, strongly suggest that the prevalence of alcholism in "ill" elderly persons seeking medical or psychiatric care is much higher than among "well" elderly persons residing in the community.

Little information is available about elderly persons who are addicted to narcotics. Schuckit notes that an estimated 1 percent of those in methadone maintenance programs are over 60 years of age; slightly more may be in hospital treatment programs; many have prior arrests and a history of previous treatment.[16] An average of 35 years of past abuse exists by the age of 60; with increasing age, income decreases and the frequency and dose of drugs also tend to decrease. The elderly addicted person often shifts the abuse from "street" drugs, such as heroin, to "legal" narcotics, such as hydromorphone (Dilaudid), morphine, or codeine. Such a person tends to be medically "sicker" than a younger counterpart and may also abuse alcohol and ancillary drugs.

A 1970 New Orleans study described 38 addicted men not in treatment, with an average age of 58.9 and a median of three past imprisonments.[21] Hydromorphone, heroin, morphine, and codeine were used most often; sources were most commonly pushers, less commonly physicians or friends. These men were typically withdrawn; all but one lived alone; reduced intake was due to decreased income. The aging of cohorts in which drug abuse has a much higher prevalence is likely to result in increasing numbers of elderly addicted persons, although the increased mortality due to the AIDS epidemic among intravenous drug users could adversely affect survival. A report from the National Institute on Drug Abuse has noted that although "there is currently no reliable documentation of the nature and extent of illicit drug abuse among the elderly. . . . the use of illicit drugs among the elderly cannot be ignored. . . . (and) is likely to increase over the next two decades."[22] More basic research, as well as evaluation of prevention and treatment programs, is needed in this population.

SCREENING AND DETECTION

When compared with younger alcoholic persons, elderly alcoholic persons are less likely to have problems such as criminal and antisocial behavior, divorce, bankruptcy, violence, and motor vehicle accidents.[19] Thus they are less likely to be identified and referred into treatment by the legal system. This "hidden" abuse is also characteristic of elderly drug-addicted persons. As has been noted, studies suggest that elderly alcoholic persons are more likely to be found among those seeking medical or psychiatric attention; thus, case finding might best be conducted through the health care system. However, Solomon notes that the diagnosis of alcoholism in an elderly person is often missed by clinicians because of a low index of suspicion, concealment by patients and families, and attribution of symptoms to advancing age.[19] Elderly alcoholic persons rarely complain of their alcoholism, because of their denial, and physicians either fail to recognize or ignore the problem. Patients also tend to underreport alcohol consumption, even when questioned directly by physicians.[23] A 1989 study revealed that only 37 percent of elderly alcoholic persons identifiable by psychosocial screening were diagnosed in a routine physician interview, and even when diagnosed were less likely to be referred for treatment.[24] White, female high school graduates were less likely to be diagnosed than non-white, male, less-educated alcoholic patients.

In order to facilitate identification of alcohol dependence, both psychosocial and biochemical markers, or a combination of the two, have been utilized. The most widely evaluated psychosocial instrument is the Michigan Alcoholism Screening Test (MAST), consisting of 25 true or false items, reasonably valid in distinguishing alcoholic from nonalcoholic persons.[25] Willenbring and his associates validated the sensitivity and specificity of the MAST, using either weighted or unit scoring, in subjects over age 60 who met *DSM* III-R criteria for alcohol abuse or dependence; briefer versions (BMAST and SMAST) were found to be less useful.[26] The CAGE items (asking whether the patient feels the need to *cut* down on drinking, is *annoyed* by criticism, feels *guilty* about drinking, and ever has an *eye*-opener) are a simple and specific screening test,[27] although use in the elderly population has not been evaluated. The CAGE is of value if positive but may not detect alcoholism in elderly patients whose drinking patterns differ from those of younger alcoholic patients. These instruments also are directed toward the later stages of alcoholism and may not detect earlier stages.

Several clinical symptoms and signs may suggest the diagnosis of alcoholism to the informed clinician. Liver and pancreatic disease, unexplained trauma, neurologic problems, sleep disturbances, and classic skin lesions may be associated with chronic alcohol use,[27] although such findings usually occur in the later stages of alcoholism. Biochemical markers such as elevations of alanine aminotransferase, aspartate aminotransferase, and alkaline phosphatase levels may be a useful adjunct in differentiating alcoholic from nonalcoholic patients.[28] A Mayo Clinic study of 216 patients over 65 who received inpatient treatment for alcoholism found a higher-than-expected frequency of serious medical problems compared with nonalcoholic patients, especially liver disease (43.1 percent), chronic obstructive pulmonary disease (30.6 percent), and peptic ulcer disease (15.3 percent).[29] Older alcoholic patients were more likely than younger ones to have abnormal mean corpuscular hemoglobin, mean corpuscular volume, aspartate aminotransferase, uric acid, and serum albumin levels. In another study of 90 psychiatric patients over the age of 65, 74 percent of chemically dependent patients had abnormal liver function tests on admission.[30]

Diagnosis of substance abuse in the elderly may be complicated by the presence of psychiatric disorders such as depression and dementia, and alcoholism appears to be a common comorbid condition among elderly persons presenting for inpatient psychiatric care. Whitcup and Miller found a 21 percent prevalence of chemical dependence in their elderly psychiatric patients.[30] Among 10 patients whose abuse was unrecognized and who were not detoxified, 7 had complicated withdrawal syndromes. Women were significantly less likely to be identified as abusers than men and were more likely to abuse prescription drugs (benzodiazepines) than alcohol.

Since the prevalence of substance abuse is higher among those elderly persons who present for medical and psychiatric care, efforts at screening should be most productive when conducted in this population. Clinicians who combine a reasonable index of suspicion, psychosocial screening instruments, careful examination for symptoms and signs of chemical dependence, and evaluation of biochemical markers may be better able to diagnose substance abuse and refer the patient to appropriate treatment.

CONSEQUENCES

A 1987 study of 270 healthy, independent, community-residing men and women over age 65 found that 8 percent drank over 30 g/day (classified as "heavy drinkers") and 48 percent consumed some alcohol daily.[31] Increased alcohol intake did not appear to be associated with decreased cognitive, psychological, or social status in this functional population. Among psychiatric patients, however, alcoholic patients frequently have organic brain syndromes usually at a younger age than nonalcoholic patients.[15,20] Alcoholism may also be an important factor in admissions of elderly persons to psychiatric institutions, nursing homes, and hospitals.[19]

In the Mayo Clinic study of 216 older alcoholic persons, concern of family and friends was the most common motivating factor for treatment, especially among late-onset alcoholic patients, who constituted 41 percent of the patients.[32] Other psychiatric diagnoses in these patients included licit drug abuse and dependence (14 percent), organic brain syndrome (25 percent), atypical organic brain syndrome (19 percent), and affective disorder (19 percent). Thus 44 percent of patients had cognitive disturbance, and alcohol could not be ruled out as a contributing factor.

Mellstrom and his associates found that elderly alcoholic, compared with nonalcoholic, patients had higher morbidity and mortality, required more care, and had lower functional ability in cognition, muscle strength, gonadal and pulmonary function, visual acuity, walking ability, and skeletal density.[17] Medical consequences of alcoholism in the elderly include sleep disturbances, diminished sexual performance, cirrhosis of the liver, pancreatitis, myopathy, Korsakoff's psychosis, nutritional and vitamin deficiencies, Wernicke's encephalopathy, and interactions with medications,[33] especially psychotropic medications, chloral hydrate, antihistamines, acetaminophen, aspirin, nitrates, and oral hypoglycemic agents.[34]

Elderly abusers of illegal drugs are susceptible to the same difficulties as younger addicted persons, including poverty, isolation, and arrest.[21] In the elderly population, chemical dependence may also contribute to difficulties in management of other medical conditions by affecting the patient's ability to seek appropriate care, comply with medications and other treatment, keep appointments for health care, and maintain the social and supportive interactions necessary for community residence.

TREATMENT

Treatment of chronic alcoholism can result in long-term improvement (abstinence over 1 year) in approximately 25 percent of all alcoholic persons. The recommended approach includes nonjudgmental confrontation and detoxification, followed by intense inpatient or outpatient educational and therapeutic experiences, including introduction into Alcoholics Anonymous (AA).[35] Elderly persons should have recovery rates at least equal to those of the general population, if they can be brought into treatment. Mishara and Kastenbaum reviewed the available literature and emphasize that although studies are limited, elderly alcoholic persons appear to have a good response to treatment in standard programs.[36] They point out that studies use different criteria for defining alcoholism and consider different populations of alcoholic persons so the results are not always comparable. They also note that criteria for successful treatment may include total abstinence, abstinence with improved functioning, or overall improved function without abstinence. Schuckit points out that elderly opiate-addicted persons are unlikely to give up drug abuse but often enter treatment voluntarily, perhaps because of health or financial considerations.[16]

Drug Treatment

Management of alcohol withdrawal is often the first step in treatment. A recent study of alcohol withdrawal comparing older (58 to 77 years) and younger (21 to 33 years) alcoholic patients indicated that the older group had more severe withdrawal syndromes and required higher doses of chlordiazepoxide for adequate treatment.[37] Drug treatment also includes the use of psychotropic drugs as an adjunct for problems such as anxiety and depression, although evidence of efficacy is lacking and the use of such drugs in the elderly involves the risk of adverse drug reactions.[36] In addition to psychotropic drugs, disulfiram (Antabuse), which causes a marked toxic response to ingested alcohol, has been used in younger alcoholic patients but should be used only with extreme caution in elderly patients, because of its severe physical effects.[38]

Although methadone maintenance is the only drug treatment available for narcotic-addicted persons, little information is available regarding its efficacy in the elderly. Pascarelli and Fischer noted that elderly addicted persons in methadone maintenance programs are least likely to request detoxification, are dissatisfied with dosage changes, and may abuse alcohol to produce euphoria.[39] Thus treatment of narcotic addiction does not appear as promising as that of alcohol alone, but more studies are needed.

Psychosocial Therapy

Individual psychotherapy and counseling are usually behavior-oriented and address the defense mechanism of denial.[38] However, the negative attitudes of therapists, the reluctance of elderly persons to seek this kind of therapy, [36] and the cost of individual psychotherapy, which is often poorly reimbursed by third-party payers, may limit the effectiveness of this form of therapy. Group therapy is usually less expensive and may be helpful in promoting insight, especially when the group is composed of other elderly alcoholic patients,[38] although this is not always possible. AA provides a free opportunity for continuation of treatment beyond the institutional setting. The AA network tends to combat the isolation of the alcoholic and provides understanding and support, using a group therapy concept.[38] Although AA encourages members of all ages, elderly people are not always well-represented. Narcotics Anonymous (NA) provides a similar program, but members may be even younger than those in AA.

Inpatient programs provide the opportunity to initiate treatment in a controlled, structured setting, with detoxification as the first concern. However, many programs have admission screening policies, usually regarding medical diagnoses, which may make it difficult for elderly persons to gain admission.[36] In addition, unless they are subsidized, inpatient programs are very expensive and thus may be limited to those clients with insurance or private funds.

Evaluations of specific programs for elderly persons with chemical dependence have not been conducted, and thus information is not readily available concerning the effectiveness of various types of treatment, especially whether elderly persons need special programs. A study by Rix compared alcoholic patients over age 60 with sex-matched younger alcoholic patients and found few differences, except for an increased prevalence of organic brain syndrome in the elderly.[40] The elderly patients consumed less alcohol, were more likely to be widowed, were less likely to have loss of control, and had onset of their alcoholism at a later age. The author concluded that elderly alcoholic patients can be treated successfully with younger ones, except that those with organic brain syndromes may need psychogeriatric services.

This conclusion was supported by an analysis of data from the National Alcoholism Program Information System, which represents 550 alcoholism treatment programs.[41] All 3163 patients over age 60 followed for 180 days were compared with 3190 patients aged 21 to 59 with regard to drinking characteristics before treatment, type of treatment received, and outcome measures. No significant differences were found between the two groups, except for slightly poorer outcomes in the age group 40 to 59, suggesting that elderly alcoholic patients do not need special programs once they have been identified and brought into the treatment system. However, a more recent retrospective, nonrandomized study compared older alcoholic veterans in a special outpatient treatment program with those treated in the same institution prior to development of the program.[42] Patients treated in the special peer group program remained in treatment significantly longer and were more likely to complete treatment than those in mixed-age groups. More research is required, perhaps including a randomized controlled trial, to determine the value of peer-group programs for elderly alcoholic patients. Problems which the elderly patients encounter may be related more to access to programs than to their actual structure. Financial limitations, transportation difficulties, physical access problems, and safety and security concerns may pose real obstacles to the elderly person's ability to enter treatment.

Therapy for chemical dependence in the elderly person must also involve family members, who may be providing important caregiving services for the dependent person. Although studies are lacking, referral to Al-Anon, Nar-Anon, and Alateen, specific programs for families of alcoholic and narcotic-addicted persons, is likely to be of benefit. In addition, Adult Children of Alcoholics (ACOA) groups have evolved from Al-Anon and may be particularly appropriate for "adult-child" caregivers. Family therapy can provide additional support for the patient and caregivers during critical periods of treatment.

The role of the physician has been clearly stated by the American College of Physicians: "recognizing and treating chemical dependence requires knowledge of the symptoms of chronic and excessive drug use and increased sensitivity to and awareness of behavior associated with such problem use."[1] Once the diagnosis is suspected, nonthreatening and nonjudgmental confrontation is appropriate. The physician should be knowledgeable about treatment modalities available in the community for both acute detoxification and chronic management and should be prepared to care for the patient over the long term. Referral for chronic treatment should include community resources such as AA or NA, which may be integrated into other rehabilitation programs.

CONCLUSION

Chemical dependence is a significant, and probably underestimated, problem in the elderly population. Decreasing prevalence of abuse with age may not occur to the extent previously surmised. Elderly alcoholic and narcotic-addicted persons tend to be more reclusive and less visible in the community than younger ones. Elderly alcoholism has been more thoroughly studied than elderly narcotic addiction, and treatment appears to be more successful for alcoholism. Physicians and other health care providers should be able to diagnose chemical dependence and make appropriate referrals for treatment. Appropriate care of chemically dependent elderly persons requires consideration of their special needs and must take into account those characteristics which distinguish this group. Research is needed to answer questions regarding prevalence, characteristics, treatment, and program evaluation, in order to design and implement necessary and effective interventions.

REFERENCES

1. *Chemical Dependence.* A position paper of the American College of Physicians. Philadelphia, American College of Physicians, 1984.
2. *Diagnostic and Statistical Manual of Mental Disorders,* 3d ed (rev). Washington, American Psychiatric Association, 1987.
3. Atkinson RM: Aging and alcohol use disorders: Diagnostic issues in the elderly. *Int Psychogeriatr* 2:55, 1990.
4. Miller NS et al: Alcohol and drug dependence among the elderly: Epidemiology, diagnosis and treatment. *Compr Psychiatry* 32:153, 1991.
5. Blazer DG, Pennybacker MR: Epidemiology of alcoholism in the elderly, in Hartford JT, Samorajski T (eds): *Alcoholism in the Elderly: Social and Biomedical Issues.* New York, Raven, 1984, p 25.
6. Drew H: Alcoholism as a self-limited disease. *Q Stud Alcohol* 29:956, 1968.
7. Barnes GM: Alcohol use among older persons: Findings from a western New York state general population survey. *J Am Geriatr Soc* 27:244, 1979.
8. Meyers AR et al: Evidence for cohort or generational differences in the drinking behavior of older adults. *Int J Aging Human Dev* 14:31, 1981.
9. Glynn RJ et al: Aging and generational effects on drinking behaviors in men: Results from the Normative Aging Study. *Am J Public Health* 75:1413, 1985.
10. Adams WL et al: Alcohol intake in the healthy elderly changes with age in a cross-sectional and longitudinal study. *J Am Geriatr Soc* 38:211, 1990.
11. Gurnack AM, Thomas JL: Behavioral factors related to elderly alcohol abuse: Research and policy issues. *Int J Addict* 24:641, 1989.
12. Vestal RE et al: Aging and ethanol metabolism. *Clin Pharmacol Ther* 21:343, 1977.
13. Vogel-Sprott M, Barret P: Age, drinking habits, and the effects of alcohol. *J Stud Alcohol* 45:517, 1984.
14. Rosin AJ, Glatt MM: Alcohol excess in the elderly. *Q J Stud Alcohol* 32:53, 1971.
15. Gaitz CM, Baer PE: Characteristics of elderly patients with alcoholism. *Arch Gen Psychiatry* 24:372, 1971.
16. Schuckit MA: Geriatric alcoholism and drug abuse. *Gerontologist* 17:168, 1977.
17. Mellstrom D et al: Previous alcohol consumption and its consequences for ageing, morbidity and mortality in men aged 70–75. *Age Ageing* 10:277, 1981.
18. Brody JA: Aging and alcohol abuse. *J Am Geriatr Soc* 30:123, 1982.
19. Solomon DH: Alcoholism and aging, in West LJ (moderator): Alcoholism, p 411. *Ann Intern Med* 100:405, 1984.
20. Simon A et al: Alcoholism in the geriatric mentally ill. *Geriatrics* 23(10):125, 1968.
21. Capel WC et al: The aging narcotic addict: An increasing problem for the next decades. *J Gerontol* 27:102, 1972.
22. Glantz MD et al (eds): *Drugs and the Elderly Adult.* Research Issues 32. Rockville, National Institute on Drug Abuse, 1983.
23. Skinner HA et al: Early identification of alcohol abuse: 1. Critical issues and psychosocial indicators for a composite index. *Can Med Assoc J* 124:1141, 1981.
24. Curtis JR et al: Characteristics, diagnosis and treatment of alcoholism in elderly patients. *J Am Geriatr Soc* 37:310, 1989.
25. Selzer ML: The Michigan Alcoholism Screening Test: The quest for a new diagnostic instrument. *Am J Psychiatry,* 127:1653, 1971.
26. Willenbring ML et al: Alcoholism screening in the elderly. *J Am Geriatr Soc* 35:864, 1987.
27. Holt S et al: Early identification of alcohol abuse: 2. Clinical and laboratory indicators. *Can Med Assoc J* 124:1279, 1981.
28. Ryback RS et al: Biochemical and hematologic correlates of alcoholism and liver disease. *JAMA* 248:2261, 1982.
29. Hurt RD et al: Alcoholism in elderly persons: Medical aspects and prognosis of 216 inpatients. *Mayo Clin Proc* 63:753, 1988.
30. Whitcup SM, Miller F: Unrecognized drug dependence in psychiatrically hospitalized elderly patients. *J Am Geriatr Soc* 35:297, 1987.
31. Goodwin JS et al: Alcohol intake in a healthy elderly population. *Am J Public Health* 77:173, 1987.
32. Finlayson RE et al: Alcoholism in elderly persons: A study of the psychiatric and psychosocial features of 216 inpatients. *Mayo Clin Proc* 63:761, 1988.
33. Hartford JT, Samorajski T: Alcoholism in the geriatric population. *J Am Geriatr Soc* 30:18, 1982.
34. Scott RB, Mitchell MC: Aging, alcohol and the liver. *J Am Geriatr Soc* 36:255, 1988.
35. West LJ: Some treatment issues in chronic alcoholism, in West LJ (moderator): Alcoholism, p 412. *Ann Intern Med* 100:405, 1984.
36. Mishara BL, Kastenbaum R: Treatment of problem drinking among the elderly, in *Alcohol and Old Age.* New York, Grune & Stratton, 1980, p 85.
37. Liskow BI et al: Alcohol withdrawal in the elderly. *J Stud Alcohol* 50:414, 1989.
38. Hartford JT, Thienhaus OJ:Psychiatric aspects of alcoholism in geriatric patients, in Hartford JT, Samorajski T (eds): *Alcoholism in the Elderly: Social and Biomedical Issues.* New York, Raven, 1984, p 253.
39. Pascarelli EF, Fischer W: Drug dependence in the elderly. *Int J Aging Human Develop* 5(4):347, 1974.
40. Rix KJB: Elderly alcoholics in the Edinburgh psychiatric services. *J R Soc Med* 75:177, 1982.
41. Janik SW, Dunham RG: A nationwide examination of the need for specific alcoholism treatment programs for the elderly. *J Stud Alcohol* 44:307, 1983.
42. Kofoed LL et al: Treatment compliance of older alcoholics: An elder-specific approach is superior to "mainstreaming." *J Stud Alcohol* 48:47, 1987.

Chapter 103

PERSONALITY DISORDERS

Suzanne Holroyd and Peter V. Rabins

Personality traits are defined as the abiding personality characteristics of individual human beings. They are characteristics shared by all individuals (i.e., they are universal). They vary in degree among individuals (i.e., they are graded or dimensional) and are relatively persistent through adulthood. Such traits influence an individual's pattern of relating to the environment and to others. An example of a personality trait is degree of emotionality. Some individuals express very little feeling even in extremely distressing situations, whereas others become emotionally upset with quite minor stressors. The vast majority of individuals fall somewhere in between these extremes. A second example of a personality trait, and one of clinical relevance, is rigidity-flexibility. At one extreme are individuals who are rigid and very inflexible. For such individuals any variation from the predicted or expected will be quite upsetting. Rigid individuals often have very high expectations of their physicians and need detailed discussions about procedures, diseases, conditions, and treatments. They may be quite compliant with treatment but are prone to anger and upset if predicted outcomes do not occur. At the other end of this dimension are individuals who are overly flexible, have very few expectations, and have little capacity to plan. These individuals have great difficulty following instructions and keeping to a schedule. They may not listen to details of a conversation. For such individuals compliance is often a significant problem. They would be vulnerable to having difficulty carrying out a multistage treatment or following a diet.

The term *personality disorder* refers to the clustering of a group of traits to an extreme that results in a maladaptive pattern of behavior. By definition, personality disorders cause significant functional impairment or subjective distress to the individual. Personality disorders often have clinical relevance to the practicing physician. Examples of clinically relevant maladaptive behaviors include interpersonal difficulties, extreme help rejection, bargaining, self-absorption, and demandingness. Hypochondriasis or self-destructive behaviors including alcoholism, drug abuse, and suicide may be features of personality disorder.

The *histrionic personality disorder,* for example, refers to the clustering of excess emotional lability, inappropriate seductiveness, overt seeking of reassurance, self-centeredness, overconcern with appearance, and being overly impressionistic or vague. Individuals with this cluster of traits are likely to present their problems in a dramatic fashion, with frequent complaints about minor somatic sensations. They frequently may direct anger at the treating physician. They are often vague and poor historians. They utilize health care facilities more frequently than others.[1]

Obsessive-compulsive personality disorder is characterized by perfectionism with unrealistically high expectations, rigidity, lack of emotionality, and a focus on details and rules. They insist others do things their way. They are indecisive and stingy. Clinically, patients with the obsessive-compulsive personality disorder give their history in excessive detail and focus on specific (sometimes minor) aspects of a general problem. They worry about minor changes in routine, have difficulty adapting to new situations, and are especially upset by the unexpected.

Figure 103-1 further illustrates the concepts of personality traits and disorders. All individuals fall somewhere on a continuum for each trait. The few individuals who fall at the extreme ends of a dimension are more vulnerable to distress. An even smaller number of individuals are at the extreme end of a group of traits which tend to cluster together to form a disorder. Thus, individual A falls at differing places on several trait dimensions but not at the extreme on

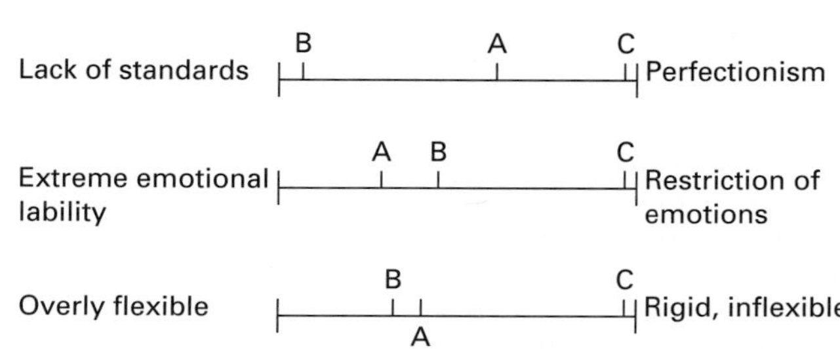

FIGURE 103-1

Schematic showing three individuals (A, B, C) whose positions on three trait dimensions vary. C would qualify for a diagnosis of obsessional personality disorder.

any of these three measures. Individual B falls toward the extreme on one dimension but on the others is more toward the mean. He or she may be more vulnerable than A to deal with certain types of situations such as extreme cleanliness or attending to details such as those required with blood sugar monitoring. Individual C, in contrast, falls to the extreme on these three traits which make up part of the obsessional cluster. Thus he or she would be considered to have an obsessive-compulsive personality disorder. Although any of these individuals could become overwhelmed in certain circumstances, individual C is at highest risk for developing problems. It should be noted that features of personality-disordered individuals will vary in intensity and frequency at different points in their lives, waning when their lives are structured and secure and emerging during chaotic disruptive periods. Personality-disordered individuals may have increased difficulty with changes in life. Changes likely to be associated with aging include physical ill health, declining mobility, and decreasing cognitive, financial, and social resources. The defenses that a younger personality-disordered individual uses during stress might be unavailable in late life. For example, having multiple relationships and "fleeing" from those relationships that turn sour is not possible for the dependent elderly person in a relationship with a caregiver. Personality-disordered behavior may thus be expressed differently in the elderly. Examples include clinging behavior, angry entitlement, and hypochondriasis.[2]

This conception of traits and disorders allows the physician to treat each patient as an individual with strengths and weaknesses. It alerts the physician to the fact that certain repeated behavior patterns indicate potential problems. Early recognition of these can help the clinician prevent or minimize problems.

EPIDEMIOLOGY AND COURSE OF PERSONALITY DISORDERS

Personality is defined as lifelong patterns of behavior. A major controversy in the study of personality is whether personality characteristics are fully established early in adulthood and then persist through life or if personality continues to "develop" or change significantly throughout the life span.

Data from the work of McCrae and Costa demonstrate that many personality characteristics measured by questionnaire are stable within individuals.[3] Correlations over a 30-year period range from 0.7 to 0.8. These are strong, particularly considering the long period of time over which the data were collected. However, this finding demonstrates that there is not complete stability of personality through the life span. It is a common observation of many clinicians that the changes in circumstances that occur as individuals age influence interpersonal relationships, usual behaviors, and day-to-day mood states. We would thus suggest that the evidence currently supports both viewpoints.

Data on the course of personality disorder in late life is lacking. A significant limitation to the study of this issue is the instability of the definitions of personality disorder. This makes it difficult to relate findings of studies done in former years to current conceptualizations of personality disorder. A review of studies from 1948 to 1964 reported that the prevalence of "character disorders" ranged from 2.2 to 12.6 percent.[4] While one study notes only 1 percent diagnosis of personality disorder in an elderly community residential program,[5] another reported that 9.8 percent of new referrals to a psychogeriatrician were diagnosed with personality disorder and usually presented because their behavior impinged on others.[6] There is disagreement whether personality disorder is always a lifelong disorder, if personality disorders may develop for the first time in late life, or, conversely, if personality disorders decline or disappear with age.[7–10] Antisocial personality disorder is an example of this debate. A large epidemiologic study carried out in the United States in the early 1980s demonstrated that the prevalence of antisocial personality disorder declined in later life.[10] The 1-month prevalence fell from 0.9 percent for individuals in the 25- to 44-year-old age group in 0.0 percent in those over age 65. Among men only, the rate fell from 1.5 percent in those aged 22 to 44 to 0.1 percent in those over age 65. Another study found the lifetime prevalence of antisocial personality disorder fell from 2.1–3.3 percent to 0.2–0.8 percent in those 65 and older.[11] Similar declines in antisocial tendencies with age have been reported with the MMPI,[12] a questionnaire presumed to measure personality characteristics. A recent study of patients seen in a forensic psychiatric center for antisocial personality disorder found some decline in criminality after age 27 but found that one-third of individuals remained criminally active throughout their lives.[13] Theories to explain this decline include improvement or "burnout" with aging, early death due to high-risk behavior, or a change in symptoms to hypochondriasis, depression, or alcoholism.[13] Since criminality is only one characteristic of an antisocial personality, it is quite possible that the disorder persists but manifests in other behaviors. Roth has argued that antisocial behavior which occurs in late life is much more likely to be the result of brain disease than a continuation of lifelong antisocial traits.[14] A study of schizotypal personality disorder revealed that all diagnosed cases began before age 40,[15] supporting the idea that some personality disorders develop only when a person is young and then are lifelong.

The prevalence of histrionic personality disorder may also decline with age. Nestadt et al. reported a community prevalence of 1.9 percent in those aged 65 and older.[1] This was lower than the prevalence of 4.2 percent in those aged 18 to 24. Interestingly, the pattern differed in men and women. They found that the prevalence of histrionic personality declined with age in men but remained constant in women. They speculated that gender differences are due to social reinforcement of such traits in women or in men the development with age of more sociopathic or aggressive features that mask the histrionic disposition.

Other studies also support the general decline of diagnosed personality disorder with aging. In one study of psychiatric consultations, the frequency of personality-related diagnoses declined over the age span.[16] A review of 2322 psychiatric hospital inpatients with major depression found the prevalence of personality disorders to be 11.2 percent in those over age 65 compared with a prevalence of 17.2 percent for those aged less than 65.[17] Interestingly, no patients over age 65 were diagnosed with borderline personality disorder. Dependent personality disorder was diagnosed in 2.4 percent. Compulsive personality disorder was diagnosed more frequently (5.5 percent) in the elderly and was the only example of an increasing prevalence of a personality disorder with age. These authors speculated, as have others, that diagnostic criteria for some personality disorders may be age-biased because certain behaviors are less likely in elderly persons despite the persistence of personality traits.[2,18,19] For example, difficulty holding a job may not be applicable to the elderly. Yet, the underlying character traits of passive-aggressiveness or unreliability that make it difficult for the young to hold a job may still be present but appear as different behaviors in the elderly. Likewise, self-destructive behavior in a young person may appear as reckless motorcycle driving, while in an elderly bedridden individual it may appear as defiantly smoking with oxygen in the room. On the other hand, dependency which may appear pathologic in a younger person may be an appropriate adjustment for an older individual with multiple physical disabilities.

Another explanation for the decrease in diagnosed personality disorder in the aged is that comorbid medical illness may bias the clinician against making a personality disorder diagnosis by masking features of personality disorder.[17] Others have speculated that some personality disorders may have a higher mortality rate because of suicide or reckless behavior, thus resulting in a decreased prevalence.[1,13,19] For example, there are only two case reports of elderly borderline personality disorder in the literature.[20,21]

DIAGNOSIS OF PERSONALITY DISORDERS

Several factors complicate the recognition of personality disorder in elderly persons. As noted above, characteristics of the aging process might interfere with the application of behavioral diagnostic criteria that have been developed for younger individuals. The presence of another psychiatric disorder such as major depression can also make diagnosis difficult. Data suggest that elderly patients with major depression have a significant increase in symptoms normally associated with personality disorder.[22] For example, depressed individuals are often dependent, avoidant, resistant, negative, and somatic. Further, elderly patients with personality disorders may be more likely to develop major depression in late life.[23]

In taking a thorough history it is important for the clinician to determine whether behavior problems developed recently or have been present lifelong. When a behavior problem is new, the behavior is more likely due to the superimposed condition, such as depression, rather than to an intrinsic personality characteristic. Such behaviors would be likely to improve with treatment of the depression. Appearing unkempt or having few friends might suggest a lifelong schizotypal disorder, but recent onset of such traits could be due to loss of social supports and family through death, and superimposition of physical and financial difficulties. Again, an accurate history including one from family or friends of the patient will aid the clinician in determining whether behaviors are lifelong or of new onset in old age.

The development of personality change in late life also requires careful assessment for developing structural brain disease or systemic illness. Such a history should raise the possibility that dementia, Parkinson's disease, stroke, other CNS disease, or a systemic illness has developed. Behavior change or an exaggeration of lifelong traits can be the first sign of Alzheimer's disease or another dementing illness. Data suggest that those with Alzheimer's disease become more passive but more irritable. They tend to become less enthusiastic, less affectionate and kind, and less spontaneous and self-reliant.[24]

CLASSIFICATION OF PERSONALITY DISORDERS

The revised third edition of the *Diagnostic and Statistical Manual of Mental Disorders* (*DSM* III-R) classifies the personality disorders into three general categories: cluster A, the odd or eccentric group (paranoid, schizoid, and schizotypal); cluster B, the dramatic, emotional, and erratic group (antisocial, borderline, histrionic, and narcissistic); and cluster C, the anxious, fearful group (avoidant, dependent, obsessive-compulsive, and passive-aggressive).

Individuals with *paranoid personality disorder* are suspicious and mistrustful. They feel victimized and shift or project blame onto others. These individuals tend to be argumentative and litigious. They bear grudges and are easily slighted. Patients with *schizoid personality disorder* are indifferent to social relationships and display a restricted range of emotions. They choose solitary activities and have no close friends except for first-degree relatives. Individuals with *schizotypal personality disorder* show a pervasive pattern of peculiarity. They feel uncomfortable in social situations and have odd beliefs. They are often eccentric, have few close friends, and may display emotions which are inappropriate for the situation.

Those with an *antisocial personality disorder* are unable to conform to social norms, rules, or laws. They are irritable or aggressive, financially irresponsible, and impulsive. They seem unable to plan ahead. They lack remorse and may repeatedly lie. They are often reckless and have little regard for their own or others' safety. They are unable to sustain relationships for more than a year. *Borderline personality disorder* is characterized by a pervasive instability of mood. *Splitting* behavior (alternating between overidealization and devaluation), impulsiveness, and anger outbursts are common. Patients with borderline personality disorder may repeatedly engage in self-injurious threats or behaviors. They may have difficulty distinguishing themselves and their emotions from those of others (identity disturbance). They have chronic feelings of emptiness and abandonment. The diagnosis of *narcissistic personality disorder* depends on the presence of an extreme sense of self-importance with entitlement ("I deserve it") and a need for constant admiration. Empathy for others is lacking, and they may exploit others. Such patients believe their problems are unique and special. Histrionic personality disorder was described earlier in this chapter.

The *avoidant personality disorder* is notable for timidity and easy embarrassment. While there is a desire for social interaction, it is accompanied by a fear of criticism. Those with *dependent personality disorder* are unable to make their own decisions. They allow others to control them and are unable to disagree with others. They feel helpless if alone and devastated when relationships end. They are frequently preoccupied with fears of being abandoned. *Passive-aggressive personality disorder* is characterized by a passive resistance to external demands with behaviors such as procrastination, working deliberately slowly, and "forgetting." They resent suggestions and believe they are doing much better than others think they are doing. Patients with passive-aggressive personality often make health practitioners angry; the anger may be directed toward the patient or toward others. It is important for the clinician to be aware that patients with these personality features induce anger; if this occurs it should be directly discussed with the patient. Obsessive-compulsive personality disorder has been discussed earlier in this chapter.

More often than not, the "pure" subtypes described above are not found, and a mix of traits is present. If so, *personality disorder not otherwise specified* may be diagnosed.

TREATMENT

Few data are available about the treatment of personality-disordered elderly patients. One should have a low threshold for treating the suspected psychiatric diagnoses such as depression or anxiety disorder that may mimic or exacerbate a personality disorder. Physical and medical problems should be investigated and treated to minimize associated somatic complaints. Psychiatric medication should be avoided unless there is a specific diagnosed condition.[21] This minimizes side effects and avoids dependency. Medications can become a power struggle between the patient and clinician. This principle is important since the elderly with abnormal personalities are at higher risk of receiving psychotropic drugs.[25]

Social and family supports should be fully maximized. Setting firm and consistent limits on inappropriate behavior is also useful for patients, their family, and their caregivers.[19,22]

Trying to determine why disordered behavior is occurring at a particular time may provide ways to restructure the individual's environment or outlook. For example, a person with an obsessive-compulsive personality may become behaviorally difficult in a changing unpredictable environment; anything done to lessen change may result in decreased distress. Psychotherapy may be helpful in aged persons and has been described elsewhere.[26] The goal of psychotherapy would not include restructuring of personality or overcoming past deficits. Rather it should focus on current life stresses and the person's vulnerabilities that make particular circumstances stressful. Adaptive strategies can be presented, and the patient can be taught to avoid or be ready for future stressful circumstances. Three clinical vignettes are provided to demonstrate management.

CLINICAL VIGNETTES

The Demanding, Dissatisfied Patient with Unexplained Symptoms

A 78-year-old woman with chronic obstructive pulmonary disease presented to the emergency room 40 times in a 1-year period with various unexplained complaints. She changed medical practitioners frequently and complained of being neglected by her physician. Her primary care physician and psychiatrist devised a plan in which she would be seen every 2 weeks for 10 minutes by the internist and on alternating weeks by a psychogeriatric nurse. Over the subsequent year her use of the emergency room decreased dramatically (two emergency room visits for documented respiratory failure). Her complaints were acknowledged by the physician and nurse, the need for medication compliance was repeatedly emphasized, and nonpharmacologic methods of treating anxiety and distress were offered. Some expression of anger was allowed, but after several months this was redirected toward more effective means of solving problems (e.g., "I know you're mad at Dr. X. However, that's no reason to stop your inhaler. Why don't you tell the doctor on your next visit about your worry but keep using the inhaler as it was prescribed").

The Obsessional, Rigid Perfectionist

A 68-year-old man admitted for treatment of a heart attack was referred for angry outbursts on the intensive care unit. He spent much time questioning multiple staff members and then comparing answers. He would then become upset if answers differed slightly. He would yell if medicines were not delivered directly on time. Past history revealed perfectionism and a rigid, unemotional personality. The patient was felt to be especially vulnerable to changes in the environment and to situations which lack a feeling of "being in control." To minimize potential problems, the patient was assigned a specific staff member who would work with him on each shift. Questions were not to be answered by all staff members but referred to a few designated ones to minimize variation. Attempts were made to keep the environment as predictable as possible by explaining all further procedures to the patient. Further control was given to the patient by allowing him to ask for medications before dosage time so that he could take them at the "exact time." Such measures resulted in marked improvement in the patient's sense of control and behavior.

The Noncompliant Self-Destructive Patient

A 78-year-old man in a nursing home was referred for agitated and noncompliant behavior. He refused medication and broke his diabetic and low-salt diet, which was felt to be the cause of at least two hospital admissions for heart failure. He also frequently cursed or threw objects at the staff. He had no social supports, either family or friends, that kept in touch. His pattern was to have an angry outburst following a pleasant interaction with a staff member, and then withdraw into his room. The patient was felt to have lifelong difficulties maintaining relationships, and his outbursts were felt to be in response to feeling uncomfortable after having a positive social interaction. Management included setting strict limits on aggressive behavior with the patient signing a contract to stop such activity or forfeit smoking privileges. Further, the staff was instructed on maintaining a distant but professional relationship with the patient to minimize angry outbursts. The patient also started seeing a therapist once every 2 weeks to explore other difficulties on an individual basis. Although verbal outbursts still occasionally occurred and dieting indiscretions as well, the staff reported significant improvement in his overall behavior.

SUMMARY

Personality traits are universally shared human characteristics. Individuals vary quantitatively along trait dimensions, and this variability makes some individuals more vulnerable to emotional upset and behavioral disorder than others. Individuals who vary to an extreme degree are said to have personality disorders. The identification of personality vulnerabilities and weaknesses by the clinician can lead to the development of treatment plans that minimize emotional and behavioral problems. Treatment rests on the explicit identification of the patient's vulnerabilities and strengths. This can help both patient and clinician to understand the behavior, give them a sense of control, and help modify the environment to meet the patient's needs.

REFERENCES

1. Nestadt G et al: An epidemiological study of histrionic personality disorder. *Psychol Med* 20:413, 1990.
2. Sadavoy J: Character pathology in the elderly. *J Geriatr Psychiatry* 20:165, 1987.
3. McCrae RR, Costa PT: *Emerging Lives, Enduring Dispositions.* Boston, Little, Brown, 1984.
4. Bergman K: The neuroses of old age, in Kay DWK, Walk A (eds): *Recent Development in Psychogeriatrics.* London, Headley Brothers, 1971, p 39.
5. Moreno C, Wile J: Community residential treatment for elderly psychiatric patients. *Hosp Community Psychiatry* 40:743, 1989.
6. Robinson JR: The natural history of mental disorder in old age. *Br J Psychiatry* 154:783, 1989.
7. Shepherd M, Gruenberg EM: The age for neuroses. *Millbank Mem Fund Q* 35:258, 1957.
8. Meyer JE: Psychoneuroses and neurotic reactions in old age. *J Am Geriatr Soc* 22:254, 1974.
9. Straker M: Adjustment disorders and personality disorders in the aged. *Psychiatric Clin North Am* 5:121, 1982.
10. Regier DA et al: One month prevalence of mental disorders in the United States. *Arch Gen Psychiatry* 45:977, 1988.
11. Robins LN et al: Lifetime prevalence of specific psychiatric disorders in three sites. *Arch Gen Psychiatry* 41:949, 1984.
12. Weiss JM: The natural history of antisocial attitudes—

What happens to psychopaths? *J Geriatr Psychiatry* 6:236, 1973.
13. Arboleda-Florez J, Holley HL: Antisocial burnout: An exploratory study. *Bull Am Acad Psychiatry Law* 19:173, 1991.
14. Roth M: Cerebral disease and mental disorders of old age as causes of antisocial behavior. *Int Psychiatry Clin* 5:35, 1968.
15. Baron M et al: Age of onset in schizophrenia and schizotypal disorders. *Neuropsychobiology* 10:199, 1983.
16. Rabins P et al: Utilization of psychiatric consultation for elderly patients. *J Am Geriatr Soc* 31:581, 1983.
17. Fogel BS, Westlake R: Personality disorder diagnoses and age in inpatients with major depression. *J Clin Psychiatry* 51:232, 1990.
18. Kroessler D: Personality disorder in the elderly. *Hosp Community Psychiatry* 41:1325, 1990.
19. Sadavoy J et al (eds): *Comprehensive Review of Geriatric Psychiatry*. Washington, American Psychiatric Press, 1991, p 377.
20. Siegel DJ, Small GW: Borderline personality disorder in the elderly: A case study. *Can J Psychiatry* 31:859, 1986.
21. Sadavoy J, Doran B: Treatment of the elderly characterologically disturbed patient in the chronic care institution. *J Geriatr Psychiatry* 16:223, 1983.
22. Thompson LW et al: Personality disorder and outcome in the treatment of late-life depression. *J Geriatr Psychiatry* 21:133, 1988.
23. Abrams RC et al: Geriatric depression and DSM-III-R personality disorder criteria. *J Am Geriatr Soc* 35:383, 1987.
24. Petry S et al: Personality alterations in dementia of the Alzheimer type. *Arch Neurol* 45:1187, 1988.
25. Mann AH et al: The twelve-month outcome of patients with neurotic illness in general practice. *Psychol Med* 11:535, 1981.
26. Yesavage JA, Karasu TB: Psychotherapy with elderly patients. *Am J Psychother* 36:41, 1982.

Chapter 104

PSYCHOPHARMACOLOGY AND PSYCHOTHERAPY

Kimberly A. Sherrill, Christopher C. Colenda, III, and Burton V. Reifler

The psychiatrist is less likely than the primary care practitioner to provide mental health services for the elderly.[1,2] According to one estimate, the elderly with mental disorders make about 4.3 visits per year to primary care providers, compared with only 1.7 visits per year to mental health specialists.[3] In addition, primary care practitioners are by far the largest prescribers of psychotropic medications in the elderly.[4]

We will discuss principles of both psychopharmacologic therapy and psychotherapy. These two areas span a broad range of therapeutic options available to the physician caring for the mental and emotional needs of the geriatric patient.

PSYCHOPHARMACOLOGY

Judicious use of psychotropic medication can benefit elderly patients greatly. Unfortunately, psychotropics also present potential hazards, the most common ones arising from unnecessary use of multiple drugs, failure to monitor side effects, and lack of understanding of the major physiologic vulnerabilities of the elderly.[5–8]

The following section presents guidelines for the use of psychotropic medicine. Patterns of drug use, patient compliance, pharmacokinetics, pharmacodynamics, and general prescribing principles are fundamental to any discussion of psychotropic drug use, and the reader is referred to Chap. 21 for more detailed discussion of these issues.

PRINCIPLES OF PSYCHOTROPIC MEDICATION MANAGEMENT

When psychiatric symptoms or disruptive behaviors arise, families usually first turn to primary care physicians, who must decide what action to take in, for example, an agitated dementia patient who is striking out at a caregiver or wandering at night. Despite the availability of behavioral management techniques, physicians are most likely to use psychotropic medications for such problems.

The first step in prescribing psychotropic medications for an elderly patient is for clinicians to ask themselves the following questions.[9–11] What are the patient's primary medical and psychiatric diagnoses? Could these symptoms or behaviors represent untreated or undetected medical problems? If these symptoms represent a primary psychiatric disorder, do they warrant medication? Is psychiatric consultation needed? And last, is there a realistic risk/benefit ratio for the medication, including factors such as compliance, polypharmacy, and side effects compared with potential benefits such as improved behavior and less caregiver stress?

The first and second questions are critical, since most geriatric patients have multiple comorbid conditions, and adding psychotropic medications may worsen one of these (e.g., benzodiazepines increase the risk of falls in a patient with osteoporosis). If the clinician can suggest alternative interventions that do not require medications, the patient may be better off.

Clinicians may feel obligated to prescribe a medication for a patient because of a caregiver's insistence that something be done. Even when this is appropriate, the physician should also address ways that caregivers may improve their capacity to handle patients. For example, if the family is struggling with a dementia patient's disruptive behavior, referral to a local dementia support group is appropriate, as well as discussion about alternative placements if the patient is being cared for at home.

Psychiatric consultation is a more delicate problem, in part due to patients' reluctance to see themselves as having emotional problems. Even if the clinician suggests referral, the patient may decline or fail to follow through, a dilemma without a clear-cut solution. However, if questions remain in a clinician's mind regarding the nature of the patient's problem, consultation is prudent, even if just a telephone contact with a psychiatric colleague.

The last question, establishing a risk/benefit ratio for medication management, involves considering the following items:

- Class of medication chosen
- Pharmacokinetic properties of the medication (absorption, distribution, metabolism, and excretion)
- Pharmacodynamic properties of the medication (CNS receptor characteristics such as number and sensitivity)
- Side effect profile
- Potential drug–drug interactions, including over-the-counter medications
- Expected length of treatment
- Compliance

These considerations are not unique to psychotropic medications. But since psychotropic medications affect peripheral and CNS functioning, keeping them in mind can prevent adverse effects. For example, choosing a potent anticholinergic antidepressant, such as amitriptyline (Elavil), for an Alzheimer's disease patient is not prudent since the anticholinergic effects may worsen cognition and increase the risk of an anticholinergic delirium.

Another element of psychotropic pharmacotherapy in the elderly is *biotitration.*[11] This means individualizing the patient's dose, remaining flexible in adapting the dose to fit the patient's clinical needs, and ensuring that a patient's dose is sufficient to achieve pharmacologic success. While *starting low and going slow* remains a sensible axiom, inadequate dosing can lead to patients' experiencing the side effects of the medication without its benefits. One way to minimize dosage uncertainties is to use plasma medication levels when appropriate. Medication levels may help clinicians determine why the patient has not responded to the medication or help determine the cause of unexpected behavioral changes in the patient. For example, monitoring plasma levels of the antidepressant nortriptyline (Pamelor), lithium, and anticonvulsants such as carbamazepine (Tegretol) is useful. Unfortunately, for medications such as benzodiazepines or neuroleptics, plasma levels do not have the same clinical or therapeutic relevance.

Medication levels in the elderly must be interpreted keeping in mind pharmacodynamic and pharmacokinetic changes that occur with age. For example, most laboratories place the threshold for lithium toxicity at a plasma level exceeding 1.5 meq/liter. For elderly patients toxic side effects (confusion, tremor, restlessness) may develop at levels below 1.0 meq/liter, a concentration young adults tolerate well. If side effects or adverse reactions develop at "normal" plasma levels, dose reduction often corrects the problem, although in some instances, alternative medications must be used. Adverse side effects may also depend on the patient's concurrent medication use, medical and physical condition, and current nutritional and fluid balance.

Another principle is to minimize polypharmacy. Polypharmacy in geriatrics is not limited to psychotropic medications; it is a generic problem. Frequently, patients are started on one medication to address certain symptoms, such as managing disruptive behavior found in dementia patients. When the first medication fails to control symptoms, other medications are sometimes prescribed without considering stopping the first one. Conscientious physicians may discontinue the original medication, but the order may not be carried through by the caregiver. Other reasons for polypharmacy include prescribing by multiple physicians, using multiple pharmacies, and poor compliance. This may lead to a vicious cycle of represcribing the medication or prescribing multiple medications for the same problem, a phenomenon physicians see repeatedly. In our opinion the best solution is coordinating medical services through one primary care physician.

Practical Treatment Options for Specific Psychiatric Disorders

While there are no universally accepted medication treatment protocols for specific psychiatric syndromes in late life, practical treatment guidelines can be recommended. First, some behavioral symptoms often found in dementia patients, such as wandering and hoarding, willful intrusiveness, or noxious repetitive behaviors, are not particularly amenable to medications. These behaviors usually escalate in response to environmental and interpersonal conflict. For example, an Alzheimer's patient's willful resistance to bathing will not respond to neuroleptic use. The patient is better served by a plan designed to minimize the perceived threat and forced confrontation. Conversely, if the observed behaviors are due to paranoia or delusions, medications may help considerably.

The remaining discussion will develop practical pharmacologic approaches for four psychiatric problems commonly found in late life: anxiety, mood disturbances, psychotic behavior, and delirium.

Anxiety Disorders in Late Life

Anxiety is a subjective psychological state of apprehension, tension, or uneasiness experienced by an individual that is not in response to a recognizable danger. These cognitive symptoms may be accompanied by somatic concerns over bodily function, depressive symptoms, and panic attacks. Anxiety is an expected human emotion in certain situations, but when it interferes with daily living or interpersonal relationships, it becomes pathological and requires treatment.

Approximately 10 percent of elderly persons show measurable symptoms of chronic anxiety, and nearly 20 percent may be expected to take prescribed antianxiety drugs within a given year. Depending on age and gender, clinical studies have found that anxiety symptoms in primary care patient populations range from 5 to 30 percent.[12] The most detailed study of anxiety disorders in the elderly is based on the Epidemiologic Catchment Area (ECA) survey.[13] The

ECA data show that the prevalence of anxiety disorders generally decreases across the life span. For individuals aged 65 and older, the prevalence of anxiety disorders is 5.5 percent compared with 7.7 percent for those aged 18 to 24, 8.3 percent for those aged 25 to 44, and 6.6 percent for those aged 45 to 64. In addition, women are almost twice as likely to report anxiety disorders than men.

Management of Anxiety Managing anxiety in late life begins with establishing an accurate diagnosis. When patients with generalized anxiety disorder, panic disorder, and somatoform disorder present to the geriatrician, they may pose a diagnostic dilemma, since so many of the symptoms could be representative of medical illnesses. Because elderly patients may find it easier to express emotional distress in terms of bodily dysfunction and because they often have medical problems that might explain their symptoms, complaints such as shakiness, restlessness, shortness of breath, chronic fatigue, and pain may not be attributed to primary anxiety disorder until late in the diagnostic workup.

The narrowness of the patient's insight may contribute to excess medication use, leading to addiction, dependence, and excess morbidity without significant reduction in the patient's level of distress. For example, although benzodiazepines are recommended for short-term use for anxiety symptoms and disorders, one study found that of those taking benzodiazepines, many reported persistence of symptoms as well as signs of psychological dependence.[14] In addition another study found that the median duration of benzodiazepine usage was 2.5 years, with 67 percent of patients taking a benzodiazepine medication for 1 year or more.[15]

Anxiolytic medications can cause complications. Elderly patients are reported to have twice the number of adverse side effects and drug interactions that younger patients have.[12] Age reduces the efficiency with which some medications, such as long-acting benzodiazepines, are metabolized and excreted. This may lead to accumulation of active metabolites, causing excess sedation, diminished sexual desire, worsening cognitive function, and reduction in the general level of energy. A recent study showed the use of sedatives to be a significant risk factor for falls in elderly persons.[16]

In light of these complications, it is important to note that some patients with anxiety disorders respond to nonpharmacologic treatment. Strategies effective in many cases include stress management, regular exercise, reduction of caffeine, relaxation techniques, and supportive psychotherapy.

In treating anxiety disorders in elderly persons, buspirone (Buspar) has shown some success. A 5-hydroxytryptamine 1a (5-HT_{1a}) partial agonist, it appears to be effective and safe for many nondemented geriatric patients with anxiety,[17] although some patients find it causes a paradoxical feeling of excitement. In addition, there are anecdotal reports that buspirone may be helpful in agitated dementia patients with a variety of disruptive behaviors.[18,19] Buspirone should be given in divided doses, with a total daily dose in the range of 45 to 60 mg/day. Like antidepressants, buspirone may take 2 weeks or longer for its full effect to be appreciated. Stopping buspirone is not associated with adverse side effects or withdrawal symptoms.

Benzodiazepines constitute another option for anxious elderly patients. Short-acting agents, such as oxazepam, lorazepam, and alprazolam, in low doses and for brief periods have been recommended.[20] Alprazolam can be started at 0.25 mg bid to tid. Doses exceeding 1.0 mg tid to qid should be avoided, if possible. If lorazepam is chosen, the starting dose can be 0.5 mg bid to tid. Doses exceeding 4 mg/day should be avoided. Hart et al. have shown in a 2-week placebo-controlled trial that alprazolam does not significantly compromise cognitive performance in healthy elders.[21] Even so, clinicians are advised not to prescribe benzodiazepines for extended periods without attempting to reduce the dose of medication or engage in drug-free trials. Because of the risk of withdrawal symptoms, these medications should not be abruptly stopped. As a general guide, they can be reduced by about 10 percent every 3 days, or slower if need be.

Antidepressants have a role in managing anxiety syndromes in elderly patients, especially those with panic disorder. Panic symptoms include intense anticipatory anxiety symptoms plus palpitations, trembling, shortness of breath, flushes, and sweating. Imipramine (Tofranil) in low doses may be an effective agent, and other antidepressants may also be effective. Generally, the starting dose is 25 to 50 mg daily, which is gradually titrated, as tolerated, to the point where symptoms are extinguished or reduced to a tolerable level. Patients may be sensitive to the anticholinergic side effects of imipramine, so changes in cognition, micturition, orthostatic blood pressure, and cardiac conduction must be monitored. Some clinicians obtain plasma imipramine levels and electrocardiograms every 4 to 6 months.

Beta blockers, particularly propranolol (Inderal), have been recognized as useful medications for somatic symptoms of anxiety in adults. However, beta blockers must be used with caution, since they may predispose susceptible patients to depression and interfere with ongoing treatment for hypertension, cardiac disease, and chronic obstructive pulmonary disease.[22] Propranolol, which is more lipid soluble than other beta blockers, is recommended as a first-choice beta blocker. Starting doses must be low, in the range of 10 to 15 mg bid to tid, with gradual dose titration. Maletta suggests that the dose should not exceed 400 mg/day.[11] Frequent electrocardiograms and blood pressure checks are recommended while the dose of propranolol is being adjusted. Atenolol, a beta-1-selective agent, and nadolol, a nonselective beta blocker, have also been reported to be beneficial.[11]

Mood Disturbances in Late Life—Mania and Depression

Mania For patients with bipolar affective disorder, which can have its onset in late life, lithium remains the treatment of choice. Where possible, elderly patients with mania are best cared for by a psychiatrist. Since elderly patients are more sensitive to lithium's side effects, the usual maintenance plasma lithium levels for manic patients are kept in the 0.3 to 0.7 meq/liter range, lower if need be.[12] For acute manic episodes, the target plasma lithium level should be 1.0 to 1.4 meq/liter.

Lithium has also been suggested for behaviors found in dementia patients, such as motor restlessness, mood fluctuations, day-night confusion, and aggression.[23] Lithium's usefulness in aggression may be related to its role as an enhancer of serotonergic function,[24] since serotonergic dysfunction has been postulated as contributing to aggressive behavior in humans. Unfortunately, the behavioral response of dementia patients to lithium is unpredictable.[11]

Carbamazepine (Tegretol) and clonazepam (Klonopin) have been recommended as alternative medications for elderly patients with hypomania or mania, especially for patients in whom lithium therapy failed or those who could not tolerate lithium.[12,25] They may also be useful in agitated dementia patients in whom therapy with other medications has failed.[26–28] For carbamazepine, plasma levels are usually kept at 4.0 to 8.0 μg/ml. Ataxia and bone marrow suppression are the major side effects to monitor when patients are on carbamazepine. Clonazepam, a benzodiazepine anticonvulsant, is recommended, but judiciously. Usual starting doses are 0.5 mg bid to tid. The dose is titrated according to how well the patient responds or tolerates the side effects. Excessive sedation, worsening memory, ataxia, and disinhibition are the major side effects. Clinical trials with carbamazepam and clonazepam in this population have not been reported to date.

Depression Antidepressants are the mainstay of treating depressed elderly patients, usually in conjunction with ongoing supportive psychotherapy. In general clinicians should choose antidepressant medications that have low anticholinergic side effects and avoid cardiovascular side effects, such as postural hypotension.

There are a number of antidepressant medications from which to choose. Newer ones, such as fluoxetine (Prozac), sertraline (Zoloft), and paroxetine (Paxil), are potent serotonin reuptake inhibitors, have few anticholinergic and cardiovascular side effects, and have been well tolerated in geriatric patients, especially sertraline and buproprion (Wellbutrin). Buproprion is a new antidepressant with noradrenergic activity, is sedating, and is usually given three times a day, which may decrease compliance. On the other hand, fluoxetine and paroxetine can be given once a day, but starting doses should be less than those recommended for young adults, in order to avoid symptoms of restlessness and increased anxiety (the so-called serotonin syndrome). The serotonin reuptake inhibitors are less likely to produce weight gain than many other antidepressants.

Most of the older antidepressants are also safe and effective. The secondary amine heterocyclic antidepressants are primarily recommended for this patient population. Nortriptyline is a secondary amine cyclic antidepressant that has the singular advantage of having a "therapeutic window" (50 to 150 ng/ml) which allows for targeted dose strategies. The usual starting dose is 10 to 25 mg daily for the frail elderly and can be increased slowly. Some clinicians recommend divided daily dosing until steady state is achieved. Another effective and well-tolerated secondary amine cyclic antidepressant is desipramine (Norpramin). It also has few anticholinergic side effects and is well tolerated by geriatric patients. The usual starting dose is 25 to 50 mg daily, and plasma levels exceeding 125 ng/ml are recommended.[12] Tertiary amine cyclic antidepressants, such as amitriptyline, imipramine, and doxepin, are not recommended as first-line antidepressants, since they have high anticholinergic side effects, and can cause orthostatic hypotension.

Trazodone (Desyrel) is an alternative choice for depression in elderly patients. Trazodone has virtually no anticholinergic side effects and is sedating, which is especially helpful for those depressed geriatric patients who complain of insomnia. However, trazodone can cause orthostatic hypotension and increase resting heart rate. The usual starting dose is 50 to 75 mg at bedtime. If necessary, the dosage can be raised by either increasing the bedtime dose to the 150- to 250-mg range or dividing the dose to a tid schedule and increasing slowly. The latter strategy is recommended for patients prone to orthostatic hypotension.

Other psychopharmacologic treatment strategies for depression, such as monoamine oxidase inhibitors, adjuvant therapy with thyroid hormone and/or lithium, dual antidepressants, or the use of psychostimulants (methylphenidate), have also been shown to be effective and safe for geriatric depressed patients. However, these strategies are probably best prescribed and monitored by a psychiatrist. If medications fail or side effects are intolerable, electroconvulsive therapy (ECT) is a safe and effective treatment for depression in elderly patients and in our opinion is underutilized.[29]

Psychosis and Delusional Behavior in Late Life

Psychotic symptoms (hallucinations, delusions, and paranoia) are seen in patients with dementia, late-life delusional disorders, and psychotic depression, with the first group most likely encountered by geriatricians (see Chap. 100). It is rare for geriatric patients to develop schizophrenia, although clinicians may be faced with elderly schizophrenic patients who developed the illness as young adults. Late-life delusional disorders are less common, but particularly vexing, since they will potentially respond to antipsychotic medication. Patients tend to see other people as the problem and do not comply with medication.

Neuroleptics (antipsychotics) are the mainstay of treating psychotic symptoms in late life. Salzman's review of controlled and uncontrolled studies of over

5000 patients finds a therapeutic response of "good to excellent" in 60 to 70 percent of them.[20] However, Schneider et al.'s meta-analytic study of controlled clinical trials, using neuroleptics for agitated dementia patients, showed modest improvement in patients receiving neuroleptics.[30] Recent clinical trials have confirmed that neuroleptics are therapeutic in controlling agitation, psychosis, restlessness, and hostility in elderly patients but are not as robust as expected.[31,32] No neuroleptic has been shown to be superior to another, and what works well for one patient may be ineffective in another.

Choosing a neuroleptic for a geriatric patient requires estimating a risk/benefit ratio. The choice may largely depend upon the medication's side-effect profile, for example low-potency neuroleptics (i.e., those requiring a higher dosage) such as thioridazine (Mellaril) cause sedation, orthostatic hypotension, and anticholinergic side effects (which may contribute to worsening of cognition). On the other hand low-potency neuroleptics are less likely to induce extrapyramidal side effects (bradykinesia, akathisia, and pseudoparkinsonian symptoms). The high-potency medications such as haloperidol (Haldol) and fluphenazine (Prolixin) are less sedating and less prone to induce orthostatic hypotension, but are more likely to cause extrapyramidal side effects. Some clinicians prefer an intermediate-potency neuroleptic that does not have extremes in side-effect potential, such as molindone (Moban) or loxapine (Loxitane).

Correct dosing of the neuroleptics is vital in order to avoid toxicity. Clinicians are divided in their opinions as to single versus divided daily dosage. The former improves compliance, while the latter gives more flexibility. Starting doses of haloperidol should be in the 0.5- to 1-mg range and gradually adjusted to control target symptoms (delusions, hallucinations, agitation) and to guard against adverse side effects, particularly extrapyramidal side effects. If thioridazine is chosen, the usual starting dose ranges from 10 to 50 mg/day, depending upon the severity of psychotic symptoms and side effects, such as orthostatic hypotension. Given the risk/benefit profile of the high-potency versus the low-potency neuroleptics, Salzman recommends high-potency agents as medications of first choice,[20] although other clinicians feel that the midpotency agents are preferable, given dose/side effect profiles.

Long-acting injectable forms of fluphenizine and haloperidol are available. Peak plasma levels of haloperidol decanoate are found about 6 days after administration, with an apparent half-life of 3 weeks. The medication is given on a weekly basis for 4 weeks and then monthly. Usual adult starting doses are 25 to 50 mg every week and 50 mg every month thereafter, although lower doses may be required to balance side effects with therapeutic efficacy for elderly patients. Long-acting decanoate neuroleptics have not been systematically studied in elderly patients, but they may be useful for psychotic geriatric patients who relapse repeatedly due to poor compliance.[33] Because of the high risk of extrapyramidal side effects, those medications are best used by clinicians experienced with administering them.

If clinicians prescribe neuroleptics, they are advised to inform patients and their families of the risk of side effects, especially tardive dyskinesia and to document in the medical record that they have done so. Additionally, for nursing home residents, the Omnibus Budget Reconciliation Act (OBRA) of 1987 requires ongoing monitoring of neuroleptic medications administered to nursing home residents. Monitoring includes yearly examination for tardive dyskinesia, documentation of dose reduction trials to see if symptoms change, and ongoing documentation justifying continued need for neuroleptics.

If neuroleptics fail to control psychotic symptoms, what other options do clinicians have? The short-acting benzodiazepines may be helpful adjuvants, but they have not been shown to be useful over prolonged periods of time or in the severely demented,[11] and in some instances administration of benzodiazepines may cause disinhibition and aggravate aggressive behavior. As stated above, carbamazepine has been shown by many investigators to be effective in controlling agitated behavior in severely demented patients.[26,27] Maletta suggests that carbamazepine be used particularly in those patients with abnormal EEGs,[11] but it has also been found effective in patients with normal EEGs. Its risks include neurotoxicity, ataxia, bone marrow suppression, and skin rashes. Clinicians treating agitated and psychotic dementia patients with carbamazepine should seek plasma levels between 4.0 and 8.0 μg/ml.[11] Patterson believes that carbamazepine has a relatively rapid onset of action when it works, usually within 24 and 36 hours.[34]

Recently, some authors have advocated using serotonergic medications to help manage belligerant psychotic dementia patients. By and large these have been case reports or small case series. Trazodone, alone or in combination with L-tryptophan, has been the primary focus of interest,[35,36] with buspirone[18] and fluoxetine[37] also having been reported as effective. Results have been modest, and clinical trials have not been conducted.

Psychopharmacologic Treatment of Delirium in Geriatric Patients

Delirium is an acute organic syndrome with impairment of cognition, perception, and behavior (see Chap. 90). It affects as many as 10 to 25 percent of all hospitalized elderly patients and up to one-third of hospitalized dementia patients.[38,39] Symptoms include rapid decline in baseline cognitive function, abrupt changes in attention, sleep-wake cycle disruption, disturbances in perception (hallucinations, delusions), emotional lability, agitation, and in some cases hypoactivity.[39] Causes of delirium range from metabolic disorders (electrolyte abnormalities, hypoxemia, azotemia, and hypoglycemia), infectious diseases (particularly urinary and respiratory tracts), alcohol, head trauma, stroke, hypothermia or hyperthermia, and environmental (recent transfer to unfamiliar surroundings).[40]

Treating delirious patients involves identifying the underlying cause of the delirium and initiating appropriate diagnostic and therapeutic measures to correct the cause. Unless the patients are dangerous to themselves or others, Beresin recommends that appropriate environmental interventions be implemented to make sure the patients are medically and physically safe, prior to medication interventions.[31] Since this may not always be possible, clinicians may need to go ahead and treat target symptoms. For example, restlessness and sleep disturbance may best be treated with a short-acting benzodiazepine like lorazepam, 1 to 2 mg every 4 to 6 hours. The benzodiazepines are also best for treating withdrawal delirium, e.g., alcohol or benzodiazepine withdrawal. However, if the patient has psychotic symptoms and severe agitation, a better choice is a neuroleptic, such as haloperidol in doses that range from 2 to 5 mg PO or IM every 3 to 4 hours until calm. In intensive care unit settings, haloperidol can be given 2.0 to 10.0 mg IV every 20 to 30 minutes until the patient is calm,[41,42] titrating based on the patient's response. Interestingly, haloperidol administered in this manner is not associated with an increased risk of acute dystonia.

PRINCIPLES OF PSYCHOTHERAPY

Elderly persons are conspicuously absent from most psychodynamic theories. Freud was not the only one, but perhaps the boldest, to express pessimistic assumptions about elderly persons.[43] He wrote, "Older people are no longer educable," and felt that late in life "the mass of material to be dealt with would prolong treatment indefinitely."[44] Fortunately, theoretical perspectives are emerging which acknowledge the value of psychotherapeutic work in the elderly.[45,46] The following sections briefly address clinical applications of certain theoretical concepts, namely, psychoanalytic stage theory, and then conclude with a discussion of psychotherapeutic modalities useful in work with the elderly.

Mechanisms of Defense

Defense mechanisms may be thought of as the different ways an individual copes with daily emotional demands.[47] Under many circumstances the use of defense mechanisms is quite appropriate, and the physician may safely support their use. For example, a patient may refer to an antidepressant as a "sleeping pill" in order to make it more psychologically palatable. In general, as long as the defense mechanism promotes healthy behavior, it may be considered appropriate. At other times, the use of defense mechanisms may become harmful, such as denial by a patient who is aware of an illness but refuses to see a physician.

Denial is a common defense mechanism because of fears of loss of independence, becoming a burden to others, or death. This may explain why elderly patients sometimes omit important bits of information and why physicians must inquire specifically, directly, and systematically about symptoms.

Transference and Countertransference

Transference and countertransference may be thought of as similar to stereotyping. When the patient unconsciously stereotypes the physician, the process is called *transference,* an example being the elderly patient who views the physician as a son or daughter. Like defense mechanisms, transference may be helpful or harmful. The patient's ability to relate warmly to the physician may be enhanced by a positive son or daughter transference, or an elderly patient who expects the physician to behave as an idealized son or daughter might make unrealistic demands and become angry at perceived slights.

Countertransference is when the physician stereotypes the patient. Although countertransference may also contribute positively to the relationship, problems can arise if the stereotypes are negative. For example, older patients are sometimes insensitively referred to as "gomers," or physicians may fail to ask elderly patients about sexual issues because of stereotypes which label older adults as asexual.

STAGES AND TASKS OF ADULT DEVELOPMENT

Erikson's theoretical formulations were among the first to consider developmental issues beyond puberty.[48] He postulated a series of developmental stages, two of which are relevant to the geriatric population: adulthood and maturity. Each stage is characterized by a unique psychosocial crisis. For the stage of adulthood, the crisis "generativity versus stagnation" involves the need to find satisfying goals, motivation, and meaning in one's work and relationships. The stage of maturity is characterized by the crisis of "ego integrity versus despair" during which one reflects back on life's accomplishments in an evaluative way.

More recent theoretical work suggests that the notion of stages may focus too much on chronological time. Since important life events do not necessarily fall in the same order for each adult, a more fitting approach might be one which considers the specific tasks themselves, regardless of chronological age.[49] This *task* rather than *stage* focus allows more flexibility in theoretical and clinical approaches.

helped by a toileting program at regular intervals. Also, simple muscle relaxation techniques which are easy to learn and apply[58] can help a patient suffering from anxiety.

THERAPEUTIC APPROACHES

Some types of therapy which are potentially useful with elderly patients are as follows.

Supportive Therapy

Support is widely held to benefit physical and psychological health.[50,51] The one-on-one, or *confidant,* relationship may be particularly important to the older adult, perhaps even more so than interaction with family and other friends.[52] Thus a physician's potential for serving as a confidant for elderly patients should not be underestimated.

Three principles may help guide the physician's supportive approach: (1) the clinician acts as an *external ego,* providing coping mechanisms which are weak or absent in the patient, (2) the counseling focuses on a specific problem which the patient helps identify, and (3) the clinician is explicit and direct, giving advice and voicing opinions about what he or she thinks is best in a given situation.[53] In this way the patient can "borrow" helpful ideas from the clinician.

Being supportive may include touching or making special efforts to overcome communication blocks such as impaired vision or hearing. The physician may need to sit nearer the older person than other adults.[54] Support may entail acknowledgment of religious values, which are an important coping resource for many elderly people, particularly those who are seriously or terminally ill.[55–57] Finally, support may mean confronting maladaptive behaviors, such as excessive use of alcohol as self-medication for depression.

Behavioral Techniques

Conditioning techniques, such as systematically reinforcing desirable behaviors while ignoring undesirable ones, may benefit certain patients who are unable to respond to other therapeutic approaches or who require a multifaceted approach. For example, a severely demented patient with incontinence may be

Group Therapy

Fundamental to all types of group therapy are the goals of decreasing alienation and social isolation. Encouragement of autonomy and control may be one of the major determinants of successful adaptation in old age.[59] For this reason, different group approaches can be beneficial to elderly patients with all kinds of psychiatric impairment. A depressed, withdrawn patient may find new interests through the socialization of a group, while a demented patient may find needed stimulation and models for appropriate behaviors.

Family Therapy

Family interventions can be important for many frail or ill elderly people. Families operate as systems, so that changes in one element of the system affect all other system components.[60,61] Caregivers themselves may be suffering from depression or other stress-related illnesses due to the strain of dealing with their parents' health or mental health problems.[62,63] Family members of patients with Alzheimer's disease can benefit from support groups such as those sponsored by a local Alzheimer's Association.[62]

CONCLUSION

This summary of pharmacologic and psychotherapeutic treatment emphasizes the importance of the primary care practitioner in providing services to the mentally ill elderly patient. A variety of effective treatment approaches are available, not only for those with mild illness who may benefit greatly from relatively simple interventions, but also for patients suffering from chronic or debilitating illnesses who can be helped through an approach that combines medical and psychotherapeutic modalities. While the psychiatrist can be called on as needed for his or her expertise, primary care physicians can incorporate many of these strategies into their own practices.

REFERENCES

1. German PS et al: Detection and management of mental health problems of older patients by primary care providers. *JAMA* 257:489, 1987.
2. George LK et al: Psychiatric disorders and mental health service use in later life: Evidence from the Epidemiologic Catchment Area program, in Brody J, Maddox G (eds): *Epidemiology and Aging*. New York, Springer, 1987.
3. Goldstrom ID et al: Mental health services use by elderly adults in a primary care setting. *J Gerontol* 42:147, 1987.
4. Larson DB et al: Psychotropics prescribed to the U.S. elderly in early and mid 1980s: Prescribing patterns of primary care practitioners, psychiatrists, and other physicians. *Int J Geriatr Psychiatry* 6:63, 1991.
5. Vestal RE: Pharmacology and aging. *J Am Geriatr Soc* 30:191, 1982.
6. Beardsley RS et al: Prescribing of psychotropics to elderly nursing home patients. *J Am Geriatr Soc* 37:327, 1989.
7. Ouslander JG: Drug therapy in the elderly. *Ann Intern Med* 95:711, 1981.
8. Thompson TL II et al: Psychotropic drug use in the elderly, I. *N Engl J Med* 308:134, 1983.
9. Colenda CC: Drug treatment of behavior problems in elderly patients with dementia: I. *Drug Ther* 21(6):15, 1991.
10. Colenda CC: Drug treatment of behavior problems in elderly patients with dementia: II. *Drug Ther* 21(7):45, 1991.
11. Maletta GJ: Pharmacologic treatment and management of the aggressive demented patient. *Psychiatr Ann* 20:446, 1990.
12. Jenike M: *Geriatric Psychiatry and Psychopharmacology: A Clinical Approach*. Chicago, Year Book Medical, 1989.
13. Reiger DA et al: One-month prevalence of psychiatric disorders in the U.S.: Based on five epidemiologic catchment area sites. *Arch Gen Psychiatry* 45:977, 1988.
14. Pinsker H, Suljaga-Petchel K: Use of benzodiazepines in primary care geriatric patients. *J Am Geriatr Soc* 8:595, 1984.
15. Nolan L, O'Malley K: Patients, prescribing, and benzodiazepines. *Eur J Clin Pharmacol* 35:225, 1988.
16. Tinetti M et al: Risk of falls among elderly persons living in the community. *N Engl J Med* 319(26):1701, 1988.
17. Bohm C et al: Buspirone therapy in anxious elderly patients: A controlled clinical trial. *J Clin Psychopharmacol* 10(suppl 3):47, 1990.
18. Colenda CC: Buspirone in treatment of agitated demented patient. *Lancet* 1 (8595):1168, 1988.
19. Tiller JWG et al: Short-term buspirone treatment in disinhibition with dementia. *Lancet* 2:510, 1988.
20. Salzman C: Treatment of agitation in the elderly, in Meltzer HY (ed): *Psychopharmacology: A Generation of Progress*. New York, Raven, 1987, p 1167.
21. Hart R et al: A placebo controlled trial comparing alprazolam and buspirone on cognitive performance in healthy elders. *Am J Psychiatry* 48:73, 1991.
22. Martin RL: Geriatric psychopharmacology: Present and future. *Psychiatric Ann* 20:682, 688, 1990.
23. Holton A, George K: The use of lithium in severely demented patients with behavioral disturbance (letter). *Br J Psychiatry* 146:99, 1985.
24. Price LH et al: Lithium treatment and serotonergic function. *Arch Gen Psychiatry* 46:13, 1989.
25. Chouinard G et al: Antimanic effect of clonazepam. *Bio Psychiatry* 18:451, 1983.
26. Leibovici A, Tariot PN: Carbamazepine treatment of agitation associated with dementia. *J Geriatr Psychiatry Neurol* 1(2):110, 1988.
27. Gleason RP, Schneider LS: Carbamazepine treatment of agitation in Alzheimer's outpatients refractory to neuroleptics. *J Clin Psychiatry* 51(3):115, 1990.
28. Smeraski PJ: Clonazepam treatment of multi-infarct dementia. *J Geriatr Psychiatry Neurol* 1(1):47, 1988.
29. Weiner RD et al (eds): *The Practice of Electroconvulsive Therapy: Recommendations for Treatment, Training, and Privileging*. Task Force Report: American Psychiatric Association. Washington, DC, American Psychiatric Press, 1990.
30. Schneider LS et al: A metaanalysis of controlled trials of neuroleptic treatment in dementia. *J Am Geriatr Soc* 38:553, 1990.
31. Raskind MA et al: Dementia and antipsychotic drugs. *J Clin Psychiatry* 48(suppl):16, 1987.
32. Barnes R et al: Efficacy of antipsychotic medications in behaviorally disturbed dementia patients. *Am J Psychiatry* 139:1170, 1982.
33. Nayak RC et al: The bioavailability and pharmacokinetics of oral and depot intramuscular haloperidol in schizophrenic patients. *J Clin Pharmacol* 27:144, 1987.
34. Patterson JF: A preliminary study of carbamazepine in the treatment of assaultive patients with dementia. *J Geriatr Psychiatry Neurol* 1(1):21, 1988.
35. Pinner E, Rich C: Effects of trazodone on aggressive behavior in seven patients with organic mental disorders. *Am J Psychiatry* 145:1295, 1988.
36. Simpson D, Foster D: Improvement in organically disturbed behavior with trazodone treatment. *J Clin Psychiatry* 47:191, 1986.
37. Sobin P et al: Fluoxetine in the treatment of agitated dementia (letter). *Am J Psychiatry* 146(12):1636, 1989.
38. Lipowski ZJ: Transient cognitive disorders (delirium, acute confusional states) in the elderly. *Am J Psychiatry* 140:1426, 1983.
39. Beresin EV: Delirium in the elderly. *J Geriatr Psychiatry Neurol* 1:127, 1988.
40. Thomas DR: Assessment and management of agitation in the elderly. *Geriatrics* 43:45, 1988.
41. Tesar GE, Stern TA: Evaluation and treatment of agitation in the intensive care unit. *J Inten Care Med* 1:137, 1986.
42. Gelfand SB et al: Psychopharmacology: Using intravenous haloperidol to control delirium. *Hosp Community Psychiatry* 43:215, 1992.
43. Larson DB et al: Geriatrics, in Wolman BB (ed): *The Therapist's Handbook: Treatment Methods of Mental Disorders,* 2d ed. New York, Van Nostrand Reinhold, 1983, p 343.
44. Freud S: On psychotherapy (1896), in Jones E (ed):

Collected Papers, London RJ (trans). London, Hogarth, vol 1, 1942.

45. Blank ML: Raising the age barrier to psychotherapy. *Geriatrics* 29:141, 1974.
46. Nemiroff RA, Colarusso CA: *The Race Against Time: Psychotherapy and Psychoanalysis in the Second Half of Life.* New York, Plenum, 1985.
47. White RB, Gilliland RM: *Elements of Psychopathology: The Mechanisms of Defense.* New York, Grune & Stratton, 1975.
48. Erikson EH: *Childhood and Society,* 2d ed. New York, Norton, 1963.
49. Colarusso CA, Nemiroff RA: Clinical implications of adult developmental theory. *Am J Psychiatry* 144:1263, 1987.
50. House JS, Kahn RL: Measures and concepts of social support, in Cohen S, Syme SL (eds): *Social Support and Health.* Orlando, FL, Academic, 1985, p 83.
51. Thoits PA: Social support and psychological well-being: Theoretical possibilities, in Sarason IG, Sarason BR (eds): *Social Support: Theory, Research and Applications.* Boston, Martinus Nijhoff, 1985, p 51.
52. Strain LA, Chappel NL: Confidants: Do they make a difference in quality of life? *Res Aging* 4:479, 1982.
53. Werman DS: *The Practice of Supportive Psychotherapy.* New York, Brunner/Mazel, 1984.
54. Blazer DG: Techniques for communicating with your elderly patient. *Geriatrics* 33:79, 1978.
55. Moberg DO: Religiosity in old age. *Gerontologist* 5:78, 1965.
56. Blazer D, Palmore E: Religion and aging in a longitudinal panel. *Gerontologist* 16:82, 1976.
57. Hadaway CK: Life satisfaction and religion: A reanalysis. *Soc Forces* 57:636, 1978.
58. Ferguson JA et al: A script for deep muscle relaxation. *Dis Nerv System* 38:703, 1977.
59. Rowe JW, Kahn RL: Human aging: Usual and successful. *Science* 237:143, 1987.
60. Minuchin S: *Families and Family Therapy.* Cambridge, Harvard University Press, 1974.
61. Miller JG, Miller JL: General living systems theory, in Kaplan HI, Sadock BJ (eds): *Comprehensive Textbook of Psychiatry/IV,* 4th ed. Baltimore, Williams & Wilkins, 1985, chaps 1 and 2.
62. Gallagher DE: Intervention strategies to assist caregivers of frail elders: Current research status and future directions, in Lawton MP, Maddox G (eds): *Annual Review of Gerontology and Geriatrics.* New York, Springer, 1985, vol 5, p 249.
63. Mace NL, Rabins PV: *The 36-Hour Day: A Family Guide to Caring for Persons with Alzheimer's Disease, Related Dementia Illnesses, and Memory Loss in Later Life.* Baltimore, Johns Hopkins University Press, 1981.

PART FOUR

GERIATRIC SYNDROMES AND SPECIAL PROBLEMS OF ELDERLY PATIENTS

Chapter 105

FRAILTY

Linda P. Fried

The identification, evaluation, and treatment of frail older adults is a cornerstone of the practice of geriatric medicine. This is the case for several reasons. First, the frail elderly are the older adults most in need of health care, community and informal support services, and long-term care. Second, given the increasing numbers and proportion of older adults that are over 75 years of age, a major concern is to prepare for the care of this group most likely to be frail. It is thought that about 10 to 20 percent of persons aged 65 and older are "frail," with the proportions increasing dramatically with increasing age.[1,2] According to the AMA White Paper on Elderly Health, "after the age of 85, 46% of those living in the community fall into this group of frail elderly."[3] Finally, much of geriatric medicine is directed toward the care of the frail older adult. A basic premise is that many geriatric interventions, such as geriatric assessment, are most cost-effectively targeted to the frail elderly; this is the subset of older adults most likely to benefit from such expertise and preventive interventions and most in need of team-based care.[4]

Geriatricians often state that the clinically expert can readily distinguish a frail from a nonfrail older person. However, there is no explicit, standard clinical definition of frailty. In fact, identification of the criteria for frailty has been found to be a highly complex and demanding task. Despite the difficulty of specifying who is frail, it is important to translate clinical instinct into explicit definitions; such definitions are needed to teach geriatric medicine, to develop useful screening tools to identify persons most likely to benefit from geriatric care, and to target interventions effectively.

It is the goal of this chapter to review the currently used definitions of frailty, to propose a framework for considering the spectrum of frailty, to consider the possible etiologies of frailty, and to review potential treatments and preventive strategies.

DEFINITION OF FRAILTY

The most widely agreed upon definition of frailty is that frail older adults are vulnerable; thus, the frail elderly are those persons at highest risk of a range of adverse health outcomes.[5,6] A recent survey of geriatricians supported this assumption. Over 90 percent of one group of academic geriatricians agreed that frail older adults are identifiable as those at high risk for dependency, institutionalization, falls, injuries, acute illness, hospitalization, slow recovery from illness, and mortality.[7]

Another approach to the definition of frailty is to identify the older individual at risk for these adverse events *before* they have occurred. Such a definition is essential to effective prevention of these outcomes. In the current literature, the frail older adult is variously identified by one or more of the following characteristics: extreme old age,[4] disability,[6,8–10] and the presence of multiple chronic diseases (comorbidity) and/or geriatric syndromes.[11–13] Each of these characteristics has been used as a measure of frailty itself, often because these characteristics are considered to predict those at highest risk of adverse outcomes.

In terms of disability, measures that have been used as indicating frailty include dependency in mobility and/or activities of daily living (ADL),[6,14] chronic limitation in instrumental activities of daily living (IADL) or ADL,[9] and high scores on an index of vulnerability which primarily assesses physical function.[2] The prevalence of physical disability increases with increasing age. It is associated with fair or poor self-assessed health or self-reported health being worse than 1 year ago. Disability is also a predictor of future risk; for example, it is associated with increased use of physician services, hospitalizations, and mortality.[10,15–17] Thus, older individuals with physical disability are clearly at high risk. A clinician is likely to assess a patient with problems ambulating as being more frail than one who has no such problems. However, it is not clear that disability is the same as frailty; clinical judgment also suggests that many frail individuals are disabled, but not all disabled individuals are frail.

Use of disability as an indicator of frailty does assist in the identification of those with special medical and service needs and in planning for service provision at an organizational level.[6,18] However, it may not sufficiently identify those who are clinically frail, particularly those who are not disabled, while including some who may not be frail.

Alternatively, it has been suggested that physical disability is an outcome of being frail.[19] That is, the term *frailty* may refer to a physiologic state that increases the risk of disability, along with the other adverse outcomes described above. Given clinical perception that there is not a one-to-one match between frail patients and those who are disabled, it appears reasonable to consider whether there is a more broadly defined clinical syndrome of frailty.

The presence of multiple chronic diseases (comorbidity) is often used as another marker of frailty. Not surprisingly, comorbidity is associated with increased risk of adverse outcomes as evidenced by higher short- and long-term mortality rates[10] and significantly increased physical disability[20] compared to those without chronic diseases. However, the presence of comorbidity may not identify the highest-risk groups or those most frail. For example, longitudinal follow-up of persons 70 years and older, surveyed in the Health Interview Survey Supplement on Aging, showed rates of new confinement to bed or chair for those with two or more chronic diseases (i.e., arthritis, heart disease, stroke, diabetes, cancer, cataracts, broken hip) was only slightly greater than that for all persons 70 and older; 24 versus 17 percent, respectively, were newly confined after 2 years. In contrast, 36 percent of those with physical disability as well as two or more chronic diseases were newly confined to a bed or chair after 2 years, as were 42 percent of those 80 years and older who also had the other characteristics of disability and comorbidity.[7] Thus, comorbidity alone does not appear to capture the group at highest risk of adverse outcomes, which is theoretically the group that would be frail. This may be because just identifying the presence of a chronic disease does not specify those with severe disease.

Therefore, the presence of comorbidity alone may not be synonymous with frailty. These population-based data are supported by conclusions from a consensus conference of geriatricians and gerontologists. This group concurred that the presence of chronic disease, in itself, is generally not sufficient to define the older adult who is frail; rather, it was thought that other physiologic processes may be more central to the development of frailty.[21] It is hypothesized that disease may worsen the health and functional status of an individual who is highly vulnerable due to a physiologic state of frailty. The following considers whether there is evidence for a clinical definition of the symptoms and signs of the physiologic state of frailty.

FRAILTY AS A CLINICAL SYNDROME

Frailty is more likely a clinical syndrome reflecting underlying physiologic changes of aging that are not disease-specific. Consistent with the definition of a syndrome, its presentation may vary across a constellation of possible manifestations. These may include nonlocalizing or constitutional symptoms such as weakness, fatigue, poor appetite, undernutrition, dehydration, and weight loss.[1,20,22–24] In addition, the presence of geriatric syndromes may help identify a frail individual. These include balance and gait abnormalities, severe deconditioning, confusion, incontinence, and depression[1,23–26] (see Fig. 105-1). These clinical characteristics have been shown to be highly predictive of a range of adverse outcomes associated with frailty, including rapid decline in function, institutionalization, and mortality.

It may be that it is the occurrence of a critical mass of physiologic changes that lead to frailty rather than any one change. Consistent with this hypothesis, 100 percent of one group of geriatricians thought that frailty was more likely to be found in individuals with *more* than one defining characteristic.[7] This has a parallel in studies on causes of falling in older adults, which show that the etiology is likely to be multifactorial. In addition, the number of risk factors present is important, in itself, in increasing risk of falls.[25,27]

Some characteristics which clinicians often associate with frailty may not necessarily be specific to being frail. For example, Speechley and Tinetti[26] have recently shown that falls occur in both frail and nonfrail, or vigorous, older individuals. They developed and applied a definition of frailty that includes a constellation of markers, with frail individuals defined as having four or more of the following characteristics: age over 80, balance and gait abnormalities, infrequent walking for exercise, depression, sedative use, decreased strength in shoulder and/or knees, lower-extremity disability, and near vision loss. This frail group fell three times more frequently than the vigorous group (52 versus 17 percent), but falls were still common among the vigorous group. However, the percentage of falls resulting in serious injury was much higher in the vigorous group than the frail group (22 versus 6 percent). Data indicated that the circumstances of falling differed between the two groups: the frail group were most likely to fall at home, while the vigorous group primarily fell in more active endeavors away from home or on stairs.[27] Thus, while the fact of falling may not adequately differentiate frail from nonfrail individuals, the history of the situations associated with falling may be important in providing insight into who is and is not frail.

The symptoms and conditions described above appear to identify many who are frail. However, it should be recognized that these factors may not always be present or clinically evident. Some older individuals may escape these definitions, be functioning well, and yet display little reserve in the face of a stressor such as a hip fracture and manifest unexpected but catastrophic decline. Data are needed to further define the clinical syndrome of frailty and to determine whether specific combinations of characteristics further improve the identification of those who are frail.

MODAL PATHWAY OF FRAILTY		
UNDERLYING ALTERATIONS	CLINICAL SYNDROME OF FRAILTY	ADVERSE OUTCOMES OF FRAILTY
DISEASE (Pathophysiology) → DECLINE IN PHYSIOLOGIC FUNCTION AND RESERVE →	SYMPTOMS •Weakness •Fatigue •Anorexia •Undernutrition •Weight loss SIGNS •Physiologic changes marking increased risk •Decreased muscle mass •Decreased bone mass •Balance and gait abnormalities •Severe deconditioning	→ •FALLS •INJURIES •ACUTE ILLNESSES •HOSPITALIZATIONS •DISABILITY •DEPENDENCY •INSTITUTIONALIZATION •DEATH

FIGURE 105-1
The modal pathway of frailty. It is necessary to distinguish the clinical syndrome, or presentation, of the frail older individual from the consequences of frailty and from its underlying etiology. Such a framework provides a basis for identifying appropriate primary, secondary, and tertiary prevention strategies.

THE TRAJECTORY AND STAGES OF FRAILTY

Recent evidence suggests that there are additional dimensions in defining the clinical status of a frail older adult besides the determination that frailty is present. First, the trajectory of decline that an individual is on may provide important insight into both the diagnosis and the severity of decline relative to the individual's baseline.[28] For example, the duration as well as severity of weight loss provides an indication of the overall debilitation of the patient relative to his or her baseline state. In addition, the long-term health status is likely to be shaped by the individual's history of exposure to adverse health practices, such as low levels of physical activity or inadequate nutritional intake over many years.[29] Clinical onset of frailty may come earlier or more severely in those with a long history of deleterious health practices; for example, a person with a sedentary lifestyle throughout adulthood may be more likely to become severely deconditioned after a brief illness than an individual of the same age who has a long history of regular exercise.

There also may be stages of frailty. Speechley and Tinetti[26] have suggested that there may be a transitional state between "vigor" and "frailty." In their study, this transitional state was characterized by having three rather than four or more of the characteristics of frailty described above, or only a few characteristics of "vigor" as defined in that study. The transition group was found to have an intermediate risk of falls between the vigorous and frail groups. This finding is supportive of the concept that clinical frailty results from a critical mass of physiologic decrements and that risk increases with the number of decrements present. It remains to be determined whether this transitional stage does, in fact, predict development of frailty. However, it is suggestive that there may be an earlier stage of frailty for which older persons should be screened and appropriate interventions instituted. Such a transitional group is one that may be optimally targeted to prevent further progression to frailty.

It has been suggested by Buchner and Wagner[19] that an important pathway to frailty may be the episodic loss of capacity due to illness or other insult which is followed by an incomplete recovery. They hypothesize that recovery can be blocked because chronic illness prevents resumption of normal activities or because depression or other psychosocial factors adversely contribute to the trajectory of decline. Recovery may also be more difficult in those with low levels of physiologic capacity prior to the insult. If it is demonstrated that lack of full recovery after an illness is a major contributor to the development of frailty, it would emphasize the need to aggressively rehabilitate at-risk individuals after an acute illness, as well as to utilize "prehabilitation" when surgery is anticipated.

There is also mounting evidence that a late stage of frailty may not be reversible. This has, with some hesitancy, been called a "failure to thrive" syndrome. This is a clinical diagnosis given to the sickest and frailest of older adults. A study[24] that evaluated the characteristics of hospitalized individuals given this diagnosis over a 1-year period in one hospital showed that their mean age was 79 years, and the patients had an average of six diagnoses. A constellation of symptoms, found on chart review, parallels the clinical syndrome defined for frailty, above. In addition, these individuals with failure to thrive generally were found to be malnourished, often dehydrated, with skin ulcers, falls, pain, and physical and cognitive disabilities. Most important, the possibility of effective intervention appeared very limited in this population, with 16 percent dying during the hospitalization, and with very limited rehabilitation potential in the remainder of the sample of patients. A separate study was done of the clinical syndrome of rapid functional decline in a population of independently ambulating older individuals.[23] Those who had nonlocalizing signs associated with a rapid decline in mobility and taking to bed were found to die within 6 months.

Clinical symptoms of the end stage of frailty are thought to have associated signs, including unintentional weight loss, low muscle mass, substantial weakness, and metabolic abnormalities including anemia of chronic disease, lymphopenia, hypoalbuminemia, hypocholesterolemia, or worsening glucose tolerance.[29] Frailty can progress to a point that it results in irreversible losses in muscle mass and the severe metabolic abnormalities associated with cachexia. Elderly patients with this presentation are the most highly vulnerable to acute illness and injury, medication side effects and iatrogenesis, with likely catastrophic decline and death.

It is possible that this irreversible end stage of frailty, with its associated rapid decline, represents the end of life, when a compression of morbidity occurs.[29] In this scenario, an individual lives independently and, when the limits of the life span are reached, decline and death occur over a brief period of time. If this is the case, then not all frailty should necessarily be treated or prevented. However, much of frailty may be premature and reversible. It is most important to recognize preventable frailty before its progression to an irreversible stage. While much remains to be done to fully characterize the constituents of frailty and the components that are reversible, it is important to recognize the syndrome as early as possible, with the goal of preventing unnecessary onset or adverse consequences. Consideration of the possible etiologies of frailty, as described below, should assist in the development of clinical interventions. In addition, ability to distinguish between those with reversible and irreversible frailty should assist in decisions about prognosis, treatment, and resource use. Given that the frail elderly utilize a substantial proportion of health care resources, a scientific basis for making decisions about which treatments are appropriate or effective is greatly needed.

POTENTIAL ETIOLOGIES OF FRAILTY

Frailty is often seen by geriatricians as "inherent vulnerability to challenge from the environment."[5] The likely physiologic basis of this vulnerability has often been conceived of as a loss of homeostatic mechanisms or of physiologic reserve. Such loss of reserves would explain the relative difficulty frail individuals have in compensating for stresses to their system while often appearing compensated in an unstressed state. While this explanation has face validity clinically, its physiologic basis has not been definitively explained. The following section will review some of the possible explanations for the physiologic basis of frailty.

Across multiple organ systems, there are strikingly similar observations about changes associated with aging. First, changes with aging are generally more notable in terms of the organism's responses to stress than in evaluation in the basal state. Second, integrative functions are slower to respond and adapt to challenges in older adults, and often slower to end the response, than in younger persons. This is thought to underlie the lower resistance of older persons to extremes of temperature or other stressing conditions. Third, at a cellular level, a frequent, though not uniform, finding is of a loss of receptors which may underlie the decrements in responding to challenges. This loss of receptors can lead to decreased responsiveness, or decreased inhibitions of response and overprolonged responsiveness, depending on the function of the receptors. Finally, decline in function in a single organ or system may not be sufficient to compromise reserve, but it may be that multiple decrements in organ or system function contribute to the syndrome of enhanced vulnerability to stressors that we call frailty.

Age-related changes in several organ systems have been specifically considered as contributing to frailty. The hypothalamic-pituitary-adrenal axis, which is a central regulator of homeostasis and of response to exogenous and endogenous stressors, is likely to be important in the pathogenesis of frailty. One theory regarding this axis is that older animals show a decreased ability to terminate the adrenocortical response to stress due to a decrease in hippocampal glucocorticoid receptors.[31] It has also been theorized that a prolongation of poststress corticosterone elevation may contribute to the presence of catabolic states often seen in frailty as well as possibly the myopathy or immunocompromise that have been proposed as components of frailty.

Recent attention has focused on decline in growth hormone levels with age. This includes decreased spontaneous growth hormone secretion and decreased amplitude of spontaneous nocturnal growth hormone pulses.[32] In addition, there are decreased basal serum levels of insulinlike growth factor I

(IGF-1), likely reflecting the decreased growth hormone levels, since plasma IGF-1 response to growth hormone is unaltered in the elderly.[33,34] These age-associated changes have been thought to potentially contribute to the decreased protein synthesis and muscle mass as well as decreased bone and diminished immunologic status in older persons. Thus, these changes appear to contribute to the syndrome of frailty. This theory has been tested in recent clinical trials of short-term exogenous administration of recombinant human growth hormone (rhGH). Of relevance in terms of frailty, one of these trials showed increases in lean body mass of 9 percent, with a 14 percent decrease in adipose tissue mass, when exogenous growth hormone was administered to 21 healthy, growth-hormone-deficient men between the ages of 61 and 81.[35] More trials are needed before clinical utility can be determined. However, these data suggest that growth hormone deficiency may play a role in the clinical syndrome of frailty.

As the individual ages, changes in the immune system occur, with loss of its effectiveness in combating newly introduced antigens. Aging is associated with an increased frequency of lymphoproliferative disorders, and susceptibility to infections and autoimmune disorders is also increased. There is ample evidence that the decline of the immune system in aged individuals is predominantly due to T-cell dysfunction, especially that of the helper T cells, whose normal functions of proliferation and cytokine production are reduced.[36] However, the biological mechanism of the decline of T-cell function is not clear. It is possible that dysregulation of the immune system could result in an imbalance in the production of inflammatory cytokines and T-cell growth factors, which, in turn, could predispose to or even cause the development of vulnerability to infection as a component of the syndrome of frailty. A better understanding of the specific changes in immunologic functioning associated with aging could lead to improved treatment and/or prevention of frailty.

Discussions of frailty often begin with recognition of the decline in muscle mass and strength that characterizes frail individuals. Many animal studies have shown a decline in structure and mass of skeletal muscle with age. Some of these studies demonstrate extensive age-related changes, including altered calcium metabolism, degeneration of nerve-muscle contact, and decreased ability to develop active tension. In contrast, other studies in healthy animals show the only age-related change to be increased muscle stiffness with age; no other functional decline was identified.[37] The suggestion from the latter studies is that decrements in muscle strength, mass, and function may not be inevitable concomitants of aging and may be more specific to the syndrome of frailty. While a change in muscle stiffness alone is important because it can affect dynamics of movement, its importance would be exacerbated with superimposed loss of muscle mass. If this line of evidence is supported in future studies, it would suggest that the causes of loss of muscle mass and function should be sought in modifiable factors of decline in physical activity level and hormonal levels that maintain muscle mass.

Clinical observation suggests that declines in energy expenditure and intake associated with aging are most pronounced in the frail older adult. In fact, a clinical indicator of the frail individual is often the history of infrequently going outside the home; that is, these are individuals with relatively little energy expenditure through physical activity. Habitual low levels of physical activity are associated with loss of muscle mass and hence also strength. Resulting declines in maximal oxygen consumption are due to alterations in muscle metabolism and loss of skeletal muscle mass as well as cardiovascular deconditioning. Such extensive deconditioning as is seen in frail older adults can well exacerbate functional problems; for example, sedentary older adults can expend 90 percent of their maximal oxygen consumption capacity in the performance of their ADLs.[38] In addition, recent evidence suggests that daily energy intake is, in part, a function of the level of physical activity in which an older individual engages.[39] Inactivity is associated with a lower intake of energy and protein, reduced whole-body protein turnover, and a resulting net loss of body protein.[40] This suggests that the inactivity resulting from frailty may further exacerbate the severity of frailty.

Thus, it appears that a number of independent physiologic processes may contribute to the syndrome of frailty, with its inherent vulnerability to stressors and decreased ability to maintain homeostasis. These processes may cause frailty by their independent presence or by a summary effect that is greater than the sum of the parts. In addition, they may contribute to each other. For example, growth hormone deficiency may contribute to a decline in muscle and bone mass and decrements in immunologic function. Growth hormone as well as independent aging effects on muscle may contribute to a decline in muscle mass and function, which then impacts on maximal oxygen consumption, exercise tolerance, and nutritional intake. This web is likely to be much more complicated than this discussion can suggest. However, it is simplistically represented by the web diagram (Fig. 105-2) which displays the hypothesized interrelationships between these physiologic changes.

TREATMENT OF FRAILTY

While there is still insufficient knowledge about the causes of frailty, therapeutic approaches can be based on our current understanding. It is important to try to recognize vulnerable, frail individuals before the occurrence of the adverse outcomes for which they are at risk. With this recognition, clinical approaches could include both careful attention to prevention of adverse outcomes, including falls and medication side effects. In addition, there is good evidence to suggest that increasing the physical activity level of a frail

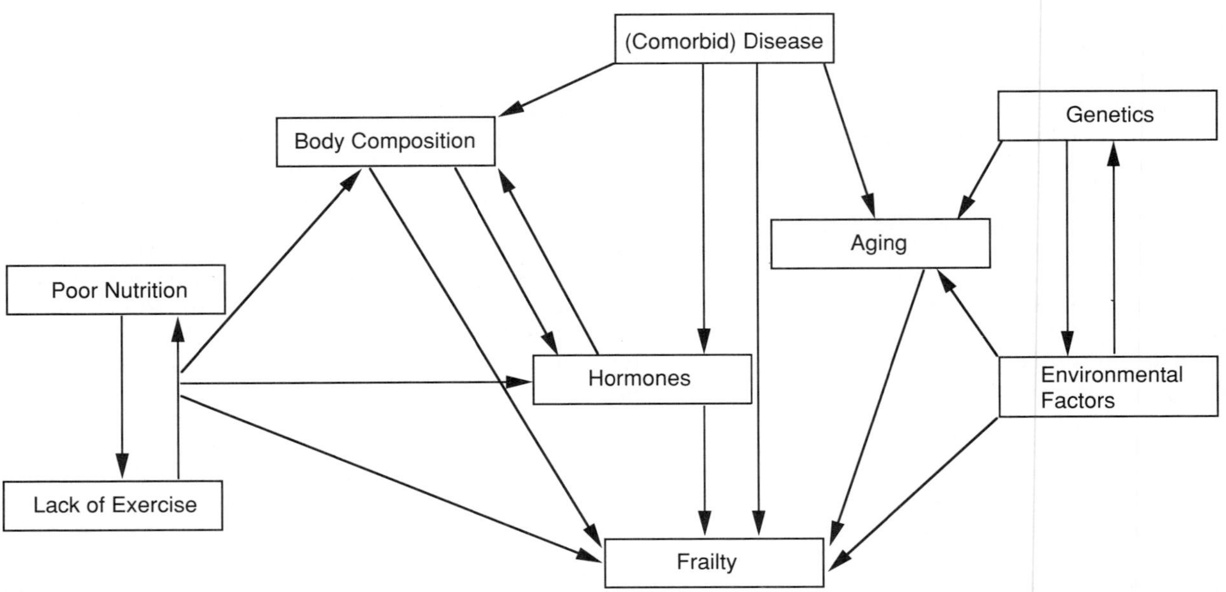

FIGURE 105-2
Physiologic contributors to frailty. Hypothetical web diagram of physiologic changes that may contribute to the onset or progression of frailty, emphasizing the potential interactions and relationships between these changes and the clinical syndrome of frailty.

older adult in small increments is likely to be an important preventive intervention resulting in improved strength, flexibility, exercise tolerance, and nutritional intake. One recent study has shown that frail nonagenarians can participate in strength training and substantially increase muscle strength.[41] A recent clinical trial in healthy older men indicates that regular moderate physical activity (1000 Kcal per week) increases resting metabolic rate and energy intake by 17 percent.[40] While such studies need to be done in frail populations of men and women, they suggest that the potential benefit of physical activity may extend well beyond exercise tolerance to maintenance of nutritional status. The use of general exercise programs may turn out to be a central intervention for the frail older adult, along with prehabilitation and rehabilitation, to prevent the marked decline that may be associated with prolonged bed rest from an illness or surgery. Use of other interventions, such as growth hormone, may turn out to be effective in improving parameters associated with frailty, such as lean body mass and strength, but further studies need to be done before such recommendations can be made on a population basis. Treatment of the frail older adult must also include improved quality of acute hospital care using individualized treatment plans. This has been shown to make an important difference in the outcomes of hospitalized frail patients, as demonstrated in randomized controlled trials of inpatient geriatric assessment units.[42]

Further studies of frailty are needed to assist not only in identifying those at risk of adverse outcomes but also in helping to select the patients most likely to benefit from interventions.[4] The clinical manifestations of frailty may be markers of increased risk in themselves. They may also identify those most vulnerable to the influence of extrinsic adverse conditions, such as loss of social support or environmental hazards. In one study that has evaluated the interaction between different patient characteristics, future institutionalization was best predicted by the combined effects of physical disability, especially dependency in ADLs, with psychosocial factors such as living alone, age over 75 years, being female, being in fair or poor health, and being cognitively impaired.[43] The interaction among factors in an already vulnerable individual may contribute to the adverse outcomes associated with frailty and may further help to target those at highest risk and the components of the problem most amenable to intervention.

REFERENCES

1. Winograd CH et al: Screening for frailty: Criteria and predictors of outcomes. *J Am Geriatr Soc* 39:778, 1991.
2. Tennstedt SL et al: Informal care for frail elders: The role of secondary caregivers. *Gerontologist* 29:677, 1989.
3. Report of the Council on Scientific Affairs: American Medical Association White Paper on Elderly Health. *Arch Intern Med* 150:2459, 1990.
4. Winograd CH: Targeting strategies: An overview of criteria and outcomes. *J Am Geriatr Soc* 39(suppl):255, 1991.
5. Fretwell MD: Acute hospital care for frail older patients, in Hazzard WR, Andres R, Bierman EL, Blass JP (eds): *Principles of Geriatric Medicine and Gerontology*, 2nd ed, 1985, pp 247–253.
6. National Institute on Aging: *Physical Frailty: A Reducible Barrier to Independence for Older Americans.* Report to US House of Representatives Committee on Appropriations, DHHS, PHS, National Institutes of Health, National Institute on Aging, Bethesda, MD, February, 1991.
7. Fried LP et al: The epidemiology of frailty: The scope of the problem, in Perry HM, Morley JE, Coe RM (eds): *Aging, Musculoskeletal Disorders and Care of the Frail Elderly.* New York, Springer, 1993, pp 3–16.
8. National Institute on Aging: *Frailty Reconsidered: Workshop on Reducing Frailty and Fall-Related Injuries in Older Persons.* Sponsored by National Institute on Aging (NIA), National Center for Nursing Research (NCNR), and Centers for Disease Control (CDC), September 27–30, 1988.
9. Soldo BJ et al: Family, households, and care arrangements of frail older women: A structural analysis. *J Gerontol Soc Sci* 45:S238, 1990.
10. Guralnik JM, Wallace RB: The conceptualization and design of intervention studies on frailty in the older populations: Insights from observational epidemiologic studies, in Weindruch R, Ory M, Hadley E (eds): *Reducing Frailty and Fall-Related Injuries in Older Persons.* Springfield, IL, Charles C Thomas, 1991, pp 29–43.
11. Jencks SF, Kay T: Do frail, disabled, poor and very old Medicare beneficiaries have higher hospital charges? *JAMA* 257:198, 1987.
12. Kellogg FR et al: Life-sustaining interventions in frail elderly persons: Talking about choices. *Arch Intern Med* 152:2317, 1992.
13. Winograd CH et al: Targeting the hospitalized elderly for geriatric consultation. *J Am Geriatr Soc* 36:1113, 1988.
14. Woodhouse KW et al: Who are the frail elderly? *QJ Med* 255:505, 1988.
15. Fried LP, Bush TL: Morbidity as a focus of preventive health care in the elderly. *Epidemiol Rev* 10:48, 1988.
16. Guralnik JM et al: Morbidity and disability in older persons in the years prior to death. *Am J Public Health* 81:443, 1991.
17. Oktay JS, Volland PJ: Post-hospital support program for the frail elderly and their caregivers. A quasi-experimental evaluation. *Am J Public Health* 80:39, 1990.
18. Gillick MR: Long-term care options for the frail elderly. *J Am Geriatr Soc* 37:1198, 1989.
19. Buchner DM, Wagner EH: Preventing frail health. *Clin Geriatr Med* 8:1, 1992.
20. Guralnik JM et al: Aging in the eighties: The prevalence of comorbidity and its association with disability. Advance data from vital and health statistics, no. 170. Hyattsville, MD, National Center for Health Statistics, 1989.
21. Fried LP: Conference on the physiologic basis of frailty: Introduction. *Aging Clin Exp Res* 4(3):251, 1992.
22. Williamson JD, Fried LP: Characteristics of frail older adults: The basis for screening and prevention. *Clin Res* 41(2):226A, 1993.
23. Clark LP et al: Taking to bed: Rapid functional decline in an independently mobile older population living in an intermediate-care facility. *J Am Geriatr Soc* 38:967, 1990.
24. Berkman B et al: Failure to thrive: Paradigm for the frail elder. *Gerontologist* 29:654, 1989.
25. Tinetti ME et al: Risk factors for falls among elderly persons living in the community. *N Engl J Med* 319:1701, 1988.
26. Speechley M, Tinetti M: Falls and injuries in frail and vigorous community elderly persons. *J Am Geriatr Soc* 39:46, 1991.
27. Nevitt ME et al: Risk factors for recurrent nonsyncopal falls: A prospective study. *JAMA* 261:2663, 1989.
28. Harris TB, Feldman JJ: Implications of health status in analysis of risk in older persons. *J Aging Health* 3(2): 262, 1991.
29. Verdery R: Malnutrition and chronic inflammation: Causes or effects of frailty? *Aging Clin Exp Res* 4:11, 1992.
30. Fries JF: Aging, natural death, and the compression of morbidity. *N Engl J Med* 303:130, 1980.
31. Martin JB, Reichlin S (eds): *Clinical Neuroendocrinology*, 2nd ed. Philadelphia, Davis, 1987.
32. Ho KY et al: Effects of sex and age on 24-hour profile of growth hormone secretion in men and women: Importance of endogenous estradiol concentrations. *J Clin Endocrinol Metab* 64:51, 1987.
33. Pavlov EP et al: Responses of growth hormone and somatomedin-C to GH-releasing hormone in healthy aging men. *J Clin Endocrinol Metab* 62:595, 1986.
34. Iranmanesh et al: Age and relative adiposity are specific negative determinants of the frequency and amplitude of growth hormone (GH) secretory bursts and the half-life of endogenous GH in healthy men. *J Clin Endocrinol Metab* 73:1081, 1991.
35. Rudman D et al: Effect of human growth hormone in men over 60 years old. *N Engl J Med* 323:1, 1990.
36. Margolick JB, Chopra RK: Relationship between the immune system and frailty: Pathogenesis of immune deficiency in HIV infection and aging. *Aging Clin Exp Res* 4(3):255, 1992.
37. McCarter RJM, Nelly NG: Decline in neuromuscular function as an index of frailty: Insights from studies in aging rodents. *Aging Clin Exp Res* 4(3):264, 1992.
38. Blessey RL: Energy cost in the physically impaired

geriatric population. *Topics Geriatr Rehab* 2(1):33, 1986.
39. Poehlman ET et al: Influence of endurance training on energy intake, norepinephrine kinetics and metabolic rate in older persons. *Metabolism* 41(9):941, 1992.
40. Poehlman ET: Metabolic deterioration with advancing age: The role of physical activity. *Aging Clin Exp Res* 4(3):260, 1992.
41. Fiatarone MA et al: High-intensity strength training in nonagenarians. *JAMA* 263:3029, 1990.
42. Rubenstein LZ et al: Impacts of geriatric evaluation and management programs on defined outcomes: Overview of the evidence. *J Am Geriatr Soc* 39(suppl):8S, 1991.
43. Shapiro E, Tate R: Who is really at risk of institutionalization? *Gerontologist* 28:237, 1988.

Chapter 106

APPROACH TO THE DIAGNOSIS AND TREATMENT OF THE INFECTED OLDER ADULT

Thomas T. Yoshikawa

EPIDEMIOLOGY

Prevalence of Important Infections

Older adults—particularly those who are 75 years and older—are at high risk for acquiring an infection.[1] Currently available data indicate that this increased susceptibility with old age is limited to select infectious diseases (Table 106-1).[2] However, several of these infections are those that are the most frequently encountered by physicians in their clinical practice, i.e., pneumonia, urinary tract infection, sepsis, intraabdominal infections, and soft-tissue infections.

Some of the important infections of the older adult (pneumonia, tuberculosis, and herpes zoster) are reviewed in depth elsewhere in this book and, therefore, will not be discussed in any detail in this chapter. Pneumonia occurs at a higher rate—up to 60 percent of all cases—in individuals 65 years or older compared with younger patients.[3] The prevalence of urinary tract infection as well as asymptomatic bacteriuria increases significantly with advancing age, in both men and women.[4] This prevalence varies from 10 to 50 percent, depending on the patient's residential status, functional limitations, underlying genitourinary disorders, and gender. Urinary tract infections alone account for 30 to 50 percent of all cases of bacteremia and sepsis in the older adult regardless of the setting.[5,6] Bacteremia and sepsis, especially gram-negative bacillary sepsis, occur predominantly in the elderly population, who account for 40 percent of all cases and 60 percent of all sepsis deaths.[6]

Acute diverticulitis and cholecystitis are important intraabdominal infections that are more common in the older adult.[7] Although acute appendicitis is primarily a surgical disease of the young, it does occur in approximately 5 percent of adults aged 60 and older.[8] The diagnosis is only infrequently considered in this age group, with resulting diagnostic and therapeutic

TABLE 106-1

Important Infectious Diseases of Older Adults

Infections	Comments
Pneumonia	Leading cause of death due to infection in elderly patients.
Urinary tract infection	Most common cause of bacteremia and sepsis in older adults.
Intraabdominal infections	Gangrene of appendix and gallbladder is highest in elderly persons; diverticulitis occurs primarily in older adults.
Soft-tissue infection	Pressure ulcers (decubitus ulcers) and postoperative wound infections are most common in older age group.
Bacteremia-sepsis	Of all cases, 40 percent occur in elderly persons; 60 percent of sepsis deaths occur in the older adult.
Infective endocarditis	Increased prevalence with old age; 30 to 50 percent of cases occur in persons over 60 years.
Tuberculosis	Approximately 25 to 30 percent of all U.S. cases occur in older adults; 60 percent of deaths due to tuberculosis are in persons 65 years and older.
Septic arthritis	Previous joint disease increases risk in the older adult.
Tetanus	Of all U.S. cases, 60 percent occur in older adults.
Herpes zoster (shingles)	Prevalence increases with age; postherpetic neuralgia occurs primarily in elderly persons.

delays; thus, morbidity and mortality are extremely high. Of all deaths due to appendicitis, 60 to 70 percent occur in persons over the age of 60 years.

In the preantibiotic era, infective endocarditis occurred predominantly in young adults. However, over the past 20 years, the demography of infective endocarditis has changed to involve more older adults (30 to 50 percent of all cases), with several studies reporting a mean age of the patients of approximately 55 years.[9] This rise in age reflects the fact that infective endocarditis involves valves with degenerative or atherosclerotic changes.[10]

Tuberculosis is evolving into an infection that is dominated by the aging population including nursing home patients.[11–14] Septic arthritis is a particularly important problem in the aged because of the high prevalence of preexisting joint disease (e.g., osteoarthritis, rheumatoid arthritis, gout, and pseudogout) as well as the common occurrence of prosthetic joints.[15,16] Of the various soft-tissue infections, infected pressure ulcers (decubitus ulcers) occur most commonly in the elderly patients,[17,18] with a frequency that varies from 5 to 10 percent. Because of waning immunity and lack of adequate immunization in the older patient, 60 percent of tetanus cases in the United States occur in persons 60 years and older.[19] Finally, herpes zoster (shingles) increases in frequency with old age,[20] most likely related to the decline in cell-mediated immunity that is associated with senescence. More importantly, the dreaded complication of postherpetic neuralgia is seen primarily in individuals over the age of 60.[20,21]

Mortality Related to Infections

Elderly persons are at increased risk for more-serious infections as well as more-severe complications including death.[22,23] Several factors related to aging contribute to poorer outcomes of older adults with infections[24]: (1) limited physiologic reserve capacities in response to stress, (2) alterations in host defense mechanisms, (3) presence of chronic and debilitating illnesses, (4) greater exposure to nosocomial pathogens, (5) delays in diagnosis and treatment, (6) higher frequency of complications from diagnostic and therapeutic procedures, (7) delayed response to chemotherapy, and (8) higher incidence of adverse reaction to antimicrobial drugs.

When comparative studies or data are available, the difference in mortality between the young and older adult is striking. The following are several examples. The mortality for hospitalized elderly patients with pneumonia is 12.8 per 100 hospital discharges compared with 1.5 per 100 hospital discharges for younger patients.[25] Elderly persons with acute appendicitis experience death at a rate 10 to 15 times that of young adults.[7] Gram-negative bacillary sepsis is associated with a mortality that is two to three times higher in older adults. Similar mortality figures are found when comparing bacterial meningitis and infective endocarditis in the young versus older adult.[26,27]

AGING AND INFECTION RISK FACTORS

Since the topic of immunity and aging is reviewed elsewhere in this book, the discussion here will focus on other factors that appear to place the older adult at greater risk or susceptibility to infectious diseases.

Environmental Factors

Not only are older adults hospitalized more frequently, but the duration of their hospitalization is generally longer than that of younger patients. This places the older adult at greater risk for acquisition of nosocomial infections. When age alone is considered, the nosocomial infection rate in elderly patients is significantly higher than in adults under 65 years old.[28] Similarly, the very old population provides the highest census in long-term care facilities. In both the acute care hospital setting and long-term care facility, urinary tract infection, pneumonia, soft-tissue infections, and bacteremia are the dominant infectious diseases.[28–30] Moreover, the attack rate for each of these infections is two to five times higher in the very old compared with young adults.[28] Unfortunately, under these circumstances, gram-negative bacilli are the most frequently isolated etiologic pathogens. They are often resistant to several antibiotics and tend to infect individuals with poor host resistance. They frequently cause bacteremia and sepsis and are associated with high mortality.

Host Factors

The Physiologic Changes of Aging

Physiologic changes include a variety of anatomic and functional alterations in tissues and organs. For example, diminished blood perfusion, alterations in permeability, decreased cough reflex, loss of cells, calcification, thinning of skin, and altered gastric motility are biological changes that might increase the risk of infection.[1]

Chronic Diseases

These diseases are common in older adults, and many of these disorders increase the susceptibility of the individual to infection. For example, dementia and strokes are associated with higher frequency of pneumonia, urinary tract infection, and pressure sores because these neurologic problems cause motor dysfunction, immobility, incontinence, poor personal hygiene, poor cough and swallowing reflexes, and diminished cognition. Similarly, tumors and cancers cause anatomic changes, obstruction, and altered blood flow, as well as compromised host defense mechanisms either from the disease or the associated therapy—all of which predispose the patient to infections.

Aberration of Host Defense Mechanisms

Changes in host defense mechanisms occur more frequently in older adults, from either the aging process or chronic underlying diseases.[1,22] Although aging alone may not be associated with dramatic changes in phagocytosis by neutrophils and macrophages and in complement function, it is likely that some of the chronic diseases that are seen in elderly patients do impact on these host defense mechanisms. Moreover, there is increasing evidence that neutrophil functions as part of the inflammation process are significantly influenced or regulated by various cytokines (which are part of the immune system).[31] With the finding of functional impairments of cell-mediated immunity with aging, the association of aging and phagocytic dysfunction may become more apparent in the future.

Clinical Features of Infections

Although the topic of altered presentations of diseases in elderly persons is discussed in Chap. 22, it is worthwhile to review some important aspects of the clinical manifestations of infection in the older adult.

Fever

Fever, whether elicited by history or determined by physical examination, is a cardinal characteristic of most infectious diseases. Although fever in children or young adults is frequently caused by relatively benign illnesses (e.g., pharyngitis, otitis media, viral syndrome), the rapid development of an elevated body temperature in an older adult is almost invariably due to a serious infectious disease, e.g., pneumonia, urinary tract infection, intraabdominal sepsis.[32] It is imperative, therefore, that the clinician carefully evaluate the febrile elderly patient for a potential serious infectious disease before the patient is released from the clinic, office, or emergency room as simply having a benign illness.

In older adults who have prolonged fever of undetermined origin (FUO), infections have been found to be the cause of FUO in approximately 40 percent of cases.[33] Neoplasms and connective tissue diseases account for the remaining cases of FUO.

Although the presence of fever in the aged person usually heralds a serious underlying problem, elderly persons when compared with younger adults more often fail to show a temperature elevation despite having a serious infectious disease.[34] In comparative studies of fever in younger versus older adults with bacteremia,[35] pneumonia,[36] infective endocarditis,[27] and tuberculosis,[12] the lack of a fever response occurred two to three times more often in elderly patients. However, in some frail elderly patients, fever response is adequate but the temperature spike is below 37.8°C (100°F) because the baseline temperature is low, e.g., 35°C (96°F).[37]

Other Features

In addition to a blunted fever response, other clinical manifestations of an infection may be atypical or nonspecific in the older adult. Like many illnesses that affect elderly persons, such nonspecific symptoms as anorexia, fatigue, and weight loss as well as atypical complaints of incontinence, falls, or mental confusion may be the primary clinical manifestation of an infection.

DIAGNOSTIC APPROACH

Differential Diagnosis

In older adults who present with typical clinical manifestations of a particular infection (e.g., fever, dysuria, frequency, and urgency for urinary tract infection), the diagnostic approach is straightforward and uncomplicated. However, in those elderly individuals who manifest only nonspecific symptoms or who have atypical complaints within a short period, an infectious disease must always be considered in the differential diagnosis.[1]

It is not practical or cost-effective to initiate an extensive diagnostic evaluation for an infectious disease in patients in whom the most likely type of infection is not clinically apparent. Certainly, determining which underlying diseases are present is often helpful in suspecting which infection and/or microorganisms might be the most probable cause. For example, chronic obstructive lung disease is most frequently complicated by pneumonia; prostatic enlargement is complicated by urinary tract infection; gallstones are complicated by bacillary sepsis; and leukemia is complicated by gram-negative bacillary sepsis.

Alternatively, a reasonably reliable differential diagnosis of various infectious diseases in the elderly patient can be made based on functional status or level of care. A differential diagnostic approach is summarized in Table 106-2. A healthy, functionally independent older adult living at home most frequently acquires respiratory tract infections (especially bacterial pneumonia), urinary tract infection, or intraabdominal sepsis (usually biliary sepsis, diverticulitis, or appendicitis). Less frequently, infective endocarditis, tuberculosis, septic arthritis, and meningitis cause infections in this group. Elderly patients in

TABLE 106-2

Differential Diagnosis of Infection in Older Adults by Functional Status or Level of Care

Functional Status or Level of Care	*Types of infection* Primary Considerations	Secondary Considerations
Independent, healthy individual living in community	Bacterial pneumonia and other respiratory tract infections Urinary tract infection Intraabdominal infections (cholecystitis, diverticulitis, appendicitis)	Infective endocarditis Tuberculosis Septic arthritis Meningitis
Hospital patient	Urinary tract infection Pneumonia Surgical wound infections	Septic thrombophlebitis Drug reactions* Pulmonary emboli* Hepatitis
Nursing home resident	Pneumonia Urinary tract infection Decubitus ulcer	Tuberculosis Drug reactions* Intraabdominal infection Gastroenteritis

*Noninfectious disorders simulating an infection or causing fever.

the hospital are at greater risk for urinary tract infection, aspiration pneumonia, surgical wound infection,[28] and septic thrombophlebitis (local intravenous site). Noninfectious disorders may cause a fever or simulate an infectious disease, and these include pulmonary emboli, drug reactions, and hepatitis (viral or toxic reaction). Patients in chronic care facilities or nursing homes are most commonly transferred to an acute care hospital because of fever or an infection.[38] The most frequent infections are pneumonia, urinary tract infection, and skin and soft tissue infections (acronym *PUS*).[29,30] These three infections account for 80 percent of proven cases of bacteremia in long-term care facilities.[5,39] Tuberculosis[11] and gastroenteritis[40] are also common in nursing homes and are associated with major outbreaks.

Diagnostic Testing

In the current modern practice of medicine, highly technical diagnostic procedures and tests are available that can diagnose or exclude, with reasonable accuracy, serious diseases or disease processes. However, many of these "high-tech" procedures are expensive. With the current enormous cost of medical care, clinicians who care for older adults must be able to select diagnostic tests judiciously. Such factors as risk versus benefits, cost versus benefits, and impact (of the test) on management must be seriously considered whenever diagnostic tests and procedures are contemplated for a geriatric patient because of the higher associated risks with certain interventions and inconclusive benefits of various treatments in older patients.

As previously discussed, based on clinical assessment, a reasonably accurate differential diagnosis for an infectious disease process can be established (see Table 106-2). The following are suggestions and guidelines for which diagnostic tests to order in older patients with a possible infection.

All Patients with Suspected Infection

If the physician suspects infection, the following tests and evaluations should be performed: blood cultures (at least two sets), complete blood count, urinalysis with culture, chest x-ray examination, and renal function tests. Leukocytosis with a left shift or leukocyte left shift alone has good predictive value for diagnosing bacterial infections in older patients.[41]

Urinary Tract Infection

Tests for urinary tract infection should be evaluated with urinalysis and culture, prostate examination, prostatic fluid culture (for recurrent urinary infections in men), residual urine volume, and possibly intravenous pyelogram or renal ultrasound (for genitourinary structure and size). Decisions on ordering more invasive procedures such as cystoscopy should be individualized.

Pulmonary Infections

Pulmonary infections are difficult to evaluate in older patients because sick elderly patients frequently are unable to cough or they are too frail to withstand a diagnostic procedure. Nevertheless, an expectorated sputum should be obtained whenever possible for staining (Gram's stain, acid-fast stain) and culture (bacterial, mycobacterial, and fungal), realizing the limited diagnostic value of these specimens for bacterial isolation because of contamination by mouth flora. Chest radiographs that include a lateral view as well as special views (e.g., apical lordotic for possible tuberculosis) should be ordered. Pleural fluid should be obtained for anaerobic and aerobic bacterial cultures (and Gram's stain) and for mycobacterial and fungal studies. Skin tests for tuberculous and fungal infections are recommended in older patients with a pulmonary lesion when a bacterial infection is an unlikely cause. Flexible bronchoscopy should be reserved for older patients in whom a cause is not determined after preliminary tests or in whom a malignancy is considered as part of the differential diagnosis. Transtracheal aspiration is generally recommended only for patients with multiple potential microbial etiologies who have failed to respond to initial chemotherapy for their pulmonary lesion.

Abdominal Infections

These infections are best assessed by initially doing an ultrasonogram, which is then followed by an abdominal computed tomographic scan. If these tests reveal nothing of significance, radionuclide scans such as a gallium-67 scintigraph may be helpful in localizing a septic focus (e.g., abscess).

ANTIBIOTICS: SPECIAL CONSIDERATIONS

Antimicrobial therapy and antibiotic usage in older patients require special considerations. Many factors and circumstances influence the approach to the selection, administration, and monitoring of antibiotics in elderly patients. These factors include limitations in obtaining diagnostic specimens, heterogeneity of microbial causes, antibiotic pharmacology, and costs.

Limitations in Diagnostic Specimens

Collection of body fluids or tissue for microbiological studies is frequently not feasible in the older patient, particularly the very old and frail elderly patient. Many are unable to expectorate sputum or to spontaneously void urine. In addition, invasive procedures (e.g., thoracentesis) are often not possible because the elderly patient is unable to cooperate or cannot tolerate the test. It is therefore more difficult to make a precise etiologic diagnosis in older patients with an infection.

Etiologic Heterogeneity

The most common infections that occur in all age groups are respiratory infection, urinary tract infection, skin and soft-tissue infections, and intraabdominal sepsis. These infections involve a variety of bacterial pathogens, including aerobic (facultative anaerobic) and obligate anaerobic strains. Moreover, etiologic diversity is greater in elderly patients compared with younger adults with the same infection. For example, pneumonia in the general population is predominantly (60 to 80 percent) caused by *Streptococcus pneumoniae.* In contrast, the elderly population experiences a lower frequency of *S. pneumoniae* (40 to 60 percent) and a higher rate of such other pathogens as *Haemophilus influenzae,* gram-negative bacilli, *Staphylococcus aureus,* and *Moraxella* (*Branhamella*) *catarrhalis.*[1]

Antibiotic Pharmacology

A detailed discussion of aging and pharmacokinetics is beyond the scope of this chapter (see Chap. 24). In terms of antibiotics, age-related changes in gastrointestinal absorption, volume distribution, and hepatic metabolism probably have little impact on the selection, administration, and dosing of these drugs.[42] However, associated with the age-related decline in renal function is a greater risk for higher serum and tissue concentration of antibiotics.[42] Antibiotics that are associated with dose-related toxicity should therefore be avoided or should be given in reduced dosages in elderly patients. The aminoglycosides are particularly relevant under these circumstances since elderly persons who already experience age-related losses in hearing and renal function are at greatest risk for oto- and nephrotoxicity of these drugs.

Costs of Antibiotic Therapy

Traditionally, the cost of antibiotic therapy has been equated to the purchasing cost of a specific drug. This is primarily the reason why physicians are reluctant to use newer and more expensive antibiotics. However, antimicrobial therapy costs include not only the acquisition cost but also the expenses related to preparation and administration of the drugs (materials and labor), and costs accrued from drug monitoring.[43] Another cost that should be (but is not) calculated as part of antibiotic costs is the added cost of adverse effects.

Drugs that are administered more frequently are often more costly because of the added staff time required. Thus, although the purchasing cost of a drug may be high, it may be less expensive overall than another drug with a cheaper purchasing price that requires more frequent dosing. In addition, drugs which require frequent laboratory monitoring or which are associated with high incidence of adverse effects become more expensive (e.g., aminoglycosides).

Costs of Hospitalization

With increasing hospital costs, it becomes imperative that elderly patients with a potential infection are diagnosed early and treated promptly. Moreover, the traditional approach to managing infectious diseases, i.e., determining a specific cause and treating with a narrow-spectrum antibiotic, is frequently not feasible in frail, ill elderly patients who cannot provide clinical specimens. Thus, the clinician has a greater chance of making errors in the initial choice of chemotherapy. These errors in diagnosis and treatment prolong the hospital stay. Thus, in severely ill older patients in whom a precise etiologic diagnosis cannot be made before culture data return, therapy should be initiated with a *broad-spectrum* antibiotic agent (or combination thereof). When the specific cause is determined, a narrower-spectrum agent may be substituted.

With the increasing availability of oral antibiotics, it becomes more feasible to treat the older patient with infection as an outpatient. This limits the number of patients who require hospitalization and permits patients to be discharged from the hospital sooner. Although many newer oral antibiotics have high retail purchasing costs (to the patient), outpatient antimicrobial chemotherapy with oral drugs is always less expensive than inpatient care.

Recommendations

Based on the above conditions and circumstances, the following recommendations are made regarding antibiotic therapy in older adults:[44]

1. Empirical antibiotic therapy should be considered earlier and more often in older patients (compared with younger patients) who appear ill or functionally incapacitated by a potential infectious disease process. Empirical therapy should be initiated only *after* all available clinical specimens for microbiological studies have been obtained.
2. Empirical therapy should be initiated with a broad-spectrum antimicrobial agent that will be effective against the most likely pathogens responsible for the infection. Generally, β-lactam antibiotics, particularly the cephalosporins, are the agent(s) of choice in older patients because of their proven efficacy, broad spectrum, safety, and favorable dosing regimens.
3. A specific narrow-spectrum antibiotic should be administered only after a precise etiologic diagnosis is made and only after determining that the causative pathogen is highly susceptible to this drug.
4. If parenteral therapy is initiated, it should be continued until the patient has clinically improved and relevant microbiological studies (e.g., cultures) have shown elimination of the causative pathogen. The patient should then be changed to oral antibiotics as soon as possible. Generally, for most serious infections, parenteral therapy is continued for 3 to 7 days in uncomplicated infections (older patients without severe underlying diseases or disabilities) and 7 to 10 days in elderly patients who are critically ill, who have immunocompromised status or other debilitating disease, and/or who fail to respond to treatment within the first 3 to 4 days. Of course, certain infections such as infective endocarditis, brain abscess, acute osteomyelitis, and abscesses require parenteral therapy for a prolonged period regardless of the patient's age or underlying health status.
5. In elderly patients, aminoglycoside antibiotics should be reserved for select circumstances, i.e., patients with septic shock without a specific etiologic diagnosis (the risk of death under these conditions is far greater than the risk of aminoglycoside toxicity); patients with serious *Pseudomonas aeruginosa* infection (endocarditis, osteomyelitis, meningitis, etc.); patients infected with an organism susceptible only to an aminoglycoside; and patients with infective endocarditis caused by a pathogen that is eradicated optimally by the principle of synergistic therapy (aminoglycoside added to a primary antibiotic).

PREVENTION

The topic of prevention of infectious diseases in the older adult is broad and beyond the scope and limitations of this chapter. However, it should be stated that immunoprophylaxis of elderly persons with influenza vaccine (yearly), pneumococcal vaccine (one dose only, except repeat dose in 6 years in patients at high risk for sepsis—e.g., asplenia—or in those who have rapid fall in antibodies to pneumococci, e.g., immunosuppression), and tetanus toxoid (three primary series followed by booster every 10 years) is an important aspect of geriatric care. Influenza-related deaths occur predominantly in elderly persons;[45] pneumococcal pneumonia and bacteremia occur most frequently and are associated with the highest mortality in persons over the age of 60 years;[46] and, as stated earlier, 60 percent of tetanus cases in the United States occur in persons over the age of 60.[19] However, the immune response or clinical efficacy of these vaccines in elderly persons has been quite variable and inconsistent.[47–49]

REFERENCES

1. Yoshikawa TT, Norman DC (eds): *Aging and Clinical Practice: Infectious Diseases. Diagnosis and Treatment.* New York, Igaku-Shoin, 1987.
2. Yoshikawa TT: Important infections in elderly persons. *West J Med* 135:441, 1981.
3. National Center for Health Statistics, Graves EJ: Utilization of short-stay hospitals, United States, 1983 Annual Summary. *Vital and Health Statistics,* ser 13, no 83, DHHS (PHS) 85-1744. Washington, Public Health Service, Government Printing Office, 1985.

4. Mims AD et al: Clinically inapparent (asymptomatic) bacteriuria in ambulatory elderly men: Epidemiological, clinical, and microbiological findings. *J Am Geriatr Soc* 38:1209, 1990.
5. Setia U et al: Bacteremia in a long-term care facility. Spectrum and mortality. *Arch Intern Med* 144:1633, 1984.
6. McCue JD: Gram-negative bacillary bacteremias in the elderly: Incidence, etiology, and mortality. *J Am Geriatr Soc* 35:213, 1987.
7. Hill AB, Meakins JL: Peritonitis, in Yoshikawa TT (ed): *Infections.* Clinics in Geriatric Medicine. Philadelphia, Saunders, 1992, p 869.
8. Norman DC, Yoshikawa TT: Acute appendicitis in the elderly, in Meakins J, McClaron J (eds): *Surgical Care of the Elderly.* Chicago, Year Book Medical, 1988, p 386.
9. Cantrell M, Yoshikawa TT: Aging and infective endocarditis. *J Am Geriatr Soc* 31:216, 1983.
10. Atkinson JB, Virmani B: Infective endocarditis: Changing trends and general approach for examination. *Hum Pathol* 18(6):603, 1987.
11. Stead WN et al: Tuberculosis as an endemic and nosocomial infection among the elderly in nursing homes. *N Engl J Med* 312:1483, 1985.
12. Alvarez S et al: Pulmonary tuberculosis in elderly men. *Am J Med* 82:602, 1987.
13. Yoshikawa TT: Elimination of tuberculosis from the United States. *J Am Geriatr Soc* 39:312, 1991.
14. Yoshikawa TT: Tuberculosis in aging adults. *J Am Geriatr Soc* 40:178, 1992.
15. Norman DC, Yoshikawa TT: Responding to septic arthritis. *Geriatrics* 38:83, 1983.
16. McGuire NM, Kauffman CA: Septic arthritis in the elderly. *J Am Geriatr Soc* 33:170,1985.
17. Allman RM: Pressure ulcers among the elderly. *N Engl J Med* 320:850, 1989.
18. Kostuik JB, Fernie G: Pressure sores in elderly patients. *J Bone Joint Surg* 67(B):1, 1985.
19. Centers for Disease Control: *Tetanus—United States, 1985–1986. MMWR* 36(29):477, July 31, 1987.
20. Watson PN, Evans RJ: Postherpetic neuralgia: A review. *Arch Neurol* 43:836, 1986.
21. Schmader KE, Studenski S: Are current therapies useful for the prevention of postherpetic neuralgia? A critical analysis of the literature. *J Gen Intern Med* 4:83, 1989.
22. Garibaldi RA, Nurse BA: Infections in the elderly. *Am J Med* 81(suppl 1A):53, 1986.
23. Jones SR: Infections in frail and vulnerable elderly patients. *Am J Med* 88(suppl 3C):3C, 1990.
24. Yoshikawa TT: Impact of aging on host response to infectious disease, in Wood WG, Strong R (eds): *Geriatric Clinical Pharmacology.* New York, Raven, 1987, p 107.
25. Utilization of short-stay hospitals. United States 1981, Annual Summary. National Center for Health Statistics, Data from the National Health Survey, ser 13, no 72, DHSS(PHS)83-1733. Washington, Government Printing Office, 1983.
26. Gorse GJ et al: Bacterial meningitis in the elderly. *Arch Intern Med* 144:1603, 1984.
27. Terpenning MS et al: Infective endocarditis: Clinical features in young and elderly patients. *Am J Med* 83:626, 1987.
28. Saviteer SM et al: Nosocomial infections in the elderly. Increased risk per hospital day. *Am J Med* 84:661, 1988.
29. Norman DC et al: Infections in the nursing home. *J Am Geriatr Soc* 35:796, 1987.
30. Alvarez S et al: Nosocomial infections in long-term facilities. *J Gerontol* 43:179, 1988.
31. Movat HZ et al: Acute inflammation in gram-negative infection: Endotoxin, interleukin 1, tumor necrosis factor, and neutrophils. *Fed Proc* 46:97, 1987.
32. Keating HJ III et al: Effect of aging on the clinical significance of fever in ambulatory adult patients. *J Am Geriatr Soc* 32:282, 1984.
33. Esposito AL, Gleckman RA: Fever of unknown origin in the elderly. *J Am Geriatr Soc* 26:498, 1978.
34. Norman DC et al: Fever and aging. *J Am Geriatr Soc* 33:859, 1985.
35. Gleckman R, Hibert D: Afebrile bacteremia: A phenomenon in geriatric patients. *JAMA* 243:1478, 1981.
36. Marrie TJ et al: Community-acquired pneumonia requiring hospitalization. Is it different in the elderly? *J Am Geriatr Soc* 38:671, 1985.
37. Castle SC et al: Fever response in elderly nursing home residents: Are the older truly colder? *J Am Geriatr Soc* 39:853, 1991.
38. Irvine PW et al: Causes for hospitalization of nursing home residents: The role of infection. *J Am Geriatr Soc* 32:103, 1984.
39. Muder RM et al: Bacteremia in a long-term care facility: A five-year prospective study of 163 consecutive episodes. *Clin Infect Dis* 14:647, 1992.
40. Choi M et al: *Salmonella* outbreak in a nursing home. *J Am Geriatr Soc* 38:531, 1990.
41. Wasserman M et al: Utility of fever, white blood cells, and differential count in predicting bacterial infections in the elderly. *J Am Geriatr Soc* 37:537, 1989.
42. Lundberg B, Nilsson-Ehle I: Pharmacokinetics of antimicrobial agents in the elderly. *Rev Infect Dis* 9:250, 1987.
43. McCue JD et al: Hospital charges for antibiotics. *Rev Infect Dis* 7:643, 1985.
44. Yoshikawa TT: Antimicrobial therapy in the elderly patient. *J Am Geriatr Soc* 38:1353, 1990.
45. Immunization Practices Advisory Committee: Prevention and control of influenza. *MMWR* 38(17):297, 1989.
46. Immunization Practices Advisory Committee: Pneumococcal polysaccharide vaccine. *MMWR* 38(5):64, 1989.
47. Levine M et al: Characterization of the immune response to trivalent influenza vaccine in elderly men. *J Am Geriatr Soc* 35:607, 1987.
48. Sims RV et al: The clinical effectiveness of pneumococcal vaccine in the elderly. *Ann Intern Med* 108:653, 1988.
49. Carbon PY et al: Serum levels of antibody to toxoid during tetanus and after specific immunization of patients with tetanus. *J Infect Dis* 145:278, 1982.

Chapter 107

DIZZINESS AND SYNCOPE

Palmi V. Jonsson and Lewis A. Lipsitz

This chapter deals with dizziness and syncope, two very important geriatric syndromes that produce falls and their morbid consequences. Dizziness and syncope may be due to cardiovascular abnormalities, in which case they differ only quantitatively, according to the degree of cerebral ischemia experienced by the patient during a cardiovascular event. However, dizziness and syncope may also differ qualitatively, dizziness being due to primary abnormalities in the central or peripheral nervous system and syncope due to cardiovascular disorders. For practical purposes, the two symptoms will be discussed separately; however, areas of overlap in their etiology, evaluation, and treatment will be highlighted.

DIZZINESS

Dizziness is one of several terms that patients use to describe an unpleasant sensation of insecure balance. Dizziness has a different meaning to different people and has multiple underlying causes. Dizziness can be separated by history into four broad categories which are useful in guiding the clinical evaluation:[1]

1. *Vertigo (spinning):* Distortion of orientation or erroneous perception of motion. Vertigo indicates a vestibular system disorder, but lack of a spinning sensation does not exclude a vestibular disorder. The vertigo may be continuous or positional only, as well as acute or chronic.
2. *Dysequilibrium (unsteadiness, imbalance):* The feeling of an imminent fall. This feeling usually indicates a neurologic disorder but may also reflect a vestibular disorder.
3. *Near-syncope (fainting, light-headedness):* The feeling of impending loss of consciousness. This feeling usually indicates a cardiovascular disorder and is best approached in a way similar to the diagnostic approach for syncope (see "Syncope").
4. *Nonspecific dizziness:* A psychogenic disease is likely when there is a vague history lacking any of the three symptom characteristics above, coupled with the presence of psychiatric symptoms and absence of known patterns of organic disease.

Epidemiology

The complaint of dizziness is common, but studies of its incidence and prevalence in the total population are scanty. A study of 1622 community-dwelling adults aged 60 and older showed a lifetime prevalence of disabling dizziness of 29.3 percent and a 1-year prevalence of 18.2 percent.[2] Dizziness was associated with a feeling of poor health but was not associated with increased risk of death or institutionalization at a 1-year follow-up.

Pathophysiology

The pathophysiology of dizziness due to cardiovascular abnormalities is discussed later, under "Syncope." Maintenance of balanced posture is accomplished through several mechanisms. Continuous afferent input from the eyes, vestibular labyrinths, muscles, and joints is processed centrally and produces the adaptive movements necessary to maintain equilibrium.

The vestibular system has several components: the vestibular labyrinth, the vestibular nerve, and the central connections. The vestibular labyrinths are spatial proprioceptors that are stimulated by gravity and rotational movement. Because the vestibular labyrinth (which is a spatial proprioceptor) and the cochlea (which is a sound receptor) lie adjacent to each other and their nerves run together to the central connections, diseases causing dizziness usually affect both balance and hearing. Visual impulses are coordinated with impulses from the vestibular labyrinths and the neck to stabilize gaze during movements of the head and body. Proprioceptive receptors around the facet joints of the cervical spine and large joints of the shoulders, hips, knees, and ankles are similarly important and lead to reflex changes in posture. Visual, proprioceptive, and labyrinthine mechanisms can generally compensate for one another to maintain balance, unless there are simultaneous defects in any two of these three sensory systems. Additionally, there is important psychophysiologic input from the cortex which modifies the interpretation of afferent stimuli. Vertigo or dysequilibrium therefore may be induced by psychological stimulation, by pathologic dysfunction in any of the sensory systems, or by impaired central processing.

Age-Related Changes

Many age-related changes have been identified within the balance system which alone or in combination with diseases of older age may result in impaired perception of where the head or the body are in space. These changes may partially explain the high prevalence of dizziness among elderly persons. Some of these changes (see Table 107-1) are diminished perception of various visual stimuli,[3] increased thresholds for vestibular and proprioceptive sensory organ responses,[4] and loss of sensory receptors such as the proprioceptive receptors of the cervical spine (mechanoreceptors).[5] While these age-related changes may predispose elderly people to clinical symptoms, such changes are not by themselves a sufficient explanation for dizziness.[6]

Disease-Related Changes

Degenerative diseases of the special sensory organs are well-known accompaniments of aging. The prevalences of cataracts, glaucoma, and macular degeneration and acquired vestibular dysfunction increase with age. Peripheral neuropathy from diabetes, alcoholism, vitamin deficiency, and idiopathic causes may produce dizziness. Cervical spondylosis, which is common in advanced age, may impair cervical mechanoreceptor function or cause cervical myelopathy with associated impairment of spacial orientation.

Etiology

Table 107-2 shows the principal diseases that cause dizziness; they can be divided into peripheral or central neurologic causes, systemic diseases, psychiatric disorders, and contributions of multiple sensory deficits. Drachman and Hart found that 38 percent of dizzy patients had peripheral neurologic disorders, 11 percent had central neurologic disorders, 8 percent had systemic diseases, 32 percent had psychiatric illness, 13 percent had multiple sensory deficits, and 9 percent had uncertain diagnoses.[1]

TABLE 107-1

Age-Related Changes Affecting the Special Senses

- I. Vision
  - Focal
    - Reduced glare tolerance
    - Reduced nocturnal acuity
  - Ambient
    - Reduced ability to perceive contrast
    - Reduced ability to fixate accurately
- II. Vestibular
  - Increased threshold of response
  - Reduction in hair cell population
- III. Peripheral proprioception
  - Increased threshold of response
  - Degeneration of cervical mechanoreceptors

TABLE 107-2

Etiology of Dizziness

Neurologic

Peripheral (labyrinth or vestibulocochlear nerve):
- Benign paroxysmal positional vertigo
- Vestibulopathy
- Ménière's disease
- Acoustic neuroma
- Medication toxic effects: aminoglycosides, diuretics, chincona alkaloids (quinidine), salicylates
- Posttraumatic

Central (brainstem, cerebellum, and cerebrum):
- Ischemia, infarcts, bleeding
- Demyelination (multiple sclerosis, postinfectious, paraneoplastic)
- Tumors (meningioma, metastasis)
- Seizures (temporal lobe)
- Medication toxic effects: phenytoin, lithium, benzodiazepines

Systemic

Cardiac, hypotension (see Table 107-4)
Toxins (lead, arsenic)
Metabolic (diabetes, hypothyroidism)
Other

Psychiatric

Anxiety, psychotic, and affective disorders

Multiple pathology

Combined visual, vestibular, and peripheral proprioceptive deficits

Neurologic Disorders

Peripheral Nervous System (PNS) Disorders Vertigo generally indicates a PNS disorder, but rarely may be due to a central lesion. PNS disorders can also present less dramatically as dysequilibrium or unsteadiness. Central and peripheral disorders generally can be distinguished by the characteristics of nystagmus induced by a rapid head-hanging maneuver (Nylen-Barany maneuver) as described later, under "Evaluation" (see Table 107-3). Peripheral disorders are characterized by a latency time of 5 to 15 seconds until the onset of vertigo or nystagmus, brief nystagmus for less than a minute, and fatigue of the response on repeated testing.[7] In central disorders there is no latency, the vertigo and nystagmus lasts more than a minute, and there is no fatigue on repeated testing.[8]

TABLE 107-3

Characteristics of Positionally Induced Vertigo and Nystagmus (the Nylen-Barany Maneuver)

	Peripheral	Central
Latency (time to onset of vertigo or nystagmus)	5–15 s	No latency
Duration	Less than 1 min	More than 1 min
Fatigability (signs and symptoms decrease after onset and on repetition of stimulus)	Yes	No
Direction of nystagmus	Same	May change
Intensity of symptoms and signs	Severe	Mild
Reproducibility	Inconsistent	More consistent
Associated symptoms or signs	Auditory	Neurologic

Benign Paroxysmal Positional Vertigo (BPPV) BPPV, the most common PNS disorder, is about twice as common as any other vestibular disorder, occurring in 10 to 30 percent of patients reporting dizziness. BPPV can have a specific cause (40 percent), such as head injury or ear disease, but it is more commonly idiopathic (60 percent). The diagnostic criteria are as follows:[9] (1) a history of episodic vertigo occurring *only* with a change in position, (2) nystagmus elicited in a head-hanging position with the Nylen-Barany maneuver (see "Evaluation"), and (3) normal caloric (oculovestibular) responses (i.e., symmetric nystagmus is induced).

The pathophysiology of BPPV probably involves the labyrinth.[6] Schuknecht hypothesized that labyrinthine degeneration causes a mass of particles (octoconia) to form within the posterior semicircular canal on one side, thus making the endolymph heavier on that side than on the opposite side.[10] This would cause an asymmetric vestibular response with posture change.

Clinically, the episodes of vertigo in BPPV are of short duration and occur when the patient turns from side to side in bed, gets out of bed, bends the head back, or moves the head rapidly horizontally or vertically. Vertigo may be associated with nausea, and the patient may complain about unsteadiness and nausea between episodes.

The incidence of BPPV peaks after age 60. The female/male ratio 2:1. Most often the symptoms subside over a period of 6 months to a year, but recurrences are common, and symptoms have been documented to last as long as 10 years.

Vestibulopathy (Vestibular Neuronitis): Acute or Recurrent Vestibulopathy is a distinctive vestibular disturbance characterized by the sudden onset of severe vertigo continuing over 5 to 24 hours and associated with a unilateral decrease in caloric response and spontaneous nystagmus in the *absence* of auditory or other neurologic abnormalities.[11] Nausea and vomiting or retching can be severe. In the recovery phase, vertigo can become positional. Vestibulopathy is a benign disorder that may occur as a single episode or be recurrent. It is thought to be due to a virus affecting the vestibular nerve between the labyrinth and the brain. It is probably less common in the elderly than in the young and middle-aged, but reliable data in the elderly population are not available.

Ménière's Disease Ménière's disease is a vestibulocochlear disorder.[12] It is associated with distension of the endolymphatic space within the cochlea and leads to degeneration of the cochlear cells. Ménière's disease is diagnosed when there is a recurrent peripheral vestibulopathy accompanied by tinnitus and hearing loss. The hearing loss has a *cochlear* sensorineural pattern, which is characterized by partial loss of perception of high-pitched sounds that can be compensated somewhat by increasing loudness (loudness recruitment). There is relative preservation of speech discrimination (i.e., the ability to distinguish similar sounds). The attacks of vertigo are typically abrupt and last minutes to hours. Nausea, vomiting and a feeling of fullness in the ear are present to a varying degree. Attacks may vary in frequency and severity. Recurrent attacks often give rise to mild chronic states of dysequilibrium. Caloric testing may or may not disclose an impairment on the involved side. Hearing loss usually begins before the first attack, fluctuates, and worsens with each attack. The disease is bilateral in 10 to 30 percent of cases. The sexes are affected equally, and the onset is most often in the fifth and sixth decades. The course of Ménière's disease is characterized by remissions and relapses.

Acoustic Neuroma Acoustic neuroma is uniformly associated with hearing loss and should be suspected in any patient with progressive unilateral hearing loss.[13] Early symptoms are tinnitus and mild sensorineural hearing loss of the *retrocochlear* type, characterized by a partial loss of high-frequency sound perception that cannot be compensated by increasing loudness (i.e., lack of loudness recruitment). There is also diminished speech discrimination that is out of proportion to the hearing loss. Caloric testing indicates decreased vestibular response on the affected side. A small number of patients complain about vertigo early on; later on it can resemble vertigo in Ménière's disease due to the associated hearing loss. The vertigo is rarely positional. Most often patients complain about dysequilibrium. Continued tumor growth may lead to frank ataxia and other associated neurologic findings, including disturbance of taste, sensory loss over the face, gait abnormality, and unilateral ataxia of the limbs.

Medication Toxicity Although medication ototoxicity is not specific to elderly patients, preexisting pathologic inner-ear conditions and the high prevalence of medication use in this population increase the risk.[6] Impaired renal function in advanced age is the dominant risk factor for ototoxicity from medications which are cleared by the kidney. Medication ototoxicity is often an overlooked cause of hearing and balance problems.[14]

The known toxic medications include antibiotics (e.g., aminoglycosides, vancomycin, and erythromycin), diuretics (e.g., ethacrynic acid and furosemide), salicylates, and quinine. *Aminoglycosides* pass the blood-perilymph barrier and bind to the sensory epithelium in the inner ear, to the hair cells, and to the striae vascularis of both the cochlea and the vestibular portions of the labyrinth. Ototoxic *diuretics* inhibit the enzyme adenosine triphosphatase, causing an increase in sodium concentration in the inner ear. Direct hair cell toxicity may also occur. *Salicylates* may cause constriction of small cochlear blood vessels, and *quinine* is believed to affect the spiral ganglion. Concurrent use of more than one toxic drug, for example, use of both gentamicin and furosemide, increases the probability of toxicity.

Gentamicin is now the principal offending toxic agent, since streptomycin and kanamycin are rarely used. It is twice as toxic to the vestibular apparatus as to the cochlear, resulting in a higher incidence of balance impairment than hearing impairment. Since a serum gentamicin level above 10 μg/ml is associated with ototoxicity, serum levels should be obtained just prior to a given dose and one hour after it, and subsequent dosages should be adjusted accordingly to avoid toxic levels.

Central Nervous System (CNS) Disorders

Cerebrovascular Disease Basilar artery insufficiency is a cerebrovascular disease in which dizziness is one of the cardinal symptoms.[15] Dizziness also can be seen in posterior cerebral artery insufficiency but is rare in association with anterior cerebral circulatory disturbances. Dizziness can present alone as a symptom of transient ischemic attack (TIA), but dizziness due to TIA is usually associated with other neurologic symptoms such as dysarthria, numbness of the face, hemiparesis, headache, and diplopia (in order of decreasing frequency). When a TIA presents as dizziness alone, an arrhythmia should be suspected.

When dizziness is due to a stroke, accompanying neurologic signs are almost always present. These signs are most frequently diplopia, dysarthria, weakness, headache, numbness of the face or limbs, ataxia of gait, cerebellar ataxia of the limbs, and visual impairment. In rare cases, sudden deafness (with or without other brainstem signs) is due to anterior inferior cerebellar artery or internal auditory artery vascular occlusion. A rotatory feeling (vertigo) is present in only 22 percent of patients with dizziness of central vascular origin in contrast to its presence in 90 percent of dizzy patients with peripheral causes.[15] Episodes of dizziness that are associated with vestibulocochlear nerve manifestations alone are highly unlikely to be vascular in origin. Episodes of dizziness that continue for more than 6 weeks without neurologic accompaniments are also rarely vascular in nature. Positional vertigo is rarely ever the result of cerebrovascular disease.

Cerebellar Disorders Cerebellar strokes (particularly those involving the flocculonodular complex and the vestibular connections of the cerebellum) or hemorrhage can present as acute vertigo, unsteadiness, nausea, vomiting, nystagmus, and truncal ataxia. Therefore, these cerebellar strokes may mimic vestibular labyrinthine disease, such as acute vestibular neuronitis or Ménière's disease.[16] Truncal ataxia is a distinguishing feature of dizziness due to cerebellar stroke. A computed tomography (CT) scan or magnetic resonance imaging (MRI) of the head with attention to the posterior fossa is an urgent test in any patient with sudden onset of these symptoms and associated ataxia.

Other Disorders Complaints of dizziness and postural instability while standing and walking are common among patients with Parkinson's disease.[17] Objective findings of vestibular dysfunction, such as reduced caloric responses, correlate highly with severity of balance impairment. These patients are diagnosed by the parkinsonian tremor, the increase in neuromuscular tone, and the typical shuffling gait.

Direct effects of medications on the CNS (as distinguished from ototoxicity) are an important cause of dizziness that often can be detected by noting the presence of a particular medication history coupled with the presence of multidirectional nystagmus. Lithium and phenytoin (Dilantin) are two good examples of drugs that cause dizziness and nystagmus. Benzodiazepines, neuroleptics, and antidepressants often cause dysequilibrium but are not associated with nystagmus.

Many other CNS diseases, such as tumors and metabolic and demyelinating disorders, can cause dizziness. They are detected by associating features of the history and physical examination with results from appropriate laboratory tests.

Systemic Causes

The major systemic causes of dizziness are the same as those that predispose to syncope and are discussed later, under "Syncope." Transient arrhythmias and hypotension are the two most common causes; only rarely does an endocrine disorder such as hypothyroidism underlie the complaint of dizziness.

Psychiatric Disease

Psychiatric disorders are the cause of dizziness in about 20 to 33 percent of all cases. This is a diagnosis made by exclusion of other potential causes, but it is suspected when the complaint of dizziness does not fit any particular recognized disease pattern.

Multiple Pathology

Drachman and Hart[1] found that multiple sensory deficits account for 13 percent of cases of dizziness. They maintain that any two or more deficits of the visual, vestibular, or somatosensory systems may cause dizziness.

Evaluation

The evaluation of dizziness is best accomplished by a systematic approach (see Fig. 107-1) in which the his-

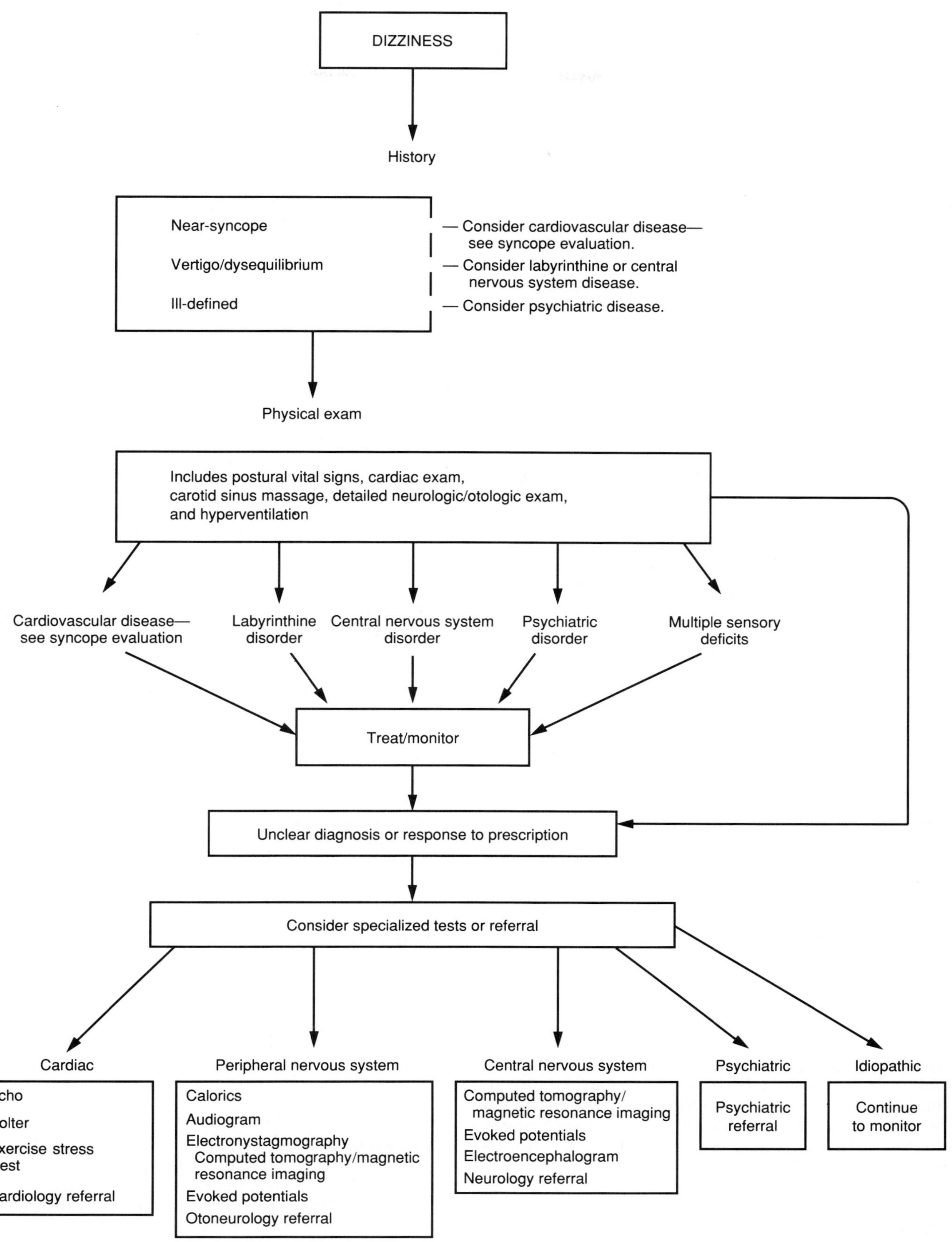

FIGURE 107-1
Algorithm for the diagnostic evaluation of the elderly dizzy patient.

tory and physical examination guide the selection of tests. This approach has been shown in one recent study to yield a diagnosis in 86.2 percent of patients studied, with BPPV (25.9 percent) and cerebrovascular disorders (21.6 percent) being the most common diagnosis.[18] The *history* should begin with an exact description of what the patient means by dizziness. Provocative factors should be sought. A spinning sensation in response to movement of the head and neck may indicate BPPV, carotid sinus syndrome, or cervical spondylosis. Faintness precipitated by standing and relieved by lying down may indicate orthostatic hypotension. Dizziness on straining at stool may indicate a posterior fossa lesion, a foramen magnum lesion, or hypotension secondary to the Valsalva maneuver. Lack of provocative factors may indicate TIAs or cardiac arrhythmias. The mode of onset of symptoms (gradual versus sudden), frequency and duration of symptoms (constant versus episodic), and symptoms between attacks all give valuable clues. When the dizziness is acute, it is more likely due to traumatic, vascular, or inflammatory causes. When it is chronic, neoplasia, demyelinating disorders, and psychiatric conditions are more likely. If symptoms are felt in the legs and there is difficulty standing and walking due to limb ataxia or dysmetria, a cerebellar lesion or a proprioceptive disorder may be the cause. Temporal-lobe seizures can present as dizziness and are suggested by automatism and amnesia. Tinnitus, hearing impairment, and fullness or pain in the ear indicate inner ear dysfunction. Nausea and vomiting are nonspecific, but when severe and sudden they may suggest a labyrinthine disorder (Ménière's disease or vestibular neuronitis) or a serious CNS disorder such as a cerebellar hemorrhage. Finally, detailed medication and toxic exposure history are important.

The *physical examination* includes postural vital signs, a cardiovascular examination, carotid sinus massage (see "Syncope"), and a careful ear and neurologic examination. Special emphasis needs to be placed on testing of the cranial nerves (e.g., hearing, corneal reflex, facial sensation, taste, eye control, spontaneous nystagmus, and swallowing), cerebellar examination (dysmetria and truncal ataxia), and gait and balance testing (Romberg and turning while walking). Deafness, hemifacial paresthesia, and unilateral limb ataxia suggest a cerebellopontine angle tumor. Diplopia, dysarthria, dysphagia, numbness of the face, weakness, and visual deficits suggest posterior circulation (vascular) causes. Any cranial nerve or brainstem sign suggests a vestibular nerve (as opposed to vestibular labyrinth) or a central cause of dizziness. If the basic evaluation is negative, psychiatric symptoms are present, and symptoms are reproduced with hyperventilation, a psychiatric disturbance is likely.

If pure tone hearing is impaired, as evidenced by reduced capacity to hear the sound of fingers rubbing together or a watch ticking, hearing should be assessed clinically with the time-honored tests of Rinne and Weber.

The *Nylen-Barany provocative maneuver*[19] is a test indicated in all patients. For this maneuver, the patient is seated on the examining table, with the head first turned 45 degrees to one side, then quickly lowered to a position with the head hanging over the edge of the table 30 degrees below horizontal. The test is repeated with the head turned 45 degrees in the opposite direction and again with the head in the straight-forward position. In each position, the patient is observed for the appearance and character of nystagmus. In a peripheral nervous system disorder, such as BPPV, there is (1) a latency period of 5 to 15 seconds before nystagmus occurs, (2) a decrease in intensity of the nystagmus after 2 to 30 seconds, (3) frequent reversal of the direction of nystagmus with assumption of the sitting position, and (4) fatigability of the nystagmus and vertigo when the subject is repeatedly put in the provocative head-hanging position. These findings are contrasted with those of a CNS disorder in Table 107-3.

The *minicaloric test* of vestibular function, modified by Nelson,[20] is a simple screening test that can be done in any outpatient setting. A tuberculin syringe is filled with ice water and 0.2 ml of the water is instilled into the ear canal with the patient supine and the patient's head positioned at approximately a 30-degree angle to the table. After the patient's head is turned to midline, the eyes are observed for nystagmus. A repeatedly negative response, i.e., the absence of induced nystagmus, indicates the presence of peripheral disease on that side.

Symptoms and signs found during history and physical examination and simple maneuvers either make the diagnosis or guide further evaluation and selection of *specialized testing*. If a peripheral vestibular disorder is suspected but cannot be confirmed clinically, caloric tests supplemented by electronystagmography (ENG) and a detailed audiometric evaluation are usually helpful. Depending on the results of these more advanced ENG studies, a CT or an MRI study may be required. When there are accompanying neurologic symptoms and signs in the initial evaluation that suggest a CNS lesion, a CT or MRI scan, an electroencephalogram (EEG), and auditory evoked potentials can help elucidate the cause. The CT should be done with contrast enhancement and closely spaced cuts through the posterior fossa. However, MRI has become the procedure of choice because of its sensitivity to brainstem lesions, such as small infarcts. An MRI with gadolinium is the diagnostic procedure of choice for identifying an acoustic neuroma.

Therapeutic Issues

Therapy for dizziness depends on the underlying disorder identified. The therapy is surgical for some diseases (e.g., acoustic neuroma). Symptomatic therapy with antihistamines or sedatives is only marginally effective, and the probability of side effects, such as falls or confusion, is markedly increased in elderly persons.

If BPPV is identified, desensitization exercises involving a series of positional movements can be helpful.[21] After the head-position change that elicits the symptom of vertigo is identified, the patient repeats the provocative maneuver five times a day until the condition improves. Elderly patients have had very satisfying results with this approach, albeit the therapeutic effect develops more slowly and is less complete than in younger patients. Use of assistive devices such as a cane or a walker can be of major benefit to the elderly patient with multiple sensory deficits. Attention to a treatable eye disease, such as cataracts, or the use of a hearing device may also benefit the patient. Finally, periodic review and support is important in the management of this prevalent and often disabling symptom.

SYNCOPE

Syncope is defined as transient loss of consciousness accompanied by loss of postural tone, with spontaneous recovery that does not require resuscitation. This common problem has multiple underlying causes and suggests an increased risk of sudden death if the cause is cardiac. Irrespective of cause, syncope can cause adverse consequences, such as falls, fractures, subdural hematomas, and loss of independent function.

Epidemiology

The information on the incidence and prevalence of syncope is fragmented. Studies of young people show a prevalence of syncope as high as 47 percent, which is primarily due to benign causes such as vasovagal reactions.[22] Data from the Framingham study show an increase in prevalence of syncope with age.[23] One percent of emergency ward visits and up to 3 percent of admissions to hospitals are for the evaluation of syncope. Most of these hospital visits are by elderly patients. A study of very elderly residents of a nursing home revealed a 10-year prevalence of 23 percent and a 1-year incidence of 6 percent. The recurrence rate for syncope is about 30 percent.[24] Patients with cardiac causes for syncope are at the highest risk for death, having a 40 percent 2-year mortality. Patients with noncardiac causes for syncope have a 20 percent 2-year mortality, which is similar to that of syncope of unknown cause.[25,26] Although syncope is associated with a high mortality rate, this high rate is probably due to the underlying diseases that cause syncope, rather than to an independent relationship between syncope and death. Recurrent syncope that remains unexplained after thorough initial evaluation is not associated with excess mortality.[24,27]

Pathophysiology

Syncope results from inadequate energy substrate delivery to the brain. The major energy substrates are oxygen and glucose. Significant hypoglycemia tends to result in coma rather than syncope, and a prolonged cessation of oxygen delivery results in death. Thus, transient cerebral hypoxia from decreased cerebral blood flow is the final common pathway in most cases of syncope. Generalized hypoxemia from cardiac or pulmonary diseases and decreased oxygen-carrying capacity of the blood from anemia are risk factors for syncope, particularly in elderly persons, but are rarely the sole cause. Infrequently, focal stenosis of arteries supplying critical areas of the brain causes syncope.

Blood pressure is determined by the product of cardiac output and peripheral arterial resistance. A reduction in either variable without an increase in the other lowers blood pressure and potentially results in syncope. Cardiac output may fall because of a reduction in stroke volume or because of extreme heart rates, either fast or slow. Reduced stroke volume may result from an obstruction to flow within the heart or pulmonary vasculature, myocardial pump failure, or a reduction in venous return. Venous return may decrease as a result of venous blood pooling or hypovolemia. Impaired arterial resistance can result from autonomic failure or medication-related effects. Cardiovascular reflexes may cause syncope by decreasing vascular resistance and/or cardiac output.

Age- and Disease-Related Changes Predisposing to Syncope in the Elderly Person

One of the characteristics of elderly people that predisposes them to syncope is the presence of multiple clinical abnormalities.[28] Additive age- and disease-related conditions that threaten cerebral blood flow or reduce oxygen content in the blood may bring oxygen delivery close to the threshold needed to maintain consciousness. A situational stress that further reduces blood pressure, such as posture change, or a Valsalva maneuver during voiding, may reduce cerebral oxygen delivery below the critical threshold and result in syncope.

Several homeostatic mechanisms that normally preserve blood pressure and cerebral oxygen delivery in the face of stress become impaired with age. These mechanisms include cerebral autoregulation,[29] baroreflexes,[30] myocardial diastolic relaxation,[31] and renal sodium conservation.[32]

Cerebral blood flow declines with normal aging.[29] In hypertension, which often accompanies advancing age, the threshold for cerebral autoregulation is shifted to higher levels of blood pressure, making elderly hypertensive patients more vulnerable to cerebral ischemia from relatively small degrees of hypotension. Baroreflex sensitivity is also impaired with advanced age. This impaired sensitivity can be demonstrated by a blunted bradycardiac response to hypertensive stimuli and diminished tachycardiac response to blood pressure reduction. At the bedside, reduced baroreceptor sensitivity is suggested by an absent or very modest cardioacceleration associated with posture change.

Changes in the diastolic properties of the heart also make the older individual more vulnerable to syncope. Due to progressive myocardial stiffness, diastolic relaxation and early diastolic ventricular filling are impaired with advancing age. As a result, the aged heart becomes more dependent on preload and atrial contraction to fill the ventricle and maintain cardiac output. A reduction in cardiac preload due to upright posture, meal digestion, or medications such as nitrates or diuretics may further reduce ventricular filling and thereby threaten cardiac output. In atrial fibrillation, the loss of atrial contraction may reduce cardiac output by as much as 50 percent. Syncope commonly occurs at the onset of rapid atrial fibrillation in the elderly patient. In addition, a rapid heart rate decreases the duration of ventricular filling and therefore may result in a fall in cardiac output and the development of hypotension.

Declines in basal and stimulated plasma renin and aldosterone concentrations and elevations in atrial natriuretic peptide levels with advancing age may predispose to volume depletion. Furthermore, many elderly persons have an impaired thirst response to hyperosmolality and therefore may not consume a sufficient quantity of fluids to prevent dehydration[33] and hypovolemia.

TABLE 107-4

Causes of Syncope

Cardiac disease (decreased cardiac output)
- Structural
  - Aortic stenosis
  - Mitral regurgitation
  - Mitral stenosis
  - Atrial myxoma
  - Cardiomyopathy
  - Pulmonary embolism
- Myocardial
  - Acute myocardial infarction
- Electrical
  - Tachyarrhythmias
  - Bradyarrhythmias
  - (Conduction disturbance, sinus node dysfunction)

Hypotension (decreased volume or peripheral vascular resistance)
- Orthostatic hypotension
  - Prolonged inactivity
  - Medications (vasodilators, antihypertensives, antidepressants, neuroleptics, diuretics, dopaminergics)
  - Central nervous system disease (Shy-Drager syndrome, Parkinson's disease)
  - Peripheral autonomic neuropathies (diabetes, alcoholism, amyloidosis)
  - Pure autonomic failure
- Postprandial hypotension
- Volume depletion (fluid or blood loss)

Reflex (decreased cardiac output or peripheral vascular resistance)
- Vasovagal
- Defecation
- Micturition
- Cough
- Swallowing
- Carotid sinus syndrome

Abnormal blood composition (reduced energy substrates)
- Hypoxemia
- Hypoglycemia
- Acute anemia

Central nervous system disease
- Seizures
- Cerebrovascular insufficiency

Etiology

Multiple studies have shown that 20 to 30 percent of syncopal episodes have cardiac causes, 10 to 20 percent have noncardiac causes, and 30 to 50 percent remain unexplained in spite of extensive evaluation.[34,35] Table 107-4 shows the common causes of syncope in the elderly population.

Structural Heart Disease

The three most common structural heart diseases that cause syncope in the elderly patient are aortic stenosis, hypertrophic cardiomyopathy, and mitral regurgitation. They all feature systolic murmurs that need to be distinguished from those attributable to the more prevalent, but benign, aortic sclerosis. About 30 percent of people over 65 years of age and 60 percent of people over 80 years of age have systolic murmurs.[36] The distinguishing features of these murmurs are often absent, making the clinical assessment difficult in the elderly patient.

Aortic Valve Disease Hemodynamically significant aortic stenosis is present in approximately 5 percent of elderly patients with a systolic murmur. Congenitally, bicuspid valves are the principal cause in the 60- to 70-year-old age group, while degenerative calcification of an otherwise normal tricuspid aortic valve is the most frequent cause of aortic stenosis in the very old.[37] Rheumatic heart disease is now an infrequent cause of aortic stenosis in the elderly patient. Most often aortic stenosis presents insidiously as congestive heart failure, but angina and syncope are still frequent manifestations.[38] The mechanism of syncope is either arrhythmia or reflex vasodilatation secondary to stimulation of ventricular vagal afferent fibers by a powerful ventricular contraction,[39] superimposed upon the structural impediment to left ventricular outflow.

Hypertrophic Cardiomyopathy (HCM) HCM is commonly overlooked in elderly patients, despite the fact that as many as 33 percent of patients with idiopathic HCM are over 60 years of age.[40] Hypertensive HCM has been described in the elderly population and appears to be most common in black women.[41] HCM can present with angina, dyspnea, or syncope.[40] Syncope is due either to left ventricular outflow obstruction or to tachyarrhythmias. Most patients with HCM have diastolic dysfunction characterized by impaired isovolumic relaxation, slow filling during the rapid-filling phase of diastole, and an excessive dependence on atrial systole to optimize ventricular volume.[42] Echocardiography is the diagnostic test of choice. It is important to think of HCM because it is exacerbated by commonly used inotropic and vasodilating medications.

Mitral Regurgitation (MR) Mitral valve prolapse, papillary muscle dysfunction, idiopathic calcification of the mitral valve annulus, and rheumatic disease are the common causes of MR. MR usually presents with congestive heart failure but can also cause syncope.

Electrical Heart Disease

Syncope is frequently the result of electrical heart disease, such as asystole, bradycardia, or tachyarrhythmia. Myocardial infarction may produce syncope via any of these mechanisms and is a common cause of syncope in the elderly patient.[43] Because arrhythmias are common in elderly people, their presence between syncopal attacks may be coincidental. Routine 24-hour ambulatory cardiac monitoring does not commonly show correlations between symptoms and rhythm disturbances.[44] A syncopal episode can be attributed to an arrhythmia only if the arrhythmia is found on an electrocardiogram at the time of the event, or if it is associated with symptoms of dizziness, near-syncope, or syncope during ambulatory monitoring. Ambulatory cardiac monitoring should be performed under the same conditions in which the syncopal episode occurred.

Since ambulatory cardiac monitoring is rarely diagnostic in the evaluation of syncope, self-activated electrocardiographic loop recorders have recently become available to capture abnormal cardiac rhythms during typical symptoms.[45] The recorder can be worn comfortably for a prolonged period of time. When it is activated by the patient after an episode of syncope or near-syncope, it can retrieve the previous 1 to 4 minutes of electrocardiographic data. In one study, the diagnostic yield of loop recorders in the evaluation of unexplained syncope was 25 percent.[45]

Rhythm Abnormalities Ventricular and supraventricular tachy- or bradyarrhythmias may produce syncope, but these rhythm abnormalities are also common in asymptomatic elderly persons. In the Baltimore Longitudinal Study on Aging, 13 percent of healthy people 60 to 85 years of age showed asymptomatic paroxysmal atrial tachycardia and 50 percent showed complex ventricular arrhythmias, including multiform ventricular premature contractions in 35 percent, couplets in 11 percent, and ventricular tachycardia in 4 percent.[46] The seriousness of ventricular ectopy correlates closely with the degree of impaired left ventricular function, with persistent ST-segment elevation, and with the extent of obstructive coronary vascular disease.[47] Thus, ventricular ectopic activity in the absence of structural or ischemic heart disease is associated with a good prognosis.[48]

Conduction Disturbances Conduction disturbances are common in the elderly population and are thought to be markers for transient heart block and associated syncope. First-degree heart block is never causally related to syncope.[49] On the other hand, second- and third-degree atrioventricular (AV) blocks are often seen in the elderly patient and may be associated with syncope, either directly through progression to complete heart block or through their close association with coexistent ventricular arrhythmias. Complete heart block is most commonly due to degenerative sclerosis of the conduction system, rather than to coronary artery disease.[50] The development of syncope in a patient with complete heart block (Stokes-Adams attack) is associated with increased mortality and should be treated with cardiac pacing.

The prevalence of left bundle-branch block in population-based studies ranges from 0.6 to 2.5 percent; right bundle-branch block prevalence ranges from 1.9 to 3.5 percent.[51] In the absence of symptoms, these forms of bundle-branch block alone do not have predictive value for syncope. Bifascicular or trifascicular conduction disease in association with syncope is of greater concern.[52] Several large studies[51,53] have shown that in asymptomatic patients with these findings, the risk of progression to high-degree AV block is low. However, in patients with transient unexplained neurologic symptoms and bi- or trifascicular block, the finding of a His-ventricular interval greater than 70 ms in an electrophysiologic study was associated with significantly greater progression to second- or third-degree AV block on follow-up. Therefore, prophylactic pacemaker implantation has been recommended in such patients for control of symptoms.[54] Syncope in patients with bifascicular block, however, is often due to causes other than heart block and does not in itself predict sudden death. Pacemaker insertion does not prevent sudden death, which presumably is due to ventricular arrhythmias, but may prevent serious morbidity associated with syncopal falls, if heart block is the cause of syncope.

Sinus Node Disease Sinus bradycardia alone in an elderly patient may be a normal finding that does not imply cardiac disease and has no effect on mortality.[55,56] However, sinus node disease (i.e., "sick sinus syndrome"), characterized by sinus bradycardia in association with paroxysmal supraventricular tachyarrhythmias, is a common cause of syncope in old people. Conduction disturbances are also common in sick sinus syndrome, occurring in approximately 50 percent of patients.[57,58] One of the major causes of syncope in sick sinus syndrome is prolonged asystole after abrupt cessation of an associated supraventricular tachycardia. Although there is potential morbidity from dizziness, falls, and syncope, the mortality rate associated with sick sinus syndrome is quite low. In one study, an 80 percent 5-year survival was found, which is similar to that for a normal age- and sex-matched population.[59] Pacemaker implantation is therefore indicated for control of symptoms and not for the prolongation of life.

Hypotension

Due to age-related abnormalities in blood pressure homeostasis, as well as superimposed conditions which reduce intravascular volume and/or peripheral vascular resistance, hypotensive syndromes are common in elderly patients.

Orthostatic Hypotension Orthostatic hypotension, defined as a systolic blood pressure decline of 20 mmHg or more on assumption of an upright posture, has been reported to occur in 10 to 30 percent of community-dwelling elderly persons.[60,61] The prevalence depends upon the characteristics of the study population and may be more related to the coexistence of hypertension, rather than age.[62,63] Many elderly patients have marked variability in orthostatic blood pressure, which may be due to impaired baroreflex function.[64] These elderly patients have normal or increased elevations in plasma norepinephrine levels in response to posture change.

The major pathologic causes of orthostatic hypotension are shown in Table 107-4. Autonomic dysfunction is commonly accompanied by a fixed heart rate, visual difficulty, incontinence, constipation, inability to sweat, heat intolerance, impotence, and fatigability.[61]

Central and peripheral autonomic insufficiency can be differentiated on the basis of plasma norepinephrine or vasopressin levels. Patients with pure autonomic failure (peripheral) have lower basal plasma norepinephrine levels while supine, no increase in norepinephrine levels with standing, a lower threshold for the pressor response to infused norepinephrine, and lower plasma norepinephrine levels in response to tyramine despite a greater pressor response to the drug.[65] These findings suggest that pure autonomic failure is characterized by depletion of norepinephrine from sympathetic nerve endings with resultant postsynaptic denervation super-sensitivity. These patients also have normal plasma vasopressin elevations in response to posture change.[66] In autonomic insufficiency with central causes (e.g., Shy-Drager syndrome), circulating norepinephrine levels and the response to infused norepinephrine and tyramine are normal,[65] but plasma norepinephrine and vasopressin levels fail to increase with standing. This syndrome is associated with degeneration of neurons in the CNS.

Postprandial Hypotension Postprandial hypotension is a common abnormality in blood pressure homeostasis in elderly people.[67,68] Institutionalized and healthy community-dwelling elderly persons have an average 11-mmHg decline in blood pressure by 1 hour after a meal. While in most older people this is an asymptomatic, age-related abnormality, individuals with postprandial syncope have more profound declines in blood pressure that are probably responsible for their fainting episodes.[69] Postprandial hypotension may be related to an inability to compensate for splanchnic blood pooling during digestion.

Volume Depletion Elderly persons are at increased risk for dehydration and associated orthostatic hypotension due to age-related impairments in renal salt and water conservation[32] and to any disease that threatens access to fluids or results in volume loss (see Chap. 108).

Abnormal Cardiovascular Reflexes

Vasovagal Syncope Vasovagal syncope is the most common form of syncope in the younger population. It is also seen in elderly persons but appears to be relatively less common. Syncope without an apparent cause is often inappropriately labeled "vasovagal." The exact prevalence is unknown. There is often a precipitant such as a painful or unpleasant experience (e.g., phlebotomy), surgical manipulation, or trauma. It is commonly associated with hunger, fatigue, crowding, or warmth. There are often premonitory signs and symptoms of intense autonomic nervous system stimulation, such as marked weakness, sweating, pallor, epigastric discomfort, nausea, yawning, sighing, hyperventilation, blurred vision, impaired hearing, a feeling of unawareness, and mydriasis.[22] Most often these symptoms occur while standing and are aborted by lying down. The circulatory changes preceding vasovagal syncope are biphasic, with initial increase in heart rate, blood pressure, total systemic resistance, and cardiac output. These changes are followed by cessation of sympathetic nervous system activity, peripheral vasodilatation, an increase in muscle blood flow, and a decrease in venous return to the heart.[70] The prognosis is good in true vasovagal syncope, although malignant forms with prolonged sinus arrest have been identified in young patients.

Carotid Sinus Syndrome Carotid sinus hypersensitivity is a common abnormality of reflex blood pressure regulation that in its pathologic extreme may result in syncope. A hypersensitive carotid sinus reflex, defined by a sinus slowing of greater than 50 percent (cardioinhibitory) or systolic blood pressure decline (vasodepressor) of over 50 mmHg or to hypotensive levels during carotid sinus massage, may identify a predisposition for syncope but does not prove that it is responsible for a given episode. Carotid sinus hypersensitivity associated with syncope is the carotid sinus syndrome.[71] A number of patients with unexplained syncope may have the carotid sinus syndrome. Unfortunately, physicians may overlook the carotid sinus syndrome by not doing carotid sinus massage on patients with syncope.

Defecation,[72] Micturition,[73] Swallowing,[74] and Cough Syncope[75,76] Syncope may occur in response to any of these activities. The mechanism of syncope may be decreased venous return during the activities, an intermittent conduction disturbance or arrhythmia, or reflex-induced bradycardia or vasodilatation. Patients with syncope during these activities may develop syncope later under different conditions. The prognosis depends on the underlying pathophysiologic mechanism.

Abnormal Blood Composition

The maintenance of consciousness depends not only on delivery of blood to the brain, but also on adequate levels of glucose and oxygen in the blood in order to support oxidative cerebral metabolism. Thus, hypoxemia (due to respiratory failure), anemia, and hypoglycemia may predispose to syncope.[28]

CNS Disease

Syncope can be attributed to CNS disease or cerebrovascular insufficiency only if transient and focal neurologic deficits are associated with the episode. The new onset of a seizure disorder may present as syncope. Conversely, syncope from other causes may be associated with seizure activity.[22]

Evaluation

The history is the most important part of the evaluation of syncope, providing a diagnosis in up to 50 percent of cases where a cause is found. The physical examination makes the diagnosis in another 20 percent of cases.[77]

The *history* includes four key questions.[78] First, was there an obvious precipitant? Emotional stress, pain, cough, micturition, defecation, swallowing, effort (aortic stenosis), neck turning (carotid sinus syndrome), change in position, recent meal, or medication are all important clues. Second, were there any associated symptoms? Hunger, sweating, odd behavior, or slow onset and recovery may suggest hypoglycemia. Flushing on recovery may suggest a Stokes-Adams attack. Palpitations, dyspnea, or chest pain may suggest pulmonary embolism, angina pectoris, or myocardial infarction. Focal neurologic symptoms suggest a neurologic disorder. Third, could medications have been responsible? Various antihypertensive and antianginal medications can cause hypotension. Digoxin and various antiarrhythmic medications can paradoxically cause arrhythmias. Fourth, how long did the symptoms last? If the symptoms last for more than 15 minutes, the physician should consider transient ischemic attack, seizure, hypoglycemia, or hysteria.

Physical examination should focus on postural vital signs, cardiovascular and neurologic systems, and a search for trauma. Blood pressure and heart rate are measured after at least a 5-minute rest in the supine position, then again after 1 minute of standing and 3 minutes of standing. If the patient cannot stand, sitting will suffice but may lead to failure to diagnose orthostatic hypotension. A symptomatic blood pressure drop focuses further evaluation on the causes of orthostatic hypotension. In the young patient, excessive acceleration of the pulse in response to posture change suggests that volume depletion, bleeding, or medications may be the cause of orthostatic hypotension. However, this finding may be absent in some elderly patients with severe baroreflex impairment. If pulse rate does not accelerate, autonomic dysfunction may also be the cause.

Careful evaluation of the carotid pulsations for contour, amplitude, and sound is important. Although the carotid upstroke is characteristically delayed in aortic stenosis, a normal upstroke does not rule out the diagnosis of aortic stenosis in the elderly patient because of an age-related increase in vascular rigidity which increases the rate of rise of the carotid pulse. When aortic stenosis develops, the rate of rise falls, but to an amplitude that may feel normal for a younger patient.[79] Also, a diminished carotid pulse or bruit may be suggestive of cerebrovascular disease, but its absence does not rule out a diagnosis of cerebral ischemia. In patients with severe aortic stenosis, simultaneous palpation of the carotid and apical impulses yields a palpable lag time between the two, which may suggest severe aortic stenosis.[80]

Cardiopulmonary examination focuses on detection of obstructive cardiovascular disorders such as aortic stenosis, hypertrophic cardiomyopathy, and pulmonary embolism. Unfortunately, cardiac murmurs become exceedingly common with advanced age, and significant murmurs in the elderly patient may be atypical in character or location.[81] Thus, associated clinical symptoms, such as congestive heart failure or angina pectoris, or signs, such as a diminished second aortic sound or left ventricular hypertrophy, should heighten the suspicion of hemodynamically significant conditions, and stimulate further studies (e.g., a Doppler echocardiogram). Stools should be checked for blood. A careful neurologic examination should include a search for focal deficits that may signify cerebral infarction, hemorrhage, or tumor.

Carotid sinus massage[82] is an important test in the evaluation of syncope if cerebrovascular disease or cardiac conduction disturbances are not present. With the electrocardiogram running and the head slightly extended and rotated to the opposite side, the carotid sinus is massaged for 5 seconds. The blood pressure is taken before and immediately after the procedure. Two to three minutes later the procedure is repeated on the other side. Only symptomatic bradycardia or hypotension can be considered truly positive responses indicating carotid sinus hypersensitivity. However, there is general agreement that a systolic blood pressure decline of more than 50 mmHg (or an absolute value less than 90 mmHg) or a sinus pause of 3 seconds or longer is sufficient to produce syncope, particularly if the patient was in an upright position at the time of the syncopal event.

An *electrocardiogram* is indicated in all patients presenting with syncope, since it can provide diagnostic clues for myocardial infarction, ischemia, or transient tachy- or bradyarrhythmias. Multifocal and frequent atrial and ventricular ectopic beats are an indication for prolonged cardiac monitoring. A short

PR interval may indicate an accessory pathway.[83] QT prolongation is associated with ventricular tachycardia and fibrillation.[84] Sinoatrial pauses or inappropriate sinus bradycardia may indicate a sinus node disorder. The presence of AV conduction abnormalities or bundle-branch block hints at transient heart block as the cause of syncope.

Tests of autonomic function are indicated in any patient with orthostatic or postprandial hypotension. The simplest tests are deep breathing and the Valsalva maneuver.[85] The cold pressor and pharmacologic tests are poorly tolerated, potentially dangerous, and usually unnecessary in elderly patients.

Since electrical cardiac disease is so common in elderly patients, telemetry is usually indicated, even without cues from the electrocardiogram, unless noncardiac causes are positively identified. Ambulatory cardiac monitoring is only indicated in those syncope patients who are still suspected, after initial evaluation and/or telemetry monitoring, to have a symptomatic and safely treatable arrhythmia or conduction disturbance. Ambulatory monitoring should be performed during the patient's usual daily activities to increase the diagnostic yield. When monitored for 24 to 48 hours, 10 to 40 percent of patients will have transient symptoms. In these patients, cause based on an arrhythmia can be confirmed or excluded in 50 to 75 percent.[86] If symptoms are infrequent and continuous ambulatory cardiac monitoring is unrevealing, the patient with unexplained syncope should wear a loop electrocardiographic recorder to capture the cardiac rhythm during typical symptoms.[45]

Laboratory tests are generally of low yield but nevertheless are useful in the elderly syncopal patient without apparent cause on history and physical examination, since syncope may be the atypical presentation of several conditions evident only on laboratory testing. Cardiac enzyme levels should be determined if there is any associated chest pain or electrocardiographic change, both of which raise the suspicion of myocardial infarction. It is important to evaluate the volume status with tests for electrolytes, blood urea nitrogen, and creatinine and to identify abnormalities that predispose to arrhythmias. Testing of arterial blood gases is indicated if there are pulmonary symptoms. A hematocrit is helpful to rule out anemia. Blood sugar values should be obtained to look for hypoglycemia and marked hyperglycemia, both of which may present with syncope in the elderly patient. Drug levels of anticonvulsants, antiarrhythmics, digoxin, or bronchodilators are useful to detect toxicity or undertreatment of a prior condition known to produce syncope.

Echocardiography is an invaluable study when structural heart disease is suspected. Doppler echocardiography is useful to identify patients with significant aortic valve gradients. Doppler echocardiography correlates well with invasive cardiac catheterization, particularly when combined with 2-D echo.[87]

An *electroencephalogram* and a *CT scan of the head* should be obtained in the presence of focal neurologic abnormalities on physical examination or signs and symptoms of seizures.[26] More invasive studies such as cerebral or coronary angiography are only indicated to confirm specific clinical diagnoses.

Electrophysiologic studies of the heart are indicated in patients with cardiovascular disease and recurrent syncope in whom there is a high suspicion of sinus node dysfunction, conduction disease, or life-threatening arrhythmias. In patients of all ages, the overall incidence of findings (sinus node dysfunction, complete AV block, or ventricular tachycardia) considered to be positively related to syncope ranges from 18 to 75 percent. Most investigators find possible causes in approximately 60 percent and an even higher yield in patients with structural heart disease.[88] During follow-up, between 70 and 90 percent of those patients who received therapy on the basis of positive electrophysiologic findings remained asymptomatic.[89] Although these results are impressive, it should also be noted that an average of 50 percent of patients not specifically treated also remain free of recurrent syncope.

Predictors for a positive electrophysiologic study include[90] organic heart disease, nonsustained ventricular tachycardia by Holter monitoring (these two are highly sensitive for serious tachyarrhythmias), sinus bradycardia, first-degree heart block, and bundle-branch block by electrocardiogram (the latter three are sensitive for bradyarrhythmias). The benefits of any invasive procedure should be balanced against the risk and cost of the procedure and the potential adverse effects of therapy (including surgery and medications).

Recently, head-up tilt studies, with or without isoproterenol infusion, have been advocated for the diagnosis of a vasovagal cause of unexplained syncope. This test is founded on the observation that a vigorous cardiac contraction around a relatively empty ventricular chamber, as occurs during sympathetic nervous system activation and upright posture, may provoke sudden bradycardia and hypotension—the *Bezold-Jarisch reflex*.[39] Recent studies report that tilt testing alone provokes vasovagal syncope in 25 to 75 percent of patients with previous unexplained syncope, while the addition of isoproterenol infusion can increase the yield to 80 percent. In elderly syncope patients up to 80 years of age, tilt testing without isoproterenol is positive in 40 to 50 percent.[91,93]

However, several considerations challenge the usefulness of this test, particularly in elderly patients. First, the use of isoproterenol, which greatly increases test sensitivity, is often contraindicated in elderly patients, especially those with known or suspected coronary artery disease. While the use of isoproterenol may possibly improve tilt test specificity, the test clearly lacks specificity without isoproterenol. As many as 50 percent of healthy young individuals without histories of syncope may experience vasodepressor responses to head-up tilt testing.[94] Furthermore, elderly patients with unexplained syncope may actually be less susceptible to symptoms during postural tilt.[95] Finally, the presence of a positive test in the laboratory does not mean that the vasodepressor reaction was responsible for a given syncopal event. Most episodes of vasovagal syncope are readily diagnosable by the history of a vagal prodrome as described above. In addition, vasovagal syncope is relatively less common among elderly patients.

Given the present state of knowledge, tilt testing for elderly syncope patients should probably be limited to the following two clinical situations: (1) the relatively healthy elderly patient without structural heart disease, who has recurrent unexplained syncope despite the work-up described above, and (2) the elderly patient in whom autonomic insufficiency with delayed orthostatic hypotension is suspected.

The diagnostic approach to the elderly syncope patient is summarized in Fig. 107-2.

Therapeutic Issues

The purpose of treating an elderly patient who presents with syncope is to prevent the morbidity and mortality associated with recurrent episodes. When the cause of a syncopal episode is readily apparent, specific therapy should be planned if the potential morbidity of the treatment is less than that of recurrent syncope. Because therapeutic interventions may be toxic to elderly patients, such interventions should be instituted with cautious attention to age- and disease-related physiologic changes that may affect response to a treatment. No persons should be denied therapy on a basis of age alone.

When the cause of a syncopal episode is not clear, the therapy should be directed toward minimizing the risk of recurrent syncope by correcting predisposing conditions and eliminating drugs that may incrementally contribute to a syncopal event.[28] For example, the risk of syncope in an older person may be substantially reduced by treating anemia with a blood transfusion, correcting hypoxemia with supplemental oxygen, improving cardiac ischemia with nitrates (while observing for orthostatic hypotension), or preventing orthostatic hypotension with a high salt intake (while observing for congestive heart failure) and support stockings. The mainstay of therapy for autonomic insufficiency is fludrocortisone and salt loading, but new pharmacologic approaches are being investigated (e.g., the use of caffeine, ergotamine, and octreotide, a synthetic somatostatin analogue.[64]

Before prescribing pharmacologic or surgical therapy for a diagnosed condition, the available safe, simple, and commonsense treatments should be implemented. Such treatments include discontinuing use of potentially harmful drugs, such as digoxin, propranolol, or alpha methyldopa, which may predispose to carotid sinus hypersensitivity or suppress the sinus node; avoiding extreme neck rotation and tight collars when there is evidence of carotid sinus hypersensitivity; arising from the supine position slowly and dorsiflexing the feet a few minutes before standing (for persons prone to postural hypotension); maintaining adequate intravascular volume through regular fluid intake (for cognitively impaired or acutely ill patients); and urinating while sitting down (for men with micturition syncope). Often a simple behavioral change or drug elimination is the only therapy necessary to prevent recurrent syncopal episodes.

Antiarrhythmic medications should be prescribed only for *symptomatic* rhythm disturbances and initially at one-half the usual dose, due to the medications' prolonged half-lives and their increased toxicity in elderly patients.[96] Clinically significant adverse reactions are seen in up to half of young patients treated with antiarrhythmic medications, with major reactions noted in one-third.[97] Proarrhythmic effects (i.e., worsening of arrhythmia as a result of therapy) are now an appreciated complication of antiarrhythmic medications in up to one-third of patients. When the high incidence of serious side effects is coupled with the fact that no controlled studies have conclusively proved that patients with arrhythmia benefit from antiarrhythmic drug therapy, a high level of reluctance for initiating this kind of therapy in the very elderly patient is justifiable. Basic monitoring of medication levels, electrolytes, the electrocardiographic QT interval, and arrhythmia frequency on the ambulatory cardiac monitor is important when antiarrhythmic medications are prescribed.

Pacemakers[98] are generally indicated for the amelioration of symptoms due to bradyarrhythmias. The most common indications for permanent pacemakers are third-degree AV block (Stokes-Adams attacks) and sick sinus syndrome. Symptomatic second-degree AV block, symptomatic bi- or trifascicular block, and carotid sinus syndrome are also indications for a permanent pacemaker. A single-chamber ventricular pacemaker is generally adequate, but in the elderly patient who is dependent on atrial contraction to generate an adequate cardiac output, a dual-chamber pacemaker should be considered. Indications for antiarrhythmic medications, pacemakers, and electrophysiologic studies are continually being reassessed, and the latest consensus should be sought and carefully considered prior to making such a prescription for an elderly patient.

Invasive therapy such as aortic valve repair, balloon valvuloplasty, coronary angioplasty, and coronary artery bypass surgery has been shown to be feasible and effective in the elderly patient and to have an acceptable (low) mortality rate in patients who are otherwise well. Experience with balloon valvuloplasty for aortic stenosis suggests that this procedure may be of benefit to the symptomatic elderly patient who is at high surgical risk.[99]

Conclusion

Age-related physiologic changes and disease-related abnormalities predispose the elderly patient to syn-

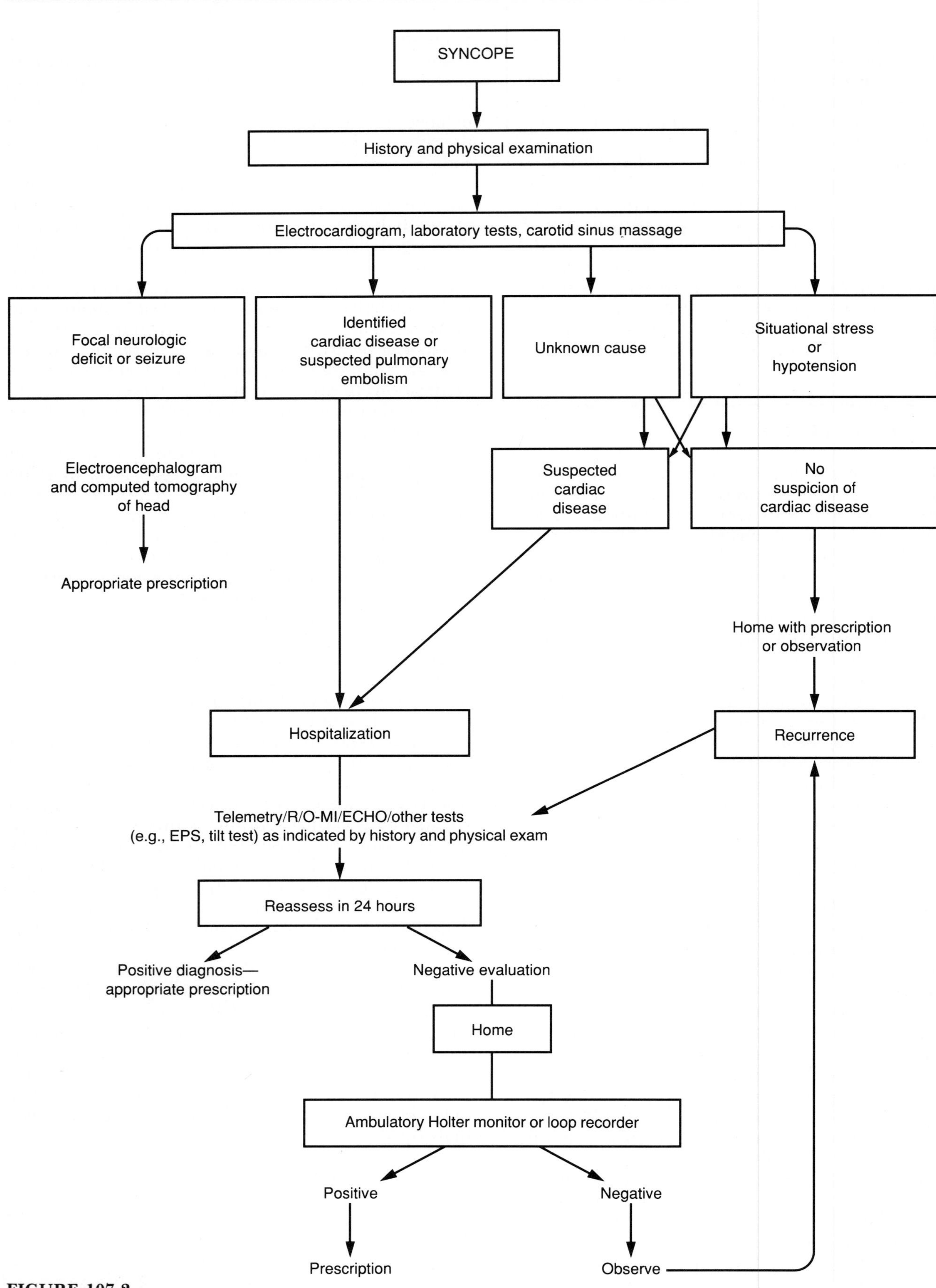

FIGURE 107-2
Algorithm for the diagnostic evaluation of the elderly syncope patient.

cope. Syncope may be the atypical manifestation of diseases or situational stresses that are usually not expected to present with syncopal episodes. Attention to situational stresses, such as posture change, meals, or drug ingestion, is likely to increase the diagnostic yield and lead to simple therapy that can reduce the morbidity and potential mortality of recurrent episodes. Therapy should be directed toward minimizing multiple risks for syncope, avoiding toxic interventions, and treating specific symptomatic diseases, while basing treatment on underlying disease rather than on age per se.

REFERENCES

1. Drachman DA, Hart CW: An approach to the dizzy patient. *Neurology* 22:323, 1972.
2. Philip S et al: Dizziness in a community elderly population. *J Am Geriatr Soc* 37:101, 1989.
3. Cohn TE, Lasley DJ: Visual depth illusion and falls in the elderly. *Clin Geriatr Med* 1:601, 1985.
4. Koken E et al: Quantitative evaluation of joint motion sensation in an aging population. *J Gerontol* 33:62, 1978.
5. Wyke B: Cervical articular contributions to posture and gait: Their relation to senile dysequilibrium. *Age Ageing* 8:251, 1979.
6. Baloh RW: Dizziness in older people. *J Am Geriatr Soc* 40:713, 1992.
7. Stanle J, Tenino J: Paroxysmal positional nystagmus: An electronystagmographic and clinical study. *Ann Otol* 74:69, 1965.
8. Cawthorne TE, Hinchcliffe R: Positional nystagmus of the central type as evidence of subtentorial metastases. *Brain* 84:415, 1961.
9. Baloh RW et al: Benign positional vertigo: Clinical and oculographic features in 240 cases. *Neurology* 37:371, 1987.
10. Schuknecht H: Cupulolithiasis. *Arch Otolaryngol* 90:765, 1969.
11. Rutka JA, Barber HO: Recurrent vestibulopathy: Third review. *J Otolaryngol* 15:105, 1986.
12. Arenberg IK: Symposium on Meniere's disease. *Otolaryngol Clin North Am* 135:4, 1984.
13. Hart R et al: Acoustic tumors: Atypical features and recent diagnostic tests. *Neurology* 33:211, 1983.
14. Hybels RL: Drug toxicity of the inner ear. *Med Clin North Am* 63:309, 1979.
15. Fisher CM: Vertigo in cerebrovascular disease. *Arch Otolaryngol* 85:529, 1967.
16. Huang C, Yu Y: Small cerebellar strokes may mimic labyrinthine lesions. *J Neurol Neurosurg Psychiatry* 48:263, 1985.
17. Reichert WH et al: Vestibular dysfunction in Parkinson's disease. *Neurology* 32:1133, 1982.
18. Sloane PD, Baloh RW: Persistent dizziness in geriatric patients. *J Am Geriatr Soc* 37:1031, 1989.
19. Dix MR, Hallpike C: The pathology, symptomatology and diagnosis of certain common disorders of the vestibular system. *Proc R Soc Med* 45:341, 1952.
20. Nelson JR: The minimal ice water caloric test. *Neurology* 19:577, 1969.
21. Norre ME, Beckers A: Benign paroxysmal positional vertigo in the elderly. Treatment by habituation exercises. *J Am Geriatr Soc* 36:425, 1988.
22. Wayne HH: Syncope: Physiological considerations and an analysis of the clinical characteristics in 510 patients. *Am J Med* 30:418, 1961.
23. Savage DD et al: Epidemiologic features of isolated syncope: The Framingham Study. *Stroke* 16:626, 1985.
24. Lipsitz LA et al: Syncope in an elderly, institutionalized population: Prevalence, incidence, and associated risk. *Q J Med* 216:45, 1985.
25. Kapoor WN et al: Syncope in the elderly. *Am J Med* 80:419, 1986.
26. Day SC et al: Evaluation and outcome of emergency room patients with transient loss of consciousness. *Am J Med* 73:15, 1982.
27. Kapoor WN et al: Diagnostic and prognostic implications of recurrences in patients with syncope. *Am J Med* 83:700, 1987.
28. Lipsitz LA: Syncope in the elderly. *Ann Intern Med* 99:92, 1983.
29. Kety SS: Human cerebral blood flow and oxygen consumption as related to aging. *J Chron Dis* 3:478, 1956.
30. Shimada K et al: Age-related changes of baroreflex function, plasma norepinephrine, and blood pressure. *Hypertension* 7:113, 1985.
31. Iskandrian AS, Hakki AH: Age-related changes in left ventricular diastolic performance. *Am Heart J* 112:75, 1986.
32. Epstein M, Hollenberg NK. Age as a determinant of renal sodium conservation in normal man. *J Lab Clin Med* 87:411, 1976.
33. Phillips PA et al: Reduced thirst after water deprivation in healthy elderly men. *N Engl J Med* 311:753, 1984.
34. Kapoor WN et al: Syncope of unknown origin: The need for a more cost-effective approach to its diagnostic evaluation. *JAMA* 247:2687, 1982.
35. Silverstein MD et al: Patients with syncope admitted to medical intensive care units. *JAMA* 248:1185, 1982.
36. Pomerance A: Cardiac pathology in the elderly, in Noble RJ, Rothbaum DA (eds): *Geriatric Cardiology.* Philadelphia, Davis, p 28.
37. Pomerance A: Pathogenesis of aortic stenosis and its relation to age. *Br Heart J* 34:569, 1972.
38. Finegan RE et al: Aortic stenosis in the elderly. *N Engl J Med* 279:225, 1968.
39. Mark AL: The Bezold-Jarisch reflex revisited: Clinical implications of inhibitory reflexes originating in the heart. *J Am Coll Cardiol* 1:90, 1983.
40. Krasnow N, Stein RA: Hypertrophic cardiomyopathy in the aged. *Am Heart J* 96:326, 1978.
41. Topol EJ et al: Hypertensive hypertrophic cardiomyopathy of the elderly. *N Engl J Med* 312:277, 1985.
42. Betocchi S et al: Isovolumic relaxation period in hyper-

trophic cardiomyopathy: Assessment by radionuclide angiography. *J Am Coll Cardiol* 7:74, 1986.
43. Cookson H: Fainting and fits in cardiac infarction. *Br Heart J* 4:163, 1942.
44. Gibson TC, Hertzman MR: Diagnostic efficacy of 24-hour electrocardiographic monitoring for syncope. *Am J Cardiol* 5:398, 1984.
45. Linzer M et al: Incremental diagnostic yield of loop electrocardiographic recorders in unexplained syncope. *Am J Cardiol* 66:214, 1990.
46. Fleg JL, Kennedy HL: Cardiac arrhythmias in a healthy elderly population. Detection by 24 hour ambulatory electrocardiography. *Chest* 81:302, 1982.
47. Horan MJ, Kennedy HL: Ventricular ectopy. History, epidemiology and clinical implications. *JAMA* 251:380, 1984.
48. Kennedy HL et al: Long-term follow-up of asymptomatic healthy subjects with frequent and complex ventricular ectopy. *N Engl J Med* 312:193, 1985.
49. Mymin D et al: The natural history of primary first-degree heart block. *N Engl J Med* 315:1183, 1986.
50. Lev M: Anatomic basis for atrioventricular block. *Am J Med* 37:742, 1964.
51. McAnulty JH et al: Natural history of "high-risk" bundle-branch block. Final report of a prospective study. *N Engl J Med* 307:137, 1982.
52. Ezri M et al: Electrophysiologic evaluation of syncope in patients with bifascicular block. *Am Heart J* 106:693, 1983.
53. Dhingra RC et al: Syncope in patients with chronic bifascicular block. Significance, causative mechanisms, and clinical implications. *Ann Intern Med* 81:302, 1974.
54. Scheinman MM et al: Prognostic value of infranodal conduction time in patients with chronic bundle branch block. *Circulation* 56:240, 1977.
55. Agruss NS et al: Significance of chronic sinus bradycardia in elderly people. *Circulation* 46:924, 1972.
56. Gann D et al: Electrophysiologic evaluation of elderly patients with sinus bradycardia. A long-term follow-up study. *Ann Intern Med* 90:24, 1979.
57. Obel IWP et al: Chronic symptomatic sinoatrial block: A review of 34 patients and their treatment. *Chest* 65:397, 1974.
58. Moss AJ, Davis RJ: Brady-tachy syndrome. *Prog Cardiovasc Dis* 16:439, 1974.
59. Shaw DB et al: Survival in sinoatrial disorder (sick-sinus syndrome). *Br Med J* 280:139, 1980.
60. Mader SL: Aging and postural hypotension. *J Am Geriatr Soc* 37:129, 1989.
61. Lipsitz LA. Orthostatic hypotension in the elderly. *N Engl J Med* 321:952, 1989.
62. Harris T et al: Postural change in blood pressure associated with age and systolic blood pressure. The national health and nutrition examination survey II. *J Gerontol* 46:M159, 1991.
63. Applegate WB et al: Prevalence of postural hypotension at baseline in the systolic hypertension in the elderly program (SHEP) cohort. *J Am Geriatr Soc* 39:1057, 1991.
64. Lipsitz LA et al: Intraindividual variability in postural blood pressure in the elderly. *Clin Sci* 69:337, 1985.
65. Polinsky RJ et al: Pharmacologic distinction of different orthostatic hypotension syndromes. *Neurology* 31:1, 1981.
66. Kaufmann H et al: Hypotension-induced vasopressin release distinguishes between pure autonomic failure and multiple system atrophy with autonomic failure. *Neurology* 42:590, 1992.
67. Vaitkevicius PV et al: Frequency and importance of postprandial blood pressure reduction in elderly nursing-home patients. *Ann Intern Med* 115:865, 1991.
68. Lipsitz LA et al: Postprandial reduction in blood pressure in the elderly. *N Engl J Med* 309:81, 1983.
69. Lipsitz LA et al: Cardiovascular and norepinephrine responses after meal consumption in elderly (older than 75 years) persons with postprandial hypotension and syncope. *Am J Cardiol* 58:810, 1986.
70. Engel GL: Psychologic stress, vasodepressor (vasovagal) syncope, and sudden death. *Ann Intern Med* 89:403, 1978.
71. Lown B, Levine SA: The carotid sinus. Clinical value of its stimulation. *Circulation* 23:766, 1961.
72. Kapoor WW et al: Defecation syncope a symptom with multiple etiologies. *Arch Intern Med* 146:2377, 1986.
73. Kapoor WW et al: Micturition syncope: A reappraisal. *JAMA* 253:796, 1985.
74. Kadish AH et al: Swallowing syncope: Observations in the absence of conduction system or esophageal disease. *Am J Med* 81:1098, 1986.
75. Sharpey-Schafer EP: The mechanism of syncope after coughing. *Br Med J* 2:860, 1953.
76. Strauss MJ et al: Case report, atypical cough syncope. *JAMA* 251:1731, 1984.
77. Kudenchuk PJ, McAnulty JH: Syncope: Evaluation and treatment. *Mod Conc Cardiovasc Dis* 54:25, 1985.
78. Ormerod AD: Syncope. *Br Med J* 288:1219, 1984.
79. Flohr KH et al: Diagnosis of aortic stenosis in older age groups using external carotid pulse recording and phonocardiography. *Br Heart J* 45:577, 1981.
80. Chun PKC, Dunn BE: Clinical clues of severe aortic stenosis. Simultaneous palpation of the carotid and apical impulses. *Arch Intern Med* 142:2284, 1982.
81. Pomerance A: Cardiac pathology and systolic murmurs in the elderly. *Br Heart J* 30:687, 1968.
82. Schweitzer P, Teichholz LE: Carotid sinus massage: Its diagnostic and therapeutic value in arrhythmias. *Am J Med* 78:645, 1985.
83. Wellens HJJ et al: The management of preexcitation syndrome. *JAMA* 257:2325, 1987.
84. Moss AJ: Prolonged QT interval syndrome. *JAMA* 256:2985, 1986.
85. Henrich WL: Autonomic insufficiency. *Arch Intern Med* 142:339, 1982.
86. Kapoor WN: Evaluation of syncope in the elderly. *J Am Geriatr Soc* 35:826, 1987.
87. Yaeger M et al: Comparison of Doppler-derived pressure gradient to that determined at cardiac catheterization in adults with aortic valve stenosis: Implications for management. *Am J Cardiol* 57:644, 1986.
88. Kapoor WN et al: Diagnosis and natural history of syncope and the role of invasive electrophysiologic testing. *Am J Cardiol* 63:730, 1989.
89. Sugrue DD et al: Impact of intracardiac electrophysiologic testing on the management of elderly patients with recurrent syncope or near syncope. *J Am Geriatr Soc* 35:1079, 1987.
90. Bachinsky WB et al: Usefulness of clinical characteristics in predicting the outcome of electrophysiologic

studies in unexplained syncope. *Am J Cardiol* 69:1044, 1992.

91. Almquist A et al: Provocation of bradycardia and hypotension by isoproterenol and upright posture in patients with unexplained syncope. *N Engl J Med* 320:346, 1989.
92. Strasberg B et al: The head-up tilt table test in patients with syncope of unknown origin. *Am Heart J* 118:923, 1989.
93. Grubb BP et al: Utility of upright tilt-table testing in the evaluation and management of syncope of unknown origin. *Am J Med* 90:6, 1991.
94. Kapoor WN, Brant N: Evaluation of syncope by upright tilt testing with isoproterenol. A nonspecific test. *Ann Intern Med* 116:358, 1992.
95. Lipsitz LA et al: Reduced susceptibility to syncope during postural tilt in old age. Is beta-blockade protective? *Arch Intern Med* 149:2709, 1989.

Chapter 108

DISORDERS OF FLUID BALANCE: DEHYDRATION AND HYPONATREMIA

Kenneth M. Davis and Kenneth L. Minaker

Disorders of water balance are common causes of morbidity and mortality in the elderly population. In this chapter, we review the age-related physiologic changes in fluid homeostasis that predispose elderly persons to disorders of fluid balance. Following this, we provide an overview of the common illnesses predisposing to dehydration and hyponatremia. Finally, we outline current therapy for these disorders.

AGE-RELATED CHANGES IN FLUID HOMEOSTASIS

In the normal young adult, neurohypophyseal-pituitary-renal axis capacity to maintain fluid balance far exceeds the ordinary demands.[1] While the functional reserve of the system is substantially diminished in old age, healthy elderly persons retain adequate homeostatic reserve for maintenance of fluid volume and composition during usual stresses.[2] However, during extremes of physiologic stress or in the course of common illness, this limited reserve may become overwhelmed, predisposing the elderly patient to clinical abnormalities of water balance.

Basal levels of electrolytes, osmolarity, and vasopressin are unchanged with age. Because of the decrease in lean body mass and the increase in percentage body fat, there is a decline in total body water with aging. The percentage of body mass as water declines from 60 percent in young men to as low as 45 percent in elderly women.

Central nervous system (CNS) control of fluid balance involves both vasopressin and thirst. Under ordinary physiologic conditions, vasopressin modulates water balance, and thirst functions as an emergency backup to repair water deficits.[3] The major physiologic stimulus for vasopressin secretion in humans is plasma osmolarity. Studies of the plasma vasopressin response of young subjects (22 to 48 years old) and older subjects (52 to 66 years old) during hypertonic saline infusions show that the threshold for vasopressin release is not influenced by age (to age 66, at least) and that vasopressin responses are even enhanced in the older group.[4] During water deprivation, greater elevations of vasopressin levels have been observed in older subjects, albeit with somewhat greater accompanying hyperosmolarity.[5] Other stimuli for vasopressin release result in distinctly different vasopressin responses with age. Volume-pressure stimulation is less likely to result in vasopressin release with age.[6]

When vasopressin and renal capacity to maintain water balance have been overwhelmed, thirst supervenes, stimulating the ingestion of water, which reduces the systemic hyperosmolarity. Thirst and drinking are stimulated by cellular dehydration in central brain osmoreceptors located in a region extending from the preoptic area of the hypothalamus and including tissue surrounding the anterocentral part of the third ventricle to the zona incerta posteriorly.[7] Following water deprivation or hypertonic saline infusion, subjective measures of thirst and objective measures of drinking behavior are decreased in the elderly.[5,8] The mechanisms for these phenomena are unclear. The renin-angiotensin system and cardiac receptors stimulate drinking when extracellular fluid volume depletion occurs. The well-described decline in renin-angiotensin levels as well as altered baroreceptor function with aging may contribute to the diminished thirst response in normal aging.[9] Oropharyngeal factors, including taste and gastric distension, are also modulators of drinking behavior. Substantial variability in the level of osmolarity producing thirst is observed in young subjects. Thirst threshold has not yet been carefully examined in elderly subjects, but it is likely that elderly persons exhibit similar variability.[10]

Changes in intrarenal vasculature and glomerular function that occur with age are associated with linear declines in renal plasma flow. Long-standing relative hypertension or high protein intake may be partially responsible for these changes. Studies of water deprivation in healthy men reveal that young subjects can decrease urine flow markedly to a minimum of 0.5 ml/min and increase urine osmolarity to a maximum of 1100 mosm/kg. Elderly subjects are only able to decrease urine flow to 1.0 ml/min and increase urine osmolarity to a maximum of 882 mosm/kg.[2] Urine-concentrating ability declines with aging even after correcting for the decreased glomerular filtration in the elderly. While Lindeman et al. were unable to demonstrate an age-related decline in response to submaximal vasopressin infusion, Miller and Shock have shown a clear diminution of maximal urinary osmolarity during high-dose vasopressin infusions in older subjects.[11,12]

A modest age-related impairment in the maximal excretion of free water after water loading has been demonstrated.[12,13] Minimal urinary concentration (urinary/plasma osmolarity) rises from 0.247 in the young to 0.418 in the elderly.[13,14] This defect in excretion of free water may predispose the elderly to hyponatremia. Finally, significant delays in adaptation to salt restriction have been documented in older subjects.[14,15]

These age-related changes in the regulation of the volume and composition of extracellular fluid increase the likelihood of developing fluid disorders during an illness or with severe physiologic stress. In addition to the normal aging-related changes, superimposed illnesses may result in a further diminution of the homeostatic capacity to regulate fluid balance.

DEHYDRATION

Common Illnesses Predisposing to Dehydration in Elderly Persons

Dehydration is the most common fluid and electrolyte problem accompanying acute illnesses in old age and is caused by one or more of the following mechanisms: excess loss of water, failure to recognize the need to increase water intake, or impaired water ingestion. The mortality of hospitalized patients with dehydration is seven times that of age-matched patients without dehydration and ranges between 40 and 70 percent.[16] Dehydration (decrease in total body water) can present in three forms:

- *Hypertonic dehydration:* Loss of water more than sodium, associated with high serum sodium levels (>145 meq/liter) and high serum osmolarity (>290 mosm/liter).
- *Isotonic dehydration:* Loss of equal amounts of sodium and water, associated with normal serum sodium levels (135 to 145 meq/liter) and normal serum osmolarity (280 to 290 mosm/liter).
- *Hypotonic dehydration:* Loss of sodium (salt) more than water, associated with low serum sodium levels (<135 meq/liter) and low serum osmolarity (<280 mosm/liter).

The electrolyte disorder classically associated with water loss is hypernatremia, which occurs in 1.1 to 1.6 percent of all acute hospital admissions in the elderly population.[17] Snyder et al.[17] studied 15,187 consecutive hospital admissions of patients over 60 years old and found that 162 (1.1 percent) had serum sodium levels greater than 148 meq/liter. Only 43 percent of these patients were hypernatremic on admission; the majority developed an elevated serum sodium level during hospitalization, one-half of them within the first 8 days. Patients who presented with hypernatremia on admission had higher sodium levels but a lower mortality rate (29 versus 52 percent) than those developing hypernatremia during acute hospitalization.

Table 108-1 lists the factors most commonly associated with hypernatremia. Forty-four percent of patients had three or more factors contributing to their hypernatremic states. This is consistent with the fact that multiple factors usually contribute to dehydration in the elderly patient. No matter what the illness, the evaluation must assess possible causes for excessive fluid loss or decreased fluid intake (Tables 108-2 and 108-3).

Increased Fluid Losses

Acute infections, such as pneumonia and urinary tract infections, are common in the elderly population, accounting for up to 20 percent of acute hospitalizations in this population. The associated fever causes increased insensible water loss from sweating, tachypnea, and increased cellular catabolism. Infection of the upper urinary tract may specifically result in reduction of the renal concentrating ability that may persist for weeks following resolution of the infection.

Excessive urinary losses of water and sodium are very common in the sick elderly patient. Continuation of diuretic drug therapy in the elderly dehydrated patient is an unfortunate yet common and prevent-

TABLE 108-1

Factors Associated with Hypernatremia

Factors	Patients, %
Febrile illness	70
Infirmity	40
Surgery	21
Nutritional supplementation	20
Intravenous solutes	18
Diabetes mellitus	15
Diarrhea	11
Gastrointestinal bleeding	9
Diuretics	9
Diabetes insipidus	7
Dialysis-related	3

SOURCE: From Snyder et al.[17]

TABLE 108-2

Causes of Increased Fluid Loss in Elderly Patients

- Chronic or acute infections
- Excessive urinary losses
  - Diuretic misuse
  - Glycosuria
  - Hypercalciuria
  - Mannitol
  - Radiographic contrast agents
  - Elevated blood urea nitrogen (BUN)
  - Diabetes insipidus
    - Central (pituitary)
    - Nephrogenic
  - Hypoaldosteronism
    - Addison's disease
    - Hyporeninemic hypoaldosteronism
  - Suppressed vasopressin
    - Alzheimer's disease
    - Phenytoin
    - Ethanol
    - Postatrial tachyarrhythmia
  - Postobstructive diuresis
- Gastrointestinal losses
  - Upper GI
    - Vomiting
    - Nasogastric drainage
  - Lower GI (diarrhea)
    - Laxative abuse or bowel preps
    - Infectious or secretory
    - Surgical bypass or fistulas
    - Ischemic bowel
    - Colectomy
- Excessive blood loss
- Environment-related fluid loss
  - Heat wave
  - Hypothermia
- Compartmental fluid shifts
  - Hypoalbuminemia
  - Pancreatitis
  - Ascites
  - Anaphylaxis
  - Burns
  - Hypertonic peritoneal dialysate

TABLE 108-3

Causes of Decreased Fluid Intake in Elderly Patients

- Limited access to fluids
  - Physical restraints
  - Mobility restriction
  - Poor visual acuity
- Fluid restriction
  - Preprocedure
  - Prevention of incontinence or nocturia or aspiration
  - Therapy for edema or hyponatremia
- Altered sensorium
  - Decreased consciousness level
    - Sedatives, neuroleptics, narcotics
    - Structural and metabolic CNS insults
    - Febrile illness
  - Decreased level of awareness
    - Dementia, delirium
    - Mania, psychosis, depression
- Gastrointestinal disorders
  - Swallowing disorders
  - Bowel obstruction
    - Mechanical
    - Metabolic
    - Ischemic
  - Anticholinergic medication
- Alteration in thirst mechanism
  - Primary adipsia
  - Medication-related
    - Cardiac glycosides
    - Amphetamines
  - Associated with focal CNS pathology

able problem. As many as 10 percent of hospitalized elderly patients in the United Kingdom are admitted with diuretic side effects such as dehydration. In addition to pharmacological diuresis, obligate diuresis is common to many prevalent illnesses of the elderly population. These include the glycosuria of diabetes mellitus, hypercalciuria of malignancy and hyperparathyroidism, and the use of intravenous mannitol and radiographic contrast agents. An obligate diuresis may result from renal absorption of excessive blood urea nitrogen (BUN) generated by increased gut protein catabolism in the setting of gastrointestinal bleeding or high-protein enteral tube feedings.[18,19]

Central diabetes insipidus is not a common disease in the elderly population, but nephrogenic diabetes insipidus is frequently seen in association with drugs such as lithium, demeclocycline, and methoxyflurane anesthesia. Hypoaldosteronism occurs in the setting of Addison's disease with inadequate mineralocorticoid replacement as well as in the hyporeninemic state associated with normal aging. This hypoaldosteronism results in impairment in the urinary salvage of sodium and water during periods of dehydration. Elderly persons with Alzheimer's disease may have an inadequate vasopressin response to hyperosmolarity.[20] Drugs such as phenytoin (Dilantin) and ethanol suppress vasopressin release, resulting in a decrease in tubular reabsorption of water. Alcohol abuse contributing to dehydration is frequently underrecognized in the elderly patient.

Urinary tract obstruction is a common affliction in the elderly man with prostatic hypertrophy (often exacerbated by anticholinergic medication). In the elderly woman, postoperative urinary retention is a frequently unrecognized cause of obstructive uropathy. The postobstructive diuresis associated with relief of urinary obstruction is physiologically similar to nephrogenic diabetes insipidus with inadequate renal responsiveness to vasopressin.

Gastrointestinal losses of fluid occur with vomiting, nasogastric drainage, diarrhea, and bleeding. In addition to the commonly recognized causes of diarrhea, laxative abuse is often present but unreported in the elderly patient. As many as 40 to 60 percent of elderly persons use laxatives regularly, and the elderly patient may continue to take regularly ordered laxatives and stool softeners in the setting of diarrhea. Older patients are often victimized by aggressive bowel-cleansing regimens before radiographic study of the bowel or kidney. A patient with previous intestinal bypass or colectomy is at further risk for dehydration due to reduced gastrointestinal water absorptive capacity.

Elderly persons are especially prone to heat-related fluid loss from excessive sweating with inadequate volume replacement. The excess mortality seen during prolonged summer heat waves disproportionately affects the elderly population. Many older persons have inadequate social and physical protective mechanisms to avoid excessive heat exposure. Elderly persons may suffer from limited access to (or recognition of the need for) salt and water and do not compensate for the increased insensible fluid loss.

Compartmental fluid shifts from conditions such as hypoalbuminemia and pancreatitis may result in a relative intravascular dehydration without clinically obvious sources of fluid loss.

Decreased Fluid Intake

Often underappreciated in elderly patients are conditions causing inadequate fluid intake (Table 108-3). Patients with physical restraints, restricted mobility, and poor vision may not have free access to fluids. Most frequently underrecognized as being at risk for fluid access problems are patients presenting with deteriorating mobility, vision, or level of consciousness who were independent in their fluid access before becoming ill.

Iatrogenic oral fluid deprivation is commonly ordered before diagnostic or surgical procedures or, inappropriately, for edema, renal insufficiency, or hyponatremia. Self- or caretaker-imposed fluid restriction is common in the older person prone to urinary incontinence, nocturia, or pulmonary aspiration. Acute and chronic alterations in sensorium are prevalent in the ill elderly patient with a resultant decrease in the perception of the need for, and access to, appropriate fluids.

Gastrointestinal problems such as swallowing disorders, bowel obstruction, and the underrecognized side effects of medication (nausea, vomiting, early satiety), often preclude adequate oral fluid intake. A common yet infrequently diagnosed cause of bowel obstruction in elderly patients is ischemic bowel disease. This condition is exacerbated by dehydration, resulting in a vicious cycle of dehydration and ischemic bowel injury.

Cardiac glycosides and amphetamines can further decrease thirst perception in elderly persons.[21] Finally, a syndrome of primary adipsia has been described in patients with a remote history of cerebral vascular accidents.[22]

Therapy for Dehydration

Prevention and early intervention are the most effective therapies for dehydration. This strategy can be accomplished by education of patients, families, and health care workers to appreciate the need for early intervention with fluid therapy in the elderly patient prone to dehydration. Specific fluid prescriptions in the home, nursing home, or acute care hospital settings can be very helpful toward this end.

For the dehydrated patient, it is essential to establish the causes of fluid loss or decreased fluid intake with history, physical examination, and appropriate laboratory studies (Tables 108-2 and 108-3) in order to direct therapy accordingly. The severity of the fluid deficit must be estimated by evaluation of blood pressure, orthostasis, skin turgor (less useful in elderly patients), and urine output. A careful measurement of weight compared with the premorbid baseline may be useful in determining the degree of fluid loss. The serum osmolarity can be measured or estimated within ±10 mosm/liter by the following formula:

$$\text{Serum osmolarity} = 2[\text{Na}] + \frac{[\text{glucose}]}{18} + \frac{[\text{BUN}]}{2.8}$$

where the sodium level is measured in milliequivalents per liter and glucose and BUN levels are measured in milligrams per deciliter. If the measured osmolarity is significantly greater than the calculated value, the presence of abnormal unmeasured solutes such as ethanol, isopropyl alcohol, ethylene glycol, methanol, or mannitol should be considered.

The magnitude of fluid deficits with primarily free water loss (hypertonic dehydration) can be estimated by the following calculation:

$$\text{Fluid deficit (liters)} = \text{desired TBW} - \text{current TBW}$$
$$\text{Current TBW} = 0.5^{*} \times \text{body weight (kg)}$$
$$\text{Desired TBW} = \frac{\text{measured serum sodium} \times \text{current TBW}}{140}$$

where TBW is the total body water in liters. In young persons, water constitutes 60 percent of the body weight compared with only 50 percent in the elderly man and 45 percent in the elderly woman. This proportional decrease in the percentage water is due to the increase in fat and decrease in lean body mass with aging.[23] The estimation of fluid deficit for patients with isotonic or hypotonic dehydration is more complex because it must take into account loss of sodium as well as water.

Three methods of fluid replacement (oral, subcutaneous, and intravenous) may be used singly or in combination, depending on the care setting and the severity of the condition. Oral rehydration is preferred; administration of free water or oral electrolyte solutions developed for use in third world countries is encouraged. Subcutaneous fluids may be very effective, safe, and easily administered, especially in the home or nursing home settings.[24,25] Three liters of isotonic fluid per day may be delivered through two subcutaneous infusion sites, each dispensing 60 ml/h. The addition of hyaluronidase (Wydase, Wyeth) may facilitate fluid absorption. The abdomen and upper

*Value for elderly men (use 0.45 for elderly women).

outer aspect of the thighs are preferred infusion sites. Intravenous fluid replacement is best reserved for the acute care setting where the dehydrated patient can be closely monitored.

The first step in the therapy of hypernatremic dehydration is correction of hemodynamic collapse, manifested by hypotension, orthostasis, and decreased urine output. The initial therapy is rapid infusions of isotonic saline until these parameters stabilize. The hemodynamically stable patient should have replacement of one-half of the fluid deficit over the first 24 hours, with the remaining volume replaced over the next 48 to 72 hours. A goal during rapid fluid replacement is to reduce serum osmolarity to 300 at a rate of no greater than 1 meq/liter per hour, followed by gradual infusion to correct the osmolar deficit over the next 48 to 72 hours. The best replacement fluid for these patients during this phase is 5 percent dextrose in half-normal saline. Patients with isotonic dehydration (normal or low serum sodium levels) should have isotonic saline as replacement fluid. In addition to correction of the fluid deficit, ongoing fluid losses must be replaced. These losses average 2 to 3 liters per day in the healthy person and may be significantly greater in illness. Continued reassessment of fluid status must be made periodically to ensure appropriate fluid replacement. This includes measurement of fluid intake and output, weight, blood pressure, pulse, serum chemistries, and osmolarities.

Overzealous rehydration, such as replacement of the entire fluid deficit over 24 hours, may result in death from cerebral edema. Dehydration of brain cells is prevented by the generation of osmotically active solute ("idiogenic osmoles"), thereby setting up an osmotic gradient to retain intracellular water in the face of systemic hyperosmolarity. If plasma hyperosmolarity is corrected too rapidly, there may be excessive movement of water into brain cells resulting in cerebral edema.[26] The fluid deficits of dehydration may be safely corrected over 72 hours, yet the associated mental status changes may persist for 2 weeks or longer.

HYPONATREMIA

The presence of hyponatremia (defined as a serum sodium level less than 135 meq/liter) also increases with age. Hyponatremia is present in 2.5 percent of hospitalized elderly patients and is associated with a sevenfold increase in mortality compared with age- and disease-matched hospitalized elderly patients without hyponatremia. In one study, hyponatremia was present in 8 percent of elderly patients seen in an outpatient setting, 11 percent of patients in a geriatric hospital unit, and 22 percent of nursing home residents.[27]

The majority of elderly patients with hyponatremia have a defect in the capacity of the kidney to excrete free water. The symptoms of hyponatremia in the elderly patient relate to the rapidity of decrease in serum sodium levels. Elderly patients may initially have nonspecific symptoms such as malaise, confusion, headache, nausea, and a decline in overall functional ability. These symptoms may progress to somnolence, seizures, or coma with lower sodium levels or more rapid decline in serum sodium levels.

The first step in the diagnosis of hyponatremia is to rule out "pseudohyponatremia," or low serum sodium levels associated with normal or elevated serum osmolarity. Serum sodium levels are low in pseudohyponatremia because of high levels of other osmotically active substances such as glucose (uncontrolled diabetes mellitus), triglycerides (hypertriglyceridemia), or plasma proteins (multiple myeloma). Serum sodium levels will return to normal with treatment of the underlying disease state.

The differential diagnosis of true hyponatremia (serum sodium less than 135 meq/liter with low serum osmolarity) requires a detailed history of diseases, medications, and fluid intake as well as physical examination to ascertain the clinical volume state.

Elderly patients with hyponatremia can be divided into two major categories: those with altered renal water excretion (relative inability to appropriately excrete free water) and those with normal renal water excretion (Table 108-4).[28]

Hyponatremia with Altered Renal Water Excretion

Patients with "effective circulating volume depletion" have normal total body water and are clinically euvolemic but have decreased tissue perfusion secondary to low cardiac output states or low plasma proteins from hepatic disease, inadequate protein intake,

TABLE 108-4

Categories of Hyponatremia

Hyponatremia with altered renal water excretion
"Effective" circulating volume depletion
Diuretics
Renal insufficiency
Euvolemic states of ADH excess
SIADH
Cortisol deficiency
Hypothyroidism
Decreased solute intake
Hyponatremia with normal renal water excretion
Primary polydipsia
Reset osmostat
"Effective" volume depletion
Psychosis
Quadriplegia
Malnutrition

or protein-losing diseases. The decrease in tissue perfusion causes hyponatremia by two primary mechanisms: enhanced vasopressin (ADH) release from decreased baroreceptive neural input, and decreased renal perfusion pressure stimulating intrarenal mechanisms of water reabsorption.[29]

Treatment of the underlying disease state is necessary to reverse the hyponatremia. In severe potassium depletion, sodium is exchanged intracellularly for potassium, resulting in hyponatremia. Sodium levels are restored with potassium replacement (or with magnesium and potassium replacement in those patients who are also magnesium deficient).

Diuretics act pharmacologically to alter free water excretion and are frequently associated with hyponatremia in the elderly patient. The thiazide diuretics cause hyponatremia more commonly than the loop diuretics. The loop diuretics (furosemide, bumetanide, ethacrynic acid) inhibit NaCl reabsorption in the thick ascending limb and tend to reduce medullary tonicity. This reduction inhibits free water reabsorption in the collecting tubule. Thiazide diuretics act in the renal cortex and distal tubule. Therefore, medullary tonicity is preserved. This intact medullary tonicity allows for enhanced reabsorption of free water without solute in the collecting tubule, and may cause hyponatremia.

Renal insufficiency may predispose the elderly person to hyponatremia. Because of the decrease in the number of kidney nephrons in elderly persons, each nephron must filter an increased solute load. This results in a relative osmotic diuresis and decreases the kidney's ability to maximally dilute the urine (excrete free water). This may contribute to the development of hyponatremia in the elderly patient with renal disease or even in the healthy elderly person during periods of excessive free water intake.

Hyponatremia may be present in patients with cortisol deficiency or hypothyroidism because of the effective volume depletion resulting from decreased cardiac output associated with these diseases. ADH levels may also be inappropriately elevated in cortisol deficiency since ADH is partially cosecreted with corticotropin-releasing factor.

The syndrome of inappropriate antidiuretic hormone (SIADH) secretion is another example of impaired water excretion in the presence of normal volume control (patients are clinically euvolemic). Patients with SIADH excrete a relatively concentrated urine when they should be excreting a dilute urine (the urine is "less than maximally dilute"). Some of the common causes of SIADH are listed in Table 108-5.

The diagnosis of SIADH is made in a patient with hyponatremia and low serum osmolarity who has normal clinical volume status; normal renal, adrenal, and thyroid function; a urine osmolarity (in a patient not taking diuretics) that is inappropriately concentrated, greater than 100 mOsm/kg; and a urine sodium level greater than 20 meq/liter. Since the maximum urinary diluting capacity declines with age, a urine osmolarity of 100 mOsm/kg may be the maximum diluting capacity of an elderly patient with normal renal function; therefore, some require that the urine osmolarity be greater than 150 mOsm/liter to diagnose SIADH in an elderly patient.

TABLE 108-5

Causes of SIADH

Increased production of ADH
- Central nervous system disorders
  - Infections, vascular disorders, neoplasm, psychosis, temporal arteritis
- Drugs
  - Intravenous cyclophosphamide (Cytoxan)
  - Carbamazepine (Tegretol)
  - Vincristine or vinblastine
  - Thiothixene (Navane)
  - Thioridazine (Mellaril)
  - Haloperidol (Haldol)
  - Amitriptyline (Elavil)
  - Monoamine oxidase inhibitors
  - Bromocriptine
- Pulmonary Disease
  - Infections
  - Chronic obstructive pulmonary disease
- Postoperative state
- Severe nausea
- Idiopathic

Ectopic production of ADH
- Carcinoma (small cell lung cancer)
- Pulmonary tuberculosis

Potentiation of ADH effect
  - Chlorpropramide (Diabinese)
  - Tolbutamide (Orinase)
  - Intravenous cyclophosphamide
  - Carbamazepine
  - Nonsteroidal anti-inflammatory drugs
- Exogenous administration
  - Intranasal vasopressin-analog (dDAVP)
  - Intravenous vasopressin (Pitressin)

The therapy for SIADH is to diagnose and treat the underlying disease and/or discontinue offending medications. The acute clinical treatment is to reverse the physiologic abnormality, making the patients' intake more concentrated than their urine output. For elderly patients with serum sodium levels greater than 120 meq/liter with few or no symptoms, this can be done by restricting free water intake and increasing solute intake to decrease the inappropriately high urine concentration. The urine can be made more dilute if necessary by the pharmacological actions of loop diuretics and/or democlocycline or lithium, which inhibit ADH action on the collecting tubule.

For patients with serum sodium levels less than 120 meq/liter with seizures, somnolence, or coma, acute intravenous sodium replacement is necessary. Normal (0.9 percent) saline has an osmolarity of 308 mOsm/liter. The patient who has a urine osmolarity of greater than 308 mOsm/liter will excrete the solute given as normal saline in less volume than it was infused and retain the remaining volume as free water with resultant worsening of the hyponatremia.

For patients with urine osmolarities greater than 308 mOsm/liter or those patients who cannot tolerate large-volume infusions, loop diuretics such as furosemide 10 to 20 mg IV every 4 to 6 hours can be used to make the urine more dilute. Another approach for patients with high urine osmolarities is to cautiously use 3% saline (1026 mOsm/liter) with the addition of a loop diuretic. Patients receiving IV sodium replacement should be monitored closely in the hospital for signs of volume overload or depletion. The rapidity of sodium replacement should be based on the clinical condition of the patient. For patients with seizures, somnolence, or coma, the serum sodium level should be raised to 120 meq/liter at approximately 0.5 to 1.0 meq/h. The amount of sodium (meq) required to raise the serum sodium level to 120 meq/liter is calculated by

$$\text{meq sodium} = 0.5 \times \text{weight (kg)} \times (120 - \text{serum sodium})$$

- 0.9% normal saline contains 154 meq of sodium per liter
- 3% saline contains 513 meq of sodium per liter

The remaining deficit should be gradually replaced over the next several days at a rate no faster than 5 to 7 meq per 24 hours. Rapid correction of the sodium deficit may result in permanent central pontine myelinolysis. The nonspecific neurological manifestations of hyponatremia in the elderly patient (confusion, lethargy, malaise) may take weeks to resolve following restoration of normal osmolarity.

Decreased solute intake may contribute to the development of hyponatremia. As noted previously, elderly patients have an inability to retain solute in times of decreased solute intake. A subset of elderly patients may become hyponatremic with clinical euvolemia from free water intake with inadequate solute intake. The treatment of hyponatremia in these patients is liberalization of salt intake with continuation of free water replacement.

Hyponatremia with Normal Renal Water Excretion

Elderly patients with primary polydipsia may have excessive fluid intake (10 to 15 liters per day) that overwhelms the kidney's ability to excrete free water, resulting in hyponatremia. This is most prevalent in elderly persons with psychiatric illness on anticholinergic medications (tricyclic antidepressants or phenothiazines) resulting in dry oral mucous membranes and secondary increase in water ingestion.[30] The treatment is to restrict free water intake and, if possible, use less anticholinergic psychotropic medication.

Many elderly patients with chronic and recurrent hyponatremia have no defect in renal water excretion, yet their hypothalamic osmostat appears to be reset at a lower level. Their ADH secretion to changing osmolarity is normal in slope but shifted to the left. Thus, vasopressin is released at a lower osmolarity. It is estimated that up to one-third of the patients with SIADH have a reset osmostat. These patients initially improve their hyponatremic state with treatment, but eventually return to their physiologic osmolarity set point. If they are asymptomatic; have normal thyroid, adrenal, and renal function; and are taking no drugs or have none of the diseases known to alter vasopressin release or action, they should be followed clinically with careful follow-up for occult malignancy, tuberculosis, or vasculitis.

REFERENCES

1. Shannon RP et al: The influence of age on water balance in man. *Semin Nephrol* 4:346, 1984.
2. Rowe JW et al: The influence of age on the renal response to water deprivation in man. *Nephron* 17:270, 1976.
3. Helderman JH: The impact of normal aging on the hypothalamic–neurohypophyseal–renal axis, in Korenman SG (ed): *Endocrine Aspects of Aging.* New York, Elsevier Biomedical, 1982, p 9.
4. Helderman JH et al: The response of arginine vasopressin to intravenous ethanol and hypertonic saline in man: The impact of aging. *J Gerontol* 33:39, 1978.
5. Phillips PA et al: Reduced thirst after water deprivation in healthy elderly men. *N Engl J Med* 12:753, 1984.
6. Rowe JW et al: Age-related failure of volume-pressure mediated vasopressin release in man. *J Clin Endocrinol Metab* 54:661, 1982.
7. Rolls BJ, Rolls ET: The control of drinking. *Br Med Bull* 37(2):127, 1981.
8. Phillips PA et al: Reduced osmotic thirst in healthy elderly men. *Am J Physiol* 261:R166, 1991.
9. Crane MG, Hornis JJ: Effect of age on renin activity and aldosterone secretion. *J Lab Clin Med* 87:947, 1976.
10. Robertson GL: Vasopressin function in health and disease. *Recent Prog Horm Res* 33:333, 1977.
11. Lindeman RD et al: Osmolar renal concentrating ability in healthy young men and hospitalized patients without renal disease. *N Engl J Med* 262:1396, 1960.
12. Miller JH, Shock NW: Age differences in the renal tubular response to antidiuretic hormone. *J Gerontol* 8:446, 1953.
13. Dontas AS et al: Mechanisms of real tubular defects in old age. *Postgrad Med J* 48:295, 1972.
14. Crowe MJ et al: Altered water excretion in healthy elderly men. *Age Ageing* 16:285, 1987.
15. Epstein M, Hollenberg NK: Age as a determinant of renal sodium conservation in normal man. *J Lab Clin Med* 87:411, 1976.

16. Lavizzo-Mourey RJ: Dehydration in the elderly. A short review. *J Natl Med Assoc* 79:1033, 1987.
17. Snyder NA et al: Hypernatremia in elderly patients. *Ann Intern Med* 107:309, 1987.
18. Berenyl M, Straus B: Hyperosmolar states in the chronically ill. *J Am Geriatr Soc* 17(7):648, 1968.
19. Rodes J et al: Hypernatremia following gastrointestinal bleeding in cirrhosis and ascites. *Am J Dig Dis* 20:127, 1975.
20. Albert SG et al: Vasopressin response to dehydration in Alzheimer's disease. *J Am Geriatr Soc* 37(9):843, 1989.
21. Hays RM, Levine SO: Pathophysiology of water metabolism, in Brenner B, Rector FC Jr (eds): *The Kidney*. Philadelphia, Saunders, 1980, p 105.
22. Miller P et al: Hypodipsia in geriatric patients. *Am J Med* 73:354, 1982.
23. Weitzman RE, Keeman CR: The clinical physiology of water metabolism: 1. The physiologic regulation of arginine vasopressin secretion and thirst. *West J Med* 13(5):373, 1979.
24. Berger EY: Nutrition by hypodermoclysis: *J Am Geriatr Soc* 32(3):199, 1984.
25. Bruera E et al: Hypodermoclysis for the administration of fluids and narcotic analgesics in patients with advanced cancer. *J Pain Symptom Manage* 5(4):218, 1990.
26. Arieff Al et al: Pathophysiology of hyperosmolar states, in Andreoli TE et al (eds): *Disturbances in Body Fluid Osmolality*. Bethesda, American Physiological Society, 1977, p 227.
27. Sunderam SG, Mankikar GD: Hyponatremia in the elderly: *Age Ageing* 12:77, 1983.
28. Rose BD: Hypoosmolal states—Hyponatremia, in Rose BD (ed): *Clinical Physiology of Acid-Base and Electrolyte Disorders,* 3d ed. New York, McGraw-Hill, 1989, p 601.
29. Schrier RW: Body fluid volume regulation in health and disease: A unifying hypothesis. *Ann Intern Med* 113(2):155, 1990.
30. Goldman MB et al: Mechanisms of altered water metabolism in psychotic patients with polydipsia and hyponatremia. *N Engl J Med* 318(7):397, 1988.

Chapter 109

DISORDERS OF TEMPERATURE REGULATION

Itamar B. Abrass

Temperature dysregulation in the elderly is an example of the narrowing of homeostatic mechanisms that occurs with advancing age. Elderly persons are less able to adjust to extremes of environmental temperatures. Hypo- and hyperthermic states are predominantly disorders of the elderly. Despite underreporting of these disorders, there is evidence that morbidity and mortality increase during particularly hot or cold periods, especially among ill elderly.[1–3] Much of this illness is caused by an increased incidence of cardiovascular disorders (myocardial infarction and stroke) or infectious diseases (pneumonia) during periods of temperature extremes.

HYPOTHERMIA

Epidemiology

Studies in the United Kingdom reveal that hypothermia is a common finding among elderly people during the winter, when homes are usually heated below 21°C (70°F).[2] As might be expected, there is a similar seasonal occurrence in the United States and Canada.[4] In Britain, as many as 3.6 percent of all patients older than 65 admitted to the hospital are hypothermic.[5] In a population study, 10 percent of elderly people living at home were found to be on the borderline of hypothermia, with a deep body temperature of less than 35.5°C.[6]

Pathophysiology

Hypothermia is defined as a core temperature (rectal, esophageal, tympanic) below 35°C. Susceptibility of the elderly to hypothermia is related to both disease and physiologic change.

The thermoregulatory center maintains body temperature through control of sweating, vasoconstriction and vasodilation, chemical thermogenesis, and shivering. Diminished sensation of cold and impaired sensitivity to change in temperature are associated with poor thermoregulation in the elderly[2,7,8] and can lead to maladaptive behavior in cold environments. Chronic cold exposure leads to a preference among older rats for cooler ambient temperatures, resulting in increased heat loss and reduced body temperature.[9] In older adults, shivering is often observed to be less intense, despite greater loss of core temperature.[2,10,11] Since maximal shivering increases heat production three- to fivefold above the resting level,[12] those elderly with a less efficient or reduced shivering process are at increased risk for hypothermia.

The mechanisms by which adrenergic deficits contribute to hypothermia in the elderly have not been defined. However, abnormal autonomic vasoconstrictor response to cold[2,11,13] is a key factor in temperature dysregulation associated with aging. This autonomic dysregulation is also manifest as a higher incidence of orthostatic hypotension in those at risk for hypothermia.[2] Diminished thermogenesis is another key factor in temperature dysregulation in the elderly. The metabolic rate is lower in older people due to a decrease in lean body mass,[14,15] thus contributing to the risk of hypothermia in these individuals. The thermic effect of feeding is also diminished in the elderly.[15–17] Since body fat contributes to insulation against heat loss,[12] thin elderly with decreased fat mass are also at increased risk.

Besides actual exposure to cold, there are a host of factors predisposing to hypothermia.[12,18,19] Disorders associated with decreased heat production include hypothyroidism, hypoglycemia, starvation, and malnutrition. The most common endocrinopathy associated with hypothermia is hypothyroidism, a condition in which as many as 80 percent of patients will have a low body temperature due to the associated depression of metabolic rate and calorigenesis.[18] Hypoglycemia reduces shivering, probably by a central effect.[20] Hypothermia may occur in 50 percent or more of patients with hypoglycemia.[21] Starvation and malnutrition may contribute to the risk of hypothermia by a decrease in lean body mass and energy stores for calorigenesis as well as by a loss of body fat and its insulating effect. Immobility and decreased activity due to such disorders as stroke, arthritis, and parkinsonism also may lead to decreased heat production. Autonomic dysfunction in Parkinson's disease may also contribute to temperature dysregulation.

Thermoregulatory impairment may occur due to hypothalamic and central nervous system dysfunction or may be drug-induced. Trauma, hypoxia, tumor, or cerebrovascular disease may impair central regulation of temperature. The drugs most commonly associated with hypothermia are ethanol, barbiturates, phenothiazines, benzodiazepines, and anesthetic agents and narcotics.[12,18] Ethanol predisposes to this problem by being a vasodilator, a central nervous system depressant, an anesthetic, a cause of hypoglycemia, and a risk factor for trauma and environmental exposure. Phenothiazines inhibit shivering by a peripheral curarizing effect.

Hypothermia in sepsis reflects an alteration in the hypothalamic set-point and overwhelmed host defenses. In cardiovascular disease, the circulatory system may not be able to respond to the stress of changes in body temperature or to the demands of such counterregulatory mechanisms as shivering.

Particularly in the elderly, living or being alone, lack of central heating, failure to use heating (whatever the type), and dementia or confusion are associated with increased risk for hypothermia.[22,23] In one survey of the elderly, only 1 elderly person in 10 was aware of the dangers of accidental hypothermia.[24]

Clinical Presentation

As stated previously, hypothermia is defined as a core temperature below 35°C. Essential to the diagnosis is early recognition with a low-recording thermometer. Ordinary thermometers will not register low temperatures. Because early signs are nonspecific and subtle, a high index of suspicion must exist to allow an early diagnosis. A history of known or potential exposure is helpful, but elderly patients can become hypothermic at modest temperatures. Early signs which occur at core temperatures of 32 to 35°C include fatigue, weakness, slowness of gait, apathy, slurred speech, confusion, and cool skin. Patients may complain of the sensation of cold and may be shivering. As hypothermia progresses (28 to 30°C), the skin becomes cold. Hypopnea and cyanosis are present, at first due to decreased metabolic demands and later due to depression of the central respiratory drive. Bradycardia, atrial and ventricular arrhythmias, and hypotension occur. Semicoma or coma and muscular rigidity are present. Consciousness is commonly lost at a brain temperature between 32° and 30°C. Reflexes are slowed and pupils are poorly reactive. Generalized edema and polyuria or oliguria may be present. Cold exposure is associated with both a water and solute diuresis.[25] Volume contraction occurs due to diuresis and also some degree of extra- and intracellular water shifts.

As core temperature falls below 28°C, the skin becomes very cold; individuals become unresponsive, rigid, and areflexive and have fixed and dilated pupils. Apnea and ventricular fibrillation are present. Patients may sometimes be mistaken for dead. Case reports reveal patients who have survived after being discovered without respiration and pulse.

The most significant early complications of severe hypothermia are arrhythmias and cardiorespiratory arrest.[19,25] Later complications include bronchopneumonia and aspiration pneumonia. The cough reflex is depressed by hypothermia, and cold results in the production of large quantities of thick, tenacious bronchial secretions, predisposing the patient to the above-mentioned complications. Pulmonary edema may occur, especially in those with prior cardiovascular disease. Pancreatitis and gastrointestinal bleeding are frequent complications, although massive hemorrhage is unusual. Acute renal failure may occur. Intravascular thrombosis is a complication of hemoconcentration and the temperature-induced changes in viscosity.

Electrocardiogram (ECG) abnormalities are common.[19] The most specific ECG finding is the J wave (Osborn wave) following the QRS complex. This abnormality disappears as temperature returns to normal. Other common abnormalities include bradycardia and prolonged PR interval, QRS complex, and QT segment as well as atrial fibrillation, premature ventricular contractions, and ventricular fibrillation.

Frequently the most difficult differential diagnosis in hypothermia is hypothyroidism. A previous history of thyroid disease, a neck scar from previous thyroid surgery, and a delay in the relaxation phase of the deep tendon reflexes may assist in the diagnosis of hypothyroidism.

Treatment

Emergency Care

In the field, the hypothermic person should immediately be removed from the cold environment, windy areas, and contact with cold objects. Wet clothing should be removed to prevent further heat loss. Top and bottom blankets should be used (covers may need to be preheated to avoid a drain of heat from the victim). The patient should be moved carefully, since the cold, bradycardic heart is extremely irritable and even minor stimuli can precipitate ventricular fibrillation or asystole.[26] Cardiac monitoring should be started as soon as possible. Patients with detectable heartbeat who are breathing spontaneously, no matter how slowly, should not be subjected to unnecessary procedures such as chest compression or placement of a pacemaker. Patients in asystole or ventricular fibrillation should be resuscitated, but the cold heart may be relatively unresponsive to drugs or electrical stimulation. Intravenous fluids, preferably D_5 normal saline without potassium, should be warmed before being used.[19,26]

General Support

In the hospital, general supportive therapy for severe hypothermia consists of intensive care management of complicated multisystem dysfunctions. Mortality is usually greater than 50 percent for severe hypothermia. It increases with age and is particularly related to underlying disease.[27,28] Every attempt should be made to assess and treat any contributing medical disorder (e.g., infection, hypothyroidism or hypoglycemia). Underlying infections are common.[29,30] Hypothermia in elderly patients should be promptly treated as sepsis unless proven otherwise. If hypothyroidism is suspected, the patient should be treated with 0.5 mg levothyroxine IV and corticosteroids. While patients should have continuous ECG monitoring, central lines should be avoided if possible because of myocardial irritability.

Because there is delayed metabolism, most drugs have little effect on a severely hypothermic patient, but they may cause problems once the patient is rewarmed. Arrhythmias are resistant to cardioversion and drug therapy. Insulin is ineffective below 30°C[12] and should be avoided in the hyperglycemic hypothermic patient. If given during hypothermia, insulin may cause hypoglycemia as the patient is rewarmed. Insulin resistance will improve spontaneously as core body temperature rises. In chronic hypothermia (lasting longer than 12 hours), volume depletion may be severe, and volume repletion may be needed as rewarming occurs.[18,19] Blood gases should be followed to assess respiratory function. Oxygen therapy, suctioning, and endotracheal intubation may be required. Serious arrhythmias, acidosis, and fluid and electrolyte disorders will usually respond to therapy only after rewarming has been accomplished. It is preferable to stabilize the patient and immediately undertake specific rewarming techniques.

Rewarming

Passive rewarming with insulating material and placement of the patient in a warm environment (>70°F) is generally adequate for those with mild (>32°C) hypothermia.[18,19,31] Active external rewarming (electric blankets, warm mattresses and bottles, submersion in a warm water bath) is a more rapid technique of rewarming than passive procedures. However, active external rewarming has been associated with increased morbidity and mortality.[32] Cold blood may suddenly be shunted to the core, further decreasing core temperature. Peripheral vasodilation resulting from external rewarming can precipitate hypovolemic shock by decreasing circulatory blood volume.[18]

For more severe hypothermia (<32°C), core rewarming is necessary. Several techniques for core rewarming have been used, but positive results have been reported only from small, uncontrolled studies. Mediastinal lavage is effective, but it is a major surgical procedure.[33] Extracorporeal circulation is a rapid method for rewarming, but this procedure requires a special hospital unit; also, there is a risk of hypotension and of bleeding from the use of heparin.[34,35] More recently continuous arteriovenous rewarming (CAVR) has been used to treat hypothermia in critically ill patients.[36] In this procedure, percutaneously placed femoral arterial and venous catheters are connected to the inflow and outflow side of a countercurrent fluid warmer to create a fistula through the heating mechanism. In a study comparing CAVR with standard rewarming techniques, CAVR was associated with an improved survival after moderately severe injury and a significant reduction in blood and fluid requirements, organ failures, and length of stay in the intensive care unit. Another approach is to use gastric lavage, in which balloons are placed in the stomach and filled with water.[37] With this method, a smaller area is rewarmed than in peritoneal dialysis, and local pharyngeal irritation may precipitate an arrhythmia.

Peritoneal dialysis and inhalation rewarming may be the most practical techniques in most institutions. However, inhalation therapy may not be as effective in moderate-to-severe hypothermia as it is in mild hypothermia. Peritoneal dialysis (40°C) implies little risk for the patient, is easy to perform, requires simple equipment, and may be performed in every hospital.[38] Dialysis with 2 liters of a potassium-free solution and rapid instillation and immediate removal is preferred.[18] Normothermia is usually accomplished within six to eight exchanges. Enemas are little used but can be used in conjunction with dialysis.

In dogs, radio wave–induced regional hyperthermia has been shown to be superior to inhalation and peritoneal lavage in the treatment of experimental hypothermia.[39,40] However, controlled studies of the treatment of hypothermia still need to be performed in humans.[36]

HYPERTHERMIA

Epidemiology

In the United States, approximately 5000 deaths occur annually as a direct result of heatstroke, and two-thirds of the victims are over 60 years old.[42] Hyperthermia can contribute to increased morbidity and mortality from various cardiovascular diseases in the elderly.[19,43] In the past, a significant number of deaths during heat waves occurred in nursing home residents.[19] Increased awareness of the problem has probably benefited this group of elderly. During the New York heat wave of 1984, the death rate for those over 75 years of age increased by almost 50 percent, but the increase was limited almost exclusively to noninstitutionalized elderly.[44]

Women appear to be more prone to the lethal effects of heatstroke. In the New York heat wave, mortality increased by 66 percent for women, compared to 39 percent for men.[44] A similar sex distribution was seen in the St. Louis and Georgia heat waves of 1983, when 77 percent of excess deaths occurred in women.[1]

Pathophysiology

Heatstroke is defined as an acute failure to maintain normal body temperature in the setting of a warm environment. Elderly people usually present with nonexertional heatstroke due to impaired heat loss and failure of homeostatic mechanisms.[19] As with hypothermia, susceptibility of the elderly to heatstroke is related to both disease and physiologic changes.

Impairment of the thermoregulatory system by diminished or absent sweating is an important cause of heat exhaustion and heatstroke in hot conditions.[14] Deaths of the elderly during heat waves can usually be ascribed to heart disease and cardiovascular disease exacerbated by heat stress.[19,45] However, some disease is directly related to primary thermoregulatory failure.[45] The sweating response to thermal and neurochemical stimulation has been found to be reduced in elderly people as compared with that in younger adults.[46,47] There is also a higher core-temperature threshold at which sweating can be initiated.[2] Delayed development of vasodilation with heating may also interfere with heat loss in elderly people.[14] Some of these changes in sweat rate and blood flow may, however, relate more to deconditioning than to aging per se. When maximum O_2 uptake is matched between younger and older men, there is no significant difference in sweat rate or forearm blood flow during exercise.[48,49] However, when the young are compared to sedentary older men, there is a decreased response in these parameters with age. Impaired sensitivity to change in temperature[2,50] may lead to maladaptive behavior in warm environments. Acclimatization to heat may be less likely to occur in the elderly as compared with the young[14] and may thus contribute to the physiologic deficits.

Inability to take appropriate measures such as removing heavy clothing, moving to a cooler environment, and increasing fluid intake increases the risk of heatstroke in elderly individuals with limited mobility. Living alone and confusion add to this risk. Elderly individuals with cardiovascular disease may not be able to adequately increase their cardiac output in response to heat stress. Congestive heart failure, diabetes mellitus, obesity, and obstructive lung disease have been associated with increased risk of death in heatstroke victims.[51] Other risk factors for death from heatstroke are alcoholism, use of tranquilizers and anticholinergics, and reduction in physical activity.[52] Elderly people are more likely to be taking multiple drugs, some of which may impair the response to a warm environment. Anticholinergics, phenothiazines, and antidepressants lead to hypohidrosis. Diuretics may be associated with hypovolemia and hypokalemia, and beta blockers may depress myocardial function.

Clinical Presentation

Heatstroke is characterized by a core temperature of greater than 40.6°C (105°F), severe central nervous system dysfunction (psychosis, delirium, coma), and anhidrosis (hot, dry skin). Earlier manifestations of heat exhaustion are nonspecific and include dizziness, weakness, sensation of warmth, anorexia, nausea, vomiting, headache, and dyspnea.

Complications of heatstroke include congestive heart failure and a host of cardiac arrhythmias, cerebral edema with seizures and diffuse and focal neurologic deficits, hepatocellular necrosis with jaundice and liver failure, hypokalemia, respiratory alkalosis and metabolic acidosis, and hypovolemia and shock. Rhabdomyolysis, disseminated intravascular coagulation, and acute renal failure are less frequent in elderly than in younger patients with exertional heatstroke.[51] The ultimate complication, death, occurs in as many as 80 percent of patients once the full syndrome of heatstroke is manifest.

Treatment

The key to treatment is rapid cooling. It should be started immediately in the field, and core body temperature should be brought to 39°C (102°F) within the first hour. The duration of hyperthermia is the major determinant of ultimate outcome. Ice packs and ice-water immersion are superior to convection cooling with alcohol sponge baths or electric fans. Complications require intensive multisystem care.

CONCLUSIONS

Prevention appears to be the most appropriate approach to the management of temperature dysregulation in the elderly. Education of older adults about their susceptibility to hypo- and hyperthermia in extremes of environmental temperature, education about appropriate behavior in such conditions, and close monitoring of the most vulnerable elderly should help reduce the morbidity and mortality from these disorders.

REFERENCES

1. Hope W et al: Illness and death due to environmental heat: Georgia and St. Louis, 1983. Leads from the MMWR. *JAMA* 252:209, 1984.
2. Collins KJ et al: Accidental hypothermia and impaired temperature homeostatis in the elderly. *Br Med J* 1:353, 1977.
3. Rango N: Exposure-related hypothermia mortality in the United States, 1970–79. *Am J Public Health* 74:1159, 1984.
4. Danzl DF et al: Multicenter hypothermia survey. *Ann Emerg Med* 16:1042, 1987.
5. Goldman A et al: A pilot study of low body temperature in old people admitted to hospital. *J R Coll Physicians Lond* 11:291, 1977.
6. Fox RH et al: Body temperature in the elderly: A national study of physiological, social and environmental conditions. *Br Med J* 1:200, 1963.
7. Collins KJ et al: Urban hypothermia: Preferred temperature and thermal perception in old age. *Br Med J* 282:175, 1981.
8. Natsume K et al: Preferred ambient temperature for old and young men in summer and winter. *Int J Biometeorol* 36:1, 1992.
9. Owen TL et al: Effect of age on cold acclimation in rats: Metabolic and behavioral responses. *Am J Physiol* 260:R284, 1991.
10. Collins KJ et al: Shivering thermogenesis and vasomotor responses with convective cooling in the elderly. *J Physiol* 320:76, 1981.
11. MacMillan AL et al: Temperature regulation in survivors of accidental hypothermia of the elderly. *Lancet* 2:165, 1967.
12. Matz R: Hypothermia: Mechanisms and countermeasures. *Hosp Pract* 21:45, 1986.
13. Richardson D et al: Attenuation of the cutaneous vasoconstrictor response to cold in elderly men. *J Gerontol Med Sci* 47:M211, 1992.
14. Collins KJ, Exton-Smith AN: Thermal homeostasis in old age. *J Am Geriatr Soc* 31:519, 1983.
15. Poehlman ET, Horton ES: Regulation of energy expenditure in aging humans. *Annu Rev Nutr* 10:255, 1990.
16. Schwartz RS et al: The thermic effect of feeding in older men: The importance of the sympathetic nervous system. *Metabolism* 39:733, 1990.
17. Thorne A, Wahren J: Diminished meal-induced thermogenesis in elderly man. *Clin Physiol* 10:427, 1990.
18. Reuler JB: Hypothermia: Pathophysiology, clinical settings, and management. *Ann Intern Med* 89:519, 1978.
19. Wongsurawat N et al: Thermoregulatory failure in the elderly. *J Am Geriatr Soc* 38:899, 1990.
20. Freinkel N et al: The hypothermia of hypoglycemia. *N Engl J Med* 287:841, 1972.
21. Strauch BS et al: Hypothermia in hypoglycemia. *JAMA* 210:345, 1969.
22. Dawson JA: A case control study of accidental hypothermia in the elderly in relation to social support and social circumstances. *Community Med* 9:141, 1987.
23. Woodhouse P et al: Factors associated with hypothermia in patients admitted to a group of inner city hospitals. *Lancet* 2:1201, 1989.
24. Avery CE, Pestle RE: Hypothermia and the elderly: Perceptions and behaviors. *Gerontologist* 27:523, 1987.
25. Granberg PO: Human physiology under cold exposure. *Arctic Med Res* 50 (suppl 6):23, 1991.
26. Treatment of hypothermia. *Med Lett Drugs Ther* 28:123, 1986.
27. Hudson LD, Conn RD: Accidental hypothermia: Associated diagnoses and prognosis in a common problem. *JAMA* 227:37, 1974.
28. O'Keeffe KM: Accidental hypothermia: A review of 62 cases. *J Am Coll Emerg Phys* 6:491, 1977.
29. Kramer MR et al: Mortality in elderly patients with thermoregulatory failure. *Arch Intern Med* 149:1521, 1989.
30. Darowski A et al: Hypothermia and infection in elderly patients admitted to hospital. *Age Ageing* 20:100, 1991.
31. Nielsen HK et al: Hypothermic patients admitted to an intensive care unit: A fifteen year survey. *Dan Med Bull* 39:190, 1992.
32. Gregory RT, Doolittle WH: Accidental hypothermia: II. Clinical implications of experimental studies. *Alaska Med* 15:48, 1973.
33. Linton AI, Ledingham IM: Severe hypothermia with barbiturate intoxication. *Lancet* 1:24, 1966.
34. Davies DM et al: Accidental hypothermia treated by extracorporeal warming. *Lancet* 1:1036, 1967.
35. Maresca L, Vasko JS: Treatment of hypothermia by extracorporeal circulation and internal rewarming. *J Trauma* 27:89, 1987.
36. Gentilello LM et al: Continuous arteriovenous rewarming: Rapid reversal of hypothermia in critically ill patients. *J Trauma* 32:316, 1992.
37. Barnard CN: Hypothermia: A method of intragastric cooling. *Br J Surg* 44:269, 1956.
38. Bristow G: Treatment of accidental hypothermia with peritoneal dialysis. *Can Med Assoc J* 118:764, 1978.
39. White JD et al: Controlled comparison of radio wave regional hyperthermia and peritoneal lavage rewarming after immersion hypothermia. *J Trauma* 25:989, 1985.
40. White JD et al: Rewarming in accidental hypothermia: Radio wave versus inhalation therapy. *Ann Emerg Med* 16:50, 1987.
41. Chinard FP: Hypothermia treatment needs controlled studies. *Ann Intern Med* 90:990, 1979.
42. Halle A, Repasy A: Classic heatstroke: A serious challenge for the elderly. *Hosp Pract* 22:26, 1987.
43. Fish PD et al: Heatwave morbidity and mortality in old age. *Age Ageing* 14:243, 1985.
44. Heat-associated mortality—New York City. *MMWR* 33:430, 1984.
45. Ellis FP: Mortality from heat illness and heat-aggravated illness in the United States. *Environ Res* 5:1, 1972.
46. Anderson RK, Kenney WL: Effect of age on heat-activated sweat gland density and flow during exercise in dry heat. *J Appl Physiol* 63:1089, 1987.
47. Inoue Y et al: Regional differences in the sweating responses of older and younger men. *J Appl Physiol* 71:2453, 1991.
48. Tankersley CG et al: Sweating and skin blood flow

during exercise: Effects of age and maximal oxygen uptake. *J Appl Physiol* 71:236, 1991.
49. Buono MJ et al: Effects of ageing and physical training on the peripheral sweat production of the human eccrine sweat gland. *Age Ageing* 20:439, 1991.
50. Miescher E, Fortney SM: Responses to dehydration and rehydration during heat exposure in young and older men. *Am J Physiol* 257:R1050, 1989.
51. Kilbourne EM et al: Risk factors for heat stroke: A case-control study. *JAMA* 247:3332, 1982.
52. Curley FJ, Irwin RS: Disorders of temperature control: I. Hyperthermia. *J Intensive Care* 1:5, 1986.

Chapter 110

SYNDROMES OF ALTERED MENTAL STATE

Marshal F. Folstein and Susan E. Folstein

In this chapter, we discuss disorders of cognition and disorders of mood because these are the most frequently encountered conditions that produce an altered mental state.

SYNDROMES OF COGNITIVE IMPAIRMENT: DELIRIUM, DEMENTIA, FOCAL SYNDROMES, SCHIZOPHRENIA, AND MENTAL RETARDATION

Delirium

Definition

Delirium (see also Chap. 90) is a global decline in cognitive function, accompanied by alteration in consciousness. Delirium is sometimes called acute confusional states, metabolic encephalopathy, or twilight states.[1,2,3] The onset may be insidious and the course chronic, as in the patient who gradually becomes intoxicated from overmedication, or the onset may be acute and the course short-lived, as in cases of drug-withdrawal syndromes. Delirious patients can recover fully if the underlying cause is reversible, but the mortality rate is high because many delirious patients suffer from irreversible organ failure.

Epidemiology

Delirium is frequent in the emergency room, inpatient services, and recovery room. Many nursing home patients are delirious from prescribed medications. Some 10 to 15 percent of elderly surgical patients and one-third of elderly medical inpatients are delirious.[4,5] Risk factors for delirium include age, drug or alcohol abuse and withdrawal, excessive dosage of prescribed drugs, seizures, or metabolic disorders. Structural brain injury due to stroke, Alzheimer's disease, trauma, and infections also predispose to delirium.

Diagnosis

The diagnosis rests on the recognition of an altered state of consciousness, which can be reliably assessed.[6] Patients may be either somnolent or hypervigilant and agitated, but they always have a decreased ability to focus attention on relevant stimuli and to remain accessible to environmental demands. The patient may appear alert and coherent one minute and confused and drowsy the next. The Mini-Mental State Examination (MMSE) score is above 23 in 30 percent of delirious patients in our practice, but such patients may report feeling clouded in their minds or in a drugged state. Mildly delirious patients often have disturbed sleep and a mild tachycardia. In more severe delirium, the patient becomes disoriented and unable to follow even the simple request to write his or her name. Maintenance of a handwriting chart is a useful way to measure daily change in the patient's condition.

In addition to cognitive impairment, other mental phenomena are common. These include illusions (shadows on the wall or folds of drapery appear to be a face or other figure) or hallucinations (commonly visual or tactile, unlike those of schizophrenia or manic depressive illness, which are typically auditory). Patients also suffer from delusions. For example, the patient may believe that the staff of the hospital are mistreating him or conspiring against him. These experiences can be frightening to patients and have led to suicide in the midst of delirium. Delirious patients are frequently anxious and depressed, even in the absence of delusions and hallucinations.

Physical signs of delirium include tachycardia, autonomic instability with either hypertension or hypotension, and diaphoresis. These symptoms are particularly common in the delirium caused by alcohol or sedative withdrawal, delirium tremens. Asterixis, or "liver flap," can be seen in delirium due to many different causes in addition to hepatic encephalopathy. It results from the patient's inability to maintain a fixed posture. When the patient is asked to extend the arms and hands for a period of a few seconds, an intermittent lapse in posture is seen, which appears as a flap or wave of the hand. Patients may also have tremor, myoclonus (repetitive, random, single muscle jerks), or purposeless movements such as picking at clothing.

Laboratory Tests

The single most useful laboratory test for delirium is the EEG, which often reveals generalized slowing. In schizophrenia, with which delirium is often confused, the EEG is normal.[7] However, several provisos must be kept in mind. First, the patient's baseline EEG alpha frequency is usually unknown. Therefore, an EEG with an alpha frequency in the low "normal" range does not exclude delirium since it may represent a fall from a higher baseline (for instance from 12 to 8 per second, both of which are within normal limits). Second, slow EEGs can be present in the absence of delirium in cognitively impaired patients with Alzheimer's disease and other diffuse cortical disorders. Finally, some forms of agitated delirium—such as those caused by alcohol or sedative withdrawal—may be unaccompanied by EEG slowing. Nevertheless, the EEG remains a useful confirmatory test for the presence of delirium.

The specific diagnostic workup depends on the patient's clinical presentation and the most likely causes of the delirium. Delirium often reflects abnormal CNS function secondary to systemic infection or metabolic disorders, such as drug toxicity, drug or alcohol withdrawal, electrolyte abnormalities, or cardiac, pulmonary, renal, or hepatic disease. Laboratory evaluation usually includes measurement of levels of electrolytes, blood urea nitrogen, creatinine, glucose, and calcium (and possibly magnesium); a complete blood cell count with differential; erythrocyte sedimentation rate; liver function tests; blood culture and other cultures, if appropriate; blood or urine levels of alcohol and any medications which can be measured; and other specific tests as suggested by the history. Drugs that contribute frequently to delirium in geriatric patients include sedatives, benzodiazepines, and medications with anticholinergic effects.[8] A lumbar puncture should be done if there is fever or nuchal rigidity, since delirium may also be caused by meningitis or encephalitis.

TREATMENT

Treatment of delirium includes treatment of the cause of the delirium and symptomatic management. Treatment of the cause should include the discontinuation whenever possible, or at least the reduction of the dosage, of psychoactive medications. In particular, medications with high anticholinergic activity such as cimetidine, ranitadine, tricyclic antidepressants, and neuroleptics should be reduced or discontinued if possible. Management of the delirious state includes the maintenance of adequate nutrition, surveillance of fluid and electrolyte balance, and the provision of a well-lighted, predictable environment. The nursing staff and family need to provide frequent reorientation, and the medical staff should provide simple explanations of any procedures or confusing stimuli. Since patients with delirium often have abnormal sleep-wake cycles, they should be encouraged to stay awake during the day to increase their chances of sleeping at night. A patient who is agitated, hallucinating, or deluded may require treatment with low doses of a neuroleptic that has low anticholinergic activity, such as haloperidol, beginning at 0.5 to 2 mg/day. Benzodiazepines are generally second-line drugs for sedation in delirium and frequently exacerbate delirium. If benzodiazepines are used, they should be those with a short half-life, such as lorazepam (which may be given intramuscularly, 0.5 to 1 mg) or oxazepam. If delirious patients are not closely observed, they frequently suffer falls, and physical restraint may be necessary to prevent the patients from falling out of bed, wandering, or harming themselves when agitated. Constant observation by family or personnel is preferable to restraint. Not only is this more humane, but physical restraints often make patients more agitated because they cannot understand why their liberty has been restricted.

Recovery from delirium may be slow, and confusion and EEG slowing may be present for some time *after* the primary cause has been attended to. Improvement can be followed by serial mental status examinations and serial EEGs. After a delirium, patients often need a period of recuperation because they feel weak and lethargic. During this period adequate support is needed to avoid secondary complications of falls, dehydration, and malnutrition. Most patients have little memory of the delirious episode, but some retain islands of memories and remain convinced of the veracity of the delusions and misperceptions that occurred during the delirious period.

Dementia

Dementia (see also Chaps. 89 and 91 to 94) is a syndrome characterized by a decline in multiple cognitive functions which occurs in clear consciousness.[9] Dementia is a syndrome defined by a group of psychological impairments and does not refer to a particular brain disease, such as Alzheimer's disease, or to aging itself. In Baltimore, 6.1 percent of the community-dwelling population over the age of 65 suffer from a dementia syndrome.[10] In nursing homes, more than 50 percent of the patients suffer from dementia.[11] The onset may be acute or insidious, and the course may be reversible or irreversible, depending on the cause. The most common diseases causing dementia are Alzheimer's disease and stroke, together accounting for more than two-thirds of cases.

Dementia syndromes can be classified into two general types, cortical and subcortical.[12] These categories are not always mutually exclusive, but can be used as a framework for thinking about the underlying diseases. Cortical dementias include Alzheimer's disease, Jakob-Creutzfeldt disease, Pick's disease, and often stroke. They are characterized by prominent *amnesia* (memory loss), *aphasia* (inability to use language), *apraxia* (inability to perform skilled movements), and *agnosia* (inability to recognize visual stimuli), and, in Alzheimer's disease, the preservation of fine motor movement and gait until late in the course. The presence of all these symptoms indicates dysfunction of wide areas of cerebral cortex. In contrast, subcortical dementias are characterized by amnesia, slowness of thought, apathy, and lack of initiative in all aspects of cognitive function but without prominent aphasia, apraxia, or agnosia.[13] Disorders of movement and gait are prominent early in the course of subcortical dementias, and depression of mood is frequent. This constellation of symptoms is seen in diseases affecting subcortical structures that have direct connections to the frontal cortex and association areas: Parkinson's disease, Huntington's disease, and hydrocephalus.

Diagnosis

The diagnosis of a patient with dementia requires two steps: (1) the documentation of a decline in cognition from a previous level, and (2) the delineation of the process causing the decline. The first step requires a history and examination of the patient's cognition. The history reveals a decline from a previous level, and the mental state examination indicates that the patient is alert, although cognitively impaired. An individual with dementia has multiple cognitive impairments, not only memory loss. The documentation of decline can be difficult in a person who has a low level of premorbid functioning, who has no close relatives or friends who can provide a history, or who reports cognitive decline but has mild or absent findings on examination. In such cases, longitudinal examinations may be needed to decide whether a cognitive decline is taking place.

For the second step, a history and examination of factors associated with neurological disease are documented. The onset and course of symptoms provide clues to the cause. Thus, a sudden onset suggests stroke; a subacute course over weeks and months suggests a tumor or Jakob-Creutzfeldt disease. The early appearance of a gait disorder suggests a subcortical disorder such as hydrocephalus or Parkinson's disease or a focal lesion of the cortex such as stroke or tumor. A dementia which increases in the weeks following a head trauma suggests a subdural hematoma. The insidious onset of cognitive decline, the absence of early motor signs, and progression to severe dementia suggest Alzheimer's disease.

The delineation of the cause of a cognitive decline may not be unequivocal. The most common dilemma is caused by finding minor neurological signs on examination or a small stroke on CT scan. This always raises the question of whether the stroke caused the patient's cognitive impairment or is an incidental finding.

Although dementia is defined by cognitive features, other psychiatric symptoms may also be present, such as abnormalities of mood, delusions, or hallucinations; and abnormal behaviors such as insomnia, wandering, incontinence, irritability, and occasionally violence. These symptoms and behaviors cause distress to patients and their families and require psychological, social, and psychopharmacological management.

Physical signs that may accompany dementia are helpful in identifying the underlying disease. In Alzheimer's disease, no abnormal motor or sensory signs are present during the first years of illness. After 3 to 4 years patients sometimes develop abnormalities of tone and gait, eventually becoming unable to move. Pathological reflexes such as suck and grasp reflexes appear in the middle to late stages of the disease, and myoclonus and seizures are late-appearing signs in a minority of patients. In stroke-related dementia, asymmetrical motor signs such as a unilateral extensor plantar response occur early. In subcortical dementias such as hydrocephalus, Parkinson's disease, and Huntington's disease, abnormal involuntary movements, bradykinesia, and disturbances of gait appear early in the illness.

Laboratory tests in the evaluation of dementia are covered elsewhere in detail. Specific tests that are particularly useful in the differential diagnosis of the more common dementias will be mentioned here. The EEG usually becomes slow in Alzheimer's disease after the first year of illness. This test is useful in differentiating Alzheimer's disease from depression, schizophrenia, and sometimes Pick's disease, in which the EEG is normal. The CT scan and MRI are useful for detecting stroke and other focal lesions. Repeated CT or MRI examinations may reveal increasing atrophy in Alzheimer's disease. Single photon emission computed tomography (SPECT) scan is a promising method for the diagnosis of Alzheimer's disease, since temporal-parietal hypometabolism is seen, as it is in positron emission tomography (PET) scans, during the first years of illness.

Treatment

Specific causes of dementia require specific treatments, but some general principles apply to all groups. First, management of the patient in all settings is made easier if any noncognitive symptoms are identified and treated. The detection of these symptoms is described in Chap. 19. Depression can be treated with nortriptyline, given at bedtime, starting with 10 mg, and titrating the dose slowly and carefully upward until the patient sleeps through the night. Hallucinations or delusions are usually successfully treated with neuroleptics. Our practice is to treat those hallucinating patients who have a sleep disturbance with thioridazine, 25 mg at bedtime. If there is no sleep disturbance, we prescribe fluphenazine, 1 or 2 mg at bedtime. Abnormalities of behavior occur in several different contexts. If they are a response to a psychopathological condition such as depression or hallucinations, those are treated. If the cause appears to be related to some specific aspect of the patient's environment, attempts are made to modify this. For example, a patient with agnosia always wandered toward the light. This behavior was made less dangerous by rearranging the lighting and furniture. Most sleep disturbances are usually seen in the context of depression, hallucinations or delusions, or behavioral disorders. Patients receiving any pharmacological treatments must be carefully monitored because of the susceptibility of demented patients to delirium. Thus, it is safer to use small dosages of neuroleptics and antidepressants and to arrange frequent follow-up to monitor both efficacy and side effects.

The second principle in caring for patients with dementia is to explain to families about the nature of amnesia, aphasia, agnosia, and apraxia and the disabilities they cause. For example, families can be taught to ask the patient to do only one thing at a time; to assist effectively with dressing, bathing, and eating; and to avoid catastrophic reactions by arranging activities within the patient's ability and by avoiding confrontations.

Third, families benefit from a discussion of diplomatic ways to gradually decrease, and eventually eliminate, the patient's access to a car, heavy machinery, and some kitchen appliances. This discussion should take place in the presence of both the patient and the family. The impact of giving up driving can be decreased by suggesting a solution that allows continued ability to travel—suggesting that someone act as "chauffeur" to take the patient where he or she wishes to go.

Fourth, patients gradually become unable to concentrate and calculate, and different arrangements for financial management need to be made; the family may need to consult a lawyer about these and other financial issues.

Fifth, the patient will remain calmer during the day and seem to sleep better at night if the family organizes a structured daily schedule that includes predictable, planned activities for the patient. One activity should be planned for each morning and each afternoon. The types of activities will vary as the patient's capacities change. When patients begin to have difficulty with continence, families and caregivers can be taught to toilet the patient every 2 to 4 hours during waking hours to prevent incontinence. If the patient has a gradually worsening dementia, such as Alzheimer's disease, the family needs help at each stage to organize social supports appropriate to the patient's changing needs. This may include day care, help at home for the spouse, and eventually 24-hour nursing care at home or in a nursing home.

Prognosis

The prognosis of dementia depends on the underlying cause. Some dementias, as, for example, those due to hypothyroidism or cerebral infections, are reversible. In others, such as Alzheimer's disease, the symptoms gradually worsen over a period of years with death occurring 7 years, on average, after the onset of memory loss. The course and prognosis of multi-infarct disease is variable and probably varies with the severity and cause of the underlying vascular disease, although studies of the course of multi-infarct dementia are few (see Chap. 91).

Focal Cognitive Syndromes

Focal cognitive syndromes involve relatively isolated deficits of memory, language, and other cognitive functions occurring in clear consciousness. These focal syndromes are to be distinguished from the multiple cognitive deficits that define dementia or mental retardation.

Amnesia, loss of memory or the inability to learn new verbal or spatial information, occurs as a focal syndrome caused by bilateral lesions of the medial temporal cortex, particularly in the hippocampal formations, or by bilateral lesions of diencephalic structures with temporal lobe connections, such as mediodorsal thalamus or mamillary bodies. Another type of amnesia, the inability to learn new procedures, is of uncertain localization but might be related to lesions of the basal ganglia and cerebellum. The physician may test for amnesia by asking the patient to learn, and then to recall, word lists (as in the MMSE) and to learn and recall diagrams or figures such as those in the Benton Visual Retention Test. Causes include hypotension or anoxia, to which hippocampal pyramidal cells are particularly susceptible. Amnesic syndromes can also be caused by thiamine deficiency, usually in the context of alcohol abuse (Korsakoff's syndrome), bilateral herpes encephalitis, head trauma, and bilateral stroke.[12]

Aphasia is the loss of the ability to use language. It is to be distinguished from difficulties in the articulation of speech such as dysarthria or stammering. Aphasia may be divided into fluent (Wernicke's) or nonfluent (Broca's) forms. Fluent aphasia is characterized by impaired comprehension of language, but the continued production of fluent speech. However, on closer listening, the speech is frequently found to be empty of content and contains word-selection errors. Such paraphasic errors consist of substitutions either in sound or sense for the intended meaning. Patients with Broca's aphasia, by contrast, are able to understand language relatively well, but have difficulty in its production. Speech is effortful, sparse, and may appear telegraphic—containing just a few nouns with high semantic content. When testing language, it is important to examine language production in both verbal and written forms, language comprehension (by asking the patient to follow commands), and word repetition (as in repeating the phrase *no ifs, ands, or buts*). Word repetition is thought to require the abilities to both comprehend and produce language. There are many causes of aphasia, but the most common is left middle cerebral artery infarction. Left hemisphere stroke usually produces a mixed aphasia. However, left anterior lesions often cause a Broca's aphasia, associated with facial apraxia and a right hemiparesis, while left posterior lesions often produce a Wernicke's aphasia with variable motor signs.[14]

Apraxia is the inability to perform previously learned motor acts in the presence of adequate motor strength. Apractic patients can neither imitate the examiner's motor performance nor sequence complicated movements to carry out useful actions such as dressing or writing. Apraxia is tested by asking the patients to perform such behaviors as miming brushing their teeth or combing their hair. The patients should be able to perform these actions as if the instruments were in their hands, i.e., they should not rub their fingers against their teeth, but should use their hands to hold the handle of the imaginary toothbrush. Another test for praxis is to have the patient mime putting a key in a lock, turning it, and opening a door using the doorknob. Apraxia generally results from damage to the parietal lobe.

A less common focal deficit is *agnosia*, or inability to recognize specific visual stimuli in the absence of visual impairment or aphasia. It may be caused by lesions, such as tumors, in the visual association areas.

The importance of routine cognitive examination is underlined in patients with focal cognitive deficits since such deficits may be missed entirely if the clinician does not test for them specifically. Some individuals with severe memory impairment could be judged cognitively normal because of their spared ability to perform certain complex procedural tasks such as typing, playing the piano, or even playing cards. Such areas of intact functioning are the hallmark of the focal deficits.

Schizophrenia

Schizophrenia in the elderly (see also Chap. 100) is an infrequent cause of altered mental state, but when it occurs it is often responsive to treatment with phenothiazines and thus should be considered in the differential diagnosis of every case with prominent delusions and hallucinations.[15,16] The characteristic presentation is an elderly person who develops intense auditory hallucinations and, sometimes, delusions of persecution. The presentation of late-life-onset schizophrenia differs from schizophrenia that begins early in life. When the onset is late in life, thought disorder does not occur, and there is preservation of the personality, i.e., there are no so-called negative symptoms such as apathy and coarsening of relationships with other people (see Chap. 100). Although the cause is not known, late-onset schizophrenia occurs in hearing-impaired individuals more often than expected. Several cases have been reported in association with parietal stroke in the nondominant hemisphere.[17]

Mental Retardation

Mental retardation (see also Chap. 101) is defined as an IQ less than 70 and the inability to adapt to social environments. It should be considered in the differential diagnosis of an abnormal mental state because many mentally retarded individuals now live into old age and present with cognitive impairment that can be misdiagnosed as a change in mental state. They may also present with a *truly* altered mental state since the retarded are vulnerable to psychological and physiological environmental changes that affect their behavior.

Many elderly individuals in the community suffer from a lifelong impairment of unknown cause. The exact prevalence is unknown, but 2 to 3 percent of all adults are thought to suffer from mental retardation, as defined by an IQ of less than 70.[18] However, 7 percent of adults in a survey of three Baltimore communities suffered from cognitive impairment as measured by a MMSE score of less than 24 (a rate similar to that of all dementia in the elderly), and, when examined, had no diagnosable psychiatric or neurological condition.[19] Many of these individuals had been reared in impoverished environments in the early 1900s and had attended school for only brief periods in a system that did not provide special educational classes. Most would be classified as having below average intelligence rather than mental retardation, and many were illiterate. Despite the high prevalence of such individuals, no studies have been published that identify the specific risk factors for their impairment. The roles of genetics, the prenatal and postnatal environments, and educational opportunity remain unexplored.[19] Furthermore, no studies exist of the prevalence of psychiatric disorder in the elderly retarded, but in younger mentally retarded individuals the rate is high relative to children with normal intelligence living in the same community.

Somewhat more is known about the mental state in elderly individuals with Down's syndrome. The neuropathological lesions of Alzheimer's disease occur in all patients with Down's syndrome after the age of 45, although not all patients appear to deteriorate clinically before death.[20] Individuals with Down's syndrome are particularly sensitive to anticholinergic agents and therefore susceptible to delirium (A. Victor, personal communication). Depression has been reported, but the rates have not yet been established.

EMOTIONAL SYNDROMES

Elderly individuals present to medical clinics with changes in their emotional state as well as in their cognitive state (see also Chaps. 99 and 103). These changes are often unrecognized by physicians who attempt to treat the patients' somatic complaints symptomatically with an accumulation of analgesics, antispasmodics, and sedatives that can produce increasing lethargy, somatic preoccupation, and sometimes delirium. The emotional syndromes of the elderly can be classified into those that are understandable reactions to the environment, called adjustment disorders by the revised third edition of the *Diagnostic and Statistical Manual of Mental Disorders* (DSM III-R) classification, and those that present the syndrome of *major depression*, which often occurs on a genetic or other somatic basis. Major depression can be divided into primary affective disorders and those that are symptomatic of, or secondary to, somatic conditions such as stroke, parkinsonism, or medication with antihypertensive agents. Physicians can screen for emotional disorders in the elderly with the General Health Questionnaire (see Chap. 19) or other scales such as the Center for Epidemiological Studies Depression Scale (CES-D) or the Yesavage Depression Scale.[21,22] These brief questionnaires were originally developed for research but are useful clinical tools. They are self-rated and require that the patient has the cognitive capacity to complete them. If the patient is cognitively impaired, the physician can complete the Hamilton Depression Scale or the Montgomery Asberg Scale based on an interview with the patient and, if necessary, an informant.[23,24]

Syndromes of Minor Depression

The minor affective syndromes are the most common emotional disorders in the elderly and rank second only to cognitive disorders in prevalence.[25] Reactive syndromes can be viewed as resulting from certain personality traits that cause an individual to be vulnerable to particular environmental stressors.[26] For example, individuals with dependent traits who were able to function in the setting of a marriage may become symptomatic when they are widowed and when their children live too far away to provide support. The symptoms vary but may appear as prolonged and unresolved grief, fears and anxieties leading to insomnia or gastrointestinal complaints, or simply demoralization and discouragement from their failure to master a changing environment. Individuals who are obsessional and perfectionistic may become preoccupied with minor aches and pains and make frequent appointments to see physicians from whom they request (demand) medications to relieve their symptoms. Such patients accumulate many unnecessary medicines that can cause other symptoms.

The management of these conditions is based on an individual formulation of each case. A detailed review of the patient's personal history will improve the physician's ability to make such a formulation. In addition, the interest shown in the patient by the physician by this detailed review will improve the patient's trust in the physician. In the context of this relationship a conversation will emerge which will help the patient put his or her symptoms into perspective and will redirect the patient's insistence on the prescription of pharmacological agents. Most importantly, the relationship will convey an attitude of hope and support.

Major Depression

Major depression (either bipolar or unipolar affective disorder) occurs in the elderly as a continuation of a process of recurrent mood disorders which began earlier in life. Occasionally, the disorder begins in old age, but there is usually a history of previous episodes and often a family history of depression.[27] There are two characteristic symptoms of depressive disorder in addition to a dysphoric mood: a change in *mood and self attitude* with feelings of hopelessness and worthlessness, and *a change in the vital sense*.[28] Patients report a new and unpleasant sensation in the body, with a draining of energy and interest. These phenomena appear to afflict the person like a dark cloud and usually appear out of the blue but are sometimes precipitated by life events. The symptoms are accompanied by a change in appetite, bowel function, and sleep pattern. There is sometimes a diurnal variation, with the mood lightening in the afternoon or evening. This syndrome is sometimes accompanied by delusions of poverty, guilt, or persecution that are congruent with the patient's low mood, or feelings of worthlessness and guilt. Patients may believe they are being persecuted because of some indiscretion or other blameworthy act they have committed. The patients' unpleasant bodily sensations and constipation can lead to a preoccupation with somatic symptoms and the belief that they have a blocked bowel, cancer, or rotting organs. These thoughts can lead to suicide. Elderly men with primary depression complicated by physical illness present the highest suicide risk.

The depressive syndrome usually occurs alone but may alternate with periods of mania, a feeling of elation or irritability accompanied by inflation of self attitude. The patients may feel they have special talents or powers and their thoughts and behaviors reflect this belief. Buying sprees, increased alcohol intake, sleeplessness, overtalkativeness, and overactivity are common.

The management of affective disorder is based on an empathic relationship with the patient which elicits the patient's cooperation. This is necessary to enable the patient to relate painful suicidal thoughts and to develop trust in the doctor, which will increase the likelihood that the patient will cooperate with the treatment plan. The empathic relationship is built as the physician spends time listening to the details of the patient's life story. The traditional medical-psychiatric history-taking framework can be used to systematically survey aspects of the patient's life from parental relationships to daily life to the present.

Pharmacological management of affective disorder includes tricyclic antidepressants, lithium, and neuroleptics. Electroconvulsive therapy (ECT) may be necessary for patients who are unresponsive to more conservative treatment. Elderly patients often suffer from conditions that complicate the use of antidepressants, which have anticholinergic effects. These conditions include glaucoma, prostatic hypertrophy, chronic constipation, gait disorders, and some cardiac arrhythmias. Patients with cerebral disorders, such as stroke or Alzheimer's disease, may develop delirium when treated with psychoactive medications. Because of these side effects, such patients require frequent checkups by the physician and small doses of medication. Psychiatric consultation and often psychiatric hospitalization are needed for these cases, and ECT may be necessary if pharmacological treatment causes too many difficulties.

Secondary or Symptomatic Depression

The syndrome of depression occurs frequently as a consequence of neurological disease. The symptoms are similar to those of primary affective disorder but may be difficult to elicit because of the patient's compromised ability to describe, remember, or clearly describe his or her mental state because of the presence of amnesia, aphasia, or dysarthria. However, with the assistance of family members, the physician can elicit the usual symptoms of depression or irritability, the associated changes in self attitude, and the vegetative symptoms of insomnia, anorexia, and loss of energy. Affective disorder associated with neurological disease might or might not be precipitated by environmental events in the life of the injured person.

A depressive syndrome occurs in perhaps 30 percent of stroke patients who have lesions in the left anterior hemisphere, 20 percent of patients with Alzheimer's disease, 40 percent of patients with Huntington's disease, and 40 to 60 percent of Parkinson's patients. Although the mechanism of the depression is not understood, all these conditions interfere with catecholaminergic pathways originating in the brainstem.[29] Patients with Alzheimer's disease who had been depressed during life had, on autopsy, fewer neurons in the locus coeruleus than patients who had not suffered from a depressive syndrome.[30] Patients with Parkinson's disease associated with depression were found to have lower levels of catechol metabolites in the CSF than Parkinson's disease patients without depression.[31] On PET, depressed Parkinson's disease patients also have lower glucose metabolism in the striatum and inferior frontal cortex compared with nondepressed Parkinson's disease patients matched for overall severity of illness.

Few clinical trials have been carried out to test the usefulness of antidepressants for depression associated with neurological disorders. Stroke patients with anterior left hemisphere lesions have been shown to respond to tricyclic antidepressants at therapeutic levels better than to placebo in a double-blind trial. Case reports indicate that patients with Parkinson's disease respond to tricyclics but often require ECT, and clinical experience suggests that patients with Alzheimer's disease and Huntington's disease respond to tricyclics and ECT.

The prognosis of depression in neurological disease is not well studied. Clinical experience suggests that the depression, even if untreated, occurs in episodes. This has been demonstrated by prospective study for stroke and by retrospective chart review for Huntington's disease.

In patients with neurological disease, the depressive syndrome is to be distinguished from other disturbances of mood such as emotional lability, pathological emotion, and catastrophic reactions. The depressive syndrome is characterized by a sustained change in mood that lasts from weeks to months, compared with the short-lived, even fleeting, changes of mood characteristic of these other conditions. Emotional lability describes a short-lived change in emotion that lasts from seconds to hours and is sometimes precipitated by thoughts or circumstances. Pathological emotion is an involuntary emotional outburst that is often ego dystonic. Patients do not know why they are laughing or crying and often do not have a congruent mood, as if the motor, but not the sensory, component of emotion were released from control. Pathological emotion occurs in patients with pseudobulbar palsy which is caused by bilateral lesions of the corticobulbar pathways, usually due to stroke in elderly patients and sometimes by multiple sclerosis in younger patients. Case reports and clinical experience suggest that these patients respond to tricyclic antidepressants. Catastrophic reactions are emotional outbursts caused by task failure and are clearly related in time to some frustrating or confusing aspect of the patient's environment.

CONCLUSION

An elderly patient who presents to a physician with an altered mental state is likely to have either a cognitive syndrome, most commonly a delirium or a dementia, or an emotional disorder, most commonly depression.

A diagnosis can usually be reached by taking a careful history from the patient and another informant and by carrying out a detailed examination of the patient's mental, physical, and neurological state, followed by selected laboratory procedures and longitudinal follow-up. Elderly patients may have several coexisting conditions that act together to alter their mental state, so that a thorough evaluation is important even when there is a clear primary diagnosis.

REFERENCES

1. Bonhoeffer C: Exogenic psychoses, in Hirsch S, Sheppard M (eds): *Themes and Variations in European Psychiatry.* Bristol, John, Right and Sons, 1974, p 47.
2. Wolf HG, Curran D: Nature of delirium in allied states: The dysergastic reaction. *Arch Neurol Psychiatry* 33:175, 1935.
3. Plum F, Posner JB: The pathologic physiology of signs and symptoms of coma, in *The Diagnosis of Stupor and Coma,* 3d ed. Philadelphia, Davis, 1982, p 1.
4. Folstein MF et al: Cognitive assessment of cancer patients. *Cancer* 53:225, 1984.
5. Tune LE, Folstein MF: Post-operative delirium. *Adv Psychosomatic Med* 15:15, 1986.
6. Leresche AJ et al: Screening for delirium on a general medical ward: The tachistoscope and a global accessibility rating. *Gen Hosp Psychiatry* 7:36, 1985.
7. Engel GL, Romano J: A syndrome of cerebral insufficiency. *J Chronic Dis* 9:260, 1959.
8. Tune L et al: Association of postoperative delirium with raised serum levels of anticholinergic drugs. *Lancet* 8248(2):651, 1981.
9. McHugh PR, Folstein MF: Organic mental disorders, in *Psychiatry.* Lippincott, 1987, p 73.
10. Folstein MF et al: Meaning of cognitive impairment in the elderly. *J Am Geriatr Soc* 33(4):228, 1985.
11. Rovner BW et al: The prevalence of mental illness in a community nursing home. *Am J Psychiatry* 143(11):1446, 1986.
12. Butters N, Milotis P: Amnesia, in Heilman KM, Valenstein E (eds): *Clinical Neuropsychology.* New York, Oxford, 1985, p 403.
13. McHugh PR, Folstein MF: Psychiatric syndromes of Huntington's chorea: A clinical and phenomenologic study, in Benson DF, Blumer (eds): *Psychiatric Aspects of Neurologic Disease.* New York, Grune & Stratton, 1975, p 267.
14. Benson F: Aphasia, in Heilman KM, Valenstein E (eds): *Clinical Neuropsychology.* New York, Oxford, 1985, p 17.
15. Post F: *Persistent Persecutory States of the Elderly.* London, Pergamon, 1966.
16. Rabins P et al: Increased ventricle-to-brain ratio in late-onset schizophrenia. *Am J Psychiatry* 144(9):1216, 1987.
17. Peroutka SJ et al: Hallucinations and delusions following a right temporoparietooccipital infarction. *Johns Hopkins Med J* 151:181, 1982.
18. Adams RD, Victor M: Disorders contingent upon deviations in development of the nervous system. *Principles Neurol* 24:381, 1977.
19. Anthony JC et al: Limits of the mini-mental state as a screening test for dementia and delirium among hospital patients. *Psychol Med* 12:397, 1982.
20. Wisniewski KE et al: Alzheimer's disease in Down's syndrome: Clinicopathologic studies. *Neurology* 35(7):957, 1985.
21. Comstock GW, Helsing KJ: Symptoms of depression in two communities. *Psychol Med* 6:551, 1976.
22. Savage JA et al: The geriatric depression rating scale in comparison with other self report and psychiatric rating scales, in Crook T et al (eds): *Assessment and Geriatric Psychopharmacology.* Mark Pally, 1983.
23. Hamilton MA: A rating scale for depression. *J Neurol, Neurosurg, Psychiatry* 23:56, 1960.
24. Montgomery SA, Asberg M: A new depression designed to be sensitive to change. *Br J Psychiatry* 134:382, 1979.
25. Slater E, Roth M: Ageing and the Mental Diseases of the Aged, in *Clinical Psychiatry* 3d ed. 1977, p 541.
26. McHugh P, Slavney P: *Perspectives of Psychiatry.* Baltimore, Johns Hopkins University Press, 1983.
27. Slater E, Roth M: Ageing and the Mental Diseases of the Aged, in *Clinical Psychiatry* 3d ed. 1977, p 569.
28. Schneider K: General psychopathology. New York, Grune & Stratton, 1959.
29. Folstein MF et al: Depression in neurological disorders: New treatment opportunities for elderly depressed patients. *J Affective Disord* 1:11, 1985.
30. Zweig R et al: The neuropathology of aminergic nuclei in Alzheimer's disease. *Ann Neurol* 24(2):233, 1988.
31. Mayeux R et al: Clinical and biochemical features of depression in Parkinson's disease. *Am J Psychiatry* 143(6):756, 1986.

Chapter 111

FAILURE TO THRIVE

Roy B. Verdery

There is little doubt that very old and oldest old people decline and eventually die and that, prior to death, many are frail and go through a period of increasing susceptibility to a variety of terminal diseases. Most people have anecdotes involving friends or family members who have gone through this process, and classical literature is replete with descriptions of frailty and decline in very old people. For example,

> . . . The sixth age shifts
> Into the lean and slippered pantaloon,
> [gait dysfunction]
> With spectacles on nose and pouch on side;
> [presbyopia]
> His youthful hose well saved, a world too wide
> [inappropriateness]
> For his shrunk shank; and his big manly voice,
> [muscle loss]
> Turning again toward childish treble, pipes
> [androgen deficiency]
> And whistles in his sound. Last scene of all, [predeath]
> That ends this strange eventful history,
> Is second childishness, and mere oblivion, [dementia]
> Sans teeth, sans eyes, sans taste, sans everything.
> [toothlessness, blindness, anorexia, poverty]
> —Shakespeare, *As You Like It,*
> Act II, Scene VII

Although this process of deterioration preceding death is common, well recognized, and widely accepted, it is difficult to define failure to thrive within a modern medical context. This difficulty arises because very old and oldest old people are very heterogenous and because many processes can cause failure to thrive.

Failure to thrive can be defined as the progressive loss of function that occurs in frail people, leading to cachexia and death. In this sense, failure to thrive is a process marked by loss of weight, strength, and the ability to perform personal and instrumental activities of daily living. The rate of failure to thrive can be measured as the rate of change of a function—for example, the rate of decline in the time a person takes to walk 50 feet. Because this definition depends on the individual's original ability to function, it is difficult to identify persons with failure to thrive without observing them over time. Semantically, it is important to distinguish between (1) frailty, the condition of being at risk for deterioration (see Chap. 105); (2) failure to thrive, the process of deterioration; and (3) the various frail states which occur after failure to thrive begins, which have been called predeath or cachexia.

One way of representing failure to thrive in an individual and relating it to expected function is shown in Fig. 111-1. This figure shows the gradual decline in some measured function (e.g., timed walking, muscle strength, cognition, cardiac output, FEV_1, etc.) that occurs due to intrinsic aging, disease, or both. At some time, the subject, who is already "frail," begins to decline at a rate greater than expected for his or her peers. Increased rate of decline often appears to be the result of a trigger (e.g., hip fracture, death of a spouse, serious illness, etc.). Subsequent to the trigger event, the rate of decline in function is greater than it had previously been, and the individual is said to be "failing to thrive." A significant question is whether the decline is reversible or not. It may proceed inexorably to death, especially if one is observing decline in a vital function such as cardiac output or if the underlying cause is irreversible (e.g., cancer or Alzheimer's disease). As described below, however, under certain circumstances failure to thrive is reversible, particularly in cases where it is due to functional and psychosocial problems. This trigger model of failure to thrive is closely related to models of loss of vigor during biological aging[1] and the progression of frailty.[2]

Research in this area has a long history. The earliest studies were cross-sectional evaluations of characteristics of people who died. This led to the concept of "predeath" as a condition which included one or more problems with cognition, continence, weight loss, or chronic disease.[3] Recent studies have been more specific, focusing on physiologic abnormalities of nursing home patients. They have led to the conclusion that risk factors for death include low weight, low muscle mass, decreased physical function, and weakness, along with laboratory markers of low albumin,[4] low cholesterol,[5] anergy, and other signs of immunodeficiency.[6] It is still true, however, that it is very difficult to identify a single "state" or syndrome in an individual elderly person with failure to thrive.

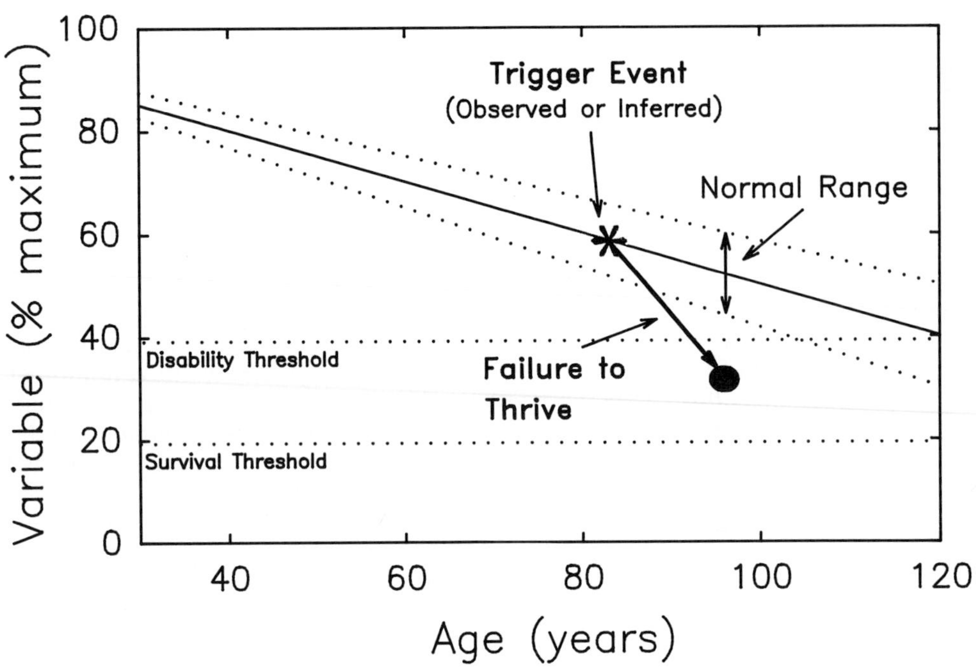

FIGURE 111-1

Trigger model for failure to thrive in elderly persons. Many functional variables decline with age, and there is a normal range for any specific age. In the context of normal changes in function, failure to thrive is defined as decline at a rate greater than expected, leading to a level of function below the age-adjusted norm. A trigger event such as a hip fracture or severe illness is often observed to occur prior to failure to thrive, but in many instances such a trigger event must be inferred.

There have been few longitudinal studies that looked at the process of moving from the state of robust good health to the state of frailty or the process of moving from mild frailty to frank cachexia.[7] These studies have focused on the development of anorexia or subsequent poor food intake. In general, the reversible causes of failure to thrive are associated with poor food intake, due to a variety of causes, and consequent starvation.[8] As described below, however, it is generally accepted that failure to thrive due to infection, cancer, and organ failure in very old people is irreversible.

WEIGHT LOSS

A hallmark of failure to thrive is unexplained weight loss and anorexia. As shown by Andres,[9] the association of mortality with weight is a U-shaped curve (Fig. 111-2), with increased mortality at both low and high weight. The nadir of U-shaped curves, the point associated with minimum mortality, increases with age and is essentially the same for both men and women. Thus, the "best weight" in terms of all-cause mortality for an elderly person is higher than the "best weight" for a younger person (Fig. 111-3). The implications of these data, derived from populations, for individuals are not certain. Even in older people, high weight is associated with increased risk for cardiovascular mortality and diabetes and its attendant problems. On the other hand, low weight is associated with occult cancer and increased risk for lung disease and certain infections such as influenza, and in people with severe low weight, weight gain often improves prognosis.

Body weight is made up of multiple components including water, fat, muscle, and bone. In older people, even when they are healthy, there is an increased proportion of fat and a decreased proportion of muscle and bone.[10] Frail older people typically have not only low weight but also low muscle mass and attendant functional problems. There is clear association of low muscle strength and decreased aerobic capacity with increased mortality from a variety of causes including cardiovascular disease. Decreased bone mass is associated with increased risk of fracture, and both

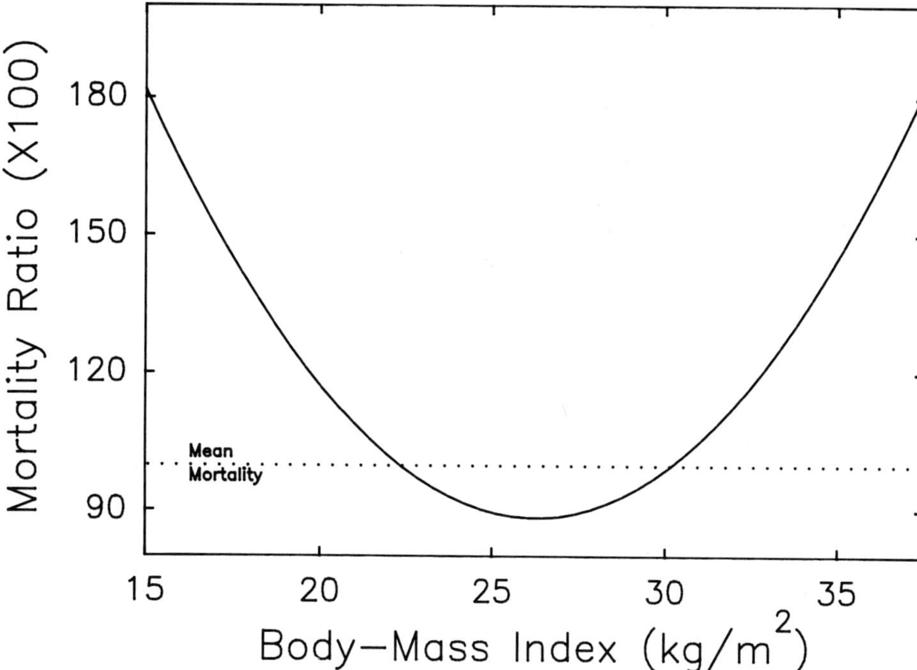

FIGURE 111-2
Relationship between weight adjusted for height, expressed as body-mass index, weight/height^2, and relative mortality for men and women 70 years old. This figure shows that mortality is a U-shaped function of weight and that there is greater mortality at weights both lower and higher than that associated with minimum mortality.[10]

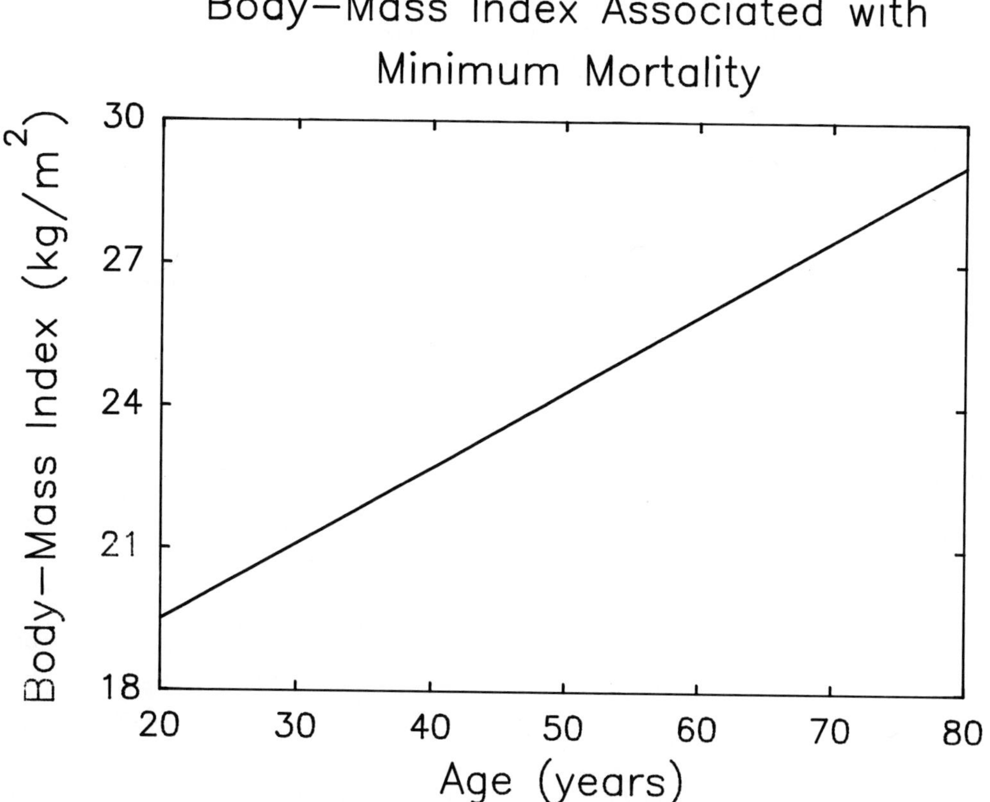

FIGURE 111-3
Relationship between age and weight associated with minimum mortality. This figure shows that the weight associated with minimum mortality increases with increasing age. At all ages, however, obesity is associated with increased risk for diabetes and cardiovascular disease and specific, disease-associated mortality.

spinal compression fractures and hip fractures are major causes of morbidity and mortality in very old and oldest old people.

Regulation of body mass changes with age. Mechanisms which regulate water and electrolyte balance and free water retention or clearance are altered in the very old and oldest old, leading to increased prevalence of hypo- and hypernatremia (Chap. 108). Diseases of increased prevalence in the very old, such as heart failure and kidney failure, also directly affect water mass.

Osteopenia and osteoporosis are extremely important in the changing body composition of very old and oldest old people (Chap. 76). The primary effectors of bone deposition, hormones and exercise, are altered with aging. Decreasing levels of estrogen in women after the menopause and the general decreased level of exercise in both men and women with age both contribute to loss of bone mass. Elderly people who become physically disabled due to illness, fracture, stroke, or other neurologic problems and "take to bed" rapidly lose bone mass.

Similar to bone mass, the metabolic components regulating muscle mass and protein balance are probably the same in older people and in younger people, but the effectors are probably altered. Declining levels of growth hormone and its effector, insulinlike growth factor I (IGF-I), lead to decreased rates of protein synthesis and muscle mass.[11] Disuse atrophy in people who have decreasing exercise levels or who take to bed for illness also leads to decreased muscle mass. Exercise clearly increases not only muscle mass but also function even in the oldest old.[12]

Fat mass and, to a lesser extent, muscle and bone mass are directly affected by food intake. The caloric content of food absorbed is either stored as fat or used as energy. There are many factors which regulate fat mass, the variable component of weight after water (Fig. 111-4). Food intake is regulated by appetite and absorption. The regulators of appetite are poorly understood. Increasing prevalence of lactose intolerance and achlorhydria often contributes to malabsorption of certain nutrients. On the other side of the equation, energy expenditure can be divided into basal energy expenditure, a factor which is well known to decline with age[13] and to change with muscle mass and energy expenditure due to exercise or disease. As noted with muscle and bone mass, decreasing levels of exercise lead to decreasing amounts of muscle and bone mass. In contrast, decreasing levels of exercise lead to increasing amounts of fat mass. Disease, on the other hand, decreases mass in all three areas due to the combination of decreased exercise level, increased energy expenditure due to the disease process, and anorexia.

PATHOPHYSIOLOGY

Failure to thrive eventually involves multiple organs. At least three hypothetical situations can be considered. The first is the general decay recognized by Shakespeare, where multiple organ systems become

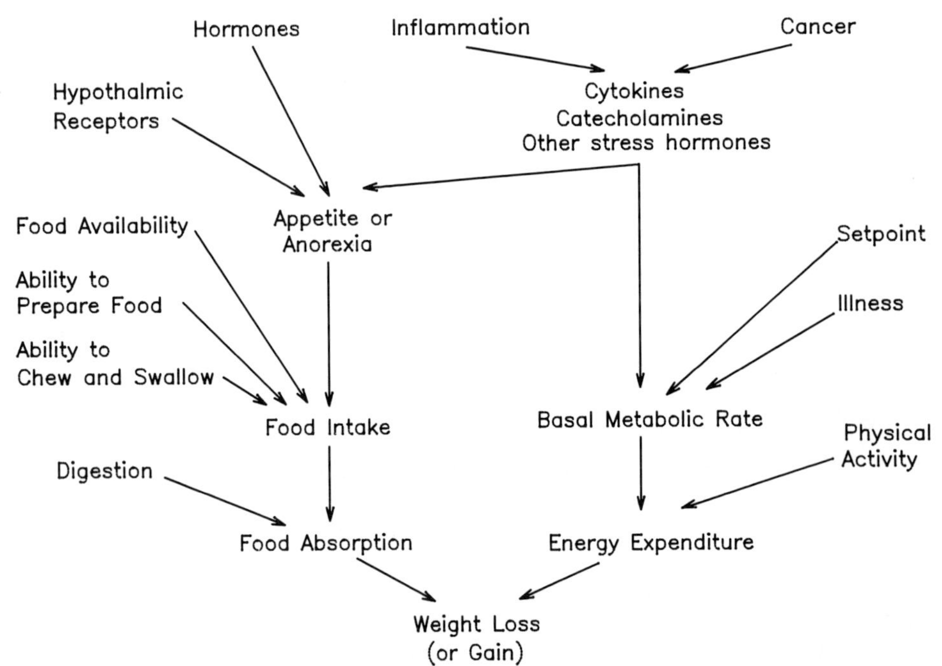

FIGURE 111-4
Relationship among some of the factors regulating weight due to inadequate food intake or excess energy expenditure. The basic equation is weight gain = absorption − expenditure, and factors regulating weight loss or gain are independent of age. However, there are important age-associated changes in food intake, absorption, and basal metabolic rate.

involved independently in some way, producing a frail old person without teeth, without vision, and without memory. A second hypothesis is epitomized by "The Deacon's Masterpiece," an analogy of human aging which runs, in part, as follows:

> You see, of course, if you're not a dunce,
> How it went to pieces all at once,
> All at once, and nothing first—
> Just as bubbles do when they burst.
>
> —Oliver Wendell Holmes
> *The Deacon's Masterpiece,*
> *or the Wonderful "One-Hoss Shay"*

In spite of the attractiveness of this model, developed by Fries and Crapo,[14] people do not usually die in old age like burst bubbles. A third hypothesis is that one organ system, such as the heart, fails before the others. This is followed by failure of other organs dependent on the first, which eventually leads to death. Indeed, organs seem to have a variety of aging schedules within the same individual.

The difficulty in distinguishing between these hypotheses includes the difficulty of relating studies of aging in animal populations to aging in human populations and in individuals, the focus of the geriatrician. There is no doubt that with increasing age in any species, there is an increasing prevalence of disease. However, diseases tend to be specific, not only for individual species but also for individual genetic groups within a single species.[15] These diseases typically involve a single organ system such as the kidney in the case of certain rat strains or the heart in the case of people living in developed countries. While the increasing prevalence of disease and the increased susceptibility to these diseases with increasing age can explain much of the population demographics of aging, this does not explain the processes of aging in individuals whose diseases might be treatable or in individuals who have managed to escape the prevalent diseases (heart disease and cancer in humans) and die of other rare conditions.

GERIATRIC PARADIGM

Geriatrics is involved not just with medical problems but also with cognitive problems, physical problems, and social problems associated with aging. Within this paradigm, geriatric problems (as compared with medical problems for old people) are those which involve dysfunction in two or more of these areas: medical and physiological, cognitive, functional, and social. This idea is the basis of the geriatric assessment, wherein a multidisciplinary group evaluates components of all four of these areas (see Chap. 17). It may well be that the ability of geriatric assessments to decrease morbidity and mortality due to degenerative processes associated with aging stems from the efficacy of geriatric assessment in dealing with failure to thrive.

Medical causes of failure to thrive are identified by the physician review; the cognitive and emotional problems associated with failure to thrive are identified by review of mental status and screen for depression; the functional causes of failure to thrive are identified in the course of a functional assessment; and social disabilities are noted by review of living circumstances. Early recognition of these disabilities which can lead to failure to thrive make early intervention possible. Early intervention, in this sense, often consists not just of medical treatment but also of the involvement of family and community resources, attention to functional deficits, and nursing and other professional assistance.

CAUSES OF FAILURE TO THRIVE

Within the multidisciplinary geriatric paradigm, causes of failure to thrive will be divided among metabolic and other diseases, functional causes, social causes, and psychological causes of failure to thrive (Table 111-1). The metabolic causes of failure to

TABLE 111-1

Causes of Failure to Thrive in the Elderly

Medical	Psychologic	Functional	Social
Cancer	Depression	Immobility	Isolation
Endocrine	Dementia	(e.g., disuse or	Poverty
(e.g., diabetes or	Psychosis	arthritis)	Caregiver fatigue
hypothyroidism)	Grief	Neurologic	Neglect
Organ failure	Intention	(e.g., stroke or	Abuse
(e.g., cardiac,	("chronic suicide")	parkinsonism)	
hepatic, or		Deafness	
renal)		Blindness	
Infection		Dental problems	
Inflammation			

thrive have been discussed in the section on weight loss and are those things which lead to changes in body composition, causing increased risk for bad outcome and making the person more "frail." These include increased fat mass, decreased muscle mass, and decreased bone mass and to a great extent are caused by poor food intake, excessive calories relative to need, decreased exercise level, and decreases in anabolic hormone levels.

Many diseases cause failure to thrive. To a great extent these are the same diseases that cause weight loss in younger people, including tuberculosis, cancer, subacute bacterial endocarditis and other infections, end-stage organ failure (such as heart, kidney, lung, or liver failure), and endocrinologic problems such as diabetes and hyperthyroidism. Some diseases, such as temporal arteritis and polymyalgia rheumatica, are associated with age. Some are not strictly diseases but are syndromes, such as polypharmacy.

Functional causes of failure to thrive are very common. Dementias make it difficult for people to obtain and prepare food or even to eat properly. Some demented individuals seem to lose all interest in food even in the absence of depression. End-stage arthritis can interfere with the ability to obtain and prepare normal meals. Blindness makes it difficult to obtain food and other services. Tooth and mouth disease makes it difficult to eat normal foods, foods which are pleasant and lead to appropriate appetite. The functional difficulties associated with the neurologic problems including dementia, paralysis after stroke, parkinsonism, and other diseases also cause failure to thrive directly. A hallmark of depression is anorexia, decreased food intake, or weight loss.

As elderly people age, many of their friends die. They are often widowed, and social disability becomes an important cause of failure to thrive. While there are no good screens for disability, it is quite clear that people who live alone, who do not have a spouse or significant other, or who are without friends and community support have an increased tendency to lose weight, become depressed, and fail to thrive. A social problem directly causing failure to thrive is that of increased prevalence in the very old of abuse. In the event of unexplained weight loss and deterioration in someone with no other problem, neglect or abuse has to be considered.

TREATMENT

Once an evaluation is obtained, many of the medical and psychosocial problems causing failure to thrive can be treated. Identified diseases can be directly treated as they would be for a younger person. Body composition is improved by exercise and appropriate food intake, and regular exercise is one of the most effective treatments if it can be employed. Because most of the psychosocial causes of failure to thrive include starvation, food supplements or enteral feeding are often an important component of treatment. Use of flavor enhancers is being promoted by some investigators. The possibility that appetite stimulants can be found which are directed at anorexia rather than depression or other functional problems needs to be further pursued. Functional deficits can be ameliorated with the help of physical therapists, occupational therapists, and aides. Social problems are alleviated by counseling, provision of services, day care, and nursing homes. The functional components of psychologic problems can be similarly alleviated by rehabilitation, if possible, and direct assistance. Estrogen replacement clearly improves bone in the immediate post-menopausal period. The role of growth hormone or IGF-I analogues is presently being investigated.[16]

REFERENCES

1. Arking R: *Biology of Aging: Observations and Principles.* Englewood Cliffs, NJ, Prentice-Hall, 1991, pp 12–19.
2. Weindruch R, Hadley EC, Ory MG (eds): *Reducing Frailty and Falls in Older Persons.* Springfield, IL, Charles C Thomas, 1991, pp 5–12.
3. Isaacs B et al: The concept of predeath. *Lancet* 1:1115, 1971.
4. Rudman D et al: A mortality risk index for men in a Veterans Administration extended care facility. *J Parenter Enter Nutr* 13:189, 1989.
5. Verdery RB, Goldberg AP: Hypocholesterolemia as a predictor of death: A prospective study of 224 nursing home residents. *J Gerontol* 46:M84, 1991.
6. Adler WH, Nagel JE: Studies of immune function in a human population, in Serge D, Smith L (eds): *Immunological Aspects of Aging.* New York, Dekker, 1981, pp 296–311.
7. Lipschitz DA, Mitchell CO: The correctability of the nutritional, immune and hematopoietic manifestations of protein calorie malnutrition in the elderly. *J Am Coll Nutr* 1:17, 1982.
8. Thomas DR et al: A prospective study of outcome from protein-energy malnutrition in nursing home residents. *J Parenter Enter Nutr* 15:400, 1991.
9. Andres R: Mortality and obesity: The rationale for age-specific height-weight tables, in Andres R, Bierman EL, Hazzard WR (eds): *Principles of Geriatric Medicine.* New York, McGraw-Hill, 1984, pp 311–318.
10. Rossman I: Anatomic and body changes with aging, in Finch CE, Hayflick L, Brody H (eds): *Handbook of the*

Biology of Aging. New York, Van Nostrand Reinhold, 1977, pp 189–221.
11. Sonntag WE et al: Growth hormone restores protein synthesis in skeletal muscle of old male rats. *J Gerontol* 40:689, 1985.
12. Fiatarone MA et al: High intensity strength training in nonagenarians. *JAMA* 263:3029, 1990.
13. Roza AM, Shizgal HM: The Harris Benedict equation reevaluated: Resting energy requirements and the body cell mass. *Am J Clin Nutr* 40:168, 1984.
14. Fries JM, Crapo LM: *Vitality and Aging*. San Francisco, Freeman, 1981.
15. Bronson RT: Rate of occurrence of lesions in 20 inbred and hybrid genotypes of rats and mice sacrificed at 6 month intervals during the first years of life, in Harrison DE (ed): *Genetic Effects on Aging*, 2d ed. Caldwell, NJ, Telford, 1990, pp 279–358.
16. Kaiser FE et al: The effect of recombinant human growth hormone on malnourished older individuals. *J Am Geriatr Soc* 39:235, 1991.

Chapter 112

SLEEP PROBLEMS

Edward F. Haponik

The recognition that alterations of sleep can produce considerable morbidity during wakefulness has been a major medical advance. Such changes considerably influence the quality of life and, in some persons, are life-threatening. In addition, there has been enhanced appreciation of secondary deleterious effects upon sleep caused by diverse acute and chronic illnesses and of untoward effects of disordered sleep upon these diseases. Nowhere is the clinical relevance of such interactions more important than in care for the elderly. The prevalence and importance of sleep problems in older people is underscored by a recent Consensus Development Conference convened by the National Institutes on Aging and the National Institutes of Health.[1] Familiarity with these conditions and with pragmatic approaches to their management is an essential component of comprehensive geriatric patient care, but most current practitioners have received little preparation to deal with this clinical challenge.

Primary considerations in older persons with sleep complaints (Table 112-1) are similar to basic principles delineated in preceding chapters. First, the clinician must attempt to differentiate disease from normal changes accompanying aging: it is often difficult to establish whether a patient's difficulties with sleep truly reflect disease. The chronicity and severity of symptoms and, most importantly, their impact upon the patient's functional status determine whether evaluation and intervention are necessary or appropriate. Second, it must be recognized that problems manifest during wakefulness might have originated in a primary sleep disorder. For example, both hypersomnolence from fragmented sleep structure and signs and symptoms of serious end-organ dysfunction may be caused by disordered breathing. Third, the clinician must exclude deleterious effects upon the quality and quantity of sleep that are due to systemic diseases, psychiatric illnesses (and their treatment), or social problems confronting the elderly patient. Acute and chronic pain, nocturia, paroxysmal dyspnea, anxiety, depression, bereavement, retirement, or institutionalization profoundly influence sleep. Failure to recognize such causes of an inability to fall asleep or of frequent nocturnal awakenings might lead to misdiagnosis and mismanagement. Fourth, one must identify treatable disease or those potentially reversible elements of what are often chronic, generally progressive conditions. Sleep apnea is a potentially curable and potentially life-threatening disorder. As another example, major depression causing early morning awakening can often be ameliorated pharmacologically. Finally and perhaps most importantly, the clinician must avoid causing iatrogenic illness. Medications prescribed by physicians are among the most common causes of sleep-related complaints in the elderly, often represent an expedient substitute for systematic diagnosis and management, and frequently lead to further pharmacologic treatment.

TABLE 112-1

Clinical Considerations in Elderly Patients with Sleep Complaints

1. Differentiate disease from normal changes with aging
2. Recognize symptoms during wakefulness that originate in sleep
3. Exclude secondary dysfunction due to systemic diseases, psychologic factors, and social factors
4. Identify treatable/reversible conditions
5. Minimize iatrogenic illness

SLEEP ALTERATIONS IN THE ELDERLY

A spectrum of subjective and objective changes of sleep occurs with aging.[1–21] Surveys reveal that from 15 to 75 percent of elderly persons residing at home or in extended-care facilities are dissatisfied with either the duration or quality of their nocturnal sleep, and physicians' accounts confirm this impression.[1–3,5–11] Subjectively, healthy elderly women experience more troubled sleep than men.[12,13] Reviews consistently identify the following complaints. Elderly persons report that although they spend relatively more total time in bed (often resting without attempting to sleep, napping, or else unable to fall asleep), their total sleep time is reduced from what it was during youth.[2–5] Sleep latency, the time it takes to fall asleep, is often increased, and older persons very commonly report that they awaken after the onset of sleep. The number of daytime naps tends to increase with age. These deteriorations of subjective sleep quality in the healthy elderly are accentuated in persons with sleep disorders.[22]

In laboratory settings, older persons' perceptions of differences in their sleep have been substantiated by objective demonstration of fundamental changes in sleep structure with aging (Table 112-2, Table 112-3, and Fig. 112-1).[2–7,14,21] Considerable variation exists among individuals and within the environments in which they have been studied. Electrophysiologic and behavioral criteria (established, for the most part, in younger populations) describe three states of active brain function: wakefulness, non–rapid eye movement (NREM) sleep, and rapid eye movement (REM) sleep.[23] NREM, or "quiet sleep," is defined by four stages. Stage 1 sleep is a transitional period of drowsiness during which electroencephalographic (EEG) activity slows, muscles, relax, and slow, rolling eye movements occur. This period is followed by stage 2, during which well-characterized sleep spindles and K complexes can be identified. Stages 3 and 4 NREM, or "deep sleep," are defined by profound EEG slowing and high-amplitude delta waves. This "slow-wave sleep" is believed to be particularly important for the restorative functions of sleep.[4] Positron emission tomography demonstrates reduced rates of cerebral glucose metabolism during slow-wave sleep in comparison to wakefulness[24]; REM sleep resembles wakefulness and is associated with increased autonomic activity and dreaming; cerebral glucose utilization during REM sleep is similar to that of wakefulness.[24] Heart rate, systemic blood pressure, and respiratory frequency vary widely during REM. Voluntary muscle tone (including that of accessory respiratory muscles) is reduced or absent except for the characteristic extraocular muscle activity. There is usually a transition from wakefulness through the four stages of NREM sleep, followed by the onset of initial REM sleep. Subsequently, NREM and REM periods alternate (Fig. 112-1). Sleep can be described by the absolute and relative durations of these stages and the distribution of cycles between NREM and REM sleep (Table 112-3).

With advancing age, there is a striking increase of stage 1 sleep, wakefulness after sleep onset, and a decrease of slow-wave sleep.[2–6] Not only the number but also the amplitude of delta waves are reduced. Increased stage 1 sleep provides a practical measure of the fragmentation or disruption of sleep. Reduced deep sleep presumably has major deleterious effects upon the restorative functions of sleep. It is likely that

TABLE 112-2

Altered Sleep in the Elderly

	Subjective Reports	Objective Monitoring
Total time in bed	Increased	Increased
Total sleep time	Decreased	Variable (usually decreased)
Sleep latency	Increased	Variable (usually increased)
Wakefulness after sleep onset	Increased	Increased
Daytime naps	Increased	Variable
Sleep efficiency	Decreased	Decreased

TABLE 112-3

Changes in Sleep Structure with Aging

Sleep Stage	Polysomnographic Findings
Non–rapid eye movement (NREM)	
Stage 1	Increased[a]
Stage 2	Variable (usually decreased)
Stage 3	Decreased
Stage 4	Decreased[a]
Rapid eye movement (REM)	
Quantity	Decreased
Distribution	Early onset; trend toward period of equal duration (rather than progressive lengthening)

[a]Common, major changes.

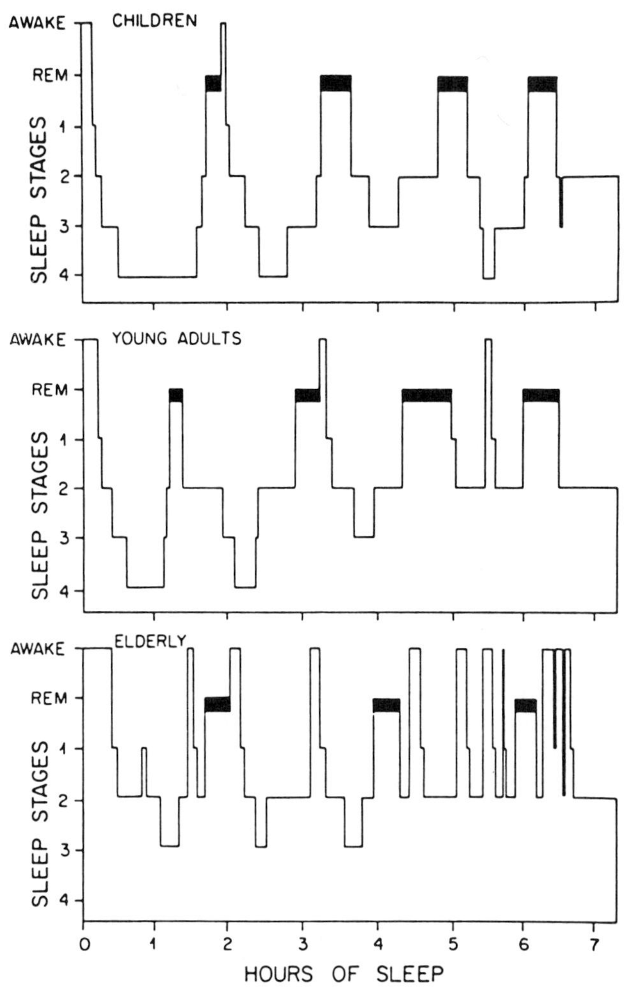

FIGURE 112-1

The structure of sleep in the elderly is characterized by increases in stages 1 and 2 sleep with marked reductions of stages 3 and 4 in NREM sleep. In addition, multiple awakenings occur, and the amount and duration of REM sleep are reduced. (*Reproduced by permission from Kales and Kales*[18] *and Baker.*[93])

sleep is disturbed even more profoundly in the elderly, since conventional scoring does not take into account very brief arousals, which are prevalent in the aged.[6] Some of the latter are due to systemic illnesses, while others have no apparent precipitant. Fatigue, irritability, impaired cognitive function, incoordination, and hallucinations have been associated with such sleep deprivation.[4] The absolute amount of REM sleep decreases in the elderly, though the percentage of total sleep time is similar to that of young individuals.[6] The distribution of sleep also changes. REM periods tend to occur earlier and to be more equal in duration, in contrast to their progressive lengthening in younger individuals. Reduced REM sleep has been associated with organic brain syndromes and altered cerebral blood flow.

In addition to these findings, even sleep posture changes with increasing age,[25] as older persons sleep less often in the prone position and markedly prefer right-sided positions. Persons over 65 years of age show longer periods of postural immobility during sleep and shift positions less often than younger individuals. The causes and effects of these changes are unclear, though the supine position is often associated with upper airway obstruction or aspiration.

The differences with age in sleep structure and, in particular, the increased stage 1 sleep, decreased stage 4 sleep, and increased wakefulness after sleep onset are more prominent in men than in women and have been thought to represent an exaggeration of gender differences seen in younger individuals.[4] Reynolds et al.[14,15] evaluated 40 healthy individuals aged 58 to 82 years and found that men were unable to maintain sleep as well as women and had reduced stage 3 sleep. Increased wakefulness during sleep was most notable during early morning hours. In an extension of this major normative study, these investigators observed stable sleep efficiency and REM sleep across three decades of late life.[26] Slow-wave sleep declined slightly among octogenarians and was better preserved in women. Eighty-year-old women had worsened sleep maintenance in contrast to eighty-year-old men when compared to 60- and 70-year-olds. A recent metaanalysis[27] of gender differences in sleep in the elderly addressed reports over the past decade and concluded that: (1) no important gender differences in total sleep time were noted, though slightly greater variability occurs among men; (2) elderly men tend to spend more time in bed than elderly women; (3) women tend to have a slightly longer objective sleep latency; (4) men tend to spend more time awake at initial sleep, but women awaken more frequently; (5) men tend to have more variable sleep efficiency, with women having higher scores on sleep efficiency and maintenance; (6) men tend to have higher percentages of stages 1 and 2 sleep, and women have more stages 3 and 4 sleep; (7) women have longer REM latencies (the strongest effect observed).

The ubiquity of clinical complaints and physiologic alterations of sleep in the elderly supports the notion that these represent expected changes, but whether they represent normal physiologic alterations or subtle manifestations of disease is unknown. Further assessment of these areas and, in particular, information about their evolution are needed. In one longitudinal study, healthy older subjects had increased but otherwise stable polygraphic measures of sleep and its quality over a 2.2-year period.[13] Excessive daytime sleepiness sufficient to cause symptoms or prompt help-seeking behavior is an important problem, but hypersomnolence does not inevitably accompany aging. Healthy "old old" persons have been found to be no more sleepy and, occasionally, were even less sleepy than young adults.[28] Older persons, however, took longer to recover from effects of acute sleep deprivation. The lack of excessive daytime sleepiness in healthy older persons suggests that their sleep needs are met despite quantitative reductions. Maintenance of well-consolidated nocturnal sleep, with sleep efficiencies of 80 percent or higher and total sleep time of about 6 hours, seems adequate to preserve daytime alertness.[28]

In institutionalized patients, disturbed sleep/wake patterns have been associated with cognitive impairment and reduced daily activity, though such changes vary markedly.[29] The similarity of EEG alterations commonly observed during sleep and wakefulness in the elderly to those seen with senile dementia of the Alzheimer's type or other chronic brain syndromes suggests that this altered electrical activity represents degenerative changes of the central nervous system.[2,6] Several investigators have shown sleep structure to be fragmented severely in such individuals. Feinberg[30,31] found that patients with dementia had reduced total sleep time, stage 4 sleep, REM sleep, and eye-movement rates as compared with age-matched controls; moreover, decreased REM sleep correlated with psychometric scores. Allen and coworkers[32] performed continuous 72-hour polygraphic recordings in residents of a geriatric unit (mean age alone 80). Individuals with Alzheimer's disease, multi-infarct dementia, and mixed/undefined dementia had less stage 2 and REM sleep and less total sleep time than controls. No differences from controls or among the dementia subgroups occurred with regard to their REM-NREM cycles. In contrast to patterns in healthy elderly individuals, no gender difference was seen in demented patients. The contributions of altered cerebral blood flow and metabolic derangements to these changes require further investigation.

MAJOR SLEEP DISORDERS

One important consequence of the recent dynamic study of sleep has been the systematic description of sleep disorders. The most recent classification of the Association of Sleep Disorder Centers in 1990 is not only comprehensive but also useful.[33] Major dyssomnias of the elderly (Table 112-4) include disturbances of initiating and maintaining sleep (DIMS), disorders of excessive somnolence (DOES), disorders of the sleep-wake cycle, and abnormal sleep behaviors (parasomnias).[1,2,23,33–35] Estimates of their relative frequencies have been derived from sleep laboratory evaluations and from ambulatory studies performed in apparently healthy elderly volunteers,[1,2,14,21] and they vary considerably with the reporting center and the characteristics of the population evaluated. Differences would be expected according to whether patients represent referrals to a sleep disorders center or are evaluated by a neurologist, psychiatrist, pulmonologist, or primary care physician. Although more comprehensive epidemiologic information is needed, clinical experience suggests that sleep disorders are common problems whose prevalence is underestimated. Of 27 elderly patients evaluated in a sleep center because of either daytime hypersomnolence or chronic insomnia, Reynolds et al.[14] found all to have organic disorders: 19 had DIMS and two-thirds had either depression or persistent psychophysiologic insomnia. This investigation confirmed the diversity of sleep distubances in the symptomatic elderly and both the need for and the feasibility of accurate characterization of illness.

TABLE 112-4

Major Sleep Disorders of the Elderly

I. Dyssomnias
   A. Intrinsic sleep disorders
      1. Psychophysiological insomnia
      2. Sleep apnea
      3. Periodic limb movements
   B. Extrinsic sleep disorders
      1. Inadequate sleep hygiene
      2. Environmental sleep disorder
      3. Adjustment sleep disorder
      4. Hypnotic-dependent sleep disorder
      5. Stimulant-dependent sleep disorder
      6. Alcohol-dependent sleep disorder
   C. Circadian rhythm sleep disorders
II. Parasomnias
III. Medical and psychiatric sleep disorders

Disorders of Initiating and Maintaining Sleep

Disorders of initiating and maintaining sleep (DIMS)[33] are characterized by the primary complaint of insomnia. Sleep apnea ("central" sleep apnea in particular) and sleep-related myoclonus (periodic limb movements, or PLMs) are important primary sleep disorders. PLMs are repetitive, stereotypical, unilateral, or bilateral sudden leg movements.[2,33,36] When this abnormal motor activity is associated with complete arousals from sleep, the patient complains of insomnia; when only partial arousals occur, sleep fragmentation and hypersomnolence ensue. Ancoli-Israel et al.[37] found PLMs (myoclonus index ≥ 5) in 45 percent of 427 community-based elderly. Although PLMs correlated with reduced satisfaction with sleep, sleeping alone, and reports of kicking at night, strengths of these associations were weak and PLMs could not be predicted reliably. Common conditions to be differentiated from PLMs are "restless legs" (uncomfortable dysthesias experienced during sleep), nocturnal leg cramps, peripheral neuropathy or myelopathy, and folate or iron deficiencies.[33]

Emotional conflicts and stresses are psychophysiologic causes of insomnia and would be expected to have an important effect on elderly persons who characteristically have impaired homeostasis. Major psychiatric illness (in particular, depression) might cause insomnia or hypersomnia and often leads to early morning awakening. The risk of developing depression appears greater in older persons with insomnia than among those without insomnia.[5] The patient might also be awakened repetitively by unrelieved pain (e.g., pain due to arthritis or malignancy); nocturia; occult thyroid, hepatic, or renal disease; paroxysmal nocturnal dyspnea caused by congestive heart failure; or nocturnal exacerbations of obstructive airways disease. Chronic brain syndromes are often associated with insomnia. Individuals with parkinsonism may exhibit disturbed sleep characterized by their awakening 2 to 3 hours into the night despite having retired at their normal hour. Patients with Alzheimer's dementia often awaken in the middle of the night, with subsequent efforts at sedation sometimes resulting in paradoxical excitement. Alcohol may cause insomnia, and other drugs often disrupt sleep. Corticosteroids, theophylline preparations, and beta blockers are common offenders. Concurrent treatment with stimulants and either withdrawal from or development of tolerance to chronically administered sedative hypnotic agents are other causes to be sought. The latter agents are administered typically in efforts to calm a patient whose awakening has disrupted the institutional or home routine.

Disorders of Excessive Somnolence

Disorders of excessive somnolence (DOES)[33] are characterized by pathologic sleepiness which interferes with activities during wakefulness. Hypersomnolence reflects reduced quality of total sleep time and interruption of the continuity of sleep. Most often due to an underlying sleep disorder and/or drugs, its onset during inappropriate times and its interference with activities define its clinical importance. Narcolepsy is infrequently a newly found cause of sleepiness among the elderly; this condition characteristically has an onset during childhood or adolescence; therefore the diagnosis is usually already established.[35] Obstructive sleep apnea (OSA) and periodic limb movements (PLMs) are the major primary sleep disorders causing hypersomnolence and are common in both asymptomatic and symptomatic elderly. Home portable sleep recordings in 145 randomly selected, healthy volunteers of age 65 or above[38,39] revealed sleep disorders in over half: 18 percent had sleep apnea, 34 percent had PLMs, and 10 percent had both disorders. Comprehensive evaluations of 83 symptomatic patients age 60 or older referred to the Stanford Sleep-Wake Disorders Clinic demonstrated sleep apnea in 39 percent and PLMs in 18 percent,[2] an incidence significantly higher than that in patients below 60 years of age. Kales et al. found that 20 to 30 percent of people over the age of 65 have either sleep apnea or nocturnal myoclonus or a combination of the two.[34,35]

Drug effects, particularly residual or "carryover" effects of sedative hypnotics, are the most common but also the most underrecognized causes of hypersomnolence in the elderly. The metabolism of drugs is altered substantially in elderly individuals, who are particularly vulnerable to their hazardous effects.[2,40–43] Despite the lack of established benefits of their chronic use and proof of their major hazards, sleeping pills are prescribed regularly (and in disproportionately high numbers) to the elderly.[1,2,40,44] From 13 to 48 percent of noninstitutionalized and 26 to 94 percent of institutionalized elderly persons receive "sleepers" regularly.[2] Although precise information regarding their impact on performance, motor coordination, and balance (particularly if the patient is required to awaken during the night) is unavailable, it is likely that these agents affect the major morbidity incurred through falls.[2] Respiratory suppression by these drugs also potentiates the effects of underlying pulmonary diseases or disorders of respiratory control. Thus, efforts either to control the patient, impose conformity to a schedule, or treat real or perceived problems with sedative hypnotics represent a formidable risk. Other commonly used drugs, such as antihistamines, major and minor tranquilizers, methyldopa, and tricyclic antidepressants may also cause excessive sleepiness. This major iatrogenic problem is reviewed in further detail in Chap. 24.

Sleep-Wake Cycle Disturbances

Disruption of the sleep-wake cycle and disturbances of the circadian rhythm cause important problems in the elderly. The "morning lark" and night-owl behaviors of older persons relate to such alterations. There is a general impression that threats to circadian rhythms by internal and external stresses increase with age, but more information is necessary to appraise their extent and impact. Resulting problems include time-zone changes, work-shift changes, irregular sleep-wake schedules, non-24-hour schedules, and both advanced and delayed sleep-phase syndromes.[4,33,45,46] While the sleep-wake cycle is a dominant rhythm, its relationship to other homeostatic rhythms (and potential disruptive effects upon them) may have a profound functional impact. Recent investigation of the circadian characteristics of healthy 80-year-olds confirmed reduced total sleep time, an early habitual time of waking, and higher "morning-type" measure of morning-evening orientation.[47] A lack of flexibility of sleep patterns and less variability in habitual sleep timing was seen in comparison to young controls.

Relationships of internal circadian rhythms to external environmental stimuli and to age-related alterations of other rhythms (e.g., reduced amplitudes of neuroendocrine rhythms and body temperature swings) also require further study. Changes such as an advanced position of the "circadian oscillator" relative to the environment probably account for the early morning wakefulness commonly observed in healthy older persons.[4] With increased age, the natural (free-running) period of the circadian system shortens, favoring earlier bedtimes and awake times, but marked heterogeneity may occur. It has been suggested that the order imposed on elderly, institutionalized patients contributes to more regular synchronous rhythms.[2] Alternatively, if the imposed schedule does not coincide with the patient's intrinsic schedule, disturbed sleep might result. Polyphasic sleep-wake patterns are particular problems among nursing home residents and persons with neurodegenerative diseases.[28] In one nursing home study, it was noted that patients were never asleep for a full hour and never awake for a full hour throughout a 24-hour day.[5]

Parasomnias

Parasomnias, such as somnambulism and night terrors, typically begin in childhood and often resolve with maturity.[33,34] A variety of other abnormal behaviors during sleep, however, have been observed in the elderly.[6] These heterogeneous problems include nocturnal confusion, wandering seizure disorders, decompensation of cardiovascular disease, enuresis, and gastroesophageal reflux. Poor general health as reflected by the Cumulative Illness Rating Scale has correlated with reduced sleep duration and efficiency and prolonged sleep latency.[47] "Sundowning," nocturnal confusion, agitation, and disruptive behavior occurs in an estimated 12 to 20 percent of demented patients.[5] Seventy percent of caregivers have noted that elders' disturbed sleep and its impact upon the caregiver was a factor in the decision to institutionalize the patient. Disturbed sleep was the strongest predictor of nursing home placement of older men.[5]

SLEEP APNEA: A PROTOTYPICAL SLEEP PROBLEM IN THE ELDERLY

TABLE 112-5

Common Sleep-Related Breathing Disorders in the Elderly

Sleep apnea
  Central (failure of rhythmnogenesis)
  Obstructive (upper airway occlusion)
  Mixed
Hypopnea
Snoring
Respiratory disease with deterioration during sleep
  Hemoglobin oxygen desaturation with:
  Chronic obstructive pulmonary disease (COPD)
  Interstitial lung disease
  Nocturnal exacerbation of COPD
Nocturnal aspiration
Paroxysmal nocturnal dyspnea (cardiogenic)

Sleep-related breathing disorders (Table 112-5) merit particular emphasis because of their prevalence, morbidity, and potential reversibility.[1,35,48–56] The most important of these, sleep apnea, is defined by cessation of airflow at the nose and mouth for at least 10 seconds. With clinically important sleep apnea, repetitive episodes permeate sleep and disrupt its structure. The prevalence of disordered breathing during sleep in the aged varies with patient assessment and definitions of the presence of a breathing disorder. Clinical diagnoses have been based arbitrarily upon the presence of more than 5 episodes per hour of sleep, but this "apnea index" (AI) is often exceeded in healthy older persons with no apparent untoward effects. Moreover, in the elderly, this widely used diagnostic criterion has variable relationships to hypersomnolence and prognosis.[52] Carskadon and Dement[53] found that 45.4 percent of men and 31.8 percent of women had more than 5 disordered breathing events per hour of sleep. There appeared to be an age-related increase in respiratory disturbances among women, most notably during the eighth decade. Disordered breathing events were associated with EEG arousals, clearly disrupting nocturnal sleep and potentially causing symptoms. Kriger et al.[58] identified frequent hypopneas and apneas in elderly individuals compared with medical students, and Niafeh et al.[59] confirmed sleep apnea and hypopnea in half of subjects over 60 years old. In Ancoli-Israel's community-based investigation of 427 randomly selected elderly (above age 65) 24 percent had an AI equal to or greater than 5 and 62 percent had a respiratory distress index equal to or greater than 10. Increased body weight, reports of snoring, observed apnea, nocturnal wandering or confusion, daytime sleepiness, and depression correlated with but did not reliably predict the presence of sleep-disordered breathing.[55] Polygraphically identified OSA and PLM in community-residing older persons tend not to be manifest in self-reported sleep-wake complaints or mood disturbances.[57]

Polygraphic distinction of three basic patterns of apnea has therapeutic implications. Central apnea results from periodic cessation of respiratory muscle activity and is associated primarily with neurologic diseases such as bulbar poliomyelitis, encephalitis, brainstem infarction, neoplasms, cervical cordotomy, other spinal surgery, and idiopathic alveolar hypoventilation. Complete EEG arousals associated with these apneic events typically cause insomnia. By contrast, OSA results from upper airway occlusion despite continued and often accentuated efforts to breathe. With mixed apnea, an initial central phase is followed by obstruction. Pharyngeal occlusion is due to an imbalance of forces collapsing the airway (negative pharyngeal pressure) and those dilating it (upper airway muscle contraction). Upper airway motor tone normally varies with sleep state and is decreased during apneic episodes. Activation of pharyngeal muscles follows EEG arousal and is associated with characteristic loud, resuscitative snoring, indicating airway patency and restored airflow. Anatomic narrowing of the upper airway is an important predisposition to OSA and both primary and secondary dysfunction of respiratory centers contribute to these dynamic events.

Normally well maintained during sleep, hemoglobin oxygen saturation (Sa_{O_2}) falls during apnea. The lower baseline Pa_{O_2} of elderly individuals makes them even more likely to desaturate hemoglobin during apnea. Repetitive hypoxemic events may have numerous sequelae, including pulmonary and systemic hypertension, nocturnal cardiac arrhythmias (especially in persons with preexisting cardiac disease), angina, stroke, and sudden death. Less often, cor pulmonale, left-ventricular failure, and erythrocytosis may ensue. Hypercapnia due to severe OSA (particularly in combination with chronic obstructive pulmonary disease) may result in morning headache. EEG arousal is associated with abnormal motor activity during sleep as the patient unknowingly struggles to open an occluded airway. Repetitive EEG arousals lead to disproportionate increases in stages 1 and 2 NREM sleep, with decreased slow-wave sleep. Thus, excessive daytime somnolence and unrefreshing sleep are major presenting complaints. Intellectual deterioration and personality changes are other prominent alterations attributed to combined effects of hypoxemia and sleep fragmentation. Because of the high prevalence of sleep apnea now recognized in asymptomatic elderly, unrecognized apnea may account for some of the changes of sleep structure previously attributed to aging in studies which did not exclude persons with clinically unsuspected breathing disorders.

Transitions from Health to Disease

Gradations in the severity of sleep-disordered breathing, the high frequency of sleep apnea in healthy older persons, and the association of these phenomena with common diseases of aging suggest a transition from health to disease (Fig. 112-2). It seems likely that subclinical, physiologic abnormalities progress to clinically recognizable stages identified by symptoms of increasing severity and/or life-threatening events. Because this course may progress insidiously through stages spanning decades, concerns about its importance in the elderly are well founded. Healthy, asymptomatic men (ages 55 to 70) with sleep-disordered breathing have reduced ventilatory responses to hypercapnia and elevated nasal airway resistance, suggesting that both anatomic abnormalities of the upper airways and altered respiratory center control of breathing had predisposed to their disorders.[60,61] Snoring, an upper-airway-occlusive event, probably represents an intermediate stage in this transition. Approximately 60 percent of men and 45 percent of women over the age of 60 snore.[62,63] Heavy snoring has been associated with systemic hypertension, coronary disease, neuropsychiatric deterioration, and embolic stroke.

It has been noted consistently that the frequency of apneas and hypopneas during sleep increases with age.[38,39,49–53,64–68] Bixler and coworkers[64] found that asymptomatic older patients often had greater "sleep apnea activity" in comparison with controls: approximately one-fourth of subjects older than age 50 had such activity, while it was present in only 8.7 percent of younger individuals. Interestingly, only one person had an AI above 5. By contrast, McGinty and coworkers[68] found that 62 percent of healthy men (ages 55 to 70) had at least 12 disordered breathing episodes per hour of sleep. Recently, Hoch et al.[69] observed that severity of sleep disordered breathing increases significantly across decades, finding an AI equal to or greater than 5 in 18.9 percent of healthy 80-year-olds, 12.1 percent of 70-year-olds and zero percent of 60-year-olds. AI was approximately four times greater in men than in women. Over one-third of 80-year-olds had significant reductions of Sa_{O_2} ($\leq$80 percent), and

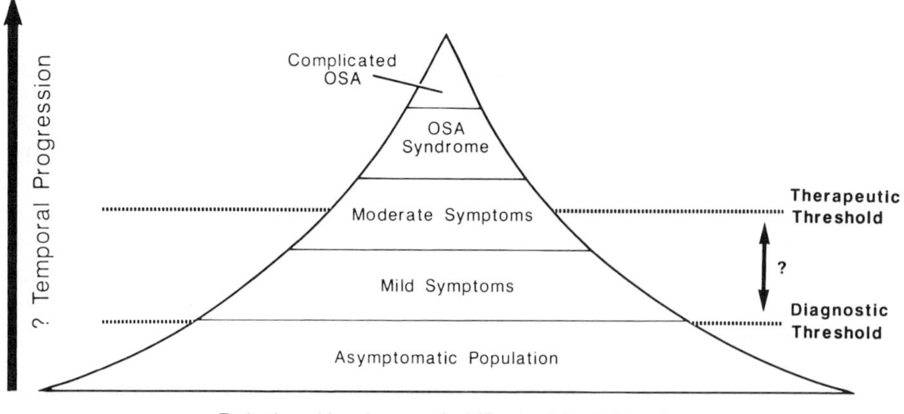

FIGURE 112-2
Sleep-disordered breathing appears to become worse with age, and the optimum diagnostic and therapeutic thresholds are continuing to evolve. The problem of identifying these thresholds is accentuated in elderly persons, who have a high prevalence of subclinical or mildly symptomatic disease. (*Reproduced from Ref. 46.*)

men experienced more prolonged episodes than women.

It is not resolved whether sleep apnea activity represents disease or is a normal concomitant of aging. As depicted in Fig. 112-2, it seems likely that there is a large population with subclinical physiologic abnormalities which progress with age and a much smaller group who develop the sleep apnea syndrome with its full constellation of manifestations. Also noted are a clinical diagnostic threshold (when physiologic changes become manifest by functional impairment recognized by the patient and, more often, by family members) and a therapeutic threshold at which intervention is necessary. The optimum points at which diagnosis and intervention are either appropriate or necessary need clarification. Resolution of this dilemma requires improved understanding of the natural history of sleep apnea and its significance in the aged.

Sleep Apnea and Mortality

Associations of sleep apnea with hypoxemia, cardiac arrhythmias, and anecdotal reports of sudden death support that it is a lethal illness,[70–74] but the precise hazard in the elderly is unknown. In one longitudinal study of elderly persons evaluated for up to 12 years, the presence of greater than 10 apneic and hypopneic episodes per hour of sleep was associated with a higher risk of death (2.7).[70] However, this relationship could not be confirmed in multivariate analysis because of the confounding effects of age. In a recent retrospective analysis, individuals with an AI above 20 had a higher mortality than those with fewer episodes, but patients who were 50 years old and over did not differ from younger individuals with regard to mortality.[71] Among seniors having mixed symptoms of cognitive impairment and depression, an excess mortality (450 percent) has been associated with sleep-disordered breathing.[73] Although sleep apnea predominates in men, among nursing home residents a lethal interaction between female gender and increased apnea index has been observed.[74]

Other intriguing observations suggest that sleep-disordered breathing contributes to sudden nocturnal death. Typically, OSA is recognized during the fifth and sixth decades and occurs in overweight men and postmenopausal women. Block found that 12 of 20 postmenopausal women had numerous sleep-disordered breathing episodes with desaturation, a finding that was rare in premenopausal women.[75] Responses to hypoxia and hypercapnia are blunted in the elderly, and such diminished sensitivity to these stimuli during sleep is especially prominent in men.[60,61,76] Whether or not the increased prevalence of sleep apnea in men (15 to 20:1) is a significant factor in the well-appreciated sex differential of mortality has not been established.[77] Chronobiologic studies underscore the hazards of early morning hours,[2,44,62,78,79] when the likelihood of cardiac death is particularly increased. Most deaths occur during nocturnal sleep, peaking immediately before morning arousal (6:00 AM). Interestingly, this timing generally coincides with REM sleep, when responsiveness to numerous physiologic stimuli is attenuated. Disordered breathing events tend to be more prolonged, and accompanying hypoxemia and hemodynamic responses are exaggerated. The diminished use of accessory respiratory muscles during these periods may exacerbate effects of underlying obstructive and restrictive lung diseases.

Sleep Apnea, Dementia, and Depression

Sleep apnea often accompanies degenerative conditions such as Alzheimer's disease, multi-infarct dementia, and depression,[80–82] but the extent to which it exacerbates and/or is caused by these conditions is unknown, and the association and its clinical implications vary widely in studies reported to date. Smallwood et al.[83] found that elderly men with Alzheimer's disease, without sleep complaints or medical problems, had more apneic and hypopneic episodes than either elderly women or young men, but the frequency of events was not higher than in age- and sex-matched controls. Reynolds et al.[81] found sleep apnea (AI $>$ 5) in 42.9 percent of patients with probable Alzheimer's disease, more often than in either healthy or depressed elderly controls. Sleep apnea was associated with Alzheimer's dementia in women but not in men, and the severity of dementia correlated with AI. Impaired performance on neuropsychological tests correlated with the presence of sleep-disordered breathing in 41 nondemented persons (mean age 69.5).[82] It has not been established whether such impairment, presumably due to "deficits in vigilance or cortical insult" from repetitive nocturnal hypoxemic events, identifies individuals who are likely to progress to more severe dementia. Hoch et al.[67] identified sleep apnea more often in subjects with Alzheimer's dementia (41.7 percent), than in healthy controls (5.5 percent), subjects with depression (11.4 percent), and individuals with symptoms of both depression and cognitive impairment (16.7 percent). In Alzheimer's patients, apnea was particularly prominent during NREM sleep, and AI correlated with the severity of dementia as graded by the Blessed Dementia Rating Scale. Erkinjuntti et al.[80] found more than 10 disordered breathing events per hour of sleep in nearly half of patients with multi-infarct dementia and Alzheimer's disease and in one-fifth of elderly controls. Disordered breathing occurred more often in patients with multi-infarct dementia than in those with Alzheimer's disease, and the frequency of events varied with the severity of dementia.

CLINICAL EVALUATION OF THE PATIENT WITH SLEEP COMPLAINTS

Clinical evaluation of the elderly patient with sleep complaints requires comprehensive, firsthand assessment, integrating efforts of all members of the health care team.[1,2,33] Maximizing the yield from history, physical examination, and other noninvasive sources is essential, with particular emphasis upon possible offending drugs, chronic diseases known to disrupt sleep, and clinical signs of the major primary sleep disorders (especially sleep apnea and nocturnal myoclonus). Classification of the predominant symptom, its duration, and whether sleep is restorative guides differential diagnosis and evaluation. For example, for patients with acute insomnia (<3 weeks), situational problems are most likely. When insomnia is prolonged, depression and effects of comorbid illnesses become paramount. Chronic hypersomnolence with nonrefreshing sleep is most often due to OSA.

Historical Clues

The sleep history (Table 112-6) can be incorporated readily into a routine review of systems and should be obtained not only from the patient but also from all potential observers. Information from bed partners, family members, or, in extended-care settings, other medical personnel,[2,6] is especially helpful and may be definitive. It should also be appreciated that this input might be distorted by the possible disruptive effects of the patient's sleep pattern upon the lifestyle of the person helping with the history. Complementary information can be obtained by means of written sleep diaries completed by the patient and/or significant others, documenting the pattern of sleep and wakefulness. The level of daytime alertness and the presence, number, and duration of awakenings from sleep are assessed. Such logs provide valuable insights about the impact of the patient's sleep complaints upon daily activities, their relationships to life stresses, and possible circadian abnormalities. With this approach, a portrait of the patient's sleep and how it either coincides with or disrupts daily routines is obtained.

The history must also be directed at the numerous external factors which might disrupt sleep, since these are often more easily treatable than internal ones. Use of prescribed and nonprescribed medications, alcohol, and caffeine is particularly important; these agents are, for many, common and removable causes. Although sleep onset may be appropriate following alcohol ingestion, awakening may occur hours later and persist. In addition, the presence of cardiopulmonary or urologic symptoms might directly implicate an etiology of troubled sleep.

TABLE 112-6

Evaluation of Elderly Patients with Sleep-Related Complaints

- Seek historical clues
  - (From patient, bed partner, family, caregivers)
- Determine characteristics of sleep
  - Time required to fall asleep (sleep latency)
  - Times of retiring and awakening
  - Total sleep time
  - Number and duration of nocturnal awakenings
  - Quality of sleep (restorative and refreshing?)
  - Level of daytime alertness (hypersomnolent?)
  - Napping pattern
  - Recent changes in pattern of sleep
  - Previous history of sleep problems/treatment
  - History of snoring, periodic breathing, abnormal motor activity
- Exclude potential external factors:
  - Use of drugs, alcohol, caffeine
  - Diets
  - Levels of activity; patterns of exercise
  - Presence of symptoms of dysfunction of other organ systems
  - Evidence of inciting situational stresses
  - General sleep hygiene
  - Consider sleep diary
- Assess impact of the problem
  - Duration of sleep disturbances
  - Degree of functional impairment by symptoms
  - Restorative nature of sleep
- Perform complete physical examination
- Observe patient during sleep
- Obtain objective physiologic testing
  - Polysomnography
  - Other monitoring studies (oximetry, Holter monitoring, actigraphy)
  - Multiple Sleep Latency Test (MSLT)

Because the continuity of sleep is vulnerable to physiologic, psychologic, and social problems present alone or in combination in the aged, this aspect of the history must be underscored. Alterations of time cues and rituals that have been familiar to the patient throughout life or altered environments due to shifts of residence commonly occur.[6] Increased napping might reflect major changes in physical activity, exercise tolerance, depression, or mere boredom rather than being a result of pathologic hypersomnolence. Threats to the patient's overall sense of well-being that are imposed by retirement or adjustments of sleep-wake schedules must all be sought. The need to conform to work-shift changes, schedules of an extended-care facility, or children's household routines can have major deleterious effects. The clinician must appreciate the life stresses affecting the patient and family. Predictably, alterations of support systems—as with the death of a spouse, separation from family members, loss of friends, or shifts to unfamiliar surroundings—alter sleep profoundly.

In this careful appraisal, the clinician's estimate of the impact of the problem is the primary determinant of the extent of evaluation. Not only the quantity and distribution of sleep but also its quality is extremely important: does the patient feel refreshed upon awakening in the morning? Nonrestorative sleep should strongly suggest a primary sleep disorder and/or depression.[84] Thus, the duration of the sleep disturbance and, most importantly, the degree of functional impairment it causes are essential data. The "normal changes" of sleep in the elderly are not known to lead to perceptible functional impairment. Severe sleep-related complaints must not be dismissed as being due to old age alone; they must be explained.

Objective Assessment

A complete physical examination and, when appropriate, laboratory tests directed at particular organ systems (e.g., thyroid function studies, electrocardiogram, chest roentgenogram, pulmonary function tests) will usually identify medical conditions which secondarily disrupt sleep. Simple bedside observation of a sleeping patient is a complementary, important source of information that is too often omitted or delegated. Nocturnal wheezing, repetitive stereotypic leg movements, or Cheyne-Stokes respirations may be diagnostic. The presence of periodic breathing, paradoxical thoracoabdominal movement indicative of upper airway obstruction, and apneic events terminated by loud resuscitative snoring has a high positive predictive value for OSA.[85] Merely watching the patient sleep may provide definitive information in a cost-effective manner. Visual monitoring of breathing[86] and of general sleep-wake patterns with recording of behavioral criteria for judging sleep[87] have been used effectively by nursing home staff. General identification of patterns as "normal," "reduced sleep," "increased sleep," and "mixed" has been related to cognitive impairment and reduced ability to handle the activities of daily living.[29] Patients who wandered tended to demonstrate the reduced sleep pattern.

When a major sleep disorder is likely or when detailed history and physical examination fail to provide a definitive diagnosis, objective physiologic testing is usually needed. Polysomnography, the simultaneous recording of multiple physiologic parameters during sleep, is the gold standard for evaluation of sleep and its disorders.[2,4] During such laboratory studies, a limited EEG, electrooculogram, and chin electromyogram (EMG) characterize sleep and its stages. Recordings of the leg EMG (to detect abnormal movements such as myoclonus), electrocardiogram (to detect cardiac arrhythmias), nasal and oral thermistors (to monitor airflow), thoracic and abdominal strain gauges (to assess breathing efforts), and an ear oximeter (to record Sa_{O_2} noninvasively) are included in typical studies. Monitoring is tailored further to evaluate other specific parameters (e.g., nocturnal seizure activity, esophageal pH, or nocturnal penile tumescence). The degree of sleepiness can also be evaluated objectively by means of multiple sleep latency testing (MSLT), during which the time it takes the patient to fall asleep in a quiet, darkened room is measured.[4,88–90] The time from "lights out" until sleep is confirmed by EEG is normally greater than 10 minutes. Such tests have shown increased sleepiness (decreased sleep latency) in elderly individuals with sleep-disordered breathing but not in aged individuals without breathing disorders.[4] In community-based, non-sleep-derived elderly, alertness/sleepiness defined by MSLT has not correlated with results of neuropsychological tests.[91]

Comprehensive evaluations are available at multidisciplinary sleep disorder centers, and extension of such facilities to community hospitals has made sleep studies increasingly accessible. Practical limitations must be recognized in the use of these resources. Pressman and Fry[6] have reviewed caveats for interpreting sleep studies in the elderly, addressing potentially confounding methodologic problems. Some biases in standard scoring criteria might underestimate the degree of sleep impairment. The need to perform these evaluations in carefully controlled laboratory environments might also hinder their applications to relatively immobile, fragile elderly patients. How well sleep in the laboratory reflects that in familiar home surroundings represents an especially important conundrum. The artificial laboratory environment itself disrupts sleep; because of a "first-night effect," a single night's evaluation may not be representative of a patient's typical sleep, and night-to-night and subject-to-subject variability are well recognized. Although a single night study often provides definitive information, conclusions about the presence and severity of sleep apnea and PLMs based upon a single test may be erroneous.[92] Thus, studies performed during several successive nights are preferable; in many instances 24- to 72-hour recordings are necessary to characterize a disorder completely. The financial cost of complete sleep studies (e.g., $2000 to $3000) makes appropriate evaluation unfeasible for elderly patients with limited economic resources.

Complete polysomnography remains the gold standard for comprehensive evaluation, but rapid technologic progress now permits reliable outpatient recordings. Such portable monitoring systems have been used to evaluate elderly persons at home and in extended-care-facilities.[50] Actigraphic recordings have been used to monitor sleep-wake cycles in nursing home patients with multi-infarct dementia and dementia of the Alzheimer type.[93] Validation of these advances will have a major impact on sleep testing of the elderly, enhancing feasibility of meaningful cost-effective evaluations in familiar surroundings.

It should be underscored that sleep laboratory studies should be used selectively, and only when the data obtained will influence management. There is little support for their role in elderly patients with insomnia; the majority of these individuals can be treated effectively without such information. Patients with hypersomnolence, nonrestorative sleep, or predispositions to OSA constitute the major group requiring polysomnography.

TREATMENT OF ELDERLY PERSONS WITH SLEEP PROBLEMS

Treatment of sleep problems in elderly persons is necessarily conservative, with emphasis upon minimizing what is done to the patient (Table 112-7). Decisions must be predicated on careful risk-benefit assessments, with appreciation that potential benefits are time-limited, that any interventions are potentially harmful, and that maintaining the patient's functional status is the prime objective. Manipulation of the environment (and potential external causes of the problem) rather than of the patient is the preferred strategy.

Nonpharmacologic measures are paramount in this approach. Accordingly, potential offending drugs are discontinued; when this is not feasible, selection of alternative agents less likely to disrupt sleep is strongly recommended. In general, the physician should avoid introducing other drugs; this may be quite difficult in view of frequent patient (and family) expectations for "a prescription in hand." In the absence of proven benefits of sedative hypnotic agents in the elderly, formulating reasonable general recommendations for their use is difficult. When selected for their limited, short-term use in treating acute situational problems, however, short-acting preparations (e.g., benzodiazepines, tricyclics) should be prescribed in low dosages and regarded as adjunctive therapy only.

Counseling the patient and establishing hygienic sleep practices often lessen the perceived need for medications considerably. Some patients and families will benefit greatly just from the physician's confirmation that minor changes in sleep (for example, earlier morning wakening, reduction of total sleep time, increased napping), when not disruptive to the patient's usual activities, are part of normal expectations with aging. This approach might not only relieve pressures to intervene but might also result in improved sleep by reducing stress for the patient. Sleep should be attempted in a comfortable environment and on a regular schedule. A patient should avoid concerted attempts to "force" himself or herself to fall asleep; this forced approach will generally be unsuccessful and may lead to psychophysiologic (conditioned or "learned") insomnia.

Kales et al.[34] have delineated the major components of a sleep hygiene program, with emphasis upon adjustments of activity schedules and environmental factors. These include standardizing times of rising and retiring, use of a later bedtime, eliminating daytime naps, increasing daytime exercise and meaningful activities, avoiding large meals and fluids before bedtime, avoiding alcohol and caffeine, use of the bedroom only for sleep and sex, and relegating arguments or problem solving sessions to early in the day rather than before retiring. Such behavioral therapy may be exceedingly effective and is best achieved through integrated efforts of family members and other support systems, as well as through education of the patient. Establishing a bedtime routine is especially important to elderly persons. In a recent investigation, sleep was found to be least disturbed in older men who followed a routine, whereas older women without a routine had the most disrupted sleep patterns.[94] Components of routines of older men differ from those of women. For men, common activities included watching television, having a light snack or drink, brushing their teeth, walking the dog, or bathing. Most often, women washed their faces, bathed, brushed their teeth, prayed, read, watched television, or listened to music. Older men with a routine were most satisfied with their sleep and tended to feel calmer at bedtime, had shorter sleep onset, fewer awakenings, were less aware of moving during sleep, slept more soundly, and felt more refreshed upon awakening.[94] Impaired sleep might reflect impaired social rhythms needed to properly entrain the circadian system. Monk and coworkers[95] have recently observed that despite subjective and objectively worsened sleep, community-based elderly volunteers (mean age 80.3 years) had a significantly greater regularity in their daily lifestyle and just as much other-person involvement and activities completed as young controls. The authors suggested that regularity in routine protects elders from unwanted somnolence that they would otherwise experience.

In efforts to identify effective, nonpharmacologic approaches, a number of behavioral approaches to the insomnia of the elderly have been investigated with varying results. Progressive relaxation training, stimulus control, education/support, attention training, and imagery training have had beneficial effects.

TABLE 112-7

Treatment of Sleep Problems in the Elderly

1. Discontinue offending drugs; avoid introducing others
2. Establish hygienic sleep practices
3. Treat specific primary sleep disorders
   - Nocturnal myoclonus: muscle relaxants (short-acting benzodiazepines, L-dopa, bromocriptine)
   - Obstructive sleep apnea: preventive measures such as weight loss (when indicated), avoidance of alcohol, sedative-hypnotics; mechanical and surgical measures such as nasal CPAP, tracheostomy, uvulopalatopharyngoplasty
   - Central sleep apnea: rocking bed, diaphragmatic pacing, oxygen
4. Treat medical and neuropsychiatric conditions secondarily disrupting sleep
5. Monitor therapeutic responses objectively

Recently, Friedman compared sleep restriction and relaxation therapy in community-residing elderly subjects (mean age 69.7 years).[96] Sleep latency and waking after sleep onset were reduced in both groups. Reduced time in bed and improved sleep efficiency persisted at 3 months of follow-up in patients receiving sleep restriction, but not in those receiving muscle tension and release/relaxation therapy. Interestingly, the authors noted perhaps the most critical ingredient of the program was the direction to the patient "to get up and out of bed in the morning."[96]

Effective therapy is available for the primary sleep disorders. Benzodiazepines, particularly clonazepam, are the treatment of choice of PLM, but L-dopa and bromocriptine are considered to be more effective by some investigators.[97] OSA is also treatable, but whether or not intervention is necessary or appropriate in asymptomatic individuals with subclinical breathing abnormalities has not been established. For practical purposes, evaluation and treatment (other than weight loss for the patient with hypertension, for instance) should be reserved for symptomatic patients. Simple measures may be all that is necessary for mild sleep apnea. Weight loss and modification of sleep posture (shifting from the supine to upright or lateral decubitus positions) may suffice. In healthy elderly volunteers, benzodiazepines and alcohol have all increased the frequency of apneic events during sleep.[41] Thus, avoidance of these agents is an important preventive measure. Significantly hypersomnolent patients must be advised to refrain from driving and other activities demanding alertness because of the increased risks of accidents.

Continuous positive airway pressure (CPAP) is the current treatment of choice for OSA. With this safe, noninvasive approach, pressure delivered by means of a mask during sleep stents open the upper airway; the pharynx remains patent, Sa_{O_2} is well maintained, and sequelae of hypoxemia and sleep fragmentation are avoided. This approach, well tolerated by even elderly individuals, avoids the morbidity of upper airway surgery. Tracheostomy is reserved for persons with life-threatening sequelae of OSA who require urgent management or in whom CPAP either cannot be tolerated or is unsuccessful. Oxygen and numerous medications have been used to treat mild OSA, but variable clinical responses do not support their general use. Protriptyline, a nonsedating tricyclic useful in selected younger individuals with mild apnea, is less often helpful in the elderly because of its anticholinergic effects and cardiac arrhythmogenic potential. Selected patients with central apnea may benefit from mechanical devices (e.g., cuirass ventilation rocking bed), diaphragmatic pacing, oxygen, or respiratory stimulants.

Management of conditions which secondarily disrupt sleep should be focused on these primary disorders rather than on the sleep complaints themselves. Treatment of nocturnal angina, congestive heart failure, exacerbated obstructive airways disease, depression, and chronic pain often has dramatic benefits. Depression, a common cause of sleep problems, may improve considerably after the initiation of a tricyclic agent, and this response may be prognostically helpful. Endogenous depression may be associated with the early onset of REM sleep (REM sleep latency). Clinical improvement with nortriyptyline has correlated with prolongation of REM sleep latency, improved sleep maintenance, and shift of slow-wave activity toward sleep onset.[98] Optimum management of circadian rhythm problems—especially in patients with severe dementia and behavioral disorders such as wandering, agitation, and/or delirium—is exceedingly challenging. In one recent report, imposed social interaction with nursing staff reduced behavioral problems and sleep-wake rhythm disorders in one-third of patients.[88,99]

In all of these instances, responses to therapy should be monitored objectively. Effective follow-up may range from counseling during an office visit, to home visits by the nurse practitioner, to repeat polysomnographic documentation of the effects of treatment. The levels of intensity and technology required are readily individualized according to the severity of dysfunction and the risks of therapy. Serial sleep studies, which are generally needed in monitoring therapeutic responses in patients with OSA, are usually well tolerated and informative.

CHALLENGES FOR PRACTITIONERS

Although experienced geriatricians confirm that disturbed sleep is a common, clinically important, and potentially treatable problem in their patients, most current practitioners have received no formal training in this area. In one survey, historical information was nearly the exclusive diagnostic tool used by clinicians, but a defined, comprehensive sleep history was often not obtained routinely.[100] Sleep complaints were usually attributed to conditions secondarily disrupting sleep and to effects of medications; primary sleep disorders were rarely diagnosed. Despite their high prevalence, neither snoring, periodic breathing, nor PLM during sleep were regarded as major patient complaints, and clinicians seldom obtained polysomnography. Hazards of drugs and pressures to prescribe them were widely acknowledged, but few clinicians used predefined nonpharmacologic sleep hygiene programs.

In another survey, only half of 501 office-based general physicians presented with a standard case of an elderly patient with insomnia actually elicited a sleep history.[101] Moreover, they asked an average of only 2.5 questions to seek other information prior to making a therapeutic recommendation. Nearly half of practitioners identified a prescription medication, rather than nonpharmacologic sleep hygiene practices, as the single most effective therapy for the older patient.[101] These observations suggest a critical need for improved education of clinicians and other health professionals about sleep problems of the elderly and for development of skills essential to their diagnosis, management, and prevention. Education of the lay public in order to promote hygienic sleep, to empower patients to communicate their concerns about problems, and to foster realistic expectations about management is another priority.

Troubled sleep is a common problem of the elderly. Primary sleep disorders, depression, iatrogenic illness, and effects of chronic diseases and life stresses are superimposed upon normative changes of sleep and frequently disrupt it. Numerous resources are available for complex patients requiring extensive evaluations, but most sleep problems in the elderly should be managed by primary care physicians. Ongoing epidemiologic studies will have substantial implications for practitioners, as the prevalence of these conditions, their relationships to normal aging, and their effects upon the patient's overall functional status become better understood. Unprecedented technologic facilities for the objective study of sleep are currently available, and further modifications will enhance their usefulness. However, the systematic approach to sleep disorders is founded upon a routinely performed sleep history and can and should be incorporated within comprehensive management programs.

REFERENCES

1. National Institutes of Health Consensus Development Conference Statement: The treatment of sleep disorders of older people. *Sleep* 14:169, 1991.
2. Dement WC et al: "White paper" on sleep and aging. *J Am Geriatr Soc* 30:25, 1982.
3. Bliwise DL: Normal aging, in Kryger MH, Roth T, Dement WC (eds): *Principles and Practice of Sleep Medicine.* Philadelphia, Saunders, 1989.
4. Dement WC et al: Changes of sleep and wakefulness with age, in Finch CE, Schneider EL (eds): *Handbook of the Biology of Aging.* New York, Van Nostrand Reinhold, 1985.
5. *Wake Up America: A National Sleep Alert.* Washington, DC, National Commission on Sleep Disorders Research, 1993.
6. Pressman MR, Fry JM: What is normal sleep in the elderly? *Clin Geriatr Med* 4:71, 1988.
7. Webb WB: Age-related changes in sleep. *Clin Geriatr Med* 5:275, 1989.
8. Thormby J et al: Subjective reports of sleep disturbance in a Houston metropolitan healthy survey. *Sleep Res* 6:180, 1977.
9. Gerard P et al: Subjective characteristics of sleep in the elderly. *Age Ageing* 7(suppl):55, 1978.
10. Karacan I et al: Prevalence of sleep disturbances in a primarily urban Florida county. *Soc Sci Med* 10:239, 1976.
11. McGhie A, Russell S: The subjective assessment of normal sleep patterns. *J Ment Sci* 108:642, 1962.
12. Hoch CC et al: Empirical note: Self-reported versus recorded sleep in healthy seniors. *Psychophysiology* 24:293, 1987.
13. Hoch CC et al: Stability of EEG sleep and sleep quality in healthy seniors. *Sleep* 11:521, 1988.
14. Reynolds CF et al: Sleep disturbances in a series of elderly patients: Polysomnographic findings. *J Am Geriatr Soc* 28:164, 1980.
15. Reynolds CF III et al: Sleep of healthy seniors: A revisit. *Sleep* 8:30, 1985.
16. Hayashi Y et al: The all-right polygraphies for healthy aged persons. *Sleep Res* 8:122, 1979.
17. Hayashi Y, Endo S: All-night sleep polygraphic recordings of healthy aged persons: REM and slow-wave sleep. *Sleep* 5:183, 1982.
18. Kales A, Kales J: Sleep disorders: Recent findings in the diagnosis and treatment of disturbed sleep. *N Engl J Med* 290:487, 1974.
19. Miles LE, Dement WC: Sleep and aging. *Sleep* 3:1, 1980.
20. Prinz P, Raskind M: Aging and sleep disorders, in Williams R, Karacan I (eds): *Sleep Disorders: Diagnosis and Treatment.* New York, Wiley, 1978, p 303.
21. Coleman RM et al: Sleep-wake disorders in the elderly: Polysomnographic analysis. *J Am Geriatr Soc* 29:289, 1981.
22. Buysse DJ et al: Quantification of subjective sleep quality in healthy elderly men and women using the Pittsburgh sleep quality index (PSQI). *Sleep* 14:331, 1991.
23. Baker TL: Introduction to sleep and sleep disorders. *Med Clin North Am* 69:1123, 1985.
24. Maquet P et al: Cerebral glucose utilization during sleep-wake cycle in man determined by positron emission tomography and [^{18}F]2-fluoro-2-deoxy-D-glucose method. *Brain Res* 513:136, 1990.
25. DeKonick J et al: Sleep positions and position shifts in five age groups: An ontogenetic picture. *Sleep* 15:143–149, 1992.
26. Reynolds CF et al: Electroencephalographic sleep in the healthy "old old": A comparison with the "young old" in visually scored and automated measures. *J Gerontol* 46(2):M39, 1991.
27. Rediehs MH et al: Sleep in old age: Focus on gender differences. *Sleep* 13:410, 1991.
28. Reynolds CF et al: Daytime sleepiness in the healthy "old old": A comparison with young adults. *J Am Geriat Soc* 39:957, 1991.
29. Meguro K et al: Disturbance in daily sleep/wake patterns in patients with cognitive impairment and decreased daily activity. *J Am Gerontol Soc* 38:1176, 1990.
30. Feinberg I et al: EEG sleep patterns as a function of normal and pathological aging in man. *J Psychiatr Res* 5:107, 1967.

31. Feinberg I: The ontogenesis of human sleep and the relationship of sleep variables to intellectual function in the aged. *Compr Psychiatry* 9:138, 1968.
32. Allen SR et al: Seventy-two hour polygraphic and behavioral recording of wakefulness and sleep in a hospital geriatric unit: Comparison between demented and nondemented patients. *Sleep* 10:143, 1987.
33. Thorpy MJ (chmn): *International Classification of Sleep Disorders: Diagnostic and Coding Manual. Diagnostic Classification Steering Committee.* Rochester, MN, American Sleep Disorders Association, 1990.
34. Kales A et al: Sleep disorders: Insomnia, sleepwalking, night terrors, nightmares, and enuresis. *Ann Intern Med* 106:582, 1987.
35. Kales A et al: Sleep disorders: Sleep apnea and narcolepsy. *Ann Intern Med* 106:434, 1987.
36. Ekbom K: Restless legs syndrome. *Neurology* 10:868, 1960.
37. Ancoli-Israel S et al: Periodic limb movements in sleep in community-dwelling elderly. *Sleep* 14:1496, 1991.
38. Ancoli-Israel S et al: Sleep apnea and nocturnal myoclonus in a senior population. *Sleep* 4:349, 1981.
39. Ancoli-Israel S et al: Sleep apnea and periodic movements in an aging sample. *J Gerontol* 40:419, 1985.
40. Roehrs TA, Roth T: Drugs, sleep disorders, and aging. *Clin Geriatr Med* 5:395, 1989.
41. Guilleminault C et al: Aging and sleep apnea: Action of benzodiazepine, acetazolamide, alcohol, and sleep deprivation in a healthy elderly group. *J Gerontol* 39:655, 1984.
42. Guilleminault C: Benzodiazepines, breathing and sleep. *Am J Med* 88:S3A, 1990.
43. Gottlieb GL: Sleep disorders and their management. Special considerations in the elderly. *Am J Med* 88:S3A, 1990.
44. Kripke DF et al: Short and long sleep and sleeping pills. *Arch Gen Psychiatry* 36:103, 1979.
45. Smolensky MH, D'Alonzo G: Biologic rhythms and medicine. *Am J Med* 85 (suppl 1B):34, 1984.
46. Monk TH: Circadian rhythm. *Clin Geriatr Med* 5:331, 1989.
47. Monk TJ et al: Circadian characteristics of healthy 80-year-olds and their relationship to objectively recorded sleep. *J Gerontol* 46(5):M171, 1991.
48. Guilleminault C et al: The sleep apnea syndromes. *Annu Rev Med* 27:465, 1976.
49. Ancoli-Israel S et al: Characteristics of obstructive and central sleep apnea in the elderly: An interim report. *Biol Psychiatry* 22:741, 1987.
50. Ancoli-Israel S et al: Comparisons of home sleep recordings and polysomnograms in older adults with sleep disorders. *Sleep* 4:183, 1981.
51. Block AJ et al: Sleep apnea, hypoapnea and oxygen desaturation in normal subjects. *N Engl J Med* 300:513, 1978.
52. Berry DTR et al: Sleep-disordered breathing in healthy aged persons: Possible daytime sequelae. *J Gerontol* 42(6):620, 1967.
53. Carskadon MA, Dement WC: Respiration during sleep in the aged human. *J Gerontol* 36:420, 1981.
54. Fleury B: Sleep apnea syndrome in the elderly. *Sleep* 15:S39, 1992.
55. Ancoli-Israel S et al: Sleep disordered breathing in community-dwelling elderly. *Sleep* 14:486, 1991.
56. Berry DT et al: Geriatric sleep apnea syndrome: A preliminary description. *J Gerontol* 45:M169, 1990.
57. Dickel MJ, Moske SS: Morbidity cut-offs for sleep apnea and periodic leg movements in predicting subjective complaints in seniors. *Sleep* 13:155, 1990.
58. Kriger J et al: Breathing during sleep in normal young and elderly subjects: Hypopneas, apneas, and correlated factors. *Sleep* 6:108, 1983.
59. Naifeh KH et al: Effect of aging on sleep-related changes in respiratory variables. *Sleep* 10:160, 1987.
60. Littner M et al: Awake abnormalities of control of breathing and of the upper airway: Occurrence in healthy older men with nocturnal disordered breathing. *Chest* 86:573, 1984.
61. Douglas NJ et al: Hypoxic ventilatory response decreases during sleep in normal men. *Am Rev Respir Dis* 125:286, 1962.
62. Lugaresi E et al: Snoring and its clinical implications, in Guilleminault C, Dement W (eds): *Sleep Apnea Syndromes.* New York, Liss, 1978.
63. Lugaresi E et al: Some epidemiological data on snoring and cardiocirculatory disturbances. *Sleep* 3:221, 1989.
64. Bixler EO et al: Sleep apneic activity in older healthy subjects. *J Appl Physiol* 58:1597, 1985.
65. Kripke DF et al: sleep apnea and nocturnal myoclonus in the elderly. *Neurobiol Aging* 3:329, 1982.
66. Bliwise DL et al: Risk factors for sleep disordered breathing in heterogeneous geriatric populations. *J Am Geriatr Soc* 35:132, 1987.
67. Hoch CC et al: Sleep-disordered breathing in normal pathologic aging. *J Clin Psychiatry* 47:499, 1986.
68. McGinty D et al: Sleep-related breathing disorders in older men: A search for underlying mechanisms. *Neurobiol Aging* 3:337, 1982.
69. Hoch CC et al: Comparison of sleep-disordered breathing among healthy elderly in the seventh, eighth, and ninth decades of life. *J Sleep* 13(6):502, 1990.
70. Bliwise DL et al: Sleep apnea and mortality in an aged cohort. *Am J Public Health* 78:544, 1988.
71. He J et al: Mortality and apnea index in obstructive sleep apnea: Experience in 385 male patients. *Chest* 94:9, 1988.
72. Partinen M et al: Long-term outcome for obstructive sleep apnea syndrome patients—Mortality. *Chest* 94:1200, 1988.
73. Hoch CC et al: Predicting mortality in mixed depression and dementia using EEG sleep variables. *J Neuropsychiatry Clin Neurosci* 1:366, 1989.
74. Ancoli-Israel S et al: Sleep apnea in female patients in a nursing home: Increased risk of mortality. *Chest* 96:1054, 1989.
75. Block AJ et al: Sleep-disordered breathing and nocturnal oxygen desaturation in postmenopausal women. *Am J Med* 69:75, 1980.
76. Kronenberg RC, Drage CW: Attenuation of the ventilatory and heart rate responses to hypoxia and hypercapnia with aging in normal men. *J Clin Invest* 52:1812, 1973.
77. Lavie P: Sleep apnea syndrome: Is it a contributing factor to the sex differential in mortality? *Med Hypotheses* 21:173, 1986.

78. Mitler M et al: When people die: Cause of death versus time of death. *Am J Med* 82:266, 1987.
79. Marshall J: Diurnal variation in occurrence of strokes. *Stroke* 8:230, 1977.
80. Erkinjuntti T et al: Sleep apnea in multiinfarct dementia and Alzheimer's disease. *Sleep* 10:419, 1987.
81. Reynolds CF III et al: Sleep apnea in Alzheimer's dementia: Correlation with mental deterioration. *J Clin Psychiatry* 46:257, 1985.
82. Yesavage J et al: Preliminary communication: Intellectual deficit and sleep-related respiratory disturbance in the elderly. *Sleep* 8:40, 1985.
83. Smallwood RG et al: Sleep apnea: Relationship of sleep apnea to age, sex, and Alzheimer's dementia. *Sleep* 6:16, 1983.
84. Ford DE, Kamerow DB: Epidemiologic study of sleep disturbances and psychiatric disorders: An opportunity for prevention? *JAMA* 262:1479–84, 1989.
85. Haponik EF et al: Evaluation of sleep disordered breathing: Is polysomnography necessary? *Am J Med* 77:671, 1984.
86. Cohen-Mansfield J et al: Validation of sleep observations in a nursing home. *Sleep* 13:512, 1991.
87. Okawa M et al: Circadian rhythm disorders in sleep-waking and body temperature in elderly patients with dementia and their treatment. *Sleep* 14:478, 1991.
88. Carskadon MA et al: Sleep fragmentation in the elderly: Relationship to daytime sleep tendency. *Neurobiol Aging* 3:321, 1982.
89. Carskadon MA et al: Sleep and daytime sleepiness in the elderly. *J Geriatr Psychiatry* 13:131, 1960.
90. Carskadon M: Nocturnal sleep and daytime alertness in the aged: A pilot study. *Sleep Res* 8:120, 1979.
91. Bliwise DL et al: MSLT-defined sleepiness and neuropsychological test performance do not correlate in the elderly. *Neurobiol Aging* 12:463, 1991.
92. Mosko SS et al: Night-to-night variability in sleep apnea and sleep-related periodic leg movements in the elderly. *Sleep* 11:340, 1988.
93. Aharon-Peretz J et al: Sleep-wake cycles in multi-infarct dementia and dementia of the Alzheimer type. *Neurology* 41:1616, 1991.
94. Johnson JE: A comparative study of the bedtime routines and sleep of older adults. *J Commun Health Nurs* 8:129, 1991.
95. Monk TH et al: Daily social rhythms in the elderly and their relation to objectively recorded sleep. *Sleep* 15:322, 1992.
96. Friedman L et al: A preliminary study comparing sleep restriction and relaxation treatments for insomnia in older adults. *J Gerontol* 46:1, 1991.
97. Montplasisis J et al: The treatment of the restless leg syndrome with or without periodic leg movements in sleep. *Sleep* 15:391, 1992.
98. Reynolds III CF et al: Sleep in late-life recurrent depression: Changes during early continuation therapy with nortriptyline. *Neuropsychopharmacology* 5:85, 1991.
99. Bliwise DL: Studies of sleep and temperature in the nursing home. *Sleep* 14:477, 1991.
100. Haponik EF: Sleep disturbances of older persons: Physicians' attitudes. *Sleep* 15:168, 1992.
101. Everitt DE et al: Clinical decision-making in the evaluation and treatment of insomnia. *Am J Med* 89:357, 1990.

Chapter 113

INCONTINENCE

Joseph G. Ouslander

URINARY INCONTINENCE

Urinary incontinence is a common, disruptive, and potentially disabling condition in elderly persons. It is defined as the involuntary loss of urine in sufficient amount or frequency to be a social and/or health problem. The prevalence of urinary incontinence increases with age, is slightly higher in women, and is more common in elderly persons in acute care hospitals and nursing homes than in those dwelling in the community (Fig. 113-1).[1–6] Incontinence is a very heterogeneous condition, ranging in severity from occasional episodes of dribbling small amounts of urine to continuous urinary incontinence with concomitant fecal incontinence.

Physical health, psychological well-being, social status, and the costs of health care can all be adversely affected by incontinence.[7–12] Urinary incontinence is curable in many elderly patients, especially those who have adequate mobility and mental functioning. Even when not curable, incontinence can always be managed in a manner that will keep patients comfortable, make life easier for caregivers, and minimize costs of caring for the condition and its complications. Since many elderly patients are embarrassed and frustrated by their incontinence and either deny it or do not discuss it with a health professional, it is essential for specific questions about incontinence to be included in periodic assessments and for incontinence to be noted as a problem when detected in institutional settings. This chapter briefly reviews the pathophysiology of incontinence in elderly persons and provides detailed information on the evaluation and management of this condition.

Normal Urination

Continence requires effective functioning of the lower urinary tract, adequate cognitive and physical functioning, motivation, and an appropriate environment (Table 113-1). Thus, the pathophysiology of incontinence in the elderly patient can relate to the anatomy and physiology of the lower urinary tract, as well as to functional, psychological, and environmental factors. At the most basic level, urination is governed by a reflex centered in the sacral micturition center. Afferent pathways (via somatic and autonomic nerves) carry information on bladder volume to the spinal cord as the bladder fills. Motor output is adjusted accordingly (Fig. 113-2). Thus, as the bladder fills, sympathetic tone closes the bladder neck, relaxes the dome of the bladder, and inhibits parasympathetic tone; somatic innervation maintains tone in the pelvic floor musculature (including striated muscle around the urethra). When urination occurs, sympathetic and somatic tone diminish, and parasympathetic cholinergically mediated impulses cause the bladder to contract. All these processes are under the influence of higher centers in the brainstem, cerebral cortex, and cerebellum. This is a very simplified description of a very complex process, and the neurophysiology of urination remains incompletely understood.[13] It appears, however, that the cerebral cortex exerts a predominantly inhibitory influence and the brainstem facilitates urination. Thus, loss of the central cortical inhibiting influences over the sacral micturition center from diseases such as dementia, stroke, and parkinsonism can produce incontinence

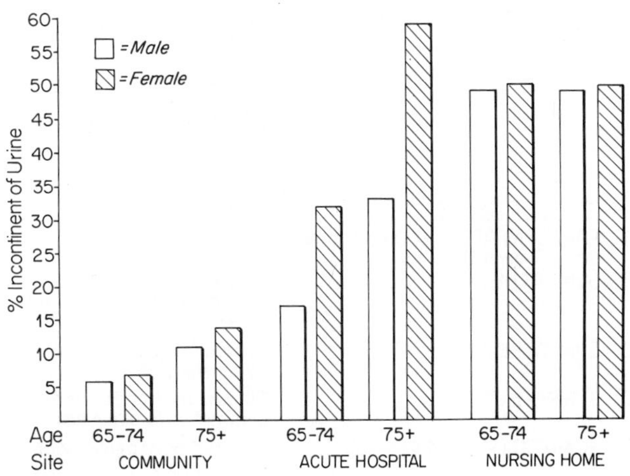

FIGURE 113-1
Prevalence of urinary incontinence by age and site. *(Reprinted with permission from Kane et al.[23])*

TABLE 113-1

Requirements for Continence

Effective lower urinary tract function
- Storage:
  - Accommodation by bladder of increasing volumes of urine under low pressure
  - Closed bladder outlet
  - Appropriate sensation of bladder fullness
  - Absence of involuntary bladder contractions
- Emptying:
  - Bladder capable of contraction
  - Lack of anatomic obstruction to urine flow
  - Coordinated lowering of outlet resistance with bladder contractions

Adequate mobility and dexterity to use toilet or toilet substitute and manage clothing

Adequate cognitive function to recognize toileting needs and find a toilet or toilet substitute

Motivation to be continent

Absence of environmental and iatrogenic barriers such as restraints and bed rails, inaccessible toilets or toilet substitutes, unavailable caregivers, or drug side effects.

SOURCE: From Kane et al,[23] with permission.

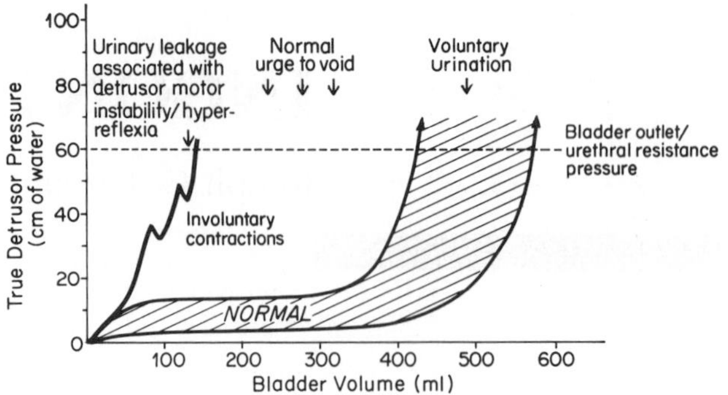

FIGURE 113-3

Simplified schematic diagram of pressure–volume relationships during bladder filling depicting the normal relationship and involuntary contractions (detrusor motor instability or hyperreflexia). True detrusor pressure is measured by subtracting intraabdominal pressure from total intravesical pressure, as would be done during a multichannel cystometrogram. *(Reprinted with permission from Kane et al.[23])*

in elderly patients. Disorders of the brainstem and suprasacral spinal cord can interfere with the coordination of bladder contraction and urethral relaxation, and interruptions of the sacral innervation can cause impaired bladder contraction and problems with continence.

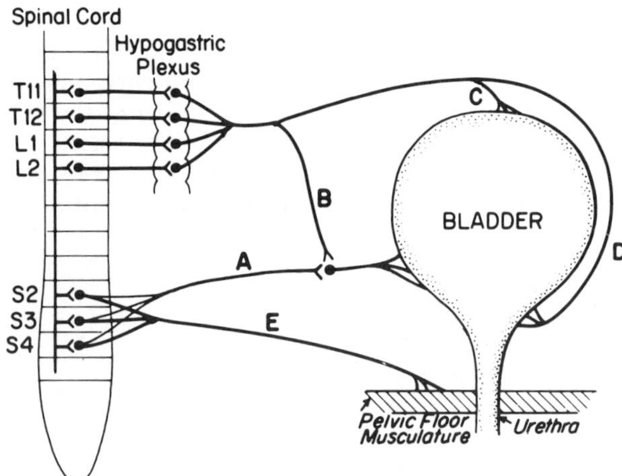

	TYPE OF NERVE	FUNCTION
A	PARASYMPATHETIC CHOLINERGIC (Nervi Erigentes)	Bladder contraction
B	SYMPATHETIC	Bladder relaxation (by inhibition of parasympathetic tone)
C	SYMPATHETIC	Bladder relaxation (β adrenergic)
D	SYMPATHETIC	Bladder neck and urethral contraction (α adrenergic)
E	SOMATIC (Pudendal nerve)	Contraction of pelvic floor musculature

FIGURE 113-2

Peripheral nerves involved in micturition. *(Reprinted with permission from Kane et al.[23])*

Normal urination is a dynamic process, requiring the coordination of several physiological processes. Figure 113-3 depicts a simplified schematic diagram of the pressure–volume relationships in the lower urinary tract, similar to measurements made in urodynamic studies (which are discussed later in this chapter). Under normal circumstances, as the bladder fills, pressure remains low (<15 cm H_2O). The first urge to void is variable, but generally occurs between 150 and 350 ml, and normal bladder capacity is 300 to 600 ml. When normal urination is initiated, true detrusor pressure (bladder pressure minus intraabdominal pressure) increases until it exceeds urethral resistance, and urine flow occurs. If at any time during bladder filling total intravesical pressure (which includes intraabdominal pressure) exceeds outlet resistance, urinary leakage occurs. This happens if, for example, intraabdominal pressure rises *without* a rise in true detrusor pressure by coughing or sneezing in someone with low outlet or urethral sphincter weakness. This would be defined as *genuine stress incontinence* in urodynamic terminology. Alternatively, the bladder can contract involuntarily and cause urinary leakage. This would be defined as *detrusor motor instability*, or *detrusor hyperreflexia* in patients with neurological disorders.[14]

Causes and Types of Urinary Incontinence

Basic Causes

There are four basic categories of causes of urinary incontinence in the elderly patient: urologic, neurological, psychological, and functional (including iatrogenic and environmental factors). Determining the cause or causes is essential to proper management. It is very important to distinguish between urologic and neurological disorders that cause incontinence and other problems (such as diminished mobility and/or mental function, inaccessible toilets, and psychological problems) that can cause or contribute to the condition. As is the case for a number of other common geriatric problems, multiple disorders often interact to cause urinary incontinence.

Aging alone does not cause urinary incontinence. Several age-related changes can, however, contribute to its development.[15] In general, bladder capacity declines with age, residual urine increases, and involuntary bladder contractions become more common. These contractions are found in 40 to 75 percent of elderly incontinent patients, 5 to 10 percent of elderly women, and in up to one-third of elderly men with no or minimal urinary symptoms.[15,16] Combined with impaired mobility, these contractions may account for a substantial proportion of incontinence in elderly functionally disabled patients.

Aging is also associated with a decline in bladder outlet and urethral resistance pressure in women. This decline, which is related to diminished estrogen influence and laxity of pelvic structures in women associated with prior childbirths, surgeries, and deconditioned muscles, predisposes to the development of stress incontinence. Decreased estrogen levels can also cause atrophic vaginitis and urethritis, which can, in turn, cause symptoms of dysuria and urgency and predispose to the development of urinary infection and urge incontinence. In men, prostatic enlargement is associated with decreased urine flow rates and detrusor motor instability and can lead to urge and/or overflow types of incontinence.

Acute (Reversible) versus Persistent Urinary Incontinence

The distinction between acute, reversible forms of incontinence and persistent incontinence is clinically important. Acute incontinence refers to those situations in which the incontinence is of sudden onset, usually related to an acute illness or an iatrogenic problem, and subsides once the illness or medication problem has been resolved. Persistent incontinence refers to incontinence that is unrelated to an acute illness and persists over time. It is important to recognize that several of the reversible factors discussed below can also contribute to persistent forms of incontinence.

Acute Incontinence The causes of acute and reversible forms of urinary incontinence can be remembered using the acronym *DRIP* (Table 113-2). Because of urinary frequency and urgency, many elderly persons, especially those limited in mobility, carefully arrange their schedules (and may even limit social activities) in order to be close to a toilet. Thus, an acute illness (e.g., pneumonia, cardiac decompensation, stroke, lower-extremity fracture) can precipitate incontinence by disrupting this delicate balance. Hospitalization, with its attendant environmental barriers (such as bed rails and poorly lit rooms), and the delirium and immobility that often accompany acute illnesses in the elderly patient can contribute to acute incontinence. Acute incontinence in these situations is likely to resolve with resolution of the underlying acute illness. Unless an indwelling or external catheter is necessary to record urine output accurately, this type of incontinence should be managed by environmental manipulations, scheduled toiletings, the appropriate use of toilet substitutes and pads, and careful attention to skin care. In a substantial proportion of patients, incontinence may persist for several weeks after hospitalization and should be further evaluated.

TABLE 113-2

Causes of Acute and Reversible Forms of Urinary Incontinence

D	Delirium
R	Restricted mobility, retention
I	Infection,* inflammation,* impaction (fecal)
P	Polyuria,† pharmaceuticals‡

*Acute symptomatic urinary tract infection, atrophic vaginitis or urethritis.
†Hyperglycemia, volume-expanded states causing excessive nocturia (e.g., congestive heart failure, venous insufficiency).
‡See Table 113-3.
SOURCE: From Kane et al,[23] with permission.

Fecal impaction is a common problem in both acutely and chronically ill elderly patients. Its role in and mechanism of producing urinary incontinence are unclear. Possibilities include mechanical obstruction of the bladder outlet with overflow-type incontinence, and reflex bladder contractions induced by rectal distension. Whatever the underlying mechanism, relief of a fecal impaction can lead to resolution of the urinary incontinence.

Urinary retention with overflow incontinence should be considered in any patient who suddenly develops urinary incontinence. Immobility; anticholinergic, narcotic, calcium channel blocking, and beta-adrenergic drugs; and fecal impaction can all precipitate overflow incontinence in an elderly patient. In addition, this condition may be a manifestation of an underlying process causing spinal cord compression presenting acutely.

Although the relationship of bacteriuria and pyuria to the pathogenesis of incontinence is unclear, any acute inflammatory condition in the lower urinary tract that causes frequency and urgency can precipitate incontinence. Thus, treatment of an acute cystitis or urethritis can help to restore continence.

Diuretics (especially the rapid-acting loop diuretics) and conditions that cause polyuria, including hyperglycemia and hypercalcemia, can precipitate acute incontinence. Patients with volume-expanded states, such as congestive heart failure and lower-extremity venous insufficiency, may have polyuria at night, which can contribute to nocturia and nocturnal incontinence. As is the case in many other conditions in geriatric patients, a wide variety of medications can

TABLE 113-3

Medications That Can Potentially Affect Continence

Type of Medication	Potential Effects on Continence
Diuretics	Polyuria, frequency, urgency
Anticholinergics	Urinary retention, overflow incontinence, impaction
Psychotropics:	
Antidepressants	Anticholinergic actions, sedation
Antipsychotics	Anticholinergic actions, sedation, rigidity, immobility
Sedative-hypnotics	Sedation, delirium, immobility, muscle relaxation
Narcotic analgesics	Urinary retention, fecal impaction, sedation, delirium
Alpha-adrenergic blockers	Urethral relaxation
Alpha-adrenergic agonists	Urinary retention
Beta-adrenergic agonists	Urinary retention
Calcium channel blockers	Urinary retention
Alcohol	Polyuria, frequency, urgency, sedation, delirium, immobility

SOURCE: From Kane et al,[23] with permission.

play a role in the development of incontinence in elderly patients (Table 113-3). Whether the incontinence is acute or persistent, the potential role of these medications in causing or contributing to a patient's incontinence should be considered. When feasible, stopping the medication, switching to an alternative, or modifying the dosage schedule can be an important component (and possibly the only one necessary) of the treatment for incontinence.

Persistent Incontinence The clinical definitions and common causes of persistent urinary incontinence are shown in Table 113-4. These types can overlap with each other, and an individual patient may have more than one type simultaneously. Three of these types of incontinence—stress, urge, and overflow—result from one or a combination of two basic abnormalities in lower genitourinary tract function:

1. Failure to store urine, caused by a hyperactive or poorly compliant bladder or by diminished outflow resistance
2. Failure to empty the bladder, caused by a poorly contractile bladder or by increased outflow resistance

Stress incontinence is common in elderly women, especially in ambulatory clinic settings.[18–20] It may be infrequent and involve very small amounts of urine and need no specific treatment in women who are not

TABLE 113-4

Basic Types and Causes of Persistent Urinary Incontinence

Type	Definition	Common Causes
Stress	Involuntary loss of urine (usually small amounts) with increases in intraabdominal pressure (e.g., cough, laugh, or exercise)	Weakness and laxity of pelvic floor musculature Bladder outlet or urethral sphincter weakness
Urge	Leakage of urine (often larger volumes, but variable) because of inability to delay voiding after sensation of bladder fullness is perceived	Detrusor motor and/or sensory instability, isolated or associated with one or more of the following: Local genitourinary condition such as cystitis, urethritis, tumors, stones, diverticuli, or outflow obstruction CNS disorders such as stroke, dementia, parkinsonism, suprasacral spinal cord injury, or disease*
Overflow	Leakage of urine (usually small amounts) resulting from mechanical forces on an overdistended bladder or from other effects of urinary retention on bladder and sphincter function	Anatomic obstruction by prostate, stricture, cystocele Acontractile bladder associated with diabetes melitus or spinal cord injury Neurogenic (detrusor-sphincter dyssynergy), associated with multiple sclerosis and other suprasacral spinal cord lesions
Functional	Urinary leakage associated with inability to toilet because of impairment of cognitive and/or physical functioning, psychological unwillingness, or environmental barriers	Severe dementia and other neurological disorders Psychological factors such as depression, regression, anger, and hostility

*When detrusor motor instability is associated with a neurological disorder, it is termed "detrusor hyperreflexia" by the International Continence Society.

SOURCE: From Kane et al,[23] with permission.

bothered by it. On the other hand, it may be so severe and/or bothersome that it requires surgical correction. It is most often associated with weakened supporting tissues surrounding the bladder outlet and urethra caused by lack of estrogen and/or previous vaginal deliveries or surgery. Obesity and chronic coughing can also contribute. Stress incontinence is unusual in men, but it can occur after transurethral surgery and/or radiation therapy for lower urinary tract malignancy when the anatomic sphincters are damaged.

Urge incontinence can be caused by a variety of lower genitourinary and neurological disorders (Table 113-4). It is most often, but not always, associated with detrusor motor instability or detrusor hyperreflexia (Fig. 113-3). Some patients have a poorly compliant bladder without involuntary contractions (e.g., in conditions of radiation or interstitial cystitis, both unusual in the elderly patient). Other patients have symptoms of urge incontinence but do not exhibit detrusor motor instability on urodynamic testing. This is sometimes termed "sensory instability" or "hypersensitive bladder"; it is likely that some of these patients do have detrusor motor instability in their everyday lives which is not documented at the time of the urodynamic study. On the other hand, there are some patients with neurological disorders who do have detrusor hyperreflexia on urodynamic testing but may not have urgency; they may instead have incontinence without any warning symptoms. Almost all the patients described above are generally treated as if they have urge incontinence if they empty their bladders and do not have other correctable genitourinary pathologic conditions (see below). A subgroup of very elderly incontinent patients with detrusor hyperreflexia who also have impaired bladder contractility, emptying less than one-third of their bladder volume with involuntary contractions on urodynamic testing, has been described.[21] The implications of this urodynamic finding for the pathophysiology and treatment of incontinence in elderly patients are unclear and currently under investigation.

Urinary retention with overflow incontinence can result from anatomic or neurogenic outflow obstruction, a hypotonic or acontractile bladder, or both. The most common causes include prostatic enlargement, diabetic neuropathic bladder, and urethral stricture. Low spinal cord injury and anatomic obstruction in women (caused by pelvic prolapse and urethral distortion) are less common causes of overflow incontinence. Several types of drugs can also contribute to this type of persistent incontinence (Table 113-3). Some patients with suprasacral spinal cord lesions (e.g., multiple sclerosis) develop detrusor-sphincter dyssynergy and consequent urinary retention, which must be treated similarly to overflow incontinence; in some instances a sphincterotomy is necessary.

Stress, urge, and overflow incontinence can occur in combination. Thus, a woman with stress incontinence or a man with obstruction may also have urge incontinence and detrusor motor instability or hyperreflexia. The coexistence of these disorders can have important therapeutic implications (see below).

Functional incontinence results when an elderly person is unable or unwilling to reach a toilet on time. Distinguishing this type of incontinence from other types of persistent incontinence is critical to appropriate management. Factors that cause functional incontinence (such as inaccessible toilets and psychological disorders) can also exacerbate other types of persistent incontinence. Patients with incontinence that appears to be predominantly related to functional factors may also have abnormalities of the lower genitourinary tract, such as detrusor hyperreflexia. In some patients it can be very difficult to determine whether the functional factors or the genitourinary factors predominate without a trial of specific types of treatment.

Evaluation

In patients with the sudden onset of incontinence (especially when associated with an acute medical condition and hospitalization), the causes of acute incontinence (Table 113-2) can be ruled out by a brief history, a physical examination, and basic laboratory studies (urinalysis, culture, and tests for serum glucose or calcium, if indicated).

Figure 113-4 summarizes the recommended approach to the diagnostic evaluation of incontinent elderly patients. The initial evaluation of urinary incontinence includes a focused history, a targeted physical examination, a urinalysis, and a postvoid residual determination. A variety of other diagnostic studies are indicated in selected patients (Table 113-5). The objectives of the basic evaluation are threefold:

1. To identify potentially reversible conditions that might be contributing to the incontinence (Table 113-2).
2. To identify conditions that require further diagnostic tests (Table 113-5) and/or referral for gynecologic or urologic evaluation.
3. To develop a management plan, which may include referral for further evaluation or a therapeutic trial of behavioral and/or pharmacologic therapy.

Detailed descriptions of the history and physical examination can be found elsewhere.[22,23] The history should focus on the characteristics of the incontinence, on current medical problems and medications, and on the impact of the incontinence on the patient and caregivers. The incontinence should be characterized in terms of frequency, timing, and amount of leakage; symptoms of urge versus stress incontinence; and symptoms of voiding difficulty (including hesitancy, intermittent stream, and straining to void). Although these symptoms are generally not specific for

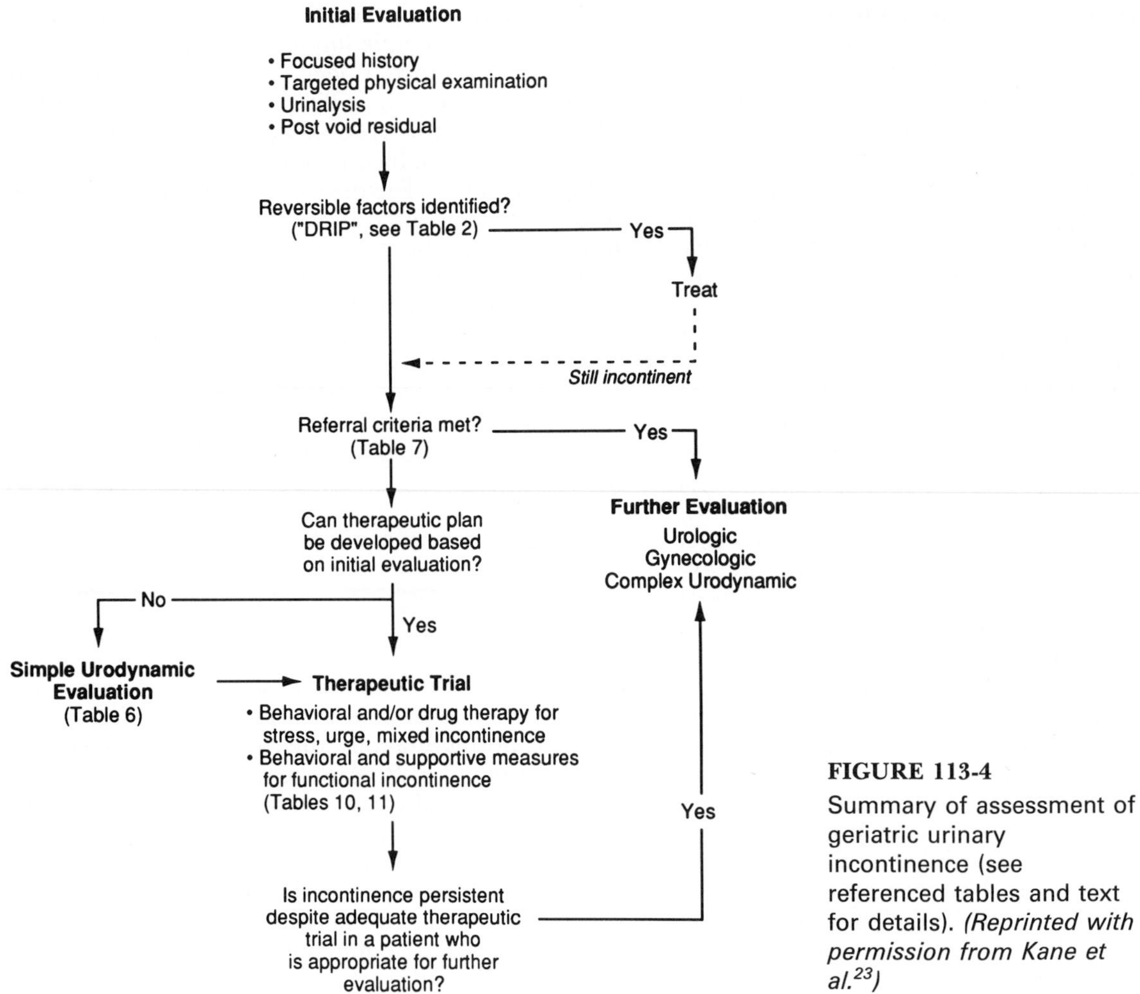

FIGURE 113-4
Summary of assessment of geriatric urinary incontinence (see referenced tables and text for details). *(Reprinted with permission from Kane et al.[23])*

the different types of incontinence, a careful history is essential in targeting the important parts of the evaluations and treatment. For example, reliably reported symptoms of voiding difficulty, especially if confirmed on clinical assessment, are an indication to consider referral for further evaluation (see below). Bladder records such as those shown in Figs. 113-5 (for outpatients) and 113-6 (for institutionalized patients[24]) can be helpful in characterizing symptoms, as well as in following the response to treatment.

Physical examination should focus on abdominal, rectal, and genital examinations, as well as an evaluation of lumbosacral innervation. During the history and physical examination, special attention should be given to factors such as mobility, mental status, medications, and accessibility of toilets that may be either causing the incontinence or interacting with urologic and neurological disorders to worsen the condition.

Urinalysis and urine culture (if indicated) are the next steps in the evaluation of incontinence—although there is controversy about how this is best done and how the results relate to incontinence. Clean urine specimens are often difficult to obtain from frail incontinent patients. For women who cannot cooperate in the collection of a clean voided specimen, catheterization may be necessary. The risk from a single bladder catheterization is small; and a postvoid residual volume can be determined at the time of specimen collection (see below). For men who cannot void spontaneously, the application of a condom catheter after cleaning the penis can be used to collect a specimen that accurately reflects bladder urine.[25] Although there is a clear relationship between acute symptomatic urinary tract infection and incontinence, the relationship between "asymptomatic" bacteriuria and incontinence is controversial. Because the prevalence of bacteriuria and incontinence roughly parallel each other in the elderly population,[26] and because the bacteriuria may resolve spontaneously and does not appear to be related to symptoms (at least in patients with minimal incontinence[27]), it is difficult to make clear recommendations. In addition, recent controlled studies of treating asymptomatic bacteriuria (including patients with incontinence), especially in nursing home settings, have not favored treatment.[28–30] Although hard data are lacking, it will still seem reasonable, when evaluating persistent incontinence in a noninstitutionalized incontinent patient, to eradicate the bacteriuria once and observe the effect on the incontinence.[31]

TABLE 113-5

Basic Components of the Diagnostic Evaluation of Persistent Urinary Incontinence

All Patients

- History
- Physical examination
- Urinalysis
- Postvoid residual determination

Selected Patients*

- Laboratory studies
  - Urine culture
  - Urine cytology
  - Blood glucose, renal function tests
  - Renal ultrasound
- Gynecologic evaluation
- Urologic evaluation
- Cystoscopy
  - Voiding cystourethrography
- Urodynamic tests
  - Simple urodynamic tests (see Table 113-6)
  - Urine flowmetry
  - Cystometrogram
  - Pressure flow study
  - Urethral pressure profilometry
  - Sphincter electromyography
  - Videourodynamics

*See text and Table 116-7.
SOURCE: From Kane et al,[23] with permission.

A postvoid residual volume determination (PVR) should be performed to exclude significant degrees of urinary retention. Neither the history nor the physical examination is sensitive or specific enough for this purpose in geriatric patients. The PVR can be done alone or in conjunction with other simple urodynamic tests (as discussed below) and can be accomplished by catheterization or by ultrasound if equipment is available and bladder filling is not going to be performed. In order to be accurate, the PVR should be obtained within a few minutes of a spontaneous continent or incontinent void. PVRs less than 100 ml in the absence of straining to void generally reflect adequate bladder emptying in geriatric patients, whereas PVRs over 200 ml are abnormal; values in between must be interpreted in light of other patient characteristics.

Most authors, as well as the clinical practice guidelines published by the Agency for Health Care Policy Research, do not recommend that all incontinent elderly patients undergo a urologic, gynecologic, or complex urodynamic evaluation. Several algorithms have been described which attempt to determine the appropriate treatment approach without the need for more complex evaluations and to identify patients who would benefit from further evaluation.[32–34] Some of these strategies depend on clinical history and physical examination alone; others include bladder catheterizations or simplified urodynamic procedures. None have been tested prospectively in large enough populations of elderly incontinent patients to make definitive recommendations about the most cost-effective diagnostic strategy.

A series of simplified tests of lower urinary tract function can be carried out in conjunction with the PVR (Table 113-6). These tests can be used with information obtained from the history and physical examination to develop a series of criteria for referral for further evaluation (Table 113-7) in the initial assessment and management of incontinent elderly patients.[34–36] These tests are especially helpful when a therapeutic plan cannot be developed based on the information gleaned from the initial evaluation. The tests take 15 to 20 minutes to complete and can in many patients be performed by a single examiner, although an extra pair of hands is usually helpful. Bladder capacity and stability, as determined by the procedures outlined in Table 113-6, have been shown to be highly correlated with results of formal multichannel cystometrograms.[32] In some settings, relatively inexpensive simple cystometric equipment and noninvasive methods of measuring urine flow rate may be available which can enhance the accuracy of the assessment. Like other diagnostic tests, these simple urodynamic tests must be performed properly and interpreted carefully in light of other clinical information and should only be performed if the results will influence the management of the patient. For example, the bladder-filling procedure may not be necessary for making a reasonable treatment plan for some patients, such as women who have sterile urine, have no atrophic vaginitis, and meet none of the criteria in Table 113-7, and who, in addition, either (1) reliably give a history of leakage with stress maneuvers without irritative or obstructive voiding symptoms and completely empty their bladder (they can be treated behaviorally and/or pharmacologically for stress-type incontinence) or (2) reliably give a history of urge incontinence without symptoms of stress incontinence, voiding difficulty, or incomplete bladder emptying (they can be treated behaviorally and/or pharmacologically for urge-type incontinence).

Management

Several therapeutic modalities are used in managing incontinent patients (Table 113-8). Although few of them have been studied in well-controlled trials in the elderly population, they can be especially helpful if specific diagnoses are made and attention is paid to all factors that may be contributing to the incontinence in a given patient. Even when cures are not possible, the comfort and satisfaction of both patients and caregivers can almost always be enhanced.

Special attention should be given to the management of acute forms of incontinence, which are most common in elderly patients in acute care hospitals. These forms of incontinence are often transient if managed appropriately; on the other hand, inappropriate management may lead to a permanent prob-

BLADDER RECORD

Day: ____________ Date: ______/______.
month day

INSTRUCTIONS:

1) In the 1st column make a mark every time during the 2-hour period you urinate into the toilet

2) Use the 2nd column to record the amount you urinate (if you are measuring amounts)

3) In the 3rd or 4th column, make a mark every time you accidentally leak urine

Time Interval	Urinated in Toilet	Amount	Leaking Accident *or*	Large Accident	Reason for Accident *
6–8 am					
8–10 am					
2–4 pm					
4–6 pm					
6–8 pm					
8–10 pm					
10–12 pm					
Overnight					

Number of pads used today: ____________

* For example, if you coughed and have a leaking accident, write "cough". If you had a large accident after a strong urge to urinate, write "urge".

FIGURE 113-5
Example of a bladder record for ambulatory care settings. *(Reprinted with permission from Kane et al.[23])*

lem. The most common approach to elderly incontinent patients in acute hospitals is indwelling catheterization. In some instances, this practice is justified by the necessity for accurate measurement of urine output during the acute phase of an illness. In many instances, however, it is unnecessary and poses a substantial and unwarranted risk of catheter-induced infection. Although other procedures may be more difficult and time-consuming, making toilets and toilet substitutes accessible and combining this accessibility with some form of scheduled toileting is probably a more appropriate approach in patients who do not require indwelling catheterization for reasons other than incontinence. Newer launderable or disposable and highly absorbent bed pads and undergarments may also be helpful in managing these patients. These products may be more costly than catheters but will probably result in less morbidity (and therefore overall cost) in the long run. All of the factors that can cause or contribute to a reversible form of incontinence (Table 113-2) should be attended to in order to maximize the potential for regaining continence.

Supportive measures are critical in managing all forms of incontinence and should be used in conjunction with other, more specific treatment modalities. Education, a positive attitude, environmental manipulations, appropriate use of toilet substitutes, avoidance of iatrogenic contributions to incontinence, modifications of diuretic and fluid intake patterns, and good skin care are all important.[8,37–39]

Specially designed incontinence undergarments and pads can be very helpful in many patients, but they must be used appropriately. They are now being marketed on television and are readily available in retail stores. Although they can be effective, several caveats should be raised:

1. Garments and pads are a nonspecific treatment. They should not be used as the first response to incontinence or before some type of diagnostic evaluation is done.
2. Many patients are curable if treated with specific therapies, and some have potentially serious factors underlying their incontinence which must be diagnosed and treated.
3. Pants and pads can interfere with attempts at certain types of behaviorally oriented therapies designed to restore a normal pattern of voiding and continence (see below).
4. Incontinence garments and pads are generally

INCONTINENCE MONITORING RECORD

INSTRUCTIONS: EACH TIME THE PATIENT IS CHECKED:
1) Mark *one* of the circles in the BLADDER section at the hour closest to the time the patient is checked.
2) Make an X in the BOWEL section if the patient has had an incontinent or normal bowel movement.

● = Incontinent, small amount	Ø = Dry	X = Incontinent BOWEL
⬤ = Incontinent, large amount	△ = Voided correctly	X = Normal BOWEL

PATIENT NAME ______________________ ROOM # __________ DATE __________

	BLADDER			BOWEL			
	INCONTINENT OF URINE	DRY	VOIDED CORRECTLY	INCONTINENT X	NORMAL X	INITIALS	COMMENTS
12 am	● ⬤	○	△ cc ____				
1	● ⬤	○	△ cc ____				
2	● ⬤	○	△ cc ____				
3	● ⬤	○	△ cc ____				
4	● ⬤	○	△ cc ____				
5	● ⬤	○	△ cc ____				
6	● ⬤	○	△ cc ____				
7	● ⬤	○	△ cc ____				
8	● ⬤	○	△ cc ____				
9	● ⬤	○	△ cc ____				
10	● ⬤	○	△ cc ____				
11	● ⬤	○	△ cc ____				
12 pm	● ⬤	○	△ cc ____				
1	● ⬤	○	△ cc ____				
2	● ⬤	○	△ cc ____				
3	● ⬤	○	△ cc ____				
4	● ⬤	○	△ cc ____				
5	● ⬤	○	△ cc ____				
6	● ⬤	○	△ cc ____				
7	● ⬤	○	△ cc ____				
8	● ⬤	○	△ cc ____				
9	● ⬤	○	△ cc ____				
10	● ⬤	○	△ cc ____				
11	● ⬤	○	△ cc ____				
TOTALS:							

FIGURE 113-6

Example of a record to monitor bladder and bowel function in institutional settings. This type of record is especially useful for implementing and following the results of various training procedures and other treatment protocols. *(Reprinted with permission from Regents of the University of California.)*

TABLE 113-6

Procedures for Simple Tests of Lower Urinary Tract Function

Procedure	Observations	Interpretation
1. Stress maneuvers If possible, start the tests when the patient feels his or her bladder is almost full. Ask the patient to cough forcefully 3 times in the standing position with a small pad over the urethral area.	a. Timing (coincident or after stress) and amount (drops or larger volumes) of any leakage	Leakage of urine coincident with stress maneuver confirms presence of stress incontinence.
2. Normal voiding Ask the patient to void privately in his or her normal fashion into a commode containing a measuring "hat" after a standard prep for clean urine specimen collection.	a. Signs of voiding difficulty (hesitancy, straining, intermittent stream) b. Voided volume	Signs of voiding difficulty may indicate obstruction or bladder contractility problem.
3. Postvoid residual determination Insert a 14 French straight catheter into the bladder using sterile technique within 5–10 minutes of the patient voiding.	a. Ease of catheter passage b. Postvoid residual volume	If there is great difficulty passing the catheter, obstruction may be present. If the residual volume is elevated (e.g., over 100 ml) after a normal void, obstruction or a bladder contractility problem may be present.
4. Bladder filling For females, position a fracture pan under their buttocks, and for males, have a urinal available to measure any leakage during filling. Attach a 50-ml catheter tip syringe without the piston to the catheter and use as a funnel to fill the bladder. Fill the bladder with room temperature sterile water, 50 ml at a time, by holding the syringe so that it is approximately 15 cm above the pubic symphysis (bladder pressure should not normally exceed 15 cm of water during filling) until the patient feels the urge to void; then instill water in 25-ml increments until bladder capacity is reached (an involuntary contraction, or "I would rush to the toilet now, I can't hold anymore"). Then remove the catheter.	a. First urge to void ("I'm starting to feel a little full") b. Presence or absence of involuntary bladder contractions—detected by continuous upward movement of the fluid column (sometimes accompanied by leaking around or expulsion of the catheter) in the absence of abdominal straining—which the patient cannot inhibit c. Amount lost with involuntary contraction and subsequent bladder emptying d. Bladder capacity—amount instilled before either an involuntary contraction or the strong urge to void is perceived	Involuntary contractions or severe urgency at relatively low bladder volume (e.g., <250–300 ml) suggests urge incontinence, especially if consistent with the patient's presenting symptoms.
5. Repeat stress maneuvers Ask the patient to cough forcefully 3 times in the supine and standing positions.	a. Timing (coincident or after stress) and amount (drops or larger volumes) of any leakage	See interpretation above for stress maneuvers. Stress maneuvers with a relatively low bladder volume are less sensitive for detecting stress incontinence.
6. Bladder emptying Ask the patient to empty his or her bladder again privately into the commode with the measuring hat.	a. Signs of voiding difficulty (see above) b. Voided volume c. Calculated postvoid residual (amount instilled minus amount voided)	See interpretation above for normal voiding. Calculated postvoid residual may be more valid if patient did not feel full at beginning of tests.

SOURCE: From Kane et al,[23] with permission.

TABLE 113-7

Criteria for Referral of Elderly Incontinent Patients for Urologic, Gynecologic, or Urodynamic Evaluation

Criteria	Definition	Rationale
History		
Recent history of lower urinary tract or pelvic surgery or irradiation	Surgery or irradiation involving the pelvic area or lower urinary tract within the past 6 months.	A structural abnormality relating to the recent procedure should be sought.
Relapse or rapid recurrence of a symptomatic urinary tract infection	Onset of dysuria, new or worsened irritative voiding symptoms, fever, suprapubic or flank pain associated with growth of $>10^5$ colony-forming units of a urinary pathogen; symptoms and bacteriuria return within 4 weeks of treatment.	A structural abnormality or pathologic condition in the urinary tract predisposing to infection should be excluded.
Physical examination		
Marked pelvic prolapse*	Pronounced uterine descensus to or through the introitus, or a prominent cystocele that descends the entire height of the vaginal vault with coughing during speculum examination.	Anatomic abnormality may underlie the pathophysiology of the incontinence and may require surgical repair.
Stress incontinence*,†	Stress incontinence demonstrated standing or supine; urine leaks, generally drops or small volumes, coincident with increasing abdominal pressure by vigorous coughing.	Bladder neck suspension procedures are generally well tolerated and successful in properly selected elderly women who have stress incontinence that respond poorly to more conservative measures.
Marked prostatic enlargement and/or suspicion of cancer	Gross enlargement of the prostate on digital exam; prominent induration or asymmetry of the lobes.	An evaluation to exclude prostate cancer that requires curative or palliative therapy should be undertaken.
Severe hesitancy, straining, and/or interrupted urinary stream	Straining to begin voiding and a dribbling or intermittent stream at a time the patient's bladder feels full.	Signs are suggestive of obstruction or poor bladder contractility.
Postvoid residual		
Difficulty passing a 14 French straight catheter	Impossible catheter passage, or passage requiring considerable force, or a larger, more rigid catheter.	Anatomic blockage of the urethra or bladder neck may be present.
Postvoid residual volume >100 ml	Volume of urine remaining in the bladder within 5–10 minutes after the patient voids spontaneously in as normal a fashion as possible.‡	Anatomic or neurogenic obstruction or poor bladder contractility may be present.
Urinalysis		
Hematuria	Greater than five red blood cells per high-power field on microscopic exam in the absence of infection.	A pathologic condition in the urinary tract should be excluded.
Uncertain diagnosis	After the history, physical exam, simple tests of lower urinary tract function, and urinalysis, none of the other referral criteria are met, and the results are not consistent with predominantly functional, urge, and/or stress incontinence.	A complex urodynamic evaluation may help better define and reproduce the symptoms associated with the patient's incontinence and target treatment.

*If medical conditions precluded surgery, or if the patient is adamantly opposed to considering surgical intervention, the patient should not be referred.

†Stress incontinence that is a prominent, bothersome symptom which has not responded to nonsurgical treatment.

‡For patients who cannot void at the time of the evaluation, postvoid residual can be calculated after filling the bladder (see Table 113-6).

SOURCE: From Kane et al,[23] with permission.

TABLE 113-8

Treatment Options for Geriatric Urinary Incontinence

Drugs (see Table 113-10)
Bladder relaxants
Alpha agonists
Estrogen
Others
Training procedures (see Table 113-11)
Pelvic muscle exercises
Biofeedback, behavioral training
Bladder retraining (see Table 113-12)
Toileting procedures
Surgery
Bladder neck suspension
Removal of obstruction or pathologic lesion
Periurethral injections
Mechanical or electrical devices
Artificial sphincters
Intravaginal electrical stimulation
Catheters (for overflow incontinence) (see Tables 113-13 and 113-14)
Intermittent
Indwelling
Nonspecific supportive measures
Toilet substitutes (e.g., commodes and urinals)
Environmental manipulations
Modifications of drug regimens and fluid intake pattern
External collection devices
Incontinence undergarments and pads
Chronic indwelling catheters

SOURCE: From Kane et al,[23] with permission.

TABLE 113-9

Primary Treatments for Different Types of Geriatric Urinary Incontinence

Type of Incontinence	*Primary Treatments*
Stress	Pelvic muscle (Kegel) exercises
	Alpha-adrenergic agonists
	Estrogen
	Biofeedback, behavioral training
	Surgical bladder neck suspension
	Periurethral injections
Urge	Bladder relaxants
	Estrogen (if vaginal atrophy present)
	Behavioral procedures (e.g., biofeedback, behavioral therapy)
	Surgical removal of obstructing or other irritating pathologic lesions
Overflow	Surgical removal of obstruction
	Intermittent catheterization (if practical)
	Indwelling catheterization
Functional	Behavioral therapies (e.g., prompted voiding, habit training, scheduled toileting)
	Environmental manipulations
	Incontinence undergarments and pads
	External collection devices
	Bladder relaxants (selected patients)*
	Indwelling catheters (selected patients)†

*Many patients with functional incontinence also have detrusor hyperreflexia, and some may benefit from bladder relaxant drug therapy (see text).

†See Table 113-13.

SOURCE: From Kane et al,[23] with permission.

not covered by third-party payers and can be expensive.

To a large extent the optimal treatment of persistent incontinence depends upon identifying the type or types. Table 113-9 outlines the primary treatments for the basic types of persistent incontinence in the geriatric population. Each treatment modality is briefly discussed below.

Drug Treatment

Table 113-10 lists the drugs used to treat various types of incontinence. The efficacy of drug treatment has not been as well studied in elderly as it has been in younger populations,[40] but for many patients, especially those with urge or stress incontinence, drug treatment may be very effective. Drug treatment can be prescribed in conjunction with one or more of the behaviorally oriented training procedures discussed in the section that follows. There are no data on the relative efficacy of drug versus behavioral versus combination treatment in the elderly population. Thus, until controlled trials are conducted, treatment decisions should be individualized and will depend in large part on the characteristics and preferences of the patient and the preferences of the health care professional.

For urge incontinence, drugs with anticholinergic and bladder smooth muscle–relaxant properties are used. All of these drugs can have bothersome systemic anticholinergic side effects, especially dry mouth, and they can precipitate urinary retention in some patients. Men with some degree of outflow obstruction, diabetic patients, and patients with impaired bladder contractility[22] may be at the highest risk for developing urinary retention and should be followed carefully when these drugs are prescribed. Patients with Alzheimer's disease must be followed for the development of drug-induced delirium, although it is unusual. Oxybutynin, starting at half the usual recommended dose (i.e., 2.5 mg three times per day), may offer some advantage over other drugs with more pronounced systemic anticholinergic side effects and does not have the potentially serious effects on blood pressure and cardiac conduction of imipramine. The latter drug has also been associated with hip fractures in elderly patients,[41] possibly due to the side effect of postural hypotension. Calcium channel blockers have been used for urge incontinence in Europe, but none are yet approved for this indication in the United States. Several studies suggest that cognitive and physical functional impairment are associated with poor responses to bladder relaxant drug therapy.[42–45] The results of these studies should not, however, preclude a treatment trial in this patient

TABLE 113-10

Drugs Used to Treat Urinary Incontinence

Drugs	Dosages	Mechanisms of Action	Types of Incontinence	Potential Adverse Effects
Anticholinergic and antispasmodic agents:				
Oxybutynin (Ditropan)	2.5–5.0 mg tid	Increase bladder capacity	Urge or stress with detrusor instability or hyperreflexia	Dry mouth, blurry vision, elevated intraocular pressure, delirium, constipation
Propantheline (Pro-Banthine)	15–30 mh tid			
Dicyclomine (Bentyl)	10–20 mg tid	Diminish involuntary bladder contractions		
Flavoxate (Urispas)	100–200 mg tid			
Imipramine (Tofranil)	25–50 mg tid			Above effects plus postural hypotension, cardiac conduction disturbances
Alpha-adrenergic agonists:				
Pseudoephedrine (Sudafed)	30–60 mg tid	Increase urethral smooth muscle contraction	Stress incontinence with sphincter weakness	Headache, tachycardia, elevation of blood pressure
Phenylpropanolamine (Ornade)	75 mg bid			
Imipramine (Tofranil)	25–50 mg tid			All effects listed above
Conjugated estrogens:*	0.625 mg/day	Increase periurethral blood flow Strengthen periurethral tissues	Stress incontinence Urge incontinence associated with atrophic vaginitis	Endometrial cancer, elevated blood pressure, gallstones
Oral (Premarin)				
Topical	0.5–1.0 g/application			
Cholinergic agonists:†				
Bethanechol (Urecholine)	10–30 mg tid	Stimulate bladder contraction	Overflow incontinence with atonic bladder	Bradycardia, hypotension, bronchoconstriction, gastric acid secretion
Alpha-adrenergic antagonist:				
Prazosin (Minipress)‡	1–2 mg tid	Relax smooth muscle of urethra and prostatic capsule	Overflow or urge incontinence associated with prostatic enlargement	Postural hypotension

*With prolonged use, cyclical administration with a progestational agent should be considered. Transdermal preparations are also available, but have not been studied for treating incontinence.
†The efficacy of chronic bethanechol therapy is controversial (see text).
‡May provide some symptomatic relief in patients who are unwilling or unable to undergo prostatectomy (see text). Other alpha antagonists, such as terazosin and doxazosin, may be effective.
SOURCE: From Kane et al,[23] with permission.

population. Some patients may respond, especially in conjunction with scheduled toileting or prompted voiding (see below). The goal of treatment in these patients may not be to cure the incontinence, but to reduce its severity and prevent discomfort and complications.

For stress incontinence, drug treatment involves a combination of an alpha-agonist and estrogen. Drug treatment is appropriate for motivated patients who (1) have mild to moderate degrees of stress incontinence, (2) do not have a major anatomic abnormality (e.g., large cystocele), and (3) do not have any contraindications to these drugs. These patients may also respond to behavioral treatments (see below), and data suggest that the two treatment modalities are roughly equivalent, with about three-fourths of patients reporting improvement;[46] a combination would also be a reasonable approach for some patients. Estrogen alone is not as effective as in combination with an alpha-agonist for stress incontinence. If either oral or vaginal estrogen is used for a prolonged period of time (more than a few months), cyclic administration and the addition of a progestational agent should be considered. Estrogen is also used, either chronically or on an intermittent basis (i.e., 1- to 2-month courses), for the treatment of irritative voiding symptoms and urge incontinence in women with atrophic vaginitis and urethritis.

Drug treatment for chronic overflow incontinence using a cholinergic agonist or an alpha-adrenergic antagonist is usually not highly efficacious. Bethanechol may be helpful when given for a brief period subcutaneously in patients with persistent bladder contractility problems after an overdistension injury, but the drug is generally not effective when given orally and long term.[47] Alpha-adrenergic blockers may be helpful in relieving symptoms associated with outflow obstruction in some patients, but they are probably not efficacious for long-term treatment of overflow incontinence in the elderly patient.[48]

Many elderly women have symptomatically and urodynamically a combination of both urge and stress incontinence. A combination of estrogen and imipramine would, at least in theory, be appropriate for these patients, because imipramine has both anticholinergic and alpha-adrenergic effects. If urge incontinence is the predominant symptom, a combination of estrogen and oxybutynin would be appropriate. Behavioral training procedures are also a reasonable approach for women with mixed incontinence (see below).

Behavioral Procedures

Many types of behavioral training procedures have been described for the management of urinary incontinence.[49,50] The nosology of these procedures has been somewhat confusing, and much of the literature has used the term *bladder training* to encompass a wide variety of techniques. It is very important to distinguish between procedures that are patient-dependent (i.e., require adequate function and motivation of the patient), in which the goal is to restore a normal pattern of voiding and continence, and procedures that are caregiver-dependent and can be used for functionally disabled patients, in which the goal is to keep the patient and the environment dry. Six of these procedures are discussed below according to the techniques used, the types of incontinence they are used for, and the characteristics of the patients for whom the techniques are most useful. This information is summarized in Table 113-11. All of the patient-dependent procedures generally involve the patient's continuous, self-monitoring use of a record such as the one depicted in Fig. 113-5, and the caregiver-dependent procedures usually involve a record such as the one in Fig. 113-6.

Pelvic muscle (Kegel) exercises are used to treat stress incontinence in women and are also used occasionally in men. Recent studies suggest that pelvic muscle exercises may also be effective for urge and mixed stress-urge incontinence.[51,52] These exercises consist of repetitive contractions of the pelvic floor muscles. This procedure is taught by having the patient interrupt voiding to get a sense of the muscles being used or by having a woman patient squeeze the examiner's finger during a vaginal exam (without doing a Valsalva maneuver, which is opposite of the intended effect). Once learned, the exercises should be practiced many times throughout the day, both during voiding and at other times. Pelvic muscle exercises may be done in conjunction with biofeedback procedures, which can be especially helpful for women who bear down (increasing intraabdominal pressure) when attempting to contract pelvic floor muscles.

Biofeedback procedures involve the use of bladder, rectal, or vaginal pressure or electrical activity recordings to train patients to contract pelvic floor muscles and relax the bladder. Studies have shown that these techniques can be very effective for managing both stress and urge incontinence, even in elderly patients.[53] The use of biofeedback techniques may be limited by their requirements for equipment and trained personnel; in addition, some of these techniques are relatively invasive and require the use of bladder or rectal catheters, or both. Vaginal cones, which are weights held in the vagina, have been used as an adjunct to pelvic muscle exercises and biofeedback. Electrical stimulation, introduced either vaginally or rectally, has also been used to help train muscles in the management of both stress and urge incontinence. Electrical stimulation techniques are not acceptable to many patients and have not been well studied or used to any great degree in the elderly population in the United States.

Other forms of patient-dependent training procedures include behavioral training and bladder retraining. Behavioral training involves the educational components taught during biofeedback, without the use of biofeedback equipment. Patients are taught pelvic muscle exercises and strategies to manage urgency and are taught to use bladder records regularly. There is some evidence that these techniques are as effective as biofeedback in a selected group of functional, motivated elderly patients.[54] Bladder retraining as described here is similar to "bladder drill," which has been used successfully to treat urge incontinence in young women. An example of a bladder-retraining protocol is shown in Table 113-12. This protocol is also applicable to patients who have had an indwelling catheter for monitoring of urinary output during a period of acute illness or for treatment of urinary retention with overflow incontinence. Such catheters should always be removed as soon as possible, and this type of bladder-retraining protocol should enable most indwelling catheters to be re-

TABLE 113-11

Examples of Behaviorally Oriented Training Procedures for Urinary Incontinence

Procedure	Definition	Types of Incontinence	Comments
Patient-dependent			
Pelvic muscle (Kegel) exercises	Repetitive contraction of pelvic floor muscles	Stress	Requires adequate function and motivation. May be done in conjunction with biofeedback.
Biofeedback	Use of bladder, rectal, or vaginal pressure recordings to train patients to contract pelvic floor muscles and relax bladder	Stress and urge	Requires equipment and trained personnel. Relatively invasive. Requires adequate cognitive and physical function and motivation.
Behavioral training	Use of educational components of biofeedback, bladder records, pelvic muscle and other behavioral exercises	Stress and urge	Requires trained therapist, adequate cognitive and physical functioning, and motivation.
Bladder retraining*	Progressive lengthening or shortening of intervoiding interval, with adjunctive techniques,† intermittent catheterization used in patients recovering from overdistension injuries with persistent retention	Acute (e.g., postcatheterization with urge or overflow, poststroke)	Goal is to restore normal pattern of voiding and continence. Requires adequate cognitive and physical function and motivation.
Caregiver-dependent			
Scheduled toileting or prompted voiding	Routine toileting at regular intervals (scheduled toileting) or offering the opportunity to toilet at regular intervals (prompted voiding); sometimes with use of adjunctive techniques	Urge and functional	Goal is to prevent wetting episodes. Can be used in patients with impaired cognitive or physical functioning. Requires staff or caregiver availability and motivation.
Habit training	Variable toileting schedule with positive reinforcement and adjunctive techniques†	Urge and functional	Goal is to prevent wetting episodes. Can be used in patients with impaired cognitive or physical functioning. Requires staff or caregiver availability and motivation.

*See Table 113-12.
† Techniques to trigger voiding (running water, stroking thigh, suprapubic tapping), completely empty bladder (bending forward, suprapubic pressure), and alterations of fluid or diuretic intake patterns.
SOURCE: From Kane et al,[23] with permission.

moved from patients in acute care hospitals as well as some in long-term care settings. A patient who continues to have difficulty voiding after 1 to 2 weeks of such a bladder-retraining protocol should be examined for other potentially reversible causes of voiding difficulties, such as those mentioned in the section above on acute incontinence. When difficulties persist, a urologic referral should be considered in order to rule out correctable lower-genitourinary pathologic conditions.

The goal of caregiver-dependent procedures such as habit training, prompted voiding, and scheduled toileting is to prevent incontinence episodes, rather than restore a normal pattern of voiding and

TABLE 113-12

Examples of a Bladder Retraining Protocol

Objective: To restore a normal pattern of voiding and continence after the removal of an indwelling catheter.*

1. Remove the indwelling catheter (clamping the catheter before removal is not necessary).
2. Treat urinary tract infection if present.†
3. Initiate a toileting schedule. Begin by toileting the patient
   a. Upon awakening
   b. Every 2 hours during the day and evening
   c. Before getting into bed
   d. Every 4 hours at night
4. Monitor the patient's voiding and continence pattern with a record‡ that allows for the recording of
   a. Frequency, timing, and amount of continent voids
   b. Frequency, timing, and amount of incontinence episodes
   c. Fluid intake pattern
   d. Postvoid or intermittent catheter volume
5. If the patient is having difficulty voiding (complete urinary retention or very low urine outputs, e.g., <240 ml in an 8-hour period while fluid intake is adequate):
   a. Perform in and out catheterization, recording volume obtained, every 6 to 8 hours until residual values are <100 ml.§
   b. Instruct the patient on techniques to trigger voiding (e.g., running water, stroking inner thigh, suprapubic tapping) and to help completely empty bladder (e.g., bending forward, suprapubic pressure, double voiding).
6. If the patient is voiding frequently (i.e., more often than every 2 hours):
   a. Perform postvoid residual determination to ensure the patient is completely emptying the bladder.
   b. Encourage the patient to delay voiding as long as possible and instruct him or her to use techniques to help completely empty bladder (above).
7. If the patient continues to have frequency and nocturia, with or without urgency and incontinence, in the absence of infection:
   a. Rule out other reversible causes (e.g., medication effects, hyperglycemia, congestive heart failure).
   b. Consider urodynamic evaluation to rule out bladder instability (unstable bladder, detrusor hyperreflexia).

*Indwelling catheters should be removed from all patients who do not have an indication for their acute or chronic use (see text and Table 113-13). Clamping routines have never been shown to be helpful and are not appropriate for patients who have had overdistended bladders.

†Significant bacteriuria with pyuria (>10 white blood cells per high power field on a spun specimen).

‡See Fig. 113-6.

§In patients who have been in urinary retention, it may take days or weeks for the bladder to regain normal function. If residuals remain high, urologic consultation should be considered before committing the patient to a chronic indwelling catheter.

SOURCE: From Kane et al,[23] with permission.

complete continence. Such procedures have also been referred to as "habit retraining," "prompted voiding," and "contingency management techniques." Scheduled toileting involves putting the patient on the toilet at regular intervals, usually every 2 hours during the day and every 4 hours during the evening and night. Prompted voiding involves offering the opportunity to toilet on a regular basis, but not automatically toileting the patient. Habit training involves a schedule of toiletings or prompted voidings that is modified according to the patient's pattern of continent voids and incontinence episodes, as demonstrated by a monitoring record such as that shown in Fig. 113-6. Positive reinforcement is offered for continent voids, and neutral reinforcement employed when incontinence occurs. Adjunctive techniques to prompt voiding (e.g., running of tap water, stroking of the inner thigh, or suprapubic tapping) and to help empty the bladder completely (e.g., having the patient bend forward after completion of voiding) may be helpful in some patients. The success of habit training and scheduled toileting procedures is largely dependent on the knowledge and motivation of the caregivers who are implementing them, rather than on the physical functional and mental status of the incontinent patient. These techniques are not feasible in home settings without available caregivers. In order for these types of training procedures to be feasible and cost-effective in the nursing home setting, the amount of time generally spent by the nursing staff in changing patients after incontinence episodes should not be exceeded by the time and effort necessary to implement such training procedures.[55] Targeting these procedures to selected patients, such as those with less frequent voiding and larger bladder capacities or voided volumes, may enhance their cost-effectiveness.[56–58]

Surgery

Surgery should be considered for elderly women with stress incontinence that continues to be bothersome after attempts at nonsurgical treatment and for women with a significant degree of pelvic prolapse. As with many other surgical procedures, patient selection and the experience of the surgeon are critical to success. Any woman being considered for surgical therapy should have a thorough evaluation, including urodynamic tests, before undergoing the procedure. Women with mixed stress incontinence and detrusor motor instability may also benefit from surgery,[59] especially if the clinical history and urodynamic findings suggest that stress incontinence is the predominant problem. In some patients this may be difficult to determine, and a trial of medical therapy as discussed above would be appropriate. Newly modified techniques of bladder neck suspension can be done with minimal risks and are highly successful in achieving continence.[60] Urinary retention can occur after surgery, but it is usually transient and can be managed by intermittent catheter drainage.

Surgery may be indicated in men in whom incontinence is associated with anatomically and/or urodynamically documented outflow obstruction. Men who have experienced an episode of complete urinary retention are likely to have another episode within a short period of time and should have a prostatic resection, as should men with incontinence associated with enough residual urine to be causing recurrent symptomatic infections or hydronephrosis. The decision about surgery in men who do not meet these criteria must be an individual one, weighing carefully the degree to which the symptoms bother the patient, the potential benefits of surgery (obstructive symptoms often respond better than irritative symptoms), and the risks of surgery (which may be minimal with newer prostate resection techniques). Several recent articles discuss these issues in detail,[61–63] and a Veterans Administration Cooperative Study involving a randomized trial of surgical versus medical follow-up for men with moderately symptomatic prostatic hyperplasia is currently underway.

A small number of elderly patients, especially men who have stress incontinence related to sphincter damage due to previous transurethral surgery, may benefit from the surgical implantation of an artificial urinary sphincter.

Catheters and Catheter Care

Three basic types of catheters and catheterization procedures are used for the management of urinary incontinence: external catheters, intermittent straight catheterization, and chronic indwelling catheterization. External catheters generally consist of some type of condom connected to a drainage system. Improvements in design and observance of proper procedure and skin care when applying the catheter decrease the risk of skin irritation, as well as the frequency with which the catheter falls off. Studies of complications associated with the use of these devices have been limited. Existing data suggest that patients with external catheters are at increased risk of developing symptomatic infection.[64] External catheters should only be used to manage intractable incontinence in male patients who do not have urinary retention and who are extremely physically dependent. As with incontinence undergarments and padding, these devices should not be used as a matter of convenience, since they may foster dependency. Contrary to popular belief, urine specimens that accurately reflect bladder urine can be collected from male patients with external catheters simply by cleaning the penis with povidone-iodine (Betadine), applying a new catheter, and collecting the first urine the patient voids.[25] Using this simple technique avoids false-positive cultures and the discomfort of straight catheterization in patients suspected of having an infection. An external catheter for use in female patients is now commercially available, but its safety and effectiveness have not been well documented in the elderly population.

Intermittent catheterization can help in the management of patients with urinary retention and overflow incontinence. The procedure can be carried out by either the patient or a caregiver and involves straight catheterization two to four times daily, depending on residual urine volumes. In the home setting, the catheter should be kept clean (but not necessarily sterile). Studies conducted largely among younger paraplegic patients have shown that this technique is practical and reduces the risk of symptomatic infection compared with the risk associated with chronic catheterization. Self-intermittent catheterization has also been shown to be feasible for elderly female outpatients who are functional and willing and able to catheterize themselves.[65] However, studies carried out in young paraplegic patients and elderly female outpatients cannot automatically be extrapolated to an elderly man or institutionalized population. The technique may be useful for certain patients in acute care hospitals or nursing homes, such as women who have undergone bladder neck suspension; it may also be useful following removal of an indwelling catheter in a bladder-retraining protocol (Table 113-12). However, the practicality and safety of this procedure in a long-term care setting have never been documented. Elderly nursing home patients, especially men, may be difficult to catheterize, and the anatomic abnormalities commonly found in elderly patients' lower urinary tracts may increase the risk of infection due to repeated straight catheterizations. In addition, using this technique in an institutional setting (which may have an abundance of organisms relatively resistant to many commonly used antimicrobial agents) may yield an unacceptable risk of nosocomial infections, and using sterile catheter trays for these procedures would be very expensive; thus it may be extremely difficult to implement such a program in a typical nursing home setting.

Chronic indwelling catheterization is overused in some settings, and when used for periods of up to 10 years has been shown to increase the incidence of a number of other complications, including chronic bacteriuria, bladder stones, periurethral abscesses, and even bladder cancer. Elderly nursing home patients managed by this technique, especially men, are at relatively high risk of developing symptomatic infections.[66,67] Given these risks, it seems appropriate to recommend that the use of chronic indwelling catheters be limited to certain specific situations (Table 113-13). When indwelling catheterization is used, cer-

TABLE 113-13

Indications for Chronic Indwelling Catheter Use

- Urinary retention that
  - Is causing persistent overflow incontinence, symptomatic infections, or renal dysfunction
  - Cannot be corrected surgically or medically
  - Cannot be managed practically with intermittent catheterization
- Skin wounds, pressure sores, or irritations that are being contaminated by incontinent urine
- Care of terminally ill or severely impaired for whom bed and clothing changes are uncomfortable or disruptive
- Preference of patient or caregiver when patient has failed to respond to more specific treatments

SOURCE: From Kane et al,[23] with permission.

TABLE 113-14

Key Principles of Chronic Indwelling Catheter Care

Maintain sterile, closed, gravity drainage system.
Avoid breaking the closed system.
Use clean techniques in emptying and changing the drainage system; wash hands between patients in institutionalized setting.
Secure the catheter to the upper thigh or lower abdomen to avoid perineal contamination and urethral irritation due to movement of the catheter.
Avoid frequent and vigorous cleaning of the catheter entry site; washing with soapy water once per day is sufficient.
Do not routinely irrigate.
If bypassing occurs in the absence of obstruction, consider the possibility of a bladder spasm, which can be treated with a bladder relaxant.
If catheter obstruction occurs frequently, increase the patient's fluid intake and acidify the urine by dilute acidic irrigations.
Do not routinely use prophylactic or suppressive urinary antiseptics or antimicrobials.
Do not do routine surveillance cultures to guide management of individual patients because all chronically catheterized patients have bacteriuria (which is often polymicrobial) and the organisms change frequently.
Do not treat infection unless the patient develops symptoms; symptoms may be nonspecific, and other possible sources of infection should be carefully excluded before attributing symptoms to the urinary tract.
If a patient develops frequent symptomatic urinary tract infections, a genitourinary evaluation should be considered to rule out pathologic lesions such as stones, periurethral or prostatic abscesses, or chronic pyelonephritis.

SOURCE: From Kane et al,[23] with permission.

tain principles of catheter care should be observed in order to attempt to minimize complications (Table 113-14).

FECAL INCONTINENCE

Fecal incontinence is less common than urinary incontinence. Its occurrence is relatively unusual in elderly patients who are continent with regard to urine; however, a large proportion (30 to 50 percent) of elderly patients with frequent urinary incontinence also have episodes of fecal incontinence, especially in institutional settings. This coexistence suggests common pathophysiological mechanisms.

Defecation, like urination, is a physiological process that involves smooth and striated muscles, central and peripheral innervation, coordination of reflex responses, mental awareness, and physical ability to get to a toilet. Disruption of any of these factors can lead to fecal incontinence.

TABLE 113-15

Causes of Fecal Incontinence

Fecal impaction
Laxative overuse or abuse
Hyperosmotic enteral feedings
Neurological disorders
  Dementia
  Stroke
  Spinal cord disease
Colorectal disorders
  Diarrheal illnesses
  Diabetic autonomic neuropathy
  Rectal sphincter damage

The most common causes of fecal incontinence are problems with constipation and laxative use, neurological disorders, and colorectal disorders (Table 113-15). In patients who are fed by enteral tubes, hyperosmotic feedings can precipitate diarrhea and fecal incontinence. Diluting the feedings or using slow continuous infusion is sometimes helpful. Constipation is extremely common in elderly persons and, when chronic, can lead to fecal impaction and incontinence. The hard stool (or scybalum) of fecal impaction irritates the rectum and results in the production of mucus and fluid. This fluid leaks around the mass of impacted stool and precipitates incontinence. Constipation is difficult to define; technically it indicates fewer than three bowel movements per week, although many patients use the term to describe difficult passage of hard stools or a feeling of incomplete evacuation. Poor dietary and toilet habits, immobility, and chronic laxative abuse are the most common causes of constipation in the elderly person (Table 113-16).

TABLE 113-16

Causes of Constipation

Diet low in bulk and fluid
Poor toilet habits
Immobility
Laxative abuse
Colorectal disorders
  Colonic tumor, stricture, volvulus
  Painful anal and rectal conditions (hemorrhoids, fissures)
Depression
Drugs
  Anticholinergic
  Calcium channel blockers
  Narcotic
Diabetic autonomic neuropathy
Endocrine or metabolic
  Hypothyroidism
  Hypercalcemia
  Hypokalemia

TABLE 113-17

Drugs Used to Treat Constipation

Type	*Examples*	*Mechanism of Action*
Stool softeners or lubricants	Dioctyl sodium succinate Mineral oil	Soften and lubricate fecal mass.
Bulk-forming agents	Bran Psyllium mucilloid	Increase fecal bulk and retain fluid in bowel lumen.
Osmotic cathartics	Milk of magnesia Magnesium sulfate or citrate	Poorly absorbed salts retain fluid in bowel lumen; increase net secretions of fluid in small intestine.
Stimulants or irritants	Cascara Senna Bisacodyl Phenolphthalein	Alter intestinal mucosal permeability; stimulate muscle activity and fluid secretions.
Enemas	Tap water Saline Sodium phosphate Oil	Induce reflex evacuations.
Suppositories	Glycerin Bisacodyl	Cause mucosal irritation.

Appropriate management of constipation prevents fecal impaction and resultant fecal incontinence. The first step in managing constipation in the elderly patient is the identification of all possible contributory factors. If the constipation is a new complaint and represents a recent change in bowel habit, colonic disease, endocrine or metabolic disorders, depression, or drug side effects should be considered. Proper diet, including adequate fluid intake and bulk, is important in preventing constipation. Crude fiber in amounts of 4 to 6 g (equivalent to 3 or 4 tablespoons of bran) a day is generally recommended. Improving mobility, body positioning during toileting, and the timing and setting of toileting are all important in managing constipation. Defecation should optimally take place in a private, unrushed atmosphere and should take advantage of the gastrocolic reflex, which occurs a few minutes after eating. These factors are often overlooked, especially in nursing home settings.

A variety of drugs can be used to treat constipation (Table 113-17). These drugs are often overused; in fact, their overuse may cause an atonic colon and contribute to chronic constipation ("cathartic colon"). Laxative drugs can also contribute to fecal incontinence. Rational use of these drugs requires knowing the nature of the constipation and quality of the stool. For example, stool softeners will not help a patient with a large mass of already soft stool in the rectum. These patients would benefit from a glycerin or irritant suppository. The use of osmotic and irritant laxatives should be limited to no more than three or four times a week.

Fecal incontinence from neurological disorders is sometimes amenable to biofeedback therapy, although many elderly demented patients are unable to cooperate. For those patients with end-stage dementia, a program of alternating constipating agents (if necessary) and laxatives in a routine schedule (such as giving laxatives and enemas three times a week) is effective in controlling defecation in many patients with fecal incontinence. Functionally dependent patients should be toileted regularly after a meal to take advantage of or possibly regain the gastrocolic reflex. Experience suggests that these measures should permit management of even severely disoriented patients. As a last resort, specially designed incontinence undergarments are sometimes helpful in managing fecal incontinence and preventing complications.

REFERENCES

1. Mohide EA: The prevalence and scope of urinary incontinence. *Clin Geriatr Med* 2:639, 1986.
2. Herzog AR, Fultz NH: Prevalence and incidence of urinary incontience in community-dwelling populations. *J Am Geriatr Soc* 38:273, 1990.
3. Diokno AC et al: Prevalence of urinary incontinence and other urological symptoms in the non-institutionalized elderly. *J Urol* 136:1022, 1986.
4. Ouslander JG et al: Urinary incontinence in elderly nursing home patients. *JAMA* 248:1194, 1982.

5. Sier H et al: Urinary incontinence among geriatric patients in an acute care hospital. *JAMA* 257:1767, 1987.
6. Ouslander et al: Incontinence among elderly community-dwelling dementia patients: Characteristics, management, and impact on caregivers. *J Am Geriatr Soc* 38:440, 1990.
7. Resnick NM, Ouslander JG (eds): NIH Consensus Conference on Urinary Incontinence. *J Am Geriatr Soc* 38:263, 1990.
8. Gartley C: *Managing Incontinence: A Guide to Living with the Loss of Bladder Control.* Ottowa, IL, Jameson Books, 1985.
9. Wyman JF et al: Psychosocial impact of urinary incontinence in the community-dwelling population. *J Am Geriatr Soc* 38:282, 1990.
10. Mitteness LS: Knowledge and beliefs about urinary incontinence in adulthood and old age. *J Am Geriatr Soc* 38:374, 1990.
11. Ouslander JG, Kane RL: The costs of urinary incontinence in nursing homes. *Med Care* 22:69, 1984.
12. Hu T-W: Impact of urinary incontinence on health-care costs. *J Am Geriatr Soc* 38:292, 1990.
13. Wein AJ: Lower urinary tract function and pharmacologic management of lower urinary tract dysfunction. *Urol Clin* 14:273, 1987.
14. Abramsi P et al: *Standardization of terminology of lower urinary tract function. Neurourol Urodynam* 7:403, 1988.
15. Ouslander JG, Bruskewitz RC: Micturition in the aging patient, in Stollerman GH (ed): *Advances in Internal Medicine.* Chicago, Year Book, 1989, vol. 34, p. 165
16. Leach GE, Yip CM: Urologic and urodynamic evaluation of the elderly population. *Clin Geriatr Med* 2:731, 1986.
17. Diokno AC et al: Clinical and cystometric characteristics of continent and incontinent noninstitutionalized elderly. *J Urol* 140:567, 1988.
18. Ouslander JG et al: Genitourinary dysfunction in a geriatric outpatient population. *J Am Geriatr Soc* 34:507, 1986.
19. Diokno et al: Urinary incontinence in elderly women: Urodynamic evaluation. *J Am Geriatr Soc* 35:940, 1987.
20. Fantl JA et al: Urinary incontinence in community-dwelling women: Clinical, urodynamic, and severity characteristics. *Am J Obstet Gynecol* 162:946, 1990.
21. Resnick NM, Yalla SV: Detrusor hyperactivity with contractile function: An unrecognized but common cause of incontinence in elderly patients. *JAMA* 257:2076, 1987.
22. Ouslander JG: Geriatric urinary incontinence. *Dis Mon* 38(2):67, 1992.
23. Kane RL et al: *Essentials of Clinical Geriatrics,* 2d ed. New York, McGraw-Hill, 1989.
24. Ouslander JG et al: Development and testing of an incontinence monitoring record. *J Am Geriatr Soc* 1986.
25. Ouslander JG et al: An accurate method to obtain urine for culture in men with external catheters. *Arch Intern Med* 147:286, 1987.
26. Boscia JA et al: Epidemiology of bacteriuria in an elderly ambulatory population. *Am J Med* 80:208, 1986.
27. Boscia JA et al: Lack of association between bacteriuria and symptoms in the elderly. *Am J Med* 81:979, 1986.
28. Boscia JA et al: Therapy vs. no therapy for bacteriuria in elderly ambulatory nonhospitalized women. *JAMA* 257:1067, 1987.
29. Nicolle LE et al: Bacteriuria in elderly institutionalized men. *N Engl J Med* 309:1420, 1983.
30. Nicolle LE et al: Prospective randomized comparison of therapy and no therapy for asymptomatic bacteriuria in institutionalized elderly women. *JAMA* 83:27, 1987.
31. Ouslander JG: Asymptomatic bacteriuria and incontinence. *J Am Geriatr Soc* 37:197, 1989.
32. Hilton P, Staton SL: Algorithmic method for assessing urinary incontinence in elderly women. *Br Med J* 282:940, 1981.
33. Resnick NM et al: An algorithmic approach to urinary incontinence in the elderly. *Clin Res* 34:832A, 1986.
34. Ouslander JG et al: Prospective evaluation of an assessment strategy for geriatric urinary incontinence. *J Am Geriatr Soc* 37:715, 1989.
35. Ouslander JG et al: Simple vs. multichannel cystometry in the evaluation of bladder function in an incontinent geriatric population. *J Urol* 140:1482, 1988.
36. Ouslander JG et al: Simplified tests of lower urinary tract function in the evaluation of geriatric urinary incontinence. *J Am Geriatr Soc* 37:706, 1989.
37. Burgio KL et al: *Staying Dry. A Practical Guide to Bladder Control.* Baltimore, Johns Hopkins University Press, 1989.
38. Brink CA, Wells TJ: Environmental support for geriatric incontinence: Toilets, toilet supplements and external equipment. *Clin Geriatr Med* 2:829, 1986.
39. Brink CA: Absorbent pads, garments, and management strategies. *J Am Geriatr Soc* 38:368, 1990.
40. Ouslander JG, Sier HC: Drug therapy for geriatric incontinence. *Clin Geriatr Med* 2:789, 1986.
41. Ray WA et al: Psychotropic drug use and the risk of hip fracture. *N Engl J Med* 316:363, 1987.
42. Zorzitto ML et al: Effectiveness on propantheline bromide in the treatment of geriatric patients with detrusor instability. *Neurourol Urodynam* 5:133, 1986.
43. Tobin GW, Brocklehurst JC: The management of urinary incontinence in local authority residential homes for the elderly. *Age Ageing* 15:292, 1986.
44. Ouslander JG et al: Habit training and oxybutynin for incontinence in nursing home patients. *J Am Geriatr Soc* 36:40, 1988.
45. Zorzitto ML et al: Oxybutynin chloride for geriatric urinary dysfunction: A double-blind placebo-controlled study. *Age Ageing* 18:195, 1989.
46. Wells T et al: Pelvic muscle exercise for stress urinary incontinence in elderly women. *J Am Geriatr Soc* 39:785, 1991.
47. Finkbeiner AE: Is bathanechol chloride clinically effective in promoting bladder emptying? A literature review. *J Urol* 134:443, 1985.
48. Caine M: The present role of alpha-adrenergic blockers in the treatment of benign prostatic hypertrophy. *J Urol* 136:1, 1986.
49. Burgio KL, Burgio LD: Behavior therapies for urinary incontinence in the elderly. *Clin Geriatr Med* 2:809, 1986.

50. Hadley E: Bladder training and related therapies for urinary incontinence in older people. *JAMA* 256(3):372, 1986.
51. Wells TJ: Pelvic (floor) muscle exercises. *J Am Geriatr Soc* 38:333, 1990.
52. Fantl JA et al: Efficacy of bladder training in older women with urinary incontinence. *JAMA* 265:609, 1991.
53. Burgio KL et al: Urinary incontinence in elderly—bladder–sphincter biofeedback and toilet skills training. *Ann Intern Med* 104:507, 1985.
54. Burton JR et al: Behavioral training for urinary incontinence in elderly patients. *J Am Geriatr Soc* 36:693, 1988.
55. McCormick KA et al: Nursing management of urinary incontinence in geriatric inpatients. *Nursing Clin North Am* 23(1):231, 1988.
56. Schnelle JF et al: Prompted voiding or urinary incontinence in nursing home patients: A behavioral management approach for nursing home staff. *J Am Geriatr Soc* 37:1051, 1989.
57. Schnelle JF et al: Management of patient continence in long term care facilities. *Gerontology* 30:373, 1990.
58. Schnelle JF et al: Reduction of urinary incontinence in nursing homes: Does it reduce or increase costs? *J Am Geriatr Soc* 36:34, 1988.
59. McGuire EJ, Savastano JA: Stress incontinence and detrusor instability/urge incontinence. *Neurourol Urodynam* 4:313, 316, 1985.
60. Schmidbauer CP et al: Surgical treatment for female geriatric incontinence. *Clin Geriatr Med* 2:759, 1986.
61. Barry MJ et al: Watchful waiting vs immediate transurethral resection for symptomatic prostatism. *JAMA* 259:3010, 1988.
62. Fowler FJ et al: Symptom status and quality of life following prostatectomy. *JAMA* 259:3018, 1988.
63. Wennberg JE et al: An assessment of prostatectomy for benign urinary tract obstruction. *JAMA* 259(20):3027, 1988.
64. Ouslander JG et al: External catheter use and urinary tract infections among male nursing home patients. *J Am Geriatr Soc* 35:1063, 1987.
65. Bennett CJ, Diokno AC: Clean intermitten self-catheterization in the elderly. *Urology* 24:43, 1984.
66. Ouslander JG et al: Complications of chronic indwelling urinary catheters among male nursing home patients: A prospective study. *J Urol* 138:1191, 1987.
67. Warren JW et al: Fever, bacteremia, and death as complications of bacteriuria in women and long-term urethral catheters. *J Infect Dis* 155(6):1151, 1987.

Chapter 114

ERECTILE DYSFUNCTION (IMPOTENCE)

Stanley G. Korenman

Erectile dysfunction or impotence commonly affects older men and is generally of organic origin and amenable to therapy. Its prevalence depends on the definition but is likely to exceed 10 million Americans, most of them over the age of 65.

DEFINITIONS

Men experience a variety of degrees of erectile failure. Erectile dysfunction may be defined as the inability to attain or sustain an erection of sufficient rigidity for vaginal penetration in 50 percent or more of sexual attempts. However, it is appropriate to consider those with a lesser degree of disability as candidates for evaluation and therapy. Other sexual dysfunctions that may occur separately or may be associated with erectile dysfunction include loss of libido and failure of ejaculation. Loss of libido characterizes severely hypogonadal men, whether due to testicular or to hypothalamic-pituitary failure. Intercurrent illness, drugs, and psychiatric problems may also be associated with a markedly reduced libido.

Nocturnal penile tumescence (NPT) denotes spontaneous erections occurring 4 to 8 times nightly, predominantly during rapid eye movement (REM) sleep. NPT declines in frequency with age, as does REM sleep. Erectile quality during NPT, as measured by penile rigidity, declines with age as well. Hypogonadism results in decreased NPT.

Early ejaculation often presages the development of full-blown impotence, so this symptom need not be attributed to an altered psychological state in men with a history of normal erectile duration. In many instances, sexual dysfunction results in withdrawal from sexual activities. Such patients should be considered impotent. Ejaculatory capability is preserved in most cases of impotence.

EPIDEMIOLOGY

A few studies have attempted to determine the age-dependent prevalence of impotence in the population. Of these 1–3 only the study of Kinsey dealt with men who were not identified through a medical source. As shown in Fig. 114-1, impotence (including an absence of sexual activity) increases rapidly after age 50. Conservative estimates of the prevalence of impotence are 5 to 10 percent in the sixth decade, 20 percent in the seventh, 30 to 40 percent in the eighth, and greater than 50 percent in the ninth.

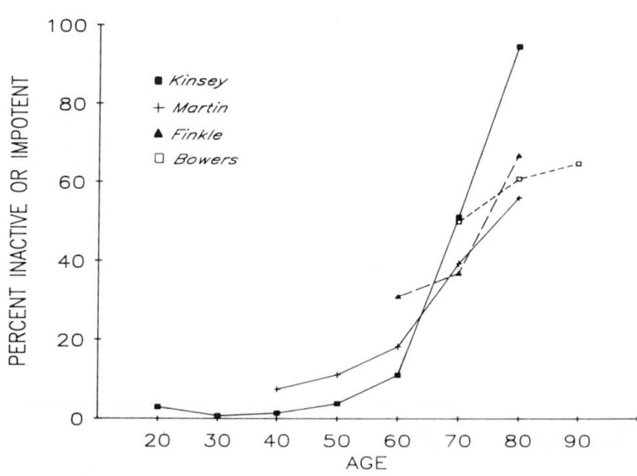

FIGURE 114-1
Reported prevalence of impotence and sexual inactivity in population studies.

TABLE 114-1

Incidence of Impotence in Various Diseases

Disorder Type	Disorder	Number	Percent Impotent
Genetic	Diabetes mellitus	541	35
	Hemochromatosis	41	22
	Cystic fibrosis	30	30
	Celiac disease	26	19
Metabolic	Uremia	256	68
	Uremia + Transplant	24	21
	Alcoholism	120	69
	Graves' disease	7	56
Vascular	Hypertension		25
	Aortoiliac disease	413	53
	Coronary HT disease	131	64
Neurologic	Stroke	78	70
	Multiple sclerosis	258	71
	Postconcussion	19	58
Inflammatory	Obstructive pulmonary	20	35
	Bowel disease	9	11
	Abdominal-perineal resection	7	55
	Rectal Anastomosis	5	40
Neoplastic	Prostate postop	152	47
	Penis postiridium	36	28
	Testis postcure	74	25
	Rectal postop	41	5
	Hodgkin's post Rx	41	58
Psychiatric	Schizophrenia on	26	54 Male
	neuroleptics	29	30 Female

MEDICAL DISEASES

A substantial level of erectile dysfunction has been reported in medical disorders (Table 114-1). Unfortunately, these analyses did not compare the prevalence in disease groups with healthy age-matched controls.

Vascular Disease

The majority of cases of secondary impotence are associated with the complications of atherosclerosis.[4–7] Myocardial infarction, stroke, and peripheral vascular disease have high impotence rates (Table 114-1). There is evidence that the penile blood pressure falls with an increasing number of cardiovascular risk factors and that low penile blood pressure significantly predicts cardiovascular events.[5,8]

Diabetes Mellitus

Erectile dysfunction in diabetes mellitus has been attributed to endocrinopathy, neuropathy, and vascular disease. The evidence of several large series suggested a prevalence of impotence of about 50 percent in unselected diabetics, rising steadily with age to reach 98 percent in a geriatric diabetes clinic.[9] In our studies, insulin-dependent diabetes mellitus (IDDM) usually resulted in erectile dysfunction years after diagnosis and was associated with normal penile blood pressure in 60 percent of cases.[9] In non-insulin-dependent diabetes mellitus (NIDDM), impotence was discovered at a variable time, from before the diagnosis to several years thereafter, depending inversely on the age at onset of diabetes. NPT was almost invariably abnormal in impotent diabetics whether compared with normal subjects or with potent diabetics.

The role of hypogonadism in diabetic impotence remains unclear. Only recently has significant evidence been adduced that older men with mild, untreated NIDDM have lower bioavailable and total testosterone levels than age-matched controls.[10] These patients were not studied for potency.[10] In IDDM, a recent report suggests that testicular infiltration with collagenous material may play a role in Leydig cell dysfunction.[11] We believe that hypogonadism, when present, contributes one more risk factor for erectile dysfunction in patients with diabetes as well as others.

Neurogenic factors in diabetic impotence were proposed on the basis of studies showing that slowed motor nerve conduction velocity correlated with secondary impotence. Clinical neuropathy, age, treatment modality, or quality of control could not distinguish impotent from potent patients.[12] However, abnormal nerve conduction velocity reached 35 percent in our series of nondiabetic impotent subjects.

The major pathogenetic role of arteriosclerotic vascular disease in diabetic impotence has become appreciated.[13–15] In patients with severe vascular disease, twice as many of the diabetic patients were impotent compared with nondiabetic patients. This is likely to be due to increased intrinsic ischemic damage to the corpus cavernosal arterial and sinusoidal smooth muscle and fibrosis of the intersinusoidal space. Renal failure, hyperlipidemia, hypertension, and peripheral vascular disease, which are so common in diabetes, all contribute to the likelihood of erectile dysfunction. Thus, diabetic persons have multiple risk factors for impotence that result in a much higher than expected prevalence for age.

Hypertension

Hypertension and its treatment result in an increased incidence of impotence. In one study, 20 percent of hypertensive patients were impotent prior to therapy, and impotence rates of greater than 30 percent occurred in all drug-treated groups.[16] Studies with age-matched controls or patients with similar conditions were not done. Patients regularly report the development of erectile dysfunction with initiation of antihypertensive therapy. Central and peripheral autonomic agents are especially implicated, but diuretics, α- and β-adrenergic blocking agents, angiotensin-converting enzyme inhibitors, and calcium channel blockers have all been reported to lead to erectile dysfunction. There is some evidence that reduction of the arterial blood pressure may accentuate the reduction in flow rate associated with vascular obstruction, so that the process of controlling the blood pressure may result in reduced penile filling.[8] It is essential to deal honestly with the possibility of erectile dysfunction in hypertensive persons initiating therapy.

Alcoholism

Alcoholism is associated with a high prevalence of impotence. Among the risk factors involved are hypogonadism with estrogen excess, autonomic neuropathy, and vascular disease associated with the smoking that almost invariably accompanies alcohol excess.

Neurologic Diseases

Neurologic diseases and pelvic surgery presumably affect potency by interrupting the autonomic fibers of the nervi erigentes that control the erectile process (see below) or the central processes responding to erotic stimuli. In the past few years those pathways have been traced in humans so that even radical prostatectomy may be carried out with preservation of potency in up to 70 percent of cases.[17]

Hypogonadism

Hypogonadism occurs frequently with increasing age. Its origin is not usually obvious, although testicular trauma, infections, irradiation, and chemical exposure are sometimes etiologically involved. Treatment with estrogens, gonadotropin releasing hormone (GnRH), cimetidine, ranitidine, and metoclopromide as well as ethanol often affect androgen availability. In older men, establishment of the hypogonadal state may be difficult because low androgen levels occur without a compensatory hypothalamic-pituitary response.[18,19] In severe cases of hypogonadism with erectile dysfunction, a gratifying response to testosterone therapy may be found.[20,21] However, the vast majority of trials with androgens demonstrated little success, because treatment solely with androgens was doomed to fail when vasculogenic factors were present.

Uremia

Uremia leads to a high prevalence of erectile dysfunction in association with many risk factors for the condition including anemia, refractory tissue hypogonadism, elevated prolactin levels, and zinc depletion. The vascular disease characterizing the underlying process in many of these patients also contributes importantly to erectile failure. The impact of erythropoietin therapy on uremic impotence has not yet been elucidated. Transplantation substantially reduces, but does not eliminate, impotence in subjects treated for uremia.

Other conditions associated with erectile dysfunction are noted in Table 114-1. In only a few cases have age-matched controls been employed to identify the specific-disease-associated risk.

MECHANISM OF ERECTION

Normal sexual function depends upon the interaction of libido and potency. Libido consists of desires (drives), thoughts (fantasies), and satisfactions (pleasures). Pelvic vasocongestion leading to erection conveys potency. Ejaculation involves separate neural and smooth muscle circuits from those responsible for erection. Over 90 percent of impotent men retain ejaculatory capacity. Androgens appear to play an important role in libido and the frequency of nonerotic or "reflex" erections including NPT and are required to stimulate the seminal vesicle and prostate to produce normal seminal fluid. Androgens do not seem to be involved acutely in erections associated with erotic stimuli.[20]

The neural, vascular, and muscular events responsible for the erectile process have become much better understood in the past few years. The central nervous system (CNS) responds to erotic signals by reversing tonic α-adrenergic suppression as well as stimulation of the thoracolumbar and sacral erection centers that activate the erectile nerves.[22] These emerge from the pelvic plexus and converge into cavernosal nerves whose postsynaptic terminals operate through the liberation of nitric oxide, to relax corpus cavernosal arterial and sinusoidal smooth muscle.[23–25] A doubling of the corporal arterial diameter provides a large increase in blood flow into the cavernosal sinuses distending them.[26] The distended sinusoids compress the subtunical venous plexus and penetrating veins that drain most of the body of the penis through the tunica albuginea, greatly reducing venous drainage.[27] Thus, an erection is caused by increased blood inflow and decreased outflow.

Detumescence may be passive or a consequence of α_1-sympathetic vasoconstrictor activity. Ejaculation occurs via both CNS and reflex arcs terminating in sympathetic nerve terminals in the testes, seminal vesicles, prostate, and pelvic smooth muscle structures.[22]

Masters and Johnson reported that with aging, erotogenic stimuli must be of greater intensity to produce a response.[28] Latency to erection increases. Penile filling slows, and there is increased venous drainage resulting in a less firm maximal erection. Often, time to ejaculation is prolonged, enhancing the quality of coitus. An increased absolute refractory period inhibits the development of the next erection. NPT declines in frequency, duration, and rigidity with age.[28,29] In many patients penile sensation decreases.

Erectile dysfunction has been shown to be associated with ultrastructural evidence of ischemic changes in the corpora cavernosa including loss of smooth muscle integrity, lipid infiltration, and intersinusoidal fibrosis.[30,31] Some investigators now believe that these intrinsic penile changes cause most impotence and that disorders of large vessels play a secondary role.[32] This tends to explain the poor therapeutic efficiency of vascular reconstruction in the treatment of impotence.

THE CLINICAL PROBLEM

The loss of erectile capacity has a debilitating effect on many men that permeates their entire lives. If impotence is associated with loss of a spouse or a divorce, then the man is apt to become socially isolated with its attendant ills. In the typical clinical scenario, secondary impotence begins slowly with loss of erectile duration during intercourse, followed by diminished erectile quality, inability to achieve a usable erection, loss of spontaneous A.M. erections, and, ultimately, inability to achieve any erection. The onset of impotence sometimes follows a major medical event such as thoracic or abdominal surgery or initiation of drug therapy for a medical condition.

The sexual partners often react predictably. The man withdraws from sexual efforts, fearing failure, and the conjugal bed becomes a place of anxiety. The couple loses intimacy. The partner may first feel unattractive and guilty, then angry at possible infidelities. Depending on the quality of the dyadic interaction, impotence can result in dissolution of the relationship, a tension-filled truce, or a resolution with determination to resolve the problem. It is important to understand the feelings and wishes of both partners by attempting to see them together and frankly discuss the problem and the diagnostic and therapeutic alternatives.

DIAGNOSTIC EVALUATION

History

The sexual and medical histories are of overwhelming importance in assessing the nature of a sexual dysfunction. The physician should determine whether erectile difficulty is indeed the problem and focus on its duration, as well as its progression over time. We determine the type and extent of current sexual activity, the presence of spontaneous (A.M.) erections, the quality and duration of best erections (full, partial, absence), their usability for coitus, and whether the erectile dysfunction is selective or with any partner. The present state should be compared with the patient's best and recent normal years. Ejaculatory capacity and alterations in penile sensation and ejaculatory volume should be recorded.

The physician should determine the level of libido expressed as interest in sex, thoughts or fantasies of a sexual nature, and the presence of spontaneous or erotogenic pelvic sensations in relation to the patient's historical norm. A substantial decline in libido suggests the possibility of hypogonadism or of clinical depression.

It should be possible from the history to determine the extent and progression of impotence, the risk factors present, and the likelihood it is organic in origin. The importance of erectile potency to the individual, the prior level of sexual satisfaction, and the impact of impotence on self-image will help to ascertain patient motivation toward diagnosis and therapy.

Erectile dysfunction is a couple's problem. Successful therapy depends to a great degree on partner-availability, interest, and health. The integrity of the sexual tissues of the partner depends on her menopausal status and its therapy. There are women, particularly in the geriatric age group, who must be prepared for a resurgence of erectile capability in their mate. It is mandatory in the evaluation to include the partner, discuss the erectile problem with her, and determine her view of sex and of the various therapeutic alternatives.

Erectile dysfunction may presage serious medical illness or be a consequence thereof.[7] A complete medical evaluation is mandatory including a psychiatric history and careful assessment of substance abuse and occupational and medication exposure. Evidence of atherosclerosis, hypertension, and diabetes would suggest a vascular cause while certain chemical agents and drugs might produce a neuropathy, inhibition of autonomic function, or hypogonadism.

Physical Examination

The physical examination should place special emphasis on evidence of hypogonadism including axillary and pubic hair loss, gynecomastia, and reduced testicular volume and density. Autonomic nervous system function may be tested by evaluating postural hypotension and heart rate responses to deep breathing. Penile size and shape and any plaque or fibrous tissue formation as well as prostate size and characteristics round out the genital examination.

Laboratory Testing

For patients who are not under medical care, there should be a full evaluation for unsuspected medical illness. The endocrine assessment should include A.M. fasting, measurements of luteinizing hormone (LH), and loosely bound or bioavailable testosterone (BT), as well as ultrasensitive thyroid-stimulating hormone (TSH). In the presence of hypogonadism a serum prolactin level should be determined. Both hyper- and hypothyroidism may be associated with impotence and are difficult to diagnose on clinical grounds, particularly in the geriatric population. The diagnosis of hypogonadism in the older man by hormone assay may be difficult. Because of increased testosterone (T) binding to sex hormone–binding globulin (SHBG), a very low concentration of non-SHBG-bound or BT may be found in the presence of a normal total T level.[19] If the LH level is elevated with a low BT level, then a presumptive diagnosis of hypogonadism may be made. However, most hypogonadal older men have low BT levels with normal to low gonadotropin levels, suggesting hypogonadotropic hypogonadism. Yet, the possibility that these men may have a pituitary adenoma and require an imaging study is remote. A normal prolactin test helps to rule out a pituitary tumor. We employ a BT level of <67 ng/dl to define hypogonadism because that figure is 2.5 standard deviations below the mean value for young men, and we suggest that similar ranges be adopted for other laboratories.[19]

SPECIFIC DIAGNOSTIC TESTS FOR ERECTILE DYSFUNCTION

Penile-Brachial Blood Pressure Index

The evaluation of impotence was advanced by the development of a simple, noninvasive method of assessing penile arterial integrity, the penile brachial pressure index (PBPI), which compares the penile and the brachial systolic blood pressures. When carefully done after relaxing the patient, the PBPI has been shown to be reasonably specific but not very sensitive.[33,34] Determination of the PBPI utilizes a portable mercury manometer connected to a 2.5-cm-wide infant cuff. A hand-held 10-MHz Doppler instrument is used to measure the systolic blood pressure at 10 and 2 o'clock on the penile shaft to get right- and left-sided corporal artery values. Brachial and penile pressures are measured after 5 minutes of rest in the supine position and remeasured after the patient performs bicycling motions with his legs in the air for 2 minutes or as long as he can. The PBPI is composed of four ratios, the ratio of penile to brachial blood pressure on each side resting and after exercise. Our criteria for abnormal responses are as follows:

1. One of the four ratios is ≤ 0.65.
2. A ≥ 0.15 decline in mean ratio between the supine and the exercise PBPI indicates a "pelvic steal" syndrome.
3. A mean ratio between 0.65 and 0.75 suggests a vascular component of impotence.

An abnormal PBPI suggests arteriogenic impotence and supports an evaluation for cardiovascular disease in patients without a known vascular condition. An abnormal test also supports the use of a full diagnostic dose of intracorporeal vasodilator solution in further testing.

Diagnostic Intracorporeal Vasodilator Injection

We employ diagnostic vasodilator injection to confirm the existence of vascular impotence, to assess the probability of major venous leakage, and to determine whether self-injection has a high probability of success in restoring erectile function.[35] Investigators have prepared a wide variety of testing solutions for this purpose utilizing various mixtures and concentrations of prostaglandin E_1 (PGE_1), phentolamine, and papaverine as well as other compounds. We employ 3 to 8 μg of PGE, with 100 to 250 μg of phentolamine, depending on the degree of vascular insufficiency and the likelihood of a neurogenic risk factor, injected laterally into the proximal penile shaft. The ensuing erection is examined at 5 minutes, and the patient asked to stimulate the penis for 5 additional minutes. The quality of erection at 10 minutes is rated as 5 (full, rigid), 4 (full, usable but not rigid), 3 (full but soft), 2 (partial), 1 (minimal), or 0 (no response). A normal sustained erection (4 and 5) suggests minimal vascular disease. Stage 3 responses suggest the presence of arterial disease. A weak or rapidly lost erection suggests severe arterial insufficiency or substantial venous leakage. The prevalence of priapism is much lower with PGE_1 than with papaverine. PGE_1 frequently causes local pain, especially in full dosage.

Nocturnal Penile Tumescence

The erections occurring during sleep (NPT) may be measured in a sleep laboratory,[29] using a Rigiscan monitor at home, or by employing techniques such as the stamp test and the Dacomed Snap Gauge, in which a ring is placed around the flaccid penis at bedtime and a broken ring in the morning indicates that at least one episode of rigidity has taken place. Normal NPT presupposes a psychogenic cause for impotence, and an abnormal response favors an organic basis. Enthusiasm for NPT measurement has declined since it was shown to relate poorly to erotic erectile capacity and to relate well to information obtained by history.[36,37] In our series, over 90 percent of impotent men over the age of 50 had abnormal NPT. Many investigators, including ourselves, no longer employ NPT testing, especially for older patients with secondary erectile dysfunction.

Duplex Scanning

Duplex scanning of penile arteries before and after vasodilator-induced erection can determine corporal arterial diameter and corporal arterial blood flow before and after intracorporeal vasodilation. It also predicts whether there will be a good response to therapeutic intracavernosal vasodilatation. It does not evaluate for pelvic steal.

Invasive Tests

Invasive diagnostic tests should be limited to unusual cases of penile trauma or total impotence in young men when arterial surgery, venous ligation, or venous sclerosis may be successful therapeutic alternatives. For other cases, especially in older men, the diagnostic value of arteriography, venography, or cavernosography remains highly questionable.

THERAPEUTIC INTERVENTIONS

Treatment for erectile dysfunction should be undertaken after thorough discussion of the alternatives with the couple. The physician must develop an understanding of the acceptability of the various alternatives to the couple. Management should be based on a risk-factor approach since the presence of hypogonadism does not rule out vascular impotence, combined arterial and veno-occlusive incompetence are not uncommon, and psychogenic factors, when present, do not preclude other diagnoses.

External Vacuum Devices

External vacuum devices have been available for treatment of impotence for over a decade and may be employed regardless of the cause of the impotence.[38–40] They generate an erection by placing a plastic cylinder around the penis and using a vacuum pump to produce cavernosal engorgement. Venous drainage is inhibited by the use of constrictor rings applied from the proximal end of the cylinder to the base of the penis. These devices provide a very satisfactory cost-effective solution to erectile dysfunction when the patient learns how to use them properly. The erection is induced only when needed. Tissues are not adversely affected. The usual coital pattern may be restored. The principal complications are reversible hematomas seen in a few patients, discomfort from the bands, and occasionally a cold temperature of the erect penis. Vacuum tumescence devices may be useful after explantation of a penile prosthesis or even with one in place to enhance the erection.[40]

Intracorporeal Pharmacotherapy

Erectile dysfunction may be treated successfully with intracorporeal injection of a vasodilator solution, self-administered by the patient prior to initiating sex play.[41] Therapy with the PGE_1-phentolamine combination described earlier at a dose of 3 to 8 μg for self-treatment, adjusted to the response to the test dose, produces excellent erections in most cases. The patient may reduce the dose to shorten the duration of the erection. Some patients cannot inject themselves, and others experience painful burning that makes PGE_1 unusable. This modality is often warmly welcomed by patients because it is unobtrusive in comparison with vacuum tumescence devices.

Penile Prostheses

Penile prostheses were the first effective universal treatment modality for impotence. Because of their expense and complications, they have been relegated to an adjunctive therapeutic role. They require surgical placement of silicone-sheathed devices into the corpora cavernosa. The prostheses consist of rigid or semirigid rods, chambers made tumescent by displacement of a liquid, soft plastic chambers filled from a prevesicular reservoir, or a mechanical device made rigid by a ratcheting mechanism.[42] While most produce good erections, they have a high incidence of complications due to mechanical problems. They also demonstrate the tissue effects of chronic silicone implantation.

Vascular Surgery

Though widely employed in Europe, arterial revascularization has not had success in impotence therapy in the United States, nor have venous ligations or sclerosis had long-term usefulness. These procedures should be reserved for special cases in young men.

Androgen Therapy

Hypogonadism should be treated with androgens. In older hypogonadal men who have a very high incidence of vascular disease, androgen therapy alone should not be expected to normalize erectile function. However, androgens improve energy, mood, and sense of well-being, and they may enhance erectile quality in some patients. Use of the available oral preparations is not warranted because of hepatic complications. A long-acting testosterone ester such as the enanthate or cypionate should be given usually at a dose of 200 mg IM every 2 weeks or preferably, if tolerated, 100 mg every week. New androgen preparations have been submitted to the FDA for approval. In the older man, the principal complication of this treatment is polycythemia, sometimes requiring phlebotomy. Concerns regarding stimulation of benign prostatic hypertrophy (BPH) and prostatic carcinoma have not been supported experimentally, nor have they been subject to rigorous scrutiny. Androgens increase the prostate-specific antigen slightly but usually not progressively.[43]

Other Drugs

At the present time no reliable study has demonstrated that an oral medication effectively treats erectile dysfunction, and none is recommended. A preliminary study suggests, however, that in selected cases, pentoxifylline may improve erectile function in men with arteriogenic sexual dysfunction, presumably by increasing the fluidity of the blood.[44]

Sex Therapy

Sex therapy techniques seem to be particularly effective in helping couples reestablish intimacy after a period of sexual dysfunction. They may improve knowledge of sexual behaviors and thus the couple's sex repertoire. Sex therapy promotes communication and experimentation. Therapy should focus on the couple. Unrealistic expectations must be dealt with and the characteristics of a more satisfactory sex life defined. Sequential goals should include (1) frequent getting together with clarity about who is to initiate, (2) showering or bathing together, (3) spending time touching each other without genital contact, (4) sharing genital touching without focus on intercourse, and (5) intercourse without pressure toward orgasm.

CONCLUSION

Recent advances in understanding the scientific basis of impotence and the development of new diagnostic tests and therapeutic alternatives have made it possible to provide the vast majority of sexually dysfunctional couples an opportunity to restore intimacy. Alleviation of this vexing emotionally and socially destructive problem provides a more vital and satisfying life to couples of all ages but particularly to elderly patients. It is mandatory for geriatricians to direct attention to sexual dysfunction.

REFERENCES

1. Kinsey AC et al: *Sexual Behavior in the Human Male.* Philadelphia, Saunders, 1948.
2. Finkle AL et al: Sexual potency and aging males. *JAMA* 170:1391, 1959.

3. Bowers LM et al: Sexual function and urologic disease in the elderly male. *J Am Geriatr Soc* 11:647, 1963.
4. Virag R, et al: Is impotence an arterial disorder? *Lancet* 1:181, 1985.
5. Lue TF et al: Vasculogenic impotence evaluated by high resolution ultrasonography and pulsed Doppler spectrum analysis. *Radiology* 155:778, 1985.
6. Kaiser FE et al: Impotence and aging: Clinical and hormonal factors. *J Am Geriatr Soc* 36:511, 1988.
7. Morley JE et al: Relationship of penile brachial pressure index to myocardial infarction and cerebrovascular accidents in older men. *Am J Med* 84:445, 1988.
8. Aboseif SR, Lue TF: Hemodynamics of penile erection. *Urol Clin North Am* 15:1, 1988.
9. Kaiser FE, Korenman SG: Impotence in diabetic men. *Am J Med* 85:147, 1988.
10. Barrett-Connor E: Lower endogenous androgen levels and dyslipidemia in men with non-insulin-dependent diabetes mellitus. *Ann Intern Med* 117:807, 1992.
11. Murray FT et al: Gonadal dysfunction in diabetic men with organic impotence. *J Clin Endocrinol Metab* 65:127, 1987.
12. Palmer JDK et al: Diabetic secondary impotence: Neuropathic factor as measured by peripheral motor nerve conduction. *Urology* 28:197, 1986.
13. Herman A et al: Vascular lesions associated with impotence in diabetic and nondiabetic arterial occlusive disease. *Diabetes* 27:975, 1978.
14. Lehman TP, Jacobs JA: Etiology of diabetic impotence. *J Urol* 129:291, 1983.
15. Jevtich MJ et al: Vascular factor in erectile failure among diabetics. *Urology* 19:163, 1982.
16. Bulpitt CJ, Dollery CT: Side effects of hypotensive agents evaluated by a self-administered questionnaire. *Br Med J* 3:485, 1973.
17. Walsh PC, Mostwin JL: Radical prostatectomy and cystoprostatectomy with preservation of potency: Results using a new nerve-sparing technique. *Br J Urol* 56:694, 1984.
18. Tenover JS et al: The effects of aging in normal men on bioavailable testosterone and luteinizing hormone secretion: Response to clomiphene citrate. *J Clin Endocrinol Metab* 65:1118, 1987.
19. Korenman SG et al: Secondary hypogonadism in older men: Its relation to impotence. *J Clin Endocrinol Metab* 71:763, 1990.
20. Davidson JM et al: Effects of androgen on sexual behavior in hypogonadal men. *J Clin Endocrinol Metab* 48:955, 1979.
21. Kwan M et al: The nature of androgen action on male sexuality: A combined laboratory-self-report study on hypogonadal men. *J Clin Endocrinol Metab* 57:557, 1983.
22. Steers WD: Neural control of penile erection. *Semin Urol* 8:66, 1990.
23. Saenz de Tejada I et al: Impaired neurogenic and endothelium-mediated relaxation of penile smooth muscle from diabetic men with impotence. *N Engl J Med* 320:1025, 1989.
24. Rajfer J et al: Nitric oxide as a mediator of relaxation of the corpus cavernosum in response to nonadrenergic, noncholinergic neurotransmission. *N Engl J Med* 326:90, 1992.
25. Burnett AL et al: Nitric oxide: A physiologic mediator of penile erection. *Science* 257:401, 1992.
26. Lue TF, Tanagho EA: Physiology of erection and pharmacological management of impotence. *J Urol* 137:829, 1987.
27. Fournier GR et al: Mechanisms of venous occlusion during canine penile erection: An anatomic demonstration. *J Urol* 137:163, 1987.
28. Masters WH, Johnson VE: *Human Sexual Inadequacy*. Boston, Little, Brown, 1970.
29. Karacan I et al: Sleep-related tumescence as a function of age. *Am J Psychiatry* 132:932, 1975.
30. Mersdorf A et al: Ultrastructural changes in impotent penile tissue: A comparison of 65 patients. *J Urol* 145:749, 1991.
31. Jevtich MJ et al: Clinical significance of ultrastructural findings in the corpora cavernosa of normal and impotent men. *J Urol* 143:289, 1991.
32. Bookstein JJ, Valji K: The arteriolar component in impotence: A possible paradigm shift. *Am J Radiol* 157:932, 1991.
33. Metz P et al: Ultrasonic Doppler pulse wave analysis versus penile blood pressure measurement in the evaluation of arteriogenic impotence. *Vasa* 12:363, 1983.
34. Chiu RCJ et al: Predictive power of penile/brachial index in diagnosing male sexual impotence. *J Vasc Surg* 4:251, 1986.
35. Virag et al: Intracavernous injection of papaverine as a diagnostic and therapeutic method in erectile failure. *Angiology* 35:79, 1984.
36. Marshall P et al: Unreliability of nocturnal penile tumescence recording and MMPI profiles in assessment of impotence. *Urology* 17:1369, 1982.
37. Ackerman MD et al: The predictive significance of patient-reported sexual functioning in rigiscan sleep evaluations. *J Urol* 146:1559, 1991.
38. Witherington R: External penile appliances for management of impotence. *Semin Urol* 8:124, 1990.
39. Korenman SG et al: Use of a vacuum tumescence device in the management of impotence. *J Am Geriatr Soc* 38:217, 1990.
40. Korenman SG, Viosca SP: Management of impotence in men with a history of penile implant or severe pelvic disease. *J Am Geriatr* 40:61, 1992.
41. Zorgniotti AW, Lefleur R: Auto-injection of the corpus cavernosum with a vasoactive drug combination for vasculogenic impotence. *J Urol* 133:39, 1985.
42. Krane RJ: Penile prosthesis. *Urol Clin North Am* 15:103, 1988.
43. Tenover JS: Effects of testosterone supplementation in the aging male. *J Clin Endocrinol Metab* 75:1092, 1992.
44. Korenman SG, Viosca SP: Treatment of vasculogenic sexual dysfunction with pentoxifylline. Unpublished.

Chapter 115

EATING AND SWALLOWING DISORDERS

Donald O. Castell

IMPORTANCE OF DYSPHAGIA IN THE ELDERLY

Dysphagia, or difficulty in swallowing, can present at any age due to a variety of disorders. Advanced age excludes none of the possibilities, and a few conditions are more likely to be seen in elderly patients (strokes, malignancies) or to occur exclusively with advancing age (Zenker's diverticulum). The oral and pharyngeal stages of swallowing involve striated muscle activity which does tend to weaken with age. Diminution of oral chemosensory perception may also contribute to impaired eating and swallowing function. In addition, eating disorders may frequently result from defects not associated with the gastrointestinal tract, such as cognitive problems or physical disability of the upper limbs. Recognition of the cause of a patient's inability to maintain adequate nutrition is crucial, since it has been shown that eating and swallowing disorders are associated with a particularly bad prognosis in elderly persons.[1] This chapter will primarily cover diagnostic considerations in the patient with dysphagia, with special emphasis on the importance of understanding and clarifying the unique historical features of the diverse abnormalities producing this symptom.

CLINICAL PRESENTATION AND CLASSIFICATION OF DYSPHAGIA

In 1959, Schatzki suggested that a strong suspicion of the right diagnosis could be obtained from a careful history in up to 85 percent of patients with dysphagia.[2] That strong statement helps to emphasize the critical importance of the medical history in clarifying the cause of this symptom.

The term *dysphagia* is derived from Greek (*dys,* "with difficulty," and *phagia,* "to eat"). It describes difficulty in swallowing and should not be confused with odynophagia (painful swallowing). The two symptoms may appear together, but dysphagia is usually not associated with pain. The patient with true dysphagia describes either difficulty initiating a swallow or a sensation of food stopping or "sticking" somewhere behind the sternum or at the suprasternal notch. When a patient complains of true difficulty with swallowing, i.e., food not passing into the stomach in the normal way, it almost always indicates some kind of organic lesion, rather than a functional problem.

Another important diagnostic distinction is that dysphagia should not be confused with a globus sensation. Globus is best described as the frequent feeling (sometimes a constant sensation) of a lump, fullness, or tickle in the throat, but which typically does not interfere with swallowing and may even be relieved by swallows. The term "globus hystericus" has often been improperly used to describe these patients. It implies, often inaccurately, that patients with the symptom have hysterical personalities. The diagnosis of globus should never be made without a thorough investigation for a lesion in the pharynx or neck and for organic esophageal disease such as reflux or a hypertensive upper esophageal sphincter. In fact, globus has been described in patients with each of these conditions.[3,4] Thus, it is essentially a diagnosis of exclusion.

Dysphagia should be categorized into two types: oropharyngeal (preesophageal) and esophageal,[5] depending on the cause. A number of specific symptoms discussed below are likely to help identify the different types and causes of dysphagia. An algorithm for the more typical symptom presentations of patients with some of the more common causes of dysphagia is illustrated in Fig. 115-1.

OROPHARYNGEAL DYSPHAGIA

Dysphagia secondary to a lesion above or proximal to the esophagus is called oropharyngeal dysphagia.

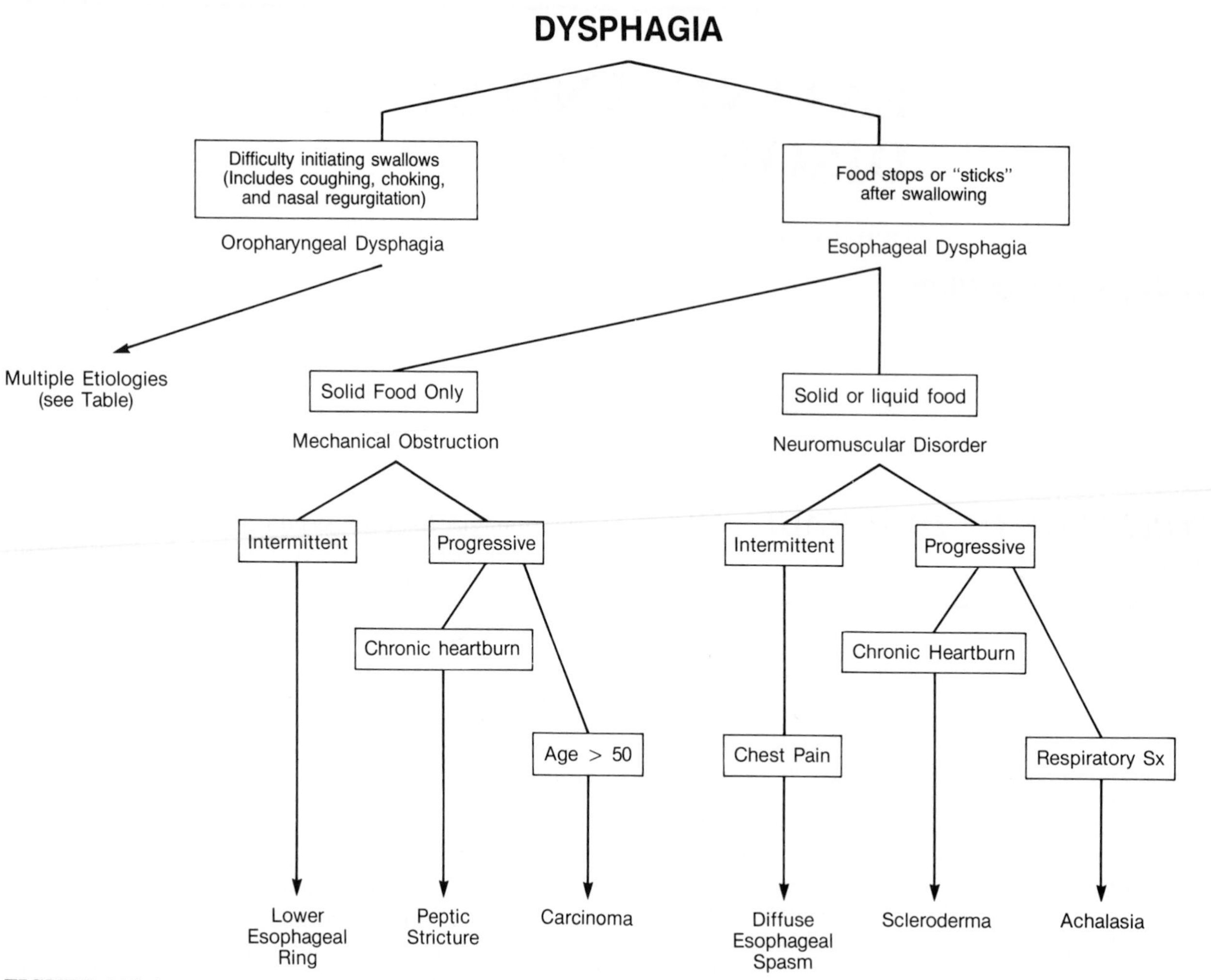

FIGURE 115-1
Diagnostic algorithm based on symptom presentation of the patient with dysphagia.

This abnormality is also called *transfer* dysphagia because the patient has trouble voluntarily transferring food from the mouth into the esophagus to initiate the involuntary phase of swallowing while protecting the airway from aspiration. Normal swallowing is accomplished by a series of finely coordinated neural and muscular phenomena, modulated through the swallowing center in the brainstem. The food bolus must be moved to the back of the mouth, the nasopharynx must be closed so that food does not go up into the nasal passages, the vocal cords must close, and the epiglottis must tilt downward to prevent food from entering the airway. Coordinated relaxation and opening of the upper esophageal sphincter must occur to allow unimpeded bolus passage. All these phenomena occur in appropriate sequence within less than 1 second during each swallow. In elderly patients, it is important to focus on the function of the oral or preparative stage. Difficulty ingesting, controlling, or delivering the food bolus to initiate the pharyngeal swallow reflex is frequently seen in individuals older than 70 years, even without a history of dysphagia.[6] Neurologic or neuromuscular degenerative disorders can produce such profound weakness of the tongue and facial muscles that the patient is unable to move food to the back of the mouth. Defects of this type which exacerbate other swallowing impairments are more likely to occur in patients with strokes or Parkinson's disease.

Table 115-1 lists the great variety of conditions that can cause oropharyngeal dysphagia, before a swallowed bolus enters the esophagus.[7] These early aspects of swallowing are produced by striated muscle, as opposed to the smooth muscle in the esophagus and the rest of the gastrointestinal tract. Thus, the lesions that cause difficulty in this region are different from those that cause esophageal dysphagia. Anything that might affect the swallowing center in the brainstem or the nerves that modulate the process—the fifth, seventh, ninth, tenth, and twelfth cranial nerves—can cause oropharyngeal dysphagia. In addition, a disorder of the striated muscles of the oropharynx, such as myasthenia gravis, or local abnormalities, such as tumors, thyroiditis, or a retropharyngeal ab-

TABLE 115-1

Causes of Oropharyngeal Dysphagia in Elderly Persons

Central nervous system
Cerebrovascular accidents (particularly with brainstem involvement)
Anterior cortical stroke
Wallenberg's syndrome
Pseudobulbar palsy
Parkinson's disease
Multiple sclerosis
Neoplasms
Other neuromuscular disorders
Amyotrophic lateral sclerosis
Polymyositis and dermatomyositis
Muscular dystrophies
Myasthenia gravis
Hypothyroidism or hyperthyroidism
Bulbar poliomyelitis
Peripheral neuropathy (secondary to diabetes mellitus)
Local structural lesions
Oropharyngeal tumors
Thyromegaly
Cervical osteoarthritis with vertebral osteophytes
Abscess
Webs
Zenker's diverticulum

scess, can cause this symptom. Decreased elasticity of the upper esophageal sphincter results in inadequate opening, as occurs in patients with Zenker's diverticulum or cricopharyngeal bar. In the patient with a Zenker's diverticulum, the pouch may fill with food and may either obstruct the esophagus by compression or result in regurgitation of previously eaten food some time following a meal.

Patients with oropharyngeal dysphagia usually describe trouble initiating a swallow and localize their symptom to the throat. Associated phenomena include nasal regurgitation, coughing during swallowing, dysarthria, or nasal speech due to weakness of palatal muscles. Other possibly associated clinical features of central nervous system defects may represent important diagnostic clues. These features include the presence of a speech disorder or evidence of any cranial nerve defects, limb weakness, or changes in sleep pattern, including sleep apnea or recent onset of snoring. Dysphagia is usually only part of the total symptom complex in oropharyngeal dysphagia; the primary diagnosis is usually quite apparent, such as a recent stroke or some form of muscular disease. In contrast, esophageal lesions often produce no symptoms other than dysphagia, and diagnosis of the cause may be more difficult. Oropharyngeal dysphagia is also more likely to affect the patient's ability to swallow liquids, while esophageal dysphagia can be expected to affect primarily the swallowing of solid foods. These distinctions are not absolutes, however, and many combinations exist.

Motility abnormalities affecting the hypopharynx are usually mild or moderate and are due to progressive weakness of the functions of mouth and pharynx combined with atrophy of the musculature. They are usually compensated, except when labial spill of saliva occurs during sleeping. Upon questioning, the patient may admit to fatigue. Gradually progressive pharyngeal dysphagia resulting from progressive impairment of motility in this area may lead to a shift in dietary preference or prolonging of meals. Weakness of the palatal muscles may cause snoring. Many symptoms in these patients are frequently not recognized as related to the swallowing difficulty and may be subtle even in the presence of significant dysphagia.[7]

Treatment of oropharyngeal dysphagia depends on the underlying cause. Dysphagia associated with systemic illnesses such as Parkinson's disease, myasthenia gravis, polymyositis, and thyroid dysfunction often improves with treatment of the underlying disorder. Neoplasm requires resection and, in some cases, chemotherapy or radiation therapy. Dysphagia after a stroke may respond to techniques aimed at rehabilitation of the physical components of swallowing. Manipulation of the diet and proper positioning of the head may facilitate swallowing in this group of patients. Consultation with a speech pathologist in conjunction with radiographic and manometric assessment of swallowing with various types of food (liquid, semisolid, solid) while maintaining different head positions may permit recommendations that lead to improved swallowing.

ESOPHAGEAL DYSPHAGIA

Esophageal dysphagia describes difficulty with the *transport* of food down the esophagus once the bolus has been successfully transferred. Normally, food is cleared from the esophagus quickly, the peristaltic wave taking approximately 8 to 10 seconds to travel from top to bottom. When liquid is swallowed while a person stands upright, the liquid traverses the esophagus in 2 or 3 seconds. Solids take longer and may require a series of peristaltic waves (primary followed by secondary peristalsis) to clear the esophagus. Normally the transport is quite efficient, and the waves sweep the esophagus clean of retained food.

Any difficulty with the coordinated contractions of the esophagus (motility disorder) or any kind of mechanical obstruction may cause abnormal transport. The patient most often describes a sensation of food "hanging up" somewhere behind the sternum.[8] If the symptom is localized to the lower part of the sternum or the epigastric area, the lesion is most likely in the distal esophagus. The symptom is often referred, however, and the patient may locate the level of dysphagia higher in the chest, giving less specificity.[9] For example, a patient with a carcinoma of the distal end of the esophagus sometimes indicates that he or she feels food stop at the suprasternal notch.

To better understand and define specific symptom components of esophageal dysphagia, three questions are most crucial: (1) What type of food causes the symptoms? (2) Is the dysphagia intermittent or progressive? (3) Does the patient have heartburn? These concerns are illustrated in Fig. 115-1.

The patient who reports that dysphagia occurs with both solids and liquids, and that even water sometimes seems to stop, most likely has a motility disorder or primary neuromuscular abnormality of the esophagus. In contrast, if dysphagia occurs only after swallowing a fairly large piece of meat or other solid food (and not when ingesting any kind of beverage), the physician should think immediately of a mechanical obstruction. Therefore, asking what kind of food causes the problem should be the initial step in sorting out the correct diagnosis.

MECHANICAL OBSTRUCTION

Features of the three most likely lesions and of a few other lesions causing mechanical obstruction are described below. An important feature is whether the dysphagia is progressive or intermittent.

Lower Esophageal Ring

In patients with a lower esophageal ring, dysphagia only occurs intermittently, when the patient is swallowing a fairly large solid bolus, such as meat or bread. This pattern may persist for years, and it may happen most often when the patient is under unusual tension. This is a typical history of a lower esophageal (Schatzki) ring. The symptom pattern should strongly suggest this diagnosis, and barium radiographic studies should confirm it. The latter will define the ring and determine the luminal diameter and the necessity for dilation, as well as show concomitant esophagitis or other pathological lesions. It may be necessary to give a solid bolus (such as a pill or a marshmallow) during the barium study to completely identify the ring.

Because the dysphagia is intermittent, a physician who is not especially attuned to the patterns of dysphagia produced by different lesions may have the impression that the symptom is psychological. A positive diagnosis of an esophageal ring may be quite satisfying to the physician and patient because many of these patients have been told that their symptoms are all "in their head" and others are worried about cancer. Effective therapy may require nothing more than allaying their apprehensions and teaching them to chew their food better. If the ring is less than 13 mm in diameter, dilation with a large (18 to 20 mm) dilator is often required.

Carcinoma

A diagnosis of carcinoma should be suspected in the elderly patient with dysphagia only for solid foods and usually of relatively short duration (less than 6 months). The swallowing disorder progressively worsens, occurring more frequently and resulting in an inability to swallow almost any kind of solid food unless it is well chewed. There is typically no trouble swallowing liquids until the last stages, when the esophageal lumen is closed by the constricting lesion. Carcinoma of the esophagus occurs frequently in this country. The older the patient, the more the physician should suspect carcinoma. Other features that point to this diagnosis are a history of heavy alcohol use and a well-established smoking habit. Excessive weight loss (greater than 15 pounds) associated with dysphagia in the elderly is an ominous sign, suggesting malignancy.

Peptic Stricture

The other lesion that might cause progressive dysphagia is peptic stricture. Most patients with this lesion have a history of chronic heartburn and/or chronic antacid use of some years' duration, but this is not always the case. The age group of patients with peptic stricture is often similar to that of patients with esophageal carcinoma. There is, however, no evidence that patients who have chronic reflux and chronic esophagitis are especially likely to develop carcinoma except in the setting of a Barrett's esophagus, i.e., metaplastic epithelial changes from squamous to columnar cell types.

Other Lesions Likely to Cause Mechanical Obstruction

Vascular Causes Dysphagia may be caused by vascular anomalies producing compression of the esophagus. The more common lesions are congenital aortic arch abnormalities ("dysphagia lusoria"), with dysphagia presenting early in childhood. Occasionally, symptoms can present in adulthood. Dysphagia aortica is a disorder of the elderly and is due to compression of the esophagus either by a large thoracic aortic aneurysm or by an atherosclerotic, rigid aorta posteriorly and the heart or esophageal hiatus anteriorly.

Mediastinal Adenopathy Adenopathy produced by lung cancer, lymphoma, tuberculosis, or sarcoid can cause dysphagia by compression of the esophagus.

Cervical Hypertrophic Osteoarthropathy In the elderly person, cervical osteoarthritis can result in dysphagia from esophageal compression due to hypertrophic spurs. Patients can present with solid food dysphagia, odynophagia, or simply discomfort in the throat. Barium-swallow radiography is usually diagnostic, but intraluminal pathological lesions should be ruled out endoscopically.

NEUROMUSCULAR (MOTILITY) DISORDERS

When a patient has dysphagia for both solids and liquids (i.e., most likely a motility disorder), the next question is whether it is progressive or intermittent. Features of the three most likely lesions are described below.

Spasm

Intermittent dysphagia for all kinds of food suggests the presence of diffuse esophageal spasm.[9] Sometimes it may be helpful to ask whether the dysphagia occurs only with particularly hot or cold foods, pills, or carbonated beverages. Another clue is the presence of intermittent chest pain which may mimic angina pectoris, even with relief from nitroglycerine. Pain of this type may result from diffuse spasm, particularly if it is associated with eating.

Achalasia

Patients with achalasia usually describe difficulty swallowing all kinds of food for considerably longer than 6 months. It is often not clear to the patient exactly when the dysphagia started, but it becomes slowly and progressively worse. The situation becomes more critical clinically with the onset of nocturnal coughing. This description is a classic history of achalasia, in which nocturnal pulmonary symptoms may be due to aspiration from an enlarged fluid-filled esophagus.[9] Occasionally these patients present initially with aspiration pneumonia, and the esophageal abnormality is only identified through careful questioning and radiographic studies. The progressive dysphagia in achalasia is often so indolent in its development that patients adapt to it. Thus, the average duration of symptoms prior to initial diagnosis and treatment in patients with achalasia is many months or even years.[10] Pneumatic dilation is the preferred treatment in most cases of achalasia, although a surgical myotomy also produces excellent results.

Scleroderma

Esophageal involvement with systemic sclerosis is characterized by progressive dysphagia for solids and liquids and a history of chronic heartburn. Other manifestations may include those typical of this entity, particularly skin tightness and/or Raynaud's phenomenon. In scleroderma, the esophagus may be involved in 70 or 80 percent of cases, with connective tissue in the wall of the esophagus squeezing out and replacing the smooth muscle. Patients so affected lose tone in the lower esophageal sphincter and also lose esophageal peristaltic contraction. Severe heartburn often develops, and complicated reflux esophagitis occurs in patients who have scleroderma esophagus. The presence of chronic heartburn and regurgitation in the patient with progressive dysphagia should help to differentiate scleroderma from achalasia, although this distinction is not an absolute rule. In contrast to scleroderma, achalasia is characterized by a strongly contracted lower esophageal sphincter with poor relaxation; therefore, reflux is highly unlikely. Some patients with achalasia, however, do describe a burning sensation similar to heartburn, believed to be due to esophageal dilatation and chronic stasis of food. An alternative explanation might be the acid pH potentially resulting from fermentation of retained food in the distal esophagus.[11]

GASTROESOPHAGEAL REFLUX

Gastroesophageal (GE) reflux and its complications are common in the elderly. Although the typical symptoms of GE reflux are heartburn and acid regurgitation, a number of other symptoms, both esophageal and nonesophageal, may be present in these patients. Dysphagia is not commonly present, but it does occur in patients with chronic GE reflux. The genesis of dysphagia may be an obstructing lesion (edema or peptic stricture) and/or a motility abnormality secondary to disordered peristalsis commonly found in patients with severe reflux disease.

As mentioned previously, a globus sensation has also been described as secondary to reflux. This clinical belief may possibly be attributed to some patients with GE reflux referring their symptoms to the region of the suprasternal notch. It is also possible that a globus symptom occurs when contents of the upper esophagus are displaced upward against the undersurface of the upper sphincter. As a result, the sphincter may contract vigorously to protect the pharynx from regurgitation of esophageal contents, causing intraluminal pressure in the sphincter segment to increase. Such a sudden contraction of the cricopharyngeal muscle might become symptomatic and result in a globus sensation.

MEDICATION-INDUCED ESOPHAGEAL INJURY

Acute esophageal injury may result from ingestion of a variety of medications (Table 115-2). The symptoms associated with acute esophageal injury include substernal pain, odynophagia, and dysphagia. Elderly patients are at particularly high risk of medication-induced esophageal injury for several reasons: They take more medications than younger patients, they are more likely to have an anatomic or motility disorder of the esophagus, they spend more time in a recumbent position, and salivary production decreases with age. In elderly patients, potassium chloride and quinidine are the drugs most frequently associated with esophageal injury, whereas in young patients antibiotics are more commonly implicated. Many patients regularly taking nonsteroidal anti-inflammatory drugs for arthritis have esophagitis. Whether this is a direct effect of the medication on the esophagus or whether such patients have chronic gastroesophageal reflux disease remains to be determined.

Factors that predispose to a drug-induced esophageal lesion may include the patient's position at the time the drug is ingested and the volume of fluid ingested. Passage of medication through the esophagus is less likely when the medication is ingested with less than 15 ml of water by a patient in a recumbent position. It is thus particularly ill-advised to administer medication at bedtime with small sips of water, as is common practice. The majority of patients with medication-induced esophageal lesions do not have underlying esophageal abnormalities. The site of injury probably relates primarily to anatomic factors, because injury occurs most frequently in the midesophagus at the level of the aortic arch or distally in the area adjacent to the left atrium or above the lower esophageal sphincter.[12]

TABLE 115-2

Medications Implicated in Esophageal Injury

Most common
- Emepronium bromide (not available in the United States)
- Tetracycline and derivatives
- Potassium chloride (especially slow-release formulations)
- Quinidine (sulfate and gluconate)

Others
- Aspirin
- Ascorbic acid
- Alprenolol
- Clindamycin
- Ferrous sulfate
- Ibuprofen
- Indomethacin
- Lincomycin
- Theophylline

DIAGNOSTIC CONSIDERATIONS

This discussion has emphasized the importance of a systemic approach to the patient with a history of dysphagia. Here and elsewhere it has been emphasized that the careful taking of a concise history of a patient's symptoms can lead to a strong suspicion of a diagnosis in the majority of cases. Some of the symptoms are directly related to the site of abnormality along the swallowing tract; others are indirect manifestations of dysphagia, such as compensation efforts, the results of complications, or a complete breakdown of swallow coordination. Aside from the major complaints, other important historical features include voice changes, sleep disorders, alterations in eating habits, respiratory malfunctions, effects of medication on swallowing functions, previous illnesses, systemic diseases, surgery, and irradiation. In one form or another, effects of these extraneous events, past or present, may adversely influence or compound existing problems with the swallowing process.

A thorough examination of the mouth and neck structures is essential. Also important is a complete neurologic exam, particularly of the cranial nerves.

Barium radiographic studies of the swallowing mechanism (both pharyngeal and esophageal) should be considered the initial screening procedure in all patients with dysphagia. It is important to remember that patients with dysphagia only for solids may require a solid bolus challenge (a marshmallow or a pill) to demonstrate the obstructing lesion. For patients with oropharyngeal dysphagia, videotaping swallows in both the anterior and the lateral aspects may be required to identify abnormalities of the rapid sequence of contractions in the pharynx and also possible aspiration. If the barium study shows an obstructing lesion, endoscopy and biopsy are usually required to establish a diagnosis. On the other hand, if the barium study suggests a motility disorder or is normal, a motility study is indicated, including both the pharyngeal and the esophageal swallowing activity. This approach should provide a clear understanding of the diagnosis in most patients with dysphagia.

REFERENCES

1. Siebens H et al: Correlates and consequences of eating dependency in institutionalized elderly. *J Am Geriatr Soc* 34:192, 1986.
2. Schatzki R: Panel discussion on diseases of the esophagus. *Am J Gastroenterol* 31:117, 1959.
3. Freeland AP et al: Globus hystericus and reflux oesophagitis. *J Laryngol Otol* 88:1025, 1974.
4. Cattau EL, Castell DO: Symptoms of esophageal dysfunction, in Stollerman GH (ed): *Advances in Internal Medicine.* Chicago, Year Book Medical, 1982, vol 27, p 151.
5. Hurwitz AL et al: Oropharyngeal dysphagia. *Am J Dig Dis* 20:313, 1975.
6. Ekberg O, Feinberg MJ: Altered swallowing function in elderly patients without dysphagia. *AJR* 156:1181, 1991.
7. Bosma JF: Sensorimotor examination of the mouth and pharynx. *Front Oral Physiol* 2:78, 1976.
8. Richter JE: Heartburn, dysphagia, odynophagia, and other esophageal symptoms, in Sleisenger MH, Fordtran JS (eds): *Gastrointestinal Disease,* 5th ed. Philadelphia, Saunders, 1993, p 331.
9. Castell DO: Dysphagia. *Gastroenterology* 76:1015, 1979.
10. Goulbourne IA, Walbaum PR: Long term results of Heller's operation for achalasia. *J R Coll Surg Edinb* 30:101, 1985.
11. Smart HL et al: Twenty-four-hour oesophageal acidity in achalasia before and after pneumatic dilatation. *Gut* 28:883, 1987.
12. Kikendahl JW et al: Pill-induced esophageal injury. *Dig Dis Sci* 228:174, 1983.

Chapter 116

CONSTIPATION

Lawrence J. Cheskin and Marvin M. Schuster

Constipation is a major problem for elderly persons in developed countries. This is evidenced by the rise in the use of laxatives with age. One British study found that 16 percent of persons between the ages of 10 and 59 used laxatives more frequently than once weekly while 30 percent of those over age 60 were regular laxative users.[1] A recent survey in the United States of community-dwelling persons over age 65 found that 30 percent of the men and 29 percent of the women considered themselves constipated. Twenty-four percent of the men and 20 percent of the women had used laxatives in the month before the survey.[2] The largest study reported to date found that 21 to 35 percent (depending on age) of 1888 women over age 65 and 9 to 26 percent of 1110 men (also over age 65) in an ambulatory health screening program reported recurrent constipation.[3]

DEFINITION

There is an important discrepancy between what physicians and elderly patients define as constipation. Many patients consider themselves constipated even if they have a bowel movement each day, particularly if defecation is difficult and associated with excessive straining, while the medical profession tends to define constipation solely by frequency of stooling and consistency of the stool. In one study, 52 percent of elderly men and 65 percent of elderly women who were constipated by self-report had a bowel movement at least once a day.[2]

In contrast to subject self-reports, the few studies of stooling frequency available have not documented differences in frequency of bowel movements[1] or whole-gut transit times[4] between elderly and young populations. This kind of evidence has led some investigators to conclude that aging is not associated with an increasing prevalence of constipation. The regularity many older people achieve, however, may be a result of laxative use. What these laxative users' bowel frequency would be were they to stop using laxatives is not known. Other indirect evidence in support of an association between increasing age and decreasing frequency of bowel movements comes from the survey of community-dwelling elderly persons mentioned previously. Thirty-six percent of male and 21 percent of female respondents reported being more constipated as they grew older.[2]

Since frequency of stooling is the most easily measured parameter of bowel function, constipation is usually defined as a frequency of fewer than three bowel movements per week. However, it is probably not advisable to work up or treat elderly patients merely because they report fewer than three bowel movements per week. Even one bowel movement per week is acceptable if it is not associated with symptoms such as painful defecation or bloating and does not represent a recent change in the patient's normal bowel habits.

LAXATIVE USE

Another issue which is difficult to assess is whether laxatives are necessary in many of the elderly persons who use them and believe they need them. Almost all laxatives are available without prescription, and there are over 700 different products sold in this country at an annual cost of $400 million. Today's elderly persons were raised during an era in which an undue emphasis was placed on the virtues of daily or more frequent bowel movements. It becomes difficult to determine whether laxatives were indicated in the first place, since chronic use of some laxatives may lead to destruction of neurons in the enteric nervous system, with resulting impairment of motility, dilatation of the colon, worsening constipation, and diminished effectiveness of laxatives.[5] Except for those with underlying diseases such as colorectal carcinoma or volvulus, which may cause a fairly sudden change in bowel habits, most elderly patients who are constipated will report being constipated for years and report a gradual, almost imperceptible shift toward constipation and increased laxative use.

ASSOCIATED FACTORS

Factors which are probably associated with constipation in the elderly include impaired general health status, increasing number of medications other than laxatives, and diminished mobility and physical activity. It is unclear what the effect of diet is on bowel habit. There is epidemiologic evidence from developing countries that greater amounts of crude dietary fiber are associated with a lesser prevalence of various gastrointestinal disorders, including diverticular disease, colorectal cancer, and constipation, but there may be intervening variables which account for these differences. Studies in which fiber was added to the diet have shown an increase in stool weight but have not shown a consistent change in whole-gut transit times, one group finding no change,[6] another a speeding of transit,[7] and a third a speeding of transit when the baseline was slow but no change or even a slowing when the baseline was rapid transit.[8,9]

Regarding the interaction of psychological illness and constipation, in one study psychological illness was significantly related to self-reported constipation in both elderly men and elderly women but was not related to average stool frequency.[2] This suggests that constipation may be among the symptoms which depressed or anxious patients are likely to exaggerate. Aside from this, patients who are being treated with antidepressants may suffer constipation as a side effect of these medications.

In summary, the increased prevalence of self-reported constipation and laxative use in elderly persons results from a complex interaction between age-related changes in lifestyle and health status. When organic causes of constipation, including unnecessary laxative use, have been ruled out, there may be little contribution from biological aging per se.

EVALUATION

Unlike constipation in young or middle-aged adults, which is usually due to spastic haustral contractions associated with the irritable bowel syndrome, most constipation in elderly persons is associated with decreased motility of the colon. This may be generalized colorectal smooth muscle dysmotility or decreased motility restricted to the anorectum. The latter is termed *dyschezia* and refers to a failure of the defecation mechanism, often due to failure of the striated muscles of the pelvic floor to relax during defecation. This is sometimes described as a functional outlet obstruction. While the processes of absorption and secretion are important in determining the consistency of the stool, hard stools are not due to excessively active absorption but are a consequence of increased exposure time of the stool to normal absorptive processes because of impaired colonic motility or dyschezia.

HISTORY

When an elderly patient complains of constipation, a careful history is the most important part of the evaluation. As noted, not all self-defined constipation is abnormal, and reassurance that there is a broad range of normal bowel frequency may be all the treatment needed in many cases. Symptoms of disorders which can impair the motility of the large bowel should be sought. These include hypothyroidism, hyperparathyroidism, scleroderma, and neurologic disorders such as Parkinson's disease, strokes, or diabetic neuropathy. Drugs, including opiates, anticholinergics, antidepressants, and calcium- or aluminum-containing antacids may also impair gut motility (see Table 116-1).

Localized colorectal diseases, such as tumors or other constricting lesions, which may cause constipation are often accompanied by other symptoms in addition to constipation. Thus, the history should include questions about abdominal pain and bleeding per rectum. In idiopathic, dietary, or drug-related constipation, there are usually no symptoms other than constipation, although a complaint of abdominal bloating sensation is common with severe constipation.

PHYSICAL EXAMINATION

The general physical examination of the elderly patient with constipation in most cases is of no value in determining cause or deciding on treatment. Exceptions include the detection of a localized mass on abdominal examination and local anorectal lesions which may contribute to constipation, such as anal fissures, fistulas, strictures, cancer, or hemorrhoids.

TABLE 116-1

Drugs Causing Constipation

- Antacids
  - Aluminum hydroxide
  - Calcium carbonate
- Anticholinergics
- Antidepressants
  - Tricyclics
  - Lithium
- Antihypertensive-antiarhythmics
  - Calcium channel blockers, especially verapamil
- Metals
  - Bismuth
  - Iron
  - Heavy metals
- Narcotic analgesics
- Nonsteroidal anti-inflammatory compounds
- Sympathomimetics
  - Pseudoephedrine

Digital rectal examination is sensitive in detecting these anal lesions, though fissures and hemorrhoids, unless they are thrombosed or large, are found more reliably with anoscopy. Thus, anoscopy should be performed routinely in newly constipated elderly persons. Digital examination of the anal canal and rectum is also useful in assessing the tone of the internal anal sphincter and the strength of the external anal sphincter and puborectalis muscles. Occasionally, the anal canal, which is normally contracted, is lax or asymmetrically contracted. This may be seen with neurologic disorders, especially strokes, peripheral neuropathies, spinal cord trauma, or postoperative scarring. The constipation in such cases is due to failure of the defecation mechanism. The amount and the consistency of stool felt in the rectum may indicate the type of constipation present. Patients with a failure of the defecation mechanism tend to have much stool in the rectal vault, while those with colonic atony or irritable bowel syndrome have little or no stool in the rectum between defecations.

SPECIAL STUDIES

The chief value of endoscopic or radiographic examinations of the colorectum in constipated elderly patients is in excluding life-threatening causes, especially carcinoma of the colon. The extent of the diagnostic evaluation must be individualized. Although for screening purposes it is justifiable to obtain a flexible or rigid sigmoidoscopy in all elderly patients because of the high incidence of colorectal carcinoma and premalignant lesions, examining the entire colon via colonoscopy or barium enema should be reserved for patients who have occult or gross rectal bleeding or who complain of a recent (within a year or two) change in bowel habits or who complain of abdominal pain or other symptoms in addition to constipation.

Other lesions which may be diagnosed by barium enema or colonoscopy include megacolon, sigmoid or cecal volvulus, and benign strictures, usually ischemic in nature. Endoscopic examination of the colon in chronically constipated elderly patients sometimes reveals a spotty or diffuse dark pigmentation of the colonic mucosa, known as melanosis coli. This is caused by chronic use of certain laxatives, especially the anthracenes such as cascara, senna, and aloe. It subsides within a year of discontinuing the offending laxatives.[10]

Additional studies which may be useful in the evaluation of constipation are tests of colonic transit and colonic motility. Transit time tests use solid radiopaque markers (Sitzmarks), which are usually enclosed 20 to a capsule and taken orally. Single abdominal radiographs are then taken 5 and 7 days after ingestion of these markers and the number and location of those remaining in the colon noted. Eighty percent of the markers are normally excreted by day 5 and all by day 7. The retention of markers in the colon or rectum is indicative of significant constipation. In addition, the pattern of retention gives information about mechanism in that holdup of markers in the rectum indicates a failure of expulsion, while holdup throughout the colon indicates generalized inertia. A refinement of this technique utilizes daily ingestion of 24 markers until a steady state is reached, at which point a single radiograph is taken; the number of markers remaining is equal to the transit time in hours.[11]

Colonic motility testing is performed only in specialized centers and involves the recording of pressure activity in the distal colon and rectum using a water-perfused or solid-state catheter introduced into the lumen via the anus. It can be used to identify different patterns of colonic activity, for example, phasic contractions (spasms) associated with the irritable bowel syndrome or the decreased response to distension seen in the atonic colon. An empiric approach to the evaluation of constipation in the elderly is diagramed in Fig. 116-1.

COMPLICATIONS OF CONSTIPATION

Although for most elderly patients constipation is just an annoyance, in a minority it has more serious consequences. Patients who are institutionalized, especially bedridden ones, are most susceptible to complications.

Fecal impaction is the result of prolonged exposure of accumulated stool to the absorptive forces of the colon and rectum. The stool may become rocklike in consistency in the rectum (70 percent), sigmoid colon (20 percent), or proximal colon (10 percent).[12] Symptoms of crampy lower abdominal and lower back pain are common. Diarrhea may paradoxically succeed the constipation which led to the impaction as watery material makes its way around the impacted mass of stool. The impaction can sometimes be evacuated by the patient after oral administration of 2 liters of a nonabsorbed solution containing polyethylene glycol (Golytely) daily for 2 days.[13] Usually, however, manual disimpaction needs to be performed. With this technique, the impacted mass is fragmented with the examining finger by pressing it against the posterior rectal wall, and the pieces are then removed. This may have to be repeated over a period of days in severe cases.

Stercoral ulcer is often an incidental finding at autopsy in the bedbound elderly patient[14] and is usually asymptomatic. It is caused by pressure necrosis of the rectal or sigmoid mucosa due to a fecal mass. In some cases the ulcer may present as rectal bleeding, and perforation can occur, though rarely.[15]

Anal fissures may result when excessive straining at stool produces tears or passive congestion of tissues near the dentate margin. The irritating effect of hard stools and toilet paper further magnifies the problem.

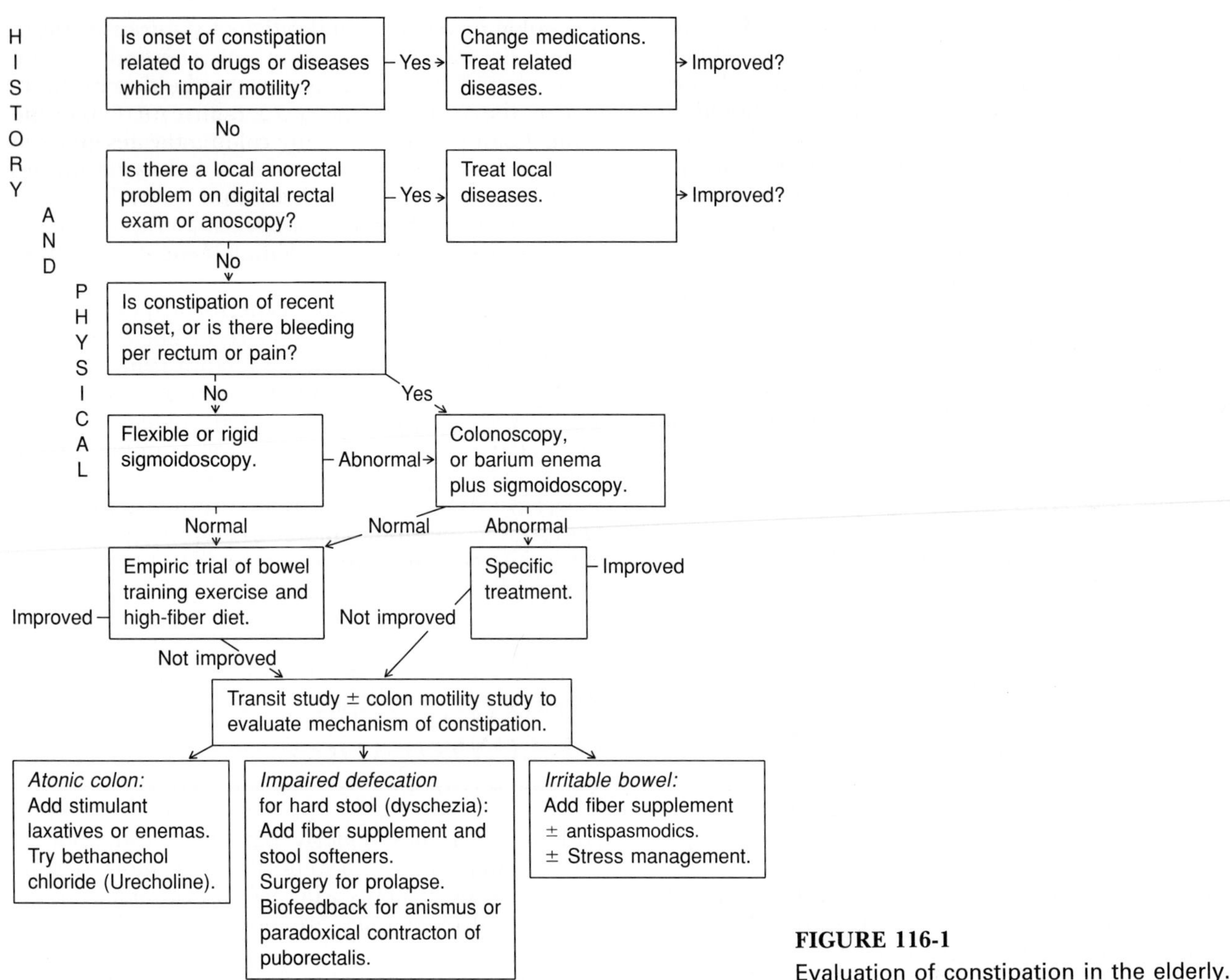

FIGURE 116-1
Evaluation of constipation in the elderly.

Intraabdominal pressures of up to 300 mmHg are generated during straining. Excessive straining at stool may cause prolapse of the anal mucosa, venous distension, and external and internal hemorrhoids.

Megacolon, while sometimes due to a congenital absence of the myenteric plexus of the colon (Hirschsprung's disease) in young patients, is almost always idiopathic when seen in elderly patients. Chronic use of cathartics over a period of many years may lead to an acquired degeneration of the colonic myenteric plexus.[5] The diagnosis of megacolon is made on a plain abdominal radiograph or barium enema, with associated findings of typanitic distension on abdominal examination and often complaints of constipation or diarrhea and fecal incontinence.

Treatment is difficult and is aimed at preventing buildup of stool and further distension of the already impaired colon by administering enemas regularly. Such patients are susceptible to bacterial overgrowth, which may require antibiotics, and to another complication of constipation, volvulus of the colon.

Volvulus, especially of the sigmoid colon, occurs most commonly in institutionalized, bedbound elderly patients and has a high mortality once the blood supply of the bowel is compromised. Although usually intermittent, the presentation may be quite insidious, and therefore a high index of suspicion is required to make an early diagnosis. Signs and symptoms include abdominal distension of variable degree, abdominal cramping, and constipation. A plain abdominal radiograph is often diagnostic. Urgent reduction of the loop is indicated, and this can be accomplished by the passage of a flexible endoscope in 85 percent of cases. In many cases, however, operative intervention is necessary.[16]

Finally, there is some evidence that chronic constipation is a risk factor for the development of carcinoma of the colon and rectum, particularly in women.[17] This might be related to increased exposure time of susceptible mucosa to potentially carcinogenic substances.

TREATMENT OF CONSTIPATION

Ideally, the treatment of constipation is based on accurate knowledge of the underlying cause or causes. Often, it is not warranted to perform an exhaustive evaluation of constipation, especially in a debilitated elderly patient. In the simplest circumstance, an underlying disease process associated with constipation can be controlled (hypothyroidism, for example) or a constipating medication can be substituted with another drug or stopped. The use of laxatives when there is an easily corrected cause is both unnecessary and potentially harmful in that the patient may become laxative-dependent or suffer side effects from the specific laxatives prescribed.

When the cause of the constipation is not obvious or readily identified and life-threatening causes such as colorectal carcinoma have been ruled out, a phased-in approach to treatment is advisable, especially in a frail elderly patient. These phases are essentially treatment trials, beginning with lifestyle interventions such as bowel retraining and dietary adjustments and proceeding, if necessary, to progressively more potent laxative treatment.

Bowel Training

Even in cognitively impaired elderly persons, it is worthwhile to impose a regular schedule of attempts at defecation. In patients who already have a regular time of day when they attempt to stool, it is best to continue on their schedule, advising the patient to make an undistracted attempt for 10 minutes only, each day, even if they do not feel the urge to defecate. When no regular schedule has been established by the patient, the best times to recommend are after breakfast and after the evening meal, to take advantage of the postprandial gastrocolic response.

The importance of establishing a regular bowel "habit" in elderly persons stems also from the frequency of diminished sensation of rectal distension. Because such patients have a less readily recognized signal, it is easy for them to ignore an urge. Such a pattern may lead to retention as the rectum accommodates to progressively greater amounts of distension. Reestablishing a logical and regular time for stooling is thus the first step in treatment.

Exercise

Competitive runners, including elderly athletes, rarely become constipated.[18] Bedfast patients are at great risk of constipation and often respond poorly to treatment. While the role of physical activity in the treatment of constipation in the elderly is unclear, patients seem often to respond favorably to a regular program of mild exercise such as walking.

Diet

In most cases of constipation in elderly persons, dietary manipulations are helpful, though they may not in isolation be sufficient treatment. Bowel training, dietary management, and regular exercise when feasible should be undertaken together as the first phase of treatment. Although certain patients may find specific foods of value as laxatives, it is not necessary to recommend, to use the most famous example, prunes to all one's constipated elderly patients. If the patient is already using a favorite "natural" laxative, however, and is convinced it is beneficial, there is usually no need to stop it.

The dietary adjustment that can be recommended to nearly all constipated elderly persons who are not obstructed is increased consumption of fiber. There are misconceptions, however, among patients and caregivers about which foods are high in fiber content. Most raw fruits and vegetables, for example, are not especially high in dietary fiber, are expensive, and are often poorly tolerated by elderly persons with functional bowel disorders or poor dentition. For instance, to provide 10 g of total dietary fiber, a minimally effective supplementary amount for constipation, the elderly person would have to eat the standard American diet plus two heads of lettuce, or six bananas, or four servings of string beans daily. A few truly high fiber foods are listed in Table 116-2. As a practical matter, it may be more efficient in many elderly patients, particularly the institutionalized, to provide additional dietary fiber in the form of supplements. Numerous preparations are available which provide 3.4 to 6.0 g of total dietary fiber per dose. For the best tolerance, each dose should be taken with liberal amounts of fluid, at least 8 ounces, and the total daily dose increased over a couple of weeks to minimize the transient bloating which occurs frequently. Ten grams is often a sufficient dose, although many patients require 20 to 30 g a day. By comparison, members of some African communities consume upward of 50 g of total dietary fiber daily. Idiopathic constipation is not reported to be a big problem for them. Although fiber is traditionally not prescribed for patients with atonic constipation, it is worth a try in all except those with severe megacolon or mechanical obstructions.

Finally, it should be recognized that a poor state of hydration may exacerbate constipation in elderly patients, particularly those who are institutionalized, demented, or receiving diuretics or nasogastric tube feedings.

TABLE 116-2

Very High Fiber Foods

Type	Total Dietary Fiber per Serving, g
100% bran cereal	8.4
Beans (baked, kidney, lima, navy)	8.5–10.0
Peas (canned)	6.0
Raspberries	4.6
Broccoli	3.2

Laxatives

When the lifestyle changes described in the initial phases of treatment fail or do not produce a sufficient improvement in symptoms, the clinician must resort to pharmacologic treatments, which have a greater risk of side effects. Because almost all laxatives and enemas are available without prescription and they represent a "quick fix" for constipation, their use is rampant and often unnecessary. Often one finds the most difficult treatment question to be which laxatives to discontinue rather than which one to start. It is also common to encounter patient resistance to stopping his or her laxatives.

Traditionally, laxatives have been divided into five categories: bulk, emollient, saline, hyperosmotic, and stimulant laxatives. Bulk laxatives include the various fiber-containing preparations and are thought to act in two ways. They are hydrophilic, so tend to increase stool mass and soften its consistency. In addition, while not digestible by pancreatic enzymes, they are acted upon by colonic bacteria, producing osmotically potent metabolites. They are the safest laxatives and are generally well tolerated by elderly patients when introduced gradually. They are contraindicated in patients with partial mechanical obstruction of any portion of the gastrointestinal tract, since there have been rare reports of complete obstruction secondary to bulk agents in patients with esophageal as well as intestinal strictures.

Emollients, or stool softeners, include mineral oil, as well as the newer docusate salts such as dioctyl sodium sulfosuccinate (Colace). Mineral oil may impair absorption of fat-soluble vitamins and may be aspirated by patients with impaired swallowing or gag reflex, with resulting lipid pneumonitis or pleuritis. It is generally not recommended since safer, effective agents are available. The newer agents work by lowering surface tension, allowing water to enter the stool more readily. They are generally well tolerated and may be particular useful in bedbound elderly patients who are at risk for fecal impaction. They are also a useful adjunct to bulk preparations in elderly patients. For idiopathic constipation, these agents are the next step in a phased-in treatment trial after bulk agents.

Saline laxatives and enemas are salts of magnesium and sodium. Those in most common use are oral milk of magnesia, oral magnesium citrate, and sodium phosphate (Fleet's) enemas. All function as hyperosmolar agents and cause net secretion of fluid into the colon. There is also evidence that colonic motility is increased by these agents via release of the hormone cholecystokinin. Chronic use of magnesium-containing saline laxatives in elderly persons may contribute to hypermagnesemia when there is impaired renal function (known or unsuspected). The phosphate-containing preparations may induce hypocalcemia when high doses are used, even in patients with normal renal function. The phosphate-containing enemas have been reported to cause damage to the rectum, both traumatic from the plastic nozzle of the enema and as a direct toxic effect of the hypertonic solution on the rectal mucosa.[19] It is advisable to use saline laxatives and enemas not as a chronic medication but as an "escape" medication when earlier phases of treatment are being tried. For example, during bowel training or a trial of fiber supplementation, one may allow the patient to take a phosphate enema after the morning attempt at stooling if no bowel movement has occurred on the trial regimen for more than 2 consecutive days. The other common use for saline laxatives is in preparing the bowels for radiographic or endoscopic examinations.

Hyperosmolar laxatives, notably lactulose, exert their effect primarily by drawing water into the gut lumen. Lactulose is a semisynthetic disaccharide which cannot be digested by pancreatic or intestinal enzymes but is metabolized by colonic bacteria to hydrogen and organic acids. This acidifies the colon, and in addition to an osmotic effect, may alter electrolyte transport and colonic motility. Lactulose is usually well tolerated but may cause transient bloating. It is used to treat hepatic encephalopathy and has been shown to be useful in treating constipation in elderly patients.[20] Lactulose is not commonly used in the United States in the treatment of constipation. As with most laxatives, there are no data on effectiveness compared with other agents.

Stimulant laxatives are in very common use in elderly patients. They are very effective but, unfortunately, have the most toxicity long term. They exert their effects primarily through direct stimulation of the myenteric plexuses of the colon, thereby increasing motility. Specific agents include the anthraquinone derivatives cascara, senna, and aloe, which are absorbed then excreted via the enterohepatic circulation into the colon, where they are converted to an active metabolite, emodine. These agents, as noted, may lead to melanosis coli and may also do permanent damage to the myenteric plexus. Phenolphthalein is a fat-soluble stimulant which may therefore have a prolonged duration of action. It has been associated with dermatitis, photosensitivity reactions, and the Stevens-Johnson syndrome.[21] Abuse of laxatives containing this substance can be demonstrated by noting a red color upon alkalinizing a stool specimen.

Castor oil, nominally but inaccurately classed with the stimulant laxatives, has as its active ingredient ricinoleic acid. It inhibits glucose and sodium absorption and stimulates water and electrolyte secretion via inhibition of Na-K-ATPase and increases in cellular cAMP. Its use can lead to fluid and electrolyte disturbances, and it generally cannot be recommended with safer agents available. Bisacodyl (Ducolax) tablets or suppositories are not absorbed but exert a stimulant effect directly on the myenteric plexus. Bisacodyl is a popular agent and probably has less toxicity than the other stimulant laxatives mentioned. All, however, affect electrolyte balance, so may precipitate hypokalemia, fluid and salt overload, or diarrhea. This category of laxatives, because of its potential for significant side effects, should be considered only after adequate trial of the categories of laxatives described earlier.

The newest category is the lavage laxatives. They include Golytely and Colyte and work by stimulating neither secretion nor motility but by passing unimpeded through the gastrointestinal tract. They are safe unless there is complete obstruction and can be used as a bowel preparation prior to procedures, as an adjunct to treatment of impactions, or as an escape laxative in the early phases of treating constipation.

Surgical Procedures

Finally, in selected cases of intractable constipation, a variety of surgical procedures have been attempted ranging from left hemicolectomy to subtotal colectomy with ileoproctostomy.[22] Surgery is rarely needed in the treatment of constipation in elderly patients and can in general be recommended only when there is an obstructing lesion of the colorectum, or recurrent volvulus due to congenital or acquired megacolon.

Thus, the treatment of constipation in elderly patients should first be directed at remediable medical and surgical conditions and the cessation of constipating medications (Fig. 116-1). When the constipation is believed to be idiopathic or related to the elderly patient's diet, mobility, dyschezia, or atonic colon, a phased-in series of treatment trials should be instituted, starting with lifestyle changes alone and adding progressively more potent laxatives over a period of weeks to months until a satisfactory outcome is achieved. Ideally, the phased-in approach will not be rigidly followed but will be adapted to the underlying pathophysiology and symptoms of the individual elderly patient. Once an effective treatment regimen is arrived at in this manner, particularly if laxatives with potentially dangerous side effects are being utilized, an attempt should be made to reduce dosages to the minimally effective range. The laxatives needed to break the cycle of severe constipation are often more potent than those needed to maintain adequate bowel movement. Thus, it may not be necessary to use more than dietary changes ultimately in most of the elderly persons suffering from this common condition.

REFERENCES

1. Connell AM et al: Variations in bowel habit in two population samples. *Br Med J* 1:1095, 1965.
2. Whitehead WE et al: Constipation and laxative use in the elderly living at home: Prevalence and relationship to exercise and dietary fiber. *J Am Geriatr Soc* 37:423, 1989.
3. Hale WE et al: Symptom prevalence in the elderly: An evaluation of age, sex, disease, and medication use. *J Am Geriatr Soc* 34:333, 1986.
4. Eastwood HDH: Bowel transit studies in the elderly. Radio-opaque markers in the investigation of constipation. *Geront Clin* 14:154, 1972.
5. Smith B: The effect of irritant purgatives on the myenteric plexus in man and mouse. *Gut* 9:139,1968.
6. Eastman MA et al: Effects of dietary supplements of wheat bran and cellulose on faeces and bowel function. *Br Med J* 4:392, 1973.
7. Cummings JH et al: Measurement of the mean transit time of dietary residue through the human gut. *Gut* 17:210, 1976.
8. Harvey RF et al: Effects of increased dietary fiber on intestinal transit. *Lancet* 1:1278, 1973.
9. Payler DK et al: The effect of wheat bran on intestinal transit. *Gut* 16:209, 1975.
10. Fine KD et al: Diarrhea, in Sleisenger MH, Fordtran JS (eds): *Gastrointestinal Disease,* 4th ed. Philadelphia, Saunders, 1988, p 307.
11. Metcalf AM et al: Simplified assessment of segmental colonic transit. *Gastroenterology* 91:1186, 1986.
12. Kaufman SA, Karin H: Fecaloma of the sigmoid flexure. *Dis Colon Rectum* 9:133, 1966.
13. Puxty JA, Fox RA: Golytely: A new approach to fecal impaction in old age. *Age Ageing* 15:182, 1982.
14. Grinvalsky HT, Bowerman CI: Stercoraceous ulcers of the colon. *JAMA* 171:1941, 1959.
15. Gekas P, Schuster MM: Stercoral perforation of the colon: Case report and review of the literature. *Gastroenterology* 80:1054, 1981.
16. Anderson JR, Lee D: The management of acute sigmoid volvulus. *Br J Surg* 68:117, 1981.
17. Vobecky J et al: A case-control study of risk factors for large bowel carcinoma. *Cancer* 51:1958, 1983.
18. Cheskin LJ et al: Constipation in the elderly: Prevalence is related to exercise. Poster, 46th Annual Meeting of the American Geriatric Society, Boston, 1989.
19. Pietsch JB et al: Injury by hypertonic phosphate enema. *Can Med J* 116:1169, 1977.
20. Wesselius-DeCasparis A et al: Treatment of chronic constipation with 'lactulose' syrup. Results of a double-blind study. *Gut* 9:84, 1968.
21. Sekas G: *Prac Gastroenterol* 1:33, 1987.
22. Gilberg K et al: Surgical treatment of constipation. *West J Med* 140:569, 1984.

Chapter 117

DIARRHEA

Richard G. Bennett and William B. Greenough

Diarrheal diseases in elderly patients represent an important problem and have been increasingly studied in the last decade. Diarrhea causes incontinence, disability, and even death in older adults. What can be a trivial illness in young persons can be catastrophic in elderly persons who do not tolerate intravascular dehydration because of atherosclerotic disease. In this chapter we will discuss the epidemiology of diarrheal diseases as it is now understood; the causes of diarrhea, with a particular emphasis on those agents that affect the elderly population preferentially; the mechanisms that result in diarrhea; host factors in elderly persons that predispose to diarrheal disease; and rational treatment and preventive considerations for gastroenteritis with an emphasis on the use of oral rehydration therapy.

SCOPE AND NATURE OF THE PROBLEM

In 1970 an outbreak of *Salmonella* enteritis resulted in the deaths of 24 individuals in a Baltimore nursing home,[1] and in 1985 a similar tragedy occurred in a Canadian facility, where 19 people died from an outbreak of verotoxin-producing *Escherichia coli.*[2] These severe outbreaks offer only a clue to the real significance of diarrheal diseases in long-term care facilities. In Maryland nursing homes, an 8 percent annual incidence rate of diarrheal outbreaks has been recognized,[3] and diarrheal diseases were among the four most common causes of infections in nursing home patients in two earlier surveys.[4,5] Recently the increased morbidity and mortality associated with diarrheal diseases in elderly persons both in nursing homes and in the community have been appreciated more fully. Several reports from the Centers for Disease Control have shown that half of diarrheal deaths in the United States occurred in adults over 74 years of age, and that the case-fatality rate and incidence of diarrhea were higher among elderly adults than among children.[6,7] Figure 117-1 shows that the incidence of death related to diarrhea is three times greater in adults over 74 years compared with children less than 4 years.[6] Despite the increasing attention that has been paid to gastrointestinal infections, there are still no reports on the epidemiology of infectious diarrhea among nursing home patients or among individuals living in the community. Furthermore, the causes of most outbreaks in nursing homes and of most cases in the community remain unidentified. Finally, oral rehydration therapy (ORT), a treatment for diarrhea that could avert many hospitalizations with their attendant costs and complications, is still rarely used to treat elderly patients with diarrhea in the United States even though experts recommend its use.[6–9] Thus, although current advances in diagnosis and treatment are still not being applied in caring for elderly patients with diarrhea, awareness of

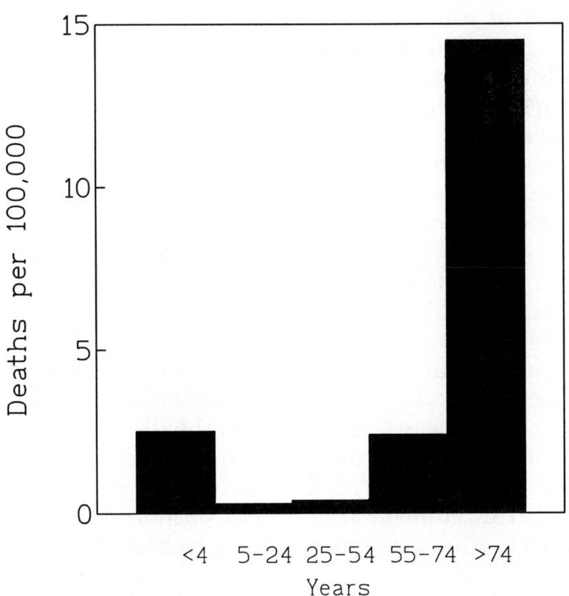

FIGURE 117-1

Diarrheal deaths per 100,000 persons per year by age group for the year 1985. (*Adapted from Lew JF et al,*[6] *Journal of the American Medical Association, June 26, 1991, Volume 265, pages 3280-3284, Copyright 1991, American Medical Association, and used with permission.*)

the problem is increasing and the scope of the problem has been better defined recently.[6]

Diarrhea is usually self-limited (24 to 48 hours), but important fluid losses can occur in a short time. In healthy individuals, such losses are partially compensated by hormonally mediated urinary concentration and by increased drinking in response to thirst. If appropriate fluids are taken, no serious consequences ensue. When fluid losses occur in elderly persons, however, a different situation exists. Maximal urinary concentration in response to dehydration is less with old age. Although the mechanisms underlying decreased renal capacity are not fully understood, the ability of the kidney to respond to disturbances in volume is clearly diminished in the elderly. More importantly, the normal mechanism whereby hyperosmolarity from volume depletion leads to thirst may decrease with age. The perception of thirst may also be impaired in patients with dementia, as may their ability to obtain fluids. Thus, dehydration from diarrhea may not be translated into a desire or opportunity to drink, and the losses of fluid may remain uncorrected. Frail elderly persons, particularly those confined in nursing homes, may have difficulty with ambulation and communication. Even if thirst is present, these individuals may be unable to replace losses because of their physical disabilities.

The loss of circulating fluid volume in elderly persons has consequences far more severe than such a loss in younger individuals. Silent atherosclerosis which results in partial occlusion of blood vessels to vital organs is common, and drugs that induce salt and potassium losses, as well as block cardiac and circulatory reflexes, are frequently prescribed. The combination of silent atherosclerosis and drug therapy increases the vulnerability to infarctions and arrhythmias. Small decrements in intravascular volume in an older person with atherosclerosis can lead directly to hypoperfusion of vital organs or the portions of vital organs served by atherosclerotic arteries. Worsening renal failure, congestive heart failure, or a decline in mental status seen after a benign episode of gastroenteritis may not be thought to be related. The important physiologic differences between the young and the old make diarrhea a life-threatening illness in elderly persons. This has been seen in Japan, where individuals over the age of 75 have a 400-fold increased mortality rate from gastrointestinal infections,[10] and it was also evident in the 1970 nursing home outbreak in Baltimore, in which patients generally did not die immediately of acute dehydration or sepsis but succumbed after a week or more from the secondary effects of myocardial, cerebral, or renal damage.[1]

Identifying the significance of volume depletion in elderly patients is important. Most of the parameters used in pediatric and adult populations are not helpful in elderly populations since age itself results in poor skin turgor, sunken eyes, and a dry tongue. About the only clinical signs of diagnostic value in elderly patients is an orthostatic change in the blood pressure. However, by the time measurable orthostasis occurs, as much as 6 to 10 percent of the intravascular volume has been lost, and serious hypoperfusion of a vital organ may have occurred. The serum electrolyte levels only identify changes in the concentration of sodium or potassium in relation to water and other solutes. Electrolyte determination tells little of the absolute status of the intravascular and extracellular fluid volume. A useful parameter which is measurable is total plasma protein or plasma specific gravity. An initial study using this measurement to estimate fluid loss in elderly patients showed that it was as useful in these patients as in younger ones.[11,12]

Unfortunately a typical scenario that occurs when a nursing home patient has diarrhea is that enteral feedings are discontinued because of the fear of osmotic diarrhea, or orders are written to encourage fluids but the type of fluids are not specified. Since both salts and water are lost with diarrhea, both intravascular depletion and electrolyte imbalance can result. Inadequate replacement of volume may lead to anuria or infarctions of vital organs. If too little fluid replacement is given, hypernatremia with hypovolemia can occur. Alternatively, if volume depletion is treated by fluids too low in salt, then hyponatremia may accompany volume depletion. Either scenario can lead to delirium or seizures, and such events typically end when the patient dies or is transferred to an acute care hospital for emergency treatment. It is now 15 years since an editorial in *Lancet* declared that understanding the physiology underlying ORT was perhaps the most important advance in medicine during the twentieth century.[13] ORT is a simple and inexpensive treatment for dehydration from diarrhea. ORT can be employed early (when diarrhea first strikes) and without any complicated technology. It can be drunk or given through enteral feeding tubes.[14] However, ORT is rarely used for adults in the United States, and there are no reports to our knowledge of its use in elderly patients in any setting, although initial metabolic balance studies have been published recently.[15] Appropriate use of ORT in nursing homes and in the community might avert many hospitalizations and prevent serious complications.

Since it has been well-documented that malnutrition is a common and serious problem among nursing home patients,[16,17] and perhaps is a problem among those living in the community as well, then any diseases that accelerate malnutrition deserve highest attention. There is now sufficient information that indicates that in both residents of developing countries and travelers to such countries an apparently trivial bout of acute diarrhea can be accompanied by rather prolonged malabsorption and anorexia.[18] It is not uncommon for travelers or long-term visitors to developing countries to experience significant weight loss as a consequence of diarrhea. There is currently only one case report of a diarrheal illness affecting the nutritional state of a nursing home patient in this country,[19] and the relationship between gastroenteritis and malnutrition among elderly persons in the United States remains to be explored more thoroughly. As in poor countries, it can be expected that diarrheal illnesses are a significant contributing factor to malnourishment within vulnerable populations in this country.

The principal change in management of diarrhea during the past 20 years has arisen from the repeated documentation that continued and early feeding, even during the acute illness, is associated with a less severe disease, a shorter disease course, and a more rapid recovery.[20] The use of early feeding and ORT in children has prevented prolonged weight loss and has accelerated a return to a normal growth curve. It is to be expected that in elderly patients, such an approach would result in prevention of accelerated malnutrition and the disorders which accompany that state (e.g., pressure sores that do not heal, anorexia, lethargy, edema, and loss of strength and muscle mass).

CAUSES

There are no thorough studies of sporadic or epidemic diarrhea in either institutionalized or community-dwelling elderly populations in which the currently available technology for diagnosing the cause of diarrhea has been applied. In settings where this technology has been used, it is possible to identify two-thirds of the causes of an episode of acute diarrhea.[21] Table 117-1 indicates some of the noninfectious and infectious causes of diarrhea that are of signal importance in elderly patients. The evaluation of patients with diarrheal illness should be directed at excluding the noninfectious causes and identifying infectious agents. Among the common noninfectious causes are laxative use and abuse, complications of prescribed medications, supplemental and tube feedings of high osmolarity, and gastrointestinal syndromes such as dysmotility with constipation and impaction, partial bowel obstruction, mesenteric vascular insufficiency, and certain neoplasms.

Of the infectious diarrheas, there are three broad categories. The first of these is acute food poisoning, in which an individual consumes preformed toxins in foods contaminated by bacteria. The most common illness of this type is associated with *Staphylococcus aureus* enterotoxins. This is an explosive illness that occurs within 2 to 8 hours of eating contaminated food and is characterized principally by vomiting.

The second category of infectious diarrheal diseases is acute watery diarrhea. These syndromes are caused by bacteria that produce several potent enterotoxins. The most dramatic of these diseases is cholera, mediated by the *Vibrio cholerae* exotoxin.[22]

TABLE 117-1

Causes of Diarrhea That Need To Be Considered in Elderly Patients

Noninfectious Causes	Infectious Agents
Iatrogenesis	Bacteria
Dietary supplements	*Campylobacter* spp.
Antacids and acid-suppressing drugs	*Clostridium difficile**
Bulk and osmotically active laxatives	*Clostridium perfringens**
(e.g., Colace, milk of magnesia, lactulose)	*Escherichia coli**
Miscellaneous drugs	*Salmonella* spp.*
(e.g., digoxin, quinidine, methyldopa)	*Shigella* spp.
	Vibrio cholerae
	Vibrio spp.
Neoplasia	Viruses
Obstructive lesions	Adenovirus*
Secretory adenomas	Astrovirus*
Hormone-secreting tumors	Calicivirus*
	Coronavirus*
	Norwalk agent*
	Rotavirus*
Gastrointestinal disease	Parasites
Obstructive lesions	*Cryptosporidium*
Dysmotility with impaction	*Entamoeba histolytica*
Inflammatory bowel disease	*Giardia**
Malabsorption	
Mesenteric atherosclerosis and ischemia	
Portal hypertension	
Systemic illness	
Diabetes mellitus	
Thyrotoxicosis	
Uremia	

*Each of these agents has been reported as the cause of an outbreak of diarrhea in a nursing home.

The pandemic of cholera in South America in the early 1990s afflicted the elderly population disproportionately, and the first death related to this epidemic in the United States was a 70-year-old man.[23] A number of other gram-negative bacteria also produce a cholera-like exotoxin, and there are several other toxins capable of producing similar diseases which are less severe and prolonged. The heat-stable toxin (ST) and heat-labile (LT) toxin of *E. coli* are examples of such toxins. Acute watery diarrhea is also caused in the absence of exotoxin production by adherence of bacteria such as enteroadherent *E. coli* to cells of the small intestine.

The third main category of infectious diarrhea is invasive or tissue-destructive diseases mediated by inflammation. The organisms that cause these illnesses also often produce enterotoxins. The most characteristic of inflammatory bacterial diarrhea is caused by *Shigella* spp., in which a dysentery-like syndrome occurs, accompanied by fever and systemic illness. Diarrheal outbreaks due to *E. coli* may share similar mechanisms.[2] Infection with *Salmonella* spp. can also result in dysentery, and salmonellosis is more common in the United States than shigellosis. However, with both salmonellosis and shigellosis it is not uncommon in young adults and children to have a dysenteric or tissue-destructive phase preceded by an acute bout of watery diarrhea, since both groups of bacteria possess enterotoxins capable of triggering the mechanism that causes acute watery diarrhea. More common than either *Shigella* or *Salmonella* diarrhea in this country, and of special note in elderly persons, is an inflammatory diarrhea caused by *Clostridium difficile*. This syndrome often follows the administration of antibiotics, and many recent reports have indicated that *C. difficile* diarrhea is very common in older hospital and nursing homes patients.[24–27] *C. difficile* is among the invasive group of organisms in that it produces a potent cytotoxin which leads to necrosis of the lining cells of the colon (and perhaps the terminal ileum) and results in severe inflammation. This inflammation can be recognized proctoscopically as pseudomembranous colitis. Occasionally inflammation from *C. difficile* colitis is diagnosed when indium-labeled white blood cell scans are ordered in patients with unexplained fevers. In these cases, affected areas of the colon and terminal ileum are visualized by the concentration of labeled white blood cells in the affected gut.

Carriage of *C. difficile* is not common in the general population or in older adults living in the community, but has been commonly found in the residents of some nursing homes. Colonization without obvious clinical symptoms may be sustained over long periods of time, but more worrisome is the observation that colonization is associated with protein-losing enteropathy which may worsen the nutritional state,[19,28] and is also associated with an increased likelihood of death.[25,29] The latter observation has parallels in work with experimental animals, particularly the hamster, in which death due to *C. difficile* infection is usually not accompanied by diarrhea but is associated with a severe and occult cecitis which might lead to systemic intoxication by *C. difficile* toxins A and B, or entry into the systemic circulation of other potent bacterial products across the damaged intestinal mucosa. We have seen cases in which nursing home patients without diarrhea died and *C. difficile* colitis was found at autopsy. Pseudomembranous colitis presenting as toxic megacolon (without diarrhea) has been increasingly recognized, and the use of antiperistaltic drugs may predispose to the development of this complication of *C. difficile* infection. Figure 117-2 shows an abdominal CT scan of a nursing home patient treated with diphenoxylate HCl–atropine sulfate who developed a high fever and was diagnosed with an obstructing colonic mass (arrow Fig. 117-2*A*). A presumptive diagnosis of *C. difficile* colitis was made when the admission cytotoxin assay returned positive, and the "mass lesion" resolved following treatment with vancomycin (Fig. 117-2*B*).

Finally, the viral diarrheas are among the group of inflammatory gastroenteridites. Many of the viruses initially identified as diarrheal agents in infants and young children have now been implicated in nursing home outbreaks of diarrhea. These include Norwalk agent, rotavirus, calicivirus, coronavirus, and astrovirus. Other enteroviruses, no doubt, will continue to be identified.

MECHANISMS

Through studies on cholera, mechanisms that underlie bacterial and viral diarrhea have been elucidated over the last two decades.[30] The final common pathway for secretion in the intestines operates through the cells of the villus crypts. These cells are influenced directly by enterotoxins and neural signals, as well as by hormones including prostaglandins, vasoactive intestinal peptides, gastrin, and others. The final stage for secretion is a chloride secretory mechanism which is linked to intracellular signals that also decrease absorption of sodium chloride. Thus, to a greater or lesser extent, in instances of diarrhea mediated either directly or indirectly through humoral signals accompanying inflammation, crypt cells secrete and villus tip cells fail to absorb fluids. The ensuing fluid accumulation that takes place principally in the duodenum and jejunum overwhelms the absorptive capacity of the ileum and colon and results in watery diarrhea.[22]

The mechanisms by which the adherence of bacteria to intestinal epithelium produces diarrhea are not as clearly defined as are those for enterotoxin-mediated diarrhea. However, it is expected that bacterial products trigger endogenous humoral signals which precipitate a secretory and nonabsorptive state of the upper intestine. Such a state, in fact, is a partial defense mechanism and operates nicely as long as the host has fluid replacement adequate to sustain the gastrointestinal fluid losses. What is in essence a

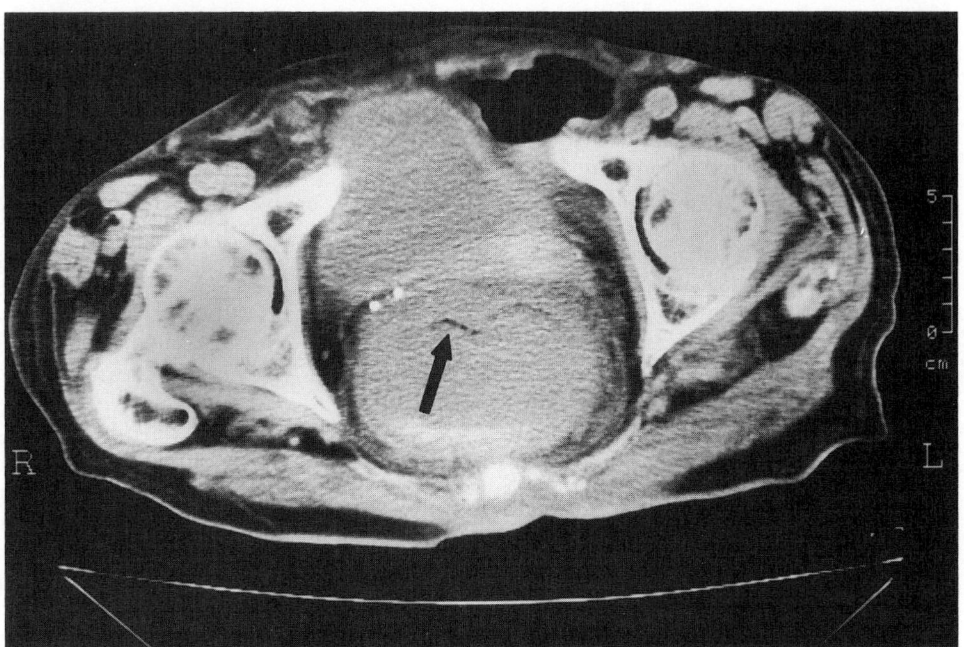

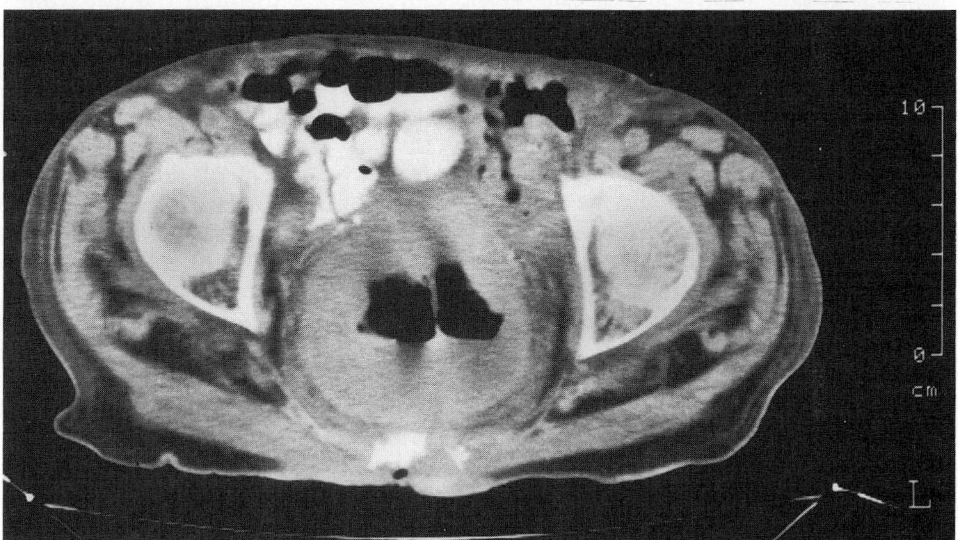

FIGURE 117-2
Computed tomography of the abdomen showing (*A*) an obstructive rectal mass with only minimal luminal gas (arrow) and (*B*) subsequent resolution of the obstruction 5 days later following treatment for pseudomembranous colitis with vancomycin. (*Originally published by the authors*[19] *and used with the permission of Geriatrics.*)

flushing mechanism removes the pathogens from the upper gut and allows normal endogenous flora to become reestablished. The precise mechanisms of invasive diarrheas are less fully studied; however, it is clear that organisms which invade possess potent substances that damage cells and allow bacterial entrance into the mucosa and even the circulation. The best studies of these factors is the verotoxin of *Shigella* and *E. coli.*[31]

HOST FACTORS

In humans, diarrhea is one of the most common causes of death before the reproductive years begin.[8] Even so, evolutionary biology has endowed humans with very effective host defenses against enteric infection. We are not aware of studies to date that investigate the change in the defense mechanisms against enteric infection with age. Since diarrhea is common and disabling in the elderly, certainly this is an important area for investigation. Clearly the most important defense against enteric infection is the intelligence of the individual which makes use of the knowledge and technologies available to prepare food and water free of parasites and microorganisms. However, especially in poor countries and institutional settings, systems preventing enteric pathogens from entering food or water often break down, engendering a risk of diarrheal diseases.

The next line of defense lies in the nose and in the mouth. The olfactory sense can detect spoiled food and produces an avoidance from eating it. Unfortunately, some enteric pathogens can proliferate in food without producing noxious odors or tastes; also, age reduces the ability to smell. The next major defense is gastric acid. Both in experimental animals and humans, the loss or diminution of gastric acid results in much higher susceptibility to all kinds of enteric infections and diarrheal diseases. Quantitative examples of this in young adults are available from research on cholera in volunteer studies. In subjects with full gastric acid, nearly a million-fold more organisms are required to create disease than in those in whom gastric acid has been neutralized.[32] Production of gastric acid may decline with age, although it is not clear whether this is a normal part of aging. The integrity of the gastric acid barrier in the elderly warrants further study. Certain bacteria, principally *Helicobacter pylori,* cause gastritis and a reduction of gastric acid and may predispose for diarrhea. Many elderly patients also take drugs that inhibit the secretion of gastric acid, e.g., histamine (H_2) receptor antagonists or proton pump inhibitors, or drugs that neutralize the stomach acid, e.g., magnesium and aluminum antacids. It would be expected that these medications would predispose individuals to developing diarrhea, particularly if the recipients of these medications travel to countries where fecal contamination of food and water supplies is common, or if they live in institutions where exposure to enteropathogens is more likely. Thus, the gastric acid has importance in that it protects against infection, and can be eliminated by common therapies.

The next line of defense is reflexive elimination from the gut by vomiting or diarrhea. The vomiting reflex occurs when certain contaminated substances are taken into the stomach and then rejected. This is particularly common with food poisonings but also occurs in other infections. Diarrhea can result from the secretory response by the upper gut, which accelerates the propulsion of infecting materials to the colon and expulsion from the anus. Diarrhea is a defense mechanism that causes disability and death when fluids are not replaced.

The most distal defense is the normal microbial flora. The anaerobic conditions of the cecum and internal ileum created by the close symbiotic relationship of intestinal microflora with these organs is a strong defense against enteric pathogens. The most striking experimental demonstration of this defense has been done in mice. A millionfold more *Salmonella* are required to generate a fatal bloodstream infection when normal intestinal flora are present compared with when antibiotics are used to destroy the intestinal flora.[33] This underscores the risks of disturbing gut microflora and permits an understanding of why infection by *C. difficile,* and potentially by *C. perfringens*[34] or *E. coli,*[2] is such a problem in the institutionalized elderly patient. The importance of the gut flora has also led to therapeutic approaches that aim to displace enteropathogens and facilitate the reestablishment of the normal intestinal microflora using microbial replacement therapy with *Lactobacillus* spp.[35] or *Saccharomyces boulardii.*[36] At the present time we are not aware of definitive studies of microfloral changes with aging. It is clear that very young infants and very old persons have certain infections in common, among them *C. difficile.* Further information on the evolution of gut microflora with age will be important for an understanding of susceptibility to invasive diarrheal diseases.

Finally, the intestine has an extremely talented and effective local immune system. Antigens passing through the gut from the earliest days of childhood are monitored by sensor cells located in the Peyer's patches. Antibodies are formed locally at the surface of the intestine where infecting organisms adhere or invade. Defense against viral and bacterial diarrheal diseases is principally through the local immune system of the intestinal tract.[37] Those growing up in countries or situations where fecal–oral pollution is great acquire at a very young age a high level of resistance to most of the diarrheal diseases and enteric infections. Few studies of the local immune system of the gut with aging are available,[38] but intestinal immunity would be expected to remain intact along with other components of the immune system except in the case of disease, severe malnutrition, immune-compromising infections, or immunosuppressive therapy. An understanding of the gut immune system is important, as all the currently effective experimental vaccines directed against enteric pathogens are administered orally. The prototypical oral vaccine is the oral poliovirus vaccine. Poliovirus enters the system through the gut, and the gut is the principal site of immune defense. Long-lasting immunity is engendered by oral polio vaccine. This also appears to be true of immunity induced by other enteric vaccines.[37]

TREATMENT

Treatment of diarrhea is very straightforward. Since acute watery diarrhea is more common than inflammatory dysentery, and since most cases are self-limited and last from 2 to 5 days, the only requirement for avoiding any complications is to replace all gastrointestinal losses with fluids of appropriate volume and composition.[8,9] Losses must be replaced early before vascular complications occur. Therapy should be initiated from the onset of the first loose stool. Although a great deal of information has been gathered on the composition of diarrheal stools in children and young adults, we are not aware of any such data in the elderly, although it is unlikely that there will be major differences with aging in the composition of secretory diarrhea. Even though most oral rehydration therapy solutions have been designed for use in children and none have been developed based on studies of diarrheal losses in older individuals, those solutions listed in Table 117-2 are appropriate for use in elderly patients. Except for the rice-based formula, these solutions are commercially available.

ORT is now the standard and best treatment for all diarrheal diseases. Neither technology nor a specialized health provider is required for the administration of ORT. What is necessary is an individual capable of offering sips of the solution to the affected patient frequently, at least every 3 to 5 minutes in patients with severe losses, and also capable of roughly estimating the volume of the diarrheal losses. The simplest rules for knowing when enough ORT has been given are that urine will be passed every 3 to 4 hours and the specific gravity of the urine will be less than 1.015. If there is concern about urinary retention, it may be necessary in debilitated patients to temporarily insert a urinary catheter to ensure that adequate replacement has been achieved. Except in patients with anuria from end-stage renal disease, urine output is the best guide to therapy. Thirst is a helpful index for guiding ORT in children and young adults, but some studies have shown the thirst mechanism to be abnormal in elderly patients, and cognitive impairment limits the usefulness of this symptom as a guide for monitoring repletion in many nursing home patients.

More precise measurements of fluid losses and gains can be carried out by accurate measurement of plasma specific gravity or plasma protein levels. This simple and inexpensive test can be used for diagnosing the severity of volume depletion in patients who are poor historians, for ensuring prompt evaluation and treatment for those involved in an outbreak, or for monitoring therapy in individuals susceptible to congestive heart failure. Careful measurements of intake and output would be ideal, but these measurements are not usually obtainable either in the community setting or in nursing homes. The principal physical finding in relation to volume loss is orthostatic hypotension. It is essential not to allow sufficient depletion to occur such that orthostasis is present. ORT should always be administered before orthostasis occurs, and in quantities sufficient to ensure that blood volume never decreases to the point of circulatory compromise.

There are risks of ORT that are greater in the elderly than in the younger age groups. The principal risk is that many older people have impaired cardiac function, and overhydration can result in congestive heart failure. Therefore it is important to observe the patient with diarrhea who is being treated with ORT and watch for signs of failure, including rales at the lung bases, jugular vein distension, and sacral or peripheral edema. In protracted illness, body weights can be measured daily, and serial weights can be used as a rough index of the state of hydration.

Feeding should accompany rehydration early in diarrheal illness. It is important, however, to avoid feedings containing a high osmolarity. Digestive enzymes of the intestinal tract are generally present in excess during diarrheal illness. Thus, proteins and starches may be given during the diarrheal illness. In

TABLE 117-2

Analysis of Six Commercially Available Oral Rehydration Therapy Solutions and a Prepared Rice-Based Solution

Oral Rehydration Therapy Solution	Na (meg)	K (meq)	Cl (meq)	Base* (meq)	Carbohydrate† (g)	Calories (kcal)
ORS‡ (Jianas Bros.)	90	20	80	30	20	80
Pedialyte (Ross)	45	20	35	30	25	100
Pediatric Electrolyte (NutraMax Products)	45	20	35	30	25	100
ElderLyte (NutraMax Products)	45	20	35	30	25	100
Rehydralyte (Ross)	75	20	65	30	25	100
Ricelyte (Mead Johnson)	50	25	45	34	30	126
Rice-based	90	20	80	30	80	320

* HCO_3 or citrate.

† ORS, Pedialyte, Pediatric Electrolyte, ElderLyte, and Rehydralyte contain glucose. Ricelyte contains rice syrup solids. Rice-based ORT can be made from precooked instant rice cereal, e.g., Gerber's Rice Cereal for Baby.

‡ This is the WHO-UNICEF formula.

fact, it can be expected that as these are degraded to component amino acids and monosaccharides, enhanced transport of sodium and absorption of water from the intestinal lumen to the bloodstream will result. Indeed, "advanced" oral rehydration solutions are made with proteins and starches, or maltidextrins. These solutions are characteristically lower in osmolarity than the present standard oral rehydration solution containing glucose and have been shown to shorten the duration of diarrhea and reduce fluid losses in young adults.[8]

From studies of food absorption in diarrheal disease, it is clear that fat is the most poorly digested food component before, during, and after diarrhea. Impairment of protein digestion and absorption is next. Carbohydrate absorption is least impaired in most diarrheal illnesses.[18] An additional safety factor in using large carbohydrate molecules or polymers in ORT is that any molecules not digested and absorbed will not worsen diarrhea because the osmotic activity of solutions of large molecules and polymers is low compared with that of solutions of simple sugars and monomers. The intestine is a very permeable membrane, and any differences in physical or osmotic pressures equilibrate extraordinarily rapidly.

When there is an inflammatory colitis, as in shigellosis, salmonellosis, or *C. difficile* disease, antibiotics may be indicated. However, the effect of antibiotics in *Salmonella* disease is controversial and disappointing, and at present antibiotics are felt to be contraindicated in this condition. Shigellosis is caused by an organism that possesses a high degree of resistance, and appropriate antibiotic therapy demands knowledge of the resistance pattern of the organism from the area where it was acquired. Treatment of *C. difficile* disease with antibiotics has been very disappointing. Relapses are frequent, and failure to eradicate toxin from the stool is not uncommon. For this reason, investigations at a number of institutions are currently being carried out which would rely on microbial competition and restoration of normal gut flora to combat colonization by *C. difficile* and formation of its toxin.[39,40] Finally, the investigation of the outbreak of dysentery-like diarrhea caused by *E. coli* in a nursing home in Toronto found that either the prior ingestion of antibiotics or the prescription of antibiotics during diarrhea significantly increased morbidity and mortality.[2] Hence the physician must proceed with great caution in treating any diarrheal illness with antibiotics.

In most instances, watery diarrhea requires no further treatment than replacement of fluid losses with ORT. In view of the risks of antibiotic therapy in elderly patients, unless there is clearly infection with an invasive organism, antibiotics are contraindicated. The risk of postantibiotic diarrhea of a more serious nature than that of the acute watery diarrhea being treated outweighs the benefit of the antibiotic. Furthermore, there are available several potentially useful antisecretory drugs that are of low cost and have few side effects. The most available of these is bismuth subsalicylate (Pepto Bismol). This very interesting remedy combines some microbicidal activity together with the antisecretory activity inherent in the salicylate moiety.[41] Except in cholera, most diarrheal diseases have a component of inflammation, which causes fluid losses through secretion of prostaglandins and other substances. Therefore, compounds that inhibit the arachidonic acid cascade can sharply reduce fluid losses in diarrhea and decrease the duration of illness. This has been nicely demonstrated in the case of traveler's diarrhea, and further studies with this agent are under way in elderly patients and in populations in poor countries. At present, it can be recommended that bismuth subsalicylate be given 30 ml every hour for up to eight doses, or until diarrhea stops, followed by a maintenance dose of 60 ml four times a day. This regimen can be prescribed without risk of toxicity and with the possibility of increasing patient comfort and shortening illness duration. Other agents that are commonly used, e.g., adsorbents like Kaopectate, charcoal, etc., have not been shown to be of significant benefit in treating diarrheal diseases. Antimotility drugs can decrease the duration of diarrhea but do not affect the amount of fluid loss. They also can have adverse effects in that they allow pooling of infected material within the intestine, delaying its expulsion from the body, have been shown to increase the severity and duration of invasive diarrheal diseases, and have led to pseudomembranous colitis in patients with *C. difficile* infection. We presently would recommend the use of ORT in all cases of diarrhea at the earliest possible time, prescription of bismuth subsalicylate, and *avoidance* of all other antidiarrheal drugs.

In approaching all cases of diarrhea in elderly patients, it is important to recognize that instances of intestinal obstruction, appendicitis, diverticulitis, and vascular insufficiency all are more common in older age groups. Each of these conditions may require surgical intervention. Except in the instance of intestinal ileus, it is still safe to administer ORT while observing the patient and carrying out further necessary investigations. It is also important to review orders and ensure that laxatives or other diarrhea-causing drugs or diets have not been introduced immediately prior to the onset of diarrhea. It is likely that many cases of diarrhea in nursing home patients are related to medications. Thus, the only indicated therapy aside from replacement of fluid would be cancellation or modification of prescribed drugs.

PREVENTIVE CONSIDERATIONS

The principal consideration in the prevention of diarrheal illness is ensuring that water and food supplies are not contaminated with fecal organisms. This means proper refrigeration, proper preparation of foods with adequate cooking, and careful handling of food by dietary workers who are well-versed in sanitary practices. Even in a wealthy and advanced society, breakdowns occur regularly in food processing, handling, and water supplies. This can be particularly true in feeding large numbers of people in institutions where food handling may be contracted out or managed with insufficient budgets and under adverse conditions. Similarly, although water supplies may be clean and safe coming into an institution, the containers in which water is placed can become contaminated if left standing for a long time. Thus, attention to the proper management of water provided to patients is essential.

Avoidance of prescription of excessive laxatives and of drugs that cause diarrhea can prevent many instances of diarrhea in the nursing home setting. Use of antibiotics only under clear indication is perhaps the single most important concern in preventing serious and disabling diarrhea related to *C. difficile* and other organisms which may multiply if the normal gut flora is disturbed. When outbreaks occur, observing basic enteric precautions of hand washing and proper handling of soiled bed linens becomes essential to avoid spread across an entire institution. The single most important measure, however, is hand washing with soap and water by all health care providers. When hand washing has been instituted even under the most adverse circumstances, there has been a marked reduction in spread of enteric infection.[42,43] Thus, education and attention to this measure deserve the greatest emphasis.[44] It is also likely, of course, that many other diseases spread by contact in handling could also be avoided in this way.

At present, there are no immunizations indicated to prevent enteric infection in elderly patients, although it is possible that in coming years this may change. Further investigations on the role of gastric acid as a defense against diarrheal disease in elderly persons are essential since there is such widespread prescription of antacid medications, and studies are needed to determine the overall morbidity and mortality of patients taking these drugs routinely. Finally, treatment regimens based on microbial replacement hold promise, and ongoing studies may provide new therapies for ameliorating and preventing infectious diarrheas.

CONCLUSION

Diarrheal diseases are very common and are an important cause of morbidity and mortality in elderly persons, particularly for older adults living in nursing homes. Outbreaks of viral gastroenteritis in long-term care facilities, and sporadic cases of *C. difficile* infection in nursing home residents, occur frequently. *C. difficile* is associated with protein-losing enteropathy, and current treatment strategies are unsatisfactory. The most important treatment for virtually all patients with diarrhea is ORT, a simple and low-cost therapy which should be initiated when diarrhea starts and continued until diarrhea resolves. ORT is the standard treatment of diarrheal diseases the world over and should be employed both at home and in institutional settings in the United States. In elderly patients, special considerations in administering ORT exist because heart failure is often present, and the hazard of fluid overload exists to a greater extent than in healthy young adults and children. Although there are few useful adjunctive agents to ORT, bismuth subsalicylate holds promise and should be used. Since antimicrobial therapy has been shown to be hazardous with respect to worsening and predisposing to gastrointestinal infections, prescription of antibiotics must be approached with great caution generally, and when treating elderly patients with diarrhea specifically. Monitoring drug regimens to minimize the use of laxatives and diarrhea-causing drugs can reduce the incidence of diarrhea in older patients. Similarly, since the use of gastric acid–inhibiting drugs such as histamine (H_2) antagonists, proton-pump inhibitors, and antacids may predispose toward diarrheal illness, their use should also be monitored. Preventive measures for diarrhea are relatively simple and are not costly. Rigorous attention to the handling of food and water, and hand washing with soap and water by all health care providers and by all food handlers will prevent many diarrheal outbreaks as well as contain the spread of enteropathogens from person to person when infected individuals are cared for at home, in a hospital, or in a nursing home.

REFERENCES

1. Farber RE et al: Salmonellosis—Baltimore, Maryland. *MMWR* 19:314, 1970.
2. Carter AO et al: A severe outbreak of *Escherichia coli* 0157:H7-associated hemorrhagic colitis in a nursing home. *N Engl J Med* 317:1496, 1987.
3. Lin FYC et al: Gastroenteritis outbreaks in nursing homes. *Abst Annu Mtg Am Soc Microbiol* 350, 1988.
4. Garibaldi RA et al: Infections among patients in nursing homes: Policies, prevalence, and problems. *N Engl J Med* 305:731, 1981.
5. Nicolle LE et al: Twelve-month surveillance of infections in institutionalized elderly men. *J Am Geriatr Soc* 32:513, 1984.
6. Lew JF et al: Diarrheal deaths in the United States: 1979 through 1987. *JAMA* 265:3280, 1991.
7. Gangarosa RE et al: Hospitalizations involving gastroenteritis in the United States, 1985: The special burden of the disease among the elderly. *Am J Epidemiol* 135:281, 1992.
8. Taylor CE, Greenough WB III: Control of diarrheal diseases. *Annu Rev Public Health* 10:221, 1989.
9. Greenough WB III: Diarrhea: Etiology and treatment

with oral rehydration therapy. *Am Assoc Ret Persons* 2(3):1, 1988.
10. *World Health Statistics Annual. Vital Statistics and Cause of Death.* Geneva, World Health Organization, 1975.
11. Dauterman KN, et al: Plasma specific gravity measures volume depletion: A common correctable and often overlooked problem in the elderly. *Clin Res* 40:394A, 1992.
12. Carpenter CCJ: Cholera diagnosis and treatment. *Bull NY Acad Med* 47:1191, 1971.
13. Water, sugar and salt (editorial). *Lancet* 2:300, 1978.
14. Nalin DR, Cash RA: Oral or nasogastric maintenance therapy for diarrhea of unknown etiology resembling cholera. *Trans R Soc Trop Med Hyg* 64(5):769, 1970.
15. Greenough WB III et al: Causes of diarrhea in the elderly: Impact on intestinal function and treatment by oral rehydration therapy. *Clin Res* 40:438A, 1992.
16. Lipschitz DA: Protein calorie malnutrition in the hospitalized elderly. *Primary Care* 9:531, 1982.
17. Rudman D, Feller AG: Protein-calorie undernutrition in the nursing home. *J Am Geriatr Soc* 37:173, 1989.
18. Molla AM et al: Food intake during and after recovery from diarrhea, in Chen L, Schrimsaw N (eds): *Diarrhea and Malnutrition.* New York, Plenum, 1983.
19. Bennett R, Greenough W: *C. difficile* diarrhea: A common and overlooked nursing home infection. *Geriatrics* 45:77, 1990.
20. Santosham M et al: Role of soy-based lactose-free formula during treatment of acute diarrhea. *Pediatrics* 76:292, 1985.
21. Stoll BJ et al: Surveillance of patients attending a diarrhoeal disease hospital in Bangladesh. *Br J Med* 285:1185, 1982.
22. Rabbani GH: Cholera. *Clin Gastroenterol* 15(3):507, 1986.
23. Swerdlow DL, Ries AM: Cholera in the Americas. *JAMA* 267:1495, 1992.
24. McFarland LV et al: Nosocomial acquisition of *Clostridium difficile* infection. *N Engl J Med* 320:204, 1989.
25. Bender BS et al: Is *Clostridium difficile* endemic in chronic-care facilities? *Lancet* 1:11, 1986.
26. Associated Press. Bacterial outbreak spurs medical alert in Chicago. *New York Times.* Sunday, September 20, 1987.
27. Bennett RG et al: *Clostridium difficile* in elderly patients. *Age Ageing* 18:354, 1989.
28. Rybolt AH et al: Protein-losing enteropathy associated with *Clostridium difficile* infection. *Lancet* 1:1353, 1989.
29. Thomas DR et al: Postantibiotic colonization with *Clostridium difficile* in nursing-home patients. *J Am Geriatr Soc* 38:415, 1990.
30. Moriarty KJ, Turnberg LA: Bacterial toxins and diarrhoea. *Clin Gastroenterol* 15(3):529, 1986.
31. O'Brien A, Holmes RK: Shiga and shiga-like toxins. *Microbiol Rev* 51:206, 1987.
32. Hornick RB et al: The Broad Street pump revisited: Response of volunteers to ingested cholera vibrios. *Bull NY Acad Med* 47:1181, 1971.
33. Bonhoff M et al: Resistance of the mouse's intestinal tract to experimental *Salmonella* infection I and II. *J Exp Med* 120:805, 1964.
34. Williams R et al: Diarrhoea due to enterotoxigenic *Clostridium perfringens:* Clinical features and management of a cluster of ten cases. *Age Ageing* 14:296, 1985.
35. Gotz A et al: Prophylaxis against ampicillin-associated diarrhea with a lactobacillus preparation. *Am J Hosp Pharm* 36:754, 1979.
36. Surawicz CM et al: Prevention of antibiotic-associated diarrhea by *Saccharomyces boulardii:* A prospective study. *Gastroenterology* 96:981, 1989.
37. Pierce NF et al: Induction of a mucosal antitoxin response and its role in immunity to experimental canine cholera. *Infect Immun* 21:185, 1978.
38. Schmucker DL, Daniels K: Aging gastrointestinal infection, and mucosal immunity. *J Am Geriatr Soc* 34:377, 1986.
39. Gorbach SL et al: Successful treatment of relapsing *Clostridium difficile* colitis with *Lactobacillus* GG. Lancet 2:1519, 1987.
40. Elmer GW, McFarland L: Suppression by *Saccharomyces boulardii* of toxigenic *Clostridium difficile* overgrowth after vancomycin treatment in hamsters. *Antimicrob Agents Chemother* 31:129, 1987.
41. Ericsson CD et al: Non-antibiotic therapy for traveler's diarrhea. *Rev Infect Dis* 8(suppl 12):S202, 1986.
42. Black RE et al: Handwashing to prevent diarrhoea in day care centers. *Am J Epidemiol* 113:445, 1981.
43. Khan MU. Interruption of shigellosis by hand-washing. *Trans R Soc Trop Med Hyg* 76:164, 1982.
44. Otherson MJ, Otherson HB Jr: A history of handwashing: Seven hundred years at a snail's pace. *Pharos,* Spring 1987, p 23.

Chapter 118

SPINAL AND PERIPHERAL NERVE SYNDROMES: BACK PAIN AND WEAKNESS

Mindy Aisen

Spinal cord dysfunction and neuropathic processes in the aging population can occur as the result of traumatic, ischemic, nutritional, malignant, or degenerative conditions; these are often complications of age-related systemic or skeletal syndromes. These conditions frequently produce profound physical and psychosocial disability, impairing voluntary movement, primary sensory perception, bowel and bladder function, sexual activity, and ventilatory capacity. Appropriate medical and rehabilitation efforts can, however, increase longevity and promote comfort and independence. The conditions affecting spinal cord and peripheral nerve function associated with aging include specific traumatic and compressive syndromes, spinal cord infarction, subacute combined degeneration, and amyotrophic lateral sclerosis.

SPINAL CORD TRAUMA

Spinal cord injury (SCI) can be a devastating experience not only because of the severity of resultant disability, but because of its acute onset. SCI occurs when the spinal cord is subjected to forces which produce excessive flexion, extension, or rotation. Such forces may disrupt bony integrity by producing vertebral fracture or dislocation. The spinal column is most often compromised at points of relative mobility abutting less mobile regions, including the atlantoaxial joint, low cervical area, and thoracolumbar and lumbosacral junctions.[1]

Cord injury occurs when compression, tension, or torsion produces hemorrhagic contusion, vascular compromise, or mechanical cell death; cord transection is a rare sequela of this sort of trauma. Experimental studies have demonstrated that immediately after impact little pathologic change is seen in acutely compressed spinal cord. Initially petechial hemorrhages are noted in central gray matter. Over hours to days, a central necrotic region develops in gray matter which gradually enlarges, involving central then peripheral white matter. This delayed progressive injury has been ascribed to several mechanisms, including phospholipases (released from disrupted lysosomes and activated by elevated levels of intracellular calcium) and free radicals, which disrupt cell membranes. Eicosanoid production, which promotes ischemia and immune-mediated cell death, has also been implicated.

Epidemiology

In the United States the yearly incidence of SCI is approximately 50 per million population with an estimated prevalence of 250,000 to 500,000.[2] Generally considered a condition of young men, the median age of onset is 25 years.[2–4] There are, however, particular syndromes associated with the aging population. For example, more than 50 percent of patients with central cord syndrome are over the age of 40, and most are in the 50- to 70-year age group.[5] The incidence of quadriplegia and that of paraplegia are approximately equivalent.[6] In the elderly population most spinal cord injuries occur as the result of motor vehicle accidents and falls.

Clinical Syndromes

The incidences of incomplete and complete syndromes are essentially equivalent.[6,7] A complete lesion refers to a condition in which there is total loss of functional motor and/or sensory function below a spinal level, while an incomplete lesion implies some preservation of function below that level. By convention, the level of injury is defined as the anatomically lowest functional segment, and motor and sensory levels and severity are often described separately.

Most patients with incomplete injuries will experience some degree of neurologic recovery, but approximately 95 percent with complete lesions will have permanent impairment.[8] Recovery tends to develop in the first months after injury. However, follow-up examinations have demonstrated improvement up to 5 years after the acute event.[9] Incomplete spinal cord patterns include the central cord, anterior spinal, and Brown-Séquard syndromes.[10] The central cord syndrome is the most common type of SCI in the aging population. It is associated with acute cervical hyperextension in those over the age of 50, particularly if underlying cervical stenosis or spondylosis is present.[11–14]

Central Cord Syndrome

Central cord injuries typically occur after minor domestic falls.[13] Abrupt cervical hyperextension may compress the cord, especially when calcified posterior ligaments buckle. Preferential central cord injury occurs because the central gray matter is exceptionally sensitive to minor trauma. Further, as the central cord is supplied by terminal branches of the anterior spinal artery with limited collateral supply, the compressive injury can be compounded by vascular insufficiency due to arterial compression.

Vertebral fracture does not uniformly complicate the central cord syndrome, but spinal column integrity must be evaluated.[13,14] If initial x-ray studies reveal no fracture or dislocation, flexion and extension views should be obtained. Magnetic resonance imaging or metrizamide myelography is necessary to ascertain whether persistent cord compression is present.

Surgical intervention (skull traction, decompression, stabilization) is necessary if there is fracture, dislocation, or unstable subluxation.[13] In the patient with a stable column but significant cervical canal narrowing whose neurologic recovery has plateaued, late decompression may be indicated.[8]

Clinically the central cord syndrome produces corticospinal and spinothalamic deficits with relative preservation of posterior column function. Disability is more severe in the upper than lower extremities, and many patients regain the ability to ambulate but are unable to use their hands effectively. Symptoms include weakness, spasticity, painful dysesthesias, and neurogenic bowel and bladder. A mix of upper motor neuron and lower motor neuron signs may be present in the upper limbs, while long tract signs predominate in the lower limbs.

Anterior Spinal Cord and Brown-Séquard Syndromes

The anterior spinal cord syndrome is associated with cervical flexion injuries. The injury occurs in the anterior two-thirds of the spinal cord in the vascular distribution of the anterior spinal artery, and vascular compromise is a likely factor in the pathogenesis. As atherosclerosis and cervical canal narrowing may be predisposing factors, elderly persons are at greater risk of developing this syndrome. Clinically, spinothalamic and corticospinal dysfunction with preserved posterior column function is observed. The patient experiences motor weakness and loss of pain and temperature perception; vibratory sensation and proprioception are unaffected.

The Brown-Séquard syndrome is associated with penetrating wounds producing mechanical cord hemitransection or rotational injuries producing physiologic hemisection. Ipsilateral corticospinal (motor) and posterior column (vibratory, proprioceptive) losses are coupled with contralateral spinothalamic (pain, temperature) signs and deficits.

VASCULAR DISORDERS

Spinal cord infarction generally occurs in the vascular distribution of the anterior spinal artery (ASA), resulting in deficits referable to the anterior two-thirds of the spinal cord. ASA ischemia results in corticospinal signs and dissociated sensory loss (impaired pain and temperature with preserved proprioceptive perception). Necrosis at the site of infarction is generally less extensive than seen in traumatic anterior SCI, and the prognosis is somewhat more favorable.[15] Sixty percent of patients with ASA syndrome experience some degree of motor recovery within the first month, plateauing after 3 months.[15] Major motor recovery is uncommon.

Blood is supplied to the anterior cord by the ASA and to the posterior cord by a pair of posterior spinal arteries which anastomose forming a posterior plexus. Cord infarction is most often due to disease in the feeder vessels of the ASA.[16,17] The ASA arises from the vertebral arteries in the foramen magnum and is fed by branches of vertebral and intercostal arteries. The artery of Ademkiewicz, which arises from the aorta, is the largest ASA supplier in the lower thoracic region. The ASA has a substantially smaller diameter above than below the entry of the artery of Ademkiewicz, creating dynamics which increase midthoracic cord vulnerability to occurrences which compromise blood flow.[18,19] ASA distribution infarction in the aged population may occur in the setting of hypotension, ASA thrombosis, vasculitis, embolism, dissecting aortic aneurysm, and operative procedures requiring cross-clamping of the aorta.[16,17]

MALIGNANCY

Spinal cord compression may be produced by intramedullary, intradural, extramedullary, or extradural tumors. Intramedullary lesions are most commonly seen in childhood and include gliomas, ependymommas, hemangioblastomas, and (rarely) metastatic carcinoma.[20] Meningiomas and neurofibromas are the most commonly encountered extramedullary primary tumors.[21] Metastatic tumors usually occur in the middle-aged and elderly population and cause extradural compression.[22]

Extramedullary Tumors

Meningiomas and neurofibromas are benign growths which cause symptoms by progressively compromising cord vascular supply and by compressing nerve roots and spinal cord. Symptomatically patients report local or radicular pain followed by slowly evolving local root and spinal cord compressive symptoms. The clinical presentation may suggest other spinal cord disorders such as degenerative arthritis, amyotrophic lateral sclerosis, syringomyelia, transverse myelitis, or arachnoiditis.

Plain x-ray films, myelography, and magnetic resonance imaging are all useful techniques which can localize and often preoperatively diagnose these tumors. A neurofibroma, for example, may produce displacement of paraspinal structures, scalloping of the posterior margin of the vertebral body, and foraminal enlargement, while meningiomas are often calcified, all evident on plain x-ray films.

The treatment is surgical excision, and adjunct chemotherapy or radiation is generally not necessary. Prognosis is related to the duration and severity of preoperative symptoms.[22] Sequelae can be similar to signs observed after traumatic injury, including motor weakness, spasticity, bowel and bladder dysfunction, and neuropathic pain.

Metastatic Lesions

Spinal cord compression is a common complication of systemic carcinoma, occurring in 5 to 10 percent of cancer patients and developing at any stage of the illness.[23] Breast, prostate, and lung tumors produce epidural compression by extension of vertebral body metastases, while lymphoma tends to access the epidural space through foraminal openings without causing bony erosion.[24,25]

The presenting symptom is local or radicular pain in more than 90 percent of patients, at times preceding other neurologic symptoms by weeks.[24,25] The development of neurologic signs signals the rapidly progressive phase of the illness. It is the time at which immediate diagnosis and intervention are critical, as irreversible paraplegia may develop within hours.[24] Therefore, it is important to maintain a very high index of suspicion for metastatic spinal cord disease in any patient with cancer and back pain.

Plain x-ray studies indicate vertebral body involvement in 90 percent of patients with epidural metastatic disease, though myelography remains the definitive technique for localizing and defining the lesion as well as determining the extent of spinal cord compromise.[26] An epidural mass producing more than an 80 percent obstruction to dye flow requires emergency therapy. The treatment includes corticosteroids and radiation therapy. Vertebrectomy is indicated when the primary tumor is unknown or when symptoms progress despite radiation therapy.

The prognosis is related to the degree of neurologic disability at the time of treatment. Reports indicate that more than 80 percent of patients who are ambulatory will remain so, while only 35 percent of nonambulatory patients will improve to an ambulatory level.[26]

CERVICAL SPONDYLOSIS

Degenerative changes of the cervical spine are common in the geriatric population. More than 80 percent of people over the age of 55 have radiographic evidence of cervical disc degeneration; half of them are symptomatic.[27] In cervical spondylosis, extensive degeneration of intervertebral bodies occurs with narrowing of disc spaces, accompanied by osteopathic lipping of vertebral bodies, thickening of ligaments, and osteoarthritic changes in posterior vertebral joints.[28] The result of these changes is generalized or focal narrowing of the cervical canal and intervertebral foramina. This can result in compression of spinal cord, nerve root, and spinal arteries. Symptoms and signs include local and radicular pain. Less often myelopathy ensues, producing spasticity, hyperreflexia, and, in advanced cases, weakness and ataxia. A well-defined segmental motor and sensory level is not generally apparent. The differential diagnosis includes subacute combined degeneration, spinal cord tumor, and early incipient pressure hydrocephalus.[29] Radiographic studies of the cervical spine are required for diagnosis.

LUMBAR STENOSIS

Pathologic changes similar to those observed in cervical spondylosis may affect the lumbar spine. As in the case of cervical spondylosis, most individuals affected are over the age of 55. Premorbid narrowing of the spinal canal makes an individual vulnerable to degenerative changes.

Symptoms include back pain and bilateral or unilateral radicular pain. Signs are indicative of a lower motor neuron problem as the lesion is caudal to the termination of the spinal cord. In severe cases, weakness of the lower extremities and urinary and bowel dysfunction are observed. On physical examination, weakness of isolated muscles, reflex loss, and pain elicited by percussion and straight leg raising may be seen. Commonly, complaints of symptoms of neurogenic ischemic claudication are elicited, and many patients assume a stooped posture in order to minimize pain.

The differential diagnosis includes all possible compressive lesions of the cauda equina including tumor. Myelography or magnetic resonance imaging are useful in distinguishing these processes. Intermittent claudication due to peripheral vascular disease may be difficult to distinguish from neurogenic claudication. Lumbar decompression is often required by patients suffering from debilitating pain or weakness.

LOW BACK PAIN

The pain-sensitive structures in the spine include nerve roots, synovial and apophyseal joints, intervertebral discs, periosteum, and vertebral arteries. Inflammation or compression of these structures can lead to local or referred pain. Paraspinal muscle spasm, which often aggravates pain, may result from poor posture, anxiety, or splinting an underlying spinal disorder. Before embarking on a rehabilitation program, it is critical to assess the degree and nature of the associated spine abnormality. Conditions such as malignancy, spinal instability, or limb weakness in association with degenerative spine disease require immediate therapy directed at the underlying lesion.

Acute radiculopathy occurs as the result of nerve root irritation producing local and referred pain in a specific distribution. Nerve inflammation in effect decreases the already compromised space between bony elements in the nerve root pathway, and previously benign limb motion more easily leads to friction and increased root irritation. Reflexively induced muscle spasm can aggravate joint compression and pain. Treatment consists of root immobilization, best achieved with bed rest, nonsteroidal anti-inflammatory medication, and relaxation of paraspinal spasm.

Chronic low back pain may respond to nonpharmacologic techniques such as massage, thermal modalities, and biofeedback. The goal of employing these therapies is relaxation of muscle spasm; as stated above, pain emanating from spinal structures can reflexively induce paraspinal muscle spasm, leading to increased joint pain and a self-sustaining pain syndrome.

Massage is a centuries-old traditional therapy which has been deemed effective by diverse cultures. It is known to relieve spasm and decrease pain. Although the mechanism of action is unknown, it has been proposed that mechanical spindle receptor stimulation leads to reflex muscle relaxation.[30] In addition, an increase in plasma beta endorphins has been demonstrated after connective tissue massage.[31] Massage consists of stroking (observed to soothe and relax deep muscle) and kneading (in which compression theoretically decreases edema and mobilizes tissue adhesions).

Thermal modalities can be useful adjuncts to massage. Superficial heating methods (heating pads, moist compresses) can raise the skin and subcutaneous tissue temperature to a depth of 2 to 3 cm, reflexively increasing superficial blood flow. The resultant cooling in underlying joint structures may contribute to pain relief.

When the pain of acute radiculopathy resolves, or in the case of chronic low back pain, it is often useful to enroll the patient in a short-term physical therapy program, with an emphasis on lumbar and paraspinal strengthening and training concerning proper body mechanics during bending, lifting, walking, and sitting. The patient with severe musculoskeletal disease may benefit from a rigid or semirigid lumbar brace to correct posture and improve mechanical alignment.

PERIPHERAL NEUROPATHY

Peripheral neuropathies are either inherited or acquired. The hereditary neuropathies almost invariably become symptomatic between infancy and young adulthood. Hereditary motor sensory neuropathy type II or neuronal Charcot-Marie-Tooth disease, however, may present in the fifties.[32] This disorder is characterized by slowly evolving motor and sensory axonopathy. Motor weakness primarily involving the peroneal nerve distribution (producing foot drop) is the prominent sign. During the later stages, an almost total loss of muscle bulk below the knee produces a "stork leg" appearance. Despite profound distal weakness, patients generally remain ambulatory, though appropriate bracing at the ankle may be indicated to enhance gait quality and safety. The diagnosis can be made by taking a careful family history, as the disease has an autosomal dominant inheritance pattern. Electrophysiologic testing should demonstrate findings consistent with generalized motor and/or sensory axonopathy.

The majority of acquired toxic and nutritional neuropathies are axonal. Symptoms often develop first in the lower extremities because longer axons are more vulnerable, and include weakness, numbness, and paresthesias in a stocking-glove pattern. A rapid onset is more suggestive of acute intoxication, while insidious progression more often accompanies chronic exposure.[33] Many pharmacologic and industrial agents have been documented to produce axonopathy.

Known neurotoxic drugs are amiodarone, chloramphenicol, cisplatin, dapsone, phenytoin, disulfiram, gold, isoniazide (on the basis of induced pyridoxine deficiency), lithium, nitrofurantoin, nitrous oxide, pyridoxine, and vincristine.[33] Chemical exposures frequently implicated in neuropathy include acrylamide, arsenic, mercury, lead, thallium, triorthocresyl phosphate, and vinyl chloride.[33] The diagnosis of acquired toxic neuropathy requires rigorous history review and appropriate toxicology screening, and symptoms may not arise until years after exposure. The electrophysiologic features are indistinguishable from inherited axonal polyneuropathy.

Nutritional neuropathies are generally associated with alcoholism but have also been described following intentional weight loss.[34] Clinical characteristics are distal limb pain, tingling, sensory loss, weakness, and areflexia. The underlying deficiency may be thiamine, pyridoxine, pantothenic acid, or folic acid. The lesion is axonal with secondary demyelination, and the treatment is nutritional supplementation.

In the aging population, common systemic illnesses which can lead to polyneuropathy include malignancy, diabetes, thyroid dysfunction, and uremia. All produce a subacute axonopathy with sensorimotor features; the condition tends to respond to treatment of the underlying condition.

Paraneoplastic polyneuropathy is predominantly sensory, though it may be sensorimotor. Distal symmetric limb atrophy, ataxia, weakness, and numbness can develop over weeks to months, associated with an elevation in cerebrospinal fluid protein. The neuropathy may precede tumor diagnosis by months to years; the most common associated malignancies are carcinoma, multiple myeloma, and lymphoma.

Amyloid neuropathy is another condition associated with malignancy (particularly multiple myeloma and medullary thyroid carcinoma), which may also be seen in association with chronic infection and in primary amyloidosis. Median neuropathy of the type seen in carpal tunnel syndrome is a common finding. Another form of amyloid neuropathy results in selective dysfunction of "small fibers," producing impairment of pain and temperature perception and autonomic instability.

SUBACUTE COMBINED DEGENERATION

Subacute combined degeneration refers to the pattern of spinal cord and peripheral nerve disease produced by systemic vitamin B_{12} deficiency. In the geriatric population it is almost invariably associated with pernicious anemia. The deficiency is unrelated to diet, but rather develops because intestinal absorption of vitamin B_{12} is impaired because of autoimmune or surgically mediated loss of gastric parietal cells which produce intrinsic factor (see Chaps. 65 and 66).[35]

Pathologically, diffuse degeneration of central and peripheral myelin occurs typically beginning in the posterior columns of the lower cervical cord, then spreading rostrally and caudally as well as anteriorly into lateral columns.[36,37] Demyelination may also occur in the brain, optic nerves, and peripheral nerves.[36] The mechanism of myelin loss may be related to decreased methionine synthesis, a B_{12}-dependent process.[38]

Neurologic manifestations reflect changes in both central and peripheral nervous systems. Initially symptoms are referable to posterior column dysfunction: paresthesias and decreased vibratory perception followed by proprioceptive deficits. Subsequently, spasticity and weakness develop. Symptoms and signs are generally symmetrical; a significant protracted asymmetry should cast doubt on the diagnosis.[36]

Objective signs on examination include early loss of vibratory and position sense coupled with corticospinal findings (weakness, spasticity, Babinski sign). Reflexes can be hyper- or hypoactive depending on the extent of accompanying lower motor neuron damage. Mental status changes are common and include irritability, apathy, cognitive decline, confusion, and depression.[39] Symptoms of optic nerve demyelination may also be seen, producing visual impairment, a centrocecal scotoma, and optic atrophy, and visual evoked potentials may be abnormal in the absence of visual symptoms.[40]

The treatment is intramuscular vitamin B_{12} supplementation. This should be administered daily for at least 3 weeks, and then once or twice weekly for the following 2 months. Monthly intramuscular vitamin B_{12} should then be continued indefinitely.

AMYOTROPHIC LATERAL SCLEROSIS (see Chap. 94 for a comprehensive review of this topic)

Amyotrophic lateral sclerosis (ALS) is a degenerative disease characterized by progressive dysfunction of corticospinal pathways, brainstem motor nuclei, and anterior horns of the spinal cord. The course is generally relentlessly progressive, culminating in death. Among sporadic cases, the mean age of onset is 56, and disease duration 2.5 years. The incidence rate increases progressively with age, suggesting that ALS is a disease of aging.[41,42]

The incidence of ALS ranges between 0.4 and 1.8 per 100,000, and the annual average death rate is one per 100,000 worldwide. ALS is a disease of adulthood which has regional (Western Pacific), familial, and sporadic presentations. Although clinically similar, the age of onset, disease duration, and male/female ratio vary among forms. The Western Pacific and familial varieties of ALS are associated with an earlier onset than is sporadic ALS.[43,44] Disease duration is generally shorter in the familial type, while a less rapidly progressive pattern of disease has been observed among individuals from high-risk areas such as Guam.

ALS is an insidiously progressive disease of the motor system. It affects upper and lower motor neuron pathways, sparing sphincteric and other autonomic functions.[45] Though brainstem involvement is common, extraocular muscle function is rarely involved. Cognitive changes have been reported in up to 10 percent of ALS patients.[46]

The symptoms of motor neuron disease include progressive dysfunction of corticospinal tracts (producing limb paresis, spasticity, and hyperreflexia), corticobulbar pathways (causing dysarthria, dysphagia, and pseudobulbar affect, i.e., exaggerated and often inappropriate emotional reactions), and motor neurons (producing progressive atrophy in limbs and bulbar musculature). In the limbs, symptoms may be symmetrical or asymmetrical, and weakness with wasting is common. Fasiculations are a prominent early clinical sign, as is cramplike pain. In most cases trunk and respiratory musculature are eventually involved. Lower motor neuron involvement of bulbar musculature causes weakness, wasting, and fasciculations in the tongue and affects palate, pharynx, larynx, and orbicularis oris functions, impairing speech and swallowing. Within an individual patient, the disease may predominantly involve either lower or upper motor neurons and either limb or bulbar musculature. Alternatively, signs and symptoms may be evenly distributed between long tracts and anterior horn cells, brainstem, and spinal cord. Though the disease is invariably progressive, the rate of progression can vary. Fifty percent of patients die within 3 years of onset, generally due to respiratory or bulbar compromise; less often a relatively benign course may be observed. Early brainstem symptoms suggest a poorer prognosis.

Differential Diagnosis

The conditions which may mimic advanced ALS, in which disseminated lower motor neuron signs (atrophy and fasciculations) are combined with upper motor neuron signs (hyperreflexia and spasticity), are subacute combined degeneration, thyrotoxicosis, and syphilis.[47,48] Appropriate serum assays should be obtained in all patients with suspected ALS, to exclude these treatable conditions.

During earlier stages of the disease, when symptoms are confined to a limited anatomic region, focal lesions must be considered. Extradural structural lesions compressing the foramen magnum or cervical spinal cord and exiting roots can produce lateral column dysfunction in association with muscle wasting and can include spondylosis and tumors. Syringomyelia is an intramedullary spinal lesion which can imitate ALS. Radiographic studies, particularly magnetic resonance imaging, distinguish structural disease from ALS in most cases.

Neuropathic processes producing progressive weakness and muscle atrophy may mimic ALS. Conditions which produce diffuse lower motor neuron signs include diabetic amyotrophy, chronic inflammatory polyradiculopathy, Charcot-Marie-Tooth disease, postpolio syndrome, and spinal muscular atrophy.[49,50]

Electromyography can be quite useful in identifying and characterizing ALS.[51] Nerve condition studies help to exclude other diagnoses and can be of prognostic value. Sensory nerve conduction velocity should be normal. Motor conduction studies show mild slowing and prolonged distal latencies, but not to the degree seen in neuropathy. Decreased amplitude of the elicited muscle action potential is seen as the muscle atrophies.

Electromyography shows fasiculations, poor motor unit potential recruitment, widespread fibrillation potentials, and large polyphasic motor unit potentials. Accepted diagnostic criteria dictate that such abnormalities must be present in three limbs, or two limbs and cranial muscles.[51] Conditions which may mimic ALS electrophysiologically include polyradiculopathy and syringomyelia.

Symptomatic Management

The major symptoms requiring treatment are weakness, spasticity, and fatigue. Commonly impaired ankle dorsiflexion produces foot drop; a polypropylene ankle-foot orthosis may be indicated to permit a safer and more effective gait pattern. Appropriate ambulation aids (canes, crutches, walkers) should be supplied as needed. Wrist cockup splints prevent median nerve compression and enhance grip strength.

The role of exercise to increase strength and decrease fatigue in ALS is controversial. There is some evidence that exhaustion predisposes motor neurons to premature death. However, prospective studies have suggested that there are beneficial effects of moderate exercise in ALS patients.[52,53]

As the disease advances, life-threatening complications develop. Malnutrition due to dysphagia often complicates the course. Early dysphagia management includes monitoring caloric intake and diet modifications (semisolids, avoiding thin liquids). Feeding gastrostomy may be required, although the ethics of such intervention have been questioned. Respiratory failure is the identifiable cause of death in most patients with ALS. Prolonged assisted ventilation in a disease which usually progresses to complete paralysis raises ethical, legal, and financial issues. Patients with prominent bulbar and respiratory dysfunction with relatively preserved limb strength are the most appropriate candidates for such support. These issues should be discussed with patients and families before the critical phase so that a rational and mutually acceptable decision can be made.

REHABILITATION: MANAGING THE SYMPTOMS AND COMPLICATIONS OF SPINAL CORD AND PERIPHERAL NERVE DISEASE

The goal of rehabilitation is to maximize functional independence, comfort, and longevity. This can be achieved by systematically assessing and treating the symptoms directly attributable to nervous system disease, which include weakness, spasticity, neurogenic bowel and bladder symptoms, and impotence. The medical and surgical complications which often develop as a result of chronic neurologic disability and that must also be addressed are urinary tract complications, respiratory compromise, decubiti, phlebitis, contractures, and shoulder-hand syndrome. For any medical intervention to be effective, the potentially devastating psychosocial and financial impact of the condition on the patient and family must be considered.

Weakness: SCI

At present there is no treatment which can reverse neurogenic paralysis. Physical and occupational therapies can increase muscle bulk, strength, and endurance in groups with preserved innervation through traditional resistive exercise and weight-lifting programs. Rehabilitation therapies also teach patients to perform functional activities by compensating for motor loss with substituted motions of preserved muscle, and to use orthotic devices and adaptive equipment.

Traditionally, SCI patients learn to use the shoulders as weight-bearing joints, using the upper extremities to perform the work of transfers and manual wheelchair propulsion. This approach often does not succeed in the geriatric population. Muscle fat content increases and conditioning potential decreases with age, limiting the results that a vigorous strengthening program can achieve. Bursitis, tendinitis, and nonspecific joint pain syndromes often complicate such efforts. Coincident medical conditions, such as atherosclerotic cardiovascular disease, may further limit the safety and efficacy of an intensive exercise program. The physical therapy program should, therefore, be tailored to the individual's premorbid capacity and condition. The strengthening program should be advanced as tolerated, and painful complications must be addressed. Vital signs and cardiorespiratory symptoms must be monitored during therapy sessions. If indicated, Holter monitoring data may provide evidence of cardiac ischemia or arrhythmia during physical activity, which can help redirect rehabilitative or medical management.

Adaptive equipment is particularly important for the aging spinal cord patient. An environmental control unit (ECU) can increase independence by interfacing with any standard electronic device, such as a television, telephone, hospital bed, lamp, or computer. ECUs can respond to any stimulus which triggers a controlling switch, including voice activation, puff and sip maneuvers, and head, shoulder, or arm movement. Simpler devices can assist the patient with impaired dexterity in writing, dressing, grooming, or eating independently, and include universal cuffs, button hooks, and adapted standard utensils.

Braces and splints can substitute for weak muscle groups, protecting vulnerable joints from injury and enhancing independence. Upper extremity braces can position limb segments more functionally and substitute for paretic or absent grasp. Bracing needs are dictated by the spinal level.[54] The C5 quadriplegic, for example, can control shoulder movement and elbow flexion, and might benefit from a mobile arm support (to permit gravity-eliminated horizontal arm movement to appropriately place the limb), a static wrist support, or an externally powered dynamic prehension splint (to add movement to hand and wrist which lack voluntary power).

The C6 quadriplegic can control wrist extension and can employ tenodesis for grasping objects; tenodesis is a mechanical phenomenon in which wrist extension results in finger flexion and thumb opposition independent of intrinsic hand musculature. C7–8 function permits elbow extension, wrist flexion, and finger extension, but a tenodesis grasp is still required. At these spinal levels universal cuffs or dynamic wrist splints, which mechanically enhance tenodesis, are often useful.

Lower extremity bracing can aid therapeutic standing and ambulation, although the energy requirements exceed four times that required for normal gait. In addition, leg braces are expensive and can lead to medical complications such as skin breakdown, particularly if there is associated spasticity or sensory impairment. In the geriatric spinal cord population, lower extremity orthotic indications are probably limited to the individual who requires only ankle stabilization. In the early phases of rehabilitation it is generally advisable to emphasize upper body conditioning, upper limb orthotics, adaptive device evaluation, and wheelchair management.

Weakness: Peripheral Nerve Disease

Rehabilitative therapies in diseases of peripheral nerve emphasize frequent range-of-motion therapy to prevent joint deformity and contracture, and sensory reeducation to prevent limb injury. As in the case of upper motor neuron lesions, the degree of strengthening which can be achieved through exercise is modest, and functional adaptation becomes the overall goal. This is accomplished through training in the use of adaptive equipment and orthotic prescription. Splinting is most often required across distal limb segments, as this is the region most often affected in peripheral neuropathy.

In nerve lesions, splints can substitute for weakened muscles, maintaining the extremity in a functional position while preventing overstretch injuries. This action is particularly important in patients with wrist and foot drop, as they are prone to such injuries.

Two types of orthoses are useful in peripheral nerve disorders: static and dynamic.[49] Static splints protect joints and position limbs functionally. Dynamic splints are generally applied to fingers and encourage active muscle contraction against counterbalancing elastic forces, to compensate for unidirectional weakness, achieve functional movements, and strengthen muscles.

In the upper limb, the static splints which are most commonly used are wrist supports which maintain the wrist in extension while allowing free hand and finger movement. They prevent median nerve compression and compensate for weakness of wrist extension. The splint is worn at night and during activities which aggravate symptoms. When weakness of hand intrinsic musculature is a prominent feature, static hand splints which prevent thumb adduction contracture (C-bar splint) or metacarpophalangeal joint hyperextension contracture (lumbrical bar) are indicated. Static splints which hold the thumb in partial abduction and opposition may provide functional assistance.

The most common lower extremity sign in motor neuropathy is foot drop due to weakness of ankle dorsiflexion. The ankle foot orthosis (AFO) is the splint of choice for this condition. It maintains the ankle in a neutral position, permitting toe clearance during the swing phase of gait. In addition, a rigid AFO provides mediolateral stability and can help prevent ankle joint injury.

Not all patients with peripheral neuropathy benefit from splinting. Even streamlined splints may "weigh down" a paretic limb, interfering with function. In patients with associated sensory neuropathy, splints may produce skin breakdown and joint injury if fit and alignment are not superb. In progressive disorders, serial evaluation and splint adjustment are necessary to ensure adequate fit and support. Similarly, the patient who is improving requires frequent reassessment to prevent overbracing, which can impede motor recovery by restricting movement.

Spasticity

Spasticity is a motor disorder which results when supraspinal influences on the cord are disrupted. Involuntary spasms, hyperreflexia, and velocity-dependent resistance to passive limb movement are all signs of spasticity.[55,56] Mild to moderate spasticity can be beneficial, as extensor tone can improve weight bearing and spasms can improve venous circulation. When spasticity interferes with voluntary movement, is painful, or appears to be leading to muscle contracture, intervention in the form of physical or pharmacologic therapy is required. The standard physical therapy measures are sustained stretching and limb cooling.[57] Pharmacologic therapies include baclofen, benzodiazepines, dantrolene sodium, and motor point blockade with phenol or botulinum toxin.

Baclofen represents the first-line spasticity pharmacotherapy. Gamma aminobutyric acid (GABA) is a major inhibitory neurotransmitter in spinal cord, and baclofen activates GABA-B receptors in primary sensory afferents.[56] It effectively decreases spasms and muscle tone, though its side effects include sedation, nausea, constipation, urinary incontinence, and fluid retention. In our experience the therapeutic/toxic ratio is lower in patients over the age of 60, with cognitive impairment (sedation, confusion, visual hallucinations) predominating as the limiting factor. Though high-dose (240 mg/day) oral baclofen has been successfully used in patients with severe spasticity, geriatric patients rarely tolerate dosages above 80 mg/day.[58] Benzodiazepines are also GABA agonists, enhancing the affinity of classic receptors for GABA. The established sedating, habituating, and addicting potential of benzodiazepines limits their clinical utility, but they are effective antispasticity agents and can be useful second-line therapies to be used alone or in combination with other medication.

Chemical denervation by motor point block is a method in which an agent (traditionally phenol and more recently botulinum toxin) is injected intramuscularly under electromyography guidance at motor points.[59,60] Selective muscle relaxation can be achieved with such techniques, and systemic side effects can be avoided. Phenol produces an immediate effect, while botulinum toxin works gradually over a 3-week period. Both drugs produce temporary relief of spasticity, reversing gradually over months. Side effects include local bruising and pain, risk of infection, and muscle weakness.

Autonomic Dysfunction: SCI

Early after SCI, abnormalities of cardiovascular function, temperature regulation, and bladder and bowel function are commonly seen, attributable to disruption between modulating influences in higher centers and sympathetic control. The sympathetic system arises from the intermediolateral columns of the thoracic cord. Postganglionic sympathetic alpha-adrenergic fibers stimulate vasoconstriction in abdominal viscera and skin, affecting blood pressure maintenance as well as thermoregulation. Postganglionic sympathetic beta-adrenergic fibers produce vasodilation in muscle fibers and accelerate heart rate in response to exercise. Postganglionic cholinergic fibers innervate sweat glands. Parasympathetic innervation is preganglionic and cholinergic and has brainstem and sacral origins.

Cardiovascular Symptoms

Sympathetic and parasympathetic influences control vascular tone and cardiac rate and contractility. Changes in blood pressure are detected by baroreceptors, and the message is transmitted to the vasomotor center in the medulla. When spinal cord disruption occurs, activation of sympathetic input to the heart and splanchnic bed does not occur. Blood pressure and heart rate are then subject essentially to vagal control, and orthostatic hypotension can result. Blood pressure regulation becomes dependent upon increased activity in the renin angiotensin and vasopressin systems.[61,62] Upright hypotension may be coupled with hypertension and rapid diuresis when the patient is supine, due to aldosterone-induced expanded intravascular volume.

Neurogenic shock refers to a syndrome observed in patients with high thoracic or cervical lesions of recent onset. Severe orthostatic hypotension, bradycardia, and hypothermia may develop. A low resting systolic pressure and pulse rate are observed. Vagal hypersensitivity is present, and exposure to vasoactive drugs, hypoxia, or maneuvers such as Valsalva can dangerously aggravate these symptoms. Surgical procedures requiring general anesthesia should be avoided. Adequate blood pressure can generally be maintained by applying firm support hosiery and an abdominal binder, in combination with gradual mobilization. A cardiac pacemaker is occasionally required for those with refractory symptomatic bradycardia.

Autonomic dysreflexia refers to a syndrome of sympathetic *hyperreflexia* leading to excessive sympathetic activity in response to often minor noxious stimuli (e.g., tight clothing, full bladder, urinary infection, bowel impaction). Sudden extreme elevation in blood pressure can occur, accompanied by tingling sensations, bradycardia, throbbing headache, and profound anxiety. Serious complications include seizures and hemorrhagic stroke. Acute treatment includes elevating the head to lower blood pressure and discontinuing the triggering stimulus. Topical nitrates may be useful in the acute phase. Recurrent dysreflexia may respond to chronic treatment with oral alpha-blocking agents.

Temperature Regulation

Thermoregulation is reliant upon connections between the anterior hypothalamus and T1. Heat is dissipated through cutaneous vasodilation and sweating and is conserved by vasoconstriction and shivering mechanisms. Quadriplegics and high paraplegics may experience poikilothermia and hyperhidrosis above the level of injury. Lesions below T8 generally allow adequate temperature regulation. Management consists of monitoring body and ambient temperatures.

Autonomic Dysfunction: Spinal Cord Disease and Neuropathy

Neurogenic Bladder

The micturition reflex is primarily affected by sacral (S3) parasympathetic pathways which promote detrusor and inhibit internal sphincter contraction. Detrusor contraction is mediated by cholinergic stimulation, while internal sphincter contraction increases with alpha-adrenergic stimulation. The external sphincter is composed of striated muscle and is under voluntary control.

Bladder dysfunction is a common complication of diseases of spinal cord and peripheral nerve, producing urinary urgency, frequency, incontinence, and retention. Complications of neurogenic bladder include urinary tract infection (UTI), hydronephrosis, and nephrolithiasis.

Disease of the spinal cord produces upper motor neuron bladder signs including incontinence, due to detrusor muscle hyperactivity coupled with sphincter insufficiency. Detrusor sphincter dyssynergia is another upper motor neuron syndrome which produces a combination of small voids, incontinence, and low volume retention and is often complicated by urinary reflux and turbulent flow. Lower motor neuron bladder signs are seen during spinal shock, following cauda equina injury, and in neuropathy. Detrusor weakness produces a low pressure retention state with large vesicular volumes; voiding occurs in the form of overflow incontinence.

Though cystometrograms can define these syndromes, adequate information for clinical management is often provided by measuring the residual retained urine volume present following spontaneous voiding, obtained by catheterizing the bladder.[63] A postvoid residual volume which is larger than either 20 percent of the total bladder volume or 100 ml indicates a need for an intermittent catheterization regimen. Intermittent catheterization can decrease the risk of infection, urolithiasis, and hydronephrosis. Patients should be catheterized at intervals which keep bladder volumes below 400 ml and should be instructed to void as frequently as possible between catheterizations.

Those who cannot self-catheterize may require surgical intervention such as suprapubic cystostomy or sphincterotomy to avoid long-term indwelling catheter management. Incontinent patients who are able to successfully intermittently catheterize or who do not require catheterization may benefit from anticholinergic agents (e.g., propranthelinе bromide, imipramine hydrochloride) which relax detrusor muscle and enhance bladder storage.

Pharmacologic agents which may be useful in treating the patient with urinary retention include cholinergic drugs, such as bethanechol, and alpha-adrenergic antagonists, such as terazosin hydrochloride.[64] These agents respectively enhance bladder emptying by stimulating detrusor contraction and relaxing the internal sphincter.

UTI is the most common complication of neurogenic bladder. Prophylactic measures include adequate bladder emptying to avoid bacterial growth in stagnant urine, preventing overdistension of the bladder, minimizing retrograde bacterial migration by avoiding indwelling catheters, and discouraging reflux and turbulent flow. Urinary acidifiers are useful to discourage bacterial growth, as is consuming cranberry juice. A UTI may be asymptomatic in the patient with impaired sensation or may produce typical symptoms such as dysesthesias or spasticity. Frequent surveillance urinalyses should be performed and are a more reliable method of distinguishing cystitis from colonization than are cultures. Antibiotic therapy should be undertaken when pyuria is evident on urinalysis. The persistent or recurrent UTI may require urological evaluation to exclude underlying structural abnormal such as tumor, diverticulum, or stone. Recurrent infection in the absence of structural abnormality often requires chronic low-dose antibiotic treatment.[65]

Neurogenic Bowel

Fecal incontinence and constipation are common and distressing symptoms of spinal cord and neuropathic disease. Complications of poorly regulated bowel function include impaction and obstruction. Incontinence can be socially disabling as well lead to skin erosion and infection. A regimen which regularly evacuates the bowel prevents impaction and incontinence. Bowel routines must be individually tailored to the needs of the patient but generally consist of a combination of daily stool softeners, high-fiber diet, laxatives, and rectal suppository. Adequate fluid intake is extremely important and must be emphasized. Patients with spinal cord disease tend to respond well to suppository treatment, while those with cauda equina or peripheral nerve lesions often require manual disimpaction.

Pulmonary Complications: Pulmonary Embolism and Pneumonia

Venous stasis and immobility are common in patients with spinal cord and peripheral nerve disease, conditions which increase the risk of developing deep vein thrombosis. Conventional prophylactic measures include low-dose subcutaneous heparin and antiembolism stockings. Sensory impairment may interfere with the patient's perception of evolving phlebitis. It is, therefore, imperative to regularly monitor lower limb diameter and to consider the diagnoses of deep vein thrombosis or pulmonary embolism when increased spasticity, unexplained fever, cough, or breathlessness occurs.

Quadriplegic patients with lesions above C4 may experience diaphragmatic paralysis. Cord lesions above T12 and peripheral neuropathy can impair intercostal muscle strength. Gastric distension may further compromise lung expansion. Systemic bacterial infections (most notably UTI) frequently seed the lungs. Respiratory fatigue, atelectasis, pneumonias, and mucus plugging therefore commonly complicate the course of such patients. Preventive measures include daily use of incentive spirometry and chest physical therapy to minimize atelectasis and mobilize secretions. It is useful to monitor vital capacities, chest x-ray films, and arterial blood gases. Influenza vaccine is recommended for patients who are at increased risk of developing pneumonia.

PAIN

Spinal cord and peripheral nerve diseases are frequently complicated by pain, which may have musculoskeletal or neuropathic origins. Mechanically induced pain is often due to abnormal joint alignment and redistribution of weight-bearing patterns, typically affecting wrists, shoulders, lumbar spine, and knees. If the precipitating behavior cannot be corrected, treatment with nonsteroidal anti-inflammatory agents, heat, massage, ultrasound, and phonophoresis often help control pain. To avoid the development of *shoulder-hand syndrome,* proper shoulder positioning, frequent range-of-motion exercises, and retrograde hand massage should be provided.

Neuropathic pain takes the form of burning, tingling, and electrical sensations which may be chronic or paroxysmal. Traditional agents used in the treatment of dysesthesias include carbamazepine, tricyclic antidepressants, phenytoin, and benzodiazepines. All have side effects to which the geriatric population is particularly susceptible, including urinary retention (carbamazepine, tricyclics), liver toxicity (carbamazepine, phenytoin), bone marrow suppression (carbamazepine), sedation (all), and nausea (all). Adjunctive therapeutic measures are counterirritant therapy, biofeedback, and transcutaneous nerve stimulation.

SOCIOECONOMIC ISSUES

Chronic neurologic disability impacts on all aspects of the patient's life. The sense of loss, increased dependency, and changes in self-image have negative emotional consequences. Limited mobility and depression can limit social contacts, leading to increasing isolation. Financial burdens can be overwhelming as the costs of home modifications, adaptive equipment, and custodial care are compounded by losses in income. A multidisciplinary and interdisciplinary approach is often required. The physician can help by maintaining a referral network involving social workers, support groups, and visiting nurse associations. Attorneys can educate patients concerning the rights of the disabled and assist them in obtaining elusive benefits. The primary care physician must monitor depressive symptoms, ask about emotional problems, and arrange treatment when emotional disturbances require clinical intervention.

REFERENCES

1. Byrne TN, Waxman SG: *Spinal Cord Compression.* Philadelphia, Davis, 1990, p 1.
2. Krauss JF: Epidemiological aspects of acute spinal cord injury: A review of incidence, prevalence, causes and outcome, in Becker DP, Povlishock JT (eds): *Central Nervous System Trauma Status Report 1985.* Washington, DC, NIH, 1985, p 313.
3. Bracken MB et al: Incidence of acute traumatic spinal cord injury in the United States, 1970–1977. *Am J Epidemiol* 133:615, 1981.
4. Fine PR et al: Spinal cord injury: An epidemiologic perspective. *Paraplegia* 17:237, 1970.
5. Shrosbee RD: Acute central cervical spinal cord syndrome—Aetiology, age incidence and relationship to the orthopedic injury. *Paraplegia* 14:351, 1977.
6. Yarkony GM et al: Benefits of rehabilitation for traumatic spinal cord injury. *Arch Neurol* 44:93, 1987.
7. Bennett C et al: Electroejaculation: New therapy for neurogenic infertility. *Contemp Urol* November 1990, p 25.
8. Green BA, Magana IA: Spinal cord trauma: Clinical aspects, in Davidoff RA (ed): *Handbook of the Spinal Cord.* New York, Dekker, 1987, p 63.
9. Piepmeier JM, Jenkins NR: Late neurological changes following traumatic spinal cord injury. *J Neurosurg* 69:399, 1988.
10. Guttmann L: *Spinal Cord Injuries Comprehensive Management and Research.* Oxford, Blackwell Scientific, 1976, p 216.
11. Schneider RC et al: The syndrome of acute central cervical spinal cord injury. *J Neurosurg* 11:564, 1954.
12. Schneider RC et al: The syndrome of acute central cervical spinal cord injury. *J Neurol Neurosurg Psychiatry* 21:216, 1956.
13. Foo D: Spinal cord injury in forty-four patients with cervical spondylosis. *Paraplegia* 24:301, 1986.
14. Hardy AG: Cervical spinal cord injury without bony injury. *Paraplegia* 14:296, 1977.
15. Foo D et al: Post-traumatic anterior spinal cord syndrome: Pathological studies of two patients. *Surg Neurol* 17:370, 1982.
16. Aminoff MJ: Vascular disorders of the spinal cord, in Davidoff M (ed): *Handbook of the Spinal Cord.* New York, Dekker, 1987, p 259.
17. Garland H et al: Infarction of the spinal cord. *Brain* 89:645, 1966.
18. Foo DM, Rossier AB: Anterior spinal artery syndrome and its natural history. *Paraplegia* 21:1, 1983.
19. Domisse GF: The blood supply of the spinal cord. *J Bone Joint Surg* 56:225, 1975.
20. Halperin EC, Burger PC: Conventional external beam radiotherapy for central nervous system malignancies. *Neurol Clin 3* 3:867, 1985.
21. Fetell MR: Spinal tumors, in Rowland LP (ed): *Merrit's Textbook of Neurology.* Lea & Febiger, 1984, p 350.
22. Bannister R: *Brain's Clinical Neurology.* Oxford University Press, 1978, p 310.
23. Rodichok LD et al: Early diagnosis of spinal epidural metastases. *Am J Med* 70:1181, 1981.
24. Patchell RA, Posner JB: Neurologic complications of systemic cancer. *Neurol Clin* 3:729, 1985.
25. Gilbert RW et al: Epidural spinal cord compression from metastatic tumor: Diagnosis and treatment. *Ann Neurol* 3:40, 1978.
26. Greenberg HS et al: Epidural spinal cord compression from metastatic tumor: Results with new treatment protocol. *Ann Neurol* 8:361, 1980.
27. Brain R, Wilkinson M: *Cervical Spondylosis.* Philadelphia, Saunders, 1967.
28. Garfield JS: Spinal lesions, in Caird FI (ed): *Neurological Disorders in the Elderly.* Littleton, MA, John Wright and Sons, 1982, p 213.
29. Adams RD: Aging and thalamic locomotion, Albert MC (ed): in *Clinical Neurology of Aging.* New York, Oxford University Press, 1984, p 381.
30. Hicks JE et al: *Handbook of Rehabilitative Rheumatology.* Bayport, NY, Contact Associates International, 1988.
31. Kaada B, Torsteinbo O: Increase of plasma beta endorphines in connective tissue massage. *Gen Pharmacol* 20:487, 1989.
32. Harding AE, Thomas PK: The clinical features of hereditary motor and sensory types I and II. *Brain* 103:259, 1980.
33. Kimura J: *Electrodiagnosis in Diseases of Nerve and Muscle: Principles and Practice.* New York, Davis, 1989.
34. Sotaniemi KA: Slimer's paralysis: Peroneal neuropathy during weight reduction. *J Neurol Neurosurg Psychiatry* 47:564, 1984.
35. Deboer WGRM et al: Pernicious anemia autoantibody to gastric parietal cells. *J Clin Pathol* 18:456, 1965.
36. Victor M: Nutrition and disease of the nervous system. *Progr Food Nutr Sci.* 1:45, 1975.
37. Dant SS et al: The myelopathy of pernicious anemia. *Acta Neurol Scand* 44 (suppl 34):1, 1968.
38. Scott JM et al: Pathogenesis of subacute combined degeneration: A result of methyl group deficiency. *Lancet* 2:334, 1981.
39. Strachan RW, Henderson JG: Psychiatric syndromes due to avitaminosis B-12 with normal blood and marrow. *Q J Med* 34:303, 1965.
40. Troncuso MD et al: Visual evoked responses in pernicious anemia. *Arch Neurol* 36:168, 1979.

41. Tandan R, Bradley WG: Amyotrophic lateral sclerosis: I. Clinical features, pathology, and ethical issues in management. *Ann Neurol* 18:271, 1985.
42. Juergens SM et al: ALS in Rochester, Minnesota, 1925–1977. *Neurology* 30:463, 1980.
43. Reed DA et al: Amyotrophic lateral sclerosis and parkinsonism-dementia on Guam, 1945–1972: I. Descriptive epidemiology. *Am J Epidemiol* 101:287, 1975.
44. Hudson AJ: Amyotrophic lateral sclerosis and its association with dementia, parkinsonism and other neurological disorders: A review. *Brain* 104:217, 1981.
45. Mulder DW: Clinical limits of amyotrophic lateral sclerosis, in Rowland LP (ed): *Human Motor Neuron Diseases.* New York, Raven, 1982, p 15.
46. Tyler HR: Nonfamilial amyotrophic lateral sclerosis with dementia or multisystem degeneration and other neurological disorders, in Rowland LP (ed): *Human Motor Neuron Diseases.* New York, Raven, 1982, p 173.
47. Victor M: *Diseases of the Nervous System Due to Nutrition Deficiency; Practice of Medicine.* Hagerstown, MD, Harper & Row, 1976, vol 10.
48. Start RJ et al: Hand wasting in spondylitic high cord compression: An electromyographic study. *Ann Neurol* 9:58, 1981.
49. Adams RD, Victor M: *Principles of Neurology.* New York, McGraw-Hill, 1986.
50. Harrington TM et al: Elevation of creatinine kinase in amyotrophic lateral sclerosis, potential confusion with polymyositis. *Arthritis Rheum* 26:201, 1983.
51. Daube RD: Electrophysiologic studies in the diagnosis of motor neuron disease, in Amnioff MJ (ed): *Neurological Clinics Symposium on Electrodiagnosis.* Philadelphia, WB Saunders, 1985, p. 473.
52. Lenman JAR: A clinical and experimental study of the effects of exercise on motor weakness in neurological disease. *J Neurol Psychiatry* 22:182, 1959.
53. Bohannon RW: Results of resistance exercise on a patient with amyotrophic lateral sclerosis: A case report. *Phys Ther* 63:965, 1983.
54. Aisen ML (ed): *Orthotics in Neurologic Disease.* New York, DEMOS, 1992.
55. Knutsson E, Martensson A: Dynamic motor capacity in spastic paresis and its relation to prime mover dysfunction, spastic reflexes and antagonist coactivation. *Scand J Rehabil Med* 12:93, 1980.
56. Davidoff RA: Antispasticity drugs: Mechanisms of action. *Neurology* 17:107, 1985.
57. Knuttson E: Topical cryotherapy in spasticity. *Scand J Rehabil Med* 2:159, 1970.
58. Aisen ML et al: Clinical and pharmacokinetic aspects of high dose oral baclofen. *J Am Paraplegia Soc* 14:211, 1992.
59. Snow BJ et al: Treatment of spasticity with botulinum toxin: A double blind study. *Ann Neurol* 28:512, 1990.
60. Jankovic J, Brin MF: Therapeutic uses of botulinum toxin. *N Engl J Med* 324:1186, 1991.
61. Sved AF et al: Release of antidiuretic hormone in quadriplegic subjects in response to head-up tilt. *Neurology* 35:78, 1985.
62. Mathias CJ et al: Plasma catecholamines, plasma renin activity and plasma aldosterone in tetraplegic man, horizontal and tilted. *Clin Sci Molec Med* 49:291, 1975.
63. Lapides J et al: Clean intermittent self-catheterization in the treatment of urinary tract disease. *Trans Am Assoc Genitourinary Surg* 63:92, 1971.
64. Lapides J: Neurogenic bladder: Principles of treatment. *Urol Clin North Am* 1:81, 1974.
65. Stamm WE: Antimicrobial prophylaxis of recurrent urinary tract infections. *Ann Intern Med* 92:770, 1980.

Chapter 119

COMMON FOOT PROBLEMS

Jeffrey A. Holman, Gary G. Poehling, and David F. Martin

GOALS

Geriatric patients must remain active physically, intellectually, and socially to preserve their sense of well-being and independence. Maintenance of proper foot care is imperative to preserving the autonomy of this special patient population. A supple, painless, plantigrade foot with adequate muscle balance and strength are the aims of the treating physician. Knowledge of proper foot maintenance, shoe prescription, and ability to diagnose and treat common foot disorders is essential for the geriatric physician.

SIMPLE FOOT CARE/PREVENTION

The elderly patient must be informed and reminded of the need for daily foot inspection and care. Thorough drying of the entire foot after bathing, especially between the toes, will limit the spread and development of fungal infections.

Nail trimming is an art and should not be taken for granted. The nail must be trimmed perpendicular to the axis of the toe. This helps maintain nail integrity and limits the potential for ingrown nails and subsequent infection.

A pumice stone softens the plantar skin, improves local circulation, and potentially improves sensation with the removal of deadened layers of skin. The stone can also soften calluses and limit pressure points.

Soft-soled leather shoes with an ample toe box, a well-padded tongue, a flexible midsole, and a well-molded Achilles pad will limit development of most pathologic foot problems.

Socks made of natural fiber are recommended for their absorbency and "breathability."

Salicylate preparations, corn pads, simple shoe modifications to compensate for biomechanical aberrancies, and simple exercise regimens are also a part of routine foot care.[1] With this approach, foot problems can be avoided in many instances. Good personal hygiene and daily care/inspection will help maintain a healthy foot. While many of the problems and conditions we will discuss are not life-threatening, they can significantly limit mobility and alter the lifestyle of the elderly patient.

THE FOOT CARE TEAM

It is important that the elderly patient with foot problems be part of the "foot care team." Proper care must involve a working team of physician, podiatrist, orthotist, physical therapist, cast technician, and patient. Good communication between the team members ensures optimal health care in each individual case.[2]

HEEL PAIN

Painful Heel/Plantar Fasciitis

Etiology

Overuse and chronic fatigue of the plantar fascia from the repetitive impact loading of heel strike can lead to failure of the fascia at the calcaneal insertion (medial tuberosity). Tightness of the Achilles tendon complex and/or insufficiency of the posterior tibial tendon can also place stress on the longitudinal arch of the foot and can lead to plantar fascial tension and stretching. The microtearing of the fascia leads to a cycle of inflammation, weakening, and retearing of the fibers.[3] The radiographic heel spur (Fig. 119-1*A*) is secondary to this pathologic cycle and is not responsible for its development.

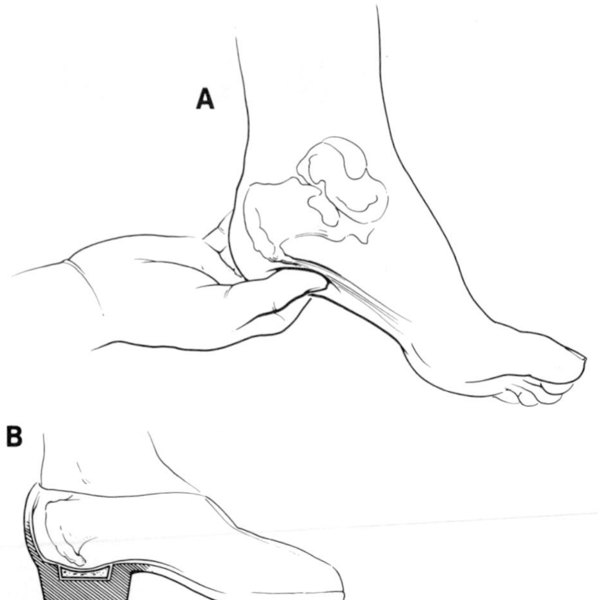

FIGURE 119-1
A. Painful plantar fasciitis with an associated heel spur. *B.* Pain relieved with Sorbathane heel pad and medial cutout.

Recently, the medial calcaneal branch of the posterior tibial nerve has been implicated in the development of plantar fasciitis (see the discussion of tarsal tunnel syndrome, below). It is postulated that isolated compression of the nerve at the origin of the flexor digitorum brevis muscle contributes to the pain complex.

In geriatric patients, the condition is often associated with atrophy of the heel pad. This leads to heightened mechanical stresses and the ensuing inflammatory process.

Signs and Symptoms

The typical patient is the middle-aged to elderly female who has undergone recent weight gain and change in activity. The patient will classically complain of medial heel pain with the first few steps upon awakening.

The patient will have point tenderness over the medial calcaneal tuberosity that may improve with activity but ultimately worsens toward the end of the day. The patient often has a tight heel cord and the foot often has a pronated (flat foot) posture. Pain can often be reproduced with forced dorsiflexion of the toes. This is due to the distal insertion of the plantar fascia at the level of the proximal phalanges of the toes.

Although the bone scan is often positive, such a scan is not necessary for diagnosis. Radiographs may demonstrate a heel spur, but this is neither a sensitive nor a specific sign.

Treatment

Conservative measures are the first line of defense in battling plantar fasciitis. Heel cups, either soft and padded or made of hard plastic, are often helpful. In more persistent cases, Sorbathane heel pads with medial cutouts (Fig. 119-1*B*)—or custom-molded inlays with a medial arch and heel cutout—in combination with soft, supportive shoes and a rigorous exercise program of heel-cord stretching will be helpful.[4] Nonsteroidal anti-inflammatory drugs (NSAIDs) are useful, but cortisone injections must be limited to prevent fat-pad atrophy, rupture of the plantar fascia, and depigmentation. Physical therapy with appropriate modalities can also be extremely helpful.

Surgical treatment is reserved for recalcitrant plantar fasciitis. Spur removal alone is not recommended. Release of the plantar fascia has brought some satisfactory results but may affect the windlass mechanism at toe-off and decrease strength. Surgery is a last resort and is often not performed until a complete course of conservative measures, over a minimum of 8 to 12 months, has failed.

Tarsal Tunnel Syndrome

Etiology

This uncommon disorder is secondary to compression of the posterior tibial nerve in its third compartment of the flexor retinaculum tunnel just posterior to the medial malleolus.[5] Fractures involving the tarsal tunnel, adjacent tendon sheath ganglions, lipomas in the area, or severe pronation (flat foot) with secondary stretch of the posterior tibial nerve may all be responsible.

Signs and Symptoms

Patients will often complain of burning in the arch, numbness in the toes, and—occasionally—proximal medial radiation of pain into the leg. The symptoms are aggravated by activity. There is usually a positive Tinel's sign with pain after percussion over the region of the posterior tibial nerve. Lumbar disk disease can contribute to symptoms and should be ruled out with electrodiagnostic studies.

Treatment

Anti-inflammatory agents coupled with a hindfoot orthosis to limit pronation of the heel and subsequent stretching of the nerve often relieve symptoms. Steroid injections have met with highly variable results.

When symptoms persist and do not respond to conservative measures, surgical release of the entire tarsal tunnel, including the calcaneal and plantar branches distally, will improve symptoms in most cases.

TOE DEFORMITIES

Bunion

Etiology

Hallux valgus involves lateral deviation of the great toe at the metatarsal phalangeal joint. As the deformity develops, the medial aspect of the first metatarsal head will be uncovered and secondary irritation will give rise to a painful callosity and underlying bursitis (Fig. 119-2*A*). Metatarsus primus varus (medial deviation of the first metatarsal) is often an associated condition, and in some cases, the head of the metatarsal is rounded or its base inclined. This deformity occurs most often in the pronated foot.

There is a familial tendency toward the development of this condition, but no true genetic link exists. Shoe wear has been shown to contribute to its development, with pointed, narrow-toe-boxed, high-heeled shoes being the primary culprit.

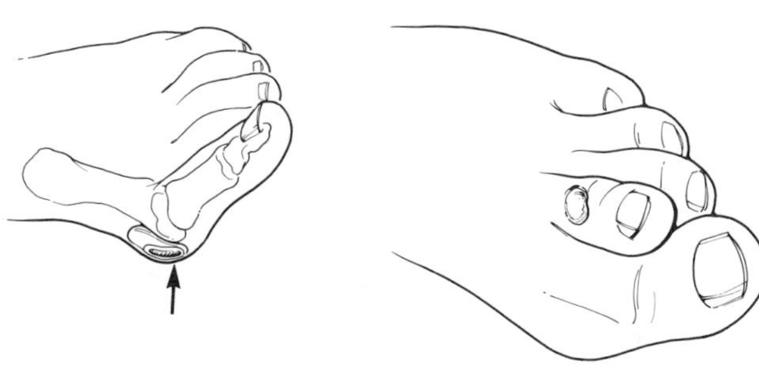

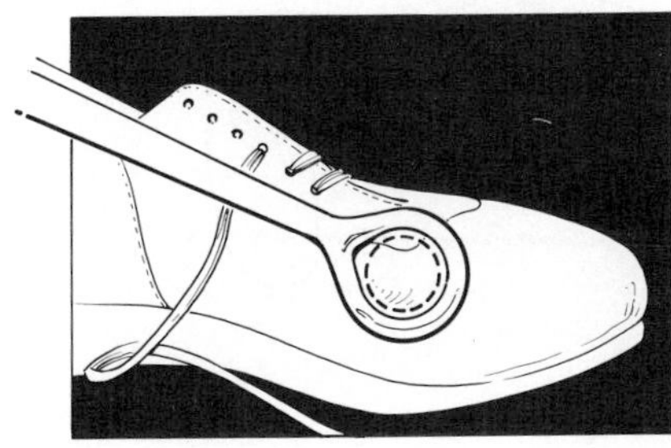

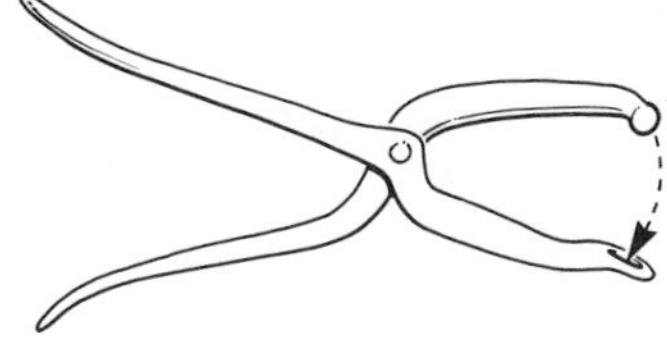

FIGURE 119-2

A. Bunion with painful callosity and bursitis. *B.* An overlapping second toe from crowding in a patient with bunion deformity of the great toe. *C.* Ball-and-ring stretcher used to accommodate the prominent first metatarsal head in a patient with a bunion.

Signs and Symptoms

Patients will complain of pain over the medial eminence of the metatarsal head and also of inability to fit into their shoes.

The deformity is obvious on physical examination, but the treating physician must also examine the foot for a transfer metatarsalgia, the degree of first metatarsophalangeal motion, and the presence of a second-toe hammer deformity (overlapping second toe). The secondary hammertoe may present with a painful dorsal corn (Fig. 119-2*B*).

Treatment

No surgical treatment is necessary if the bunion deformity is asymptomatic and the patient accepts required footwear modifications. Initial management steps include conservative measures of patient education and acceptance, shoe modification, and occasionally bunion pads. The shoe should have a wide, high toe box to accommodate the deformity. A ball-and-ring stretcher (Fig. 119-2*C*) may mold the leather over the prominence to provide even further space. The shoe may occasionally need to be cut out to accept the deformity.

One must be willing to address the problems often associated with a bunion. The second-toe hammertoe can be addressed with daily filing of the dorsal proximal interphalangeal joint (PIP) corn and soft pads. Transfer metatarsalgia is often responsive to a metatarsal pad.

Surgical treatment is reserved for those cases unresponsive to conservative measures and in those feet with significant deformity.

Hallux Rigidus

Etiology

This disorder is characterized by painful and limited range of motion of the first metatarsophalangeal joint, predominantly in dorsiflexion.[6] Repetitive microtrauma leads to a degenerative process that manifests itself with a proliferation of dorsal bone, limiting toe dorsiflexion (Fig. 119-3*A*).

Signs and Symptoms

Patients will complain of pain in the first metatarsophalangeal joint with walking and an inability to wear heels. They may note an oblique shoe crease that is secondary to decreased first metatarsophalangeal joint motion (Fig. 119-3*B*). A palpable dorsal osteophyte is often present, and the patient will have pain with forced plantar flexion of the great toe. Secondary lateral ankle pain from a shifting of weight away from the great toe and toward the lesser digits during toe-off may develop.

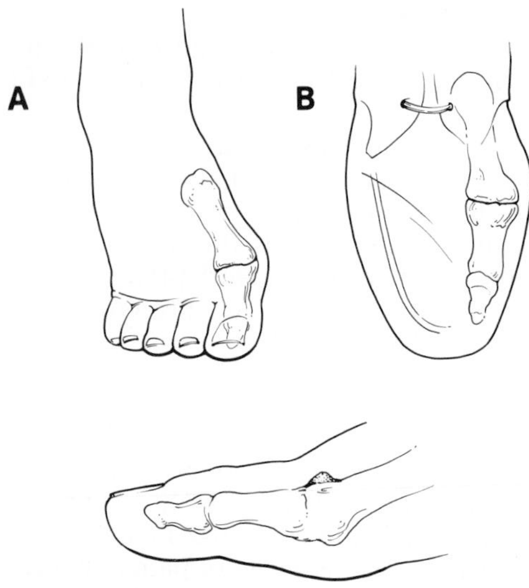

FIGURE 119-3
A. Hallux rigidus with dorsal osteophyte formation on the first metatarsal head. *B.* Oblique shoe crease from transfer of weight to the lateral side of the foot.

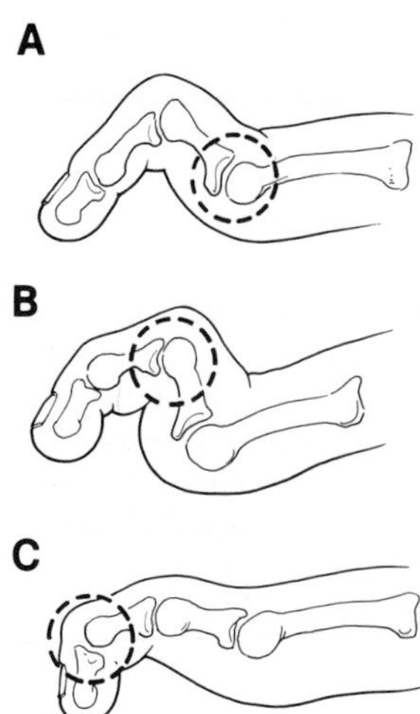

FIGURE 119-4
A. Hammertoe with primary hyperextension deformity of the metatarsal phalangeal joint. *B.* Claw toe with primary hyperflexion deformity of the distal interphalangeal joint. *C.* Mallet toe with primary hyperflexion deformity of the distal interphalangeal joint.

Treatment

The initial aims of treatment should include conversion to a rocker-bottom soled shoe to allow easier transition from stance into toe-off. A steel shank in the sole of the shoe may also dissipate the need for the great toe to achieve plantar flexion forcibly in walking. An enlarged toe box may limit excessive pressure on the dorsal bone.

Surgical intervention should be entertained if other measures fail. Cheilectomy (removal of the bump), fusion, and arthroplasty (resection versus Silastic implant) are all options.

Hammer Toe/Claw Toe/Mallet Toe

Etiology

Lesser toe deformities (Fig. 119-4) are often the result of crowding inside the shoe. There are, however, many other etiologies for the development of these conditions. Muscle imbalance following a neurologic event (cerebrovascular accident, head injury), peripheral nerve damage, diabetes, rheumatoid arthritis, or traumatic tendon disruption can all lead to the development of these conditions.

Signs and Symptoms

The hammertoe (Fig. 119-5*A*) is primarily a hyperextension deformity at the metatarsophalangeal joint plus a flexion deformity of the proximal interphalangeal joint. Early in the development of these deformities, patients may have a mildly painful metatarsophalangeal synovitis. As the disease progresses, painful corns above the proximal interphalangeal joint de-

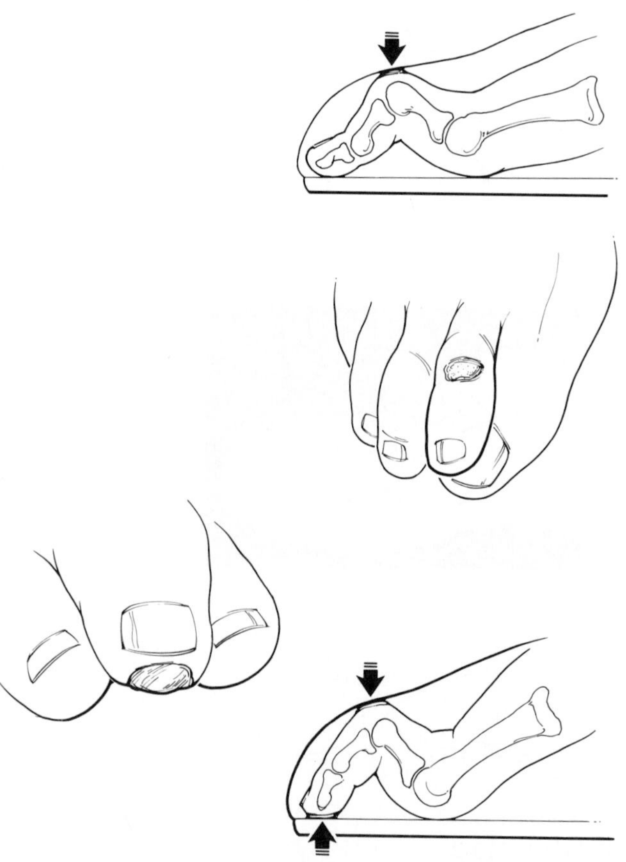

FIGURE 119-5
A. Hammering of the second toe with dorsal proximal interphalangeal callosity secondary to bunion deformity. Arrow illustrates callosity formation. *B.* Clawing of the toe with painful distal phalangeal corn. Arrow illustrates callosity formation.

velop as a result of continuous rubbing against the overlying shoe. Development of intractable plantar keratosis is often not far behind.

The claw toe (Fig. 119-5*B*) is primarily a hyperextension deformity at the metatarsophalangeal joint, with flexion of both the distal interphalangeal and proximal interphalangeal joints. Corns form both over the dorsal proximal interphalangeal and at the tip of the distal phalanx.

The mallet toe is primarily a flexion contracture of the distal interphalangeal joint. This deformity results in weight being borne by the tip of the toe and may result in an exquisitely tender end-bearing callus.

Treatment

When the lesser toe deformity is flexible, conservative measures may suffice. Shoe modification with inlay orthotics, callus soaking and filing, metatarsal pads for associated intractable plantar keratoses, comma crest pads for distal calluses, and passive stretching with taping are all modes of attack in treatment.

Surgical intervention of these lesser toe deformities is reserved for cases of intractable flexible toe deformities or symptomatic rigid lesser toe pathology.

Bunionette

Etiology

The flat splayfoot with associated bunion deformity of the great toe may predispose to the development of a tailor's bunion or bunionette of the fifth metatarsal. The prominent fifth metatarsal head prompts irritation from the overlying shoe and a secondary callus and bursa develop (Fig. 119-6). As in the more common great-toe bunion deformity, the overgrown, inflamed tissue can be either bony or soft in origin.

Signs and Symptoms

Patients will have pain over the fifth metatarsal head with a prominent callus over the lateral aspect of the toe. Occasionally the metatarsal head will be plantarflexed and an area of intractable plantar keratosis may present on the sole of the foot.

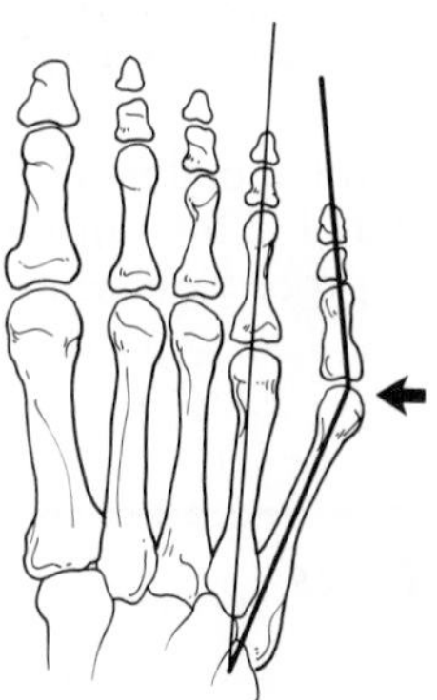

FIGURE 119-6
Bunionette deformity with deviated fifth metatarsal in a splay foot. Arrow illustrates callosity formation.

Treatment

Conservative measures are aimed at accommodating the deformity. A ball-and-hook stretcher can soften leather shoes over the prominence. Simple shoe modification to include a wide toe box is often all that is necessary.

Many surgeries ranging from simple bone and soft-tissue removal to metatarsal shaft osteotomy have been advocated in unresponsive cases. By way of an oblique osteotomy, the metatarsal head may be shifted both medially and dorsally to relieve associated intractable plantar keratosis.

METATARSALGIA

There is a constellation of foot problems that present to the physician with metatarsalgia (pain under the forefoot).[7] The following is a discussion of the more common causes of metatarsalgia in elderly patients. Not included in this section are discussions of systemic inflammatory processes and the cavus or high-arched foot, which can also contribute to or cause metatarsalgia.

Morton's Neuroma

Etiology

Repetitive microtrauma of the common digital nerves leads to a cycle of inflammation, accumulation of perineural fibrosis, and enlargement of the neurolemma. This is not a true neuroma but an irritation and scarring of tissue surrounding the nerve.

The microtrauma is thought to originate from traction of the interdigital nerve as it passes around the intermetatarsal ligament. Compression from adjacent metatarsal heads may also initiate the pathologic process, and often the swelling is located adjacent to the metatarsal heads as the nerve bifurcates (Fig. 119-7).

Signs and Symptoms

Women are affected four times more commonly than males because they more often wear tight, confining shoes (pumps). The neuromas are unilateral in 85 percent of cases, are most frequent in the third web space (over 85 percent), but are occasionally found in the second web space (less than 15 percent). The problem rarely if ever occurs in the first or fourth web space.

Patients complain of a burning type of pain at the third or second web space, with radiation into the tips

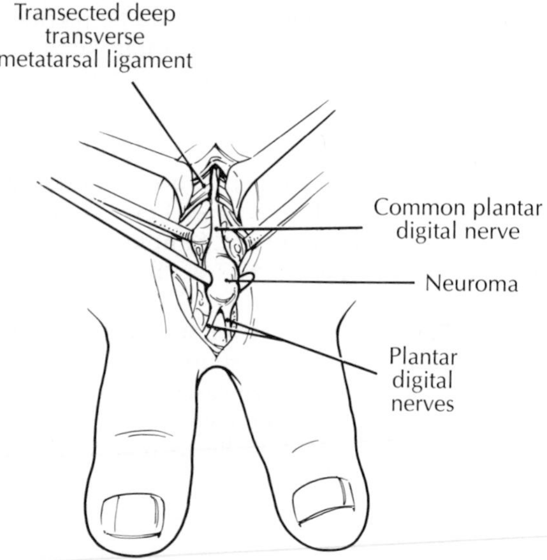

FIGURE 119-7
Intraoperative diagram of a Morton's neuroma between two adjacent metatarsal heads. The neuroma is adjacent to the nerve bifurcation.

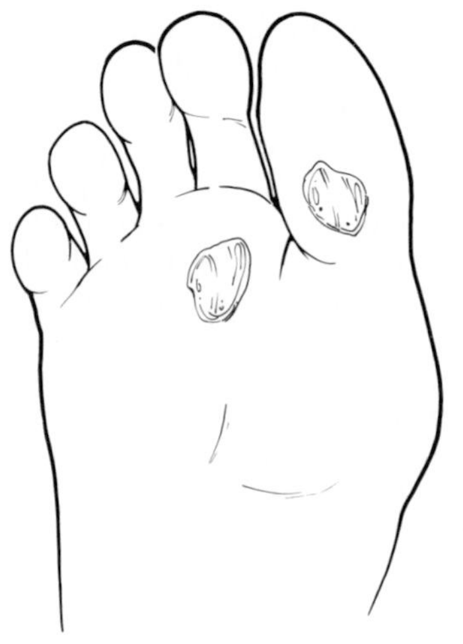

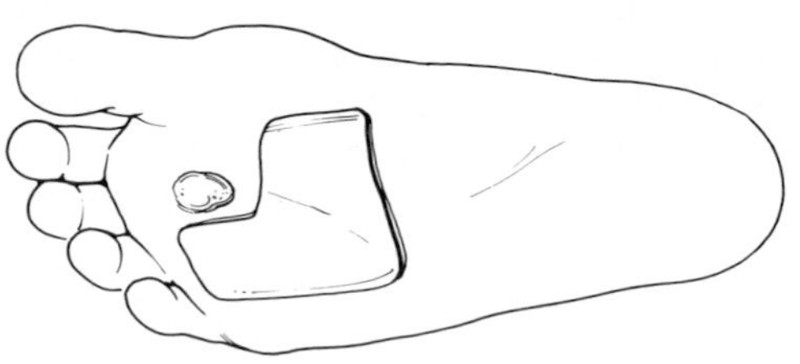

FIGURE 119-8
A. Transfer metatarsalgia (second-toe metatarsalgia) in a patient with bunion deformity. *B.* Padding to alleviate point pressure on the prominent second metatarsal head.

of the involved toes. Weight bearing exacerbates the symptoms, while shoe removal and massage often relieves the pain.

Physical exam reveals tenderness to palpation at the involved web space and symptoms with compression of the involved metatarsals. The neuroma may be palpable and may often be "pushed" back and forth between the involved toes, causing a clinching sensation. Symmes-Weinstein monofilament testing may demonstrate diminished interdigital toe sensation. Symptomatic relief can result from common digital nerve block with local anaesthetic. This also serves as an excellent diagnostic test.

Treatment

Metatarsal pads are the first line of defense. By acting to spread the metatarsal heads and decompress the nerve, they may bring relief. Steroid injection and antiinflammatory medications may interrupt the cycle of chronic inflammation/fibrosis.

Neuroma resection is advised in recalcitrant cases that meet diagnostic criteria. The procedure does cause some loss of sensation, and it is important that patients be aware of this preoperatively.

Second-Toe Metatarsalgia

Etiology

The foot with a relatively long second metatarsal is predisposed to excessive plantar forces with ambulation. The disorder is often associated with a great-toe bunion and the classic "transfer metatarsalgia" (Fig. 119-8*A*).

Signs and Symptoms

There is a large diffuse plantar callus centered over the second metatarsal head. The first metatarsal cuneiform joint is often hypermobile, and occasionally there is an associated bunion. Radiographs may show an elongated second metatarsal.

Treatment

The first line of treatment is a metatarsal pad or custom inlays (Fig. 119-8*B*) with a medial forefoot post. In addition, treatment should include attention to the great-toe bunion deformity.

Surgical osteotomy of the second metatarsal is the preferred treatment when pads fail. This can be combined with a corrective bunion procedure when indicated.

Intractable Plantar Keratosis

Etiology

Often a pressure point on the plantar surface leads to a callosity on the sole of the foot. When this hypertrophied skin becomes trapped, a discrete seed callus develops. The condition is associated with prominent fibular condyles of the lesser metatarsal heads, prominent tibial sesamoid under the first ray, tailor's bunion, hammertoe, or a prominent whole metatarsal head adjacent to a previously osteotomized metatarsal.

Signs and Symptoms

The sole of the foot will have a discrete, isolated callus. There is associated pain, which can be exquisite. Paring of these lesions seldom causes bleeding. Radiographs may demonstrate a bony prominence as the source of the point pressure.

Treatment

Callus shaving will sometimes reveal a keratin pearl. Metatarsal pads, custom inlays, and felt relief pads may be satisfactory treatment. When this fails, operative correction of the primary process (i.e., bony abnormality) is the goal of interventional treatment.

Sesamoiditis

Etiology

The sesamoid bones are contained in the two tendons of the short great-toe flexor muscle (flexor hallucis brevis). They articulate with the underface of the great-toe metatarsal head. Symptoms involving the great toe sesamoids may originate from osteochondritis, microfracture, or avascular necrosis. Inflammation and irritation in this weight-bearing area that is a source of toe-off power can result in a constellation of symptoms.

Signs and Symptoms

Patients will often have vague complaints of pain over the involved sesamoid that is worsened with activity. The pain may be quite severe and radiate into the great toe. Tenderness can be elicited with direct palpation and pain can occur with forced dorsiflexion of the great toe. The exam will demonstrate point tenderness under the involved sesamoid, with occasional associated metatarsophalangeal joint swelling. Radiographic evidence of fragmentation or collapse of the sesamoid can often be demonstrated on special views. The bone scan is frequently positive and can be used to pinpoint areas of inflammation with pinhole columnation.

Treatment

Nonoperative treatment may take 2 years to improve the condition and should be pursued as a first line of therapy. Metatarsal pads or cutout inlays can relieve pressure under the sesamoid.

Operative removal of the involved sesamoid is associated with a significant complication rate and should be considered a last resort. Medial sesamoid removal may lead to hallux valgus deformity, lateral removal to hallux varus, and removal of both to a "cock-up" deformity.

Plantar Warts (Verrucae)

Etiology

The papovaviruses are etiologic in the formation of plantar warts. Subacute viral infection leads to scarring and papule formation with heaping of the skin.[8]

Signs and Symptoms

These well-circumscribed, hyperkeratotic papules may be exquisitely tender. The pain is associated with weight bearing. The lesions may be isolated or in clusters. They bleed freely with attempts at paring (unlike intractable plantar keratoses).

Treatment

Many plantar warts will resolve with time (50 percent at 1 year, 75 percent at 2 years) and no treatment. Preparations containing salicylic acid may alleviate symptoms, and local lidocaine injection may also be of benefit.

Surgical removal of plantar warts is contraindicated in most cases, since this process can replace the painful wart with a painful scar. Cryotherapy or CO_2 laser are ways of removing the warts with minimal scarring.

Atrophy of Transverse Metatarsal Arch Fat Pad

Etiology

The cause of metatarsalgia is often not identifiable. Atrophy of the metatarsal fat pad is a diagnosis of exclusion and is not associated with other pathologic processes, such as claw toes.

Signs and Symptoms

Metatarsal discomfort without a concrete diagnosis puts the patient into this category. Atrophy of the fat pad is relative and should not lead the physician to abandon the search for other sources of the patient's pain.

Treatment

Patient education with calm reassurance and shoe modification are the mainstays of treatment. Surgical intervention is not indicated.

SOFT PARTS

Clavus (Soft Corn)

Etiology

A clavus forms in response to the abutment of one toe against a prominent bony condyle of the opposing toe. A hyperkeratotic lesion forms on the inner surface (web space) between the toes (Fig. 119-9*A*). The skin will often macerate and cause problems with local infection and tenderness. The underlying digital nerve may become compressed by the same process. Tight shoes have been implicated in the etiology of this process.

The two most common locations for clavuses to occur are (1) deep in the fourth web space, where a prominent lateral base of the fourth proximal phalanx abuts with a prominent fifth proximal interphalangeal joint (Fig. 119-9*B*), and (2) on the medial side of the second proximal interphalangeal joint as it rubs against the great-toe interphalangeal joint.

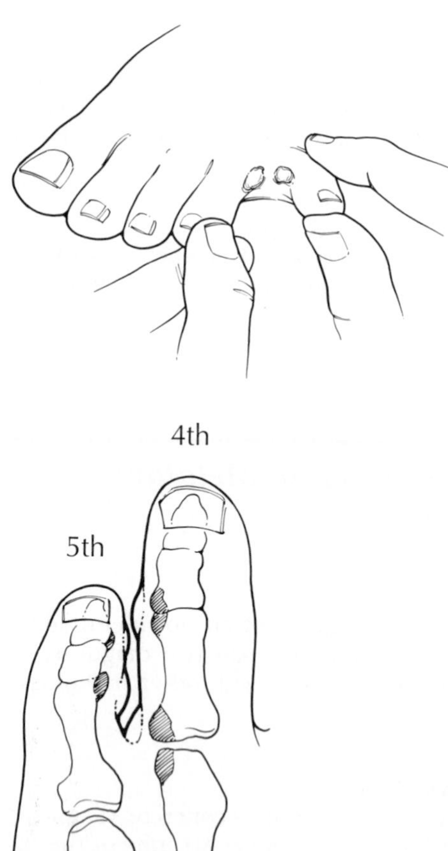

FIGURE 119-9

A. Soft corns in the fourth web space. *B.* Areas of bony abutment between the fourth and fifth toes predisposing to formation of soft corns.

Signs and Symptoms

An area of raised skin in the web space is apparent on clinical exam. The overlying skin may be macerated, and complaints of local infection are not uncommon. Patients will have extremely painful soft corns when the underlying digital nerve becomes involved.

Treatment

Primary treatment is directed at reducing pressure on the overlying skin by padding with lamb's wool. Shoes with a wide toe box relieve lateral compression. Trimming of the corn may also be of benefit.

If conservative therapy fails, surgical intervention through decompression of bony prominences by condylectomy is often indicated. This is a modest but very successful procedure.

Posterior Tibial Tendinitis/Tendon Rupture

Etiology

Chronic and recurrent tenosynovitis of the posterior tibial tendon leads to its attenuation and degeneration with age. Attritional rupture of the tendon is not uncommon. The attenuation or rupture is commonly located at the level of the medial malleolus, where its blood supply is limited and the tendon tunnel is narrowest.

Signs and Symptoms

Patients complain of pain and swelling over the medial aspect of the ankle. They may also complain of a change in the shape of the foot or instability with ambulation.

When the tendon is significantly attenuated or ruptured, the patient will demonstrate a significant valgus deflection of the heel, loss in height of the medial longitudinal arch, and abduction of the forefoot, with a positive "too-many-toes sign" (appearance of more toes lateral to the ankle when comparing the feet from behind).[9]

Radiographs can demonstrate a flat foot with talonavicular sag and valgus deflection of the os calcis. Magnetic resonance imaging is most helpful in diagnosing rupture or degeneration of the posterior tibial tendon.

Treatment

Conservative treatment includes shoe modification with a ¼-inch medial heel wedge and a medial arch support. Anti-inflammatory medication and patient education on limiting activity are also helpful.

Surgical reconstruction of the posterior tibial tendon in the elderly patient is rarely indicated. In selected long-standing cases, limited fusions including tarsonavicular and triple arthrodesis may be warranted.

TOENAILS

Ingrown Toenail

Etiology

Extrinsic pressure on the toe can trap the sharp corner of an improperly cut nail into the medial or lateral soft tissues. Continuous irritation of the soft parts by the nail leads to inflammation, infection, and hypertrophic granulation tissue. Factors predisposing to the development of ingrown toenails include improper trimming, heredity, improper shoe fit, and obesity. The nail of the great toe is most commonly involved (Fig. 119-10*A*).

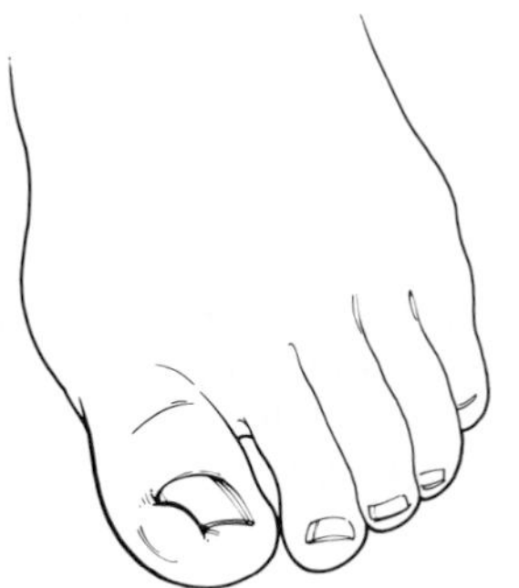

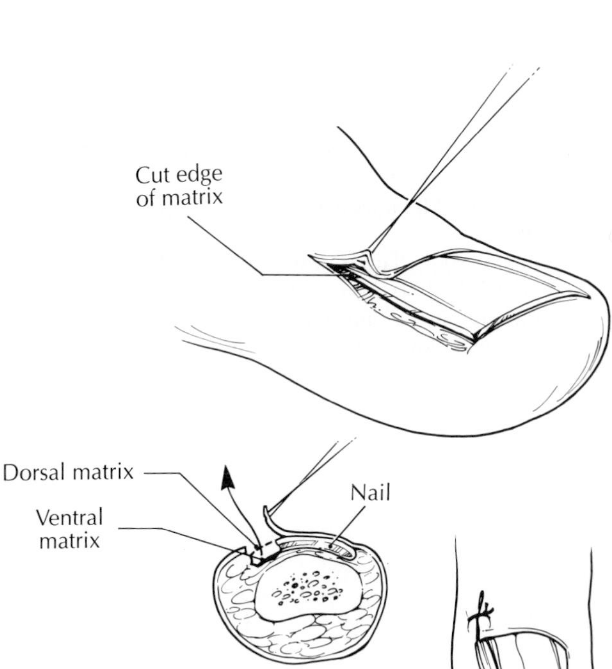

FIGURE 119-10

A. Ingrown toenail with hypertrophic granulation tissue. *B.* Removal of involved nail plate and underlying matrix in patient with ingrown toenail.

Signs and Symptoms

Patients will complain of pain of the involved toe while walking or wearing tight shoes. They may occasionally have drainage associated with local bacterial infection.

Treatment

Early, local cases may respond to warm soaks, antibiotics, and elevation of the nail corner with collodion-soaked wisps of cotton placed beneath the spicule of nail. Most cases, however, require that the offending nail be removed. This can be combined with matrixectomy (Fig. 119-10*B*).

Onychomycosis

Etiology

Fungal or dermatophyte infections of the toenail begin with an area of localized discoloration beneath the nail that begins at the tip, moves proximally, and ultimately enters through the nail plate itself. The etiologic agents are *Trichophyton mentagrophytes, Candida albicans,* or *Trichophyton rubrum.* As the nail bed becomes chronically irritated from persistent local inflammation, an accumulation of hyperkeratotic debris leads to thickening, cracking, and brownish-yellow discoloration.

Signs and Symptoms

The enlarged nail may make it difficult for patients to find comfortable shoes. Patients may also express concern about local spread to other toenails as well as the cosmetic appearance of the foot. The infection itself is asymptomatic.

Treatment

Nail trimming is the mainstay of treatment for the enlarged, thickened nail. Medical management including oral griseofulvin for 12 months coupled with a local antifungal agent (e.g., clotrimazole) applied beneath the nail plate may eliminate the infection. Resistant cases should be managed with nail removal and nail matrix destruction.

SPECIAL CONSIDERATIONS

Care of the Diabetic Foot

The prevention and early detection of foot problems in the diabetic patient population is critical. The number of elderly diabetic patients continues to increase. Secondary manifestations of the diabetic disease process are also becoming more prevalent. It is the responsibility of the treating physician to emphasize the importance of daily foot care in this patient population. Periodic examination by the physician and daily exam by the patient must be encouraged. Selection of proper shoe wear including ample toe box, soft rocker-bottom sole, padded shoe tongue, leather construction, light weight, and a well-molded Achilles pad should be recommended.

Peripheral diabetic neuropathy predisposes the foot to clawing of the toes and loss of sensation. This contributes to the development of malperforans ulceration adjacent to the prominent metatarsal heads. These ulcers are painless, rimmed by callus, and less necrotic than vascular ulcerations.

The diabetic patient is also vulnerable to infection. Altered chemotaxis and other factors predispose the diabetic to prolonged, multiorganism, and often anaerobic bacterial processes.[10] The location of malperforans ulceration predisposes the metatarsal heads to the development of osteomyelitis. Broad-spectrum antibiotics with aggressive incision and debridement, including amputation in advanced cases, is the recommended treatment of such cases.

Fragile defense mechanisms coupled with the potential for disastrous foot problems in the diabetic population mandate the need for early detection and active participation of the foot care team. When inspection discovers early malperforans ulceration, wound care, orthotics, total contact casting, patellar-tendon-bearing (PTB) bracing (Fig. 119-11), and ultimately surgery may be required. Infected ulcers need even more aggressive treatment. Most important in this population is taking the time to educate the patient in daily foot care and prevention.

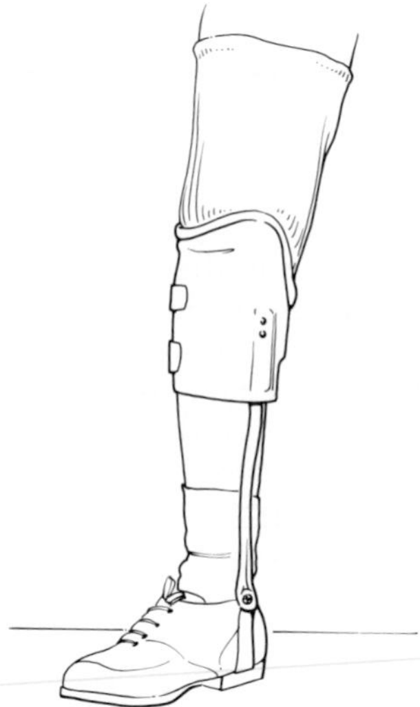

FIGURE 119-11
Double upright patellar-tendon-bearing (PTB) in patient with chronic malperforans ulcerations.

REFERENCES

1. Bordelon RL: Orthotics, shoes and braces. *Clin Orthop* 20:751, 1989.
2. Jahss MH: *Disorders of the Foot and Ankle: Medical and Surgical Management.* Philadelphia, Saunders, 1991.
3. Kwong PK et al: Plantar fasciitis: Mechanics and pathomechanics of treatment. *Clin Sports Med* 7:119, 1988.
4. Baxter DE et al: Chronic heel pain. *Orthop Clin North Am* 20:563, 1989.
5. Cimino WR: Tarsal tunnel syndrome: Review of the literature. *Foot Ankle* 11:47, 1990.
6. Hawkins BJ, Haddad RJ: Hallux rigidus. *Clin Sports Med* 7:37, 1988.
7. Gould JS: Metatarsalgia. *Orthop Clin North Am* 20:553, 1989.
8. Glover MG: Plantar warts. *Foot Ankle* 11:172, 1990.
9. Kade RA, Jahs MH: Tibialis posterior: A review of anatomy and biomechanics in relation to support of the medial longitudinal arch. *Foot Ankle* 11:244, 1991.
10. Harrelson JM: Management of the diabetic foot. *Orthop Clin North Am* 20:605, 1989.

Chapter 120

IMMOBILITY

Walter H. Ettinger, Jr.

Mobility is the ability to move around in one's environment and is a complex, integrated function measured in multiple interrelated domains. However, from a clinical perspective, mobility can be conceptualized as encompassing three functions: walking, climbing stairs, and transferring from the seated to the standing position.

Immobility, defined as difficulty with or inability to perform mobility tasks, is an important outcome of disease in older people. Immobility adversely affects the quality of life of older people, threatens independent living and personal autonomy, and increases both formal and informal care needs. Persons with difficulty in mobility tasks use a disproportionate share of health care, and the costs of caring for such persons will rise dramatically over the next two decades.[1] Immobility has adverse effects on physical health, since inactivity increases the risks of osteoporosis, diabetes, and cardiovascular disease. Abnormal gait and poor balance are important risk factors for falls and injury in older people. Persons confined to a bed or chair are at increased risk for incontinence, skin breakdown, deep venous thrombosis, and pulmonary embolism. Finally, "immobility begets immobility." Persons who are sedentary develop muscle weakness and low aerobic power, which further compromise physical capacity.[2]

EPIDEMIOLOGY

Immobility is a highly prevalent problem in older people. As noted above, mobility can be assessed in three domains: walking, climbing stairs, and transferring. Within each of these domains, there are hierarchies of tasks based on the physical demands of each activity. For example, the walking domain includes low-level activities such as walking across a small room, moderate-level activities such as walking a mile, and highly demanding activities such as long-distance running. Thus, the prevalence of immobility depends on assessment of difficulty with specific tasks. This point is illustrated in Fig. 120-1, which shows the prevalence of immobility among older community-

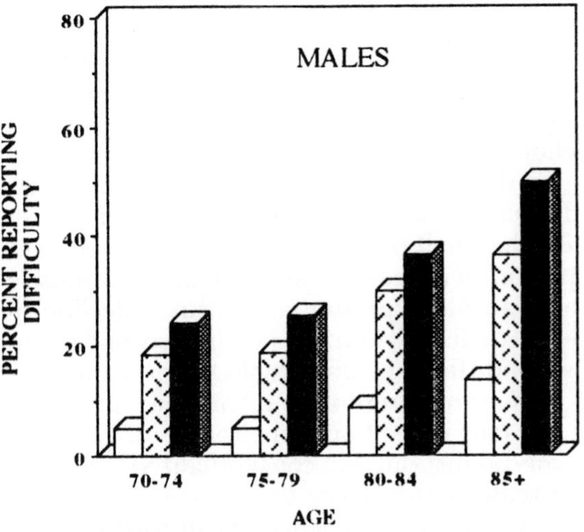

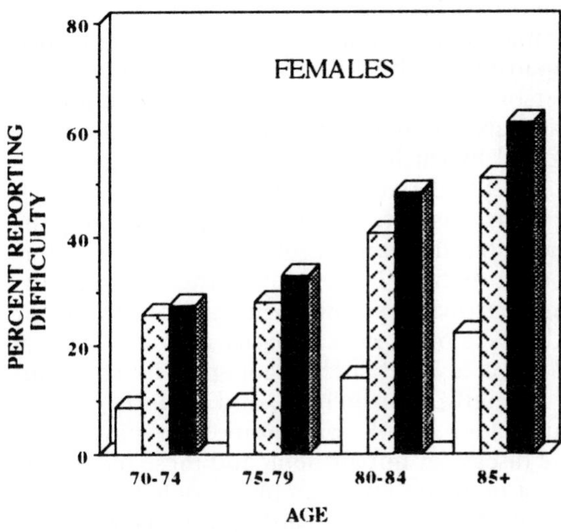

FIGURE 120-1

The prevalence of self-reported difficulty in three mobility tasks: transferring from bed to chair □, climbing steps ▨, and walking ¼ mile ■. (*From National Center for Health Statistics.*[3])

dwelling persons who participated in the Longitudinal Study on Aging (LSOA).[3] Difficulty with walking 1/4 mile was most prevalent, followed by difficulty climbing stairs, and then transferring from bed to chair. The prevalence of difficulty increased with age, and women reported more difficulty than men among all age groups and tasks. Additionally, people with lower incomes and less education reported higher levels of difficulty with mobility tasks.

The prevalence of immobility and other physical disabilities is more dynamic than had previously been realized. In the LSOA and other studies, up to 25 percent of people who reported difficulty with mobility tasks reported no difficulty 2 years later.[3,4] The reasons for this are unclear, but these data suggest that a significant proportion of immobility is self-limited and/or responds to treatment.

PATHOGENESIS OF IMMOBILITY

Acute and chronic diseases are the causes of immobility in older people. However, mobility is a highly complex, integrated function; to understand the pathogenesis of immobility, one must use a model which focuses on capacity and function as well as disease. A modification of the World Health Organization's topology of disease outcomes is a useful construct, helping us to understand the pathogenesis and treatments of immobility.[5] In this model, chronic or acute *diseases* lead to physiological abnormalities termed *impairments,* which can be temporary or permanent. The impairments lead to *disability,* or the inability to perform an activity such as walking or climbing stairs in a manner that falls within the normal range. The relationship among diseases, impairment, and disability is modified by a number of factors including physiological age, environment, psychosocial factors, health habits, and treatment.

Common and treatable diseases and their associated impairments which cause loss of mobility in the older person are listed in Table 120-1. Musculoskeletal diseases are the most important causes of immobility, followed by cardiovascular and neurological diseases. Conceptually, it is important to note that each disease exerts its effect through different impairments, and that the patterns of immobility are different for each disease. For example, the main impairment from arthritis is pain, whereas cardiovascular disease limits aerobic work capacity and neurological diseases affect a variety of physiological functions including strength, coordination, and balance.

Many older people with immobility have more than one disease or impairment, and these may interact to limit mobility. For example, people with osteoarthritis of the knee and cardiopulmonary disease have more severe disability than would be expected from a simple additive effect of these diseases.[6] The reasons for this are not known, but it may be that impairment from one disease increases the impairment from another; the inefficiency of gait in a person with osteoarthritis may be made worse by the low work capacity caused by cardiovascular disease.

TABLE 120-1

Diseases and Impairments which are Important Causes of Immobility in Older People

Diseases	Impairments
Musculoskeletal disease	Pain, limited range of motion, muscle weakness, deconditioning
Osteoarthritis	
Osteoporosis (fractures)	
Polymalgia rheumatica	
Bursitis-tendonitis	
Degenerative spine disease	
Heart disease	Pain, shortness of breath, low aerobic work capacity
Congestive heart failure	
Coronary heart disease	
Valvular heart disease	
Neurological disease	Muscle weakness, loss of proprioceptive and other sensory input, abnormalities of gait, vertigo, apraxia
Parkinson's disease	
Stroke	
Dementias	
Peripheral neuropathy	
Spinal stenosis	
Benign positional vertigo	
Pulmonary diseases	Shortness of breath, low aerobic work capacity
Chronic obstructive pulmonary disease	
Restrictive lung disease	
Other	
Peripheral vascular disease	Pain
Hyper- and hypothyroidism	Muscle weakness, fatigue
Retinopathies and other eye diseases	Low visual acuity
Postural hypotension	Instability
Anemia	Low work capacity

Several factors modify the disease-impairment-disability relationship. Physiological aging is associated with decreased capacity in a number of organ systems which are important for mobility: loss of muscle strength, decreased aerobic power, blunted baroreceptor responses, slowed reaction times, etc. Physiological aging rarely causes immobility but does result in a decline in maximum capacity, which may come close to the threshold of physical performance below which disability will occur.[2] Thus, a task which requires less than half of maximal muscle strength in a young person may require nearly maximum muscle strength in an older person, and a small decline in capacity due to disease or other factors may make simple activities difficult or impossible to carry out.

An important component of mobility problems in older persons is the home environment. Environmental conditions can be conceptualized as those which decrease performance (barriers such as stairs) and those which maintain activity performance (supports such as grab bars). In the context of the conceptual scheme of disability illustrated in Fig. 120-2, environmental factors modify the impact of an impairment on the level of disability experienced.[7]

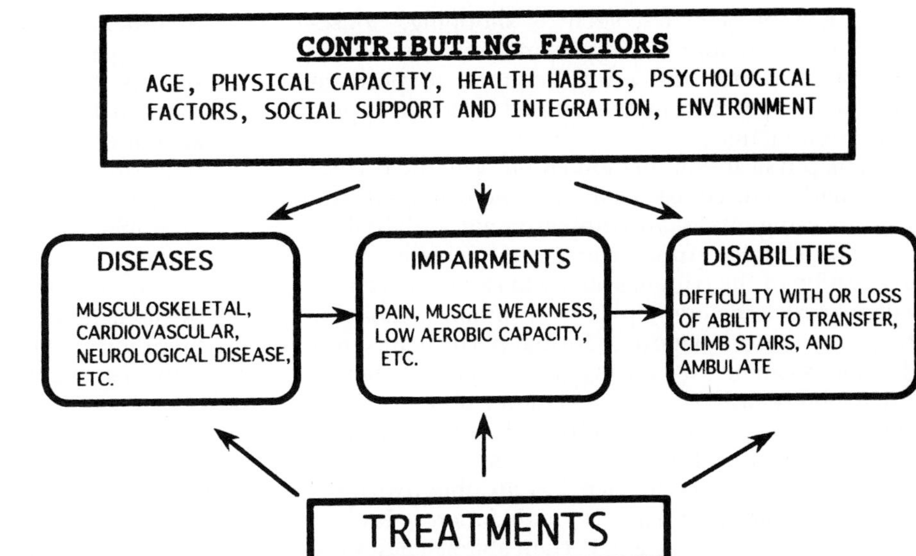

FIGURE 120-2
A conceptual model of immobility based on the World Health Organization's classification of impairments, disabilities, and handicaps. (*From World Health Organization.*[5])

Thus, the physical environment influences disability by moderating performance parameters of an activity or task, such as physical ability and amount of pain elicited. Some level of environmental stress may be beneficial, as it forces the individual to be more physically active, thus preserving physical capacity.

Psychological variables including personality traits, (neuroticism, self-regulation, etc.), and coping skills are important modifiers of the disease-impairment-disability relationship.[8,9] Neuroticism is the disposition to experience unpleasant emotional states over time and across situations. It is associated with physical complaints and help-seeking behavior and thus may be directly related to self-reported disability. Self-regulatory skilfullness—actions taken by an individual to control the disruptive effects which emotional arousal, undesired thoughts, and pain can have on desired behavior—modulates the effects of impairments on physical performance. This term also refers to actions a person takes to establish and maintain adaptive and healthy habits. Thus, individuals with good self-control can learn adaptive ways of managing or reducing their disabilities.

Social support is a third factor which modifies the disease-disability relationship.[10] A large body of data has accumulated linking social support to physical health outcomes. Insufficient social support appears to be an important risk factor for morbidity and mortality in a wide range of diseases. Thus, persons with little social support and limited social integration will have more problems with mobility tasks.

Interactions among these domains are also important in modulating the physiological age/environment/psychological/social effects on mobility, especially among older persons. For example, impaired balance secondary to diminished proprioception and reduced bone mass, coupled with an environment containing hazards such as low lighting and stairs, may produce a fall and injury, increasing both social dependence and fear of falling.

ASSESSMENT AND EVALUATION OF MOBILITY PROBLEMS

Both performance of and capacity to perform mobility tasks should be assessed regularly in all older patients. Mobility is assessed by both self-report of performance and direct observation. Several standardized questionnaires have been developed to measure mobility and other physical functions in a clinical setting.[11] At a minimum, patients should be queried about their ability to walk in their homes and outside their homes, to climb stairs, and to transfer (activities such as getting in and out of a car, a chair, the bathtub, and so on).

The duration and severity of mobility problems should be established. Patients who have long-standing disabilities are less likely to respond to treatment than are patients whose mobility has changed recently. Obtaining details about specific activities is helpful: "Do you walk out to the mailbox at the end of your driveway?" "How far is the mailbox from your house?" "How many times a day do you walk to the end of the driveway?" "Do you have to stop to rest part way?" "Has there been any change in your ability to walk to the mailbox in the past month?" "In the past 6 months?" "Do you require the use of a cane or walker?" When it is determined that a patient has limited mobility, the reasons for the limitations should be elucidated. For example, "Do you have difficulty walking to the mailbox because of pain in your knees?" "Do you get short of breath, weak, or unsteady?" "Are you afraid you will fall?" Finally, the importance of the task to the patient should be explored. What sort of loss has the patient suffered because of the inability to walk or perform specific activities? What are the implications for caregivers or other people for whom the patient is responsible, such as a disabled spouse? Mobility is an important component of activities, such as shopping, housework, and so on, and it is important to determine the level of assistance and effort required to perform these tasks. This information is used to devise appropriate treatments.

The physical examination emphasizes the cardiopulmonary, musculoskeletal, and neurological systems, focusing on diseases, impairments, and disabilities. The simplest functional test of mobility is an observation of the patient's ability to rise from a chair, walk toward, and climb up on the examining table for the physical examination. A formal performance test of mobility can be used if the patient reports difficulty with mobility tasks or if the examiner observes difficulty when the patient moves from chair to examining table. A formal performance test of mobility has several advantages: the clinician has an objective measure of mobility performance, ambulation is broken down into components, and certain abnormalities are revealed which are predictive of susceptibility to falling. A practical and well-planned performance test was designed by Tinneti.[12] To begin, the patient arises from a firm armchair and stands, feet close together, for 30 seconds; difficulty rising from a chair is most often caused by proximal weakness or pain in the large joints. If the patient becomes light-headed, pulse and blood pressure should be monitored. Unsteadiness while upright and a propensity to fall are indicated by the inability to perform a semitandem gait or the inability to compensate after a firm tug on the patient's waistband from behind. The examiner watches the patient walk across the room and notes any abnormalities of gait. The patient turns 180°, returns, and sits down in a chair. Two other tasks can be added to the examination which are physically demanding: stair climbing and walking endurance. During an observed stair climb, the examiner notes fatigue, unsteadiness, and improper technique. In the 5-minute walk test, the total distance covered as well as the limiting symptoms are noted.

TREATMENT OF IMMOBILITY

Three principles guide the treatment of mobility problems:

1. Therapy is multifactorial and focuses on treating diseases, impairments, and other factors which affect disability.
2. The patient should be actively involved in decisions regarding therapy, and the patient's preferences will guide the specific goals of therapy. Setting priorities with the patient and focusing treatment on the tasks which are most important to the patient will lead to greater satisfaction and success. Supporters of the patient should also participate in the therapeutic strategy, including, at times, urging the patient to perform activities requiring mobility rather than doing tasks for the patient. Clearly the latter course risks reinforcing immobility and dependency.
3. Therapy is to be aimed at restoration of function and improvement of quality of life; the treatment of diseases or impairments without an improvement in function adds unnecessary costs and may cause iatrogenic complications.

Disease-specific treatment should be initiated when improvement in the disease will lead to improvement in function. For example, total joint replacement for the treatment of painful lower-extremity arthritis dramatically improves functional ability. Similarly, pharmacological treatment of Parkinson's disease or angina pectoris will improve physical function. Treatment of capacity-limiting impairments can be effective in improving mobility. For example, therapeutic exercise to increase muscle strength and/or aerobic power is an important tool in improving physical function. Weakness and poor conditioning contribute to mobility limitations in many older people regardless of the diseases which have caused their immobility. Recent studies indicate that older people, including the very old and frail, show dramatic increases in muscle strength and work capacity from vigorous exercise.[13] Initially, exercise should be done under the supervision of an exercise or physical therapist. However, to achieve a substantial increase in muscle strength or aerobic power requires exercise designed to achieve a training effect. Therapists may not prescribe exercise of sufficient intensity, frequency, and duration to effect a meaningful improvement in physical capacity. Therefore, it is important for the physician to discuss the therapeutic goals of exercise and the necessity of obtaining a training effect with the therapist.

Environmental manipulation is an important component of therapy for immobility. The best way to assess the environment is for the physician or an occupational therapist to make a home visit. Direct observation is a powerful tool in determining how the environment affects a person's physical ability. Manipulations of the environment include the use of adaptive devices (such as a raised toilet seat, grab bars, etc.) and/or manipulations and rearrangement of the home so that all the essential functions can be done on one floor. Physical therapists will also recommend the use of assistive devices such as a cane, walker, or brace to help correct specific impairments. Occupational therapists will teach adaptive strategies in performing daily activities.

SUMMARY

Immobility is an important disease outcome and public health problem in older people. The pathogenesis of immobility is complex. The degree of immobility is determined by the severity and progression of disease and impairments. However, the disease-impairment-disability relationship is modified by several factors including physiological, psychological, social, and environmental factors. Treatment is multifactorial and should be focused on factors which will improve function and quality of life. Successful treatment of immobility may substantially improve the quality of life of older people.

REFERENCES

1. Rice DP, LaPlante MP: Chronic disease, disability, and increasing longevity, in Sullivan S, Lewin M (eds): *Ethics and Economics of Long Term Care.* Washington, DC, American Enterprise Institute, 1988, pp 9–55.
2. Ettinger WH: Immobility in the Elderly, in Kelly WN, DeVita VT, Dupont HL, et al (eds): *Textbook of Internal Medicine,* Philadelphia, Lippincott, 1992, pp 2399–2404.
3. National Center for Health Statistics, Fitti JE, Kovar MG: *The Supplement on Aging to the 1984 National Health Interview Survey.* Vital and Health Statistics, series 1, no. 21, DHHS pub. no. (PHS) 87-1323. Washington, DC, US Public Health Service, US Government Printing Office, October 1987.
4. Harris T et al: Longitudinal study of physical ability in the oldest-old. *Am J Public Health* 79:698, 1989.
5. World Health Organization: *The International Classification of Impairments, Disabilities, and Handicaps.* Geneva, World Health Organization, 1980.
6. Ettinger WH et al: Long term physical functioning in persons with knee osteoarthritis from NHANES I: Effects of comorbid medical conditions. *J Clin Epidemiol* (in press).
7. Jette A, Branch L: Impairment and disability in the aged. *J Chronic Dis* 38:59, 1985.
8. Costa P, McRae R: Hypochondriasis, neuroticism, and aging: When are somatic complaints unfounded? *Am Psychol* 40:19, 1985.
9. Rosenbaum M: *Learned Resourcefulness: On Coping Skill, Self-Control, and Adaptive Behavior.* New York, Springer, 1990.
10. Shumaker SA, Hill DR: Gender differences in social support and physical health. *Health Psychol* 10:102, 1991.
11. Applegate WB: Instruments for the assessment of function in older patients. *N Engl J Med* 332:1207, 1990.
12. Tinetti ME: Performance-oriented assessment of mobility problems in elderly patients. *J Am Geriatr Soc* 34:119, 1986.
13. Fiatarone MA et al: High-intensity strength training in nonagenarians: Effects on skeletal muscle. *JAMA* 263:3029, 1990.

Chapter 121

FALLS

Mary E. Tinetti

Falling is a common and potentially preventable source of mortality and morbidity in elderly patients. While some falls have an overwhelming intrinsic cause, such as syncope (discussed in Chap. 107), or an overwhelming extrinsic cause, such as being hit by a bus, most falls by elderly patients are multifactorial in origin, resulting from an interaction between stability-impairing characteristics of the host and hazards or demands of the environment.

Falls by institutionalized and community-dwelling persons are considered separately in this chapter because of significant differences in levels of impairment, as well as in environmental demands and hazards. The topics discussed in this chapter include prevalence, morbidity, risk factors, and possible preventive strategies.

FALLS AMONG COMMUNITY-LIVING ELDERLY PERSONS

Prevalence

According to several community-based surveys, about 30 percent of persons over age 65 experience falls each year in situations where there are no overwhelming intrinsic causes such as syncope or extrinsic causes such as sports activities.[1–3] About one-half of these fallers have multiple falling episodes. The likelihood of falling increases with age.[1–4] Results have been contradictory as to whether older women fall more frequently than older men or whether whites fall more frequently than nonwhites. While falling is more common among frail elderly persons, healthy elderly persons fall as well during ordinary daily activities, suggesting that falling is not merely a marker of functional decline.

Morbidity

Known fall-related morbidity includes death, serious injury, consequences of long lies from inability to get up, and fear or loss of confidence. Unintentional injury is the sixth leading cause of death in persons aged over 65 years.[1] The majority of these deaths are attributed to falls, especially among persons 85 years of age or older.

Perhaps the most feared morbid outcome of falling is a fractured hip, suffered by over 200,000 Americans every year, most of whom are elderly women.[1] Hip fractures are discussed in Chap. 122. While injury to any bone may result from a fall, humeral, wrist, pelvic, and hip fractures are the most common age-related fractures, resulting from the combined effects of osteoporosis and falling.[5] Serious soft tissue injuries, such as joint dislocations, sprains, and strains, may also result from falls.[1,3] Fortunately, the most serious injuries, such as subdural hematomas and cervical fractures, are rare. Certainly, the majority of falls do not result in serious physical injury. An estimated 1 percent of falls by elderly persons result in a hip fracture, 5 percent in other fractures, and an additional 5 percent in serious soft tissue injuries.[1,3] Approximately one-half of falls result in minor injuries such as abrasions or contusions.

Women appear to have a higher rate of both fracture and nonfracture injuries than men, while whites have a higher rate than nonwhites.[1,4] There is also some evidence that healthier, more active elderly persons are at greater risk of injury per fall than are frailer individuals.[6]

The inability to get up without help is a sequela which occurs in almost one-half of falls, although fewer than 10 percent result in lies of greater than 1 hour.[7] These long lies may result in dehydration, pressure sores, rhabdomyolysis, and pneumonia.

Fear of falling or loss of confidence is another important fall-related morbidity. Up to one-half of fallers admit to being afraid, and one-quarter report that because of fear they avoid even essential activities such as mobility within the home, bathing, and dressing.[3]

Falls and their sequelae constitute important clinical and public health problems which contribute to death, functional decline, and increased health care utilization. Recent studies have shown that fallers experience greater declines in activities of daily living and physical and social activities, report more restricted activity days, and have a greater chance of institutionalization than nonfallers, independent of other contributing physical, psychological, and social factors.[8,9] Elderly persons who report at least one fall also utilize more health care services including physician visits and hospital days than nonfallers.[9,10]

Risk Factors

The risk factors associated with falling include both chronic risk factors that predispose to falling and situational factors that are present at the time of falls.

Predisposing Risk Factors

Predisposing risk factors are best understood by considering that stability requires input from sensory, central integrative, cognitive, and musculoskeletal components in a highly integrated manner. Diseases and disabilities impacting on these components often are superimposed on age-related physiologic changes. Furthermore, cardiac, respiratory, metabolic, and other systemic disorders may compromise the functioning of any (or all) of these components. Gait disorders (Chap. 120) are especially important contributors to the risk of falling in elderly persons. Therefore, it is the cumulative effect of multiple age-related changes, diseases, and disabilities that appears to predispose to falling.

Sensory Vision, hearing, vestibular function, and proprioception are the major sensory modalities related to stability. Age-related visual changes are discussed in Chap. 39. Falling has been associated with both structural diseases of the eye, such as cataracts, and functional impairments in visual perception, acuity, glare tolerance, and dark adaptation.[1–4,11] The question of age-related changes in the vestibular system remains unresolved. Certainly, benign positional vertigo is seen more frequently in older persons. Factors predisposing to vestibular dysfunction, including previous ear infections, ear surgery, aminoglycosides, quinidine, and furosemide, are common among elderly patients.[12] Peripheral neuropathy and cervical degenerative disease probably are the most common causes of proprioceptive dysfunctions in elderly patients.[13] Almost one-third of elderly patients have abnormal position sense when tested clinically.[14]

Central Nervous System Sensory inputs are integrated in the central nervous system, and appropriate signals are then sent to the effector components of the musculoskeletal system. Therefore, any altered central nervous system process will predispose to falling. Falling has been associated with many central nervous system diseases, including stroke, Parkinson's disease, and normal-pressure hydrocephalus.

Cognitive Dementia has been associated with an increased risk of falling in several studies.[1–4] Dementia may be an especially important risk factor for falling among patients with other impairments because of their greater need for problem-solving ability.

Musculoskeletal The effector component of stability includes the efferent peripheral nervous system, bones, joints, and muscles. Patients with lower-extremity disabilities such as severe arthritis or weakness have a severalfold increase in the risk of falling.[3] The feet are an often-unrecognized source of morbidity in elderly patients. Thick nails, callouses, bunions, and toe deformities, as well as ill-fitting shoes, may give misleading proprioceptive information.[15]

Other Predisposing Risk Factors In several community studies, depression has been associated with an increased risk of falling. This risk appears to be independent of medication effect or other diseases. Postural hypotension has been postulated as a fall risk factor, although recent studies have found no association with falling. Unfortunately, the lack of blood pressure measurements at the time of the fall is a major limitation in determining the contribution of postural hypotension to falls in community-dwelling persons.

Medications appear to be a major predisposing risk factor for falls. Although results have been contradictory, most studies have shown that sedatives such as benzodiazepines, phenothiazines, and antidepressants increase the risk of falling, independent of the effect of the dementia or depression for which they are usually prescribed.[1–4] There is evidence suggesting a dose-response relationship, and the risk appears to be greater for the longer-acting medications.[16] The independent role of other medications that may impair postural regulation of blood pressure, such as diuretics, antihypertensives, or cardiac medications, is not yet clear. There does appear to be an increased risk of falling among patients receiving four or more prescription medications. This risk seems to be independent of the impairments and diseases for which the medications are prescribed.

The results of studies concerning the role of alcohol have been contradictory, with some studies showing an association with falls and injury and others showing no such association. One problem is that the self-report of alcohol consumption may not have been reliable.

Situational Factors

Patients who are predisposed to falling because of the above characteristics do so only intermittently. Therefore, in understanding fall etiology, it is also necessary to identify factors that may precipitate falls.

Activity The majority of falls occur during only mildly or moderately displacing activities such as walking, stepping up or down, or changing position. Only a minority of falls, probably about 5 percent, occur during clearly hazardous activities such as climbing on ladders or chairs.[3] However, compared with sedentary older persons, there is an increased incidence of falls among elderly persons who participate in more physical activity and exercise, probably because of exposure to severe displacement and hazards.

Environment More than 70 percent of falls occur at home. Perhaps 10 percent of falls occur on stairs, with descending being more hazardous than ascending.[13] Environmental hazards may be present in over one-half of all falls. Most commonly, these hazards are objects that are tripped over, such as cords, furniture, and small objects left on the floor. The role of other potential environmental hazards such as poor lighting, improperly fitting shoes, and surfaces with glare are more difficult to assess. A recent area of research in environmental hazards concerns optical patterns on escalators, stairs, and floor surfaces that may be important contributors to falls because of visual perceptual problems in elderly persons.[17] The contribution of environmental factors to falls is particularly difficult to assess both because many environmental factors such as tripping hazards or lighting vary over time and because the severity of the hazard depends on individual patients' combinations of impairments.

Acute Host Factors Dizziness and syncope, other obvious causes of falls, are discussed in Chap. 107. Acute illnesses or exacerbations of chronic illnesses are known to precipitate falls. In fact, falling is a well-recognized nonspecific presentation for illnesses such as pneumonias, urinary tract infections, and congestive heart failure among elderly patients.

Risk Factors for Fall Injuries

Recent attention has focused on identifying risk factors for suffering a serious injury during a fall.[7] While still under active investigation, postulated factors that contribute to an increased risk of injury include orientation of the body at impact; location of impact; energy-absorption capability of tissue including muscle, fat, and bone; and protective responses such as reaction time, muscle strength, and level of alertness and cognition.

Prevention

While controlled studies of fall prevention in community-dwelling elderly persons are not yet available, the risk factor for falls, as described above, are well detailed. Many of these risk factors respond to medical or rehabilitative interventions. The optimal fall-prevention strategy that can be recommended with present knowledge, therefore, is the identification and treatment of modifiable risk factors. These preventive strategies should address both the predisposing and the precipitating factors and should also address both intrinsic and environmental factors. As greater information becomes available concerning specific risk factors for fall sequelae such as injury or fear, these risk factors should be the target of preventive interventions. Until then, however, it must be assumed that all fallers are at risk for suffering fall morbidity. Known fall risk factors should be the target of intervention strategies.

Identifying Predisposing Risk Factors

Because elderly fallers are predisposed to fall based on the cumulative effects of multiple disabilities, the primary aim of the clinical evaluation is to identify the modifiable factors. The optimal fall evaluation involves assessing sensory, neurologic, musculoskeletal, and systemic processes in order to identify all possible contributors in individual patients (Table 121-1). The evaluation should include observing directly the patient's balance and gait (Table 121-2).

TABLE 121-1

Predisposing Risk Factors and Potential Interventions

Risk Factor	Potential Interventions
Sensory	
Vision: close-range and distance perception, dark adaptation	Appropriate refraction; surgery; medications; good lighting
Hearing	Cerumen removal; hearing aid
Vestibular	
Drugs, previous infections, surgery, benign positional vertigo	Avoidance of toxic drugs; surgery; balance exercises, good lighting
Proprioceptive	
Peripheral nerves, spinal cord	Treatment of underlying disease; good lighting; appropriate walking aid and footwear
Cervical: arthritis, spondylosis	Balance exercises; surgery
Central neurologic	
Any central nervous system disease impairing problem solving and judgment	Treatment of underlying disease; supervised, structured, safe environment
Musculoskeletal	
Arthritides, especially lower extremities	Medical and possibly surgical treatment of underlying disease
Muscle weakness, contractures	Strengthening exercises; balance and gait training; appropriate adaptive devices
Foot disorders: bunions, callouses, deformities	Podiatry; appropriate footwear
Systemic diseases	
Postural hypotension	Hydration; lowest effective dosage of necessary medications; reconditioning exercises; elevation of head of bed; stockings
Cardiac, respiratory, metabolic diseases	Treatment of underlying diseases
Depression	Careful consideration to risk/benefit ratio of antidepressant medication
Medications	
All—especially sedating medications	Lowest effective dosage of essential medications, starting low and increasing slowly
Environment	Environmental hazard checklist; appropriate adaptations and manipulations

TABLE 121-2

Performance-Oriented Evaluation of Balance and Gait

Abnormal Maneuver	Possible Causes	Possible Therapeutic or Rehabilitative Measures†	Possible Preventive or Adaptive Measures†
Difficulty arising from chair	Proximal muscle weakness (many causes) Arthritides (especially involving hip and knees) Parkinson's syndrome Hemiparesis or paraparesis Deconditioning	Treatment of specific disease states (e.g., with steroids, L-dopa) Hip and quadricep exercises Transfer training	High, firm chair with arms Raised toilet seats Ejection chairs
Instability on first standing	Postural hypotension Cerebellar disease Multisensory deficits Lower-extremity weakness or pain Foot pain causing reduced weight bearing	Treatment of specific diseases (e.g., adequate salt and fluid status, flucortisone) Jobst stockings Hip and knee exercises Foot problem correction	Slow rising Head of bed on blocks Supportive aid (e.g., walker, quadcane)
Instability with nudge on sternum or pull test	Parkinson's syndrome Back problems Normal pressure hydrocephalus ? Peripheral neuropathy Deconditioning	Treatment of specific diseases (e.g., with L-dopa, shunt) ? Back exercises Analgesia ? Balance exercises (e.g., Frankel's)	Obstacle-free environment Appropriate walking aid (cane, walker) Night-lights (less likely to fall if bump into object) Close observation with acute illness (high risk of falling) Avoidance of slippers
Instability with eyes closed (stable with eyes open)	Multisensory deficits Reduced proprioception, position sense (e.g., B_{12} deficiency, diabetes mellitus, etc.)	Treatment of specific diseases (e.g., B_{12} deficiency) Visual, hearing problem correction	Bright lights Night-lights Cane
Instability on neck turning or extension	Cervical arthritis Cervical spondylosis Vertebral-basilar insufficiency	? Balance exercises ? Antiarthritic medication ? Cervical collar ? Neck exercises	Avoidance of quick turns Turning of body, not just head Storage of objects in home low enough to avoid need to look up
Instability on turning	Cerebellar disease Hemiparesis Visual field cut Reduced proprioception Mild ataxia	Gait training ? Proprioceptive exercises	Appropriate walking aid Obstacle-free environment Properly fitting shoes
Unsafeness on sitting down (misjudges distance or falls into chair)	Reduced vision Proximal myopathies Apraxia	Treatment of specific diseases ? Coordination training Leg-strengthening exercises	High, firm chairs with arms, in good repair Transfer training
Decreased step height and length (bilateral)‡	Parkinson's syndrome Pseudobulbar palsy Myelopathy (usually spastic gait) Normal pressure hydrocephalus Advanced Alzheimer's disease (frontal lobe gait) Compensation for reduced vision or proprioception Fear of falling Habit	Treatment of specific diseases (e.g., with L-dopa) Vision correction Gait training (correct problems, suggest compensations, increase confidence)	Avoidance of throw rugs Good lighting Proper footwear (good fit, not too much friction or slipperiness) Appropriate walking aid

*This is not an exhaustive list.
†Most of these measures have not been subjected to clinical trials; evidence for effectiveness is usually anecdotal at best.
‡There will often be a flexed posture with all of these conditions.
SOURCE: From Tinetti.[20]

Because the risk of falling increases with the number of impairments, the clinician can estimate the risk of falling based on the results of the routine clinical evaluation suggested in Table 121-1. More importantly, if the risk of falling increases with the number of disabilities, risk may be minimized by ameliorating or eliminating even a few contributing factors.

As shown in Table 121-1, potential interventions may be medical, surgical, rehabilitative, or environmental. In most cases, the treatment of identified risk factors should include components of each of these types of intervention. Examples include surgery for cataracts; recommendations concerning good lighting; podiatric care, adaptive footwear, or surgery for foot problems; and physical therapy, exercise programs, and appropriate walking aids for musculoskeletal problems. Several investigators have seen benefit from balance exercises for vestibular or proprioceptive problems.[18,19] Further examples of recommended interventions for fall-related impairments are listed in Table 121-1 and are described elsewhere.[1,15,20,21] Obviously, all interventions need to be considered within the context of overall health and not merely fall prevention. Furthermore, the risk and benefit of each intervention need to be considered because of possible opposing effects. For example, while depression is associated with an increased risk of falling, antidepressants also contribute to the risk of falling.

Medications need to be assessed carefully. In an evaluation of an individual's risk of falling, the use of sedative drugs, tranquilizers, and antidepressants requires particular attention because of strong evidence supporting the role of such drugs in causing falls. Recommendations concerning medications and their contribution to falling include careful review of risks and benefits of each medication, consideration of the combination of drugs and their total doses consumed, maintenance of the lowest dose possible, and frequent review of the continued need for each medication.

The complex relationship between activity level and falling highlights the opposing goals of independence and safety in health care of elderly persons. On the one hand, regular exercise can lead to improved musculoskeletal strength, flexibility, and endurance. On the other hand, those who regularly engage in more strenuous activity are at increased risk of falling and at increased risk of injury during a fall.[6] Given these conflicting effects, educational emphasis should be on avoiding clearly hazardous and probably unnecessary activities such as climbing on chairs. Other activities, such as climbing stairs or exercising, while increasing risk of falling, probably should be encouraged given their contributions to functional independence and overall health.

Observing Balance and Gait

Directly observing how the patient performs the position changes and movements used during daily activity serves the following three purposes: (1) it identifies how the disabilities and impairments described above impact on mobility, (2) it identifies the situations under which the patient is at risk of falling, and (3) it provides a standardized, qualitative assessment of balance and gait that can be used to monitor change over time or with treatment. While computerized and specialized assessments are available, clinically useful tests of balance and gait have been developed that require no equipment and little expertise.[14,22,23] Most clinical tests of balance assess two of the three components of functional balance, namely ability to maintain positions and ability to respond to voluntary position changes or movements. The third component, ability to respond to anticipated or unanticipated perturbations—important in situations such as being bumped in a crowd or sudden stop of an elevator—are not easily testable with simple clinical tests.[23] Examples of position changes and movements tested include getting up and down from a chair or bed, turning, reaching up, and bending over. Ability to maintain stability with decreasing base of support is tested with positions such as side-by-side, tandem, and one-legged stands with eyes opened and closed. Gait maneuvers that can be observed include initiation, step height, length, continuity, and symmetry as well as alignment of head, trunk, and extremities, path deviation, stability on turns, usual walking speed, and ability to pick up walking speed. Potential fall situations and preventive measures can be identified by using these balance and gait observations. For example, the individual who has difficulty getting up from a chair is at risk for falling during this maneuver. Possible interventions include leg-strengthening exercises, balance training, and the use of high, firm chairs with arms. Further examples are included in Table 121-2.

Addressing Situational Factors

Preventive strategies need to address factors present at the time of the fall, as well as the chronic predisposing factors discussed above. Situational factors may be intrinsic to the individual or related to the activity engaged in at the time of the fall, or they may represent hazards within the environment. A careful review of the fall situation may identify interventions aimed at preventing recurrence.[15] If the activity was an essential one, such as walking, performing a basic activity of daily living, changing positions, or climbing up or down stairs, the preventive strategy should be to ensure that these activities are performed in a safer, more effective manner. A short course in balance and gait training by a physical therapist may be effective for this purpose. As noted above, only if the activity was clearly hazardous, such as climbing on stools or chairs, should avoidance of the activity be recommended.

Environmental hazard assessment is an integral part of any fall-prevention strategy. Potential hazards can be identified through the use of environmental hazard checklists.[24] These checklists, developed for use at home, include assessment of floor surfaces and lighting and the presence of obstacles, as well as careful review of high-risk areas such as bathrooms and stairs. These checklists can be completed by home health nurses or therapists and perhaps by patients and families themselves. Specific environmental recommendations follow from the environmental assessments. The greatest attention should be given to environmental hazards that directly impact on patients' impairments or disabilities such as tripping hazards, if a gait disorder is present, or poor lighting if proprioception is diminished. Because of some elderly people's reluctance to making even minor environmental changes (such as removing throw rugs), careful education and close follow-up are needed to improve compliance with recommendations. In addition to an environmental hazard assessment, environmental contributors to individual falls should be ascertained using both open- and closed-ended questions. The closed-ended questions ensure thoroughness, while an open-ended approach, that is, asking patients to identify the environmental hazards themselves, has an important advantage in that adherence to recommended environmental changes may be higher if the faller identifies the environmental hazards as contributing to the fall.

FALLS AMONG INSTITUTIONALIZED ELDERLY

Prevalence

Over one-half of ambulatory nursing home patients fall each year. The estimated annual incidence is 1600 falls per 1000 beds.[15] The higher frequency of falling among institutionalized elderly persons probably results both from the greater frailty of these patients compared with community-living elderly persons and from the better reliability of fall reporting because of closer observation. The evidence is conflicting concerning fall frequency in women versus men.

Morbidity

As with community-living elderly persons, about 5 percent of falls by institutionalized persons result in fracture. Another 10 percent of falls result in serious soft tissue injuries and 20 percent in minor soft tissue injuries such as lacerations or abrasions.[25,26] Women are more likely than men to suffer a serious injury. Other factors associated with an increased risk of injury during a fall are lower-extremity weakness, greater independence in activities of daily living, and a history of fewer falls.[26] These factors suggest that both components of injury, namely, increased force of impact of the fall and impaired protective responses of the faller, contribute to likelihood of injury.[18]

Clustering of falls, that is, a sudden increase in number over a short time, is associated with a high 6-month mortality.[25] Most likely, this clustering of falling is a marker for decline rather than a direct cause of death.

Risk Factors

Predisposing and Situational Intrinsic Risk Factors

As with falls experienced by community-living elderly persons, the majority of falls in institutionalized elderly persons are multifactorial. Only about 3 percent of falls experienced by institutionalized elderly persons result from an overwhelming intrinsic event such as syncope, seizure, or stroke. The chronic disabilities and impairments predisposing institutionalized elderly persons to falls are similar to those of community-living elderly persons. Dementia, sensory impairments, musculoskeletal and neurologic disorders, postural instability, and depression have all been associated with falling in institutionalized elderly persons.[1,27,28] The proportion of institutionalized elderly persons who fall increases with the number of these risk factors present.

Acute problems are more readily identified in institutionalized elderly persons, who are often observed at or near the time of the fall. Approximately one-fifth of falls among a cohort of nursing home residents were attributed primarily to an acute cardiovascular problem including drug-related hypotension, postural hypotension, postprandial hypotension, and bradycardia.[28] In another group of nursing home patients, about 5 percent of falls occurred during acute illnesses such as pneumonias, other febrile illness, urinary tract infections, or exacerbations of chronic diseases such as congestive heart failure.[27] In addition to the acute effect of medications, the chronic use of sedatives, tranquilizers, and antidepressants increases the risk of falling among nursing home residents.[27,28] Risk increases with the number of these medications consumed.

Environmental Risk Factors

Fall etiology appears to be predominantly intrinsic among institutionalized elderly persons, with less contribution from environmental factors than among community-dwelling elderly persons. The reasons for this difference are several. First, their greater frailty and larger number of disabilities predispose institutionalized elderly persons to fall under situations where healthier, more functional community-dwelling elderly persons would not. Second, institutions in general are safer environments with many of the fall hazards already identified and removed. Furthermore, institutionalized elderly persons have fewer opportunities and lesser need to engage in hazardous activities such as climbing on ladders or walking on ice.

Although perhaps less important than in community-dwellers' falls, environmental contributors to falls in the institutionalized elderly do exist. These environmental hazards may be more subtle, such as cluttered pathways, ill-fitting shoes, untied shoe laces, long pants, or a floor slippery from water or urine.[15] Furniture may constitute a hazard. Beds that are too high or too short, bed rails that can be climbed over, and chairs that are too low, too soft, or unstable are responsible for some falls by institutionalized patients. Walking aids may also contribute to falls. Canes and walkers may be tripped over. Wheelchairs may be a hazard if not locked when the patient is getting in or out, and footrests may be tripped over.

The contribution of staffing patterns remains unclear. Some studies show a higher fall incidence during shift change or during hours of lower staff-to-patient ratios, while other studies show no such effect.

Prevention

As in community-dwelling elderly persons, the first step in fall prevention in institutionalized elderly persons is establishing appropriate goals. In nursing homes where persons are more closely observed, where prevalence of falling, but not injury, is higher, and where personal mobility may be an important index of remaining autonomy, perhaps the primary goal should be preventing injury rather than preventing falls.

Identification of Intrinsic Risk Factors

A thorough clinical evaluation aimed at identifying all contributing risk factors is the cornerstone of the evaluation in nursing home residents. As with community-living elderly persons, the risk of falling increases with the number of disabilities, suggesting again that ameliorating or eliminating as many risk factors as possible may decrease risk.[27]

Directly observing balance and gait has proved to be effective in identifying residents at risk for falling. As discussed earlier, this direct observation has the added benefit of identifying potential causes of problems, as well as potential interventions within the resident and in the environment.

Interventions aimed at minimizing chronic predisposing factors can be recommended based on results of the evaluation. Exercise programs may increase strength and flexibility or improve balance. Careful review of medications should ensure the use of the least number of drugs at the lowest effective dose. Balance and gait training should target problem maneuvers such as getting in and out of chairs or turning while walking.

A careful review of fall situations may identify problem situations to be avoided in the future. The patient who falls during acute illnesses needs closer observation during future episodes. Falls soon after meals or upon getting up suggest postural hypotension. Remedies include advising the resident to rise more slowly and having companions available to help during these high-risk times. For subjects with persistent hypotension, sleeping with the head of the bed elevated, wearing support stockings, and avoiding exacerbating medications may be helpful.

Environmental Prevention

General environmental measures include ensuring adequate lighting without glare, and dry, nonslippery floors which are free of obstacles (and urine). High, firm chairs and beds at appropriate levels for individual residents (feet should touch the floor with the knees bent at 90 degrees) and raised toilet seats are preventive measures appropriate for all residents.

Footwear that fits properly, provides good support and proprioceptive input, and has soles that are neither too slippery nor too high in friction are simple fall-prevention measures. Pant legs should not be long enough or loose enough to trip over.

Given the contribution of walking aids to falls, ensuring that the patient has the appropriate walking aid and uses it correctly is very important. This education should be an ongoing process.

Use of Restraints

Restraints are perhaps the most frequently used fall-prevention measure in nursing homes. It is not yet known whether recent federal regulations will result in reduced, or altered patterns of, restraint use. Restraints include side rails in bed, geriatric chairs that residents cannot get out of alone, and vest and waist restraints. Although restraint use is frequent enough to be considered almost routine, no study has ever shown a decrease in falls, or, more importantly, injuries, with restraint use.[30] Potential complications of restraints include strangulation, vascular and neurologic damage, and skin tears. Complications occur when the restraints are applied inappropriately, when the incorrect type of restraint is used, or when the resident is not observed closely. Falls and injuries do occur with restraints when the resident slips out of or removes the restraints. A resident may tip over a chair or wheelchair while wearing restraints. The role of restraints in fall and injury prevention remains undefined. Restraints should not take the place of close supervision and attention to the risk factors discussed in this chapter. Alternatives to restraints, including wedges in chairs for maintenance of position, or organized walking and grid barriers for prevention of wandering, are being investigated; their effectiveness at preventing falls and injuries and wandering is not yet established.

SUMMARY

In summary, falling is a common and potentially morbid problem among community-living and institutionalized elderly persons. Potential morbidity includes fractures, other physical injuries, long lies because of inability to get up, and restriction of activity because of fear or discouragement from care providers. The risk factors include predisposing factors and situational factors present at the time of the fall. The goal of preventive strategies should be to maximize confidence and minimize risk of falls and injuries without compromising autonomy and mobility. Preventive strategies include a combination of medical, surgical, rehabilitative, social, and environmental components.

REFERENCES

1. Sattin RW: Falls among older persons: A public health perspective. *Annu Rev Public Health* 13:489, 1992.
2. Blake AJ et al: Falls by elderly persons at home. *Age Ageing* 17:365, 1988.
3. Tinetti ME et al: Risk factors for falls among elderly persons living in the community. *N Engl J Med* 319:1701, 1988.
4. Nevitt MC et al: Risk factors for recurrent nonsyncopal falls in older persons. *JAMA* 261:2663, 1989.
5. Melton LJ, Riggs BL: Risk factors for injury after a fall. *Clin Geriatr Med* 1:525, 1985.
6. Speechley M, Tinetti ME: Falls and injuries in frail and vigorous community elderly persons. *J Am Geriatr Soc* 39:46, 1991.
7. Nevitt MC et al: Risk factors for injurious falls. A prospective study. *J Gerontol* 46:M164, 1991.
8. Dunn JE et al: Mortality, disability, and falls in older persons: The role of underlying disease and disability. *Am J Public Health* 82:395, 1992.
9. Kiel DP et al: Health care utilization and functional status in the aged following a fall. *Med Care* 29:221, 1991.
10. Wolinsky F et al: Falling, health status and the use of health services by older adults. *Med Care* 30:587, 1992.
11. Lord SR et al: Physiological factors associated with falls in an elderly population. *J Am Geriatr Soc* 39:1194, 1991.
12. Hazell JWP: Vestibular problems of balance. *Age Ageing* 8:258, 1979.
13. Wyke B: Cervical articular contributions to posture and gait: Their relation to senile disequilibrium. *Age Ageing* 8:251, 1979.
14. Tinetti ME, Ginter SF: Identifying mobility dysfunctions in elderly patients. *JAMA* 259:1190, 1988.
15. Rubenstein LZ et al: Falls and instability in the elderly. *J Am Geriatr Soc* 36:266, 1988.
16. Ray WA et al: Psychotropic drug use and the risk of hip fracture. *N Engl J Med* 316:363, 1987.
17. Archea JC: Environmental factors associated with stair accidents by the elderly. *Clin Geriatr Med* 1:555, 1985.
18. Norré ME, Beckers A: Benign positional vertigo in the elderly: Treatment by habituation exercises. *J Am Geriatr Soc* 36:425, 1988.
19. Kottke FJ: Exercises to develop neuromuscular coordination, in Kottke FJ et al (eds): *Krusens Handbook of Physical Medicine and Rehabilitation*. Philadelphia, Saunders, 1982, p 403.
20. Tinetti ME: Performance-oriented assessment of mobility problems in elderly patients. *J Am Geriatr Soc* 34:119, 1986.
21. Tinetti ME, Speechley M: Prevention of falls among the elderly. *N Engl J Med* 320:1055, 1989.
22. Mathias S et al: Balance in elderly patients: The "get up and go" test. *Arch Phys Med Rehabil* 67:387, 1986.
23. Berg K et al: Measuring balance in the elderly: Preliminary development of an instrument. *Physiotherapy Canada* 41:304, 1989.
24. Tideiksaar R: Preventing falls: Home hazard checklists to help older patients protect themselves. *Geriatrics* 41:26, 1986.
25. Gryfe CI et al: A longitudinal study of falls in an elderly population: I. Incidence and morbidity. *Age Ageing* 6:201, 1977.
26. Tinetti ME: Factors associated with serious injury during falls by ambulatory nursing home residents. *J Am Geriatr Soc* 35:644, 1987.
27. Tinetti ME et al: Fall risk index for elderly patients based on number of chronic disabilities. *Am J Med* 80:429, 1986.
28. Lipsitz LA et al: Causes and correlates of recurrent falls in ambulatory frail elderly. *J Gerontol* 46:M114, 1991.
29. Granek E et al: Medications and diagnoses in relation to falls in a long term care facility. *J Am Geriatr Soc* 35:503, 1987.
30. Tinetti ME et al: Mechanical restraint use and fall-related injuries among residents of skilled nursing facilities. *Ann Intern Med* 116:369, 1992.

Chapter 122

HIP FRACTURES

Jeane Ann Grisso and Frederick Kaplan

Hip fractures are associated with more deaths, disability, and medical costs than all other osteoporotic fractures combined. Of those who live to the age of 90, an estimated 33 percent of women and 17 percent of men will have a hip fracture.[1] The annual cost of hip fractures was estimated to be $8.7 billion in 1988.[2] Thus, the prevention and treatment of hip fractures are a major public health and clinical concern.

EPIDEMIOLOGY

Approximately 250,000 persons were hospitalized in the United States for hip fractures in 1988.[2] Studies have documented rising age-specific hip fracture incidence rates in England, northern Europe, and Hong Kong. Although hip fracture rates may be increasing in the United States, the dramatic rise in the number of hip fractures each year appears to be primarily a result of the increasing number of elderly persons.[1] By the year 2000 it is estimated that more than 340,000 hip fractures will occur annually; the current number of hip fractures can be expected to double or triple by the middle of the next century.

After age 50, the incidence of hip fractures increases exponentially with age, doubling every 5 years. Thus, more than 85 percent of all hip fractures occur in persons 65 years of age or older. Most hip fractures (75 percent) occur in women. The female predominance is due to both the greater life expectancy of women compared with men and higher age-specific hip fracture rates in women. In the United States the rate of hip fractures in women is about twice that of men. By the time a woman reaches 80 years of age, she has about a 15 percent chance of suffering a hip fracture before she dies compared with an 80-year-old man, who has an 8 percent chance.[1]

Hip fracture rates vary markedly by ethnic and racial group. Whites have age-adjusted hip fracture rates that are two to three times higher than those of Latinos, African Americans, or Asians. In the United States, the high female/male ratios in hip fracture risk appear to be present in whites, Latinos, and Asians (Table 122-1). Whether there is a gender difference in hip fracture rates among African Americans is uncertain, although most studies have observed higher rates in African American women compared with African American men after 70 to 80 years of age (Table 122-1).

TABLE 122-1

Hip Fracture Incidence Rates in California by Age, Gender, and Ethnic Group*

Age (years)	*Women*				*Men*			
	White	**Latino**	**African American**	**Asian**	**White**	**Latino**	**African American**	**Asian**
<50	6.2	2.6	5.3	2.7	11.5	5.6	12.4	6.3
50–59	65.3	15.7	35.2	17.4	37.3	15.0	46.4	16.4
60–69	212.9	59.6	80.7	91.8	91.5	34.3	83.6	49.1
70–79	726.0	246.0	267.8	321.6	334.1	145.9	189.2	155.0
80+	2502.3	958.7	988.8	1912.7	1209.6	595.1	816.4	738.7
TOTAL	**140.7**	**49.7**	**57.3**	**85.4**	**48.9**	**22.2**	**38.7**	**26.3**

*Hospital discharges per 100,000 patients per year.
SOURCE: Silverman SL, Madison RE: Decreased incidence of hip fracture in Hispanics, Asians, and Blacks: California hospital discharge data. *Am J Public Health* 78:1482, 1988.

Morbidity and Mortality

The consequences of hip fracture are often devastating. Mortality during hospitalization approximates 5 percent, and 1-year mortality rates are approximately 23 percent.[3] Although the 1-year mortality rates are 12 to 20 percent higher than are mortality rates in persons of similar age and gender who have not suffered hip fractures, it is unclear how much of the excess mortality can be attributed to underlying conditions that preceded the fracture.

Those who survive hip fracture often suffer permanent disability and dependency. More than 50 percent of all patients who endure hip fractures are discharged to nursing homes, and, of that 50 percent, nearly half remain in nursing homes 1 year after hospitalization.[4] Fewer than 50 percent of patients are able to walk independently 1 year after hip fracture, and fewer than 30 percent regain their prefracture levels of physical functioning.[5]

Several studies have documented that hospital lengths of stay for hip fractures have been significantly reduced since Congress enacted the prospective payment system for diagnostic related groups (DRGs) in 1983. The impact of the reduced hospital length of stay on hip fracture recovery is controversial. Although hip fracture mortality rates have not been affected by the shorter hospitalization stays, some studies have reported that since DRGs were introduced, long-term institutionalization rates have increased for patients with hip fractures, particularly for those who were not discharged to a setting with active rehabilitation programs.[4,6–8]

DEFINITION OF HIP FRACTURE

Hip fractures can be classified into two major types of fractures involving the proximal femur: intracapsular fractures, occurring in approximately one-third of cases, and intertrochanteric fractures, occurring in the remaining two-third of cases. Intracapsular fractures can be subclassified as subcapital, transcervical, and basicervical fractures based on the exact location of the fracture. Intertrochanteric fractures are subclassified by degree of comminution and displacement. Treatment and prognosis are based upon location and degree of displacement for both types. Few studies have been conducted to assess whether risk factors for hip fracture vary by fracture site.

RISK FACTORS

A great deal of progress has been achieved in our understanding of the pathogenesis of hip fractures. Determinants of hip fracture include factors that affect osteoporosis, factors that affect the propensity to fall, and, possibly, factors that affect protective responses during a fall (see Fig. 122-1). Table 122-2 lists well-established risk factors for hip fracture, which are grouped according to possible pathogenetic mechanisms.

Osteoporosis

Although bone mass measurements in patients with hip fracture overlap considerably with bone mass measurements in persons of the same age and gender, several prospective studies in white women have reported that bone mass values predict the likelihood of subsequent hip fracture.[9,10] The importance of bone mass as a determinant of hip fracture is further strengthened by the established associations of hip fracture with factors known to affect bone mass. For example, age, sex, and race are perhaps the best-established predictors of hip fracture. It is known that bone mass declines with age, is greater in men than in women, and is greater in African Americans than in Caucasians. Thus, differences in bone mass probably account for some of the ethnic and gender differences in hip fracture rates.

Several other well-established risk factors for hip fracture are thought to primarily affect bone mass. These factors include gonadal steroid status, thiazide diuretic use, dietary habits, smoking, alcohol use, body build, and physical activity.

In women, the performance of a bilateral oophorectomy predisposes to osteoporosis, and estrogen therapy begun in the perimenopausal period (regard-

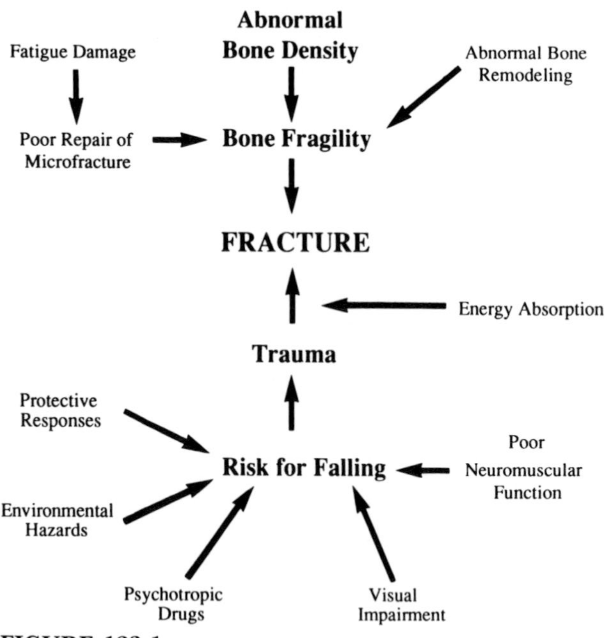

FIGURE 122-1
Risk factors for hip fracture.

TABLE 122-2

Risk Factors for Hip Fracture*

Factors associated with decreased bone mass
- Increasing age
- Female sex
- White race
- Bilateral oophorectomy
- Thin body build
- Prolonged immobility
- Family history of osteoporosis
- Heavy alcohol use
- Smoking
- Hyperthyroidism
- Chronic glucocorticoid therapy

Factors associated with preservation of bone mass
- Postmenopausal estrogen therapy
- Weight-bearing exercise
- Adequate calcium and vitamin D intake

Factors increasing the risk of falls
- Gait and mobility abnormalities
- Psychotropic medications
- Visual impairment

*The factors included in this list are those that have been best documented as associated with hip fractures. See Chaps. 76 and 121 for extensive reviews of established risk factors for falls and osteoporosis.

less of whether it was a surgical or natural menopause) prevents or retards bone loss. Numerous case-control studies and several cohort studies have reported that the use of estrogen therapy reduces the risk of hip fracture by about 50 percent.[1] Although most of these observational studies are based on periods in which unopposed estrogens had been used, subsequent studies have reported that the addition of progestins (for protection against endometrial carcinoma) did not reduce the efficacy of estrogens in preventing bone loss. In addition, transdermal estrogen preparations have been approved for the prevention and treatment of osteoporosis.

The importance of dietary calcium or calcium supplementation in preventing hip fractures has not been consistently demonstrated although several case-control studies of hip fracture have reported protective effects with dietary calcium intakes of 800 mg or more daily. The addition of calcium supplements to the diet appears to slow bone loss in women although not to the same extent as does estrogen therapy.[1,11] Calcium supplements may be particularly useful in older persons whose diets are chronically low in calcium.[12]

The use of thiazide diuretics lowers the urinary excretion of calcium and has been associated with increased bone mass. Several studies have reported reductions in hip fractures of 40 to 50 percent with thiazide diuretic use.[13,14] This association needs to be confirmed in additional studies, and more information is needed regarding the effects of timing and duration of use.

Alcohol use and cigarette smoking have not been consistently found to be associated with hip fracture risk. Most studies have suggested that persons who smoke cigarettes have reduced cortical bone mass and a greater risk of hip fractures than do nonsmokers.[1,11] In women, smoking may increase the risk of hip fracture through antiestrogen effects and reduced levels of endogenous estrogens[1,11] Heavy alcohol use appears to be associated with lower bone mass, and, in some studies, an increased risk of hip fractures—although moderate alcohol use has not been demonstrated to have an effect.[15] The association between alcoholism and hip fractures could be a consequence of poor nutrition, reduced body weight, liver disease, or an increased risk of falling.[1]

Perhaps the most consistently identified risk factor for hip fractures is body build. Both men and women who are thin have reduced cortical bone mass and markedly increased risk of hip fracture.[1,16] Thin body build may not, however, increase hip fracture risk solely through causing osteoporosis. Thus, for example, body build has not been consistently shown to increase the risk of Colles' fractures, which are known to result from osteoporosis (personal communication, J. Bernstein).[17] Increased body weight might afford protection from hip fractures through padding around the hips, which could help to absorb some of the energy of the impact of the fall. More studies are needed to understand the mechanism by which body weight is such a powerful predictor of hip fracture risk.

Prolonged immobility or weightlessness brings about reduction in bone mass. Studies of young athletes have shown increased bone mass in the limb(s) involved in the athletic activity. Although no prospective studies have reported that exercise reduces the risk of hip fracture, trials of exercise interventions have documented a positive impact on bone mass.[1,11] Results of epidemiologic studies of hip fracture are consistent with the hypothesis that the low levels of physical activity associated with Western lifestyles may increase hip fracture risk. Hip fracture risk has been found to be higher in urban than in rural areas in Europe and Japan,[1] and decreased physical activity has also been reported to be associated with increased hip fracture risk in Hong Kong and England.[18,19]

Falls

Factors other than bone mass must contribute to the overall risk of hip fracture because the majority of white women have significant osteoporosis by the age of 75 years, yet only 2 to 3 percent of this population suffer a hip fracture each year. Although only 1 to 14 percent of falls in women result in hip fracture, more than 90 percent of hip fractures occur as a result of a fall, which usually occurs from a standing height. Lotz and Hayes have documented that a fall from a standing height has the potential energy to fracture even a normal hip.[20]

Only recently have studies been conducted to assess whether established risk factors for falls are also associated with an increased risk of hip fracture.[21–25] Fall risk factors that have been best documented as increasing the risk of hip fractures include the use of psychotropic medications, visual impairment, and gait and mobility abnormalities.

Psychotropic medications are commonly prescribed for older persons, and changing medication use may be a promising way to prevent hip fracture. Increased risks of hip fracture have been reported among older persons receiving hypnotic, anxiolytic, antidepressant, and antipsychotic agents. Benzodiazepines are the psychotropic agent prescribed most frequently to elderly persons, and it appears that benzodiazepines with half-lives of 24 hours or greater are associated with an increased risk of hip fractures, whereas shorter-acting preparations may not increase this risk.[22] In one recent study, the risk of hip fracture in persons concurrently receiving psychotropic drugs and opioids was reported to be nearly three times that for nonusers of these drugs.[24] This finding is consistent with findings from experimental studies that have shown additive psychomotor impairment in subjects following the ingestion of codeine and diazepam. Physicians thus should be especially cautious in the use of multiple centrally acting drugs in elderly persons.[25]

The prevalence of visual impairment among older persons is very high. Visual acuity, adaptation to dark, peripheral vision, contrast sensitivity, and accommodation may be affected by age-related changes as well as by conditions such as cataracts, macular degeneration, and glaucoma. Studies have documented that impaired visual function predisposes elderly persons to falls,[21] and a few recent studies have reported an increased risk of hip fractures among elderly persons with visual impairment.[23,26]

Gait and mobility disturbances may result from neurologic conditions, vestibular and proprioceptive function abnormalities, and any disease or disability that affects the bones, muscles, and joints. Abnormalities in balance and gait have been repeatedly associated with falling.[21] Studies have reported increased risks of hip fracture in older persons with a previous stroke, Parkinson's disease, or previous gait and mobility disturbances. Mobility problems may increase the risk of hip fracture through predisposing to falls as well as leading to accelerated bone loss because of immobility.

Type of Fall and Protective Responses

Osteoporosis and an increased risk of falling still do not fully account for the strikingly increased risk of hip fracture with age. Among white women in the United States, the risk of falling approximately doubles from age 60 to 80 years, whereas the risk of hip fractures increases almost 100-fold during the same interval.[27] Osteoporosis also cannot explain why the incidence of hip fractures increases exponentially with age while the incidence of Colles' fractures reaches a plateau after age 65. Cummings and Nevitt argue that the differences in the age-related incidence of these fractures might be due to changes in the mechanics of falls with advancing age.[27] They hypothesize that for a fall from a standing height to cause a hip fracture, a sequence of four conditions must be satisfied: (1) the fall must be oriented so that the person lands on or near the hip, (2) protective responses must be inadequate to reduce the energy of the fall below the critical threshold, (3) local shock absorbers, such as fat and muscles around the hip, must be inadequate to absorb enough of the energy of the fall to prevent the fracture, and (4) bone strength in the proximal femur must be insufficient to resist the residual energy of the fall that is transmitted to the hip. Figure 122-2 illustrates that for elderly persons who may be walking slowly with little forward momentum, the principal point of impact may be near the hip, whereas those who fall while moving at a more rapid gait are most likely to fall forward and fracture the distal forearm. Thus, the orientation of the fall may help determine the fracture site and explain the differences in the age-related risks for fractures of the hip and distal forearm.

FIGURE 122-2

A. A fall occurring while standing still, walking slowly, or slowly descending a step has little forward momentum. With little forward momentum, the principal point of impact will be near the hip. *B.* A fall occurring during rapid walking has enough forward momentum to carry the faller onto her hands or knees instead of her hip. *(Reproduced by permission from Cummings and Nevitt.[27])*

Protective responses also may be important in changing the orientation of the fall or reducing the energy of a fall if it occurs. Once a fall is inevitable, the grabbing of nearby objects could substantially slow the rate of falling, and by quickly extending the arms, the person falling can absorb the energy of the fall with the arms and hands and minimize the force of impact on the hip. These responses may explain why the risk of suffering a fracture of any type is four times greater during a syncopal compared with a nonsyncopal fall.

Studies are under way to evaluate whether the orientation of the fall and protective responses are important determinants of whether a fall results in hip fracture. If these factors are confirmed, promising preventive interventions might include upper arm strengthening exercise as well as gait and mobility training programs. Environmental modifications, such as grab bars, might also assist in breaking falls.

TREATMENT

Surgical treatment of hip fractures that permits rapid remobilization of patients has led to a dramatic decrease in early mortality due to hip fractures over the past 30 years. The location of the hip fracture (intracapsular vs. intertrochanteric) and the degree of initial displacement are the most important factors in determining the appropriate surgical treatment. Nondisplaced or minimally displaced intracapsular fractures are most effectively treated by closed reduction and internal fixation. Severely displaced intracapsular fractures are most effectively treated by endoprosthetic replacement of the femoral head. Such treatment is particularly effective for rapid postoperative mobilization and precludes any concern for fracture healing. Nondisplaced and displaced intertrochanteric fractures pose very little threat to the viability of the femoral head but are associated with greater initial blood loss and pain and are most effectively treated by open reduction and internal fixation with a hip compression screw and femoral side plate. Such treatment also permits early postoperative mobilization with protected weight bearing until the fracture heals.

RECOVERY

Elderly patients with hip fracture present a complex array of medical and functional problems. Given the high prevalence of chronic medical conditions and the catastrophic nature of a hip fracture, the risk of medical complications during hospitalization is high.[28]

In one prospective study, complications during the hospital stay included confusion (49 percent), urinary tract infection (33 percent), heart rhythm disturbances (26 percent), pneumonia (19 percent), depression (15 percent), and congestive heart failure (7 percent).[28] Cognitive impairment, depression, and transient mental status changes are major predictors of prolonged lengths of hospital stays and are extremely common in the elderly population.[5,29] Preliminary evidence suggests that a comprehensive evaluation and continued follow-up may be effective in preventing and treating conditions such as heart failure, metabolic disorders, and infections, as well as in obviating the use of excessive and unnecessary medication.[25]

Studies are just beginning to identify factors important to long-term recovery after hip fracture. Surprisingly, advanced age may not predict survival, whereas gender and race do. Men are two to three times more likely than women to die within the first year after a hip fracture, and African Americans may also be at a higher risk for death.[29] Whether these differences are due to a higher prevalence of chronic medical illnesses among men and African Americans compared with white women is uncertain. Illnesses, functional level, and psychosocial factors have also been found to affect survival after hip fracture.[5,29] Magaziner et al. found that the most important factors to predict mortality are the presence of serious concomitant illness and marked delirium.[29] Prefracture physical function, cognitive status, and depression have also been found to be predictors of recovery among patients with hip fracture who survive the perioperative period.[5] High postsurgery depression scores (present in 51 percent of patients with hip fracture) are associated with poorer recovery in both functional and psychosocial domains. Considering the importance of motivation for physical therapy, it seems probable that the systematic screening of all patients with hip fracture for symptoms of depression and the early institution of treatment may improve the outcome in many of these patients. Given the trend toward decreased lengths of hospital stays, studies are needed to evaluate both institutional and home rehabilitation programs to improve recovery after hip fractures.

PREVENTION

Measures to prevent hip fractures can be categorized as those that target bone loss and those that target falls. To date, no randomized controlled trial has demonstrated the protective efficacy of any measure to prevent hip fractures. Such a trial would require very large sample sizes and, depending on the preventive modality, might have to be carried out over a long period. The Women's Health Initiative, a prospective clinical trial involving more than 140,000 postmenopausal women, has recently been authorized by the National Institutes of Health to evaluate the impact of vitamin D, progestins, and estrogen therapy on the prevention of hip fractures. Definitive results will not be available for 15 years; nevertheless, several measures to prevent osteoporosis and falls show great promise and entail relatively few risks. Measures to prevent bone loss are discussed in detail in Chap. 76. For patients who are perimenopausal or recently postmenopausal, adequate calcium intake, an exercise program, and, in the absence of contraindications, estrogen therapy should be strongly considered. Fall-prevention programs may be especially relevant in elderly women whose proximal femoral bone density is already considerably below the fracture threshold and for whom measures to prevent bone loss may be of little benefit. Interventions to prevent falls are discussed in detail in Chap. 121. General fall-prevention measures include medical, rehabilitation, and environmental interventions.[21] The most promising measures are (1) balance training, gait training, and strengthening exercises for gait and mobility disturbances, (2) appropriate refraction and medical-surgical care for visual problems, and (3) reduction in the use of psychoactive medications. A recent study reported that an educational program targeted to physicians, nurses, and aides resulted in a significant reduction in the use of psychoactive drugs in nursing homes without having adversely affected the overall behavior and level of functioning of the residents.[25]

Although general fall-prevention measures may be effective in preventing hip fractures, specific measures to decrease the transmission of energy from the impact of the fall to the proximal femur may be theoretically even more protective. These measures might include padding devices around the hip, or carpeting or other measures to reduce the hardness of surfaces.

CONCLUSION

Hip fractures are a major public health problem in the United States. In recent years a great deal of progress has been achieved in our understanding of the pathogenesis of hip fractures. Determinants of hip fracture include factors that affect osteoporosis, factors that affect the propensity to fall, and, possibly, factors that affect protective responses during a fall. Measures to prevent bone loss that have been documented in women include an adequate calcium intake, an exercise program, and, in the absence of contraindications, estrogen therapy. The most promising measures to prevent falls include balance and gait training, appropriate care for visual problems, and reduction in the use of psychoactive medications.

Although measures to prevent bone loss and falls may be effective in preventing many hip fractures, serious attention should also be given to optimizing recovery after a hip fracture occurs. Studies have just begun to identify factors that predict poor recovery. Mortality rates are highest in men and African Americans. Poor functional recovery is highest in those with cognitive impairment, chronic illness, and depression. More studies are needed to evaluate interventions to improve functional status after hip fracture occurrence.

REFERENCES

1. Cummings SR et al: Epidemiology of osteoporotic fractures. *Epidemiol Rev* 7:178, 1985.
2. Praemer A et al: *Musculoskeletal Conditions in the United States.* Chicago, American Academy of Orthopaedic Surgeons, 1992.
3. Fisher ES et al: Hip fracture incidence and mortality in New England. *Epidemiology* 2:116, 1991.
4. Fitgerald JF et al: The care of elderly patients with hip fracture. *N Engl J Med* 319:1392, 1988.
5. Mossey JM et al: Determinants of recovery 12 months after hip fracture: The importance of psychosocial factors. *Am J Public Health* 79:279, 1989.
6. Palmer RM et al: The impact of the prospective payment system on the treatment of hip fractures in the elderly. *Arch Intern Med* 149:2237, 1989.
7. Gerety MB et al: Impact of prospective payment and discharge location on the outcome of hip fracture. *J Gen Intern Med* 4:388, 1989.
8. Ray WA et al: Mortality following hip fracture before and after implementation of the prospective payment system. *Arch Intern Med* 150:2109, 1990.
9. Hui SL et al: Baseline measurement of bone mass predicts fracture in white women. *Ann Intern Med* 111:355, 1989.
10. Cummings SR et al: Appendicular bone density and age predict hip fracture in women. *JAMA* 263:665, 1990.
11. Kelsey JL, Hoffman S: Risk factors for hip fracture. *N Engl J Med* 316:404, 1987.
12. Dawson-Hughes B et al: A controlled trial of the effect of calcium supplementation on bone density in postmenopausal women. *N Engl J Med* 323:878, 1990.
13. Felson DT et al: Thiazide diuretics and the risk of hip fracture. *JAMA* 265:370, 1991.
14. LaCroix AZ et al: Thiazide diuretic agents and the incidence of hip fracture. *N Engl J Med* 322:286, 1990.
15. Felson DT et al: Alcohol consumption and hip fractures: The Framingham Study. *Am J Epidemiol* 128:1102, 1988.
16. Grisso JA et al: Risk factors for hip fractures in men: A preliminary study. *J Bone Min Res* 6:865, 1991.
17. Kelsey JL et al: Risk factors for fractures of the distal forearm and proximal humerus. *Am J Epidemiol* 135:477, 1992.
18. Wickham CAC et al: Dietary calcium, physical activity, and risk of hip fracture: A prospective study. *Br Med J* 299:889, 1989.
19. Donnan EL et al: Physical activity and calcium intake

in fracture of the proximal femur in Hong Kong. *Br Med J* 297:1441, 1988.

20. Lotz JC, Hayes WC: The use of quantitative computed tomography to estimate risk of fracture of the hip from falls. *J Bone Joint Surg* 72A:689, 1990.
21. Tinetti ME, Speechley M: Prevention of falls among the elderly. *N Engl J Med* 320:1055, 1989.
22. Ray WA et al: Benzodiazepines of long and short elimination half-life and the risk of hip fracture. *JAMA* 262:3303, 1989.
23. Felson DT et al: Impaired vision and hip fracture: The Framingham study. *J Am Geriatr Soc* 37:495, 1989.
24. Shorr RI et al: Opioid analgesics and the risk of hip fracture in the elderly. Codeine and propoxyphene. *J Gerontol* 47:M111, 1992.
25. Avorn J et al: A randomized trial of a program to reduce the use of psychoactive drugs in nursing homes. *N Engl J Med* 327:168, 1992.
26. Grisso JA et al: Risk factors for falls as a cause of hip fracture in women. *N Engl J Med* 324:1326, 1991.
27. Cummings SR, Nevitt MC: A hypothesis: The causes of hip fractures. *J Gerontol* 44:M107, 1989.
28. Campion EW et al: Hip fracture: A prospective study of hospital course, complications, and costs. *J Gen Intern Med* 2:78, 1987.
29. Magaziner et al: Survival experience of aged hip fracture patients. *Am J Public Health* 79:274, 1989.

Chapter 123

PRESSURE ULCERS

Richard M. Allman

EPIDEMIOLOGY

Prevalence and Incidence

Pressure ulcers are a common and serious problem for older people suffering from immobility. They may present as nonblanchable erythema over a bony prominence or as areas of epithelial loss, skin breakdown, blisters, or skin necrosis manifested by eschar formation. Synonymous terms include *pressure ulcers, decubitus ulcers,* or *bedsores,* but since pressure is the primary pathophysiologic factor in the development of these lesions, *pressure ulcer* has become the preferred term. The terms *decubitus ulcer* and *bedsore* imply that the lesions occur only when lying down, but some of the most severe pressure-induced cutaneous injury may occur as a result of prolonged sitting, and hence these terms are misleadingly narrow.

Stage 1 lesions present as nonblanchable erythema of intact skin. Partial thickness skin loss involving epidermis and/or dermis is stage 2. Stage 3 ulcers extend into the subcutaneous tissues to the deep fascia and typically show undermining. Stage 4 lesions involve muscle and or bone.[1] Full-thickness injury manifested by eschar frequently involves muscle and bone but cannot be staged until the eschar is removed. Pressure-induced subepidermal blisters typically occur on the heels. Their depth cannot be determined by clinical examination.

The prevalence of stage 2 and greater pressure ulcers among patients in acute care hospitals ranges from 3 to 11 percent, and the incidence during hospitalization is between 1 and 3 percent. Among patients expected to be hospitalized and confined to bed or chair for at least 1 week, the prevalence of stage 2 and greater pressure ulcers is as high as 28 percent, and the incidence within 3 weeks is 7.7 percent. Pressure ulcers generally occur within the first 2 weeks of hospitalization, and of those patients with an ulcer, 60 percent develop them after admission. More than 50 percent of pressure ulcers occur in persons over 70.[2]

The prevalence of pressure ulcers in nursing homes is very similar to that reported in acute care hospitals. As many as 20 to 33 percent of patients admitted to nursing homes have a stage 2 or greater pressure ulcer.[2,3] The incidence of pressure ulcers among newly admitted residents who remain in a nursing home for 3 months is about 5 percent.[4]

Complications

Sepsis is the most serious complication of pressure ulcers. One study found that there were 3.5 episodes of pressure ulcer–associated bacteremia per 10,000 discharges among four major hospitals. Of the episodes of pressure ulcer–associated bacteremia, the pressure ulcer met criteria for being the probable source in 49 percent of the cases. Among patients with the pressure ulcer being the probable source of infection, the in-hospital mortality was 56.9 percent. Sixty-two percent of the deaths were attributed to the infection in these cases.[5] In another study, transient bacteremia occurred after débridement of pressure ulcers in 50 percent of subjects.[6] Other infectious complications of pressure ulcers include local infection, cellulitis, and osteomyelitis. Infected pressure ulcers were the most common infection found in a survey of seven skilled nursing facilities and were found in 6 percent of patients.[7] Among patients with nonhealing pressure ulcers, one study found that 26.3 percent of ulcers had underlying pathologic bone lesions consistent with osteomyelitis.[8] Infected pressure ulcers may be deeply undermined and lead to pyarthrosis or penetrate into the abdominal cavity. Secondary amyloidosis can also be a complication of chronic suppurative pressure ulcers.[9] Infected pressure ulcers also can serve as reservoirs for nosocomial infections with antibiotic-resistant bacteria.[10]

Pressure ulcers are associated with prolonged and expensive hospitalizations. The mean length of stay for hospitalized patients with pressure ulcers was nearly five times that noted for other patients in one study. After adjusting for other factors associated with increased length of stay, the association remained significant.[11]

Mortality

Increased death rates have been consistently observed in elderly individuals who develop pressure ulcers.[3,4,11,12] In addition, failure of an ulcer to heal or improve has been associated with a higher rate of death in nursing home residents.[3,13,14] In-hospital death rates for patients with pressure ulcers range from 23 to 36 percent.[11,13] Most of these deaths are in patients with severe, underlying disease, so the contribution of the pressure ulcers themselves to the outcome is difficult to define.

Risk Factors

Any disease process leading to immobility and limited activity levels, such as a spinal cord injury, dementia, Parkinson's disease, severe congestive heart failure, or lung disease, increases the risk of pressure ulcers. In one study of geriatric patients the spontaneous nocturnal movements were counted using a device attached to the patients' mattresses. No patients with 51 or more spontaneous movements during the night developed a pressure ulcer, but 90 percent of patients with 20 or fewer spontaneous movements developed an ulcer.[15]

Other risk factors for stage 2 and greater pressure ulcers consistently identified by prospective studies include incontinence, nutritional factors, and altered level of consciousness.[16] Two prospective studies have suggested that fecal incontinence, but not urinary incontinence, is a risk factor among patients in the acute care hospital.[11,17] Nutritional factors found to be associated significantly with pressure ulcer development include a decreased lymphocyte count,[12,17] hypoalbuminemia,[12] inadequate dietary intake,[12,18] decreased body weight,[17] and a depleted triceps skin fold.[17]

Potential risk factors identified in prospective studies include dry skin,[17,19] increased body temperature,[12] decreased blood pressure,[12] and increased age.[12,17,18] The functional impairment associated with the age-related increase in disease prevalence may explain the association of age with increased risk of pressure ulcers in part, but the age-related changes in the skin described in Chap. 37 may predispose the elderly to pressure-induced cutaneous injury independent of immobility.

PATHOGENESIS AND PATHOPHYSIOLOGY

Role of Pressure

Four factors have been implicated in the pathogenesis of pressure ulcers: pressure, shearing forces, friction, and moisture. Animal studies have repeatedly shown that muscle and subcutaneous tissues are more sensitive to pressure-induced injury than the epidermis. Contact pressures of 60 to 70 mmHg for 1 to 2 hours lead to degeneration of muscle fibers. In the dog, skin ulceration occurred over the greater trochanter after exposure to contact pressures of 150 mmHg for 9 to 12 hours, or pressures of 500 mmHg for 2 to 6 hours. Since dogs do not have a layer of subcutaneous tissue comparable to that of humans, investigators have studied the effect of pressure over the trochanter of pigs. Pigs have tissue layers more comparable to human skin. In these latter experiments, full-thickness injury required exposure to higher pressures: 600 mmHg for 11 hours, or 200 mmHg for 16 hours. Depending on the methodology used, pressures measured under bony prominences such as the sacrum and greater trochanter can be as high as 100 to 150 mmHg when subjects are lying on a regular hospital mattress. The pressures obtained are sufficient to decrease the transcutaneous oxygen tension to nearly zero. In seated subjects, the pressures measured under the ischial tuberosities may easily reach 300 mmHg. Although the magnitude of these pressures may not be sufficient to cause full-thickness tissue injury without prolonged exposure to pressure, other factors can lower the pressure or time required to cause the full-thickness injury observed clinically. Repeated exposures to pressure will cause skin necrosis at lower pressures. Other data suggest that loss of subcutaneous tissue can also lower the threshold for skin breakdown due to pressure.[20]

Role of Shearing Forces, Friction, and Moisture

Shearing forces lower the amount of pressure required to cause damage to the epidermis. Shearing forces are tangential forces that are exerted when a person is seated or the head of the bed is elevated and the person slides toward the floor or the foot of the bed. The sacral skin is held in place by friction while the gluteal vessels are angulated and elongated. Such forces decrease the amount of pressure required to occlude blood vessels and are likely important in the development of deep tissue injury. One study found that the shearing forces of seated elderly and paraplegic patients are threefold greater and blood flow is about one-third that of healthy young adults, although the contact pressures are similar.[21]

In experimental studies, friction has been shown to cause intraepidermal blisters. When unroofed, these lesions result in superficial erosions. This kind of injury can occur when a patient is pulled across a sheet or the patient has repetitive movements that expose a bony prominence to such frictional forces. Intermediate degrees of moisture increase the amount of friction produced at the rubbing interface, while extremes of moisture or dryness decrease the frictional forces between two surfaces rubbing against each other. In addition to its impact on frictional forces, skin moisture may directly lead to maceration and epidermal injury.[16]

Relative Importance of Pathophysiologic Factors

The effects of pressure on tissues overlying bony prominences are likely due to ischemia associated with the occlusion of blood and lymphatic vessels rather than mechanical injury. Injury due to pressure alone typically begins in deeper tissues and spreads toward the skin surface. If relieved, the normal response to pressure is hyperemia, but if persistent, pressure-induced ischemia leads to endothelial swelling and vessel leak. As plasma leaks into the interstitium, diffusing distances between the cellular elements of skin and blood vessels increase. Ultimately, hemorrhage occurs and leads to nonblanchable erythema of the skin. In bacteremic experimental animals, bacteria are deposited at sites of pressure-induced injury and set up a deep suppurative process. This may explain the occurrence of deep pressure ulcers with apparently normal overlying skin or simply a draining sinus. The accumulation of edema fluid, blood, inflammatory cells, toxic wastes, and possibly bacteria ultimately and progressively leads to the death of muscle, subcutaneous tissue, and, finally, epidermal tissue. The damage caused by shearing forces probably is mediated by pressure-induced ischemia in deep tissues as well as direct mechanical injury to subcutaneous tissue. Friction and moisture are most important in the development of superficial lesions, but their effects are likely to be greatest when excessive pressures are also present.[22]

PREVENTION OF PRESSURE ULCERS

Clinical Practice Guideline

The Agency for Health Care Policy and Research sponsored a multidisciplinary panel to develop recommendations for the prevention of pressure ulcers. The resulting clinical practice guideline, *Pressure Ulcers in Adults: Prediction and Prevention,* was released in May 1992 and contains recommendations for risk assessment, skin care, early treatment of pressure ulcers, and protection against the adverse effects of pressure, friction, and shear, and recommendations for the utilization of educational programs about pressure ulcers.[16]

Risk Assessment

The guideline recommends that bed- and chair-bound individuals or those with impaired ability to reposition should be assessed for additional risk factors that increase risk for developing pressure ulcers on admission to acute care and rehabilitation hospitals, nursing homes, home care programs, and other health care facilities. A systematic risk assessment can be accomplished by using a validated risk assessment tool such as the Braden Scale or Norton Scale.[16] Pressure ulcer risk should be reassessed when there is a change in activity or mobility levels.

Skin Care and Early Treatment

A number of recommendations were made in the clinical practice guideline for prevention of pressure ulcers based upon expert opinion due to the lack of research-based evidence. These recommendations are outlined in Table 123-1. In addition to these recommendations, the panel noted that studies are available to suggest that massage over bony prominences should be avoided since it may decrease blood flow and result in deep tissue injury.[16]

Prevention against the Adverse Effects of Pressure, Friction, and Shear

Positioning

Frequent repositioning historically has been the primary method of preventing pressure ulcers. One

TABLE 123-1

Skin Care and Early Treatment Recommendations Based on Expert Opinion

Systematically inspect skin daily.
Clean skin with a mild cleansing agent at the time of soiling and at routine intervals, avoiding hot water, and minimizing force and friction applied to the skin.
Minimize skin drying due to low humidity and exposure to cold and use moisturizers for dry skin.
Minimize skin exposure to moisture due to incontinence, perspiration, or wound drainage. If incontinence cannot be controlled after appropriate assessment and treatment, use an absorptive brief or underpad. Topical agents that act as barriers to moisture can also be used.
Minimize skin injury due to friction and shear using proper positioning, transferring, and turning techniques; lubricants such as cornstarch and creams; and protective films, dressings, and pads over bony prominences.
Ensure adequate dietary intake and correct nutritional deficiencies in a way consistent with overall goals of therapy.
Institute rehabilitation efforts if consistent with overall goals of therapy.
Document all interventions and outcomes.

study demonstrated that the incidence of pressure ulcers was one-third that observed in historical controls when elderly at-risk patients were repositioned on a regular schedule. Patients at highest risk were repositioned every 2 to 3 hours, while lower-risk patients were repositioned two to four times per day. The nurse/patient ratio was higher and greater attention was paid to the problem of incontinence in the study group than in the control patients. In addition to a lower incidence, the ulcers that developed in the study group were less severe than those observed in the group not repositioned on a regular schedule. These beneficial effects were noted, although the patients who were repositioned were generally at higher risk than the historical controls.[23] Although the study group did not have a concurrent control group, and the independent role of repositioning on patient outcome is uncertain, these data support the recommendation that at-risk patients should be repositioned every 2 hours if consistent with overall patient goals.[16] Pressure-reducing support surfaces may reduce the frequency of repositioning required in some patients.[13,24] Controlled trials are required to define the optimal repositioning schedules for patients on such surfaces.

Repositioning should be performed so that a person at risk is positioned without pressure on vulnerable bony prominences. Most of these sites are avoided by positioning patients with the back at a 30-degree angle to the support surface, alternatively from the right to left sides and the supine position. At-risk patients should never be repositioned with the back at a 90-degree angle to the support surface because such a position exposes the greater trochanter and lateral malleolus to excessive pressure. The use of pillows between the legs, behind the back, and supporting the arms aids in maintaining optimal positioning.[16,24] A person with limited ability to change position who needs to sit in a chair or to have the head of the bed elevated should not remain in the chair for more than 1 hour at a time. When possible, individuals should be taught to shift weight every 15 minutes while seated. The head of the bed should be maintained at the lowest degree of elevation consistent with medical conditions and other restrictions, and the amount of time the head of the bed is elevated also should be limited.[16] This decreases exposure of the sacral area to shearing forces that may predispose to deep tissue injury.

Pressure-Reducing Devices

Despite nurses' best efforts, the use of proper positioning techniques frequently is not sufficient or possible, and pressure ulcers occur. While one should not rely on a pressure-reducing device to substitute for good nursing care, such a mattress or support surface is indicated for persons at high risk for pressure ulcers. Unfortunately, no controlled trials have been performed in the United States to test which available products are most effective for the prevention of pressure ulcers. One randomized, controlled trial in Europe showed that the use of water mattresses or alternating air mattresses decreased the incidence of pressure ulcers by one-half compared with the use of conventional hospital mattresses.[25] The comparability of these devices to those used in the United States is uncertain.

A number of products and devices are marketed for the prevention and treatment of pressure ulcers in the United States. Sheepskins and 2-inch convoluted foam pad products are very popular and relatively inexpensive. Unfortunately, they do not have the capability to decrease pressure enough to eliminate risk of cutaneous injury. Alternating air mattresses consist of interconnecting air cells that are alternately inflated and deflated with a bedside pump. Alternating air mattresses are prone to mechanical breakdowns and unreliably lower pressure under bony prominences. The alternating air mattresses shown to be effective in Europe have larger-diameter air cells than devices marketed in the United States. Some air mattresses have interconnecting air cells that may deflate or inflate when a person changes position on them and do not require a bedside pump. These air mattresses and some thicker foam products with different configurations or densities than the typical "egg crate" foam mattress are reportedly capable of decreasing skin pressures to below capillary filling pressure under most bony prominences. Water mattresses are heavy, they can leak, and they theoretically increase the risk of maceration since they are made of impermeable materials. Moreover, nursing tasks are made more difficult when a water mattress is used. The use of foam-padded chairs, stretchers, and wheelchairs also may be helpful in lowering the incidence of pressure ulcers. Pillows under the length of the lower leg can totally relieve pressure on the heels of immobile individuals. Doughnut cushions should not be used because they decrease blood flow to the skin in the center of the cushion.[16] However, a foam, static air, alternating air, gel, or water mattress is indicated for any individual found to be at risk for developing pressure ulcers. Lifting devices such as a trapeze or bed linen to move (rather than drag) can minimize friction- and shear-induced injuries during transfers and position changes.[16] Air-fluidized and low-air-loss beds are most commonly used for the treatment of pressure ulcers and are discussed later.

Education and Multidisciplinary Teams

Several studies have shown a significant decrease in pressure ulcer incidence after an educational program and a multidisciplinary team approach to the problem of pressure ulcers are implemented.[26] Such educational programs should be directed at all levels of health care providers, patients, and family or caregivers.[16]

ASSESSMENT OF PATIENTS WITH PRESSURE ULCERS

General Assessment

The appropriate management of patients with pressure ulcers requires assessment and treatment of underlying diseases and conditions that have put the person at risk for development of a pressure ulcer and may prevent the lesion from healing. Nutritional assessment is particularly important (see Chaps. 4, 29, and 111). The size, stage, number, location, and wound character of pressure ulcers should be recorded. The most common sites for pressure ulcers are the sacrum, the buttocks over the ischium, the trochanters, the heels, and the lateral malleoli. Eighty percent of pressure ulcers occur at these sites.[24] The most severe ulcers are generally found in the pelvic area. Surrounding erythema may represent cellulitis, while purulent drainage suggests local wound infection. The presence of necrotic tissue or a darkly pigmented eschar identifies a wound unlikely to heal without débridement. Sinograms may be required to delineate the extent of pressure ulcers associated with a sinus tract.[27]

Assessment of Associated Infection

Bacterial counts of greater than 100,000 colonies per gram of tissue in pressure ulcers correlate well with poor wound healing and wound graft failure.[28] In particular, *Pseudomonas aeruginosa, Providencia,* and *Proteus* species and anaerobic bacteria have been reported to be associated with poorly healing ulcers.[29,30] Despite this, bacteriologic studies are not indicated unless there is evidence for sepsis, osteomyelitis, or cellulitis. When performed, bacteriologic studies of infected pressure ulcers often identify multiple organisms. The most common isolates include gram-negative aerobic rods. These accounted for 45 percent of isolates in one study of sepsis due to pressure ulcers. Gram-positive aerobic cocci also were frequent and accounted for 39 percent of isolates. *Bacteroides* species were the most common anaerobic isolates, accounting for 16 percent of the total. This study also found that isolation of *Bacteroides,* the presence of multiple pressure ulcers, and surgical débridement were associated with having a pressure ulcer as the probable source of the bacteremia.[5] The frequency of polymicrobial sepsis in patients with bacteremia due to a pressure ulcer ranges from 19.6 to 38 percent.[5,31] Foul-smelling lesions are very likely to be infected with anaerobic organisms, but the absence of odor does not exclude infection with anaerobes. Stage 3 and 4 lesions also are more likely to be infected with anaerobes.[32]

Underlying osteomyelitis may also lead to a nonhealing pressure ulcer. The diagnosis of osteomyelitis beneath a pressure ulcer can be difficult because there may be radiographic changes in the underlying bone due to pressure that may mimic changes seen in osteomyelitis. However, in one study in which 23 percent of subjects had osteomyelitis confirmed by bone biopsy, an abnormal plain bone radiograph *or* a leukocyte count of more than 15.0×10^9/liter *or* an erythrocyte sedimentation rate of 120 mm/h or higher was associated with a probability of osteomyelitis of 69 percent. When all three tests were normal, the probability of osteomyelitis was 4 percent.[33] Thus, any of these abnormalities in an individual with a nonhealing pressure ulcer should prompt consideration of a bone biopsy and culture to confirm the diagnosis and to guide therapy.

TREATMENT OF PRESSURE ULCERS

Systemic Measures

Systemic measures are critical in the management of individuals with pressure ulcers. Nutritional factors seem to be particularly important. In one randomized, placebo-controlled trial of vitamin C at a dose of 500 mg PO bid, the patients receiving vitamin C showed an 84 percent reduction of pressure ulcer surface area, while those receiving placebo showed only a 43 percent reduction in ulcer area ($p < .005$).[34] In another study, protein intake was one of the most important predictors of pressure ulcer improvement.[13] The use of zinc sulfate 200 mg tid may be helpful for the treatment of recalcitrant ulcers.[22]

Systemic antibiotics are indicated for patients with sepsis, cellulitis, or osteomyelitis, or for the prevention of bacterial endocarditis in persons with valvular heart disease and who require débridement of a pressure ulcer. A first-generation cephalosporin, cefazolin, does not penetrate into the tissue surrounding pressure ulcers,[35] while clindamycin and gentamicin do.[35,36] Because of the high mortality of sepsis associated with pressure ulcers despite appropriate antibiotics,[5,31] broad-spectrum coverage for aerobic gram-negative rods, gram-positive cocci, and anaerobes is indicated pending culture results in patients with suspected bacteremia. Ampicillin sulbactim, imipenem, ticarcillin clavulanate, or a combination of clindamycin and an aminoglycoside is an appropriate choice for initial antibiotic therapy. In septic patients, vigorous surgical débridement of necrotic tissue is necessary to remove the source of the bacteremia.[27]

Specialized Beds and Mattresses

Treatment of pressure ulcers includes the use of all the preventive measures needed for individuals at risk for pressure ulcers, including the use of a pressure-reducing device. Some of the air or foam products used for prevention probably are adequate for many patients with pressure ulcers, but some patients may require the use of one of the more expensive, specialized beds available.

One such specialized device is the air-fluidized bed. Air-fluidized beds contain microspheres of ceramic glass, and warm, pressurized air is forced up through the beads so that they take on the characteristics of a fluid. The beads are covered by a filter sheet that allows air, but not the beads, to escape. Patients then float on the beads, with pressures reduced under prominences.

Air-fluidized bed therapy was compared with conventional therapy (repositioning every 2 hours on a regular bed covered with an alternating air mattress and foam pad) for the treatment of pressure ulcers in one randomized, controlled trial. In that study, pressure ulcers showed a decrease in surface area on air-fluidized therapy and an increase in size on conventional therapy. The effect of treatment was greater for pressure ulcers 7.8 cm^2 or larger. After adjusting for other factors associated with a masked assessment of improvement, air-fluidized therapy was associated with a greater than fivefold increase in the odds of pressure ulcer improvement compared with conventional therapy. Although air-fluidized therapy increased the odds of improvement, only 13 percent of patients achieved healing of all pressure ulcers. About 25 percent of affected patients died in the hospital regardless of pressure ulcer treatment, and improved pressure ulcer outcome did not result in a significantly shorter hospital stay.[13]

While these data suggest that air-fluidized therapy is more effective than conventional therapy for treatment of pressure ulcers, the clinical impact of this difference in effectiveness may be limited by the underlying disease severity of patients hospitalized with pressure ulcers. On the other hand, failure of a pressure ulcer to improve was associated with a fourfold increased risk of death. An effective treatment may lower this risk for some pressure ulcer patients.

Other specialized beds are available for treatment of patients with pressure ulcers. Low-air-loss beds consist of large fabric cushions that are constantly inflated with air. In contrast to air-fluidized beds, the cushions of low-air-loss beds are fitted on a regular hospital bed frame. This allows the head of these beds and the beds themselves to be raised or lowered. These features facilitate patient transfers and eliminate the difficulties associated with trying to keep a patient's head elevated when he or she is on an air-fluidized bed. In a randomized, controlled trial among nursing home residents, the decrease in pressure ulcer area was three times faster when low-air-loss beds were compared with conventional care. Despite the faster rate of healing observed on the low-air-loss beds, the proportion of residents showing complete healing of the study ulcer was not significantly different in the two treatment groups.[37]

The clinical effectiveness of low-air-loss beds has not been compared with that of air-fluidized beds. Air-fluidized beds may be better able to reduce damage due to pressure, shear, and friction, and the warm environment of air-fluidized beds may reduce catabolism. On the other hand, air-fluidized beds are more expensive than low-air-loss beds and have a drying effect on tissues that may or may not be desired in certain clinical situations. The use of air-fluidized or low-air-loss beds should be considered when there are large, multiple, or full-thickness (stage 3 or 4) pressure ulcers; when an individual has fewer than two turning surfaces free of pressure ulcers; after reconstructive surgery for pressure ulcers; or when an individual has experienced recurrent ulceration and inability to heal on a less-expensive pressure-reducing device.[22]

Other specialized beds have been developed that automatically reposition immobilized subjects. A low-air-loss bed with this capability is available, while other devices automatically turn patients from side to side on a more traditional support surface. These beds are generally more expensive than both the air-fluidized and regular low-air-loss beds. Without more data to suggest that these beds with automatic repositioning capability improve clinical outcome, there appears little justification to use them for treatment or prevention of pressure-induced cutaneous injury. On the other hand, they may be useful in preventing the pulmonary complications of immobility, particularly in spinal cord injury patients.

Local Wound Care

Stage 1 and 2 ulcers infrequently require the use of any specific topical therapy, but data are available to suggest that deeper ulcers, particularly when there is evidence of local infection, may benefit from topical antibiotics. One controlled trial reported improved healing with topical gentamicin when compared with saline gauze dressings.[38] Another study showed that silver sulfadiazine, normal saline, and povidone-iodine are all able to lower pressure ulcer bacterial counts, but suggested that silver sulfadiazine is significantly better than povidone-iodine, but not better than saline. Clinical outcome seem to reflect changes in bacterial counts.[39] Topical antiseptics such as hypochlorite solutions, povidone-iodine, acetic acid, and hydrogen peroxide should be avoided because of the potential for inhibiting wound healing. Iodine compounds may cause systemic toxicity if applied to large ulcers.[20,22]

Surgical débridement augmented with wet-to-dry dressings using normal saline usually is sufficient to remove necrotic tissue in a pressure ulcer and thereby lower bacterial counts and allow healing to occur. Whirlpool therapy or the use of a 19-gauge 35-ml syringe for irrigation may be used to facilitate wound cleansing in some cases. The débridement of moist, exudative wounds may be augmented by using hydrophilic polymers like dextranomer. Enzymatic agents such as collagenase, fibrinolysin and deoxyribonuclease, streptokinase, and streptodornase may be helpful in aiding débridement but should not be used when an ulcer bed becomes clean and begins to granulate. Additional randomized, controlled trials are needed to determine the precise role of these and other topical agents.

Once an ulcer is clean and granulation or epithelialization begins to occur, then a moist wound environment should be maintained without disturbing the healing tissue. Superficial lesions heal by migration of epithelial cells from the borders of an ulcer, while deep lesions heal as granulation tissue fills the base of the wound. Controlled trials have suggested that the use of occlusive dressings such as transparent films and hydrocolloid dressings improves healing of stage 2 pressure ulcers.[40,41] These dressings may remain in place for several days and allow a layer of serous exudate to form underneath the dressing, facilitating epithelial migration. Such occlusive dressings have not proved to be more effective in healing deep ulcers but reduce the nursing time required for treatment. Generally, clean stage 3 and 4 ulcers should be dressed with a gauze dressing kept moistened with normal saline. Moist dressings should be kept off surrounding intact skin to avoid macerating normal tissues.

Surgery

A multitude of surgical procedures are available for the treatment of pressure ulcers. These include primary closure, skin grafts and myocutaneous flaps, and removal of underlying bony prominences. Radical procedures, such as amputation and hemicorporectomy, are sometimes required in complicated and extensive, infected pressure ulcers. Removal of ischial tuberosities can be complicated by urethral fistula formation.

One study has compared the outcome of flap surgeries in 21 traumatic paraplegic patients (mean age = 32 years) and in a group of 16 nontraumatic, nonparaplegic patients (mean age = 73 years). The latter group's immobility was attributed to cerebral dysfunction and chronic illness. Both groups had an operative complication rate of greater than 30 percent. Complications included dehiscence, flap infection, necrosis, and hematoma. One of the younger patients required prolonged intubation and tracheostomy. Two of the older patients experienced cardiopulmonary complications. More than 70 percent of the ulcers were healed at discharge from the hospital in both groups. The mean length of stay for younger patients was 40 days, compared with 60 days for the older patients.[42]

After a mean follow-up of 11 months, the traumatic paraplegic group had a 79 percent ulcer recurrence rate, compared with 40 percent in the older group after a mean follow-up of 8 months. On the other hand, none of the younger patients developed new ulcers, while 29 percent of the older patients did. Mortality was less than 5 percent for the younger group but reached 50 percent in the older group.[42] These data raise questions about the benefits of surgical closure for pressure ulcers. Randomized, controlled trials are needed to define the appropriate use of such procedures in geriatric patients.

Potential or Experimental Treatments

Multitudes of treatments have been advocated for the treatment of pressure ulcers without sufficient data to support their use. Such treatments include the use of hyperbaric oxygen. A number of topical agents and growth factors are being developed that may stimulate wound healing. Preliminary trial data suggest that recombinant platelet-derived growth factor may improve healing of stage 3 pressure ulcers.[43] Despite the potential development of more effective treatments in the future, the best approach to pressure ulcers will remain prevention.

REFERENCES

1. National Pressure Ulcer Advisory Panel: Pressure ulcers: Prevalence, cost, and risk assessment. Consensus Development Conference Statement. *Decubitus* 2:24, 1989.
2. Allman RM: Epidemiology of pressure ulcers in different populations. *Decubitus* 2:30, 1989.
3. Berlowitz DR, Wilking SVB: The short term outcome of pressure ulcers. *J Am Geriatr Soc* 38:748, 1990.
4. Brandeis GH et al: The epidemiology and natural history of pressure ulcers in elderly nursing home residents. *JAMA* 264:2905, 1990.
5. Bryan LS et al: Bacteremia associated with decubitus ulcers. *Arch Intern Med* 143:2093, 1983.
6. Glenchor H et al: Transient bacteremia associated with débridement of decubitus ulcers. *Milit Med* 146:432, 1981.
7. Garibaldi RA et al: Infections among patients in nursing homes: Policies, prevalence, and problems. *N Engl J Med* 305:731, 1981.
8. Sugarman B: Pressure ulcers and underlying bone infection. *Arch Intern Med* 147:553, 1987.

9. Dalton JJ et al: Amyloidosis in the paraplegic: Incidence and significance. *J Urol* 93:553, 1965.
10. Haley RW et al: The emergence of methicillin-resistant *Staphylococcus aureus* infections in United States hospitals: Possible roles of the housestaff-patient transfer circuit. *Ann Intern Med* 97:297, 1982.
11. Allman RM et al: Pressure ulcers among hospitalized patients. *Ann Intern Med* 105:337, 1986.
12. Bergstrom N, Braden B: A prospective study of pressure ulcers risk among institutionalized elderly. *J Am Geriatr Soc* 40:747, 1992.
13. Allman RM et al: Air-fluidized beds or conventional therapy for pressure ulcers: A randomized trial. *Ann Intern Med* 107:641, 1987.
14. Bennett RG et al: Air-fluidized bed treatment of nursing home patients with pressure ulcers. *J Am Geriatr Soc* 37:235, 1989.
15. Exton-Smith AN, Sherwin RW: The prevention of pressure ulcers: Significance of spontaneous bodily movements. *Lancet* 2:1124, 1961.
16. Panel for the Prediction and Prevention of Pressure Ulcers in Adults. *Pressure Ulcers in Adults: Prediction and Prevention. Clinical Practice Guideline, Number 3* AHCPR Publication No. 92-0047. Rockville, MD, Agency for Health Care Policy and Research, Public Health Service, U.S. Department of Health and Human Services, May 1992.
17. Allman RM et al: Predictors of time to pressure ulcer development (abstract). *Clin Res* 40:302A, 1992.
18. Berlowitz DR, Wilking SVB: Risk factors for pressure ulcers: A comparison of cross-sectional and cohort-derived data. *J Am Geriatr Soc* 37:1043, 1989.
19. Guralnik JM et al: Occurrence and predictors of pressure ulcers in the National Health and Nutrition Examination Survey Follow-up. *J Am Geriatr Soc* 36:807, 1988.
20. Allman RM: Pressure ulcers among the elderly. *N Engl J Med* 320:850, 1989.
21. Bennett L et al: Skin stress and blood flow in sitting paraplegic patients. *Arch Phys Med Rehabil* 65:186, 1984.
22. Goode PS, Allman RM: The prevention and management of pressure ulcers. *Med Clin North Am* 73:1511, 1989.
23. Norton et al: A study of factors concerned in the production of pressure ulcers and their prevention, in *An Investigation of Geriatric Nursing Problems in Hospital,* 2d ed. Edinburgh, Churchill Livingstone, 1975, p 194.
24. Seiler WO, Stähelin HB: Decubitus ulcers: Preventive techniques for the elderly patient. *Geriatrics* 40:53, 1985.
25. Anderson KE et al: Decubitus prophylaxis: A prospective trial on the efficiency of alternating-pressure air-mattresses and water-mattresses. *Acta Derm Venereol (Stockh)* 63:227, 1982.
26. Smith DM et al: Pressure ulcers in the elderly: Can this outcome be improved? *J Gen Intern Med* 6:81, 1991.
27. Reuler JB, Cooney TG: The pressure ulcers: Pathophysiology and principles of management. *Ann Intern Med* 94:661, 1981.
28. Robson MC, Heggers TP: Bacterial quantification of open wounds. *Milit Med* 134:19, 1969.
29. Daltrey DC et al: Investigation into the microbial floral of healing and non-healing decubitus ulcers. *J Clin Pathol* 34:701, 1981.
30. Seiler WO, Stähelin HB: Recent findings on decubitus ulcer pathology: Implications for care. *Geriatrics* 41:47, 1986.
31. Galpin JE et al: Sepsis associated with decubitus ulcers. *Am J Med* 61:346, 1976.
32. Sapico FL et al: Quantitative microbiology of pressure ulcers in different stages of healing. *Diagn Microbiol Infect Dis* 5:31, 1986.
33. Lewis VL et al: The diagnosis of osteomyelitis in patients with pressure ulcers. *Plast Reconstr Surg* 81:229, 1988.
34. Taylor TV et al: Ascorbic acid supplementation in the treatment of pressure ulcers. *Lancet* 2:544, 1974.
35. Berger SA et al: Penetration of antibiotics in decubitus ulcers. *J Antimicrob Chemother* 7:193, 1981.
36. Berger SA et al: Penetration of clindamycin into decubitus. *Antimicrob Agents Chemother* 14:498, 1978.
37. Ferrell BA et al: A randomized trial of low-air-loss beds for treatment of pressure ulcers. *JAMA* 269:494, 1993.
38. Bendy RH et al: Relationship of quantitative wound bacterial counts for healing of decubiti: Effect of topical gentamicin. *Antimicrob Agents Chemother* 4:147, 1965.
39. Kucan JO et al: Comparison of silver sulfadiazine, povidone-iodine and physiologic saline in the treatment of chronic pressure ulcers. *J Am Geriatr Soc* 29:232, 1981.
40. Oleske DM et al: A randomized clinical trial of two dressing methods for the treatment of low-grade pressure ulcers. *J Enterostom Ther* 13:90, 1986.
41. Sebern MD: Pressure ulcer management in home health care: Efficacy and cost effectiveness of moisture vapor permeable dressing. *Arch Phys Med Rehabil* 67:726, 1986.
42. Disa JJ et al: Efficacy of operative cure in pressure ulcer patients. *Plast Reconstr Surg* 89:272, 1992.
43. Cutler N et al: Recombinant PDGF-BB in chronic pressure ulcers. Presented at the 1992 National Wound Healing Society Meeting, Richmond, VA, April 1992.

INDEX

Note: Page numbers in italics indicate figures; page numbers followed by an italic *t* indicate tabular material.

Abandonment, issue of, 405
Abdominal aneurysms, 313, 534–535
Abdominal disorders:
  etiology, 302*t*
  surgical procedures, 301–302
Abdominal infections, diagnostictesting, 1161
Abdominal pain, management, *370*
Abdominal wall hernia, 309–310, *310*
Abscesses:
  CNS, 1076–1077
  diverticular disease and, 724
  pyogenic liver, sepsis and, 710
  renal, 630, 632
Absence seizures, 1089
Absolute white cell count, defined, 750, 751*t*
Abuse, elder, 392–393
Acalculous cholecystitis, 712
Accelerated aging, 500
ACE inhibitors (*see* Angiotensin converting enzyme inhibitors)
Acetaminophen, 324, 948, 950
Acetanilid, 676
Acetylcholine, neurotransmission and, 1008, 1024
Acetylcholinesterase (AChE), 1008
Achalasia, 687–688, 1263
Achlorhydria, 567, 668
Achondroplasia, 31
Acid-base balance:
  chronic renal failure, 649
  esophagus, 24-hour pH monitoring, 685
  tubular function, 617
Acid excretion, renal, 617
Acid-fast bacillus cultures, 576, 577, 580
Acid perfusion test, 684
Acidification:
  of stool, 727–728
  of urine, 632
Acoustic neuroma, 1167
Acquired immune deficiency syndrome (AIDS):
  candidiasis, 420–421
  hypergammaglobulinemia, 69
  Kaposi's sarcoma, 426–427
  non-Hodgkin's lymphoma, 763
  sex differential and, 40
  transmission, 122
Acromegaly, 800
Actinic keratoses, 425
Actinic purpura, 418
Activated partial thromboplastin time, 778
Activation phase, immune response, 63
Active euthanasia, defined, 402
Activities of daily living (ADLs):
  assessment, 204–205, 208–209
  limitations of, 375
Acuity, examination, 442
Acute bacterial pyelonephritis, 644–645
Acute cholecystitis, 711–712
Acute confusional state, 284, 1021–1025
Acute fulminant hepatitis, 708
Acute glomerulonephritis, 641–642
Acute interstitial nephritis, 645
Acute lymphoblastic leukemia (ALL), 759
Acute myeloblastic leukemia (AML), 758–759
Acute myocardial infarction (*see* Myocardial infarction)
Acute renal failure:
  acute tubular necrosis, 647
  interference with renal autoregulation, 647–648
  obstructive uropathy, 648
  prerenal azotemia, 646–647
Acute (reversible) urinary incontinence, 1231, 1231*t*
Acute tubular necrosis, 647
Acute tubulointerstitial nephritis, 644–645
Adaptive equipment, rehabilitation, 1291–1292
Addiction (*see* Chemical dependence)
Addison's disease, 802, 1185
Adenocarcinoma:
  endometrium, 477
  esophagus, 691
  gallbladder/biliary tract, 712–713
  gastric, 701–702
  lung, 607–608, 612
Adhesive capsulitis, 1000
Adie's syndrome, 442
Adjustment disorders, 1106
Adrenal glands:
  disorders, 801–802
  hypothalamic-pituitary-adrenal axis, 792–794
Adrenal hormones, secretion, 793–794
Adrenocorticotropic hormone (ACTH), 608, 618, 793
Adriamycin, 487, 611, 612
Adult day care, 379–380
Adult respiratory distress syndrome, 576, 644–645
Advance care planning directives:
  ethical aspects, 405*t*, 406
  importance of, 245
  legal aspects, 393–394
Advanced glycosylated end product (AGE proteins), 511
Advanced maternal age, defined, 31
Aerobic capacity, defined, 97
Aerobic exercise, 91–94
Aerobic power, maximal, 91
Aerosol vaccines, 66
Affect, impairment of, 207

Ageism:
  defined, 197
  delivery of health care and, 301, 401
Agency for Health Care Policy Research (AHCPR), 253
Aggressive-type lymphomas, 766
Aging:
  cultural aspects, 177–184
  defined, 3
  evolutional model, 8–11, *10*, *12*
  exercise and, 91–96
  experimental gerontology, topics in, 11–16
  fundamental observations, 4–6
  lifestyle/environment and, 179
  modification of process, 130–132
  preventing functional impairment, 184
  as risk factor, morbidity/mortality, 154
  sociological aspects, 125–133
  theories of, 6–8
Aging, physiology of:
  anesthesia, drug response, 292–293
  articular cartilage, 937, 937*t*
  atherogenesis, 512–513
  brain, neurochemistry, 1005–1006
  cardiovascular system, *494*
  eye, 441–442
  fluid homeostasis, 1183–1184
  hematopoietic system, 749, 783–785
  infection risk factors, 1158–1159
  interstitial disease, 646
  lipoprotein metabolism, 857–858, 858*t*–859*t*
  liver, 707
  normal, 195–196, *196*
  pancreas, 717
  pharmacodynamics, 268–270
  pharmacokinetics, 260–261, 263–264, 265
  respiratory system, 555–563
  skin, 411–414
  surgical risk, 277, 278*t*, 301
Agitated depression, 1106
Agitation, control of, 284
Agnosia:
  dementia, 1199, 1200
  focal cognitive syndromes, 1201
Agranulocytosis, 951–952
Agreeableness, personality trait, 108
AIDS (*see* Acquired immune deficiency syndrome (AIDS))
Air-bone gap, defined, 463
Air conduction, audiologic testing, 462
Albert's test, 349–350
Alcohol abuse (*See also* Chemical dependence)
  depression and, 1106
  epidemiology, 148
  esophageal disorders, 691
  hepatic toxicity, 708
  incidence, 1125–1126
  nutritional aspects, 57
  preventive gerontology and, 189–190
  as risk factor, falls, 1314
  screening/detection, 1127
  secondary impotence, 1253
Alcohol withdrawal delirium, 1023
Alcoholics Anonymous (AA), 1128, 1129
Aldosterone, 618, 620
Alginic acid, gastroesophageal reflux disease, 685
Alimentation:
  enteral, 333–336
  parenteral, 333
Alkaline phosphatase, 638, 649, 931–932
Allele, defined, 20
Allergic contact dermatitis, 416
Allergic reactions:
  immune response and, 63, 66, 71
  NSAIDs, 951
Allergy, diagnosis, 67
Allopurinol, 991
Aloe, 1272
Alpha-adrenergic blocking agents, 659
Altered mental state:
  defined, 221
  neuropsychiatric assessment, 221–228
  syndromes of, 1197–1203
Aluminum accumulation, 649, 651
Aluminum-containing phosphate binders, 649
Aluminum hydroxide, 649
Alveolar hypoxemia, 603
Alzheimer amyloid precursor protein, 1006
Alzheimer's disease:
  assessment, 205
  biochemistry, 1010, 1010*t*, 1043–1044
  characteristics, 1036*t*
  cholinergic hypothesis, 1044
  clinical diagnosis, 1035–1036, 1037*t*
  corticotropin-releasing hormone system, 794
  delirium and, 1023, 1024
  dementia and, 1198–1200
  depression with, 1203
  differential diagnosis, 1056–1057
  epidemiology, 148, 1039*t*, 1039–1040
  familial, 27–29
  genetic linkages to familial forms, 28*t*
  head injury and, 1085
  incidence, *1040*, 1040*t*
  laboratory studies, 1038–1039
  management, 1044–1045
  manifestations
    cognitive/behavioral, 1036*t*, 1036–1037
  manifestations, cognitive/behavioral, *1037t*
  manifestations, physical, 1037–1038
  neuropathology, similarities with Down's, 26, 1120, 1201
  nutritional support and, 336
  pathology, 1041–1043, *1042*
  rehabilitation, 352–353
  risk factors, 1040*t*, 1040–1041
  sleep apnea and, 1220
Alzheimer's Disease and Related Disorders Association (ADRDA), 233
Amantadine:
  influenza, 569, 570, 575
  Parkinson's, 1057–1058
Amaurosis fugax, 956, 1028
Ambulatory cardiac monitoring, 1173
American Cancer Society, 81, 82
American College of Physicians (ACP), 400
American Geriatric Society, 400
American Medical Association (AMA), 402
American Nurses Association (ANA), 249, 251, 252
Ametropia, 443
Amicar, 781
Amino acid transport, 617
Aminoglycosides:
  nephrotoxicity, 629, 647, 650, 1161, 1162
  ototoxicity, 1168
  pneumonia, 570
  sepsis, antibiotic drug resistance, 71
Amitriptyline, 328, 1140
Amnesia:
  dementia, 1199, 1200
  focal cognitive syndromes, 1200
  transient global, TIAs and, 1028
Amphotericin B, 647, 1075
Ampicillin, 629, 725
Ampullary disequilibrium of aging, 470
Amsler grid, 443
Amyloid (congophilic) angiopathy, 1028–1029
Amyloid deposition, Alzheimer's disease, 1041, 1042, 1043
Amyloid neuropathy, 1289
Amyloidosis, 27, 643, 771
Amyotrophic lateral sclerosis (ALS):
  clinical features, 1066
  differential diagnosis, 1290
  incidence, 1289–1290
  management, symptomatic, 1290
Anabolic steroids, 45, 907
Anaerobic bacteria, 566, 567–568
Anal fissures, 1269
Analgesics (*See also* Nonopioids; Nonsteroidal anti-inflammatory drugs; Opioids)

Analgesics (*Cont.*)
adjuvant drugs, 322, 323, 327–328
alternatives to NSAIDs, 948
guidelines, 323–329
mild-moderate pain, 324*t*
nephropathy, 645
pharmacologic considerations, 322–323
side effects, 328–329
Androgen ablation therapy, prostatic cancer, 663
Androgens:
benign prostatic hyperplasia and, 657
bone resorption and, 893, *893*
hypogonadism, 1257
libido and, 117
Androstenedione, 869
Anemia:
age-related changes and, 742*t*
chronic disease and, 745
chronic renal failure, 650
classification, 743*t*
clinical presentation, 746–747
diagnosis, *744*, 746*t*
evaluation, 742–743
hemolytic, 746
hypoproliferative, 743–745, *744*
ineffective erythropoiesis, *744*, 745–746
prevalence, 741–742
Anergy, 577, 581
Anesthesia (*See also* Spinal anesthesia)
basic principles, 292
blood replacement, 296
changing physiologic states, 293
complications, 291–292, 292*t*
drug response, *292*, 292–293
hemodynamic instability, *293*, 293–294
hypothermia, 294–295
hypothyroidism and, 816
informed consent, *289*, 296–297
management, basic principles, 292
mortality, 280
perioperative risk factors, *287*, 287–288, *288*
postoperative care, 296
regional, 295, 387
risk factors, 288–291, *291*
Anesthesia-related complications (ARCs), 287, *290*, 290–292
Anesthesiologists, 288
Anesthetist, 288
Aneuploidy, 26, 31
Aneurysms:
aortic, 313
clinical evaluation, 535–536
clinical features of, 535
common sites of, 534–535
diagnostic aids, ancillary, 536
treatment, 537
Angina pectoris, 517–518
Angiodysplasia, 308
Angiography, pulmonary, 604–605
Angiokeratoma corporis diffusum, 418
Angiokeratomas of Fordyce, 418
Angiomas, 418
Angiotensin converting enzyme (ACE) inhibitors:
drug interactions, NSAIDs, 947
hyperkalemia, 622
hypertension, 550–551
pharmacokinetics, 262
renal disease and, 637–638, 647–648
use in diabetic patients, 840
Angiotensin II-induced vasoconstriction, 647
Angle-closure glaucoma, 452
Anisocoria, 442
Ankle/arm index, arterial pressure, 536
Ankle foot orthosis, 1292
Anorectal function, 672–673
Anorexia:
defined, 434
dying patient, 387
salt depletion with, 620
Anserine bursitis, 996
Antabuse, 1128
Antacids:
drug interactions, NSAIDs, 947
gastroesophageal reflux disease, 685
pneumonia, prevention and, 567, 575
Anterior spinal artery, 1286
Anterior spinal cord syndrome, 1286
Anthraquinone derivatives, 1272
Anthropometric measures, nutritional status and, 334
Anti-idiotype antibodies, 69, 72
Anti-inflammatory agents (*see* Nonsteroidal anti-inflammatory drugs (NSAIDs))
Anti-RNP antibodies, rheumatic disease, 972
Anti-Sm (Smith) antibodies, rheumatic disease, 972
Antiarrhythmic agents, 519, 1177
Antibiotics:
diarrhea, 1282
economic aspects, 1161
endocarditis, prophylaxis, 282, 283*t*
infections, special considerations, 1161–1162
neurosyphilis, 1075
pneumonia, 570, 571*t*, 576
pressure ulcers, infected, 1333, 1334
resistance to, 576
selection, 71
Antibody testing, rheumatic disease, 971*t*, 971–973
Anticholinergic agents:
as cause of delirium, 1024
contraindications, 1198
COPD, 587
Parkinson's, 1057–1058
preoperative management, 281
Anticoagulant functions, 776–777, *777*
Anticoagulant therapy:
cerebral infarction, 1029
drug interactions, NSAIDs, 947
pulmonary embolism, 605
thromboembolic disease
renal, 639
venous, 784–785
Antidepressants:
anxiety, 1139
dementia, 1199–1200
depression, 1140
Parkinson's, 1060
Antidiuretic hormone (ADH), 619, 621, 816
Antiemetics, 328, 388
Antiepileptic agents, 1091, 1092
Antifungal agents, 388
Antigens, intradermal injection, 67
Antigeroid syndromes, 30–31
Antiglomerular basement membrane antibody, 641
Antihistamines, 416, 424, 1060
Antihypertensive agents:
actions/uses, 549–551, 550*t*
as cause of depression, 1106
drug interactions, NSAIDs, 947
evidence for efficacy of therapy, 544–547
risk/benefit ratio, 543–544
Antimicrobial agents:
urinary tract infections, 629–630
Antimicrobial agents, urinary tract infections, 630*t*
Antineutrophil cytoplasmic antibodies (ANCA), 642
Antinuclear autoantibodies (ANA), 971–972
Antiplatelet agents, 1029
Antipsychotic agents, 1140–1141
Antipyretic agents, 948
Antisocial personality, 1132, 1133
Antistreptolysin O (ASO) titers, 642
Antithrombin III, 776, 781
Antithyroid agents, 812
Antituberculosis agents, 579*t*, *580*
Antiubiquitin immunohistochemistry, 1064
Antral gastritis, 695
Anxiety:
personality stability and, 110
treatment, 1138–1139
Anxiolytic agents, 388, 1106, 1139
Aorta, coarctation of, 522
Aortic aneurysm, 313, 534–535, 537
Aortic arch abnormalities, 1262
Aortic regurgitation, acute/chronic, 524–525

Aortic stenosis:
diagnosis, 522–524
nonsurgical management, 524
as preoperative risk factor, 281
valve replacement, 524
Aortic valve disease:
surgery for, 311–312
syncope and, 1172
Aortic valvuloplasty, 524
Aphasia:
dementia, 1199, 1200
focal cognitive syndromes, 1200–1201
Pick's disease, 1063
Apnea index (AI), 1218
Apocrine glands, 414
Apomorphine, 1060
Appendicitis, 304
Appetite, loss of (*see* Anorexia)
Apraxia:
dementia, 1199, 1200
focal cognitive syndromes, 1201
Arginine vasopressin (AVP), 619, 620
Arrhythmias:
hypokalemia and, 623
management, 529
ventricular, 284
Arterial occlusion:
aneurysms, 534–535
epidemiology, 145
lower limb, 534
pathophysiology, 533–534
Arterial oxygen tension, 557–558
Arterial pressure:
measurement, 536
regional anesthesia and, 294
Arterial thromboembolism:
myocardial infarction, 786
peripheral, 787
reversible ischemic neurologic deficits, 786–787
risk factors for, 785–786
stroke, 786–787
Arterial wall, atherogenesis and, 512
Arteriography:
peripheral vascular disease, 536
renal, 638–639
Arteriosclerosis:
age-related risk factors, 510
defined, 509
nonatheromatous, 510
ophthalmopathy, 453
Arteriosclerosis obliterans:
clinical features, 534–536
pathogenesis, 533
pathophysiology, 533–534
treatment, 536–537
Arteriovenous fistulas, dialysis, 652
Arthritis (*See also* Osteoarthritis; Rheumatoid arthritis)
epidemiology, 142
exercise, benefits of, 100–101
Articular cartilage:
aging and, 937
biochemistry, 936, 937
components, 935–936
mechanical properties, 936–937
osteoarthritis and, 937, 937*t*
Articular temporomandibular joint (TMJ) disorders, 437
Artificial hydration/nutrition:
dying patient, 384–385
ethical aspects, 405–406
Ascorbic acid, 632
Aspiration pneumonia, 567, 683
Aspirin:
anti-platelet action, 219, 520, 536, 786, 787, 788, 1029
pain, 324
pharmacology, age-related, 947
preoperative management, 281
Assessment (*See also* Geriatric assessment; Nutritional assessment)
balance/gait, 1316*t*
dying patient, 384–385
immune function, 66*t*, 66–70
incontinence, 246
neuropsychiatric, 221–228
nursing home admission, 359–361, 360*t*, 362*t*–364*t*, 371–373
pain, 320–322
perioperative, 277–280
pressure ulcers, infections of, 1333
stroke, 350–351
Assistive Listening Devices (ALDs), 467
Asteotic eczema, 415
Asterixis, 1197
Asthma:
corticosteroids, 593*t*
management, 591–593
pulmonary function tests, 560
signs/symptoms, 591–593
Asymptomatic bacteriuria, 625, 628, 633
Ataxia telangiectasia, 25, 66
Atheroembolic renal disease, 639
Atherogeneis, 512–513
Atherosclerosis:
exercise, benefits of, 100
hyperlipidemia, 862–864
incidence, 509
pathobiology, 513–514
pathogenesis, 533, 835–836
prevention, 189, 515
renovascular disease and, 637–638
reversibility/regression of, 514–515
as risk factor, thromboembolism, 785
risk factors, 510*t*, 510–512, 513–514, 860–861
sex differential in, 42–46
Ativan, 389
Atlantoaxial subluxation, 970
Atrial natriuretic peptide (ANP), 618
Atrial septal defect, 521
Atrioventricular (AV) node, 495
Atrophic gastritis, 669
Atrophic vaginitis, 475
Atrophy of transverse metatarsal arch fat pad, 1303
Attention, impairment of, 1013–1014, 1022
Atypical hyperplasia (dysplasia), 481
Audiograms, *462*, 462–465
Audiological tests:
general considerations, 462–463
interpretation, 463–464
site-of-lesion evaluation, 463
Audiometers, use of, 461–465, 468
Audioscope, 208, 461, *461*
Auditory dysfunction, 457–458 (*See also* Hearing loss)
Auditory training, 467
Autoantibodies, 69
Autoimmune diseases, 39 (*See also* Rheumatic diseases; Rheumatoid arthritis)
Autoimmune theory of aging, 69
Autologous anti-idiotype antibodies, 69
Automated peritoneal dialysis (APD), 652
Automobile driving (*see* Driving, automobile)
Autonomic dysfunction, spinal cord disease, 1292–1294
Autonomic dysreflexia, 1293
Autosomal dominant disorders, 29
Autosomal recessive disorders, 23
Avoidant personality disorder, 1134
Azathioprine, 963
Azorean motor system degeneration, 997
Azotemia, 620, 646–647
Azothioprine, 642

B cells:
augmenting activity of, 72
classification, 62
function, 62–64, 68
Back pain, 903, 904, 1288
Baclofen, 1292
Bacteremia, 627, 629
Bacterial endocarditis, prophylaxis, 283*t*
Bacterial meningitis, 1071–1073, 1073*t*
Bacterial virulence factors, UTIs and, 626
Bacteriuria (*See also* Urinary tract infection)
asymptomatic, 633
catheter-assisted, 631–632

Balance:
- age/disease related changes, 1166
- evaluation, 208*t*, 468–470, 1316*t*, 1317
- mechanisms of, 1165–1166
- as risk factor, hip fracture, 1324

Balloon dilatation of prostatic urethra, 659
Barbiturates, indications, 1092
Barium enema:
- colorectal cancer, 728
- diverticular disease, 724

Barium esophagram, 684
Barrett's esophagus, 686–687, 1262
Basal cell carcinoma, skin, 425
Basal metabolic rate (BMR), 333
Basophilia, 752
Basophils:
- decreased, significance of, 756
- function, 749
- increased, significance of, 752

Bayes' theorem of probability, 237
Beck Depression Inventory, 207
Beds, pressure-relieving, 1333–1334
Bedsores (*see* Pressure ulcers)
Behavioral techniques:
- cognitive, 1108
- urinary incontinence, 1242–1244

Behçet's disease, 691
Behind-the-ear (BTE) hearing aids, 465
Bell's palsy, 445
Bence Jones proteins, 646
Beneficence, defined, 399
Benign monoclonal gammopathy (BMG), 69, 771, 772*t*
Benign paroxysmal positional vertigo (BPPV), 1167
Benign positional vertigo (BPV), 469
Benign prostatic hyperplasia (BPH):
- diagnostic tests, 658–659
- etiology, 657–658
- incidence, 657
- pathogenesis, 658
- physical examination, 659
- symptoms, 659
- treatment, 659–660

Benoxaprofen, 950
Benton Visual Retention Test, 1200
Benzbromarone, 991
Benzodiazepines:
- Alzheimer's disease, 1045
- anxiety, 284, 1139
- delirium, 1198
- pharmacodynamics, 269
- preoperative management, 281
- psychosis, 1141
- reversal agents, 293
- spasticity, 1292
- status epilepticus, 1092
- withdrawal delirium, 1142

Benzonatate, 387
Bereavement, 110–111, 389–390
Bernstein acid perfusion test, 684
Beta blockers:
- acute MI, 519, 520
- adjuvant therapy, hyperthyroidism, 812
- hypercalcemia, 926
- hypertension, 549–550
- preoperative management, 281

Beta-lactam derivatives, 645
β-adrenergic stimulation, cardiovascular response, 503–504, *504*, *505*
β -amyloid precursor gene, Alzheimer's disease and, 28
β-amyloidogenesis, unified hypothesis of, 28
β-carotene, 73
17β-estradiol, 868–869
Bethanechol, 686
Bezold-Jarisch reflex, 1176
Bicipital tendinitis, 999–1000
Bile-salt sequestering agents, 819
Biliary disorders, 302–303, 707, 710–713
Biliary function, age-related, 674–677
Bimanual pelvic examination, 473
Binswanger's disease, 1031
Bioavailability, pharmacokinetics, *259*, 259–260
Biofeedback procedures, urinary incontinence, 1242
Biogenic amines, defined, 791
Biopsy:
- bone, 900, 902, 915, 924
- brain tumor, 1098
- breast mass, 483
- esophagus, 684–685
- muscle, 963, 964
- prostate, 660–661
- renal, 642, 643
- temporal artery, 957
- vulva, 473

Biotitration, defined, 1138
Bipolar affective disorder, 207, 1139–1140, 1202–1203
Birth control pills, 785
Bisacodyl, 1272
Bismuth subsalicylate, 1282
Bisphosphonates, 906, 932
Bladder, neurogenic, 1293–1294
Bladder control records, 1234, *1236*
Bladder training/retraining, 1242–1244, 1244*t*
Bleeding, gastrointestinal, 700–701, 724, 726
Bleeding disorders:
- assessment, 777–778
- presurgical risk assessment, 778
- treatment, 778–779

Bleeding time, 778
Blepharitis, 444
Blepharoptosis, 445
Blessed Dementia Rating Scale, 223, 1107
Blessed Information-Memory Concentration Test, 206
Blindness, transient monocular, 1028
Blistering skin diseases, 423–424
Blood pressure (*see* Hypertension)
Blood transfusion, indications, 296
Blood urea nitrogen (BUN), 646, 650
Bloom's syndrome, 24
Body composition:
- changes in, 50–51, 195
- failure to thrive and, 1206–1208
- fat distribution, importance of, 852

Body hearing aids, 465–466
Body mass index (BMI) (*See also* Lean body mass (LBM))
- computation, 848
- malnutrition, 208
- mortality and, *851*
- nutritional assessment, 54, *56*, 56*t*

Body weight (*See also* Obesity)
- actuarial data, 850–852
- cholesterol/triglyceride, age and, *42*, 43
- effect on mortality, 848–852
- failure to thrive and, 1206–1208
- gain patterns, sex differential and, 43
- height/weight tables, 852*t*
- standards of normal, 847–848

Bone biopsy, osteomalacia, 915
Bone cancer, 930, 931
Bone cells, types, 883–885
Bone conduction, audiologic testing, 462–464
Bone density (*See also* Osteoporosis)
- defined, 879
- evaluation, 871
- fracture risk and, *893*

Bone formation/resorption, 179–180, 881, 887, *889*, 889–891
Bone marrow:
- function, age-related, 735
- function, normal, 733
- transplantation, 785

Bone mass deficiency:
- measurement, 900–903, 901*t*
- osteoporosis, 897–899
- PTH and, 924
- skin synthesis/vitamin D, 51
- treatment, *904*, 904*t*, 904–905, 905*t*

Bone metabolism:
- bone cells, 883–885, *884*, *885*
- bone remodeling/volume, regulation, 885–889, *888*, *889*
- bone structure, 883, *883*
- bone volume, men, *891*, *893*, 893–894
- bone volume, women, *889*, 889-891, *890*, *891*
- hyperparathyroidism, 923

Bone metabolism (*Cont.*)
normal, 879
Bone scan:
metastatic prostatic cancer, 662
osteomalacia, 915–916
Paget's disease, 931
Bone volume:
defined, 879
exercise and, *892*
regulation, 883, 889, *889*
women, major determinants of, 889–891
Borderline personality disorder, 1134
Boston Naming Test, 225, *1014*
Botulinum toxin, motor point block, 1292
Bouchard's nodes, 983
Bowel function (*See also* Constipation)
assessment, 246
colorectal cancer and, 728
diverticular disease and, 724
normal, 672–673
Bowen's disease, 425, 447
BPH (*see* Benign prostatic hyperplasia)
Braces/splints:
peripheral neuropathy, 1292
spinal cord injury, 1291
Brachytherapy, 1099, 1100
Braden Scale, 1331
Bradykinesia, 1054
Brain:
chemical constituents, 1006–1007
conduction/neurotransmission, 1007–1008
morphologic considerations, 1063–1064
related diseases, 1009–1010
Brain abscess, 1076
Brain tumors:
biopsy, 1098
classification, 1095*t*, 1095–1096
clinical presentation, 1096*t*, 1096–1097
diagnosis, 1096–1098, 1097–1098
epidemiology, 1095–1096
prognosis, 1100
radiologic imaging, 1097
treatment
chemotherapy, 1099–1101
corticosteroids, 1098–1099
radiation, 1099–1101
surgery, 1099
types, 1100
Brainstem Auditory Evoked Potentials (BAEPs), 463
Breast cancer:
biology, 481–482
diagnosis, 483
estrogen replacement therapy and, 874
incidence, *481*
male, 489–490
mortality rates, *481*
pathogenesis, 481–482
prevention, 482
risk factors, 476, 477, 481–482
screening, 217, 482–483, 483*t*
staging, 485, 486*t*
survival, *485*
treatment
adjuvant systemic, 485–488, 487*t*, 488*t*
early localized lesions, 483–484, 489*t*
follow-up, 485, 486*t*
metastatic disease, 488–489
tamoxifen, 484
Breast reconstruction, 484
Broad spectrum antibiotics, 1162
Broca's aphasia, 1200–1201
Bromocriptine, 1059
Bromsulphalein (BSP) test, 676
Bronchitis, chronic, 584–585
Bronchoalveolar lavage, 599
Bronchodilator therapy, COPD, 586*t*, 586–587, 587*t*, 591
Bronchoscopy, fiberoptic, 608
Brown-Séquard syndrome, 1286
Bruits, 535, 538, 539
Brush-border enzyme activity, 670
Bulk laxatives, 1272
Bullous pemphigoid, 423
Bunion, 1299, *1299*
Bunionette, 1301, *1301*
Buprenorphine, 325
Buproprion, 1140
Burkitt's lymphoma, 766
Burnet's clonal selection theory, 69
Burns:
chemical, conjunctiva, 446
epidemiology, 141–142
prevention, 219
Bursitis, 948, 995–997
Burst-forming unit-erythroid (BFU-E), 733, 735
Buspirone (Buspar), 1139

C_{19}-steroids, 868–869
CAGE screening test, 1127
Calcitonin:
serum calcium regulation, 882–883, 899
therapy
osteoporosis, 906
Paget's disease, 932–933
Calcitriol, 927
Calcium acetate, 649
Calcium carbonate, 649
Calcium channel blockers:
acute MI, 519
cerebral infarction, 1030
hypertension, 550
Calcium chloride, 927
Calcium deficiency, bone loss and, *889*, *891*, 891, 893
Calcium metabolism:
hormonal regulation, 881–883, 882*t*
hyperparathyroidism, 923
normal, 879
organs of, *880*, 880–881
renal disease and, 649
Calcium pyrophosphate dihydrate crystal deposition disease (*see* Pyrophosphate gout)
Calcium supplementation:
age-related, 73
menopause and, 872
osteoporosis and, 905
Paget's disease, 933
prevention, hip fractures, 1325
Calculus, 433, 630
California Death with Dignity Act, 395
Caloric requirements, 334
Caloric restriction, 4, 5, *6*
Caloric testing, vestibular lesions, 469
Campylobacter pylori (*see Helicobacter pylori*)
Cancer:
aging and neoplasia, 79–81
bile ducts, 713
biologic behavior in elderly, 83
breast, 481–490
chemotherapy, 86–87
clinical presentation, 81–84, 83*t*
colorectal, 309, 726–730
cornea, 447
epidemiology, 147
esophageal, 312–313, 690–691, 1262
eye lids, 445
gallbladder, 712–713
gastric, 306–307, 701–702
hematologic, 756–759
hormonal therapy, 86–87
incidence, 77–78, *78*, *183*, 183
interstitial nephritis and, 646
lung, 312, 607–613
management, 84–87, *85*
oral, 436
pancreatic, 304, 719–720
preventive gerontology and, 188
prostate, 660–663
radiation therapy, 85–86
risk factors, 162–163, *163*
screening, 81–82, 82*t*, 216–218
spinal cord, 1286–1287
supportive care, 87
surgery, 85
thyroid, 821–822
vagina, 475
vulvar, 474–475

Cancer, female genital:
epidemiology, 476, 476*t*
screening for, 476–477
sexual dysfunction after treatment, 473–474
types, 477–478
Cancer pain syndrome, 321
Candidiasis:
cutaneous, 420–421
dentures and, 433, 436
esophagus, 689–690
oral, 388, 420–421, 433, 436
Capsulitis, adhesive, 1000
Captopril, 638
Carbamazepine:
adjuvant analgesia, 327
agitation, 1141
epileptic seizures, 1092
mood disorders, 1140
rapid-cycling depression, 1105
Carbidopa, 1058–1059
Carbohydrate absorption, small intestine, 671
Carboplatinum, 478
Carcinoembryonic antigen (CEA), 729
Carcinoma (*see* Cancer)
Cardiac complications, preoperative risk factors, 279, 281
Cardiac function, age-related, 499*t*, 499–500, *500*
Cardiac monitoring, ambulatory, 1173
Cardiac output:
age-related changes, 494
maximal, exercise and, 92
Cardiac rehabilitation, 353, 519–520
Cardiac Risk Index, 279, 279*t*
Cardiac surgery, 310–312
Cardiomyopathy:
dilated or congestive, 527–528
hypertrophic, 528
restrictive, 528
Cardiopulmonary resuscitation (CPR), 394 (*See also* "Do not resuscitate")
Cardiovascular disease:
autonomic dysfunction, SCI, 1293
epidemiology, 142–146
exercise, benefits of, 100
hypothyroidism, 815
sex differential in, 43
Cardiovascular function:
abnormal reflexes, syncope and, 1174–1175
β-adrenergic stimulation, 503–504
cardiac pump/myocardial contractile function, 498–499
dynamic exercise and, 502–503
failure, ischemic hepatic injury and, 710
heart rate/rhythm, 494–495
orthostatic stress, 501–502
physical work capacity, aging and, 504–505
preload or filling, 495–496
pressor stress, 502
at rest, structure and, 493–494, *494*, 499–500
stress response, 500–504
structure and, 497–498
Caregivers (*see* Family as caregivers; Nursing homes)
Caries, dental, 431, 432–433
Carmustine, 1100
Carotid endarterectomy, 539
Carotid sinus massage, 1175
Carotid sinus syndrome, 1174
Carpal tunnel syndrome, 1001, *1001*
Cascara, 1272
Castor oil, 1272
Castration:
benign prostatic hyperplasia and, 657
prostatic cancer and, 660, 663
Cataracts, 53–54, 442, 447–448
Catechol-*o*-methyltransferase (COMT), 1007
Catecholamines, neurotransmission and, 1007–1008
"Cathartic colon," 1247
Caval filters, 605, 784
CD T cells (cluster designation), 67
Cecal vascular ectasia, *307*
Celibacy, 115, 121
Cell culture, immune function and, 66
Cell-mediated immunity, 67
Center for Epidemiological Studies Depression Scale, 1202
Central auditory processing disorder (CAPD), 458
Central nervous system disorders:
dizziness and, 1168
hypernatremia and, 622
hyponatremia and, 621
hypothyroidism, 814
Central nervous system infections:
abscess
brain, 1076
epidural, 1076–1077
meningitis
bacterial, 1071–1073, 1073*t*
fungal, 1074–1075
tuberculous, 1074
meningoencephalitis, viral, 1073–1074
neurosyphilis, 1075
subdural empyema, 1076–1077
types, 1071–1073, 1072*t*
Central pontine myelinolysis (CPM), 621
Central sleep apnea, 1218, 1224
Central spinal cord syndrome, 1286
Cephalosporins:
drug-resistance organisms, 71
pneumonia, 568, 570
urinary tract infection, 629
Cerebral artery disease, screening, 216
Cerebral edema, 1187
Cerebral infarction, pharmacotherapy, 1029–1030
Cerebrospinal fluid, 577
Cerebrovascular disease (*See also* Stroke)
sex differential in, 42
surgery for, 313
vascular dementia, 1030–1031
Certified registered nurse anesthetists (CRNAs), 288
Cerumen glands, 459
Cervical cancer, 217, 476–477, 478
Cervical caries, 432
Cervical esophageal webs, 688
Cervical hypertrophic osteoarthropathy, 1263
Cervical intraepithelial neoplasia (CIN), 475
Cervical spondylosis, 1287
CHAMPUS, reimbursement structure, 252
Charcot-Marie-Tooth disease, 1288
Charting (*see* Documentation, medical)
Cheilectomy, 1300
Chemical dependence:
characteristics, 1125–1126
consequences, 1127–1128
definitions, 1125
detection, 1127
diagnostic criteria, 1125
drug treatment, 1128
opioids, 329, 386
psychosocial therapy, 1128–1129
screening, 1127
Chemical restraints (*see* Restraints, chemical/physical)
Chemotherapy:
brain tumors, 1099–1101
breast cancer, 485–488
colorectal cancer, 729
endometrial cancer, 477
female genital organ cancer, 476
Hodgkin's disease, 768
indications, 86–87
lung cancer, 611*t*, 611–612
multiple myeloma, 771
non-Hodgkin's lymphomas, 765–766
ovarian cancer, 477–478
platinum-based, 477–478
prostatic cancer, 663
Chenodeoxycholic acid, 711
Cherry angiomas, 418
Chest pain, esophageal disorders and, 688
Cheyne-Stokes respirations, 1222
Chlamydia pneumoniae, 569
Chlorambucil, 643
Chlordiazepoxide, 1128
Chlorpropamide, 281
Chlorthalidone, 933

Cholecystectomy, 303, 710
Cholecystitis, 711–712
Choledocholithiasis, 712
Cholelithiasis, 710–711
Cholera, 1277–1278
Cholesterol:
estrogen replacement therapy and, 44–46, 872–874
hearing loss and, 459
as risk factor, CHD, 158
sex differential, atherosclerosis, heart disease and, 42–46
triglyceride and relative body weight, *42*, 43
Cholestyramine, 819, 947
Choline acetyltransferase (CAT), 1008
Cholinergic hypothesis, Alzheimer's disease, 1044
Chondrocalcinosis (*see* Pyrophosphate gout)
Chondrocytes, 935, 937–940
Chondroitin sulfate, decrease in OA, 981
Chondrosarcoma, 930
Choroid:
aging of, 442
diseases of, 449
Chromolyn sodium, 593
Chronic bronchitis, 584–585
Chronic disease:
age-related statistics, 344*t*
surgical risk assessment and, 277–280
Chronic hepatitis, 709
Chronic interstitial nephritis, 645–646
Chronic lymphocytic leukemia (CLL), 752, 757–758
Chronic myelocytic leukemia (CML), 752, 756–757
Chronic neuropsychological impairments (CNI):
classification, 1119
coexisting medical conditions, 1120*t*, 1120–1122, 1122*t*
Down's syndrome, 1120
epidemiology, 1119
prevalence, 1119–1120
Chronic obstructive pulmonary disease (COPD):
bronchodilator therapy, 586*t*, 586–587, 587*t*
chronic bronchitis, 584–585
clinical assessment, 585
corticosteroids, 589–590
emphysema, 584
exacerbation/respiratory failure in, 590–591
exercise reconditioning, 588
grading, severity of FEV/FVC defects, 583*t*
immunization, 586
management, 585, *585*, 590–591
nutritional therapy, 587–598
oxygen therapy, 588–589, *590*
prognosis, 583–584, 591
pulmonary function test pattern, 560
rehabilitation, 588
risk factors, 583, *584*
survival rates, *589*
therapeutic considerations, 561–563
Chronic renal failure:
acid-base status, 649
anemia of, 650
calcium and phosphorus metabolism, 649
dialysis, indications for, 650
dietary protein intake, 650
drug dosages, 650
potassium homeostasis, 648–649
sodium and water, 648
vitamins, 650
Chvostek sign, 927
Ciliary neurotrophic factor, 1067
Cimetidine, 264, 645
Ciprofloxacin, 631
Circadian rhythms, 1104, 1217–1218
Circulating neutrophil pool (CNP), 753
Circulatory system (*see* Cardiovascular function)
Cirrhosis, 709–710
Cisplatin:
endometrial cancer, 477
lung cancer, 611, 612
malignant gliomas, 1100
Civilian Health and Medical Program of the Uniformed Service (CHAMPUS), 252
Claudication, intermittent, 956–957
Clavus (soft corn), 1304, *1304*
Claw toe, 1300–1301
Clean-catch midstream urine specimens, 628
Clearance, pharmacokinetics and, 261–264
Climacteric, female (*see* Menopause)
Climacteric, male, 118
Clindamycin, 568
Clinical management (*See also* Geriatric assessment)
case study, 199–200
clinical differences, young and old people, 195–196
clinical perspective, changes in, 197–198
function, importance of, 199
physical examination, 200–201
presentation of illness in, 196–197
Clinical pharmacology:
adverse drug effects, 270
drug development/approval process, *271*, 271–272
pharmacodynamics, 265–270
pharmacokinetics, 259–265
Clonal senescence, focal, atherogenesis and, 512
Clonazepam, 1140
Clonidine, 281
Closed urinary catheter system, 626, 631
Clostridium difficile, 1278
Clotrimazole, 421
Cluster designation of T cells, 67
Coagulation cascade, 775–776, *776*
Coarctation of the aorta, 522
Cochlear conductive presbycusis, 460
Cockcroft formula, 617
Codman's exercises, 999
Cognitive-behavioral therapy, 1108
Cognitive Capacity Screening Examination, 206
Cognitive impairment (*See also* Alzheimer's disease)
assessment, 205–207, 224, 225–227, 246
attention, 1012–1014
conceptualization, 1016
delirium, 1197–1198
dementia, 1198–1200
focal cognitive syndromes, 1200–1201
as function of aging, 180–181, 1016–1017
general intelligence, 1016
global disorder of, 1022
language, 1014
memory, 1014–1015
mental retardation, 1201
nutritional aspects, 53, 53*t*
Parkinson's, 1055
as risk factor, falls, 1314
schizophrenia, 1201
studies of, methodology, 1013
visuospatial ability, 1015
Colace, 1272
Colchicine, 989, 990
Cold agglutinin disease, 788
"Cold" thyroid nodules, 819
Colectomy, 308, 726
Colestipol, 819
Collagen, 936, 942–943
Collagen vascular disorders, 600
Colon cancer, screening, 217
Colonic disorders:
colorectal cancer, 726–730
diverticular disease, 723–726
Colonic function, age-related, 672
Colonic motility, 1269
Colonic transit time, 672, 1269
Colonoscopy:
colorectal cancer, 727, 728, 729–730
diverticular disease, 726
indications, 1269
Colony forming unit-culture (CFU-C), 733, 735

Colony forming unit-erythroid (CFU-E), 733, 735
Colony forming unit-granulocyte/macrophage (CFU-GM), 733
Colony forming unit-spleen (CFU-S), 733, 734, *734*
Colorectal cancer:
  clinical features, 728
  epidemiology, 726–728
  pathogenesis, 726–728
  screening, 729–730
  surgery, 309
  treatment, 309, 728–729
Colostomy, diverticular disease and, 725–726
Colyte, 1273
Coma, myxedema, 816
Communication, hearing loss and, 458, 467*t*
Community (*see* Long-term care, community based)
Compensated incontinence, defined, 246
Competency:
  defined, 222, 392
  ethical aspects, 406
  legal aspects, 391–392
Complex partial seizures, 1089
Comprehensive geriatric assessment (CGA), 244*t*, 244–245 (*See also* Geriatric assessment)
Comprehensive Older Persons' Evaluation (COPE) scale, 209
Compulsions, defined, 224
Computer tomography (CT):
  bone mass measurement, 900, 901–902
  brain tumors, 1097
  chronic subdural hematoma, 1081–1082, *1082*
  Paget's disease, 931
  pelvic, prostatic cancer, 662
  vestibular dysfunction, 469
Conceptualization, impairment of, 1016, *1016*
Condom urinary catheters, 632
Conduction, neuronal, 1007–1009
Conduction system disease:
  syncope and, 1173
  types, 1173
Conductive hearing loss, 463–464, *464*
Condyloma acuminatum, 421
Confusion, acute, 284, 1021–1025
Congenital heart disease, 521–522
Congestive cardiomyopathy, 527–528
Congestive heart failure:
  diagnosis, 526
  differential diagnosis, 526
  epidemiology, 145, *146*
  management, 527
  postoperative risk factors, 282
Congregate housing, defined, 381
Conjunctiva:
  aging of, 441
  diseases of, 445–446
Conjunctivitis, 446
Conn's syndrome, 802
Conscientiousness, personality trait, 108
Consciousness:
  disorders of, 1023
  loss of, 1082–1083
Conservatorship, legal aspects, 393
Constipation:
  associated factors, 1268
  autonomic dysfunction, SCI, 328
  colorectal cancer and, 728
  complications, 1269–1270
  defined, 1267
  dietary prevention, 1271
  diverticular disease and, 724
  endoscopic/radiographic studies, 1269
  etiology, 1246*t*
  evaluation, 1268, *1270*
  history, 1268
  hypokalemia and, 622
  medications as cause of, 328–329, 1267, 1268*t*
  physical examination, 1268–1269
  treatment, 388, 1247*t*, 1270–1273
Contact dermatitis, 416
Continence (*see* Incontinence)
Continuing-care retirement communities, 255–256, 380
Continuous ambulatory peritoneal dialysis (CAPD), 652
Continuous arteriovenous rewarming (CAVR), 1193
Convulsions (*see* Seizures)
Convulsive status epilepticus, 1091–1092
Coomb's test, 746
COOP Chart, 209
COPD (*see* Chronic obstructive pulmonary disease (COPD))
Core rewarming, hypothermia and, 1193
Cornea:
  aging of, 441
  diseases of, 446–447
Cornea guttata, 447
Cornell Scale, 207
Corns, soft (clavus), 1304
Coronal caries, 432
Coronary artery bypass surgery:
  incidence, 310–311
  indications, 520–521
  mortality, 281, 311*t*
Coronary artery disease:
  acute MI, 518–520
  angina pectoris, 517–518
  diabetes mellitus and, 835
  epidemiology, 142–143, *143*, 143*t*, *860*
  estrogen replacement therapy and, 872–874, *873*, 873*t*
  hyperlipidemia, *863*, *865*
  hypertension, 543, 547
  occult, identifying, 279*t*
  risk factors, 157–161, 158*t*, 543
  screening, 215–216
  sex differential in, 42–46
  sex mortality rates, 41–42, *860*, *862*
  treatment, 520–521
  type A behavior pattern, effect of, 111
Corporate-sponsored health care programs, 380
Cortical bone, 883, *883*
Cortical dementia, 1198–1199
Corticosteroids:
  asthma, 593, 593*t*
  brain tumors, 1098–1099
  COPD, 589–590, 591
  giant cell arteritis, 958
  glomerulonephritis, 642
  neutrophilia, as cause of, 751
  ophthalmopathy of, 456
  polymyalgia rheumatica, 958
  preoperative management, 281
  tuberculosis, extrapulmonary, 580
Corticotropin-releasing hormone (CRH), 793
Cortisol, 793–794
"Cotton-wool" appearance (skull), Paget's disease, 930
Cotton-wool spots, 449, 453
Cough:
  management, 387
  reflex, 558–559
  syncope, 1174–1175
Coumadin, 570, 947
Countertransference, defined, 1142
Coupling, bone formation/resorption, 889, *889*, 889–891
Courvoisier's sign, 720
CPR (*see* Cardiopulmonary resuscitation (CPR))
Creatinine, serum, 650
Creatinine clearance:
  glomerular filtration rate and, 616–617
  pharmacokinetics and, 261–262, *262*
Creatinine concentration, 646
Creatinine-height index, 282
CREST variant, rheumatic disease, 972, 976
Creutzfeldt-Jakob disease, 29
Crocodile shagreen, 441
Cryoprecipitate, 779, 782
Cryoproteinemia, 788
Cryptococcal meningitis, 1074–1075
CSAT monoclonal antibody, 941
Cupulolithiasis of aging, 470

Cushing's disease, 801–802, 897, 902
Cutaneous disorders (*see* Skin disorders)
Cutaneous hypersensitivity vasculitis, 640
Cutaneous T-cell lymphoma, 427
Cyanotic heart disease, 522
Cyclophosphamide:
  breast cancer, 487
  lung cancer, 612
  renal disease, 642, 643
Cyclophosphamine:
  polyarteritis nodosa, 640
Cyclosporine A, 652
Cycloxygenase, 947
Cyklocapron, 781
Cystitis, 118, 626
Cystocele, 475
Cystoid macular edema, 448
Cystometrograms, 659, 1235, 1293
Cystourethroscopy, 659
Cytokines, 63, 64*t*, 71
Cytomel, 1109
Cytotoxic-suppressor T cells, 62–64, 67

Day care, adult, 379–380
DDAVP administration, 779
Death and dying (*See also* Dying patient, care of; Suicide)
  family bereavement, 389–390
  home care, 390
Decubitus ulcers (*see* Pressure ulcers)
Deep-breathing maneuvers, 282
Deep vein thrombosis:
  prevention, 282
  risk factors, 295
Defecation (*See also* Fecal incontinence)
  mechanism, failure of, 1268, 1269
  normal function, 672
  syncope, 1174–1175
Defense mechanisms, 1142
Dehydration (*See also* Diarrhea)
  decreased fluid intake, 1186
  hypernatremia and, 621–622, 1184*t*
  increased fluid losses, 1184–1186
  predisposing factors, 1184
  treatment, 1186–1187
Deinstitutionalization, CNI and, 1120
Delayed hypersensitivity reactions, 67, 577
Delayed traumatic intracerebral hematoma, 1081
Deliberate thyroid ablation, 812
Delirium:
  Alzheimer's disease, 1038
  anticipated outcomes, 255*t*
  clinical features, 1021–1023
  defined, 1021, 1197
  diagnosis, 1024–1025, 1197–1198
  differential diagnosis, 1024–1025
  epidemiology, 1197
  etiology, 1023–1024
  frequency, 1021
  laboratory tests, 1198
  management, 1025
  pathogenesis, 1024
  postoperative, 284
  treatment, 1141–1142, 1198
Delirium tremens, 1023, 1197
Delusional (paranoid) disorder, 1111–1116
Delusions:
  Alzheimer's disease, 1036
  assessment, 223–224
  defined, 1022
  delirium and, 1197
  paraphrenia, 1113–1114
  treatment, 1140–1141
Dementia:
  assessment, 205
  defined, 1198–1199
  diagnosis, 207, 1199
  diagnostic tests, 239*t*
  dialysis and, 651
  epidemiology, 148
  hypothyroidism, 814
  prognosis, 1200
  rehabilitation, 352–353
  sleep apnea and, 1220
  treatment, 1199–1200
  vascular, 1030–1031
Dementia praecox, 1111
Dementia Rating Scale, 207
Demographics:
  health and elderly, 135, *136*
  life expectancy, 177–179
Denial, as defense mechanism, 1142
Dental care, utilization of, 433
Dental caries, 431, 432
Dental plaque, 432–433
Dental status of adults, demographics, 432*t*
Dentition, 431–432
Dentures, 433, 436, 1120
Deontological principles, defined, 399
Dependent personality disorder, 1134
Depression:
  assessment, 207
  course/prognosis, 1108
  diagnosis, 1105*t*, 1105–1107
  differential diagnosis, 1105–1107, 1106*t*
  dying patient, 388
  epidemiology, 148, 1103–1104
  etiology, 1104–1105
  hearing loss and, 458
  laboratory studies, 1107, 1107*t*
  major, 1202–1203
  management, clinical, 1108–1110
  minor, syndromes of, 1202
  Parkinson's, 1060
  personality stability and, 110
  secondary/symptomatic, 1203
  sleep apnea and, 1220
  treatment, 1109*t*, 1139–1140
  underreporting of illness and, 197
Dermatitis:
  contact, 416
  seborrheic, 422–423
  stasis, venous ulcers, 415–416
Dermatomyositis, 961–964
Dermatoses, inflammatory, 415–418
Dermis, components, 412–414, *413*
Desipramine, 1108, 1140
Desyrel, 1140
Detoxification, 1128
Detrusor hyperreflexia, defined, 1230, 1293
Detrusor motor instability, defined, 1230
Di Guglielmo's syndrome, 746
Diabetes:
  atherosclerosis and, 511, 513–514
  epidemiology, 146–147
  foot care, 1305–1306
  ophthalmopathy, 453–454, *454*
  peripheral vascular disease and, 535, 536–537
  as risk factor, stroke, 162
  urinary tract infections and, 627
Diabetes insipidus, 1185
Diabetes mellitus:
  classification, 832–834
  clinical manifestations, 836*t*
  complications, 834–838, 837*t*
  diagnostic criteria, 829–832, *831*
  drug interaction/glucose tolerance, 832*t*
  epidemiology, 829
  exercise and, 102
  implications, 833–834
  incidence, 826*t*
  management
    dietary, 840, 841
    drug therapy, 841–843, 842*t*
    exercise, 840–841
    general, 838–840, 841*t*
  metabolic defect of, 828–829
  normal glucose metabolism, 825–826, *827*
  pathophysiology, 751
  secondary impotence, 1252–1253
  signs/symptoms, 828*t*
Diabetic ketoacidosis (DKA), 837–839
Diabetic retinopathy, 834–835
Diagnosis-related groups (DRGs), 169, 400
Diagnostic intracorporeal vasodilator injection, 1255–1256
Diagnostic tests:
  characteristics/definitions, *237*
  dementia, 239*t*
  performance, features of, 236–237
  predictive value

Diagnostic tests (*Cont.*)
calculation, 237
prevalence and, 238
purpose, 235–236
results, relationship with disease occurrence, *237*
selection, guidelines, 236*t*
selection, new tests, 238–239
technology assessment, principles of, 238
Dialysis:
dementia of, 651
hemodialysis, 651–652
indications, 650
peritoneal, 652
Diaper dermatitis, 416
Diarrhea:
colorectal cancer and, 728
diverticular disease and, 724
etiology, 1277*t*, 1277–1278
host factors, 1279–1280
hyponatremia and, 621
mechanisms, 1278–1279
morbidity/mortality, 1275, *1275*
NSAIDs and, 950
nutritional support and, 338
prevention, 1282–1283
salt losses with, 620
treatment, 1280–1282
volume depletion, 1276
Diarthrodial joint:
articular cartilage, 935–937, 937–940
meniscus, 941
synovial fluid, 941
synovial membrane, 940–941
Diastolic blood pressure, 541, 542–543
Diazepam, 1092
Diclofenac, 947, 951
Didronel, 926, 932–933
Diet (*See also* Nutritional assessment)
colorectal cancer and, 727–728
constipation and, 1271
diabetic, 840, 841
immune response and, 73
as risk factor, cancer, 162–163
Diethylstilbestrol (DES), 663
Differential blood count, 750
Diffuse goiter, 819
Diffuse mixed lymphomas, 765
Diffusion, alveolar, 557
Digestive function, age-related, 666*t*
Digitalis, 570, 623
Digoxin, 620, 650
Dihydrotestosterone (DHT), 657
Dilantin, 1168
Dilated cardiomyopathy, 527–528
Dilaudid, 386
Diminished-supply neutropenia, 754–755
Dioctyl sodium sulfosuccinate, 1272
Diphosphonates, 932–933
Diplopia, 455–456
Dipyridamole, 788, 1029
Disability:
classification, WHO, 271, 343, *1309*
defined, 203, 222
exercise and, 96–98
rating scales, 222–223
risk factors, epidemiologic aspects, 153–164
severe, age-related causes, 345*t*
Disability rates, 137–138, *141*, 142*t*
Disk edema, 451
Disodium etidronate, 926, 932–933
Disorders of excessive somnolence (DOES), 1216, 1217
Disorders of initiating and maintaining sleep (DIMS), 1216–1217
Disorientation, time/place/person, 1022
Disseminated intravascular coagulation (DIC), 644–645, 780–781, 781*t*, 787–788
Disseminated tuberculosis, 577
Distribution, pharmacokinetics and, 260–261
Disulfiram, 1128
Diuretics:
as cause of incontinence, 1231–1232
dehydration and, 1184–1185
drug interactions, NSAIDs, 947
hypercalcemia and, 1031
hypertension, 549
ototoxicity, 1168
potassium metabolism and, 623
preoperative management, 281
sodium metabolism and, 621, 1188
Diverticular disease:
clinical features
bleeding, 726
diverticulitis, 724–726
symptomatic diverticular disease, 724
defined, 723
epidemiology, 723–724
esophageal, 689
pathogenesis, 723–724
Diverticulitis:
clinical features, 724
defined, 723
diagnosis, 724–725
surgery for, *308*, 308–309
treatment, 725–726
Diverticulosis, 723, 724
Dizziness:
age/disease-related changes, 1166
categories, 1165
epidemiology, 1165
etiology, 1166*t*, 1166–1168
evaluation, 468–470, 1168–1170, *1169*
pathophysiology, 1165–1166
treatment, 1170–1171
"Do not resuscitate" (DNR) orders:
anesthesia-related issues, 297
dying patient, 384
ethical aspects, 403*t*, 403–405
legal aspects, 394, 395
Documentation, medical, 364–365, *366*
Dopamine, neurotransmission and, 791–792, 1007–1009
Doppler sonography, 783
"Dowager's hump" deformity, 900
Down's syndrome:
genetics of, 25
maternal age and, 31
neuropathology, similarities with Alzheimer's, 26, 1120, 1201
Doxepin, 1108, 1140
Doxorubicin:
breast cancer, 487
endometrial cancer, 477
lung cancer, 611, 612
Driving, automobile, 141, 219, 392, 1200
Drop attacks, TIAs and, 1027
"Drop fingers," 969
Drug eruptions, skin, 417*t*, 417–418
Drugs (*see* Medications)
Dry mouth (xerostomia), 434
Dual-energy x-ray absorptiometry (DEXA), 900, 901–902
Dual-photon absorptiometry (DPA), 900, 901–902
Ducolax, 1272
Ductal carcinoma in situ, 484
Duke's staging, colorectal cancer, 727, 729
Duodenal disorders, 693
Duodenal ulcers, 304–305, 305*t*, 950
Duplex scanning, penile arteries, 1256
Durable powers of attorney, 393–394, 403, 406
Dying patient, care of (*See also* Death and dying)
assessment, 384–385
decision making, 384–385
family, bereavement and, 389–390
gastrointestinal problems, 387–388
genitourinary tract, 389
home care, 390
medications, 385
mental status changes, 388
pain relief, 385–386
pulmonary symptoms, 387
seizures, 389
skin care, 388–389
Dynamic exercise stress, cardiovascular response, 502–503
Dynamic orthoses, 1292
Dyschezia, defined, 1268
Dysequilibrium, defined, 1165
Dysfibrinogenemia, 782
Dyslipidemia, exercise and, 99

Dyslipoproteinemia:
aging and, 858*t*–859*t*
defined, 855
hyperlipidemia, 862–864
hypocholesterolemia, 861–862
lipoprotein metabolism, 855–857
Dyspareunia, 118
Dysphagia:
causes, 962
classification, 1259
clinical features, 1259
diagnosis, *1260*, 1264
esophageal, 1261–1262
gastroesophageal reflux, 1263
mechanical obstruction, 1262–1264
medication-induced esophageal injury, 1264
neuromuscular (motility) disorders, 1263
oropharyngeal, 1259–1261
Dysphagia lusoria, 1262
Dyspnea, treatment, 387
Dysuria, 627

Eaton-Lambert syndrome, 608
Ebstein's disease, 522
Ecchymoses, 779
Eccrine glands, 414
Edema, body sodium and, 620, 621
Ego, defined, 107
Ejaculation, 1251, 1253
Ejection fraction, 498
Elder abuse, legal aspects, 392–393
Elder housing, 381
Elderly:
demographics, 177*t*, 177–179, *178*
income levels, 131*t*
Electrical heart disease, syncope and, 1173–1174
Electrocardiography (EKG):
abnormalities, epidemiology, 143, 143*t*
monitoring, postoperatively, 284
syncope and, 1175–1176
Electrocochleography (ECoG), 463
Electroconvulsive therapy (ECT):
depression, 1105, 1108, 1109–1110, 1140, 1203
paraphrenia, 1114, 1115
Electroencephalogram (EEG):
Alzheimer's disease, 1039
delirium, 1024, 1198
seizures, 1090
syndromes of altered mental state, 227
Electrolyte disorders (*see* Fluid-electrolyte disorders)
Electromyography (EMG), 963
Electronystagmography (ENG), 469
Elimination half-life, pharmacokinetics and, 264–265
ELISA (*see* Enzyme-linked immunosorbent assay (ELISA))
E_{max} model, pharmacodynamics, 265, 267
Embolectomy, 639
Embolism:
arterial occlusion, 533–534
prevention, 784
pulmonary, 604–605
Emergency care:
diabetic metabolic disorders, 836–838
hyperthermia, 1194
hypothermia, 1192–1193
Emollient laxatives, 1272
Emotional syndromes (*see* Mood disorders)
Emphysema, 584
Encephalitis, 1071–1073
Encephalopathy, spongiform, 29–30
End-diastolic volume index (EDVI), *495*, 495–496, 498, 499–500
End-stage renal disease:
clinical presentation, 651
hemodialysis, 651–652
incidence, 650–651
peritoneal dialysis, 652
transplantation, 652
End-systolic volume (ESV), 498
Endarterectomy, 313
Endocarditis:
infective, 584
postoperative risk factors, 282, 283*t*
Endocrine disorders:
adrenal, 801–802
hypothalamic-pituitary, 799–801
testicular, 801
Endocrine system:
female, menopause and, 867–869, *868*, 869*t*
growth hormone axis, 794–797, *795*
hypothalamic-pituitary-adrenal axis, *792*, 792–794
hypothalamic-pituitary-testicular axis, 797–799, *798*
neurotransmitter regulation, 791–792, *792*
Endometrial cancer:
estrogen, exogenous and, 46, 874
management, 477
Endoscopic retrograde cholangiopancreatography (ERCP), 707, 717
Endoscopy:
colorectal cancer, 727, 729–730
esophagus, 684–685
Endurance exercise, physiology of, 91–94
Enemas, 1272
Energy requirements/expenditures, 337*t*
Enophthalmos, 441
Enteral alimentation:
feeding products, choice of, 335–336, 336*t*
long-term routes, 336
short-term routes, 335
Enterobacter, 627
Enterococcus, 629
Entrapment neuropathies, 1000–1002
Entropion/ectropion, senile, 441
Environmental control/manipulation:
nursing home care and, 370
rehabilitative therapy and, 1291, 1310
Environmental hazards:
as risk factor, falls, 1314–1315, 1317–1318, 1319
Enzyme-linked immunosorbent assay (ELISA), 62, 709
Eosinophilia, 752
Eosinophils:
decreased, significance of, 756
function, 749
increased, significance of, 752
Epidemiological Studies Depression Scale, 207
Epidemiology of aging:
Alzheimer's disease, 148
arthritis, 142
automobile crashes, 141
burns, 141–142
cancer, 147
cardiovascular disease, 142–146
dementia, 148
depression, 148
diabetes, 146–147
disability, 137–138
falls, 138
fractures, 138
genital organ cancer, female, 476
health habits and, 148–149
hypertension, 146
incontinence, 142
influenza, 147
morbidity/mortality, 135–137
non-fall injury, 138, 141
osteoporosis, 138
Parkinson's disease, 148
pneumonia, 147
study of, challenges to, 149–150
suicide, 141
Epidermis, components, 412, *413*
Epidermolysis esophagus, 691
Epidural abscess, 1076–1077
Epidural anesthesia, 293–294
Epidural hematoma, 1081
Epilepsy:
myoclonic, ragged red fibers and, 30
status epilepticus, 1091–1092
Epileptic seizures:
classification, 1089
etiology, 1089–1090
evaluation, 1090

Epileptic seizures (*Cont.*)
incidence, 1089
treatment, 1090–1091, 1092
Epinephrine, neurotransmission and, 1007–1008
Epiphenomena of gene action, defined, 19
Epiphora, 441
Epistaxis, 779
Epitope, defined, 63
Epsilon aminocaproic acid (EACA, Amicar), 781
Epstein-Barr virus, 766
Erection, penile:
dysfunction, 1251–1257
mechanisms of, 1253–1254
"Error catastrophe" model of aging, 7
Erysipelas (St. Anthony's fire), 421
Erythema craquelé, 415
Erythema multiforme, 417–418
Erythrocyte sedimentation rate (ESR), 966, *966*
Erythroid stem cells, 733
Erythromycin, 568, 569, 570
Erythroplasia of Queyrat, 426
Erythropoiesis, 735, *736*, 745–746
Erythropoietin, 650, 735
Escherichia coli, 626, 627, 629
Esophageal cancer, 312–313, 690–691
Esophageal disorders:
diverticula, 689
gastroesophageal reflux disease, 683–687
infections, 689–690
Mallory-Weiss syndrome, 689
medication-induced injury, 690
motor disorders, 687*t*, 687–688
rings and webs, 688–689
Esophageal dysphagia, 1261–1262
Esophageal function, age-related, 665–667
Esophageal manometry, 685
Esophageal pH monitoring, 24-hour, 685
Esophageal (Schatzki) ring, lower, 688–689
Esophageal spasm, 688, 1263
Essential tremor, 1056
Estrogen:
intravaginal, 626, 632
libido and, 117
lipoprotein metabolism, 44–46, *45*, 857, 860
secretion, menopause and, 867–869
therapy, prostatic cancer, 660
topical, 473
Estrogen deficiency, osteoporosis and, *889*, 889–891, *890*, 899
Estrogen replacement therapy:
cardioprotective effects of, 872*t*, 872–874
contraindications/precautions, 874–875, 875*t*
coronary heart disease and, 161
endometrial cancer and, 477
osteoporosis and, 870–872, *872*, 906
regimens for, 875, 875*t*
Ethacrinic acid, 648
Ethambutol (EMB), 578–580, 581
Ethical issues:
guiding principles, 398–399
informed consent, 399–400
institutional setting, challenges of, 406
life-support systems, withholding/withdrawing, 401–406, 405*t*
artificial hydration/nutrition, 405–406
CPR and DNR orders, 397–399, 403*t*
general recommendations, 402–403
medical resources, equitable distribution of, 400
mental incapacitation, 406
moral dilemmas, reasoning about, 398–399
nursing home care, 371, 372*t*
physician values: old age/quality of life, 401
problems in geriatrics and, 397–398
suggestions, 406–407
Ethosuximide, 1091
Etidronate disodium, 926, 932–933
Etodolac, 947
Etoposide, 612
Euthanasia, 384, 395, 402–403
Euthyroid hyperthyroxinemia, 811
Euthyroid sick syndrome, 811, 816, 817–818
Exercise:
benefits of
arthritis, 100–101
atherosclerotic cardiovascular disease, 100
constipation, 1271
COPD, 588
coronary heart disease, 160
diabetes, 840–841
dyslipidemia, 99
hypertension, 99–100
osteoarthritis, 891–892
osteoporosis, 101, 891–892, *950*
Parkinson's, 1060–1061
rheumatoid arthritis, 969
cardiovascular response, 92–94, *93*, 502–503
functional status and, 96–98, *97*
insulin resistance/glucose intolerance, *98*, 98–99
physiologic effect, strength training, 95–96
prevalence of, 148
risks, 101–102
skeletal muscle strength, 94–95, 941–942
tendon, 942–943
Exercise capacity, aging and, 91–94, *93*, 504–505, 558
Exercise programs:
osteoarthritis, 984
post-MI, 520
recommendations, 102, 218
rotator cuff tendinitis, 999, *999*
Exophthalmos, 443, 810
External ear, hearing loss and, 459
External vacuum devices, penile, 1256
Extracellular fluid, sodium handling and, 620
Extracranial arterial disease, 538–539
Extramedullary tumors, 1287
Extrapulmonary tuberculosis, 580–581
Extraversion, personality trait, 107–108
Eye (*See also* Ocular diseases)
aging, physiology of, 441–442
clinical evaluation, 442–443, 453*t*
Eyeglass hearing aids, 465

Fabry's disease, 418
Facet joints, 943
Factor IX, 775, 778
Factor VIII, 775, 778
Failure to thrive:
defined, 1152, 1205–1206
etiology, 1152–1154, *1154*, 1209*t*, 1209–1210
geriatric paradigm, 1209
pathophysiology, 1208–1209
treatment, 1153–1154, 1210
trigger model, *1206*
weight loss, 1206–1208, *1207*
Fainting (*see* Syncope)
Fairley washout technique, 629
Falls:
as cause of hip fractures, 1325–1327
institutionalized persons, 1318–1319
morbidity, 1313–1314, 1318
osteoporosis, 138
prevalence, 1313, 1318
prevention, 219, 351, 1315*t*, 1315–1318, 1316*t*, 1319
risk factors, 163–164, 182–183, 1065, 1314, 1315*t*, 1318–1319
types/protective responses, *1324*
Familial Alzheimer's disease, 27–29, 28*t*
Familial cervical lipodysplasia, 26
Familial dyslipidemic hypertension, 857
Familial hypercholesterolemia, 26–27
Familial hypocalciuria hypercalcemia (FHH), 925

Family as caregivers:
availability of, 229–230, 230, 357, 375–376
dementia, 1200
emotional/physical/economic aspects, 232
impact of chemical dependence, 1129
preoperative management and, 280
role of, 230–231, 376–377
support for, 232–233, 347, 380
Family therapy, 1108, 1110, 1143
Famotidine, 264
Fast-twitch muscle fibers, 95, 942
Fasting plasma glucose concentration, 830
Fat, dietary, as cancer risk factor, 163
Fat absorption, small intestine, 671
Fat free mass (FFM), 92, 94
Fatal familial insomnia, 30
Feasibility Scale for Predicting Hearing Aid Use, 466–467
Fecal impaction, 622, 1231, 1269
Fecal incontinence:
anorectal function, age-related, 673
autonomic dysfunction, SCI, 1294
causes, 1246–1247
epidemiology, 142
Felty's syndrome, 754
Fentanyl, 386
Fetal tissue transplantation, 73, 1060
Fever of undetermined origin (FUO), 1159
Fiber, dietary:
anorectal function and, *673*
bowel function and, 1268, 1271
colorectal cancer and, 73, 723, 727
diverticular disease and, 725
sources, 1271*t*
Fiberoptic bronchoscopy, 608
Fibrin, 776
Fibrinogen, 776, 782
Fibrinolytic system, 777, 777
Fibrosarcoma, 930
Filling, left ventricular, 495–496, *496*, 500
Filters, caval, 605, 784
Financial abuse of elderly, 393
Finasteride, 659
Fistulas, diverticular disease and, 724
Fitness, functional status and, *97*, 97–98
Five-factor model, personality traits, 107–108
5-hydroxyindoleacetic acid (5-HIAA), neurotransmission and, 1104
Fixed drug reactions, 417
Fixed resistance exercise, 96
Flashes, ocular, 442, 450–451
Fleet's enema, 1272
Floaters, ocular, 442, 450–451
Fluconazole, 1075
Fludrocortisone, 1065
Fluid-electrolyte disorders:
age-related changes, 1183–1184
dehydration, 1184–1187, 1185*t*
hyponatremia, 1187*t*, 1187–1189
hypothyroidism, 815–816
potassium, 622–623
sodium, 620–622
water metabolism, 621–622
Fluid intake (*See also* Oral rehydration therapy)
decreased, causes of, 1185*t*, 1186
forcing, 632
Fluid loss (*See also* Diarrhea)
calculation of, 1186
increased, causes of, 1184–1186, 1185*t*
Fluid replacement (*see* Oral rehydration therapy)
Fluoride administration, 906–907
Fluoroquinolones, 630, 631
Fluorouracil, 487
Fluoxetine, 1108, 1140
Fluphenazine, 1141
Focal calcific arteriosclerosis, 510
Focal cognitive syndromes, 1200–1201
Folate deficiency, 650, 745–746
Folic acid deficiency, 754–755
Follicle-stimulating hormone (FSH), 797–799, 868
Food (*see* Nutrition)
Food and Drug Administration (FDA), 271–272
Food poisoning, 1277
Foot care, 1297, 1305–1306
Foot drop, 1292
Foot problems:
diabetes, foot care and, 1305–1306, *1306*
heel pain, 1297–1298, *1298*
metatarsalgia, 1301–1303, *1302*
prevention, 1297
soft parts, 1304, *1304*
toe deformities, *1299*, 1299–1301, *1300, 1301*
toe nails, 1305, *1305*
Forced expiratory volume (FEV), 583*t*, 583–584
Forced vital capacity (FVC), 583
Forcing fluids, urinary tract infection and, 632
Foster homes, 381
Foster-Kennedy syndrome, 451
Fractures (*See also* Hip fractures; Vertebral compression fractures)
osteoporosis and, 138, *871*, 900, 902–903
risk factors, 163–164
Frailty:
as clinical syndrome, 1150
defined, 96, 1149–1150
etiology, 1152–1154
modal pathway, *1151*
risk factors, *214*
stages, 1151–1152
treatment, 1153–1154
Frailty, acute hospital care and:
cascade of illness, 243
complications, development of, *243*, *244*
defined, 241–242
functional decline, prevention of, 245–246
quality of care, improving, 244–245
treatment/environment, description of, 242–243
"Free radical" theory of aging, 8
Free T_4 (FT_4), 807–808, 810–811
Free thyroxine index (FT_4 index), 807–808, 810–811, 816–817
Fresh-frozen plasma preparations, 71
Friction, pressure ulcers and, 1330–1331
Frozen shoulder, 1000
Function:
importance of, 196, 199, 200, 232
preventing loss of, 214*t*
promoting health and, 213–220
Functional Assessment Instrument (FAI), 209
Functional impairment:
assessment, 206*t*, 208–209, 280, 345
exercise and, 96–98
as operative risk, 280
Functional residual capacity, 555–557
Functional Status Questionnaire, 209
Functional urinary incontinence, 1233
Fundal gastritis, 694–695
Fungal meningitis, 1074–1075
Fungating tumors, 389
Furosemide, 621, 648

G-CSF (*see* Granulocyte colony stimulating factor (G-CSF))
G proteins (guanine nucleotide-binding regulatory), 68
Gait:
evaluation, 208*t*, 1316*t*, 1317
as risk factor, hip fracture, 1324
Gallbladder disease:
adenocarcinoma, 712–713
cholecystitis, 711–712
choledocholithiasis, 712
cholelithiasis, 710–711
estrogen replacement therapy and, 874
gallstones, 302–303
jaundice and, 707
Gallbladder function, age-related, 674–677, *733*

Gallium 67 uptake:
lung scans, 599
Paget's disease, 931
Gallstone pancreatitis, 718
Gallstones:
dissolution, 711
formation, 710–711
treatment, surgical, 302–303, *303*
Gamma aminobutyric acid (GABA):
neurotransmission and, 1008
spasticity, 1292
Gamma benzene hexachloride (Lindane, Kwell), 419
Gangrene, 537
Gardner's syndrome, 727
Gastrectomy, 306–307
Gastric acid output, 668
Gastric cancer, 306–307
Gastric emptying, *667*, 667–668, *668*, 698–700
Gastric neoplasms, 701–702
Gastric stasis syndromes, 699
Gastric ulcers, treatment, 305–306, *306*
Gastritis:
acute, 694
chronic, 694–696
classification, 694*t*
hypertrophic, 696
Gastroduodenal function, age-related, 667–669
Gastroesophageal reflux disease:
complications, 686–687
diagnosis, 684–685
pathophysiology, 683
symptoms, 683, *684*, 1263
treatment, 685–686
Gastrointestinal bleeding, 700–701
Gastrointestinal disorders (*See also* Stomach disorders)
duodenal, 693
fluid losses of, 1185–1186
hypothyroidism, 815
potassium deficiency and, 622
sodium depletion and, 620
Gastrointestinal system:
anorectal function, 672–673
colonic function, 672
digestion, age-related changes, 666*t*
gastroduodenal function, 667–669
hepatobiliary function, 674–677
pancreatic function, 673–674
pharyngoesophageal function, 665–667
small intestinal function, 669–671
Gastrointestinal toxicity, NSAIDs, 950
Gastroparesis, 699
Gaviscon, 685
Gene transfer, viral-mediated, 73
General Health Questionnaire (GHQ), 225, 1202
Generalized seizures, 1089
Genetics:
aging and, 22–23
Alzheimer's disease, 1041
antigeroid syndromes, 30–31
epiphenomena of, 20
heritability of longevity, 19–20
interspecific/intraspecific life span variations, 19
mechanisms of MLSP, 22–23
number of genetic loci, estimated, 20–21
progeroid syndromes
segmental, 23–26
unimodal, 26–30
sex differences, longevity and, 21–22, 37–46
Genital organ cancer, female, 476–477, 874
Genital warts, 421
Genitourinary system, female, 869–870
Gentamicin:
diverticulitis, 725
toxicity, 620, 1168
Genuine stress incontinence, defined, 1230
Geriatric assessment:
benefits, 204*t*, 209
components, 204–205
evidence of effectiveness, 203–204
procedure, 200
rationale, 203–204
screening methods
cognitive impairment, 205–207
depression, 207
functional disability, 208–209
malnutrition, 208
musculoskeletal impairment/immobility, 207–208, 208*t*
procedure, 206*t*
visual/hearing impairment, 208
Geriatric Depression Scale, 207
Geriatric medicine:
experimental topics, 11–16
legal aspects
advance directives, 393–394
competency, 391–392
drivers licenses, 392
elder abuse/neglect, 392–393
guardianship/conservatorship, 393
Medicaid planning, 396
nursing homes, 395–396
physician-assisted death, 395
surrogates, 394–395
Geriatric nursing:
educational preparation, 249–252, 250*t*
future direction, 256–257
interdisciplinary mandate, 256
practice models, specialization in, 253–256
research, 252–253
Gerontological nursing (*see* Geriatric nursing)
Gerontological rehabilitation (*see* Rehabilitation)
Gerontology (*see* Geriatric medicine; Preventive gerontology)
Gerstmann-Straussler-Scheinker disease, 29, 1064
Gestational diabetes, 833
Giant cell arteritis (GCA):
clinical presentation, 956*t*, 956–957
differential diagnosis, 957–958
etiology, 955
laboratory studies, 957
ophthalmopathy, 454
pathogenesis, 955
pathology, 957
treatment, 958
Gingivitis, 432
Glasgow Coma Scale (GCS), 1083
Glaucoma:
low-tension, 451
screening, 208
symptoms, 452–453
Gliomas, 1100
Global Assessment Scale, 1107
Global disorders:
of attention, 1022
of cognition, 1022
"Globus hystericus," 1259
Globus sensation, 1259, 1263
Glomerular diseases:
acute glomerulonephritis, 641–642
clinical presentation, 641
nephrotic syndrome, 643–644
prevalence, 640–641, 641*t*
tubulointerstitial nephritis, 644–646
Glomerular filtration rate (GFR), 616–617
Glomerular kidney disease, multiple myeloma and, 770, 770*t*
Glomerulonephritis, acute, 641–642
Glucocorticoid excess, 801–802
"Glucocorticoid" hypothesis of aging, 7
Glucose intolerance:
exercise, benefits of, *98*, 98–99
nutritional support and, 338
Glucose metabolism:
insulin response, *827*
measurement, fasting plasma levels, 830
normal, 825–826
Glucose tolerance test, intravenous (IVGTT), 832
Glucose transport mechanisms, 617
Glutamic acid decarboxylase (GAD), 1008
Glycosaminoglycans, 936–937, 981
Glycosylated hemoglobin (HbA_{1c}), 832
"Glycosylation" theory of aging, 8

GM-CSF (*see* Granulocyte macrophage colony stimulating factor (GM-CSF))
Goiter:
  diagnosis, 819–820
  multinodular, cancer in, 820
  treatment, nontoxic, 820
Goldman's Cardiac Risk Index, 279, 280, 281
Golytely, 1273
Gonadal hormones, 798
Gonadotropin-releasing hormone (GnRH), 797, 799, 868
Gonadotropins, 798
Gonioscopy, 443
Goodpasture's disease, 641
Gottron's sign, 962
Gout:
  associated disorders, 988–989
  classification, 990–991
  diagnosis, 989–990
  hyperuricemia, 988
  precipitating factors, 987–988
  pyrophosphate (chondrocalcinosis), 991–992
  signs/symptoms, 987–988
  treatment, 990
Grafts:
  dialysis, 651
  lower-extremity, occlusive disease and, 314
Gram-negative bacteremia, 70–71
Gram-negative organisms:
  pneumonia, 566, 567
  urinary tract infection, 630
Gram-positive organisms, urinary tract infection, 627, 630
Granulocyte colony-stimulating factor (G-CSF), 71, 72, 478
Granulocyte macrophage colony stimulating factor (GM-CSF), 72, 478
Granulocytes:
  evaluation, 750
  immune response and, 62–66, 69–70
Granulovacuolar degeneration, Alzheimer's disease, 1041, 1043
Grave's disease, 455, 810, 811, 819
Greenfield filters, 605
Group psychotherapy, 1143
Growth factors:
  evaluation, 66
  musculoskeletal system and, 939
  as therapy, ovarian cancer, 478
  uses of, 72
Growth hormone (GH):
  action, 795
  secretion, 72, 794–795
Growth hormone-releasing hormone (GHRH), 796
Guaiac, occult testing for, 658, 729
Guaifenesin syrup, 387
Guamanian Parkinson-amyotrophic lateral sclerosis (ALS)-dementia complex, 1051
Guanine nucleotide-binding regulatory proteins (G proteins), 68
Guardianship, legal aspects, 393
Guilford-Zimmerman Temperament Survey, 109
Gum bleeding, 779
Gynecologic care:
  cancer
    cervical, 476–477, 478
    endometrium, 477
    ovarian, 477–478
    vaginal, 475
    vulvar, 474
  general considerations, 473
  history and physical examination, 473–474
  vagina, 475
  vulva, 474–475
Gynecomastia, 800–801

H_2 blocking agents, 567, 575, 686
Haemophilus influenzae, 565, 568, 1161
Hair follicles, 414
Hair growth, 414
Hairy cell leukemia (HCL), 758
Haldol, 388, 1141
Hallervorden-Spatz disease, 1052
Hallpike maneuvers, 469
Hallucinations:
  Alzheimer's disease, 1036
  assessment, 224
  cognitive disorders and, 1022
  delirium, 1197
  drug therapy, 388
  paraphrenia, 1113–1114
  post-operative delirium, 284
Hallux rigidus, 1299–1300, *1300*
Hallux valgus, 1299
Haloperidol:
  Alzheimer's disease, 1045
  delirium, 284, 1025, 1198
  hallucinations, 388
  psychoses, 1141
Hamilton Depression Rating Scale, 1107, 1202
Hammer toe, *1300*, 1300–1301
Hampton's hump, 604
Handicaps (*See also* Disability)
  classification, WHO, *1309*
  defined, 343
Handwriting, changes in, 1054, 1197
Harris-Benedict equation, 337, 337*t*
Hartmann's procedure, *308*
Hashimoto's thyroiditis, 815, 819
Hassall-Henle bodies, 441, 447
Hayflick model of growth potential, 12, 22
Head-hanging maneuver, 1166
Head injury:
  chronic subdural hematoma, 1081–1082
  clinical pathology, 1080–1081
  etiology, *1080*
  evaluation, 1085–1086
  hypoxia/hypotension, *1084*
  incidence, *1079*, 1079–1080, *1080*
  minor, 1082–1083
  prognosis, *1083*, 1083–1085, *1084*, *1085*, 1085*t*
  treatment, 1085–1086
Head-up tilt studies, syncope and, 1176–1177
Headache, differential diagnosis, 455
Health care:
  ageism in delivery of, 401
  allocation of resources, 175
  cost-quality trade-offs and, 175
  distribution of resources, ethical aspects, 400
  expenditures
    causes of increasing, 169–170
    distribution of, 170
    future trends, 170
  financing, 170–174, *171*
  personnel and organization, 174
  quality of, 174–175
  reform issues, 400
  sociological aspects, 125–133
  utilization, 167–168, *168*, 168*t*, 196–197, 433
Health Care Financing Administration, 377
Health habits:
  epidemiology, 148
  promotion of, 213–220
  sexuality, effect on, 119
Health maintenance organizations (HMOs), 174, 377
Healthy People 2000, 216
Hearing aids:
  candidacy for, 466
  prognostic factors, 466–467
  types, 465–466
Hearing Handicap Inventory for the Elderly (HHIE), 462
Hearing loss:
  anatomic/physiologic correlates of, 459–460
  assessment, 208
  clinical evaluation, 460–465, *462*, 463*t*, *464*, *465*
  etiology, 457
  general considerations, 457–458
  prevalence, 457
  psychosocial implications, 458–459
  rehabilitation, 465–468

Heart disease (*See also* Congestive heart failure; Coronary artery disease)
- arrhythmias, 529
- cardiomyopathy, 527–528
- congenital, 521–522
- cyanotic, 522
- epidemiology, 517
- sodium metabolism and, 620
- syncope and, 1172–1174
- valvular, 522–526

Heart rate, 494–495
Heart rhythm, 494–495, 1173
Heartburn (pyrosis), 683–687
Heatstroke, 1193–1194
Heavy chain B cells, 62
Heavy chain disease, 68, 771
Heberden's nodes, 983
Heel pain, 1297–1298
Height/weight tables, 852*t*
Helicobacter pylori, 668, 693
Heller myotomy, 688
Helper-inducer T cells, 62–64, 67
Hematologic disorders, hypothyroidism, 816
Hematologic toxicity, NSAIDs, 951–952
Hematoma, subdural, 1081–1082
Hematopoietic system:
- effect of aging, *736*, 736*t*, 783–785
- immune function, protein-energy malnutrition, 742*t*
- malignancies of, 756–759

Hemodialysis, 651–652
Hemoglobin:
- anemia and, 741, 742–743
- blood replacement and, 296
- postoperative monitoring, 284

Hemoglobin oxygen saturation, 1219
Hemolytic anemias, 746
Hemolytic uremic syndrome, 788
Hemophilia, 775
Hemorrhage (*See also* Bleeding disorders)
- diverticular disease and, 724, 726
- etiology, 779
- lower gastrointestinal, *307*, 307–308

Hemorrhagic stroke, 1028–1029
Hemostasis:
- anticoagulant functions
  - antithrombin III, 776
  - natural system, 776–777
  - resolution, 777
- disorders of, 779–782
- fibrinolysis, 777
- precoagulant functions
  - coagulation cascade, 775–776
  - platelets, 776

Heparin:
- cerebral infarction, 1029
- disseminated intravascular coagulation, 780–781
- peripheral artery embolism/thrombosis, 787
- preoperative, 282
- thromboembolic disorders, 639, 784–785

Hepatic drug clearance, 262–264
Hepatic dysfunction, bleeding disorders and, 781–782
Hepatic injury:
- alcohol-induced, 708
- circulatory failure, 710
- drug-induced, 708
- INH, 581
- NSAIDs, 950–951

Hepatic pyogenic abscess, sepsis and, 710
Hepatic vein thrombosis, 785
Hepatitis:
- chronic, 709
- viral, 708–709

Hepatitis B, 708, 782
Hepatitis C, 709, 782
Hepatobiliary disorders, 707–713
Hepatobiliary function, age-related, 674–677
Hereditary amyloidosis, 27
Hernia, abdominal wall, 309–310, *310*
Herniorrhaphy, 309–310
Herpes simplex, esophagus, 690
Herpes zoster, 421–422
Herpesviruses, 74, 446–447
Heterogametic, defined, 21
High-density lipoproteins:
- atherosclerosis and, 510, 512
- CHD and, 158–159
- sex differential and, 43–46, *44*, 44–46

Hill equation, 267
Hip fractures:
- defined, 1322
- epidemiology, 1321
- incidence, 1321*t*
- morbidity/mortality, 1322
- prevention, 1325–1326
- recovery, 1325
- rehabilitation, 351–352
- risk factors, *1322*, 1322–1325, 1325*t*
- treatment, 1325

Hirano bodies, Alzheimer's disease, 1041, 1043
Histamine-stimulated gastric acid secretion, 668, 685–686
History, taking:
- gynecologic, 473–474
- neuropsychiatric, 221–222
- preoperative management, 280

Histrionic personality disorder:
- defined, 1131
- prevalence, 1132–1133

HIV infection:
- transmission, 782
- tuberculosis and, 575, 576, 580

"Hives," 417
HMG CoA reductase inhibitors, 863, 864
Hodgkin's disease:
- etiology, 766–767
- histology, 767*t*, 767–768
- management, 772*t*
- presentation, 767
- staging, 767
- survival, 768–769
- therapy, 768, 768*t*

Hodgkin's lymphomas, staging, 764*t*
Hollenhorst plaques, 1028
Home health agencies, defined, 375
Home health care:
- defined, 375
- oxygen, COPD and, 589
- respiratory disease, 561–563
- services, 232, 375–376
- utilization of, 167

Homemaker services, 377
Homocysteine, 52–53
Homogametic, defined, 21
Homosexuality, 120
Hormonal therapy (*See also* Estrogen replacement therapy)
- breast cancer, 485–488
- indications, 86–87
- prostatic cancer, 663

Horner's syndrome, 442, 608, 612
Hospice care, 384
Hospitalization:
- acute, nursing home interface, 370–371
- economic aspects, 1161–1162
- frail patients, 241–247
- geriatric nurse practitioners, role of, 254–255
- improving quality of care, 244

Host defense mechanisms (*see* Immune system)
Hot flushes, 869, 870
"Hot" thyroid nodules, 819
House calls, physician, 378–379
Housing, special elderly, 380–381
Human leukocyte cell surface antigens, 63*t*
Human papillomavirus (HPV), 421, 474, 476
Huntington's disease, 29, 1199, 1203
Hutchinson-Gilford syndrome, 15, 22, 24–25
Hyaline cartilage, 935
Hyaluronic acid, 935–937, 981
Hyaluronidase, 1186
Hydralazine, 551
Hydration, artificial, ethical aspects, 405–406
Hydrocephalus, dementia, 1199
Hydromorphone HCl, 386
Hydroxychloroquine, 969

Hyperactive behavior, 1023
Hyperacute therapy, cerebral infarction, 1030
Hyperalphalipoproteinemia, neonatal familial, 31
Hypercalcemia, 608, 649
Hypercalcemic nephropathy, 645–646
Hypercapnic respiratory failure, 593–594
Hypercholesterolemia:
  atherosclerosis and, 511–512
  familial, 26–27
Hypercoagulable states, 608
Hyperglycemia:
  atherosclerosis and, 511, 513–514
  diabetic ketoacidosis, 838
Hyperinsulinism, 857
Hyperkalemia, 618, 622
Hyperlipidemia:
  atherosclerosis and, 511–512, 514
  defined, 855
  pancreatitis and, 45, 718–719
  treatment, 862–864
Hyperlipoproteinemia, defined, 855
Hypernatremia:
  factors associated with, 1184*t*
  fluid balance and, 621–622, 1184
  treatment, 1187
Hyperosmolar hyperglycemic nonketotic coma (HHNC):
  precipitating factors, 837*t*
  treatment, 837–838
Hyperosmotic laxatives, 1272
Hyperparathyroidism:
  diagnosis, 925
  differential diagnosis, 925–926, 926*t*
  etiology, 649, 923–924
  pathology, 923–924
  signs/symptoms, 924–925
  treatment, 926–927
Hyperprolactinemia, 800
Hyperreflexia, sympathetic, 1293
Hypersensitivity pneumonitis:
  clinical features, 601–602
  diagnosis/treatment, 602
  examples, 601*t*
Hypersensitivity reactions (*see* Allergic reactions)
Hypertension:
  atherosclerosis and, 511, 513
  diagnosis, 547–548
  epidemiology, 146, 146*t*
  estrogen replacement therapy and, 874
  evidence for efficacy of therapy, 544–547, 545*t*, 546*t*
  exercise, benefits of, 99–100
  morbidity/mortality, 545*t*, 546*t*
  ophthalmopathy, 453
  physiology, 541–542, 542*t*
  prevalence, 542–543
  pulmonary, 602–604
  renovascular disease and, 637–638
  risk/benefit ratio of therapy, 543–544
  as risk factor, CHD, 159–160
  as risk factor, stroke, 162
  risk factors, 542–543
  secondary impotence, 1253
  treatment, 548–551, 550*t*
Hyperthermia, 1193–1194
Hyperthyroidism:
  incidence, 809
  laboratory studies, 810–811
  signs/symptoms, 809–810
  therapy, 811–813
  variants in the elderly, 811
Hypertonic dehydration, 1184, 1186
Hypertriglyceridemia:
  atherosclerosis and, 511–512
  estrogen, effect of, 45
Hypertrophic cardiomyopathy (HCM), 528, 1173
Hypertrophic gastritis, 696
Hypertrophic pulmonary osteoarthropathy, 608
Hyperuricemia, 988, 989
Hypoactive behavior, 1023
Hypoaldosteronism, 1185
Hypobetalipoproteinemia, neonatal familial, 31
Hypocholesterolemia, 855, 861–862
Hypochondriasis, as cause of depression, 1106–1107
Hypodipsia, age-related, 619–620
Hypoglycemia:
  clinical signs, 836*t*
  emergency treatment, 836–838
  etiology, 836*t*
  exercise and, 102
Hypogonadism, 1252, 1253, 1257
Hypokalemia, 618, 622–623
Hyponatremia:
  diagnosis, 1187
  fluid balance/renal function and, 621, 1187*t*, 1187–1189, 1189
  nutritional support and, 338
Hypophosphatemia, osteomalacia and, 917
Hypopituitarism, 799–800
Hypoproliferative anemias, 743–745
Hypostatic pneumonia, 568
Hypotension, syncope and, 1174
Hypothalamic hormones, secretion, 791–792
Hypothalamic-pituitary-adrenal axis, 792–794, 1104
Hypothalamic-pituitary disorders, 799–801
Hypothalamic-pituitary-testicular axis, 797–799
Hypothermia, 294–295, 1191–1193
Hypothyroidism:
  clinical features, 813–814, 814–816
  etiology, 812, 813
  laboratory studies, 816–817
  myxedema coma, 816
  therapy, 818–819
Hypotonic dehydration, 1184
Hypovolemia:
  diuretic-induced, hyponatremia and, 621
  symptoms, 620
Hypoxanthine guanine phosphoribosyltransferase (HPRT), 988
Hypoxemia, COPD, oxygen therapy and, 588–589
Hypoxemic respiratory failure, 594
Hysterectomy, sexuality and, 119
Hytrin, 659

Iatrogenesis, 242
Iatrogenic conditions, medications and, 434, 437
Ibuprofen, 947, 951
Id, defined, 107
Idiogenic osmoles, 622, 1187
Idiopathic diabetes mellitus, type II, 833
Idiopathic orthostatic hypotension, 1065
Idiopathic pulmonary fibrosis, 600
Idiotype, defined, 69
IF-ANA assay, rheumatic disease antibodies, 971
Ileus, hypokalemia and, 622
Iliac aneurysms, 534
Iliac crest bone biopsy, 900, 902
Illness:
  presentation in older persons, 196–197
  sexuality, effect on, 119
  underreporting of, 196–197
Illusions, defined, 1022
Imipramine, 1139, 1140
Immobility (*see* Mobility, impairment of)
Immune system:
  assessment, 66–70, 70*t*
  augmentation of response, 70–74
  clinical applications, infectious disease, 70–74
  function, normal, 62–66
  hematopoietic function, protein-energy malnutrition, 742*t*
  host defense mechanisms, 62–66, 1159
  nutritional aspects, 51–52, *52*
  organization of, 61–62
  respiratory system, 559
  testing/evaluation, 66*t*
  urinary tract infection and, 626–627

Immunizations, 68, 182 (*See also* Influenza immunization; Pneumococcal immunization)
Immunoblastic lymphoma, 765
Immunodeficiency:
  age-related, 62
  augmenting immune response, 70–74
Immunoglobulins:
  IgA, 66, 68
  IgD, 68
  IgE, 68
  IgG, 63
  IgM, 68
  intravenous, 71
  serum levels, 68
Immunosenescence, defined, 61
Immunosuppression:
  indications, 71
  renal transplantation, 652
Immunotherapy, breast cancer, 487–489
Impairments (*See also* Functional impairment)
  as cause of immobility, 1308*t*
  classification, WHO, 319, 343, *1309*
  defined, 203, 222
Impotence:
  after prostatectomy, 663
  causes, 119, 121
  diagnostic tests, 1255–1256
  epidemiology, 1251
  history and physical examination, 1254–1255
  incidence, 1252*t*
  mechanisms of erection, 1253–1254
  secondary to medical disease, 1252–1253
  terminology, 1251
  treatment, 1256–1257
In-home care services, 232
In-the-canal (ITC) hearing aids, 465
In-the-ear (ITE) hearing aids, 465
Incentive spirometry, 282
Inclusion body myositis, 961–964
Incompetence (*see* Competency)
Incontinence, 246 (*See also* Fecal incontinence; Urinary incontinence)
Incontinence monitoring record, *1237*
Incontinence undergarments/pads, 1236, 1240
Independence, of living (*see* Function)
Inderal, 1139
Indoleacetic acid derivatives, 647
Indomethacin, 947, 953
Inducer-helper T cells, 62–64, 67
Indwelling urinary catheters:
  care principles, 1246*t*
  indications, 1236, 1245*t*, 1245–1246
  postoperative complications and, 283–284
Infection (*See also* Urinary tract infection)
  antibiotic therapy, 1161–1162
  conjunctiva, 446
  COPD, 590
  diagnosis, 1159–1161
  differential diagnosis, 1159–1161, 1160*t*
  epidemiology, 1157*t*, 1157–1158
  esophagus, 689–690
  mortality, 1158
  nursing home care and, 370
  pressure ulcers and, 1333
  prevalence, 1157*t*, 1157–1158
  prevention, 370, 1162
  risk factors, 1158–1159
  skin, 420–422
Infectious diarrheal diseases:
  host factors, 1279–1280
  mechanisms, 1278–1279
  types, 1277–1278
Infectious diseases:
  common, adults, 1157*t*
  epidemiology, 147*t*
  immune response and, 70–74
  prevention, 182
  risk factors, 71*t*
Infective endocarditis, 526
Infestations, skin, 418–419
Infiltrative ophthalmopathy, 810
Inflammatory dermatoses, 415–418
Inflammatory-immune reaction, 63, 66
Influenza:
  epidemiology, 147
  pneumonia and, 566, 569
Influenza immunization:
  effectiveness, 219, 570, 575
  recommendations, 74, 586
Informed consent:
  anesthesia, 296–297
  ethical aspects, 399–400
  legal aspects, 391–392
  sample form, *289*
Ingrown toenails, 1305, *1305*
INH (Isoniazid), 578–580, 581, 582
Inhalation therapy:
  asthma, 593*t*
  COPD, 586–587
Injuries (*See also* Falls; Head injury; Spinal cord injury)
  non-fall, 138, 141
  prevention, 219
  risk factors, exercise and, 101–102
Inner ear, hearing loss and, 459–460
Insomnia, 30, 1023 (*See also* Sleep disturbances)
Instrumental activities of daily living (IADLs):
  assessment, 204–205, 208–209
  limitations of, incidence of, 375
Insulin:
  preoperative management, 281
  regimens, 842–843
  renal function and, 650
Insulin-dependent diabetes mellitus, type I, 832–833
Insulin resistance, exercise and, *98*, 98–99
Insulin resistance syndrome, *827*, 857
Insulinlike growth factor I, 795, 797
Insurance, private health, 172–173
Intelligence test performance, 225, 1016, *1017*
Intensity of service, defined, 169
Interferon-γ, 66, 70
Interferon therapy, ovarian cancer, 478
Interleukin 1 (IL-1), 66, 70, 71
Interleukin 2 (IL-2), 72
Interleukin 6 (IL-6), 66, 70
Intermediate care facilities (ICFs) (*see* Nursing homes)
Intermediate-grade lymphomas, 764*t*, 765–766
Intermittent claudication, 535–536
Intermittent urinary catheterization, 632
Interstitial lung disease:
  blood tests, 598
  bronchoalveolar lavage, 599
  clinical manifestations, 597
  diagnosis, 599–600
  gallium 67 lung scans, 599
  pulmonary function, 597–598, 598*t*
  radiography, 598, *599*
  treatment, 600–601
Interstitial nephritis, 644–646
Intertriginous candidiasis, 421
Intervertebral discs, 943
Intestinal function, age-related, 669–671
Intestinal obstruction, management, 388
Intracellular fluid, sodium handling and, 620
Intracorporeal pharmacotherapy, 1256
Intracorporeal vasodilator injection, diagnostic, 1255–1256
Intracranial hemorrhage, 786–787
Intracranial tumors, 1095–1101
Intractable plantar keratosis, 1302–1303
Intradermal injection of antigens, 67
Intraocular tension, 443
Intraperitoneal (IP) chemotherapy, 478
Intrarenal abscess, 630, 632
Intravenous fluids, ethical aspects, 405–406
Intravenous glucose tolerance test (IVGTT), 832
Intravenous pyelogram, 638–639
Intrinsic cutaneous aging:
  changes of, 412*t*
  defined, 411

Investigational New Drug Application (IND), 271
Iodide-induced thyrotoxicosis (IIT), 811
Iodide therapy, hyperthyroidism, 811–812
Iron absorption, small intestine, 671
Iron deficiency, 743–745
Iron supplementation, 284
Irritant contact dermatitis, 416
Ischemia:
  chronic, treatment, 536–537
  lower limb, 534
Ischemic optic neuropathy, 451
Ischemic score, defined, 1031
Ischiogluteal bursitis, 996
Isokinetic strength, defined, 94
Isolated systolic hypertension:
  defined, 541
  evidence for efficacy of therapy, 546–547
  as hypertension risk factor, 542–543
Isometric strength, defined, 94
Isoniazid (INH), 578–580, 581, 582
Isoniazid-resistant bacilli, 578, 580
Isotonic dehydration, 1184
Isotonic strength, defined, 94

Jakob-Creutzfeldt disease, 1199
Jaundice, etiology, 707–709
Jerne's network theory, 69

Kaopectate, 1282
Kaposi's sarcoma, 426–427
Katz Scale of ADLs, 209
Kayexalate, 649
Kayser-Fleischer ring, 447
Kegel exercises, 1242
Kenyoun staining method, 577
Keratan sulfate, 935–937, 981
Keratoses:
  actinic, 425
  seborrheic, 425
Ketoconazole, 421
Ketoprofen, 947
Ketorolac tromethamine, 324, 386
Kinsey study of sexuality, 115
Klebsiella, 627
Klinefelter's syndrome, 26, 489
Klonopin, 1140
Korsakoff's psychosis, 1128
Kuru disease, 29
Kwell, 419
Kyphosis, 900

Labetalol, 551
Laboratory studies:
  Alzheimer's disease, 1038–1039
  delirium, 1198
  dementia, 239*t*
  depression, 1107*t*
  giant cell arteritis, 957
  immune function, 66*t*, 66–67
  inflammatory myopathies, 962–963
  neuropsychiatric assessment, 227
  osteomalacia, 916–917
  polymyalgia rheumatica, 957
  preoperative management, 282
  rheumatoid arthritis, 966
  thyroid diseases, 807–808, 810–811, 816–817
  vestibular dysfunction, 469
Lacrimal function, 441, 447
Lactate dehydrogenase (LDH), 638, 639
Lactulose, 1272
Lacune infarcts, 1031
Langsmuir saturation isotherm equation, 265
Language, impairment of:
  Alzheimer's disease, 1036
  dementia, 1199
  focal cognitive syndromes, 1200–1201
  Pick's disease, 1063
  testing, 225, 1014, *1014*
Lanthanic (asymptomatic) pyrophosphate gout, 993
Laparoscopic cholecystectomy, 303
Large cell lung cancer:
  clinical presentation, 607–608
  treatment, 612
Large unstained cells, significance of increase, 752
Laryngeal obstruction, 970
Laser prostatectomy, transurethral, 659
Lavage laxatives, 1273
Laxatives:
  diarrhea and, 1283
  role in constipation, 1246–1247, 1267
  types, 1272–1273
Lean body mass (LBM):
  exercise and, 92, 94
  loss of, age-related, *50*, 50–51, 333, 510, 942
Left shift, WBC differential, 751
Left-to-right shunt, 522
Left ventricular pump function, preload and, 495–496
Left ventricular wall thickness, 498
Legal issues:
  advance directives, 393–394
  competency, 391–392
  drivers licenses, 392
  elder abuse/neglect, 392–393
  guardianship/conservatorship, 393
  Medicaid planning, 396
  nursing homes, 395–396
  patient autonomy/self-determination, 399
  physician-assisted death, 395
  surrogates, 394–395
Legionella pneumophila, 565, 568–569
Legionnaires' disease, 568–569
Lens, ocular:
  aging of, 441–442
  diseases of, 447–448
Lentigines, 425, 444
Lesch-Nyhan disease, 988, 991
Leu designations, T cell monoclonal antibodies, 67
Leukemia, types, 756–759
Leukemoid reaction, 751–752
Leukoaraiosis, defined, 1031
Leukocytes:
  cell surface antigens, 63*t*
  decreased, significance of, 752–756, 754*t*
  increased, significance of, 750–752, 751*t*
  total/absolute, adults, 751*t*
  types, 750*t*
Leukocytosis, defined, 751
Levodopa:
  Lewy body disease, 1064, 1065
  Parkinson's, 1058–1059
Lewy body disease, 1064–1065
Lexical knowledge, 1014
Leydig cells, 798
Liability, physician, 392
Libido, 117–118, 119, 1251, 1253
Lice, 418–419
Lichen simplex chronicus, 416
Lidocaine, 519
Lids, diseases of, 444–445
Life-care retirement communities, 380
Life expectancy (*See also* Genetics; Maximum life span potential)
  adult whites, 37*t*
  demographics, 127*t*, 177*t*, 177–179, 179*t*
  neuropsychologic impairment and, 1119–1120
Life-sustaining treatment:
  refusal of, 394
  withholding/withdrawing of, 401–406, 405*t* artificial hydration/nutrition, 405–406 CPR and DNR orders, 397–399, 403*t* general recommendations, 402–403
Lifestyle:
  changes in, disease prevention, 188*t*, 195
  environment and aging, demographics of, 179
  exercise and bone formation, 891–892

Light chain B cells, 62
Light chain disease, 68
Likelihood ratio statistics, 238
Lindane, 419
Linguistic ability (*see* Language, impairment of)
Lip reading, 467
Lipase, 674
Lipids:
  as brain constituent, 1006-1007
  epidemiology, 143, *145*
  as risk factor, CHD, 158
Lipoprotein metabolism:
  aging and, 858*t*–859*t*, 861
  exercise, benefits of, 99
  regulation, 855, *856*, 857, 860-861
  as risk factor, CHD, 158
Lithium:
  depression, 1105, 1109, 1203
  hypercalcemia and, 923
  mood disturbances, 1139-1140
  toxicity, 1168
Livedo reticularis, 639
"Liver flap," 1197
Liver spots, 444
Living wills, 394, 403
Lobectomy, 312, 580, 609, 611
Lobular carcinoma in situ, 484
Long-term care:
  community-based
    adult day care, 379-380
    corporate-sponsored, 380
    costs, effectiveness of, 376-377
    demand for, 375
    housing, special elderly, 380-381
    physician house-call programs, 378-379
    public programs, 377-378
    respite care, 380
  defined, 375
  ethical issues, 406
  financing, 128
Long-term memory (*see* Memory, impairment of)
Longevity (*See also* Sex differential in longevity)
  biochemical/physiologic measurements, *9*
  body mass and, *11*
  effect of bereavement, 110-111
  evolutionary model, 8-9
  heritability of, 19-20
  number of genetic loci, estimated, 20-21
  terminology/definitions, 3-4
Loop diuretics, 621, 648, 1188
Lorazepam, 284, 389, 1092
Lou Gehrig's disease, 1066-1067
Low back pain, 1288
Low-density lipoproteins:
  atherosclerosis and, 512, 514
  CHD and, 158-159
  familial hypercholesterolemia, 26-27
  familial lipid disorders, 857
  sex differential and, 43-46, *44*, 44-46
Low-grade gliomas, 1100
Low-grade lymphomas, 764*t*, 764-765
Low-sodium diet, hyperkalemia and, 622
Lower esophageal (Schatzki) ring, 1262
Lower esophageal sphincter (LES) relaxations, 666-667
Lower-extremity:
  arterial disease, 145
  ischemia, 534
  mobility, assessment, 207-208
  occlusive disease and, 314
Lower gastrointestinal hemorrhage, *307*, 307-308
Lower-tract urinary infection:
  diagnosis, 630
  symptoms, 627
  treatment, 630-631
Lumbar puncture:
  Alzheimer's disease, 1038
  brain tumors, 1098
  CNS infections, 1072*t*
  contraindications, 1076
  meningitis, 1072
  neurosyphilis, 1075
  tuberculosis meningitis, 577
Lumbar stenosis, 1287-1288
Lung cancer:
  characteristics, 607*t*
  clinical presentation, 607-608
  diagnosis, 608
  epidemiology, 607
  histologic patterns, 607-608
  local/regional/metastatic disease, 608
  mortality rates, 41-42, *163*
  pancoast (superior sulcus) tumors, 612
  pathogenesis, 607
  screening, 217, 607
  signs/symptoms, 608*t*
  staging, 609, 610*t*
  superior vena cava syndrome, 612
  survival, 612-613
  treatment
    chemotherapy, 611*t*, 611-612
    radiation, 611
    by stage/histology, 612
    surgical, 312, 609, 611
Lung disease (*see* Pulmonary disorders)
Lung scans, 599, 604
Lupus (*see* Systemic lupus erythematosus (SLE))
Lupus-like syndrome, 974, 974*t*
Luteinizing hormone (LH), 797-799, 868
Luteinizing hormone-releasing hormone (LH-RH) analogs, 663
Lymph nodes, immune response, 62-64
Lymphadenectomy, prostatectomy and, 662
Lymphangiography, prostatic cancer, 662
Lymphocytes:
  decreased, significance of, 756
  function, 62-64, 749
  increased, significance of, 752
Lymphocytic "silent" ("painless") thyroiditis, 811
Lymphocytosis, 752
Lymphokines, 63, 70
Lymphomas:
  cutaneous T-cell, 427
  gastric, 702
  malignant, 763-766
  treatment, 1100
Lymphopenia, 756
Lysosomal theory, atherogenesis and, 513
Lysozyme, *737*, 737, *738*

Macroangiopathy of diabetes, 835-836
Macrocytic anemia, 745-746
Macrocytosis, 742-743
Macrophages, 70, 749
Macrosocial (societal) effects, resource allocation and, 126-127
Macular degeneration, 450, *450*
Macular disequilibrium of aging, 470
Magnesium citrate, oral, 1272
Magnesium deficiency, hyponatremia and, 1188
Magnesium supplementation, 73, 927
Magnetic resonance imaging (MRI):
  altered mental state, 227
  brain tumors, 1097
  Paget's disease, 931
  prostatic cancer, 662
  vestibular dysfunction, 469
Magnetic resonance spectroscopy (MRS), 1097
Malabsorption, nutrients, small intestine, 671
Male breast cancer, 489-490
Male climacteric syndrome, 118
Malignant gliomas, 1100
Malignant lymphocytosis, 752
Malignant melanoma, 426
Malignant neutrophilia, 752
Mallet toe, 1300-1301
Mallory-Weiss syndrome, 689, 700
Malnutrition:
  assessment, 208
  immune and hematopoietic function, 742, 742*t*
  as risk factor, preoperatively, 281-282
Malperforans ulcerations, 1306

Malpractice, anesthesia risk and, *291*
Mammography, 482–483
Mandelate, 632
Mania, treatment, 1139–1140
Manual dexterity, assessment, 207-208
MAO inhibitors, 1109
Marcus Gunn pupil, 442–443
Marginal neutrophil pool (MNP), 753
Massage, therapeutic, 1288
"Master clock" theory of aging, 7
Mastication, 436–437, 683
Masturbation, 115, 119, 120
Maternal age and aneuploidy, 31
Mattresses, pressure-relieving, 1333–1334
Maximal aerobic power, defined, 91
Maximum life span potential (MLSP):
  defined, 5
  gene action and, 22–23
  number of genetic loci, estimated, 20–21
  sex differences and, 21–22
Maximum oxygen consumption (VO_{2max}):
  circulatory function, age-related, 504–505
  exercise and, 91–93, *92*
  pulmonary function, age-related, 558
Mazepine, 1091
MDS protocol, nursing home assessments, 372
Mean arterial pressure, regional anesthesia and, 294
"Mechanic's hand," 962
Mediastinal adenopathy, 1262
Mediastinal lavage, hypothermia and, 1193
Medical care, compared to long-term care, 375
Medicare/Medicaid:
  catastrophic expenses, 172–173, 173
  eligibility, 133, 396
  expenditures, *169*, 169–170
  financing, 170–174
  health care utilization and, 167
  home health care, 375
  provisions, 128, 171
  reimbursement structure
    breast cancer screening, 482–483
    colorectal screening, 730
    community-based long-term care, 377–378
    hospice care, 384
    nurse practitioners, 252
    nursing homes, 361, 371–373
    rehabilitation, 346, 352
  social/health maintenance organizations and, 377
Medications (*See also* Psychopharmacology)
  assessment
    acute hospital admission, 245–246
    preoperative use, 281
  development/approval process, 271–272
  dosage nomogram, 617
  dying patient, administration to, 385
  hypothyroidism and, 816
  interactions
    antibiotics, 570
    bile-salt sequestering agents, 819
    NSAIDs, 947, 949*t*
  pancreatitis and, 719
  pharmacodynamics, 270
  renal function and, 620, 650
  as risk factor, falls, 1314, 1317, 1318
  side effects
    constipation, 1268*t*
    depression, 1106
    drug eruptions, 417–418
    esophageal injury, 690, 1264, 1264*t*
    excessive somnolence, 1217
    fluid homeostasis, 1185, 1186, 1189
    gastric emptying, 668
    glucose tolerance alteration, 832*t*
    hepatic toxicity, 708
    interstitial lung disease, 600
    lupus-like syndrome, 974, 974*t*
    neurotoxicity, 1288–1289
    neutropenia, 755–756
    nutritional deficiency, 55*t*
    ophthalmopathy, 447, 456
    sexuality, 119
    SIADH, 621
    sodium/potassium metabolism, 622–623
    tardive dyskinesia, 437
    urinary incontinence, 1231–1232, 1232*t*
    vertigo, 1167–1168
    xerostomia, 434
"Medigap" insurance, 172
Medroxyprogesterone acetate, 46
Megacolon, 1270
Megaloblastic anemia, 745–746
Melancholic depression, 1105
Melanoma:
  ocular, 447, 449, *449*
  skin, 426
Melphalan, 643
Membranous nephropathy, 643
Memory, impairment of (*See also* Alzheimer's disease)
  delirium, 1022
  dementia, 1199
  focal cognitive syndromes, 1200
  testing, 225, 1014–1015, *1015*
Ménierè's disease, 1167
Meningiomas, 1100–1101, 1287
Meningitis:
  bacterial, 1071–1073
  fungal, 1074–1075
  tubercular, 576, 577, 1074
Meningoencephalitis, viral, 1073–1074
Meniscus, 941
Menopausal syndrome, 869
Menopause:
  age at, frequency distribution, *867*
  atherosclerosis disease and, 43
  cardiovascular system, effect on, 872–874
  defined, 867
  endocrine changes, 867–869
  estrogen therapy, 870–874
  genitourinary changes, 869–870
  male, 118–119
  osteoporosis and, 870–872, 897–899, 902
  sexuality and, 117–118, 121
  structural/physiologic changes, 869, *870*
  vasomotor symptoms, 869–870
Mental retardation, 1201 (*See also* Chronic neuropsychological impairments)
Mental state, altered:
  defined, 221
  screening tests, 224–225
  syndromes of, 1197–1203
Mental status examination, depression, 1107
Mental Status Questionnaire, 206
Meperidine, 283, 329
Mesosocial (institutional) effects, resource allocation and, 127–128
Metabolic complications:
  diabetes, 836–838
  nutritional support, 337–338
Metastatic disease:
  brain, 1100
  lung, 608
  spinal cord, 1287
Metatarsalgia, 1301–1303
Metatarsus primus varus, *1299*
Metered-dose inhalers (MDI), 586*t*, 586–587, 593
Methadone maintenance, 1128
Methenamine, 632
Methenamine hippurate, 632
Methicillin, 568, 645
Methimazole, 812
Methionine, 632
Methotrexate:
  breast cancer, 487
  inflammatory myopathies, 963
  rheumatoid arthritis, 968
Methyldopa, 551
Methylphenidate, 388, 1109
Methylprednisone, 642
Metronidazole, 725
METS, energy measurement unit, 97
MI (*see* Myocardial infarction)
Michaelis-Menten equation, 265
Michigan Alcoholism Screening Test (MAST), 1127

Microangiopathic hemolytic anemia, 746
Microangiopathy of diabetes, 834–835
Microcytosis, 742–743
Microemboli, 536
Microscopic polyarteritis nodosa, 640
Microsocial (milieu) effects, resource allocation and, 127
Microvascular thrombosis, 787–788
Micturition (*see* Urination)
Micturition syncope, 1174–1175
Mid-life crisis, 108
Middle ear, hearing loss and, 459
Mikulicz syndrome, 443
Miliary tuberculosis, 576
Milk of magnesia, 1272
Mineral absorption, small intestine, 671
Mineral oil, 1272
Mineralocorticoid excess, 802
Mini-Mental State Examination (MMSE), 206, 224, 227, 1197
Minicaloric test, vestibular function, 1170
Minimal change disease, 643
Minimum Data Set (MDS), 359
Mithramycin, 933
Mitochondrial disease, 30
Mitogen assay, 67–68
Mitral annular calcification, 526
Mitral regurgitation, 525–526, 1173
Mitral stenosis, 525
Mitral valve disease, 312
Mitral valve prolapse, 525
Mixed hearing loss, 464, *465*
Mixed sleep apnea, 1218
Mobility, impairment of:
  assessment, 207–208, 247, 1309–1310
  decreased bone mass, 1325
  epidemiology, 1307–1308
  pathogenesis, 1308*t*, 1308–1309
  pressure ulcers and, 1329–1333
  prevalence, *1307*
  treatment, 1310
Mobilization, postoperative, 283
Moisture, pressure ulcers and, 1330–1331
Mönckeberg's sclerosis, 509, 510
Monitoring, cardiac, 1173
Monoamine oxidase inhibitors, 1058
Monoamine oxidase (MAO), 1007, 1104
Monoclonal antibodies:
  identifying membrane markers, 62
  identifying T cell markers, 67
  treatment of sepsis, 71
Monoclonal antibody CSAT, 941
Monoclonal gammopathy of uncertain significance (MGUS), 69
Monoclonal hypothesis, atherogenesis and, 512
Monoclonal immunoglobulin, 68–69
Monocyte-macrophage cells, 63
Monocytes:
  decreased, significance of, 756
  function, 62–66, 70, 749
  increased, significance of, 752
Monocytosis, 752
Mononeuritis multiplex, 640
Monozygotic twins, aging in, 20
Montgomery-Asberg Depression Rating Scale, 1107, 1202
Mood disorders:
  assessment, 223–225
  depression
    major, 1202–1203
    minor, 1202
    secondary/symptomatic, 1203
  diagnosis, 1201–1202
  NOS (not otherwise specified), 1106
  prevalence, 1103
  treatment, 1139–1140
  types, 1106
Moraxella (Branhamella) catarrhalis, 1161
Morbidity/mortality rates:
  anesthesia, 288–291, 295*t*
  epidemiology, age-related, 135, 137, *137*, 138*t*, 139*t*, 140*t*
  gender-related, *156*
  hip fractures, 1322
  as measure of aging, 5, *6*
  obesity and, 847–852
  perioperative, 287–288
  postoperative, 280
  pulmonary function assessment and, 560
  risk factors, epidemiologic aspects, 153–164, *155*, *156*, *157*
Morphine, 386
Morton's neuroma, 1301–1302, *1302*
Motor function:
  assessment, 226–227
  esophageal, 687–688
  oral cavity, 436–437
  Parkinson's, 1054
Motor function, impairment of:
  dementia, 1199
  focal cognitive syndromes, 1201
Motor neuron diseases, 1066–1067
Motor point blockade, 1292
Motor vehicles (*see* Driving, automobile)
Mourning (*see* Bereavement)
Mucosa, oral, 435–436
Multi-infarct dementia, 1031, 1056–1057, 1220
Multifocal myoclonus, 329
Multinodular goiter, 820
Multiple myeloma:
  clinical presentation, 770–771
  compared with BMG, 772*t*
  epidemiology, 769
  etiology, 769
  immunological aspects, 68, 69, 72
  interstitial nephritis and, 646
  pathogenesis, 769–770, 770*t*
  therapy, 771
Multiple organ system failure, microvascular thrombi, 788
Multiple system atrophy, 1065–1066
Muscae volitantes, 442
Muscle biopsy, inflammatory myopathies, 963, 964
Muscle fibers, 95
Muscle strength, skeletal, 94–96
Musculoskeletal disorders:
  giant cell arteritis, 955–958
  hypothyroidism and, 815
  impairment, assessment, 207–208
  polymyalgia rheumatica, 955–958
Musculoskeletal system:
  diarthrodial joints, 935–941
  skeletal muscle, 941–942
  spine, 943
  tendon, 942–943
Mutant allele, expression of, 20
Mutation, parental age and, 31
Muted hypertension, 500
Myasthenia gravis, 456
Mycosis fungoides, 427
Myeloblasts, 733
Myelodysplastic syndrome, 755
Myobacterium tuberculosis, 575, 577
Myocardial infarction:
  diagnosis, 518–519
  etiology, 786
  incidence, *509*
  rehabilitation, 519-520
  sexuality and, 121
  treatment, 519
Myochosis, defined, 723, 724
Myoclonic epilepsy, ragged red fibers and, 30
Myoclonus, 329, 1197–1198
Myopathy:
  inflammatory, 961, 962*t*
  ocular, 30
Myotonic dystrophy, 26
Myxedema, 814, 1106
Myxedema coma, 816

Nafcillin, 568
Naloxone (Narcan), 328, 387
Naproxen, 947
Narcissistic personality disorder, 1134
Narcolepsy, 1217
Narcotics (*see* Opioids)
Narcotics Anonymous (NA), 1129
National Center for Nursing Research (NCNR), 252–253
National Institute of Mental Health (NIMH), 253
National Institute on Aging (NIA), 253

National Institutes of Health-Traumatic Coma Data Bank, 1083–1084
Natural Death Acts, 403
Natural killer cells, 62–64, 69
Nausea:
as side effect
chemotherapy, 87
opioids, 328
treatment, 388
Near-syncope, defined, 1165
NEO Personality Survey, 109
Neomycin, 630
Neonatal familial hyperalphalipoproteinemia, 31
Neonatal familial hypobetalipoproteinemia, 31
Neonatal progeroid syndrome, 25
Neoplasms (*See also* Cancer)
skin, 425–427
thyroid, 820–822
Nephritis, tubulointerstitial, 644–646
Nephrolithiasis, 1028
Nephropathy:
analgesics, 645
diabetic, 834
hypercalcemic, 645–646
Nephrostomy, percutaneous, 630
Nephrotic syndrome, 643–644, 645
Nephrotoxic acute tubular necrosis, 647
"Nerve deafness," 466
Nervous system disorders:
degenerative
late onset, 29–30
Lewy body disease, 1064–1065
motor neuron diseases, 1066–1067
multiple system atrophy, 1065–1066
Pick's disease, 1063–1064
primary autonomic failure, 1065–1066
progressive supranuclear palsy, 1065
Shy-Drager syndrome, 1065–1066
spinocerebellar atrophy, 1065–1066
Neural presbycusis, 460
Neurinomas, treatment, 1101
Neurochemistry, age-related, 1005–1006
Neurodermatitis circumscripta, 416
Neurofibrillary tangles, Alzheimer's disease, 1041, 1042–1043
Neurofibromas, 1287
Neurogenic bladder, 1293–1294
Neurogenic bowel, 1293–1294
Neurogenic shock, 1293
Neuroleptics:
Alzheimer's disease, 1045
contraindications, 1198
dementia, 1199–1200
depression, 1203
paraphrenia, 1115
psychoses, 1140–1141
Neurological disorders, dizziness and, 1166–1168
Neurological examination:
cognitive impairment, 225–227
pain assessment and, 320–321
seizure evaluation, 1090
Neuromuscular disorders:
esophagus, 1263
hypothyroidism, 814
Neuronal loss, Alzheimer's disease, 1041, 1043
Neuroophthalmic disorders, 455–456
Neuropathic pain, 318, 1294
Neuropathy:
diabetic, 536–537, 835
entrapment, 1000–1002
peripheral, 1288–1289
Neuropeptides, neurotransmission and, 791, 1008–1009
Neuropsychiatric assessment:
cognitive impairment and, 225–227
disability status, 222–223
history taking, 221–222
laboratory studies, 227
mental state examination, 223–224, 227
mental state screening tests, 224–225, 227
psychological status, 225
Neurosyphilis, 1075
Neuroticism, personality trait, 107–108
Neurotoxicity, medications, 1288–1289
Neurotransmitter regulation:
biochemical aspects, 1007–1009, 1043–1044
dopamine, 791–792
norepinephrine, 792
opioids, 792
serotonin, 792
Neutra-Phos-K, 919, 926
Neutropenia, etiology, 752–756, 755*t*
Neutrophil function, age-related, *737*, 737–738
Neutrophil storage pool (NSP), 753, *753*
Neutrophilia, etiology, 751–752
Neutrophils:
decreased, significance of, 752–756
function, 749
increased, significance of, 751–752
production/kinetics/distribution, *753*, 753–754
New Drug Application (NDA), 271
Nicotine replacement therapy, 585
Night vision, 441
Nikolsky sign, 423
Nitrates, 519
Nitrofurantoin, 631
NMDA receptor blockers, 1030
Nocturnal penile tumescence (NPT), 1251, 1256
Noise, environmental and hearing loss, 459
Nolvadex, 415, 484, 487
Nomograms:
creatinine clearance, 617
water deficit, hypernatremia, 622
Non-A hepatitis, 709
Non-B hepatitis, 709
Non-Hodgkin's lymphomas:
classification, 763, 764*t*
clinical features, 764–765
epidemiology, 763
evaluation, 763–764
management, 772*t*
staging, 763–764, 764*t*
treatment
aggressive lymphomas, 766
intermediate lymphomas, 765–766
low-grade lymphomas, 764–765
Non-insulin-dependent diabetes (NIDDM):
atherosclerosis and, 511
clinical features, 833
incidence, 828–829
management, 838–843
Non-rapid eye movement (NREM) sleep, 1214–1216, *1215*
Non-small cell lung cancer:
clinical presentation, 608
treatment, 611, 611*t*, 612
Nonarticular temporomandibular joint (TMJ) disorders, 437
Nonatheromatous arteriosclerosis, 510
Nonconvulsive seizures, 1089
Nonmaleficence, defined, 399
Nonmalignant lymphocytosis, 752
Nonmalignant neutrophilia, 751
Nonmammalian model systems, longevity study, 20
Nonmelancholic depression, 1105
Nonopioids (*See also* Nonsteroidal anti- inflammatory drugs (NSAIDs))
dying patient, 386
guidelines, 323–329
pharmacologic considerations, 322–323
Nonpsychotic depression, 1105
Nonspecific dizziness, defined, 1165
Nonspecific esophageal motor disorders, 688
Nonsteroidal anti-inflammatory drugs (NSAIDs):
adverse effects
diverticular disease, 724
gastrointestinal, 305, 694, 950
hematologic, 951–952
hepatic, 950–951
hyperkalemia, 622
hypersensitivity reactions, 951

Nonsteroidal anti-inflammatory drugs (NSAIDs):
- adverse effects (*Cont.*)
- alternative therapies, 948, 950
- characteristics, 948*t*
- drug interactions, 947, 949*t*
- efficacy of, 948
- nephrotoxicity, 645, 647, 650, 951
- osteoarthritis, 983–984
- pain, 324–325
- pharmacology of, 262, 947–949
- preoperative management, 281
- principles of use, 952
- rheumatoid arthritis, 968
- rotator cuff tendinitis, 998–999

Nontoxic goiter, 820
Norepinephrine, neurotransmission and, 792, 1007–1008, 1104
Normeperidine, 283
Norpramin, 1140
Norton Scale, 1331
Nortriptyline, 1108, 1140
Norwegian scabies, 419–420
Nosocomial infections, 1158, 1333
Nosocomial pneumonia, 567, 568, 570–572, 572
NSAIDs (*see* Nonsteroidal anti-inflammatory drugs (NSAIDs))
Nucleic acids as brain constituent, 1006
Nurse practitioners, role of, 252, 370
Nursing, geriatric (*see* Geriatric nursing)
Nursing home care:
- acute care hospital interface, 370–371
- clinical aspects, 359–361, 360*t*
- documentation, 364–365, *366*
- ethical issues, 371, 372*t*
- falls, prevention, 1318–1319
- goals, 358–359, 359*t*
- improvement strategies, 364–365
- patient assessment/treatment factors, 359–361, 360*t*, 362*t*–364*t*, 371–373
- pneumonia and, 568, 570–572, 572
- pressure ulcers, incidence of, 1329
- preventative measures, 367*t*–369*t*, 370, 1318–1319
- process of, 361, 364
- tuberculosis infections and, 581–582

Nursing home residents:
- basic types, *359*, 359
- common clinical disorders, 360*t*
- demographics, *358*

Nursing homes:
- characteristics, 357–358, 358*t*
- expenditures for, 376, 378
- financing, 128
- geriatric nurse practitioners, role of, 253–254
- government regulations, 395–396
- privacy and sexuality in, 116, 119

"Nutcracker esophagus," 688
Nutritional assessment:
- appetite loss, etiology, 434–435
- body composition changes, 54–56, 57*t*, 208, 334
- laboratory studies, 335*t*
- preoperatively, 281–282

Nutritional deficiency:
- anemia and, 741–742, 745
- correction, 57–58
- hematopoietic function, 742
- immune response and, 73–74, 742
- neuropathy and, 1289
- risk factors, 54*t*, 55*t*
- signs/symptoms, 56*t*

Nutritional requirements, geriatric:
- changes of body composition/lean mass, 50–51
- changes of physiologic function and, 49, 49*t*
- cognitive function and, 53
- declining bone density, 51
- declining skin synthesis/vitamin D, 51
- immune response and, 51–52, *52*, 73–74
- recommendations, 181, 333*t*, 333–334, 337*t*
- vascular system and, 52–53
- vision and, 53–54

Nutritional support:
- acute hospital care and, 246
- basic concepts, 333, 338–340
- case studies, 338–340
- COPD and, 587–598
- dying patient, 384–385
- ethical aspects, 405–406
- formulating a plan, 56–58
- goals, 336
- intervention in, 334–337
- metabolic complications of, 337–338
- monitoring, 336–337
- pressure ulcers and, 1333

Nylen-Barany maneuver, 1166, 1167, 1167*t*, 1170
Nystagmus, 468–469, 1166, 1167, 1167*t*
Nystatin, 421

Obesity:
- atherosclerosis and, 510–511, 513
- mortality and, 847–852
- preventive gerontology and, 188–189
- as risk factor, CHD, 160–161
- as risk factor, osteoarthritis, 982

Obesity hypoventilation (pickwickian) syndrome, 603
Obesity index, defined, 848
Obligate diuresis, 1185
OBRA (*see* Omnibus Reconciliation Act (OBRA))
Obsessions, defined, 224
Obsessive-compulsive personality disorder, 1131, 1133
Obstructive disorders (*See also* Chronic obstructive pulmonary disease (COPD))
Obstructive esophageal disorders, 1262–1264
Obstructive sleep apnea (OSA), 1217, 1220, 1222, 1224
Obstructive uropathy, acute renal failure, 648
Occlusion:
- arterial, 533–534
- retinal circulation, *450*

Occult blood testing, stool, *309*, 658, 729
Occupations as risk factor:
- osteoarthritis, 982
- pulmonary diseases, 599

Ocular diseases:
- conjunctiva, 445–446
- cornea, 446–447
- differential diagnosis, 452*t*
- glaucoma, 452–453
- lens, 447–448
- lids, 444–445, *445*
- optic nerve, 451–452
- orbital, 443–444
- retina, 449–450, *450*, *451*
- signs/symptoms, 453*t*
- systemic aspects, 453–456, *454*
- uveal tract, 448–449, *449*

Ocular myopathy, 30
Odynophagia, defined, 1259
OKT designations, T cell monoclonal antibodies, 67
Older Americans' Act, 377, 378
Older American's Resources and Services Multidimensional Functional Assessment Questionnaire (OMFAQ), 209
Olecranon bursitis, 995–996
Olfactory function, age-related, 435
Oliguria, 620
Olivopontocerebellar degeneration, 1057, 1066
Omentopexy, 305
Omeprazole, 686
Omnibus Reconciliation Act (OBRA):
- regulations
  - neuroleptic agents, 1141
  - nursing homes, 175, 371–373
  - patient assessment, 359, 372
- reimbursement structure, nurse practitioners, 252

Oncogenes, 79–80
1,25-dihydroxy-vitamin D:
  calcium metabolism, renal disease, 649
  hyperparathyroidism, 926, 927
  osteomalacia, 911–913, 917–919
Onychomycosis, *1305*
Open-angle glaucoma, 452
Openness, personality trait, 107–108
Opioids:
  addiction, 1126–1127
  dying patient, 386*t*, 386–387
  guidelines, 323–329
  hypothalamic-pituitary-testicular axis, 799
  moderate-to-severe pain, 326*t*
  neurotransmitter regulation, 792
  pharmacologic considerations, 322–323
  reversal agents, 293, 328, 387
  side effects, 328–329
  tolerance, 329
Opportunistic infections, 566
Optic nerve, diseases of, 451
Oral cavity:
  cancer, 217
  dentition, 431–432
  gum bleeding, 779
  motor function, 436–437
  mucosa, 435–436
  periodontium, 431–432
  salivary glands, 433–434
  sensory function, 434*t*, 434–435
Oral contraceptives, cholesterol levels and, 44, *45*
Oral glucose tolerance test (OGTT):
  clinical applications, 826, 830–832
  interpretation, *831*
  survey results, 826*t*
Oral health, age-related, 181–182
Oral hypoglycemic agents, preoperative management, 281
Oral mucosa, 435–436
Oral rehydration therapy (ORT):
  clinical application, diarrhea, 1275, 1276, 1281, 1281*t*
  methods, 1186–1187
Oral sulfonylureas, 841–842, 842*t*
Oral thrush, 388, 420–421
Orbital diseases, 443–444
Organ of Corti, 459–460
Orgasm, male and female, 117
Oropharyngeal dysphagia, 437, 1259–1261, 1261*t*
Orthoses, types, 1292
Orthostatic hypotension:
  fluid depletion, 1276, 1281
  primary autonomic failure, 1065
  syncope, 1174
Orthostatic stress, cardiovascular response, 501–502
Orthotic prescription, rehabilitation, 1291–1292
Osler maneuver, 548
Osteitis fibrosa cystica, 924, 927
Osteoarthritis (OA):
  articular cartilage and, 937, 937*t*
  cartilage
    age-related change, 981
    normal/aging, compared, 982*t*
  contributing factors, *880*
  diarthrodial joints, 935–941, 937
  differential diagnosis, 966–967, 967*t*
  facet, 943
  pathophysiology, 982, 982*t*
  rehabilitation, 353
  risk factors, 982–983
  synovial fluid, *941*
  treatment, 948, 983–984
Osteoblasts, 884–885, *885*
Osteoclasts, 884–885, *886*
Osteocytes, 884
Osteomalacia:
  case study, 919–920
  diagnosis, *914*, 914–918, *915*
  etiology, 911*t*, 911–914
  laboratory studies, 916*t*, 916–917, *917*
  pathogenesis, 911–914, *914*
  renal failure, 917
  treatment, 918–919
Osteopenia, 897, 899*t*, 904–905
Osteoporosis:
  bone mineral content, age and, *872*
  classification, 898*t*
  clinical presentation, 900
  defined, 897
  diagnosis, 900–903
  epidemiology, 138, 897
  estrogen replacement therapy and, 870–872, *872*
  exercise, benefits of, 101, 891–892, *892*
  pathogenesis, 897–899, *898*
  prevention, 189
  as risk factor, hip fracture, 1322–1323
  risk factors, 163–164, *871*, 899*t*, 899–900
  treatment, 903–907, *904*, 904*t*, 905*t*
Osteoporosis circumscripta, 930
Osteosarcoma, 930
Osteosclerosis, 924
Otoscopy, 468
Ototoxicity, medications, 1167–1168
Outpatient care, respiratory disease, 563*t*
Ovarian cancer, 477–478
Ovarian function:
  menopause and, 867–869
  neuroendocrine control, experimental topics, 14
Over-the-counter medications, effect on sexuality, 119
Overuse injuries, 101, 982
"Oxford" technique, strength training, 96
Oxygen consumption, 97 (*See also* Maximum oxygen consumption (VO_{2max}))
Oxygen therapy, COPD and, 588–589, *590*, 591

Pacemakers, syncope and, 1177
Paget's disease:
  clinical manifestations, 930, 930*t*
  complications, 930
  epidemiology, 929
  etiology, 929*t*, 929–930
  laboratory studies, 930–931
  pathology, 929
  treatment
    drug therapy, 932*t*, 932–933, 933*t*
    surgery, 933–934
Pain:
  assessment, 320*t*, 320–322
  epidemiology, 317–318
  low back, 1288
  management
    approaches, 321*t*–322*t*, 321–322
    drug therapy, 322–329
    for dying patient, 385–386
    mild-moderate pain, 324*t*
    moderate-to-severe, 326*t*
    postoperative, 283
  nonmalignant, sites of, 319*t*
  spinal cord/peripheral nerve diseases, 1294
  temporal aspects, 319
  types, 318
  types of patients with, 319*t*, 319–320
Painful diverticular disease, defined, 723
Pancoast (superior sulcus) tumors, 612
Pancoast's syndrome, 608
Pancreatic cancer, 304, 719–720
Pancreatic disorders, 303–304, 717–719
Pancreatic function, age-related, 673–674, 717
Pancreatitis:
  acute, 717–718
  chronic, 719
  gallstone, 718
  hyperlipemic, 45
  hyperlipidemia and, 718–719
  medications as cause, 719
  surgical procedures, 303–304
Panic disorder, 1139
Pap smear test, 476–477
Papillitis, 451
Papillomas, corneal, 447
Papulosquamous disorders, 422–423

Paraneoplastic polyneuropathy, 1289
Paraneoplastic syndromes, 608
Paranoia, defined, 1111
Paranoid disorder, 1111–1116
Paranoid personality disorder, 1133
Paraphrenias:
biological markers, 1114
defined, 1111
drug therapy, 1114–1115
family history, 1112–1113
prognosis, 1114
symptoms, 1113–1114
terminology, 1111–1112
Parasomnias, 1216, 1218
Parathyroid hormone (PTH):
ectopic, paraneoplastic syndromes and, 608
hyperparathyroidism, 923–927
increased, renal disease, 649
serum calcium regulation, 879, 881
Parathyroidectomy, 926–927
Parenteral alimentation, 333
Parkinsonian syndromes, 1051–1052
Parkinson's disease:
biochemical pathology, 1009, 1009*t*, 1089–1090
classification, 1051*t*, 1051–1052
clinical features/course, 1054–1055
dementia with, 1199
depression with, 1203
diagnosis, 1052*t*
differential diagnosis, 1056–1057
epidemiology, 148, 1052
examination, 1055–1056
pathology, 1043, 1052–1053
prognosis, 1056
treatment
drug therapy, 1057*t*, 1057–1060
physical therapy, 1060–1061
Paroxetine, 1140
Partial seizures, 1089
Partial thromboplastin time, 778
Passive-aggressive personality disorder, 1134
Passive euthanasia, defined, 402
Patent ductus arteriosus, 522
Paternal age, point mutation and, 31
Patient Self-Determination Act (1991), 245, 394, 403
Patterson-Kelly syndrome, 688
Paxil, 1140
Peak expiratory flow (PEFR) measurements, 587
Pediculosis infestation, 418–419
Peer review organizations (PROs), 169
Pelvic examination, 473
Pelvic floor:
muscle exercises, 1242
muscle relaxation, 475
Pemphigoid bullosa, esophagus, 691
Pemphigus vulgaris, 423–424
Pendulum exercises, *999*
Penicillin:
antipseudomonas, 570
pneumonia, 568
toxicity, 1090
Penile-brachial blood pressure index (PBPI), 1255
Penile prostheses, 1257
Pentoxifylline, 536
Peptic strictures, 686, 1262
Peptic ulcer:
clinical signs, 697
complications, 697–698
diagnosis, 697
incidence, 696
treatment, 698
Peptidergic hormones, function, 791
Pepto Bismol, 1282
Perception, disorder of, 1022
Percutaneous balloon dilation, aortic stenosis, 524
Percutaneous cholangiography, 707
Percutaneous transluminal coronary angioplasty (PTCA), 311, 521, 816
Percutaneous transluminal renal angioplasty (PTRA), 638
Perforated ulcer, 305
Perfusion lung scan, 784
Pergolide, 1059–1060
Perimetry, indications, 442
Perineal prostatectomy, 662–663, *663*
Perinephric abscess, 630, 632
Periodic limb movements (PLMs), 1216, 1217, 1222
Periodontal disease, 431
Periodontitis, 432
Periodontium, 431–432
Perioperative management:
assessment of risk, 277–280
mortality, *287*, *288*
postoperative, 282–285
preoperative, 280–282
Peripheral nervous system disorders:
dizziness and, 1166
hypothyroidism, 814–815
Peripheral neuropathy:
ALS, 1289–1290
complications, 1291–1294
etiology, 1288–1289
pain management, 1294
rehabilitation, 1291–1294
socioeconomic issues, 1294
subacute combined degeneration, 1289
Peripheral vascular disease:
arteriosclerosis obliterans, 533–537
extracranial arterial disease, 538–539
postthrombotic syndrome, 537–538
rehabilitation, 353
sex differential in, 42
thromboembolism, 788
Peripheral vascular resistance (PVR), 494, 497, 499–500
Peritoneal dialysis, 652
Peritonitis, diverticular disease and, 725
Permethrins (Nix, Elemite), 419, 420
Pernicious anemia, 695, 745–746, 1289
Persistent urinary incontinence, 1231, 1232*t*, 1232–1233, 1235*t*
Personality:
defined, 107
stability, implications of, 110–111
testing, 108, 109
Personality disorders:
case studies, 1134–1135
classification, 1133–1134
diagnosis, 1133
epidemiology/course, 1132–1133
NOS (not otherwise specified), 1134
terminology, 1131–1132
treatment, 1134
Personality traits:
defined, 107, 1131
differences, mean level of, 108–109
differences, stability of individual, *109*, 109–110
five-factor model, 107–108, 108*t*
types, *1131*
Pessaries, 475
Petechiae, 778–779
pH (*see* Acid-base balance)
Phagocytosis, 69–70
Phalen's sign, 1001, *1002*
Pharmacodynamics:
adverse drug effects, 270
age-related changes, 266*t*–267*t*, 268–270, *269*
defined, 259
drug development/approval process, *271*, 271–272
E_{max} model, 265, 267, *267*, *269*
indirect drug effects-reflex responses, 268
linear model, 268
Pharmacokinetics:
bioavailability, *259*, 259–260
clearance, 261–264, *262*, *264*
distribution, 260–261
elimination half-life, 264–265, *265*
terminology, 259
Pharyngoesophageal function, age-related, 665–667
Phenacetin, 645
Phenobarbital, 1091, 1092
Phenol, motor point block, 1292
Phenolphthalein, 1272
Phenothiazines, 437
Phenylbutazone, 951–952
Phenytoin:
adjuvant analgesia, 327
epileptic seizures, 1091
status epilepticus, 1092
toxicity, 1121, 1168
Phobias, assessment, 224

Phonologic knowledge, 1014
Phosphate binders, 649
Phosphate-deficiency osteomalacia, 913–914, 917, 919
Phosphate metabolism, *913*
Phosphate supplementation, 926
Phosphorus metabolism, 649, 923
Photoaging, skin, 411, 414, 415
Photoallergic drug reactions, 417
Physical activity (*see* Exercise)
Physical examination:
  eye, 442–443
  gynecologic, 473–474
  hearing loss, 460–465
  mental state, 223–224
  neurological, 1090
  performing, 200–201
  preoperative management, 280
Physical therapy:
  Parkinson's, 1060–1061
  spinal cord/peripheral neuropathy, 1291–1294
Physician assistants, role of, 370
Physician-assisted suicide (PAS), 384, 395, 402–403
Physician house-call programs, 378–379
Physicians:
  house calls, 378–379
  reimbursement, nursing home visits, 361
  relationship, dying patient, 384
  reporting laws, unsafe drivers and, 392
  role in rehabilitation, 347
  values, old age/quality of life, 401
Physiologic neutrophilia, 751
Physiologic reserve, defined, 97
Pick's disease, 1063–1064, 1199
Pilosebaceous units, 414
Piroxicam, 947
Pituitary adenomas, 1101
Pituitary function:
  hypothalamic-pituitary-adrenal axis, 792–794
  hypothalamic-pituitary-testicular axis, 797–799
  pituitary-hypothalamic disorders, 799–801
  water homeostasis and, 619, 1183
Pituitary hormone, secretion, 791
Placebos, 329
Plantar fasciitis, 1297–1298, *1298*
Plantar keratosis, intractable, 1302–1303
Plantar warts, 421, 1303
Plasma cell dyscrasias, 769*t*, 769–772
Plasma renin activity, 618, 638
Plasma transfusion, 782
Plasmin, 777
Plasmin inhibitor, 781
Plasminogen activator, 777
Platelet transfusion, 780
Platelets, 776
Platinum-based chemotherapy, 477–478
Pleural effusion, 576, 577
Pleural tuberculosis:
  diagnosis, 576–577
  treatment, 577–578, 579*t*, 580, *580*
Plicamycin, 933
Plummer-Vision syndrome, 688
Pluripotent hematopoietic stem cells, *734*
Pneumococcal immunization, 73–74, 219, 571, 586
Pneumococci, 567
Pneumocystis carinii, 566
Pneumonectomy, 312, 609, 611
Pneumonia:
  atypical, 569
  autonomic dysfunction, SCI, 1294
  drug therapy, 571*t*
  epidemiology, 147
  etiology, 566–568
  incidence, 565
  prevention, 570–572
  prognosis, 565
  risk factors, 560–561, 565–566
  treatment, 569–570, 571*t*
Pneumonitis, hypersensitivity, 601–602
Podospora anserina, 30
Polyarteritis nodosa, 640
Polycythemia vera (PV), 752, 757
Polymorphisms, genetic, longevity study, 20
Polymyalgia rheumatica (PMR):
  clinical presentation, 956–957
  diagnosis, 967–968
  differential diagnosis, 957–958
  etiology, 955
  laboratory studies, 957
  pathogenesis, 955
  pathology, 957
  treatment, 958
Polymyositis, 961–964
Polypharmacy, 1138
Polyps, colorectal, 727, 728–729, 729
Polysomnography, 1222–1223
Polytetrafluoroethylene (PTFE) grafts, 314
Pontiac fever, 568
Population pharmacokinetic screen, defined, 214
Positioning, pressure ulcer prevention and, 1331–1332
Positive nitrogen balance, 336
Positron emission tomography (PET):
  altered mental state, 227
  Alzheimer's disease, 1038
  brain tumors, 1097
Posterior tibial tendinitis, 1304
Postoperative management:
  acute confusion/delirium, 284
  analgesia, 296
  cardiac complications, 284
  catheters, 283–284
  hemoglobin, decrease in, 284
  mobilization, 283
  pain control, 283
Postprandial hypotension, syncope and, 1174
Postthrombotic syndrome, 537–538
Postural hypotension:
  hypovolemia, 620
  as risk factor, falls, 1314, 1318
Posture:
  oral muscular, 436–437
  Parkinson's disease, 1054
Postvoid residual volume determination (PVR), 1235
Potassium, dietary, 649
Potassium homeostasis, 618, 648–649, 1188
Powers of attorney, 393–394
PPD (Purified protein derivative), 67, 581
PR interval, 495
Prazosin, 551
Prednisone:
  glomerulonephritis, 642, 643
  inflammatory myopathies, 963–964
  nephritis, 646
  systemic vasculitis, 640
  thrombotic thrombocytopenic purpura, 788
Preferred provider organizations, 174
Preload, resting, 495–496
Premarin, 44
Preoperative management:
  history and physical, 280
  laboratory studies, 281
  medications, 281
  nutrition, 281–282
  preventive measures, 282
  risk assessment
    bleeding disorders, 778
    cardiac, 281
    thromboembolism, 783
Prerenal azotemia, 646–647
Presbycusis:
  clinical manifestations, 459–460
  defined, 457
  etiology, 459
  types, 459–460
Presbyopia, 441, 443
Pressor stress, cardiovascular response, 502
Pressure-reducing devices, 1332, 1333–1334
Pressure ulcers:
  assessment, 1333
  complications, 1329
  dying patient, care of, 388–389
  epidemiology, 1329–1330
  incidence, 1329

Pressure ulcers (*Cont.*)
mortality, 1329–1330
pathogenesis/pathophysiology, 1330–1331
prevalence, 1329
prevention, 1331*t*, 1331–1332
risk factors, 1330
treatment, 1333–1335
Preventive gerontology:
alcohol, 189–190
atherosclerosis, 189
cancer, 189
chronic disease, attenuation of, 187–190, 188*t*
conceptual framework, 213–214
health habits, modification, 218–219
obesity, 188–189
osteoporosis, 189
physiologic capacity
acute/subacute losses, 219
modifying loss of, 215–218
tobacco smoking and, 188
Priapism, 1256
Primary amyloidosis, 68
Primary autonomic failure, 1065–1066
Primary epilepsy, 1090
Primary lateral sclerosis, 1066
Primary memory, 1015
Primary osteoporosis, defined, 897
Primidone, 1091
Prion diseases, 29–30
"Private markers", genetics of aging and, 20
Probenecid, 991
Procainamide:
acute MI, 519
lupus-like syndrome, 974*t*
Proctoscopy, diverticular disease and, 726
Prodromal symptoms, acute confusion and, 1022
Proerythroblasts, 733
Progeria, 15, 24–25
Progeroid syndromes:
defined, 23
experimental topics, 15
identification criteria, 24*t*
segmental, 23–26
unimodal, 26–30
Progesterone therapy:
estrogen replacement therapy and, 477
libido and, 117
Progestin, 46
Progress notes (*see* Documentation, medical)
Progressive rate training, 96
Progressive resistance exercise, 96
Progressive supranuclear palsy, 1056, 1065
Progressive systemic sclerosis (scleroderma), 976–977
Prolactin, hypothalamic-pituitary-testicular axis, 799
Proliferating cell nuclear antigen (PCNA) antibodies, 972
Prolixin, 1141
Promotility agents, 686
Proopiomelanocortin (POMC), 792, 793
Propionic acid derivatives, 647
Propranolol:
adjuvant therapy, hyperthyroidism, 812
as anti-anxiety agent, 1139
preoperative management, 281
Proprioceptive receptors, 1165
Proptosis, 443
Propylthiouracil, 812
Proscar, 659
Prospective payment system, Medicare, 169
Prostaglandin synthase inhibitors, 647
Prostaglandins, 947, 950
Prostate anatomy, normal, 657, *657*, *658*
Prostate-specific antigen (PSA), 661–662
Prostatectomy, 119, 659, 662–663
Prostatic acid phosphatase (PAP), 662
Prostatic cancer:
diagnosis, 660–663
etiology, 660
incidence, 660
pathogenesis, 660
physical examination, 660
screening, 217, 658
staging, *661*, 661–662
symptoms, 660
treatment, 662–663
Prostatic enlargement, 632
Prostatic hyperplasia, benign, 657–658
Protein, dietary, 334, 648, 650
Protein, serum, multiple myeloma and, 769–770
Protein absorption, small intestine, 671
Protein C, 776, 782, 783
Protein-energy malnutrition, 742
Protein S, 782, 783
Proteins as brain constituent, 1006
Proteoglycans (PG), 935–937, *936*
Proteus, 626, 627
Prothrombin, 782
Prothrombin time, 282, 778
Proton pump inhibitors, 686
Provera, 46
Proximal tubular reabsorption, 617
Prozac, 1140
Pruritus:
causes, 424*t*
external ear, 459
treatment, 389, 424
Pseudo-arthritis, 993
Pseudofractures, 915, *915*, 918
Pseudogout, 987, 991, 992–993
Pseudohypertension, 548
Pseudohyponatremia, 1187
Pseudomonas, 627
Pseudomonas aeruginosa, 629, 1162
Pseudoneuropathic pyrophosphate gout, 993
Pseudoneutropenia, 753–754
Psoriasis, 423
Psychiatric complications:
Alzheimer's disease, 1045
frailty, acute hospital care and, 242
hypothyroidism, 814
Psychiatric consultation, indications, 1137
Psychiatry (*See also* Psychopharmacology)
personality traits/stability and, 108, 110–111
Psychogeriatric Dependency Rating Scale (PGDRS), 223
Psychomotor behavior, disorder of, 1023
Psychopharmacology:
depression, 1108–1109, 1109*t*, 1199–1200, 1203
principles of, 1137–1138
as risk factor, hip fracture, 1324
treatment options, 1138–1142
Psychoses, 1111–1116, 1140–1141
Psychosocial function:
depression and, 1105
hearing loss and, 458
immobility and, 1309
importance of, 183, 280
pain assessment and, 320
rheumatoid arthritis, 970
Psychotherapy:
adult developmental stages/tasks, 1142–1143
chemical dependence, 1128–1129
depression, 1108
principles, 1142
types/approaches, 1143
Psychotic depression, 1105
Psychotropic agents (*see* Psychopharmacology)
Ptosis, 444–445
Public policy, health care delivery and, 132–133
Public programs, long-term care and, 377–378
Pulmonary complications, surgical risk and, 279, 282
Pulmonary disorders (*See also* Chronic obstructive pulmonary disease (COPD); Interstitial lung disease)
infection, diagnostic testing, 1160
inflammatory myopathies and, 962
pathophysiology, age-related, 555–557

Pulmonary edema, 620, 621
Pulmonary embolism:
  autonomic dysfunction, SCI, 1294
  clinical features, 604
  diagnosis, 604–605, 783–784
  prevention, 282
  risk factors, 295
  treatment, 605
Pulmonary function tests:
  COPD, 583
  interstitial lung disease, 597–598, 598*t*
  use of, 556*t*, *557*, 559–560, *561*, *562*, 562*t*
Pulmonary hypertension:
  clinical findings, 603
  etiology, 603
  pathophysiology, 602
  treatment, 603–604
Pulmonary sarcoidosis, 600
Purified protein derivative (PPD), 67, 581
Purine synthesis, disorders of, 988
Purple toe syndrome, 787
Purpura, 418
Purpura fulminans, 787
Pyelonephritis, 626, 629, 644–645
Pyogenic liver abscess, sepsis and, 710
Pyrazinamide (PZA), 578, 581
Pyrethrins (Rid), 419
Pyridoxine, 73, 650
Pyrophosphate gout (chondrocalcinosis):
  clinical presentation, 992–993
  compared, gouty arthritis, 991–992
  incidence, 987
  management, 993
  terminology, 991
Pyrosis, 683–687
Pyuria, 628, 630

Quality of life issues, 401, 544
Quetelet index, 848
Quinine, toxicity of, 1168

Radiation therapy:
  brain tumors, 1099–1101
  colorectal cancer, 729
  endometrial cancer, 477
  female genital cancer, 476
  Hodgkin's disease, 768
  indications, 85–86
  multiple myeloma, 771
  prostatic cancer, 662–663
Radioactive iodide, hyperthyroidism, 811–812, 813
Radioiodinated contrast agents, toxicity of, 647
Radiologic imaging:
  Alzheimer's disease, 1038
  barium esophagram, 684
  bone loss, 871
  brain tumors, 1097
  constipation, 1269
  dysphagia, 1264
  interstitial lung disease, 598
  osteomalacia, 915
  Paget's disease, 930–931, *931*
  rheumatoid arthritis, 965–966
  urinary tract disorders, 632–633
Radionuclide ventilation, 784
Ranitidine, 264
Rapid-cycling depression, 1105
Rapid-eye movement (REM) sleep, 1214–1216, *1215*
"Rate of living" model of aging, 7
RDAs (*see* Recommended dietary allowances)
Reaction to injury hypothesis, atherogenesis and, 512
Reading tests, 225
Recognition phase, immune response, 63
Recombinant human erythropoietin, 650, 651
Recombinant human growth hormone, 72
Recommended dietary allowances (RDAs), 49, 333–334, 337*t*
Rectal bleeding, diverticular disease and, 725
Rectal cancer (*see* Colorectal cancer)
Rectal examination:
  benign prostatic hyperplasia and, 658
  colorectal cancer and, 729
  constipation, 1269
  prostatic cancer, 660, 661–662
Rectal function, age-related, 672–673
Rectocele, 475
Rectovaginal examination, 473
Red blood cells, growth factors for, 72
Red eyes, differential diagnosis, 452*t*
Reed-Sternberg cell, 767
Referred pain, 320
Refraction, examination, 443
Refusal of treatment, 391–392
Regional anesthesia:
  complications, 295–296
  hemodynamic instability, 293–294
Regurgitation, defined, 683
Rehabilitation:
  aural, 467
  cardiac, 353, 519–520
  care needs, 347
  COPD, 588
  dementia, 352–353
  geriatric conditions, 353–354
  hearing loss, 465–468
  hip fracture, 351–352
  osteoarthritis, 353
  peripheral neuropathy, 1291–1294
  peripheral vascular disease, 353
  physician's role, 347
  principles of, 343*t*, 343–345, 345
  site of, 345–347
  spinal cord disease, 1291–1294
  steps in approach to, 345*t*
  stroke, 349–351
Rehydration (*see* Oral rehydration therapy)
Relative weight, defined, 848
Relaxed selection, defined, 31
Renal artery embolism, 638–639
Renal autoregulation, interference with, 647–648
Renal blood flow, 616, 638
Renal calculi, prevention, 991
Renal disease:
  glomerular, 640–644
  hypothyroidism, 815–816
  systemic necrotizing vasculitis, 639–640
  tubulointerstitial nephritis, 644–646
  vascular, 637–639
Renal failure (*See also* Acute renal failure; Chronic renal failure; End- stage renal disease)
  multiple myeloma and, 770, 770*t*
  osteomalacia, 917, 919
  risk factors, 620
Renal function:
  anatomic changes, 615–616
  calcium metabolism and, 880–881
  drug clearance, 261–262
  fluid homeostasis, 1183–1184
  glomerular filtration rate, 616–617
  hyperkalemia, 622
  hypernatremia, 621–622
  hypokalemia, 622–623
  hyponatremia, 621
  physiologic changes, clinical consequences of, 542, 620
  potassium homeostasis, 618
  potassium metabolism, disorders of, 622–623
  renal blood flow, 616
  sodium handling, 618, 1187–1189
  sodium metabolism, disorders of, 620–622
  tubular functions, 617
  water homeostasis, 618–619
  water metabolism, disorders of, 621
Renal hypoperfusion, 647
Renal insufficiency, anesthesia and, 294
Renal toxicity, NSAIDs, 951
Renal transplantation, 652
Renal vein thrombosis, 785
Renin-aldosterone axis, 618, 620

Renin-angiotensin system:
- fluid homeostasis, 1183
- hypertension and, 542
- renal autoregulation, 647–648

Renography, 638–639
Renovascular disease, 637–638
Reporting laws:
- elder abuse, 392–393
- unsafe elderly drivers, 392

Reserpine, 551
Resident assessment protocols (RAPs), 372
Residual volume, 556–557
Resistance exercise, 95–96
Resource-based relative value system, Medicare, 169
Respiratory depression, opioids and, 328
Respiratory failure:
- COPD, 590–591
- hypercapnic, 593–594
- hypoxemic, 594

Respiratory system:
- arterial oxygen tension, 557–558
- control of, 558
- defense mechanisms, 558–559
- diffusing capacity, 557
- distribution of ventilation, 557
- exercise capacity, 558
- immunity, humoral/cellular, 559
- lung/chest wall interaction, 555–557, *557*
- outpatient care, need for, 563*t*
- pathophysiology, 555, 556*t*
- pulmonary function tests, 556*t*, 559–560
- treatment approaches, 560–563, 563*t*

Respite care programs, 232, 380
Restraints, chemical/physical, 372–373, 1319
Restriction fragment length polymorphisms (RFLPs), 1041
Restrictive cardiomyopathy, 528
Restrictive pulmonary diseases, pulmonary function tests, 560
Resuscitation (*see* Cardiopulmonary resuscitation (CPR))
Retarded depression, compared to agitated depression, 1106
Retina:
- aging of, 442
- diseases of, 449–450, *450*, *454*
- hypertensive changes, 548

Retinal detachment, 451
Retinopathy:
- diabetic, 834–835
- exercise and, 102

Retrocalcaneal bursitis, 996–997
Retrograde urethrogram, 659
Retropubic prostatectomy, 662–663, *663*
Retroviruses, 73
Reversible acute urinary incontinence, 1231, 1231*t*
Reversible ischemic neurologic deficits, 538, 786–787
Rewarming, hypothermia and, 1193
Rey-Osterich test, 225
Rheumatic diseases:
- drug-induced lupus, 974, 974*t*
- hypothyroidism, 815
- inflammatory myopathies and, 961, 962
- scleroderma, 976–977
- serologic tests, 971*t*, 971–973
- Sjögren's syndrome, 974–976
- systemic lupus erythematosus, *973*, 973–974

Rheumatoid arthritis:
- clinical features, 965
- complications, 970
- differential diagnosis, 966–967, 967*t*
- laboratory studies, 966, *966*
- management, long-standing RA, 970–971
- management, new-onset RA, 968–969
- pseudo, 993
- psychosocial support, 970
- radiologic findings, 965–966
- treatment
  - drug therapy, 948
  - nonpharmacologic, 969
  - surgical, 969–970

Ribosomal nucleoprotein (rRNP) antibodies, 972
Rifamate, 578
Rifampin, 264, 578–580, 581
Right-to-left shunt, 522
"Ringworm," 420
Rip Van Winkle syndrome, 1031
Ritalin, 388
Romberg test, 469
Rosacea, 416–417
Rotator cuff:
- tear, *998*
- tendinitis, 997–999

Ruptured abdominal aortic aneurysms, 535, 537
Rural Health Act, 252

Salicylates:
- contraindications, 991
- ototoxicity, 1168
- rheumatoid arthritis, 968

Saline laxatives, 1272
Saliva, functions of, 433, 433*t*
Salivary glands:
- age-related changes, 434
- dysfunction, medications and, 434
- function, 433–434

Salt metabolism, 620
Salt substitute, 622
Scabies, 419–420
Schatzki (lower esophageal) ring, 688–689, 1262
Schilling test, 745
Schirmer's test, 975
Schizoid personality disorder, 1133
Schizophrenia, 1111, 1201
Schizotypal personality disorder, 1134
Sclera, aging of, 441
Scleroderma, 976–977, 1263
Scoliosis, 1120
Screening tests:
- breast cancer, 482–483
- cancer, 81–82, 82*t*, 216–218
- cerebral artery disease, 216
- chemical dependence, 1127
- colorectal cancer, 729–730
- coronary artery disease, 215–216
- genital organ cancer, female, 476–477
- hearing loss, 461–465
- lung cancer, 607
- mental state, 224–225
- prostatic cancer, 658
- recommendations, 215, 216*t*–217*t*, 218
- thyroid diseases, 808–809

Seasonal affective disorders, 1105–1106
Sebaceous glands, 414
Seborrheic dermatitis, 422–423
Seborrheic keratoses, 425
Second-toe metatarsalgia, 1302, *1302*
Secondarily generalized tonic-clonic seizures, 1089
Secondary epilepsy, 1090
Secondary hyperparathyroidism, 923
Secondary memory, 1015
Secondary osteoporosis:
- defined, 897
- pathogenesis, 897–898, 898*t*
- treatment, 907

Segmental progeroid syndromes:
- ataxia telangiectasia, 25
- Down's syndrome, 25–26
- Hutchinson-Gilford, 24–25
- Werner's, 23–24

Seip syndrome, 26
Seizures (*See also* Epileptic seizures)
- antiepileptic agents, 1092
- classification of types, 1089
- etiology, 1089–1090
- evaluation, 1090
- incidence, 1089
- as side effect, opioids, 329
- status epilepticus, 1091–1092
- treatment, 389, 1090–1091

Selegiline, 1057–1058
Self Help for Hard of Hearing People (SHHH) organization, 467
Semantic knowledge, 1014
Senescence, defined, 3

Senile dementia:
Alzheimer type, 27–28
vascular basis, 1030
Senile (neuritic) plaques, Alzheimer's disease, 1041–1042, *1042*
Senile purpura, 418
Senna, 1272
Sensorineural hearing loss, 463–464, *464*, 466
Sensory deprivation:
delirium and, 1023
effect of aging, 180
as risk factor, falls, 1314
Sensory function:
auditory, 457–470
taste/oral cavity, 434–435
vestibular, 469–470
Sensory memory, 1015
Sensory presbycusis, 460
Sepsis (*See also* Infection)
immune response and, 70–74
pressure ulcers, 1329
prevalence, 1157*t*
Sepsis syndrome, microvascular thrombi, 788
Septic shock, 70–71
Serial impedance plethysmography, 783
Serine protease, 775, 776
Serotonin, neurotransmission and, 792, 1007–1008, 1104
Serotonin syndrome, 1140
Serratia, 627
Sertoli cells, 798
Sertraline, 1140
Serum CA 125, 477
Serum glutamic oxaloacetic transaminase (SGOT), 581, 638, 639
Serum osmolarity, calculation of, 1186
Serum thyroxine (T_4), 807–808, 810–811, 816–817
Serum triiodothyronine (T_3), 807–808, 810–811
Sesamoiditis, 1303
Set Test, 206
Sex differential in longevity:
atherosclerosis and, *42*, 42–46, *44*, *45*
biological basis, 38–39
dimensions of, *37*, 37–38, *38*
genetic aspects, 21–22
implications of, 46
morbidity/mortality, 39–42, *40*, 40*t*, *41*, 154–155
Sexual behavior:
biological factors affecting, 116–117
counseling, 120–122
health, illness, medications and, 119
in later life, 115–116
menopause, female, 117–118
menopause, male, 118–119
normal response cycle, 116–117
social factors affecting, 116
Sexual dysfunction (*See also* Impotence)
counseling, 120–122, 1257
diagnosing, female, 473–474
Sexual intercourse, urinary tract infections and, 118, 626
Sexually transmitted diseases (STDs), 121–122
Sézary syndrome, 427
Shearing forces, pressure ulcers and, 1330–1331
Sheltered housing, defined, 381
Shingles, 421–422
Short Portable Mental Status Questionnaire, 206
Short Test of Mental Status, 206
Shoulder-hand syndrome, 1294
Shy-Drager syndrome, 1051, 1057, 1065–1066
SIADH (*see* Syndrome of inappropriate antidiuretic hormone (SIADH))
Sick sinus syndrome, 529
Sickness Impact Profile, 223, 458
Sideroblastic anemia, 746
Sigmoidoscopy, colorectal cancer, 727, 728, 729–730
"Silent gallstones," 302–303
Simon foci, 576
Simple goiter, 819
Simple partial seizures, 1089
Sinemet, 1058–1059
Single-photon absorptiometry (SPA), 900, 901–902
Sinoatrial (SA) node, 495
Sinus node disease, syncope and, 1173–1174
Sipple's syndrome, 923
Sjögren's syndrome, 434, 974–976
Skeletal muscle:
age-related changes, 179–180
exercise and, 94–96
function, 941–942
Skeletal osteopenia, defined, 897
Skilled nursing facilities (SNFs) (*see* Nursing homes)
Skin:
components, 412–414, *413*
functional/morphologic changes, 411–414
functions, 411
Skin cancer:
etiology, 414
screening, 217
types, 425–427
Skin disorders:
benign neoplasms, 425
blistering diseases, 423–424
decubitus ulcer breakdown, 388–389
evaluation, 414–415
hypothyroidism, 815
infections, 420–422
infestations, 418–419
inflammatory dermatoses, 415–418
management, 414–415
papulosquamous disorders, 422–423
pruritus, 424
terminology, 411*t*
vascular lesions, 418
Skin hypersensitivity antigen reaction, 67
Skin testing, tuberculosis, 577
SLE (*see* Systemic lupus erythematosus (SLE))
Sleep apnea syndrome:
clinical features, 1218–1219
dementia/depression and, 1220
gradations in severity of, *1219*, 1219–1220
hypothyroidism, 814
mortality and, 1220
Sleep disturbances:
age-related, 1213*t*, *1215*
classification, 1216*t*
clinical evaluation, 1213*t*, 1221*t*, 1221–1223
excessive somnolence, 1217
initiating/maintaining sleep, 1216–1217
menopause, 121, 870
parasomnias, 1218
related breathing disorders, 1218*t*
sleep-wake cycle, 1023, 1217–1218
treatment, 1223*t*, 1223–1225
Sleep-wake cycle disturbances, 1023, 1217–1218
Slow-twitch muscle fibers, 95, 942
Small cell lung cancer:
clinical presentation, 607–608
treatment, 611*t*, 612
Small intestinal function:
age-related changes, 669–671
calcium metabolism and, 880
Smoking (*see* Tobacco smoking)
Smoldering multiple myeloma, 69
Snellen test, 208
Snoring, 1219, 1222
SOAP notes, format of, 365, 365*t*
Social/health maintenance organization (SHMO), 377
Social Security policy, 131 (*See also* Medicare)
Social Services Block Grants, 377, 378
Social support system, 183, 280 (*See also* Psychosocial function)
Socioeconomic issues, allocation of resources and, 126–127
Sociology of aging, 125–133
Sodium, dietary restriction, 622, 648
Sodium bicarbonate, 649
Sodium fluoride, osteoporosis and, 906–907

Sodium homeostasis:
- disorders of, 620–622, 1188–1189
- renal excretion/conservation, 618, 648

Sodium phosphate (Fleet's) enema, 1272
Sodium polystyrene sulfonate, 649
Somatic pain, 318
Somatomedin C, 795, 797
Somatostatin, 794–795, 796–797
Somnambulism, 1218
Somnolence, disorders of excessive, 1216, 1217
Sorbitol, 514
Spasticity, spinal cord/peripheral neuropathy, 1292
Speech production, 436–437
Speech reading, 467
Speech Reception Threshold (SRT), 462
Spider angiomas, 418
Spinal anesthesia, 280, 293–294
Spinal compression fractures (*see* Vertebral compression fractures)
Spinal cord disorders:
- autonomic dysfunction neuropathy, 1293–1294
- cervical spondylosis, 1287
- complications, 1291–1294
- infarction, 1286
- low back pain, 1288
- lumbar stenosis, 1287–1288
- malignancy, 1286–1287

Spinal cord injury (SCI):
- clinical syndromes, 1285–1286
- complications, 1291–1294
- pain management, 1294
- pulmonary complications, 1294
- rehabilitation, 1291–1294
- socioeconomic issues, 1294

Spinal muscular atrophy, 1066
Spine, joints and discs, 943
Spinocerebellar atrophy, 1065–1066
Spirometry, 559, 583
Splay foot, *1301*
Splints, braces and, 1291, 1292
Splitting behavior, 1134
Spondylosis, cervical, 1287
Spongiform encephalopathies, 29–30
Sputum cultures:
- contamination, 566
- diagnosing pneumonia, 569–570

Sputum cytology, 608
Squamous cell carcinoma:
- esophagus, 690–691
- lung, 607–608, 612
- skin, 425–426

St. Anthony's fire, 421
Staging system, malignancies:
- breast cancer, 485, 486*t*
- colorectal cancer, 727
- lung cancer, 609, 610*t*
- non-Hodgkin's lymphomas, 763–764
- prostatic cancer, 661–662

Standard of competency, defined, 392
Stanozolol, 45, 907
Staphylococcus aureus, 568, 1161
Staphylococcus saprophyticus, 627
Stasis dermatitis/venous ulcers, 415–416
Static orthoses, 1292
Status epilepticus, 1091–1092
Steatorrhea, 719
Steele-Richardson-Olszewski syndrome, 1065
Steinert disease, 26
Stem cells, transplantation of, 73
Stents, intraurethral, 659–660
Stercoral ulcer, 1269
Stereotactic interstitial radiosurgery, 1099
Stevens-Johnson syndrome, 417–418, 1272
Stimulant laxatives, 1272
Stokes-Adams attack, 1173, 1177
Stomach disorders:
- bleeding, 700–701
- gastric-emptying, 698–700
- gastric neoplasms, 701–702
- gastritis, acute/chronic, 694*t*, 694–696
- *Helicobacter pylori*, 693
- NSAIDs and, 694
- peptic ulcer, 696–698

Stool (*see* Constipation; Diarrhea; Fecal incontinence)
Stool softeners, 1272
Strength, muscle, 94–96
Strength training, 95–96
Streptococcus mutans, 432
Streptococcus pneumoniae, 566, 567, 1161
Streptokinase, 605, 639, 786
Streptomycin, 578–580
Stress, cardiovascular response, 500–504
Stress urinary incontinence, 475, 1230, 1232–1233, 1240
Strial (metabolic) presbycusis, 460
Striatonigral degeneration, 1057
Stroke:
- assessment, 350–351
- as cause of depression, 1106
- cerebral infarction, pharmacotherapy, 1029–1030
- clinical presentation, 538–539
- dementia of, 1198–1200
- depression with, 1203
- epidemiology, 143, 145, 145*t*
- hemorrhagic, 1028–1029
- management, 313, 786–787, 1030
- pathogenesis, 538
- rehabilitation, 349–351
- risk factors, 161–162, 162*t*
- transient ischemic attacks, 1027–1028
- treatment, 539, 1029–1030
- vascular dementia, 1030–1031

Stroke volume index (SVI), 495–496, *496*, 498, 499–500
Stroop Test, 225
Subacromial bursitis, 995
Subacute combined degeneration, spinal/peripheral nerve disease, 1289
Subarachnoid space, infection of, 1071
Subcortical dementia, 1198–1199
Subdural empyema, 1076–1077
Subdural hematoma, chronic, 1081–1082
Subluxation, cervical vertebrae, 970
Substance abuse/dependence, 1125 (*See also* Chemical dependence)
Substituted judgment family as, 394–395
Sucralfate, 686
Suicide:
- epidemiology, 141
- physician-assisted, 384, 395, 402–403
- risk of, depression and, 1103–1104, 1107, 1108, 1202

Sulfinpyrazone, 991
Sulfonamides, 630
Sulindac, 947
Sun exposure, skin, 412, 414–415, 417 (*See also* Photoaging, skin; Skin cancer)
Sunscreens, 415
Superego, defined, 107
Superior sulcus tumors (Pancoast syndrome), 612
Superior vena cava syndrome, 612, 785
Superoxide dismutase (SOD), 677
Support groups, family caregivers, 232
Supportive psychotherapy, 1143
Suppressor-cytotoxic T cells, 62–64, 67
Suprapubic catheterization, 632
Suprathreshold taste functions, 434
Supraventricular arrhythmias, 529
Suramin, 663
Surgery:
- abdominal disorders, 301–302
- aortic aneurysm, 313
- appendicitis, 304
- biliary tract, 302–303
- brain tumors, 1099
- cancer
  - colorectal, 309
  - esophageal, 312–313
  - gastric, 306–307
  - gynecologic, 476
  - lung, 312, 609, 611
- cardiac and thoracic, 310–313
- cerebral infarction, 1030

Surgery (*Cont.*)
  cerebrovascular disease, 313
  coronary artery bypass grafting, 310–311
  disfiguring, sexuality and, 119, 121
  diverticulitis, 308–309
  hemorrhage, lower gastrointestinal, 307–308
  hernia, abdominal wall, 309–310
  hip fracture, 1325
  hypothyroidism and, 816
  intractable constipation, 1273
  occlusive disease, 314
  pancreatic disorders, 303–304
  Parkinson's, 1060
  pressure ulcers, 1334–1335
  procedures performed, elderly, 302*t*
  rheumatoid arthritis, 969–970
  ulcers
    duodenal, 304–305
    gastric, 305–306
  vascular, 313–314
Surgical risk:
  age-related, 278*t*
  assessment, bleeding disorders, 778
  assessment, thromboembolism, 783
  cardiac complications, 279, 279*t*
  functional impairment, operative risk and, 280
  mortality, overall, 277–278
  period of, 280
  pulmonary complications, 279
Surrogates:
  family as, 384, 394–395, 404*t*, 404–405
  informed consent and, 391–392
Swallowing (*See also* Dysphagia)
  function of, 436–437, 683
  syncope and, 1174–1175
Sweat glands, 414
Symmes-Weinstein monofilament testing, 1302
Syncope:
  age/disease-related changes, 1171–1172
  epidemiology, 1171
  etiology, 1172*t*, 1172–1175
  evaluation, 1175–1177, *1178*
  pathophysiology, 1171
  primary autonomic failure, 1065
  TIAs and, 1027–1028
  treatment, 1177
Syndrome of inappropriate antidiuretic hormone (SIADH):
  diagnosis, 1188
  differential diagnosis, 816
  etiology, 1188, 1188*t*
  paraneoplastic syndromes, 608
  treatment, 1188–1189
  water metabolism disorders, hyponatremia and, 621
Syneresis (vitreous), 442
Synovial fluid, 941, 941*t*
Synovial membrane, 940–941
Syntactic knowledge, 1014
Syphilis, 1075
Systemic lupus erythematosus (SLE), 640, *973*, 973–974
Systemic necrotizing vasculitis, 639–640
Systolic blood pressure, 541, 542–543
Systolic cardiac function, 498–499
Systolic-diastolic hypertension:
  defined, 541
  evidence for efficacy of therapy, 545–546
Systolic pressure, ankle measurements, 536

T cell monoclonal antibodies, designation of, 67
T cells:
  age-related changes, 61, 67–68, 566
  augmenting activity of, 71–72
  cell mediated immunity and, 67
  classes/subdivisions, 62
  compromised function, pneumonia and, 559, 570
  membrane markers, 62, 63*t*
T_4 (serum thyroxine), 807–808, 810–811, 816–817
T_3 (serum triiodothyronine), 807–808, 810–811
Tachyarrhythmia, hypokalemia and, 623
Tamm-Horsfall protein, 627
Tamoxifen, 484, 487, 489
Tardive dyskinesia, 437, 1141
Tarsal tunnel syndrome, 1001–1002, 1298
Taste, function of, 434–435
Tears (*see* Lacrimal function)
Technological advances:
  geriatric care, ethical aspects, 397
  health care utilization and, 168, 169
Teeth:
  components of, 432
  loss of, 431–432
Tegretol, 1140, 1141
Telephone devices for the deaf (TDDs), 468
Telomere shortening, experimental topics, 14–15
Temperature regulation:
  autonomic dysfunction, SCI, 1293
  hyperthermia, 1193–1194
  hypothermia, 1191–1193
Temporal artery biopsy, 957
Temporomandibular joint (TMJ), 437
Tendinitis, 997–1000
Tendon, components of, 942–943
Tendon rupture, posterior tibial, 1304
Tendonitis, 948
Terazosin, 659
Tertiary hyperparathyroidism, 923
Tessalon, 387
Testicular disorders, 797–799, 801
Testosterone:
  libido and, 117
  osteoporosis and, 900, 907
Testosterone propionate, 474
Tetracycline, 569
Tetralogy of Fallot, 522
Thalassemia, 746
Theophylline:
  asthma, 591, 593
  COPD, 587, 587*t*
  toxicity, 1090
Thermal control, age-related loss of, 1159
Thermal treatment modalities, 1288
Thiazide diuretics:
  as cause of hypercalcemia, 1031
  decreased bone mass with, 1325
  hypertension, 549
Thirst, 619–620, 1183, 1189, 1276
Thoracic surgery, 310, 312–313
Threshold taste functions, 434
Thrombectomy, 639
Thrombin, 776
Thrombocytopenia, 778–779
Thromboembolic disorders:
  arterial, 785–787
  estrogen replacement therapy and, 874
  microvascular thrombosis, 787–788
  renal artery, 638–639
  venous, 783–785
Thrombogenesis, 782–783
Thrombolytic agents:
  acute MI, 519
  arterial thromboembolism, 786–787
  cerebral infarction, 1029
  pulmonary embolism, 605
Thrombomodulin, 776
Thrombosis:
  arterial obstruction and, 533–534
  deep venous, prevention, 282
  hemostasis and, 775–777
  physiology, 782
  venous, 537–538
Thrombotic thrombocytopenic purpura (TTP), 788
Thrush, oral, 388, 420–421
Thymic hormone preparations, 72
Thymic involution, 68, 72
Thymus transplantation, 73
Thyroid cancer, 821–822
Thyroid disorders:
  as cause of depression, 1106
  goiter, 819–820
  hyperthyroidism, 809–813
  hypothyroidism, 813–819
  laboratory tests, 807–808
  neoplasms, 820–822

Thyroid disorders (*Cont.*)
  screening, 808–809
Thyroid hormone-binding ratio (THBR), 807–808
Thyroid nodules, 820–821
Thyroid ophthalmopathy, 455
Thyroiditis, 811
Thyrotoxicosis, iodide-induced, 811
Thyrotropin (TSH), 807–808, 810–811, 816–817
Thyroxine, 818–819
Tibial osteotomy, Paget's disease, 933–934
Tibial tendinitis, posterior, 1304
Ticlid, 539
Ticlopidine, 539, 1029
Tilt testing, syncope and, 1176–1177
Timed manual performance test, 207
Tinea (dermatophytes), 420
Tinel's sign, 1001, *1001*
Tinnitus, 457
Tissue plasminogen activator, 786
TMJ disorders (temporomandibular joint), 437
Tobacco smoking:
  cessation, benefits of, 182, 218–219
  COPD, *584*, 585
  epidemiology, 148, 149*t*
  female genital cancer and, 476
  lung cancer, 607
  menopause and, 867
  peripheral vascular disease and, 536
  preoperative management of, 282
  as risk factor
    cancer, 162, 188
    CHD, 159
  sex mortality rates, 41–42
Toe deformities, 1299–1301
Toenails, disorders of, 1305
Tofranil, 1139
Token Test, 225
Tolosa-Hunt syndrome, 444
Tonometry, ocular, 443
Tooth (*see* Teeth)
Toradol, 324, 386
Total blood neutrophil pool (TBNP), 753, *753*
Total hip replacement, Paget's disease, 933–934
Total lung capacity, 555–556
Total white cell count, defined, 750, 751*t*
Toxic epidermal necrolysis (TEN), 417–418
Toxic neuropathy, 1288–1289
Trabecular bone, 883, *883*
Trace elements, RDAs for, 337*t*
Tranexamic acid, 781
Transcutaneous electrical nerve stimulation (TENS), 387, 984
Transfer dysphagia, 1260
Transference, defined, 1142
Transient global amnesia (TGA), 1028
Transient ischemic attacks (TIAs):
  ophthalmopathy, 455
  stroke and, 313, 538–539, 1027–1028
  symptoms, 1168
Transient monocular blindness, 1028
Transit time tests, colonic, 1269
Transperineal prostatic biopsy, 660–661
Transplantation (organs, tissues, etc.):
  fetal adrenal, 1060
  fetal thymus, 73
  renal, 652
Transrectal prostatic biopsy, 660–661
Transrectal ultrasonography (TRUS), 662
Transthyretin gene, amyloidosis and, 27
Transurethral prostate resection, 659
Transvaginal sonography, 477
Tranylcypromine, 1109
Trauma (*see* Injuries)
Traveler's diarrhea, 1282
Trazodone, 1108, 1140
Treatment, refusal of, 391–392, 394, 395
Tremor, differential diagnosis, 809–810, 1052, 1054, 1056
Treponema pallidum, 1075
Tretinoin, topical, 425
Triceps skinfold test, 208, 282
Tricyclic antidepressants:
  adjuvant analgesia, 328
  contraindications, 1198
  depression, 1108, 1109, 1203
Trifascicular block, 529
Triglyceride, cholesterol, body weight, age and, *42*, 43
Triiodothyronine resin uptake (T_3U), 807–808
Trimethoprim-sulfamethoxazole, 630, 631, 632
Trisomy 21, 25–26, 1120
Trochanteric bursitis, 996
Trousseau's sign, 608, 927
Trypsin, 674
TSH assays, 807–809, 810–811, 816–817
Tuberculin skin testing, 67
Tuberculosis:
  chronic pulmonary, 576
  clinical, 576
  etiology, 575–576
  extrapulmonary, 580–581
  pathogenesis, 575–576
  pleural disease, 576–580
  prevention, 369, 581–582
  primary infection, 576
  resistance to, 575
  special problems of, 581
  transmission, 575–576
Tuberculous meningitis, 1074
Tubular transport mechanisms, age-related changes, 617
Tubulointerstitial nephritis, 644–646
Tubulointerstitial nephropathy, 646
Tumor growth factor-β (TGF-β), 70
Tumor growth factor (TGF), 65
Tumor necrosis factor-α (TNF-α), 65, 71
Tumor necrosis factor (TNF), 70
Tumor suppressor genes, defined, 80
Tuning fork tests, 468
Turner's syndrome, 26, 31, 870
24-hour urine collection, 648, 650
Twins, monozygotic, aging in, 20
Type A behavior pattern, 111

Ulcers:
  corneal, 446
  duodenal, 304–305, 305*t*
  gastric, 305–306, *306*, 950
  venous/stasis dermatitis, 415–416
Ultrasound:
  abdominal, 659
  arterial occlusion, 536
  bone mass measurement, 900
Ultraviolet light, decontamination with, 576
Ultraviolet radiation (UVR), 414, 415
Undernutrition (*see* Nutritional deficiency)
Unimodal progeroid syndromes:
  familial Alzheimer's disease, 27–29
  familial hypercholesterolemia, 26–27
  hereditary amyloidosis, 27
  Huntington's disease, 29
  mitochondrial disease, 30
  spongiform encephalopathies, 29–30
Unipolar affective disorder, 1202–1203
University of Pennsylvania Smell Identification Test, 435
Up & Go test, 207
Upper-extremity mobility, assessment, 207–208
Upper-tract urinary infection:
  diagnosis, 629–630
  symptoms, 627
  treatment, 629–630
Ureidopenicillin, 629
Uremia:
  as cause of impotence, 1253
  symptoms, 650
"Uremic threshold," 620
Ureteral catheterization, 629
Urethral obstruction, 632, 657–658
Urge urinary incontinence, 1233, 1240
Urinalysis, 628, 1234

Urinary catheters (*See also* Indwelling urinary catheters)
bacteriuria and, 631–632
external, 632, 1245
intermittent, 632, 1245, 1293
management of incontinence, 1245–1246
postoperative complications and, 283–284
as risk factor, UTI, 625–626, 627–628
suprapubic, 632
ureteral, 629
Urinary frequency, 627
Urinary hydroxyproline excretion, Paget's disease, 931–932
Urinary incontinence:
autonomic dysfunction, SCI, 1293–1294
catheters/catheter care, 1245–1246
epidemiology, 142
etiology, 1230–1231
evaluation, 1233–1235, *1234*, 1239*t*
incidence, 1229, *1229*
management, 1235–1237, 1240
post-prostatectomy, 663
stress, 475
terminally ill, 389
treatment
behavioral procedures, 1242–1244, 1243*t*
drug therapy, 1240*t*, 1240–1242, 1241*t*
surgery, 1244–1245
types, 1230–1235, 1232*t*, 1240*t*
Urinary retention:
with overflow incontinence, 1231, 1233, 1293
as side effect, opioids, 329
treatment, drug therapy, 1293–1294
Urinary system:
menopause and, 869–870
simple tests of function, 1235, 1238*t*
Urinary tract infection:
adjunctive therapy, 632
as cause of incontinence, 1231
clinical features, 627–628
diagnosis, 628–629, 1160
epidemiology, 625–626
lower-tract infection, 630–631
management, 629–633
microbiology, 627
neurogenic bladder, 1294
pathogenesis, 626–627
radiologic imaging, 632–633
relapse/reinfection, 631
treatment, 389
upper-tract infection, 629–630
Urinary tract obstruction:
acute renal failure and, 648
benign prostatic hyperplasia and, 657–658
postobstructive diuresis, renal function and, 1185
prostatic cancer and, 660
urinary tract infection and, 632
Urinary urgency, 627
Urination:
autonomic dysfunction, SCI, 1293–1294
difficulty with, BPH and, 658
normal, 1229–1230, *1230*, 1230*t*
Urine concentration, 617, 618–619
Urine culture, 628–629, 1234
Urine dilution, 617, 620
Urodynamic testing, 658–659, 1235
Uroflowmetry, 658–659
Urokinase:
arterial thromboembolic disorders, 786, 787
fibrinolysis, physiologic, 777
pulmonary embolism, 605
thromboembolic disorders, 639
Urticaria, 417
Uveitis, 448–449

Vaccines:
booster doses, 68
with IL-2, 73
immunologic aspects, 73–74
topical aerosol, 66
Vacuum penile tumescence devices, 1256
Vagina:
dryness of, 473
examination, 473
intraepithelial neoplasia, 475
pelvic relaxation, 475
Vaginal cancer, 475
Vaginismus, 118
Vaginitis, atrophic, 475, 870
Valproate, 1091, 1092
Valvular heart disease:
aortic, 522–526
endocarditis, infective, 526
mitral, 525–526
treatment, surgical, 311–312
Vancomycin, 629
Varicella virus, 422
Varicella-zoster vaccine, 74
Vascular dementia, 1030–1031
Vascular disease:
diabetes mellitus and, 834–836
pulmonary embolism, 604–605
pulmonary hypertension, 602–604
renal, 637–639
secondary impotence, 1252
spinal cord infarction, 1286
Vascular skin lesions, 418
Vascular surgery, 313–314
Vascular system:
aging, effects of, 499–500, *500*
changes, hypertension and, 497–498, 541–542
nutritional aspects, 52–53
Vasculitis, systemic, 639–640
Vasomotor symptoms, menopause, 869–870
Vasopressin, 619, 793, 1183
Vasovagal syncope, 1174
VDRL (Venereal Disease Research Laboratory), 1075
Vena caval filters, 605, 784
Venography, 783
Venous lakes, 418
Venous stasis, 782
Venous thromboembolism:
diagnosis, 783–784
hepatic vein, 785
postthrombotic syndrome, 537–538
preoperative risk assessment, 783
prevention, 283
renal vein, 785
risk factors, 783
superior vena caval syndrome, 785
treatment, 784–785, 785*t*
Venous ulcers/stasis dermatitis, 415–416
Ventilation, distribution of, 557
Ventilatory hypoxic response, 558
Ventricular arrhythmias, 284, 529
Ventricular septal defect, 522
Verrucae, 421, 1303
Vertebral compression fractures, 871, 903, 924
Vertical nystagmus, 469
Vertigo:
defined, 1165
evaluation, 468–470
syncope and, 1165–1171
TIAs and, 1028
Very low-density lipoprotein (VLDL), 857
Vestibular ataxia of aging, 470
Vestibular dysfunction:
anatomic/physiologic correlates of, 469–470
clinical evaluation, 468–469
general considerations, 457–458, 468
minicaloric test, 1170
neuronitis, acute/recurrent, 1167
Vestibular labyrinth, 1165
Villous adenoma polyps, 728
Vincristine, 611, 612, 788
Viral antigens, 73
Viral diarrheas, 1278
Viral hepatitis, 708–709
Viral-mediated gene transfer, 73
Viral meningoencephalitis, 1073–1074
Virchow's node, 728
Visceral pain, 318
Vision:
acuity, testing for, 208
impairment

Vision (*Cont.*)
- assessment, 208
- as risk factor, falls, 1324
- nutritional aspects, 53–54

Visuospatial ability, impairment of:
- Alzheimer's disease, 1036
- dementia, 1199
- focal cognitive syndromes, 1201
- testing, 225, 1015

Vital capacity, 557
Vitamin A, 73, 650
Vitamin B_{12} deficiency, 671, 745–746, 754–755, 1289
Vitamin C, 1333
Vitamin D:
- bone density and, 51
- calcium/phosphorus metabolism, 649
- calcium regulation, 881–882
- deficiency, causes, 882*t*
- intoxication, 925
- metabolism, *912*
- osteoporosis and, 73, 899, 905–906
- renal disease and, 649–650
- skin synthesis, 51, 412

Vitamin D-deficiency osteomalacia, 911–914, 916–917, 918
Vitamin deficiencies:
- neurologic/behavioral effects, 53*t*
- treatment, 57–58, 58*t*

Vitamin E, 73, 121, 650
Vitamin K, 776–777, 779–780, 787
Vitamins:
- absorption, small intestine, 671
- chronic renal failure, 650
- requirements for, 334

Vitreous, ocular, 442
Voiding (*see* Urination)
Volume depletion:
- clinical signs, 1276
- hyponatremia and, 620, 621
- syncope and, 1174

Volume performance standard, Medicare, 169–170
Volvulus, 1270
VO_{2max} (*see* Maximum oxygen consumption (VO_{2max}))
Vomiting:
- salt losses with, 620
- as side effect
  - chemotherapy, 87
  - opioids, 328
- treatment, 388

Von Willebrand factor, 957
Von Willebrand's disease, 779
Vulva:
- cancer, 474–475
- dermatological conditions, 474
- examination, 473
- human papillomavirus lesions, 474

Vulvar intraepithelial neoplasia (VIN), 476

Waist-hip ratio, 94, 188, 852
Waldenström's macroglobulinemia, 68, 770, 771
Waldeyer's ring, 765
Walking pneumonia, 568, 569
Warfarin:
- as cause of skin necrosis, 787
- cerebral infarction, 1029
- drug interactions, 570, 947
- overdosage, 780
- thromboembolic disorders, 639
- thromboembolic disorders, arterial, 787
- thromboembolic disorders, venous, 784–785

Warts, 421
Water brash, defined, 683
Water deficit, hypernatremia and, 622
Water homeostasis, 618–619, 648
Water metabolism, disorders of, 621–622
Weakness, spinal cord/peripheral neuropathy, 1291–1292
Wechsler intelligence/memory tests, 225, 1014, *1015*
"Weeping lubrication," 937
Wegener's granulomatosis, 640, 642
Wellbutrin, 1140
Werner's syndrome, 15, 23–24, 923
Wernicke's encephalopathy, 1128
Westergren sedimentation rate, 957
Westermark's sign, 604
White blood count (WBC), 750
White cells:
- decreased, significance of, 752–756
- effect of aging, 749
- evaluation, 749–750
- functions, 749
- increased, significance of, 750–752, 751*t*
- malignancy/clonal disorders, 756–759

Whitmore staging system, prostatic cancer, *661*, 661–662
Wiedemann-Rautenstrauch syndrome, 25
Wilson's disease, 447, 1052
Winter itch, 415
Wisconsin Card Sorting Test, 225
World Health Organization (WHO), classification, impairments, 213–214, 343, *1309*
Wydase (Wyeth), 1186

X chromosome, longevity and, 38–39
X-linked diseases, enzyme defects, 988
Xanthelasma, 444
Xerosis, 415
Xerostomia, 434

Y chromosome, longevity and, 21–22, 38–39
Yergason's sign, 999, *1000*
Yesavage Depression Scale, 1202

Zenker's diverticulum, 689, 1261
Ziehl-Neelsen staining, 577
Zinc, 73
Zinc sulfate, 1333
Zollinger-Ellison syndrome, 696
Zoloft, 1140
Zomepirac, 951
Zung Depression Scale, 225

ISBN 0-07-027501-7